THE 1995
INFORMATION PLEASE®
SPORTS
ALMANAC

D1517742

Mike Meserole

EDITOR

Project Manager
Andrew Roberts

Production Coordinator
Nancy Priest

Research assistance by
**Bob Baggett, Gerry Brown,
Mike Coffey, Ed Ryan**
and **Howie Schwab**

HOUGHTON MIFFLIN COMPANY
Boston   New York

The Information Please Sports Almanac

ISSN: 1045-4980
ISBN: 0-395-66565-5

Cover photographs:
Simpson: 1994 Wide World Photographs; **Major League Bummer**: 1994 Wide World Photographs; **Harding and Kerrigan**: 1994 Wide World Photographs; **Mark Messier**: 1994 Canapress Photo Service; **Dunga**: 1994 Billy Stickland/Allsport USA; **Jones and Johnson**: 1994 Wide World Photographs; **Bonnie Blair**: 1994 Clive Brunskill/Allsport USA; **Nick Price**: 1994 David Cannon/Allsport USA; **Unser and Penske**: 1994 Wide World Photographs; **Corliss Williamson**: 1994 David Gottschalk/Arkansas Democrat-Gazette; **Madden and Summerall**: 1994 Aaron Rapoport/Fox; **Navratilova**: 1993 Glenn Cratty/Allsport USA.

Comments and Suggestions

Comments and suggestions from readers are invited. Because of the many letters received, however, its not possible to respond personally to every correspondent. Nevertheless, all letters are welcome and each will be carefully considered. **The Information Please Sports Almanac** does not rule on bets or wagers. Address all correspondence to Houghton Mifflin Company, 222 Berkeley Street, Boston, Massachusetts 02116.

Additional copies of The **1995 Information Please Sports Almanac** may be ordered directly by mail from:

Customer Service Department
Houghton Mifflin Company
Burlington, MA 01803

Phone toll-free (800) 225-3362 for price and shipping information. In Massachusetts, phone (617) 272-1500.

Information Please is a registered trademark of Houghton Mifflin Company.

Printed in the United States of America

WP 10 9 8 7 6 5 4 3 2 1

The 1995 Information Pleas
Sports Almanac

Now in its 6th year as America's
favorite sports reference book.
Ranked as one of journalism's
"50 Basic Reference Books"
by *The Essential Researcher*.

Sports history at your fingertips. A complete and reliable record
of the past 12 months and the last 125 years.
The winners, losers and all-time leaders.
Year by year and sport by sport.
Hundreds of photos, charts and directories.
Easy to find and understand.

With Year in Review essays by many of the country's top sports writers:

Tony Barnhart
Atlanta Constitution
on College Sports

Jerry Crasnick
The Denver Post
on Baseball

Eric Duhatschek
Calgary Herald
on Hockey

Bernard Fernandez
The Philadelphia Daily News
on Boxing

Tom Gaffney
Akron Beacon Journal
on Bowling

Paul Gardner
Soccer America
on Soccer

Mike Harris
Associated Press
on Auto Racing

Philip Hersh
Chicago Tribune
on the Olympic Games
and International Sports

Ivan Maisel
Newsday
on College Football

Skip Myslenski
Chicago Tribune
on College Basketball

Scott Ostler
San Francisco Chronicle
on The Year in Sports

Marino Parascenzo
Pittsburgh Post-Gazette
on Golf

Diane Pucin
The Philadelphia Inquirer
on Tennis

Bob Ryan
The Boston Globe
on Pro Basketball

Richard Sandomir
The New York Times
on Business & Media

Sharon Smith
Author and commentator
on Horse Racing

Vito Stellino
The Baltimore Sun
on Pro Football

Plus an exclusive cartoon
by the *Atlanta Constitution's*
Mike Luckovich

"This is a remarkable book—complete, accurate and interesting. After my over 60 years
announcing sports, I should know a great record book. This is certainly it."
—Red Barber (1908-92)

The Champions of 1994

Auto Racing

NASCAR Circuit
Daytona 500 ....Sterling Marlin
Winston 500 ....Dale Earnhardt
Coca-Cola 600 ....Jeff Gordon
Southern 500 ....Bill Elliot
Winston Cup Champion ....Dale Earnhardt

IndyCar Circuit
Indianapolis 500 ....Al Unser Jr.
PPG Cup Champion ....Al Unser Jr.

Formula One Circuit
World Driving Championship ....undecided

Baseball

Division Winners
American League
East ....New York (70-43)
Central ....Chicago (67-46)
West ....Texas (52-62)
National League
East ....Montreal (74-40)
Central ....Cincinnati (66-48)
West ....Los Angeles (58-56)

All-Star Game ......National League, (8-7, 10 inn) at Pitt.
MVP ....Fred McGriff, Atlanta, OF
College World Series ....Oklahoma 13, Georgia Tech 5
MVP ....Chip Glass, Oklahoma, CF

College Basketball

Men's NCAA Final Four
Championship ....Arkansas 76, Duke 72
Semifinals ....Arkansas 91, Arizona 82
Duke 70, Florida 65
MVP ....Corliss Williamson, Arkansas, F
Women's NCAA Final Four
Championship ....North Carolina 70, Louisiana Tech 69
Semifinals ....Louisiana Tech 69, Alabama 66
North Carolina 89, Purdue 74
MVP ....Charlotte Smith, North Carolina, F

Pro Basketball

NBA Finals ....Houston def. New York, 4 games to 3
MVP ....Hakeem Olajuwon, Houston, C
Eastern Final ....New York def. Indiana, 4 games to 3
Western Final ....Houston def. Utah, 4 games to 1
All-Star Game ....East, 127-116 at Minnesota
MVP ....Scottie Pippen, Chicago, F

College Football (1993)

National Champions
AP and Coaches ....Florida St. (12-1)
Major Bowls
Sugar ....Florida 41, West Virigina 7
Orange ....Florida St. 18, Nebraska 16
Cotton ....Notre Dame 24, Texas A&M 21
Rose ....Wisconsin 21, UCLA 16
Fiesta ....Arizona 29, Miami 0
Heisman Trophy ....Charlie Ward, Florida St., QB

Pro Football (1993)

Super Bowl XXVIII ....Dallas 30, Buffalo 13
MVP ....Emmitt Smith, Dallas, RB
AFC Championship ....Buffalo 30, Kansas City 13
NFC Championship ......Dallas 38, San Francisco 21
Pro Bowl ....NFC, 17-3
MVP ....Andre Rison, Atlanta, WR
CFL Grey Cup Final ....Edmonton 33, Winnipeg 23
MVP ....Damon Allen, Edmonton, QB

Golf

Men's Major Championships
Masters ....Jose Maria Olazabal
U.S. Open ....Ernie Els
British Open ....Nick Price
PGA Championship ....Nick Price
Seniors Major Championships
The Tradition ....Ray Floyd
PGA Seniors ....Lee Trevino
Senior Players Championship ....Dave Stockton
U.S. Senior Open ....Jim Colbert
Women's Major Championships
Nabisco Dinah Shore ....Donna Andrews
LPGA Championship ....Laura Davies
U.S. Women's Open ....Pattie Sheehan
du Maurier Classic ....Martha Nause
National Team Competition
Solheim Cup (Women) ....United States

Hockey

Stanley Cup ....NY Rangers def. Vancouver, 4 games to 3
MVP ....Brian Leetch, NYR, D
Western Final ....Vancouver def. Toronto, 4 games to 1
Eastern Final .NY Rangers def. New Jersey, 4 games to 3
All-Star Game ....Eastern Conf. 9-8 (at New York City)
MVP ....Mike Richter, NY Rangers, G
NCAA Div. I Final ....Lake Superior St. 9, Boston Univ. 1
MVP ....Sean Tallaire, Lake Superior State, RW
Olympics ....Sweden 3, Canada 2 (shootout)
World Championship ...Canada 2, Finland 1 (shootout)

Horse Racing

Triple Crown Champions
Kentucky Derby ....Go for Gin (Chris McCarron)
Preakness Stakes ....Tabasco Cat (Pat Day)
Belmont Stakes ....Tabasco Cat (Pat Day)

Soccer

1994 World Cup final ....Brazil 0, Italy 0
(Brazil wins shootout, 3-2)
MVP ....Romario, Brazil, F

Tennis

Men's Grand Slam Championships
Australian Open ....Pete Sampras
French Open ....Sergi Bruguera
Wimbledon ....Pete Sampras
U.S. Open ....Andre Agassi
Women's Grand Slam Championships
Australian Open ....Steffi Graf
French Open ....Arantxa Sanchez Vicario
Wimbledon ....Conchita Martinez
U.S. Open ....Arantxa Sanchez Vicario
National Team Competition
1992 Davis Cup (Men) ....Germany
1993 Federation Cup (Women) ....Spain

Winter Olympics
(at Lillehammer, Norway)

Most Medals Won:
Top 3 Countries ....26 Norway (10-11-5)
....24 Germany (9-7-8)
....23 Russia (11-8-4)
Men ....4 Bjorn Dahlie, Norway (2-2-0)
Five tied with 3 each
Women ....5 Manuela Di Centa, Italy (2-2-1)
4 Lyubov Egorova, Russia (3-1-0)

I found out early that you can't count on big league sports.

On June 13, 1957, three weeks shy of my seventh birthday, my Dad took me and my two older brothers to see the Dodgers play the Milwaukee Braves at Ebbets Field in Brooklyn. It was my first major league baseball game and I clearly remember how exciting it all was. I also remember lead-off batter Billy Bruton of the Braves hitting two home runs off Don Drysdale in his first two at bats and Drysdale drilling number two hitter Johnny Logan and Bruton's second homer. A bench-clearing brawl ensued with Drysdale fending off Logan and then getting pummeled by Eddie Mathews. The Dodgers lost the game but what a show!

The next day I graduated from the comics to the sports section, reading about the game in every morning and afternoon newspaper I could lay my grubby little hands on. *The Herald-Tribune, New York Times, Daily News, the Mirror, Journal-American, World-Telegram & Sun* and *Bergen Evening Record.* Game reports, box scores, sidebars, photographs, the Willard Mullin cartoon, you name it. I was hooked. The Dodgers were my team: Drysdale, Podres, Campy, Duke, Hodges and a 21-year-old flamethrower with a control problem named Koufax, who, according to my favorite barber Fred, just might be great if he learned to throw a curve.

Then, just like that, the Dodgers moved to the West Coast. In all the reading I'd done on the team I hadn't noticed that owner Walter O'Malley had been busy buying up real estate in Los Angeles. I still rooted for the Dodgers, of course— especially Koufax— but it wasn't the same.

When the baseball players went out on strike this summer and the World Series was eventually called off, I wondered if there was a 7-year-old kid in Cleveland somewhere, who felt as confused as I did when the Dodgers left Brooklyn 37 years ago. Who went with his Dad and his brothers to his first Indians' game at Jacobs Field this season and got hooked only to have all the fun of being a new fan pulled out from under him.

Welcome to the majors, kid.

As grim a year as this was to cover sports, putting the almanac together for the sixth time was made easier by moving the entire operation up to Boston and producing it under one roof at Houghton Mifflin. It meant moving away from friends in Connecticut and ending an enjoyable collaboration with Michael Michaud, but at 896 pages the book had gotten too big to do out of my bedroom any longer.

My thanks to Andy Roberts and Nancy Priest, who kept me and the project on course all year; to Pat McTiernan, Margaret Anne Miles and Christina Granados; to Michael Rosenstein, Miriam Palmerola, Susan Harkins, Lori Galvin and Jane Ellin; to Steve Lewers, Marnie Patterson, Mark Caleb, Steve Frail, Greg Mroczek, Chris Leonesio; to Jim Murphy and Paul Schaefer; to Charley and Marcia Monagan, Bruce and Allie Delventhal, Lynn Michaud, Mindy Keskinen and Eddie Kramer and friends down in the Houghton mailroom; to Nat Andriani at Wide World Photos and Jonathan Braun at Allsport; to Paul Kennedy at Soccer America, Jim Callis at Baseball America, and Rick Campbell and Gary Johnson at the NCAA; and all the communications and public relations folks who returned my calls and provided needed information.

I hope we can all find the intestinal fortitude to do this again next year.

—Mike Meserole

Boston
Oct. 28, 1994

Major League Cities & Teams

As of Oct. 28, 1994, there were 125 major league teams playing or scheduled to play baseball, basketball, football and hockey in 55 cities in the United States and Canada. Listed below are the cities and the teams that play there.

Anaheim
AL	California Angels
NFL	Los Angeles Rams
NHL	Mighty Ducks of Anaheim

Arlington
| AL | Texas Rangers |

Atlanta
NL	Braves
NBA	Hawks
NFL	Falcons

Baltimore
| AL | Orioles |
| CFL | Football Club |

Boston
AL	Red Sox
NBA	Celtics
NFL	N.E. Patriots (Foxboro)
NHL	Bruins

Buffalo
| NFL | Bills (Orchard Park) |
| NHL | Sabres |

Calgary
| CFL | Stampeders |
| NHL | Flames |

Charlotte
| NBA | Hornets |
| NFL | Carolina Panthers (1995) |

Chicago
AL	White Sox
NL	Cubs
NBA	Bulls
NFL	Bears
NHL	Blackhawks

Cincinnati
| NL | Reds |
| NFL | Bengals |

Cleveland
AL	Indians
NBA	Cavaliers
NFL	Browns

Dallas
NBA	Mavericks
NFL	Cowboys (Irving)
NHL	Stars

Denver
NL	Colorado Rockies
NBA	Nuggets
NFL	Broncos

Detroit
AL	Tigers
NBA	Pistons (Auburn Hills)
NFL	Lions (Pontiac)
NHL	Red Wings

East Rutherford
NBA	New Jersey Nets
NFL	New York Giants
NFL	New York Jets
NHL	New Jersey Devils

Edmonton
| CFL | Eskimos |
| NHL | Oilers |

Green Bay
| NFL | Packers |

Hamilton
| CFL | Tiger-Cats |

Hartford
| NHL | Whalers |

Houston
NL	Astros
NBA	Rockets
NFL	Oilers

Indianapolis
| NBA | Pacers |
| NFL | Colts |

Jacksonville
| NFL | Jaguars (1995) |

Kansas City
| AL | Royals |
| NFL | Chiefs |

Las Vegas
| CFL | Posse |

Los Angeles
NL	Dodgers
NBA	Clippers
NBA	Lakers (Inglewood)
NFL	Raiders
NHL	Kings (Inglewood)

Miami
NL	Florida Marlins
NBA	Heat
NFL	Dolphins
NHL	Florida Panthers

Milwaukee
| AL | Brewers |
| NBA | Bucks |

Minneapolis
AL	Minn. Twins
NBA	Minn. Timberwolves
NFL	Minn. Vikings

Montreal
| NL | Expos |
| NHL | Canadiens |

New Orleans
| NFL | Saints |

New York
AL	Yankees
NL	Mets
NBA	Knicks
NHL	Rangers

Oakland
| AL | Athletics |
| NBA | Golden St. Warriors |

Orlando
| NBA | Magic |

Ottawa
| CFL | Rough Riders |
| NHL | Senators |

Philadelphia
NL	Phillies
NBA	76ers
NFL	Eagles
NHL	Flyers

Phoenix
| NBA | Suns |
| NFL | Cardinals (Tempe) |

Pittsburgh
NL	Pirates
NFL	Steelers
NHL	Penguins

Portland
| NBA | Trail Blazers |

Quebec City
| NHL | Nordiques |

Regina
| CFL | Saskatchewan Roughriders |

Sacramento
| CFL | Gold Miners |
| NBA | Kings |

St. Louis
| NL | Cardinals |
| NHL | Blues |

Salt Lake City
| NBA | Jazz |

San Antonio
| NBA | Spurs |

San Diego
| NL | Padres |
| NFL | Chargers |

San Francisco
| NL | Giants |
| NFL | 49ers |

San Jose
| NHL | Sharks |

Seattle
AL	Mariners
NBA	SuperSonics
NFL	Seahawks

Shreveport
| CFL | Pirates |

Tampa
| NFL | Buccaneers |
| NHL | Lightning |

Toronto
AL	Blue Jays
CFL	Argonauts
NBA	Raptors (1995-96)
NHL	Maple Leafs

Uniondale
| NHL | New York Islanders |

Vancouver
CFL	B.C. Lions
NBA	Grizzlies (1995-96)
NHL	Canucks

Washington
NBA	Bullets (Landover)
NFL	Redskins
NHL	Capitals (Landover)

Winnipeg
| NHL | Jets |
| CFL | Blue Bombers |

The 1994 baseball strike stretched into November with acting commissioner **Bud Selig** and his fellow owners still determined to install a salary cap.

UPDATES

$alary Cap

*First came free agency, then salary arbitration, now there's
a new issue and it has shut down both baseball and the NHL.*

Baseball has struck out. Again. This past summer, for the eighth time in eight tries since 1972, the players and the owners failed to agree on a new Basic Agreement, and the games stopped.

What was unprecedented and especially sad about 1994, of course, was that the games never got started again. The season ended without ever ending. There were no pennant races, no playoffs, and no World Series. There was no champion. Everybody lost.

Past strikes have taught us much (against our will) about arcane subjects such as free agency and salary arbitration, topics so far removed from our pure enjoyment of the game that I hate to even bring them up; I apologize for having to. But that's reality, baseball fans. And this year we have a new reality to grasp, a new hot-button issue, one you probably thought was no concern of yours, until now: the salary cap.

The salary cap was born a decade ago in the NBA. It was a different league then, a different era, symbolized for me by the memory of a cold midwinter's night at Madison Square Garden in 1982. I was there with a buddy, watching the Knicks play the San Diego Clippers. Even though we had great seats, right behind the Clippers' bench, it turned out to be a dull, depressing evening. The action was flat, the

crowd was indifferent. The poor Clipper subs were as bored as we were. They kept turning away from the game, scanning the crowd for women who seemed willing, and calling out their hotel room numbers. "What we're seeing tonight," I remember my friend saying, "is what's wrong with the NBA."

The bright success of the NBA today—the overflowing arenas, the wildly popular licensed merchandise, the astounding $125 million per team expansion fees, the average player salary (despite the cap) of $1.4 million—is perhaps the best argument in favor of the salary cap anyone can make.

In 1983-84, the last season before the cap was put in place, a lot of NBA teams were losing money; at least four were on the brink of insolvency. League vice president Gary Bettman (remember that name) came up with the cap to staunch the flow of red ink—and, by the way, give somebody besides members of the Lakers and the Celtics an opportunity to win a championship ring.

The concept was a simple one: total the league revenues, multiply by 53%, divide by the number of franchises, and voila, you have a number that equals the maximum player payroll per team. That number has grown dramatically over the years, from $3.6 million at the outset to $16 million today—but then so have revenues, that's the point. Last year, the league's 27 franchises took in more than a billion dollars. Is correlation the same as causation?

David Whitford writes for *Inc.* magazine and is the author of *Playing Hardball: The High Stakes Battle for Baseball's New Franchises.*

Five days after his appointment by President Clinton as special mediator, **W.J. Usery** (center) meets with players' union executive director **Donald Fehr** (left) and owners' negotiator **Richard Ravitch** on Oct. 19 in Washington, D.C. It was the first formal meeting between the two sides since Sept. 9.

Hard to prove. Gene Orza, counsel to the Major League Baseball Players Association, is one who would argue no, not in this case. "The salary cap had nothing to do with the NBA's success," he has said. "Their success can be summed up in six words: Magic Johnson, Larry Bird, Michael Jordan."

Right or wrong, that's an argument we're not likely to settle here. Even if we could convince the players that a salary cap was somehow in their best long-term interest, it probably wouldn't make any difference. That's because there's a world of difference between the NBA 10 years ago and Major League Baseball today. And it's that difference—not logic, not power—that has made the salary cap such a hard sell in 1994.

"With the NBA, there was a sense of urgency on both sides, a crisis," says Charles Euchner, assistant professor of political science at The College of the Holy Cross in Worcester, Mass., and author of *Playing the Field: Why Sports Teams Move and Cities Fight to Keep Them.* "None of the national broadcasting networks would touch the NBA. Both sides thought they needed to come up with a social contract, some way of controlling the game so they could package it better. Stabilizing the game's finances was the critical first step, and the cap did that. But baseball is not in a crisis. Baseball is very healthy, very secure. The players therefore view the cap as guaranteeing profits for the owners, rather than guaranteeing the survival of the game."

The owners argue otherwise, of course—that survival is precisely what's at stake. "The game's ills cannot be cured without substantial change in the player compensation system," is how Bud Selig—owner of the Milwaukee Brewers and acting commissioner of baseball—justified the cap to members of Congress at a hearing in September. "It became painfully clear to the clubs during the term of our last labor agreement...that we finally had to confront the problems we have been avoiding for years."

What's lacking in Selig's case is evidence. The owners refuse to open their books. They're asking the players to trust them. And the players, understandably, find that

Wide World Photos

NHL commissioner **Gary Bettman**, who devised the NBA's salary cap in the mid-1980s, closed the 1994-95 hockey season down before it started when the league's players refused to accept a cap on their salaries.

hard to do. Look at the long history of the reserve clause; at the way the owners fought free agency; at the failed experiment with collusion (that wound up costing the owners $280 million in fines); and it's easy to conclude, along with Marvin Miller, former head of the players union, that in the baseball business, "The mechanism has always been, 'Let's not compete.'"

Everyone accepts the fact—even without seeing the books—that there are vast economic discrepancies among the franchises.

We know, for example, that the New York Yankees began the 1994 season counting on $47 million in local TV and radio revenues, while the Colorado Rockies stood to make just $4 million from the same sources; and that the Toronto Blue Jays are among a handful of teams (including the Rockies) that sell about $40 million worth of tickets every year, while smaller-market franchises such as the San Diego Padres and Pittsburgh Pirates have had to make do with about $15 million in ticket sales.

Those differences account, in part, for the wide differences in player payrolls: seven teams had 1994 contract obligations total-

ing at least $40 million each, or enough to pay all the Padres this year, next year, and the year after that.

Numbers like those are what Bud Selig had in mind when he told Congress in September: "Our economic problems had become so serious that in many of our cities the 'competitive hope' that is the very essence of our game was being eroded."

Well, maybe. We could remind Selig, if we wanted to, of the success of the Montreal Expos, who had the best record in baseball on Aug. 12, the day the strike began, despite also having the second lowest player payroll ($18.6 million).

Or we could compare records over the past several seasons of the Minnesota Twins ($4.6 million in local TV/radio revenue) with the New York Mets ($30 million) and the Chicago Cubs ($20 million). But that would be beside the point. The fact is, baseball's small-market teams have been demanding for years that big-market teams share more of the pie with them. And those cries were heard, finally, when the owners met this past January in Fort Lauderdale.

The plan the owners settled on called for annual transfers of as much as $10 million from the wealthy franchises to their poorer league brethren. But there was a catch: The only way the big-market teams would agree to do that—take money out of their pockets and hand it over to small-market teams—was if the players agreed first to limit their salaries.

The owners' aim was obvious: To make the players pay for revenue sharing. The mechanism they proposed was a salary cap—50% of revenues—which then became the owners' central demand in negotiations with the players for a new Basic Agreement to replace the one that expired at the end of the '94 season. The players said no way, and walked off the job, just as the races were starting to get interesting.

And so Cleveland lost all hope for its first pennant since 1954. Matt Williams lost his shot at 60 homers. Tony Gwynn lost his at chance at batting .400. Ticket-takers, beer-sellers and front-office workers lost their jobs. Young fans lost their innocence, then lost interest (sales of licensed baseball merchandise dropped 50% at Sears in the first few weeks after the strike).

Back to the cap. Wherever you looked in

With baseball on strike and hockey locked out, the NFL had the fall to itself, thanks to a collective bargaining agreement that included a salary cap and was signed on June 29, 1993, by players' union executive director **Gene Upshaw** (right) and **Harold Henderson**, the chairmen of the NFL management council. Pittsburgh Steelers president **Dan Rooney** (standing left), NFL commissioner **Paul Tagliabue** and **Mike Kenn** of the Atlanta Falcons look on.

the sports pages this fall, there was no escaping it. Bettman, well into his second year as commissioner of the National Hockey League, tried to get NHL players to agree to one in their new collective bargaining agreement with the owners.

Bad timing. Long the weak sister in the family of major pro sports, hockey has suddenly come into its own. Attendance last season was a record 17.5 million. League revenues hit $717 million, another record. And over the summer, the upstart Fox network decided to give the NHL one more shot at attracting a national following, signing the league to a five-year, $155 million deal.

Why now of all times should we give the owners a break on salaries, the hockey players asked themselves. When they couldn't answer that question, they arrived at an impasse, leading to a lockout, resulting in a very strange, very quiet fall, when for more than two months—until the NBA season got rolling in November—the NFL

was the only big-time pro game in town.

The NFL, meanwhile, was having its own problems with the salary cap. The NFL version, agreed to by a crippled players association two years ago, took effect with the start of the 1994 season. It caps salaries at 64% of league revenues.

This year, that works out to $34.6 million per team. Unlike the NBA's soft cap, which has more holes in it than the federal tax code, the NFL cap is hard, like a helmet. That made for some ugly situations this summer, as teams scrambled to make it under the cap by Opening Day.

Because of the cap, quarterback Phil Simms wound up at an ESPN anchor desk instead of the New York Giants' huddle and wide receiver Art Monk joined the New York Jets for about half the $1.1 million he made last year with the Washington Redskins, among countless other calamities.

Players howled, blaming union chief and former All-Pro Gene Upshaw for the fix they were in—conveniently forgetting for the

Wide World Photos

The NBA players union agreed to a salary cap in 1984 when times were tough. Now that the league enjoys immense success, commissioner **David Stern** (right) has to negotiate a new contract with a union determined to make the cap history.

leagues in baseball and hockey, NBA commissioner David Stern and union chief Charles Grantham announced a no-strike, no-lockout agreement on Oct. 27, that would allow the 1994-95 season to proceed uninterrupted through the NBA Finals in June.

While both Stern and Grantham recognized that hammering out a new labor contract would be difficult, they were hopeful that the eight-month truce would foster a productive atmosphere for negotiation and some kind of lasting peace.

"We each know the capacity that we have to damage the game and each other," Grantham told *The New York Times*. "We're not interested in getting into that."

One thing is clear: in the NBA, at least, there can be no cap without a new agreement. For the cap is, by definition, restraint of trade. And for the owners to simply cap salaries on their own would eventually leave them vulnerable to tough legal challenges under the nation's antitrust laws.

In baseball, the situation is a little different. There the owners operate under the protection—unique among professional sports—of an ancient antitrust exemption. Theoretically they could, if they chose, impose a cap immediately and hope the players would capitulate in time for Opening Day, 1995. That seems unlikely, and not just because the owners are afraid of the players' resolve. They're mindful of Congress, too, which has threatened so many times in the past to take away baseball's cherished exemption and would no doubt act, finally, if the owners ever dared to play that kind of hardball.

In October, shortly after he was appointed by President Clinton to end the strike, veteran federal mediator and former Labor Secretary W. J. Usery brought both sides together for the first time in weeks, raising the possibility, however slim, of a settlement before Christmas. But whenever the strike ends, under whatever terms, the cap may soon be a thing of the past, remembered one day as nothing more than another failed management fad.

"It's been sold as a mechanical quick-fix, but it's not," says Prof. Euchner. "It's an artificial device, and both sides have to agree on the need for it to get it to work. That's why it won't work in baseball. And if it gets imposed, it won't last." ❑

moment that 98% of them had approved the contract that contained the cap when it had come up for a vote. "Yeah," a philosophical Upshaw told *The Sporting News*, "and no one voted for Nixon, either."

Does the cap have a future in pro sports? If the owners have anything to say about it, definitely. Suddenly it's an issue in all four sports at once, a situation Prof. Euchner describes as "at the least, very curious." Either it's an idea whose time has come, separately and simultaneously, to all the members of the sports barons' fraternity, or, alternatively, we could be looking at the mother of all collusion cases somewhere down the road.

But the players, for their part, are fed up with it, even the basketball players who supported it for so long. While most still concede it was the right solution for the times, times have changed. And now that the NBA's labor agreement has expired, the union is clamoring to remove the cap and let salaries rise to market levels. But not at the expense of the regular season.

Showing remarkably clear thinking given the stubbornness exhibited by their col-

AUTO RACING

Dale Earnhardt caught up with Richard Petty on Oct. 23, winning the AC Delco 500 at Rockingham, N.C., to join the king as the only NASCAR drivers to capture seven Winston Cup championships.

Earnhardt clinched the title for the fourth time in the last five years when the engine of his closest pursuer, Rusty Wallace, went dead with 192 laps remaining. Wallace finished 35th.

"It's great to be No. 1 all the way around on race day," said a jubilant Earnhardt, who dedicated the victory to his great friend, the late Neil Bonnett. "We've won seven titles, but Richard Petty is still the king."

Before the race, Geoff Bodine clinched the Busch Pole Award by virtue of his five pole positions in 1994. He donated the $25,000 winner's check to injured colleague Ernie Irvan, who also won five poles in '94, but lost the tie-breaker with only one outside pole to Bodine's four. "With Ernie not competing, this is a bogus way to win the thing," said Bodine.

On the Formula One circuit, Michael Schumacher of Germany returned from a two-race suspension to win the European Grand Prix from the pole in Jerez, Spain. Damon Hill of Britain finished second, but fell five points behind Schumacher with two races to go in their duel for the world championship.

Former world champion Nigel Mansell, back with Williams-Renault after two years on the Indy-car circuit in the U.S., spun out with 92 laps to go and did not finish. Meanwhile, Michael Andretti and Paul Tracy will replace Mansell and the recently-retired Mario Andretti as drivers for the Newman-Haas Inday-car racing team in 1994.

BASEBALL

While the players' strike cancelled the World Series for the first time in 90 years, there were a number of other moves made in September and October.

The managerial ax fell in Boston, Chicago, Texas, Kansas City, and Baltimore. Butch Hobson, Tom Trebelhorn, Kevin Kennedy, Hal McRae, Johnny Oates were canned, although the latter two had winning records before the work stoppage.

Bob Boone was hired as Kansas City's

Wide World Photos

Dale Earnhardt hugs his 7th Winston Cup after clinching NASCAR title Oct. 23.

manager on Oct. 7. Boone concluded his 19-year playing career with the Royals from 1989-90. Kennedy was hired by Boston just six days after being dismissed by Texas, while Oates replaced Kennedy in Texas on Oct. 19. Jim Riggleman left San Diego for the Chicago Cubs on Oct. 21, but the Padres filled the void by promoting third-base coach Bruce Bochy.

With no postseason to report on the Baseball Writers announced their 1994 regular season award-winners a few weeks early.

Buck Showalter of the New York Yankees and Montreal's Felipe Alou were the Managers of the Year, while the top rookies were Kansas City designated hitter Bob Hamelin and Los Angeles outfielder Paul Mondesi. Hamelin is the first DH to get the nod and the first Royal since Lou Piniella in 1969, while Mondesi is the third straight Dodger to win the prize.

Atlanta righthander Greg Maddux became the sixth pitcher to win three Cy Young Awards but the first to win three in a row when he topped the NL vote. The AL Cy Young went to Kansas City right-hander David Cone, who edged out Yankee hurler

Jimmy Key. Both Cone and Maddux won 16 games, but Maddux had the ERA advantage, 1.56 to 2.94.

First basemen swept Most Valuable Player honors, with Frank Thomas of the White Sox repeating in the AL and Houston's Jeff Bagwell winning unanimously in the NL. Thomas hit .353 with 38 HRs and 101 RBI and garnered 24 of 28 first place votes to beat out Seattle's Ken Griffey. Bagwell, who also put up big offensive numbers (.368, 39, 116), led the majors in runs batted in and trailed only the Padres' Tony Gwynn (.394) in batting and the Giants' Matt Williams (43) in homers.

1994 Sporting News Awards

Voted on by the players of each league and released Oct. 25, 1994. All players are eligible to vote for Player of the Year but only managers eligible to vote for Manager of the Year.

Player of the Year: Jeff Bagwell, Houston, 1B. **Pitchers of the Year:** AL—Jimmy Key, New York and NL— Greg Maddux, Atlanta.

Rookies of the Year: AL—Bob Hamelin, Kansas City, DH and NL—Raul Mondesi, Los Angeles, OF.

Comebacks of the Year: AL—Jose Canseco, Texas, DH and NL—Tim Wallach, Los Angeles, 3B.

Firemen of the Year: AL—Lee Smith, Baltimore and NL—John Franco, New York.

Managers of the Year: AL—Buck Showalter, New York and NL—Felipe Alou, Montreal.

Executive of the Year: John Hart, Cleveland.

AL All-Star Team: C—Ivan Rodriguez, Texas; 1B—Frank Thomas, Chicago; 2B—Chuck Knoblauch, Minnesota; 3B—Wade Boggs, New York; SS—Cal Ripken, Baltimore; OF—Ken Griffey, Seattle, Kirby Puckett, Minnesota and Albert Belle, Cleveland; DH—Paul Molitor, Toronto; RHP—David Cone, Kansas City; LHP—Jimmy Key, New York.

NL All-Star Team: C—Mike Piazza, Los Angeles; 1B— Jeff Bagwell, Houston; 2B—Craig Biggio, Houston; 3B—Matt Williams, San Francisco; SS—Barry Larkin, Cincinnati; OF—Moises Alou, Montreal, Tony Gwynn, San Diego and Barry Bonds, San Francisco; RHP—Greg Maddux, Atlanta; LHP—Danny Jackson, Philadelphia.

COLLEGE BASKETBALL

UNLV interim president Kenny Guinn and Runnin' Rebels' head coach Rollie Massimino reached an agreement on Oct. 14, in which Massimino resigned in exchange for a $1.8 million buyout. Massimino lost favor with the university after it was learned that he had a "secret" contract paying him $375,000 a year on top of his base salary of $511,000. He was quickly replaced by former Jerry Tarkanian assistant Tim Grgurich.

Howard University, after months of searching for a replacement for Butch Beard—who left to take over the NBA's New Jersey Nets— opted for Mike McLeese, a highly-successful District of Columbia high school coach.

PRO BASKETBALL

The Los Angeles Clippers hired Bill Fitch as their new head coach on July 27. Fitch, who spent the past two seasons out of the NBA, entered the 1994-95 season having coaching more games than anyone else (1,722). His record was 845-877.

The San Antonio Spurs named Bob Hill as head coach on Aug. 29, replacing John Lucas, who resigned to become head coach and GM in Philadelphia. Hill was the assistant coach with Orlando.

Bill Blair with 13 years NBA assistant coaching experience, was named head coach of the Minnesota Timberwolves on Aug. 29. Blair replaced Sidney Lowe. The Timberwolves were also sold in the off-season to Mankato, Minn., businessman Glen Taylor for $88 million. Earlier in the summer, a New Orleans syndicate headed by boxing promoter Bob Arum tried to buy the team for $152 million, but was turned down by the NBA's board of governors.

There were also a number of trades and player signings prior to the start of training camps. The Boston Celtics signed free agent Dominique Wilkins and let go of aging (41) center Robert Parish, who later caught on with Charlotte.

Orlando dealt guard Scott Skiles to the Washington, then signed a pair of veteran free agents—Horace Grant and Brian Shaw. Grant had been with Chicago and Shaw with Miami last season.

The Phoenix Suns kept busy, adding Danny Manning from Atlanta and Waymon Tisdale from the Kings as free agents. They

A Season To Savor

by Ivan Maisel
Newsday

Wide World Photos

Colorado's **Michael Westbrook** makes The Catch against Michigan with 0:00 left.

College football in the fall of 1994 brought to bear a philosophical question. Is it really this good, or are we so hungry for sports that it only seems like it?

Baseball and hockey disappeared. Notre Dame, which lost three of its first seven, disappeared with them. Yet college football's hold on the national attention span has never been tighter, thanks to some of the most dramatic finishes in recent years.

Michigan went to Notre Dame on Sept. 10, surrendered the lead in the final minute, then drove quickly downfield to kick a game-winning field goal. The Wolverines, who had been 1-6 in close games under Gary Moeller, appeared to break the spell.

Instead, the victory only set up Michigan for a greater fall two weeks later.

A decade ago, an undersized quarterback from Boston College flung a "Hail Mary" pass in the dying seconds against Miami. When it came down a touchdown, Doug Flutie had won the game, the Heisman Trophy and a permanent place in college football's all-time highlight film.

"I saw it when it happened," said Colorado senior quaterback Kordell Stewart. "They show that play all the time. Every team in the country works that play. Who would say it would happen to me my last year against one of the top two teams in the country?"

With :06 to play at Michigan Stadium, Stewart threw a 64-yard touchdown pass that passed through more hands than a one-dollar bill before Michael Westbrook cradled it in his long arms. Colorado, which trailed Michigan 26-14 with 2:30 to play, won, 27-26.

"I kissed the end zone," Stewart said. "I kissed the grass. I kissed players on the lips. I kissed anybody who was close to me."

The Buffaloes headed toward a late-season showdown with Big Eight Conference archrival Nebraska. The winner would appear on any short list of national championship candidates along with Penn State. The Nittany Lions, 6-0 through Oct. 22 with a 31-24 Big Ten win over Michigan, unleashed an offense that belied their dull, traditional uniforms. Quarterback Kerry Collins and tailback Ki-Jana Carter both put themselves in All-America contention.

For some reason, however, no one appeared interested in captivating the Heisman voters, other than record-setting Division I-AA quarterback Steve McNair of Alcorn State. Injuries slowed wide receiver J.J. Stokes of UCLA and tailback Tyrone Wheatley of Michigan.

Senior tailback Napoleon Kaufman of Washington received a boost when the Huskies ended Miami's 58-game winning streak in the Orange Bowl by defeating the Hurricanes, 38-20, on Sept. 24. Miami coach Dennis Erickson, who in five-plus seasons has won two national titles and nearly 90% of his games, nonetheless endured two weeks of catcalls from the locals. He shut them up when the 'Canes beat Florida State, 34-20.

Florida appeared to take up the mantle for the Sunshine State before collapsing in the final minute at home to lose to Auburn, 36-33. on Oct. 15. The victory wrote yet another amazing chapter in the Terry Bowden Story. He arrived in Auburn in 1993 to coach a team dispirited by two years of mediocrity and an NCAA bowl probation. Yet the Tigers ran up a school-record winning streak under Bowden.

"I don't feel AP will give the national championship to an 11-0 team that's not playing in January," said Bowden, the eldest son of a Florida State head coach Bobby Bowden. "I do believe, however, that they will give it to a team that's 22-0."

also sent forward Cedric Ceballos to the Los Angeles Lakers for a future first-round draft choice. Another Sun setting elsewhere was free agent Oliver Miller, who signed with Detroit.

The Chicago Bulls added guard Ron Harper from the Clippers via free agency, while the team lost both Grant (to the Magic) and Bill Cartwright (to the Sonics). Meanwhile, Atlanta traded forward Adam Keefe, a former first round draft pick, to Utah for forward Tyrone Corbin.

With No. 1 pick Glenn Robinson holding out for $100 million in his negotiations with the Milwaukee Bucks, the richest rookie contract went to Dallas first pick, former Cal point guard Jason Kidd. Kidd, the second player drafted overall, signed a nine-year deal worth $54 million with the Mavericks. No. 3 pick Grant Hill played a fiscally-fit second fiddle, signing for eight seasons and $45 million with Detroit.

Several injuries marred the NBA preseason. LA Clippers center Stanley Roberts, who hadn't played since he ruptured his right Achilles tendon last December, ruptured his left Achilles in his first game back in '94 and had to be carried of the floor. Philadelphia center Shawn Bradley re-injured his left knee in an exhibition game with Minnesota and could miss the first month and half of the season.

Golden State once again started the year with assorted injuries. Chris Mullin hurt his knee, Tim Hardaway hurt his wrist and Billy Owens strained a hamstring.

Portland sharpshooter Terry Porter needed surgery on his right ankle, Milwaukee point guard Eric Murdock suffered a badly bruised eye and Cleveland forward Larry Nance's ailing right knee forced the three-time NBA All-Star to retire on Sept. 27.

Finally, a couple of former NBA big men were hired as assistant coaches: Dave Cowens joined the Spurs and Bob Lanier was added to the Warriors staff.

BOWLING

Norm Duke won his fifth tournament of the season and his first of the PBA fall tour with a 216-190 victory over Doug Kent in the championship round of the Greater Rochester (N.Y.) Open on Oct. 26. Other fall winners included John Mazza in the Dick Webber Classic, Walter Ray Williams Jr. in the Touring Players Championships

and Bryuan Goebel at the Greater Detroit Open.

On the Women's tour, Aleta Sill won the BPAA U.S. Open on Oct. 9, beating Anne Marie Duggan in the final, 229-170. Sill won again on Oct. 27, beating Tish Johnson, 219-195, in the finals of the Delaware Open. Sill and Duggan were the only LPBT regulars with earnings over $100,000 heading into November.

Meanwhile, Barry Gurney, Gary Dickinson and Larry Laub each won once on the PBA Seniors tour.

BOXING

The $13 million Hong Kong card scheduled for Oct. 23— featuring bouts between WBO heavyweight champion Herbie Hide and Tommy Morrison, heavyweights Frank Bruno and Ray Mercer, IBF lightweight champ Rafael Ruelas and Billy Schwar, and WBO middleweight champ Steve Collins and Lonny Beasely— was called off on Oct. 22, when Hide's manager withdrew his group of fighters because they hadn't been paid.

Promoter Bob Arum said the four-fight card would rescheduled within 60 days.

COLLEGE SPORTS

Florida State fired suspended athletic director Bob Goin on Oct. 18, five days after the state's ethics commission recommended that he be censured for accepting a new roof for his home from the construction company that worked on FSU's $96 million stadium expansion. Goin, who has denied any wrong-doing, had been on paid leave since July.

On Oct. 13, the Big West invited four institutions— Boise State, Cal Poly-SLO, Idaho and North Texas— to join then conference, effective with the 1996-97 school year. UNLV and San Jose State will be leaving the Big West for the Western Athletic Conference in 1996-97.

On Sept. 27, the NCAA slapped the Coastal Carolina basketball program with four years' probation for various recruiting violations. The Chanticleers were also banned from postseason play and television for one year and will be allowed fewer scholarships over the next two seasons.

DePaul's basketball program was also put on probation for one year, but will still be eligible for the postseason and TV.

PRO FOOTBALL

Montana Still The Master

by Vito Stellino
The Baltimore Sun

Don Shula proved father does know best, Joe Montana showed he hasn't lost his touch, the Dallas Cowboys appeared to still be the best team and the San Diego Chargers emerged as the surprise challenger.

Those were the most significant developments of the first half of the NFL's 75th season as the league celebrated the anniversary by having its players wear "throwback" uniforms.

The season, though, featured something new: The first father-son coaching matchup in any major American pro sport. On Oct. 2, Don Shula, the winningest coach in NFL history at age 64, paced the sideline against his 35-year-old son David. Dad won as Miami beat Cincinnati, 23-7. It was a typical result for both Shulas as the Dolphins started out 5-2 and Bengals began 0-7.

In another emotional matchup on Sept. 11, Montana passed for two touchdowns to give the Kansas City Chiefs a 24-17 victory over his former San Francisco 49er teammates.

Steve Young, who followed in Montana's footsteps with the Niners, said, "In a lot of ways, it shows the master still had some more to teach the student." John Elway was saying much the same thing five weeks later when Montana outdueled him in the final eight seconds of a Monday night game to beat the Broncos, 31-28, in Denver.

Despite the loss to the Chiefs, the 49ers got off to a 6-2 start and still appeared to be the main roadblock in a Dallas bid to become the first team to win three straight Super Bowls. Even with Barry Switzer replacing Jimmy Johnson as head coach, the Cowboys got off to a 6-1 start.

In the AFC West, San Diego, sporting the best of the throwback uniforms, jumped out to a 6-0 record before losing at home to Denver, 20-15, on Oct. 23. Quarterback Stan Humphries and running back Natrone Means keyed the Chargers' quick start, which included a 20-6 win over Montana and the Chiefs. Denver, meanwhile, had four last-minute losses and a 2-5 record.

The only other 6-1 team was the Cleveland Browns, who were cruising through a rela-

Wide World Photos

Quarterbacks **Steve Young** (left) and **Joe Montana** before the 49ers-Chiefs game.

tively easy first half, while the four-time defending AFC champion Buffalo Bills struggled to win four of its first seven games.

One of the most disappointing teams had to be the Arizona Cardinals. Bombastic new coach Buddy Ryan promised fans a winner, but got off to the same 2-5 start the team had under Joe Bugel last year.

Jerry Rice, the San Francisco wide receiver, scored seven touchdowns in his first eight games to become the NFL's all-time touchdown leader with 131. He topped Jim Brown's mark of 126.

Off the field, Gene Upshaw, the head of the NFL Players Association, spent most of the fall defending the league's controversial new salary cap.

Although San Francisco displayed some creative bookkeeping by squeezing high-priced players like Deion Sanders, Rickey Jackson and Richard Dent under the cap, many veterans around the league were forced to take paycuts and some—New York Giants' quarterback Phil Simms was the primary example—were forced out of the game.

Upshaw countered that the cap, which expires with the current collective bargaining agreement in 1999, gave the players free agency and 64 per cent of the gross revenues.

Besides, through October, NFL players were playing while baseball and hockey players were either on strike or locked out.

21

COLLEGE FOOTBALL

In the first two months of the season, there were a number of exciting games. Two of the best involved the University of Michigan, who upset Notre Dame, 26-24, on Sept. 10 on a Remy Hamilton 42-yard field goal with two seconds left, and then lost to Colorado in the final second (see page 19).

Miami, which saw its 58-game home win streak ended by Washington on Sept. 24, went on to upend defending national champion Florida State, 34-20 on Oct. 8. Dennis Erickson called the win the biggest of his career, impressive considering he has two national championship rings.

LaVell Edwards of BYU earned career win number 200 on September 24th as the Cougars edged New Mexico, 49-47.

Randy Gatewood of UNLV decimated the Division I-A receiving portion of the record book in a Sept. 17 loss to Idaho. Gatewood caught 23 passes to shatter BYU receiver Jay Miller's 21-year old mark of 22 catches. His 363-yard total broke the 29-year-old record of 349 by Chuck Hughes of UTEP.

Alcorn State superstar quarterback Steve McNair racked up numbers that numbed the senses. On Oct. 22, against Southern, the top-rated Division I-AA defense in the nation, the surprise Heisman candidate broke his own I-AA single-game record with 649 total yards. He also broke Ty Detmer's NCAA career record of 14,665 yards total offense, finishing the afternoon with 15,049.

Penn State's Nittany Lions remained undefeated and cast a cloud on a possible Bowl Coalition national champion, beating Michigan, 31-24, on Oct. 15, and taking a step further toward their first Rose Bowl bid since 1923.

Rice shocked No. 9 Texas on Oct. 16 beating the Longhorns, 19-17, for the first time since 1965.

Meanwhile, Colorado, behind tailback Rashaan Salaam's 179 yards a game, climbed up the polls to sit at No. 2 on the eve of a Big Eight showdown with No. 3 Nebraska.

PRO FOOTBALL

San Francisco signed flamboyant defensive back Deion Sanders on Sept. 15, and he scored a key touchdown just 10 days later in a 49er win over New Orleans.

The two-point conversion became a reality in the NFL as Tom Tupa scored the first one against Cincinnati on Sept. 4.

On Oct. 23, New Orleans and the Los Angeles Rams played one of the stranger games of the year. Special teams ruled the day in a 37-34 Saints' victory at the Superdome. LA's Robert Bailey set an NFL record when he ran back a 103-yard punt return. The Saints thought the ball went through the back of the end zone and as their defense came on to the field Bailey picked up the ball and ran, all alone, into the other end zone.

The Saints' Tyrone Hughes also set a new NFL mark. Hughes piled up a single-game record 347 combined kick return yards, which included kickoff runbacks of 98 and 92 yards for scores. Toby Wright also got into the long distance act with a Rams' club-record 98-yard touchdown off a fumble.

While Doug Flutie cranked it up a notch north of the border, the Canadian Football League did the same south of their border, fielding three more U.S. expansion teams—Baltimore, Las Vegas and Shreveport (La.). Flutie, the Calgary Stampeders' quarterback who is gunning for four straight MVP awards, led the CFL in every passing category and his team to a league-best 13-3 record as of Oct. 29.

In Baltimore, owner Jim Speros had hoped to call his team the Colts, but the NFL slapped an injunction on the use of the name saying that confusion between the CFL Colts and the NFL's Indianapolis Colts would hurt sales of their merchandise. The injunction is still pending and Speros must decide next season whether to continue his fight for the nickname Baltimore made famous.

GOLF

On Oct. 23, the U.S. women's team reclaimed the Solheim Cup, winning eight of ten singles matches on the final day of competition to beat Europe, 13-7, at White Sulphur Springs, W.Va.

"I'm so happy for the way all of them played," said a teary U.S. captain JoAnne Carner. "We really wanted to bring the Cup back here, and they did it. They did it."

The U.S. lost the Solheim Cup, the women's equivalent of the Ryder Cup, to the Europeans in 1992 at Dalmahoy in Scotland.

The China Syndrome

by Christine Brennan
The Washington Post

So, are the Chinese women on performance-enhancing drugs, or aren't they?

That is the question that has riveted the international sports community, especially vanquished U.S. athletes and coaches, as the 1996 Atlanta Summer Olympics approach.

It's difficult to say what has been more intriguing the past few years, the performance of China's women athletes or the outside world's reaction to them. Are we seeing the emergence of the next great superpower in women's sports or, simply, another East Germany?

First came the Chinese runners and their incredible world records in 1993. Then there were the swimmers—winning an amazing 12 of 16 women's events at the 1994 world championships in Rome. Finally, the 1994 Asian Games turned into a Chinese rout, led, of course, by the women. China won 137 of a possible 337 gold medals. They swept women's weightlifting and swimming, dominated diving, as usual, and won 11 of 12 rowing events, among other results.

Athletes and coaches from the United States as well as many other Western athletic powers officially questioned the tactics of the Chinese women, inferring that they are chemically aiding their performances.

China's coaches react by saying the Americans are sore losers, or, even worse, racist or anti-Asian.

Not so, say U.S. swimmers, who voice two basic concerns. First, they wonder how the Chinese could have become so good so fast. Prior to 1988, no Chinese woman swimmer was ranked in the top 10 in any event. Six years later, they dominated nearly every race. Their athletes also come and go quickly: None of their 1992 Olympic gold medalists won a world title in 1994. Meanwhile, Dai Guohong, whose name couldn't be found in the top 150 in the world in 1992, won the 400 individual medley in 1994.

Second, in the words of U.S. legend Mary T. Meagher: "Where are the men?" Not one Chinese male swimmer finished in the top eight of any event at the world championships. It is widely accepted that anabolic steroids,

Wide World Photos

Chinese weightlifter **Hua Ju** winning the women's 167½-lb class at the Asian Games.

which build up the level of testosterone in the body, can have a stronger impact on a female athlete than a male. Four Chinese women swimmers have tested positive for anabolic steroids in the past two years.

The Chinese say, however, that they are producing their results with rigorous training (a marathon a day for the distance runners) and an inventive diet including caterpillar fungus and stewed soft-shell turtle.

However, "toxicological problems," revealed by track coach Ma Junren at the Asian Games, slowed the runners in 1994. He said 11 of them—nearly half the team—required appendectomies, furthering Western concerns about Chinese methods.

All this sounds very familiar to U.S. athletes. In the 1970s and '80s, East German women burst onto the scene in track and field and swimming, spoiling the gold-medal hopes of many, especially U.S. swimmer Shirley Babashoff, who finished second four times to East Germans at the 1976 Olympics. At the time, Babashoff was labeled a whiner for complaining that East German swimmers like Kornelia Ender and Petra Thumer were cheating. When the Berlin Wall came down, widespread steroid use was confirmed by former East German officials, even though no East German star ever tested positive.

"We can't put our heads in the sand again," said U.S. Swimming national team director Dennis Pursley, "and pretend what we know is happening isn't happening."

Canada surprised the U.S., 2-1, to win the Dunhill Cup at St. Andrews, Scotland on Oct. 9. In the final, Tom Kite, of the defending champion U.S. squad, double-bogeyed at No. 17 while Fred Couples, missed a 3-foot putt on the 16th, and each lost their matches by a single stroke.

Beth Daniel continued her stellar play with her fourth win of the year at the LPGA World Championship of Golf in Naples, Fla. on Oct. 16. Daniel shot a bogey-free, 7-under-par 65 final round to edge third-round leader Elaine Crosby for the $105,000 top prize.

HOCKEY

While the start of the regular season was delayed by the owners' lockout, there were still a number of developments leading into the campaign.

On Aug. 29, Pittsburgh Penguins' superstar Mario Lemieux announced that he will sit out the entire 1994-95 season because of recurring back problems and fatigue brought on by the radiation treatments for his Hodgkin's disease.

A month earlier, the Pens' moved to shore up their offensive punch by trading right wing Rick Tocchet to Los Angeles for five-time All-NHL left winger Luc Robitaille.

The New York Rangers replaced the departed Mike Keenan on Aug. 9, with his 1993-94 assistant Colin Campbell.

Meanwhile, Keenan's new team in St. Louis traded for veterans— picking up center up veteran center Guy Carbonneau from Montreal (for Jim Montgomery) and defenseman Al MacInness from Calgary (for Phil Housley).

Philadelphia re-acquired goaltender Ron Hextall in a trade with the New York Islanders with the Isles getting goaltender Tommy Soderstrom.

Ed Jovanovski, the league's top draft choice made by the Florida Panthers, was returned to Windsor of the Ontario Hockey League after he failed to sign a contract.

And Vezina Trophy-winning goaltender Dominik Hasek of Buffalo signed a three-year contract extension worth $8 million plus incentives.

SOCCER

Major League Soccer, the proposed first division league that hoped to get off the ground in April 1995, may have to wait a year.

U.S. Soccer Federation president Alan Rothenberg, attending year-end FIFA meetings in New York, hinted strongly on Oct. 25 that a postponement was possible. "The key thing is doing it right, not the when," said Rothenberg.

MLS, which has announced only seven of its proposed 12 franchise cities, offered the existing American Professional Soccer League a chance to merge into one "super league," but the APSL turned it down on Oct. 5.

England shut out the United States, 2-0, Sept. 7, at London's Wembley Stadium in the first meeting between the two national teams since the Americans upset the English, 2-0, in US Cup '93. Striker Alan Shearer scored both goals for the home side. It was the first time a U.S. team had played at Wembley.

American World Cup star Alexi Lalas, in his first season as a defender in Division I Italian soccer, led underdog Padova to a 2-0 win over mighty AC Milan on Oct. 16. Lalas scored the first goal of the game for his previously winless club.

The University of North Carolina women's socccer team played to a scoreless tie with Notre Dame to end their 92-game winning streak on Oct. 2. Two weeks later, the Tarheels lost to Duke, 3-2, ending their 101-game unbeaten streak that dated back to Sept. 22, 1990.

TENNIS

By Oct. 24, Wimbledon finalists Pete Sampras and Goran Ivanisevic and French Open champion Sergi Bruguera had clinched three of the eight berths in the IBM/ATP Tour World Championship. With three weeks to go before the tournament, Michael Stich, Stefan Edberg, Boris Becker, Michael Chang and Andre Agassi appeared likely to qualify, unless any overtaken by Alberto Berasategui, Todd Martin or Wayne Ferreira.

On the women's tour, Arantxa Sanchez Vicario and Steffi Graf topped a list of 11 players who have clinched berths in the 16-player field that will compete in the year-end Virginia Slims Championships in New York. The other nine qualifiers included Conchita Martinez, Mary Pierce, Martina Navratilova, Jana Novotna, Gabriela Sabatini, Lindsay Davenport, Natalia Zvereva, Kimiko Date and Magdalena Maleeva.

COLLEGE FOOTBALL

AP Top 25 Poll
(as of Oct. 23, 1994)

Sportswriters and broadcasters poll, including games through Oct. 23, 1994. First place votes in parentheses, followed by record, total points (based on 25 for 1st, 24 for 2nd, etc.) and preseason rank.

	Record	Pts	Preseason		Record	Pts	Preseason
1 Penn St. (19)	6-0-0	1486	9	14 Syracuse	6-1-0	703	32
2 Colorado (16)	7-0-0	1482	8	15 Washington	5-2-0	591	23
3 Nebraska (24)	8-0-0	1461	4	16 Duke	7-0-0	564	NR
4 Auburn (3)	7-0-0	1397	11	17 Colorado St.	7-1-0	543	NR
5 Florida	5-1-0	1246	1	18 Virginia	6-1-0	484	29
6 Miami	5-1-0	1187	6	19 Texas	5-2-0	409	18
7 Texas A&M	7-0-0	1171	15	20 BYU	7-1-0	363	27
8 Alabama	8-0-0	1165	12	21 Ohio St.	6-2-0	330	20
9 Florida St.	5-1-0	1076	3	22 Washington St.	5-2-0	306	NR
10 Michigan	5-2-0	998	5	23 Kansas St.	4-2-0	269	31
11 Arizona	6-1-0	890	7	24 North Carolina	5-2-0	204	19
12 Utah	7-0-0	831	43	25 USC	5-2-0	91	17
13 Virginia Tech	7-1-0	709	22				

Others receiving votes: N.C. State (80); Oregon (30); Mississippi St. (27); Illinois (17); Boston College (11); Notre Dame (10); Bowling Green (9); Indiana (5); Rice (5).

PRO FOOTBALL

NFL Standings
(as of Oct. 24, 1994)

American Football Conference

Eastern Division

	W	L	T	Pct.	PF	PA
Miami	5	2	0	.714	180	146
Buffalo	4	3	0	.571	134	143
NY Jets	4	3	0	.571	116	122
New England	3	4	0	.429	175	183
Indianapolis	3	5	0	.375	167	186

Central Division

	W	L	T	Pct.	PF	PA
Cleveland	6	1	0	.857	166	79
Pittsburgh	5	2	0	.714	124	117
Houston	1	6	0	.143	93	155
Cincinnati	0	7	0	.000	101	180

Western Division

	W	L	T	Pct.	PF	PA
San Diego	6	1	0	.857	185	126
Kansas City	5	2	0	.714	159	131
LA Raiders	3	4	0	.429	163	178
Seattle	3	4	0	.429	153	124
Denver	2	5	0	.286	156	192

National Football Conference

Eastern Division

	W	L	T	Pct.	PF	PA
Dallas	6	1	0	.857	187	90
Philadelphia	5	2	0	.714	161	112
NY Giants	3	4	0	.429	127	144
Arizona	2	5	0	.286	89	155
Washington	2	6	0	.250	169	211

Central Division

	W	L	T	Pct.	PF	PA
Minnesota	5	2	0	.714	147	105
Chicago	4	3	0	.571	129	129
Detroit	3	4	0	.429	127	145
Green Bay	3	4	0	.429	117	97
Tampa Bay	2	5	0	.286	96	159

Western Division

	W	L	T	Pct.	PF	PA
San Francisco	6	2	0	.750	237	150
Atlanta	4	4	0	.500	158	184
LA Rams	3	5	0	.375	135	156
New Orleans	3	5	0	.375	156	208

CFL Standing
(as of Oct. 23, 1994)

(*) indicates playoff qualifiers.

Eastern Division

	W	L	T	Pct.	PF	PA
*Winnipeg	12	4	0	.750	606	477
*Baltimore	11	5	0	.688	504	403
*Toronto	7	9	0	.438	449	514
Ottawa	4	12	0	.250	427	573
Hamilton	4	12	0	.250	411	508
Shreveport	1	15	0	.063	273	610

Western Division

	W	L	T	Pct.	PF	PA
*Calgary	13	3	0	.813	626	312
*Edmonton	11	5	0	.688	444	375
*B.C. Lions	10	5	1	.656	536	425
Saskatchewan	9	7	0	.563	450	411
Sacramento	8	7	1	.531	402	414
Las Vegas	5	11	0	.313	430	526

Playoffs begin Nov. 12.
Grey Cup: Nov. 27 (at Vancouver)

TENNIS

Late 1994 Tournament Results
Men's Tour

Finals	Tournament	Winner	Earnings	Loser	Score
Sept. 18	Club Colombia Open	Nicholas Pereira	$42,000	M. Hadad	63 36 64
Oct. 2	Championship of Sicily	Alberto Berasategui	42,000	A. Corretja	26 76 64
Oct. 2	Salem Open (Malaysia)	Jacco Eltingh	54,000	A. Olhovskiy	76 26 64
Oct. 2	Swiss Indoors	Wayne Ferreira	110,500	P. McEnroe	46 62 76 63
Oct. 9	Athens International	Alberto Berasategui	27,000	O. Martinez	46 76 63
Oct. 9	Toulouse Grand Prix (France)	Magnus Larsson	54,000	J. Palmer	61 63
Oct. 9	Australian Indoors	Richard Krajicek	150,000	B. Becker	76 76 26 63
Oct. 16	Eisenberg Israel Open	Wayne Ferreira	36,000	A. Mansdorf	76 63
Oct. 16	IPB Czech Indoors	MaliVai Washington	42,000	A. Boetsch	46 63 63
Oct. 16	Seiko Super Tennis (Tokyo)	Goran Ivanisevic	147,000	S. Edberg	64 64
Oct. 23	Lion Grand Prix (France)	Marc Rosset	82,000	J. Courier	64 76
Oct. 23	CA Tennis Trophy (Vienna)	Andre Agassi	54,000	M. Stich	76 46 62 63
Oct. 23	Salem Open (Beijing)	Michael Chang	42,600	A. Jarryd	75 75

Remaining ATP Events (10): Stockholm Open and Helmann's Cup (Oct. 24-30); Paris Indoor and Topper Open (Oct. 31-Nov. 6); Topper South American Open, European Community Championships and Kremlin Cup (Nov. 7-13); ATP World Championship (at Frankfurt, Nov. 14-20); ATP Doubles World Championship (at Jakarta, Nov. 21-27); Davis Cup Final (at Moscow, Dec. 2-4).

Women's Tour

Finals	Tournament	Winner	Earnings	Loser	Score
Sept. 24	Moscow Ladies Open	Magdalena Maleeva	$27,000	S. Cecchini	75 61
Sept. 25	Nichirei International (Tokyo)	A. Sanchez Vicario	80,000	A. Frazier	61 62
Oct. 2	International Damen Grand Prix (Germany)	Jana Novotna	80,000	M. Pierce	75 61
Oct. 9	European Indoors (Zurich)	Magdalena Maleeva	150,000	N. Zvereva	75 36 64
Oct. 16	Porsche Grand Prix (Germany)	Anke Huber	80,000	M. Pierce	64 62
Oct. 23	Brighton International (England)	Jana Novotna	80,000	H. Sukova	67 63 64

Remaining WTA Events (5): Nokia Grand Prix (Oct. 24-30); Bank of the West Classic (Oct. 31-Nov. 6); Bell Challenge Championship (Oct. 31-Nov. 6); Va. Slims/Philadelphia (Nov. 7-13); Va. Slims Championships/New York (Nov. 14-23).

GOLF

Late 1994 Tournament Results
PGA Tour

Last Rd	Tournament	Winner	Earnings	Runner-Up
Oct. 2	Buick Southern Open	Steve Elkington (200)	$144,000	Steve Rintoul (205)
Oct. 9	Disney World/Olds Classic	Rick Fehr (269)	198,000	Fuzzy Zoeller (271)
Oct. 16	Texas Open	Bob Estes (265)	180,000	Gil Morgan (266)
Oct. 23	Las Vegas Invitational	Bruce Lietzke (332)	270,000	Robert Gamez (333)

Remaining Events (8): PGA Tour Championship (Oct. 27-30); Kapalua International (Nov. 3-6); PGA Grand Slam (Nov. 8-9); World Cup of Golf (Nov. 10-13); Shark Shootout (Nov. 17-20); Skins Game (Nov. 26-27); JC Penney Classic (Dec. 1-4); Diners Club Matches (Dec. 8-11).

European PGA Tour

Last Rd	Tournament	Winner	Earnings	Runner-Up
Oct. 3	Mercedes German Masters	Seve Ballesteros (270)*	£ 104,125	Ernie Els & J.M. Olazabal (270)
Oct. 16	Toyota World Match Play Championship	Ernie Els (4 & 2)	160,000	Colin Montgomerie
Oct. 23	Chemapol Trophy Czech Open	Per-Ulrik Johansson (237)	83,330	Klas Ericksson (240)

*Playoffs: **German Masters**—Ballesteros won on the 1st hole.
Remaining Events (3): Volvo Masters (Oct. 27-30); World Cup of Golf (Nov. 10-13); The Johnnie Walker World Championship (Dec. 15-18).

Seniors Tour

Last Rd	Tournament	Winner	Earnings	Runner-Up
Oct. 2	Vantage Championship	Larry Gilbert (198)	$ 22,500	Ray Floyd (199)
Oct. 9	The TransAmerica	Kermit Zarley (204)*	90,000	Isao Aoki (204)
Oct. 16	Raley's Senior Gold Rush	Bob Murphy (208)*	97,500	D. Eichelberger (208)
Oct. 23	Ralph's Senior Classic	Jack Kiefer (197)	112,500	Dale Douglass (198)

*Playoffs: **TransAmerica**—Zarley won on the 1st hole; Gold Rush-Murphy won on the 5th hole.
Remaining Events (4): Kaanapali Classic (Oct. 27-30); Shoot-Out Championship (Oct. 31-Nov. 1); Golf Magazine Tour Championship (Nov. 10-13); Diners Club Matches (Dec. 9-11).

LPGA

Last Rd	Tournament	Winner	Earnings	Runner-Up
Oct. 2	Heartland Classic	Liselotte Neumann (278)	$ 75,000	Elaine Crosby (281)
Oct. 16	World Championship of Golf	Beth Daniel (274)	105,000	Elaine Crosby (277)

Remaining Events (5): Nichirei International (Oct. 28-30); Toray Japan Queens Cup (Nov. 4-6); JC Penney Classic (Dec. 1-4); Diners Club Matches (Dec. 9-11); Wendy's Three-Tour Challenge (Dec. 17-18).

Team Competition
Dunhill Cup
at St. Andrews, Scotland (Oct. 6-9)

Semifinals (USA def. England, 3-0): Tom Kite (USA) def. Mark Roe (ENG), 69-70; Fred Couples (USA) def. Howard Clark (ENG), 68-74; Curtis Strange (USA) def. Barry Lane (ENG), 70-71.

Semifinals (Canada def. South Africa, 2-1): Ray Stewart (CAN) def. David Frost (SAF), 70-75; Rick Gibson (CAN) def. Wayne Westner (SAF), 70-74; Ernie Els (SAF) def. Dave Bahr (CAN), 68-72.

Final (Canada def. USA, 2-1): Dave Bahr (CAN) def. Tom Kite (USA), 70-71; Curtis Strange (USA) def. Rick Gibson (CAN), 67-74; Ray Stewart (CAN) def. Fred Couples (USA), 71-72.

Solheim Cup
at White Sulphur Springs, W. Va. (Oct. 20-23)
USA def. Europe, 13-7

Day One (foursomes): Dottie Mochrie & Brandie Burton (USA) def. Liselotte Neumann & Helen Alfredsson (EUR) 3 & 2; Annika Sorenstam & Catrin Nilsmark (EUR) def. Beth Daniel & Meg Mallon (USA) 1 up at 18th; Dale Reid & Lora Fairclough (EUR) def. Tammie Green & Kelly Robbins (USA) 2 & 1; Patty Sheehan & Sherri Steinhauer (USA) def. Pam Wright & Trish Johnson (EUR) 2 up at 18th. Europe leads 3-2.

Day Two (four-ball): Mochrie & Burton def. Davis & Alison Nicholas (EUR) 2 & 1; Daniel & Mallon def. Nilsmark & Sorenstam 6 & 5; Reid & Fairclough def. Green & Robbins 4 & 3; Donna Andrews & Betsy King (USA) def. Johnson & Wright 3 & 2; Neumann & Alfredsson def. Sheehan & Steinhauer 1 up at 18th. USA & Europe tied 5-5.

Day Three (singles): Alfredsson def. King 2 & 1; Mochrie def. Nilsmark 6 & 5; Daniel def. Johnson 2 up at 18th; Robbins def. Fairclough 4 & 2; Mallon def. Wright 1 up at 18th; Nicholas def. Sheehan 3 & 2; Burton def. Laura Davies (EUR) 2 up at 18th; Green def. Sorenstam 3 & 2; Steinhauer def. Reid 2 up at 18th; Andrews def. Neumann 3 & 2.

THOROUGHBRED RACING

Late 1994 Major Stakes Races

Date	Race	Location	Miles	Winner	Jockey	Purse
Oct. 1	Super Derby XV	La. Downs	$1\frac{1}{4}$	Soul of the Matter	Kent Desormeaux	$ 750,000
Oct. 2	L'Arc de Triomphe	Longchamp	$1\frac{1}{2}$ (T)	Carnegie	Thierry Jarnet	1,275,080
Oct. 8	Turf Classic	Belmont	$1\frac{1}{2}$ (T)	Tikkanen	Cash Asmussen	500,000
Oct. 8	Jockey Club Gold Cup	Belmont	$1\frac{1}{4}$	Colonial Affair	Jose Santos	750,000
Oct. 8	Champagne Stakes	Belmont	$1\frac{1}{16}$	Timber Country	Pat Day	500,000
Oct. 8	Frizzette Stakes	Belmont	$1\frac{1}{16}$	Flanders	Pat Day	250,000
Oct. 9	Oak Tree Invitational	Santa Anita	$1\frac{1}{2}$ (T)	Sandpit	Corey Nakatani	300,000
Oct. 14	Meadowlands Cup	Meadowlands	$1\frac{1}{8}$	Conveyor	Mike Smith	500,000
Oct. 15	My Dear Girl Stakes	Calder	$1\frac{1}{16}$	Fortune Pending	Jorge Velasquez	400,000
Oct. 15	In Reality Stakes	Calder	$1\frac{1}{16}$	Sea Emperor	Wigberto Ramos	400,000
Oct. 15	Wash. D.C. Int'l Mile	Laurel	$1\frac{1}{4}$ (T)	Paradise Creek	Pat Day	600,000
Oct. 15	Goodwood Handicap	Santa Anita	$1\frac{1}{8}$	Bertrando	Gary Stevens	200,000
Oct. 16	Rothmans International	Woodbine	$1\frac{1}{2}$ (T)	Raintrap	Robbie Davis	1,000,000
Oct. 16	Spinster Stakes	Keeneland	$1\frac{1}{8}$	Dispute	Pat Day	300,000

Remaining major events (7): Breeders' Cup at Churchill Downs (Nov. 5); Hollywood Derby Day (Nov. 20); HolidayFest Day (Nov. 26); Japan Cup (Nov. 27); Hollywood Turf Cup (Dec. 11); Hollywood Starlet Stakes (Dec. 17); Hollywood Futurity (Dec. 18).

HARNESS RACING

Late 1994 Major Stakes Races

Date	Race	Raceway	Winner	Driver	Purse
Oct. 7	Kentucky Futurity	The Red Mile	Bullville Victory	John Campbell	$ 89,485*
Oct. 15	BC Horse and Gelding Pace	Freehold Raceway	Village Jiffy	Paul MacDonell	334,000
Oct. 15	BC Mare Pace	Freehold Raceway	Shady Daisy	Michel Lachance	250,000
Oct. 15	BC Horse and Gelding Trot	Freehold Raceway	Pine Chip	John Campbell	300,000
Oct. 15	BC Mare Trot	Freehold Raceway	Ambro Keepsake	Stig Johansson	250,000
Oct. 21	BC 3-Yr-Old Colt Pace	Garden State Park	Magical Mike	Michel Lachance	400,000
Oct. 21	BC 3-Yr-Old Filly Pace	Garden State Park	Hardie Hanover	Tim Twaddle	325,000
Oct. 21	BC 3-Yr-Old Colt Trot	Garden State Park	Incredible Abe	Italo Tamborrino	400,000
Oct. 21	BC 3-Yr-Old Filly Trot	Garden State Park	Imageofa Clear Day	Bill O'Donnell	325,000

*Includes bonus purse for beating Victory Dream in race-off.
Remaining Events (5): BC 2-Yr-Old Colt Pace (Oct. 28); BC 2-Yr-Old Filly Trot (Oct. 28); Governor's Cup (Nov. 19); Gold Smith Maid (Nov. 24); Provincial Cup (Dec. 4).

AUTO RACING

Late 1994 Results

NASCAR

Date	Event	Location	Winner (Pos.)	Avg.mph	Earnings	Pole	Qual.mph
Oct. 23	AC Delco 500........Rockingham		Dale Earnhardt (20)	126.407	$60,600	R. Rudd	157.099

Winning Cars: Chevy Lumina
Remaining Races (2): Slick-50 500 (Oct. 30); Hooters 500 (Nov. 13)

Indy Car

Season ended Oct. 3rd. (see Auto Racing chapter)

Formula 1

Date	Event	Location	Winner (Pos.)	Time	Avg.mph	Pole	Qual.mph
Oct. 16	European GP......Jerez, Spain		Michael Schumacher (1)	1:40:26.289	113.43	M. Schumacher	119.664

Winning Constructors: Benneton-Ford
Remaining race (2): Japanese Grand Prix (Nov. 6); Australian Grand Prix (Nov. 13)

BOWLING

1994 Fall Tour Results

PBA

Final	Event	Winner	Earnings	Final	Runner-Up
Oct. 5	Dick Weber Classic	John Mazza	$60,000	216-183	Parker Bohn III
Oct. 12	Touring Players Champs.	Walter Ray Williams Jr.	16,000	259-206	Butch Soper
Oct. 19	Greater Detroit Open	Bryan Goebel	14,000	257-190	Eric Forkel
Oct. 26	Rochester Open	Norm Duke	16,000	216-190	Doug Kent

Remaining Events (3): Great Lakes PBA Classic (Oct. 29-Nov. 2); Brunswick Memorial World Open (Nov. 3-9); PBA/LPBT Merit Mixed Doubles (Dec. 8-11)

Seniors

Final	Event	Winner	Earnings	Final	Runner-Up
Sept. 20	Naples Senior Open	Barry Gurney	$10,000	255-225	Richard Beattie
Sept. 27	St. Pete/Clearwater PBA Open	Gary Dickinson	15,000	238-180	Bobby Knipple
Oct. 5	Palm Beach PBA Senior Classic	Larry Laub	8,000	247-233	Barry Gurney

Season completed

LPBT

Final	Event	Winner	Earnings	Final	Runner-Up
Oct. 9	PBAA Women's U.S. Open	Aleta Sill	$18000	229-170	Anne Marie Duggan
Oct. 13	Hammer Midwest Open	Kim Canady	13,500	213-167	Marianne DiRupo
Oct. 20	Brunswick Three Rivers Open	Kim Straub	13,500	265-216	Nikki Gianulias
Oct. 27	Columbia 300 Delaware Open	Aleta Sill	13,500	219-195	Tish Johnson

Remaining Events (4): Hammer Eastern Open (Oct. 29-Nov. 3); South Bend Open (Nov. 6-10); Sam's Town Invitational (Nov. 12-19); PBA/LPBT Merit Mixed Doubles (Dec. 8-11)

BOXING

Late 1994 Major Bouts

(from Oct. 2-22)

WBA, WBC and IBF champions are listed in **bold** type. Note the following Result column abbreviations: KO (knockout); TKO (technical knockout) Wu (won by unanimous decision).

Heavyweights

Date	Winner	Loser	Result	Title	Site
Oct. 1	Buster Mathis Jr.	Michael Faulkner	Wu 10	non-title	Boston
Oct. 22	John Carlo	Leon Spinks	KO 1	non-title	Washington, D.C.

Super Middleweights

Date	Winner	Loser	Result	Title	Site
Oct. 18	Roberto Duran	Heath Todd	TKO 6	non-title	Bay St. Louis, Miss.

Welterweights

Date	Winner	Loser	Result	Title	Site
Oct. 1	**Ike Quartey**	Alberto Cortes	TKO 5	**WBA**	Carpentras, FRA

Featherweights

Date	Winner	Loser	Result	Title	Site
Oct. 22	**Tom Johnson**	Francisco Segura	Wu 12	**IBF**	Atlantic City

Junior Bantamweights

Date	Winner	Loser	Result	Title	Site
Oct. 13	Johnny Tapia	Henry Martinez	TKO 11	(vacant WBO)	Albuquerque

Phil Coale

Football coaches **Bobby** and **Terry Bowden** achieved a unique, father-son double in 1993-94, Bobby won a national championship and Terry went undefeated.

THE SWEET SIXTEEN

Top Personalities of the Year
by Bob Ley

What, you may ask, was so sweet about a year when Baseball bit down on a cyanide pill, and Hockey sipped hemlock? The editors of *The Sports Almanac* can find sweetness and light anywhere. This year was the acid test. Any exclusive group finds others in the ante-room, anxiously awaiting word. Be advised Ken Burns got a long look, as the only purveyor of baseball in September. Bruce McNall's precipitous fall from NHL Board of Governors president to Federal defendant-to-be was breathtaking. And Nolan Richardson's use of the Final Four bully pulpit stirred the mind.

The Sports Almanac Sweet Sixteen includes an entire country (not America) and a non-sportsman from a country (not America) who displays the sort of cheek we used to admire in the State. There are a pair of entries: two men linked by blood, and two women linked by a blood feud. Our sole repeater from last year is Michael Jordan. But then, he has a way of doing things singularly. That's the quality which got all these folks past the doorman.

The Sports Almanac Sweet 16
(in alphabetical order)

Bonnie Blair	Nancy Kerrigan & Tonya Harding	Nick Price
The Bowdens	Don King	O.J. Simpson
Brazil	Mark Messier	Emmitt Smith
Miguel Indurain	Rupert Murdoch	Tiger Woods
Michael Jordan	Martina Navratilova	The U.S. Sports Fan
	Hakeem Olajuwon	

Bob Ley is the principal reporter for ESPN's Emmy Award-winning "Outside The Lines" series and has been a SportsCenter anchor since the sports cable network started in 1979.

Bonnie Blair

Bonnie Blair's abilities and spirits define this sport which only sporadically captures our fancy. In Lillehammer, she wrote American history.

Blair's Gold at 500 meters was her third consecutive at that distance. Four days later she embellished that with a 1,000-meter Gold, passing Eric Heiden as the all-time winningest U.S. Winter Olympian, with six medals. For good measure, a month later, Blair broke her 500-meter world record once again.

The Bowdens

Bobby's national title quest was finally realized in the Orange Bowl, with Florida State's win over Nebraska. By summer, tales of sports agents' dealings with FSU players had stripped much of the luster from that title.

Terry called his father at halftime from Gainesville, Oct. 15. "Don't change a thing," advised Bobby. And Auburn went on to beat #1 Florida, forcing consideration of Terry's probationary Auburn team to succeed his father's as champion.

Tom Knutsen

Brazil

No nation knew the extremes of grief and exultation, as did Brazil. Millions of Brazilians wept after Ayrton Senna's fatal crash in San Marino, May 1st. The funeral for the three-time F-1 World Driving champion surpassed that of any head of state.

Two months later, moments after the Brazilian team outlasted Italy in the World Cup final, the team unfurled a banner on the steamy floor of the Rose Bowl, dedicating its global victory to Senna's memory.

Gerald Vandystadt

Miguel Indurain

So dominant is Miguel Indurain that nine months before the 1995 Tour De France, his competitors considered the new schedule of stages and disciplines. The question for them became, who will finish second to Spain's "Big Mig?"

Indurain won his fourth straight Tour without winning any single stage. He took the leader's yellow jersey on the 9th stage, and never gave it up. He attempts this year to be the fourth man to win five Tours, but the first to do it consecutively.

Birmingham Barons

Michael Jordan

The purists had the first word, denouncing his quixotic spring training. By summer's end, Michael Jordan's baseball was not only the purest form; for many people, it was all they had left.

Jordan wanted so badly to finish over the "Mendoza Line." A .300 push the final three weeks lifted his first Double A year to a .202 average. The largest irony came July 30th when he finally went deep. Only a tourist's video camera captured Jordan's first professional home run.

UPI/Bettmann

Don King

His mantra is "Only in America", and Don King's Yankee ingenuity continued to astound. A 63-year-old promoter, newly-indicted on Federal insurance fraud charges (King pleaded innocent) should be on the ropes.

But Oliver McCall's WBC upset put King back in the heavyweight picture. Julio Cesar Chavez remains a lucrative commodity. And King awaits the springtime prison release of the man who may yet make him his greatest fortune: Mike Tyson.

Bruce Bennett Studios

Mark Messier

Neither his name on the Stanley Cup nor the "C" on his jersey were new. But Mark Messier's New York Rangers' season brought new dimension to those experiences, as he led the exorcism of 54 years of demons.

The numbers say 30 points in 23 playoff games. The mind recalls Messier's Namath-like guarantee of victory in Game 6 of the Eastern Finals against New Jersey. Messier not only delivered, he made good with a third-period hat trick.

Fox Broadcasting Co.

Rupert Murdoch

Crazy like a Fox? The father of the newest network spent often and well to acquire rights to the NFL and the NHL, and make a run at Wimbledon. Rupert Murdoch's characteristic boldness was etched in each of the $1.58 billion he paid to outbid CBS for his football deal.

It was a strategy to boost the Fox Network. But, for the first time in 15 years NBC's AFC games outrated the NFC and Fox Sunday's primetime ratings were down over 10 percent.

Wide World Photos

Nancy & Tonya

It was tabloid warmup for O.J. From Nancy Kerrigan's assault on Jan. 6 to March 16 when Tonya Harding pleaded guilty, America reveled in the lurid desire and bizarre turns of a story that included everything from nude photos to a perceived slight of Mickey Mouse.

If there was poetic justice in Harding's 8th place Lillehammer showing, what to make of Kerrigan's silver medal 'defeat'? The rest of the world celebrated the young champion Oksana Baiul.

Reuters/Bettmann

Martina Navratilova

"The only good thing about Communism," observed Martina Navratilova, "was that it rewarded female athletes as well as the men." Her rewards in this land would total 167 career titles, and universal respect as the best women's player of all-time.

Forever synonymous with Wimbledon, she reached the final in '94 only to lose in three sets. Before leaving, Navratilova stooped for a keepsake pinch of Center Court grass. Her legend continues to grow.

Houston Rockets

Hakeem Olajuwon

'Dignity' and 'stature' demand inclusion in any description of Hakeem Olajuwon. No one works harder in the NBA. Yet the truest measure of stature in this league is a championship ring.

In a season of personal vindication and celebration, Olajuwon scored a personal best 27.3 ppg, increased that in the post season, and won both the regular season and playoff MVP's. But most importantly, he has the ring to prove he is a champion of his game.

PGA Tour

Nick Price

Perhaps most decisively among all athletes, Nick Price stands as the best in his profession. He won two majors in '94: his second PGA championship, and his first British Open. He also won the Honda Classic, Colonial, Western Open and Canadian Open all before mid-September. There was no competition, as in 1993, for PGA Player of the Year.

Golf 's many variables reduce expectations to vague hopes. Price elevated that hope to near certainty.

Reuters/Bettmann

O.J. Simpson

Style and speed. From his 1968 Heisman Trophy, to an NFL career that included 5 Pro Bowls and a single-season rushing record, O.J. Simpson's public life encompassed those qualities.

A month short of his 47th birthday, Simpson's sports celebrity and media personality became the instruments of his passage to a singular place in American culture. Almost incidental was the question of his innocence or guilt, in the murder of his ex-wife and her friend.

Dallas Cowboys

Emmitt Smith

There are backs who run well, but only one is vital for the two-time SuperBowl champions. Emmitt Smith sat out the first two games of the '93 season, yet still won his third straight NFL rushing title.

Smith was the Super Bowl MVP, with 132 yards and 2 TDs. But the day of legend was the final regular season game. Against the Giants, Smith stayed in the game with a separated shoulder, ran for 168 yards, and sealed Dallas' home field advantage for the playoffs.

Clive Mason/Allsport

Tiger Woods

Don't pigeonhole Tiger Woods as a rare black golf star. He is that other rare commodity: a fresh American golf prodigy. His skills have met every expectation and then some.

Woods came from six strokes back Aug. 28 to win the U.S. Amateur championship at the age of 18, the youngest champion in the 94 years of the event. Later, he interrupted his freshman year at Stanford to help the U.S. team win the World Amateur Team Championship in France.

Wide World Photos

U.S. Sports Fan

Battered but brave describes the U.S. sports fan, teased by a remarkable 1993. On the heels of record years at the gate in baseball and hockey, both sports smacked Everyfan in the face. No World Series, and a less than full NHL 1994-95 regular season.

But his finest hour came in the World Cup, when the rest of the world couldn't believe its eyes. U.S. fans comprised the largest part of the record 3.6 million who turned a soccer ticket into a hot property.

Also Receiving Votes
(In alphabetical order)

Andre Agassi (tennis)
Troy Aikman (football)
Roberto Baggio (soccer)
Jeff Bagwell (baseball)
Gary Bettman (hockey)
Ken Burns (TV and radio)
Leroy Burrell (track and field)
Andres Cantor (TV and radio)
Juilo Cesar Chavez (boxing)
Bjorn Dahlie (skiing)
Dominique Dawes (gymnastics)
Manuela Di Centa (skiing)
Dale Earnhardt (auto racing)

Luybov Egorova (skiing)
Sergei Fedorov (hockey)
Donald Fehr (baseball)
Wayne Gretzky (hockey)
Tony Gwynn (baseball)
Dan Jansen (speed skating)
Le Jingyi (swimming)
Mike Keenan (hockey)
Johann Olav Koss (speed skating)
Julie Krone (horse racing)
Alexi Lalas (soccer)
John Madden (TV and radio)
Greg Maddux (baseball)

Oliver McCall (boxing)
Bruce McNall (hockey)
Shannon Miller (gymnastics)
Tommy Moe (skiing)
Ty Murray (rodeo)
Paula Newby-Fraser (triathlon)
Roger Penske (auto racing)
Uta Pippig (marathon)
Jerry Rice (football)
Nolan Richardson (basketball)
Glenn Robinson (basketball)
Romario (soccer)
Alan Rothenberg (soccer)

Pete Sampras (tennis)
Arantxa Sanchez Vicario (tennis)
Vreni Schneider (skiing)
Michael Schumacher (auto racing)
Bud Selig (baseball)
Pat Smith (wrestling)
Frank Thomas (baseball)
James Toney (boxing)
U.S. Solheim Cup team (golf)
Al Unser Jr. (auto racing)
Erick Walder (track and field)
Pernell Whitaker (boxing)
Corliss Williamson (basketball)

Mike Luckovich

THE YEAR IN REVIEW

Soap Opera

What else can you call a year plagued by murder, mayhem, a strike, a lockout and more grim lawyers than happy fans?

One spring day a goose flew over a driving range in Lakeville, Mass., spotted a pile of golf balls in a bin, landed and tried to hatch the balls.

After two weeks under warm feathers, the balls had not even begun to hatch, so the silly goose saw the handwriting on the wall ("Titleist") and flew off to get a life. But not before being named the year's MVP, Most Vexed Poultry, the very symbol of sports in 1994, a year in which many of our silly-goose heroes sat on their balls, and bats, and pucks, and in courtrooms and conference rooms. It was The Year of the Suit—ballplayers in ties sitting with grim attorneys and waiting for nothing to happen.

Not that there weren't glorious battles! Looking back years from now, or maybe next week, we will blink a tear when we recall baseball's Battle of the Wallet Bulge, where snippy words and economic gibberish flew back and forth between players and owners like spit-wads, only less effective....And the raw courage of Tonya Harding, skating in the Olympics despite the handicap of her rival having two healthy legs....And O.J. Simpson, crawling to daylight behind a phalanx of lawyers who opened loopholes and knocked down evidence, like the Electric Company of the '70s, trying to spring loose the Juice.

Through it all, the suits and sitters remained unmoved. The only visible tears were those of Marlins' second baseman Brett Barberie, who cried like a baby when he ate some jalapeño peppers with his fingers, then put in his contact lenses. Lave sus manos, dude!

Fortunately, a significant number of sportsmen and sportswomen clung to the quaint belief that the show must go on. Thus we had the best Winter Olympics ever, the happiest World Cup ever, and fun-filled NFL and NBA seasons with hardly any strike/lockout grumbling/rumbling.

It was a vintage year for MVPs Hakeem Olajuwon and Emmitt Smith, surging vets Nick Price and Andre Agassi, warhorses Martina Navratilova and Wayne Gretzky, and inspirational comebackers Paul Azinger and Ernie Irvan.

The folks who played the games, though, played second fiddle to the three major mysteries that remained unsolved as we tried to slam the door on '94:

First, who killed baseball—the players or the owners? "I don't know who is right," Harry Caray said, "but they're both wrong." Second, did Harding mastermind (we use the word very advisedly) the attack on Nancy Kerrigan? And third, was O.J. involved in the gruesome murder of his ex-wife and her friend, or is he just a messy shaver?

We do have a motive in the first two crimes: Money. Baseball choked to death

Scott Ostler is a sports columnist for the *San Francisco Chronicle.*

Mike Luckovich is the editorial cartoonist for the *Atlanta Constitution.*

O.J. Simpson (right) in a Los Angeles courtroom with attorney **Robert Shapiro**, during a preliminary hearing leading up to his September trial for the double murder of ex-wife Nicole Brown Simpson and her friend Ronald Goldman.

on it, crushed beneath the sheer weight of its own profits. And Harding's pals wanted Kerrigan out of the way so Tonya could cash in by endorsing products, like maybe cigarettes and billiard cues.

Baseball was great while it lasted. On opening day in Chicago, Hillary Clinton and Harry Caray sang "Take Me Out to the Ballgame," rekindling memories of Sonny and Cher.

And when the year's first sacrifice bunt went for a double in the gap, we knew we were dealing with baseballs that had more bounce and pep than the Dallas Cowboy cheerleaders. Baseball's leaders swore the '94 balls were not juiced, but you were better off heeding Sparky Anderson, who warned, "Don't take a baseball to bed with you. It will keep you up all night."

Matt Williams, Junior Griffey, Frank Thomas and other boppers kept baseballs up in the air all night, and were on pace to erase all the old slugging records.

Then: Cloutus interruptus, as one scribe called the walkout. The only positive glimmer from the situation was the hope it offered for universal peace, if somehow negotiators Richard Ravitch (owners) and Donald Fehr (players) could be placed in command of the world's generals and soldiers, respectively.

In "Baseball," the epic Ken Burns documentary, Ty Cobb says (through a narrator) that baseball is a tough game, and "mollycoddles had better stay out!" Seventy years later the Georgia Peach's warning was heeded. The mollycoddles walked out and stayed out, falling back on a strike kitty of $200 million.

The players drummed up some public sympathy, though not enough to cork a bat. Detroit infielder Lou Whitaker arrived at a union meeting in a stretch limo, raised his palms and said, "I'm rich. What am I supposed to do, hide it?" Many helpful fans were quick to suggest a place Lou and his pals could shove their bankrolls.

As greed-stricken as the players appeared, it was the owners, specifically the small-market-team owners, who strangled the goose that layed the $2 billion-a-year egg (no relation to the golf-ball-sitting goose). The owners refused to open their books, yet demanded protection from the real world. And when they couldn't extort it, they shut down the World Series. A bitter fan noted that even Hitler hadn't been able to stop the Fall Classic.

"The strike is like a death in the family," Dodger pitcher Orel Hershiser said.

Not quite, because dead men don't wear plaid, as players and owners were doing in the late summer and fall on golf courses.

Hockey had the same problem as baseball: Plenty of money for everyone, but no way to spread it around to everyone's satisfaction. The game was like Little Jack Horner's pie, and everyone had a thumb the size of a goaltender's catching glove. The NHL had a great 1993-94 season, with the lowly San Jose Sharks making a plucky run at the title and the New York Rangers breaking an ancient curse by winning the Stanley Cup. The last time the Rangers ruled the NHL was 1940, when the Cup was so small that it came with a Stanley Saucer.

But the start of the 1994-95 season was delayed when the owners, shrewdly electing not to cash in on baseball's absence, locked out the players.

Strike fever almost trickled down to kiddie baseball at the Little League World Series in Williamsport. Northridge, Calif., parents were angry at their lousy ticket locations and briefly threatened to hold their boys out of the championship game.

"I'm morally opposed to capital punishment," one sportswriter said, "but had those parents carried out their threat, I would have been forced to re-think my stand."

Gee, the seasons keep getting longer, and in '94 the overlapping was more dramatic than ever. The baseball strike season spilled over into the O.J. Simpson trial season, and both threatened to go on forever.

Los Angeles police sought to arrest Simpson in connection with the double murder of his ex-wife Nicole and her friend,

Ronald Goldman. But when the cops closed in on O.J., he audiblized and ran out a back door, leaving behind what looked like a suicide note.

The police finally caught up with O.J. on an L.A. freeway. His pal Al Cowlings was driving and Simpson had a gun, and if someone had been quick enough to sell tickets along the freeway route, or offer the chase on pay-per-view TV, they would have been right in sync with the spirit of commercial exploitation that pervaded the year.

The surrealistic low-speed chase lasted two hours and fans dashed to fences and overpasses to gawk, wave and hold up "Run, Juice, Run!" signs, as Los Angeles lurched one step closer to breaking off from Planet Earth. Finally O.J. surrendered, after first stopping at his Brentwood home for a glass of orange juice. No doubt Simpson realized that the cops' patience might have snapped had Cowlings driven him through a Jack-in-the-Box.

The body of evidence that piled up against O.J. was balanced by botched police work and crime-lab testing. To find field work this sloppy, you'd have to go back three decades to Marv Throneberry, although Throneberry at least had a hazy notion of what to do when he found a glove.

Behind bars awaiting trial, O.J. got busy. He signed and dated 2,500 trading cards, and helped design a bronze bust of himself to be sold for $3,395 a copy. His popularity rating soared to an all-time high in opinion polls, he got named to the NFL's all-time team, and he began assembling his own all-star team of attorneys, which marched into court and challenged everything but the infield fly rule.

"O.J. hired a fifth lawyer today," David Letterman noted. "He's going to the nickel defense."

But it was no joke that one of America's all-time athletic heroes was either a psychopathic killer with no remorse, or had been brilliantly framed by a murderer still on the loose.

The daily barrage of ugly O.J. updates and revelations made sports fans yearn for the sweet, innocent days of the previous winter, when the worst imaginable sports-related crime was the blackjack attack on Nancy Kerrigan at the U.S. Figure Skating Championships in Detroit.

Kerrigan recovered and skated in the

Baseball owners' negotiator **Richard Ravitch** (left) and players' union executive director **Donald Fehr** during a joint appearance on NBC's "Meet the Press," a week before the players went out on strike Aug. 12.

Olympics, but left unresolved was the question of whether Tonya Harding, the chain-smoking, pool-shooting ice babe from Oregon, had approved of the plot, as a grand jury decided she had. Tonya pled guilty to a minor charge of obstructing an investigation, sounding like a Hallmark greeting card when she said, "I'm sorry I interfered."

Even sorrier was Harding's gang: Boyfriend and ex-hubby Jeff (The Stoolie) Gillooly, who tried to rat on Tonya; porky motormouth Shawn Eckardt, who could botch an escape from a phone booth; and blackjack swinger Shane Stant, who wanted sympathy because he hadn't broken any of Kerrigan's bones. The boys added getaway driver Derrick Smith to the mix mainly to avoid charges of blatantly ripping off the Three Stooges.

Whatever damage Skategate did to the collective American psyche, it was a roaring commercial success. Tonya sold TV, book and movie rights. Kerrigan sold trading cards and her diary, and cavorted at Disney World with Mickey Mouse. Stant and Eckardt got a 900 phone number and sold t-shirts and replicas of their blackjack. And loverboy Gillooly launched a career selling naked photos and videos of Tonya.

What could be stupider than the crime? How about the U.S. Olympic Committee's clumsy attempt to ban Harding from the Games despite the lack of smoking-gun evidence to link her to the attack? Tonya's lawyers swatted aside the USOC's flimsy roadblock and Tonya went to Norway, where her presence threatened to turn one of the world's most dignified sporting events into a two-week version of "Hard Copy Meets Oprah Winfrey."

One Norwegian newsperson said of the American media's feverish blanket coverage of Nancy & Tonya, "You people are boiling the same potato every day."

Wrong. The media were also baking, hash-browning, french-frying and au gratin-ing the same potato. But the craziest thing happened: American TV viewers couldn't get enough of Nancy and Tonya.

They saw Kerrigan finish second (silver) and Tonya finish eighth (pig iron), then stayed to watch the rest of the show—creating record TV ratings for the entire Olympics.

"We like the story," a Norwegian news bureau chief said of Skategate. "We see it as an American soap opera. And it has increased awareness of the Games."

The Games were worthy of the attention. In fact, they were incandescent. Every athlete seemed to have brought a dramatic story and a clutch performance and jaded journalists got goose-bumps even in well-heated arenas. Prices in town were high, but so were the hospitality and spirit of the Norwegians. They were stunningly gracious hosts and had a dandy time themselves—cheering every nation's athletes and swooning over their own Norse gods, like speed skater Johan Olav Koss. Koss, who made Huck Finn look like Johnny Depp, won three golds and signed over his huge bonus check to war relief efforts in Sarajevo.

The Norwegians also fell in love with American speed skaters Bonnie Blair and Dan Jansen, who closed out their careers with gold medals to highlight a surprisingly strong U.S. showing in the Games.

Say this for '94: It was a year that knew how to throw a world party.

When the United States was awarded the '94 World Cup, there were only two fears: That visiting English hooligans would pillage and raze every major city, and that Americans would react to great soccer with the kind of enthusiasm usually reserved for great rutabaga.

Not to worry. The English team failed to qualify, making America a lout-free zone. And U.S. sports fans, despite only a vague grasp of the game, jam-packed the huge stadiums and were swept up in the intensity and joy. The final game was a showdown between superpowers Brazil and Italy, resulting in a scoreless tie that led to a sudden-death penalty kickoff. It became Italian superstar Roberto Baggio's Cup to win or lose and his kick missed. The streets of Rio are still rocking in celebration and Cup officials are still counting the gate receipts.

But even the World Cup had a tragedy. Columbian fullback Andres Escobar accidentally scored a goal for the Americans, and his team lost, 2-1. Soon after he

Air Jordan Decides To Take The Bus

Minor league baseball, for Michael Jordan, was strictly BYOB— buy your own bus.

When Jordan decided to try his hand at pro baseball, and was assigned to the Chicago White Sox' Birmingham farm team, he took one look at the Barons' clunky bus and said, "Do I have to ride that?"

"No," said Michael's accountant.

So Jordan bought the Barons a new bus. Actually he paid the difference between the lease cost of the old bus and the lease cost of a bus the Rolling Stones would have been proud to tour in. It had rocker seats, a superb VCR/stereo setup, a wet bar and lounge.

Cynics sneered that the bus helped Jordan cement a spot in the starting lineup. For sure he was never going to be a Phil Linz, the Yankees' infielder who was kicked off the team bus by manager Yogi Berra in 1964 for playing "Mary Had a Little Lamb" on a harmonica after a tough loss. If Jordan wanted to play "A Hundred Bottles of Beer on the Wall" on a tuba, the rest of the Barons would sing along.

It turned out that Jordan had more to offer the Barons and baseball than a bus, and this would come as a surprise to the many cynics (them again). When Air Jordan, who had retired from basketball after the '92-'93 season, showed up at the White Sox major league spring training camp, the reaction ranged from disbelief to outright anger.

"Bag It, Michael!" screamed *Sports Illustrated* on its cover, over a photo of Jordan whiffing awkwardly. "Jordan and The White Sox Are Embarrassing Baseball."

Some saw Michael as a shoddy version of the Famous Chicken, a novelty act to boost minor-league ticket sales. But he worked hard and kept cool, even when opposing pitchers would strike him out, then ask him to autograph the ball.

"I'm mature, I'm 31 and I can accept failure," Jordan said.

But not without a fight, which included extra batting practice and fielding work every day, and a complete involvement with his teammates and the game.

When the season was over, Barons' manager Terry Francona said, "Even if he quits tomorrow, this will not have been a hoax. By

Wide World Photos

While he may not have hit much more than his weight with Double-A Birmingham, **Michael Jordan** proved he could play.

the end of the year, he was a baseball player."

Other managers were also impressed, pointing out that Jordan showed an enthusiasm for the game and a willingness to work that few younger players could begin to match.

"His intensity is unbelievable," said Dave Trembley of the Orlando Cubs. "I wish every one of my guys played as hard as he did. He's a professional."

Sports Illustrated even ate a sliver of humble pie with a tiny story headlined, "He Made the Grade."

Jordan hit .202, just under his weight of 205 pounds, in the Class AA Southern League. He had 51 RBIs and 30 steals (fifth in the league), one of only six players in all of Double-A ball in the 50-30 Club. He heated up in August, hitting .260 with 12 RBIs, and only two of his 11 outfield errors came in the second half of the season. And everywhere he went people wanted to watch him play. Lots of people. The Southern League never saw such big crowds. The Barons, who ranked a respectable third in attendance in 1993 with

277,096 paying customers, saw their turnstiles buckle against the waistlines of a league record 467,867 fans in '94.

Jordan went 353 at-bats without hitting a home run, then went on a power binge, hitting three round-trippers in his last 83 at-bats. He seemed to be getting the idea.

And when the season was over, Jordan headed West to suit up with the Scottsdale Scorpions of the Arizona Fall League, vowing to learn to hit the slider.

Through it all, Michael put basketball behind him, sort of. He rooted for his old Chicago Bulls teammates during the playoffs, even though they had greeted his retirement with something approaching glee.

It turned out that Scottie Pippen and Horace Grant could carry Jordan's jock. They just couldn't wear it. Lacking the ultimate go-to guy, the Bulls were knocked out of the playoffs by the Knicks, and Jordan, fed up with the junk he kept hearing, finally exploded.

"I covered their asses when they got tight at the end of games," Jordan seethed, "and I had to overcome fourth quarter deficits all by myself. It bothered my father a lot, just as it bothers me, to hear them bitching about not geting enough credit or not getting enough shots, or squawking about the supposed preferential treatment I was getting from (coach) Phil (Jackson)."

Jordan swore he would never return to the NBA, although in June he bragged, "I think I could go out in a week's [practice] time and be in regular-season form. Say it this way: I think I could get my average [32.3 ppg, career]."

There was even talk of Jordan and his `92 Olympics Dream Team teammates coming back to play Dream Team II in a grudge match. The young-uns were popping off about how good they were and Jordan finally said, "If they think they could beat us, they are dreaming."

And Reggie Miller shot back, "Michael really means that, just like he meant it when he said he could hit .300."

Good line, but Reggie and the boys of Dream Team Lite wouldn't have wanted any of Baseball Mike. Jordan kept his shooting eye sharp by playing Nerf basketball in a clubhouse trash can with the Barons' bat boys. Then he did return to basketball one night, on Sept. 9, closing down Chicago Stadium forever in an exhibition game.

Fifty-two points and several soaring dunks later, Jordan waved and headed right back to baseball. Who wants to play in the NBA and ride those rickety busses?

Tonya Harding stands in court with her attorney **Bob Weaver** after pleading guilty to a conspiracy charge in the Jan. 6 attack on rival Nancy Kerrigan.

returned to his home town of Medellín, he was murdered by an unknown gunman.

American athletes didn't quite master soccer, but did continue to own basketball, as demonstrated drearily at the World Basketball Championships in Toronto. The U.S. team won the gold medal, but came in dead last in the Mr. Congeniality competition. Players on Dream Team Lite trash-talked, taunted and ridiculed overmatched opponents.

"I don't like it, but I can't control it," said U.S. coach Don Nelson.

Other teams had even uglier years than the Dreamers, including the Buffalo Bills, who four-peated as losers of the Super Bowl. The Dallas Cowboys won their second straight title, proving they can walk the walk and talk the talk, but the Bills still can't walk the walk while they chew the gum. "We weren't able to capitalize," Bills' QB Jim Kelly explained. No lie. When it comes to the Super Bowl, the Bills have more trouble capitalizing than e.e. cummings.

The U.S. Olympic bobsled team was disqualified for heating its sled runners. One rumor pegged the problem to a pre-race mix-up. Seeking inspiration, the team was to watch "Cool Runnings," but accidently saw "Chariots of Fire."

Florida State copped its first national football title by defeating Nebraska in the Orange Bowl. But the Seminoles never met a law or NCAA guideline they couldn't break. Their last shred of dignity fled with the news that nine players took part in a frenzied, agent-financed shopping spree in a Foot Locker store. Florida coach Steve Spurrier couldn't resist referring to FSU as Free Shoes University.

Meanwhile, the sports world seemed to seek a cosmic balance. In golf, John Daly left to get his head straight and Paul Azinger returned, having fought off cancer; Arnold Palmer played in his last U.S. Open, while teen phenom Tiger Woods qualified for his first by winning the U.S. Amateur. In tennis, Martina Navratilova bowed out and 14-year-old Martina Hingus arrived.

Elsewhere, Jimmy Johnson tired of bickering with Cowboys' owner Jerry Jones and got out of coaching, while Buddy Ryan tired of not bickering and slugged his way back to a head coaching job. Former bad-boy Andre Agassi made a comeback, winning the U.S. Open, while former teen queen Jennifer Capriati was rounded up in a cheap hotel drug bust and steered to rehab. And Wayne Gretzky broke Gordie Howe's career goals record, but Kings' team owner Bruce McNall was implicated in a massive illegal bank-loan scheme.

Nothing, however, could fill the void made by the retirement of the Super Mario Brothers—auto racing's Andretti and hockey's Lemieux. Andretti got out of Indy-car racing before he became broken down and Lemieux took an indefinite leave from hockey because he was broken down.

And no amount of good news could ease the grief after the deaths of racing ace Ayrton Senna and former tennis champ Vitas Gerulaitis.

Looking back on '94, we didn't know whether to laugh or cry. We were like Karch Kiraly, the famed volleyball player. He and his doubles partner won a major beach tournament then Karch tripped and tumbled off the awards platform, thus becoming the first athlete ever to punctuate a victory by spiking himself.

At least he didn't just sit there. ❐

Wide World Photos

TOP OF THE WORLD, MA!
Hometown heavyweight **Mahmut Demir** exults as he sits atop a vanquished **Bruce Baumgartner** after defeating the American in the World Freestyle Wrestling Championships in Istanbul in August.

EXTRA POINTS

EXTRA POINTS
by Charles A. Monagan

Wide World Photos

Wide World Photos

MAKEOUT ARTISTS OF THE YEAR
Chicago Cubs broadcaster **Harry Carey** (left) gives First Lady Hillary Rodham Clinton a big kiss on Opening Day at Wrigley Field, while tennis star **Andre Agassi** smooches his reflection in the winner's trophy after capturing his first U.S. Open.

ON THE REBOUND
Denver Nuggets center Dikembe Mutombo not only popped the question to Michelle Roberts, but then presented her with a prenuptial agreement that stipulated she bear him a child within two years, return to work four months after the baby is born—and also forget about alimony or child support should she and Mutombo divorce. And that was the end of that romance.

GREAT BY ANY NAME
Thai junior bantamweight champ Samson Elitegym got his last name from the gym where he trains in Bangkok. His real name? Saenmuangnoi Lookchaopormahesak.

While we're at it, three players on the basketball team for Rice High in New York City were named Angel Ponce de Leon, Souvenir Callwood and the improbable Scientific Mapp.

And how about one more—rising Israeli tennis star Anna Smashnova.

Charles A. Monagan has been the editor of *Connecticut* magazine since 1989.

FISH THE RAFT
At least one group of Floridians was happy to see the boatloads of refugees headed their way from Cuba. Fishermen discovered that good fish were to be found lurking in the shadows beneath the jerry-built rafts. "If you see a Cuban raft, the first thing you do is fish the raft," said Steve Hartman, owner of a marina in Key Largo. "That's where you find the dolphin and the tuna."

LOSING IT
Now that the New York Rangers have brought home the NHL's Stanley Cup after 54 years of wandering in the hockey wilderness, let's update the major league teams with the longest dry spells between league championships. In baseball: the Chicago Cubs (1908) in the NL and the Chicago White Sox (1917) in the AL. In football: the Chicago-St. Louis-Phoenix-Arizona Cardinals (1947). In basketball: the Rochester-Cincinnati-Kansas City-Omaha-Sacramento Royals-Kings (1951). And in hockey: the Detroit Red Wings (1955).

QUOTES OF THE YEAR, PART I

"I loved *Candide*. That was also about the world and how you start up one thing and end up another, 'cause the world don't let you do the right thing most of the time."

> —Mike Tyson, on one of the books he's read while serving prison time for his rape conviction.

"It's youth. But that youth thing gets old after a while."

> —San Francisco Giants pitching coach Dick Pole, on the troubles of 22-year-old Salomon Torres.

"I guess it was just a matter of time before she grew tired of picking up guys one at a time."

> —David Letterman, on Madonna's stated intention to buy an NBA franchise.

"I resent being tabbed as greedy. I could handle dumb."

> —Detroit Tigers owner Mike Illitch, during the baseball strike.

"I'd probably be in the middle. I'm not wack, but I'm not on the level with Heavy D. . . . I'm okay. I ain't wack. I have rhythm. I sound okay. All my beats are dope. I'm okay. I'm just glad I'm not wack."

> —Shaquille O'Neal, rating himself as a rap singer.

Wide World Photos   PGA Tour

Shaquille O'Neal   Ray Floyd

"Well, it is outdoors, I'll say that for it."

> —Golf pro Ray Floyd, when asked to comment on the new Jack Nicklaus layout at Desert Mountain.

"At the moment, my best surface is my bed."

> —Slumping tennis star Jim Courier, before dropping off the circuit.

HEY, JIM KELLY! SHOW US HOW MANY SUPER BOWLS RINGS YOU HAVE!

Wide World Photos

BIRD IN THE BUSH

Following the weird tradition of Texas politicians, gubernatorial aspirant George W. Bush was out at dawn on the first day of dove hunting season, looking to bag himself a bird—and some publicity in the Texas press. After firing seven times, Bush did kill a bird, but the publicity wasn't the kind he wanted. He shot a killdeer, a Texas songbird whose killing is a crime under state law, punishable by a fine up to $500. After paying his fine, Bush said simply, "I thought it was a dove."

TELLING IT LIKE IT IS

All but one minute of Michael Moorer's victory over Evander Holyfield was shown on HBO. The missing 60 seconds? The segment in which color commentator George Foreman implied promoter Dan Duva had fixed the fight. "It's not based on any fact, and we're journalists here," said HBO executive producer and vice president Ross Greenburg.

THE YEAR IN GOLF

Noted low-handicapper Jack Nicholson used his overlapping grip and a two-iron to smash the windshield and dent the roof of a Mercedes that had cut him off in traffic.

Presidential aide David Watkins was fired after comandeering the White House helicopter to fly out for a quick 18 holes on a course in Frederick, Md.

And the round of the year for a pro belonged to Swede Anders Forsbrand who had to withdraw from the French Open after running out of golf balls during the second round. Standing on the 18th tee with his score already at 93, he hit his last two balls (pros are allowed "only" nine per round) into the water and walked off the course. His bogey count? One sextuple, a quintuple, two quadruples, a triple, a double and three regular old bogeys.

THE FACES OF SPORT, 1994

Wide World Photos

Wide World Photos

Allsport

Humorless baseball union boss **Donald Fehr** (left), and trash talkin' Knicks' fan **Spike Lee**.

Wide World Photos

Bettmann Archive

Hockey defenseman **Mathieu Schneider** (left) and pro football's **Red Grange** (you want throwbacks to the old days? To begin with, take off the face masks).

YOU ARE CORRECT, SIR

President Clinton set the pace for political correctness on Opening Day in Cleveland, when he wore an Indians cap without the controversial Chief Wahoo logo. The trend continued at the University of Iowa, where American Indian mascots were banned, at Marquette, where the Warriors became the Golden Eagles, and at St. John's, where the Redmen became the Red Storm.

Maybe the trend should continue on to schools with obviously sexist nicknames, such as:

SCHOOL	NICKNAME
Centenary	Gentleman
Fairfield	Stags
Illinois College	Blueboys
Massachusetts	Minutemen
Navy	Midshipmen
Oberlin	Yeomen
Ohio Wesleyan	Battling Bishops
Providence	Friars
Syracuse	Orangemen
Wake Forest	Demon Deacons

And even a case of extreme reverse sexism (not to mention ageism):

SCHOOL	NICKNAME
Mississippi	Ole Miss

QUOTES OF THE YEAR, PART II

"I didn't bet him anything. New York doesn't have anything I want."
> —Texas Gov. Ann Richards, on wagering with New York Gov. Mario Cuomo before the Cowboys and Bills met in the Super Bowl.

"At first I thought it was defamation of character, and then I realized I had no character."
> —Charles Barkley, on how he felt hearing Tonya Harding referring to herself as the "Charles Barkley of figure skating."

"On July 4, wherever we are, you are rooming with me."
> —Royals manager Hal McRae, after the team acquired fireworks-loving Vince Coleman.

"I'll take down every former child star in the country one at a time."
> —Danny Bonaduce, after bloodying Donny Osmond in a boxing match and then pinning Chris Knight (formerly of "The Brady Bunch") in a wrestling match.

ABC-TV   ABC-TV

Danny Bonaduce   **Donny Osmond**

"None of us are real good around the house."
> —Fired Falcons coach Jerry Glanville, on how hard it is for former coaches to deal with life after football.

"We have a marriage, like a father and son."
> —Don King, on his relationship with lightweight champ Julio Cesar Chavez.

Wide World Photos

FUN COUPLES

Neil Smith and Mike Keenan (above)
Scottie Pippen and Tony Kukoc
Jerry Jones and Jimmy Johnson
Geoff and Brett Bodine
Donald Fehr and Richard Ravitch
Tonya Harding and Jeff Gillooly
Phil Simms and Paul Tagliabue
Gary McCord and Masters officials
Robert Shapiro and Marcia Clark

OFFICIALS SPIKE SCAM

The best scam of the year goes to a group of 34 men and 22 women who showed up at the Asian Games in Hiroshima, Japan, posing as the Philippines National Volleyball Team. Wearing convincing uniforms and carrying Philippine flags, the group appeared ready to play until officials, thinking the players suspiciously short, looked into their luggage and found lots of fake IDs and no volleyball gear. Apparently, the 56 had left the Philippines separately earlier in the week, rendezvoused in Seoul and traveled forward into Japan as a "team." Best of all, they didn't have to worry about bumping into the real Philippines team, because there isn't one. Asian Games officials, however, sent them packing back to Manila.

INJURY OF THE YEAR

Luke Jensen, half of tennis's loopy Jensen twins, broke his right thumb while smashing his racquet on Late Night With Conan O'Brien, where he and his brother Murphy had been trying to imitate rock guitarists going crazy and destroying their instruments. The injury really didn't faze Luke, though; he's ambidextrous.

COACHES' CORNER

—Temple University suspended basketball coach John Chaney after a spectacular outburst in which he publicly threatened UMass coach John Calipari after the Owls' 56-55 loss to UMass in February. After the game, Chaney charged the podium where Calipari was talking to the press and screamed, "I'll kill you! You remember that!" Chaney had to be restrained by the crowd, which included his own players.

—In Illinois, a high school football coach tried to motivate his players by staging a fake shooting. Hours before his Libertyville team was to play Loyola Academy, coach Dale Christensen participated in the school pep rally. At one point, he interceded in a fake fight he had set up between two students. Shots rang out and Christensen fell to the floor. When police arrived, Chistensen admitted it had all been a set-up. He later resigned.

—Finally, Iowa State coach Jim Walden (below) went to his knees to plead with field judge Cliff Hendrick, claiming the ground caused a fumble by one of his players in the Kansas State game.

David Cannon/Allsport

BAD MOON RISING DEPT.

—Swedish golfer Jesper Parnevik (above) revolutionized the logo potential for his sport by flipping up the bill of his cap so that the word "Titleist" was visible twice. So what if he looked like a dork.

—If they want to (and they do), it is now possible for television stations to electronically superimpose their own advertising messages over billboards at the stadiums so that home viewers get only the ads they're supposed to get.

—Jockeys in New York State can now wear advertising logos on their boots, pants and turtlenecks. No word yet on the horses, although branding with a nice corporate logo is always a possibility.

Wide World Photos

HEADS OF THE CLASS

Bonehead—California judge George Taylor ruled to halve the family support payments Barry Bonds had to pay his estranged wife from $15,000 to $7,500 a month. After the decision, he asked Bonds for his autograph.

Airhead—ESPN II's Jim Rome goaded Rams' quarterback Jim Everett by repeatedly calling him "Chris Evert" during a telecast. Everett finally went after Rome on the air, thus providing the fledgling network with some free publicity.

Snackhead—Among the products in Pete Rose's new line of prepared foods: Hit King Frozen Pizza, Batters Box Bar-B-Que Sauce, and Charlie Hustle Cheese Dip.

Fathead—Cincinnati Reds' owner Marge Schott voted against the decision to cancel the World Series. She wanted minor leaguers to play in the fall classic.

Hosehead—Parachutist Jim Miller, who came crashing down into the ring ropes during the fight between Evander Holyfield and Riddick Bowe in Las Vegas.

Pothead—Jennifer Capriati was arrested on a marijuana charge after police busted her in a Florida motel room.

Pinheads—After several scuffles among players, the Marmonte League in Ventura County, Calif., banned the tradition of having players line up and shake hands at the end of games.

Hothead—Utah Jazz owner Larry Miller screamed at coach Jerry Sloan and climbed into the stands to fight with a Denver fan during Game 6 in the playoff series against the Nuggets.

Greedhead—New Jersey Nets forward Derrick Coleman turned down a long-term $94 million contract, believing he could do better elsewhere.

MAKEOVERS OF THE YEAR

Arizona Cardinals—Buddy Ball revealed as Buddy Bull.

Dennis Rodman—an endless search for the perfect do.

Whatizit—Atlanta's Olympic mascot still looks stupid.

SEPARATED AT BIRTH

Senior PGA Tour

Simon Hobday
U.S. Sr. Open Champ

Wide World Photos

Jim Lambright
Huskies head coach

ESPN

Peter Gammons
Baseball analyst

Leon Kuzmanoff

Norman Rockwell
Beloved illustrator

GETTING A HEAD

Japan's Sumo Association was forced into action after discovering some wrestlers were injecting silicon under their scalps to meet height requirements. One aspirant, Koji Harada, described as sporting a "box-shaped head topped by a large hairy lump," was rejected after officials found a 6-inch layer of silicon beneath his scalp.

TWO MINUTES FOR INTERFERENCE

Chicago Blackhawks' defenseman Chris Chelios on the NHL lockout:

"If I was Gary Bettman, I'd be worrying about my family, my well-being. Some crazed fan or even a player, who knows, might take it in his hands and figure if they'd got him out of the way, then this thing might get settled."

49

Wide World Photos

YOU'RE OUTTA HERE!

Thirty-three major league head coaches and managers found themselves looking for new jobs between Nov. 1, 1993 to Oct. 28, 1994. The list:

NFL

Joe Bugel, Cardinals (fired)
Bruce Coslet, Jets (fired)
Jerry Glanville, Falcons (fired)
Jimmy Johnson, Cowboys (quit)
Richie Petitbon, Redskins (fired)

NBA

Rick Adelman, Trail Blazers (fired)
Quinn Buckner, Mavericks (fired)
Fred Carter, 76ers (fired)
Chuck Daly, Nets (retired)
Magic Johnson, Lakers (quit)
Sidney Lowe, Timberwolves (fired)
John Lucas, Spurs (quit)
Randy Pfund, Lakers (fired)
Wes Unseld, Bullets (quit)
Bob Weiss, Clippers (fired)

NHL

Al Arbour, Islanders (retired)
Bob Berry, Blues (fired)
Ted Green, Oilers (fired)
Paul Holmgren, Whalers (fired)
Mike Keenan, Rangers (quit)
Pierre Maguire, Whalers (fired)
Terry Murray, Capitals (fired)
Pierre Page, Nordiques (fired)
Pat Quinn, Canucks (GM only)
Glen Sather, Oilers (GM only)
Terry Simpson, Flyers (fired)

Baseball

Butch Hobson, Red Sox (fired)
Kevin Kennedy, Rangers (fired)
Hal McRae, Royals (fired)
Johnny Oates, Orioles (fired)
Jim Riggleman, Padres (quit)
Buck Rodgers, Angels (fired)
Tom Trebelhorn, Cubs (fired)

THE DALY LINE

It was another tough year for golf's John Daly, who doesn't seem to know what an easy year is.

Trouble began at the British Open, where he claimed that drug use was common on the PGA tour. Although he could provide neither evidence nor examples, the British press ran with the story. Daly's allegations were met with disbelief and scorn from his fellow tour players.

Then, at the World Series of Golf, Daly got into a parking-lot fight with the father of another pro, into whose group Daly had repeatedly hit during the just-completed round.

By season's end, Daly had dropped out of play and out of sight and had in turn been dropped, at least until he gets his act together, by Reebok and Wilson.

WHATEVER HAPPENED TO TOYS FOR TOTS?

The first 300 people who turned over a firearm to Denver officials received a pair of Adidas sneakers and two tickets to a Nuggets-Bulls game.

Wide World Photos

WHAT DID YOU EXPECT?

Nancy Kerrigan passed up the closing ceremonies at the Winter Olympics in Lillehammer to hurry back to the U.S. for a parade in her honor at Disney World. Trouble was they made her wear her silver medal.

"This is corny," she muttered sitting next to Mickey Mouse and waving to her fans. "This is so dumb. I hate it. It's the corniest thing I've ever done."

Kenya's **Cosmas Ndeti** celebrates his second straight victory in the Boston Marathon with one-year-old son **Gabriel Boston** after receiving the laurel wreath from race officials.

1993-1994 CALENDAR

NOV '93

Sun	Mon	Tue	Wed	Thu	Fri	Sat
	1	2	3	4	5	6
7	8	9	10	11	12	13
14	15	16	17	18	19	20
21	22	23	24	25	26	27
28	29	30				

Big Games

NOV. 13—Notre Dame, ranked second in the polls, beats No. 1 Florida State at South Bend, 31-24.
NOV. 14—Miami Dolphins' head coach Don Shula is carried off the field after breaking George Halas' career record for victories. The win over Phialdelphia was Shula's 325th.

Big Mess

NOV. 25—Leon Lett lives in infamy! His blunder allows Miami to upset Dallas on Thanksgiving, 16-14. Lett touches the ball after a last-second 41-yard Pete Stoyanovich field goal attempt is blocked. When Miami recovers on the one-yard line, Stoyanovich is given another try and makes it.

Big Deals

NOV. 4—The NBA grants 1995-96 expansion franchise to Toronto group headed by John Bitove Jr. for $125 million.
NOV. 30—The NFL tabs long-shot Jacksonville, Fla., as second 1995 expansion team. The Jaguars join the Carolina Pathers as NFL's first new teams since 1976.

Big Fight

NOV. 6—Evander Holyfield regains both the WBA and IBF heavyweight titles by beating Riddick Bowe in a 12-round decision in Las Vegas. The fight is marred by an interruption of bizarre proportions as a parachutist crash-lands at ringside, disrupting the seventh round and overshadowing Holyfield's victory.

Big Upset

NOV. 6—Arcangues, the French-based horse scores the most stunning upset in Breeders' Cup history by winning the $3 million Classic at Santa Anita. Arcangues, at odds of 133-1, rallies to stun favorite Bertrando by two lengths.

1 Seattle SuperSonics acquire all-star forward Detlef Schrempf from Indiana for forward Derrick McKey and guard Gerald Paddio.
Boston Bruins defenseman Ray Bourque, a four-time Norris Trophy winner, settles an earlier contract dispute that led to an arbitration ruling favoring the Bruins, by signing a five-year, $12 million contract.

2 Chicago White Sox right-hander Jack McDowell, who led the American League with 22 victories, wins Cy Young Award for 1993.
Chicago Blackhawks holdout Steve Larmer is traded to Hartford and then shipped to the New York Rangers to complete a three-way deal involving eight players.

3 Atlanta pitcher Greg Maddux, who led the majors with a 2.36 ERA becomes the first pitcher to win back-to-back NL Cy Young Awards since Sandy Koufax did it in 1966.

4 NBA grants a 1995-96 expansion franchise to Toronto at the cost of $125 million.
Chicago Bulls superstar Michael Jordan makes his retirement official via a letter of resignation to the NBA league office.

5 The Bulls open their Michael Jordan-less NBA title defense with a 124-123 overtime win over the Charlotte Hornets.
The NCAA names Arizona athletic director Cedric Dempsey to replace Dick Schultz as executive director.

6 Evander Holyfield becomes only the fourth man in boxing history to regain the heavyweight championship, pounding out a 12-round majority decision over Riddick Bowe in Las Vegas for the WBA/IBF titles.
A propeller-driven parachutist named James Miller is arrested and hospitalized after disrupting the Bowe-Holyfield bout in the seventh round by landing in the ring at the outdoor arena.
France's Arcangues, a 133-1 shot, stuns the field in the $3 million Breeder's Cup Classic at Santa Anita Park with a two-length victory over favorite Bertrando.
Brazil's Ayrton Senna wins the Australian Grand Prix by 9.2 seconds over long-time rival and four-time world champion Alain Prost of France. Prost retires after the race.

7 Troubled golfer John Daly is suspended from the PGA Tour for failing to complete play in the second round of the Kapalua International in Hawaii.

9 Barry Bonds of the San Francisco Giants wins his third National League MVP award in four years after hitting .336 with 46 homers and 123 RBI.
The NCAA ends its 17-year battle with UNLV by placing the Runnin' Rebels' basketball program on three year's probation.

10 Chicago White Sox first baseman Frank Thomas becomes the eighth player in AL history to be unanimously voted MVP after batting .317 with 41 HRs and 128 RBI.
Ex-Cleveland Browns QB Bernie Kosar signs on with Dallas and his former college coach at Miami-FL, Jimmy Johnson.

12 Pittsburgh Penguins center Mario Lemieux confirms that he will be out indefinitely in order to rehabilitate his surgically repaired back.

13 Second-ranked Notre Dame withstands a last-second comeback by No. 1 Florida St. for a 31-24 victory in South Bend.
Defending NCAA champion North Carolina is ranked No. 1 in the AP preseason college basketball poll with 61 of 65 first place votes.

Wide World Photos

Arcangues (left), a 133-to-1 shot with **Jerry Bailey** aboard, thunders down the stretch ahead of **Bertrando** (right) to win the Breeders' Cup Classic at Santa Anita on Nov. 6.

14 Miami head coach Don Shula wins his NFL-record 325th game, as the Dolphins beat Philadelphia, 19-14. Shula replaces George Halas as the all-time leader in career coaching victories.

Mexico's Andres Espinosa captures the New York City Marathon men's division in a time of 2:10:04. Uta Pippig of Germany wins the women's race in 2:26:24.

NHL referees and linesmen reject the league's final offer and vote, unanimously, to strike at midnight. The league says it will use substitute officials.

15 Rusty Wallace notches his 10th NASCAR victory of the season in the Hooters 500 in Atlanta, but Dale Earnhardt drives off with his sixth Winston Cup championship.

Regular NHL referees and linesmen give way to replacement officials on the first night of their league-wide strike.

16 Detroit Pistons guard Isiah Thomas will miss 4-6 weeks with a broken hand suffered during a fight with teammate Bill Laimbeer.

The Hartford Whalers name assistant Pierre McGuire as head coach, replacing Paul Holmgren who will remain as general manager.

17 On the final day of qualifying for the 1994 World Cup, Argentina, Italy and Ireland make the 24-team field. England and France are both eliminated.

Former Pittsburgh Pirates bullpen coach Terry Collins is named manager of the Houston Astros, replacing Art Howe.

18 Nigel Mansell of Great Britain, who successfully moved from Formula One to Winston Cup racing, is named Driver of the Year by a national panel of motor sports journalists.

19 The Los Angeles Dodgers send pitcher Pedro Martinez to Montreal for second baseman Delino DeShields.

Buffalo Sabres center Pat LaFontaine is scheduled to undergo season-ending knee surgery.

20 Boston College stuns No. 1 Notre Dame, 41-39, in South Bend on a last-second field goal while No. 2 Florida St. trounces North Carolina State, 62-3.

21 Steffi Graf defeats Arantxa Sanchez Vicario in four sets to win the Virginia Slims Championship at New York's Madison Square Garden.

Michael Stich upsets Wimbledon and U.S. Open champion Pete Sampras, to capture the ATP Tour Championship in Frankfurt, Germany.

22 The Texas Rangers sign former San Francisco first baseman Will Clark to a five-year, $30 million free-agent contract.

23 Monica Seles, sidelined since her Apr. 30 stabbing by a deranged Steffi Graf fan, finishes eighth in the final 1993 Women's Tennis rankings.

25 Edmonton Oilers president and general manager Glen Sather returns to the bench as head coach, replacing Ted Green.

The Dutch doubles team of Jacco Eltingh and Paul Haarhuis defeats Todd Woodbridge and Mark Woodforde in straight sets to capture the World Doubles Championships in Johannesburg.

30 The NFL says 'yes' to Jacksonville and 'no' to St. Louis, Baltimore and Memphis as it grants its 30th expansion franchise. Jacksonville and fellow expansion team in Charlotte, N.C. will pay $140 million each to join the league in 1995.

DEC '93

Sun	Mon	Tue	Wed	Thu	Fri	Sat
			1	2	3	4
5	6	7	8	9	10	11
12	13	14	15	16	17	18
19	20	21	22	23	24	25
26	27	28	29	30.	31	

Big Game

DEC. 23—Dallas Mavericks avoid setting an NBA-record 21-game losing streak by beating Minnesota, 93-89, on the road.

Big Hurt

DEC. 12—Sacramento Kings guard Bobby Hurley is critically injured in an automobile accident following a home loss to the LA Clippers. He is thrown 20 feet from his vehicle and suffers broken ribs, collapsed lungs, a fractured shoulder blade and other injuries. He will eventually return to training camp in October.

Big Deals

DEC. 17—Upstart Fox Television gains instant credibility by outbidding CBS for the rights to NFC football games. The $1.58 billion, four-year deal is $100 million more than CBS put on the table to maintain its 38-year relationship with the NFL.

DEC. 22—Running back Barry Sanders of the Detroit Lions agrees to a four-year deal worth $17.2 million to stay with the club through 1997.

DEC. 23—Dallas quarterback Troy Aikman signs eight-year, $50 million deal with the Cowboys, making him the highest-paid player in the NFL.

Big Upset

DEC. 18—Simon Brown KO's Terry Norris to win the WBC super welterweight title. Norris was considered by many to be the best pound-for-pound fighter before this stunner. He will later avenge the loss in a 12-round decision over Brown.

Big Margin

DEC. 11—Florida State quarterback Charlie Ward wins the Heisman Trophy by the second-largest margin ever, beating out Tennessee QB Heath Shuler by 1,622 points.

1 **Detroit Pistons' center** Bill Laimbeer, 36, ends his 14-year NBA career as one of only 19 players to accumulate 10,000 points and 10,000 rebounds.

2 **Houston wins** its 15th consecutive game since opening night, beating New York, 94-85, at Madison Square Garden. The Rockets share the NBA's best start record with the 1948 Washington Capitols.

The Cleveland Indians reach into the free agent pool and sign up veteran first baseman and DH Eddie Murray and righthander Dennis Martinez.

Philadelphia Phillies trade relief pitcher and World Series goat Mitch Williams to Houston for pitchers Doug Jones and Jeff Juden.

Notre Dame offensive tackle Aaron Taylor wins the Lombardi Award as the nation's top college football lineman.

NHL officials end their 17-day walkout after reaching an agreement with the league on a four-year contract.

3 **Atlanta beats** Houston, 133-111, halting the Rockets' bid for a record-breaking 16th straight season opening victory.

4 **Seventh-ranked Wisconsin** clinches its first Rose Bowl appearance since 1963 with a 41-20 victory over Michigan State in Tokyo.

5 **Nebraska** (11-0) and Florida St. (11-1) grab the top two slots in the final Bowl Coalition poll, setting up a showdown in the Orange Bowl on New Year's night.

For the second straight year basketball's Michael Jordan tops the list of Forbes magazine's richest athletes with an estimated $36 million in earnings for 1993.

Michael Stich's 6-4, 6-2, 6-2 victory over Australia's Richard Fromberg gives Germany its third Davis Cup title.

Virginia becomes the first team in the 34-year history of the NCAA Division I soccer tournament to win three consecutive titles. The Cavaliers beat South Carolina, 2-0, before a record crowd of 10,549 in Davidson, N.C.

6 **Harvard names** 37-year-old Tim Murphy, who had led the University of Cincinnati to its first winning season in 11 years, head football coach, replacing the retired Joe Restic.

7 **The NCAA appoints** a task force to study the possibility of a Division 1-A team football playoff system after the bowl season of 1995.

South Carolina names Florida St. offensive coordinator Brad Scott as its new head football coach.

8 **Paul Azinger**, who won his first major title at the 1993 PGA Championship, is diagnosed with lymphoma in his right shoulder blade. He is expected to miss at least seven months while being treated.

10 **Indiana suspends** head basketball coach Bob Knight for one game following Knight's unsportsmanlike conduct during the Indiana-Notre Dame game on Dec. 7.

Teenage tennis star Jennifer Capriati receives a citation for shoplifting at a Tampa mall after walking away from a booth wearing a $15 ring.

11 **Florida St. QB Charlie Ward** wins the Heisman Trophy by the second largest margin (1,622 points) in the award's 59-year history. Tennessee QB Heath Shuler is runner-up.

12 **Sacramento rookie** guard Bobby Hurley is in serious condition following an auto accident that occurs when Hurley's truck was hit broadside by a station wagon travelling without headlights.

Michael Stich (center), with teammates **Bernd Karbacher** (left) and **Carl Uwe Steeb**, pose around Davis Cup after teaming with Marc Goellner and Patrick Kuehnen to beat Australia, 4-1.

13 Baltimore signs former Texas first baseman Rafael Palmeiro to a five-year, $30.35 million contract that includes a record $12 million signing bonus.

14 Houston Oilers defensive lineman Jeff Alm commits suicide after his best friend dies in a car accident involving the vehicle Alm was driving.

15 Thoroughbred trainer Jeff Lukas, the son of D. Wayne Lukas, suffers a severe head injury after being trampled by 2-year-old Tabasco Cat at Santa Anita.

17 The Fox Network outbids CBS by $100 million for the TV broadcast rights to the NFL's National Conference beginning in 1994. Fox will pay the NFL $395 million a year for four years.

18 Youngstown St. (13-2) scores 17 first-quarter points defeating Marshall (11-4), 17-5, to win the Division 1-AA championship at Huntington, W.Va. for the second time in three years.

19 At the World Cup soccer draw in Las Vegas, the U.S. joins Switzerland, Romania and Columbia in Group A of the 24-team field. The World Cup will be played June 17 to July 17, 1994.
Italian forward Roberto Baggio outpoints Brazilian forward Romario, 152-84, in the voting for FIFA's 1993 World Player of the Year.

20 NBC retains broadcast rights to the NFL's American Conference for $220 million a year over four years, thwarting a late challenge by CBS, which will be left without pro football for the first time in 38 years.

22 Barry Sanders of the Detroit Lions signs a four-year, $17.2 million contract extension making him the highest paid running back in the NFL.

The NBA's Dallas Mavericks lose their record-tying 20th in a row to Milwaukee, 96-86. The league mark of futility was established by the 1972-73 Philadelphia 76ers.

23 Dallas QB Troy Aikman signs an eight-year, $50 million contract making him the highest-paid player in NFL history. The deal is made on the day before the new NFL salary cap takes effect.
Bobby Hurley is released from the hospital almost two weeks after sustaining multiple injuries in an auto accident.
The Dallas Mavericks (2-23) avert an NBA-record 21st consecutive loss with a 93-89 win over the Timberwolves in Minnesota.

24 Tennis star Boris Becker says there is drug use on the ATP tour, suggesting that the authorities have been able to cover it up.

26 Mike Gartner of the New York Rangers scores his 600th career goal, becoming just the sixth player in league history to reach the milestone.
Green Bay wide receiver Sterling Sharpe catches seven passes in the Packers' regular season finale to become the NFL's first player with two 100 reception seasons.

27 A number of Russian born NHL players, including superstar Pavel Bure of Vancouver, admit to extortion attempts by organized crime groups in their homeland.

30 A federal judge refuses to order the Washington Redskins to suspend 34 players from their final regular season game for failure to pay $5,000 each in union dues. The players' union had requested the suspension.

JAN '94

Sun	Mon	Tue	Wed	Thu	Fri	Sat
						1
2	3	4	5	6	7	8
9	10	11	12	13	14	15
16	17	18	19	20	21	22
23/30	24/31	25	26	27	28	29

Big Games

JAN. 1—Bobby Bowden finally gets his first national title, but barely. Florida State wins the Orange Bowl and the championship in a surprisingly close 18-16 decision over Nebraska. The Seminoles win on a 22-yard field goal by Scott Bentley with 21 seconds left.
JAN. 30—Dallas Cowboys win their second straight Super Bowl, 30-13, over the Buffalo Bills, who become the first team to four-peat as Super Bowl losers. Emmitt Smith rushes for 132 yards on 30 carries to earn MVP.

Big Mess

JAN. 6—Nancy Kerrigan suffers leg injuries when she is assaulted after a practice session prior to the U.S. Skating Championships in Detroit. This is the beginning of a saga which goes through the Olympics (see page 590).

Big Deal

JAN. 24—John Madden joins Fox network as football commentator for a reported $32 million over four years, making him the highest paid performer in football on field or off.

Big Upset

JAN. 29—Frankie Randall, a 15-1 underdog, wins WBC super lightweight title by upsetting Julio Cesar Chavez. In the 11th round, Chavez is knocked down for the first time in his career. The defeat is also his first in 91 fights.

Big Honor

JAN. 29—Pro Football Hall of Fame announces 1994 inductees, who include former Dallas teammates Tony Dorsett and Randy White and former Vikings coach Bud Grant. Grant becomes first man elected to both NFL and CFL halls of fame.

1 Freshman Scott Bentley's 4th field goal of the game with 21 seconds left gives No. 1 Florida St. an 18-16 win over No. 2 Nebraska in the Orange Bowl.
Elsewhere, No. 3 West Virginia falls from the ranks of the unbeaten in the Sugar Bowl, No. 4 Notre Dame wins the Cotton and No. 9 Wisconsin wins the Rose Bowl for the first time ever.

2 Florida St. (12-1) is ranked No. 1 in the final USA Today/CNN coaches and AP media polls. The national title is the first for the Seminoles and head coach Bobby Bowden.
Green Bay wide receiver Sterling Sharpe breaks his own single season reception record of 108 with a 6-catch performance against Detroit. He finishes the season with 112.

4 Atlanta fires head coach Jerry Glanville after his second consecutive 6-10 NFL season, while Washington dismisses beleaguered rookie head coach Richie Petitbon after a 4-12 campaign—the Redskins' worst since 1963.

5 Texas A&M football program receives five years probation from the NCAA but manages to avert the "death penalty" as a result of major violations.

6 Defending women's figure skating national champion Nancy Kerrigan is clubbed on the right kneecap in an off-ice attack by an unidentified assailant at the U.S. Olympic trials in Detroit.
The Los Angeles Rams invoke an escape clause in their 35-year stadium lease at Anaheim to explore the option of leaving Southern California.

7 Nancy Kerrigan, hobbled by a bruised and swollen right knee, withdraws from the U.S. Figure Skating Championships.
The New York Jets fire fourth-year head coach Bruce Coslet (26-39), and replace him with defensive coordinator Pete Carroll.

8 NFL playoffs open with Kansas City beating Pittsburgh on a late field goal and Green Bay edging Detroit on a 40-yard, Brett Favre to Sterling Sharpe TD pass with :55 left.
Tonya Harding wins the U.S. Figure Skating title. Nancy Kerrigan, unable to compete in the nationals, is named to the U.S. Olympic team by the USFSA's international committee.

10 NBC announces a five-year, $37.5 million renewal of its exclusive contract to televise Notre Dame home football games.

12 Lefthander Steve Carlton, winner of 329 games and four Cy Young Awards, is the only player voted into the baseball Hall of Fame. Slugging first baseman Orlando Cepeda misses entry by seven votes.
Bill Polian, architect of Buffalo's AFC championship reign, is named general manager of the NFL's expansion Carolina Panthers.

13 Figure skater Tonya Harding's bodyguard Shawn Eckardt is arrested for his alleged role in the attack on skater Nancy Kerrigan.

14 The Black Coaches Association postpones its threatened boycott of NCAA basketball games in protest of several issues, most recently the loss of a 14th scholarship for men's Division I schools.

15 New York Giants linebacker Lawrence Taylor, who appeared in a record 10 straight Pro Bowls, announces his retirement after 13 seasons, two Super Bowl rings, an MVP award (1986), and 132½ career sacks.

The outfield scoreboard at **Anaheim Stadium** after it collapsed under its own weight on Jan. 17 following a California earthquake that measured 6.7 on the Richter scale.

San Antonio extends the Dallas Mavericks' home losing streak to an NBA-record 17 with a 104-87 victory.

16 Tonya Harding, through a statement read by her attorney, denies any involvement in the attack on Nancy Kerrigan despite the arrest of her bodyguard and the alleged assailant.

17 An earthquake measuring 6.7 on the Richter scale rocks southern California, resulting in considerable damage to Anaheim Stadium and Los Angeles Memorial Coliseum. The NBA game between the L.A. Lakers and visiting Sacramento is called off, but horse racing continues at Santa Anita.

18 Major league baseball owners end months of bitter negotiations by approving a revenue-sharing plan designed to allow small-market teams to remain financially competitive with the large-market clubs.

19 Tonya Harding's estranged husband Jeff Gillooly is arrested and charged with planning the attack on Nancy Kerrigan at the U.S. Figure Skating Championships.
CBS Sports purchases the rights to the 1998 Winter Olympics in Nagano, Japan for $375 million, a 27% increase over what the network doled out for next month's Winter Games in Lillehammer, Norway.

20 Thoroughbred racing's Eclipse Awards are announced with male turf horse Kotashaan, jockey Mike Smith and trainer John Franks among the winners. Horse of the Year will be announced Feb. 4.

21 Bob Kraft, owner of Foxboro Stadium, purchases the New England Patriots from James Orthwein for $170 million.

The East beats the West, 9-8, in the NHL All-Star game at Madison Square Garden. N.Y. Rangers' goalie Mike Richter is named MVP.

23 Dallas beats San Francisco, 38-21, to win the NFC championship and Buffalo defeats Kansas City, 30-13, to take the AFC, setting up the first-ever rematch of the previous year's Super Bowl participants.

24 Despite victories in four of their last five regular season games, the Phoenix Cardinals fire fourth year head coach Joe Bugel. Atlanta names offensive coordinator June Jones as head coach.
Blockbuster Video owner Wayne Huizenga reaches an agreement with the family of the late Joe Robbie to purchase controlling interest in the NFL's Miami Dolphins.
Former CBS pro football analyst John Madden signs a four-year, $32 million-contract with the Fox Network, making him the highest-paid performer in football.

27 In a prepared statement to the media, Tonya Harding admits that she did not report details regarding the assault on Nancy Kerrigan after the fact, but says she had no prior knowledge of the attack.
Former NHL head coach and present ESPN hockey analyst Jim Schoenfeld is named head coach of the Washington Capitals, replacing Terry Murray.

29 Julio Cesar Chavez suffers the first defeat of his pro boxing career, losing his WBC super lightweight crown on a split decision to 32-year-old Frankie Randall in Las Vegas.

30 Dallas wins its second straight Super Bowl with a 30-13 victory over Buffalo in Atlanta. The Bills have now lost four Super Bowls in a row.

FEB '94

Sun	Mon	Tue	Wed	Thu	Fri	Sat
		1	2	3	4	5
6	7	8	9	10	11	12
13	14	15	16	17	18	19
20	21	22	23	24	25	26
27	28					

Golden Moments

FEB. 18—Dan Jansen ends 10 years of frustration by winning the 1,000-meter speed skating event in world record time at the Winter Olympics in Lillehammer.

FEB. 19—Bonnie Blair wins her third straight 500-meter speed skating gold medal, giving her a career total of five Olympic golds.

FEB. 25—Ukranian figure skater Oksana Baiul edges Nancy Kerrigan in the finals of the women's Olympic skating competition.

Big Deals

FEB. 7—Following a workout in front of the media, former Chicago Bulls superstar Michael Jordan signs a minor league contract with the Chicago White Sox.

FEB. 24—In a rare in-season exchange of NBA stars (and free agents at season's end), the Atlanta Hawks send Dominique Wilkins to the LA Clippers for Danny Manning.

Big Upset

FEB. 19—Humberto (Chiquita) Gonzalez wins back world flyweight title, beating previously-undefeated Michael Carbajal in a split decision at Inglewood. Carbajal had knocked out Gonzalez in the seventh round to win the title on Mar. 13, 1993.

FEB. 26—Steve Little captures WBA super middleweight crown with a stunning majority decision over Michael Nunn in London.

Hired

FEB. 2—Washington Redskins name Norv Turner as head coach. Turner was offensive coordinator for the rival Dallas Cowboys.

FEB. 3—Phoenix (soon to be Arizona) Cardinals hire Buddy Ryan as head coach.

FEB. 21—Expansion Jacksonville Jaguars hire Tom Coughlin as head coach and general manager. Coughlin heads south after two seasons at Boston College and a big upset over Notre Dame.

1   **Jeff Gillooly implicates** his ex-wife Tonya Harding and pleads guilty to a racketeering charge for his role in masterminding the attack on skater Nancy Kerrigan.

2   **Nancy Kerrigan**, her knee injury healed, is declared ready for the Olympics after her performance for the U.S. Figure Skating Association review panel.

    Washington names Dallas Cowboys' offensive coordinator Norv Turner head coach, signing him to a five-year contract.

    Atlanta's Lenny Wilkens earns his 900th regular season NBA coaching win, with a 118-99 victory over Orlando.

3   **Phoenix Cardinals name** Buddy Ryan as their new head coach and general manager.

4   **Texas Rangers sign** slugging left-fielder and 2-time HR champion Juan Gonzalez to a seven-year contract potentially worth $45.5 million.

    French-bred Kotashaan, a 5-year-old in 1993, wins the Eclipse award as Horse of the Year.

6   **NFC defeats** AFC, 17-3, at the annual NFL Pro Bowl in Honolulu.

    Johnny Miller, 46, climbs down from the TV tower and captures his first tour victory since 1987 with a one-stroke win at the Pebble Beach National Pro-Am.

7   **Seven-time** NBA scoring champion Michael Jordan signs a minor league baseball contract with the Chicago White Sox.

8   **Coaches Chuck Daly and Denny Crum** are among five named to the Basketball Hall of Fame, in Springfield, Mass.

9   **Tonya Harding files** a $20 million lawsuit against the U.S. Olympic Committee, seeking a temporary restraining order to block a Feb. 15 hearing on her Olympic eligibility.

    Former Oklahoma football coach Bud Wilkinson, who lead the Sooners to three national titles and an NCAA-record 47 consecutive wins from 1953-57, dies of congestive heart failure at 77 .

10   **Ontario's government agrees** to drop wagering on NBA games from its sports lottery, thereby clearing the way for an NBA expansion franchise in Toronto.

11   **Veteran Winston Cup driver** Neil Bonnett dies from massive head injuries suffered in a crash during a Daytona 500 practice session at Daytona International Speedway.

    Robin Yount, a two-time league MVP with the Milwaukee Brewers, announces his retirement from baseball after 20 seasons in the majors.

12   **King Harald V** of Norway officially opens the XVII Winter Olympics in Lillehammer.

    Tonya Harding strikes a deal with the U.S. Olympic Committee and will skate in Lillehammer Olympics.

    Pittsburgh Penguins' captain Mario Lemieux returns from back surgery to score a goal and an assist in a 9-3 Pens' loss to Dallas.

    Britain's Colin Jackson breaks the 60-meter hurdles world indoor record with a time of 7.35.

13   **Alaska's Tommy Moe** wins the Olympic gold medal in the men's downhill, making him the first U.S. male alpine skiing medalist in 10 years.

    Scottie Pippen leads the East over the West, 127-118 at the NBA All-Star game in Minneapolis.

    Temple basketball coach John Chaney interrupts a postgame press conference screaming "I'll kill you" at UMass coach John Calipari after a one-point Owls' loss in which Chaney felt Calipari had tried to verbally intimidate the referees.

Wide World Photos

Olympic men's downhill champion **Tommy Moe** of the U.S. reacts to his victory with silver medal winner **Kjetil Andre Aamodt** of Norway (left) and bronze medalist **Edward Podivinsky** of Canada.

14 **Speed skater Dan Jansen** fails again to win an Olympic medal, slipping on the final turn of the 500-meter event to finish eighth.

Former No. 1-ranked player Monica Seles is officially dropped from the WTA women's tennis rankings.

Temple coach John Chaney is suspended for one game by school president Peter Liacouras for his shouting match with UMass head coach John Calipari.

More than 300 players are awarded $59.5 million in claims against baseball owners found guilty of collusion in the mid-1980s. Biggest individual winner is retired Jack Clark, who reportedly gets $2.1 million.

15 **American skier** Diann Roffe-Steinrotter wins the gold medal in the Olympic Super G, besting Russia's Svetlana Gladischeva by three-tenths of a second.

18 **Dan Jansen ends** 10 years of Olympic heartache with a gold medal in 1,000 meter event, finishing with a world record time of 1:12.43.

19 **Bonnie Blair makes** Olympic history with her record third straight gold medal in the 500-meter speed skating event. U.S. skier Picabo Street takes the silver medal in the women's downhill.

Humberto (Chiquita) Gonzalez beats previously-undefeated Michael Carbajal in a 12-round split decision to regain the world junior flyweight title.

Philadelphia 76ers' 7-foot-6 rookie center Shawn Bradley dislocates his left knee cap against Portland and will miss the rest of the season.

20 **Norwegian speed skater** Johan Olav Koss sets his third world record of the Olympics, winning the 10,000 meters in 13:30.55.

Sterling Marlin, a 17-year NASCAR veteran, records his first Winston Cup victory ever, winning the Daytona 500.

21 **The U.S. Olympic hockey** team advances to the medal round with a 7-1 win over Italy.

The NFL expansion Jacksonville Jaguars name Boston College head coach Tom Coughlin head coach and general manager.

Heavyweight champion Evander Holyfield fires trainer Emmanuel Stewart and hires Don Turner two months before his Apr. 22 defense against Michael Moorer.

22 **Kentucky basketball coach** Rick Pitino suspends three of his players for participating in a free throw swapping scheme.

23 **Baylor University** announces it will leave the Southwest Conference for the Big Eight. Before the week is out, Texas, Texas A&M and Texas Tech will join the exodus from the SWC.

24 **Cathy Turner wins** her second straight Olympic gold medal in the 500-meter short-track speed skating event.

The Atlanta Hawks trade veteran All-Star Dominique Wilkins to the Los Angeles Clippers for Danny Manning.

25 **Ukranian Oskana Baiul** edges American Nancy Kerrigan by one-tenth of a point for the Olympic gold medal in women's figure skating. Tonya Harding finishes in eighth place.

27 **Sweden defeats Canada**, 3-2, in a sudden death shootout for the hockey gold medal as the Lillehammer Olympic Games come to a close.

MAR '94

Sun	Mon	Tue	Wed	Thu	Fri	Sat
		1	2	3	4	5
6	7	8	9	10	11	12
13	14	15	16	17	18	19
20	21	22	23	24	25	26
27	28	29	30	31		

Big Mess

MAR. 16—Tonya Harding pleads guilty on hindering charges in the Kerrigan caper. She draws a $100,000 fine and is forced to withdraw from the U.S. Figure Skating Association.

Big Deal

MAR. 21—At the NHL trade deadline, there are a number of big deals. The most noteworthy sees the Washington Capitals send defenseman Al Iafrate go to Boston for the Bruins' Joe Juneau, and the New York Rangers deal 600+ goal-scorer Mike Gartner to Toronto for Glen Anderson.

Big Departures

MAR. 22—It's a departure from conservative football as the NFL owners approve the two-point conversion for the 1994 season.

MAR. 29—The Jimmy and Jerry Show comes to an end in Dallas as Jimmy Johnson resigns as head coach of the two-time defending Super Bowl champion Cowboys. One day later, Jones hires former University of Oklahoma coach Barry Switzer, who hasn't coached football since 1988.

Milestone

MAR. 23—Wayne Gretzky breaks Gordie Howe's NHL record for career goals, scoring No. 802 on a power play against Vancouver's Kirk McLean at 14:47 of the second period at the Great Western Forum in Inglewood.

Hired

MAR. 1—National League owners elect Leonard Coleman to replace Bill White as president.

MAR. 23—Magic Johnson is named coach of the Los Angeles Lakers for the rest of the season, replacing Randy Pfund.

1 **Leonard Coleman is elected** the 14th president of the National League, succeeding outgoing NL boss Bill White.

PGA commissioner Deane Beman announces he will step down when his contract expires in Dec. 1995.

2 **Former NFL head coach** Dan Henning is named head football coach at Boston College.

3 **Alan Eagleson**, founder of the NHL Players Association, is indicted on 32 separate counts, including charges of racketeering, fraud and embezzlement.

4 **The Washington St. athletic department** is placed on three years probation by the NCAA for athletic financial aid violations.

6 **Britain's Colin Jackson** sets another world indoor record in the 60-meters hurdles with a time of 7.30 in Sindelfingen, Germany.

7 **The U.S. Supreme Court rejects** imprisoned boxer Mike Tyson's appeal of his Feb. rape conviction.

9 **Philadelphia Phillies'** first baseman John Kruk expected to make a full recovery following surgery for testicular cancer.

The Big East invites Rutgers and West Virginia to join as conference all-sports members in 1995. The two schools currently play Big East football only.

New York Rangers forward Mike Gartner scores his 611th career goal in a 7-5 victory over Washington. He moves past Bobby Hull into fifth place on the NHL's all-time list.

A Superior court judge clears defending national champion Maine to play in the Hockey East postseason tournament. The conference had tried to ban the Black Bears for using an ineligible player.

14 **The North Carolina** men (27-6) and Tennessee women (29-1) are ranked first in the final AP regular season college basketball polls.

15 **Xavier of Ohio accepts** an invitation from the Atlantic 10 Conference to enter the league as a full-time, all-sport member.

Martin Buser captures his second Iditarod Trail Sled Dog Race in the record time of 10 days, 13 hours, 2 minutes and 39 seconds.

Atlanta releases outfielder Ron Gant. The Braves signed Gant to a record one-year contract of $5.5 million, but Gant broke his right leg in two places Feb. 3, in a dirt-bike accident.

16 **Tonya Harding pleads** guilty to conspiring to hinder the investigation into the attack on rival Nancy Kerrigan. Harding is fined $100,000 and agrees to resign membership in the U.S. Figure Skating Association.

Yugoslavian-born international tennis star Monica Seles becomes a United States citizen.

17 **NFL's Phoenix Cardinals announce** they are changing their name to the Arizona Cardinals.

20 **Wayne Gretzky scores** his 801st career goal with 49 seconds left in regulation to garner a 6-6 tie with the San Jose Sharks. The goal moves Gretzky, who reached the milestone in just 15 seasons, into a tie with all-time NHL goals leader Gordie Howe, who played 26 seasons.

Eight-point underdog Boston College shocks top seed North Carolina, 75-72, to join Indiana, Duke, Tulsa, Marquette, Arizona, Arkansas and Louisville in NCAA basketball tournament Sweet 16.

Michael Andretti returns to Indy-car racing with a win in the Australian Grand Prix at Surfers Paradise. He beats out Emerson Fittipaldi by 1.33 seconds.

New Dallas Cowboys' head coach **Barry Switzer** (right) holds court on Mar. 30, alongside his new employer **Jerry Jones**. Switzer took the job the day after old coach Jimmy Johnson quit.

21 **A record 18 deals** are made before the NHL trading deadline. The New York Rangers stock up for the playoffs by sending Mike Gartner to Toronto for Glenn Anderson; Todd Marchant to Edmonton for Craig MacTavish; and Tony Amonte to Chicago for Brian Noonan and Stephane Matteau. Also, Boston ships Joe Juneau to Washington for Al Iafrate.
Boston Bruins' star right wing Cam Neely will sit out for the rest of the season with a torn ligament in his right knee. He suffered the injury in a game against New Jersey, Mar. 19.

22 **NFL owners vote**, 23-4, to approve the two-point conversion after touchdowns in the league's first scoring change in 75 seasons.

23 **Wayne Gretzky scores** his 802nd career goal in front of a sellout crowd of 16,005 at the Great Western Forum, to break the legendary Gordie Howe's NHL all-time goal record.
Magic Johnson is named head coach of the Los Angeles Lakers, replacing Randy Pfund for the remainder of 1993-94 season. The Lakers are currently 10 games below .500 and scrambling for a position in the playoffs.
NFL owners approve the sale of the Miami Dolphins to Wayne Huizenga on an interim basis, despite the league's rule against cross-ownership. Huizenga already owns baseball's Florida Marlins and hockey's Florida Panthers as well as Joe Robbie Stadium.

24 **NFL owners end** annual meetings by voting to increase the league's first salary cap to $34.2 million per club.

Olympic silver medalist Elvis Stojko of Canada wins the men's gold medal at the World Figure Skating Championships in Chiba, Japan.

25 **Yuka Sato**, of Japan, captures the women's gold medal at the World Figure Skating Championships. Oksana Baiul and Nancy Kerrigan, the Olympic gold and silver medalists, do not compete.

26 **Bonnie Blair breaks** her own speed skating world record in the 500 meters with a time of 38.99 at the Calgary Olympic Oval.

27 **Arkansas beats** Michigan, 76-68, and Florida downs Boston College, 74-66, to join Duke and Arizona in the NCAA Final Four.
Purdue forward Glenn Robinson and Southern Cal's Lisa Leslie win the James Naismith award as college basketball's Players of the Year.
Magic Johnson's NBA coaching debut is a successful one as the Lakers defeat Milwaukee, 110-101, in L.A.

29 **Two months after** winning his second straight Super Bowl, Jimmy Johnson resigns as head coach of the Dallas Cowboys because of a long-running feud with team owner Jerry Jones.

30 **Former University of Oklahoma coach** Barry Switzer is named head coach of the Dallas Cowboys. Switzer, who won three national championships in 16 years with the Sooners, has not coached football since 1988.

31 **Chicago White Sox assign** retired NBA legend Michael Jordan to the class AA Birmingham Barons of the Southern League.

APRIL '94

Sun	Mon	Tue	Wed	Thu	Fri	Sat
					1	2
3	4	5	6	7	8	9
10	11	12	13	14	15	16
17	18	19	20	21	22	23
24	25	26	27	28	29	30

Big Game

APR. 4—Arkansas wins its first Div. I basketball championship with a 76-72 win over Duke. Corliss Williamson scores 23 points to lead the Razorbacks. Grant Hill is held to 12 points in his final game as a Blue Devil.

Big Deals

APR. 6—Norman Braman agrees to sell Philadelphia Eagles to Hollywood movie producer Jeff Lurie for a pro sports-record $185 million.
APR. 14—The Houston Oilers, with two high-priced quarterbacks and a salary cap problem looming, trade Warren Moon to Minnesota.
APR. 21—San Francisco 49ers sign free agent linebacker Ken Norton Jr. away from the Dallas Cowboys.

Big Win

APR. 10—Golfer Jose Maria Olazabal captures the Masters with a two-stroke win over Tom Lehman. Olazabal finishes at nine-under-par 279 to earn the $360,000 first prize.

Big Upset

APR. 22—Michael Moorer decisions Evander Holyfield to win the world heavyweight title, becoming the first left-hander in history to win the title.
APR. 30—The San Jose Sharks, playing in their first Stanley Cup playoffs, continue a magical season by shocking Western Conference top-seed Detroit, 3-2, in Game 7 of their first round series.

Big Effort

APR. 24—David Robinson clinches the first NBA scoring title of the post-Jordan era with a 71-point performance against the LA Clippers.

1 **Minnesota-Duluth senior** left wing Chris Marinucci wins the 14th annual Hobey Baker Award as college hockey's Player of the Year.

2 **Arkansas beats** Arizona, 91-82, and Duke edges Florida, 70-65, to advance to the finals of the NCAA basketball tournament in Charlotte.
Louisiana Tech edges Alabama, 69-66, and North Carolina downs Purdue, 89-74, to advance to the finals of the NCAA Women's basketball tournament.
Lake Superior St. routs Boston University, 9-1, to win its second NCAA hockey championship in three years.

3 **The St. Louis Cardinals beat** Cincinnati, 6-4, at Riverfront Stadium in the first Sunday night season opener in major league history.
North Carolina beats Louisiana Tech, 60-59, on a buzzer-beating three-pointer by Charlotte Smith to win the NCAA women's basketball title.

4 **Arkansas beats** Duke, 76-72, to win the school's first NCAA basketball championship. Razorbacks' forward Corliss Williamson scores 23 points and is named tournament MVP.
President Clinton plays hooky from the pressures of the Oval Office by traveling to Cleveland to throw out the first pitch of the Indians' opener at new Jacobs Field and then winging to Charlotte to watch his home state Arkansas team defeat Duke in the NCAA basketball final.

6 **Norman Braman reaches** an agreement to sell the NFL's Philadelphia Eagles to movie mogul Jeffrey Lurie for a record $185 million. The previous record price tag for a big league ballclub was $173 million paid for baseball's Baltimore Orioles in 1993.
New Orleans quarterback Jim Everett trottles ESPN2 personality Jim Rome during a talk show after Rome repeatedly calls him "Chris" Everett.

8 **Atlanta Braves pitcher** Kent Mercker, in only his 12th major league start, hurls a 6-0, no-hitter against the Dodgers in L.A.
With a crowd of 10,359 sqeezing into tiny Hoover Metropolitan Stadium in Birmingham, Ala., Michael Jordan goes hitless in his minor league baseball debut with the Double A Barons.
Purdue forward Glenn Robinson wins the John Wooden Award as college basketball's top player.

9 **Wayne Messmer**, whose rendition of "The Star-Spangled Banner" has revved up Blackhawks' fans at Chicago Stadium for 15 years, is shot in the neck and seriously wounded while driving home from a restaurant after a Blackhawks game. He will eventually make a full recovery.
Pernell Whitaker retains his WBC welterweight belt with a unanimous decision victory over Puerto Rican challenger Santos Cardona.

10 **Jose Maria Olazabal** of Spain wins the 58th Masters golf tournament by two strokes, becoming the sixth foreign-born player fitted for a green blazer in the last seven years.

11 **Philadelphia** first baseman John Kruk, activated just six hours after radiation treatment, returns to the Phillies' lineup for the home opener and collects three hits.

12 **Senate majority leader** George Mitchell (D., Maine) turns down a Supreme Court nomination, but leaves the door open for an offer to become baseball's next commissioner.

14 **Houston Oiler** quarterback Warren Moon is traded to Minnesota for several draft picks.

An Opening Day crowd of 41,459 in Cleveland watched the Indians baptize new **Jacobs Field** with a 4-3 win over Seattle. President Clinton threw out the first ball then left for the NCAA basketball final.

15 Magic Johnson announces he won't return as head coach of the Lakers. In 16 games under Johnson, the Lakers are 5-11 and out of the playoffs.

17 Lee Trevino wins the PGA Senior Golf Championship after Ray Floyd quadruple-bogies the par 3 15th hole.
The Santa Monica Track Club relay team of Carl Lewis, Michael Marsh, Leroy Burrell and Floyd Heard break their 4 x 200-meter world record with a timing of 1:18.68 at a meet in Walnut, Calif.

18 Taking advantage of 20-mph tailwinds and temperatures in the 50s, Cosmas Ndeti of Kenya (2:07:15) and Germany's Uta Pippig (2:21:45) set course records at the 98th Boston Marathon.

19 Detroit Pistons All-Star Isiah Thomas suffers a career-ending injury when he tears his Achilles tendon in a 132-104 loss to Orlando.

21 Former Dallas coach Jimmy Johnson joins the Fox network as a studio analyst for football broadcasts.

22 Michael Moorer becomes the first southpaw to claim the heavyweight championship when he wins a majority 12-round decision over Evander Holyfield for the IBF and WBA titles in Las Vegas.
American Shannon Miller wins her second all-around title at the World Gymnastics Championships in Brisbane, Australia.

23 Montreal goaltender Patrick Roy leaves his hospital bed (a flared appendix) to lead the Canadiens to a 5-2 playoff victory over the Boston Bruins. The Eastern Conference first round series is tied, 2-2.

24 Ohio St. defensive lineman Dan Wilkinson (Bengals) and San Diego St. running back Marshall Faulk (Colts) are the first two players selected in the NFL Draft.
San Antonio center David Robinson scores 71 points in a 112-97 win against the L.A. Clippers to edge Shaquille O'Neal for the NBA scoring title. O'Neal scores 32 against New Jersey.
Washington Bullets coach Wes Unseld resigns after six consecutive losing seasons.

25 Florida St. QB Charlie Ward becomes the first Heisman Trophy winner in 35 years not to be taken in the NFL's Draft. Ward, who also plays basketball at FSU, will eventually be a first round pick of the N.Y. Knicks in the NBA Draft.

26 Evander Holyfield announces his retirement from boxing at age 31 after learning he has a "non-compliant" left ventrical, or "stiff heart."

27 Minnesota pitcher Scott Erickson pitches the Twins' first no-hitter since 1967 (Dean Chance) with a 6-0 victory over Milwaukee.
Goaltenders Dominik Hasek of Buffalo and Martin Brodeur of New Jersey excel as the Sabres beat the Devils, 1-0, in four overtimes in Game 6 of their NHL playoff series. Dave Hannan scores the game-winner at 5:47 of the fourth OT.
NBA awards a second Canadian expansion franchise. For a $125 million entry fee Vancouver will join Toronto as a new member in 1995-96.

29 Los Angeles Kings owner Bruce McNall, under investigation by a federal grand jury, resigns his post as chairman of the NHL's Board of Governors.

MAY '94

Sun	Mon	Tue	Wed	Thu	Fri	Sat
1	2	3	4	5	6	7
8	9	10	11	12	13	14
15	16	17	18	19	20	21
22	23	24	25	26	27	28
29	30	31				

Big Tragedy

MAY 1—Formula One race car driver Ayrton Senna of Brazil is killed at the San Marino Grand Prix in Imola, Italy, when his car slams into a wall. Senna, 34, had won 41 races and 65 poles in his 10 year career.

Big Game

MAY 22—The Chicago Bulls see their dreams of a four-peat go down the drain as New York eliminates them, 87-77, in Game 7 of the Eastern Conference semifinals.

Big Wins

MAY 7—Julio Cesar Chavez earns a technical decision over Frankie Randall to regain his WBC junior lightweight title. Terry Norris also regains his WBC junior middleweight title with a convincing win over Simon Brown.

Big Comeback

MAY 25—Jockey Julie Krone makes her return to racing after suffering an ankle injury back in August of 1993.

Big Upset

MAY 7—The Denver Nuggets, seeded eighth in the NBA Western Conference playoffs, stun top-seeded Seattle in the decisive fifth game of their first round series. The Sonics, with a league-best regular season record of 63-19, become the first No. 1 seed to lose in the first round since the playoffs went to a 16-team field.

MAY 23—Martina Navratilova, playing in her final French Open, is beaten by Holland's Miriam Oremans in the first round.

Big Trophy

MAY 24—Houston center Hakeem Olajuwon is named MVP of the NBA, with 66 first-place votes to beat out David Robinson of the Spurs.

1 **Three-time world driving champion** Ayrton Senna, 34, dies from massive head injuries at the San Marino Grand Prix in Imola, Italy. His car slammed head-on into a barrier at 185-mph while leading the Formula One race.
Arantxa Sanchez Vicario ends Steffi Graf's 36-match winning streak with a 4-6, 7-6 (7-3), 7-6 (8-6) victory in the Citizen Cup singles final in Hamburg.

2 **Purdue's Glenn Robinson** announces he will forego his final year of college eligibility and enter the NBA draft.
NFL files suit against the Candian Football League and their new Baltimore franchise over the use of the name "Colts." The NFL Indianapolis Colts moved out of Baltimore after the 1983 season.

3 **Dallas fires** head coach Quinn Buckner after the Mavericks post a league-worst 13-69 regular season mark.
Golden State forward Chris Webber is named the NBA Rookie of the Year.

4 **Washington names** Philadelphia 76er GM Jim Lynam head coach.
Formula One officials announce new safety procedures, including reduced speeds on pit road, at emergency meeting.
U.S. beats Russia, 3-1, for the first time since 1980, in the quarterfinals of the World Hockey Championships in Milan.
Thoroughbred Racing Hall of Fame elects jockey Steve Cauthen, 34, and trainer Jimmy Croll, 74.

5 **Cincinnati Bengals** sign top draft pick Dan Wilkinson to a six-year deal worth $14.4 million plus an NFL-record $5 million signing bonus.
Financially troubled Bruce McNall sells the CFL's Toronto Argonauts to the John Labatt Broadcast Group.

6 **Lennox Lewis defends** his WBC Heavyweight belt with an eight-round TKO of Phil Jackson in Atlantic City.

7 **Go for Gin,** a 9-1 underdog, captures the 120th Kentucky Derby with Chris McCarron in the saddle. Favorite Holy Bull finishes 12th on sloppy track.
Julio Cesar Chavez wins a technical split decision over Frankie Randall to regain his WBC super lightweight title after Randall's unintentional head butt opens a deep cut over Chavez's eye.
The Denver Nuggets stun top-seeded Seattle, 98-94 in OT, to win decisive Game 5 and oust the Sonics from the NBA playoffs.

8 **Canada beats** Finland, 2-1, in a shootout to win its first World Hockey Championship since 1961. Sweden beats U.S., 7-2, for third place.

9 **PGA Tour names** Deane Beman lieutenant Tim Finchem as commissioner.

11 **Detroit Pistons** All-Star point guard Isiah Thomas, 33, officially announces his retirement.

12 **Easy Goer,** who won the Belmont Stakes and finished second in both the Kentucky Derby and Preakness in 1989, dies of natural causes at age eight.

13 **Los Angeles Lakers name** Del Harris to replace Magic Johnson as head coach.

15 **Al Unser Jr. wins** the pole at the Indianapolis 500 for the first time with a qualifying speed of 228.011 mph in his Penske-Mercedes.
England's Laura Davies wins LPGA Championship by three strokes.

16 **Troubled tennis star** Jennifer Capriati, 18, is arrested in a Florida hotel room for possession of marijuana.

Wide World Photos

The May 29 Coca-Cola 600 featured **Jeff Gordon** (right) winning from the pole, while **John Andretti** became the first driver to compete in the Indianapolis 500 and Coke 600 in the same day.

17 **California fires** manager Buck Rodgers, replacing him with Florida Marlins' pitching coach Marcel Lachemann.
Dick Motta is named head coach of the Dallas Mavericks. Motta coached the team previously from 1980-87.
Veteran Indy-car driver Al Unser Sr. announces his retirement.
A federal appeals court reverses a $27.3 million decision awarded to runner Butch Reynolds over a 1990 IAAF two-year suspension, stemming from a disputed steroids test.

18 **Cincinnati Reds owner** Marge Schott makes derogatory comments about men who wear earrings just two months after her probation for using racial slurs ended.

19 **Portland fires** head coach Rick Adelman after the Trail Blazers fail to get past the first round of the playoffs for the second straight season.
In the NHL, Hartford fires Pierre McGuire, 32, formerly the league's youngest coach.
Monica Seles, citing lack of security, files a $10 million claim against the German Tennis Federation for losses caused by her 1993 stabbing in Hamburg.

20 **Philadelphia fires** first-year head coach Terry Simpson, after the Flyers fail to make the NHL playoffs for the fifth straight year.

21 **Tabasco Cat edges** Kentucky Derby winner Go for Gin by three-quarters of a length to win the 119th Preakness.

22 **New York eliminates** the Chicago Bulls, 87-77, in decisive seventh game of a heated NBA Eastern finals.

Milwaukee wins NBA Draft lottery, and the chance to draft Purdue's Glen Robinson.

24 **Houston Rockets'** center Hakeem Olajuwon is voted the NBA's Most Valuable Player.
The new expansion Toronto Raptors of the NBA name Isiah Thomas vice-president of basketball operations.
The Quebec Nordiques fire coach and general manager Pierre Page.
Mark Messier, who guaranteed a New York victory before the game, scores three times in the third period to lead the Rangers to a 4-2 win over New Jersey in Game 6 of the Eastern Conference final.

25 **Julie Krone**, the first female jockey to win a Triple Crown race, returns to racing for first time since a career-threatening ankle injury in 1993.

26 **Chuck Daly quits** as head coach of the New Jersey Nets. And Atlanta's Lenny Wilkens is named NBA coach of the year.

29 **Al Unser Jr. wins** the 78th Indianapolis 500 after taking the lead with 16 laps remaining when defending champion Emerson Fittipaldi crashes.
John Andretti finishes 10th at Indy then hurries to Charlotte Motor Speedway to drive in Coca-Cola 600, becoming first driver to run in both races in same day.

30 **Cincinnati acquires** outfielder Deion Sanders from Atlanta for outfielder Roberto Kelly and pitcher Roger Etheridge.

31 **Jim Courier ends** Australian Open champion Pete Sampras's quest for the Grand Slam with a 6-4, 5-7, 6-4, 6-4 win in the quarterfinals of the French Open.

JUNE '94

Sun	Mon	Tue	Wed	Thu	Fri	Sat
			1	2	3	4
5	6	7	8	9	10	11
12	13	14	15	16	17	18
19	20	21	22	23	24	25
26	27	28	29	30		

Big Games

JUNE 14—New York Rangers win the Stanley Cup for the first time since 1940, beating Vancouver, 3-2, in Game 7 of the Finals at Madison Square Garden. Defenseman Brian Leetch wins Conn Smythe trophy as playoff MVP.

JUNE 22—Houston Rockets win first major league title in city's history, defeating New York, 90-84 in Game 7 of the NBA Finals. Hakeem Olajuwon is named playoff MVP.

JUNE 22—U.S. national soccer team upsets Columbia, 2-1, at the Rose Bowl in first round of World Cup play. It is the first U.S. victory in a World Cup since shocking England, 1-0, in 1950.

Big Story

JUNE 12—O.J. Simpson's ex-wife Nicole and friend Ronald Goldman are found murdered near her condo in suburban L.A.

Big Messes

JUNE 15—In another move influenced by the new NFL salary cap, the New York Giants released quarterback Phil Simms.

JUNE 28—New York Mets pitcher Dwight Gooden is suspended for 60 days for failure to comply with his drug aftercare program.

Majors

JUNE 5—Due to rain, the men's and women's singles finals of French open occur on the same day and Spain dominates. With King Carlos looking on at Stade Roland Garros, Arantxa Sanchez Vicario beats Mary Pierce in the women's final while Sergi Bruguera defeats countryman Alberto Berasategui for the men's title.

JUNE 20—Ernie Els wins the U.S. Open golf championship in three-way playoff, defeating Loren Roberts on second extra hole. Colin Montgomerie was eliminated after 18 holes.

1 **Al Arbour**, 61, who led the New York Islanders to four consecutive Stanley Cups from 1980-83, resigns after 22 seasons behind the bench (19 in New York) and 902 career victories during the regular season and playoffs.

2 **Mary Pierce shocks** No. 1-ranked Steffi Graf in straight sets to reach the French Open final where she will meet Spain's Arantxa Sanchez Vicario. Sanchez Vicario beats countrywoman Conchita Martinez, 6-3, 6-2.
Florida St. righthander Paul Wilson is selected by N.Y. Mets as the first pick in baseball's annual amateur draft.

5 **New York Knicks** come from behind to edge Reggie Miller and the Indiana Pacers, 94-90, in Game 7 of the Eastern Conference finals. The Knicks will face Western Conference champion Houston in the NBA Finals.

8 **Baseball owners**, meeting in Cincinnati, unanimously agree to seek a salary cap from the players' union and that in the event of a strike, any collective bargaining agreement must be approved by 75% of the owners instead of the previous simple majority. University of Kansas chancellor Gene Budig is named AL president, replacing Bobby Brown.

11 **Tabasco Cat**, with Pat Day aboard, wins the 126th Belmont Stakes, beating Kentucky Derby winner Go for Gin by two lengths.
Oklahoma routs Georgia Tech, 13-5, in Omaha to win baseball's College World Series for the first time since 1951. Sooners' outfielder Chip Glass is named MVP.

12 **The bodies** of O.J. Simpson's former wife, Nicole Brown Simpson, and friend Ronald Goldman are found outside her condominium in suburban Los Angeles. Both were stabbed.

13 **Ryne Sandberg announces** his retirement from baseball. The 10-time All-Star second baseman with the Chicago Cubs leaves the game and the $16.1 million remaining in his contract with 245 career homeruns and over 2,000 hits.
Los Angeles police question O.J. Simpson in connection with the murder of his ex-wife, Nicole Brown Simpson. Investigators also search Simpson's Brentwood estate for evidence.

14 **The New York Rangers** finally win their first Stanley Cup in 54 years, beating Vancouver, 3-2, in Game 7 at Madison Square Garden. New York defenseman Brian Leetch wins Conn Smythe Trophy as playoff MVP.
Baseball owners present players' union with seven-year economic deal that includes a salary cap, revenue sharing, and elimination of salary arbitration.
In Philadelphia, the NHL Flyers welcome back Hall of Famer Bob Clark as team president and the NBA 76ers name John Lucas as head coach and GM.

15 **Phil Simms**, who refused to retire, is released by the New York Giants largely because of NFL's new salary cap. Simms, a 15-year veteran quarterback, led the Giants to their first Super Bowl victory in 1987.
Major League Soccer, the newly-formed pro outdoor league, announces the first seven cities in its proposed 12-team circuit set for 1995. The cities include Boston, Columbus (Ohio), East Rutherford (N.J.), Los Angeles, San Jose, Uniondale (N.Y.) and Washington, D.C.

16 **Sergei Fedorov** of the Detroit Red Wings becomes the first Russian player to win the NHL's Hart Trophy as regular season MVP.

New York Rangers' coach **Mike Keenan** (center) joins his players for a Stanley Cup photo opportunity after defeating Vancouver, 4-3, on June 15, to win the Cup for the first time since 1940.

17 O.J. Simpson, charged with the murders of ex-wife Nicole Brown Simpson and Ronald Goldman, finally surrenders, after leading L.A. police on a bizarre, nationally-televised car chase.
World Cup USA '94 officially opens at Chicago's Soldier Field where defending champion Germany beats Bolivia, 1-0.

18 The United States ties Switzerland (1-1), while Ireland upsets Italy (1-0) and Romania stuns Colombia (3-1) in World Cup soccer.

20 O.J. Simpson pleads not guilty to the murders of ex-wife Nicole Brown Simpson and Ronald Goldman and is held without bail.
South African golfer Ernie Els defeats Loren Roberts and Colin Montgomerie to win three-way extra-round playoff for U.S. Open Championship in Oakmont, Pa. Els beats Roberts on second hole of sudden death after they tie at 74.

21 Lori McNeil, ranked 22nd in the world, stuns top seed and defending champion Steffi Graf, 7-5, 7-6 (7-5), in first round at Wimbledon.
Cincinnati Reds sign injured free agent outfielder Ron Gant to two-year contract. Gant was released Mar. 15 by Atlanta.
Wake Forest men's basketball program is placed on one-year probation by NCAA for recruiting violations.

22 Houston Rockets beat New York, 90-84, in Game 7 of the NBA Finals, to capture the city's first professional sports title. Rockets' center Hakeem Olajuwon is named MVP.
United States shocks Colombia, 2-1, in World Cup before 93,194 at Rose Bowl. Win is first for USA since upsetting England in 1950 Cup tournament.

23 P.J. Carlesimo is named head coach of the Portland Trail Blazers, signing a five-year, $7.8 million contract to leave Seton Hall.
Terry Murray is named head coach of the Philadelphia Flyers.
Ohio State basketball and track and field programs are placed on probation by NCAA for a variety of recruiting violations.

25 Vinny Pazienza wins a unanimous 12-round decision over Roberto Duran in Las Vegas.

26 Romania defeats the U.S., 1-0, to reach Round of 16 in World Cup soccer. Americans expect to advance after ending first round with 1-1-1 record.

27 NBA players union files suit asking that the league's salary cap, college draft and right of first refusal be declared illegal.
Magic Johnson buys a $10 million share of the Los Angeles Lakers.

28 Toronto Maple Leafs trade captain Wendel Clark to Quebec for Mats Sundin in six-player deal. Florida makes Windsor defenseman Ed Jovanovski the first pick of NHL Draft in Hartford.
New Hartford GM Jim Rutherford announces Paul Holmgren will serve second stint as Whalers' head coach.

29 Purdue's Glenn Robinson is selected by Milwaukee as the first overall pick in NBA Draft.

30 Argentina's Diego Maradona is banned from World Cup play after testing positive for banned drugs.
Tonya Harding is stripped of her 1994 U.S. Figure Skating title and banned for life by U.S. Skating Federation.

JULY '94

Sun	Mon	Tue	Wed	Thu	Fri	Sat
					1	2
3	4	5	6	7	8	9
10	11	12	13	14	15	16
17	18	19	20	21	22	23
24/31	25	26	27	28	29	30

Big Games

JULY 4—Brazil defeats the United States, 1-0, in the World Cup round of 16. A crowd of 84,147 sees the game in Stanford, Calif.
JULY 12—Montreal's Moises Alou's doubles in San Diego's Tony Gwynn for the winning run in the bottom of the 10th inning, as the National League beats the AL, 8-7. The game is witnessed by a crown of 59,568 at Pittsburgh's Three Rivers Stadium.

Big Story

JULY 2—Just days after Colombia was eliminated from the first round of the World Cup, team member Andres Escobar is gunned down outside a bar in Medellín. Escobar accidentally scored a goal against his own team in a 2-1 loss to the U.S. on June 22.

Big Mess

JULY 15—Mike Keenan decides to leave his position as head coach of the New York Rangers, claiming a breach of contract. Two days later he's named head coach and general manager of the St. Louis Blues.

Majors

JULY 2-3—Conchita Martinez and Pete Sampras win at Wimbledon. Martinez denies Martina Navratilova a 10th singles title while Sampras wins for the second year in a row.
JULY 17—Golfer Nick Price rallies to beat Jasper Parnevik and win the British Open.
JULY 24—Patty Sheehan wins her second U.S. Women's Open.

Big Mig

JULY 24—Miguel Indurain of Spain earns his fourth consecutive Tour de France cycling title.

Big Effort

JULY 28—Texas pitcher Kenny Rogers is the first lefty in AL history to throw a perfect game, beating California, 4-0.

2 **Conchita Martinez** denies Martina Navratilova a 10th Wimbledon singles title, winning the women's final, 6-4, 3-6, 6-3.
Andres Escobar, the Colombian soccer player who accidently kicked the ball into his own net in a World Cup loss to the USA, is shot to death outside a bar in Medellin. The Colombian team was eliminated in the first round.

3 **Pete Sampras beats** Goran Ivanisevic, 7-6 (7-2), 7-6 (7-5), 6-0, for his second straight men's title at Wimbledon.
Michael Schumacher defeats Damon Hill by 12.642 seconds to win the French Grand Prix at Magny Cours. Former world champion and current Indy-car regular Nigel Mansell returns to F-1 racing for the weekend but does not finish.

4 **Brazil ousts** the USA, 1-0, before 84,147 at Stanford, while Holland eliminates Ireland, 2-0, in World Cup soccer.
The St. Louis Blues move to acquire two big-name defensemen, sending Phil Housley to Calgary for Al MacInnis and signing New Jersey's Scott Stevens to an offer sheet worth $16 million.

6 **American Leroy Burrell breaks** the 100-meter world record with a time of 9.85 seconds. The previous mark of 9.86 belonged to Carl Lewis.
NHL's Quebec Nordiques name Marc Crawford coach.

7 **Darryl Strawberry goes** 0 for 3 in his debut with the San Francisco Giants.

8 **O.J. Simpson is ordered** by judge Kathleen Kennedy-Powell to stand trial on two counts of murder.

9 **Brazil edges** Holland, 3-2, and Italy knocks off Spain, 2-1, to advance to World Cup semifinals.

10 **Bulgaria upsets** defending champion Germany, 2-1, and after playing to a 1-1 tie, Sweden beats Romania, 5-4, on penalty kicks to advance to World Cup semifinals.

11 **Notre Dame announces** it will join the Big East, as a non-football playing member, starting in the 1995-1996 season.
Tonya Harding's bodyguard Shawn Eckardt is sentenced to 18 months in prison for his role in the Nancy Kerrigan assault.

12 **The National League wins** the 65th All-Star game, 8-7, in Pittsburgh as Montreal's Moises Alou doubles in Tony Gwynn of San Diego in the bottom of the 10th. Atlanta's Fred McGriff, who tied the game with a two-run, pinch-hit HR in the 9th is named MVP.
The University of Mississippi fires head football coach Billy Brewer in the wake of an announcement that the NCAA is investigating the Ole Miss football program.
NCAA puts the University of Washington football program on two years probation for paying players for work not actually performed. Huskies opt to have penalties imposed in 1995.

13 **Brazil and Italy**, each seeking a fourth championship, advance to the World Cup final. In the semifinals: Brazil edges Sweden, 1-0, and Italy downs Bulgaria, 2-1.
Jeff Gillooly, Tonya Harding's ex-husband, is sentenced to two years in prison and given a $100,000 fine for masterminding the Jan. 6 attack on Nancy Kerrigan.

14 **Boxing promoter Don King** is indicted on nine counts of insurance fraud by a federal grand. King allegedly submitted a false insurance claim for $350,000 with Lloyd's of London.

United States goalkeeper **Tony Meola** looks on helplessly as a ball kicked by Brazilian forward **Bebeto** (center) becomes the winning goal in Brazil's 1-0 win over the U.S., July 4 at Stanford Stadium.

15 Mike Keenan, who coached the New York Rangers to their first Stanley Cup since 1940, accuses the Rangers of breaching his contract and announces he's leaving with four years remaining on his five-year pact.

17 Brazil wins an unprecedented fourth World Cup, defeating Italy, 3-2, at the Rose Bowl in the first final decided by penalty kicks. The teams were knotted in a scoreless tie after 120 minutes.
Nick Price sinks 50-foot eagle putt at the 17th hole on his way to winning his first British Open.
Two days after declaring himself a free agent and bolting the New York Rangers, Mike Keenan signs a five-year deal as head coach and GM of the St. Louis Blues. The Rangers say they intend to fight the move.

18 Federal judge Kevin Duffy deals NBA players' union a setback, ruling that the league's salary cap, college draft and right of first refusal do not violate antitrust law. He also urges both sides to work out a new collective bargaining agreement.
The baseball players' union emphatically rejects the owners' salary cap proposal.

20 The Kingdome is closed in Seattle due to falling ceiling tiles. Mariner baseball games and Seahawk NFL games will have to be rescheduled until the ceiling is completely renovated.

22 O.J. Simpson, in response to double murder charges, issues a plea of not guilty.
All-Star free agent Dominique Wilkins agrees to a three-year, $11 million deal with the Boston Celtics.
Vancouver's NBA expansion franchise names former New York Knicks and current Wisconsin head coach Stu Jackson as general manager.

23 The third Goodwill Games open in St. Petersburg, Russia, with five weightlifting world records set on first day of competition.

24 NHL commissioner Gary Bettman suspends former New York Rangers coach Mike Keenan until Sept. 24 and fines him $100,000 for breaking his contract to sign with St. Louis. Rangers deal Esa Tikkanen and Doug Lidster to Blues for Petr Nedved as part of settlement.
Spanish cyclist Miguel Indurain wins his fourth straight Tour de France by more than five minutes, even though he didn't win a single road stage.
Patty Sheehan wins her second U.S. Women's Open golf title in three years, beating Tammie Green by one stroke.

28 Kenny Rogers of the Texas Rangers becomes first left-hander in American League history to pitch a perfect game, blanking California, 4-0, at The Ballpark in Arlington.
Players' union sets Aug. 12 as baseball strike deadline.
Bill Fitch agrees to become the Los Angeles Clippers' ninth head coach since they moved to L.A. in 1984.

29 Los Angeles Kings send left wing Luc Robitaille to Pittsburgh for right wing Rick Tocchet and a second-round draft pick.

30 Michael Jordan hits the first home run of his professional baseball career with a solo shot in the eighth inning as Birmingham beats Carolina, 6-1, in the Double A Southern League.

31 Sergey Bubka scales 20 feet, 1¾ inches to break his world pole vault record for the 17th time.

AUG '94

Sun	Mon	Tue	Wed	Thu	Fri	Sat
	1	2	3	4	5	6
7	8	9	10	11	12	13
14	15	16	17	18	19	20
21	22	23	24	25	26	27
28	29	30	31			

Big Mess

AUG. 12—Major league baseball players go out on strike in protest of owners' plans for a salary cap. The move will eventually end the season and cancel the World Series for the first time in 90 years.

Big Game

AUG. 14—Dream Team II wins the World Championship of Basketball, 137-91, over Russia.
AUG. 27—Venezuela edges Northridge, Calif., 4-3, to win Little League World Series after three hour rain delay

Big Deal

AUG. 28—Madison Square Garden, the Knicks and the Rangers are sold as part of a $1.1 billion deal with Cablevision and ITT.

Major

AUG. 14—Nick Price earns his second major tournament title of the year by capturing the PGA championship at Southern Hills in Tulsa.

Big Upset

AUG. 26—Hector Acero Sanchez wins the WBC junior featherweight title, beating champion Tracy Patterson. Patterson is the adopted son of former heavyweight champion Floyd Patterson.
AUG. 29—Boris Becker and Goran Ivanisevic are each knocked out of the first round of the U.S. Open. Becker loses to Richey Reneberg in five sets while Ivanisevic falls to Marcus Zoecke.

Hired

AUG. 2—Edmonton Oilers name George Burnett as head coach, replacing Glen Sather, who returns to his position in the front office.
AUG. 9—New York Rangers name Colin Campbell to replace Mike Keenan as coach.

1 **Baltimore shortstop** Cal Ripken Jr. plays in his 2,000th consecutive game, 130 short of Lou Gehrig's record.

2 **NBA rejects** contracts signed by forwards A.C. Green of Phoenix and Horace Grant of Orlando, saying deals circumvent salary cap.
Algeria's Nourredine Morceli sets a world record in 3,000 meters with a time of 7:25.11 in Monte Carlo meet.

3 **Baseball owners refuse** to make a $7.8 million pension payment. Angered players consider moving up strike date.

4 **Dream Team II beats** scrappy Spaniards, 115-100, in opener of World Basketball Championships in Hamilton, Ontario.
The Cotton Bowl will cease to be a major college football bowl game in 1996 as the new bowl alliance picks Fiesta, Sugar and Orange bowls to host national championship game on a rotating basis.

5 **Phoenix Suns** and A.C. Green file suit against NBA for the league's invalidation of Green's contract.
NBA's Minnesota Timberwolves are sold for $88 million to a group led by former state senator Glen Taylor.
Toni Kukoc signs six-year deal worth $26 million with the Chicago Bulls, surpassing Michael Jordan as the highest-paid player in Bulls' history.
Paul Azinger, absent from the PGA Tour since late 1993 when cancer was found in his shoulder, returns to action with a 4-over-par 76 at the Buick Open in Grand Blanc, Mich.

6 **Jeff Gordon wins** the inaugural NASCAR Brickyard 400 at the Indianapolis Motor Speedway, picking up a winner's check worth $613,000.

7 **U.S. Women's basketball beats** France, 87-63 to win the gold medal at the Goodwill Games.

9 **New York Rangers promote** former Keenan assistant Colin Campbell to head coach.

10 **Baseball talks** are broken off without any agreement between the players and owners, setting the stage for a strike.
Vancouver Canucks' president Pat Quinn steps down as head coach, naming assistant Rick Ley to replace him.
CFL announces that 1997 Grey Cup will be played at Baltimore's Memorial Stadium.

12 **Baseball strike begins** at 12:45 a.m. EDT after final out of Seattle-Oakland game. President Clinton urges owners and players to return to bargaining table.

13 **Former world heavyweight champ** Riddick Bowe knocks out a kneeling Buster Mathis in the 4th round. The bout is judged a no contest.

14 **Nick Price wins** his second PGA Championship in three years, shooting a tournament record 11-under 269 at Southern Hills Country Club in Tulsa.
Dream Team II demolishes Russia, 137-91, for the World Basketball Championship gold medal in Toronto.

15 **The largest crowd** in NFL history (112,376) turns out in Mexico City to see Houston beat Dallas, 6-0, in the mud of Azteca Stadium.

16 **Ole Miss admits** to nine of 15 NCAA allegations relating to the Mississippi football program.

17 **Minnesota Timberwolves fire** head coach Sidney Lowe and his staff. Lowe's record with Minnesota was 33-102 in two years.

Jonathan Daniel/Allsport

The plaintive cry of baseball fans across the country went unheeded on Aug. 12 when the most exciting season in 25 years was shut down by a players strike over the owners desire for a salary cap.

18 **Florida ranked No. 1** in both AP media and USA Today/CNN coaches preseason college football polls. AP picks Notre Dame No. 2, while coaches tab Florida St. second.

19 **NBA rejects** Toni Kukoc's big money contract with Chicago, saying it violates the salary cap.

20 **Holy Bull wins** the 125th Travers Stakes at Saratoga by a neck over Concern. Tabasco Cat is third.
  George Foreman wins his suit against the World Boxing Association when a federal judge rules that the WBA "acted capriciously" in denying an official sanction to Foreman's Nov. 5 bout with heavyweight champion Michael Moorer.

21 **NASCAR driver** Ernie Irvan is in critical condition and on life-support systems after suffering collapsed lungs and a broken skull in a crash while practicing at Michigan International Speedway.

23 **O.J. Simpson is** one of 48 players named to the NFL's all-time team (see page 464).

24 **Baseball owners** and players resume their labor talks in New York for the first time since start of strike, but no progress is made.
  Argentine soccer legend Diego Maradona is suspended for 15 months by FIFA for failing the drug test that got him tossed from the World Cup.

25 **Baseball labor talks** break off after just two days of negotiation.

27 **Venezuela nips Northridge,** Calif., 4-3, after a three-hour rain delay to capture its first Little League World Series championship. Northridge represents the community hit hardest in the Jan. 17 California earthquake.

28 **The New York Knicks** and Rangers as well as Madison Square Garden and the MSG cable network are sold to Cablevision Systems and ITT Corp. for $1.1 billion.
  The college football season gets underway as Nebraska routs West Virginia, 31-0, in the Kickoff Classic at East Rutherford, N.J.
  Eighteen-year-old Tiger Woods becomes the youngest winner of the U.S. Amateur golf championship and the first black player to win as he rallies from six holes back to beat Oklahoma St. junior Trip Kuehne, 2-up.
  Michael Schumacher of Germany is disqualified for an illegal skid plate after placing first in the Belgian Grand Prix. Runner-up Damon Hill of England is declared the winner.

29 **Pittsburgh Penguins captain** and two-time league MVP Mario Lemieux announces he will sit out the 1994-95 NHL season because of recurring back woes and fatigue brought on by his radiation treatments for Hodgkin's disease.
  Minnesota Timberwolves name former Indiana Pacers assistant Bill Blair as head coach.
  San Antonio Spurs name former Orlando Magic assistant Bob Hill head coach.
  Nigel Mansell announces his intention to leave the Indy-car circuit at the end of the 1994 season and return to Formula One racing.

30 **NHL owners and players resume** negotiations on a collective bargaining agreement while the league denies reports of a player lockout.

31 **Superior Court Judge** Lance Ito postpones O.J. Simpson's murder trial until Sept. 26.

SEPT '94

Sun	Mon	Tue	Wed	Thu	Fri	Sat
				1	2	3
4	5	6	7	8	9	10
11	12	13	14	15	16	17
18	19	20	21	22	23	24
25	26	27	28	29	30	

Big Messes

SEPT. 14—The baseball season is officially cancelled due to the player's strike. This guarantees there will be no World Series for the first time since 1904.
SEPT. 30—NHL commissioner Gary Bettman announces the delay of the start of the 1994-95 regular season for two weeks, while owners and players bicker over a new collective bargaining agreement.

Big Game

SEPT. 9—Michael Jordan returns for one last hoop game at Chicago Stadium, scoring 52 points in Scottie Pippen's charity exhibition.

Big Deals

SEPT. 8—Phoenix Suns sign forward Danny Manning, squeezing him under the cap for 20 percent of his market value.
SEPT. 13—Fox network strikes again, signing five-year, $155 million deal for NHL broadcast rights. Observers estimate Fox overbid by $60 million.

Majors

SEPT. 10—Arantxa Sanchez Vicario upsets Steffi Graf in three sets to win U.S. Open.
SEPT. 11—Andre Agassi becomes the first unseeded player in the Open era to win the U.S. men's title, defeating Michael Stich.

Big Upset

SEPT. 24—Oliver McCall scores a second-round TKO over Lennox Lewis to win the WBC heavyweight title at London's Wembley Arena.

Milestone

SEPT. 5—San Francisco wide receiver Jerry Rice passes NFL great Jim Brown to become the league's all-time touchdown leader with 127. Rice scores three times as the 49ers rout the Raiders, 44-14, at Candlestick Park.

1 **Mighty Ducks** of Anaheim sign 1993 first round pick Paul Kariya to a three-year deal worth $6.5 million. Kariya, the 1993 Hobey Baker Award winner, led Maine to the '93 NCAA title, then starred on Canada's 1994 Olympic (silver medal) and World Championship (gold medal) teams.

2 **Ginger Helgeson** of the U.S. jolts third-seeded Conchita Martinez, 3-6, 6-4, 6-1, in the second round of U.S. Open.
Acting baseball commissioner Bud Selig threatens to cancel the remainder of the season if a resolution to the strike isn't found by Sept. 9.

3 **Dallas Mavericks sign** top draft pick, guard Jason Kidd, to a 9-year contract worth a reported $60 million.

4 **The NFL opens** its 75th anniverary season as defending Super Bowl champion Dallas beats Pittsburgh, 26-9, in coach Barry Switzer's pro debut.
Bill Elliott ends 52-race NASCAR winless streak by capturing the Southern 500 at Darlington (S.C.). He passes leader Dale Earnhardt with 13 laps remaining.

5 **All-Pro receiver Jerry Rice** of San Francisco scores three times to break the NFL career touchdown record of 126 set by Jim Brown as the 49ers whip the L.A. Raiders, 44-14, on Monday night. Rice's three TDs push his career total to 127.

6 **Unseeded Jaime Yzaga** of Peru upsets defending champion Pete Sampras in five sets in the fourth round of the U.S. Open. The match lasts three hours and 38 minutes.
American swimmer Tom Dolan, 19, sets a world record in 400-meter individual medley with a time of 4:12.3 at the World Championships in Rome.

7 **China shatters** the women's 4 x 100-meter relay world record with a time of 3:37.91 at the World Aquatic Championships in Rome. Two day's earlier, China's Le Jingyi broke the world record in the 100-meter freestyle.

8 **NBA free agent** forward Danny Manning signs one-year contract with Phoenix for $1 million—roughly 20 percent of his market value. He takes less to fit under the salary cap.

9 **Michael Jordan shakes** off the rust and pours in 52 points as he returns to Chicago Stadium to play in a charity game hosted by former Bulls' teammate Scottie Pippen. It is the final game played at the Stadium.
Acting commissioner Bud Selig's season cancellation deadline passes as baseball negotiations break off again.
Chicago Cubs name Minnesota general manager Andy MacPhail as club president.

10 **Arantxa Sanchez Vicario beats** Steffi Graf in three sets to add the U.S. Open championship to her '94 French Open trophy.

11 **Andre Agassi completes** a remarkable run in the U.S. Open, beating Michael Stich in straight sets to become the first unseeded player to win the men's title since Fred Stolle in 1966.
Al Unser Jr. clinches IndyCar driving championship with second place in Texaco-Havoline 200 at Elkhart Lake, Wis. PPG Cup is second for Unser and ninth for team owner Roger Penske.
Nick Price wins the Canadian Open, becoming the first golfer on the PGA Tour to win six times in a year since Tom Watson in 1980.

12 **National Labor Relations Board** awards NFL players $30 million in back pay stemming from a lockout by owners at the end of the 1987 players' strike.

John Gichigi/Allsport

Challenger **Oliver McCall** (right), a 5½-to-1 underdog, jumps for joy after realizing that WBC heavyweight champion **Lennox Lewis** has been counted out in the second round of their Sept. 24 bout.

13 **The NHL announces** new five-year TV deals with Fox and ESPN. Fox outbids CBS to secure broadcast rights for $155 million.
NBA competition committee moves to create more offense by shortening three-point line to 22 feet and award three free throws for a foul on a three-point attempt. Several new rules are also passed to curb the recent increase in violent play.

14 **The World Series is cancelled** for the first time since 1904 as baseball owners call off the remainder of the season. Vote is 26-2 with Baltimore and Cincinnati dissenting. No hope seen for ending 34-day-old players' strike.

15 **Kansas City manager** Hal McRae and his coaching staff are sent packing by the Royals after going 64-41 in the AL Central.
With the baseball season over, Cincinnati Reds outfielder Deion Sanders signs a one-year deal worth a potential $1.85 million, to play cornerback for the San Francisco 49ers.

17 **Julio Cesar Chavez knocks out** Meldrick Taylor with a left hook in the eighth round in the rematch of their controversial 1990 fight.
Buffalo Sabres sign All-Star center Pat LaFontaine to a five-year, $22.5 million contract extension.

20 **Boston Red Sox fire** manager Butch Hobson after three straight losing seasons.

21 **NHL commissioner** Gary Bettman says the league will push back the start of the 1994-95 season if a collective bargaining agreement isn't reached by opening night on Oct. 1.

24 **Oliver McCall**, a 5½-to-1 underdog, wins WBC heavyweight title by stopping champion Lennox Lewis 31 seconds into the second round in London.

25 **Sweden rallies** to beat the U.S., 3-2, and Russia upsets defending champion Germany, 4-1, in Davis Cup semifinal matches. The Swedes and Russians will play for the Cup in Moscow, Dec. 2-4.

26 **The O.J. Simpson murder** trial begins with the jury selection process. Strangely, the first prospective juror is No. 0032, the number Simpson wore in college and the NFL.
Baltimore fires manager Johnny Oates. The Orioles were 63-49 and 6 1/2 games out of first in AL East when the strike began.

28 **NHL players reject** owners' contract proposal, saying it is little more than a salary cap.
NFL owners decide on details of mid-February expansion draft for new Carolina and Jacksonville franchises. Panthers and Jaguars will also get No. 1 and 2 picks in each round of regular draft and seven extra picks in 1995 and '96 drafts.

29 **In an 11th hour attempt** to avert a lockout, NHL players offer a no-strike pledge, if league owners will call off the expected lockout announcement on Oct. 1. Owners reject offer.
NBA increases salary cap to $15,964,000.

30 **NHL commissioner** Gary Bettman postpones start of the 1994-95 season until Oct. 15, in hopes of getting players back to bargaining table.
Roy Tarpley, banned from the NBA for life just three years ago for repeated drug problems, is reinstated by the league.

OCT '94

Sun	Mon	Tue	Wed	Thu	Fri	Sat
						1
2	3	4	5	6	7	8
9	10	11	12	13	14	15
16	17	18	19	20	21	22
23 / 30	24 / 31	25	26	27	28	29

Big Game

OCT. 15—Penn State defeats Michigan at Ann Arbor, 31-24, a win that elevates the Nittany Lions to the top of both college polls. Ki-Jana Carter rushes for 165 yards on 26 carries.

Big Plays

OCT. 23—The New Orleans-LA Rams game is one of the wildest ever, with the Saints prevailing, 37-34, at the Superdome. Robert Bailey sets an NFL record with a 103-yard punt return. Tyrone Hughes sets another NFL record for kickoff return yardage in one game with 347 yards, including runbacks of 92 and 98 yards for scores. Toby Wright also returned a fumble 98 yards for a Rams TD.

Big Upset

OCT. 15—Auburn, a 17-point underdog, stuns No. 1 Florida, 36-33, at Florida Field in Gainesville. The loss is the first league home setback under coach Steve Spurrier. Meanwhile, Auburn coach Terry Bowden is still undefeated in 18 Div. 1-A games.
OCT. 19—Duke snaps the North Carolina women's soccer team unbeaten streak at 101 games, beating the Tar Heels, 3-2.

Shula Bowl I

OCT. 2—Miami beats Cincinnati in first NFL father vs. son coaching battle. Don Shula and the Dolphins beat David Shula and the Bengals, 23-7.

Big Fight

OCT. 1—Pernell Whitaker defends his WBC welterweight title with a unanimous decision over Buddy Mc Girt at Norfolk, Va.

Big Debut

OCT. 4—Martina Hingis makes her pro debut at age 14 a successful one by beating Patty Fendick in a tournament in Switzerland.

1 **Pernell Whitaker** (34-1-1) defends his WBC welterweight title against Buddy McGirt, scoring a unanimous 12-round decision in Norfolk, Va.

2 **Don Shula** (496 games coached), faces off against his son Dave (37 games coached), in the first father-son coaching matchup in NFL history. Don proves father knows best when his Miami Dolphins beat Dave's Cincinnati Bengals, 23-7.
University of North Carolina women's soccer team, winners of eight consecutive championships, sees its 92-game winning streak end at the collegiate America Cup with a scoreless tie against Notre Dame.

4 **Martina Hingis**, 14, beats veteran Patty Fendick, 6-4, 6-3 in her professional tennis debut at the Swiss Indoor in Zurich.

5 **NBA Commissioner** David Stern promises season will start on time despite the lack of a new collective bargaining agreement.
Judge Lance Ito denies a motion by O.J. Simpson's defense team to suppress evidence in the case.
Roy Tarpley, just recently reinstated by the NBA, signs a multi-year deal with his old team the Dallas Mavericks.

7 **Kansas City Royals name** former Royals catcher Bob Boone manager.

8 **No. 13 Miami surprises** the No. 3 Florida State Seminoles, 34-20, and unranked Boston College shocks No. 8 Notre Dame, 30-11 in college football.

9 **Mario Andretti places** 18th in the last race of his long career at the Grand Prix of Monterey (Calif.) Andretti's engine blew with three laps to go. Paul Tracy takes the checkered flag.

10 **NHL's Players Association** present a new contract proposal to the owners in hopes of playing a full 84-game schedule.

11 **NHL owners reject** the player's new contract proposal, indefinitely postponing the start of the regular season.
The Orange Bowl Committee votes to relocate the annual New Year's Day game to Joe Robbie Stadium followin the 1996 season.

12 **Texas Rangers dismiss** two-year manager Kevin Kennedy. Kennedy compiled a symmetrical 138-138 record at Texas.

14 **The White House** appoints W.J. Usery as a mediator in the continuing baseball strike talks.
Rollie Massimino resigns as the head basketball coach at UNLV in exchange for a reported $1.8 million buyout after stories of a secret supplementary $375,000 annual contract surfaced. UNLV asks permission of the Seattle Supersonics to talk with assistant Tim Grgurich.

15 **No. 1 Florida loses** to No. 6 Auburn, 36-33, on a Tiger touchdown with 30 seconds to play. No. 3 Penn State downs No. 5 Michigan, 31-24.
Orlando Magic sign hold-out guard Anfernee Hardaway to a nine-year, $70 million deal.

16 **Penn State jumps** to No. 1 in the AP football poll and Colorado is ranked second after their win over Oklahoma.
Baltimore Orioles name Cleveland Indians pitching coach Phil Regan manager.
Michael Schumacher returns from a two-race suspension to win the European Grand Prix in Spain.

17 **Felipe Alou** of the Montreal Expos is named National League Manager of the Year. The Chicago Cubs ax manager Tom Trebelhorn.

Wide World Photos

The winning United States team gathers around captain **JoAnne Carner** after defeating Europe, 13-7, to recapture the Solheim Cup on Oct. 23, at White Sulphur Springs, West Va.

Milwaukee Bucks call a press conference to announce the team and the draft's No. 1 pick, Glenn Robinson, are four years and $40 million apart in contract negotiations.

18 **Buck Showalter** of the New York Yankees is named American League Manager of the Year. Tony LaRussa signs a three-year contract extension with the Oakland Athletics and the Boston Red Sox name former Texas Ranger Kevin Kennedy manager.

19 **University of North Carolina's** women's soccer team falls to Duke, 3-2, ending their amazing 101-game unbeaten streak. It was only their second loss in 206 games, dating back eight years.
Texas Rangers hire former Baltimore skipper Johnny Oates as their new manager replacing the fired Kevin Kennedy.

21 **Jim Riggleman**, formerly of the San Diego Padres, is named manager of the Chicago Cubs. He becomes the 12th Cubs manager in 13 years.
Tim Grgurich, a former assistant to Jerry Tarkanian at UNLV, agrees to take over the head coaching duties at Nevada-Las Vegas in the wake of Rollie Massimino's dismisssal.

22 **Heisman hopeful** Steve McNair of tiny Alcorn State breaks former BYU quarterback Ty Detmer's NCAA career total offense record of 14,665 yards with a 1-AA single-game record 649-yard performance in a 41-37 win over league rival Southern. MacNair has amassed 15,049 yards in four years at Alcorn State.

23 **United States wins** the Solheim Cup with a 13-7 victory over the European team. The U.S. women win eight of 10 singles matches on the final day to reclaim the women's version of the Ryder Cup.

Dale Earnhardt clinches his record-tying seventh Winston Cup championship with a victory in the AC Delco 500 at Rockingham, N.C. Earnhardt ties racing legend Richard Petty on the all-time list.

24 **Atlanta right-hander** Greg Maddux wins his third consecutive Cy Young award, becoming the first pitcher in major league history to ever do so. Maddux compiled a 16-6 mark and an astounding 1.56 ERA to become the sixth pitcher in history to win three Cy Young awards.
NHL announces it will shorten each team's schedule by four games, cancelling two home and two away contests because of the labor dispute that has pushed back the start of the season.

25 **Kansas City right-hander** David Cone wins the American League Cy Young award edging Yankee hurler Jimmy Key. Cone tallied a 16-4 mark with a 2.94 ERA.

26 **Chicago first baseman** Frank Thomas repeats as American League MVP receiving 24 of 28 first place votes. Thomas hit .353 with 38 HRs and a 101 RBI. Seattle's Ken Griffey finishes second.
NHL players union announces it will stage a "four-on-four" charity tournament Nov. 10-12 in Hamilton, Ont. All-Star teams representing Quebec, Alberta, Ontario and the U.S. are expected to compete.

27 **NBA owners** and players reach no-strike, no-lockout agreement, clearing way for opening of regular season on schedule, Nov. 4. Deal assures uninterrupted 1994-95 season.
Houston first baseman Jeff Bagwell is unanimous choice for National League MVP award. Bagwell hit .368 with 39 HRs and a major league-leading 116 RBI in 110 games. S.F. Giant Matt Williams is runner-up.

JANUARY

1 NFL Playoff (2): AFC/NFC wild card game.
1 Major bowl games (3): Gator (Gainsville); Orange (Miami); Peach (Atlanta).
2 Major bowl games (7): Car Quest Bowl (Miami); Citrus (Orlando); Cotton (Dallas); Fiesta (Tempe); Hall of Fame (Tampa); Rose (Pasadena) and Sugar (New Orleans).
7 NCAA Convention begins (San Antonio).
7 NFL playoffs (2): AFC/NFC semifinal games.
8 NFL playoffs (2): AFC/NFC semifinal games.
15 NFL playoffs (2): AFC/NFC championship games.
16 Australian Open tennis begins (Melbourne).
21 NHL All-Star Game (San Jose).*
29 Super Bowl XXIX

FEBRUARY

3 Davis Cup first round begins (eight sites).
4 24 Hours at Daytona begins (Daytona Beach).
5 NFL Pro Bowl (Honolulu).
6 U.S. Figure Skating Championships (Providence).
12 NBA All-Star Game (Phoenix).
19 Daytona 500 (Daytona Beach).
19 PBA National bowling begins (Toledo).*

MARCH

4 Iditarod Trail Sled Dog race begins (Anchorage to Nome).
6 World Figure Skating Championships begin (Birmingham, England).
10 NCAA Indoor Track & Field Championships begin (Indianapolis).
10 IAAF World Indoor Championships (Barcelona, Spain).
11 XIIth Pan American Games begin (Argentina).
12 NFL Annual Meeting begins (Phoenix).
16 NCAA Women's Division I Basketball tournament begins.
16 NCAA Men's Division I Basketball tournament begins.
23 LPGA Dinah Shore golf begins (Rancho Mirage, Calif.).
30 NCAA Div. I Hockey Final Four begins (Providence).
31 Davis Cup second round begins (four sites).

APRIL

1 NCAA Women's Basketball Final Four begins (Minneapolis).
1 NCAA Men's Basketball Final Four begins (Seattle).
2 U.S. Men's Open bowling begins (Troy, Mich.).
2 Baseball Opening Night.
6 Masters golf begins (Augusta).
9 NHL regular season ends.*
11 NHL Stanley Cup playoffs begin.*
17 Boston Marathon.
17 PBA Tournament of Champions bowling begins (Fairlong, Ohio).
22 Women's Federation Cup tennis first round begins.
23 NBA regular season ends.
23 NFL Draft begins (New York).
26 Tour DuPont cycling race begins (Eastern U.S.).
27 NBA playoffs begin.

MAY

1 ABC Masters bowling begins (Reno, Nev.).
6 Kentucky Derby (Louisville).
11 LPGA McDonald's Championship golf begins (Wilmington, Del.).
20 Preakness Stakes (Baltimore).
22 French Open tennis begins (Paris).
27 NCAA Men's Div. I Lacrosse Final Four begins (College Park, Md.).
28 Indianapolis 500.
31 NCAA Men's and Women's Track & Field Championships begin (Knoxville, Tenn.).

JUNE

2 NCAA College World Series begins (Omaha, Neb.).
10 Belmont Stakes (Elmont, N.Y.).
15 U.S. Open golf begins (Southampton, N.Y.).
15 IOC meeting in Budapest (will announce site of 2002 Winter Olympics.
17 NHL Draft (Winnipeg).*
18 24 Hours of Le Mans auto race begins (France).
19 Wimbledon tennis begins.
28 NBA Draft (Toronto).
29 U.S. Senior Open golf begins (Bethesda, Md.).

JULY

1 Tour de France cycling race begins (through July 23).
11 Baseball All-Star Game (Arlington, Texas).
13 U.S. Women's Open golf begins (Colorado Springs).
15 Davis Cup tennis second round begins (four sites).
20 British Open golf begins (St. Andrews).
21 U.S. Olympic Festival begins (Colorado).
22 Women's Federation Cup tennis semifinals-finals begin.

AUGUST

4 IAAF World Track & Field Championships (Göteburg, Sweden).
5 Hambletonian harness race (E. Rutherford, N.J.).
6 All-American Soap Box Derby (Akron, Ohio).
10 PGA Championship golf begins (Pacific Palisades, Calif.).
16 U.S. Gymnastics Championships begin (New Orleans).
21 Little League Baseball World Series begins (Williamsport, Pa).
24 LPGA du Maurier Classic begins (Montreal).
28 U.S. Open tennis begins (Flushing, N.Y.).

SEPTEMBER

3 NFL regular season opens.
22 Davis Cup tennis semifinal round begins (two sites).
22 Ryder Cup golf (Rochester, N.Y.).

OCTOBER

1 Baseball regular season ends.
1 World Gymnastics Team Champs. begin (Sabae, Japan).
1 U.S. Women's Open bowling begins (Wichita, Kan.).
3 Baseball playoffs begin (first round).
7 College football: Miami at Florida State.
8 Ironman Triathlon Championship (Hawaii).
10 Baseball League Championship Series begin.
21 World Series begins (in city of AL champion).
21 College football: USC at Notre Dame.
28 Breeders' Cup horse racing (Louisville).

NOVEMBER

5 Triathlon World Championship (Cancun, Mexico).*
12 New York City Marathon.
13 ATP Men's Tennis Championships begin (Frankfurt).
13 WTA Tour Tennis Championships begin (New York).
18 College Football: Harvard at Yale; Oklahoma at Nebraska; UCLA at USC.
19 CFL Grey Cup (Regina, Sask.).
25 Women's Federation Cup tennis finals begin.
25 College Football: Alabama at Auburn; Florida State at Florida; Ohio State at Michigan.

DECEMBER

1 Davis Cup tennis final begins.
1 National Finals Rodeo begins (Las Vegas).
2 College football: SEC Championship Game (Atlanta); Army vs. Navy (Philadelphia).
8 NCAA Men's Soccer Final Four (Richmond, Va.).
9 Heisman Trophy winner announced (New York).
25 NFL regular season ends.

*tentative date

This denizen of Yankee Stadium spoke for most baseball fans in midsummer as the Aug. 12 deadline for the threatened players' strike approached.

BASEBALL

Cancelled

*One of the best seasons in years is called off on Sept. 14
as baseball suffers its 8th work stoppage since 1972.*

The 1994 baseball season is destined to go down in history as an unfinished symphony. For all its high notes and low notes, its pratfalls and pitfalls, its tricks and its treats, the historians will duly note that Wednesday, Sept. 14, was the day the music died.

After consulting with his peers and acknowledging the irreconcilable differences that existed between players and owners in baseball's latest labor dispute, acting commissioner Bud Selig cranked up the faxes and spread the unfortunate news: The remainder of the regular season was being cancelled, and with it, the playoffs and World Series.

"This is a sad day," Selig said. "Nobody wanted this to happen, but the continuing player strike leaves us no choice but to take this action. We have reached the point where it is no longer practical to complete the remainder of the season or to preserve the integrity of postseason play."

Fans will remember the 1994 season for a lot of things. Integrity isn't one of them. On Aug. 12, just about the time pennant races and record chases were likely to heat up in earnest, the players went on strike rather than accept management's proposal of a salary cap. It was baseball's eighth work stoppage since 1972 (see page 85).

On the 34th day of the strike, Selig and

the owners decreed there would be no World Series for the first time since 1904. The great October tradition, which had survived World Wars, scandals, a depression, an earthquake, Marge Schott and George Steinbrenner, had finally succumbed to a dispute over the almighty dollar.

While an industry shutdown can never be beneficial, the latest labor meltdown came at a particularly inopportune time for baseball. After losing ground to basketball and football, particularly among the youth of America, the game seemed primed for a turnaround.

An array of charismatic young stars, led by Ken Griffey Jr. and Frank Thomas, had begun making an impact everywhere from Main Street to Madison Avenue. If kids weren't wearing their hats backward like Junior, they were fighting over who could carry the designation of The Big Hurt in neighborhood pickup games.

New ballparks opened in Texas and Cleveland, and fans responded by coming out in droves. The new six-division realignment, scorned by purists, had the desired effect of keeping more teams in contention.

In the American League Central, Chicago, Cleveland and Kansas City were separated by a mere four games at the time of the strike. In the AL West—christened the AL Worst—the California Angels were 47-68 at the time of the strike. Last in the division, they stood a mere 5½ games behind the first-place Rangers.

In the final aborted standings, the best

Jerry Crasnick is the national baseball writer for *The Denver Post* and a columnist for *Baseball America*.

Wide World Photos

Wide World Photos

Ken Griffey Jr. (left) of Seattle and **Frank Thomas** of the Chicago White Sox were only two of the six young stars in both leagues who had a shot at 50 home runs before the strike. Junior and The Big Hurt, along with Albert Belle of Cleveland, were also the American League's prime MVP candidates.

record in the game belonged to the Montreal Expos, who, in the course of going 74-40, landed smack in the middle of the raging big market/small market debate.

The Players Association cited the Expos as a paragon of front office acumen. The union pointed out that Montreal won despite a miniscule $18.5 million payroll. They did it with quality scouting, foresight and a strong farm system.

And the owners? They claimed the Expos are destined to emulate the Pittsburgh Pirates, who were forced to part company with Barry Bonds, Bobby Bonilla and Doug Drabek in the early '90s when it became clear those stars would receive more enticing offers from the big boys.

Money was at the core of minor disputes as well as momentous ones. Purists cringed over the presence of billboard advertisements behind home plate, and in the ultimate affront to fans' sensibilities, the Florida Marlins sold their outfield foul poles to Office Depot. Each pole at Joe Robbie Stadium resembled a 30-foot-tall pencil. "If there's any question about a ball being a home run, they can just check for lead

marks," said Marlins' outfielder Jeff Conine.

The biggest bombshell of the summer came courtesy of a player who walked away from gobs of money. Cubs second baseman Ryne Sandberg threw the baseball world for a loop when he announced his retirement on June 13. Sandberg, 34, claimed he couldn't be satisfied in giving any less than a complete effort. In walking away, Sandberg gave up a guaranteed $12.7 million over the final three years of his contract, and an additional $3.4 million if the Cubs exercised their option for 1997.

While Sandberg was hitting a mere .238 at the time of his announcement, Cubs fans will remember him for his 10 All-Star appearances and nine Gold Gloves. Sandberg ranks fourth on the all-time home run list for second basemen behind Joe Morgan, Rogers Hornsby and Joe Gordon. He finished with five errorless streaks of 50 games or more in his career, and was the best second baseman of his era, by a mile.

Sandberg didn't hit much in 1994, but he was in the minority. The season was all about offense from the moment Karl (Tuffy) Rhodes, an unheralded outfielder with the Cubs, homered three times off Dwight

Gooden on opening day at Wrigley Field. Rhodes went deep only five more times in his next 94 games, and shaved his head at one point in hopes of breaking a 1-for-22 slump. "I did it so I'd be more aerodynamically sound," he said.

In contrast to Rhodes, baseball's boppers never let up. Griffey outhomered the Montreal Expos 15-14 in the month of May. In early June, he vowed not to re-sign with the Seattle Mariners after the 1996 season —because, he claims, he has had his fill of losing in the Great Northwest. Apprised of Griffey's comments, manager Lou Piniella walked up to his young star in the clubhouse and comforted him. "Junior's disgusted with losing, and if I had enough players who were as disgusted with losing, we wouldn't be losing," Piniella said.

For all his accomplishments—a .323 average, 40 homers and 90 RBI—Griffey was in a three-man race for MVP when the season ended. Cleveland's Albert Belle hit .357, led the league in total bases and ranked in the top 10 in 11 offensive categories. He was also the focus of a bizarre incident in Chicago on July 15, when White Sox manager Gene Lamont confiscated his bat to see if it had been corked. The following day, an unknown perpetrator sneaked into the umpires' room at Comiskey Park and replaced Belle's bat with a substitute. The incident came to be known as "Batgate." When the dust from the bat shavings finally settled, Belle received a 10-game suspension that was later reduced to six.

Thomas, coming off an MVP season, enhanced his reputation as baseball's most dangerous hitter. Even with his staggering numbers—a .353 average, 101 RBI, 109 walks and 106 runs scored in 113 games—Thomas made his biggest imprint in the home run hitting contest at the All-Star Game in Pittsburgh. Thomas' best bolt traveled 519 feet, landing in the upper deck an incredible nine sections over from the left field foul pole.

In retrospect, the entire season was an ongoing game of home run derby. At the time of the strike, Thomas, Griffey, Belle, Matt Williams, Jeff Bagwell and Barry Bonds all were on a pace to surpass 50 home runs. That's six players shooting for a target that has been reached only 18 times in baseball history.

Bagwell, who suffered a broken left hand when he was hit by an Andy Benes pitch in August, was destined to fall by the wayside. But the magnitude of the 1994's power onslaught was still unprecedented by historical standards.

Only three times in history have two players managed to hit 50 home runs in a season. In 1938, Hank Greenberg hit 58 and Jimmie Foxx 50. In 1947, Ralph Kiner and Johnny Mize each hit 51. Then there was 1961, the year that set the standard for power hitting, when Roger Maris broke Babe Ruth's record with 61 and teammate Mickey Mantle hit 54.

In the minds of many, the current crop of young stars compares favorably with the killer constellation of the 1950s. Frank Thomas, Ken Griffey, Jeff Bagwell & Co., say hello to Willie Mays, Hank Aaron, Roberto Clemente, Mickey Mantle, Ernie Banks and Frank Robinson.

"Ten years down the line, people will look at the players in today's game and put them in the same class as Mays, Aaron and Mantle," said Phillies manager Jim Fregosi. "They beat to their own drum, so to speak. They're individuals. There are a lot of glamorous players in today's game. When you're in the middle of it, you don't really see how good they are."

Not that the geezers rolled over and played dead. At the time of the strike, San Diego's 34-year-old Tony Gwynn was hitting .394 and trying to become the first player to bat .400 since Ted Williams in 1941. When Gwynn missed the final month of the 1993 season with a knee injury, his detractors suggested he put down that knife and fork and get back to work. Funny thing. Gwynn's weight was never an issue this season. He simply hit a ton.

Gwynn was center stage in one of the summer's most stirring moments. At the All-Star Game, Fred McGriff of Atlanta hit a two-run, pinch-hit homer off Baltimore reliever Lee Smith in the bottom of the ninth to pull the National League even at 7-7. In the 10th, Moises Alou lined a double to the gap and Gwynn slid under an Ivan Rodriguez tag to give the Nationals an 8-7 victory.

The climactic play touched off a wild celebration at home plate, in which Bonds, the personification of cool, rushed onto the field wearing a suit and tie to slap backs with his

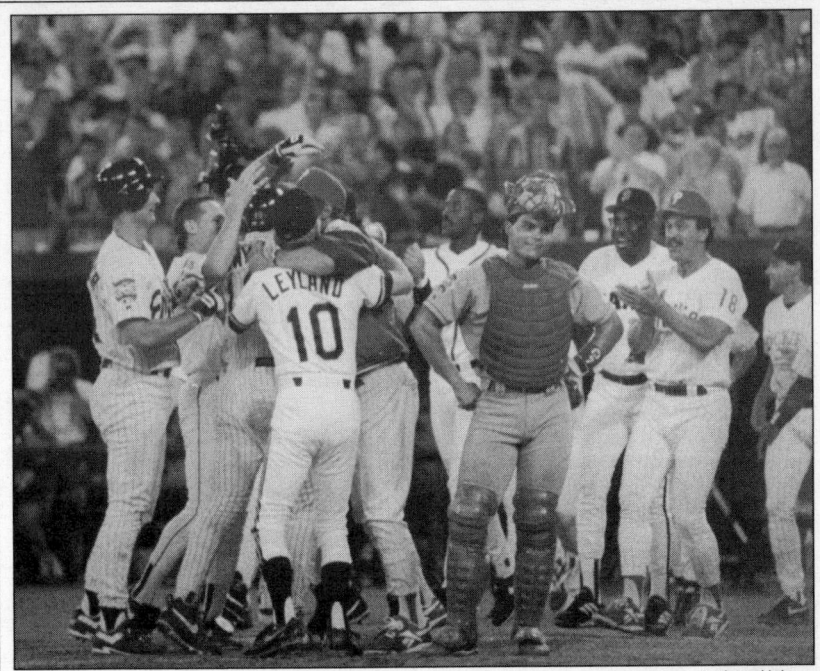

Texas catcher **Ivan Rodriguez** can manage only a weak smile as the National League dugout empties to congratulate San Diego's **Tony Gwynn**, who scored the winning run of the All-Star Game in the bottom of the 10th inning on a single by Atlanta's Fred McGriff. The NL won the game, 8-7, in Pittsburgh.

teammates. For sheer hold-your-breath excitement, the last All-Star Games to end on such a scintillating note were a pair of NL extra-inning victories in 1970 (4-3) and '72 (5-4). In 1972, the Reds' Joe Morgan knocked in the winning run with one out in the bottom of the 10th. And in '70, Pete Rose scored on a Jim Hickman single in the bottom of the 12th, crossing the plate after a violent collision with Cleveland catcher Ray Fosse.

Pitchers were so thoroughly used and abused during the season that those who managed to persevere deserve special mention. The Mets' Bret Saberhagen walked 13 batters in 177⅓ innings. His strikeout-to-walk ratio of 11-to-1 was easily the best in the 20th century. And Atlanta's Greg Maddux, on his way to an unprecedented third straight Cy Young Award, continued to prove that a 95-mph fastball takes a backseat to control, smarts and chutzpah. Maddux's 1.56 ERA was the

third lowest for an ERA qualifier since 1920.

On Apr. 8, Atlanta's Kent Mercker threw the season's first no-hitter in a 6-0 victory over the Dodgers. Manager Bobby Cox rewarded Mercker by giving him seven days rest before his next start. Less than three weeks later, Minnesota's Scott Erickson tossed a no-hitter in a 6-0 victory over Milwaukee.

But the season's undisputed gem was turned in by Texas lefty Kenny Rogers, who threw the 14th perfect game in baseball history in a 4-0 victory over California on July 28. Rogers needed a lift from rookie center fielder Rusty Greer, who made a diving catch on a sinking liner by Rex Hudler to lead off the ninth inning. Said Rogers, "I don't think I'm going to top this. I'm on the downside of my career now."

It was a summer to forget for the 1993 World Series participants. In Philadelphia, John Kruk began the season on the disabled list with testicular cancer. When he

81

wasn't undergoing treatment, Kruk was ripping teammate Curt Schilling in his book. Resident catalyst Lenny Dykstra missed 31 games with an assortment of injuries, and the Phillies' pitching staff was such a disaster that general manager Lee Thomas resorted to signing Fernando Valenzuela—whose official age evoked guffaws from teammates and opponents alike. "Yeah, he's 33," said Marlins' 46-year-old pitcher Charlie Hough. "And he broke in when he was 11, after 10 years in the Mexican League."

The good news in Philadelphia: With no pennant winner to take the Phillies' place, the league championship trophy will remain at Veterans Stadium for another year. When the NL office made it official, fans in Montreal were beyond miffed. The Expos weren't too thrilled, either. Team president Claude Brochu suggested the fairest solution would be to move the trophy to a neutral site for a year. "If they want to consider the Phillies champions, I have one four-letter answer to that," said Montreal outfielder Larry Walker. "J-o-k-e. Knowing the guys on that team, they'd still tell you they were the best team in the world regardless of how low they finished in the standings."

After two straight World Championships, the Toronto Blue Jays crashed and burned. Their pitching staff bordered on respectable, ranking seventh in the American League with a 4.70 ERA. But for some inexplicable reason, Toronto's star-studded offense hit only .269 and ranked ninth in the league in runs scored. The Blue Jays bottomed out with a 10-game losing streak in June, during which they scored 18 runs and hit two homers—both by backup catcher Randy Knorr.

Sandberg wasn't the only marquee player to take an unexpected hike. Mitch Williams, hoping for a new start in Houston, was back at the 3 & 2 Ranch in Hico, Texas, by June. Williams' replacement, John Hudek, had 15 saves by July 10 and made the All-Star team.

Most notable among the season's comebacks was Jose Canseco, who swore off pitching after blowing out his elbow at Fenway Park in 1993 and returned to hit 31 homers in 111 games for the Rangers. Maybe the highlight-show guys can finally cut Jose some slack and stop airing the tape

Strike Hurts The Most In Cleveland

The Cleveland Indians lost more than a postseason berth when the baseball season was called on account of labor disharmony. They lost an opportunity for redemption.

You know Cleveland. Home of Bob Feller and Rocky Colavito and the butt of jokes for more years than the locals care to remember. The movie "Major League" was popular for its oddball slant on a fantasy—the Indians actually winning a pennant.

Until Don Fehr and Richard Ravitch began dominating the headlines, life was doing a passable impersonation of art. On Aug. 12, the Indians were 66-47 and one game behind the first-place Chicago White Sox in the American League's Central Division. If the regular season had ended that day, the Indians would have been a wild-card team and opposing the New York Yankees in the opening round of the playoffs.

And they would have been tough to beat—with Albert Belle (.357, 36 HRs, 101 RBI), Kenny Lofton (.349, 160 hits, 60 SBs) and Carlos Baerga (.314, 139 hits, 32 doubles) at the plate and Charles Nagy (10-8, 3.45), Dennis Martinez (11-6, 3.52) and Mark Clark (11-3, 3.82) on the mound.

That's heady stuff for a franchise that hadn't made a postseason appearance since the team won 111 games in 1954 (and lost the Series to the New York Giants in four straight). The last time Cleveland was remotely this excited about its baseball team was in 1980 when a rookie outfielder named Joe Charboneau was hitting home runs and guzzling beer through his nose.

The Indians, playing at beautiful, new Jacobs Field, drew 1,995,174 fans in 51 home dates. Had the season gone the distance, they would have surpassed 3 million in attendance. The club record, set in 1948 when Bill Veeck owned the team, is 2.6 million.

"My friends used to give me a hard time about Cleveland," said starting pitcher Charles Nagy, who was the Indians' first round draft pick in 1988. "Then when they came out to visit me they had a great time. Now I have to tell them no, they can't come, because they're all coming here in droves."

Some of the current Indians were around in

Stephen Dunn/Allsport   Otto Greule/Allsport   Otto Greule/Allsport

Much of the Indians' success can be traced to management's willingness to gamble on young stars like **Albert Belle** (left), **Kenny Lofton** (center) and **Carlos Baerga** and sign them to multiyear contracts. That gamble has paid off.

1991 when the club went 57-105 and finished 34 games out of first place in the American League East. They could relate to the fans' angst. But with redemption close enough so that entire city could feel it, baseball shut it down in a dispute over the salary cap.

There was no cap on the sense of disappointment in Cleveland.

"What we did this year wasn't a mirage," said Indians general manager John Hart. "These could have been magical times for the fans and us. These could have been dramatic times—especially for a team that hasn't been in the playoffs for 40 years."

Said Cleveland third baseman Jim Thome: "To me this season was like one long dream. It was like a storybook, but we looked at only three-fourths of it. Now it's like a soap opera—to be continued."

If Hart is right, and the magic returns, it will be a tribute to foresight, careful planning and some risk-taking. While the Montreal Expos are the consummate example of a small-market club succeeding by conducting business the right way, the Indians stand as a role model in their own right.

In the span of a year, from 1992 to '93, the front office made a commitment to several young players they thought could serve as the nucleus of the franchise for years to come. They agreed to multiyear deals with outfielders Albert Belle and Kenny Lofton, second baseman Carlos Baerga, first baseman Paul Sorrento, catcher Sandy Alomar Jr. and Nagy.

While none of the players had more than three years of big-league experience at the time, the Indians hoped the approach would foster chemistry, cost control and loyalty among their top players. Under the best-case scenario, management thought they would learn to win as a unit.

"At the time, everybody thought it was a gamble," Hart said. "I said this isn't a model for anybody else. It's just our way to survive and compete."

While the Indians didn't look so astute by signing pitchers Jack Armstrong and Scott Scudder to multiyear deals, the approach was, as a rule, successful. Lofton, baseball's premier leadoff man, is under contract through 1997. Belle's deal runs through 1996 and Baerga's through '99. The Indians know what they'll cost, and those nasty contract hassles are a thing of the past.

Hart has made some nice trades in his tenure with the club. His Lofton-for-Eddie Taubensee deal with Houston in 1991 qualifies as one of baseball's all-time great swindles. The Indians picked up Mark Clark for Mark Whiten, and Sorrento for Oscar Munoz and Curtis Leskanic.

The Indians could boast of baseball's fifth best record in 1994 despite a relatively sane payroll of $28.5 million. That's less than the New York Mets, Chicago Cubs, Detroit Tigers and Boston Red Sox invested in also-rans.

Poor Cleveland, baseball's perennial doormat, had it all figured out. The Indians made only one mistake: They picked the worst possible year to do things right.

Chicago Cubs' second baseman **Ryne Sandberg** purses his lips at a June 13 press conference after stunning the baseball world with his decision to retire immediately at age 34 and walk away from over $12 million in salary.

of that fly ball bouncing off his noggin and over the fence for a home run.

Darryl Strawberry entered the Betty Ford Clinic in April, and spent 28 days undergoing treatment for a substance abuse problem. The Dodgers released him, and he subsequently signed with the Giants. San Francisco ripped off nine straight victories upon Strawberry's arrival. But when the initial hoopla faded and the players went on strike, Strawberry was hitting .239.

Jimmie Reese, the California Angels' 92-year-old conditioning coach, died on July 13. Reese, who once roomed with Babe Ruth in New York, was a legend with a fungo bat and a source of inspiration to many. "You couldn't help but fall in love with the guy," said Angels' pitcher Chuck Finley. "He was so warm and positive."

Steve Carlton entered the Hall of Fame, but was upstaged by a humorous, heartfelt speech from the Scooter, Phil Rizzuto. Sparky Anderson passed Joe McCarthy to become the fourth winningest manager of all-time. With 2,134 regular season wins, he needs 26 more to pass Bucky Harris and move into third behind Connie Mack

(3,731) and John McGraw (2,784).

Some milestones fell, while others hit a wall. On Aug. 10, Cal Ripken Jr. played in his 2,009th consecutive game to move within 121 of Lou Gehrig's record. Ripken, adhering to principals over personal goals, vowed not to participate in replacement games in the spring, if it came to that. His pursuit of Gehrig could end without nature taking its course.

Eddie Murray, whose Hall of Fame prospects are no longer in doubt, finished the season with 2,930 career hits. Murray would have already passed 3,000 if not for the work stoppages in 1981 and '84. Paul Molitor, who turns 39 in August, entered the strike with 2,647 career hits. Every day lost makes Molitor's Cooperstown quest that much more difficult.

Some losses can't be measured with statistics. Don Mattingly, the New York Yankees' spiritual leader, was on the verge of playing in the postseason for the first time in his career. By mid-August, he was back home in Evansville, Ind., sticking with the union and thinking wistfully about what might have been.

Baseball 1994 was the Colorado Rockies, on pace to break their single season attendance record of 4,483,350 before losing out on their final 24 home games. It was Montreal's Pedro Martinez carrying a perfect game into the eighth inning, only to hit Reggie Sanders with a pitch and watch in shock as Sanders charged the mound.

It was tiles falling from the ceiling of the Kingdome in Seattle, and Larry Walker losing track of the outs at Chavez Ravine and innocently handing the ball to a young fan in the stands. It was Paul O'Neill coming of age, Chuck Knoblauch doubling to the gap and Charlie Hough wobbling his final knuckleball plateward.

It was relief pitchers Robb Nen of Florida and Dave Otto of the Cubs making history on Aug. 3, by becoming the first two players whose last names are palindromes to appear in the same game. A palindrome is a word spelled the same way forward and backward. "It's not exactly the greatest piece of history to be a part of," said Nen. "I'd rather be celebrating my 6,000th strikeout." No word on whether Toby Harrah was at the game.

It was a wild, wonderful ride, while it lasted. It simply didn't last long enough. ❒

THE 1995 INFORMATION PLEASE SPORTS ALMANAC

BASEBALL STATISTICS

THE SEASON IN REVIEW
1994
LEAGUE LEADERS • POST SEASON

SEC A
PAGE 85

Final Major League Standings

Division champions are unofficial. Number of seasons listed after each manager refers to latest tenure with club.

American League

East Division

	W	L	Pct	GB	Home	Away
New York	70	43	.619	—	33-24	37-19
Baltimore	63	49	.563	6½	28-27	35-22
Toronto	55	60	.478	16	33-26	22-34
Boston	54	61	.470	17	31-33	23-28
Detroit	53	62	.461	18	34-24	19-38

1994 Managers: NY—Buck Showalter (3rd season); **Bal**—Johnny Oates (4th); **Tor**—Cito Gaston (6th); **Bos**—Butch Hobson (3rd); **Det**—Sparky Anderson (16th).

1993 Standings: 1. Toronto (95-67); 2. New York (88-74); 3. Baltimore (85-77) and Detroit (85-77); 5. Boston (80-82); 6. Cleveland (76-86); 7. Milwaukee (69-93).

Central Division

	W	L	Pct	GB	Home	Away
Chicago	67	46	.593	—	34-19	33-27
Cleveland	66	47	.584	1	35-16	31-31
Kansas City	64	51	.557	4	35-24	29-27
Minnesota	53	60	.469	14	32-27	21-33
Milwaukee	53	62	.461	15	24-32	29-30

1994 Managers: Chi—Gene Lamont (3rd season); **Cle**—Mike Hargrove (4th); **KC**—Hal McRae (4th); **Min**—Tom Kelly (9th); **Mil**—Phil Garner (3rd). There was no Central Division in 1993.

West Division

	W	L	Pct	GB	Home	Away
Texas	52	62	.456	—	31-32	21-30
Oakland	51	63	.447	1	24-32	27-31
Seattle	49	63	.438	2	22-22	27-41
California	47	68	.409	5½	23-40	24-28

1994 Managers: Tex—Kevin Kennedy (2nd season); **Oak**—Tony La Russa (9th); **Sea**—Lou Piniella (2nd); **Cal**—replaced Buck Rodgers (4th, 16-23) with coach Bobby Knoop (1-1) on May 17 and then with Florida pitching coach Marcel Lachemann (30-44) on May 19.

1993 Standings: 1. Chicago (94-68); 2. Texas (86-76); 3. Kansas City (84-78); 4. Seattle (82-80); 5. California (71-91) and Minnesota (71-91); 7. Oakland (68-94).

National League

East Division

	W	L	Pct	GB	Home	Away
Montreal	74	40	.649	—	32-20	42-20
Atlanta	68	46	.596	6	31-24	37-22
New York	55	58	.487	18½	29-30	32-28
Philadelphia	54	61	.470	20½	34-26	20-35
Florida	51	64	.443	23½	25-34	26-30

1994 Managers: Mon—Felipe Alou (3rd season); **Atl**—Bobby Cox (5th); **NY**—Dallas Green (2nd); **Phi**—Jim Fregosi (4th); **Fla**—Rene Lachemann (2nd).

1993 Standings: 1. Philadelphia (97-65); 2. Montreal (94-68); 3. St Louis (87-75); 4. Chicago (84-78); 5. Pittsburgh (75-87); 6. Florida (64-98); 7. New York (59-103).

Central Division

	W	L	Pct	GB	Home	Away
Cincinnati	66	48	.579	—	37-22	29-26
Houston	66	49	.574	½	37-22	29-27
Pittsburgh	53	61	.465	13	32-29	21-32
St. Louis	53	61	.465	13	23-33	30-28
Chicago	49	64	.434	16½	20-39	29-25

1994 Managers: Cin—Davey Johnson (2nd season); **Hou**—Terry Collins (1st); **Pit**—Jim Leyland (9th); **St.L**—Joe Torre (5th); **Chi**—Tom Trebelhorn (1st). There was no Central Division in 1993.

West Division

	W	L	Pct	GB	Home	Away
Los Angeles	58	56	.509	—	33-22	25-34
San Francisco	55	60	.478	3½	29-31	26-29
Colorado	53	64	.453	6½	25-33	28-31
San Diego	47	70	.402	12½	26-31	21-39

1994 Managers: LA—Tommy Lasorda (19th season); **SF**—Dusty Baker (2nd); **Col**—Don Baylor (2nd); **SD**—Jim Riggleman (3rd).

1993 Standings: 1. Atlanta (104-58); 2. San Francisco (103-59); 3. Houston (85-77); 4. Los Angeles (81-81); 5. Cincinnati (73-89); 6. Colorado (67-95); 7. San Diego (61-101).

Baseball's Eight Work Stoppages

Year	Work Stoppage	Games Missed	Length	Dates	Issue
1972	Strike	86	13 days	April 1-13	Pensions
1973	Lockout	0	17 days	February 8-25	Salary arbitration
1976	Lockout	0	17 days	March 1-17	Free agency
1980	Strike	0	8 days	April 1-8	Free-agent compensation
1981	Strike	712	50 days	June 12-July 31	Free-agent compensation
1985	Strike	0	2 days	August 6-7	Salary arbitration
1990	Lockout	0	32 days	Feb. 15-March 18	Salary arbitration and salary cap
1994	Strike	669*	81 days†	Aug. 12—	Salary cap and revenue sharing

*Through end of regular season (owners cancelled remainder of regular season and entire postseason on Sept. 14, 1994).
†As of Oct. 31, 1994.

Chicago White Sox
Frank Thomas

Wide World Photos
Jimmy Key

Houston Astros
Jeff Bagwell

Atlanta Braves
Greg Maddux

American League Leaders
Batting

Minimum of 3.1 plate appearances multiplied by number of games played by team.

	Bat	Gm	AB	R	H	Avg	TB	2B	3B	HR	RBI	BB	Int BB	SO	SB	Slg Pct	OB Pct
Paul O'Neill, NY	L	103	368	68	132	.359	222	25	1	21	83	72	56	5	4	.603	.460
Albert Belle, Cle	R	106	412	90	147	.357	294	35	2	36	101	58	71	9	6	.714	.438
Frank Thomas, Chi	R	113	399	106	141	.353	291	34	1	38	101	109	61	2	3	.729	.487
Kenny Lofton, Cle	L	112	459	105	160	.349	246	32	9	12	57	52	56	60	12	.536	.412
Wade Boggs, NY	L	97	366	61	125	.342	179	19	1	11	55	61	29	2	1	.489	.433
Paul Molitor, Tor	R	115	454	86	155	.341	235	30	4	14	75	55	48	20	0	.518	.410
Will Clark, Tex	L	110	389	73	128	.329	195	24	2	13	80	71	59	5	1	.501	.431
Ken Griffey, Sea	L	111	433	94	140	.323	292	24	4	40	90	56	73	11	3	.674	.402
Rafael Palmeiro, Bal	L	111	436	82	139	.319	240	32	0	23	76	54	63	7	3	.550	.392
Julio Franco, Chi	R	112	433	72	138	.319	221	19	2	20	98	62	75	8	1	.510	.406
Kirby Puckett, Min	R	108	439	79	139	.317	237	32	3	20	112	28	47	6	3	.540	.362
Felix Fermin, Sea	R	101	379	52	120	.317	144	21	0	1	35	11	22	4	4	.380	.338
Cal Ripken, Bal	R	112	444	71	140	.315	204	19	3	13	75	32	41	1	0	.459	.364
Carlos Baerga, Cle	S	103	442	81	139	.314	232	32	2	19	80	10	45	8	2	.525	.333
Chuck Knoblauch, Min	R	109	445	85	139	.312	205	45	3	5	51	41	56	35	6	.461	.381

Home Runs

Griffey, Sea	40
Thomas, Chi	38
Belle, Cle	36
Canseco, Tex	31
Fielder, Det	28
Carter, Tor	27
Davis, Cal	26
Vaughn, Bos	26
Hamelin, KC	24
Four tied with 23.	

Runs Batted In

Puckett, Min	112
Carter, Tor	103
Belle, Cle	101
Thomas, Chi	101
Franco, Chi	98
Sierra, Oak	92
Canseco, Tex	90
Fielder, Det	90
Griffey, Sea	90
Two tied with 85.	

Hits

Lofton, Cle	160
Molitor, Tor	155
Belle, Cle	147
Thomas, Chi	141
Griffey, Sea	140
Ripken, Bal	140
Baerga, Cle	139
Knoblauch, Min	139
Palmiero, Bal	139
Puckett, Min	139

Stolen Bases

	SB	CS
Lofton, Cle	60	12
Coleman, KC	50	8
Nixon, Bos	42	10
Knoblauch, Min	35	6
Anderson, Bal	31	1
Cole, Min	29	8
McRae, KC	28	8
L. Johnson, Chi	26	6
Curtis, Cal	25	11

Triples

L. Johnson, Chi	14
Coleman, KC	12
Lofton, Cle	9
Diaz, Mil	7
McRae, KC	6
Polonia, NY	6
White, Tor	6
Six tied with 5.	

Doubles

Knoblauch, Min	45
Belle, Cle	35
Fryman, Det	34
Thomas, Chi	34
Baerga, Cle	32
Lofton, Cle	32
Palmeiro, Bal	32
Puckett, Min	32

Runs

Thomas, Chi	106
Lofton, Cle	105
Griffey, Sea	94
Phillips, Det	91
Belle, Cle	90
Canseco, Tex	88
Molitor, Tor	86
Knoblauch, Min	85

Total Bases

Belle, Cle	294
Griffey, Sea	292
Thomas, Chi	291
Lofton, Cle	246
Palmeiro, Bal	240
Canseco, Tex	237
Puckett, Min	237
Molitor, Tor	235

On Base Pct.

Thomas, Chi	.487
O'Neill, NY	.460
Belle, Cle	.438
Boggs, NY	.433
Clark, Tex	.431
Tettleton, Det	.419
Lofton, Cle	.412

Slugging Pct.

Thomas, Chi	.729
Belle, Cle	.714
Griffey, Sea	.674
O'Neill, NY	.603
Hamelin, KC	.599
Vaughn, Bos	.576
Davis, Cal	.561

Walks

Thomas, Chi	109
Tettleton, Det	97
Phillips, Det	95
Henderson, Oak	72
O'Neill, NY	72
Clark, Tex	71
Two tied with 69.	

Strikeouts

Fryman, Det	128
Canseco, Tex	114
Vaughn, Bos	112
Tartabull, NY	111
Fielder, Det	110
Phillips, Det	105
Salmon, Cal	102

Pitching

Minimum of one inning pitched multiplied by number of games played by team.

	Arm	W	L	ERA	Gm	GS	CG	ShO	Sv	IP	H	R	ER	HR	HB	BB	SO	WP
Steve Ontiveros, Oak	R	6	4	2.65	27	13	2	0	0	115.1	93	39	34	7	6	26	56	5
Roger Clemens, Bos	R	9	7	2.85	24	24	3	1	0	170.2	124	62	54	15	4	71	168	4
David Cone, KC	R	16	5	2.94	23	23	4	3	0	171.2	130	60	56	15	7	54	132	5
Mike Mussina, Bal	R	16	5	3.06	24	24	3	0	0	176.1	163	63	60	19	1	42	99	0
Randy Johnson, Sea	L	13	6	3.19	23	23	9	4	0	172.0	132	65	61	14	6	72	204	5
Jimmy Key, NY	L	17	4	3.27	25	25	1	0	0	168.0	177	68	61	10	3	52	97	8
Pat Hentgen, Tor	R	13	8	3.40	24	24	6	3	0	174.2	158	74	66	21	3	59	147	5
Ricky Bones, Mil	R	10	9	3.43	24	24	4	1	0	170.2	166	76	65	17	0	45	57	8
Wilson Alvarez, Chi	L	12	8	3.45	24	24	2	1	0	161.2	147	72	62	16	0	62	108	3
Charles Nagy, Cle	R	10	8	3.45	23	23	3	0	0	169.1	175	76	65	15	5	48	108	5
Dennis Martinez, Cle	R	11	6	3.52	24	24	7	3	0	176.2	166	75	69	14	7	44	92	4
Jack McDowell, Chi	R	10	9	3.73	25	25	6	2	0	181.0	186	82	75	12	5	42	127	4
Scott Kamieniecki, NY	R	8	6	3.76	22	16	1	0	0	117.1	115	53	49	13	3	59	71	4
Jason Bere, Chi	R	12	2	3.81	24	24	0	0	0	141.2	119	65	60	17	1	80	127	2
Mark Clark, Cle	R	11	3	3.82	20	20	4	1	0	127.1	133	61	54	14	4	40	60	9

Wins

Key, NY 17-4
Cone, KC 16-5
Mussina, Bal 16-5
McDonald, Bal 14-7
Johnson, Sea 13-6
Hentgen, Tor 13-8
Bere, Chi 12-2
Alvarez, Chi 12-8
Guzman, Tor 12-11
Eight tied with 11.

Appearances

Wickman, NY 53
Mesa, Cle 51
Brewer, KC 50
Guthrie, Min 50
Willis, Min 49

Saves

	SV	BS
Le. Smith, Bal	33	6
Montgomery, KC	27	5
Aguilera, Min	23	6
Eckersley, Oak	19	6
Ayala, Sea	18	6

Complete Games

Johnson, Sea 9
Finley, Cal 7
Martinez, Cle 7
Eldred, Mil 6

Shutouts

Johnson, Sea 4
Five tied with 3.

Strikeouts

Johnson, Sea 204
Clemens, Bos 168
Finley, Cal 148
Hentgen, Tor 147
Appier, KC 145
Cone, KC 132
Bere, Chi 127
McDowell, Chi 127
Gordon, KC 126
Guzman, Tor 124

Walks

Moore, Det 89
Van Poppel, Oak 89
Gordon, KC 87
Eldred, Mil 84
Bere, Chi 80

Losses

Belcher, Det 7-15
Deshaies, Min 6-12
Four tied with 11.

Innings

Finley, Cal 183.1
McDowell, Chi 181.0
Eldred, Mil 179.0
Martinez, Cle 176.2
Mussina, Bal 176.1
Hentgen, Tor 174.2

HRs Given Up

Deshaies, Min 30
S. Fernandez, Bal 27
Moore, Det 27
Stewart, Tor 26

National League Leaders

Batting

Minimum of 3.1 plate appearances multiplied by number of games played by team.

	Bat	Gm	AB	R	H	Avg	TB	2B	3B	HR	RBI	BB	Int BB	SO	SB	Slg Pct	OB Pct
Tony Gwynn, SD	L	110	419	79	165	.394	238	35	1	12	64	48	19	5	0	.568	.454
Jeff Bagwell, Hou	R	110	400	104	147	.368	300	32	2	39	116	65	65	15	4	.750	.451
Moises Alou, Mon	R	107	422	81	143	.339	250	31	5	22	78	42	63	7	6	.592	.397
Hal Morris, Cin	L	112	436	60	146	.335	214	30	4	10	78	34	62	6	2	.491	.385
Kevin Mitchell, Cin	R	95	310	57	101	.326	211	18	1	30	77	59	62	2	0	.681	.429
Gregg Jefferies, St.L	S	103	397	52	129	.325	194	27	1	12	55	45	26	12	5	.489	.391
Larry Walker, Mon	L	103	395	76	127	.322	232	44	2	19	86	47	74	15	5	.587	.394
Bret Boone, Cin	R	108	381	59	122	.320	187	25	2	12	68	24	74	3	4	.491	.368
Bip Roberts, SD	S	105	403	52	129	.320	160	15	5	2	31	39	57	21	7	.397	.383
Jeff Conine, Fla	R	115	451	60	144	.319	237	27	6	18	82	40	92	1	2	.525	.373
Andres Galarraga, Col	R	103	417	77	133	.319	247	21	0	31	85	19	93	8	3	.592	.356
Mike Piazza, LA	R	107	405	64	129	.319	219	18	0	24	92	33	65	1	3	.541	.370
Fred McGriff, Atl	L	113	424	81	135	.318	264	25	1	34	94	50	76	7	3	.623	.389
Craig Biggio, Hou	R	114	437	88	139	.318	211	44	5	6	56	62	58	39	4	.483	.411
Brett Butler, LA	L	111	417	79	131	.314	186	13	9	8	33	68	52	27	8	.446	.411

Home Runs

Williams, SF 43
Bagwell, Hou 39
Bonds, SF 37
McGriff, Atl 34
Galarraga, Col 31
Mitchell, Cin 30
Bichette, Col 27
Sheffield, Fla 27
Sosa, Chi 25
Piazza, LA 24

Runs Batted In

Bagwell, Hou 116
Williams, SF 96
Bichette, Col 95
McGriff, Atl 94
Piazza, LA 92
Walker, Mon 86
Galarraga, Col 85
Conine, Fla 82
Bonds, SF 81
4 tied 78

Hits

Gywnn, SD 165
Bagwell, Hou 147
Bichette, Col 147
Morris, Cin 146
Conine, Fla 144
Alou, Mon 143
Biggio, Hou 139
Grissom, Mon 137
Bell, SD 135
McGriff, Atl 135

Stolen Bases

	SB	CS
Biggio, Hou	39	4
D. Sanders, Atl-Cin	38	16
Grissom, Mon	36	6
Carr, Fla	32	8
Lewis, SF	30	13
Bonds, SF	29	5
Butler, LA	27	8
DeShields, LA	27	7
Larkin, Cin	26	2

National League Leaders (Cont.)
Batting

Triples

Butler, LA	9
Lewis, SF	9
Kingery, Col	8
Mondesi, LA	8
R. Sanders, Cin	8
Clayton, SF	6
Connie, Fla	6
Fernandez, Cin	6
Sosa, Chi	6

Doubles

Biggio, Hou	44
Walker, Mon	44
Bell, Pit	35
Gwynn, SD	35
Bichette, Col	33
Bagwell, Hou	32
Alou, Mon	31
Cordero, Mon	30
Morris, Cin	30

Runs

Bagwell, Hou	104
Grissom, Mon	96
Bonds, SF	89
Lankford, St.L	89
Biggio, Hou	88
Alou, Mon	81
McGriff, Atl	81
Butler, LA	79
Gwynn, SD	79

Total Bases

Bagwell, Hou	300
Williams, SF	270
Bichette, Col	265
McGriff, Atl	264
Bonds, SF	253
Alou, Mon	250
Galarraga, Col	247
Gwynn, SD	238
Conine, Fla	237

On Base Pct.

Gwynn, SD	.454
Bagwell, Hou	.451
Mitchell, Cin	.429
Justice, Atl	.427
Bonds, SF	.426
Biggio, Hou	.411
Butler, LA	.411

Slugging Pct.

Bagwell, Hou	.750
Mitchell, Cin	.681
Bonds, SF	.647
McGriff, Atl	.623
Williams, SF	.607
Alou, Mon	.592
Galarraga, Col	.592

Walks

Bonds, SF	74
Justice, Atl	69
Butler, LA	68
Dykstra, Phi	68
Bagwell, Hou	65
Larkin, Cin	64
Biggio, Hou	62

Strikeouts

R. Sanders, Cin	114
Lankford, St.L	113
Bonilla, NY	101
Abbott, Fla	98
Thompson, NY	94
Galarraga, Col	93
Two tied with 92.	

Pitching

Minimum of one inning pitched multiplied by number of games played by team.

	Arm	W	L	ERA	Gm	GS	CG	ShO	Sv	IP	H	R	ER	HR	HB	BB	SO	WP
Greg Maddux, Atl	R	16	6	1.56	25	25	10	3	0	202.0	150	44	35	4	6	31	156	3
Bret Saberhagen, NY	R	14	4	2.74	24	24	4	0	0	177.1	169	58	54	13	4	13	143	0
Doug Drabek, Hou	R	12	6	2.84	23	23	6	2	0	164.2	132	58	52	14	2	45	121	2
Jeff Fassero, Mon	L	8	6	2.99	21	21	1	0	0	138.2	119	54	46	13	1	40	119	6
Shane Reynolds, Hou	R	8	5	3.05	33	14	0	0	0	124.0	128	46	42	10	6	21	110	3
Jose Rijo, Cin	R	9	6	3.08	26	26	2	0	0	172.1	177	73	59	16	4	52	171	1
Bobby Jones, NY	R	12	7	3.15	24	24	1	1	0	160.0	157	75	56	10	4	56	80	1
Steve Trachsel, Chi	R	9	7	3.21	22	22	1	0	0	146.0	133	57	52	19	3	54	108	6
Danny Jackson, Phi	L	14	6	3.26	25	25	4	1	0	179.1	183	71	65	13	2	46	129	2
Zane Smith, Pit	L	10	8	3.27	25	24	2	1	0	157.0	162	67	57	18	0	34	57	2
Ken Hill, Mon	R	16	5	3.32	23	23	2	1	0	154.2	145	61	57	12	6	44	85	3
Andy Ashby, SD	R	6	11	3.40	24	24	4	0	0	164.1	145	75	62	16	3	43	121	5
Pedro Martinez, Mon	R	11	5	3.42	24	23	1	1	1	144.2	115	58	55	11	11	45	142	6
Kevin Gross, LA	R	9	7	3.60	25	23	1	0	1	157.1	162	64	63	11	2	43	124	4
John Burkett, SF	R	6	8	3.62	25	25	0	0	0	159.1	176	72	64	14	7	36	85	2

Wins

Hill, Mon	16-5
Maddux, Atl	16-6
Saberhagen, NY	14-4
Jackson, Phi	14-6
Glavine, Atl	13-9
Drabek, Hou	12-6
Jones, NY	12-7
Martinez, LA	12-7
Tewksbury, St.L	12-10
Two tied with 11.	

Appearances

Reed, Col	61
Bautista, Chi	58
Rojas, Mon	58
Burba, SF	57
Munoz, Col	57

Saves

	SV	BS
Franco, NY	30	6
Beck, SF	28	0
Jones, Phi	27	2
Wetteland, Mon	25	10
McMichael, Atl	21	10
Myers, Chi	21	5

Complete Games

Maddux, Atl	10
Drabek, Hou	6
Candiotti, LA	5
Five tied with 4.	

Shutouts

Maddux, Atl	3
Martinez, LA	3

Strikeouts

Benes, SD	189
Rijo, Cin	171
Maddux, Atl	156
Saberhagen, NY	143
Martinez, Mon	142
Glavine, Atl	140
Jackson, Phi	129
Gross, LA	124
Avery, Atl	122
Neagle, Pit	122

Losses

Benes, SD	6-14
Harris, Col	3-12
Weathers, Fla	8-12

Innings

Maddux, Atl	202.0
Jackson, Phi	179.1
Saberhagen, NY	177.1
Benes, SD	172.1
Rijo, Cin	172.1

Walks

Kile, Hou	82
Glavine, Atl	70
Rapp, Fla	69
West, Phi	61
Weathers, Fla	59

HRs Given Up

Smith, NY	25
Harris, Col	22
Cooke, Pitt	21
Three tied with 20.	

Annual Awards

Voting done by Baseball Writers Association of America.

American League

MVP	Frank Thomas, Chi.,	1B
Cy Young	David Cone, KC,	P
Rookie	Bob Hamelin, KC,	DH
Manager	Buck Showalter,	NY

National League

MVP	Jeff Bagwell, Hou.,	1B
Cy Young	Greg Maddux, Atl.,	P
Rookie	Raul Mondesi, LA,	OF
Manager	Felipe Alou, Mon.	

1994 All-Star Game

65th Baseball All-Star Game. Date: July 12 at Three Rivers Stadium in Pittsburgh; **Managers:** Jim Fregosi, Philadelphia (NL) and Cito Gaston, Toronto (AL); **Most Valuable Player**: PH-1B Fred McGriff, Atlanta (NL): 1-for-1, 2-run pinch hit HR in 9th tied game, 7-7.

American League

	AB	R	H	BI	BB	SO	Avg
Roberto Alomar, Tor, 2b	3	1	1	0	0	0	.333
Chuck Knoblauch, Min, 2b	3	1	0	0	0	2	.000
Wade Boggs, NY, 3b	3	1	1	0	0	2	.333
Scott Cooper, Bos, 3b	2	1	1	1	0	0	.500
Ken Griffey Jr, Sea, cf	3	0	2	1	0	0	.667
Kenny Lofton, Cle, cf	2	0	1	2	0	1	.500
Frank Thomas, Chi, 1b	2	1	2	1	1	0	1.000
Will Clark, Tex, 1b	2	0	2	0	0	0	1.000
Joe Carter, Tor, lf	3	1	0	0	0	0	.000
Albert Belle, Cle, lf	2	0	0	0	0	0	.000
Kirby Puckett, Min, rf	3	0	1	1	0	0	.333
Ruben Sierra, Oak, rf	2	0	1	0	0	0	.500
Cal Ripken Jr Bal, ss	5	0	1	0	0	2	.200
Ivan Rodriguez, Tex, c	5	1	2	0	0	1	.400
Paul Molitor, Tor, ph	1	0	0	0	0	0	.000
Chili Davis, Cal, ph	1	0	0	0	0	0	.000
Mickey Tettleton, Det, ph	0	0	0	0	0	0	.000
Paul O'Neill, NY, ph	1	0	0	0	0	0	.000
Travis Fryman, Det, ph	1	0	0	0	0	0	.000
TOTALS	44	7	15	6	2	8	.341

National League

	AB	R	H	BI	BB	SO	Avg
Gregg Jefferies, St.L, 1b	1	2	1	0	0	0	1.000
Dante Bichette, Col, ph	1	0	1	0	0	0	1.000
Wil Cordero, Mon, ss	2	0	0	0	0	0	.000
Tony Gwynn, SD, cf-rf	5	2	2	2	0	0	.400
Barry Bonds, SF, lf	3	0	0	1	0	2	.000
Moises Alou, Mon, lf	1	0	1	0	0	0	1.000
Mike Piazza, LA, c	4	0	1	1	0	0	.250
Darren Fletcher, Mon, c	0	0	0	0	0	0	—
Matt Williams, SF, 3b	3	0	0	0	0	0	.000
Dave Caminiti, Hou, 3b	1	0	0	0	0	0	.000
David Justice, Atl, rf	2	0	0	0	0	0	.000
Marquis Grissom, Mon, cf	1	1	1	1	1	0	1.000
Mariano Duncan, Cin, 2b	1	0	0	0	0	0	.000
Carlos Garcia, Pit, 2b	2	0	1	0	0	0	.500
Craig Biggio, Hou, 2b	1	0	0	0	0	0	.000
Ozzie Smith, St.L, ss	3	0	1	0	0	0	.333
Fred McGriff, Atl, ph-1b	1	1	1	2	0	0	1.000
Jeff Bagwell, Hou, 1b	4	1	2	0	0	1	.500
TOTALS	36	8	12	8	1	5	.333

	1	2	3		4	5	6		7	8	9	10		R	H	E
American League	1	0	0		0	0	3		3	0	0	0—		7	15	0
National League	1	0	3		0	0	1		0	0	2	1—		8	12	1

No outs when winning run scored. **E**—Williams, NL. **LOB**—American 9, National 4. **2B**—Cooper, Griffey, Ripken, AL; Alou, Gwynn, Jefferies, NL. **HR**—Grissom (off Johnson), McGriff (off L. Smith), NL. **SB**—Alomar, Clark, Lofton, AL. **SF**—Bonds, NL. **GIDP**—Cordero, NL. **DP**—AL (1), NL (1).

AL Pitching

	IP	H	R	ER	BB	SO	NP
Jimmy Key, NY	2.0	1	1	1	0	1	18
David Cone, KC	2.0	4	3	3	0	3	40
Mike Mussina, Bal	1.0	1	0	0	0	1	17
Randy Johnson, Sea	1.0	2	1	1	0	0	20
Pat Hentgen, Tor	1.0	1	0	0	0	0	10
Wilson Alvarez, Chi	1.0	0	0	0	0	0	6
Lee Smith, Bal	1.0	1	2	2	1	0	28
Jason Bere, Chi (L)	0.0	2	1	1	0	0	5
TOTALS	9.0	12	8	8	1	5	144

NL Pitching

	IP	H	R	ER	BB	SO	NP
Greg Maddux, Atl	3.0	3	1	1	0	2	35
Ken Hill, Mon	2.0	0	0	0	1	0	21
Doug Drabek, Hou	0.2	4	3	1	0	1	20
John Hudek, Hou	0.2	1	2	2	1	1	15
Danny Jackson, Phi	0.0	3	1	1	0	0	12
Rod Beck, SF	1.2	1	0	0	0	1	21
Randy Myers, Chi	1.0	1	0	0	0	1	10
Doug Jones, Phi (W)	1.0	2	0	0	0	2	16
TOTALS	9.0	15	7	5	2	8	138

HBP—Jefferies (by Cone, AL). **Umpires**—Paul Runge (NL) plate; John Shulock (AL) 1b; Jerry Layne (NL) 2b; Rocky Roe (AL) 3b; Bill Hohn (NL) lf; Jim Joyce (AL) rf. **Attendance**—59,568. Time—3:14. **TV Rating**—15.7/28 (NBC).

Home Attendance

Overall 1994 regular season attendance in Major League Baseball was 50,009,024 in 1,582 games for an average per game crowd of 31,611; numbers in parentheses indicate ranking in 1993; HD indicates home dates.

American League
Based on tickets sold.

	Attendance	HD	Average
1 Toronto (1)	2,907,933	59	49,287
2 Baltimore (2)	2,535,359	54	46,951
3 Texas (6)	2,502,538	62	40,364
4 Cleveland (7)	1,995,174	51	39,121
5 Chicago (3)	1,697,398	53	32,026
6 New York (5)	1,675,557	57	29,396
7 Boston (4)	1,775,826	61	29,112
8 Seattle (9)	1,103,798	44	25,086
9 Kansas City (13)	1,400,494	57	24,570
10 California (8)	1,512,622	63	24,010
11 Minnesota (10)	1,398,565	59	23,704
12 Milwaukee (14)	1,268,397	56	22,650
13 Oakland (11)	1,242,692	56	22,191
14 Detroit (12)	1,184,783	57	20,786
AL Totals	24,201,136	789	30,673

National League
Based on tickets sold.

	Attendance	HD	Average
1 Colorado (1)	3,281,511	56	58,598
2 Atlanta (2)	2,539,240	54	47,023
3 Los Angeles (3)	2,279,421	55	41,444
4 Philadelphia (4)	2,290,971	58	39,500
5 St. Louis (6)	1,866,544	54	34,566
6 Florida (5)	1,937,467	59	32,838
7 Chicago (7)	1,845,208	58	31,814
8 Cincinnati (9)	1,897,681	60	31,628
9 San Francisco (8)	1,704,614	59	28,892
10 Houston (10)	1,561,136	59	26,460
11 Montreal (11)	1,276,250	52	24,543
12 New York (11)	1,151,471	52	22,144
13 Pittsburgh (12)	1,222,517	60	20,375
14 San Diego (14)	953,857	57	16,734
NL Totals	25,807,888	793	32,545

AL Team by Team Statistics

At least 120 at bats or 25 innings pitched during the regular season. Players who competed for more than one AL team are listed with their final club. Players traded from the NL are listed with AL team only if they have 120 AB or 25 IP. Note that (*) indicates rookie.

Baltimore Orioles

Batting (120 AB)	Avg	AB	R	H	HR	RBI	SB
Rafael Palmeiro	.319	436	82	139	23	76	7
Cal Ripken	.315	444	71	140	13	75	1
Jeffrey Hammonds*	.296	250	45	74	8	31	5
Harold Baines	.294	326	44	96	16	54	0
Dwight Smith	.281	196	31	55	8	30	2
Leo Gomez	.274	285	46	78	15	56	0
Brady Anderson	.263	453	78	119	12	48	31
Mark McLemore	.257	343	44	88	3	29	20
Chris Sabo	.256	258	41	66	11	42	1
Chris Hoiles	.247	332	45	82	19	53	2
Jack Voigt	.241	141	15	34	3	20	0
Mike Devereaux	.203	301	35	61	9	33	1

Pitching (25 IP)	ERA	W-L	Gm	IP	BB	SO
Mark Eichhorn	2.15	6-5	43	71.0	19	35
Mike Mussina	3.06	16-5	24	176.1	42	99
Lee Smith	3.29	1-4	41	38.1	11	42
Mark Williamson	4.01	3-1	28	67.1	17	28
Ben McDonald	4.06	14-7	24	157.1	54	94
Jamie Moyer	4.77	5-7	23	149.0	38	87
Sid Fernandez	5.15	6-6	19	115.1	46	95
Alan Mills	5.16	3-3	47	45.1	24	44
Arthur Rhodes	5.81	3-5	10	52.2	30	47
Mike Oquist	6.17	3-3	15	58.1	30	39

Saves: Smith (33); Mills (2); Eichhorn and Williamson (1). **Complete games:** McDonald (5); Mussina and Rhodes (3); Fernandez (2). **Shutouts:** Rhodes (2); McDonald (1).

Boston Red Sox

Batting (120 AB)	Avg	AB	R	H	HR	RBI	SB
John Valentin	.316	301	53	95	9	49	3
Mo Vaughn	.310	394	65	122	26	82	4
Carlos Rodriguez*	.287	174	15	50	1	13	1
Scott Cooper	.282	369	49	104	13	53	0
Tim Naehring	.276	297	41	82	7	42	1
Otis Nixon	.274	398	60	109	0	25	42
Mike Greenwell	.269	327	60	88	11	45	2
Damon Berryhill	.263	255	30	67	6	34	0
Wes Chamberlain	.256	164	13	42	4	20	0
Billy Hatcher	.244	164	24	40	1	18	4
Andre Dawson	.240	292	34	70	16	48	2
Tom Brunansky	.234	205	24	48	10	34	0
Scott Fletcher	.227	185	31	42	3	11	8
Lee Tinsley*	.222	144	27	32	2	14	13

Acquired: OF Chamberlain and P Mike Sullivan from Phil. (May 31) for OF Billy Hatcher and P Paul Quantrill; OF Brunansky from Milw. (Jun 16) for C Dave Valle; P Farr and P Nabholz from Clev. (July 1) for P Jeff Russell.

Pitching (30 IP)	ERA	W-L	Gm	IP	BB	SO
Ken Ryan	2.44	2-3	42	48.0	17	32
Roger Clemens	2.85	9-7	24	170.2	71	168
Chris Howard	3.63	1-0	37	39.2	12	22
Aaron Sele	3.83	8-7	22	143.1	60	105
Joe Hesketh	4.26	8-5	25	114.0	46	83
Scott Bankhead	4.54	3-2	27	37.2	12	25
Frank Viola	4.65	1-1	6	31.0	17	9
Tony Fossas	4.76	2-0	44	34.0	15	31
Gar Finnvold	5.94	0-4	8	36.1	15	17
Danny Darwin	6.30	7-5	13	75.2	24	54
Tim Vanegmond*	6.34	2-3	7	38.1	21	22
Chris Nabholz	7.64	3-5	14	53.0	38	28

Saves: Ryan (13); Steve Farr (4); Fossas, Todd Frohwirth and Howard (1). **Complete Games:** Clemens (3); Sele (2); Vanegmond (1). **Shutouts:** Clemens (1).

California Angels

Batting (120 AB)	Avg	AB	R	H	HR	RBI	SB
Chili Davis	.311	392	72	122	26	84	3
Spike Owen	.310	268	30	83	3	37	2
Rex Hudler	.298	124	17	37	8	20	2
Tim Salmon	.287	373	67	107	23	70	1
Jorge Fabregas	.283	127	12	36	0	16	2
Bo Jackson	.279	201	23	56	13	43	1
Jim Edmonds*	.273	289	35	79	5	37	4
Gary DiSarcina	.260	389	53	101	3	33	3
Chad Curtis	.256	453	67	116	11	50	25
Greg Myers	.246	126	10	31	2	8	0
Chris Turner*	.242	149	23	36	1	12	3
Harold Reynolds	.232	207	33	48	0	11	10
J.T. Snow	.220	223	22	49	8	30	0
Damion Easley	.215	316	41	68	6	30	4
Eduardo Perez	.209	129	10	27	5	16	3

Pitching (25 IP)	ERA	W-L	Gm	IP	BB	SO
Bob Patterson	4.07	2-3	47	42.0	15	30
Chuck Finley	4.32	10-10	25	183.1	71	148
Craig Lefferts	4.67	1-1	30	34.2	12	27
Mark Langston	4.68	7-8	18	119.1	54	109
Mark Leiter	4.72	4-7	40	95.1	35	71
Brian Anderson*	5.22	7-5	18	101.2	27	47
Russ Springer	5.52	2-2	18	45.2	14	28
Phil Leftwich	5.68	5-10	20	114.0	42	67
Scott Lewis	6.10	0-1	20	31.0	10	10
John Dopson	6.14	1-4	21	58.2	26	33
Joe Grahe	6.65	2-5	40	43.1	18	26
Mike Butcher	6.67	2-1	33	29.2	23	19
Joe Magrane	7.30	2-6	20	74.0	51	33

Saves: Grahe (13); Leiter and Springer (2); Butcher, Dopson, Lefferts and Patterson (1). **Complete Games:** Finley (7); Langston (2); Leftwich and Magrane (1). **Shutouts:** Finley (2); Langston (1).

Chicago White Sox

Batting (120 AB)	Avg	AB	R	H	HR	RBI	SB
Frank Thomas	.353	399	106	141	38	101	2
Julio Franco	.319	433	72	138	20	98	8
Darrin Jackson	.312	369	43	115	10	51	7
Ozzie Guillen	.288	365	46	105	1	39	5
Robin Ventura	.282	401	57	113	18	78	3
Mike Lavalliere	.281	139	6	39	1	24	0
Lance Johnson	.277	412	56	114	3	54	26
Joey Cora	.276	312	55	86	2	30	8
Norberto Martin*	.275	131	19	36	1	16	4
Tim Raines	.266	384	80	102	10	52	13
Ron Karkovice	.213	207	33	44	11	29	0

Pitching (25 IP)	ERA	W-L	Gm	IP	BB	SO
Jose Deleon	3.36	3-2	42	67.0	31	67
Kirk McCaskill	3.42	1-4	40	52.2	22	37
Wilson Alvarez	3.45	12-8	24	161.2	62	108
Paul Assenmacher	3.55	1-2	44	33.0	13	29
Dennis Cook	3.55	3-1	38	33.0	14	26
Jack McDowell	3.73	10-9	25	181.0	42	127
Jason Bere	3.81	12-2	24	141.2	80	127
Alex Fernandez	3.86	11-7	24	170.1	50	122
Roberto Hernandez	4.91	4-4	45	47.2	19	50
Scott Sanderson	5.09	8-4	18	92.0	12	36

Saves: Hernandez (14); McCaskill (3); Deleon (2); Assenmacher (1). **Complete Games:** McDowell (6); Fernandez (4); Alvarez (2); Sanderson (1). **Shutouts:** Fernandez (3); McDowell (2); Alvarez (1).

Cleveland Indians

Batting (120 AB)	Avg	AB	R	H	HR	RBI	SB
Albert Belle	.357	412	90	147	36	101	9
Kenny Lofton	.349	459	105	160	12	57	60
Carlos Baerga	.314	442	81	139	19	80	8
Wayne Kirby	.293	191	33	56	5	23	11
Sandy Alomar	.288	292	44	84	14	43	8
Paul Sorrento	.280	322	43	90	14	62	0
Omar Vizquel	.273	286	39	78	1	33	13
Manny Ramirez*	.269	290	51	78	17	60	4
Jim Thome	.268	321	58	86	20	52	3
Eddie Murray	.254	433	57	110	17	76	8
Alvaro Espinoza	.238	231	27	55	1	19	1

Acquired: P Russell from Bos. (July 1) for P Steve Farr and P Chris Nabholz. Claimed: P Casian off waivers from Minn. (July 14).

Pitching (25 IP)	ERA	W-L	Gm	IP	BB	SO
Eric Plunk	2.54	7-2	41	71.0	37	73
Charles Nagy	3.45	10-8	23	169.1	48	108
Dennis Martinez	3.52	11-6	24	176.2	44	92
Mark Clark	3.82	11-3	20	127.1	40	60
Jose Mesa	3.82	7-5	51	73.0	26	63
Jason Grimsley	4.57	5-2	14	82.2	34	59
Derek Lilliquist	4.91	1-3	36	29.1	8	15
Jeff Russell	5.09	1-6	42	40.2	16	28
Jack Morris	5.60	10-6	23	141.1	67	100
Larry Casian	7.35	1-5	40	49.0	16	20

Saves: Russell (17); Paul Shuey (5); Plunk (3); Mesa (2); Casian, Lilliquist and Turner (1). **Complete Games:** Martinez (7); Clark (4); Nagy (3); Grimsley, Albie Lopez and Morris (1). **Shutouts:** Martinez (3); Clark and Lopez (1).

Detroit Tigers

Batting (120 AB)	Avg	AB	R	H	HR	RBI	SB
Juan Samuel	.309	136	32	42	5	21	5
Junior Felix	.306	301	54	92	13	49	1
Lou Whitaker	.301	322	67	97	12	43	2
Tony Phillips	.281	438	91	123	19	61	13
Kirk Gibson	.276	330	71	91	23	72	4
Alan Trammell	.267	292	38	78	8	28	3
Travis Fryman	.263	464	66	122	18	85	2
Cecil Fielder	.259	425	67	110	28	90	0
Chris Gomez*	.257	296	32	76	8	53	5
Mickey Tettleton	.248	339	57	84	17	51	0
Chad Kreuter	.224	170	17	38	1	19	0
Eric Davis	.183	120	19	22	3	13	5

Signed: Free agent P Cadaret (June 17).

Pitching (25 IP)	ERA	W-L	Gm	IP	BB	SO
Storm Davis	3.56	2-4	35	48.0	34	38
Buddy Groom	3.94	0-1	40	32.0	13	27
David Wells	3.96	5-7	16	111.1	24	71
Joe Boever	3.98	9-2	46	81.1	37	49
Mike Gardiner	4.14	2-2	38	58.2	23	31
Greg Gohr	4.50	2-2	8	34.0	21	21
Greg Cadaret	4.73	1-1	38	40.0	33	29
Mike Henneman	5.19	1-3	30	34.2	17	21
Mike Moore	5.42	11-10	25	154.1	89	62
Tim Belcher	5.89	7-15	25	162.0	78	76
Bill Gullickson	5.93	4-5	21	115.1	25	65
John Doherty	6.48	6-7	18	101.1	26	28

Saves: Henneman (8); Gardiner (5); Boever (3); Cadaret (2); Groom and Gene Harris (1). **Complete Games:** Wells (5); Moore (4); Belcher (3); Doherty (2); Gullickson (1). **Shutouts:** Wells (1).

Kansas City Royals

Batting (120 AB)	Avg	AB	R	H	HR	RBI	SB
Wally Joyner	.311	363	52	113	8	57	3
Felix Jose	.303	366	56	111	11	55	10
Gary Gaetti	.287	327	53	94	12	57	0
Bob Hamelin*	.282	312	64	88	24	65	4
Brian McRae	.273	436	71	119	4	40	28
Jose Lind	.269	290	34	78	1	31	9
Greg Gagne	.259	375	39	97	7	51	10
Brent Mayne	.257	144	19	37	2	20	1
Mike Macfarlane	.255	314	53	80	14	47	1
Dave Henderson	.247	198	27	49	5	31	2
Terry Shumpert	.240	183	28	44	8	24	18
Vince Coleman	.240	438	61	105	2	33	50

Pitching (25 IP)	ERA	W-L	Gm	IP	BB	SO
Billy Brewer	2.56	4-1	50	38.2	16	25
David Cone	2.94	16-5	23	171.2	54	132
Rusty Meacham	3.73	3-3	36	50.2	12	36
Kevin Appier	3.83	7-6	23	155.0	63	145
Jeff Montgomery	4.03	2-3	42	44.2	15	50
Tom Gordon	4.35	11-7	24	155.1	87	126
Mark Gubicza	4.50	7-9	22	130.0	26	59
Mike Magnante	4.60	2-3	36	47.0	16	21
Jose DeJesus	4.73	3-1	5	26.2	13	12
Hipolito Pichardo	4.92	5-3	45	67.2	24	36
Stan Belinda	5.14	2-2	37	49.0	24	37
Bob Milacki	6.14	0-5	10	55.2	20	17
Chris Haney	7.31	2-2	6	28.1	11	18

Saves: Montgomery (27); Meacham (4); Brewer and Pichardo (3); Belinda (1). **Complete games:** Cone (4); Appier (1). **Shutouts:** Cone (3).

Milwaukee Brewers

Batting (120 AB)	Avg	AB	R	H	HR	RBI	SB
Kevin Seitzer	.314	309	44	97	5	49	2
Brian Harper	.291	251	23	73	4	32	0
Dave Nilsson	.275	397	51	109	12	69	1
Jody Reed	.271	399	48	108	2	37	5
Darryl Hamilton	.262	141	23	37	1	13	3
B.J. Surhoff	.261	134	20	35	5	22	0
Matt Mieske*	.259	259	39	67	10	38	3
Greg Vaughn	.254	370	59	94	19	55	9
Bill Spiers	.252	214	27	54	0	17	7
Alex Diaz	.251	187	17	47	1	17	5
John Jaha	.241	291	45	70	12	39	3
Jose Valentin*	.239	285	47	68	11	46	12
Jeff Cirillo*	.238	126	17	30	3	12	0
Turner Ward	.232	367	55	85	9	45	6

Pitching (25 IP)	ERA	W-L	Gm	IP	BB	SO
Jose Mercedes*	2.32	2-0	19	31.0	16	11
Mike Fetters	2.54	1-4	42	46.0	27	31
Ricky Bones	3.43	10-9	24	170.2	45	57
Bob Scanlan	4.11	2-6	30	103.0	28	65
Bill Wegman	4.51	8-4	19	115.2	26	59
Mike Ignasiak	4.53	3-1	23	47.2	13	24
Doug Henry	4.60	2-3	25	31.1	23	20
Cal Eldred	4.68	11-11	25	179.0	84	98
Jesse Orosco	5.08	3-1	40	39.0	26	36
Graeme Lloyd	5.17	2-3	43	47.0	15	31
Angel Miranda	5.28	2-5	8	46.0	27	24
Jaime Navarro	6.62	4-9	29	89.2	35	65
Ted Higuera	7.06	1-5	17	58.2	36	35

Saves: Fetters (17); Lloyd (3); Scanlan (2); Jeff Bronkey (1). **Complete games:** Eldred (6); Bones (4); Miranda (1). **Shutouts:** Bones (1).

Minnesota Twins

Batting (120 AB)

	Avg	AB	R	H	HR	RBI	SB
Shane Mack	.333	303	55	101	15	61	4
Kirby Puckett	.317	439	79	139	20	112	6
Chuck Knoblauch	.312	445	85	139	5	51	35
Alex Cole	.296	345	68	102	4	23	29
Pedro Munoz	.295	244	35	72	11	36	0
Kent Hrbek	.270	274	34	74	10	53	0
Pat Meares	.266	229	29	61	2	24	5
Dave McCarty	.260	131	21	34	1	12	2
Jeff Reboulet	.259	189	28	49	3	23	0
Dave Winfield	.252	294	35	74	10	43	2
Scott Leius	.246	350	57	86	14	49	2
Matt Walbeck*	.204	338	31	69	5	35	1

Pitching (25 IP)

	ERA	W-L	Gm	IP	BB	SO
Rick Aguilera	3.63	1-4	44	44.2	10	46
Kevin Tapani	4.62	11-7	24	156.0	39	91
Pat Mahomes	4.73	9-5	21	120.0	62	53
Scott Erickson	5.44	8-11	23	144.0	59	104
Carl Willis	5.92	2-4	49	59.1	12	37
Carlos Pulido*	5.98	3-7	19	84.1	40	32
Mark Guthrie	6.14	4-2	50	51.1	18	38
Mike Trombley	6.33	2-0	24	48.1	18	32
Dave Stevens*	6.80	5-2	24	45.0	23	24
Jim Deshaies	7.39	6-12	25	130.1	54	78

Saves: Aguilera (23); Willis (3); Guthrie and Erik Schullstrom (1).
Complete games: Tapani (4); Erickson (2). **Shutouts:** Erickson and Tapani (1).

Oakland Athletics

Batting (120 AB)

	Avg	AB	R	H	HR	RBI	SB
Geronimo Berroa	.306	340	55	104	13	65	7
Terry Steinbach	.285	369	51	105	11	57	2
Brent Gates	.283	233	29	66	2	24	3
Stan Javier	.272	419	75	114	10	44	24
Ruben Sierra	.268	426	71	114	23	92	8
Troy Neel	.266	278	43	74	15	48	2
Rickey Henderson	.260	296	66	77	6	20	22
Mike Bordick	.253	391	38	99	2	37	7
Mark McGwire	.252	135	26	34	9	25	0
Mike Aldrete	.242	178	23	43	4	18	2
Scott Brosius	.238	324	31	77	14	49	2
Scott Hemond	.222	198	23	44	3	20	7

Pitching (25 IP)

	ERA	W-L	Gm	IP	BB	SO
Steve Karsay	2.57	1-1	4	28.0	8	15
Steve Ontiveros	2.65	6-4	27	115.1	26	56
Mark Acre*	3.41	5-1	34	34.1	23	21
Bill Taylor	3.50	1-3	41	46.1	18	48
John Briscoe	4.01	4-2	37	49.1	39	45
Carlos Reyes*	4.15	0-3	27	78.0	44	57
Dennis Eckersley	4.26	5-4	45	44.1	13	47
Ron Darling	4.50	10-11	25	160.0	59	108
Vince Horsman	4.91	0-1	33	29.1	11	20
Bobby Witt	5.04	8-10	24	135.2	70	111
Todd Van Poppel	6.09	7-10	23	116.2	89	83
Bob Welch	7.08	3-6	25	68.2	43	44
Miguel Jimenez	7.41	1-4	8	34.0	32	22

Saves: Eckersley (19); Briscoe, Dave Leiper, Reyes and Taylor (1).
Complete games: Wit (5); Darling (4); Ontiveros (2); Karsay (1). **Shutouts:** Witt (3).

New York Yankees

Batting (120 AB)

	Avg	AB	R	H	HR	RBI	SB
Paul O'Neill	.359	368	68	132	21	83	5
Wade Boggs	.342	366	61	125	11	55	2
Luis Polonia	.311	350	62	109	1	36	20
Don Mattingly	.304	372	62	113	6	51	0
Mike Stanley	.300	290	54	87	17	57	0
Bernie Williams	.289	408	80	118	12	57	16
Pat Kelly	.280	286	35	80	3	41	6
Randy Velarde	.279	280	47	78	9	34	4
Jim Leyritz	.265	249	47	66	17	58	0
Danny Tartabull	.256	399	68	102	19	67	1
Mike Gallego	.239	306	39	73	6	41	0

Signed: Free agent P Harris (July 3).

Pitching (25 IP)

	ERA	W-L	Gm	IP	BB	SO
Steve Howe	1.80	3-0	40	40.0	7	18
Bob Wickman	3.09	5-4	53	70.0	27	56
Jimmy Key	3.27	17-4	25	168.0	52	97
Donn Pall	3.60	1-2	26	35.0	9	21
Scott Kamieniecki	3.76	8-6	22	117.1	59	71
Melido Perez	4.10	9-4	22	151.1	58	109
Sterling Hitchcock*	4.20	4-1	23	49.1	29	37
Jim Abbott	4.55	9-8	24	160.1	64	90
Paul Gibson	4.97	1-1	30	29.0	17	21
Xavier Hernandez	5.85	4-4	31	40.0	21	37
Terry Mulholland	6.49	6-7	24	120.2	37	72
Greg Harris	7.99	3-5	38	50.2	26	48

Saves: Howe (15); Hernandez and Wickman (6); Harris, Hitchcock and Jeff Reardon (2). **Complete games:** Abbott and Mulholland (2); Hitchcock, Kamieniecki, Key and Perez (1). **Shutouts:** None.

Seattle Mariners

Batting (120 AB)

	Avg	AB	R	H	HR	RBI	SB
Reggie Jefferson	.327	162	24	53	8	32	0
Ken Griffey	.323	433	94	140	40	90	11
Felix Fermin	.317	379	52	120	1	35	4
Mike Blowers	.289	270	37	78	9	49	2
Edgar Martinez	.285	326	47	93	13	51	6
Jay Buhner	.279	358	74	100	21	68	0
Luis Sojo	.277	213	32	59	6	22	2
Rich Amaral	.263	228	37	60	4	18	5
Tino Martinez	.261	329	42	86	20	61	1
Eric Anthony	.237	262	31	62	10	30	6
Keith Mitchell*	.227	128	21	29	5	15	0
Dan Wilson	.216	282	24	61	3	27	1

Pitching (25 IP)

	ERA	W-L	Gm	IP	BB	SO
Jeff Nelson	2.76	0-0	28	42.1	20	44
Bobby Ayala	2.86	4-3	46	56.2	26	76
Randy Johnson	3.19	13-6	23	172.0	72	204
Bill Risley*	3.44	9-6	37	52.1	19	61
Tim Davis*	4.01	2-2	42	49.1	25	28
Rich Gossage	4.18	3-0	36	47.1	15	29
Chris Bosio	4.32	4-10	19	125.0	40	67
John Cummings	5.63	2-4	17	64.0	37	33
Dave Fleming	6.46	7-11	23	117.0	65	65
Greg Hibbard	6.69	1-5	15	80.2	31	39
Roger Salkeld*	7.17	2-5	13	59.0	45	46
Jim Converse*	8.69	0-5	13	48.2	40	39

Saves: Ayala (18); Davis (2); Gossage (1). **Complete games:** Johnson (9); Bosio (4). **Shutouts:** Johnson (4).

Texas Rangers

Batting (120 AB)	Avg	AB	R	H	HR	RBI	SB
Will Clark	.329	389	73	128	13	80	5
Jeff Frye	.327	205	37	67	0	18	6
Rusty Greer*	.314	277	36	87	10	46	0
Ivan Rodriguez	.298	363	56	108	16	57	6
Esteban Beltre	.282	131	12	37	0	12	2
Jose Canseco	.282	429	88	121	31	90	15
Manny Lee	.278	335	41	93	2	38	3
Juan Gonzalez	.275	422	57	116	19	85	6
Oddibe McDowell	.262	183	34	48	1	15	14
Chris James	.256	133	28	34	7	19	0
David Hulse	.255	310	58	79	1	19	18
Dean Palmer	.246	342	50	84	19	59	3
Doug Strange	.212	226	26	48	5	26	1

Bought: P Hurst from Okla. City of AAA (May 10).

Pitching (25 IP)	ERA	W-L	Gm	IP	BB	SO
Darren Oliver*	3.42	4-0	43	50.0	35	50
Tom Henke	3.79	3-6	37	38.0	12	39
John Dettmer*	4.33	0-6	11	54.0	20	27
Kenny Rogers	4.46	11-8	24	167.1	52	120
Kevin Brown	4.82	7-9	26	170.0	50	123
Matt Whiteside	5.02	2-2	47	61.0	28	37
Cris Carpenter	5.03	2-5	47	59.0	20	39
Jay Howell	5.44	4-1	40	43.0	16	22
Rick Helling	5.88	3-2	9	52.0	18	25
Hector Fajardo	6.91	5-7	18	83.1	26	45
Bruce Hurst	7.11	2-1	8	38.0	16	24
Rick Honeycutt	7.20	1-2	42	25.0	9	18
Brian Bohanon	7.23	2-2	11	37.1	8	26
Roger Pavlik	7.69	2-5	11	50.1	30	31

Saves: Henke (15); Carpenter (5); Howell and Oliver (2); Honeycutt and Whiteside (1). **Complete games:** Rogers (6); Brown (3); Helling (1). **Shutouts:** Rogers (2); Helling (1).

Toronto Blue Jays

Batting (120 AB)	Avg	AB	R	H	HR	RBI	SB
Paul Molitor	.341	454	86	155	14	75	20
Roberto Alomar	.306	392	78	120	8	38	19
Mike Huff	.304	207	31	63	3	25	2
John Olerud	.297	384	47	114	12	67	1
Joe Carter	.271	435	70	118	27	103	11
Devon White	.270	403	67	109	13	49	11
Dick Schofield	.255	325	38	83	4	32	7
Pat Borders	.247	295	24	73	3	26	1
Randy Knorr	.242	124	20	30	7	19	0
Ed Sprague	.240	405	38	97	11	44	1
Carlos Delgado	.215	130	17	28	9	24	1
Darnell Coles	.210	143	15	30	4	15	0

Pitching (25 IP)	ERA	W-L	Gm	IP	BB	SO
Tony Castillo	2.51	5-2	41	68.0	28	43
Pat Hentgen	3.40	13-8	24	174.2	59	147
Darren Hall*	3.41	2-3	30	31.2	14	28
Woody Williams	3.64	1-3	38	59.1	33	56
Todd Stottlemyre	4.22	7-7	26	140.2	48	105
Al Leiter	5.08	6-7	20	111.2	65	100
Mike Timlin	5.18	0-1	34	40.0	20	38
Juan Guzman	5.68	12-11	25	147.1	76	124
Dave Stewart	5.87	7-8	22	133.1	62	111
Scott Brow	5.90	0-3	18	29.0	19	15
Brad Cornett*	6.68	1-3	9	31.0	11	22

Saves: Hall (17); Danny Cox (3); Brow and Timlin (2); Castillo and Stottlemyre (1). **Complete games:** Hentgen (6); Stottlemyre (3); Guzman (2); Leiter and Stewart (1). **Shutouts:** Hentgen (3); Stottlemyre (1).

Team Leaders
AL

Batting

	Avg	AB	R	H	HR	RBI	SB
New York	.290	3986	670	1155	139	632	55
Cleveland	.290	4022	679	1165	167	647	131
Chicago	.287	3942	633	1133	121	602	77
Texas	.280	3983	613	1114	124	582	82
Minnesota	.276	3952	594	1092	103	556	94
Baltimore	.272	3856	589	1047	139	557	69
Seattle	.269	3883	569	1045	153	549	48
Kansas City	.269	3911	574	1051	100	538	140
Toronto	.269	3962	566	1064	115	534	79
Detroit	.265	3955	652	1048	161	622	46
California	.264	3943	543	1042	120	518	65
Boston	.263	3940	552	1038	120	523	81
Milwaukee	.263	3978	547	1045	99	510	59
Oakland	.260	3885	549	1009	113	515	91

Pitching

	ERA	W	Sv	CG	ShO	HR	BB	SO
Chicago	3.96	67	20	13	9	115	377	754
Kansas	4.23	64	38	5	6	95	392	717
Baltimore	4.31	63	37	13	4	131	351	666
New York	4.34	70	31	8	2	120	398	656
Cleveland	4.36	66	21	17	5	94	404	666
Milwaukee	4.62	53	23	11	3	127	421	577
Toronto	4.70	55	26	13	4	127	482	832
Oakland	4.80	51	23	12	9	128	510	732
Boston	4.93	54	30	6	3	120	450	729
Seattle	4.99	49	21	13	7	109	486	763
Detroit	5.38	53	20	15	1	148	449	560
California	5.42	47	21	11	4	150	436	682
Texas	5.45	52	26	10	4	157	394	682
Minnesota	5.68	53	29	6	4	153	388	602

NL

Batting

	Avg	AB	R	H	HR	RBI	SB
Cincinnati	.286	3999	609	1142	124	569	119
Houston	.278	3955	602	1099	120	573	124
Montreal	.278	4000	585	1111	108	542	137
San Diego	.275	4068	479	1117	92	445	79
Colorado	.274	4006	573	1098	125	540	91
Los Angeles	.270	3904	532	1055	115	505	74
Atlanta	.267	3861	542	1031	137	510	48
Florida	.266	3926	468	1043	94	451	65
St. Louis	.263	3902	535	1026	108	506	76
Philadelphia	.262	3927	521	1028	80	484	67
Chicago	.259	3918	500	1015	109	464	69
Pittsburgh	.259	3864	466	1001	80	435	53
New York	.250	3869	506	966	117	477	25
San Francisco	.249	3869	504	963	123	472	114

Pitching

	ERA	W	Sv	CG	ShO	HR	BB	SO
Montreal	3.56	74	46	4	8	100	288	805
Atlanta	3.57	68	26	16	6	76	378	865
Cincinnati	3.78	66	27	6	6	117	339	799
Philadelphia	3.85	54	30	7	6	98	377	699
Houston	3.97	66	29	9	6	102	367	739
San Francisco	3.99	55	33	2	4	122	372	655
San Diego	4.08	47	27	8	6	99	393	862
New York	4.13	55	35	7	3	117	332	640
Los Angeles	4.17	58	20	14	5	90	354	732
Chicago	4.47	49	27	5	5	120	392	710
Florida	4.50	51	30	5	7	120	428	649
Pittsburgh	4.64	53	24	8	2	117	370	650
St. Louis	5.14	53	29	7	7	134	355	622
Colorado	5.15	53	28	4	5	120	448	703

NL Team by Team Statistics

At least 120 at bats or 25 innings pitched during the regular season. Players who competed for more than one NL team are listed with their final club. Players traded from the AL are listed with NL team only if they have 120 AB or 25 IP. Note that (*) indicates rookie.

Atlanta Braves

Batting (120 AB)	Avg	AB	R	H	HR	RBI	SB
Fred McGriff	.318	424	81	135	34	94	7
David Justice	.313	352	61	110	19	59	2
Mark Lemke	.294	350	40	103	3	31	0
Roberto Kelly	.293	434	73	127	9	45	19
Ryan Klesko	.278	245	42	68	17	47	1
Tony Tarasco*	.273	132	16	36	5	19	5
Jeff Blauser	.258	380	56	98	6	45	1
Terry Pendleton	.252	309	25	78	7	30	2
Javier Lopez*	.245	277	27	68	13	35	0
Charlie O'Brien	.243	152	24	37	8	28	0
Rafael Belliard	.242	120	9	29	0	9	0
Dave Gallagher	.224	152	27	34	2	14	0

Acquired: OF Kelly from Cinc. (May 29) for OF Deion Sanders and P Roger Etheridge.

Pitching (25 IP)	ERA	W-L	Gm	IP	BB	SO
Greg Maddux	1.56	16-6	25	202.0	31	156
Steve Bedrosian	3.33	0-2	46	46.0	18	43
Kent Mercker	3.45	9-4	20	112.1	45	111
Mike Stanton	3.55	3-1	49	45.2	26	35
Greg McMichael	3.84	4-6	51	58.2	19	47
Tom Glavine	3.97	13-9	25	165.1	70	140
Mike Bielecki	4.00	2-0	19	27.0	12	18
Steve Avery	4.04	8-3	24	151.2	55	122
John Smoltz	4.14	6-10	21	134.2	48	113
Mark Wohlers	4.59	7-2	51	51.0	33	58

Saves: McMichael (21); Stanton (3); Greg Olson and Wohlers (1). **Complete games:** Maddux (10); Glavine and Mercker (2); Avery and Smoltz (1). **Shutouts:** Maddux (3); Mercker (1).

Cincinnati Reds

Batting (120 AB)	Avg	AB	R	H	HR	RBI	SB
Hal Morris	.335	436	60	146	10	78	6
Kevin Mitchell	.326	310	57	101	30	77	2
Bret Boone	.320	381	59	122	12	68	3
Jacob Brumfield	.311	122	36	38	4	11	6
Eddie Taubensee	.283	187	29	53	8	21	2
Deion Sanders	.283	375	58	106	4	28	38
Tony Fernandez	.279	366	50	102	8	50	12
Barry Larkin	.279	427	78	119	9	52	26
Thomas Howard	.264	178	24	47	5	24	4
Reggie Sanders	.263	400	66	105	17	62	21
Brian Dorsett	.245	216	21	53	5	26	0
Brian Hunter	.234	256	34	60	15	57	0

Claimed: P Schourek on waivers from N.Y. Mets (April 7). **Acquired:** C Taubensee from Hou. (April 19) for P Ross Powell and P Marty Lister; OF D. Sanders and P Roger Etheridge from Atl. (May 29) for OF Roberto Kelly; 1B Hunter from Pitt. (July 27) for player to be named later.

Pitching (25 IP)	ERA	W-L	Gm	IP	BB	SO
Hector Carrasco*	2.24	5-6	45	56.1	30	41
Chuck McElroy	2.34	1-2	52	57.2	15	38
Jeff Brantley	2.48	6-6	50	65.1	28	63
Jose Rijo	3.08	9-6	26	172.1	52	171
Johnny Ruffin*	3.09	7-2	51	70.0	27	44
John Smiley	3.86	11-10	24	158.2	37	112
Pete Schourek	4.09	7-2	22	81.1	29	69
Erik Hanson	4.11	5-5	22	122.2	23	101
Tim Fortugno	4.20	1-0	25	30.0	14	29
Tom Browning	4.20	3-1	7	40.2	13	22
John Roper	4.50	6-2	16	92.0	30	51
Tim Pugh	6.04	3-3	10	47.2	26	24

Saves: Brantley (15); Carrasco (6); McElroy (5); Ruffin (1). **Complete games:** Browning and Rijo (2); Pugh and Smiley (1). **Shutouts:** Browning and Smiley (1).

Chicago Cubs

Batting (120 AB)	Avg	AB	R	H	HR	RBI	SB
Sammy Sosa	.300	426	59	128	25	70	22
Mark Grace	.298	403	55	120	6	44	0
Glenallen Hill	.297	269	48	80	10	38	19
Rey Sanchez	.285	291	26	83	0	24	2
Derrick May	.284	345	43	98	8	51	3
Shawon Dunston	.278	331	38	92	11	35	3
Jose Hernandez*	.242	132	18	32	1	9	2
Steve Buechele	.242	339	33	82	14	52	1
Ryne Sandberg	.238	223	36	53	5	24	2
Karl Rhodes	.234	269	39	63	8	19	6
Rick Wilkins	.227	313	44	71	7	39	4

Pitching (25 IP)	ERA	W-L	Gm	IP	BB	SO
Kevin Foster*	2.89	3-4	13	81.0	35	75
Steve Trachsel*	3.21	9-7	22	146.0	54	108
Jim Bullinger	3.60	6-2	33	100.0	34	72
Randy Myers	3.79	1-5	38	40.1	16	32
Dave Otto	3.80	0-1	36	45.0	22	19
Jose Bautista	3.89	4-5	58	69.1	17	45
Anthony Young	3.92	4-6	20	114.2	46	65
Chuck Crim	4.48	5-4	49	64.1	24	43
Dan Plesac	4.61	2-3	54	54.2	13	53
Willie Banks	5.40	8-12	23	138.1	56	91
Mike Morgan	6.69	2-10	15	80.2	35	57

Saves: Myers (21); Bullinger and Crim (2); Bautista and Plesac (1). **Complete games:** Banks, Bullinger, Castillo, Morgan and Trachsel (1). **Shutouts:** Banks (1).

Colorado Rockies

Batting (120 AB)	Avg	AB	R	H	HR	RBI	SB
Mike Kingery	.349	301	56	105	4	41	5
Vinny Castilla	.331	130	16	43	3	18	2
Ellis Burks	.322	149	33	48	13	24	3
Andres Galarraga	.319	417	77	133	31	85	8
Dante Bichette	.304	484	74	147	27	95	21
Charlie Hayes	.288	423	46	122	10	50	3
Joe Girardi	.276	330	47	91	4	34	3
Eric Young	.272	228	37	62	7	30	18
Nelson Liriano	.255	255	39	65	3	31	0
Walt Weiss	.251	423	58	106	1	32	12
Howard Johnson	.211	227	30	48	10	40	11

Pitching (25 IP)	ERA	W-L	Gm	IP	BB	SO
Marvin Freeman	2.80	10-2	19	112.2	23	67
Mike Munoz	3.74	4-2	57	45.2	31	32
Steve Reed	3.94	3-2	61	64.0	26	51
Bruce Ruffin	4.04	4-5	56	55.2	30	65
David Nied	4.80	9-7	22	122.0	47	74
Armando Reynoso	4.82	3-4	9	52.1	22	25
Kevin Ritz	5.62	5-6	15	73.2	35	53
Mike Harkey	5.79	1-6	24	91.2	35	39
Willie Blair	5.79	0-5	47	77.2	39	68
Lance Painter*	6.11	4-6	15	73.2	26	41
Marcus Moore	6.15	1-1	29	33.2	21	33
Darren Holmes	6.35	0-3	29	28.1	24	33
Greg Harris	6.65	3-12	29	130.0	52	82

Saves: Ruffin (16); Blair, Holmes and Reed (3); Harris and Munoz (1). **Complete Games:** Nied (2); Harris and Reynoso (1). **Shutouts:** Nied (1).

Florida Marlins

Batting (120 AB)	Avg	AB	R	H	HR	RBI	SB
Jeff Conine	.319	451	60	144	18	82	1
Greg Colbrunn	.303	155	17	47	6	31	1
Bret Barberie	.301	372	40	112	5	31	2
Jerry Browne	.295	329	42	97	3	30	3
Gary Sheffield	.276	322	61	89	27	78	12
Dave Magadan	.275	211	30	58	1	17	0
Benito Santiago	.273	337	35	92	11	41	1
Chuck Carr	.263	433	61	114	2	30	32
Matias Carrillo*	.250	136	13	34	0	9	3
Kurt Abbott*	.249	345	41	86	9	33	3
Orestes Destrade	.208	130	12	27	5	15	1

Pitching (25 IP)	ERA	W-L	Gm	IP	BB	SO
Robb Nen	2.95	5-5	44	58.0	17	60
Chris Hammond	3.07	4-4	13	73.1	23	40
Rich Scheid*	3.34	1-3	8	32.1	8	17
Terry Mathews	3.35	2-1	24	43.0	9	21
Yorkis Perez*	3.54	3-0	44	40.2	14	41
Luis Aquino	3.73	2-1	29	50.2	22	22
Pat Rapp	3.85	7-8	24	133.1	69	75
Mark Gardner	4.87	4-4	20	92.1	30	57
Ryan Bowen	4.94	1-5	8	47.1	19	32
Charlie Hough	5.15	5-9	21	113.2	52	65
Dave Weathers	5.27	8-12	24	135.0	59	72
Jeff Mutis	5.40	1-0	35	38.1	15	30
Richie Lewis	5.67	1-4	45	54.0	38	45

Saves: Nen (15); Hernandez (9); Bryan Harvey (6). **Complete games:** Rapp (2); Bowen, Hammond and Hough (1). **Shutouts:** Hammond, Hough and Rapp (1).

Los Angeles Dodgers

Batting (120 AB)	Avg	AB	R	H	HR	RBI	SB
Mike Piazza	.319	405	64	129	24	92	1
Brett Butler	.314	417	79	131	8	33	27
Raul Mondesi*	.306	434	63	133	16	56	11
Tim Wallach	.280	414	68	116	23	78	0
Henry Rodriguez	.268	306	33	82	8	49	0
Eric Karros	.266	406	51	108	14	46	2
Delino DeShields	.250	320	51	80	2	33	27
Cory Snyder	.235	153	18	36	6	18	1
Jose Offerman	.210	243	27	51	1	25	2

Pitching (25 IP)	ERA	W-L	Gm	IP	BB	SO
Ismael Valdes*	3.18	3-1	21	28.1	10	28
Kevin Gross	3.60	9-7	25	157.1	43	124
Orel Hershiser	3.79	6-6	21	135.1	42	72
Ramon Martinez	3.97	12-7	24	170.0	56	119
Tom Candiotti	4.12	7-7	23	153.0	54	102
Todd Worrell	4.29	6-5	38	42.0	12	44
Pedro Astacio	4.29	6-8	23	149.0	47	108
Roger McDowell	5.23	0-3	32	41.1	22	29
Jim Gott	5.94	5-3	37	36.1	20	29
Darren Dreifort	6.21	0-5	27	29.0	15	22

Saves: Worrell (11); Dreifort (6); Gott (2); Gross (1). **Complete games:** Candiotti (5); Martinez (4); Astacio (3); Gross and Hershiser (1). **Shutouts:** Martinez (3); Astacio (1).

Houston Astros

Batting (120 AB)	Avg	AB	R	H	HR	RBI	SB
Jeff Bagwell	.368	400	104	147	39	116	15
Craig Biggio	.318	437	88	139	6	56	39
Kevin Bass	.310	203	37	63	6	35	2
Tony Eusebio*	.296	159	18	47	5	30	0
Ken Caminiti	.283	406	63	115	18	75	4
Steve Finley	.276	373	64	103	11	33	13
Milt Thompson	.274	241	34	66	4	33	9
Luis Gonzalez	.273	392	57	107	8	67	15
Andujar Cedeno	.263	342	38	90	9	49	1
James Mouton*	.245	310	43	76	2	16	24
Scott Servais	.195	251	27	49	9	41	0

Acquired: OF Milt Thompson from Phil. (July 31) for P Tom Edens.

Pitching (25 IP)	ERA	W-L	Gm	IP	BB	SO
Dave Veres*	2.41	3-3	32	41.0	7	28
Todd Jones	2.72	5-2	48	72.2	26	63
Doug Drabek	2.84	12-6	23	164.2	45	121
John Hudek*	2.97	0-2	42	39.1	18	39
Shane Reynolds*	3.05	8-5	33	124.0	21	110
Mike Hampton	3.70	2-1	44	41.1	16	24
Greg Swindell	4.37	8-9	24	148.1	26	74
Darryl Kile	4.57	9-6	24	147.2	82	105
Pete Harnisch	5.40	8-5	17	95.0	39	62
Brian Williams	5.74	6-5	20	78.1	41	49

Saves: Hudek (16); Williams (6); Jones (5); Veres (1). **Complete games:** Drabek (6); Harnisch, Reynolds and Swindell (1). **Shutouts:** Drabek (2); Reynolds (1).

Montreal Expos

Batting (120 AB)	Avg	AB	R	H	HR	RBI	SB
Moises Alou	.339	422	81	143	22	78	7
Larry Walker	.322	395	76	127	19	86	15
Wil Cordero	.294	415	65	122	15	63	16
Marquis Grissom	.288	475	96	137	11	45	36
Cliff Floyd*	.281	334	43	94	4	41	10
Sean Berry	.278	320	43	89	11	41	14
Lenny Webster	.273	143	13	39	5	23	0
Lou Frazier	.271	140	25	38	0	14	20
Mike Lansing	.266	394	44	105	5	35	12
Darrin Fletcher	.260	285	28	74	10	57	0

Pitching (25 IP)	ERA	W-L	Gm	IP	BB	SO
Butch Henry	2.43	8-3	24	107.1	20	70
Tim Scott	2.70	5-2	40	53.1	18	37
John Wetteland	2.83	4-6	52	63.2	21	68
Jeff Fassero	2.99	8-6	21	138.2	40	119
Ken Hill	3.32	16-5	23	154.2	44	85
Mel Rojas	3.32	3-2	58	84.0	21	84
Pedro Martinez	3.42	11-5	24	144.2	45	142
Gil Heredia	3.46	6-3	39	75.1	13	62
Jeff Shaw	3.88	5-2	46	67.1	15	47
Kirk Rueter	5.17	7-3	20	92.1	23	50

Saves: Wetteland (25); Rojas (16); Henry, Martinez, Scott, Shaw and Gabe White (1). **Complete games:** Hill (2); Fassero and Martinez (1). **Shutouts:** Hill and Martinez (1).

New York Mets

Batting (120 AB)

	Avg	AB	R	H	HR	RBI	SB
Rico Brogna*	.351	131	16	46	7	20	1
Jeff Kent	.292	415	53	121	14	68	1
Bobby Bonilla	.290	403	60	117	20	67	1
Jim Lindeman	.270	137	18	37	7	20	0
Joe Orsulak	.260	292	39	76	8	42	4
Jose Vizcaino	.256	410	47	105	3	33	1
Kevin McReynolds	.256	180	23	46	4	21	2
Kelly Stinnett*	.253	150	20	38	2	14	2
Fernando Vina	.250	124	20	31	0	6	3
David Segui	.241	336	46	81	10	43	0
Jeromy Burnitz	.238	143	26	34	3	15	1
Todd Hundley	.237	291	45	69	16	42	2
Ryan Thompson	.225	334	39	75	18	59	1

Bought: P Mason from Scranton of AAA (Apr. 29).

Pitching (25 IP)

	ERA	W-L	Gm	IP	BB	SO
Josias Manzanillo	2.66	3-2	37	47.1	13	48
Jason Jacome*	2.67	4-3	8	54.0	17	30
John Franco	2.70	1-4	47	50.0	19	42
Bret Saberhagen	2.74	14-4	24	177.1	13	143
Bobby Jones	3.15	12-7	24	160.0	56	80
Roger Mason	3.75	3-5	47	60.0	25	33
Doug Linton	4.47	6-2	32	50.1	20	29
Mike Remlinger*	4.61	1-5	10	54.2	35	33
Mauro Gozzo	4.83	3-5	23	69.0	28	33
Mike Maddux	5.11	2-1	27	44.0	13	32
Pete Smith	5.55	4-10	21	131.1	42	62
Dwight Gooden	6.31	3-4	7	41.1	15	40
Eric Hillman	7.79	0-3	11	34.2	11	20

Saves: Franco (30); Maddux and Manzanillo (2); Mason (1).
Complete games: Saberhagen (4); Jacome, Jones and Smith (1). **Shutouts:** Jacome and Jones (1).

Pittsburgh Pirates

Batting (120 AB)

	Avg	AB	R	H	HR	RBI	SB
Dave Clark	.296	223	37	66	10	46	2
Don Slaught	.288	240	21	69	2	21	0
Al Martin	.286	276	48	79	9	33	15
Carlos Garcia	.277	412	49	114	6	28	18
Jay Bell	.276	424	68	117	9	45	2
Orlando Merced	.272	386	48	105	9	51	4
Lance Parrish	.270	126	10	34	3	16	1
Jeff King	.263	339	36	89	5	42	3
Andy Van Slyke	.246	374	41	92	6	30	7
Tom Foley	.236	123	17	29	3	15	0
Kevin Young	.205	122	15	25	1	11	0

Signed: Free agent C Parrish (Apr. 30).

Pitching (25 IP)

	ERA	W-L	Gm	IP	BB	SO
Zane Smith	3.27	10-8	25	157.0	34	57
Mark Dewey	3.68	2-1	45	51.1	19	30
Jon Lieber*	3.73	6-7	17	108.2	25	71
Rick White*	3.82	4-5	43	75.1	17	38
Ravelo Manzanillo*	4.14	4-2	46	50.0	42	39
Paul Wagner	4.59	7-8	29	119.2	50	86
Alejandro Pena	5.02	3-2	22	28.2	10	27
Steve Cooke	5.02	4-11	25	134.1	46	74
Denny Neagle	5.12	9-10	24	137.0	49	122
Dan Miceli*	5.93	2-1	28	27.1	11	27

Saves: Pena (7); White (6); Mike Dyer (4); Jeff Ballard and Miceli (2); Dewey, Manzanillo and Blas Minor (1). **Complete games:** Cooke, Neagle and Smith (2); Lieber and Wagner (1). **Shutouts:** Smith (1).

Philadelphia Phillies

Batting (120 AB)

	Avg	AB	R	H	HR	RBI	SB
John Kruk	.302	255	35	77	5	38	4
Jim Eisenreich	.300	290	42	87	4	43	6
Darren Daulton	.300	257	43	77	15	56	4
Mickey Morandini	.292	274	40	80	2	26	10
Ricky Jordan	.282	220	29	62	8	37	0
Kevin Stocker	.273	271	38	74	2	28	2
Lenny Dykstra	.273	315	68	86	5	24	15
Mariano Duncan	.268	347	49	93	8	48	10
Billy Hatcher	.246	134	15	33	2	13	4
Tony Longmire*	.237	139	10	33	0	17	2
Kim Batiste	.234	209	17	49	1	13	1
Pete Incaviglia	.230	244	28	56	13	32	1
Dave Hollins	.222	162	28	36	4	26	1

Acquired: P Boskie from Chi. N. (Apr. 12) for P Kevin Foster; OF Hatcher and P Quantrill from Bos. (May 31) for OF Wes Chamberlin and P Mike Sullivan; 1B Fred McNair from Sea. (July 21) for P Boskie; P Tom Edens from Hou. (July 31) for OF Milt Thompson. **Signed:** Free agent P Valenzuela (June 24).

Pitching (35 IP)

	ERA	W-L	Gm	IP	BB	SO
Doug Jones	2.17	2-4	47	54.0	6	38
Bobby Munoz	2.67	7-5	21	104.1	35	59
Heathcliff Slocumb	2.86	5-1	52	72.1	28	58
Fernando Valenzuela	3.00	1-2	8	45.0	7	19
Danny Jackson	3.26	14-6	25	179.1	46	129
David West	3.55	4-10	31	99.0	61	83
Tom Edens	4.33	5-1	42	54.0	18	39
Curt Schilling	4.48	2-8	13	82.1	28	58
Tommy Greene	4.54	2-0	7	35.2	22	28
Mike Williams	5.01	2-4	12	50.1	20	29
Shawn Boskie	5.01	4-6	20	88.0	29	61
Ben Rivera	6.87	3-4	9	38.0	22	19

Saves: Jones (27); Toby Borland, Edens, Munoz and Paul Quantrill (1). **Complete games:** Jackson (4); Boskie, Munoz and Schilling (1). **Shutouts:** Jackson (1).

St. Louis Cardinals

Batting (120 AB)

	Avg	AB	R	H	HR	RBI	SB
Gregg Jefferies	.325	397	52	129	12	55	12
Mark Whiten	.293	334	57	98	14	53	10
Luis Alicea	.278	205	32	57	5	29	4
Tom Pagnozzi	.272	243	21	66	7	40	0
Todd Zeile	.267	415	62	111	19	75	1
Ray Lankford	.267	416	89	111	19	57	11
Jose Oquendo	.264	129	13	34	0	9	1
Ozzie Smith	.262	381	51	100	3	30	6
Brian Jordan	.258	178	14	46	5	15	4
Geronimo Pena	.254	213	33	54	11	34	9
Bernard Gilkey	.253	380	52	96	6	45	15

Pitching (25 IP)

	ERA	W-L	Gm	IP	BB	SO
John Habyan	3.23	1-0	52	47.1	20	46
Rob Murphy	3.79	4-3	50	40.1	13	26
Rene Arocha	4.01	4-4	45	83.0	21	62
Rich Rodriguez	4.03	3-5	56	60.1	26	43
Vicente Palacios	4.44	3-8	31	117.2	43	95
Bryan Eversgerd*	4.52	2-3	40	67.2	20	47
Tom Urbani	5.15	3-7	20	80.1	21	43
Bob Tewksbury	5.32	12-10	24	155.2	22	79
Rheal Cormier	5.45	3-2	7	39.2	7	26
Allen Watson	5.52	6-5	22	115.2	53	74
Omar Olivares	5.74	3-4	14	73.2	37	26
Rick Sutcliffe	6.52	6-4	16	67.2	32	26
Mike Perez	8.71	2-3	36	31.0	10	20

Saves: Perez (12); Arocha (11); Murphy (2); Frank Cimorelli, Habyan, Olivares and Palacios (1). **Completed games:** Tewksbury (4); Arocha, Olivares and Palacios (1). **Shutouts:** Arocha, Palacios and Tewksbury (1).

San Diego Padres

Batting (120 AB)	Avg	AB	R	H	HR	RBI	SB
Tony Gwynn	.394	419	79	165	12	64	5
Craig Shipley	.333	240	32	80	4	30	6
Eddie Williams	.331	175	32	58	11	42	0
Bip Roberts	.320	403	52	129	2	31	21
Derek Bell	.311	434	54	135	14	54	24
Luis Lopez*	.277	235	29	65	2	20	3
Scott Livingstone	.272	180	11	49	2	10	2
Brad Ausmus	.251	327	45	82	7	24	5
Ricky Gutierrez	.240	275	27	66	1	28	2
Phil Plantier	.220	341	44	75	18	41	3
Archi Cianfrocco	.219	146	9	32	4	13	2
Billy Bean	.215	135	7	29	0	14	0
Phil Clark	.215	149	14	32	5	20	1

Acquired: 3B Livingstone from Det. (May 11) for P Gene Harris.
Claimed: P Tabaka on waivers from Pitt. (May 12).

Pitching (25 IP)	ERA	W-L	Gm	IP	BB	SO
Trevor Hoffman	2.57	4-4	47	56.0	20	68
Pedro Martinez	2.90	3-2	48	68.1	49	52
Joey Hamilton*	2.98	9-6	16	108.2	29	61
Donnie Elliott	3.27	0-1	30	33.0	21	24
Andy Ashby	3.40	6-11	24	164.1	43	121
Tim Mauser	3.49	2-4	35	49.0	19	32
Andy Benes	3.86	6-14	25	172.1	51	189
Scott Sanders	4.78	4-8	23	111.0	48	109
Bill Krueger	4.83	3-2	8	41.0	7	30
Wally Whitehurst	4.92	4-7	13	64.0	26	43
Jeff Tabaka*	5.27	3-1	39	41.0	27	32
A.J. Sager	5.98	1-4	22	46.2	16	26

Saves: Hoffman (20); Martinez (3); Mauser (2); Sanders and Tabaka (1). **Complete games:** Ashby (4); Benes (2); Hamilton and Krueger (1). **Shutouts:** Benes (2); Hamilton (1).

San Francisco Giants

Batting (120 AB)	Avg	AB	R	H	HR	RBI	SB
Barry Bonds	.312	391	89	122	37	81	29
Willie McGee	.282	156	19	44	5	23	3
Matt Williams	.267	445	74	119	43	96	1
Todd Benzinger	.265	328	32	87	9	31	2
Darren Lewis	.257	451	70	116	4	29	30
Kirt Manwaring	.250	316	30	79	1	29	1
Dave Martinez	.247	235	23	58	4	27	3
John Patterson*	.238	240	36	57	3	32	13
Royce Clayton	.236	385	38	91	3	30	23
Robby Thompson	.209	129	13	27	2	7	3

Pitching (25 IP)	ERA	W-L	Gm	IP	BB	SO
Mike Jackson	1.49	3-2	36	42.1	11	51
Rod Beck	2.77	2-4	48	48.2	13	39
Rich Monteleone	3.18	4-3	39	45.1	13	16
Bill Swift	3.38	8-7	17	109.1	31	62
Bill VanLandingham*	3.54	8-2	16	84.0	43	56
John Burkett	3.62	6-8	25	159.1	36	85
Pat Gomez*	3.78	0-1	26	33.1	20	14
Mark Portugal	3.93	10-8	21	137.1	45	87
Dave Burba	4.38	3-6	57	74.0	45	84
Bud Black	4.47	4-2	10	54.1	16	28
Steve Frey	4.94	1-0	44	31.0	15	20
Bryan Hickerson	5.40	4-8	28	98.1	38	59
Salomon Torres	5.44	2-8	16	84.1	34	42
Kent Bottenfield	6.15	3-1	16	26.1	10	15

Saves: Beck (28); Jackson (4); Bottenfield and Hickerson (1). **Completed games:** Portugal and Torres (1). **Shutouts:** None.

Atlanta Braves

Kent Mercker

April 8
Atlanta at Los Angeles
Dodger Stadium (att: 36,546)

	R	H	E
Atl .... 020 100 102—6	6	0
LA ..... 000 000 000—0	0	0

4 BB, 10 SO, Record (1-0)
catcher: Javy Lopez
Time-2:28

Minnesota Twins

Scott Erickson

April 27
Milwaukee at Minnesota
Metrodome (att: 17,988)

	R	H	E
Mil ..... 000 000 000—0	0	0
Min .... 111 200 01x—6	13	0

4 BB, 5 SO, Record (2-3)
catcher: Matt Walbeck
Time-2:42

Texas Rangers

Kenny Rogers

July 28
California at Texas
The Ballpark (att: 46,581)

	R	H	E
Cal .... 000 000 000—0	0	0
Tex .... 202 000 00x—4	6	0

0 BB, 8 SO, Record (11-6)
catcher: Ivan Rodriguez
Time-2:08

No-Hitter   **No-Hitter**   **Perfect Game**

COLLEGE

Final *Baseball America* Top 25

Final 1994 Division I Top 25, voted on by the editors of *Baseball America* and released June 13, following the NCAA College World Series. Given are final records and winning percentages (including all postseason games); records in College World Series and team eliminated by (DNP indicates team did not play in tourney); head coach (career years and record including 1994 postseason) preseason ranking and rank before start of CWS.

		Final Record	Pct	CWS Recap	Head Coach	Jan 20 Rank	May 23 Rank
1	Oklahoma	50-17	.746	4-0	Larry Cochell (28 yrs: 960-546-2)	NR	13
2	Georgia Tech	50-17	.746	3-1 (Oklahoma)	Danny Hall (7 yrs: 258-134)	1	6
3	CS-Fullerton	47-16	.746	2-2 (Ga.Tech)	Augie Garrido (26 yrs: 1050-499-7)	6	7
4	Clemson	57-18	.760	DNP	Jack Leggett (15 yrs: 434-305)	NR	1
5	Arizona St	45-18	.714	2-2 (Oklahoma)	Jim Brock (23 yrs: 1100-440)	13	10
6	Miami-FL	49-14	.778	1-2 (Ariz.St.)	Jim Morris (13 yrs: 553-258-1)	18	4
7	Florida St	53-22	.707	1-2 (CS-Full)	Mike Martin (15 yrs: 814-280-3)	2	8
8	Tennessee	52-14	.788	DNP	Rod Delmonico (5 yrs: 201-104)	10	2
9	Oklahoma St	49-17	.742	DNP	Gary Ward (17 yrs: 862-273-1)	9	3
10	LSU	46-20	.697	0-2 (CS-Full)	Skip Bertman (11 yrs: 529-202-1)	4	12
11	USC	41-20	.672	DNP	Mike Gillespie (8 yrs: 299-193-1)	5	9
12	Ohio St	49- 9	.845	DNP	Bob Todd (11 yrs: 408-228-1)	16	5
13	Auburn	44-21	.677	0-2 (Miami-FL)	Hal Baird (15 yrs: 514-283)	23	NR
14	Texas	43-21	.672	DNP	Cliff Gustafson (27 yrs: 1344-330-2)	11	17
15	Stanford	36-24	.600	DNP	Mark Marquess (18 yrs: 727-389-5)	12	11
16	Washington	46-18	.719	DNP	Ken Knutson (2 yrs: 85-37)	NR	NR
17	Nevada	41-15	.732	DNP	Gary Powers (12 yrs: 349-284)	NR	15
18	Long Beach St	41-19	.683	DNP	Dave Snow (10 yrs: 413-200-3)	21	16
19	Wichita St	45-17	.726	DNP	Gene Stephenson (17 yrs: 951-292-3)	3	14
20	Notre Dame	46-16	.742	DNP	Pat Murphy (10 yrs: 373-171-3)	20	23
21	Texas Tech	40-17	.702	DNP	Larry Hays (24 yrs: 967-560-2)	NR	18
22	TCU	38-22	.633	DNP	Lance Brown (8 yrs: 246-220)	NR	20
23	Memphis	52-11	.825	DNP	Bob Kilpatrick (23 yrs: 747-367-2)	NR	24
24	Kansas	40-18	.690	DNP	Dave Bingham (21 yrs: 783-462-2)	25	19
25	Minnesota	42-21	.667	DNP	John Anderson (13 yrs: 469-291-2)	17	22

College World Series

CWS Seeds: 1. Miami-FL (48-12); **2.** Georgia Tech (47-16); **3.** LSU (46-18); **4.** Oklahoma (46-17); **5.** Auburn (44-19); **6.** Florida St. (52-20); **7.** Cal St. Fullerton (45-14); **8.** Arizona St. (43-16).

Bracket One

June 3— Georgia Tech 2...............................CS-Fullerton 0
June 3— Florida St. 6..LSU 3
June 5— Georgia Tech 12.................................Florida St. 4*
June 5— CS-Fullerton 20 ....LSU 6 (out)
June 7— CS-Fullerton 10 ....Florida St. 3 (out)
June 8— Georgia Tech 3 ....CS-Fullerton 2 (out)**
*10 innings; **12 innings.

Bracket Two

June 4— Arizona St. 4.......................................Miami-FL 0
June 4— Oklahoma 5...Auburn 4
June 6— Miami-FL 7......................................Auburn 5 (out)
June 6— Oklahoma 4.....................................Arizona St. 3*
June 7— Arizona St. 9.................................Miami-FL 5 (out)
June 9— Oklahoma 6..................................Arizona St. 1 (out)
*11 innings.

CWS Championship Game

Saturday, June 11, at Rosenblatt Stadium in Omaha.

	1 2 3	4 5 6	7 8 9	R	H	E
Georgia Tech	0 1 1	0 0 2	0 1 0—	5	10	4
Oklahoma	2 0 0	5 0 4	2 0 x—	13	16	0

Win: OU—Tim Walton (7-3). **Save:** OU—Bucky Buckles (14). **Loss:** GT—Al Gagolin (12-3). Starters: OU—Kevin Lovingier; GT—Gogolin. **Strikeouts:** OU—Buckles 2, Lovingier 2, Walton 1; GT—Chris Myers 3, Carlos Cason 1. **WP:** GT—Shane McGill. **2B:** OU—Rich Hills, GT—Jay Payton, Michael Sorrow. **3B:** OU—Darvin Traylor. **HR:** OU—Damon Minor (14), Chip Glass (6); GT—Jason Varitek (17), Nomar Garciaparra (16). **RBI:** OU—Rick Gutierrez, D. Minor 3, Hills 2, M.J. Mariani 2, Glass, Aric Thomas, Traylor; GT—Sorrow 2, Garciaparra, Michael Smith, Varitek. **SB:** OU—Glass (26). **CS:** OU—Mariani; GT—Garciaparra. **HBP:** OU—Hills (by Myers). **Attendance**—21,503. Time—2:50.

Most Outstanding Player

Chip Glass, Oklahoma, OF

Avg	AB	R	H	2B	3B	HR	RBI	SB
.389	18	6	7	0	0	3	4	4

All-Tournament Team

C—Jason Varitek, Georgia Tech. **1B**—Ryan Minor, Oklahoma. **2B**—Rick Gutierrez, Oklahoma. **SS**—Nomar Garciaparra, Georgia Tech. **3B**—Antone Williamson, Arizona St. **OF**—Chip Glass and Darvin Traylor, Oklahoma; Mark Katsay, CS-Fullerton. **DH**—Todd Walker, LSU. **P**—Mark Redman, Oklahoma; Brad Rigby, Georgia Tech.

Annual Awards

Chosen by *Baseball America* and the American Baseball Coaches Association.

Player of the Year

Jason Varitek, Georgia Tech.....................BA, Coaches

Coaches of the Year

Jim Morris, Miami-FL...BA
Larry Cochell, Oklahoma...............................Coaches

Ignored Early, Sooners Gain Respect Later

by Jim Callis

Oklahoma's 13-4 victory over Georgia Tech on June 11 not only gave the Sooners the 1994 College World Series championship but something they craved even more: Respect.

Oklahoma wasn't ranked in any of the pre-season polls, and Sooners' coach Larry Cochell and his staff hung signs in each player's locker to make sure they didn't forget.

They didn't.

After thrashing the Yellow Jackets with a championship-game record total of runs, Rick Gutierrez, a senior second baseman and the soul of the Sooners, spoke for the entire team.

"We knew we were going to win," Gutierrez said. "We got no respect all year, and now we've got it. We knew who was the best team out here."

Oklahoma won four straight games in Omaha, trailing for only one inning, and its heroes were many. Sophomore lefthander Mark Redman won the opener against Auburn and the semifinal against Arizona State. Junior closer Bucky Buckles saved the first and last wins, and picked up the victory in a pivotal 4-3, 11-inning win over Arizona State in the second round. Gutierrez, who batted .563 to lead all players, sparked several rallies and played solid defense.

The most improbable hero was senior center fielder Chip Glass, who choked up on his bat during the CWS in order to keep the ball on the ground and better utilize his speed. So, of course, he led all players with three home runs. He also batted .389 and stole four bases—a performance that earned him Most Outstanding Player honors. Defensively, he saved the first win over Arizona State with a spectacular diving catch in the gap to end the sixth inning with the bases loaded.

Georgia Tech fell one game short of becoming the first team since Minnesota in 1956 to win the championship in its first CWS appearance, which also would have made Danny Hall the first coach to win the title in his first year at a school.

The Yellow Jackets did claim the honor of having college baseball's consensus Player of

Wide World Photos
Oklahoma pitcher **Mark Redman** celebrates after his complete game victory over Arizona State put the Sooners in the College World Series championship game against Georgia Tech.

the Year in senior catcher Jason Varitek. A two-time All-America and first-round draft pick of the Seattle Mariners, Varitek batted .426 with 17 home runs and 86 RBIs for the season. He returned for his senior year after turning down a reported $400,000 to sign with the Minnesota Twins, who made him their first round pick in the '93 amateur draft.

The championship game drew a record 21,503 fans to Rosenblatt Stadium and overall attendance reached 161,638.

Sadly, the 1994 CWS will be remembered as Jim Brock's farewell. The legendary Arizona State coach, who won 1,100 games and two national titles in 23 seasons, had been battling liver and colon cancer for a year when he became ill and had to leave his team on June 6 in the middle of the tournament. He flew home to Arizona, where he died in a Mesa hospital on June 12 at age 57.

On a more positive coaching note, Texas's Cliff Gustafson became the all-time NCAA Division I victory leader. Gustafson passed the 1,332 wins of former Southern California coach Rod Dedeaux with a 10-1 rout of Grand Canyon University on April 22, and finished the year with a 1,344-330 record over 27 seasons.

Jim Callis is managing editor of *Baseball America*.

Consensus All-America Team

NCAA Division I players cited most frequently by the following three selectors: *Baseball America*, the American College Coaches Assn. (ACCA) and the National Collegiate Baseball Writers Assn. (NCBWA). Holdovers from 1993 All-America first team are in **bold** type.

First Team

Pos		Cl	Avg	HR	RBI
C—	**Jason Varitek**, Ga. Tech	Sr.	.426	17	86
1B—	Tommy Davis, Southern Miss	Jr.	.409	19	82
2B—	**Todd Walker**, LSU	Jr.	.393	18	68
SS—	Nomar Garciaparra, Ga. Tech	Jr.	.427	16	73
3B—	**Antone Williamson**, Ariz. St.	Jr.	.371	15	74
OF—	Jose Cruz Jr., Rice	So.	.401	14	68
OF—	Shane Monahan, Clemson	So.	.415	11	53
OF—	Jay Payton, Georgia Tech	Jr.	.434	20	102
DH—	Ryan Hall, BYU	Jr.	.421	26	75

Pos		Cl	W-L	Sv	ERA
P—	R.A. Dickey, Tennessee	Fr.	15-2	0	3.00
P—	Danny Graves, Miami-FL	Jr.	1-1	21	0.89
P—	Paul Wilson, Florida St.	Jr.	13-5	0	2.08
P—	Gary Rath, Miss. St.	Jr.	10-3	0	1.71
P—	Jason Bell, Oklahoma St.	So.	14-2	0	3.30

Second Team

Pos		Cl	Avg	HR	RBI
C—	A.J. Hinch, Stanford	So.	.309	7	36
1B—	Mark Landers, West Va	Sr.	.416	19	81
2B—	Mark Merila, Minnesota	Sr.	.452	7	61
SS—	Mark Lewis, Nevada	Sr.	.372	10	63
3B—	Mike Hampton, Clemson	Sr.	.380	11	70
OF—	Jeff Abbott, Kentucky	Jr.	.445	23	64
OF—	Jacob Cruz, Arizona St	Jr.	.393	15	69
OF—	Mark Little, Memphis	Jr.	.435	21	86
DH—	Todd Helton, Tennessee	So.	.355	7	80

Pos		Cl	W-L	Sv	ERA
P—	Matt Beaumont, Ohio St	Jr.	11-1	0	3.56
P—	Jason Beverlin, W. Car.	Jr.	11-4	0	2.39
P—	Randy Flores, USC	Fr.	11-1	0	1.66
P—	Ryan Nye, Texas Tech	Jr.	11-3	0	2.25
P—	Brad Rigby, Ga. Tech	Jr.	14-4	0	3.46
P—	Scott Rivette, L.Beach St	So.	14-1	0	2.50

NCAA Division I Leaders

Batting

Average

(At least 110 AB)

	Cl	Gm	AB	H	Avg
Adrian Price, Coppin St	Jr.	41	137	65	.474
Erik Sauve, VCU	Sr.	56	203	95	.468
Mike Merila, Minnesota	Sr.	54	177	80	.452
Jeff Abbott, Kentucky	Jr.	55	229	102	.445
Brian Church, Hofstra	Jr.	37	129	57	.442

Home Runs

(At least 15)

	Cl	Gm	HR	Avg
Shane Jones, Utah	Sr.	54	26*	0.48
Cookie Massey, N. Carolina	Sr.	46	22	0.48
Ryan Hall, BYU	Jr.	55	26*	0.47
Jeff Abbott, Kentucky	Jr.	55	23	0.42
Ryan Jackson, Duke	Sr.	53	22	0.42
*led nation.				

Runs Batted In

(At least 50)

	Cl	Gm	RBI	Avg
Mike Miller, Hofstra	Jr.	36	57	1.58
Jay Payton, Georgia Tech	Jr.	67	102*	1.52
Glenn Harris, Air Force	Jr.	49	72	1.47
Jeff Vallillo, Hofstra	Jr.	36	50	1.39
Mark Little, Memphis	Sr.	63	86	1.37
*led nation.				

Pitching

Earned Run Avg. (50 inn)

(At least 50 inn.)

	Cl	Gm	IP	ERA
Danny Graves, Miami-FL	Jr.	40	61.0	0.89
Mike Manning, W. Carolina	Sr.	40	55.2	0.97
Jay Tessmer, Miami-FL	Jr.	40	70.0	1.16
Gabe Gonzalez, L. Beach St	Jr.	28	50.2	1.24
Shane Dennis, Wichita St	Sr.	16	113.2	1.35

Wins

	Cl	Gm	IP	W-L
R.A. Dickey, Tennessee	Fr.	21	147.0	15-2
Scott Rivette, Long Beach St	So.	16	111.2	14-1
Jason Bell, Oklahoma St	So.	19	128.0	14-2
Mark Redman, Oklahoma	So.	23	135.1	14-3
Brad Rigby, Georgia Tech	Jr.	24	143.0	14-4
Mark Guerra, Jacksonville	Jr.	23	144.0	14-4
Tom Price, Notre Dame	Sr.	20	140.1	14-5

Strikeouts (per 9 inn.)

(At least 50 inn.)

	Cl	IP	So	Avg
John Powell, Auburn	Sr.	89.1	130	13.1
Yates Hall, Virginia	Jr.	72.2	104	12.9
J. O'Shaughnessy, N'eastern	Fr.	55.0	76	12.4
Todd Dyess, Tulane	Jr.	80.0	110	12.4
Joe Mamott, Canisius	Jr.	64.0	85	12.0

MLB Amateur Draft

First round selections at the 30th Amateur Draft held on June 2, 1994.

First Round

No			Pos
1	NY Mets	Paul Wilson, Florida St.	rhp
2	Oakland	Ben Grieve, HS—Arlington, TX	of
3	San Diego	Dustin Hermanson, Kent Univ.	rhp
4	Milwaukee	Antone Williamson, Arizona St.	3b
5	Florida	Josh Booty, HS—Shreveport, LA	ss
6	California	McKay Christensen, HS—Fresno, CA	of
7	Colorado	Doug Million, HS—Sarasota, FL	lhp
8	Minnesota	Todd Walker, LSU	2b
9	Cincinnati	C.J. Nitkowski, St. John's	lhp
10	Cleveland	Jaret Wright, HS—Anaheim, CA	rhp
11	Pittsburgh	Mark Farris, HS—Angleton, TX	ss
12	Boston	Nomar Garciaparra, Georgia Tech	ss
13	Los Angeles	Paul Konerko, HS—Scottsdale, AZ	c
14	Seattle	Jason Varitek, Georgia Tech	c

No			Pos
15	Chicago-NL	Jayson Peterson, HS—Denver	rhp
16	Kansas City	Matt Smith, HS—Grants Pass, OR	1b
17	Houston	Ramon Castro, HS—Vega Baja, P.R.	c
18	Detroit	Cade Gaspar, Pepperdine	rhp
19	St. Louis	Bret Wagner, Wake Forest	lhp
20	a-NY Mets	Terrence Long, HS—Millbrook, AL	1b
21	Montreal	Hiram Bocachica, HS—Bayamon P.R.	ss
22	b-San Fran	Dante Powell, CS-Fullerton	of
23	Philadelphia	Carlton Loewer, Mississippi St.	rhp
24	NY Yankees	Brian Buchanan, Virginia	1b-of
25	c-Houston	Scott Elarton, HS—Lamar, CO	rhp
26	Chicago-AL	Mark Johnson, HS—W. Robins, GA	c
27	Atlanta	Jacob Shumate, HS—Hartsville, SC	rhp
28	Toronto	Kevin Witt, HS—Jacksonville	3b

Acquired picks: a—from Baltimore for signing Type A free agent Sid Fernandez; **b**—from Texas for signing Type A Will Clark; **c**—from San Francisco for signing Type A Mark Portugal.

THE 1995 INFORMATION PLEASE SPORTS ALMANAC

BASEBALL STATISTICS

SEC B

THROUGH THE YEARS
1900-1994
WORLD SERIES • ALL-TIMERS

PAGE 101

The World Series

The World Series began in 1903 when Pittsburgh of the older National League (founded in 1876) invited Boston of the American League (founded in 1901) to play a best-of-9 game series to determine which of the two league champions was the best. Boston was the surprise winner, 5 games to 3. The 1904 NL champion New York Giants refused to play Boston the following year, so there was no series. Giants' owner John T. Brush and his manager John McGraw both despised AL president Ban Johnson and considered the junior circuit to be a minor league. By the following year, however, Brush and Johnson had smoothed out their differences and the Giants agreed to play Philadelphia in a best-of-7 game series. Since then the World Series has been best-of-7 format, except from 1919-21 when it returned to best-of-9.

After surviving two world wars and an earthquake in 1989, the World Series was cancelled for only the second time in 1994 when the players went out on strike Aug. 12 to protest the owners' call for revenue sharing and a salary cap. On Sept. 14, with no hope of reaching a labor agreement to end the 34-day strike, the owners called off the remainder of the regular season and the entire postseason.

In the chart below, the National League teams are listed in CAPITAL letters. Also, each World Series champion's wins and losses are noted in parentheses after the Series score in games.

Multiple champions: New York Yankees (22); Philadelphia-Oakland A's and St. Louis Cardinals (9); Brooklyn-Los Angeles Dodgers (6); Boston Red Sox, Cincinnati Reds, New York-San Francisco Giants and Pittsburgh Pirates (5); Detroit Tigers (4); Baltimore Orioles and Washington Senators-Minnesota Twins (3); Boston-Milwaukee Braves, Chicago Cubs, Chicago White Sox, Cleveland Indians, New York Mets and Toronto Blue Jays (2).

Year	Winner	Manager	Series	Loser	Manager
1903	Boston Red Sox	Jimmy Collins	5-3 (LWLLWWWW)	PITTSBURGH	Fred Clarke
1904	Not held				
1905	NY GIANTS	John McGraw	4-1 (WLWWW)	Philadelphia A's	Connie Mack
1906	Chicago White Sox	Fielder Jones	4-2 (WLWLWW)	CHICAGO CUBS	Frank Chance
1907	CHICAGO CUBS	Frank Chance	4-0-1 (TWWWW)	Detroit	Hughie Jennings
1908	CHICAGO CUBS	Frank Chance	4-1 (WWLWW)	Detroit	Hughie Jennings
1909	PITTSBURGH	Fred Clarke	4-3 (WLWLWLW)	Detroit	Hughie Jennings
1910	Philadelphia A's	Connie Mack	4-1 (WWWLW)	CHICAGO CUBS	Frank Chance
1911	Philadelphia A's	Connie Mack	4-2 (LWWWLW)	NY GIANTS	John McGraw
1912	Boston Red Sox	Jake Stahl	4-3-1 (WTLWWLLW)	NY GIANTS	John McGraw
1913	Philadelphia A's	Connie Mack	4-1 (WLWWW)	NY GIANTS	John McGraw
1914	BOSTON BRAVES	George Stallings	4-0	Philadelphia A's	Connie Mack
1915	Boston Red Sox	Bill Carrigan	4-1 (LWWWW)	PHILA. PHILLIES	Pat Moran
1916	Boston Red Sox	Bill Carrigan	4-1 (WWLWW)	BKLN. DODGERS	Wilbert Robinson
1917	Chicago White Sox	Pants Rowland	4-2 (WWLLWW)	NY GIANTS	John McGraw
1918	Boston Red Sox	Ed Barrow	4-2 (WLWLWW)	CHICAGO CUBS	Fred Mitchell
1919	CINCINNATI	Pat Moran	5-3 (WWLWWLLW)	Chicago White Sox	Kid Gleason
1920	Cleveland	Tris Speaker	5-2 (WLLWWWW)	BKLN. DODGERS	Wilbert Robinson
1921	NY GIANTS	John McGraw	5-3 (LLWWWLWW)	NY Yankees	Miller Huggins
1922	NY GIANTS	John McGraw	4-0-1 (WTWWW)	NY Yankees	Miller Huggins
1923	NY Yankees	Miller Huggins	4-2 (LWLWWW)	NY GIANTS	John McGraw
1924	Washington	Bucky Harris	4-3 (LWLWLWW)	NY GIANTS	John McGraw
1925	PITTSBURGH	Bill McKechnie	4-3 (LWLLWWW)	Washington	Bucky Harris
1926	ST.L. CARDINALS	Rogers Hornsby	4-3 (LWWLLWW)	NY Yankees	Miller Huggins
1927	NY Yankees	Miller Huggins	4-0	PITTSBURGH	Donie Bush
1928	NY Yankees	Miller Huggins	4-0	ST.L. CARDINALS	Bill McKechnie
1929	Philadelphia A's	Connie Mack	4-1 (WWLWW)	CHICAGO CUBS	Joe McCarthy
1930	Philadelphia A's	Connie Mack	4-2 (WWLLWW)	ST.L. CARDINALS	Gabby Street
1931	ST.L. CARDINALS	Gabby Street	4-3 (LWWLWLW)	Philadelphia A's	Connie Mack
1932	NY Yankees	Joe McCarthy	4-0	CHICAGO CUBS	Charlie Grimm
1933	NY GIANTS	Bill Terry	4-1 (WWLWW)	Washington	Joe Cronin
1934	ST.L. CARDINALS	Frankie Frisch	4-3 (WLWLLWW)	Detroit	Mickey Cochrane
1935	Detroit	Mickey Cochrane	4-2 (LWWWLW)	CHICAGO CUBS	Charlie Grimm
1936	NY Yankees	Joe McCarthy	4-2 (LWWWLW)	NY GIANTS	Bill Terry
1937	NY Yankees	Joe McCarthy	4-1 (WWWLW)	NY GIANTS	Bill Terry
1938	NY Yankees	Joe McCarthy	4-0	CHICAGO CUBS	Gabby Hartnett
1939	NY Yankees	Joe McCarthy	4-0	CINCINNATI	Bill McKechnie

World Series (Cont.)

Year	Winner	Manager	Series	Loser	Manager
1940	CINCINNATI	Bill McKechnie	4-3 (LWLWLWW)	Detroit	Del Baker
1941	NY Yankees	Joe McCarthy	4-1 (WLWWW)	BKLN. DODGERS	Leo Durocher
1942	ST.L. CARDINALS	Billy Southworth	4-1 (LWWWW)	NY Yankees	Joe McCarthy
1943	NY Yankees	Joe McCarthy	4-1 (LWWWW)	ST.L. CARDINALS	Billy Southworth
1944	ST.L. CARDINALS	Billy Southworth	4-2 (LWLWWW)	St. Louis Browns	Luke Sewell
1945	Detroit	Steve O'Neill	4-3 (LWLWLW)	CHICAGO CUBS	Charlie Grimm
1946	ST.L. CARDINALS	Eddie Dyer	4-3 (LWLWLWW)	Boston Red Sox	Joe Cronin
1947	NY Yankees	Bucky Harris	4-3 (WWLLWLW)	BKLN. DODGERS	Burt Shotton
1948	Cleveland	Lou Boudreau	4-2 (LWWWLW)	BOSTON BRAVES	Billy Southworth
1949	NY Yankees	Casey Stengel	4-1 (WLWWW)	BKLN. DODGERS	Burt Shotton
1950	NY Yankees	Casey Stengel	4-0	PHILA. PHILLIES	Eddie Sawyer
1951	NY Yankees	Casey Stengel	4-2 (LWLWWW)	NY GIANTS	Leo Durocher
1952	NY Yankees	Casey Stengel	4-3 (LWLWWLW)	BKLN. DODGERS	Charlie Dressen
1953	NY Yankees	Casey Stengel	4-2 (WWLLWW)	BKLN. DODGERS	Charlie Dressen
1954	NY GIANTS	Leo Durocher	4-0	Cleveland	Al Lopez
1955	BKLN. DODGERS	Walter Alston	4-3 (LLWWWLW)	NY Yankees	Casey Stengel
1956	NY Yankees	Casey Stengel	4-3 (LLWWWLW)	BKLN. DODGERS	Walter Alston
1957	MILW. BRAVES	Fred Haney	4-3 (WLWWLW)	NY Yankees	Casey Stengel
1958	NY Yankees	Casey Stengel	4-3 (LLWLWWW)	MILW. BRAVES	Fred Haney
1959	LA DODGERS	Walter Alston	4-2 (LWWWLW)	Chicago White Sox	Al Lopez
1960	PITTSBURGH	Danny Murtaugh	4-3 (WLLWWLW)	NY Yankees	Casey Stengel
1961	NY Yankees	Ralph Houk	4-1 (WLWWW)	CINCINNATI	Fred Hutchinson
1962	NY Yankees	Ralph Houk	4-3 (WLWLWLW)	SF GIANTS	Alvin Dark
1963	LA DODGERS	Walter Alston	4-0	NY Yankees	Ralph Houk
1964	ST.L. CARDINALS	Johnny Keane	4-3 (WLLWWLW)	NY Yankees	Yogi Berra
1965	LA DODGERS	Walter Alston	4-3 (LLWWWLW)	Minnesota	Sam Mele
1966	Baltimore	Hank Bauer	4-0	LA DODGERS	Walter Alston
1967	ST.L. CARDINALS	Red Schoendienst	4-3 (WLWWLLW)	Boston Red Sox	Dick Williams
1968	Detroit	Mayo Smith	4-3 (LWLLWWW)	ST.L. CARDINALS	Red Schoendienst
1969	NY METS	Gil Hodges	4-1 (LWWWW)	Baltimore	Earl Weaver
1970	Baltimore	Earl Weaver	4-1 (WWWLW)	CINCINNATI	Sparky Anderson
1971	PITTSBURGH	Danny Murtaugh	4-3 (LLWWWLW)	Baltimore	Earl Weaver
1972	Oakland A's	Dick Williams	4-3 (WWLWLLW)	CINCINNATI	Sparky Anderson
1973	Oakland A's	Dick Williams	4-3 (WLWLLWW)	NY METS	Yogi Berra
1974	Oakland A's	Alvin Dark	4-1 (WLWWW)	LA DODGERS	Walter Alston
1975	CINCINNATI	Sparky Anderson	4-3 (LWWLWLW)	Boston Red Sox	Darrell Johnson
1976	CINCINNATI	Sparky Anderson	4-0	NY Yankees	Billy Martin
1977	NY Yankees	Billy Martin	4-2 (WLWLW)	LA DODGERS	Tommy Lasorda
1978	NY Yankees	Bob Lemon	4-2 (LLWWWW)	LA DODGERS	Tommy Lasorda
1979	PITTSBURGH	Chuck Tanner	4-3 (LWLLWWW)	Baltimore	Earl Weaver
1980	PHILA. PHILLIES	Dallas Green	4-2 (WWLLWW)	Kansas City	Jim Frey
1981	LA DODGERS	Tommy Lasorda	4-2 (LLWWWW)	NY Yankees	Bob Lemon
1982	ST.L. CARDINALS	Whitey Herzog	4-3 (WLLWWLW)	Milwaukee Brewers	Harvey Kuenn
1983	Baltimore	Joe Altobelli	4-1 (LWWWW)	PHILA. PHILLIES	Paul Owens
1984	Detroit	Sparky Anderson	4-1 (WLWWW)	SAN DIEGO	Dick Williams
1985	Kansas City	Dick Howser	4-3 (LLWLWWW)	ST.L. CARDINALS	Whitey Herzog
1986	NY METS	Davey Johnson	4-3 (WWLLLWW)	Boston Red Sox	John McNamara
1987	Minnesota	Tom Kelly	4-3 (WWLLLWW)	ST.L. CARDINALS	Whitey Herzog
1988	LA DODGERS	Tommy Lasorda	4-1 (WWLWW)	Oakland A's	Tony La Russa
1989	Oakland A's	Tony La Russa	4-0	SF GIANTS	Roger Craig
1990	CINCINNATI	Lou Piniella	4-0	Oakland A's	Tony La Russa
1991	Minnesota	Tom Kelly	4-3 (WWLLLWW)	ATLANTA BRAVES	Bobby Cox
1992	Toronto	Cito Gaston	4-2 (LWWWLW)	ATLANTA BRAVES	Bobby Cox
1993	Toronto	Cito Gaston	4-2 (WLWWLW)	PHILA. PHILLIES	Jim Fregosi
1994	Not held				

Most Valuable Players

Currently selected by media panel made up of representatives of CBS Sports, CBS Radio, AP, UPI, and World Series official scorers. Presented by *Sport* magazine from 1955-88 and by Major League Baseball since 1989. Winners who did not play for World Series champions are in **bold** type.

Multiple winners: Bob Gibson, Reggie Jackson and Sandy Koufax (2).

Year		Year		Year	
1955	Johnny Podres, Bklyn, P	1960	**Bobby Richardson**, NY, 2B	1965	Sandy Koufax, LA, P
1956	Don Larsen, NY, P	1961	Whitey Ford, NY, P	1966	Frank Robinson, Bal., OF
1957	Lew Burdette, Mil., P	1962	Ralph Terry, NY, P	1967	Bob Gibson, St.L., P
1958	Bob Turley, NY, P	1963	Sandy Koufax, LA, P	1968	Mickey Lolich, Det., P
1959	Larry Sherry, LA, P	1964	Bob Gibson, St.L., P	1969	Donn Clendenon, NY, 1B

Year		Year		Year	
1970	Brooks Robinson, Bal., 3B	1980	Mike Schmidt, Phi., 3B	1988	Orel Hershiser, LA, P
1971	Roberto Clemente, Pit., OF	1981	Pedro Guerrero, LA, OF;	1989	Dave Stewart, Oak., P
1972	Gene Tenace, Oak., C		Ron Cey, LA, 3B;	1990	Jose Rijo, Cin., P
1973	Reggie Jackson, Oak., OF		& Steve Yeager, LA, C	1991	Jack Morris, Min., P
1974	Rollie Fingers, Oak., P	1982	Darrell Porter, St.L., C	1992	Pat Borders, Tor., C
1975	Pete Rose, Cin., 3B	1983	Rick Dempsey, Bal., C	1993	Paul Molitor, Tor., DH/1B/3B
1976	Johnny Bench, Cin., C	1984	Alan Trammell, Det., SS	1994	No award
1977	Reggie Jackson, NY, OF	1985	Bret Saberhagen, KC, P		
1978	Bucky Dent, NY, SS	1986	Ray Knight, NY, 3B		
1979	Willie Stargell, Pit., 1B	1987	Frank Viola, Min., P		

All-Time World Series Leaders
CAREER

World Series leaders through 1994. Years listed indicate number of World Series appearances.

Hitting

Games

	Yrs	Gm
Yogi Berra, NY Yankees	14	75
Mickey Mantle, NY Yankees	12	65
Elston Howard, NY Yankees-Boston	10	54
Hank Bauer, NY Yankees	9	53
Gil McDougald, NY Yankees	8	53

At Bats

	Yrs	AB
Yogi Berra, NY Yankees	14	259
Mickey Mantle, NY Yankees	12	230
Joe DiMaggio, NY Yankees	10	199
Frankie Frisch, NY Giants-St.L Cards	8	197
Gil McDougald, NY Yankees	8	190

Batting Avg. (minimum 50 AB)

	AB	H	Avg
Pepper Martin, St.L Cards	55	23	.418
Lou Brock, St. Louis	87	34	.391
Thurman Munson, NY Yankees	67	25	.373
George Brett, Kansas City	51	19	.373
Hank Aaron, Milw. Braves	55	20	.364

Hits

	AB	H	Avg
Yogi Berra, NY Yankees	259	71	.274
Mickey Mantle, NY Yankees	230	59	.257
Frankie Frisch, NYG-St.L Cards	197	58	.294
Joe DiMaggio, NY Yankees	199	54	.271
Hank Bauer, NY Yankees	188	46	.245
Pee Wee Reese, Brooklyn	169	46	.272

Runs

	Gm	R
Mickey Mantle, NY Yankees	65	42
Yogi Berra, NY Yankees	75	41
Babe Ruth, NY Yankees	41	37
Lou Gehrig, NY Yankees	34	30
Joe DiMaggio, NY Yankees	51	27

Home Runs

	AB	HR
Mickey Mantle, NY Yankees	230	18
Babe Ruth, NY Yankees	129	15
Yogi Berra, NY Yankees	259	12
Duke Snider, Brooklyn-LA	133	11
Lou Gehrig, NY Yankees	119	10
Reggie Jackson, Oakland-NY Yankees	98	10

Runs Batted In

	Gm	RBI
Mickey Mantle, NY Yankees	65	40
Yogi Berra, NY Yankees	75	39
Lou Gehrig, NY Yankees	34	35
Babe Ruth, NY Yankees	41	33
Joe DiMaggio, NY Yankees	51	30

Stolen Bases

	Gm	SB
Lou Brock, St. Louis	21	14
Eddie Collins, Phi. A's-Chisox	34	14
Frank Chance, Chi. Cubs	20	10
Davey Lopes, Los Angeles	23	10
Phil Rizzuto, NY Yankees	52	10

Total Bases

	Gm	TB
Mickey Mantle, NY Yankees	65	123
Yogi Berra, NY Yankees	75	117
Babe Ruth, NY Yankees	41	96
Lou Gehrig, NY Yankees	34	87
Joe DiMaggio, NY Yankees	51	84

Slugging Pct. (50 AB)

	AB	Avg
Reggie Jackson, Oakland-NY Yankees	98	.755
Babe Ruth, NY Yankees	129	.744
Lou Gehrig, NY Yankees	119	.731
Al Simmons, Phi. A's-Cincinnati	73	.658
Lou Brock, St. Louis	87	.655

World Series Appearances

In the 90 years that the World Series has been contested, American League teams have won 53 championships while National League teams have won 37.

The following teams are ranked by number of appearances through the 1993 World Series; (*) indicates AL teams.

	App	W	L	Pct.	Last Series	Last Title
NY Yankees*	33	22	11	.667	1981	1978
Bklyn/LA Dodgers	18	6	12	.333	1988	1988
NY/SF Giants	16	5	11	.313	1989	1954
St.L.Cardinals	15	9	6	.600	1987	1982
Phi/KC/Oak.A's*	14	9	5	.643	1990	1989
Chicago Cubs	10	2	8	.200	1945	1908
Boston Red Sox*	9	5	4	.556	1986	1918
Cincinnati Reds	9	5	4	.556	1990	1990
Detroit Tigers*	9	4	5	.444	1984	1984
Pittsburgh Pirates	7	5	2	.714	1979	1979
St.L/Bal.Orioles*	7	3	4	.429	1983	1983
Wash./Min.Twins*	6	3	3	.500	1991	1991
Bos/Mil/Atl.Braves	6	2	4	.333	1992	1957
Chi.White Sox*	4	2	2	.500	1959	1917
Phi.Phillies	5	1	4	.200	1993	1980
Cle.Indians*	3	2	1	.667	1954	1948
NY Mets	3	2	1	.667	1986	1986
Tor. Blue Jays	2	2	0	1.000	1993	1993
KC Royals*	2	1	1	.500	1985	1985
Sea./Mil.Brewers*	1	0	1	.000	1982	—
SD Padres	1	0	1	.000	1984	—

All-Time World Series Leaders (Cont.)
Pitching

Games

	Yrs	Gm
Whitey Ford, NY Yankees	11	22
Rollie Fingers, Oakland	3	16
Allie Reynolds, NY Yankees	6	15
Bob Turley, NY Yankees	5	15
Clay Carroll, Cincinnati	3	1

Wins

	Gm	W-L
Whitey Ford, NY Yankees	22	10-8
Bob Gibson, St. Louis	9	7-2
Allie Reynolds, NY Yankees	15	7-2
Red Ruffing, NY Yankees	10	7-2
Lefty Gomez, NY Yankees	7	6-0
Chief Bender, Philadelphia A's	10	6-4
Waite Hoyt, NY Yankees-Phi. A's	12	6-4

ERA (minimum 25 IP)

	Gm	IP	ERA
Jack Billingham, Cincinnati	7	25	0.36
Harry Brecheen, St. Louis	7	33	0.83
Babe Ruth, Boston Red Sox	3	31	0.87
Sherry Smith, Brooklyn	3	30	0.89
Sandy Koufax, Los Angeles	8	57	0.95

Saves

	Gm	IP	Sv
Rollie Fingers, Oakland	16	33	6
Allie Reynolds, NY Yankees	15	77	4
Johnny Murphy, NY Yankees	8	16	4
Seven pitchers tied with 3 each.			

Shutouts

	GS	CG	ShO
Christy Mathewson, NY Giants	11	10	4
Three Finger Brown, Chi. Cubs	7	5	3
Whitey Ford, NY Yankees	22	7	3
Seven pitchers tied with 2 each.			

Innings Pitched

	Gm	IP
Whitey Ford, NY Yankees	22	146
Christy Mathewson, NY Giants	11	102
Red Ruffing, NY Yankees	10	86
Chief Bender, Philadelphia A's	10	85
Waite Hoyt, NY Yankees-Phi. A's	12	84

Complete Games

	GS	CG	W-L
Christy Mathewson, NY Giants	11	10	5-5
Chief Bender, Philadelphia A's	10	9	6-4
Bob Gibson, St. Louis	9	8	7-2
Whitey Ford, NY Yankees	22	7	10-8
Red Ruffing, NY Yankees	10	7	7-2

Strikeouts

	Gm	IP	SO
Whitey Ford, NY Yankees	22	146	94
Bob Gibson, St. Louis	9	81	92
Allie Reynolds, NY Yankees	15	77	62
Sandy Koufax, Los Angeles	8	57	61
Red Ruffing, NY Yankees	10	86	61

Bases on Balls

	Gm	IP	BB
Whitey Ford, NY Yankees	22	146	34
Allie Reynolds, NY Yankees	15	77	32
Art Nehf, NY Giants-Chi.Cubs	12	79	32
Jim Palmer, Baltimore	9	65	31
Bob Turley, NY Yankees	15	54	29

Losses

	Gm	W-L
Whitey Ford, NY Yankees	22	10-8
Christy Mathewson, NY Giants	11	5-5
Joe Bush, Phi. A's-Bosox-NY Yankees	9	2-5
Rube Marquard, NY Giants-Brooklyn	11	2-5
Eddie Plank, Philadelphia A's	7	2-5
Schoolboy Rowe, Detroit	8	2-5

League Championship Series

Division play came to the major leagues in 1969 when both the American and National Leagues expanded to 12 teams. With an East and West Division in each league, League Championship Series (LCS) became necessary to determine the NL and AL pennant winners. In the charts below, the East Division champions are noted by the letter E and the West Division champions by W. Also, each playoff winner's wins and losses are noted in parentheses after the series score. The LCS changed from best-of-5 to best-of-7 in 1985. Each league's LCS was cancelled in 1994 due to the players' strike.

National League

Multiple champions: Cincinnati and LA Dodgers (5); NY Mets, Philadelphia and St. Louis (3); Atlanta and Pittsburgh (2).

Year	Winner	Manager	Series	Loser	Manager
1969	E- New York	Gil Hodges	3-0	W- Atlanta	Lum Harris
1970	W- Cincinnati	Sparky Anderson	3-0	E- Pittsburgh	Danny Murtaugh
1971	E- Pittsburgh	Danny Murtaugh	3-1 (LWWW)	W- San Francisco	Charlie Fox
1972	W- Cincinnati	Sparky Anderson	3-2 (LWLWW)	E- Pittsburgh	Bill Virdon
1973	E- New York	Yogi Berra	3-2 (LWWLW)	W- Cincinnati	Sparky Anderson
1974	W- Los Angeles	Walter Alston	3-1 (WWLW)	E- Pittsburgh	Danny Murtaugh
1975	W- Cincinnati	Sparky Anderson	3-0	E- Pittsburgh	Danny Murtaugh
1976	W- Cincinnati	Sparky Anderson	3-0	E- Philadelphia	Danny Ozark
1977	W- Los Angeles	Tommy Lasorda	3-1 (LWWW)	E- Philadelphia	Danny Ozark
1978	W- Los Angeles	Tommy Lasorda	3-1 (WWLW)	E- Philadelphia	Danny Ozark
1979	E- Pittsburgh	Chuck Tanner	3-0	W- Cincinnati	John McNamara
1980	E- Philadelphia	Dallas Green	3-2 (WLLWW)	W- Houston	Bill Virdon
1981	W- Los Angeles	Tommy Lasorda	3-2 (WLLWW)	E- Montreal	Jim Fanning

Year	Winner	Manager	Series	Loser	Manager
1982	E- St. Louis	Whitey Herzog	3-0	W- Atlanta	Joe Torre
1983	E- Philadelphia	Paul Owens	3-1 (WLWW)	W- Los Angeles	Tommy Lasorda
1984	W- San Diego	Dick Williams	3-2 (LLWWW)	E- Chicago	Jim Frey
1985	E- St. Louis	Whitey Herzog	4-2 (LLWWWW)	W- Los Angeles	Tommy Lasorda
1986	E- New York	Davey Johnson	4-2 (LWWWW)	W- Houston	Hal Lanier
1987	E- St. Louis	Whitey Herzog	4-3 (WLWLLWW)	W- San Francisco	Roger Craig
1988	W- Los Angeles	Tommy Lasorda	4-3 (LWLWWLW)	E- New York	Davey Johnson
1989	W- San Francisco	Roger Craig	4-1 (WLWWW)	E- Chicago	Don Zimmer
1990	W- Cincinnati	Lou Piniella	4-2 (LWWWLW)	E- Pittsburgh	Jim Leyland
1991	W-Atlanta	Bobby Cox	4-3 (LWWLLWW)	E- Pittsburgh	Jim Leyland
1992	W-Atlanta	Bobby Cox	4-3 (WWLWLLLW)	E-Pittsburgh	Jim Leyland
1993	E-Philadelphia	Jim Fregosi	4-2 (WLLWWW)	W-Atlanta	Bobby Cox
1994	Not held				

NLCS Most Valuable Players

Winners who did not play for NLCS champions are in **bold** type.

Year		Year		Year	
1977	Dusty Baker, LA, OF	1984	Steve Garvey, SD, 1B	1990	Rob Dibble, Cin., P
1978	Steve Garvey, LA, 1B	1985	Ozzie Smith, St.L., SS		& Randy Myers, Cin., P
1979	Willie Stargell, Pit., 1B	1986	**Mike Scott,** Hou., P	1991	Steve Avery, Atl., P
1980	Manny Trillo, Phi., 2B	1987	**Jeff Leonard,** SF, OF	1992	John Smoltz, Atl., P
1981	Burt Hooton, LA, P	1988	Orel Hershiser, LA, P	1993	Curt Schilling, Phi., P
1982	Darrell Porter, St.L., C	1989	Will Clark, SF, 1B	1994	No award
1983	Gary Matthews, Phi., OF				

American League

Multiple champions: Oakland (6); Baltimore (5); NY Yankees (4); Boston, Kansas City, Minnesota and Toronto (2).

Year	Winner	Manager	Series	Loser	Manager
1969	E- Baltimore	Earl Weaver	3-0	W- Minnesota	Billy Martin
1970	E- Baltimore	Earl Weaver	3-0	W- Minnesota	Bill Rigney
1971	E- Baltimore	Earl Weaver	3-0	W- Oakland	Dick Williams
1972	W- Oakland	Dick Williams	3-2 (WWLLW)	E- Detroit	Billy Martin
1973	W- Oakland	Dick Williams	3-2 (LWWLW)	E- Baltimore	Earl Weaver
1974	W- Oakland	Alvin Dark	3-1 (LWWW)	E- Baltimore	Earl Weaver
1975	E- Boston	Darrell Johnson	3-0	W- Oakland	Alvin Dark
1976	E- New York	Billy Martin	3-2 (WLWLW)	W- Kansas City	Whitey Herzog
1977	E- New York	Billy Martin	3-2 (LWLWW)	W- Kansas City	Whitey Herzog
1978	E- New York	Bob Lemon	3-1 (WLWW)	W- Kansas City	Whitey Herzog
1979	E- Baltimore	Earl Weaver	3-1 (WWLW)	W- California	Jim Fregosi
1980	W- Kansas City	Jim Frey	3-0	E- New York	Dick Howser
1981	E- New York	Bob Lemon	3-0	W- Oakland	Billy Martin
1982	E- Milwaukee	Harvey Kuenn	3-2 (LLWWW)	W- California	Gene Mauch
1983	E- Baltimore	Joe Altobelli	3-1 (LWWW)	W- Chicago	Tony La Russa
1984	E- Detroit	Sparky Anderson	3-0	W- Kansas City	Dick Howser
1985	W- Kansas City	Dick Howser	4-3 (LLWLWWW)	E- Toronto	Bobby Cox
1986	E- Boston	John McNamara	4-3 (LWLLWWW)	W- California	Gene Mauch
1987	W- Minnesota	Tom Kelly	4-1 (WWLWW)	E- Detroit	Sparky Anderson
1988	W- Oakland	Tony La Russa	4-0	E- Boston	Joe Morgan
1989	W- Oakland	Tony La Russa	4-1 (WWLWW)	E- Toronto	Cito Gaston
1990	W- Oakland	Tony La Russa	4-0	E- Boston	Joe Morgan
1991	W-Minnesota	Tom Kelly	4-1 (WLWWW)	E-Toronto	Cito Gaston
1992	E-Toronto	Cito Gaston	4-2 (LWWWLW)	W-Oakland	Tony La Russa
1993	E-Toronto	Cito Gaston	4-2 (WWLLWW)	W-Chicago	Gene Lamont
1994	Not held				

ALCS Most Valuable Players

Winners who did not play for ALCS champions are in **bold** type.

Multiple winners: Dave Stewart (2).

Year		Year		Year	
1980	Frank White, KC, 2B	1985	George Brett, KC, 3B	1990	Dave Stewart, Oak., P
1981	Graig Nettles, NY, 3B	1986	Marty Barrett, Bos., 2B	1991	Kirby Puckett, Min., OF
1982	**Fred Lynn,** Cal., OF	1987	Gary Gaetti, Min., 3B	1992	Roberto Alomar, Tor., 2B
1983	Mike Boddicker, Bal., P	1988	Dennis Eckersley, Oak., P	1993	Dave Stewart, Tor., P
1984	Kirk Gibson, Det., OF	1989	Rickey Henderson, Oak., OF	1994	No award

Other Playoffs

Seven times from 1946-80, playoffs were necessary to decide league or division championships when two teams tied for first place at the end of the regular season. In the strike year of 1981, there were playoffs between the first and second half-season champions in both leagues.

National League

Year	NL	W	L	Manager	Year	NL West	W	L	Manager
1946	Brooklyn	96	58	Leo Durocher	1980	Houston	92	70	Bill Virdon
	St. Louis	96	58	Eddie Dyer		Los Angeles	92	70	Tommy Lasorda
	Playoff: (Best-of-3) St. Louis, 2-0					Playoff: (1 game) Houston, 7-1 (at LA)			

Year	NL	W	L	Manager	Year	NL East	W	L	Manager
1951	Brooklyn	96	58	Charlie Dressen	1981	(1st Half) Phila	34	21	Dallas Green
	New York	96	58	Leo Durocher		(2nd Half) Montreal	30	23	Jim Fanning
	Playoff: (Best-of-3) New York, 2-1 (WLW)					Playoff: (Best-of-5) Montreal, 3-2 (WWLLW)			

Year	NL	W	L	Manager		NL West	W	L	Manager
1959	Milwaukee	86	68	Fred Haney		(1st Half) Los Ang	36	21	Tommy Lasorda
	Los Angeles	86	68	Walter Alston		(2nd Half) Houston	33	20	Bill Virdon
	Playoff: (Best-of-3) Los Angeles, 2-0					Playoff: (Best-of-5) Los Angeles, 3-2 (LLWWW)			

Year	NL	W	L	Manager
1962	Los Angeles	101	61	Walter Alston
	San Francisco	101	61	Alvin Dark
	Playoff: (Best-of-3) San Francisco, 2-1 (WLW)			

American League

Year	AL	W	L	Manager	Year	AL East	W	L	Manager
1948	Boston	96	58	Joe McCarthy	1981	(1st Half) N.Y.	34	22	Bob Lemon
	Cleveland	96	58	Lou Boudreau		(2nd Half) Milw.	31	23	Buck Rodgers
	Playoff: (1 game) Cleveland, 8-3 (at Boston)					Playoff: (Best-of-5) New York, 3-2 (WWLLW)			

Year	AL East	W	L	Manager		AL West	W	L	Manager
1978	Boston	99	63	Don Zimmer		(1st Half) Oakland	37	23	Billy Martin
	New York	99	63	Bob Lemon		(2nd Half) Kan.City	30	23	Jim Frey
	Playoff: (1 game) New York, 5-4 (at Boston)					Playoff: (Best-of-5), Oakland, 3-0			

Regular Season League & Division Winners

Regular season National and American League pennant winners from 1900-68, as well as West and East divisional champions from 1969-93. In 1994, both leagues went to three divisions—West, Central and East. However, due to the players' strike that resulted in the cancelling of the season after games played on Aug. 11, division leaders at the time of the strike are not considered official champions by either league. Note that (*) indicates 1994 divisional champion is unofficial and that **GA** column indicates games ahead of the second place club.

National League

Multiple pennant winners: Brooklyn-LA (19); New York-SF Giants (17); St. Louis (15); Chicago (10); Cincinnati and Pittsburgh (9); Boston-Milwaukee-Atlanta (6); Philadelphia (5); New York Mets (3). **Multiple division winners:** WEST—Cincinnati and Los Angeles (7); Atlanta (5); San Francisco (3); Houston (2). EAST—Pittsburgh (9); Philadelphia (6); NY Mets (4); St. Louis (3); Chicago (2).

Year		W	L	Pct	GA	Year		W	L	Pct	GA
1900	Brooklyn	82	54	.603	4½	1924	New York	93	60	.608	1½
1901	Pittsburgh	90	49	.647	7½	1925	Pittsburgh	95	58	.621	8½
1902	Pittsburgh	103	36	.741	27½	1926	St. Louis	89	65	.578	2
1903	Pittsburgh	91	49	.650	6½	1927	Pittsburgh	94	60	.610	1½
1904	New York	106	47	.693	13	1928	St. Louis	95	59	.617	2
1905	New York	105	48	.686	9	1929	Chicago	98	54	.645	10½
1906	Chicago	116	36	.763	20	1930	St. Louis	92	62	.597	2
1907	Chicago	107	45	.704	17	1931	St. Louis	101	53	.656	13
1908	Chicago	99	55	.643	1	1932	Chicago	90	64	.584	4
1909	Pittsburgh	110	42	.724	6½	1933	New York	91	61	.599	5
1910	Chicago	104	50	.675	13	1934	St. Louis	95	58	.621	2
1911	New York	99	54	.647	7½	1935	Chicago	100	54	.649	4
1912	New York	103	48	.682	10	1936	New York	92	62	.597	5
1913	New York	101	51	.664	12½	1937	New York	95	57	.625	3
1914	Boston	94	59	.614	10½	1938	Chicago	89	63	.586	2
1915	Philadelphia	90	62	.592	7	1939	Cincinnati	97	57	.630	4½
1916	Brooklyn	94	60	.610	2½	1940	Cincinnati	100	53	.654	12
1917	New York	98	56	.636	10	1941	Brooklyn	100	54	.649	2½
1918	Chicago	84	45	.651	10½	1942	St. Louis	106	48	.688	2
1919	Cincinnati	96	44	.686	9	1943	St. Louis	105	49	.682	18
1920	Brooklyn	93	61	.604	7	1944	St. Louis	105	49	.682	14½
1921	New York	94	59	.614	4	1945	Chicago	98	56	.636	3
1922	New York	93	61	.604	7	1946	St. Louis†	98	58	.628	2
1923	New York	95	58	.621	4½	1947	Brooklyn	94	60	.610	5

Year		W	L	Pct	GA
1948	Boston	91	62	.595	6½
1949	Brooklyn	97	57	.630	1
1950	Philadelphia	91	63	.591	2
1951	New York†	98	59	.624	1
1952	Brooklyn	96	57	.627	4½
1953	Brooklyn	105	49	.682	13
1954	New York	97	57	.630	5
1955	Brooklyn	98	55	.641	13½
1956	Brooklyn	93	61	.604	1
1957	Milwaukee	95	59	.617	8
1958	Milwaukee	92	62	.597	8
1959	Los Angeles†	88	68	.564	2
1960	Pittsburgh	95	59	.617	7
1961	Cincinnati	93	61	.604	4
1962	San Francisco†	103	62	.624	1
1963	Los Angeles	99	63	.611	6
1964	St. Louis	93	69	.574	1
1965	Los Angeles	97	65	.599	2
1966	Los Angeles	95	67	.586	1½
1967	St. Louis	101	60	.627	10½
1968	St. Louis	97	65	.599	9
1969	West—Atlanta	93	69	.574	3
	East—N.Y. Mets	100	62	.617	8
1970	West—Cincinnati	102	60	.630	14½
	East—Pittsburgh	89	73	.549	5
1971	West—San Francisco	90	72	.556	1
	East—Pittsburgh	97	65	.599	7
1972	West—Cincinnati	95	59	.617	10½
	East—Pittsburgh	96	59	.619	11
1973	West—Cincinnati	99	63	.611	3½
	East—N.Y. Mets	82	79	.509	1½
1974	West—Los Angeles	102	60	.630	4
	East—Pittsburgh	88	74	.543	1½
1975	West—Cincinnati	108	54	.667	20
	East—Pittsburgh	92	69	.571	6½
1976	West—Cincinnati	102	60	.630	10
	East—Philadelphia	101	61	.623	9
1977	West—Los Angeles	98	64	.605	10
	East—Philadelphia	101	61	.623	5
1978	West—Los Angeles	95	67	.586	2½
	East—Philadelphia	90	72	.556	1½
1979	West—Cincinnati	90	71	.559	1½
	East—Pittsburgh	98	64	.605	2
1980	West—Houston	93	70	.571	1
	East—Philadelphia	91	71	.562	1
1981	West—Los Angeles†	63	47	.573	—
	East—Montreal†	60	48	.556	—
1982	West—Atlanta	89	73	.549	1
	East—St. Louis	92	70	.568	3
1983	West—Los Angeles	91	71	.562	3
	East—Philadelphia	90	72	.556	6
1984	West—San Diego	92	70	.568	12
	East—Chicago	96	65	.596	6½
1985	West—Los Angeles	95	67	.586	5½
	East—St. Louis	101	61	.623	3
1986	West—Houston	96	66	.593	10
	East—N.Y. Mets	108	54	.667	21½
1987	West—San Francisco	90	72	.556	6
	East—St. Louis	95	67	.586	3
1988	West—Los Angeles	94	67	.584	7
	East—N.Y. Mets	100	60	.625	15
1989	West—San Francisco	92	70	.568	3
	East—Chicago	93	69	.574	6
1990	West—Cincinnati	91	71	.562	5
	East—Pittsburgh	95	67	.586	4
1991	West—Atlanta	94	68	.580	1
	East—Pittsburgh	98	64	.605	14
1992	West—Atlanta	98	64	.605	8
	East—Pittsburgh	96	66	.593	9
1993	West—Atlanta	104	58	.642	1
	East—Philadelphia	97	65	.599	3
1994	West—Los Angeles*	58	56	.509	3½
	Central—Cincinnati*	66	48	.579	½
	East—Montreal*	74	40	.649	6

†Regular season playoffs: 1946—St. Louis def. Brooklyn (2 games to 1); 1951—New York def. Brooklyn (2 games to 1); 1959—Los Angeles def. Milwaukee (2 games to none); 1962—San Francisco def. Los Angeles (2 games to 1); 1981—East: Philadelphia def. Montreal (3 games to 2) and West: Los Angeles def. Houston (3 games to 2).

American League

Multiple pennant winners: NY Yankees (32); Philadelphia-Oakland A's (15); Boston (10); Detroit (9); Baltimore and Washington-Minnesota (6); Chicago (5); Cleveland (3); KC Royals and Toronto (2). Multiple division winners: WEST—Oakland (10); Kansas City (6); Minnesota (4); California (3); Chicago (2). EAST—Baltimore (7); NY Yankees and Toronto (5); Boston (4); Detroit (3).

Year		W	L	Pct	GA
1901	Chicago	83	53	.610	4
1902	Philadelphia	83	53	.610	5
1903	Boston	91	47	.659	14½
1904	Boston	95	59	.617	1½
1905	Philadelphia	92	56	.622	2
1906	Chicago	93	58	.616	3
1907	Detroit	92	58	.613	1½
1908	Detroit	90	63	.588	½
1909	Detroit	98	54	.645	3½
1910	Philadelphia	102	48	.680	14½
1911	Philadelphia	101	50	.669	13½
1912	Boston	105	47	.691	14
1913	Philadelphia	96	57	.627	6½
1914	Philadelphia	99	53	.651	8½
1915	Boston	101	50	.669	2½
1916	Boston	91	63	.591	2
1917	Chicago	100	54	.649	9
1918	Boston	75	51	.595	2½
1919	Chicago	88	52	.629	3½
1920	Cleveland	98	56	.636	2
1921	New York	98	55	.641	4½
1922	New York	94	60	.610	1
1923	New York	98	54	.645	16
1924	Washington	92	62	.597	2
1925	Washington	96	55	.636	8½
1926	New York	91	63	.591	3
1927	New York	110	44	.714	19
1928	New York	101	53	.656	2½
1929	Philadelphia	104	46	.693	18
1930	Philadelphia	102	52	.662	8
1931	Philadelphia	107	45	.704	13½
1932	New York	107	47	.695	13
1933	Washington	99	53	.651	7
1934	Detroit	101	53	.656	7
1935	Detroit	93	58	.616	3
1936	New York	102	51	.667	19½
1937	New York	102	52	.662	13
1938	New York	99	53	.651	9½
1939	New York	106	45	.702	17
1940	Detroit	90	64	.584	1
1941	New York	101	53	.656	17
1942	New York	103	51	.669	9
1943	New York	98	56	.636	13½
1944	St. Louis	89	65	.578	1

Regular Season League & Division Winners (Cont.)
American League

Year		W	L	Pct	GA	Year		W	L	Pct	GA
1945	Detroit	88	65	.575	1½	1976	West—Kansas City	90	72	.556	2½
1946	Boston	104	50	.675	12		East—New York	97	62	.610	10½
1947	New York	97	57	.630	12	1977	West—Kansas City	102	60	.630	8
1948	Cleveland†	97	58	.626	1		East—New York	100	62	.617	2½
1949	New York	97	57	.630	1	1978	West—Kansas City	92	70	.568	5
							East—New York†	100	63	.613	1
1950	New York	98	56	.636	3	1979	West—California	88	74	.543	3
1951	New York	98	56	.636	5		East—Baltimore	102	57	.642	8
1952	New York	95	59	.617	2						
1953	New York	99	52	.656	8½	1980	West—Kansas City	97	65	.599	14
1954	Cleveland	111	43	.721	8		East—New York	103	59	.636	3
1955	New York	96	58	.623	3	1981	West—Oakland†	64	45	.587	—
1956	New York	97	57	.630	9		East—New York†	59	48	.551	—
1957	New York	98	56	.636	8	1982	West—California	93	69	.574	3
1958	New York	92	62	.597	10		East—Milwaukee	95	67	.586	1
1959	Chicago	94	60	.610	5	1983	West—Chicago	99	63	.611	20
							East—Baltimore	98	64	.605	6
1960	New York	97	57	.630	8	1984	West—Kansas City	84	78	.519	3
1961	New York	109	53	.673	8		East—Detroit	104	58	.642	15
1962	New York	96	66	.593	5	1985	West—Kansas City	91	71	.562	1
1963	New York	104	57	.646	10½		East—Toronto	99	62	.615	2
1964	New York	99	63	.611	1	1986	West—California	92	70	.568	5
1965	Minnesota	102	60	.630	7		East—Boston	95	66	.590	5½
1966	Baltimore	97	63	.606	9	1987	West—Minnesota	85	77	.525	2
1967	Boston	92	70	.568	1		East—Detroit	98	64	.605	2
1968	Detroit	103	59	.636	12	1988	West—Oakland	104	58	.642	13
1969	West—Minnesota	97	65	.599	9		East—Boston	89	73	.549	1
	East—Baltimore	109	53	.673	19	1989	West—Oakland	99	63	.611	7
							East—Toronto	89	73	.549	2
1970	West—Minnesota	98	64	.605	9						
	East—Baltimore	108	54	.667	15	1990	West—Oakland	103	59	.636	9
1971	West—Oakland	101	60	.627	16		East—Boston	88	74	.543	2
	East—Baltimore	101	57	.639	12	1991	West—Minnesota	95	67	.586	8
1972	West—Oakland	93	62	.600	5½		East—Toronto	91	71	.562	7
	East—Detroit	86	70	.551	½	1992	West—Oakland	96	66	.593	6
1973	West—Oakland	94	68	.580	6		East—Toronto	96	66	.593	4
	East—Baltimore	97	65	.599	8	1993	West—Chicago	94	68	.580	8
1974	West—Oakland	90	72	.556	5		East—Toronto	95	67	.586	7
	East—Baltimore	91	71	.562	2	1994	West—Texas*	52	62	.456	1
1975	West—Oakland	98	64	.605	7		Central—Chicago*	67	46	.593	1
	East—Boston	95	65	.594	4½		East—New York*	70	43	.619	6½

†**Regular season playoffs: 1948**—Cleveland def. Boston, 2-1 (one game); **1978**—New York def. Boston, 5-4 (one game); **1981**—East: New York def. Milwaukee (3 games to 2) and West: Oakland def. Kansas City (3 games to none).

The All-Star Game

Baseball's first All-Star Game was held on July 6, 1933, before 47,595 at Comiskey Park in Chicago. From that year on, the All-Star Game has matched the best players in the American League against the best in the National. From 1959-62, two All-Star Games were played. The only year an All-Star Game wasn't played was 1945, when World War II travel restrictions made it necessary to cancel the meeting (see page 109). The NL leads the series, 38-26-1. In the chart below, the American League is listed in **bold** type.

Year		Host (Ballpark)	AL Manager	NL Manager
1933	**American,** 4-2	Chicago (Comiskey Park)	Connie Mack	John McGraw
1934	**American,** 9-7	New York (Polo Grounds)	Joe Cronin	Bill Terry
1935	**American,** 4-1	Cleveland (Cleveland Stadium)	Mickey Cochrane	Frankie Frisch
1936	National, 4-3	Boston (Braves Field)	Joe McCarthy	Charlie Grimm
1937	**American,** 8-3	Washington (Griffith Stadium)	Joe McCarthy	Bill Terry
1938	National, 4-1	Cincinnati (Crosley Field)	Joe McCarthy	Bill Terry
1939	**American,** 3-1	New York (Yankee Stadium)	Joe McCarthy	Gabby Hartnett
1940	National, 4-0	St. Louis (Sportsman's Park)	Joe Cronin	Bill McKechnie
1941	**American,** 7-5	Detroit (Briggs Stadium)	Del Baker	Bill McKechnie
1942	**American,** 3-1	New York (Polo Grounds)	Joe McCarthy	Leo Durocher
1943	**American,** 5-3	Philadelphia (Shibe Park)	Joe McCarthy	Billy Southworth
1944	National, 7-1	Pittsburgh (Forbes Field)	Joe McCarthy	Billy Southworth
1945	No Game			
1946	**American,** 12-0	Boston (Fenway Park)	Steve O'Neill	Charlie Grimm
1947	**American,** 2-1	Chicago (Wrigley Field)	Joe Cronin	Eddie Dyer
1948	**American,** 5-2	St. Louis (Sportsman's Park)	Bucky Harris	Leo Durocher
1949	**American,** 11-7	Brooklyn (Ebbets Field)	Lou Boudreau	Billy Southworth

The Year The All-Star Game Was Cancelled

by Bill Deane

If you check the record books for the result of the 1945 All-Star Game, you will see something like "Game cancelled due to wartime travel restrictions." But, who decided that there would be no game? And when? And was anything held in its stead?

The 1945 All-Star Game was scheduled. It was to be played at Boston's Fenway Park on Tuesday, July 10. Even after the game was nixed in February, schedule-makers left the dates of July 9, 10 and 11 open in hopes that circumstances might change by then, permitting the contest.

During the winter of 1944-45, America's involvement in World War II was at its most critical stage. Although President Franklin Roosevelt had given the "green light" for baseball to continue three years earlier, times had changed, and there was serious doubt as to whether the 1945 season would be held at all. The game had no commissioner (sound familiar?), following Kenesaw Landis's death on Nov. 25, 1944, and most of its biggest stars—Williams, Musial, Feller, DiMaggio, et al—were in military service.

On Feb. 21, 1945, league presidents Ford Frick of the NL and William Harridge of the AL met with Col. J. Monroe Johnson, Director of the Office of Defense Transportation (ODT). By the end of the meeting, the baseball season was still alive, but the World Series appeared doubtful and the All-Star Game was dead.

"The transportation situation this year is so critical," announced Johnson, "that I am asking baseball to effect such further economies as will permit the continuation of the national game." Johnson "requested" that baseball cut travel by 25% in comparison with 1944, and Frick and Harridge volunteered to eliminate the mid-summer classic, estimating that "500,000 man-miles" would be saved. Spring Training was also curtailed again; no team trained any further south than Cairo, Illinois.

The March 8 edition of *The Sporting News* had a column from *Boston Post* writer Jack

The Bettmann Archive

After Germany surrendered in 1945, New York theatrical impresario **Mike Todd** talked Supreme Allied Headquarters into agreeing to stage the All-Star Game in Nuremberg. Baseball officials however, said the plan was impractical.

Malaney. Malaney, former president of the Baseball Writers' Association, and future member of the Hall of Fame Veterans' Committee, introduced what came to be known as the "Jack Malaney Plan." He proposed that each of the 16 major league teams play interleague exhibition games on July 10, scheduled to minimize travel. The five cities that had teams in each league—Boston, Chicago, New York, Philadelphia, and St. Louis—would host games between the cross-town rivals, while the other six teams would play in cities en route to regularly-scheduled games. Proceeds from the games would be split between the American Red Cross and the National War Fund (in 1942-44, regular league games had been designated for the same cause).

On April 24, club owners—meeting in Cleveland to select a new commissioner, who turned out to be U.S. Senator Happy Chandler—approved the Malaney Plan. Besides the same-city games, Cincinnati would play at Cleveland, Brooklyn at Washington and Detroit at Pittsburgh. The Tigers-Pirates contest, however, 110 ➤

Bill Deane is a baseball researcher, writer and editor based near Cooperstown, N.Y.

would later be scrapped when the ODT refused to grant Detroit permission to detour 62 miles to get to Forbes Field.

After Germany's surrender on May 7, baseball followers wondered if the All-Star Game might be exhumed. Col. Johnson, however, quickly burst that bubble, citing the need to move troops from the European theater of operations to the Pacific. "Conditions are far worse now than at any time since we began going over transportation problems with various sports groups," he said on May 12.

On June 1 came a surprise twist to the story. Brig. Gen. Mike Todd, the New York theatrical impresario and consultant for the Army Special Services on Entertainment, announced an All-Star Game plan of his own—approved by Supreme Allied Headquarters—to stage the mid-summer classic at Germany's Nuremberg Stadium (capacity 120,000). "GI's want American entertainment," said Todd, "and there isn't anything more American than the All-Star Game … we'll have a game right here where Hitler used to strut."

Todd offered to arrange the transportation and suggested that the likes of Babe Ruth and Ty Cobb be brought over to act as coaches or managers. The plan provided for two games between league All-Stars and servicemen, leading up to the main event.

Major league officials, upon hearing of the grandiose scheme, quickly pronounced it wholly impractical, due to traveling and scheduling red tape. Todd's brainstorm never got off the ground.

The seven benefit games were held on July 9 and 10. At old Comiskey Park, the White Sox edged the Cubs, 5-4, in ten innings, before Chicago's biggest crowd (47,144) since 1941. At Cleveland, the Reds blanked the Indians, 6-0. At New York's Polo Grounds, Hershel Martin's grand slam helped the Yankees trounce the Giants, 7-1, in a rain-shortened game. At Philadelphia, slugger Jimmie Foxx was the starting pitcher for the Phillies (or Bluejays) as they defeated the Athletics, 7-6.

At St. Louis, the Browns avenged their 1944 World Series loss to the Cardinals with a 3-0 triumph. The Browns had nine different pitchers hurl one shutout inning each, while the Cards had four pitchers work two innings apiece. Despite the 11 pitching changes, the game took only one hour, 31 minutes to play!

At Fenway Park, the Red Sox topped the Braves, 8-1, in the only day game of the series. Dave Ferriss, discarding plans to pitch both right and left-handed, stayed with his right in subduing the Braves. The Sox' Jack Tobin singled off his brother, Jim, while Tommy Holmes managed a safety for the Braves. Holmes entered the All-Star break with a .401 average and a NL-record 37-game hitting streak, but the skein was snapped the day the regular schedule was resumed.

Finally, at Washington, the Senators beat the Dodgers, 4-3, in a game marred by the career-ending knee injury suffered by Brooklyn's rookie pitcher, Lee Pfund. Ironically, the game's winning pitcher was Bert Shepard, who had lost a leg in military service.

The games raised a total of $244,778 for charity. The Boston game, though it had the third-lowest attendance of the games, contributed the most: $73,000. The reason: 44 box seats were sold at the price of $1,000 each. The New York and Chicago games each netted $50,000-plus.

On July 12, it was back to business as usual. By 1946, the war was over, baseball was back in full swing and the All-Star Game was again an annual event.

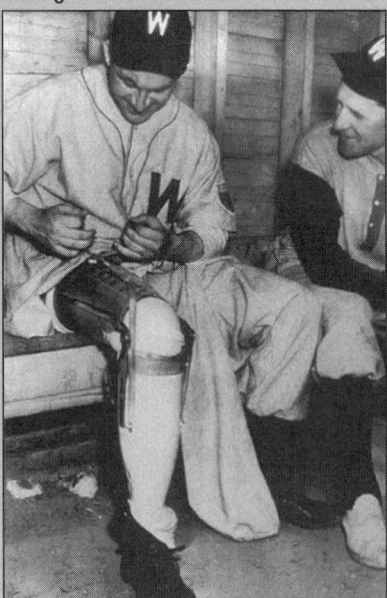

Bert Shepard of the Washington Senators, seen here strapping on his artificial right leg, was one of the winning pitchers in the 1945 midsummer series of inter-league exhibition games.

The All-Star Game (Cont.)

Year			Host (Ballpark)	AL Manager	NL Manager
1950		National, 4-3 (14)	Chicago (Comiskey Park)	Casey Stengel	Burt Shotton
1951		National, 8-3	Detroit (Briggs Stadium)	Casey Stengel	Eddie Sawyer
1952		National, 3-2 (5, rain)	Philadelphia (Shibe Park)	Casey Stengel	Leo Durocher
1953		National, 5-1	Cincinnati (Crosley Field)	Casey Stengel	Charlie Dressen
1954		**American, 11-9**	Cleveland (Cleveland Stadium)	Casey Stengel	Walter Alston
1955		National, 6-5 (12)	Milwaukee (County Stadium)	Al Lopez	Leo Durocher
1956		National, 7-3	Washington (Griffith Stadium)	Casey Stengel	Walter Alston
1957		**American, 6-5**	St. Louis (Busch Stadium)	Casey Stengel	Walter Alston
1958		**American, 4-3**	Baltimore (Memorial Stadium)	Casey Stengel	Fred Haney
1959	Game 1	National, 5-4	Pittsburgh (Forbes Field)	Casey Stengel	Fred Haney
	Game 2	**American, 5-3**	Los Angeles (Memorial Coliseum)	Casey Stengel	Fred Haney
1960	Game 1	National, 5-3	Kansas City (Municipal Stadium)	Al Lopez	Walter Alston
	Game 2	National, 6-0	New York (Yankee Stadium)	Al Lopez	Walter Alston
1961	Game 1	National, 5-4 (10)	San Francisco (Candlestick Park)	Paul Richards	Danny Murtaugh
	Game 2	TIE, 1-1 (9, rain)	Boston (Fenway Park)	Paul Richards	Danny Murtaugh
1962	Game 1	National, 3-1	Washington (D.C.Stadium)	Ralph Houk	Fred Hutchinson
	Game 2	**American, 9-4**	Chicago (Wrigley Field)	Ralph Houk	Fred Hutchinson
1963		National, 5-3	Cleveland (Cleveland Stadium)	Ralph Houk	Alvin Dark
1964		National, 7-4	New York (Shea Stadium)	Al Lopez	Walter Alston
1965		National, 6-5	Minnesota (Metropolitan Stadium)	Al Lopez	Gene Mauch
1966		National, 2-1 (10)	St. Louis (Busch Memorial Stadium)	Sam Mele	Walter Alston
1967		National, 2-1 (15)	California (Anaheim Stadium)	Hank Bauer	Walter Alston
1968		National, 1-0	Houston (The Astrodome)	Dick Williams	Red Schoendienst
1969		National, 9-3	Washington (RFK Stadium)	Mayo Smith	Red Schoendienst
1970		National, 5-4 (12)	Cincinnati (Riverfront Stadium)	Earl Weaver	Gil Hodges
1971		**American, 6-4**	Detroit (Tiger Stadium)	Earl Weaver	Sparky Anderson
1972		National, 4-3 (10)	Atlanta (Atlanta Stadium)	Earl Weaver	Danny Murtaugh
1973		National, 7-1	Kansas City (Royals Stadium)	Dick Williams	Sparky Anderson
1974		National, 7-2	Pittsburgh (Three Rivers Stadium)	Dick Williams	Yogi Berra
1975		National, 6-3	Milwaukee (County Stadium)	Alvin Dark	Walter Alston
1976		National, 7-1	Philadelphia (Veterans Stadium)	Darrell Johnson	Sparky Anderson
1977		National, 7-5	New York (Yankee Stadium)	Billy Martin	Sparky Anderson
1978		National, 7-3	San Diego (San Diego Stadium)	Billy Martin	Tommy Lasorda
1979		National, 7-6	Seattle (The Kingdome)	Bob Lemon	Tommy Lasorda
1980		National, 4-2	Los Angeles (Dodger Stadium)	Earl Weaver	Chuck Tanner
1981		National, 5-4	Cleveland (Cleveland Stadium)	Jim Frey	Dallas Green
1982		National, 4-1	Montreal (Olympic Stadium)	Billy Martin	Tommy Lasorda
1983		**American, 13-3**	Chicago (Comiskey Park)	Harvey Kuenn	Whitey Herzog
1984		National, 3-1	San Francisco (Candlestick Park)	Joe Altobelli	Paul Owens
1985		National, 6-1	Minnesota (HHH Metrodome)	Sparky Anderson	Dick Williams
1986		**American, 3-2**	Houston (The Astrodome)	Dick Howser	Whitey Herzog
1987		National, 2-0 (13)	Oakland (Oakland Coliseum)	John McNamara	Davey Johnson
1988		**American, 2-1**	Cincinnati (Riverfront Stadium)	Tom Kelly	Whitey Herzog
1989		**American, 5-3**	California (Anaheim Stadium)	Tony La Russa	Tommy Lasorda
1990		**American, 2-0**	Chicago (Wrigley Field)	Tony La Russa	Roger Craig
1991		**American, 4-2**	Toronto (SkyDome)	Tony La Russa	Lou Piniella
1992		**American, 13-6**	San Diego (SD/Murphy Stadium)	Tom Kelly	Bobby Cox
1993		**American, 9-3**	Baltimore (Camden Yards)	Cito Gaston	Bobby Cox
1994		National, 8-7 (10)	Pittsburgh (Three Rivers Stadium)	Cito Gaston	Jim Fregosi

Arch Ward Memorial Award

The All-Star Game MVP award is named after Arch Ward, the *Chicago Tribune* sports editor who founded the game in 1933. First given at the two All-Star games in 1962, the name of the award was changed to the Commissioner's Trophy in 1970 and back to the Ward Memorial Award in 1985. **Multiple winners:** Gary Carter, Steve Garvey and Willie Mays.

Year		Year		Year	
1962-a	Maury Wills, LA (NL), SS	1973	Bobby Bonds, SF, OF	1984	Gary Carter, Mon., C
1962-b	Leon Wagner, LA (AL), OF	1974	Steve Garvey, LA, 1B	1985	LaMarr Hoyt, SD, P
1963	Willie Mays, SF, OF	1975	Bill Madlock, Chi.(NL), 3B	1986	Roger Clemens, Bos., P
1964	Johnny Callison, Phi., OF		& Jon Matlack, NY (NL), P	1987	Tim Raines, Mon., OF
1965	Juan Marichal, SF, P	1976	George Foster, Cin., OF	1988	Terry Steinbach, Oak., C
1966	Brooks Robinson, Bal., 3B	1977	Don Sutton, LA, P	1989	Bo Jackson, KC, OF
1967	Tony Perez, Cin., 3B	1978	Steve Garvey, LA, 1B		
1968	Willie Mays, SF, OF	1979	Dave Parker, Pit, OF	1990	Julio Franco, Tex., 2B
1969	Willie McCovey, SF, 1B			1991	Cal Ripken, Jr., Bal., SS
		1980	Ken Griffey, Cin., OF	1992	Ken Griffey, Sea., OF
1970	Carl Yastrzemski, Bos., OF-1B	1981	Gary Carter, Mon., C	1993	Kirby Puckett, Min., OF
1971	Frank Robinson, Bal., OF	1982	Dave Concepcion, Cin., SS	1994	Fred McGriff, Atl., 1B
1972	Joe Morgan, Cin., 2B	1983	Fred Lynn, Cal., OF		

Major League Franchise Origins

Here is what the current 28 teams in Major League Baseball have to show for the years they have put in as members of the National League (NL) and American League (AL). Pennants and World Series championships are since 1901.

National League

	1st Year	Pennants & World Series	Franchise Stops

Atlanta Braves	1876	6 NL (1914,48,57-58,91-92)
		2 WS (1914,57)
			• Boston (1876-1952)
			  Milwaukee (1953-65)
			  Atlanta (1966—)

Chicago Cubs	1876	10 NL (1906-08,10,18,29,32,35,38,45) 2 WS (1907-08)	• Chicago (1876—)
Cincinnati Reds	1876	9 NL (1919,39-40,61,70,72,75-76,90) 5 WS (1919,40,75-76,90)	• Cincinnati (1876-80) Cincinnati (1890—)
Colorado Rockies	1993	None	• Denver (1993—)
Florida Marlins	1993	None	• Miami (1993—)
Houston Astros	1962	None	• Houston (1962—)

Los Angeles Dodgers	1890	18 NL (1916,20,41,47,49,52-53,55-56,59,63,
		  65-66,74,77-78, 81,88)
		6 WS (1955,59,63,65,81,88)
			• Brooklyn (1890-1957)
			  Los Angeles (1958—)

Montreal Expos	1969	None	• Montreal (1969—)
New York Mets	1962	3 NL (1969,73,86) 2 WS (1969,86)	• New York (1962—)
Philadelphia Phillies	1883	5 NL (1915,50,80,83,93) 1 WS (1980)	• Philadelphia (1883—)
Pittsburgh Pirates	1887	7 NL (1903,09,25,27,60,71,79) 5 WS (1909,25,60,71,79)	• Pittsburgh (1887—)
St. Louis Cardinals	1892	15 NL (1926,28,30-31,34,42-44,46,64, 67-68,82,85,87) 9 WS (1926,31,34,42,44,46,64,67,82)	• St. Louis (1892—)
San Diego Padres	1969	1 NL (1984)	• San Diego (1969—)

San Francisco Giants	1883	16 NL (1905,11-13,17,21-24,33,36-37,51,
		  54,62,89)
		5 WS (1905,21-22,33,54)
			• New York (1883–1957)
			  San Francisco (1958—)

American League

	1st Year	Pennants & World Series	Franchise Stops

Baltimore Orioles	1901	7 AL (1944,66,69-71,79,83)
		3 WS (1966,70,83)
			• Milwaukee (1901)
			  St. Louis (1902-53)
			  Baltimore (1954—)

Boston Red Sox	1901	9 AL (1903,12,15-16,18,46,67,75,86) 5 WS (1903,12,15-16,18)	• Boston (1901—)
California Angels	1961	None	• Los Angeles (1961-65) Anaheim, CA (1966—)
Chicago White Sox	1901	4 AL (1906,17,19,59) 2 WS (1906,17)	• Chicago (1901—)
Cleveland Indians	1901	3 AL (1920,48,54) 2 WS (1920,48)	• Cleveland (1901—)
Detroit Tigers	1901	9 AL (1907-09,34-35,40,45,68,84) 4 WS (1935,45,68,84)	• Detroit (1901—)
Kansas City Royals	1969	2 AL (1980,85) 1 WS (1985)	• Kansas City (1969—)
Milwaukee Brewers	1969	1 AL (1982)	• Seattle (1969) Milwaukee (1970—)

Minnesota Twins	1901	6 AL (1924-25,33,65,87,91)
		3 WS (1924,87,91)
			• Washington, DC (1901-60)
			  Bloomington, MN (1961-81)
			  Minneapolis (1982—)

New York Yankees	1901	33 AL (1921-23,26-28,32,36-39,41-43,47,
		  49-53,55-58,60-64,76-78,81)
		22 WS (1923,27-28,32,36-39,41,43,47,49-53,
		  56,58,61-62,77-78)
			• Baltimore (1901-02)
			  New York (1903—)

Oakland Athletics	1901	14 AL (1905,10-11,13-14,29-31,72-74,88-90)
		9 WS (1910-11,13,29-30,72-74,89)
			• Philadelphia (1901-54)
			  Kansas City (1955-67)
			  Oakland (1968—)

	1st Year	Pennants & World Series	Franchise Stops
Seattle Mariners	1977	None	• Seattle (1977—)
Texas Rangers	1961	None	• Washington, DC (1961-71) Arlington, TX (1972—)
Toronto Blue Jays	1977	2 AL (1992-93) 2 WS (1992-93)	• Toronto (1977—)

The Growth of Major League Baseball

The National League (founded in 1876) and the American League (founded in 1901) were both eight-team circuits at the turn of the century and remained that way until expansion finally came to Major League Baseball in the 1960s. The AL added two teams in 1961 and the NL did the same a year later. Both leagues went to 12 teams and split into two divisions in 1969. The AL then grew by two more teams in 1977, but the NL didn't follow suit until adding its 13th and 14th clubs in 1993.

Expansion Timetable (Since 1901)

1961—Los Angeles Angels (now California) and Washington Senators (now Texas Rangers) join AL; **1962**—Houston Colt .45s (now Astros) and New York Mets join NL; **1969**—Kansas City Royals and Seattle Pilots (now Milwaukee Brewers) join AL, while Montreal Expos and San Diego Padres join NL; **1977**—Seattle Mariners and Toronto Blue Jays join AL; **1993**—Colorado Rockies and Florida Marlins join NL.

City and Nickname Changes
National League

1953—Boston Braves move to Milwaukee; **1958**—Brooklyn Dodgers move to Los Angeles and New York Giants move to San Francisco; **1965**—Houston Colt .45s renamed Astros; **1966**—Milwaukee Braves move to Atlanta.
Other nicknames: Boston (Beaneaters and Doves through 1908, and Bees from 1936-40); **Brooklyn** (Superbas through 1926, then Robins from 1927-31; then Dodgers from 1932-57); **Cincinnati** (Red Legs from 1944-45, then Redlegs from 1954-60, then Reds since 1961); **Philadelphia** (Blue Jays from 1943-44).

American League

1902—Milwaukee Brewers move to St. Louis and become Browns; **1903**—Baltimore Orioles move to New York and become Highlanders; **1913**—NY Highlanders renamed Yankees; **1954**—St. Louis Browns move to Baltimore and become Orioles; **1955**—Philadelphia Athletics move to Kansas City; **1961**—Washington Senators move to Bloomington, Minn., and become Minnesota Twins; **1965**—LA Angels renamed California Angels; **1966**—California Angels move to Anaheim; **1968**—KC Athletics move to Oakland and become A's; **1970**—Seattle Pilots move to Milwaukee and become Brewers; **1972**—Washington Senators move to Arlington, Texas, and become Rangers; **1982**—Minnesota Twins move to Minneapolis; **1987**—Oakland A's renamed Athletics.
Other nicknames: Boston (Pilgrims, Puritans, Plymouth Rocks and Somersets through 1906); **Cleveland** (Broncos, Blues, Naps and Molly McGuires through 1914); **Washington** (Senators through 1904, then Nationals from 1905-44, then Senators again from 1945-60).

National League Pennant Winners from 1876-99

Founded in 1876, the National League played 24 seasons before the turn of the century and its eventual rivalry with the younger American League. **Multiple winners:** Boston (8); Chicago (6); Baltimore (3); Brooklyn and New York (2).

Year		Year		Year		Year	
1876	Chicago	1882	Chicago	1888	New York	1894	Baltimore
1877	Boston	1883	Boston	1889	New York	1895	Baltimore
1878	Boston	1884	Providence	1890	Brooklyn	1896	Baltimore
1879	Providence	1885	Chicago	1891	Boston	1897	Boston
1880	Chicago	1886	Chicago	1892	Boston	1898	Boston
1881	Chicago	1887	Detroit	1893	Boston	1899	Brooklyn

Champions Leagues That No Longer Exist

A Special Baseball Records Committee appointed by the commissioner found in 1968 that four extinct leagues qualified for major league status—the American Association (1882-91), the Union Association (1884), the Players' League (1890) and the Federal League (1914-15). The first years of the American League (1900) and Federal League (1913) were not recognized.

American Association

Year	Champion	Manager	Year	Champion	Manager	Year	Champion	Manager
1882	Cincinnati	Pop Snyder	1886	St. Louis	Charlie Comiskey	1889	Brooklyn	Bill McGunnigle
1883	Philadelphia	Lew Simmons	1887	St. Louis	Charlie Comiskey	1890	Louisville	Jack Chapman
1884	New York	Jim Mutrie	1888	St. Louis	Charlie Comiskey	1891	Boston	Arthur Irwin
1885	St. Louis	Charlie Comiskey						

Union Association

Year	Champion	Manager
1884	St. Louis	Henry Lucas

Players' League

Year	Champion	Manager
1890	Boston	King Kelly

Federal League

Year	Champion	Manager
1914	Indianapolis	Bill Phillips
1915	Chicago	Joe Tinker

Annual Batting Leaders (since 1900)
Batting Average
National League

Multiple winners: Honus Wagner (8); Rogers Hornsby and Stan Musial (7); Tony Gwynn (5); Roberto Clemente and Bill Madlock (4); Pete Rose and Paul Waner (3); Hank Aaron, Richie Ashburn, Jake Daubert, Tommy Davis, Ernie Lombardi, Willie McGee, Lefty O'Doul, Dave Parker and Edd Roush (2).

Year		Avg	Year		Avg	Year		Avg
1900	Honus Wagner, Pit	.381	1932	Lefty O'Doul, Bklyn	.368	1964	Roberto Clemente, Pit	.339
1901	Jesse Burkett, St.L	.382	1933	Chuck Klein, Phi	.368	1965	Roberto Clemente, Pit	.329
1902	Ginger Beaumont, Pit	.357	1934	Paul Waner, Pit	.362	1966	Matty Alou, Pit	.342
1903	Honus Wagner, Pit	.355	1935	Arkie Vaughan, Pit	.385	1967	Roberto Clemente, Pit	.357
1904	Honus Wagner, Pit	.349	1936	Paul Waner, Pit	.373	1968	Pete Rose, Cin	.335
1905	Cy Seymour, Cin	.377	1937	Joe Medwick, St.L	.374	1969	Pete Rose, Cin	.348
1906	Honus Wagner, Pit	.339	1938	Ernie Lombardi, Cin	.342			
1907	Honus Wagner, Pit	.350	1939	Johnny Mize, St.L	.349	1970	Rico Carty, Atl	.366
1908	Honus Wagner, Pit	.354				1971	Joe Torre, St.L	.363
1909	Honus Wagner, Pit	.339	1940	Debs Garms, Pit	.355	1972	Billy Williams, Chi	.333
			1941	Pete Reiser, Bklyn	.343	1973	Pete Rose, Cin	.338
1910	Sherry Magee, Phi	.331	1942	Ernie Lombardi, Bos	.330	1974	Ralph Garr, Atl	.353
1911	Honus Wagner, Pit	.334	1943	Stan Musial, St.L	.357	1975	Bill Madlock, Chi	.354
1912	Heinie Zimmerman, Chi	.372	1944	Dixie Walker, Bklyn	.357	1976	Bill Madlock, Chi	.339
1913	Jake Daubert, Bklyn	.350	1945	Phil Cavarretta, Chi	.355	1977	Dave Parker, Pit	.338
1914	Jake Daubert, Bklyn	.329	1946	Stan Musial, St.L	.365	1978	Dave Parker, Pit	.334
1915	Larry Doyle, NY	.320	1947	Harry Walker, St.L-Phi	.363	1979	Keith Hernandez, St.L	.344
1916	Hal Chase, Cin	.339	1948	Stan Musial, St.L	.376			
1917	Edd Roush, Cin	.341	1949	Jackie Robinson, Bklyn	.342	1980	Bill Buckner, Chi	.324
1918	Zack Wheat, Bklyn	.335				1981	Bill Madlock, Pit	.341
1919	Edd Roush, Cin	.321	1950	Stan Musial, St.L	.346	1982	Al Oliver, Mon	.331
			1951	Stan Musial, St.L	.355	1983	Bill Madlock, Pit	.323
1920	Rogers Hornsby, St.L	.370	1952	Stan Musial, St.L	.336	1984	Tony Gwynn, SD	.351
1921	Rogers Hornsby, St.L	.397	1953	Carl Furillo, Bklyn	.344	1985	Willie McGee, St.L	.353
1922	Rogers Hornsby, St.L	.401	1954	Willie Mays, NY	.345	1986	Tim Raines, Mon	.334
1923	Rogers Hornsby, St.L	.384	1955	Richie Ashburn, Phi	.338	1987	Tony Gwynn, SD	.370
1924	Rogers Hornsby, St.L	.424	1956	Hank Aaron, Mil	.328	1988	Tony Gwynn, SD	.313
1925	Rogers Hornsby, St.L	.403	1957	Stan Musial, St.L	.351	1989	Tony Gwynn, SD	.336
1926	Bubbles Hargrave, Cin	.353	1958	Richie Ashburn, Phi	.350			
1927	Paul Waner, Pit	.380	1959	Hank Aaron, Mil	.355	1990	Willie McGee, St.L	.335
1928	Rogers Hornsby, Bos	.387				1991	Terry Pendleton, Atl	.319
1929	Lefty O'Doul, Phi	.398	1960	Dick Groat, Pit	.325	1992	Gary Sheffield, SD	.330
1930	Bill Terry, NY	.401	1961	Roberto Clemente, Pit	.351	1993	Andres Galarraga, Col	.370
1931	Chick Hafey, St.L	.349	1962	Tommy Davis, LA	.346	1994	Tony Gwynn, SD	.394
			1963	Tommy Davis, LA	.326			

American League

Multiple winners: Ty Cobb (12); Rod Carew (7); Ted Williams (6); Wade Boggs (5); Harry Heilmann (4); George Brett, Nap Lajoie, Tony Oliva and Carl Yastrzemski (3); Luke Appling, Joe DiMaggio, Ferris Fain, Jimmie Foxx, Pete Runnels, Al Simmons, George Sisler and Mickey Vernon (2).

Year		Avg	Year		Avg	Year		Avg
1901	Nap Lajoie, Phi	.422	1924	Babe Ruth, NY	.378	1947	Ted Williams, Bos	.343
1902	Ed Delahanty, Wash	.376	1925	Harry Heilmann, Det	.393	1948	Ted Williams, Bos	.369
1903	Nap Lajoie, Cle	.355	1926	Heinie Manush, Det	.378	1949	George Kell, Det	.343
1904	Nap Lajoie, Cle	.381	1927	Harry Heilmann, Det	.398			
1905	Elmer Flick, Cle	.306	1928	Goose Goslin, Wash	.379	1950	Billy Goodman, Bos	.354
1906	George Stone, St.L	.358	1929	Lew Fonseca, Cle	.369	1951	Ferris Fain, Phi	.344
1907	Ty Cobb, Det	.350				1952	Ferris Fain, Phi	.327
1908	Ty Cobb, Det	.324	1930	Al Simmons, Phi	.381	1953	Mickey Vernon, Wash	.337
1909	Ty Cobb, Det	.377	1931	Al Simmons, Phi	.390	1954	Bobby Avila, Clev	.341
			1932	Dale Alexander, Det-Bos	.367	1955	Al Kaline, Det	.340
1910	Ty Cobb, Det	.385	1933	Jimmie Foxx, Phi	.356	1956	Mickey Mantle, NY	.353
1911	Ty Cobb, Det	.420	1934	Lou Gehrig, NY	.363	1957	Ted Williams, Bos	.388
1912	Ty Cobb, Det	.410	1935	Buddy Myer, Wash	.349	1958	Ted Williams, Bos	.328
1913	Ty Cobb, Det	.390	1936	Luke Appling, Chi	.388	1959	Harvey Kuenn, Det	.353
1914	Ty Cobb, Det	.368	1937	Charlie Gehringer, Det	.371			
1915	Ty Cobb, Det	.369	1938	Jimmie Foxx, Bos	.349	1960	Pete Runnels, Bos	.320
1916	Tris Speaker, Cle	.386	1939	Joe DiMaggio, NY	.381	1961	Norm Cash, Det	.361
1917	Ty Cobb, Det	.383				1962	Pete Runnels, Bos	.326
1918	Ty Cobb, Det	.382	1940	Joe DiMaggio, NY	.352	1963	Carl Yastrzemski, Bos	.321
1919	Ty Cobb, Det	.384	1941	Ted Williams, Bos	.406	1964	Tony Oliva, Min	.323
			1942	Ted Williams, Bos	.356	1965	Tony Oliva, Min	.321
1920	George Sisler, St.L	.407	1943	Luke Appling, Chi	.328	1966	Frank Robinson, Bal	.316
1921	Harry Heilmann, Det	.394	1944	Lou Boudreau, Clev	.327	1967	Carl Yastrzemski, Bos	.326
1922	George Sisler, St.L	.420	1945	Snuffy Stirnweiss, NY	.309	1968	Carl Yastrzemski, Bos	.301
1923	Harry Heilmann, Det	.403	1946	Mickey Vernon, Wash	.353	1969	Rod Carew, Min	.332

Year	Avg	Year	Avg	Year	Avg
1970 Alex Johnson, Cal	.329	1980 George Brett, KC	.390	1988 Wade Boggs, Bos	.366
1971 Tony Oliva, Min	.337	1981 Carney Lansford, Bos	.336	1989 Kirby Puckett, Min	.339
1972 Rod Carew, Min	.318	1982 Willie Wilson, KC	.332	1990 George Brett, KC	.329
1973 Rod Carew, Min	.350	1983 Wade Boggs, Bos	.361	1991 Julio Franco, Tex	.341
1974 Rod Carew, Min	.364	1984 Don Mattingly, NY	.343	1992 Edgar Martinez, Sea	.343
1975 Rod Carew, Min	.359	1985 Wade Boggs, Bos	.368	1993 John Olerud, Tor	.363
1976 George Brett, KC	.333	1986 Wade Boggs, Bos	.357	1994 Paul O'Neill, NY	.359
1977 Rod Carew, Min	.388	1987 Wade Boggs, Bos	.363		
1978 Rod Carew, Min	.333				
1979 Fred Lynn, Bos	.333				

Home Runs
National League

Multiple winners: Mike Schmidt (8); Ralph Kiner (7); Gavvy Cravath and Mel Ott (6); Hank Aaron, Chuck Klein, Willie Mays, Johnny Mize, Cy Williams and Hack Wilson (4); Willie McCovey (3); Ernie Banks, Johnny Bench, George Foster, Rogers Hornsby, Tim Jordan, Dave Kingman, Eddie Mathews, Dale Murphy, Bill Nicholson, Dave Robertson, Wildfire Schulte and Willie Stargell (2).

Year	HR	Year	HR	Year	HR
1900 Herman Long, Bos	12	1932 Chuck Klein, Phi	38	1962 Willie Mays, SF	49
1901 Sam Crawford, Cin	16	& Mel Ott, NY	38	1963 Hank Aaron, Mil	44
1902 Tommy Leach, Pit	6	1933 Chuck Klein, Phi	28	& Willie McCovey, SF	44
1903 Jimmy Sheckard, Bklyn	9	1934 Rip Collins, St.L	35	1964 Willie Mays, SF	47
1904 Harry Lumley, Bklyn	9	& Mel Ott, NY	35	1965 Willie Mays, SF	52
1905 Fred Odwell, Cin	9	1935 Wally Berger, Bos	34	1966 Hank Aaron, Atl	44
1906 Tim Jordan, Bklyn	12	1936 Mel Ott, NY	33	1967 Hank Aaron, Atl	39
1907 Dave Brain, Bos	10	1937 Joe Medwick, St.L	31	1968 Willie McCovey, SF	36
1908 Tim Jordan, Bklyn	12	& Mel Ott, NY	31	1969 Willie McCovey, SF	45
1909 Red Murray, NY	7	1938 Mel Ott, NY	36	1970 Johnny Bench, Cin	45
1910 Fred Beck, Bos	10	1939 Johnny Mize, St.L	28	1971 Willie Stargell, Pit	48
& Wildfire Schulte, Chi	10	1940 Johnny Mize, St.L	43	1972 Johnny Bench, Cin	40
1911 Wildfire Schulte, Chi	21	1941 Dolf Camilli, Bklyn	34	1973 Willie Stargell, Pit	44
1912 Heinie Zimmerman, Chi	14	1942 Mel Ott, NY	30	1974 Mike Schmidt, Phi	36
1913 Gavvy Cravath, Phi	19	1943 Bill Nicholson, Chi	29	1975 Mike Schmidt, Phi	38
1914 Gavvy Cravath, Phi	19	1944 Bill Nicholson, Chi	33	1976 Mike Schmidt, Phi	38
1915 Gavvy Cravath, Phi	24	1945 Tommy Holmes, Bos	28	1977 George Foster, Cin	52
1916 Cy Williams, Chi	12	1946 Ralph Kiner, Pit	23	1978 George Foster, Cin	40
& Dave Robertson, NY	12	1947 Ralph Kiner, Pit	51	1979 Dave Kingman, Chi	48
1917 Gavvy Cravath, Phi	12	& Johnny Mize, NY	51	1980 Mike Schmidt, Phi	48
& Dave Robertson, NY	12	1948 Ralph Kiner, Pit	40	1981 Mike Schmidt, Phi	31
1918 Gavvy Cravath, Phi	8	& Johnny Mize, NY	40	1982 Dave Kingman, NY	37
1919 Gavvy Cravath, Phi	12	1949 Ralph Kiner, Pit	54	1983 Mike Schmidt, Phi	40
1920 Cy Williams, Phi	15	1950 Ralph Kiner, Pit	47	1984 Dale Murphy, Atl	36
1921 George Kelly, NY	23	1951 Ralph Kiner, Pit	42	& Mike Schmidt, Phi	36
1922 Rogers Hornsby, St.L	42	1952 Ralph Kiner, Pit	37	1985 Dale Murphy, Atl	37
1923 Cy Williams, Phi	41	& Hank Sauer, Chi	37	1986 Mike Schmidt, Phi	37
1924 Jack Fournier, Bklyn	27	1953 Eddie Mathews, Mil	47	1987 Andre Dawson, Chi	49
1925 Rogers Hornsby, St.L	39	1954 Ted Kluszewski, Cin	49	1988 Darryl Strawberry, NY	39
1926 Hack Wilson, Chi	21	1955 Willie Mays, NY	51	1989 Kevin Mitchell, SF	47
1927 Cy Williams, Phi	30	1956 Duke Snider, Bklyn	43	1990 Ryne Sandberg, Chi	40
& Hack Wilson, Chi	30	1957 Hank Aaron, Mil	44	1991 Howard Johnson, NY	38
1928 Jim Bottomley, St.L	31	1958 Ernie Banks, Chi	47	1992 Fred McGriff, SD	35
& Hack Wilson, Chi	31	1959 Eddie Mathews, Mil	46	1993 Barry Bonds, SF	46
1929 Chuck Klein, Phi	43	1960 Ernie Banks, Chi	41	1994 Matt Williams, SF	43
1930 Hack Wilson, Chi	56	1961 Orlando Cepeda, SF	46		
1931 Chuck Klein, Phi	31				

American League

Multiple winners: Babe Ruth (12); Harmon Killebrew (6); Home Run Baker, Harry Davis, Jimmie Foxx, Hank Greenberg, Reggie Jackson, Mickey Mantle and Ted Williams (4); Lou Gehrig and Jim Rice (3); Dick Allen, Tony Armas, Jose Canseco, Joe DiMaggio, Larry Doby, Cecil Fielder, Juan Gonzalez, Frank Howard, Wally Pipp, Al Rosen and Gorman Thomas (2).

Year	HR	Year	HR	Year	HR
1901 Nap Lajoie, Phi	14	1908 Sam Crawford, Det	7	1914 Home Run Baker, Phi	9
1902 Socks Seybold, Phi	16	1909 Ty Cobb, Det	9	1915 Braggo Roth, Chi-Cle	7
1903 Buck Freeman, Bos	13	1910 Jake Stahl, Bos	10	1916 Wally Pipp, NY	12
1904 Harry Davis, Phi	10	1911 Home Run Baker, Phi	11	1917 Wally Pipp, NY	9
1905 Harry Davis, Phi	8	1912 Home Run Baker, Phi	10	1918 Babe Ruth, Bos	11
1906 Harry Davis, Phi	12	& Tris Speaker, Bos	10	& Tilly Walker, Phi	11
1907 Harry Davis, Phi	8	1913 Home Run Baker, Phi	12	1919 Babe Ruth, Bos	29

Annual Batting Leaders (Cont.)
Home Runs
American League

Year	Player	HR
1920	Babe Ruth, NY	54
1921	Babe Ruth, NY	59
1922	Ken Williams, St.L	39
1923	Babe Ruth, NY	41
1924	Babe Ruth, NY	46
1925	Bob Meusel, NY	33
1926	Babe Ruth, NY	47
1927	Babe Ruth, NY	60
1928	Babe Ruth, NY	54
1929	Babe Ruth, NY	46
1930	Babe Ruth, NY	49
1931	Lou Gehrig, NY	46
	& Babe Ruth, NY	46
1932	Jimmie Foxx, Phi	58
1933	Jimmie Foxx, Phi	48
1934	Lou Gehrig, NY	49
1935	Jimmie Foxx, Phi	36
	& Hank Greenberg, Det	36
1936	Lou Gehrig, NY	49
1937	Joe DiMaggio, NY	46
1938	Hank Greenberg, Det	58
1939	Jimmie Foxx, Bos	35
1940	Hank Greenberg, Det	41
1941	Ted Williams, Bos	37
1942	Ted Williams, Bos	36
1943	Rudy York, Det	34
1944	Nick Etten, NY	22
1945	Vern Stephens, St.L	24
1946	Hank Greenberg, Det	44
1947	Ted Williams, Bos	32
1948	Joe DiMaggio, NY	39
1949	Ted Williams, Bos	43
1950	Al Rosen, Cle	37
1951	Gus Zernial, Chi-Phi	33
1952	Larry Doby, Cle	32
1953	Al Rosen, Cle	43
1954	Larry Doby, Cle	32
1955	Mickey Mantle, NY	37
1956	Mickey Mantle, NY	52
1957	Roy Sievers, Wash	42
1958	Mickey Mantle, NY	42
1959	Rocky Colavito, Cle	42
	& Harmon Killebrew, Wash.	42
1960	Mickey Mantle, NY	40
1961	Roger Maris, NY	61
1962	Harmon Killebrew, Min	48
1963	Harmon Killebrew, Min	45
1964	Harmon Killebrew, Min	49
1965	Tony Conigliaro, Bos	32
1966	Frank Robinson, Bal	49
1967	Harmon Killebrew, Min	44
	& Carl Yastrzemski, Bos	44
1968	Frank Howard, Wash	44
1969	Harmon Killebrew, Min	49
1970	Frank Howard, Wash	44
1971	Bill Melton, Chi	33
1972	Dick Allen, Chi	37
1973	Reggie Jackson, Oak	32
1974	Dick Allen, Chi	32
1975	Reggie Jackson, Oak	36
	& George Scott, Mil	36
1976	Graig Nettles, NY	32
1977	Jim Rice, Bos	39
1978	Jim Rice, Bos	46
1979	Gorman Thomas, Mil	45
1980	Reggie Jackson, NY	41
	& Ben Oglivie, Mil	41
1981	Tony Armas, Oak	22
	Dwight Evans, Bos	22
	Bobby Grich, Cal	22
	& Eddie Murray, Bal	22
1982	Reggie Jackson, Cal	39
	& Gorman Thomas, Mil	39
1983	Jim Rice, Bos	39
1984	Tony Armas, Bos	43
1985	Darrell Evans, Det	40
1986	Jesse Barfield, Tor	40
1987	Mark McGwire, Oak	49
1988	Jose Canseco, Oak	42
1989	Fred McGriff, Tor	36
1990	Cecil Fielder, Det	51
1991	Jose Canseco, Oak	44
	& Cecil Fielder, Det	44
1992	Juan Gonzalez, Tex	43
1993	Juan Gonzalez, Tex	46
1994	Ken Griffey, Sea	40

Runs Batted In
National League

Multiple winners: Hank Aaron, Rogers Hornsby, Sherry Magee, Mike Schmidt and Honus Wagner (4); Johnny Bench, George Foster, Joe Medwick, Johnny Mize and Heinie Zimmerman (3); Ernie Banks, Jim Bottomley, Orlando Cepeda, Gavvy Cravath, George Kelly, Chuck Klein, Willie McCovey, Dale Murphy, Stan Musial, Bill Nicholson and Hack Wilson (2).

Year	Player	RBI
1900	Elmer Flick, Phi	110
1901	Honus Wagner, Pit	126
1902	Honus Wagner, Pit	91
1903	Sam Mertes, NY	104
1904	Bill Dahlen, NY	80
1905	Cy Seymour, Cin	121
1906	Jim Nealon, Pit	83
	& Harry Steinfeldt, Chi	83
1907	Sherry Magee, Phi	85
1908	Honus Wagner, Pit	109
1909	Honus Wagner, Pit	100
1910	Sherry Magee, Phi	123
1911	Wildfire Schulte, Chi	121
1912	Heinie Zimmerman, Chi	103
1913	Gavvy Cravath, Phi	128
1914	Sherry Magee, Phi	103
1915	Gavvy Cravath, Phi	115
1916	Heinie Zimmerman, Chi-NY	83
1917	Heinie Zimmerman, NY	102
1918	Sherry Magee, Cin	76
1919	Hy Myers, Bklyn	73
1920	Rogers Hornsby, St.L	94
	& George Kelly, NY	94
1921	Rogers Hornsby, St.L	126
1922	Rogers Hornsby, St.L	152
1923	Irish Meusel, NY	125
1924	George Kelly, NY	136
1925	Rogers Hornsby, St.L	143
1926	Jim Bottomley, St.L	120
1927	Paul Waner, Pit	131
1928	Jim Bottomley, St.L	136
1929	Hack Wilson, Chi	159
1930	Hack Wilson, Chi	190
1931	Chuck Klein, Phi	121
1932	Don Hurst, Phi	143
1933	Chuck Klein, Phi	120
1934	Mel Ott, NY	135
1935	Wally Berger, Bos	130
1936	Joe Medwick, St.L	138
1937	Joe Medwick, St.L	154
1938	Joe Medwick, St.L	122
1939	Frank McCormick, Cin	128
1940	Johnny Mize, St.L	137
1941	Dolph Camilli, Bklyn	120
1942	Johnny Mize, NY	110
1943	Bill Nicholson, Chi	128
1944	Bill Nicholson, Chi	122
1945	Dixie Walker, Bklyn	124
1946	Enos Slaughter, St.L	130
1947	Johnny Mize, NY	138
1948	Stan Musial, St.L	131
1949	Ralph Kiner, Pit	127
1950	Del Ennis, Phi	126
1951	Monte Irvin, NY	121
1952	Hank Sauer, Chi	121
1953	Roy Campanella, Bklyn	142
1954	Ted Kluszewski, Cin	141
1955	Duke Snider, Bklyn	136
1956	Stan Musial, St.L	109
1957	Hank Aaron, Mil	132
1958	Ernie Banks, Chi	129
1959	Ernie Banks, Chi	143
1960	Hank Aaron, Mil	126
1961	Orlando Cepeda, SF	142
1962	Tommy Davis, LA	153
1963	Hank Aaron, Mil	130
1964	Ken Boyer, St.L	119
1965	Deron Johnson, Cin	130
1966	Hank Aaron, Atl	127
1967	Orlando Cepeda, St.L	111
1968	Willie McCovey, SF	105
1969	Willie McCovey, SF	126
1970	Johnny Bench, Cin	148
1971	Joe Torre, St.L	137
1972	Johnny Bench, Cin	125
1973	Willie Stargell, Pit	119

Year		RBI	Year		RBI	Year		RBI
1974	Johnny Bench, Cin	129	1982	Dale Murphy, Atl	109	1988	Will Clark, SF	109
1975	Greg Luzinski, Phi	120		& Al Oliver, Mon	109	1989	Kevin Mitchell, SF	125
1976	George Foster, Cin	121	1983	Dale Murphy, Atl	121	1990	Matt Williams, SF	122
1977	George Foster, Cin	149	1984	Gary Carter, Mon	106	1991	Howard Johnson, NY	117
1978	George Foster, Cin	120		& Mike Schmidt, Phi	106	1992	Darren Daulton, Phi	109
1979	Dave Winfield, SD	118	1985	Dave Parker, Cin	125	1993	Barry Bonds, SF	123
1980	Mike Schmidt, Phi	121	1986	Mike Schmidt, Phi	119	1994	Jeff Bagwell, Hou	116
1981	Mike Schmidt, Phi	91	1987	Andre Dawson, Chi	137			

American League

Multiple winners: Babe Ruth (6); Lou Gehrig (5); Ty Cobb, Hank Greenberg and Ted Williams (4); Sam Crawford, Cecil Fielder, Jimmie Foxx, Jackie Jensen, Harmon Killebrew, Vern Stephens and Bobby Veach (3); Home Run Baker, Cecil Cooper, Harry Davis, Joe DiMaggio, Buck Freeman, Nap Lajoie, Roger Maris, Jim Rice, Al Rosen, and Bobby Veach (2).

Year		RBI	Year		RBI	Year		RBI
1901	Nap Lajoie, Phi	125	1933	Jimmie Foxx, Phi	163	1964	Brooks Robinson, Bal	118
1902	Buck Freeman, Bos	121	1934	Lou Gehrig, NY	165	1965	Rocky Colavito, Cle	108
1903	Buck Freeman, Bos	104	1935	Hank Greenberg, Det	170	1966	Frank Robinson, Bal	122
1904	Nap Lajoie, Cle	102	1936	Hal Trosky, Cle	162	1967	Carl Yastrzemski, Bos	121
1905	Harry Davis, Phi	83	1937	Hank Greenberg, Det	183	1968	Ken Harrelson, Bos	109
1906	Harry Davis, Phi	96	1938	Jimmie Foxx, Bos	175	1969	Harmon Killebrew, Min	140
1907	Ty Cobb, Det	116	1939	Ted Williams, Bos	145			
1908	Ty Cobb, Det	108	1940	Hank Greenberg, Det	150	1970	Frank Howard, Wash	126
1909	Ty Cobb, Det	107	1941	Joe DiMaggio, NY	125	1971	Harmon Killebrew, Min	119
1910	Sam Crawford, Det	120	1942	Ted Williams, Bos	137	1972	Dick Allen, Chi	113
1911	Ty Cobb, Det	144	1943	Rudy York, Det	118	1973	Reggie Jackson, Oak	117
1912	Home Run Baker, Phi	133	1944	Vern Stephens, St.L	109	1974	Jeff Burroughs, Tex	118
1913	Home Run Baker, Phi	126	1945	Nick Etten, NY	111	1975	George Scott, Mil	109
1914	Sam Crawford, Det	104	1946	Hank Greenberg, Det	127	1976	Lee May, Bal	109
1915	Sam Crawford, Det	112	1947	Ted Williams, Bos	114	1977	Larry Hisle, Min	119
	& Bobby Veach, Det	112	1948	Joe DiMaggio, NY	155	1978	Jim Rice, Bos	139
1916	Del Pratt, St.L	103	1949	Ted Williams, Bos	159	1979	Don Baylor, Cal	139
1917	Bobby Veach, Det	103		& Vern Stephens, Bos	159	1980	Cecil Cooper, Mil	122
1918	Bobby Veach, Det	78	1950	Walt Dropo, Bos	144	1981	Eddie Murray, Bal	78
1919	Babe Ruth, Bos	114		& Vern Stephens, Bos	144	1982	Hal McRae, KC	133
1920	Babe Ruth, NY	137	1951	Gus Zernial, Chi-Phi	129	1983	Cecil Cooper, Mil	126
1921	Babe Ruth, NY	171	1952	Al Rosen, Cle	105		& Jim Rice, Bos	126
1922	Ken Williams, St.L	155	1953	Al Rosen, Cle	145	1984	Tony Armas, Bos	123
1923	Babe Ruth, NY	131	1954	Larry Doby, Cle	126	1985	Don Mattingly, NY	145
1924	Goose Goslin, Wash	129	1955	Ray Boone, Det	116	1986	Joe Carter, Cle	121
1925	Bob Meusel, NY	138		& Jackie Jensen, Bos	116	1987	George Bell, Tor	134
1926	Babe Ruth, NY	145	1956	Mickey Mantle, NY	130	1988	Jose Canseco, Oak	124
1927	Lou Gehrig, NY	175	1957	Roy Sievers, Wash	114	1989	Ruben Sierra, Tex	119
1928	Lou Gehrig, NY	142	1958	Jackie Jensen, Bos	122	1990	Cecil Fielder, Det	132
	& Babe Ruth, NY	142	1959	Jackie Jensen, Bos	112	1991	Cecil Fielder, Det	133
1929	Al Simmons, Phi	157	1960	Roger Maris, NY	112	1992	Cecil Fielder, Det	124
1930	Lou Gehrig, NY	174	1961	Roger Maris, NY	142	1993	Albert Belle, Cle	129
1931	Lou Gehrig, NY	184	1962	Harmon Killebrew, Min	126	1994	Kirby Puckett, Min	112
1932	Jimmie Foxx, Phi	169	1963	Dick Stuart, Bos	118			

Batting Triple Crown Winners

Players who led either league in Batting Average, Home Runs and Runs Batted In over a single season.

National League

	Year	Avg	HR	RBI
Paul Hines, Providence	1878	.358	4	50
Hugh Duffy, Boston	1894	.438	18	145
Heinie Zimmerman, Chicago	1912	.372	14	103
Rogers Hornsby, St. Louis	1922	.401	42	152
Rogers Hornsby, St. Louis	1925	.403	39	143
Chuck Klein, Philadelphia	1933	.368	28	120
Joe Medwick, St. Louis	1937	.374	31*	154

*Tied for league lead in HRs with Mel Ott, NY.

American League

	Year	Avg	HR	RBI
Nap Lajoie, Philadelphia	1901	.422	14	125
Ty Cobb, Detroit	1909	.377	9	115
Jimmie Foxx, Philadelphia	1933	.356	48	163
Lou Gehrig, New York	1934	.363	49	165
Ted Williams, Boston	1942	.356	36	137
Ted Williams, Boston	1947	.343	32	114
Mickey Mantle, New York	1956	.353	52	130
Frank Robinson, Baltimore	1966	.316	49	122
Carl Yastrzemski, Boston	1967	.326	44*	121

*Tied for league lead in HRs with Harmon Killebrew, Min.

Annual Batting Leaders (Cont.)
Stolen Bases
National League

Multiple winners: Max Carey (10); Lou Brock (8); Vince Coleman and Maury Wills (6); Honus Wagner (5); Bob Brescher, Kiki Cuyler, Willie Mays and Tim Raines (4); Bill Bruton, Frankie Frisch and Pepper Martin (3); George Burns, Frank Chance, Augie Galan, Marquis Grissom, Stan Hack, Sam Jethroe, Davey Lopes, Omar Moreno, Pete Reiser and Jackie Robinson (2).

Year		SB	Year		SB	Year		SB
1900	Patsy Donovan, St.L	45	1930	Kiki Cuyler, Chi	37	1962	Maury Wills, LA	104
	& George Van Haltren, NY	45	1931	Frankie Frisch, St.L	28	1963	Maury Wills, LA	40
1901	Honus Wagner, Pit	49	1932	Chuck Klein, Phi	20	1964	Maury Wills, LA	53
1902	Honus Wagner, Pit	42	1933	Pepper Martin, St.L	26	1965	Maury Wills, LA	94
1903	Frank Chance, Chi	67	1934	Pepper Martin, St.L	23	1966	Lou Brock, St.L	74
	& Jimmy Sheckard, Bklyn	67	1935	Augie Galan, Chi	22	1967	Lou Brock, St.L	52
1904	Honus Wagner, Pit	53	1936	Pepper Martin, St.L	23	1968	Lou Brock, St.L	62
1905	Art Devlin, NY	59	1937	Augie Galan, Chi	23	1969	Lou Brock, St.L	53
	& Billy Maloney, Chi	59	1938	Stan Hack, Chi	16			
1906	Frank Chance, Chi	57	1939	Stan Hack, Chi	17	1970	Bobby Tolan, Cin	57
1907	Honus Wagner, Pit	61		& Lee Handley, Pit	17	1971	Lou Brock, St.L	64
1908	Honus Wagner, Pit	53				1972	Lou Brock, St.L	63
1909	Bob Bescher, Cin	54	1940	Lonny Frey, Cin	22	1973	Lou Brock, St.L	70
			1941	Danny Murtaugh, Phi	18	1974	Lou Brock, St.L	118
1910	Bob Bescher, Cin	70	1942	Pete Reiser, Bklyn	20	1975	Davey Lopes, LA	77
1911	Bob Bescher, Cin	81	1943	Arky Vaughan, Bklyn	20	1976	Davey Lopes, LA	63
1912	Bob Bescher, Cin	67	1944	Johnny Barrett, Pit	28	1977	Frank Tavares, Pit	70
1913	Max Carey, Pit	61	1945	Red Schoendienst, St.L	26	1978	Omar Moreno, Pit	71
1914	George Burns, NY	62	1946	Pete Reiser, Bklyn	34	1979	Omar Moreno, Pit	77
1915	Max Carey, Pit	36	1947	Jackie Robinson, Bklyn	29			
1916	Max Carey, Pit	63	1948	Richie Ashburn, Phi	32	1980	Ron LeFlore, Mon	97
1917	Max Carey, Pit	46	1949	Jackie Robinson, Bklyn	37	1981	Tim Raines, Mon	71
1918	Max Carey, Pit	58				1982	Tim Raines, Mon	78
1919	George Burns, NY	40	1950	Sam Jethroe, Bos	35	1983	Tim Raines, Mon	90
			1951	Sam Jethroe, Bos	35	1984	Tim Raines, Mon	75
1920	Max Carey, Pit	52	1952	Pee Wee Reese, Bklyn	30	1985	Vince Coleman, St.L	110
1921	Frankie Frisch, NY	49	1953	Bill Bruton, Mil	26	1986	Vince Coleman, St.L	107
1922	Max Carey, Pit	51	1954	Bill Bruton, Mil	34	1987	Vince Coleman, St.L	109
1923	Max Carey, Pit	51	1955	Bill Bruton, Mil	25	1988	Vince Coleman, St.L	81
1924	Max Carey, Pit	49	1956	Willie Mays, NY	40	1989	Vince Coleman, St.L	66
1925	Max Carey, Pit	46	1957	Willie Mays, NY	38			
1926	Kiki Cuyler, Pit	35	1958	Willie Mays, SF	31	1990	Vince Coleman, St.L	77
1927	Frankie Frisch, St.L	48	1959	Willie Mays, SF	27	1991	Marquis Grissom, Mon	76
1928	Kiki Cuyler, Chi	37				1992	Marquis Grissom, Mon	78
1929	Kiki Cuyler, Chi	43	1960	Maury Wills, LA	50	1993	Chuck Carr, Fla	58
			1961	Maury Wills, LA	35	1994	Craig Baggio, Hou	39

American League

Multiple winners: Rickey Henderson (11); Luis Aparicio (9); Bert Campaneris, George Case and Ty Cobb (6); Ben Chapman, Eddie Collins and George Sisler (4); Bob Dillinger, Kenny Lofton, Minnie Minoso and Bill Werber (3); Elmer Flick, Tommy Harper, Clyde Milan, Johnny Mostil, Bill North and Snuffy Stirnweiss (2).

Year		SB	Year		SB	Year		SB
1901	Frank Isbell, Chi	52	1920	Sam Rice, Wash	63	1939	George Case, Wash	51
1902	Topsy Hartsel, Phi	47	1921	George Sisler, St.L	35			
1903	Harry Bay, Cle	45	1922	George Sisler, St.L	51	1940	George Case, Wash	35
1904	Elmer Flick, Cle	42	1923	Eddie Collins, Chi	47	1941	George Case, Wash	33
1905	Danny Hoffman, Phi	46	1924	Eddie Collins, Chi	42	1942	George Case, Wash	44
1906	John Anderson, Wash	39	1925	Johnny Mostil, Chi	43	1943	George Case, Wash	61
	& Elmer Flick, Cle	39	1926	Johnny Mostil, Chi	35	1944	Snuffy Stirnweiss, NY	55
1907	Ty Cobb, Det	49	1927	George Sisler, St.L	27	1945	Snuffy Stirnweiss, NY	33
1908	Patsy Dougherty, Chi	47	1928	Buddy Myer, Bos	30	1946	George Case, Cle	28
1909	Ty Cobb, Det	76	1929	Charlie Gehringer, Det	2	1947	Bob Dillinger, St.L	34
						1948	Bob Dillinger, St.L	28
1910	Eddie Collins, Phi	81	1930	Marty McManus, Det	23	1949	Bob Dillinger, St.L	20
1911	Ty Cobb, Det	83	1931	Ben Chapman, NY	61			
1912	Clyde Milan, Wash	88	1932	Ben Chapman, NY	38	1950	Dom DiMaggio, Bos	15
1913	Clyde Milan, Wash	75	1933	Ben Chapman, NY	27	1951	Minnie Minoso, Cle-Chi	31
1914	Fritz Maisel, NY	74	1934	Bill Werber, Bos	40	1952	Minnie Minoso, Chi	22
1915	Ty Cobb, Det	96	1935	Bill Werber, Bos	29	1953	Minnie Minoso, Chi	25
1916	Ty Cobb, Det	68	1936	Lyn Lary, St.L	37	1954	Jackie Jensen, Bos	22
1917	Ty Cobb, Det	55	1937	Ben Chapman, Wash-Bos	35	1955	Jim Rivera, Chi	25
1918	George Sisler, St.L	45		& Bill Werber, Phi	35	1956	Luis Aparicio, Chi	21
1919	Eddie Collins, Chi	33	1938	Frank Crosetti, NY	27	1957	Luis Aparicio, Chi	28

Year		SB	Year		SB	Year		SB
1958	Luis Aparicio, Chi	29	1972	Bert Campaneris, Oak	52	1986	Rickey Henderson, NY	87
1959	Luis Aparicio, Chi	56	1973	Tommy Harper, Bos	54	1987	Harold Reynolds, Sea	60
1960	Luis Aparicio, Chi	51	1974	Bill North, Oak	54	1988	Rickey Henderson, NY	93
1961	Luis Aparicio, Chi	53	1975	Mickey Rivers, CA	70	1989	R.Henderson, NY-Oak	77
1962	Luis Aparicio, Chi	31	1976	Bill North, Oak	75			
1963	Luis Aparicio, Bal	40	1977	Freddie Patek, KC	53	1990	Rickey Henderson, Oak	65
1964	Luis Aparicio, Bal	57	1978	Ron LeFlore, Det	68	1991	Rickey Henderson, Oak	58
1965	Bert Campaneris, KC	51	1979	Willie Wilson, KC	83	1992	Kenny Lofton, Cle	62
1966	Bert Campaneris, KC	52				1993	Kenny Lofton, Cle	70
1967	Bert Campaneris, KC	55	1980	Rickey Henderson, Oak	100	1994	Kenny Lofton, Cle	60
1968	Bert Campaneris, Oak	62	1981	Rickey Henderson, Oak	56			
1969	Tommy Harper, Sea	73	1982	Rickey Henderson, Oak	130			
1970	Bert Campaneris, Oak	42	1983	Rickey Henderson, Oak	108			
1971	Amos Otis, KC	52	1984	Rickey Henderson, Oak	66			
			1985	Rickey·Henderson, NY	80			

30 Homers & 30 Stolen Bases in One Season
National League

	Year	Gm	HR	SB
Willie Mays, NY Giants	1956	152	36	40
Willie Mays, NY Giants	1957	152	35	38
Hank Aaron, Milwaukee	1963	161	44	31
Bobby Bonds, San Francisco	1969	158	32	45
Bobby Bonds, San Francisco	1973	160	39	43
Dale Murphy, Atlanta	1983	162	36	30
Eric Davis, Cincinnati	1987	129	37	50
Howard Johnson, NY Mets	1987	157	36	32
Darryl Strawberry, NY Mets	1987	154	39	36
Howard Johnson, NY Mets	1989	153	36	41
Ron Gant, Atlanta	1990	152	32	33
Barry Bonds, Pittsburgh	1990	151	33	52
Ron Gant, Atlanta	1991	154	32	34

	Year	Gm	HR	SB
Howard Johnson, NY Mets	1991	156	38	30
Barry Bonds, Pittsburgh	1992	140	34	39
Sammy Sosa, Chicago	1993	159	33	36

American League

	Year	Gm	HR	SB
Kenny Williams, St. Louis	1922	153	39	37
Tommy Harper, Milwaukee	1970	154	31	38
Bobby Bonds, New York	1975	145	32	30
Bobby Bonds, California	1977	158	37	41
Bobby Bonds, Chicago-Texas	1978	156	31	43
Joe Carter, Cleveland	1987	149	32	31
Jose Canseco, Oakland	1988	158	42	40

Consecutive Game Streaks
Regular season games through 1994.

Games Played
Active streak in **bold** type.

Gm		Dates of Streak		
2130	Lou Gehrig, NY	6/1/25	to	4/30/39
2009	**Cal Ripken, Jr.,** Bal	5/30/82	to	—
1307	Everett Scott, Bos-NY	6/20/16	to	5/5/25
1207	Steve Garvey, LA-SD	9/3/75	to	7/29/83
1117	Billy Williams, Cubs	9/22/63	to	9/2/70
1103	Joe Sewell, Cle	9/13/22	to	4/30/30
895	Stan Musial, St.L	4/15/52	to	8/23/57
829	Eddie Yost, Wash	4/30/49	to	5/11/55
822	Gus Suhr, Pit	9/11/31	to	6/4/37
798	Nellie Fox, Chisox	8/8/55	to	9/3/60
745	Pete Rose, Cin-Phi	9/2/78	to	8/23/83
740	Dale Murphy, Atl	9/26/81	to	7/8/86
730	Richie Ashburn, Phi	6/7/50	to	4/13/55
717	Ernie Banks, Cubs	8/28/56	to	6/22/61
678	Pete Rose, Cin	9/28/73	to	5/7/78

Others

Gm		Gm	
673	Earl Averill	565	Aaron Ward
652	Frank McCormick	540	Candy LaChance
648	Sandy Alomar, Sr.	535	John Freeman
618	Eddie Brown	533	Fred Luderus
585	Roy McMillan	511	Clyde Milan
577	George Pinckney	511	Charlie Gehringer
574	Steve Brodie	508	Vada Pinson

Hitting

	Gm	Year
Joe DiMaggio, New York (AL)	56	1941
Willie Keeler, Baltimore (NL)	44	1897
Pete Rose, Cincinnati (NL)	44	1978
Bill Dahlen, Chicago (NL)	42	1894
George Sisler, St. Louis (AL)	41	1922
Ty Cobb, Detroit (AL)	40	1911
Paul Molitor, Milwaukee (AL)	39	1987
Tommy Holmes, Boston (NL)	37	1945
Billy Hamilton, Philadelphia (NL)	36	1894
Fred Clarke, Louisville (NL)	35	1895
Ty Cobb, Detroit (AL)	35	1917
George Sisler, St. Louis (AL)	34	1925
John Stone, Detroit (AL)	34	1930
George McQuinn, St. Louis (AL)	34	1938
Dom DiMaggio, Boston (AL)	34	1949
Benito Santiago, San Diego (NL)	34	1987
George Davis, New York (NL)	33	1893
Hal Chase, New York (AL)	33	1907
Rogers Hornsby, St. Louis (NL)	33	1922
Heinie Manush, Washington (AL)	33	1933
Ed Delahanty, Philadelphia (NL)	31	1899
Nap Lajoie, Cleveland (AL)	31	1906
Sam Rice, Washington, (AL)	31	1924
Willie Davis, Los Angeles (NL)	31	1969
Rico Carty, Atlanta (NL)	31	1970
Ken Landreaux, Minnesota (AL)	31	1980

Annual Pitching Leaders (since 1900)
Winning Percentage

At least 15 wins, except in strike years of 1981 (when the minimum was 10) and 1994 (when the minimum was eight).

National League

Multiple winners: Ed Reulbach and Tom Seaver (3); Larry Benton, Harry Brecheen, Jack Chesbro, Paul Derringer, Freddie Fitzsimmons, Don Gullet, Claude Hendrix, Carl Hubbell, Sandy Koufax, Bill Lee, Christy Mathewson, Don Newcombe and Preacher Roe (2).

Year		W-L	Pct	Year		W-L	Pct
1900	Jesse Tannehill, Pittsburgh	20-6	.769	1950	Sal Maglie, New York	18-4	.818
1901	Jack Chesbro, Pittsburgh	21-10	.677	1951	Preacher Roe, Brooklyn	22-3	.880
1902	Jack Chesbro, Pittsburgh	28-6	.824	1952	Hoyt Wilhelm, New York	15-3	.833
1903	Sam Leever, Pittsburgh	25-7	.781	1953	Carl Erskine, Brooklyn	20-6	.769
1904	Joe McGinnity, New York	35-8	.814	1954	Johnny Antonelli, New York	21-7	.750
1905	Christy Mathewson, New York	31-8	.795	1955	Don Newcombe, Brooklyn	20-5	.800
1906	Ed Reulbach, Chicago	19-4	.826	1956	Don Newcombe, Brooklyn	27-7	.794
1907	Ed Reulbach, Chicago	17-4	.810	1957	Bob Buhl, Milwaukee	18-7	.720
1908	Ed Reulbach, Chicago	24-7	.774	1958	Warren Spahn, Milwaukee	22-11	.667
1909	Howie Camnitz, Pittsburgh	25-6	.806		& Lew Burdette, Milwaukee	20-10	.667
	& Christy Mathewson, New York	25-6	.806	1959	Roy Face, Pittsburgh	18-1	.947
1910	King Cole, Chicago	20-4	.833	1960	Ernie Broglio, St. Louis	21-9	.700
1911	Rube Marquard, New York	24-7	.774	1961	Johnny Podres, Los Angeles	18-5	.783
1912	Claude Hendrix, Pittsburgh	24-9	.727	1962	Bob Purkey, Cincinnati	23-5	.821
1913	Bert Humphries, Chicago	16-4	.800	1963	Ron Perranoski, Los Angeles	16-3	.842
1914	Bill James, Boston	26-7	.788	1964	Sandy Koufax, Los Angeles	19-5	.792
1915	Grover Alexander, Phila.	31-10	.756	1965	Sandy Koufax, Los Angeles	26-8	.765
1916	Tom Hughes, Boston	16-3	.842	1966	Juan Marichal, San Francisco	25-6	.806
1917	Ferdie Schupp, New York	21-7	.750	1967	Dick Hughes, St. Louis	16-6	.727
1918	Claude Hendrix, Chicago	19-7	.731	1968	Steve Blass, Pittsburgh	18-6	.750
1919	Dutch Ruether, Cincinnati	19-6	.760	1969	Tom Seaver, New York	25-7	.781
1920	Burleigh Grimes, Brooklyn	23-11	.676	1970	Bob Gibson, St. Louis	23-7	.767
1921	Bill Doak, St. Louis	15-6	.714	1971	Don Gullett, Cincinnati	16-6	.727
1922	Pete Donohue, Cincinnati	18-9	.667	1972	Gary Nolan, Cincinnati	15-5	.750
1923	Dolf Luque, Cincinnati	27-8	.771	1973	Tommy John, Los Angeles	16-7	.696
1924	Emil Yde, Pittsburgh	16-3	.842	1974	Andy Messersmith, Los Angeles	20-6	.769
1925	Bill Sherdel, St. Louis	15-6	.714	1975	Don Gullett, Cincinnati	15-4	.789
1926	Ray Kremer, Pittsburgh	20-6	.769	1976	Steve Carlton, Philadelphia	20-7	.741
1927	Larry Benton, Boston-NY	17-7	.708	1977	John Candelaria, Pittsburgh	20-5	.800
1928	Larry Benton, New York	25-9	.735	1978	Gaylord Perry, San Diego	21-6	.778
1929	Charlie Root, Chicago	19-6	.760	1979	Tom Seaver, Cincinnati	16-6	.727
1930	Freddie Fitzsimmons, NY	19-7	.731	1980	Jim Bibby, Pittsburgh	19-6	.760
1931	Paul Derringer, St. Louis	18-8	.692	1981	Tom Seaver, Cincinnati	14-2	.875
1932	Lon Warneke, Chicago	22-6	.786	1982	Phil Niekro, Atlanta	17-4	.810
1933	Ben Cantwell, Boston	20-10	.667	1983	John Denny, Philadelphia	19-6	.760
1934	Dizzy Dean, St. Louis	30-7	.811	1984	Rick Sutcliffe, Chicago	16-1	.941
1935	Bill Lee, Chicago	20-6	.769	1985	Orel Hershiser, Los Angeles	19-3	.864
1936	Carl Hubbell, New York	26-6	.813	1986	Bob Ojeda, New York	18-5	.783
1937	Carl Hubbell, New York	22-8	.733	1987	Dwight Gooden, New York	15-7	.682
1938	Bill Lee, Chicago	22-9	.710	1988	David Cone, New York	20-3	.870
1939	Paul Derringer, Cincinnati	25-7	.781	1989	Mike Bielecki, Chicago	18-7	.720
1940	Freddie Fitzsimmons, Bklyn	16-2	.889	1990	Doug Drabek, Pittsburgh	22-6	.786
1941	Elmer Riddle, Cincinnati	19-4	.826	1991	John Smiley, Pittsburgh	20-8	.714
1942	Larry French, Brooklyn	15-4	.789		& Jose Rijo, Cincinnati	15-6	.714
1943	Mort Cooper, St. Louis	21-8	.724	1992	Bob Tewksbury, St. Louis	16-5	.762
1944	Ted Wilks, St. Louis	17-4	.810	1993	Mark Portugal, Houston	18-4	.818
1945	Harry Brecheen, St. Louis	14-4	.778	1994	Marvin Freeman, Colorado	10-2	.833
1946	Murray Dickson, St. Louis	15-6	.714				
1947	Larry Jansen, New York	21-5	.808				
1948	Harry Brecheen, St. Louis	20-7	.741				
1949	Preacher Roe, Brooklyn	15-6	.714				

Note: In 1984, Sutcliffe was also 4-5 with Cleveland for a combined AL-NL record of 20-6 (.769).

American League

Multiple winners: Lefty Grove (5); Chief Bender and Whitey Ford (3); Johnny Allen, Eddie Cicotte, Roger Clemens, Mike Cuellar, Lefty Gomez, Catfish Hunter, Walter Johnson, Jim Palmer, Pete Vuckovich and Smokey Joe Wood (2).

Year		W-L	Pct	Year		W-L	Pct
1901	Clark Griffith, Chicago	24-7	.774	1904	Jack Chesbro, New York	41-12	.774
1902	Bill Bernhard, Phila-Cleve	18-5	.783	1905	Andy Coakley, Philadelphia	20-7	.741
1903	Cy Young, Boston	28-9	.757	1906	Eddie Plank, Philadelphia	19-6	.760

Year		W-L	Pct	Year		W-L	Pct
1907	Wild Bill Donovan, Detroit	25-4	.862	1952	Bobby Shantz, Philadelphia	24-7	.774
1908	Ed Walsh, Chicago	40-15	.727	1953	Ed Lopat, New York	16-4	.800
1909	George Mullin, Detroit	29-8	.784	1954	Sandy Consuegra, Chicago	16-3	.842
				1955	Tommy Byrne, New York	16-5	.762
1910	Chief Bender, Philadelphia	23-5	.821	1956	Whitey Ford, New York	19-6	.760
1911	Chief Bender, Philadelphia	17-5	.773	1957	Dick Donovan, Chicago	16-6	.727
1912	Smokey Joe Wood, Boston	34-5	.872		& Tom Sturdivant, New York	16-6	.727
1913	Walter Johnson, Washington	36-7	.837	1958	Bob Turley, New York	21-7	.750
1914	Chief Bender, Philadelphia	17-3	.850	1959	Bob Shaw, Chicago	18-6	.750
1915	Smokey Joe Wood, Boston	15-5	.750				
1916	Eddie Cicotte, Chicago	15-7	.682	1960	Jim Perry, Cleveland	18-10	.643
1917	Reb Russell, Chicago	15-5	.750	1961	Whitey Ford, New York	25-4	.862
1918	Sad Sam Jones, Boston	16-5	.762	1962	Ray Herbert, Chicago	20-9	.690
1919	Eddie Cicotte, Chicago	29-7	.806	1963	Whitey Ford, New York	24-7	.774
				1964	Wally Bunker, Baltimore	19-5	.792
1920	Jim Bagby, Cleveland	31-12	.721	1965	Mudcat Grant, Minnesota	21-7	.750
1921	Carl Mays, New York	27-9	.750	1966	Sonny Siebert, Cleveland	16-8	.667
1922	Joe Bush, New York	26-7	.788	1967	Joe Horlen, Chicago	19-7	.731
1923	Herb Pennock, New York	19-6	.760	1968	Denny McLain, Detroit	31-6	.838
1924	Walter Johnson, Washington	23-7	.767	1969	Jim Palmer, Baltimore	16-4	.800
1925	Stan Coveleski, Washington	20-5	.800				
1926	George Uhle, Cleveland	27-11	.711	1970	Mike Cuellar, Baltimore	24-8	.750
1927	Waite Hoyt, New York	22-7	.759	1971	Dave McNally, Baltimore	21-5	.808
1928	General Crowder, St. Louis	21-5	.808	1972	Catfish Hunter, Oakland	21-7	.750
1929	Lefty Grove, Philadelphia	20-6	.769	1973	Catfish Hunter, Oakland	21-5	.808
				1974	Mike Cuellar, Baltimore	22-10	.688
1930	Lefty Grove, Philadelphia	28-5	.848	1975	Mike Torrez, Baltimore	20-9	.690
1931	Lefty Grove, Philadelphia	31-4	.886	1976	Bill Campbell, Minnesota	17-5	.773
1932	Johnny Allen, New York	17-4	.810	1977	Paul Splittorff, Kansas City	16-6	.727
1933	Lefty Grove, Philadelphia	24-8	.750	1978	Ron Guidry, New York	25-3	.893
1934	Lefty Gomez, New York	26-5	.839	1979	Mike Caldwell, Milwaukee	16-6	.727
1935	Eldon Auker, Detroit	18-7	.720				
1936	Monte Pearson, New York	19-7	.731	1980	Steve Stone, Baltimore	25-7	.781
1937	Johnny Allen, Cleveland	15-1	.938	1981	Pete Vuckovich, Milwaukee	14-4	.778
1938	Red Ruffing, New York	21-7	.750	1982	Pete Vuckovich, Milwaukee	18-6	.750
1939	Lefty Grove, Boston	15-4	.789		& Jim Palmer, Baltimore	15-5	.750
				1983	Rich Dotson, Chicago	22-7	.759
1940	Schoolboy Rowe, Detroit	16-3	.842	1984	Doyle Alexander, Toronto	17-6	.739
1941	Lefty Gomez, New York	15-5	.750	1985	Ron Guidry, New York	22-6	.786
1942	Ernie Bonham, New York	21-5	.808	1986	Roger Clemens, Boston	24-4	.857
1943	Spud Chandler, New York	20-4	.833	1987	Roger Clemens, Boston	20-9	.690
1944	Tex Hughson, Boston	18-5	.783	1988	Frank Viola, Minnesota	24-7	.774
1945	Hal Newhouser, Detroit	25-9	.735	1989	Bret Saberhagen, Kansas City	23-6	.793
1946	Boo Ferriss, Boston	25-6	.806				
1947	Allie Reynolds, New York	19-8	.704	1990	Bob Welch, Oakland	27-6	.818
1948	Jack Kramer, Boston	18-5	.783	1991	Scott Erickson, Minnesota	20-8	.714
1949	Ellis Kinder, Boston	23-6	.793	1992	Mike Mussina, Baltimore	18-5	.783
				1993	Jimmy Key, New York	18-6	.750
1950	Vic Raschi, New York	21-8	.724	1994	Jason Bere, Chicago	12-2	.857
1951	Bob Feller, Cleveland	22-8	.733				

Earned Run Average

Earned Run Averages were based on at least 10 complete games pitched (1900-50), at least 154 innings pitched (1950-60), and at least 162 innings pitched since 1961 in the AL and 1962 in the NL. In the strike year of 1981, qualifiers had to pitch at least as many innings as the total number of games their team played that season.

National League

Multiple winners: Grover Alexander, Sandy Koufax and Christy Mathewson (5); Carl Hubbell, Tom Seaver, Warren Spahn and Dazzy Vance (3); Bill Doak, Ray Kremer, Dolf Luque, Greg Maddux, Howie Pollet, Nolan Ryan, Bill Walker and Bucky Walters (2).

Year		ERA	Year		ERA	Year		ERA
1900	Rube Waddell, Pit	2.37	1909	Christy Mathewson, NY	1.14	1917	Grover Alexander, Phi	1.86
1901	Jesse Tannehill, Pit	2.18	1910	George McQuillan, Phi	1.60	1918	Hippo Vaughn, Chi	1.74
1902	Jack Taylor, Chi	1.33				1919	Grover Alexander, Chi	1.72
1903	Sam Leever, Pit	2.06	1911	Christy Mathewson, NY	1.99			
1904	Joe McGinnity, NY	1.61	1912	Jeff Tesreau, NY	1.96	1920	Grover Alexander, Chi	1.91
1905	Christy Mathewson, NY	1.27	1913	Christy Mathewson, NY	2.06	1921	Bill Doak, St.L	2.59
1906	Three Finger Brown, Chi	1.04	1914	Bill Doak, St.L	1.72	1922	Rosy Ryan, NY	3.01
1907	Jack Pfiester, Chi	1.15	1915	Grover Alexander, Phi	1.22	1923	Dolf Luque, Cin	1.93
1908	Christy Mathewson, NY	1.43	1916	Grover Alexander, Phi	1.55	1924	Dazzy Vance, Bklyn	2.16

Annual Pitching Leaders (Cont.)
Earned Run Average
National League

Year		ERA	Year		ERA	Year		ERA
1925	Dolf Luque, Cin	2.63	1950	Jim Hearn, St.L-NY	2.49	1975	Randy Jones, SD	2.24
1926	Ray Kremer, Pit	2.61	1951	Chet Nichols, Bos	2.88	1976	John Denny, St.L	2.52
1927	Ray Kremer, Pit	2.47	1952	Hoyt Wilhelm, NY	2.43	1977	John Candelaria, Pit	2.34
1928	Dazzy Vance, Bklyn	2.09	1953	Warren Spahn, Mil	2.10	1978	Craig Swan, NY	2.43
1929	Bill Walker, NY	3.09	1954	Johnny Antonelli, NY	2.30	1979	J.R. Richard, Hou	2.71
1930	Dazzy Vance, Bklyn	2.61	1955	Bob Friend, Pit	2.83			
1931	Bill Walker, NY	2.26	1956	Lew Burdette, Mil	2.70	1980	Don Sutton, LA	2.21
1932	Lon Warneke, Chi	2.37	1957	Johnny Podres, Bklyn	2.66	1981	Nolan Ryan, Hou	1.69
1933	Carl Hubbell, NY	1.66	1958	Stu Miller, SF	2.47	1982	Steve Rogers, Mon	2.40
1934	Carl Hubbell, NY	2.30	1959	Sam Jones, SF	2.83	1983	Atlee Hammaker, SF	2.25
1935	Cy Blanton, Pit	2.58				1984	Alejandro Pena, LA	2.48
1936	Carl Hubbell, NY	2.31	1960	Mike McCormick, SF	2.70	1985	Dwight Gooden, NY	1.53
1937	Jim Turner, Bos	2.38	1961	Warren Spahn, Mil	3.02	1986	Mike Scott, Hou	2.22
1938	Bill Lee, Chi	2.66	1962	Sandy Koufax, LA	2.54	1987	Nolan Ryan, Hou	2.76
1939	Bucky Walters, Cin	2.29	1963	Sandy Koufax, LA	1.88	1988	Joe Magrane, St.L	2.18
1940	Bucky Walters, Cin	2.48	1964	Sandy Koufax, LA	1.74	1989	Scott Garrelts, SF	2.28
1941	Elmer Riddle, Cin	2.24	1965	Sandy Koufax, LA	2.04			
1942	Mort Cooper, St.L	1.78	1966	Sandy Koufax, LA	1.73	1990	Danny Darwin, Hou	2.21
1943	Howie Pollet, St.L	1.75	1967	Phil Niekro, Atl	1.87	1991	Dennis Martinez, Mon	2.39
1944	Ed Heusser, Cin	2.38	1968	Bob Gibson, St.L	1.12	1992	Bill Swift, SF	2.08
1945	Hank Borowy, Chi	2.13	1969	Juan Marichal, SF	2.10	1993	Greg Maddux, Atl	2.36
1946	Howie Pollet, St.L	2.10				1994	Greg Maddux, Atl	1.56
1947	Warren Spahn, Bos	2.33	1970	Tom Seaver, NY	2.81			
1948	Harry Brecheen, St.L	2.24	1971	Tom Seaver, NY	1.76			
1949	Dave Koslo, NY	2.50	1972	Steve Carlton, Phi	1.98			
			1973	Tom Seaver, NY	2.08			
			1974	Buzz Capra, Atl	2.28			

Note: In 1945, Borowy had a 3.13 ERA in 18 games with New York (AL) for a combined ERA of 2.65.

American League

Multiple winners: Lefty Grove (9); Walter Johnson (5); Roger Clemens (4); Spud Chandler, Stan Coveleski, Red Faber, Whitey Ford, Lefty Gomez, Ron Guidry, Addie Joss, Hal Newhouser, Jim Palmer, Gary Peters, Luis Tiant and Ed Walsh (2).

Year		ERA	Year		ERA	Year		ERA
1901	Cy Young, Bos	1.62	1933	Monte Pearson, Cle	2.33	1965	Sam McDowell, Cle	2.18
1902	Ed Siever, Det	1.91	1934	Lefty Gomez, NY	2.33	1966	Gary Peters, Chi	1.98
1903	Earl Moore, Cle	1.77	1935	Lefty Grove, Bos	2.70	1967	Joe Horlen, Chi	2.06
1904	Addie Joss, Cle	1.59	1936	Lefty Grove, Bos	2.81	1968	Luis Tiant, Cle	1.60
1905	Rube Waddell, Phi	1.48	1937	Lefty Gomez, NY	2.33	1969	Dick Bosman, Wash	2.19
1906	Doc White, Chi	1.52	1938	Lefty Grove, Bos	3.08			
1907	Ed Walsh, Chi	1.60	1939	Lefty Grove, Bos	2.54	1970	Diego Segui, Oak	2.56
1908	Addie Joss, Cle	1.16				1971	Vida Blue, Oak	1.82
1909	Harry Krause, Phi	1.39	1940	Bob Feller, Cle	2.61	1972	Luis Tiant, Bos	1.91
			1941	Thornton Lee, Chi	2.37	1973	Jim Palmer, Bal	2.40
1910	Ed Walsh, Chi	1.27	1942	Ted Lyons, Chi	2.10	1974	Catfish Hunter, Oak	2.49
1911	Vean Gregg, Cle	1.81	1943	Spud Chandler, NY	1.64	1975	Jim Palmer, Bal	2.09
1912	Walter Johnson, Wash	1.39	1944	Dizzy Trout, Det	2.12	1976	Mark Fidrych, Det	2.34
1913	Walter Johnson, Wash	1.09	1945	Hal Newhouser, Det	1.81	1977	Frank Tanana, Cal	2.54
1914	Dutch Leonard, Bos	1.01	1946	Hal Newhouser, Det	1.94	1978	Ron Guidry, NY	1.74
1915	Smokey Joe Wood, Bos	1.49	1947	Spud Chandler, NY	2.46	1979	Ron Guidry, NY	2.78
1916	Babe Ruth, Bos	1.75	1948	Gene Bearden, Bos	2.43			
1917	Eddie Cicotte, Chi	1.53	1949	Mel Parnell, Bos	2.77	1980	Rudy May, NY	2.47
1918	Walter Johnson, Wash	1.27				1981	Steve McCatty, Oak	2.32
1919	Walter Johnson, Wash	1.49	1950	Early Wynn, Cle	3.20	1982	Rick Sutcliffe, Cle	2.96
			1951	Saul Rogovin, Det-Chi	2.78	1983	Rick Honeycutt, Tex	2.42
1920	Bob Shawkey, NY	2.45	1952	Allie Reynolds, NY	2.06	1984	Mike Boddicker, Bal	2.79
1921	Red Faber, Chi	2.48	1953	Ed Lopat, NY	2.42	1985	Dave Stieb, Tor	2.48
1922	Red Faber, Chi	2.80	1954	Mike Garcia, Cle	2.64	1986	Roger Clemens, Bos	2.48
1923	Stan Coveleski, Cle	2.76	1955	Billy Pierce, Chi	1.97	1987	Jimmy Key, Tor	2.76
1924	Walter Johnson, Wash	2.72	1956	Whitey Ford, NY	2.47	1988	Allan Anderson, Min	2.45
1925	Stan Coveleski, Wash	2.84	1957	Bobby Shantz, NY	2.45	1989	Bret Saberhagen, KC	2.16
1926	Lefty Grove, Phi	2.51	1958	Whitey Ford, NY	2.01			
1927	Wilcy Moore, NY	2.28	1959	Hoyt Wilhelm, Bal	2.19	1990	Roger Clemens, Bos	1.93
1928	Garland Braxton, Wash	2.51				1991	Roger Clemens, Bos	2.62
1929	Lefty Grove, Phi	2.81	1960	Frank Baumann, Chi	2.67	1992	Roger Clemens, Bos	2.41
			1961	Dick Donovan, Wash	2.40	1993	Kevin Appier, KC	2.56
1930	Lefty Grove, Phi	2.54	1962	Hank Aguirre, Det	2.21	1994	Steve Ontiveros, Oak	2.65
1931	Lefty Grove, Phi	2.06	1963	Gary Peters, Chi	2.33			
1932	Lefty Grove, Phi	2.84	1964	Dean Chance, LA	1.65			

Note: In 1940, Ernie Bonham of NY had a 1.90 ERA and 10 complete games, but appeared in only a total of 12 games and 99 innings.

Strikeouts
National League

Multiple winners: Dazzy Vance (7); Grover Alexander (6); Steve Carlton, Christy Mathewson and Tom Seaver (5); Dizzy Dean, Sandy Koufax and Warren Spahn (4); Don Drysdale, Sam Jones and Johnny Vander Meer (3); David Cone, Dwight Gooden, Bill Hallahan, J.R. Richard, Robin Roberts, Nolan Ryan and Hippo Vaughn (2).

Year		SO	Year		SO	Year		SO
1900	Rube Waddell, Pit	130	1933	Dizzy Dean, St.L	199	1964	Bob Veale, Pit	250
1901	Noodles Hahn, Cinn	239	1934	Dizzy Dean, St.L	195	1965	Sandy Koufax, LA	382
1902	Vic Willis, Bos	225	1935	Dizzy Dean, St.L	182	1966	Sandy Koufax, LA	317
1903	Christy Mathewson, NY	267	1936	Van Lingle Mungo,Bklyn	238	1967	Jim Bunning, Phi	253
1904	Christy Mathewson, NY	212	1937	Carl Hubbell, NY	159	1968	Bob Gibson, St.L	268
1905	Christy Mathewson, NY	206	1938	Clay Bryant, Chi	135	1969	Ferguson Jenkins, Chi	273
1906	Fred Beebe, Chi-St.L	171	1939	Claude Passeau,Phi-Chi	137			
1907	Christy Mathewson, NY	178		& Bucky Walters, Cin	137	1970	Tom Seaver, NY	283
1908	Christy Mathewson, NY	259				1971	Tom Seaver, NY	289
1909	Orval Overall, Chi	205	1940	Kirby Higbe, Phi	137	1972	Steve Carlton, Phi	310
			1941	John Vander Meer,Cin	202	1973	Tom Seaver, NY	251
1910	Earl Moore, Phi	185	1942	John Vander Meer,Cin	186	1974	Steve Carlton, Phi	240
1911	Rube Marquard, NY	237	1943	John Vander Meer,Cin	174	1975	Tom Seaver, NY	243
1912	Grover Alexander, Phi	195	1944	Bill Voiselle, NY	161	1976	Tom Seaver, NY	235
1913	Tom Seaton, Phi	168	1945	Preacher Roe, Pitt	148	1977	Phil Niekro, Atl	262
1914	Grover Alexander, Phi	214	1946	Johnny Schmitz, Chi	135	1978	J.R. Richard, Hou	303
1915	Grover Alexander, Phi	241	1947	Ewell Blackwell, Cin	193	1979	J.R. Richard, Hou	313
1916	Grover Alexander, Phi	167	1948	Harry Brecheen, St.L	149			
1917	Grover Alexander, Phi	201	1949	Warren Spahn, Bos	151	1980	Steve Carlton, Phi	286
1918	Hippo Vaughn, Chi	148				1981	F. Valenzuela,LA	180
1919	Hippo Vaughn, Chi	141	1950	Warren Spahn, Bos	191	1982	Steve Carlton, Phi	286
			1951	Don Newcombe, Bklyn	164	1983	Steve Carlton, Phi	275
1920	Grover Alexander, Chi	173		& Warren Spahn, Bos	164	1984	Dwight Gooden, NY	276
1921	Burleigh Grimes, Bklyn	136	1952	Warren Spahn, Bos	183	1985	Dwight Gooden, NY	268
1922	Dazzy Vance, Bklyn	134	1953	Robin Roberts, Phi	198	1986	Mike Scott, Hou	306
1923	Dazzy Vance, Bklyn	197	1954	Robin Roberts, Phi	185	1987	Nolan Ryan, Hou	270
1924	Dazzy Vance, Bklyn	262	1955	Sam Jones, Chi	198	1988	Nolan Ryan, Hou	228
1925	Dazzy Vance, Bklyn	221	1956	Sam Jones, Chi	176	1989	Jose DeLeon, St.L	201
1926	Dazzy Vance, Bklyn	140	1957	Jack Sanford, Phi	188			
1927	Dazzy Vance, Bklyn	184	1958	Sam Jones, St.L	225	1990	David Cone, NY	233
1928	Dazzy Vance, Bklyn	200	1959	Don Drysdale, LA	242	1991	David Cone, NY	241
1929	Pat Malone, Chi	166				1992	John Smoltz, Atl	215
			1960	Don Drysdale, LA	246	1993	Jose Rijo, Cin	227
1930	Bill Hallahan, St.L	177	1961	Sandy Koufax, LA	269	1994	Andy Benes, SD	189
1931	Bill Hallahan, St.L	159	1962	Don Drysdale, LA	232			
1932	Dizzy Dean, St.L	191	1963	Sandy Koufax, LA	306			

American League

Multiple winners: Walter Johnson (12); Nolan Ryan (9); Bob Feller and Lefty Grove (7); Rube Waddell (6); Sam McDowell (5); Lefty Gomez, Randy Johnson, Mark Langston and Camilo Pascual (3); Len Barker, Tommy Bridges, Jim Bunning, Roger Clemens, Hal Newhouser, Allie Reynolds, Herb Score, Ed Walsh and Early Wynn (2).

Year		SO	Year		SO	Year		SO
1901	Cy Young, Bos	158	1920	Stan Coveleski, Cle	133	1939	Bob Feller, Cle	246
1902	Rube Waddell, Phi	210	1921	Walter Johnson, Wash	143			
1903	Rube Waddell, Phi	302	1922	Urban Shocker, St.L	149	1940	Bob Feller, Cle	261
1904	Rube Waddell, Phi	349	1923	Walter Johnson, Wash	130	1941	Bob Feller, Cle	260
1905	Rube Waddell, Phi	287	1924	Walter Johnson, Wash	158	1942	Tex Hughson, Bos	113
1906	Rube Waddell, Phi	196	1925	Lefty Grove, Phi	116		& Bobo Newsom,Wash	113
1907	Rube Waddell, Phi	232	1926	Lefty Grove, Phi	194	1943	Allie Reynolds, Cle	151
1908	Ed Walsh, Chi	269	1927	Lefty Grove, Phi	174	1944	Hal Newhouser, Det	187
1909	Frank Smith, Chi	177	1928	Lefty Grove, Phi	183	1945	Hal Newhouser, Det	212
			1929	Lefty Grove, Phi	170	1946	Bob Feller, Cle	348
1910	Walter Johnson, Wash	313				1947	Bob Feller, Cle	196
1911	Ed Walsh, Chi	255	1930	Lefty Grove, Phi	209	1948	Bob Feller, Cle	164
1912	Walter Johnson, Wash	303	1931	Lefty Grove, Phi	175	1949	Virgil Trucks, Det	153
1913	Walter Johnson, Wash	243	1932	Red Ruffing, NY	190			
1914	Walter Johnson, Wash	225	1933	Lefty Gomez, NY	163	1950	Bob Lemon, Cle	170
1915	Walter Johnson, Wash	203	1934	Lefty Gomez, NY	158	1951	Vic Raschi, NY	164
1916	Walter Johnson, Wash	228	1935	Tommy Bridges, Det	163	1952	Allie Reynolds, NY	160
1917	Walter Johnson, Wash	188	1936	Tommy Bridges, Det	175	1953	Billy Pierce Chi	186
1918	Walter Johnson, Wash	162	1937	Lefty Gomez, NY	194	1954	Bob Turley, Bal	185
1919	Walter Johnson, Wash	147	1938	Bob Feller, Cle	240	1955	Herb Score, Cle	245

Annual Pitching Leaders (Cont.)
Strikeouts
American League

Year		SO	Year		SO	Year		SO
1956	Herb Score, Cle	263	1970	Sam McDowell, Cle	304	1984	Mark Langston, Sea	204
1957	Early Wynn, Cle	184	1971	Mickey Lolich, Det	308	1985	Bert Blyleven,Cle-Min	206
1958	Early Wynn, Chi	179	1972	Nolan Ryan, Cal	329	1986	Mark Langston, Sea	245
1959	Jim Bunning, Det	201	1973	Nolan Ryan, Cal	383	1987	Mark Langston, Sea	262
1960	Jim Bunning, Det	201	1974	Nolan Ryan, Cal	367	1988	Roger Clemens, Bos	291
1961	Camilo Pascual, Min	221	1975	Frank Tanana, Cal	269	1989	Nolan Ryan, Tex	301
1962	Camilo Pascual, Min	206	1976	Nolan Ryan, Cal	327			
1963	Camilo Pascual, Min	202	1977	Nolan Ryan, Cal	341	1990	Nolan Ryan, Tex	232
1964	Al Downing, NY	217	1978	Nolan Ryan, Cal	260	1991	Roger Clemens, Bos	241
1965	Sam McDowell, Cle	325	1979	Nolan Ryan, Cal	223	1992	Randy Johnson, Sea	241
1966	Sam McDowell, Cle	225	1980	Len Barker, Cle	187	1993	Randy Johnson, Sea	308
1967	Jim Lonborg, Bos	246	1981	Len Barker, Cle	127	1994	Randy Johnson, Sea	204
1968	Sam McDowell, Cle	283	1982	Floyd Bannister, Sea	209			
1969	Sam McDowell, Cle	279	1983	Jack Morris, Det	232			

Pitching Triple Crown Winners

Pitchers who led either league in Earned Run Average, Wins and Strikeouts over a single season.

National League

	Year	ERA	W-L	SO
Tommy Bond, Bos	1877	2.11	40-17	170
Hoss Radbourn, Prov	1884	1.38	60-12	441
Tim Keefe, NY	1888	1.74	35-12	333
John Clarkson, Bos	1889	2.73	49-19	284
Amos Rusie, NY	1894	2.78	36-13	195
Christy Mathewson, NY	1905	1.27	31-8	206
Christy Mathewson, NY	1908	1.43	37-11	259
Grover Alexander, Phi	1915	1.22	31-10	241
Grover Alexander, Phi	1916	1.55	33-12	167
Grover Alexander, Phi	1917	1.86	30-13	201
Hippo Vaughn, Chi	1918	1.74	22-10	148
Grover Alexander, Chi	1920	1.91	27-14	173
Dazzy Vance, Bklyn	1924	2.16	28-6	262
Bucky Walters, Cin	1939	2.29	27-11	137
Sandy Koufax, LA	1963	1.88	25-5	306
Sandy Koufax, LA	1965	2.04	26-8	382
Sandy Koufax, LA	1966	1.73	27-9	317
Steve Carlton, Phi	1972	1.97	27-10	310
Dwight Gooden, NY	1985	1.53	24-4	268

Ties: In 1894, Rusie tied for league lead in wins with Jouett Meekin, NY (36-10); in 1939, Walters tied for league lead in strikeouts with Claude Passeau, Phi-Chi; in 1963, Koufax tied for the league lead in wins with Juan Marichal, SF.

American League

	Year	ERA	W-L	SO
Cy Young, Bos	1901	1.62	33-10	158
Rube Waddell, Phi	1905	1.48	26-11	287
Walter Johnson, Wash	1913	1.09	36-7	243
Walter Johnson, Wash	1918	1.27	23-13	162
Walter Johnson, Wash	1924	2.72	23-7	158
Lefty Grove, Phi	1930	2.54	28-5	209
Lefty Grove, Phi	1931	2.06	31-4	175
Lefty Gomez, NY	1934	2.33	26-5	158
Lefty Gomez, NY	1937	2.33	21-11	194
Hal Newhouser, Det	1945	1.81	25-9	212

Perfect Games

Sixteen pitchers have thrown perfect games (27 up, 27 down) in major league history. However, the games pitched by Harvey Haddix and Ernie Shore are not considered to be official.

National League

	Game	Date	Score
Lee Richmond	Wor. vs Cle.	6/12/1880	1-0
Monte Ward	Prov. vs Bos.	6/17/1880	5-0
Harvey Haddix	Pit. at Mil.	5/26/1959	0-1*
Jim Bunning	Phi. at NY	6/21/1964	6-0
Sandy Koufax	LA vs Chi.	9/9/1965	1-0
Tom Browning	Cin. vs LA	9/16/1988	1-0
Dennis Martinez	Mon. at LA	7/28/1991	2-0

*Haddix pitched 12 perfect innings before losing in the 13th. Braves' lead-off batter Felix Mantilla reached on a throwing error by Pirates 3B Don Hoak, Eddie Mathews sacrificed Mantilla to 2nd, Hank Aaron was walked intentionally, and Joe Adcock hit a 3-run HR. Adcock, however, passed Aaron on the bases and was only credited with a 1-run double.

American League

	Game	Date	Score
Cy Young	Bos. vs Phi.	5/5/1904	3-0
Adrian Joss	Cle. vs Chi.	10/2/1908	1-0
Ernie Shore	Bos. vs Wash.	6/23/1917	4-0*
Charlie Robertson	Chi. at Det.	4/30/1922	2-0
Catfish Hunter	Oak. vs Min.	5/8/1968	4-0
Len Barker	Cle. vs Tor.	5/15/1981	3-0
Mike Witt	Cal. at Tex.	9/30/1984	1-0
Kenny Rogers	Tex. vs Cal.	6/28/1994	4-0

*Babe Ruth started for Boston, walking Senators' lead-off batter Ray Morgan, then was thrown out of game by umpire Brick Owens for arguing the call. Shore came on in relief. Morgan was caught stealing and Shore retired the next 26 batters in a row. While technically not a perfect game—since he didn't start—Shore gets credit anyway.

World Series

Pitcher	Game	Date	Score
Don Larsen	NY vs Bklyn	10/8/1956	2-0

All-Time Major League Leaders

Based on statistics compiled by *The Baseball Encyclopedia* (9th ed.); through 1994 regular season.

CAREER

Players active in 1994 in **bold** type.

Batting

Note that (*) indicates left-handed hitter and (†) indicates switch-hitter.

Batting Average

		Yrs	AB	H	Avg
1	Ty Cobb*	24	11,429	4191	.367
2	Rogers Hornsby	23	8,137	2930	.358
3	Joe Jackson*	13	4,981	1774	.356
4	Ed Delahanty	16	7,509	2597	.346
5	Tris Speaker*	22	10,197	3514	.345
6	Ted Williams*	19	7,706	2654	.344
7	Billy Hamilton*	14	6,284	2163	.344
8	Willie Keeler*	19	8,585	2947	.343
9	Dan Brouthers*	19	6,711	2296	.342
10	Babe Ruth*	22	8,399	2873	.342
11	Harry Heilmann	17	7,787	2660	.342
12	Pete Browning	13	4,820	1646	.341
13	Bill Terry*	14	6,428	2193	.341
14	George Sisler*	15	8,267	2812	.340
15	Lou Gehrig*	17	8,001	2721	.340
16	Jesse Burkett*	16	8,413	2853	.339
17	Nap Lajoie	21	9,592	3244	.338
18	Riggs Stephenson	14	4,508	1515	.336
19	**Wade Boggs***	13	7,139	2392	.335
20	Al Simmons	20	8,761	2927	.334
21	Paul Waner*	20	9,459	3152	.333
22	Eddie Collins*	25	9,951	3313	.333
23	Stan Musial*	22	10,972	3630	.331
24	Sam Thompson*	14	6,005	1986	.331
25	Heinie Manush*	17	7,653	2524	.330

Hits

		Yrs	AB	H	Avg
1	Pete Rose†	24	14,053	4256	.303
2	Ty Cobb*	24	11,429	4191	.367
3	Hank Aaron	23	12,364	3771	.305
4	Stan Musial*	22	10,972	3630	.331
5	Tris Speaker*	22	10,197	3514	.345
6	Carl Yastrzemski*	23	11,988	3419	.285
7	Honus Wagner	21	10,443	3418	.327
8	Eddie Collins*	25	9,951	3313	.333
9	Willie Mays	22	10,881	3283	.302
10	Nap Lajoie	21	9,592	3244	.338
11	George Brett*	21	10,349	3154	.305
12	Paul Waner*	20	9,459	3152	.333
13	Robin Yount	20	11,008	3142	.285
14	**Dave Winfield**	21	10,888	3088	.284
15	Rod Carew*	19	9,315	3053	.328
16	Lou Brock*	19	10,332	3023	.293
17	Al Kaline	22	10,116	3007	.297
18	Cap Anson	22	9,108	3000	.329
	Roberto Clemente	18	9,454	3000	.317
20	Sam Rice	20	9,269	2987	.322
21	Sam Crawford*	19	9,580	2964	.309
22	Willie Keeler*	19	8,585	2947	.343
23	Frank Robinson	21	10,006	2943	.294
24	Jake Beckley*	20	9,527	2931	.308
25	Rogers Hornsby	23	8,173	2930	.358
	Eddie Murray†	18	10,167	2930	.288

Players Active in 1994

		Yrs	AB	H	Avg
1	Wade Boggs*	13	7,139	2392	.335
2	Tony Gwynn*	13	6,609	2204	.333
3	Frank Thomas	5	2,271	741	.326
4	Kirby Puckett	11	6,706	2135	.318
5	Hal Morris*	7	2,035	637	.313
6	Jeff Bagwell	4	2,075	641	.309
7	Don Mattingly*	13	6,545	2021	.309
8	Paul Molitor	17	8,610	2647	.307
9	Ken Griffey, Jr.*	6	3,180	972	.306
10	Mike Greenwell*	10	3,847	1170	.304
11	Mark Grace	7	3,804	1153	.303
12	Carlos Baerga†	5	2,628	796	.303
13	Will Clark*	9	4,658	1406	.302

Players Active in 1994

		Yrs	AB	H	Avg
1	Dave Winfield	21	10,888	3088	.284
2	Eddie Murray†	18	10,167	2930	.288
3	Andre Dawson	19	9,643	2700	.280
4	Paul Molitor	17	8,610	2647	.307
5	Wade Boggs*	13	7,139	2392	.335
6	Ozzie Smith†	17	9,013	2365	.262
7	Lou Whitaker*	18	8,320	2296	.276
8	Alan Trammell	18	7,872	2260	.287
9	Cal Ripken, Jr.*	14	8,027	2227	.277
10	Rickey Henderson	16	7,656	2216	.289
11	Willie Wilson†	19	7,731	2207	.285
12	Tony Gwynn*	13	6,609	2204	.333
13	Harold Baines	15	7,486	2156	.288

Games Played

1	Pete Rose	3562
2	Carl Yastrzemski	3308
3	Hank Aaron	3298
4	Ty Cobb	3034
5	Stan Musial	3026
6	Willie Mays	2992
7	Rusty Staub	2951
8	**Dave Winfield**	2927
9	Brooks Robinson	2896
10	Robin Yount	2856
11	Al Kaline	2834
12	Eddie Collins	2826
13	Reggie Jackson	2820
14	Frank Robinson	2808
15	Tris Speaker	2789
	Honus Wagner	2789
17	Tony Perez	2777
18	Mel Ott	2734
19	George Brett	2707
20	**Eddie Murray**	2706

At Bats

1	Pete Rose	14,053
2	Hank Aaron	12,364
3	Carl Yastrzemski	11,988
4	Ty Cobb	11,429
5	Robin Yount	11,008
6	Stan Musial	10,972
7	**Dave Winfield**	10,888
8	Willie Mays	10,881
9	Brooks Robinson	10,654
10	Honus Wagner	10,441
11	George Brett	10,349
12	Lou Brock	10,332
13	Luis Aparicio	10,230
14	Tris Speaker	10,197
15	**Eddie Murray**	10,167
16	Al Kaline	10,116
17	Rabbit Maranville	10,078
18	Frank Robinson	10,006
19	Eddie Collins	9,951
20	Reggie Jackson	9,864

Total Bases

1	Hank Aaron	6856
2	Stan Musial	6134
3	Willie Mays	6066
4	Ty Cobb	5863
5	Babe Ruth	5793
6	Pete Rose	5752
7	Carl Yastrzemski	5539
8	Frank Robinson	5373
9	**Dave Winfield**	5186
10	Tris Speaker	5103
11	Lou Gehrig	5059
12	George Brett	5044
13	Mel Ott	5041
14	Jimmie Foxx	4956
15	Ted Williams	4884
16	**Eddie Murray**	4883
17	Honus Wagner	4868
18	Al Kaline	4852
19	Reggie Jackson	4834
20	Robin Yount	4730

All-Time Major League Leaders (Cont.)
Batting

Home Runs

		Yrs	AB	HR	AB/HR
1	Hank Aaron	23	12,364	755	16.4
2	Babe Ruth*	22	8,399	714	11.8
3	Willie Mays	22	10,881	660	16.5
4	Frank Robinson	21	10,006	586	17.1
5	Harmon Killebrew	22	8,147	573	14.2
6	Reggie Jackson*	21	9,864	563	17.5
7	Mike Schmidt	18	8,352	548	15.2
8	Mickey Mantle†	18	8,102	536	15.1
9	Jimmie Foxx	20	8,134	534	15.2
10	Ted Williams*	19	7,706	521	14.8
	Willie McCovey*	22	8,197	521	15.7
12	Ed Mathews*	17	8,537	512	16.7
	Ernie Banks	19	9,421	512	18.4
14	Mel Ott*	22	9,456	511	18.5
15	Lou Gehrig*	17	8,001	493	16.2
16	Willie Stargell*	21	7,927	475	16.7
	Stan Musial*	22	10,972	475	23.1
18	**Dave Winfield**	21	10,888	463	23.5
19	**Eddie Murray†**	18	10,167	458	22.2
20	Carl Yastrzemski*	23	11,988	452	26.5
21	Dave Kingman	16	6,677	442	15.1
22	**Andre Dawson**	19	9,643	428	22.5
23	Billy Williams*	18	9,350	426	22.0
24	Darrell Evans	21	8,973	414	21.7
25	Duke Snider	18	7,161	407	17.6

Runs Batted In

		Yrs	Gm	RBI	P/G
1	Hank Aaron	23	3298	2297	.70
2	Babe Ruth*	22	2503	2211	.88
3	Lou Gehrig*	17	2164	1990	.92
4	Ty Cobb*	24	3034	1961	.65
5	Stan Musial*	22	3026	1951	.64
6	Jimmie Foxx	20	2317	1921	.83
7	Willie Mays	22	2992	1903	.64
8	Mel Ott*	22	2732	1861	.68
9	Carl Yastrzemski*	23	3308	1844	.56
10	Ted Williams*	19	2292	1839	.80
11	**Dave Winfield**	21	2927	1829	.62
12	Al Simmons	20	2215	1827	.82
13	Frank Robinson	21	2808	1812	.65
14	**Eddie Murray†**	18	2706	1738	.64
15	Honus Wagner	21	2786	1732	.62
16	Cap Anson	22	2276	1715	.75
17	Reggie Jackson*	21	2820	1702	.60
18	Tony Perez	23	2777	1652	.59
19	Ernie Banks	19	2528	1636	.65
20	Goose Goslin	18	2287	1609	.70
21	Nap Lajoie	21	2475	1599	.65
22	Mike Schmidt	18	2404	1595	.66
	George Brett	21	2707	1595	.59
24	Rogers Hornsby	23	2259	1584	.70
	Harmon Killebrew	22	2435	1584	.65

Players Active in 1994

		Yrs	AB	HR	AB/HR
1	Dave Winfield	21	10,888	463	23.5
2	Eddie Murray†	18	10,167	458	22.2
3	Andre Dawson	19	9,643	428	22.5
4	Cal Ripken	14	8,027	310	25.9
5	Joe Carter	12	6,239	302	20.7
6	Darryl Strawberry*	12	4,756	294	16.2
7	Kent Hrbek*	14	6,192	293	21.1
8	Harold Baines	15	7,486	277	27.0
9	Jose Canseco	10	4,315	276	15.6
10	Tom Brunansky	14	6,289	271	23.2
11	Fred McGriff	9	3,984	262	15.2
12	Barry Bonds	9	4,514	259	17.4
13	Gary Gaetti	14	6,689	257	26.0
14	Kirk Gibson	16	5,571	246	22.6
15	Ryne Sandberg	14	7,384	245	30.1

Players Active in 1994

		Yrs	Gm	RBI	P/G
1	Dave Winfield	21	2927	1829	.62
2	Eddie Murray†	18	2706	1738	.64
3	Andre Dawson	19	2506	1540	.61
4	Harold Baines*	15	2056	1198	.58
5	Cal Ripken, Jr.	14	2074	1179	.57
6	Joe Carter	12	1610	1097	.68
7	Kent Hrbek*	14	1747	1086	.62
8	Don Mattingly*	13	1657	1050	.63
9	Tim Wallach	15	2013	1045	.52
10	Lou Whitaker	18	2306	1040	.45
11	Chili Davis	14	1850	1014	.55
12	Kirby Puckett	11	1646	986	.60
13	Gary Gaetti	14	1835	979	.53
14	Paul Molitor	17	2131	976	.46
15	Alan Trammell	18	2153	964	.45

Runs

1	Ty Cobb	2245
2	Babe Ruth	2174
	Hank Aaron	2174
4	Pete Rose	2165
5	Willie Mays	2062
6	Stan Musial	1949
7	Lou Gehrig	1888
8	Tris Speaker	1882
9	Mel Ott	1859
10	Frank Robinson	1829
11	Eddie Collins	1820
12	Carl Yastrzemski	1816
13	Ted Williams	1798
14	Charlie Gehringer	1774
15	Jimmie Foxx	1751
16	Honus Wagner	1735
17	Willie Keeler	1727
18	Cap Anson	1719
19	Jesse Burkett	1718
20	Billy Hamilton	1692

Extra Base Hits

1	Hank Aaron	1477
2	Stan Musial	1377
3	Babe Ruth	1356
4	Willie Mays	1323
5	Lou Gehrig	1190
6	Frank Robinson	1186
7	Carl Yastrzemski	1157
8	Ty Cobb	1139
9	Tris Speaker	1132
10	George Brett	1119
11	Ted Williams	1117
	Jimmie Foxx	1117
13	**Dave Winfield**	1086
14	Reggie Jackson	1075
15	Mel Ott	1071
16	Pete Rose	1041
17	Mike Schmidt	1015
18	**Andre Dawson**	1014
19	Rogers Hornsby	1011
20	**Eddie Murray**	1003

Slugging Average

1	Babe Ruth	.690
2	Ted Williams	.634
3	Lou Gehrig	.632
4	Jimmie Foxx	.609
5	Hank Greenberg	.605
6	Joe DiMaggio	.579
7	Rogers Hornsby	.577
8	Johnny Mize	.562
9	Stan Musial	.559
10	Willie Mays	.557
11	Mickey Mantle	.557
12	Hank Aaron	.555
13	Ralph Kiner	.548
14	Hack Wilson	.545
15	Chuck Klein	.543
16	Duke Snider	.540
17	Frank Robinson	.537
18	Al Simmons	.535
19	Dick Allen	.534
20	Earl Averill	.533

Stolen Bases

1	**Rickey Henderson**	1117
2	Lou Brock	938
3	Billy Hamilton	915
4	Ty Cobb	892
5	**Tim Raines**	764
6	Eddie Collins	743
7	Max Carey	738
8	Honus Wagner	720
9	**Vince Coleman**	698
10	Joe Morgan	689
11	Arlie Latham	679
12	**Willie Wilson**	668
13	Bert Campaneris	649
14	Tom Brown	627
15	George Davis	615
16	Dummy Hoy	597
17	Maury Wills	586
18	Hugh Duffy	583
	George Van Haltren	583
20	**Ozzie Smith**	569

Walks

1	Babe Ruth	2056
2	Ted Williams	2019
3	Joe Morgan	1865
4	Carl Yastrzemski	1845
5	Mickey Mantle	1734
6	Mel Ott	1708
7	Eddie Yost	1614
8	Darrell Evans	1605
9	Stan Musial	1599
10	Pete Rose	1566
11	Harmon Killebrew	1559
12	Lou Gehrig	1508
13	Mike Schmidt	1507
14	Eddie Collins	1503
15	**Rickey Henderson**	1478
16	Willie Mays	1463
17	Jimmie Foxx	1452
18	Eddie Mathews	1444
19	Frank Robinson	1420
20	Hank Aaron	1402

Strikeouts

1	Reggie Jackson	2597
2	Willie Stargell	1936
3	Mike Schmidt	1883
4	Tony Perez	1867
5	Dave Kingman	1816
6	Bobby Bonds	1757
7	Dale Murphy	1748
8	Lou Brock	1730
9	Mickey Mantle	1710
10	Harmon Killebrew	1699
11	Dwight Evans	1697
12	**Dave Winfield**	1660
13	Lee May	1570
14	Dick Allen	1556
15	Willie McCovey	1550
16	Dave Parker	1537
17	Frank Robinson	1532
18	Willie Mays	1526
19	Rick Monday	1513
20	Greg Luzinski	1495

Pitching

Note that (*) indicates left-handed pitcher. Active pitcher leaders are listed for wins, strikeouts and saves.

Wins

		Yrs	GS	W	L	Pct
1	Cy Young	22	815	511	316	.618
2	Walter Johnson	21	666	416	279	.599
3	Christy Mathewson	17	551	373	188	.665
	Grover Alexander	20	598	373	208	.642
5	Warren Spahn*	21	665	363	245	.597
6	Kid Nichols	15	561	361	208	.634
	Pud Galvin	14	682	361	308	.540
8	Tim Keefe	14	594	342	225	.603
9	Steve Carlton*	24	709	329	244	.574
10	Eddie Plank*	17	527	327	193	.629
11	John Clarkson	12	518	326	177	.648
12	Don Sutton	23	756	324	256	.559
13	Nolan Ryan	27	773	324	292	.526
14	Phil Niekro	24	716	318	274	.537
15	Gaylord Perry	22	690	314	265	.542
16	Old Hoss Radbourn	12	503	311	194	.616
	Tom Seaver	20	647	311	205	.603
18	Mickey Welch	13	549	308	209	.596
19	Lefty Grove*	17	456	300	141	.680
	Early Wynn	23	612	300	244	.551
21	Tommy John*	26	700	288	231	.555
22	Bert Blyleven	22	685	287	250	.534
23	Robin Roberts	19	609	286	245	.539
24	Tony Mullane	13	505	285	220	.564
25	Ferguson Jenkins	19	594	284	226	.557
26	Jim Kaat*	25	625	283	237	.544
27	Red Ruffing	22	536	273	225	.548
28	Burleigh Grimes	19	495	270	212	.560
29	Jim Palmer	19	521	268	152	.638
30	Bob Feller	18	484	266	162	.621

Strikeouts

		Yrs	IP	SO	P/9
1	Nolan Ryan	27	5387.0	5714	9.54
2	Steve Carlton*	24	5217.1	4136	7.13
3	Bert Blyleven	22	4970.1	3701	6.70
4	Tom Seaver	20	4782.2	3640	6.85
5	Don Sutton	23	5282.1	3574	6.09
6	Gaylord Perry	22	5350.1	3534	5.94
7	Walter Johnson	21	5923.2	3508	5.33
8	Phil Niekro	24	5404.1	3342	5.57
9	Ferguson Jenkins	19	4500.2	3192	6.38
10	Bob Gibson	17	3884.1	3117	7.22
11	Jim Bunning	17	3760.1	2855	6.83
12	Mickey Lolich*	16	3638.1	2832	7.01
13	Cy Young	22	7354.2	2796	3.42
14	Frank Tanana*	21	4186.2	2773	5.96
15	Warren Spahn*	21	5243.2	2583	4.43
16	Bob Feller	18	3827.0	2581	6.07
17	Jerry Koosman*	19	3839.1	2556	5.99
18	Tim Keefe	14	5061.1	2527	4.50
19	Christy Mathewson	17	4781.0	2502	4.71
20	Don Drysdale	14	3432.0	2486	6.52
21	**Jack Morris**	18	3824.2	2478	5.83
22	Jim Kaat*	25	4530.1	2461	4.89
23	Sam McDowell*	15	2492.1	2453	8.86
24	Luis Tiant	19	3486.1	2416	6.24
25	Sandy Koufax*	12	2324.1	2396	9.28
26	**Charlie Hough**	25	3799.1	2363	5.60
27	Robin Roberts	19	4688.2	2357	4.52
28	Early Wynn	23	4564.0	2334	4.60
29	Rube Waddell*	13	2961.1	2316	7.04
30	Juan Marichal	16	3507.1	2303	5.91

Pitchers Active in 1994

		Yrs	GS	W	L	Pct
1	Jack Morris	18	527	254	186	.577
2	Dennis Martinez	19	499	219	170	.563
3	Charlie Hough	25	440	216	216	.500
4	Bob Welch	17	462	211	146	.591
5	Dennis Eckersley	20	361	188	153	.551
6	Frank Viola	13	411	175	146	.545
7	Roger Clemens	11	325	172	93	.649
8	Dave Stewart	15	332	165	122	.575
9	Bill Gullickson	14	390	162	136	.544
	Scott Sanderson	17	396	162	138	.540

Pitchers Active in 1994

		Yrs	IP	SO	P/9
1	Jack Morris	18	3824.2	2478	5.83
2	Charlie Hough	25	3799.1	2363	5.60
3	Dennis Eckersley	20	3082.2	2245	6.56
4	Roger Clemens	11	2393.1	2201	8.27
5	Mark Langston	11	2448.1	2110	7.76
6	Bob Welch	17	3091.1	1969	5.74
7	Dennis Martinez	19	3561.1	1923	4.86
8	Dwight Gooden	11	2169.2	1875	7.78
9	Fernando Valenzuela	14	2579.0	1861	6.48
10	Frank Viola	13	2791.2	1822	5.88

All-Time Major League Leaders (Cont.)
Pitching

Winning Pct.

		Yrs	W-L	Pct
1	Bob Caruthers	9	218-97	.692
2	Dave Foutz	11	147-66	.690
3	Whitey Ford*	16	236-106	.690
4	Lefty Grove*	17	300-141	.680
5	Vic Raschi	10	132-66	.667
6	Christy Mathewson	17	373-188	.665
7	Larry Corcoran	8	177-90	.663
8	Sam Leever	13	194-101	.658
9	Sal Maglie	10	119-62	.657
10	Sandy Koufax*	12	165-87	.655
11	Johnny Allen	13	142-75	.654
12	Ron Guidry*	14	170-91	.651
13	Lefty Gomez*	14	189-102	.649
	Roger Clemens	11	172-93	.649
	Dwight Gooden	11	157-85	.649

Losses

		Yrs	GS	W	L	Pct
1	Cy Young	22	815	511	316	.618
2	Pud Galvin	14	682	361	308	.540
3	Nolan Ryan	27	773	324	292	.526
4	Walter Johnson	21	666	416	279	.599
5	Phil Niekro	24	716	318	274	.537
6	Gaylord Perry	22	690	314	265	.542
7	Jack Powell	16	517	245	256	.489
	Don Sutton	23	756	324	256	.559
9	Eppa Rixey*	21	552	266	251	.515
10	Bert Blyleven	22	685	287	250	.534
11	Robin Roberts	19	609	286	245	.539
	Warren Spahn*	21	665	363	245	.597
13	Early Wynn	23	612	300	244	.551
	Steve Carlton*	24	709	329	244	.574
15	Jim Kaat*	25	625	283	237	.544

Appearances

1	Hoyt Wilhelm	1070
2	Kent Tekulve	1050
3	**Rich Gossage**	1002
4	Lindy McDaniel	987
5	Rollie Fingers	944
6	Gene Garber	931
7	Cy Young	906
8	Sparky Lyle	899
9	Jim Kaat	898
10	**Lee Smith**	891
11	**Jeff Reardon**	880
12	Don McMahon	874
13	Phil Niekro	864
14	**Charlie Hough**	858
15	Roy Face	848

Innings Pitched

1	Cy Young	7356.0
2	Pud Galvin	5941.1
3	Walter Johnson	5923.2
4	Phil Niekro	5404.1
5	Nolan Ryan	5387.0
6	Gaylord Perry	5350.1
7	Don Sutton	5282.1
8	Warren Spahn	5243.2
9	Steve Carlton	5217.1
10	Grover Alexander	5189.1
11	Tim Keefe	5061.1
12	Kid Nichols	5057.1
13	Bert Blyleven	4970.1
14	Mickey Welch	4802.0
15	Tom Seaver	4782.2

Earned Run Avg.

1	Ed Walsh	1.82
2	Addie Joss	1.88
3	Three Finger Brown	2.06
4	Monte Ward	2.10
5	Christy Mathewson	2.13
6	Rube Waddell	2.16
7	Walter Johnson	2.17
8	Orval Overall	2.24
9	Tommy Bond	2.25
10	Will White	2.28
11	Ed Reulbach	2.28
12	Jim Scott	2.32
13	Eddie Plank	2.34
14	Larry Corcoran	2.36
15	Eddie Cicotte	2.37

Shutouts

1	Walter Johnson	110
2	Grover Alexander	90
3	Christy Mathewson	80
4	Cy Young	76
5	Eddie Plank	69
6	Warren Spahn	63
7	Nolan Ryan	61
	Tom Seaver	61
9	Bert Blyleven	60
10	Don Sutton	58
11	Three Finger Brown	57
	Pud Galvin	57
	Ed Walsh	57
14	Bob Gibson	56
15	Steve Carlton	55

Walks Allowed

1	Nolan Ryan	2795
2	Steve Carlton	1833
3	Phil Niekro	1809
4	Early Wynn	1775
5	Bob Feller	1764
6	Bobo Newsom	1732
7	Amos Rusie	1704
8	**Charlie Hough**	1665
9	Gus Weyhing	1566
10	Red Ruffing	1541
11	Bump Hadley	1442
12	Warren Spahn	1434
13	Earl Whitehill	1431
14	Tony Mullane	1409
15	Sad Sam Jones	1396

HRs Allowed

1	Robin Roberts	505
2	Ferguson Jenkins	484
3	Phil Niekro	482
4	Don Sutton	472
5	Frank Tanana	448
6	Warren Spahn	434
7	Bert Blyleven	430
8	Steve Carlton	414
9	Gaylord Perry	399
10	Jim Kaat	395
11	**Jack Morris**	389
12	**Charlie Hough**	383
13	Tom Seaver	380
14	Jim Hunter	374
15	Jim Bunning	372

Saves

1	**Lee Smith**	434
2	**Jeff Reardon**	367
3	Rollie Fingers	341
4	**Rich Gossage**	310
5	Bruce Sutter	300
6	**Dennis Eckersley**	294
7	**Tom Henke**	275
8	**John Franco**	266
9	**Dave Righetti**	252
10	Dan Quisenberry	244
11	Sparky Lyle	238
12	Hoyt Wilhelm	227
13	Gene Garber	218
14	**Doug Jones**	217
15	Dave Smith	216
16	**Randy Myers**	205
17	**Bobby Thigpen**	201
18	Roy Face	193
19	**Mitch Williams**	192
20	**Jeff Montgomery**	187
21	**Steve Bedrosian**	184
	Kent Tekulve	184
23	Tug McGraw	180
24	**Rick Aguilera**	179
	Ron Perranoski	179
26	**Bryan Harvey**	177
27	Lindy McDaniel	172
28	**Jeff Russell**	163
29	**Gregg Olson**	161
30	**Jay Howell**	155

SINGLE SEASON

Through 1994 regular season.

Batting

Home Runs

		Year	Gm	AB	HR
1	Roger Maris, NY-AL	1961	162	590	61
2	Babe Ruth, NY-AL	1927	151	540	60
3	Babe Ruth, NY-AL	1921	152	540	59
4	Hank Greenberg, Det	1938	155	556	58
	Jimmie Foxx, Phi-AL	1932	154	585	58
6	Hack Wilson, Chi-NL	1930	155	585	56
7	Babe Ruth, NY-AL	1920	142	458	54
	Mickey Mantle, NY-AL	1961	153	514	54
	Babe Ruth, NY-AL	1928	154	536	54
	Ralph Kiner, Pit	1949	152	549	54
11	Mickey Mantle, NY-AL	1956	150	533	52
	Willie Mays, SF	1965	157	558	52
	George Foster, Cin	1977	158	615	52
14	Ralph Kiner, Pit	1947	152	565	51
	Cecil Fielder, Det	1990	159	573	51
	Willie Mays, NY-NL	1955	152	580	51
	Johnny Mize, NY-NL	1947	154	586	51
18	Jimmie Foxx, Bos-AL	1938	149	565	50

Hits

		Year	AB	H	Avg
1	George Sisler, StL-AL	1920	631	257	.407
2	Bill Terry, NY-NL	1930	633	254	.401
	Lefty O'Doul, Phi-NL	1929	638	254	.398
4	Al Simmons, Phi-AL	1925	658	253	.384
5	Rogers Hornsby, StL-NL	1922	623	250	.401
6	Chuck Klein, Phi-NL	1930	648	250	.386
7	Ty Cobb, Det	1911	591	248	.420
8	George Sisler, StL-AL	1922	586	246	.420
9	Babe Herman, Bklyn	1930	614	241	.393
	Heinie Manush, StL-AL	1928	638	241	.378
11	Wade Boggs, Bos	1985	653	240	.368
12	Rod Carew, Min	1977	616	239	.388
13	Don Mattingly, NY-AL	1986	677	238	.352
14	Harry Heilmann, Det	1921	602	237	.394
	Paul Waner, Pit	1927	623	237	.380
	Joe Medwick, StL-NL	1937	633	237	.374
17	Jack Tobin, StL-AL	1921	671	236	.352
18	Rogers Hornsby, StL-NL	1921	592	235	.397

Batting Average

From 1900-49

		Year	AB	H	Avg
1	Rogers Hornsby, StL-NL	1924	536	227	.424
2	Nap Lajoie, Phi-AL	1901	543	229	.422
3	George Sisler, StL-AL	1922	586	246	.420
	Ty Cobb, Det	1911	591	248	.420
5	Ty Cobb, Det	1912	533	227	.410
6	Joe Jackson, Cle	1911	571	233	.408
7	George Sisler, StL-AL	1920	631	257	.407
8	Ted Williams, Bos-AL	1941	456	185	.406
9	Rogers Hornsby, StL-NL	1925	504	203	.403
10	Harry Heilmann, Det	1923	524	211	.403

Since 1950

		Year	AB	H	Avg
1	Tony Gwynn	1994	419	175	.394
2	George Brett, KC	1980	449	175	.390
3	Ted Williams, Bos	1957	420	163	.388
	Rod Carew, Min	1977	616	239	.388
5	Tony Gwynn, SD	1987	589	218	.370
	Andres Galarraga, Col	1993	470	174	.370
7	Wade Boggs, Bos	1985	653	240	.368
8	Wade Boggs, Bos	1988	584	214	.366
	Rico Carty, Atl	1970	478	175	.366
10	Mickey Mantle, NY-AL	1957	474	173	.365

Total Bases

From 1900-49

		Year	TB
1	Babe Ruth, New York-AL	1921	457
2	Rogers Hornsby, St. Louis-NL	1922	450
3	Lou Gehrig, New York-AL	1927	447
4	Chuck Klein, Philadelphia-NL	1930	445
5	Jimmie Foxx, Philadelphia-AL	1932	438
6	Stan Musial, St. Louis-NL	1948	429
7	Hack Wilson, Chicago-NL	1930	423
8	Chuck Klein, Philadelphia-NL	1932	420
9	Lou Gehrig, New York-AL	1930	419
10	Joe DiMaggio, New York-AL	1937	418

Since 1950

		Year	TB
1	Jim Rice, Boston	1978	406
2	Hank Aaron, Milwaukee	1959	400
3	George Foster, Cincinnati	1977	388
	Don Mattingly, New York-AL	1986	388
5	Willie Mays, New York-NL	1955	382
	Willie Mays, San Francisco	1962	382
	Jim Rice, Boston	1977	382
8	Frank Robinson, Cincinnati	1962	380
9	Ernie Banks, Chicago-NL	1958	379
10	Duke Snider, Brooklyn	1954	378

Runs Batted In

From 1900-49

		Year	Avg	HR	RBI
1	Hack Wilson, Chi-NL	1930	.356	56	190
2	Lou Gehrig, NY-AL	1931	.341	46	184
3	Hank Greenberg, Det	1937	.337	40	183
4	Lou Gehrig, NY-AL	1927	.373	47	175
	Jimmie Foxx, Bos-AL	1938	.349	50	175
6	Lou Gehrig, NY-AL	1930	.379	41	174
7	Babe Ruth, NY-AL	1921	.378	59	171
8	Chuck Klein, Phi-NL	1930	.386	40	170
	Hank Greenberg, Det	1935	.328	36	170
10	Jimmie Foxx, Phi-AL	1932	.364	58	169

Since 1950

		Year	Avg	HR	RBI
1	Tommy Davis, LA-NL	1962	.346	27	153
2	George Foster, Cin	1977	.320	52	149
3	Johnny Bench, Cin	1970	.293	45	148
4	Al Rosen, Cle	1953	.336	43	145
	Don Mattingly, NY-AL	1985	.324	35	145
6	Walt Dropo, Bos-AL	1950	.322	34	144
	Vern Stephens, Bos-AL	1950	.295	30	144
8	Ernie Banks, Chi-NL	1959	.304	45	143
9	Roy Campanella, Bklyn	1953	.312	41	142
	Orlando Cepeda, SF	1961	.311	46	142
	Roger Maris, NY-AL	1961	.269	61	142

All-Time Major League Leaders (Cont.)
Batting

Runs

		Year	Runs
1	Babe Ruth, New York-AL	1921	177
2	Lou Gehrig, New York-AL	1936	167
3	Babe Ruth, New York-AL	1928	163
	Lou Gehrig, New York-AL	1931	163
5	Babe Ruth, New York-AL	1920	158
	Babe Ruth, New York-AL	1927	158
	Chuck Klein, Philadelphia-NL	1930	158
8	Rogers Hornsby, Chicago-NL	1929	156
9	Kiki Cuyler, Chicago-NL	1930	155
10	Lefty O'Doul, Philadelphia-NL	1929	152
	Woody English, Chicago-NL	1930	152
	Al Simmons, Philadelphia-AL	1930	152
	Chuck Klein, Philadelphia-NL	1932	152
14	Babe Ruth, New York-AL	1923	151
	Jimmie Foxx, Philadelphia-AL	1932	151
	Joe DiMaggio, New York-AL	1937	151
17	Babe Ruth, New York-AL	1930	150
	Ted Williams, Boston-AL	1940	150
19	Lou Gehrig, New York-AL	1927	149
	Babe Ruth, New York-AL	1931	149

Walks

		Year	BB
1	Babe Ruth, New York-AL	1923	170
2	Ted Williams, Boston-AL	1947	162
	Ted Williams, Boston-AL	1949	162
4	Ted Williams, Boston-AL	1946	156
5	Eddie Yost, Washington	1956	151
6	Eddie Joost, Philadelphia-AL	1949	149
7	Babe Ruth, New York-AL	1920	148
	Eddie Stanky, Brooklyn	1945	148
	Jimmy Wynn, Houston	1969	148
10	Jimmy Sheckard, Chicago-NL	1911	147

Extra Base Hits

		Year	EBH
1	Babe Ruth, New York-AL	1921	119
2	Lou Gehrig, New York-AL	1927	117
3	Chuck Klein, Philadelphia-NL	1930	107
4	Chuck Klein, Philadelphia-NL	1932	103
	Hank Greenberg, Detroit	1937	103
	Stan Musial, St. Louis-NL	1948	103
7	Rogers Hornsby, St. Louis-NL	1922	102
8	Lou Gehrig, New York-AL	1930	100
	Jimmie Foxx, Philadelphia-AL	1933	100
10	Three tied with 99.		

Slugging Percentage
From 1900-49

		Year	Pct
1	Babe Ruth, New York-AL	1920	.847
2	Babe Ruth, New York-AL	1921	.846
3	Babe Ruth, New York-AL	1927	.772
4	Lou Gehrig, New York-AL	1927	.765
5	Babe Ruth, New York-AL	1923	.764
6	Rogers Hornsby, St. Louis-NL	1925	.756
7	Jimmie Foxx, Philadelphia-AL	1932	.749
8	Babe Ruth, New York-AL	1924	.739
9	Babe Ruth, New York-AL	1926	.737
10	Ted Williams, Boston-AL	1941	.735

Since 1950

		Year	Pct
1	Ted Williams, Boston-AL	1957	.731
2	Mickey Mantle, New York-AL	1956	.705
3	Mickey Mantle, New York-AL	1961	.687
4	Barry Bonds, San Francisco	1993	.677
5	Hank Aaron, Atlanta	1971	.669

Stolen Bases

		Year	SB
1	Rickey Henderson, Oakland	1982	130
2	Lou Brock, St. Louis	1974	118
3	Vince Coleman, St. Louis	1985	110
4	Vince Coleman, St. Louis	1987	109
5	Rickey Henderson, Oakland	1983	108
6	Vince Coleman, St. Louis	1986	107
7	Maury Wills, Los Angeles-NL	1962	104
8	Rickey Henderson, Oakland	1980	100
9	Ron LeFlore, Montreal	1980	97
10	Ty Cobb, Detroit	1915	96
11	Omar Moreno, Pittsburgh	1980	96
12	Maury Wills, Los Angeles	1965	94
13	Rickey Henderson, New York-AL	1988	93
14	Tim Raines, Montreal	1983	90
15	Clyde Milan, Washington	1912	88
16	Rickey Henderson, New York-AL	1986	87
17	Ty Cobb, Detroit	1911	83
	Willie Wilson, Kansas City	1979	83
19	Bob Bescher, Cincinnati	1911	81
	Eddie Collins, Philadelphia-AL	1910	81
	Vince Coleman, St. Louis	1988	81

Strikeouts

		Year	SO
1	Bobby Bonds, San Francisco	1970	189
2	Bobby Bonds, San Francisco	1969	187
3	Rob Deer, Milwaukee	1987	186
4	Pete Incaviglia, Texas	1986	185
5	Cecil Fielder, Detroit	1990	182
6	Mike Schmidt, Philadelphia	1975	180
7	Rob Deer, Milwaukee	1986	179
8	Dave Nicholson, Chicago-AL	1963	175
	Gorman Thomas, Milwaukee	1979	175
	Jose Canseco, Oakland	1986	175
	Rob Deer, Detroit	1991	175

Pinch Hits

Career pinch hits in parentheses.

		Year	PH	
1	Jose Morales, Montreal	1976	25	(123)
2	Dave Philley, Baltimore	1961	24	(93)
	Vic Davalillo, St. Louis	1970	24	(95)
	Rusty Staub, New York-NL	1983	24	(100)
5	Wallace Johnson, Montreal	1988	22	(78)
	Peanuts Lowrey, St. Louis	1953	22	(62)
	Sam Leslie, New York-NL	1932	22	(59)
	Red Schoendienst, St. Louis	1962	22	(56)

Note: The all-time career pinch hit leader is Manny Mota (150).

Four Home Runs in One Game
National League

	Date	H/A	Inn
Bobby Lowe, Boston	5/30/1894	H	9
Ed Delahanty, Philadelphia	7/13/1896	A	9
Chuck Klein, Philadelphia	7/10/1936	A	10
Gil Hodges, Brooklyn	8/31/1950	H	9
Joe Adcock, Milwaukee	7/31/1954	A	9
Willie Mays, San Francisco	4/30/1961	A	9
Mike Schmidt, Philadelphia	4/17/1976	A	10
Bob Horner, Atlanta	7/6/1986	H	9
Mark Whiten, St. Louis	9/7/1993	A	9

American League

	Date	H/A	Inn
Lou Gehrig, New York	6/3/1932	A	9
Pat Seerey, Chicago	7/18/1948	A	11
Rocky Colavito, Cleveland	6/10/1959	A	9

Pitching
Wins

From 1900-49

	Year	W	L	Pct
1 Jack Chesbro, NY-AL	1904	41	12	.774
2 Ed Walsh, Chi-AL	1908	40	15	.727
3 Christy Mathewson, NY-NL	1908	37	11	.771
4 Walter Johnson, Wash	1913	36	7	.837
5 Joe McGinnity, NY-NL	1904	35	8	.814
6 Smokey Joe Wood, Bos-AL	1912	34	5	.872
7 Cy Young, Bos-AL	1901	33	10	.767
Grover Alexander, Phi-NL	1916	33	12	.733
Christy Mathewson, NY-NL	1904	33	12	.733

Since 1950

	Year	W	L	Pct
1 Denny McLain, Det	1968	31	6	.838
2 Robin Roberts, Phi-NL	1952	28	7	.800
3 Bob Welch, Oak	1990	27	6	.818
4 Don Newcombe, Bklyn	1956	27	7	.794
Sandy Koufax, LA	1966	27	9	.750
6 Steve Carlton, Phi	1972	27	10	.730
7 Sandy Koufax, LA	1965	26	8	.765
Juan Marichal, SF	1968	26	9	.743

Note: 11 pitchers tied with 25 wins, including Marichal twice.

Earned Run Average

From 1900-49

	Year	ShO	ERA
1 Dutch Leonard, Bos-AL	1914	7	1.01
2 Three Finger Brown,	1906	10	1.04
3 Walter Johnson, Wash	1913	11	1.09
4 Bob Gibson, St.L	1968	13	1.12
5 Christy Mathewson, NY-NL	1909	8	1.14
6 Jack Pfiester, Chi-NL	1907	3	1.15
7 Addie Joss, Cle	1908	9	1.16
8 Carl Lundgren, Chi-NL	1907	7	1.17
9 Grover Alexander, Phi-NL	1915	12	1.22
10 Cy Young, Bos-AL	1908	3	1.26

Since 1950

	Year	ShO	ERA
1 Bob Gibson, St.L	1968	13	1.12
2 Dwight Gooden, NY-NL	1985	8	1.53
3 Greg Maddux, Atl	1994	3	1.56
4 Luis Tiant, Cle	1968	9	1.60
5 Dean Chance, LA-AL	1964	11	1.65
6 Nolan Ryan, Cal	1981	3	1.69
7 Sandy Koufax, LA	1966	5	1.73
8 Sandy Koufax, LA	1964	7	1.74
9 Ron Guidry, NY-AL	1978	9	1.74
10 Tom Seaver, NY-NL	1971	4	1.76

Winning Pct.

	Year	W-L	Pct
1 Roy Face, Pit	1959	18-1	.947
2 Rick Sutcliffe, Chi-NL*	1984	16-1	.941
3 Johnny Allen, Cle	1937	15-1	.938
4 Ron Guidry, NY-AL	1978	25-3	.893
5 Freddie Fitzsimmons, Bklyn	1940	16-2	.889
6 Lefty Grove, Phi-AL	1931	31-4	.886
7 Bob Stanley, Bos	1978	15-2	.882
8 Preacher Roe, Bklyn	1951	22-3	.880
9 Tom Seaver, Cin	1981	14-2	.875
10 Smokey Joe Wood, Bos-AL	1912	34-5	.872

*Sutcliffe began 1984 with Cleveland and was 4-5 before being traded to the Cubs; his overall winning pct. was .769 (20-6).

Strikeouts

	Year	SO	P/G
1 Nolan Ryan, Cal	1973	383	10.57
2 Sandy Koufax, LA	1965	382	10.24
3 Nolan Ryan, Cal	1974	367	9.92
4 Rube Waddell, Phi-AL	1904	349	8.12
5 Bob Feller, Cle	1946	348	8.45
6 Nolan Ryan, Cal	1977	341	10.26
7 Nolan Ryan, Cal	1972	329	10.43
8 Nolan Ryan, Cal	1976	327	10.36
9 Sam McDowell, Cle	1965	325	10.71
10 Sandy Koufax, LA	1966	317	8.83

Appearances

	Year	App	Sv
1 Mike Marshall, LA	1974	106	21
2 Kent Tekulve, Pit	1979	94	31
3 Mike Marshall, LA	1973	92	31
4 Kent Tekulve, Pit	1978	91	31
5 Wayne Granger, Cin	1969	90	27
Mike Marshall, Min	1979	90	32
Kent Tekulve, Phi	1987	90	3

Saves

	Year	App	Sv
1 Bobby Thigpen, Chi-AL	1990	77	57
2 Randy Myers, Chi-NL	1993	73	53
3 Dennis Eckersley, Oak	1992	69	51
4 Dennis Eckersley, Oak	1990	63	48
Rod Beck, SF	1993	76	48
6 Lee Smith, St.L	1991	67	47

Innings Pitched (since 1920)

	Year	IP	W-L
1 Wilbur Wood, Chi-AL	1972	377	24-17
2 Mickey Lolich, Det	1971	376	25-14
3 Bob Feller, Cle	1946	371	26-15
4 Grover Alexander, Chi-NL	1920	363	27-14
5 Wilbur Wood, Chi-AL	1973	359	24-20

Shutouts

	Year	ShO	ERA
1 Grover Alexander, Phi-NL	1916	16	1.55
2 Jack Coombs, Phi-AL	1910	13	1.30
Bob Gibson, St.L	1968	13	1.12
4 Christy Mathewson, NY-NL	1908	12	1.43
Grover Alexander, Phi-NL	1915	12	1.22

Walks Allowed

	Year	BB	SO
1 Bob Feller, Cle	1938	208	240
2 Nolan Ryan, Cal	1977	204	341
3 Nolan Ryan, Cal	1974	202	367
4 Bob Feller, Cle	1941	194	260
5 Bobo Newsom, St.L-AL	1938	192	226

Home Runs Allowed

	Year	HRs
1 Bert Blyleven, Minnesota	1986	50
2 Robin Roberts, Philadelphia	1956	46
Bert Blyleven, Minnesota	1987	46
4 Pedro Ramos, Washington	1957	43
5 Denny McLain, Detroit	1966	42

All-Time Winningest Managers

Top 20 Major League career victories through the 1994 season. Career, regular season and postseason (playoffs and World Series) records are noted along with AL and NL pennants and World Series titles won. Managers active during 1994 season in **bold** type.

		Career			Regular Season			Postseason			
	Yrs	W	L	Pct	W	L	Pct	W	L	Pct	Titles
1 Connie Mack	53	**3755**	3967	.486	3731	3948	.486	24	19	.558	9 AL, 5 WS
2 John McGraw	33	**2810**	1987	.586	2784	1959	.587	26	28	.482	10 NL, 2 WS
3 **Sparky Anderson**	25	**2178**	1771	.552	2134	1750	.549	34	21	.618	4 NL, 1 AL, 3 WS
4 Bucky Harris	29	**2168**	2228	.493	2157	2218	.493	11	10	.524	3 AL, 2 WS
5 Joe McCarthy	24	**2155**	1346	.616	2125	1333	.615	30	13	.698	1 NL, 8 AL, 7 WS
6 Walter Alston	23	**2063**	1634	.558	2040	1613	.558	23	21	.523	7 NL, 4 WS
7 Leo Durocher	24	**2015**	1717	.540	2008	1709	.540	7	8	.467	3 NL, 1 WS
8 Casey Stengel	25	**1942**	1868	.510	1905	1842	.508	37	26	.587	10 AL, 7 WS
9 Gene Mauch	26	**1907**	2044	.483	1902	2037	.483	5	7	.417	—None—
10 Bill McKechnie	25	**1904**	1737	.523	1896	1723	.524	8	14	.364	4 NL, 2 WS
11 Ralph Houk	20	**1627**	1539	.514	1619	1531	.514	8	8	.500	3 AL, 2 WS
12 Fred Clarke	19	**1609**	1189	.575	1602	1181	.576	7	8	.467	2 NL, 1 WS
13 Dick Williams	21	**1592**	1474	.519	1571	1451	.520	21	23	.477	3 AL, 1 NL, 2 WS
14 **Tommy Lasorda**	19	**1511**	1365	.525	1480	1338	.525	31	27	.534	4 NL, 2 WS
15 Earl Weaver	17	**1506**	1080	.582	1480	1060	.583	26	20	.565	4 AL, 1 WS
16 Clark Griffith	20	**1491**	1367	.522	1491	1367	.522	0	0	.000	1 AL (1901)
17 Miller Huggins	17	**1431**	1149	.555	1413	1134	.555	18	15	.545	6 AL, 3 WS
18 Al Lopez	17	**1412**	1012	.583	1410	1004	.584	2	8	.200	2 AL
19 Jimmy Dykes	21	**1406**	1541	.477	1406	1541	.477	0	0	.000	—None—
20 Wilbert Robertson	19	**1402**	1407	.499	1399	1398	.500	3	9	.250	2 NL

Notes: John McGraw's postseason record also includes two World Series tie games (1912,'22); Miller Huggins postseason record also includes one World Series tie game (1922).

Where They Managed

Alston—Brooklyn/Los Angeles NL (1954-76); **Anderson**—Cincinnati NL (1970-78), Detroit AL (1979—); **Clarke**—Louisville NL (1897-99), Pittsburgh NL (1900-15); **Durocher**—Brooklyn NL (1939-46,48), New York NL (1948-55), Chicago NL (1966-72), Houston NL (1972-73); **Dykes**—Chicago AL (1934-46), Philadelphia AL (1951- 53), Baltimore AL (1954), Cincinnati NL (1958), Detroit AL (1959-60), Cleveland AL (1960-61); **Griffith**—Chicago AL (1901-02), New York AL (1903-08), Cincinnati NL (1909-11), Washington AL (1912-20); **Harris**—Washington AL (1924-28,35-42,50-54), Detroit AL (1929-33,55-56), Boston AL (1934), Philadelphia NL (1943), New York AL (1947-48); **Houk**—New York AL (1961-63,66,73), Detroit AL (1974-78), Boston AL (1981-84); **Huggins**—St. Louis NL (1913-17), New York AL (1918-29); **Lasorda**—Los Angeles NL (1976—); **Lopez**—Cleveland AL (1951-56), Chicago AL (1957-65,68-69).

Mack—Pittsburgh NL (1894-96), Philadelphia AL (1901-50); **Mauch**—Philadelphia NL (1960-68), Montreal NL (1969-75), Minnesota NL (1976-80), California AL (1981-82,85-87); **McCarthy**—Chicago NL (1926-30), New York AL (1931-46), Boston AL (1948-50); **McGraw**—Baltimore NL (1899), Baltimore AL (1901-02), New York NL (1902-32); **McKechnie**—Newark FL (1915), Pittsburgh NL (1922-26), St. Louis NL (1928-29), Boston NL (1930- 37), Cincinnati NL (1938-46); **Robertson**—Baltimore NL (1902), Brooklyn NL (1914-31); **Stengel**—Brooklyn NL (1934-36), Boston NL (1938-43), New York AL (1949-60), New York NL (1962-65); **Weaver**—Baltimore AL (1968-82,85-86); **Williams**—Boston AL (1967-69), Oakland AL (1971-73), California AL (1974-76), Montreal NL (1977-81), San Diego NL (1982-85), Seattle AL (1986-88).

Regular Season Winning Pct.

Minimum of 750 victories.

	Yrs	W	L	Pct	Pen
1 Joe McCarthy	24	2125	1333	.614	9
2 Charlie Comiskey	12	838	541	.608	4
3 Frank Selee	16	1284	862	.598	5
4 Billy Southworth	13	1044	704	.597	4
5 Frank Chance	11	946	648	.593	4
6 John McGraw	33	2784	1959	.587	9
7 Al Lopez	17	1410	1004	.584	2
8 Earl Weaver	17	1480	1060	.583	4
9 Cap Anson	21	1296	947	.578	5
10 Fred Clarke	19	1602	1181	.576	2
11 Steve O'Neill	14	1040	821	.559	1
12 Walter Alston	23	2040	1613	.558	7
13 Bill Terry	10	823	661	.555	3
14 Miller Huggins	17	1413	1134	.555	6
15 Billy Martin	16	1253	1013	.553	2
16 **Sparky Anderson**	25	2134	1750	.549	5
17 Harry Wright	18	1000	825	.548	3
18 Charlie Grimm	19	1287	1067	.547	3
19 Hugh Jennings	15	1163	984	.542	3
20 Three tied at .540 each.					

World Series Victories

	App	W	L	T	Pct	WS
1 Casey Stengel	10	37	26	0	.587	7
2 Joe McCarthy	9	30	13	0	.698	7
3 John McGraw	9	26	28	2	.482	2
4 Connie Mack	8	24	19	0	.558	5
5 Walter Alston	7	20	20	0	.523	4
6 Miller Huggins	6	18	15	1	.544	3
7 **Sparky Anderson**	5	16	12	0	.571	3
8 **Tommy Lasorda**	4	12	11	0	.522	2
	Dick Williams	4	12	14	0	.462	2
10 Frank Chance	4	11	9	1	.548	2
	Bucky Harris	3	11	10	0	.524	2
	Billy Southworth	4	11	11	0	.500	2
	Earl Weaver	4	11	13	0	.458	1
14 Whitey Herzog	3	10	11	0	.476	1
15 Bill Carrigan	2	8	2	0	.800	2
	Danny Murtaugh	2	8	6	0	.571	2
	Ralph Houk	3	8	5	0	.500	2
	Bill McKechnie	4	8	14	0	.364	2
	Tom Kelly	2	8	6	0	.571	2
20 Seven tied with 7 wins each.						

Active Managers' Records

Regular season games only; through 1994.

National League

		Yrs	W	L	Pct
1	Tommy Lasorda, LA	19	1480	1338	.525
2	Bobby Cox, Atl	13	1025	908	.530
3	Joe Torre, St.L	12	874	976	.472
4	Jim Fregosi, Phi	11	725	768	.486
5	Jim Leyland, Pit	9	720	688	.511
6	Davey Johnson, Cin	9	714	530	.574
7	Dallas Green, NY	6	326	331	.496
8	Rene Lachemann, Fla	6	322	436	.425
9	Felipe Alou, Mon	3	238	163	.594
10	Dusty Baker, SF	2	158	119	.570
11	Don Baylor, Col	2	120	159	.430
12	Jim Riggleman, Chi	3	112	179	.385
13	Terry Collins, Hou	1	66	49	.574
14	Bruce Bochy, SD	0	0	0	.000

American League

		Yrs	W	L	Pct
1	Sparky Anderson, Det	25	2134	1750	.549
2	Tony LaRussa, Oak	16	1253	1106	.531
3	Tom Kelly, Min	9	651	619	.513
4	Lou Piniella, Sea	8	610	567	.518
5	Cito Gaston, Tor	6	481	375	.562
6	Johnny Oates, Tex	3	291	270	.519
7	Mike Hargrove, Cle	4	250	272	.479
8	Gene Lamont, Chi	3	247	190	.565
9	Buck Showalter, NY	3	234	203	.535
10	Phil Garner, Mil	3	214	225	.487
11	Kevin Kennedy, Bos	2	138	138	.500
12	Marcel Lachemann, Cal	1	30	44	.405
13	Bob Boone, KC	0	0	0	.000
	Phil Regan, Balt.	0	0	0	.000

Annual Awards

MOST VALUABLE PLAYER

There have been three different Most Valuable Player awards in baseball since 1911—the Chalmers Award (1911-14), presented by the Detroit-based automobile company; the League Award (1922-29), presented by the National and American Leagues; and the Baseball Writers' Award (since 1931), presented by the Baseball Writers' Association of America. Statistics for winning players are provided below. Stats for winning pitchers are listed on page 135.

Multiple winners: NL—Barry Bonds, Roy Campanella, Stan Musial and Mike Schmidt (3); Ernie Banks, Johnny Bench, Rogers Hornsby, Carl Hubbell, Willie Mays, Joe Morgan and Dale Murphy (2). **AL**—Yogi Berra, Joe DiMaggio, Jimmie Foxx and Mickey Mantle (3); Mickey Cochrane, Lou Gehrig, Hank Greenberg, Walter Johnson, Roger Maris, Hal Newhouser, Cal Ripken Jr., Frank Thomas and Ted Williams (2). **NL & AL**—Frank Robinson (2, one in each).

Chalmers Award

National League

Year		Pos	HR	RBI	Avg
1911	Wildfire Schulte, Chi	OF	21	121	.300
1912	Larry Doyle, NY	2B	10	90	.330
1913	Jake Daubert, Bklyn	1B	2	52	.350
1914	Johnny Evers, Bos	2B	1	40	.279

American League

Year		Pos	HR	RBI	Avg
1911	Ty Cobb, Det	OF	8	144	.420
1912	Tris Speaker, Bos	OF	10	98	.383
1913	Walter Johnson, Wash	P	—	—	—
1914	Eddie Collins, Phi	2B	2	85	.344

League Award

National League

Year		Pos	HR	RBI	Avg
1922	No selection				
1923	No selection				
1924	Dazzy Vance, Bklyn	P	—	—	—
1925	Rogers Hornsby, St.L	2B-Mgr	29	143	.403
1926	Bob O'Farrell, St.L	C	7	68	.293
1927	Paul Waner, Pit	OF	9	131	.380
1928	Jim Bottomley, St.L	1B	31	136	.325
1929	Rogers Hornsby, Chi	2B	39	149	.380

American League

Year		Pos	HR	RBI	Avg
1922	George Sisler, St.L	1B	8	105	.420
1923	Babe Ruth, NY	OF	41	131	.393
1924	Walter Johnson, Wash	P	—	—	—
1925	Roger Peckinpaugh, Wash	SS	4	64	.294
1926	George Burns, Cle	1B	4	114	.358
1927	Lou Gehrig, NY	1B	47	175	.373
1928	Mickey Cochrane, Phi	C	10	57	.293
1929	No selection				

Wide World Photos

Walter Johnson

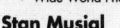

Wide World Photos

Stan Musial

Wide World Photos

Roy Campanella

Wide World Photos

Barry Bonds

Annual Awards (Cont.)

Most Valuable Player
Baseball Writers' Award

Winning pitchers' statistics on page 135.

National League

Year		Pos	HR	RBI	Avg
1930	Hack Wilson, Chi	OF	56	190	.356
1931	Frankie Frisch, St.L	2B	4	82	.311
1932	Chuck Klein, Phi	OF	38	137	.348
1933	Carl Hubbell, NY	P	—	—	—
1934	Dizzy Dean, St.L	P	—	—	—
1935	Gabby Hartnett, Chi	C	13	91	.344
1936	Carl Hubbell, NY	P	—	—	—
1937	Joe Medwick, St.L	OF	31	154	.374
1938	Ernie Lombardi, Cin	C	19	95	.342
1939	Bucky Walters, Cin	P	—	—	—
1940	Frank McCormick, Cin	1B	19	127	.309
1941	Dolf Camilli, Bklyn	1B	34	120	.285
1942	Mort Cooper, St.L	P	—	—	—
1943	Stan Musial, St.L	OF	13	81	.357
1944	Marty Marion, St.L	SS	6	63	.267
1945	Phil Cavarretta, Chi	1B	6	97	.355
1946	Stan Musial, St.L	1B-OF	16	103	.365
1947	Bob Elliott, Bos	3B	22	113	.317
1948	Stan Musial, St.L	OF	39	131	.376
1949	Jackie Robinson, Bklyn	2B	16	124	.342
1950	Jim Konstanty, Phi	P	—	—	—
1951	Roy Campanella, Bklyn	C	33	108	.325
1952	Hank Sauer, Chi	OF	37	121	.270
1953	Roy Campanella, Bklyn	C	41	142	.312
1954	Willie Mays, NY	OF	41	110	.345
1955	Roy Campanella, Bklyn	C	32	107	.318
1956	Don Newcombe, Bklyn	P	—	—	—
1957	Hank Aaron, Mil	OF	44	132	.322
1958	Ernie Banks, Chi	SS	47	129	.313
1959	Ernie Banks, Chi	SS	45	143	.304
1960	Dick Groat, Pit	SS	2	50	.325
1961	Frank Robinson, Cin	OF	37	124	.323
1962	Maury Wills, LA	SS	6	48	.299
1963	Sandy Koufax, LA	P	—	—	—
1964	Ken Boyer, St.L	3B	24	119	.295
1965	Willie Mays, SF	OF	52	112	.317
1966	Roberto Clemente, Pit	OF	29	119	.317
1967	Orlando Cepeda, St.L	1B	25	111	.325
1968	Bob Gibson, St.L	P	—	—	—
1969	Willie McCovey, SF	1B	45	126	.320
1970	Johnny Bench, Cin	C	45	148	.293
1971	Joe Torre, St.L	3B	45	137	.363
1972	Johnny Bench, Cin	C	40	125	.270
1973	Pete Rose, Cin	OF	5	64	.338
1974	Steve Garvey, LA	1B	21	111	.312
1975	Joe Morgan, Cin	2B	17	94	.327
1976	Joe Morgan, Cin	2B	27	111	.320
1977	George Foster, Cin	OF	52	149	.320
1978	Dave Parker, Pit	OF	30	117	.334
1979	Keith Hernandez, St.L	1B	11	105	.344
	& Willie Stargell, Pit	1B	32	82	.281
1980	Mike Schmidt, Phi	3B	48	121	.286
1981	Mike Schmidt, Phi	3B	31	91	.316
1982	Dale Murphy, Atl	OF	36	109	.281
1983	Dale Murphy, Atl	OF	36	121	.302
1984	Ryne Sandberg, Chi	2B	19	84	.314
1985	Willie McGee, St.L	OF	10	82	.353

American League

Year		Pos	HR	RBI	Avg
1930	Joe Cronin, Wash	SS	13	126	.346
1931	Lefty Grove, Phi	P	—	—	—
1932	Jimmie Foxx, Phi	1B	58	169	.364
1933	Jimmie Foxx, Phi	1B	48	163	.356
1934	Mickey Cochrane, Det	C-Mgr	2	76	.320
1935	Hank Greenberg, Det	1B	36	170	.328
1936	Lou Gehrig, NY	1B	49	152	.354
1937	Charlie Gehringer, Det	2B	14	96	.371
1938	Jimmie Foxx, Bos	1B	50	175	.349
1939	Joe DiMaggio, NY	OF	30	126	.381
1940	Hank Greenberg, Det	OF	41	150	.340
1941	Joe DiMaggio, NY	OF	30	125	.357
1942	Joe Gordon, NY	2B	18	103	.322
1943	Spud Chandler, NY	P	—	—	—
1944	Hal Newhouser, Det	P	—	—	—
1945	Hal Newhouser, Det	P	—	—	—
1946	Ted Williams, Bos	OF	38	123	.342
1947	Joe DiMaggio, NY	OF	20	97	.315
1948	Lou Boudreau, Cle	SS-Mgr	18	106	.355
1949	Ted Williams, Bos	OF	43	159	.343
1950	Phil Rizzuto, NY	SS	7	66	.324
1951	Yogi Berra, NY	C	27	88	.294
1952	Bobby Shantz, Phi	P	—	—	—
1953	Al Rosen, Cle	3B	43	145	.336
1954	Yogi Berra, NY	C	22	125	.307
1955	Yogi Berra, NY	C	27	108	.272
1956	Mickey Mantle, NY	OF	52	130	.353
1957	Mickey Mantle, NY	OF	34	94	.365
1958	Jackie Jensen, Bos	OF	35	122	.286
1959	Nellie Fox, Chi	2B	2	70	.306
1960	Roger Maris, NY	OF	39	112	.283
1961	Roger Maris, NY	OF	61	142	.269
1962	Mickey Mantle, NY	OF	30	89	.321
1963	Elston Howard, NY	C	28	85	.287
1964	Brooks Robinson, Bal	3B	28	118	.317
1965	Zoilo Versalles, Min	SS	19	77	.273
1966	Frank Robinson, Bal	OF	49	122	.316
1967	Carl Yastrzemski, Bos	OF	44	121	.326
1968	Denny McLain, Det	P	—	—	—
1969	Harmon Killebrew, Min	3B-1B	49	140	.276
1970	Boog Powell, Bal	1B	35	114	.297
1971	Vida Blue, Oak	P	—	—	—
1972	Dick Allen, Chi	1B	37	113	.308
1973	Reggie Jackson, Oak	OF	32	117	.293
1974	Jeff Burroughs, Tex	OF	25	118	.301
1975	Fred Lynn, Bos	OF	21	105	.331
1976	Thurman Munson, NY	C	17	105	.302
1977	Rod Carew, Min	1B	14	100	.388
1978	Jim Rice, Bos	OF-DH	46	139	.315
1979	Don Baylor, Cal	OF-DH	36	139	.296
1980	George Brett, KC	3B	24	118	.390
1981	Rollie Fingers, Mil	P	—	—	—
1982	Robin Yount, Mil	SS	29	114	.331
1983	Cal Ripken, Jr., Bal	SS	27	102	.318
1984	Willie Hernandez, Det	P	—	—	—
1985	Don Mattingly, NY	1B	35	145	.324

National League

Year		Pos	HR	RBI	Avg
1986	Mike Schmidt, Phi	3B	37	119	.290
1987	Andre Dawson, Chi	OF	49	137	.287
1988	Kirk Gibson, LA	OF	25	76	.290
1989	Kevin Mitchell, SF	OF	47	125	.291
1990	Barry Bonds, Pit	OF	33	114	.301
1991	Terry Pendleton, Atl	3B	22	86	.319
1992	Barry Bonds, Pit	OF	34	103	.311
1993	Barry Bonds, SF	OF	46	123	.336
1994	Jeff Bagwell, Hou	1B	39	116	.368

American League

Year		Pos	HR	RBI	Avg
1986	Roger Clemens, Bos	P	—	—	—
1987	George Bell, Tor	OF	47	134	.308
1988	Jose Canseco, Oak	OF	42	124	.307
1989	Robin Yount, Mil	OF	21	103	.318
1990	Rickey Henderson, Oak	OF	28	61	.325
1991	Cal Ripken, Jr., Bal	SS	34	114	.323
1992	Dennis Eckersley, Oak	P	—	—	—
1993	Frank Thomas, Chi	1B	41	128	.317
1994	Frank Thomas, Chi	1B	38	101	.353

MVP Pitchers' Statistics

Pitchers have been named Most Valuable Player on 23 occasions, 10 times in the NL and 13 in the AL. Four have been relief pitchers—Jim Konstanty, Rollie Fingers, Willie Hernandez and Dennis Eckersley.

National League

Year		Gm	W-L	SV	ERA
1924	Dazzy Vance, Bklyn	35	28-6	0	2.16
1933	Carl Hubbell, NY	45	23-12	5	1.66
1934	Dizzy Dean, St.L	50	30-7	7	2.65
1936	Carl Hubbell, NY	42	26-6	3	2.31
1939	Bucky Walters, Cin	39	27-11	0	2.29
1942	Mort Cooper, St.L	37	22-7	0	1.77
1950	Jim Konstanty, Phi	74	16-7	22	2.66
1956	Don Newcombe, Bklyn	38	27-7	0	3.06
1963	Sandy Koufax, LA	40	25-5	0	1.88
1968	Bob Gibson, St.L	34	22-9	0	1.12

American League

Year		Gm	W-L	SV	ERA
1913	Walter Johnson, Wash	47	36-7	2	1.09
1924	Walter Johnson, Wash	38	23-7	0	2.72
1931	Lefty Grove, Phi	41	31-4	5	2.05
1943	Spud Chandler, NY	30	20-4	0	1.64
1944	Hal Newhouser, Det	47	29-9	2	2.22
1945	Hal Newhouser, Det	40	25-9	0	1.81
1952	Bobby Shantz, Phi	33	24-7	0	2.48
1968	Denny McLain, Det	41	31-6	0	1.96
1971	Vida Blue, Oak	39	24-8	0	1.82
1981	Rollie Fingers, Mil	47	6-3	28	1.04
1984	Willie Hernandez, Det	80	9-3	32	1.92
1986	Roger Clemens, Bos	33	24-4	0	2.48
1992	Dennis Eckersley, Oak	69	7-1	51	1.91

CY YOUNG AWARD

Voted on by the Baseball Writers Association of America. One award was presented from 1956-66, two since 1967. Pitchers who won the MVP and Cy Young awards in the same season are in **bold** type.

Multiple winners: NL—Steve Carlton (4); Sandy Koufax, Greg Maddux and Tom Seaver (3); Bob Gibson (2). **AL**—Jim Palmer and Roger Clemens (3); Denny McLain (2). **NL & AL**—Gaylord Perry (2, one in each).

NL and AL Combined

Year	National League	Gm	W-L	SV	ERA
1956	**Don Newcombe**, Bklyn	38	27-7	0	3.06
1957	Warren Spahn, Mil	39	21-11	3	2.69
1960	Vernon Law, Pit	35	20-9	0	3.08
1962	Don Drysdale, LA	43	25-9	1	2.83
1963	**Sandy Koufax**, LA	40	25-5	0	1.88
1965	Sandy Koufax, LA	43	26-8	2	2.04
1966	Sandy Koufax, LA	41	27-9	0	1.73

Year	American League	Gm	W-L	SV	ERA
1958	Bob Turley, NY	33	21-7	1	2.97
1959	Early Wynn, Chi	37	22-10	0	3.17
1961	Whitey Ford, NY	39	25-4	0	3.21
1964	Dean Chance, LA	46	20-9	4	1.65

Separate League Awards

National League

Year		Gm	W-L	SV	ERA
1967	Mike McCormick, SF	40	22-10	0	2.85
1968	**Bob Gibson**, St.L	34	22-9	0	1.12
1969	Tom Seaver, NY	36	25-7	0	2.21
1970	Bob Gibson, St.L	34	23-7	0	3.12
1971	Ferguson Jenkins, Chi	39	24-13	0	2.77
1972	Steve Carlton, Phi	41	27-10	0	1.97
1973	Tom Seaver, NY	36	19-10	0	2.08
1974	Mike Marshall, LA	106	15-12	21	2.42
1975	Tom Seaver, NY	36	22-9	0	2.38
1976	Randy Jones, SD	40	22-14	0	2.74
1977	Steve Carlton, Phi	36	23-10	0	2.64
1978	Gaylord Perry, SD	37	21-6	0	2.72
1979	Bruce Sutter, Chi	62	6-6	37	2.23

American League

Year		Gm	W-L	SV	ERA
1967	Jim Lonborg, Bos	39	22-9	0	3.16
1968	**Denny McLain**, Det	41	31-6	0	1.96
1969	Denny McLain, Det	42	24-9	0	2.80
	& Mike Cuellar, Bal	39	23-11	0	2.38
1970	Jim Perry, Min	40	24-12	0	3.03
1971	**Vida Blue**, Oak	39	24-8	0	1.82
1972	Gaylord Perry, Cle	41	24-16	1	1.92
1973	Jim Palmer, Bal	38	22-9	1	2.40
1974	Catfish Hunter, Oak	41	25-12	0	2.49
1975	Jim Palmer, Bal	39	23-11	1	2.09
1976	Jim Palmer, Bal	40	22-13	0	2.51
1977	Sparky Lyle, NY	72	13-5	26	2.17
1978	Ron Guidry, NY	35	25-3	0	1.74
1979	Mike Flanagan, Bal	39	23-9	0	3.08

Annual Awards (Cont.)
Cy Young Award

National League

Year		Gm	W-L	SV	ERA
1980	Steve Carlton, Phi	38	24-9	0	2.34
1981	Fernando Valenzuela, LA	25	13-7	0	2.48
1982	Steve Carlton, Phi	38	23-11	0	3.10
1983	John Denny, Phi	36	19-6	0	2.37
1984	Rick Sutcliffe, Chi	20*	16-1	0	2.69
1985	Dwight Gooden, NY	35	24-4	0	1.53
1986	Mike Scott, Hou	37	18-10	0	2.22
1987	Steve Bedrosian, Phi	65	5-3	40	2.83
1988	Orel Hershiser, LA	35	23-8	1	2.26
1989	Mark Davis, SD	70	4-3	44	1.85
1990	Doug Drabek, Pit	33	22-6	0	2.76
1991	Tom Glavine, Atl	34	20-11	0	2.55
1992	Greg Maddux, Chi	35	20-11	0	2.18
1993	Greg Maddux, Atl	36	20-10	0	2.36
1994	Greg Maddux, Atl	25	16-6	0	1.56

American League

Year		Gm	W-L	SV	ERA
1980	Steve Stone, Bal	37	25-7	0	3.23
1981	**Rollie Fingers**, Mil	47	6-3	28	1.04
1982	Pete Vuckovich, Mil	30	18-6	0	3.34
1983	LaMarr Hoyt, Chi	36	24-10	0	3.66
1984	**Willie Hernandez**, Det	80	9-3	32	1.92
1985	Bret Saberhagen, KC	32	20-6	0	2.87
1986	**Roger Clemens**, Bos	33	24-4	0	2.48
1987	Roger Clemens, Bos	36	20-9	0	2.97
1988	Frank Viola, Min	35	24-7	0	2.64
1989	Bret Saberhagen, KC	36	23-6	0	2.16
1990	Bob Welch, Oak	35	27-6	0	2.95
1991	Roger Clemens, Bos	35	18-10	0	2.62
1992	**Dennis Eckersley**, Oak	69	7-1	51	1.91
1993	Jack McDowell, Chi	34	22-10	0	3.37
1994	David Cone, KC	23	16-5	0	2.94

*NL games only, Sutcliffe pitched 15 games with Cleveland before being traded to the Cubs.

ROOKIE OF THE YEAR

Voted on by the Baseball Writers Assn. of America. One award was presented from 1947-48. Two awards (one for each league) have been presented since 1949. Winners who were also named MVP are in **bold** type.

NL and AL Combined

Year		Pos	Year		Pos
1947	Jackie Robinson, Brooklyn	1B	1948	Alvin Dark, Boston-NL	SS

National League

Year		Pos
1949	Don Newcombe, Bklyn	P
1950	Sam Jethroe, Bos	OF
1951	Willie Mays, NY	OF
1952	Joe Black, Bklyn	P
1953	Jim Gilliam, Bklyn	2B
1954	Wally Moon, St.L	OF
1955	Bill Virdon, St.L	OF
1956	Frank Robinson, Cin	OF
1957	Jack Sanford, Phi	P
1958	Orlando Cepeda, SF	1B
1959	Willie McCovey, SF	1B
1960	Frank Howard, LA	OF
1961	Billy Williams, Chi	OF
1962	Ken Hubbs, Chi	2B
1963	Pete Rose, Cin	2B
1964	Richie Allen, Phi	3B
1965	Jim Lefebvre, LA	2B
1966	Tommy Helms, Cin	3B
1967	Tom Seaver, NY	P
1968	Johnny Bench, Cin	C
1969	Ted Sizemore, LA	2B
1970	Carl Morton, Mon	P
1971	Earl Williams, Atl	C
1972	Jon Matlack, NY	P
1973	Gary Matthews, SF	OF
1974	Bake McBride, St.L	OF
1975	John Montefusco, SF	P
1976	Butch Metzger, SD & Pat Zachry, Cin	P
1977	Andre Dawson, Mon	OF
1978	Bob Horner, Atl	3B
1979	Rick Sutcliffe, LA	P
1980	Steve Howe, LA	P
1981	Fernando Valenzuela, LA	P
1982	Steve Sax, LA	2B
1983	Darryl Strawberry, NY	OF
1984	Dwight Gooden, NY	P
1985	Vince Coleman, St.L	OF
1986	Todd Worrell, St.L	P
1987	Benito Santiago, SD	C
1988	Chris Sabo, Cin	3B
1989	Jerome Walton, Chi	OF
1990	David Justice, Atl	OF
1991	Jeff Bagwell, Hou	1B
1992	Eric Karros, LA	1B
1993	Mike Piazza, LA	C
1994	Raul Mondesi, LA	OF

American League

Year		Pos
1949	Roy Sievers, St.L	OF
1950	Walt Dropo, Bos	1B
1951	Gil McDougald, NY	3B
1952	Harry Byrd, Phi	P
1953	Harvey Kuenn, Det	SS
1954	Bob Grim, NY	P
1955	Herb Score, Cle	P
1956	Luis Aparicio, Chi	SS
1957	Tony Kubek, NY	INF-OF
1958	Albie Pearson, Wash	OF
1959	Bob Allison, Wash	OF
1960	Ron Hansen, Bal	SS
1961	Don Schwall, Bos	P
1962	Tom Tresh, NY	SS-OF
1963	Gary Peters, Chi	P
1964	Tony Oliva, Min	OF
1965	Curt Blefary, Bal	OF
1966	Tommie Agee, Chi	OF
1967	Rod Carew, Min	2B
1968	Stan Bahnsen, NY	P
1969	Lou Piniella, KC	OF
1970	Thurman Munson, NY	C
1971	Chris Chambliss, Cle	1B
1972	Carlton Fisk, Bos	C
1973	Al Bumbry, Bal	OF
1974	Mike Hargrove, Tex	1B
1975	**Fred Lynn**, Bos	OF
1976	Mark Fidrych, Det	P
1977	Eddie Murray, Bal	DH-1B
1978	Lou Whitaker, Det	2B
1979	John Castino, Min & Alfredo Griffin, Tor	3B SS
1980	Joe Charboneau, Cle	OF-DH
1981	Dave Righetti, NY	P
1982	Cal Ripken, Jr., Bal	SS-3B
1983	Ron Kittle, Chi	OF
1984	Alvin Davis, Sea	1B
1985	Ozzie Guillen, Chi	SS
1986	Jose Canseco, Oak	OF
1987	Mark McGwire, Oak	1B
1988	Walt Weiss, Oak	SS
1989	Gregg Olson, Bal	P
1990	Sandy Alomar, Jr., Cle	C
1991	Chuck Knoblauch, Min	2B
1992	Pat Listach, Mil	SS
1993	Tim Salmon, Cal	OF
1994	Bob Hamelin, KC	DH

The Sporting News' MVP Awards

When the major leagues temporarily discontinued their Most Valuable Player awards in 1929 (AL) and 1930 (NL), *The Sporting News* stepped in to present its own league honors—for MVP from 1929-45, for Player and Pitcher of the Year from 1948-91 and Major League Player of the Year in 1992. There were no awards given in 1946 and '47.

National League

Multiple winners: Carl Hubbell and Chuck Klein (2).

Year		Pos	Year		Pos	Year		Pos
1929	No selection		1935	Arky Vaughan, Pit	SS	1941	Dolf Camilli, Bklyn	1B
1930	Bill Terry, NY	1B	1936	Carl Hubbell, NY	P	1942	Mort Cooper, St.L	P
1931	Chuck Klein, Phi	OF	1937	Joe Medwick, St.L	OF	1943	Stan Musial, St.L	OF
1932	Chuck Klein, Phi	OF	1938	Ernie Lombardi, Cin	C	1944	Marty Marion, St.L	SS
1933	Carl Hubbell, NY	P	1939	Bucky Walters, Cin	P	1945	Tommy Holmes, Bos	OF
1934	Dizzy Dean, St.L	P	1940	Frank McCormick, Cin	1B			

American League

Multiple winners: Jimmie Foxx and Lou Gehrig (3); Joe DiMaggio and Hank Greenberg (2).

Year		Pos	Year		Pos	Year		Pos
1929	Al Simmons, Phi	OF	1935	Hank Greenberg, Det	1B	1941	Joe DiMaggio, NY	OF
1930	Joe Cronin, Wash	SS	1936	Lou Gehrig, NY	1B	1942	Joe Gordon, NY	2B
1931	Lou Gehrig, NY	1B	1937	Charlie Gehringer, Det	2B	1943	Spud Chandler, NY	P
1932	Jimmie Foxx, Phi	1B	1938	Jimmie Foxx, Bos	1B	1944	Bobby Doerr, Bos	2B
1933	Jimmie Foxx, Phi	1B	1939	Joe DiMaggio, NY	OF	1945	Eddie Mayo, Det	2B
1934	Lou Gehrig, NY	1B	1940	Hank Greenberg, Det	OF			

The Sporting News' Player of the Year

National League

Multiple winners: Hank Aaron, Ernie Banks, Barry Bonds, Andre Dawson, George Foster, Willie Mays, Dale Murphy, Stan Musial and Mike Schmidt (2).

Year		Pos	Year		Pos	Year		Pos
1948	Stan Musial, St.L	OF-1B	1963	Hank Aaron, Mil	OF	1978	Dave Parker, Pit	OF
1949	Enos Slaughter, St.L	OF	1964	Ken Boyer, St.L	3B	1979	Keith Hernandez, St.L	1B
1950	Ralph Kiner, Pit	OF	1965	Willie Mays, SF	OF	1980	Mike Schmidt, Phi	3B
1951	Stan Musial, St.L	OF	1966	Roberto Clemente, Pit	OF	1981	Andre Dawson, Mon	OF
1952	Hank Sauer, Chi	OF	1967	Orlando Cepeda, St.L	1B	1982	Dale Murphy, Atl	OF
1953	Roy Campanella, Bklyn	C	1968	Pete Rose, Cin	OF	1983	Dale Murphy, Atl	OF
1954	Willie Mays, NY	OF	1969	Willie McCovey, SF	1B	1984	Ryne Sandberg, Chi	2B
1955	Duke Snider, Bklyn	OF				1985	Willie McGee, St.L	OF
1956	Hank Aaron, Mil	OF	1970	Johnny Bench, Cin	C	1986	Mike Schmidt, Phi	3B
1957	Stan Musial, St.L	1B	1971	Joe Torre, St.L	3B	1987	Andre Dawson, Chi	OF
1958	Ernie Banks, Chi	SS	1972	Billy Williams, Chi	OF	1988	Andy Van Slyke, St.L	OF
1959	Ernie Banks, Chi	SS	1973	Bobby Bonds, SF	OF	1989	Kevin Mitchell, SF	OF
1960	Dick Groat, Pit	SS	1974	Lou Brock, St.L	OF			
1961	Frank Robinson, Cin	OF	1975	Joe Morgan, Cin	2B	1990	Barry Bonds, Pit	OF
1962	Maury Wills, LA	SS	1976	George Foster, Cin	OF	1991	Barry Bonds, Pit	OF
			1977	George Foster, Cin	OF			

American League

Multiple winners: Don Mattingly (3); Al Kaline, Harmon Killebrew, Mickey Mantle, Roger Maris, Tony Oliva, Cal Ripken, Jr. and Ted Williams (2).

Year		Pos	Year		Pos	Year		Pos
1948	Lou Boudreau, Cle	SS	1963	Al Kaline, Det	OF	1978	Jim Rice, Bos	OF
1949	Ted Williams, Bos	OF	1964	Brooks Robinson, Bal	3B	1979	Don Baylor, Cal	OF-DH
1950	Phil Rizzuto, NY	SS	1965	Tony Oliva, Min	OF	1980	George Brett, KC	3B
1951	Ferris Fain, Phi	1B	1966	Frank Robinson, Bal	OF	1981	Tony Armas, Oak	OF
1952	Luke Easter, Cle	1B	1967	Carl Yastrzemski, Bos	OF	1982	Robin Yount, Mil	SS
1953	Al Rosen, Cle	3B	1968	Ken Harrelson, Bos	OF	1983	Cal Ripken, Jr., Bal	SS
1954	Bobby Avila, Cle	2B	1969	Harmon Killebrew, Min	INF	1984	Don Mattingly, NY	1B
1955	Al Kaline, Det	OF				1985	Don Mattingly, NY	1B
1956	Mickey Mantle, NY	OF	1970	Harmon Killebrew, Min	INF	1986	Don Mattingly, NY	1B
1957	Ted Williams, Bos	OF	1971	Tony Oliva, Min	OF	1987	George Bell, NY	OF
1958	Jackie Jensen, Bos	OF	1972	Dick Allen, Chi	1B	1988	Jose Canseco, Oak	OF
1959	Nellie Fox, Chi	2B	1973	Reggie Jackson, Oak	OF	1989	Ruben Sierra, Tex	OF
1960	Roger Maris, NY	OF	1974	Jeff Burroughs, Tex	OF			
1961	Roger Maris, NY	OF	1975	Fred Lynn, Bos	OF	1990	Cecil Fielder, Det	1B
1962	Mickey Mantle, NY	OF	1976	Thurman Munson, NY	C	1991	Cal Ripken, Jr., Bal	SS
			1977	Rod Carew, Min	1B			

NL and AL Combined

1992	Gary Sheffield, SD	3B	1993	Frank Thomas, Chi	1B	1994	Jeff Bagwell, Hou	1B

Annual Awards (Cont.)

The Sporting News' Pitchers of the Year

National League

Multiple winners: Steve Carlton, Sandy Koufax and Warren Spahn (4); Greg Maddux (3); Bob Gibson, Robin Roberts, Tom Seaver and Rick Sutcliffe (2).

Year		Year		Year		Year	
1948	Johnny Sain, Bos.	1960	Vernon Law, Pit.	1972	Steve Carlton, Phi.	1984	Rick Sutcliffe, Chi.
1949	Howie Pollet, St.L.	1961	Warren Spahn, Mil.	1973	Ron Bryant, SF	1985	Dwight Gooden, NY
1950	Jim Konstanty, Phi.	1962	Don Drysdale, LA	1974	Mike Marshall, LA	1986	Mike Scott, Hou.
1951	Preacher Roe, Bklyn.	1963	Sandy Koufax, LA	1975	Tom Seaver, NY	1987	Rick Sutcliffe, Chi.
1952	Robin Roberts, Phi.	1964	Sandy Koufax, LA	1976	Randy Jones, SD	1988	Orel Hershiser, LA
1953	Warren Spahn, Mil.	1965	Sandy Koufax, LA	1977	Steve Carlton, Phi.	1989	Mark Davis, SD
1954	Johnny Antonelli, NY	1966	Sandy Koufax, LA	1978	Vida Blue, SF	1990	Doug Drabek, Pit.
1955	Robin Roberts, Phi.	1967	Mike McCormick, SF	1979	Joe Niekro, Hou.	1991	Tom Glavine, Atl.
1956	Don Newcombe, Bklyn.	1968	Bob Gibson, St.L.	1980	Steve Carlton, Phi.	1992	Greg Maddux, Chi.
1957	Warren Spahn, Mil.	1969	Tom Seaver, NY	1981	Fernando Valenzuela, LA	1993	Greg Maddux, Atl.
1958	Warren Spahn, Mil.	1970	Bob Gibson, St.L.	1982	Steve Carlton, Phi.	1994	Greg Maddux, Atl.
1959	Sam Jones, SF	1971	Ferguson Jenkins, Chi.	1983	John Denny, Phi.		

American League

Multiple winners: Whitey Ford, Bob Lemon and Jim Palmer (3); Roger Clemens, Denny McLain, Billy Pierce and Bret Saberhagen (2).

Year		Year		Year		Year	
1948	Bob Lemon, Cle.	1960	Chuck Estrada, Bal.	1972	Wilbur Wood, Chi.	1984	Willie Hernandez, Det.
1949	Ellis Kinder, Bos.	1961	Whitey Ford, NY	1973	Jim Palmer, Bal.	1985	Bret Saberhagen, KC
1950	Bob Lemon, Cle.	1962	Dick Donovan, Cle.	1974	Catfish Hunter, Oak.	1986	Roger Clemens, Bos.
1951	Bob Feller, Cle.	1963	Whitey Ford, NY	1975	Jim Palmer, Bal.	1987	Jimmy Key, Tor.
1952	Bobby Shantz, Phi.	1964	Dean Chance, LA	1976	Jim Palmer, Bal.	1988	Frank Viola, Min.
1953	Bob Porterfield, Wash.	1965	Mudcat Grant, Min.	1977	Nolan Ryan, Cal.	1989	Bret Saberhagen, KC
1954	Bob Lemon, Cle.	1966	Jim Kaat, Min.	1978	Ron Guidry, NY	1990	Bob Welch, Oak.
1955	Whitey Ford, NY.	1967	Jim Lonborg, Bos.	1979	Mike Flanagan, Bal.	1991	Roger Clemens, Bos.
1956	Billy Pierce, Chi.	1968	Denny McLain, Det.	1980	Steve Stone, Bal.	1992	Dennis Eckersley, Oak.
1957	Billy Pierce, Chi.	1969	Denny McLain, Det.	1981	Jack Morris, Det.	1993	Jack McDowell, Chi.
1958	Bob Turley, NY	1970	Sam McDowell, Cle	1982	Dave Stieb, Tor.	1994	Jimmy Key, NY
1959	Early Wynn, Chi.	1971	Vida Blue, Oak.	1983	LaMarr Hoyt, Chi.		

The Sporting News' Rookies of the Year

One award was presented from 1946-48 and in 1950. Two awards (one for each league) were presented in 1949 and from 1951-62. And four awards (best rookie player and pitcher in each league) have been regularly presented since 1963.

NL and AL Combined

Year			Year		
1946	Del Ennis, Philadelphia, NL	OF	1948	Richie Ashburn, Philadelphia, NL	OF
1947	Jackie Robinson, Brooklyn	1B	1950	Whitey Ford, New York, AL	P

National League

Year		Pos	Year	Pos	Year		Pos
1949	Don Newcombe, Bklyn	P	1964	Richie Allen, Phi 3B	1974	Greg Gross, Hou ....OF
1950	Combined pick (see above)			& Billy McCool, Cin ....P		& John D'Acquisto, SF ....P
1951	Willie Mays, NY	OF	1965	Joe Morgan, Hou 2B	1975	Gary Carter, Mon ....OF-C
1952	Joe Black, Bklyn	P		& Frank Linzy, SF ....P		& John Montefusco, SF ....P
1953	Jim Gilliam, Bklyn	2B	1966	Tommy Helms, Cin 3B	1976	Larry Herndon, SF ....OF
1954	Wally Moon, St.L	OF		& Don Sutton, LA ....P		Butch Metzger, SD.........P
1955	Bill Virdon, St.L	OF	1967	Lee May, Cin 1B	1977	Andre Dawson, Mon ....OF
1956	Frank Robinson, Cin	OF		& Dick Hughes, St.L ....P		Bob Owchinko, SD ....P
1957	Ed Bouchee, Phi	1B	1968	Johnny Bench, Cin C	1978	Bob Horner, Atl...........3B
	& Jack Sanford, Phi	P		Jerry Koosman, NY ....P		& Don Robinson, Pit ....P
1958	Orlando Cepeda, SF	1B	1969	Coco Laboy, Mon 3B	1979	Jeff Leonard, Hou ....OF
	& Carlton Willey, Mil	P		Tom Griffin, Hou ....P		Rick Sutcliffe, LA.........P
1959	Willie McCovey, SF	1B	1970	Bernie Carbo, Cin ....OF	1980	Lonnie Smith, Phi ....OF
1960	Frank Howard, LA	OF		& Carl Morton, Mon.........P		& Bill Gullickson, Mon ....P
1961	Billy Williams, Chi	OF	1971	Earl Williams, Atl C	1981	Tim Raines, Mon ....OF
	& Ken Hunt, Cin	P		& Reggie Cleveland, St.L........P		& Fernando Valenzuela, LA ...P
1962	Ken Hubbs, Chi	2B	1972	Dave Rader, SF C	1982	Johnny Ray, Pit 2B
1963	Pete Rose, Cin	2B		& Jon Matlack, NY ....P		Steve Bedrosian, Atl ....P
	& Ray Culp, Phi	P	1973	Gary Matthews, SF ....OF	1983	Darryl Strawberry, NY.......OF
				& Steve Rogers, Mon ....P		Craig McMurtry, Atl ....P

Year		Pos
1984	Juan Samuel, Phi	2B
	& Dwight Gooden, NY	P
1985	Vince Coleman, St.L	OF
	& Tom Browning, Cin	P
1986	Robby Thompson, SF	2B
	Todd Worrell, St.L	P
1987	Benito Santiago, SD	C
	& Mike Dunne, Pit	P
1988	Mark Grace, Chi	1B
	Tim Belcher, LA	P
1989	Jerome Walton, Chi	OF
	& Andy Benes, SD	P
1990	David Justice, Atl	OF
	Mike Harkey, Chi	P
1991	Jeff Bagwell, Hou	1B
	Al Osuna, Hou	P
1992	Eric Karros, LA	1B
	& Tim Wakefield, Pit	P
1993	Mike Piazza, LA	C
	& Kirk Rueter, Mon	P
1994	Raul Mondesi, LA	OF
	Steve Trachsel, Chi	P

American League

Year		Pos
1949	Roy Sievers, St.L	OF
1950	Combined pick (see p.138)	
1951	Minnie Minoso, Chi	OF
1952	Clint Courtney, St.L	C
1953	Harvey Kuenn, Det	SS
1954	Bob Grim, NY	P
1955	Herb Score, Cle	P
1956	Luis Aparicio, Chi	SS
1957	Tony Kubek, NY	INF-OF
1958	Albie Pearson, Wash	OF
	& Ryne Duren, NY	P
1959	Bob Allison, Wash	OF
1960	Ron Hansen, Bal	SS
1961	Dick Howser, KC	SS
	& Don Schwall, Bos	P
1962	Tom Tresh, NY	OF-SS
1963	Pete Ward, Chi	3B
	& Gary Peters, Chi	P
1964	Tony Oliva, Min	OF
	& Wally Bunker, Bal	P
1965	Curt Blefary, Bal	OF
	& Marcelino Lopez, Cal.	P
1966	Tommie Agee, Chi	OF
	& Jim Nash, KC	P
1967	Rod Carew, Min	2B
	& Tom Phoebus, Bal	P
1968	Del Unser, Wash	OF
	& Stan Bahnsen, NY	P
1969	Carlos May, Chi	OF
	& Mike Nagy, Bos	P
1970	Roy Foster, Cle	OF
	& Bert Blyleven, Min	P
1971	Chris Chambliss, NY	1B
	& Bill Parsons, Mil	P
1972	Carlton Fisk, Bos	C
	& Dick Tidrow, Cle	P
1973	Al Bumbry, Bal	OF
	& Steve Busby, KC	P
1974	Mike Hargrove, Tex	1B
	& Frank Tanana, Cal	P
1975	Fred Lynn, Bos	OF
	& Dennis Eckersley, Cle	P
1976	Butch Wynegar, Min	C
	& Mark Fidrych, Det	P
1977	Mitchell Page, Oak	OF
	& Dave Rozema, Det	P
1978	Paul Molitor, Mil	2B
	& Rich Gale, KC	P
1979	Pat Putnam, Tex	1B
	& Mark Clear, Cal	P
1980	Joe Charboneau, Cle	OF
	& Britt Burns, Chi	P
1981	Rich Gedman, Bos	C
	& Dave Righetti, NY	P
1982	Cal Ripken, Jr., Bal	SS-3B
	& Ed Vande Berg, Sea	P
1983	Ron Kittle, Chi	OF
	& Mike Boddicker, Bal	P
1984	Alvin Davis, Sea	1B
	& Mark Langston, Sea	P
1985	Ozzie Guillen, Chi	SS
	& Teddy Higuera, Mil	P
1986	Jose Canseco, Oak	OF
	& Mark Eichhorn, Tor	P
1987	Mark McGwire, Oak	1B
	& Mike Henneman, Det	P
1988	Walt Weiss, Oak	SS
	& Bryan Harvey, Cal	P
1989	Craig Worthington, Bal	3B
	& Tom Gordon, KC	P
1990	Sandy Alomar, Jr., Cle	C
	& Kevin Appier, KC	P
1991	Chuck Knoblauch, Min	2B
	& Juan Guzman, Tor	P
1992	Pat Listach, Mil	SS
	& Cal Eldred, Mil	P
1993	Tim Salmon, Cal	OF
	& Aaron Sele, Bos	P
1994	Bob Hamelin, KC	DH
	Brian Anderson, Cal	P

The Sporting News' Manager of the Year

One award was presented from 1936-85. Two awards (one for each league) have been presented since 1986. Note that (*) indicates a league pennant (1936-68) or division championship (since 1969).

Multiple winners: Walter Alston, Leo Durocher, Joe McCarthy and Casey Stengel (3); Tony La Russa, Jim Leyland, Bill McKechnie, Danny Murtaugh, Billy Southworth, Bill Virdon and Earl Weaver (2).

NL and AL Combined

Year		Improvement		
1936	Joe McCarthy, NY (AL)	89-60	to	102-51*
1937	Bill McKechnie, Bos.(NL)	71-83	to	79-73
1938	Joe McCarthy, NY (AL)	102-52*	to	99-53*
1939	Leo Durocher, Bklyn.(NL)	69-80	to	84-69
1940	Bill McKechnie, Cin	97-57*	to	100-53*
1941	Billy Southworth, St.L.(NL)	84-69	to	97-56
1942	Billy Southworth, St.L.(NL)	97-56	to	106-48*
1943	Joe McCarthy, NY (AL)	103-51*	to	98-56*
1944	Leo Durocher, St.L.(AL)	72-80	to	89-65*
1945	Ossie Bluege, Wash.	64-90	to	87-67
1946	Eddie Dyer, St.L.(NL)	95-59	to	98-58*
1947	Bucky Harris, NY (AL)	87-67	to	97-57*
1948	Bill Meyer, Pit.	62-92	to	83-71
1949	Casey Stengel, NY (AL)	94-60	to	97-57*
1950	Red Rolfe, Det.	87-67	to	95-59
1951	Leo Durocher, NY (NL)	86-68	to	98-59*
1952	Eddie Stanky, St.L.	81-73	to	88-66
1953	Casey Stengel, NY (AL)	95-59*	to	99-52*
1954	Leo Durocher, NY (NL)	70-84	to	97-57*
1955	Walter Alston, Bklyn	92-62	to	98-55*
1956	Birdie Tebbetts, Cin	75-79	to	91-63
1957	Fred Hutchinson, St.L.	76-78	to	87-67
1958	Casey Stengel, NY (AL)	98-56*	to	92-62*
1959	Walter Alston, LA	71-83	to	88-68*
1960	Danny Murtaugh, Pit	78-76	to	95-59*
1961	Ralph Houk, NY (AL)	97-57*	to	109-53*
1962	Bill Rigney, LA (AL)	70-91	to	86-76
1963	Walter Alston, LA	102-63	to	99-63*
1964	Johnny Keane, St.L.	93-69	to	93-69*
1965	Sam Mele, Min	79-83	to	102-60*
1966	Hank Bauer, Bal	94-68	to	97-63*
1967	Dick Williams, Bos	72-90	to	92-70*
1968	Mayo Smith, Det	91-71	to	103-59*
1969	Gil Hodges, NY (NL)	73-89	to	100-62*
1970	Danny Murtaugh, Pit	88-74	to	89-73*
1971	Charlie Fox, SF	86-76	to	90-72*
1972	Chuck Tanner, Chi. (AL)	79-83	to	87-67
1973	Gene Mauch, Mon	70-86	to	79-83

Annual Awards (Cont.)
The Sporting News' Manager of the Year
NL and AL Combined

Year		Improvement		Year		Improvement	
1974	Bill Virdon, NY (AL)	80-82	to 89-73	1980	Bill Virdon, Hou	89-73	to 93-70*
1975	Darrell Johnson, Bos.	84-78	to 95-65*	1981	Billy Martin, Oak	83-79	to 64-45*
1976	Danny Ozark, Phi	86-76	to 101-61*	1982	Whitey Herzog, St.L.	59-43	to 92-70*
1977	Earl Weaver, Bal	88-74	to 97-64	1983	Tony La Russa, Chi. (AL)	87-75	to 99-63*
1978	George Bamberger, Mil.	67-95	to 93-69	1984	Jim Frey, Chi. (NL)	71-91	to 96-75*
1979	Earl Weaver, Bal	90-71	to 102-57*	1985	Bobby Cox, Tor.	89-73	to 99-62*

Note: In 1981, both league seasons were reduced to 110 games or less due to a players' strike.

National League

Year		Improvement	
1986	Hal Lanier, Hou	83-79	to 96-66*
1987	Buck Rodgers, Mon	78-83	to 91-71
1988	Tommy Lasorda, LA	73-89	to 94-67*
	& Jim Leyland, Pit.	80-82	to 85-75
1989	Don Zimmer, Chi	77-85	to 93-69*
1990	Jim Leyland, Pit	74-88	to 95-67
1991	Bobby Cox, Atl.	65-97	to 94-68*
1992	Jim Leyland, Pit	98-64	to 96-66*
1993	Bobby Cox, Atl	98-64	to 104-58*
1994	Felipe Alou, Mon	74-40	to 74-40

American League

Year		Improvement	
1986	John McNamara, Bos.	81-81	to 95-66*
1987	Sparky Anderson, Det	87-75	to 98-64*
1988	Tony La Russa, Oak	81-81	to 104-58*
1989	Frank Robinson, Bal	54-107	to 87-75
1990	Jeff Torborg, Chi	69-92	to 94-68
1991	Tom Kelly, Min.	74-88	to 95-67*
1992	Tony LaRussa, Oak	84-78	to 96-66*
1993	Johnny Oates, Bal	89-73	to 85-77
1994	Buck Showalter, NY	88-74	to 70-43

The Sporting News' Executive of the Year

Multiple winners: George Weiss (4); Branch Rickey (3); Ed Barrow, Harry Dalton, Bing Devine, Roland Hemond, Dick O'Connell, Gabe Paul, Hank Peters and Bill Veeck (2).

AL and NL Combined

Year			Year			Year		
1936	Branch Rickey, St.L	NL	1956	Gabe Paul, Cin	NL	1975	Dick O'Connell, Bos.	AL
1937	Ed Barrow, NY	AL	1957	Frank Lane, St.L	NL	1976	Joe Burke, KC	AL
1938	Warren Giles, Cin	NL	1958	Joe Brown, Pit	NL	1977	Bill Veeck, Chi.	AL
1939	Larry MacPhail, Bklyn	NL	1959	Buzzie Bavasi, LA	NL	1978	Spec Richardson, SF	NL
						1979	Hank Peters, Bal	AL
1940	W.O. Briggs Sr., Det	AL	1960	George Weiss, NY	AL			
1941	Ed Barrow, NY	AL	1961	Dan Topping, NY	AL	1980	Tal Smith, Hou	NL
1942	Branch Rickey, St.L	NL	1962	Fred Haney, LA	AL	1981	John McHale, Mon	NL
1943	Clark Griffith, Wash	AL	1963	Bing Devine, St.L	NL	1982	Harry Dalton, Mil	AL
1944	William DeWitt, St.L	AL	1964	Bing Devine, St.L	NL	1983	Hank Peters, Bal	AL
1945	Philip Wrigley, Chi	NL	1965	Calvin Griffith, Min	AL	1984	Dallas Green, Chi	NL
1946	Thomas Yawkey, Bos	AL	1966	Lee MacPhail, Commissioner's Office		1985	John Schuerholz, KC	AL
1947	Branch Rickey, Bklyn	NL				1986	Frank Cashen, NY	NL
1948	Bill Veeck, Cle	AL	1967	Dick O'Connell, Bos.	AL	1987	Al Rosen, SF	NL
1949	Robert Carpenter, Phi	NL	1968	James Campbell, Det	AL	1988	Fred Claire, LA	NL
			1969	John Murphy, NY	NL	1989	Roland Hemond, Bal	AL
1950	George Weiss, NY	AL						
1951	George Weiss, NY	AL	1970	Harry Dalton, Bal	AL	1990	Bob Quinn, Cin	NL
1952	George Weiss, NY	AL	1971	Cedric Tallis, KC	AL	1991	Andy MacPhail, Min	AL
1953	Louis Perini, Mil	NL	1972	Roland Hemond, Chi	AL	1992	Dan Duquette, Mon	NL
1954	Horace Stoneham, NY	NL	1973	Bob Howsam, Cin	NL	1993	Lee Thomas, Phi	NL
1955	Walter O'Malley, Bklyn	NL	1974	Gabe Paul, NY	AL	1994	John Hart, Cle	AL

Wide World Photos
Branch Rickey

Wide World Photos
George Weiss

Wide World Photos
Gabe Paul

Wide World Photos
Bill Veeck

COLLEGE BASEBALL

College World Series

The NCAA Division I College World Series has been held in Kalamazoo, Mich. (1947-48), Wichita, Kan. (1949) and Omaha, Neb. (since 1950).

Multiple winners: USC (11); Arizona St. (5); Texas (4); Arizona and Minnesota (3); CS-Fullerton, California, LSU, Miami-FL, Michigan, Oklahoma and Stanford (2).

Year	Winner	Coach	Score	Loser	Year	Winner	Coach	Score	Loser
1947	California	Clint Evans	8-7	Yale	1973	USC	Rod Dedeaux	4-3	Ariz. St.
1948	USC	Sam Barry	9-2	Yale	1974	USC	Rod Dedeaux	7-3	Miami, FL
1949	Texas	Bibb Falk	10-3	W. Forest	1975	Texas	Cliff Gustafson	5-1	S. Carolina
1950	Texas	Bibb Falk	3-0	Wash. St.	1976	Arizona	Jerry Kindall	7-1	E. Michigan
1951	Oklahoma	Jack Baer	3-2	Tennessee	1977	Arizona St.	Jim Brock	2-1	S. Carolina
1952	Holy Cross	Jack Barry	8-4	Missouri	1978	USC	Rod Dedeaux	10-3	Ariz. St.
1953	Michigan	Ray Fisher	7-5	Texas	1979	CS-Fullerton	Augie Garrido	2-1	Arkansas
1954	Missouri	Hi Simmons	4-1	Rollins	1980	Arizona	Jerry Kindall	5-3	Hawaii
1955	Wake Forest	Taylor Sanford	7-6	W. Mich.	1981	Arizona St.	Jim Brock	7-4	Okla. St.
1956	Minnesota	Dick Siebert	12-1	Arizona	1982	Miami-FL	Ron Fraser	9-3	Wichita St.
1957	California	Geo. Wolfman	1-0	Penn St.	1983	Texas	Cliff Gustafson	4-3	Alabama
1958	USC	Rod Dedeaux	8-7	Missouri	1984	CS-Fullerton	Augie Garrido	3-1	Texas
1959	Oklahoma St.	Toby Greene	5-3	Arizona	1985	Miami-FL	Ron Fraser	10-6	Texas
1960	Minnesota	Dick Siebert	2-1	USC	1986	Arizona	Jerry Kindall	10-2	Fla. St.
1961	USC	Rod Dedeaux	1-0	Okla. St.	1987	Stanford	M.Marquess	9-5	Okla. St.
1962	Michigan	Don Lund	5-4	S. Clara	1988	Stanford	M.Marquess	9-4	Ariz. St.
1963	USC	Rod Dedeaux	5-2	Arizona	1989	Wichita St.	G.Stephenson	5-3	Texas
1964	Minnesota	Dick Siebert	5-1	Missouri	1990	Georgia	Steve Webber	2-1	Okla. St.
1965	Arizona St.	Bobby Winkles	2-1	Ohio St.	1991	LSU	Skip Bertman	6-3	Wichita St.
1966	Ohio St.	Marty Karow	8-2	Okla. St.	1992	Pepperdine	Andy Lopez	3-2	CS-Fullerton
1967	Arizona St.	Bobby Winkles	11-2	Houston	1993	LSU	Skip Bertman	8-0	Wichita St.
1968	USC	Rod Dedeaux	4-3	So. Ill.	1994	Oklahoma	Larry Cochell	13-5	Ga. Tech
1969	Arizona St.	Bobby Winkles	10-1	Tulsa					
1970	USC	Rod Dedeaux	2-1	Fla. St.					
1971	USC	Rod Dedeaux	7-2	So. Ill.					
1972	USC	Rod Dedeaux	1-0	Ariz. St.					

Most Outstanding Players

The Most Outstanding Player has been selected every year of the College World Series since 1949. Winners who did not play for the CWS champion are listed in **bold** type. No player has won the award more than once.

Year		Year		Year	
1949	**Charles Teague,** W. Forest	1965	Sal Bando, Ariz. St.	1980	Terry Francona, Arizona
		1966	Steve Arlin, Ohio St.	1981	Stan Holmes, Ariz. St.
1950	**Ray VanCleef,** Rutgers	1967	Ron Davini, Ariz. St.	1982	Dan Smith, Miami-FL
1951	**Sidney Hatfield,** Tenn.	1968	Bill Seinsoth, USC	1983	Calvin Schiraldi, Texas
1952	James O'Neill, Holy Cross	1969	John Dolinsek, Ariz. St.	1984	John Fishel, CS-Fullerton
1953	**J.L. Smith,** Texas	1970	**Gene Ammann,** Fla. St.	1985	Greg Ellena, Miami-FL
1954	**Tom Yewcic,** Mich. St.	1971	**Jerry Tabb,** Tulsa	1986	Mike Senne, Arizona
1955	**Tom Borland,** Okla. St.	1972	Russ McQueen, USC	1987	Paul Carey, Stanford
1956	Jerry Thomas, Minn.	1973	**Dave Winfield,** Minn.	1988	Lee Plemel, Stanford
1957	**Cal Emery,** Penn St.	1974	George Milke, USC	1989	Greg Brummett, Wich. St.
1958	Bill Thom, USC	1975	Mickey Reichenbach, Texas		
1959	Jim Dobson, Okla. St.	1976	Steve Powers, Arizona	1990	Mike Rebhan, Georgia
1960	John Erickson, Minn.	1977	Bob Horner, Ariz. St.	1991	Gary Hymel, LSU
1961	**Littleton Fowler,** Okla. St.	1978	Rod Boxberger, USC	1992	**Phil Nevin,** CS-Fullerton
1962	**Bob Garibaldi,** Santa Clara	1979	Tony Hudson, CS-Fullerton	1993	Todd Walker, LSU
1963	Bud Hollowell, USC			1994	Chip Glass, Oklahoma
1964	**Joe Ferris,** Maine				

Annual Awards
Golden Spikes Award

First presented in 1978 by USA Baseball, honoring the nation's best amateur player. Alex Fernandez, the 1990 winner, was the first junior college player chosen.

Year		Year		Year	
1978	Bob Horner, Ariz. St, 2B	1984	Oddibe McDowell, Ariz. St., OF	1990	Alex Fernandez, Miami-Dade, P
1979	Tim Wallach, CS-Fullerton, 1B	1985	Will Clark, Miss. St., 1B	1991	Mike Kelly, Ariz. St., OF
1980	Terry Francona, Arizona, OF	1986	Mike Loynd, Fla. St., P	1992	Phil Nevin, CS-Fullerton, 3B
1981	Mike Fuentes, Fla. St., OF	1987	Jim Abbott, Michigan, P	1993	Darren Dreifort, Wichita St., P
1982	Augie Schmidt, N. Orleans, SS	1988	Robin Ventura, Okla. St., 3B	1994	TBA
1983	Dave Magadan, Alabama, 1B	1989	Ben McDonald, LSU, P		

Annual Awards (Cont.)
Baseball America Player of the Year

Presented to the College Player of the Year since 1981 by *Baseball America*.

Year		Year		Year	
1981	Mike Sodders, Ariz. St., 3B	1986	Casey Close, Michigan, OF	1991	David McCarty, Stanford, 1B
1982	Jeff Ledbetter, Fla. St., OF/P	1987	Robin Ventura, Okla. St., 3B	1992	Phil Nevin, CS-Fullerton, 3B
1983	Dave Magadan, Alabama, 1B	1988	John Olerud, Wash. St., 1B/P	1993	Brooks Kieschnick, Texas, DH/P
1984	Oddibe McDowell, Ariz. St., OF	1989	Ben McDonald, LSU, P	1994	Jason Varitek, Ga. Tech, C
1985	Pete Incaviglia, Okla. St., OF	1990	Mike Kelly, Ariz. St., OF		

Dick Howser Trophy

Presented to the College Player of the Year since 1987 by the American Baseball Coaches Association. Named after the late two-time All-America shortstop and college coach at Florida St., Howser was also a major league manager with Kansas City and the New York Yankees.
Multiple winner: Brooks Kieschnick (2).

Year		Year		Year	
1987	Mike Fiore, Miami-FL, OF	1990	Paul Ellis, UCLA, C	1993	Brooks Kieschnick, Texas, DH/P
1988	Robin Ventura, Okla. St., 3B	1991	Bobby Jones, Fresno St., P	1994	Jason Varitek, Ga. Tech, C
1989	Scott Bryant, Texas, DH	1992	Brooks Kieschnick, Texas, DH/P		

Baseball America Coach of the Year

Presented to the College Player of the Year since 1981 by *Baseball America*.
Multiple winner: Dave Snow and Gene Stephenson (2).

Year		Year		Year	
1981	Ron Fraser, Miami-FL	1986	Skip Bertman, LSU	1990	Steve Webber, Georgia
1982	Gene Stephenson, Wichita St.		& Dave Snow, Loyola-CA	1991	Jim Hendry, Creighton
1983	Barry Shollenberger, Alabama	1987	Mark Marquess, Stanford	1992	Andy Lopez, Pepperdine
1984	Augie Garrido, CS-Fullerton	1988	Jim Brock, Arizona St.	1993	Gene Stephenson, Wichita St.
1985	Ron Polk, Mississippi St.	1989	Dave Snow, Long Beach St.	1994	Jim Morris, Miami-FL

All-Time Winningest Coaches
Coaches active in 1994 in **bold** type.

Top 10 Winning Percentage
(Minimum 10 years in Division I)

		Yrs	W	L	T	Pct
1	John Barry	40	619	147	6	.806
2	**Cliff Gustafson**	27	1344	330	2	.803
3	W.J. Disch	29	465	115	0	.802
4	Harry Carlson	17	143	41	0	.777
5	**Gene Stephenson**	17	951	292	3	.765
6	**Gary Ward**	17	862	273	1	.760
7	George Jacobs	11	76	25	0	.752
	Bobby Winkles	13	524	173	0	.752
9	**Mike Martin**	15	814	280	3	.744
	Frank Sancet	23	831	283	8	.744

Top 10 Victories

		Yrs	W	L	T	Pct
1	**Cliff Gustafson**	27	1344	330	2	.803
2	Rod Dedeaux	45	1332	571	11	.699
3	Ron Fraser	30	1271	438	9	.742
4	**Bobo Brayton**	33	1162	523	8	.690
5	**Bill Wilhelm**	36	1161	536	10	.683
6	**Al Ogletree**	37	1145	624	10	.647
7	Jim Brock	23	1100	440	0	.714
8	**Jack Stallings**	34	1092	673	5	.619
9	**Chuck Hartman**	35	1069	511	3	.677
10	**Augie Garrido**	26	1050	499	7	.678

Other NCAA Champions
Divison II

Multiple winner: Florida Southern (7); Cal Poly Pomona (3); CS-Northridge, Jacksonville St., Tampa, Troy St., UC-Irvine and UC-Riverside (2).

Year		Year		Year		Year	
1968	Chapman, CA	1975	Florida Southern	1982	UC-Riverside	1990	Jacksonville St., AL
1969	Illinois St.	1976	Cal Poly Pomona	1983	Cal Poly Pomona	1991	Jacksonville St., AL
1970	CS-Northridge	1977	UC-Riverside	1984	CS-Northridge	1992	Tampa
1971	Florida Southern	1978	Florida Southern	1985	Florida Southern	1993	Tampa
1972	Florida Southern	1979	Valdosta St., GA	1986	Troy St., AL	1994	Central Missouri St.
1973	UC-Irvine	1980	Cal Poly Pomona	1987	Troy St., AL		
1974	UC-Irvine	1981	Florida Southern	1988	Florida Southern		
				1989	Cal Poly SLO		

Divison III

Multiple winner: Marietta (3); CS-Stanislaus, Eastern Conn. St., Glassboro St., Ithaca and Montclair St. (2).

Year		Year		Year		Year	
1976	CS-Stanislaus	1981	Marietta, OH	1986	Marietta, OH	1991	Southern Maine
1977	CS-Stanislaus	1982	Eastern Conn. St.	1987	Monclair St., NJ	1992	Wm. Paterson, NJ
1978	Glassboro St., NJ	1983	Marietta, OH	1988	Ithaca, NY	1993	Montclair St., NJ
1979	Glassboro St., NJ	1984	Ramapo, NJ	1989	NC-Wesleyan	1994	Wisconsin-Oshkosh
1980	Ithaca, NY	1985	Wisconsin-Oshkosh	1990	Eastern Conn. St.		

Florida State quarterback **Charlie Ward** became the first Heisman Trophy winner to lead his team to the national championship since Pitt's Tony Dorsett in 1976.

COLLEGE FOOTBALL

COLLEGE FOOTBALL

by Ivan Maisel

Seminoles!

Heisman-winning QB Charlie Ward leads Florida St. to elusive national title despite losing to second-ranked Notre Dame.

Perhaps by the time you read this, the argument will have expired. Naaah. The case of Florida State vs. Notre Dame will remain a part of college football lore as long as there are echoes to be awakened, or at least as long as it took FSU coach Bobby Bowden to win his first national championship (28 years).

Proponents of the New Year's Day bowl games believe that postseason "Who's Number One?" debates such as *Colorado vs. Georgia Tech* (1990) and *Miami vs. Washington* (1991) actually promote college football. The 1993 season provided the ultimate test of whether the fuzzy nature of the bowls benefit the sport.

If you snack on "Who's No. 1?" arguments like artery-clogging theater popcorn, this one came in a No. 10 washtub, drowned in butter. Five teams— Florida State, Notre Dame, Nebraska, West Virginia and Auburn— went into the new year claiming the national title. The furor grew so loud that one voter in the Associated Press media poll, Loren Tate of the Champaign, Ill., *News-Gazette*, surrendered his ballot before the regular season ended.

Under the revised terms of the two-year-old Bowl Coalition, the combined wis-dom of the AP media and *USA Today*-CNN coaches polls at the end of the regular season decided which two schools squared off for the national championship on Jan. 1. Florida State (11-1) won the final regular season AP poll, but placed second to *USA Today*/CNN champ Nebraska (11-0) in the Bowl Poll.

The Seminoles and Cornhuskers met in the 60th edition of the Orange Bowl game, and any playoff matchup, no matter how arrived at, would have had trouble equaling the unruly excitement of FSU's last-second, 18-16 victory.

Missed field goals had cost Florida State the opportunity to play for a national championship in 1991 and 1992, so Bowden recruited Scott Bentley out of Aurora, Colo., to remedy the situation. And the freshman delivered— kicking a 22-yard field goal with 24 seconds left to regain the lead. Nebraska placekicker Byron Bennett had put the Huskers in front 16-15 less than a minute earlier from 27 yards out.

Twenty-four seconds can be an eternity in college football. A celebration penalty forced Florida State to kick off from its own 20. Barron Miles then returned the ball 23 yards to the Nebraska 43. After an incomplete pass, Nebraska quarterback Tommie Frazier pitched a 29-yard strike down the middle of the field to tight end Truman Bell.

No sooner had the scoreboard clock ticked down to 0:00 than Bowden underwent the now-traditional icy sideline shower and made the soggy trot toward midfield.

Ivan Maisel covers national college sports for *Newsday* in New York and is a columnist for *The Sporting News*. He was the national college football writer for *The Dallas Morning News* from 1987-94.

Brian Masck/Allsport

Tailback **Lee Becton** of Notre Dame scampers for the end zone on one of his two touchdown runs against Florida State. Becton gained 122 yards in the game as the Irish upset FSU, 31-24, in their No. 1 vs. No. 2 battle in South Bend on Nov. 13.

But the officials, after conferring with their cohorts in the press box, put one second back on the clock and cleared the field. Nebraska then called its final time-out.

The only person less prepared than Bowden for the game to continue may have been Bennett. He rushed out to attempt a 45-yard field goal and hooked it badly to the left.

"We've lost national championships, we thought, by missing kicks," Bowden said after the game. "Tonight, we won a national championship by making a kick." A few months later, Bowden altered that analysis somewhat. "We won," he said, "because somebody else missed a kick."

Bentley's field goal and Bennett's miss were only the final touches, however. The Seminoles won their first national title behind their trademark brand of fast defense and the unmatchable talents of quarterback Charlie Ward.

The senior from Thomasville, Ga., could run, throw and get out of the way so efficiently that he rarely played in a fourth quarter. He finished fourth in the nation in passing efficiency with 3,032 yards in the air, a completion percentage of .695 (264-for-380), 27 touchdowns and only four interceptions.

Ward's efforts earned him seven player and quarterback of the year awards in the postseason, including two that bordered on the historic. He became the first player since Tony Dorsett in 1976 to win the Heisman Trophy and a national championship in the same year, and the first football player to capture the Sullivan Award as the country's top amateur athlete since Army's Doc Blanchard and Arnold Tucker did it back-to-back in 1945 and '46.

He is also the third Heisman winner, along with Army halfback Pete Dawkins in 1958 and Nebraska tailback Mike Rozier in 1984 not to be chosen in the regular NFL Draft. Dawkins had a military obligation after his senior year while Rozier signed with the USFL and was later picked in the NFL supplemental draft. Ward, a four-year starter on the FSU basketball team, scared NFL teams off with a wait-and-see attitude about the NBA Draft (the New York Knicks later picked him in the first round).

That Bentley, who came from a Notre

Dame family and turned down a Notre Dame scholarship offer, would cost the Fighting Irish a national title added drama to a story already dripping with it.

Notre Dame head coach Lou Holtz went to bed New Year's Night secure in the belief that he had won his second national championship in eight years at South Bend.

Of the Bowl Poll Top 5, only FSU (12-1) and Notre Dame (11-1) had won their bowl games— the Irish edging Texas A&M, 24-21, in the Cotton Bowl. More importantly, at least in Holtz's mind, was the fact that on Nov. 13, Notre Dame had upset Florida State, 31-24.

Four years earlier, the Irish had finished 12-1 against the toughest schedule in the nation. Miami, however, had beaten Notre Dame, 27-10, so the pollsters awarded the 11-1 Hurricanes the national title.

"There's no way in this world that you can convince me after the criteria that they used in 1989, that they can possibly deny this football team in 1993," Holtz said.

"The first criteria for a tiebreaker in the NFL or any conference," Holtz argued, "is 'How did they do head-to-head?' And we won the football game."

While his logic was impeccable, Holtz was alone with his thoughts on Jan. 2. Florida State swept the major postseason polls, receiving 46 first place votes to Notre Dame's 12 in the final AP vote, and winning by margins of 36-25 in the Coaches poll, by 43-28 in the Hall of Fame vote for the MacArthur Bowl, and by 3-2 in the five-man Football Writers vote. The final *New York Times* computer ratings had Notre Dame fourth behind FSU, Florida and Auburn.

The year was a rollercoaster ride for Holtz. Early on he not only had to replace his entire offensive backfield (i.e., quarterback Rick Mirer and running backs Jerome Bettis and Reggie Brooks), but also weather the negative publicity generated by "Under the Tarnished Dome," an expose of his tenure at Notre Dame. The book, which painted Holtz as a man willing to cut ethical and NCAA corners in order to win football games, appeared in bookstores just as the season began.

Holtz stonewalled questions raised by authors Douglas S. Looney and Don Yaeger, but he responded more effectively by developing a winning team. With a sim-

Money Chase Has Game In State Of Flux

Though the pursuit of money has been an integral part of intercollegiate athletics since the first pig was skinned, the past year has been unprecedented in the brazen moves taken to fill Division I-A conference coffers.

The College Football Association television package with ABC and ESPN unraveled in February when the CFA's main attraction, the Southeastern Conference, walked out to make its own five-year, $125 million deal with CBS. The SEC-CBS pact will cover football and basketball beginning in 1996.

The Southwest Conference, founded in 1914, broke up in late February when its four healthiest members— Baylor, Texas, Texas A&M and Texas Tech— bolted for the Big Eight effective in 1996.

The move represented a compromise for the two biggest guns in the SWC, Texas and Texas A&M. The Pac-10, outwardly noncommittal about expansion, had reached agreements with the two schools in 1993 to issue invitations at the right moment.

That moment never arrived. To maneuver through the political shoals back home, the two universities had to take Baylor and Texas Tech with them wherever they went. That put the Pac-10 out of the picture.

The Big Eight's move to expand to 12 teams was topped on April 21 when the Western Athletic Conference announced it would grow to 16 schools beginning in 1996. The six new WAC members will include Rice, Southern Methodist and Texas Christian from the SWC, independent Tulsa and Big West defectors San Jose State and Nevada-Las Vegas.

The Big Eight will be renamed the Big 12 and split into two divisions while the WAC will divide itself into four "Quads." Both conference championships figure to be decided with well-hyped (and nationally-televised) playoff games like the SEC has done since 1992. By April, the Big Eight had signed contracts worth a total of $100 million with ABC and Liberty Media, Inc., which operates several regional cable networks.

The Big East's eight-team football conference followed the SEC to CBS, signing a five-year contract for $65 million. It also inked a cable deal with ESPN and ESPN2 for an additional $35 million.

The beginning of the end of the 79-year-old Southwest Conference came on Feb. 23, when Baylor president **Herbert Reynolds** (left), Board of Regents Chairman **Thomas Powers** (center) and athletic director **Dick Ellis** announced that the school would be joining the Big Eight in 1996. Texas, Texas A&M and Texas Tech joined the exodus from the SWC two days later.

Then there's the often-discussed possibility of a Division I-A national championship playoff to replace the Bowl Coalition—the four major Jan. 1 bowls, five conferences and Notre Dame who banded together three years ago in an attempt to stave off the demise of the bowl system.

In fact, the coalition may have hastened it. The controversy engendered by the debate over who was really No. 1 in 1993 gave resolve to NCAA officials to pursue what they perceive to be the last untouched gold mine in college sports.

The NCAA would love to duplicate the phenomenal success of its men's basketball tournament with a football version of the Final Four. March Madness is earning the NCAA $1 billion in TV money over seven years. While football won't generate quite those dollars, proponents believe a four-team, post-bowl playoff would earn close to $100 million annually.

That should be enough of a windfall to win over most reluctant university presidents. Indeed, none other than UCLA chancellor Charles Young, a long-standing playoff foe, has chaired two NCAA fact-finding groups looking into a playoff.

Young changed his mind, he said, because of former NCAA executive director Dick Schultz's State of the Association speech in 1993. Schultz suggested a I-A playoff may be the best method of financing gender equity.

The projected $100 million per year would be a lot of "new" money. But no one knows how accurate that projection is or what shape the final playoff would take.

"I think a four-team playoff maximizes the playoff revenue," Young says. "Beyond that, I think it may get smaller. At some point, there is a finite amount of advertising dollars, sponsorship dollars and community support."

The bowls use those same three criteria to rake in $70 million every year. Unfortunately, that's gross, not net. Net is about $39 million.

"A great deal of that money is poured right back into the bowls, and the hotels and airlines that support the bowls," says Ohio State athletic director Andy Geiger.

Update: The NCAA Presidents Commission, meeting June 28-29 in Kansas City, denied Young's committee permission to continue hashing out a playoff proposal, saying it was "an idea whose time has not come." The sentiment came as no surprise after a report in May that the study was producing more questions than answers.

"If there was any significant level of interest among the NCAA membership in a championship, it would make sense to continue working," said NCAA president Joseph Crowley. "However, the level of interest simply isn't there."

Meanwhile, major bowl committees and conference commissioners have set about revising the current Division I-A bowl coalition that expires after the 1994 season. See "College Sports" chapter for further details.

147

Placekickers **David Gordon** of Boston College (left) and **Scott Bentley** of Florida State celebrate after their last-second field goals won two of the year's biggest games. Gordon's 41-yard effort enabled BC to topple No. 1 Notre Dame on Nov. 20, while Bentley's 22-yarder upended Nebraska in the Orange Bowl.

ple, physical rushing attack and a much-improved defense, Notre Dame stunned Michigan, 27-23, in Ann Arbor on Sept. 11 and continued to win. The questions about the book ceased.

Two months later, No. 2 Notre Dame and No. 1 Florida State carried 9-0 records into their showdown before 59,075 at Notre Dame Stadium and millions more on national TV. It was easily the most bally-hooed 1 vs. 2 regular season game since Oklahoma and Nebraska met on Thanksgiving Day, 1971.

The Irish wore down the smaller, quicker Seminoles. Ward, bamboozled by a brisk wind, didn't sharpen his passes until the visitors trailed, 31-17, in the fourth quarter. With only 2:26 to play, he threw a fourth-down, 20-yard deflected touchdown pass to wide receiver Kez McCorvey to get Florida State within a touchdown.

Ward got one more chance from the Seminoles' 37 with 0:51 left on the clock.

After taking 41 seconds to move the ball to the Notre Dame 14, he had time left for only two passes into the end zone and both were batted down. As time ran out, Notre Dame took over as the nation's top team and FSU slipped to No. 2.

But the Irish weren't on top for long. One week later, Boston College, ranked 17th and itching to avenge a 54-7 pounding at the hands of Notre Dame a year earlier, came to South Bend as a 14½-point under-dog and upset their hosts, 41-39.

The hero for the Eagles was a senior placekicker named David Gordon, who booted the winning 41-yard field goal with time running out. Before the game, Gordon, the son of the owner of the NHL's Hartford Whalers, was best known for missing a 40-yard field goal with a minute to go that would have beaten lowly Northwestern on Sept. 18.

On Nov. 20, Gordon's moment in the autumn sun came after B.C. blew a 38-17 fourth quarter lead, allowing Notre Dame to pull ahead 39-38 with 1:10 to play.

Rallying around senior quarterback Glenn Foley, the Eagles mounted one last drive, marching from their own 10-yard-line to the Irish 24. It was there that Gordon stared down the ghosts of America's most famous college football stadium and split the uprights as time expired.

The defeat opened the door for Florida State to regain the No. 1 spot and revived the championship hopes of the three remaining unbeaten teams— Nebraska, West Virginia and Auburn.

The Cornhuskers withstood a rash of early season injuries in their backfield to finish 11-0 for the first time in 10 years. Two differences existed between this Nebraska team and recent ones that stumbled. These 'Huskers withstood their stumble, edging a mediocre Kansas team, 21-20, on Nov. 6, when the Jayhawks missed a two-point conversion in the final minute. Also, Nebraska played tough defense, an attribute that hadn't been seen in Lincoln in years.

Coach Tom Osborne, a late convert to speed, switched to a 3-4 alignment that highlighted the talents of linebacker Trev Alberts. The 6-4, 230-pound senior All-America went on to win the Butkus Award by dominating opponents with a combination of speed, strength and smarts.

Osborne, who has 206 wins in only 21 years as a head coach, hasn't been very successful in the postseason. His teams are 8-13 in bowl games, 5-8 in major bowls and have yet to win a national title. Nevertheless, Nebraska earned overdue respect by playing Florida State, a 16½-point favorite, beyond the final second.

"As far as I'm concerned, we won," Osborne said. "The main thing is playing like champions and we did that."

FSU's Bowden didn't disagree. "I guess it was just our time," he said, "because Nebraska played as good or better than we did."

Five months later, Bowden was fending off accusations by *Sports Illustrated* that several of his players had taken money and gifts from agents and phony jobs from boosters in violation of NCAA rules (see "College Sports" chapter).

West Virginia, picked before the season to finish in the middle of the Big East Conference, combined a roster loaded with seniors with a schedule loaded with patsies to go 11-0. They closed out the regular season with consecutive 17-14 victories over once-mighty Miami and Boston College to win the Big East title. In the second game, the Mountaineers caught the Eagles only six days after B.C.'s upset at Notre Dame.

Despite going undefeated, West Virginia never climbed higher than fourth in the polls. The local populace, sensitive to the appearance of any slight from the rest of the nation, bombarded the AP voters with postcards and faxes urging higher votes. *The Daily Athenaeum,* the student newspaper on the Morgantown campus, printed the phone and fax numbers of the 21 AP voters who ranked West Virginia lower than third in the final regular-season poll.

The West Virginia campaign died a quick, yet painful, death in the Louisiana Superdome on New Year's Night when Southeastern Conference champion Florida routed them, 41-7, in the Sugar Bowl.

Florida (10-2) may have been the official SEC champion, but try selling that at Toomer's Corner, the main intersection in the lovely college town of Auburn, Ala., where the hometown Tigers went 11-0.

Auburn's surprising success proved that the only clear champion in college football in 1993 was the Bowden family. While Bobby finally won a national title at age 64, son Terry was the consensus Division I-A Coach of the Year at 37.

Terry took over a discredited Tigers program following the forced resignation of head coach Pat Dye on Nov. 25, 1992. Dye's last two seasons had been rendered mediocre by the Eric Ramsey affair, a debacle that led the NCAA to hand down a two-year probation on Aug. 18, 1993. Without the possibility of a national championship— and the national scrutiny that accompanies the chase— Bowden and his players quickly and quietly bonded with one another and won every game.

It helped that Auburn played a schedule that made West Virginia's look Herculean— facing only two top-quality opponents and both of them at Jordan-Hare Stadium. The Tigers came from behind to beat both Florida (38-35) on Oct. 16 and archrival Alabama (22-14) in the final game of the regular season.

The Crimson Tide, the defending national champion, suffered through a season ham-

Wide World Photos

While his father finally won a national title in his 28th season, rookie Auburn coach **Terry Bowden** led his Tigers to a surprising 11-0 record and won Coach of the Year honors.

pered by injuries— the worst to starting quarterback Jay Barker— and ineligibility— All-America cornerback Antonio Langham, burned by an agent, missed the last three games of the year.

Had it not been for the exciting antics of junior flanker-quarterback David Palmer, who single-handedly salvaged a 17-17 tie against Tennessee, Alabama would have been hard-pressed to finish even 8-3-1. The Tide didn't beat a team with a winning record until it upset North Carolina, 24-10, in the Gator Bowl.

With Auburn removed from the postseason picture, Alabama represented the Western Division in the SEC championship game. In a rematch of the inaugural playoff, Eastern Division champion Florida evened the score by winning, 28-13. A sub-capacity crowd (76,345) at Legion Field gave SEC officials an excuse to move the game from Birmingham to the Georgia Dome in Atlanta, beginning in 1994.

Out west, the Rose Bowl stayed in Pasadena, but even the ancient matchup of Big 10 and Pac-10 champions sported a new look on New Year's Day: cheeseheads.

Wisconsin returned to the Rose Bowl for the first time since 1963, when the then No. 2 Badgers lost to top-ranked Southern Cal,

42-37, in the oldest bowl's wildest game ever. Thirty-one years later, Wisconsin beat UCLA, 21-16, to finish the season ranked No. 6 with a record of 10-1-1.

On-campus enthusiasm for the Badgers' revival under fourth-year coach Barry Alvarez got out of control in the final seconds of their 20-13 home victory over Big Ten power Michigan on Oct. 30. When hundreds of students seated in one corner of the Camp Randall Stadium end zone spilled through a chain link fence onto the turf, the resulting crush left 69 people injured, several critically.

The incident stunned the school, the team and the nation one week before the Badgers' Nov. 6 showdown at home with unbeaten Ohio State. Yet, with vastly increased security, the Badgers tied the Buckeyes, 14-14. They also tied OSU for the Big Ten championship, but gained the Rose Bowl berth because of their longer absence from Pasadena.

The Badgers' best player, junior tailback Brent Moss—1,479 yards and 11 straight 100-yard games— labored without acclaim throughout the season. So, too, did Northern Illinois running back LeShon Johnson, who won the I-A rushing title with 1,976 yards.

San Diego State junior tailback Marshall Faulk, bedeviled with an inexperienced offensive line, never mounted a challenge to Ward in the Heisman Trophy race. Faulk gained 1,530 yards and scored 21 touchdowns but faltered against the 6-5 Aztecs' toughest opponents.

Within days of San Diego State firing head coach Al Luginbill, Faulk announced he would enter the NFL draft. Other All-America players who left early included Palmer of Alabama, Ohio State sophomore defensive tackle Dan Wilkinson, Texas A&M junior defensive tackle Sam Adams, UCLA junior linebacker Jamir Miller and Florida State junior cornerback Corey Sawyer (see page 160).

Two players who might have been All-Americas in other years, quarterbacks Heath Shuler of Tennessee and Trent Dilfer of Fresno State, left early for the NFL, too. Despite their enormous talent, no one questioned their absence on the All-America team. Charlie Ward of Florida State left no room for debate.

If only that were true for his team.   ◻

COLLEGE FOOTBALL
S T A T I S T I C S

THE SEASON IN REVIEW
1993-1994
TOP 25 • BOWLS • STANDINGS

THE 1995 INFORMATION PLEASE SPORTS ALMANAC

SEC A

PAGE 151

Final AP Top 25 Poll

Voted on by panel of 62 sportswriters & broadcasters following Jan. 1, 1994 bowl games: winning team receives the Bear Bryant Trophy, given since 1983; first place votes in parentheses, records, total points (based on 25 for 1st, 24 for 2nd, etc.) bowl game result, head coach and career record, preseason rank (released on Aug.21) and final regular season rank (released Dec. 5).

		Final Record	Points	Bowl Game	Head Coach	Aug.21 Rank	Dec.5 Rank
1	Florida St. (46)	12-1-0	1532	Won Orange	Bobby Bowden (28 yrs: 239-78-3)	1	1
2	Notre Dame (12)	11-1-0	1478	Won Cotton	Lou Holtz (24 yrs: 193-84-6)	7	4
3	Nebraska	11-1-0	1418	Lost Orange	Tom Osborne (21 yrs: 206-47-3)	8	2
4	Auburn (4)	11-0-0	1375	On probation	Terry Bowden (10 yrs: 75-36-1)	44	5
5	Florida	11-2-0	1307	Won Sugar	Steve Spurrier (7 yrs: 59-23-1)	9	8
6	Wisconsin	10-1-1	1228	Won Rose	Barry Alvarez (4 yrs: 21-23-1)	33t	9
7	West Virginia	11-1-0	1090	Lost Sugar	Don Nehlen (23 yrs: 156-91-8)	49	3
8	Penn St	10-2-0	1074	Won Citrus	Joe Paterno (28 yrs: 257-69-3)	16	13
9	Texas A&M	10-2-0	1043	Lost Cotton	R.C. Slocum (5 yrs: 49-12-1)	4	7
10	Arizona	10-2-0	992	Won Fiesta	Dick Tomey (17 yrs: 109-77-7)	14	16
11	Ohio St.	10-1-1	971	Won Holiday	John Cooper (17 yrs: 126-63-6)	17	11
12	Tennessee	9-2-1	870	Lost Citrus	Phillip Fulmer (2 yrs: 13-2-1)	10	6
13	Boston College	9-3-0	817	Won Carquest	Tom Coughlin (5 yrs: 28-23-2)	21	15
14	Alabama	9-3-1	685	Won Gator	Gene Stallings (11 yrs: 67-54-2)	2	18
15	Miami-FL	9-3-0	611	Lost Fiesta	Dennis Erickson (12 yrs: 103-38-1)	5	10
16	Colorado	8-3-1	574	Won Aloha	Bill McCartney (12 yrs: 82-54-5)	11	17
17	Oklahoma	9-3-0	521	Won Hancock	Gary Gibbs (5 yrs: 38-17-2)	22	19
18	UCLA	8-4-0	460	Lost Rose	Terry Donahue (18 yrs: 139-63-8)	33t	14
19	North Carolina	10-3-0	447	Lost Gator	Mack Brown (10 yrs: 51-62-1)	20	12
20	Kansas St.	9-2-1	444	Won Copper	Bill Snyder (5 yrs: 27-28-1)	NR	20
21	Michigan	8-4-0	397	Won Hall of Fame	Gary Moeller (7 yrs: 42-33-6)	3	23
22	Virginia Tech	9-3-0	321	Won Independence	Frank Beamer (13 yrs: 75-66-4)	NR	22
23	Clemson	9-3-0	164	Won Peach	Ken Hatfield (15 yrs: 113-62-3) & Tommy West (1 yr: 5-7-0)	23	24
24	Louisville	9-3-0	159	Won Liberty	H. Schnellenberger (14 yrs: 89-67-2)	33t	25t
25	California	9-4-0	79	Won Alamo	Keith Gilbertson (5 yrs: 41-20-0)	NR	31

Note: Clemson named West head coach on Nov. 29, after Hatfield (8-3-0) resigned following the regular season. West, a former Clemson assistant, was 4-7 in his first year as head coach at Tenn-Chattanooga in 1993.

Other teams receiving votes: 26. **USC** (8-5-0, 46 points, won Freedom); 27. **Indiana** (8-4-0, 21 pts, lost Independence); 28. **Cincinnati** (8-3-0, 9 pts, no bowl); 29. **Fresno St.** (8-4-0, 5 pts, lost Aloha); 30. **Michigan St.** (6-6-0, 4 pts, lost Liberty); 31. **Arizona St.** (6-5-0, 2 pts, no bowl), **Virginia** (7-5-0, 2 pts, lost Carquest) and **Washington** (7-4-0, 2 pts, ineligible for bowl); 34. **Kentucky** (6-6-0, 1 pt, lost Peach) and **Utah St.** (7-5-0, 1 pt, won Las Vegas).

AP Preseason and Final Regular Season Polls

First place votes in parentheses.

Top 25 (Aug. 21, 1993)

		Pts			Pts
1	Florida St. (42)	1522	14	Arizona	695
2	Alabama (14)	1472	15	Stanford (1)	660
3	Michigan (3)	1413	16	Penn St.	598
4	Texas A&M	1261	17	Ohio St.	470
5	Miami-FL	1245	18	USC	436
6	Syracuse (2)	1180	19	BYU	323
7	Notre Dame	1137	20	North Carolina	322
8	Nebraska	1050	21	Boston College	299
9	Florida	998	22	Oklahoma	269
10	Tennessee	976	23	Clemson	262
11	Colorado	961	24	Mississippi St.	165
12	Washington	890	25	N.C. State	162
13	Georgia	725			

Top 25 (Dec. 5, 1993)

		Pts			Pts
1	Florida St. (41)	1507	14	UCLA	739
2	Nebraska (15)	1468	15	Boston College	695
3	West Virginia (3)	1420	16	Arizona	583
4	Notre Dame (1)	1353	17	Colorado	508
5	Auburn (1)	1343	18	Alabama	474
6	Tennessee	1255	19	Oklahoma	438
7	Texas A&M	1126	20	Kansas St.	403
8	Florida	1099	21	Indiana	334
9	Wisconsin	1033	22	Virginia Tech	263
10	Miami-FL	1030	23	Michigan	238
11	Ohio St.	874	24	Clemson	148
12	North Carolina	840	25	Fresno St.	34
13	Penn St.	808		Louisville	34

1993-94 Bowl Games

Listed by bowls matching highest-ranked teams as of final AP regular season poll taken Dec. 5th.

Bowl		Winner	Regular Season	Loser		Regular Season	Score	Date	Attendance
Orange	# 1	Florida St.	11-1-0	# 2	Nebraska	11-0-0	18-16	Jan. 1	81,536
Sugar	# 8	Florida	10-2-0	# 3	West Virginia	11-0-0	41- 7	Jan. 1	75,437
Cotton	# 4	Notre Dame	10-1-0	# 7	Texas A&M	10-1-0	24-21	Jan. 1	69,855
Citrus	#13	Penn St.	9-2-0	# 6	Tennessee	9-1-1	31-13	Jan. 1	72,456
Rose	# 9	Wisconsin	9-1-1	#14	UCLA	8-3-0	21-16	Jan. 1	101,237
Fiesta	#16	Arizona	9-2-0	#10	Miami-FL	9-2-0	29- 0	Jan. 1	72,260
Holiday	#11	Ohio St.	9-1-1		BYU	6-5-0	28-21	Dec.30	52,108
Gator	#18	Alabama	8-3-1	#12	North Carolina	10-2-0	24-10	Dec.31	67,205
Carquest	#15	Boston College	8-3-0		Virginia	7-4-0	31-13	Jan. 1	38,516
Aloha	#17	Colorado	7-3-1	#25	Fresno St.	8-3-0	41-30	Dec.25	44,009
Hancock	#19	Oklahoma	8-3-0		Texas Tech	6-5-0	41-10	Dec.24	43,848
Copper	#20	Kansas St.	8-2-1		Wyoming	8-3-0	52-17	Dec.29	49,075
Independence	#22	Virginia Tech	8-3-0	#21	Indiana	8-3-0	45-20	Dec.31	33,819
Hall of Fame	#23	Michigan	7-4-0		N.C. State	7-4-0	42- 7	Jan. 1	52,649
Peach	#24	Clemson	8-3-0		Kentucky	6-5-0	14-13	Dec.31	63,416
Liberty	#25	Louisville	8-3-0		Michigan St.	6-5-0	18- 7	Dec.28	21,097
Freedom		USC	7-5-0		Utah	7-5-0	28-21	Dec.30	37,203
Alamo		California	8-4-0		Iowa	6-5-0	37- 3	Dec.31	45,716
Las Vegas		Utah St.	6-5-0		Ball St.	8-2-1	42-33	Dec.17	15,508

Per Team Payouts

Rose ($6.5 million each); **Federal Express Orange** ($4.2 million); **USF&G Sugar** ($4.15 million); **Mobil Cotton** ($3.1 million); **IBM OS/2 Fiesta** ($3 million); **CompUSA Florida Citrus** ($2.5 million); **Thrifty Car Rental Holiday** ($1.7 million); **Outback Steakhouse Gator** ($1.5 million); **Peach** ($1.125 million); **John Hancock** ($1.1 million); **Carquest**, **Hall of Fame** and **St. Jude Liberty** ($1 million); **Jeep Eagle Aloha** ($750,000); **Builders Square Alamo, Freedom, Poulan/Weed Eater Independence** and **Weiser Lock Copper** ($700,000); **Las Vegas** ($228,000).

Final Bowl Coalition Poll

Combined point totals of AP media and USA/CNN coaches polls to determine bowl match-ups and released Dec. 5, 1993. Although Auburn was on probation and ineligible for coaches poll, its AP points total was doubled in the coalition poll.

		AP Poll		Coaches		Total
		No.	Pts	No.	Pts	Pts
1	Nebraska	2	(1468)	1	(1519)	2987
2	Florida St.	1	(1507)	3	(1446)	2953
3	West Virginia	3	(1420)	2	(1469)	2889
4	Notre Dame	4	(1353)	4	(1369)	2722
5	Auburn	5	(1343)		—	2686
6	Tennessee	6	(1255)	5	(1278)	2533
7	Texas A&M	7	(1126)	6	(1238)	2364
8	Florida	8	(1099)	8	(1075)	2174
9	Wisconsin	9	(1033)	7	(1089)	2122
10	Miami-FL	10	(1030)	9	(1049)	2079
11	Ohio St.	11	(874)		(951)	1825
12	N. Carolina	12	(840)	11	(901)	1741
13	Penn St.	13	(808)	12	(884)	1692
14	UCLA	14	(739)	13	(808)	1547
15	Boston Col.	15	(695)	15	(654)	1349
16	Arizona	16	(583)	14	(728)	1311
17	Colorado	17	(508)	17	(490)	998
18	Alabama	18	(474)	18	(481)	955
19	Oklahoma	19	(438)	16	(501)	939
20	Kansas St	20	(403)	19	(443)	846
21	Indiana	21	(334)	20	(394)	728
22	Virginia Tech	22	(263)	20	(394)	657
23	Michigan	23	(238)	22	(306)	544
24	Clemson	24	(148)	23	(257)	405
25	Fresno St	25	(34)	24	(95)	129

NO. 1 vs. NO. 2
Irish upset Seminoles

Florida State and Notre Dame, both unbeaten and untied in nine games, met Saturday afternoon Nov. 13 at South Bend in the first of the 1993 season's two games between the AP poll's Number 1 and 2 teams. The Irish won, 31-24, but then lost at home the following weekend to Boston College by a 41-39 score. FSU then reclaimed the top spot and defeated No. 2 Nebraska in the Orange Bowl on Jan. 1 (see next page).

Notre Dame, 31-24

Nov. 13, 1993, at South Bend.

#1 Florida St. (9-0)	7	0	7	10—24
#2 Notre Dame (9-0)	7	14	3	7—31

Scoring summary

1st Quarter: FSU— Kevin Knox 12-yd pass from Charlie Ward at 7:09 (Scott Bentley kick); ND— Adrian Jarrell 32-yd run at 4:30 (Kevin Pendergast kick).

2nd Quarter: ND— Lee Becton 26-yd run at 10:42 (Pendergast kick); ND— Jeff Burris 6-yd run at 7:48 (Pendergast kick).

3rd Quarter: ND— Pendergast 47-yd FG at 9:41; FSU— Warrick Dunn 6-yd pass from Ward at 4:45 (Bentley kick).

4th Quarter: FSU— Bentley 24-yd FG at 10:40; ND— Burris 11-yd run at 6:53 (Pendergast kick); FSU— Kez McCorvey 20-yd pass from Ward at 2:26 (Bentley kick).

Favorite: FSU by 7   **Attendance:** 59,075
Field: Grass   **Time:** 3:45
Weather: 59, Cloudy   **TV Rating:** 16.0/39 share (NBC)

National Championship Game

Florida State, AP's No. 1 team at the end of the regular season, and Nebraska, the top-ranked choice of the Coaches, met for the national championship on New Year's Night at the Orange Bowl. Seminoles won, 18-16, in their second No. 1 vs No. 2 showdown of the season. The Final 1993 seasonrecords of both teams are listed below; AP rank and records of opponents are day of game.

Florida St. Seminoles (12-1-0)

Date	AP Rank	Opponent	Result
Aug. 28	#1	vs Kansas* (0-0)	42- 0
Sept. 4	#1	at Duke (0-0)	45- 7
Sept.11	#1	#21 Clemson (1-0)	57- 0
Sept.18	#1	#13 at North Carolina (3-0)	33- 7
Oct. 2	#1	Georgia Tech (1-2)	51- 0
Oct. 9	#1	#3 Miami-FL (4-0)	28-10
Oct.16	#1	#15 Virginia (5-0)	40-14
Oct.30	#1	Wake Forest (2-5)	54- 0
Nov. 6	#1	at Maryland (1-7)	49-20
Nov.13	#1	at #2 Notre Dame (9-0)	24-31
Nov.20	#2	N.C. State (7-3)	62- 3
Nov.27	#1	at #7 Florida (9-1)	33-21
Jan. 1	#1	vs #2 Nebraska† (11-0)	18-16

*Kickoff Classic (at E. Rutherford, N.J.)   †Orange Bowl (at Miami)

Nebraska Cornhuskers (11-1-0)

Date	AP Rank	Opponent	Result
Sept. 4	#9	North Texas* (0-0)	76-14
Sept.11	#9	Texas Tech (1-0)	50-27
Sept.18	#8	at UCLA (0-1)	14-13
Sept.25	#6	Colorado St. (1-2)	48-13
Oct. 7	#7	at Oklahoma St. (3-1)	27-13
Oct.16	#6	Kansas St. (5-0)	45-28
Oct.23	#5	Missouri (2-3-1)	49- 7
Oct.30	#6	at #20 Colorado (4-2-1)	21-17
Nov. 6	#6	at Kansas (3-6)	21-20
Nov.13	#6	Iowa St. (3-6)	49-17
Nov.26	#2	#16 Oklahoma (8-2)	27- 7
Jan. 1	#2	vs #1 Florida St.† (11-1)	16-18

*Division I-AA opponent.   †Orange Bowl (at Miami)

Regular Season Statistics

Passing (5 Att)

	Att	Cmp	Pct	Yds	TD	Rate
Danny Kanell	49	36	73.5	499	7	206.2
Jon Stark	35	25	71.4	328	3	167
Charlie Ward	380	264	69.5	3032	27	157.8

Interceptions: Ward 4, Stark 2.

Top Receivers

	No	Yds	Avg	Long	TD
Kez McCorvey	74	966	13.1	37	6
Matt Frier	45	598	13.3	72-td	3
Tamarick Vanover	45	542	12	86-td	3
Kevin Knox	42	575	13.7	40	7
Sean Jackson	32	184	5.8	15-td	3

Top Rushers

	Car	Yds	Avg	Long	TD
Sean Jackson	134	825	6.2	69-td	6
Warrick Dunn	68	511	7.5	63-td	4
Charlie Ward	65	339	5.2	28	4
William Floyd	63	321	5.1	19	5
Marquette Smith	62	297	4.8	21	2

Most Touchdowns

	TD	Run	Rec	Ret	Pts
Warrick Dunn	10	4	6	0	60
Sean Jackson	8	5	3	0	48
Kevin Knox	7	0	7	0	42
Kez McCorvey	6	0	6	0	36

Kicking

	FG/Att	Lg	PAT/Att	Pts
Scott Bentley	13/20	47	56/64	95
Dan Mowrey	0/0	—	3/4	3

Punting (10 or more)

	No	Yds	Long	Blk	Avg
Sean Liss	32	1256	55	1	39.3

Most Interceptions
Corey Sawyer 6

Most Sacks
Chris Cowart 7½

Regular Season Statistics

Passing (5 Att)

	Att	Cmp	Pct	Yds	TD	Rate
Tony Veland	9	6	66.7	76	1	152
Brook Berringer	27	17	63.0	222	2	149.1
Tommie Frazier	162	77	47.5	1159	12	127.1

Interceptions: Frazier 4, Berringer 1, Veland 1.

Top Receivers

	No	Yds	Avg	Long	TD
Abdul Muhammad	25	383	15.3	41-td	3
Corey Dixon	17	320	18.8	60-td	2
Trumane Bell	12	187	15.6	33	2
Gerald Armstrong	11	145	13.2	31	5
Clester Johnson	8	96	12.0	18	1

Top Rushers

	Car	Yds	Avg	Long	TD
Calvin Jones	185	1043	5.6	64	12
Tommie Frazier	126	704	5.6	58	9
Lawrence Phillips	92	508	5.5	46-td	6
Damon Benning	55	324	5.9	51	4
Cory Schlesinger	48	192	4	16	1

Most Touchdowns

	TD	Run	Rec	Ret	Pts
Calvin Jones	13	12	1	0	78
Tommie Frazier	9	9	0	0	54
Gerald Armstrong	5	0	5	0	30
Lawrence Phillips	5	5	0	0	30

Kicking

	FG/Att	Lg	PAT/Att	Pts
Byron Bennett	6/11	48	53/55	71
Tom Sieler	0/0	—	2/2	2

Punting (10 or more)

	No	Yds	Long	Blk	Avg
Byron Bennett	46	1896	61	0	41.2

Most Interceptions
Toby Wright 3

Most Sacks
Trev Alberts 15

Florida St., 18-16

Saturday, Jan. 1 at the Orange Bowl in Miami.

#2 Nebraska (Big 8)	0	7	0	9	**16**
#1 Florida St. (ACC)	0	6	9	3	**18**

Favorite: FSU by 6½
Field: Grass
Weather: 75, Cloudy

Attendance: 81,536
Time: 4:00
TV Rating: 18.2/31 share (ABC)

Most Valuable Players

QBs Charlie Ward, Florida St. (passing— 24 for 43, 286 yds; rushing— 8 for minus 3 yds) and Tommie Frazier, Nebraska (passing— 13 for 24, 206 yds, 1 TD, 2 INT; rushing— 14 for 77 yds).

Scoring Summary

2nd Quarter: FSU—Scott Bentley 34-yd FG at 7:06; NEB—Reggie Baul 34-yd pass from Tommie Frazier at 9:01 (Byron Bennett kick); FSU—Bentley 25-yd FG at 14:38.

3rd Quarter: FSU—William Floyd 1-yd run at 2:10 (pass failed); FSU—Bentley 39-yd FG at 11:54.

4th Quarter: NEB—Lawrence Phillips 12-yd run at 0:05 (run failed); NEB—Bennett 27-yd FG at 13:44; FSU—Bentley 22-yd FG at 14:39. **Note:** Nebraska's Bennett missed 45-yd FG as time expired.

Other Division I-A Final Polls

USA Today/CNN Coaches Poll

Voted on by panel of 60 Division I-A head coaches; winning team receives the Sears Trophy (originally the McDonald's Trophy, 1991-93); first place votes in parentheses with total points (based on 25 for 1st, 24 for 2nd, etc.).

	Pts			Pts
1 Florida St. (36)	1523	14 Oklahoma		636
2 Notre Dame (25)	1494	15 Miami-FL		604
3 Nebraska (1)	1441	16 Colorado		586
4 Florida	1313	17 UCLA		539
5 Wisconsin	1271	18 Kansas St.		523
6 West Virginia	1142	19 Michigan		496
7 Penn St.	1132	20 Virginia Tech		472
8 Texas A&M	1107	21 North Carolina		452
9 Arizona	1094	22 Clemson		240
10 Ohio St.	960	23 Louisville		214
11 Tennessee	891	24 California		158
12 Boston College	828	25 USC		121
13 Alabama	742			

Other teams receiving votes: Indiana (79 pts); Fresno St. (40); Virginia (19); Cincinnati (15); BYU (8); Kentucky (3); Michigan St., Utah St. and Wyoming (2); N.C. State (1). Teams on probation (and ineligible to receive votes): Auburn and Washington.

USA Today/Hall of Fame Poll

Voted on by panel of 72 members of the National Football Foundation and College Hall of Fame; winning team receives the NFF's MacArthur Bowl, given since 1959: first place votes in parentheses with total points (based on 25 for 1st, 24 for 2nd, etc.).

	Pts			Pts
1 Florida St. (43)	1745	14 Miami-FL		836
2 Notre Dame (28)	1712	15 Oklahoma		712
3 Nebraska (1)	1642	16 UCLA		653
4 Florida	1520	17 Colorado		651
5 Wisconsin	1467	18 Michigan		614
6 Penn St.	1358	19 Kansas St.		501
7 West Virginia	1297	20 North Carolina		457
8 Arizona	1263	21 Virginia Tech		411
9 Texas A&M	1193	22 Louisville		312
10 Ohio St.	1170	23 Clemson		205
11 Tennessee	1059	24 California		176
12 Boston College	1021	25 USC		125
13 Alabama	944			

Teams on probation (and ineligible to receive votes): Auburn and Washington.

FWAA Poll

Voted on by five-man panel including Roy Exum, *Chattanooga* (Tenn.) *News-Free Press*; Bob Hentzen, *The Topeka* (Kan.) *Capital-Journal*; Mike Lopresti, Gannett News Service; Thomas O'Toole, Scripps-Howard News Service; and Blackie Sherrod, *The Dallas Morning News*. Each selector selects three teams in order of preference (three points for 1st, two for 2nd and one for 3rd); winning team receives the Grantland Rice Award, given since 1954.

	1st	2nd	3rd	Pts
1 Florida St	3	2	0 — 13
2 Notre Dame	2	3	0 — 12
3 Nebraska	0	0	4 — 4
4 Auburn	0	0	1 — 1

Top 30 Teams Over Last 5 Years

Division I-A schools with the best overall winning percentage over the last five seasons (1989-93), through the bowl games of Jan. 1, 1994.
National Championships: National champions: 1989—Miami-FL; 1990—Colorado (AP, FWAA, NFF) and Georgia Tech (UPI); 1991—Miami-FL (AP) and Washington (FWAA, NFF, USA Today/CNN); 1992—Alabama; 1993—Florida St.

	Overall Record	Bowls Record	Overall Win Pct
1 Miami-FL	53- 7-0	3-2-0	.883
2 Florida St	54- 8-0	5-0-0	.871
3 Notre Dame	52- 9-1	4-1-0	.847
4 Alabama	50-11-1	3-2-0	.815
5 Nebraska	48-11-1	0-5-0	.808
6 Colorado	47-10-4	2-3-0	.803
7 Texas A&M	49-12-1	1-4-0	.798
8 Tennessee	47-11-3	3-2-0	.795
9 Michigan	46-11-3	3-2-0	.792
10 Washington	46-13-0	3-1-0	.780
11 Fresno St	46-13-1	2-2-0	.775
12 Florida	46-15-0	2-2-0	.754
13 Penn St	45-15-1	3-2-0	.746
14 Clemson	43-15-1	3-1-0	.737
15 Syracuse	41-16-3	4-0-0	.708
Ohio St	41-16-3	1-4-0	.708
17 Auburn	39-16-2	2-0-0	.702
18 Oklahoma	38-17-2	2-0-0	.684
19 Virginia	40-19-1	0-4-0	.675
20 BYU	42-20-2	0-4-1	.672
21 N.C.State	39-21-1	1-4-0	.648
22 Georgia Tech	36-21-1	2-0-0	.629
23 West Virginia	34-20-3	0-2-0	.623
24 Mississippi	36-22-0	2-1-0	.621
25 Hawaii	37-23-1	1-1-0	.615
26 Arizona	35-23-1	2-2-0	.602
Illinois	35-23-1	1-3-0	.602
28 Air Force	36-24-1	2-2-0	.598
29 Georgia	34-24-0	2-1-0	.586
30 California	34-24-1	3-0-0	.585
Iowa	34-24-1	0-2-1	.585

NY Times Computer Ratings

Based on an analysis of each team's scores with emphasis on three factors: who won, by what margin, and against what quality of opposition. Computer balances lop-sided scores, notes home field advantage and gives late-season games more weight than those played earlier in the schedule. The top team is assigned a rating of 1.000, ratings of all other teams reflect their strength relative to strength of No.1 team.

	Rating		Rating
1 Florida St	1.000	13 Boston College	.802
2 Florida	.951	Michigan	.802
3 Auburn	.918	15 Arizona	.801
4 Notre Dame	.900	Miami-FL	.801
5 Nebraska	.893	17 Colorado	.796
6 Ohio St	.839	18 Virginia Tech	.778
Penn St	.839	19 UCLA	.772
8 Tennessee	.836	20 Kansas St	.771
9 Texas A&M	.833	21 USC	.763
10 West Virginia	.825	22 Louisville	.751
11 Wisconsin	.824	23 Alabama	.737
12 Oklahoma	.804	24 California	.710
		25 N. Carolina	.703

☞ See pages 163-165 for list of all national championship teams since 1883. Also, see pages 166-180 for every Associated Press Final Top 20 poll since 1936.

NCAA Division I-A Final Standings

Standings based on conference games only; overall records include postseason games.

Atlantic Coast Conference

	Conference					Overall			
	W	L	T	PF	PA	W	L	T	PF	PA
*Florida St.........8	0	0	391	51	12	1	0	536	129
*N.Carolina 6	2	0	259	168	10	3	0	431	253
*Clemson 5	3	0	117	152	9	3	0	198	192
*Virginia............5	3	0	208	159	7	5	0	317	217
*N.C.State 4	4	0	191	227	7	5	0	278	327
Georgia Tech....3	5	0	176	213	5	6	0	260	286
Maryland 2	6	0	171	312	2	9	0	243	479
Duke 2	6	0	115	237	3	8	0	214	349
Wake Forest 1	7	0	153	262	2	9	0	199	318

*Bowls (2-3): Florida St. (won Orange); North Carolina (lost Gator); Clemson (won Peach); Virginia (lost Carquest); N.C. State (lost Hall of Fame).

Big East Conference

	Conference					Overall			
	W	L	T	PF	PA	W	L	T	PF	PA
*West Virginia ...7	0	0	240	91	11	1	0	408	212
*Miami-FL..........6	1	0	215	57	9	3	0	331	167
*Boston Col 5	2	0	232	138	9	3	0	408	240
*Virginia Tech 4	3	0	261	177	9	3	0	445	270
Syracuse 3	4	0	160	212	6	4	1	281	288
Pittsburgh 2	5	0	119	225	3	8	0	168	371
Rutgers 1	6	0	192	221	4	7	0	351	334
Temple 0	7	0	56	354	1	10	0	115	527

*Bowls (2-2): West Virginia (lost Sugar); Miami-FL (lost Fiesta); Boston College (won Carquest); Virginia Tech (won Independence).

Big Eight Conference

	Conference					Overall			
	W	L	T	PF	PA	W	L	T	PF	PA
*Nebraska 7	0	0	233	109	11	1	0	437	194
*Colorado 5	1	0	180	109	8	3	1	368	250
*Kansas St 4	2	1	150	142	9	2	1	340	227
*Oklahoma 4	3	0	159	122	9	3	0	358	186
Kansas 3	4	0	142	133	5	7	0	242	256
Missouri 2	5	0	148	223	3	7	1	192	344
Iowa St.............2	5	0	141	206	3	8	0	251	324
Oklahoma St 0	7	0	76	185	3	8	0	174	236

*Bowls (3-1): Nebraska (lost Orange); Colorado (won Aloha); Kansas St. (won Copper); Oklahoma (won Hancock).

Big Ten Conference

	Conference					Overall			
	W	L	T	PF	PA	W	L	T	PF	PA
*Wisconsin 6	1	1	246	139	10	1	1	354	195
*Ohio St 6	1	1	205	125	10	1	1	351	193
*Penn St 6	2	0	235	168	10	2	0	388	215
*Indiana 5	3	0	160	134	8	4	0	259	197
*Michigan 5	3	0	194	91	8	4	0	342	160
Illinois 5	3	0	180	150	5	6	0	204	210
*Michigan St 4	4	0	177	187	6	6	0	277	289
*Iowa 3	5	0	100	183	6	6	0	214	293
Minnesota 3	5	0	184	266	4	7	0	253	354
Northwestern 0	8	0	125	273	2	9	0	185	335
Purdue 0	8	0	186	276	1	10	0	221	326

Tiebreaker: The co-champion with the longest wait between Rose Bowls goes to Pasadena. Wisconsin last appeared in 1963 and Ohio St. in '85. The Badgers and Buckeyes played to a 14-14 tie (Nov. 6).

*Bowls (4-3): Wisconsin (won Rose); Ohio St. (won Holiday); Penn St. (won Citrus); Indiana (lost Independence); Michigan (won Hall of Fame); Michigan St. (lost Liberty); Iowa (lost Alamo).

Big West Conference

	Conference					Overall			
	W	L	T	PF	PA	W	L	T	PF	PA
*Utah St 5	1	0	179	138	7	5	0	363	354
SW Louisiana 5	1	0	141	100	8	3	0	249	227
Nevada 4	2	0	237	195	7	4	0	419	315
N. Mexico St......4	2	0	155	171	5	6	0	231	350
Northern Ill 3	3	0	142	139	4	7	0	227	334
Pacific 2	4	0	127	129	3	8	0	184	260
UNLV 2	4	0	150	202	3	8	0	259	347
Louisiana Tech ..2	4	0	93	123	2	9	0	143	332
San Jose St 2	4	0	175	141	2	9	0	282	337
Arkansas St 1	5	0	61	122	2	8	1	122	274

Tiebreaker: Utah St. beat SW Louisiana, 34-13 (Sept. 4).

*Bowl (1-0): Utah St. (won Las Vegas).

Mid-American Conference

	Conference					Overall			
	W	L	T	PF	PA	W	L	T	PF	PA
*Ball St 7	0	1	199	114	8	3	1	301	165
Western Mich 6	1	1	190	135	7	3	1	236	187
Bowl. Green 5	1	2	211	106	6	3	2	268	173
Central Mich 4	4	0	221	163	5	6	0	275	244
Akron 4	4	0	147	161	5	6	0	192	222
Ohio Univ..........4	5	0	124	197	4	7	0	134	282
Toledo 3	5	0	179	184	4	7	0	252	270
Eastern Mich 3	5	0	113	127	4	7	0	163	220
Miami-OH 3	6	0	134	190	4	7	0	186	248
Kent 0	9	0	132	273	0	11	0	149	357

*Bowl (0-1): Ball St. (lost Las Vegas).

Pacific-10 Conference

	Conference					Overall			
	W	L	T	PF	PA	W	L	T	PF	PA
*UCLA 6	2	0	219	168	8	4	0	368	230
*Arizona............6	2	0	209	128	10	2	0	294	161
*USC 6	2	0	229	141	8	5	0	348	252
Washington 5	3	0	189	160	7	4	0	288	198
Arizona St 4	4	0	215	203	6	5	0	282	248
*California..........4	4	0	183	244	9	4	0	411	303
Wash. St 3	5	0	191	193	5	6	0	271	248
Stanford 2	6	0	199	276	4	7	0	291	389
Oregon St 2	6	0	125	223	4	7	0	224	294
Oregon 2	6	0	207	230	5	6	0	278	276

Tiebreakers: UCLA beat Arizona, 37-17 (Oct. 30) and USC, 27-21 (Nov. 20); and Arizona beat USC, 38-7 (Oct. 2).

*Bowls (3-1): UCLA (lost Rose); Arizona (won Fiesta); USC (won Freedom); California (won Alamo).

Note: Washington ineligible for bowl games while on Pac-10 probation.

Conference Bowling Results

Postseason records for 1993 season.

	W-L		W-L
Big Ten 4-3		SEC 2-2
Big Eight 3-1		ACC 2-3
Pac-10...................3-1		Mid-American 0-1
Independents 2-0		SWC 0-2
Big West 1-0		WAC 0-4
Big East..................2-2		

Conference Moves

In 1993, Penn St. joined the Big Ten; and Arkansas St., Louisiana Tech, Northern Illinois and SW Louisiana joined the Big West as football members only. (See "College Sports" chapter for 1995 conference moves.)

NCAA Division I-A Final Standings (Cont.)

Southeastern Conference

Eastern	Conference W L T PF PA				Overall W L T PF PA				
*Florida	8	1	0	346 184	11	2	0	513	244
*Tennessee	6	1	1	324 115	9	2	1	484	175
*Kentucky	4	4	0	158 168	6	6	0	220	209
S. Carolina	2	6	0	114 192	4	7	0	188	214
Georgia	2	6	0	179 218	5	6	0	328	289
Vanderbilt	1	7	0	52 264	4	7	0	137	290

Western	Conference W L T PF PA				Overall W L T PF PA				
Auburn	8	0	0	228 147	11	0	0	353	192
*Alabama	5	3	1	189 138	9	3	1	340	168
Arkansas	3	4	1	131 185	5	5	1	165	208
LSU	3	5	0	128 257	5	6	0	190	308
Mississippi	3	5	0	155 116	5	6	0	242	142
Mississippi St	2	5	1	155 175	3	6	2	241	245

SEC Championship: Florida beat Alabama, 28-13 (Dec. 4).

*Bowls (2-2): Florida (won Sugar); Tennessee (lost Citrus); Alabama (won Gator); Kentucky (lost Peach).

Note: Auburn ineligible for bowl games while on NCAA probation.

Southwest Conference

	Conference W L T PF PA				Overall W L T PF PA				
*Texas A&M	7	0	0	251 68	10	2	0	425	143
*Texas Tech	5	2	0	256 149	6	6	0	419	335
Texas	5	2	0	219 133	5	5	1	281	269
Baylor	3	4	0	147 186	5	6	0	265	331
Rice	3	4	0	180 226	6	5	0	284	294
TCU	2	5	0	127 210	4	7	0	201	313
SMU	1	5	1	132 220	2	7	2	206	277
Houston	1	5	1	102 222	1	9	1	171	392

*Bowls (0-2): Texas A&M (lost Cotton); Texas Tech (lost Hancock).

Western Athletic Conference

	Conference W L T PF PA				Overall W L T PF PA				
*BYU	6	2	0	300 236	6	6	0	411	435
*Fresno St	6	2	0	320 223	8	4	0	467	350
*Wyoming	6	2	0	243 183	8	4	0	357	329
*Utah	5	3	0	280 257	7	6	0	390	396
Colorado St	5	3	0	202 173	5	6	0	230	268
San Diego St	4	4	0	293 261	6	6	0	413	392
New Mexico	4	4	0	220 201	6	5	0	335	256
Hawaii	3	5	0	235 267	6	6	0	393	357
Air Force	1	7	0	149 236	4	8	0	296	291
UTEP	0	8	0	120 325	1	11	0	220	449

Tiebreaker: Since BYU, Fresno St. and Wyoming did not all play each other, the Holiday Bowl berth was decided by how each fared against Colorado St. (the highest WAC finisher that all three teams played). BYU beat the Rams, 27-22 (Sept. 18), but Fresno St. lost, 34-32 (Oct. 9) and so did Wyoming, 41-21 (Nov. 20).

*Bowls (0-4): BYU (lost Holiday); Fresno St. (lost Aloha); Wyoming (lost Copper); Utah (lost Freedom).

I-A Independents

	W	L	T	PF	PA
*Notre Dame	11	1	0	427	215
*Louisville	9	3	0	350	243
Cincinnati	8	3	0	302	197
Army	6	5	0	289	243
Memphis St	6	5	0	268	215
Tulsa	4	6	1	262	273
Navy	4	7	0	203	307
Tulane	3	9	0	154	355
Southern Mississippi	2	8	1	214	311
East Carolina	2	9	0	175	329

*Bowls (2-0): Notre Dame (won Cotton); Louisville (won Liberty).

NCAA Division I-A Individual Leaders

REGULAR SEASON
Total Offense

		Rushing				Passing			Total Offense			
	Cl	Car	Gain	Loss	Net	Att	Yds	Plays	Yds	YdsPP	TDR	YdsPG
Chris Vargas, Nevada	Sr.	45	140	73	67	490	4265	535	4332	8.10	35	393.82
Mike McCoy, Utah	Jr.	99	356	247	109	430	3860	529	3969	7.50	21	330.75
Eric Zeier, Georgia	Jr.	59	161	204	-43	425	3525	484	3482	7.19	25	316.55
Scott Milanovich, Maryland	So.	91	208	270	-62	431	3499	522	3437	6.58	29	312.45
John Walsh, BYU	So.	83	70	377	-307	397	3727	480	3420	7.13	31	310.91
Steve Stenstrom, Stanford	Sr.	57	39	268	-229	455	3627	512	3398	6.64	27	308.91
Charlie Ward, Florida St	Sr.	65	452	113	339	380	3032	445	3371	7.58	31	306.45
Glenn Foley, Boston Col	Sr.	26	38	82	-44	363	3397	389	3353	8.62	25	304.82
Anthony Calvillo, Utah St	Sr.	89	298	186	112	469	3148	558	3260	5.84	23	296.36
Trent Dilfer, Fresno St	Jr.	36	74	138	-64	333	3276	369	3212	8.70	29	292

Games: All played 11, except McCoy (12).

All-Purpose Running

	Cl	Gm	Rush	Rec	PR	KOR	Total Yds	YdsPG
LeShon Johnson, Northern Ill	Sr.	11	1976	106	0	0	2082	189.27
Terrell Willis, Rutgers	Fr.	11	1261	61	0	704	2026	184.18
Marshall Faulk, San Diego St	Jr.	12	1530	644	0	0	2174	181.17
Bam Morris, Texas Tech	Jr.	11	1752	150	0	0	1902	172.91
Mike Adams, Texas	So.	11	68	908	256	622	1854	168.55
Napoleon Kaufman, Washington	Jr.	11	1299	139	25	388	1851	168.27
David Palmer, Alabama	Jr.	12	278	1000	244	439	1961	163.42
Tyrone Wheatley, Michigan	Jr.	9	1005	192	0	246	1403	155.89
Chris Penn, Tulsa	Sr.	11	2	1578	134	0	1714	155.82
John Leach, Wake Forest	Sr.	11	1089	340	9	253	1691	153.73

Northern Illinois

Fresno St.

Texas Tech

Tulsa

LeShon Johnson
Rushing,
All-Purpose Running

Trent Dilfer
Passing Efficiency

Bam Morris
Points Per Game

Chris Penn
Receptions

Passing Efficiency
(Minimum 15 attempts per game)

	Cl	Gm	Att	Cmp	Cmp Pct	Int	Int Pct	Yds	Yds/ Att	TD	TD Pct	Rating Points
Trent Dilfer, Fresno St.	Jr.	11	333	217	65.17	4	1.20	3276	9.84	28	8.41	173.1
Dave Barr, California	Jr.	11	275	187	68.00	12	4.36	2619	9.52	21	7.64	164.5
Darrell Bevell, Wisconsin	So.	11	256	177	69.14	10	3.91	2294	8.96	19	7.42	161.1
Charlie Ward, Florida St	Sr.	11	380	264	69.47	4	1.05	3032	7.98	27	7.11	157.8
Maurice DeShazo, Va. Tech	Jr.	11	230	129	56.09	7	3.04	2080	9.04	22	9.57	157.5
Heath Shuler, Tennessee	Jr.	11	285	184	64.56	8	2.81	2354	8.26	25	8.77	157.3
Glenn Foley, Boston Col	Sr.	11	363	222	61.16	10	2.75	3397	9.36	25	6.89	157.0
Chris Vargas, Nevada	Sr.	11	490	331	67.55	18	3.67	4265	8.70	34	6.94	156.2
John Walsh, BYU	So.	11	397	244	61.46	15	3.78	3727	9.39	28	7.05	156.0
Rob Johnson, USC	Jr.	12	405	278	68.64	5	1.23	3285	8.11	26	6.42	155.5
Tim Gutierrez, S. Diego St	Jr.	10	341	208	61.00	10	2.93	3033	8.89	24	7.04	153.1
Kevin McDougal, N. Dame	Sr.	10	159	98	61.64	5	3.14	1541	9.69	7	4.40	151.3
Mike McCoy, Utah	Jr.	12	430	276	64.19	10	2.33	3860	8.98	21	4.88	151.1
Robert Hall, Texas Tech	Sr.	11	341	216	63.34	7	2.05	2894	8.49	21	6.16	150.8
Todd Collins, Michigan	Jr.	11	274	178	64.96	7	2.55	2320	8.47	16	5.84	150.2

Rushing

	Cl	Car	Yds	TD	YdsPG
LeShon Johnson, No. Ill	Sr.	327	1976	12	179.64
Bam Morris, Texas Tech	Jr.	298	1752	22	159.27
Brent Moss, Wisconsin	Jr.	276	1479	14	134.45
Ron Rivers, Fresno St	Sr.	216	1440	14	130.91
Marshall Faulk, S. Diego St	Jr.	300	1530	21	127.50
Junior Smith, E. Carolina	Jr.	278	1352	9	122.91
Napoleon Kaufman, Wash.	Jr.	226	1299	14	118.09
David Small, Cincinnati	Sr.	223	1180	17	118.00
Calvin Jones, Nebraska	Jr.	185	1043	12	115.89
Terrell Willis, Rutgers	Fr.	195	1261	13	114.64
Ki-Jana Carter, Penn St	So.	155	1026	7	114.00
Tyrone Wheatley, Michigan	Jr.	189	1005	11	111.67

Games: All played 11, except Faulk (12); Small (10); and Jones, Carter and Wheatley (9).

Receptions

	Cl	Ct	Yds	TD	CPG
Chris Penn, Tulsa	Sr.	105	1578	12	9.55
Bryan Reeves, Nevada	Sr.	91	1362	17	9.10
Michael Stephens, Nevada	Sr.	80	1062	7	7.27
Brice Hunter, Georgia	So.	76	970	9	6.91
Darnay Scott, S. Diego St	Jr.	75	1262	10	6.82
Isaac Bruce, Memphis St	Sr.	74	1054	10	6.73
Brian Dusho, Kent	Sr.	72	890	1	6.55
Johnnie Morton, USC	Sr.	78	1373	12	6.50
Mike Lee, Utah St	Sr.	70	715	5	6.36
Mike Jones, Wyoming	Sr.	69	763	5	6.27
Russ Weaver, Maryland	Jr.	69	606	2	6.27
J.J. Stokes, UCLA	Jr.	68	1005	17	6.18

Games: All played 11, except Morton (12); and Douglas and Reeves (10).

Scoring

Non-Kickers

	Cl	TD	Pts	P/Gm
Bam Morris, Texas Tech	Jr.	22	134*	12.18
Marshall Faulk, San Diego St	Jr.	24	144	12.00
Darnell Campbell, Boston Col	Sr.	21	126	11.45
Bryan Reeves, Nevada	Sr.	17	102	10.20
David Small, Cincinnati	Sr.	17	102	10.20
Lindsey Chapman, California	Sr.	17	102	9.27
J.J. Stokes, UCLA	Jr.	17	102	9.27
Ryan Yarborough, Wyoming	Sr.	16	98*	8.91
Calvin Jones, Nebraska	Jr.	13	78	8.67
Leon Johnson, North Carolina	Fr.	16	100*	8.33

*Includes one 2-point conversion.

Games: All played 11 except Faulk and Johnson (12); Reeves and Small (10); and Jones (9).

Kickers

	Cl	FG/Att	PAT/Att	Pts
Michael Proctor, Alabama	So.	22/29	31/31	97
Judd Davis, Florida	Jr.	15/19	51/53	96
Scott Bentley, Fla. St	Fr.	13/20	56/64	95
John Becksvoort, Tenn	Jr.	12/13	59/59	95
Peter Holt, San Diego St	Fr.	16/23	45/46	93
Derek Mahoney, Fresno St	Sr.	14/20	51/54	93
Kanon Parkman, Georgia	So.	19/27	35/36	92
Bjorn Merten, UCLA	Fr.	20/25	31/34	91
Nathan Morreale, Utah St	Fr.	19/27	33/34	90
T. Venetoulias, Texas A&M	Sr.	13/19	51/51	90

Games: All played 11, except Proctor, Davis and Bentley (12).

NCAA Division I-A Individual Leaders (Cont.)

Field Goals

	Cl	FG/Att	Pct	FGPG
Michael Proctor, Alabama	So.	22/29	759	1.83
Bjorn Merten, UCLA	Fr.	20/25	800	1.82
Nathan Morreale, Utah St	Fr.	19/27	704	1.73
Kanon Parkman, Georgia	So.	19/27	704	1.73
Jon Baker, Arizona St	Jr.	18/26	692	1.64
Tom Dallen, Cincinnati	Jr.	17/22	773	1.55
Tom Burke, Miss. St	Sr.	17/23	739	1.55
Aaron Price, Wash. St	Sr.	17/31	548	1.55
Tommy Thompson, Oregon	Sr.	16/21	762	1.45
Chris Boniol, La. Tech	Sr.	16/22	727	1.45
Scott Szeredy, Texas	Sr.	16/22	727	1.45

Games: All played 11, except Proctor (12).

Interceptions

	Cl	No	Yds	TD	IPG
Orlanda Thomas, SW La	Jr.	9	84	1	0.82
Anthony Bridges, L'ville	Jr.	7	184	2	0.64
Alundis Brice, Mississippi	Jr.	7	98	2	0.64
Antonio Langham, Alabama	Sr.	7	67	1	0.64
Troy Jensen, San Jose St	Sr.	7	60	0	0.64

Nine tied with 6 INTs each.

Games: All played 11.

Punting

(Minimum of 3.6 per game)

	Cl	No	Yds	Avg
Chris MacInnis, Air Force	Sr.	49	2303	47.00
Terry Daniel, Auburn	Jr.	51	2393	46.92
Mike Nesbitt, New Mexico	Sr.	53	2387	45.04
Brad Faunce, UNLV	Jr.	61	2745	45.00
Pat O'Neill, Syracuse	Sr.	44	1950	44.32

Punt Returns

(Minimum of 1.2 per game)

	Cl	No	Yds	TD	Avg
Aaron Glenn, Texas A&M	Sr.	17	339	2	19.94
Shawn Summers, Tennessee	So.	18	255	1	14.17
Lee Gissendaner, N'western	Sr.	16	223	0	13.94
Scott Gumina, Miss. St	Jr.	13	180	1	13.85
Andre Coleman, Kansas St	Sr.	27	362	1	13.41

Kickoff Returns

(Minimum of 1.2 per game)

	Cl	No	Yds	TD	Avg
Leeland McElroy, Texas A&M	Fr.	15	590	3	39.33
Chris Hewitt, Cincinnati	Fr.	14	441	1	31.50
Tyler Anderson, BYU	Sr.	19	568	1	29.89
Andre Coleman, Kansas St	Sr.	15	434	0	28.93
Jack Jackson, Florida	So.	17	480	1	28.24

NCAA Division I-A Team Leaders
REGULAR SEASON

Scoring Offense

	Gm	Record	Pts	Avg
Florida St	12	11-1-0	518	43.2
Tennessee	11	9-1-1	471	42.8
Fresno St	11	8-3-0	437	39.7
Florida	12	10-2-0	472	39.3
Nebraska	11	11-0-0	421	38.3
Nevada	11	7-4-0	419	38.1
Texas Tech	11	6-5-0	409	37.2
Texas A&M	11	10-1-0	404	36.7
Notre Dame	11	10-1-0	403	36.6
West Virginia	11	11-0-0	401	36.5

Scoring Defense

	Gm	Record	Pts	Avg
Florida St	12	11-1-0	113	9.4
Texas A&M	11	10-1-0	119	10.8
Miami-FL	11	9-2-0	138	12.5
Mississippi	11	5-6-0	142	12.9
Tennessee	11	9-1-1	144	13.1
Alabama	12	8-3-1	158	13.2
Indiana	11	8-3-0	152	13.8
Michigan	11	7-4-0	153	13.9
Arizona	11	9-2-0	161	14.6
West Virginia	11	11-0-0	171	15.5

Total Offense

	Gm	Plays	Yds	Avg	TD	YdsPG
Nevada	11	955	6260	6.6	56	569.09
Florida St	12	939	6576	7	63	548.00
Fresno St	11	808	5863	7.3	53	533.00
Boston College	11	827	5570	6.7	51	506.36
Utah	12	906	5815	6.4	43	484.58
Tennessee	11	762	5286	6.9	58	480.55
Florida	12	888	5719	6.4	59	476.58
Texas Tech	11	854	5225	6.1	51	475.00
BYU	11	853	5222	6.1	51	474.73
Colorado	11	841	5175	6.2	40	470.45

Note: Touchdowns scored by rushing and passing only.

Total Defense

	Gm	Plays	Yds	Avg	TD	YdsPG
Mississippi	11	727	2580	3.5	13	234.5
Arizona	11	739	2606	3.5	14	236.9
Texas A&M	11	740	2724	3.7	10	247.6
Miami-FL	11	723	2814	3.9	15	255.8
Alabama	12	738	3104	4.2	19	258.7
Florida St	12	773	3414	4.4	15	284.5
Bowling Green	11	715	3285	4.6	22	298.6
Washington St	11	773	3287	4.3	27	298.8
Ohio St	11	744	3293	4.4	19	299.4
Indiana	11	747	3336	4.5	18	303.3

Note: Opponents' TDs scored by rushing and passing only.

Single Game Highs
INDIVIDUAL

Rushing Yards

Yds
329 John Leach, Wake Forest vs Maryland (Nov. 20)
322 LeShon Johnson, Northern Ill. vs Southern Ill. (Oct. 2)
306 LeShon Johnson, Northern Ill. vs Iowa (Nov. 6)

Rushing Attempts

Att
46 John Leach, Wake Forest vs Maryland (Nov. 20)
22 LeShon Johnson, Northern Ill. vs Southern Ill. (Oct. 2)
41 Errict Rhett, Florida vs Georgia (Oct. 30)

Passes Completed

No
38 Charlie Ward, Florida St. vs Florida (Nov. 27)
37 Chris Vargas, Nevada vs Weber St. (Oct. 23)
37 Scott Milanovich, Maryland vs Wake Forest (Nov. 20)

Passes Attempted

Att
66 Tim Schade, Minnesota vs Penn St. (Sept. 4)
66 Chuck Clements, Houston vs Cincinnati (Nov. 13)
65 Eric Zeier, Georgia vs Florida (Oct. 30)

Passing Yards

Yds
619 John Walsh, BYU vs Utah St. (Oct. 30)
544 Eric Zeier, Georgia vs Southern Miss. (Oct. 9)
538 Chris Vargas, Nevada vs UNLV (Oct. 2)

Passes Caught

No
16 Chris Penn, Tulsa vs East Carolina (Nov. 6)
15 Daryl Rodgers, Pacific vs Arkansas St. (Nov. 13)
15 Johnnie Morton, USC vs Houston (Sept. 4)
15 Shannon Mitchell, Georgia vs Florida (Oct. 30)

Receiving Yards

Yds
297 Brian Oliver, Ball St. vs Toledo (Oct. 9)
285 Thomas Lewis, Indiana vs Penn St. (Nov. 6)
259 Chris Penn, Tulsa vs East Carolina (Nov. 6)

TEAM

Points Scored

Pts
76 Nebraska (76-14) vs North Texas* (Sept. 4)
73 Texas A&M (73-0) vs Missouri (Sept. 18)
70 Penn St. (70-7) at Maryland (Oct. 2)
68 Rutgers (68-6) vs Colgate* (Sept. 4)
68 UCLA (68-14) vs BYU (Oct. 9)
66 Boston College (66-14) vs Temple (Sept. 25)
63 Air Force (63-21) vs Indiana St.* (Sept. 4)
63 Virginia Tech (63-21) at Pittsburgh (Sept. 11)
63 Ohio St. (63-28) at Pittsburgh (Sept. 18)
63 Nevada (63-13) vs Texas Southern* (Sept. 18)
63 Fresno St. (63-37) vs San Diego St. (Nov. 20)

*Division I-AA opponent.

Annual Awards

Player of the Year

Charlie Ward, Florida St ....Camp, Heisman, Maxwell,
The Sporting News, UPI

Position Players of the Year

Davey O'Brien (QB).........................Charlie Ward, Fla. St.
Johnny Unitas (Senior QB) ....Charlie Ward, Fla. St.
Doak Walker (RB) ....Bam Morris, Texas Tech
UPI Back of Year............................LeShon Johnson, No. Ill.
Lou Groza (PK)...................................Judd Davis, Florida
Outland Trophy (Int. Lineman)..........Rob Waldrop, Arizona
FWAA Defensive Player of Year......Rob Waldrop, Arizona
UPI Lineman of Year.......................Rob Waldrop, Arizona
Butkus Award (LB) ....Trev Alberts, Nebraska
Lombardi Award (Lineman)........Aaron Taylor, Notre Dame
Thorpe Award (Def. Back)........Antonio Langham, Alabama

Coaches of the Year

Terry Bowden, Auburn ....Camp, FWAA, UPI,
The Sporting News
Barry Alvarez, Wisconsin ....AFCA, Dodd

Heisman Trophy Vote

Presented since 1935 by the Downtown Athletic of New York City and named after former college coach and DAC athletic director John W. Heisman. Voting done by national media and former Heisman winners. Each ballot allows for three names (points based on 3 for 1st, 2 for 2nd and 1 for 3rd).

Top 10 Vote-Getters

	Pos	1st	2nd	3rd	Pts
Charlie Ward, Fla. St	QB	740	39	12	2310
Heath Shuler, Tennessee	QB	10	274	110	688
David Palmer, Alabama	RB	16	78	88	292
Marshall Faulk, S.D. St	RB	7	74	81	250
Glenn Foley, Boston Col	QB	5	47	71	180
LeShon Johnson, No. Ill	RB	5	51	59	176
J.J. Stokes, UCLA	WR	3	37	48	131
Tyrone Wheatley, Mich	RB	2	31	32	100
Trent Dilfer, Fresno St	QB	2	28	29	91
Eric Zeier, Georgia	QB	0	24	37	85

Note: All players were juniors except seniors Ward, Foley and Johnson.

Consensus All-America Team

NCAA Division I-A players cited most frequently by the following five selectors: AFCA (Kodak), AP, FWAA, UPI and Walter Camp Foundation. Holdovers from 1992 All-America team are in **bold** type; (*) indicates unanimous selection.

Offense

Pos	Class	Hgt	Wgt
WR— J.J. Stokes*, UCLA	Jr.	6-4	215
WR— Johnnie Morton, USC	Sr.	6-0	195
L— **Aaron Taylor***, Notre Dame	Sr.	6-4	299
L— Mark Dixon, Virginia	Sr.	6-4	283
L— Wayne Gandy, Auburn	Sr.	6-5	275
L— Rich Braham, West Virginia	Sr.	6-5	260
L— Stacy Seegars, Clemson	Sr.	6-4	320
C— Jim Pyne*, Virginia Tech	Sr.	6-2	280
QB— Charlie Ward*, Florida St	Sr.	6-1	185
RB— **Marshall Faulk***, S. Diego St	Jr.	5-10	200
RB— LeShon Johnson*, No. Illinois	Sr.	6-0	201
AP— David Palmer, Alabama	Jr.	5-9	170
K— Bjorn Merten, UCLA	Fr.	6-1	203

Defense

Pos	Class	Hgt	Wgt
L— **Rob Waldrop***, Arizona	Sr.	6-2	274
L— Sam Adams, Texas A&M	Jr.	6-4	282
L— Dan Wilkinson, Ohio St	So.	6-5	310
L— Kevin Patrick, Miami-Fl	Sr.	6-4	255
LB— Trev Alberts*, Nebraska	Sr.	6-4	230
LB— Derrick Brooks*, Florida St	Jr.	6-1	225
LB— Dana Howard, Illinois	Jr.	6-0	240
LB— Jamir Miller, UCLA	Jr.	6-4	245
B— Aaron Glenn*, Texas A&M	Sr.	5-10	180
B— Antonio Langham, Alabama	Sr.	6-1	170
B— Jeff Burris, Notre Dame	Sr.	6-0	204
P— Terry Daniel, Auburn	Jr.	6-1	226

Underclassmen Who Declared For 1994 NFL Draft

Twenty-nine players— all of whom have been out of high school for at least three seasons— forfeited the remainder of their college eligibility and declared for the NFL Draft in 1994. Players listed in alphabetical order; first round selections in **bold** type. NFL teams drafted 26 underclassmen.

	Pos	Drafted By	Overall Pick		Pos	Drafted By	Overall Pick
Sam Adams, Texas A&M	DL	Philadelphia	8	Chuck Levy, Arizona	RB	Arizona	38
Mario Bates, Arizona St.	RB	New Orleans	44	**Thomas Lewis**, Indiana	WR	NY Giants	24
Donnell Bennett, Miami-FL	RB	Kansas City	58	Dwight McFadden, USC	RB	Not selected	—
James Bostic, Auburn	RB	LA Rams	83	**Jamir Miller**, UCLA	LB	Arizona	10
Tim Bowens, Mississippi	DT	Miami	20	Bam Morris, Texas Tech	RB	Pittsburgh	91
Trent Dilfer, Fresno St.	QB	Tampa Bay	6	A.J. Ofodile, Missouri	TE	Buffalo	158
Marshall Faulk, S.Diego St.	RB	Indianapolis	2	David Palmer, Alabama	WR	Minnesota	40
William Floyd, Florida St.	RB	San Francisco	28	Corey Sawyer, Florida St.	CB	Cincinnati	104
Marvin Goodwin, UCLA	S	Philadelphia	144	Darnay Scott, San Diego St.	WR	Cincinnati	30
Rodney Harrison, Western Ill.	DB	San Diego	145	**Heath Shuler**, Tennessee	QB	Washington	3
George Hegamin, N.C State	OT	Dallas	102	Bruce Walker, UCLA	DT	Philadelphia	37
Greg Hill, Texas A&M	RB	Kansas City	25	Lamont Warren, Colorado	RB	Indianapolis	164
Joe Johnson, Louisville	DE	New Orleans	13	**Dan Wilkinson**, Ohio St.	DT	Cincinnati	1
Calvin Jones, Nebraska	RB	LA Raiders	80	Rodney Woodard, West Va.	RB	Not selected	—
Jimmy Klingler, Houston	QB	Not selected	—				

Note: Florida St. true sophomore WR Tamarick Vanover also left school for the pros. Ineligible for the NFL Draft, however, he signed with Las Vegas of the CFL.

Final NCAA Division I-AA Standings

Standings based on conference games only; overall records include postseason games.

American West Conference

	Conference W L T PF PA	Overall W L T PF PA
UC-Davis	3 1 0 159 124	10 2 0 460 297
Southern Utah	3 1 0 77 99	3 7 1 262 303
CS-Sacramento	2 2 0 115 133	4 6 0 231 319
Cal Poly-SLO	1 3 0 111 100	6 4 0 365 201
CS-Northridge	1 3 0 107 113	4 6 0 229 222

Playoffs: No teams invited.
Note: New to Division I-AA in 1993 and included Div. II school UC-Davis and Cal Poly in 1993. UC-Davis, 1-1 in Div. II playoffs, left conference after '93 season. Cal Poly will move up to Div. I-AA in '94.

Big Sky Conference

	Conference W L T PF PA	Overall W L T PF PA
*Montana	7 0 0 280 164	10 2 0 501 310
*Idaho	5 2 0 313 154	11 2 0 577 318
Eastern Wash	5 2 0 186 163	7 3 0 285 225
Montana St	4 3 0 178 171	7 4 0 311 292
Weber St	3 4 0 158 210	7 4 0 315 319
Northern Ariz	3 4 0 182 221	7 4 0 315 293
Boise St	1 6 0 135 228	3 8 0 210 319
Idaho St	0 7 0 133 234	2 9 0 264 307

*Playoffs (2-2): Montana (0-1); Idaho (2-1).

Gateway Athletic Conference

	Conference W L T PF PA	Overall W L T PF PA
*Northern Iowa	5 1 0 160 112	8 4 0 350 238
SW Missouri St	4 2 0 141 139	7 4 0 271 249
Western Ill	4 2 0 108 99	4 7 0 189 247
Illinois St	2 3 1 137 113	6 4 1 256 219
Eastern Ill	2 3 1 159 151	3 7 1 250 310
Indiana St	2 4 0 103 140	4 7 0 234 267
Southern Ill	1 5 0 133 187	2 9 0 252 373

*Playoffs (0-1): Northern Iowa (0-1).

Ivy League

	Conference W L T PF PA	Overall W L T PF PA
Penn	7 0 0 202 77	10 0 0 308 131
Dartmouth	6 1 0 213 148	7 3 0 258 188
Princeton	5 2 0 151 106	8 2 0 241 136
Cornell	3 4 0 146 95	4 6 0 213 158
Brown	3 4 0 127 183	4 6 0 190 267
Yale	2 5 0 99 199	3 7 0 172 293
Harvard	1 6 0 154 193	3 7 0 233 279
Columbia	1 6 0 118 209	2 8 0 155 294

Playoffs: League does not play postseason games.

Metro Atlantic Athletic Conference

	Conference W L T PF PA	Overall W L T PF PA
Iona	5 0 0 172 103	9 2 0 304 212
Canisius	4 1 0 114 90	5 5 0 186 165
St. John's	3 2 0 130 123	8 3 0 298 229
Georgetown	2 3 0 114 91	4 5 0 161 141
St. Peter's	1 4 0 126 119	3 7 0 249 228
Siena	0 5 0 52 182	0 10 0 91 365

Playoffs: No teams invited.
Note: New to Division I-AA in 1993. Duquesne and Marist will join league in '94.

Mid-Eastern Athletic Conference

	Conference W L T PF PA	Overall W L T PF PA
*Howard	6 0 0 243 139	11 1 0 438 270
†S.C. State	4 2 0 216 158	8 4 0 384 239
Delaware St	4 2 0 211 192	6 5 0 371 352
N.Carolina A&T	3 3 0 225 184	8 3 0 420 259
Florida A&M	3 3 0 129 144	5 6 0 216 257
Beth-Cookman	1 5 0 137 189	3 8 0 255 321
Morgan St	0 6 0 156 311	2 9 0 315 496

*Playoffs (0-1): Howard (0-1).
†Heritage Bowl: South Carolina St. lost to SWAC Champion Southern-Baton Rouge, 11-0 (Jan. 1).

Ohio Valley Conference

	Conference					Overall				
	W	L	T	PF	PA	W	L	T	PF	PA
*Eastern Ky	8	0	0	273	95	8	4	0	331	190
Tenn. Tech	7	1	0	197	87	8	3	0	263	154
Tenn-Martin	5	3	0	142	153	6	5	0	169	201
Tennessee St	4	4	0	157	173	4	7	0	218	253
Mid. Tenn. St	4	4	0	253	149	5	6	0	354	235
Murray St	4	4	0	167	172	4	7	0	201	279
Morehead St	2	6	0	56	212	3	8	0	122	334
SE Missouri St	2	6	0	114	167	3	8	0	176	245
Austin Peay St	0	8	0	114	265	1	10	0	179	354

Playoffs (0-1): Eastern Kentucky (0-1).

Patriot League

	Conference					Overall				
	W	L	T	PF	PA	W	L	T	PF	PA
Lehigh	4	1	0	143	94	7	4	0	309	336
Lafayette	3	1	1	131	99	5	4	2	270	214
Bucknell	3	2	0	114	115	4	7	0	193	302
Holy Cross	2	3	0	115	128	3	8	0	205	326
Colgate	1	3	1	79	95	3	7	1	149	284
Fordham	1	4	0	68	119	1	10	0	145	315

Playoffs: League does not play postseason games.

Pioneer League

	Conference					Overall				
	W	L	T	PF	PA	W	L	T	PF	PA
Dayton	5	1	0	163	63	9	1	0	298	114
Drake	3	2	0	87	116	8	2	0	304	239
Butler	3	3	0	112	102	4	6	0	183	206
Evansville	2	3	0	106	105	6	4	0	251	175
San Diego	2	4	0	139	150	6	4	0	252	227
Valparaiso	1	4	0	85	138	5	5	0	239	280

Note: New to Division I-AA in 1993.
Playoffs: No teams invited.

Southern Conference

	Conference					Overall				
	W	L	T	PF	PA	W	L	T	PF	PA
*Ga. Southern	7	1	0	236	108	10	3	0	357	200
*Marshall	6	2	0	221	96	11	4	0	414	206
W. Carolina	5	3	0	215	145	6	5	0	281	235
The Citadel	4	4	0	178	193	5	6	0	246	255
Furman	4	4	0	204	164	5	5	1	247	232
Appalachian St	4	4	0	180	190	4	7	0	207	252
E. Tenn. St	3	5	0	145	178	5	6	0	213	222
Tenn-Chatt	2	6	0	158	295	4	7	0	250	376
VMI	1	7	0	110	278	1	10	0	139	396

Playoffs (4-2): Georgia Southern (1-1); Marshall (3-1).

Southland Conference

	Conference					Overall				
	W	L	T	PF	PA	W	L	T	PF	PA
*McNeese St	7	0	0	198	94	10	3	0	366	233
*NE Louisiana	6	1	0	278	160	9	3	0	462	275
*S.F. Austin St	5	2	0	198	142	8	4	0	362	272
Northwestern St	3	4	0	173	218	5	6	0	264	314
North Texas	2	5	0	224	219	4	7	0	328	365
Sam Houston St	2	5	0	149	187	4	7	0	260	259
Nicholls St	2	5	0	176	267	3	8	0	269	377
SW Texas St	1	6	0	135	244	2	9	0	220	375

Playoffs (1-3): McNeese St. (1-1); Northeast Louisiana (0-1); Stephen F. Austin St. (0-1).

Southwestern Athletic Conference

	Conference					Overall				
	W	L	T	PF	PA	W	L	T	PF	PA
Southern-BR	7	0	0	225	87	11	1	0	320	142
Alcorn St	6	1	0	218	189	8	3	0	347	350
Grambling St	4	3	0	194	131	7	4	0	333	206
Jackson St	3	3	1	138	108	5	5	1	238	213
Alabama St	3	3	1	149	124	5	4	1	190	192
Miss.Valley St	2	3	2	156	124	4	4	2	225	182
Texas Southern	1	6	0	177	257	2	9	0	243	417
Prairie View	0	7	0	43	280	0	11	0	77	423

Playoffs: No teams invited.
†**Heritage Bowl:** Southern-Baton Rouge beat MEAC Runner-up South Carolina St. 11-0 (Jan. 1).

Yankee Conference

	Conference					Overall				
Mid-Atlantic	W	L	T	PF	PA	W	L	T	PF	PA
*Wm. & Mary	7	1	0	320	173	9	3	0	442	240
*Delaware	6	2	0	257	190	9	4	0	485	366
James Madison	4	5	0	285	236	6	5	0	375	253
Richmond	4	6	0	170	259	5	6	0	208	273
Villanova	2	7	0	97	259	3	8	0	135	291
Northeastern	2	8	0	182	254	2	9	0	195	281

	Conference					Overall				
New England	W	L	T	PF	PA	W	L	T	PF	PA
*Boston Univ	9	0	0	290	118	12	1	0	436	211
Massachusetts	7	3	0	247	214	8	3	0	284	221
Connecticut	5	3	0	192	149	6	5	0	261	217
New Hampshire	5	5	0	296	225	6	5	0	310	232
Maine	2	7	0	145	277	3	8	0	190	331
Rhode Island	1	7	0	134	261	3	8	0	211	331

Playoffs (2-3): William & Mary (0-1); Delaware (1-1); Boston University (1-1).

I-AA Independents

	W	L	T	PF	PA
*Troy St	12	0	1	484	203
*Youngstown St	13	2	0	448	232
Alabama-Birmingham	9	2	0	356	213
Wagner	9	2	0	292	187
Towson St	8	2	0	381	223
*Central Florida	9	3	0	413	277
Western Kentucky	8	3	0	310	228
Hofstra	6	3	1	271	189
St. Mary's-CA	6	3	1	298	221
Davidson	6	4	0	258	184
Liberty	6	5	0	259	286
Marist	5	5	0	222	194
Central Connecticut St	5	5	0	220	265
Samford	5	6	0	191	255
Duquesne	4	6	0	169	213
St. Francis-PA	3	7	0	182	241
Charleston Southern	3	8	0	135	381
Buffalo	1	10	0	190	359

Playoffs (6-2): Troy St. (2-1); Youngstown St. (4-0); Central Florida (0-1).

Division I-AA Adds 23

Beginning with the 1993-1994 academic year, all NCAA Division I schools must classify all sports in Division I. As a result, 23 schools upgraded their football programs to Div. I-AA; eight from Div. II and 15 from Div. III.

NCAA Playoffs

Division I-AA

First Round (Nov. 27)

at Boston Univ. 27	2OT	Northern Iowa 21
Delaware 49		at Montana 48
at Georgia Southern 14		Eastern Kentucky 12
Idaho 34		at NE Louisiana 31
at Marshall 28		Howard 14
at McNeese St. 34		William & Mary 28
at Troy St. 42		Stephen F. Austin 20
at Youngstown St. 56		Central Florida 30

Quarterfinals (Dec. 4)

at Marshall 34	Delaware 31
at Idaho 21	Boston Univ. 14
Troy St. 35	at McNeese St. 28
at Youngstown St. 34	Georgia Southern 14

Semifinals (Dec. 11)

at Marshall 24	Troy St. 21
at Youngstown St. 35	Idaho 16

Championship Game

Dec. 18 at Huntington, W. Va. (Att: 29,218)

Youngstown St. 17	Marshall 5
(13-2-0)	(11-4-0)

Division II

First Round (Nov. 20)

at Hampton (Va.) 33	Albany St. (Ga.) 7
at Indiana (Pa.) 28	Ferris St. (Mich.) 21
Mankato St. (Minn.) 34	at Mo. Southern St. 13
at New Haven (Conn.) 48	Edinboro (Pa.) 28
at North Alabama 38	Carson-Newman (Tenn.) 28
at North Dakota 17	Pittsburg St. (Kan.) 14
Texas A&M-Kingsville 50	at Portland St. 15
at UC-Davis 37	Fort Hays St. (Kan.) 34

Quarterfinals (Nov. 27)

Indiana (Pa.) 38	at New Haven 35
at North Alabama 45	Hampton 20
at North Dakota 54	Mankato St. 21
Texas A&M-Kingsville 51	at UC-Davis 28

Semifinals (Dec. 4)

at Indiana (Pa.) 21	North Dakota 6
at North Alabama 27	Texas A&M-Kingsville 25

Championship Game

Dec. 11 at Florence, Ala. (Att: 15,631)

North Alabama 41	Indiana (Pa.) 34
(14-0-0)	(13-1-0)

Division I-AA, II and III Awards

Players of the Year

Payton Award (Div. I-AA)	Doug Nussmeier, QB Idaho (Sr.)
Hill Trophy (Div. II)	Roger Graham, RB New Haven (Jr.)
Gagliardi Trophy (Div. III)	Jim Ballard, QB Mount Union (Sr.)

Coaches of the Year

Eddie Robinson Award	Dan Allen, Boston Univ.
AFCA (NCAA Div. I-AA)	Dan Allen, Boston Univ.
AFCA (College Div. I)	Bobby Wallace, No. Alabama
AFCA (College Div. II)	Larry Kehres, Mount Union

Division III

First Round (Nov. 20)

at Albion (Mich.) 41	Anderson (Ind.) 21
Frostburg St. (Md.) 26	at Wilkes (Pa.) 25
at Mount Union (Ohio) 40	Allegheny (Pa.) 7
at Rowan (N.J.) 29	Buffalo St. (N.Y.) 6
at St. John's (Minn.) 32	Coe (Iowa) 14
at Wash. & Jeff. (Pa.) 27	Moravian (Pa.) 7
Wm. Patterson (N.J.) 17	at Union (N.Y.) 7
at Wisconsin-La Cross 55	Wartburg (Iowa) 26

Quarterfinals (Nov. 27)

at Mount Union 30	Albion 16
Rowan 37	at Wm. Patterson 0
St. John's (Minn.) 47	at WI-La Crosse 25
Washington & Jefferson 28	at Frostburg St. 7

Semifinals (Dec. 4)

at Mount Union 56	St. John's (Minn.) 8
Rowan 23	at Washington & Jefferson 16

Amos Alonzo Stagg Bowl

Dec. 11 at Salem, Va. (Att: 7,304)

Mount Union 34	Rowan 24
(14-0-0)	(11-2-0)

NAIA Playoffs

Division I

First Round (Nov. 20)

at Arkansas-Monticello 26	Langston (Okla.) 13
Central St. (Ohio) 58	at Winona St. (Minn.) 7
East Central (Okla.) 24	at W. New Mexico 22
Glenville St. (W.Va.) 41	at Carroll (Mont.) 24

Semifinals (Dec. 4)

at East Central 27	Arkansas-Monticello 0
at Glenville St. 13	Central St. 12

Championship

Dec. 11 at Ada, Okla. (Att: 5,750)

East Central 49	Glenville St. 35
(10-3-0)	(10-3-0)

Division II

First Round (Nov. 20)

at Baker (Kan.) 39	Hastings (Neb.) 19
Central Washington 28	at Linfield (Ore.) 26
at Doane (Neb.) 17	Bethany (Kan.) 10
at Findlay (Ohio) 28	Tiffin (Ohio) 14
at Hardin-Simmons (Texas) 42	Evangel (Mo.) 21
Mary (N.D.) 31	at Minot (N.D.) 20
at Pacific Lutheran (Wash.) 61	Cumberland (Tenn.) 7
Westminster (Pa.) 25	at Georgetown (Ky.) 13

Quarterfinals (Dec. 4)

at Baker 28	Doane 21
Hardin-Simmons 30	Mary 20
at Pacific Lutheran 35	Central Washington 17
Westminster 24	at Findlay 0

Semifinals (Dec. 11)

at Pacific Lutheran 52	Baker 14
at Westminster 10	Hardin-Simmons 0

Championship

Dec. 18 at Portland, Ore. (Att: 7,262)

Pacific Lutheran 50	Westminster 20
(12-0-1)	(10-3-0)

COLLEGE FOOTBALL

S T A T I S T I C S

THE 1995 INFORMATION PLEASE SPORTS ALMANAC

THROUGH THE YEARS

1883-1994

BOWLS • ALL-TIME LEADERS

SEC
B

PAGE
163

National Champions

Over the years, 23 different national selectors have chosen college football's Number One team by way of polls (12), mathematical rating systems (10) and historical research (1). The list below has been culled from eight of those groups: the Helms Athletic Foundation (1883–1935), the Dickinson System (1924–40), Associated Press (since 1936), United Press (1950–57), International News Service (1952–57), United Press International (1958–90), the Football Writers Association of America (since 1954), the National Football Foundation and Hall of Fame (since 1959), and USA Today/CNN (since 1991). In 1991, the American Football Coaches Association switched its poll from UPI to USA Today/CNN, and UPI merged with the NFF-Hall of Fame poll.

Bowl game results were counted in the Helms selections but not in the Dickinson picks. The final AP sportswriters and broadcasters poll was taken following the bowl games for the first time in 1965. After returning to a pre-bowls final vote in 1966 and '67, the AP poll has been taken following the bowls since 1968. The FWAA has selected its champion after the bowl games since 1955, the NFF-Hall of Fame since 1971, UPI after 1974, and USA Today/CNN since 1982.

Originally the AP Trophy, the Associated Press its championship prize in honor of Alabama coach Bear Bryant after his death in 1983. The Football Writers' championship trophy is called the Grantland Rice Award (in honor of the legendary sportswriter) and the NFF-Hall of Fame trophy is called the MacArthur Bowl (in honor of Gen. Douglas MacArthur).

Whenever more than one champion is listed in the chart below, the selector's initials are given.

Multiple champions (1883–1935): Yale (11); Princeton and Harvard (7); Michigan and Penn (4); Cornell, Notre Dame and USC (3); Alabama, Georgia Tech, Illinois, Minnesota and Pittsburgh (2).

Multiple champions (since 1936): Notre Dame (9); Alabama (7); Ohio St. and Oklahoma (6); USC (5); Miami-FL and Minnesota (4); Michigan St. and Texas (3); Army, Georgia Tech, Nebraska, Penn St. and Pittsburgh (2).

Year		Record	Year		Record	Year		Record
1883	**Yale**	8-0-0	1889	**Princeton**	10-0-0	1895	**Penn**	14-0-0
1884	**Yale**	9-0-0	1890	**Harvard**	11-0-0	1896	**Princeton**	10-0-1
1885	**Princeton**	9-0-0	1891	**Yale**	13-0-0	1897	**Penn**	15-0-0
1886	**Yale**	9-0-1	1892	**Yale**	13-0-0	1898	**Harvard**	11-0-0
1887	**Yale**	9-0-0	1893	**Princeton**	11-0-0	1899	**Harvard**	10-0-1
1888	**Yale**	13-0-0	1894	**Yale**	16-0-0			

Year		Record	Bowl Game	Head Coach	Outstanding Player
1900	**Yale**	12-0-0	No bowl	Malcolm McBride	Perry Hale, HB
1901	**Michigan**	11-0-0	Won Rose	Hurry Up Yost	Willie Heston, HB
1902	**Michigan**	11-0-0	No bowl	Hurry Up Yost	Willie Heston, HB
1903	**Princeton**	11-0-0	No bowl	Art Hillebrand	John DeWitt, G
1904	**Penn**	12-0-0	No bowl	Carl Williams	Andy Smith, HB
1905	**Chicago**	11-0-0	No bowl	Amos Alonzo Stagg	Walter Eckersall, QB
1906	**Princeton**	9-0-1	No bowl	Bill Roper	Ed Dillon, HB
1907	**Yale**	9-0-1	No bowl	Bill Knox	T.A.D. Jones, HB
1908	**Penn**	11-0-1	No bowl	Sol Metzger	Hunter Scarlett, E
1909	**Yale**	10-0-0	No bowl	Howard Jones	Ted Coy, FB
1910	**Harvard**	8-0-1	No bowl	Percy Haughton	Percy Wendell, HB
1911	**Princeton**	8-0-2	No bowl	Bill Roper	Sanford White, E
1912	**Harvard**	9-0-0	No bowl	Percy Haughton	Charley Brickley, HB
1913	**Harvard**	9-0-0	No bowl	Percy Haughton	Eddie Mahan, FB
1914	**Army**	9-0-0	No bowl	Charley Daly	John McEwan, C
1915	**Cornell**	9-0-0	No bowl	Al Sharpe	Charley Barrett, HB
1916	**Pittsburgh**	8-0-0	No bowl	Pop Warner	Bob Peck, C
1917	**Georgia Tech**	9-0-0	No bowl	John Heisman	George Strupper, HB
1918	**Pittsburgh**	4-1-0	No bowl	Pop Warner	Tom Davies, HB
1919	**Harvard**	9-0-1	Won Rose	Bob Fisher	Ed Casey, HB
1920	**California**	9-0-0	Won Rose	Andy Smith	Brick Muller, E
1921	**Cornell**	8-0-0	No bowl	Gil Dobie	Eddie Kaw, HB
1922	**Cornell**	8-0-0	No bowl	Gil Dobie	George Pfann, QB
1923	**Illinois**	8-0-0	No bowl	Bob Zuppke	Red Grange, HB
1924	**Notre Dame**	10-0-0	Won Rose	Knute Rockne	"The Four Horsemen"*

*Notre Dame's **Four Horsemen** were Harry Stuhldreher (QB), Jim Crowley (HB), Don Miller (HB-P) and Elmer Layden (FB).

National Champions (Cont.)

Year		Record	Bowl Game	Head Coach	Outstanding Player
1925	**Alabama** (H)	10-0-0	Won Rose	Wallace Wade	Johnny Mack Brown, HB
	& Dartmouth (D)	8-0-0	No bowl	Jesse Hawley	Andy Oberlander, HB
1926	**Alabama**	9-0-1	Tied Rose	Wallace Wade	Hoyt Winslett, E
	& Stanford (D)	10-0-1	Tied Rose	Pop Warner	Ted Shipkey, E
1927	**Illinois**	7-0-1	No bowl	Bob Zuppke	Russ Crane, G
1928	**Georgia Tech** (H)	10-0-0	Won Rose	Bill Alexander	Pete Pund, C
	& USC (D)	9-0-1	No bowl	Howard Jones	Lloyd Thomas, HB
1929	**Notre Dame**	9-0-0	No bowl	Knute Rockne	Frank Carideo, QB
1930	**Notre Dame**	10-0-0	No bowl	Knute Rockne	Frank Carideo, QB
1931	**USC**	10-1-0	Won Rose	Howard Jones	Ernie Pinckert, HB
1932	**USC** (H)	10-0-0	Won Rose	Howard Jones	Ernie Smith, T-K
	& Michigan (D)	8-0-0	No bowl	Harry Kipke	Harry Newman, QB
1933	**Michigan**	7-0-1	No bowl	Harry Kipke	Frank Wistert, T
1934	**Minnesota**	8-0-0	No bowl	Bernie Bierman	Pug Lund, HB
1935	**Minnesota** (H)	8-0-0	No bowl	Bernie Bierman	Dick Smith, T
	& SMU (D)	12-1-0	Lost Rose	Matty Bell	Bobby Wilson, HB
1936	**Minnesota**	7-1-0	No bowl	Bernie Bierman	Ed Widseth, T
1937	**Pittsburgh**	9-0-1	No bowl	Jock Sutherland	Marshall Goldberg, HB
1938	**TCU**	11-0-0	Won Sugar	Dutch Meyer	Davey O'Brien, QB
1939	**Texas A&M**	11-0-0	Won Sugar	Homer Norton	John Kimbrough, FB
1940	**Minnesota**	8-0-0	No Bowl	Bernie Bierman	George Franck, FB
1941	**Minnesota**	8-0-0	No bowl	Bernie Bierman	Bruce Smith, HB
1942	**Ohio St.**	9-1-0	No bowl	Paul Brown	Gene Fekete, FB
1943	**Notre Dame**	9-1-0	No bowl	Frank Leahy	Angelo Bertelli, QB
1944	**Army**	9-0-0	No bowl	Red Blaik	Glenn Davis, HB
1945	**Army**	9-0-0	No bowl	Red Blaik	Doc Blanchard, FB
1946	**Notre Dame**	8-0-1	No bowl	Frank Leahy	Johnny Lujack, QB
1947	**Notre Dame**	9-0-0	No bowl	Frank Leahy	Johnny Lujack, QB
1948	**Michigan**	9-0-0	No bowl	Bennie Oosterbaan	Dick Rifenburg, E
1949	**Notre Dame**	10-0-0	No bowl	Frank Leahy	Leon Hart, E
1950	**Oklahoma**	10-1-0	Lost Sugar	Bud Wilkinson	Leon Heath, FB
1951	**Tennessee**	10-0-0	Lost Sugar	Bob Neyland	Hank Lauricella, QB
1952	**Michigan St.** (AP, UP)	9-0-0	No bowl	Biggie Munn	Don McAuliffe, HB
	& Georgia Tech (INS)	12-0-0	Won Sugar	Bobby Dodd	Hal Miller, T
1953	**Maryland**	10-1-0	Lost Orange	Jim Tatum	Bernie Faloney, QB
1954	**Ohio St.** (AP, INS)	10-0-0	Won Rose	Woody Hayes	Howard Cassady, HB
	& UCLA (UP, FW)	9-0-0	No bowl	Red Sanders	Bob Davenport, FB
1955	**Oklahoma**	11-0-0	Won Orange	Bud Wilkinson	Jerry Tubbs, C
1956	**Oklahoma**	10-0-0	No bowl	Bud Wilkinson	Tommy McDonald, HB
1957	**Auburn** (AP)	10-0-0	No bowl	Shug Jordan	Jimmy Phillips, E
	& Ohio St. (UP, FW, INS)	9-1-0	Won Rose	Woody Hayes	Bob White, FB
1958	**LSU** (AP, UPI)	11-0-0	Won Sugar	Paul Dietzel	Billy Cannon, HB
	& Iowa (FW)	8-1-1	Won Rose	Forest Evashevski	Randy Duncan, QB
1959	**Syracuse**	11-0-0	Won Cotton	Ben Schwartzwalder	Ernie Davis, HB
1960	**Minnesota** (AP, UPI, NFF)	8-2-0	Lost Rose	Murray Warmath	Tom Brown, G
	& Mississippi (FW)	10-0-0	Won Sugar	Johnny Vaught	Jake Gibbs, QB
1961	**Alabama** (AP, UPI, NFF)	11-0-0	Won Sugar	Bear Bryant	Billy Neighbors, T
	& Ohio St. (FW)	8-0-1	No bowl	Woody Hayes	Bob Ferguson, FB
1962	**USC**	11-0-0	Won Rose	John McKay	Hal Bedsole, E
1963	**Texas**	11-0-0	Won Cotton	Darrell Royal	Scott Appleton, T
1964	**Alabama** (AP, UPI)	10-1-0	Lost Orange	Bear Bryant	Joe Namath, QB
	Arkansas (FW)	11-0-0	Won Cotton	Frank Broyles	Ronnie Caveness, LB
	& Notre Dame (NFF)	9-1-0	No bowl	Ara Parseghian	John Huarte, QB
1965	**Alabama** (AP, FW-tie)	9-1-1	Won Orange	Bear Bryant	Paul Crane, C
	& Michigan St. (UPI, NFF, FW-tie)	10-1-0	Lost Rose	Duffy Daugherty	George Webster, LB
1966	**Notre Dame** (AP, UPI, FW, NFF-tie)	9-0-1	No bowl	Ara Parseghian	Jim Lynch, LB
	& Michigan St. (NFF-tie)	9-0-1	No bowl	Duffy Daugherty	Bubba Smith, DE
1967	**USC**	10-1-0	Won Rose	John McKay	O.J. Simpson, HB
1968	**Ohio St.**	10-0-0	Won Rose	Woody Hayes	Rex Kern, QB
1969	**Texas**	11-0-0	Won Cotton	Darrell Royal	James Street, QB
1970	**Nebraska** (AP, FW)	11-0-1	Won Orange	Bob Devaney	Jerry Tagge, QB
	Texas (UPI, NFF-tie)	10-1-0	Lost Cotton	Darrell Royal	Steve Worster, RB
	& Ohio St. (NFF-tie)	9-1-0	Lost Rose	Woody Hayes	Jim Stillwagon, MG
1971	**Nebraska**	13-0-0	Won Orange	Bob Devaney	Johnny Rodgers, WR
1972	**USC**	12-0-0	Won Rose	John McKay	Charles Young, TE
1973	**Notre Dame** (AP, FW, NFF)	11-0-0	Won Sugar	Ara Parseghian	Mike Townsend, DB
	& Alabama (UPI)	11-1-0	Lost Sugar	Bear Bryant	Buddy Brown, OT

1974	**Oklahoma** (AP) 11-0-0	No bowl	Barry Switzer	Joe Washington, RB
	& USC (UPI, FW, NFF) 10-1-1	Won Rose	John McKay	Anthony Davis, RB
1975	**Oklahoma**...................................11-1-0	Won Orange	Barry Switzer	Lee Roy Selmon, DT
1976	**Pittsburgh**..................................12-0-0	Won Sugar	Johnny Majors	Tony Dorsett, RB
1977	**Notre Dame**................................11-1-0	Won Cotton	Dan Devine	Ross Browner, DE
1978	**Alabama** (AP, FW, NFF).............11-1-0	Won Sugar	Bear Bryant	Marty Lyons, DT
	& USC (UPI).............................12-1-0	Won Rose	John Robinson	Charles White, RB
1979	**Alabama**....................................12-0-0	Won Sugar	Bear Bryant	Steadman Shealy, QB
1980	**Georgia**.....................................12-0-0	Won Sugar	Vince Dooley	Herschel Walker, RB
1981	**Clemson**.....................................12-0-0	Won Orange	Danny Ford	Jeff Davis, LB
1982	**Penn St.**.....................................11-1-0	Won Sugar	Joe Paterno	Todd Blackledge, QB
1983	**Miami-FL**....................................11-1-0	Won Orange	H. Schnellenberger	Bernie Kosar, QB
1984	**BYU**...13-0-0	Won Holiday	LaVell Edwards	Robbie Bosco, QB
1985	**Oklahoma**...................................11-1-0	Won Orange	Barry Switzer	Brian Bosworth, LB
1986	**Penn St.**.....................................12-0-0	Won Fiesta	Joe Paterno	D.J. Dozier, RB
1987	**Miami-FL**....................................12-0-0	Won Orange	Jimmy Johnson	Steve Walsh, QB
1988	**Notre Dame**................................12-0-0	Won Fiesta	Lou Holtz	Tony Rice, QB
1989	**Miami-FL**....................................11-1-0	Won Sugar	Dennis Erickson	Craig Erickson, QB
1990	**Colorado** (AP, FW, NFF).............11-1-1	Won Orange	Bill McCartney	Eric Bieniemy, RB
	& Georgia Tech (UPI)................11-0-1	Won Citrus	Bobby Ross	Shawn Jones, QB
1991	**Miami-FL** (AP)............................12-0-0	Won Orange	Dennis Erickson	Gino Torretta, QB
	& Washington (USA, FW, NFF)....12-0-0	Won Rose	Don James	Steve Emtman, DT
1992	**Alabama**....................................13-0-0	Won Sugar	Gene Stallings	Eric Curry, DE
1993	**Florida St.**.................................12-1-0	Won Orange	Bobby Bowden	Charlie Ward, QB

Number 1 vs Number 2

Since the Associated Press writers poll started keeping track of such things in 1936, the No.1 and No.2 ranked teams in the country have met 29 times; 19 during the regular season and 10 in bowl games. Since the first showdown in 1943, the No.1 team has beaten the No.2 team 17 times, lost 10 and there have been two ties. Each showdown is listed below with the date, the match-up, the final score, the stadium and site.

Date	Match-up	Stadium
Oct. 9 1943	#1 Notre Dame (2-0) 35	Michigan
	#2 Michigan (3-0) 12	(Ann Arbor)
Nov. 20 1943	#1 Notre Dame (8-0).........14	Notre Dame
	#2 Iowa Pre-Flight (8-0).....13	(South Bend)
Dec. 2 1944	#1 Army (8-0) 23	Municipal
	#2 Navy (6-2)......................7	(Baltimore)
Nov. 10 1945	#1 Army (6-0) 48	Yankee
	#2 Notre Dame (5-0-1) 0	(New York)
Dec. 1 1945	#1 Army (8-0) 32	Municipal
	#2 Navy (7-0-1) 13	(Philadelphia)
Nov. 9 1946	#1 Army (7-0) 0	Yankee
	#2 Notre Dame (5-0)...........0	(New York)
Jan. 1 1963	#1 USC (10-0) 42	ROSE BOWL
	#2 Wisconsin (8-1) 37	(Pasadena)
Oct. 12 1963	#2 Texas (3-0) 28	Cotton Bowl
	#1 Oklahoma (2-0) 7	(Dallas)
Jan. 1 1964	#1 Texas (10-0) 28	COTTON BOWL
	#2 Navy (9-1)......................6	(Dallas)
Nov. 19 1966	#1 Notre Dame (8-0).........10	Spartan
	#2 Michigan St. (9-0) 10	(East Lansing)
Sept. 28 1968	#1 Purdue (1-0) 37	Notre Dame
	#2 Notre Dame (1-0)..........22	(South Bend)
Jan. 1 1969	#1 Ohio St. (9-0) 27	ROSE BOWL
	#2 USC (9-0-1)..................16	(Pasadena)
Dec. 6 1969	#1 Texas (9-0) 15	Razorback
	#2 Arkansas (9-0)..............14	(Fayetteville)
Nov. 25 1971	#1 Nebraska (10-0) 35	Owen Field
	#2 Oklahoma (9-0)............31	(Norman)
Jan. 1 1972	#1 Nebraska (12-0)...........38	ORANGE BOWL
	#2 Alabama (11-0).............6	(Miami)
Jan. 1 1979	#2 Alabama (10-1)...........14	SUGAR BOWL
	#1 Penn St. (11-0)..............7	(New Orleans)
Sept. 26 1981	#1 USC (2-0) 28	Coliseum
	#2 Oklahoma (1-0)............24	(Los Angeles)
Jan. 1 1983	#2 Penn St. (10-1)............27	SUGAR BOWL
	#1 Georgia (11-0) 23	(New Orleans)
Oct. 19 1985	#1 Iowa (5-0) 12	Kinnick
	#2 Michigan (5-0).............10	(Iowa City)
Sept. 27 1986	#2 Miami-FL (3-0) 28	Orange Bowl
	#1 Oklahoma (2-0)............16	(Miami)
Jan. 2 1987	#2 Penn St. (11-0)............14	FIESTA BOWL
	#1 Miami-FL (11-0)...........10	(Tempe)
Nov. 21 1987	#2 Oklahoma (10-0)..........17	Memorial
	#1 Nebraska (10-0).............7	(Lincoln)
Jan. 1 1988	#2 Miami-FL (11-0)...........20	ORANGE BOWL
	#1 Oklahoma (11-0)...........14	(Miami)
Nov. 26 1988	#1 Notre Dame (10-0)........27	Coliseum
	#2 USC (10-0)..................10	(Los Angeles)
Sept. 16 1989	#1 Notre Dame (1-0).........24	Michigan
	#2 Michigan (0-0).............19	(Ann Arbor)
Nov. 16 1991	#2 Miami-FL (8-0) 17	Doak Campbell
	#1 Florida St. (10-0).........16	(Tallahassee)
Jan. 1 1993	#2 Alabama (12-0-0).........34	SUGAR BOWL
	#1 Miama-FL (11-0-0).......13	(New Orleans)
Nov. 13 1993	#2 Notre Dame (9-0)........31	Notre Dame
	#1 Florida St. (9-0)...........24	(South Bend)
Jan. 1 1994	#1 Florida St. (11-1).........18	ORANGE BOWL
	#2 Nebraska (11-0)...........16	(Miami)

Associated Press Final Polls

The Associated Press introduced its weekly college football poll of sportswriters (later, sportswriters and broadcasters) in 1936. The final AP poll was released at the end of the regular season until 1965, when bowl results were included for one year. After a two-year return to regular season games only, the final poll has come out after the bowls since 1968.

1936

Final poll released Nov. 30. Top 20 regular season results after that: **Dec.5**—#8 Notre Dame tied USC, 13-13; #17 Tennessee tied Ole Miss, 0-0; #18 Arkansas over Texas, 6-0. **Dec.12**—#16 TCU over #6 Santa Clara, 9-0.

		As of Nov. 30	Head Coach	After Bowls
1	Minnesota	7-1-0	Bernie Bierman	same
2	LSU	9-0-1	Bernie Moore	9-1-1
3	Pittsburgh	7-1-1	Jock Sutherland	8-1-1
4	Alabama	8-0-1	Frank Thomas	same
5	Washington	7-1-1	Jimmy Phelan	7-2-1
6	Santa Clara	7-0-0	Buck Shaw	8-1-0
7	Northwestern	7-1-0	Pappy Waldorf	same
8	Notre Dame	6-2-0	Elmer Layden	6-2-1
9	Nebraska	7-2-0	Dana X. Bible	same
10	Penn	7-1-1	Harvey Harman	same
11	Duke	9-1-0	Wallace Wade	same
12	Yale	7-1-0	Ducky Pond	same
13	Dartmouth	7-1-1	Red Blaik	same
14	Duquesne	7-2-0	John Smith	8-2-0
15	Fordham	5-1-2	Jim Crowley	same
16	TCU	7-2-2	Dutch Meyer	9-2-2
17	Tennessee	6-2-1	Bob Neyland	6-2-2
18	Arkansas	6-3-0	Fred Thomsen	7-3-0
	Navy	6-3-0	Tom Hamilton	same
20	Marquette	7-1-0	Frank Murray	7-2-0

Key Bowl Games

Sugar—#6 Santa Clara over #2 LSU, 21-14; **Rose**—#3 Pitt over #5 Washington, 21-0; **Orange**—#14 Duquesne over Mississippi St., 13-12; **Cotton**—#16 TCU over #20 Marquette, 16-6.

1937

Final poll released Nov.29. Top 20 regular season results after that: **Dec.4**—#18 Rice over SMU, 15-7.

		As of Nov. 29	Head Coach	After Bowls
1	Pittsburgh	9-0-1	Jock Sutherland	same
2	California	9-0-1	Stub Allison	10-0-1
3	Fordham	7-0-1	Jim Crowley	same
4	Alabama	9-0-0	Frank Thomas	9-1-0
5	Minnesota	6-2-0	Bernie Bierman	same
6	Villanova	8-0-1	Clipper Smith	same
7	Dartmouth	7-0-2	Red Blaik	same
8	LSU	9-1-0	Bernie Moore	9-2-0
9	Notre Dame	6-2-1	Elmer Layden	same
	Santa Clara	8-0-0	Buck Shaw	9-0-0
11	Nebraska	6-1-2	Biff Jones	same
12	Yale	6-1-1	Ducky Pond	same
13	Ohio St.	6-2-0	Francis Schmidt	same
14	Holy Cross	8-0-2	Eddie Anderson	same
	Arkansas	6-2-2	Fred Thomsen	same
16	TCU	4-2-2	Dutch Meyer	same
17	Colorado	8-0-0	Bunnie Oakes	8-1-0
18	Rice	4-3-2	Jimmy Kitts	6-3-2
19	North Carolina	7-1-1	Ray Wolf	same
20	Duke	7-2-1	Wallace Wade	same

Key Bowl Games

Rose—#2 Cal over #4 Alabama, 13-0; **Sugar**—#9 Santa Clara over #8 LSU, 6-0; **Cotton**—#18 Rice over #17 Colorado, 28-14; **Orange**—Auburn over Michigan St., 6-0.

1938

Final poll released Dec.5. Top 20 regular season results after that: **Dec.26**—#14 Cal over Georgia Tech, 13-7.

		As of Dec. 5	Head Coach	After Bowls
1	TCU	10-0-0	Dutch Meyer	11-0-0
2	Tennessee	10-0-0	Bob Neyland	11-0-0
3	Duke	9-0-0	Wallace Wade	9-1-0
4	Oklahoma	10-0-0	Tom Stidham	10-1-0
5	Notre Dame	8-1-0	Elmer Layden	same
6	Carnegie Tech	7-1-0	Bill Kern	7-2-0
7	USC	8-2-0	Howard Jones	9-2-0
8	Pittsburgh	8-2-0	Jock Sutherland	same
9	Holy Cross	8-1-0	Eddie Anderson	same
10	Minnesota	6-2-0	Bernie Bierman	same
11	Texas Tech	10-0-0	Pete Cawthon	10-1-0
12	Cornell	5-1-1	Carl Snavely	same
13	Alabama	7-1-1	Frank Thomas	same
14	California	9-1-0	Stub Allison	10-1-0
15	Fordham	6-1-2	Jim Crowley	same
16	Michigan	6-1-1	Fritz Crisler	same
17	Northwestern	4-2-2	Pappy Waldorf	same
18	Villanova	8-0-1	Clipper Smith	same
19	Tulane	7-2-1	Red Dawson	same
20	Dartmouth	7-2-0	Red Blaik	same

Key Bowl Games

Sugar—#1 TCU over #6 Carnegie Tech, 15-7; **Orange**—#2 Tennessee over #4 Oklahoma, 17-0; **Rose**—#7 USC over #3 Duke, 7-3; **Cotton**—St. Mary's over #11 Texas Tech 20-13.

1939

Final poll released Dec.11. Top 20 regular season results after that: None.

		As of Dec. 11	Head Coach	After Bowls
1	Texas A&M	10-0-0	Homer Norton	11-0-0
2	Tennessee	10-0-0	Bob Neyland	10-1-0
3	USC	7-0-2	Howard Jones	8-0-2
4	Cornell	8-0-0	Carl Snavely	same
5	Tulane	8-0-1	Red Dawson	8-1-1
6	Missouri	8-1-0	Don Faurot	8-2-0
7	UCLA	6-0-4	Babe Horrell	same
8	Duke	8-1-0	Wallace Wade	same
9	Iowa	6-1-1	Eddie Anderson	same
10	Duquesne	8-0-1	Buff Donelli	same
11	Boston College	9-1-0	Frank Leahy	9-2-0
12	Clemson	8-1-0	Jess Neely	9-1-0
13	Notre Dame	7-2-0	Elmer Layden	same
14	Santa Clara	5-1-3	Buck Shaw	same
15	Ohio St.	6-2-0	Francis Schmidt	same
16	Georgia Tech	7-2-0	Bill Alexander	8-2-0
17	Fordham	6-2-0	Jim Crowley	same
18	Nebraska	7-1-1	Biff Jones	same
19	Oklahoma	6-2-1	Tom Stidham	same
20	Michigan	6-2-0	Fritz Crisler	same

Key Bowl Games

Sugar—#1 Texas A&M over #5 Tulane, 14-13; **Rose**—#3 USC over #2 Tennessee, 14-0; **Orange**—#16 Georgia Tech over #6 Missouri, 21-7; **Cotton**—#12 Clemson over #11 Boston College, 6-3.

1940

Final poll released Dec.2. Top 20 regular season results after that: **Dec.7**—#16 SMU over Rice, 7-6.

	As of Dec. 2	Head Coach	After Bowls
1 Minnesota	8-0-0	Bernie Bierman	same
2 Stanford	9-0-0	Clark Shaughnessy	10-0-0
3 Michigan	7-1-0	Fritz Crisler	same
4 Tennessee	10-0-0	Bob Neyland	10-1-0
5 Boston College	10-0-0	Frank Leahy	11-0-0
6 Texas A&M	8-1-0	Homer Norton	9-1-0
7 Nebraska	8-1-0	Biff Jones	8-2-0
8 Northwestern	6-2-0	Pappy Waldorf	same
9 Mississippi St.	9-0-1	Allyn McKeen	10-0-1
10 Washington	7-2-0	Jimmy Phelan	same
11 Santa Clara	6-1-1	Buck Shaw	same
12 Fordham	7-1-0	Jim Crowley	7-2-0
13 Georgetown	8-1-0	Jack Hagerty	8-2-0
14 Penn	6-1-1	George Munger	same
15 Cornell	6-2-0	Carl Snavely	same
16 SMU	7-1-1	Matty Bell	8-1-1
17 Hardin-Simmons	9-0-0	Warren Woodson	same
18 Duke	7-2-0	Wallace Wade	same
19 Lafayette	9-0-0	Hooks Mylin	same
20 —			

Note: Only 19 teams ranked.

Key Bowl Games

Rose—#2 Stanford over #7 Nebraska, 21-13; **Sugar**—#5 Boston College over #4 Tennessee, 19-13; **Cotton**—#6 Texas A&M over #12 Fordham, 13-12; **Orange**—#9 Mississippi St. over #13 Georgetown, 14-7.

1941

Final poll released Dec.1. Top 20 regular season results after that: **Dec.6**—#4 Texas over Oregon, 71-7; #9 Texas A&M over #19 Washington St., 7-0; #16 Mississippi St. over San Francisco, 26-13.

	As of Dec. 1	Head Coach	After Bowls
1 Minnesota	8-0-0	Bernie Bierman	same
2 Duke	9-0-0	Wallace Wade	9-1-0
3 Notre Dame	8-0-1	Frank Leahy	same
4 Texas	7-1-1	Dana X. Bible	8-1-1
5 Michigan	6-1-1	Fritz Crisler	same
6 Fordham	7-1-0	Jim Crowley	8-1-0
7 Missouri	8-1-0	Don Faurot	8-2-0
8 Duquesne	8-0-0	Buff Donelli	same
9 Texas A&M	8-1-0	Homer Norton	9-2-0
10 Navy	7-1-1	Swede Larson	same
11 Northwestern	5-3-0	Pappy Waldorf	same
12 Oregon St.	7-2-0	Lon Stiner	8-2-0
13 Ohio St.	6-1-1	Paul Brown	same
14 Georgia	8-1-1	Wally Butts	9-1-1
15 Penn	7-1-1	George Munger	same
16 Mississippi St.	7-1-1	Allyn McKeen	8-1-1
17 Mississippi	6-2-1	Harry Mehre	same
18 Tennessee	8-2-0	John Barnhill	same
19 Washington St.	6-3-0	Babe Hollingbery	6-4-0
20 Alabama	8-2-0	Frank Thomas	9-2-0

Note: 1942 Rose Bowl moved to Durham, N.C., for one year after outbreak of World War II.

Key Bowl Games

Rose—#12 Oregon St. over #2 Duke, 20-16; **Sugar**—#6 Fordham over #7 Missouri, 2-0; **Cotton**—#20 Alabama over #9 Texas A&M, 29-21; **Orange**—#14 Georgia over TCU, 40-26.

1942

Final poll released Nov.30. Top 20 regular season results after that: **Dec.5**—#6 Notre Dame tied Great Lakes Naval Station, 13-13; #13 UCLA over Idaho, 40-13; #14 William & Mary over Oklahoma, 14-7; #17 Washington St. lost to Texas A&M, 21-0; #18 Mississippi St. over San Francisco, 19-7. **Dec.12**—#13 UCLA over USC, 14-7.

	As of Nov. 30	Head Coach	After Bowls
1 Ohio St.	9-1-0	Paul Brown	same
2 Georgia	10-1-0	Wally Butts	11-1-0
3 Wisconsin	8-1-1	Harry Stuhldreher	same
4 Tulsa	10-0-0	Henry Frnka	10-1-0
5 Georgia Tech	9-1-0	Bill Alexander	9-2-0
6 Notre Dame	7-2-1	Frank Leahy	7-2-2
7 Tennessee	8-1-1	John Barnhill	9-1-1
8 Boston College	8-1-0	Denny Myers	8-2-0
9 Michigan	7-3-0	Fritz Crisler	same
10 Alabama	7-3-0	Frank Thomas	8-3-0
11 Texas	8-2-0	Dana X. Bible	9-2-0
12 Stanford	6-4-0	Marchie Schwartz	same
13 UCLA	5-3-0	Babe Horrell	7-4-0
14 William & Mary	8-1-1	Carl Voyles	9-1-1
15 Santa Clara	7-2-0	Buck Shaw	same
16 Auburn	6-4-1	Jack Meagher	same
17 Washington St.	6-1-2	Babe Hollingbery	6-2-2
18 Mississippi St.	7-2-0	Allyn McKeen	8-2-0
19 Minnesota	5-4-0	George Hauser	same
Holy Cross	5-4-1	Ank Scanlon	same
Penn St.	6-1-1	Bob Higgins	same

Key Bowl Games

Rose—#2 Georgia over #13 UCLA, 9-0; **Sugar**—#7 Tennessee over #4 Tulsa, 14-7; **Cotton**—#11 Texas over #5 Georgia Tech, 14-7; **Orange**—#10 Alabama over #8 Boston College, 37-21.

1943

Final poll released Nov.29. Top 20 regular season results after that: **Dec.11**—#10 March Field over #19 Pacific, 19-0.

	As of Nov. 29	Head Coach	After Bowls
1 Notre Dame	9-1-0	Frank Leahy	same
2 Iowa Pre-Flight	9-1-0	Don Faurot	same
3 Michigan	8-1-0	Fritz Crisler	same
4 Navy	8-1-0	Billick Whelchel	same
5 Purdue	9-0-0	Elmer Burnham	same
6 Great Lakes Naval Station	10-2-0	Tony Hinkle	same
7 Duke	8-1-0	Eddie Cameron	same
8 Del Monte Pre-Flight	7-1-0	Bill Kern	same
9 Northwestern	6-2-0	Pappy Waldorf	same
10 March Field	8-1-0	Paul Schissler	9-1-0
11 Army	7-2-1	Red Blaik	same
12 Washington	4-0-0	Ralph Welch	4-1-0
13 Georgia Tech	7-3-0	Bill Alexander	8-3-0
14 Texas	7-1-0	Dana X. Bible	7-1-1
15 Tulsa	6-0-1	Henry Frnka	6-1-1
16 Dartmouth	6-1-0	Earl Brown	same
17 Bainbridge Navy Training School	7-0-0	Joe Maniaci	same
18 Colorado College	7-0-0	Hal White	same
19 Pacific	7-1-0	Amos A. Stagg	7-2-0
20 Penn	6-2-1	George Munger	same

Key Bowl Games

Rose—USC over #12 Washington, 29-0; **Sugar**—#13 Georgia Tech over #15 Tulsa, 20-18; **Cotton**—#14 Texas tied Randolph Field, 7-7; **Orange**—LSU over #4 Texas A&M, 19-14.

Associated Press Final Polls (Cont.)

1944

Final poll released Dec.4. Top 20 regular season results after that: **Dec.10**—#3 Randolph Field over #10 March Field, 20-7; #18 Fort Pierce over Kessler Field, 34-7; Morris Field over #20 Second Air Force, 14-7.

	As of Dec. 4	Head Coach	After Bowls
1 Army	9-0-0	Red Blaik	same
2 Ohio St.	9-0-0	Carroll Widdoes	same
3 Randolph Field	10-0-0	Frank Tritico	12-0-0
4 Navy	6-3-0	Oscar Hagberg	same
5 Bainbridge Navy Training School	10-0-0	Joe Maniaci	same
6 Iowa Pre-Flight	10-1-0	Jack Meagher	same
7 USC	7-0-2	Jeff Cravath	8-0-2
8 Michigan	8-2-0	Fritz Crisler	same
9 Notre Dame	8-2-0	Ed McKeever	same
10 March Field	7-0-2	Paul Schissler	7-1-2
11 Duke	5-4-0	Eddie Cameron	6-4-0
12 Tennessee	7-0-1	John Barnhill	7-1-1
13 Georgia Tech	8-2-0	Bill Alexander	8-3-0
14 Norman Pre-Flight	6-0-0	John Gregg	same
15 Illinois	5-4-1	Ray Eliot	same
16 El Toro Marines	8-1-0	Dick Hanley	same
17 Great Lakes Naval Station	9-2-1	Paul Brown	same
18 Fort Pierce	8-0-0	Hamp Pool	9-0-0
19 St.Mary's Pre-Flight	4-4-0	Jules Sikes	same
20 Second Air Force	10-2-1	Bill Reese	10-4-1

Key Bowl Games

Treasury—#3 Randolph Field over #20 Second Air Force, 13-6; **Rose**—#7 USC over #12 Tennessee, 25-0; **Sugar**—#11 Duke over Alabama, 29-26; **Orange**—Tulsa over #13 Georgia Tech, 26-12; **Cotton**—Oklahoma A&M over TCU, 34-0.

1945

Final poll released Dec.3. Top 20 regular season results after that: None.

	As of Dec. 3	Head Coach	After Bowls
1 Army	9-0-0	Red Blaik	same
2 Alabama	9-0-0	Frank Thomas	10-0-0
3 Navy	7-1-1	Oscar Hagberg	same
4 Indiana	9-0-1	Bo McMillan	same
5 Oklahoma A&M	8-0-0	Jim Lookabaugh	9-0-0
6 Michigan	7-3-0	Fritz Crisler	same
7 St. Mary's-CA	7-1-0	Jimmy Phelan	7-2-0
8 Penn	6-2-0	George Munger	same
9 Notre Dame	7-2-1	Hugh Devore	same
10 Texas	9-1-0	Dana X. Bible	10-1-0
11 USC	7-3-0	Jeff Cravath	7-4-0
12 Ohio St.	7-2-0	Carroll Widdoes	same
13 Duke	6-2-0	Eddie Cameron	same
14 Tennessee	8-1-0	John Barnhill	same
15 LSU	7-2-0	Bernie Moore	same
16 Holy Cross	8-1-0	John DeGrosa	8-2-0
17 Tulsa	8-2-0	Henry Frnka	8-3-0
18 Georgia	8-2-0	Wally Butts	9-2-0
19 Wake Forest	4-3-1	Peahead Walker	5-3-1
20 Columbia	8-1-0	Lou Little	same

Key Bowl Games

Rose—#2 Alabama over #11 USC, 34-14; **Sugar**—#5 Oklahoma A&M over #7 St. Mary's, 33-13; **Cotton**—#10 Texas over Missouri, 40-27; **Orange**—Miami-FL over #16 Holy Cross, 13-6.

1946

Final poll released Dec.2. Top 20 regular season results after that: None.

	As of Dec. 2	Head Coach	After Bowls
1 Notre Dame	8-0-1	Frank Leahy	same
2 Army	9-0-1	Red Blaik	same
3 Georgia	10-0-0	Wally Butts	11-0-0
4 UCLA	10-0-0	Bert LaBrucherie	10-1-0
5 Illinois	7-2-0	Ray Eliot	8-2-0
6 Michigan	6-2-1	Fritz Crisler	same
7 Tennessee	9-1-0	Bob Neyland	9-2-0
8 LSU	9-1-0	Bernie Moore	9-1-1
9 North Carolina	8-1-1	Carl Snavely	8-2-1
10 Rice	8-2-0	Jess Neely	9-2-0
11 Georgia Tech	8-2-0	Bobby Dodd	9-2-0
12 Yale	7-1-1	Howard Odell	same
13 Penn	6-2-0	George Munger	same
14 Oklahoma	7-3-0	Jim Tatum	8-3-0
15 Texas	8-2-0	Dana X. Bible	same
16 Arkansas	6-3-1	John Barnhill	6-3-2
17 Tulsa	9-1-0	J.O. Brothers	same
18 N.C. State	8-2-0	Beattie Feathers	8-3-0
19 Delaware	9-0-0	Bill Murray	10-0-0
20 Indiana	6-3-0	Bo McMillan	same

Key Bowl Games

Sugar—#3 Georgia over #9 N.Carolina, 20-10; **Rose**—#5 Illinois over #4 UCLA, 45-14; **Orange**—#10 Rice over #7 Tennessee, 8-0; **Cotton**—#8 LSU tied #16 Arkansas, 0-0.

1947

Final poll released Dec.8. Top 20 regular season results after that: None.

	As of Dec. 8	Head Coach	After Bowls
1 Notre Dame	9-0-0	Frank Leahy	same
2 Michigan	9-0-0	Fritz Crisler	10-0-0
3 SMU	9-0-1	Matty Bell	9-0-2
4 Penn St.	9-0-0	Bob Higgins	9-0-1
5 Texas	9-1-0	Blair Cherry	10-1-0
6 Alabama	8-2-0	Red Drew	8-3-0
7 Penn	7-0-1	George Munger	same
8 USC	7-1-1	Jeff Cravath	7-2-1
9 North Carolina	8-2-0	Carl Snavely	same
10 Georgia Tech	9-1-0	Bobby Dodd	10-1-0
11 Army	5-2-2	Red Blaik	same
12 Kansas	8-0-2	George Sauer	8-1-2
13 Mississippi	8-2-0	Johnny Vaught	9-2-0
14 William & Mary	9-1-0	Rube McCray	9-2-0
15 California	9-1-0	Pappy Waldorf	same
16 Oklahoma	7-2-1	Bud Wilkinson	same
17 N.C. State	5-3-1	Beattie Feathers	same
18 Rice	6-3-1	Jess Neely	same
19 Duke	4-3-2	Wallace Wade	same
20 Columbia	7-2-0	Lou Little	same

Key Bowl Games

Rose—#2 Michigan over #8 USC, 49-0; **Cotton**—#3 SMU tied #4 Penn St., 13-13; **Sugar**—#5 Texas over #6 Alabama, 27-7; **Orange**—#10 Georgia Tech over #12 Kansas, 20-14.

1948

Final poll released Nov.29. Top 20 regular season results after that: **Dec.3**—#12 Vanderbilt over Miami-FL, 33-6. **Dec.4**—#2 Notre Dame tied USC, 14-14; #11 Clemson over The Citadel, 20-0.

	As of Nov.29	Head Coach	After Bowls
1 Michigan	9-0-0	Bennie Oosterbaan	same
2 Notre Dame	9-0-0	Frank Leahy	9-0-1
3 North Carolina	9-0-1	Carl Snavely	9-1-1
4 California	10-0-0	Pappy Waldorf	10-1-0
5 Oklahoma	9-1-0	Bud Wilkinson	10-1-0
6 Army	8-0-1	Red Blaik	same
7 Northwestern	7-2-0	Bob Voigts	8-2-0
8 Georgia	9-1-0	Wally Butts	9-2-0
9 Oregon	9-1-0	Jim Aiken	9-2-0
10 SMU	8-1-1	Matty Bell	9-1-1
11 Clemson	9-0-0	Frank Howard	11-0-0
12 Vanderbilt	7-2-1	Red Sanders	8-2-1
13 Tulane	9-1-0	Henry Frnka	same
14 Michigan St.	6-2-2	Biggie Munn	same
15 Mississippi	8-1-0	Johnny Vaught	same
16 Minnesota	7-2-0	Bernie Bierman	same
17 William & Mary	6-2-2	Rube McCray	7-2-2
18 Penn St.	7-1-1	Bob Higgins	same
19 Cornell	8-1-0	Lefty James	same
20 Wake Forest	6-3-0	Peahead Walker	6-4-0

Note: Big Nine "no-repeat" rule kept Michigan from Rose Bowl.

Key Bowl Games

Sugar—#5 Oklahoma over #3 North Carolina, 14-6; **Rose**—#7 Northwestern over #4 Cal, 20-14; **Orange**—Texas over #8 Georgia, 41-28; **Cotton**—#10 SMU over #9 Oregon, 21-13.

1949

Final poll released Nov.28. Top 20 regular season results after that: **Dec.2**—#14 Maryland over Miami-FL, 13-0. **Dec.3**—#1 Notre Dame over SMU, 27-20; #10 Pacific over Hawaii, 75-0.

	As of Nov. 28	Head Coach	After Bowls
1 Notre Dame	9-0-0	Frank Leahy	10-0-0
2 Oklahoma	10-0-0	Bud Wilkinson	11-0-0
3 California	10-0-0	Pappy Waldorf	10-1-0
4 Army	9-0-0	Red Blaik	same
5 Rice	9-1-0	Jess Neely	10-1-0
6 Ohio St.	6-1-2	Wes Fesler	7-1-2
7 Michigan	6-2-1	Bennie Oosterbaan	same
8 Minnesota	7-2-0	Bernie Bierman	same
9 LSU	8-2-0	Gaynell Tinsley	8-3-0
10 Pacific	10-0-0	Larry Siemering	11-0-0
11 Kentucky	9-2-0	Bear Bryant	9-3-0
12 Cornell	8-1-0	Lefty James	same
13 Villanova	8-1-0	Jim Leonard	same
14 Maryland	7-1-0	Jim Tatum	9-1-0
15 Santa Clara	7-2-1	Len Casanova	8-2-1
16 North Carolina	7-3-0	Carl Snavely	7-4-0
17 Tennessee	7-2-1	Bob Neyland	same
18 Princeton	6-3-0	Charlie Caldwell	same
19 Michigan St.	6-3-0	Biggie Munn	same
20 Missouri	7-3-0	Don Faurot	7-4-0
Baylor	8-2-0	Bob Woodruff	same

Key Bowl Games

Sugar—#2 Oklahoma over #9 LSU, 35-0; **Rose**—#6 Ohio St. over #3 Cal, 17-14; **Cotton**—#5 Rice over #16 North Carolina, 27-13; **Orange**—#15 Santa Clara over #11 Kentucky, 21-13.

1950

Final poll released Nov.27. Top 20 regular season results after that: **Nov.30**—#3 Texas over Texas A&M, 17-0. **Dec.1**—#15 Miami-FL over Missouri, 27—9. **Dec.2**—#1 Oklahoma over Okla. A&M, 41-14; Navy over #2 Army, 14-2; #4 Tennessee over Vanderbilt, 43-0; #16 Alabama over Auburn, 34-0; #19 Tulsa over Houston, 28-21; #20 Tulane tied LSU, 14-14. **Dec.9**—#3 Texas over LSU, 21-6.

	As of Nov. 27	Head Coach	After Bowls
1 Oklahoma	9-0-0	Bud Wilkinson	10-1-0
2 Army	8-0-0	Red Blaik	8-1-0
3 Texas	7-1-0	Blair Cherry	9-2-0
4 Tennessee	9-1-0	Bob Neyland	11-1-0
5 California	9-0-1	Pappy Waldorf	9-1-1
6 Princeton	9-0-0	Charlie Caldwell	same
7 Kentucky	10-1-0	Bear Bryant	11-1-0
8 Michigan St.	8-1-0	Biggie Munn	same
9 Michigan	5-3-1	Bennie Oosterbaan	6-3-1
10 Clemson	8-0-1	Frank Howard	9-0-1
11 Washington	8-2-0	Howard Odell	same
12 Wyoming	9-0-0	Bowden Wyatt	10-0-0
13 Illinois	7-2-0	Ray Eliot	same
14 Ohio St.	6-3-0	Wes Fesler	same
15 Miami-FL	8-0-1	Andy Gustafson	9-1-1
16 Alabama	8-2-0	Red Drew	9-2-0
17 Nebraska	6-2-1	Bill Glassford	same
18 Wash. & Lee	8-2-0	George Barclay	8-3-0
19 Tulsa	8-1-1	J.O. Brothers	9-1-1
20 Tulane	6-2-0	Henry Frnka	6-2-1

Key Bowl Games

Sugar—#7 Kentucky over #1 Oklahoma, 13-7; **Cotton**—#4 Tennessee over #3 Texas, 20-14; **Rose**—#9 Michigan over #5 Cal, 14-6; **Orange**—#10 Clemson over #15 Miami-FL, 15-14.

1951

Final poll released Dec.3. Top 20 regular season results after that: None.

	As of Dec. 3	Head Coach	After Bowls
1 Tennessee	10-0-0	Bob Neyland	10-1-0
2 Michigan St.	9-0-0	Biggie Munn	same
3 Maryland	9-0-0	Jim Tatum	10-0-0
4 Illinois	8-0-1	Ray Eliot	9-0-1
5 Georgia Tech	10-0-1	Bobby Dodd	11-0-1
6 Princeton	9-0-0	Charlie Caldwell	same
7 Stanford	9-1-0	Chuck Taylor	9-2-0
8 Wisconsin	7-1-1	Ivy Williamson	same
9 Baylor	8-1-1	George Sauer	8-2-1
10 Oklahoma	8-2-0	Bud Wilkinson	same
11 TCU	6-4-0	Dutch Meyer	6-5-0
12 California	8-2-0	Pappy Waldorf	same
13 Virginia	8-1-0	Art Guepe	same
14 San Francisco	9-0-0	Joe Kuharich	same
15 Kentucky	7-4-0	Bear Bryant	8-4-0
16 Boston Univ.	6-4-0	Buff Donelli	same
17 UCLA	5-3-1	Red Sanders	same
18 Washington St.	7-3-0	Forest Evashevski	same
19 Holy Cross	8-2-0	Eddie Anderson	same
Clemson	7-2-0	Frank Howard	7-3-0

Key Bowl Games

Sugar—#3 Maryland over #1 Tennessee, 28-13; **Rose**—#4 Illinois over #7 Stanford, 40-7; **Orange**—#5 Georgia Tech over #9 Baylor, 17-14; **Cotton**—#15 Kentucky over #11 TCU, 20-7.

Associated Press Final Polls (Cont.)

1952

Final poll released Dec.1. Top 20 regular season results after that: **Dec.6**—#15 Florida over #20 Kentucky, 27-20.

		As of Dec. 1	Head Coach	After Bowls
1	Michigan St.	9-0-0	Biggie Munn	same
2	Georgia Tech	11-0-0	Bobby Dodd	12-0-0
3	Notre Dame	7-2-1	Frank Leahy	same
4	Oklahoma	8-1-1	Bud Wilkinson	same
5	USC	9-1-0	Jess Hill	10-1-0
6	UCLA	8-1-0	Red Sanders	same
7	Mississippi	8-0-2	Johnny Vaught	8-1-2
8	Tennessee	8-1-1	Bob Neyland	8-2-1
9	Alabama	9-2-0	Red Drew	10-2-0
10	Texas	8-2-0	Ed Price	9-2-0
11	Wisconsin	6-2-1	Ivy Williamson	6-3-1
12	Tulsa	8-1-1	J.O. Brothers	8-2-1
13	Maryland	7-2-0	Jim Tatum	same
14	Syracuse	7-2-0	Ben Schwartzwalder	7-3-0
15	Florida	6-3-0	Bob Woodruff	8-3-0
16	Duke	8-2-0	Bill Murray	same
17	Ohio St.	6-3-0	Woody Hayes	same
18	Purdue	4-3-2	Stu Holcomb	same
19	Princeton	8-1-0	Charlie Caldwell	same
20	Kentucky	5-3-2	Bear Bryant	5-4-2

Note: Michigan St. would officially join Big Ten in 1953.

Key Bowl Games

Sugar—#2 Georgia Tech over #7 Ole Miss, 24-7; **Rose**—#5 USC over #11 Wisconsin, 7-0; **Cotton**—#10 Texas over #8 Tennessee, 16-0; **Orange**—#9 Alabama over #14 Syracuse, 61-6.

1953

Final poll released Nov.30. Top 20 regular season results after that: **Dec.5**—#2 Notre Dame over SMU, 40-14.

		As of Nov. 30	Head Coach	After Bowls
1	Maryland	10-0-0	Jim Tatum	10-1-0
2	Notre Dame	8-0-1	Frank Leahy	9-0-1
3	Michigan St.	8-1-0	Biggie Munn	9-1-0
4	Oklahoma	8-1-1	Bud Wilkinson	9-1-1
5	UCLA	8-1-0	Red Sanders	8-2-0
6	Rice	8-2-0	Jess Neely	9-2-0
7	Illinois	7-1-1	Ray Eliot	same
8	Georgia Tech	8-2-1	Bobby Dodd	9-2-1
9	Iowa	5-3-1	Forest Evashevski	same
10	West Virginia	8-1-0	Art Lewis	8-2-0
11	Texas	7-3-0	Ed Price	same
12	Texas Tech	10-1-0	DeWitt Weaver	11-1-0
13	Alabama	6-2-3	Red Drew	6-3-3
14	Army	7-1-1	Red Blaik	same
15	Wisconsin	6-2-1	Ivy Williamson	same
16	Kentucky	7-2-1	Bear Bryant	same
17	Auburn	7-2-1	Shug Jordan	7-3-1
18	Duke	7-2-1	Bill Murray	same
19	Stanford	6-3-1	Chuck Taylor	same
20	Michigan	6-3-0	Bennie Oosterbaan	same

Key Bowl Games

Orange—#4 Oklahoma over #1 Maryland, 7-0; **Rose**—#3 Michigan St. over #5 UCLA, 28-20; **Cotton**—#6 Rice over #13 Alabama, 28-6; **Sugar**—#8 Georgia Tech over #10 West Virginia, 42-19.

1954

Final poll released Nov.29. Top 20 regular season results after that: **Dec.4**—#4 Notre Dame over SMU, 26-14.

		As of Nov. 29	Head Coach	After Bowls
1	Ohio St.	9-0-0	Woody Hayes	10-0-0
2	UCLA	9-0-0	Red Sanders	same
3	Oklahoma	10-0-0	Bud Wilkinson	same
4	Notre Dame	8-1-0	Terry Brennan	9-1-0
5	Navy	7-2-0	Eddie Erdelatz	8-2-0
6	Mississippi	9-1-0	Johnny Vaught	9-2-0
7	Army	7-2-0	Red Blaik	same
8	Maryland	7-2-1	Jim Tatum	same
9	Wisconsin	7-2-0	Ivy Williamson	same
10	Arkansas	8-2-0	Bowden Wyatt	8-3-0
11	Miami-FL	8-1-0	Andy Gustafson	same
12	West Virginia	8-1-0	Art Lewis	same
13	Auburn	7-3-0	Shug Jordan	8-3-0
14	Duke	7-2-1	Bill Murray	8-2-1
15	Michigan	6-3-0	Bennie Oosterbaan	same
16	Virginia Tech	8-0-1	Frank Moseley	same
17	USC	8-3-0	Jess Hill	8-4-0
18	Baylor	7-3-0	George Sauer	7-4-0
19	Rice	7-3-0	Jess Neely	same
20	Penn St.	7-2-0	Rip Engle	same

Note: PCC and Big Seven "no-repeat" rules kept UCLA and Oklahoma from Orange and Rose bowls, respectively.

Key Bowl Games

Rose—#1 Ohio St. over #17 USC, 20-7; **Sugar**—#5 Navy over #6 Ole Miss, 21-0; **Cotton**—Georgia Tech over #10 Arkansas, 14-6; **Orange**—#14 Duke over Nebraska, 34-7.

1955

Final poll released Nov.28. Top 20 regular season results after that: None.

		As of Nov. 28	Head Coach	After Bowls
1	Oklahoma	10-0-0	Bud Wilkinson	11-0-0
2	Michigan St.	8-1-0	Duffy Daugherty	9-1-0
3	Maryland	10-0-0	Jim Tatum	10-1-0
4	UCLA	9-1-0	Red Sanders	9-2-0
5	Ohio St.	7-2-0	Woody Hayes	same
6	TCU	9-1-0	Abe Martin	9-2-0
7	Georgia Tech	8-1-1	Bobby Dodd	9-1-1
8	Auburn	8-1-1	Shug Jordan	8-2-1
9	Notre Dame	8-2-0	Terry Brennan	same
10	Mississippi	9-1-0	Johnny Vaught	10-1-0
11	Pittsburgh	7-3-0	John Michelosen	7-4-0
12	Michigan	7-2-0	Bennie Oosterbaan	same
13	USC	6-4-0	Jess Hill	same
14	Miami-FL	6-3-0	Andy Gustafson	same
15	Miami-OH	9-0-0	Ara Parseghian	same
16	Stanford	6-3-1	Chuck Taylor	same
17	Texas A&M	7-2-1	Bear Bryant	same
18	Navy	6-2-1	Eddie Erdelatz	same
19	West Virginia	8-2-0	Art Lewis	same
20	Army	6-3-0	Red Blaik	same

Note: Big Ten "no-repeat" rule kept Ohio St. from Rose Bowl.

Key Bowl Games

Orange—#1 Oklahoma over #3 Maryland, 20-6; **Rose**—#2 Michigan St. over #4 UCLA, 17-14; **Cotton**—#10 Ole Miss over #6 TCU, 14-13; **Sugar**—#7 Georgia Tech over #11 Pitt, 7-0; **Gator**—Vanderbilt over #8 Auburn, 25-13.

1956

Final poll released Dec.3. Top 20 regular season results after that: **Dec.8**—#13 Pitt over #6 Miami-FL, 14-7.

	As of Dec. 3	Head Coach	After Bowls
1 Oklahoma	10-0-0	Bud Wilkinson	same
2 Tennessee	10-0-0	Bowden Wyatt	10-1-0
3 Iowa	8-1-0	Forest Evashevski	9-1-0
4 Georgia Tech	9-1-0	Bobby Dodd	10-1-0
5 Texas A&M	9-0-1	Bear Bryant	same
6 Miami-FL	8-0-1	Andy Gustafson	8-1-1
7 Michigan	7-2-0	Bennie Oosterbaan	same
8 Syracuse	7-1-0	Ben Schwartzwalder	7-2-0
9 Michigan St.	7-2-0	Duffy Daugherty	same
10 Oregon St.	7-2-1	Tommy Prothro	7-3-1
11 Baylor	8-2-0	Sam Boyd	9-2-0
12 Minnesota	6-1-2	Murray Warmath	same
13 Pittsburgh	6-2-1	John Michelosen	7-3-1
14 TCU	7-3-0	Abe Martin	8-3-0
15 Ohio St.	6-3-0	Woody Hayes	same
16 Navy	6-1-2	Eddie Erdelatz	same
17 G. Washington	7-1-1	Gene Sherman	8-1-1
18 USC	8-2-0	Jess Hill	same
19 Clemson	7-1-2	Frank Howard	7-2-2
20 Colorado	7-2-1	Dallas Ward	8-2-1

Note: Big Seven "no-repeat" rule kept Oklahoma from Orange Bowl and Texas A&M was on probation.

Key Bowl Games

Sugar—#11 Baylor over #2 Tennessee, 13-7; **Rose**—#3 Iowa over #10 Oregon St., 35-19; **Gator**—#4 Georgia Tech over #13 Pitt, 21-14; **Cotton**—#14 TCU over #8 Syracuse, 28-27; **Orange**—#20 Colorado over #19 Clemson, 27-21.

1957

Final poll released Dec.2. Top 20 regular season results after that: **Dec.7**—#10 Notre Dame over SMU, 54-21.

	As of Dec. 2	Head Coach	After Bowls
1 Auburn	10-0-0	Shug Jordan	same
2 Ohio St.	8-1-0	Woody Hayes	9-1-0
3 Michigan St.	8-1-0	Duffy Daugherty	same
4 Oklahoma	9-1-0	Bud Wilkinson	10-1-0
5 Navy	8-1-1	Eddie Erdelatz	9-1-1
6 Iowa	7-1-1	Forest Evashevski	same
7 Mississippi	8-1-1	Johnny Vaught	9-1-1
8 Rice	7-3-0	Jess Neely	7-4-0
9 Texas A&M	8-2-0	Bear Bryant	8-3-0
10 Notre Dame	6-3-0	Terry Brennan	7-3-0
11 Texas	6-3-1	Darrell Royal	6-4-1
12 Arizona St.	10-0-0	Dan Devine	same
13 Tennessee	7-3-0	Bowden Wyatt	8-3-0
14 Mississippi St.	6-2-1	Wade Walker	same
15 N.C. State	7-1-2	Earle Edwards	same
16 Duke	6-2-2	Bill Murray	6-3-2
17 Florida	6-2-1	Bob Woodruff	same
18 Army	7-2-0	Red Blaik	same
19 Wisconsin	6-3-0	Milt Bruhn	same
20 VMI	9-0-1	John McKenna	same

Note: Auburn on probation, ineligible for bowl game.

Key Bowl Games

Rose—#2 Ohio St. over Oregon, 10-7; **Orange**—#4 Oklahoma over #16 Duke, 48-21; **Cotton**—#5 Navy over #8 Rice, 20-7; **Sugar**—#7 Ole Miss over #11 Texas, 39-7; **Gator**—#13 Tennessee over #9 Texas A&M, 3-0.

1958

Final poll released Dec.1. Top 20 regular season results after that: None.

	As of Dec. 1	Head Coach	After Bowls
1 LSU	10-0-0	Paul Dietzel	11-0-0
2 Iowa	7-1-1	Forest Evashevski	8-1-1
3 Army	8-0-1	Red Blaik	same
4 Auburn	9-0-1	Shug Jordan	same
5 Oklahoma	9-1-0	Bud Wilkinson	10-1-0
6 Air Force	9-0-1	Ben Martin	9-0-2
7 Wisconsin	7-1-1	Milt Bruhn	same
8 Ohio St.	6-1-2	Woody Hayes	same
9 Syracuse	8-1-0	Ben Schwartzwalder	8-2-0
10 TCU	8-2-0	Abe Martin	8-2-1
11 Mississippi	8-2-0	Johnny Vaught	9-2-0
12 Clemson	8-2-0	Frank Howard	8-3-0
13 Purdue	6-1-2	Jack Mollenkopf	same
14 Florida	6-3-1	Bob Woodruff	6-4-1
15 South Carolina	7-3-0	Warren Giese	same
16 California	7-3-0	Pete Elliott	7-4-0
17 Notre Dame	6-4-0	Terry Brennan	same
18 SMU	6-4-0	Bill Meek	same
19 Oklahoma St.	7-3-0	Cliff Speegle	8-3-0
20 Rutgers	8-1-0	John Stiegman	same

Key Bowl Games

Sugar—#1 LSU over #12 Clemson, 7-0; **Rose**—#2 Iowa over #16 Cal, 38-12; **Orange**—#5 Oklahoma over #9 Syracuse, 21-6; **Cotton**—#6 Air Force tied #10 TCU, 0-0.

1959

Final poll released Dec.7. Top 20 regular season results after that: None.

	As of Dec. 7	Head Coach	After Bowls
1 Syracuse	10-0-0	Ben Schwartzwalder	11-0-0
2 Mississippi	9-1-0	Johnny Vaught	10-1-0
3 LSU	9-1-0	Paul Dietzel	9-2-0
4 Texas	9-1-0	Darrell Royal	9-2-0
5 Georgia	9-1-0	Wally Butts	10-1-0
6 Wisconsin	7-2-0	Milt Bruhn	7-3-0
7 TCU	8-2-0	Abe Martin	8-3-0
8 Washington	9-1-0	Jim Owens	10-1-0
9 Arkansas	8-2-0	Frank Broyles	9-2-0
10 Alabama	7-1-2	Bear Bryant	7-2-2
11 Clemson	8-2-0	Frank Howard	9-2-0
12 Penn St.	8-2-0	Rip Engle	9-2-0
13 Illinois	5-3-1	Ray Eliot	same
14 USC	8-2-0	Don Clark	same
15 Oklahoma	7-3-0	Bud Wilkinson	same
16 Wyoming	9-1-0	Bob Devaney	same
17 Notre Dame	5-5-0	Joe Kuharich	same
18 Missouri	6-4-0	Dan Devine	6-5-0
19 Florida	5-4-1	Bob Woodruff	same
20 Pittsburgh	6-4-0	John Michelosen	same

Note: Big Seven "no-repeat" rule kept Oklahoma from Orange Bowl.

Key Bowl Games

Cotton—#1 Syracuse over #4 Texas, 23-14; **Sugar**—#2 Ole Miss over #3 LSU, 21-0; **Orange**—#5 Georgia over #18 Missouri, 14-0; **Rose**—#8 Washington over #6 Wisconsin, 44-8; **Bluebonnet**—#11 Clemson over #7 TCU, 23-7; **Gator**—#9 Arkansas over Georgia Tech, 14-7; **Liberty**—#12 Penn St. over #10 Alabama, 7-0.

Associated Press Final Polls (Cont.)

AP ranked only 10 teams from 1962-67.

1960

Final poll released Nov.28. Top 20 regular season results after that: **Dec.3**—UCLA over #10 Duke, 27-6.

		As of Nov. 28	Head Coach	After Bowls
1	Minnesota	8-1-0	Murray Warmath	8-2-0
2	Mississippi	9-0-1	Johnny Vaught	10-0-1
3	Iowa	8-1-0	Forest Evashevski	same
4	Navy	9-1-0	Wayne Hardin	9-2-0
5	Missouri	9-1-0	Dan Devine	10-1-0
6	Washington	9-1-0	Jim Owens	10-1-0
7	Arkansas	8-2-0	Frank Broyles	8-3-0
8	Ohio St.	7-2-0	Woody Hayes	same
9	Alabama	8-1-1	Bear Bryant	8-1-2
10	Duke	7-2-0	Bill Murray	8-3-0
11	Kansas	7-2-1	Jack Mitchell	same
12	Baylor	8-2-0	John Bridgers	8-3-0
13	Auburn	8-2-0	Shug Jordan	same
14	Yale	9-0-0	Jordan Olivar	same
15	Michigan St.	6-2-1	Duffy Daugherty	same
16	Penn St.	6-3-0	Rip Engle	7-3-0
17	New Mexico St.	10-0-0	Warren Woodson	11-0-0
18	Florida	8-2-0	Ray Graves	9-2-0
19	Syracuse	7-2-0	Ben Schwartzwalder	same
	Purdue	4-4-1	Jack Mollenkopf	same

Key Bowl Games

Rose—#6 Washington over #1 Minnesota, 17-7; **Sugar**—#2 Ole Miss over Rice, 14-6; **Orange**—#5 Missouri over #4 Navy, 21-14; **Cotton**—#10 Duke over #7 Arkansas, 7-6; **Bluebonnet**—#9 Alabama tied Texas, 3-3.

1961

Final poll released Dec.4. Top 20 regular season results after that: None.

		As of Dec. 4	Head Coach	After Bowls
1	Alabama	10-0-0	Bear Bryant	11-0-0
2	Ohio St.	8-0-1	Woody Hayes	same
3	Texas	9-1-0	Darrell Royal	10-1-0
4	LSU	9-1-0	Paul Dietzel	10-1-0
5	Mississippi	9-1-0	Johnny Vaught	9-2-0
6	Minnesota	7-2-0	Murray Warmath	8-2-0
7	Colorado	9-1-0	Sonny Grandelius	9-2-0
8	Michigan St.	7-2-0	Duffy Daugherty	same
9	Arkansas	8-2-0	Frank Broyles	8-3-0
10	Utah St.	9-0-1	John Ralston	9-1-1
11	Missouri	7-2-1	Dan Devine	same
12	Purdue	6-3-0	Jack Mollenkopf	same
13	Georgia Tech	7-3-0	Bobby Dodd	7-4-0
14	Syracuse	7-3-0	Ben Schwartzwalder	8-3-0
15	Rutgers	9-0-0	John Bateman	same
16	UCLA	7-3-0	Bill Barnes	7-4-0
17	Rice	7-3-0	Jess Neely	7-4-0
	Penn St.	7-3-0	Rip Engle	8-3-0
	Arizona	8-1-1	Jim LaRue	same
20	Duke	7-3-0	Bill Murray	same

Note: Ohio St. faculty council turned down Rose Bowl invitation citing concern with OSU's overemphasis on sports.

Key Bowl Games

Sugar—#1 Alabama over #9 Arkansas, 10-3; **Cotton**—#3 Texas over #5 Ole Miss, 12-7; **Orange**—#4 LSU over #7 Colorado, 25-7; **Rose**—#6 Minnesota over #16 UCLA, 21-3; **Gotham**—Baylor over #10 Utah St., 24-9.

1962

Final poll released Dec.3. Top 10 regular season results after that: None.

		As of Dec. 3	Head Coach	After Bowls
1	USC	10-0-0	John McKay	11-0-0
2	Wisconsin	8-1-0	Milt Bruhn	8-2-0
3	Mississippi	9-0-0	Johnny Vaught	10-0-0
4	Texas	9-0-1	Darrell Royal	9-1-1
5	Alabama	9-1-0	Bear Bryant	10-1-0
6	Arkansas	9-1-0	Frank Broyles	9-2-0
7	LSU	8-1-1	Charlie McClendon	9-1-1
8	Oklahoma	8-2-0	Bud Wilkinson	8-3-0
9	Penn St.	9-1-0	Rip Engle	9-2-0
10	Minnesota	6-2-1	Murray Warmath	same

Key Bowl Games

Rose—#1 USC over #2 Wisconsin, 42-37; **Sugar**—#3 Ole Miss over #6 Arkansas, 17-13; **Cotton**—#7 LSU over #4 Texas, 13-0; **Orange**—#5 Alabama over #8 Oklahoma, 17-0; **Gator**—Florida over #9 Penn St.,17-7.

1963

Final poll released Dec.9. Top 10 regular season results after that: **Dec.14**—#8 Alabama over Miami-FL, 17-12.

		As of Dec. 9	Head Coach	After Bowls
1	Texas	10-0-0	Darrell Royal	11-0-0
2	Navy	9-1-0	Wayne Hardin	9-2-0
3	Illinois	7-1-1	Pete Elliott	8-1-1
4	Pittsburgh	9-1-0	John Michelosen	same
5	Auburn	9-1-0	Shug Jordan	9-2-0
6	Nebraska	9-1-0	Bob Devaney	10-1-0
7	Mississippi	7-0-2	Johnny Vaught	7-1-2
8	Alabama	7-2-0	Bear Bryant	9-2-0
9	Michigan St.	6-2-1	Duffy Daugherty	same
10	Oklahoma	8-2-0	Bud Wilkinson	same

Key Bowl Games

Cotton—#1 Texas over #2 Navy, 28-6; **Rose**—#3 Illinois over Washington, 17-7; **Orange**—#6 Nebraska over #5 Auburn, 13-7; **Sugar**—#8 Alabama over #7 Ole Miss, 12-7.

1964

Final poll released Nov.30. Top 10 regular season results after that: **Dec.5**—Florida over #7 LSU, 20-6.

		As of Nov. 30	Head Coach	After Bowls
1	Alabama	10-0-0	Bear Bryant	10-1-0
2	Arkansas	10-0-0	Frank Broyles	11-0-0
3	Notre Dame	9-1-0	Ara Parseghian	same
4	Michigan	8-1-0	Bump Elliott	9-1-0
5	Texas	9-1-0	Darrell Royal	10-1-0
6	Nebraska	9-1-0	Bob Devaney	9-2-0
7	LSU	7-1-1	Charlie McClendon	8-2-1
8	Oregon St.	8-2-0	Tommy Prothro	8-3-0
9	Ohio St.	7-2-0	Woody Hayes	same
10	USC	7-3-0	John McKay	same

Key Bowl Games

Orange—#5 Texas over #1 Alabama, 21-17; **Cotton**—#2 Arkansas over #6 Nebraska, 10-7; **Rose**— #4 Michigan over #8 Oregon St., 34-7; **Sugar**—#7 LSU over Syracuse, 13-10.

1965

Final poll taken after bowl games for the first time.

	After Bowls	Head Coach	Regular Season
1 Alabama	9-1-1	Bear Bryant	8-1-1
2 Michigan St.	10-1-0	Duffy Daugherty	10-0-0
3 Arkansas	10-1-0	Frank Broyles	10-0-0
4 UCLA	8-2-1	Tommy Prothro	7-1-1
5 Nebraska	10-1-0	Bob Devaney	10-0-0
6 Missouri	8-2-1	Dan Devine	7-2-1
7 Tennessee	8-1-2	Doug Dickey	6-1-2
8 LSU	8-3-0	Charlie McClendon	7-3-0
9 Notre Dame	7-2-1	Ara Parseghian	same
10 USC	7-2-1	John McKay	same

Key Bowl Games

Rankings below reflect final regular season poll, released Nov.29. No bowls for then #8 USC or #9 Notre Dame. **Rose**—#5 UCLA over #1 Michigan St., 14-12; **Cotton**—LSU over #2 Arkansas, 14-7; **Orange**—#4 Alabama over #3 Nebraska, 39-28; **Sugar**—#6 Missouri over Florida, 20-18; **Bluebonnet**—#7 Tennessee over Tulsa, 27-6; **Gator**—Georgia Tech over #10 Texas Tech, 31-21.

1966

Final poll released Dec.5, returning to pre-bowl status. Top 10 regular season results after that: None.

	As of Dec. 5	Head Coach	After Bowls
1 Notre Dame	9-0-1	Ara Parseghian	same
2 Michigan St.	9-0-1	Duffy Daugherty	same
3 Alabama	10-0-0	Bear Bryant	11-0-0
4 Georgia	9-1-0	Vince Dooley	10-1-0
5 UCLA	9-1-0	Tommy Prothro	same
6 Nebraska	9-1-0	Bob Devaney	9-2-0
7 Purdue	8-2-0	Jack Mollenkopf	9-2-0
8 Georgia Tech	9-1-0	Bobby Dodd	9-2-0
9 Miami-FL	7-2-1	Charlie Tate	8-2-1
10 SMU	8-2-0	Hayden Fry	8-3-0

Key Bowl Games

Sugar—#3 Alabama over #6 Nebraska, 34-7; **Cotton**—#4 Georgia over #10 SMU, 24-9; **Rose**—#7 Purdue over USC, 14-13; **Orange**—Florida over #8 Georgia Tech, 27-12; **Liberty**—#9 Miami-FL over Virginia Tech, 14-7.

1967

Final poll released Nov.27. Top 10 regular season results after that: Dec.2—#2 Tennessee over Vanderbilt, 41-14; #3 Oklahoma over Oklahoma St., 38-14; #8 Alabama over Auburn, 7-3.

	As of Nov. 27	Head Coach	After Bowls
1 USC	9-1-0	John McKay	10-1-0
2 Tennessee	8-1-0	Doug Dickey	9-2-0
3 Oklahoma	8-1-0	Chuck Fairbanks	10-1-0
4 Indiana	9-1-0	John Pont	9-2-0
5 Notre Dame	8-2-0	Ara Parseghian	same
6 Wyoming	10-0-0	Lloyd Eaton	10-1-0
7 Oregon St.	7-2-1	Dee Andros	same
8 Alabama	7-1-1	Bear Bryant	8-2-1
9 Purdue	8-2-0	Jack Mollenkopf	same
10 Penn St.	8-2-0	Joe Paterno	8-2-1

Key Bowl Games

Rose—#1 USC over #4 Indiana, 14-3; **Orange**—#3 Oklahoma over #2 Tennessee, 26-24; **Sugar**—LSU over #6 Wyoming, 20-13; **Cotton**—Texas A&M over #8 Alabama, 20-16; **Gator**—#10 Penn St. tied Florida St. 17-17.

1968

Final poll taken after bowl games for first time since close of 1965 season.

	After Bowls	Head Coach	Regular Season
1 Ohio St.	10-0-0	Woody Hayes	9-0-0
2 Penn St.	11-0-0	Joe Paterno	10-0-0
3 Texas	9-1-1	Darrell Royal	8-1-1
4 USC	9-1-1	John McKay	9-0-1
5 Notre Dame	7-2-1	Ara Parseghian	same
6 Arkansas	10-1-0	Frank Broyles	9-1-0
7 Kansas	9-2-0	Pepper Rodgers	9-1-0
8 Georgia	8-1-2	Vince Dooley	8-0-2
9 Missouri	8-3-0	Dan Devine	7-3-0
10 Purdue	8-2-0	Jack Mollenkopf	same
11 Oklahoma	7-4-0	Chuck Fairbanks	7-3-0
12 Michigan	8-2-0	Bump Elliott	same
13 Tennessee	8-2-1	Doug Dickey	8-1-1
14 SMU	8-3-0	Hayden Fry	7-3-0
15 Oregon St.	7-3-0	Dee Andros	same
16 Auburn	7-4-0	Shug Jordan	6-4-0
17 Alabama	8-3-0	Bear Bryant	8-2-0
18 Houston	6-2-2	Bill Yeoman	same
19 LSU	8-3-0	Charlie McClendon	7-3-0
20 Ohio Univ.	10-1-0	Bill Hess	10-0-0

Key Bowl Games

Rankings below reflect final regular season poll, released Dec.2. No bowls for then #7 Notre Dame and #11 Purdue. **Rose**—#1 Ohio St. over #2 USC, 27-16; **Orange**—#3 Penn St. over #6 Kansas, 15-14; **Sugar**—#9 Arkansas over #4 Georgia, 16-2; **Cotton**—#5 Texas over #8 Tennessee, 36-13; **Bluebonnet**—#20 SMU over #10 Oklahoma, 28-27; **Gator**—#16 Missouri over #12 Alabama, 35-10.

1969

Final poll taken after bowl games.

	After Bowls	Head Coach	Regular Season
1 Texas	11-0-0	Darrell Royal	10-0-0
2 Penn St.	11-0-0	Joe Paterno	10-0-0
3 USC	10-0-1	John McKay	9-0-1
4 Ohio St.	8-1-0	Woody Hayes	same
5 Notre Dame	8-2-1	Ara Parseghian	8-1-1
6 Missouri	9-2-0	Dan Devine	9-1-0
7 Arkansas	9-2-0	Frank Broyles	9-1-0
8 Mississippi	8-3-0	Johnny Vaught	7-3-0
9 Michigan	8-3-0	Bo Schembechler	8-2-0
10 LSU	9-1-0	Charlie McClendon	same
11 Nebraska	9-2-0	Bob Devaney	8-2-0
12 Houston	9-2-0	Bill Yeoman	8-2-0
13 UCLA	8-1-1	Tommy Prothro	same
14 Florida	9-1-1	Ray Graves	8-1-1
15 Tennessee	9-2-0	Doug Dickey	9-1-0
16 Colorado	8-3-0	Eddie Crowder	7-3-0
17 West Virginia	10-1-0	Jim Carlen	9-1-0
18 Purdue	8-2-0	Jack Mollenkopf	same
19 Stanford	7-2-1	John Ralston	same
20 Auburn	8-3-0	Shug Jordan	8-2-0

Key Bowl Games

Rankings below reflect final regular season poll, released Dec.8. No bowls for then #4 Ohio St., #8 LSU and #10 UCLA. **Cotton**—#1 Texas over #9 Notre Dame, 21-17; **Orange**—#2 Penn St. over #6 Missouri, 10-3; **Sugar**—#13 Ole Miss over #3 Arkansas, 27-22; **Rose**—#5 USC over #7 Michigan, 10-3.

Associated Press Final Polls (Cont.)

1970

Final poll taken after bowl games.

		After Bowls	Head Coach	Regular Season
1	Nebraska	11-0-1	Bob Devaney	10-0-1
2	Notre Dame	10-1-0	Ara Parseghian	9-0-1
3	Texas	10-1-0	Darrell Royal	10-0-0
4	Tennessee	11-1-0	Bill Battle	10-1-0
5	Ohio St.	9-1-0	Woody Hayes	9-0-0
6	Arizona St.	11-0-0	Frank Kush	10-0-0
7	LSU	9-3-0	Charlie McClendon	9-2-0
8	Stanford	9-3-0	John Ralston	8-3-0
9	Michigan	9-1-0	Bo Schembechler	same
10	Auburn	9-2-0	Shug Jordan	8-2-0
11	Arkansas	9-2-0	Frank Broyles	same
12	Toledo	12-0-0	Frank Lauterbur	11-0-0
13	Georgia Tech	9-3-0	Bud Carson	8-3-0
14	Dartmouth	9-0-0	Bob Blackman	same
15	USC	6-4-1	John McKay	same
16	Air Force	9-3-0	Ben Martin	9-2-0
17	Tulane	8-4-0	Jim Pittman	7-4-0
18	Penn St.	7-3-0	Joe Paterno	same
19	Houston	8-3-0	Bill Yeoman	same
20	Oklahoma	7-4-1	Chuck Fairbanks	7-4-0
	Mississippi	7-4-0	Johnny Vaught	7-3-0

Key Bowl Games

Rankings below reflect final regular season poll, released Dec.7. No bowls for then #4 Arkansas and #7 Michigan.
Cotton—#6 Notre Dame over #1 Texas, 24-11; **Rose**—#12 Stanford over #2 Ohio St., 27-17; **Orange**—#3 Nebraska over #8 LSU, 17-12; **Sugar**—#5 Tennessee over #11 Air Force, 34-13; **Peach**—#9 Ariz. St. over N. Carolina, 48-26.

1972

Final poll taken after bowl games.

		After Bowls	Head Coach	Regular Season
1	USC	12-0-0	John McKay	11-0-0
2	Oklahoma	11-1-0	Chuck Fairbanks	10-1-0
3	Texas	10-1-0	Darrell Royal	9-1-0
4	Nebraska	9-2-1	Bob Devaney	8-2-1
5	Auburn	10-1-0	Shug Jordan	9-1-0
6	Michigan	10-1-0	Bo Schembechler	same
7	Alabama	10-2-0	Bear Bryant	10-1-0
8	Tennessee	10-2-0	Bill Battle	9-2-0
9	Ohio St.	9-2-0	Woody Hayes	9-1-0
10	Penn St.	10-2-0	Joe Paterno	10-1-0
11	LSU	9-2-1	Charlie McClendon	9-1-1
12	North Carolina	11-1-0	Bill Dooley	10-1-0
13	Arizona St.	10-2-0	Frank Kush	9-2-0
14	Notre Dame	8-3-0	Ara Parseghian	8-2-0
15	UCLA	8-3-0	Pepper Rodgers	same
16	Colorado	8-4-0	Eddie Crowder	8-3-0
17	N.C. State	8-3-1	Lou Holtz	7-3-1
18	Louisville	9-1-0	Lee Corso	same
19	Washington St.	7-4-0	Jim Sweeney	same
20	Georgia Tech	7-4-1	Bill Fulcher	6-4-1

Key Bowl Games

Rankings below reflect final regular season poll, released Dec.4. No bowl for then #8 Michigan.
Rose—#1 USC over #3 Ohio St., 42-17; **Sugar**—#2 Oklahoma over #5 Penn St., 14-0; **Cotton**—#7 Texas over #4 Alabama, 17-13; **Orange**—#9 Nebraska over #12 Notre Dame, 40-6; **Gator**—#6 Auburn over #13 Colorado, 24-3; **Bluebonnet**—#11 Tennessee over #10 LSU, 24-17.

1971

Final poll taken after bowl games.

		After Bowls	Head Coach	Regular Season
1	Nebraska	13-0-0	Bob Devaney	12-0-0
2	Oklahoma	11-1-0	Chuck Fairbanks	10-1-0
3	Colorado	10-2-0	Eddie Crowder	9-2-0
4	Alabama	11-1-0	Bear Bryant	11-0-0
5	Penn St.	11-1-0	Joe Paterno	10-1-0
6	Michigan	11-1-0	Bo Schembechler	11-0-0
7	Georgia	11-1-0	Vince Dooley	10-1-0
8	Arizona St.	11-1-0	Frank Kush	10-1-0
9	Tennessee	10-2-0	Bill Battle	9-2-0
10	Stanford	9-3-0	John Ralston	8-3-0
11	LSU	9-3-0	Charlie McClendon	8-3-0
12	Auburn	9-2-0	Shug Jordan	9-1-0
13	Notre Dame	8-2-0	Ara Parseghian	same
14	Toledo	12-0-0	John Murphy	11-0-0
15	Mississippi	10-2-0	Billy Kinard	9-2-0
16	Arkansas	8-3-1	Frank Broyles	8-2-1
17	Houston	9-3-0	Bill Yeoman	9-2-0
18	Texas	8-3-0	Darrell Royal	8-2-0
19	Washington	8-3-0	Jim Owens	same
20	USC	6-4-1	John McKay	same

Key Bowl Games

Rankings below reflect final regular season poll, released Dec.6.
Orange—#1 Nebraska over #2 Alabama, 38-6; **Sugar**—#3 Oklahoma over #5 Auburn, 40-22; **Rose**—#16 Stanford over #4 Michigan, 13-12; **Gator**—#6 Georgia over N.Carolina, 7-3; **Bluebonnet**—#7 Colorado over #15 Houston, 29-17; **Fiesta**—#8 Ariz. St. over Florida St., 45-38; **Cotton**—#10 Penn St. over #12 Texas, 30-6.

1973

Final poll taken after bowl games.

		After Bowls	Head Coach	Regular Season
1	Notre Dame	11-0-0	Ara Parseghian	10-0-0
2	Ohio St.	10-0-1	Woody Hayes	9-0-1
3	Oklahoma	10-0-1	Barry Switzer	same
4	Alabama	11-1-0	Bear Bryant	11-0-0
5	Penn St.	12-0-0	Joe Paterno	11-0-0
6	Michigan	10-0-1	Bo Schembechler	same
7	Nebraska	9-2-1	Tom Osborne	8-2-1
8	USC	9-2-1	John McKay	9-1-1
9	Arizona St.	11-1-0	Frank Kush	10-1-0
	Houston	11-1-0	Bill Yeoman	10-1-0
11	Texas Tech	11-1-0	Jim Carlen	10-1-0
12	UCLA	9-2-0	Pepper Rodgers	same
13	LSU	9-3-0	Charlie McClendon	9-2-0
14	Texas	8-3-0	Darrell Royal	8-2-0
15	Miami-OH	11-0-0	Bill Mallory	10-0-0
16	N.C. State	9-3-0	Lou Holtz	8-3-0
17	Missouri	8-4-0	Al Onofrio	7-4-0
18	Kansas	7-4-1	Don Fambrough	7-3-1
19	Tennessee	8-4-0	Bill Battle	8-3-0
20	Maryland	8-4-0	Jerry Claiborne	8-3-0
	Tulane	9-3-0	Bennie Ellender	9-2-0

Key Bowl Games

Rankings below reflect final regular season poll, released Dec.3. No bowls for then #2 Oklahoma (probation), #5 Michigan and #9 UCLA.
Sugar—#3 Notre Dame over #1 Alabama, 24-23; **Rose**—#4 Ohio St. over #7 USC, 42-21; **Orange**—#6 Penn St. over #13 LSU, 16-9; **Cotton**—#12 Nebraska over #8 Texas, 19-3; **Fiesta**—#10 Ariz. St. over Pitt, 28-7; **Bluebonnet**—#14 Houston over #17 Tulane, 47-7.

1974

Final poll taken after bowl games.

	After Bowls	Head Coach	Regular Season
1 Oklahoma	11-0-0	Barry Switzer	same
2 USC	10-1-1	John McKay	9-1-1
3 Michigan	10-1-0	Bo Schembechler	same
4 Ohio St.	10-2-0	Woody Hayes	10-1-0
5 Alabama	11-1-0	Bear Bryant	11-0-0
6 Notre Dame	10-2-0	Ara Parseghian	9-2-0
7 Penn St.	10-2-0	Joe Paterno	9-2-0
8 Auburn	10-2-0	Shug Jordan	9-2-0
9 Nebraska	9-3-0	Tom Osborne	8-3-0
10 Miami-OH	10-0-1	Dick Crum	9-0-1
11 N.C. State	9-2-1	Lou Holtz	9-2-0
12 Michigan St.	7-3-1	Denny Stolz	same
13 Maryland	8-4-0	Jerry Claiborne	8-3-0
14 Baylor	8-4-0	Grant Teaff	8-3-0
15 Florida	8-4-0	Doug Dickey	8-3-0
16 Texas A&M	8-3-0	Emory Ballard	same
17 Mississippi St.	9-3-0	Bob Tyler	8-3-0
Texas	8-4-0	Darrell Royal	8-3-0
19 Houston	8-3-1	Bill Yeoman	8-3-0
20 Tennessee	7-3-2	Bill Battle	6-3-2

Key Bowl Games

Rankings below reflect final regular season poll, released Dec.2. No bowls for #1 Oklahoma (probation) and then #4 Michigan.
Orange—#9 Notre Dame over #2 Alabama, 13-11; **Rose**—#5 USC over #3 Ohio St., 18-17; **Gator**—#6 Auburn over #11 Texas, 27-3; **Cotton**—#7 Penn St. over #12 Baylor, 41-20; **Sugar**—#8 Nebraska over #18 Florida, 13-10; **Liberty**—Tennessee over #10 Maryland, 7-3.

1975

Final poll taken after bowl games.

	After Bowls	Head Coach	Regular Season
1 Oklahoma	11-1-0	Barry Switzer	10-1-0
2 Arizona St.	12-0-0	Frank Kush	11-0-0
3 Alabama	11-1-0	Bear Bryant	10-1-0
4 Ohio St.	11-1-0	Woody Hayes	11-0-0
5 UCLA	9-2-1	Dick Vermeil	8-2-1
6 Texas	10-2-0	Darrell Royal	9-2-0
7 Arkansas	10-2-0	Frank Broyles	9-2-0
8 Michigan	8-2-2	Bo Schembechler	8-1-2
9 Nebraska	10-2-0	Tom Osborne	10-1-0
10 Penn St.	9-3-0	Joe Paterno	9-2-0
11 Texas A&M	10-2-0	Emory Bellard	10-1-0
12 Miami-OH	11-1-0	Dick Crum	10-1-0
13 Maryland	9-2-1	Jerry Claiborne	8-2-1
14 California	8-3-0	Mike White	same
15 Pittsburgh	8-4-0	Johnny Majors	7-4-0
16 Colorado	9-3-0	Bill Mallory	9-2-0
17 USC	8-4-0	John McKay	7-4-0
18 Arizona	9-2-0	Jim Young	same
19 Georgia	9-3-0	Vince Dooley	9-2-0
20 West Virginia	9-3-0	Bobby Bowden	8-3-0

Key Bowl Games

Rankings below reflect final regular season poll, released Dec.1. Texas A&M was unbeaten and ranked 2nd in that poll, but lost to #18 Arkansas, 31-6, in its final regular season game on Dec.6.
Rose—#11 UCLA over #1 Ohio St., 23-10; **Liberty**—#17 USC over #2 Texas A&M, 20-0; **Orange**—#3 Oklahoma over #5 Michigan, 14-6; **Sugar**—#4 Alabama over #8 Penn St., 13-6; **Fiesta**—#7 Ariz. St. over #6 Nebraska, 17-14; **Bluebonnet**—#9 Texas over #10 Colorado, 38-21; **Cotton**—#18 Arkansas over #12 Georgia, 31-10.

1976

Final poll taken after bowl games.

	After Bowls	Head Coach	Regular Season
1 Pittsburgh	12-0-0	Johnny Majors	11-0-0
2 USC	11-1-0	John Robinson	10-1-0
3 Michigan	10-2-0	Bo Schembechler	10-1-0
4 Houston	10-2-0	Bill Yeoman	9-2-0
5 Oklahoma	9-2-1	Barry Switzer	8-2-1
6 Ohio St.	9-2-1	Woody Hayes	8-2-1
7 Texas A&M	10-2-0	Emory Bellard	9-2-0
8 Maryland	11-1-0	Jerry Claiborne	11-0-0
9 Nebraska	9-3-1	Tom Osborne	8-3-1
10 Georgia	10-2-0	Vince Dooley	10-1-0
11 Alabama	9-3-0	Bear Bryant	8-3-0
12 Notre Dame	9-3-0	Dan Devine	8-3-0
13 Texas Tech	10-2-0	Steve Sloan	10-1-0
14 Oklahoma St.	9-3-0	Jim Stanley	8-3-0
15 UCLA	9-2-1	Terry Donahue	9-1-1
16 Colorado	8-4-0	Bill Mallory	8-3-0
17 Rutgers	11-0-0	Frank Burns	same
18 Kentucky	8-4-0	Fran Curci	7-4-0
19 Iowa St.	8-3-0	Earle Bruce	same
20 Mississippi St.	9-2-0	Bob Tyler	same

Key Bowl Games

Rankings below reflect final regular season poll, released Nov.29. No bowl for #20 Miss. St. (probation).
Sugar—#1 Pitt over #5 Georgia, 27-3; **Rose**—#3 USC over #2 Michigan, 14-6; **Cotton**—#6 Houston over #4 Maryland, 30-21; **Liberty**—#16 Alabama over #20 UCLA, 36-6; **Fiesta**—#8 Oklahoma over Wyoming, 41-7; **Bluebonnet**—#13 Nebraska over #9 Texas Tech, 27-24; **Sun**—#10 Texas A&M over Florida, 37-14; **Orange**—#11 Ohio St. over #12 Colorado, 27-10.

1977

Final poll taken after bowl games.

	After Bowls	Head Coach	Regular Season
1 Notre Dame	11-1-0	Dan Devine	10-1-0
2 Alabama	11-1-0	Bear Bryant	10-1-0
3 Arkansas	11-1-0	Lou Holtz	10-1-0
4 Texas	11-1-0	Fred Akers	11-0-0
5 Penn St.	11-1-0	Joe Paterno	10-1-0
6 Kentucky	10-1-0	Fran Curci	same
7 Oklahoma	10-2-0	Barry Switzer	10-1-0
8 Pittsburgh	9-2-1	Jackie Sherrill	8-2-1
9 Michigan	10-2-0	Bo Schembechler	10-1-0
10 Washington	8-4-0	Don James	7-4-0
11 Ohio St.	9-3-0	Woody Hayes	9-2-0
12 Nebraska	9-3-0	Tom Osborne	8-3-0
13 USC	8-4-0	John Robinson	7-4-0
14 Florida St.	10-2-0	Bobby Bowden	9-2-0
15 Stanford	9-3-0	Bill Walsh	8-3-0
16 San Diego St.	10-1-0	Claude Gilbert	same
17 North Carolina	8-3-1	Bill Dooley	8-2-1
18 Arizona St.	9-3-0	Frank Kush	9-2-0
19 Clemson	8-3-1	Charley Pell	8-2-1
20 BYU	9-2-0	LaVell Edwards	same

Key Bowl Games

Rankings below reflect final regular season poll, released Nov.28. No bowl for #7 Kentucky (probation).
Cotton—#5 Notre Dame over #1 Texas, 38-10; **Orange**—#6 Arkansas over #2 Oklahoma, 31-6; **Sugar**—#3 Alabama over #9 Ohio St., 35-6; **Rose**—#13 Washington over #4 Michigan, 27-20; **Fiesta**—#8 Penn St. over #15 Ariz. St., 42-30; **Gator**—#10 Pitt over #11 Clemson, 34-3.

Associated Press Final Polls (Cont.)

1978

Final poll taken after bowl games.

		After Bowls	Head Coach	Regular Season
1	Alabama	11-1-0	Bear Bryant	10-1-0
2	USC	12-1-0	John Robinson	11-1-0
3	Oklahoma	11-1-0	Barry Switzer	10-1-0
4	Penn St.	11-1-0	Joe Paterno	11-0-0
5	Michigan	10-2-0	Bo Schembechler	10-1-0
6	Clemson	11-1-0	Charley Pell	10-1-0
7	Notre Dame	9-3-0	Dan Devine	8-3-0
8	Nebraska	9-3-0	Tom Osborne	9-2-0
9	Texas	9-3-0	Fred Akers	8-3-0
10	Houston	9-3-0	Bill Yeoman	9-2-0
11	Arkansas	9-2-1	Lou Holtz	9-2-0
12	Michigan St.	8-3-0	Darryl Rogers	same
13	Purdue	9-2-1	Jim Young	8-2-1
14	UCLA	8-3-1	Terry Donahue	8-3-0
15	Missouri	8-4-0	Warren Powers	7-4-0
16	Georgia	9-2-1	Vince Dooley	9-1-1
17	Stanford	8-4-0	Bill Walsh	7-4-0
18	N.C. State	9-3-0	Bo Rein	8-3-0
19	Texas A&M	8-4-0	Emory Bellard (4-2) & Tom Wilson (4-2)	7-4-0
20	Maryland	9-3-0	Jerry Claiborne	9-2-0

Key Bowl Games

Rankings below reflect final regular season poll, released Dec. 4. No bowl for then #12 Michigan St. (probation). **Sugar**—#2 Alabama over #1 Penn St., 14-7; **Rose**—#3 USC over #5 Michigan, 17-10; **Orange**—#4 Oklahoma over #6 Nebraska, 31-24; **Gator**—#7 Clemson over #20 Ohio St., 17-15; **Fiesta**—#8 Arkansas tied #15 UCLA, 10-10; **Cotton**—#10 Notre Dame over #9 Houston, 35-34.

1979

Final poll taken after bowl games.

		After Bowls	Head Coach	Regular Season
1	Alabama	12-0-0	Bear Bryant	11-0-0
2	USC	11-0-1	John Robinson	10-0-1
3	Oklahoma	11-1-0	Barry Switzer	10-1-0
4	Ohio St.	11-1-0	Earle Bruce	11-0-0
5	Houston	11-1-0	Bill Yeoman	10-1-0
6	Florida St.	11-1-0	Bobby Bowden	11-0-0
7	Pittsburgh	11-1-0	Jackie Sherrill	10-1-0
8	Arkansas	10-2-0	Lou Holtz	10-1-0
9	Nebraska	10-2-0	Tom Osborne	10-1-0
10	Purdue	10-2-0	Jim Young	9-2-0
11	Washington	9-3-0	Don James	8-3-0
12	Texas	9-3-0	Fred Akers	9-2-0
13	BYU	11-1-0	LaVell Edwards	11-0-0
14	Baylor	8-4-0	Grant Teaff	7-4-0
15	North Carolina	8-3-1	Dick Crum	7-3-1
16	Auburn	8-3-0	Doug Barfield	same
17	Temple	10-2-0	Wayne Hardin	9-2-0
18	Michigan	8-4-0	Bo Schembechler	8-3-0
19	Indiana	8-4-0	Lee Corso	7-4-0
20	Penn St.	8-4-0	Joe Paterno	7-4-0

Key Bowl Games

Rankings below reflect final regular season poll, released Dec.3. No bowl for then #17 Auburn (probation). **Sugar**—#2 Alabama over #6 Arkansas, 24-9; **Rose**—#3 USC over #1 Ohio St., 17-16; **Orange**—#5 Oklahoma over #4 Florida St., 24-7; **Sun**—#13 Washington over #11 Texas, 14-7; **Cotton**—#8 Houston over #7 Nebraska, 17-14; **Fiesta**—#10 Pitt over Arizona, 16-10.

1980

Final poll taken after bowl games.

		After Bowls	Head Coach	Regular Season
1	Georgia	12-0-0	Vince Dooley	11-0-0
2	Pittsburgh	11-1-0	Jackie Sherrill	10-1-0
3	Oklahoma	10-2-0	Barry Switzer	9-2-0
4	Michigan	10-2-0	Bo Schembechler	9-2-0
5	Florida St.	10-2-0	Bobby Bowden	10-1-0
6	Alabama	10-2-0	Bear Bryant	9-2-0
7	Nebraska	10-2-0	Tom Osborne	9-2-0
8	Penn St.	10-2-0	Joe Paterno	9-2-0
9	Notre Dame	9-2-1	Dan Devine	9-1-1
10	North Carolina	11-1-0	Dick Crum	10-1-0
11	USC	8-2-1	John Robinson	same
12	BYU	12-1-0	LaVell Edwards	11-1-0
13	UCLA	9-2-0	Terry Donahue	same
14	Baylor	10-2-0	Grant Teaff	10-1-0
15	Ohio St.	9-3-0	Earle Bruce	9-2-0
16	Washington	9-3-0	Don James	9-2-0
17	Purdue	9-3-0	Jim Young	8-3-0
18	Miami-FL	9-3-0	H. Schnellenberger	8-3-0
19	Mississippi St.	9-3-0	Emory Bellard	9-2-0
20	SMU	8-4-0	Ron Meyer	8-3-0

Key Bowl Games

Rankings below reflect final regular season poll, released Dec.8. **Sugar**—#1 Georgia over #7 Notre Dame, 17-10; **Orange**—#4 Oklahoma over #2 Florida St., 18-17; **Gator**—#3 Pitt over #18 S. Carolina, 37-9; **Rose**—#9 Michigan over #16 Washington, 23-6; **Cotton**—#9 Alabama over #6 Baylor, 30-2; **Sun**—#8 Nebraska over #17 Miss. St., 31-17; **Fiesta**—#10 Penn St. over #11 Ohio St., 31-19; **Bluebonnet**—#13 N. Carolina over Texas, 16-7.

1981

Final poll taken after bowl games.

		After Bowls	Head Coach	Regular Season
1	Clemson	12-0-0	Danny Ford	11-0-0
2	Texas	10-1-1	Fred Akers	9-1-1
3	Penn St.	10-2-0	Joe Paterno	9-2-0
4	Pittsburgh	11-1-0	Jackie Sherrill	10-1-0
5	SMU	10-1-0	Ron Meyer	same
6	Georgia	10-2-0	Vince Dooley	10-1-0
7	Alabama	9-2-1	Bear Bryant	9-1-1
8	Miami-FL	9-2-0	H. Schnellenberger	same
9	North Carolina	10-2-0	Dick Crum	9-2-0
10	Washington	10-2-0	Don James	9-2-0
11	Nebraska	9-3-0	Tom Osborne	9-2-0
12	Michigan	9-3-0	Bo Schembechler	8-3-0
13	BYU	11-2-0	LaVell Edwards	10-2-0
14	USC	9-3-0	John Robinson	9-2-0
15	Ohio St.	9-3-0	Earle Bruce	8-3-0
16	Arizona St.	9-2-0	Darryl Rogers	same
17	West Virginia	9-3-0	Don Nehlen	8-3-0
18	Iowa	8-4-0	Hayden Fry	8-3-0
19	Missouri	8-4-0	Warren Powers	7-4-0
20	Oklahoma	7-4-1	Barry Switzer	6-4-1

Key Bowl Games

Rankings below reflect final regular season poll, released Nov.30. No bowl for then #5 SMU (probation), #9 Miami-FL (probation), and #17 Ariz. St. (probation). **Orange**—#1 Clemson over #4 Nebraska, 22-15; **Sugar**—#10 Pitt over #2 Georgia, 24-20; **Cotton**—#6 Texas over #3 Alabama, 14-12; **Fiesta**—#7 Penn St. over #8 USC, 26-10; **Gator**—#11 N. Carolina over Arkansas, 31-27; **Rose**—#12 Washington over #13 Iowa, 28-0.

1982

Final poll taken after bowl games.

	After Bowls	Head Coach	Regular Season
1 Penn St.	11-1-0	Joe Paterno	10-1-0
2 SMU	11-0-1	Bobby Collins	10-0-0
3 Nebraska	12-1-0	Tom Osborne	11-1-0
4 Georgia	11-1-0	Vince Dooley	11-0-0
5 UCLA	10-1-1	Terry Donahue	9-1-1
6 Arizona St.	10-2-0	Darryl Rogers	9-2-0
7 Washington	10-2-0	Don James	9-2-0
8 Clemson	9-1-1	Danny Ford	same
9 Arkansas	9-2-1	Lou Holtz	8-2-1
10 Pittsburgh	9-3-0	Foge Fazio	9-2-0
11 LSU	8-3-1	Jerry Stovall	8-2-1
12 Ohio St.	9-3-0	Earle Bruce	8-3-0
13 Florida St.	9-3-0	Bobby Bowden	8-3-0
14 Auburn	9-3-0	Pat Dye	8-3-0
15 USC	8-3-0	John Robinson	same
16 Oklahoma	8-4-0	Barry Switzer	8-3-0
17 Texas	9-3-0	Fred Akers	9-2-0
18 North Carolina	8-4-0	Dick Crum	7-4-0
19 West Virginia	9-3-0	Don Nehlen	8-3-0
20 Maryland	8-4-0	Bobby Ross	8-3-0

Key Bowl Games

Rankings below reflect final regular season poll, released Dec.6. No bowl for then #7 Clemson (probation) and #15 USC (probation).

Sugar—#2 Penn St. over #1 Georgia, 27-23; **Orange**—#3 Nebraska over #13 LSU, 21-20; **Cotton**—#4 SMU over #6 Pitt, 7-3; **Rose**—#5 UCLA over #19 Michigan, 24-14; **Aloha**—#9 Washington over #16 Maryland, 21-20; **Fiesta**—#11 Ariz. St. over #12 Oklahoma, 32-21; **Bluebonnet**—#14 Arkansas over Florida, 28-24.

1983

Final poll taken after bowl games.

	After Bowls	Head Coach	Regular Season
1 Miami-FL	11-1-0	H. Schnellenberger	10-1-0
2 Nebraska	12-1-0	Tom Osborne	12-0-0
3 Auburn	11-1-0	Pat Dye	10-1-0
4 Georgia	10-1-1	Vince Dooley	9-1-1
5 Texas	11-1-0	Fred Akers	11-0-0
6 Florida	9-2-1	Charley Pell	8-2-1
7 BYU	11-1-0	LaVell Edwards	10-1-0
8 Michigan	9-3-0	Bo Schembechler	9-2-0
9 Ohio St.	9-3-0	Earle Bruce	8-3-0
10 Illinois	10-2-0	Mike White	10-1-0
11 Clemson	9-1-1	Danny Ford	same
12 SMU	10-2-0	Bobby Collins	10-1-0
13 Air Force	10-2-0	Ken Hatfield	9-2-0
14 Iowa	9-3-0	Hayden Fry	9-2-0
15 Alabama	8-4-0	Ray Perkins	7-4-0
16 West Virginia	9-3-0	Don Nehlen	8-3-0
17 UCLA	7-4-1	Terry Donahue	6-4-1
18 Pittsburgh	8-3-1	Foge Fazio	8-2-1
19 Boston College	9-3-0	Jack Bicknell	9-2-0
20 East Carolina	8-3-0	Ed Emory	same

Key Bowl Games

Rankings below reflect final regular season poll, released Dec.5. No bowl for then #12 Clemson (probation).

Orange—#5 Miami-FL over #1 Nebraska, 31-30; **Cotton**—#7 Georgia over #2 Texas, 10-9; **Sugar**—#3 Auburn over #8 Michigan, 9-7; **Rose**—UCLA over #4 Illinois, 45-9; **Holiday**—#9 BYU over Missouri, 21-17; **Gator**—#11 Florida over #10 Iowa, 14-6; **Fiesta**—#14 Ohio St. over #15 Pitt, 28-23.

1984

Final poll taken after bowl games.

	After Bowls	Head Coach	Regular Season
1 BYU	13-0-0	LaVell Edwards	12-0-0
2 Washington	11-1-0	Don James	10-1-0
3 Florida	9-1-1	Charley Pell (0-1-1) & Galen Hall (9-0)	same
4 Nebraska	10-2-0	Tom Osborne	9-2-0
5 Boston College	10-2-0	Jack Bicknell	9-2-0
6 Oklahoma	9-2-1	Barry Switzer	9-1-1
7 Oklahoma St.	10-2-0	Pat Jones	9-2-0
8 SMU	10-2-0	Bobby Collins	9-2-0
9 UCLA	9-3-0	Terry Donahue	8-3-0
10 USC	9-3-0	Ted Tollner	8-3-0
11 South Carolina	10-2-0	Joe Morrison	10-1-0
12 Maryland	9-3-0	Bobby Ross	8-3-0
13 Ohio St.	9-3-0	Earle Bruce	9-2-0
14 Auburn	9-4-0	Pat Dye	8-4-0
15 LSU	8-3-1	Bill Arnsparger	8-2-1
16 Iowa	8-4-1	Hayden Fry	7-4-1
17 Florida St.	7-3-2	Bobby Bowden	7-3-1
18 Miami-FL	8-5-0	Jimmy Johnson	8-4-0
19 Kentucky	9-3-0	Jerry Claiborne	8-3-0
20 Virginia	8-2-2	George Welsh	7-2-2

Key Bowl Games

Rankings below reflect final regular season poll, released Dec.3. No bowl for then #3 Florida (probation).

Holiday—#1 BYU over Michigan, 24-17; **Orange**—#4 Washington over Oklahoma, 28-17; **Sugar**—#5 Nebraska over #11 LSU, 28-10; **Rose**—#18 USC over #6 Ohio St., 20-17; **Gator**—#9 Okla. St. over #7 S. Carolina, 21-14; **Cotton**—#8 BC over Houston, 45-28; **Aloha**—#10 SMU over #17 Notre Dame, 27-20.

1985

Final poll taken after bowl games.

	After Bowls	Head Coach	Regular Season
1 Oklahoma	11-1-0	Barry Switzer	10-1-0
2 Michigan	10-1-1	Bo Schembechler	9-1-1
3 Penn St.	11-1-0	Joe Paterno	11-0-0
4 Tennessee	9-1-2	Johnny Majors	8-1-2
5 Florida	9-1-1	Galen Hall	same
6 Texas A&M	10-2-0	Jackie Sherrill	9-2-0
7 UCLA	9-2-1	Terry Donahue	8-2-1
8 Air Force	12-1-0	Fisher DeBerry	11-1-0
9 Miami-FL	10-2-0	Jimmy Johnson	10-1-0
10 Iowa	10-2-0	Hayden Fry	10-1-0
11 Nebraska	9-3-0	Tom Osborne	9-2-0
12 Arkansas	10-2-0	Ken Hatfield	9-2-0
13 Alabama	9-2-1	Ray Perkins	8-2-1
14 Ohio St.	9-3-0	Earle Bruce	8-3-0
15 Florida St.	9-3-0	Bobby Bowden	8-3-0
16 BYU	11-3-0	LaVell Edwards	11-2-0
17 Baylor	9-3-0	Grant Teaff	8-3-0
18 Maryland	9-3-0	Bobby Ross	8-3-0
19 Georgia Tech	9-2-1	Bill Curry	8-2-1
20 LSU	9-2-1	Bill Arnsparger	9-1-1

Key Bowl Games

Rankings below reflect final regular season poll, released Dec. 9. No bowl for then #6 Florida (probation).

Orange—#3 Oklahoma over #1 Penn St., 25-10; **Sugar**—#8 Tennessee over #2 Miami-FL, 35-7; **Rose**—#13 UCLA over #4 Iowa, 45-28; **Fiesta**—#5 Michigan over #7 Nebraska, 27-23; **Bluebonnet**—#10 Air Force over Texas, 24-16; **Cotton**—#11 Texas A&M over #16 Auburn, 36-16.

Associated Press Final Polls (Cont.)

1986

Final poll taken after bowl games.

	After Bowls	Head Coach	Regular Season
1 Penn St.	12-0-0	Joe Paterno	11-0-0
2 Miami-FL	11-1-0	Jimmy Johnson	11-0-0
3 Oklahoma	11-1-0	Barry Switzer	10-1-0
4 Arizona St.	10-1-1	John Cooper	9-1-1
5 Nebraska	10-2-0	Tom Osborne	9-2-0
6 Auburn	10-2-0	Pat Dye	9-2-0
7 Ohio St.	10-3-0	Earle Bruce	9-3-0
8 Michigan	11-2-0	Bo Schembechler	11-1-0
9 Alabama	10-3-0	Ray Perkins	9-3-0
10 LSU	9-3-0	Bill Arnsparger	9-2-0
11 Arizona	9-3-0	Larry Smith	8-3-0
12 Baylor	9-3-0	Grant Teaff	8-3-0
13 Texas A&M	9-3-0	Jackie Sherrill	9-2-0
14 UCLA	8-3-1	Terry Donahue	7-3-1
15 Arkansas	9-3-0	Ken Hatfield	9-2-0
16 Iowa	9-3-0	Hayden Fry	8-3-0
17 Clemson	8-2-2	Danny Ford	7-2-2
18 Washington	8-3-1	Don James	8-2-1
19 Boston College	9-3-0	Jack Bicknell	8-3-0
20 Virginia Tech	9-2-1	Bill Dooley	8-2-1

Key Bowl Games

Rankings below reflect final regular season poll, released Dec.1.

Fiesta—#2 Penn St. over #1 Miami-FL, 14-10; **Orange**—#3 Oklahoma over #9 Arkansas, 42-8; **Rose**— #7 Ariz. St. over #4 Michigan, 22-15; **Sugar**—#6 Nebraska over #5 LSU, 30-15; **Cotton**—#11 Ohio St. over #8 Texas A&M, 28-12; **Citrus**—#10 Auburn over USC, 16-7; **Sun**—#13 Alabama over #12 Washington, 28-6.

1987

Final poll taken after bowl games.

	After Bowls	Head Coach	Regular Season
1 Miami-FL	12-0-0	Jimmy Johnson	11-0-0
2 Florida St.	11-1-0	Bobby Bowden	10-1-0
3 Oklahoma	11-1-0	Barry Switzer	11-0-0
4 Syracuse	11-0-1	Dick MacPherson	11-0-0
5 LSU	10-1-1	Mike Archer	9-1-1
6 Nebraska	10-2-0	Tom Osborne	10-1-0
7 Auburn	9-1-2	Pat Dye	9-1-1
8 Michigan St.	9-2-1	George Perles	8-2-1
9 UCLA	10-2-0	Terry Donahue	9-2-0
10 Texas A&M	10-2-0	Jackie Sherrill	9-2-0
11 Oklahoma St.	10-2-0	Pat Jones	9-2-0
12 Clemson	10-2-0	Danny Ford	9-2-0
13 Georgia	9-3-0	Vince Dooley	8-3-0
14 Tennessee	10-2-1	Johnny Majors	9-2-1
15 South Carolina	8-4-0	Joe Morrison	8-3-0
16 Iowa	10-3-0	Hayden Fry	9-3-0
17 Notre Dame	8-4-0	Lou Holtz	8-3-0
18 USC	8-4-0	Larry Smith	8-3-0
19 Michigan	8-4-0	Bo Schembechler	7-4-0
20 Arizona St.	7-4-1	John Cooper	6-4-1

Key Bowl Games

Rankings below reflect final regular season poll, released Dec.7.

Orange—#2 Miami-FL over #1 Oklahoma, 20-14; **Fiesta**—#3 Florida St. over #5 Nebraska, 31-28; **Sugar**—#4 Syracuse tied #6 Auburn, 16-16; **Gator**—#7 LSU over #9 S.Carolina, 30-13; **Rose**—#8 Mich. St. over #16 USC, 20-17; **Aloha**—#10 UCLA over Florida, 20-16; **Cotton**—#13 Texas A&M over #12 Notre Dame, 35-10.

1988

Final poll taken after bowl games.

	After Bowls	Head Coach	Regular Season
1 Notre Dame	12-0-0	Lou Holtz	11-0-0
2 Miami-FL	11-1-0	Jimmy Johnson	10-1-0
3 Florida St.	11-1-0	Bobby Bowden	10-1-0
4 Michigan	9-2-1	Bo Schembechler	8-2-1
5 West Virginia	11-1-0	Don Nehlen	11-0-0
6 UCLA	10-2-0	Terry Donahue	9-2-0
7 USC	10-2-0	Larry Smith	10-1-0
8 Auburn	10-2-0	Pat Dye	10-1-0
9 Clemson	10-2-0	Danny Ford	9-2-0
10 Nebraska	11-2-0	Tom Osborne	11-1-0
11 Oklahoma St.	10-2-0	Pat Jones	9-2-0
12 Arkansas	10-2-0	Ken Hatfield	10-1-0
13 Syracuse	10-2-0	Dick MacPherson	9-2-0
14 Oklahoma	9-3-0	Barry Switzer	9-2-0
15 Georgia	9-3-0	Vince Dooley	8-3-0
16 Washington St.	9-3-0	Dennis Erickson	8-3-0
17 Alabama	9-3-0	Bill Curry	8-3-0
18 Houston	9-3-0	Jack Pardee	9-2-0
19 LSU	8-4-0	Mike Archer	8-3-0
20 Indiana	8-3-1	Bill Mallory	7-3-1

Key Bowl Games

Rankings below reflect final regular season poll, released Dec.5.

Fiesta—#1 Notre Dame over #3 West Va., 34-21; **Orange**—#2 Miami-FL over #6 Nebraska, 23-3; **Sugar**—#4 Florida St. over #7 Auburn, 13-7; **Rose**—#11 USC over #5 Michigan, 22-14; **Cotton**—#9 UCLA over #8 Arkansas, 17-3; **Citrus**—#13 Clemson over #10 Oklahoma, 13-6.

1989

Final poll taken after bowl games.

	After Bowls	Head Coach	Regular Season
1 Miami-FL	11-1-0	Dennis Erickson	10-1-0
2 Notre Dame	12-1-0	Lou Holtz	11-1-0
3 Florida St.	10-2-0	Bobby Bowden	9-2-0
4 Colorado	11-1-0	Bill McCartney	11-0-0
5 Tennessee	11-1-0	Johnny Majors	10-1-0
6 Auburn	10-2-0	Pat Dye	9-2-0
7 Michigan	10-2-0	Bo Schembechler	10-1-0
8 USC	9-2-1	Larry Smith	8-2-1
9 Alabama	10-2-0	Bill Curry	10-1-0
10 Illinois	10-2-0	John Mackovic	9-2-0
11 Nebraska	10-2-0	Tom Osborne	10-1-0
12 Clemson	10-2-0	Danny Ford	9-2-0
13 Arkansas	10-2-0	Ken Hatfield	10-1-0
14 Houston	9-2-0	Jack Pardee	same
15 Penn St.	8-3-1	Joe Paterno	7-3-1
16 Michigan St.	8-4-0	George Perles	7-4-0
17 Pittsburgh	8-3-1	Mike Gottfried (7-3-1) & Paul Hackett (1-0)	7-3-1
18 Virginia	10-3-0	George Welsh	10-2-0
19 Texas Tech	9-3-0	Spike Dykes	8-3-0
20 Texas A&M	8-4-0	R.C. Slocum	8-3-0

Key Bowl Games

Rankings below reflect final regular season poll, released Dec.11. No bowl for then #13 Houston (probation).

Orange—#4 Notre Dame over #1 Colorado, 21-6; **Sugar**—#2 Miami-FL over #7 Alabama, 33-25; **Rose**— #12 USC over #3 Michigan, 17-10; **Fiesta**—#5 Florida St. over #6 Nebraska, 41-17; **Cotton**—#8 Tennessee over #10 Arkansas, 31-27; **Hall of Fame**—#9 Auburn over #21 Ohio St., 31-14; **Citrus**—#11 Illinois over #15 Virginia, 31-21.

1990

Final poll taken after bowl games.

	After Bowls	Head Coach	Regular Season
1 Colorado	11-1-1	Bill McCartney	10-1-1
2 Georgia Tech	11-0-1	Bobby Ross	10-0-1
3 Miami-FL	10-2-0	Dennis Erickson	9-2-0
4 Florida St.	10-2-0	Bobby Bowden	9-2-0
5 Washington	10-2-0	Don James	9-2-0
6 Notre Dame	9-3-0	Lou Holtz	9-2-0
7 Michigan	9-3-0	Gary Moeller	8-3-0
8 Tennessee	9-2-2	Johnny Majors	8-2-2
9 Clemson	10-2-0	Ken Hatfield	9-2-0
10 Houston	10-1-0	John Jenkins	same
11 Penn St.	9-3-0	Joe Paterno	9-2-0
12 Texas	10-2-0	David McWilliams	10-1-0
13 Florida	9-2-0	Steve Spurrier	same
14 Louisville	10-1-1	H. Schnellenberger	9-1-1
15 Texas A&M	9-3-1	R.C. Slocum	8-3-1
16 Michigan St.	8-3-1	George Perles	7-3-1
17 Oklahoma	8-3-0	Gary Gibbs	same
18 Iowa	8-4-0	Hayden Fry	8-3-0
19 Auburn	8-3-1	Pat Dye	7-3-1
20 USC	8-4-1	Larry Smith	8-3-1

Key Bowl Games

Rankings below reflect final regular season poll, released Dec.3. No bowl for then #9 Houston (probation), #11 Florida (probation) and #20 Oklahoma (probation).

Orange—#1 Colorado over #5 Notre Dame, 10-9; **Citrus**—#2 Ga. Tech over #19 Nebraska, 45-21; **Cotton**—#4 Miami-FL over #3 Texas, 46-3; **Blockbuster**—#6 Florida St. over #7 Penn St., 24-17; **Rose**—#8 Washington over #17 Iowa, 46-34; **Sugar**—#10 Tennessee over Virginia, 23-22; **Gator**—#12 Michigan over #15 Ole Miss, 35-3.

1991

Final poll taken after bowl games.

	After Bowls	Head Coach	Regular Season
1 Miami-FL	12-0-0	Dennis Erickson	11-0-0
2 Washington	12-0-0	Don James	11-0-0
3 Penn St.	11-2-0	Joe Paterno	10-2-0
4 Florida St.	11-2-0	Bobby Bowden	10-2-0
5 Alabama	11-1-0	Gene Stallings	10-1-0
6 Michigan	10-2-0	Gary Moeller	10-1-0
7 Florida	10-2-0	Steve Spurrier	10-1-0
8 California	10-2-0	Bruce Snyder	9-2-0
9 East Carolina	11-1-0	Bill Lewis	10-1-0
10 Iowa	10-1-1	Hayden Fry	10-1-0
11 Syracuse	10-2-0	Paul Pasqualoni	9-2-0
12 Texas A&M	10-2-0	R.C. Slocum	10-1-0
13 Notre Dame	10-3-0	Lou Holtz	9-3-0
14 Tennessee	9-3-0	Johnny Majors	9-2-0
15 Nebraska	9-2-1	Tom Osborne	9-1-1
16 Oklahoma	9-3-0	Gary Gibbs	8-3-0
17 Georgia	9-3-0	Ray Goff	8-3-0
18 Clemson	9-2-1	Ken Hatfield	9-1-1
19 UCLA	9-3-0	Terry Donahue	8-3-0
20 Colorado	8-3-1	Bill McCartney	8-2-1

Key Bowl Games

Rankings below reflect final regular season poll, taken Dec.2.

Orange—#1 Miami-FL over #11 Nebraska, 22-0; **Rose**—#2 Washington over #4 Michigan, 34-14; **Sugar**—#18 Notre Dame over #3 Florida, 39-28; **Cotton**—#5 Florida St. over #9 Texas A&M, 10-2; **Fiesta**—#6 Penn St. over #10 Tennessee, 42-17; **Holiday**—#7 Iowa tied BYU, 13-13; **Blockbuster**—#8 Alabama over #15 Colorado, 30-25; **Citrus**—#14 California over #13 Clemson, 37-13; **Peach**—#12 East Carolina over #21 N.C. State, 37-34.

1992

Final poll taken after bowl games.

	After Bowls	Head Coach	Regular Season
1 Alabama	13-0-0	Gene Stallings	12-0-0
2 Florida St.	11-1-0	Bobby Bowden	0-1-0
3 Miami-FL	11-1-0	Dennis Erickson	11-0-0
4 Notre Dame	10-1-1	Lou Holtz	9-1-1
5 Michigan	9-0-3	Gary Moeller	8-0-3
6 Syracuse	10-2-0	Paul Pasqualoni	9-2-0
7 Texas A&M	12-1-0	R.C. Slocum	12-0-0
8 Georgia	10-2-0	Ray Goff	9-2-0
9 Stanford	10-3-0	Bill Walsh	9-3-0
10 Florida	9-4-0	Steve Spurrier	8-4-0
11 Washington	9-3-0	Don James	9-2-0
12 Tennessee	9-3-0	Johnny Majors (5-3) & Phillip Fulmer (4-0)	8-3-0
13 Colorado	9-2-1	Bill McCartney	9-1-1
14 Nebraska	9-3-0	Tom Osborne	9-2-0
15 Washington St.	9-3-0	Mike Price	8-3-0
16 Mississippi	9-3-0	Billy Brewer	8-3-0
17 N.C. State	9-3-1	Dick Sheridan	9-2-1
18 Ohio St.	8-3-1	John Cooper	8-2-1
19 North Carolina	9-3-0	Mack Brown	8-3-0
20 Hawaii	11-2-0	Bob Wagner	10-2-0

Key Bowl Games

Rankings below reflect final regular season poll, taken Dec. 5.

Sugar—#2 Alabama over #1 Miami-FL, 34-13; **Orange**—#3 Florida St. over #11 Nebraska, 27-14; **Cotton**—#5 Notre Dame over #4 Texas A&M, 28-3; **Fiesta**—#6 Syracuse over #10 Colorado, 26-22; **Rose**—#7 Michigan over #9 Washington, 38-31; **Citrus**—#8 Georgia over #15 Ohio St., 21-14.

1993

Final poll taken after bowl games.

	After Bowls	Head Coach	Regular Season
1 Florida St	12-1-0	Bobby Bowden	11-1-0
2 Notre Dame	11-1-0	Lou Holtz	10-1-0
3 Nebraska	11-1-0	Tom Osborne	11-0-0
4 Auburn	11-0-0	Terry Bowden	11-0-0
5 Florida	11-2-0	Steve Spurrier	10-2-0
6 Wisconsin	10-1-1	Barry Alvarez	9-1-1
7 West Virginia	11-1-0	Don Nehlen	11-0-0
8 Penn St	10-2-0	Joe Paterno	9-2-0
9 Texas A&M	10-2-0	R.C. Slocum	10-1-0
10 Arizona	10-2-0	Dick Tomey	9-2-0
11 Ohio St	10-1-1	John Cooper	9-1-1
12 Tennessee	9-2-1	Phillip Fulmer	9-1-1
13 Boston College	9-3-0	Tom Coughlin	8-3-0
14 Alabama	9-3-1	Gene Stallings	8-3-1
15 Miami-FL	9-3-0	Dennis Erickson	9-2-0
16 Colorado	8-3-1	Bill McCartney	7-3-1
17 Oklahoma	9-3-0	Gary Gibbs	8-3-0
18 UCLA	8-4-0	Terry Donahue	8-3-0
19 North Carolina	10-3-0	Mack Brown	10-2-0
20 Kansas St	9-2-1	Bill Snyder	8-2-1

Key Bowl Games

Rankings below reflect final regular season poll, taken Dec.5. No bowl for then #5 Auburn (probation).

Orange—#1 Florida St. over #2 Nebraska, 18-16; **Sugar**—#8 Notre Dame over #3 West Virginia, 41-7; **Cotton**—#4 Notre Dame over #7 Texas A&M, 24-21; **Citrus**—#13 Penn St. over #6 Tennessee, 31-13; **Rose**—#9 Wisconsin over #14 UCLA, 21-16; **Fiesta**—#6 Syracuse over #10 Colorado, 26-22; **Holiday**—#11 Ohio St. over BYU, 28-21; **Gator**—#18 Alabama over #12 North Carolina, 24-10; **Carquest**—#15 Boston College over Virginia, 31-13.

Associated Press Final Polls (Cont.)

All-Time AP Top 20

The composite AP Top 20 from 1936 season through the 1993 season, based on the final rankings of each year. The final AP poll has been taken after the bowl games in 1965 and since 1968. Team point totals are based on 20 points for all 1st place finishes, 19 for each 2nd, etc. Also listed are the number of times named national champion by AP, and times ranked in the final Top 10 and Top 20.

	Pts	No.1	Top 10	Top 20			Pts	No.1	Top 10	Top 20
1 Notre Dame	614	8	34	42		11 UCLA	293	0	14	27
2 Oklahoma	558	6	29	41		12 LSU	260	1	14	23
3 Michigan	532	1	32	41		13 Auburn	259	1	13	24
4 Alabama	525	6	29	39		Arkansas	259	0	13	23
5 Ohio St.	449	3	21	36		15 Miami-FL	241	4	12	18
6 Nebraska	426	2	23	33		16 Georgia	238	1	13	20
7 USC	397	3	20	34		Michigan St	238	1	12	19
8 Texas	393	2	19	30		18 Pittsburgh	194	2	10	16
9 Tennessee	357	1	17	31		Washington	194	0	10	16
10 Penn St	343	2	19	29		20 Mississippi	193	0	10	17

The Special Election That Didn't Count

There was one No. 1 vs No. 2 confrontation not noted on page 165. It came in a special election or re-vote of AP selectors following the 1948 Rose Bowl. Here's what happened: Unbeaten Notre Dame was declared 1947 national champion by AP on Dec. 8, two days after closing out an undefeated season with a 38-7 rout of then third-ranked USC in Los Angeles. Twenty-four days later, however, unbeaten Michigan, AP's final No. 2 team, clobbered now 8th-ranked USC, 49-0, in the Rose Bowl. An immediate cry went up for an unprecedented two-team, "Who's No. 1" ballot and AP gave in. Michigan won the election, 226-119, with 12 voters calling it even. However, AP ruled that the Dec. 8 final poll won by Notre Dame would be the vote of record.

Top 50 Rivalries

Top Division I series records, including games through the 1993 season. Note that the Boston College-Holy Cross series ended after the 1986 season, Notre Dame and Miami-FL concluded their series in 1990, while Arkansas and Texas ended theirs in 1991. The series between Miami-FL and Florida was suspended after the 1987 season and formally cancelled in 1991. Penn St. and Pitt played each other annually from 1935-92 and 91 times from 1893-1992, but are not scheduled to meet again until 1997.

	Gm	Series Leader			Gm	Series Leader
Air Force-Army	28	Air Force (16-11-1)		**Kansas-Kansas St**	91	Kansas (61-25-5)
Air Force-Navy	26	Air Force (17-9-0)		**Kentucky-Tennessee**	89	Tennessee (57-23-9)
Alabama-Auburn	58	Alabama (33-24-1)		**Lafayette-Lehigh**	129	Lafayette (70-54-5)
Alabama-Tennessee	76	Alabama (41-27-8)		**LSU-Tulane**	91	LSU (62-22-7)
Arizona-Arizona St	67	Arizona (38-28-1)		**Miami,FL-Notre Dame**	23	Notre Dame (15-7-1)
Arkansas-Texas	73	Texas (54-19-0)		**Michigan-Michigan St**	86	Michigan (56-25-5)
Army-Navy	94	Army (44-43-7)		**Michigan-Notre Dame**	25	Michigan (14-10-1)
Auburn-Georgia	97	Auburn (46-44-7)		**Michigan-Ohio St**	90	Michigan (51-33-6)
Baylor-TCU	100	TCU (47-46-7)		**Minnesota-Wisconsin**	103	Minnesota (56-39-8)
Boston Col-Holy Cross	79	BC (48-31-0)		**Mississippi-Miss. St**	90	Ole Miss (52-32-6)
BYU-Utah	69	Utah (41-24-4)		**Nebraska-Oklahoma**	74	Oklahoma (39-32-3)
California-Stanford	96	Stanford (47-38-11)		**N.Carolina-N.C. State**	83	N. Carolina (53-24-6)
Cincinnati-Miami,OH	98	Miami (53-39-6)		**Notre Dame-Purdue**	65	Notre Dame (42-21-2)
Clemson-S. Carolina	91	Clemson (54-33-4)		**Notre Dame-USC**	65	Notre Dame (38-23-4)
Colorado-Colorado St	67	Colorado (49-16-2)		**Oklahoma-Okla. St**	88	Oklahoma (70-11-7)
Duke-North Carolina	79	N. Carolina (40-35-4)		**Oklahoma-Texas**	88	Texas (51-33-4)
Florida-Florida St	36	Florida (23-12-1)		**Oregon-Oregon St**	97	Oregon (47-40-10)
Florida-Miami,FL	49	Florida (25-24-0)		**Penn St.-Pittsburgh**	92	Penn St.(47-41-4)
Florida-Georgia	72	Georgia (44-26-2)		**Pittsburgh-West Va**	86	Pitt (55-28-3)
Florida St.-Miami,FL	37	Miami (22-15-0)		**Princeton-Yale**	116	Yale (63-43-10)
Georgia-Georgia Tech	88	Georgia (48-35-5)		**Richmond-Wm.& Mary**	103	Wm. & Mary (51-47-5)
Harvard-Yale	110	Yale (54-34-8)		**Tennessee-Vanderbilt**	87	Tennessee (56-26-5)
Indiana-Purdue	96	Purdue (58-32-6)		**Texas-Texas A&M**	100	Texas (64-31-5)
Iowa-Iowa St	41	Iowa (29-12-0)		**UCLA-USC**	63	USC (34-22-7)
Kansas-Missouri	102	Missouri (48-45-9)		**Washington-Wash. St**	86	Washington (55-25-6)

All-Time Winningest Division I-A Teams

Schools classified as Divison I-A for at least 10 years; through 1993 season (including bowl games).

Top 25 Winning Percentage

		Yrs	Gm	W	L	T	Pct	Bowls App	Bowls Record	1993 Season Bowl	1993 Season Record
1	Notre Dame	105	975	723	211	41	.763	19	13-6-0	won Cotton	11-1-0
2	Michigan	114	1017	739	242	36	.744	25	12-13-0	won Hall of Fame	8-4-0
3	Alabama	99	972	691	237	44	.734	46	26-17-3	won Gator	9-3-1
4	Oklahoma	99	951	659	240	52	.720	31	20-10-1	won Hancock	9-3-0
5	Texas	101	992	687	273	32	.709	34	16-16-2	none	5-5-1
6	Ohio St	104	977	659	265	53	.702	26	12-14-0	won Holiday	10-1-1
7	USC	101	936	630	254	52	.701	36	23-13-0	won Freedom	8-5-0
8	Nebraska	104	1003	673	290	40	.691	32	14-18-0	lost Orange	11-1-0
9	Penn St	107	1006	674	291	41	.690	30	18-10-2	won Citrus	10-2-0
10	Tennessee	97	965	636	276	53	.687	34	18-16-0	lost Citrus	9-2-1
11	Central Michigan	93	771	480	255	36	.646	4	3-1-0	none	5-6-0
12	Florida St	47	508	316	176	16	.638	23	14-7-2	won Orange	12-1-0
13	Washington	104	921	562	310	49	.637	21	12-8-1	on probation	7-4-0
14	Army	104	965	588	327	50	.635	3	2-1-0	none	6-5-0
15	Miami-OH	105	896	546	308	42	.633	7	5-2-0	none	4-7-0
16	LSU	100	944	573	325	46	.631	28	11-16-1	none	5-6-0
	Georgia	100	975	589	333	53	.631	31	15-13-3	none	5-6-0
	Arizona St	81	723	444	255	24	.631	15	9-5-1	none	6-5-0
19	Auburn	101	939	558	335	46	.619	23	12-9-2	on probation	11-0-0
20	Colorado	104	941	557	348	36	.611	18	6-12-0	won Aloha	8-3-1
21	Miami-FL	67	687	411	260	19	.612	20	10-10-0	lost Fiesta	9-3-0
22	Michigan St	97	892	521	328	43	.608	11	5-6-0	lost Liberty	6-6-0
23	Bowling Green	75	684	389	243	52	.607	5	2-3-0	none	6-3-2
24	UCLA	75	754	437	280	37	.604	19	10-8-1	lost Rose	8-4-0
25	Minnesota	110	957	555	359	43	.602	5	2-3-0	none	4-7-0
	Fresno St	72	739	431	280	28	.602	9	6-3-0	lost Aloha	8-4-0

Top 50 Victories

		Wins
1	Michigan	739
2	Notre Dame	723
3	Alabama	691
4	Texas	687
5	Penn St	674
6	Nebraska	673
7	Ohio St	659
	Oklahoma	659
9	Tennessee	636
10	USC	630
11	Georgia	589
12	Army	588
13	Syracuse	583
14	LSU	573
15	Pittsburgh	566
16	Washington	562
17	Auburn	558
18	Colorado	557
	West Virginia	557
20	Georgia Tech	555
	Minnesota	555
22	Arkansas	550
23	Texas A&M	549
24	North Carolina	548
25	Miami-OH	546
	Navy	546
27	California	530
	Rutgers	530
29	Clemson	526
30	Michigan St	521
31	Mississippi	513
	Virginia Tech	513
33	Missouri	507
34	Maryland	505
35	Vanderbilt	502
36	Virginia	501
37	Boston College	497
38	Illinois	496
39	Kentucky	490
40	Florida	491
41	Central Michigan	480
	Stanford	480
43	Wisconsin	478
44	Kansas	477
45	Tulsa	474
46	Utah	473
47	Purdue	471
48	Baylor	468
49	Iowa	465
50	Arizona	459

Note: Division I-AA schools with 500 or more wins through 1993: Yale (773); Princeton (706); Harvard (701); Penn (694); Fordham (671); Dartmouth (591); Lafayette (564); Cornell (548); Holy Cross (522); Lehigh (509) and Delaware (506).

Top 25 Bowl Appearances

		Overall App	Overall W	Overall L	Overall T	Big Four W	Big Four L	Big Four T
1	Alabama	46	26	17	3	18	12	1
2	USC	36	23	13	0	19	8	0
3	Tennessee	34	18	16	0	7	9	0
	Texas	34	16	16	2	12	10	1
5	Nebraska	32	14	18	0	9	13	0
6	Oklahoma	31	20	10	1	15	6	0
	Georgia	31	15	13	3	7	6	0
8	Penn St	30	18	10	2	6	5	1
9	LSU	28	11	16	1	7	10	1
10	Arkansas	27	9	15	3	4	10	1
11	Ohio St	26	12	14	0	7	8	0
12	Georgia Tech	25	17	8	0	9	3	0
	Mississippi	25	14	11	0	6	5	0
	Michigan	25	12	13	0	7	11	0
15	Auburn	23	12	9	2	2	4	1
16	Florida St	22	13	7	2	4	2	0
17	Washington	21	12	8	1	7	6	1
	Texas A&M	21	11	10	0	5	6	0
	Florida	21	11	10	0	2	3	0
20	Miami-FL	20	10	10	0	7	4	0
21	Notre Dame	19	13	6	0	11	5	0
	Clemson	19	12	7	0	3	2	0
	UCLA	19	10	8	1	6	6	0
	Missouri	19	8	11	0	2	5	0
	Texas Tech	19	4	14	1	0	1	0

Note: The "Big Four" bowls are the Rose, Orange, Sugar and Cotton. Only Alabama, Georgia, Georgia Tech and Notre Dame have won all four.

Bowl Games

From Jan. 1, 1902 through Jan. 1, 1994. Corporate title sponsors and automatic berths updated through June 1, 1994.

Rose Bowl

City: Pasadena, Calif.; **Stadium:** Rose Bowl; **Capacity:** 104,000; **Playing surface:** Grass; **First year:** 1902;
Playing sites: Tournament Park (1902, 1916-22); Rose Bowl (1923-41 and since 1943); Duke Stadium in Durham,
NC (1942, due to wartime restrictions following Japan's attack on Pearl Harbor on Dec. 7, 1941).

   Automatic berths: Pacific Coast Conference champion vs opponent selected by PCC (1924-45 seasons); Big Ten
champion vs Pac-10 champion (since 1946 season).

   Multiple wins: USC (19); Michigan (7); Washington (6); Ohio St., Stanford and UCLA (5); Alabama (4); Illinois
and Michigan St. (3); California and Iowa (2).

Year		Year		Year	
1902*	Michigan 49, Stanford 0	1942	Oregon St. 20, Duke 16	1969	Ohio St. 27, USC 16
1916	Washington 9, Brown 0	1943	Georgia 9, UCLA 0		
1917	Oregon 14, Penn 0	1944	USC 29, Washington 0	1970	USC 10, Michigan 3
1918	Mare Island 19, Camp Lewis 7	1945	USC 25, Tennessee 0	1971	Stanford 27, Ohio St. 17
1919	Great Lakes 17, Mare Island 0	1946	Alabama 34, USC 14	1972	Stanford 13, Michigan 12
		1947	Illinois 45, UCLA 14	1973	USC 42, Ohio St. 17
1920	Harvard 7, Oregon 6	1948	Michigan 49, USC 0	1974	Ohio St. 42, USC 21
1921	California 28, Ohio St. 0	1949	Northwestern 20, California 14	1975	USC 18, Ohio St. 17
1922	0-0, California vs Wash. & Jeff.			1976	UCLA 23, Ohio St. 10
1923	USC 14, Penn St. 0	1950	Ohio St. 17, California 14	1977	USC 14, Michigan 6
1924	14-14, Navy vs Washington	1951	Michigan 14, California 6	1978	Washington 27, Michigan 20
1925	Notre Dame 27, Stanford 10	1952	Illinois 40, Stanford 7	1979	USC 17, Michigan 10
1926	Alabama 20, Washington 19	1953	USC 7, Wisconsin 0		
1927	7-7, Alabama vs Stanford	1954	Michigan St. 28, UCLA 20	1980	USC 17, Ohio St. 16
1928	Stanford 7, Pittsburgh 6	1955	Ohio St. 20, USC 7	1981	Michigan 23, Washington 6
1929	Georgia Tech 8, California 7	1956	Michigan St. 17, UCLA 14	1982	Washington 28, Iowa 0
		1957	Iowa 35, Oregon St. 19	1983	UCLA 24, Michigan 14
1930	USC 47, Pittsburgh 14	1958	Ohio St. 10, Oregon 7	1984	UCLA 45, Illinois 9
1931	Alabama 24, Washington St. 0	1959	Iowa 38, California 12	1985	USC 20, Ohio St. 17
1932	USC 21, Tulane 12			1986	UCLA 45, Iowa 28
1933	USC 35, Pittsburgh 0	1960	Washington 44, Wisconsin 8	1987	Arizona St. 22, Michigan 15
1934	Columbia 7, Stanford 0	1961	Washington 17, Minnesota 7	1988	Michigan St. 20, USC 17
1935	Alabama 29, Stanford 13	1962	Minnesota 21, UCLA 3	1989	Michigan 22, USC 14
1936	Stanford 7, SMU 0	1963	USC 42, Wisconsin 37		
1937	Pittsburgh 21, Washington 0	1964	Illinois 17, Washington 7	1990	USC 17, Michigan 10
1938	California 13, Alabama 0	1965	Michigan 34, Oregon St. 7	1991	Washington 46, Iowa 34
1939	USC 7, Duke 3	1966	UCLA 14, Michigan St. 12	1992	Washington 34, Michigan 14
		1967	Purdue 14, USC 13	1993	Michigan 38, Washington 31
1940	USC 14, Tennessee 0	1968	USC 14, Indiana 3	1994	Wisconsin 21, UCLA 16
1941	Stanford 21, Nebraska 13				

*January game since 1902.

Orange Bowl

City: Miami, Fla.; **Stadium:** Orange Bowl; **Capacity:** 74,224; **Playing surface:** Grass; **First year:** 1935;
Playing site: Orange Bowl (since 1935). **Corporate title sponsor:** Federal Express (since 1990).

   Automatic berths: Big Eight champion vs at-large opponent (1953-63 and 1975-91 seasons); Big Eight champion
vs one of first five picks from 8-team bowl coalition pool (since 1992 season).

   Multiple wins: Oklahoma (11); Miami-FL and Nebraska (5); Alabama (4); Georgia Tech and Penn St. (3);
Clemson, Colorado, Florida St., Georgia, LSU, Notre Dame and Texas (2).

Year		Year		Year	
1935*	Bucknell 26, Miami-FL 0	1955	Duke 34, Nebraska 7	1975	Notre Dame 13, Alabama 11
1936	Catholic U. 20, Mississippi 19	1956	Oklahoma 20, Maryland 6	1976	Oklahoma 14, Michigan 6
1937	Duquesne 13, Mississippi St. 12	1957	Colorado 27, Clemson 21	1977	Ohio St. 27, Colorado 10
1938	Auburn 6, Michigan St. 0	1958	Oklahoma 48, Duke 21	1978	Arkansas 31, Oklahoma 6
1939	Tennessee 17, Oklahoma 0	1959	Oklahoma 21, Syracuse 6	1979	Oklahoma 31, Nebraska 24
1940	Georgia Tech 21, Missouri 7	1960	Georgia 14, Missouri 0	1980	Oklahoma 24, Florida St. 7
1941	Mississippi St. 14, Georgetown 7	1961	Missouri 21, Navy 14	1981	Oklahoma 18, Florida St. 17
1942	Georgia 40, TCU 26	1962	LSU 25, Colorado 7	1982	Clemson 22, Nebraska 15
1943	Alabama 37, Boston College 21	1963	Alabama 17, Oklahoma 0	1983	Nebraska 21, LSU 20
1944	LSU 19, Texas A&M 14	1964	Nebraska 13, Auburn 7	1984	Miami-FL 31, Nebraska 30
1945	Tulsa 26, Georgia Tech 12	1965†	Texas 21, Alabama 17	1985	Washington 28, Oklahoma 17
1946	Miami-FL 13, Holy Cross 6	1966	Alabama 39, Nebraska 28	1986	Oklahoma 25, Penn St. 10
1947	Rice 8, Tennessee 0	1967	Florida 27, Georgia Tech 12	1987	Oklahoma 42, Arkansas 8
1948	Georgia Tech 20, Kansas 14	1968	Oklahoma 26, Tennessee 24	1988	Miami-FL 20, Oklahoma 14
1949	Texas 41, Georgia 28	1969	Penn St. 15, Kansas 14	1989	Miami-FL 23, Nebraska 3
1950	Santa Clara 21, Kentucky 13	1970	Penn St. 10, Missouri 3	1990	Notre Dame, 21, Colorado 6
1951	Clemson 15, Miami-FL 14	1971	Nebraska 17, LSU 12	1991	Colorado 10, Notre Dame 9
1952	Georgia Tech 17, Baylor 14	1972	Nebraska 38, Alabama 6	1992	Miami-FL 22, Nebraska 0
1953	Alabama 61, Syracuse 6	1973	Nebraska 40, Notre Dame 6	1993	Florida St. 27, Nebraska 14
1954	Oklahoma 7, Maryland 0	1974	Penn St. 16, LSU 9	1994	Florida St. 18, Nebraska 16

*January game since 1935.   †Night game since 1965.

Sugar Bowl

City: New Orleans, La.; **Stadium:** Louisiana Superdome; **Capacity:** 73,468; **Playing surface:** AstroTurf; **First year:** 1935; **Playing sites:** Tulane Stadium (1935-74); Superdome (since 1975); **Corporate title sponsor:** USF&G Financial Services (since 1987).

Automatic berths: SEC champion vs at-large opponent (1976-91 seasons); SEC champion vs one of first five picks from 8-team bowl coalition pool (since 1992 season).

Multiple wins: Alabama (8); Mississippi (5); Georgia Tech, Oklahoma and Tennessee (4); LSU and Nebraska (3); Georgia, Notre Dame, Pittsburgh, Santa Clara and TCU (2).

Year		Year		Year	
1935*	Tulane 20, Temple 14	1955	Navy 21, Mississippi 0	1974	Nebraska 13, Florida 10
1936	TCU 3, LSU 2	1956	Georgia Tech 7, Pittsburgh 0	1975	Alabama 13, Penn St. 6
1937	Santa Clara 21, LSU 14	1957	Baylor 13, Tennessee 7	1977*	Pittsburgh 27, Georgia 3
1938	Santa Clara 6, LSU 0	1958	Mississippi 39, Texas 7	1978	Alabama 35, Ohio St. 6
1939	TCU 15, Carnegie Tech 7	1959	LSU 7, Clemson 0	1979	Alabama 14, Penn St. 7
1940	Texas A&M 14, Tulane 13	1960	Mississippi 21, LSU 0	1980	Alabama 24, Arkansas 9
1941	Boston College 19, Tennessee 13	1961	Mississippi 14, Rice 6	1981	Georgia 17, Notre Dame 10
1942	Fordham 2, Missouri 0	1962	Alabama 10, Arkansas 3	1982	Pittsburgh 24, Georgia 20
1943	Tennessee 14, Tulsa 7	1963	Mississippi 17, Arkansas 13	1983	Penn St. 27, Georgia 23
1944	Georgia Tech 20, Tulsa 18	1964	Alabama 12, Mississippi 7	1984	Auburn 9, Michigan 7
1945	Duke 29, Alabama 26	1965	LSU 13, Syracuse 10	1985	Nebraska 28, LSU 10
1946	Okla. A&M 33, St.Mary's 13	1966	Missouri 20, Florida 18	1986	Tennessee 35, Miami-FL 7
1947	Georgia 20, N.Carolina 10	1967	Alabama 34, Nebraska 7	1987	Nebraska 30, LSU 15
1948	Texas 27, Alabama 7	1968	LSU 20, Wyoming 13	1988	16-16, Syracuse vs Auburn
1949	Oklahoma 14, N.Carolina 6	1969	Arkansas 16, Georgia 2	1989	Florida St. 13, Auburn 7
1950	Oklahoma 35, LSU 0	1970	Mississippi 27, Arkansas 22	1990	Miami-FL 33, Alabama 25
1951	Kentucky 13, Oklahoma 7	1971	Tennessee 34, Air Force 13	1991	Tennessee 23, Virginia 22
1952	Maryland 28, Tennessee 13	1972	Oklahoma 40, Auburn 22	1992	Notre Dame 39, Florida 28
1953	Georgia Tech 24, Mississippi 7	1972†	Oklahoma 14, Penn St. 0	1993	Alabama 34, Miami-FL 13
1954	Georgia Tech 42, West Va. 19	1973	Notre Dame 24, Alabama 23	1994	Florida 41, West Va. 7

*January game from 1935-72 and since 1977.   †Game played on Dec. 31 from 1972-75.

The Bowl Coalition

Until plans for a national championship playoff are presented and approved, Division I-A football remains the only NCAA sport on any level that does not have a sanctioned postseason tournament. The Bowl Coalition, which was formalized on Jan. 23, 1992 and expires after the 1994 season, is a three-year alliance of six bowl committees, six conferences and independent Notre Dame. The Coalition has produced national title games in each of its first two seasons— at the 1993 Sugar Bowl (Alabama 34, Miami-FL 13) and '94 Orange Bowl (Florida St. 18, Nebraska 16).

As of June 1, members of the coalition for the 1994 season included the following: **Major bowls**— Cotton, Fiesta, Orange and Sugar; **Secondary bowls**— Gator and John Hancock; **Conferences**— ACC, Big East, Big Eight, Pac-10, Southeastern and Southwest; **Independent**— Notre Dame.

How The Coalition Works

1. After automatic berths are filled by the Cotton (SWC champion), Orange (Big Eight champ) and Sugar (SEC champ) following the SEC championship game on Dec. 3, 1994, those three bowls will select at-large opponents from a coalition pool of eight teams. The bowl with the highest-ranked automatic qualifier selects first. The ACC and Big East champions are each guaranteed berths in one of these three bowls, but can refuse an invitation in order to play in the Fiesta.

2. If any combination of the ACC champion, the Big East champion and Notre Dame are ranked 1-2 in the final regular season Bowl Poll Top 25, then those two teams must meet in the Fiesta.

3. Final regular season national rankings will be determined by the Coalition Bowl Poll which will combine the point totals of the AP (media) and USA Today/CNN (coaches) Top 25 polls.

4. A coalition team can refuse an invitation to a coalition bowl in one of three ways— a) the offer results in a rematch with a regular season opponent; b) it can make significantly more money playing in another bowl; or c) it has already played in that particular bowl the last two seasons.

5. Once the four major bowls have filled their eight slots with three automatic qualifiers (the Big Eight, SEC and SWC champs) and five at-large choices (from an eight-team pool that includes the ACC and Big East champs, Notre Dame, and second picks out of the ACC, Big East, Big Eight, Pac-10 and Southwest conferences), the Gator and John Hancock bowls then select from the three teams remaining in the pool.

Note that the coalition pool of teams does not include the second pick out of the Southeastern Conference, which has an outside deal with the Florida Citrus Bowl. The Citrus gets to choose any SEC it wants after the Sugar Bowl gets the conference champion. The Gator has a similar deal for third choice out of the SEC.

The coalition cannot arrange a game for the national title if either the No. 1 or No. 2 teams come from the Big Ten or Pac-10. The Big Ten and Pac-10 champions are both committed to the Rose Bowl, which is not a coalition member. While the Big Ten has no involvement whatever with the coalition, the Pac-10 does allow its runner-up to participate.

Bowl Games (Cont.)

Cotton Bowl

City: Dallas, Tex.; **Stadium:** Cotton Bowl; **Capacity:** 71,615; **Playing surface:** Grass; **First year:** 1937; **Playing sites:** Fair Park Stadium (1937), Cotton Bowl (since 1938). **Corporate title sponsor:** Mobil Corporation (since 1989).

    Automatic berths: SWC champion vs at-large opponent (1941-91 seasons); SWC champion vs one of first five picks from 8-team bowl coalition pool (since 1992 season).

    Multiple wins: Texas (9); Notre Dame (5); Texas A&M (4); Rice (3); Alabama, Arkansas, Georgia, Houston, LSU, Penn St., SMU, Tennessee and TCU (2).

Year		Year		Year	
1937*	TCU 16, Marquette 6	1957	TCU 28, Syracuse 17	1977	Houston 30, Maryland 21
1938	Rice 28, Colorado 14	1958	Navy 20, Rice 7	1978	Notre Dame 38, Texas 10
1939	St. Mary's 20, Texas Tech 13	1959	0-0, TCU vs Air Force	1979	Notre Dame 35, Houston 34
1940	Clemson 6, Boston College 3	1960	Syracuse 23, Texas 14	1980	Houston 17, Nebraska 14
1941	Texas A&M 13, Fordham 12	1961	Duke 7, Arkansas 6	1981	Alabama 30, Baylor 2
1942	Alabama 29, Texas A&M 21	1962	Texas 12, Mississippi 7	1982	Texas 14, Alabama 12
1943	Texas 14, Georgia Tech 7	1963	LSU 13, Texas 0	1983	SMU 7, Pittsburgh 3
1944	7-7, Texas vs Randolph Field	1964	Texas 28, Navy 6	1984	Georgia 10, Texas 9
1945	Oklahoma A&M 34, TCU 0	1965	Arkansas 10, Nebraska 7	1985	Boston College 45, Houston 28
1946	Texas 40, Missouri 27	1966	LSU 14, Arkansas 7	1986	Texas A&M 36, Auburn 16
1947	0-0, Arkansas vs LSU	1966†	Georgia 24, SMU 9	1987	Ohio St. 28, Texas A&M 12
1948	13-13, SMU vs Penn St.	1968*	Texas A&M 20, Alabama 16	1988	Texas A&M 35, Notre Dame 10
1949	SMU 21, Oregon 13	1969	Texas 36, Tennessee 13	1989	UCLA 17, Arkansas 3
1950	Rice 27, N. Carolina 13	1970	Texas 21, Notre Dame 17	1990	Tennessee 31, Arkansas 27
1951	Tennessee 20, Texas 14	1971	Notre Dame 24, Texas 11	1991	Miami-FL 46, Texas 3
1952	Kentucky 20, TCU 7	1972	Penn St. 30, Texas 6	1992	Florida St. 10, Texas A&M 2
1953	Texas 16, Tennessee 0	1973	Texas 17, Alabama 13	1993	Notre Dame 28, Texas A&M 3
1954	Rice 28, Alabama 6	1974	Nebraska 19, Texas 3	1994	Notre Dame 24, Texas A&M 21
1955	Georgia Tech 14, Arkansas 6	1975	Penn St. 41, Baylor 20		
1956	Mississippi 14, TCU 13	1976	Arkansas 31, Georgia 10		

*January game from 1937-66 and since 1968.   †Game played on Dec. 31, 1966.

Fiesta Bowl

City: Tempe, Ariz.; **Stadium:** Sun Devil; **Capacity:** 74,865; **Playing surface:** Grass; **First year:** 1971; **Playing site:** Sun Devil Stadium (since 1971). **Corporate title sponsor:** Sunkist Citrus Growers (1986-91); IBM OS/2 (since 1993).

    Automatic berths: Two of first five picks from 8-team bowl coalition pool (since 1992 season).

    Multiple wins: Arizona St. and Penn St. (5); Florida St. (2).

Year		Year		Year	
1971†	Arizona St. 45, Florida St. 38	1980	Penn St. 31, Ohio St. 19	1990	Florida St. 41, Nebraska 17
1972	Arizona St. 49, Missouri 35	1982*	Penn St. 26, USC 10	1991	Louisville 34, Alabama 7
1973	Arizona St. 28, Pittsburgh 7	1983	Arizona St. 32, Oklahoma 21	1992	Penn St. 42, Tennessee 17
1974	Oklahoma St. 16, BYU 6	1984	Ohio St. 28, Pittsburgh 23	1993	Syracuse 26, Colorado 22
1975	Arizona St. 17, Nebraska 14	1985	UCLA 39, Miami-FL 37	1994	Arizona 29, Miami-FL 0
1976	Oklahoma 41, Wyoming 7	1986	Michigan 27, Nebraska 23		
1977	Penn St. 42, Arizona St. 30	1987	Penn St. 14, Miami-FL 10		
1978	10-10, Arkansas vs UCLA	1988	Florida St. 31, Nebraska 28		
1979	Pittsburgh 16, Arizona 10	1989	Notre Dame 34, West Va. 21		

†December game from 1971-80.   *January game since 1982.

Bowl Matchups of Unbeaten Teams

Date	Bowl	Winner	Head Coach	Score	Loser	Head Coach
1/1/21	Rose	California (8-0)	Andy Smith	28-0	Ohio St. (7-0)	John Wilce
1/2/22	Rose	Wash. & Jeff.(10-0)	Greasy Neale	0-0	California (9-0)	Andy Smith
1/1/27	Rose	Stanford (10-0)	Pop Warner	7-7	Alabama (9-0)	Wallace Wade
1/1/31	Rose	Alabama (9-0)	Wallace Wade	24-0	Washington St. (9-0)	Babe Hollingbery
1/2/39	Orange	Tennessee (10-0)	Bob Neyland	17-0	Oklahoma (10-0)	Tom Stidham
1/1/41	Sugar	Boston College (10-0)	Frank Leahy	19-13	Tennessee (10-0)	Bob Neyland
1/1/52	Sugar	Maryland (9-0)	Jim Tatum	28-13	Tennessee (10-0)	Bob Neyland
1/2/56	Orange	Oklahoma (10-0)	Bud Wilkinson	20-6	Maryland (10-0)	Jim Tatum
1/1/72	Orange	Nebraska (12-0)	Bob Devaney	38-6	Alabama (11-0)	Bear Bryant
12/31/73	Sugar	Notre Dame (10-0)	Ara Parseghian	24-23	Alabama (11-0)	Bear Bryant
1/2/87	Fiesta	Penn St. (11-0)	Joe Paterno	14-10	Miami-FL (11-0)	Jimmy Johnson
1/1/88	Orange	Miami-FL (11-0)	Jimmy Johnson	20-14	Oklahoma (11-0)	Barry Switzer
1/2/89	Fiesta	Notre Dame (11-0)	Lou Holtz	34-21	West Va. (11-0)	Don Nehlen
1/1/93	Sugar	Alabama (12-0)	Gene Stallings	34-13	Miami-FL. (11-0)	Dennis Erickson

Gator Bowl

City: Jacksonville, Fla.; **Stadium:** Gator Bowl; **Capacity:** 80,128; **Playing surface:** Grass; **First year:** 1946; **Playing site:** Gator Bowl (since 1946). **Corporate title sponsor:** Mazda Motor of America, Inc. (1986-Jan. '91); Outback Steakhouse (since 1992).

    Automatic berths: Third pick from SEC vs sixth pick from 8-team bowl coalition pool (since 1992 season).

    Multiple wins: Florida (6); Auburn and Clemson (4); Florida St. and North Carolina (3); Georgia, Georgia Tech, Maryland, Oklahoma, Pittsburgh, Tennessee and Texas Tech (2).

Year	Year	Year
1946* Wake Forest 26, S. Carolina 14	1961 Penn St. 30, Georgia Tech 15	1978 Clemson 17, Ohio St. 15
1947 Oklahoma 34, N.C. State 13	1962 Florida 17, Penn St. 7	1979 N. Carolina 17, Michigan 15
1948 20-20, Maryland vs Georgia	1963 N. Carolina 35, Air Force 0	1980 Pittsburgh 37, S. Carolina 9
1949 Clemson 24, Missouri 23	1965* Florida St. 36, Oklahoma 19	1981 N. Carolina 31, Arkansas 27
	1965† Georgia Tech 31, Texas Tech 21	1982 Florida St. 31, West Va. 12
1950 Maryland 20, Missouri 7	1966 Tennessee 18, Syracuse 12	1983 Florida 14, Iowa 6
1951 Wyoming 20, Wash. & Lee 7	1967 17-17, Florida St. vs Penn St.	1984 Oklahoma St. 21, S. Carolina 14
1952 Miami-FL 14, Clemson 0	1968 Missouri 35, Alabama 10	1985 Florida St. 34, Oklahoma St. 23
1953 Florida 14, Tulsa 13	1969 Florida 14, Tennessee 13	1986 Clemson 27, Stanford 21
1954 Texas Tech 35, Auburn 13		1987 LSU 30, S. Carolina 13
1954† Auburn 33, Baylor 13	1971* Auburn 35, Mississippi 28	1989* Georgia 34, Michigan St. 27
1955 Vanderbilt 25, Auburn 13	1971† Georgia 7, N. Carolina 3	1989† Clemson 27, West Va. 7
1956 Georgia Tech 21, Pittsburgh 14	1972 Auburn 24, Colorado 3	
1957 Tennessee 3, Texas A&M 0	1973 Texas Tech 28, Tennessee 19	1991* Michigan 35, Mississippi 3
1958 Mississippi 7, Florida 3	1974 Auburn 27, Texas 3	1991† Oklahoma 48, Virginia 14
	1975 Maryland 13, Florida 0	1992 Florida 27, N.C. State 10
1960* Arkansas 14, Georgia Tech 7	1976 Notre Dame 20, Penn St. 9	1993 Alabama 24, N. Carolina 10
1960† Florida 13, Baylor 12	1977 Pittsburgh 34, Clemson 3	

*January game from 1946-54, 1960, 1965, 1971, 1989 and 1991.
†December game from 1954-58, 1960-63, 1965-69, 1971-87, 1989 and since 1991.

Liberty Bowl

City: Memphis, Tenn.; **Stadium:** Liberty Bowl Memorial; **Capacity:** 63,424; **Playing surface:** Grass; **First year:** 1959; **Playing sites:** Municipal Stadium in Philadelphia (1959-63); Convention Hall in Atlantic City, N.J. (1964); Memphis Memorial Stadium (1965-75); Liberty Bowl Memorial Stadium (since 1976). Memphis Memorial Stadium renamed Liberty Bowl Memorial in 1976. **Civic title sponsor:** St. Jude's Hospital (since 1993).

    Automatic berths: Commander-in-Chief's Trophy winner (Army, Navy or Air Force) vs at-large opponent (1989-92 seasons); none (1993 season); best team from independent group of Cincinnati, East Carolina, Louisville, Memphis St., Southern Miss., Tulane and Tulsa vs at-large opponent (beginning with 1994 season).

    Multiple wins: Mississippi (4); Penn St. and Tennessee (3); Air Force, Alabama and N.C. State (2).

Year	Year	Year
1959† Penn St. 7, Alabama 0	1970 Tulane 17, Colorado 3	1982 Alabama 21, Illinois 15
	1971 Tennessee 14, Arkansas 13	1983 Notre Dame 19, Boston Col. 18
1960 Penn St. 41, Oregon 12	1972 Georgia Tech 31, Iowa St. 30	1984 Auburn 21, Arkansas 15
1961 Syracuse 15, Miami-FL 14	1973 N.C. State 31, Kansas 18	1985 Baylor 21, LSU 7
1962 Oregon St. 6, Villanova 0	1974 Tennessee 7, Maryland 3	1986 Tennessee 21, Minnesota 14
1963 Mississippi St. 16, N.C. State 12	1975 USC 20, Texas A&M 0	1987 Georgia 20, Arkansas 17
1964 Utah 32, West Virgina 6	1976 Alabama 36, UCLA 6	1988 Indiana 34, S. Carolina 10
1965 Mississippi 13, Auburn 7	1977 Nebraska 21, N. Carolina 17	1989 Mississippi 42, Air Force 29
1966 Miami-FL 14, Virginia Tech 7	1978 Missouri 20, LSU 15	
1967 N.C. State 14, Georgia 7	1979 Penn St. 9, Tulane 6	1990 Air Force 23, Ohio St. 11
1968 Mississippi 34, Virginia Tech 17		1991 Air Force 38, Mississippi St. 15
1969 Colorado 47, Alabama 33	1980 Purdue 28, Missouri 25	1992 Mississippi 13, Air Force 0
	1981 Ohio St. 31, Navy 28	1993 Louisville 18, Michigan St. 7

†December game since 1959.

Peach Bowl

City: Atlanta, Ga.; **Stadium:** Georgia Dome; **Capacity:** 71,500; **Playing surface:** AstroTurf; **First year:** 1968; **Playing sites:** Grant Field (1968-70); Atlanta Stadium (1971-92); Georgia Dome (since 1993).

    Automatic berth: Third pick from ACC vs at-large opponent (1992 season); third pick from ACC vs fourth pick from SEC (since 1993 season).

    Multiple wins: N.C. State and West Virginia (3).

Year	Year	Year
1968† LSU 31, Florida St. 27	1977 N.C. State 24, Iowa St. 14	1986 Va. Tech 25, N.C. State 24
1969 West Va. 14, S. Carolina 3	1978 Purdue 41, Georgia Tech 21	1988* Tennessee 27, Indiana 22
	1979 Baylor 24, Clemson 18	1988† N.C. State 28, Iowa 23
1970 Arizona St. 48, N. Carolina 26		1989 Syracuse 19, Georgia 18
1971 Mississippi 41, Georgia Tech 18	1981* Miami-FL 20, Va. Tech 10	
1972 N.C. State 49, West Va. 13	1981† West Va. 26, Florida 6	1990 Auburn 27, Indiana 23
1973 Georgia 17, Maryland 16	1982 Iowa 28, Tennessee 22	1992* E. Carolina 37, N.C. State 34
1974 6-6, Vanderbilt vs Texas Tech	1983 Florida St. 28, N. Carolina 3	1993 N. Carolina 21, Miss. St. 17
1975 West Va. 13, N.C. State 10	1984 Virginia 27, Purdue 24	1993† Clemson 14, Kentucky 13
1976 Kentucky 21, N. Carolina 0	1985 Army 31, Illinois 29	

†December game from 1968-79, 1981-86, 1988-90, and since 1993.   *January game in 1981, 1988 and 1992-93.

Bowl Games (Cont.)

John Hancock Bowl

City: El Paso, Tex.; **Stadium:** Sun Bowl; **Capacity:** 52,000; **Playing surface:** AstroTurf; **First year:** 1936; **Name changes:** Sun Bowl (1936-85), John Hancock Sun Bowl (1986-88) and John Hancock Bowl (since 1989); **Playing sites:** Kidd Field (1936-62) and Sun Bowl (since 1963). **Corporate title sponsor:** John Hancock Financial Services (since 1986).

Automatic berths: Eighth pick from 8-team bowl coalition pool vs at-large opponent (1992 season); seventh and eighth picks from 8-team bowl coalition pool (since 1993 season).

Multiple wins: Texas Western/UTEP (5); Alabama and Wyoming (3); Nebraska, New Mexico St., North Carolina, Oklahoma, Pittsburgh, Southwestern-Texas, West Texas St. and West Virginia (2).

Year		Year		Year	
1936*	14-14, Hardin-Simmons vs New Mexico St.	1954	Tex. Western 37, So. Miss. 14	1974	Miss. St. 26, N. Carolina 24
1937	Hardin-Simmons 34, Texas Mines 6	1955	Tex. Western 47, Florida St. 20	1975	Pittsburgh 33, Kansas 19
		1956	Wyoming 21, Texas Tech 14	1977*	Texas A&M 37, Florida 14
1938	West Va. 7, Texas Tech 6	1957	Geo. Wash. 13, Tex. Western 0	1977†	Stanford 24, LSU 14
1939	Utah 26, New Mexico 0	1958	Louisville 34, Drake 20	1978	Texas 42, Maryland 0
		1958*	Wyoming 14, Hardin-Simmons 6	1979	Washington 14, Texas 7
1940	0-0, Catholic U. vs Arizona St.	1959	New Mexico St. 28, N. Texas 8	1980	Nebraska 31, Miss. St. 17
1941	W. Reserve 26, Arizona St. 13	1960	New Mexico St. 20, Utah St. 13	1981	Oklahoma 40, Houston 14
1942	Tulsa 6, Texas Tech 0	1961	Villanova 17, Wichita 9	1982	N. Carolina 26, Texas 10
1943	Second Air Force 13, Hardin-Simmons 7	1962	West Texas 15, Ohio U. 14	1983	Alabama 28, SMU 7
		1963	Oregon 21, SMU 14	1984	Maryland 28, Tennessee 27
1944	SW Texas 7, New Mexico 0	1964	Gergia 7, Gergia Tech 0	1985	13-13, Georgia vs Arizona
1945	SW Texas 35, U. of Mexico 0	1965	Texas Western 13, TCU 12	1986	Alabama 28, Washington 6
1946	New Mexico 34, Denver 24	1966	Wyoming 28, Florida St. 20	1987	Oklahoma 35, West Va. 33
1947	Cincinnati 18, Va. Tech 6	1967	UTEP 14, Mississippi 7	1988	Alabama 29, Army 28
1948	Miami-OH 13, Texas Tech 12	1968	Auburn 34, Arizona 10	1989	Pittsburgh 31, Texas A&M 28
1949	West Va. 21, Texas Mines 12	1969	Nebraska 45, Georgia 6	1990	Michigan St. 17, USC 16
1950	Tex. Western 33, Georgetown 20	1970	Georgia Tech 17, Texas Tech 9	1991	UCLA 6, Illinois 3
1951	West Texas 14, Cincinnati 13	1971	LSU 33, Iowa St. 15	1992	Baylor 20, Arizona 15
1952	Texas Tech 25, Pacific 14	1972	N. Carolina 32, Texas Tech 28	1993	Oklahoma 41, Texas Tech 10
1953	Pacific 26, Southern Miss. 7	1973	Missouri 34, Auburn 17		

*January game from 1936-58 and in 1977.   †December game from 1958-75 and since 1977.

Florida Citrus Bowl

City: Orlando, Fla.; **Stadium:** Florida Citrus Bowl; **Capacity:** 70,363; **Playing surface:** Grass; **First year:** 1947; **Name changes:** Tangerine Bowl (1947-82); Florida Citrus Bowl (since 1983); **Playing sites:** Tangerine Bowl (1947-72, 1974-82), Florida Field in Gainesville (1973), Orlando Stadium (1983-85); Florida Citrus Bowl (since 1986). The Tangerine Bowl, Orlando Stadium and Florida Citrus Bowl are all the same stadium. **Corporate title sponsors:** Florida Department of Citrus (since 1983) and CompUSA (since 1993).

Automatic berths: Championship game of Atlantic Coast Regional Conference (1964-67 seasons); Mid-American Conference champion vs Southern Conference champion (1968-75) seasons; ACC champion vs at-large opponent (1987-91 seasons); second pick from SEC vs second pick from Big Ten (since 1992 season).

Multiple wins: East Texas St., Miami-OH and Toledo (3); Auburn, Catawba, Clemson, East Carolina (2).

Year		Year		Year	
1947*	Catawba 31, Maryville 6	1962	Houston 49, Miami-OH 21	1978	N.C. State 30, Pittsburgh 17
1948	Catawba 7, Marshall 0	1963	Western Ky. 27, Coast Guard 0	1979	LSU 34, Wake Forest 10
1949	21-21, Murray St. vs Sul Ross St.	1964	E. Carolina 14, Massachusetts 13	1980	Florida 35, Maryland 20
1950	St. Vincent 7, Emory & Henry 6	1965	E. Carolina 31, Maine 0	1981	Missouri 19, Southern Miss. 17
1951	M. Harvey 35, Emory & Henry 14	1966	Morgan St. 14, West Chester 6	1982	Auburn 33, Boston College 26
1952	Stetson 35, Arkansas St. 20	1967	Tenn-Martin 25, West Chester 8	1983	Tennessee 30, Maryland 23
1953	E. Texas St. 33, Tenn. Tech 0	1968	Richmond 49, Ohio U. 42	1984	17-17, Florida St. vs Georgia
1954	7-7, E. Texas St. vs Arkansas St.	1969	Toledo 56, Davidson 33	1985	Ohio St. 10, BYU 7
1955	Neb.-Omaha 7, Eastern Ky. 6	1970	Toledo 40, Wm. & Mary 12	1987*	Auburn 16, USC 7
1956	6-6, Juniata vs Missouri Valley	1971	Toledo 28, Richmond 3	1988	Clemson 35, Penn St. 10
1957	W. Texas St. 20, So. Miss. 13	1972	Tampa 21, Kent St. 18	1989	Clemson 13, Oklahoma 6
1958	E. Texas St. 10, So. Miss. 9	1973	Miami-OH 16, Florida 7	1990	Illinois 31, Virginia 21
1958†	E. Texas St. 26, Mo. Valley 7	1974	Miami-OH 21, Georgia 10	1991	Georgia Tech 45, Nebraska 21
1960*	Mid. Tenn. 21, Presbyterian 12	1975	Miami-OH 20, S. Carolina 7	1992	California 37, Clemson 13
1960†	Citadel 27, Tenn. Tech 0	1976	Oklahoma 49, BYU 21	1993	Georgia 21, Ohio St. 14
1961	Lamar 21, Middle Tenn. 14	1977	Florida St. 40, Texas Tech 17	1994	Penn St. 31, Tennessee 13

*January game from 1947-58, in 1960 and since 1987.   †December game from 1958 and 1960-85.

Independence Bowl

City: Shreveport, La.; **Stadium:** Independence; **Capacity:** 50,459; Playing surface: **Grass;** First year: 1976;
Playing sites: Independence Stadium (since 1976). **Corporate title sponsor:** Poulan/Weed Eater (since 1990).
   Automatic berths: None (since 1976 season).
   Multiple wins: Air Force and Southern Miss. (2).

Year	Year	Year
1976† McNeese St. 20, Tulsa 16	1982 Wisconsin 14, Kansas St. 3	1988 Southern Miss 38, UTEP 18
1977 La. Tech 24, Louisville 14	1983 Air Force 9, Mississippi 3	1989 Oregon 27, Tulsa 24
1978 E. Carolina 35, La. Tech 13	1984 Air Force 23, Va. Tech 7	1990 34-34, La. Tech vs Maryland
1979 Syracuse 31, McNeese St. 7	1985 Minnesota 20, Clemson 13	1991 Georgia 24, Arkansas 15
1980 So. Miss. 16, McNeese St. 14	1986 Mississippi 20, Texas Tech 17	1992 Wake Forest 39, Oregon 35
1981 Texas A&M 33, Oklahoma St.16	1987 Washington 24, Tulane 12	1993 Va. Tech 45, Indiana 20

†December game since 1976.

Holiday Bowl

City: San Diego, Calif.; **Stadium:** San Diego/Jack Murphy; **Capacity:** 60,000; **Playing surface:** Grass; **First year:** 1978; **Playing sites:** San Diego/Jack Murphy Stadium (since 1978). **Corporate title sponsors:** Sea World (1986-90); Thrifty Car Rental (since 1991).
   Automatic berths: WAC champion vs at-large opponent (1978-84, 1986-90 seasons); WAC champ vs second pick from Big Ten (1991 season); WAC champ vs third pick from Big Ten (since 1992 season).
   Multiple wins: BYU (4); Iowa and Ohio St. (2).

Year	Year	Year
1978† Navy 23, BYU 16	1984 BYU 24, Michigan 17	1990 Texas A&M 65, BYU 14
1979 Indiana 38, BYU 37	1985 Arkansas 18, Arizona St. 17	1991 13-13, Iowa vs BYU
1980 BYU 46, SMU 45	1986 Iowa 39, San Diego St. 38	1992 Hawaii 27, Illinois 17
1981 BYU 38, Washington St. 36	1987 Iowa 20, Wyoming 19	1993 Ohio St. 28, BYU 21
1982 Ohio St. 47, BYU 17	1988 Oklahoma St. 62, Wyoming 14	
1983 BYU 21, Missouri 17	1989 Penn St. 50, BYU 39	

†December game since 1978.

Las Vegas Bowl

City: Las Vegas, Nev.; **Stadium:** Sam Boyd Silver Bowl; **Capacity:** 32,000; **Playing surface:** Turf; **First year:** 1992; **Playing site:** Silver Bowl (since 1992);
   Automatic berths: Mid-American champion vs Big West champion (since 1992 season).
   Note: the MAC and Big West champs have met in a bowl game since 1981— originally in Fresno at the California Bowl (1981-88, 1992) and California Raisin Bowl (1989-91). The results from 1981-91 are included below.
   Multiple wins: Fresno St. (4); Bowling Green, San Jose St. and Toledo (2).

Year	Year	Year
1981† Toledo 27, San Jose St. 25	1986 San Jose St. 37, Miami-OH 7	1991 Bowling Green 28, Fresno St. 21
1982 Fresno St. 29, Bowling Green 28	1987 E. Michigan 30, San Jose St. 27	1992 Bowling Green 35, Nevada 34
1983 Northern Ill. 20, CS-Fullerton 13	1988 Fresno St. 35, W. Michigan 30	1993 Utah St. 42, Ball St. 33
1984 UNLV 30, Toledo 13	1989 Fresno St. 27, Ball St. 6	
1985 Fresno St. 51, Bowling Green 7	1990 San Jose St. 48, C. Michigan 24	

†December game since 1981. **Note:** Toledo later ruled winner of 1984 game by forfeit when UNLV was found to have used ineligible players.

Aloha Bowl

City: Honolulu, Hawaii; **Stadium:** Aloha; **Capacity:** 50,000; **Playing surface:** AstroTurf; **First year:** 1982; **Playing site:** Aloha Stadium (since 1982). **Corporate title sponsor:** Jeep Eagle Division of Chrysler (since 1987).
   Automatic berth: Second pick from WAC vs third-place team from Big Eight (since 1992 season).
   Multiple wins: None.

Year	Year	Year
1982† Washington 21, Maryland 20	1986 Arizona 30, N. Carolina 21	1990 Syracuse 28, Arizona 0
1983 Penn St. 13, Washington 10	1987 UCLA 20, Florida 16	1991 Georgia Tech 18, Stanford 17
1984 SMU 27, Notre Dame 20	1988 Washington St. 24, Houston 22	1992 Kansas 23, BYU 20
1985 Alabama 24, USC 3	1989 Michigan St. 33, Hawaii 13	1993 Colorado 41, Fresno St. 30

†December game since 1982.

Freedom Bowl

City: Anaheim, Calif.; **Stadium:** Anaheim; **Capacity:** 69,001; **Playing surface:** Grass; **First year:** 1984; **Playing site:** Anaheim Stadium (since 1984).
   Automatic berth: Third pick from Pac-10 vs at-large opponent (1992 season); third pick from Pac-10 vs fourth pick from WAC (1993 season); WAC second place team vs Pac-10 third place team (beginning with 1994 season).
   Multiple wins: Washington (2).

Year	Year	Year
1984† Iowa 55, Texas 17	1988 BYU 20, Colorado 17	1992 Fresno St. 24, USC 7
1985 Washington 20, Colorado 17	1989 Washington 34, Florida 7	1993 USC 28, Utah 21
1986 UCLA 31, BYU 10	1990 Colorado St. 32, Oregon 31	
1987 Arizona St. 33, Air Force 28	1991 Tulsa 28, San Diego St. 17	

†December game since 1984.

Bowl Games (Cont.)

Hall of Fame Bowl

City: Tampa, Fla.; **Stadium:** Tampa; **Capacity:** 74,314; **Playing surface:** Grass; **First year:** 1986; **Playing site:** Tampa Stadium (since 1986).
   Automatic berths: Fourth pick from ACC vs fourth pick from Big Ten (since 1993 season).
   Multiple wins: Michigan and Syracuse (2).

Year		Year		Year	
1986† Boston College 27, Georgia 24		1990	Auburn 31, Ohio St. 14	1993	Tennessee 38, Boston Col. 23
1988* Michigan 28, Alabama 24		1991	Clemson 30, Illinois 0	1994	Michigan 42, N.C. State 7
1989 Syracuse 23, LSU 10		1992	Syracuse 24, Ohio St. 17		

†December game in 1986.   *January game since 1988.

Copper Bowl

City: Tucson, Ariz.; **Stadium:** Arizona; **Capacity:** 56,136; **Playing surface:** Grass; **First year:** 1989; **Playing site:** Arizona Stadium (since 1989). **Corporate title sponsor:** Domino's Pizza (1990-91); Weiser Lock (since 1992).
   Automatic berth: Third pick from WAC vs at-large opponent (1992 season); third pick from WAC vs fourth pick from Big Ten (since 1993 season).
   Multiple wins: None.

Year		Year		Year	
1989† Arizona 17, N.C. State 10		1991	Indiana 24, Baylor 0	1993	Kansas St. 52, Wyoming 17
1990 California 17, Wyoming 15		1992	Washington St. 31, Utah 28		

†December game since 1989.

Carquest Bowl

City: Miami, Fla.; **Stadium:** Joe Robbie; **Capacity:** 73,000; **Playing surface:** Grass; **First year:** 1990; **Name change:** Blockbuster Bowl (1990-93) and Carquest Bowl since 1994; **Playing site:** Joe Robbie Stadium (since 1990). **Corporate title sponsor:** Blockbuster Video (1990-1993); Carquest Auto Parts (since 1994).
   Automatic berths: Penn St. vs seventh pick from 8-team bowl coalition pool (1992 season); third pick from Big East vs fifth pick from SEC (since 1993 season).
   Multiple wins: None.

Year		Year		Year	
1990† Florida St. 24, Penn St. 17		1993* Stanford 24, Penn St. 3		1994	Boston College 31, Virginia 13
1991 Alabama 30, Colorado 25					

†December game from 1990-91.   *January game since 1993.

Alamo Bowl

City: San Antonio, Tex.; **Stadium:** Alamodome; **Capacity:** 65,000; **Playing surface:** Turf; **First year:** 1993; **Playing site:** Alamodome (since 1993). **Corporate title sponsor:** Builders Square (since 1993).
   Automatic berths: Third pick from SWC vs fourth pick from Pac-10 (since 1993 season).

Year	
1993† California 37, Iowa 3	

†December game since 1993.

Bluebonnet Bowl
Discontinued in 1988.

Years: 1959-87; **City:** Houston, Tex.; **Name changes:** Bluebonnet Bowl (1959-67, 1977-87); Astro-Bluebonnet Bowl (1968-76); **Playing sites:** Rice Stadium (1959-67, 1985-86), Astrodome (1968-84, 1987); **Dates:** December game every year.
   Automatic berths: None.
   Multiple wins: Texas (3); Baylor, Colorado, Houston and Tennessee (2).

Year		Year		Year	
1959	Clemson 23, TCU 7	1969	Houston 36, Auburn 7	1979	Purdue 27, Tennessee 22
1960	3-3, Alabama vs Texas	1970	24-24, Alabama vs Oklahoma	1980	N. Carolina 16, Texas 7
1961	Kansas 33, Rice 7	1971	Colorado 29, Houston 17	1981	Michigan 33, UCLA 14
1962	Missouri 14, Georgia Tech 10	1972	Tennessee 24, LSU 17	1982	Arkansas 28, Florida 24
1963	Baylor 14, LSU 7	1973	Houston 47, Tulane 7	1983	Oklahoma St. 24, Baylor 14
1964	Tulsa 14, Mississippi 7	1974	31-31, Houston vs N.C. State	1984	West Va. 31, TCU 14
1965	Tennessee 27, Tulsa 6	1975	Texas 38, Colorado 21	1985	Air Force 24, Texas 16
1966	Texas 19, Mississippi 0	1976	Nebraska 27, Texas Tech 24	1986	Baylor 21, Colorado 9
1967	Colorado 31, Miami-FL 21	1977	USC 47, Texas A&M 28	1987	Texas 32, Pittsburgh 27
1968	SMU 28, Oklahoma 27	1978	Stanford 25, Georgia 22		

Major Conference Champions

Atlantic Coast Conference

Founded in 1953 when charter members all left Southern Conference to form ACC. **Charter members** (7): Clemson, Duke, Maryland, North Carolina, North Carolina St., South Carolina and Wake Forest. **Admitted later** (3): Virginia in 1953 (began play in '54); Georgia Tech in 1978 (began play in '83); Florida St. (began play in '92). **Withdrew later** (1): South Carolina in 1971.

Current playing membership (9): Clemson, Duke, Florida St., Georgia Tech, Maryland, North Carolina, N.C. State, Virginia and Wake Forest.

Multiple titles: Clemson (13); Maryland (8); Duke and N.C. State (7); North Carolina (5); Florida St. (2).

Year		Year		Year		Year	
1953	Duke (4-0) & Maryland (3-0)	1963	North Carolina (6-1) & N.C. State (6-1)	1973	N.C. State (6-0)	1984	Maryland (5-0)
1954	Duke (4-0)	1964	N.C. State (5-2)	1974	Maryland (6-0)	1985	Maryland (6-0)
1955	Maryland (4-0) & Duke (4-0)	1965	Clemson (5-2) & N.C. State (5-2).	1975	Maryland (5-0)	1986	Clemson (5-1-1)
1956	Clemson (4-0-1)	1966	Clemson (6-1)	1976	Maryland (5-0)	1987	Clemson (6-1)
1957	N.C. State (5-0-1)	1967	Clemson (6-0)	1977	North Carolina (5-0-1)	1988	Clemson (6-1)
1958	Clemson (5-1)	1968	N.C. State (6-1)	1978	Clemson (6-0)	1989	Virginia (6-1) & Duke (6-1)
1959	Clemson (6-1)	1969	South Carolina (6-0)	1979	N.C. State (5-1)		
1960	Duke (5-1)	1970	Wake Forest (5-1)	1980	North Carolina (6-0)	1990	Georgia Tech (6-0-1)
1961	Duke (5-1)	1971	North Carolina (6-0)	1981	Clemson (6-0)	1991	Clemson (6-0-1)
1962	Duke (6-0)	1972	North Carolina (6-0)	1982	Clemson (6-0)	1992	Florida St. (8-0)
				1983	Clemson (7-0) † & Maryland (5-0)	1993	Florida St. (8-0)

†On probation, ineligible for championship.

Big East Conference

Founded in 1991 when charter members all gave up independent football status to form Big East. **Charter members** (8): Boston College, Miami of Florida, Pittsburgh, Rutgers, Syracuse, Temple, Virginia Tech and West Virginia. **Note:** Temple and Virginia Tech are Big East members in football only.

Current playing membership (8): Boston College, Miami-FL, Pittsburgh, Rutgers, Syracuse, Temple, Virginia Tech and West Virginia.

Conference champion: For 1991 and '92, team with highest ranking in final regular season *USA Today*/CNN coaches poll won title. Championship decided by full 7-game round robin schedule sine 1993.

Multiple titles: Miami-FL (2).

Year		Year		Year	
1991	Miami-FL (2-0, #1) & Syracuse (5-0, #16)	1992	Miami-FL (4-0, #1)	1993	West Virginia (7-0)

Big Eight Conference

Originally founded in 1907 as Missouri Valley Intercollegiate Athletic Assn. **Charter members** (5): Iowa, Kansas, Missouri, Nebraska and Washington University of St. Louis. **Admitted later** (6): Drake and Iowa St. (then Ames College) in 1908; Kansas St. in 1913; Grinnell in 1919; Oklahoma in 1920; Oklahoma St. (then Oklahoma A&M) in 1925. **Withdrew later** (1): Iowa in 1911. **Note:** Iowa belonged to both the MVIAA and Western Conference from 1907-10.

Big Six founded in 1928 when charter members left MVIAA. **Charter members** (6): Iowa St., Kansas, Kansas St., Missouri, Nebraska and Oklahoma. **Admitted later** (6): Colorado in 1947 (began play in '48); Oklahoma St. in 1957 (began play in '60); Baylor, Texas, Texas A&M, and Texas Tech in 1994 (all four will begin play in '96). Renamed **Big Seven** in 1948, **Big Eight** in 1958, and will become **Big Twelve** in 1996.

Current playing membership (8): Colorado, Iowa St., Kansas, Kansas St., Missouri, Nebraska, Oklahoma and Oklahoma St.

Multiple titles: Nebraska (39); Oklahoma (33); Missouri (12); Kansas (6); Colorado (5); Iowa St. and Oklahoma St. (2).

Year		Year		Year		Year	
1907	Iowa (1-0) & Nebraska (1-0)	1916	Nebraska (3-1)	1928	Nebraska (4-0)	1940	Nebraska (5-0)
1908	Kansas (4-0)	1917	Nebraska (2-0)	1929	Nebraska (3-0-2)	1941	Missouri (5-0)
1909	Missouri (4-0-1)	1918	Vacant (WW I)	1930	Kansas (4-1)	1942	Missouri (4-0-1)
		1919	Missouri (4-0-1)	1931	Nebraska (5-0)	1943	Oklahoma (5-0)
1910	Nebraska (2-0)	1920	Oklahoma (4-0-1)	1932	Nebraska (5-0)	1944	Oklahoma (4-0-1)
1911	Iowa St. (2-0-1) & Nebraska (2-0-1)	1921	Nebraska (3-0)	1933	Nebraska (5-0)	1945	Missouri (5-0)
1912	Iowa St. (2-0) & Nebraska (2-0)	1922	Nebraska (5-0)	1934	Kansas St. (5-0)	1946	Oklahoma (4-1) & Kansas (4-1)
		1923	Nebraska (3-0-2) & Kansas (3-0-3)	1935	Nebraska (4-0-1)	1947	Kansas (4-0-1) & Oklahoma (4-0-1)
1913	Missouri (4-0) & Nebraska (3-0)	1924	Missouri (5-1)	1936	Nebraska (5-0)		
1914	Nebraska (3-0)	1925	Missouri (5-1)	1937	Nebraska (3-0-2)	1948	Oklahoma (5-0)
1915	Nebraska (4-0)	1926	Okla. A&M (3-0-1)	1938	Oklahoma (5-0)	1949	Oklahoma (5-0)
		1927	Missouri (5-1)	1939	Missouri (5-0)		

Major Conference Champions (Cont.)
Big Eight Conference

Year		Year		Year		Year	
1950	Oklahoma (6-0)	1963	Nebraska (7-0)	1974	Oklahoma (7-0)	1983	Nebraska (7-0)
1951	Oklahoma (6-0)	1964	Nebraska (6-1)	1975	Nebraska (6-1)	1984	Oklahoma (6-1)
1952	Oklahoma (5-0-1)	1965	Nebraska (7-0)		& Oklahoma (6-1)		& Nebraska (6-1)
1953	Oklahoma (6-0)	1966	Nebraska (6-1)	1976	Colorado (5-2),	1985	Oklahoma (7-0)
1954	Oklahoma (6-0)	1967	Oklahoma (7-0)		Oklahoma (5-2)	1986	Oklahoma (7-0)
1955	Oklahoma (6-0)	1968	Kansas (6-1)		& Oklahoma St. (5-2)	1987	Oklahoma (7-0)
1956	Oklahoma (6-0)		& Oklahoma (6-1)	1977	Oklahoma (7-0)	1988	Nebraska (7-0)
1957	Oklahoma (6-0)	1969	Missouri (6-1)	1978	Nebraska (6-1)	1989	Colorado (7-0)
1958	Oklahoma (6-0)		& Nebraska (6-1)		& Oklahoma (6-1)	1990	Colorado (7-0)
1959	Oklahoma (5-1)	1970	Nebraska (7-0)	1979	Oklahoma (7-0)	1991	Nebraska (6-0-1)
1960	Missouri (7-0)	1971	Nebraska (7-0)	1980	Oklahoma (7-0)		& Colorado (6-0-1)
1961	Colorado (7-0)	1972	Nebraska (5-1-1)*	1981	Nebraska (7-0)	1992	Nebraska (6-1)
1962	Missouri (7-0)	1973	Oklahoma (7-0)	1982	Nebraska (7-0)	1993	Nebraska (7-0)

*Oklahoma (6-1) forfeited title in 1972.

Big Ten Conference

Originally founded in 1895 as the Intercollegiate Conference of Faculty Representatives, better known as the Western Conference. **Charter members** (7): Chicago, Illinois, Michigan, Minnesota, Northwestern, Purdue and Wisconsin. **Admitted later** (5): Indiana and Iowa in 1899; Ohio St. in 1912; Michigan St. in 1950 (began play in '53); Penn St. in 1990 (began play in '93). **Withdrew later** (2): Michigan in 1907 (rejoined in '17); Chicago in 1940. **Note:** Iowa belonged to both the Western and Missouri Valley conferences from 1907-10.

Unofficially called **Big Ten** from 1912 until Chicago withdrew after 1939 season, then **Big Nine** from 1940 until Michigan St. began conference play in 1953. Formally renamed **Big Ten** in 1984 and has kept name with Penn St. as 11th member.

Current playing membership (11): Illinois, Indiana, Iowa, Michigan, Michigan St., Minnesota, Northwestern, Ohio St., Penn St., Purdue and Wisconsin.

Multiple titles: Michigan (37); Ohio St. (26); Minnesota (18); Illinois (14); Iowa and Wisconsin (9); Purdue (7); Chicago and Michigan St. (6); Northwestern (5); Indiana (2).

Year		Year		Year		Year	
1896	Wisconsin (2-0-1)	1920	Ohio St. (5-0)	1944	Ohio St. (6-0)	1972	Ohio St. (8-0)
1897	Wisconsin (3-0)	1921	Iowa (5-0)	1945	Indiana (5-0-1)		& Michigan (7-1)
1898	Michigan (3-0)	1922	Iowa (5-0)	1946	Illinois (6-1)	1973	Ohio St. (7-0-1)
1899	Chicago (4-0)		& Michigan (4-0)	1947	Michigan (6-0)		& Michigan (7-0-1)
1900	Iowa (3-0-1)	1923	Illinois (5-0)	1948	Michigan (6-0)	1974	Ohio St. (7-1)
	& Minnesota (3-0-1)		& Michigan (4-0)	1949	Ohio St. (4-1-1)		& Michigan (7-1)
1901	Michigan (4-0)	1924	Chicago (3-0-3)		& Michigan (4-1-1)	1975	Ohio St. (8-0)
	& Wisconsin (2-0)	1925	Michigan (5-1)	1950	Michigan (4-1-1)	1976	Michigan (7-1)
1902	Michigan (5-0)	1926	Michigan (5-0)	1951	Illinois (5-0-1)		& Ohio St. (7-1)
1903	Michigan (3-0-1),		& Northwestern (5-0)	1952	Wisconsin (4-1-1)	1977	Michigan (7-1)
	Minnesota (3-0-1)	1927	Illinois (5-0)		& Purdue (4-1-1)		& Ohio St. (7-1)
	& Northwestern (1-0-2)		& Minnesota (3-0-1)	1953	Michigan St. (5-1)	1978	Michigan (7-1)
1904	Minnesota (3-0)	1928	Illinois (4-1)		& Illinois (5-1)		& Michigan St. (7-1)
	& Michigan (2-0)	1929	Purdue (5-0)	1954	Ohio St. (7-0)	1979	Ohio St. (8-0)
1905	Chicago (7-0)	1930	Michigan (5-0)	1955	Ohio St. (6-0)	1980	Michigan (8-0)
1906	Wisconsin (3-0),		& Northwestern (5-0)	1956	Iowa (5-1)	1981	Iowa (6-2)
	Minnesota (2-0)	1931	Purdue (5-1),	1957	Ohio St. (7-0)		& Ohio St. (6-2)
	& Michigan (1-0)		Michigan (5-1)	1958	Iowa (5-1)	1982	Michigan (8-1)
1907	Chicago (4-0)		& Northwestern (5-1)	1959	Wisconsin (5-2)	1983	Illinois (9-0)
1908	Chicago (5-0)	1932	Michigan (6-0)	1960	Minnesota (5-1)	1984	Ohio St. (7-2)
1909	Minnesota (3-0)		& Purdue (5-0-1)		& Iowa (5-1)	1985	Iowa (7-1)
1910	Illinois (4-0)	1933	Michigan (5-0-1)	1961	Ohio St. (6-0)	1986	Michigan (7-1)
	& Minnesota (2-0)		& Minnesota (2-0-4)	1962	Wisconsin (6-1)		& Ohio St. (7-1)
1911	Minnesota (3-0-1)	1934	Minnesota (5-0)	1963	Illinois (5-1-1)	1987	Michigan St. (7-0-1)
1912	Wisconsin (6-0)	1935	Minnesota (5-0)	1964	Michigan (6-1)	1988	Michigan (7-0-1)
1913	Chicago (7-0)		& Ohio St. (5-0)	1965	Michigan St. (7-0)	1989	Michigan (8-0)
1914	Illinois (6-0)	1936	Northwestern (6-0)	1966	Michigan St. (7-0)	1990	Iowa (6-2),
1915	Minnesota (3-0-1)	1937	Minnesota (5-0)	1967	Indiana (6-1),		Michigan (6-2),
	& Illinois (3-0-2)	1938	Minnesota (4-1)		Purdue (6-1)		Michigan St. (6-2)
1916	Ohio St. (4-0)	1939	Ohio St. (5-1)		& Minnesota (6-1)		& Illinois (6-2)
1917	Ohio St. (4-0)	1940	Minnesota (6-0)	1968	Ohio St. (7-0)	1991	Michigan (8-0)
1918	Illinois (4-0),	1941	Minnesota (5-0)	1969	Ohio St. (6-1)	1992	Michigan (6-0-2)
	Michigan (2-0)	1942	Ohio St. (5-1)		& Michigan (6-1)	1993	Wisconsin (6-1-1)
	& Purdue (1-0)	1943	Purdue (6-0)	1970	Ohio St. (7-0)		& Ohio St. (6-1-1)
1919	Illinois (6-1)		& Michigan (6-0)	1971	Michigan (8-0)		

Big West Conference

Originally founded in 1969 as Pacific Coast Athletic Assn. **Charter members** (7): Cal-Santa Barbara, Cal St.-Los Angeles, Fresno St., Long Beach St., Pacific, San Diego St. and San Jose St. **Admitted later** (9): Cal St.-Fullerton in 1974; Utah St. in 1977 (began play in '78); Nevada-Las Vegas in 1982; New Mexico St. in 1983 (began play in '84); Nevada-Reno in 1991 (began play in '92); Arkansas St., Louisiana Tech, Northern Illinois and SW Louisiana in 1992 (all four began play in '93 in football only). **Withdrew later** (7): UC-Santa Barbara in 1972; CS-Los Angeles in 1974; San Diego St. in 1976; Fresno St. in 1991 (left for WAC after '91 season); Long Beach St. in 1991 (dropped football after '91 season); San Jose St. and UNLV in 1994 (both will leave for WAC after '95 season). Renamed **Big West** in 1988.

Current playing membership (11): Arkansas St., CS-Fullerton, Louisiana Tech., Nevada, New Mexico St., Northern Illinois, Pacific, San Jose St., SW Louisiana, UNLV and Utah St.

Multiple titles: San Jose St. (8); Fresno St. (6); San Diego St. (5); Long Beach St. and Utah St. (3); CS-Fullerton St. (2).

Year		Year		Year		Year	
1969	San Diego St. (6-0)	1976	San Jose St. (4-0)	1983	CS-Fullerton (5-1)	1991	Fresno St. (6-1)
1970	Long Beach St. (5-1)	1977	Fresno St. (4-0)	1984	CS-Fullerton (6-1)†		& San Jose St. (6-1)
	& San Diego St. (5-1)	1978	San Jose St. (4-1)	1985	Fresno St. (7-0)	1992	Nevada (5-1)
1971	Long Beach St. (5-1)		& Utah St. (4-1)	1986	San Jose St. (7-0)	1993	Utah St. (5-1)
1972	San Jose St. (4-0)	1979	Utah St. (4-0-1)*	1987	San Jose St. (7-0)		& SW Louisiana (5-1)
1973	San Diego St. (3-0-1)	1980	Long Beach St. (5-0)	1988	Fresno St. (7-0)		
1974	San Diego St. (4-0)	1981	San Jose St. (5-0)	1989	Fresno St. (7-0)		
1975	San Jose St. (5-0)	1982	Fresno St. (6-0)	1990	San Jose St. (7-0)		

*San Jose St. (4-0-1) forfeited share of title in 1979.   †UNLV (7-0) forfeited title in 1984.

Mid-American Conference

Founded in 1946. **Charter members** (6): Butler, Cincinnati, Miami of Ohio, Ohio University, Western Michigan and Western Reserve (Miami and WMU began play in '48). **Admitted later** (9): Kent St. (now Kent) and Toledo in 1951 (Toledo began play in '52); Bowling Green in 1952; Marshall in 1954; Central Michigan and Eastern Michigan in 1972 (CMU began play in '75, EMU in '76); Ball St. and Northern Illinois in 1973 (both began play in '75); Akron in 1991 (began play in '92). **Withdrew later** (5): Butler in 1950; Cincinnati in 1953; Western Reserve in 1955; Marshall in 1969; Northern Ill. in 1986.

Current playing membership (10): Akron, Ball St., Bowling Green, Central Michigan, Eastern Michigan, Kent, Miami-OH, Ohio University, Toledo and Western Michigan.

Multiple titles: Miami-OH (15); Bowling Green (10); Toledo (7); Ohio University (5); Cincinnati (4); Ball St. and Central Michigan (3); Western Michigan (2).

Year		Year		Year		Year	
1947	Cincinnati (3-1)	1959	Bowling Green (6-0)	1970	Toledo (5-0)	1984	Toledo (7-1-1)
1948	Miami-OH (4-0)	1960	Ohio Univ. (6-0)	1971	Toledo (5-0)	1985	Bowling Green (9-0)
1949	Cincinnati (4-0)	1961	Bowling Green (5-1)	1972	Kent St. (4-1)	1986	Miami-OH (6-2)
1950	Miami-OH (4-0)	1962	Bowling Green (5-0-1)	1973	Miami-OH (5-0)	1987	Eastern Mich. (7-1)
1951	Cincinnati (3-0)	1963	Ohio Univ. (5-1)	1974	Miami-OH (5-0)	1988	Western Mich. (7-1)
1952	Cincinnati (3-0)	1964	Bowling Green (5-1)	1975	Miami-OH (6-0)	1989	Ball St. (6-1-1)
1953	Ohio Univ. (5-0-1)	1965	Bowling Green (5-1)	1976	Ball St. (4-1)		
	& Miami-OH (3-0-1)		& Miami-OH (5-1)	1977	Miami-OH (5-0)	1990	Central Mich. (7-1)
1954	Miami-OH (4-0)	1966	Miami-OH (5-1)	1978	Ball St. (8-0)		& Toledo (7-1)
1955	Miami-OH (5-0)		& Western Mich. (5-1)	1979	Central Mich. (8-0-1)	1991	Bowling Green (8-0)
1956	Bowling Green (5-0-1)	1967	Toledo (5-1)	1980	Central Mich. (7-2)	1992	Bowling Green (8-0)
	& Miami-OH (4-0-1)		& Ohio Univ. (5-1)	1981	Toledo (8-1)	1993	Ball St. (7-0-1)
1957	Miami-OH (5-0)	1968	Ohio Univ. (6-0)	1982	Bowling Green (7-2)		
1958	Miami-OH (5-0)	1969	Toledo (5-0)	1983	Northern Ill. (8-1)		

Pacific-10 Conference

Originally founded in 1915 as Pacific Coast Conference. **Charter members** (4): California, Oregon, Oregon St. and Washington. **Admitted later** (6): Washington St. in 1917; Stanford in 1918; Idaho and USC (Southern Cal) in 1922; Montana in 1924; UCLA in 1928. **Withdrew later** (1): Montana in 1950.

The **PCC** dissolved in 1959 and the **AAWU** (Athletic Assn. of Western Universities) was founded. **Charter members** (5): California, Stanford, UCLA, USC and Washington. **Admitted later** (5): Washington St. in 1962, Oregon and Oregon St. in 1964, Arizona and Arizona St. in 1978. Conference renamed **Pac-8** in 1968 and **Pac-10** in 1978.

Current playing membership (10): Arizona, Arizona St., California, Oregon, Oregon St., Stanford, UCLA, USC, Washington and Washington St.

Multiple titles: USC (29); UCLA (16); California (13); Washington (13); Stanford (11); Oregon and Oregon St. (4); Washington St. (2).

Year		Year		Year		Year	
1916	Washington (3-0-1)	1923	California (5-0)	1930	Washington St. (6-0)	1936	Washington (6-0-1)
1917	Washington St. (3-0)	1924	Stanford (3-0-1)	1931	USC (7-0)	1937	California (6-0-1)
1918	California (3-0)	1925	Washington (5-0)	1932	USC (6-0)	1938	USC (6-1)
1919	Oregon (2-1)	1926	Stanford (4-0)	1933	Oregon (4-1)		& California (6-1)
	& Washington (2-1)	1927	USC (4-0-1)		& Stanford (4-1)	1939	USC (5-0-2)
			& Stanford (4-0-1)	1934	Stanford (5-0)		& UCLA (5-0-3)
1920	California (3-0)	1928	USC (4-0-1)	1935	California (4-1),		
1921	California (5-0)	1929	USC (6-1)		Stanford (4-1)	1940	Stanford (7-0)
1922	California (3-0)				& UCLA (4-1)	1941	Oregon St. (7-2)

Major Conference Champions (Cont.)
Pacific-10 Conference

Year	Year	Year	Year
1942 UCLA (6-1)	1957 Oregon (6-2)	1968 USC (6-0)	1982 UCLA (5-1-1)
1943 USC (4-0)	& Oregon St. (6-2)	1969 USC (6-0)	1983 UCLA (6-1-1)
1944 USC (3-0-2)	1958 California (6-1)	1970 Stanford (6-1)	1984 USC (7-1)
1945 USC (5-1)	1959 Washington (3-1),	1971 Stanford (6-1)	1985 UCLA (6-2)
1946 UCLA (7-0)	USC (3-1)	1972 USC (7-0)	1986 Arizona St. (5-1-1)
1947 USC (6-0)	& UCLA (3-1)	1973 USC (7-0)	1987 USC (7-1)
1948 California (6-0)	1960 Washington (4-0)	1974 USC (6-0-1)	& UCLA (7-1)
& Oregon (6-0)	1961 UCLA (3-1)	1975 UCLA (6-1)	1988 USC (8-0)
1949 California (7-0)	1962 USC (4-0)	& California (6-1)	1989 USC (6-0-1)
1950 California (5-0-1)	1963 Washington (4-1)	1976 USC (7-0)	1990 Washington (7-1)
1951 Stanford (6-1)	1964 Oregon St. (3-1)	1977 Washington (6-1)	1991 Washington (8-0)
1952 USC (6-0)	& USC (3-1)	1978 USC (6-1)	1992 Washington (6-2)
1953 UCLA (6-1)	1965 UCLA (4-0)	1979 USC (6-0-1)	& Stanford (6-2)
1954 UCLA (6-0)	1966 USC (4-1)	1980 Washington (6-1)	1993 UCLA (6-2),
1955 UCLA (6-0)	1967 USC (6-1)	1981 Washington (6-2)	Arizona (6-2)
1956 Oregon St. (6-1-1)			& USC (6-2)

Southeastern Conference

Founded in 1933 when charter members all left Southern Conference to form SEC. **Charter members** (13): Alabama, Auburn, Florida, Georgia, Georgia Tech, Kentucky, LSU (Louisiana St.), Mississippi, Mississippi St., Sewanee, Tennessee, Tulane and Vanderbilt. **Admitted later** (2): Arkansas and South Carolina in 1990 (both began play in '92). **Withdrew later** (3): Sewanee in 1940; Georgia Tech in 1964; Tulane in 1966.

Current playing membership (12): Alabama, Arkansas, Auburn, Florida, Georgia, Kentucky, LSU, Mississippi, Mississippi St., South Carolina, Tennessee and Vanderbilt.

Multiple titles: Alabama (20); Tennessee (11); Georgia (10); LSU (7); Mississippi (6); Auburn and Georgia Tech (5); Kentucky and Tulane (3); Florida (3, one vacated).

Year	Year	Year	Year
1933 Alabama (5-0-1)	1948 Georgia (6-0)	1965 Alabama (6-1-1)	1981 Georgia (6-0)
1934 Tulane (8-0)	1949 Tulane (5-1)	1966 Alabama (6-0)	& Alabama (6-0)
& Alabama (7-0)	1950 Kentucky (5-1)	& Georgia (6-0)	1982 Georgia (6-0)
1935 LSU (5-0)	1951 Georgia Tech (7-0)	1967 Tennessee (6-0)	1983 Auburn (6-0)
1936 LSU (6-0)	& Tennessee (5-0)	1968 Georgia (5-0-1)	1984 Florida (5-0-1)*
1937 Alabama (6-0)	1952 Georgia Tech (6-0)	1969 Tennessee (5-1)	1985 Florida (5-1)†
1938 Tennessee (7-0)	1953 Alabama (4-0-3)	1970 LSU (5-0)	& Tennessee (5-1)
1939 Tennessee (6-0),	1954 Mississippi (5-1)	1971 Alabama (7-0)	1986 LSU (5-1)
Georgia Tech (6-0)	1955 Mississippi (5-1)	1972 Alabama (7-1)	1987 Auburn (5-0-1)
& Tulane (5-0)	1956 Tennessee (6-0)	1973 Alabama (8-0)	1988 Auburn (6-1)
1940 Tennessee (5-0)	1957 Auburn (7-0)	1974 Alabama (6-0)	& LSU (6-1)
1941 Mississippi St. (4-0-1)	1958 LSU (6-0)	1975 Alabama (6-0)	1989 Alabama (6-1),
1942 Georgia (6-1)	1959 Georgia (7-0)	1976 Georgia (5-1)	Tennessee (6-1)
1943 Georgia Tech (3-0)		& Kentucky (5-1)	& Auburn (6-1)
1944 Georgia Tech (4-0)	1960 Mississippi (5-0-1)	1977 Alabama (7-0)	1990 Florida (6-1)†
1945 Alabama (6-0)	1961 Alabama (7-0)	& Kentucky (6-0)	& Tennessee (5-1-1)
1946 Georgia (5-0)	& LSU (6-0)	1978 Alabama (6-0)	1991 Florida (7-0)
& Tennessee (5-0)	1962 Mississippi (6-0)	1979 Alabama (6-0)	1992 Alabama (9-0)
1947 Mississippi (6-1)	1963 Mississippi (5-0-1)	1980 Georgia (6-0)	1993 Florida (8-1)
	1964 Alabama (8-0)		

*Title vacated. †On probation, ineligible for championship.

Southwest Conference

Founded in 1914 as Southwest Athletic Conference. **Charter members** (8): Arkansas, Baylor, Oklahoma, Oklahoma A&M (now Oklahoma St.), Rice, Southwestern, Texas, Texas A&M. **Admitted later** (5): SMU (Southern Methodist) in 1918; Phillips in 1920; TCU (Texas Christian) in 1923; Texas Tech in 1956 (began play in 1960); Houston in 1971 (began play in 1976). **Withdrew later** (9): Southwestern in 1917; Oklahoma in 1920; Phillips in 1921; Oklahoma A&M in 1925; Arkansas in 1990 (left for SEC after '91 season); Baylor, Texas, Texas A&M and Texas Tech in 1994 (all will leave for Big Eight after '95 season); Rice, SMU and TCU in 1994 (all will leave for WAC after '95 season); Houston in 1994 (undecided about conference affiliation after '95 season).

Current playing membership (8): Baylor, Houston, Rice, SMU, Texas, Texas A&M, TCU and Texas Tech.

Multiple titles: Texas (24); Texas A&M (17); Arkansas (14, one vacated); SMU (10); TCU (8); Rice (6); Baylor and Houston (4).

Year	Year	Year	Year
1914 No champion	1919 Texas A&M (4-0)	1924 Baylor (4-0-1)	1929 TCU (4-0-1)
1915 Oklahoma (3-0)	1920 Texas (5-0)	1925 Texas A&M (4-1)	1930 Texas (4-1)
1916 No champion	1921 Texas A&M (3-0-2)	1926 SMU (5-0)	1931 SMU (5-0-1)
1917 Texas A&M (2-0)	1922 Baylor (5-0)	1927 Texas A&M (4-0-1)	1932 TCU (6-0)
1918 No champion	1923 SMU (5-0)	1928 Texas (5-1)	1933 Arkansas (4-1)*

Year		Year		Year		Year	
1934	Rice (5-1)	1950	Texas (6-0)	1965	Arkansas (7-0)	1979	Houston (7-1)
1935	SMU (6-0)	1951	TCU (5-1)	1966	SMU (6-1)		& Arkansas (7-1)
1936	Arkansas (5-1)	1952	Texas (6-0)	1967	Texas A&M (6-1)		
1937	Rice (4-1-1)	1953	Rice (5-1)	1968	Arkansas (6-1)	1980	Baylor (8-0)
1938	TCU (6-0)		& Texas (5-1)		& Texas (6-1)	1981	SMU (7-1)†
1939	Texas A&M (6-0)	1954	Arkansas (5-1)	1969	Texas (7-0)		& Texas (6-1-1)
		1955	TCU (5-1)			1982	SMU (7-0-1)
1940	Texas A&M (5-1)	1956	Texas A&M (6-0)	1970	Texas (7-0)	1983	Texas (8-0)
	& SMU (5-1)	1957	Rice (5-1)	1971	Texas (6-1)	1984	SMU (6-2)
1941	Texas A&M (5-1)	1958	TCU (5-1)	1972	Texas (7-0)		& Houston (6-2)
1942	Texas (5-1)	1959	Texas (5-1),	1973	Texas (7-0)	1985	Texas A&M (7-1)
1943	Texas (5-0)		TCU (5-1)	1974	Baylor (6-1)	1986	Texas A&M (7-1)
1944	TCU (3-1-1)		& Arkansas (5-1)	1975	Arkansas (6-1),	1987	Texas A&M (6-1)
1945	Texas (5-1)	1960	Arkansas (6-1)		Texas (6-1)	1988	Arkansas (7-0)
1946	Rice (5-1)	1961	Texas (6-1)		& Texas A&M (6-1)	1989	Arkansas (7-1)
	& Arkansas (5-1)		& Arkansas (6-1)	1976	Houston (7-1)		
1947	SMU (5-0-1)	1962	Texas (6-0-1)		& Texas Tech (7-1)	1990	Texas (8-0)
1948	SMU (5-0-1)	1963	Texas (7-0)	1977	Texas (8-0)	1991	Texas A&M (8-0)
1949	Rice (6-0)	1964	Arkansas (7-0)	1978	Houston (7-1)	1992	Texas A&M (7-0)
						1993	Texas A&M (7-0)

*Title vacated. †On probation, ineligible for championship.

Western Athletic Conference

Founded in 1962 when charter members left the Skyline and Border Conferences to form the WAC. **Charter members** (6): Arizona (independent); Arizona St. (from Border); BYU (Brigham Young), New Mexico, Utah and Wyoming (from Skyline). **Admitted later** (12): Colorado St. and UTEP (Texas-El Paso) in 1967 (both began play in '68); San Diego St. in 1978; Hawaii in 1979; Air Force in 1980; Fresno St. in 1991 (began play in '92); Rice, San Jose St., SMU (Southern Methodist), TCU (Texas Christian), Tulsa and UNLV (Nevada - Las Vegas) in 1994 (all will begin play in '96). **Withdrew later** (2): Arizona and Arizona St. in 1978.
   Current playing membership (10): Air Force, BYU, Colorado St., Fresno St., Hawaii, New Mexico, San Diego St., UTEP, Utah and Wyoming.
   Multiple titles: BYU (17); Arizona St. (7); Wyoming (7); New Mexico (3); Arizona and Fresno St. (2).

Year		Year		Year		Year	
1962	New Mexico (2-1-1)	1970	Arizona St. (7-0)	1978	BYU (5-1)	1987	Wyoming (8-0)
1963	New Mexico (3-1)	1971	Arizona St. (7-0)	1979	BYU (7-0)	1988	Wyoming (8-0)
1964	Utah (3-1),	1972	Arizona St. (5-1)			1989	BYU (8-0)
	New Mexico (3-1)	1973	Arizona St. (6-1)	1980	BYU (6-1)		
	& Arizona (3-1)		& Arizona (6-1)	1981	BYU (7-1)	1990	BYU (6-1)
1965	BYU (4-1)	1974	BYU (6-0-1)	1982	BYU (7-1)	1991	BYU (7-0-1)
1966	Wyoming (5-0)	1975	Arizona St. (7-0)	1983	BYU (7-0)	1992	Hawaii (6-2),
1967	Wyoming (5-0)	1976	BYU (6-1)	1984	BYU (8-0)		BYU (6-2)
1968	Wyoming (6-1)		& Wyoming (6-1)	1985	Air Force (7-1)		& Fresno St. (6-2)
1969	Arizona St. (6-1)	1977	Arizona St. (6-1)		& BYU (7-1)	1993	BYU (6-2),
			& BYU (6-1)	1986	San Diego St. (7-1)		Fresno St. (6-2)
							& Wyoming (6-2)

Ivy League

First called the "Ivy League" in 1937 by sportswriter Caswell Adams of the *New York Herald Tribune*. Unofficial conference of 10 eastern teams was occasionally referred to as the "Old 10" and included: Army, Brown, Columbia, Cornell, Dartmouth, Harvard, Navy, Pennsylvania, Princeton and Yale. Army and Navy were dropped from the group after 1940. **League formalized** in 1954 for play beginning in 1956. **Charter members** (8): Brown, Columbia, Cornell, Dartmouth, Harvard, Pennsylvania, Princeton, and Yale. League downgraded from Division I to Division I-AA after 1977 season. **Current playing membership:** the same.
   Multiple titles: Dartmouth (16); Yale (12); Harvard and Penn (8); Princeton (7); Cornell (3).

Year		Year		Year		Year	
1955	Princeton (6-1)	1967	Yale (7-0)	1976	Brown (6-1)	1985	Penn (6-1)
1956	Yale (7-0)	1968	Harvard (6-0-1)		& Yale (6-1)	1986	Penn (7-0)
1957	Princeton (6-1)		& Yale (6-0-1)	1977	Yale (6-1)	1987	Harvard (6-1)
1958	Dartmouth (6-1)	1969	Dartmouth (6-1),	1978	Dartmouth (6-1)	1988	Penn (6-1)
1959	Penn (6-1)		Yale (6-1)	1979	Yale (6-1)		& Cornell (6-1)
1960	Yale (7-0)		& Princeton (6-1)	1980	Yale (6-1)	1989	Princeton (6-1)
1961	Columbia (6-1)	1970	Dartmouth (7-0)	1981	Yale (6-1)		& Yale (6-1)
	& Harvard (6-1)	1971	Cornell (6-1)		& Dartmouth (6-1)	1990	Cornell (6-1)
1962	Dartmouth (7-0)		& Dartmouth (6-1)	1982	Harvard (5-2),		& Dartmouth (6-1)
1963	Dartmouth (5-2)	1972	Dartmouth (5-1-1)		Penn (5-2)	1991	Dartmouth (6-0-1)
	& Princeton (5-2)	1973	Dartmouth (6-1)		& Dartmouth (5-2)	1992	Dartmouth (6-1)
1964	Princeton (7-0)	1974	Harvard (6-1)	1983	Harvard (5-1-1)		& Princeton (6-1)
1965	Dartmouth (7-0)		& Yale (6-1)		& Penn (5-1-1)	1993	Penn (7-0)
1966	Dartmouth (6-1),	1975	Harvard (6-1)	1984	Penn (7-0)		
	Harvard (6-1)						
	& Princeton (6-1)						

Longest Division I Streaks

Winning Streaks
(Including bowl games)

No		Seasons	Spoiler	Score
47	Oklahoma	1953-57	Notre Dame	7-0
39	Washington	1908-14	Oregon St.	0-0
37	Yale	1890-93	Princeton	6-0
37	Yale	1887-89	Princeton	10-0
35	Toledo	1969-71	Tampa	21-0
34	Penn	1894-96	Lafayette	6-4
31	Oklahoma	1948-50	Kentucky	13-7*
31	Pittsburgh............	1914-18	Cleve. Naval	10-9
31	Penn	1896-98	Harvard	10-0
30	Texas....................	1968-70	Notre Dame	24-11*
29	Michigan	1901-03	Minnesota	6-6
28	Alabama	1978-80	Mississippi St.	6-3
28	Oklahoma	1973-75	Kansas	23-3
28	Michigan St.	1950-53	Purdue	6-0
27	Nebraska...............	1901-04	Colorado	6-0
26	Cornell	1921-24	Williams	14-7
26	Michigan	1903-05	Chicago	2-0
25	BYU......................	1983-85	UCLA	27-24
25	Michigan	1946-49	Army	21-7
25	Army	1944-46	Notre Dame	0-0
25	USC	1931-33	Oregon St.	0-0

*Note: Kentucky beat Oklahoma in 1951 Sugar Bowl and Notre Dame beat Texas in 1971 Cotton Bowl.

Unbeaten Streaks
(Including bowl games)

No	W-T	Seasons	Spoiler	Score
63	59-4	Washington ...	1907-17	California	27-0
56	55-1	Michigan	1901-05	Chicago	2-0
50	46-4	California......	1920-25	Olympic Club	15-0
48	47-1	Oklahoma	1953-57	N. Dame	7-0
48	47-1	Yale..............	1885-89	Princeton	10-0
47	42-5	Yale..............	1879-85	Princeton	6-5
44	42-2	Yale..............	1894-96	Princeton	24-6
42	39-3	Yale..............	1904-08	Harvard	4-0
39	37-2	N. Dame........	1946-50	Purdue	28-14
37	36-1	Oklahoma	1972-75	Kansas	23-3
35	34-1	Minnesota......	1903-05	Wisconsin	16-12

Losing Streaks

No		Seasons	Victim	Score
44	Columbia..............	1983-88	Princeton	16-14
34	Northwestern	1979-82	No. Illinois	31-6
28	Virginia	1958-60	Wm. & Mary	21-6*
28	Kansas St.............	1945-48	Arkansas St.	37-6
27	Eastern Mich.	1980-82	Kent St.	9-7
27	New Mexico St.......	1988-90	CS-Fullerton	43-9

*Note: Virginia ended its losing streak in the opening game of the 1961 season.

Annual NCAA Division I-A Leaders

Rushing

Individual championship decided on Rushing Yards (1937-69), and on Yards Per Game (since 1970).
Multiple winners: Marshall Faulk, Art Lupino, Ed Marinaro, Rudy Mobley, Jim Pilot and O.J. Simpson (2).

Year		Car	Yards
1937	Byron (Whizzer) White, Colorado........	181	1121
1938	Len Eshmont, Fordham	132	831
1939	John Polansky, Wake Forest	137	882
1940	Al Ghesquiere, Detroit.......................	146	957
1941	Frank Sinkwich, Georgia....................	209	1103
1942	Rudy Mobley, Hardin-Simmons............	187	1281
1943	Creighton Miller, Notre Dame............	151	911
1944	Red Williams, Minnesota....................	136	911
1945	Bob Fenimore, Oklahoma A&M*	142	1048
1946	Rudy Mobley, Hardin-Simmons............	227	1262
1947	Wilton Davis, Hardin-Simmons	193	1173
1948	Fred Wendt, Texas Mines*..................	184	1570
1949	John Dottley, Ole Miss.......................	208	1312
1950	Wilford White, Arizona St..................	199	1502
1951	Ollie Matson, San Francisco	245	1566
1952	Howie Waugh, Tulsa..........................	164	1372
1953	J.C. Caroline, Illinois.......................	194	1256
1954	Art Luppino, Arizona.........................	179	1359
1955	Art Luppino, Arizona	209	1313
1956	Jim Crawford, Wyoming.....................	200	1104
1957	Leon Burton, Arizona St.	117	1126
1958	Dick Bass, Pacific............................	205	1361
1959	Pervis Atkins, New Mexico St..............	130	971
1960	Bob Gaiters, New Mexico St...............	197	1338
1961	Jim Pilot, New Mexico St	191	1278
1962	Jim Pilot, New Mexico St	208	1247
1963	Dave Casinelli, Memphis St.................	219	1016
1964	Brian Piccolo, Wake Forest................	252	1044
1965	Mike Garrett, USC	267	1440

Year		Car	Yards
1966	Ray McDonald, Idaho	259	1329
1967	O.J. Simpson, USC	266	1415
1968	O.J. Simpson, USC	355	1709
1969	Steve Owens, Oklahoma	358	1523

Year		Car	Yards	P/Gm
1970	Ed Marinaro, Cornell	285	1425	158.3
1971	Ed Marinaro, Cornell	356	1881	209.0
1972	Pete VanValkenburg, BYU	232	1386	138.6
1973	Mark Kellar, Northern Ill	291	1719	156.3
1974	Louie Giammona, Utah St.	329	1534	153.4
1975	Ricky Bell, USC.......................	357	1875	170.5
1976	Tony Dorsett, Pittsburgh............	338	1948	177.1
1977	Earl Campbell, Texas................	267	1744	158.5
1978	Billy Sims, Oklahoma................	231	1762	160.2
1979	Charles White, USC..................	293	1803	180.3
1980	George Rogers, S. Carolina	297	1781	161.9
1981	Marcus Allen, USC...................	403	2342	212.9
1982	Ernest Anderson, Okla. St.	353	1877	170.6
1983	Mike Rozier, Nebraska	275	2148	179.0
1984	Keith Byars, Ohio St.	313	1655	150.5
1985	Lorenzo White, Mich. St.	386	1908	173.5
1986	Paul Palmer, Temple	346	1866	169.6
1987	Ickey Woods, UNLV	259	1658	150.7
1988	Barry Sanders, Okla. St.	344	2628	238.9
1989	Anthony Thompson, Ind	358	1793	163.0
1990	Gerald Hudson, Okla. St..........	279	1642	149.3
1991	Marshall Faulk, S. Diego St.	201	1429	158.8
1992	Marshall Faulk, S. Diego St.......	265	1630	163.0
1993	LeShon Johnson, No. Ill............	327	1976	179.6

*Oklahoma A&M is now Oklahoma St. and Texas Mines is now UTEP.

All-Purpose Running

Championship decided on Running Yards Per Game.

Multiple winners: Marcus Allen, Pervis Atkins, Ryan Benjamin, Louie Giammona, Tom Harmon, Art Lupino, Napolean McCallum, O.J. Simpson, Charles White and Gary Wood (2).

Year		Yards	P/Gm
1937	Byron (Whizzer) White, Colorado	1970	246.3
1938	Parker Hall, Ole Miss	1420	129.1
1939	Tom Harmon, Michigan	1208	151.0
1940	Tom Harmon, Michigan	1312	164.0
1941	Bill Dudley, Virginia	1674	186.0
1942	Complete records not available		
1943	Stan Koslowski, Holy Cross	1411	176.4
1944	Red Williams, Minnesota	1467	163.0
1945	Bob Fenimore, Oklahoma A&M	1577	197.1
1946	Rudy Mobley, Hardin-Simmons	1765	176.5
1947	Wilton Davis, Hardin-Simmons	1798	179.8
1948	Lou Kusserow, Columbia	1737	193.0
1949	Johnny Papit, Virginia	1611	179.0
1950	Wilford White, Arizona St.	2065	206.5
1951	Ollie Matson, San Francisco	2037	226.3
1952	Billy Vessels, Oklahoma	1512	151.2
1953	J.C. Caroline, Illinois	1470	163.3
1954	Art Lupino, Arizona	2193	219.3
1955	Jim Swink, TCU	1702	170.2
	& Art Lupino, Arizona	1702	170.2
1956	Jack Hill, Utah St.	1691	169.1
1957	Overton Curtis, Utah St.	1608	160.8
1958	Dick Bass, Pacific	1878	187.8
1959	Pervis Atkins, New Mexico St	1800	180.0
1960	Pervis Atkins, New Mexico St	1613	161.3
1961	Jim Pilot, New Mexico St	1606	160.6
1962	Gary Wood, Cornell	1395	155.0
1963	Gary Wood, Cornell	1508	167.6
1964	Donny Anderson, Texas Tech	1710	171.0
1965	Floyd Little, Syracuse	1990	199.0
1966	Frank Quayle, Virginia	1616	161.6
1967	O.J. Simpson, USC	1700	188.9
1968	O.J. Simpson, USC	1966	196.6
1969	Lynn Moore, Army	1795	179.5
1970	Don McCauley, North Carolina	2021	183.7
1971	Ed Marinaro, Cornell	1932	214.7
1972	Howard Stevens, Louisville	2132	213.2
1973	Willard Harrell, Pacific	1777	177.7
1974	Louie Giammona, Utah St.	1984	198.4
1975	Louie Giammona, Utah St.	2045	185.9
1976	Tony Dorsett, Pittsburgh	2021	183.7
1977	Earl Campbell, Texas	1855	168.6
1978	Charles White, USC	2096	174.7
1979	Charles White, USC	1941	194.1
1980	Marcus Allen, USC	1794	179.4
1981	Marcus Allen, USC	2559	232.6
1982	Carl Monroe, Utah	2036	185.1
1983	Napoleon McCallum, Navy	2385	216.8
1984	Keith Byars, Ohio St	2284	207.6
1985	Napoleon McCallum, Navy	2330	211.8
1986	Paul Palmer, Temple	2633	239.4
1987	Eric Wilkerson, Kent St	2074	188.6
1988	Barry Sanders, Oklahoma St.	3250	295.5
1989	Mike Pringle, CS-Fullerton	2690	244.6
1990	Glyn Milburn, Stanford	2222	202.0
1991	Ryan Benjamin, Pacific	2995	249.6
1992	Ryan Benjamin, Pacific	2597	236.1
1993	LeShon Johnson, No. Ill.	2082	189.3

Total Offense

Individual championship decided on Total Yards (1937-69), and on Yards Per Game (since 1970).

Multiple winners: Johnny Bright, Bob Fenimore and Jim McMahon (2).

Year		Plays	Yards	P/Gm
1937	Byron (Whizzer) White, Colorado	224	1596	
1938	Davey O'Brien, TCU	291	1847	
1939	Kenny Washington, UCLA	259	1370	
1940	Johnny Knolla, Creighton	298	1420	
1941	Bud Schwenk, Washington-MO	354	1928	
1942	Frank Sinkwich, Georgia	341	2187	
1943	Bob Hoernschemeyer, Indiana	355	1648	
1944	Bob Fenimore, Oklahoma A&M	241	1758	
1945	Bob Fenimore, Oklahoma A&M	203	1641	
1946	Travis Bidwell, Auburn	339	1715	
1947	Fred Enke, Arizona	329	1941	
1948	Stan Heath, Nevada-Reno	233	1992	
1949	Johnny Bright, Drake	275	1950	
1950	Johnny Bright, Drake	320	2400	
1951	Dick Kazmaier, Princeton	272	1827	
1952	Ted Marchibroda, Detroit	305	1813	
1953	Paul Larson, California	262	1572	
1954	George Shaw, Oregon	276	1536	
1955	George Welsh, Navy	203	1348	
1956	John Brodie, Stanford	295	1642	
1957	Bob Newman, Washington St	263	1444	
1958	Dick Bass, Pacific	218	1440	
1959	Dick Norman, Stanford	319	2018	
1960	Bill Kilmer, UCLA	292	1889	
1961	Dave Hoppmann, Iowa St	320	1638	
1962	Terry Baker, Oregon St	318	2276	
1963	George Mira, Miami-FL	394	2318	
1964	Jerry Rhome, Tulsa	470	3128	
1965	Bill Anderson, Tulsa	580	3343	
1966	Virgil Carter, BYU	388	2545	
1967	Sal Olivas, New Mexico St	368	2184	
1968	Greg Cook, Cincinnati	507	3210	
1969	Dennis Shaw, San Diego St	388	3197	
1970	Pat Sullivan, Auburn	333	2856	285.6
1971	Gary Huff, Florida St	386	2653	241.2
1972	Don Strock, Va. Tech	480	3170	288.2
1973	Jesse Freitas, San Diego St.	410	2901	263.7
1974	Steve Joachim, Temple	331	2227	222.7
1975	Gene Swick, Toledo	490	2706	246.0
1976	Tommy Kramer, Rice	562	3272	297.5
1977	Doug Williams, Grambling	377	3229	293.5
1978	Mike Ford, SMU	459	2957	268.8
1979	Marc Wilson, BYU	488	3580	325.5
1980	Jim McMahon, BYU	540	4627	385.6
1981	Jim McMahon, BYU	487	3458	345.8
1982	Todd Dillon, Long Beach St	585	3587	326.1
1983	Steve Young, BYU	531	4346	395.1
1984	Robbie Bosco, BYU	543	3932	327.7
1985	Jim Everett, Purdue	518	3589	326.3
1986	Mike Perez, San Jose St	425	2969	329.9
1987	Todd Santos, San Diego St.	562	3688	307.3
1988	Scott Mitchell, Utah	589	4299	390.8
1989	Andre Ware, Houston	628	4661	423.7
1990	David Klingler, Houston	704	5221	474.6
1991	Ty Detmer, BYU	478	4001	333.4
1992	Jimmy Klingler, Houston	544	3768	342.6
1993	Chris Vargas, Nevada	535	4332	393.8

Annual NCAA Division I-A Leaders (Cont.)

Passing

Individual championship decided on Completions (1937-69), on Completions Per Game (1970-78), and on Passing Efficiency rating points (since 1979).

Multiple winners: Elvis Grbac, Don Heinrich, Jim McMahon, Davey O'Brien and Don Trull (2).

Year		Cmp	Pct	TD	Yds
1937	Davey O'Brien, TCU	94	.402	—	969
1938	Davey O'Brien, TCU	93	.557	—	1457
1939	Kay Eakin, Arkansas	78	.404	—	962
1940	Billy Sewell, Wash. St.	86	.494	—	1023
1941	Bud Schwenk, Wash.-MO	114	.487	—	1457
1942	Ray Evans, Kansas	101	.505	—	1117
1943	Johnny Cook, Georgia	73	.465	—	1007
1944	Paul Rickards, Pittsburgh	84	.472	—	997
1945	Al Dekdebrun, Cornell	90	.464	—	1227
1946	Travis Tidwell, Auburn	79	.500	5	943
1947	Charlie Conerly, Ole Miss	133	.571	18	1367
1948	Stan Heath, Nev-Reno	126	.568	22	2005
1949	Adrian Burk, Baylor	110	.576	14	1428
1950	Don Heinrich, Washington	134	.606	14	1846
1951	Don Klosterman, Loyola-CA	159	.505	9	1843
1952	Don Heinrich, Washington	137	.507	13	1647
1953	Bob Garrett, Stanford	118	.576	17	1637
1954	Paul Larson, California	125	.641	10	1537
1955	George Welsh, Navy	94	.627	8	1319
1956	John Brodie, Stanford	139	.579	12	1633
1957	Ken Ford, H-Simmons	115	.561	14	1254
1958	Buddy Humphrey, Baylor	112	.574	7	1316
1959	Dick Norman, Stanford	152	.578	11	1963
1960	Harold Stephens, H-Simm.	145	.566	3	1254
1961	Chon Gallegos, S. Jose St.	117	.594	14	1480
1962	Don Trull, Baylor	125	.546	11	1627
1963	Don Trull, Baylor	174	.565	12	2157
1964	Jerry Rhome, Tulsa	224	.687	32	2870
1965	Bill Anderson, Tulsa	296	.582	30	3464
1966	John Eckman, Wichita St.	195	.426	7	2339

Year		Cmp	Pct	TD	Yds
1967	Terry Stone, N. Mexico	160	.476	9	1946
1968	Chuck Hixon, SMU	265	.566	21	3103
1969	John Reaves, Florida	222	.561	24	2896

Year		Cmp	P/Gm	TD	Yds
1970	Sonny Sixkiller, Wash	186	18.6	15	2303
1971	Brian Sipe, S. Diego St.	196	17.8	17	2532
1972	Don Strock, Va. Tech	228	20.7	16	3243
1973	Jesse Freitas, S. Diego St.	227	20.6	21	2993
1974	Steve Bartkowski, Cal	182	16.5	12	2580
1975	Craig Penrose, S. Diego St.	198	18.0	15	2660
1976	Tommy Kramer, Rice	269	24.5	21	3317
1977	Guy Benjamin, Stanford	208	20.8	19	2521
1978	Steve Dils, Stanford	247	22.5	22	2943

Year		Cmp	TD	Yds	Rating
1979	Turk Schonert, Stanford	148	19	1922	163.0
1980	Jim McMahon, BYU	284	47	4571	176.9
1981	Jim McMahon, BYU	272	30	3555	155.0
1982	Tom Ramsey, UCLA	191	21	2824	153.5
1983	Steve Young, BYU	306	33	3902	168.5
1984	Doug Flutie, BC	233	27	3454	152.9
1985	Jim Harbaugh, Michigan	139	18	1913	163.7
1986	V. Testaverde, Miami-FL	175	26	2557	165.8
1987	Don McPherson, Syracuse	129	22	2341	164.3
1988	Timm Rosenbach, Wash. St.	199	23	2791	162.0
1989	Ty Detmer, BYU	265	32	4560	175.6
1990	Shawn Moore, Virginia	144	21	2262	160.7
1991	Elvis Grbac, Michigan	152	24	1955	169.0
1992	Elvis Grbac, Michigan	112	15	1465	154.2
1993	Trent Dilfer, Fresno St.	217	28	3276	173.1

Receptions

Championship decided on Passes Caught (1937-69), and on Catches Per Game (since 1970). Touchdown totals unavailable in 1939 and 1941-45.

Multiple winners: Neil Armstrong, Hugh Campell, Manny Hazard, Reid Mosely, Jason Phillips and Howard Twilley (2).

Year		No	TD	Yds
1937	Jim Benton, Arkansas	47	7	754
1938	Sam Boyd Baylor	32	5	537
1939	Ken Kavanaugh, LSU	30	—	467
1940	Eddie Bryant, Virginia	30	2	222
1941	Hank Stanton, Arizona	50	—	820
1942	Bill Rogers, Texas A&M	39	—	432
1943	Neil Armstrong, Okla. A&M	39	—	317
1944	Reid Moseley, Georgia	32	—	506
1945	Reid Moseley, Georgia	31	—	662
1946	Neil Armstrong, Okla. A&M	32	1	479
1947	Barney Poole, Ole Miss.	52	8	513
1948	Red O'Quinn, Wake Forest	39	7	605
1949	Art Weiner, N. Carolina	52	7	762
1950	Gordon Cooper, Denver	46	8	569
1951	Dewey McConnell, Wyoming	47	9	725
1952	Ed Brown, Fordham	57	6	774
1953	John Carson, Georgia	45	4	663
1954	Jim Hanifan, California	44	7	569
1955	Hank Burnine, Missouri	44	2	594
1956	Art Powell, San Jose St	40	5	583
1957	Stuart Vaughan, Utah	53	5	756
1958	Dave Hibbert, Arizona	61	4	606

Year		No	TD	Yds
1959	Chris Burford, Stanford	61	6	756
1960	Hugh Campbell, Wash. St	66	10	881
1961	Hugh Campbell, Wash. St	53	5	723
1962	Vern Burke, Oregon St	69	10	1007
1963	Lawrence Elkins, Baylor	70	8	873
1964	Howard Twilley, Tulsa	95	13	1178
1965	Howard Twilley, Tulsa	134	16	1779
1966	Glenn Meltzer, Wichita St.	91	4	1115
1967	Bob Goodridge, Vanderbilt	79	6	1114
1968	Ron Sellers, Florida St	86	12	1496
1969	Jerry Hendren, Idaho	95	12	1452

Year		No	P/Gm	TD	Yds
1970	Mike Mikolayunas, Davidson	87	8.7	8	1128
1971	Tom Reynolds, San Diego St	67	6.7	7	1070
1972	Tom Forzani, Utah St	85	7.7	8	1169
1973	Jay Miller, BYU	100	9.1	8	1181
1974	D. McDonald, San Diego St	86	7.8	7	1157
1975	Bob Farnham, Brown	56	6.2	2	701
1976	Billy Ryckman, La. Tech	77	7.0	10	1382
1977	W. Tolleson, W. Carolina	73	6.6	7	1101
1978	Dave Petzke, Northern Ill	91	8.3	11	1217
1979	Rick Beasley, Appalach. St	74	6.7	12	1205

Year		No	P/Gm	TD	Yds
1980	Dave Young, Purdue	67	6.1	8	917
1981	Pete Harvey, N.Texas St	57	6.3	3	743
1982	Vincent White, Stanford	68	6.8	8	677
1983	Keith Edwards, Vanderbilt	97	8.8	8	909
1984	David Williams, Illinois	101	9.2	8	1278
1985	Rodney Carter, Purdue	98	8.9	4	1099
1986	Mark Templeton, L. Beach St	99	9.0	2	688
1987	Jason Phillips, Houston	99	9.0	3	875
1988	Jason Phillips, Houston	108	9.8	15	1444
1989	Manny Hazard, Houston	142	12.9	22	1689
1990	Manny Hazard, Houston	78	7.8	9	946
1991	Fred Gilbert, Houston	106	9.6	7	957
1992	Sherman Smith, Houston	103	9.4	6	923
1993	Chris Penn, Tulsa	105	9.6	12	1578

Scoring

Championship decided on Total Points (1937-69), and on Points Per Game (since 1970).

Multiple winners: Tom Harmon and Billy Sims (2).

Year		TD	XP	FG	Pts
1937	Byron (Whizzer) White, Colo	16	23	1	122
1938	Parker Hall, Ole Miss	11	7	0	73
1939	Tom Harmon, Michigan	14	15	1	102
1940	Tom Harmon, Michigan	16	18	1	117
1941	Bill Dudley, Virginia	18	23	1	134
1942	Bob Steuber, Missouri	18	13	0	121
1943	Steve Van Buren, LSU	14	14	0	98
1944	Glenn Davis, Army	20	0	0	120
1945	Doc Blanchard, Army	19	1	0	115
1946	Gene Roberts, Tenn-Chatt	18	9	0	117
1947	Lou Gambino, Maryland	16	0	0	96
1948	Fred Wendt, Texas Mines*	20	32	0	152
1949	George Thomas, Oklahoma	19	3	0	117
1950	Bobby Reynolds, Nebraska	22	25	0	157
1951	Ollie Matson, San Francisco	21	0	0	126
1952	Jackie Parker, Miss. St.	16	24	0	120
1953	Earl Lindley, Utah St.	13	3	0	81
1954	Art Luppino, Arizona	24	22	0	166
1955	Jim Swink, TCU	20	5	0	125
1956	Clendon Thomas, Oklahoma	18	0	0	108
1957	Leon Burton, Ariz. St.	16	0	0	96
1958	Dick Bass, Pacific	18	8	0	116
1959	Pervis Atkins, N. Mexico St.	17	5	0	107
1960	Bob Gaiters, N. Mexico St.	23	7	0	145
1961	Jim Pilot, N. Mexico St.	21	12	0	138
1962	Jerry Logan, W. Texas St.	13	32	0	110
1963	Cosmo Iacavazzi, Princeton	14	0	0	84
	& Dave Casinelli, Memphis St.	14	0	0	84
1964	Brian Piccolo, Wake Forest	17	9	0	111
1965	Howard Twilley, Tulsa	16	31	0	127

Year		TD	XP	FG	Pts
1966	Ken Hebert, Houston	11	41	2	113
1967	Leroy Keyes, Purdue	19	0	0	114
1968	Jim O'Brien, Cincinnati	12	31	13	142
1969	Steve Owens, Oklahoma	23	0	0	138

Year		TD	XP	FG	Pts	P/Gm
1970	Brian Bream, Air Force	20	0	0	120	12.0
	& Gary Kosins, Dayton	18	0	0	108	12.0
1971	Ed Marinaro, Cornell	24	4	0	148	16.4
1972	Harold Henson, Ohio St	20	0	0	120	12.0
1973	Jim Jennings, Rutgers	21	2	0	128	11.6
1974	Bill Marek, Wisconsin	19	0	0	114	12.7
1975	Pete Johnson, Ohio St	25	0	0	150	13.6
1976	Tony Dorsett, Pitt	22	2	0	134	12.2
1977	Earl Campbell, Texas	19	0	0	114	10.4
1978	Billy Sims, Oklahoma	20	0	0	120	10.9
1979	Billy Sims, Oklahoma	22	0	0	132	12.0
1980	Sammy Wilder, So. Miss.	20	0	0	120	10.9
1981	Marcus Allen, USC	23	0	0	138	12.5
1982	Greg Allen, Fla. St.	21	0	0	126	11.5
1983	Mike Rozier, Nebraska	29	0	0	174	14.5
1984	Keith Byars, Ohio St	24	0	0	144	13.1
1985	Bernard White, B. Green	19	0	0	114	10.4
1986	Steve Bartalo, Colo. St.	19	0	0	114	10.4
1987	Paul Hewitt, S. Diego St	24	0	0	144	12.0
1988	Barry Sanders, Okla. St.	39	0	0	234	21.3
1989	Anthony Thompson, Ind	25	4	0	154	14.0
1990	Stacey Robinson, No. Ill	19	6	0	120	10.9
1991	Marshall Faulk, S.D. St.	23	2	0	140	15.6
1992	Garrison Hearst, Georgia	21	0	0	126	11.5
1993	Bam Morris, Texas Tech	22	2	0	134	12.2

*Texas Mines is now UTEP.

All-Time NCAA Division I-A Leaders

Through the 1993 regular season. The NCAA does not recognize active players among career Per Game leaders.

CAREER

Passing

(Minimum 500 Completions)

Passing Efficiency	Years	Rating
1 Ty Detmer, BYU	1988-91	162.7
2 Jim McMahon, BYU	1977-78,80-81	156.9
3 Steve Young, BYU	1982,84-86	149.8
4 Robbie Bosco, BYU	1981-83	149.4
5 Chuck Long, Iowa	1981-85	147.8

Yards Gained	Years	Yards
1 Ty Detmer, BYU	1988-91	15,031
2 Todd Santos, San Diego St	1984-87	11,425
3 Alex Van Pelt, Pitt	1989-92	10,913
4 Kevin Sweeney, Fresno St	1983-86	10,623
5 Doug Flutie, Boston College	1981-84	10,579

Completions	Years	No
1 Ty Detmer, BYU	1988-91	958
2 Todd Santos, San Diego St	1984-87	910
3 Brian McClure, Bowling Green	1982-85	900
4 Ben Bennett, Duke	1980-83	820
5 Troy Kopp, Pacific	1989-92	798

Receptions

Catches	Years	No
1 Aaron Turner, Pacific	1989-92	266
2 Terance Mathis, New Mexico	1985-87,89	263
3 Mark Templeton, Long Beach St	1983-86	262
4 Howard Twilley, Tulsa	1963-65	261
5 David Williams, Illinois	1983-85	245

Catches Per Game	Years	No	P/Gm
1 Manny Hazard, Houston	1989-90	220	10.5
2 Howard Twilley, Tulsa	1963-65	261	10.0
3 Jason Phillips, Houston	1987-88	207	9.4
4 Bryan Reeves, Nevada	1991-93	234	7.6
5 David Williams, Illinois	1983-85	245	7.4

Yards Gained	Years	No	Yards
1 Ryan Yarborough, Wyoming	1990-93	229	4357
2 Aaron Turner, Pacific	1989-92	266	4345
3 Terance Mathis, N. Mexico	1985-87,89	263	4254
4 Marc Zeno, Tulane	1984-87	236	3725
5 Ron Sellers, Florida St	1966-68	212	3598

All-Time NCAA Division I-A Leaders (Cont.)

Rushing

Yards Gained	Years	Yards
1 Tony Dorsett, Pitt	1973-76	6082
2 Charles White, USC	1976-79	5598
3 Herschel Walker, Georgia	1980-82	5259
4 Archie Griffin, Ohio St.	1972-75	5177
5 Darren Lewis, Texas A&M	1987-90	5012

Yards Per Game	Years	Yards	P/Gm
1 Ed Marinaro, Cornell	1969-71	4715	174.6
2 O.J. Simpson, USC	1967-68	3124	164.4
3 Herschel Walker, Georgia	1980-82	5259	159.4
4 LeShon Johnson, No. Ill.	1992-93	3314	150.6
5 Marshall Faulk, S. Diego St.	1991-93	4589	148.0

Total Offense

Yards Gained	Years	Yards
1 Ty Detmer, BYU	1988-91	14,665
2 Doug Flutie, Boston College	1981-84	11,317
3 Alex Van Pelt, Pitt	1989-92	10,814
4 Todd Santos, San Diego St	1984-87	10,513
5 Kevin Sweeney, Fresno St.	1983-86	10,252

Yards Per Game	Years	Yards	P/Gm
1 Ty Detmer, BYU	1988-91	14,665	318.8
2 Mike Perez, San Jose St	1986-87	6,182	309.1
3 Doug Gaynor, L. Beach St.	1984-85	6,710	305.0
4 Tony Eason, Illinois	1981-82	6,589	299.5
5 David Klingler, Houston	1988-91	9,327	291.5

All-Purpose Running

Yards Gained	Years	Yards
1 Napoleon McCallum, Navy	1981-85	7172
2 Darrin Nelson, Stanford	1977-78,80-81	6885
3 Terance Mathis, N. Mexico	1985-87,89	6691
4 Tony Dorsett, Pitt	1973-76	6615
5 Paul Palmer, Temple	1983-86	6609

Yards Per Game	Years	Yards	P/Gm
1 Ryan Benjamin, Pacific	1989-92	5707	237.8
2 Sheldon Canley, S. Jose St.	1988-90	5146	205.8
3 Howard Stevens, Louisville	1971-72	3873	193.7
4 O.J. Simpson, USC	1967-68	3666	192.9
5 Ed Marinaro, Cornell	1969-71	4940	183.0

Scoring

NON-KICKERS

Points	Years	TD	Xpt	FG	Pts
1 Anthony Thompson, Ind	1986-89	65	4	0	394
2 Marshall Faulk, S.D. St.	1991-93	62	4	0	376
3 Tony Dorsett, Pitt	1973-76	59	2	0	356
4 Glenn Davis, Army	1943-46	59	0	0	354
5 Art Luppino, Ariz	1953-56	48	49	0	337

	Years				
1 Aaron Turner, Pacific	1989-92				43
2 Ryan Yarborough, Wyoming	1990-93				42
3 Clarkston Hines, Duke	1986-89				38
4 Terance Mathis, N. Mexico	1985-87,89				36
5 Elmo Wright, Houston	1968-70				34

Points Per Game	Years	Pts	P/Gm
1 Marshall Faulk, S.Diego St.	1991-93	376	12.1
2 Bob Gaiters, N. Mexico St	1959-60	203	11.9
3 Ed Marinaro, Cornell	1969-71	318	11.8
4 Bill Burnett, Arkansas	1968-70	294	11.3
5 Steve Owens, Oklahoma	1967-69	336	11.2

KICKERS

Points	Years	FG	XP	Pts
1 Roman Anderson, Hou	1988-91	70	213	423
2 Carlos Huerta, Mia	1988-91	73	178	397
3 Jason Elam, Hawaii	1988-89, 91-92	79	158	395
4 Derek Schmidt, Fla. St.	1984-87	73	174	393
5 Luis Zendejas, Ariz. St	1981-84	78	134	368
6 Jeff Jaeger, Wash	1983-86	80	118	358
7 John Lee, UCLA	1982-85	79	116	353
Max Zendejas, Arizona	1982-85	77	122	353
Kevin Butler, Georgia	1981-84	77	122	353

Touchdowns Rushing	Years	No
1 Marshall Faulk, S.Diego St.	1991-93	57
2 Steve Owens, Oklahoma	1967-69	56
3 Tony Dorsett, Pitt	1973-76	55
4 Anthony Thompson, Indiana	1986-89	54
5 Ed Marinaro, Cornell	1969-71	50
Mike Rozier, Nebraska	1981-83	50

Field Goals	Years	No
1 Jeff Jaeger, Wash	1983-86	80
2 John Lee, UCLA	1982-85	79
Jason Elam, Hawaii	1988-89, 91-92	79
4 Philip Doyle, Alabama	1987-90	78
Luis Zendejas, Ariz. St.	1981-84	78

Touchdowns Passing	Years	No
1 Ty Detmer, BYU	1988-91	121
2 David Klingler, Houston	1988-91	91
3 Troy Kopp, Pacific	1989-92	87
4 Jim McMahon, BYU	1977-78,80-81	84
5 Joe Adams, Tenn. St	1977-80	81

Touchdown Catches	Years	No

Miscellaneous

Interceptions	Years	No
1 Al Brosky, Illinois	1950-52	29
2 John Provost, Holy Cross	1972-74	27
Martin Bayless, Bowling Green	1980-83	27
4 Tom Curtis, Michigan	1967-69	25
Tony Thurman, Boston College	1981-84	25
Tracy Saul, Texas Tech	1989-92	25

Punt Return Average*	Years	Avg
1 Jack Mitchell, Oklahoma	1946-48	23.6
2 Gene Gibson, Cincinnati	1949-50	20.5
3 Eddie Macon, Pacific	1949-51	18.9
4 Jackie Robinson, UCLA	1939-40	18.8
Two tied at 17.7 each.		

*At least 1.2 punt returns per game.

Punting Average*	Years	Avg
1 Reggie Roby, Iowa	1979-82	45.6
2 Greg Montgomery, Mich. St	1985-87	45.4
3 Tom Tupa, Ohio St	1984-87	45.2

*At least 150 punts kicked.

Kickoff Return Average*	Years	Avg
1 Forrest Hall, San Francisco	1946-47	36.2
2 Anthony Davis, USC	1972-74	35.1
3 Overton Curtis, Utah St	1957-58	31.0

*At least 1.2 kickoff returns per game.

SINGLE SEASON

Rushing

Yards Gained

	Year	Gm	Car	Yards
Barry Sanders, Okla. St	1988	11	344	2628
Marcus Allen, USC	1981	11	403	2342
Mike Rozier, Nebraska	1983	12	275	2148
LeShon Johnson, No. Ill.	1993	11	327	1976
Tony Dorsett, Pitt	1976	11	338	1948

Yards Per Game

	Year	Gm	Yards	P/Gm
Barry Sanders, Okla. St	1988	11	2628	238.9
Marcus Allen, USC	1981	11	2342	212.9
Ed Marinaro, Cornell	1971	9	1881	209.0
Charles White, USC	1979	10	1803	180.3
LeShon Johnson, No. Ill.	1993	11	1976	179.6

Total Offense

Yards Gained

	Year	Gm	Plays	Yards
David Klingler, Houston	1990	11	704	5221
Ty Detmer, BYU	1990	12	635	5022
Andre Ware, Houston	1989	11	628	4661
Jim McMahon, BYU	1980	12	540	4627
Ty Detmer, BYU	1989	12	497	4433

Yards Per Game

	Year	Gm	Yards	P/Gm
David Klingler, Houston	1990	11	5221	474.6
Andre Ware, Houston	1989	11	4661	423.7
Ty Detmer, BYU	1990	12	5022	418.5
Steve Young, BYU	1983	11	4346	395.1
Chris Vargas, Nevada	1993	11	4332	393.8

All-Purpose Running

Yards Gained

	Year	Yards
Barry Sanders, Okla. St	1988	3250
Ryan Benjamin, Pacific	1991	2995
Mike Pringle, CS-Fullerton	1989	2690
Paul Palmer, Temple	1986	2633
Ryan Benjamin, Pacific	1992	2597

Yards Per Game

	Year	Yards	P/Gm
Barry Sanders, Okla. St	1988	3250	295.5
Ryan Benjamin, Pacific	1991	2995	249.6
Byron (Whizzer) White, Colo	1937	1970	246.3
Mike Pringle, CS-Fullerton	1989	2690	244.6
Paul Palmer, Temple	1986	2633	239.4

Scoring

Points

	Year	TD	Xpt	FG	Pts
Barry Sanders, Okla. St	1988	39	0	0	234
Mike Rozier, Nebraska	1983	29	0	0	174
Lydell Mitchell, Penn St	1971	29	0	0	174
Art Luppino, Arizona	1954	24	22	0	166
Bobby Reynolds, Nebraska	1950	22	25	0	157

Points Per Game

	Year	Pts	P/Gm
Barry Sanders, Okla. St	1988	234	21.3
Bobby Reynolds, Nebraska	1950	157	17.4
Art Luppino, Arizona	1954	166	16.6
Ed Marinaro, Cornell	1971	148	16.4
Lydell Mitchell, Penn St	1971	174	15.8

Touchdowns Rushing

	Year	No
Barry Sanders, Okla. St	1988	37
Mike Rozier, Nebraska	1983	29
Ed Marinaro, Cornell	1971	24
Anthony Thompson, Indiana	1988	24
Anthony Thompson, Indiana	1989	24

Passing

(Minimum 15 Attempts Per Game)

Passing Efficiency

	Year	Rating
Jim McMahon, BYU	1980	176.9
Ty Detmer, BYU	1989	175.6
Trent Dilfer, Fresno St.	1993	173.1
Jerry Rhome, Tulsa	1964	172.6
Elvis Grbac, Michigan	1991	169.0

Yards Gained

	Year	Yards
Ty Detmer, BYU	1990	5188
David Klingler, Houston	1990	5140
Andre Ware, Houston	1989	4699
Jim McMahon, BYU	1980	4571
Ty Detmer, BYU	1989	4560

Completions

	Year	Att	No
David Klingler, Houston	1990	643	374
Andre Ware, Houston	1989	578	365
Ty Detmer, BYU	1990	562	361
Robbie Bosco, BYU	1985	511	338
Chris Vargas, Nevada	1993	490	331

Receptions

Catches

	Year	Gm	No
Manny Hazard, Houston	1989	11	142
Howard Twilley, Tulsa	1965	10	134
Jason Phillips, Houston	1988	11	108
Fred Gilbert, Houston	1991	11	106
Chris Penn, Tulsa	1993	11	105

Catches Per Game

	Year	No	P/Gm
Howard Twilley, Tulsa	1965	134	13.4
Manny Hazard, Houston	1989	142	12.9
Jason Phillips, Houston	1988	108	9.8
Fred Gilbert, Houston	1991	106	9.6
Chris Penn, Tulsa	1993	105	9.6
Jerry Hendren, Idaho	1969	95	9.5
Howard Twilley, Tulsa	1964	95	9.5

Yards Gained

	Year	No	Yards
Howard Twilley, Tulsa	1965	134	1779
Manny Hazard, Houston	1989	142	1689
Aaron Turner, Pacific	1991	92	1604
Chris Penn, Tulsa	1993	106	1578
Chuck Hughes, UTEP*	1965	80	1519

*UTEP was Texas Western in 1965.

Scoring

Touchdowns Passing

	Year	No
David Klingler, Houston	1990	54
Jim McMahon, BYU	1980	47
Andre Ware, Houston	1989	46
Ty Detmer, BYU	1990	41
Dennis Shaw, San Diego St	1969	39

Touchdown Catches

	Year	No
Manny Hazard, Houston	1989	22
Desmond Howard, Michigan	1991	19
Tom Reynolds, San Diego St	1969	18
Dennis Smith, Utah	1989	18
Aaron Turner, Pacific	1991	18

Field Goals

	Year	No
John Lee, UCLA	1984	29
Paul Woodside, West Virginia	1982	28
Luis Zendejas, Arizona St	1983	28
Fuad Reveiz, Tennessee	1982	27
Three tied with 25 each.		

All-Time NCAA Division I-A Leaders (Cont.)

Miscellaneous

Interceptions		Year	No
Al Worley, Washington		1968	14
George Shaw, Oregon		1951	13
Eight tied with 12 each.			

Punt Return Average*		Year	Avg
Bill Blackstock, Tennessee		1951	25.9
George Sims, Baylor		1948	25.0
Gene Derricotte, Michigan		1947	24.8
*At least 1.2 returns per game.			

Punting Average*		Year	Avg
Reggie Roby, Iowa		1981	49.8
Kirk Wilson, UCLA		1956	49.3
Zack Jordan, Colorado		1950	48.2
Ricky Anderson, Vanderbilt		1984	48.2
*Qualifiers for championship.			

Kickoff Return Average*		Year	Avg
Leeland McElroy, Texas A&M		1993	39.3
Forrest Hall, San Francisco		1946	38.2
Tony Ball, Tenn-Chattanooga		1977	36.4
Rocket Ismail, Notre Dame		1988	36.1
*At least 1.2 kickoff returns per game.			

SINGLE GAME

Rushing

Yards Gained	Opponent	Year	Yds
Tony Sands, Kansas	Missouri	1991	396
Marshall Faulk, San Diego St	Pacific	1991	386
Anthony Thompson, Indiana	Wisconsin	1989	377
Rueben Mayes, Wash.St.	Oregon	1984	357
Mike Pringle, CS-Fullerton	N. Mex. St.	1989	357

Total Offense

Yards Gained	Opponent	Year	Yds
David Klingler, Houston	Arizona St.	1990	732
Matt Vogler, TCU	Houston	1990	696
David Klingler, Houston	TCU	1990	625
Scott Mitchell, Utah	Air Force	1988	625
Jimmy Klinger, Houston	Rice	1992	612

Passing

Yards Gained	Opponent	Year	Yds
David Klingler, Houston	Arizona St.	1990	716
Matt Vogler, TCU	Houston	1990	690
Scott Mitchell, Utah	Air Force	1988	631
Jeremy Leach, New Mexico	Utah	1989	622
Dave Wilson, Illinois	Ohio St.	1980	621

Completions	Opponent	Year	No
David Klingler, Houston	SMU	1990	48
Jimmy Klingler, Houston	Rice	1992	46
Sandy Schwab, Northwestern	Michigan	1982	45
Chuck Hartlieb, Iowa	Indiana	1988	44
Jim McMahon, BYU	Colo. St.	1981	44
Matt Vogler, TCU	Houston	1990	44

Receptions

Catches	Opponent	Year	No
Miller, BYU	New Mexico	1973	22
Rick Eber, Tulsa	Idaho St.	1967	20
Howard Twilley, Tulsa	Colo. St.	1965	19
Ron Fair, Arizona St	Wash.St.	1989	19
Manny Hazard, Houston	TCU	1989	19
Manny Hazard, Houston	Texas	1989	19

Yards Gained	Opponent	Year	Yds
Chuck Hughes, UTEP*	N. Texas St.	1965	349
Rick Eber, Tulsa	Idaho St.	1967	322
Harry Wood, Tulsa	Idaho St.	1967	318
Jeff Evans, N. Mexico St	So.Ill.	1978	316
Brian Oliver, Ball St	Toledo	1993	297
*UTEP was Texas Western in 1965.			

Longest Plays (since 1941)

Rushing	Opponent	Year	Yds
Gale Sayers, Kansas	Nebraska	1963	99
Max Anderson, Ariz. St.	Wyoming	1967	99
Ralph Thompson, W. Texas St	Wich. St.	1970	99
Kelsey Finch, Tennessee	Florida	1977	99
Jerald Sowell, Tulane	Alabama	1993	99

Passing	Opponent	Year	Yds
Fred Owens			
to Jack Ford, Portland	St. Mary's	1947	99
Bo Burris			
to Warren McVea, Houston	Wash. St.	1966	99
Colin Clapton			
to Eddie Jenkins, Holy Cross	Boston U.	1970	99
Terry Peel			
to Robert Ford, Houston	Syracuse	1970	99
Terry Peel			
to Robert Ford, Houston	S. Diego St.	1972	99
Cris Collinsworth			
to Derrick Gaffney, Florida	Rice	1977	99
Scott Ankrom			
to James Maness, TCU	Rice	1984	99
Gino Torretta			
to Horace Copeland, Miami-FL	Ark.	1991	99
John Paci			
to Thomas Lewis, Indiana	Penn St.	1993	99

Field Goals	Opponent	Year	Yds
Steve Little, Arkansas	Texas	1977	67
Russell Erxleben, Texas	Rice	1977	67
Joe Williams, Wichita St	So. Ill.	1978	67

Scoring

Points	Opponent	Year	Pts
Howard Griffith, Illinois	So. Ill.	1990	48
Marshall Faulk, S. Diego St	Pacific	1991	44
Jim Brown, Syracuse	Colgate	1956	43
Showboat Boykin, Ole Miss	Miss. St.	1951	42
Fred Wendt, UTEP*	N. Mex. St.	1948	42
*UTEP was Texas Mines in 1948.			

Touchdowns Rushing	Opponent	Year	No
Howard Griffith, Illinois	So. Ill	1990	8
Showboat Boykin, Ole Miss	Miss. St.	1951	7
Note: Griffith's TD runs (5-51-7-41-5-18-5-3).			

Touchdowns Passing	Opponent	Year	No
David Klingler, Houston	E. Wash.	1990	11
Dennis Shaw, S. Diego St	N. Mex. St.	1969	9
Note: Klingler's TD passes (5-48-29-7-3-7-40-8-7-8-51).			

Touchdown Catches	Opponent	Year	No
Tim Delaney, S. Diego St	N. Mex. St.	1969	6
Note: Delaney TD catches (2-22-34-31-30-9).			

Field Goals	Opponent	Year	No
Dale Klein, Nebraska	Missouri	1985	7
Mike Prindle, W. Mich	Marshall	1984	7
Note: Klein's FGs (32-22-43-44-29-43-43); Prindle's FGs (32-44-42-23-48-41-27).			

Extra Points (Kick)	Opponent	Year	No
Terry Leiweke, Houston	Tulsa	1968	13
Derek Mahoney, Fresno St	New Mexico	1991	13

Annual Awards

Heisman Trophy

Originally presented in 1935 as the DAC Trophy by the Downtown Athletic Club of New York City to the best college football player east of the Mississippi. In 1936, players across the country were eligible and the award was renamed the Heisman Trophy following the death of former college coach and DAC athletic director John W. Heisman. Top three vote getters for each year are listed with point totals.

Multiple winner: Archie Griffin (2).

Winners in junior year (11): Doc Blanchard (1945), Ty Detmer (1990); Archie Griffin (1974), Desmond Howard (1991), Vic Janowicz (1950), Barry Sanders (1988), Billy Sims (1978), Roger Staubach (1963), Doak Walker (1948), Herschel Walker (1982), Andre Ware (1989).

Winners on AP national champions (8): Angelo Bertelli (Notre Dame, 1943); Doc Blanchard (Army, 1945); Tony Dorsett (Pittsburgh, 1976); Leon Hart (Notre Dame, 1949); Johnny Lujack (Notre Dame, 1947); Davey O'Brien (TCU, 1938); Bruce Smith (Minnesota, 1941); Charlie Ward (Florida St., 1993).

Year		Points
1935	**Jay Berwanger,** Chicago, HB	84
	2nd—Monk Meyer, Army, HB	29
	3rd—Bill Shakespeare, Notre Dame, HB	23
	4th—Pepper Constable, Princeton, FB	20
1936	**Larry Kelley,** Yale, E	219
	2nd—Sam Francis, Nebraska, FB	47
	3rd—Ray Buivid, Marquette, HB	43
	4th—Sammy Baugh, TCU, HB	39
1937	**Clint Frank,** Yale, HB	524
	2nd—Byron (Whizzer) White, Colo., HB	264
	3rd—Marshall Goldberg, Pitt, HB	211
	4th—Alex Wojciechowicz, Fordham, C	85
1938	**Davey O'Brien,** TCU, QB	519
	2nd—Marshall Goldberg, Pitt, HB	294
	3rd—Sid Luckman, Columbia, QB	154
	4th—Bob MacLeod, Dartmouth, HB	78
1939	**Nile Kinnick,** Iowa, HB	651
	2nd—Tom Harmon, Michigan, HB	405
	3rd—Paul Christman, Missouri, QB	391
	4th—George Cafego, Tennessee, QB	296
1940	**Tom Harmon,** Michigan, HB	1303
	2nd—John Kimbrough, Texas A&M, FB	841
	3rd—George Franck, Minnesota, HB	102
	4th—Frankie Albert, Stanford, QB	90
1941	**Bruce Smith,** Minnesota, HB	554
	2nd—Angelo Bertelli, N.Dame, QB	345
	3rd—Frankie Albert, Stanford, QB	336
	4th—Frank Sinkwich, Georgia, HB	249
1942	**Frank Sinkwich,** Georgia, TB	1059
	2nd—Paul Governali, Columbia, QB	218
	3rd—Clint Castleberry, Ga.Tech, HB	99
	4th—Mike Holovak, Boston College, FB	95
1943	**Angelo Bertelli,** Notre Dame, QB	648
	2nd—Bob Odell, Penn, HB	177
	3rd—Otto Graham, Northwestern, QB	140
	4th—Creighton Miller, Notre Dame, HB	134
1944	**Les Horvath,** Ohio St., TB-QB	412
	2nd—Glenn Davis, Army, HB	287
	3rd—Doc Blanchard, Army, FB	237
	4th—Don Whitmore, Navy, T	115
1945	**Doc Blanchard,** Army, FB	860
	2nd—Glenn Davis, Army, HB	638
	3rd—Bob Fenimore, Oklahoma A&M, HB	187
	4th—Herman Wedemeyer, St. Mary's, HB	152
1946	**Glenn Davis,** Army, HB	792
	2nd—Charlie Trippi, Georgia, HB	435
	3rd—Johnny Lujack, Notre Dame, QB	379
	4th—Doc Blanchard, Army, FB	267
1947	**Johnny Lujack,** Notre Dame, QB	742
	2nd—Bob Chappius, Michigan, HB	555
	3rd—Doak Walker, SMU, HB	196
	4th—Charlie Conerly, Mississippi, QB	186
1948	**Doak Walker,** SMU, HB	778
	2nd—Charlie Justice, N. Carolina, HB	443
	3rd—Chuck Bednarik, Penn, C	336
	4th—Jackie Jensen, California, HB	143

Year		Points
1949	**Leon Hart,** Notre Dame, E	995
	2nd—Charlie Justice, N. Carolina, HB	272
	3rd—Doak Walker, SMU, HB	229
	4th—Arnold Galiffa, Army QB	196
1950	**Vic Janowicz,** Ohio St., HB	633
	2nd—Kyle Rote, SMU, HB	280
	3rd—Reds Bagnell, Penn, HB	231
	4th—Babe Parilli, Kentucky, QB	214
1951	**Dick Kazmaier,** Princeton, TB	1777
	2nd—Hank Lauricella, Tennessee, HB	424
	3rd—Babe Parilli, Kentucky, QB	344
	4th—Bill McColl, Stanford, E	313
1952	**Billy Vessels,** Oklahoma, HB	525
	2nd—Jack Scarbath, Maryland, QB	367
	3rd—Paul Giel, Minnesota, HB	329
	4th—Donn Moomaw, UCLA, C	257
1953	**Johnny Lattner,** Notre Dame, HB	1850
	2nd—Paul Giel, Minnesota, HB	1794
	3rd—Paul Cameron, UCLA, HB	444
	4th—Bernie Faloney, Maryland, QB	258
1954	**Alan Ameche,** Wisconsin, FB	1068
	2nd—Kurt Burris, Oklahoma, C	838
	3rd—Howard Cassady, Ohio St., HB	810
	4th—Ralph Guglielmi, Notre Dame, QB	691
1955	**Howard Cassady,** Ohio St., HB	2219
	2nd—Jim Swink, TCU, HB	742
	3rd—George Welsh, Navy, QB	383
	4th—Earl Morrall, Michigan St., QB	323
1956	**Paul Hornung,** Notre Dame, QB	1066
	2nd—Johnny Majors, Tennessee, HB	994
	3rd—Tommy McDonald, Oklahoma, HB	973
	4th—Jerry Tubbs, Oklahoma, C	724
1957	**John David Crow,** Texas A&M, HB	1183
	2nd—Alex Karras, Iowa, T	693
	3rd—Walt Kowalczyk, Mich. St., HB	630
	4th—Lou Michaels, Kentucky, T	330
1958	**Pete Dawkins,** Army, HB	1394
	2nd—Randy Duncan, Iowa, QB	1021
	3rd—Billy Cannon, LSU, HB	975
	4th—Bob White, Ohio St., HB	365
1959	**Billy Cannon,** LSU, HB	1929
	2nd—Richie Lucas, Penn St., QB	613
	3rd—Don Meredith, SMU, QB	286
	4th—Bill Burrell, Illinois, G	196
1960	**Joe Bellino,** Navy, HB	1793
	2nd—Tom Brown, Minnesota, G	731
	3rd—Jake Gibbs, Mississippi, QB	453
	4th—Ed Dyas, Auburn, HB	319
1961	**Ernie Davis,** Syracuse, HB	824
	2nd—Bob Ferguson, Ohio St., HB	771
	3rd—Jimmy Saxton, Texas, HB	551
	4th—Sandy Stephens, Minnesota, QB	543
1962	**Terry Baker,** Oregon St., QB	707
	2nd—Jerry Stovall, LSU, HB	618
	3rd—Bobby Bell, Minnesota, T	429
	4th—Lee Roy Jordan, Alabama, C	321

Annual Awards (Cont.)
Heisman Trophy

Year		Points
1963	**Roger Staubach,** Navy, QB	1860
	2nd—Billy Lothridge, Ga.Tech, QB	504
	3rd—Sherman Lewis, Mich. St., HB	369
	4th—Don Trull, Baylor, QB	253
1964	**John Huarte,** Notre Dame, QB	1026
	2nd—Jerry Rhome, Tulsa, QB	952
	3rd—Dick Butkus, Illinois, C	505
	4th—Bob Timberlake, Michigan, QB	361
1965	**Mike Garrett,** USC, HB	926
	2nd—Howard Twilley, Tulsa, E	528
	3rd—Jim Grabowski, Illinois, FB	481
	4th—Donny Anderson, Texas Tech, HB	408
1966	**Steve Spurrier,** Florida, QB	1679
	2nd—Bob Griese, Purdue, QB	816
	3rd—Nick Eddy, Notre Dame, HB	456
	4th—Gary Beban, UCLA, QB	318
1967	**Gary Beban,** UCLA, QB	1968
	2nd—O.J. Simpson, USC, HB	1722
	3rd—Leroy Keyes, Purdue, HB	1366
	4th—Larry Csonka, Syracuse, FB	136
1968	**O.J. Simpson,** USC, HB	2853
	2nd—Leroy Keyes, Purdue, HB	1103
	3rd—Terry Hanratty, Notre Dame, QB	387
	4th—Ted Kwalick, Penn St., TE	254
1969	**Steve Owens,** Oklahoma, HB	1488
	2nd—Mike Phipps, Purdue, QB	1344
	3rd—Rex Kern, Ohio St., QB	856
	4th—Archie Manning, Mississippi, QB	582
1970	**Jim Plunkett,** Stanford, QB	2229
	2nd—Joe Theismann, Notre Dame, QB	1410
	3rd—Archie Manning, Mississippi, QB	849
	4th—Steve Worster, Texas, RB	398
1971	**Pat Sullivan,** Auburn, QB	1597
	2nd—Ed Marinaro, Cornell, RB	1445
	3rd—Greg Pruitt, Oklahoma, RB	586
	4th—Johnny Musso, Alabama, RB	365
1972	**Johnny Rodgers,** Nebraska, FL	1310
	2nd—Greg Pruitt, Oklahoma, RB	966
	3rd—Rich Glover, Nebraska, MG	652
	4th—Bert Jones, LSU, QB	351
1973	**John Cappelletti,** Penn St., RB	1057
	2nd—John Hicks, Ohio St., OT	524
	3rd—Roosevelt Leaks, Texas, RB	482
	4th—David Jaynes, Kansas, QB	394
1974	**Archie Griffin,** Ohio St., RB	1920
	2nd—Anthony Davis, USC, RB	819
	3rd—Joe Washington, Oklahoma, RB	661
	4th—Tom Clements, Notre Dame, QB	244
1975	**Archie Griffin,** Ohio St., RB	1800
	2nd—Chuck Muncie, California, RB	730
	3rd—Ricky Bell, USC, RB	708
	4th—Tony Dorsett, Pitt, RB	616
1976	**Tony Dorsett,** Pittsburgh, RB	2357
	2nd—Ricky Bell, USC, RB	1346
	3rd—Rob Lytle, Michigan, RB	413
	4th—Terry Miller, Oklahoma St., RB	197
1977	**Earl Campbell,** Texas, RB	1547
	2nd—Terry Miller, Oklahoma, RB	812
	3rd—Ken MacAfee, Notre Dame, TE	343
	4th—Doug Williams, Grambling, QB	266
1978	**Billy Sims,** Oklahoma, RB	827
	2nd—Chuck Fusina, Penn St., QB	750
	3rd—Rick Leach, Michigan, QB	435
	4th—Charles White, USC, RB	354
1979	**Charles White,** USC, RB	1695
	2nd—Billy Sims, Oklahoma, RB	773
	3rd—Marc Wilson, BYU, QB	589
	4th—Art Schlichter, Ohio St., QB	251

Year		Points
1980	**George Rogers,** South Carolina, RB	1128
	2nd—Hugh Green, Pittsburgh, DE	861
	3rd—Herschel Walker, Georgia, RB	683
	4th—Mark Herrmann, Purdue, QB	405
1981	**Marcus Allen,** USC, RB	1797
	2nd—Herschel Walker, Georgia, RB	1199
	3rd—Jim McMahon, BYU, QB	706
	4th—Dan Marino, Pitt, QB	256
1982	**Herschel Walker,** Georgia, RB	1926
	2nd—John Elway, Stanford, QB	1231
	3rd—Eric Dickerson, SMU, RB	465
	4th—Anthony Carter, Michigan, WR	142
1983	**Mike Rozier,** Nebraska, RB	1801
	2nd—Steve Young, BYU, QB	1172
	3rd—Doug Flutie, Boston College, QB	253
	4th—Turner Gill, Nebraska, QB	190
1984	**Doug Flutie,** Boston College, QB	2240
	2nd—Keith Byers, Ohio St., RB	1251
	3rd—Robbie Bosco, BYU, QB	443
	4th—Bernie Kosar, Miami-FL, QB	320
1985	**Bo Jackson,** Auburn, RB	1509
	2nd—Chuck Long, Iowa, QB	1464
	3rd—Robbie Bosco, BYU, QB	459
	4th—Lorenzo White, Michigan St., RB	391
1986	**Vinny Testaverde,** Miami-FL, QB	2213
	2nd—Paul Palmer, Temple, RB	672
	3rd—Jim Harbaugh, Michigan, QB	458
	4th—Brian Bosworth, Oklahoma, LB	395
1987	**Tim Brown,** Notre Dame, WR	1442
	2nd—Don McPherson, Syracuse, QB	831
	3rd—Gordie Lockbaum, Holy Cross, WR-DB	657
	4th—Lorenzo White, Michigan St., RB	632
1988	**Barry Sanders,** Oklahoma St., RB	1878
	2nd—Rodney Peete, USC, QB	912
	3rd—Troy Aikman, UCLA, QB	582
	4th—Steve Walsh, Miami-FL, QB	341
1989	**Andre Ware,** Houston, QB	1073
	2nd—Anthony Thompson, Ind., RB	1003
	3rd—Major Harris, West Va., QB	709
	4th—Tony Rice, Notre Dame, QB	523
1990	**Ty Detmer,** BYU, QB	1482
	2nd—Rocket Ismail, Notre Dame, FL	1177
	3rd—Eric Bieniemy, Colorado, RB	798
	4th—Shawn Moore, Virginia, QB	465
1991	**Desmond Howard,** Michigan, WR	2077
	2nd—Casey Weldon, Florida St., QB	503
	3rd—Ty Detmer, BYU, QB	445
	4th—Steve Emtman, Washington, DT	357
1992	**Gino Torretta,** Miami-FL, QB	1400
	2nd—Marshall Faulk, S. Diego St., RB	1080
	3rd—Garrison Hearst, Georgia, RB	982
	4th—Marvin Jones, Florida St., LB	392
1993	**Charlie Ward,** Florida St., QB	2310
	2nd—Heath Shuler, Tennessee, QB	688
	3rd—David Palmer, Alabama, RB	292
	4th—Marshall Faulk, S. Diego St., RB	250

Colleges With Three Winners

Notre Dame (7)—Bertelli (1943), Brown (1987), Hart (1949), Hornung (1956), Huarte (1964), Lattner (1953) and Lujack (1947). **Ohio St.** (5)—Cassady (1955), Griffin (1974-75), Horvath (1944) and Janowicz (1950). **USC** (4)—Allen (1981), Garrett (1965), Simpson (1968) and White (1979). **Army** (3)—Blanchard (1945), Davis (1946) and Dawkins (1958). **Oklahoma** (3)—Owens (1969), Sims (1978) and Vessels (1952).

Maxwell Award

First presented in 1937 by the Maxwell Memorial Football Club of Philadelphia, the award is named after Robert "Tiny" Maxwell, a Philadelphia native who was a standout lineman at the University of Chicago at the turn of the century. Like the Heisman, the Maxwell is given to the outstanding college player in the nation. Both awards have gone to the same player in the same season 30 times. Those players are preceded by (#). Glenn Davis of Army and Doak Walker of SMU won both but in different years.

Multiple winner: Johnny Lattner (2).

Year	Year	Year
1937 #Clint Frank, Yale, HB	1956 Tommy McDonald, Okla., HB	1975 #Archie Griffin, Ohio St., RB
1938 #Davey O'Brien, TCU, QB	1957 Bob Reifsnyder, Navy, T	1976 #Tony Dorsett, Pitt, RB
1939 #Nile Kinnick, Iowa, HB	1958 #Pete Dawkins, Army, HB	1977 Ross Browner, Notre Dame, DE
1940 #Tom Harmon, Michigan, HB	1959 Rich Lucas, Penn St., QB	1978 Chuck Fusina, Penn St., QB
1941 Bill Dudley, Virginia, HB		1979 #Charles White, USC, RB
1942 Paul Governali, Columbia, QB	1960 #Joe Bellino, Navy, HB	
1943 Bob Odell, Penn, HB	1961 Bob Ferguson, Ohio St., HB	1980 Hugh Green, Pitt, DE
1944 Glenn Davis, Army, HB	1962 #Terry Baker, Oregon St., QB	1981 #Marcus Allen, USC, RB
1945 #Doc Blanchard, Army, FB	1963 #Roger Staubach, Navy, QB	1982 #Herschel Walker, Georgia, RB
1946 Charley Trippi, Georgia, HB	1964 Glenn Ressler, Penn St., G	1983 #Mike Rozier, Nebraska, RB
1947 Doak Walker, SMU, HB	1965 Tommy Nobis, Texas, LB	1984 #Doug Flutie, Boston Col., QB
1948 Chuck Bednarik, Penn, C	1966 Jim Lynch, Notre Dame, LB	1985 Chuck Long, Iowa, QB
1949 #Leon Hart, Notre Dame, E	1967 #Gary Beban, UCLA, QB	1986 #V. Testaverde, Miami-FL, QB
	1968 #O.J. Simpson, USC, HB	1987 Don McPherson, Syracuse, QB
1950 Reds Bagnell, Penn, HB	1969 Mike Reid, Penn St., DT	1988 #Barry Sanders, Okla. St., RB
1951 #Dick Kazmaier, Princeton, TB		1989 Anthony Thompson, Indiana, RB
1952 Johnny Lattner, Notre Dame, HB	1970 #Jim Plunkett, Stanford, QB	
1953 #Johnny Lattner, N. Dame, HB	1971 Ed Marinaro, Cornell, RB	1990 #Ty Detmer, BYU, QB
1954 Ron Beagle, Navy, E	1972 Brad Van Pelt, Michigan St., DB	1991 #Desmond Howard, Mich., WR
1955 #Howard Cassady, Ohio St., HB	1973 #John Cappelletti, Penn St., RB	1992 #Gino Torretta, Miami-FL, QB
	1974 Steve Joachim, Temple, QB	1993 #Charlie Ward, Florida St., QB

Outland Trophy

First presented in 1946 by the Football Writers Association of America, honoring the the nation's outstanding interior lineman. The award is named after its benefactor, Dr. John H. Outland (Kansas, Class of 1898). Players listed in **bold** type helped lead their team to a national championship (according to AP).

Multiple winner: Dave Rimmington (2). **Winners in junior year:** Ross Browner (1976), Steve Emtman (1991) and Rimmington (1981).

Year	Year	Year
1946 **George Connor,** N. Dame, T	1962 Bobby Bell, Minnesota, T	1978 Greg Roberts, Oklahoma, G
1947 Joe Steffy, Army, G	1963 **Scott Appleton,** Texas, T	1979 Jim Richter, N.C. State, C
1948 Bill Fischer, Notre Dame, G	1964 Steve DeLong, Tennessee, T	
1949 Ed Bagdon, Michigan St., G	1965 Tommy Nobis, Texas, G	1980 Mark May, Pittsburgh, OT
	1966 Loyd Phillips, Arkansas, T	1981 Dave Rimmington, Nebraska, C
1950 Bob Gain, Kentucky, T	1967 **Ron Yary,** USC, T	1982 Dave Rimmington, Nebraska, C
1951 Jim Weatherall, Oklahoma, T	1968 Bill Stanfill, Georgia, T	1983 Dean Steinkuhler, Nebraska, G
1952 Dick Modzelewski, Maryland, T	1969 Mike Reid, Penn St., DT	1984 Bruce Smith, Virginia Tech, DT
1953 J.D. Roberts, Oklahoma, G		1985 Mike Ruth, Boston College, NG
1954 Bill Brooks, Arkansas, G	1970 Jim Stillwagon, Ohio St., MG	1986 Jason Buck, BYU, DT
1955 Calvin Jones, Iowa, G	1971 **Larry Jacobson,** Neb., DT	1987 Chad Hennings, Air Force, DT
1956 Jim Parker, Ohio St., G	1972 Rich Glover, Nebraska, MG	1988 Tracy Rocker, Auburn, DT
1957 Alex Karras, Iowa, T	1973 John Hicks, Ohio St., OT	1989 Mohammed Elewonibi, BYU, G
1958 Zeke Smith, Auburn, G	1974 Randy White, Maryland, DT	
1959 Mike McGee, Duke, T	1975 **Lee Roy Selmon,** Okla., DT	1990 Russell Maryland, Miami-FL, NT
	1976 Ross Browner, Notre Dame, DE	1991 Steve Emtman, Washington, DT
1960 **Tom Brown,** Minnesota, G	1977 Brad Shearer, Texas, DT	1992 Will Shields, Nebraska, G
1961 Merlin Olsen, Utah St., T		1993 Rob Waldrop, Arizona, NG

Butkus Award

First presented in 1985 by the Downtown Athletic Club of Orlando, Fla., to honor the nation's outstanding linebacker. The award is named after Dick Butkus, two-time consensus All-America at Illinois and six-time All-Pro with the Chicago Bears.

Multiple winner: Brian Bosworth (2).

Year	Year	Year
1985 Brian Bosworth, Oklahoma	1988 Derrick Thomas, Alabama	1991 Erick Anderson, Michigan
1986 Brian Bosworth, Oklahoma	1989 Percy Snow, Michigan St.	1992 Marvin Jones, Florida St.
1987 Paul McGowan, Florida St.	1990 Alfred Williams, Colorado	1993 Trev Alberts, Nebraska

Annual Awards (Cont.)

Lombardi Award

First presented in 1970 by the Rotary Club of Houston, honoring the nation's best lineman. The award is named after pro football coach Vince Lombardi, who, as a guard, was a member of the famous "Seven Blocks of Granite" at Fordham in the 1930s. The Lombardi and Outland awards have gone to the same player in the same year nine times. Those players are preceded by (#). Ross Browner of Notre Dame won both, but in different years.

Year
1970 #Jim Stillwagon, Ohio St., MG
1971 Walt Patulski, Notre Dame, DE
1972 #Rich Glover, Nebraska, MG
1973 #John Hicks, Ohio St., OT
1974 #Randy White, Maryland, DT
1975 #Lee Roy Selmon, Okla., DT
1976 Wilson Whitley, Houston, DT
1977 Ross Browner, Notre Dame, DE
1978 Bruce Clark, Penn St., DT

Year
1979 Brad Budde, USC, G
1980 Hugh Green, Pitt, DE
1981 Kenneth Sims, Texas, DT
1982 #Dave Rimmington, Neb., C
1983 #Dean Steinkuhler, Neb., G
1984 Tony Degrate, Texas, DT
1985 Tony Casillas, Oklahoma, NG
1986 Cornelius Bennett, Alabama, LB

Year
1987 Chris Spielman, Ohio St., LB
1988 #Tracy Rocker, Auburn, DT
1989 Percy Snow, Michigan St., LB
1990 Chris Zorich, Notre Dame, NT
1991 #Steve Emtman, Wash., DT
1992 Marvin Jones, Florida St., LB
1993 Aaron Taylor, Notre Dame, OT

O'Brien Quarterback Award

First presented in 1977 as the O'Brien Memorial Trophy, the award went to the outstanding player in the Southwest. In 1981, however, the Davey O'Brien Educational and Charitable Trust of Ft. Worth renamed the prize the O'Brien National Quarterback Award and now honors the nation's best quarterback. The award is named after 1938 Heisman Trophy-winning QB Davey O'Brien of Texas Christian.
    Multiple winners: Ty Detmer and Mike Singletary (2).

Memorial Trophy

Year
1977 Earl Campbell, Texas, RB
1978 Billy Sims, Oklahoma, RB

Year
1979 Mike Singletary, Baylor, LB

Year
1980 Mike Singletary, Baylor, LB

National QB Award

Year
1981 Jim McMahon, BYU
1982 Todd Blackledge, Penn St.
1983 Steve Young, BYU
1984 Doug Flutie, Boston College
1985 Chuck Long, Iowa

Year
1986 Vinny Testaverde, Miami,FL
1987 Don McPherson, Syracuse
1988 Troy Aikman, UCLA
1989 Andre Ware, Houston

Year
1990 Ty Detmer, BYU
1991 Ty Detmer, BYU
1992 Gino Torretta, Miami-FL
1993 Charlie Ward, Florida St.

Thorpe Award

First presented in 1986 by the Jim Thorpe Athletic Club of Oklahoma City to honor the nation's outstanding defensive back. The award is named after Jim Thorpe—Olympic champion, two-time consensus All-America HB at Carlisle, and pro football pioneer.

Year
1986 Thomas Everett, Baylor
1987 Bennie Blades, Miami-FL
    & Rickey Dixon, Oklahoma

Year
1988 Deion Sanders, Florida St.
1989 Mike Carrier, USC
1990 Darryl Lewis, Arizona

Year
1991 Terrell Buckley, Florida St.
1992 Deon Figures, Colorado
1993 Antonio Langham, Alabama

Payton Award

First presented in 1987 by the Sports Network and Division I-AA sports information directors to honor the nation's outstanding Division I-AA player. The award is named after Walter Payton, the NFL's all-time leading rusher who was an All-America RB at Jackson St.

Year
1987 Kenny Gamble, Colgate, RB
1988 Dave Meggett, Towson St., RB
1989 John Friesz, Idaho, QB

Year
1990 Walter Dean, Grambling, RB
1991 Jamie Martin, Weber St., QB

Year
1992 Michael Payton, Marshall, QB
1993 Doug Nussmeier, Idaho, QB

Hill Trophy

First presented in 1986 by the Harlon Hill Awards Committee in Florence, AL, to honor the nation's outstanding Division II player. The award is named after three-time NFL All-Pro Harlon Hill who played college ball at North Alabama.
    Multiple winner: Johnny Bailey (3).

Year
1986 Jeff Bentrim, N.Dakota St., QB
1987 Johnny Bailey, Texas A&I, RB
1988 Johnny Bailey, Texas A&I, RB

Year
1989 Johnny Bailey, Texas A&I, RB
1990 Chris Simdorn, N.Dakota St., QB
1991 Ronnie West, Pittsburg St., WR

Year
1992 Ronald Moore, Pittsburg St., RB
1993 Roger Graham, New Haven, RB

All-Time Winningest Division I-A Coaches

Minimum of 10 years in Division I-A through 1993 season. Regular season and bowl games included. Coaches active in 1993 in **bold** type.

Top 25 Winning Percentage

		Yrs	W	L	T	Pct
1	Knute Rockne	13	105	12	5	.881
2	Frank Leahy	13	107	13	9	.864
3	George Woodruff	12	142	25	2	.846
4	Barry Switzer	16	157	29	4	.837
5	Percy Haughton	13	96	17	6	.832
6	Bob Neyland	21	173	31	12	.829
7	Hurry Up Yost	29	196	36	12	.828
8	Bud Wilkinson	17	145	29	4	.826
9	Jock Sutherland	20	144	28	14	.812
10	Bob Devaney	16	136	30	7	.806
11	**Tom Osborne**	21	206	47	3	.811
12	Frank Thomas	19	141	33	9	.795
13	Henry Williams	23	141	34	12	.786
14	**Joe Paterno**	28	257	69	3	.786
15	Gil Dobie	33	180	45	15	.781
16	Bear Bryant	38	323	85	17	.780
17	Fred Folsom	19	106	28	6	.779
18	Bo Schembechler	27	234	65	8	.775
19	Fritz Crisler	18	116	32	9	.768
20	Charley Moran	18	122	33	12	.766
21	Wallace Wade	24	171	49	10	.765
22	Frank Kush	22	176	54	1	.764
23	Dan McGugin	30	197	55	19	.762
24	Jim Crowley	13	78	21	10	.761
25	Andy Smith	17	116	32	13	.761

Top 25 Victories

		Yrs	W	L	T	Pct
1	Bear Bryant	38	323	85	17	.780
2	Pop Warner	44	319	106	32	.733
3	Amos Alonzo Stagg	57	314	199	35	.605
4	**Joe Paterno**	28	257	69	3	.786
5	**Bobby Bowden**	28	239	78	3	.752
6	Woody Hayes	33	238	72	10	.759
7	Bo Schembechler	27	234	65	8	.775
8	Jess Neely	40	207	176	19	.539
9	**Tom Osborne**	21	206	47	3	.811
10	Warren Woodson	31	203	95	14	.673
11	Vince Dooley	25	201	77	10	.715
	Eddie Anderson	39	201	128	15	.606
13	**Hayden Fry**	32	200	153	9	.565
14	Dana X. Bible	33	198	72	23	.715
15	Dan McGugin	30	197	55	19	.762
	LaVell Edwards	22	197	73	3	.727
17	Hurry Up Yost	29	196	36	12	.828
18	Howard Jones	29	194	64	21	.733
19	**Lou Holtz**	24	193	84	6	.693
20	Johnny Vaught	25	190	61	12	.745
21	**Jim Sweeney**	29	186	133	3	.582
22	John Heisman	36	185	70	17	.711
23	Darrell Royal	23	184	60	5	.749
24	Gil Dobie	33	180	45	15	.781
	Carl Snavely	32	180	96	16	.644

Note: Eddie Robinson of Division I-AA Grambling (1941-42, 1945—) is the all-time NCAA leader in coaching wins with a 388-140-15 record and .728 winning pct. over 51 seasons.

Where They Coached

Anderson—Loras (1922-24), DePaul (1925-31), Holy Cross (1933-38), Iowa (1939-42), Holy Cross (1950-64); **Bible**—Mississippi College (1913-15), LSU (1916), Texas A&M (1917, 1919-28), Nebraska (1929-36), Texas (1937-46); **Bowden**—Samford (1959-62), West Virginia (1970-75), Florida St. (1976—); **Bryant**—Maryland (1945), Kentucky (1946-53), Texas A&M (1954-57), Alabama (1958-82); **Crisler**—Minnesota (1930-31), Princeton (1932-37), Michigan (1938-47); **Crowley**—Michigan St. (1929-32), Fordham (1933-41); **Devaney**—Wyoming (1957-61), Nebraska (1962-72); **Dobie**—North Dakota St. (1906-07), Washington (1908-16), Navy (1917-19), Cornell (1920-35), Boston College (1936-38); **V.Dooley**—Georgia (1964-88); **Edwards**—BYU (1972—); **Folsom**—Colorado (1895-99, 1901-02), Dartmouth (1903-06), Colorado (1908-15).

Fry—SMU (1962-72), North Texas (1973-78), Iowa (1979—); **Haughton**—Cornell (1899-1900), Harvard (1908-16), Columbia (1923-24); **Hayes**—Denison (1946-48), Miami-OH (1949-50), Ohio St. (1951-78); **Heisman**—Oberlin (1892), Akron (1893), Oberlin (1894), Auburn (1895-99), Clemson (1900-03), Georgia Tech (1904-19), Penn (1920-22), Washington & Jefferson (1923), Rice (1924-27); **Holtz**—William & Mary (1969-71), N.C. State (1972-75), Arkansas (1977-83), Minnesota (1984-85), Notre Dame (1986—); **Jones**—Syracuse (1908), Yale (1909), Ohio St. (1910), Yale (1913), Iowa (1916-23), Duke (1924), USC (1925-40); **Kush**—Arizona St. (1958-79); **Leahy**—Boston College (1939- 40), Notre Dame (1941-43, 1946-53); **McGugin**—Vanderbilt (1904-17, 1919-34); **Moran**—Texas A&M (1909-14), Centre (1919-23), Bucknell (1924-26), Catawba (1930-33).

Neely—Rhodes (1924-27), Clemson (1931-39), Rice (1940-66); **Neyland**—Tennessee (1926-34, 1936-40, 1946-52); **Osborne**—Nebraska (1973—); **Paterno**—Penn St. (1966—); **Rockne**—Notre Dame (1918-30); **Royal**—Mississippi St. (1954-55), Washington (1956), Texas (1957-76); **Schembechler**—Miami-OH (1963-68), Michigan (1969-89); **Smith**—Penn (1909-12), Purdue (1913-15), California (1916-25); **Snavely**—Bucknell (1927-33), North Carolina (1934-35), Cornell (1936-44), North Carolina (1945-52), Washington-MO (1953-58); **Stagg**—Springfield College (1890-91), Chicago (1892-1932), Pacific (1933-46); **Sutherland**—Lafayette (1919-23), Pittsburgh (1924-38); **Sweeney**—Montana St. (1963-67), Washington St. (1968-75), Fresno St. (1976—); **Switzer**—Oklahoma (1973-88).

Thomas—Chattanooga (1925-28), Alabama (1931-42, 1944-46); **Vaught**—Mississippi (1947-70); **Wade**—Alabama (1923-30), Duke (1931-41, 1946-50); **Warner**—Georgia (1895-96), Cornell (1897-98), Carlisle (1899-1903), Cornell (1904-06), Carlisle (1907-13), Pittsburgh (1915-23), Stanford (1924-32), Temple (1933-38); **Wilkinson**—Oklahoma (1947-63); **Williams**—Army (1891), Minnesota (1900-21); **Woodruff**—Penn (1892-1901), Illinois (1903), Carlisle (1905); **Woodson**—Central Arkansas (1935-39), Hardin-Simmons (1941-42, 1946-51), Arizona (1952-56), New Mexico St. (1958-67), Trinity-TX (1972-73); **Yost**—Ohio Wesleyan (1897), Nebraska (1898), Kansas (1899), Stanford (1900), Michigan (1901-23, 1925-26).

Winningest Division I-A Coaches (Cont.)

All-Time Bowl Appearances

Active coaches in **bold** type.

		Overall			Big Four		
		App	W	L	T	W	L	T
1	Bear Bryant	29	15	12	2	12	8	0
2	**Joe Paterno**	24	15	8	1	6	4	0
3	Vince Dooley	20	8	10	2	3	5	0
	Tom Osborne	21	8	13	0	5	8	0
5	Johnny Vaught	18	10	8	0	6	4	0
6	**Lou Holtz**	18	10	6	2	5	3	0
	LaVell Edwards	18	5	12	1	0	0	0
	Bo Schembechler	17	5	12	0	2	10	0
9	**Bobby Bowden**	17	13	3	1	4	2	0
	Johnny Majors	16	9	7	0	4	0	0
	Darrell Royal	16	8	7	1	6	6	0
12	Don James	15	10	5	0	5	2	0
13	Bobby Dodd	13	9	4	0	6	1	0
	Barry Switzer	13	8	5	0	6	3	0
	Charlie McClendon	13	7	6	0	4	2	0
	Hayden Fry	14	5	8	1	0	4	0
17	**Terry Donahue**	12	8	3	1	4	1	0
	Earle Bruce	12	7	5	0	1	2	0
	Woody Hayes	12	6	6	0	5	5	0
	Shug Jordan	12	5	7	0	0	2	0

Active Coaches' Victories

Minimum 5 years in Division I-A.

		Yrs	W	L	T	Pct
1	Joe Paterno, Penn St.	28	257	69	3	786
2	Bobby Bowden, Fla.St	28	239	78	3	752
3	Tom Osborne, Nebraska	21	206	47	3	811
4	Hayden Fry, Iowa	32	200	153	9	565
5	LaVell Edwards, BYU	22	197	73	3	727
6	Lou Holtz, Notre Dame	24	193	84	6	693
7	Jim Sweeney, Fresno St	29	186	133	3	582
8	Johnny Majors, Pitt	26	176	113	10	605
9	Don Nehlen, West Va	23	156	91	8	627
	Bill Mallory, Indiana	24	156	108	4	590
11	Al Molde, Western Mich	23	152	87	8	632
12	Jim Wacker, Minnesota	23	150	107	3	583
13	Terry Donahue, UCLA	18	139	63	8	681
14	George Welsh, Virginia	21	135	102	4	568
15	John Cooper, Ohio St	17	126	63	6	662
16	Billy Brewer, Mississippi	20	124	95	6	564
17	Jackie Sherrill, Miss.St	16	122	61	4	663
18	Ken Hatfield, Rice	15	113	62	3	643
19	Herb Deromedi, Cent.Mich	16	110	55	10	657
20	Dick Tomey, Arizona	17	109	77	7	583

Note: The "Big Four" bowls are the Rose, Orange, Sugar and Cotton. Only three coaches—**Bill Alexander** of Georgia Tech (1920-44); **Bob Neyland** of Tennessee (1926-34,36-40,46-52); and **Frank Thomas** of Alabama (1931-42,44-46)—have taken teams to all four. Alexander and Thomas won three of the Big Four, Neyland two.

AFCA Coach of the Year

First presented in 1935 by the American Football Coaches Association.
Multiple winners: Joe Paterno (4), Bear Bryant (3), John McKay and Darrell Royal (2).

Year

1935 Pappy Waldorf, Northwestern
1936 Dick Harlow, Harvard
1937 Hooks Mylin, Lafayette
1938 Bill Kern, Carnegie Tech
1939 Eddie Anderson, Iowa
1940 Clark Shaughnessy, Stanford
1941 Frank Leahy, Notre Dame
1942 Bill Alexander, Georgia Tech
1943 Amos Alonzo Stagg, Pacific
1944 Carroll Widdoes, Ohio St.
1945 Bo McMillin, Indiana
1946 Red Blaik, Army
1947 Fritz Crisler, Michigan
1948 Bennie Oosterbaan, Michigan
1949 Bud Wilkinson, Oklahoma
1950 Charlie Caldwell, Princeton
1951 Chuck Taylor, Stanford
1952 Biggie Munn, Michigan St.
1953 Jim Tatum, Maryland
1954 Red Sanders, UCLA
1955 Duffy Daugherty, Michigan St.

1956 Bowden Wyatt, Tennessee
1957 Woody Hayes, Ohio St.
1958 Paul Dietzel, LSU
1959 Ben Schwartzwalder, Syracuse
1960 Murray Warmath, Minnesota
1961 Bear Bryant, Alabama
1962 John McKay, USC
1963 Darrell Royal, Texas
1964 Frank Broyles, Arkansas & Ara Parseghian, Notre Dame
1965 Tommy Prothro, UCLA
1966 Tom Cahill, Army
1967 John Pont, Indiana
1968 Joe Paterno, Penn St.
1969 Bo Schembechler, Michigan
1970 Charlie McClendon, LSU & Darrell Royal, Texas
1971 Bear Bryant, Alabama
1972 John McKay, USC
1973 Bear Bryant, Alabama
1974 Grant Teaff, Baylor

1975 Frank Kush, Arizona St.
1976 Johnny Majors, Pittsburgh
1977 Don James, Washington
1978 Joe Paterno, Penn St.
1979 Earle Bruce, Ohio St.
1980 Vince Dooley, Georgia
1981 Danny Ford, Clemson
1982 Joe Paterno, Penn St.
1983 Ken Hatfield, Air Force
1984 LaVell Edwards, BYU
1985 Fisher DeBerry, Air Force
1986 Joe Paterno, Penn St.
1987 Dick MacPherson, Syracuse
1988 Don Nehlen, West Virginia
1989 Bill McCartney, Colorado
1990 Bobby Ross, Georgia Tech
1991 Bill Lewis, East Carolina
1992 Gene Stallings, Alabama
1993 Barry Alvarez, Wisconsin

FWAA Coach of the Year

First presented in 1957 by the Football Writers Association of America. The FWAA and AFCA awards have both gone to the same coach in the same season 25 times. Those double winners are preceded by (#).
Multiple winners: Woody Hayes and Joe Paterno (3); Lou Holtz, Johnny Majors and John McKay (2).

Year

1957 #Woody Hayes, Ohio St.
1958 #Paul Dietzel, LSU
1959 #Ben Schwartzwalder, Syracuse
1960 #Murray Warmath, Minnesota
1961 Darrell Royal, Texas
1962 #John McKay, USC
1963 #Darrell Royal, Texas

1964 #Ara Parseghian, Notre Dame
1965 #Duffy Daugherty, Michigan St.
1966 #Tom Cahill, Army
1967 #John Pont, Indiana
1968 Woody Hayes, Ohio St.
1969 #Bo Schembechler, Michigan
1970 Alex Agase, Northwestern
1971 Bob Devaney, Nebraska

1972 #John McKay, USC
1973 Johnny Majors, Pitt
1974 #Grant Teaff, Baylor
1975 Woody Hayes, Ohio St.
1976 #Johnny Majors, Pitt
1977 Lou Holtz, Arkansas
1978 #Joe Paterno, Penn St.
1979 #Earle Bruce, Ohio St.

Year
1980 #Vince Dooley, Georgia
1981 #Danny Ford, Clemson
1982 #Joe Paterno, Penn St.
1983 Howard Schnellenberger, Miami-FL
1984 #LaVell Edwards, BYU

Year
1985 #Fisher DeBerry, Air Force
1986 #Joe Paterno, Penn St.
1987 #Dick MacPherson, Syracuse
1988 Lou Holtz, Notre Dame
1989 #Bill McCartney, Colorado

Year
1990 #Bobby Ross, Georgia Tech
1991 Don James, Washington
1992 #Gene Stallings, Alabama
1993 Terry Bowden, Auburn

Active Division I-AA Coaches

Minimum of 5 years as a Division I-A and/or Division I-AA through 1993 season.

Top 5 Winning Percentage

	Yrs	W	L	T	Pct
1 Roy Kidd, Eastern Ky	30	247	88	8	.731
2 Eddie Robinson, Gram	51	388	140	15	.728
3 Tubby Raymond, Del	28	232	92	2	.715
4 Jim Tressel, Yngstwn St	8	70	33	1	.678
5 Houston Markham, Ala. St	7	49	23	4	.671

Top 5 Victories

	Yrs	W	L	T	Pct
1 Eddie Robinson, Gram	51	388	140	15	.728
2 Roy Kidd, Eastern Ky	30	247	88	8	.731
3 Tubby Raymond, Del	28	232	92	2	.715
4 Carmen Cozza, Yale	29	169	99	5	.628
5 Ron Randleman, S.Hous.St	25	155	105	6	.594

Division I-AA Coach of the Year

First presented in 1983 by the American Football Coaches Association.
Multiple winners: Mark Duffner and Erk Russell (2).

Year
1983 Rey Dempsey, Southern Ill.
1984 Dave Arnold, Montana St.
1985 Dick Sheridan, Furman
1986 Erk Russell, Ga. Southern

Year
1987 Mark Duffner, Holy Cross
1988 Jimmy Satterfield, Furman
1989 Erk Russell, Ga. Southern
1990 Tim Stowers, Ga. Southern

Year
1991 Mark Duffner, Holy Cross
1992 Charlie Taafe, Citadel
1993 Dan Allen, Boston Univ.

NCAA Playoffs

The NCAA has decided its Division I-AA national championship with a postseason playoff since 1978. Divisions II and III have had national championship playoffs since 1973.

Division I-AA

Established in 1978 as a four-team playoff. Tournament field increased to eight teams in 1981, 12 teams in 1982 and 16 teams in 1986. Automatic berths have been awarded to champions of the Big Sky, Gateway, Ohio Valley, Southern, Southland and Yankee conferences since 1992.
Multiple winners: Georgia Southern (4); Eastern Kentucky and Youngstown St. (2).

Year	Winner	Score	Loser
1978	Florida A&M	35-28	Massachusetts
1979	Eastern Kentucky	30-7	Lehigh, PA
1980	Boise St., ID	31-29	Eastern Kentucky
1981	Idaho St.	34-23	Eastern Kentucky
1982	Eastern Kentucky	17-14	Delaware
1983	Southern Illinois	43-7	Western Carolina
1984	Montana St.	19-6	Louisiana Tech
1985	Georgia Southern	44-42	Furman, SC

Year	Winner	Score	Loser
1986	Georgia Southern	48-21	Arkansas St.
1987	NE Louisiana	43-42	Marshall, WV
1988	Furman, SC	17-12	Georgia Southern
1989	Georgia Southern	37-34	S.F. Austin St.
1990	Georgia Southern	36-13	Nevada-Reno
1991	Youngstown St.	25-17	Marshall
1992	Marshall	31-28	Youngstown St.
1993	Youngstown St.	17-5	Marshall

Division II

Established in 1973 as an eight-team playoff. Tournament field increased to 16 teams in 1988. From 1964-72, eight qualifying NCAA College Division member institutions competed in four regional bowl games, but there was no tournament and no national championship until 1973.
Multiple winners: North Dakota St. (5); Southwest Texas St. and Troy St. (2).

Year	Winner	Score	Loser
1973	Louisiana Tech	34-0	Western Kentucky
1974	Central Michigan	54-14	Delaware
1975	Northern Michigan	16-14	Western Kentucky
1976	Montana St.	24-13	Akron, OH
1977	Lehigh, PA	33-0	Jacksonville St., AL
1978	Eastern Illinois	10-9	Delaware
1979	Delaware	38-21	Youngstown St., OH
1980	Cal Poly-SLO	21-13	Eastern Illinois
1981	SW Texas St.	42-13	North Dakota St.
1982	SW Texas St.	34-9	UC-Davis
1983	North Dakota St.	41-21	Central St., OH

Year	Winner	Score	Loser
1984	Troy St., AL	18-17	North Dakota St.
1985	North Dakota St.	35-7	North Alabama
1986	North Dakota St.	27-7	South Dakota
1987	Troy St., AL	31-17	Portland St., OR
1988	North Dakota St.	35-21	Portland St., OR
1989	Mississippi Col.	3-0	Jacksonville St., AL
1990	North Dakota St.	51-11	Indiana, PA
1991	Pittsburg St., KS	23-6	Jacksonville St., AL
1992	Jacksonville St., AL	17-13	Pittsburg St., KS
1993	North Alabama	41-34	Indiana, PA

NCAA Playoffs (Cont.)

Division III

Established in 1973 as a four-team playoff. Tournament field increased to eight teams in 1975 and 16 teams in 1985. From 1969-72, four qualifying NCAA College Division member institutions competed in two regional bowl games, but there was no tournament and no national championship until 1973.

Multiple winners: Augustana (4); Ithaca (3); Dayton, Widener and Wittenberg (2).

Year	Winner	Score	Loser	Year	Winner	Score	Loser
1973	Wittenberg, OH	41-0	Juniata, PA	1984	Augustana, IL	21-12	Central, IA
1974	Central, IA	10-8	Ithaca, NY	1985	Augustana, IL	20-7	Ithaca, NY
1975	Wittenberg, OH	28-0	Ithaca, NY	1986	Augustana, IL	31-3	Salisbury St., MD
1976	St.John's, MN	31-28	Towson St., MD	1987	Wagner, NY	19-3	Dayton, OH
1977	Widener, PA	39-36	Wabash, IN	1988	Ithaca, NY	39-24	Central, IA
1978	Baldwin-Wallace	24-10	Wittenberg, OH	1989	Dayton, OH	17-7	Union, NY
1979	Ithaca, NY	14-10	Wittenberg, OH	1990	Allegheny, PA*	21-14	Lycoming, PA
1980	Dayton, OH	63-0	Ithaca, NY	1991	Ithaca, NY	34-20	Dayton, OH
1981	Widener, PA	17-10	Dayton, OH	1992	WI-La Crosse	16-12	Wash. & Jeff., PA
1982	West Georgia	14-0	Augustana, IL	1993	Mt. Union, OH	34-24	Rowan, NJ
1983	Augustana, IL	21-17	Union, NY		*Overtime		

NAIA Playoffs

The NAIA has held national championship playoffs in Division I since 1956 and Division II since 1970.

Division I

Established in 1956 as two-team playoff.Tournament field increased to four teams in 1958, eight teams in 1978 and 16 teams in 1987 before cutting back to eight teams in 1989. The title game has ended in a tie four times (1956, '64, '84 and '85).

Multiple winners: Texas A&I (7); Carson-Newman (5); Central Arkansas (3); Abilene Christian, Central St-OH, Central St-OK, Elon, Pittsburg St. and St. John's-MN (2).

Year	Winner	Score	Loser	Year	Winner	Score	Loser
1956	Montana St.	0-0	St. Joseph's, IN	1975	Texas A&I	37-0	Salem, WV
1957	Pittsburg St., KS	27-26	Hillsdale, MI	1976	Texas A&I	26-0	Central Arkansas
1958	NE Oklahoma	19-13	Northern Arizona	1977	Abilene Christian	24-7	SW Oklahoma
1959	Texas A&I	20-7	Lenoir-Rhyne, NC	1978	Angelo St., TX	24-14	Elon, NC
1960	Lenoir-Rhyne, NC	15-14	Humboldt St., CA	1979	Texas A&I	20-14	Central St., OK
1961	Pittsburg St., KS	12-7	Linfield, OR	1980	Elon, NC	17-10	NE Oklahoma
1962	Central St., OK	28-13	Lenoir-Rhyne, NC	1981	Elon, NC	3-0	Pittsburg St., KS
1963	St.John's, MN	33-27	Prairie View, TX	1982	Central St., OK	14-11	Mesa, CO
1964	Concordia, MN	7-7	Sam Houston, TX	1983	Car-Newman, TN	36-28	Mesa, CO
1965	St.John's, MN	33-0	Linfield, OR	1984	Car-Newman, TN	19-19	Central Arkansas
1966	Waynesburg, PA	42-21	WI-Whitewater	1985	Hillsdale, MI	10-10	Central Arkansas
1967	Fairmont St., WV	28-21	Eastern Wash.	1986	Car-Newman, TN	17-0	Cameron, OK
1968	Troy St., AL	43-35	Texas A&I	1987	Cameron, OK	30-2	Car-Newman, TN
1969	Texas A&I	32-7	Concordia, MN	1988	Car-Newman, TN	56-21	Adams St., CO
1970	Texas A&I	48-7	Wofford, SC	1989	Car-Newman, TN	34-20	Emporia St., KS
1971	Livingston, AL	14-12	Arkansas Tech	1990	Central St., OH	38-16	Mesa, CO
1972	East Texas St.	21-18	Car-Newman, TN	1991	Central Arkansas	19-16	Central St., OH
1973	Abilene Christian	42-14	Elon, NC	1992	Central St., OH	19-16	Gardner-Webb, NC
1974	Texas A&I	34-23	Henderson St., AR	1993	E. Central, OH	49-35	Glenville St., WV

Division II

Established in 1970 as four-team playoff. Tournament field increased to eight teams in 1978 and 16 teams in 1987. The title game has ended in a tie twice (1981 and '87). Multiple winners: Westminster (5); Linfield and Pacific Lutheran (3); Concordia-MN, Findlay, Northwestern-IA and Texas Lutheran (2).

Year	Winner	Score	Loser	Year	Winner	Score	Loser
1970	Westminster, PA	21-16	Anderson, IN	1983	Northwestern, IA	25-21	Pacific Lutheran
1971	Calif. Lutheran	30-14	Westminster, PA	1984	Linfield, OR	33-22	Northwestern, IA
1972	Missouri Southern	21-14	Northwestern, IA	1985	WI-La Crosse	24-7	Pacific Lutheran
1973	Northwestern, IA	10-3	Glenville St., WV	1986	Linfield, OR	17-0	Baker, KS
1974	Texas Lutheran	42-0	Missouri Valley	1987	Pacific Lutheran	16-16	WI-Stevens Pt.*
1975	Texas Lutheran	34-8	Calif.Lutheran	1988	Westminster, PA	21-14	WI-La Crosse
1976	Westminster, PA	20-13	Redlands, CA	1989	Westminster, PA	51-30	WI-La Crosse
1977	Westminster, PA	17-9	Calif.Lutheran	1990	Peru St., NE	17-7	Westminster, PA
1978	Concordia, MN	7-0	Findlay, OH	1991	Georgetown-KY	28-20	Pacific Lutheran
1979	Findlay, OH	51-6	Northwestern, IA	1992	Findlay, OH	26-13	Linfield, OR
1980	Pacific Lutheran	38-10	Wilmington, OH	1993	Pacific Lutheran	50-20	Westminster, PA
1981	Austin College, TX	24-24	Concordia, MN		*Wisconsin-Stevens Point forfeited its entire 1987 schedule due to		
1982	Linfield, OR	33-15	Wm. Jewell, MO		its use of an ineligible player.		

Dallas owner **Jerry Jones** (left) and head coach **Jimmy Johnson** are all smiles on Jan. 30 after their Cowboys beat Buffalo to repeat as Super Bowl champions.

PRO FOOTBALL

PRO FOOTBALL
by Vito Stellino

Saddle Sore

*Cowboys repeat as Super Bowl champs, but the cattle drive ends
for owner Jerry Jones and head coach Jimmy Johnson.*

The 1993 NFL season will be remembered as Jerry and Jimmy's last roundup.

Jerry Jones and Jimmy Johnson, the onetime college roommates at the University of Arkansas whose king-sized egos were ultimately too big to coexist even in a state as large as Texas, built the Dallas Cowboys from worst to first in just four seasons and then couldn't stop squabbling over which one of them deserved most of the credit.

The JJs finally went pfft just two months after the Cowboys beat the Buffalo Bills at the Georgia Dome on Jan. 30 to become the fifth franchise (along with Green Bay, Miami, Pittsburgh and San Francisco) to win back-to-back Super Bowls.

Their bizarre parting culminated a tumultuous year in which the Cowboys overcame a bitter holdout by running back Emmitt Smith, made peace with legendary first coach Tom Landry, weathered injuries to both Smith and quarterback Troy Aikman, and then routed the Bills, 30-13, to win their fourth Super Bowl in three decades.

The Jones-Johnson split upstaged an eventful year in pro football that saw the NFL negotiate a record $4.3 billion TV contract, implement a new collective bargaining agreement that brought the sport free agency tied to a salary cap, and

expand for the first time since 1976 by awarding franchises to Charlotte, N.C. and Jacksonville, Fla. (see sidebar).

Meanwhile, back at the ranch, the Cowboys' chances of becoming the first team to win three straight Super Bowls suffered a jolt when the 52-year-old owner and his 50-year-old coach agreed to go their separate ways.

Their long-simmering feud exploded on March 21 at the NFL owners meetings in Orlando, Fla., when Jones, annoyed after he felt he had been snubbed by Johnson and several former Dallas colleagues at a league party, told several reporters in a hotel bar that he was thinking of firing Johnson and hiring former Oklahoma coach (and Johnson rival) Barry Switzer.

When Jones' comments were relayed to Johnson, he confronted Jones and then stormed out of the meetings.

"I'm deeply hurt," Johnson said before leaving.

Actually, Johnson may have been more delighted than hurt because the incident gave him a chance to get out of the remaining five years of his 10-year, $1 million a year contract. He had long chafed at the way Jones meddled in football decisions and claimed credit for the team's success. But Johnson didn't want to quit because he wouldn't then be free to coach another team.

When Jones, who wanted a coach who would respect his football acumen, offered to release Johnson and provide a $2 million

Vito Stellino is the national pro football writer for *The Baltimore Sun* and has covered six Super Bowl championship seasons in Pittsburgh and Washington since 1974.

Wide World Photos

Two months after winning their second straight Super Bowl title, Dallas head coach **Jimmy Johnson** and owner **Jerry Jones** can manage only a handshake at the March 29 press conference announcing Johnson's decision to leave the team after five years of squabbling with Jones.

settlement, Johnson agreed to leave and exited after holding an amicable joint press conference with Jones on March 29. There were no bitter words from Johnson, who figures to be coaching again in 1995.

"We're going through a little transition here," Johnson told the assembled media. When reporters laughed, Johnson smiled and said, "Maybe it's a *big* transition, but, hey, the Cowboys will be right on top."

It will be the 55-year-old Switzer's job to keep them there. Named as Cowboys head coach the day after Johnson's departure, Switzer, who has never coached in the pros, emerged from the football wilderness five years after being forced out at Oklahoma when several of his players were charged with assault and drug offenses in 1989.

Switzer has the fourth best winning percentage (.837) of any coach in modern college history, rolling up three national titles and a record of 157-29-4 in 16 seasons with the Sooners. He is also an Arkansas grad (Class of '60) and was an assistant coach on the 1964 Razorbacks' national championship team that Jones and Johnson played on.

He will bring an energetic, gung-ho style to the job. At his introductory press conference on March 30, he practically oozed enthusiasm for the task at hand, shouting, "We've got a job to do and we're going to do it, bay-bee!"

While several Dallas players voiced their displeasure at the change in command, Aikman and Smith were quick to make the adjustment publicly.

Aikman, who was recruited by Switzer but transfered to UCLA in 1986, said Switzer was the best motivator he'd ever been around and added, "There's no reason why Barry can't be a great NFL head coach."

Smith called Switzer a "player's coach," but that came a few days after he said, "We could win without Jerry...I'm not certain we could win without Jimmy."

Ultimately, the NFL salary cap may determine how successful the Cowboys will be. Dallas lost six valuable players in the off-season, including Pro Bowl linebacker Ken Norton and defensive lineman Tony Casillas, but Jones sent a message after Johnson left that he wants to keep the nucleus together by re-signing fullback Daryl Johnston and guard Nate Newton.

The Cowboys also have Smith under contract for three more years and Aikman for the rest of the decade. Aikman, who signed a record eight-year, $50 million deal, is the league's highest paid player. Smith ended his holdout on Sept. 16 after agreeing to a four-year deal worth $13.6 million. The deal made him the league's highest paid running back until it was topped by the four-year, $17.2 million contract the Detroit Lions gave Barry Sanders.

At those prices, Smith was a bargain. Seldom has one player dominated a season the way Emmitt dominated the NFL in 1993. He didn't just lead the league in rushing for the third straight year, he gained his 1,486 yards playing two fewer games than everyone else. With Smith sitting out the first two games in his contract dispute with Jones, the Cowboys opened with consecutive losses to Washington (35-16) and Buffalo (13-10). With Smith back in uniform on Sept. 19 (eight carries for 45 yards against Phoenix), Dallas proceeded to win 15 of its next 17 games.

Aikman, who sat out three exhibition games after undergoing back surgery in June, then missed two regular season starts with a pulled hamstring and suffered a concussion in the NFC title game against San Francisco, saluted Smith when he said, "If you look at the first two games this year and how we did without him, that should say it all. I can't put into words what he means to us."

Smith's finest hour came in the final game of the regular season on the road against the New York Giants with the Eastern Division title on the line. Despite separating his left shoulder late in the second quarter, he rushed 32 times for 168 yards and caught 10 passes for 61 yards to lead the Cowboys to a dramatic 16-13 victory.

After the game, wide receiver Alvin Harper said, "In the huddle, you could see his eyes watering. I asked him how he felt and he said, 'Man, you don't want to know.' "

Smith was the unanimous choice as Most Valuable Player of the regular season and picked up Super Bowl MVP as well with 132 yards in 30 carries and two touchdowns. Dallas safety James Washington probably deserved the trip to Disney World more by virtue of making the game's three key plays— forcing a Thurman Thomas fumble, running another Thomas fumble back 46 yards for a touchdown and intercepting a Jim Kelly pass. But Washington had no complaints about Smith getting the honor. "If it wasn't for Emmitt," he said, "we wouldn't have been here in the first place."

While the Cowboys finished on top for the second straight season, the Bills suffered the frustration of losing the Super Bowl for a record fourth year in a row. They joined the Denver Broncos and Minnesota Vikings as the only four-time Super Bowl losers although neither the Broncos nor the Vikings lost four straight.

Bills coach Marv Levy joined Miami's Don Shula and former Vikings coach Bud Grant as the only losers of four Super Bowls. Not bad company. On Nov. 14, 1993, Shula won his 325th game to surpass George Halas as the NFL's all-time career victory leader. Grant was voted into the Hall of Fame on Jan. 30, 1994, along with five former players, including running backs Tony Dorsett and Leroy Kelly, tight end Jackie Smith, defensive tackle Randy White and defensive back Jimmy Johnson (no relation to the ex-Cowboys coach).

Thomas, the hard luck Buffalo running back, had another nightmarish Super Bowl gaining only 37 yards and fumbling twice to set up 10 Dallas points. After gaining 135 yards in his first Super Bowl against the Giants in 1991, he has rushed for only 13, 19 and 37 yards in the last three.

"Why did I pick this time to have one of my worst games?" Thomas said afterward. Forgotten in this latest Super defeat was the fact that Thomas led the AFC in rushing (1,315 yards) for the third time in four years.

The playoffs had a familiar look as eight of 1992's 12 postseason teams returned. Two of the newcomers, the Giants and Detroit Lions, had the best turnarounds of the year. New York went from 6-10 to 11-5 and the Lions rebounded from 5-11 to 10-6. Giants coach Dan Reeves, who was fired by the Broncos after the 1992 season for not getting on with owner Pat Bowlen and quarterback John Elway, was vindicated by winning Coach of the Year honors. Back in Denver, Elway led the AFC in passing and returned to the playoffs under new coach Wade Phillips.

Jonathan Daniel/Allsport

Dallas running back **Emmitt Smith** began the season as a holdout and ended it as the Most Valuable Player of the regular season and the Super Bowl.

Steve Young, who led all NFL quarterbacks with a 101.5 passing rating, guided the 49ers to a lackluster (for them) 10-6 record. The Niners ended the Giants season in the second round of the playoffs as running back Ricky Watters scored five times to key a 44-3 victory. The next week, San Francisco fell in the NFC title game for the third time in four years, losing to the Cowboys, 38-21. It was George Seifert's worst loss in five years as a head coach.

The other two playoff newcomers were the Green Bay Packers, who posted a 9-7 record for the second straight year, and the Los Angeles Raiders, who went from 7-9 to 10-6. The Packers were led by defensive end Reggie White, the league's richest free agent ($4.25 million a year) and wide receiver Sterling Sharpe, who caught a single season-record 112 passes.

The Kansas City Chiefs (11-5) improved by only one game, but were one of the most talked about teams in the league after trad-

ing for four-time Super Bowl winner Joe Montana and signing former Super Bowl MVP Marcus Allen as a free agent.

Although Montana had the AFC's second highest quarterback rating, he was sidelined for five games with injuries and played in only 38 of 64 regular season quarters. Nevertheless, he led the Chiefs to the AFC title game where he was knocked out with a concussion in the third period of a 20-6 loss to Buffalo. Allen also earned his keep, rushing for 764 yards on 206 carries and scoring 12 touchdowns.

The Indianapolis Colts and Washington Redskins, took the year's biggest steps backward— both slipping from 9-7 to 4-12. The Colts kept head coach Ted Marchibroda and fired general manager (and owner's son) Jim Irsay, while the Redskins fired first-year coach Richie Petitbon and retained GM Charley Casserly.

Meanwhile, Phoenix owner Bill Bidwill reacted to the Cardinals' ninth straight losing season by firing both GM Larry Wilson and coach Joe Bugel and hiring 59-year-old Buddy Ryan to take both jobs. Bidwill also clinched alphabetical first place in the NFC East by changing his club's name to the *Arizona* Cardinals.

The feisty Ryan's return to the head coaching ranks came three years after his dismissal in Philadelphia and four weeks after he traded punches with fellow Houston assistant coach Kevin Gilbride. The exchange took place during the Oilers' 24-0 drubbing of the New York Jets in the regular season finale.

Houston's roller coaster ride through the 1993 campaign also included starting out 1-4 and losing defensive lineman Jeff Alm when he committed suicide on Dec. 14 after accidently killing a friend in a car crash. Management struck by head coach Jack Pardee and the team responded by winning its last 11 in a row before losing to Kansas City in the first round of the playoffs.

Elsewhere, Cowboys assistant Norv Turner took the Washington job, the Jets fired Bruce Coslet and promoted defensive coordinator Pete Carroll, and Atlanta fired Jerry Glanville and promoted offensive coordinator June Jones.

While Emmitt Smith was the named MVP by the Associated Press, AP's Offensive and Defensive Players of the Year were San Francisco wide receiver Jerry Rice and cornerback Rod Woodson of Pittsburgh. Rice caught 98 passes for 1,503 yards— an NFL-record eighth straight season of 1,000 yards or more. He also led the NFL in touchdowns with 16 to boost his career total to 124, two shy of Jim Brown's all-time mark. As for Woodson, even though quarterbacks were reluctant to throw in his direction, he intercepted eight passes and was regarded the best cover corner in the league.

The consensus Rookie of the Year was running back Jerome Bettis of the Los Angeles Rams, who ran for 1,429 yards on 294 carries and scored seven touchdowns. Other top first year players included San Francisco defensive tackle Dana Stubblefield and Bettis' former Notre Dame teammate, quarterback Rick Mirer of Seattle.

An even more celebrated Golden Domer in his first NFL season was Raghib (Rocket) Ismail, who passed up the 1991 NFL Draft for greater riches with the Toronto Argonauts of the Canadian Football League. Migrating south of the border after two seasons, Ismail suited up for the L.A. Raiders and the led the AFC in kickoff returns with a 24.2 average. His brother Qadry, a rookie with Minnesota, had the seventh best kickoff return average (21.5) in the NFC.

Speaking of brothers, the Sharpes— Sterling of Green Bay and Shannon of Denver— both made All-Pro. Sterling led the NFC in receptions for the third time in five years, even though he wasn't able to practice after Nov. 7 because of a turf toe. Shannon was third among AFC pass catchers with 81.

Injuries sidelined two of the game's best quarterbacks— Dan Marino of Miami and Randall Cunningham of Philadelphia. Cunningham broke his left leg in the fourth game and Marino snapped his right Achilles tendon in the fifth week. Both their teams missed the playoffs without them. Another big name quarterback, Bernie Kosar, lost his job when Cleveland coach Bill Belichick waived him after nine seasons on Nov. 8, 1993. Kosar signed on with Dallas two days later and got a Super Bowl ring as Aikman's backup.

Four of the best players of the 1980s, linebackers Lawrence Taylor and Andre Tippett, defensive end Howie Long and run-

Fox Network's NFL Invasion Costs Plenty

In a year that witnessed the arrival of a salary cap in the NFL, who do you suppose was the most sought after and, once signed, highest paid individual in pro football?

Hint: he's making nearly $2 million more than Troy Aikman.

Give up?

BOOM! TV analyst John Madden, who will make $8 million a year analyzing NFC games at the Fox Network for the next four years.

The Fox network?

Desperate to establish its string of 139 affiliated stations as the country's fourth major TV network, Fox came out of nowhere on Dec. 17, 1993, to blindside CBS and run off with the NFC package for a staggering $1.58 billion (with a B). That comes to $395 million a year for four years, a jump of 49% over the annual $265 million CBS paid from 1990-93 (see "Business & Media" chapter).

"This changes a lot; it makes us a network in the real sense of the word," Fox chairman Rupert Murdoch told The Wall Street Journal. "It is all part of a long-term term strategy. You can have 500 channels, but no one will have this but Fox."

Fox's raid on the NFL hen house followed two years of complaints by the other networks that they were losing money on their existing contracts and wanted to negotiate lower fees the next time around. NFL owners, led by TV Committee member Jerry Jones of the Dallas Cowboys, would have none of it.

"The incumbents were focusing on their expenses over the last contract," said Jones. "Fox was addressing how things are going to be in the media over the next five to 10 years."

The key to the deal was that Fox was willing to lose more than $100 million a year, if necessary, to promote itself. Their original plan was to bid either $210 million for the AFC package or $300 million for the NFC. When NBC offered $217 million a year to keep the AFC, Fox made a preemptive strike of $395 million a year for the NFC package.

CBS, which couldn't justify keeping the NFC at that price, dropped out and made a bid $250 million a year for the AFC. Despite their 38 continuous years together, the NFL turned

Wide World Photos

Former CBS analyst **John Madden** became pro football's highest-paid performer on Jan. 24, when he signed a four-year, $32 million deal with the Fox network. Fox intercepted the broadcast rights to NFC games for a staggering $1.58 billion, ending a CBS-NFL partnership that dated back to 1957.

CBS down saying it had a gentlemen's agreement to accept the lower NBC offer.

The infusion of TV money means more income for the players, who get 64 percent of the designated gross revenue this year under the salary cap. Each team can spend $34.6 million on player salaries this year. Six days after the Fox deal was announced, Dallas owner Jones made Aikman the league's highest-paid player ever with a eight-year contract worth $50 million. The pact included an $11 million signing bonus and base salaries that escalate to $7.5 million in the year 2000.

Back in 1989, Jones bought the Cowboys for $65 million and ponied up another $75 million for Texas Stadium. Five years and two Super Bowls later, his franchise is worth $190 million (according to *Financial World* magazine) and his quarterback alone is worth $50 million.

By contrast, on Sept. 16, 1993 — three months before the new TV contracts with Fox, NBC, ESPN and TNT were negotiated for an overall $4.3 billion — Dallas running back and league MVP Emmitt Smith had to sit out two games to get a four-year deal worth a total of $13.6 million.

Smith's reign as the NFL's highest-paid running back ended on Dec. 22, 1993, when the Detroit Lions inked Barry Sanders for four years and $17.2 million.

But as salaries escalate with free agency, many teams had problems staying under the cap. The result was that several teams had to cut veterans with big salaries to make room under the cap to sign free agents.

Meanwhile, the 28 current teams are getting a $280 million windfall from the two new expansion teams, the Carolina Panthers of Charlotte, N.C., and Jacksonville (Fla.) Jaguars, that they won't have to share with the players.

Carolina and Jacksonville each paid $140 million to get into the league although their actual cost will be closer to $200 million. That's because each will pay about $17 million in interest while getting only half a share of the TV revenue for the first three seasons they field teams starting in 1995.

The expansion fees raised the worth of existing franchises as Boston businessman Bob Kraft paid $170 million to buy the New England Patriots, Hollywood producer Jeffrey Lurie paid $185 million for the Philadephia Eagles, and Wayne Huizenga, who already owned 15 percent of the Miami Dolphins, paid $138 million for the remaining 85 per cent of the team.

Former Super Bowl heroes **Marcus Allen** and **Joe Montana** helped lead Kansas City to a division title, but they could only get as far as the AFC title game where the Chiefs were stopped 30-13, by four-time conference champion Buffalo.

ning back Eric Dickerson, all retired. Taylor got an emotional farewell at the Meadowlands as New York Giants fans chanted "LT, LT, LT..." during his final home game. Dickerson was unceremoniously waived by Atlanta early in the season after rushing for just 91 yards in 26 carries. Long and Tippett announced their retirements after the season ended. The quartet made All-Pro a combined 18 times from 1981-89, led by Taylor's eight selections.

Taylor's old coach, Bill Parcells, who retired after the Giants' second Super Bowl-winning season in 1990, resurfaced in New England to rebuild a Patriots team that had won only nine games in the 90's. With overall No. 1 draft pick Drew Bledsoe at quarterback, the Pats lost 11 of their first 12 games, then kicked into gear and won their last four in a row to finish at 5-11 (a three-game improvement).

In an attempt to put more touchdowns on the scoreboard— 24 per cent of the points were accounted by field goals last year— the owners approved a package of rule changes to help the offense in 1994, including the two-point conversion.

There's evidence that the fans aren't concerned about all the field goals. For the fifth straight year, the NFL total paid attendance reached a record level. The NFL attracted a total of 17,951,831 fans for all games and 13,966,843 for 224 regular season games — an average of 62,352 per game.

Pro football is so popular in the U.S. that the Canadian Football League has decided to win over American fans. The CFL's first American-based team, the Sacramento Gold Miners, finished 6-12 in its inaugural 1993 season. Three more teams from the States— the Las Vegas Posse, Baltimore "CFL Colts" and Shreveport (La.) Pirates— began league play in July.

The CFL has ambitious plans to add five more U.S. teams and one Montreal franchise by 1998. The 18-member league would then divide into separate nine-team Canadian and American conferences.

The 1993 Grey Cup was played Nov. 28 in Calgary where the Edmonton Eskimos beat the Winnipeg Blue Bombers, 33-23, as Sean Fleming kicked six field goals. The Eskimos quarterback Damon Allen, the brother of Marcus Allen, was the game's MVP. The regular season MVP for the third straight season was former USFL and NFL quarterback and Heisman Trophy winner Doug Flutie of Calgary. ❑

PRO FOOTBALL
STATISTICS
THE SEASON IN REVIEW
1993-1994
STANDINGS • PLAYOFFS • DRAFT

SEC **A**
PAGE **217**

THE 1995 INFORMATION PLEASE SPORTS ALMANAC

Final NFL Standings

Division champions (*) and Wild Card playoff qualifiers (†) are noted; division champions with two best records received first round byes. Number of seasons listed after each head coach refers to latest tenure with club through 1993 season.

American Football Conference
Eastern Division

	W	L	T	PF	PA	vs Div	vs AFC
*Buffalo	12	4	0	329	242	7-1-0	8-4-0
Miami	9	7	0	349	351	4-4-0	6-6-0
NY Jets	8	8	0	270	247	5-3-0	6-6-0
New England	5	11	0	238	286	2-6-0	4-10-0
Indianapolis	4	12	0	189	378	2-6-0	4-8-0

1993 Head coaches: Buf— Marv Levy (8th season); **Mia**— Don Shula (24th); **NY**— Bruce Coslet (4th); **NE**— Bill Parcells (1st); **Ind**— Ted Marchibroda (2nd).
1992 Standings: 1. Miami (11-5); 2. Buffalo (11-5); 3. Indianapolis (9-7); 4. NY Jets (4-12); 5. New England (2-14).

Central Division

	W	L	T	PF	PA	vs Div	vs AFC
*Houston	12	4	0	368	238	6-0-0	10-2-0
†Pittsburgh	9	7	0	308	281	3-3-0	7-5-0
Cleveland	7	9	0	304	307	3-3-0	4-8-0
Cincinnati	3	13	0	187	319	0-6-0	1-11-0

1993 Head coaches: Hou— Jack Pardee (4th season); **Pit**— Bill Cowher (2nd); **Cle**— Bill Belichick (3rd); **Cin**— David Shula (2nd).
1992 Standings: 1. Pittsburgh (11-5); 2. Houston (10-6); 3. Cleveland (7-9); 4. Cincinnati (5-11).

Western Division

	W	L	T	PF	PA	vs Div	vs AFC
*Kansas City	11	5	0	328	291	7-1-0	9-3-0
†LA Raiders	10	6	0	306	326	5-3-0	7-5-0
†Denver	9	7	0	373	284	4-4-0	8-4-0
San Diego	8	8	0	322	290	3-5-0	6-6-0
Seattle	6	10	0	280	314	1-7-0	6-8-0

1993 Head coaches: KC— Marty Schottenheimer (5th season); **LA**— Art Shell (5th); **Den**— Wade Phillips (1st); **SD**— Bobby Ross (2nd); **Sea**— Tom Flores (2nd).
1992 Standings: 1. San Diego (11-5); 2. Kansas City (10-6); 3. Denver (8-8); 4. LA Raiders (7-9); 5. Seattle (2-14).

National Football Conference
Eastern Division

	W	L	T	PF	PA	vs Div	vs NFC
*Dallas	12	4	0	376	229	7-1-0	10-2-0
†NY Giants	11	5	0	288	205	5-3-0	9-3-0
Philadelphia	8	8	0	293	315	3-5-0	6-6-0
Phoenix	7	9	0	326	269	4-4-0	6-8-0
Washington	4	12	0	230	345	1-7-0	3-9-0

1993 Head coaches: Dal— Jimmy Johnson (5th season); **NY**— Dan Reeves (1st); **Phi**— Rich Kotite (3rd); **Pho**— Joe Bugel (4th); **Wash**— Richie Petitbon (1st).
1992 Standings: 1. Dallas (13-3); 2. Philadelphia (11-5); 3. Washington (9-7); 4. NY Giants (6-10); 5. Phoenix (4-12).

Central Division

	W	L	T	PF	PA	vs Div	vs NFC
*Detroit	10	6	0	298	292	4-4-0	8-6-0
†Minnesota	9	7	0	277	290	6-2-0	7-5-0
†Green Bay	9	7	0	340	282	4-4-0	6-6-0
Chicago	7	9	0	234	230	3-5-0	5-7-0
Tampa Bay	5	11	0	237	376	3-5-0	4-8-0

1993 Head Coaches: Det— Wayne Fontes (6th season); **Min**— Dennis Green (2nd); **GB**— Mike Holmgren (2nd); **Chi**— Dave Wannstedt (1st); **TB**— Sam Wyche (2nd).
1992 Standings: 1. Minnesota (11-5); 2. Green Bay (9-7); 3. Tampa Bay (5-11); 4. Chicago (5-11); 5. Detroit (5-11).

Western Division

	W	L	T	PF	PA	vs Div	vs NFC
*San Francisco	10	6	0	473	297	4-2-0	8-4-0
New Orleans	8	8	0	317	343	3-3-0	6-6-0
Atlanta	6	10	0	316	385	4-2-0	5-7-0
LA Rams	5	11	0	221	367	1-5-0	3-9-0

1992 Head Coaches: SF— George Seifert (5th season); **NO**— Jim Mora (8th); **Atl**— Jerry Glanville (4th); **LA**— Chuck Knox (2nd).
1992 Standings: 1. San Francisco (14-2); 2. New Orleans (12-4); 3. Atlanta (6-10); 4. LA Rams (6-10).

Playoff Tiebreakers
Wild Card Berth

AFC: Denver (9-7) and Pittsburgh (9-7) qualified over Miami (9-7) with better conference records (the Broncos were 8-4, the Steelers were 7-5 and the Dolphins were 6-6).

NFL Regular Season Individual Leaders

(* indicates rookies)

Passing Efficiency

(Minimum of 224 attempts)

AFC	Att	Cmp	Cmp Pct	Yds	Avg Gain	TD	Long	Int	Sack	Yds Lost	Rating
John Elway, Den	551	348	63.2	4030	7.31	25	63	10	39	293	92.8
Joe Montana, KC	298	181	60.7	2144	7.19	13	50-td	7	12	61	87.4
Vinny Testaverde, Cle	230	130	56.5	1797	7.81	14	62-td	9	17	101	85.7
Boomer Esiason, NY	473	288	60.9	3421	7.23	16	77	11	18	139	84.5
Scott Mitchell, Mia	233	133	57.1	1773	7.61	12	77-td	8	7	49	84.2
Jeff Hostetler, LA	419	236	56.3	3242	7.74	14	74-td	10	38	206	82.5
Jim Kelly, Buf	470	288	61.3	3382	7.20	18	65-td	18	25	171	79.9
Neil O'Donnell, Pit	486	270	55.6	3208	6.60	14	71-td	7	41	331	79.5
Jeff George, Ind	407	234	57.5	2526	6.21	8	72-td	6	26	190	76.3
Steve DeBerg, TB-Mia	227	136	59.9	1707	7.52	7	47	10	18	143	75.3
Warren Moon, Hou	520	303	58.3	3485	6.70	21	80-td	21	34	218	75.2
John Friesz, SD	238	128	53.8	1402	5.89	6	66-td	4	14	98	72.8
Stan Humphries, SD	324	173	53.4	1981	6.11	12	48-td	10	18	142	71.5
Rick Mirer*, Sea	486	274	56.4	2833	5.83	12	53-td	17	47	235	67.0
David Klingler, Cin	343	190	55.4	1935	5.64	6	51	9	40	202	66.6
Drew Bledsoe*, NE	429	214	49.9	2494	5.81	15	54-td	15	16	99	65.0

NFC	Att	Cmp	Cmp Pct	Yds	Avg Gain	TD	Long	Int	Sack	Yds Lost	Rating
Steve Young, SF	462	314	68.0	4023	8.71	29	80-td	16	31	160	101.5
Troy Aikman, Dal	392	271	69.1	3100	7.91	15	80-td	6	26	153	99.0
Phil Simms, NY	400	247	61.8	3038	7.60	15	62	9	37	217	88.3
Bubby Brister, Phi	309	181	58.6	1905	6.17	14	58	5	19	148	84.9
Bobby Hebert, Atl	430	263	61.2	2978	6.93	24	98-td	17	29	190	84.0
Steve Beuerlein, Pho	418	258	61.7	3164	7.57	18	65-td	17	29	206	82.5
Jim McMahon, Min	331	200	60.4	1967	5.94	9	58	8	23	104	76.2
Brett Favre, GB	522	318	60.9	3303	6.33	19	66-td	24	30	199	72.2
Jim Harbaugh, Chi	325	200	61.5	2002	6.16	7	48	11	43	210	72.1
Wade Wilson, NO	388	221	57.0	2457	6.33	12	42-td	15	37	225	70.1
Rodney Peete, Det	252	157	62.3	1670	6.63	6	93-td	14	34	174	66.4
Craig Erickson, TB	457	233	51.0	3054	6.68	18	67-td	21	35	236	66.4
Jim Everett, LA	274	135	49.3	1652	6.03	8	60-td	12	18	125	59.7
Mark Rypien, Wash	319	166	52.0	1514	4.75	4	43	10	16	87	56.3

Receptions

AFC	No	Yds	Avg	Long	TD
Reggie Langhorne, Ind	85	1038	12.2	72-td	3
Anthony Miller, SD	84	1162	13.8	66-td	7
Shannon Sharpe, Den	81	995	12.3	63	9
Tim Brown, LA	80	1180	14.8	71-td	7
Brian Blades, Sea	80	945	11.8	41	3
Webster Slaughter, Hou	77	904	11.7	41	5
Terry Kirby*, Mia	75	874	11.7	47	3
Ronnie Harmon, SD	73	671	9.2	37	2
Ernest Givins, Hou	68	887	13.0	80-td	4
Pete Metzelaars, Buf	68	609	9.0	51	4
Johnny Johnson, NY	67	641	9.6	48	1
Haywood Jeffires, Hou	66	753	11.4	66-td	6

NFC	No	Yds	Avg	Long	TD
Sterling Sharpe, GB	112	1274	11.4	54	11
Jerry Rice, SF	98	1503	15.3	80-td	15
Michael Irvin, Dal	88	1330	15.1	61-td	7
Andre Rison, Atl	86	1242	14.4	53-td	15
Cris Carter, Min	86	1071	12.5	58	9
Herschel Walker, Phi	75	610	8.1	55	3
Mike Pritchard, Atl	74	736	9.9	34	7
Michael Haynes, Atl	72	778	10.8	98-td	4
Brent Jones, SF	68	735	10.8	29	3
Eric Martin, NO	66	950	14.4	54-td	3
Larry Centers, Pho	66	603	9.1	29	3
Ricky Proehl, Pho	65	877	13.5	51-td	7

Rushing

AFC	Car	Yds	Avg	Long	TD
Thurman Thomas, Buf	355	1315	3.7	27	6
Leonard Russell, NE	300	1088	3.6	21	7
Chris Warren, Sea	273	1072	3.9	45-td	7
Gary Brown, Hou	195	1002	5.1	26	6
Johnny Johnson, NY	198	821	4.1	57-td	3
Rod Bernstine, Den	223	816	3.7	24	4
Marcus Allen, KC	206	764	3.7	39	12
Leroy Thompson, Pit	205	763	3.7	36	3
Marion Butts, SD	185	746	4.0	27	4
Barry Foster, Pit	177	711	4.0	38	8
Roosevelt Potts*, Ind	179	711	4.0	34	0
Mark Higgs, Mia	186	693	3.7	31	3

NFC	Car	Yds	Avg	Long	TD
Emmitt Smith, Dal	283	1486	5.3	62-td	9
Jerome Bettis*, LA	294	1429	4.9	71-td	7
Erric Pegram, Atl	292	1185	4.1	29	3
Barry Sanders, Det	243	1115	4.6	42	3
Rodney Hampton, NY	292	1077	3.7	20	5
Reggie Brooks*, Wash	223	1063	4.8	85-td	3
Ron Moore*, Pho	263	1018	3.9	20	9
Ricky Watters, SF	208	950	4.6	39	10
Herschel Walker, Phi	174	746	4.3	35	1
Derek Brown*, NO	180	705	3.9	60	2
Reggie Cobb, TB	221	658	3.0	16	3
Darrell Thompson, GB	169	654	3.9	60-td	3

San Francisco 49ers
Steve Young
Passing Efficiency

Green Bay Packers
Sterling Sharpe
Receptions

Dallas Cowboys
Emmitt Smith
Rushing

San Francisco 49ers
Jerry Rice
Touchdowns

All-Purpose Running

AFC	Rush	Rec	Ret	Total	NFC	Rush	Rec	Ret	Total
Eric Metcalf, Cle	611	539	782	1932	Emmitt Smith, Dal	1486	414	0	1900
Thurman Thomas, Buf	1315	387	0	1702	Jerome Bettis*, LA	1429	244	0	1673
Tim Brown, LA	7	1180	465	1652	Jerry Rice, SF	69	1503	0	1572
Johnny Johnson, NY	821	641	0	1462	Erric Pegram, Atl	1185	302	63	1550
Terry Kirby*, Mia	390	874	85	1349	Herschel Walker, Phi	746	610	184	1540
Leonard Russell, NE	1088	245	0	1333	Johnny Bailey, Pho	253	243	981	1477
Clarence Verdin, Ind	33	20	1223	1276	David Meggett, NY	329	319	734	1382
Gary Brown, Hou	1002	240	29	1271	Michael Irvin, Dal	6	1330	0	1336
O.J. McDuffie*, Mia	—4	197	1072	1265	Barry Sanders, Det	1115	205	0	1320
Anthony Miller, SD	0	1162	42	1204	Rodney Hampton, NY	1077	210	0	1287
Rod Bernstine, Den	816	372	0	1188	Sterling Sharpe, GB	8	1274	0	1282
Chris Warren, Sea	1072	99	0	1171	Ricky Watters, SF	950	326	0	1276

Note: Returns (Ret) includes kickoffs, punts, fumbles and interceptions returned.

Scoring

Kickers

AFC	PAT	FG	Long	Pts
Jeff Jaeger, LA	27/29	35/44	53	132
Al Del Greco, Hou	39/40	29/34	52	126
John Carney, SD	31/33	31/40	51	124
Jason Elam*, Den	41/42	26/35	54	119
Gary Anderson, Pit	32/32	28/30	46	116
Pete Stoyanovich, Mia	37/37	24/32	52	109
Nick Lowery, KC	37/37	23/29	52	106
Steve Christie, Buf	36/37	23/32	59	105
John Kasay, Sea	29/29	23/28	55	98
Dean Biasucci, Ind	15/16	26/31	53	93
Doug Pelfrey*, Cin	13/16	24/31	53	85
Matt Stover, Cle	36/36	16/22	53	84
Cary Blanchard, NY	31/31	17/26	45	82

NFC	PAT	FG	Long	Pts
Jason Hanson, Det	28/28	34/43	53	130
Chris Jacke, GB	35/35	31/37	54	128
Eddie Murray, Dal	38/38	28/33	52	122
Morten Andersen, NO	33/33	28/35	56	117
Norm Johnson, Atl	34/34	26/27	54	112
Mike Cofer, SF	59/61	16/26	46	107
Fuad Reveiz, Min	27/28	26/35	51	105
David Treadwell, NY	28/29	25/31	46	103
Kevin Butler, Chi	21/22	27/36	55	102
Greg Davis, Pho	37/37	21/28	55	100
Michael Husted, TB	27/27	16/22	57	75
Chip Lohmiller, Wash	24/26	16/28	51	72
Tony Zendejas, LA	23/25	16/23	54	71

Touchdowns

AFC	TD	Rush	Rec	Ret	Pts
Marcus Allen, KC	15	12	3	0	90
Barry Foster, Pit	9	8	1	0	54
Shannon Sharpe, Den	9	0	9	0	54
Gary Brown, Hou	8	6	2	0	48
Tim Brown, LA	8	0	7	1	48
Ben Coates, NE	8	0	8	0	48
Robert Delpino, Den	8	8	0	0	48
Michael Jackson, Cle	8	0	8	0	48
Natrone Means*, SD	8	8	0	0	48
Brad Baxter, NY	7	7	0	0	42
Willie Davis, KC	7	0	7	0	42
Anthony Miller, SD	7	0	7	0	42
Leonard Russell, NE	7	7	0	0	42
Chris Warren, Sea	7	7	0	0	42

NFC	TD	Rush	Rec	Ret	Pts
Jerry Rice, SF	16	1	15	0	96
Andre Rison, Atl	15	0	15	0	90
Sterling Sharpe, GB	11	0	11	0	66
Ricky Watters, SF	11	10	1	0	66
Edgar Bennett, GB	10	9	1	0	60
Emmitt Smith, Dal	10	9	1	0	60
Calvin Williams, Phi	10	0	10	0	60
Cris Carter, Min	9	0	9	0	54
Ron Moore*, Pho	9	9	0	0	54
Jerome Bettis*, LA	7	7	0	0	42
Michael Irvin, Dal	7	0	7	0	42
Marc Logan, SF	7	7	0	0	42
Mike Pritchard, Atl	7	0	7	0	42
Ricky Proehl, Pho	7	0	7	0	42

NFL Regular Season Individual Leaders (Cont.)

Interceptions

AFC	No	Yds	Long	TD
Eugene Robinson, Sea	9	80	28	0
Nate Odomes, Buf	9	65	25	0
Rod Woodson, Pit	8	138	63-td	1
Marcus Robertson, Hou	7	137	69	0
Darren Carrington, SD	7	104	28	0

NFC	No	Yds	Long	TD
Deion Sanders, Atl	7	91	41	0
Eric Allen, Phi	6	201	94-td	4
LeRoy Butler, GB	6	131	39	0
Kevin Smith, Dal	6	56	32-td	1
Tom Carter*, Wash	6	54	29	0

Sacks

AFC	No
Neil Smith, Kansas City	15
Simon Fletcher, Denver	13½
Bruce Smith, Buffalo	13½
Sean Jones, Houston	13
Kevin Greene, Pittsburgh	12½
Anthony Smith, LA Raiders	12½

NFC	No
Renaldo Turnbull, New Orleans	13
Reggie White, Green Bay	13
Richard Dent, Chicago	12½
Chris Doleman, Minnesota	12½
John Randle, Minnesota	12½

Punting

AFC	No	Yds	Long	Avg	In 20
Greg Montgomery, Hou	54	2462	77	45.6	13
Tom Rouen, Den	67	3017	62	45.0	17
Rick Tuten, Sea	90	4007	64	44.5	21
Brian Hansen, Cle	82	3632	72	44.3	15
Lee Johnson, Cin	90	3954	60	43.9	24

NFC	No	Yds	Long	Avg	In 20
Jim Arnold, Det	72	3207	68	44.5	15
Reggie Roby, Wash	78	3447	60	44.2	15
Rich Camarillo, Pho	73	3189	61	43.7	23
Tommy Barnhardt, NO	77	3356	58	43.6	26
Harold Alexander*, Atl	72	3114	75	43.3	21

Punt Returns

AFC	No	Yds	Avg	Long	TD
Eric Metcalf, Cle	36	464	12.9	91-td	2
Darrien Gordon*, SD	31	395	12.7	54	0
Tim Brown, LA	40	465	11.6	74-td	1
O.J. McDuffie*, Mia	28	317	11.3	72-td	2
Glyn Milburn*, Den	40	425	10.6	54	0

NFC	No	Yds	Avg	Long	TD
Tyrone Hughes*, NO	37	503	13.6	83-td	2
Dexter Carter, SF	34	411	12.1	72-td	1
Kevin Williams*, Dal	36	381	10.6	64-td	2
David Meggett, NY	32	331	10.3	75-td	1
Mel Gray, Det	23	197	8.6	35	0

Kickoff Returns

AFC	No	Yds	Avg	Long	TD
Rocket Ismail, LA	25	605	24.2	66	0
O.J. McDuffie*, Mia	32	755	23.6	48	0
Eric Ball, Cin	23	501	21.8	45	0
Clarence Verdin, Ind	50	1050	21.0	38	0
Ray Crittenden, NE	23	478	20.8	44	0

NFC	No	Yds	Avg	Long	TD
Robert Brooks, GB	23	611	26.6	95-td	1
Tyrone Hughes*, NO	30	753	25.1	99-td	1
Tony Smith, Atl	38	948	24.9	97-td	1
Mel Gray, Det	28	688	24.6	95-td	1
Johnny Bailey, Pho	31	699	22.5	48	0

Single Game Highs

(*) indicates overtime game.

Passing

AFC	Att/Cmp	Yds	TD
Jeff Hostetler, LA vs SD (10/31)	32/20	424	2
Jeff George, Ind at Wash (11/7)	59/37	376	3
Boomer Esiason, NYJ vs Den (9/5)	40/29	371	2
Warren Moon, Hou vs Sea (11/7)	55/36	369	2
John Elway, Den at GB (10/10)	59/33	367	1

NFC	Att/Cmp	Yds	TD
Steve Young, SF at Rams (11/28)	32/26	462	4
Steve Beuerlein, Pho at Sea (12/19)*	53/34	431	3
Brett Favre, GB at Chi (12/5)	54/36	402	2
Sean Salisbury, Min at Den (11/14)	37/19	366	2
R. Cunningham, Phi vs Wash (9/19)	39/25	360	3

Rushing

AFC	Car	Yds	TD
Gary Brown, Hou at Cle (11/21)	34	194	1
Chris Warren, Sea at NE (9/19)	36	174	1
Chris Warren, Sea vs Pho (12/19)*	27	168	1
Gary Brown, Hou at Cin (11/14)	26	166	1
Johnny Johnson, NYJ at Wash (12/11)	32	155	0

NFC	Car	Yds	TD
Emmitt Smith, Dal at Phi (10/31)	30	237	1
Jerome Bettis, Rams at NO (12/12)	28	212	1
Erric Pegram, Atl at SF (9/19)	27	192	0
Barry Sanders, Det vs TB (11/7)	29	187	0
Erric Pegram, Atl at Cin (12/26)	37	180	1

Reception Yards

AFC	No	Yds	TD
Reggie Langhorne, Ind at Wash (11/7)	12	203	1
Jeff Graham, Pit vs Hou (12/19)	7	192	0
Tim Brown, Raiders at Buf (12/5)	10	183	1
Tim Brown, Raiders vs Den (1/2)*	11	173	2
Andre Reed, Buf vs Wash (11/1)	7	159	1

NFC	No	Yds	TD
Michael Hayes, Atl vs NO (9/12)	7	182	2
Calvin Williams, Phi vs Wash (9/19)	8	181	3
Jerry Rice, SF at TB (11/14)	8	172	4
Michael Irvin, Dal vs SF (10/17)	12	168	1
Jerry Rice, SF at Rams (11/28)	8	166	2

NFL Bests

Longest Field Goal
59 yds .... Steve Christie, Buf vs Mia (9/26)

Longest Run from Scrimmage
85 yds .... Reggie Brooks, Wash at Phi (9/19), TD

Longest Pass Play
98 yds .... Hebert to Haynes, Atl vs NO (9/12), TD

Longest Interception Return
102 yds .... Donald Frank, SD at Raiders (10/31), TD

Longest Punt Return
91 yds .... Eric Metcalf, Cle vs Pit (10/24), TD

Longest Kickoff Return
99 yds .... Tyrone Hughes, NO at Min (11/28), TD

NFL Regular Season Team Leaders

Offense

AFC	Points		Yardage			
	For	Avg	Rush	Pass	Total	Avg
Miami	349	21.8	1459	4353	5812	363.3
Houston	368	23.0	1792	3866	5658	353.6
Denver	373	23.3	1693	3768	5461	341.3
Buffalo	329	20.6	1943	3317	5260	328.8
Pittsburgh	308	19.3	2003	3232	5235	327.2
New York	270	16.8	1880	3332	5212	325.8
New England	238	14.9	1780	3285	5065	316.6
Los Angeles	306	19.1	1425	3589	5014	313.4
San Diego	322	20.1	1824	3143	4967	310.4
Kansas City	328	20.5	1655	3180	4835	302.2
Cleveland	304	19.0	1701	3039	4740	296.3
Indianapolis	189	11.8	1288	3417	4705	294.1
Seattle	280	17.5	2015	2654	4669	291.8
Cincinnati	187	11.7	1511	2541	4052	253.3

NFC	Points		Yardage			
	For	Avg	Rush	Pass	Total	Avg
San Francisco	473	29.6	2133	4302	6435	402.2
Dallas	376	23.5	2161	3454	5615	350.9
Phoenix	326	20.4	1809	3404	5213	325.8
New York	288	18.0	2210	2935	5145	321.6
Atlanta	316	19.8	1590	3520	5110	319.4
Philadelphia	293	18.3	1761	3161	4922	307.6
Minnesota	277	17.3	1623	3199	4822	301.4
Los Angeles	221	13.8	2014	2790	4804	300.3
Green Bay	340	21.3	1619	3131	4750	296.9
New Orleans	317	19.8	1766	2941	4707	294.2
Detroit	298	18.6	1944	2714	4658	291.1
Tampa Bay	237	14.8	1290	3021	4311	269.4
Washington	230	14.4	1726	2545	4271	266.9
Chicago	234	14.6	1677	2040	3717	232.3

Defense

AFC	Points		Yardage			
	Opp	Avg	Rush	Pass	Total	Avg
Pittsburgh	281	17.6	1368	3163	4531	283.2
New York	247	15.4	1473	3239	4712	294.5
Los Angeles	326	20.4	1865	2858	4723	295.2
Kansas City	291	18.2	1620	3151	4771	298.2
Cleveland	307	19.2	1654	3124	4778	298.6
New England	286	17.9	1951	2845	4796	299.8
Houston	238	14.9	1273	3601	4874	304.6
Cincinnati	319	19.9	2220	2798	5018	313.6
San Diego	290	18.1	1314	3752	5066	316.6
Denver	284	17.8	1418	3731	5149	321.8
Miami	351	21.9	1665	3485	5150	321.9
Seattle	314	19.6	1660	3653	5313	332.1
Buffalo	242	15.1	1921	3633	5554	347.1
Indianapolis	378	23.6	2521	3117	5638	352.4

NFC	Points		Yardage			
	Opp	Avg	Rush	Pass	Total	Avg
Minnesota	290	18.1	1534	2870	4404	275.3
Green Bay	282	17.6	1582	2900	4482	280.1
Chicago	230	14.4	1835	2818	4653	290.8
New York	205	12.8	1547	3116	4663	291.4
Detroit	292	18.3	1649	3020	4669	291.8
New Orleans	343	21.4	2090	2606	4696	293.5
Dallas	229	14.3	1651	3116	4767	297.9
San Francisco	295	18.4	1800	3197	4997	312.3
Philadelphia	315	19.7	2080	2939	5019	313.7
Phoenix	269	16.8	1861	3306	5167	322.9
Tampa Bay	376	23.5	1994	3252	5246	327.9
Los Angeles	367	22.9	1851	3560	5411	338.2
Atlanta	385	24.1	1784	3637	5421	338.8
Washington	345	21.6	2111	3386	5497	343.6

Takeaways / Giveaways

AFC	Takeaways			Giveaways			Net Diff
	Int	Fum	Tot	Int	Fum	Tot	
San Diego	22	12	34	14	5	19	+15
Buffalo	23	24	47	18	17	35	+12
Pittsburgh	24	14	38	12	15	27	+11
Kansas City	21	17	38	10	18	28	+10
New York	19	18	37	12	16	28	+9
Cincinnati	12	14	26	11	9	20	+6
Seattle	22	15	37	18	13	31	+6
Denver	18	13	31	10	18	28	+3
Houston	26	17	43	25	20	45	-2
Los Angeles	14	9	23	14	11	25	-2
Miami	13	14	27	18	16	34	-7
New England	13	9	22	24	10	34	-12
Cleveland	13	9	22	19	17	36	-14
Indianapolis	10	11	21	15	20	35	-14
TOTALS	250	196	446	220	205	425	+21

NFC	Takeaways			Giveaways			Net Diff
	Int	Fum	Tot	Int	Fum	Tot	
New York	18	10	28	9	8	17	+11
Minnesota	24	10	34	14	10	24	+10
Dallas	14	14	28	6	16	22	+6
Detroit	19	16	35	19	13	32	+3
Philadelphia	20	15	35	13	21	34	+1
San Francisco	19	11	30	17	13	30	0
Washington	17	14	31	21	10	31	0
Chicago	18	12	30	16	14	30	0
Green Bay	18	15	33	24	10	34	-1
New Orleans	10	20	30	21	13	34	-4
Phoenix	9	17	26	20	11	31	-5
Los Angeles	11	9	20	19	11	30	-10
Tampa Bay	9	13	22	25	11	36	-14
Atlanta	13	11	24	25	17	42	-18
TOTALS	219	187	406	249	178	427	-21

Overall Club Rankings

Combined AFC and NFC rankings by yards gained on offense and yards given up on defense.

	Offense			Defense		
	Rush	Pass	Rank	Rush	Pass	Rank
Atlanta	23	6	11	15	25	25
Buffalo	8	11	6	21	24	27
Chicago	19	28	28	17	3	4
Cincinnati	24	27	27	27	2	16
Cleveland	17	19	20	12	13	12
Dallas	2	7	4	11	10t	10
Denver	18	4	5	4	27	19
Detroit	7	24	24	10	9	6
Green Bay	22	18	19	8	7	2
Houston	12	3	3	1	23	14
Indianapolis	28	8	22	28	12	28
Kansas City	20	15	16	9	14	11
LA Raiders	26	5	13	20	5	9
LA Rams	5	23	18	18	22	24
Miami	25	1	2	14	21	20
Minnesota	21	14	17	6	6	1
New England	13	12	12	22	4	13
New Orleans	14	21	21	25	1	7
NY Giants	1	22	10	7	10t	5
NY Jets	9	10	9	5	17	8
Philadelphia	15	16	15	24	8	17
Phoenix	11	9	8	19	19	21
Pittsburgh	6	13	7	3	15	3
San Diego	10	17	14	2	28	18
San Francisco	3	2	1	16	16	15
Seattle	4	25	23	13	26	23
Tampa Bay	27	20	25	23	18	22
Washington	16	26	26	26	20	26

AFC Team by Team Statistics

Players with more than one team during the regular season are listed with second club; (*) indicates rookies.

Buffalo Bills

Passing (5 Att)	Att	Cmp	Pct	Yds	TD	Rate
Frank Reich	26	16	61.5	153	2	103.5
Jim Kelly	470	288	61.3	3382	18	79.9

Interceptions: Kelly 18.

Top Receivers	No	Yds	Avg	Long	TD
Pete Metzelaars	68	609	9.0	51	4
Bill Brooks	60	714	11.9	32	5
Andre Reed	52	854	16.4	65-td	6
Thurman Thomas	48	387	8.1	37	0
Don Beebe	31	504	16.3	65-td	3
Kenneth Davis	21	95	4.5	28	0

Top Rushers	Car	Yds	Avg	Long	TD
Thurman Thomas	355	1315	3.7	27	6
Kenneth Davis	109	391	3.6	19	6
Jim Kelly	36	102	2.8	17	0
Carwell Gardner	20	56	2.8	8	0
Nate Turner	11	36	3.3	10	0

Most Touchdowns	TD	Run	Rec	Ret	Pts
Kenneth Davis	6	6	0	0	36
Andre Reed	6	0	6	0	36
Thurman Thomas	6	6	0	0	36
Bill Brooks	5	0	5	0	30
Pete Metzelaars	4	0	4	0	24

Kicking	PAT/Att	FG/Att	Lg	Pts
Steve Christie	36/37	23/32	59	105

Punts (10 or more)	No	Yds	Long	Avg	In 20
Chris Mohr	74	2991	58	40.4	19

Most Interceptions		Most Sacks	
Nate Odomes	9	Bruce Smith	13½

Cincinnati Bengals

Passing (5 Att)	Att	Cmp	Pct	Yds	TD	Rate
Erik Wilhelm	6	4	66.7	63	0	101.4
Jay Schroeder	159	78	49.1	832	5	70.0
David Klingler	343	190	55.4	1935	6	66.6

Interceptions: Klingler 9, Schroeder 2.

Top Receivers	No	Yds	Avg	Long	TD
Jeff Query	56	654	11.7	51	4
Derrick Fenner	48	427	8.9	40	0
Tony McGee*	44	525	11.9	37	0
Carl Pickens	43	565	13.1	36	6
Harold Green	22	115	5.2	16	0

Top Rushers	Car	Yds	Avg	Long	TD
Harold Green	215	589	2.7	25	0
Derrick Fenner	121	482	4.0	26	1
David Klingler	41	282	6.9	29	0
Ostell Miles	22	56	2.5	15	1
Jay Schroeder	10	41	4.1	20	0

Most Touchdowns	TD	Run	Rec	Ret	Pts
Carl Pickens	6	0	6	0	36
Jeff Query	4	0	4	0	24

Six tied with one TD each.

Kicking	PAT/Att	FG/Att	Lg	Pts
Doug Pelfrey*	13/16	24/31	53	85

Punts (10 or more)	No	Yds	Long	Avg	In 20
Lee Johnson	90	3954	60	43.9	24

Most Interceptions		Most Sacks	
Mike Brim	3	Daniel Stubbs	5

Cleveland Browns

Passing (5 Att)	Att	Cmp	Pct	Yds	TD	Rate
Vinny Testaverde	230	130	56.5	1797	14	85.7
Todd Philcox	108	52	48.1	699	4	54.5

Interceptions: Testaverde 9, Philcox 7.
Released: Bernie Kosar (Nov. 8).

Top Receivers	No	Yds	Avg	Long	TD
Eric Metcalf	63	539	8.6	49-td	2
Mark Carrier	43	746	17.3	55	3
Michael Jackson	41	756	18.4	62-td	8
Leroy Hoard	35	351	10.0	41	0
Brian Kinchen	29	347	12.0	40	2

Top Rushers	Car	Yds	Avg	Long	TD
Tommy Vardell	171	644	3.8	54	3
Eric Metcalf	129	611	4.7	55	1
Leroy Hoard	56	227	4.1	30	0
Vinny Testaverde	18	74	4.1	14	0
Randy Baldwin	18	61	3.4	11	0

Most Touchdowns	TD	Run	Rec	Ret	Pts
Michael Jackson	8	0	8	0	48
Mark Carrier	5	1	3	1	30
Eric Metcalf	5	1	2	2	30
Keenan McCardell	4	0	4	0	24
Tommy Vardell	4	3	1	0	24

Kicking	PAT/Att	FG/Att	Lg	Pts
Matt Stover	36/36	16/22	53	84

Punts (10 or more)	No	Yds	Long	Avg	In 20
Brian Hansen	82	3632	72	44.3	15

Most Interceptions		Most Sacks	
Eric Turner	5	Anthony Pleasant	11

Denver Broncos

Passing (5 Att)	Att	Cmp	Pct	Yds	TD	Rate
John Elway	551	348	63.2	4030	25	92.8

Interceptions: Elway 10.

Top Receivers	No	Yds	Avg	Long	TD
Shannon Sharpe	81	995	12.3	63	9
Derek Russell	44	719	16.3	43	3
Rod Bernstine	44	372	8.5	41	0
Glyn Milburn*	38	300	7.9	50	3
Vance Johnson	36	517	14.4	56	5
Arthur Marshall	28	360	12.9	40	2
Robert Delpino	26	195	7.5	25	0

Top Rushers	Car	Yds	Avg	Long	TD
Rod Bernstine	223	816	3.7	24	4
Robert Delpino	131	445	3.4	18	8
Glyn Milburn*	52	231	4.4	26	0
John Elway	44	153	3.5	18	0
Reggie Rivers	15	50	3.3	14	1

Most Touchdowns	TD	Run	Rec	Ret	Pts
Shannon Sharpe	9	0	9	0	54
Robert Delpino	8	8	0	0	48
Vance Johnson	5	0	5	0	30
Rod Bernstine	4	4	0	0	24
Derek Russell	4	0	3	1	24

Kicking	PAT/Att	FG/Att	Lg	Pts
Jason Elam*	41/42	26/35	54	119

Punts (10 or more)	No	Yds	Long	Avg	In 20
Tom Rouen	67	3017	62	45.0	17

Most Interceptions		Most Sacks	
Tyrone Braxton	3	Simon Fletcher	13½
Dennis Smith	3		

Houston Oilers

Passing (5 Att)

	Att	Cmp	Pct	Yds	TD	Rate
Warren Moon	520	303	58.3	3485	21	75.2
Cody Carlson	90	51	56.7	605	2	66.2

Interceptions: Moon 21, Carlson 4.

Top Receivers

	No	Yds	Avg	Long	TD
Webster Slaughter	77	904	11.7	41	5
Ernest Givins	68	887	13.0	80-td	4
Haywood Jeffries	66	753	11.4	66-td	6
Curtis Duncan	41	456	11.1	47	3
Lorenzo White	34	229	6.7	20	0
Gary Wellman	31	430	13.9	44	1

Top Rushers

	Car	Yds	Avg	Long	TD
Gary Brown	195	1002	5.1	26	6
Lorenzo White	131	465	3.5	14	2
Warren Moon	48	145	3.0	35	1
Spencer Tillman	9	94	10.4	34	0

Most Touchdowns

	TD	Run	Rec	Ret	Pts
Gary Brown	8	6	2	0	48
Haywood Jeffries	6	0	6	0	36
Webster Slaughter	5	0	5	0	30
Ernest Givins	4	0	4	0	24
Curtis Duncan	3	0	3	0	18

Kicking

	PAT/Att	FG/Att	Lg	Pts
Al Del Greco	39/40	29/34	52	126

Punts (10 or more)

	No	Yds	Long	Avg	In20
Greg Montgomery	54	2462	77	45.6	13
Kent Sullivan	15	614	50	40.9	4
SD	13	541	50	41.6	3
HOU	2	73	37	36.5	1

Signed: Sullivan (Nov. 13).
Released: Sullivan (Nov. 30).

Most Interceptions
Marcus Robertson 7

Most Sacks
Sean Jones 13

Indianapolis Colts

Passing (5 Att)

	Att	Cmp	Pct	Yds	TD	Rate
Jeff George	407	234	57.5	2526	8	76.3
Jack Trudeau	162	85	52.5	992	2	57.4
Don Majkowski	24	13	54.2	105	0	48.1

Interceptions: Trudeau 7, George 6, Majkowski 1.

Top Receivers

	No	Yds	Avg	Long	TD
Reggie Langhorne	85	1038	12.2	72-td	3
Jessie Hester	64	835	13.0	58	1
Anthony Johnson	55	443	8.1	36	0
Kerry Cash	43	402	9.3	37	3
Sean Dawkins*	26	430	16.5	68	1
Roosevelt Potts*	26	189	7.3	24	0

Top Rushers

	Car	Yds	Avg	Long	TD
Roosevelt Potts*	179	711	4.0	34	0
Anthony Johnson	95	331	3.5	14	1
Rodney Culver	65	150	2.3	9	3
Jeff George	13	39	3.0	14	0

Most Touchdowns

	TD	Run	Rec	Ret	Pts
Rodney Culver	5	3	1	1	30
Kerry Cash	3	0	3	0	18
Reggie Langhorne	3	0	3	0	18

Five tied with 1 TD each.

Kicking

	PAT/Att	FG/Att	Lg	Pts
Dean Biasucci	15/16	26/31	53	93

Punts (10 or more)

	No	Yds	Long	Avg	In20
Rohn Stark	83	3595	65	43.3	18

Most Interceptions
Ray Buchanan* 4

Most Sacks
Jon Hand 5

Kansas City Chiefs

Passing (5 Att)

	Att	Cmp	Pct	Yds	TD	Rate
Joe Montana	298	181	60.7	2144	13	87.4
Dave Krieg	189	105	55.6	1238	7	81.4

Interceptions: Montana 7, Kreig 3.

Top Receivers

	No	Yds	Avg	Long	TD
Willie Davis	52	909	17.5	66-td	7
J.J. Birden	51	721	14.1	50-td	2
Kimble Anders	40	326	8.2	27	1
Marcus Allen	34	238	7.0	18-td	3
Jonathan Hayes	24	331	13.8	49	1
Keith Cash	24	242	10.1	24	4

Top Rushers

	Car	Yds	Avg	Long	TD
Marcus Allen	206	764	3.7	39	12
Kimble Anders	75	291	3.9	18	0
Todd McNair	51	278	5.5	47	2
John Stephens	54	191	3.5	22	1
GB	48	173	3.6	22	1
KC	6	18	3.0	7	0
Harvey Williams	42	149	3.5	19	0
Joe Montana	25	64	2.6	17	0

Signed: Stephens (Nov. 3).

Most Touchdowns

	TD	Run	Rec	Ret	Pts
Marcus Allen	15	12	3	0	90
Willie Davis	7	0	7	0	42
Keith Cash	4	0	4	0	24
J.J. Birden	2	0	2	0	12
Todd McNair	2	2	0	0	12

Kicking

	PAT/Att	FG/Att	Lg	Pts
Nick Lowery	37/37	23/29	52	106

Punts (10 or more)

	No	Yds	Long	Avg	In20
Bryan Barker	76	3240	59	42.6	19

Most Interceptions
Albert Lewis 6

Most Sacks
Neil Smith 15

Los Angeles Raiders

Passing (5 Att)

	Att	Cmp	Pct	Yds	TD	Rate
Jeff Hostetler	419	236	56.3	3242	14	82.5
Vince Evans	76	45	59.2	640	3	77.7

Interceptions: Hostetler 10, Evans 4.

Top Receivers

	No	Yds	Avg	Long	TD
Tim Brown	80	1180	14.8	71-td	7
Ethan Horton	43	467	10.9	32	1
James Jett*	33	771	23.4	74-td	3
Alexander Wright	27	462	17.1	68-td	4
Rocket Ismail	26	353	13.6	43-td	1

Top Rushers

	Car	Yds	Avg	Long	TD
Greg Robinson*	156	591	3.8	16	1
Jeff Hostetler	55	202	3.7	19	5
Nick Bell	67	180	2.7	12	1
Steve Smith	47	156	3.3	13	0
Napoleon McCallum	37	114	3.1	14	3
Tyrone Montgomery	37	106	2.9	15	0

Most Touchdowns

	TD	Run	Rec	Ret	Pts
Tim Brown	8	0	7	1	48
Jeff Hostetler	5	5	0	0	30
Alexander Wright	4	0	4	0	24
James Jett*	3	0	3	0	18
Napoleon McCallum	3	3	0	0	18

Kicking

	PAT/Att	FG/Att	Lg	Pts
Jeff Jaeger	27/29	35/44	53	132

Punts (10 or more)

	No	Yds	Long	Avg	In20
Jeff Gossett	71	2971	61	41.8	19

Most Interceptions
Terry McDaniel 5

Most Sacks
Anthony Smith 12½

Miami Dolphins

Passing (5 Att)	Att	Cmp	Pct	Yds	TD	Rate
Dan Marino	150	91	60.7	1218	8	95.9
Scott Mitchell	233	133	57.1	1773	12	84.2
Steve DeBerg	227	136	59.9	1707	7	75.3
TB	39	23	59.0	186	1	47.6
MIA	188	113	60.1	1521	6	81.0

Interceptions: DeBerg 10, Mitchell 8, Marino 3.
Signed: DeBerg (Nov. 10).

Top Receivers	No	Yds	Avg	Long	TD
Terry Kirby*	75	874	11.7	47	3
Irving Fryar	64	1010	15.8	65-td	5
Keith Byars	61	613	10.0	27	3
Mark Ingram	44	707	16.1	77-td	6
Keith Jackson	39	613	15.7	57-td	6

Top Rushers	Car	Yds	Avg	Long	TD
Mark Higgs	186	693	3.7	31	3
Terry Kirby*	119	390	3.3	20	3
Keith Byars	64	269	4.2	77-td	3
Scott Mitchell	21	89	4.2	32	0

Most Touchdowns	TD	Run	Rec	Ret	Pts
Keith Byars	6	3	3	0	36
Mark Ingram	6	0	6	0	36
Keith Jackson	6	0	6	0	36
Terry Kirby*	6	3	3	0	36
Irving Fryar	5	0	5	0	30

Kicking	PAT/Att	FG/Att	Lg	Pts
Pete Stoyanovich	37/37	24/32	52	109

Punts (10 or more)	No	Yds	Long	Avg	In20
Dale Hatcher	58	2304	56	39.7	13

Most Interceptions		Most Sacks	
J.B. Brown	5	Jeff Cross	10½

New York Jets

Passing (5 Att)	Att	Cmp	Pct	Yds	TD	Rate
Boomer Esiason	473	288	60.9	3421	16	84.5
Browning Nagle	14	6	42.9	71	0	58.9

Interceptions: Esiason 11.

Top Receivers	No	Yds	Avg	Long	TD
Johnny Johnson	67	641	9.6	48	1
Rob Moore	64	843	13.2	51	1
Chris Burkett	40	531	13.3	77	4
Johnny Mitchell	39	630	16.2	65-td	6
Terance Mathis	24	352	14.7	46	0

Top Rushers	Car	Yds	Avg	Long	TD
Johnny Johnson	198	821	4.1	57-td	3
Brad Baxter	174	559	3.2	16	7
Blair Thomas	59	221	3.7	24	1
Adrian Murrell*	34	157	4.6	37-td	1
Boomer Esiason	45	118	2.6	17	1

Most Touchdowns	TD	Run	Rec	Ret	Pts
Brad Baxter	7	7	0	0	42
Johnny Mitchell	6	0	6	0	36
Chris Burkett	4	0	4	0	24
Johnny Johnson	4	3	1	0	24
James Thornton	2	0	2	0	12

Kicking	PAT/Att	FG/Att	Lg	Pts
Cary Blanchard	31/31	17/26	45	82

Punts (10 or more)	No	Yds	Long	Avg	In20
Louie Aguiar	73	2806	71	38.4	21

Most Interceptions		Most Sacks	
Brian Washington	6	Jeff Lageman	8½

New England Patriots

Passing (5 Att)	Att	Cmp	Pct	Yds	TD	Rate
Drew Bledsoe*	429	214	49.9	2494	15	65.0
Scott Secules	75	56.0	918	2	54.3	

Interceptions: Bledsoe 15, Secules 9.

Top Receivers	No	Yds	Avg	Long	TD
Ben Coates	53	659	12.4	54-td	8
Vincent Brisby*	45	626	13.9	39	2
Michael Timpson	42	654	15.6	48	2
Kevin Turner	39	333	8.5	26	2
Leonard Russell	26	245	9.4	69	0

Top Rushers	Car	Yds	Avg	Long	TD
Leonard Russell	300	1088	3.6	21	7
Kevin Turner	50	231	4.6	49	0
Corey Croom*	60	198	3.3	22	1
Sam Gash	48	149	3.1	14	1
Drew Bledsoe*	32	82	2.6	15	0

Most Touchdowns	TD	Run	Rec	Ret	Pts
Ben Coates	8	0	8	0	48
Leonard Russell	7	7	0	0	42
Vincent Brisby*	2	0	2	0	12
Michael Timpson	2	0	2	0	12
Kevin Turner	2	0	2	0	12

Kicking	PAT/Att	FG/Att	Lg	Pts
Matt Bahr	28/29	13/18	48	67
PHI	18/19	8/13	48	42
NE	10/10	5/5	37	25
Scott Sisson*	15/15	14/26	40	57

Signed: Bahr (Dec 15).

Punts (10 or more)	No	Yds	Long	Avg	In20
Mike Saxon	73	3096	59	42.4	25

Most Interceptions		Most Sacks	
Maurice Hurst	4	Chris Slade*	9

Pittsburgh Steelers

Passing (5 Att)	Att	Cmp	Pct	Yds	TD	Rate
Neil O'Donnell	486	270	55.6	3208	14	79.5
Mike Tomczak	54	29	53.7	398	2	51.3

Interceptions: O'Donnell 7, Tomczak 5.

Top Receivers	No	Yds	Avg	Long	TD
Eric Green	63	942	15.0	71-td	5
Dwight Stone	41	587	14.3	44	2
Jeff Graham	38	579	15.2	51	0
Leroy Thompson	38	259	6.8	28	0
Merril Hoge	33	247	7.5	18	4
Ernie Mills	29	386	13.3	30	1
Barry Foster	27	217	8.0	21	1

Top Rushers	Car	Yds	Avg	Long	TD
Leroy Thompson	205	763	3.7	36	3
Barry Foster	177	711	4.0	38	8
Merril Hoge	51	249	4.9	30	1
Dwight Stone	12	121	10.1	38-td	1
Neil O'Donnell	26	111	4.3	27	0

Most Touchdowns	TD	Run	Rec	Ret	Pts
Barry Foster	9	8	1	0	54
Eric Green	5	0	5	0	30
Merril Hoge	5	1	4	0	30
Dwight Stone	3	0	3	0	18
Yancey Thigpen	3	0	3	0	18
Leroy Thompson	3	3	0	0	18

Kicking	PAT/Att	FG/Att	Lg	Pts
Gary Anderson	32/32	28/30	46	116

Punts (10 or more)	No	Yds	Long	Avg	In20
Mark Royals	89	3781	61	42.5	28

Most Interceptions		Most Sacks	
Rod Woodson	8	Kevin Greene	12½

San Diego Chargers

Passing (5 Att)	Att	Cmp	Pct	Yds	TD	Rate
John Friesz	238	128	53.8	1402	6	72.8
Stan Humphries	324	173	53.4	1981	12	71.5

Interceptions: Humphries 10, Friesz 4.

Top Receivers	No	Yds	Avg	Long	TD
Anthony Miller	84	1162	13.8	66-td	7
Ronnie Harmon	73	671	9.2	37	2
Nate Lewis	38	463	12.2	47	4
Shawn Jefferson	30	391	13.0	39-td	2
Derrick Walker	21	212	10.1	25-td	1

Top Rushers	Car	Yds	Avg	Long	TD
Marion Butts	185	746	4.0	27	4
Natrone Means*	160	645	4.0	65-td	8
Ronnie Harmon	46	216	4.7	19	0
Eric Bieniemy	33	135	4.1	12	1

Most Touchdowns	TD	Run	Rec	Ret	Pts
Natrone Means*	8	8	0	0	48
Anthony Miller	7	0	7	0	42
Marion Butts	4	4	0	0	24
Nate Lewis	4	0	4	0	24

Three tied with two TDs each.

Kicking	PAT/Att	FG/Att	Lg	Pts
John Carney	31/33	31/40	51	124

Punts (10 or more)	No	Yds	Long	Avg	In20
John Kidd	57	2431	67	42.6	16

Most Interceptions
Darren Carrington ... 7

Most Sacks
Leslie O'Neal ... 12

Seattle Seahawks

Passing (5 Att)	Att	Cmp	Pct	Yds	TD	Rate
Dan McGwire	5	3	60.0	24	1	111.7
Rick Mirer*	486	274	56.4	2833	12	67.0
Stan Gelbaugh	5	3	60.0	39	0	45.0

Interceptions: Mirer 17, Gelbaugh 1.

Top Receivers	No	Yds	Avg	Long	TD
Brian Blades	80	945	11.8	41	3
John L. Williams	58	450	7.8	25	1
Kelvin Martin	57	798	14.0	53-td	5
Ferrell Edmunds	24	239	10.0	32	2
Paul Green	23	178	7.7	20	1

Top Rushers	Car	Yds	Avg	Long	TD
Chris Warren	273	1072	3.9	45-td	7
John L. Williams	82	371	4.5	38	3
Rick Mirer*	68	343	5.0	33	3
Jon Vaughn	36	153	4.3	37	0
Brian Blades	5	52	10.4	26	0

Most Touchdowns	TD	Run	Rec	Ret	Pts
Chris Warren	7	7	0	0	42
Kelvin Martin	5	0	5	0	30
John L. Williams	4	3	1	0	24
Brian Blades	3	0	3	0	18
Rick Mirer*	3	3	0	0	18

Kicking	PAT/Att	FG/Att	Lg	Pts
John Kasay	29/29	23/28	55	98

Punts (10 or more)	No	Yds	Long	Avg	In20
Rick Tuten	90	4007	64	44.5	21

Most Interceptions
Eugene Robinson ... 9

Most Sacks
Michael Sinclair ... 8

NFC Team by Team Statistics

Players with more than one team during the regular season are listed with second club; (*) indicates rookies.

Atlanta Falcons

Passing (5 Att)	Att	Cmp	Pct	Yds	TD	Rate
Bobby Hebert	430	263	61.2	2978	24	84.0
Billy Joe Tolliver	76	39	51.3	464	3	56.0
Chris Miller	66	32	48.5	345	1	50.4

Interceptions: Hebert 17, Tolliver 5, Miller 3.

Top Receivers	No	Yds	Avg	Long	TD
Andre Rison	86	1242	14.4	53-td	15
Mike Pritchard	74	736	9.9	34	7
Michael Haynes	72	778	10.8	98-td	4
Drew Hill	34	384	11.3	30	0
Erric Pegram	33	302	9.2	30	0

Top Rushers	Car	Yds	Avg	Long	TD
Erric Pegram	292	1185	4.1	29	3
Steve Broussard	39	206	5.3	26	1
Eric Dickerson	26	91	3.5	10	0

Released: John Stephens (Oct. 26).
Retired: Dickerson (Oct. 20).

Most Touchdowns	TD	Run	Rec	Ret	Pts
Andre Rison	15	0	15	0	90
Mike Pritchard	7	0	7	0	42
Michael Haynes	4	0	4	0	24
Erric Pegram	3	3	0	0	18

Kicking	PAT/Att	FG/Att	Lg	Pts
Norm Johnson	34/34	26/27	54	112
Lin Elliott	2/3	2/4	43	8
DAL	2/3	2/4	43	8
ATL	0/0	0/0	—	0

Signed: Elliott (Oct. 13). **Released:** Elliott (Oct. 18).

Punts (10 or more)	No	Yds	Long	Avg	In20
Harold Alexander*	72	3114	75	43.3	21

Most Interceptions
Deion Sanders ... 7

Most Sacks
Pierce Holt ... 6½

Chicago Bears

Passing (5 Att)	Att	Cmp	Pct	Yds	TD	Rate
Jim Harbaugh	325	200	61.5	2002	7	72.1
Peter Tom Willis	60	30	50.0	268	0	27.6

Interceptions: Harbaugh 11, Willis 5.

Top Receivers	No	Yds	Avg	Long	TD
Tom Waddle	44	552	12.5	38	1
Neal Anderson	31	160	5.2	35	0
Terry Obee	26	351	13.5	48	3
Curtis Conway*	19	231	12.2	38-td	2

Top Rushers	Car	Yds	Avg	Long	TD
Neal Anderson	202	646	3.2	45	4
Tim Worley	110	437	4.0	28	2
Jim Harbaugh	60	277	4.6	25	0
Ironhead Heyward	68	206	3.0	11	0

Most Touchdowns	TD	Run	Rec	Ret	Pts
Neal Anderson	4	4	0	0	24
Jim Harbaugh	4	4	0	0	24
Terry Obee	3	0	3	0	18
Myron Baker*	2	0	0	2	12
Chris Conway*	2	0	2	0	12
Tim Worley	2	2	0	0	12

Kicking	PAT/Att	FG/Att	Lg	Pts
Kevin Butler	21/22	27/36	55	102

Punts (10 or more)	No	Yds	Long	Avg	In20
Chris Gardocki	80	3080	58	38.5	28

Most Interceptions
Mark Carrier ... 4
Dante Jones ... 4

Most Sacks
Richard Dent ... 12½

Dallas Cowboys

Passing (5 Att)	Att	Cmp	Pct	Yds	TD	Rate
Troy Aikman	392	271	69.1	3100	15	99.0
Bernie Kosar	201	115	57.2	1217	8	82.0
DAL	63	36	57.1	410	3	92.7
CLE	138	79	57.2	807	5	77.2
Jason Garrett	19	9	47.4	61	0	54.9

Interceptions: Aikman 6, Kosar 3.
Signed: Kosar (Nov. 10).

Top Receivers	No	Yds	Avg	Long	TD
Michael Irvin	88	1330	15.1	61-td	7
Emmitt Smith	57	414	7.3	86	1
Daryl Johnston	50	372	7.4	20	1
Jay Novacek	44	445	10.1	30	1
Alvin Harper	36	777	21.6	80-td	5

Top Rushers	Car	Yds	Avg	Long	TD
Emmitt Smith	283	1486	5.3	62-td	9
Derrick Lassic*	75	269	3.6	15	3
Lincoln Coleman	34	132	3.9	16	2
Troy Aikman	32	125	3.9	20	0
Daryl Johnston	24	74	3.1	11	3

Most Touchdowns	TD	Run	Rec	Ret	Pts
Emmitt Smith	10	9	1	0	60
Michael Irvin	7	0	7	0	42
Kevin Williams*	6	2	2	2	36
Alvin Harper	5	0	5	0	30
Daryl Johnston	4	3	1	0	24

Kicking	PAT/Att	FG/Att	Lg	Pts
Eddie Murray	38/38	28/33	52	122

Released: Lin Elliott (Sept. 14).
Signed: Murray (Sept. 14).

Punts (10 or more)	No	Yds	Long	Avg	In20
John Jett	56	2342	59	41.8	22

Most Interceptions		Most Sacks	
Kevin Smith	6	Tony Tolbert	7½

Detroit Lions

Passing (5 Att)	Att	Cmp	Pct	Yds	TD	Rate
Erik Kramer	138	87	63.0	1002	8	95.1
Rodney Peete	252	157	62.3	1670	6	66.4
Andre Ware	45	20	44.4	271	1	53.1

Interceptions: Peete 14, Kramer 3, Ware 2.

Top Receivers	No	Yds	Avg	Long	TD
Herman Moore	61	935	15.3	93-td	6
Brett Perriman	49	496	10.1	34	2
Barry Sanders	36	205	5.7	17	0
Willie Green	28	462	16.5	47	2
Rodney Holman	25	244	9.8	28-td	2

Top Rushers	Car	Yds	Avg	Long	TD
Barry Sanders	243	1115	4.6	42	3
Derrick Moore	88	405	4.6	48	3
Eric Lynch	53	207	3.9	15	2
Rodney Peete	45	165	3.7	28	1

Most Touchdowns	TD	Run	Rec	Ret	Pts
Herman Moore	6	0	6	0	36
Derrick Moore	4	3	1	0	24
Barry Sanders	3	3	0	0	18

Six tied with two TDs each.

Kicking	PAT/Att	FG/Att	Lg	Pts
Jason Hanson	28/28	34/43	53	130

Punts (10 or more)	No	Yds	Long	Avg	In20
Jim Arnold	72	3207	68	44.5	15

Most Interceptions		Most Sacks	
Pat Swilling	3	Robert Porcher	8½

Green Bay Packers

Passing (5 Att)	Att	Cmp	Pct	Yds	TD	Rate
Ty Detmer	5	3	60.0	26	0	73.8
Brett Favre	522	318	60.9	3303	19	72.2

Interceptions: Favre 24.

Top Receivers	No	Yds	Avg	Long	TD
Sterling Sharpe	112	1274	11.4	54	11
Edgar Bennett	59	457	7.7	39-td	1
Jackie Harris	42	604	14.4	66-td	4
Mark Clayton	32	331	10.3	32	3
Ed West	25	253	10.1	24	0

Top Rushers	Car	Yds	Avg	Long	TD
Darrell Thompson	169	654	3.9	60-td	3
Edgar Bennett	159	550	3.5	19	9
Brett Favre	58	216	3.7	27	1

Traded: John Stephens to Atlanta for DB Bruce Pickens (Oct.14).

Most Touchdowns	TD	Run	Rec	Ret	Pts
Sterling Sharpe	11	0	11	0	66
Edgar Bennett	10	9	1	0	60
Jackie Harris	4	0	4	0	24
Mark Clayton	3	0	3	0	18
Darrell Thompson	3	3	0	0	18

Kicking	PAT/Att	FG/Att	Lg	Pts
Chris Jacke	35/35	31/37	54	128

Punts (10 or more)	No	Yds	Long	Avg	In20
Bryan Wagner	74	3174	60	42.9	19

Most Interceptions		Most Sacks	
LeRoy Butler	6	Reggie White	13

Los Angeles Rams

Passing (5 Att)	Att	Cmp	Pct	Yds	TD	Rate
T.J. Rubley	189	108	57.1	1338	8	80.1
Jim Everett	274	135	49.3	1652	8	59.7
Mike Pagel	9	3	33.3	23	0	2.8

Interceptions: Everett 12, Rubley 6, Pagel 1.

Top Receivers	No	Yds	Avg	Long	TD
Henry Ellard	61	945	15.5	54	2
Willie Anderson	37	552	14.9	56-td	4
Cleveland Gary	36	289	8.0	60-td	1
Troy Drayton*	27	319	11.8	27	4
Jerome Bettis*	26	244	9.4	28	0

Top Rushers	Car	Yds	Avg	Long	TD
Jerome Bettis*	294	1429	4.9	71-td	7
Cleveland Gary	79	293	3.7	15	1
T.J. Rubley	29	102	3.5	13	0
Tim Lester	11	74	6.7	26	0
Jim Everett	19	38	2.0	14	0

Most Touchdowns	TD	Run	Rec	Ret	Pts
Jerome Bettis*	7	7	0	0	42
Willie Anderson	4	0	4	0	24
Troy Drayton*	4	0	4	0	24

Three tied with 2 TDs each.

Kicking	PAT/Att	FG/Att	Lg	Pts
Tony Zendejas	23/25	16/23	54	71

Punts (10 or more)	No	Yds	Long	Avg	In20
Sean Landeta	75	3215	66	42.9	18
NYG	33	1390	57	42.1	11
RAMS	42	1825	66	43.5	7
Don Bracken	17	651	51	38.3	5
Paul McJulien	21	795	56	37.9	5

Released: McJulien (Nov. 12).
Signed: Landeta (Nov. 12).

Most Interceptions		Most Sacks	
Four tied with 2 each.		Sean Gilbert	10½

Minnesota Vikings

Passing (5 Att)	Att	Cmp	Pct	Yds	TD	Rate
Sean Salisbury	195	115	59.0	1413	9	84.0
Jim McMahon	331	200	60.4	1967	9	76.2

Interceptions: McMahon 8, Salisbury 6.

Top Receivers	No	Yds	Avg	Long	TD
Cris Carter	86	1071	12.5	58	9
Anthony Carter	60	774	12.9	39	5
Steve Jordan	56	542	9.7	53	1
Robert Smith*	24	111	4.6	12	0
Qadry Ismail*	19	212	11.2	37	1

Top Rushers	Car	Yds	Avg	Long	TD
Scottie Graham	118	487	4.1	31	3
Barry Word	142	458	3.2	14	2
Robert Smith*	82	399	4.9	26-td	2
Roger Craig	38	119	3.1	11	1
Jim McMahon	33	96	2.9	16	0

Most Touchdowns	TD	Run	Rec	Ret	Pts
Cris Carter	9	0	9	0	54
Anthony Carter	5	0	5	0	30
Scottie Graham	3	3	0	0	18
Roger Craig	2	1	1	0	12
Robert Smith*	2	2	0	0	12
Barry Word	2	2	0	0	12

Kicking	PAT/Att	FG/Att	Lg	Pts
Fuad Reveiz	27/28	26/35	51	105

Punts (10 or more)	No	Yds	Long	Avg	In20
Harry Newsome	90	3864	64	42.9	25

Most Interceptions		Most Sacks	
Vencie Glenn	5	Chris Doleman	12½
		John Randle	12½

New York Giants

Passing (5 Att)	Att	Cmp	Pct	Yds	TD	Rate
Phil Simms	400	247	61.8	3038	15	88.3
Kent Graham	22	8	36.4	79	0	47.3

Interceptions: Simms 9.

Top Receivers	No	Yds	Avg	Long	TD
Mark Jackson	58	708	12.2	40-td	4
Dave Meggett	38	319	8.4	50	0
Chris Calloway	35	513	14.7	47	3
Ed McCaffrey	27	335	12.4	31	2
Mike Sherrard	24	433	18.0	55-td	2
Howard Cross	21	272	13.0	32	5

Top Rushers	Car	Yds	Avg	Long	TD
Rodney Hampton	292	1077	3.7	20	5
Lewis Tillman	121	585	4.8	58	3
Dave Meggett	69	329	4.8	23	0
Jarrod Bunch	33	128	3.9	13	2

Most Touchdowns	TD	Run	Rec	Ret	Pts
Howard Cross	5	0	5	0	30
Rodney Hampton	5	5	0	0	30
Mark Jackson	4	0	4	0	24
Jarrod Bunch	3	2	1	0	18
Chris Calloway	3	0	3	0	18
Lewis Tillman	3	3	0	0	18

Kicking	PAT/Att	FG/Att	Lg	Pts
David Treadwell	28/29	25/31	46	103
Brad Daluiso	0/0	1/3	54	3

Punts (10 or more)	No	Yds	Long	Avg	In20
Mike Horan	44	1882	60	42.8	13

Released: Sean Landeta (Nov. 9).
Signed: Horan (Nov. 9).

Most Interceptions		Most Sacks	
Mark Collins	4	Keith Hamilton	11½
Greg Jackson	4		

New Orleans Saints

Passing (5 Att)	Att	Cmp	Pct	Yds	TD	Rate
Mike Buck	54	32	59.3	448	4	87.6
Wade Wilson	388	221	57.0	2457	12	70.1
Steve Walsh	38	20	52.6	271	2	60.3

Interceptions: Wilson 15, Buck 3, Walsh 3.

Top Receivers	No	Yds	Avg	Long	TD
Eric Martin	66	950	14.4	54-td	3
Quinn Early	45	670	14.9	63-td	6
Dalton Hilliard	40	296	7.4	34	1
Brad Muster	23	195	8.5	31	0
Derek Brown*	21	170	8.1	19	1

Top Rushers	Car	Yds	Avg	Long	TD
Derek Brown*	180	705	3.9	60	2
Wade Wilson	31	230	7.4	44	0
Brad Muster	64	214	3.3	18	3
Lorenzo Neal*	21	175	8.3	74-td	1
Dalton Hilliard	50	165	3.3	16	2
Fred McAfee	51	160	3.1	27	1

Most Touchdowns	TD	Run	Rec	Ret	Pts
Quinn Early	6	0	6	0	36
Derek Brown*	3	2	1	0	18
Dalton Hilliard	3	2	1	0	18
Tyrone Hughes*	3	0	0	3	18
Eric Martin	3	0	3	0	18
Brad Muster	3	3	0	0	18

Kicking	PAT/Att	FG/Att	Lg	Pts
Morten Andersen	33/33	28/35	56	117

Punts (10 or more)	No	Yds	Long	Avg	In20
Tommy Barnhardt	77	3356	58	43.6	26

Most Interceptions		Most Sacks	
Gene Atkins	3	Renaldo Turnbull	13

Philadelphia Eagles

Passing (5 Att)	Att	Cmp	Pct	Yds	TD	Rate
R. Cunningham	110	76	69.1	850	5	88.1
Bubby Brister	309	181	58.6	1905	14	84.9
Ken O'Brien	137	71	51.8	708	4	67.4

Interceptions: Cunningham 5, Brister 5, O'Brien 3.

Top Receivers	No	Yds	Avg	Long	TD
Herschel Walker	75	610	8.1	55	3
Calvin Williams	60	725	12.1	80-td	10
Mark Bavaro	43	481	11.2	27	6
Victor Bailey*	41	545	13.3	58	1
James Joseph	29	291	10.0	48	1

Top Rushers	Car	Yds	Avg	Long	TD
Herschel Walker	174	746	4.3	35	1
Heath Sherman	115	406	3.5	19	2
Vaughn Hebron*	84	297	3.5	33	3
James Joseph	39	140	3.6	12	0
Randall Cunningham	18	110	6.1	26	1

Most Touchdowns	TD	Run	Rec	Ret	Pts
Calvin Williams	10	0	10	0	60
Mark Bavaro	6	0	6	0	36
Eric Allen	4	0	0	4	24
Herschel Walker	4	1	3	0	24
Vaughn Hebron*	3	3	0	0	18

Kicking	PAT/Att	FG/Att	Lg	Pts
Roger Ruzek	13/16	8/10	46	37

Released: Matt Bahr (Dec. 13).

Punts (10 or more)	No	Yds	Long	Avg	In20
Jeff Feagles	83	3323	60	40.0	31

Most Interceptions		Most Sacks	
Eric Allen	6	Andy Harmon	11½

Phoenix Cardinals

Passing (5 Att)	Att	Cmp	Pct	Yds	TD	Rate
Steve Beuerlein	418	258	61.7	3164	18	82.5
Chris Chandler	103	52	50.5	471	3	64.8

Interceptions: Beuerlein 17, Chandler 2.

Top Receivers	No	Yds	Avg	Long	TD
Larry Centers	66	603	9.1	29	3
Ricky Proehl	65	877	13.5	51-td	7
Gary Clark	63	818	13.0	55	4
Randal Hill	35	519	14.8	58-td	4
Johnny Bailey	32	243	7.6	30	0

Top Rushers	Car	Yds	Avg	Long	TD
Ron Moore*	263	1018	3.9	20	9
Garrison Hearst*	76	264	3.5	57	1
Johnny Bailey	49	253	5.2	31	1
Larry Centers	25	152	6.1	33	0

Most Touchdowns	TD	Run	Rec	Ret	Pts
Ron Moore*	9	9	0	0	54
Ricky Proehl	7	0	7	0	42
Gary Clark	4	0	4	0	24
Randal Hill	4	0	4	0	24
Larry Centers	3	0	3	0	18

Kicking	PAT/Att	FG/Att	Lg	Pts
Greg Davis	37/37	21/28	55	100

Punts (10 or more)	No	Yds	Long	Avg	In20
Rich Camarillo	73	3189	61	43.7	23

Most Interceptions		Most Sacks	
Lorenzo Lynch	3	Ken Harvey	9½

Tampa Bay Buccaneers

Passing (5 Att)	Att	Cmp	Pct	Yds	TD	Rate
Craig Erickson	457	233	51.0	3054	18	66.4
Casey Weldon	11	6	54.5	55	0	30.5

Interceptions: Erickson 21, Weldon 1.
Released: Steve DeBerg (Nov. 2).

Top Receivers	No	Yds	Avg	Long	TD
Courtney Hawkins	62	933	15.0	67	5
Vince Workman	54	411	7.6	42-td	4
Horace Copeland*	30	633	21.1	67-td	4
Ron Hall	23	268	11.7	37-td	1
Charles Wilson	15	225	15.0	24	0
Lawrence Dawsey	15	203	13.5	24	0

Top Rushers	Car	Yds	Avg	Long	TD
Reggie Cobb	221	658	3.0	16	3
Vince Workman	78	284	3.6	21	2
Mazio Royster	33	115	3.5	19	1
Craig Erickson	26	96	3.7	15	0

Most Touchdowns	TD	Run	Rec	Ret	Pts
Courtney Hawkins	5	0	5	0	30
Reggie Cobb	4	3	1	0	24
Horace Copeland*	4	0	4	0	24
Vince Workman	4	2	2	0	24
Lamar Thomas*	2	0	2	0	12

Kicking	PAT/Att	FG/Att	Lg	Pts
Michael Husted*	27/27	16/22	57	75

Punts (10 or more)	No	Yds	Long	Avg	In20
Dan Stryzinski	93	3772	57	40.6	24

Most Interceptions		Most Sacks	
Joe King	3	Ray Seals	8½

San Francisco 49ers

Passing (5 Att)	Att	Cmp	Pct	Yds	TD	Rate
Steve Young	462	314	68.0	4023	29	101.5
Steve Bono	61	39	63.9	416	0	76.9

Interceptions: Young 16, Bono 1.

Top Receivers	No	Yds	Avg	Long	TD
Jerry Rice	98	1503	15.3	80-td	15
Brent Jones	68	735	10.8	29	3
John Taylor	56	940	16.8	76-td	5
Marc Logan	37	348	9.4	24	0
Ricky Watters	31	326	10.5	48-td	1

Top Rushers	Car	Yds	Avg	Long	TD
Ricky Watters	208	950	4.6	39	10
Steve Young	69	407	5.9	35	2
Marc Logan	58	280	4.8	45	7
Amp Lee	72	230	3.2	13	1
Tom Rathman	19	80	4.2	19	3

Most Touchdowns	TD	Run	Rec	Ret	Pts
Jerry Rice	16	1	15	0	96
Ricky Watters	11	10	1	0	66
Marc Logan	7	7	0	0	42
John Taylor	5	0	5	0	30

Three tied with three TDs each.

Kicking	PAT/Att	FG/Att	Lg	Pts
Mike Cofer	59/61	16/26	46	107

Punts (10 or more)	No	Yds	Long	Avg	In20
Klaus Wilmsmeyer	42	1718	61	40.9	11

Most Interceptions		Most Sacks	
Michael McGruder	5	Dana Stubblefield*	10½

Washington Redskins

Passing (5 Att)	Att	Cmp	Pct	Yds	TD	Rate
Cary Conklin	87	46	52.9	496	4	70.9
Rich Gannon	125	74	59.2	704	3	59.6
Mark Rypien	319	166	52.0	1514	4	56.3

Interceptions: Rypien 10, Gannon 7, Conklin 3.

Top Receivers	No	Yds	Avg	Long	TD
Ricky Sanders	58	638	11.0	50	4
Art Monk	41	398	9.7	29	2
Tim McGee	39	500	12.8	54	3
Earnest Byner	27	194	7.2	20	0
Ron Middleton	24	154	6.4	18	2
Desmond Howard	23	286	12.4	27	0

Top Rushers	Car	Yds	Avg	Long	TD
Reggie Brooks*	223	1063	4.8	85-td	3
Brian Mitchell	63	246	3.9	29-td	3
Ricky Ervins	50	201	4.0	18	0
Earnest Byner	23	105	4.6	16	1
Rich Gannon	21	88	4.2	12	1

Most Touchdowns	TD	Run	Rec	Ret	Pts
Ricky Sanders	4	0	4	0	24
Reggie Brooks*	3	3	0	0	18
Tim McGee	3	0	3	0	18
Brian Mitchell	3	3	0	0	18
Mark Rypien	3	3	0	0	18

Kicking	PAT/Att	FG/Att	Lg	Pts
Chip Lohmiller	24/26	16/28	51	72

Punts (10 or more)	No	Yds	Long	Avg	In20
Reggie Roby	78	3447	60	44.2	25

Signed: Roby (Sept. 8).

Most Interceptions		Most Sacks	
Tom Carter*	6	Monte Coleman	6
		Andre Collins	6

NFL PLAYOFFS

1ST ROUND	SEMIFINALS	FINAL		FINAL	SEMIFINALS	1ST ROUND

XXVIII

† Denver 24
† LA Raiders 42
LA Raiders 23
Buffalo 30
Buffalo 29
AFC
Dallas 30
Buffalo 13
† Pittsburgh 24
(OT)
Kansas City 27
Kansas City 28
Kansas City 13
Houston 20

San Francisco 21
NFC
Dallas 38
Dallas 27

† Minnesota 16
NY Giants 19
NY Giants 3
San Francisco 44
† Green Bay 28
† Detroit 24
Green Bay 17

Jan. 30, 1994
Georgia Dome, Atlanta

† Wild Card Team

† Wild Card Team

Game Summaries

Team records listed in parentheses indicate records before game.

WILD CARD ROUND

AFC

Chiefs, 27-24 (OT)

Pittsburgh (9-7)	7	10	0	7	0— **24**
Kansas City (11-5)	7	0	3	14	3— **27**

Date— Jan. 8. **Att**— 74,515. **Time**— 3:32.

1st Quarter: PIT— Adrian Cooper 10-yd pass from Neil O'Donnell (Gary Anderson kick), 6:15. KC— J.J. Birden 23-yd pass from Dave Krieg (Nick Lowery kick), 13:21.

2nd Quarter: PIT— Anderson 30-yd FG, 5:26. PIT— Ernie Mills 26-yd pass from O'Donnell (Anderson kick), 14:42.

3rd Quarter: KC— Lowery 23-yd FG, 13:51.

4th Quarter: KC— Marcus Allen 2-yd run (Lowery kick), 6:02. PIT— Eric Green 22-yd pass from O'Donnell (Anderson kick), 10:49. KC— Tim Barnett 7-yd pass from Joe Montana (Lowery kick), 13:17.

Overtime: KC— Lowery 32-yd FG, 11:03.

Raiders, 42-24

Denver (9-7)	7	14	0	3— **24**
LA Raiders (10-6)	14	7	14	7— **42**

Date— Jan. 9. **Att**— 65,314. **Time**— 3:34.

1st Quarter: LA— Ethan Horton 9-yd pass from Jeff Hostetler (Jeff Jaeger kick), 5:34. DEN— Shannon Sharpe 23-yd pass from John Elway (Jason Elam kick), 8:48. LA— Tim Brown 65-yd pass from Hostetler (Jaeger kick), 12:35.

2nd Quarter: DEN— Reggie Johnson 16-yd pass from Elway (Elam kick), 4:54. LA— James Jett 54-yd pass from Hostetler (Jaeger kick), 7:32. DEN—Derek Russell 6-yd pass from Elway (Elam kick), 14:28.

3rd Quarter: LA— Napoleon McCallum 26-yd run (Jaeger kick), 6:52. LA— McCallum 2-yd run (Jaeger kick), 10:33.

4th Quarter: DEN— Elam 33-yd FG, 2:24. LA— McCallum 1-yd run (Jaeger kick), 8:17.

NFC

Packers, 28-24

Green Bay (9-7)	0	7	14	7— **28**
Detroit (10-6)	3	7	7	7— **24**

Date— Jan. 8. **Att**— 68,479. **Time**— 2:53.

1st Quarter: DET— Jason Hanson 47-yd FG, 15:00.

2nd Quarter: GB— Sterling Sharpe 12-yd pass from Brett Favre (Chris Jacke kick), 7:04. DET— Brett Perriman 1-yd pass from Erik Kramer (Hanson kick), 12:56.

3rd Quarter: DET— Melvin Jenkins 15-yd interception return (Hanson kick), 6:40. GB— Sharpe 28-yd pass from Favre (Jacke kick), 10:25. GB—George Teague 101-yd interception return (Jacke kick), 13:20.

4th Quarter: DET— Derrick Moore 5-yd run (Hanson kick), 6:33. GB— Sharpe 40-yd pass from Favre (Jacke kick), 14:05.

Giants, 17-10

Minnesota (9-7)	0	10	0	0— **10**
NY Giants (11-5)	3	0	14	0— **17**

Date— Jan. 9. **Att**— 75,089. **Time**— 3:01.

1st Quarter: NY— David Treadwell 26-yd FG, 6:25.

2nd Quarter: MIN— Cris Carter 40-yd pass from Jim McMahon (Fuad Reveiz kick), 13:07. MIN— Reveiz 52-yd FG, 14:58.

3rd Quarter: NY— Rodney Hampton 51-yd run (Treadwell kick), 2:54. NY— Hampton 2-yd run (Treadwell kick), 9:23.

NFL Playoffs (Cont.)
DIVISIONAL SEMIFINALS

AFC

🏈 Bills, 29-23

LA Raiders (11-6) ....0 17 6 0— **23**
Buffalo (12-4) ....0 13 9 7— **29**
Date— Jan. 15. **Att**— 61,923. **Time**— 3:07.

2nd Quarter: LA— Jeff Jaeger 30-yd FG, 1:13. BUF— Kenneth Davis 1-yd run (kick failed), 1:30. LA— Napoleon McCallum 1-yd run (Jaeger kick), 6:50. LA— McCallum 1-yd run (Jaeger kick), 13:03. BUF— Thurman Thomas 8-yd run (Steve Christie kick), 14:10.

3rd Quarter: BUF— Bill Brooks 25-yd pass from Jim Kelly (kick failed), 11:37. BUF— Christie 29-yd FG, 14:01. LA— Tim Brown 86-yd pass from Jeff Hostetler (kick failed), 14:30.

4th Quarter: BUF— Brooks 22-yd pass from Kelly (Christie kick), 2:55.

🏈 Chiefs, 28-20

Kansas City (12-5) ....0 0 7 21— **28**
Houston (12-4) ....10 0 0 10— **20**
Date— Jan. 16. **Att**— 64,011. **Time**— 3:13.

1st Quarter: HOU— Al Del Greco 49-yd FG, 3:50. HOU— Gary Brown 2-yd run (Del Greco kick), 13:01.

3rd Quarter: KC— Keith Cash 7-yd pass from Joe Montana (Nick Lowery kick), 4:41.

4th Quarter: HOU— Del Greco 43-yd FG, 5:23. KC— J.J. Birden 11-yd pass from Montana (Lowery kick), 6:22. KC— Willie Davis 18-yd pass from Montana (Lowery kick), 7:16. HOU— Ernest Givins 7-yd pass from Warren Moon (Del Greco kick), 11:15. KC— Marcus Allen 21-yd run (Lowery kick), 13:05.

NFC

🏈 49ers, 44-3

NY Giants (12-5) ....0 3 0 0— **3**
San Francisco (10-6) ....9 14 14 7— **44**
Date— Jan. 15. **Att**— 67,143. **Time**— 2:50.

1st Quarter: SF— Ricky Watters 1-yd run (kick failed), 4:27. SF— Mike Cofer 29-yd FG, 10:07.

2nd Quarter: SF— Watters 1-yd run (Cofer kick), 0:02. SF— Watters 2-yd run (Cofer kick), 10:57. NY— David Treadwell 25-yd FG, 15:00.

3rd Quarter: SF— Watters 6-yd run (Cofer kick), 7:22. SF— Watters 2-yd run (Cofer kick), 13:51.

4th Quarter: SF— Marc Logan 2-yd run (Cofer kick), 2:34.

🏈 Cowboys, 27-17

Green Bay (10-7) ....3 0 7 7— **17**
Dallas (12-4) ....0 17 7 3— **27**
Date— Jan. 16. **Att**— 64,790. **Time**— 3:00.

1st Quarter: GB— Chris Jacke 30-yd FG, 11:40.

2nd Quarter: DAL— Alvin Harper 25-yd pass from Troy Aikman (Eddie Murray kick), 5:53. DAL— Murray 41-yd FG, 14:37. DAL— Jay Novacek 6-yd pass from Aikman (Murray kick), 14:55.

3rd Quarter: DAL— Michael Irvin 19-yd pass from Aikman (Murray kick), 9:05. GB— Robert Brooks 13-yd pass from Brett Favre (Jacke kick), 13:28.

4th Quarter: DAL— Murray 38-yd FG, 7:22. GB— Sterling Sharpe 29-yd pass from Favre (Jacke kick), 14:38.

CONFERENCE CHAMPIONSHIPS

AFC

🏈 Bills, 30-13

Kansas City (13-5) ....6 0 7 0— **13**
Buffalo (13-4) ....7 13 0 10— **30**
Date— Jan. 23. **Att**— 76,642. **Time**— 3:10.

1st Quarter: BUF— Thurman Thomas 12-yd run (Steve Christie kick), 8:11. KC— Nick Lowery 31-yd FG, 12:46. KC— Lowery 31-yd FG, 14:21.

2nd Quarter: BUF— Thomas 3-yd run (Christie kick), 2:58. BUF— Christie 23-yd FG, 7:56. BUF— Christie 25-yd FG, 12:59.

3rd Quarter: KC— Marcus Allen 1-yd run (Lowery kick), 11:54.

4th Quarter: BUF— Christie 18-yd FG, 3:05. BUF— Thomas 3-yd run (Christie kick), 9:30.

NFC

🏈 Cowboys, 38-21

San Francisco (11-6) ....0 7 7 7— **21**
Dallas (13-4) ....7 21 7 3— **38**
Date— Jan. 23. **Att**— 64,902. **Time**— 3:11.

1st Quarter: DAL— Emmitt Smith 5-yd run (Eddie Murray kick), 6:19.

2nd Quarter: SF— Tom Rathman 7-yd pass from Steve Young (Mike Cofer kick), 0:05. DAL— Daryl Johnston 4-yd run (Murray kick), 5:12. DAL— E. Smith 11-yd pass from Troy Aikman (Murray kick), 8:56. DAL— Jay Novacek 19-yd pass from Aikman (Murray kick), 14:02.

3rd Quarter: SF— Ricky Watters 4-yd run (Cofer kick), 9:13. DAL— Alvin Harper 42-yd pass from Bernie Kosar (Murray kick), 12:36.

4th Quarter: DAL— Murray 50-yd FG, 5:08. SF— Young 1-yd run (Cofer kick), 10:54.

Super Bowl XXVIII
Sunday, Jan. 30 at the Georgia Dome in Atlanta.

Dallas (15-4) 6   0 14 10— **30**
Buffalo (14-5) ....3 10   0   0— **13**

1st Quarter: DAL— Eddie Murray 41-yd FG, 2:19. Drive: 24 yards in 5 plays. BUF— Steve Christie 54-yd FG, 4:41. Drive: 43 yards in 8 plays. DAL— Murray 24-yd FG, 11:05. Drive: 43 yards in 7 plays.
2nd Quarter: BUF— Thurman Thomas 4-yd run (Christie kick), 2:34. Drive: 80 yards in 17 plays. BUF— Christie 28-yd FG, 15:00. Drive: 38 yards in 7 plays.
3rd Quarter: DAL— James Washington 46-yd fumble return (Murray kick), 0:55. Fumble caused when Leon Lett stripped ball from Thomas. DAL—Emmitt Smith 15-yd run (Murray kick), 6:18. Drive: 64 yards on 8 plays.
4th Quarter: DAL— E. Smith 1-yd run (Murray kick), 5:10. Drive: 34 yards in 9 plays. DAL— Murray 20-yd FG, 12:10. Drive: 49 yards in 10 plays.

Favorite: Dallas, 10½   **Attendance:** 72,817
Field: Turf   **Time:** 3:16
Weather: Indoors   **TV Rating:** 45.5/66 share (NBC)

Officials: Bob McElwee (referee); Art Demmas (umpire); Sid Semon (HL); Tom Barnes (LJ); Al Jury (BJ); Nate Jones (SJ); Don Orr (FJ).

Most Valuable Player
Emmitt Smith, Dallas, RB (30 carries for 132 yds, 4 catches for 26 yds, 2 TDs)

Team Statistics

	Cowboys	Bills
Touchdowns	3	1
Rushing	2	1
Passing	0	0
Returns	1	0
Time of possession	34:29	25:31
First downs	20	22
Rushing	6	6
Passing	14	15
Penalties	0	1
3rd down efficiency	5/13	5/17
4th down efficiency	1/1	2/3
Total offense (net yards)	341	314
Plays	64	80
Average Gain	5.3	3.9
Rushes/yards	35/137	27/87
Passing yards	204	227
Completions/attempts	19/27	31/50
Times intercepted	1	0
Times sacked/yards lost	2/3	3/33
Return yardage	89	119
Punt returns/yards	1/5	1/5
Kickoff returns/yards	2/72	6/144
Interceptions/yards	1/12	1/41
Fumbles/lost	0/0	3/2
Penalties/yards	6/50	1/10
Punts/average	4/43.8	5/37.6
Punts blocked	0	

Individual Statistics

Dallas Cowboys

Passing	Att	Cmp	Pct	Yds	TD	Int
Troy Aikman	27	19	70.1	207	0	1
Bernie Kosar	0	0	0.0	0	0	0

Receiving	No	Yds	Avg	Long	TD
Michael Irvin	5	66	13.2	20	0
Jay Novacek	5	26	5.2	9	0
Emmitt Smith	4	26	6.5	10	0
Alvin Harper	3	75	25.0	35	0
Daryl Johnston	2	14	7.0	11	0
TOTAL	19	207	10.9	35	0

Rushing	Car	Yds	Avg	Long	TD
Emmitt Smith	30	132	4.4	15-td	2
Kevin Williams	1	6	6.0	6	0
Troy Aikman	1	3	3.0	3	0
Daryl Johnston	1	0	0.0	0	0
Bernie Kosar	1	-1	-1.0	-1	0
Lincoln Coleman	1	-3	-3.0	-3	0
TOTAL	35	137	3.9	15	2

Field Goals	20-29	30-29	40-49	50-59	Total
Eddie Murray	2-2	0-0	1-1	0-0	3-3

Punting	No	Yds	Long	Avg	In 20
John Jett	4	175	47	43.8	2

Punt Returns	FC	Ret	Yds	Long	Avg	TD
Kevin Williams	1	1	5	5	5.0	0

Kickoff Returns	No	Yds	Long	Avg	TD
Kevin Williams	1	50	50	50.0	0
Kenneth Gant	1	22	22	22.0	0

Interceptions	No	Yds	Long	Avg	TD
James Washington	1	12	12	12.0	0

Sacks		Most Tackles	
Jimmie Jones	1	James Washington	11
Four tied with ½ each.		Thomas Everett	8

Buffalo Bills

Passing	Att	Cmp	Pct	Yds	TD	Int
Jim Kelly	50	31	62.0	260	0	1

Receiving	No	Yds	Avg	Long	TD
Bill Brooks	7	63	9.0	15	0
Thurman Thomas	7	52	7.4	24	0
Andre Reed	6	75	12.5	22	0
Don Beebe	6	60	10.0	18	0
Kenneth Davis	3	-5	-1.7	7	0
Pete Metzelaars	1	8	8.0	8	0
Keith McKeller	1	7	7.0	7	0
TOTAL	31	260	8.4	24	0

Rushing	Car	Yds	Avg	Long	TD
Kenneth Davis	9	38	4.2	11	0
Thurman Thomas	16	37	2.3	6	1
Jim Kelly	2	12	6.0	8	0
TOTAL	27	87	3.2	11	1

Field Goals	20-29	30-29	40-49	50-59	Total
Steve Christie	1-1	0-0	0-0	1-1	2-2

Punting	No	Yds	Long	Avg	In 20
Chris Mohr	5	188	52	37.6	1

Punt Returns	FC	Ret	Yds	Long	Avg	TD
Russell Copeland	1	1	5	5	5.0	0

Kickoff Returns	No	Yds	Long	Avg	TD
Russell Copeland	4	82	22	20.5	0
Don Beebe	2	62	34	30.5	0
TOTAL	6	144	34	24.0	0

Interceptions	No	Yds	Long	Avg	TD
Nate Odomes	1	41	41	41.0	0

Sacks		Most Tackles	
Jeff Wright	2	Cornelius Bennett	10
		James Patton	9

Super Bowl Finalists' Playoff Statistics

Dallas (3-0)

Passing (5 Att)	Att	Cmp	Pct	Yds	TD	Rate
Bernie Kosar 9	5	55.6	83	1	123.8
Troy Aikman 82	61	74.4	686	5	104.0
TOTAL 92	66	71.7	769	6	104.8

Interceptions: Aikman 3.

Receiving	No	Yds	Avg	Long	TD
Michael Irvin 16	215	13.4	27	1
Jay Novacek 15	142	9.5	20	2
Emmitt Smith 13	138	10.6	28	1
Daryl Johnston 10	74	7.4	12	0
Alvin Harper 9	186	20.7	42-td	2
Lincoln Coleman 2	6	3.0	6	0
Derrick Lassic 1	8	8.0	8	0
TOTAL................................66	769	11.7	42-td	6

Rushing	Car	Yds	Avg	Long	TD
Emmitt Smith 66	280	4.2	15-td	3
Troy Aikman 7	28	4.0	12	0
Daryl Johnston 8	25	3.1	5	1
Lincoln Coleman 6	16	2.7	9	0
Derrick Lassic 3	7	2.3	7	0
Kevin Williams....................1	6	6.0	6	0
Bill Bates 1	0	0.0	0	0
Bernie Kosar 3	−4	−1.3	−1	0
TOTAL................................95	358	3.8	14	4

Touchdowns	TD	Run	Rec	Ret	Pts
Emmitt Smith.....................4	3	1	0	24
Alvin Harper......................2	0	2	0	12
Jay Novacek......................2	0	2	0	12
Michael Irvin 1	0	1	0	6
Daryl Johnston 1	1	0	0	6
James Washington 1	0	0	1	6
TOTAL................................11	4	6	1	66

Kicking	PAT/Att	FG/Att	Lg	Pts
Eddie Murray 11/11	6/6	50	29

Punts	No	Yds	Long	Avg	In20
John Jett 11	470	48	42.7	3

Most Interceptions
Four tied with 1 each.

Most Sacks
Jim Jeffcoat...................2½
Tony Tolbert 2½

Buffalo (2-1)

Passing (5 Att)	Att	Cmp	Pct	Yds	TD	Rate
Jim Kelly 114	75	65.8	707	2	84.9

Interceptions: Kelly 1.

Receiving	No	Yds	Avg	Long	TD
Bill Brooks 17	193	11.4	25-td	2
Thurman Thomas 15	122	8.1	24	0
Andre Reed 14	177	12.6	28	0
Pete Metzelaars 10	80	8.0	17	0
Keith McKeller 5	35	7.0	8	0
Don Beebe 9	88	9.8	18	0
Kenneth Davis 4	11	2.8	16	0
Carwell Gardner 1	1	1.0	1	0
TOTAL................................75	707	9.4	28	2

Rushing	Car	Yds	Avg	Long	TD
Thurman Thomas 63	267	4.2	33	5
Kenneth Davis 30	106	3.5	15	1
Andre Reed 1	8	8.0	8	0
Jim Kelly 9	11	1.2	8	0
TOTAL..............................103	392	3.8	33	6

Touchdowns	TD	Run	Rec	Ret	Pts
Thurman Thomas 5	5	0	0	30
Bill Brooks 2	0	2	0	12
Kenneth Davis 1	1	0	0	6
TOTAL...............................8	6	2	0	48

Kicking	PAT/Att	FG/Att	Lg	Pts
Steve Christie 6/8	6/7	54	24

Punts	No	Yds	Long	Avg	In20
Chris Mohr 12	430	52	35.8	3

Most Interceptions
Henry Jones 1
Nate Odomes 1
James Williams 1

Most Sacks
Bruce Smith 3
Jeff Wright.........................3
Phil Hanson.......................1

Cowboys' 1993 Schedule

Date	Regular Season	Result	W-L
Sept. 6*	at Washington (0-0)	L, 16-35	0-1
Sept.12	Buffalo (1-0)	L, 10-13	0-2
Sept.19	at Phoenix (1-1)	W, 17-10	1-2
Sept.26	Open date	—	—
Oct. 3	Green Bay (1-2)	W, 36-14	2-2
Oct. 10	at Indianapolis (2-2)	W, 27-3	3-2
Oct. 17	San Francisco (3-2)	W, 26-17	4-2
Oct. 24	Open date	—	—
Oct. 31	at Philadelphia (4-2)	W, 23-10	5-2
Nov. 7	NY Giants (5-2)	W, 31-9	6-2
Nov. 14	Phoenix (3-6)	W, 20-15	7-2
Nov. 21	at Atlanta (3-6)	L, 14-27	7-3
Nov. 25	Miami (8-2)	L, 14-16	7-4
Dec. 6*	Philadelphia (5-6)	W, 23-17	8-4
Dec. 12	at Minnesota (6-6)	W, 37-20	9-4
Dec. 18	at NY Jets (8-5)	W, 28-7	10-4
Dec. 26	Washington (4-10)	W, 38-3	11-4
Jan. 2	at NY Giants (11-4)	W, 16-13 (OT)	12-4

Date	Playoffs	Result	W-L
Jan. 8	Bye	—	—
Jan. 16	Green Bay (10-7)	W, 27-17	13-4
Jan. 23	San Francisco (11-6)	W, 38-21	14-4
Jan. 30	vs Buffalo (14-4)	W, 30-13	15-4

Bills' 1993 Schedule

Date	Regular Season	Result	W-L
Sept. 5	New England (0-0)	W, 38-14	1-0
Sept.12	at Dallas (0-1)	W, 34-10	2-0
Sept.19	Open date	—	—
Sept.26	Miami (1-1)	L, 13-22	2-1
Oct. 3	NY Giants (3-0)	W, 17-14	3-1
Oct. 11*	Houston (1-3)	W, 35-7	4-1
Oct. 17	Open date	—	—
Oct. 24	at NY Jets (2-3)	W, 19-10	5-1
Nov. 1*	Washington (1-5)	W, 24-10	6-1
Nov. 7	at New England (1-7)	W, 13-10 (OT)	7-1
Nov. 15*	at Pittsburgh (5-3)	L, 0-23	7-2
Nov. 21	Indianapolis (3-6)	W, 23-9	8-2
Nov. 28	at Kansas City (7-3)	L, 7-23	8-3
Dec. 5	LA Raiders (6-5)	L, 24-25	8-4
Dec. 12	at Philadelphia (5-7)	W, 10-7	9-4
Dec. 19	at Miami (9-4)	W, 47-34	10-4
Dec. 26	NY Jets (8-6)	W, 16-14	11-4
Jan. 2	at Indianapolis (4-11)	W, 30-10	12-4

Date	Playoffs	Result	W-L
Jan. 8	Bye	—	—
Jan. 16	LA Raiders (11-6)	W, 29-23	13-4
Jan. 23	Kansas City (13-5)	W, 30-13	14-4
Jan. 30	vs Dallas (14-4)	L, 13-30	14-5

Note: (*) indicates Monday Night game; listed records of opponents are day of game.

NFL Pro Bowl

44th NFL Pro Bowl Game and 24th AFC-NFC contest (NFC leads series, 14-10). **Date:** Feb. 6 at Aloha Stadium in Honolulu. **Coaches:** Marty Schottenheimer, Kansas City (AFC) and George Seifert, San Francisco (NFC). **Player of the Game:** WR Andre Rison of Atlanta, who had six catches for 86 yards, including a 32-yard toss from teammate Bobby Hebert to spark the NFC's go-ahead touchdown drive in the third quarter.

NFC ....3 0 7 7— **17**
AFC ....0 3 0 0— **3**

1st Quarter: NFC— Norm Johnson 35-yd FG, 10:28.

2nd Quarter: AFC— Gary Anderson 25-yd FG, 13:51.

3rd Quarter: NFC— Jerome Bettis 4-yd run (Johnson kick), 13:33.

4th Quarter: NFC— Cris Carter 15-yd pass from Bobby Hebert (Johnson kick), 0:53.

Attendance— 50,026; **Time**— 3:19; **TV Rating**— 6.2/9 share (ESPN).

STARTING LINEUPS

As voted on by NFL players and coaches.

American Conference

Pos Offense	Pos Defense
WR–Tim Brown, LA	E–Bruce Smith, Buf.
WR–Webster Slaughter, Hou.	E–Neil Smith, KC
TE–Shannon Sharpe, Den.	T–Ray Childress, Hou.
T–Howard Ballard, Buf.	T–Cortez Kennedy, Sea.
T–Richmond Webb, Mia.	LB–Greg Lloyd, Pit.
G–Mike Munchak, Hou.	LB–Junior Seau, SD
G–Steve Wisniewski, LA	LB–Derrick Thomas, KC
C–Bruce Matthews, Hou.	CB–Nate Odomes, Buf.
QB–John Elway, Den.	CB–Rod Woodson, Pit.
RB–Thurman Thomas, Buf.	S–Steve Atwater, Den.
RB–Marcus Allen, KC	S–Dennis Smith, Den.
K–Gary Anderson, Pit.	P–Greg Montgomery, Hou.
KR Eric Metcalf, Cle.	ST–Steve Tasker, Buf.

Note: WR Slaughter, OG Munchak and DE B.Smith were injured and unable to play.

Reserves

Offense: WR— Anthony Miller, SD and Andre Reed, Buf.; **TE**— Keith Jackson, Mia.; **T**— John Alt, KC; **G**— Max Montoya, LA and Keith Sims, Mia.; **C**— Dermontti Dawson, Pit.; **QB**— Joe Montana, KC and Warren Moon, Hou.; **RB**— Keith Byars, Mia. and Barry Foster, Pit.

Defense: E— Howie Long, LA and Leslie O'Neal, SD; **L**— Michael Dean Perry, Cle.; **LB**— Cornelius Bennett, Buf. and Karl Mecklenburg, Den.; **CB**— Terry McDaniel, LA; **S**— Eugene Robinson, Sea.

Replacements: Offense— WR Irving Fryar, Mia. for Slaughter; WR Haywood Jeffires, Hou. for Reed; TE Eric Green, Pit. for Jackson; QB Boomer Esiason, NY for Montana; RB Chris Warren, Sea. for Foster. **Defense**— DE Sean Jones, Hou. for B. Smith.

National Conference

Pos Offense	Pos Defense
WR–Michael Irvin, Dal.	E–Richard Dent, Chi.
WR–Jerry Rice, SF	E–Reggie White, GB
TE–Jay Novacek, Dal.	L–Sean Gilbert, LA
T–Harris Barton, SF	L–John Randle, Min.
T–Erik Williams, Dal.	LB–Rickey Jackson, NO
G–Randall McDaniel, Min.	LB–Hardy Nickerson, TB
G–Nate Newton, Dal.	LB–Renaldo Turnbull, NO
C–Mark Stepnoski, Dal.	CB–Eric Allen, Phi.
QB–Troy Aikman, Dal.	CB–Deion Sanders, Atl.
RB–Barry Sanders, Det.	S–Mark Carrier, Chi.
RB–Emmitt Smith, Dal.	S–Tim McDonald, SF
K–Norm Johnson, Atl.	P–Rich Camarillo, Pho.
KR–Tyrone Hughes, NO	ST–Elbert Shelley, Atl.

Note: C Stepnoski, QB Aikman, RB B.Sanders and RB E.Smith were injured and unable to play.

Reserves

Offense: WR— Andre Rison, Atl. and Sterling Sharpe, GB; **TE**—Brent Jones, SF; **T**— Jumbo Elliott, NY (injured, not replaced); **G**—Guy McIntyre, SF; **C**— Jesse Sapolu, SF; **QB**— Steve Young, SF and Phil Simms, NY; **RB**— Jerome Bettis, LA and Daryl Johnston, Dal.

Defense: E— Chris Doleman, Min.; **L**— Russell Maryland, Dal.; **LB**— Seth Joyner, Phi., Ken Norton, Dal. and Pat Swilling, Det.; **CB**—Donnell Woolford, Chi.; **S**— Thomas Everett, Dal.

Replacements: Offense— WR Cris Carter, Min. for S. Sharpe; C Bart Oates, NY for Stepnoski; QB Brett Favre for Aikman; QB Bobby Hebert, Atl. for Simms; RB Ricky Watters, SF for B. Sanders; RB Rodney Hampton, NY for E. Smith. **Defense**— S LeRoy Butler, GB for Everett.

Annual Awards

The NFL does not sanction any postseason awards for players or coaches, but many are given out. Among the presenters for the 1993 regular season were AP, UPI, *The Sporting News* and the Pro Football Writers of America. MVP awards are also given out by the Maxwell Club of Philadelphia (Bert Bell Award) and the NFL Players Association.

Most Valuable Player   **Selectors**
    NFL Emmitt Smith, Dallas, RB ....AP, MC, PFWA, TSN
    AFC John Elway, Denver, QB ....NFLPA
    NFC Jerry Rice, San Francisco, WR ....NFLPA

Offensive Players of the Year
    NFL Jerry Rice, San Francisco, WR ....AP
    AFC John Elway, Denver, QB ....UPI
    NFC Emmitt Smith, Dallas, RB ....UPI

Defensive Players of the Year
    NFL Rod Woodson, Pittsburgh, CB ....AP
    AFC Rod Woodson, Pittsburgh, CB ....UPI
    NFC Eric Allen, Philadelphia, CB ....UPI

Rookies of the Year
    NFL Jerome Bettis, LA Rams, RB ....PFWA, TSN
    AFC Rick Mirer, Seattle, QB ....UPI
    NFC Jerome Bettis, LA Rams, RB............................UPI
    Offense Jerome Bettis, LA Rams, RB ....AP
    Defense Dana Stubblefield, San Francisco, DT ....AP

Coaches of the Year
    NFL Dan Reeves, NY Giants.................AP, PFWA, TSN
    AFC Marv Levy, Buffalo.......................................UPI
    NFC Dan Reeves, NY Giants..................................UPI

All-NFL Team

The 1993 All-NFL team combining the All-Pro selections of the Associated Press and the Pro Football Writers of America (PFWA). Holdovers from the 1992 All-NFL team in **bold** type; (*) indicates rookie.

Offense

Pos		Selectors
WR	**Jerry Rice**, San Francisco	AP,PFWA
WR	**Sterling Sharpe**, Green Bay	AP,PFWA
TE	Shannon Sharpe, Denver	AP,PFWA
T	**Harris Barton**, San Francisco	AP,PFWA
T	Erik Williams, Dallas	AP,PFWA
G	**Randall McDaniel**, Minnesota	AP,PFWA
G	Chris Hinton, Atlanta	AP
G	**Steve Wisniewski**, LA Raiders	PFWA
C	Dermontti Dawson, Pittsburgh	AP
C	**Bruce Matthews**, Houston	PFWA
QB	**Steve Young**, San Francisco	AP,PFWA
RB	**Emmitt Smith**, Dallas	AP,PFWA
RB	Jerome Bettis*, LA Rams	AP,PFWA

Defense

Pos		Selectors
DE	Bruce Smith, Buffalo	AP,PFWA
DE	Neil Smith, Kansas City	AP,PFWA
DT	**Cortez Kennedy**, Seattle	AP,PFWA
DT	John Randle, Minnesota	AP,PFWA
OLB	Greg Lloyd, Pittsburgh	AP,PFWA
OLB	Seth Joyner, Philadelphia	PFWA
OLB	Renaldo Turnbull, New Orleans	AP
ILB	**Junior Seau**, San Diego	AP,PFWA
ILB	Hardy Nickerson, Tampa Bay	AP,PFWA
CB	**Deion Sanders**, Atlanta	AP,PFWA
CB	**Rod Woodson**, Pittsburgh	AP,PFWA
S	LeRoy Butler, Green Bay	AP,PFWA
S	Marcus Robertson, Houston	AP
S	Eugene Robinson, Seattle	PFWA

Note: Sanders made team as a kick return specialist in 1992.

Specialists

PK	Chris Jacke, Green Bay	AP	R	Tyrone Hughes, New Orleans	PFWA
PK	Norm Johnson, Atlanta	PFWA	KR	Eric Metcalf, Cleveland	AP
P	Greg Montgomery, Houston	AP,PFWA	ST	Steve Tasker, Buffalo	PFWA

NFL College Draft

First and second round selections at the 59th annual NFL College Draft held April 24-25, 1994, in New York City. Seventeen underclassmen were among the first 65 players chosen and are listed in capital LETTERS.

First Round

	Team		Pos
1	Cincinnati	DAN WILKINSON, Ohio St.	DT
2	Indianapolis	MARSHALL FAULK, San Diego St.	RB
3	Washington	HEATH SHULER, Tennessee	QB
4	New England	Willie McGinest, USC	DE
5	a-Indianapolis	Trev Alberts, Nebraska	LB
6	Tampa Bay	TRENT DILFER, Fresno St.	QB
7	b-San Francisco	Bryant Young, Notre Dame	DT
8	Seattle	SAM ADAMS, Texas A&M	DT
9	Cleveland	Antonio Langham, Alabama	DB
10	Arizona	JAMIR MILLER, UCLA	LB
11	Chicago	John Thierry, Alcorn St.	LB
12	c-NY Jets	Aaron Glenn, Texas A&M	DB
13	d-New Orleans	JOE JOHNSON, Louisville	DE
14	Philadelphia	Bernard Williams, Georgia	OT
15	e-LA Rams	Wayne Gandy, Auburn	OT
16	f-Green Bay	Aaron Taylor, Notre Dame	OT
17	Pittsburgh	Charles Johnson, Colorado	WR
18	g-Minnesota	Dewayne Washington, N.C. State	DB
19	Minnesota	Todd Steussie, California	OT
20	h-Miami	TIM BOWENS, Mississippi	DT
21	Detroit	Johnnie Morton, USC	WR
22	LA Raiders	Rob Fredrickson, Mich. St.	LB
23	i-Dallas	Shante Carver, Arizona St.	DE
24	NY Giants	THOMAS LEWIS, Indiana	WR
25	Kansas City	GREG HILL, Texas A&M	RB
26	Houston	Henry Ford, Arkansas	DE
27	Buffalo	Jeff Burris, Notre Dame	DB
28	j-San Francisco	WILLIAM FLOYD, Florida St.	FB
29	k-Cleveland	Derrick Alexander, Michigan	WR

Second Round

	Team		Pos
30	Cincinnati	DARNAY SCOTT, San Diego St.	WR
31	Washington	Tre Johnson, Temple	OG
32	Indianapolis	Eric Mahlum, California	C
33	LA Rams	Isaac Bruce, Memphis St.	WR
34	Tampa Bay	Errict Rhett, Florida	RB
35	New England	Kevin Lee, Alabama	WR
36	Seattle	Kevin Mawae, LSU	C
37	l-Philadelphia	BRUCE WALKER, UCLA	DT
38	Arizona	CHUCK LEVY, Arizona	RB
39	Chicago	Marcus Spears, N'western St.	OT
40	m-Minnesota	DAVID PALMER, Alabama	WR
41	NY Jets	Ryan Yarborough, Wyoming	WR
42	Philadelphia	Charlie Garner, Tennessee	RB
43	San Diego	Isaac Davis, Arkansas	OG
44	New Orleans	MARIO BATES, Arizona St.	RB
45	n-Atlanta	Bert Emanuel, Rice	WR
46	Dallas	Larry Allen, Sonoma St.	OG
47	NY Giants	Thomas Randolph, Kansas St.	DB
48	Buffalo	Bucky Brooks, N. Carolina	WR
49	LA Rams	Toby Wright, Nebraska	DB
50	Pittsburgh	Brentson Buckner, Clemson	DE
51	Denver	Allen Aldridge, Houston	LB
52	o-LA Raiders	James Folston, NE Louisiana	LB
53	p-San Francisco	Kevin Mitchell, Syracuse	LB
54	Miami	Aubrey Beavers, Oklahoma	LB
55	q-Minnesota	Fernando Smith, Jackson St.	DE
56	r-LA Rams	Brad Ottis, Wayne St.	DT
57	Detroit	Van Malone, Texas	DB
58	Kansas City	DONNELL BENNETT, Miami-FL	RB
59	NY Giants	Jason Sehorn, USC	DB
60	Houston	Jeremy Nunley, Alabama	DE
61	Buffalo	Lonnie Johnson, Florida St.	TE
62	s-San Francisco	Tyronne Drakeford, Va. Tech	DB
63	San Diego	Vaughn Parker, UCLA	OG
64	Buffalo	Sam Rogers, Colorado	LB
65	t-Miami	Tim Ruddy, Notre Dame	C

Acquired picks: a—from LA Rams; **b**—Atlanta thru Indianapolis and LA Rams; **c**—from New Orleans; **d**—from NY Jets; **e**—from San Diego thru San Francisco; **f**—from Miami; **g**—from Denver; **h**—from Green Bay; **i**—from San Francisco; **j**—from Dallas; **k**—from Philadelphia, which received a compensatory pick for Green Bay's signing of Reggie White in 1993; **l**—from Atlanta; **m**—from Cleveland thru Philadelphia and Atlanta; **n**—from Minnesota; **o**—from Minnesota; **p**—from Green Bay; **q**—from LA Raiders; **r**—from San Francisco; **s**—from Dallas; **t**—from Arizona.

Postseason Player Movement

The 1993 settlement of the NFL players' lawsuit against the league provided for genuine free agency by directing that all players with five or more years of NFL experience whose contracts expire on Feb. 1 can negotiate with any NFL club, including their own, from March 1 through July 15. All free agent signings and key acquisitions from the close of the 1993 season through June 1, 1994 are listed below. Under "Key Acquisitions," note that the team listed is the last club played for; (T) indicates acquired in trade; (S) indicates signed off waivers. See "Updates" for further developments.

AFC

BUFFALO
Free Agents Signed
Rick Strom, Pit................................QB
Key Acquisitions
None.

CINCINNATI
Free Agents Signed
Darrick Brilz, Sea...........................G
Eric Moore, NY Giants ....OT
Louis Oliver, Mia ....DB
Troy Sadowski, NY Jets................TE
Key Acquisitions
Tim McGee, Wash (S)................WR
Santo Stephens, KC (S) ....LB

CLEVELAND
Free Agents Signed
Earnest Byner, Wash ....RB
Don Griffin, SF ....CB
Walter Reeves, Ariz......................TE
Mike Withycombe, SD..................G
Key Acquisitions
Donald Frank, SD (T) ....CB
Mark Rypien, Wash (S) ....QB

DENVER
Free Agents Signed
Jeff Campbell, Det.......................WR
Ray Crockett, Det..........................DB
Richard Harvey, Buf......................LB
Randy Hilliard, Cle ....DB
Anthony Miller, SD ....WR
Key Acquisitions
Mike Pritchard, Atl (t)..................WR
Ben Smith, Phi (t)...........................DB
Ted Washington, SF (t) ....DT

HOUSTON
Free Agents Signed
Rich Camarillo, Ariz.......................P
Pat Carter, LA Rams......................TE
Kenny Davidson, Pit.....................DE
Sean Salisbury, Min ....QB
Key Acquisition
None.

INDIANAPOLIS
Free Agents Signed
Tony Bennett, GB ....LB
Wesley Carroll, Cin ....WR
Floyd Turner, NO ....WR
Key Acquisition
Jim Harbaugh, Chi (S).................QB

KANSAS CITY
Free Agents Signed
Louie Aguiar, NY Jets ....P
Tony Casillas, Dal ....NT
Mark Collins, NY Giants ....CB
Key Acquisition
Steve Bono, SF (T) ....QB

LA RAIDERS
Free Agents Signed
Kevin Gogan, Dal ....G
Albert Lewis, KC ....DB
Jamie Williams, SF ....TE
Key Acquisitions
Derrick Gainer, Dal (T) ....RB
Harvey Williams, KC (S)...............RB

MIAMI
Free Agents Signed
Jim Arnold, Det...............................P
Gene Atkins, NO...........................DB
Tyrone Braxton, Den ....CB
Bernie Kosar, Dal ....QB
Michael Stewart, LA Rams.............DB
Key Acquisitions
None.

NEW ENGLAND
Free Agents Signed
Steve DeOssie, NY Jets ....LB
Myron Guyton, NY Giants.............DB
Bob Kratch, NY Giants ....G
Ricky Reynolds, TB.......................DB
Blair Thomas, NY Jets...................RB
Key Acquisition
Marion Butts, SD (T) ....RB

NY JETS
Free Agents Signed
Donald Evans, Pit ....DE
Brian Hansen, Cle...........................P
Pat Terrell, LA Rams........................S
Perry Williams, NYG ....CB
Key Acquisition
Jack Trudeau, Ind (S) ....QB

PITTSBURGH
Free Agents Signed
Ray Seals, TB................................DE
John L. Williams, Sea...................RB
Key Acquisitions.
None.

SAN DIEGO
Free Agents Signed
Reuben Davis, Ariz ....DT
Dennis Gibson, Det........................LB
Gale Gilbert, Buf...........................QB
David Griggs, Mia..........................LB
Dwayne Harper, Sea......................DB
Vance Johnson, Den ....WR
Key Acquisition
Tony Martin, Mia (T) ....WR

SEATTLE
Free Agents Signed
Howard Ballard, Buf.....................OT
Nate Odomes, Buf.........................DB
Brent Williams, NE ....DE
Key Acquisition
Reggie Barrett, Det (T)..................WR

All-Time Blockbuster NFL Trades

Twelve for one (Oct. 12, 1989)— The Dallas Cowboys trade RB Herschel Walker to Minnesota for five players (LB Jesse Solomon, LB David Howard, CB Issiac Holt, DE Alex Stewart and RB Darrin Nelson) and seven draft picks (1st in 1992 and six conditional picks over next three years).

Eleven for one (June 13, 1952)— The LA Rams trade 11 players (FB Dick Hoerner, DB Tom Keane, DB George Sims, C Joe Reid, HB Billy Baggett, T Jack Halliday, FB Dick McKissack, LB Vic Vasicek, Richard Wilkins, Aubrey Phillips and Dave Anderson) to the Dallas Texans for the draft rights to LB Les Richter.

Nine for one (Mar. 23, 1959)— The LA Rams trade seven players (DT Frank Fuller, DT Glenn Holtzman, DT Ken Panfil, G Art Hauser, LB John Tracey, FB Larry Hickman and Don Brown), a 2nd round pick in the 1960 Draft and a player to named during training camp in 1959 for All-Pro HB Ollie Matson.

Eight for one (Oct. 31, 1987)— The LA Rams trade RB Eric Dickerson to the Indianapolis Colts for two players and six draft picks in a three-way deal involving the Buffalo Bills. The Colts send the draft rights to DE Cornelius Bennett for RB Greg Bell and three draft picks (1st in 1988 plus 1st and 2nd round picks in '89). The Colts then send Bell and the three Buffalo picks to the Rams along with RB Owen Gill and three more draft picks (the Colts 1st and 2nd in 1988 and 1st rounder in '89) for Dickerson.

NFC

ARIZONA
Free Agents Signed
Jeff Feagles, Phi ....P
Seth Joyner, Phi ....LB
Randy Kirk, Cin ....LB
Clyde Simmons, Phi ....DE
Key Acquisition
James Williams, Buf (T) ....DB

ATLANTA
Free Agents Signed
D.J. Johnson, Pit ....DB
Terance Mathis. NY Jets ....WR
Kevin Ross, KC ....DB
Ricky Sanders, Wash ....WR
Mike Zandofsky, SD ....G
Key Acquisitions
Chris Doleman, Min (T) ....DE
Jeff George, Ind (T) ....QB

CHICAGO
Free Agents Signed
Andy Heck, Sea ....LB
Merril Hoge, Pit ....RB
Erik Kramer, Det............................QB
Lewis Tillman, NY Giants ....RB
Key Acquisitions
Marv Cook, NE (S) ....TE
Jeff Graham, Pit (T) ....WR
Steve Walsh, NO (S) ....QB

DALLAS
Free Agents Signed
Derek Kennard, NO ....G
Rodney Peete, Det ....QB
Key Acquisitions
None.

DETROIT
Free Agents Signed
Ron Hall, TB...................................TE
Mike Johnson, Cle ....LB
Dave Krieg, KC.............................QB
Robert Massey, Ariz......................DB
Scott Mitchell, Mia ....QB
Greg Montgomery, Hou ....P
Key Acquisitions
None.

GREEN BAY
Free Agents Signed
Reggie Cobb, TB ....RB
Sean Jones, Hou ....DL
Key Acquisition
Scott Mersereau, NY Jets (S) ....DT

LA RAMS
Free Agents Signed
Chris Chandler, Ariz ....QB
Jimmie Jones, Dal ....DE
Greg McMurtry, NE ....WR
Chris Miller, Atl ....QB
Key Acquisitions
Joe Kelly, LA Raiders (S) ....LB
Nate Lewis, SD (T) ....WR
Marquez Pope, SD (T) ....DB

MINNESOTA
Free Agents Signed
Chris Hinton, Atl ....OT
David Pool, Den ....DB
Key Acquisitions
Adrian Cooper, Pit (T) ....TE
Warren Moon, Hou (T) ....QB
Andre Ware, Det (S) ....QB

NEW ORLEANS
Free Agents Signed
Mike Haynes, Atl...........................WR
Jeff Uhlenhake, Mia........................C
Wesley Walls, SF ....TE
Key Acquisition
Jim Everett, LA Rams (T) ....QB

NY GIANTS
Free Agents Signed
Lance Smith, Ariz............................G
Key Acquisition
Arthur Marshall, Den (T) ....WR

PHILADELPHIA
Free Agents Signed
William Fuller, Hou ....DE
Eddie Murray, Dal.........................PK
Key Acquisitions
Burt Grossman, SD (T) ....DL
Bill Romanowski, SF (T) ....LB

SAN FRANCISCO
Free Agents Signed
Ken Norton, Dal.............................LB
Gary Plummer, SD.........................LB
Key Acquisitions
None.

TAMPA BAY
Free Agents Signed
Jeff Hunter, Mia ....DL
Tim Irwin, Min................................OL
Lonnie Marts, KC ....LB
Tony Stargell, Ind ....CB
Key Acquisitions
Thomas Everett, Dal (T) ....S
Blaise Winter, SD (T) ....DT

WASHINGTON
Free Agents Signed
Henry Ellard, LA Rams.................WR
John Friesz, SD...............................QB
John Gesek, Dal...............................G
Ken Harvey, Ariz............................LB
Ethan Horton, LA Raiders ....TE
Trevor Matich, Ind C
Keith Taylor, NO............................DB
Tony Woods, LA Rams ....DE
Key Acquisitions
None.

Retired
(Following 1993 season)

		Yrs
Jeff Bostic, Wash	C	14
Hobey Brenner, NO	TE	13
Chris Burkett, NYJ	WR	9
Danny Copeland, Wash	S	5
Dave Duerson, Ariz	S	11
Grant Feasel, Sea	C	11
Tim Green, Atl	DE	8
Bryan Hinkle, Pit	LB	13
Howie Long, LA Raiders	DE	13
Reuben Mayes, Sea	RB	7
Anthony Munoz, TB	OT	14
Brian Noble, GB	LB	9
Vai Sikahema, Phi	KR	8
Lawrence Taylor, NYG	LB	13
Andre Tippett, NE	LB	11

Coaching Changes
NFL teams that changed head coaches after the 1993 regular season.

AFC
NY Jets—fired Bruce Coslet and promoted defensive coordinator Pete Carroll (both Jan. 7).

NFC
Arizona (Phoenix)—fired Joe Bugel (Jan. 24), hired Houston defensive coordinator Buddy Ryan (Feb. 3); **Atlanta**—fired Jerry Glanville (Jan. 4), promoted offensive coordinator June Jones (Jan. 24); **Dallas**—accepted Jimmy Johnson's resignation (Mar. 29), hired former Oklahoma coach Barry Switzer (Mar. 30). **Washington**—fired Petitbon (Jan. 4), hired Dallas offensive coordinator Norv Turner (Feb. 2).

Canadian Football League
Final 1993 Standings

Division champions (*) and other playoff qualifiers (†) are noted. Number of seasons listed after each head coach refers to latest tenure with club through 1993 season.

Western Division

	W	L	T	Pts	PF	PA	vs Div
*Calgary	15	3	0	30	646	418	7-3-0
†Edmonton	12	6	0	24	507	372	7-3-0
†Saskatchewan	11	7	0	22	511	495	5-5-0
†B.C. Lions	10	8	0	20	574	583	3-7-0
Sacramento	6	12	0	12	498	509	3-7-0

1993 Head Coaches: Calg— Wally Buono (4th season); **Edm**— Ron Lancaster (3rd); **Sask**— Don Matthews (3rd); **BC**— Dave Ritchie (1st); **Sac**— Kay Stephenson (1st).
1992 Standings: 1. Calgary (13-5); 2. Edmonton (10-8); 3. Saskatchewan (9-9); 4. B.C. Lions (3-15).

Eastern Division

	W	L	T	Pts	PF	PA	vs Div
*Winnipeg	14	4	0	28	646	421	7-1-0
†Hamilton	6	12	0	12	316	567	4-4-0
†Ottawa	4	14	0	8	387	517	3-5-0
Toronto	3	15	0	6	390	593	2-6-0

1993 Head Coaches: Win— Cal Murphy (1st season); **Ham**— John Gregory (3rd); **Ott**— Ron Smeltzer (2nd); **Tor**— replaced Dennis Meyer (2nd, 1-9) with former coach Bill O'Billovich (2-6) on Sept. 10.
1992 Standings: 1. Winnipeg (11-7); 2. Hamilton (11-7); 3. Ottawa (9-9); 4. Toronto (6-12).

All-CFL Team

The 1993 All-CFL team as selected by a Football Writers of Canada panel.

Pos Offense	Pos Defense
WR–David Williams, Win.	E –Tim Cofield, Ham.
WR–Rod Harris, Sac.	E –Will Johnson, Calg.
T –Bruce Covernton, Calg.	T –Jearld Baylis, Sask
T –Chris Walby, Win.	T –H. Hasselbach, Calg.
G –David Black, Win.	LB –Elfrid Payton, Win.
G –Rob Smith, BC	LB –Willie Pless, Edm.
C –Rod Connop, Edm.	LB –John Motton, Ham.
QB–Doug Flutie, Calg.	CB –Karl Anthony, Calg.
FB–Sean Millington, BC	CB –Barry Wilburn, Sask.
RB–Mike Richardson, Win.	HB –Darryl Sampson, Win.
SB–Ray Elgaard, Sask.	HB –Don Wilson, Edm.
SB–David Sapunjis, Calg	S –Glen Suitor, Sask.

Specialists

Kicker— David Ridgway, Sask.; Punter— Bob Cameron, Win.; Kick Returns— Henry Williams, Edm.

1993 CFL Playoffs
Division Semifinals (Nov. 14)

Western: at Calgary 17 ............................B.C. Lions 9
at Edmonton 51 ....Saskatchewan 13
Eastern: at Hamilton 21............................Ottawa 10

Division Championships (Nov. 21)

Western: Edmonton 29 ....at Calgary 15
Eastern: at Winnipeg 20......................Hamilton 19

81st Grey Cup Championship

Nov. 28 at McMahon Stadium, Calgary
(Att: 50,035)

Winnipeg (15-4)	0	10	7	6—	23
Edmonton (14-6)	17	7	0	9—	33

Most Outstanding Player

Damon Allen, Edmonton, QB: (passing— 17 for 29, 226 yds, 1 TD, 1 Int.; rushing— 14 for 90 yds).

CFL Regular Season Individual Leaders
Passing Efficiency

(Minimum of 400 attempts)

	Att	Cmp	Pct	Yds	Gain	TD	Long	Int	Rating
Doug Flutie, Calg	703	416	59.2	6092	8.67	44	75-td	17	98.5
Damon Allen, Edm	400	214	53.5	3394	8.49	25	102-td	10	92.6
Danny Barrett, BC	513	293	57.1	4097	7.99	24	70-td	12	89.0
David Archer, Sac	701	403	57.5	6023	8.59	35	90-td	23	88.7
Matt Dunigan, Win	600	334	55.7	4682	7.80	36	75-td	18	88.5

All-Purpose Running

	Rush	Rec	Ret	Total
Henry Williams, Edm	115	950	1538	2603
Derrick Crawford, Calg	155	1007	1051	2213
Mike Clemons, Tor	481	344	1320	2145
Earl Winfield, Ham	53	1076	812	1941
Freeman Baysinger, Sac-BC	114	833	889	1836
Mike Saunders, Sask	683	612	535	1830

Note: Returns (Ret) includes kickoffs, punts and missed field goals returned.

Touchdowns

	TD	Rush	Rec	Ret	Pts
David Williams, Win	15	0	15	0	90
David Sapunjis, Calg	15	0	15	0	90
Eddie Brown, Edm	15	0	15	0	90
Mike Oliphant, Sac	13	8	5	0	78
Cory Philpot, BC	12	8	3	1	72
Mike Trevathan, BC	12	0	12	0	72
Will Moore, Calg	12	0	12	0	72

Other Individual Leaders

Points (Kicking)	215	Mark McLoughlin, Calg.
Rushing Yards	925	Mike Richardson, Win.
Passing Yards	6092	Doug Flutie, Calg.
Receptions	103	David Sapunjis, Calg.
Interceptions	8	Andre Francis, BC
Sacks	22	Elfrid Payton, Win.
Punting Average	45.5	Terry Baker, Ott.

Most Outstanding Players

Top Player	Doug Flutie, Calgary, QB
Canadian	Dave Sapunjis, Calgary, SB
Offensive Lineman	Chris Walby, Winnipeg, OT
Defensive Player	Jearld Baylis, Saskatch., DT
Rookie	Michael O'Shea, Hamilton, DT
Coach	Wally Buono, Calgary

THE 1995 INFORMATION PLEASE SPORTS ALMANAC

PRO FOOTBALL STATISTICS

THROUGH THE YEARS
1920-1994
SUPER BOWLS • NFL LEADERS

SEC B

PAGE 238

The Super Bowl

The first AFL-NFL World Championship Game, as it was originally called, was played seven months after the two leagues agreed to merge in June of 1966. It became the Super Bowl (complete with roman numerals) by the third game in 1969. The Super Bowl winner has been presented the Vince Lombardi Trophy since 1971. Lombardi, whose Green Bay teams won the first two title games, died in 1970. NFL champions (1966-69) and NFC champions (since 1970) are listed in CAPITAL letters.

Multiple winners: Dallas, Pittsburgh and San Francisco (4); Oakland-LA Raiders and Washington (3); Green Bay, Miami and NY Giants (2).

Bowl	Date	Winner	Head Coach	Score	Loser	Head Coach	Site
I	1/15/67	GREEN BAY	Vince Lombardi	35-10	Kansas City	Hank Stram	Los Angeles
II	1/14/68	GREEN BAY	Vince Lombardi	33-14	Oakland	John Rauch	Miami
III	1/12/69	NY Jets	Weeb Ewbank	16- 7	BALTIMORE	Don Shula	Miami
IV	1/11/70	Kansas City	Hank Stram	23- 7	MINNESOTA	Bud Grant	New Orleans
V	1/17/71	Baltimore	Don McCafferty	16-13	DALLAS	Tom Landry	Miami
VI	1/16/72	DALLAS	Tom Landry	24- 3	Miami	Don Shula	New Orleans
VII	1/14/73	Miami	Don Shula	14- 7	WASHINGTON	George Allen	Los Angeles
VIII	1/13/74	Miami	Don Shula	24- 7	MINNESOTA	Bud Grant	Houston
IX	1/12/75	Pittsburgh	Chuck Noll	16- 6	MINNESOTA	Bud Grant	New Orleans
X	1/18/76	Pittsburgh	Chuck Noll	21-17	DALLAS	Tom Landry	Miami
XI	1/ 9/77	Oakland	John Madden	32-14	MINNESOTA	Bud Grant	Pasadena
XII	1/15/78	DALLAS	Tom Landry	27-10	Denver	Red Miller	New Orleans
XIII	1/21/79	Pittsburgh	Chuck Noll	35-31	DALLAS	Tom Landry	Miami
XIV	1/20/80	Pittsburgh	Chuck Noll	31-19	LA RAMS	Ray Malavasi	Pasadena
XV	1/25/81	Oakland	Tom Flores	27-10	PHILADELPHIA	Dick Vermeil	New Orleans
XVI	1/24/82	SAN FRANCISCO	Bill Walsh	26-21	Cincinnati	Forrest Gregg	Pontiac, MI
XVII	1/30/83	WASHINGTON	Joe Gibbs	27-17	Miami	Don Shula	Pasadena
XVIII	1/22/84	LA Raiders	Tom Flores	38- 9	WASHINGTON	Joe Gibbs	Tampa
XIX	1/20/85	SAN FRANCISCO	Bill Walsh	38-16	Miami	Don Shula	Stanford
XX	1/26/86	CHICAGO	Mike Ditka	46-10	New England	Raymond Berry	New Orleans
XXI	1/25/87	NY GIANTS	Bill Parcells	39-20	Denver	Dan Reeves	Pasadena
XXII	1/31/88	WASHINGTON	Joe Gibbs	42-10	Denver	Dan Reeves	San Diego
XXIII	1/22/89	SAN FRANCISCO	Bill Walsh	20-16	Cincinnati	Sam Wyche	Miami
XXIV	1/28/90	SAN FRANCISCO	George Seifert	55-10	Denver	Dan Reeves	New Orleans
XXV	1/27/91	NY GIANTS	Bill Parcells	20-19	Buffalo	Marv Levy	Tampa
XXVI	1/26/92	WASHINGTON	Joe Gibbs	37-24	Buffalo	Marv Levy	Minneapolis
XXVII	1/31/93	DALLAS	Jimmy Johnson	52-17	Buffalo	Marv Levy	Pasadena
XXVIII	1/30/94	DALLAS	Jimmy Johnson	30-13	Buffalo	Marv Levy	Atlanta

Pete Rozelle Award (MVP)

The Most Valuable Player in the Super Bowl. Currently selected by an 11-member panel made up of national pro football writers and broadcasters chosen by the NFL. Presented by Sport magazine from 1967-89 and by the NFL since 1990. Named after former NFL commissioner Pete Rozelle in 1990. Winner who did not play for Super Bowl champion is in **bold** type.

Multiple winners: Joe Montana (3); Terry Bradshaw and Bart Starr (2).

Bowl		Bowl		Bowl	
I	Bart Starr, Green Bay, QB	XI	Fred Biletnikoff, Oakland, WR	XX	Richard Dent, Chicago, DE
II	Bart Starr, Green Bay, QB	XII	Harvey Martin, Dallas, DE	XXI	Phil Simms, NY Giants, QB
III	Joe Namath, NY Jets, QB		& Randy White, Dallas, DT	XXII	Doug Williams, Washington, QB
IV	Len Dawson, Kansas City, QB	XIII	Terry Bradshaw, Pittsburgh, QB	XXIII	Jerry Rice, San Francisco, WR
V	**Chuck Howley**, Dallas, LB	XIV	Terry Bradshaw, Pittsburgh, QB	XXIV	Joe Montana, San Francisco, QB
VI	Roger Staubach, Dallas, QB	XV	Jim Plunkett, Oakland, QB	XXV	Ottis Anderson, NY Giants, RB
VII	Jake Scott, Miami, S	XVI	Joe Montana, San Francisco, QB	XXVI	Mark Rypien, Washington, QB
VIII	Larry Csonka, Miami, RB	XVII	John Riggins, Washington, RB	XXVII	Troy Aikman, Dallas, QB
IX	Franco Harris, Pittsburgh, RB	XVIII	Marcus Allen, LA Raiders, RB	XXVIII	Emmitt Smith, Dallas, RB
X	Lynn Swann, Pittsburgh, WR	XIX	Joe Montana, San Francisco, QB		

All-Time Super Bowl Leaders
Through Jan. 30, 1994; participants in Super Bowl XXVIII in **bold** type.

CAREER
Passing Efficiency

Ratings based on performance standards established for completion percentage, average gain, touchdown percentage and interception percentage. Quarterbacks are allocated points according to how their statistics measure up to those standards. Minimum 25 passing attempts.

		Gm	Att	Cmp	Cmp%	Yards	Avg Gain	TD	TD%	Int	Int%	Rating
1	Phil Simms, NYG	1	25	22	88.0	268	10.72	3	12.0	0	0.0	150.9
2	Doug Williams, Wash	1	29	18	62.1	340	11.72	4	13.8	1	3.4	128.1
3	Joe Montana, SF	4	122	83	68.0	1142	9.36	11	9.0	0	0.0	127.8
4	Jim Plunkett, Oak-LA	2	46	29	63.0	433	9.41	4	8.7	0	0.0	122.8
5	**Troy Aikman**, Dal	2	57	41	71.9	480	8.42	4	7.0	1	1.8	113.2
6	Terry Bradshaw, Pit	4	84	49	58.3	932	11.10	9	10.7	4	4.8	112.6
7	Ken Anderson, Cin	1	34	25	73.5	300	8.82	2	5.9	2	5.9	95.2
8	Roger Staubach, Dal	4	98	61	62.2	734	7.49	8	8.2	4	4.1	95.4
9	Bart Starr, GB	2	47	29	61.7	452	9.62	3	6.4	1	2.1	95.1
10	Jeff Hostetler, NYG	1	32	20	62.5	222	6.94	1	3.1	0	0.0	93.4

Passing Yards

		Gms	Att	Cmp	Pct	Yds
1	Joe Montana, SF	4	122	83	68.0	1142
2	Terry Bradshaw, Pit	4	84	49	58.3	932
3	**Jim Kelly**, Buf	4	145	81	55.9	829
4	Roger Staubach, Dal	4	98	61	62.2	734
5	John Elway, Den	3	101	46	45.5	669
6	Fran Tarkenton, Min	3	89	46	51.7	489
7	**Troy Aikman**, Dal	2	57	41	71.9	480
8	Bart Starr, GB	2	47	29	61.7	452
9	Jim Plunkett, Raiders	2	46	29	63.0	433
10	Joe Theismann, Wash	2	58	31	53.4	386
11	Len Dawson, KC	2	44	28	63.6	353
12	Doug Williams, Wash	1	29	18	62.1	340
13	Dan Marino, Mia	1	50	29	58.0	318
14	Ken Anderson, Cin	1	34	25	73.5	300
15	Bob Griese, Mia	3	41	26	63.4	295

Receptions

		Gm	No	Yds	Avg	TD
1	**Andre Reed**, Buf	4	27	323	12.0	0
2	Roger Craig, SF	3	20	212	10.6	3
	Thurman Thomas, Buf	4	20	144	7.2	0
4	Jerry Rice, SF	2	18	363	20.2	4
5	Lynn Swann, Pit	4	16	364	22.8	3
6	Chuck Foreman, Min	3	15	139	9.3	0
7	Cliff Branch, Raiders	3	14	181	12.9	3
8	**Don Beebe**, Buf	3	12	171	14.3	2
	Preston Pearson, Bal-Pit-Dal	5	12	105	8.8	0
	Jay Novacek, Dal	2	12	98	8.2	1
	Kenneth Davis, Buf	4	12	72	6.0	0
12	John Stallworth, Pit	4	11	268	24.4	3
	Michael Irvin, Dal	2	11	180	16.4	2
	Dan Ross, Cin	1	11	104	9.5	2

Six tied with 10 catches each.

Super Bowl Appearances

Through Super Bowl XXVIII, nine NFL teams have yet to play for the Vince Lombardi Trophy. In alphabetical order, they are: Atlanta, Cleveland, Detroit, Houston, New Orleans, Phoenix, San Diego, Seattle and Tampa Bay. Of the 19 teams that have participated, Dallas has the most appearances (7) and is tied for the most titles (4) with Pittsburgh and San Francisco.

App		W	L	Pct	PF	PA
7	Dallas	4	3	.571	194	115
5	Washington	3	2	.600	122	103
5	Miami	2	3	.400	74	103
4	Pittsburgh	4	0	1.00	103	73
4	San Francisco	4	0	1.00	139	63
4	Oak/LA Raiders	3	1	.750	111	66
4	Buffalo	0	4	.000	73	139
4	Denver	0	4	.000	50	163
4	Minnesota	0	4	.000	34	95
2	Green Bay	2	0	1.00	68	24
2	NY Giants	2	0	1.00	59	39
2	Baltimore Colts	1	1	.500	23	29
2	Kansas City	1	1	.500	33	42
2	Cincinnati	0	2	.000	37	46
1	Chicago	1	0	1.00	46	10
1	NY Jets	1	0	1.00	16	7
1	LA Rams	0	1	.000	19	31
1	New England	0	1	.000	10	46
1	Philadelphia	0	1	.000	10	27

Rushing Yards

		Gm	Car	Yds	Avg	TD
1	Franco Harris, Pit	4	101	354	3.5	4
2	Larry Csonka, Mia	3	57	297	5.2	2
3	**Emmitt Smith**, Dal	2	52	240	4.6	3
4	John Riggins, Wash	2	64	230	3.6	2
5	Timmy Smith, Wash	1	22	204	9.3	2
	Thurman Thomas, Buf	4	52	204	3.9	4
7	Roger Craig, SF	3	52	201	3.9	2
8	Marcus Allen, Raid	1	20	191	9.5	2
9	Tony Dorsett, Dal	2	31	162	5.2	1
10	Mark van Eeghen, Raiders	2	37	153	4.1	0
11	**Kenneth Davis**, Buf	4	30	145	4.8	0
12	Rocky Bleier, Pit	4	44	144	3.3	0
13	Walt Garrison, Dal	2	26	139	5.3	0
14	Clarence Davis, Raiders	1	16	137	8.6	0
15	Duane Thomas, Dal	2	37	130	3.5	1

All-Purpose Running

		Gm	Rush	Rec	Ret	Total
1	Franco Harris, Pit	4	354	114	0	468
2	Roger Craig, SF	3	201	212	0	413
3	Lynn Swann, Pit	4	−7	364	34	391
4	Jerry Rice, SF	2	5	363	0	368
5	**T. Thomas**, Buf	4	204	144	0	348
6	**Andre Reed**, Buf	3	0	323	0	323
7	Larry Csonka, Mia	3	297	17	0	314
8	Fulton Walker, Mia	2	0	0	298	298
9	**Emmitt Smith**, Dal	2	240	53	0	293
10	Ricky Sanders, Wash	2	−3	234	46	277

Scoring

Points

		Gm	TD	FG	PAT	Pts
1	Roger Craig, SF	3	4	0	0	24
	Franco Harris, Pit	4	4	0	0	24
	Jerry Rice, SF	2	4	0	0	24
	Thurman Thomas, Buf	4	4	0	0	24
5	Ray Wersching, SF	2	0	5	7	22
6	Don Chandler, GB	2	0	4	8	20
7	Cliff Branch, Raiders	3	3	0	0	18
	John Stallworth, Pit	4	3	0	0	18
	Emmitt Smith, Dal	2	3	0	0	18
	Lynn Swann, Pit	4	3	0	0	18
11	Chris Bahr, Raiders	2	0	3	8	17
12	Matt Bahr, Pit-NYG	2	0	3	6	15
	Mike Cofer, SF	2	0	2	9	15
	Uwe von Schamann, Mia	2	0	4	3	15
15	Kevin Butler, Chi	1	0	3	5	14
	Roy Gerela, Pit	3	0	2	8	14
	Jim Turner, NYJ-Den	2	0	4	2	14

Punting Average
(Minimum 10 Punts)

		Gm	No	Yds	Avg.
1	Jerrel Wilson, KC	2	11	511	46.5
2	Ray Guy, Raiders	3	14	587	41.9
3	Larry Seiple, Mia	3	15	620	41.3
4	Mike Eischeid, Oak-Min	3	17	698	41.1
5	Danny White, Dal	2	10	406	40.6

Punt Return Average
(Minimum 4 returns)

		Gm	No	Yds	Avg.	TD
1	John Taylor, SF	2	6	94	15.7	0
2	Neal Colzie, Oak	1	4	43	10.8	0
3	Dana McLemore, SF	1	5	51	10.2	0
4	Mike Fuller, Cin	1	4	35	8.8	0
5	Mike Nelms, Wash	1	6	52	8.7	0

Kickoff Return Average
(Minimum 4 returns)

		Gm	No	Yds	Avg.	TD
1	Fulton Walker, Mia	2	8	283	35.4	1
2	Larry Anderson, Pit	2	8	207	25.9	0
3	Darren Carrington, Den	1	6	146	24.3	1
4	Jim Duncan, Bal	1	4	90	22.5	0
5	Stephen Starring, NE	1	7	153	21.9	0

Touchdowns

		Gm	Rush	Rec	Ret	TD
1	Roger Craig, SF	3	2	2	0	4
	Franco Harris, Pit	4	4	0	0	4
	Jerry Rice, SF	2	0	4	0	4
	Thurman Thomas, Buf	4	4	0	0	4
5	Cliff Branch, Raiders	3	0	3	0	3
	Emmitt Smith, Dal	2	3	0	0	3
	John Stallworth, Pit	4	0	3	0	3
	Lynn Swann, Pit	4	0	3	0	3

9 Twenty-three tied with 2 TDs each.
Marcus Allen, Raiders; Ottis Anderson, NYG; Pete Banaszak, Raiders; **Don Beebe**, Buf.; Gary Clark, Wash.; Larry Csonka, Mia.; John Elway, Den.; **Michael Irvin**, Dal.; Butch Johnson, Dal.; Jim Kiick, Mia.; Max McGee, GB; Jim McMahon, Chi.; Bill Miller, Raiders; Joe Montana, SF; Elijah Pitts, GB; Tom Rathman, SF; John Riggins, Wash.; Gerald Riggs, Wash.; Dan Ross, Cin.; Ricky Sanders, Wash.; Timmy Smith, Wash.; John Taylor, SF and Duane Thomas, Dal.

Interceptions

		Gm	No	Yds	TD
1	Chuck Howley, Dal	2	3	63	0
	Rod Martin, Raiders	2	3	44	0
3	Randy Beverly, NYJ	1	2	0	0
	Mel Blount, Pit	4	2	23	0
	Brad Edwards, Wash	1	2	56	0
	Thomas Everett, Dal	1	2	22	0
	Jake Scott, Mia	3	2	63	0
	Mike Wagner, Pit	3	2	45	0
	James Washington, Dal	2	2	25	0
	Barry Wilburn, Wash	1	2	11	0
	Eric Wright, SF	4	2	25	0

Sacks

		Gm	No
1	Charles Haley, SF-Dal	4	3½
2	Leonard Marshall, NYG	2	3
	Danny Stubbs, SF	2	3
	Jeff Wright, Buf.	4	3
5	Jim Jeffcoat, Dal	2	2½
	Dexter Manley, Wash	3	2½

Four-Time Super Bowl Winners

Pittsburgh Steelers

Year	Bowl	Head Coach	Quarterback	MVP	Opponent	Score	Location
1975	IX	Chuck Noll	Terry Bradshaw	Franco Harris	Minnesota	16-6	New Orleans
1976	X	Chuck Noll	Terry Bradshaw	Lynn Swann	Dallas	21-17	Miami
1979	XIII	Chuck Noll	Terry Bradshaw	Bradshaw	Dallas	35-31	Miami
1980	XIV	Chuck Noll	Terry Bradshaw	Bradshaw	LA Rams	31-19	Pasadena

San Francisco

Year	Bowl	Head Coach	Quarterback	MVP	Opponent	Score	Location
1982	XVI	Bill Walsh	Joe Montana	Montana	Cincinnati	26-21	Pontiac
1985	XIX	Bill Walsh	Joe Montana	Montana	Miami	38-16	Stanford
1989	XXIII	Bill Walsh	Joe Montana	Jerry Rice	Cincinnati	20-16	Miami
1990	XXIV	George Seifert	Joe Montana	Montana	Denver	55-10	New Orleans

Dallas

Year	Bowl	Head Coach	Quarterback	MVP	Opponent	Score	Location
1972	VI	Tom Landry	Roger Staubach	Staubach	Miami	24-3	New Orleans
1978	XII	Tom Landry	Roger Staubach	Harvey Martin & Randy White	Denver	27-10	New Orleans
1993	XXVII	Jimmy Johnson	Troy Aikman	Aikman	Buffalo	52-17	Pasadena
1994	XXVIII	Jimmy Johnson	Troy Aikman	Emmitt Smith	Buffalo	30-13	Atlanta

SINGLE GAME

Passing

Yards Gained	Year	Att/Cmp	Yds
Joe Montana, SF vs Cin	1989	36/23	357
Doug Williams, Wash vs Den	1988	29/18	340
Joe Montana, SF vs Mia	1985	35/24	331
Terry Bradshaw, Pit vs Dal	1979	30/17	318
Dan Marino, Mia vs SF	1985	50/29	318
Terry Bradshaw, Pit vs Rams	1980	21/14	309
John Elway, Den vs NYG	1987	37/22	304
Ken Anderson, Cin vs SF	1982	34/25	300
Joe Montana, SF vs Den	1990	29/22	297
Mark Rypien, Wash vs Buf	1992	33/18	292

Touchdown Passes	Year	TD	Int
Joe Montana, SF vs Den	1990	5	0
Terry Bradshaw, Pit vs Dal	1979	4	1
Doug Williams, Wash vs Den	1988	4	1
Troy Aikman, Dal vs Buf	1993	4	0
Roger Staubach, Dal vs Pit	1979	3	1
Jim Plunkett, Raiders vs Phi	1981	3	0
Joe Montana, SF vs Mia	1985	3	0
Phil Simms, NYG vs Den	1987	3	0
Eleven tied with 2 TD passes each.			

Rushing

Yards Gained	Year	Car	Yds	TD
Timmy Smith, Wash vs Den	1988	22	204	2
Marcus Allen, Raiders vs Wash	1984	20	191	2
John Riggins, Wash vs Mia	1983	38	166	1
Franco Harris, Pit vs Min	1975	34	158	1
Larry Csonka, Mia vs Min	1974	33	145	2
Clarence Davis, Raiders vs Min	1977	16	137	0
Thurman Thomas, Buf vs NYG	1991	15	135	1
Emmitt Smith, Dal vs Buf	1994	30	132	2
Matt Snell, NYJ vs Bal	1969	30	121	1
Tom Matte, Bal vs NYJ	1969	11	116	0
Larry Csonka, Mia vs Wash	1973	15	112	1
Emmitt Smith, Dal vs Buf	1993	22	108	1
Ottis Anderson, NYG vs Buf	1991	21	102	1
Tony Dorsett, Dal vs Pit	1979	16	96	0
Duane Thomas, Dal vs Mia	1972	19	95	1

Scoring

Points	Year	TD	FG	PAT	Pts
Roger Craig, SF vs Mia	1985	3	0	0	18
Jerry Rice, SF vs Den	1990	3	0	0	18
Don Chandler, GB vs Raiders	1968	0	4	3	15
Ray Wersching, SF vs Cin	1982	0	4	2	14
Kevin Butler, Chi vs NE	1986	0	3	5	14
Chip Lohmiller, Wash vs Buf	1992	0	3	4	13
Seventeen tied with 12 points each.					

Touchdowns	Year	TD	Rush	Rec
Roger Craig, SF vs Mia	1985	3	1	2
Jerry Rice, SF vs Den	1990	3	0	3
Max McGee, GB vs KC	1967	2	0	2
Elijah Pitts, GB vs KC	1967	2	2	0
Bill Miller, Raiders vs GB	1968	2	0	2
Larry Csonka, Mia vs Min	1974	2	2	0
Pete Banaszak, Raiders vs Min.	1977	2	2	0
John Stallworth, Pit vs Dal	1979	2	0	2
Franco Harris, Pit vs Rams	1980	2	2	0
Cliff Branch, Raiders vs Phi	1981	2	0	2
Dan Ross, Cin vs SF	1982	2	0	2
Marcus Allen, Raiders vs Wash	1984	2	2	0
Jim McMahon, Chi vs NE	1986	2	2	0
Ricky Sanders, Wash vs Den	1988	2	0	2
Timmy Smith, Wash vs Den	1988	2	2	0
Tom Rathman, SF vs Den	1990	2	2	0
Gerald Riggs, Wash vs Buf	1992	2	2	0
Michael Irvin, Dal vs Buf	1993	2	0	2
Emmitt Smith, Dal vs Buf	1994	2	2	0

Receptions

Catches	Year	No	Yds	TD
Dan Ross, Cin vs SF	1982	11	104	2
Jerry Rice, SF vs Cin	1989	11	215	1
Tony Nathan, Mia vs SF	1985	10	83	0
Ricky Sanders, Wash vs Den	1988	9	193	2
George Sauer, NYJ vs Bal	1969	8	133	0
Roger Craig, SF vs Cin	1989	8	101	0
Andre Reed, Buf vs NYG	1991	8	62	0
Andre Reed, Buf vs Dal	1993	8	152	0
Nine tied with 7 catches each.				

Yards Gained	Year	No	Yds	TD
Jerry Rice, SF vs Cin	1989	11	215	1
Ricky Sanders, Wash vs Den	1988	9	193	2
Lynn Swann, Pit vs Dal	1976	4	161	1
Andre Reed, Buf vs Dal	1993	8	152	0
Jerry Rice, SF vs Den	1990	7	148	3
Max McGee, GB vs KC	1967	7	138	2
George Sauer, NYJ vs Bal	1969	8	133	0
Willie Gault, Chi vs NE	1986	4	129	0
Lynn Swann, Pit vs Dal	1979	7	124	1
John Stallworth, Pit vs Rams	1980	3	121	1
Vance Johnson, Den vs NYG	1987	5	121	1

All-Purpose Running

Yards Gained	Year	Run	Rec	Tot
Ricky Sanders, Wash vs Den	1988	193	-4	235*
Jerry Rice, SF vs Cin	1989	215	5	220
Timmy Smith, Wash vs Den	1988	204	9	213
Marcus Allen, Raiders vs Wash	1984	191	18	209
Stephen Starring, NE vs Chi	1986	0	39	192†
Fulton Walker, Mia vs Wash	1983	0	0	190#
Thurman Thomas, Buf vs NYG	1991	135	55	190
John Riggins, Wash vs Mia	1983	166	15	181
Roger Craig, SF vs Cin	1989	74	101	175
Lynn Swann, Pit vs Dal	1976	0	161	161
Matt Snell, NYJ vs Bal	1969	121	40	161

*Sanders also returned three kickoffs for 48 yards.
†Starring also returned seven kickoffs for 153 yards.
#Walker gained all his yards on four kickoff returns.

Interceptions

	Year	No	Yds	TD
Rod Martin, Raiders vs Phi	1981	3	44	0
Six tied with two interceptions each.				

Punting

(Minimum 4 punts)

	Year	No	Yds	Avg
Jerrel Wilson, KC vs Min	1970	4	194	48.5
Jim Miller, SF vs Cin	1982	4	185	46.3
Jerrel Wilson, KC vs GB	1967	7	317	45.3

Punt Returns

(Minimum 3 returns)

	Year	No	Yds	Avg
John Taylor, SF vs Cin	1989	3	56	18.7
John Taylor, SF vs Den	1990	3	38	12.7
Kelvin Martin, Dal. vs Buf	1993	3	35	11.7

Kickoff Returns

(Minimum 3 returns)

	Year	No	Yds	Avg
Fulton Walker, Mia.vs Wash	1983	4	109	47.5
Larry Anderson, Pit.vs Rams	1980	5	162	32.4
Rick Upchurch, Den.vs Dal	1978	3	94	31.3

Super Bowl Playoffs

The Super Bowl forced the NFL to set up pro football's first guaranteed multiple-game playoff format. Over the years, the NFL-AFL merger, the creation of two conferences comprised of three divisions each and the proliferation of Wild Card entries has seen the postseason field grow from four teams (1966), to six (1967-68), to eight (1969-77), to 10 (1978-81, 1983-89), to the present 12 (since 1990).

In 1982, when a 57-day players' strike shortened the regular season to just nine games, playoff berths were extended to 16 teams (eight from each conference) and a 15-game tournament was played.

Note that in the following year-by-year summary, records of finalists include all games leading up to the Super Bowl; (*) indicates Wild Card teams.

1966 Season

AFL Playoffs
Championship.........................Kansas City 31, at Buffalo 7

NFL Playoffs
Championship.........................Green Bay 34, at Dallas 27

Super Bowl I
Jan. 15, 1967
Memorial Coliseum, Los Angeles
Favorite: Packers by 14   Attendance: 61,946

Kansas City (12-2-1).................0 10   0   0— **10**
Green Bay (13-2).......................7   7 14   7— **35**
MVP: Green Bay QB Bart Starr (16 for 23, 250 yds, 2 TD, 1 Int)

1967 Season

AFL Playoffs
Championship ....at Oakland 40, Houston 7

NFL Playoffs
Eastern Conference....................at Dallas 52, Cleveland 14
Western Conference...............at Green Bay 28, LA Rams 7
Championship..........................at Green Bay 21, Dallas 17

Super Bowl II
Jan. 14, 1968
Orange Bowl, Miami
Favorite: Packers by 13½   Attendance: 75,546

Green Bay (11-4-1)...................3 13 10   7— **33**
Oakland (14-1) 0   7   0   7— **14**
MVP: Green Bay QB Bart Starr (13 for 24, 202 yds, 1 TD)

1968 Season

AFL Playoffs
Western Div. Playoff ....at Oakland 41, Kansas City 6
AFL Championship ....at NY Jets 27, Oakland 23

NFL Playoffs
Eastern Conference....................at Cleveland 31, Dallas 20
Western Conference.............at Baltimore 24, Minnesota 14
NFL Championship ....Baltimore 34, at Cleveland 0

Super Bowl III
Jan. 12, 1969
Orange Bowl, Miami
Favorite: Colts by 18   Attendance: 75,389

NY Jets (12-3)............................0   7   6   3— **16**
Baltimore (15-1)........................0   0   0   7— **7**
MVP: NY Jets QB Joe Namath (17 for 28, 206 yds)

1969 Season

AFL Playoffs
Inter-Division ....*Kansas City 13, at NY Jets 6
............................at Oakland 56, *Houston 7
AFL Championship...............Kansas City 17, at Oakland 7

NFL Playoffs
Eastern Conference....................Cleveland 38, at Dallas 14
Western Conference ....at Minnesota 23, LA Rams 20
NFL Championship ....at Minnesota 27, Cleveland 7

Super Bowl IV
Jan. 11, 1970
Tulane Stadium, New Orleans
Favorite: Vikings by 12   Attendance: 80,562

Minnesota (14-2) 0   0   7   0— **7**
Kansas City (13-3)....................3 13   7   0— **23**
MVP: KC QB Len Dawson (12 for 17, 142 yds, 1 TD, 1 Int)

1970 Season

AFC Playoffs
First Round...........................at Baltimore 17, Cincinnati 0
................................at Oakland 21, *Miami 14
Championship.......................at Baltimore 27, Oakland 17

NFC Playoffs
First Round ....at Dallas 5, *Detroit 0
...................San Francisco 17, at Minnesota 14
Championship....................Dallas 17, at San Francisco 10

Super Bowl V
Jan. 17, 1971
Orange Bowl, Miami
Favorite: Cowboys by 2½   Attendance: 79,204

Baltimore (13-2-1).....................0   6   0 10— **16**
Dallas (12-4).............................3 10   0   0— **13**
MVP: Dallas LB Chuck Howley (2 Interceptions for 22 yds)

1971 Season

AFC Playoffs
First Round ....Miami 27, at Kansas City 24 (OT)
............................*Baltimore 20, at Cleveland 3
Championship ....at Miami 21, Baltimore 0

NFC Playoffs
First Round ....Dallas 20, at Minnesota 12
...............at San Francisco 24, *Washington 20
Championship.......................at Dallas 14, San Francisco 3

Super Bowl VI
Jan. 16, 1972
Tulane Stadium, New Orleans
Favorite: Cowboys by 6   Attendance: 81,023

Dallas (13-3)..............................3   7   7   7— **24**
Miami (12-3-1)...........................0   3   0   0— **3**
MVP: Dallas QB Roger Staubach (12 for 19, 119 yds, 2TD)

1972 Season

AFC Playoffs

First Round ....at Pittsburgh 13, Oakland 7
...................................at Miami 20, *Cleveland 14
Championship.........................Miami 21, at Pittsburgh 17

NFC Playoffs

First Round ....*Dallas 30, at San Francisco 28
.............................at Washington 16, Green Bay 3
Championship.........................at Washington 26, Dallas 3

Super Bowl VII

Jan. 14, 1973
Memorial Coliseum, Los Angeles
Favorite: Redskins by 1½   Attendance: 90,182

Miami (16-0)....................7   7   0   0— **14**
Washington (13-3) 0   0   0   7— **7**
MVP: Miami safety Jake Scott (2 interceptions for 63 yds)

1973 Season

AFC Playoffs

First Round..........................at Oakland 33, *Pittsburgh 14
...............................at Miami 34, Cincinnati 16
Championship ....at Miami 27, Oakland 10

NFC Playoffs

First Round ....at Minnesota 27, *Washington 20
...........................at Dallas 27, LA Rams 16
Championship ....Minnesota 27, at Dallas 10

Super Bowl VIII

Jan. 13, 1974
Rice Stadium, Houston
Favorite: Dolphins by 6½   Attendance: 71,882

Minnesota (14-2) 0   0   0   7— **7**
Miami (12-4)...........................14   3   7   0— **24**
MVP: Miami FB Larry Csonka (33 carries, 145 yds, 2 TD)

1974 Season

AFC Playoffs

First Round ....at Oakland 28, Miami 26
...............................at Pittsburgh 32, *Buffalo 14
Championship ....Pittsburgh 24, at Oakland 13

NFC Playoffs

First Round ....at Minnesota 30, St.Louis 14
.....................at LA Rams 19, *Washington 10
Championship ....at Minnesota 14, LA Rams 10

Super Bowl IX

Jan. 12, 1975
Tulane Stadium, New Orleans
Favorite: Steelers by 3   Attendance: 80,997

Pittsburgh (12-3-1) 0   2   7   7— **16**
Minnesota (12-4) 0   0   0   6— **6**
MVP: Pittsburgh RB Franco Harris (34 carries, 158 yds, 1 TD)

1975 Season

AFC Playoffs

First Round ....at Pittsburgh 28, Baltimore 10
..........................at Oakland 31, *Cincinnati 28
Championship ....at Pittsburgh 16, Oakland 10

NFC Playoffs

First Round............................at LA Rams 35, St. Louis 23
..........................*Dallas 17, at Minnesota 14
Championship...............................Dallas 37, at LA Rams 7

Super Bowl X

Jan. 18, 1976
Orange Bowl, Miami
Favorite: Steelers by 6½   Attendance: 80,187

Dallas (12-4)........................7   3   0   7— **17**
Pittsburgh (14-2)........................7   0   0   14— **21**
MVP: Pittsburgh WR Lynn Swann (4 catches, 161 yds, 1 TD)

1976 Season

AFC Playoffs

First Round ....at Oakland 24, *New England 21
..........................Pittsburgh 40, at Baltimore 14
Championship ....at Oakland 24, Pittsburgh 7

NFC Playoffs

First Round ....at Minnesota 35, *Washington 20
...................................LA Rams 14, at Dallas 12
Championship ....at Minnesota 24, LA Rams 13

Super Bowl XI

Jan. 9, 1977
Rose Bowl, Pasadena
Favorite: Raiders by 4½   Attendance: 103,438

Oakland (15-1) 0   16   3   13— **32**
Minnesota (13-2-1) 0   0   7   7— **14**
MVP: Oakland WR Fred Biletnikoff (4 catches, 79 yds)

1977 Season

AFC Playoffs

First Round............................at Denver 34, Pittsburgh 21
...................*Oakland 37, at Baltimore 31 (OT)
Championship ....at Denver 20, Oakland 17

NFC Playoffs

First Round ....at Dallas 37, *Chicago 7
..............................Minnesota 14, at LA Rams 7
Championship ....at Dallas 23, Minnesota 6

Super Bowl XII

Jan. 15, 1978
Louisiana Superdome, New Orleans
Favorite: Cowboys by 6   Attendance: 75,583

Dallas (14-2)...........................10   3   7   7— **27**
Denver (14-2)..............................0   0   10   0— **10**
MVPs: Dallas DE Harvey Martin and DT Randy White
(Cowboys' defense forced 8 turnovers)

A Year Later...

Super Bowl champions who did not qualify for the playoffs the following season.

Season		Record	Finish	Season		Record	Finish
1968	Green Bay	6-7-1	3rd in NFL Central	1982	San Francisco	3-6-0*	11th in overall NFC
1970	Kansas City	7-5-2	2nd in AFC West	1987	NY Giants	6-9-0*	5th in NFC East
1980	Pittsburgh	9-7-0	3rd in AFC Central	1988	Washington	7-9-0	3rd in NFC East
1981	Oakland	7-9-0	4th in AFC West	1991	NY Giants	8-8-0	4th in NFC East

*Seasons when player strikes interrupted schedule.

Super Bowl Playoffs (Cont.)

1978 Season

AFC Playoffs

First Round ....*Houston 17, at *Miami 9
Second Round.....................Houston 31, at New England 14
...............................at Pittsburgh 33, Denver 10
Championship ....at Pittsburgh 34, Houston 5

NFC Playoffs

First Round..........................at *Atlanta 14, *Philadelphia 13
Second Round................................at Dallas 27, Atlanta 20
.........................at LA Rams 34, Minnesota 10
Championship.................................Dallas 28, at LA Rams 0

Super Bowl XIII

Jan. 21, 1979
Orange Bowl, Miami
Favorite: Steelers by 3½   Attendance: 79,484

Pittsburgh (16-2)	7	14	0	14—	**35**
Dallas (14-4)	7	7	3	14—	**31**

MVP: Pittsburgh QB Terry Bradshaw (17 for 30, 318 yds,
4 TD, 1 Int)

1979 Season

AFC Playoffs

First Round ....at *Houston 13, *Denver 7
Second Round ....Houston 17, at San Diego 14
.............................at Pittsburgh 34, Houston 14
Championship ....at Pittsburgh 27, Houston 13

NFC Playoffs

First Round....................at *Philadelphia 27, *Chicago 17
Second Round ....at Tampa Bay 24, Philadelphia 17
.............................LA Rams 21, at Dallas 19
Championship ....LA Rams 9, at Tampa Bay 0

Super Bowl XIV

Jan. 20, 1980
Rose Bowl, Pasadena
Favorite: Steelers by 10½   Attendance: 103,985

LA Rams (11-7)	7	6	6	0—	**19**
Pittsburgh (14-4)	3	7	7	14—	**31**

MVP: Pittsburgh QB Terry Bradshaw (14 for 21, 309 yds,
2 TD, 3 Int)

1980 Season

AFC Playoffs

First Round ....at *Oakland 27, *Houston 7
Second Round ....at San Diego 20, Buffalo 14
.........................Oakland 14, at Cleveland 12
Championship ....Oakland 34, at San Diego 27

NFC Playoffs

First Round ....at *Dallas 34, *LA Rams 13
Second Round ....at Philadelphia 31, Minnesota 16
...........................Dallas 30, at Atlanta 27
Championship ....at Philadelphia 20, Dallas 7

Super Bowl XV

Jan. 25, 1981
Louisiana Superdome, New Orleans
Favorite: Eagles by 3   Attendance: 76,135

Oakland (14-5)	14	0	10	3—	**27**
Philadelphia (14-4)	0	3	0	7—	**10**

MVP: Oakland QB Jim Plunkett (13 for 21, 261 yds, 3 TD)

1981 Season

AFC Playoffs

First Round ....*Buffalo 31, at *NY Jets 27
Second Round ....San Diego 41, at Miami 38 (OT)
...........................at Cincinnati 28, Buffalo 21
Championship ....at Cincinnati 27, San Diego 7

NFC Playoffs

First Round ....*NY Giants 27, at *Philadelphia 21
Second Round ....at Dallas 38, Tampa Bay 0
...............at San Francisco 38, NY Giants 24
Championship.....................at San Francisco 28, Dallas 27

Super Bowl XVI

Jan. 24, 1982
Pontiac Silverdome, Pontiac, Mich.
Favorite: Pick'em   Attendance: 81,270

San Francisco (15-3)	7	13	0	6—	**26**
Cincinnati (14-4)	0	0	7	14—	**21**

MVP: San Francisco QB Joe Montana (14 for 22, 157
yds, 1 TD; 6 carries, 18 yds, 1 TD)

1982 Season

A 57-day players' strike shortened the regular season from
16 games to nine. The playoff format was changed to a 16-
team tournament open to the top eight teams in each
conference.

AFC Playoffs

First Round ....at LA Raiders 27, Cleveland 10
...........................at Miami 28, New England 3
...........................NY Jets 44, at Cincinnati 17
...........................San Diego 31, at Pittsburgh 28
Second Round ....NY Jets 17, at LA Raiders 14
...........................at Miami 34, San Diego 13
Championship ....at Miami 14, NY Jets 0

NFC Playoffs

First Round ....at Washington 31, Detroit 7
...........................at Dallas 30, Tampa Bay 17
...........................at Green Bay 41, St. Louis 16
...........................at Minnesota 30, Atlanta 24
Second Round ....at Washington 21, Minnesota 7
...........................at Dallas 37, Green Bay 26
Championship......................at Washington 31, Dallas 17

Super Bowl XVII

Jan. 30, 1983
Rose Bowl, Pasadena
Favorite: Dolphins by 3   Attendance: 103,667

Miami (10-2)	7	10	0	0—	**17**
Washington (11-1)	0	10	3	14—	**27**

MVP: Washington RB John Riggins (38 carries, 166 yds,
1 TD; 1 catch, 15 yds)

Most Popular Playing Sites

Stadiums hosting more than one Super Bowl.

No	Stadium	Years
5	Orange Bowl (Miami)	1968-69, 71, 76, 79
5	Rose Bowl (Pasadena)	1977, 80, 83, 87, 93
4	Superdome (N.Orleans)	1978, 81, 86, 90
3	Tulane Stadium (N.Orleans)	1970, 72, 75
2	LA Memorial Coliseum	1967, 73
2	Tampa Stadium	1984, 91

1983 Season

AFC Playoffs

First Round ....at *Seattle 31, *Denver 7
Second Round ....Seattle 27, at Miami 20
.....................at LA Raiders 38, Pittsburgh 10
Championship ....at LA Raiders 30, Seattle 14

NFC Playoffs

First Round ....*LA Rams 24, at *Dallas 17
Second Round ....at San Francisco 24, Detroit 23
.....................at Washington 51, LA Rams 7
Championship ....at Washington 24, San Francisco 21

Super Bowl XVIII

Jan. 22, 1984
Tampa Stadium, Tampa
Favorite: Redskins by 3   Attendance: 72,920

Washington (16-2) 0   3   6   0— **9**
LA Raiders (14-4) 7   14   14   3— **38**
MVP: LA Raiders RB Marcus Allen (20 carries, 191 yds,
2 TD; 2 catches, 18 yds)

1984 Season

AFC Playoffs

First Round ....at *Seattle 13, *LA Raiders 7
Second Round ....at Miami 31, Seattle 10
.....................Pittsburgh 24, at Denver 17
Championship ....at Miami 45, Pittsburgh 28

NFC Playoffs

First Round ....*NY Giants 16, at *LA Rams 13
Second Round ....at San Francisco 21, NY Giants 10
.....................Chicago 23, at Washington 19
Championship ....at San Francisco 23, Chicago 0

Super Bowl XIX

Jan. 20, 1985
Stanford Stadium, Stanford, Calif.
Favorite: 49ers by 3   Attendance: 84,059

Miami (16-2) 10   6   0   0— **16**
San Francisco (17-1) 7   21   10   0— **38**
MVP: San Francisco QB Joe Montana (24 for 35, 331
yds, 2 TD; 5 carries, 59 yards, 1 TD)

1985 Season

AFC Playoffs

First Round ....*New England 26, at *NY Jets 14
Second Round ....at Miami 24, Cleveland 21
..............New England 27, at LA Raiders 20
Championship ....New England 31, at Miami 14

NFC Playoffs

First Round...................at *NY Giants 17, *San Francisco 3
Second Round..............................at LA Rams 20, Dallas 0
.....................at Chicago 21, NY Giants 0
Championship ....at Chicago 24, LA Rams 0

Super Bowl XX

Jan. 26, 1986
Louisiana Superdome, New Orleans
Favorite: Bears by 10   Attendance: 73,818

Chicago Bears (17-1) 13   10   21   2— **46**
New England (14-5) 3   0   0   7— **10**
MVP: Chicago DE Richard Dent (Bears defense: 7 sacks, 6
turnovers, 1 safety and gave up just 123 total yards)

1986 Season

AFC Playoffs

First Round ....at *NY Jets 35, *Kansas City 15
Second Round..................at Cleveland 23, NY Jets 20 (OT)
.....................at Denver 22, New England 17
Championship ....Denver 23, at Cleveland 20 (OT)

NFC Playoffs

First Round.....................at *Washington 19, *LA Rams 7
Second Round...................Washington 27, at Chicago 13
..................at NY Giants 49, San Francisco 3
Championship ....at NY Giants 17, Washington 0

Super Bowl XXI

Jan. 25, 1987
Rose Bowl, Pasadena
Favorite: Giants by 9½   Attendance: 101,063

Denver (13-5) 10   0   0   10— **20**
NY Giants (16-2).........................7   2   17   13— **39**
MVP: NY Giants QB Phil Simms (22 for 25, 268 yds, 3
TD; 3 carries, 25 yds)

1987 Season

A 24-day players' strike shortened the regular season to 15
games with replacement teams playing for three weeks.

AFC Playoffs

First Round ....at *Houston 23, *Seattle 20 (OT)
Second Round ....at Cleveland 38, Indianapolis 21
.............................at Denver 34, Houston 10
Championship ....at Denver 38, Cleveland 33

NFC Playoffs

First Round ....*Minnesota 44, at *New Orleans 10
Second Round..............Minnesota 36, at San Francisco 24
..............................Washington 21, at Chicago 17
Championship ....at Washington 17, Minnesota 10

Super Bowl XXII

Jan. 31, 1988
San Diego/Jack Murphy Stadium
Favorite: Broncos by 3½   Attendance: 73,302

Washington (13-4) 0   35   0   7— **42**
Denver (12-4-1) 10   0   0   0— **10**
MVP: Washington QB Doug Williams (18 for 29, 340
yds, 4 TD, 1 Int)

1988 Season

AFC Playoffs

First Round........................*Houston 24, at *Cleveland 23
Second Round ....at Buffalo 17, Houston 10
.............................at Cincinnati 21, Seattle 13
Championship ....at Cincinnati 21, Buffalo 10

NFC Playoffs

First Round ....at *Minnesota 28, *LA Rams 17
Second Round ....at San Francisco 34, Minnesota 9
.....................at Chicago 20, Philadelphia 12
Championship...................San Francisco 28, at Chicago 3

Super Bowl XXIII

Jan. 22, 1989
Joe Robbie Stadium, Miami
Favorite: 49ers by 7   Attendance: 75,129

Cincinnati (17-1)........................0   3   10   3— **16**
San Francisco (14-5)..................3   0   3   14— **20**
MVP: San Francisco WR Jerry Rice (11 catches, 215 yds,
1 TD; 1 carry, 5 yds)

Super Bowl Playoffs (Cont.)

1989 Season

AFC Playoffs

First Round ....*Pittsburgh 26, at *Houston 23
Second Round.....................at Cleveland 34, Buffalo 30
..........................at Denver 24, Pittsburgh 23
Championship ....at Denver 37, Cleveland 21

NFC Playoffs

First Round ....*LA Rams 21, at *Philadelphia 7
Second Round...............LA Rams 19, NY Giants 13 (OT)
................at San Francisco 41, Minnesota 13
Championship ....at San Francisco 30, LA Rams 3

Super Bowl XXIV

Jan. 28, 1990
Louisiana Superdome, New Orleans
Favorite: 49ers by 12½   Attendance: 72,919

San Francisco (17-2)...............13	14	14	14—	**55**
Denver (13-6) 3	0	7	0—	**10**

MVP: San Francisco QB Joe Montana (22 for 29, 297 yds, 5 TD, 0 Int)

1990 Season

AFC Playoffs

First Round.........................at *Miami 17, *Kansas City 16
.............................at Cincinnati 41, *Houston 14
Second Round................................at Buffalo 44, Miami 34
....................at LA Raiders 20, Cincinnati 10
Championship ....at Buffalo 51, LA Raiders 3

NFC Playoffs

First Round..................*Washington 20, at *Philadelphia 6
........................at Chicago 16, *New Orleans 6
Second Round ....at San Francisco 28, Washington 10
.........................at NY Giants 31, Chicago 3
Championship...............NY Giants 15, at San Francisco 13

Super Bowl XXV

Jan. 27, 1991
Tampa Stadium, Tampa
Favorite: Bills by 7   Attendance: 73,813

Buffalo (15-4) 3	9	0	7—	**19**
NY Giants (16-3)........................3	7	7	3—	**20**

MVP: NY Giants RB Ottis Anderson (21 carries, 102 yds, 1 TD; 1 catch, 7 yds)

1991 Season

AFC Playoffs

First Round ....at *Kansas City 10, *LA Raiders 6
....................................at Houston 17, *NY Jets 10
Second Round ....at Denver 26, Houston 24
........................at Buffalo 37, Kansas City 14
Championship..................................at Buffalo 10, Denver 7

NFC Playoffs

First Round........................*Atlanta 27, at New Orleans 20
....................................*Dallas 17, at *Chicago 13
Second Round ....at Washington 24, Atlanta 7
....................................at Detroit 38, Dallas 6
Championship ....at Washington 41, Detroit 10

Super Bowl XXVI

Jan. 26, 1992
Hubert Humphrey Metrodome, Minneapolis
Favorite: Redskins by 7   Attendance: 63,130

Washington (16-2) 0	17	14	6—	**37**
Buffalo (15-3) 0	0	10	14—	**24**

MVP: Washington QB Mark Rypien (18 for 33, 292 yds, 2 TD, 1 Int)

1992 Season

AFC Playoffs

First Round.........................at *Buffalo 41, *Houston 38 (OT)
......................................at San Diego 17, *Kansas City 0
Second Round ....Buffalo 24, at Pittsburgh 3
........................at Miami 31, San Diego 0
Championship..................................Buffalo 29, at Miami 10

NFC Playoffs

First Round ....*Washington 24, at Minnesota 7
...............*Philadelphia 36, at *New Orleans 20
Second Round ....at San Francisco 20, Washington 13
....................................at Dallas 34, Philadelphia 10
Championship.....................Dallas 30, at San Francisco 20

Super Bowl XXVII

Jan. 31, 1993
Rose Bowl, Pasadena
Favorite: Cowboys by 7   Attendance: 98,374

Buffalo (14-5) 7	3	7	0—	**17**
Dallas (15-3)............................14	14	3	21—	**52**

MVP: Dallas QB Troy Aikman (22 for 30, 273 yds, 4 TD, 0 Int)

1993 Season

AFC Playoffs

First Round...............at Kansas City 27, *Pittsburgh 24 (OT)
..........................at *LA Raiders 42, *Denver 24
Second Round.......................at Buffalo 29, LA Raiders 23
......................Kansas City 28, at Houston 20
Championship......................at Buffalo 30, Kansas City 13

NFC Playoffs

First Round ....*Green Bay 28, at Detroit 24
.......................at *NY Giants 17, *Minnesota 10
Second Round ....at San Francisco 44, NY Giants 3
...........................at Dallas 27, Green Bay 17
Championship.....................at Dallas 38, San Francisco 21

Super Bowl XXVIII

Jan. 30, 1994
Georgia Dome, Atlanta
Favorite: Cowboys by 10½   Attendance: 72,817

Dallas (15-4)...............................6	0	14	10—	**30**
Buffalo (14-5) 3	10	0	0—	**13**

MVP: Dallas RB Emmitt Smith (30 carries, 132 yds, 2 TDs; 4 catches, 26 yds)

Before the Super Bowl

The first NFL champion was the Akron Pros in 1920, when the league was called the American Professional Football Association (APFA) and the title went to the team with the best regular season record. The APFA changed its name to the National Football League in 1922.

The first playoff game with the championship at stake came in 1932, when the Chicago Bears (6-1-6) and Portsmouth (Ohio) Spartans (6-1-4) ended the regular season tied for first place. The Bears won the subsequent playoff. Due to a snowstorm and cold weather, the game was moved from Wrigley Field to an improvised 80-yard dirt field at Chicago Stadium, making it the first indoor title game as well.

The NFL Championship Game decided the league title until the NFL merged with the AFL and the first Super Bowl was played following the 1966 season.

NFL Champions, 1920-32

Multiple winners: Green Bay (3); Canton (2).

Year	Champion	Head Coach
1920	Akron Pros	Fritz Pollard, HB
		& Elgie Tobin, QB
1921	Chicago Staleys	George Halas, E
	(Staleys renamed Bears in 1922)	
1922	Canton Bulldogs	Guy Chamberlin, E
1923	Canton Bulldogs	Guy Chamberlin, E
1924	Cleveland Bulldogs	Guy Chamberlin, E
1925	Chicago Cardinals	Norm Barry
1926	Frankford Yellow Jackets	Guy Chamberlin, E
1927	New York Giants	Earl Potteiger, QB
1928	Providence Steam Roller	Jimmy Conzelman, HB
1929	Green Bay Packers	Curly Lambeau, QB
1930	Green Bay Packers	Curly Lambeau
1931	Green Bay Packers	Curly Lambeau
1932	Chicago Bears	Ralph Jones
	(Bears beat Portsmouth-OH in playoff, 9-0)	

NFL-NFC Championship Game

NFL Championship games from 1933-69 and NFC Championship games since the completion of the NFL-AFL merger following the 1969 season.

Multiple winners: Green Bay (8); Chicago Bears, Dallas and Washington (7); NY Giants (5); Cleveland Browns, Detroit, Minnesota, Philadelphia and San Francisco (4); Baltimore (3); Cleveland-LA Rams (2).

Season	Winner	Head Coach	Score	Loser	Head Coach	Site
1933	Chicago Bears	George Halas	23-21	New York	Steve Owen	Chicago
1934	New York	Steve Owen	30-13	Chicago Bears	George Halas	New York
1935	Detroit	Potsy Clark	26- 7	New York	Steve Owen	Detroit
1936	Green Bay	Curly Lambeau	21- 6	Boston Redskins	Ray Flaherty	New York
1937	Washington Redskins	Ray Flaherty	28-21	Chicago Bears	George Halas	Chicago
1938	New York	Steve Owen	23-17	Green Bay	Curly Lambeau	New York
1939	Green Bay	Curly Lambeau	27- 0	New York	Steve Owen	Milwaukee
1940	Chicago Bears	George Halas	73- 0	Washington	Ray Flaherty	Washington
1941	Chicago Bears	George Halas	37- 9	New York	Steve Owen	Chicago
1942	Washington	Ray Flaherty	14- 6	Chicago Bears	Hunk Anderson & Luke Johnsos	Washington
1943	Chicago Bears	Hunk Anderson & Luke Johnsos	41-21	Washington	Arthur Bergman	Chicago
1944	Green Bay	Curly Lambeau	14- 7	New York	Steve Owen	New York
1945	Cleveland Rams	Adam Walsh	15-14	Washington	Dudley DeGroot	Cleveland
1946	Chicago Bears	George Halas	24-14	New York	Steve Owen	New York
1947	Chicago Cardinals	Jimmy Conzelman	28-21	Philadelphia	Greasy Neale	Chicago
1948	Philadelphia	Greasy Neale	7- 0	Chicago Cardinals	Jimmy Conzelman	Philadelphia
1949	Philadelphia	Greasy Neale	14- 0	Los Angeles Rams	Clark Shaughnessy	Los Angeles
1950	Cleveland Browns	Paul Brown	30-28	Los Angeles	Joe Stydahar	Cleveland
1951	Los Angeles	Joe Stydahar	24-17	Cleveland	Paul Brown	Los Angeles
1952	Detroit	Buddy Parker	17- 7	Cleveland	Paul Brown	Cleveland
1953	Detroit	Buddy Parker	17-16	Cleveland	Paul Brown	Detroit
1954	Cleveland	Paul Brown	56-10	Detroit	Buddy Parker	Cleveland
1955	Cleveland	Paul Brown	38-14	Los Angeles	Sid Gillman	Los Angeles
1956	New York	Jim Lee Howell	47- 7	Chicago Bears	Paddy Driscoll	New York
1957	Detroit	George Wilson	59-14	Cleveland	Paul Brown	Detroit
1958	Baltimore	Weeb Ewbank	23-17*	New York	Jim Lee Howell	New York
1959	Baltimore	Weeb Ewbank	31-16	New York	Jim Lee Howell	Baltimore
1960	Philadelphia	Buck Shaw	17-13	Green Bay	Vince Lombardi	Philadelphia
1961	Green Bay	Vince Lombardi	37- 0	New York	Allie Sherman	Green Bay
1962	Green Bay	Vince Lombardi	16- 7	New York	Allie Sherman	New York
1963	Chicago	George Halas	14-10	New York	Allie Sherman	Chicago
1964	Cleveland	Blanton Collier	27- 0	Baltimore	Don Shula	Cleveland
1965	Green Bay	Vince Lombardi	23-12	Cleveland	Blanton Collier	Green Bay
1966	Green Bay	Vince Lombardi	34-27	Dallas	Tom Landry	Dallas
1967	Green Bay	Vince Lombardi	21-17	Dallas	Tom Landry	Green Bay
1968	Baltimore	Don Shula	34- 0	Cleveland	Blanton Collier	Cleveland
1969	Minnesota	Bud Grant	27- 7	Cleveland	Blanton Collier	Minnesota
1970	Dallas	Tom Landry	17-10	San Francisco	Dick Nolan	San Francisco
1971	Dallas	Tom Landry	14- 3	San Francisco	Dick Nolan	Dallas
1972	Washington	George Allen	26- 3	Dallas	Tom Landry	Washington

*Sudden death overtime

NFL-NFC Championship Game (Cont.)

Season	Winner	Head Coach	Score	Loser	Head Coach	Site
1973	Minnesota	Bud Grant	27-10	Dallas	Tom Landry	Dallas
1974	Minnesota	Bud Grant	14-10	Los Angeles	Chuck Knox	Minnesota
1975	Dallas	Tom Landry	37- 7	Los Angeles	Chuck Knox	Los Angeles
1976	Minnesota	Bud Grant	24-13	Los Angeles	Chuck Knox	Minnesota
1977	Dallas	Tom Landry	23- 6	Minnesota	Bud Grant	Dallas
1978	Dallas	Tom Landry	28- 0	Los Angeles	Ray Malavasi	Los Angeles
1979	Los Angeles	Ray Malavasi	9- 0	Tampa Bay	John McKay	Tampa Bay
1980	Philadelphia	Dick Vermeil	20- 7	Dallas	Tom Landry	Philadelphia
1981	San Francisco	Bill Walsh	28-27	Dallas	Tom Landry	San Francisco
1982	Washington	Joe Gibbs	31-17	Dallas	Tom Landry	Washington
1983	Washington	Joe Gibbs	24-21	San Francisco	Bill Walsh	Washington
1984	San Francisco	Bill Walsh	23- 0	Chicago	Mike Ditka	San Francisco
1985	Chicago	Mike Ditka	24- 0	Los Angeles	John Robinson	Chicago
1986	New York	Bill Parcells	17- 0	Washington	Joe Gibbs	New York
1987	Washington	Joe Gibbs	17-10	Minnesota	Jerry Burns	Washington
1988	San Francisco	Bill Walsh	28- 3	Chicago	Mike Ditka	Chicago
1989	San Francisco	George Seifert	30- 3	Los Angeles	John Robinson	San Francisco
1990	New York	Bill Parcells	15-13	San Francisco	George Seifert	San Francisco
1991	Washington	Joe Gibbs	41-10	Detroit	Wayne Fontes	Washington
1992	Dallas	Jimmy Johnson	30-20	San Francisco	George Seifert	San Francisco
1993	Dallas	Jimmy Johnson	38-21	San Francisco	George Seifert	Dallas

NFL-NFC Championship Game Appearances

App		W	L	Pct	PF	PA	App		W	L	Pct	PF	PA
16	NY Giants	5	11	.313	240	322	10	San Francisco	4	6	.400	197	171
14	Dallas Cowboys	7	7	.500	295	254	6	Minnesota	4	2	.667	108	80
13	Chicago Bears	7	6	.538	286	245	6	Detroit	4	2	.667	139	141
12	Boston-Wash.Redskins	7	5	.583	222	255	5	Philadelphia	4	1	.800	79	48
12	Cleveland-LA Rams	3	9	.250	123	270	4	Baltimore Colts	3	1	.750	88	60
11	Cleveland Browns	4	7	.364	224	253	2	Chicago Cardinals	1	1	.500	28	28
10	Green Bay	8	2	.800	223	116	1	Tampa Bay	0	1	.000	0	9

AFL-AFC Championship Game

AFL Championship games from 1960-69 and AFC Championship games since the completion of the NFL-AFL merger following the 1969 season.

Multiple winners: Buffalo (6); Miami (5); Denver, Oakland-LA Raiders and Pittsburgh (4); Dallas Texans-KC Chiefs (3); Cincinnati and Houston (2).

Season	Winner	Head Coach	Score	Loser	Head Coach	Site
1960	Houston	Lou Rymkus	24-16	LA Chargers	Sid Gillman	Houston
1961	Houston	Wally Lemm	10- 3	SD Chargers	Sid Gillman	San Diego
1962	Dallas	Hank Stram	20-17*	Houston	Pop Ivy	Houston
1963	San Diego	Sid Gillman	51-10	Boston Patriots	Mike Holovak	San Diego
1964	Buffalo	Lou Saban	20- 7	San Diego	Sid Gillman	Buffalo
1965	Buffalo	Lou Saban	23- 0	San Diego	Sid Gillman	San Diego
1966	Kansas City	Hank Stram	31- 7	Buffalo	Joel Collier	Buffalo
1967	Oakland	John Rauch	40- 7	Houston	Wally Lemm	Oakland
1968	NY Jets	Webb Ewbank	27-23	Oakland	John Rauch	New York
1969	Kansas City	Hank Stram	17- 7	Oakland	John Madden	Oakland
1970	Baltimore	Don McCafferty	27-17	Oakland	John Madden	Baltimore
1971	Miami	Don Shula	21- 0	Baltimore	Don McCafferty	Miami
1972	Miami	Don Shula	21-17	Pittsburgh	Chuck Noll	Pittsburgh
1973	Miami	Don Shula	27-10	Oakland	John Madden	Miami
1974	Pittsburgh	Chuck Noll	24-13	Oakland	John Madden	Oakland
1975	Pittsburgh	Chuck Noll	16-10	Oakland	John Madden	Pittsburgh
1976	Oakland	John Madden	24- 7	Pittsburgh	Chuck Noll	Oakland
1977	Denver	Red Miller	20-17	Oakland	John Madden	Denver
1978	Pittsburgh	Chuck Noll	34- 5	Houston	Bum Phillips	Pittsburgh
1979	Pittsburgh	Chuck Noll	27-13	Houston	Bum Phillips	Pittsburgh
1980	Oakland	Tom Flores	34-27	San Diego	Don Coryell	San Diego
1981	Cincinnati	Forrest Gregg	27- 7	San Diego	Don Coryell	Cincinnati
1982	Miami	Don Shula	14- 0	NY Jets	Walt Michaels	Miami
1983	LA Raiders	Tom Flores	30-14	Seattle	Chuck Knox	Los Angeles
1984	Miami	Don Shula	45-28	Pittsburgh	Chuck Noll	Miami
1985	NE Patriots	Raymond Berry	31-14	Miami	Don Shula	Miami
1986	Denver	Dan Reeves	23-20*	Cleveland	Marty Schottenheimer	Cleveland

*Sudden death overtime

Season	Winner	Head Coach	Score	Loser	Head Coach	Site
1987	Denver	Dan Reeves	38-33	Cleveland	Marty Schottenheimer	Denver
1988	Cincinnati	Sam Wyche	21-10	Buffalo	Marv Levy	Cincinnati
1989	Denver	Dan Reeves	37-21	Cleveland	Bud Carson	Denver
1990	Buffalo	Marv Levy	51- 3	LA Raiders	Art Shell	Buffalo
1991	Buffalo	Marv Levy	10- 7	Denver	Dan Reeves	Buffalo
1992	Buffalo	Marv Levy	29-10	Miami	Don Shula	Miami
1993	Buffalo	Marv Levy	30-13	Kansas City	Marty Schottenheimer	Buffalo

AFL-AFC Championship Game Appearances

App		W	L	Pct	PF	PA	App		W	L	Pct	PF	PA
12	Oakland-LA Raiders	4	8	.333	228	264	4	Dallas Texans/KC Chiefs	3	1	.750	81	61
8	Buffalo	6	2	.750	180	92	3	Cleveland	0	3	.000	74	98
7	Miami	5	2	.714	152	115	2	Cincinnati	2	0	1.000	48	17
7	Pittsburgh	4	3	.571	153	131	2	Baltimore Colts	1	1	.500	27	38
7	LA-San Diego Chargers	1	6	.143	111	148	2	Boston-NE Patriots	1	1	.500	41	65
6	Houston	2	4	.333	76	140	2	NY Jets	1	1	.500	27	37
5	Denver	4	1	.800	125	101	1	Seattle	0	1	.000	14	30

NFL Divisional Champions

The NFL adopted divisional play for the first time in 1967, splitting both conferences into two four-team divisions—the Capitol and Century divisions in the East and the Central and Coastal divisions in the West. Merger with the AFL in 1970 increased NFL membership to 26 teams and made it necessary for the league to realign. Two 13-team conferences—the AFC and NFC—were formed by moving established NFL clubs in Baltimore, Cleveland and Pittsburgh to the AFC and rearranging both conferences into Eastern, Central and Western divisions.

Division champions are listed below; teams that went on to win the Super Bowl are in **bold** type. Note that in 1980, Oakland won the Super Bowl as a wild card team; and in 1982, the players' strike shortened the regular season to nine games and eliminated divisional play for one season.

Multiple champions (since 1970): **AFC**—Miami and Pittsburgh (10); Oakland-LA Raiders (9); Denver (7); Buffalo and Cleveland (6); Baltimore-Indianapolis Colts and Cincinnati (5); San Diego (4); Houston, Kansas City and New England (3). **NFC**—San Francisco (13); Dallas and Minnesota (11); LA Rams (8); Chicago (6); Washington (5); Detroit and NY Giants (3); Philadelphia, St. Louis Cardinals and Tampa Bay (2).

American Football League

Season	East	West
1966	Buffalo	Kansas City

Season	East	West
1967	Houston	Oakland
1968	**NY Jets**	Oakland
1969	NY Jets	Oakland

Note: Kansas City, an AFL Wild Card team, won the Super Bowl in 1969.

National Football League

Season	East	West
1966	Dallas	Green Bay

Season	Capitol	Century	Central	Coastal
1967	Dallas	Cleveland	**Green Bay**	LA Rams
1968	Dallas	Cleveland	Minnesota	Baltimore
1969	Dallas	Cleveland	Minnesota	LA Rams

American Football Conference

Season	East	Central	West
1970	**Baltimore**	Cincinnati	Oakland
1971	Miami	Cleveland	Kansas City
1972	**Miami**	Pittsburgh	Oakland
1973	**Miami**	Cincinnati	Oakland
1974	Miami	**Pittsburgh**	Oakland
1975	Baltimore	**Pittsburgh**	Oakland
1976	Baltimore	Pittsburgh	**Oakland**
1977	Baltimore	Pittsburgh	Denver
1978	New England	**Pittsburgh**	Denver
1979	Miami	**Pittsburgh**	San Diego
1980	Buffalo	Cleveland	San Diego
1981	Miami	Cincinnati	San Diego
1982	—	—	—
1983	Miami	Pittsburgh	**LA Raiders**
1984	Miami	Pittsburgh	Denver
1985	Miami	Cleveland	LA Raiders
1986	New England	Cleveland	Denver
1987	Indianapolis	Cleveland	Denver
1988	Buffalo	Cincinnati	Seattle
1989	Buffalo	Cleveland	Denver
1990	Buffalo	Cincinnati	LA Raiders
1991	Buffalo	Houston	Denver
1992	Miami	Pittsburgh	San Diego
1993	Buffalo	Houston	Kansas City

National Football Conference

Season	East	Central	West
1970	Dallas	Minnesota	San Francisco
1971	**Dallas**	Minnesota	San Francisco
1972	Washington	Green Bay	San Francisco
1973	Dallas	Minnesota	LA Rams
1974	St. Louis	Minnesota	LA Rams
1975	St. Louis	Minnesota	LA Rams
1976	Dallas	Minnesota	LA Rams
1977	**Dallas**	Minnesota	LA Rams
1978	Dallas	Minnesota	LA Rams
1979	Dallas	Tampa Bay	LA Rams
1980	Philadelphia	Minnesota	Atlanta
1981	Dallas	Tampa Bay	**San Francisco**
1982	—	—	—
1983	Washington	Detroit	San Francisco
1984	Washington	Chicago	**San Francisco**
1985	Dallas	**Chicago**	LA Rams
1986	**NY Giants**	Chicago	San Francisco
1987	**Washington**	Chicago	San Francisco
1988	Philadelphia	Chicago	**San Francisco**
1989	NY Giants	Minnesota	**San Francisco**
1990	**NY Giants**	Chicago	San Francisco
1991	**Washington**	Detroit	New Orleans
1992	**Dallas**	Minnesota	San Francisco
1993	**Dallas**	Detroit	San Francisco

Note: Oakland, an AFC Wild Card team, won the Super Bowl in 1980.

Overall Postseason Games

The postseason records of all 28 teams in the NFL, ranked by number of playoff games participated in from 1933 through the 1993 season.

Gm		W	L	Pct	PF	PA	Gm		W	L	Pct	PF	PA
44	Dallas Cowboys	27	17	.614	1039	789	19	Denver Broncos	9	10	.474	380	502
35	Boston-Wash. Redskins	21	14	.600	738	625	17	Philadelphia Eagles	8	9	.471	287	288
36	Oakland-LA Raiders	21	15	.583	855	659	16	Balt-Indianapolis Colts	8	8	.500	285	300
33	Cleveland-LA Rams	13	20	.394	501	697	16	Dallas Texans/KC Chiefs	8	8	.500	267	333
32	New York Giants	14	18	.438	529	593	14	LA-San Diego Chargers	5	9	.357	247	310
30	Minnesota Vikings	13	17	.433	535	611	13	Detroit Lions	7	6	.538	293	283
29	San Francisco 49ers	18	11	.621	712	536	12	Cincinnati Bengals	5	7	.417	246	257
28	Miami Dolphins	16	12	.571	627	557	11	New York Jets	5	6	.455	216	200
28	Cleveland Browns	10	18	.357	567	660	10	Boston-NE Patriots	4	6	.400	195	258
27	Pittsburgh Steelers	16	11	.593	609	545	7	Seattle Seahawks	3	4	.429	128	139
26	Chicago Bears	13	13	.500	529	490	6	Atlanta Falcons	2	4	.333	119	144
24	Buffalo Bills	13	11	.542	563	520	5	Chi-St.L-Ariz Cards	1	4	.200	81	134
22	Houston Oilers	9	13	.409	371	533	4	Tampa Bay Buccaneers	1	3	.250	41	94
20	Green Bay Packers	14	6	.700	461	310	4	New Orleans Saints	0	4	.000	56	123

All-Time Postseason Leaders

Through Super Bowl XXVIII, Jan. 30, 1994.

CAREER
Quarterback Ratings

Ratings based on performance standards established for completion percentage, average gain, touchdown percentage and interception percentage. Quarterbacks are allocated points according to how their statistics measure up to those standards. Minimum 100 passing attempts.

		Gm	Att	Cmp	Cmp%	Yards	Avg Gain	TD	TD%	Int	Int%	Rating
1	**Troy Aikman**, Dal	7	187	133	71.1	1595	8.53	13	7.0	4	2.1	111.2
2	Bart Starr, GB	10	213	130	61.0	1753	8.23	15	7.0	3	1.4	104.8
3	**Joe Montana**, SF-KC	22	697	434	62.3	5458	7.83	43	6.2	20	2.9	95.2
4	Ken Anderson, Cin	6	166	110	66.3	1321	7.96	9	5.4	6	3.6	93.5
5	Joe Theismann, Wash	10	211	128	60.7	1782	8.45	11	5.2	7	3.3	91.4
6	**Warren Moon**, Hou	9	351	230	65.5	2578	7.34	15	4.3	12	3.4	87.3
7	Ken Stabler, Oak	13	351	203	57.8	2641	7.52	19	5.4	13	3.7	84.2
8	**Bernie Kosar**, Cle-Dal	9	269	151	56.1	1943	7.22	16	5.9	10	3.7	83.2
9	Terry Bradshaw, Pit	19	456	261	57.2	3833	8.41	30	6.6	26	5.7	83.0
10	Jim Plunkett, Raiders	10	272	162	59.6	2293	8.43	11	4.0	12	4.4	81.9

Passing

(Minimum 100 Attempts)

Efficiency	Gm	Cmp%	Yds	TD	Int	Rate
1 **Troy Aikman**	4	68.6	909	8	1	116.7
2 Bart Starr	10	61.0	1753	15	3	104.8
3 **Joe Montana**	22	62.3	5458	43	20	95.2

Yards Gained	Gm	Att	Cmp	Cmp%	Yds
1 **Joe Montana**	22	697	434	62.3	5458
2 Terry Bradshaw	19	456	261	57.2	3833
3 John Elway	14	431	229	53.1	3321

Completions	Gm	Att	Cmp	Yds	TD
1 **Joe Montana**	22	697	434	5458	43
2 Terry Bradshaw	19	456	261	3833	30
3 Roger Staubach	20	410	223	2791	24

Touchdown Passes	Gm	Att	Cmp	Yds	TD
1 **Joe Montana**	22	697	434	5458	43
2 Terry Bradshaw	19	456	261	3833	30
3 Roger Staubach	20	410	223	2791	24

Receiving

Catches	Gm	No	Yds	Avg
1 **Jerry Rice**	15	84	1306	15.5
2 Cliff Branch	22	73	1289	17.7
3 Fred Biletnikoff	19	70	1167	16.7

Yards Gained	Gm	No	Yds	Avg
2 **Jerry Rice**	15	84	1306	15.5
1 Cliff Branch	22	73	1289	17.7
3 Fred Biletnikoff	19	70	1167	16.7

Rushing

Yards Gained	Gm	Car	Yds	Avg
1 Franco Harris	19	400	1556	3.89
2 Tony Dorsett	17	302	1383	4.58
3 John Riggins	9	251	996	3.97

Yards Per Carry	Gm	Car	Yds	Avg
1 Timmy Smith	3	51	342	6.71
2 Paul Lowe	5	57	380	6.67
3 **Marcus Allen**	13	220	1152	5.24

Scoring

Points	Gm	TD	FG	PAT	Pts
1 George Blanda	19	0	22	49	115
2 Franco Harris	19	17	0	0	102
3 Matt Bahr	13	0	19	39	96

Touchdowns	Gm	Run	Rec	Ret	No
1 Franco Harris	19	16	1	0	17
2 **Jerry Rice**	15	0	13	0	13
3 John Riggins	9	12	0	0	12
John Stallworth	18	0	12	0	12

Field Goals	Gm	Att	FG	Pct
1 George Blanda	19	39	22	.564
2 Toni Fritsch	14	28	20	.714
3 Matt Bahr	13	23	19	.826

Champions Of Leagues That No Longer Exist

No professional league in American sports has had to contend with more pretenders to the throne than the NFL. Seven times in as many decades a rival league has risen up to challenge the NFL and six of them went under in less than five seasons. Only the fourth American Football League (1960-69) succeeded, forcing the older league to sue for peace and a full partnership in 1966.

Of the six leagues that didn't make it, only the All-America Football Conference (1946-49) lives on—the Cleveland Browns and San Francisco 49ers joined the NFL after the AAFC folded in 1949.

The champions of leagues past are listed below.

American Football League I

Year		Head Coach
1926	Philadelphia Quakers (7-2)	Bob Folwell

Note: Philadelphia was challenged to a postseason game by the 7th place New York Giants (8-4-1) of the NFL. The Giants won, 31-0, in a snowstorm.

American Football League II

Year		Head Coach
1936	Boston Shamrocks (8-3)	George Kenneally
1937	Los Angeles Bulldogs (8-0)	Gus Henderson

Note: Boston was scheduled to play 2nd place Cleveland (5-2-2) in the '36 championship game, but the Shamrock players refused to participate because they were owed pay for past games.

American Football League III

Year		Head Coach
1940	Columbus Bullies (8-1-1)	Phil Bucklew
1941	Columbus Bullies (5-1-2)	Phil Bucklew

All-America Football Conference

Year	Winner	Head Coach	Score	Loser	Head Coach	Site
1946	Cleveland Browns	Paul Brown	14-9	NY Yankees	Ray Flaherty	Cleveland
1947	Cleveland Browns	Paul Brown	14-3	NY Yankees	Ray Flaherty	New York
1948	Cleveland Browns	Paul Brown	49-7	Buffalo Bills	Red Dawson	Cleveland
1949	Cleveland Browns	Paul Brown	21-7	S.F. 49ers	Buck Shaw	Cleveland

World Football League

Year	Winner	Head Coach	Score	Loser	Head Coach	Site
1974	Birmingham Americans	Jack Gotta	22-21	Florida Blazers	Jack Pardee	Birmingham
1975	WFL folded Oct. 22.					

United States Football League

Year	Winner	Head Coach	Score	Loser	Head Coach	Site
1983	Michigan Panthers	Jim Stanley	24-22	Philadelphia Stars	Jim Mora	Denver
1984	Philadelphia Stars	Jim Mora	23-3	Arizona Wranglers	George Allen	Tampa
1985	Baltimore Stars	Jim Mora	28-24	Oakland Invaders	Charlie Sumner	E. Rutherford

Defunct Leagues

AFL I (1926): Boston Bulldogs, Brooklyn Horseman, Chicago Bulls, Cleveland Panthers, Los Angeles Wildcats, New York Yankees, Newark Bears, Philadelphia Quakers, Rock Island Independents.

AFL II (1936-37): Boston Shamrocks (1936-37); Brooklyn Tigers (1936); Cincinnati Bengals (1937); Cleveland Rams (1936); Los Angeles Bulldogs (1937); New York Yankees (1936-37); Pittsburgh Americans (1936-37); Rochester Tigers (1936-37).

AFL III (1940-41): Boston Bears (1940); Buffalo Indians (1940-41); Cincinnati Bengals (1940-41); Columbus Bullies (1940-41); Milwaukee Chiefs (1940-41); New York Yankees (1940) renamed Americans (1941).

AAFC (1946-49): Brooklyn Dodgers (1946-48) merged to become Brooklyn-New York Yankees (1949); Buffalo Bisons (1946) renamed Bills (1947-49); Chicago Rockets (1946-48) renamed Hornets (1949); Cleveland Browns (1946-49); Los Angeles Dons (1946-49); Miami Seahawks (1946) became Baltimore Colts (1947-49); New York Yankees (1946-48) merged to become Brooklyn-New York Yankees (1949); San Francisco 49ers (1946-49).

WFL (1974-75): Birmingham Americans (1974) renamed Vulcans (1975); Chicago Fire (1974) renamed Winds (1975); Detroit Wheels (1974); Florida Blazers (1974) became San Antonio Wings (1975); The Hawaiians (1974-75); Houston Texans (1974) became Shreveport (La.) Steamer (1974-75); Jacksonville Sharks (1974) renamed Express (1975); Memphis Southmen (1974) also known as Grizzlies (1975); New York Stars (1974) became Charlotte Hornets (1974-75); Philadelphia Bell (1974-75); Portland Storm (1974) renamed Thunder (1975); Southern California Sun (1974-75).

USFL (1983-85): Arizona Wranglers (1983-84) merged with Oklahoma to become Arizona Outlaws (1985); Birmingham Stallions (1983-85); Boston Breakers (1983) became New Orleans Breakers (1984) and then Portland Breakers (1985); Chicago Blitz (1983-84); Denver Gold (1983-85); Houston Gamblers (1984-85); Jacksonville Bulls (1984-85); Los Angeles Express (1983-85); Memphis Showboats (1984-85); Michigan Panthers (1983-84) merged with Oakland (1985); New Jersey Generals (1983-85); Oakland Invaders (1983-85); Oklahoma Outlaws (1984) merged with Arizona to become Arizona Outlaws (1985); Philadelphia Stars (1983-84) became Baltimore Stars (1985); Pittsburgh Maulers (1984); San Antonio Gunslingers (1984-85); Tampa Bay Bandits (1983-85); Washington Federals (1983-84) became Orlando Renegades (1985).

NFL Pro Bowl

A postseason All-Star game between the new league champion and a team of professional all-stars was added to the NFL schedule in 1939. In the first game at Wrigley Field in Los Angeles, the NY Giants beat a team made up of players from NFL teams and two independent clubs in Los Angeles (the LA Bulldogs and Hollywood Stars). An all-NFL All-Star team provided the opposition over the next four seasons, but the game was cancelled in 1943.

The Pro Bowl was revived in 1951 as a contest between conference all-star teams: American vs National (1951-53), Eastern vs Western (1954-70), and AFC vs NFC (since 1971). The NFC leads the current series with the AFC, 14-10.

The MVP trophy was named the Dan McGuire Award in 1984 after the late SF 49ers publicist and Honolulu Advertiser sports columnist.

Year	Winner	Score	Loser
1939	NY Giants	13-10	All-Stars
1940	Green Bay	16- 7	All-Stars
1940	Chicago Bears	28-14	All-Stars
1942	Chcago Bears	35-24	All-Stars
1942	All-Stars	17-14	Washington
1943-50		No game	

Year	Winner	MVP
1951	American, 28-27	Otto Graham, Cle., QB
1952	National, 30-13	Dan Towler, LA, HB
1953	National, 27-7	Don Doll, Det., DB
1954	East, 20-9	Chuck Bednarik, Phi., LB
1955	West, 26-19	Billy Wilson, SF, E
1956	East, 31-30	Ollie Matson, Cards, HB
1957	West, 19-10	Back—Bert Rechichar, Bal.
		Line—Ernie Stautner, Pit.
1958	West, 26-7	Back—Hugh McElhenny, SF
		Line—Gene Brito, Wash.
1959	East, 28-21	Back—Frank Gifford, NY
		Line—Doug Atkins, Chi.
1960	West, 38-21	Back—Johnny Unitas, Bal.
		Line—Big Daddy Lipscomb, Pit.
1961	West, 35-31	Back—Johnny Unitas, Bal.
		Line—Sam Huff, NY
1962	West, 31-30	Back—Jim Brown, Cle.
		Line—Henry Jordan, GB
1963	East, 30-20	Back—Jim Brown, Cle.
		Line—Big Daddy Lipscomb, Pit.
1964	West, 31-17	Back—Johnny Unitas, Bal.
		Line—Gino Marchetti, Bal.
1965	West, 34-14	Back—Fran Tarkenton, Min.
		Line—Terry Barr, Det.
1966	East, 36-7	Back—Jim Brown, Cle.
		Line—Dale Meinhart, St.L.
1967	East, 20-10	Back—Gale Sayers, Chi.
		Line—Floyd Peters, Phi.

Year	Winner	MVP
1968	West, 38-20	Back—Gale Sayers, Chi.
		Line—Dave Robinson, GB
1969	West, 10-7	Back—Roman Gabriel, LA
		Line—Merlin Olsen, LA
1970	West, 16-13	Back—Gale Sayers, Chi.
		Line—George Andrie, Dal.
1971	NFC, 27-6	Back—Mel Renfro, Dal.
		Line—Fred Carr, GB
1972	AFC, 26-13	Off—Jan Stenerud, KC
		Def—Willie Lanier, KC
1973	AFC, 33-28	O.J. Simpson, Buf., RB
1974	AFC, 15-13	Garo Yepremian, Mia., PK
1975	NFC, 17-10	James Harris, LA Rams, QB
1976	NFC, 23-20	Billy Johnson, Hou., KR
1977	AFC, 24-14	Mel Blount, Pit., CB
1978	NFC, 14-13	Walter Payton, Chi., RB
1979	NFC, 13-7	Ahmad Rashad, Min., WR
1980	NFC, 37-27	Chuck Muncie, NO, RB
1981	NFC, 21-7	Eddie Murray, Det., PK
1982	AFC, 16-13	Kellen Winslow, SD, WR
		& Lee Roy Selmon, TB, DE
1983	NFC, 20-19	Dan Fouts, SD, QB
		& John Jefferson, GB, WR
1984	NFC, 45-3	Joe Theismann, Wash., QB
1985	AFC, 22-14	Mark Gastineau, NYJ, DE
1986	NFC, 28-24	Phil Simms, NYG, QB
1987	AFC, 10-6	Reggie White, Phi., DE
1988	AFC, 15-6	Bruce Smith, Buf., DE
1989	NFC, 34-3	Randall Cunningham, Phi., QB
1990	NFC, 27-21	Jerry Gray, LA Rams, CB
1991	AFC, 23-21	Jim Kelly, Buf., QB
1992	NFC, 21-15	Michael Irvin, Dal., WR
1993	AFC, 23-20 (OT)	Steve Tasker, Buf., Sp. Teams
1994	NFC, 17-3	Andre Rison, Atl., WR

Playing sites: Wrigley Field in Los Angeles (1939); Gilmore Stadium in Los Angeles (both games); Polo Grounds in New York (Jan., 1942); Shibe Park in Philadelphia (Dec., 1942); Memorial Coliseum in Los Angeles (1951-72 and 1979); Texas Stadium in Irving, TX (1973); Arrowhead Stadium in Kansas City (1974); Orange Bowl in Miami (1975); Superdome in New Orleans (1976); Kingdome in Seattle (1977); Tampa Stadium in Tampa (1978) and Aloha Stadium in Honolulu (since 1980).

AFL All-Star Game

The AFL did not play an All-Star game after its first season in 1960 but did stage All-Star games from 1962-70. All-Star teams from the Eastern and Western divisions played each other every year except 1966 with the West winning the series, 6-2. In 1966, the league champion Buffalo Bills met an elite squad made up of the best players from the league's other eight clubs and lost, 30-19.

Year	Winner	MVP
1962	West, 47-27	Cotton Davidson, Oak., QB
1963	West, 21-14	Off—Curtis McClinton, Dal.
		Def—Earl Faison, SD
1964	West, 27-24	Off—Keith Lincoln, SD
		Def—Archie Matsos, Oak.
1965	West, 38-14	Off—Keith Lincoln, SD
		Def—Willie Brown, Den.
1966	All-Stars 30	Off—Joe Namath, NY
	Buffalo 19	Def—Frank Buncom, SD

Year	Winner	MVP
1967	East, 30-23	Off—Babe Parilli, Bos.
		Def—Verlon Biggs, NY
1968	East, 25-24	Off—Joe Namath, NY
		& Don Maynard, NY
		Def—Speedy Duncan, SD
1969	West, 38-25	Off—Len Dawson, KC
		Def—George Webster, Hou.
1970	West, 26-3	John Hadl, SD, QB

Playing sites: Balboa Stadium in San Diego (1962-64); Jeppesen Stadium in Houston (1965); Rice Stadium in Houston (1966); Oakland Coliseum (1967); Gator Bowl in Jacksonville (1968-69) and Astrodome in Houston (1970).

NFL Franchise Origins

Here is what the current 28 teams in the National Football League have to show for the years they have put in as members of the American Professional Football Association (APFA), the NFL, the All-America Football Conference (AAFC) and the American Football League (AFL). Years given for league titles indicate seasons championships were won.

American Football Conference

	First Season	League Titles	Franchise Stops
Buffalo Bills	1960 (AFL)	2 AFL (1964-65)	• Buffalo (1960-72) Orchard Park, NY (1973–)
Cincinnati Bengals	1968 (AFL)	None	• Cincinnati (1968–)
Cleveland Browns	1946 (AAFC)	4 AAFC (1946-49) 4 NFL (1950,54-55,64)	• Cleveland (1946–)
Denver Broncos	1960 (AFL)	None	• Denver (1960—)
Houston Oilers	1960 (AFL)	2 AFL (1960-61)	• Houston (1960—)
Indianapolis Colts	1953 (NFL)	3 NFL (1958-59,68) 1 Super Bowl (1970)	• Baltimore (1953-83) Indianapolis (1984—)
Kansas City Chiefs	1960 (AFL)	3 AFL (1962,66,69) 1 Super Bowl (1969)	• Dallas (1960-62) Kansas City (1963—)
Los Angeles Raiders	1960 (AFL)	1 AFL (1967) 3 Super Bowls (1976,80,83)	• Oakland (1960-81) Los Angeles (1982—)
Miami Dolphins	1966 (AFL)	2 Super Bowls (1972-73)	• Miami (1966—)
New England Patriots	1960 (AFL)	None	• Boston (1960-70) Foxboro, MA (1971—)
New York Jets	1960 (AFL)	1 AFL (1968) 1 Super Bowl (1968)	• New York (1960-83) E. Rutherford, NJ (1984—)
Pittsburgh Steelers	1933 (NFL)	4 Super Bowls (1974-75,78-79)	• Pittsburgh (1933—)
San Diego Chargers	1960 (AFL)	1 AFL (1963)	• Los Angeles (1960) San Diego (1961—)
Seattle Seahawks	1976 (NFL)	None	• Seattle (1976—)

National Football Conference

	First Season	League Titles	Franchise Stops
Arizona Cardinals	1920 (APFA)	2 NFL (1925,47)	• Chicago (1920-59) St. Louis (1960-87) Tempe, AZ (1988—)
Atlanta Falcons	1966 (NFL)	None	• Atlanta (1966—)
Chicago Bears	1920 (APFA)	8 NFL (1921, 32-33,40-41,43, 46,63) 1 Super Bowl (1985)	• Decatur, IL (1920) Chicago (1921—)
Dallas Cowboys	1960 (NFL)	4 Super Bowls (1971,77,92-93)	• Dallas (1960-70) Irving, TX (1971—)
Detroit Lions	1930 (NFL)	4 NFL (1935,52-53,57)	• Portsmouth, OH (1930-33) Detroit (1934-74) Pontiac, MI (1975—)
Green Bay Packers	1921 (APFA)	11 NFL (1929-31,36,39,44, 61-62,65-67) 2 Super Bowls (1966-67)	• Green Bay (1921—)
Los Angeles Rams	1937 (NFL)	2 NFL (1945,51)	• Cleveland (1937-45) Los Angeles (1946-79) Anaheim (1980—)
Minnesota Vikings	1961 (NFL)	1 NFL (1969)	• Bloomington, MN (1961-81) Minneapolis, MN (1982—)
New Orleans Saints	1967 (NFL)	None	• New Orleans (1967—)
New York Giants	1925 (NFL)	4 NFL (1927,34,38,56) 2 Super Bowls (1986,90)	• New York (1925-73,75) New Haven, CT (1973-74) E. Rutherford, NJ (1976—)
Philadelphia Eagles	1933 (NFL)	3 NFL (1948-49,60)	• Philadelphia (1933—)
San Francisco 49ers	1946 (AAFC)	4 Super Bowls (1981,84,88-89)	• San Francisco (1946—)
Tampa Bay Buccaneers	1976 (NFL)	None	• Tampa, FL (1976—)
Washington Redskins	1932 (NFL)	2 NFL (1937,42) 3 Super Bowls (1982,87,91)	• Boston (1932-36) Washington, DC (1937—)

☞ The expansion **Carolina Panthers** (based in Charlotte, N.C.) and **Jacksonville** (Fla.) **Jaguars** will ☜ begin play in 1995. Their conference affiliations had not been announced as of July 1, 1994.

The Growth of the NFL

Of the 14 franchises that comprised the American Professional Football Association in 1920, only two remain—the Chicago Bears (originally the Decatur-IL Staleys) and the Phoenix Cardinals (then the Chicago Cardinals). Green Bay joined the APFC in 1921 and the league changed its name to the NFL in 1922. Since then, 52 NFL clubs have come and gone, five rival leagues have expired and two other leagues have been swallowed up.

The NFL merged with the **All-America Football Conference** (1946-49) following the 1949 season and adopted three of its seven clubs—the Baltimore Colts, Cleveland Browns and San Francisco 49ers. The four remaining AAFC teams—the Brooklyn/NY Yankees, Buffalo Bills, Chicago Hornets and Los Angeles Dons—did not survive. After the 1950 season, the financially troubled Colts were sold back to the NFL. The league folded the team and added its players to the 1951 college draft pool. A new Baltimore franchise, also named the Colts, joined the NFL in 1953.

The formation of the **American Football League** (1960-69) was announced in 1959 with ownership lined up in eight cities—Boston, Buffalo, Dallas, Denver, Houston, Los Angeles, Minneapolis and New York. Set to begin play in the autumn of 1960, the AFL was stunned early that year when Minneapolis withdrew to accept an offer to join the NFL as an expansion team in 1961. The new league responded by choosing Oakland to replace Minneapolis and inherit the departed team's draft picks. Since no AFL team actually played in Minneapolis, it is not considered the original home of the Oakland (now Los Angeles) Raiders.

In 1966, the NFL and AFL agreed to a merger that resulted in the first Super Bowl (originally called the AFL-NFL World Championship Game) following the 1966 season. In 1970, the now 10-member AFL officially joined the NFL, forming a 26-team league made up of two conferences of three divisions each.

Expansion/Merger Timetable

For teams currently in NFL.

1921—Green Bay Packers; **1925**—New York Giants; **1930**—Portsmouth-OH Spartans (now Detroit Lions); **1932**—Boston Braves (now Washington Redskins); **1933**—Philadelphia Eagles and Pittsburgh Pirates (now Steelers); **1937**—Cleveland Rams (now Los Angeles); **1950**—added AAFC's Cleveland Browns and San Francisco 49ers; **1953**—Baltimore Colts (now Indianapolis).

1960—Dallas Cowboys; **1961**—Minnesota Vikings; **1966**—Atlanta Falcons; **1967**—New Orleans Saints; **1970**—added AFL's Boston Patriots (now New England), Buffalo Bills, Cincinnati Bengals (1968 expansion team), Denver Broncos, Houston Oilers, Kansas City Chiefs, Miami Dolphins (1966 expansion team), New York Jets, Oakland Raiders (now Los Angeles) and San Diego Chargers (the AFL-NFL merger divided the league into two 13-team conferences with old-line NFL clubs Baltimore, Cleveland and Pittsburgh moving to the AFC); **1976**—Seattle Seahawks and Tampa Bay Buccaneers (Seattle was originally in the NFC West and Tampa Bay in the AFC West, but were switched to their current divisions in 1977). **1993**—New franchises awarded to Charlotte, N.C. and Jacksonville, Fla. The Carolina Cougars and Jacksonville Jaguars will begin play in 1995.

City and Nickname Changes

1921—Decatur Staleys move to Chicago; **1922**—Chicago Staleys renamed Bears; **1933**—Boston Braves renamed Redskins; **1937**—Boston Redskins move to Washington; **1934**—Portsmouth (Ohio) Spartans move to Detroit and become Lions; **1941**—Pittsburgh Pirates renamed Steelers; **1943**—Philadelphia and Pittsburgh merge for one season and become Phil-Pitt, or the "Steagles"; **1944**—Chicago Cardinals and Pittsburgh merge for one season and become Card-Pitt; **1946**—Cleveland Rams move to Los Angeles.

1960—Chicago Cardinals move to St. Louis; **1961**—Los Angeles Chargers (AFL) move to San Diego; **1963**—New York Titans (AFL) renamed Jets and Dallas Texans (AFL) move to Kansas City and become Chiefs; **1971**—Boston Patriots become New England Patriots; **1982**—Oakland Raiders move to Los Angeles; **1984**—Baltimore Colts move to Indianapolis; **1988**—St. Louis Cardinals move to Phoenix; **1994**—Phoenix Cardinals become Arizona Cardinals.

Defunct NFL Teams

Teams that once played in the APFA and NFL, but no longer exist.

Akron-OH—Pros (1920-25) and Indians (1926); **Baltimore**—Colts (1950); **Boston**—Bulldogs (1926) and Yanks (1944-48); **Brooklyn**—Lions (1926), Dodgers (1930-43) and Tigers (1944); **Buffalo**—All-Americans (1921-23), Bisons (1924-25), Rangers (1926), Bisons (1927,1929); **Canton-OH**—Bulldogs (1920-23,1925-26); **Chicago**—Tigers (1920); **Cincinnati**—Celts (1921) and Reds (1933-34); **Cleveland**—Tigers (1920), Indians (1921), Indians (1923), Bulldogs (1924-25,1927) and Indians (1931); **Columbus-OH**—Panhandles (1920-22) and Tigers (1923-26); **Dallas**—Texans (1952); **Dayton-OH**—Triangles (1920-29).

Detroit—Heralds (1920-21), Panthers (1925-26) and Wolverines (1928); **Duluth-MN**—Kelleys (1923-25) and Eskimos (1926-27); **Evansville-IN**—Crimson Giants (1921-22); **Frankford-PA**—Yellow Jackets (1924-31); **Hammond-IN**—Pros (1920-26); **Hartford**—Blues (1926); **Kansas City**—Blues (1924) and Cowboys (1925-26); **Kenosha-WI**—Maroons (1924); **Los Angeles**—Buccaneers (1926); **Louisville**—Brecks (1921-23) and Colonels (1926); **Marion-OH**—Oorang Indians (1922-23); **Milwaukee**—Badgers (1922-26); **Minneapolis**—Marines (1922-24) and Red Jackets (1929-30); **Muncie-IN**—Flyers (1920-21).

New York—Giants (1921), Yankees (1927-28), Bulldogs (1949) and Yankees (1950-51); **Newark-NJ**—Tornadoes (1930); **Orange-NJ**—Tornadoes (1929); **Pottsville-PA**—Maroons (1925-28); **Providence-RI**—Steam Roller (1925-31); **Racine-WI**—Legion (1922-24) and Tornadoes (1926); **Rochester-NY**—Jeffersons (1920-25); **Rock Island-IL**—Independents (1920-26); **Staten Island-NY**—Stapletons (1929-32); **St. Louis**—All-Stars (1923) and Gunners (1934); **Toledo-OH**—Maroons (1922-23); **Tonawanda-NY**—Kardex (1921), also called Lumbermen; **Washington**—Senators (1921).

Annual NFL Leaders

Individual leaders in NFL (1932-69), NFC (since 1970), AFL (1960-69) and AFC (since 1970).

Passing
NFL-NFC

Since 1932, the NFL has used several formulas to determine passing leadership, from Total Yards alone (1932-37), to the current rating system—adopted in 1973—that takes Completions, Completion Pct., Yards Gained, TD Passes, Interceptions, Interception Pct. and other factors into account. The quarterbacks listed below all led the league according to the system in use at the time.

Multiple winners: Sammy Baugh (6); Joe Montana and Roger Staubach (5); Arnie Herber, Sonny Jurgensen, Bart Starr, Norm Van Brocklin and Steve Young (3); Ed Danowski, Otto Graham, Cecil Isbell, Milt Plum and Bob Waterfield (2).

Year		Att	Cmp	Yds	TD
1932	Arnie Herber, GB	101	37	639	9
1933	Harry Newman, NY	136	53	973	11
1934	Arnie Herber, GB	115	42	799	8
1935	Ed Danowski, NY	113	57	794	10
1936	Arnie Herber, GB	173	77	1239	11
1937	Sammy Baugh, Wash	171	81	1127	8
1938	Ed Danowski, NY	129	70	848	7
1939	Parker Hall, Cle. Rams	208	106	1227	9
1940	Sammy Baugh, Wash	177	111	1367	12
1941	Cecil Isbell, GB	206	117	1479	15
1942	Cecil Isbell, GB	268	146	2021	24
1943	Sammy Baugh, Wash	239	133	1754	23
1944	Frank Filchock, Wash	147	84	1139	13
1945	Sammy Baugh, Wash	182	128	1669	11
	& Sid Luckman, Chi. Bears	217	117	1725	14
1946	Bob Waterfield, LA	251	127	1747	18
1947	Sammy Baugh, Wash	354	210	2938	25
1948	Tommy Thompson, Phi	246	141	1965	25
1949	Sammy Baugh, Wash	255	145	1903	18
1950	Norm Van Brocklin, LA	233	127	2061	18
1951	Bob Waterfield, LA	176	88	1566	13
1952	Norm Van Brocklin, LA	205	113	1736	14
1953	Otto Graham, Cle	258	167	2722	11
1954	Norm Van Brocklin, LA	260	139	2637	13
1955	Otto Graham, Cle	185	98	1721	15
1956	Ed Brown, Chi. Bears	168	96	1667	11
1957	Tommy O'Connell, Cle	110	63	1229	9
1958	Eddie LeBaron, Wash	145	79	1365	11
1959	Charlie Conerly, NY	194	113	1706	14
1960	Milt Plum, Cle	250	151	2297	21
1961	Milt Plum, Cle	302	177	2416	16
1962	Bart Starr, GB	285	178	2438	12
1963	Y.A.Tittle, NY	367	221	3145	36
1964	Bart Starr, GB	272	163	2144	15
1965	Rudy Bukich, Chi	312	176	2641	20
1966	Bart Starr, GB	251	156	2257	14
1967	Sonny Jurgensen, Wash	508	288	3747	31
1968	Earl Morrall, Bal	317	182	2909	26
1969	Sonny Jurgensen, Wash	442	274	3102	22
1970	John Brodie, SF	378	223	2941	24
1971	Roger Staubach, Dal	211	126	1882	15
1972	Norm Snead, NY	325	196	2307	17
1973	Roger Staubach, Dal	286	179	2428	23
1974	Sonny Jurgensen, Wash	167	107	1185	11
1975	Fran Tarkenton, Min	425	273	2994	25
1976	James Harris, LA	158	91	1460	8
1977	Roger Staubach, Dal	361	210	2620	18
1978	Roger Staubach, Dal	413	231	3190	25
1979	Roger Staubach, Dal	461	267	3586	27
1980	Ron Jaworski, Phi	451	257	3529	27
1981	Joe Montana, SF	488	311	3565	19
1982	Joe Theismann, Wash	252	161	2033	13
1983	Steve Bartkowski, Atl	432	274	3167	22
1984	Joe Montana, SF	432	279	3630	28
1985	Joe Montana, SF	494	303	3653	27
1986	Tommy Kramer, Min	372	208	3000	24
1987	Joe Montana, SF	398	266	3054	31
1988	Wade Wilson, Min	332	204	2746	15
1989	Don Majkowski, GB	599	353	4318	27
1990	Joe Montana, SF	520	321	3944	26
1991	Steve Young, SF	279	180	2517	17
1992	Steve Young, SF	402	268	3465	25
1993	Steve Young, SF	462	314	4023	29

Note: In 1945, **Sammy Baugh** and **Sid Luckman** tied with 8 points on an inverse rating system.

AFL-AFC

Multiple winners: Ken Anderson, Len Dawson, Dan Marino (4); Bob Griese, Daryle Lamonica, Warren Moon and Ken Stabler (2).

Year		Att	Cmp	Yds	TD
1960	Jack Kemp, LA	406	211	3018	20
1961	George Blanda, Hou	362	187	3330	36
1962	Len Dawson, Dal	310	189	2759	29
1963	Tobin Rote, SD	286	170	2510	20
1964	Len Dawson, KC	354	199	2879	30
1965	John Hadl, SD	348	174	2798	20
1966	Len Dawson, KC	284	159	2527	26
1967	Daryle Lamonica, Oak	425	220	3228	30
1968	Len Dawson, KC	224	131	2109	17
1969	Greg Cook, Cin	197	106	1854	15
1970	Daryle Lamonica, Oak	356	179	2516	22
1971	Bob Griese, Mia	263	145	2089	19
1972	Earl Morrall, Mia	150	83	1360	11
1973	Ken Stabler, Oak	260	163	1997	14
1974	Ken Anderson, Cin	328	213	2667	18
1975	Ken Anderson, Cin	377	228	3169	21
1976	Ken Stabler, Oak	291	194	2737	27
1977	Bob Griese, Mia	307	180	2252	22
1978	Terry Bradshaw, Pit	368	207	2915	28
1979	Dan Fouts, SD	530	332	4082	24
1980	Brian Sipe, Cle	554	337	4132	30
1981	Ken Anderson, Cin	479	300	3753	29
1982	Ken Anderson, Cin	309	218	2495	12
1983	Dan Marino, Mia	296	173	2210	20
1984	Dan Marino, Mia	564	362	5084	48
1985	Ken O'Brien, NY	488	297	3888	25
1986	Dan Marino, Mia	623	378	4746	44
1987	Bernie Kosar, Cle	389	241	3033	22
1988	Boomer Esiason, Cin	388	223	3572	28
1989	Dan Marino, Mia	550	308	3997	24
1990	Warren Moon, Hou	584	362	4689	33
1991	Jim Kelly, Buf	474	304	3844	33
1992	Warren Moon, Hou	346	224	2521	18
1993	John Elway, Den	551	348	4030	25

Annual NFL Leaders (Cont.)

Receptions
NFL-NFC

Multiple winners: Don Hutson (8); Raymond Berry, Tom Fears, Pete Pihos, Sterling Sharpe and Billy Wilson (3); Dwight Clark, Ahmad Rashad, Jerry Rice and Charley Taylor (2).

Year	Player	No	Yds	Avg	TD
1932	Ray Flaherty, NY	21	350	16.7	3
1933	Shipwreck Kelly, Bklyn	22	246	11.2	3
1934	Joe Carter, Phi	16	238	14.9	4
	& Red Badgro, NY	16	206	12.9	1
1935	Tod Goodwin, NY	26	432	16.6	4
1936	Don Hutson, GB	34	536	15.8	8
1937	Don Hutson, GB	41	552	13.5	7
1938	Gaynell Tinsley, Chi. Cards	41	516	12.6	1
1939	Don Hutson, GB	34	846	24.9	6
1940	Don Looney, Phi	58	707	12.2	4
1941	Don Hutson, GB	58	739	12.7	10
1942	Don Hutson, GB	74	1211	16.4	17
1943	Don Hutson, GB	47	776	16.5	11
1944	Don Hutson, GB	58	866	14.9	9
1945	Don Hutson, GB	47	834	17.7	9
1946	Jim Benton, LA	63	981	15.6	6
1947	Jim Keane, Chi. Bears	64	910	14.2	10
1948	Tom Fears, LA	51	698	13.7	4
1949	Tom Fears, LA	77	1013	13.2	9
1950	Tom Fears, LA	84	1116	13.3	7
1951	Elroy Hirsch, LA	66	1495	22.7	17
1952	Mac Speedie, Cle	62	911	14.7	5
1953	Pete Pihos, Phi	63	1049	16.7	10
1954	Pete Pihos, Phi	60	872	14.5	10
	& Billy Wilson, SF	60	830	13.8	5
1955	Pete Pihos, Phi	62	864	13.9	7
1956	Billy Wilson, SF	60	889	14.8	5
1957	Billy Wilson, SF	52	757	14.6	6
1958	Raymond Berry, Bal	56	794	14.2	9
	& Pete Retzlaff, Phi	56	766	13.7	2
1959	Raymond Berry, Bal	66	959	14.5	14
1960	Raymond Berry, Bal	74	1298	17.5	10
1961	Red Phillips, LA	78	1092	14.0	5
1962	Bobby Mitchell, Wash	72	1384	19.2	11
1963	Bobby Joe Conrad, St.L	73	967	13.2	10
1964	Johnny Morris, Chi. Bears	93	1200	12.9	10
1965	Dave Parks, SF	80	1344	16.8	12
1966	Charley Taylor, Wash	72	1119	15.5	12
1967	Charley Taylor, Wash	70	990	14.1	9
1968	Clifton McNeil, SF	71	994	14.0	7
1969	Dan Abramowicz, NO	73	1015	13.9	7
1970	Dick Gordon, Chi	71	1026	14.5	13
1971	Bob Tucker, NY	59	791	13.4	4
1972	Harold Jackson, Phi	62	1048	16.9	4
1973	Harold Carmichael, Phi	67	1116	16.7	9
1974	Charle Young, Phi	63	696	11.0	3
1975	Chuck Foreman, Min	73	691	9.5	9
1976	Drew Pearson, Dal	58	806	13.9	6
1977	Ahmad Rashad, Min	51	681	13.4	2
1978	Rickey Young, Min	88	704	8.0	5
1979	Ahmad Rashad, Min	80	1156	14.5	9
1980	Earl Cooper, SF	83	567	6.8	4
1981	Dwight Clark, SF	85	1105	13.0	4
1982	Dwight Clark, SF	60	913	12.2	5
1983	Roy Green, St.L	78	1227	15.7	14
	Charlie Brown, Wash	78	1225	15.7	8
	& Earnest Gray, NY	78	1139	14.6	5
1984	Art Monk, Wash	106	1372	12.9	7
1985	Roger Craig, SF	92	1016	11.0	6
1986	Jerry Rice, SF	86	1570	18.3	15
1987	J.T. Smith, St.L	91	1117	12.3	8
1988	Henry Ellard, LA	86	1414	16.4	10
1989	Sterling Sharpe, GB	90	1423	15.8	12
1990	Jerry Rice, SF	100	1502	15.0	13
1991	Michael Irvin, Dal	93	1523	16.4	8
1992	Sterling Sharpe, GB	108	1461	13.5	13
1993	Sterling Sharpe, GB	112	1274	11.4	11

AFL-AFC

Multiple winners: Lionel Taylor (5); Lance Alworth, Haywood Jeffires, Lydell Mitchell and Kellen Winslow (3); Fred Biletnikoff, Todd Christensen and Al Toon (2).

Year	Player	No	Yds	Avg	TD
1960	Lionel Taylor, Den	92	1235	13.4	12
1961	Lionel Taylor, Den	100	1176	11.8	4
1962	Lionel Taylor, Den	77	908	11.8	4
1963	Lionel Taylor, Den	78	1101	14.1	10
1964	Charley Hennigan, Hou	101	1546	15.3	8
1965	Lionel Taylor, Den	85	1131	13.3	6
1966	Lance Alworth, SD	73	1383	18.9	13
1967	George Sauer, NY	75	1189	15.9	6
1968	Lance Alworth, SD	68	1312	19.3	10
1969	Lance Alworth, SD	64	1003	15.7	4
1970	Marlin Briscoe, Buf	57	1036	18.2	8
1971	Fred Biletnikoff, Oak	61	929	15.2	9
1972	Fred Biletnikoff, Oak	58	802	13.8	7
1973	Fred Willis, Hou	57	371	6.5	1
1974	Lydell Mitchell, Bal	72	544	7.6	2
1975	Reggie Rucker, Cle	60	770	12.8	3
	& Lydell Mitchell, Bal	60	544	9.1	4
1976	MacArthur Lane, KC	66	686	10.4	1
1977	Lydell Mitchell, Bal	71	620	8.7	4
1978	Steve Largent, Sea	71	1168	16.5	8
1979	Joe Washington, Bal	82	750	9.1	3
1980	Kellen Winslow, S.D	89	1290	14.5	9
1981	Kellen Winslow, S.D	88	1075	12.2	10
1982	Kellen Winslow, S.D	54	721	13.4	6
1983	Todd Christensen, LA	92	1247	13.6	12
1984	Ozzie Newsome, Cle	89	1001	11.2	5
1985	Lionel James, SD	86	1027	11.9	6
1986	Todd Christensen, LA	95	1153	12.1	8
1987	Al Toon, NY	68	976	14.4	5
1988	Al Toon, NY	93	1067	11.5	5
1989	Andre Reed, Buf	88	1312	14.9	9
1990	Haywood Jeffires, Hou	74	1048	14.2	8
	& Drew Hill, Hou	74	1019	13.8	5
1991	Haywood Jeffires, Hou	100	1181	11.8	7
1992	Haywood Jeffires, Hou	90	913	10.1	9
1993	Reggie Langhorne, Ind	85	1038	12.2	3

Rushing
NFL-NFC

Multiple winners: Jim Brown (8); Walter Payton (5); Steve Van Buren (4); Eric Dickerson and Emmitt Smith (3); Cliff Battles, John Brockington, Larry Brown, Bill Dudley, Leroy Kelly, Bill Paschal, Joe Perry, Barry Sanders, Gale Sayers and Whizzer White (2).

Year		Car	Yds	Avg	TD	Year		Car	Yds	Avg	TD
1932	Cliff Battles, Bos	148	576	3.9	3	1963	Jim Brown, Cle	291	1863	6.4	12
1933	Jim Musick, Bos	173	809	4.7	5	1964	Jim Brown, Cle	280	1446	5.2	7
1934	Beattie Feathers, Chi. Bears	119	1004	8.4	8	1965	Jim Brown, Cle	289	1544	5.3	17
1935	Doug Russell, Chi. Cards	140	499	3.6	0	1966	Gale Sayers, Chi	229	1231	5.4	8
1936	Tuffy Leemans, NY	206	830	4.0	2	1967	Leroy Kelly, Cle	235	1205	5.1	11
1937	Cliff Battles, Wash	216	874	4.0	5	1968	Leroy Kelly, Cle	248	1239	5.0	16
1938	Whizzer White, Pit	152	567	3.7	4	1969	Gale Sayers, Chi	236	1032	4.4	8
1939	Bill Osmanski, Chi. Bears	121	699	5.8	7						
1940	Whizzer White, Det	146	514	3.5	5	1970	Larry Brown, Wash	237	1125	4.7	5
1941	Pug Manders, Bklyn	111	486	4.4	5	1971	John Brockington, GB	216	1105	5.1	4
1942	Bill Dudley, Pit	162	696	4.3	5	1972	Larry Brown, Wash	285	1216	4.3	8
1943	Bill Paschal, NY	147	572	3.9	10	1973	John Brockington, GB	265	1144	4.3	3
1944	Bill Paschal, NY	196	737	3.8	9	1974	Lawrence McCutcheon, LA	236	1109	4.7	3
1945	Steve Van Buren, Phi	143	832	5.8	15	1975	Jim Otis, St.L	269	1076	4.0	5
1946	Bill Dudley, Pit	146	604	4.1	3	1976	Walter Payton, Chi	311	1390	4.5	13
1947	Steve Van Buren, Phi	217	1008	4.6	13	1977	Walter Payton, Chi	339	1852	5.5	14
1948	Steve Van Buren, Phi	201	945	4.7	10	1978	Walter Payton, Chi	333	1395	4.2	11
1949	Steve Van Buren, Phi	263	1146	4.4	11	1979	Walter Payton, Chi	369	1610	4.4	14
1950	Marion Motley, Cle	140	810	5.8	3	1980	Walter Payton, Chi	317	1460	4.6	6
1951	Eddie Price, NY Giants	271	971	3.6	7	1981	George Rogers, NO	378	1674	4.4	13
1952	Dan Towler, LA	156	894	5.7	10	1982	Tony Dorsett, Dal	177	745	4.2	5
1953	Joe Perry, SF	192	1018	5.3	10	1983	Eric Dickerson, LA	390	1808	4.6	18
1954	Joe Perry, SF	173	1049	6.1	8	1984	Eric Dickerson, LA	379	2105	5.6	14
1955	Alan Ameche, Bal	213	961	4.5	9	1985	Gerald Riggs, Atl	397	1719	4.3	10
1956	Rick Casares, Chi. Bears	234	1126	4.8	12	1986	Eric Dickerson, LA	404	1821	4.5	11
1957	Jim Brown, Cle	202	942	4.7	9	1987	Charles White, LA	324	1374	4.2	11
1958	Jim Brown, Cle	257	1527	5.9	17	1988	Herschel Walker, Dal	361	1514	4.2	5
1959	Jim Brown, Cle	290	1329	4.6	14	1989	Barry Sanders, Det	280	1470	5.3	14
1960	Jim Brown, Cle	215	1257	5.8	9	1990	Barry Sanders, Det	255	1304	5.1	13
1961	Jim Brown, Cle	305	1408	4.6	8	1991	Emmitt Smith, Dal	365	1563	4.3	12
1962	Jim Taylor, GB	272	1474	5.4	19	1992	Emmitt Smith, Dal	373	1713	4.6	18
						1993	Emmitt Smith, Dal	283	1486	5.3	9

Note: Jim Brown led the NFL in rushing eight of his nine years in the league. The one season he didn't win (1962) he finished fourth (996 yds) behind Jim Taylor, John Henry Johnson of Pittsburgh (1,141 yds) and Dick Bass of the LA Rams (1,033 yds).

AFL-AFC

Multiple winners: Earl Campbell and O.J. Simpson (4); Thurman Thomas (3); Cookie Gilchrist, Eric Dickerson, Floyd Little, Jim Nance and Curt Warner (2).

Year		Car	Yds	Avg	TD	Year		Car	Yds	Avg	TD
1960	Abner Haynes, Dal	157	875	5.6	9	1978	Earl Campbell, Hou	302	1450	4.8	13
1961	Billy Cannon, Hou	200	948	4.7	6	1979	Earl Campbell, Hou	368	1697	4.6	19
1962	Cookie Gilchrist, Buf	214	1096	5.1	13	1980	Earl Campbell, Hou	373	1934	5.2	13
1963	Clem Daniels, Oak	215	1099	5.1	3	1981	Earl Campbell, Hou	361	1376	3.8	10
1964	Cookie Gilchrist, Buf	230	981	4.3	6	1982	Freeman McNeil, NY	151	786	5.2	6
1965	Paul Lowe, SD	222	1121	5.0	7	1983	Curt Warner, Sea	335	1449	4.3	13
1966	Jim Nance, Bos	299	1458	4.9	11	1984	Earnest Jackson, SD	296	1179	4.0	8
1967	Jim Nance, Bos	269	1216	4.5	7	1985	Marcus Allen, LA	380	1759	4.6	11
1968	Paul Robinson, Cin	238	1023	4.3	8	1986	Curt Warner, Sea	319	1481	4.6	13
1969	Dickie Post, SD	182	873	4.8	6	1987	Eric Dickerson, Ind	223	1011	4.5	5
1970	Floyd Little, Den	209	901	4.3	3	1988	Eric Dickerson, Ind	388	1659	4.3	14
1971	Floyd Little, Den	284	1133	4.0	6	1989	Christian Okoye, KC	370	1480	4.0	12
1972	O.J. Simpson, Buf	292	1251	4.3	6	1990	Thurman Thomas, Buf	271	1297	4.8	11
1973	O.J. Simpson, Buf	332	2003	6.0	12	1991	Thurman Thomas, Buf	288	1407	4.9	7
1974	Otis Armstrong, Den	263	1407	5.3	9	1992	Barry Foster, Pit	390	1690	4.3	11
1975	O.J. Simpson, Buf	329	1817	5.5	16	1993	Thurman Thomas, Buf	355	1315	3.7	6
1976	O.J. Simpson, Buf	290	1503	5.2	8						
1977	Mark van Eeghen, Oak	324	1273	3.9	7						

Note: Eric Dickerson was traded to Indianapolis from the NFC's LA Rams during the 1987 season. In three games with the Rams, he carried the ball 60 times for 277 yds, a 4.6 avg and 1 TD. His official AFC statistics above came in nine games with the Colts.

Annual NFL Leaders (Cont.)

Scoring

NFL-NFC

Multiple winners: Don Hutson (5); Dutch Clark, Pat Harder, Paul Hornung, Chip Lohmiller and Mark Moseley (3); Kevin Butler, Mike Cofer, Fred Cox, Jack Manders, Chester Marcol, Eddie Murray, Gordy Soltau and Doak Walker (2).

Year		TD	FG	PAT	Pts	Year		TD	FG	PAT	Pts
1932	Dutch Clark, Portsmouth	6	3	10	55	1963	Don Chandler, NY	0	18	52	106
1933	Glenn Presnell, Portsmouth	6	6	10	64	1964	Lenny Moore, Bal	20	0	0	120
	& Ken Strong, NY	6	5	13	64	1965	Gale Sayers, Chi	22	0	0	132
1934	Jack Manders, Chi. Bears	3	10	31	79	1966	Bruce Gossett, LA	0	28	29	113
1935	Dutch Clark, Det	6	1	16	55	1967	Jim Bakken, St.L	0	27	36	117
1936	Dutch Clark, Det	7	4	19	73	1968	Leroy Kelly, Cle	20	0	0	120
1937	Jack Manders, Chi. Bears	5	8	15	69	1969	Fred Cox, Min	0	26	43	121
1938	Clarke Hinkle, GB	7	3	7	58						
1939	Andy Farkas, Wash	11	0	2	68	1970	Fred Cox, Min	0	30	35	125
						1971	Curt Knight, Wash	0	29	27	114
1940	Don Hutson, GB	7	0	15	57	1972	Chester Marcol, GB	0	33	29	128
1941	Don Hutson, GB	12	1	20	95	1973	David Ray, LA	0	30	40	130
1942	Don Hutson, GB	17	1	33	138	1974	Chester Marcol, GB	0	25	19	94
1943	Don Hutson, GB	12	3	26	117	1975	Chuck Foreman, Min	22	0	0	132
1944	Don Hutson, GB	9	0	31	85	1976	Mark Moseley, Wash	0	22	31	97
1945	Steve Van Buren, Phi	18	0	2	110	1977	Walter Payton, Chi	16	0	0	96
1946	Ted Fritsch, GB	10	9	13	100	1978	Frank Corral, LA	0	29	31	118
1947	Pat Harder, Chi. Cards	7	7	39	102	1979	Mark Moseley, Wash	0	25	39	114
1948	Pat Harder, Chi. Cards	6	7	53	110						
1949	Gene Roberts, NY Giants	17	0	0	102	1980	Eddie Murray, Det	0	27	35	116
	& Pat Harder, Chi. Cards	8	3	45	102	1981	Rafael Septien, Dal	0	27	40	121
							& Eddie Murray, Det	0	25	46	121
1950	Doak Walker, Det	11	8	38	128	1982	Wendell Tyler, LA	13	0	0	78
1951	Elroy Hirsch, LA	17	0	0	102	1983	Mark Moseley, Wash	0	33	62	161
1952	Gordy Soltau, SF	7	6	34	94	1984	Ray Wersching, SF	0	25	56	131
1953	Gordy Soltau, SF	6	10	48	114	1985	Kevin Butler, Chi	0	31	51	144
1954	Bobby Walston, Phi	11	4	36	114	1986	Kevin Butler, Chi	0	28	36	120
1955	Doak Walker, Det	7	9	27	96	1987	Jerry Rice, SF	23	0	0	138
1956	Bobby Layne, Det	5	12	33	99	1988	Mike Cofer, SF	0	27	40	121
1957	Sam Baker, Wash	1	14	29	77	1989	Mike Cofer, SF	0	29	49	136
	& Lou Groza, Cle	0	15	32	77						
1958	Jim Brown, Cle	18	0	0	108	1990	Chip Lohmiller, Wash	0	30	41	131
1959	Paul Hornung, GB	7	7	31	94	1991	Chip Lohmiller, Wash	0	31	56	149
						1992	Chip Lohmiller, Wash	0	30	30	120
1960	Paul Hornung, GB	15	15	41	176		& Morten Andersen, NO	0	29	33	120
1961	Paul Hornung, GB	10	15	41	146	1993	Jason Hanson, Det	0	34	28	130
1962	Jim Taylor, GB	19	0	0	114						

AFL-AFC

Multiple winners: Gino Cappelletti (5); Gary Anderson (3); Jim Breech, Roy Gerela, Gene Mingo, Nick Lowery, John Smith, Pete Stoyanovich and Jim Turner (2).

Year		TD	FG	PAT	Pts	Year		TD	FG	PAT	Pts
1960	Gene Mingo, Den	6	18	33	123	1978	Pat Leahy, NY	0	22	41	107
1961	Gino Cappelletti, Bos	8	17	48	147	1979	John Smith, NE	0	23	46	115
1962	Gene Mingo, Den	4	27	32	137						
1963	Gino Cappelletti, Bos	2	22	35	113	1980	John Smith, NE	0	26	51	129
1964	Gino Cappelletti, Bos	7	25	36	155	1981	Nick Lowery, KC	0	26	37	115
1965	Gino Cappelletti, Bos	9	17	27	132		& Jim Breech, Cin	0	22	49	115
1966	Gino Cappelletti, Bos	6	16	35	119	1982	Marcus Allen, LA	14	0	0	84
1967	George Blanda, Oak	0	20	56	116	1983	Gary Anderson, Pit	0	27	38	119
1968	Jim Turner, NY	0	34	43	145	1984	Gary Anderson, Pit	0	24	45	117
1969	Jim Turner, NY	0	32	33	129	1985	Gary Anderson, Pit	0	33	40	139
						1986	Tony Franklin, NE	0	32	44	140
1970	Jan Stenerud, KC	0	30	26	116	1987	Jim Breech, Cin	0	24	25	97
1971	Garo Yepremian, Mia	0	28	33	117	1988	Scott Norwood, Buf	0	32	33	129
1972	Bobby Howfield, NY	0	27	40	121	1989	David Treadwell, Den	0	27	39	120
1973	Roy Gerela, Pit	0	29	36	123						
1974	Roy Gerela, Pit	0	20	33	93	1990	Nick Lowery, KC	0	34	37	139
1975	O.J. Simpson, Buf	23	0	0	138	1991	Pete Stoyanovich, Mia	0	31	28	121
1976	Toni Linhart, Bal	0	20	49	109	1992	Pete Stoyanovich, Mia	0	30	34	124
1977	Errol Mann, Oak	0	20	39	99	1993	Jeff Jaeger, LA	0	35	27	132

All-Time NFL Leaders

Through 1993 regular season.

CAREER

Players active in 1993 in **bold** type.

Passing Efficiency

Ratings based on performance standards established for completion percentage, average gain, touchdown percentage and interception percentage. Quarterbacks are allocated points according to how their statistics measure up to those standards. Minimum 1500 passing attempts.

		Yrs	Att	Cmp	Cmp%	Yards	Avg Gain	TD	TD%	Int	Int%	Rating
1	**Joe Montana**	14	4898	3110	63.5	37,268	7.61	257	5.2	130	2.7	93.1
2	**Steve Young**	9	1968	1222	62.1	15,900	8.08	105	5.3	58	2.9	93.0
3	**Dan Marino**	11	5434	3219	59.2	40,720	7.49	298	5.5	168	3.1	88.1
4	**Jim Kelly**	8	3494	2112	60.4	26,413	7.56	179	5.1	126	3.6	86.0
5	Roger Staubach	11	2958	1685	57.0	22,700	7.67	153	5.2	109	3.7	83.4
6	Neil Lomax	8	3153	1817	57.6	22,771	7.22	136	4.3	90	2.9	82.7
7	Sonny Jurgensen	18	4262	2433	57.1	32,224	7.56	255	6.0	189	4.4	82.63
8	Len Dawson	19	3741	2136	57.1	28,711	7.67	239	6.4	183	4.9	82.56
9	**Boomer Esiason**	10	3851	2185	56.7	29,092	7.55	190	4.9	140	3.6	82.1
10	Dave Krieg	14	4178	2431	58.2	30,485	7.30	217	5.2	163	3.9	82.0
11	Ken Anderson	16	4475	2654	59.3	32,838	7.34	197	4.4	160	3.6	81.858
12	**Bernie Kosar**	9	3213	1889	58.8	22,314	6.94	119	3.7	81	2.5	81.856
13	Danny White	13	2950	1761	59.7	21,959	7.44	155	5.3	132	4.5	81.7
14	**Troy Aikman**	5	1920	1191	62.0	13,627	7.10	69	3.6	66	3.4	81.0
15	Bart Starr	16	3149	1808	57.4	24,718	7.85	152	4.8	138	4.4	80.5
16	Ken O'Brien	10	3602	2110	58.6	25,094	6.97	128	3.6	98	2.7	80.44
17	**Warren Moon**	10	4546	2632	57.9	33,685	7.41	196	4.3	166	3.7	80.36
18	Fran Tarkenton	18	6467	3686	57.0	47,003	7.27	342	5.3	266	4.1	80.35
19	**Randall Cunningham**	9	2751	1540	56.0	19,043	6.92	131	4.8	87	3.2	80.3
20	Dan Fouts	15	5604	3297	58.8	43,040	7.68	254	4.5	242	4.3	80.23
21	**Mark Rypien**	6	2207	1244	56.4	15,928	7.22	101	4.6	75	3.4	80.22
22	**Bobby Hebert**	8	2485	1465	59.0	17,608	7.09	109	4.4	92	3.7	79.9
23	Tony Eason	8	1564	911	58.2	11,142	7.12	61	3.9	51	3.3	79.7
24	**Jim McMahon**	12	2525	1465	58.0	17,883	7.08	99	3.9	87	3.4	78.7
25	Phil Simms	14	4647	2576	55.4	33,462	7.20	199	4.3	157	3.4	78.5

Note: The NFL does not recognize records from the All-America Football Conference (1946-49). If it did, **Otto Graham** would rank 5th (after Kelly) with the following stats: 10 Yrs; 2,626 Att; 1,464 Cmp; 55.8 Cmp Pct; 23,584 Yards; 8.98 Avg Gain; 174 TD; 6.6 TD Pct; 135 Int; 5.1 Int Pct; and 86.6 Rating Pts.

Touchdown Passes

		No
1	Fran Tarkenton	342
2	**Dan Marino**	298
3	Johnny Unitas	290
4	**Joe Montana**	257
5	Sonny Jurgensen	255
6	Dan Fouts	254
7	John Hadl	244
8	Len Dawson	239
9	George Blanda	236
10	**Dave Krieg**	217
11	John Brodie	214
12	Terry Bradshaw	212
	Y.A. Tittle	212
14	Jim Hart	209
15	Roman Gabriel	201
16	**Phil Simms**	199
17	Ken Anderson	197
18	Joe Ferguson	196
	Bobby Layne	196
	Warren Moon	196
	Norm Snead	196
22	Ken Stabler	194
23	**Steve DeBerg**	193
24	Bob Griese	192
25	**Boomer Esiason**	190
26	Sammy Baugh	187
27	**John Elway**	183
	Craig Morton	183
29	Steve Grogan	182
30	Ron Jaworski	179
	Jim Kelly	179
31	Babe Parilli	178
32	Charlie Conerly	173
	Joe Namath	173
	Norm Van Brocklin	173
35	Charley Johnson	170
36	Daryle Lamonica	164
	Jim Plunkett	164
38	Earl Morrall	161
39	Joe Theismann	160
40	Tommy Kramer	159
41	Steve Bartkowski	156
42	Danny White	155
44	Brian Sipe	154
45	Roger Staubach	153

Note: The NFL does not recognize records from the All-American Football Conference (1946-49). If it did, **Y.A. Tittle** would rank 8th (after Hadl) with 242 TDs and **Otto Graham** would rank 32nd (after Parilli) with 174 TD's.

Passes Intercepted

		No
1	George Blanda	277
2	John Hadl	268
3	Fran Tarkenton	266
4	Norm Snead	253
	Johnny Unitas	253
6	Jim Hart	247
7	Bobby Layne	243
8	Dan Fouts	242
9	John Brodie	224
10	Ken Stabler	222
11	Y.A. Tittle	221
12	Joe Namath	220
	Babe Parilli	220
14	Terry Bradshaw	210
15	Joe Ferguson	209
16	Steve Grogan	208
17	Sammy Baugh	203
	Steve DeBerg	203
19	Jim Plunkett	198
20	Tobin Rote	191

All-Time NFL Leaders (Cont.)

Passing Yards

		Yrs	Att	Comp	Pct	Yards
1	Fran Tarkenton	18	6467	3686	57.0	47,003
2	Dan Fouts	15	5604	3297	58.8	43,040
3	Dan Marino	12	5434	3219	59.2	40.720
4	Johnny Unitas	18	5186	2830	54.6	40,239
5	Joe Montana	14	4898	3110	63.5	37,268
6	Jim Hart	19	5076	2593	51.1	34,665
7	John Elway	11	4890	2723	55.7	34,246
8	Steve DeBerg	16	4965	2844	57.3	33,872
9	Warren Moon	10	4546	2632	57.9	33,685
10	John Hadl	16	4687	2363	50.4	33,513
11	Phil Simms	14	4647	2576	55.4	33,462
12	Ken Anderson	16	4475	2654	59.3	32,838
13	Sonny Jurgensen	18	4262	2433	57.1	32,224
14	John Brodie	17	4491	2469	55.0	31,548
15	Norm Snead	16	4353	2276	52.3	30,797
16	Dave Krieg	14	4178	2431	58.2	30,485
17	Joe Ferguson	18	4519	2369	52.4	29,817
18	Roman Gabriel	16	4498	2366	52.6	29,444
19	Boomer Esiason	10	3851	2185	56.7	29,092
20	Len Dawson	19	3741	2136	57.1	28,711
21	Y.A. Tittle	15	3817	2118	55.5	28,339
22	Ron Jaworski	16	4117	2187	53.1	28,190
23	Terry Bradshaw	14	3901	2025	51.9	27,989
24	Ken Stabler	15	3793	2270	59.8	27,938
25	Craig Morton	18	3786	2053	54.2	27,908

Note: The NFL does not recognize records from the All-American Football Conference (1946-49). If it did, **Y.A. Tittle** would rank 8th (after Simms) with the following stats: 17 Yrs; 4,395 Att; 2,427 Comp; 55.2 Pct; and 33,070 Yards.

Receptions

		Yrs	No	Yards	Avg	TD
1	Art Monk	14	888	12,026	13.5	65
2	Steve Largent	14	819	13,089	16.0	100
3	James Lofton	16	764	14,004	18.3	75
4	Charlie Joiner	18	750	12,146	16.2	65
5	Jerry Rice	9	708	11,776	16.6	118
6	Ozzie Newsome	13	662	7,980	12.1	47
7	Charley Taylor	13	649	9,110	14.0	79
8	Drew Hill	14	634	9,831	15.5	60
9	Don Maynard	15	633	11,834	18.7	88
10	Raymond Berry	13	631	9,275	14.7	68
11	Gary Clark	9	612	9,560	15.6	62
12	Henry Ellard	11	593	9,761	16.5	48
13	Harold Carmichael	14	590	8,985	15.2	79
14	Fred Biletnikoff	14	589	8,974	15.2	76
15	Andre Reed	9	586	8,233	14.0	58
16	Mark Clayton	11	582	8,974	15.4	84
17	Harold Jackson	16	579	10,372	17.9	76
18	Lionel Taylor	10	567	7,195	12.7	45
19	Roger Craig	11	566	4,911	8.7	17
20	Wes Chandler	11	559	8,966	16.0	56
	Roy Green	14	559	8,965	16.0	66
22	Stanley Morgan	14	557	10,716	19.2	72
23	J.T. Smith	13	544	6,974	12.8	35
24	Lance Alworth	11	542	10,266	18.9	85
25	Kellen Winslow	10	541	6,741	12.5	45

Rushing Yards

		Yrs	Car	Yards	Avg	TD
1	Walter Payton	13	3838	16,726	4.4	110
2	Eric Dickerson	11	2996	13,259	4.4	90
3	Tony Dorsett	12	2936	12,739	4.3	77
4	Jim Brown	9	2359	12,312	5.2	106
5	Franco Harris	13	2949	12,120	4.1	91
6	John Riggins	14	2916	11,352	3.9	104
7	O.J. Simpson	11	2404	11,236	4.7	61
8	Ottis Anderson	14	2562	10,273	4.0	81
9	Earl Campbell	8	2187	9,407	4.3	74
10	Marcus Allen	12	2296	9,309	4.1	91
11	Jim Taylor	10	1941	8,597	4.4	83
12	Joe Perry	14	1737	8,378	4.8	53
13	Roger Craig	11	1991	8,189	4.1	56
14	Gerald Riggs	10	1989	8,188	4.1	69
15	Larry Csonka	11	1891	8,081	4.3	64
16	Freeman McNeil	12	1798	8,074	4.5	38
17	James Brooks	12	1685	7,962	4.7	49
18	Thurman Thomas	6	1731	7,631	4.4	41
19	Herschel Walker	8	1794	7,468	4.2	55
20	Mike Pruitt	11	1844	7,378	4.0	51
21	Leroy Kelly	10	1727	7,274	4.2	74
22	George Rogers	7	1692	7,176	4.2	54
23	Curt Warner	8	1698	6,844	4.0	56
24	John H. Johnson	13	1571	6,803	4.3	48
25	Barry Sanders	5	1432	6,789	4.7	55
	Wilbert Montgomery	9	1540	6,789	4.4	45

Note: The NFL does not recognize records from the All-American Football Conference (1946-49). If it did, **Joe Perry** would rank 9th (after Anderson) with the following stats: 16 Yrs; 1,929 Att; 9,723 Yards; 5.0 Avg; and 71 TD.

All-Purpose Running

		Rush	Rec	Ret	Total
1	Walter Payton	16,726	4,538	539	21,803
2	Tony Dorsett	12,739	3,554	33	16,326
3	Jim Brown	12,312	2,499	648	15,459
4	Eric Dickerson	13,259	2,137	15	15,411
5	James Brooks	7,962	3,621	3,327	14,910
6	Franco Harris	12,120	2,287	215	14,622
7	O.J. Simpson	11,236	2,142	990	14,368
8	James Lofton	246	14,004	27	14,277
9	Bobby Mitchell	2,735	7,954	3,389	14,078
10	Marcus Allen	9,309	4,496	-6	13,799
11	John Riggins	11,352	2,090	-7	13,435
12	Steve Largent	83	13,089	224	13,396
13	Ottis Anderson	10,273	3,062	29	13,364
14	Drew Hill	19	9,831	3,487	13,337
15	Greg Pruitt	5,672	3,069	4,521	13,262
16	Roger Craig	8,189	4,911	43	13,143
17	Herschel Walker	7,468	3,887	1,676	13,031
18	Ollie Matson	5,173	3,285	4,426	12,884
19	Tim Brown	3,862	3,399	5,423	12,684
20	Lenny Moore	5,174	6,039	1,238	12,451
21	Don Maynard	70	11,834	475	12,379
22	Charlie Joyner	22	12,146	199	12,367
23	Leroy Kelly	7,274	2,281	2,775	12,330
24	Floyd Little	6,323	2,418	3,432	12,173
25	Abner Haynes	4,630	3,535	3,900	12,065

Note: The NFL does not recognize records from the All-American Football Conference (1946-49). If it did, **Joe Perry** would rank 20th (after Tim Brown) with the following stats: 9,723 Rush; 2,021 Rec; 788 Ret; 12,532 Total in 16 years.

Years played: Allen (12); Anderson (14); Brooks (12); J. Brown (9); T. Brown (10); Craig (11); Dickerson (11); Dorsett (12); Harris (13); Haynes (8); Hill (14); Joiner (18); Kelly (10); Largent (14); Little (9); Lofton (16); Matson (14); Maynard (15); B. Mitchell (11); Moore (12); Payton (13); Pruitt (12); Riggins (14); Simpson (11); Walker (8).

Scoring

Points

		Yrs	TD	FG	PAT	Total
1	George Blanda	26	9	335	943	2002
2	Jan Stenerud	19	0	373	580	1699
3	**Nick Lowery**	15	0	329	486	1473
4	Pat Leahy	18	0	304	558	1470
5	Jim Turner	16	1	304	521	1439
6	Mark Moseley	16	0	300	482	1382
7	Jim Bakken	17	0	282	534	1380
8	Fred Cox	15	0	282	519	1365
9	Lou Groza	17	1	234	641	1349
10	**Eddie Murray**	14	0	277	432	1263
11	Jim Breech	14	0	243	517	1246
12	**Gary Anderson**	12	0	285	384	1239
13	Chris Bahr	14	0	241	490	1213
14	**Matt Bahr**	15	0	250	459	1209
15	**Morten Andersen**	12	0	274	380	1202
16	Gino Cappelletti	11	42	176	350	1130†
17	Ray Wersching	15	0	222	456	1122
18	**Norm Johnson**	12	0	222	444	1110
19	Don Cockroft	13	0	216	432	1080
20	Garo Yepremian	14	0	210	444	1074
21	Bruce Gossett	11	0	219	374	1031
22	Sam Baker	15	2	179	428	977
23	Rafael Septien	10	0	180	420	960
24	Lou Michaels	13	1	187	386	955†
25	**Kevin Butler**	9	0	199	318	915

†Cappelletti's total includes four 2-point conversions, and Michaels' total includes one safety.

Note: The NFL does not recognize records from the All-American Football Conference (1946-49). If it did, **Lou Groza** would move up to 3rd (after Stenerud) with the following stats: 21 Yrs; 1 TD; 264 FG, 810 PAT; 1,608 Pts.

Touchdowns

		Yrs	Rush	Rec	Ret	Total
1	Jim Brown	9	106	20	0	126
2	Walter Payton	13	110	15	0	125
3	**Jerry Rice**	9	6	118	0	124
4	John Riggins	14	104	12	0	116
5	**Marcus Allen**	12	91	21	1	113
	Lenny Moore	12	63	48	2	113
7	Don Hutson	11	3	99	3	105
8	Steve Largent	14	1	100	0	101
9	Franco Harris	13	91	9	0	100
10	**Eric Dickerson**	10	90	6	0	96
11	Jim Taylor	10	83	10	0	93
12	Tony Dorsett	12	77	13	1	91
	Bobby Mitchell	11	18	65	8	91
14	Leroy Kelly	10	74	13	3	90
	Charley Taylor	13	11	79	0	90
16	Don Maynard	15	0	88	0	88
17	Lance Alworth	11	2	85	0	87
18	Ottis Anderson	14	81	5	0	86
	Paul Warfield	13	1	85	0	86
20	**Mark Clayton**	10	0	84	1	85
	Tommy McDonald	12	0	84	1	85
22	Pete Johnson	8	76	6	0	82
23	Art Powell	10	0	81	1	82
24	Harold Carmichael	14	0	79	0	79
25	Frank Gifford	12	34	43	1	78

Note: The NFL does not recognize records from the All-American Football Conference (1946-49). If it did, **Joe Perry** would rank 23rd (after McDonald) with the following stats: 16 Yrs; 71 Rush; 12 Rec; 1 Ret; 84 TDs.

Interceptions

		Yrs	No	Yards	TD
1	Paul Krause	16	81	1185	3
2	Emlen Tunnell	14	79	1282	4
3	Dick (Night Train) Lane	14	68	1207	5
4	Ken Riley	15	65	596	5
5	Dick LeBeau	13	62	762	3
	Dave Brown	15	62	698	5

Sacks

		Yrs	No
1	Deacon Jones	14	172
2	Jack Youngblood	14	150½
3	Alan Page	15	148
4	**Lawrence Taylor**	13	142
5	Claude Humphrey	14	139½

Kickoff Returns

Minimum 75 returns.

		Yrs	No	Yards	Avg	TD
1	Gale Sayers	7	91	2781	30.6	6
2	Lynn Chandnois	7	92	2720	29.6	3
3	Abe Woodson	9	193	5538	28.7	5
4	Buddy Young	6	90	2514	27.9	2
5	Travis Williams	5	102	2801	27.5	6

Punting

Minimum 300 punts.

		Yrs	No	Yards	Avg
1	Sammy Baugh	16	338	15,245	45.1
2	Tommy Davis	11	511	22,833	44.7
3	Yale Lary	11	503	22,279	44.3
4	**Rohn Stark**	12	912	40,070	43.9
5	Horace Gillom	7	385	16,872	43.8
	Jerry Norton	11	358	15,671	43.8

Punt Returns

Minimum 75 returns.

		Yrs	No	Yards	Avg	TD
1	George McAfee	8	112	1431	12.8	2
	Jack Christiansen	8	85	1084	12.8	8
3	Claude Gibson	5	110	1381	12.6	3
4	Bill Dudley	9	124	1515	12.2	3
5	Rick Upchurch	9	248	3008	12.1	8

Safeties

		Yrs	No
1	Ted Hendricks	15	4
	Doug English	10	4
2	Eleven players tied with three.		

Long-Playing Records

Seasons

		No
1	George Blanda, QB-K	26
2	Earl Morrall, QB	21
3	Jim Marshall, DE	20

Games

		No
1	George Blanda, QB-K	340
2	Jim Marshall, DE	282
3	Jan Stenerud, K	263

Consecutive Games

		No
1	Jim Marshall, DE	282
2	Mick Tingelhoff, C	240
3	Jim Bakken, K	234

All-Time NFL Leaders (Cont.)
SINGLE SEASON

Passing

Yards Gained	Year	Att	Cmp	Pct	Yds
Dan Marino, Mia	1984	564	362	64.2	5084
Dan Fouts, SD	1981	609	360	59.1	4802
Dan Marino, Mia	1986	623	378	60.7	4746
Dan Fouts, SD	1980	589	348	59.1	4715
Warren Moon, Hou	1991	655	404	61.7	4690
Warren Moon, Hou	1990	584	362	62.0	4689
Neil Lomax, St.L	1984	560	345	61.6	4614
Lynn Dickey, GB	1983	484	289	59.7	4458
Dan Marino, Mia	1988	606	354	58.4	4434
Bill Kenney, KC	1983	603	346	57.4	4348

Rushing

Yards Gained	Year	Att	Yds	Avg
Eric Dickerson, LA Rams	1984	379	2105	5.6
O.J. Simpson, Buf	1973	332	2003	6.0
Earl Campbell, Hou	1980	373	1934	5.2
Jim Brown, Cle	1963	291	1863	6.4
Walter Payton, Chi	1977	339	1852	5.5
Eric Dickerson, LA Rams	1986	404	1821	4.5
O.J. Simpson, Buf	1975	329	1817	5.5
Eric Dickerson, LA Rams	1983	390	1808	4.6
Marcus Allen, LA Raiders	1985	380	1759	4.6
Gerald Riggs, Atl	1985	397	1719	4.3

Receptions

Catches	Year	No	Yds
Sterling Sharpe, GB	1993	112	1274
Sterling Sharpe, GB	1992	108	1461
Art Monk, Wash	1984	106	1372
Charley Hennigan, Hou	1964	101	1546
Jerry Rice, SF	1990	100	1502
Haywood Jeffires, Hou	1991	100	1181
Lionel Taylor, Den	1961	100	1176
Jerry Rice, SF	1993	98	1503
Todd Christensen, LA Raiders	1986	95	1153
Four tied with 93 each.			

All-Purpose Running

	Year	Run	Rec	Ret	Total
Lionel James, SD	1985	516	1027	992	2535
Terry Metcalf, St.L	1975	816	378	1268	2462
Mack Herron, NE	1974	824	474	1146	2444
Gale Sayers, Chi	1966	1231	447	762	2440
Timmy Brown, Phi	1963	841	487	1100	2428
Tim Brown, Raiders	1988	50	725	1542	2317
Marcus Allen, Raiders	1985	1759	555	-6	2308
Timmy Brown, Phi	1962	545	849	912	2306
Gale Sayers, Chi	1965	867	507	898	2272
Eric Dickerson, Rams	1984	2105	139	15	2259
O.J. Simpson, Buf	1975	1817	426	0	2243

Scoring

Points

	Year	TD	PAT	FG	Pts
Paul Hornung, GB	1960	15	41	15	176
Mark Moseley, Wash	1983	0	62	33	161
Gino Cappelletti, Bos	1964	7	38	25	155
Chip Lohmiller, Wash	1991	0	56	31	149
Gino Cappelletti, Bos	1961	8	48	17	147
Paul Hornung, GB	1961	10	41	15	146
Jim Turner, Jets	1968	0	43	34	145
John Riggins, Wash	1983	24	0	0	144
Kevin Butler, Chi	1985	0	51	31	144
Tony Franklin, NE	1986	0	44	32	140

Touchdowns

	Year	Rush	Rec	Ret	Total
John Riggins, Wash	1983	24	0	0	24
O.J. Simpson, Buf	1975	16	7	0	23
Jerry Rice, SF	1987	1	22	0	23
Gale Sayers, Chi	1966	14	6	2	22
Chuck Foreman, Min	1975	13	9	0	22
Jim Brown, Cle	1965	17	4	0	21
Joe Morris, NY Giants	1985	21	0	0	21
Lenny Moore, Bal	1964	16	3	1	20
Leroy Kelly, Cle	1968	16	4	0	20
Eric Dickerson, LA Rams	1983	18	2	0	20

Note: The NFL regular season schedule grew from 12 games (1947-60) to 14 (1961-77) to 16 (1978-present). The AFL regular season schedule was always 14 games (1960-69).

Touchdowns Rushing

	Year	No
John Riggins, Washington	1983	24
Joe Morris, NY Giants	1985	21
Jim Taylor, Green Bay	1962	19
Earl Campbell, Houston	1979	19
Chuck Muncie, San Diego	1981	19
Eric Dickerson, LA Rams	1983	18
George Rogers, Washington	1986	18
Emmitt Smith, Dallas	1992	18
Jim Brown, Cleveland	1958	17
Jim Brown, Cleveland	1965	17

Touchdowns Receiving

	Year	No
Jerry Rice, San Francisco	1987	22
Mark Clayton, Miami	1984	18
Don Hutson, Green Bay	1942	17
Elroy (Crazylegs) Hirsch, LA Rams	1951	17
Bill Groman, Houston	1961	17
Jerry Rice, San Francisco	1989	17
Art Powell, Oakland	1963	16
Jerry Rice, San Francisco	1986	15
Jerry Rice, San Francisco	1993	15
Andre Rison, Atlanta	1993	15

Touchdowns Passing

	Year	No
Dan Marino, Miami	1984	48
Dan Marino, Miami	1986	44
George Blanda, Houston	1961	36
Y.A. Tittle, NY Giants	1963	36
Y.A. Tittle, NY Giants	1962	33
Dan Fouts, San Diego	1981	33
Warren Moon, Houston	1990	33
Jim Kelly, Buffalo	1991	33
Four tied with 32 each.		

Field Goals

	Year	Att	No
Ali Haji-Sheikh, NY Giants	1983	42	35
Jeff Jaeger, LA Rams	1993	44	35
Nick Lowery, Kansas City	1990	37	34
Jim Turner, NY Jets*	1968	46	34
Jason Hanson, Detroit	1993	43	34
Gary Anderson, Pittsburgh	1985	42	33
Mark Moseley, Washington*	1983	47	33
Chester Marcol, Green Bay	1972	48	33
Three tied with 32 each.			

*Old-style, straight ahead kicker.

Interceptions

	Year	No
Dick (Night Train) Lane, Detroit	1952	14
Dan Sandifer, Washington	1948	13
Spec Sanders, NY Yanks	1950	13
Lester Hayes, Oakland	1980	13

Kickoff Returns

	Year	Avg
Travis Williams, Green Bay	1967	41.1
Gale Sayers, Chicago	1967	37.7
Ollie Matson, Chicago Cards	1958	35.5

Sacks

	Year	No		Year	No
Coy Bacon, Cincinnati	1976	26	Reggie White, Philadelphia	1987	21
Mark Gastineau, NY Jets	1984	22	Chris Doleman, Minnesota	1989	21

Punting

Qualifiers	Year	Avg
Sammy Baugh, Washington	1940	51.4
Yale Lary, Detroit	1963	48.9
Sammy Baugh, Washington	1941	48.7

Punt Returns

	Year	Avg
Herb Rich, Baltimore	1950	23.0
Jack Christiansen, Detroit	1952	21.5
Dick Christy, NY Titans	1961	21.3
Bob Hayes, Dallas	1968	20.8

SINGLE GAME

Passing

Yards Gained	Date	Yds
Norm Van Brocklin, LA vs NY Yanks	9/28/51	554
Warren Moon, Hou at KC	12/16/90	527
Dan Marino, Mia vs NYJ	10/23/88	521
Phil Simms, NYG vs Cin	10/13/85	513
Vince Ferragamo, Rams vs Chi	12/26/82	509

Completions	Date	No
Richard Todd, NYJ vs SF	9/21/80	42
Warren Moon, Hou vs Dal	11/10/91	41
Ken Anderson, Cin vs SD	12/20/82	40
Phil Simms, NYG vs Cin	10/13/85	40
Dan Marino, Mia vs Buf	11/16/86	39

Rushing

Yards Gained	Date	Yds
Walter Payton, Chi vs Min	11/20/77	275
O.J. Simpson, Buf vs Det	11/25/76	273
O.J. Simpson, Buf vs NE	9/16/73	250
Willie Ellison, LA Rams vs NO	12/ 5/71	247
Cookie Gilchrist, Buf vs NYJ	12/ 8/63	243

Receptions

Catches	Date	No
Tom Fears, LA vs GB	12/ 3/50	18
Clark Gaines, NYJ vs SF	9/21/80	17
Sonny Randle, St.L vs NYG	11/ 4/62	16
Five tied with 15 each.		

Yards Gained	Date	Yds
Flipper Anderson, LA Rams vs NO	11/26/89	336
Stephone Paige, KC vs SD	12/22/85	309
Jim Benton, Cle vs Det	11/22/45	303
Cloyce Box, Det vs Bal	12/ 3/50	302
John Taylor, SF vs LA Rams	12/11/89	286

All-Purpose Running

	Date	Yds
Billy Cannon, Hou vs NY Titans	12/10/61	373
Lionel James, SD vs Raiders	11/10/85	345
Timmy Brown, Phi vs St.L	12/16/62	341
Gale Sayers, Chi vs Min	12/18/66	339
Gale Sayers, Chi vs SF	12/12/65	336

Scoring

Points

	Date	Pts
Ernie Nevers, Chi. Cards vs Chi. Bears	11/28/29	40
Dub Jones, Cle vs Chi. Bears	11/25/51	36
Gale Sayers, Chi vs SF	12/12/65	36
Paul Hornung, GB vs Bal	10/ 8/61	33
Bob Shaw, Chi. Cards vs Bal	10/ 2/50	30
Jim Brown, Cle vs Bal	11/ 1/59	30
Abner Haynes, Dal. Texans vs Oak	11/26/61	30
Billy Cannon, Hou vs NY Titans	12/10/61	30
Cookie Gilchrist, Buf vs NY Jets	12/ 8/63	30
Kellen Winslow, SD vs Oak	11/22/81	30
Jerry Rice, SF at Atl	10/14/90	30

Note: Nevers celebrated Thanksgiving, 1929, by scoring all the Chicago Cardinals' points on six rushing TDs and four PATs. The Cards beat Red Grange and the Chicago Bears, 40-6.

Touchdowns Passing

	Date	No
Sid Luckman, Chi. Bears vs NYG	11/14/43	7
Adrian Burk, Phi vs Wash	10/17/54	7
George Blanda, Hou vs NY Titans	11/19/61	7
Y.A. Tittle, NYG vs Wash	10/28/62	7
Joe Kapp, Min vs Bal	9/28/69	7

Touchdowns Receiving

	Date	No
Bob Shaw, Chi. Cards vs Bal	10/ 2/50	5
Kellen Winslow, SD vs Oak	11/22/81	5
Jerry Rice, SF vs Atl	10/14/90	5

Touchdowns Rushing

	Date	No
Ernie Nevers, Chi. Cards vs Chi. Bears	11/28/29	6
Jim Brown, Cle vs Bal	11/ 1/59	5
Cookie Gilchrist, Buf vs NY Jets	12/ 8/63	5

Field Goals

	Date	No
Jim Bakken, St.L vs Pit	9/24/67	7
Rich Karlis, Min vs Rams	11/ 5/89	7
Eight players tied with 6 FGs.		

Note: Bakken was 7-for-9, Karlis 7-for-7.

Extra Point Kicks

	Date	No
Pat Harder, Cards vs NYG	10/17/48	9
Bob Waterfield, LA vs Bal	10/22/50	9
Charlie Gogolak, Wash vs NYG	11/27/66	9

All-Time NFL Leaders (Cont.)
LONGEST PLAYS

Passing (all for TDs)	Date	Yds
Frank Filchock to Andy Farkas, Wash vs Pit	10/15/39	99
George Izo to Bobby Mitchell, Wash vs Cle	9/15/63	99
Karl Sweetan to Pat Studstill, Det vs Bal	10/16/66	99
Sonny Jurgensen to Gerry Allen, Wash vs Chi	9/15/68	99
Jim Plunkett to Cliff Branch, LA Raiders vs Wash	10/2/83	99
Ron Jaworski to Mike Quick, Phi vs Atl	11/10/85	99

Runs from Scrimmage (all for TDs)	Date	Yds
Tony Dorsett, Dal vs Min	1/3/83	99
Andy Uram, GB vs Chi. Cards	10/8/39	97
Bob Gage, Pit vs Bears	12/4/49	97

Field Goals	Date	Yds
Tom Dempsey, NO vs Det	11/8/70	63
Steve Cox, Cle vs Cin	10/21/84	60
Morten Andersen, NO vs Chi	10/27/91	60

Punt Returns (all for TDs)	Date	Yds
Gil LeFebvre, Cin vs Bklyn	12/3/33	98
Charlie West, Min vs Wash	11/3/68	98
Dennis Morgan, Dal vs St.L	10/13/74	98
Terance Mathis, NYJ vs Dal	11/4/90	98

Kickoff Returns (all for TDs)	Date	Yds
Al Carmichael, GB vs Chi. Bears	10/7/56	106
Noland Smith, KC vs Den	12/17/67	106
Roy Green, St.L vs Dal	10/21/79	106

Interception Returns (for TDs)	Date	Yds
Vencie Glenn, SD vs Den	11/29/87	103
Four players tied with 102-yd returns.		

Chicago College All-Star Game

On Aug.31, 1934, a year after sponsoring Major League Baseball's first All-Star Game, Chicago *Tribune* sports editor Arch Ward presented the first Chicago College All-Star Game at Soldier Field. A crowd of 79,432 turned out to see an all-star team of graduated college seniors battle the 1933 NFL champion Chicago Bears to a scoreless tie. The preseason game was played annually at Soldier Field until it was cancelled in 1977. The NFL champs won the series, 32-9-1.

Year		Year		Year	
1934	Chi. Bears 0, All-Stars 0	1950	All-Stars 17, Philadelphia 7	1965	Cleveland 24, All-Stars 16
1935	Chi. Bears 5, All-Stars 0	1951	Cleveland 33, All-Stars 0	1966	Green Bay 38, All-Stars 0
1936	Detroit 7, All-Stars 0	1952	LA Rams 10, All-Stars 7	1967	Green Bay 27, All-Stars 0
1937	All-Stars 6, Green Bay 0	1953	Detroit 24, All-Stars 10	1968	Green Bay 34, All-Stars 17
1938	All-Stars 28, Washington 16	1954	Detroit 31, All-Stars 6	1969	NY Jets 26, All-Stars 24
1939	NY Giants 9, All-Stars 0	1955	All-Stars 30, Cleveland 27		
		1956	Cleveland 26, All-Stars 0	1970	Kansas City 24, All-Stars 3
1940	Green Bay 45, All-Stars 28	1957	NY Giants 22, All-Stars 12	1971	Baltimore 24, All-Stars 17
1941	Chi. Bears 37, All-Stars 13	1958	All-Stars 35, Detroit 19	1972	Dallas 20, All-Stars 7
1942	Chi. Bears 21, All-Stars 7	1959	Baltimore 29, All-Stars 0	1973	Miami 14, All-Stars 3
1943	All-Stars 27, Washington 7			1974	No Game (NFLPA Strike)
1944	Chi. Bears 24, All-Stars 21	1960	Baltimore 32, All-Stars 7	1975	Pittsburgh 21, All-Stars 14
1945	Green Bay 19, All-Stars 7	1961	Philadelphia 28, All-Stars 14	1976	Pittsburgh 24, All-Stars 0*
1946	All-Stars 16, LA Rams 0	1962	Green Bay 42, All-Stars 20		
1947	All-Stars 16, Chi. Bears 0	1963	All-Stars 20, Green Bay 17	*Downpour flooded field, game called
1948	Chi. Cards 28, All-Stars 0	1964	Chi. Bears 28, All-Stars 17	with 1:22 left in 3rd quarter.
1949	Philadelphia 38, All-Stars 0				

Number One Draft Choices

In an effort to blunt the dominance of the Chicago Bears and New York Giants in the 1930s and distribute talent more evenly throughout the league, the NFL established the college draft in 1936. The first player chosen in the first draft was Jay Berwanger, who was also college football's Heisman Trophy winner. In all, 16 Heisman winners have also been the NFL's No.1 draft choice. They are noted in **bold** type. The American Football League (formed in 1960) held its own draft for six years before agreeing to merge with the NFL and select players in a common draft starting in 1967.

Year	Team		Year	Team	
1936	Philadelphia	**Jay Berwanger**, HB, Chicago	1953	San Francisco	Harry Babcock, E, Georgia
1937	Philadelphia	Sam Francis, FB, Nebraska	1954	Cleveland	Bobby Garrett, QB, Stanford
1938	Cleveland Rams	Corbett Davis, FB, Indiana	1955	Baltimore	George Shaw, QB, Oregon
1939	Chicago Cards	Ki Aldrich, C, TCU	1956	Pittsburgh	Gary Glick, DB, Colo. A&M
			1957	Green Bay	**Paul Hornung**, QB, N. Dame
1940	Chicago Cards	George Cafego, HB, Tennessee	1958	Chicago Cards	King Hill, QB, Rice
1941	Chicago Bears	**Tom Harmon**, HB, Michigan	1959	Green Bay	Randy Duncan, QB, Iowa
1942	Pittsburgh	Bill Dudley, HB, Viginia			
1943	Detroit	**Frank Sinkwich**, HB, Georgia	1960	NFL—LA Rams	**Billy Cannon**, HB, LSU
1944	Boston Yanks	**Angelo Bertelli**, QB, N. Dame		AFL—No choice	
1945	Chicago Cards	Charley Trippi, HB, Georgia	1961	NFL—Minnesota	Tommy Mason, HB, Tulane
1946	Boston Yanks	Frank Dancewicz, QB, N. Dame		AFL—Buffalo	Ken Rice, G, Auburn
1947	Chicago Bears	Bob Fenimore, HB, Okla. A&M	1962	NFL—Washington	**Ernie Davis**, HB, Syracuse
1948	Washington	Harry Gilmer, QB, Alabama		AFL—Oakland	Roman Gabriel, QB, N.C. State
1949	Philadelphia	Chuck Bednarik, C, Penn	1963	NFL—LA Rams	**Terry Baker**, QB, Oregon St.
				AFL—Kan.City	Buck Buchanan, DT, Grambling
1950	Detroit	**Leon Hart**, E, Notre Dame	1964	NFL—San Fran	Dave Parks, E, Texas Tech
1951	NY Giants	Kyle Rote, HB, SMU		AFL—Boston	Jack Concannon, QB, Boston Col.
1952	LA Rams	Bill Wade, QB, Vanderbilt			

Year	Team			Year	Team	
1965	NFL—NY Giants	Tucker Frederickson, HB, Auburn		1980	Detroit	**Billy Sims**, RB, Oklahoma
	AFL—Houston	Lawrence Elkins, E, Baylor		1981	New Orleans	**George Rogers**, RB, S. Carolina
1966	NFL—Atlanta	Tommy Nobis, LB, Texas		1982	New England	Kenneth Sims, DT, Texas
	AFL—Miami	Jim Grabowski, FB, Illinois		1983	Baltimore	John Elway, QB, Stanford
1967	Baltimore	Bubba Smith, DT, Michigan St.		1984	New England	Irving Fryar, WR, Nebraska
1968	Minnesota	Ron Yary, T, USC		1985	Buffalo	Bruce Smith, DE, Va. Tech
1969	Buffalo	**O.J. Simpson**, RB, USC		1986	Tampa Bay	**Bo Jackson**, RB, Auburn
				1987	Tampa Bay	**V. Testaverde**, QB, Miami-FL
1970	Pittsburgh	Terry Bradshaw, QB, La.Tech		1988	Atlanta	Aundray Bruce, LB, Auburn
1971	New England	**Jim Plunkett**, QB, Stanford		1989	Dallas	Troy Aikman, QB, UCLA
1972	Buffalo	Walt Patulski, DE, Notre Dame				
1973	Houston	John Matuszak, DE, Tampa		1990	Indianapolis	Jeff George, QB, Illinois
1974	Dallas	Ed (Too Tall) Jones, Tenn. St.		1991	Dallas	Russell Maryland, DL, Miami-FL
1975	Atlanta	Steve Bartkowski, QB, Calif.		1992	Indianapolis	Steve Emtman, DL, Washington
1976	Tampa Bay	Lee Roy Selmon, DE, Oklahoma		1993	New England	Drew Bledsoe, QB, Washington St.
1977	Tampa Bay	Ricky Bell, RB, USC		1994	Cincinnati	Dan Wilkinson, DT, Ohio St.
1978	Houston	**Earl Campbell**, RB, Texas				
1979	Buffalo	Tom Cousineau, LB, Ohio St.				

All-Time Winningest NFL Coaches

NFL career victories through the 1993 season. Career, regular season and playoff records are noted along with NFL, AFL and Super Bowl titles won. Coaches active during 1993 season in **bold** type.

		Career				Regular Season				Playoffs			
		Yrs	W	L	T	Pct	W	L	T	Pct	W	L	Pct.	League Titles
1	**Don Shula**	31	**327**	158	6	672	309	143	6	681	18	15	545	2 Super Bowls and 1 NFL
2	George Halas	40	**324**	151	31	671	318	148	31	681	6	3	667	5 NFL
3	Tom Landry	29	**270**	178	6	601	250	162	6	605	20	16	556	2 Super Bowls
4	Curly Lambeau	33	**229**	134	22	623	226	132	22	624	3	2	600	6 NFL
5	Chuck Noll	23	**209**	156	1	572	193	148	1	566	16	8	667	4 Super Bowls
6	**Chuck Knox**	21	**189**	146	1	564	182	135	1	574	7	11	389	None
7	Paul Brown	21	**170**	108	6	609	166	100	6	621	4	8	333	3 NFL
8	Bud Grant	18	**168**	108	5	607	158	96	5	620	10	12	455	1 NFL
9	Steve Owen	23	**153**	108	17	581	151	100	17	595	2	8	200	2 NFL
10	Joe Gibbs	12	**140**	65	0	683	124	60	0	674	16	5	762	3 Super Bowls
11	Hank Stram	17	**136**	100	10	573	131	97	10	571	5	3	625	1 Super Bowl and 3 AFL
12	Weeb Ewbank	20	**134**	130	7	507	130	129	7	502	4	1	800	1 Super Bowl, 2 NFL and 1 AFL
13	**Dan Reeves**	13	**129**	85	1	602	121	78	1	608	8	7	533	None
14	Sid Gillman	18	**123**	104	7	541	122	99	7	550	1	5	167	1 AFL
15	**Marv Levy**	13	**120**	87	0	580	110	81	0	576	10	6	625	None
16	George Allen	12	**118**	54	5	681	116	47	5	705	2	7	222	None
17	Don Coryell	14	**114**	89	1	561	111	83	1	572	3	6	333	None
18	John Madden	10	**112**	39	7	731	103	32	7	750	9	7	563	1 Super Bowl
	Mike Ditka	11	**112**	68	0	622	106	62	0	631	6	6	500	1 Super Bowl
20	Buddy Parker	15	**107**	76	9	581	104	75	9	577	3	1	750	2 NFL
21	Vince Lombardi	10	**105**	35	6	740	96	34	6	728	9	1	900	2 Super Bowls and 5 NFL
22	Bill Walsh	10	**102**	63	1	617	92	59	1	609	10	4	714	3 Super Bowls
23	**Tom Flores**	11	**99**	80	0	553	91	77	0	542	8	3	727	2 Super Bowls
	M.Schottenheimer	10	**99**	64	1	607	94	56	1	626	5	8	385	None
25	Lou Saban	16	**97**	101	7	490	95	100	7	488	2	1	667	2 AFL

Notes: The NFL does not recognize records from the All-American Football Conference (1946-49). If it did, **Paul Brown** (52-4-3 in four AAFC seasons) would move up to 5th on the all-time list with the following career stats—25 Yrs; 222 Wins; 112 Losses; 9 Ties; .660 Pct; 9-8 playoff record; and 4 AAFC titles.

The NFL also considers the Playoff Bowl or Runner-up Bowl (officially: the Bert Bell Benefit Bowl) as a post-season exhibition game.The Playoff Bowl was contested every year from 1960-69 in Miami between Eastern and Western Conference second place teams. While the games did not count, six of the coaches above went to the Playoff Bowl at least once and came away with the following records— Allen (2-0), Brown (0-1), Grant (0-1), Landry (1-2), Lombardi (1-1) and Shula (2-0).

Where They Coached

Allen— LA Rams (1966-70), Washington (1971-77); **Brown**—Cleveland (1950-62), Cincinnati (1968-75); **Coryell**— St.Louis (1973-77), San Diego (1978-86); **Ditka**— Chicago (1982-92); **Ewbank**—Baltimore (1954-62), NY Jets (1963-73); **Flores**— Oakland-LA Raiders (1979-87), Seattle (1992—); **Gibbs**— Washington (1981-92); **Gillman**—LA Rams (1955-59), LA-San Diego Chargers (1960-69), Houston (1973-74).

Grant— Minnesota (1967-83,1985); **Halas**— Chicago Bears (1920-29,33-42,46-55,58-67); **Knox**— LA Rams (1973-77, 1992—); Buffalo (1978-82), Seattle (1983-91); **Lambeau**— Green Bay (1921-49), Green Bay Cards (1950-51), Washington (1952-53); **Landry**— Dallas (1960-88); **Levy**— Kansas City (1978-82), Buffalo (1986—); **Lombardi**— Green Bay (1959-67), Washington (1969); **Madden**— Oakland (1969-78).

Noll— Pittsburgh (1969-91); **Owen**— NY Giants (1931-53); **Parker**—Chicago Cards (1949), Detroit (1951-56), Pittsburgh (1957-64); **Reeves**— Denver (1981-92), NY Giants (1993—); **Saban**— Boston Patriots (1960-61), Buffalo (1962-65,72-76), Denver (1967-71); **Schottenheimer**— Cleveland (1984-88), Kansas City (1989—); **Shula**— Baltimore (1963-69), Miami (1970—); **Stram**— Dallas-Kansas City (1960-74), New Orleans (1976-77); **Walsh**— San Francisco (1979-88).

All-Time Winningest NFL Coaches (Cont.)

Top Winning Percentages

Minimum of 85 NFL victories, including playoffs.

		Yrs	W	L	T	Pct
1	Vince Lombardi	10	105	35	6	.740
2	John Madden	10	112	39	7	.731
3	Joe Gibbs	12	140	65	0	.683
4	George Allen	12	118	54	5	.681
5	Don Shula	31	327	158	6	.672
6	George Halas	40	324	151	31	.671
7	Curly Lambeau	33	229	134	22	.623
8	Mike Ditka	11	112	68	0	.622
9	Bill Walsh	10	102	63	1	.617
10	Paul Brown	21	170	108	6	.609
11	Bud Grant	18	168	108	5	.607
12	M. Schottenheimer	10	99	64	1	.607
13	Dan Reeves	13	129	85	1	.602
14	Tom Landry	29	270	178	6	.601
15	Bill Parcells	9	90	63	1	.588
16	Steve Owen	23	153	108	17	.581
17	Buddy Parker	15	107	76	9	.581
18	Marv Levy	13	120	87	0	.580
19	Hank Stram	17	136	100	10	.573
20	Chuck Noll	23	209	156	1	.572
21	Chuck Knox	21	189	146	1	.564
22	Don Coryell	14	114	89	1	.561
23	Jimmy Conzelman	15	89	68	17	.560
24	Jack Pardee	10	86	69	0	.555
25	Tom Flores	11	99	80	0	.553

Note: If AAFC records are included, **Paul Brown** moves to 7th with a percentage of .660 (25 yrs, 222-112-9) and Buck Shaw would be 9th at .619 (8 yrs, 91-55-5).

Active Coaches' Victories

Through 1993 season, including playoffs.

		Yrs	W	L	T	Pct
1	Don Shula, Miami	31	327	158	6	.672
2	Chuck Knox, LA Rams	21	189	146	1	.564
3	Dan Reeves, NY Giants	13	129	85	1	.602
4	Marv Levy, Buffalo	13	120	87	0	.580
5	Marty Schottenheimer, KC	10	99	64	1	.607
	Tom Flores, Seattle	11	99	80	0	.553
7	Bill Parcells, New England	9	90	63	1	.588
8	Jack Pardee, Houston	10	86	69	0	.555
9	Jim Mora, New Orleans	8	77	54	0	.588
10	Sam Wyche, Tampa Bay	10	74	90	0	.451
11	George Seifert, San Fran	5	68	21	0	.764
12	Ted Marchibroda, Ind	7	54	55	0	.495
13	Art Shell, LA Raiders	5	47	34	0	.580
14	Buddy Ryan, Phoenix	5	43	38	1	.530
	Wayne Fontes, Detroit	6	43	45	0	.489
16	Rich Kotite, Philadelphia	3	30	20	0	.600
17	Bill Cowher, Pittsburgh	2	20	14	0	.588
	Dennis Green, Minnesota	2	20	14	0	.588
	Bobby Ross, San Diego	2	20	14	0	.588
	Bill Belichick, Cleveland	3	20	28	0	.417
21	Mike Holmgren, Green Bay	2	19	15	0	.559
22	Wade Phillips, Denver	2	10	11	0	.476
23	David Shula, Cincinnati	2	8	24	0	.250
24	Dave Wannstedt, Chicago	1	7	9	0	.438
25	Pete Carroll, NY Jets	0	0	0	0	.000
	June Jones, Atlanta	0	0	0	0	.000
	Barry Switzer, Dallas	0	0	0	0	.000
	Norv Turner, Washington	0	0	0	0	.000

Annual Awards
NFL Player of the Year

Unlike the other major pro team sports, the NFL no longer sanctions a Most Valuable Player award. The league gave out the Joe F. Carr Trophy (Carr was NFL president from 1921-39) for nine years but discontinued it in 1947. Since then, four principal MVP awards have been given out: UPI (1953-69), AP (since 1957), the Maxwell Club of Philadelphia's Bert Bell Trophy (since 1959) and the Pro Football Writers Assn. (since 1976). UPI switched to AFC and NFC Player of the Year awards in 1970.

Multiple winners (named in more than one season): Jim Brown (4); Johnny Unitas and Y.A. Tittle (3); Earl Campbell, Randall Cunningham, Otto Graham, Don Hutson, Joe Montana, Walter Payton, Ken Stabler and Joe Theismann (2).

Year		Awards
1938	Mel Hein, NY Giants, C	Carr
1939	Parker Hall, Cleveland Rams, HB	Carr
1940	Ace Parker, Brooklyn, HB	Carr
1941	Don Hutson, Green Bay, E	Carr
1942	Don Hutson, Green Bay, E	Carr
1943	Sid Luckman, Chicago Bears, QB	Carr
1944	Frank Sinkwich, Detroit, HB	Carr
1945	Bob Waterfield, Cleveland Rams, QB	Carr
1946	Bill Dudley, Pittsburgh, HB	Carr
1947-49	No award	
1950-52	No award	
1953	Otto Graham, Cleveland Browns, QB	UPI
1954	Joe Perry, San Francisco, FB	UPI
1955	Otto Graham, Cleveland, QB	UPI
1956	Frank Gifford, NY Giants, HB	UPI
1957	Y.A. Tittle, San Francisco, QB	UPI
	& Jim Brown, Cleveland, FB	AP
1958	Jim Brown, Cleveland, FB	UPI
	& Gino Marchetti, Baltimore, DE	AP
1959	Johnny Unitas, Baltimore, QB	UPI, Bell
	& Charley Conerly, NY Giants, QB	AP
1960	Norm Van Brocklin, Phi., QB	UPI, AP (tie), Bell
	& Joe Schmidt, Detroit, LB	AP (tie)
1961	Paul Hornung, Green Bay, HB	UPI, AP, Bell

Year		Awards
1962	Y.A. Tittle, NY Giants, QB	UPI
	Jim Taylor, Green Bay, FB	AP
	& Andy Robustelli, NY Giants, DE	Bell
1963	Jim Brown, Cleveland, FB	UPI, AP, Bell
	& Y.A. Tittle, NY Giants, QB	AP
1964	Johnny Unitas, Baltimore, QB	UPI, AP, Bell
1965	Jim Brown, Cleveland, FB	UPI, AP
	& Pete Retzlaff, Philadelphia, TE	Bell
1966	Bart Starr, Green Bay, QB	UPI, AP, Bell
	& Don Meredith, Dallas, QB	Bell
1967	Johnny Unitas, Baltimore, QB	UPI, AP, Bell
1968	Earl Morrall, Baltimore, QB	UPI, AP, Bell
	& Leroy Kelly, Cleveland, RB	Bell
1969	Roman Gabriel, LA Rams, QB	UPI, AP, Bell
1970	John Brodie, San Francisco, QB	AP
	& George Blanda, Oakland, QB-PK	Bell
1971	Alan Page, Minnesota, DT	AP
	& Roger Staubach, Dallas, QB	Bell
1972	Larry Brown, Washington, RB	AP, Bell
1973	O.J. Simpson, Buffalo, RB	AP, Bell
1974	Ken Stabler, Oakland, QB	AP
	& Merlin Olsen, LA Rams, DT	Bell
1975	Fran Tarkenton, Minnesota, QB	AP, Bell
1976	Bert Jones, Baltimore, QB	AP, PFWA
	& Ken Stabler, Oakland, QB	Bell

Year		Awards	Year		Awards
1977	Walter Payton, Chicago, RB	AP, PFWA	1985	Marcus Allen, LA Raiders, RB	AP, PFWA
	& Bob Griese, Miami, QB	Bell		& Walter Payton, Chicago, RB	Bell
1978	Terry Bradshaw, Pittsburgh, QB	AP, Bell	1986	Lawrence Taylor, NY Giants, LB	AP, Bell, PFWA
	& Earl Campbell, Houston, RB	PFWA	1987	Jerry Rice, San Francisco, WR	Bell, PFWA
1979	Earl Campbell, Houston, RB	AP, Bell, PFWA		& John Elway, Denver, QB	AP
1980	Brian Sipe, Cleveland, QB	AP, PFWA	1988	Boomer Esiason, Cincinnati, QB	AP, PFWA
	& Ron Jaworski, Philadelphia, QB	Bell		& Randall Cunningham, Phila, QB	Bell
1981	Ken Anderson, Cincinnati, QB	AP, Bell, PFWA	1989	Joe Montana, San Francisco, QB	AP, Bell, PFWA
1982	Mark Moseley, Washington, PK	AP	1990	Randall Cunningham, Phila., QB	Bell, PFWA
	Joe Theismann, Washington, QB	Bell		& Joe Montana, San Francisco, QB	AP
	& Dan Fouts, San Diego, QB	PFWA	1991	Thurman Thomas, Buffalo, RB	AP, PFWA
1983	Joe Theismann, Washington, QB	AP, PFWA		& Barry Sanders, Detroit, RB	Bell
	& John Riggins, Washington, RB	Bell	1992	Steve Young, San Francisco, QB	Bell, PFWA
1984	Dan Marino, Miami, QB	AP, Bell, PFWA	1993	Emmitt Smith, Dallas, RB	AP, Bell, PFWA

NFC Player of the Year

Given out by UPI since 1970. Offensive and defensive players have been honored since 1983. Rookie winners are in **bold** type.
  Multiple winners: Eric Dickerson and Mike Singletary (3); Walter Payton, Lawrence Taylor and Reggie White (2).

Year		Pos	Year		Pos
1970	John Brodie, San Francisco	QB	1986	Off—Eric Dickerson, Los Angeles	RB
1971	Alan Page, Minnesota	DT		Def—Lawrence Taylor, New York	LB
1972	Larry Brown, Washington	RB	1987	Off—Jerry Rice, San Francisco	WR
1973	John Hadl, Los Angeles	QB		Def—Reggie White, Philadelphia	DE
1974	Jim Hart, St. Louis	QB	1988	Off—Roger Craig, San Francisco	RB
1975	Fran Tarkenton, Minnesota	QB		Def—Mike Singletary, Chicago	LB
1976	Chuck Foreman, Minnesota	RB	1989	Off—Joe Montana, San Francisco	QB
1977	Walter Payton, Chicago	RB		Def—Keith Millard, Minnesota	DT
1978	Archie Manning, New Orleans	QB	1990	Off—Randall Cunningham, Philadelphia	QB
1979	**Ottis Anderson**, St. Louis	RB		Def—Charles Haley, San Francisco	LB
1980	Ron Jaworski, Philadelphia	QB	1991	Off—Mark Rypien, Washington	QB
1981	Tony Dorsett, Dallas	RB		Def—Reggie White, Philadelphia	DE
1982	Mark Moseley, Washington	PK	1992	Off—Steve Young, San Francisco	QB
1983	Off—**Eric Dickerson**, Los Angeles	RB		Def—Chris Dolman, Minnesota	DE
	Def—Lawrence Taylor, New York	LB	1993	Off—Emmitt Smith, Dallas	RB
1984	Off—Eric Dickerson, Los Angeles	RB		Def—Eric Allen, Philadelphia	CB
	Def—Mike Singletary, Chicago	LB			
1985	Off—Walter Payton, Chicago	RB			
	Def—Mike Singletary, Chicago	LB			

AFL-AFC Player of the Year

Presented by UPI to the top player in the AFL (1960-69) and AFC (since 1970). Offensive and defensive players have been honored since 1983. Rookie winners are in **bold** type.
  Multiple winners: O.J. Simpson and Bruce Smith (3); Cornelius Bennett, George Blanda, John Elway, Dan Fouts, Daryle Lamonica and Curt Warner (2).

Year		Pos	Year		Pos
1960	**Abner Haynes**, Dallas Texans	HB	1983	Off—**Curt Warner**, Seattle	RB
1961	George Blanda, Houston	QB		Def—Rod Martin, Los Angeles	LB
1962	Cookie Gilchrist, Buffalo	FB	1984	Off—Dan Marino, Miami	QB
1963	Lance Alworth, San Diego	FL		Def—Mark Gastineau, New York	DE
1964	Gino Cappelletti, Boston	FL-PK	1985	Off—Marcus Allen, Los Angeles	RB
1965	Paul Lowe, San Diego	HB		Def—Andre Tippett, New England	LB
1966	Jim Nance, Boston	FB	1986	Off—Curt Warner, Seattle	RB
1967	Daryle Lamonica, Oakland	QB		Def—Rulon Jones, Denver	DE
1968	Joe Namath, New York	QB	1987	Off—John Elway, Denver	QB
1969	Daryle Lamonica, Oakland	QB		Def—Bruce Smith, Buffalo	DE
1970	George Blanda, Oakland	QB-PK	1988	Off—Boomer Esiason, Cincinnatti	QB
1971	Otis Taylor, Kansas City	WR		Def—Bruce Smith, Buffalo	DE
1972	O.J. Simpson, Buffalo	RB		& Cornelius Bennett, Buffalo	LB
1973	O.J. Simpson, Buffalo	RB	1989	Off—Christian Okoye, Kansas City	RB
1974	Ken Stabler, Oakland	QB		Def—Michael Dean Perry, Cleveland	NT
1975	O.J. Simpson, Buffalo	RB	1990	Off—Warren Moon, Houston	QB
1976	Bert Jones, Baltimore	QB		Def—Bruce Smith, Buffalo	DE
1977	Craig Morton, Denver	QB	1991	Off—Thurman Thomas, Buffalo	RB
1978	**Earl Campbell**, Houston	RB		Def—Cornelius Bennett, Buffalo	LB
1979	Dan Fouts, San Diego	QB	1992	Off—Barry Foster, Pittsburgh	RB
1980	Brian Sipe, Cleveland	QB		Def—Junior Seau, San Diego	LB
1981	Ken Anderson, Cincinnati	QB	1993	Off—John Elway, Denver	QB
1982	Dan Fouts, San Diego	QB		Def—Rod Woodson, Pittsburgh	CB

Annual Awards (Cont.)

NFL-NFC Rookie of the Year

Presented by UPI to the top rookie in the NFL (1955-69) and NFC (since 1970). Players who were the overall first pick in the NFL draft are in **bold** type.

Year		Pos	Year		Pos	Year		Pos
1955	Alan Ameche, Bal	FB	1970	Bruce Taylor, SF	DB	1985	Jerry Rice, SF	WR
1956	Lenny Moore, Bal	HB	1971	John Brockington, GB	RB	1986	Reuben Mayes, NO	RB
1957	Jim Brown, Cle	FB	1972	Chester Marcol, GB	PK	1987	Robert Awalt, St.L	TE
1958	Jimmy Orr, Pit	FL	1973	Charle Young, Phi	TE	1988	Keith Jackson, Phi	TE
1959	Boyd Dowler, GB	FL	1974	John Hicks, NY	G	1989	Barry Sanders, Det	RB
1960	Gail Cogdill, Det	FB	1975	Mike Thomas, Wash	RB	1990	Mark Carrier, Chi	S
1961	Mike Ditka, Chi	TE	1976	Sammy White, Min	WR	1991	Lawrence Dawsey, TB	WR
1962	Ronnie Bull, Chi	FB	1977	Tony Dorsett, Dal	RB	1992	Robert Jones, Dal	LB
1963	Paul Flatley, Min	FL	1978	Bubba Baker, Det	DE	1993	Jerome Bettis, LA	RB
1964	Charley Taylor, Wash	FB	1979	Ottis Anderson, St.L	RB			
1965	Gale Sayers, Chi	HB	1980	**Billy Sims**, Det	RB			
1966	Johnny Roland, St.L	HB	1981	**George Rogers**, NO	RB			
1967	Mel Farr, Det	RB	1982	Jim McMahon, Chi	QB			
1968	Earl McCullough, Det	FL	1983	Eric Dickerson, LA	RB			
1969	Calvin Hill, Dal	RB	1984	Paul McFadden, Phi	PK			

AFL-AFC Rookie of the Year

Presented by UPI to the top rookie in the AFL (1960-69) and AFC (since 1970). Players who were the overall first pick in the AFL or NFL draft are in **bold** type.

Year		Pos	Year		Pos	Year		Pos
1960	Abner Haynes, Dal	HB	1972	Franco Harris, Pit	RB	1984	Louis Lipps, Pit	WR
1961	Earl Faison, SD	DE	1973	Boobie Clark, Cin	RB	1985	Kevin Mack, Cle	RB
1962	Curtis McClinton, Dal	FB	1974	Don Woods, SD	RB	1986	Leslie O'Neal, SD	DE
1963	Billy Joe, Den	FB	1975	Robert Brazile, Hou	LB	1987	Shane Conlan, Buf	LB
1964	Matt Snell, NY	FB	1976	Mike Haynes, NE	DB	1988	John Stephens, NE	RB
1965	Joe Namath, NY	QB	1977	A.J. Duhe, Mia	DE	1989	Derrick Thomas, KC	LB
1966	Bobby Burnett, Buf	HB	1978	**Earl Campbell**, Hou	RB	1990	Richmond Webb, Mia	OT
1967	George Webster, Hou	LB	1979	Jerry Butler, Buf	WR	1991	Mike Croel, Den	LB
1968	Paul Robinson, Cin	RB	1980	Joe Cribbs, Buf	RB	1992	Dale Carter, KC	CB
1969	Greg Cook, Cin	QB	1981	Joe Delaney, KC	RB	1993	Rick Mirer, Sea	QB
1970	Dennis Shaw, Buf	QB	1982	Marcus Allen, LA	RB			
1971	**Jim Plunkett**, NE	QB	1983	Curt Warner, Sea	RB			

NFL-NFC Coach of the Year

Presented by UPI to the top coach in the NFL (1955-69) and NFC (since 1970). Records indicate how much coach's team improved over one season.

Multiple winners: George Allen, Leeman Bennett, Mike Ditka, George Halas, Tom Landry, Jack Pardee, Allie Sherman, Don Shula and Bill Walsh (2).

Year		Improvement	Year		Improvement
1955	Joe Kuharich, Washington	3-9 to 8-4	1976	Jack Pardee, Chicago	4-10 to 7-7
1956	Buddy Parker, Detroit	3-9 to 9-3	1977	Leeman Bennett, Atlanta	4-10 to 7-7
1957	Paul Brown, Cleveland	5-7 to 9-2-1	1978	Dick Vermeil, Philadelphia	5-9 to 9-7
1958	Weeb Ewbank, Baltimore	7-5 to 9-3	1979	Jack Pardee, Washington	8-8 to 10-6
1959	Vince Lombardi, Green Bay	1-10-1 to 7-5	1980	Leeman Bennett, Atlanta	6-10 to 12-4
1960	Buck Shaw, Philadelphia	7-5 to 10-2	1981	Bill Walsh, San Francisco	6-10 to 13-3
1961	Allie Sherman, New York	6-4-2 to 10-3-1	1982	Joe Gibbs, Washington	8-8 to 8-1
1962	Allie Sherman, New York	10-3-1 to 12-2	1983	John Robinson, Los Angeles	2-7 to 9-7
1963	George Halas, Chicago	9-5 to 11-1-2	1984	Bill Walsh, San Francisco	10-6 to 15-1
1964	Don Shula, Baltimore	8-6 to 12-2	1985	Mike Ditka, Chicago	10-6 to 15-1
1965	George Halas, Chicago	5-9 to 9-5	1986	Bill Parcells, New York	10-6 to 14-2
1966	Tom Landry, Dallas	7-7 to 10-3-1	1987	Jim Mora, New Orleans	7-9 to 12-3
1967	George Allen, Los Angeles	8-6 to 11-1-2	1988	Mike Ditka, Chicago	11-4 to 12-4
1968	Don Shula, Baltimore	11-1-2 to 13-1	1989	Lindy Infante, Green Bay	4-12 to 10-6
1969	Bud Grant, Minnesota	8-6 to 12-2	1990	Jimmy Johnson, Dallas	1-15 to 7-9
1970	Alex Webster, New York	6-8 to 9-5	1991	Wayne Fontes, Detroit	6-10 to 12-4
1971	George Allen, Washington	6-8 to 9-4-1	1992	Dennis Green, Minnesota	8-8 to 11-5
1972	Dan Devine, Green Bay	4-8-2 to 10-4	1993	Dan Reeves, New York	6-10 to 11-5
1973	Chuck Knox, Los Angeles	6-7-1 to 12-2			
1974	Don Coryell, St. Louis	4-9-1 to 10-4			
1975	Tom Landry, Dallas	8-6 to 10-4			

AFL-AFC Coach of the Year

Presented by UPI to the top coach in the AFL (1960-69) and AFC (since 1970). Records indicate how much coach's team improved over one season. The AFC began play in 1960.

Multiple winners: Chuck Knox, Marv Levy, Sam Rutigliano, Lou Saban, Dan Reeves and Don Shula (2)

Year		Improvement	Year		Improvement
1960	Lou Rymkus, Houston	10-4	1978	Walt Michaels, New York	3-11 to 8-8
1961	Wally Lemm, Houston	10-4 to 10-3-1	1979	Sam Rutigliano, Cleveland	8-8 to 9-7
1962	Jack Faulkner, Denver	3-11 to 7-7			
1963	Al Davis, Oakland	1-13 to 10-4	1980	Sam Rutigliano, Cleveland	9-7 to 11-5
1964	Lou Saban, Buffalo	7-6-1 to 12-2	1981	Forrest Gregg, Cincinnati	6-10 to 12-4
1965	Lou Saban, Buffalo	12-2 to 10-3-1	1982	Tom Flores, Los Angeles	7-9 to 8-1
1966	Mike Holovak, Boston	4-8-2 to 8-4-2	1983	Chuck Knox, Seattle	4-5 to 9-7
1967	John Rauch, Oakland	8-5-1 to 13-1	1984	Chuck Knox, Seattle	9-7 to 12-4
1968	Hank Stram, Kansas City	9-5 to 12-2	1985	Raymond Berry, New England	9-7 to 11-5
1969	Paul Brown, Cincinnati	3-11 to 4-9-1	1986	Marty Schottenheimer, Cleveland	8-8 to 12-4
			1987	Ron Meyer, Indianapolis	3-13 to 9-6
1970	Don Shula, Miami	3-10-1 to 10-4	1988	Marv Levy, Buffalo	7-8 to 12-4
1971	Don Shula, Miami	10-4 to 10-3-1	1989	Dan Reeves, Denver	8-8 to 11-5
1972	Chuck Noll, Pittsburgh	6-8 to 11-3			
1973	John Ralston, Denver	5-9 to 7-5-2	1990	Art Shell, Los Angeles	8-8 to 12-4
1974	Sid Gillman, Houston	1-13 to 7-7	1991	Dan Reeves, Denver	5-11 to 12-4
1975	Ted Marchibroda, Baltimore	2-12 to 10-4	1992	Bobby Ross, San Diego	4-12 to 11-5
1976	Chuck Fairbanks, New England	3-11 to 11-3	1993	Marv Levy, Buffalo	11-5 to 12-4
1977	Red Miller, Denver	9-5 to 12-2			

Canadian Football
The Grey Cup

Earl Grey, the Governor-General of Canada (1904-11) donated a trophy in 1909 for the Rugby Football Championship of Canada. The trophy, which later became known as the Grey Cup, was originally open to competition for teams registered with the Canada Rugby Union. Since 1954, the Cup has gone to the champion of the Canadian Football League (CFL).

Overall multiple winners: Toronto Argonauts (12); Edmonton Eskimos (11); Winnipeg Blue Bombers (9); Hamilton Tiger-Cats and Ottawa Rough Riders (7); Hamilton Tigers (5); Montreal Alouettes and University of Toronto (4); Calgary Stampeders and Queen's University (3); B.C. Lions, Ottawa Senators, Sarnia Imperials, Saskatchewan Roughriders and Toronto Balmy Beach (2).

CFL multiple winners (since 1954): Edmonton (11); Winnipeg (7); Hamilton (6); Ottawa (5); Montreal (3); B.C. Lions, Calgary, Saskatchewan and Toronto (2).

Year	Cup Final	Year	Cup Final
1909	Univ. of Toronto 26, Toronto Parkdale 6	1934	Sarnia Imperials 20, Regina Roughriders 12
1910	Univ. of Toronto 16, Hamilton Tigers 7	1935	Winnipeg 'Pegs 18, Hamilton Tigers 12
1911	Univ. of Toronto 14, Toronto Argonauts 7	1936	Sarnia Imperials 26, Ottawa Rough Riders 20
1912	Hamilton Alerts 11, Toronto Argonauts 4	1937	Toronto Argonauts 4, Winnipeg Blue Bombers 3
1913	Hamilton Tigers 44, Toronto Parkdale 2	1938	Toronto Argonauts 30, Winnipeg Blue Bombers 7
1914	Toronto Argonauts 14, Univ. of Toronto 2	1939	Winnipeg Blue Bombers 8, Ottawa Rough Riders 7
1915	Hamilton Tigers 13, Toronto Rowing 7		
1916-19	Not held (WWI)	1940	Gm 1: Ottawa Rough Riders 8, Toronto B-Beach 2
			Gm 2: Ottawa Rough Riders 12, Toronto B-Beach 5
1920	Univ. of Toronto 16, Toronto Argonauts 3	1941	Winnipeg Blue Bombers 18, Ottawa Rough Riders 16
1921	Toronto Argonauts 23, Edmonton Eskimos 0	1942	Toronto RACF 8, Winnipeg RACF 5
1922	Queens Univ. 13, Edmonton Elks 1	1943	Hamilton Wildcats 23, Winnipeg RACF 14
1923	Queens Univ. 54, Regina Roughriders 0	1944	Montreal HMCS 7, Hamilton Wildcats 6
1924	Queens Univ. 11, Toronto Balmy Beach 3	1945	Toronto Argonauts 35, Winnipeg Blue Bombers 0
1925	Ottawa Senators 24, Winnipeg Tigers 1	1946	Toronto Argonauts 28, Winnipeg Blue Bombers 6
1926	Ottawa Senators 10, Univ. of Toronto 7	1947	Toronto Argonauts 10, Winnipeg Blue Bombers 9
1927	Toronto Balmy Beach 9, Hamilton Tigers 6	1948	Calgary Stampeders 12, Ottawa Rough Riders 7
1928	Hamilton Tigers 30, Regina Roughriders 0	1949	Montreal Alouettes 28, Calgary Stampeders 15
1929	Hamilton Tigers 14, Regina Roughriders 3		
		1950	Toronto Argonauts 13, Winnipeg Blue Bombers 0
1930	Toronto Balmy Beach 11, Regina Roughriders 6	1951	Ottawa Rough Riders 21, Saskatch. Roughriders 14
1931	Montreal AAA 22, Regina Roughriders 0	1952	Toronto Argonauts 21, Edmonton Eskimos 11
1932	Hamilton Tigers 25, Regina Roughriders 6	1953	Hamilton Tiger-Cats 12, Winnipeg Blue Bombers 6
1933	Toronto Argonauts 4, Sarnia Imperials 3		

Year	Winner	Head Coach	Score	Loser	Head Coach	Site
1954	Edmonton	Frank (Pop) Ivy	26-25	Montreal	Doug Walker	Toronto
1955	Edmonton	Frank (Pop) Ivy	34-19	Montreal	Doug Walker	Vancouver
1956	Edmonton	Frank (Pop) Ivy	50-27	Montreal	Doug Walker	Toronto
1957	Hamilton	Jim Trimble	32- 7	Winnipeg	Bud Grant	Toronto
1958	Winnipeg	Bud Grant	35-28	Hamilton	Jim Trimble	Vancouver
1959	Winnipeg	Bud Grant	21- 7	Hamilton	Jim Trimble	Toronto

Canadian Football (Cont.)

The Grey Cup

Year	Winner	Head Coach	Score	Loser	Head Coach	Site
1960	Ottawa	Frank Clair	16- 6	Edmonton	Eagle Keys	Vancouver
1961	Winnipeg	Bud Grant	21-14*	Hamilton	Jim Trimble	Toronto
1962	Winnipeg	Bud Grant	28-27**	Hamilton	Jim Trimble	Toronto
1963	Hamilton	Ralph Sazio	21-10	B.C. Lions	Dave Skrien	Vancouver
1964	B.C. Lions	Dave Skrien	34-24	Hamilton	Ralph Sazio	Toronto
1965	Hamilton	Ralph Sazio	22-16	Winnipeg	Bud Grant	Toronto
1966	Saskatchewan	Eagle Keys	29-14	Ottawa	Frank Clair	Vancouver
1967	Hamilton	Ralph Sazio	24- 1	Saskatchewan	Eagle Keys	Ottawa
1968	Ottawa	Frank Clair	24-21	Calgary	Jerry Williams	Toronto
1969	Ottawa	Frank Clair	29-11	Saskatchewan	Eagle Keys	Montreal
1970	Montreal	Sam Etcheverry	23-10	Calgary	Jim Duncan	Toronto
1971	Calgary	Jim Duncan	14-11	Toronto	Leo Cahill	Vancouver
1972	Hamilton	Jerry Williams	13-10	Saskatchewan	Dave Skrien	Hamilton
1973	Ottawa	Jack Gotta	22-18	Edmonton	Ray Jauch	Toronto
1974	Montreal	Marv Levy	20- 7	Edmonton	Ray Jauch	Vancouver
1975	Edmonton	Ray Jauch	9- 8	Montreal	Marv Levy	Calgary
1976	Ottawa	George Brancato	23-20	Saskatchewan	John Payne	Toronto
1977	Montreal	Marv Levy	41- 6	Edmonton	Hugh Campbell	Montreal
1978	Edmonton	Hugh Campbell	20-13	Montreal	Joe Scannella	Toronto
1979	Edmonton	Hugh Campbell	17- 9	Montreal	Joe Scannella	Montrea
1980	Edmonton	Hugh Campbell	48-10	Hamilton	John Payne	Toronto
1981	Edmonton	Hugh Campbell	26-23	Ottawa	George Brancato	Montreal
1982	Edmonton	Hugh Campbell	32-16	Toronto	Bob O'Billovich	Toronto
1983	Toronto	Bob O'Billovich	18-17	B.C. Lions	Don Matthews	Vancouver
1984	Winnipeg	Cal Murphy	47-17	Hamilton	Al Bruno	Edmonton
1985	B.C. Lions	Don Matthews	37-24	Hamilton	Al Bruno	Montreal
1986	Hamilton	Al Bruno	39-15	Edmonton	Jack Parker	Vancouver
1987	Edmonton	Joe Faragalli	38-36	Toronto	Bob O'Billovich	Vancouver
1988	Winnipeg	Mike Riley	22-21	B.C. Lions	Larry Donovan	Ottawa
1989	Saskatchewan	John Gregory	43-40	Hamilton	Al Bruno	Toronto
1990	Winnipeg	Mike Riley	50-11	Edmonton	Joe Faragalli	Vancouver
1991	Toronto	Adam Rita	36-21	Calgary	Wally Buono	Winnipeg
1992	Calgary	Wally Buono	24-10	Winnipeg	Urban Bowman	Toronto
1993	Edmonton	Ron Lancaster	33-23	Winnipeg	Cal Murphy	Calgary

*Overtime. **Halted by fog in 4th quarter, final 9:29 played the following day.

CFL Most Outstanding Player

Regular season Player of the Year as selected by The Football Reporters of Canada since 1953.
Multiple winners: Doug Flutie, Russ Jackson and Jackie Parker (3); Dieter Brock, Ron Lancaster (2).

Year	
1953	Billy Vessels, Edmonton, RB
1954	Sam Etcheverry, Montreal, QB
1955	Pat Abbruzzi, Montreal, RB
1956	Hal Patterson, Montreal, E-DB
1957	Jackie Parker, Edmonton, RB
1958	Jackie Parker, Edmonton, QB
1959	Johnny Bright, Edmonton, RB
1960	Jackie Parker, Edmonton, QB
1961	Bernie Faloney, Hamilton, QB
1962	George Dixon, Montreal, RB
1963	Russ Jackson, Ottawa, QB
1964	Lovell Coleman, Calgary, RB
1965	George Reed, Saskatchewan, RB
1966	Russ Jackson, Ottawa, QB
1967	Peter Liske, Calgary, QB
1968	Bill Symons, Toronto, RB
1969	Russ Jackson, Ottawa, QB
1970	Ron Lancaster, Saskatch., QB
1971	Don Jonas, Winnipeg, QB
1972	Garney Henley, Hamilton, WR
1973	Geo. McGowan, Edmonton, WR
1974	Tom Wilkinson, Edmonton, QB
1975	Willie Burden, Calgary, RB
1976	Ron Lancaster, Saskatch., QB
1977	Jimmy Edwards, Hamilton, RB
1978	Tony Gabriel, Ottawa, TE
1979	David Green, Montreal, RB
1980	Dieter Brock, Winnipeg, QB
1981	Dieter Brock, Winnipeg, QB
1982	Condredge Holloway, Tor., QB
1983	Warren Moon, Edmonton, QB
1984	Willard Reaves, Winnipeg, RB
1985	Merv Fernandez, B.C. Lions, WR
1986	James Murphy, Winnipeg, WR
1987	Tom Clements, Winnipeg, QB
1988	David Williams, B.C. Lions, WR
1989	Tracy Ham, Edmonton, QB
1990	Mike Clemons, Toronto, RB
1991	Doug Flutie, B.C. Lions, QB
1992	Doug Flutie, Calgary, QB
1993	Doug Flutie, Calgary, QB

CFL Most Outstanding Rookie

Regular season Rookie of the Year as selected by The Football Reporters of Canada since 1972.

Year	
1972	Chuck Ealey, Hamilton, QB
1973	Johnny Rodgers, Montreal, WR
1974	Sam Cvijanovich, Toronto, LB
1975	Tom Clements, Ottawa, QB
1976	John Sciarra, B.C. Lions, QB
1977	Leon Bright, B.C. Lions, WR
1978	Joe Poplawski, Winnipeg, WR
1979	Brian Kelly, Edmonton, WR
1980	William Miller, Winnipeg, RB
1981	Vince Goldsmith, Saskatch., LB
1982	Chris Issac, Ottawa, QB
1983	Johnny Shepherd, Hamilton, RB
1984	Dwaine Wilson, Montreal, RB
1985	Mike Gray, B.C. Lions, DT
1986	Harold Hallman, Calgary, DT
1987	Gill Fenerty, Toronto, RB
1988	Orville Lee, Ottawa, RB
1989	Stephen Jordan, Hamilton, DB
1990	Reggie Barnes, Ottawa, RB
1991	Jon Volpe, B.C. Lions, RB
1992	Mike Richardson, Winnipeg, RB
1993	Michael O'Shea, Hamilton, DT

Arkansas forward and tournament MVP **Corliss Williamson** scores two over Duke's **Grant Hill** during the Razorbacks' 76-72 victory in the NCAA championship game.

COLLEGE BASKETBALL

Boss Hogs

Arkansas beats Duke, 76-72, to capture its first NCAA title and complete a year-long mission to command respect.

G rant Hill, the fluid Duke forward, rose from just beyond the top of the circle and softly offered up a three-pointer. He had, in this national championship game, missed his previous five field goal attempts. But all through the chaotic 1993-94 college basketball season, he had also proven himself to be a special performer, and so it was no surprise here that his sixth shot was true and nestled home.

Now, with just 89 seconds remaining, the table was fittingly set for the climax of this climactic meeting between Hill's Blue Devils and Arkansas. The score was tied at 70. The 23,674 fans jammed into the Charlotte Coliseum were in full cry. And all the words, all the analyses, all the conjectures that had preceded this game were about to be played out.

Duke, in its fourth NCAA title game in five years, was familiar with the cauldron of pressure bubbling around it and appeared to have a distinct advantage despite entering the game as a six-point underdog. The Blue Devils, went this line of thinking, were smart and experienced and to them the challenge in the seconds ahead was just another plaything. They stood in stark contrast to Arkansas, which was in its first title game ever and conventionally viewed as very talented but basically undisciplined.

Skip Myslenski has been the national college basketball writer for the *Chicago Tribune* since 1988.

That thinking, of course, was too simplistic, yet it had long rankled both Razorbacks' coach Nolan Richardson and his players. Richardson had, in fact, moved through the tournament like some itinerant preacher or zealous crusader. From Oklahoma City to Dallas and on to this moment in Charlotte he had spread his message with evangelical fervor.

His team, which had been ranked No. 1 more frequently than any other, did not get enough respect. His team, which counted the President of the United States among its biggest fans, did not get enough recognition. That had been his message and it didn't matter whether he believed it or was just using it as a ploy.

What mattered was that his players believed it and that had caused them to transform their season into a mission. Any number of them had used that term while accompanying their coach through the tourney, and now, with the table set in the ultimate game, they had their opportunity to bring their mission to a successful close.

With 75 seconds remaining— and 21 on the shot clock— Richardson called a time-out to settle his players. When play resumed, the ball was in the hands of Hog guard Corey Beck under the Duke basket. Beck had been a dervish this evening, which he would end with 15 points and 10 rebounds, but here he played it smart and kicked it out toward Dwight Stewart at the top of the circle.

"I was squaring up [to shoot], but I fum-

Coach **Nolan Richardson** holds up the national championship trophy after guiding Arkansas to an overall 31-3 record and the school's first NCAA basketball title.

bled the ball," Stewart would later remember, and then he spotted teammate Scotty Thurman to his right and wide open. Thurman, who can be as smooth as cream spilling across a dance floor, accepted Stewart's hurried pass, and knew that just a tick, maybe two, remained on the shot clock.

Duke forward Antonio Lang knew that too, and as Thurman rose to shoot a three-pointer, Lang flew at him with his right hand reaching for the clouds. "I saw the shot clock going down," Thurman said later, "so when the ball came to me, I had no choice but to put it up. But his whole body was in my face."

"I thought I could tip it," said Lang. "That's how close I was."

But the arc Thurman put on his shot was extreme— a rainbow for the ages— clearing Lang's hand before floating slowly toward the basket and finding nothing but net with 50.7 seconds left. Arkansas by three, 73-70.

"I still don't know how it went in," Lang said afterward. "It was just a big-time play on Scotty's part."

"You're surprised, huh?" Thurman yelled at the Hog doubters on press row as he hurried back up the court.

Hard on his heels were the attacking Blue Devils, who knew just how to play in these final, frantic moments. But here Chris Collins, their sophomore guard, inexplicably launched a 26-footer with some 20 seconds left on the shot clock and 35 seconds on the game clock. It rattled in-and-out and was rebounded by Thurman.

"It felt good when I shot it," said Collins. "It probably felt as good as any shot I took in the game."

"It was a tough shot, but Chris hits shots like that," said Duke coach Mike Krzyzewski. "I wouldn't say the game was won or lost on one shot. They just had a little more firepower than us."

But now all that firepower needed tempering, needed only to play smart and make the foul shots the Hogs were sure to get in these last seconds. Clint McDaniel, another of their guards, made one-of-two, and then after Collins missed a twisting, driving layup, Beck also made one-of-two. That pushed Arkansas' lead to five, but after an offensive rebound by Duke center Cherokee

Parks, it was back down to three with 10.2 seconds yet remaining.

Duke still had a chance to weave its magic, but Arkansas was not about to fumble this one away. The Hogs inbounded the ball to McDaniel, Duke fouled him and he made the back end of a one and one. Stewart then stripped Hill of the ball to finally pull down the curtain on the game, the season, and conventional images. Arkansas wins, 76-72.

Bill Clinton, a President who knows all about images, was soon congratulating Richardson and his players. Richardson then showed up for his press conference in a t-shirt that bore the words: "National Champions." He had gotten it made up days earlier, that's how confident he was, and had laid it on the locker room floor just before the game, once more stoking the flames he had long ago ignited. The anger and the fury he had exhibited, he had used intelligently to spur his players to the pinnacle, and now he would revel in the moment.

A day earlier, after hearing a media oracle say the smarter team, the Duke team, would win, he had bristled, saying, "No question Mike has done a tremendous job. I'll say he's one of the greatest coaches there is. I'm not on an ego trip, so I don't have a problem with that. What you perceive, that's what I have a problem with."

Now, those perceptions shattered, he said, "It was a battle of a couple heavyweights. Your turn. My turn. Your turn. My turn."

And right in the thick of it was sophomore forward Corliss Williamson, the SEC Player of the Year and the Final Four's Most Outstanding Player. In the semifinals against Arizona, he led the way to a 91-82 win with 29 points, 13 rebounds and five assists. Against Duke he scored 23 points, grabbed eight boards and helped drag the Hogs back from 10 points down early in the second half. "Us coming back from a 10-point deficit, I think that's what really broke Duke's back," he said. "I don't think they expected us to come back."

"All we wanted was a little respect," added Thurman, who contributed 15 points in the final. "But we won the whole thing, so I guess we got a lot of respect."

"What a great championship game," said Krzyzewski. "It was a game somebody won and nobody lost, that's the way I look at it.

It's hard for me to be disappointed."

It would have been hard to script a more fitting climax to the 1993-94 college basketball season, which was every bit as rambunctious and contentious as the game for the championship had been.

During the season six teams— Arkansas, Duke, Kansas, Kentucky, North Carolina and UCLA— took turns atop the polls, and from Jan. 3 to Feb. 14, the No. 1 ranking in the AP Top 25 changed hands seven consecutive weeks. Along the way upsets were as frequent as complaints about officiating and teams from so-called minor conferences regularly whacked those from conferences considered major.

It was a season during which the Black Coaches Association threatened to boycott games, and the actions of countless coaches belied all those speeches they give on the need for self-discipline and control in stressful situations.

Examples from that last category stretched from the ridiculous to the dangerous. There was Temple coach John Chaney crashing the postgame press conference of Massachusetts coach John Calipari, and threatening to both "kill him" and "kick his ass" because he thought Calipari had been trying to verbally intimidate the referees after a one-point Atlantic 10 victory over Temple on Feb. 13. Chaney later apologized and served a one-game suspension for his intemperate remarks. There was Texas A&M coach Tony Barone joining some of his Aggies in an assault on Texas Tech fans, and Rollie Massimino of Nevada-Las Vegas challenging one of his own supporters to a fist fight.

Arizona's Lute Olson and Todd Bozeman of California screamed at each other during their Pac-10 meeting in Berkeley, while Cincinnati's Bob Huggins refused to shake hands with Xavier's Pete Gillen after their intra-city contest in Cincinnati. Krzyzewski, Kentucky's Rick Pitino, Roy Williams of Kansas and Indiana icon Bob Knight each took time out during the season to chastise his own fans for one shortcoming or another, and Knight garnered additional headlines after berating his son Pat for a turnover near the end of 101-82 Hoosier rout of Notre Dame.

Then there was Dale Brown and Ricky Byrdsong. Brown, the tightly-wrapped LSU coach, had to be restrained by campus

After leading the nation in scoring and sweeping the Player of the Year awards, Purdue junior **Glenn Robinson** declared for the NBA Draft and was the overall first choice.

police in Tuscaloosa after trying to bring a particularly abusive Alabama supporter to justice. According to Brown, the "psycho" fan had showered his bench with obscenities and spit. "I said I wanted to make a citizen's arrest," said Brown, "and they (the cops) just laughed."

Byrdsong, the Northwestern coach, also

left his bench for the stands on a Feb. 5th visit to Minnesota. Only instead of trying to bust opposition fans he was seen shaking hands with them as his team lost its eighth game in a row. Two days later, he was granted a leave of absence to clear his head and returned as coach two weeks later. The Wildcats finished at 15-13 and made it to the second round of the NIT.

But all these contretemps were ultimately overshadowed by the controversy that erupted between the Black Coaches Association and the NCAA [see sidebar]. After the restoration of a 14th scholarship to Division I men's basketball was voted down at the NCAA Convention in January, the BCA threatened to boycott regular season games and hinted it might stage some unspecified demonstration in Charlotte during the Final Four. None of the threats came to pass, however, thanks to the intervention of the Congressional Black Caucus.

Out on the court, Purdue junior forward Glenn Robinson was everyone's choice for Player of the Year, leading the nation in scoring (30.3 points per game) as he carried the Boilermakers to a 26-4 regular season record and the Big 10 championship. In the NCAA's, Robinson & Co. reached the Southeast Regional final where they lost to Duke, 69-60.

After announcing his decision to give up his final year of college eligibility and turn pro, Robinson was selected by the Milwaukee Bucks as the first overall pick of the NBA Draft. He thus became the first collegian to win the scoring title, be named Player of the Year and get picked first in the NBA Draft all in the same year.

Robinson was a unanimous All-America choice along with Hill of Duke (a senior), sophomore guard Jason Kidd of California and Connecticut junior forward Donyell Marshall. Louisville junior forward Clifford Rozier rounded out the consensus first team. Kidd, Marshall and Rozier all joined Robinson in declaring early for the draft.

In all, 20 underclassmen went pro, including Michigan juniors Juwan Howard and Jalen Rose, leaving only Jimmy King and Ray Jackson of the original Fab Five. The fifth member, Chris Webber, bolted for the pros in 1993 and became the NBA's Rookie of the Year with Golden State. Three other noteworthy early exits were Cal junior and Pac-10 scoring champ Lamond Murray, Cincinnati freshman Dontonio Wingfield and George Washington's 7-foot-1 sophomore Yinka Dare.

Back to the season. The parade of upsets began in the second week when UMass upset No. 1 North Carolina in overtime, 91-86, in the semifinals of the Pre-Season NIT. The defending NCAA champion Tar

Black Coaches Back Off Their Boycott Threat

Boycotts recall another era, an era when the Civil Rights movement was in full flower and unconventional methods nudged a nation toward racial equality. But last basketball season, more than a quarter of a century after the death of Martin Luther King Jr., the Black Coaches Association [BCA] raised the spectre of civil disobedience to draw attention to its many concerns.

"Simply stated," said Southern Cal coach George Raveling, "this is about African-American children. There is a growing body of evidence that the system has lost respect for African-Americans."

"It wasn't any one thing that pushed us to the brink," added Ohio State coach Randy Ayers. "It's been a growing thing, something we've talked about over the last two, three years. The association felt it was finally time to take a stand."

"Anyone who thinks this is about one scholarship, that's an insult," concluded Wisconsin coach Stu Jackson. "It's about a number of issues and philosophies held by the NCAA, and how they deal with student-athletes across the board."

Jackson spoke near mid-season, shortly after January's NCAA Convention refused to restore a 14th basketball scholarship at 297 Division I schools. Nearly two-thirds of all Division I players on scholarship are black. While the scholarship issue was the catalyst that made the boycott a real possibility, it wasn't the only problem.

The BCA was also concerned about coaches' access to players, which is now limited by NCAA rules; about the lack of opportunities for minority students, whom it felt are disproportionately effected by the NCAA's ever-increasing academic standards; and about the NCAA's abolishment of an entry-level coaching position, which diminishes opportunities for young-and-aspiring coaches [both male and female]. Added to that were issues regarding the scarcity of black female coaches in women's basketball and the few number of black administrators in decision-making positions.

In short, the 3,000-member BCA was concerned about equity and fairness and having its grievances listened to by the NCAA. That's

Congressional Black Caucus

Southern Cal coach **George Raveling** answers questions during Jan. 14 press conference in Washington convened by the Black Coaches Association and the Congressional Black Caucus. To the left of Raveling is Cong. **Kweisi Mfume** (D., Md.) and to the right are Cong. **Cardiss Collins** (D., Ill.) and Cong. **John Conyers Jr**. (D., Mich.).

why it met in Norfolk, Va., in mid-August of 1993 and again in Chicago in early October. It's also why it boycotted an Oct. 19-21 issues forum sponsored by the National Association of Basketball Coaches.

"Marching, boycotts, things that changed America— we've looked at them. They were very effective," said Drake coach Rudy Washington, the BCA's executive director. "We have a lot of actions like that planned, but we're not talking about them. We know exactly what we're going to do and how we're going to do it. But when you go to war, you don't tell the enemy what you're doing."

The boycott of the NABC forum and statements like Washington's captured some headlines, but the conflict soon faded from public consciousness. Until the NCAA Convention in San Antonio, Jan. 8-12.

The refusal by the NCAA's rank and file to restore a 14th scholarship lit an already short BCA fuse and threatened to blow up the season. The BCA talked aloud of boycotting games as soon as Jan. 15 (Martin Luther King Jr.'s birthday), reportedly targeting those games that matched minority coaches. Some coaches even implied that they would take their players out on strike with them, effec- tively forfeiting games and TV money. And down the road, the BCA pointedly declared, were possible demonstrations in Charlotte during the Final Four.

Prominent white coaches like Duke's Mike Krzyzewski, Denny Crum of Louisville and Roy Williams of Kansas hinted broadly that they would support any BCA action a devel- opment that, not surprisingly, led to a flurry of activity. There were calls between the BCA and the NCAA. There was a Jan. 13 meeting involving representatives of the BCA and the Congressional Black Caucus. And finally, just a day before the first boycotts were to occur came the announcement that the Justice Department, in some unspecified manner, was going to intervene in the dispute.

That was enough to momentarily pull the dispute back from the brink and to assure that the season would be completed without inter- ruption. Yet nothing was actually resolved, so the BCA's concerns still exist and boycotts in the future are still a real possibility.

"Maybe the Justice Department will give some justice," said Nolan Richardson of Arkansas. "Maybe that's where we need to go. How did civil rights come about? The gov- ernment had to step in."

277

Heels, with four returning starters and a trio of heralded frosh, had looked invincible until that moment. But their stumble in New York presaged the rude treatment both they and other favorites would receive throughout the year.

It seemed like the only surprising thing about all the upsets was when one didn't occur.

Alabama lost to Tennessee-Chattanooga, the College of Charleston and South Carolina, then defeated Arkansas, 66-64. And how about the Big South? Towson State beat St. John's of the Big East; Radford beat LSU of the SEC; Coastal Carolina beat South Carolina of the SEC; and Campbell beat both South Carolina and the ACC's North Carolina State.

Meanwhile, N.C. State beat tourney-bound Maryland on a Wednesday, and lost to Division I newcomer Florida Atlantic the following Monday. Wake Forest lost to Alaska-Anchorage and beat Duke twice; Clemson lost to Davidson and defeated North Carolina; Arizona State lost to Northeastern Illinois and defeated Arizona; and Notre Dame defeated Missouri and UCLA and lost to Duquesne, St. Bonaventure, Manhattan and Loyola of Chicago.

Georgia Tech, which upset North Carolina twice, was itself victimized by enough upsets to miss its first NCAA tourney in a decade. The Yellow Jackets (16-13) may have been the NCAA's best-known absentee, but there were 18 other schools which did not get tournament invitations despite winning 20 games or more.

Liberty University, which finished a modest 18-11, did get its first bid by winning the Big South tourney, and that gave its founder— the Rev. Jerry Falwell— the opportunity to cut down the nets. Others that would make their first tourney appearances were Loyola of Maryland, Southwest Texas State and Central Florida.

All four tournament first-timers lost their opening games, but there were still some first round shockers. The most notable early exits were by Pac-10 powers California (beaten by Wisconsin-Green Bay) and UCLA (sent packing by Tulsa). And Big Eight tournament champion Nebraska lost to Ivy champ Penn.

The trend continued in the second round with Boston College upsetting No. 1 North Carolina, Marquette ousting No. 7 Kentucky and Maryland tripping No. 8 UMass.

Form took over in the later rounds, however, producing a Final Four of one top-seed (Arkansas), two No. 2 seeds (Duke and Arizona) and a third seed (Florida).

By getting his team to Charlotte in just his fourth year at Florida, Gator coach Lon Kruger stamped himself as one of the season's surprising success stories. Missouri's Norm Stewart was another, guiding his Tigers through their Big Eight schedule undefeated after they lost by 52 to Arkansas in early December.

Maryland's Gary Williams, with a starting lineup composed of three sophomores and two freshmen, returned the Terps to the spotlight and Charlie Spoonhour did the same at Saint Louis, which opened the year with 14 straight wins and ended it in the tourney for the first time since 1957.

Kevin O'Neill resurrected memories of Al McGuire's glory days at Marquette with a 24-9 season, then skipped off to Tennessee to replace Wade Houston, who had resigned after five unsuccessful seasons. O'Neill was replaced by Siena's Mike Deane, in what was just the start of a wild game of postseason musical chairs.

By the first of June, 48 Division I schools had changed coaches. Two legends, Iowa State's Johnny Orr and Hofstra's Butch van Breda Kolff, retired. Billy Tubbs left Oklahoma for Texas Christian; Rick Barnes left Providence for Clemson; Xavier's Gillen moved to Providence and Clemson's Cliff Ellis to Auburn; Western Kentucky lost Ralph Willard to Pittsburgh; and former Alabama coach Wimp Sanderson resurfaced at Arkansas-Little Rock.

In women's basketball, where coaches tend to stay put, Tennessee's Pat Summitt won her 500th game in her 20th season in Knoxville. The Vols ended the regular season ranked No. 1, but were beaten by Louisiana Tech in the third round of the NCAAs. Tech lost to North Carolina, 60-59, in the NCAA Final on a last-second three-pointer by Charlotte Smith (see page 291).

A day later, Thurman's trey with less than a minute left won the men's title for Arkansas and with that the college basketball year exhaled and was finally over. ❑

THE 1995 SPORTS ALMANAC — INFORMATION PLEASE

COLLEGE BASKETBALL
S T A T I S T I C S

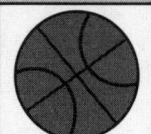

THE SEASON IN REVIEW
1993-1994
TOP 25 • NCAA'S • STANDINGS

SEC
A

PAGE
279

Final Regular Season AP Men's Top 25 Poll
Taken **before** start of NCAA tournament.

The sportswriters & broadcasters poll: first place votes in parentheses; records through March 13; total points (based on 25 for 1st, 24 for 2nd, etc.); record in 1994 NCAA tourney and team lost to; head coach (career years and record including '94 postseason), and preseason ranking. Teams in **bold** type went on to reach NCAA Final Four.

		Mar.13 Record	Points	NCAA Recap	Head Coach	Preseason Rank
1	North Carolina (37)	27-6	1576	1-1 (Boston Col.)	Dean Smith (33 yrs: 802-230)	1
2	**Arkansas** (16)	25-3	1546	6-0	Nolan Richardson (14 yrs: 339-112)	3
3	Purdue (11)	26-4	1493	3-1 (Duke)	Gene Keady (16 yrs: 335-154)	21
4	Connecticut	27-4	1400	2-1 (Florida)	Jim Calhoun (22 yrs: 410-228)	21
5	Missouri	25-3	1352	3-1 (Arizona)	Norm Stewart (33 yrs: 640-310)	34
6	**Duke**	23-5	1252	5-1 (Arkansas)	Mike Krzyzewski (19 yrs: 422-183)	4
7	Kentucky	26-6	1236	1-1 (Marquette)	Rick Pitino (12 yrs: 255-112)	2
8	Massachusetts (1)	27-6	1229	1-1 (Maryland)	John Calipari (6 yrs: 129-64)	22
9	**Arizona**	25-5	1095	4-1 (Arkansas)	Lute Olson (21 yrs: 458-179)	18
10	Louisville	26-5	1039	2-1 (Arizona)	Denny Crum (23 yrs: 546-198)	7
11	Michigan	21-7	996	3-1 (Arkansas)	Steve Fisher (6 yrs: 123-45)	5
12	Temple	22-7	840	1-1 (Indiana)	John Chaney (22 yrs: 501-164)	8
13	Kansas	25-7	777	2-1 (Purdue)	Roy Williams (6 yrs: 159-45)	9
14	**Florida**	25-7	758	4-1 (Duke)	Lon Kruger (12 yrs: 208-156)	NR
15	Syracuse	21-6	743	2-1 (Missouri)	Jim Boeheim (18 yrs: 434-140)	20
16	California	22-7	574	0-1 (Wisc-GB)	Todd Bozeman (2 yrs: 33-10)	6
17	UCLA	21-6	559	0-1 (Tulsa)	Jim Harrick (15 yrs: 304-150)	13
18	Indiana	19-8	396	2-1 (Boston Col.)	Bob Knight (29 yrs: 640-223)	12
19	Oklahoma St	23-9	384	1-1 (Tulsa)	Eddie Sutton (24 yrs: 526-199)	11
20	Texas	25-7	291	1-1 (Michigan)	Tom Penders (23 yrs: 402-273)	30
21	Marquette	22-8	265	2-1 (Duke)	Kevin O'Neill (6 yrs: 103-76)	27
22	Nebraska	20-9	217	0-1 (Penn)	Danny Nee (14 yrs: 253-170)	39
23	Minnesota	20-11	202	1-1 (Louisville)	Clem Haskins (14 yrs: 233-185)	10
24	Saint Louis	23-5	192	0-1 (Maryland)	Charlie Spoonhour (11 yrs: 232-104)	NR
25	Cincinnati	22-9	188	0-1 (Wisconsin)	Bob Huggins (13 yrs: 284-118)	19

Others receiving votes: 26. **Penn** (24-2, 126 pts); 27. **Wake Forest** (20-11, 119); 28. **Ala-Birmingham** (22-7, 88); 29. Providence (20-9, 72); 30. **Virginia** (17-12, 36); 31. **Boston College** (20-10, 17); 32. **Alabama** (19-9, 15) and **Michigan St.** (19-11, 15); 34. **Illinois** (17-10, 9); 35. **Ohio Univ.** (25-7, 7); 36. **New Mexico St.** (23-7, 6); 37. **WI-Green Bay** (26-6, 5); 38. **SW Louisiana** (22-7, 4); 39. **Washington St.** (20-10, 2); 40. **College of Charleston** (24-3, 1), **Murray St.** (23-5, 1), **Western Ky.** (20-10, 1) and **Wisconsin** (17-10, 1).

NCAA Men's Division I Tournament Seeds

	WEST		MIDWEST		SOUTHEAST		EAST
1	Missouri (25-3)	1	**Arkansas** (25-3)	1	Purdue (26-4)	1	North Carolina (27-6)
2	**Arizona** (25-5)	2	UMass (27-6)	2	**Duke** (23-5)	2	UConn (27-4)
3	Louisville (26-5)	3	Michigan (21-7)	3	Kentucky (26-6)	3	**Florida** (25-7)
4	Syracuse (21-6)	4	Oklahoma St. (23-9)	4	Kansas (25-7)	4	Temple (22-7)
5	California (22-7)	5	UCLA (21-6)	5	Wake Forest (20-11)	5	Indiana (19-8)
6	Minnesota (20-11)	6	Texas (25-7)	6	Marquette (22-8)	6	Nebraska (20-9)
7	Virginia (17-12)	7	Saint Louis (23-5)	7	Michigan St. (19-11)	7	Ala-Birmingham (22-7)
8	Cincinnati (22-9)	8	Illinois (17-10)	8	Providence (20-9)	8	Washington St. (20-10)
9	Wisconsin (17-10)	9	Georgetown (18-11)	9	Alabama (19-9)	9	Boston College (20-10)
10	New Mexico (23-7)	10	Maryland (16-11)	10	Seton Hall (17-12)	10	Geo.Washington (17-11)
11	Southern Ill. (23-6)	11	Western Ky. (20-10)	11	SW Louisiana (22-7)	11	Penn (24-2)
12	WI-Green Bay (26-6)	12	Tulsa (21-7)	12	Charleston (24-3)	12	Ohio Univ. (25-7)
13	Hawaii (18-14)	13	New Mexico St. (23-7)	13	Tenn-Chatt. (23-6)	13	Drexel (25-4)
14	Boise St. (17-12)	14	Pepperdine (19-8)	14	Tennessee St. (19-11)	14	James Madison (20-9)
15	Loyola-MD (17-12)	15	SW Texas St. (25-6)	15	TX Southern (19-10)	15	Rider (21-8)
16	Navy (17-12)	16	N. Car. A&T (16-13)	16	Central Fla. (21-8)	16	Liberty (18-11)

1994 NCAA BASKETBALL MEN'S DIVISION I

EAST

1ST ROUND — March 17-18

Seed / Team	Score
1 North Carolina	71
16 Liberty	51
8 Washington St.	64
9 Boston College	67
5 Indiana	84
12 Ohio Univ.	72
4 Temple	61
13 Drexel	39
6 Nebraska	80
11 Penn	90
3 Florida	64
14 James Madison	46
7 Al-Birmingham	46
10 G. Washington	51
2 Connecticut	64
15 Rider	46

2ND ROUND — March 19-20

- N. Carolina 72
- Boston Col. 75
- Indiana 67
- Temple 58
- Penn 58
- Florida 70
- G. Washington 63
- UConn 75

REGIONALS — March 24-27 / MIAMI

- Boston Col. 77
- Indiana 68
- Florida 69 (OT)
- UConn 60
- Boston Col. 66
- Florida 74
- Florida 65

SOUTHEAST

1ST ROUND — March 17-18

Seed / Team	Score
1 Purdue	98
16 Central Fla.	67
8 Providence	70
9 Alabama	76
5 Wake Forest	68
12 Charleston	58
4 Kansas	102
13 Tenn-Chatt.	73
6 Marquette	81
11 SW Louisiana	59
3 Kentucky	83
14 Tennessee St.	70
7 Michigan St.	84
10 Seton Hall	73
2 Duke	82
15 TX Southern	70

2ND ROUND — March 19-20

- Purdue 83
- Alabama 73
- Wake Forest 58
- Kansas 69
- Marquette 75
- Kentucky 63
- Michigan St. 74
- Duke 85

REGIONALS / KNOXVILLE

- Purdue 83
- Kansas 78
- Marquette 49
- Duke 59
- Purdue 60
- Duke 69
- Duke 70

MIDWEST

1ST ROUND — March 17-18

Seed / Team	Score
1 Arkansas	94
16 N.C. A&T	79
8 Illinois	77
9 Georgetown	84
5 UCLA	102
12 Tulsa	112
4 Oklahoma St.	65
13 N. Mexico St.	55
6 Texas	91
11 Western Ky.	77
3 Michigan	78
14 Pepperdine (OT)	74
7 Saint Louis	66
10 Maryland	74
2 Massachusetts	78
15 SW Texas St.	60

2ND ROUND — March 19-20

- Arkansas 85
- Georgetown 73
- Tulsa 82
- Oklahoma St. 80
- Texas 79
- Michigan 84
- Maryland 95
- UMass 87

REGIONALS — March 25 and 27 / DALLAS

- Arkansas 103
- Tulsa 84
- Michigan 78
- Maryland 71
- Arkansas 76
- Michigan 68
- Arkansas 91

WEST

1ST ROUND — March 17-18

Seed / Team	Score
1 Missouri	76
16 Navy	53
8 Cincinnati	72
9 Wisconsin	80
5 California	57
12 Wi-Green Bay	61
4 Syracuse	92
13 Hawaii	78
6 Minnesota	74
11 Southern Ill.	60
3 Louisville	67
14 Boise St.	58
7 Virginia	57
10 New Mexico	54
2 Arizona	81
15 Loyola-MD	55

2ND ROUND — March 19-20

- Missouri 109
- Wisconsin 96
- Wi-Green Bay 59
- Syracuse 64
- Minnesota 55
- Louisville 60
- Virginia 58
- Arizona 71

REGIONALS / LOS ANGELES

- Missouri 98 (OT)
- Syracuse 88
- Louisville 70
- Arizona 82
- Missouri 72
- Arizona 92
- Arizona 82

NATIONAL CHAMPIONSHIP

Arkansas 76 — Duke 72

NCAA FINAL FOUR 1994 CHARLOTTE

FINAL FOUR
at the Charlotte (N.C.) Coliseum

Semifinals: April 2
Final: April 4

NCAA Men's Championship Game

56th NCAA Division I Championship Game **Date:** Monday, April 4, at the Charlotte (N.C.) Coliseum. **Coaches:** Nolan Richardson of Arkansas and Mike Krzyzewski of Duke. **Favorite:** Arkansas by 4. **Attendance:** 23,674; **Officials:** Jim Burr, Jody Silvestri and Ted Valentine; **TV Rating:** 21.6/33 share (CBS).

Duke 72

	Min	FG M-A	FT M-A	Pts	Reb O-T	A	PF
Grant Hill	38	4-11	3-5	12	1-14	6	3
Antonio Lang	34	6-9	3-3	15	3-5	3	5
Cherokee Parks	30	7-10	0-1	14	3-7	0	3
Jeff Capel	35	6-16	0-0	14	1-5	4	3
Chris Collins	34	4-11	0-0	12	0-0	1	1
Marty Clark	15	1-6	1-2	3	1-1	3	2
Eric Meek	14	1-2	0-0	2	3-7	0	1
TOTALS	200	29-65	7-11	72	12-39	17	18

Three-point FG: 7-20 (Collins 4-8, Capel 2-6, Hill 1-4, Clark 0-2); **Team Rebounds:** 5 (not listed above); **Blocked Shots:** 7 (Hill 3, Parks 2, Lang, Collins); **Turnovers:** 23 (Hill 9, Capel 6, Lang 5, Clark 2, Collins); **Steals:** 5 (Hill 3, Capel, Collins) **Percentages:** 2-Pt FG (.489), 3-Pt FG (.350), Total FG (.446), Free Throws (.636).

Arkansas 76

	Min	FG M-A	FT M-A	Pts	Reb O-T	A	PF
Corliss Williamson	35	10-24	3-5	23	7-8	3	3
Ken Biley	3	0-0	0-0	0	0-0	0	1
Dwight Stewart	29	3-11	0-0	6	4-9	4	3
Corey Beck	35	5-11	5-8	15	2-10	4	3
Scotty Thurman	36	6-13	0-0	15	1-5	1	2
Clint McDaniel	32	2-5	2-4	7	0-2	3	2
Darnell Robinson	12	1-5	0-0	2	1-2	0	1
Al Dillard	8	1-5	1-2	4	1-1	0	1
Davor Rimac	5	0-1	0-0	0	0-0	0	0
Lee Wilson	5	2-2	0-0	4	1-4	0	1
TOTALS	200	30-77	11-19	76	17-41	15	17

Three-point FG: 5-18 (Thurman 3-5, McDaniel 1-3, Dillard 1-4, Beck 0-1, Stewart 0-5); **Team Rebounds:** 3 (not listed above); **Blocked Shots:** 3 (Williamson 2, Rimac); **Turnovers:** 12 (Williamson 5, Beck 3, Wilson, McDaniel, Robinson, Stewart); **Steals:** 11 (Stewart 4, McDaniel 3, Williamson 2, Beck, Thurman); **Percentages:** 2-Pt FG (.424), 3-Pt FG (.278), Total FG (.390), Free Throws (.579).

Duke (ACC) .... 33 39— **72**
Arkansas (SEC) .... 34 42— **76**

THE FINAL FOUR

Charlotte (N.C.) Coliseum (April 2-4)

Most Outstanding Player

Corliss Williamson, Arkansas sophomore forward. SEMIFINAL— 37 minutes, 29 points, 13 rebounds, 5 assists; FINAL— 35 minutes, 23 points, 8 rebounds, 3 assists.

All-Tournament Team

Williamson and guards Corey Beck and Scotty Thurman of Arkansas; forwards Grant Hill and Antonio Lang of Duke.

Semifinal—Game One

Midwest Regional champion Arkansas vs. West Regional champ Arizona; Saturday, April 2 (5:42 p.m tipoff). Coaches: Nolan Richardson, Arkansas and Lute Olson, Arizona. Favorite: Arkansas by 2½.
Arizona (Pac-10) 41   41— **82**
Arkansas (SEC) 41   50— **91**
High scorers—Corliss Williamson, Ark (29) and Khalid Reeves, Ariz (20); **Att**—23,674; **TV rating**—13.2/31 share (CBS).

Semifinal—Game Two

Southeast Regional champion Duke vs. East Regional champ Florida; Saturday, April 2 (8:15 p.m tipoff). Coaches: Mike Krzyzewski, Duke and Lon Kruger, Florida. Favorite: Duke by 6½.
Florida (SEC) 39   26— **65**
Duke (ACC) 32   38— **70**
High scorers—Grant Hill, Duke (25) and Dametri Hill, Florida (16); **Att**—23,674; **TV rating**—14.0/26 share (CBS).

Final USA Today/CNN Coaches Poll

Taken **after** NCAA Tournament.

Voted on by a panel of 34 Division I head coaches following the NCAA tournament; first place votes in parentheses with total points (based on 25 for 1st, 24 for 2nd, etc.). Schools on major probation are ineligible to be ranked.

		After NCAAs		Before NCAAs	
		W-L	Pts	W-L	Rank
1	Arkansas (34)	31-3	850	25-3	1
2	Duke	28-6	816	23-5	6
3	Arizona	29-6	773	25-5	10
4	Florida	29-8	737	25-7	15
5	Purdue	29-5	702	26-4	4
6	Missouri	28-4	656	25-3	5
7	Connecticut	29-5	635	27-4	3
8	Michigan	24-8	618	21-7	11
9	North Carolina	28-7	547	27-6	2
10	Louisville	28-6	512	26-5	9
11	Boston College	23-11	496	20-10	30
12	Kansas	27-8	468	25-7	13
13	Kentucky	27-7	407	26-6	8
14	Syracuse	23-7	388	21-6	14
15	Massachusetts	28-7	373	27-6	7
16	Indiana	21-9	359	19-8	18
17	Marquette	24-9	324	22-8	22
18	Temple	23-8	274	22-7	12
19	Tulsa	23-8	216	21-7	31
20	Maryland	18-12	176	16-11	45t
21	Oklahoma St	24-10	150	23-9	19
22	UCLA	21-7	128	21-6	16
23	Minnesota	21-12	112	20-11	20
24	Texas	26-8	75	25-7	24
25	Penn	25-3	47	24-2	27

NCAA Finalists' Tournament and Season Statistics

At least 10 games played during the overall season.

Arkansas (31-3)

| | | NCAA Tournament | | | | | | Overall Season | | | |
| | | | Per Game | | | | | | Per Game | | |
	Gm	FG%	TPts	Pts	Reb	Ast	Gm	FG%	TPts	Pts	Reb	Ast
Corliss Williamson	6	.618	130	21.7	8.2	3.3	34	.626	695	20.4	7.7	2.2
Scotty Thurman	6	.500	97	16.2	3.5	3.5	34	.469	539	15.9	4.5	3.0
Corey Beck	6	.486	60	10.0	5.7	4.7	34	.506	299	8.8	3.9	5.0
Clint McDaniel	6	.514	56	9.3	4.0	1.5	31	.407	252	8.1	2.8	1.9
Darnell Robinson	6	.535	55	9.2	3.0	1.3	27	.457	205	7.6	4.7	1.9
Dwight Stewart	6	.486	52	8.7	5.5	2.5	34	.453	271	8.0	5.0	1.4
Al Dillard	6	.344	34	5.7	0.5	1.5	34	.404	302	8.9	1.1	1.4
Lee Wilson	6	.533	18	3.0	3.2	0.2	30	.493	103	3.4	3.1	0.4
Roger Crawford	2	.400	5	2.5	0.5	1.0	30	.556	221	7.4	1.9	2.0
Davor Rimac	6	.333	13	2.2	0.3	0.7	34	.455	163	4.8	1.9	0.9
Elmer Martin	4	.500	3	0.8	1.0	0.3	27	.308	35	1.3	1.2	0.5
Ken Biley	3	1.000	2	0.7	0.0	0.3	18	.655	50	2.8	2.1	0.2
Ray Biggers	3	.000	0	0.0	0.0	0.0	18	.172	19	1.1	2.2	0.9
ARKANSAS	6	.513	525	87.5	37.8	19.8	34	.488	3176	93.4	41.6	20.2
OPPONENTS	6	.388	458	76.3	41.5	15.5	34	.402	2569	75.6	40.5	14.1

Three-pointers: NCAA TOURNEY—Thurman (14-for-34), Stewart (11-20), McDaniel (9-22), Dillard (9-25), Rimac (2-9), Crawford (1-2), Beck (1-3), Robinson (0-2), Team (47-117 for .402 Pct.); OVERALL—Thurman (85-for-198), Dillard (75-183), McDaniel (38-108), Stewart (37-95), Rimac (32-79), Crawford (15-43), Robinson (7-23), Beck (5-11), Engskov (2-3), Biggers (2-15), Martin (2-17), Merritt (1-2), Team (301-777 for .387 Pct.).

Duke (28-6)

| | | NCAA Tournament | | | | | | Overall Season | | | |
| | | | Per Game | | | | | | Per Game | | |
	Gm	FG%	TPts	Pts	Reb	Ast	Gm	FG%	TPts	Pts	Reb	Ast
Grant Hill	6	.500	106	17.7	8.3	5.7	34	.462	591	17.4	6.9	5.2
Antonio Lang	6	.560	87	14.5	6.2	0.8	34	.588	424	12.5	5.4	1.0
Cherokee Parks	6	.471	87	14.5	9.2	0.7	34	.536	490	14.4	8.4	0.9
Jeff Capel	6	.431	70	11.7	3.8	3.8	34	.458	292	8.6	2.7	3.2
Chris Collins	6	.318	46	7.7	1.5	1.0	34	.400	341	10.0	2.0	2.3
Marty Clark	6	.260	20	3.3	1.3	2.0	33	.450	267	8.1	1.9	1.8
Eric Meek	6	.500	17	2.8	3.8	0.2	34	.545	120	3.5	4.2	0.4
Greg Newton	4	.000	0	0.0	0.3	0.0	21	.364	23	1.1	1.3	0.4
Carmen Wallace	0	—	—	—	—	—	17	.563	28	1.6	0.5	0.1
Joey Beard	0	—	—	—	—	—	16	.500	21	1.3	0.5	0.2
Tony Moore	0	—	—	—	—	—	18	.600	19	1.1	0.8	0.2
DUKE	6	.452	437	72.8	37.2	14.3	34	.486	2639	77.6	36.1	15.6
OPPONENTS	6	.405	394	65.7	37.3	14.3	34	.415	2289	67.3	35.2	12.9

Three-pointers: NCAA TOURNEY—Collins (10-for-32), Hill (8-16), Capel (8-18), Clark (3-11), Team (29-77 for .377 Pct.); OVERALL—Collins (76-for-202), Hill (39-100), Capel (32-76), Clark (18-64), Parks (3-17), Blakeney (2-3), Wallace (2-5), Beard (0-2), Lang (0-2), Team (172-471 for .365 Pct.).

Arkansas' Schedule

Regular Season (24-2)

W	Murray St	93-67
W	Missouri	120-68
W	N'western St	111-76
W	at Memphis St	96-78
W	Delaware St	123-66
W	Jackson St	96-80
W	at Tulsa (OT)	93-91
W	TX Southern	129-63
W	SMU	96-70
W	Mississippi	87-61
L	at Alabama	64-66
W	LSU	84-83
W	at Auburn	117-105
L	at Miss. St	71-72
W	S. Carolina	79-53
W	at Tennessee	65-64
W	Vanderbilt	89-76
W	Montevallo	131-63
W	at Kentucky	90-82
W	Florida	99-87
W	Alabama	102-81
W	at Mississippi	90-73
W	at Georgia	74-65
W	Auburn	91-81
W	at LSU (OT)	108-105
W	Miss. St	80-62

SEC Tourney (1-1)

W	Georgia	95-83
L	Kentucky	78-90

NCAA Tourney (6-0)

W	N.C. A&T	94-79
W	Georgetown	85-73
W	Tulsa	103-84
W	Michigan	76-68
W	Arizona	91-82
W	Duke	76-72

Duke's Schedule

Regular Season (23-5)

W	Northeastern	86-72
W	The Citadel	78-63
W	Xavier-OH	82-60
W	S.C. State	97-61
W	at Michigan	73-63
W	at Iowa	79-76
W	W. Carolina	87-67
W	at Clemson	71-65
W	Georgia Tech	88-71
W	Brown	89-71
L	Wake Forest	68-69
W	at Virginia	66-58
W	at N.C. State	92-65
W	Florida St	106-79
W	Notre Dame	74-72
W	Maryland	75-62
L	at N. Carolina	78-89
W	Clemson	78-74
W	at Ga. Tech	66-63
L	at Wake Forest	69-78
W	Virginia	84-54
W	N.C. State	85-58
W	at Florida St	84-72
W	Temple	59-47
W	at Maryland	73-69
L	N. Carolina	77-87
W	Clemson	77-64

ACC Tourney (1-1)

W	Clemson	77-64
L	Virginia	61-66

NCAA Tourney (5-1)

W	TX Southern	82-70
W	Michigan St	85-74
W	Marquette	59-49
W	Purdue	69-60
W	Florida	70-65
L	Arkansas	76-72

Final NCAA Men's Division I Standings

Conference records include regular season games only. Overall records include all postseason tournament games.

Atlantic Coast Conference

	Conference			Overall		
	W	L	Pct	W	L	Pct
*Duke	12	4	.750	28	6	.824
*North Carolina	11	5	.688	28	7	.800
*Wake Forest	9	7	.563	21	12	.636
*Maryland	8	8	.500	18	12	.600
*Virginia	8	8	.500	18	13	.581
†Georgia Tech	7	9	.438	16	13	.552
†Clemson	6	10	.375	18	16	.529
Florida St	6	10	.375	13	14	.481
N.C. State	5	11	.313	11	19	.367

Conf. Tourney Final: North Carolina 73, Virginia 66.
***NCAA Tourney (10-5):** Duke (5-1), Maryland (2-1), North Carolina (1-1), Virginia (1-1), Wake Forest (1-1).
†NIT Tourney (2-2): Clemson (2-1), Georgia Tech (0-1).

Atlantic 10 Conference

	Conference			Overall		
	W	L	Pct	W	L	Pct
*Massachusetts	14	2	.875	28	7	.800
*Temple	12	4	.750	23	8	.742
*George Washington	8	8	.500	18	12	.600
†West Virginia	8	8	.500	17	12	.586
†Duquesne	8	8	.500	17	13	.567
Rhode Island	7	9	.438	11	16	.407
Rutgers	6	10	.375	11	16	.407
St. Joseph's	5	11	.313	14	14	.500
St. Bonaventure	4	12	.250	10	17	.370

Conf. Tourney Final: Massachusetts 70, Temple 59.
***NCAA Tourney (3-3):** George Washington (1-1), Massachusetts (1-1), Temple (1-1).
†NIT Tourney (2-2): Duquesne (1-1), West Virginia (1-1).

Big East Conference

	Conference			Overall		
	W	L	Pct	W	L	Pct
*Connecticut	16	2	.889	29	5	.853
*Syracuse	13	5	.722	23	7	.767
*Boston College	11	7	.611	23	11	.676
*Providence	10	8	.556	20	10	.667
*Georgetown	10	8	.556	19	12	.613
†Villanova	10	8	.556	20	12	.625
*Seton Hall	8	10	.444	17	13	.567
Pittsburgh	7	11	.389	13	14	.481
St. John's	5	13	.278	12	17	.414
Miami-FL	0	18	.000	7	20	.259

Conf. Tourney Final: Providence 74, Georgetown 64.
***NCAA Tourney (8-6):** Boston College (3-1), UConn (2-1), Syracuse (2-1), Georgetown (1-1), Providence (0-1), Seton Hall (0-1).
†NIT Tourney (5-0): Villanova (5-0).

Big Eight Conference

	Conference			Overall		
	W	L	Pct	W	L	Pct
*Missouri	14	0	1.000	28	4	.875
*Oklahoma St	10	4	.714	24	10	.706
*Kansas	9	5	.643	27	8	.771
*Nebraska	7	7	.500	20	10	.667
†Oklahoma	6	8	.429	15	13	.536
†Kansas St	4	10	.286	20	14	.588
Iowa St	4–10		.286	14	13	.519
Colorado	2	12	.143	10	17	.370

Conf. Tourney Final: Nebraska 77, Oklahoma St. 68.
***NCAA Tourney (6-4):** Missouri (3-1), Kansas (2-1), Oklahoma St. (1-1), Nebraska (0-1).
†NIT Tourney (3-3): Kansas St. (3-2), Oklahoma (0-1).

Big Sky Conference

	Conference			Overall		
	W	L	Pct	W	L	Pct
Weber St	10	4	.714	20	10	.667
Idaho St	10	4	.714	18	9	.667
Idaho	9	5	.643	18	10	.643
Montana St	8	6	.571	16	11	.593
*Boise St	7	7	.500	17	13	.567
Montana	6	8	.429	19	9	.679
Northern Arizona	6	8	.429	13	13	.500
Eastern Washington	0	14	.000	5	21	.192

Conf. Tourney Final: Boise St. 85, Idaho St. 81.
***NCAA Tourney (0-1):** Boise St. (0-1).

Big South Conference

	Conference			Overall		
	W	L	Pct	W	L	Pct
Towson St	16	2	.889	22	8	.733
Campbell	14	4	.778	21	8	.724
Radford	13	5	.722	20	8	.714
*Liberty	13	5	.722	19	11	.633
NC-Greensboro	11	7	.611	15	12	.556
Charleston Southern	8	10	.444	10	17	.370
MD-Balt. County	6	12	.333	7	20	.259
Winthrop	5	13	.278	6	21	.222
NC-Asheville	3	15	.167	5	22	.185
Coastal Carolina	1	17	.056	6	20	.231

Probation: NC-Greensboro ineligible for postseason.
Conf. Tourney Final: Liberty 76, Campbell 62.
***NCAA Tourney (0-1):** Liberty (0-1).

Big Ten Conference

	Conference			Overall		
	W	L	Pct	W	L	Pct
*Purdue	14	4	.778	29	5	.853
*Michigan	13	5	.722	24	8	.750
*Indiana	12	6	.667	21	9	.700
*Minnesota	10	8	.556	21	12	.636
*Michigan St	10	8	.556	20	12	.625
*Illinois	10	8	.556	17	11	.607
*Wisconsin	8	10	.444	18	11	.621
Penn St	6	12	.333	13	14	.481
Ohio St	6	12	.333	13	16	.448
†Northwestern	5	13	.278	15	14	.517
Iowa	5	13	.278	11	16	.407

Conf. Tourney Final: Big Ten has no tournament.
***NCAA Tourney (11-7):** Michigan (3-1), Purdue (3-1), Indiana (2-1), Michigan St. (1-1), Minnesota (1-1), Wisconsin (1-1), Illinois (0-1).
†NIT Tourney (1-1): Northwestern (1-1).

Big West Conference

	Conference			Overall		
	W	L	Pct	W	L	Pct
*New Mexico St	12	6	.667	23	8	.742
Long Beach St	11	7	.611	17	10	.630
San Jose St	11	7	.611	15	12	.556
Utah St	11	7	.611	14	13	.519
Pacific	10	8	.556	17	14	.548
UNLV	10	8	.556	15	13	.536
UC-Santa Barbara	9	9	.500	13	17	.433
Nevada	6	12	.333	11	17	.393
CS-Fullerton	6	12	.333	8	19	.296
UC-Irvine	4	14	.222	10	20	.333

Conf. Tourney Final: New Mexico St. 70, UC-Irvine 64.
***NCAA Tourney (0-1):** New Mexico St. (0-1).

Final NCAA Men's Division I Standings (Cont.)

Colonial Athletic Association

	Conference			Overall		
	W	L	Pct	W	L	Pct
*James Madison	10	4	.714	20	10	.667
†Old Dominion	10	4	.714	21	10	.677
NC-Wilmington	9	5	.643	18	10	.643
Richmond	8	6	.571	14	14	.500
East Carolina	7	7	.500	15	12	.556
George Mason	5	9	.357	10	17	.370
American	5	9	.357	8	19	.296
William & Mary	2	12	.143	4	23	.148

Conf. Tourney Final: James Madison 77, Old Dominion 76.
***NCAA Tourney (0-1):** James Madison (0-1).
†NIT Tourney (1-1): Old Dominion (1-1).

East Coast Conference

	Conference			Overall		
	W	L	Pct	W	L	Pct
Troy St	5	0	1.000	13	14	.481
NE Illinois	4	1	.800	17	11	.607
Buffalo	3	2	.600	9	18	.333
Chicago St	2	3	.400	4	23	.148
Hofstra	1	4	.200	9	20	.310
Central Conn	0	5	.000	4	21	.160

Conf. Tourney Final: Hofstra 88, NE Illinois 86 (2 OT).

Great Midwest Conference

	Conference			Overall		
	W	L	Pct	W	L	Pct
*Marquette	10	2	.833	24	9	.727
*Saint Louis	8	4	.667	23	6	.793
*Ala-Birmingham	8	4	.667	22	8	.733
*Cincinnati	7	5	.583	22	10	.688
†DePaul	4	8	.333	16	12	.571
Memphis St	4	8	.333	13	16	.448
Dayton	1	11	.083	6	21	.222

Conf. Tourney Final: Cincinnati 68, Memphis St. 47.
***NCAA Tourney (2-4):** Marquette (2-1), Cincinnati (0-1), Ala-Birmingham (0-1), Saint Louis (0-1).
†NIT Tourney (0-1): DePaul (0-1).

Ivy League

	Conference			Overall		
	W	L	Pct	W	L	Pct
*Penn	14	0	1.000	25	3	.893
Princeton	11	3	.786	18	8	.692
Yale	7	7	.500	10	16	.385
Brown	6	8	.429	12	14	.462
Dartmouth	6	8	.429	10	16	.385
Harvard	5	9	.357	9	17	.346
Columbia	4	10	.286	6	20	.231
Cornell	3	11	.214	8	18	.308

Conf. Tourney Final: Ivy League has no tournament.
***NCAA Tourney (1-1):** Penn (1-1).

Metro Conference

	Conference			Overall		
	W	L	Pct	W	L	Pct
*Louisville	10	2	.833	28	6	.824
†Tulane	7	5	.583	18	11	.621
†NC-Charlotte	7	5	.583	16	13	.552
Virginia Tech	6	6	.500	18	10	.643
VCU	5	7	.417	14	13	.519
Southern Miss	5	7	.417	15	14	.517
South Florida	2	10	.167	10	17	.370

Conf. Tourney Final: Louisville 69, Southern Miss. 61.
***NCAA Tourney (2-1):** Louisville (2-1).
†NIT Tourney (1-2): Tulane (1-1), NC-Charlotte (0-1).

Metro Atlantic Conference

	Conference			Overall		
	W	L	Pct	W	L	Pct
†Canisius	12	2	.857	22	7	.759
†Siena	10	4	.714	25	8	.758
†Manhattan	10	4	.714	19	11	.633
St. Peter's	8	6	.571	14	13	.519
*Loyola-MD	6	8	.429	17	13	.567
Fairfield	4	10	.286	8	19	.296
Iona	3	11	.214	7	20	.259
Niagara	3	11	.214	6	21	.222

Conf. Tourney Final: Loyola-MD 80, Manhattan 75.
***NCAA Tourney (0-1):** Loyola-MD (0-1).
†NIT Tourney (4-3): Siena (4-1), Canisius (0-1), Manhattan (0-1).

Mid-American Conference

	Conference			Overall		
	W	L	Pct	W	L	Pct
*Ohio University	14	4	.778	25	8	.758
†Miami-OH	12	6	.667	19	11	.633
Bowling Green	12	6	.667	18	10	.643
Ball St	11	7	.611	16	12	.571
Eastern Michigan	10	8	.556	15	12	.556
Toledo	10	8	.556	15	12	.556
Kent	8	10	.444	13	14	.481
Western Michigan	7	11	.389	14	14	.500
Central Michigan	4	14	.222	5	21	.192
Akron	2	16	.111	8	18	.308

Conf. Tourney Final: Ohio University 89, Miami-OH 66.
***NCAA Tourney (0-1):** Ohio University (0-1).
†NIT Tourney (0-1): Miami-OH (0-1).

Mid-Continent Conference

	Conference			Overall		
	W	L	Pct	W	L	Pct
*WI-Green Bay	15	3	.833	27	7	.794
Valparaiso	14	4	.778	20	8	.714
Illinois-Chicago	14	4	.778	20	9	.690
Cleveland St	9	9	.500	14	15	.483
Wright St	9	9	.500	12	18	.400
Eastern Illinois	7	11	.389	12	15	.444
Northern Illinois	7	11	.389	10	17	.370
WI-Milwaukee	7	11	.389	10	17	.370
Western Illinois	5	13	.278	7	20	.259
Youngstown St	3	15	.167	5	21	.192

Conf. Tourney Final: WI-Green Bay 61, IL-Chicago 56.
***NCAA Tourney (1-1):** WI-Green Bay (1-1).

Mid-Eastern Athletic Conference

	Conference			Overall		
	W	L	Pct	W	L	Pct
Coppin St	16	0	1.000	22	8	.733
MD-Eastern Shore	10	6	.625	16	12	.571
*N. Carolina A&T	10	6	.625	16	14	.533
South Carolina St	10	6	.625	16	13	.552
Bethune-Cookman	8	8	.500	9	18	.333
Howard	7	9	.438	10	17	.370
Delaware St	5	11	.313	8	19	.296
Morgan St	4	12	.250	8	21	.276
Florida A&M	2	14	.125	4	23	.148

Conf. Tourney Final: N. Carolina A&T 87, S. Carolina St. 70.
NCAA Tourney (0-1): North Carolina A&T (0-1).

Midwestern Collegiate Conference

	Conference			Overall		
	W	L	Pct	W	L	Pct
†Xavier-OH	8	2	.800	22	8	.733
†Evansville	6	4	.600	21	11	.656
Butler	6	4	.600	16	13	.552
Detroit Mercy	5	5	.500	16	13	.552
La Salle	4	6	.400	11	16	.407
Loyola-IL	1	9	.100	8	19	.296

Conf. Tourney Final: Detroit Mercy 70, Evansville 65.
†NIT Tourney (2-2): Xavier-OH (2-1), Evansville (0-1).

Missouri Valley Conference

	Conference			Overall		
	W	L	Pct	W	L	Pct
*Tulsa	15	3	.833	23	8	.742
*Southern Illinois	14	4	.778	23	7	.767
†Bradley	14	4	.778	23	8	.742
Illinois St	12	6	.667	16	11	.593
Northern Iowa	10	8	.556	16	13	.552
SW Missouri St	7	11	.389	12	15	.444
Drake	6	12	.333	11	16	.407
Wichita St	6	12	.333	9	18	.333
Creighton	3	15	.167	7	22	.241
Indiana St	3	15	.167	4	22	.154

Conf. Tourney Final: Southern Illinois 77, Northern Iowa 74.
NCAA Tourney (2-2): Tulsa (2-1), Southern Illinois (0-1).
†NIT Tourney (2-1): Bradley (2-1).

North Atlantic Conference

	Conference			Overall		
	W	L	Pct	W	L	Pct
*Drexel	12	2	.857	25	5	.833
Maine	11	3	.786	20	9	.690
Hartford	9	5	.643	16	12	.571
New Hampshire	8	6	.571	15	13	.536
Delaware	7	7	.500	14	13	.519
Boston University	4	10	.286	11	16	.407
Vermont	3	11	.214	12	15	.444
Northeastern	2	12	.143	5	22	.185

Conf. Tourney Final: Drexel 86, Maine 78.
NCAA Tourney (0-1): Drexel (0-1).

Northeast Conference

	Conference			Overall		
	W	L	Pct	W	L	Pct
*Rider	14	4	.778	21	9	.700
Monmouth	13	5	.722	18	11	.621
Wagner	11	7	.611	16	12	.571
Robert Morris	11	7	.611	14	14	.500
Fairleigh Dickinson	10	8	.556	14	13	.519
Marist	10	8	.556	14	13	.519
Mt. St. Mary's	9	9	.500	14	14	.500
St. Francis-PA	9	9	.500	13	15	.464
Long Island	2	16	.111	3	24	.111
St. Francis-NY	1	17	.056	1	26	.037

Conf. Tourney Final: Rider 62, Monmouth 56.
NCAA Tourney (0-1): Rider (0-1).

Ohio Valley Conference

	Conference			Overall		
	W	L	Pct	W	L	Pct
Murray St	15	1	.938	23	6	.793
*Tennessee St	12	4	.750	19	12	.633
Austin Peay St	10	6	.625	11	16	.407
Eastern Kentucky	9	7	.563	13	14	.481
Morehead St	8	8	.500	14	14	.500
SE Missouri St	5	11	.313	10	17	.370
Tennessee Tech	5	11	.313	10	21	.323
Middle Tenn. St	5	11	.313	8	19	.296
Tennessee-Martin	3	13	.188	5	22	.185

Conf. Tourney Final: Tennessee St. 73, Murray St. 72.
NCAA Tourney (0-1): Tennessee St. (0-1).
†NIT Tourney (0-1): Murray St. (0-1).

Pacific-10 Conference

	Conference			Overall		
	W	L	Pct	W	L	Pct
*Arizona	14	4	.778	29	6	.829
*UCLA	13	5	.722	21	7	.750
*California	13	5	.722	22	8	.733
*Washington St	10	8	.556	20	11	.645
†Stanford	10	8	.556	17	11	.607
†Arizona St	10	8	.556	15	13	.536
†USC	9	9	.500	16	12	.571
Oregon	6	12	.333	10	17	.370
Washington	3	15	.167	5	22	.185
Oregon St	2	16	.111	6	21	.222

Conf. Tourney Final: Pac-10 has no tournament.
NCAA Tourney (4-4): Arizona (4-1), California (0-1), UCLA (0-1), Washington St. (0-1).
†NIT Tourney (0-3): Arizona St. (0-1), Stanford (0-1), USC (0-1).

Patriot League

	Conference			Overall		
	W	L	Pct	W	L	Pct
*Navy	9	5	.643	17	13	.560
Colgate	9	5	.643	17	12	.586
Holy Cross	9	5	.643	14	14	.500
Fordham	9	5	.643	12	15	.444
Bucknell	6	8	.429	10	17	.370
Lehigh	6	8	.429	10	17	.370
Lafayette	4	10	.286	9	19	.321
Army	4	10	.286	7	20	.259

Conf. Tourney Final: Navy 78, Colgate 76.
NCAA Tourney (0-1): Navy (0-1).

Final NCAA Men's Division I Standings (Cont.)

Southeastern Conference

Eastern Div.	Conference			Overall		
	W	L	Pct	W	L	Pct
*Florida	12	4	.750	29	8	.784
*Kentucky	12	4	.750	27	7	.794
†Vanderbilt	9	7	.563	20	12	.625
Georgia	7	9	.438	14	16	.467
South Carolina	4	12	.250	9	19	.321
Tennessee	2	14	.125	5	22	.185

Western Div.	Conference			Overall		
	W	L	Pct	W	L	Pct
*Arkansas	14	2	.875	31	3	.912
*Alabama	12	4	.750	20	10	.667
†Mississippi St	9	7	.563	18	11	.621
Mississippi	7	9	.438	14	13	.519
LSU	5	11	.313	11	16	.407
Auburn	3	13	.188	11	17	.393

Conf. Tourney Final: Kentucky 73, Florida 60.
***NCAA Tourney (12-3):** Arkansas (6-0), Florida (4-1), Kentucky (1-1), Alabama (1-1).
†NIT Tourney (4-2): Vanderbilt (4-1), Mississippi St. (0-1).

Southern Conference

	Conference			Overall		
	W	L	Pct	W	L	Pct
*Tenn-Chattanooga	14	4	.778	23	7	.767
†Davidson	13	5	.722	22	8	.733
East Tennessee St.	13	5	.722	16	14	.533
Appalachian St	12	6	.667	16	11	.593
Georgia Southern	9	9	.500	14	14	.500
Western Carolina	8	10	.444	12	16	.429
Marshall	7	11	.389	9	18	.333
The Citadel	6	12	.333	11	16	.407
Furman	6	12	.333	10	18	.357
VMI	2	16	.111	5	23	.179

Conf. Tourney Final: Tenn-Chattanooga 65, Davidson 64.
***NCAA Tourney (0-1):** Tenn-Chattanooga (0-1).
†NIT Tourney (0-1): Davidson (0-1).

Southland Conference

	Conference			Overall		
	W	L	Pct	W	L	Pct
NE Louisiana	15	3	.833	19	9	.679
*SW Texas St	14	4	.778	25	7	.781
Nicholls St.	12	6	.667	19	9	.679
North Texas	9	9	.500	14	15	.483
McNeese St.	9	9	.500	11	16	.407
Texas-San Antonio	8	10	.444	12	15	.444
Sam Houston St	7	11	.389	7	20	.259
NW Louisiana	6	12	.333	11	15	.423
Stephen F. Austin	6	12	.333	9	18	.333
Texas-Arlington	4	14	.222	7	22	.241

Conf. Tourney Final: Southwest Texas St. 69, North Texas 60.
***NCAA Tourney (0-1):** SW Texas St. (0-1).

Best In Show

Conferences with at least three victories in 1994 NCAA Tournament.

	W-L		W-L
SEC	12-3	Big Eight	6-4
Big Ten	11-7	Pac-10	4-4
ACC	10-5	Atlantic	3-3
Big East	8-6		

Southwest Conference

	Conference			Overall		
	W	L	Pct	W	L	Pct
*Texas	12	2	.857	26	8	.765
†Texas A&M	10	4	.714	19	11	.655
Texas Tech	10	4	.714	17	11	.607
Baylor	7	7	.500	16	11	.593
Rice	6	8	.429	15	14	.517
Houston	5	9	.357	8	19	.296
TCU	3	11	.214	7	20	.259
SMU	3	11	.214	6	21	.222

Conf. Tourney Final: Texas 87, Texas A&M 62.
***NCAA Tourney (1-1):** Texas (1-1).
†NIT Tourney (0-1): Texas A&M (0-1).

Southwestern Athletic Conference

	Conference			Overall		
	W	L	Pct	W	L	Pct
*Texas Southern	12	2	.857	19	11	.633
Jackson St	11	3	.786	19	10	.655
Alabama St	10	4	.714	19	10	.655
Southern-BR	8	6	.571	15	11	.577
Miss. Valley St	6	8	.429	10	17	.370
Grambling St	4	10	.286	9	18	.333
Alcorn St	3	11	.214	3	24	.111
Prairie View A&M	2	12	.143	5	22	.185

Conf. Tourney Final: Texas Southern 70, Jackson St. 67.
***NCAA Tourney (0-1):** Texas Southern (0-1).

Sun Belt Conference

	Conference			Overall		
	W	L	Pct	W	L	Pct
*Western Kentucky	14	4	.778	20	11	.645
*SW Louisiana	13	5	.722	22	8	.733
†New Orleans	12	6	.667	20	10	.667
Jacksonville	11	7	.611	17	11	.607
Arkansas St	10	8	.556	15	12	.556
Texas-Pan Am	9	9	.500	16	12	.571
South Alabama	9	9	.500	13	14	.481
Ark-Little Rock	6	12	.333	13	15	.464
Lamar	6	12	.333	10	17	.370
Louisiana Tech	0	18	.000	2	25	.074

Conf Tourney Final: SW Louisiana 78, Western Kentucky 72.
***NCAA Tourney (0-2):** SW Louisiana (0-1), Western Kentucky (0-1).
†NIT Tourney (1-1): New Orleans (1-1).

Trans America Athletic Conference

	Conference			Overall		
	W	L	Pct	W	L	Pct
Col. of Charleston	14	2	.875	24	4	.857
Central Florida	11	5	.688	21	9	.700
Stetson	9	7	.563	14	15	.483
Georgia St	9	7	.563	13	14	.481
Centenary	8	8	.500	16	12	.571
Florida Int'l	7	9	.438	11	16	.407
SE Louisiana	7	9	.438	10	17	.370
Samford	4	12	.250	10	18	.357
Mercer	3	13	.188	5	24	.172
Florida Atlantic	0	0	.000	3	24	.111

Note: Florida Atlantic will play first full TAAC schedule in 1995-96.
Conf. Tourney Final: Central Florida 70, Stetson 67.
***NCAA Tourney (0-2):** Central Florida (0-1), College of Charleston (0-1).

West Coast Conference

	Conference			Overall		
	W	L	Pct	W	L	Pct
†Gonzaga	12	2	.857	22	8	.733
*Pepperdine	8	6	.571	19	11	.633
San Francisco	8	6	.571	17	11	.607
San Diego	7	7	.500	18	11	.621
Santa Clara	6	8	.429	13	14	.481
Portland	6	8	.429	13	17	.433
St. Mary's	5	9	.357	13	14	.481
Loyola-CA	4	10	.286	6	21	.222

Conf. Tourney Final: Pepperdine 56, San Diego 53.
***NCAA Tourney (0-1):** Pepperdine (0-1).
†NIT Tourney (1-1): Gonzaga (1-1).

Western Athletic Conference

	Conference			Overall		
	W	L	Pct	W	L	Pct
*New Mexico	14	4	.778	23	8	.742
†Fresno St	13	5	.722	21	11	.656
†BYU	12	6	.667	22	10	.688
*Hawaii	11	7	.611	18	15	.545
UTEP	8	10	.444	18	12	.600
Colorado St	8	10	.444	15	13	.536
Utah	8	10	.444	14	14	.500
Wyoming	7	11	.389	14	14	.500
San Diego St	6	12	.333	12	16	.429
Air Force	3	15	.167	8	18	.308

Conf. Tourney Final: Hawaii 73, BYU 66.
***NCAA Tourney (0-2):** Hawaii (0-1), New Mexico (0-1).
†NIT Tourney (3-2): Fresno St. (2-1), BYU (1-1).

Division I Independents

	W	L	Pct
Southern Utah	16	11	.593
Missouri-Kansas City	12	17	.414
Notre Dame	12	17	.414
CS-Northridge	8	18	.308
Oral Roberts	6	21	.222
CS-Sacramento	1	26	.037

Annual Awards
Player of the Year

Glenn Robinson, Purdue ....AP, Eastman, Naismith, UPI,
USBWA, Wooden.

Wooden Award Voting

Presented since 1977 by the Los Angeles Athletic Club
and named after the former Purdue All-America and
UCLA coach John Wooden. Voting done by 980-
member panel of national media; candidates must have
a cumulative college grade point average of 2.0 (out of
4.0).

		Cl	Pos	Pts
1	Glenn Robinson, Purdue	Jr.	F	4930
2	Grant Hill, Duke	Sr.	F/G	3862
3	Donyell Marshall, UConn	Jr.	F	3585
4	Jason Kidd, California	So.	G	3461
5	Clifford Rozier, Louisville	Jr.	C/F	1818
6	Jalen Rose, Michigan	Jr.	G	1802
7	Corliss Williamson, Arkansas	So.	F	1683
8	Khalid Reeves, Arizona	Sr.	G	1319
9	Eric Montross, N. Carolina	Sr.	C	1313
10	Damon Bailey, Indiana	Sr.	G	1285

Other nominees (6): Aaron McKie, Temple (745 pts); Lou
Roe, UMass (660); Ed O'Bannon, UCLA (613); Billy McCaffrey,
Vanderbilt (519); Lamond Murray, California (513); Michael
Finley, Wisconsin (272).

Wide World Photos

Former UCLA coach **John Wooden** (left) presents
the Wooden Award to 1994 Player of the Year
Glenn Robinson of Purdue. Wooden was a three-
time All-America guard at Purdue from 1930-32 and
is generally regarded as Player of the Year in '32.

Consensus All-America Team

The NCAA Division I players cited most frequently by the
following All-America selectors: AP, U.S. Basketball
Writers, National Assn. of Basketball Coaches and UPI.
There were no holdovers from the 1992-93 first team; (*)
indicates unanimous first team selection.

First Team

	Class	Hgt	Pos
Grant Hill, Duke*	Sr.	6-8	F/G
Jason Kidd, California*	So.	6-4	G
Donyell Marshall, UConn*	Jr.	6-9	F
Glenn Robinson, Purdue*	Jr.	6-8	F
Clifford Rozier, Louisville	Jr.	6-9	C/F

Second Team

	Class	Hgt	Pos
Jalen Rose, Michigan	Jr.	6-8	G
Corliss Williamson, Arkansas	So.	6-7	F
Melvin Booker, Missouri	Sr.	6-2	G
Khalid Reeves, Arizona	Sr.	6-2	G
Eric Montross, N. Carolina	Sr.	7-0	C

Third Team

	Class	Hgt	Pos
Lamond Murray, California	Jr.	6-7	F
Damon Bailey, Indiana	Sr.	6-3	G
Juwan Howard, Michigan	Jr.	6-9	C
Bryant Reeves, Oklahoma St	Jr.	7-0	C
Joe Smith, Maryland	Fr.	6-9	C/F

Coaches of the Year

Nolan Richardson, Arkansas	co-NABC, Naismith
Norm Stewart, Missouri	AP, UPI
Gene Keady, Purdue	co-NABC
Charlie Spoonhour, Saint Louis	USBWA

NCAA Men's Division I Leaders
Includes games through NCAA and NIT tourneys.

INDIVIDUAL

Scoring

	Cl	Gm	FG%	3Pt/Att	FT%	Reb	Ast	Stl	Blk	Pts	Avg	Hi
Glenn Robinson, Purdue	Jr.	34	.483	79/208	.796	344	66	56	31	1030	30.3	49
Rob Feaster, Holy Cross	Jr.	28	.472	42/101	.702	183	59	43	22	785	28.0	46
Jervaughn Scales, Southern-BR	Sr.	27	.594	0/3	.576	38	43	31	55	733	27.1	52
Frankie King, Western Carolina	Jr.	28	.490	29/96	.737	211	59	61	10	752	26.9	41
Tucker Neale, Colgate	Jr.	29	.475	95/238	.832	120	84	48	6	771	26.6	45
Eddie Benton, Vermont	So.	26	.385	68/210	.833	66	99	22	1	687	26.4	54
Tony Dumas, Missouri-KC	Sr.	29	.421	74/205	.757	166	87	49	19	753	26.0	44
Doremus Bennerman, Siena	Sr.	33	.440	102/249	.867	137	182	50	5	858	26.0	51
Otis Jones, Air Force	Jr.	26	.447	77/201	.770	93	48	36	2	663	25.5	32
Gary Trent, Ohio Univ	So.	33	.576	9/33	.722	377	65	28	53	837	25.4	46
Orlando Lightfoot, Idaho	Sr.	28	.456	71/204	.673	214	24	22	9	710	25.4	50
Izett Buchanan, Marist	Sr.	27	.427	41/127	.734	255	39	63	8	685	25.4	51
Donyell Marshall, UConn	Jr.	34	.511	41/132	.752	302	56	43	111	853	25.1	42
Reggie Smith, NE Illinois	Sr.	27	.436	61/175	.813	147	89	53	9	678	25.1	41
Carlos Rogers, Tennessee St	Sr.	31	.614	4/13	.649	358	47	21	93	759	24.5	38
Lamond Murray, California	Jr.	30	.476	46/139	.764	236	63	44	31	729	24.3	38
Shawn Respert, Michigan St	Jr.	32	.484	92/205	.840	127	81	43	5	778	24.3	43
Eric Kubel, Northwestern St	Sr.	26	.485	1/8	.757	341	31	22	24	632	24.3	34
Sherell Ford, IL-Chicago	Jr.	29	.498	26/87	.698	254	32	54	45	704	24.3	32
Khalid Reeves, Arizona	Sr.	35	.483	85/224	.799	150	103	64	4	848	24.2	40

Rebounds

	Cl	Gm	No	Avg
Jerome Lambert, Baylor	Jr.	24	355	14.8
Jervaughn Scales, Southern-BR	Sr.	27	384	14.2
Eric Kubel, Northwestern St	Sr.	26	341	13.1
Kendrick Warren, VCU	Sr.	27	336	12.4
Malik Rose, Drexel	So.	30	371	12.4
David Vaughn, Memphis St	So.	28	335	12.0
Reggie Jackson, Nicholls St	Jr.	26	311	12.0
Melvin Simon, New Orleans	Sr.	30	355	11.8
Kebu Stewart, UNLV	So.	22	256	11.6
Carlos Rogers, Tennessee St	Sr.	31	358	11.5
Michael Smith, Providence	Sr.	30	344	11.5
Gary Trent, Ohio Univ	So.	33	377	11.4
Carlin Warley, St. Joseph's-PA	Sr.	28	318	11.4
Cliff Rozier, Louisville	Jr.	34	377	11.1
Neville Dyson, Lamar	Sr.	27	298	11.0
Steve Payne, Ball St	Jr.	26	286	11.0

Assists

	Cl	Gm	No	Avg
Jason Kidd, California	So.	30	272	9.1
David Edwards, Texas A&M	Sr.	30	265	8.8
Tony Miller, Marquette	Jr.	33	274	8.3
Eathan O'Bryant, Nevada	Jr.	28	232	8.3
Abdul Abdullah, Providence	Sr.	30	241	8.0
Howard Nathan, NE Louisiana	So.	23	179	7.8
Orlando Smart, San Francisco	Sr.	27	204	7.6
Dan Pogue, Campbell	So.	28	207	7.4
Dedan Thomas, UNLV	Sr.	28	205	7.3
Nelson Haggerty, Baylor	Jr.	22	161	7.3
Greg Black, Texas-Pan Am	Sr.	28	202	7.2
Travis DeCuire, Montana	Sr.	28	200	7.1
John Woolery, Santa Clara	Sr.	27	190	7.0
Jerry McCullough, Pittsburgh	Jr.	25	175	7.0
Brian Santiago, Fresno St	Sr.	32	223	7.0

Field Goal Percentage
Minimum 5 Field Goals made per game.

	Cl	Gm	FG	FTA	Pct
Mike Atkinson, L. Beach St	Jr.	26	141	203	.695
Lynwood Wade, SW Texas St	Sr.	32	232	356	.652
Anthony Miller, Mich. St	Sr.	32	162	249	.651
Deon Thomas, Illinois	Sr.	28	207	327	.633
Aaron Swinson, Alabama	Sr.	28	234	371	.631
Clayton Ritter, J. Madison	Sr.	30	230	366	.628
Corliss Williamson, Arkansas	So.	34	273	436	.626
David Ardayfio, Army	Sr.	27	180	289	.623
Jimmy Lunsford, Alabama St	So.	28	163	263	.620
Cliff Rozier, Louisville	Jr.	34	247	400	.618

3-Pt Field Goal Percentage
Minimum 1.5 Three-Point FG made per game.

	Cl	Gm	FG	FGA	Pct
Brent Kell, Evansville	So.	29	62	123	.504
Brian Santiago, Fresno St	Sr.	32	64	128	.500
Brandon Born, Tenn-Chatt	Jr.	30	67	135	.496
Chris Young, Canisius	So.	29	53	109	.486
Howard Eisley, Boston Col	Sr.	34	91	188	.484
Marc Blucas, Wake Forest	Jr.	33	52	109	.477
Brooks Thompson, Okla. St	Sr.	34	110	233	.472
Brooks Barnhard, San Diego	Sr.	29	59	125	.472
Bubba Donnelly, Robt. Morris	Jr.	28	65	138	.471
Scott Neely, Campbell	Jr.	29	81	173	.468

Free Throw Percentage
Minimum 2.5 Free Throws made per game.

	Cl	Gm	FT	FTA	Pct
Danny Basile, Marist	So.	27	84	89	.944
Dandrea Evans, Troy St	Sr.	27	72	77	.935
Casey Schmidt, Valparaiso	Sr.	25	75	81	.926
Matthew Hildebrand, Liberty	Sr.	30	149	161	.925
Kent Culuko, J. Madison	Sr.	30	117	127	.921
Ryan Yoder, Colorado St	Sr.	28	107	117	.915
Travis Ford, Kentucky	Sr.	33	103	113	.912
Ryan Hoover, Notre Dame	So.	29	76	84	.905

3-Pt Field Goals Per Game

	Cl	Gm	No	Avg
Chris Brown, UC-Irvine	Jr.	26	122	4.7
Keke Hicks, Coastal Carolina	Jr.	26	115	4.4
Lazelle Durden, Cincinnati	Jr.	25	102	4.1
Bernard Haslett, Southern Miss	Sr.	30	112	3.7
Kareem Townes, La Salle	Jr.	27	100	3.7
Donald Ross, Geo. Mason	Sr.	27	99	3.7
Keith Carmichael, Coppin St	Sr.	30	108	3.6
B.J. Tyler, Texas	Sr.	28	99	3.5

Baylor
Jerome Lambert
Rebounds

Wide World
Jason Kidd
Assists

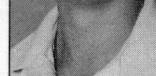
Long Beach St.
Mike Atkinson
Field Goal Pct.

SW Louisiana
Shawn Griggs
Steals

Blocked Shots

	Cl	Gm	No	Avg
Grady Livingston, Howard	Jr.	26	115	4.4
Jim McIlvaine, Marquette	Sr.	33	142	4.3
Theo Ratliff, Wyoming	Jr.	28	114	4.1
David Vaughn, Memphis St.	So.	28	107	3.8
Tim Duncan, Wake Forest	Fr.	33	124	3.8
Marcus Camby, UMass	Fr.	29	105	3.6
Kelvin Cato, South Alabama	So.	24	85	3.5
Donyell Marshall, UConn	Jr.	34	111	3.3
Michael McDonald, New Orleans	Sr.	30	96	3.2
Pascal Fleury, MD-Balt. County	Jr.	25	80	3.2

Steals

	Cl	Gm	No	Avg
Shawn Griggs, SW Louisiana	Sr.	30	120	4.0
Gerald Walker, San Francisco	So.	28	109	3.9
Andre Cradle, LIU-Brooklyn	Sr.	21	79	3.8
Jason Kidd, California	So.	30	94	3.1
B.J. Tyler, Texas	Sr.	28	87	3.1
Clarence Ceasar, LSU	Jr.	27	80	3.0

Five tied at 2.9 each.

Single Game Highs
Individual Points

No		Opponent	Date
62	Askia Jones, Kansas St.	Fresno St.	3/24
54	Eddie Benton, Vermont	Drexel	1/29
52	J. Scales, Southern-BR	Patten	11/26
51	Izett Buchanan, Marist	LIU-Brooklyn	2/12
51	D. Bennerman, Siena	Kansas St.	3/30
50	Orlando Lightfoot, Idaho	Gonzaga	12/21
49	J. Conic, Southern-BR	Louisiana Col.	12/13
49	Glenn Robinson, Purdue	Illinois	3/13
46	Paul Queen, Prairie View	Alabama St.	2/5
46	Rob Feaster, Holy Cross	Navy	2/19
46	Gary Trent, Ohio Univ.	Bowl. Green	2/19
46	Donnie Boyce, Colorado	Oklahoma St.	3/5

Team Points

No		Opponent	Date
154	Southern-BR	Patten (NAIA I)	11/26
148	Tennessee St.	Fisk (NCAA III)	12/6
148	Southern-BR	La Christian (NCCAA)	12/13
142	Southern-BR	Paul Quinn (NSCAA)	11/29
140	Nicholls St.	Baptist Christian (NSCAA)	12/16
132	Louisville	George Mason (NCAA I)	1/4
131	Charleston So.	Warner Southern (NAIA II)	12/11
131	Arkansas	Montevallo (NAIA I)	2/5
130	Connecticut	Tennessee Tech (NCAA I)	12/30

TEAM
Scoring Offense

	Gm	W-L	Pts	Avg
Southern-Baton Rouge	27	16-11	2727	101.0
Troy St	27	13-14	2634	97.6
Arkansas	34	31-3	3176	93.4
Texas	34	26-8	3119	91.7
Murray St	29	23-6	2611	90.0
Arizona	35	29-6	3124	89.3
Nicholls St	28	19-9	2492	89.0
San Francisco	28	17-11	2488	88.9
Oklahoma	28	15-13	2477	88.5
George Mason	27	10-17	2385	88.3
Nebraska	30	20-10	2620	87.3
Kentucky	34	27-7	2952	86.8
UCLA	28	21-7	2410	86.1
North Carolina	35	28-7	2996	85.6

Scoring Defense

	Gm	W-L	Pts	Avg
Princeton	26	18-8	1361	52.3
Temple	31	23-8	1697	54.7
Wisconsin-Green Bay	34	27-7	1872	55.1
Alabama-Birmingham	30	22-8	1806	60.2
Marquette	33	24-9	2040	61.8
Southwest Missouri St	27	12-15	1690	62.6
Coppin St	30	22-8	1924	64.1
Pennsylvania	28	25-3	1799	64.3
Pepperdine	30	19-11	1935	64.5
Southwest Texas St	32	25-7	2070	64.7
Bradley	31	23-8	2008	64.8
New Orleans	30	20-10	1958	65.3
College of Charleston	28	24-4	1833	65.5
Wake Forest	33	21-12	2162	65.5

Scoring Margin

	Off	Def	Margin
Arkansas	93.4	75.6	+17.9
Connecticut	84.9	68.6	+16.3
Arizona	89.3	74.4	+14.9
Southern-Baton Rouge	101.0	87.7	+13.3
North Carolina	85.6	72.4	+13.2
Kentucky	86.8	74.6	+12.2
Kansas	80.5	68.3	+12.1
Pennsylvania	76.4	64.3	+12.1
Texas	91.7	79.6	+12.1
Oklahoma St	80.5	68.8	+11.7
Coppin St	75.8	64.1	+11.7
Ohio University	80.8	69.2	+11.7
Princeton	64.0	52.3	+11.7
Louisville	80.2	68.8	+11.4

Other Men's Tournaments

NIT Tourney

The 57th annual National Invitational Tournament had a 32-team field. First three rounds played on home courts of higher seeded teams. Semifinal, Third Place and Championship games played March 28-30 at Madison Square Garden, N.Y.

1st Round

at Duquesne 75	NC-Charlotte 73
at Siena 76	Georgia Tech 68
at Clemson 96	Southern Miss. 85
at Old Dominion 76	Manhattan 74
at West Virginia 85	Davidson 69
at Villanova 103	Canisius 79
Tulane 76	Evansville 63
at Bradley 66	Murray St. 58
at Northwestern 69	DePaul 68
at Xavier-OH 80	Miami-OH 68
at Kansas St. 78	Mississippi St. 67
at New Orleans 79 ..... OT	Texas A&M 73
Vanderbilt 77	at Oklahoma 67
at Fresno St. 79	USC 76
at BYU 74	Arizona St. 67
Gonzaga 80	at Stanford 76

2nd Round

Clemson 96	at West Virginia 79
Xavier-OH 83	at Northwestern 79
Villanova 82	at Duquesne 67
at Vanderbilt 78	New Orleans 59
at Siena 89	Tulane 79
at Kansas St. 66	Gonzaga 64
at Bradley 79	Old Dominion 75
at Fresno St. 68	BYU 66

Quarterfinals

at Villanova 76	Xavier-OH 74
at Vanderbilt 89	Clemson 74
at Siena 75	Bradley 62
at Kansas St. 115	Fresno St. 77

Semifinals

Vanderbilt 82	Kansas St. 76
Villanova 66	Siena 58

Third Place

Siena 92	Kansas St. 79

Championship

Villanova 80	Vanderbilt 73

Most Valuable Players

NIT
Doremus Bennerman
Siena guard

NCAA Division II
Stan Gourard
Southern Indiana forward

NCAA Division III
Mike Rhoades and Adam Crawford
Lebanon Valley guards

NAIA Division I	**NAIA Division II**
Kevin Franklin	Chris Peterson
Oklahoma City guard	Eureka guard

NCAA Division II

The eight regional winners of the 32-team Division II tournament: NORTHEAST—New Hampshire College (27-4); EAST—Indiana-PA (27-2); SOUTH ATLANTIC—Norfolk St., VA (27-5); SOUTH—Alabama A&M (27-4); SOUTH CENTRAL—Washburn, KS (28-3); GREAT LAKES—Southern Indiana (26-3); NORTH CENTRAL—South Dakota (24-5); WEST—CS-Bakersfield (24-6).

The Elite Eight played for the Division II championship, March 23-26, in Springfield, Mass. There was no Third Place game.

Quarterfinals

Washburn 69	Norfolk St. 58
CS-Bakersfield 87	Indiana-PA 69
Southern Ind. 98	South Dakota 77
N.H. College 100	Alabama A&M 90

Semifinals

CS-Bakersfield 67	Washburn 64
Southern Ind. 111	N.H. College 89

Championship

CS-Bakersfield 92	Southern Ind. 86

NCAA Division III

The four sectional winners of the 40-team Division II tournament: ATLANTIC/EAST—NYU (24-4); MID-ATLANTIC/NORTHEAST—Lebanon Valley-PA (26-4); GREAT LAKES/MIDWEST—Wittenberg-OH (29-1); SOUTH/WEST—St. Thomas-MN (24-5).

The Final Four played for the Division III championship, March 18-19, in Buffalo, N.Y.

Semifinals

NYU 75	St. Thomas 68
Lebanon Valley 83 ..... OT	Wittenberg 73

Third Place

Wittenberg 73	St. Thomas 62

Championship

Lebanon Valley 66 ..... OT	NYU 59

NAIA Division I

The quarterfinalists, in alphabetical order, after two rounds of the 32-team NAIA tournament: Belmont, TN (30-6); Benedict, SC (29-2); Drury, MO (27-3); Hawaii Pacific (27-7); Life, GA (25-9); Midwestern St., TX (22-11); Oklahoma Baptist (28-7); Oklahoma City (25-7). All tournament games played, March 15-21, at the Mabee Center in Tulsa. There was no Third Place game.

Quarterfinals: Life 96, Hawaii Pacific 77; Midwestern St. 68, Benedict 60; Oklahoma City 90, Drury 70; Oklahoma Baptist 89, Belmont 76.

Semifinals: Life 85, Midwestern St. 67; Oklahoma City 86, Oklahoma Baptist 85.

Championship: Oklahoma City 99, Life 81.

NAIA Division II

The semifinalists, in alphabetical order, after two rounds of the 24-team NAIA tournament: Eureka, IL (25-4); Lewis & Clark OR (23-8); Northern St. SD (24-8); Northwest Nazarene, ID (26-7). All tournament games played, March 10-15, at Nampa, Idaho. There was no Third Place game.

Semifinals: Northern St. 106, Lewis & Clark 96; Eureka 83, NW Nazarene 67.

Championship: Eureka 98-95 (OT).

They Love Charlotte In Chapel Hill

by Wendy Parker

Jim Gund/Allsport

North Carolina's **Charlotte Smith** lets go of her winning, three-point buzzer beater to give the UNC women their first-ever NCAA basketball title.

There's a new Smith in town at Chapel Hill and her name is Charlotte.

With seven-tenths of a second remaining in the women's NCAA final between North Carolina and Louisiana Tech, Tar Heels' junior forward Charlotte Smith threw in a three-point basket to earn UNC a spectacular 60-59 victory before a capacity crowd of 11,966 at the Richmond (Va.) Coliseum. The winning shot topped off a 20-point, 23-rebound performance that earned her Most Outstanding Player honors.

Even those accustomed to the remarkable success of men's coach Dean Smith won't soon forget the shot that earned for North Carolina the distinction of being the only school to have men's and women's national basketball champions.

Not only did the women's victory provide a madcap ending to an unpredictable season, but it was a symbol of the turning tide in women's college basketball. Most of the nation's top ranked teams were missing from this Final Four, having fallen victim to upsets that just a few years ago were highly unlikely.

Tennessee rolled to the top spot in the final regular season polls for the second straight year, but could not survive regional play. Neither could No. 2 Penn State, defending champion Texas Tech and three other Top 10 occupants: USC, Stanford and Connecticut.

Even though the teams that did advance to the Final Four— North Carolina, Purdue, Louisiana Tech and Alabama— also were among the nation's elite, they were considered either too young or darkhorses.

The Tar Heels in particular came from abject basketball poverty in a relatively short period. In 1991, they finished last in the ACC with a 2-12 record (12-16 overall). Later that fall, coach Sylvia Hatchell signed Smith, a 6-1 forward from Shelby, N. C.

While she wasn't projected to be a major Division I player, Smith's bloodlines couldn't be ignored. Her uncle, former N.C. State star David Thompson, led the Wolfpack to the 1974 national title.

With Smith in the lineup, North Carolina improved to 22-9 in 1992 and 23-7 in '93, when they were routed, 74-54, by a physical Tennessee team in the regional semifinals of the NCAA tournament.

Resolving to better utilize their athletic skills, the Tar Heels hit the weight room during the off-season and converted a world-class sprinter, freshman Marion Jones, to point guard. They went 27-2 through the 1993-94 regular season, losing twice to ACC champ Virginia and winning five straight to gain the NCAA final.

As the title game wound down to its final seconds, North Carolina trailed Louisiana Tech, 59-57. UNC's Tonya Sampson missed on a drive and a scramble ensued under the basket, resulting in a jump ball. The Tar Heels retained possession, but only 0.7 seconds showed on the clock.

After a UNC time-out, Smith got the ball on an inbounds play and immediately lofted her three-pointer through the basket.

"I was praying the whole time," said Smith. "And God answered my prayers."

Wendy Parker is the women's basketball correspondent for *Basketball Times*.

Final Regular Season AP Women's Top 25 Poll

Taken **before** start of NCAA tournament.

Compiled by Mel Greenberg of the *Philadelphia Inquirer*: first place votes in parentheses; records through March 13; total points (based on 25 for 1st, 24 for 2nd, etc.); in 1994 NCAA tourney and team lost to; head coach (career years and record including '94 postseason), and preseason ranking. Teams in **bold type** went on to reach NCAA Final Four.

		Mar.13 Record	Points	NCAA Recap	Head Coach	Preseason Rank
1	Tennessee (64)	29-1	1624	2-1 (La. Tech)	Pat Summitt (20 yrs: 530-126)	1
2	Penn St.	25-2	1510	3-1 (Alabama)	Rene Portland (18 yrs: 412-135)	7
3	Connecticut	27-2	1488	3-1 (N. Carolina)	Geno Auriemma (9 yrs: 192-81)	18
4	**North Carolina**	27-2	1387	6-0	Sylvia Hatchell (19 yrs: 414-176)	9
5	Colorado	25-4	1288	2-1 (Stanford)	Ceal Barry (15 yrs: 293-160)	12
6	**Louisiana Tech**	26-3	1227	5-1 (N. Carolina)	Leon Barmore (12 yrs: 338-56)	4
7	USC	23-3	1204	3-1 (La. Tech)	Cheryl Miller (1 yr: 26-4)	11
8	**Purdue** (1)	25-4	1170	4-1 (N. Carolina)	Lin Dunn (23 yrs: 403-238)	25
9	Texas Tech	26-4	1141	2-1 (Alabama)	Marsha Sharp (12 yrs: 269-102)	14
10	Virginia	25-4	1092	2-1 (USC)	Debbie Ryan (17 yrs: 386-135)	10
11	Stanford	22-5	1084	3-1 (Purdue)	Tara VanDerveer (16 yrs: 373-110)	6
12	Vanderbilt	23-7	918	2-1 (N. Carolina)	Jim Foster (16 yrs: 325-146)	2
13	Iowa	20-6	740	1-1 (Alabama)	Vivian Stringer (22 yrs: 509-118)	3
14	Seton Hall	25-4	731	2-1 (Penn St.)	Phyllis Mangina (9 yrs: 139-120)	45
15	Kansas	21-5	639	1-1 (Penn St.)	Marian Washington (21 yrs: 390-231)	16
16	**Alabama**	22-6	610	4-1 (La. Tech)	Rick Moody (5 yrs: 104-47)	19
17	Montana	24-4	473	1-1 (Stanford)	Robin Selvig (16 yrs: 382-93)	47
18	Washington	20-7	465	1-1 (Purdue)	Chris Gobrecht (15 yrs: 286-159)	28
19	Florida Int'l	25-3	383	0-1 (Clemson)	Cindy Russo (17 yrs: 340-144)	46
20	Florida	22-6	347	0-1 (Texas A&M)	Carol Ross (3 yrs: 54-31)	56
21	Boise St	23-5	262	0-1 (Washington)	June Daugherty (4 yrs: 75-41)	42
22	Southern Miss	24-4	252	2-1 (UConn)	Kay James (22 yrs: 407-183)	34
23	Mississippi	23-8	196	1-1 (La. Tech)	Van Chancellor (16 yrs: 384-124)	22
24	Bowling Green	26-3	143	0-1 (Creighton)	Jaci Clark (3 yrs: 75-14)	43
25	Texas	21-8	114	1-1 (Seton Hall)	Jody Conradt (25 yrs: 642-162)	27

Others receiving votes: 26. **Rutgers** (22-7, 92 pts); 27. **Virginia Tech** (24-5, 73); 28. **SW Missouri St.** (23-5, 71); 29. **Oregon** (19-8, 52); 30. **San Diego St.** (25-4, 48); 31. **Hawaii** (25-4, 44); 32. **Minnesota** (17-10, 41); 33. **UNLV** (23-6, 40); 34. **Old Dominion** (24-5, 29); 35. **Western Ky.** (23-9, 26); 36. **Clemson** (19-9, 16); 37. **Notre Dame** (22-6, 15); 38. **Auburn** (19-9, 14) 39. **Ala-Birmingham** (23-5, 11); 40. **Georgia** (17-11, 9), **New Mexico St.** (23-6, 9) and **Santa Clara** (21-6, 9); 43. **Northern Ill.** (24-5, 7); 44. **Missouri** (12-17, 6); 45. **Oklahoma St.** (21-8, 5); 46. **Geo Washington** (22-7, 4), **Indiana** (19-8, 4) and **S.F. Austin** (23-6, 4); 49. **Texas A&M** (21-7, 3); 50. **Kent** (20-8, 2) and **Oregon St** (17-10, 2); 52. **Marquette** (22-6, 1).

NCAA Women's Division I Leaders

Includes games through NCAA tournament.

Scoring

	Cl	Gm	Pts	Avg
Kristy Ryan, CS-Sacramento	Sr.	26	727	28.0
Patty Stoffey, Loyola-MD	Jr.	29	757	26.1
Cornelia Gayden, LSU	Jr.	27	647	24.0
Sheri Turnbull, Vermont	Sr.	30	714	23.8
Shannon Johnson, S. Carolina	So.	27	634	23.5
Carol Ann Shudlick, Minnesota	Sr.	29	678	23.4
Natalie Williams, UCLA	Sr.	24	561	23.4
Mary Lowry, Baylor	So.	27	626	23.2
Trenia Tillis, S.F. Austin	Sr.	29	669	23.1
Tera Sheriff, Jackson St	Jr.	20	454	22.7
Anjinea Hopson, Grambling St	Jr.	30	677	22.6
Dawn Beachler, Texas-Pan Am	Sr.	27	606	22.4
Angela Crosby, Appalachian St	Sr.	28	623	22.3
Kerry Curran, Boston College	Sr.	27	599	22.2
Katie Smith, Ohio St	So.	28	616	22.0
E.C. Hill, Northern Ill	Sr.	30	659	22.0

Rebounds

	Cl	Gm	No	Avg
DeShawne Blocker, E. Tenn St	Jr.	26	450	17.3
Joskeen Garner, N'western St	So.	28	387	13.8
Kristy Ryan, CS-Sacramento	Sr.	26	347	13.3
Travesa Gant, Lamar	Sr.	27	357	13.2
Tammy Butler, Harvard	Jr.	26	343	13.2
Natalie Williams, UCLA	Sr.	24	314	13.1
Oberon Pitterson, Western Ill	Jr.	28	362	12.9
Tera Sheriff, Jackson St	Jr.	20	252	12.6
Sheri Turnbull, Vermont	Sr.	30	376	12.5
Lisa Leslie, USC	Sr.	30	369	12.3

Assists

	Cl	Gm	No	Avg
Andrea Nagy, Florida Int'l	Jr.	29	298	10.3
Bozana Vidic, Oregon St	So.	21	176	8.4
Sharee Mitchum, Oklahoma	Jr.	30	242	8.1
Carol Madsen, Xavier-OH	Sr.	29	212	7.3
Moira Kennelly, Northwestern	Sr.	27	196	7.3
Niesa Johnson, Alabama	Jr.	33	237	7.2
Kelly Pilcher, Montana	Sr.	30	215	7.2
Tina Robbins, SW Missouri St	Sr.	30	213	7.1
Tamika Matlock, Arizona St	So.	25	174	7.0
Lisa Branch, Texas A&M	So.	31	214	6.9
Karen Lewis, Wichita St	Jr.	27	186	6.9

Single Game Highs

No		Opponent	Date
54	Mary Lowry, Baylor	Texas	2/16
54	Anjinea Hopson, Grambling St.	Jackson St.	2/21
48	Danielle Viglione, Texas	Houston	1/29
46	Carol Madsen, Xavier-OH	La Salle	2/10
45	Kristy Ryan, CS-Sacramento	UC-Irvine	12/4

1994 NCAA BASKETBALL WOMEN'S DIVISION I

Column headers (outer to inner): 1ST ROUND March 16 · 2ND ROUND March 19-20 · REGIONALS March 24 and 26

MIDEAST

1ST ROUND	2ND ROUND	REGIONALS
1 Tennessee 111		
16 N.C. A&T 37	Tennessee 78	
8 Florida Int'l 64		Tennessee 68
9 Clemson 65	Clemson 66	
5 Mississippi 83		
12 Indiana 61	Mississippi 67	
4 Louisiana Tech 96		La. Tech 71
13 SMU 62	La. Tech 82	La. Tech 75
6 SW Mo. St. 75		
11 Northern Ill. 56	SW Mo. St. 63	
3 Virginia 72		Virginia 66
14 Loyola-MD 47	Virginia 67	
7 G. Washington 74		
10 Al-Birmingham 66	G. Washington 72	USC 66
2 USC 77		USC 85
15 Portland 62	USC 76	

FAYETTEVILLE

EAST

1ST ROUND	2ND ROUND	REGIONALS
1 Connecticut 79		
16 Brown 60	Connecticut 81	
8 Va. Tech 51		Connecticut 78
9 Auburn 60	Auburn 59	
5 Rutgers 73		
12 Western Ky. 84	Western Ky. 69	
4 So. Miss. 86		So. Miss. 64
13 Tenn. St. 72	So. Miss. 72	Connecticut 69
6 Old Dominion 56		
11 St. Joseph's 55	Old Dominion 52	
3 N. Carolina 101		N. Carolina 73
14 Go. Southern 53	N. Carolina 63	
7 Notre Dame 76		
10 Minnesota 81	Minnesota 72	N. Carolina 81
2 Vanderbilt 95		Vanderbilt 69
15 Grambling 85	Vanderbilt 98	

PISCATAWAY

MIDWEST

1ST ROUND	2ND ROUND	REGIONALS
1 Penn St. 94		
16 Fordham 41	Penn St. 85	
8 S.F. Austin 63		Penn St. 64
9 Kansas 72	Kansas 68	
5 Texas 75		
12 Oklahoma St. 67	Texas 66	
4 Seton Hall 60		Seton Hall 60
13 Vermont 60	Seton Hall 71	Penn St. 82
6 Alabama 96		
11 Oregon St. 86	Alabama 84	
3 Iowa 70		Alabama 73
14 Mt. St. Mary's 47	Iowa 78	
7 Bowling Green 73		
10 Creighton 84	Creighton 65	Alabama 96
2 Texas Tech 75		Texas Tech 68
15 Missouri 61	Texas Tech 75	

AUSTIN

WEST

1ST ROUND	2ND ROUND	REGIONALS
1 Purdue 103		
16 Radford 56	Purdue 86	
8 Washington 89		Purdue 82
9 Boise St. 61	Washington 59	
5 San Diego St. 81		
12 Hawaii 75	San Diego St. 72 (OT)	
4 Florida 76		Texas A&M 56
13 Texas A&M 78	Texas A&M 75	Purdue 82
6 Oregon 74		
11 Santa Clara 59	Oregon 71	
3 Colorado 77		Colorado 62
14 Marquette 74	Colorado 92	
7 Montana 77		
10 UNLV 67	Montana 62	Stanford 78
2 Stanford 81		Stanford 65
15 Wi-Green Bay 56	Stanford 66	

STANFORD

Regional Finals / Final Four

- MIDEAST final: La. Tech 69
- MIDWEST final: Alabama 66
- EAST final: N. Carolina 89
- WEST final: Purdue 74

NATIONAL CHAMPIONSHIP
- N. Carolina 60
- La. Tech 59

FINAL FOUR

at the Richmond (Va.) Coliseum

Semifinals: April 2
Final: April 3

WOMEN'S FINAL FOUR
at Richmond (Va.) Coliseum (April 2-3).

Semifinals
Louisiana Tech 69 ....Alabama 66
North Carolina 89 ....Purdue 74

Championship
North Carolina 60 ....Louisiana Tech 59

Final Records: North Carolina (33-2), Louisiana Tech (31-4), Purdue (29-5), Alabama (26-7).

Most Outstanding Player: Charlotte Smith, North Carolina junior forward. SEMIFINAL—39 minutes, 23 points, 8 rebounds, 8 assists, 1 steal, 2 blocked shots; FINAL—40 minutes, 20 points, 23 rebounds, 2 steals, 2 blocked shots.

All-Tournament Team: Smith and guard Tonya Sampson of North Carolina; guards Vickie Johnson and Pam Thomas of Louisiana Tech; and guard Betsy Harris of Alabama.

NCAA Championship Game
Louisiana Tech 59

	Min	FG M-A	FT M-A	Pts	Rb	A	F
Amy Brown	13	2-6	0-0	4	2	0	3
Vickie Johnson	40	6-15	0-0	12	10	1	2
Racquel Spurlock	29	1-4	0-0	2	6	0	4
Pam Thomas	24	6-14	2-2	15	4	1	3
Debra Williams	27	4-19	0-1	8	6	1	0
Kendra Neal	26	0-3	6-8	6	2	2	2
Joletta Riser	3	0-0	0-0	0	1	0	0
Maquisha Walker	20	5-7	0-0	10	5	0	0
LaShawn Brown	18	1-2	0-0	2	2	0	5
TOTALS	200	25-70	8-11	59	38	5	19

Three-point FG: 1-8 (Thomas 1-1, A. Brown 0-1, Johnson 0-2, Williams 0-4); **Team Rebounds:** 6; Blocked Shots: 3 (Neal, Riser, Spurlock); **Turnovers:** 15 (Neal 4, Johnson 3, Spurlock 2, Thomas 2, Williams 2, L. Brown, Walker); **Steals:** 12 (Neal 4, L. Brown 2, Spurlock 2, Thomas 2, Johnson, Williams). **Percentages:** 2-Pt FG (.387); 3-Pt FG (.125); Total FG (.357); Free Throws (.727).

North Carolina 60

	Min	FG M-A	FT M-A	Pts	Rb	A	F
Charlotte Smith	40	7-19	5-7	20	23	2	2
Tonya Sampson	38	9-25	0-0	21	8	1	4
Sylvia Crawley	39	4-7	6-8	14	4	1	2
Marion Jones	22	0-5	2-3	2	2	3	3
Steph. Lawrence	40	1-2	0-0	3	4	5	1
Jill Suddreth	2	0-0	0-0	0	0	0	1
Carrie McKee	1	0-0	0-0	0	0	0	0
Tonya Cooper	12	0-2	0-1	0	0	0	0
Lori Gear	6	0-1	0-0	0	1	1	1
TOTALS	200	21-61	13-19	60	42	13	14

Three-point FG: 5-13 (Sampson 3-7, Lawrence 1-1, Smith 1-3, Cooper 0-1, Jones 0-1); **Team Rebounds:** 6; **Blocked Shots:** 6 (Crawley 3, Smith 2, Jones); **Turnovers:** 21 (Crawley 6, Smith 6, Jones 4, Cooper 2, Lawrence, Sampson, Suddreth); **Steals:** 5 (Sampson 2, Cooper, Crawley, Lawrence). **Percentages:** 2-Pt FG (.333); 3-Pt FG (.385); Total FG (.344); Free Throws (.684).

Louisiana Tech (Sun Belt).........................32 27— 59
North Carolina (ACC)..............................32 28— 60

Technical Fouls: None. **Officials:** June Courteau, John Morningstar. **Attendance:** 11,966. **TV Rating:** 3.7/12 share (CBS).

Final *USA Today*/CNN Coaches Poll
Taken **after** NCAA Tourney.

Voted on by panel of 35 women's coaches and media following the NCAA tourney: first place votes in parentheses with final overall records:

		Record			Record
1	N.Carolina (35)	..33-2	14	Seton Hall	..27-5
2	Louisiana Tech	31-4	15	Iowa	..21-7
3	Purdue	29-5	16	Southern Miss	..26-5
4	Alabama	26-7	17	Kansas	22-6
5	Tennessee	31-2	18	Montana	25-5
6	Penn St	28-3	19	Texas A&M	23-8
7	UConn	30-3	20	Mississippi	..24-9
8	Stanford	25-6	21	Washington	..21-8
9	USC	26-4	22	Clemson	20-10
10	Colorado	27-5	23	Texas	22-9
11	Texas Tech	28-5	24	Florida Int'l	25-4
12	Virginia	27-5	25	Florida	22-7
13	Vanderbilt	25-8			

Annual Awards
Players of the Year
Lisa Leslie, USC ....Naismith, USBWA, WBCA, WBNS
Carol Ann Shudlick, Minnesota.................................Wade

Coaches of the Year
Ceal Barry, Colorado..USBWA
Cheryl Miller, USC..WBNS
Marsha Sharp, Texas Tech ....WBCA
Pat Summitt, Tennessee ....Naismith

Consensus All-America
The NCAA Division I players cited most frequently by the U.S. Basketball Writers Assn., the Women's Basketball Coaches Assn.(Kodak) and the Women's Basketball News Service. There were no holdovers from the 1992-93 All-America first team.

First Team

	Class	Hgt	Pos
Niesa Johnson, Alabama	Jr.	5-9	G
Lisa Leslie, USC	Sr.	6-5	C
Rebecca Lobo, UConn	Jr.	6-4	C
Nikki McCray, Tennessee	Jr.	5-11	F
Andrea Nagy, Florida Int'l	Jr.	5-7	G
Natalie Williams, UCLA	Sr.	6-1	F

Second Team

	Class	Hgt	Pos
Jessica Barr, Clemson	Sr.	6-2	F
Janice Felder, Southern Miss	Sr.	6-0	F
E.C. Hill, Northern Ill	Sr.	5-7	G
Staci Reed, Kentucky	So.	5-7	G
Tonya Sampson, N. Carolina	Sr.	5-9	G
Carol Ann Shudlick, Minnesota	Sr.	6-0	C/F
Shelly Sheetz, Colorado	Sr.	5-6	G
Necole Tunsil, Iowa	Sr.	6-1	F

Other Women's Tournaments
NIT (Mar. 26 at Amarillo, Texas): Final—Oklahoma 69, Arkansas St. 65.

NCAA Division II (Mar. 26 at Fargo, N.D.): Final—North Dakota St. 89, CS-San Bernardino 56.

NCAA Division III (Mar. 19 Eau Claire, WI): Final—Capital (OH) 82, Washington (MO) 63.

NAIA Division I (Mar. 22 at Jackson, Tenn.): Final—Southern Nazarene (OK) 97, David Lipscomb (TN) 74.

NAIA Division II (Mar. 15 at Monmouth, Ore.): Final—Northern St. (SD) 48, Western Oregon 45.

THE 1995 INFORMATION PLEASE SPORTS ALMANAC

COLLEGE BASKETBALL
S T A T I S T I C S

THROUGH THE YEARS
1901-1994

NCAA'S • ALL-TIME LEADERS

SEC B

PAGE 295

National Champions

The Helms Foundation of Los Angeles, under the direction of founder Bill Schroeder, selected national college basketball champions from 1942-82 and researched retroactive picks from 1901-41. The first NIT tournament and then the NCAA tournament have settled the national championship since 1938, but there are four years (1939, '40, '44 and '54) where the Helms selections differ.

Multiple champions (1901-37): Chicago, Columbia and Wisconsin (3); Kansas, Minnesota, Notre Dame, Penn, Pittsburgh, Syracuse and Yale (2).

Multiple champions (since 1938): UCLA (10); Kentucky (6); Indiana (5); North Carolina (3); Cincinnati, Duke, Kansas, Louisville, N.C. State, Oklahoma A&M and San Francisco (2).

Year		Record	Head Coach	Outstanding Player
1901	Yale	10-4	No coach	G.M. Clark, F
1902	Minnesota	11-0	Louis Cooke	W.C. Deering, F
1903	Yale	15-1	W.H. Murphy	R.B. Hyatt, F
1904	Columbia	17-1	No coach	Harry Fisher, F
1905	Columbia	19-1	No coach	Harry Fisher, F
1906	Dartmouth	16-2	No coach	George Grebenstein, F
1907	Chicago	22-2	Joseph Raycroft	John Schommer, C
1908	Chicago	21-2	Joseph Raycroft	John Schommer, C
1909	Chicago	12-0	Joseph Raycroft	John Schommer, C
1910	Columbia	11-1	Harry Fisher	Ted Kiendl, F
1911	St. John's-NY	14-0	Claude Allen	John Keenan, F/C
1912	Wisconsin	15-0	Doc Meanwell	Otto Stangel, F
1913	Navy	9-0	Louis Wenzell	Laurence Wild, F
1914	Wisconsin	15-0	Doc Meanwell	Gene Van Gent, C
1915	Illinois	16-0	Ralph Jones	Ray Woods, G
1916	Wisconsin	20-1	Doc Meanwell	George Levis, F
1917	Washington St	25-1	Doc Bohler	Roy Bohler, G
1918	Syracuse	16-1	Edmund Dollard	Joe Schwarzer, G
1919	Minnesota	13-0	Louis Cooke	Arnold Oss, F
1920	Pennsylvania	22-1	Lon Jourdet	George Sweeney, F
1921	Pennsylvania	21-2	Edward McNichol	Danny McNichol, G
1922	Kansas	16-2	Phog Allen	Paul Endacott, G
1923	Kansas	17-1	Phog Allen	Paul Endacott, G
1924	North Carolina	25-0	Bo Shepard	Jack Cobb, F
1925	Princeton	21-2	Al Wittmer	Art Loeb, G
1926	Syracuse	19-1	Lew Andreas	Vic Hanson, F
1927	Notre Dame	19-1	George Keogan	John Nyikos, C
1928	Pittsburgh	21-0	Doc Carlson	Chuck Hyatt, F
1929	Montana St.	36-2	Schubert Dyche	John (Cat) Thompson, F
1930	Pittsburgh	23-2	Doc Carlson	Chuck Hyatt, F
1931	Northwestern	16-1	Dutch Lonborg	Joe Reiff, C
1932	Purdue	17-1	Piggy Lambert	John Wooden, G
1933	Kentucky	20-3	Adolph Rupp	Forest Sale, F
1934	Wyoming	26-3	Willard Witte	Les Witte, G
1935	NYU	19-1	Howard Cann	Sid Gross, F
1936	Notre Dame	22-2-1	George Keogan	John Moir, F
1937	Stanford	25-2	John Bunn	Hank Luisetti, F

Year		Record	Winner	Head Coach	Outstanding Player
1938	Temple	23-2	NIT	James Usilton	Meyer Bloom, G
1939	Oregon	29-5	NCAA	Howard Hobson	Slim Wintermute, C
	& LIU-Brooklyn (Helms)	24-0	NIT	Clair Bee	Irv Torgoff, F
1940	Indiana	20-3	NCAA	Branch McCracken	Marv Huffman, G
	& USC (Helms)	20-3	*	Sam Barry	Ralph Vaughn, F

*USC was beaten by Kansas in the West regional of the NCAA tournament.

National Champions (Cont.)

Year		Record	Winner	Head Coach	Outstanding Player
1941	**Wisconsin**	20-3	NCAA	Bud Foster	Gene Englund, F
1942	**Stanford**	27-4	NCAA	Everett Dean	Jim Pollard, F
1943	**Wyoming**	31-2	NCAA	Everett Shelton	Kenny Sailors, G
1944	**Utah**	21-4	NCAA	Vadal Peterson	Arnie Ferrin, F
	& Army (Helms)	15-0	**	Ed Kelleher	Dale Hall, F
1945	**Oklahoma** A&M	27-4	NCAA	Hank Iba	Bob Kurland, C
1946	**Oklahoma** A&M	31-2	NCAA	Hank Iba	Bob Kurland, C
1947	**Holy Cross**	27-3	NCAA	Doggie Julian	George Kaftan, F
1948	**Kentucky**	36-3	NCAA	Adolph Rupp	Ralph Beard, G
1949	**Kentucky**	32-2	NCAA	Adolph Rupp	Alex Groza, C
1950	**CCNY**	24-5	NCAA & NIT	Nat Holman	Irwin Dambrot, G
1951	**Kentucky**	32-2	NCAA	Adolph Rupp	Bill Spivey, C
1952	**Kansas**	28-3	NCAA	Phog Allen	Clyde Lovellette, C
1953	**Indiana**	23-3	NCAA	Branch McCracken	Don Schlundt, C
1954	**La Salle**	26-4	NCAA	Ken Loeffler	Tom Gola, F
	& Kentucky (Helms)	25-0	***	Adolph Rupp	Cliff Hagan, G
1955	**San Francisco**	28-1	NCAA	Phil Woolpert	Bill Russell, C
1956	**San Francisco**	29-0	NCAA	Phil Woolpert	Bill Russell, C
1957	**North Carolina**	32-0	NCAA	Frank McGuire	Lennie Rosenbluth, F
1958	**Kentucky**	23-6	NCAA	Adolph Rupp	Vern Hatton, G
1959	**California**	24-4	NCAA	Pete Newell	Darrall Imhoff, C
1960	**Ohio St**	25-3	NCAA	Fred Taylor	Jerry Lucas, C
1961	**Cincinnati**	27-3	NCAA	Ed Jucker	Bob Wiesenhahn, F
1962	**Cincinnati**	29-2	NCAA	Ed Jucker	Paul Hogue, C
1963	**Loyola-IL**	29-2	NCAA	George Ireland	Jerry Harkness, F
1964	**UCLA**	30-0	NCAA	John Wooden	Walt Hazzard, G
1965	**UCLA**	28-2	NCAA	John Wooden	Gail Goodrich, G
1966	**Texas Western**	28-1	NCAA	Don Haskins	Bobby Joe Hill, G
1967	**UCLA**	30-0	NCAA	John Wooden	Lew Alcindor, C
1968	**UCLA**	29-1	NCAA	John Wooden	Lew Alcindor, C
1969	**UCLA**	29-1	NCAA	John Wooden	Lew Alcindor, C
1970	**UCLA**	28-2	NCAA	John Wooden	Sidney Wicks, F
1971	**UCLA**	29-1	NCAA	John Wooden	Sidney Wicks, F
1972	**UCLA**	30-0	NCAA	John Wooden	Bill Walton, C
1973	**UCLA**	30-0	NCAA	John Wooden	Bill Walton, C
1974	**N.C. State**	30-1	NCAA	Norm Sloan	David Thompson, F
1975	**UCLA**	28-3	NCAA	John Wooden	Dave Meyers, F
1976	**Indiana**	32-0	NCAA	Bob Knight	Scott May, F
1977	**Marquette**	25-7	NCAA	Al McGuire	Butch Lee, G
1978	**Kentucky**	30-2	NCAA	Joe B. Hall	Jack Givens, F
1979	**Michigan St**	26-6	NCAA	Jud Heathcote	Magic Johnson, G
1980	**Louisville**	33-3	NCAA	Denny Crum	Darrell Griffith, G
1981	**Indiana**	26-9	NCAA	Bob Knight	Isiah Thomas, G
1982	**North Carolina**	32-2	NCAA	Dean Smith	James Worthy, F
1983	**N.C. State**	26-10	NCAA	Jim Valvano	Sidney Lowe, G
1984	**Georgetown**	34-3	NCAA	John Thompson	Patrick Ewing, C
1985	**Villanova**	25-10	NCAA	Rollie Massimino	Ed Pinckney, C
1986	**Louisville**	32-7	NCAA	Denny Crum	Pervis Ellison, C
1987	**Indiana**	30-4	NCAA	Bob Knight	Steve Alford, G
1988	**Kansas**	27-11	NCAA	Larry Brown	Danny Manning, C
1989	**Michigan**	30-7	NCAA	Steve Fisher	Glen Rice, F
1990	**UNLV**	35-5	NCAA	Jerry Tarkanian	Larry Johnson, F
1991	**Duke**	32-7	NCAA	Mike Krzyzewski	Christian Laettner, F/C
1992	**Duke**	34-2	NCAA	Mike Krzyzewski	Christian Laettner, C
1993	**North Carolina**	34-4	NCAA	Dean Smith	Eric Montross, C
1994	**Arkansas**	31-3	NCAA	Nolan Richardson	Corliss Williamson, F

**Army did not lift its policy against postseason play until accepting a bid to the 1961 NIT.
***Unbeaten Kentucky turned down a bid to the 1954 NCAA tournament after the NCAA declared seniors Cliff Hagan, Frank Ramsey and Lou Tsioropoulos ineligible for postseason play.

The Red Cross Benefit Games, 1943-45

For three seasons during World War II, the NCAA and NIT champions met in a benefit game at Madison Square Garden in New York to raise money for the Red Cross. The NCAA champs won all three games.

Year	Winner	Score	Loser
1943	Wyoming (NCAA)	52-47	St. John's (NIT)
1944	Utah (NCAA)	43-36	St. John's (NIT)
1945	Oklahoma A&M (NCAA)	52-44	DePaul (NIT)

NCAA Final Four

The NCAA basketball tournament began in 1939 under the sponsorship of the National Association of Basketball Coaches, but was taken over by the NCAA in 1940. From 1939-51, the winners of the Eastern and Western Regionals played for the national championship, while regional runners-up shared third place. The concept of a Final Four originated in 1952 when four teams qualified for the first national semifinals. Consolation games to determine overall third place were held between regional finalists from 1946-51 and then national semifinalists from 1952-81. Consolation games were discontinued in 1982.

Multiple champions: UCLA (10); Indiana and Kentucky (5); North Carolina (3); Cincinnati, Duke, Kansas, Louisville, N.C. State, Oklahoma A&M (now Oklahoma St.) and San Francisco (2).

Year	Champion	Runner-up	Score	Final Two	Third Place	
1939	Oregon	Ohio St.	46-33	@ Evanston, IL	Oklahoma	Villanova
1940	Indiana	Kansas	60-42	@ Kansas City	Duquesne	USC
1941	Wisconsin	Washington St.	39-34	@ Kansas City	Arkansas	Pittsburgh
1942	Stanford	Dartmouth	53-38	@ Kansas City	Colorado	Kentucky
1943	Wyoming	Georgetown	46-34	@ New York	DePaul	Texas
1944	Utah	Dartmouth	42-40	@ New York	Iowa St.	Ohio St.
1945	Oklahoma A&M	NYU	49-45	@ New York	Arkansas	Ohio St.

Year	Champion	Runner-up	Score	Final Two	Third Place	Fourth Place
1946	Oklahoma A&M	North Carolina	43-40 (OT)	@ New York	Ohio St.	California
1947	Holy Cross	Oklahoma	58-47	@ New York	Texas	CCNY
1948	Kentucky	Baylor	58-42	@ New York	Holy Cross	Kansas St.
1949	Kentucky	Oklahoma A&M	46-36	@ Seattle	Illinois	Oregon St.
1950	CCNY	Bradley	71-68	@ New York	N.C. State	Baylor
1951	Kentucky	Kansas St.	68-58	@ Minneapolis	Illinois	Oklahoma A&M

Year	Champion	Runner-up	Score	Third Place	Fourth Place	Final Four
1952	Kansas	St. John's	80-63	Illinois	Santa Clara	@ Seattle
1953	Indiana	Kansas	69-68	Washington	LSU	@ Kansas City
1954	La Salle	Bradley	92-76	Penn St.	USC	@ Kansas City
1955	San Francisco	La Salle	77-63	Colorado	Iowa	@ Kansas City
1956	San Francisco	Iowa	83-71	Temple	SMU	@ Evanston, IL
1957	North Carolina	Kansas	54-53 (3OT)	San Francisco	Michigan St.	@ Kansas City
1958	Kentucky	Seattle	84-72	Temple	Kansas St.	@ Louisville
1959	California	West Virginia	71-70	Cincinnati	Louisville	@ Louisville
1960	Ohio St.	California	75-55	Cincinnati	NYU	@ San Francisco
1961	Cincinnati	Ohio St.	70-65 (OT)	St. Joseph's-PA	Utah	@ Kansas City
1962	Cincinnati	Ohio St.	71-59	Wake Forest	UCLA	@ Louisville
1963	Loyola-IL	Cincinnati	60-58 (OT)	Duke	Oregon St.	@ Louisville
1964	UCLA	Duke	98-83	Michigan	Kansas St.	@ Kansas City
1965	UCLA	Michigan	91-80	Princeton	Wichita St.	@ Portland, OR
1966	Texas Western	Kentucky	72-65	Duke	Utah	@ College Park, MD
1967	UCLA	Dayton	79-64	Houston	North Carolina	@ Louisville
1968	UCLA	North Carolina	78-55	Ohio St.	Houston	@ Los Angeles
1969	UCLA	Purdue	92-72	Drake	North Carolina	@ Louisville
1970	UCLA	Jacksonville	80-69	New Mexico St.	St. Bonaventure	@ College Park, MD
1971	UCLA	Villanova	68-62	Western Ky.	Kansas	@ Houston
1972	UCLA	Florida St.	81-76	North Carolina	Louisville	@ Los Angeles
1973	UCLA	Memphis St.	87-66	Indiana	Providence	@ St. Louis
1974	N.C. State	Marquette	76-64	UCLA	Kansas	@ Greensboro, NC
1975	UCLA	Kentucky	92-85	Louisville	Syracuse	@ San Diego
1976	Indiana	Michigan	86-68	UCLA	Rutgers	@ Philadelphia
1977	Marquette	North Carolina	67-59	UNLV	NC-Charlotte	@ Atlanta
1978	Kentucky	Duke	94-88	Arkansas	Notre Dame	@ St. Louis
1979	Michigan St.	Indiana St.	75-64	DePaul	Penn	@ Salt Lake City
1980	Louisville	UCLA	59-54	Purdue	Iowa	@ Indianapolis
1981	Indiana	North Carolina	63-50	Virginia	LSU	@ Philadelphia

Year	Champion	Runner-up	Score	Third Place		Final Four
1982	North Carolina	Georgetown	63-62	Houston	Louisville	@ New Orleans
1983	N.C. State	Houston	54-52	Georgia	Louisville	@ Albuquerque
1984	Georgetown	Houston	84-75	Kentucky	Virginia	@ Seattle
1985	Villanova	Georgetown	66-64	Memphis St.	St. John's	@ Lexington
1986	Louisville	Duke	72-69	Kansas	LSU	@ Dallas
1987	Indiana	Syracuse	74-73	Providence	UNLV	@ New Orleans
1988	Kansas	Oklahoma	83-79	Arizona	Duke	@ Kansas City
1989	Michigan	Seton Hall	80-79 (OT)	Duke	Illinois	@ Seattle
1990	UNLV	Duke	103-73	Arkansas	Georgia Tech	@ Denver
1991	Duke	Kansas	72-65	North Carolina	UNLV	@ Indianapolis
1992	Duke	Michigan	71-51	Cincinnati	Indiana	@ Minneapolis
1993	North Carolina	Michigan	77-71	Kansas	Kentucky	@ New Orleans
1994	Arkansas	Duke	77-72	Arizona	Florida	@ Charlotte

Note: Five teams have had their standing in the Final Four vacated for using ineligible players: 1961—St. Joseph's-PA (3rd place); 1971—Villanova (Runner-up) and Western Kentucky (3rd place); 1980—UCLA (Runner-up); 1985—Memphis St. (3rd place).

Most Outstanding Player

A Most Outstanding Player has been selected every year of the NCAA tournament. Winners who did not play for the tournament champion are listed in **bold** type. The 1939 and 1951 winners are unofficial and not recognized by the NCAA.
Multiple winners: Lew Alcindor (3); Alex Groza, Bob Kurland, Jerry Lucas and Bill Walton (2).

Year		Year		Year	
1939	**Jimmy Hull**, Ohio St.	1958	**Elgin Baylor**, Seattle	1977	Butch Lee, Marquette
1940	Marv Huffman, Indiana	1959	**Jerry West**, West Virginia	1978	Jack Givens, Kentucky
1941	John Kotz, Wisconsin	1960	Jerry Lucas, Ohio St.	1979	Magic Johnson, Michigan St.
1942	Howie Dallmar, Stanford	1961	**Jerry Lucas**, Ohio St.	1980	Darrell Griffith, Louisville
1943	Kenny Sailors, Wyoming	1962	Paul Hogue, Cincinnati	1981	Isiah Thomas, Indiana
1944	Arnie Ferrin, Utah	1963	**Art Heyman**, Duke	1982	James Worthy, N. Carolina
1945	Bob Kurland, Okla. A&M	1964	Walt Hazzard, UCLA	1983	**Akeem Olajuwon**, Houston
1946	Bob Kurland, Okla. A&M	1965	**Bill Bradley**, Princeton	1984	Patrick Ewing, Georgetown
1947	George Kaftan, Holy Cross	1966	**Jerry Chambers**, Utah	1985	Ed Pinckney, Villanova
1948	Alex Groza, Kentucky	1967	Lew Alcindor, UCLA	1986	Pervis Ellison, Louisville
1949	Alex Groza, Kentucky	1968	Lew Alcindor, UCLA	1987	Keith Smart, Indiana
1950	Irwin Dambrot, CCNY	1969	Lew Alcindor, UCLA	1988	Danny Manning, Kansas
1951	Bill Spivey, Kentucky	1970	Sidney Wicks, UCLA	1989	Glen Rice, Michigan
1952	Clyde Lovellette, Kansas	1971	**Howard Porter**, Villanova	1990	Anderson Hunt, UNLV
1953	**B.H. Born**, Kansas	1972	Bill Walton, UCLA	1991	Christian Laettner, Duke
1954	Tom Gola, La Salle	1973	Bill Walton, UCLA	1992	Bobby Hurley, Duke
1955	Bill Russell, San Francisco	1974	David Thompson, N.C. State	1993	Donald Williams, N. Carolina
1956	**Hal Lear**, Temple	1975	Richard Washington, UCLA	1994	Corliss Williamson, Arkansas
1957	**Wilt Chamberlain**, Kansas	1976	Kent Benson, Indiana		

Note: Howard Porter (1971) was declared ineligible by the NCAA after the tournament and his award was vacated.

Final Four All-Decade Teams

To celebrate the 50th anniversary of the NCAA tournament in 1989, five All-Decade teams were selected by a blue ribbon panel of coaches and administrators. An All-Time Final Four team was also chosen.
Selection panel: Vic Bubas, Denny Crum, Wayne Duke, Dave Gavitt, Joe B. Hall, Jud Heathcote, Hank Iba, Pete Newell, Dean Smith, John Thompson and John Wooden.

All-Time Team

	Years
Lew Alcindor, UCLA	1967-69
Larry Bird, Indiana St.	1979
Wilt Chamberlain, Kansas	1957
Magic Johnson, Mich.St	1979
Michael Jordan, N. Carolina	1982

All-1950s

	Years
Elgin Baylor, Seattle	1958
Wilt Chamberlain, Kansas	1957
Tom Gola, La Salle	1954
K.C. Jones, San Francisco	1955
Clyde Lovellette, Kansas	1952
Oscar Robertson, Cinn.	1959-60
Guy Rodgers, Temple	1958
Lennie Rosenbluth, N. Carolina	1957
Bill Russell, San Francisco	1955-56
Jerry West, West Virginia	1959

All-1970s

	Years
Kent Benson, Indiana	1976
Larry Bird, Indiana St	1979
Jack Givens, Kentucky	1978
Magic Johnson, Mich. St.	1979
Marques Johnson, UCLA	1975-76
Scott May, Indiana	1976
David Thompson, N.C. State	1974
Bill Walton, UCLA	1972-74
Sidney Wicks, UCLA	1969-71
Keith Wilkes, UCLA	1972-74

All-1940s

	Years
Ralph Beard, Kentucky	1948-49
Howie Dallmar, Stanford	1942
Dwight Eddleman, Illinois	1949
Arnie Ferrin, Utah	1944
Alex Groza, Kentucky	1948-49
George Kaftan, Holy Cross	1947
Bob Kurland, Okla. A&M	1945-46
Jim Pollard, Stanford	1942
Kenny Sailors, Wyoming	1943
Gerry Tucker, Oklahoma	1947

All-1960s

	Years
Lew Alcindor, UCLA	1967-69
Bill Bradley, Princeton	1965
Gail Goodrich, UCLA	1964-65
John Havlicek, Ohio St	1961-62
Elvin Hayes, Houston	1967
Walt Hazzard, UCLA	1964
Jerry Lucas, Ohio St	1960-61
Jeff Mullins, Duke	1964
Cazzie Russell, Michigan	1965
Charlie Scott, N. Carolina	1968-69

All-1980s

	Years
Steve Alford, Indiana	1987
Johnny Dawkins, Duke	1986
Patrick Ewing, Georgetown	1982-84
Darrell Griffith, Louisville	1980
Michael Jordan, N. Carolina	1982
Rodney McCray, Louisville	1980
Akeem Olajuwon, Houston	1983-84
Ed Pinckney, Villanova	1985
Isiah Thomas, Indiana	1981
James Worthy, N. Carolina	1982

Note: Lew Alcindor later changed his name to Kareem Abdul-Jabbar; Keith Wilkes later changed his first name to Jamaal; and Akeem Olajuwon later changed the spelling of his first name to Hakeem.

Collegiate Commissioners Association Tournament

The Collegiate Commissioners Association staged an eight-team tournament for teams that didn't make the NCAA tournament in 1974 and '75.
Most Valuable Players: 1974—Kent Benson, Indiana: 1975—Bob Elliot, Arizona.

Year	Winner	Score	Loser	Site	Year	Winner	Score	Loser	Site
1974	Indiana	85-60	USC	St. Louis	1975	Drake	83-76	Arizona	Louisville

NCAA Tournament Appearances

Through 1994; listed are schools with most appearances, overall tournament records, times reaching Final Four, and number of NCAA championships.

App		W-L	F4	Championships	App		W-L	F4	Championships
36	Kentucky	63-33	10	5 (1948-49,51,58,78)	18	Ohio St	31-17	8	1 (1960)
30	UCLA	68-24	14	10 (1964-65,67-73,75)	18	Georgetown	31-17	4	1 (1984)
28	North Carolina	63-28	11	3 (1957,82,93)	18	Temple	22-18	2	None
24	Louisville	43-26	7	2 (1980,86)	18	Houston	26-23	5	None
24	Notre Dame	25-28	1	None	18	Princeton	11-22	1	None
23	Indiana	50-18	7	5 (1940,53,76,81,87)	17	Michigan	40-16	6	1 (1989)
23	Kansas	49-23	10	2 (1952,88)	17	N.C. State	27-16	3	2 (1974,83)
23	St. John's	23-25	2	None	17	Connecticut	12-18	0	None
21	Villanova	35-21	3	1 (1985)	17	West Virginia	11-17	1	None
21	Syracuse	29-22	2	None	17	BYU	11-20	0	None
21	Kansas St	27-25	4	None	16	Illinois	21-17	4	None
20	Arkansas	30-20	5	1 (1994)	16	Iowa	22-18	3	None
20	DePaul	20-23	2	None	16	Utah	19-19	3	1 (1944)
19	Duke	56-17	11	2 (1991-92)	16	Oregon St	12-19	2	None
19	Marquette	27-20	2	1 (1977)					

Note: Although all NCAA tournament appearances are included above, the NCAA has officially voided the records of Villanova (4-1) in 1971, UCLA (5-1) in 1980, Oregon St. (2-3) from 1980-82, N.C. State (0-2) from 1987-88, Kentucky (2-1) in 1988.

All-Time NCAA Division I Tournament Leaders

Through 1993-94; minimum of six games; **Last** column indicates final year played.

CAREER

Scoring

	Points	Yrs	Last	Gm	Pts
1	Christian Laettner, Duke	4	1992	23	407
2	Elvin Hayes, Houston	3	1968	13	358
3	Danny Manning, Kansas	4	1988	16	328
4	Oscar Robertson, Cincinnati	3	1960	10	324
5	Glen Rice, Michigan	4	1989	13	308
6	Lew Alcindor, UCLA	3	1969	12	304
7	Bill Bradley, Princeton	3	1965	9	303
8	Austin Carr, Notre Dame	3	1971	7	289
9	Juwan Howard, Michigan	3	1994	16	280
10	Jerry West, West Virginia	3	1960	9	275

	Average	Yrs	Last	Pts	Avg
1	Austin Carr, Notre Dame	3	1971	289	41.3
2	Bill Bradley, Princeton	3	1965	303	33.7
3	Oscar Robertson, Cincinnati	3	1960	324	32.4
4	Jerry West, West Virginia	3	1960	275	30.6
5	Bob Pettit, LSU	2	1954	183	30.5
6	Dan Issel, Kentucky	3	1970	176	29.3
7	Jim McDaniels, Western Ky	2	1971	176	29.3
8	Dwight Lamar, SW Louisiana	2	1973	175	29.2
9	Bo Kimble, Loyola-CA	3	1990	204	29.1
10	David Robinson, Navy	3	1987	200	28.6

Rebounds

	Total	Yrs	Last	Gm	No
1	Elvin Hayes, Houston	3	1968	13	222
2	Lew Alcindor, UCLA	3	1969	12	201
3	Jerry Lucas, Ohio St.	3	1962	12	197
4	Bill Walton, UCLA	3	1974	12	176
5	Christian Laettner, Duke	4	1992	23	169
6	Paul Hogue, Cincinnati	3	1962	12	160
7	Sam Lacey, New Mexico St	3	1970	11	157
8	Derrick Coleman, Syracuse	4	1990	14	155
9	Akeem Olajuwon, Houston	3	1984	15	153
10	Patrick Ewing, Georgetown	4	1985	18	144

	Average	Yrs	Last	Reb	Avg
1	Johnny Green, Michigan St	2	1959	118	19.7
2	Artis Gilmore, Jacksonville	2	1971	115	19.2
3	Paul Silas, Creighton	3	1964	111	18.5
4	Len Chappell, Wake Forest	2	1962	137	17.1
5	Elvin Hayes, Houston	3	1968	222	17.1
6	Lew Alcindor, UCLA	3	1969	201	16.8
7	Jerry Lucas, Ohio St.	3	1962	197	16.4
8	Bill Walton, UCLA	3	1974	176	14.7
9	Sam Lacey, New Mexico St	3	1970	157	14.3
10	Bob Lanier, St. Bonaventure	3	1970	85	14.2

3-Pt Field Goals

	Total	Yrs	Last	Gm	No
1	Bobby Hurley, Duke	4	1993	20	42
2	Jeff Fryer, Loyola-CA	3	1990	7	38
3	Glen Rice, Michigan	4	1989	13	35
4	Anderson Hunt, UNLV	3	1991	15	34
5	Dennis Scott, Georgia Tech	3	1990	8	33

Assists

	Total	Yrs	Last	Gm	No
1	Bobby Hurley, Duke	4	1993	20	145
2	Sherman Douglas, Syracuse	4	1989	14	106
3	Greg Anthony, UNLV	3	1991	15	100
4	Mark Wade, UNLV	2	1987	8	93
	Rumeal Robinson, Michigan	3	1990	11	93

SINGLE TOURNAMENT

Scoring

	Points	Year	Gm	Pts
1	Glen Rice, Michigan	1989	6	184
2	Bill Bradley, Princeton	1965	5	177
3	Elvin Hayes, Houston	1968	5	167
4	Danny Manning, Kansas	1988	6	163
5	Hal Lear, Temple	1956	5	160
	Jerry West, West Virginia	1959	5	160

	Average	Year	Gm	Pts	Avg
1	Austin Carr, Notre Dame	1970	3	158	52.7
2	Austin Carr, Notre Dame	1971	3	125	41.7
3	Jerry Chambers, Utah	1966	4	143	35.8
4	Bo Kimble, Loyola-CA	1990	4	143	35.8
5	Bill Bradley, Princeton	1965	5	177	35.4
6	Clyde Lovellette, Kansas	1952	4	141	35.3

All-Time NCAA Division I Tourney Leaders (Cont.)

Rebounds

Total	Year	Gm	No	Avg
1 Elvin Hayes, Houston	1968	5	97	19.4
2 Artis Gilmore, Jacksonville	1970	5	93	18.6
3 Elgin Baylor, Seattle	1958	5	91	18.2
4 Sam Lacey, New Mexico St.	1970	5	90	18.0
5 Clarence Glover, Western Ky	1971	5	89	17.8

Assists

Total	Year	Gm	No	Avg
1 Mark Wade, UNLV	1987	5	61	12.2
2 Rumeal Robinson, Michigan	1989	6	56	9.3
3 Sherman Douglas, Syracuse	1987	6	49	8.2
4 Bobby Hurley, Duke	1992	6	47	7.8
5 Michael Jackson, Georgetown	1985	6	45	7.5

SINGLE GAME

Scoring

Points	Year	Pts
1 Austin Carr, Notre Dame vs Ohio Univ	1970	61
2 Bill Bradley, Princeton vs Wichita St.	1965	58
3 Oscar Robertson, Cincinnati vs Arkansas	1958	56
4 Austin Carr, Notre Dame vs Kentucky	1970	52
Austin Carr, Notre Dame vs TCU	1971	52
6 David Robinson, Navy vs Michigan	1987	50
7 Elvin Hayes, Houston vs Loyola-IL	1968	49
8 Hal Lear, Temple vs SMU	1956	48
9 Austin Carr, Notre Dame vs Houston	1971	47
10 Dave Corzine, DePaul vs Louisville	1978	46
11 Bob Houbregs, Washington vs Seattle	1953	45
Austin Carr, Notre Dame vs Iowa	1970	45
Bo Kimble, Loyola-CA vs New Mexico St.	1990	45
14 Seven players tied with 44 each.		

Rebounds

Total	Year	No
1 Fred Cohen, Temple vs UConn	1956	34
2 Nate Thurmond, Bowling Green vs Miss. St.	1963	31
3 Jerry Lucas, Ohio St. vs Kentucky	1961	30
4 Toby Kimball, UConn vs St. Joseph's-PA	1965	29
5 Elvin Hayes, Houston vs Pacific	1966	28

Assists

Total	Year	No
1 Mark Wade, UNLV vs Indiana	1987	18
2 Sam Crawford, N. Mexico St. vs Nebraska	1993	16
3 Kenny Patterson, DePaul vs Syracuse	1985	15
4 Keith Smart, Indiana vs Auburn	1987	15
5 Five players tied with 14 each.		

SINGLE FINAL FOUR GAME

Letters in the **Year** column indicate the following: C for Consolation Game, F for Final and S for Semifinal.

Scoring

Total	Year	Pts
1 Bill Bradley, Princeton vs Wichita St	1965-C	58
2 Hal Lear, Temple vs SMU	1956-C	48
3 Bill Walton, UCLA vs Memphis St	1973-F	44
4 Bob Houbregs, Washington vs LSU	1953-C	42
Jack Egan, St. Joseph's-PA vs Utah	1961-C	42*
Gail Goodrich, UCLA vs Michigan	1965-C	42
7 Jack Givens, Kentucky vs Duke	1978-F	41
8 Oscar Robertson, Cincinnati vs L'ville	1959-C	39
Al Wood, N. Carolina vs Virginia	1981-S	39
10 Jerry West, West Va. vs Louisville	1959-S	38
Jerry Chambers, Utah vs Texas Western	1966-S	38
Freddie Banks, UNLV vs Indiana	1987-S	38

* Four overtimes.

Rebounds

Total	Year	No
1 Bill Russell, San Francisco vs Iowa	1956-F	27
2 Elvin Hayes, Houston vs UCLA	1967-S	24
3 Bill Russell, San Francisco vs SMU	1956-S	23
4 Four players tied with 22 each.		

Assists

Total	Year	No
1 Mark Wade, UNLV vs Indiana	1987-S	18
2 Rumeal Robinson, Michigan vs Illinois	1989-S	12
3 Michael Jackson, G'town vs St. John's	1985-S	11
4 Milt Wagner, Louisville vs LSU	1986-S	11
5 Rumeal Robinson, Mich. vs Seton Hall	1989-F	11*

*Overtime.

Teams in both NCAA and NIT

Fourteen teams played in both the NCAA and NIT tournaments from 1940-52. Colorado (1940), Utah (1944), Kentucky (1949) and BYU (1951) won one of the titles, while CCNY won two in 1950, beating Bradley in both championship games.

Year		NIT	NCAA
1940	Colorado	**Won Final**	Lost 1st Rd
	Duquesne	Lost Final	Lost 2nd Rd
1944	Utah	Lost 1st Rd	**Won Final**
1949	Kentucky	Lost 2nd Rd	**Won Final**
1950	CCNY	**Won Final**	**Won Final**
	Bradley	Lost Final	Lost Final
1951	BYU	**Won Final**	Lost 2nd Rd
	St. John's	Lost 3rd Rd	Lost 2nd Rd
	N.C. State	Lost 2nd Rd	Lost 2nd Rd
	Arizona	Lost 2nd Rd	Lost 1st Rd
1952	St. John's	Lost Final	Lost 2nd Rd
	Dayton	Lost 1st Rd	Lost Final
	Duquesne	Lost 2nd Rd	Lost 2nd Rd
	Saint Louis	Lost 2nd Rd	Lost 2nd Rd

Most Popular Final Four Sites

The NCAA has staged its Men's Division I championship—the Final Two (1939-51) and Final Four (since 1952)—at 29 different arenas and indoor stadiums in 24 different cities. The following facilities have all hosted the event more than once.

No	Arena	Years
9	Municipal Auditorium (KC)	1940-42, 53-55, 57, 61, 64
7	Madison Sq. Garden (NYC)	1943-48, 50
6	Freedom Hall (Louisville)	1958-59, 62-63, 67, 69
3	Superdome (New Orleans)	1982, 87, 93
2	Edmundson Pavilion (Seattle)	1949, 52
	Kingdome (Seattle)	1984, 89
	Cole Field House (College Park, Md.)	1966, 70
	LA Sports Arena	1968, 72
	St. Louis Arena	1973, 78
	Spectrum (Philadelphia)	1976, 81

NIT Championship

The National Invitation Tournament began under the sponsorship of the Metropolitan New York Basketball Writers Association in 1938. The NIT is now administered by the Metropolitan Intercollegiate Basketball Association. All championship games have been played at Madison Square Garden.

Multiple winners: St. John's (5); Bradley (4); BYU, Dayton, Kentucky, LIU-Brooklyn, Providence, Temple and Virginia (2).

Year	Winner	Score	Loser	Year	Winner	Score	Loser
1938	Temple	60-36	Colorado	1968	Dayton	61-48	Kansas
1939	LIU-Brooklyn	44-32	Loyola-IL	1969	Temple	89-76	Boston College
1940	Colorado	51-40	Duquesne	1970	Marquette	65-53	St. John's
1941	LIU-Brooklyn	56-42	Ohio Univ.	1971	North Carolina	84-66	Georgia Tech
1942	West Virginia	47-45	Western Ky.	1972	Maryland	100-69	Niagara
1943	St. John's	48-27	Toledo	1973	Virginia Tech	92-91 (OT)	Notre Dame
1944	St. John's	47-39	DePaul	1974	Purdue	97-81	Utah
1945	DePaul	71-54	Bowling Green	1975	Princeton	80-69	Providence
1946	Kentucky	46-45	Rhode Island	1976	Kentucky	71-67	NC-Charlotte
1947	Utah	49-45	Kentucky	1977	St. Bonaventure	94-91	Houston
1948	Saint Louis	65-52	NYU	1978	Texas	101-93	N.C. State
1949	San Francisco	48-47	Loyola-IL	1979	Indiana	53-52	Purdue
1950	CCNY	69-61	Bradley	1980	Virginia	58-55	Minnesota
1951	BYU	62-43	Dayton	1981	Tulsa	86-84 (OT)	Syracuse
1952	La Salle	75-64	Dayton	1982	Bradley	67-58	Purdue
1953	Seton Hall	58-46	St. John's	1983	Fresno St.	69-60	DePaul
1954	Holy Cross	71-62	Duquesne	1984	Michigan	83-63	Notre Dame
1955	Duquesne	70-58	Dayton	1985	UCLA	65-62	Indiana
1956	Louisville	93-80	Dayton	1986	Ohio St.	73-63	Wyoming
1957	Bradley	84-83	Memphis St.	1987	Southern Miss.	84-80	La Salle
1958	Xavier-OH	78-74 (OT)	Dayton	1988	Connecticut	72-67	Ohio St.
1959	St. John's	76-71 (OT)	Bradley	1989	St. John's	73-65	Saint Louis
1960	Bradley	88-72	Providence	1990	Vanderbilt	74-72	Saint Louis
1961	Providence	62-59	Saint Louis	1991	Stanford	78-72	Oklahoma
1962	Dayton	73-67	St. John's	1992	Virginia	81-76 (OT)	Notre Dame
1963	Providence	81-66	Canisius	1993	Minnesota	62-61	Georgetown
1964	Bradley	86-54	New Mexico	1994	Villanova	80-73	Vanderbilt
1965	St. John's	55-51	Villanova				
1966	BYU	97-84	NYU				
1967	Southern Illinois	71-56	Marquette				

Most Valuable Player

A Most Valuable Player has been selected every year of the NIT tournament. Winners who did not play for the tournament champion are listed in **bold** type.

Multiple winners: None. However, Tom Gola is the only player to be named MVP in both the NIT (1952) and NCAA (1954) tournaments.

Year		Year		Year	
1938	Don Shields, Temple	1957	**Win Wilfong**, Memphis St.	1977	Greg Sanders, St. Bonaventure
1939	**Bill Lloyd**, St. John's	1958	Hank Stein, Xavier-OH	1978	Ron Baxter, Texas
		1959	Tony Jackson, St. John's		& Jim Krivacs, Texas
1940	Bob Doll, Colorado			1979	Clarence Carter, Indiana
1941	**Frank Baumholtz**, Ohio U.	1960	**Lenny Wilkens**, Providence		& Ray Tolbert, Indiana
1942	Rudy Baric, West Virginia	1961	Vin Ernst, Providence		
1943	Harry Boykoff, St. John's	1962	Bill Chmielewski, Dayton	1980	Ralph Sampson, Virginia
1944	Bill Kotsores, St. John's	1963	Ray Flynn, Providence	1981	Greg Stewart, Tulsa
1945	George Mikan, DePaul	1964	Lavern Tart, Bradley	1982	Mitchell Anderson, Bradley
1946	**Ernie Calverley**, Rhode Island	1965	Ken McIntyre, St. John's	1983	Ron Anderson, Fresno St.
1947	Vern Gardner, Utah	1966	**Bill Melchionni**, Villanova	1984	Tim McCormick, Michigan
1948	Ed Macauley, Saint Louis	1967	Walt Frazier, So. Illinois	1985	Reggie Miller, UCLA
1949	Don Lofgran, San Francisco	1968	Don May, Dayton	1986	Brad Sellers, Ohio St.
		1969	**Terry Driscoll**, Boston College	1987	Randolph Keys, So. Miss.
1950	Ed Warner, CCNY			1988	Phil Gamble, Connecticut
1951	Roland Minson, BYU	1970	Dean Meminger, Marquette	1989	Jayson Williams, St. John's
1952	Tom Gola, La Salle	1971	Bill Chamberlain, N. Carolina		
	& Norm Grekin, La Salle	1972	Tom McMillen, Maryland	1990	Scott Draud, Vanderbilt
1953	Walter Dukes, Seton Hall	1973	**John Shumate**, Notre Dame	1991	Adam Keefe, Stanford
1954	Togo Palazzi, Holy Cross	1974	**Mike Sojourner**, Utah	1992	Bryant Stith, Virginia
1955	**Maurice Stokes**, St. Francis-PA	1975	**Ron Lee**, Oregon	1993	Voshon Lenard, Minnesota
1956	Charlie Tyra, Louisville	1976	**Cedric Maxwell**, NC-Charlotte	1994	**Doremus Bennerman**, Siena

All-Time Winningest Division I Teams

Top 25 Winning Percentage

Division I schools with best winning percentages through 1993-94 season (including tournament games). Years in Division I only; minimum 20 years. NCAA tournament columns indicate years in tournament, record and number of championships.

		First Year	Yrs	Games	Won	Lost	Tied	Pct	NCAA Tourney Yrs	W-L	Titles
1	UNLV	1961	34	1002	762	240	0	.760	12	30-11	1
2	Kentucky	1903	91	2102	1588	513	1	.756	36	63-33	5
3	North Carolina	1911	84	2169	1598	571	0	.737	36	63-28	3
4	St. John's	1908	87	2146	1494	652	0	.696	23	23-25	0
5	UCLA	1920	75	1899	1315	584	0	.692	30	68-24	10
6	Kansas	1899	96	2239	1542	697	0	.689	23	49-23	2
7	Syracuse	1901	93	2034	1383	651	0	.680	21	29-22	0
8	Western Kentucky	1915	75	1920	1304	616	0	.679	15	14-16	0
9	Duke	1906	89	2172	1463	709	0	.674	19	56-17	2
10	DePaul	1924	71	1719	1150	569	0	.669	20	20-23	0
11	Notre Dame	1898	89	2093	1374	718	1	.657	24	25-28	0
12	Louisville	1912	80	1919	1258	661	0	.656	24	43-26	2
13	Indiana	1901	94	2070	1350	720	0	.6522	23	50-18	5
14	Arkansas	1924	71	1798	1172	626	0	.6518	20	30-20	1
15	Temple	1895	98	2185	1416	769	0	.648	18	22-18	0
16	La Salle	1931	64	1631	1056	575	0	.6475	11	11-10	1
17	Weber St.	1963	32	903	584	319	0	.6467	10	4-11	0
18	Houston	1946	49	1361	875	486	0	.64291	18	26-23	0
19	Illinois	1906	89	1963	1262	701	0	.64289	16	21-17	0
20	Utah	1909	86	1973	1262	711	0	.640	16	19-19	1
21	Purdue	1897	96	2011	1286	725	0	.639	13	16-13	0
22	North Carolina St	1913	82	1982	1265	717	0	.6382	17	27-16	2
23	Penn	1902	93	2175	1387	788	0	.6377	15	13-17	0
24	Villanova	1921	74	1861	1181	680	0	.635	21	35-21	1
25	UTEP	1947	48	1298	819	479	0	.631	14	14-13	1

Top 35 Victories

Division I schools with most victories through 1993-94 (including postseason tournaments). Minimum 20 years in Division I.

	Wins		Wins		Wins		Wins
1 North Carolina	1598	10 Notre Dame	1374	19 N.C. State	1265	28 Montana St.	1208
2 Kentucky	1588	11 Indiana	1350	20 Illinois	1262	29 Cincinnati	1207
3 Kansas	1542	12 Washington	1323	Utah	1262	30 Arizona	1203
4 St. John's	1494	13 UCLA	1315	22 Bradley	1259	31 Kansas St	1195
5 Duke	1463	14 Western Ky	1304	23 Louisville	1257	32 Alabama	1192
6 Oregon St	1421	15 Princeton	1297	24 Washington St	1252	33 St. Joseph's-PA	1184
7 Temple	1416	16 Fordham	1287	25 Texas	1240	34 Villanova	1181
8 Penn	1387	17 Purdue	1286	26 Ohio St	1230	35 Iowa	1179
9 Syracuse	1383	18 West Virginia	1279	27 USC	1210		

Top 50 Single-Season Victories

Division I schools with most victories in a single season through 1993-94 (including postseason tournaments). NCAA champions in **bold** type.

	Year	Record		Year	Record		Year	Record
1 UNLV	1987	37-2	18 **N. Carolina**	1957	32-0	36 Indiana	1975	31-1
Duke	1986	37-3	**Indiana**	1976	32-0	**Wyoming**	1943	31-2
3 **Kentucky**	1948	36-3	**Kentucky**	1949	32-2	**Okla. A&M**	1946	31-2
4 Georgetown	1985	35-3	**Kentucky**	1951	32-2	Seton Hall	1953	31-2
Arizona	1988	35-3	**N. Carolina**	1982	32-2	Houston	1968	31-2
Kansas	1986	35-4	Temple	1988	32-2	Rutgers	1976	31-2
Oklahoma	1988	35-4	Arkansas	1978	32-3	Houston	1983	31-3
UNLV	1990	35-5	Bradley	1986	32-3	**Arkansas**	1994	31-3
9 UNLV	1991	34-1	Louisville	1983	32-4	Memphis St	1985	31-4
Duke	1992	34-2	Kentucky	1986	32-4	St. John's	1985	31-4
Kentucky	1947	34-3	N. Carolina	1987	32-4	Indiana	1993	31-4
Georgetown	1984	34-3	Temple	1987	32-4	LSU	1981	31-5
Arkansas	1991	34-4	Bradley	1950	32-5	St. John's	1986	31-5
N. Carolina	1993	34-4	Marshall	1947	32-5	Illinois	1989	31-5
15 Indiana St	1979	33-1	Houston	1984	32-5	Michigan	1993	31-5
Louisville	1980	33-3	Bradley	1951	32-6	Oklahoma	1985	31-6
UNLV	1986	33-5	**Louisville**	1986	32-7	Connecticut	1990	31-6
			Duke	1991	32-7	Syracuse	1987	31-7
						Seton Hall	1989	31-7

Associated Press Final Polls

The Associated Press introduced its weekly college basketball poll of sportswriters (later, sportswriters and broadcasters) during the 1948-49 season.

Since the NCAA Division I tournament has determined the national champion since 1939, the final AP poll ranks the nation's best teams through the regular season and conference tournaments.

Except for 1974 and '75, the final AP poll has always been released prior to the NCAA and NIT tournaments and has gone from a Top 10 (1949 and 1963-67) to a Top 20 (1950-62 and 1968-89) to a Top 25 (since 1990).

Tournament champions are in **bold** type.

1949

	Before Tourns	Head Coach	Final Record
1 **Kentucky**	29-1	Adolph Rupp	32-2
2 Oklahoma A&M	21-4	Hank Iba	23-5
3 Saint Louis	22-3	Eddie Hickey	22-4
4 Illinois	19-3	Harry Combes	21-4
5 Western Ky.	25-3	Ed Diddle	25-4
6 Minnesota	18-3	Ozzie Cowles	same
7 Bradley	25-6	Forddy Anderson	27-8
8 **San Francisco**	21-5	Pete Newell	25-5
9 Tulane	24-4	Cliff Wells	same
10 Bowling Green	21-6	Harold Anderson	24-7

NCAA Final Four (at Edmundson Pavilion, Seattle): **Third Place**—Illinois 57, Oregon St. 53. **Championship**—Kentucky 46, Oklahoma A&M 36.

NIT Final Four (at Madison Square Garden): **Semifinals**—San Francisco 49, Bowling Green 39; Loyola-IL 55, Bradley 50. **Third Place**—Bowling Green 82, Bradley 77. **Championship**—San Francisco 48, Loyola-IL 47.

1950

	Before Tourns	Head Coach	Final Record
1 Bradley	28-3	Forddy Anderson	32-5
2 Ohio St.	21-3	Tippy Dye	22-4
3 Kentucky	25-4	Adolph Rupp	25-5
4 Holy Cross	27-2	Buster Sheary	27-4
5 N.C. State	25-5	Everett Case	27-6
6 Duquesne	22-5	Dudey Moore	23-6
7 UCLA	24-5	John Wooden	24-7
8 Western Ky.	24-5	Ed Diddle	25-6
9 St. John's	23-4	Frank McGuire	24-5
10 La Salle	20-3	Ken Loeffler	21-4
11 Villanova	25-4	Al Severance	same
12 San Francisco	19-6	Pete Newell	19-7
13 LIU-Brooklyn	20-4	Clair Bee	20-5
14 Kansas St.	17-7	Jack Gardner	same
15 Arizona	26-4	Fred Enke	26-5
16 Wisconsin	17-5	Bud Foster	same
17 San Jose St.	21-7	Walter McPherson	same
18 Washington St.	19-13	Jack Friel	same
19 Kansas	14-11	Phog Allen	same
20 Indiana	17-5	Branch McCracken	same

Note: Unranked CCNY, coached by Nat Holman, won both the NCAAs and NIT. The Beavers entered the postseason at 17-5 and had a final record of 24-5.

NCAA Final Four (at Madison Square Garden): **Third Place**—N. Carolina St. 53, Baylor 41. **Championship**—CCNY 71, Bradley 68.

NIT Final Four (at Madison Square Garden): **Semifinals**—Bradley 83, Duquesne 72; CCNY 62, Duquesne 52. **Third Place**—St. John's 69, Duquesne 67 (OT). **Championship**—CCNY 69, Bradley 61.

1951

	Before Tourns	Head Coach	Final Record
1 **Kentucky**	28-2	Adolph Rupp	32-2
2 Oklahoma A&M	27-4	Hank Iba	29-6
3 Columbia	22-0	Lou Rossini	22-1
4 Kansas St.	22-3	Jack Gardner	25-4
5 Illinois	19-4	Harry Combes	22-5
6 Bradley	32-6	Forddy Anderson	same
7 Indiana	19-3	Branch McCracken	same
8 N.C. State	29-4	Everett Case	30-7
9 St. John's	22-3	Frank McGuire	26-5
10 Saint Louis	21-7	Eddie Hickey	22-8
11 **BYU**	22-8	Stan Watts	26-10
12 Arizona	24-4	Fred Enke	24-6
13 Dayton	24-4	Tom Blackburn	27-5
14 Toledo	23-8	Jerry Bush	same
15 Washington	22-5	Tippy Dye	24-6
16 Murray St.	21-6	Harlan Hodges	same
17 Cincinnati	18-3	John Wiethe	18-4
18 Siena	19-8	Dan Cunha	same
19 USC	21-6	Forrest Twogood	same
20 Villanova	25-6	Al Severance	25-7

NCAA Final Four (at Williams Arena, Minneapolis): **Third Place**—Illinois 61, Oklahoma St. 46. **Championship**—Kentucky 68, Kansas St. 58.

NIT Final Four (at Madison Sq. Garden): **Semifinals**—Dayton 69, St. John's 62 (OT); BYU 69, Seton Hall 59. **Third Place**—St. John's 70, Seton Hall 68 (2 OT). **Championship**—BYU 62, Dayton 43.

1952

	Before Tourns	Head Coach	Final Record
1 Kentucky	28-2	Adolph Rupp	29-3
2 Illinois	19-3	Harry Combes	22-4
3 Kansas St.	19-5	Jack Gardner	same
4 Duquesne	21-1	Dudey Moore	23-4
5 Saint Louis	22-6	Eddie Hickey	23-8
6 Washington	25-6	Tippy Dye	same
7 Iowa	19-3	Bucky O'Connor	same
8 **Kansas**	24-3	Phog Allen	28-3
9 West Virginia	23-4	Red Brown	same
10 St. John's	22-3	Frank McGuire	25-5
11 Dayton	24-3	Tom Blackburn	28-5
12 Duke	24-6	Harold Bradley	same
13 Holy Cross	23-3	Buster Sheary	24-4
14 Seton Hall	25-2	Honey Russell	25-3
15 St. Bonaventure	19-5	Ed Melvin	21-6
16 Wyoming	27-6	Everett Shelton	28-7
17 Louisville	20-5	Peck Hickman	20-6
18 Seattle	29-7	Al Brightman	29-8
19 UCLA	19-10	John Wooden	19-12
20 SW Texas St.	30-1	Milton Jowers	same

Note: Unranked La Salle, coached by Ken Loefler, won the NIT. The Explorers entered the postseason at 21-7 and had a final record of 25-7.

NCAA Final Four (at Edmundson Pavillion, Seattle): **Semifinals**—St. John's 61, Illinois 59; Kansas 74, Santa Clara 59. **Third Place**—Illinois 67, Santa Clara 64. **Championship**—Kansas 80, St. John's 63.

NIT Final Four (at Madison Sq. Garden): **Semifinals**—La Salle 59, Duquesne 46; Dayton 69, St. Bonaventure 62. **Third Place**—St. Bonaventure 48, Duquesne 34. **Championship**—La Salle 75, Dayton 64.

Associated Press Final Polls (Cont.)

Taken before NCAA and NIT tournaments

1953

	Before Tourns	Head Coach	Final Record
1 **Indiana**	19-3	Branch McCracken	23-3
2 **Seton Hall**	28-2	Honey Russell	31-2
3 Kansas	16-5	Phog Allen	19-6
4 Washington	27-2	Tippy Dye	30-3
5 LSU	22-1	Harry Rabenhorst	24-3
6 La Salle	25-2	Ken Loeffler	25-3
7 St. John's	14-5	Al DeStefano	17-6
8 Oklahoma A&M	22-6	Hank Iba	23-7
9 Duquesne	18-7	Dudey Moore	21-8
10 Notre Dame	17-4	John Jordan	19-5
11 Illinois	18-4	Harry Combes	same
12 Kansas St.	17-4	Jack Gardner	same
13 Holy Cross	18-5	Buster Sheary	20-6
14 Seattle	27-3	Al Brightman	29-4
15 Wake Forest	21-6	Murray Greason	22-7
16 Santa Clara	18-6	Bob Feerick	20-7
17 Western Ky.	25-5	Ed Diddle	25-6
18 N.C. State	26-6	Everett Case	same
19 DePaul	18-7	Ray Meyer	19-9
20 SW Missouri St.	19-4	Bob Vanatta	24-4

NCAA Final Four (at Municipal Auditorium, Kansas City): **Semifinals**—Indiana 80, LSU 67; Kansas 79, Washington 53. **Third Place**—Washington 88, LSU 69. **Championship**—Indiana 69, Kansas 68.
NIT Final Four (at Madison Sq. Garden): **Semifinals**—Seton Hall 74, Manhattan 56; St. John's 64, Duquesne 55. **Third Place**—Duquesne 81, Manhattan 67. **Championship**—Seton Hall 58, St. John's 46.

1955

	Before Tourns	Head Coach	Final Record
1 **San Francisco**	23-1	Phil Woolpert	28-1
2 Kentucky	22-2	Adolph Rupp	23-3
3 La Salle	22-4	Ken Loeffler	26-5
4 N.C. State	28-4	Everett Case	same
5 Iowa	17-5	Bucky O'Connor	19-7
6 **Duquesne**	19-4	Dudey Moore	22-4
7 Utah	23-3	Jack Gardner	24-4
8 Marquette	22-2	Jack Nagle	24-3
9 Dayton	23-3	Tom Blackburn	25-4
10 Oregon St.	21-7	Slats Gill	22-8
11 Minnesota	15-7	Ozzie Cowles	same
12 Alabama	19-5	Johnny Dee	same
13 UCLA	21-5	John Wooden	same
14 G. Washington	24-6	Bill Reinhart	same
15 Colorado	16-5	Bebe Lee	19-6
16 Tulsa	20-6	Clarence Iba	21-7
17 Vanderbilt	16-6	Bob Polk	same
18 Illinois	17-5	Harry Combes	same
19 West Virginia	19-10	Fred Schaus	19-11
20 Saint Louis	19-7	Eddie Hickey	20-8

NCAA Final Four (at Municipal Auditorium, Kansas City): **Semifinals**—La Salle 76, Iowa 73; San Francisco 62, Colorado 50. **Third Place**—Colorado 75, Iowa 74. **Championship**—San Francisco 77, La Salle 63.
NIT Final Four (at Madison Square Garden): **Semifinals**—Dayton 79, St. Francis-PA 73 (OT); Duquesne 65, Cincinnati 51. **Third Place**—Cincinnati 96, St. Francis-PA 91 (OT). **Championship**—Duquesne 70, Dayton 58.

1954

	Before Tourns	Head Coach	Final Record
1 Kentucky	25-0	Adolph Rupp	same
2 **La Salle**	21-4	Ken Loeffler	26-4
3 **Holy Cross**	23-2	Buster Sheary	26-2
4 Indiana	19-3	Branch McCracken	20-4
5 Duquesne	24-2	Dudey Moore	26-3
6 Notre Dame	20-2	John Jordan	22-3
7 Bradley	15-12	Forddy Anderson	19-13
8 Western Ky.	28-1	Ed Diddle	29-3
9 Penn St.	14-5	Elmer Gross	18-6
10 Oklahoma A&M	23-4	Hank Iba	24-5
11 USC	17-12	Forrest Twogood	19-14
12 G. Washington	23-2	Bill Reinhart	23-3
13 Iowa	17-5	Bucky O'Connor	same
14 LSU	21-3	Harry Rabenhorst	21-5
15 Duke	22-6	Harold Bradley	same
16 Niagara	22-5	Taps Gallagher	24-6
17 Seattle	26-1	Al Brightman	26-2
18 Kansas	16-5	Phog Allen	same
19 Illinois	17-5	Harry Combes	17-5
20 Maryland	23-7	Bud Millikan	same

NCAA Final Four (at Municipal Auditorium, Kansas City): **Semifinals**—La Salle 69, Penn St. 54; Bradley 74, USC 72. **Third Place**—Penn St. 70, USC 61. **Championship**—La Salle 92, Bradley 76.
NIT Final Four (at Madison Square Garden): **Semifinals**—Duquesne 66, Niagara 51; Holy Cross 75, Western Ky. 69. **Third Place**—Niagara 71, Western Ky. 65. **Championship**—Holy Cross 71, Duquesne 62.

1956

	Before Tourns	Head Coach	Final Record
1 San Francisco	25-0	Phil Woolpert	29-0
2 N.C. State	24-3	Everett Case	24-4
3 Dayton	23-3	Tom Blackburn	25-4
4 Iowa	17-5	Bucky O'Connor	20-6
5 Alabama	21-3	Johnny Dee	same
6 **Louisville**	23-3	Peck Hickman	26-3
7 SMU	22-2	Doc Hayes	25-4
8 UCLA	21-5	John Wooden	22-6
9 Kentucky	19-5	Adolph Rupp	20-6
10 Illinois	18-4	Harry Combes	same
11 Oklahoma City	18-6	Abe Lemons	20-7
12 Vanderbilt	19-4	Bob Polk	same
13 North Carolina	18-5	Frank McGuire	same
14 Holy Cross	22-4	Roy Leenig	22-5
15 Temple	23-3	Harry Litwack	27-4
16 Wake Forest	19-9	Murray Greason	same
17 Duke	19-7	Harold Bradley	same
18 Utah	21-5	Jack Gardner	22-6
19 Oklahoma A&M	18-8	Hank Iba	18-9
20 West Virginia	21-8	Fred Schaus	21-9

NCAA Final Four (at McGaw Hall, Evanston, IL): **Semifinals**—Iowa 83, Temple 76; San Francisco 86, SMU 68. **Third Place**—Temple 90, SMU 81. **Championship**—San Francisco 83, Iowa 71.
NIT Final Four (at Madison Square Garden): **Semifinals**—Dayton 89, St. Francis-NY 58; Louisville 89, St. Joseph's-PA 79. **Third Place**—St. Joseph's-PA 93, St. Francis-NY 82. **Championship**—Louisville 93, Dayton 80.

1957

		Before Tourns	Head Coach	Final Record
1	North Carolina	27-0	Frank McGuire	32-0
2	Kansas	21-2	Dick Harp	24-3
3	Kentucky	22-4	Adolph Rupp	23-5
4	SMU	21-3	Doc Hayes	22-4
5	Seattle	24-2	John Castellani	24-3
6	Louisville	21-5	Peck Hickman	same
7	West Va.	25-4	Fred Schaus	25-5
8	Vanderbilt	17-5	Bob Polk	same
9	Oklahoma City	17-8	Abe Lemons	19-9
10	Saint Louis	19-7	Eddie Hickey	19-9
11	Michigan St.	14-8	Forddy Anderson	16-10
12	Memphis St.	21-5	Bob Vanatta	24-6
13	California	20-4	Pete Newell	21-5
14	UCLA	22-4	John Wooden	same
15	Mississippi St.	17-8	Babe McCarthy	same
16	Idaho St.	24-2	John Grayson	25-4
17	Notre Dame	18-7	John Jordan	20-8
18	Wake Forest	19-9	Murray Greason	same
19	Canisius	20-5	Joe Curran	22-6
20	Oklahoma A&M	17-9	Hank Iba	same

Note: Unranked Bradley, coached by Chuck Orsborn, won the NIT. The Braves entered the tourney at 19-7 and had a final record of 22-7.

NCAA Final Four (at Municipal Auditorium, Kansas City): **Semifinals**—North Carolina 74, Michigan St. 70 (3 OT); Kansas 80, San Francisco 56. **Third Place**—San Francisco 67, Michigan St. 60. **Championship**—North Carolina 54, Kansas 53 (3 OT).

NIT Final Four (at Madison Square Garden): **Semifinals**—Memphis St. 80, St. Bonaventure 78; Bradley 78, Temple 66. **Third Place**—Temple 67, St. Bonaventure 50. **Championship**—Bradley 84, Memphis St. 83.

1959

		Before Tourns	Head Coach	Final Record
1	Kansas St.	24-1	Tex Winter	25-2
2	Kentucky	23-2	Adolph Rupp	24-3
3	Mississippi St.	24-1	Babe McCarthy	same*
4	Bradley	23-3	Chuck Orsborn	25-4
5	Cincinnati	23-3	George Smith	26-4
6	N.C. State	22-4	Everett Case	same
7	Michigan St.	18-3	Forddy Anderson	19-4
8	Auburn	20-2	Joel Eaves	same
9	North Carolina	20-4	Frank McGuire	20-5
10	West Virginia	25-4	Fred Schaus	29-5
11	California	20-4	Pete Newell	24-4
12	Saint Louis	20-5	John Benington	20-6
13	Seattle	23-6	Vince Cazzetta	same
14	St. Joseph's-PA	22-3	Jack Ramsay	22-5
15	St. Mary's-CA	18-5	Jim Weaver	19-6
16	TCU	19-5	Buster Brannon	20-6
17	Oklahoma City	20-6	Abe Lemons	20-7
18	Utah	21-5	Jack Gardner	21-7
19	St. Bonaventure	20-2	Eddie Donovan	20-3
20	Marquette	22-4	Eddie Hickey	23-6

*Turned down invitation to NCAA tournament because it was an integrated event.
Note: Unranked St.John's, coached by Joe Lapchick, won the NIT. The Redmen entered the tourney at 16-6 and had a final record of 20-6.

NCAA Final Four (at Freedom Hall, Louisville): **Semifinals**—West Virginia 94, Louisville 79; California 64, Cincinnati 58. **Third Place**—Cincinnati 98, Louisville 85. **Championship**—California 71, West Virginia 70.

NIT Final Four (at Madison Square Garden): **Semifinals**—Bradley 59, NYU 57; St. John's 76, Providence 55. **Third Place**—NYU 71, Providence 57. **Championship**—St. John's 76, Bradley 71 (OT).

1958

		Before Tourns	Head Coach	Final Record
1	West Virginia	26-1	Fred Schaus	26-2
2	Cincinnati	24-2	George Smith	25-3
3	Kansas St.	20-3	Tex Winter	22-5
4	San Francisco	24-1	Phil Woolpert	25-2
5	Temple	24-2	Harry Litwack	27-3
6	Maryland	20-6	Bud Millikan	22-7
7	Kansas	18-5	Dick Harp	same
8	Notre Dame	22-4	John Jordan	24-5
9	Kentucky	19-6	Adolph Rupp	23-6
10	Duke	18-7	Harold Bradley	same
11	Dayton	23-3	Tom Blackburn	25-4
12	Indiana	12-10	Branch McCracken	13-11
13	North Carolina	19-7	Frank McGuire	same
14	Bradley	20-6	Chuck Orsborn	20-7
15	Mississippi St.	20-5	Babe McCarthy	same
16	Auburn	16-6	Joel Eaves	same
17	Michigan St.	16-6	Forddy Anderson	same
18	Seattle	20-6	John Castellani	24-7
19	Oklahoma St.	19-7	Hank Iba	21-8
20	N.C. State	18-6	Everett Case	same

Note: Unranked Xavier-OH, coached by Jim McCafferty, won the NIT. The Musketeers entered the tourney at 15-11 and had a final record of 19-11.

NCAA Final Four (at Freedom Hall, Louisville): **Semifinals**—Kentucky 61, Temple 60; Seattle 73, Kansas St. 51. **Third Place**—Temple 67, Kansas St. 57. **Championship**—Kentucky 84, Seattle 72.

NIT Final Four (at Madison Square Garden): **Semifinals**—Dayton 80, St. John's 56; Xavier-OH 72, St. Bonaventure 53. **Third Place**—St. Bonaventure 84, St. John's 69. **Championship**—Xavier-OH 78, Dayton 74 (OT).

1960

		Before Tourns	Head Coach	Final Record
1	Cincinnati	25-1	George Smith	28-2
2	California	24-1	Pete Newell	28-2
3	Ohio St.	21-3	Fred Taylor	25-3
4	Bradley	24-2	Chuck Orsborn	27-2
5	West Virginia	24-4	Fred Schaus	26-5
6	Utah	24-2	Jack Gardner	26-3
7	Indiana	20-4	Branch McCracken	same
8	Utah St.	22-4	Cecil Baker	24-5
9	St. Bonaventure	19-3	Eddie Donovan	21-5
10	Miami-FL	23-3	Bruce Hale	23-4
11	Auburn	19-3	Joel Eaves	same
12	NYU	19-4	Lou Rossini	22-5
13	Georgia Tech	21-5	Whack Hyder	22-6
14	Providence	21-4	Joe Mullaney	24-5
15	Saint Louis	19-7	John Benington	19-8
16	Holy Cross	20-5	Roy Leenig	20-6
17	Villanova	19-5	Al Severance	20-6
18	Duke	15-10	Vic Bubas	17-11
19	Wake Forest	21-7	Bones McKinney	same
20	St. John's	17-7	Joe Lapchick	17-8

NCAA Final Four (at the Cow Palace, San Fran.): **Semifinals**—Ohio St. 76, NYU 54; California 77, Cincinnati 69. **Third Place**—Cincinnati 95, NYU 71. **Championship**—Ohio St. 75, California 55.

NIT Final Four (at Madison Square Garden): **Semifinals**—Bradley 82, St. Bonaventure 71; Providence 68, Utah St. 62. **Third Place**—Utah St. 99, St. Bonaventure 93. **Championship**—Bradley 88, Providence 72.

Associated Press Final Polls (Cont.)

Taken before NCAA and NIT tournaments

1961

		Before Tourns	Head Coach	Final Record
1	Ohio St.	24-0	Fred Taylor	27-1
2	**Cincinnati**	23-3	Ed Jucker	27-3
3	St. Bonaventure	22-3	Eddie Donovan	24-4
4	Kansas St.	22-3	Tex Winter	23-4
5	North Carolina	19-4	Frank McGuire	same
6	Bradley	21-5	Chuck Orsborn	same
7	USC	20-6	Forrest Twogood	21-8
8	Iowa	18-6	S. Scheuerman	same
9	West Virginia	23-4	George King	same
10	Duke	22-6	Vic Bubas	same
11	Utah	21-6	Jack Gardner	23-8
12	Texas Tech	14-9	Polk Robison	15-10
13	Niagara	16-4	Taps Gallagher	16-5
14	Memphis St.	20-2	Bob Vanatta	20-3
15	Wake Forest	17-10	Bones McKinney	19-11
16	St. John's	20-4	Joe Lapchick	20-5
17	St. Joseph's-PA	22-4	Jack Ramsay	25-5
18	Drake	19-7	Maury John	same
19	Holy Cross	19-4	Roy Leenig	22-5
20	Kentucky	18-8	Adolph Rupp	19-9

Note: Unranked Providence, coached by Joe Mullaney, won the NIT. The Friars entered the tourney at 20-5 and had a final record of 24-5.

NCAA Final Four (at Municipal Auditorium, Kansas City): **Semifinals**—Ohio St. 95, St. Joseph's-PA 69; Cincinnati 82, Utah 67. **Third Place**—St. Joseph's-PA 127, Utah 120 (4 OT). **Championship**—Cincinnati 70, Ohio St. 65 (OT).

NIT Final Four (at Madison Square Garden) **Semifinals**—St. Louis 67, Dayton 60; Providence 90, Holy Cross 83 (OT). **Third Place**—Holy Cross 85, Dayton 67. **Championship**—Providence 62, St. Louis 59.

1962

		Before Tourns	Head Coach	Final Record
1	Ohio St.	23-1	Fred Taylor	26-2
2	**Cincinnati**	25-2	Ed Jucker	29-2
3	Kentucky	22-2	Adolph Rupp	23-3
4	Mississippi St.	19-6	Babe McCarthy	same
5	Bradley	21-6	Chuck Orsborn	21-7
6	Kansas St.	22-3	Tex Winter	same
7	Utah	23-3	Jack Gardner	same
8	Bowling Green	21-3	Harold Anderson	same
9	Colorado	18-6	Sox Walseth	19-7
10	Duke	20-5	Vic Bubas	same
11	Loyola-IL	21-3	George Ireland	23-4
12	St. John's	19-4	Joe Lapchick	21-5
13	Wake Forest	18-8	Bones McKinney	22-9
14	Oregon St.	22-4	Slats Gill	24-5
15	West Virginia	24-5	George King	24-6
16	Arizona St.	23-3	Ned Wulk	23-4
17	Duquesne	20-5	Red Manning	22-7
18	Utah St.	21-5	Ladell Andersen	22-7
19	UCLA	16-9	John Wooden	18-11
20	Villanova	19-6	Jack Kraft	21-7

Note: Unranked Dayton, coached by Tom Blackburn, won the NIT. The Flyers entered the tourney at 20-6 and had a final record of 24-6.

NCAA Final Four (at Freedom Hall, Louisville): **Semifinals**—Ohio St. 84, Wake Forest 68; Cincinnati 72, UCLA 70. **Third Place**—Wake Forest 82, UCLA 80. **Championship**—Cincinnati 71, Ohio St. 59.

NIT Final Four (at Madison Square Garden): **Semifinals**—Dayton 98, Loyola-IL 82; St. John's 76, Duquesne 65. **Third Place**—Loyola-IL 95, Duquesne 84. **Championship**—Dayton 73, St. John's 67.

1963

AP ranked only 10 teams from the 1962-63 season through 1967-68.

		Before Tourns	Head Coach	Final Record
1	Cincinnati	23-1	Ed Jucker	26-2
2	Duke	24-2	Vic Bubas	27-3
3	**Loyola-IL**	24-2	George Ireland	29-2
4	Arizona St.	24-2	Ned Wulk	26-3
5	Wichita	19-7	Ralph Miller	19-8
6	Mississippi St.	21-5	Babe McCarthy	22-6
7	Ohio St.	20-4	Fred Taylor	same
8	Illinois	19-5	Harry Combes	20-6
9	NYU	17-3	Lou Rossini	18-5
10	Colorado	18-6	Sox Walseth	19-7

Note: Unranked Providence, coached by Joe Mullaney, won the NIT. The Friars entered the tourney at 21-4 and had a final record of 24-4.

NCAA Final Four (at Freedom Hall, Louisville): **Semifinals**—Loyola-IL 94, Duke 75; Cincinnati 80, Oregon St. 46. **Third Place**—Duke 85, Oregon St. 63. **Championship**—Loyola-IL 60, Cincinnati 58 (OT).

NIT Final Four (at Madison Square Garden): **Semifinals**—Providence 70, Marquette 64; Canisius 61, Villanova 46. **Third Place**—Marquette 66, Villanova 58. **Championship**—Providence 81, Canisius 66.

1964

AP ranked only 10 teams from the 1962-63 season through 1967-68.

		Before Tourns	Head Coach	Final Record
1	UCLA	26-0	John Wooden	30-0
2	Michigan	20-4	Dave Strack	23-5
3	Duke	23-4	Vic Bubas	26-5
4	Kentucky	21-4	Adolph Rupp	21-6
5	Wichita St.	22-5	Ralph Miller	23-6
6	Oregon St.	25-3	Slats Gill	25-4
7	Villanova	22-3	Jack Kraft	24-4
8	Loyola-IL	20-5	George Ireland	22-6
9	DePaul	21-3	Ray Meyer	21-4
10	Davidson	22-4	Lefty Driesell	same

Note: Unranked Bradley, coached by Chuck Orsborn, won the NIT. The Braves entered the tourney at 20-6 and finished with a record of 23-6.

NCAA Final Four (at Municipal Auditorium, Kansas City): **Semifinals**—Duke 91, Michigan 80; UCLA 90, Kansas St. 84. **Third Place**—Michigan 100, Kansas St. 90. **Championship**—UCLA 98, Duke 83.

NIT Final Four (12 at Madison Square Garden): **Semifinals**—New Mexico 72, NYU 65; Bradley 67, Army 52. **Third Place**—Army 60, NYU 59. **Championship**—Bradley 86, New Mexico 54.

Undefeated National Champions

The 1964 UCLA team is one of only seven NCAA champions to win the title with an undefeated record.

Year		W-L	Year		W-L
1956	San Francisco	29-0	1972	UCLA	30-0
1957	North Carolina	32-0	1973	UCLA	30-0
1964	UCLA	30-0	1976	Indiana	32-0
1967	UCLA	30-0			

1965

AP ranked only 10 teams from the 1962-63 season through 1967-68.

	Before Tourns	Head Coach	Final Record
1 Michigan	21-3	Dave Strack	24-4
2 **UCLA**	24-2	John Wooden	28-2
3 St. Joseph's-PA	25-1	Jack Ramsay	26-3
4 Providence	22-1	Joe Mullaney	24-2
5 Vanderbilt	23-3	Roy Skinner	24-4
6 Davidson	24-2	Lefty Driesell	same
7 Minnesota	19-5	John Kundla	same
8 Villanova	21-4	Jack Kraft	23-5
9 BYU	21-5	Stan Watts	21-7
10 Duke	20-5	Vic Bubas	same

Note: Unranked St. John's, coached by Joe Lapchick, won the NIT. The Redmen entered the tourney at 17-8 and finished with a record of 21-8.

NCAA Final Four (at Memorial Coliseum, Portland, OR): **Semifinals**—Michigan 93, Princeton 76; UCLA 108, Wichita St. 89. **Third Place**—Princeton 118, Wichita St. 82. **Championship**—UCLA 91, Michigan 80.

NIT Final Four (at Madison Square Garden): **Semifinals**—Villanova 91, NYU 69; St. John's 67, Army 60. **Third Place**—Army 75, NYU 74. **Championship**—St. John's 55, Villanova 51.

1966

AP ranked only 10 teams from the 1962-63 season through 1967-68.

	Before Tourns	Head Coach	Final Record
1 Kentucky	24-1	Adolph Rupp	27-2
2 Duke	23-3	Vic Bubas	26-4
3 **Texas Western**	23-1	Don Haskins	28-1
4 Kansas	22-3	Ted Owens	23-4
5 St. Joseph's-PA	22-4	Jack Ramsay	24-5
6 Loyola-IL	22-2	George Ireland	22-3
7 Cincinnati	21-5	Tay Baker	21-7
8 Vanderbilt	22-4	Roy Skinner	same
9 Michigan	17-7	Dave Strack	18-8
10 Western Ky.	23-2	Johnny Oldham	25-3

Note: Unranked BYU, coached by Stan Watts, won the NIT. The Cougars entered the tourney at 17-5 and had a final record of 20-5.

NCAA Final Four (at Cole Fieldhouse, College Park, MD): **Semifinals**—Kentucky 83, Duke 79; Texas Western 85, Utah 78. **Third Place**—Duke 79, Utah 77. **Championship**—Texas Western 72, Kentucky 65.

NIT Final Four (at Madison Square Garden): **Semifinals**—BYU 66, Army 60; NYU 69, Villanova 63. **Third Place**—Villanova 76, Army 65. **Championship**—BYU 97, NYU 84.

1967

AP ranked only 10 teams from the 1962-63 season through 1967-68.

	Before Tourns	Head Coach	Final Record
1 **UCLA**	26-0	John Wooden	30-0
2 Louisville	23-3	Peck Hickman	23-5
3 Kansas	22-3	Ted Owens	23-4
4 North Carolina	24-4	Dean Smith	26-6
5 Princeton	23-2	B.vanBreda Kolff	25-3
6 Western Ky.	23-2	Johnny Oldham	23-3
7 Houston	23-3	Guy Lewis	27-4
8 Tennessee	21-5	Ray Mears	21-7
9 Boston College	19-2	Bob Cousy	21-3
10 Texas Western	20-5	Don Haskins	22-6

Note: Unranked Southern Illinois, coached by Jack Hartman, won the NIT. The Salukis entered the tourney at 20-2 and had a final record of 24-2.

NCAA Final Four (at Freedom Hall, Louisville): **Semifinals**—Dayton 76, N. Carolina 62; UCLA 73, Houston 58. **Third Place**—Houston 84, N. Carolina 62. **Championship**—UCLA 79, Dayton 64.

NIT Final Four (at Madison Square Garden): **Semifinals**—Marquette 83, Marshall 78; Southern Ill. 79, Rutgers 70. **Third Place**—Rutgers 93, Marshall 76. **Championship**—Southern Ill. 71, Marquette 56.

1968

AP ranked only 10 teams from the 1962-63 season through 1967-68.

	Before Tourns	Head Coach	Final Record
1 Houston	28-0	Guy Lewis	31-2
2 **UCLA**	25-1	John Wooden	29-1
3 St. Bonaventure	22-0	Larry Weise	23-2
4 North Carolina	25-3	Dean Smith	28-4
5 Kentucky	21-4	Adolph Rupp	22-5
6 New Mexico	23-3	Bob King	23-5
7 Columbia	21-4	Jack Rohan	23-5
8 Davidson	22-4	Lefty Driesell	24-5
9 Louisville	20-6	John Dromo	21-7
10 Duke	21-5	Vic Bubas	22-6

Note: Unranked Dayton, coached by Don Donoher, won the NIT. The Flyers entered the tourney at 17-9 and had a final record of 21-9.

NCAA Final Four (at the Sports Arena, Los Angeles): **Semifinals**—N. Carolina 80, Ohio St. 66; UCLA 101, Houston 69. **Third Place**—Ohio St. 89, Houston 85. **Championship**—UCLA 78, N. Carolina 55.

NIT Final Four (at Madison Square Garden): **Semifinals**—Dayton 76, Notre Dame 74 (OT); Kansas 58, St. Peter's 46. **Third Place**—Notre Dame 81, St. Peter's 78. **Championship**—Dayton 61, Kansas 48.

Highest-Rated College Games on TV

The dozen highest-rated college basketball games seen on U.S. television have been NCAA tournament championship games, led by the 1979 Michigan State-Indiana State final that featured Magic Johnson and Larry Bird. The 1994 final between Arkansas and Duke is sixth.

Listed below are the finalists (winning team first), date of game, TV network, and TV rating and audience share (according to Nielson Media Research).

	Date	Net	Rtg/Sh			Date	Net	Rtg/Sh
1 Michigan St.-Indiana St.	3/26/79	NBC	24.1/38		7 N. Carolina-Georgetown	3/29/82	CBS	21.6/31
2 Villanova-Georgetown	4/1/85	CBS	23.3/33		8 UCLA-Kentucky	3/31/75	NBC	21.3/33
3 Duke-Michigan	4/6/92	CBS	22.7/35		9 Michigan-Seton Hall	4/3/89	CBS	21.3/33
4 N.C. State-Houston	4/4/83	CBS	22.3/32		10 Louisville-Duke	3/32/86	CBS	20.7/31
5 N. Carolina-Michigan	4/5/93	CBS	22.2/34		11 Indiana-N. Carolina	3/30/81	NBC	20.7/29
6 Arkansas-Duke	4/4/94	CBS	21.6/33		12 UCLA-Memphis St.	3/26/73	NBC	20.5/32

Associated Press Final Polls (Cont.)

Taken before NCAA, NIT and Collegiate Commissioner's Assn. (1974-75) tournaments; (*) indicates on probation.

1969

	Before Tourns	Head Coach	Final Record
1 UCLA	25-1	John Wooden	29-1
2 La Salle	23-1	Tom Gola	same*
3 Santa Clara	26-1	Dick Garibaldi	27-2
4 North Carolina	25-3	Dean Smith	27-5
5 Davidson	24-2	Lefty Driesell	26-3
6 Purdue	20-4	George King	23-5
7 Kentucky	22-4	Adolph Rupp	23-5
8 St. John's	22-4	Lou Carnesecca	23-6
9 Duquesne	19-4	Red Manning	21-5
10 Villanova	21-4	Jack Kraft	21-5
11 Drake	23-4	Maury John	26-5
12 New Mexico St.	23-3	Lou Henson	24-5
13 South Carolina	20-6	Frank McGuire	21-7
14 Marquette	22-4	Al McGuire	24-5
15 Louisville	20-5	John Dromo	21-6
16 Boston College	21-3	Bob Cousy	24-4
17 Notre Dame	20-6	Johnny Dee	20-7
18 Colorado	20-6	Sox Walseth	21-7
19 Kansas	20-6	Ted Owens	20-7
20 Illinois	19-5	Harvey Schmidt	same

Note: NIT champ Temple, coached by Harry Litwak, entered the tourney unranked at 18-8 and had a final record of 22-8.

NCAA Final Four (at Freedom Hall, Louisville): **Semifinals**—Purdue 92, N. Carolina 65; UCLA 85, Drake 82. **Third Place**—Drake 104, N. Carolina 84. **Championship**—UCLA 92, Purdue 72.

NIT Final Four (at Madison Square Garden): **Semifinals**—Temple 63, Tennessee 58; Boston College 73, Army 61. **Third Place**—Tennessee 64, Army 52. **Championship**—Temple 89, Boston College 76.

1970

	Before Tourns	Head Coach	Final Record
1 Kentucky	25-1	Adolph Rupp	26-2
2 UCLA	24-2	John Wooden	28-2
3 St. Bonaventure	22-1	Larry Weise	25-3
4 Jacksonville	23-1	Joe Williams	27-2
5 New Mexico St.	23-2	Lou Henson	27-3
6 South Carolina	25-3	Frank McGuire	25-3
7 Iowa	19-4	Ralph Miller	20-5
8 Marquette	22-3	Al McGuire	26-3
9 Notre Dame	20-6	Johnny Dee	21-8
10 N.C. State	22-6	Norm Sloan	23-7
11 Florida St.	23-3	Hugh Durham	23-3
12 Houston	24-3	Guy Lewis	25-5
13 Penn	25-1	Dick Harter	25-2
14 Drake	21-6	Maury John	22-7
15 Davidson	22-4	Terry Holland	22-5
16 Utah St.	20-6	Ladell Andersen	22-7
17 Niagara	21-5	Frank Layden	22-7
18 Western Ky.	22-2	John Oldham	22-3
19 Long Beach St.	23-3	Jerry Tarkanian	24-5
20 USC	18-8	Bob Boyd	18-8

NCAA Final Four (at Cole Fieldhouse, College Park, MD): **Semifinals**—Jacksonville 91, St. Bonaventure 83; UCLA 93, New Mexico St. 77. **Third Place**—N. Mexico St. 79, St. Bonaventure 73. **Championship**—UCLA 80, Jacksonville 69.

NIT Final Four (at Madison Square Garden): **Semifinals**—St. John's 60, Army 59; Marquette 101, LSU 79. **Third Place**—Army 75, LSU 68. **Championship**—Marquette 65, St. John's 53.

1971

	Before Tourns	Head Coach	Final Record
1 UCLA	25-1	John Wooden	29-1
2 Marquette	26-0	Al McGuire	28-1
3 Penn	26-0	Dick Harter	28-1
4 Kansas	25-1	Ted Owens	27-3
5 USC	24-2	Bob Boyd	24-2
6 South Carolina	23-4	Frank McGuire	23-6
7 Western Ky.	20-5	John Oldham	24-6
8 Kentucky	22-4	Adolph Rupp	22-6
9 Fordham	25-1	Digger Phelps	26-3
10 Ohio St.	19-5	Fred Taylor	20-6
11 Jacksonville	22-3	Tom Wasdin	22-4
12 Notre Dame	19-7	Johnny Dee	20-9
13 North Carolina	22-6	Dean Smith	26-6
14 Houston	20-6	Guy Lewis	22-7
15 Duquesne	21-3	Red Manning	21-4
16 Long Beach St.	21-4	Jerry Tarkanian	23-5
17 Tennessee	20-6	Ray Mears	21-7
18 Villanova	19-5	Jack Kraft	23-6
19 Drake	20-7	Maury John	21-8
20 BYU	18-9	Stan Watts	18-11

NCAA Final Four (at The Astrodome, Houston): **Semifinals**—Villanova 92, Western Ky. 89 (2 OT); UCLA 68, Kansas 60. **Third Place**—Western Ky. 77, Kansas 75. **Championship**—UCLA 68, Villanova 62.

NIT Final Four (at Madison Square Garden): **Semifinals**—N. Carolina 73, Duke 69; Ga. Tech 76, St. Bonaventure 71 (2 OT). **Third Place**—St. Bonaventure 92, Duke 88 (OT). **Championship**—N. Carolina 84, Ga. Tech 66.

1972

	Before Tourns	Head Coach	Final Record
1 UCLA	26-0	John Wooden	30-0
2 North Carolina	23-4	Dean Smith	26-5
3 Penn	23-2	Chuck Daly	25-3
4 Louisville	23-4	Denny Crum	26-5
5 Long Beach St.	23-3	Jerry Tarkanian	25-4
6 South Carolina	22-4	Frank McGuire	24-5
7 Marquette	24-2	Al McGuire	25-4
8 SW Louisiana	23-3	Beryl Shipley	25-4
9 BYU	21-4	Stan Watts	21-5
10 Florida St.	23-5	Hugh Durham	27-6
11 Minnesota	17-6	Bill Musselman	18-7
12 Marshall	23-3	Carl Tacy	23-4
13 Memphis St.	21-6	Gene Bartow	21-7
14 Maryland	23-5	Lefty Driesell	27-5
15 Villanova	19-6	Jack Kraft	20-8
16 Oral Roberts	25-1	Ken Trickey	26-2
17 Indiana	17-7	Bob Knight	17-8
18 Kentucky	20-6	Adolph Rupp	21-7
19 Ohio St.	18-6	Fred Taylor	same
20 Virginia	21-6	Bill Gibson	21-7

NCAA Final Four (at the Sports Arena, Los Angeles): **Semifinals**—Florida St. 79, N. Carolina 75; UCLA 96, Louisville 77. **Third Place**—N. Carolina 105, Louisville 91. **Championship**—UCLA 81, Florida St. 76.

NIT Final Four (at Madison Square Garden): **Semifinals**—Maryland 91, Jacksonville 77; Niagara 69, St. John's 67. **Third Place**—Jacksonville 83, St. John's 80. **Championship**—Maryland 100, Niagara 69.

1973

	Before Tourns	Head Coach	Final Record
1 **UCLA**	26-0	John Wooden	30-0
2 N.C. State	27-0	Norm Sloan	same*
3 Long Beach St.	24-2	Jerry Tarkanian	26-3
4 Providence	24-2	Dave Gavitt	27-4
5 Marquette	23-3	Al McGuire	25-4
6 Indiana	19-5	Bob Knight	22-6
7 SW Louisiana	23-2	Beryl Shipley	24-5
8 Maryland	22-6	Lefty Driesell	23-7
9 Kansas St.	22-4	Jack Hartman	23-5
10 Minnesota	20-4	Bill Musselman	21-5
11 North Carolina	22-7	Dean Smith	25-8
12 Memphis St.	21-5	Gene Bartow	24-6
13 Houston	23-3	Guy Lewis	23-4
14 Syracuse	22-4	Roy Danforth	24-5
15 Missouri	21-5	Norm Stewart	21-6
16 Arizona St.	18-7	Ned Wulk	19-9
17 Kentucky	19-7	Joe B. Hall	20-8
18 Penn	20-5	Chuck Daly	21-7
19 Austin Peay	21-5	Lake Kelly	22-7
20 San Francisco	22-4	Bob Gaillard	23-5

*Ineligible for NCAA tournament for using improper methods to recruit David Thompson.

Note: NIT champ Va. Tech, coached by Don DeVoe, entered the tourney unranked at 18-5 and had a final record of 22-5.

NCAA Final Four (at The Arena, St. Louis): **Semifinals**—Memphis St. 98, Providence 85; UCLA 70, Indiana 59. **Third Place**—Indiana 97, Providence 79. **Championship**—UCLA 87, Memphis St. 66.

NIT Final Four (at Madison Square Garden): **Semifinals**—Va. Tech 74, Alabama 73; Notre Dame 78, N. Carolina 71. **Third Place**—N. Carolina 88, Alabama 69. **Championship**—Va. Tech 92, Notre Dame 91 (OT).

1974

	Before Tourns	Head Coach	Final Record
1 **N.C. State**	26-1	Norm Sloan	30-1
2 UCLA	23-3	John Wooden	26-4
3 Notre Dame	24-2	Digger Phelps	26-3
4 Maryland	23-5	Lefty Driesell	same
5 Providence	26-3	Dave Gavitt	28-4
6 Vanderbilt	23-3	Roy Skinner	23-5
7 Marquette	22-4	Al McGuire	26-5
8 North Carolina	22-5	Dean Smith	22-6
9 Long Beach St.	24-2	Lute Olson	same
10 **Indiana**	20-5	Bob Knight	23-5
11 Alabama	22-4	C.M. Newton	same
12 Michigan	21-4	Johnny Orr	22-5
13 Pittsburgh	23-3	Buzz Ridl	25-4
14 Kansas	21-5	Ted Owens	23-7
15 USC	22-4	Bob Boyd	24-5
16 Louisville	21-6	Denny Crum	21-7
17 New Mexico	21-6	Norm Ellenberger	22-7
18 South Carolina	22-4	Frank McGuire	22-5
19 Creighton	22-6	Eddie Sutton	23-7
20 Dayton	19-7	Don Donoher	20-9

NCAA Final Four (at Greensboro, NC, Coliseum): **Semifinals**—N.C. State 80, UCLA 77 (2 OT); Marquette 64, Kansas 51. **Third Place**—UCLA 78, Kansas 61. **Championship**—N.C. State 76, Marquette 64.

NIT Final Four (at Madison Square Garden): **Semifinals**—Purdue 78, Jacksonville 63; Utah 117, Boston Col. 93. **Third Place**—Boston Col. 87, Jacksonville 77. **Championship**—Purdue 87, Utah 81.

CCA Final Four (at The Arena, St. Louis): **Semifinals**—Indiana 73, Toledo 72; USC 74, Bradley 73. **Championship**—Indiana 85, USC 60.

1975

	Before Tourns	Head Coach	Final Record
1 Indiana	29-0	Bob Knight	31-1
2 **UCLA**	23-3	John Wooden	28-3
3 Louisville	24-2	Denny Crum	28-3
4 Maryland	22-4	Lefty Driesell	24-5
5 Kentucky	22-4	Joe B. Hall	26-5
6 North Carolina	21-7	Dean Smith	23-8
7 Arizona St.	23-3	Ned Wulk	25-4
8 N.C. State	22-6	Norm Sloan	22-6
9 Notre Dame	18-8	Digger Phelps	19-10
10 Marquette	23-3	Al McGuire	23-4
11 Alabama	22-4	C.M. Newton	22-5
12 Cincinnati	21-5	Gale Catlett	23-6
13 Oregon St.	18-10	Ralph Miller	19-12
14 **Drake**	16-10	Bob Ortegel	19-10
15 Penn	23-4	Chuck Daly	23-5
16 UNLV	22-4	Jerry Tarkanian	24-5
17 Kansas St.	18-8	Jack Hartman	20-9
18 USC	18-7	Bob Boyd	18-8
19 Centenary	25-4	Larry Little	same
20 Syracuse	20-7	Roy Danforth	23-9

NCAA Final Four (at San Diego Sports Arena): **Semifinals**—Kentucky 95, Syracuse 79; UCLA 75, Louisville 74 (OT). **Third Place**—Louisville 96, Syracuse 88 (OT). **Championship**—UCLA 92, Kentucky 85.

NIT Championship (at Madison Sq. Garden): Princeton 80, Providence 69. No Top 20 teams played in NIT.

CCA Championship (at Freedom Hall, Louisville): Drake 83, Arizona 76. No.14 Drake and No.18 USC were only Top 20 teams in CCA.

Post-Tournament Polls

The final AP Top 20 poll has been released after the postseason tournaments only twice—in 1974 and '75. Those two polls are listed below; teams not included in the last regular season poll are in *CAPITAL* italic letters.

1974	Final Record	**1975**	Final Record
1 N.C. State	30-1	1 UCLA	28-3
2 UCLA	26-4	2 Kentucky	26-5
3 Marquette	26-5	3 Indiana	31-1
4 Maryland	23-5	4 Louisville	28-3
5 Notre Dame	26-3	5 Maryland	24-5
6 Michigan	22-5	6 Syracuse	23-9
7 Kansas	23-7	7 N.C. State	22-6
8 Providence	28-4	8 Arizona St.	25-4
9 Indiana	23-5	9 North Carolina	23-8
10 Long Beach St.	24-2	10 Alabama	22-5
11 *PURDUE*	22-8	11 Marquette	23-4
12 North Carolina	22-6	12 *PRINCETON*	22-8
13 Vanderbilt	23-5	13 Cincinnati	23-6
14 Alabama	22-4	14 Notre Dame	19-10
15 *UTAH*	22-8	15 Kansas St.	20-9
16 Pittsburgh	25-4	16 Drake	19-10
17 USC	24-5	17 UNLV	24-5
18 *ORAL ROBERTS*	23-6	18 Oregon St.	19-12
19 South Carolina	22-5	19 *MICHIGAN*	19-8
20 Dayton	20-9	20 Penn	23-5

Pre-Tournament Records

1974—Purdue (Fred Schaus, 18-8), Utah (Bill Foster, 19-7), Oral Roberts (Ken Trickey, 21-5).

1975—Princeton (Pete Carril, 18-8), Michigan (Johnny Orr, 19-7).

Associated Press Final Polls (Cont.)

Taken before NCAA and NIT Tournaments; (*) indicates on probation.

1976

	Before Tourns	Head Coach	Final Record
1 **Indiana**	27-0	Bob Knight	32-0
2 Marquette	25-1	Al McGuire	27-2
3 UNLV	28-1	Jerry Tarkanian	29-2
4 Rutgers	28-0	Tom Young	31-2
5 UCLA	24-3	Gene Bartow	28-4
6 Alabama	22-4	C.M. Newton	23-5
7 Notre Dame	22-5	Digger Phelps	23-6
8 North Carolina	25-3	Dean Smith	25-4
9 Michigan	21-6	Johnny Orr	25-7
10 Western Mich.	24-2	Eldon Miller	25-3
11 Maryland	22-6	Lefty Driesell	same
12 Cincinnati	25-5	Gale Catlett	25-6
13 Tennessee	21-5	Ray Mears	21-6
14 Missouri	24-4	Norm Stewart	26-5
15 Arizona	22-8	Fred Snowden	24-9
16 Texas Tech	24-5	Gerald Myers	25-6
17 DePaul	19-8	Ray Meyer	20-9
18 Virginia	18-11	Terry Holland	18-12
19 Centenary	22-5	Larry Little	same
20 Pepperdine	21-5	Gary Colson	22-6

NCAA Final Four (at The Spectrum, Phila.); **Semifinals**—Michigan 86, Rutgers 70; Indiana 65, UCLA 51. **Third Place**—UCLA 106, Rutgers 92. **Championship**—Indiana 86, Michigan 68.

NIT Championship (at Madison Square Garden): Kentucky 71, NC-Charlotte 67. No Top 20 teams played in NIT.

1977

	Before Tourns	Head Coach	Final Record
1 Michigan	24-3	Johnny Orr	26-4
2 UCLA	24-3	Gene Bartow	25-4
3 Kentucky	24-3	Joe B. Hall	26-4
4 UNLV	25-2	Jerry Tarkanian	29-3
5 North Carolina	24-4	Dean Smith	28-5
6 Syracuse	25-3	Jim Boeheim	26-4
7 **Marquette**	20-7	Al McGuire	25-7
8 San Francisco	29-1	Bob Gaillard	29-2
9 Wake Forest	20-7	Carl Tacy	22-8
10 Notre Dame	21-6	Digger Phelps	22-7
11 Alabama	23-4	C.M. Newton	25-6
12 Detroit	24-3	Dick Vitale	25-4
13 Minnesota	24-3	Jim Dutcher	same*
14 Utah	22-6	Jerry Pimm	23-7
15 Tennessee	22-5	Ray Mears	22-6
16 Kansas St.	23-6	Jack Hartman	24-7
17 NC-Charlotte	25-3	Lee Rose	28-5
18 Arkansas	26-1	Eddie Sutton	26-2
19 Louisville	21-6	Denny Crum	21-7
20 VMI	25-3	Charlie Schmaus	26-4

NCAA Final Four (at The Omni, Atlanta): **Semifinals**—Marquette 51, NC-Charlotte, 49; N. Carolina 84, UNLV 83. **Third Place**—UNLV 106, NC-Charlotte 94. **Championship**—Marquette 67, N. Carolina 59.

NIT Championship (at Madison Square Garden): St. Bonaventure 94, Houston 91. No.11 Alabama was only Top 20 team in NIT.

1978

	Before Tourns	Head Coach	Final Record
1 **Kentucky**	25-2	Joe B. Hall	30-2
2 UCLA	24-2	Gary Cunningham	25-3
3 DePaul	25-2	Ray Meyer	27-3
4 Michigan St.	23-4	Jud Heathcote	25-5
5 Arkansas	28-3	Eddie Sutton	32-3
6 Notre Dame	20-6	Digger Phelps	23-8
7 Duke	23-6	Bill Foster	27-7
8 Marquette	24-3	Hank Raymonds	24-4
9 Louisville	22-6	Denny Crum	23-7
10 Kansas	24-4	Ted Owens	24-5
11 San Francisco	22-5	Bob Gaillard	23-6
12 New Mexico	24-3	Norm Ellenberger	24-4
13 Indiana	20-7	Bob Knight	21-8
14 Utah	22-5	Jerry Pimm	23-6
15 Florida St.	23-5	Hugh Durham	23-6
16 North Carolina	23-7	Dean Smith	23-8
17 **Texas**	22-5	Abe Lemons	26-5
18 Detroit	24-3	Dave Gaines	25-4
19 Miami-OH	18-8	Darrell Hedric	19-9
20 Penn	19-7	Bob Weinhauer	20-8

NCAA Final Four (at The Checkerdome, St. Louis): **Semifinals**—Kentucky 64, Arkansas 59; Duke 90, Notre Dame 86. **Third Place**—Arkansas 71, Notre Dame 69. **Championship**—Kentucky 94, Duke 88.

NIT Championship (at Madison Square Garden): Texas 101, N.C. State 93. No.17 Texas and No.18 Detroit were only Top 20 teams in NIT.

1979

	Before Tourns	Head Coach	Final Record
1 Indiana St.	29-0	Bill Hodges	33-1
2 UCLA	23-4	Gary Cunningham	25-5
3 **Michigan St.**	21-6	Jud Heathcote	26-6
4 Notre Dame	22-5	Digger Phelps	24-6
5 Arkansas	23-4	Eddie Sutton	25-5
6 DePaul	22-5	Ray Meyer	26-6
7 LSU	22-5	Dale Brown	23-6
8 Syracuse	25-3	Jim Boeheim	26-4
9 North Carolina	23-5	Dean Smith	23-6
10 Marquette	21-6	Hank Raymonds	22-7
11 Duke	22-7	Bill Foster	22-8
12 San Francisco	21-6	Dan Belluomini	22-7
13 Louisville	23-7	Denny Crum	24-8
14 Penn	21-5	Bob Weinhauer	25-7
15 Purdue	23-7	Lee Rose	27-8
16 Oklahoma	20-9	Dave Bliss	21-10
17 St. John's	18-10	Lou Carnesecca	21-11
18 Rutgers	21-8	Tom Young	22-9
19 Toledo	21-6	Bob Nichols	22-7
20 Iowa	20-7	Lute Olson	20-8

NCAA Final Four (at Special Events Center, Salt Lake City): **Semifinals**—Michigan St. 101, Penn 67; Indiana St. 76, DePaul 74. **Third Place**—DePaul 96, Penn 93. **Championship**—Michigan St. 75, Indiana St. 64.

NIT Championship (at Madison Square Garden): Indiana 53, Purdue 52. No.15 Purdue was only Top 20 team in NIT.

1980

	Before Tourns	Head Coach	Final Record
1 DePaul	26-1	Ray Meyer	26-2
2 **Louisville**	28-3	Denny Crum	33-3
3 LSU	24-5	Dale Brown	26-6
4 Kentucky	28-5	Joe B. Hall	29-6
5 Oregon St.	26-3	Ralph Miller	26-4
6 Syracuse	25-3	Jim Boeheim	26-4
7 Indiana	20-7	Bob Knight	21-8
8 Maryland	23-6	Lefty Driesell	24-7
9 Notre Dame	20-7	Digger Phelps	20-8
10 Ohio St.	24-5	Eldon Miller	21-8
11 Georgetown	24-5	John Thompson	26-6
12 BYU	24-4	Frank Arnold	24-5
13 St. John's	24-4	Lou Carnesecca	24-5
14 Duke	22-8	Bill Foster	24-9
15 North Carolina	21-7	Dean Smith	21-8
16 Missouri	23-5	Norm Stewart	25-6
17 Weber St.	26-2	Neil McCarthy	26-3
18 Arizona St.	21-6	Ned Wulk	22-7
19 Iona	28-4	Jim Valvano	29-5
20 Purdue	19-9	Lee Rose	23-10

NCAA Final Four (at Market Square Arena, Indianapolis): **Semifinals**—Louisville 80, Iowa 72; UCLA 67, Purdue 62; **Championship**—Louisville 59, UCLA 54.
NIT Championship (at Madison Square Garden): Virginia 58, Minnesota 55. No Top 20 teams played in NIT.

1981

	Before Tourns	Head Coach	Final Record
1 DePaul	27-1	Ray Meyer	27-2
2 Oregon St.	26-1	Ralph Miller	26-2
3 Arizona St.	24-3	Ned Wulk	24-4
4 LSU	28-3	Dale Brown	31-5
5 Virginia	25-3	Terry Holland	29-4
6 North Carolina	25-7	Dean Smith	29-8
7 Notre Dame	22-5	Digger Phelps	23-6
8 Kentucky	22-5	Joe B. Hall	22-6
9 **Indiana**	21-9	Bob Knight	26-9
10 UCLA	20-6	Larry Brown	20-7
11 Wake Forest	22-6	Carl Tacy	22-7
12 Louisville	21-8	Denny Crum	21-9
13 Iowa	21-6	Lute Olson	21-7
14 Utah	24-4	Jerry Pimm	25-5
15 Tennessee	20-7	Don DeVoe	21-8
16 BYU	22-6	Frank Arnold	25-7
17 Wyoming	23-5	Jim Brandenburg	24-6
18 Maryland	20-9	Lefty Driesell	21-10
19 Illinois	20-7	Lou Henson	21-8
20 Arkansas	22-7	Eddie Sutton	24-8

NCAA Final Four (at The Spectrum, Phila.): **Semifinals**—N. Carolina 78, Virginia 65; Indiana 67, LSU 49. **Third Place**—Virginia 78, LSU 74. **Championship**—Indiana 63, N. Carolina 50.
NIT Championship (at Madison Square Garden): Tulsa 86, Syracuse 84. No Top 20 teams played in NIT.

1982

	Before Tourns	Head Coach	Final Record
1 **North Carolina**	27-2	Dean Smith	32-2
2 DePaul	26-1	Ray Meyer	26-2
3 Virginia	29-3	Terry Holland	30-4
4 Oregon St.	23-4	Ralph Miller	25-5
5 Missouri	26-3	Norm Stewart	27-4
6 Georgetown	26-6	John Thompson	30-7
7 Minnesota	22-5	Jim Dutcher	23-6
8 Idaho	26-2	Don Monson	27-3
9 Memphis St.	23-4	Dana Kirk	24-5
10 Tulsa	24-5	Nolan Richardson	24-6
11 Fresno St.	26-2	Boyd Grant	27-3
12 Arkansas	23-5	Eddie Sutton	23-6
13 Alabama	23-6	Wimp Sanderson	24-7
14 West Virginia	26-3	Gale Catlett	27-4
15 Kentucky	22-7	Joe B. Hall	22-8
16 Iowa	20-7	Lute Olson	21-8
17 Ala-Birmingham	23-5	Gene Bartow	25-6
18 Wake Forest	20-8	Carl Tacy	21-9
19 UCLA	21-6	Larry Farmer	21-6
20 Louisville	20-9	Denny Crum	23-10

NCAA Final Four (at The Superdome, New Orleans): **Semifinals**—N. Carolina 68, Houston 63; Georgetown 50, Louisville 46. **Championship**—N. Carolina 63, Georgetown 62.
NIT Championship (at Madison Square Garden): Bradley 67, Purdue 58. No Top 20 teams played in NIT.

1983

	Before Tourns	Head Coach	Final Record
1 Houston	27-2	Guy Lewis	31-3
2 Louisville	29-3	Denny Crum	32-4
3 St. John's	27-4	Lou Carnesecca	28-5
4 Virginia	27-4	Terry Holland	29-5
5 Indiana	23-5	Bob Knight	24-6
6 UNLV	28-2	Jerry Tarkanian	28-3
7 UCLA	23-5	Larry Farmer	23-6
8 North Carolina	26-7	Dean Smith	28-8
9 Arkansas	25-3	Eddie Sutton	26-4
10 Missouri	26-7	Norm Stewart	26-8
11 Boston College	24-6	Gary Williams	25-7
12 Kentucky	22-7	Joe B. Hall	23-8
13 Villanova	22-7	Rollie Massimino	24-8
14 Wichita St.	25-3	Gene Smithson	same*
15 Tenn-Chatt.	26-3	Murray Arnold	26-4
16 **N.C. State**	20-10	Jim Valvano	26-10
17 Memphis St.	22-7	Dana Kirk	23-8
18 Georgia	21-9	Hugh Durham	24-10
19 Oklahoma St.	24-6	Paul Hansen	24-7
20 Georgetown	21-9	John Thompson	22-10

NCAA Final Four (at The Pit, Albuquerque, NM): **Semifinals**—N.C. State 67, Georgia 60; Houston 94, Louisville 81. **Championship**—N.C. State 54, Houston 52.
NIT Championship (at Madison Square Garden): Fresno St. 69, DePaul 60. No Top 20 teams played in NIT.

Associated Press Final Polls (Cont.)

Taken before NCAA and NIT Tournaments; (*) indicates on probation.

1984

		Before Tourns	Head Coach	Final Record
1	North Carolina	27-2	Dean Smith	28-3
2	**Georgetown**	29-3	John Thompson	34-3
3	Kentucky	26-4	Joe B. Hall	29-5
4	DePaul	26-2	Ray Meyer	27-3
5	Houston	28-4	Guy Lewis	32-5
6	Illinois	24-4	Lou Henson	26-5
7	Oklahoma	29-4	Billy Tubbs	29-5
8	Arkansas	25-6	Eddie Sutton	25-7
9	UTEP	27-3	Don Haskins	27-4
10	Purdue	22-6	Gene Keady	22-7
11	Maryland	23-7	Lefty Driesell	24-8
12	Tulsa	27-3	Nolan Richardson	27-4
13	UNLV	27-5	Jerry Tarkanian	29-6
14	Duke	24-9	Mike Krzyzewski	24-10
15	Washington	22-6	Marv Harshman	24-7
16	Memphis St.	24-6	Dana Kirk	26-7
17	Oregon St.	22-6	Ralph Miller	22-7
18	Syracuse	22-8	Jim Boeheim	23-9
19	Wake Forest	21-8	Carl Tacy	23-9
20	Temple	25-4	John Chaney	26-5

NCAA Final Four (at The Kingdome, Seattle): **Semifinals**—Houston 49, Virginia 47 (OT); Georgetown 53, Kentucky 40. **Championship**—Georgetown 84, Houston 75.

NIT Championship (at Madison Square Garden): Michigan 83, Notre Dame 63. No Top 20 teams played in NIT.

1985

		Before Tourns	Head Coach	Final Record
1	Georgetown	30-2	John Thompson	35-3
2	Michigan	25-3	Bill Frieder	26-4
3	St. John's	27-3	Lou Carnesecca	31-4
4	Oklahoma	28-5	Billy Tubbs	31-6
5	Memphis St.	27-3	Dana Kirk	31-4
6	Georgia Tech	24-7	Bobby Cremins	27-8
7	North Carolina	24-8	Dean Smith	27-9
8	Louisiana Tech	27-2	Andy Russo	29-3
9	UNLV	27-3	Jerry Tarkanian	28-4
10	Duke	22-7	Mike Krzyzewski	23-8
11	VCU	25-5	J.D. Barnett	26-6
12	Illinois	24-8	Lou Henson	26-9
13	Kansas	25-7	Larry Brown	26-8
14	Loyola-IL	25-5	Gene Sullivan	27-6
15	Syracuse	21-8	Jim Boeheim	22-9
16	N.C. State	20-9	Jim Valvano	23-10
17	Texas Tech	23-7	Gerald Myers	23-8
18	Tulsa	23-7	Nolan Richardson	23-8
19	Georgia	21-8	Hugh Durham	22-9
20	LSU	19-9	Dale Brown	19-10

Note: Unranked Villanova, coached by Rollie Massimino, won the NCAAs. The Wildcats entered the tourney at 19-10 and had a final record of 25-10.

NCAA Final Four (at Rupp Arena, Lexington, KY): **Semifinals**— Georgetown 77, St. John's 59; Villanova 52, Memphis St. 45. **Championship**—Villanova 66, Georgetown 64.

NIT Championship (at Madison Square Garden): UCLA 65, Indiana 62. No Top 20 teams played in NIT.

1986

		Before Tourns	Head Coach	Final Record
1	Duke	32-2	Mike Krzyzewski	37-3
2	Kansas	31-3	Larry Brown	35-4
3	Kentucky	29-3	Eddie Sutton	32-4
4	St. John's	30-4	Lou Carnesecca	31-5
5	Michigan	27-4	Bill Frieder	28-5
6	Georgia Tech	25-6	Bobby Cremins	27-7
7	**Louisville**	26-7	Denny Crum	32-7
8	North Carolina	26-5	Dean Smith	28-6
9	Syracuse	25-5	Jim Boeheim	26-6
10	Notre Dame	23-5	Digger Phelps	23-6
11	UNLV	31-4	Jerry Tarkanian	33-5
12	Memphis St.	27-5	Dana Kirk	28-6
13	Georgetown	23-7	John Thompson	24-8
14	Bradley	31-2	Dick Versace	32-3
15	Oklahoma	25-8	Billy Tubbs	26-9
16	Indiana	21-7	Bob Knight	21-8
17	Navy	27-4	Paul Evans	30-5
18	Michigan St.	21-7	Jud Heathcote	23-8
19	Illinois	21-9	Lou Henson	22-10
20	UTEP	27-5	Don Haskins	27-6

NCAA Final Four (at Reunion Arena, Dallas): **Semifinals**—Duke 71, Kansas 67; Louisville 88, LSU 77. **Championship**—Louisville 72, Duke 69.

NIT Championship (at Madison Square Garden): Ohio St. 73, Wyoming 63. No Top 20 teams played in NIT.

1987

		Before Tourns	Head Coach	Final Record
1	UNLV	33-1	Jerry Tarkanian	37-2
2	North Carolina	29-3	Dean Smith	32-4
3	**Indiana**	24-4	Bob Knight	30-4
4	Georgetown	26-4	John Thompson	29-5
5	DePaul	26-2	Joey Meyer	28-3
6	Iowa	27-4	Tom Davis	30-5
7	Purdue	24-4	Gene Keady	25-5
8	Temple	31-3	John Chaney	32-4
9	Alabama	26-4	Wimp Sanderson	28-5
10	Syracuse	26-6	Jim Boeheim	31-7
11	Illinois	23-7	Lou Henson	23-8
12	Pittsburgh	24-7	Paul Evans	25-8
13	Clemson	25-5	Cliff Ellis	25-6
14	Missouri	24-9	Norm Stewart	24-10
15	UCLA	24-6	Walt Hazzard	25-7
16	New Orleans	25-3	Benny Dees	26-4
17	Duke	22-8	Mike Krzyzewski	24-9
18	Notre Dame	22-7	Digger Phelps	24-8
19	TCU	23-6	Jim Killingsworth	24-7
20	Kansas	23-10	Larry Brown	25-11

NCAA Final Four (at The Superdome, New Orleans): **Semifinals**—Syracuse 77, Providence 63; Indiana 97, UNLV 93. **Championship**—Indiana 74, Syracuse 73.

NIT Championship (at Madison Square Garden): Southern Miss. 84, La Salle 80. No Top 20 teams played in NIT.

1988

		Before Tourns	Head Coach	Final Record
1	Temple	29-1	John Chaney	32-2
2	Arizona	31-2	Lute Olson	35-3
3	Purdue	27-3	Gene Keady	29-4
4	Oklahoma	30-3	Billy Tubbs	35-4
5	Duke	24-6	Mike Krzyzewski	28-7
6	Kentucky	25-5	Eddie Sutton	27-6
7	North Carolina	24-6	Dean Smith	27-7
8	Pittsburgh	23-6	Paul Evans	24-7
9	Syracuse	25-8	Jim Boeheim	26-9
10	Michigan	24-7	Bill Frieder	26-8
11	Bradley	26-4	Stan Albeck	26-5
12	UNLV	27-5	Jerry Tarkanian	28-6
13	Wyoming	26-5	Benny Dees	26-6
14	N.C. State	24-7	Jim Valvano	24-8
15	Loyola-CA	27-3	Paul Westhead	28-4
16	Illinois	22-9	Lou Henson	23-10
17	Iowa	22-9	Tom Davis	24-10
18	Xavier-OH	26-3	Pete Gillen	26-4
19	BYU	25-5	Ladell Andersen	26-6
20	Kansas St.	22-8	Lon Kruger	25-9

Note: Unranked Kansas, coached by Larry Brown, won the NCAAs. The Jayhawks entered the tourney at 21-11 and had a final record of 27-11.

NCAA Final Four (at Kemper Arena, Kansas City): **Semifinals**—Kansas 66, Duke 59; Oklahoma 86, Arizona 78. **Championship**—Kansas 83, Oklahoma 79.

NIT Championship (at Madison Square Garden): Connecticut 72, Ohio St. 67. No Top 20 teams played in NIT.

1990

		Before Tourns	Head Coach	Final Record
1	Oklahoma	26-4	Billy Tubbs	27-5
2	**UNLV**	29-5	Jerry Tarkanian	35-5
3	Connecticut	28-5	Jim Calhoun	31-6
4	Michigan St.	26-5	Jud Heathcote	28-6
5	Kansas	29-4	Roy Williams	30-5
6	Syracuse	24-6	Jim Boeheim	26-7
7	Arkansas	26-4	Nolan Richardson	30-5
8	Georgetown	23-6	John Thompson	24-7
9	Georgia Tech	24-6	Bobby Cremins	28-7
10	Purdue	21-7	Gene Keady	22-8
11	Missouri	26-5	Norm Stewart	26-6
12	La Salle	29-1	Speedy Morris	30-2
13	Michigan	22-7	Steve Fisher	23-8
14	Arizona	24-6	Lute Olson	25-7
15	Duke	24-8	Mike Krzyzewski	29-9
16	Louisville	26-7	Denny Crum	27-8
17	Clemson	24-8	Cliff Ellis	26-9
18	Illinois	21-7	Lou Henson	21-8
19	LSU	22-8	Dale Brown	23-9
20	Minnesota	20-8	Clem Haskins	23-9
21	Loyola-CA	23-5	Paul Westhead	26-6
22	Oregon St.	22-6	Jim Anderson	22-7
23	Alabama	24-8	Wimp Sanderson	26-9
24	New Mexico St.	26-4	Neil McCarthy	26-5
25	Xavier-OH	26-4	Pete Gillen	28-5

NCAA Final Four (at McNichols Sports Arena, Denver): **Semifinals**—Duke 97, Arkansas 83; UNLV 90, Georgia Tech 81. **Championship**—UNLV 103, Duke 73.

NIT Championship (at Madison Square Garden): Vanderbilt 74, St. Louis 72. No Top 25 teams played in NIT.

1989

		Before Tourns	Head Coach	Final Record
1	Arizona	27-3	Lute Olson	29-4
2	Georgetown	26-4	John Thompson	29-5
3	Illinois	27-4	Lou Henson	31-5
4	Oklahoma	28-5	Billy Tubbs	30-6
5	North Carolina	27-7	Dean Smith	29-8
6	Missouri	27-7	Norm Stewart & Rich Daly	29-8
7	Syracuse	27-7	Jim Boeheim	30-8
8	Indiana	25-7	Bob Knight	27-8
9	Duke	24-7	Mike Krzyzewski	28-8
10	**Michigan**	24-7	Bill Frieder & Steve Fisher	30-7
11	Seton Hall	26-6	P.J. Carlesimo	31-7
12	Louisville	22-8	Denny Crum	24-9
13	Stanford	26-6	Mike Montgomery	26-7
14	Iowa	22-9	Tom Davis	23-10
15	UNLV	26-7	Jerry Tarkanian	29-8
16	Florida St.	22-7	Pat Kennedy	22-8
17	West Virginia	25-4	Gale Catlett	26-5
18	Ball State	28-2	Rick Majerus	29-3
19	N.C. State	20-8	Jim Valvano	22-9
20	Alabama	23-7	Wimp Sanderson	23-8

NCAA Final Four (at The Kingdome, Seattle): **Semifinals**—Seton Hall 95, Duke 78; Michigan 83, Illinois 81. **Championship**—Michigan 80, Seton Hall 79 (OT).

NIT Championship (at Madison Square Garden): St. John's 73, St. Louis 65. No Top 20 teams played in NIT.

1991

		Before Tourns	Head Coach	Final Record
1	UNLV	30-0	Jerry Tarkanian	34-1
2	Arkansas	31-3	Nolan Richardson	34-4
3	Indiana	27-4	Bob Knight	29-5
4	North Carolina	25-5	Dean Smith	29-6
5	Ohio St.	25-3	Randy Ayers	27-4
6	**Duke**	26-7	Mike Krzyzewski	32-7
7	Syracuse	26-5	Jim Boeheim	26-6
8	Arizona	26-6	Lute Olson	28-7
9	Kentucky	22-6	Rick Pitino	same*
10	Utah	28-3	Rick Majerus	30-4
11	Nebraska	26-7	Danny Nee	26-8
12	Kansas	22-7	Roy Williams	27-8
13	Seton Hall	22-8	P.J. Carlesimo	25-9
14	Oklahoma St.	22-7	Eddie Sutton	24-8
15	New Mexico St.	23-5	Neil McCarthy	23-6
16	UCLA	23-8	Jim Harrick	23-9
17	E. Tennessee St.	28-4	Alan LaForce	28-5
18	Princeton	24-2	Pete Carril	24-3
19	Alabama	21-9	Wimp Sanderson	23-10
20	St. John's	20-8	Lou Carnesecca	23-9
21	Mississippi St.	20-8	Richard Williams	20-9
22	LSU	20-9	Dale Brown	20-10
23	Texas	22-8	Tom Penders	23-9
24	DePaul	20-8	Joey Meyer	20-9
25	So. Mississippi	21-7	M.K. Turk	21-8

NCAA Final Four (at the Hoosier Dome, Indianapolis): **Semifinals**—Kansas 79, North Carolina 73; Duke 79, UNLV 77. **Championship**—Duke 72, Kansas 65.

NIT Championship (at Madison Square Garden): Stanford 78, Oklahoma 72. No Top 25 teams played in NIT.

Associated Press Final Polls (Cont.)

Taken before NCAA and NIT Tournaments; (*) indicates on probation.

1992

	Before Tourns	Head Coach	Final Record
1 **Duke**	28-2	Mike Krzyzewski	34-2
2 Kansas	26-4	Roy Williams	27-5
3 Ohio St.	23-5	Randy Ayers	26-6
4 UCLA	25-4	Jim Harrick	28-5
5 Indiana	23-6	Bob Knight	27-7
6 Kentucky	26-6	Rick Pitino	29-7
7 UNLV	26-2	Jerry Tarkanian	same*
8 USC	23-5	George Raveling	24-6
9 Arkansas	25-7	Nolan Richardson	26-8
10 Arizona	24-6	Lute Olson	24-7
11 Oklahoma St.	26-7	Eddie Sutton	28-8
12 Cincinnati	25-4	Bob Huggins	29-5
13 Alabama	25-8	Wimp Sanderson	26-9
14 Michigan St.	21-7	Jud Heathcote	22-8
15 Michigan	20-8	Steve Fisher	25-9
16 Missouri	20-8	Norm Stewart	21-9
17 Massachusetts	28-4	John Calipari	30-5
18 North Carolina	21-9	Dean Smith	23-10
19 Seton Hall	21-8	P.J. Carlesimo	23-9
20 Florida St.	20-9	Pat Kennedy	22-10
21 Syracuse	21-9	Jim Boeheim	22-10
22 Georgetown	21-9	John Thompson	22-10
23 Oklahoma	21-8	Billy Tubbs	21-9
24 DePaul	20-8	Joey Meyer	20-9
25 LSU	20-9	Dale Brown	21-10

NCAA Final Four (at Metrodome in Minneapolis): **Semifinals**—Michigan 76, Cincinnati 72; Duke 81, Indiana 78. **Championship**—Duke 71, Michigan 51.

NIT Championship (at Madison Square Garden): Virginia 81, Notre Dame 76 (OT). No Top 25 teams in NIT.

1993

	Before Tourns	Head Coach	Final Record
1 Indiana	28-3	Bob Knight	31-4
2 Kentucky	26-3	Rick Pitino	30-4
3 Michigan	26-4	Steve Fisher	31-5
4 **North Carolina**	28-4	Dean Smith	34-4
5 Arizona	24-3	Lute Olson	24-4
6 Seton Hall	27-6	P.J. Carlesimo	28-7
7 Cincinnati	24-4	Bob Huggins	27-5
8 Vanderbilt	26-5	Eddie Fogler	28-6
9 Kansas	25-6	Roy Williams	29-7
10 Duke	23-7	Mike Krzyzewski	24-8
11 Florida St.	22-9	Pat Kennedy	25-10
12 Arkansas	20-8	Nolan Richardson	22-9
13 Iowa	22-8	Tom Davis	23-9
14 Massachusetts	23-6	John Calipari	24-7
15 Louisville	20-8	Denny Crum	22-9
16 Wake Forest	19-8	Dave Odom	21-9
17 New Orleans	26-3	Tim Floyd	26-4
18 Georgia Tech	19-10	Bobby Cremins	19-11
19 Utah	23-6	Rick Majerus	24-7
20 Western Ky.	24-5	Ralph Willard	26-6
21 New Mexico	24-6	Dave Bliss	24-7
22 Purdue	18-9	Gene Keady	18-10
23 Oklahoma St.	19-8	Eddie Sutton	20-9
24 New Mexico St.	25-7	Neil McCarthy	26-8
25 UNLV	21-7	Rollie Massimino	21-8

NCAA Final Four (at Superdome in New Orleans): **Semifinals**—North Carolina 78, Kansas 68; Michigan 81, Kentucky 78 (OT). **Championship**—North Carolina 77, Michigan 71.

NIT Championship (at Madison Square Garden): Minnesota 62, Georgetown 61. No. 25 UNLV was only Top 25 team in NIT.

1994

	Before Tourns	Head Coach	Final Record
1 North Carolina	27-6	Dean Smith	28-7
2 **Arkansas**	25-3	Nolan Richardson	31-3
3 Purdue	26-4	Gene Keady	29-5
4 Connecticut	27-4	Jim Calhoun	29-5
5 Missouri	25-3	Norm Stewart	28-4
6 Duke	23-5	Mike Krzyzewski	28-6
7 Kentucky	26-6	Rick Pitino	27-7
8 Massachusetts	27-6	John Calipari	28-7
9 Arizona	25-5	Lute Olson	29-6
10 Louisville	26-5	Denny Crum	28-6
11 Michigan	21-7	Steve Fisher	24-8
12 Temple	22-7	John Chaney	23-8
13 Kansas	25-7	Roy Williams	27-8
14 Florida	25-7	Lon Kruger	29-8
15 Syracuse	21-6	Jim Boeheim	23-7
16 California	22-7	Todd Bozeman	22-8
17 UCLA	21-6	Jim Harrick	21-7
18 Indiana	19-8	Bob Knight	21-9
19 Oklahoma St.	23-9	Eddie Sutton	24-10
20 Texas	25-7	Tom Penders	26-8
21 Marquette	22-8	Kevin O'Neill	24-9
22 Nebraska	20-9	Danny Nee	20-10
23 Minnesota	20-11	Clem Haskins	21-12
24 Saint Louis	23-5	Charlie Spoonhour	23-6
25 Cincinnati	22-9	Bob Huggins	22-10

NCAA Final Four (at Charlotte, NC Coliseum): **Semifinals**— Arkansas 91, Arizona 82; Duke 70, Florida 65. **Championship**— Arkansas 76, Duke 72.

NIT Championship (at Madison Square Garden): Villanova 80, Vanderbilt 73. No top 25 teams in NIT.

All-Time AP Top 20

The composite AP Top 20 from the 1948-49 season through 1993-94, based on the final regular season rankings of each year. The final AP poll has been taken before the NCAA and NIT tournaments each season since 1949 except 1974 and '75 when the final poll came out after the postseason. Team point totals are based on 20 points for all 1st place finishes, 19 for each 2nd and so on. Also listed are the number of times ranked No.1 by AP going into the tournaments, and times ranked in the pre-tournament Top 10 and Top 20.

	Pts	No.1	Top10	Top20
1 Kentucky	514	7	29	34
2 North Carolina	433	4	24	31
3 UCLA	393	6	20	28
4 Duke	301	2	17	26
5 Indiana	288	4	16	22
6 Kansas	233	0	12	20
7 Louisville	226	0	11	21
8 Notre Dame	195	0	13	17
9 Michigan	191	2	10	14
10 UNLV	173	2	8	13
11 Cincinnati	172	2	8	12
12 N.C. State	166	1	9	15
13 Marquette	165	0	11	14
14 Illinois	156	0	7	17
15 Bradley	152	1	8	11
16 Ohio St	149	2	9	10
17 Syracuse	144	0	9	14
18 Arkansas	143	0	8	12
DePaul	143	2	8	10
Kansas St.	143	1	7	12
St. John's	143	0	8	14

Annual NCAA Division I Leaders
Scoring

The NCAA did not begin keeping individual scoring records until the 1947-48 season. All averages include postseason games where applicable.

Multiple winners: Pete Maravich and Oscar Robertson (3); Darrell Floyd, Harry Kelly, Frank Selvy and Freeman Williams (2).

Year	Gm	Pts	Avg	Year	Gm	Pts	Avg
1948 Murray Wier, Iowa	19	399	21.0	1972 Dwight Lamar, SW La	29	1054	36.3
1949 Tony Lavelli, Yale	30	671	22.4	1973 Bird Averitt, Pepperdine	25	848	33.9
				1974 Larry Fogle, Canisius	25	835	33.4
1950 Paul Arizin, Villanova	29	735	25.3	1975 Bob McCurdy, Richmond	26	855	32.9
1951 Bill Mlkvy, Temple	25	731	29.2	1976 Marshall Rodgers, Texas-Pan Am	25	919	36.8
1952 Clyde Lovellette, Kansas	28	795	28.4	1977 Freeman Williams, Portland St.	26	1010	38.8
1953 Frank Selvy, Furman	25	738	29.5	1978 Freeman Williams, Portland St.	27	969	35.9
1954 Frank Selvy, Furman	29	1209	41.7	1979 Lawrence Butler, Idaho St.	27	812	30.1
1955 Darrell Floyd, Furman	25	897	35.9				
1956 Darrell Floyd, Furman	28	946	33.8	1980 Tony Murphy, Southern-BR	29	932	32.1
1957 Grady Wallace, S. Carolina	29	906	31.2	1981 Zam Fredrick, S. Carolina	27	781	28.9
1958 Oscar Robertson, Cincinnati	28	984	35.1	1982 Harry Kelly, Texas Southern	29	862	29.7
1959 Oscar Robertson, Cincinnati	30	978	32.6	1983 Harry Kelly, Texas Southern	29	835	28.8
				1984 Joe Jakubick, Akron	27	814	30.1
1960 Oscar Robertson, Cincinnati	30	1011	33.7	1985 Xavier McDaniel, Wichita St	31	844	27.2
1961 Frank Burgess, Gonzaga	26	842	32.4	1986 Terrance Bailey, Wagner	29	854	29.4
1962 Billy McGill, Utah	26	1009	38.8	1987 Kevin Houston, Army	29	953	32.9
1963 Nick Werkman, Seton Hall	22	650	29.5	1988 Hersey Hawkins, Bradley	31	1125	36.3
1964 Howie Komives, Bowling Green	23	844	36.7	1989 Hank Gathers, Loyola-CA	31	1015	32.7
1965 Rick Barry, Miami-FL	26	973	37.4				
1966 Dave Schellhase, Purdue	24	781	32.5	1990 Bo Kimble, Loyola-CA	32	1131	35.3
1967 Jimmy Walker, Providence	28	851	30.4	1991 Kevin Bradshaw, US Int'l	28	1054	37.6
1968 Pete Maravich, LSU	26	1138	43.8	1992 Brett Roberts, Morehead St	29	815	28.1
1969 Pete Maravich, LSU	26	1148	44.2	1993 Greg Guy, Texas-Pan Am	19	556	29.3
1970 Pete Maravich, LSU	31	1381	44.5	1994 Glenn Robinson, Purdue	34	1030	30.3
1971 Johnny Neumann, Ole Miss	23	923	40.1				

Note: Sixteen underclassmen have won the title. **Sophomores** (4)—Robertson (1958), Maravich (1968), Neumann (1971), Fogle (1974); **Juniors** (12)—Selvy (1953), Floyd (1955), Robertson (1959), Werkman (1963), Maravich (1969), Lamar (1972), Williams (1977), Kelly (1982), Bailey (1986), Gathers (1989), Guy (1993), Robinson (1994).

Rebounds

The NCAA did not begin keeping individual rebounding records until the 1950-51 season. From 1956-62, the championship was decided on highest percentage of recoveries out of all rebounds made by both teams in all games. All averages include postseason games where applicable; (*) indicates also led nation in scoring.

Multiple winners: Artis Gilmore, Jerry Lucas, Xavier McDaniel, Kermit Washington and Leroy Wright (2).

Year	Gm	No	Avg	Year	Gm	No	Avg
1951 Ernie Beck, Penn	27	556	20.6	1974 Marvin Barnes, Providence	32	597	18.7
1952 Bill Hannon, Army	17	355	20.9	1975 John Irving, Hofstra	21	323	15.4
1953 Ed Conlin, Fordham	26	612	23.5	1976 Sam Pellom, Buffalo	26	420	16.2
1954 Art Quimby, Connecticut	26	588	22.6	1977 Glenn Moseley, Seton Hall	29	473	16.3
1955 Charlie Slack, Marshall	21	538	25.6	1978 Ken Williams, N. Texas	28	411	14.7
1956 Joe Holup, G. Washington	26	604	.256	1979 Monti Davis, Tennessee St.	26	421	16.2
1957 Elgin Baylor, Seattle	25	508	.235				
1958 Alex Ellis, Niagara	25	536	.262	1980 Larry Smith, Alcorn State	26	392	15.1
1959 Leroy Wright, Pacific	26	652	.238	1981 Darryl Watson, Miss. Valley St.	27	379	14.0
				1982 LaSalle Thompson, Texas	27	365	13.5
1960 Leroy Wright, Pacific	17	380	.234	1983 Xavier McDaniel, Wichita St.	28	403	14.4
1961 Jerry Lucas, Ohio St.	27	470	.198	1984 Akeem Olajuwon, Houston	37	500	13.5
1962 Jerry Lucas, Ohio St.	28	499	.211	1985 Xavier McDaniel, Wichita St.*	31	460	14.8
1963 Paul Silas, Creighton	27	557	20.6	1986 David Robinson, Navy	35	455	13.0
1964 Bob Pelkington, Xavier-OH	26	567	21.8	1987 Jerome Lane, Pittsburgh	33	444	13.5
1965 Toby Kimball, Connecticut	23	483	21.0	1988 Kenny Miller, Loyola-IL	29	395	13.6
1966 Jim Ware, Oklahoma City	29	607	20.9	1989 Hank Gathers, Loyola-CA*	31	426	13.7
1967 Dick Cunningham, Murray St.	22	479	21.8				
1968 Neal Walk, Florida	25	494	19.8	1990 Anthony Bonner, St. Louis	33	456	13.8
1969 Spencer Haywood, Detroit	22	472	21.5	1991 Shaquille O'Neal, LSU	28	411	14.7
				1992 Popeye Jones, Murray St.	30	431	14.4
1970 Artis Gilmore, Jacksonville	28	621	22.2	1993 Warren Kidd, Mid. Tenn. St.	26	386	14.8
1971 Artis Gilmore, Jacksonville	26	603	23.2	1994 Jerome Lambert, Baylor	24	355	14.8
1972 Kermit Washington, American	23	455	19.8				
1973 Kermit Washington, American	22	439	20.0				

Annual NCAA Division I Individual Leaders (Cont.)

Assists

The NCAA did not begin keeping individual assist records until the 1983-84 season. All averages include postseason games where applicable.

Multiple winner: Avery Johnson (2).

Year		Gm	No	Avg
1984	Craig Lathen, IL-Chicago	29	274	9.45
1985	Rob Weingard, Hofstra	24	228	9.50
1986	Mark Jackson, St. John's	36	328	9.11
1987	Avery Johnson, Southern-BR	31	333	10.74
1988	Avery Johnson, Southern-BR	30	399	13.30
1989	Glenn Williams, Holy Cross	28	278	9.93
1990	Todd Lehmann, Drexel	28	260	9.29
1991	Chris Corchiani, N.C. State	31	299	9.65
1992	Van Usher, Tennessee Tech	29	254	8.76
1993	Sam Crawford, N. Mexico St	34	310	9.12
1994	Jason Kidd, California	30	272	9.06

Blocked Shots

The NCAA did not begin keeping individual assist records until the 1985-86 season. All averages include postseason games where applicable.

Multiple winner: David Robinson (2).

Year		Gm	No	Avg
1986	David Robinson, Navy	35	207	5.91
1987	David Robinson, Navy	32	144	4.50
1988	Rodney Blake, St. Joe's-PA	29	116	4.00
1989	Alonzo Mourning, G'town	34	169	4.97
1990	Kenny Green, Rhode Island	26	124	4.77
1991	Shawn Bradley, BYU	34	177	5.21
1992	Shaquille O'Neal, LSU	30	157	5.23
1993	Theo Ratliff, Wyoming	28	124	4.43
1994	Grady Livingston, Howard	26	115	4.42

All-Time NCAA Division I Individual Leaders

Through 1992-93; includes regular season and tournament games; **Last** column indicates final year played.

CAREER
Scoring

	Points	Yrs	Last	Gm	Pts
1	Pete Maravich, LSU	3	1970	83	3667
2	Freeman Williams, Port. St.	4	1978	106	3249
3	Lionel Simmons, La Salle	4	1990	131	3217
4	Alphonzo Ford, Miss. Val. St.	4	1993	109	3165
5	Harry Kelly, Texas-Southern	4	1983	110	3066
6	Hersey Hawkins, Bradley	4	1988	125	3008
7	Oscar Robertson, Cincinnati	3	1960	88	2973
8	Danny Manning, Kansas	4	1988	147	2951
9	Alfredrick Hughes, Loyola-IL	4	1985	120	2914
10	Elvin Hayes, Houston	3	1968	93	2884
11	Larry Bird, Indiana St.	3	1979	94	2850
12	Otis Birdsong, Houston	4	1977	116	2832
13	Kevin Bradshaw, US Int'l	4	1991	111	2804
14	Allan Houston, Tennessee	4	1993	128	2801
15	Hank Gathers, USC/Loyola-CA	4	1990	117	2723
16	Reggie Lewis, N'eastern	4	1987	122	2708
17	Daren Queenan, Lehigh	4	1988	118	2703
18	Byron Larkin, Xavier-OH	4	1988	121	2696
19	David Robinson, Navy	4	1987	127	2669
20	Wayman Tisdale, Oklahoma	3	1985	104	2661

	Average	Yrs	Last	Pts	Avg
1	Pete Maravich, LSU	3	1970	3667	44.2
2	Austin Carr, Notre Dame	3	1971	2560	34.6
3	Oscar Robertson, Cinn.	3	1960	2973	33.8
4	Calvin Murphy, Niagara	3	1970	2548	33.1
5	Dwight Lamar, SW La	2	1973	1862	32.7
6	Frank Selvy, Furman	3	1954	2538	32.5
7	Rick Mount, Purdue	3	1970	2323	32.3
8	Darrell Floyd, Furman	3	1956	2281	32.1
9	Nick Werkman, Seton Hall	3	1964	2273	32.0
10	Willie Humes, Idaho St.	2	1971	1510	31.5
11	William Averitt, Pepperdine	2	1973	1541	31.4
12	Elgin Baylor, Idaho/Seattle	3	1958	2500	31.3
13	Elvin Hayes, Houston	3	1968	2884	31.0
14	Freeman Williams, Port. St.	4	1978	3249	30.7
15	Larry Bird, Indiana St.	3	1979	2850	30.3
16	Bill Bradley, Princeton	3	1965	2503	30.2
17	Rich Fuqua, Oral Roberts	2	1973	1617	29.9
18	Wilt Chamberlain, Kansas	2	1958	1433	29.9
19	Rick Barry, Miami-FL	3	1965	2298	29.8
20	Doug Collins, Illinois St.	3	1973	2240	29.1

	Field Goal Pct.	Yrs	Last	FG	FGA	Pct
1	Ricky Nedd, Appalach. St.	4	1994	412	597	.690
2	Stephen Scheffler, Purdue	4	1990	408	596	.685
3	Steve Johnson, Ore. St.	4	1981	828	1222	.678
4	Murray Brown, Fla. St.	4	1980	566	847	.668
5	Lee Campbell, SW Mo. St.	3	1990	411	618	.665
6	Warren Kidd, Mid. Tenn. St.	3	1993	496	747	.664
7	Joe Senser, West Chester	4	1979	476	719	.662
8	Kevin McGee, UC-Irvine	2	1982	552	841	.656
9	O. Phillips, Pepperdine	2	1983	404	618	.654
10	Bill Walton, UCLA	3	1974	747	1147	.651

Note: minimum 400 FGs made.

	Free Throw Pct.	Yrs	Last	FG	FGA	Pct
1	Greg Starrick, Ky/So. Ill	4	1972	341	375	.909
2	Jack Moore, Nebraska	4	1982	446	495	.901
3	Steve Henson, Kansas St.	4	1990	361	401	.900
4	Steve Alford, Indiana	4	1987	535	596	.898
5	Bob Lloyd, Rutgers	3	1967	543	605	.898
6	Jim Barton, Dartmouth	4	1989	394	440	.895
7	Tommy Boyer, Arkansas	3	1963	315	353	.892
8	Rob Robbins, N. Mexico	4	1991	309	348	.888
9	Sean Miller, Pitt	4	1992	317	358	.885
10	Ron Perry, Holy Cross	4	1980	680	768	.885
	Joe Dykstra, Western Ill.	4	1983	587	663	.885

Note: minimum 300 FTs made.

	3-Pt Field Goals	Yrs	Last	Gm	3FG
1	Doug Day, Radford	4	1993	117	401
2	Ronnie Schmitz, Missouri-KC	4	1993	112	378
3	Mark Alberts, Akron	4	1993	107	375
4	Jeff Fryer, Loyola-CA	4	1990	112	363
5	Dennis Scott, Ga. Tech	3	1990	99	351

	3-Pt Field Goal Pct.	Yrs	Last	3FG	Att	Pct
1	Tony Bennett, Wisc-GB	4	1992	290	584	.497
2	Keith Jennings, E. Tenn. St.	4	1991	223	452	.493
3	Kirk Manns, Michigan St.	4	1990	212	446	.475
4	Tim Locum, Wisconsin	4	1991	227	481	.472
5	David Olson, Eastern Ill	4	1992	262	562	.466

Note: minimum 200 3FGs made.

Rebounds

Total (before 1973)	Yrs	Last	Gm	No
1 Tom Gola, La Salle	4	1955	118	2201
2 Joe Holup, G. Washington	4	1956	104	2030
3 Charlie Slack, Marshall	4	1956	88	1916
4 Ed Conlin, Fordham	4	1955	102	1884
5 Dickie Hemric, Wake Forest	4	1955	104	1802
6 Paul Silas, Creighton	3	1964	81	1751
7 Art Quimby, UConn	4	1955	80	1716
8 Jerry Harper, Alabama	4	1956	93	1688
9 Jeff Cohen, Wm. & Mary	4	1961	103	1679
10 Steve Hamilton, Morehead St.	4	1958	102	1675

Total (since 1973)	Yrs	Last	Gm	No
1 Derrick Coleman, Syracuse	4	1990	143	1537
2 Ralph Sampson, Virginia	4	1983	132	1511
3 Pete Padgett, Nevada-Reno	4	1976	104	1464
4 Lionel Simmons, La Salle	4	1990	131	1429
5 Anthony Bonner, St. Louis	4	1990	133	1424
6 Tyrone Hill, Xavier-OH	4	1990	126	1380
7 Popeye Jones, Murray St.	4	1992	123	1374
8 Michael Brooks, La Salle	4	1980	114	1372
9 Xavier McDaniel, Wichita St.	4	1985	117	1359
10 John Irving, Ariz./Hofstra	4	1977	103	1348

Average (before 1973)	Yrs	Last	No	Avg
1 Artis Gilmore, Jacksonville	2	1971	1224	22.7
2 Charlie Slack, Marshall	4	1956	1916	21.8
3 Paul Silas, Creighton	3	1964	1751	21.6
4 Leroy Wright, Pacific	3	1960	1442	21.5
5 Art Quimby, UConn	4	1955	1716	21.5

Note: minimum 800 rebounds.

Average (since 1973)	Yrs	Last	No	Avg
1 Glenn Mosley, Seton Hall	4	1977	1263	15.2
2 Bill Campion, Manhattan	3	1975	1070	14.2
3 Pete Padgett, Nevada-Reno	4	1976	1464	14.1
4 Bob Warner, Maine	4	1976	1304	13.6
5 Shaquille O'Neal, LSU	3	1992	1217	13.5

Note: minimum 650 rebounds.

Assists

Total	Yrs	Last	Gm	No
1 Bobby Hurley, Duke	4	1993	140	1076
2 Chris Corchiani, N.C. State	4	1991	124	1038
3 Keith Jennings, E. Tenn. St.	4	1991	127	983
4 Sherman Douglas, Syracuse	4	1989	138	960
5 Greg Anthony, Portland/UNLV	4	1991	138	950
6 Gary Payton, Oregon St.	4	1990	120	939
7 Orlando Smart, San Fran	4	1994	116	902
8 Andre LaFleur, N'eastern	4	1987	128	894
9 Jim Les, Bradley	4	1986	118	884
10 Frank Smith, Old Dominion	4	1988	120	883

Average	Yrs	Last	No	Avg
1 A. Johnson, Cameron/Southern	3	1988	838	8.91
2 Sam Crawford, N. Mexico St.	2	1993	592	8.84
3 Mark Wade, Okla/UNLV	3	1987	693	8.77
4 Chris Corchiani, N.C. State	4	1991	1038	8.37
5 Taurence Chisholm, Delaware	4	1988	877	7.97
6 Van Usher, Tennessee Tech	3	1992	676	7.95
7 Anthony Manuel, Bradley	3	1989	855	7.92
8 Gary Payton, Oregon St.	4	1990	938	7.82
9 Orlando Smart, San Fran	4	1994	902	7.78
10 Keith Jennings, E. Tenn. St.	4	1991	983	7.74

Note: minimum 550 assists.

Blocked Shots

Average	Yrs	Last	No	Avg
1 David Robinson, Navy	2	1987	351	5.24
2 Shaquille O'Neal, LSU	3	1992	412	4.58
3 Alonzo Mourning, Georgetown	4	1992	453	3.78
4 Lorenzo Williams, Stetson	2	1991	234	3.71
5 Dikembe Mutombo, Georgetown	3	1991	354	3.69

Note: minimum 200 blocked shots.

Steals

Average	Yrs	Last	No	Avg
1 Mookie Blaylock, Oklahoma	2	1989	281	3.80
2 Ronn McMahon, Eastern Wash.	3	1990	225	3.52
3 Jason Kidd, California	2	1994	204	3.46
4 Eric Murdock, Providence	4	1991	376	3.21
5 Van Usher, Tennessee Tech	3	1992	270	3.18

Note: minimum 200 steals.

2000 Points/1000 Rebounds

For a combined total of 4000 or more.

	Gm	Pts	Reb	Total
1 Tom Gola, La Salle	118	2462	2201	4663
2 Lionel Simmons, La Salle	131	3217	1429	4646
3 Elvin Hayes, Houston	93	2884	1602	4486
4 Dickie Hemric, W. Forest	104	2587	1802	4389
5 Oscar Robertson, Cinn	88	2973	1338	4311
6 Joe Holup, G. Washington	104	2226	2030	4256
7 Harry Kelly, TX-Southern	110	3066	1085	4151
8 Danny Manning, Kansas	147	2951	1187	4138
9 Larry Bird, Indiana St.	94	2850	1247	4097
10 Elgin Baylor, Col.Idaho/Seattle	80	2500	1559	4059
11 Michael Brooks, La Salle	114	2628	1372	4000

Years Played— Baylor (1956-58); Bird (1977-79); Brooks (1977-80); Gola (1952-55); Hayes (1966-68); Hemric (1952-55); Holup (1953-56); Kelly (1980-83); Manning (1985-88); Robertson (1958-60); Sampson (1980-83); Simmons (1987-90).

SINGLE SEASON
Scoring

Points	Year	Gm	Pts
1 Pete Maravich, LSU	1970	31	1381
2 Elvin Hayes, Houston	1968	33	1214
3 Frank Selvy, Furman	1954	29	1209
4 Pete Maravich, LSU	1969	26	1148
5 Pete Maravich, LSU	1968	26	1138
6 Bo Kimble, Loyola-CA	1990	32	1131
7 Hersey Hawkins, Bradley	1988	31	1125
8 Austin Carr, Notre Dame	1970	29	1106
9 Austin Carr, Notre Dame	1971	29	1101
10 Otis Birdsong, Houston	1977	36	1090

Average	Year	Gm	Pts	Avg
1 Pete Maravich, LSU	1970	31	1381	44.5
2 Pete Maravich, LSU	1969	26	1148	44.2
3 Pete Maravich, LSU	1968	26	1138	43.8
4 Frank Selvy, Furman	1954	29	1209	41.7
5 Johnny Neumann, Ole Miss	1971	23	923	40.1
6 Freeman Williams, Port. St.	1977	26	1010	38.8
7 Billy McGill, Utah	1962	26	1009	38.8
8 Calvin Murphy, Niagara	1968	24	916	38.2
9 Austin Carr, Notre Dame	1970	29	1106	38.1
10 Austin Carr, Notre Dame	1971	29	1101	38.0

All-Time NCAA Division I Individual Leaders (Cont.)

Scoring

Field Goal Pct.

		Year	FG	FGA	Pct
1	Steve Johnson, Oregon St.	1981	235	315	.746
2	Dwayne Davis, Florida	1989	179	248	.722
3	Keith Walker, Utica	1985	154	216	.713
4	Steve Johnson, Oregon St.	1980	211	297	.710
5	Oliver Miller, Arkansas	1991	254	361	.704

Free Throw Pct.

		Year	FT	FTA	Pct
1	Craig Collins, Penn St.	1985	94	98	.959
2	Rod Foster, UCLA	1982	95	100	.950
3	Carlos Gibson, Marshall	1978	84	89	.944
4	Danny Basile, Marist	1994	84	89	.944
5	Jim Barton, Dartmouth	1986	65	69	.942

3-Pt Field Goal Pct.

		Year	3FG	3FGA	Pct
1	Glenn Tropf, Holy Cross	1988	52	82	.634
2	Sean Wightman, W. Mich.	1992	48	76	.632
3	Keith Jennings, E. Tenn. St.	1991	84	142	.592
4	Dave Calloway, Monmouth	1989	48	82	.585
5	Steve Kerr, Arizona	1988	114	199	.573

Assists

Average

		Year	Gm	No	Avg
1	Avery Johnson, Southern-BR	1988	30	399	13.3
2	Anthony Manuel, Bradley	1988	31	373	12.0
3	Avery Johnson, Southern-BR	1987	31	333	10.7
4	Mark Wade, UNLV	1987	38	406	10.7
5	Glenn Williams, Holy Cross	1989	28	278	9.9

Rebounds

Average (before 1973)

		Year	Gm	No	Avg
1	Charlie Slack, Marshall	1955	21	538	25.6
2	Leroy Wright, Pacific	1959	26	652	25.1
3	Art Quimby, Connecticut	1955	25	611	24.4
4	Charlie Slack, Marshall	1956	22	520	23.6
5	Ed Conlin, Fordham	1953	26	612	23.5

Average (since 1973)

		Year	Gm	No	Avg
1	Kermit Washington, American	1973	25	511	20.4
2	Marvin Barnes, Providence	1973	30	571	19.0
3	Marvin Barnes, Providence	1974	32	597	18.7
4	Pete Padgett, Nevada	1973	26	462	17.8
5	Jim Bradley, Northern Ill	1973	24	426	17.8

Blocked Shots

Average

		Year	Gm	No	Avg
1	David Robinson, Navy	1986	35	207	5.91
2	Shaquille O'Neal, LSU	1992	30	157	5.23
3	Shawn Bradley, BYU	1991	34	177	5.21
4	Cedric Lewis, Maryland	1991	28	143	5.11
5	Shaquille O'Neal, LSU	1991	28	140	5.00
	Alonzo Mourning, G'town	1992	32	160	5.00

Steals

Average

		Year	Gm	No	Avg
1	Darron Brittman, Chicago St.	1986	28	139	4.96
2	Aldwin Ware, Florida A&M	1988	29	142	4.90
3	Ronn McMahon, East Wash.	1990	29	130	4.48
4	Jim Paguaga, St. Francis-NY	1986	28	120	4.29
5	Marty Johnson, Towson St.	1988	30	124	4.13

SINGLE GAME

Scoring

Points vs Div. I Team

		Year	Pts
1	Kevin Bradshaw, US Int'l vs Loyola-CA	1991	72
2	Pete Maravich, LSU vs Alabama	1970	69
3	Calvin Murphy, Niagara vs Syracuse	1969	68
4	Jay Handlan, Wash. & Lee vs Furman	1951	66
	Pete Maravich, LSU vs Tulane	1969	66
	Anthony Roberts, Oral Rbts vs N.C.A&T	1977	66
7	Anthony Roberts, Oral Rbts vs Ore	1977	65
	Scott Haffner, Evansville vs Dayton	1989	65
9	Pete Maravich, LSU vs Kentucky	1970	64
10	Johnny Neumann, Ole Miss vs LSU	1971	63
	Hersey Hawkins, Bradley vs Detroit	1988	63

Points vs Non-Div. I Team

		Year	Pts
1	Frank Selvy, Furman vs Newberry	1954	100
2	Paul Arizin, Villanova vs Phi. NAMC	1949	85
3	Freeman Williams, Port. St. vs Rocky Mt	1978	81
4	Bill Mlkvy, Temple vs Wilkes	1951	73
5	Freeman Williams, Port. St. vs So. Ore	1977	71

Note: Bevo Francis of Division II Rio Grande (Ohio) scored an overall collegiate record 113 points against Hillsdale in 1954. He also scored 84 against Alliance and 82 against Bluffton that same season.

Assists

		Year	No
1	Tony Fairley, Baptist vs Armstrng St.	1987	22
	Avery Johnson, Southern-BR vs TX-South	1988	22
	Sherman Douglas, Syracuse vs Providence	1989	22
4	Mark Wade, UNLV vs Navy	1986	21
	Kelvin Scarborough, N. Mexico vs Hawaii	1987	21
	Anthony Manuel, Bradley vs UC-Irvine	1987	21
	Avery Johnson, Southern-BR vs Ala. St.	1988	21

3-Pt Field Goals

		Year	No
1	Dave Jamerson, Ohio U. vs Charleston	1989	14
	Askia Jones, Kansas St. vs Fresno St.	1994	14
3	Gary Bosserd, Niagara vs Siena	1987	12
	Darrin Fitzgerald, Butler vs Detroit	1987	12
	Al Dillard, Arkansas vs Delaware St.	1993	12

Rebounds

Total (before 1973)

		Year	No
1	Bill Chambers, Wm. & Mary vs Virginia	1953	51
2	Charlie Slack, Marshall vs M. Harvey	1954	43
3	Tom Heinsohn, Holy Cross vs BC	1955	42
4	Art Quimby, UConn vs BU	1955	40
5	Three players tied with 39 each.		

Total (since 1973)

		Year	No
1	David Vaughn, Oral Roberts vs Brandeis	1973	34
2	Robert Parish, Centenary vs So. Miss	1973	33
3	Durand Macklin, LSU vs Tulane	1976	32
	Jervaughn Scales, South-BR vs Grambling	1994	32
5	Jim Bradley, Northern Ill. vs WI-Milw	1973	31
	Calvin Natt, NE La. vs Ga. Southern	1976	31

Blocked Shots

		Year	No
1	David Robinson, Navy vs NC-Wilmington	1986	14
2	Shawn Bradley, BYU vs Eastern Ky	1990	14
3	Jim McIlvaine, Marquette vs No. Ill	1993	13
4	Nine players tied with 12 each.		

Steals

		Year	No
1	Mookie Blaylock, Oklahoma vs Centenary	1987	13
	Mookie Blaylock, Oklahoma vs Loyola-CA	1988	13
3	Kenny Robertson, Cleve. St. vs Wagner	1988	12
	Terry Evans, Oklahoma vs Florida A&M	1993	12
5	Seven players tied with 11 each.		

Division I Winning Streaks

Full Season
(Including tournaments)

Regular Season
(Not including tournaments)

No		Seasons	Broken by	Score	No		Seasons	Broken by	Score
88	UCLA	1971-74	Notre Dame	71-70	76	UCLA	1971-74	Notre Dame	71-70
60	San Francisco	1955-57	Illinois	62-33	57	Indiana	1975-77	Toledo	59-57
47	UCLA	1966-68	Houston	71-69	56	Marquette	1970-72	Detroit	70-49
45	UNLV	1990-91	Duke	79-77	54	Kentucky	1952-55	Georgia Tech	59-58
44	Texas	1913-17	Rice	24-18	51	San Francisco	1955-57	Illinois	62-33
43	Seton Hall	1939-41	LIU-Bklyn	49-26	48	Penn	1970-72	Temple	57-52
43	LIU-Brooklyn	1935-37	Stanford	45-31	47	Ohio St	1960-62	Wisconsin	86-67
41	UCLA	1968-69	USC	46-44	44	Texas	1913-17	Rice	24-18
39	Marquette	1970-71	Ohio St.	60-59	43	UCLA	1966-68	Houston	71-69
37	Cincinnati	1962-63	Wichita St.	65-64	43	LIU-Brooklyn	1935-37	Stanford	45-31
37	North Carolina	1957-58	West Virginia	75-64	42	Seton Hall	1939-41	LIU-Bklyn	49-26
36	N.C. State	1974-75	Wake Forest	83-78					
35	Arkansas	1927-29	Texas	26-25					

All-Time Highest Scoring Teams

SINGLE SEASON
Scoring

	Year	Gm	Pts	Avg
Loyola-CA	1990	32	3918	122.4
Loyola-CA	1989	31	3486	112.5
UNLV	1976	31	3426	110.5
Loyola-CA	1988	32	3528	110.3
UNLV	1977	32	3426	107.1

SINGLE GAME
Scoring

	Score	Opponent	Date
Loyola-CA	186-140	US Int'l	1/5/91
Loyola-CA	181-150	US Int'l	1/31/89
Oklahoma	173-101	US Int'l	11/29/89
Oklahoma	172-112	Loyola-CA	12/15/90
Arkansas	166-101	US Int'l	12/9/89

Annual Awards

UPI picked the first national Division I Player of the Year in 1955. Since then, the U.S.Basketball Writers Assn.(1959), the Commonwealth Athletic Club of Kentucky's Adolph Rupp Trophy (1961), the Atlanta Tip-Off Club (1969), the National Assn. of Basketball Coaches (1975), and the LA Athletic Club's John Wooden Award (1977) have joined in.

Since 1977, the first year all six awards were given out, the same player has won all of them in the same season eight times: Marques Johnson in 1977, Larry Bird in 1979, Ralph Sampson in both 1982 and '83, Michael Jordan in 1984, David Robinson in 1987, Lionel Simmons in 1990, Calbert Cheaney in 1993 and Glenn Robinson in 1994.

Wooden Award

Voted on by a panel of coaches, sportswriters and broadcasters and first presented in 1977 by the Los Angeles Athletic Club in the name of former Purdue All-America and UCLA coach John Wooden. Unlike the other five Player of the Year awards, candidates for the Wooden must have a minimum grade point average of 2.00 (out of 4.00).

Multiple winner: Ralph Sampson (2).

Year		Year		Year	
1977	Marques Johnson, UCLA	1983	Ralph Sampson, Virginia	1990	Lionel Simmons, La Salle
1978	Phil Ford, North Carolina	1984	Michael Jordan, N. Carolina	1991	Larry Johnson, UNLV
1979	Larry Bird, Indiana St.	1985	Chris Mullin, St. John's	1992	Christian Laettner, Duke
		1986	Walter Berry St. John's	1993	Calbert Cheaney, Indiana
1980	Darrell Griffith, Louisville	1987	David Robinson, Navy	1994	Glenn Robinson, Purdue
1981	Danny Ainge, BYU	1988	Danny Manning, Kansas		
1982	Ralph Sampson, Virginia	1989	Sean Elliott, Arizona		

Rupp Trophy

Voted on by AP sportswriters and broadcasters and first presented in 1961 by the Commonwealth Athletic Club of Kentucky in the name of former University of Kentucky coach Adolph Rupp.

Multiple winners: Ralph Sampson (3); Lew Alcindor, Jerry Lucas, David Thompson and Bill Walton (2).

Year		Year		Year	
1961	Jerry Lucas, Ohio St.	1973	Bill Walton, UCLA	1985	Patrick Ewing, Georgetown
1962	Jerry Lucas, Ohio St.	1974	David Thompson, N.C. State	1986	Walter Berry, St. John's
1963	Art Heyman, Duke	1975	David Thompson, N.C. State	1987	David Robinson, Navy
1964	Gary Bradds, Ohio St.	1976	Scott May, Indiana	1988	Hersey Hawkins, Bradley
1965	Bill Bradley, Princeton	1977	Marques Johnson, UCLA	1989	Sean Elliott, Arizona
1966	Cazzie Russell, Michigan	1978	Butch Lee, Marquette		
1967	Lew Alcindor, UCLA	1979	Larry Bird, Indiana St.	1990	Lionel Simmons, La Salle
1968	Elvin Hayes, Houston			1991	Shaquille O'Neal, LSU
1969	Lew Alcindor, UCLA	1980	Mark Aguirre, DePaul	1992	Christian Laettner, Duke
		1981	Ralph Sampson, Virginia	1993	Calbert Cheaney, Indiana
1970	Pete Maravich, LSU	1982	Ralph Sampson, Virginia	1994	Glenn Robinson, Purdue
1971	Austin Carr, Notre Dame	1983	Ralph Sampson, Virginia		
1972	Bill Walton, UCLA	1984	Michael Jordan, N. Carolina		

Annual Awards (Cont.)

United Press International

Voted on by a panel of UPI college basketball writers and first presented in 1955.
Multiple winners: Oscar Robertson, Ralph Sampson and Bill Walton (3); Lew Alcindor and Jerry Lucas (2).

Year		Year		Year	
1955	Tom Gola, La Salle	1970	Pete Maravich, LSU	1985	Chris Mullin, St. John's
1956	Bill Russell, San Francisco	1971	Austin Carr, Notre Dame	1986	Walter Berry, St. John's
1957	Chet Forte, Columbia	1972	Bill Walton, UCLA	1987	David Robinson, Navy
1958	Oscar Robertson, Cincinnati	1973	Bill Walton, UCLA	1988	Hersey Hawkins, Bradley
1959	Oscar Robertson, Cincinnati	1974	Bill Walton, UCLA	1989	Danny Ferry, Duke
1960	Oscar Robertson, Cincinnati	1975	David Thompson, N.C. State	1990	Lionel Simmons, La Salle
1961	Jerry Lucas, Ohio St.	1976	Scott May, Indiana	1991	Shaquille O'Neal, LSU
1962	Jerry Lucas, Ohio St.	1977	Marques Johnson, UCLA	1992	Jim Jackson, Ohio St.
1963	Art Heyman, Duke	1978	Butch Lee, Marquette	1993	Calbert Cheaney, Indiana
1964	Gary Bradds, Ohio St.	1979	Larry Bird, Indiana St.	1994	Glenn Robinson, Purdue
1965	Bill Bradley, Princeton	1980	Mark Aguirre, DePaul		
1966	Cazzie Russell, Michigan	1981	Ralph Sampson, Virginia		
1967	Lew Alcindor, UCLA	1982	Ralph Sampson, Virginia		
1968	Elvin Hayes, Houston	1983	Ralph Sampson, Virginia		
1969	Lew Alcindor, UCLA	1984	Michael Jordan, N. Carolina		

U.S. Basketball Writers Association

Voted on by the USBWA and first presented in 1959.
Multiple winners: Ralph Sampson and Bill Walton (3); Lew Alcindor, Jerry Lucas, Oscar Robertson (2).

Year		Year		Year	
1959	Oscar Robertson, Cincinnati	1972	Bill Walton, UCLA	1985	Chris Mullin, St. John's
1960	Oscar Robertson, Cincinnati	1973	Bill Walton, UCLA	1986	Walter Berry, St. John's
1961	Jerry Lucas, Ohio St.	1974	Bill Walton, UCLA	1987	David Robinson, Navy
1962	Jerry Lucas, Ohio St.	1975	David Thompson, N.C. State	1988	Hersey Hawkins, Bradley
1963	Art Heyman, Duke	1976	Adrian Dantley, Notre Dame	1989	Danny Ferry, Duke
1964	Walt Hazzard, UCLA	1977	Marques Johnson, UCLA		
1965	Bill Bradley, Princeton	1978	Phil Ford, North Carolina	1990	Lionel Simmons, La Salle
1966	Cazzie Russell, Michigan	1979	Larry Bird, Indiana St.	1991	Larry Johnson, UNLV
1967	Lew Alcindor, UCLA	1980	Mark Aguirre, DePaul	1992	Christian Laettner, Duke
1968	Elvin Hayes, Houston	1981	Ralph Sampson, Virginia	1993	Calbert Cheaney, Indiana
1969	Lew Alcindor, UCLA	1982	Ralph Sampson, Virginia	1994	Glenn Robinson, Purdue
1970	Pete Maravich, LSU	1983	Ralph Sampson, Virginia		
1971	Sidney Wicks, UCLA	1984	Michael Jordan, N. Carolina		

Naismith Award

Voted on by a panel of coaches, sportswriters and broadcasters and first presented in 1969 by the Atlanta Tip-Off Club in 1969 in the name of the inventor of basketball, Dr. James Naismith.
Multiple winners: Ralph Sampson and Bill Walton (3).

Year		Year		Year	
1969	Lew Alcindor, UCLA	1978	Butch Lee, Marquette	1987	David Robinson, Navy
1970	Pete Maravich, LSU	1979	Larry Bird, Indiana St.	1988	Danny Manning, Kansas
1971	Austin Carr, Notre Dame	1980	Mark Aguirre, DePaul	1989	Danny Ferry, Duke
1972	Bill Walton, UCLA	1981	Ralph Sampson, Virginia	1990	Lionel Simmons, La Salle
1973	Bill Walton, UCLA	1982	Ralph Sampson, Virginia	1991	Larry Johnson, UNLV
1974	Bill Walton, UCLA	1983	Ralph Sampson, Virginia	1992	Christian Laettner, Duke
1975	David Thompson, N.C. State	1984	Michael Jordan, N. Carolina	1993	Calbert Cheaney, Indiana
1976	Scott May, Indiana	1985	Patrick Ewing, Georgetown	1994	Glenn Robinson, Purdue
1977	Marques Johnson, UCLA	1986	Johnny Dawkins, Duke		

Eastman Award

Voted on by the National Assn. of Basketball Coaches and first presented by the Eastman Kodak Co. in 1975.
Multiple winner: Ralph Sampson (2).

Year		Year		Year	
1975	David Thompson, N.C. State	1982	Ralph Sampson, Virginia	1990	Lionel Simmons, La Salle
1976	Scott May, Indiana	1983	Ralph Sampson, Virginia	1991	Larry Johnson, UNLV
1977	Marques Johnson, UCLA	1984	Michael Jordan, N. Carolina	1992	Christian Laettner, Duke
1978	Phil Ford, North Carolina	1985	Patrick Ewing, Georgetown	1993	Calbert Cheaney, Indiana
1979	Larry Bird, Indiana St.	1986	Walter Berry, St. John's	1994	Glenn Robinson, Purdue
1980	Michael Brooks, La Salle	1987	David Robinson, Navy		
1981	Danny Ainge, BYU	1988	Danny Manning, Kansas		
		1989	Sean Elliott, Arizona		

All-Time Winningest Division I Coaches

Minimum of 10 seasons as Division I head coach; regular season and tournament games included; coaches active during 1993-94 in **bold** type.

Top 30 Winning Percentage

		Yrs	W	L	Pct
1	Jerry Tarkanian	24	625	122	.837
2	Clair Bee	21	412	87	.826
3	Adolph Rupp	41	876	190	.822
4	John Wooden	29	664	162	.804
5	**Dean Smith**	33	802	230	.777
6	Harry Fisher	13	147	44	.770
7	Frank Keaney	27	387	117	.768
8	George Keogan	24	385	117	.767
9	Jack Ramsay	11	231	71	.765
10	Vic Bubas	10	213	67	.761
11	**Jim Boeheim**	18	434	140	.756
12	**John Chaney**	22	501	164	.753
13	**Nolan Richardson**	14	339	112	.752
14	Chick Davies	21	314	106	.748
15	Ray Mears	21	399	135	.747
16	**Bob Knight**	29	640	223	.742
17	Al McGuire	20	405	143	.739
	Everett Case	18	376	133	.739
	Phog Allen	48	746	264	.739
20	Walter Meanwell	22	280	101	.735
21	**Denny Crum**	23	546	198	.734
22	Cam Henderson	35	583	216	.730
23	Lew Andreas	25	355	134	.726
	John Thompson	22	503	190	.726
	Eddie Sutton	24	526	199	.726
26	Lou Carnesecca	24	526	200	.725
27	Fred Schaus	12	251	96	.723
28	Hugh Greer	17	290	112	.721
29	Joe Lapchick	20	335	130	.720
30	**Lute Olson**	21	458	179	.719

Top 30 Victories

		Yrs	W	L	Pct
1	Adolph Rupp	41	876	190	.822
2	**Dean Smith**	33	802	230	.777
3	Hank Iba	41	767	338	.694
4	Ed Diddle	42	759	302	.715
5	Phog Allen	48	746	264	.739
6	Ray Meyer	42	724	354	.672
7	John Wooden	29	664	162	.804
8	Ralph Miller	38	657	382	.632
9	**Don Haskins**	33	645	288	.691
10	Marv Harshman	40	642	448	.589
11	**Lefty Driesell**	32	641	289	.689
12	**Bob Knight**	29	640	223	.742
	Norm Stewart	33	640	310	.674
14	**Lou Henson**	32	626	306	.672
15	Jerry Tarkanian	24	625	122	.837
16	Norm Sloan	37	624	393	.614
17	**Gene Bartow**	32	617	323	.656
18	Slats Gill	36	599	392	.604
19	Abe Lemons	34	597	344	.634
20	Guy Lewis	30	592	279	.680
21	Cam Henderson	35	583	216	.730
22	**Glenn Wilkes**	37	565	451	.556
23	Tony Hinkle	41	557	393	.586
24	Frank McGuire	30	550	235	.701
	Gary Colson	33	550	369	.598
26	**Denny Crum**	23	546	198	.734
27	Harry Miller	34	534	374	.588
28	**Eddie Sutton**	24	526	199	.726
	Lou Carnesecca	24	526	200	.725
30	Fred Enke	38	525	341	.606

Note: Clarence (Bighouse) Gaines of Division II Winston-Salem St. (1947-93) retired after the 1992-93 season to finish his 47-year career ranked No. 2 on the all-time NCAA list of all coaches regardless of division. His record is 828-446 with a .650 winning percentage.

Where They Coached

Allen—Kansas & Baker (1908-09), & Haskell (1909), Central Mo. St.(1913-19), Kansas (1920-56); **Andreas**—Syracuse (1925-43; 45-50); **Bartow**—Central Mo. St. (1962-64), Valparaiso (1965-70), Memphis St. (1971-74), Illinois (1975), UCLA (1976-77), UAB (1979—); **Bee**—Rider (1929-31), LIU-Brooklyn (1932-45, 46-51); **Boeheim**—Syracuse (1977—); **Bubas**—Duke (1960-69); **Carnesecca**—St. John's (1966-70, 74-92); **Case**—N.C. State (1947-64); **Colson**—Valdosta St. (1959-68), Pepperdine (1969-79), New Mexico (1981-88), Fresno St. (1991—); **Crum**—Louisville (1972—); **Davies**—Duquesne (1925-43, 47-48); **Diddle**—Western Ky. (1923-64); **Driesell**—Davidson (1961-69), Maryland (1970-86), J. Madison (1989—); **Enke**—Louisville (1924-25), Arizona (1926-61); **Fisher**—Columbia (1907-16), Army (1922-23, 25).

Gill—Oregon St. (1929-64); **Greer**—Connecticut (1947-63); **Harshman**—Pacific Lutheran (1946-58), Wash. St. (1959-71), Washington (1972-85); **Haskins**—UTEP (1962—); **Henderson**—Muskingum (1920-22), Davis & Elkins (1923-35), Marshall (1936-55); **Henson**—Hardin-Simmons (1963-66), N. Mexico St. (1967-75), Illinois (1976—); **Hinkle**—Butler (1927-42, 46-70); **Iba**—NW Missouri St. (1930-33), Colorado (1934), Oklahoma St. (1935-70); **Keaney**—Rhode Island (1921-48); **Knight**—Army (1966-71), Indiana (1972—); **Koegan**—St. Louis (1916), Allegheny (1919), Valparaiso (1920-21), Notre Dame (1924-43).

Lapchick—St. John's (1937-47,57-65); **Lemons**—Okla. City (1956-73), Pan American (1974-76), Texas (1977-82), Okla. City (1984-90); **Lewis**—Houston (1957-86); **A. McGuire**—Belmont Abbey (1958-64), Marquette (1965-77); **F. McGuire**—St. John's (1948-52), North Carolina (1953-61), South Carolina (1965-80); **Meanwell**—Wisconsin (1912-17, 21-34), Missouri (1918-20); **Mears**—Wittenberg (1957-62), Tennessee (1963-77); **R. Meyer**—DePaul (1943-84); **H. Miller**—Western St. (1953-58), Fresno St. (1961-65), E. New Mexico (1966-70), North Texas (1971), Wichita St. (1972-78), S.F. Austin (1979-88); **R. Miller**—Wichita St. (1952-64), Iowa (1965-70), Oregon St. (1971-89); **Olson**—Long Beach St. (1974), Iowa (1975-83), Arizona (1984—).

Ramsay—St. Joseph's-PA (1956-66); **Richardson**—Tulsa (1981-85), Arkansas (1986—); **Schaus**—West Va. (1955-60), Purdue (1973-78); **Sloan**—Presbyterian (1952-55), Citadel (1957-60), Florida (1961-66), N.C. State (1967-80), Florida (1981-89); **Smith**—North Carolina (1962—); **Stewart**—No. Iowa (1962-67), Missouri (1968—); **Sutton**—Creighton (1970-74), Arkansas (1975-85), Kentucky (1986-89), Oklahoma St. (1991—); **Tarkanian**—Long Beach St. (1969-73), UNLV (1974-92); **Thompson**—Georgetown (1973—); **Wilkes**—Stetson (1958—); **Wooden**—Indiana St. (1947-48), UCLA (1949-75).

All-Time Winningest Division I Coaches (Cont.)

Most NCAA Tournaments

Through 1994; listed are number of appearances, overall tournament record, times reaching Final Four, and number of NCAA championships.

App		W-L	F4	Championships
24	**Dean Smith**	56-24	9	2 (1982,93)
20	Adolph Rupp	30-18	6	4 (1948-89, 51,58)
18	**Bob Knight**	40-15	5	3 (1976,81,87)
18	**Denny Crum**	37-18	6	2 (1980,86)
18	Lou Carnesecca	17-20	1	None
17	**John Thompson**	29-16	3	1 (1984)
17	**Eddie Sutton**	23-17	1	None
17	**Lou Henson**	19-18	2	None
16	John Wooden	47-10	12	10 (1964-65, 67-73,75)
16	Jerry Tarkanian	37-16	4	1 (1990)
15	**Jim Boeheim**	21-15	1	None
15	**Lute Olson**	20-16	3	None
15	Digger Phelps	17-17	1	None
14	**Don Haskins**	14-13	1	1 (1966)
14	Guy Lewis	26-18	5	None
14	**Norm Stewart**	11-14	0	None

Active Coaches' Victories

Minimum five seasons in Division I.

		Yrs	W	L	Pct
1	Dean Smith, N. Carolina	33	802	230	.777
2	Jim Phelan, Mt. St. Mary's	40	720	379	.655
3	Don Haskins, UTEP	33	645	288	.691
4	Lefty Driesell, J. Madison	32	641	289	.689
5	Bob Knight, Indiana	29	640	223	.742
	Norm Stewart, Missouri	33	640	310	.674
7	Lou Henson, Illinois	32	626	306	.672
8	Gene Bartow, UAB	32	617	323	.656
9	Glenn Wilkes, Stetson	37	565	451	.556
10	Gary Colson, Fresno St	33	550	369	.598
11	Denny Crum, Louisville	23	546	198	.734
12	Eddie Sutton, Oklahoma St	24	526	199	.726
13	Eldon Miller, Northern Iowa	32	520	357	.593
14	Hugh Durham, Georgia	28	509	300	.629
15	John Thompson, Georgetown	22	503	190	.726
16	John Chaney, Temple	22	501	164	.753
17	Pete Carril, Princeton	28	487	256	.655
18	Bill Foster, Virginia Tech	27	469	293	.615
19	Bob Hallberg, IL-Chicago	23	456	246	.650
20	Calvin Luther, Tenn-Martin	33	448	374	.545

Annual Awards

UPI picked the first national Division I Coach of the Year in 1955. Since then, The U.S. Basketball Writers Assn. (1959), AP (1967), the National Assn. of Basketball Coaches (1969), and the Atlanta Tip-Off Club (1987) have joined in. Since 1987, the first year all five awards were given out, no coach has won all of them in the same season.

United Press International

Voted on by a panel of UPI college basketball writers and first presented in 1955.

Multiple winners: John Wooden (6); Bob Knight, Ray Meyer, Adolph Rupp, Norm Stewart, Fred Taylor and Phil Woopert (2).

Year		Year		Year	
1955	Phil Woolpert, San Francisco	1970	John Wooden, UCLA	1985	Lou Carnesecca, St. John's
1956	Phil Woolpert, San Francisco	1971	Al McGuire, Marquette	1986	Mike Krzyzewski, Duke
1957	Frank McGuire, North Carolina	1972	John Wooden, UCLA	1987	John Thompson, Georgetown
1958	Tex Winter, Kansas St.	1973	John Wooden, UCLA	1988	John Chaney, Temple
1959	Adolph Rupp, Kentucky	1974	Digger Phelps, Notre Dame	1989	Bob Knight, Indiana
1960	Pete Newell, California	1975	Bob Knight, Indiana		
1961	Fred Taylor, Ohio St.	1976	Tom Young, Rutgers	1990	Jim Calhoun, Connecticut
1962	Fred Taylor, Ohio St.	1977	Bob Gaillard, San Francisco	1991	Rick Majerus, Utah
1963	Ed Jucker, Cincinnati	1978	Eddie Sutton, Arkansas	1992	Perry Clark, Tulane
1964	John Wooden, UCLA	1979	Bill Hodges, Indiana St.	1993	Eddie Fogler, Vanderbilt
1965	Dave Strack, Michigan			1994	Norm Stewart, Missouri
1966	Adolph Rupp, Kentucky	1980	Ray Meyer, DePaul		
1967	John Wooden, UCLA	1981	Ralph Miller, Oregon St.		
1968	Guy Lewis, Houston	1982	Norm Stewart, Missouri		
1969	John Wooden, UCLA	1983	Jerry Tarkanian, UNLV		
		1984	Ray Meyer, DePaul		

U.S. Basketball Writers Association

Voted on by the USBWA and first presented in 1959.

Multiple winners: John Wooden (5); Bob Knight (3); Lou Carnesecca, John Chaney and Ray Meyer (2).

Year		Year		Year	
1959	Eddie Hickey, Marquette	1972	John Wooden, UCLA	1986	Dick Versace, Bradley
1960	Pete Newell, California	1973	John Wooden, UCLA	1987	John Chaney, Temple
1961	Fred Taylor, Ohio St.	1974	Norm Sloan, N.C. State	1988	John Chaney, Temple
1962	Fred Taylor, Ohio St.	1975	Bob Knight, Indiana	1989	Bob Knight, Indiana
1963	Ed Jucker, Cincinnati	1976	Bob Knight, Indiana		
1964	John Wooden, UCLA	1977	Eddie Sutton, Arkansas	1990	Roy Williams, Kansas
1965	Butch van Breda Kolff, Princeton	1978	Ray Meyer, DePaul	1991	Randy Ayers, Ohio St.
1966	Adolph Rupp, Kentucky	1979	Dean Smith, North Carolina	1992	Perry Clark, Tulane
1967	John Wooden, UCLA			1993	Eddie Fogler, Vanderbilt
1968	Guy Lewis, Houston	1980	Ray Meyer, DePaul	1994	Charlie Spoonhour, St. Louis
1969	Maury John, Drake	1981	Ralph Miller, Oregon St.		
		1982	John Thompson, Georgetown		
1970	John Wooden, UCLA	1983	Lou Carnesecca, St. John's		
1971	Al McGuire, Marquette	1984	Gene Keady, Purdue		
		1985	Lou Carnesecca, St. John's		

Associated Press

Voted on by AP sportswriters and broadcasters and first presented in 1967.
Multiple winners: John Wooden (5); Bob Knight (3); Guy Lewis, Ray Meyer, Ralph Miller and Eddie Sutton (2).

Year		Year		Year	
1967	John Wooden, UCLA	1977	Bob Gaillard, San Francisco	1987	Tom Davis, Iowa
1968	Guy Lewis, Houston	1978	Eddie Sutton, Arkansas	1988	John Chaney, Temple
1969	John Wooden, UCLA	1979	Bill Hodges, Indiana St.	1989	Bob Knight, Indiana
1970	John Wooden, UCLA	1980	Ray Meyer, DePaul	1990	Jim Calhoun, Connecticut
1971	Al McGuire, Marquette	1981	Ralph Miller, Oregon St.	1991	Randy Ayers, Ohio St.
1972	John Wooden, UCLA	1982	Ralph Miller, Oregon St.	1992	Roy Williams, Kansas
1973	John Wooden, UCLA	1983	Guy Lewis, Houston	1993	Eddie Fogler, Vanderbilt
1974	Norm Sloan, N.C. State	1984	Ray Meyer, DePaul	1994	Norm Stewart, Missouri
1975	Bob Knight, Indiana	1985	Bill Frieder, Michigan		
1976	Bob Knight, Indiana	1986	Eddie Sutton, Kentucky		

National Association of Basketball Coaches

Voted on by NABC membership and first presented in 1969.
Multiple winner: John Wooden (3).

Year		Year		Year	
1969	John Wooden, UCLA	1979	Ray Meyer, DePaul	1987	Rick Pitino, Providence
				1988	John Chaney, Temple
1970	John Wooden, UCLA	1980	Lute Olson, Iowa	1989	P.J. Carlesimo, Seton Hall
1971	Jack Kraft, Villanova	1981	Ralph Miller, Oregon St.		
1972	John Wooden, UCLA		& Jack Hartman, Kansas St.	1990	Jud Heathcote, Michigan St.
1973	Gene Bartow, Memphis St.	1982	Don Monson, Idaho	1991	Mike Krzyzewski, Duke
1974	Al McGuire, Marquette	1983	Lou Carnesecca, St. John's	1992	George Raveling, USC
1975	Bob Knight, Indiana	1984	Marv Harshman, Washington	1993	Eddie Fogler, Vanderbilt
1976	Johnny Orr, Michigan	1985	John Thompson, Georgetown	1994	Nolan Richardson, Arkansas
1977	Dean Smith, North Carolina	1986	Eddie Sutton, Kentucky		& Gene Keady, Purdue
1978	Bill Foster, Duke				
	& Abe Lemons, Texas				

Naismith Award

Voted on by a panel of coaches, sportswriters and broadcasters and first presented by the Atlanta Tip-Off Club in 1987 in the name of the inventor of basketball, Dr. James Naismith.
Multiple winner: Mike Krzyzewski (2).

Year		Year		Year	
1987	Bob Knight, Indiana	1990	Bobby Cremins, Georgia Tech	1993	Dean Smith, North Carolina
1988	Larry Brown, Kansas	1991	Randy Ayers, Ohio St.	1994	Nolan Richardson, Arkansas
1989	Mike Krzyzewski, Duke	1992	Mike Krzyzewski, Duke		

Other Men's Champions

The NCAA has sanctioned national championship tournaments for Division II since 1957 and Division III since 1975. The NAIA sanctioned a single tournament from 1937-91, then split into two divisions in 1992.

NCAA Div. II Finals

Multiple winners: Kentucky Wesleyan (6); Evansville (5); CS-Bakersfield, North Alabama and Virginia Union (2).

Year	Winner	Score	Loser	Year	Winner	Score	Loser
1957	Wheaton, IL	89-65	Ky. Wesleyan	1976	Puget Sound, WA	83-74	Tennessee-Chatt.
1958	South Dakota	75-53	St. Michael's, VT	1977	Tennessee-Chatt.	71-62	Randolph-Macon
1959	Evansville, IN	83-67	SW Missouri St.	1978	Cheyney, PA	47-40	WI-Green Bay
				1979	North Alabama	64-50	WI-Green Bay
1960	Evansville, IN	90-69	Chapman, CA	1980	Virginia Union	80-74	New York Tech
1961	Wittenberg, OH	42-38	SE Missouri St.	1981	Florida Southern	73-68	Mt. St. Mary's, MD
1962	Mt. St. Mary's, MD	58-57*	CS-Sacramento	1982	Dist. of Columbia	73-63	Florida Southern
1963	South Dakota St.	42-40	Wittenberg, OH	1983	Wright St., OH	92-73	Dist. of Columbia
1964	Evansville, IN	72-59	Akron, OH	1984	Central Mo. St.	81-77	St. Augustine's, NC
1965	Evansville, IN	85-82*	Southern Illinois	1985	Jacksonville St.	74-73	South Dakota St.
1966	Ky. Wesleyan	54-51	Southern Illinois	1986	Sacred Heart, CT	93-87	SE Missouri St.
1967	Winston-Salem, NC	77-74	SW Missouri St.	1987	Ky. Wesleyan	92-74	Gannon, PA
1968	Ky. Wesleyan	63-52	Indiana St.	1988	Lowell, MA	75-72	AK-Anchorage
1969	Ky. Wesleyan	75-71	SW Missouri St.	1989	N.C. Central	73-46	SE Missouri St.
1970	Phila. Textile	76-65	Tennessee St.	1990	Ky. Wesleyan	93-79	CS-Bakersfield
1971	Evansville, IN	97-82	Old Dominion, VA	1991	North Alabama	79-72	Bridgeport, CT
1972	Roanoke, VA	84-72	Akron, OH	1992	Virginia Union	100-75	Bridgeport, CT
1973	Ky. Wesleyan	78-76*	Tennessee St.	1993	CS-Bakersfield	85-72	Troy St., AL
1974	Morgan St., MD	67-52	SW Missouri St.	1994	CS-Bakersfield	92-86	Southern Ind.
1975	Old Dominion, VA	76-74	New Orleans				

*Overtime

NCAA Div. III Finals

Multiple winners: North Park (5); Potsdam St., Scranton and WI-Whitewater (2).

Year	Winner	Score	Loser	Year	Winner	Score	Loser
1975	LeMoyne-Owen, TN	57-54	Glassboro St., NJ	1985	North Park, IL	72-71	Potsdam St., NY
1976	Scranton, PA	60-57	Wittenberg, OH	1986	Potsdam St., NY	76-73	LeMoyne-Owen, TN
1977	Wittenberg, OH	79-66	Oneonta St., NY	1987	North Park, IL	106-100	Clark, MA
1978	North Park, IL	69-57	Widener, PA	1988	Ohio Wesleyan	92-70	Scranton, PA
1979	North Park, IL	66-62	Potsdam St., NY	1989	WI-Whitewater	94-86	Trenton St., NJ
1980	North Park, IL	83-76	Upsala, NJ	1990	Rochester, NY	43-42	DePauw, IN
1981	Potsdam St., NY	67-65*	Augustana, IL	1991	WI-Platteville	81-74	Franklin Marshall
1982	Wabash, IN	83-62	Potsdam St., NY	1992	Calvin, MI	62-49	Rochester, NY
1983	Scranton, PA	64-63	Wittenberg, OH	1993	Ohio Northern	71-68	Augustana, IL
1984	WI-Whitewater	103-86	Clark, MA	1994	Lebanon Valley, PA	66-59*	NYU

*Overtime

NAIA Finals, 1937-91

Multiple winners: Grand Canyon, Hamline, Kentucky St. and Tennessee St. (3); Central Missouri, Central St., Fort Hays St. and SW Missouri St. (2).

Year	Winner	Score	Loser	Year	Winner	Score	Loser
1937	Central Missouri	35-24	Morningside, IA	1965	Central St., OH	85-51	Oklahoma Baptist
1938	Central Missouri	45-30	Roanoke, VA	1966	Oklahoma Baptist	88-59	Georgia Southern
1939	Southwestern, KS	32-31	San Diego St.	1967	St. Benedict's, KS	71-65	Oklahoma Baptist
				1968	Central St., OH	51-48	Fairmont St., WV
1940	Tarkio, MO	52-31	San Diego St.	1969	Eastern New Mexico	99-76	MD-Eastern Shore
1941	San Diego St.	36-32	Murray St., KY				
1942	Hamline, MN	33-31	SE Oklahoma	1970	Kentucky St.	79-71	Central Wash.
1943	SE Missouri St.	34-32	NW Missouri St.	1971	Kentucky St.	102-82	Eastern Michigan
1944	Not held			1972	Kentucky St.	71-62	WI-Eau Claire
1945	Loyola-LA	49-36	Pepperdine, CA	1973	Guilford, NC	99-96	MD-Eastern Shore
1946	Southern Illinois	49-40	Indiana St.	1974	West Georgia	97-79	Alcorn St., MS
1947	Marshall, WV	73-59	Mankato St., MN	1975	Grand Canyon, AZ	65-54	M'western St., TX
1948	Louisville, KY	82-70	Indiana St.	1976	Coppin St., MD	96-91	Henderson St., AR
1949	Hamline, MN	57-46	Regis, CO	1977	Texas Southern	71-44	Campbell, NC
				1978	Grand Canyon, AZ	79-75	Kearney St., NE
1950	Indiana St.	61-47	East Central, OK	1979	Drury, MO	60-54	Henderson St., AR
1951	Hamline, MN	69-61	Millikin, IL				
1952	SW Missouri St.	73-64	Murray St., KY	1980	Cameron, OK	84-77	Alabama St.
1953	SW Missouri St.	79-71	Hamline, MN	1981	Beth. Nazarene, OK	86-85*	AL-Huntsville
1954	St. Benedict's, KS	62-56	Western Illinois	1982	SC-Spartanburg	51-38	Biola, CA
1955	East Texas St.	71-54	SE Oklahoma	1983	Charleston, SC	57-53	WV-Wesleyan
1956	McNeese St., LA	60-55	Texas Southern	1984	Fort Hays St., KS	48-46*	WI-Stevens Pt.
1957	Tennessee St.	92-73	SE Oklahoma	1985	Fort Hays St., KS	82-80*	Wayland Bapt., TX
1958	Tennessee St.	85-73	Western Illinois	1986	David Lipscomb, TN	67-54	AR-Monticello
1959	Tennessee St.	97-87	Pacific-Luth., WA	1987	Washburn, KS	79-77	West Virginia St.
				1988	Grand Canyon, AZ	88-86*	Auburn-Montg, AL
1960	SW Texas St.	66-44	Westminster, PA	1989	St. Mary's, TX	61-58	East Central, OK
1961	Grambling, LA	95-75	Georgetown, KY				
1962	Prairie View, TX	62-53	Westminster, PA	1990	Birm-Southern, AL	88-80	WI-Eau Claire
1963	Pan American, TX	73-62	Western Carolina	1991	Oklahoma City	77-74	Central Arkansas
1964	Rockhurst, MO	66-56	Pan American, TX				

*Overtime

NAIA Div. I Finals

NAIA split tournament into two divisions in 1992.
Multiple winner: Oklahoma City (2).

Year	Winner	Score	Loser
1992	Oklahoma City	82-73*	Central Arkansas
1993	Hawaii Pacific	88-83	Okla. Baptist
1994	Oklahoma City	99-81	Life, GA

*Overtime

NAIA Div. II Finals

NAIA split tournament into two divisions in 1992.

Year	Winner	Score	Loser
1992	Grace,IN	85-79*	Northwestern-IA
1993	Williamette, OR	63-56	Northern St., SD
1994	Eureka, IL	98-95*	Northern St., SD

*Overtime

Player of the Year and NBA MVP

College basketball Players of the Year who have gone on to win the Most Valuable Player award (the Maurice Podoloff Trophy) in the NBA.
Bill Russell: COLLEGE—San Francisco (1956); PROS—Boston Celtics (1958, 1961, 1962, 1963 and 1965).
Oscar Robertson: COLLEGE—Cincinnati (1958, 1959 and 1960); PROS—Cincinnati Royals (1964).
Kareem Abdul-Jabbar: COLLEGE—UCLA (1967 and 1968); PROS—Milwaukee Bucks (1971 and 1972) and LA Lakers (1974, 1976, 1977 and 1980).
Bill Walton: COLLEGE—UCLA (1972, 1973 and 1974); PROS—Portland Trail Blazers (1978).
Larry Bird: COLLEGE—Indiana St. (1979); PROS—Boston Celtics (1984, 1985, and 1986).
Michael Jordan: COLLEGE—North Carolina (1984); PROS—Chicago Bulls (1988, 1991 and 1992).

WOMEN

NCAA Final Four

Replaced the Association of Intercollegiate Athletics for Women (AIAW) tournament in 1982 as the official playoff for the national championship.
Multiple winners: Tennessee (3); Louisiana Tech, Stanford and USC (2).

Year	Champion	Head Coach	Score	Runner-up	Third Place	
1982	Louisiana Tech	Sonya Hogg	76-62	Cheyney	Maryland	Tennessee
1983	USC	Linda Sharp	69-67	Louisiana Tech	Georgia	Old Dominion
1984	USC	Linda Sharp	72-61	Tennessee	Cheyney	Louisiana Tech
1985	Old Dominion	Marianne Stanley	70-65	Georgia	NE Louisiana	Western Ky.
1986	Texas	Jody Conradt	97-81	USC	Tennessee	Western Ky.
1987	Tennessee	Pat Summitt	67-44	Louisiana Tech	Long Beach St.	Texas
1988	Louisiana Tech	Leon Barmore	56-54	Auburn	Long Beach St.	Tennessee
1989	Tennessee	Pat Summitt	76-60	Auburn	Louisiana Tech	Maryland
1990	Stanford	Tara VanDerveer	88-81	Auburn	Louisiana Tech	Virginia
1991	Tennessee	Pat Summitt	70-67 (OT)	Virginia	Connecticut	Stanford
1992	Stanford	Tara VanDerveer	78-62	Western Kentucky	SW Missouri St.	Virginia
1993	Texas Tech	Marsha Sharp	84-82	Ohio St.	Iowa	Vanderbilt
1994	North Carolina	Sylvia Hatchell	60-59	Louisiana Tech	Alabama	Purdue

Final Four sites: 1982 (Norfolk, VA.), **1983** (Norfolk, Va.), **1984** (Los Angeles), **1985** (Austin), **1986** (Lexington), **1987** (Austin), **1988** (Tacoma), **1989** (Tacoma), **1990** (Knoxville), **1991** (New Orleans), **1992** (Los Angeles), **1993** (Atlanta), **1994** (Richmond).

Most Outstanding Player

A Most Outstanding Player has been selected every year of the NCAA tournament. Winner who did not play for the tournament champion is listed in **bold** type.
Multiple winner: Cheryl Miller (2).

Year		Year		Year	
1982	Janice Lawrence, La. Tech	1987	Tonya Edwards, Tennessee	1992	Molly Goodenbour, Stanford
1983	Cheryl Miller, USC	1988	Erica Westbrooks, La. Tech	1993	Sheryl Swoopes, Texas Tech
1984	Cheryl Miller, USC	1989	Bridgette Gordon, Tennessee	1994	Charlotte Smith, N. Carolina
1985	Tracy Claxton, Old Dominion	1990	Jennifer Azzi, Stanford		
1986	Clarissa Davis, Texas	1991	**Dawn Staley,** Virginia		

Associated Press Final Top 10 Polls

The Associated Press introduced its weekly college basketball poll of women's coaches, compiled by Mel Greenberg of the Philadelphia Inquirer, during the 1976-77 season. The Assn. of Incollegiate Athletics for Women (AIAW) tournament determined the Division I national champion from 1972-81. The NCAA tournament began its women's tournament in 1982. Eventual national champions are in **bold** type.

	1977		**1979**		**1981**		**1983**
1	**Delta St.**	1	**Old Dominion**	1	**Louisiana Tech**	1	**USC**
2	Immaculata	2	Louisiana Tech	2	Tennessee	2	Louisiana Tech
3	St. Joseph's-PA	3	Tennessee	3	Old Dominion	3	Texas
4	CS-Fullerton	4	Texas	4	USC	4	Old Dominion
5	Tennessee	5	S.F. Austin St.	5	Cheyney	5	Cheyney
6	Tennessee Tech	6	UCLA	6	Long Beach St.	6	Long Beach St.
7	Wayland Baptist	7	Rutgers	7	UCLA	7	Maryland
8	Monclair St.	8	Maryland	8	Maryland	8	Penn St.
9	S.F. Austin St.	9	Cheyney	9	Rutgers	9	Georgia
10	N.C. State	10	Wayland Baptist	10	Kansas	10	Tennessee

	1978		**1980**		**1982**		**1984**
1	Tennessee	1	**Old Dominion**	1	**Louisiana Tech**	1	Texas
2	Wayland Baptist	2	Tennessee	2	Cheyney	2	Louisiana Tech
3	N.C. State	3	Louisiana Tech	3	Maryland	3	Georgia
4	Monclair St.	4	South Carolina	4	Tennessee	4	Old Dominion
5	**UCLA**	5	S.F. Austin St.	5	Texas	5	**USC**
6	Maryland	6	Maryland	6	USC	6	Long Beach St.
7	Queens-NY	7	Texas	7	Old Dominion	7	Kansas St.
8	Valdosta St.	8	Rutgers	8	Rutgers	8	LSU
9	Delta St.	9	Long Beach St.	9	Long Beach St.	9	Cheyney
10	LSU	10	N.C. State	10	Penn St.	10	Mississippi

Associated Press Final Top 10 Polls (Cont.)

1985
1 Texas
2 NE Louisiana
3 Long Beach St.
4 Louisiana Tech
5 **Old Dominion**
6 Mississippi
7 Ohio St.
8 Georgia
9 Penn St.
10 Auburn

1986
1 **Texas**
2 Georgia
3 USC
4 Louisiana Tech
5 Western Ky.
6 Virginia
7 Auburn
8 Long Beach St.
9 LSU
10 Rutgers

1987
1 Texas
2 Auburn
3 Louisiana Tech
4 Long Beach St.
5 Rutgers
6 Georgia
7 **Tennessee**
8 Mississippi
9 Iowa
10 Ohio St.

1988
1 Tennessee
2 Iowa
3 Auburn
4 Texas
5 **Louisiana Tech**
6 Ohio St.
7 Long Beach St.
8 Rutgers
9 Maryland
10 Virginia

1989
1 **Tennessee**
2 Auburn
3 Louisiana Tech
4 Stanford
5 Maryland
6 Texas
7 Long Beach St.
8 Iowa
9 Colorado
10 Georgia

1990
1 **Louisiana Tech**
2 Stanford
3 Washington
4 Tennessee
5 UNLV
6 S.F. Austin St.
7 Georgia
8 Texas
9 Auburn
10 Iowa

1991
1 Penn St.
2 Virginia
3 Georgia
4 **Tennessee**
5 Purdue
6 Auburn
7 N.C. State
8 LSU
9 Arkansas
10 Western Ky.

1992
1 Virginia
2 Tennessee
3 **Stanford**
4 S.F. Austin St.
5 Mississippi
6 Miami-FL
7 Iowa
8 Maryland
9 Penn St.
10 SW Missouri St.

1993
1 Vanderbilt
2 Tennessee
3 Ohio St.
4 Iowa
5 **Texas Tech**
6 Stanford
7 Auburn
8 Penn St.
9 Virginia
10 Colorado

1994
1 Tennessee
2 Penn St.
3 Connecticut
4 **North Carolina**
5 Colorado
6 Louisiana Tech
7 USC
8 Purdue
9 Texas Tech
10 Virginia

All-Time Winningest Division I Teams

Division I schools with best winning percentages and most victories through 1993-94 (including postseason tournaments).

Top 10 Winning Percentage

		Yrs	W	L	T	Pct
1	Louisiana Tech	20	555	102	0	.845
2	Texas	20	563	117	0	.828
3	Tennessee	20	530	126	0	.808
4	Mount St. Mary's	20	403	126	0	.762
5	S.F. Austin St.	22	524	167	0	.758
6	Long Beach St.	32	575	188	0	.754
7	UNLV	20	427	142	0	.750
8	Montana	20	416	141	0	.747
9	Rutgers	20	428	150	0	.740
10	Mississippi	20	462	163	0	.739

Top 10 Victories

		Yrs	W	L	T	Pct
1	Long Beach St.	32	575	188	0	.754
2	Texas	20	563	117	0	.828
3	Louisiana Tech	20	555	102	0	.845
4	James Madison	72	554	303	5	.646
5	Tennessee Tech	24	536	204	0	.724
6	Tennessee	20	530	126	0	.808
7	S.F. Austin St.	22	524	167	0	.758
8	Old Dominion	25	503	199	0	.717
9	Ohio St.	29	493	194	0	.718
10	Kansas St.	26	475	274	0	.634

All-Time NCAA Division I Individual Leaders

Through 1993-94; includes regular season and tournament games; **Last** column indicates final year played.

CAREER

Scoring

	Average	Yrs	Last	Pts	Pts
1	Patricia Hoskins, Miss.Valley St.	4	1989	3122	28.4
2	Sandra Hodge, New Orleans	4	1984	2860	26.7
3	Lorri Bauman, Drake	4	1984	3115	26.0
4	Valorie Whiteside, Appalach. St.	4	1988	2944	25.4
5	Joyce Walker, LSU	4	1984	2906	24.8
6	Tarcha Hollis, Grambling	4	1991	2058	24.2
7	Karen Pelphrey, Marshall	4	1986	2746	24.1
8	Erma Jones, Bethune-Cookman	3	1984	2095	24.1
9	Cheryl Miller, USC	4	1986	3018	23.6
10	Chris Starr, Nevada	4	1986	2356	23.3

Rebounds

	Average	Yrs	Last	Reb	Avg
1	Wanda Ford, Drake	4	1986	1887	16.1
2	Patricia Hoskins, Miss. Valley	4	1989	1662	15.1
3	Tarcha Hollis, Grambling	4	1991	1185	13.9
4	Katie Beck, East Tenn. St.	4	1988	1404	13.4
5	Marilyn Stephens, Temple	4	1984	1519	13.0
6	Cheryl Taylor, Tenn. Tech	4	1987	1532	12.8
7	Olivia Bradley, West Virginia	4	1985	1484	12.7
8	Judy Mosley, Hawaii	4	1990	1441	12.6
9	Chana Perry, NE La./S.Diego St.	4	1989	1286	12.5
10	Three players tied at 12.2 each.				

SINGLE SEASON
Scoring

Average	Year	Gm	Pts	Avg
1 Patricia Hoskins, Miss.Valley St.	1989	27	908	33.6
2 Andrea Congreaves, Mercer	1992	28	925	33.0
3 Deborah Temple, Delta St.	1984	28	873	31.2
4 Andrea Congreaves, Mercer	1993	26	805	31.0
5 Wanda Ford, Drake	1986	30	919	30.6
6 Anucha Browne, Northwestern	1985	28	855	30.5
7 LeChandra LeDay, Grambling	1988	28	850	30.4
8 Kim Perrot, SW Louisiana	1990	28	839	30.0
9 Tina Hutchinson, San Diego St.	1984	30	898	29.9
10 Jan Jensen, Drake	1991	30	888	29.6

SINGLE GAME
Scoring

Average	Year	Pts
1 Cindy Brown, Long Beach St. vs San Jose St.	1987	60
2 Lorri Bauman, Drake vs SW Missouri St.	1984	58
Kim Perrot, SW La. vs SE La	1990	58
4 Patricia Hoskins, Miss.Valley vs Southern-BR.	1989	55
Patricia Hoskins, Miss.Valley vs Alabama St.	1989	55
6 Wanda Ford, Drake vs SW Missouri St.	1986	54
7 Chris Starr, Nevada vs CS-Sacramento	1983	53
Felisha Edwards, NE La. vs Southern Miss	1991	53
Sheryl Swoopes, Texas Tech vs Texas	1993	53
10 Three players tied at 52 points each.		

Winningest Active Division I Coaches

Minimum of five seasons as Division I head coach; regular season and tournament games included.

Top 10 Winning Percentage

	Yrs	W	L	Pct
1 Leon Barmore, La. Tech	12	338	56	.858
2 Bill Sheahan, Mt. St. Mary's	13	297	64	.823
3 Vivian Stringer, Iowa	22	509	118	.812
4 Pat Summitt, Tennessee	20	530	126	.808
5 Robin Selvig, Montana	16	382	93	.804
6 Jody Conradt, Texas	25	642	162	.799
7 Joe Ciampi, Auburn	17	409	111	.787
8 Jim Bolla, UNLV	12	285	84	.772
9 Tara VanDerveer, Stanford	16	373	110	.772
10 Andy Landers, Georgia	15	361	114	.760

Top 10 Victories

	Yrs	W	L	Pct
1 Jody Conradt, Texas	25	642	162	.799
2 Pat Summitt, Tennessee	20	530	126	.808
3 Vivian Stringer, Iowa	22	509	118	.812
4 Sue Gunter, LSU	24	494	209	.703
5 Marynell Meadors, Florida St	24	479	249	.658
6 Kay Yow, N.C. State	23	467	182	.720
7 Theresa Grentz, Rutgers	20	444	141	.759
8 Sylvia Hatchell, N. Carolina	19	414	176	.693
9 Rene Portland, Penn St	18	412	135	.753
10 Joe Ciampi, Auburn	17	409	111	.787

Annual Awards

The Broderick Award was first given out to the Women's Division I or Large School Player of the Year in 1977. Since then, the National Assn. for Girls and Women in Sports (1978), the Women's Basketball Coaches Assn. (1983) and the Atlanta Tip-Off Club (1983) have joined in.

Since 1983, the first year all four awards were given out, the same player has won all of them in the same season once: Cheryl Miller of USC in 1985.

Broderick Award

Voted on by a national panel of women's collegiate athletic directors and first presented by the late Thomas Broderick, an athletic outfitter, in 1976. Honda has presented the award since 1987. Basketball Player of the Year is one of 10 nominated for Collegiate Woman Athlete of the Year; (*) indicates player also won Athlete of the Year.
Multiple winners: Nancy Lieberman, Cheryl Miller and Dawn Staley (2).

Year		Year		Year	
1977	Lucy Harris, Delta St.*	1983	Anne Donovan, Old Dominion	1989	Bridgette Gordon, Tennessee
1978	Anne Meyers, UCLA*	1984	Cheryl Miller, USC*	1990	Jennifer Azzi, Stanford
1979	Nancy Lieberman, Old Dominion*	1985	Cheryl Miller, USC	1991	Dawn Staley, Virginia
1980	Nancy Lieberman, Old Dominion*	1986	Kamie Ethridge, Texas*	1992	Dawn Staley, Virginia
1981	Lynette Woodward, Kansas	1987	Katrina McClain, Georgia	1993	Sheryl Swoopes, Texas Tech
1982	Pam Kelly, La. Tech.	1988	Teresa Weatherspoon, La. Tech*	1994	TBA in fall

Wade Trophy

Voted on by the National Assn. for Girls and Women in Sports (NAGWS) and awarded for academics and community service as well as player performance. First presented in 1978 in the name of former Delta St. coach Margaret Wade.
Multiple winner: Nancy Lieberman (2).

Year		Year		Year	
1978	Carol Blazejowski, Montclair St.	1984	Janice Lawrence, La. Tech	1990	Jennifer Azzi, Stanford
1979	Nancy Lieberman, Old Dominion	1985	Cheryl Miller, USC	1991	Daedra Charles, Tennessee
1980	Nancy Lieberman, Old Dominion	1986	Kamie Ethridge, Texas	1992	Susan Robinson, Penn St.
1981	Lynette Woodward, Kansas	1987	Shelly Pennefather, Villanova	1993	Karen Jennings, Nebraska
1982	Pam Kelly, La. Tech	1988	Teresa Weatherspoon, La. Tech	1994	Carol Ann Shudlick, Minnesota
1983	LaTaunya Pollard, L. Beach St.	1989	Clarissa Davis, Texas		

Annual Awards (Cont.)
Naismith Trophy

Voted on by a panel of coaches, sportwriters and broadcasters and first presented in 1983 by the Atlanta Tip-Off Club in the name of the inventor of basketball, Dr. James Naismith.

Multiple winners: Cheryl Miller (3); Clarissa Davis and Dawn Staley (2).

Year		Year		Year	
1983	Anne Donovan, Old Dominion	1987	Clarissa Davis, Texas	1991	Dawn Staley, Virginia
1984	Cheryl Miller, USC	1988	Sue Wicks, Rutgers	1992	Dawn Staley, Virginia
1985	Cheryl Miller, USC	1989	Clarissa Davis, Texas	1993	Sheryl Swoopes, Texas Tech
1986	Cheryl Miller, USC	1990	Jennifer Azzi, Stanford	1994	Lisa Leslie, USC

Women's Basketball Coaches Association

Voted on by the WBCA and first presented by Champion athletic outfitters in 1983.

Multiple winners: Cheryl Miller and Dawn Staley (2).

Year		Year		Year	
1983	Anne Donovan, Old Dominion	1987	Katrina McClain, Georgia	1991	Dawn Staley, Virgina
1984	Janice Lawrence, La. Tech	1988	Michelle Edwards, Iowa	1992	Dawn Staley, Virginia
1985	Cheryl Miller, USC	1989	Clarissa Davis, Texas	1993	Sheryl Swoopes, Texas Tech
1986	Cheryl Miller, USC	1990	Venus Lacey, La. Tech	1994	Lisa Leslie, USC

Coach of the Year Award

Voted on by the Women's Basketball Coaches Assn. and first presented by Converse athletic outfitters in 1983.

Multiple winner: Jody Conradt (2).

Year		Year		Year	
1983	Pat Summitt, Tennessee	1987	Theresa Grentz, Rutgers	1991	Rene Portland, Penn St.
1984	Jody Conradt, Texas	1988	Vivian Stringer, Iowa	1992	Ferne Labati, Miami-FL
1985	Jim Foster, St. Joseph's-PA	1989	Tara VanDerveer, Stanford	1993	Vivian Stringer, Iowa
1986	Jody Conradt, Texas	1990	Kay Yow, N.C. State	1994	Marsha Sharp, Texas Tech

Other Women's Champions

NCAA Div. II Finals

Year	Winner	Score	Loser
1982	Cal Poly Pomona	93-74	Tuskegee, AL
1983	Virginia Union	73-60	Cal Poly Pomona
1984	Central Mo. St.	80-73	Virginia Union
1985	Cal Poly Pomona	80-69	Central Mo. St.
1986	Cal Poly Pomona	70-63	North Dakota St.
1987	New Haven, CT	77-75	Cal Poly Pomona
1988	Hampton, VA	65-48	West Texas St.
1989	Delta St., MS	88-58	Cal Poly Pomona
1990	Delta St., MS	77-43	Bentley, MA
1991	North Dakota St.	81-74	SE Missouri St.
1992	Delta St., MS	65-63	North Dakota St.
1993	North Dakota St.	95-63	Delta St., MS
1994	North Dakota St.	89-56	CS-San Bernadino

NCAA Div. III Finals

Year	Winner	Score	Loser
1982	Elizabethtown, PA	67-66*	NC-Greensboro
1983	North Central, IL	83-71	Elizabethtown, PA
1984	Rust College, MS	51-49	Elizabethtown, PA
1985	Scranton, PA	68-59	New Rochelle, NY
1986	Salem St., MA	89-85	Bishop, TX
1987	WI-Stevens Pt.	81-74	Concordia, MN
1988	Concordia, MN	65-57	St. John Fisher, NY
1989	Elizabethtown, PA	66-65	CS-Stanislaüs
1990	Hope, MI	65-63	St. John Fisher
1991	St. Thomas, MN	73-55	Muskingum, OH
1992	Alma, MI	79-75	Moravian, PA
1993	Central Iowa	71-63	Capital, OH
1994	Capital, OH	82-63	Washington, MO

*Overtime

AIAW Finals

The Association of Intercollegiate Athletics for Women Large College tournament determined the women's national champion for 10 years until supplanted by the NCAA. In 1982, most Division I teams entered the first NCAA tournament rather than the last one staged by the AIAW.

Year	Winner	Score	Loser
1972	Immaculata, PA	52-48	West Chester, PA
1973	Immaculata, PA	59-52	Queens College, NY
1974	Immaculata, PA	68-53	Mississippi College
1975	Delta St., MS	90-81	Immaculata, PA
1976	Delta St., MS	69-64	Immaculata, PA
1977	Delta St., MS	68-55	LSU
1978	UCLA	90-74	Maryland
1979	Old Dominion	75-65	Louisiana Tech
1980	Old Dominion	68-53	Tennessee
1981	Louisiana Tech	79-59	Tennessee
1982	Rutgers	83-77	Texas

NAIA Finals

Year	Winner	Score	Loser
1981	Kentucky St.	73-67	Texas Southern
1982	SW Oklahoma	80-45	Mo. Southern
1983	SW Oklahoma	80-68	AL-Huntsville
1984	NC-Asheville	72-70*	Portland, OR
1985	SW Oklahoma	55-54	Saginaw Val., MI
1986	Francis Marion, SC	75-65	Wayland Baptist, TX
1987	SW Oklahoma	60-58	North Georgia
1988	Oklahoma City	113-95	Claflin, SC
1989	So. Nazarene	98-96	Claflin, SC
1990	SW Oklahoma	82-75	AR-Monticello
1991	Ft. Hays St., KS	57-53	SW Oklahoma
1992	I— Arkansas Tech	84-68	Wayland Baptist, TX
	II— Northern St., SD	73-56	Tarleton St., TX
1993	I— Arkansas Tech	76-75	Union, TN
	II— No. Montana	71-68	Northern St., SD
1994	I— So. Nazarene	97-74	David Lipscomb, TN
	II— Northern St., SD	48-45	Western Oregon

*Overtime

Wide World Photos

Regular season and playoff MVP **Hakeem Olajuwon** holds up the Larry O'Brien Trophy during a parade honoring the Houston Rockets as 1994 NBA champions.

PRO BASKETBALL

329

PRO BASKETBALL

by Bob Ryan

Rocket Science

Without Michael Jordan, defense becomes the NBA's formula for success and no team is more successful than Houston.

Pity the poor cryogenically-frozen NBA fan who last saw a game in the world's greatest basketball league 30 years ago.

He had left behind a league whose *raison d'etre* was offense. Put the ball in the basket. Take 99 shots a game. Minimum. To play it safe, you'd better squeeze off 110. Defense, such as it was, took place in little bursts.

Back in 1963-64, the two lowest scoring clubs in the nine-team NBA— San Francisco and Detroit— averaged 107.8 and 107.7 points a game, respectively. And no one gave up less than 102 points a night. Simply put, the way to win in those rootin'-tootin' days of yore was to play like Boston— take 110 shots a game and have Bill Russell on your side.

And that was a slowdown era compared to the 1966-67 season. The NBA had 10 teams that year and all of them scored at least 111 points a game. Three clubs— Philadelphia, San Francisco and Los Angeles— all averaged over 120 while Boston was the only club to hold opponents to less than 115 points per night.

Fast forward to 1993-94. This past season the Phoenix Suns led the 27-team NBA in scoring by ringing up 108.2 points a game and Portland averaged the most shots per outing with 91. Meanwhile, seven

Bob Ryan is a columnist for *The Boston Globe* and has covered the NBA for 20 years. He is also a regular on ESPN's "Sports Reporters."

teams failed to average 100 points a game and 11 others couldn't reach 102.

What's going on here?

They like to say the NBA is a players' league, but the truth is that the coaches dictate the flow of the game nowadays, and what coaches want is defense. The latent athleticism of these magnificent players is being channeled into defense. If you aren't willing to play defense, you won't get into the game.

The NBA had been ever so slowly throttling back on offense throughout the 1970s and '80s when along came Chuck Daly and the Detroit Pistons, winning back-to-back titles in 1989 and '90 with some of the best defense the league has ever seen. That did it. Anyone sitting on the fence was now leaping onto the side marked "D," not the one labeled "O."

What we now have is a nightly tooth-pull. And it all came to a head in the 1994 NBA Finals, in which the Houston Rockets and New York Knicks played seven jarring games in which neither team scored as many as 94 points on any given night. The last time neither finalist broke 100 was back in the spring of 1954 and the 24-clock was introduced the following season.

While the NBA had clearly been slowing down for years, few people noticed as long as Michael Jordan, the league's one-man entertainment conglomerate, was around leading the Chicago Bulls to three straight NBA titles.

But in 1993-94, Michael Jordan was else-

Anne Ryan/USA TODAY

Wide World Photos

With scoring machine **Michael Jordan** (right) forsaking the NBA and the Bulls for a minor league baseball career, Chicago fans (left) weren't alone in protesting the post-Michael era of roughhouse defensive tactics epitomized by the New York Knicks.

where. Talk about bombshells. On Oct. 5, Jordan throws out the first ball before Game 1 of the American League playoffs between the Toronto Blue Jays and the hometown White Sox. The next day, he throws in the towel on his nine-year NBA career— four weeks before the start of the new season.

No one in Chicago was ready for this. A basketball season without Michael Jordan? Why not pizza without the cheese?

"We went from predictable, with probably a 99 percent chance of winning for the fourth time, to a let's-see-how-far-we-can-make-it type of season," said center Will Perdue. "All of a sudden, it's like driving a train into a dark tunnel. You don't know what to expect."

Perdue spoke from the perspective of the Bulls, but he might as well have been speaking for the whole league. For Michael Jordan was more than just Michael Jordan. He was the last active member of a hallowed Big Three who had elevated the NBA to unprecedented heights.

Jordan, Magic Johnson and Larry Bird were the Holy Trinity of Hoop, a magnetic threesome who had brought attention to the league by virtue of their magnificent talents and special swagger. From 1979, when Magic and Bird broke in, through the end of the 1992-93 season, when Jordan led the Bulls to their third championship, the NBA had led a charmed life.

Suddenly, they were all gone. Bird was forced to quit at the end of the 1991-92 season due to back miseries. Magic had retired in November of 1992 with the shocking revelation that he was HIV-positive. Now Jordan, a vigorous 30 years of age at the time of his announcement, was exiting the sport. The NBA felt adrift.

Since Jordan has become one of the most recognizable sports figures in the world, the story was hardly confined to the United States. International reaction was formidable. The story took up the first three pages of the French national sports daily, *L'Equipe*, with the page one headline playing off a Jacques Brel song title: "Don't Leave Us." Said *L'Equipe*'s Francois Brassemin, "Michael Jordan is the most popular athlete among young people in France."

The sentiment was echoed next door.

"Even people interested in soccer wanted to see him in action," said the normally-staid *Frankfurter Allgemeine*. "People who knew nothing about German basketball knew about Michael Jordan."

The story was the same in Argentina, Kenya, Spain, Japan and even China, where it is not the custom to comment on events for a day or two. But this time both the *Beijing Daily* and *Guangming Daily* were moved to comment. "Jordan left the biggest impact of all players," said the man from *Guanming Daily*.

What the NBA needed to fill the void was an influx of new stars and central casting was ready with a few. The 1993 NBA Draft yielded new barely-shaving zillionaires such as Chris Webber, Anfernee Hardaway, Shawn Bradley and Jamal Mashburn, early draft entries all, and each gifted with a fabulous contract.

The reported numbers were truly staggering— Webber: 15 years, $74.4 million; Bradley: eight years, $44.3 million; Hardaway: 13 years, $65 million; and Mashburn: seven years, $32 million.

"You've got to pay the going rate," shrugged Golden State president Dan Finnane.

Webber appeared to be worth something, but whether or not it's $74.4 million is yet to be determined. The former Michigan star came through with 17.5 points and 9.1 rebounds a game while shooting .552 from the floor. Those figures, plus his team's surprising (in the face of severe injury losses) 50-win season, were good enough to earn him Rookie of the Year honors.

As for his first-year colleagues, the 7-foot-6 inch Bradley was sidelined halfway through the season after sustaining a knee injury; Hardaway earned the requisite raves as a point guard for his Orlando team (finishing second to Webber in the rookie balloting); and Mashburn scored 19 points a game for a beleagured Dallas team.

Houston had no marquee rookie but its first round pick, dynamic Sam Cassell (the overall 24th choice), grew in stature as the season progressed. You might say the same about the entire team, since they are the NBA champions.

While the headlines belonged to the Bulls and New York Knicks in the East and Phoenix and Seattle in the West, the Rockets sailed sublimely on, winning their first 15 games, taking a second consecutive Midwest Division title and then bringing home Houston's first major professional championship of any kind (the AFL Oilers of 1960 and '61 and the WHA Aeros of 1974 and '75 excepted).

Houston was not the pre-playoff favorite, Seattle was. Houston wasn't supposed to defeat Phoenix, either. But when the last basket was scored, the record revealed that since Jan. 8, 1993, the Rockets had gone 120-49, playoffs and regular season combined, and that was the best record in basketball over that prolonged stretch.

The Houston linchpin was the regal Hakeem Olajuwon. The 31-year-old Nigerian, who didn't take up the game in his native country until he was 17, was named the Most Valuable Player for both the regular season and the playoffs. He finished third in scoring (27.3), fourth in rebounding (11.9) and 10th in field goal percentage (.528). From the field, he and Indiana's Rik Smits were the only members of the Top 10 whose calling card shot is the turnaround jumper; the rest were all dunkmeisters. Olajuwon also was second in the league in blocked shots, and his overall expertise at the so-called "other" end of the floor led to his selection as the Defensive Player of the Year for the second season in a row.

The Rockets' coach was Rudy Tomjanovich, a franchise lifer. Popularly known as "Rudy T," the friendly Tomjanovich was a five-time All-Star and eight-year assistant coach before being named to the head job 52 games into the 1991-92 season. He has bought into the defensive philosophy so prevalent in the league, and has been able to sell his message with great effectiveness.

The New York Knicks battled— literally— their way to the seventh game of the Finals. No team expended more energy or overcame more continual adversity in the form of injury and overall frustration than Pat Riley's club. At one point in the season, both members of his original starting backcourt were out with knee injuries, but the Knicks battled on, thanks to an amazing defense which limited opponents to 91.5 points a game, the lowest such total since 1954-55, the first year of the 24-second clock. The Knicks kept their opponents under 100 a whopping 62 times. With a defense like that, it hardly mattered that the New Yorkers only averaged 98.5 points a game themselves.

Rookies **Chris Webber** of Golden State (left) and **Anfernee Hardaway** of Orlando after being picked first and second in the 1993 NBA Draft. They also finished 1-2 in the 1994 Rookie of the Year voting after signing for a combined 28 years and $139.4 million.

Another Eastern Conference overachiever was Chicago. After suffering through some early post-Jordan trauma, the Bulls started to realize that in Dream Teamer Scottie Pippen and solid power forward Horace Grant they still owned the league's best forward duo. It was also evident that point guard B.J. Armstrong was ready to be a star and that with Phil Jackson on the bench there was no danger of ever being out-coached.

After a shaky first month, Chicago began to roll. The Bulls engaged in a great three-way duel with New York and equally-surprising Atlanta for the best record in the East. In the end, the Central Division champion Hawks (57-25) won out over the Atlantic Division champion Knicks (57-25) by virtue of a tiebreaker, while the Bulls (55-27) came in third. The home court didn't do much for Atlanta when it was knocked out of the playoffs by Indiana in the second round, but it proved crucial to the Knicks, who needed it to squeeze past Chicago in a taut, seven-game Eastern Conference semifinal.

The playoffs' most controversial moment came at the end of Game 3 in the brawling Knicks-Bulls series. Tied at 102 with just 1.8 seconds remaining and the Bulls in danger of falling behind three games to none, Jackson called a timeout. In the huddle, he

decided to run a last-shot play not for Pippen but for Toni Kukoc. Pippen, who openly resented the 26-year-old rookie from Croatia, refused to re-enter the game. Kukoc, nevertheless, knocked in the winning fallaway jumper from 18 feet. Although Pippen later apologized for his snit, he may forever be labeled a quitter.

The most newsworthy trade of the season came on Feb. 24, when Atlanta shipped perennial All-Star Dominique Wilkins to the Los Angeles Clippers for Danny Manning. Seldom does a first place team unload its leading scorer, but the Hawks had transmogrified under veteran coach Lenny Wilkens— improving 14 games in the standings by changing from an indifferent defensive team into a very good one. Wilkens, in his 21st year as an NBA coach, also became only the second coach in league history (Red Auerbach was the first) to post 900 regular season victories.

During the summer Dominique exercised his right as a free agent and signed with Boston while Manning, also a free agent, appeared headed to Phoenix.

Atlanta was tripped up in the Eastern semifinals by Indiana, which had established itself as the NBA's quintessential mediocre franchise by going 42-40, 41-41,

Indiana guard **Reggie Miller** made a name for himself with 39 points against New York in Game 5 of the Eastern Conference final, but the Knicks came back to win the series.

the '94 post-season watching on TV, mainly because star Larry Johnson (who had signed a 12-year, $84 million contract), came up with the Great American Bad Back which sidelined him for 31 games.

Seattle was the regular season story in the West. George Karl's team, adjudged to be the league's deepest, rang up a franchise-best 63 wins, featuring pressure defense and two-platoon offense. But the season came to a stunning end in the first round of the playoffs when the unheralded Denver Nuggets beat the Sonics in five games. It was the first time a No. 8 seed had ever toppled a No. 1 in either conference since the current format was adopted in 1984.

"I feel we have a two or three-year window of opportunity," Karl said early in the year. "If we don't win a championship, then there are questions that should be asked."

One man kept San Antonio in the headlines all season, and it wasn't All-Star center David Robinson. Dennis Rodman established himself as a member of the All-Time, All-Eccentric team as he played the entire season in a variety of hair dyes, primarily red and yellow. He also led the league in rebounding again.

The Spurs (55-27) overachieved for coach John Lucas, but their lack of bench strength caught up with them in a first round playoff loss to Utah. Robinson, the league's leading scorer (29.8), was Olajuwon's chief MVP rival. He also added his name to an exclusive list on the final day of the regular season when he scored 71 points against the Clippers in L.A.

Phoenix (56-26) struggled with injuries, losing Kevin Johnson for 15 games and dealing with Charles Barkley's back woes. Sir Charles was something less than his dynamic MVP self of the previous year, and when the season was over announced grimly he would not be returning if he could not get relief from his back pain. (He finally decided he would return, afterall.)

Denver established itself as the Team of the Future, qualifying for the playoffs with a 42-40 record and then proceeding to upset Seattle in the first round before losing a wild seven-gamer to Utah after falling behind, 3-0. In shot blocking king Dikembe Mutombo, LaPhonso Ellis and free throw shooter extraordinaire Mahmoud Abdul-Rauf (formerly Chris Jackson) coach Dan Issel has a solid foundation.

40-42 and 41-41 in the preceding four years. The Pacers finally began to assert themselves under first-year coach Larry Brown, the vagabond genius. They won 31 of their last 43 games to finish the regular season at 47-35 and then went down to the final minute of the seventh game at Madison Square Garden before falling to the Knicks in the Eastern Conference finals.

Pacer guard Reggie Miller established himself as a superstar in the series and it was yet another notch in the coaching belt for Brown, who had previously produced winners at Carolina and Denver in the ABA, with New Jersey, San Antonio and the L.A. Clippers in the NBA, and at UCLA and Kansas in the college ranks.

Shaquille O'Neal and Hardaway led Orlando into the playoffs for the first time, but were eliminated in three straight by the Pacers. Charlotte, which made it to the second round of the playoffs in 1993, spent

Whatever Happened To "Showtime?"

Remember fast breaks? Remember the Old Celtics, the Sizzling Sixers, the Bombastic (Baltimore) Bullets?

Remember "Showtime?"

None of that in the 1994 playoffs where all we saw from most teams was boring, slug-it-out, half court basketball, especially in the East, where in only two of 35 games did both teams score 100 points simultaneously (those scores being 103-101 and 104-102). And it all culminated in the NBA Finals where neither Houston nor New York could score 100 points, period.

Cause for concern? Not according to NBA commissioner David Stern.

"I feel we've had one of our great years," says Stern, who points out that the league broke its single-season attendance mark for the ninth time in 11 seasons and announced that Toronto and Vancouver have agreed to fork over $125 million apiece to become the NBA's 28th and 29th teams in 1995.

And as for the preponderance of 91-87 and 83-78 games?

"I don't understand the fascination with the scores of games," says Stern. "I've seen a lot of baseball and I enjoy pitchers' duels. A baseball game doesn't have to be 13-12 to be exciting. The same with basketball. If a coach wants to take the air out of the ball, that demonstrates the flexibility of the game."

That's his public stance. But there is little doubt the commissioner really is concerned, if only because media perception of his league is negative and the NBA is nothing if not highly responsive to the media.

Stern has admitted there is great concern about the way hand-checking has crept back into the game. A second problem is impeded cutters. Anyone trying to run from Point A to Point B in an NBA game must negotiate an obstacle course consisting of knees, elbows, forearms and chests. Stern promised a summer review of the current officiating philosophy.

Something must also be done to open up the game. After watching the Knicks and Bulls suffocate each other in the Eastern semifinals, former Knicks' scoring great Bernard King observed, "If I were playing in that game, I wouldn't even be able to use my basketball

Mike Powell/Allsport

The NBA's shift to slug-it-out, half court basketball is a far cry from the excitement generated during the **Magic Johnson** and **Pat Riley** era in Los Angeles.

skills." This, from one of the great low post operators of all-time.

But the crisis transcends mere rough play. Coaches are reluctant to employ fast-paced offenses. Whereas once teams routinely took 100 shots a game, the average club now takes 82 or 83 shots. NBA coaches have grown conservative and cautious.

This is a true crisis, because the NBA now faces stiff competition in many markets from a rejuvenated National Hockey League (e.g., the NHL's transplanted Dallas Stars stole the town away from the once-untouchable, now-woeful Mavericks). If the perception persists that the NBA is merely arena football in shorts and that the game's grace and beauty has been expunged, dark days lie ahead.

No team exemplifies the new NBA style more than the New York Knicks, who last season held opponents to 91.5 points a game. It is difficult to imagine that Pat Riley is the same coach who presided over the famed Los Angeles Laker "Showtime" a decade ago.

But Riley understands the problem. Asked if he agreed that the league could never have attained its great popularity with a steady diet of dull games such as the ones his Knicks play on a regular basis, he replied: "I won't argue with that premise."

Denver center **Dikembe Mutombo** (left) rejects an attempted layup by Seattle's **Detlef Schrempf** in overtime of Game 5. The Nuggets upset the heavily-favored Sonics, 3 games to 2, in the first round of the playoffs.

No team raised more questioning eyebrows than Dallas, which picked up a nice rookie prospect like Mashburn and then proceeded to win just two more games than the year before. In other words, 13. First-year coach Quinn Buckner managed to alienate his best veteran, guard Derek Harper (who was traded to New York in January), and his two young stars, Jimmy Jackson and Mashburn, and was dismissed at the season's end with four years remaining on his contract.

Long faces were not confined to Dallas. Minnesota continued to flounder aimlessly (105-305 since joining the NBA in 1989-90) and when the season was over its loyal fans had to read about a proposed franchise shift to New Orleans (since voted down by league owners). The Timberwolves are the only one of the four recent expansion teams not to have made the playoffs.

It is said that the NBA system is designed to elevate the weak and punish the strong. Thus the plight of the L.A. Lakers, Boston,

Detroit and Philadelphia. Those four teams won every NBA title from 1980 to 1990, but in 1993-94 they could manage a combined record of only 110-218 for a winning percentage of .335. None of the four made the playoffs. Even Magic Johnson couldn't elevate the Lakers. Magic tried his hand at coaching for 16 games (5-11), liked it for about one week and then announced he would resign after the season was over.

The Lakers and 76ers were two of eight teams to replace coaches by mid-summer. The Lakers hired former Houston and Milwaukee coach Del Harris, while the Sixers signed the Spurs' John Lucas as coach and general manager. The Philadelphia jobs opened up when coach Fred Carter was fired and GM Jim Lynam returned to the bench as Wes Unseld's replacement in Washington. In Portland, the Trail Blazers fired Rick Adelman and hired college coach P.J. Carlesimo of Seton Hall.

Two of the NBA's all-time winningest coaches, Dick Motta and Bill Fitch, will resume their active careers in 1994-95. The 63-year-old Motta, who has won 912 regular season and playoff games in 22 years with Chicago, Washington, Dallas and Sacramento, will return to Reunion Arena where he was the Mavs' first coach from 1980-87. Fitch, 60, a 900-game winner in 21 seasons with Cleveland, Boston, Houston and New Jersey, assumes control of the Los Angeles Clippers.

Another coaching greybeard, 64-year-old Chuck Daly, was inducted into the Hall of Fame on May 9, then elected to retire as Nets coach on May 26 to accept an analyst's job with TNT. His 12-year tenure included those two NBA titles with Detroit in 1989 and '90 and the Dream Team's 1992 Olympic romp on Barcelona.

Finally, the league announced plans to expand into Canada in 1995, awarding franchises to Toronto and Vancouver. The Toronto Raptors named Isiah Thomas as their vice president of basketball operations on May 24, two weeks after the 12-time Piston All-Star retired following a year-ending Achilles tendon injury. The Vancouver Grizzlies named University of Wisconsin coach Stu Jackson as its general manager in July. Jackson coached the Knicks from 1989-90 and was the NBA's Director of Basketball Operations from 1991-92. ❏

THE 1995 INFORMATION PLEASE SPORTS ALMANAC

PRO BASKETBALL STATISTICS

SEC A

THE SEASON IN REVIEW
1993-1994
STANDINGS • PLAYOFFS • DRAFT

PAGE 337

Final NBA Standings

Division champions (*) and playoff qualifiers (†) are noted. Number of seasons listed after each head coach refers to latest tenure with club through 1993-94 season.

Western Conference

Pacific Division

	W	L	Pct	GB	—Per Game—For	Opp
* Seattle	63	19	.768	—	105.9	96.9
† Phoenix	56	26	.683	7	108.2	103.4
† Golden St	50	32	.610	13	107.9	106.1
† Portland	47	35	.573	16	107.3	104.6
LA Lakers	33	49	.402	30	100.4	104.7
Sacramento	28	54	.341	35	101.1	106.9
LA Clippers	27	55	.329	36	103.0	108.7

Head Coaches: Sea— George Karl (3rd season); **Pho**— Paul Westphal (2nd); **GS**— Don Nelson (6th); **Por**— Rick Adelman (6th); **LAL**— replaced Randy Pfund (2nd, 27-37) with assistant Bill Bertka (1-1) on Mar. 22 and Magic Johnson (5-11) on Mar. 26; **Sac**— Garry St. Jean (2nd); **LAC**— Bob Weiss (1st).
1992-93 Standings: 1. Phoenix (62-20); 2. Seattle (55-27); 3. Portland (51-31); 4. LA Clippers (41-41); 5. LA Lakers (39-43); 6. Golden St. (34-48); 7. Sacramento (25-57).

Midwest Division

	W	L	Pct	GB	—Per Game—For	Opp
* Houston	58	24	.707	—	101.1	96.8
† San Antonio	55	27	.671	3	100.0	94.8
† Utah	53	29	.646	5	101.9	97.7
† Denver	42	40	.512	16	100.3	98.8
Minnesota	20	62	.244	38	96.7	103.6
Dallas	13	69	.159	45	95.1	103.8

Head Coaches: Hou— Rudy Tomjanovich (3rd season); **SA**— John Lucas (2nd); **Utah**— Jerry Sloan (6th); **Den**— Dan Issel (2nd); **Min**— Sidney Lowe (2nd); **Dal**— Quinn Buckner (1st).
1992-93 Standings: 1. Houston (55-27); 2. San Antonio (49-33); 3. Utah (47-35); 4. Denver (36-46); 5. Minnesota (19-63); 6. Dallas (11-71).

Eastern Conference

Central Division

	W	L	Pct	GB	—Per Game—For	Opp
* Atlanta	57	25	.695	—	101.4	96.2
† Chicago	55	27	.671	2	98.0	94.9
† Indiana	47	35	.573	10	101.0	97.5
† Cleveland	47	35	.573	10	101.2	97.1
Charlotte	41	41	.500	16	106.5	106.7
Detroit	20	62	.244	37	96.9	104.7
Milwaukee	20	62	.244	37	96.9	103.4

Head Coaches: Atl— Lenny Wilkens (1st season); **Chi**— Phil Jackson (5th); **Ind**— Larry Brown (1st); **Cle**— Mike Fratello (1st); **Char**— Allan Bristow (3rd); **Det**— Don Chaney (1st); **Mil**— Mike Dunleavy (2nd).
1992-93 Standings: 1. Chicago (57-25); 2. Cleveland (54-28); 3. Charlotte (44-38); 4. Atlanta (43-39); 5. Indiana (41-41); 6. Detroit (40-42); 7. Milwaukee (28-54).

Atlantic Division

	W	L	Pct	GB	—Per Game—For	Opp
* New York	57	25	.695	—	98.5	91.5
† Orlando	50	32	.610	7	105.7	101.8
† New Jersey	45	37	.549	12	103.2	101.0
† Miami	42	40	.512	15	103.4	100.7
Boston	32	50	.390	25	100.8	105.1
Philadelphia	25	57	.305	32	98.0	105.6
Washington	24	58	.293	33	100.4	107.7

Head Coaches: NY— Pat Riley (3rd season); **Orl**— Brian Hill (1st); **NJ**— Chuck Daly (3rd); **Mia**— Kevin Loughery (3rd); **Bos**— Chris Ford (4th); **Phi**— Fred Carter (2nd); **Wash**— Wes Unseld (7th).
1992-93 Standings: 1. New York (60-22); 2. Boston (48-34); 3. New Jersey (43-39); 4. Orlando (41-41); 5. Miami (36-46); 6. Philadelphia (26-56); 7. Washington (22-60).

Overall Conference Standings

Sixteen teams—eight from each conference—qualify for the NBA Playoffs; (*) indicates division champions.

Western Conference

	W	L	Home	Away	Div	Conf
1 Seattle*	63	19	37-4	26-15	25-5	44-10
2 Houston*	58	24	35-6	23-18	15-11	38-16
3 Phoenix	56	26	36-5	20-21	19-11	37-17
4 San Antonio	55	27	32-9	23-18	16-10	32-22
5 Utah	53	29	33-8	20-21	21-5	36-18
6 Golden St	50	32	29-12	21-20	19-11	33-21
7 Portland	47	35	30-11	17-24	17-13	29-25
8 Denver	42	40	28-13	14-27	14-12	27-27
LA Lakers	33	49	21-20	12-29	7-23	18-36
Sacramento	28	54	20-21	8-33	9-21	17-37
LA Clippers	27	55	17-24	10-31	9-21	17-37
Minnesota	20	62	13-28	7-34	5-21	13-41
Dallas	13	69	6-35	7-34	7-19	10-44

Eastern Conference

	W	L	Home	Away	Div	Conf
1 Atlanta*	57	25	36-5	21-20	21-7	42-14
2 New York*	57	25	32-9	25-16	18-10	40-16
3 Chicago	55	27	31-10	24-17	21-7	38-18
4 Orlando	50	32	31-10	19-22	20-8	35-21
5 Indiana	47	35	29-12	18-23	15-13	32-24
6 Cleveland	47	35	31-10	16-25	16-12	31-25
7 New Jersey	45	37	29-12	16-25	17-11	32-24
8 Miami	42	40	29-12	13-28	11-16	32-24
Charlotte	41	41	28-13	13-28	12-16	29-27
Boston	32	50	18-23	14-27	12-16	21-35
Philadelphia	25	57	15-26	10-31	7-21	17-39
Washington	24	58	17-24	7-34	8-20	17-39
Detroit	20	62	10-31	10-31	4-24	12-44
Milwaukee	20	62	11-30	9-32	9-19	14-42

Tiebreakers: Atlanta and New York split their four regular season games, but the Hawks had a better conference record; Indiana won its season series against Cleveland, 3 games to 2.

1994 NBA All-Star Game
East, 127-118

44th NBA All-Star Game. **Date:** Feb. 13, at the Target Center in Minneapolis; **Coaches:** Lenny Wilkens, Atlanta (East) and George Karl, Seattle (West); **MVP:** Scottie Pippen, Chicago (31 minutes, 29 points, 11 rebounds).

Starters chosen by fan vote; bench chosen by conference coaches vote. Team replacements: EAST— reserve center Alonzo Mourning of Charlotte by Charles Oakley; WEST— starting forward Charles Barkley of Phoenix by Gary Payton.

Eastern Conference

Pos	Starters	Min	FG M-A	Pts	Rb	A
F	Scottie Pippen, Chi	31	9-15	29	11	2
G	B.J. Armstrong, Chi	22	5-9	11	1	4
C	Shaquille O'Neal, Orl	26	2-12	8	10	0
G	Kenny Anderson, NJ	16	3-10	6	4	3
F	Derrick Coleman, NJ	18	1-6	2	3	1
	Bench					
C	Patrick Ewing, NY	24	7-15	20	8	1
G	Mark Price, Cle	22	8-10	20	2	5
F	Dominique Wilkins, Atl	17	4-9	11	2	4
G	John Starks, NY	20	4-9	9	3	3
G	Mookie Blaylock, Atl	16	2-5	5	1	2
F	Horace Grant, Chi	17	2-8	4	8	2
C	Charles Oakley, NY	11	1-3	2	3	3
	Totals	240	48-111	127	56	30

Three-Point FG: 10-24 (Pippen 5-9, Price 2-3, Armstrong 1-2, Blaylock 1-2, Starks 1-3, Anderson 0-1, Coleman 0-2, Wilikns 0-2); **Free Throws:** 21-36 (Ewing 6-7, Pippen 6-10, O'Neal 4-11, Wilkins 3-6, Price 2-2); **Percentages:** FG (.432), Three-Pt. FG (.417), Free Throws: (.583); **Turnovers:** 13 (Anderson 4, Pippen 2, Starks 2, Armstrong, Blaylock, Ewing, Grant, O'Neal); **Steals:** 11 (Pippen 4, Blaylock 2, Coleman, Grant, O'Neal, Price, Starks); **Blocked Shots:** 9 (O'Neal 4, Grant 2, Coleman, Pippen, Price); **Fouls:** 21 (Blaylock 3, Coleman 3, Oakley 3, Anderson 2, Ewing 2, O'Neal 2, Pippen 2, Armstrong, Price, Starks, Wilkins); **Team Rebounds:** 16.

Western Conference

Pos	Starters	Min	FG M-A	Pts	Rb	A
C	Hakeem Olajuwon, Hou	30	8-15	19	11	2
G	Mitch Richmond, Sac	24	5-16	10	2	3
G	Clyde Drexler, Port	15	3-7	6	3	1
F	Shawn Kemp, Sea	22	3-11	6	12	4
F	Karl Malone, Utah	21	3-9	6	7	2
	Bench					
C	David Robinson, SA	21	6-13	19	5	0
G	John Stockton, Utah	26	6-10	13	5	10
F	Cliff Robinson, Port	18	5-8	10	2	5
G	Latrell Sprewell, GS	15	3-8	9	7	1
F	Danny Manning, LAC	17	4-7	8	4	2
G	Kevin Johnson, Pho	14	3-6	6	1	2
F	Gary Payton, Sea	17	3-4	6	6	9
	Totals	240	52-114	118	65	41

Three-Point FG: 1-6 (Stockton 1-1, C.Robinson 0-1, Drexler 0-2, Sprewell 0-2); **Free Throws:** 13-24 (D.Robinson 7-10, Olajuwon 3-6, Sprewell 3-3, Johnson 0-1); **Percentages:** FG (.456), Three-Pt. FG (.167), **Free Throws:** (.542); **Turnovers:** 22 (Kemp 6, Stockton 4, Olajuwon 3, Johnson 2, Richmond 2, Sprewell 2, Drexler, Malone, D.Robinson); **Steals:** 7 (Olajuwon 2, Drexler, Johnson, Malone, C.Robinson, Stockton); **Blocked Shots:** 12 (Olajuwon 6, Kemp 3, D.Robinson 2, Drexler, Manning); **Fouls:** 23 (Kemp 4, Manning 4, Olajuwon 4, Malone 2, Payton 2, D.Robinson 2, Stockton 2, Drexler, Johnson, Sprewell); **Team Rebounds:** 14.

	1	2	3	4	F
East	33	39	29	26	127
West	28	36	26	28	118

Halftime— East, 72-64; **Third Quarter**— East, 101-90; **Technical Fouls**— none; **Officials**— Jake O'Donnell, Jess Kersey, Joe Crawford; **Attendance**— 17,096; **Time**— 2:18; **TV Rating**— 9.1/14 share (NBC).

NBA Regular Season Team Leaders

Offense

— Per Game —

WEST	Pts	Reb	Ast	FG%	3Pt%	FT%
Phoenix	108.2	44.8	27.6	.484	.330	.728
Golden St.	107.9	43.6	26.8	.492	.339	.664
Portland	107.3	45.9	25.2	.454	.353	.743
Seattle	105.9	41.2	25.8	.484	.335	.745
LA Clippers	103.0	43.0	26.5	.467	.303	.709
Utah	101.9	42.0	26.6	.477	.320	.740
Houston	101.1	43.2	25.4	.475	.334	.743
Sacramento	101.1	42.3	24.7	.452	.353	.731
LA Lakers	100.4	42.2	24.2	.450	.300	.717
Denver	100.3	44.7	21.5	.465	.285	.718
San Antonio	100.0	46.2	23.1	.475	.349	.742
Minnesota	96.7	40.6	24.0	.457	.329	.772
Dallas	95.1	41.7	19.9	.432	.312	.747

— Per Game —

EAST	Pts	Reb	Ast	FG%	3Pt%	FT%
Charlotte	106.5	42.6	27.0	.476	.367	.764
Orlando	105.7	43.1	25.2	.485	.347	.678
Miami	103.4	44.4	22.6	.464	.338	.785
New Jersey	103.2	47.0	23.2	.445	.327	.762
Atlanta	101.4	44.8	25.1	.461	.323	.752
Cleveland	101.2	42.0	25.0	.465	.362	.770
Indiana	101.0	43.2	25.1	.486	.368	.738
Boston	100.8	41.7	23.5	.472	.289	.730
Washington	100.4	39.8	22.2	.468	.297	.748
New York	98.5	45.3	25.2	.460	.348	.746
Philadelphia	98.0	41.5	22.3	.455	.338	.714
Chicago	98.0	43.1	25.6	.476	.354	.705
Detroit	96.9	40.8	21.5	.452	.344	.731
Milwaukee	96.9	40.0	23.7	.447	.325	.702

Defense

— Per Game —

WEST	Pts	Reb	Ast	FG%	3Pt%	FT%
San Antonio	94.8	39.5	21.6	.446	.333	.719
Houston	96.8	43.6	23.2	.440	.306	.736
Seattle	96.9	39.9	22.0	.453	.345	.741
Utah	97.7	41.8	22.0	.448	.299	.725
Denver	98.8	42.1	21.3	.438	.290	.750
Phoenix	103.4	40.6	26.3	.474	.328	.720
Minnesota	103.6	41.4	25.7	.472	.308	.727
Dallas	103.8	44.0	24.0	.494	.362	.737
Portland	104.6	42.6	25.5	.469	.357	.750
LA Lakers	104.7	46.5	26.4	.476	.315	.717
Golden St.	106.1	45.5	26.6	.468	.351	.731
Sacramento	106.9	45.9	25.0	.479	.359	.722
LA Clippers	108.7	47.8	27.1	.473	.349	.717

— Per Game —

EAST	Pts	Reb	Ast	FG%	3Pt%	FT%
New York	91.5	39.8	20.5	.431	.307	.719
Chicago	94.9	39.3	22.4	.463	.323	.740
Atlanta	96.2	42.9	23.1	.455	.315	.742
Cleveland	97.1	41.4	24.5	.464	.354	.735
Indiana	97.5	40.1	23.2	.450	.335	.730
Miami	100.7	40.7	22.2	.457	.331	.748
New Jersey	101.0	44.8	23.4	.458	.318	.745
Orlando	101.8	42.7	25.6	.458	.349	.745
Milwaukee	103.4	43.7	25.5	.491	.362	.737
Detroit	104.7	46.1	25.6	.473	.334	.736
Boston	105.1	44.4	25.5	.477	.347	.754
Philadelphia	105.6	46.5	28.7	.484	.331	.744
Charlotte	106.7	44.9	25.8	.471	.346	.740
Washington	107.7	42.5	25.8	.508	.349	.723

San Antonio Spurs

David Robinson
Scoring

Utah Jazz

John Stockman
Assists

San Antonio Spurs

Dennis Rodman
Rebounds

Denver Nuggets

Mahoud Abdul-Raul
Free Throw Pct.

NBA Regular Season Individual Leaders

Minimum of 70 games or 1400 points, 800 rebounds, 400 assists, 100 blocked shots, 300 field goals, 125 steals, 125 free throws made, and 50 three-point field goals; (*) indicates rookie.

Scoring

	Gm	Min	FG	FG%	3Pt/Att	FT	FT%	Reb	Ast	Stl	Blk	Pts	Avg	Hi
David Robinson, SA	80	3241	840	.507	10/29	693	.749	855	381	139	265	2383	29.8	71
Shaquille O'Neal, Orl	81	3224	953	.599	0/2	471	.554	1072	195	76	231	2377	29.3	53
Hakeem Olajuwon, Hou	80	3277	894	.528	8/19	388	.716	955	287	128	297	2184	27.3	45
Domnq. Wilkins, Atl-LAC	74	2635	698	.440	85/295	442	.847	481	169	92	30	1923	26.0	42
Karl Malone, Utah	82	3329	772	.497	8/32	511	.694	940	328	125	126	2063	25.2	38
Patrick Ewing, NY	79	2972	745	.496	4/14	445	.765	885	179	90	217	1939	24.5	44
Mitch Richmond, Sac	78	2897	635	.445	127/312	426	.834	286	313	103	17	1823	23.4	40
Scottie Pippen, Chi	72	2759	627	.491	63/197	270	.660	629	403	211	58	1587	22.0	39
Charles Barkley, Pho	65	2298	518	.495	48/178	318	.704	727	296	101	37	1402	21.6	38
Glen Rice, Mia	81	2999	663	.467	132/346	250	.880	434	184	110	32	1708	21.1	40
Latrell Sprewell, GS	82	3533	613	.433	141/391	353	.774	401	385	180	76	1720	21.0	41
Danny Manning, LAC-Atl	68	2520	586	.488	3/17	228	.669	465	261	99	82	1403	20.6	43
Joe Dumars, Det	69	2591	505	.452	124/320	276	.836	151	261	63	4	1410	20.4	44
Derrick Coleman, NJ	77	2778	541	.447	38/121	439	.774	870	262	68	142	1559	20.2	36
Ron Harper, LAC	75	2856	569	.426	71/236	299	.715	460	344	144	54	1508	20.1	39
Cliff Robinson, Port	82	2853	641	.457	13/53	352	.765	550	159	118	111	1647	20.1	34
Reggie Miller, Ind	79	2638	524	.503	123/292	403	.908	212	248	119	24	1574	19.9	38
Jim Jackson, Dal	82	3066	637	.445	17/60	285	.821	388	374	87	25	1576	19.2	37
Jamal Mashburn*, Dal	79	2896	561	.406	85/299	306	.699	353	266	89	14	1513	19.2	37
Kevin Willis, Atl	80	2867	627	.499	9/24	268	.713	963	150	79	38	1531	19.1	34
Kenny Anderson, NJ	82	3135	576	.417	40/132	346	.818	322	784	158	15	1538	18.8	45
Clar. Weatherspoon, Phi	82	3147	602	.483	4/17	298	.693	832	192	100	116	1506	18.4	31
Don MacLean, Wash	75	2487	517	.502	3/21	328	.824	467	160	47	22	1365	18.2	38
Shawn Kemp, Sea	79	2597	533	.538	1/4	364	.741	851	207	142	166	1431	18.1	32
Mahmoud Abdul-Rauf, Den	80	2617	588	.460	42/133	219	.956	168	362	82	10	1437	18.0	33

Rebounds

	Gm	Off	Def	Total	Avg
Dennis Rodman, SA	79	453	914	1367	17.3
Shaquille O'Neal, Orl	81	384	688	1072	13.2
Kevin Willis, Atl	80	335	628	963	12.0
Hakeem Olajuwon, Hou	80	229	726	955	11.9
Olden Polynice, Det-Sac	68	299	510	809	11.9
Dikembe Mutombo, Den	82	286	685	971	11.8
Charles Oakley, NY	82	349	616	965	11.8
Karl Malone, Utah	82	235	705	940	11.5
Derrick Coleman, NJ	77	262	608	870	11.3
Patrick Ewing, NY	79	219	666	885	11.2
Horace Grant, Chi	70	306	463	769	11.0
Vlade Divac, LAL	79	282	569	851	10.8
Shawn Kemp, Sea	79	312	539	851	10.8
David Robinson, SA	80	241	614	855	10.7
Otis Thorpe, Hou	82	271	599	870	10.6

Assists

	Gm	No	Avg
John Stockton, Utah	82	1031	12.6
Muggsy Bogues, Char	77	780	10.1
Mookie Blaylock, Atl	81	789	9.7
Kenny Anderson, NJ	82	784	9.6
Kevin Johnson, Pho	67	637	9.5
Rod Strickland, Port	82	740	9.0
Sherman Douglas, Bos	78	683	8.8
Mark Jackson, LAC	79	678	8.6
Mark Price, Cle	76	589	7.8
Micheal Williams, Min	71	512	7.2
Michael Adams, Wash	70	480	6.9
Spud Webb, Sac	79	528	6.7
Eric Murdock, Mil	82	546	6.7
Anfernee Hardaway*, Orl	82	544	6.6
Haywoode Workman, Ind	65	404	6.2

NBA Regular Season Individual Leaders (Cont.)

Field Goal Pct.

	Gm	FG	Att	Avg
Shaquille O'Neal, Orl	81	953	1591	.599
Dikembe Mutombo, Den	82	365	642	.569
Otis Thorpe, Hou	82	449	801	.561
Chris Webber*, GS	76	572	1037	.552
Shawn Kemp, Sea	79	533	990	.538
Loy Vaught, LAC	75	373	695	.537
Cedric Ceballos, Pho	53	425	795	.535
Rik Smits, Ind	78	493	923	.534
Dale Davis, Ind	66	308	582	.529
Hakeem Olajuwon, Hou	80	894	1694	.528
John Stockton, Utah	82	458	868	.528

Free Throw Pct.

	Gm	FG	Att	Avg
Mahmoud Abdul-Rauf, Den	80	219	229	.956
Reggie Miller, Ind	79	403	444	.908
Ricky Pierce, Sea	51	189	211	.896
Sedale Threatt, LAL	81	138	155	.890
Mark Price, Cle	76	238	268	.888
Glen Rice, Mia	81	250	284	.880
Jeff Hornacek, Phi-Utah	80	260	296	.878
Scott Skiles, Orl	82	195	222	.878
Terry Porter, Port	77	204	234	.872
Kenny Smith, Hou	78	135	155	.871

3-Point Field Goal Pct.

	Gm	FG	Att	Avg
Tracy Murray, Port	66	50	109	.459
B.J. Armstrong, Chi	82	60	135	.444
Reggie Miller, Ind	79	123	292	.421
Steve Kerr, Chi	82	52	124	.419
Scott Skiles, Orl	82	68	165	.412
Eric Murdock, Mil	82	69	168	.411
Mitch Richmond, Sac	78	127	312	.407
Kenny Smith, Hou	78	89	220	.405
Dell Curry, Char	82	152	378	.402
Hubert Davis, NY	56	53	132	.402

Game High Points

	Opp	Date	FG-FT—Pts
David Robinson, SA	at LAC	4/24	26-18—71
Shaquille O'Neal, Orl	vs Min.	4/20	22- 9—53
David Robinson, SA	at Min.	2/21	18-13—50
Shaquille O'Neal, Orl	at Ind.	12/9	17-15—49
David Robinson, SA	vs Sac.	3/19	17-14—48
David Robinson, SA	vs Bos.	12/26	16-14—46
Hakeem Olajuwon, Hou	at Wash.	1/13	16-13—45
Kenny Anderson, NJ	vs Det.	4/15	12-20—45*
Patrick Ewing, NY	at Cle.	11/7	17-10—44*
Joe Dumars, Det	vs NJ	3/9	16- 9—44

*Overtime.

Blocked Shots

	Gm	No	Avg
Dikembe Mutombo, Den	82	336	4.10
Hakeem Olajuwon, Hou	80	297	3.71
David Robinson, SA	80	265	3.31
Alonzo Mourning, Char	60	188	3.13
Shawn Bradley*, Phi	49	147	3.00
Shaquille O'Neal, Orl	81	231	2.85
Patrick Ewing, NY	79	217	2.75
Oliver Miller, Pho	69	156	2.26
Chris Webber*, GS	76	164	2.16
Shawn Kemp, Sea	79	166	2.10

Steals

	Gm	No	Avg
Nate McMillan, Sea	73	216	2.96
Scottie Pippen, Chi	72	211	2.93
Mookie Blaylock, Atl	81	212	2.62
John Stockton, Utah	82	199	2.43
Eric Murdock, Mil	82	197	2.40
Anfernee Hardaway*, Orl	82	190	2.32
Gary Payton, Sea	82	188	2.29
Tom Gugliotta, Wash	78	172	2.21
Latrell Sprewell, GS	82	180	2.20
Dee Brown, Bos	77	156	2.03

Rookie Leaders

Scoring

	Gm	FG	FT	Pts	Avg
Jamal Mashburn, Dal	79	561	306	1513	19.2
Chris Webber, GS	76	572	189	1333	17.5
Isaiah Rider, Min	79	522	215	1313	16.6
Anfernee Hardaway, Orl	82	509	245	1313	16.0
Dino Radja, Bos	80	491	226	1208	15.1

Field Goal Pct.

	Gm	FG	Att	Pct
Chris Webber, GS	76	572	1037	552
Dino Radja, Bos	80	491	942	521
Vin Baker, Mil	82	435	869	501
Popeye Jones, Dal	81	195	407	479
Calbert Cheaney, Wash	65	327	696	470

Rebounds

	Gm	Off	Def	Tot	Avg
Chris Webber, GS	76	305	389	694	9.1
Vin Baker, Mil	82	277	344	621	7.6
Popeye Jones, Dal	81	299	306	605	7.5
Dino Radja, Bos	80	191	386	577	7.2
P.J. Brown, NJ	79	188	305	493	6.2

Assists

	Gm	No	Avg
Anfernee Hardaway, Orl	82	544	6.6
Nick Van Exel, LAL	81	466	5.8
Lindsey Hunter, Det	82	390	4.8
Chris Webber, GS	76	272	3.6
Jamal Mashburn, Dal	79	266	3.4

Personal Fouls

Shawn Kemp, Sea	312
Terry Mills, Det	309
LaPhonso Ellis, Den	304
Felton Spencer, Utah	304
Charles Oakley, NY	293

Disqualifications

Shawn Kemp, Sea	11
Rik Smits, Ind	11
Rony Seikaly, Mia	8
Six tied with 6 each.	

Turnovers

Jim Jackson, Dal	334
Anfernee Hardaway*, Orl	292
Hakeem Olajuwon, Hou	271
Kenny Anderson, NJ	266
John Stockton, Utah	266

Triple Doubles

David Robinson, SA	5
Kenny Anderson, NJ	3
Dikembe Mutombo, Den	3
Five tied with 2 each.	

Minutes Played

Latrell Sprewell, GS	3533
Karl Malone, Utah	3329
Hakeem Olajuwon, Hou	3277
David Robinson, SA	3241
Shaquille O'Neal, Orl	3224

Assist/Turnover Ratio

Muggsy Bogues, Char	4.56
Mookie Blaylock, Atl	4.03
John Stockton, Utah	3.88
Steve Kerr, Chi	3.68
Sedale Threatt, LAL	3.25

Note: David Robinson had the season's only Quadruple Double (34 pts, 10 reb, 10 ast, 10 blk, vs Detroit on 2/17).

Team by Team Statistics

At least 16 games played. Players who competed for more than one team during the regular season are listed with their final club; (*) indicates rookies.

Atlanta Hawks

	Gm	FG%	TPts	—Per Game—Pts	Reb	Ast
Danny Manning	68	.488	1403	20.6	6.8	3.8
LAC	42	.493	994	23.7	7.0	4.2
ATL	26	.476	409	15.7	6.5	3.3
Kevin Willis	80	.499	1531	19.1	12.0	1.9
Stacey Augmon	82	.510	1212	14.8	4.8	2.3
Mookie Blaylock	81	.411	1118	13.8	5.2	9.7
Craig Ehlo	82	.446	821	10.0	3.4	3.3
Duane Ferrell	72	.485	513	7.1	1.8	0.9
Andrew Lang	82	.469	504	6.1	3.8	0.6
Adam Keefe	63	.451	273	4.3	3.2	0.5
Jon Koncak	82	.431	342	4.2	4.5	1.2
Ennis Whatley	82	.508	292	3.6	1.2	2.2
Paul Graham	21	.368	58	2.8	0.6	0.6
Doug Edwards	16	.347	43	2.7	1.1	0.5

Triple doubles: Blaylock (2) and Manning (1 with LAC). **3-pt FG leader:** Blaylock (114). **Steals leader:** Blaylock (212). **Blocks leader:** Koncak (125).

Acquired: F Manning from LA Clippers for F Dominique Wilkins and future draft pick (Feb. 24).

Boston Celtics

	Gm	FG%	TPts	—Per Game—Pts	Reb	Ast
Dee Brown	77	.480	1192	15.5	3.9	4.5
Dino Radja	80	.521	1208	15.1	7.2	1.4
Sherman Douglas	78	.462	1040	13.3	2.5	8.8
Roberts Parish	74	.491	866	11.7	7.3	1.1
Kevin Gamble	75	.458	864	11.5	2.1	2.0
Xavier McDaniel	82	.461	928	11.3	4.9	1.5
Rick Fox	82	.467	887	10.8	4.3	2.6
Acie Earl	74	.406	410	5.5	3.3	0.2
Ed Pinckney	76	.522	394	5.2	6.3	0.8
Jimmy Oliver	44	.416	216	4.9	1.0	0.8
Chris Corchiani	51	.426	117	2.3	0.9	1.7

Triple doubles: none. **3-pt FG leader:** Fox (33). **Steals leader:** Brown (156). **Blocks leader:** Parish (96).

Charlotte Hornets

	Gm	FG%	TPts	—Per Game—Pts	Reb	Ast
Alonzo Mourning	60	.505	1287	21.5	10.2	1.4
Larry Johnson	51	.515	834	16.4	8.8	3.6
Dell Curry	82	.455	1335	16.3	3.2	2.7
Hersey Hawkins	82	.460	1180	14.4	4.6	2.6
Frank Brickowski	71	.488	935	13.2	5.7	3.1
MIL	43	.482	653	15.2	6.5	3.8
CHAR	28	.502	282	10.1	4.5	2.0
Eddie Johnson	73	.459	836	11.5	3.1	1.7
Muggsy Bogues	77	.471	835	10.8	4.1	10.1
Kenny Gattison	77	.524	592	7.7	4.6	1.2
David Wingate	50	.481	310	6.2	2.7	2.1
Scott Burrell	51	.419	244	4.8	2.6	1.2
LeRon Ellis	50	.484	221	4.4	3.8	0.5
Rumeal Robinson	31	.362	131	4.2	1.0	2.0
NJ	17	.353	101	5.9	1.4	2.6
CHAR	14	.394	30	2.1	0.6	1.3
Tony Bennet	74	.399	248	3.4	1.2	2.2

Triple doubles: L. Johnson (1). **3-pt FG leader:** Curry (152). **Steals leader:** Hawkins (135). **Blocks leader:** Mourning (188).

Acquired: G Robinson from New Jersey for F Johnny Newman (Dec. 10); F/C Brickowski from Milwaukee for C Mike Gminski and future 1st round draft pick (Feb. 24).

Chicago Bulls

	Gm	FG%	TPts	—Per Game—Pts	Reb	Ast
Scottie Pippen	72	.491	1587	22.0	8.7	5.6
Horace Grant	70	.524	1057	15.1	11.0	3.4
B.J. Armstrong	82	.476	1212	14.8	2.1	3.9
Toni Kukoc	75	.431	814	10.9	4.0	3.4
Steve Kerr	82	.497	709	8.6	1.6	2.6
Pete Myers	82	.455	650	7.9	2.2	3.0
Scott Williams	38	.483	289	7.6	4.8	1.0
Bill Wennington	76	.488	542	7.1	4.6	0.9
Luc Longley	76	.471	528	6.9	5.7	1.4
MIN	49	.464	324	6.6	6.0	0.9
CHI	27	.483	204	7.6	5.1	2.3
Bill Cartwright	42	.513	235	5.6	3.6	1.4
JoJo English	36	.434	130	3.6	1.3	1.1
Corie Blount	67	.437	198	3.0	2.9	0.8
Dave Johnson	17	.315	47	2.8	0.9	0.2
Will Perdue	43	.420	117	2.7	2.9	0.8
John Paxson	27	.441	70	2.6	0.7	1.2

Triple doubles: Pippen (2). **3-pt FG leader:** Pippen (63). **Steals leader:** Pippen (211). **Blocks leader:** Grant (84).

Acquired: C Longley from Minnesota for F/C Stacey King (Feb. 23).

Cleveland Cavaliers

	Gm	FG%	TPts	Pts	Reb	Ast
Mark Price	76	.478	1316	17.3	3.0	7.8
Brad Daugherty	50	.488	848	17.0	10.2	3.0
Gerald Wilkins	82	.457	1170	14.3	3.7	3.1
John Williams	76	.478	1040	13.7	7.6	2.5
Larry Nance	33	.487	370	11.2	6.9	1.5
Tyrone Hill	57	.543	603	10.6	8.8	0.8
Chris Mills	79	.419	743	9.4	5.1	1.6
Bobby Phills	72	.471	598	8.3	2.9	1.8
Terrell Brandon	73	.420	606	8.3	2.2	3.8
John Battle	51	.476	338	6.6	0.8	1.6
Rod Higgins	36	.436	195	5.4	2.3	1.0
Danny Ferry	70	.446	350	5.0	2.0	1.1
Gerald Madkins	22	.355	35	1.6	0.5	0.9
Jay Guidinger	32	.500	47	1.5	1.0	0.1

Triple doubles: none. **3-pt FG leader:** Price (118). **Steals leader:** Wilkins (105). **Blocks leader:** Williams (130).

Dream Team II

The 12-member NBA All-Star roster picked to represent the USA at the 12th World Championship tournament scheduled for Aug. 4-14, 1994, in Toronto. See "International Sports" chapter.

Centers: Alonzo Mourning, Charlotte and Shaquille O'Neal, Orlando.

Forwards: Derrick Coleman, New Jersey; Larry Johnson, Charlotte; Shawn Kemp, Seattle and Dominique Wilkins, Boston (signed as free agent on July 22).

Guards: Joe Dumars, Detroit; Kevin Johnson, Phoenix; Dan Majerle, Phoenix; Reggie Miller, Indiana; Mark Price, Cleveland and Steve Smith, Miami.

Injured and unable to compete: guards Tim Hardaway, Golden St. (knee) and Isiah Thomas, Detroit (Achilles tendon).

Dallas Mavericks

	Gm	FG%	TPts	—Per Game— Pts	Reb	Ast
Jim Jackson	82	.445	1576	19.2	4.7	4.6
Jamal Mashburn	79	.406	1513	19.2	4.5	3.4
Sean Rooks	47	.491	536	11.4	5.5	1.0
Doug Smith	79	.435	698	8.8	4.4	1.5
Tony Campbell	63	.443	555	8.8	3.0	1.3
NY	22	.492	157	7.1	2.7	1.4
DAL	41	.427	398	9.7	3.1	1.2
Tim Legler	79	.438	656	8.3	1.6	1.5
Fat Lever	81	.408	555	6.9	3.5	2.6
Randy White	18	.402	115	6.4	4.6	0.6
Popeye Jones	81	.479	468	5.8	7.5	1.2
Lucious Harris	77	.421	418	5.4	2.0	1.4
Terry Davis	15	.407	56	3.7	4.9	0.4
Lorenzo Williams	38	.445	110	2.9	5.7	0.7
ORL	3	.167	2	0.7	1.3	0.7
CHAR	1	.000	0	0.0	4.0	0.0
DAL	34	.466	108	3.2	6.1	0.7
Donald Hodge	50	.455	136	2.7	1.9	0.6
Greg Dreiling	54	.500	132	2.4	3.1	0.6
Morlon Wiley	16	.310	21	1.3	0.6	1.4
MIA	4	.375	7	1.8	1.0	1.8
DAL	12	.286	14	1.2	0.5	1.3

Triple doubles: none. **3-pt FG leader:** Mashburn (85). **Steals leader:** Lever (159). **Blocks leader:** Williams (46).
Acquired: F/G Campbell and 1997 1st round draft pick from New York for G Derek Harper (Jan. 6). **Signed:** F/G Williams (Feb. 14) and G Wiley (Apr. 1) as free agents.

Denver Nuggets

	Gm	FG%	TPts	—Per Game— Pts	Reb	Ast
Mahmoud Abdul-Rauf	80	.460	1437	18.0	2.1	4.5
LaPhonso Ellis	79	.502	1215	15.4	8.6	2.1
Reggie Williams	82	.412	1065	13.0	4.8	3.7
Bryant Stith	82	.450	1023	12.5	4.3	2.4
Dikembe Mutombo	82	.569	986	12.0	11.8	1.5
Robert Pack	66	.443	631	9.6	1.9	5.4
Rodney Rogers	79	.439	640	8.1	2.9	1.3
Brian Williams	80	.541	639	8.0	5.6	0.6
Tom Hammonds	74	.500	301	4.1	2.7	0.5
Kevin Brooks	34	.364	85	2.5	0.6	0.1
Mark Randall	28	.340	58	2.1	0.8	0.4
Darnell Mee	38	.318	73	1.9	0.9	0.4

Triple doubles: Mutombo (3). **3-pt FG leader:** R. Williams (64). **Steals leader:** R. Williams (117). **Blocks leader:** Mutombo (336).

Individual Highs

Most Field Goals Made
Season: 953 ....Shaquille O'Neal, Orlando
Game: 26................David Robinson, SA at LAC (4/24)

Most Field Goals Attempted
Season: 1,694 ....Hakeem Olajuwon, Houston
Game: 41................David Robinson, SA at LAC (4/24)

Most 3-Pt Field Goals Made
Season: 192.......................Dan Majerle, Phoenix
Game: 8 ....Dan Marjerle, Pho at LAC (11/9)
  8 ....Mitch Richmond, Sac at LAC (2/25)

Most 3-Pt Field Goals Attempted
Season: 503 ....Dan Majerle, Phoenix
Game: 16................Nick Van Exel, LAL vs Utah (4/24)

Detroit Pistons

	Gm	FG%	TPts	—Per Game— Pts	Reb	Ast
Joe Dumars	69	.452	1410	20.4	2.2	3.8
Terry Mills	80	.511	1381	17.3	8.4	2.2
Isiah Thomas	58	.417	856	14.8	2.7	6.9
Sean Elliot	73	.455	885	12.1	3.6	2.7
Lindsey Hunter	82	.375	843	10.3	2.3	4.8
Bill Laimbeer	11	.522	108	9.8	5.1	1.3
Allan Houston	79	.405	668	8.5	1.5	1.3
Greg Anderson	77	.543	491	6.4	7.4	0.7
Pete Chilcutt	76	.453	450	5.9	4.9	1.1
SAC	46	.463	335	7.3	5.9	1.5
DET	30	.425	115	3.8	3.3	0.5
David Wood	78	.459	322	4.1	3.1	0.7
Mark Macon	42	.375	163	3.9	1.0	1.6
DEN	7	.311	36	5.1	1.0	1.6
DET	35	.396	127	3.6	1.0	1.1
Marcus Liberty	38	.325	109	2.9	1.6	0.4
DEN	3	.571	9	3.0	1.7	0.7
DET	35	.310	100	2.9	1.6	0.4
Charles Jones	42	.462	91	2.2	5.6	0.7

Triple doubles: none. **3-pt FG leader:** Dumars (124). **Steals leader:** Hunter (121). **Blocks leader:** Anderson (68).
Acquired: G Macon and F Liberty from Denver for G Alvin Robertson and 1995 2nd round draft pick (Nov. 19); F/C Chilcutt from Sacramento for C Olden Polynice (Feb. 20).
Retired: Bill Laimbeer (Dec. 1).

Golden State Warriors

	Gm	FG%	TPts	—Per Game— Pts	Reb	Ast
Latrell Sprewell	82	.433	1720	21.0	4.9	4.7
Chris Webber	76	.552	1333	17.5	9.1	3.6
Chris Mullin	62	.472	1040	16.8	5.6	5.1
Billy Owens	79	.507	1186	15.0	8.1	4.1
Avery Johnson	82	.492	890	10.9	2.1	5.3
Victor Alexander	69	.530	602	8.7	4.5	1.0
Chris Gatling	82	.588	671	8.2	4.8	0.5
Jeff Grayer	67	.526	455	6.8	2.9	0.9
Keith Jennings	76	.404	432	5.7	1.2	2.9
Josh Grant	53	.404	157	3.0	1.7	0.5
Jud Buechler	36	.500	106	2.9	0.9	0.4
Byron Houston	71	.458	196	2.8	2.7	0.5

Triple doubles: Mullin (1) and Webber (1). **3-pt FG leader:** Sprewell (141). **Steals leader:** Sprewell (180). **Blocks leader:** Webber (164).

Houston Rockets

	Gm	FG%	TPts	—Per Game— Pts	Reb	Ast
Hakeem Olajuwon	80	.528	2184	27.3	11.9	3.6
Otis Thorpe	82	.561	1149	14.0	10.6	2.3
Vernon Maxwell	75	.389	1023	13.6	3.1	5.1
Kenny Smith	78	.480	906	11.6	1.8	4.2
Robert Horry	81	.459	803	9.9	5.4	2.9
Mario Elie	67	.446	626	9.3	2.7	3.1
Sam Cassell	66	.418	440	6.7	2.0	2.9
Scott Brooks	73	.491	381	5.2	1.4	2.0
Carl Herrera	75	.458	353	4.7	3.8	0.5
Matt Bullard	65	.345	226	3.5	1.3	1.0
Richard Petruska	22	.435	53	2.4	1.4	0.0
Eric Riley	47	.486	88	1.9	1.3	0.2

Triple doubles: Olajuwon (1). **3-pt FG Leader**: Maxwell (120). **Steals leader:** Olajuwon (128). **Blocks leader:** Olajuwon (297).

Indiana Pacers

	Gm	FG%	TPts	Pts	Reb	Ast
				—Per Game—		
Reggie Miller	79	.503	1574	19.9	2.7	3.1
Rik Smits	78	.534	1224	15.7	6.2	2.0
Derrick McKey	76	.500	911	12.0	5.3	4.3
Dale Davis	66	.529	771	11.7	10.9	1.5
Byron Scott	67	.467	696	10.4	1.6	2.0
Pooh Richardson	37	.452	370	10.0	3.0	6.4
Antonio Davis	81	.508	626	7.7	6.2	0.7
Haywoode Workman	65	.424	501	7.7	3.1	6.2
Malik Sealy	43	.405	285	6.6	2.7	1.1
Vern Fleming	55	.462	358	6.5	2.2	3.1
Ken Williams	68	.488	427	6.3	3.0	0.8
Sam Mitchell	75	.458	362	4.8	2.5	0.9
LaSalle Thompson	30	.351	70	2.3	2.5	0.5
Scott Haskin	27	.467	55	2.0	2.0	0.2

Triple doubles: none. **3-pt FG leader:** Miller (123). **Steals leader:** Miller (119). **Blocks leader:** D. Davis (106).

Los Angeles Clippers

	Gm	FG%	TPts	Pts	Reb	Ast
				—Per Game—		
Dominique Wilkins	74	.440	1923	26.0	6.5	2.3
ATL	49	.432	1196	24.4	6.2	2.3
LAC	25	.453	727	29.1	7.0	2.2
Ron Harper	75	.426	1508	20.1	6.1	4.6
Loy Vaught	75	.537	877	11.7	8.7	1.0
Mark Jackson	79	.452	865	10.9	4.4	8.6
Mark Aguirre	39	.468	413	10.6	3.0	2.7
Elmore Spencer	76	.533	673	8.9	5.5	1.0
Harold Ellis	49	.545	424	8.7	3.1	0.6
Gary Grant	78	.449	588	7.5	1.8	3.7
Charles Outlaw	37	.587	257	6.9	5.7	1.0
John Williams	34	.431	191	5.6	3.7	2.9
Terry Dehere	64	.377	342	5.3	1.1	1.2
Tom Tolbert	49	.418	187	3.8	2.2	0.6
Randy Woods	40	.368	145	3.6	0.7	1.8
Bob Martin	53	.455	111	2.1	2.2	0.3

Triple doubles: Harper (2) and Jackson (1). **3-pt FG leader:** Wilkins (85). **Steals leader:** Harper (144). **Blocks leader:** Spencer (127).

Acquired: F Wilkins from Atlanta for F Danny Manning (Feb. 24).

Los Angeles Lakers

	Gm	FG%	TPts	Pts	Reb	Ast
				—Per Game—		
Vlade Divac	79	.506	1123	14.2	10.8	3.9
Anthony Peeler	30	.430	423	14.1	3.6	3.1
Nick Van Exel	81	.394	1099	13.6	2.9	5.8
Elden Campbell	76	.462	934	12.3	6.8	1.1
Sedale Threatt	81	.482	965	11.9	1.9	4.2
Doug Christie	65	.434	672	10.3	3.6	2.1
James Worthy	80	.406	812	10.2	2.3	1.9
George Lynch	71	.508	681	9.6	5.8	1.4
Sam Bowie	25	.436	223	8.9	5.2	1.9
Tony Smith	73	.441	645	8.8	2.7	2.0
Reggie Jordan	23	.427	125	5.4	2.9	1.1
James Edwards	45	.464	210	4.7	1.4	0.5
Kurt Rambis	50	.518	164	3.3	3.8	0.6
Antonio Harvey	27	.367	70	2.6	2.2	0.2
Dan Schayes	36	.333	85	2.4	2.2	0.4
MIL	23	.304	49	2.1	2.0	0.2
LAL	13	.368	36	2.8	2.6	0.6

Triple doubles: Divac (2). **3-pt FG leader:** Van Exel (123). **Steals leader:** Threatt (110). **Blocks leader:** Campbell (146).

Acquired: C Schayes from Milwaukee for 1995 2nd round draft pick (Feb. 24).

Miami Heat

	Gm	FG%	TPts	Pts	Reb	Ast
				—Per Game—		
Glen Rice	81	.467	1708	21.1	5.4	2.3
Steve Smith	78	.456	1346	17.3	4.5	5.1
Rony Seikaly	72	.488	1088	15.1	10.3	1.9
Grant Long	69	.446	788	11.4	7.2	2.5
Harold Miner	63	.477	661	10.5	2.5	1.5
Brian Shaw	77	.417	693	9.0	4.5	5.0
Bimbo Coles	76	.449	588	7.7	2.1	3.5
John Salley	76	.477	582	7.7	5.4	1.8
Matt Geiger	72	.574	521	7.2	4.2	0.4
Willie Burton	53	.438	371	7.0	2.6	0.7
Keith Askins	37	.409	85	2.3	2.2	0.4
Alec Kessler	15	.440	33	2.2	0.7	0.1

Triple doubles: none. **3-pt FG leader:** Rice (132). **Steals leader:** Rice (110). Blocks leader: Seikaly (100).

Milwaukee Bucks

	Gm	FG%	TPts	Pts	Reb	Ast
				—Per Game—		
Eric Murdock	82	.468	1257	15.3	3.2	6.7
Vin Baker	82	.501	1105	13.5	7.6	2.0
Todd Day	76	.415	966	12.7	4.1	1.8
Ken Norman	82	.448	979	11.9	6.1	2.7
Theodore Edwards	82	.478	953	11.6	4.0	2.1
Derek Strong	67	.413	444	6.6	4.2	0.7
Jon Barry	72	.414	445	6.2	2.0	2.3
Lee Mayberry	82	.415	433	5.3	1.2	2.6
Brad Lohaus	67	.363	270	4.0	2.2	0.9
Joe Courtney	52	.453	168	3.2	1.1	0.3
PHO	33	.513	103	3.1	0.8	0.3
MIL	19	.386	65	3.4	1.5	0.3
Mike Gminski	29	.350	86	3.0	2.6	0.4
CHAR	21	.392	73	3.5	2.8	0.5
MIL	8	.208	13	1.6	1.9	0.0
Anthony Cook	25	.481	62	2.5	2.2	0.2
ORL	2	.000	0	0.0	0.0	0.0
MIL	23	.491	62	2.7	2.4	0.2

Triple doubles: none. **3-pt FG leader:** Murdock (69). **Steals leader:** Murdock (197). **Blocks leader:** Baker (114).

Acquired: C/F Cook from Orlando for F Anthony Avent and 1994 1st round draft pick (Jan. 15); C Gminski from Charlotte for F/C Frank Brickowski (Feb. 24). **Signed:** F Courtney (Mar. 2) as free agent.

Minnesota Timberwolves

	Gm	FG%	TPts	Pts	Reb	Ast
				—Per Game—		
Christian Laettner	70	.448	1173	16.8	8.6	4.4
Isaiah Rider	79	.468	1313	16.6	4.0	2.6
Doug West	72	.487	1056	14.7	3.2	2.4
Micheal Williams	71	.457	971	13.7	3.1	7.2
Chuck Person	77	.422	894	11.6	3.3	2.4
Stacey King	49	.428	385	7.9	4.9	1.2
CHI	31	.398	172	5.5	4.3	1.3
MIN	18	.459	213	11.8	6.1	1.1
Thurl Bailey	79	.510	583	7.4	2.7	0.7
Chris Smith	80	.435	473	5.9	1.5	3.6
Marlon Maxey	55	.533	248	4.5	3.6	0.2
Mike Brown	82	.427	299	3.6	5.5	0.9
Tellis Frank	67	.419	188	2.8	3.3	0.9
Stanley Jackson	17	.515	38	2.2	1.6	0.9
Brian Davis	68	.317	131	1.9	0.8	0.3

Triple doubles: none. **3-pt FG leader:** Person (100). **Steals leader:** M. Williams (118). **Blocks leader:** Laettner (86).

Acquired: F/C King from Chicago for C Luc Longley (Feb. 23).

New Jersey Nets

	Gm	FG%	TPts	Pts	Reb	Ast
Derrick Coleman	77	.447	1559	20.2	11.3	3.4
Kenny Anderson	82	.417	1538	18.8	3.9	9.6
Kevin Edwards	82	.458	1144	14.0	3.4	2.8
Armon Gilliam	82	.510	970	11.8	6.1	0.8
Chris Morris	50	.447	544	10.9	4.6	1.7
Johnny Newman	81	.471	832	10.3	2.2	0.9
CHAR	18	.523	234	13.0	3.2	1.6
NJ	63	.453	598	9.5	1.9	0.7
Benoit Benjamin	77	.480	718	9.3	6.5	0.6
P.J. Brown	79	.415	450	5.7	6.2	1.2
Jayson Williams	70	.427	322	4.6	3.8	0.4
Rex Walters	48	.522	162	3.4	0.8	1.5
David Wesley	60	.368	183	3.1	0.7	2.1
Dwayne Schintzius	30	.345	68	2.3	3.0	0.4
Rick Mahorn	28	.489	59	2.1	1.9	0.2

Triple doubles: Anderson (3) and Coleman (2). **3-pt FG leader:** Morris (53). **Steals leader:** Anderson (158). **Blocks leader:** Coleman (142).

Acquired: F Newman from Charlotte for G Rumeal Robinson (Dec. 10).

New York Knickerbockers

	Gm	FG%	TPts	Pts	Reb	Ast
Patrick Ewing	79	.496	1939	24.5	11.2	2.3
John Starks	59	.420	1120	19.0	3.1	5.9
Charles Oakley	82	.478	969	11.8	11.8	2.7
Hubert Davis	56	.471	614	11.0	1.2	2.9
Charles Smith	43	.443	447	10.4	3.8	1.2
Derek Harper	82	.407	791	9.6	1.7	4.1
DAL	28	.380	325	11.6	2.0	3.5
NY	54	.430	466	8.6	1.6	4.4
Greg Anthony	80	.394	628	7.9	2.4	4.6
Doc Rivers	19	.433	143	7.5	2.1	5.3
Rolando Blackman	55	.436	400	7.3	1.7	1.4
Anthony Mason	73	.476	528	7.2	5.8	2.1
Anthony Bonner	73	.563	374	5.1	4.7	1.2
Herb Williams	70	.442	233	3.3	2.6	0.4
Corey Gaines	18	.450	33	1.8	0.7	1.7

Triple doubles: none. **3-pt FG leader:** Starks (113). **Steals leader:** Harper (125). **Blocks leader:** Ewing (217).

Acquired: G Harper from Dallas for F Tony Campbell and 1994 1st round draft pick (Jan. 6).

Orlando Magic

	Gm	FG%	TPts	Pts	Reb	Ast
Shaquille O'Neal	81	.599	2377	29.3	13.2	2.4
Anfernee Hardaway	82	.466	1313	16.0	5.4	6.6
Nick Anderson	81	.478	1277	15.8	5.9	3.6
Dennis Scott	82	.405	1046	12.8	2.7	2.6
Scott Skiles	82	.429	815	9.9	2.3	6.1
Donald Royal	74	.501	547	7.4	3.4	0.8
Jeff Turner	68	.467	447	6.6	4.0	0.9
Anthony Avent	74	.377	389	5.3	4.6	0.9
MIL	33	.404	245	7.4	4.7	1.0
ORL	41	.341	144	3.5	4.5	0.8
Larry Krystkowiak	34	.480	173	5.1	3.6	1.0
Anthony Bowie	70	.481	320	4.6	1.7	1.5
Litterial Green	29	.386	73	2.5	0.4	0.3
Tree Rollins	45	.547	76	1.7	2.1	0.2
Greg Kite	29	.371	34	1.2	2.4	0.1

Triple doubles: Hardaway (1) and O'Neal (1). **3-pt FG leader:** Scott (155). **Steals leader:** Hardaway (190). **Blocks leader:** O'Neal (231).

Acquired: F Avent from Milwaukee for C/F Anthony Cook and 1994 1st round draft pick (Jan. 15).

Philadelphia 76ers

	Gm	FG%	TPts	Pts	Reb	Ast
Clar. Weatherspoon	82	.483	1506	18.4	10.1	2.3
Jeff Malone	77	.486	1262	16.4	2.6	1.6
UTAH	50	.488	808	16.2	2.3	1.3
PHI	27	.481	454	16.8	3.1	2.2
Dana Barros	81	.469	1075	13.3	2.4	5.2
Orlando Woolridge	74	.471	937	12.7	4.0	1.9
Shawn Bradley	49	.409	504	10.3	6.2	2.0
Tim Perry	80	.435	719	9.0	5.1	1.2
Johnny Dawkins	72	.418	475	6.6	1.7	3.7
Moses Malone	55	.440	294	5.3	4.1	0.6
Eric Leckner	71	.486	362	5.1	4.0	1.2
Greg Graham	70	.400	338	4.8	1.2	0.9
Warren Kidd	68	.592	247	3.6	3.4	0.3
Manute Bol	14	.211	8	0.6	1.3	0.1
MIA	8	.083	2	0.3	1.4	0.0
WASH	2	—	0	0.0	0.5	0.5
PHI	4	.429	6	1.5	1.5	0.0

Triple doubles: Weatherspoon (1). **3-pt FG leader:** Barros (135). **Steals leader:** Barros (107). **Blocks leader:** Bradley (147).

Acquired: G Jeff Malone and 1994 1st round draft pick from Utah for G Jeff Hornacek, G Sean Green and future 2nd round pick (Feb. 24). **Signed:** C Manute Bol (Mar. 9) as free agent.

Phoenix Suns

	Gm	FG%	TPts	Pts	Reb	Ast
Charles Barkley	65	.495	1402	21.6	11.2	4.6
Kevin Johnson	67	.487	1340	20.0	2.5	9.5
Cedric Ceballos	53	.535	1010	19.1	6.5	1.7
Dan Majerle	80	.418	1320	16.5	4.4	3.4
A.C. Green	82	.502	1204	14.7	9.2	1.7
Oliver Miller	69	.609	636	9.2	6.9	3.5
Danny Ainge	68	.417	606	8.9	1.9	2.6
Mark West	82	.566	382	4.7	3.6	0.4
Frank Johnson	70	.448	324	4.6	1.2	2.1
Elliott Perry	27	.372	105	3.9	1.4	4.6
Joe Kleine	74	.488	285	3.9	2.6	0.6
Jerrod Mustaf	33	.357	73	2.2	1.7	0.2
Duane Cooper	23	.439	48	2.1	0.4	1.2
Malcolm Mackey	22	.378	32	1.5	1.1	0.0

Triple doubles: Barkley (1), K. Johnson (1) and Miller (1). **3-pt FG leader:** Majerle (192). **Steals leader:** Majerle (129). **Blocks leader:** Miller (156).

More Individual Highs

Most Assists
Season: 1,031 .... John Stockton, Utah
Game: 25 .... Kevin Johnson, Pho vs SA (4/6)

Most Offensive Rebounds
Season: 453 .... Dennis Rodman, San Antonio
Game: 14 .... Shaquille O'Neal, Orl vs Bos (2/15)
14 .... Olden Polynice, Sac vs Mil (3/11)

Most Defensive Rebounds
Season: 914 .... Dennis Rodman, San Antonio
Game: 23 .... Dennis Rodman, SA vs Dal (1/22)

Most Blocked Shots
Season: 336 .... Dikembe Mutombo, Denver
Game: 15 .... Shaquille O'Neal, Orl at NJ (11/20)

Most Steals
Season: 216 .... Nate McMillan, Seattle
Game: 10 .... Kevin Johnson, Pho vs Wash (12/9)

Portland Trail Blazers

	Gm	FG%	TPts	—Per Game— Pts	Reb	Ast
Clifford Robinson	82	.457	1647	20.1	6.7	1.9
Clyde Drexler	68	.428	1303	19.2	6.5	4.9
Rod Strickland	82	.483	1411	17.2	4.5	9.0
Terry Porter	77	.416	1010	13.1	2.8	5.2
Harvey Grant	77	.460	798	10.4	4.6	1.4
Buck Williams	81	.555	783	9.7	10.4	1.0
Tracy Murray	66	.470	434	6.6	1.7	0.5
Jerome Kersey	78	.433	508	6.5	4.2	1.0
Mark Bryant	79	.482	442	5.6	4.0	0.5
James Robinson	58	.365	276	4.8	1.3	1.2
Jaren Jackson	29	.391	80	2.8	0.6	0.9
Reggie Smith	43	.403	76	1.8	2.3	0.1

Triple doubles: none. **3-pt FG leader:** Porter (110). **Steals leader:** Strickland (147). **Blocks leader:** C. Robinson (111).

Sacramento Kings

	Gm	FG%	TPts	—Per Game— Pts	Reb	Ast
Mitch Richmond	78	.445	1823	23.4	3.7	4.0
Wayman Tisdale	79	.501	1319	16.7	7.1	1.8
Lionel Simmons	75	.438	1129	15.1	7.5	4.1
Anthony Webb	79	.460	1005	12.7	2.8	6.7
Olden Polynice	68	.523	789	11.6	11.9	0.6
DET	37	.547	486	13.1	12.3	0.6
SAC	31	.484	303	9.8	11.4	0.6
Walt Williams	57	.390	638	11.2	4.1	2.3
Trevor Wilson	57	.482	466	8.2	4.8	1.3
LAL	5	.487	51	10.2	5.6	2.4
SAC	52	.481	415	8.0	4.7	1.2
Bobby Hurley	19	.370	134	7.1	1.8	6.1
Andre Spencer	28	.441	159	5.7	2.6	0.8
GS	5	.500	21	4.2	2.4	0.6
SAC	23	.430	138	6.0	2.7	0.8
LaBradford Smith	66	.405	332	5.0	1.3	1.7
WASH	7	.444	31	4.4	1.1	0.7
SAC	59	.403	301	5.1	1.3	1.8
Randy Brown	61	.438	273	4.5	1.8	2.2
Duane Causewell	41	.518	182	4.4	4.5	0.3
Mike Peplowski	55	.539	176	3.2	3.1	0.4
Jim Les	18	.382	45	2.5	0.7	2.2
Evers Burns	23	.400	56	2.4	1.3	0.4
Randy Breuer	26	.308	19	0.7	2.2	0.3

Triple doubles: Richmond (1) and Simmons (1). **3-pt FG leader:** Richmond (127). **Steals leader:** Simmons (104). **Blocks leader:** Polynice (67).

Acquired: C Polynice from Detroit for F/C Pete Chilcutt, a future 1st round draft pick and 1994 2nd round pick (Feb. 20). **Signed:** G Smith (Dec. 8), F Wilson (Dec. 15) and F Spencer (Mar. 3) as free agents.

San Antonio Spurs

	Gm	FG%	TPts	—Per Game— Pts	Reb	Ast
David Robinson	80	.507	2383	29.8	10.7	4.8
Dale Ellis	77	.494	1170	15.2	3.3	1.0
Willie Anderson	80	.471	955	11.9	3.0	4.3
Vinny Del Negro	77	.487	773	10.0	2.1	4.2
Negele Knight	65	.474	595	9.2	1.6	3.0
PHO	1	.250	2	2.0	0.0	0.0
SA	64	.476	593	9.3	1.6	3.1
J.R. Reid	70	.491	627	9.0	3.1	1.0
Terry Cummings	59	.428	429	7.3	5.0	0.8
Antoine Carr	34	.488	198	5.8	1.5	0.4
Lloyd Daniels	65	.376	370	5.7	1.7	1.4
Dennis Rodman	79	.534	370	4.7	17.3	2.3
Sleepy Floyd	53	.335	200	3.8	1.3	1.9
Jack Haley	28	.438	59	2.1	0.9	0.0
Chris Whitney	40	.305	72	1.8	0.7	1.3

Triple doubles: Robinson (5). **3-pt FG leader:** Ellis (131). **Steals leader:** Robinson (139). **Blocks leader:** Robinson (265).

Acquired: G Knight from Phoenix for 2nd round draft pick (Nov. 8).

Seattle Supersonics

	Gm	FG%	TPts	—Per Game— Pts	Reb	Ast
Shawn Kemp	79	.538	1431	18.1	10.8	2.6
Gary Payton	82	.504	1349	16.5	3.3	6.0
Detlef Schrempf	81	.493	1212	15.0	5.6	3.4
Ricky Pierce	51	.471	739	14.5	1.6	1.8
Kendall Gill	79	.443	1111	14.1	3.4	3.5
Sam Perkins	81	.438	999	12.3	4.5	1.4
Vincent Askew	80	.481	727	9.1	2.3	2.4
Nate McMillan	73	.447	437	6.0	3.9	5.3
Michael Cage	82	.545	378	4.6	5.4	0.5
Ervin Johnson	45	.415	117	2.6	2.6	0.2
Steve Scheffler	35	.609	75	2.1	0.7	0.2
Rich King	27	.441	41	1.5	0.7	0.3

Triple doubles: Kemp (1). **3-pt FG leader:** Perkins (99). **Steals leader:** McMillan (216). **Blocks leader:** Kemp (166).

Utah Jazz

	Gm	FG%	TPts	—Per Game— Pts	Reb	Ast
Karl Malone	82	.497	2063	25.2	11.5	4.0
Jeff Hornacek	80	.470	1274	15.9	3.5	5.2
PHI	53	.455	880	16.6	4.0	5.9
UTAH	27	.509	394	14.6	2.5	3.9
John Stockton	82	.528	1236	15.1	3.1	12.6
Tom Chambers	80	.440	893	11.2	4.1	1.0
Felton Spencer	79	.505	677	8.6	8.3	0.5
Tyrone Corbin	82	.456	659	8.0	4.7	1.5
Jay Humphries	75	.436	561	7.5	1.7	2.9
David Benoit	55	.385	358	6.5	4.7	0.4
Bryon Russell	67	.484	334	5.0	2.7	0.8
Darren Morningstar	23	.476	96	4.2	3.5	0.7
DAL	22	.469	94	4.3	3.6	0.7
UTAH	1	1.000	2	2.0	1.0	0.0
Sean Green	36	.344	149	4.1	0.9	0.4
PHI	35	.346	149	4.3	1.0	0.5
UTAH	1	.000	0	0.0	0.0	0.0
Walter Bond	56	.404	176	3.1	1.1	0.6
John Crotty	45	.455	132	2.9	0.7	1.7

Triple doubles: none. **3-pt FG leader:** Hornacek (70). **Steals leader:** Stockton (199). **Blocks leader:** Malone (126).

Acquired: G Hornacek, G Green and future 2nd round draft pick from Philadelphia for G Jeff Malone and 1994 1st round pick (Feb. 24). **Signed:** F/C Morningstar (Feb. 21) as free agent.

Washington Bullets

	Gm	FG%	TPts	—Per Game— Pts	Reb	Ast
Rex Chapman	60	.498	1094	18.2	2.4	3.1
Don MacLean	75	.502	1365	18.2	6.2	2.1
Tom Gugliotta	78	.466	1333	17.1	9.3	3.5
Michael Adams	70	.408	849	12.1	2.6	6.9
Calbert Cheaney	65	.470	779	12.0	2.9	1.9
Marty Conlon	30	.576	233	7.8	4.6	1.1
CHAR	16	.606	163	10.2	5.6	1.8
WASH	14	.518	70	5.0	3.6	0.4
Pervis Ellison	47	.469	344	7.3	5.1	1.5
Mitchell Butler	75	.495	518	6.9	3.0	1.0
Kevin Duckworth	69	.417	456	6.6	4.7	0.8
Brent Price	65	.433	400	6.2	1.4	3.3
Gheorghe Muresan	54	.545	304	5.6	3.6	0.3
Kenny Walker	73	.482	351	4.8	4.0	0.5
Ron Anderson	21	.407	96	4.6	2.5	0.4
NJ	11	.349	44	4.0	2.4	0.5
WASH	10	.465	52	5.2	2.7	1.1
Doug Overton	61	.403	218	3.6	1.1	1.5
Gerald Paddio	18	.367	53	2.9	0.9	0.6
IND	7	.391	19	2.7	0.7	0.6
NY	3	.400	4	1.3	0.0	0.0
WASH	8	.344	30	3.8	1.4	0.9

Triple doubles: none. **3-pt FG leader:** Chapman (64). **Steals leader:** Gugliotta (172). **Blocks leader:** Walker (59).

Signed: G/F Paddio (Jan. 27), F Anderson (Feb. 16) and F Conlon (Mar. 25) as free agents.

Series Summaries
WESTERN CONFERENCE

FIRST ROUND (Best of 5)

	W-L	Avg.	Leading Scorer
Denver	3 2	94.2	Ellis (16.0)
Seattle	2 3	95.0	Schrempf (18.6)

Date	Winner	Home Court
Apr. 28	Sonics, 106-82	at Seattle
Apr. 30	Sonics, 97-87	at Seattle
May 2	Nuggets, 110-93	at Denver
May 5	Nuggets, 94-85 (OT)	at Denver
May 7	Nuggets, 98-94 (OT)	at Seattle

	W-L	Avg.	Leading Scorer
Utah	3 1	96.3	K. Malone (29.3)
San Antonio	1 3	88.0	Robinson (20.0)

Date	Winner	Home Court
Apr. 28	Spurs, 106-89	at San Antonio
Apr. 30	Jazz, 96-84	at San Antonio
May 3	Jazz, 105-72	at Utah
May 5	Jazz, 95-90	at Utah

	W-L	Avg.	Leading Scorer
Phoenix	3 0	122.7	Barkley (37.3)
Golden St	0 3	116.0	Mullin (25.3)

Date	Winner	Home Court
Apr. 29	Suns, 111-104	at Phoenix
May 1	Suns, 117-111	at Phoenix
May 4	Suns, 140-133	at Golden St.

	W-L	Avg.	Leading Scorer
Houston	3 1	109.0	Olajuwon (34.0)
Portland	1 3	103.8	Strickland (23.5)

Date	Winner	Home Court
Apr. 29	Rockets, 114-104	at Houston
May 1	Rockets, 115-104	at Houston
May 3	Blazers, 118-115	at Portland
May 6	Rockets, 92-89	at Portland

SEMIFINALS (Best of 7)

	W-L	Avg.	Leading Scorer
Utah	4 3	97.1	K. Malone (26.7)
Denver	3 4	94.4	Abdul-Rauf (15.7)

Date	Winner	Home Court
May 10	Jazz, 100-91	at Utah
May 12	Jazz, 104-94	at Utah
May 14	Jazz, 111-109 (OT)	at Denver
May 15	Nuggets, 83-82	at Denver
May 17	Nuggets, 109-101 (2OT)	at Utah
May 19	Nuggets, 94-91	at Denver
May 21	Jazz, 91-81	at Utah

	W-L	Avg.	Leading Scorer
Houston	4 3	104.4	Olajuwon (28.7)
Phoenix	3 4	99.4	K. Johnson (26.6)

Date	Winner	Home Court
May 8	Suns, 91-87	at Houston
May 11	Suns, 124-117 (OT)	at Houston
May 13	Rockets, 118-102	at Phoenix
May 15	Rockets, 107-96	at Phoenix
May 17	Rockets, 109-86	at Houston
May 19	Suns, 103-89	at Phoenix
May 21	Rockets, 104-94	at Houston

CHAMPIONSHIP (Best of 7)

	W-L	Avg.	Leading Scorer
Houston	4 1	92.8	Olajuwon (27.8)
Utah	1 4	88.6	K. Malone (26.0)

Date	Winner	Home Court	Date	Winner	Home Court
May 23	Rockets, 100-88	at Houston	May 29	Rockets, 80-78	at Utah
May 25	Rockets, 104-99	at Houston	May 31	Rockets, 94-83	at Houston
May 27	Jazz, 95-86	at Utah			

EASTERN CONFERENCE

FIRST ROUND (Best of 5)

	W-L	Avg.	Leading Scorer
Atlanta	3 2	96.6	Manning (18.0)
Miami	2 3	89.8	S. Smith (19.2)

Date	Winner	Home Court
Apr. 28	Heat, 93-88	at Atlanta
Apr. 30	Hawks, 104-86	at Atlanta
May 3	Heat, 90-86	at Miami
May 5	Hawks, 103-89	at Miami
May 8	Hawks, 102-91	at Atlanta

	W-L	Avg.	Leading Scorer
New York	3 1	93.8	Ewing (24.8)
New Jersey	1 3	86.5	Coleman (24.5)

Date	Winner	Home Court
Apr. 29	Knicks, 91-80	at New York
May 1	Knicks, 90-81	at New York
May 4	Nets, 93-92 (OT)	at New Jersey
May 6	Knicks, 102-92	at New Jersey

	W-L	Avg.	Leading Scorer
Indiana	3 0	97.0	Miller (29.0)
Orlando	0 3	91.7	O'Neal (20.7)

Date	Winner	Home Court
Apr. 28	Pacers, 89-88	at Orlando
Apr. 30	Pacers, 103-101	at Orlando
May 2	Pacers, 99-86	at Indiana

	W-L	Avg.	Leading Scorer
Chicago	3 0	101.3	Pippen (25.3)
Cleveland	0 3	94.7	Wilkins (20.3)

Date	Winner	Home Court
Apr. 29	Bulls, 104-96	at Chicago
May 1	Bulls, 105-96	at Chicago
May 3	Bulls, 95-92 (OT)	at Cleveland

SEMIFINALS (Best of 7)

	W-L	Avg.	Leading Scorer
Indiana	4 2	90.2	Miller (18.5)
Atlanta	2 4	85.2	Manning (21.7)

Date	Winner	Home Court
May 10	Pacers, 96-85	at Atlanta
May 12	Hawks, 92-69	at Atlanta
May 14	Pacers, 101-81	at Indiana
May 15	Pacers, 102-86	at Indiana
May 17	Hawks, 88-76	at Atlanta
May 19	Pacers, 98-79	at Indiana

	W-L	Avg.	Leading Scorer
New York	4 3	89.1	Ewing (22.9)
Chicago	3 4	90.3	Pippen (21.7)

Date	Winner	Home Court
May 8	Knicks, 90-86	at New York
May 11	Knicks, 96-91	at New York
May 13	Bulls, 104-102	at Chicago
May 15	Bulls, 95-83	at Chicago
May 18	Knicks, 87-86	at New York
May 20	Bulls, 93-79	at Chicago
May 22	Knicks, 87-77	at New York

CHAMPIONSHIP (Best of 7)

	W-L	Avg.	Leading Scorer
New York	4 3	87.4	Ewing (22.3)
Indiana	3 4	87.4	Miller (24.7)

Date	Winner	Home Court
May 24	Knicks, 100-89	at New York
May 26	Knicks, 89-78	at New York
May 28	Pacers, 88-68	at Indiana
May 30	Pacers, 83-77	at Indiana
June 1	Pacers, 93-86	at New York
June 3	Knicks, 98-91	at Indiana
June 5	Knicks, 94-90	at New York

NBA FINALS

	W-L	Avg.	Leading Scorer
Houston	4 3	86.1	Olajuwon (26.9)
New York	3 4	86.9	Ewing (18.9)

Date	Winner	Home Court
June 8	Rockets, 85-78	at Houston
June 10	Knicks, 91-83	at Houston
June 12	Rockets, 93-89	at New York
June 15	Knicks, 91-82	at New York
June 17	Knicks, 91-84	at New York
June 19	Rockets, 86-84	at Houston
June 22	Rockets, 90-84	at Houston

Most Valuable Player

Hakeem Olajuwon, Houston, C
26.9 pts, 9.1 rebs, 3.9 blocks, 3.6 assists.

Scoring Leaders

	Gm	FG	FT	Pts	Avg
Hakeem Olajuwon, Hou	23	267	128	664	28.9
Charles Barkley, Pho	10	110	42	276	27.6
Karl Malone, Utah	16	158	118	434	27.1
Kevin Johnson, Pho	10	97	69	266	26.6
Chris Mullin, GS	3	30	10	76	25.3
Derrick Coleman, NJ	4	27	39	98	24.5
Rod Strickland, Port	4	36	22	94	23.5
Reggie Miller, Ind	16	121	94	371	23.2
Scottie Pippen, Chi	10	85	46	228	22.8
Latrell Sprewell, GS	3	26	8	68	22.7
Patrick Ewing, NY	25	210	123	547	21.9
Clyde Drexler, Pho	4	31	19	84	21.0

High-Point Games

	Date	FG-FT—Pts
Charles Barkley, Pho at GS	5/4	23-7—56
Hakeem Olajuwon, Hou vs Port	5/1	16-13—46
Hakeem Olajuwon, Hou vs Utah	5/25	14-13—41
Reggie Miller, Ind at NY	6/1	14-5—39
Kevin Johnson, Pho vs GS	5/1	15-8—38
Kevin Johnson, Pho vs Hou	5/13	12-13—38
Kevin Johnson, Pho vs Hou	5/15	15-6—38

Final Playoff Standings

(Ranked by victories)

	Gm	W	L	Pct	Per Game For	Per Game Opp
Houston	23	15	8	.652	97.1	94.0
New York	25	14	11	.560	88.8	87.7
Indiana	16	10	6	.625	90.3	87.4
Utah	16	8	8	.500	94.3	92.3
Chicago	10	6	4	.600	93.6	90.8
Phoenix	10	6	4	.600	106.4	107.9
Denver	12	6	6	.500	94.3	96.3
Atlanta	11	5	6	.455	90.4	90.0
Seattle	5	2	3	.400	95.0	94.2
Miami	5	2	3	.400	89.8	96.6
Portland	4	1	3	.250	103.8	109.0
New Jersey	4	1	3	.250	86.5	93.8
San Antonio	4	1	3	.250	88.0	96.3
Orlando	3	0	3	.000	91.7	97.0
Golden St.	3	0	3	.000	116.0	122.7
Cleveland	3	0	3	.000	94.7	101.3

NBA Finalists' Composite Box Scores
Houston Rockets (15-8)

	Overall Playoffs						Finals vs New York					
				—Per Game—						—Per Game—		
	Gm	FG%	TPts	Pts	Reb	Ast	Gm	FG%	TPts	Pts	Reb	Ast
Hakeem Olajuwon	23	.519	664	28.9	11.0	4.3	7	.500	188	26.9	9.1	3.6
Vernon Maxwell	23	.376	318	13.8	3.5	4.2	7	.365	94	13.4	3.3	2.9
Robert Horry	23	.434	269	11.7	6.1	3.6	7	.324	72	10.3	6.1	3.7
Otis Thorpe	23	.572	261	11.3	9.9	2.3	7	.519	65	9.3	11.3	3.3
Kenny Smith	23	.455	248	10.8	2.3	4.1	7	.389	39	5.6	1.4	3.1
Sam Cassell	22	.394	207	9.4	2.7	4.2	7	.422	70	10.0	3.1	2.9
Mario Elie	23	.396	134	5.8	1.7	1.7	7	.250	17	2.4	1.0	1.0
Carl Herrera	16	.534	75	4.7	2.8	0.2	7	.579	50	7.1	3.6	0.4
Scott Brooks	5	.833	11	2.2	0.4	0.6	0	—	0	0.0	0.0	0.0
Earl Cureton	10	.800	18	1.8	2.9	0.2	1	—	0	0.0	0.0	0.0
Matt Bullard	10	.211	16	1.6	1.0	0.0	2	.200	8	4.0	3.0	0.0
Chris Jent	11	.250	13	1.2	0.8	0.6	3	.000	0	0.0	0.3	0.0
ROCKETS	23	.461	2234	97.1	41.4	24.8	7	.426	603	86.1	40.0	20.9
OPPONENTS	23	.422	2162	94.0	44.0	22.2	7	.407	608	86.9	43.0	21.7

Three-pointers: PLAYOFFS— Maxwell (45-for-138), Smith (34-76), Horry (34-89), Cassell (17-45), Elie (10-32), Jent (3-13), Olajuwon (2-4), Bullard (2-10), Brooks (1-1), Thorpe (1-2), Team (149-410 for .363 pct.); FINALS— Horry (11-for-36), Maxwell (9-40), Smith (5-14), Elie (2-5), Bullard (2-7), Olajuwon (1-1), Jent 0-2); Team (37-121 for .306 pct.).

New York Knicks (14-11)

	Overall Playoffs						Finals vs Houston					
				—Per Game—						—Per Game—		
	Gm	FG%	TPts	Pts	Reb	Ast	Gm	FG%	TPts	Pts	Reb	Ast
Patrick Ewing	25	.437	547	21.9	11.7	2.6	7	.363	132	18.9	12.4	1.7
John Starks	25	.381	364	14.6	2.3	4.6	7	.368	124	17.7	3.1	5.9
Charles Oakley	25	.477	329	13.2	11.7	2.4	7	.484	77	11.0	11.9	2.4
Derek Harper	23	.429	263	11.4	2.3	4.5	7	.467	115	16.4	3.0	6.0
Charles Smith	25	.480	221	8.8	3.8	1.0	7	.441	65	9.3	4.3	1.7
Anthony Mason	25	.489	189	7.6	5.8	1.8	7	.468	60	8.6	6.9	1.3
Hubert Davis	23	.364	121	5.3	0.9	1.1	5	.200	8	1.6	0.4	0.4
Greg Anthony	25	.352	122	4.9	1.1	2.4	7	.323	23	3.3	0.9	2.4
Anthony Bonner	13	.455	27	2.1	2.2	0.2	2	1.000	4	2.0	1.0	0.0
Herb Williams	19	.419	28	1.5	1.1	0.2	4	.000	0	0.0	0.0	0.0
Rolando Blackman	6	.273	8	1.3	0.5	0.5	0	—	0	0.0	0.0	0.0
Corey Gaines	4	.000	0	0.0	0.0	0.0	0	—	0	0.0	0.0	0.0
KNICKS	25	.428	2219	88.8	41.6	20.3	7	.407	608	86.9	43.0	21.7
OPPONENTS	25	.425	2193	87.7	39.2	20.1	7	.426	603	86.1	40.0	20.9

Three-pointers: PLAYOFFS— Starks (47-for-132), Harper (29-85), Anthony (18-61), Davis (10-35), Ewing (4-11), Blackman (2-4), Gaines (0-1), Smith 0-3); Team (110-332 for .331 pct.); FINALS— Harper (17-for-39), Starks (16-50), Davis (1-1), Ewing (1-5), Anthony (1-8), Smith (0-2), Team (36-105 for .343 pct.).

Annual Awards

Most Valuable Player

The Maurice Podoloff Trophy; voting by 101-member panel of local and national pro basketball writers and broadcasters. Each ballot has five entries; points awarded on 10-7-5-3-1 basis.

	1st	2nd	3rd	4th	5th	Pts
Hakeem Olajuwon, Hou	66	28	6	1	0	889
David Robinson, SA	24	57	17	2	0	730
Scottie Pippen, Chi	7	9	37	18	18	390
Shaquille O'Neal, Orl	3	3	21	36	25	289
Patrick Ewing, NY	1	3	19	34	27	255

Also receiving votes: Gary Payton, Sea. (20 pts); Shawn Kemp, Sea. (17 pts); Karl Malone, Utah (17 pts); Mark Price, Cle. (7pts); and Charles Barkley, Pho. (5 pts).

Rookie of the Year

The Eddie Gottlieb Trophy; voting by 101-member panel of local and national pro basketball writers and broadcasters. Each ballot has one entry.

	Pos	Votes
Chris Webber, Golden St	C	53
Anfernee Hardaway, Orlando	G	47
Jamal Washburn, Dallas	F	1

All-NBA Teams

Voting by a 101-member panel of local and national pro basketball writers and broadcasters. Each ballot has entries for three teams; points awarded on 5-3-1 basis. First Team repeaters from 1992-93 are in **bold** type.

Pos First Team	1st	Pts
F Scottie Pippen, Chicago	94	485
F **Karl Malone, Utah**	65	417
C **Hakeem Olajuwon, Houston**	68	433
G John Stockton, Utah	56	356
G Latrell Sprewell, Golden St.	29	252

Pos Second Team	1st	Pts
F Shawn Kemp, Seattle	17	211½
F Charles Barkley, Phoenix	15	204
C David Robinson, San Antonio	29	341
G Mitch Richmond, Sacramento	24	198
G Kevin Johnson, Phoenix	23	190

Pos Third Team	1st	Pts
F Derrick Coleman, New Jersey	4	139
F Dominique Wilkins, Atl-LAC	3	106
C Shaquille O'Neal, Orlando	3	94½
G Mark Price, Cleveland	22	182
G Gary Payton, Seattle	21	175

All-Rookie Team

Voting by NBA's 27 head coaches, who cannot vote players on their team. Each ballot has entries for two five-man teams, regardless of position; two points given for 1st team, one for 2nd. First team votes in parentheses.

First Team	College	Pts
Chris Webber, Golden St. (26)	Michigan	52
Anfernee Hardaway, Orlando (26)	Memphis St.	52
Vin Baker, Milwaukee (20)	Hartford	46
Jamal Mashburn, Dallas (20)	Kentucky	44
Isaiah Rider, Minnesota (14)	UNLV	38

Second Team	College	Pts
Dino Radja, Boston (11)	Croatia	35
Nick Van Exel, LA Lakers (4)	Cincinnati	26
Shawn Bradley, Philadelphia (3)	BYU	21
Toni Kukoc, Chicago (2)	Croatia	19
Lindsey Hunter, Detroit (1)	Jackson St.	15

Coach of the Year

The Red Auerbach Trophy; voting by 101-member panel of local and national pro basketball writers and broadcasters. Each ballot has one entry.

	Votes	Record	Div
Lenny Wilkens, Atlanta	71	57-25	1st
Phil Jackson, Chicago	16	55-27	2nd
George Karl, Seattle	8	63-19	1st

Also receiving votes: Rudy Tomjanovich, Hou. (3); Chuck Daly, NJ (1); Don Nelson, GS (1); Pat Riley, NY (1).

All-Defensive Teams

Voting by NBA head coaches. Each ballot has entries for two teams; two points given for 1st team, one for 2nd. Coaches cannot vote for own players. First Team repeaters from 1992-93 are in **bold** type.

Pos	First Team	1st	Pts
F	Scottie Pippen, Chicago	20	45
F	Charles Oakley, New York	12	35
C	**Hakeem Olajuwon,** Houston	13	35
G	Gary Payton, Seattle	19	42
G	Mookie Blaylock, Atlanta	13	35

Pos	Second Team	1st	Pts
F	Dennis Rodman, San Antonio	14	34
F	Horace Grant, Chicago	5	20
C	David Robinson, San Antonio	10	33
G	Nate McMillan, Seattle	4	23
G	Latrell Sprewell, Golden St	3	14

Other Awards

Defensive Player of the Year— Hakeem Olajuwon, Houston; **Most Improved Player**— Don MacLean, Washington; **Sixth Man Award**— Dell Curry, Charlotte; **IBM Award** (for contributing most to team's success)— David Robinson, San Antonio; **Kennedy Citizenship Award**— Joe Dumars, Detroit; **Executive of the Year** (chosen by *The Sporting News*)— Bob Whitsitt, Seattle.

NBA Draft

First and second round picks at the 48th annual NBA College Draft held June 29, 1994, at the Hoosier Dome in Indianapolis. The order of the first 11 positions determined by a Draft Lottery held May 22, in Secaucus, N.J. Positions 12 through 27 reflect regular season records in reverse order. Underclassmen selected are noted in CAPITAL letters.

First Round

	Team		Pos
1	Milwaukee	GLENN ROBINSON, Purdue	F
2	Dallas	JASON KIDD, California	G
3	Detroit	Grant Hill, Duke	F/G
4	Minnesota	DONYELL MARSHALL, Connecticut	F
5	Washington	JUWAN HOWARD, Michigan	F
6	Philadelphia	SHARONE WRIGHT, Clemson	F/C
7	LA Clippers	LAMOND MURRAY, California	F
8	Sacramento	Brian Grant, Xavier-OH	F
9	Boston	Eric Montross, North Carolina	C
10	LA Lakers	Eddie Jones, Temple	G
11	**a**-Seattle	Carlos Rogers, Tennessee St.	F/C
12	Miami	Khalid Reeves, Arizona	G
13	Denver	JALEN ROSE, Michigan	G
14	New Jersey	YINKA DARE, George Washington	C
15	Indiana	Eric Piatkowski, Nebraska	F/G
16	**b**-Golden St	CLIFFORD ROZIER, Louisville	F
17	Portland	Aaron McKie, Temple	G
18	**c**-Milwaukee	Eric Mobley, Pittsburgh	F/C
19	**d**-Dallas	Tony Dumas, Missouri-KC	G
20	**e**-Philadelphia	B.J. Tyler, Texas	G
21	Chicago	Dickey Simpkins, Providence	F
22	San Antonio	Bill Curley, Boston College	F
23	Phoenix	Wesley Person, Auburn	G
24	New York	Monty Williams, Notre Dame	F
25	**f**-LA Clippers	Greg Minor, Louisville	G/F
26	**g**-New York	Charlie Ward, Florida St.	G
27	**h**-Orlando	Brooks Thompson, Oklahoma St.	G

Second Round

	Team		Pos
28	Dallas	Deon Thomas, Illinois	F
29	**i**-Phoenix	Antonio Lang, Duke	F
30	Minnesota	Howard Eisley, Boston College	G
31	**j**-Orlando	Rodney Dent, Kentucky	C
32	Washington	Jim McIlvaine, Marquette	C
33	Philadelphia	Derrick Alston, Duquesne	C
34	**k**-Atlanta	Gaylon Nickerson, NW Okla. St.	G
35	Sacramento	Michael Smith, Providence	F
36	Boston	Andrei Fetisov, Russia	C
37	**l**-Seattle	DONTONIO WINGFIELD, Cincinnati	F
38	Charlotte	Darrin Hancock, Kansas	G
39	**m**-Golden St	Anthony Miller, Michigan St.	F
40	Miami	Jeff Webster, Oklahoma	F
41	**n**-Indiana	William Njoku, Canada	F
42	Cleveland	Gary Collier, Tulsa	G
43	Portland	Shawnelle Scott, St. John's	C
44	Indiana	Damon Bailey, Indiana	G
45	Golden St	Dwayne Morton, Louisville	F
46	**o**-Milwaukee	VOSHON LENARD, Minnesota	G
47	Utah	Jamie Watson, South Carolina	F
48	**p**-Detroit	Jevon Crudup, Missouri	F
49	Chicago	Kris Bruton, Benedict-SC	G
50	Phoenix	CHARLES CLAXTON, Georgia	C
51	**q**-Sacramento	Lawrence Funderburke, Ohio St.	F
52	**r**-Phoenix	Anthony Goldwire, Houston	G
53	Houston	Albert Burditt, Texas	F
54	Seattle	Zeljko Rebraca, Yugoslavia	C

Acquired Picks

FIRST ROUND: **a**- from Charlotte; **b**- from Cleveland; **c**- from Orlando; **d**- from Golden St.; **e**- from Utah; **f**- from Atlanta; **g**- from Houston via Atlanta; **h**- from Seattle via LA Clippers.

SECOND ROUND: **i**- from Detroit via San Antonio; **j**- from Washington via Milwaukee and Denver; **k**- from LA Clippers; **l**- from LA Lakers; **m**- from Denver; **n**- from New Jersey via Philadelphia; **o**- from Orlando; **p**- from San Antonio via Sacramento; **q**- from Atlanta; **r**- from New York.

THE 1995 INFORMATION PLEASE SPORTS ALMANAC

PRO BASKETBALL STATISTICS

THROUGH THE YEARS 1947-1994

CHAMPIONS • NBA LEADERS

SEC B

PAGE 350

The NBA Finals

Although the National Basketball Association traces its first championship back to the 1946-47 season, the league was then called the Basketball Association of America (BAA). It did not become the NBA until after the 1948-49 season when the BAA and the National Basketball League (NBL) agreed to merge.

In the chart below, the Eastern finalists (representing the NBA Eastern Division from 1947-70, and the NBA Eastern Conference since 1971) are listed in CAPITAL letters. Also, each NBA champion's wins and losses are noted in parentheses after the series score.

Multiple winners: Boston (16); Minneapolis-LA Lakers (11); Chicago Bulls, Phi-SF-Golden St. Warriors and Syracuse Nats-Phi. 76ers (3); Detroit and New York (2).

Year	Winner	Head Coach	Series	Loser	Head Coach
1947	PHILADELPHIA WARRIORS	Eddie Gottlieb	4-1 (WWWLW)	Chicago Stags	Harold Olsen
1948	Baltimore Bullets	Buddy Jeannette	4-2 (LWWWLW)	PHILA. WARRIORS	Eddie Gottlieb
1949	Minneapolis Lakers	John Kundla	4-2 (LWWWLLW)	WASH. CAPITOLS	Red Auerbach
1950	Minneapolis Lakers	John Kundla	4-2 (WLWWLW)	SYRACUSE	Al Cervi
1951	Rochester	Les Harrison	4-3 (WWWWLLLW)	NEW YORK	Joe Lapchick
1952	Minneapolis Lakers	John Kundla	4-3 (WLWLWLW)	NEW YORK	Joe Lapchick
1953	Minneapolis Lakers	John Kundla	4-1 (LWWWW)	NEW YORK	Joe Lapchick
1954	Minneapolis Lakers	John Kundla	4-3 (WLWLWLW)	SYRACUSE	Al Cervi
1955	SYRACUSE	Al Cervi	4-3 (WWLLLWW)	Ft. Wayne Pistons	Charles Eckman
1956	PHILADELPHIA WARRIORS	George Senesky	4-1 (WLWWW)	Ft. Wayne Pistons	Charles Eckman
1957	BOSTON	Red Auerbach	4-3 (LWLWLWW)	St. Louis Hawks	Alex Hannum
1958	St. Louis Hawks	Alex Hannum	4-2 (WLWLWW)	BOSTON	Red Auerbach
1959	BOSTON	Red Auerbach	4-0	Mpls. Lakers	John Kundla
1960	BOSTON	Red Auerbach	4-3 (WLWLWLW)	St. Louis Hawks	Ed Macauley
1961	BOSTON	Red Auerbach	4-1 (WWLWW)	St. Louis Hawks	Paul Seymour
1962	BOSTON	Red Auerbach	4-3 (WLLWLWW)	LA Lakers	Fred Schaus
1963	BOSTON	Red Auerbach	4-2 (WWLWLW)	LA Lakers	Fred Schaus
1964	BOSTON	Red Auerbach	4-1 (WWLWW)	SF Warriors	Alex Hannum
1965	BOSTON	Red Auerbach	4-1 (WWLWW)	LA Lakers	Fred Schaus
1966	BOSTON	Red Auerbach	4-3 (LWWWLLW)	LA Lakers	Fred Schaus
1967	PHILADELPHIA 76ERS	Alex Hannum	4-2 (WWLWLW)	SF Warriors	Bill Sharman
1968	BOSTON	Bill Russell	4-2 (WLWLWW)	LA Lakers	B.van Breda Kolff
1969	BOSTON	Bill Russell	4-3 (LLWWWLWW)	LA Lakers	B.van Breda Kolff
1970	NEW YORK	Red Holzman	4-3 (WLWLWLW)	LA Lakers	Joe Mullaney
1971	Milwaukee	Larry Costello	4-0	BALT. BULLETS	Gene Shue
1972	LA Lakers	Bill Sharman	4-1 (LWWWW)	NEW YORK	Red Holzman
1973	NEW YORK	Red Holzman	4-1 (LWWWW)	LA Lakers	Bill Sharman
1974	BOSTON	Tommy Heinsohn	4-3 (WLWLWLW)	Milwaukee	Larry Costello
1975	Golden St. Warriors	Al Attles	4-0	WASH. BULLETS	K.C. Jones
1976	BOSTON	Tommy Heinsohn	4-2 (WWLLWW)	Phoenix	John MacLeod
1977	Portland	Jack Ramsay	4-2 (LLWWWW)	PHILA. 76ERS	Gene Shue
1978	WASHINGTON BULLETS	Dick Motta	4-3 (LWLWLWW)	Seattle	Lenny Wilkens
1979	Seattle	Lenny Wilkens	4-1 (LWWWW)	WASH. BULLETS	Dick Motta
1980	LA Lakers	Paul Westhead	4-2 (WLWLWW)	PHILA. 76ERS	Billy Cunningham
1981	BOSTON	Bill Fitch	4-2 (WLWLWW)	Houston	Del Harris
1982	LA Lakers	Pat Riley	4-2 (WLWLWW)	PHILA. 76ERS	Billy Cunningham
1983	PHILADELPHIA 76ERS	Billy Cunningham	4-0	LA Lakers	Pat Riley
1984	BOSTON	K.C. Jones	4-3 (LWLWWWLW)	LA Lakers	Pat Riley
1985	LA Lakers	Pat Riley	4-2 (LWWWLW)	BOSTON	K.C. Jones
1986	BOSTON	K.C. Jones	4-2 (WWLWLW)	Houston	Bill Fitch
1987	LA Lakers	Pat Riley	4-2 (WWLWLW)	BOSTON	K.C. Jones
1988	LA Lakers	Pat Riley	4-3 (LWWLLWW)	DETROIT PISTONS	Chuck Daly
1989	DETROIT PISTONS	Chuck Daly	4-0	LA Lakers	Pat Riley

Year	Winner	Head Coach	Series	Loser	Head Coach
1990	DETROIT	Chuck Daly	4-1 (WLWWW)	Portland	Rick Adelman
1991	CHICAGO	Phil Jackson	4-1 (LWWWW)	LA Lakers	Mike Dunleavy
1992	CHICAGO	Phil Jackson	4-2 (WLWLWW)	Portland	Rick Adelman
1993	CHICAGO	Phil Jackson	4-2 (WWLWLW)	Phoenix	Paul Westphal
1994	Houston	Rudy Tomjanovich	4-3 (WLWLLWW)	NEW YORK	Pat Riley

Note: Four Finalists were led by player-coaches: **1948**—Buddy Jeannette (guard) of Baltimore; **1950**—Al Cervi (guard) of Syracuse; **1968**—Bill Russell (center) of Boston; **1969**—Bill Russell (center) of Boston.

Most Valuable Player

Selected by an 11-member media panel. Winner who did not play for the NBA champion is in **bold** type.
   Multiple winners: Magic Johnson and Michael Jordan (3); Kareem Abdul-Jabbar, Larry Bird and Willis Reed (2).

Year		Year		Year	
1969	**Jerry West**, LA Lakers, G	1978	Wes Unseld, Washington, C	1987	Magic Johnson, LA Lakers, G
		1979	Dennis Johnson, Seattle, G	1988	James Worthy, LA Lakers, F
1970	Willis Reed, New York, C			1989	Joe Dumars, Detroit, G
1971	Lew Alcindor, Milwaukee, C	1980	Magic Johnson, LA Lakers, G/C		
1972	Wilt Chamberlain, LA Lakers, C	1981	Cedric Maxwell, Boston, F	1990	Isiah Thomas, Detroit, G
1973	Willis Reed, New York, C	1982	Magic Johnson, LA Lakers, G	1991	Michael Jordan, Chicago, G
1974	John Havlicek, Boston, F	1983	Moses Malone, Philadelphia, C	1992	Michael Jordan, Chicago, G
1975	Rick Barry, Golden State, F	1984	Larry Bird, Boston, F	1993	Michael Jordan, Chicago, G
1976	Jo Jo White, Boston, G	1985	K. Abdul-Jabbar, LA Lakers, C	1994	Hakeem Olajuwon, Houston, C
1977	Bill Walton, Portland, C	1986	Larry Bird, Boston, F		

Note: Alcindor changed his name to Kareem Abdul-Jabbar after the 1970-71 season.

All-Time NBA Playoff Leaders

Through the 1994 playoffs.

CAREER

Years listed indicate number of playoff appearances. Players active in 1994 in **bold** type; (DNP) indicates active player who did not participate in '94 playoffs.

Points

		Yrs	Gm	Pts	Avg
1	Kareem Abdul-Jabbar	18	237	5762	24.3
2	Jerry West	13	153	4457	29.1
3	Larry Bird	12	164	3897	23.8
4	Michael Jordan	9	111	3850	34.7
5	John Havlicek	13	172	3776	22.0
6	Magic Johnson	12	186	3640	19.6
7	Elgin Baylor	12	134	3623	27.0
8	Wilt Chamberlain	13	160	3607	22.5
9	Kevin McHale	13	169	3182	18.8
10	Dennis Johnson	13	180	3116	17.3
11	Julius Erving	11	141	3088	21.9
12	**James Worthy** (DNP)	9	143	3022	21.1
13	Sam Jones	12	154	2909	18.9
14	**Robert Parish** (DNP)	14	178	2804	15.8
15	Bill Russell	13	165	2673	16.2
16	**Hakeem Olajuwon**	9	85	2298	27.0
17	Byron Scott	11	158	2297	14.5
18	**Isiah Thomas** (DNP)	9	111	2261	20.4
19	Bob Pettit	9	88	2240	25.5
20	Elvin Hayes	10	96	2194	22.9

Scoring Average

Minimum of 25 games or 700 points.

		Yrs	Gm	Pts	Avg
1	Michael Jordan	9	111	3850	34.7
2	Jerry West	13	153	4457	29.1
3	**Karl Malone**	9	74	2018	27.3
4	Elgin Baylor	12	134	3623	27.0
5	**Hakeem Olajuwon**	9	85	2298	27.0
6	George Gervin	9	59	1592	27.0
7	**Dominique Wilkins** (DNP)	8	51	1345	26.4
8	Bob Pettit	9	88	2240	25.5
9	Rick Barry	7	74	1833	24.8
10	Bernard King	5	28	687	24.5
11	Alex English	10	68	1661	24.4
12	Kareem Abdul-Jabbar	18	237	5762	24.3
13	**Charles Barkley**	8	85	2058	24.2
14	Paul Arizin	8	49	1186	24.2
15	Larry Bird	12	164	3897	23.8
16	George Mikan	9	91	2141	23.5
17	**Patrick Ewing**	7	78	1799	23.1
18	Bob Love	6	47	1076	22.9
19	Elvin Hayes	10	96	2194	22.9
20	Wilt Chamberlain	13	160	3607	22.5

Field Goals

		Yrs	FG	Att	Pct
1	Kareem Abdul-Jabbar	18	2356	4422	.533
2	Jerry West	13	1622	3460	.469
3	Larry Bird	12	1458	3090	.472
4	John Havlicek	13	1451	3329	.436
5	Wilt Chamberlain	13	1425	2728	.522
6	Michael Jordan	9	1411	2818	.501
7	Elgin Baylor	12	1388	3161	.439
8	Magic Johnson	12	1276	2513	.508
9	**James Worthy** (DNP)	9	1267	2329	.544
10	Kevin McHale	13	1204	2145	.561

Free Throws

		Yrs	FT	Att	Pct
1	Jerry West	13	1213	1507	.805
2	Kareem Abdul-Jabbar	18	1050	1419	.740
3	Magic Johnson	12	1040	1241	.838
4	Michael Jordan	9	942	1129	.834
5	Larry Bird	12	901	1012	.891
6	John Havlicek	13	874	1046	.836
7	Elgin Baylor	12	847	1101	.769
8	Kevin McHale	13	766	972	.788
9	Wilt Chamberlain	13	757	1627	.465
10	Dennis Johnson	13	756	943	.802

All-Time NBA Playoff Leaders (Cont.)

Assists

		Yrs	Gm	No	Avg
1	Magic Johnson	12	186	2320	12.5
2	Larry Bird	12	164	1062	6.5
3	Dennis Johnson	13	180	1006	5.6
4	**Isiah Thomas** (DNP)	9	111	987	8.9
5	Jerry West	13	153	970	6.3

Rebounds

		Yrs	Gm	Reb	Avg
1	Bill Russell	13	165	4104	24.9
2	Wilt Chamberlain	13	160	3913	24.5
3	Kareem Abdul-Jabbar	18	237	2481	10.5
4	Wes Unseld	12	119	1777	14.9
5	**Robert Parish** (DNP)	14	178	1752	9.8

Appearances

	No		No
Kareem Abdul-Jabbar	18	Hal Greer	13
Dolph Schayes	15	John Havlicek	13
Robert Parish	14	Kevin McHale	13
Paul Silas	14	Dennis Johnson	13
Wilt Chamberlain	13	Bill Russell	13
Maurice Cheeks	13	Chet Walker	13
Bob Cousy	13	Jerry West	13

Games Played

	No		No
K. Abdul-Jabbar	237	Michael Cooper	168
Magic Johnson	186	Bill Russell	165
Danny Ainge	183	Larry Bird	164
Dennis Johnson	180	Paul Silas	163
Robert Parish	178	Wilt Chamberlain	160
John Havlicek	172	**Byron Scott**	158
Kevin McHale	169	Sam Jones	154

SINGLE GAME

Points

	Date	FG-FT—Pts
Michael Jordan, Chi at Bos*	4/20/86	22-19—63
Elgin Baylor, LA at Bos	4/14/62	22-17—61
Wilt Chamberlain, Phi vs Syr	3/22/62	22-12—56
Michael Jordan, Chi at Mia	4/29/92	20-16—56
Charles Barkley, Pho vs GS	5/4/94	23- 7—56
Rick Barry, SF vs Phi	4/18/67	22-11—55
Michael Jordan, Chi vs Cle	5/1/88	24- 7—55
Michael Jordan, Chi vs Pho	4/16/93	21-13—55

*Double overtime.

Field Goals

	Date	FG	Att
Wilt Chamberlain, Phi vs Syr	3/14/60	24	42
John Havlicek, Bos vs Atl	4/1/73	24	36
Michael Jordan, Chi vs Cle	5/1/88	24	45
Seven tied with 22 each.			

Miscellaneous

3-Pt Field Goals

	Date	No
Dan Majerle, Pho vs Sea	6/1/93	8
Chuck Person, Ind at Bos	4/28/91	7
Ten tied with 6 each.		

Assists

	Date	No
Magic Johnson, LA vs Pho	5/15/84	24
John Stockton, Utah at LA Lakers	5/17/88	24
Magic Johnson, LA Lakers at Port	5/3/85	23
Doc Rivers, Atl vs Bos	5/16/88	22
Four tied with 21 each.		

Rebounds

	Date	No
Wilt Chamberlain, Phi vs Bos	4/5/67	41
Bill Russell, Bos vs Phi	3/23/58	40
Bill Russell, Bos vs St.L.	3/29/60	40
Bill Russell, Bos vs LA*	4/18/62	40
Three tied with 39 each.		

*Overtime.

Appearances in NBA Finals

Standings of all NBA teams that have reached the NBA Finals since 1947.

App		Titles	Last Won
24	Minneapolis-LA Lakers	11	1988
19	Boston Celtics	16	1986
8	Syracuse Nats-Phila. 76ers	3	1983
7	New York Knicks	2	1973
6	Phila-SF-Golden St. Warriors	3	1975
4	Ft. Wayne-Detroit Pistons	2	1990
4	St. Louis Hawks	1	1958
4	Baltimore-Washington Bullets	1	1978
3	Chicago Bulls	3	1993
3	Portland Trail Blazers	1	1977
3	Houston Rockets	1	1994
2	Milwaukee Bucks	1	1971
2	Seattle SuperSonics	1	1979
2	Phoenix Suns	0	—
1	Baltimore Bullets	1	1948
1	Chicago Stags	0	—
1	Rochester Royals	1	1951
1	Washington Capitols	0	—

Change of address: The St. Louis Hawks now play in Atlanta and the Rochester Royals are now the Sacramento Kings.

Teams now defunct: Baltimore Bullets (1947-55), Chicago Stags (1946-50) and Washington Capitols (1946-51).

NBA FINALS

Points

Series		Year	Pts
4-Gm	Rick Barry, GS vs Wash	1975	118
5-Gm	Jerry West, LA vs Bos	1965	169
6-Gm	Michael Jordan, Chi vs Pho	1993	246
7-Gm	Elgin Baylor, LA vs Bos	1962	284

Field Goals

Series		Year	No
4-Gm	K. Abdul-Jabbar, Mil vs Bal	1971	46
5-Gm	Michael Jordan, Chi vs LAL	1991	63
6-Gm	Michael Jordan, Chi vs Pho	1993	101
7-Gm	Elgin Baylor, LA vs Bos	1962	101

Assists

Series		Year	No
4-Gm	Bob Cousy, Bos vs Mpls	1959	51
5-Gm	Magic Johnson, LAL vs Chi	1991	62
6-Gm	Magic Johnson, LAL vs Bos	1985	84
7-Gm	Magic Johnson, LA vs Bos	1984	95

Rebounds

Series		Year	No
4-Gm	Bill Russell, Bos vs Mpls	1959	118
5-Gm	Bill Russell, Bos vs St.L.	1961	144
6-Gm	Wilt Chamberlain, Phi vs SF	1967	171
7-Gm	Bill Russell, Bos vs LA	1962	189

The National Basketball League

Formed in 1937 by three corporations— General Electric and the Firestone and Goodyear rubber companies of Akron, Ohio— who were interested in moving up from their midwestern industrial league origins and backing a fully professional league. The NBL started with 13 previously independent teams in 1937-38 and although GE, Firestone and Goodyear were gone by late 1942, ran 12 years before merging with the three-year-old Basketball Association of America in 1949 to form the NBA.

Multiple champions: Akron Firestone Non-Skids, Fort Wayne Zollner Pistons, Oshkosh All-Stars (2).

Year	Winner	Series	Loser	Year	Winner	Series	Loser
1938	Goodyear Wingfoots	2-1	Oshkosh All-Stars	1944	Ft. Wayne Pistons	3-0	Sheboygan Redskins
1939	Firestone Non-Skids	3-2	Oshkosh All-Stars	1945	Ft. Wayne Pistons	3-2	Sheboygan Redskins
1940	Firestone Non-Skids	3-2	Oshkosh All-Stars	1946	Rochester Royals	3-0	Sheboygan Redskins
1941	Oshkosh All-Stars	3-0	Sheboygan Redskins	1947	Chicago Gears	3-2	Rochester Royals
1942	Oshkosh All-Stars	2-1	Ft. Wayne Pistons	1948	Minneapolis Lakers	3-1	Rochester Royals
1943	Sheboygan Redskins	2-1	Ft. Wayne Pistons	1949	Anderson Packers	3-0	Oshkosh All-Stars

NBA All-Star Game

The NBA staged its first All-Star Game before 10,094 at Boston Garden on March 2, 1951. From that year on, the game has matched the best players in the East against the best in the West. Winning coaches are listed first. East leads series, 28-16.

Multiple MVP winners: Bob Pettit (4); Oscar Robertson (3); Bob Cousy, Julius Erving, Magic Johnson, Karl Malone and Isiah Thomas (2).

Year		Host	Coaches	Most Valuable Player
1951	East 111, West 94	Boston	Joe Lapchick, John Kundla	Ed Macauley, Boston
1952	East 108, West 91	Boston	Al Cervi, John Kundla	Paul Arizin, Philadelphia
1953	West 79, East 75	Ft. Wayne	John Kundla, Joe Lapchick	George Mikan, Minneapolis
1954	East 98, West 93 (OT)	New York	Joe Lapchick, John Kundla	Bob Cousy, Boston
1955	East 100, West 91	New York	Al Cervi, Charley Eckman	Bill Sharman, Boston
1956	West 108, East 94	Rochester	Charley Eckman, George Senesky	Bob Pettit, St. Louis
1957	East 109, West 97	Boston	Red Auerbach, Bobby Wanzer	Bob Cousy, Boston
1958	East 130, West 118	St. Louis	Red Auerbach, Alex Hannum	Bob Pettit, St. Louis
1959	West 124, East 108	Detroit	Ed Macauley, Red Auerbach	Bob Pettit, St. Louis & Elgin Baylor, Minneapolis
1960	East 125, West 115	Philadelphia	Red Auerbach, Ed Macauley	Wilt Chamberlain, Philadelphia
1961	West 153, East 131	Syracuse	Paul Seymour, Red Auerbach	Oscar Robertson, Cincinnati
1962	West 150, East 130	St. Louis	Fred Schaus, Red Auerbach	Bob Pettit, St. Louis
1963	East 115, West 108	Los Angeles	Red Auerbach, Fred Schaus	Bill Russell, Boston
1964	East 111, West 107	Boston	Red Auerbach, Fred Schaus	Oscar Robertson, Cincinnati
1965	East 124, West 123	St. Louis	Red Auerbach, Alex Hannum	Jerry Lucas, Cincinnati
1966	East 137, West 94	Cincinnati	Red Auerbach, Fred Schaus	Adrian Smith, Cincinnati
1967	West 135, East 120	San Francisco	Fred Schaus, Red Auerbach	Rick Barry, San Francisco
1968	East 144, West 124	New York	Alex Hannum, Bill Sharman	Hal Greer, Philadelphia
1969	East 123, West 112	Baltimore	Gene Shue, Richie Guerin	Oscar Robertson, Cincinnati
1970	East 142, West 135	Philadelphia	Red Holzman, Richie Guerin	Willis Reed, New York
1971	West 108, East 107	San Diego	Larry Costello, Red Holzman	Lenny Wilkens, Seattle
1972	West 112, East 110	Los Angeles	Bill Sharman, Tom Heinsohn	Jerry West, Los Angeles
1973	East 104, West 84	Chicago	Tom Heinsohn, Bill Sharman	Dave Cowens, Boston
1974	East 134, West 123	Seattle	Larry Costello, Tom Heinsohn	Bob Lanier, Detroit
1975	East 108, West 102	Phoenix	K.C. Jones, Al Attles	Walt Frazier, New York
1976	East 123, West 109	Philadelphia	Tom Heinsohn, Al Attles	Dave Bing, Washington
1977	West 125, East 124	Milwaukee	Larry Brown, Gene Shue	Julius Erving, Philadelphia
1978	East 133, West 125	Atlanta	Billy Cunningham, Jack Ramsay	Randy Smith, Buffalo
1979	West 134, East 129	Detroit	Lenny Wilkens, Dick Motta	David Thompson, Denver
1980	East 144, West 135 (OT)	Washington	Billy Cunningham, Len Wilkens	George Gervin, San Antonio
1981	East 123, West 120	Cleveland	Billy Cunningham, John MacLeod	Nate Archibald, Boston
1982	East 120, West 118	New Jersey	Bill Fitch, Pat Riley	Larry Bird, Boston
1983	East 132, West 123	Los Angeles	Billy Cunningham, Pat Riley	Julius Erving, Philadelphia
1984	East 154, West 145 (OT)	Denver	K.C. Jones, Frank Layden	Isiah Thomas, Detroit
1985	West 140, East 129	Indiana	Pat Riley, K.C. Jones	Ralph Sampson, Houston
1986	East 139, West 132	Dallas	K.C. Jones, Pat Riley	Isiah Thomas, Detroit
1987	West 154, East 149 (OT)	Seattle	Pat Riley, K.C. Jones	Tom Chambers, Seattle
1988	East 138, West 133	Chicago	Mike Fratello, Pat Riley	Michael Jordan, Chicago
1989	West 143, East 134	Houston	Pat Riley, Lenny Wilkens	Karl Malone, Utah
1990	East 130, West 113	Miami	Chuck Daly, Pat Riley	Magic Johnson, LA Lakers
1991	East 116, West 114	Charlotte	Chris Ford, Rick Adelman	Charles Barkley, Philadelphia
1992	West 153, East 113	Orlando	Don Nelson, Phil Jackson	Magic Johnson, LA Lakers
1993	West 135, East 132 (OT)	Salt Lake City	Paul Westphal, Pat Riley	Karl Malone, Utah & John Stockton, Utah
1994	East 127, West 118	Minneapolis	Lenny Wilkens, George Karl	Scottie Pippen, Chicago

NBA Franchise Origins

Here is what the current 27 teams in the National Basketball Association have to show for the years they have put in as members of the National Basketball League (NBL), Basketball Association of America (BAA), the NBA, and the American Basketball Association (ABA). League titles are noted by year won.

Western Conference

	First Season		League Titles	Franchise Stops
Dallas Mavericks	1980-81	(NBA)	None	•Dallas (1980—)
Denver Nuggets	1967-68	(ABA)	None	•Denver (1967—)
Golden St. Warriors	1946-47	(BAA)	1 BAA (1947) 2 NBA (1956,75)	•Philadelphia (1946-62) San Francisco (1962-71) Oakland (1971—)
Houston Rockets	1967-68	(NBA)	1 NBA (1994)	•San Diego (1967-71) Houston (1971—)
Los Angeles Clippers	1970-71	(NBA)	None	•Buffalo (1970-78) San Diego (1978-84) Los Angeles (1984—)
Los Angeles Lakers	1947-48	(NBL)	1 NBL (1947) 1 BAA (1949) 10 NBA (1950,52-54,72, 80,82,85,87-88)	•Minneapolis (1947-60) Los Angeles (1960-67) Inglewood, CA (1967—)
Minnesota Timberwolves	1989-90	(NBA)	None	•Minneapolis (1989—)
Phoenix Suns	1968-69	(NBA)	None	•Phoenix (1968—)
Portland Trail Blazers	1970-71	(NBA)	1 NBA (1977)	•Portland (1970—)
Sacramento Kings	1945-46	(NBL)	1 NBL (1946) 1 NBA (1951)	•Rochester, NY (1945-58) Cincinnati (1958-72) KC-Omaha (1972-75) Kansas City (1975-85) Sacramento (1985—)
San Antonio Spurs	1967-68	(ABA)	None	•Dallas (1967-73) San Antonio (1973—)
Seattle SuperSonics	1967-68	(NBA)	1 NBA (1979)	•Seattle (1967—)
Utah Jazz	1974-75	(NBA)	None	•New Orleans (1974-79) Salt Lake City (1979—)

Eastern Conference

	First Season		League Titles	Franchise Stops
Atlanta Hawks	1946-47	(NBL)	1 NBA (1958)	•Tri-Cities (1946-51) Milwaukee (1951-55) St. Louis (1955-68) Atlanta (1968—)
Boston Celtics	1946-47	(BAA)	16 NBA (1957,59-66,68-69 74,76,81,84,86)	•Boston (1946—)
Charlotte Hornets	1988-89	(NBA)	None	•Charlotte (1988—)
Chicago Bulls	1966-67	(NBA)	3 NBA (1991-92)	•Chicago (1966—)
Cleveland Cavaliers	1970-71	(NBA)	None	•Cleveland (1970-74) Richfield, OH (1974-94) Cleveland (1994—)
Detroit Pistons	1941-42	(NBL)	2 NBL (1944-45) 2 NBA (1989-90)	•Ft. Wayne, IN (1941-57) Detroit (1957-78) Pontiac, MI (1978-88) Auburn Hills, MI (1988—)
Indiana Pacers	1967-68	(ABA)	3 ABA (1970,72-73)	•Indianapolis (1967—)
Miami Heat	1988-89	(NBA)	None	•Miami (1988—)
Milwaukee Bucks	1968-69	(NBA)	1 NBA (1971)	•Milwaukee (1968—)
New Jersey Nets	1967-68	(ABA)	2 ABA (1974,76)	•Teaneck, NJ (1967-68) Commack, NY (1968-69) W. Hempstead, NY (1969-71) Uniondale, NY (1971-77) Piscataway, NJ (1977-81) E. Rutherford, NJ (1981—)
New York Knicks	1946-47	(BAA)	2 NBA (1970,73)	•New York (1946—)
Orlando Magic	1989-90	(NBA)	None	•Orlando, FL (1989—)
Philadelphia 76ers	1949-50	(NBA)	3 NBA (1955,67,83)	•Syracuse, NY (1949-63) Philadelphia (1963—)
Washington Bullets	1961-62	(NBA)	1 NBA (1978)	•Chicago (1961-63) Baltimore (1963-73) Landover, MD (1973—)

Note: The Tri-Cities Blackhawks represented Moline and Rock Island, Ill., and Davenport, Iowa.

☞ Two Canadian expansion teams, the Toronto Raptors and Vancouver Grizzlies, will begin play in 1995-96. ☜

The Growth of the NBA

Of the 11 franchises that comprised the Basketball Association of America (BAA) at the start of the 1946-47 season, only three remain—the Boston Celtics, New York Knickerbockers and Golden State Warriors (originally Philadelphia Warriors).

Just before the start of the 1948-49 season, four teams from the more established **National Basketball League** (NBL)—the Ft. Wayne Pistons (now Detroit), Indianapolis Jets, Minneapolis Lakers (now Los Angeles) and Rochester Royals (now Sacramento Kings)—joined the BAA.

A year later, the six remaining NBL franchises—Anderson (Ind.), Denver, Sheboygan (Wisc.), the Syracuse Nationals (now Philadelphia 76ers), Tri-Cities Blackhawks (now Atlanta Hawks) and Waterloo (Iowa)—joined along with the new Indianapolis Olympians and the BAA became the 17-team **National Basketball Association**.

The NBA was down to 10 teams by the 1950-51 season and slipped to eight by 1954-55 with Boston, New York, Philadelphia and Syracuse in the Eastern Division, and Ft. Wayne, Milwaukee (formerly Tri-Cities), Minneapolis and Rochester in the West.

By 1960, five of those surviving eight teams had moved to other cities but by the end of the decade the NBA was a 14-team league. It also had a rival, the **American Basketball Association**, which began play in 1967 with a red, white and blue ball, a three-point line and 11 teams. After a nine-year run, the ABA merged four clubs—the Denver Nuggets, Indiana Pacers, New York Nets and San Antonio Spurs—with the NBA following the 1975-76 season. The NBA adopted the three-point play in 1979-80.

Expansion/Merger Timetable

For teams currently in NBA.

1948—Added NBL's Ft. Wayne Pistons (now Detroit), Minneapolis Lakers (now Los Angeles) and Rochester Royals (now Sacramento Kings); **1949**—Syracuse Nationals (now Philadelphia 76ers) and Tri-Cities Blackhawks (now Atlanta Hawks).
1961—Chicago Packers (now Washington Bullets); **1966**—Chicago Bulls; **1967**—San Diego Rockets (now Houston) and Seattle SuperSonics; **1968**—Milwaukee Bucks and Phoenix Suns.
1970—Buffalo Braves (now Los Angeles Clippers), Cleveland Cavaliers and Portland Trail Blazers; **1974**—New Orleans Jazz (now Utah); **1976**—added ABA's Denver Nuggets, Indiana Pacers, New York Nets (now New Jersey) and San Antonio Spurs.
1980—Dallas Mavericks; **1988**—Charlotte Hornets and Miami Heat; **1989**—Minnesota Timberwolves and Orlando Magic.
1994—New franchises awarded to Toronto and Vancouver for play beginning with the 1995-96 season.

City and Nickname Changes

1951—Tri-Cities Blackhawks, who divided home games between Moline and Rock Island, Ill., and Davenport, Iowa, move to Milwaukee and become the Hawks; **1955**—Milwaukee Hawks move to St. Louis; **1957**—Ft. Wayne Pistons move to Detroit, while Rochester Royals move to Cincinnati.
1960—Minneapolis Lakers move to Los Angeles; **1962**—Chicago Packers renamed Zephyrs, while Philadelphia Warriors move to San Francisco; **1963**—Chicago Zephyrs move to Baltimore and become Bullets, while Syracuse Nationals move to Philadelphia and become 76ers; **1968**—St. Louis Hawks move to Atlanta.
1971—San Diego Rockets move to Houston, while San Francisco Warriors move to Oakland and become Golden State Warriors; **1972**—Cincinnati Royals move to Midwest, divide home games between Kansas City, Mo., and Omaha, Neb., and become Kings; **1973**—Baltimore Bullets move to Landover, Md., outside Washington and become Capital Bullets; **1974**—Capital Bullets renamed Washington Bullets; **1975**—KC-Omaha Kings settle in Kansas City; **1977**—New York Nets move from Uniondale, N.Y., to Piscataway, N.J. (later East Rutherford) and become New Jersey Nets; **1978**—Buffalo Braves move to San Diego and become Clippers.
1980—New Orleans Jazz move to Salt Lake City and become Utah Jazz; **1984**—San Diego Clippers move to Los Angeles; **1985**—Kansas City Kings move to Sacramento.

Defunct NBA Teams

Teams that once played in the BAA and NBA, but no longer exist.

Anderson (Ind.)—Packers (1949-50); **Baltimore**—Bullets (1947-55); **Chicago**—Stags (1946-50); **Cleveland**—Rebels (1946-47); **Denver**—Nuggets (1949-50); **Detroit**—Falcons (1946-47); **Indianapolis**—Jets (1948-49) and Olympians (1949-53). **Pittsburgh**—Ironmen (1946-47); **Providence**—Steamrollers (1946-49); **St. Louis**—Bombers (1946-50); **Sheboygan (Wisc.)**—Redskins (1949-50); **Toronto**—Huskies (1946-47); **Washington**—Capitols (1946-51); **Waterloo (Iowa)**—Hawks (1949-50).

ABA Teams (1967-76)

Anaheim—Amigos (1967-68, moved to LA); **Baltimore**—Claws (1975, never played); **Carolina**—Cougars (1969-74, moved to St. Louis); **Dallas**—Chaparrals (1967-73, called Texas Chaparrals in 1970-71, moved to San Antonio); **Denver**—Rockets (1967-76, renamed Nuggets in 1974-76); **Miami**—Floridians (1968-72, called simply Floridians from 1970-72).
Houston—Mavericks (1967-69, moved to North Carolina); **Indiana**—Pacers (1967-76); **Kentucky**—Colonels (1967-76); **Los Angeles**—Stars (1968-70, moved to Utah); **Memphis**—Pros (1970-75, renamed Tams in 1972 and Sounds in 1974, moved to Baltimore); **Minnesota**—Muskies (1967-68, moved to Miami) and Pipers (1968-69, moved back to Pittsburgh); **New Jersey**—Americans (1967-68, moved to New York).
New Orleans—Buccaneers (1967-70, moved to Memphis); **New York**—Nets (1968-76); **Oakland**—Oaks (1967-69, moved to Washington); **Pittsburgh**—Pipers (1967-68, moved to Minnesota), Pipers (1969-72, renamed Condors in 1970); **St. Louis**—Spirits of St. Louis (1974-76); **San Antonio**—Spurs (1973-76); **San Diego**—Conquistadors (1972-75, renamed Sails in 1975); **Utah**—Stars (1970-75); **Virginia**—Squires (1970-76); **Washington**—Caps (1969-70, moved to Virginia).

Annual NBA Leaders
Scoring

Decided by total points from 1947-69, and per game average since 1970.

Multiple winners: Wilt Chamberlain and Michael Jordan (7); George Gervin (4); Neil Johnston, Bob McAdoo and George Mikan (3); Kareem Abdul-Jabbar, Paul Arizin, Adrian Dantley and Bob Pettit (2).

Year		Gm	Pts	Avg	Year		Gm	Pts	Avg
1947	Joe Fulks, Phi	60	1389	23.2	1972	Kareem Abdul-Jabbar, Mil	81	2822	34.8
1948	Max Zaslofsky, Chi	48	1007	21.0	1973	Nate Archibald, KC-Omaha	80	2719	34.0
1949	George Mikan, Mpls	60	1698	28.3	1974	Bob McAdoo, Buf	74	2261	30.6
1950	George Mikan, Mpls	68	1865	27.4	1975	Bob McAdoo, Buf	82	2831	34.5
1951	George Mikan, Mpls	68	1932	28.4	1976	Bob McAdoo, Buf	78	2427	31.1
1952	Paul Arizin, Phi	66	1674	25.4	1977	Pete Maravich, NO	73	2273	31.1
1953	Neil Johnston, Phi	70	1564	22.3	1978	George Gervin, SA	82	2232	27.2
1954	Neil Johnston, Phi	72	1759	24.4	1979	George Gervin, SA	80	2365	29.6
1955	Neil Johnston, Phi	72	1631	22.7	1980	George Gervin, SA	78	2585	33.1
1956	Bob Pettit, St.L	72	1849	25.7	1981	Adrian Dantley, Utah	80	2452	30.7
1957	Paul Arizin, Phi	71	1817	25.6	1982	George Gervin, SA	79	2551	32.3
1958	George Yardley, Det	72	2001	27.8	1983	Alex English, Den	82	2326	28.4
1959	Bob Pettit, St.L	72	2105	29.2	1984	Adrian Dantley, Utah	79	2418	30.6
1960	Wilt Chamberlain, Phi	72	2707	37.6	1985	Bernard King, NY	55	1809	32.9
1961	Wilt Chamberlain, Phi	79	3033	38.4	1986	Dominique Wilkins, Atl	78	2366	30.3
1962	Wilt Chamberlain, Phi	80	4029	50.4	1987	Michael Jordan, Chi	82	3041	37.1
1963	Wilt Chamberlain, SF	80	3586	44.8	1988	Michael Jordan, Chi	82	2868	35.0
1964	Wilt Chamberlain, SF	80	2948	36.9	1989	Michael Jordan, Chi	81	2633	32.5
1965	Wilt Chamberlain, SF-Phi	73	2534	34.7	1990	Michael Jordan, Chi	82	2753	33.6
1966	Wilt Chamberlain, Phi	79	2649	33.5	1991	Michael Jordan, Chi	82	2580	31.5
1967	Rick Barry, SF	78	2775	35.6	1992	Michael Jordan, Chi	80	2404	30.1
1968	Dave Bing, Det	79	2142	27.1	1993	Michael Jordan, Chi	78	2541	32.6
1969	Elvin Hayes, SD	82	2327	28.4	1994	David Robinson, SA	80	2383	29.8
1970	Jerry West, LA	74	2309	31.2					
1971	Lew Alcindor, Mil	82	2596	31.7					

Note: Alcindor changed his name to Kareem Abdul-Jabbar after the 1970-71 season.

Rebounds

Decided by total rebounds from 1951-69 and per game average since 1970.

Multiple winners: Wilt Chamberlain (11); Moses Malone (6); Bill Russell (4); Dennis Rodman (3); Elvin Hayes and Hakeem Olajuwon (2).

Year		Gm	No	Avg	Year		Gm	No	Avg
1951	Dolph Schayes, Syr	66	1080	16.4	1973	Wilt Chamberlain, LA	82	1526	18.6
1952	Larry Foust, Ft. Wayne	66	880	13.3	1974	Elvin Hayes, Cap*	81	1463	18.1
	& Mel Hutchins, Mil	66	880	13.3	1975	Wes Unseld, Wash	73	1077	14.8
1953	George Mikan, Mpls	70	1007	14.4	1976	Kareem Abdul-Jabbar, LA	82	1383	16.9
1954	Harry Gallatin, NY	72	1098	15.3	1977	Bill Walton, Port	65	934	14.4
1955	Neil Johnston, Phi	72	1085	15.1	1978	Len Robinson, NO	82	1288	15.7
1956	Bob Pettit, St.L	72	1164	16.2	1979	Moses Malone, Hou	82	1444	17.6
1957	Maurice Stokes, Roch	72	1256	17.4	1980	Swen Nater, SD	81	1216	15.0
1958	Bill Russell, Bos	69	1564	22.7	1981	Moses Malone, Hou	80	1180	14.8
1959	Bill Russell, Bos	70	1612	23.0	1982	Moses Malone, Hou	81	1188	14.7
1960	Wilt Chamberlain, Phi	72	1941	27.0	1983	Moses Malone, Phi	78	1194	15.3
1961	Wilt Chamberlain, Phi	79	2149	27.2	1984	Moses Malone, Phi	71	950	13.4
1962	Wilt Chamberlain, Phi	80	2052	25.7	1985	Moses Malone, Phi	79	1031	13.1
1963	Wilt Chamberlain, SF	80	1946	24.3	1986	Bill Laimbeer, Det	82	1075	13.1
1964	Bill Russell, Bos	78	1930	24.7	1987	Charles Barkley, Phi	68	994	14.6
1965	Bill Russell, Bos	78	1878	24.1	1988	Michael Cage, LA Clippers	72	938	13.0
1966	Wilt Chamberlain, Phi	79	1943	24.6	1989	Hakeem Olajuwon, Hou	82	1105	13.5
1967	Wilt Chamberlain, Phi	81	1957	24.2	1990	Hakeem Olajuwon, Hou	82	1149	14.0
1968	Wilt Chamberlain, Phi	82	1952	23.8	1991	David Robinson, SA	82	1063	13.0
1969	Wilt Chamberlain, LA	81	1712	21.1	1992	Dennis Rodman, Det	82	1530	18.7
1970	Elvin Hayes, SD	82	1386	16.9	1993	Dennis Rodman, Det	62	1232	18.3
1971	Wilt Chamberlain, LA	82	1493	18.2	1994	Dennis Rodman, SA	79	1367	17.3
1972	Wilt Chamberlain, LA	82	1572	19.2					

*The Baltimore Bullets moved to Landover, MD in 1973-74 and became first the Capital Bullets, then the Washington Bullets in 1974-75.

Assists

Decided by total assists from 1952-69 and per game average since 1970.
Multiple winners: Bob Cousy (8); John Stockton (7); Oscar Robertson (6); Magic Johnson and Kevin Porter (4); Andy Phillip and Guy Rodgers (2).

Year		No	Year		No	Year		Avg
1947	Ernie Calverley, Prov	202	1964	Oscar Robertson, Cin	868	1980	M.R. Richardson, NY	10.1
1948	Howie Dallmar, Phi	120	1965	Oscar Robertson, Cin	861	1981	Kevin Porter, Wash	9.1
1949	Bob Davies, Roch	321	1966	Oscar Robertson, Cin	847	1982	Johnny Moore, SA	9.6
			1967	Guy Rodgers, Chi	908	1983	Magic Johnson, LA	10.5
1950	Dick McGuire, NY	386	1968	Wilt Chamberlain, Phi	702	1984	Magic Johnson, LA	13.1
1951	Andy Phillip, Phi	414	1969	Oscar Robertson, Cin	772	1985	Isiah Thomas, Det	13.9
1952	Andy Phillip, Phi	539				1986	Magic Johnson, Lakers	12.6
1953	Bob Cousy, Bos	547	Year		Avg	1987	Magic Johnson, Lakers	12.2
1954	Bob Cousy, Bos	518	1970	Lenny Wilkens, Sea	9.1	1988	John Stockton, Utah	13.8
1955	Bob Cousy, Bos	557	1971	Norm Van Lier, Chi	10.1	1989	John Stockton, Utah	13.6
1956	Bob Cousy, Bos	642	1972	Jerry West, LA	9.7			
1957	Bob Cousy, Bos	478	1973	Nate Archibald, KC-O	11.4	1990	John Stockton, Utah	14.5
1958	Bob Cousy, Bos	463	1974	Ernie DiGregorio, Buf	8.2	1991	John Stockton, Utah	14.2
1959	Bob Cousy, Bos	557	1975	Kevin Porter, Wash	8.0	1992	John Stockton, Utah	13.7
1960	Bob Cousy, Bos	715	1976	Slick Watts, Sea	8.1	1993	John Stockton, Utah	12.0
1961	Oscar Robertson, Cin	690	1977	Don Buse, Ind	8.5	1994	John Stockton, Utah	12.6
1962	Oscar Robertson, Cin	899	1978	Kevin Porter, Det-NJ	10.2			
1963	Guy Rodgers, SF	825	1979	Kevin Porter, Det	13.4			

Field Goal Pct.

Multiple winners: Wilt Chamberlain (9); Artis Gilmore (4); Neil Johnston (3); Bob Feerick, Johnny Green, Alex Groza, Cedric Maxwell, Kevin McHale, Ken Sears and Buck Williams (2).

Year		Pct	Year		Pct	Year		Pct
1947	Bob Feerick, Wash	.401	1963	Wilt Chamberlain, SF	.528	1980	Cedric Maxwell, Bos	.609
1948	Bob Feerick, Wash	.340	1964	Jerry Lucas, Cin	.527	1981	Artis Gilmore, Chi.	.670
1949	Arnie Risen, Roch	.423	1965	W.Chamberlain, SF-Phi	.510	1982	Artis Gilmore, Chi.	.652
1950	Alex Groza, Indpls	.478	1966	Wilt Chamberlain, Phi	.540	1983	Artis Gilmore, SA	.626
1951	Alex Groza, Indpls	.470	1967	Wilt Chamberlain, Phi	.683	1984	Artis Gilmore, SA	.631
1952	Paul Arizin, Phi	.448	1968	Wilt Chamberlain, Phi	.595	1985	James Donaldson, LAC	.637
1953	Neil Johnston, Phi	.452	1969	Wilt Chamberlain, LA	.583	1986	Steve Johnson, SA	.632
1954	Ed Macauley, Bos	.486				1987	Kevin McHale, Bos	.604
1955	Larry Foust, Ft.W	.487	1970	Johnny Green, Cin	.559	1988	Kevin McHale, Bos	.604
1956	Neil Johnston, Phi	.457	1971	Johnny Green, Cin	.587	1989	Dennis Rodman, Det.	.595
1957	Neil Johnston, Phi	.447	1972	Wilt Chamberlain, LA	.649			
1958	Jack Twyman, Cin	.452	1973	Wilt Chamberlain, LA	.727	1990	Mark West, Pho	.625
1959	Ken Sears, NY	.490	1974	Bob McAdoo, Buf	.547	1991	Buck Williams, Port	.602
1960	Ken Sears, NY	.477	1975	Don Nelson, Bos	.539	1992	Buck Williams, Port	.604
1961	Wilt Chamberlain, Phi	.509	1976	Wes Unseld, Wash	.561	1993	Cedric Ceballos, Pho	.576
1962	Walt Bellamy, Chi	.519	1977	K. Abdul-Jabbar, LA	.579	1994	Shaquille O'Neal, Orl	.599
			1978	Bobby Jones, Den	.578			
			1979	Cedric Maxwell, Bos	.584			

Free Throw Percentage

Multiple leaders: Bill Sharman (7); Rick Barry (6); Larry Bird (4); Dolph Schayes (3); Larry Costello, Ernie DiGregorio, Bob Feerick, Kyle Macy, Calvin Murphy, Price, Oscar Robertson and Larry Siegfried (2).

Year		Pct	Year		Pct	Year		Pct
1947	Fred Scolari, Wash	.811	1963	Larry Costello, Syr	.881	1980	Rick Barry, Hou	.935
1948	Bob Feerick, Wash	.788	1964	Oscar Robertson, Cin	.853	1981	Calvin Murphy, Hou	.958
1949	Bob Feerick, Wash	.859	1965	Larry Costello, Phi	.877	1982	Kyle Macy, Pho	.899
1950	Max Zaslofsky, Chi	.843	1966	Larry Siegfried, Bos	.881	1983	Calvin Murphy, Hou	.920
1951	Joe Fulks, Phi	.855	1967	Adrian Smith, Cin	.903	1984	Larry Bird, Bos	.888
1952	Bob Wanzer, Roch	.904	1968	Oscar Robertson, Cin	.873	1985	Kyle Macy, Pho	.907
1953	Bill Sharman, Bos	.850	1969	Larry Siegfried, NY	.864	1986	Larry Bird, Bos	.896
1954	Bill Sharman, Bos	.844				1987	Larry Bird, Bos	.910
1955	Bill Sharman, Bos	.897	1970	Flynn Robinson, Mil	.898	1988	Jack Sikma, Mil	.922
1956	Bill Sharman, Bos	.867	1971	Chet Walker, Chi	.859	1989	Magic Johnson, LAL	.911
1957	Bill Sharman, Bos	.905	1972	Jack Marin, Bal	.894			
1958	Dolph Schayes, Syr	.904	1973	Rick Barry, GS	.902	1990	Larry Bird, Bos	.930
1959	Bill Sharman, Bos	.932	1974	Ernie DiGregorio, Buf	.902	1991	Reggie Miller, Ind	.918
1960	Dolph Schayes, Syr	.892	1975	Rick Barry, GS	.904	1992	Mark Price, Cle	.947
1961	Bill Sharman, Bos	.921	1976	Rick Barry, GS	.923	1993	Mark Price, Cle	.948
1962	Dolph Schayes, Syr	.896	1977	Ernie DiGregorio, Buf	.945	1994	M. Abdul-Rauf, Den	.956
			1978	Rick Barry, GS	.924			
			1979	Rick Barry, Hou	.947			

Note: Mahmoud Abdul-Rauf changed his name from Chris Jackson after the 1992-93 season.

Annual NBA Leaders (Cont.)

Blocked Shots

Decided by per game average since 1973-74 season.

Multiple winners: Kareem Abdul-Jabbar and Mark Eaton (4); George Johnson and Hakeem Olajuwon (3); Manute Bol (2).

Year		Gm	No	Avg
1974	Elmore Smith, LA	81	393	4.85
1975	Kareem Abdul-Jabbar, Mil	65	212	3.26
1976	Kareem Abdul-Jabbar, LA	82	338	4.12
1977	Bill Walton, Port	65	211	3.25
1978	George Johnson, NJ	81	274	3.38
1979	Kareem Abdul-Jabbar, LA	80	316	3.95
1980	Kareem Abdul-Jabbar, LA	82	280	3.41
1981	George Johnson, SA	82	278	3.39
1982	George Johnson, SA	75	234	3.12
1983	Tree Rollins, Atl	80	343	4.29
1984	Mark Eaton, Utah	82	351	4.28
1985	Mark Eaton, Utah	82	456	5.56
1986	Manute Bol, Wash	80	397	4.96
1987	Mark Eaton, Utah	79	321	4.06
1988	Mark Eaton, Utah	82	304	3.71
1989	Manute Bol, GS	80	345	4.31
1990	Akeem Olajuwon, Hou	82	376	4.59
1991	Hakeem Olajuwon, Hou	56	221	3.95
1992	David Robinson, SA	68	305	4.49
1993	Hakeem Olajuwon, Hou	82	342	4.17
1994	Dikembe Mutombo, Den	82	336	4.10

Note: Olajuwon changed the spelling of his first name to Hakeem during the 1990-91 season.

Steals

Decided by per game average since 1973-74 season.

Multiple winners: Michael Jordan, Micheal Ray Richardson and Alvin Robertson (3); Magic Johnson and John Stockton (2).

Year		Gm	No	Avg
1974	Larry Steele, Port	81	217	2.68
1975	Rick Barry, GS	80	228	2.85
1976	Slick Watts, Sea	82	261	3.18
1977	Don Buse, Ind	81	281	3.47
1978	Ron Lee, Pho	82	225	2.74
1979	M.L. Carr, Det	80	197	2.46
1980	Micheal Ray Richardson, NY	82	265	3.23
1981	Magic Johnson, LA	37	127	3.43
1982	Magic Johnson, LA	78	208	2.67
1983	Micheal Ray Richardson, GS-NJ	64	182	2.84
1984	Rickey Green, Utah	81	215	2.65
1985	Micheal Ray Richardson, NJ	82	243	2.96
1986	Alvin Robertson, SA	82	301	3.67
1987	Alvin Robertson, SA	81	260	3.21
1988	Michael Jordan, Chi	82	259	3.16
1989	John Stockton, Utah	82	263	3.21
1990	Michael Jordan, Chi	82	227	2.77
1991	Alvin Robertson, SA	81	246	3.04
1992	John Stockton, Utah	82	244	2.98
1993	Michael Jordan, Chi	78	221	2.83
1994	Nate McMillan, Sea	73	216	2.96

All-Time NBA Regular Season Leaders

Through the 1993-94 regular season.

CAREER

Players active in 1993-94 in **bold** type.

Points

		Yrs	Gm	Pts	Avg
1	Kareem Abdul-Jabbar	20	1560	38,387	24.6
2	Wilt Chamberlain	14	1045	31,419	30.1
3	**Moses Malone**	18	1312	27,360	20.9
4	Elvin Hayes	16	1303	27,313	21.0
5	Oscar Robertson	14	1040	26,710	25.7
6	John Havlicek	16	1270	26,395	20.8
7	Alex English	15	1193	25,613	21.5
8	Jerry West	14	932	25,192	27.0
9	**Dominique Wilkins**	12	907	24,019	26.5
10	Adrian Dantley	15	955	23,177	24.3
11	Elgin Baylor	14	846	23,149	27.4
12	**Robert Parish**	18	1413	22,494	15.9
13	Larry Bird	13	897	21,791	24.3
14	Hal Greer	15	1122	21,586	19.2
15	Michael Jordan	9	667	21,541	32.3
16	Walt Bellamy	14	1043	20,941	20.1
17	Bob Pettit	11	792	20,880	26.4
18	George Gervin	10	791	20,708	26.2
19	Bernard King	14	874	19,655	22.5
20	**Tom Chambers**	13	1013	19,521	19.3
	Walter Davis	15	1033	19,521	18.9
22	Dolph Schayes	16	1059	19,249	18.2
23	Bob Lanier	14	959	19,248	20.1
24	Gail Goodrich	14	1031	19,181	18.6
25	**Karl Malone**	9	734	19,050	26.0
26	Reggie Theus	13	1026	19,015	18.5
27	Chet Walker	13	1032	18,831	18.2
28	**Isiah Thomas**	13	979	18,822	19.2
29	Bob McAdoo	14	852	18,787	22.1
30	**Mark Aguirre**	13	923	18,458	20.0

Scoring Average

Minimum of 400 games or 10,000 points.

		Yrs	Gm	Pts	Avg
1	Michael Jordan	9	667	21,541	32.3
2	Wilt Chamberlain	14	1045	31,419	30.1
3	Elgin Baylor	14	846	23,149	27.4
4	Jerry West	14	932	25,192	27.0
5	**Dominique Wilkins**	12	907	24,019	26.5
6	Bob Pettit	11	792	20,880	26.4
7	George Gervin	10	791	20,708	26.2
8	**Karl Malone**	9	734	19,050	26.0
9	Oscar Robertson	14	1040	26,710	25.7
10	Kareem Abdul-Jabbar	20	1560	38,387	24.6
11	Larry Bird	13	897	21,791	24.3
12	Adrian Dantley	15	955	23,177	24.3
13	Pete Maravich	10	658	15,948	24.2
14	**Patrick Ewing**	9	680	16,191	23.8
15	**Hakeem Olajuwon**	10	756	17,899	23.7
16	**Charles Barkley**	10	751	17,530	23.3
17	Rick Barry	10	794	18,395	23.2
18	Paul Arizin	10	713	16,266	22.8
19	George Mikan	9	520	11,764	22.6
20	Bernard King	14	874	19,655	22.5
21	David Thompson	8	509	11,264	22.1
22	Bob McAdoo	14	852	18,787	22.1
23	Julius Erving	11	836	18,364	22.0
24	**Chris Mullin**	9	628	13,767	21.9
25	Alex English	15	1193	25,613	21.5
26	Elvin Hayes	16	1303	27,313	21.0
27	**Moses Malone**	18	1312	27,360	20.9
28	Billy Cunningham	9	654	13,626	20.8
29	John Havlicek	16	1270	26,395	20.8
30	**Clyde Drexler**	11	826	17,136	20.7

NBA-ABA Top 20
Points

All-Time combined regular season scoring leaders, including ABA service (1968-76). NBA players with ABA experience are listed in CAPITAL letters. Players active during 1993-94 are in **bold** type.

		Yrs	Pts	Avg
1	Kareem Abdul-Jabbar	20	38,387	24.6
2	Wilt Chamberlain	14	31,419	30.1
3	JULIUS ERVING	16	30,026	24.2
4	**MOSES MALONE**	20	29,531	20.5
5	DAN ISSEL	15	27,482	22.6
6	Elvin Hayes	16	27,313	21.0
7	Oscar Robertson	14	26,710	25.7
8	GEORGE GERVIN	14	26,595	25.1
9	John Havlicek	16	26,395	20.8
10	Alex English	15	25,613	21.5
11	RICK BARRY	14	25,279	24.8
12	Jerry West	14	25,192	27.0
13	ARTIS GILMORE	17	24,941	18.8
14	**Dominique Wilkins**	12	24,019	26.5
15	Adrian Dantley	15	23,177	24.3
16	Elgin Baylor	14	23,149	27.4
17	**Robert Parish**	18	22,494	15.9
18	Larry Bird	13	21,791	24.3
19	Hal Greer	15	21,586	19.2
20	Michael Jordan	9	21,541	32.3

ABA Totals: BARRY (4 yrs, 226 gm, 6884 pts, 30.5 avg); ERVING (5 yrs, 407 gm, 11,662 pts, 28.7 avg); GERVIN (4 yrs, 269 gm, 5887 pts, 21.9 avg); GILMORE (5 yrs, 420 gm, 9362 pts, 22.3 avg); ISSEL (6 yrs, 500 gm, 12,823 pts, 25.6 avg); MALONE (2 yrs, 126 gm, 2171 pts, 17.2 avg).

Field Goals

		Yrs	FG	Att	Pct
1	Kareem Abdul-Jabbar	20	15,837	28,307	.559
2	Wilt Chamberlain	14	12,681	23,497	.540
3	Elvin Hayes	16	10,976	24,272	.452
4	Alex English	15	10,659	21,036	.507
5	John Havlicek	16	10,513	23,930	.439
6	Oscar Robertson	14	9,508	19,620	.485
7	**Moses Malone**	18	9,422	19,190	.491
8	**Robert Parish**	18	9,265	17,158	.540
9	**Dominique Wilkins**	12	9,020	19,335	.467
10	Jerry West	14	9,016	19,032	.474

Note: If field goals made in the ABA are included, consider these NBA-ABA totals: Julius Erving (11,818), Dan Issel (10,431), George Gervin (10,368), Moses Malone (10,264), Rick Barry (9,695) and Artis Gilmore (9,403).

Free Throws

		Yrs	FG	Att	Pct
1	**Moses Malone**	18	8509	11,058	.769
2	Oscar Robertson	14	7694	9,185	.838
3	Jerry West	14	7160	8,801	.814
4	Dolph Schayes	16	6979	8,273	.844
5	Adrian Dantley	15	6832	8,351	.818
6	Kareem Abdul-Jabbar	20	6712	9,304	.721
7	Bob Pettit	11	6182	8,119	.761
8	Wilt Chamberlain	14	6057	11,862	.511
9	Elgin Baylor	14	5763	7,391	.780
10	Lenny Wilkens	15	5394	6,973	.774

Note: If free throws made in the ABA are included, consider these totals: Moses Malone (8,996), Dan Issel (6,591), Julius Erving (6,256) and Artis Gilmore (6,132).

Assists

		Yrs	Gm	Ast	Avg
1	Magic Johnson	12	874	9921	11.4
2	Oscar Robertson	14	1040	9887	9.5
3	**John Stockton**	10	816	9383	11.5
4	**Isiah Thomas**	13	979	9061	9.3
5	Maurice Cheeks	15	1101	7392	6.7
6	Lenny Wilkens	15	1077	7211	6.7
7	Bob Cousy	14	924	6955	7.5
8	Guy Rodgers	12	892	6917	7.8
9	Nate Archibald	13	876	6476	7.4
10	John Lucas	14	928	6454	7.0

Rebounds

		Yrs	Gm	Reb	Avg
1	Wilt Chamberlain	14	1045	23,924	22.9
2	Bill Russell	13	963	21,620	22.5
3	Kareem Abdul-Jabbar	20	1560	17,440	11.2
4	Elvin Hayes	16	1303	16,279	12.5
5	**Moses Malone**	18	1312	16,166	12.3
6	Nate Thurmond	14	964	14,464	15.0
7	Walt Bellamy	14	1043	14,241	13.7
8	**Robert Parish**	18	1413	13,973	9.9
9	Wes Unseld	13	984	13,769	14.0
10	Jerry Lucas	11	829	12,942	15.6

Note: If rebounds pulled down in the ABA are included, consider the following totals: Moses Malone (17,788) and Artis Gilmore (16,330).

Years Played

		Yrs	Career	Gm
1	Kareem Abdul-Jabbar	20	1969-89	1560
2	**Robert Parish**	18	1976—	1413
	Moses Malone	18	1976—	1312
4	**James Edwards**	17	1977—	1112
5	Four tied with 16 each.			

Note: If ABA records are included, consider the following year totals: Moses Malone (20, 1974—); Artis Gilmore (17, 1971-88); Caldwell Jones (17, 1973-90); Julius Erving (16, 1971-87); Dan Issel (15, 1970-85); Billy Paultz (15, 1970-85).

Games Played

		Yrs	Career	Gm
1	Kareem Abdul-Jabbar	20	1970-89	1560
2	**Robert Parish**	18	1976—	1413
3	**Moses Malone**	18	1976—	1312
4	Elvin Hayes	16	1969-84	1303
5	John Havlicek	16	1963-78	1270

Note: If ABA records are included, consider the following game totals: Moses Malone (1,438); Artis Gilmore (1,329); Caldwell Jones (1,299); Julius Erving (1,243); Dan Issel (1,218); Billy Paultz (1,124).

Personal Fouls

		Yrs	Gm	Fouls	DQ
1	Kareem Abdul-Jabbar	20	1560	4657	48
2	Elvin Hayes	16	1303	4193	53
3	**Robert Parish**	18	1413	4191	86
4	**James Edwards**	17	1112	3937	95
5	Jack Sikma	14	1107	3879	80

Note: If ABA records are included, consider the following personal foul totals: Artis Gilmore (4,529) and Caldwell Jones (4,436).

Disqualifications

		Yrs	Gm	No
1	Vern Mikkelsen	10	699	127
2	Walter Dukes	8	553	121
3	Charlie Share	8	555	105
4	Paul Arizin	10	713	101
5	Darryl Dawkins	14	726	100

All-Time NBA Regular Season Leaders (Cont.)
SINGLE SEASON

Scoring Average

		Season	Avg
1	Wilt Chamberlain, Phi	1961-62	50.4
2	Wilt Chamberlain, SF	1962-63	44.8
3	Wilt Chamberlain, Phi	1960-61	38.4
4	Elgin Baylor, LA	1961-62	38.3
5	Wilt Chamberlain, Phi	1959-60	37.6
6	Michael Jordan, Chi	1986-87	37.1
7	Wilt Chamberlain, SF	1963-64	36.9
8	Rick Barry, SF	1966-67	35.6
9	Michael Jordan, Chi	1987-88	35.0
10	Elgin Baylor, LA	1960-61	34.8
	Kareem Abdul-Jabbar, Mil	1971-72	34.8

Field Goal Pct.

		Season	Pct
1	Wilt Chamberlain, LA	1972-73	.727
2	Wilt Chamberlain, SF	1966-67	.683
3	Artis Gilmore, Chi	1980-81	.670
4	Artis Gilmore, Chi	1981-82	.652
5	Wilt Chamberlain, LA	1971-72	.649

Free Throw Pct.

		Season	Pct
1	Calvin Murphy, Hou	1980-81	.958
2	Mahmond Abdul-Rauf, Den	1993-94	.956
3	Mark Price, Cle	1992-93	.948
4	Mark Price, Cle	1991-92	.947
	Rick Barry, Hou	1978-79	.947

3-Pt Field Goal Pct.

		Season	Pct
1	Jon Sundvold, Mia	1988-89	.522
2	Steve Kerr, Cle	1989-90	.507
3	Craig Hodges, Mil-Pho	1987-88	.491
4	Mark Price, Cle	1987-88	.486
5	Kiki Vandeweghe, Port	1986-87	.481
	Craig Hodges, Chi	1989-90	.481

Assists

		Season	Avg
1	John Stockton, Utah	1989-90	14.5
2	John Stockton, Utah	1990-91	14.2
3	Isiah Thomas, Det	1984-85	13.9
4	John Stockton, Utah	1987-88	13.8
5	John Stockton, Utah	1991-92	13.7
6	John Stockton, Utah	1988-89	13.6
7	Kevin Porter, Det	1978-79	13.4
8	Magic Johnson, LA Lakers	1983-84	13.1
9	Magic Johnson, LA Lakers	1988-89	12.8
10	Magic Johnson, LA Lakers	1984-85	12.6
	John Stockton, Utah	1993-94	12.6

Rebounds

		Season	Avg
1	Wilt Chamberlain, Phi	1960-61	27.2
2	Wilt Chamberlain, Phi	1959-60	27.0
3	Wilt Chamberlain, Phi	1961-62	25.7
4	Bill Russell, Bos	1963-64	24.7
5	Wilt Chamberlain, Phi	1965-66	24.6

Blocked Shots

		Season	Avg
1	Mark Eaton, Utah	1984-85	5.56
2	Manute Bol, Wash	1985-86	4.96
3	Elmore Smith, LA	1973-74	4.85
4	Mark Eaton, Utah	1985-86	4.61
5	Hakeem Olajuwon, Hou	1989-90	4.59

Steals

		Season	Avg
1	Alvin Robertson, SA	1985-86	3.67
2	Don Buse, Ind	1976-77	3.47
3	Magic Johnson, LA Lakers	1980-81	3.43
4	Micheal Ray Richardson, NY	1979-80	3.23
5	Alvin Robertson, SA	1986-87	3.21

SINGLE GAME

Points

	Date	FG-FT	Pts
Wilt Chamberlain, Phi vs NY	3/2/62	36-28—	100
Wilt Chamberlain, Phi vs LA***	12/8/61	31-16—	78
Wilt Chamberlain, Phi vs Chi	1/13/62	29-15—	73
Wilt Chamberlain, SF at NY	11/16/62	29-15—	73
David Thompson, Den at Det	4/9/78	28-17—	73
Wilt Chamberlain, SF at LA	11/3/62	29-14—	72
Elgin Baylor, LA at NY	11/15/60	28-15—	71
David Robinson, SA at LAC	4/24/94	26-18—	71
Wilt Chamberlain, SF at Syr	3/10/63	27-16—	70
Michael Jordan, Chi at Cle*	3/28/90	23-21—	69
Wilt Chamberlain, Phi at Chi	12/16/67	30- 8—	68
Pete Maravich, NO vs NYK	2/25/77	26-16—	68
Wilt Chamberlain, Phi vs NY	3/9/61	27-13—	67
Wilt Chamberlain, Phi at St. L	2/17/62	26-15—	67
Wilt Chamberlain, Phi vs NY	2/25/62	25-17—	67
Wilt Chamberlain, SF vs LA	1/11/63	28-11—	67
Wilt Chamberlain, LA vs Pho	2/9/69	29- 8—	66
Wilt Chamberlain, Phi at Cin	2/13/62	24-17—	65
Wilt Chamberlain, Phi at St. L	2/27/62	25-15—	65
Wilt Chamberlain, Phi vs LA	2/7/66	28- 9—	65
Elgin Baylor, Mpls at Bos	11/8/59	25-14—	64
Rick Barry, GS vs Port	3/26/74	30- 4—	64
Michael Jordan, Chi vs Orl	1/16/93	27- 9—	64

*Overtime; ***Triple overtime.
Note: Chamberlain's 100-point game vs New York was played at Hershey, Pa.

Field Goals

	Date	FG	Att
Wilt Chamberlain, Phi vs NY	3/2/62	36	63
Wilt Chamberlain, Phi vs LA***	12/8/61	31	62
Wilt Chamberlain, Phi at Chi	12/16/67	30	40
Rick Barry, GS vs Port	2/26/74	30	45
Four players tied with 29 each.			

***Triple overtime.

Free Throws

	Date	FT	Att
Wilt Chamberlain, Phi vs NY	3/2/62	28	32
Adrian Dantley, Utah vs Hou	1/4/84	28	29
Adrian Dantley, Utah vs Den	11/25/83	27	31
Adrian Dantley, Utah vs Dal	10/31/80	26	29
Michael Jordan, Chi vs NJ	2/26/87	26	27

3-Pt Field Goals

	Date	No
Brian Shaw, Mia at Mil	4/8/93	10
Dale Ellis, Sea vs LA Clippers	4/20/90	9
Michael Adams, Den at LA Clippers	4/12/91	9
Seven tied with 8 each.		

Assists

	Date	No
Scott Skiles, Orl vs Den	12/30/90	30
Kevin Porter, NJ vs Hou	2/24/78	29
Bob Cousy, Bos vs Mpls	2/27/59	28
Guy Rodgers, SF vs St. L	3/14/63	28
John Stockton, Utah vs SA	1/15/91	28

Rebounds

	Date	No
Wilt Chamberlain, Phi vs Bos	11/24/60	55
Bill Russell, Bos vs Syr	2/5/60	51
Bill Russell, Bos vs Phi	11/16/57	49
Bill Russell, Bos vs Det	3/11/65	49
Wilt Chamberlain, Phi vs Syr	2/6/60	45
Wilt Chamberlain, Phi vs LA	1/21/61	45

Blocked Shots

	Date	No
Elmore Smith, LA vs Port	10/28/73	17
Manute Bol, Wash vs Atl	1/25/86	15
Manute Bol, Wash vs Ind	2/26/87	15
Shaquille O'Neal, Orl at NJ	11/20/93	15

Steals

	Date	No
Larry Kenon, San Antonio vs KC	2/9/80	11

11 different players tied with 10 each, including Alvin Robertson who has had 10 steals in a game four times.

All-Time Winningest NBA Coaches

Top 25 NBA career victories through the 1993-94 season. Career, regular season and playoff records are noted along with NBA titles won. Coaches active during 1993-94 season in **bold** type.

		Career			Regular Season			Playoffs			
	Yrs	W	L	Pct	W	L	Pct	W	L	Pct	NBA Titles
1 Red Auerbach	20	1037	548	.654	938	479	.662	99	69	.589	9 (1957,59-66)
2 **Lenny Wilkens**	21	986	835	.541	926	774	.545	60	61	.496	1 (1979)
3 Dick Motta	22	912	933	.494	856	863	.498	56	70	.444	1 (1978)
4 Jack Ramsay	21	908	841	.519	864	783	.525	44	58	.431	1 (1977)
5 Bill Fitch	21	900	928	.492	845	877	.491	55	51	.519	1 (1981)
6 **Don Nelson**	17	854	634	.574	803	573	.584	51	61	.455	None
7 Cotton Fitzsimmons	19	839	791	.515	805	745	.519	34	46	.425	None
8 **Pat Riley**	12	832	342	.709	701	272	.720	131	70	.652	4 (1982,85,87-88)
9 Gene Shue	22	814	908	.473	784	861	.477	30	47	.390	None
10 Red Holzman	18	754	651	.537	696	604	.535	58	47	.552	2 (1970,73)
John MacLeod	18	754	711	.515	707	657	.518	47	54	.465	None
12 Doug Moe	15	661	579	.533	628	529	.543	33	50	.398	None
13 **Chuck Daly**	12	638	427	.599	564	379	.598	74	48	.607	2 (1989-90)
14 K.C. Jones	10	603	309	.661	522	252	.674	81	57	.587	2 (1984,86)
15 Al Attles	14	588	548	.518	557	518	.518	31	30	.508	1 (1975)
16 Billy Cunningham	8	520	235	.689	454	196	.698	66	39	.629	1 (1983)
17 Alex Hannum	12	516	446	.536	471	412	.533	45	34	.570	2 (1958,67)
18 **Larry Brown**	11	510	409	.555	481	377	.561	29	32	.475	None
19 John Kundla	11	483	337	.589	423	302	.583	60	35	.632	5 (1949-50,52-54)
20 Tommy Heinsohn	9	474	296	.616	427	263	.619	47	33	.588	2 (1974,76)
21 Larry Costello	10	467	323	.591	430	300	.589	37	23	.617	1 (1971)
22 **Kevin Loughery**	16	463	654	.415	457	633	.419	6	21	.222	None
23 **Jerry Sloan**	9	425	325	.567	398	292	.577	27	33	.450	None
24 **Mike Fratello**	9	389	313	.554	371	288	.563	18	25	.419	None
25 Bill Russell	8	375	317	.542	341	290	.540	34	27	.557	2 (1968-69)

Note: The NBA does not recognize records from the National Basketball League (1937-49), the American Basketball League (1961-62) or the American Basketball Assn. (1968-76), so the following NBL, ABL and ABA overall coaching records are not included above: NBL— **Kundla** (51-19 and a title in 1 year). ABA— **Brown** (249-129 in 4 yrs), **Hannum** (194-164 and one title in 4 yrs), **Jones** (30-58 in 1 yr); **Loughery** (189-95 and one title in 3 yrs).

Where They Coached

Attles—Golden St. (1970-80,80-83); **Auerbach**—Washington (1946-49); Tri-Cities (1949-50); Boston (1950-66); **Brown**—Denver (1976-79), New Jersey (1981-83), San Antonio (1988-92), LA Clippers (1992-93), Indiana (1993—); **Costello**—Milwaukee (1968-76), Chicago (1978-79); **Cunningham**—Philadelphia (1977-85); **Daly**—Cleveland (1981-82), Detroit (1983-92), New Jersey (1992-94); **Fitch**—Cleveland (1970-79), Boston (1979-83), Houston (1983-88), New Jersey (1989-92), LA Clippers (1994—); **Fitzsimmons**—Phoenix (1970-72), Atlanta (1972-76), Buffalo (1977-78), Kansas City (1978-84), San Antonio (1984-86), Phoenix (1988-92); **Fratello**—Atlanta (1980-90), Cleveland (1993—).
Hannum—St. Louis (1957-58), Syracuse (1960-63), San Francisco (1963-66), Phila. 76ers (1966-68), Houston (1970-71); **Heinsohn**—Boston (1969-77); **Holzman**—Milwaukee-St. Louis Hawks (1954-57), NY Knicks (1968-77,78-82); **Jones**—Washington (1973-76), Boston (1983-88), Seattle (1990-92); **Kundla**—Minneapolis (1948-57,58-59); **Loughery**—Philadelphia (1972-73), NY-NJ Nets (1976-81), Atlanta (1981-83), Chicago (1983-85), Washington (1985-88), Miami (1991—); **MacLeod**—Phoenix (1973-87), Dallas (1987-89), NY Knicks (1990-91); **Moe**—San Antonio (1976-80), Denver (1981-90), Philadelphia (1992-93).
Motta—Chicago (1968-76), Washington (1976-80), Dallas (1980-87), Sacramento (1990-91), Dallas (1994—); **Nelson**—Milwaukee (1976-87), Golden St. (1988—); **Ramsay**—Philadelphia (1968-72), Buffalo (1972-76), Portland (1976-86), Indiana (1986-89); **Riley**—LA Lakers (1981-90), New York (1991—); **Russell**—Boston (1966-68), Seattle (1973-77), Sacramento (1987-88); **Shue**—Baltimore (1967-73), Philadelphia (1973-77), San Diego Clippers (1978-80), Washington (1980-86), LA Clippers (1987-89); **Sloan**—Chicago (1979-82), Utah (1988—); **Wilkens**—Seattle (1969-72), Portland (1974-76), Seattle (1977-85), Cleveland (1986-93), Atlanta (1993—).

All-Time Winningest NBA Coaches (Cont.)

Top Winning Percentages

Minimum of 350 victories, including playoffs; coaches active during 1993-94 season in **bold** type.

		Yrs	W	L	Pct
1	**Phil Jackson**	5	356	138	.721
2	**Pat Riley**	12	832	342	.709
3	Billy Cunningham	8	520	235	.689
4	K.C. Jones	10	603	309	.661
5	Red Auerbach	20	1037	548	.654
6	Tommy Heinsohn	9	474	296	.616
7	**Chuck Daly**	12	638	427	.599
8	Larry Costello	10	467	323	.591
9	John Kundla	11	483	337	.589
10	Bill Sharman	7	368	267	.580
11	**Don Nelson**	17	854	634	.574
12	Al Cervi	9	359	267	.573
13	**Jerry Sloan**	9	425	325	.567
14	Joe Lapchick	9	356	277	.562
15	**Larry Brown**	11	510	409	.555
16	**Mike Fratello**	9	389	313	.554
17	Bill Russell	8	375	317	.542
18	**Lenny Wilkens**	21	986	835	.541
19	Red Holzman	18	754	651	.537
20	Alex Hannum	12	516	446	.536
21	Doug Moe	15	661	579	.533
22	Richie Guerin	8	353	325	.521
23	Jack Ramsay	21	908	841	.519
24	Al Attles	14	588	548	.518
25	Cotton Fitzsimmons	19	839	791	.515
	John MacLeod	18	754	711	.515

Active Coaches' Victories

Through 1993-94 season, including playoffs.

		Yrs	W	L	Pct
1	Lenny Wilkens, Atlanta	21	986	835	.541
2	Dick Motta, Dallas	22	912	933	.494
3	Bill Fitch, LA Clippers	21	900	928	.492
4	Don Nelson, Golden St	17	854	634	.574
5	Pat Riley, New York	12	832	342	.709
6	Larry Brown, Indiana	11	510	409	.555
7	Kevin Loughery, Miami	16	463	654	.415
8	Jerry Sloan, Utah	9	425	325	.567
9	Mike Fratello, Cleveland	9	389	313	.554
10	Phil Jackson, Chicago	5	356	138	.721
11	Del Harris, LA Lakers	9	353	372	.487
12	George Karl, Seattle	7	285	263	.520
13	Jim Lynam, Washington	7	254	277	.478
14	Don Chaney, Detroit	8	239	337	.415
15	Chris Ford, Boston	4	199	154	.564
16	Mike Dunleavy, Milwaukee	4	162	189	.462
17	Rudy Tomjanovich, Houston	3	150	79	.655
18	Allan Bristow, Charlotte	2	120	135	.471
19	Paul Westphal, Phoenix	2	137	61	.692
20	Bob Hill, San Antonio	4	136	163	.455
21	John Lucas, Philadelphia	2	100	57	.637
22	Dan Issel, Denver	2	84	92	.477
23	Garry St. Jean, Sacramento	2	53	111	.323
24	Brian Hill, Orlando	1	50	35	.588
25	Butch Beard, New York	0	0	0	.000
	Bill Blair, Minnesota	0	0	0	.000
	P.J. Carlesimo, Portland	0	0	0	.000

Annual Awards
Most Valuable Player

The Maurice Podoloff Trophy for regular season MVP. Named after the first commissioner (then president) of the NBA. Winners first selected by the NBA players (1956-80) then a national panel of pro basketball writers and broadcasters (since 1981). Winners' scoring averages are provided; (*) indicates led league.

Multiple winners: Kareem Abdul-Jabbar (6); Bill Russell (5); Wilt Chamberlain (4); Larry Bird, Magic Johnson, Michael Jordan and Moses Malone (3); Bob Pettit (2).

Year		Avg	Year		Avg
1956	Bob Pettit, St. Louis, F	25.7*	1976	Kareem Abdul-Jabbar, LA, C	27.7
1957	Bob Cousy, Boston, G	20.6	1977	Kareem Abdul-Jabbar, LA, C	26.2
1958	Bill Russell, Boston, C	16.6	1978	Bill Walton, Portland, C	18.9
1959	Bob Pettit, St. Louis, F	29.2*	1979	Moses Malone, Houston, C	24.8
1960	Wilt Chamberlain, Philadelphia, C	37.6*	1980	Kareem Abdul-Jabbar, LA, C	24.8
1961	Bill Russell, Boston, C	16.9	1981	Julius Erving, Philadelphia, F	24.6
1962	Bill Russell, Boston, C	18.9	1982	Moses Malone, Houston, C	31.1
1963	Bill Russell, Boston, C	16.8	1983	Moses Malone, Philadelphia, C	24.5
1964	Oscar Robertson, Cincinnati, G	31.4	1984	Larry Bird, Boston, F	24.2
1965	Bill Russell, Boston, C	14.1	1985	Larry Bird, Boston, F	28.7
1966	Wilt Chamberlain, Philadelphia, C	33.5*	1986	Larry Bird, Boston, F	25.8
1967	Wilt Chamberlain, Philadelphia, C	24.1	1987	Magic Johnson, LA Lakers, G	23.9
1968	Wilt Chamberlain, Philadelphia, C	24.3	1988	Michael Jordan, Chicago, G	35.0*
1969	Wes Unseld, Baltimore, C	13.8	1989	Magic Johnson, LA Lakers, G	22.5
1970	Willis Reed, New York, C	21.7	1990	Magic Johnson, LA Lakers, G	22.3
1971	Lew Alcindor, Milwaukee, C	31.7*	1991	Michael Jordan, Chicago, G	31.5*
1972	Kareem Abdul-Jabbar, Milwaukee, C	34.8*	1992	Michael Jordan, Chicago, G	30.1*
1973	Dave Cowens, Boston, C	20.5	1993	Charles Barkley, Phoenix, F	25.6
1974	Kareem Abdul-Jabbar, LA, C	27.0	1994	Hakeem Olajuwon, Houston, C	27.3
1975	Bob McAdoo, Buffalo, F	34.5*			

Note: Alcindor changed his name to Kareem Abdul-Jabbar after the 1970-71 season.

Defensive Player of the Year

Awarded to the Best Defensive Player for the regular season. Winners selected by a national panel of pro basketball writers and broadcasters.

Multiple winners: Mark Eaton, Sidney Moncrief, Hakeem Olajuwon and Dennis Rodman (2).

Year		Year		Year	
1983	Sidney Moncrief, Mil., G	1987	Michael Cooper, LAL, F	1991	Dennis Rodman, Det., F
1984	Sidney Moncrief, Mil., G	1988	Michael Jordan, Chi., G	1992	David Robinson, SA, C
1985	Mark Eaton, Utah, C	1989	Mark Eaton, Utah, C	1993	Hakeem Olajuwon, Hou., C
1986	Alvin Robertson, SA, G	1990	Dennis Rodman, Det., F	1994	Hakeem Olajuwon, Hou., C

Rookie of the Year

The Eddie Gottlieb Trophy for outstanding rookie of the regular season. Named after the pro basketball pioneer and owner-coach of the first NBA champion Philadelphia Warriors. Winners selected by a national panel of pro basketball writers and broadcasters. Winners' scoring averages provided; (*) indicates led league; winners who were also named MVP are in **bold** type.

Year		Year		Year	
1953	Don Meineke, Ft.Wayne, F	1968	Earl Monroe, Bal., G	1981	Darrell Griffith, Utah, G
1954	Ray Felix, Bal., C	1969	**Wes Unseld**, Bal., C	1982	Buck Williams, NJ, F
1955	Bob Pettit, Mil., F			1983	Terry Cummings, SD, F
1956	Maurice Stokes, Roch., F/C	1970	Lew Alcindor, Mil., C	1984	Ralph Sampson, Hou., C
1957	Tommy Heinsohn, Bos., F	1971	Dave Cowens, Bos., C	1985	Michael Jordan, Chi., G
1958	Woody Sauldsberry, Phi., F/C		& Geoff Petrie, Port., F	1986	Patrick Ewing, NY, C
1959	Elgin Baylor, Mpls., F	1972	Sidney Wicks, Port., F	1987	Chuck Person, Ind., F
		1973	Bob McAdoo, Buf., C/F	1988	Mark Jackson, NY, G
1960	**Wilt Chamberlain**, Phi., C	1974	Ernie DiGregorio, Buf., G	1989	Mitch Richmond, G.St., G
1961	Oscar Robertson, Cin., G	1975	Keith Wilkes, GS, F		
1962	Walt Bellamy, Chi., C	1976	Alvan Adams, Pho., C	1990	David Robinson, SA, C
1963	Terry Dischinger, Chi., F	1977	Adrian Dantley, Buf., F	1991	Derrick Coleman, NJ, F
1964	Jerry Lucas, Cin., F/C	1978	Walter Davis, Pho., G	1992	Larry Johnson, Char., F
1965	Willis Reed, NY, C	1979	Phil Ford, KC, G	1993	Shaquille O'Neal, Orl., C
1966	Rick Barry, SF, F			1994	Chris Webber, GS, C
1967	Dave Bing, Det., G	1980	Larry Bird, Bos., F		

Note: Alcindor changed his name to Kareem Abdul-Jabbar after the 1970-71 season.

Coach of the Year

The Red Auerbach Trophy for outstanding coach of the year. Renamed in 1967 for the former Boston coach who led the Celtics to nine NBA titles. Winners selected by a national panel of pro basketball writers and broadcasters. Previous season and winning season records are provided; (*) indicates division title.

Multiple winners: Don Nelson (3); Bill Fitch, Cotton Fitzsimmons, Pat Riley and Gene Shue (2).

Year		Improvement		Year		Improvement	
1963	Harry Gallatin, St. L	29-51	to 48-32	1980	Bill Fitch, Bos	29-53	to 61-21*
1964	Alex Hannum, SF	31-49	to 48-32*	1981	Jack McKinney, Ind	37-45	to 44-38
1965	Red Auerbach, Bos	59-21*	to 61-18*	1982	Gene Shue, Wash	39-43	to 43-39
1966	Dolph Schayes, Phi	40-40	to 55-25*	1983	Don Nelson, Mil	55-27*	to 51-31*
1967	Johnny Kerr, Chi	Expan.	to 33-48	1984	Frank Layden, Utah	30-52	to 45-37*
1968	Richie Guerin, St. L	39-42	to 56-26*	1985	Don Nelson, Mil	50-32*	to 59-23*
1969	Gene Shue, Balt	36-46	to 57-25*	1986	Mike Fratello, Atl	34-48	to 50-32
1970	Red Holzman, NY	54-28	to 60-22*	1987	Mike Schuler, Port	40-42	to 49-33
1971	Dick Motta, Chi	39-43	to 51-31	1988	Doug Moe, Den	37-45	to 54-28*
1972	Bill Sharman, LA	48-34*	to 69-13*	1989	Cotton Fitzsimmons, Pho	28-54	to 55-27
1973	Tommy Heinsohn, Bos	56-26*	to 68-14*	1990	Pat Riley, LA Lakers	57-25*	to 63-19*
1974	Ray Scott, Det	40-42	to 52-30	1991	Don Chaney, Hou	41-41	to 52-30
1975	Phil Johnson, KC-Omaha	33-49	to 44-38	1992	Don Nelson, GS	44-38	to 55-27
1976	Bill Fitch, Cle	40-42	to 49-33*	1993	Pat Riley, NY	51-31	to 60-22
1977	Tom Nissalke, Hou	40-42	to 49-33*	1994	Lenny Wilkens, Atl	43-39	to 57-25*
1978	Hubie Brown, Atl	31-51	to 41-41				
1979	Cotton Fitzsimmons, KC	31-51	to 48-34*				

Number One Draft Choices

Overall first choices in the NBA Draft since the abolition of the Territorial Draft in 1966. Players who became Rookie of the Year are in **bold** type.

Year		Overall 1st Pick	Year		Overall 1st Pick
1966	New York	Cazzie Russell, Michigan	1982	LA Lakers	James Worthy, N. Carolina
1967	Detroit	Jimmy Walker, Providence	1983	Houston	**Ralph Sampson**, Virginia
1968	San Diego	Elvin Hayes, Houston	1984	Houston	Akeem Olajuwon, Houston
1969	Milwaukee	**Lew Alcindor,** UCLA	1985	New York	**Patrick Ewing**, Georgetown
1970	Detroit	Bob Lanier, St. Bonaventure	1986	Cleveland	Brad Daugherty, N. Carolina
1971	Cleveland	Austin Carr, Notre Dame	1987	San Antonio	**David Robinson**, Navy
1972	Portland	LaRue Martin, Loyola-Chicago	1988	LA Clippers	Danny Manning, Kansas
1973	Philadelphia	Doug Collins, Illinois St.	1989	Sacramento	Pervis Ellison, Louisville
1974	Portland	Bill Walton, UCLA			
1975	Atlanta	David Thompson, N.C. State	1990	New Jersey	**Derrick Coleman**, Syracuse
1976	Houston	John Lucas, Maryland	1991	Charlotte	**Larry Johnson**, UNLV
1977	Milwaukee	Kent Benson, Indiana	1992	Orlando	**Shaquille O'Neal**, LSU
1978	Portland	Mychal Thompson, Minnesota	1993	Orlando	**Chris Weber**, Michigan
1979	LA Lakers	Magic Johnson, Michigan St.	1994	Milwaukee	Glenn Robinson, Purdue
1980	Golden St	Joe Barry Carroll, Purdue			
1981	Dallas	Mark Aguirre, DePaul			

Note: Alcindor changed his name to Kareem Abdul-Jabbar after the 1970-71 season; Olajuwon changed his first name to Hakeem in 1991; and Robinson joined NBA for 1989-90 season after fulfilling military obligation.

American Basketball Association
ABA Finals

The American Basketball Assn. began play in 1967-68 as a 10-team rival of the 21-year-old NBA. The ABA, which introduced the three-point basket, a multi-colored ball and the All-Star Game Slam Dunk Contest, lasted nine seasons before folding following the 1975-76 season. Four ABA teams—Denver, Indiana, New York and San Antonio—survived to enter the NBA in 1976-77. The NBA also adopted the 3-pt basket (in 1979-80) and the All-Star Game Slam Dunk Contest. The older league, however, refused to take in the ABA ball.

Multiple winners: Indiana (3); New York (2).

Year	Winner	Head Coach	Series	Loser	Head Coach
1968	Pittsburgh Pipers	Vince Cazetta	4-2 (WLLWLWW)	New Orleans Bucs	Babe McCarthy
1969	Oakland Oaks	Alex Hannum	4-1 (WLWWW)	Indiana Pacers	Bob Leonard
1970	Indiana Pacers	Bob Leonard	4-2 (WWLWLW)	Los Angeles Stars	Bill Sharman
1971	Utah Stars	Bill Sharman	4-3 (WWLLWLW)	Kentucky Colonels	Frank Ramsey
1972	Indiana Pacers	Bob Leonard	4-2 (WLWLWW)	New York Nets	Lou Carnesecca
1973	Indiana Pacers	Bob Leonard	4-3 (WLLWWLW)	Kentucky Colonels	Joe Mullaney
1974	New York Nets	Kevin Loughery	4-1 (WWWLW)	Utah Stars	Joe Mullaney
1975	Kentucky Colonels	Hubie Brown	4-1 (WWWLW)	Indiana Pacers	Bob Leonard
1976	New York Nets	Kevin Loughery	4-2 (WLWWLW)	Denver Nuggets	Larry Brown

Most Valuable Player

Winners' scoring averages provided; (*) indicates led league.

Multiple winners: Julius Erving (3); Mel Daniels (2).

Year		Pts
1968	Connie Hawkins, Pittsburgh, C	26.8*
1969	Mel Daniels, Indiana, C	24.0
1970	Spencer Haywood, Denver, C	30.0*
1971	Mel Daniels, Indiana, C	21.0
1972	Artis Gilmore, Kentucky, C	23.8
1973	Billy Cunningham, Carolina, F	24.1
1974	Julius Erving, New York, F	27.4*
1975	George McGinnis, Indiana, F	29.8*
	& Julius Erving, New York, F	27.9
1976	Julius Erving, New York, F	29.3*

Rookie of the Year

Winners' scoring averages provided; (*) indicates led league. Rookies who were also named Most Valuable Player are in bold type.

Year		Pts
1968	Mel Daniels, Minnesota, C	22.2
1969	Warren Armstrong, Oakland, G	21.5
1970	**Spencer Haywood, Denver, C**	30.0*
1971	Dan Issel, Kentucky, C	29.8*
	& Charlie Scott, Virginia, G	27.1
1972	Artis Gilmore, Kentucky, C	23.8
1973	Brian Taylor, New York, G	15.3
1974	Swen Nater, Virginia-SA, C	14.1
1975	Marvin Barnes, St. Louis, C	24.0
1976	David Thompson, Denver, F	26.0

Note: Armstrong changed his name to Warren Jabali after the 1970-71 season.

Coach of the Year

Previous season and winning season records are provided; (*) indicates division title.

Multiple winner: Larry Brown (3).

Year		Improvement
1968	Vince Cazetta, Pittsburgh	54-24*
1969	Alex Hannum, Oakland	22-56 to 60-18*
1970	Joe Belmont, Denver	44-34 to 51-33*
	& Bill Sharman, LA Stars	33-45 to 43-41
1971	Al Bianchi, Virginia	44-40 to 55-29*
1972	Tom Nissalke, Dallas	30-54 to 42-42
1973	Larry Brown, Carolina	35-49 to 57-27*
1974	Babe McCarthy, Kentucky	56-28 to 53-31
	& Joe Mullaney, Utah	55-29* to 51-33*
1975	Larry Brown, Denver	37-47 to 65-19*
1976	Larry Brown, Denver	65-19* to 60-24*

Scoring Leaders

Scoring championship decided by per game point average.
Multiple winner: Julius Erving (3).

Year		Gm	Avg	Pts
1968	Connie Hawkins, Pittsburgh	70	1875	26.8
1969	Rick Barry, Oakland	35	1190	34.0
1970	Spencer Haywood, Denver	84	2519	30.0
1971	Dan Issel, Kentucky	83	2480	29.8
1972	Charlie Scott, Virginia	73	2524	34.6
1973	Julius Erving, Virginia	71	2268	31.9
1974	Julius Erving, NY Mets	84	2299	27.4
1975	George McGinnis, Indiana	79	2353	29.8
1976	Julius Erving, NY Nets	84	2462	29.3

ABA All-Star Game

The ABA All-Star Game was an Eastern Division vs Western Division contest from 1968-75. League membership had dropped to seven teams by 1976, the ABA's last season, so the team in first place at the break (Denver) played an All-Star team made up from the other six clubs.

Series: East won 5, West 3 and Denver 1.

Year	Result	Host	Coaches	Most Valuable Player
1968	East 126, West 120	Indiana	Jim Pollard, Babe McCarthy	Larry Brown, New Orleans
1969	West 133, East 127	Louisville	Alex Hannum, Gene Rhodes	John Beasley, Dallas
1970	West 128, East 98	Indiana	Babe McCarthy, Bob Leonard	Spencer Haywood, Denver
1971	East 126, West 122	Carolina	Al Bianchi, Bill Sharman	Mel Daniels, Indiana
1972	East 142, West 115	Louisville	Joe Mullaney, Ladell Andersen	Dan Issel, Kentucky
1973	West 123, East 111	Utah	Ladell Andersen, Larry Brown	Warren Jabali, Denver
1974	East 128, West 112	Virginia	Babe McCarthy, Joe Mullaney	Artis Gilmore, Kentucky
1975	East 151, West 124	San Antonio	Kevin Loughery, Larry Brown	Freddie Lewis, St. Louis
1976	Denver 144, ABA 138	Denver	Larry Brown, Kevin Loughery	David Thompson, Denver

New York Rangers' captain **Mark Messier** gleefully accepts the Stanley Cup following his club's thrilling Game 7 victory over Vancouver at Madison Square Garden.

HOCKEY

by Eric Duhatschek

Garden Party

Cursed for 54 years, the New York Rangers finally win back the Stanley Cup, hanging on to defeat Vancouver in Game 7.

Legend has it that shortly after the New York Rangers won the Stanley Cup for the third time in 1940, they were cursed. Not once but twice.

In 1941, Gen. John Reed Kilpatrick, president of both the Rangers and Madison Square Garden, incurred the wrath of the hockey gods when he celebrated paying off the Garden's mortgage by burning the papers in the Cup.

In 1942, the New York Americans, the Garden's original National Hockey League tenant, went bust and their embittered coach and general manager Red Dutton blamed the Rangers for running the Amerks out of business. Dutton, who vowed that the Rangers would never win the Cup again in his lifetime, died in 1987.

He was right and then some.

Entering the 1993-94 NHL season, the Rangers had not only failed to win the Cup in 53 years, they had been to the finals just three times (in 1950, '72 and '79). Uncannily poor luck dogged the club for decades. In the 24 years from 1943 to 1966, they missed the playoffs 18 times. Fan favorites like Andy Bathgate and Gump Worsley didn't play for a Cup winner until they were traded away. Proven champions like Doug Harvey, Jacques Plante and Phil Esposito were acquired past their prime, but to no avail.

Eric Duhatschek has covered the NHL for the *Calgary Herald* since 1980. He is also a columnist for *The Hockey News*.

To make matters worse, the New York Islanders had come along as an expansion team in 1972 and skated off with consecutive Cup titles from 1980-83. The Islanders made it look easy and their fans rubbed it in, taunting the Rangers with the chant, "1940," at every opportunity. No NHL team had ever gone longer between championships.

Somewhere, Red Dutton was smiling.

Enter Mark Messier. The Rangers acquired the former Edmonton captain and catalyst of five Stanley Cup championships on Oct. 4, 1991. And Messier provided immediate results. After being named captain, he won his second Hart Trophy as MVP and led his new club to the league's best regular season record. But then the Rangers reverted to form, losing in the second round of the 1992 playoffs and missing the postseason altogether in '93.

The curse.

"Right from the start of this season, we knew if we tried to take on the 54-year history of the Rangers [since 1940], it would be too much," said Messier. "When you put on a Ranger sweater, you buy into the fact that you are involved in all the things that have gone on in the past."

Mike Keenan, who signed a five-year contract to coach the Rangers on April, 17, 1993, encouraged his players to feed off 1940, not run from it. If they could put an end to all the bad karma, they would be the talk of the town.

The Rangers' mystique made their 1994

New York goaltender **Mike Richter** stops Vancouver's **Pavel Bure** on a penalty shot attempt during the second period of Game 4 of the Stanley Cup Final. The Rangers won the game for a 3-1 series lead, but the Canucks extended them to seven games.

Stanley Cup Final with Vancouver one of the most compelling in years. So did the quality of the hockey. Only once in the previous 23 seasons did the Final go seven games. That was in 1987 (Edmonton vs. Philadephia), and several of the same players were back seven years later.

Six members of the '87 Oilers— Messier, Glenn Anderson, Jeff Beukeboom, Kevin Lowe, Craig MacTavish and Esa Tikkanen— were now Rangers. Keenan coached the Flyers in '87 and one of his players then, Murray Craven, was now with the Canucks.

After turning in the NHL's best regular season record (52-24-8, 112 points), the Rangers cruised through the opening two playoff rounds in just nine games— shaking off the Islanders in four straight and the Washington Capitals in five. Goaltender Mike Richter, who led the NHL in regular season wins with 42, showed the way with three shutouts.

The Eastern Conference finals were a different story, however, as the New Yorkers fell behind the New Jersey Devils and their Rookie of the Year goalie Martin Brodeur, 3 games to 2. Before Game 6, Messier

stepped forward and guaranteed a victory at the Meadowlands. He then went out and scored three third-period goals to erase a two-goal Devils' lead and win the game 4-2. It was easily the most memorable night of the playoffs.

Afterwards, Messier said: "No one man wins a hockey game or a championship or anything in team sports. It [his prediction] wasn't about being cocky or arrogant. It was one of those things you have to do to get the team to believe in itself."

Added Devils' center Bernie Nicholls: "He leads and they follow. That's why, in my opinion, Messier is the best money player in the game. When the chips are down and there is a big game to be won, there is nobody better."

In Game 7, which went into double overtime, the Ranger hero was winger Stephane Matteau, a mid-season pick-up from Chicago, who thrilled the Madison Square Garden faithful by scoring the game winner at 4:24 of the extra period.

In the Cup Final, New York faced overachieving Vancouver. Little more than a .500 team during the regular season (41-

40-3, 85 points) and seeded seventh in the West, the Canucks nevertheless rallied from a 3-games-to-1 deficit to upset Calgary then knocked off Dallas and Toronto in five games each.

Against the Rangers, Vancouver took Game 1 in overtime, then lost three straight to fall behind three games to one. New York was one victory away from recapturing the Cup. The drought was over. Game 5 was at the Garden and a foregone conclusion. All that remained was the ticker-tape parade up Broadway.

Instead of finishing the Canucks off, however, the Rangers lost Games 5 and 6 by three goals each, 6-3 in New York and 4-1 in Vancouver. The series was suddenly and incredibly tied.

As MacTavish put it the day before the climatic Game 7: Despite 52 regular-season wins and 15 more in the playoffs, the Rangers' season would be judged on the basis of one game. Win and they go down in history as the team that finally broke the curse. Lose and they were chokers, only the second team in the history of the Stanley Cup Final to blow a 3-1 series lead.

On June 14, the Rangers completed the longest NHL season ever (253 days) in memorable, heart-stopping fashion. Messier lived up to his reputation as one of the game's great clutch players, by scoring the winning goal in a 3-2 victory.

For the final 20 minutes of the game, the Canucks pressed the attack relentlessly, memories of their 11th-hour comeback against Calgary dancing in their heads. The Rangers looked like an aging heavyweight, ahead on the scorecard, but just hanging on the ropes, waiting to be saved by the bell.

In the last minute, defenseman Brian Leetch slid across the front of the Ranger net to block Jyrki Lumme's path to the goal, maybe the best chance the Canucks had to tie it and force overtime. Messier then tied up Craven twice in the face-off circle and time finally ran out on the curse.

The long-suffering denizens of the Garden let out a cheer they (and their ancestors) had been holding back since before World War II.

"I've been in the game 16 years and won five Stanley Cups," said Messier afterward, "but I've never experienced anything like the last two months. I wasn't saying much,

802nd Goal By Gretzky Passes Howe

The watch began in early March when Wayne Gretzky edged to within four goals of Gordie Howe's all-time National Hockey League goalscoring record by putting No. 797 past the Hartford Whalers' Sean Burke.

Gretzky once scored five goals in a game and even if his numbers had been dropping off in recent years, everybody knew it was only a matter of time before he broke the one NHL record that had seemed beyond even his reach.

Baseball saw Babe Ruth's career home run record of 714 fall to Hank Aaron on April 8, 1974. Two weeks shy of 20 years later, on March 23, 1994, Gretzky completed the hockey equivalent to Aaron's historic feat— scoring the 802nd goal of his NHL career to pass the legendary Howe.

For the record, the Great One scored the Big One off Vancouver goalie Kirk McLean at 14:47 of the second period in a 6-3 loss to the Canucks at the Great Western Forum in Los Angeles. NHL officials stopped the game at that point for a brief ceremony. Gretzky's family and friends were there, everybody that mattered to him in fact, except Howe.

Howe and Gretzky share a lot of history. Growing up in Brantford, Ontario, Gretzky idolized Howe, the great right wing of the Detroit Red Wings. And even if some coolness developed in the relationship over the years, the two share a healthy respect for one another's accomplishments.

In the days leading up to his record-breaking night, Gretzky wasn't sure if this— the 62nd record of his career— would be the most enduring. He figured there was a pretty good chance. Historically, hockey is a game of ebb and flow. With the current 84-game schedule, it's possible that someone will eventually come along to challenge Gretzky's record, but it doesn't seem likely.

If he plays two more seasons, Gretzky could easily score 850 career goals.

"That's 17 years at 50 goals a year," he says. There are people who are talented enough to do it, but you have to be on the right team, you have to be healthy and you have to stay around a long time.

"Sports have changed so much now that fewer and fewer athletes are staying that 15

Gordie Howe (left) playfully highsticks 11-year-old **Wayne Gretzky** at a 1972 banquet in Toronto. Twenty-two years later, Gretzky holds up record book presented to him after he scored his 802nd career goal to break Howe's all-time NHL scoring record.

to 20 years that they used to in the fifties, sixties and seventies."

The record was especially pleasing because Gretzky is not known for scoring goals.

"My forte was playmaking," says Gretzky. "When people ask: 'If you saw Wayne Gretzky play, what would you be watching for?' The first thing everybody says is: 'Watch how he passes the puck and sees the ice.' You rarely hear people say: 'Watch out for his slapshot, it's pretty quick.'

"If you were to ask me who the three best goal scorers in history were, I'd be the first to say Howe, Phil Esposito and Rocket Richard. I wouldn't make any bones about it. That's what makes breaking this record so unique."

Howe insists that the key career goal scoring record is his all-time professional total of 975, which includes 174 goals scored in the World Hockey Association from 1973-79. Even so, it doesn't diminish what Gretzky has accomplished.

The 33-year-old Kings' center has set so many records during his 15-year NHL career (see page 406) that your eyes glaze over whenever you hear he's established another one. That, too, is unfortunate. Gretzky's 802nd NHL goal was not just any record. It was THE record. And he did it in 1,117 games— 650 fewer than the 1,767 Howe needed to score 801.

Can you compare hockey across the generations? Maybe not. Many people believe that in the old six-team league, Gretzky wouldn't have been as productive a scorer because he wouldn't have been as durable. There were also no expansion teams to beat up on prior to 1967. A last-place team in 1966 would have been a playoff contender in 1994.

On the other hand, players weren't as fit back then and travel wasn't nearly as difficult. It's a moot point anyway. You can argue that other players have been more spectacular or more complete players. But you cannot argue that anyone has been more prolific than Gretzky.

What made the record bittersweet was that in March, as Gretzky closed in on Howe, it became increasingly clear that the Kings would miss the playoffs. For a team that went all the way to the Cup Final in 1993, that was a shocking comeuppance. For a player who had never missed the playoffs in 14 previous NHL seasons, the disappointment hit hard.

"We just weren't very consistent," he said.

Things were even worse for Bruce McNall, the man who brought Gretzky to L.A. in 1988. Debt-ridden and under federal investigation for allegedly falsifying loan documents, McNall was obliged to sell 72 percent of the Kings for $60 million and declare bankruptcy.

but in my own mind, I was saying: 'This is absolutely incredible.'"

Complicating matters was the fact that between Games 6 and 7, rumors spread that Rangers' coach Mike Keenan would bolt from New York following the series to become general manager of the Detroit Red Wings. On the morning before Game 7, Keenan awoke to a *New York Post* headline that likened him to Benedict Arnold, the legendary traitor.

"I can deny the rumors entirely," said Keenan. "I am not going to Detroit. I signed a five-year deal with the New York Rangers last year. There is no escape clause and I am not looking for an escape clause."

The ensuing uproar could have had a negative effect on a less poised team. However, for three years, Rangers' GM Neil Smith had been assembling the best team money could buy, wishing and hoping that if a Stanley Cup Final ever came down to a single game, the composure that Messier and the five other ex-Oilers could provide would prove decisive. It was.

Leetch, the team's mercurial defenseman, led all scorers with 34 points and won the Conn Smythe Trophy as playoff MVP. As the first American player so honored, he was saluted by a phone call from President Clinton, another Stanley Cup first.

The Rangers' dramatic victory topped off a very good year for the NHL— on the ice, in the boardroom and at the cash register. There were signs that, under new, 42-year-old commissioner Gary Bettman, hockey was winning the battle for acceptance in the U.S. For starters, the message about violence was finally sinking in. Hockey doesn't have bench-clearing brawls anymore— a stereotype perpetuated by talking heads on TV that does not jibe with reality. Baseball and basketball annually feature more ugly brawls than hockey.

Bettman also managed to tap dance around the issue of a possible players' strike all season long. The players were in a legal strike position from Sept. 15 on, but Bettman kept the lines of communication open with Bob Goodenow, head of the players' union. Nothing was resolved, but they were able to get the season in without a repeat of the 10-day strike that occurred two years previously.

There was one work stoppage that Bettman did have to deal with, however.

NHL referees and linesmen walked off the job in mid-November to protest low salaries. Anticipating the strike, the league set up training camps for replacement officials well in advance. So when the regular officials went out, the league was ready and no games had to be cancelled. The work of the replacements was erratic— sometimes good, usually adequate, occasionally horrific. Eventually, after a 17-day strike, the league and the officials settled their dispute.

Hockey's two most durable stars, Wayne Gretzky of Los Angeles and Ray Bourque of Boston, each marked his 15th NHL season in style. Gretzky broke Gordie Howe's all-time NHL goal-scoring record (see sidebar) and led the league in points for the 10th time, while Bourque led all defensemen in points and won his fifth Norris Trophy.

Pittsburgh's Mario Lemieux, however, missed 62 games following back surgery a year after his remarkable comeback from radiation treatments for Hodgkin's disease. The Penguins lost to Washington in the first round of the playoffs due, in part, to a tired and leg-weary Lemieux who was later said to be suffering from anemia— a deficiency in the oxygen-carrying material of the blood that can occur as long as two years after radiation therapy.

Elsewhere, the year also saw the debut of two more expansion franchises, the Mighty Ducks of Anaheim and the Florida Panthers, both of which were wildly successful. It helped that, in addition to the usual castoffs, the league made quality goaltenders available in the expansion draft. Florida chose ex-Ranger and Vezina Trophy winner John Vanbiesbrouck with their No. 1 pick, while the Ducks relied on the tandem of Guy Hebert and Ron Tugnutt most of the season.

With Vanbiesbrouck leading the way— he ended up as a finalist for the Hart Trophy as the league's MVP— the Panthers stayed in the playoff race until the final weekend. Only a late-season collapse kept them from edging the Islanders for the eighth seed in the East. Florida finished with 33 wins, the same as the Ducks, a record for a first-year NHL expansion team.

The only thing more amazing than their play was the performance by the San Jose Sharks in their third season. The Sharks, whose 1992-93 record was a toothless 11-

The **San Jose Sharks** went from toothless to terrifying in 1993-94, finishing third behind Calgary and Vancouver in the Pacific Division with 82 points and upsetting Detroit in the first round of the playoffs.

71-2 for 24 points, went 33-35-16 for 82 points and a playoff berth under rookie coach Kevin Constantine. Their 58-point turnaround was the largest in NHL history. Then, in the opening round of the playoffs, they knocked off the top-seeded team in the Western Conference, the Detroit Red Wings, in one of the biggest upsets in Stanley Cup history.

The Sharks were led by Latvian goaltender Arturs Irbe, who established an NHL record by playing 4,412 minutes, breaking a 22-year-old mark held by former Flyers' great Bernie Parent.

Irbe's strong play in goal was mirrored around the NHL in what became known as the year of the goaltender. In 1992-93, only two goaltenders with 25 or more games played finished with a goals-against averages under 3.00. A year later, 19 goalies did it, led by Buffalo's Dominik Hasek, who became the first netminder since Parent to register a goals-against aveage under 2.00.

Part of the improvement in team defense could be traced to the "neutral zone trap," popularized by coaches like Constantine and Florida's Roger Neilson.

Buffalo's John Muckler earned a nomination for Coach of the Year, mainly because his team used the trap so well. Forced to play much of the season without scoring threats Pat LaFontaine and Craig Simpson, Muckler, who used to coach the free-wheeling Oilers in their glory days, convinced his team that the only way to be competitive was to play defense first.

The Sabres qualified as the No. 6 seed in the East and took the Devils to seven games before losing in the opening round. The best example of the trap at work came in Game 6 of that series which featured six scoreless periods before Buffalo emerged with a 1-0 win in quadruple overtime.

The year also marked another step forward for the internationalization of the NHL. For the first time in history, a Russian— Detroit center Sergei Fedorov— won the Hart Trophy as league MVP and a Czech— Hasek of Buffalo— won the Vezina Trophy as the league's top goaltender. Also, for the second year in a row, a

Detroit center **Sergei Fedorov** (right) takes puck away from Winnipeg's **Teemu Selanne** during a regular season game. Fedorov was runner-up to Wayne Gretzky in the scoring race with 120 points and became the first Russian winner of the Hart Trophy as MVP.

European— this time, Russian Pavel Bure of Vancouver— led the league in goalscoring.

Moreover, the myth that Europeans do not perform well in the playoffs was pretty much shattered in 1994. Five of the Top 15 scoring leaders in the playoffs were Russians, led by the 23-year-old Bure, who had 16 goals. And four members of the Rangers— Alexander Karpovtsev, Alexei Kovalev, Sergei Nemchinov and Sergei Zubov— became the first Russian-trained players to win the Stanley Cup.

In the end, the Rangers' win was as much about New York as it was about hockey. Even by pro sports standards, the scene inside the Garden was wild. Spectators chanted "We want the Cup." Ticket scalpers were getting upwards of $2,000 for a choice seat. One report, confirmed by a Rangers' front office source, said a Wall St. brokerage firm paid $17,000 for four tickets to Game 5 of the Cup Final.

New Yorkers treated the win as a cathartic experience. After so many failures, finally success. After so many heartaches, sweet release.

The good feeling lasted exactly 31 days.

On July 15, Keenan announced the Rangers were a day late with his playoff bonus and he was leaving. Two days after that, he signed a five-year deal as coach and GM in St. Louis.

New York went ballistic. "It Stinks!" screamed the front page of the *New York Post*. "He's a Liar" claimed *Newsday*. The Rangers sued Keenan in federal court, calling him a "faithless employee," who had betrayed the team and its millions of fans.

By the time Bettman stepped in on July 24 to resolve the mess, the damage was done. Keenan could go, but he was suspended 60 days (through Sept. 24) and fined $100,000. The Rangers had to pay him his $608,00 playoff bonus, but Keenan had to give back $400,000 in repayment of his 1993 signing bonus. The Blues were fined $250,000 for signing Keenan and the Red Wings were out $25,000 for talking to him about coming to Detroit.

Finally, the Blues were allowed to trade center Petr Nedved as compensation to New York in exchange for Tikkanen and defenseman Doug Lidster.

No word on any curses. ❑

Final NHL Standings

Division champions (*) and playoff qualifiers (†) are noted. Number of seasons listed after each head coach refers to latest tenure with club through 1993-94 season. Note that Anaheim (Pacific) and Florida (Atlantic) were expansion teams.

Western Conference
Pacific Division

	W	L	T	Pts	For	Opp	Dif
*Calgary	42	29	13	97	302	256	+46
†Vancouver	41	40	3	85	279	276	+3
†San Jose	33	35	16	82	252	265	–13
Anaheim	33	46	5	71	229	251	–22
Los Angeles	27	45	12	66	294	322	–28
Edmonton	25	45	14	64	261	305	–44

Head Coaches: Calg— Dave King (2nd season); **Van**—Pat Quinn (4th); **SJ**—Kevin Constantine (1st season); **Ana**— Ron Wilson (1st); **LA**— Barry Melrose (2nd); **Edm**— replaced Ted Green (3rd, 3-18-3) with president-GM Glen Sather (22-27-11) on Nov 25.

1992-93 Standings (Smythe): 1. Vancouver (46-29-9, 101 points); 2. Calgary (43-30-11, 97 pts); 3. Los Angeles (39-35-10, 88 pts); 4. Winnipeg (40-37-7, 87 pts); 5. Edmonton (26-50-8, 60 pts); 6. San Jose (11-71-2, 24 pts).

Central Division

	W	L	T	Pts	For	Opp	Dif
*Detroit	46	30	8	100	356	275	+81
†Toronto	43	29	12	98	280	243	+37
†Dallas	42	29	13	97	286	265	+21
St. Louis	40	33	11	91	270	283	–13
†Chicago	39	36	9	87	254	240	+14
Winnipeg	24	51	9	57	245	344	–99

Head Coaches: Det— Scotty Bowman (1st season); **Tor**— Pat Burns (2nd); **Dal**— Bob Gainey (4th); **St.L**— Bob Berry (2nd); **Chi**— Darryl Sutter (2nd); **Win**— John Paddock (3rd).

1992-93 Standings (Norris): 1. Chicago (47-25-12, 106 points); 2. Detroit (47-28-9, 103 pts); 3. Toronto (44-29-11, 99 pts); 4. St. Louis (37-36-11, 85 pts); 5. Minnesota (36-38-10, 82 pts); 6. Tampa Bay (23-54-7, 53 pts).

Eastern Conference
Northeast Division

	W	L	T	Pts	For	Opp	Dif
*Pittsburgh	44	27	13	101	299	285	+14
†Boston	42	29	13	97	289	252	+37
†Montreal	41	29	14	96	283	248	+35
†Buffalo	43	32	9	95	282	218	+64
Quebec	34	42	8	76	277	292	–15
Hartford	27	48	9	63	227	288	–61
Ottawa	14	61	9	37	201	397	196

Head Coaches: Pit— Eddie Johnston (1st season); **Bos**— Brian Sutter (2nd); **Mon**— Jacques Demers (2nd); **Buf**— John Muckler (3rd); **Que**— Pierre Page (3rd); **Hart**— replaced Paul Holmgren (2nd, 4-11-2) with assistant Pierre Maguire (23-37-7) on Nov 16; **Ott**— Rick Bowness (2nd).

1992-93 Standings (Adams): 1. Boston (51-26-7, 109 points); 2. Quebec (47-27-10, 104 pts); 3. Montreal (48-30-6, 102 pts); 4. Buffalo (38-36-10, 86 pts); 5. Hartford (26-52-6, 58 pts); 6. Ottawa (10-70-4, 24 pts).

Atlantic Division

	W	L	T	Pts	For	Opp	Dif
*NY Rangers	52	24	8	112	299	231	+68
†New Jersey	47	25	12	106	306	220	+86
†Washington	39	35	10	88	277	263	+14
†NY Islanders	36	36	12	84	282	264	+18
Florida	33	34	17	83	233	233	E
Philadelphia	35	39	10	80	294	314	–20
Tampa Bay	30	43	11	71	224	251	–27

Head Coaches: NYR— Mike Keenan (1st season); **NJ**— Jacques Lemaire (1st); **Wash**— replaced Terry Murray (5th, 20-23-4) with ESPN analyst Jim Schoenfeld (19-12-6) on Jan. 27; **NYI**— Al Arbour (6th, 34-35-10) served 5-game suspension (Jan. 7-15) during which assistant Lorne Henning went 2-1-2; **Fla**— Roger Neilson (1st); **Phi**— Terry Simpson (1st); **TB**— Terry Crisp (2nd).

1992-93 Standings (Patrick): 1. Pittsburgh (56-21-7, 119 points); 2. Washington (43-34-7, 93 pts); 3. NY Islanders (40-37-7, 87 pts); 4. New Jersey (40-37-7, 87 pts); 5. Philadelphia (36-37-11, 83 pts); 6. NY Rangers (34-39-11, 79 pts).

Old NHL Alignment Overhauled

The NHL renamed its two conferences and four divisions along geographical lines before the start of the 1993-94 season. The old Clarence Campbell and Prince of Wales conferences dated back to 1974-75. The league also did away with mandatory intra-divisional competition in the first two rounds of the Stanley Cup playoffs, which guaranteed each division four qualifiers. Here's how the NHL was aligned in 1992-93:

Campbell Conference

Smythe Division		Norris Division	
Calgary	San Jose	Chicago	St. Louis
Edmonton	Vancouver	Detroit	Tampa Bay
Los Angeles	Winnipeg	Minnesota	Toronto

Wales Conference

Adams Division		Patrick Division	
Boston	Montreal	New Jersey	Philadelphia
Buffalo	Ottawa	NY Islanders	Pittsburgh
Hartford	Quebec	NY Rangers	Washington

Home & Away, Division Records

Sixteen teams— eight from each conference— qualify for the Stanley Cup Playoffs; (*) indicates division champions.

Western Conference

		Pts	Home	Away	Div
1	Detroit*	100	23-13-6	23-17-2	13-13-4
2	Calgary*	97	25-12-5	17-17-8	20-8-4
3	Toronto	98	23-15-4	20-14-8	18-8-4
4	Dallas	97	23-12-7	19-17-6	12-13-5
5	St. Louis	91	23-11-8	17-22-3	12-13-5
6	Chicago	87	21-16-5	18-20-4	14-15-1
7	Vancouver	85	20-19-3	21-21-0	17-14-1
8	San Jose	82	19-13-10	14-22-6	14-11-5
	Anaheim	71	14-26-2	19-20-3	11-18-1
	Los Angeles	66	18-19-5	9-26-7	12-14-6
	Edmonton	64	17-22-3	8-23-11	9-18-5
	Winnipeg	57	15-23-4	9-28-5	10-17-3

Eastern Conference

		Pts	Home	Away	Div
1	NY Rangers*	112	28-8-6	24-16-2	21-8-3
2	Pittsburgh*	101	25-9-8	19-18-5	21-9-2
3	New Jersey	106	29-11-2	18-14-10	17-11-3
4	Boston	97	20-14-8	22-15-5	14-13-4
5	Montreal	96	26-12-4	15-17-10	17-10-4
6	Buffalo	95	22-17-3	21-15-6	19-9-3
7	Washington	88	17-16-9	22-19-1	13-15-4
8	NY Islanders	84	23-15-4	13-21-8	14-13-3
	Florida	83	15-18-9	18-16-8	13-11-6
	Philadelphia	80	19-20-3	16-19-7	11-16-4
	Quebec	76	19-17-6	15-25-2	13-15-3
	Tampa Bay	71	14-22-6	16-21-5	5-20-5
	Hartford	63	14-22-6	13-26-3	9-18-3
	Ottawa	37	8-30-4	6-31-5	4-23-3

1994 NHL All-Star Game

East, 9-8

45th NHL All-Star Game. **Date:** Jan. 22, at Madison Square Garden in New York; **Coaches:** Jacques Demers, Montreal (East) and Barry Melrose, Los Angeles (West); **MVP:** Mike Richter, NY Rangers goalie (East)— 21 shots, 19 saves in 2nd period.

Starters chosen in fan vote. Team replacements: WEST— Courtnall for Dallas C Mike Modano; Irbe for Calgary G Mike Vernon, Shanahan for Toronto LW Wendel Clark; EAST— Mullen for Detroit D Mark Howe Benches chosen by 5-man panel of league general managers; senior stars Dave Taylor and Mark Howe selected in recognition of career accomplishments Ottawa's Yashin added to East squad after Senators traded Kudelski to Florida (Jan. 6). East inserted C Messier into starting line-up and moved Lindros to RW after Pittsburgh's Jaromir Jagr was injured in skills competition.

Western Conference

Starters	G	A	Pts	PM
LW Pavel Bure, Vancouver	0	2	2	0
C Wayne Gretzky, Los Angeles	0	2	2	0
D Paul Coffey, Detroit	1	0	1	0
RW Brett Hull, St. Louis	0	1	1	0
D Chris Chelios, Chicago	0	1	1	0
G Felix Potvin, Toronto	0	0	0	0
Bench				
D Sandis Ozolinsh, San Jose	2	1	3	0
W Brendan Shanahan, St. Louis	2	0	2	0
W Dave Andreychuk, Toronto	1	1	2	0
C Sergei Fedorov, Detroit	1	1	2	0
C Jeremy Roenick, Chicago	1	1	2	0
D Rob Blake, Los Angeles	0	1	1	0
C Doug Gilmour, Toronto	0	1	1	0
D Al MacInnis, Calgary	0	1	1	0
C Joe Nieuwendyk, Calgary	0	1	1	0
W Dave Taylor, Los Angeles	0	1	1	0
W Shayne Corson, Edmonton	0	0	0	0
W Russ Courtnall, Dallas	0	0	0	0
D Alexei Kasatonov, Anaheim	0	0	0	0
W Teemu Selanne, Winnipeg	0	0	0	0
TOTALS	8	15	23	0

Goaltenders	Mins	Shots	Saves	GA
Felix Potvin, Tor	20:00	19	16	3
Arturs Irbe, SJ	20:00	18	16	2
Curtis Joseph, St.L	19:00	19	15	4
TOTALS	59:00	56	47	9

Eastern Conference

Starters	G	A	Pts	PM
C Mark Messier, NY Rangers	1	2	3	0
RW Eric Lindros, Philadelpha	1	0	1	0
D Ray Bourque, Boston	0	1	1	0
D Brian Leetch, NY Rangers	0	0	0	0
LW Alexander Mogilny, Buffalo	0	0	0	0
G Patrick Roy, Montreal	0	0	0	0
Bench				
C Pierre Turgeon, NY Islanders	0	4	4	0
C Joe Sakic, Quebec	1	2	3	0
W Bob Kudelski, Florida	2	0	2	0
C Alexei Yashin, Ottawa	2	0	2	0
W Joey Mullen, Pittsburgh	1	1	2	0
D Scott Stevens, New Jersey	1	1	2	0
W Adam Graves, NY Rangers	0	2	2	0
C Adam Oates, Boston	0	1	1	0
C Geoff Sanderson, Hartford	0	1	1	0
C Brian Bradley, Tampa Bay	0	0	0	0
D Garry Galley, Philadelphia	0	0	0	0
D Al Iafrate, Washington	0	0	0	0
D Larry Murphy, Pittsburgh	0	0	0	0
W Mark Ricchi, Philadelphia	0	0	0	0
TOTALS	9	15	24	0

Goaltenders	Mins	Shots	Saves	GA
Patrick Roy, Mon	20:00	17	13	4
Mike Richter, NYR	20:00	21	19	2
John Vanbiesbrouck, Fla	20:00	8	6	2
TOTALS	60:00	46	38	8

Score by Periods

	1	2	3	Final
West	4	2	2	8
East	3	2	4	9

Power plays— none; **Officials**— Bill McCreary (referee), Gord Broseker and Pat Dapuzzo (linesmen). **Attendance**— 18,200; **TV Rating**— 2.5/7 share (NBC).

Vancouver Canucks
Pavel Bure
Goals

Boston Bruins
Ray Bourque
Defensemen Points

N.J. Devils
Scott Stevens
Plus/Minus

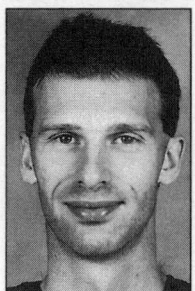
Buffalo Sabres
Dominik Hasek
Goals Against Avg.

NHL Regular Season Individual Leaders

Scoring

	Pos	Gm	G	A	Pts	+/-	PM	PP	SH	GW	GT	Shots	Pct
Wayne Gretzky, Los Angeles	C	81	38	92	130	−25	20	14	4	0	1	233	16.3
Sergei Federov, Detroit	C	82	56	64	120	+48	34	13	4	10	0	337	16.6
Adam Oates, Boston	C	77	32	80	112	+10	45	16	2	3	0	197	16.2
Doug Gilmour, Toronto	C	83	27	84	111	+25	105	10	1	3	2	167	16.2
Pavel Bure, Vancouver	RW	76	60	47	107	+1	86	25	4	9	0	374	16.0
Jeremy Roenick, Chicago	C	84	46	61	107	+21	125	24	5	5	1	281	16.4
Mark Recchi, Philadelphia	C	84	40	67	107	−2	46	11	0	5	0	217	18.4
Brendan Shanahan, St. Louis	LW	81	52	50	102	−9	211	15	7	8	1	397	13.1
Jaromir Jagr, Pittsburgh	RW	80	32	67	99	+15	61	9	0	6	2	298	10.7
Dave Andreychuk, Toronto	LW	83	53	45	98	+22	98	21	5	8	0	333	15.9
Brett Hull, St. Louis	RW	81	57	40	97	−3	38	25	3	6	1	392	14.5
Eric Lindros, Philadelphia	C	65	44	53	97	+16	103	13	2	9	1	197	22.3
Rod Brind'Amour, Philadelphia	C	84	35	62	97	−9	85	14	1	4	0	230	15.2
Pierre Turgeon, NY Islanders	C	69	38	56	94	+14	18	10	4	6	0	254	15.0
Ray Sheppard, Detroit	RW	82	52	41	93	+13	26	19	0	5	0	260	20.0
Mike Modano, Dallas	C	76	50	43	93	−8	54	18	0	4	2	281	17.8
Robert Reichel, Calgary	C	84	40	53	93	+20	58	14	0	6	0	249	16.1
Ron Francis, Pittsburgh	C	82	27	66	93	−3	62	8	0	2	1	216	12.5
Joe Sakic, Quebec	C	84	28	64	92	−8	18	10	1	9	1	279	10.0
Vincent Damphousse, Montreal	LW	84	40	51	91	E	75	13	0	10	1	274	14.6
Ray Bourque, Boston	D	72	20	71	91	+26	58	10	3	1	1	386	05.2

Goals

Bure, Van	60
Hull, St.L	57
Fedorov, Det	56
Andreychuk, Tor	53
Graves, NYR	52
Shanahan, St.L	52
Sheppard, Det	52
Neely, Bos	50
Modano, Dal	50
Clark, Tor	46
Roenick, Chi	46
Lindros, Phi	44
Robitaille, LA	44
Thomas, NYI	42
Four tied with 41 each.	

Assists

Gretzky, LA	92
Gilmour, Tor	84
Oates, Bos	80
Zubov, NYR	77
Bourque, Bos	71
Janney, St.L	68
Jagr, Pit	67
Recchi, Phi	67
Francis, Pit	66
Juneau, Bos-Wash	66
Fedorov, Det	64
Sakic, Que	64
Coffey, Det	63
Brind'Amour, Phi	62
Roenick, Chi	61

Defensemen Points

Bourque, Bos	91
Zubov, NYR	89
MacInnis, Calg	82
Leetch, NYR	79
Stevens, NJ	78
Coffey, Det	77
Murphy, Pit	73
Galley, Phi	70
Blake, LA	68
Brown, St.L-Van	66

Power Play Goals

Hull, St.L	25
Bure, Van	25
Robitaille, LA	24
Roenick, Chi	24
Tkachuk, Win	22
Andeychuk, Tor	21
Clark, Tor	21
Stevens, Pit	21
Graves, NYR	20
Neely, Bos	20

Rookie Points

Renberg, Phi	82
Yashin, Ott	79
Arnott, Edm	68
Plante, Buf	56
Smolinski, Bos	51
Daigle, Ott	51
Belanger, Fla	50
Gratton, TB	42
Fraser, Que	37
Mironov, Win-Edm	31

Short-Handed Goals

Shanahan, St.L	7
Andreychuk, Tor	5
Emerson, Win	5
Gartner, NYR-Tor	5
Hogue, NYI	5
McEachern, LA-Pit	5
McInnis, NYI	5
Presley, Buf	5
Roenick, Chi	5
Eight tied with 4 each.	

Plus/Minus

Stevens, NJ	+53
Fedorov, Det	+48
Lidstrom, Det	+43
Musil, Calg	+38
Roberts, Calg	+37

Penalty Minutes

Domi, Win	347
Churla, Dal	333
Rychel, LA	322
Berube, Wash	305
Chase, St.L	278

NHL Regular Season Individual Leaders (Cont.)

Goaltending
(Minimum 25 games)

	Gm	Min	GAA	GA	Shots	Sv%	EN	SO	Record	Offense G	A	Pts	PM
Dominik Hasek, Buffalo	58	3358	1.95	109	1552	.930	3	7	30-20-6	0	3	3	6
Martin Brodeur,* N. Jersey	47	2625	2.40	105	1238	.915	0	3	27-11-8	0	0	0	2
Patrick Roy, Montreal	68	3867	2.50	161	1956	.918	4	7	35-17-11	0	1	1	30
John VanBiesbrouck, Fla	57	3440	2.53	145	1912	.924	4	1	21-25-11	0	0	0	38
Mike Richter, NY Rangers	68	3710	2.57	159	1758	.910	1	5	42-12-6	0	0	0	2
Darcy Wakaluk, Dallas	36	2000	2.64	88	978	.910	0	3	18-9-6	0	2	2	34
Ed Belfour, Chicago	70	3998	2.67	178	1892	.906	0	7	37-24-6	0	4	4	61
Daren Puppa, Tampa Bay	63	3653	2.71	165	1637	.899	4	4	22-33-6	0	1	1	2
Chris Terreri, N. Jersey	44	2340	2.72	106	1141	.907	2	2	20-11-4	0	2	2	4
Mark Fitzpatrick, Florida	28	1603	2.73	73	844	.914	3	1	12-8-6	0	2	2	4
Mike Vernon, Calgary	48	2798	2.81	131	1209	.892	4	3	26-17-5	0	0	0	14
Guy Hebert, Anaheim	52	2991	2.83	141	1513	.907	5	2	20-27-3	0	0	0	0
Arturs Irbe, San Jose	74	4412	2.84	209	2064	.899	4	3	30-28-16	0	2	2	16
Don Beaupre, Washington	53	2853	2.84	135	1122	.880	3	2	24-16-8	0	1	1	16
Chris Osgood,* Detroit	41	2206	2.86	105	999	.895	0	2	23-8-5	0	0	0	2

Wins
Richter, NYR 42
Belfour, Chi 37
Joseph, St. L 36
Roy, Mon 35
Potvin, Tor 34
Casey, Bos 30
Hasek, Buf 30
Irbe, SJ 30
Roussel, Phi 29
Two tied with 27 each.

Shutouts
Belfour, Chi 7
Hasek, Buf 7
Roy, Mon 7
Hextall, NYI 5
Richter, NYR 5
Casey, Bos 4
Puppa, TB 4
Six tied with 3 each.

Save Pct.
Hasek, Buf 930
VanB'brouck, Fla 924
Roy, Mon 918
Brodeur,* NJ 915
Fitzpatrick, Fla 913
Joseph, St. L 911
Richter, NYR 910
Wakaluk, Dal 910
Three tied at .907.

Losses
Billington, Ott 41
Essensa, Win-Det 37
Ranford, Edm 34
Puppa, TB 33
Hrudey, LA 31
Irbe, SJ 28
Hebert, Ana 27
Hextall, NYI 26
McLean, Van 26

Power Play/Penalty Killing

Power play and penalty killing conversions. Power play: No— number of opportunities; GF— goals for; Pct— percentage. Penalty killing: No— number of times shorthanded; GA— goals against; Pct— percentage of penalties killed; SH— shorthanded goals for.

WESTERN	Power Play No	GF	Pct	Penalty Killing No	GA	Pct	SH
Calgary	410	87	21.2	465	90	80.6	16
Detroit	408	85	20.8	383	73	80.9	22
Los Angeles	444	92	20.7	462	90	80.5	19
St. Louis	420	86	20.5	388	73	81.2	17
Winnipeg	423	82	19.4	445	91	79.6	13
Toronto	459	88	19.2	409	74	81.9	8
Vancouver	441	83	18.8	458	84	81.7	14
Dallas	440	81	18.4	428	68	84.1	8
Edmonton	402	74	18.4	401	78	80.5	2
Chicago	383	67	17.5	427	71	83.4	15
San Jose	424	68	16.0	360	77	78.6	6
Anaheim	376	54	14.4	388	67	82.7	9

EASTERN	Power Play No	GF	Pct	Penalty Killing No	GA	Pct	SH
NY Rangers	417	96	23.0	435	67	84.6	20
Buffalo	424	96	22.6	380	58	84.7	21
Boston	387	84	21.7	378	58	84.7	17
Philadelphia	385	80	20.8	414	80	80.7	9
NY Islanders	369	74	20.1	417	79	81.1	15
Montreal	388	78	20.1	390	68	82.6	8
Pittsburgh	404	76	18.8	401	72	82.0	6
New Jersey	333	61	18.3	376	71	81.1	10
Washington	386	70	18.1	403	74	81.6	8
Florida	409	65	15.9	396	69	82.6	8
Quebec	430	67	15.6	426	87	79.6	10
Hartford	408	61	15.0	416	88	78.8	8
Tampa Bay	388	57	14.7	335	58	82.7	7
Ottawa	435	63	14.5	412	110	73.3	9

Team Goaltending

WESTERN	GAA	Mins	GA	Shots	Sv%	EN	SO
Chicago	2.82	5099	240	2458	.902	0	7
Toronto	2.85	5115	243	2554	.905	3	3
Anaheim	2.97	5079	251	2616	.904	10	3
Calgary	3.00	5124	256	2311	.889	5	5
Dallas	3.10	5132	265	2589	.898	7	5
San Jose	3.10	5125	265	2389	.889	6	3
Detroit	3.24	5094	275	2303	.881	7	4
Vancouver	3.27	5070	276	2285	.879	7	3
St. Louis	3.32	5107	283	2946	.904	1	1
Edmonton	3.57	5121	305	2891	.895	8	1
Los Angeles	3.77	5124	322	3046	.894	13	2
Winnipeg	4.05	5098	344	2798	.877	6	2

EASTERN	GAA	Mins	GA	Shots	Sv%	EN	SO
Buffalo	2.57	5097	218	2462	.911	3	9
New Jersey	2.59	5104	220	2437	.910	3	5
Florida	2.72	5144	233	2808	.917	7	2
NY Rangers	2.72	5089	231	2328	.901	3	7
Montreal	2.91	5122	248	2533	.902	5	7
Tampa Bay	2.94	5116	251	2296	.891	5	5
Boston	2.96	5116	252	2113	.881	2	5
NY Islanders	3.09	5119	264	2561	.897	3	5
Washington	3.09	5099	263	2172	.879	4	4
Pittsburgh	3.34	5118	285	2676	.893	2	3
Hartford	3.39	5099	288	2588	.889	14	3
Quebec	3.45	5080	292	2572	.886	11	2
Philadelphia	3.69	5102	314	2663	.882	10	3
Ottawa	4.67	5105	397	2776	.857	9	0

Team by Team Statistics

High scorers and goaltenders with at least 10 games played. Players who competed for more than one team during the regular season are listed with their final club; (*) indicates rookies eligible for Calder Trophy.

Mighty Ducks of Anaheim

Top Scorers	Gm	G	A	Pts	+/-	PM	PP
Terry Yake	82	21	31	52	+2	44	5
Bob Corkum	76	23	28	51	+4	18	3
Garry Valk	78	18	27	45	+8	100	4
Tim Sweeney	78	16	27	43	+3	49	6
Bill Houlder	80	14	25	39	-18	40	3
Joe Sacco	84	19	18	37	-11	61	3
Peter Douris	74	12	22	34	-5	21	1
Shaun Van Allen	80	8	25	33	E	64	2
Anatoli Semenov	49	11	19	30	-4	12	4
Sean Hill	68	7	20	27	-12	78	2
Stephan LeBeau	56	15	11	26	-4	22	6
MON	34	9	7	16	+1	8	4
ANA	22	6	4	10	-5	14	2
Patrik Carnback*	73	12	11	23	-8	54	3
Bobby Dollas	77	9	11	20	+20	55	1
David Williams	56	5	15	20	+8	42	2
Troy Loney	62	13	6	19	-5	88	6
Todd Ewen	76	9	9	18	-7	272	0
Don McSween	32	3	9	12	+4	39	1
Steven King*	36	8	3	11	-7	44	3
Randy Ladouceur	81	1	9	10	+7	74	0

Acquired: BeBeau from Mon. (Mar. 20).

Goalies (10 Gm)	Gm	Min	GAA	Sv%	Record
Mikhail Shtalenko	10	543	2.65	.909	3-4-1
Guy Hebert	52	2991	2.83	.907	20-27-3
ANAHEIM	84	5079	2.97	.904	33-46-5

Shutouts: Hebert (2); **Assists:** none; **PM:** Hebert (2).

Boston Bruins

Top Scorers	Gm	G	A	Pts	+/-	PM	PP
Adam Oates	77	32	80	112	+10	45	16
Ray Bourque	72	20	71	91	+26	58	10
Cam Neely	49	50	24	74	+12	54	20
Al Iafrate	79	15	43	58	+16	163	6
WASH	67	10	35	45	+10	143	4
BOS	12	5	8	13	+6	20	2
Glen Wesley	81	14	44	58	+1	64	6
Ted Donato	84	22	32	54	E	59	9
Bryan Smolinski*	83	31	20	51	+4	82	4
Glen Murray	81	18	13	31	-1	48	0
Brent Hughes	77	13	11	24	+10	143	1
Jozef Stumpel*	59	8	15	23	+4	14	0
Dave Reid	83	6	17	23	+10	25	0
Stephen Heinze	77	10	11	21	-2	32	0
Don Sweeney	75	6	15	21	+29	50	1
Dmitri Kvartalnov	39	12	7	19	-9	10	4
Stephen Leach	42	5	10	15	-10	74	1
Dan Marois	22	7	3	10	-4	18	3
Paul Stanton	71	3	7	10	-7	54	1
David Shaw	55	1	9	10	-11	85	0
Cameron Stewart*	57	3	6	9	-6	66	0
Glen Featherstone	58	1	8	9	-5	152	0
Gordie Roberts	59	1	6	7	-13	40	0

Acquired: Iafrate from Wash. (Mar. 21).

Goalies (10 Gm)	Gm	Min	GAA	Sv%	Record
Jon Casey	57	3192	2.88	.881	30-15-9
John Blue	18	944	2.99	.885	5-8-3
Vincent Riendeau	26	1321	3.32	.866	9-10-1
DET	8	345	4.00	.824	2-4-0
BOS	18	976	3.07	.880	7-6-1
BOSTON	84	5116	2.96	.881	42-29-13

Shutouts: Casey (4), Riendeau (1); **Assists:** Casey (2), Riendeau (1); **PM:** Casey (14), Blue (7).
Acquired: Riendeau from Det. (Jan. 17).

Buffalo Sabres

Top Scorers	Gm	G	A	Pts	+/-	PM	PP
Dale Hawerchuk	81	35	51	86	+10	91	13
Alexander Mogilny	66	32	47	79	+8	22	17
Donald Audette	77	29	30	59	+2	41	16
Yuri Khmylev	72	27	31	58	+13	49	11
Derek Plante*	77	21	35	56	+4	24	8
Brad May	84	18	27	45	-6	171	3
Richard Smehlik	84	14	27	41	+22	69	3
Doug Bodger	75	7	32	39	+8	76	5
Randy Wood	84	22	16	38	+11	71	2
Wayne Presley	65	17	8	25	+18	103	1
Bob Sweeney	60	11	14	25	+3	94	3
Ken Sutton	78	4	20	24	-6	71	1
Dave Hannan	83	6	15	21	+10	53	0
Pat LaFontaine	16	5	13	18	-4	2	1
Craig Simpson	22	8	8	16	-3	8	2
Petr Svoboda	60	2	14	16	+11	89	1
Philippe Boucher*	38	6	8	14	-1	29	4
Craig Muni	82	2	12	14	+31	66	0
CHI	9	0	4	4	+3	4	0
BUF	73	2	8	10	+28	62	0

Acquired: Muni from Chi. (Oct. 28).

Goalies (10 Gm)	Gm	Min	GAA	Sv%	Record
Dominik Hasek	58	3358	1.95	.930	30-20-6
Grant Fuhr	32	1726	3.68	.883	13-12-3
BUFFALO	84	5097	2.57	.911	43-32-9

Shutouts: Hasek (7), Fuhr (2); **Assists:** Fuhr (4), Hasek (3);
PM: Fuhr (16), Hasek (6).

Calgary Flames

Top Scorers	Gm	G	A	Pts	+/-	PM	PP
Robert Reichel	84	40	53	93	+20	58	14
Theoren Fleury	83	40	45	85	+30	186	16
Gary Roberts	73	41	43	84	+37	145	12
Al Macinnis	75	28	54	82	+35	95	12
Joe Nieuwendyk	64	36	39	75	+19	51	14
Michael Nylander	73	13	42	55	+8	30	4
HART	58	11	33	44	-2	24	4
CALG	15	2	9	11	+10	6	0
Zarley Zalapski	69	10	37	47	-6	74	1
HFD	56	7	30	37	-6	56	0
CGY	13	3	7	10	E	18	1
German Titov	76	27	18	45	+20	28	8
Wes Walz	53	11	27	38	+20	16	1
James Patrick	68	10	25	35	-5	40	2
NYR	6	0	3	3	+1	2	0
HART	47	8	20	28	-12	32	4
CALG	15	2	2	4	+6	6	1
Kelly Kisio	51	7	23	30	-6	28	1
Ronnie Stern	71	9	20	29	+6	243	0
Joel Otto	81	11	12	23	-17	92	3
Michel Petit	63	2	21	23	+5	110	0
Dan Keczmer	69	1	21	22	-8	60	0
HART	12	0	1	1	-6	12	0
CALG	57	1	20	21	-2	48	0
Trent Yawney	58	6	15	21	+21	60	1

Acquired: Keczmer from Hart. (Nov. 19); Nylander, Patrick and Zalapski from Hart. (Mar. 10).

Goalies (10 Gm)	Gm	Min	GAA	Sv%	Record
Andrei Trefilov	11	623	2.50	.915	3-4-2
Mike Vernon	48	2798	2.81	.892	26-17-5
Trevor Kidd	31	1614	3.16	.887	13-7-6
CALGARY	84	5124	3.00	.889	42-29-13

Shutouts: Vernon (3), Trefilov (2); **Assists:** Kidd (4); **PM:** Vernon (14), Kidd (4), Trefilov (4).

Chicago Blackhawks

Top Scorers	Gm	G	A	Pts	+/-	PM	PP
Jeremy Roenick	84	46	61	107	+21	125	24
Joe Murphy	81	31	39	70	+1	111	7
Chris Chelios	76	16	44	60	+12	212	7
Tony Amonte	79	17	25	42	E	37	4
NYR	72	16	22	38	+5	31	3
CHI	7	1	3	4	-5	6	1
Brent Sutter	73	9	29	38	+17	43	3
Paul Ysebaert	71	14	21	35	-7	26	3
WIN	60	9	18	27	-8	18	1
CHI	11	5	3	8	+1	8	2
Dirk Graham	67	15	18	33	+13	45	0
Michel Goulet	56	16	14	30	+1	26	3
Christian Ruuttu	54	9	20	29	-4	68	1
Patrick Poulin	67	14	14	28	-8	51	2
HART	9	2	1	3	-8	11	1
CHI	58	12	13	25	E	40	1
Eric Weinrich	62	4	24	28	+1	35	2
HFD	8	1	1	2	-5	2	1
CHI	54	3	23	26	+6	33	1
Steve Smith	57	5	22	27	-5	174	1
Rich Sutter	83	12	14	26	-8	108	0
Randy Cunneyworth	79	13	11	24	-1	100	0
HART	63	9	8	17	-2	87	0
CHI	16	4	3	7	+1	13	0
Gary Suter	41	6	12	18	-12	38	4
CALG	25	4	9	13	-3	20	2
CHI	16	2	3	5	-9	18	2

Acquired: Poulin and Weinrich from Hart. (Nov. 2); Cunneyworth from Hart. (Mar. 11); Suter from Calg. (Mar. 11); Amonte from NYR (Mar. 21); Ysebaert from Win. (Mar. 21).

Goalies (10 Gm)	Gm	Min	GAA	Sv%	Record
Ed Belfour	70	3998	2.67	.906	37-24-6
Jeff Hackett	22	1084	3.43	.890	2-12-3
CHICAGO	84	5099	2.82	.902	39-36-9

Shutouts: Belfour (7); **Assists:** Belfour (4), Hackett (1); **PM:** Belfour (61), Hackett (2).

Dallas Stars

Top Scorers	Gm	G	A	Pts	+/-	PM	PP
Mike Modano	76	50	43	93	-8	54	18
Russ Courtnall	84	23	57	80	+6	59	5
Dave Gagner	76	32	29	61	+13	83	10
Neal Broten	79	17	35	52	+10	62	2
Grant Ledyard	84	9	37	46	+7	42	6
Paul Cavallini	74	11	33	44	+13	82	6
Dean Evason	80	11	33	44	-12	66	3
Trent Klatt	61	14	24	38	+13	30	3
Mike Craig	72	13	24	37	-14	139	3
Mike McPhee	79	20	15	35	+8	36	1
Brent Gilchrist	76	17	14	31	E	31	3
Derian Hatcher	83	12	19	31	+19	211	2
Paul Broten	64	12	12	24	+18	30	0
Mark Tinordi	61	6	18	24	+6	143	1
Pelle Eklund	53	3	17	20	-2	10	0
PHI	48	1	16	17	-1	8	0
DAL	5	2	1	3	-1	2	0
Craig Ludwig	84	1	13	14	-1	123	1
Shane Churla	69	6	7	13	-8	333	3
Alan May	51	5	7	12	-3	115	0
WASH	43	4	7	11	-2	97	0
DAL	8	1	0	1	-1	18	0

Acquired: Eklund from Phi. (Mar. 21); May from Wash. (Mar. 21).

Goalies (10 Gm)	Gm	Min	GAA	Sv%	Record
Darcy Wakaluk	36	2000	2.64	.910	18-9-6
Andy Moog	55	3121	3.27	.894	24-20-7
DALLAS	84	5132	3.10	.898	42-29-13

Shutouts: Wakaluk (3), Moog (2); **Assists:** Wakaluk (2), Moog (1); **PM:** Wakaluk (34), Moog (16).

Detroit Red Wings

Top Scorers	Gm	G	A	Pts	+/-	PM	PP
Sergei Fedorov	82	56	64	120	+48	34	13
Ray Sheppard	82	52	41	93	+13	26	19
Steve Yzerman	58	24	58	82	+11	36	7
Paul Coffey	80	14	63	77	+28	106	5
Vyacheslav Kozlov	77	34	39	73	+27	50	8
Keith Primeau	78	31	42	73	+34	173	7
Dino Ciccarelli	66	28	29	57	+10	73	12
Nicklas Lidstrom	84	10	46	56	+43	26	4
Steve Chiasson	82	13	33	46	+17	122	4
Vlad. Konstantinov	80	12	21	33	+30	138	1
Mike Sillinger	62	8	21	29	+2	10	0
Darren McCarty*	67	9	17	26	+12	181	0
Mark Howe	44	4	20	24	+16	8	1
Shawn Burr	51	10	12	22	+12	31	0
Bob Probert	66	7	10	17	-1	275	1
Greg Johnson*	52	6	11	17	-7	22	1
Martin Lapointe*	50	8	8	16	+7	55	2
Sheldon Kennedy	61	6	7	13	-2	30	0
Kris Draper	39	5	8	13	+11	31	0
Micah Aivazoff*	59	4	4	8	-1	38	0
Terry Carkner	68	1	6	7	+13	130	0
Sergei Bautin	60	0	7	7	-12	78	0
WIN	59	0	7	7	-13	78	0
DET	1	0	0	0	+1	0	0

Acquired: Bautin from Win. (Mar. 8).

Goalies (10 Gm)	Gm	Min	GAA	Sv%	Record
Bob Essensa	69	3914	3.60	.885	23-37-8
WIN	56	3136	3.85	.883	19-30-6
DET	13	778	2.62	.899	4-7-2
Chris Osgood	41	2206	2.86	.895	23-8-5
DETROIT	84	5094	3.24	.881	46-30-8

Shutouts: Essensa (2), Osgood (2); **Assists:** Essensa (2); **PM:** Essensa (6), Osgood (2).
Acquired: Essensa from Win. (Mar. 8).

Edmonton Oilers

Top Scorers	Gm	G	A	Pts	+/-	PM	PP
Doug Weight	84	24	50	74	-22	47	4
Jason Arnott*	78	33	35	68	+1	104	10
Zdeno Ciger	84	22	35	57	-11	8	8
Shayne Corson	64	25	29	54	-8	118	11
Igor Kravchuk	81	12	38	50	-12	16	5
Bob Beers	82	11	32	43	-22	86	6
TB	16	1	5	6	-11	12	1
EDM	66	10	27	37	-11	74	5
Scott Pearson	72	19	18	37	-4	165	3
Fredrik Olausson	73	11	24	35	-7	30	7
WIN	18	2	5	7	-3	10	1
EDM	55	9	19	28	-4	20	6
Steven Rice	63	17	15	32	-10	36	6
Boris Mironov*	79	7	24	31	-33	110	5
WIN	65	7	22	29	-29	96	5
EDM	14	0	2	2	-4	14	0
Ilya Byakin	44	8	20	28	-3	30	6
Dean McAmmond*	45	6	21	27	+12	16	2
Mike Stapleton	81	12	13	25	-5	46	4
PIT	58	7	4	11	-4	18	3
EDM	23	5	9	14	-1	28	1
Kelly Buchberger	84	3	18	21	-20	199	0
Kirk Maltby*	68	11	8	19	-2	74	0
Vladimir Vujtek	40	4	15	19	-7	14	0

Acquired: Beers from T.B. (Nov. 12); Olausson from Win. (Dec. 6); Stapleton on waivers from Pit. (Feb. 19); Mironov from Win. (Mar. 15).

Goalies (10 Gm)	Gm	Min	GAA	Sv%	Record
Bill Ranford	71	4070	3.48	.898	22-34-11
Fred Brathwaite	19	982	3.54	.889	3-10-3
EDMONTON	84	5121	3.57	.895	25-45-14

Shutout: Ranford (1); **Assists:** Ranford (2); **PM:** Ranford (2).

Florida Panthers

Top Scorers	Gm	G	A	Pts	+/-	PM	PP
Bob Kudelski	86	40	30	70	-33	24	17
OTT	42	26	15	41	-25	14	12
FLA	44	14	15	29	-8	10	5
Scott Mellanby	80	30	30	60	E	149	17
Jesse Belanger*	70	17	33	50	-4	16	11
Stu Barnes	77	23	24	47	+4	38	8
WIN	18	5	4	9	-1	8	2
FLA	59	18	20	38	+5	30	6
Andrei Lomakin	76	19	28	47	+1	26	3
Gord Murphy	84	14	29	43	-11	71	9
Brian Skrudland	79	15	25	40	+13	136	0
Dave Lowry	80	15	22	37	-4	64	3
Tom Fitzgerald	83	18	14	32	-3	54	0
Brian Benning	73	6	24	30	-7	107	2
Mike Hough	78	6	23	29	+3	62	0
Jody Hull	69	13	13	26	+6	8	0
Rob Niedermayer*	65	9	17	26	-11	51	3
Bill Lindsay	84	6	6	12	-2	97	0
Keith Brown	51	4	8	12	+11	60	1
Brent Severyn	67	4	7	11	-1	156	1
Joe Cirella	63	1	9	10	+8	99	0

Acquired: Barnes from Win. (Nov. 26); Kudelski from Ott. (Jan. 6).

Goalies (10 Gm)	Gm	Min	GAA	Sv%	Record
John Vanbiesbrouck	57	3440	2.53	.924	21-25-11
Mark Fitzpatrick	28	1603	2.73	.914	12-8-6
FLORIDA	84	5144	2.72	.917	33-34-17

Shutouts: Fitzpatrick (1), Vanbiesbrouck (1); **Assists:** Fitzpatrick (2); **PM:** Vanbiesbrouck (38), Fitzpatrick (4).

Hartford Whalers

Top Scorers	Gm	G	A	Pts	+/-	PM	PP
Pat Verbeek	84	37	38	75	-15	177	15
Geoff Sanderson	82	41	26	67	-13	42	15
Andrew Cassels	79	16	42	58	-21	37	8
Robert Kron	77	24	26	50	E	8	2
Chris Pronger*	81	5	25	30	-3	113	2
Brian Propp	65	12	17	29	+3	44	3
Jocelyn Lemieux	82	18	9	27	-3	82	0
CHI	66	12	8	20	+5	63	0
HART	16	6	1	7	-8	19	0
Paul Ranheim	82	10	17	27	-18	22	0
CGY	67	10	14	24	-7	20	0
HART	15	0	3	3	-11	2	0
Alex. Godynyuk	69	3	19	22	+13	75	0
FLA	26	0	10	10	+5	35	0
HART	43	3	9	12	+8	40	0
Frantisek Kucera	76	5	16	21	-3	48	3
CHI	60	4	13	17	+9	34	2
HART	16	1	3	4	-12	14	1
Darren Turcotte	32	4	15	19	-13	17	0
NYR	13	2	4	6	-2	13	0
HART	19	2	11	13	-11	4	0
Ted Drury*	50	6	12	18	-15	36	0
CALG	34	5	7	12	-5	26	0
HART	16	1	5	6	-10	10	0
Adam Burt	63	1	17	18	-4	75	0

Acquired: Turcotte from NYR (Nov. 2); Godynuk from Fla. (Dec. 16); Drury and Ranheim from Calg. (Mar. 10); Kucera and Lemieux from Chi. (Mar. 11).

Goalies (10 Gm)	Gm	Min	GAA	Sv%	Record
Sean Burke	47	2750	2.99	.906	17-24-5
Jeff Reese	19	1086	3.09	.893	5-9-3
Frank Pietrangelo	19	984	3.60	.875	5-11-1
HARTFORD	84	5099	3.39	.889	27-48-9

Shutouts: Burke (2), Reese (1); **Assists:** Reese (1); **PM:** Burke (16), Pietrangelo (2).

Los Angeles Kings

Top Scorers	Gm	G	A	Pts	+/-	PM	PP
Wayne Gretzky	81	38	92	130	-25	20	14
Luc Robitaille	83	44	42	86	-20	86	24
Jari Kurri	81	31	46	77	-24	48	14
Rob Blake	84	20	48	68	-7	137	7
Alexei Zhitnik	81	12	40	52	-11	101	11
Mike Donnelly	81	21	21	42	+2	34	4
Darryl Sydor	84	8	27	35	-9	94	1
John Druce	55	14	17	31	+16	50	1
Marty McSorley	65	7	24	31	-12	194	1
PIT	47	3	18	21	-9	139	0
LA	18	4	6	10	-3	55	1
Pat Conacher	77	15	13	28	E	71	0
Kevin Todd	47	8	14	22	-3	24	4
CHI	35	5	6	11	-2	16	1
LA	12	3	8	11	-1	8	3
Tony Granato	50	7	14	21	-2	150	2
Warren Rychel	80	10	9	19	-19	322	0
Robert Lang*	32	9	10	19	+7	10	0
Charlie Huddy	79	5	13	18	+4	71	1
Dixon Ward	67	12	3	15	-22	82	4
VAN	33	6	1	7	-14	37	2
LA	34	6	2	8	-8	45	2
Tim Watters	60	1	9	10	-11	67	0

Acquired: Ward from Van. (Jan. 8); McSorley from Pit. (Mar. 15); Todd from Chi. (Mar. 21).

Goalies (10 Gm)	Gm	Min	GAA	Sv%	Record
Robb Stauber	22	1144	3.41	.908	4-11-5
Kelly Hrudey	64	3713	3.68	.897	22-31-7
LOS ANGELES	84	5124	3.77	.894	27-45-12

Shutouts: Hrudey (1), Stauber (1); **Assists:** Hrudey (1); **PM:** Stauber (18), Hrudey (6).

Montreal Canadiens

Top Scorers	Gm	G	A	Pts	+/-	PM	PP
Vincent Damphousse	84	40	51	91	E	75	13
Brian Bellows	77	33	38	71	+9	36	13
Kirk Muller	76	23	34	57	-1	96	9
Matt Schneider	75	20	32	52	+15	62	11
Mike Keane	80	16	30	46	+6	119	6
Gilbert Dionne	74	19	26	45	-9	31	3
John Leclair	74	19	24	43	+17	32	1
Lyle Odelein	79	11	29	40	+8	276	6
Guy Carbonneau	79	14	24	38	+16	48	0
Eric Desjardins	84	23	35	58	-1	97	6
Paul Di Pietro	70	13	20	33	-2	37	2
Benoit Brunet	71	10	20	30	+14	20	0
Oleg Petrov*	55	12	15	27	+7	2	1
Patrice Brisebois	53	2	21	23	+5	63	1
Gary Leeman	31	4	11	15	+5	17	0
Ed Ronan	61	6	8	14	+3	42	0
Peter Popovic*	47	2	12	14	+10	26	1
J.J. Daigneault	68	2	12	14	+16	73	0
Kevin Haller	68	4	9	13	+3	118	0
Ron Wilson	48	2	10	12	-2	12	0
Pierre Sevigny*	43	4	5	9	+6	42	1
Donald Brashear*	14	2	2	4	E	34	0

Acquired: Tugnutt from Ana. (Feb. 20).

Goalies (10 Gm)	Gm	Min	GAA	Sv%	Record
Patrick Roy	68	3867	2.50	.918	35-17-11
Ron Tugnutt	36	1898	3.16	.900	12-18-2
ANA	28	1520	3.00	.908	10-15-1
MON	8	378	3.81	.860	2-3-1
Andre Racicot	11	500	4.44	.850	2-6-2
MONTREAL	84	5122	2.91	.902	41-29-14

Shutouts: Roy (7), Tugnutt (1); **Assists:** Roy (1); **PM:** Roy (30), Tugnutt (2).

New Jersey Devils

Top Scorers	Gm	G	A	Pts	+/-	PM	PP
Scott Stevens	83	18	60	78	+53	112	5
Stephane Richer	80	36	36	72	+31	16	7
John Maclean	80	37	33	70	+30	95	8
Valeri Zelepukin	82	26	31	57	+36	70	8
Corey Millen	78	20	30	50	+24	52	4
Bernie Nicholls	61	19	27	46	+24	86	3
Scott Niedermayer	81	10	36	46	+34	42	5
Bill Guerin	81	25	19	44	+14	101	2
Claude Lemieux	79	18	26	44	+13	86	5
Tom Chorske	76	21	20	41	+14	32	1
Bobby Holik	70	13	20	33	+28	72	2
Bob Carpenter	76	10	23	33	+7	51	0
Bruce Driver	66	8	24	32	+29	63	3
Alexander Semak	54	12	17	29	+6	22	2
Randy McKay	78	12	15	27	+24	244	0
Mike Peluso	69	4	16	20	+19	238	0
Tommy Albelin	62	2	17	19	+20	36	1
Jaroslav Modry*	41	2	15	17	+10	18	2
Jim Dowd*	15	5	10	15	+8	0	2
Viacheslav Fetisov	52	1	14	15	+14	30	0
David Emma*	15	5	5	10	E	2	1
Ken Daneyko	78	1	9	10	+27	176	0
Jason Smith*	41	0	5	5	+7	43	0

Goalies (10 Gm)	Gm	Min	GAA	Sv%	Record
Martin Brodeur	47	2625	2.40	.915	27-11-8
Chris Terreri	44	2340	2.72	.907	20-11-4
NEW JERSEY	84	5104	2.59	.910	47-25-12

Shutouts: Brodeur (3), Terreri (2); **Assists:** Terreri (2); **PM:** Terreri (4), Brodeur (2).

New York Islanders

Top Scorers	Gm	G	A	Pts	+/-	PM	PP
Pierre Turgeon	69	38	56	94	+14	18	10
Steve Thomas	78	42	33	75	-9	139	17
Derek King	78	30	40	70	+18	59	10
Benoit Hogue	83	36	33	69	-7	73	9
Vladimir Malakhov	76	10	47	57	+29	80	4
Marty McInnis	81	25	31	56	+31	24	3
Ray Ferraro	82	21	32	53	+1	83	5
Patrick Flatley	64	12	30	42	+12	40	2
Travis Green	83	18	22	40	+16	44	1
Tom Kurvers	66	9	31	40	+7	47	5
Brad Dalgarno	73	11	19	30	+14	62	3
Uwe Krupp	41	7	14	21	+11	30	3
Dave Volek	32	5	9	14	E	10	2
Scott Lachance	74	3	11	14	-5	70	0
Dennis Vaske	65	2	11	13	+21	76	0
Darius Kasparaitis	76	1	10	11	-6	142	0
Keith Acton	77	2	7	9	-5	71	0
WASH	6	0	0	0	-4	21	0
NYI	71	2	7	9	-1	50	0
David Maley	56	0	6	6	-7	104	0
SJ	19	0	0	0	-1	30	0
NYI	37	0	6	6	-6	74	0
Richard Pilon	28	1	4	5	-4	75	0
Mick Vukota	72	3	1	4	-5	237	0
Chris Luongo	17	1	3	4	-1	13	0
Dean Chynoweth	39	0	4	4	+3	122	0

Acquired: Acton on waivers from Wash. (Oct. 22); Maley from S.J. (Jan. 24).

Goalies (10 Gm)	Gm	Min	GAA	Sv%	Record
Jamie McLennan	22	1287	2.84	.905	8-7-6
Ron Hextall	65	3581	3.08	.898	27-26-6
NEW YORK	84	5119	3.09	.897	36-36-12

Shutouts: Hextall (5); **Assists:** Hextall (3), McLennan (1); **PM:** Hextall (52), McLennan (6).

New York Rangers

Top Scorers	Gm	G	A	Pts	+/-	PM	PP
Sergei Zubov	78	12	77	89	+20	39	9
Mark Messier	76	26	58	84	+25	76	6
Adam Graves	84	52	27	79	+27	127	20
Brian Leetch	84	23	56	79	+28	67	17
Steve Larmer	68	21	39	60	+14	41	6
Alexei Kovalev	76	23	33	56	+18	154	7
Esa Tikkanen	83	22	32	54	+5	114	5
Sergei Nemchinov	76	22	27	49	+13	36	4
Glenn Anderson	85	21	20	41	-5	62	7
TOR	73	17	18	35	-6	50	5
NYR	12	4	2	6	+1	12	2
Brian Noonan	76	18	23	41	+7	69	10
CHI	64	14	21	35	+2	57	8
NYR	12	4	2	6	+5	12	2
Stephane Matteau	77	19	19	38	+15	57	3
CHI	65	15	16	31	+10	55	2
NYR	12	4	3	7	+5	2	1
Craig MacTavish	78	20	13	33	-14	91	1
EDM	66	16	10	26	-20	80	0
NYR	12	4	3	7	+6	11	1
Kevin Lowe	71	5	14	19	+4	70	0
A. Karpovtsev*	67	3	15	18	+12	58	1
Jeff Beukeboom	68	8	8	16	+18	170	1
Greg Gilbert	76	4	11	15	-3	29	1
Mike Hudson	48	4	7	11	-5	47	0

Acquired: Larmer from Hart. (Nov. 2); Anderson from Tor. (Mar. 21); McTavis from Edm. (Mar. 21); Matteau and Noonan from Chi. (Mar. 21).

Goalies (10 Gm)	Gm	Min	GAA	Sv%	Record
Mike Richter	68	3710	2.57	.910	42-12-6
Glenn Healy	29	1368	3.03	.878	10-12-2
NEW YORK	84	5089	2.72	.901	52-24-8

Shutouts: Richter (5), Healy (2); **Assists:** Healy (2); **PM:** Healy (2), Richter (2).

Ottawa Senators

Top Scorers	Gm	G	A	Pts	+/-	PM	PP
Alexei Yashin*	83	30	49	79	-49	22	11
Alexandre Daigle*	84	20	31	51	-45	40	4
Dave McLlwain	66	17	26	43	-40	48	1
Sylvain Turgeon	47	11	15	26	-25	52	7
Troy Mallette	82	7	16	23	-33	166	0
Brad Shaw	66	4	19	23	-41	59	1
Norm Maciver	53	3	20	23	-26	26	0
Gord Dineen	77	0	21	21	-52	89	0
Evgeny Davydov	61	7	13	20	-9	46	1
FLA	21	2	6	8	-3	8	1
OTT	40	5	7	12	-6	38	0
Andrew McBain	55	11	8	19	-41	64	8
Scott Levins*	62	8	11	19	-26	162	4
FLA	29	5	6	11	E	69	2
OTT	33	3	5	8	-26	93	2
David Archibald	33	10	8	18	-7	14	2
Vladimir Ruzicka	42	5	13	18	-21	14	4
Kerry Huffman	62	4	14	18	-28	40	2
QUE	28	0	6	6	+2	28	0
OTT	34	4	8	12	-30	12	2
Darren Rumble	70	6	9	15	-50	116	0

Acquired: Davydov and Levins from Fla. (Jan. 6); Huffman on waivers from Que. (Jan. 15).

Goalies (10 Gm)	Gm	Min	GAA	Sv%	Record
Darrin Madeley	32	1583	4.36	.868	3-18-5
Craig Billington	63	3319	4.59	.859	11-41-4
OTTAWA	84	5105	4.67	.857	14-61-9

Shutouts: none; **Assists:** none; **PM:** Billington (8).

Philadelphia Flyers

Top Scorers	Gm	G	A	Pts	+/-	PM	PP
Mark Recchi	84	40	67	107	-2	46	11
Eric Lindros	65	44	53	97	+16	103	13
Rod Brind'Amour	84	35	62	97	-9	85	14
Mikael Renberg*	83	38	44	82	+8	36	9
Garry Galley	81	10	60	70	-11	91	5
Yves Racine	67	9	43	52	-11	48	5
Josef Beranek	80	28	21	49	-2	85	6
Kevin Dineen	71	19	23	42	-9	113	5
Brent Fedyk	72	20	18	38	-14	74	5
Mark Lamb	85	12	24	36	-44	72	4
OTT	66	11	18	29	-41	56	4
PHI	19	1	6	7	-3	16	0
Dimitri Yushkevich	75	5	25	30	-8	86	1
Rob DiMaio	53	11	12	23	-4	46	2
TB	39	8	7	15	-5	40	2
PHI	14	3	5	8	+1	6	0
Dave Tippett	73	4	11	15	-20	38	0
Andre Faust*	37	8	5	13	-1	10	0
Jeff Finley	55	1	8	9	+16	24	0
Allan Conroy	62	4	3	7	-12	65	0
Rob Zettler	75	0	7	7	-26	134	0
SJ	42	0	3	3	-7	65	0
PHI	33	0	4	4	-19	69	0
Jason Bowen*	56	1	5	6	+12	87	0
Dave Brown	71	1	4	5	-12	137	0

Acquired: Zettler from S.J. (Feb. 1); Lamb from Ott. (Mar. 5); DiMaio from T.B. (Mar. 18).

Goalies (10 Gm)	Gm	Min	GAA	Sv%	Record
Dominic Roussel	60	3285	3.34	.896	29-20-5
Tommy Soderstrom	34	1736	4.01	.864	6-18-4
PHILADELPHIA	84	5102	3.69	.882	35-39-10

Shutouts: Soderstrom (2), Roussel (1); **Assists:** Roussel (1); **PM:** Roussel (4).

Pittsburgh Penguins

Top Scorers	Gm	G	A	Pts	+/-	PM	PP
Jaromir Jagr	80	32	67	99	+15	61	9
Ron Francis	82	27	66	93	-3	62	8
Kevin Stevens	83	41	47	88	-24	155	21
Larry Murphy	84	17	56	73	+10	44	7
Joe Mullen	84	38	32	70	+9	41	6
Martin Straka	84	30	34	64	+24	24	2
Tomas Sandstrom	78	23	35	58	-7	83	4
LA	51	17	24	41	-12	59	4
PIT	27	6	11	17	+5	24	0
Doug Brown	77	18	37	55	+19	18	2
Shawn McEachern	76	20	22	42	+14	34	0
LA	49	8	13	21	+1	24	0
PIT	27	12	9	21	+13	10	0
Rick Tocchet	51	14	26	40	-15	134	5
Mario Lemieux	22	17	20	37	-2	32	7
Greg Hawgood	64	6	28	34	+9	36	4
PHI	19	3	12	15	+2	19	3
FLA	33	2	14	16	+8	9	0
PIT	12	1	2	3	-1	8	1
Ulf Samuelsson	80	5	24	29	+23	199	1
Bryan Trottier	41	4	11	15	-12	36	0
Peter Taglianetti	60	2	12	14	+5	142	0
Kjell Samuelsson	59	5	8	13	+18	118	1
Markus Naslund*	71	4	7	11	-3	27	1
Greg Brown	36	3	8	11	+1	28	1

Acquired: McEachern and Sanstrom from L.A. (Feb. 15); Hawgood from Fla. (Mar. 19).

Goalies (10 Gm)	Gm	Min	GAA	Sv%	Record
Tom Barrasso	44	2482	3.36	.893	22-15-5
Ken Wregget	42	2456	3.37	.893	21-12-7
PITTSBURGH	84	5118	3.34	.893	44-27-13

Shutouts: Barrasso (2), Wregget (1); **Assists:** Barrasso (1), Wregget (1); **PM:** Barrasso (42), Wregget (8).

Quebec Nordiques

Top Scorers	Gm	G	A	Pts	+/-	PM	PP
Joe Sakic	84	28	64	92	-8	18	10
Mats Sundin	84	32	53	85	+1	60	6
Valeri Kamensky	76	28	37	65	+12	42	6
Mike Ricci	83	30	21	51	-9	113	13
Scott Young	76	26	25	51	-4	14	6
Ron Sutter	73	15	25	40	+2	90	5
ST.L.	36	6	12	18	-1	46	1
QUE	37	9	13	22	+3	44	4
Iain Fraser*	60	17	20	37	-5	23	2
Andrei Kovalenko	58	16	17	33	-5	46	5
Martin Rucinsky	60	9	23	32	+4	58	4
Bob Bassen	83	13	15	28	-17	99	1
ST.L.	46	2	7	9	-14	44	0
QUE	37	11	8	19	-3	55	1
Claude Lapointe	59	11	17	28	+2	70	1
Alexei Gusarov	76	5	20	25	+3	38	0
Curtis Leschyshyn	72	5	17	22	-2	65	3
Garth Butcher	77	4	15	19	-7	143	0
ST.L.	43	1	6	7	-6	76	0
QUE	34	3	9	12	-1	67	0
Dave Karpa*	60	5	12	17	E	148	2
Steven Finn	80	4	13	17	-9	159	0
Craig Wolanin	63	6	10	16	+16	80	0
Mike McKee*	48	3	12	15	+5	41	2

Acquired: Bassen, Butcher and Sutter from St.L. (Jan. 23).

Goalies (10 Gm)	Gm	Min	GAA	Sv%	Record
Jacques Cloutier	14	475	3.03	.897	3-2-1
Jocelyn Thibault	29	1504	3.31	.892	8-13-3
Stephane Fiset	50	2798	3.39	.890	20-25-4
QUEBEC	84	5080	3.45	.886	34-42-8

Shutouts: Fiset (2); **Assists:** Fiset (3); **PM:** Fiset (8), Cloutier (2), Thibault (2).

St. Louis Blues

Top Scorers	Gm	G	A	Pts	+/-	PM	PP
Brendan Shanahan	81	52	50	102	-9	211	15
Brett Hull	81	57	40	97	-3	38	25
Craig Janney	69	16	68	84	-14	24	8
Kevin Miller	75	23	25	48	+6	83	6
Steve Duchesne	36	12	19	31	+1	14	8
Vitali Prokhorov	55	15	10	25	-6	20	3
Philippe Bozon	80	9	16	25	+4	42	0
Alexei Kasatonov	63	4	20	24	-3	62	1
ANA	55	4	18	22	-8	43	1
ST.L.	8	0	2	2	+5	19	0
Phil Housley	26	7	15	22	-5	12	4
Vitali Karamnov*	59	9	12	21	-3	51	2
Petr Nedved	19	6	14	20	+2	8	2
Jim Montgomery*	67	6	14	20	-1	44	0
Igor Korolev	73	6	10	16	-12	40	0
Peter Stastny	17	5	11	16	-2	4	2
Murray Baron	77	5	9	14	-14	123	0
Tony Hrkac	36	6	5	11	-11	8	1
Rick Zombo	74	2	8	10	-15	85	0
Doug Crossman	50	2	7	9	+1	10	1
Tom Tilley	48	1	7	8	+3	32	0
Kelly Chase	68	5	5	7	-5	278	0
Dave Mackey	30	3	5	4	-4	56	0
Daniel Laperriere*	20	1	3	4	-1	8	1
Basil McRae	40	1	2	3	-7	103	0

Acquired: Duchesne from Que (Jan. 23); Kasatonov from Ana. (Mar. 21).

Goalies (10 Gm)	Gm	Min	GAA	Sv%	Record
Curtis Joseph	71	4127	3.10	.911	36-23-11
Jim Hrivnak	23	970	4.27	.877	4-10-0
ST. LOUIS	84	5107	3.32	.904	40-33-11

Shutout: Joseph (1); **Assists:** Joseph (3), Hrivnak (1); **PM:** Joseph (4), Hrivnak (2).

San Jose Sharks

Top Scorers	Gm	G	A	Pts	+/-	PM	PP
Ulf Dahlen	78	25	44	69	−1	10	15
DAL	65	19	38	57	−1	10	12
SJ	13	6	6	12	E	0	3
Sergei Makarov	80	30	38	68	+11	78	10
Todd Elik	79	25	41	66	−3	95	9
EDM	4	0	0	0	E	6	0
SJ	75	25	41	66	−3	89	9
Sandis Ozolinsh	81	26	38	64	+16	24	4
Igor Larionov	60	18	38	56	+20	40	3
Pat Falloon	83	22	31	53	−3	18	6
Johan Garpenlov	80	18	35	53	+9	28	7
Ray Whitney	61	14	26	40	+2	14	1
Jeff Norton	64	7	33	40	+16	36	1
Rob Gaudreau	84	15	20	35	−10	28	6
Bob Errey	64	12	18	30	−11	126	5
Gaetan Duchesne	84	12	18	30	+8	28	0
Tom Pederson	74	6	19	25	+3	31	3
Viacheslav Butsayev	59	12	11	23	E	68	2
PHI	47	12	9	21	+2	58	2
SJ	12	0	2	2	−2	10	0
Jeff Odgers	81	13	8	21	−13	222	7
Jamie Baker	65	12	5	17	+2	38	0
Mike Rathje*	47	1	9	10	−9	59	1
Dale Craigwell	58	3	6	9	−13	16	0

Acquired: Elik on waivers from Edm. (Oct. 26); Butsayev from Phi. (Feb. 1); Dahlen (Mar. 19).

Goalies (10 Gm)	Gm	Min	GAA	Sv%	Record
Arturs Irbe	74	4412	2.84	.899	30-28-16
Jim Waite	15	697	4.30	.843	3-7-0
SAN JOSE	84	5125	3.10	.889	33-35-16

Shutouts: Irbe (3); **Assists:** Irbe (2); **PM:** Irbe (16), Waite (6).

Toronto Maple Leafs

Top Scorers	Gm	G	A	Pts	+/-	PM	PP
Doug Gilmour	83	27	84	111	+25	105	10
Dave Andreychuk	83	53	45	98	+22	98	21
Wendel Clark	64	46	30	76	+10	115	21
Mike Gartner	81	34	30	64	+20	62	11
NYR	71	28	24	52	+11	58	10
TOR	10	6	6	12	+9	4	1
Dave Ellett	68	7	36	43	+6	42	5
Dmitri Mironov	76	9	27	36	+5	78	3
Nikolai Borschevsky	45	14	21	35	+6	10	7
John Cullen	53	13	17	30	−2	67	2
Rob Pearson	67	12	18	30	−6	189	1
Jamie Macoun	82	3	27	30	−5	115	1
Todd Gill	45	4	23	27	+8	44	2
Mark Osborne	73	9	16	25	+2	145	1
Bill Berg	83	8	11	19	−3	93	0
Mike Eastwood	54	8	10	18	+2	28	1
Peter Zezel	41	8	8	16	+5	19	0
Kent Manderville	67	7	9	16	+5	63	0
Bob Rouse	63	5	11	16	+8	101	1
Mark Greig	44	6	7	13	−5	41	0
HART	31	4	5	9	−6	31	0
TOR	13	2	2	4	+1	10	0
Mike Krushelnyski	54	5	6	11	−5	28	1
Sylvain Lefebvre	84	2	9	11	+33	79	0

Acquired: Greig from Hart. (Jan. 25); Gartner from NYR (Mar. 21).

Goalies (10 Gm)	Gm	Min	GAA	Sv%	Record
Damian Rhodes	22	1213	2.62	.902	9-7-3
Felix Potvin	66	3883	2.89	.907	34-22-9
TORONTO	84	5115	2.85	.905	43-29-12

Shutouts: Potvin (3); **Assists:** Potvin (4); **PM:** Potvin (4), Rhodes (2).

Tampa Bay Lightning

Top Scorers	Gm	G	A	Pts	+/-	PM	PP
Brian Bradley	78	24	40	64	−8	56	6
Petr Klima	75	28	27	55	−15	76	10
Denis Savard	74	18	28	46	−1	106	2
Danton Cole	81	20	23	43	+7	32	8
Chris Gratton*	84	13	29	42	−25	123	5
John Tucker	66	17	23	40	+9	28	2
Shawn Chambers	66	11	23	34	−6	23	6
Chris Joseph	76	11	20	31	−21	136	8
EDM	10	1	1	2	−8	28	1
TB	66	10	19	29	−13	108	7
Pat Elynuik	67	13	15	28	−21	64	4
WASH	4	1	1	2	−3	0	1
TB	63	12	14	26	−18	64	3
Mikael Andersson	76	13	12	25	+8	23	1
Roman Hamrlik	64	3	18	21	−14	135	0
Adam Creighton	53	10	10	20	−7	37	2
Marc Bergevin	83	1	15	16	−5	87	0
Marc Bureau	75	8	7	15	−9	30	0
Gerard Gallant	51	4	9	13	−6	74	1
Rob Zamuner	59	6	6	12	−9	42	0
Rudy Poeschek	71	3	6	9	+3	118	0
Bill McDougall	22	3	3	6	−4	8	1
Chris LiPuma*	27	0	4	4	+1	77	0

Acquired: Elynuik from Wash. (Oct. 24); Joseph from Edm. (Nov. 12).

Goalies (10 Gm)	Gm	Min	GAA	Sv%	Record
Daren Puppa	63	3653	2.71	.899	22-33-6
Pat Jablonski	15	834	3.88	.856	5-6-3
TAMPA BAY	84	5116	2.94	.891	30-43-11

Shutouts: Puppa (4); **Assists:** Puppa (1); **PM:** Puppa (2).

Vancouver Canucks

Top Scorers	Gm	G	A	Pts	+/-	PM	PP
Pavel Bure	76	60	47	107	+1	86	25
Geoff Courtnall	82	26	44	70	+15	123	12
Cliff Ronning	76	25	43	68	+2	42	10
Jeff Brown	74	14	52	66	−11	56	7
ST. L	63	13	47	60	−13	46	7
VAN	11	1	5	6	+2	10	0
Trevor Linden	84	32	29	61	+6	73	10
Murray Craven	78	15	40	55	+5	30	2
Jyrki Lumme	83	13	42	55	+3	50	1
Jiri Slegr	78	5	33	38	E	86	1
Greg Adams	68	13	24	37	−1	20	5
Dave Babych	73	4	28	32	E	52	0
Gino Odjick	76	16	13	29	+13	271	4
Martin Gelinas	64	14	14	28	−8	34	3
QUE	31	6	6	12	−2	8	0
VAN	33	8	8	16	−6	26	3
Jimmy Carson	59	11	17	28	−15	24	3
LA	25	4	7	11	−2	2	1
VAN	34	7	10	17	−13	22	2
Sergio Momesso	68	14	13	27	−2	149	4
Dana Murzyn	80	6	14	20	+4	109	0
Brian Glynn	64	2	13	15	−19	53	1
OTT	48	2	13	15	−15	41	1
VAN	16	0	0	0	−4	12	0
Jose Charbonneau	30	7	7	14	−3	49	1

Acquired: Carson from L.A. (Jan. 8); Gelinas on waivers from Que. (Jan. 15); Glynn on waivers from Ott. (Feb. 5); Brown and Bret Hedican from St.L. (Mar. 21).

Goalies (10 Gm)	Gm	Min	GAA	Sv%	Record
Kirk McLean	52	3128	2.99	.891	23-26-3
Kay Whitmore	32	1921	3.53	.867	18-14-0
VANCOUVER	84	5070	3.27	.879	41-40-3

Shutouts: McLean (3); **Assists:** McLean (4); **PM:** Whitmore (6), McLean (2).

Washington Capitals

Top Scorers	Gm	G	A	Pts	+/-	PM	PP
Joe Juneau	74	19	66	85	+11	41	6
BOS	63	14	58	72	11	35	4
WASH	11	5	8	13	E	6	2
Mike Ridley	81	26	44	70	+15	24	10
Dimitri Khristich	83	29	29	58	−2	73	10
Sylvain Cote	84	16	35	51	+30	66	3
Michal Pivonka	82	14	36	50	+2	38	5
Peter Bondra	69	24	19	43	+22	40	4
Randy Burridge	78	25	17	42	−1	73	8
Calle Johansson	84	9	33	42	+3	59	4
Kevin Hatcher	72	16	24	40	−13	108	6
Kelly Miller	84	14	25	39	+8	32	0
Dale Hunter	52	9	29	38	−4	131	1
Keith Jones	68	16	19	35	+4	149	5
Todd Krygier	66	12	18	30	−4	60	0
Pat Peake*	49	11	18	29	+1	39	3
Steve Konowalchuk	62	12	14	26	+9	33	0
Dave Poulin	63	6	19	25	−1	52	0
Joe Reekie	85	1	16	17	+15	156	0
TB	73	1	11	12	+8	127	0
WASH	12	0	5	5	+7	29	0
John Slaney*	47	7	9	16	+3	27	3

Acquired: Juneau from Bos. and Reekie from T.B. (Mar. 21).

Goalies (10 Gm)	Gm	Min	GAA	Sv%	Record
Don Beaupre	53	2853	2.84	.880	24-16-8
Rick Tabaracci	32	1770	3.08	.889	13-14-2
WASHINGTON	84	5099	3.09	.879	39-35-10

Shutouts: Beaupre (2), Tabaracci (2); **Assists:** Beaupre (1); **PM:** Beaupre (16), Tabaracci (6).

Winnipeg Jets

Top Scorers	Gm	G	A	Pts	+/-	PM	PP
Keith Tkachuk	84	41	40	81	−12	255	22
Nelson Emerson	83	33	41	74	−38	80	4
Alexei Zhamnov	61	26	45	71	−20	62	7
Darrin Shannon	77	21	37	58	−18	87	9
Teemu Selanne	51	25	29	54	−23	22	11
Thomas Steen	76	19	32	51	−38	32	6
Dallas Drake	62	13	27	40	−1	49	1
DET	47	10	22	32	+5	37	0
WIN	15	3	5	8	−6	12	1
Stephane Quintal	81	8	18	26	−25	119	1
Teppo Numminen	57	5	18	23	−23	28	4
Dave Manson	70	4	17	21	−14	191	1
EDM	57	3	13	16	−4	140	0
WIN	13	1	4	5	−10	51	1
Tie Domi	81	8	11	19	−8	347	1
Luciano Borsato	75	5	13	18	−11	28	1
Igor Ulanov	74	0	17	17	−11	165	

Acquired: Drake from Det. (Mar. 8); Manson from Edm. (Mar. 15).

Goalies (10 Gm)	Gm	Min	GAA	Sv%	Record
Tim Cheveldae	44	2360	3.64	.882	21-17-2
DET	30	1572	3.47	.875	16-9-1
WIN	14	788	3.96	.893	5-8-1
Michael O'Neill	17	738	4.15	.866	0-9-1
Steph Beauregard	13	418	4.88	.839	0-4-1
WINNIPEG	84	5098	4.05	.877	24-51-9

Shutouts: Cheveldae (2); **Assists:** Cheveldae (1); **PM:** Cheveldae (2).
Acquired: Cheveldae from Det. (Mar. 8).

World Championship

Canada captured its first World Hockey Championship since 1961 on May 8, defeating Finland when Luc Robitaille of the LA Kings scored the deciding goal in a dramatic sudden death shootout. Tied at 1-1 following regulation time and a scoreless overtime period, the game then went to a shootout (five players from each team alternating shots) which ended at 2-2. A sudden death shootout followed with Robitaille scored for Canada and the Finns' Mika Nieminen missing. At the Winter Olympics in February, Canada lost the gold medal game to Sweden in a shootout (see "Olympics" chapter).

The 47th World Hockey Championships were held in Alba di Canazei and Bolzano, Italy, from April 25 to May 8, 1994. Top four teams in Groups A and B after preliminary round-robin advanced to the quarterfinals. NHL personnel available for tournament was limited to players on teams not participating in Stanley Cup playoffs.

Final Round Robin Standings

(Overall records in parentheses)

Group A	Gm	W-L-T	Pts	GF	GA
*Canada (8-0-0)	5	5-0-0	10	24	7
*Russia (4-2-0)	5	4-1-0	8	30	7
*Italy (3-3-0)	5	3-2-0	6	17	16
*Austria (1-4-1)	5	1-3-1	2	15	15
Germany (1-3-1)	5	1-3-1	2	10	14
Great Britain (0-6-0)	5	0-5-0	0	7	44

Note: Austria tied Germany, 2-2, but qualified for medal round on goal differential.

Group B	Gm	W-L-T	Pts	GF	GA
*Finland (6-1-1)	5	4-0-1	9	29	11
*Sweden (5-2-1)	5	3-1-1	7	22	11
*United States (4-4-0)	5	3-2-0	6	21	19
*Czech Republic (1-3-2)	5	1-2-2	4	15	17
France (1-4-0)	5	1-4-0	2	8	25
Norway (1-3-2)	5	0-3-2	2	9	21

Quarterfinals

United States 3, Russia 1   Sweden 7, Italy 2
Canada 3, Czech Republic 2   Finland 10, Austria 0

Semifinals

Finland 8, United States 0   Canada 6, Sweden 0

Third Place

Sweden 7 .... United States 2

Championship Game

Canada 1 .... OT .... Finland 1

Note: (Canada won sudden death shootout, 1-0.)

Leading Scorers

	Gm	G	A	Pts	PM
Mats Sundin, Sweden	8	5	9	14	4
Paul Kariya, Canada	8	5	7	12	2
Saku Koivu, Finland	8	5	6	11	4
Valeri Kamensky, Russia	5	5	5	10	12
Jari Kurri, Finland	8	4	6	10	2
Magnus Svensson, Sweden	8	8	1	9	8
Mikko Makela, Finland	8	5	4	9	6
Igor Fedulov, Russia	6	4	5	9	6
Andrei Kovalenko, Russia	6	3	5	8	2
Jonas Bergkvist, Sweden	8	3	5	8	4
Jere Lehtinen, Finland	8	3	5	8	4

Leading Goaltenders

	Gm	Min	GA	Avg	Sv%
Mikhail Shtalenkov, Rus	6	294	5	1.02	.962
Bill Ranford, Can	7	360	7	1.17	.956
Jarmo Myllys, Fin	7	400	9	1.35	.942
Roger Nordstrom, Swe	5	300	11	2.20	.875
Michael Puschacher, Aut	5	271	12	2.65	.926

All-Tournament

First Team (picked by media): **G**— Bill Ranford, Canada; **D**— Timo Jutila, Finland and Magnus Svensson, Sweden; **C**— Saku Koivu, Finland; **LW**— Paul Kariya, Canada; **RW**— Jari Kurri, Finland.

STANLEY CUP PLAYOFFS

| FIRST ROUND | SEMIFINALS | FINAL | | FINAL | SEMIFINALS | FIRST ROUND |

Detroit 3
San Jose 4

Toronto 4 (#1)

Calgary 3
Vancouver 4

San Jose 3 (#4)

Toronto 1

WESTERN CONFERENCE

NY Rangers 4
Vancouver 3

Toronto 4
Chicago 2

Dallas 1 (#2)

Dallas 4
St. Louis 0

Vancouver 4 (#3)

Vancouver 4

NY Rangers 4

EASTERN CONFERENCE

New Jersey 3

NY Rangers 4 (#1)

Washington 1 (#4)

New Jersey 4 (#2)

Boston 2 (#3)

NY Rangers 4
NY Islanders 0

Pittsburgh 2
Washington 4

New Jersey 4
Buffalo 3

Boston 4
Montreal 3

Note: teams surviving 1st round are reseeded in conference semi-finals.

Series Summaries

WESTERN CONFERENCE

FIRST ROUND (Best of 7)

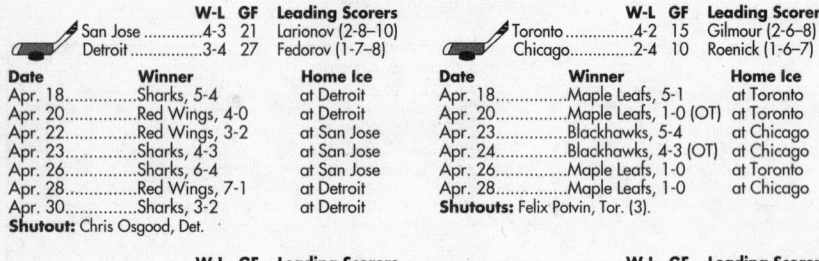

	W-L	GF	Leading Scorers
San Jose	4-3	21	Larionov (2-8-10)
Detroit	3-4	27	Fedorov (1-7-8)

Date	Winner	Home Ice
Apr. 18	Sharks, 5-4	at Detroit
Apr. 20	Red Wings, 4-0	at Detroit
Apr. 22	Red Wings, 3-2	at San Jose
Apr. 23	Sharks, 4-3	at San Jose
Apr. 26	Sharks, 6-4	at San Jose
Apr. 28	Red Wings, 7-1	at Detroit
Apr. 30	Sharks, 3-2	at Detroit

Shutout: Chris Osgood, Det.

	W-L	GF	Leading Scorers
Toronto	4-2	15	Gilmour (2-6-8)
Chicago	2-4	10	Roenick (1-6-7)

Date	Winner	Home Ice
Apr. 18	Maple Leafs, 5-1	at Toronto
Apr. 20	Maple Leafs, 1-0 (OT)	at Toronto
Apr. 23	Blackhawks, 5-4	at Chicago
Apr. 24	Blackhawks, 4-3 (OT)	at Chicago
Apr. 26	Maple Leafs, 1-0	at Toronto
Apr. 28	Maple Leafs, 1-0	at Chicago

Shutouts: Felix Potvin, Tor. (3).

	W-L	GF	Leading Scorers
Vancouver	4-3	23	Courtnall (4-4-8)
			& Bure (3-5-8)
Calgary	3-4	20	Fleury (6-4-10)

Date	Winner	Home Ice
Apr. 18	Canucks, 5-0	at Calgary
Apr. 20	Flames, 7-5	at Calgary
Apr. 22	Flames, 4-2	at Vancouver
Apr. 24	Flames, 3-2	at Vancouver
Apr. 26	Canucks, 2-1 (OT)	at Calgary
Apr. 28	Canucks, 3-2 (OT)	at Vancouver
Apr. 30	Canucks, 4-3 (2OT)	at Calgary

Shutout: Kirk McLean, Van.

	W-L	GF	Leading Scorers
Dallas	4-0	16	Modano (5-3-8)
St. Louis	0-4	10	Shanahan(2-5-7)

Date	Winner	Home Ice
Apr. 17	Stars, 5-3	at Dallas
Apr. 20	Stars, 4-2	at Dallas
Apr. 22	Stars, 5-4 (OT)	at St. Louis
Apr. 24	Stars, 2-1	at St. Louis

SEMIFINALS (Best of 7)

	W-L	GF	Leading Scorers
Toronto	4-3	26	Gilmour (3-11-14)
San Jose	3-4	21	Larionov (3-4-7)

Date	Winner	Home Ice
May 2	Sharks, 3-2	at Toronto
May 4	Maple Leafs, 5-1	at Toronto
May 6	Sharks, 5-2	at San Jose
May 8	Maple Leafs, 8-3	at San Jose
May 10	Sharks, 5-2	at San Jose
May 12	Maple Leafs, 3-2 (OT)	at Toronto
May 14	Maple Leafs, 4-2	at Toronto

	W-L	GF	Leading Scorers
Vancouver	4-1	18	Bure (6-2-8)
Dallas	1-4	11	Four tied with 3 pts.

Date	Winner	Home Ice
May 2	Canucks, 6-4	at Dallas
May 4	Canucks, 3-0	at Dallas
May 6	Stars, 4-3	at Vancouver
May 8	Canucks, 2-1 (OT)	at Vancouver
May 10	Canucks, 4-2	at Vancouver

Shutout: Kirk McLean, Van.

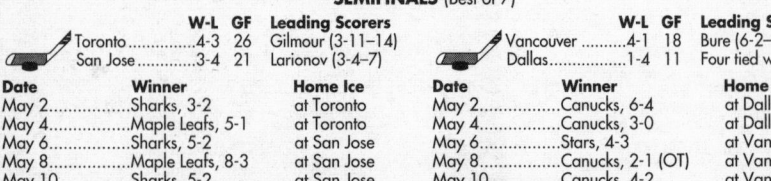

CHAMPIONSHIP (Best of 7)

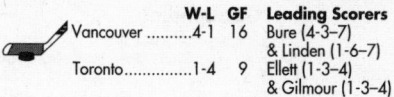

	W-L	GF	Leading Scorers
Vancouver	4-1	16	Bure (4-3–7)
			& Linden (1-6–7)
Toronto	1-4	9	Ellett (1-3–4)
			& Gilmour (1-3–4)

Date	Winner	Home Ice
May 16	Maple Leafs, 3-2 (OT)	at Toronto
May 18	Canucks, 4-3	at Toronto
May 20	Canucks, 4-0	at Vancouver
May 22	Canucks, 2-0	at Vancouver
May 24	Canucks, 4-3 (2OT)	at Vancouver

Shutouts: Kirk McLean, Van. (2).

EASTERN CONFERENCE

FIRST ROUND (Best of 7)

	W-L	GF	Leading Scorers
NY Rangers	4-0	22	Leetch (2-6–8)
NY Islanders	0-4	3	Nine tied with 1 pt.

Date	Winner	Home Ice
Apr. 17	Rangers, 6-0	at New York
Apr. 18	Rangers, 6-0	at New York
Apr. 21	Rangers, 5-1	at Long Island
Apr. 24	Rangers, 5-2	at Long Island

Shutouts: Mike Richter, NYR (2).

	W-L	GF	Leading Scorers
Washington	4-2	20	Juneau (3-4–7)
			& Pivonka (3-4–7)
Pittsburgh	2-4	12	Lemieux (4-3–7)

Date	Winner	Home Ice
Apr. 17	Capitals, 5-3	at Pittsburgh
Apr. 19	Penguins, 2-1	at Pittsburgh
Apr. 21	Capitals, 2-0	at Washington
Apr. 23	Capitals, 4-1	at Washington
Apr. 25	Penguins, 3-2	at Pittsburgh
Apr. 27	Capitals, 6-3	at Washington

Shutout: Don Beaupre, Wash.

	W-L	GF	Leading Scorers
New Jersey	4-3	14	Lemieux (4-2–6),
			MacLean (3-3–6)
			& Stevens (2-5–7)
Buffalo	3-4	14	Hawerchuk (0-7–7)

Date	Winner	Home Ice
Apr. 17	Sabres, 2-0	at New Jersey
Apr. 19	Devils, 2-1	at New Jeresy
Apr. 21	Devils, 2-1	at Buffalo
Apr. 23	Sabres, 5-3	at Buffalo
Apr. 25	Devils, 5-3	at New Jersey
Apr. 27	Sabres, 1-0 (4OT)	at Buffalo
Apr. 29	Devils, 2-1	at New Jersey

Shutouts: Dominik Hasek, Buf. (2).

	W-L	GF	Leading Scorers
Boston	4-3	22	Bourque (1-5–6)
Montreal	3-4	20	Muller (6-2–8)

Date	Winner	Home Ice
Apr. 16	Bruins, 3-2	at Boston
Apr. 18	Canadiens, 3-2	at Boston
Apr. 21	Bruins, 6-3	at Montreal
Apr. 23	Canadiens, 5-2	at Montreal
Apr. 25	Canadiens, 2-1 (OT)	at Boston
Apr. 27	Bruins, 3-2	at Montreal
Apr. 29	Bruins, 5-3	at Boston

SEMIFINALS (Best of 7)

	W-L	GF	Leading Scorers
NY Rangers	4-1	20	Leetch (3-6–9)
Washington	1-4	12	Cote (1-6–7)

Date	Winner	Home Ice
May 1	Rangers, 6-3	at New York
May 3	Rangers, 5-2	at New York
May 5	Rangers, 3-0	at Washington
May 7	Capitals, 4-2	at Washington
May 9	Rangers, 4-3	at New York

Shutout: Mike Richter, NYR.

	W-L	GF	Leading Scorers
New Jersey	4-2	22	Lemieux (1-6–7)
Boston	2-4	17	Oates (0-7–7)

Date	Winner	Home Ice
May 1	Bruins, 2-1	at New Jersey
May 3	Bruins, 6-5 (OT)	at New Jersey
May 5	Devils, 4-2	at Boston
May 7	Devils, 5-4 (OT)	at Boston
May 9	Devils, 2-0	at New Jersey
May 11	Devils, 5-3	at Boston

Shutout: Martin Brodeur, NJ.

CHAMPIONSHIP (Best of 7)

	W-L	GF	Leading Scorers
NY Rangers	4-3	18	Messier (4-7–11)
New Jersey	3-4	16	Lemieux (2-3–5)
			& Nicholls (2-3–5)

Date	Winner	Home Ice
May 16	Devils, 4-3 (2OT)	at New York
May 17	Rangers, 4-0	at New York
May 19	Rangers, 3-2 (2OT)	at New Jersey
May 21	Devils, 3-1	at New Jersey
May 23	Devils, 4-1	at New York
May 25	Rangers, 4-2	at New Jersey
May 27	Rangers, 2-1 (2OT)	at New York

Shutout: Mike Richter, NYR.

STANLEY CUP FINAL

	W-L	GF	Leading Scorers
NY Rangers	4-3	21	Leetch (5-6–11)
Vancouver	3-4	19	Bure (3-4–7)
			& Ronning (1-6–7)

Date	Winner	Home Ice
May 31	Canucks, 3-2 (OT)	at New York
June 2	Rangers, 3-1	at New York
June 4	Rangers, 5-1	at Vancouver
June 7	Rangers, 4-2	at Vancouver
June 9	Canucks, 6-3	at Vancouver
June 11	Canucks, 4-1	at Vancouver
June 14	Rangers, 3-2	at New York

Conn Smythe Trophy (MVP)

Brian Leetch, NY Rangers, D
23 games, 11 goals, 23 assists, 34 points

Stanley Cup Leaders

Scoring

	Pos	Gm	G	A	Pts	+/-	PM
Brian Leetch, NYR ....D		23	11	23	**34**	+19	6
Pavel Bure, Van..............R		24	16	14	**30**	+7	40
Mark Messier, NYR C		23	12	18	**30**	+14	33
Doug Gilmour, Tor C		18	6	22	**28**	+3	42
Trevor Linden, Van C		24	12	13	**25**	+3	18
Alexei Kovalev, NYR C		23	9	12	**21**	+5	18
Geoff Courtnall, Van L		24	9	10	**19**	+10	51
Sergei Zubov, NYR ....D		22	5	14	**19**	+10	0
Claude Lemieux, NJ L		20	7	11	**18**	+4	44
Igor Larionov, SJ C		14	5	13	**18**	−1	10
Dave Ellett, Tor ....D		18	3	15	**18**	+5	31
Adam Graves, NYR L		23	10	7	**17**	+12	24
Wendel Clark, Tor...........L		18	9	7	**16**	E	24
Steve Larmer, NYR ....R		23	9	7	**16**	+8	14
John MacLean, NJ ....R		20	6	10	**16**	−2	22

Goaltending

(Minimum 420 minutes)

	Gm	Min	W-L	ShO	GAA
Dominik Hasek, Buf.........7		484	3-4	2	**1.61**
Martin Brodeur*, NJ 17		1171	8-9	1	**1.95**
Mike Richter, NYR.................23		1417	16-7	4	**2.07**
Kirk McLean, Van 24		1544	15-9	4	**2.29**
Felix Potvin, Tor 18		1124	9-9	3	**2.46**
Ed Belfour, Chi 6		360	2-4	1	**2.50**
Patrick Roy, Mon 6		375	3-3	0	**2.56**

Wins

Richter, NYR 16-7	
McLean, Van 15-9	
Potvin, Tor 9-9	
Brodeur*, NJ 8-9	
Irbe, SJ 7-7	

Save Pct.

Hasek, Buf..............	.950
Roy, Mon	.930
McLean, Van	.928
Brodeur*, NJ	.928
Richter, NYR	.921

Goals

Bure, Van	16
Linden, Van	12
Messier, NYR	12
Leetch, NYR	11
Graves, NYR	10

Assists

Leetch, NYR	23
Gilmour, Tor	22
Messier, NYR	18
Ellet, Tor	15
Bure, Van	14
Zubov, NYR	14

Power Play Goals

Mironov, Tor	6
Gilmour, Tor	5
Kovalev, NYR.............	5
Linden, Van	5
Leetch, NYR	4

Overtime Goals

Adams, Van	2
Matteau, NYR	2
Richer, NJ	2
12 tied with one each.	

Plus/Minus

Leetch, NYR	+19
Beukeboom, NYR .....+17	
Messier, NYR	+14
LaFayette*, Van........	+13
Hedican, Van	+13

Penalty Minutes

Peluso, NJ	64
Momesso, Van	56
Osborne, Tor	52
Courtnall, Van	51
Beukeboom, NYR.......50	

Final Stanley Cup Standings

					Goals		
	Gm	W	L	Pts	For	Opp	Dif
NY Rangers.............	23	16	7	32	50	+31	
Vancouver...............	24	15	9	30	76	61	+15
New Jersey..............	20	11	9	22	52	49	+3
Toronto..................	18	9	9	18	50	47	+3
San Jose.................	14	7	7	14	42	53	−11
Boston....................	13	6	7	12	39	42	−3
Washington..............	11	5	6	10	32	32	E
Dallas.....................	9	5	4	10	27	28	−1
Detroit....................	7	3	4	6	27	21	+6
Buffalo....................	7	3	4	6	14	14	E
Montreal.................	7	3	4	6	20	22	−2
Calgary...................	7	3	4	6	20	23	−3
Chicago..................	6	2	4	4	10	15	−5
Pittsburgh...............	6	2	4	4	12	20	−8
St. Louis.................	4	0	4	0	10	16	−6
NY Islanders............	4	0	4	0	3	22	−19

Finalists' Composite Box Scores
New York Rangers (16-7)

		Overall Playoffs								Finals vs Vancouver						
Top Scorers	Pos	Gm	G	A	Pts	+/-	PM	PP	S	Gm	G	A	Pts	+/-	PM	PP	S
Brian Leetch ....D		23	11	23	**34**	+19	6	4	88	7	5	6	**11**	−1	4	0	29
Mark Messier C		23	12	18	**30**	+14	33	2	75	7	2	5	**7**	E	17	1	25
Alexei Kovalev C		23	9	12	**21**	+5	18	5	71	7	4	3	**7**	−4	2	3	24
Sergei Zubov ....D		22	5	14	**19**	+10	0	2	60	6	1	5	**6**	+2	0	1	17
Adams Graves L		23	10	7	**17**	+12	24	3	93	7	1	3	**4**	E	4	1	24
Steve Larmer ....R		23	9	7	**16**	+8	14	3	54	7	4	0	**4**	+3	2	0	26
Brian Noonan ....R		22	4	7	**11**	+2	17	2	45	7	0	1	**1**	−2	0	0	15
Stephane Matteau L		23	6	3	**9**	+5	20	1	36	7	0	1	**1**	−1	6	0	7
Esa Tikkanen L		23	4	4	**8**	+1	34	0	56	7	1	1	**1**	−2	12	0	24
Sergei Nemchinov C		23	2	5	**7**	+1	6	0	33	7	0	2	**2**	E	2	0	6
Glenn Anderson ....R		23	3	3	**6**	+5	42	0	31	7	2	1	**3**	E	4	0	11
Jeff Beukeboom ....D		23	0	6	**6**	+17	50	0	22	7	0	2	**2**	+3	25	0	8
Craig MacTavish C		23	1	4	**5**	E	22	0	15	7	0	1	**1**	+1	6	0	4
Greg Gilbert L		23	1	3	**4**	−2	8	0	23	7	0	1	**1**	E	2	0	7
Alexander Karpovtsev* ....D		17	0	4	**4**	−6	12	0	14	2	0	0	**0**	−1	0	0	0
Doug Lidster ....D		9	2	0	**2**	−4	0	0	9	7	2	0	**2**	−3	10	0	8
Joey Kocur ....R		20	1	1	**2**	−1	17	0	16	7	0	0	**0**	E	2	0	5
Kevin Lowe ....D		22	1	0	**1**	+6	20	0	15	6	0	0	**0**	E	6	0	4
Jay Wells ....D		23	0	0	**0**	−6	20	0	12	7	0	0	**0**	−2	8	0	4

Overtime goals—OVERALL (Matteau 2); FINALS (none). **Shorthanded goals**—OVERALL (Anderson, Messier); FINALS (Anderson).

Goaltending	Gm	Min	GAA	GA	SA	Sv%	W-L	Gm	Min	GAA	GA	SA	Sv%	W-L
Glenn Healy	2	68	**0.88**	1	17	.941	0-0	—	—	—	—	—	—	—
Mike Richter	23	1417	**2.07**	49	623	.921	16-7	7	439	**2.60**	19	213	.911	4-3
TOTAL..................................	23	1485	**2.02**	50	640	.922	16-7	7	439	**2.60**	19	213	.911	4-3

Empty Net Goals—OVERALL (0); **Shutouts**—OVERALL (Richter 4), FINALS (none); **Assists**—OVERALL (none); **Penalty Minutes:** OVERALL (Richter 2), FINALS (Richter 2); **Power Play conversions**—6 for 28 (21.4%).

Vancouver Canucks (15-9)

Top Scorers	Pos	Overall Playoffs								Finals vs NY Rangers							
		Gm	G	A	Pts	+/-	PM	PP	S	Gm	G	A	Pts	+/-	PM	PP	S
Pavel Bure	R	24	16	14	30	+7	40	3	101	7	3	4	7	−1	15	0	30
Trevor Linden	C	24	12	13	25	+3	18	5	67	7	3	2	5	+2	6	2	18
Geoff Courtnall	L	24	9	10	19	+10	51	0	77	7	4	1	5	+3	11	0	24
Jeff Brown	D	24	6	9	15	+7	37	3	76	7	3	1	4	+1	8	1	19
Cliff Ronning	C	24	5	10	15	−2	16	2	69	7	1	6	7	+4	6	0	21
Greg Adams	L	23	6	8	14	+1	2	2	46	7	1	2	3	−3	2	0	15
Murray Craven	R	22	4	9	13	+10	18	0	38	7	0	2	2	−1	4	0	7
Jyrki Lumme	D	24	2	11	13	+8	16	2	53	7	0	4	4	+3	6	0	20
Martin Gelinas	R	24	5	4	9	−1	14	2	35	7	1	0	1	E	4	0	8
Nathan LaFayette*	C	20	2	7	9	+13	4	0	24	7	0	3	3	+4	0	0	7
Dave Babych	D	24	3	5	8	+4	12	0	26	7	0	1	1	−4	2	0	8
Gerald Diduck	D	24	1	7	8	+1	22	0	32	7	0	1	1	−4	6	0	6
Sergio Momesso	L	24	3	4	7	+7	56	0	38	7	1	1	2	+2	17	0	13
Bret Hedican	D	24	1	6	7	+13	16	0	22	7	1	3	4	+5	4	0	8
Brian Glynn	D	17	0	3	3	+5	10	0	11	7	0	1	1	+2	0	0	3
Jose Charbonneau	R	3	1	0	1	+1	4	0	4	—	—	—	—	—	—	—	—
Jimmy Carson	C	2	0	1	1	+1	0	0	2	—	—	—	—	—	—	—	—
Shawn Antoski*	L	16	0	1	1	−3	36	0	4	7	0	1	1	−3	8	0	2
Tim Hunter	R	24	0	1	1	−2	26	0	8	7	0	1	1	−2	18	0	1
John McIntyre	C	24	0	1	1	−3	16	0	12	7	0	0	0	−3	6	0	3

Overtime goals—OVERALL (Adams 2, Bure, Courtnall, Linden, Momesso); FINALS (Adams). **Shorthanded goals**—OVERALL (Courtnall, Linden); FINALS (Linden); **Power Play conversions**—3 for 35 (8.6%).

Goaltending	Gm	Min	GAA	GA	SA	Sv%	W-L	Gm	Min	GAA	GA	SA	Sv%	W-L
Kirk McLean	24	1544	2.29	59	820	.928	15-9	7	436	2.75	20	248	.919	3-4
TOTAL	24	1554	2.36	61	822	.926	15-9	7	439	2.87	21	249	.916	3-4

Empty Net Goals—OVERALL (2), FINALS (1); **Shutouts**—OVERALL (McLean 4), FINALS—(none); **Assists**—OVERALL (McLean), FINALS (none); **Penalty Minutes:** OVERALL (none).

NHL Draft

First and second round selections at the 32nd annual NHL Entry Draft held June 28-29, 1994, in Hartford. League and national affiliations are listed below.

First Round				Second Round		
	Team		Pos		Team	Pos
1	Florida	Ed Jovanovski, Windsor	D	27	Florida	Rhett Warrener, Saskatoon	D
2	Anaheim	Oleg Tverdovsky, Krylja (RUS)	D	28	Anaheim	Johan Davidsson, HV 71 (SWE)	C
3	Ottawa	Radek Bonk, Las Vegas	C	29	Ottawa	Stanislav Nackar, Budejovice (CZE)	D
4	**a**-Edmonton	Jason Bonsignore, Niagara Falls	C	30	Winnipeg	Deron Quint, Seattle	D
5	Hartford	Jeff O'Neill, Guelph	C	31	**g**-Florida	Jason Podollan, Spokane	R
6	Edmonton	Ryan Smyth, Moose Jaw	L	32	Edmonton	Mike Watt, Stratford (Jr.B)	L
7	Los Angeles	Jamie Storr, Owen Sound	G	33	Los Angeles	Matt Johnson, Peterborough	L
8	Tampa Bay	Jason Weimer, Portland	L	34	Tampa Bay	Colin Cloutier, Brandon	C
9	**b**-NY Isles	Brett Lindros, Kingston	R	35	Quebec	Josef Marha, Jihlava (CZE)	C
10	**c**-Washington	Nolan Baumgartner, Kamloops	D	36	**h**-Florida	Ryan Johnson, Thunder Bay	C
11	San Jose	Jeff Friesen, Regina	L	37	San Jose	Angel Nikulov, Chemopetrol (CZE)	C
12	**d**-Quebec	Wade Belak, Saskatoon	D	38	NY Islanders	Jason Holland, Kamloops	D
13	Vancouver	Mattias Ohlund, Pitea (SWE)	D	39	Vancouver	Robb Gordon, Powell River (Jr.A)	C
14	Chicago	Ethan Moreau, Niagara Falls	L	40	Chicago	Jean-Yves Leroux, Beauport	L
15	Washington	Alex. Kharlamov, Cska Moscow	L	41	Washington	Scott Cherrey, North Bay	L
16	**e**-Toronto	Eric Fichaud, Chicoutimi	G	42	**i**-Vancouver	Dave Scatchard, Portland	C
17	Buffalo	Wayne Primeau, Owen Sound	C	43	Buffalo	Curtis Brown, Moose Jaw	C
18	Montreal	Brad Brown, North Bay	D	44	Montreal	Jose Theodore, St. Jean	G
19	Calgary	Chris Dingman, Brandon	L	45	Calgary	Dimitri Riabykin, Dynamo Moscow	D
20	Dallas	Jason Botterill, U. of Michigan	L	46	Dallas	Lee Jinman, North Bay	C
21	Boston	Yevgeni Ryabchikov, Molot-Perm (RUS)	G	47	Boston	Daniel Goneau, Laval	L
22	**f**-Quebec	Jeff Kealty, Catholic H.S. (MA)	D	48	Toronto	Sean Haggerty, Detroit	L
23	Detroit	Yan Golubovsky, Cska Moscow	D	49	Detroit	Mathieu Dandenault, Sherbrooke	R
24	Pittsburgh	Chris Wells, Seattle	C	50	Pittsburgh	Richard Park, Belleville	C
25	New Jersey	Vadim Sharifjanov, Salavat (RUS)	R	51	New Jersey	Patrik Elias, Kladno (CZE)	F
26	New York	Dan Cloutier, Sault Ste. Marie	G	52	NY Rangers	Rudolf Vercik, Bratislava (SVK)	F

Acquired picks: FIRST ROUND: **a**— from Winnipeg; **b**— from Quebec; **c**— from Quebec through Toronto; **d**— from NY Islanders; **e**— from Washington; **f**— from Toronto. SECOND ROUND: **g**— from Hartford; **h**— from Philadelphia; **i**— from St. Louis.

Affiliations: Czech Republic— Budejovice, Chemopetrol, Dukla Jihlava, Kladno; **IHL** (International Hockey League)— Las Vegas; **Junior A**— Powell River; **Junior B**— Stratford; **OHL** (Ontario Hockey League)— Belleville, Detroit, Guelph, Kingston, Niagara Falls, North Bay, Owen Sound, Peterborough, Sault Ste. Marie, Windsor; **QMJHL** (Quebec Major Jr. Hockey League)— Beauport, Chicoutimi, Laval, St. Jean, Sherbrooke; **Russia**— Cska Moscow, Dynamo-Moscow, Krylja Sovetov, Molot-Perm, Ufa Salavat; **Slovakia**— Bratislava; **Sweden**— HV 71, Pitea; **U.S. College**— Michigan (CCHA); **U.S. High School**— Catholic Memorial (Boston); **USHL** (U.S. Hockey League)— Thunder Bay; **WHL** (Western Hockey League)— Brandon, Kamloops, Moose Jaw, Portland, Regina, Saskatoon, Seattle, Spokane.

Annual Awards

Except for Vezina Trophy and Adams Award, voting by 50-member panel of the Pro Hockey Writers Assn., while full PHWA membership voted for Masterton Trophy. Vezina Trophy voted on by NHL general managers and Adams Award by NHL broadcasters. Points awarded on 5-3-1 basis.

Hart Trophy

For Most Valuable Player.

	Pos	1st	2nd	3rd	Pts
Sergei Fedorov, Det	C	31	11	6—	194
Dominik Hasek, Buf	G	6	15	11—	86
John Vanbiesbrouck, Fla	G	7	11	6—	74
Doug Gilmour, Tor	C	4	7	9—	50
Patrick Roy, Mon	G	3	3	2—	26

Calder Trophy

For Rookie of the Year.

	Pos	1st	2nd	3rd	Pts
Martin Brodeur, NJ	G	21	16	11—	164
Jason Arnott, Edm	C	15	18	8—	137
Mikael Renberg, Phi	R	9	16	16—	109
Alexei Yashin, Ott	C	9	4	16—	73

Three tied with one 3rd place vote each.

Norris Trophy

For Best Defenseman.

	1st	2nd	3rd	Pts
Ray Bourque, Bos	26	21	6—	199
Scott Stevens, NJ	24	23	6—	195
Al MacInnis, Calg	4	6	22—	60
Sergei Zubov, NYR	0	2	9—	15
Brian Leetch, NYR	0	2	4—	10

Vezina Trophy

For Outstanding Goaltender.

	1st	2nd	3rd	Pts
Dominik Hasek, Buf	15	8	0—	99
John Vanbiesbrouck, Fla	6	10	4—	64
Patrick Roy, Mon	3	3	10—	34
Curtis Joseph, St. L	1	1	2—	10
Arturs Irbe, SJ	1	1	1—	9

Lady Byng Trophy

For Sportsmanship and Gentlemanly Play.

	Pos	1st	2nd	3rd	Pts
Wayne Gretzky, LA	C	23	7	9—	145
Adam Oates, Bos	C	9	9	9—	81
Pierre Turgeon, NYI	C	6	12	5—	71
Sergei Fedorov, Det	C	10	6	2—	70
Ray Sheppard, Det	R	2	6	4—	32

Selke Trophy

For Best Defensive Forward.

	Pos	1st	2nd	3rd	Pts
Sergei Fedorov, Det	C	32	6	3—	181
Doug Gilmour, Tor	C	8	20	7—	107
Brian Skrudland, Fla	C	4	3	8—	37
Guy Carbonneau, Mon	C	1	5	9—	29
Adam Graves, NYR	L	2	2	3—	19

Adams Award

For Coach of the Year.

	1st	2nd	3rd	Pts
Jacques Lemiere, NJ	28	18	8—	202
Kevin Constantine, SJ	14	16	18—	136
John Muckler, Buf	12	10	8—	98
Roger Neilson, Fla	5	9	16—	68
Mike Keenan, NYR	3	5	6—	36

Wide World Photos

Detroit center **Sergei Fedorov** poses with his two trophies, the Selke (left) and the Hart.

Other Awards

Lester Pearson Award (NHL Players Assn. MVP)— Sergei Fedorov, Detroit, C; **Jennings Trophy** (goaltender with fewest goals against)— Dominik Hasek and Grant Fuhr, Buffalo; **Masterton Trophy** (for perserverence and dedication to hockey)—Cam Neely, Boston, RW; **King Clancy Trophy** (for leadership and humanitarian contribution to community)—Adam Graves, NY Rangers, LW; **Executive of the Year** (chosen by *The Hockey News*)—Neil Smith, NY Rangers.

All-NHL

Voting by Pro Hockey Writers' Association (PHWA). Holdover from 1992-93 All-NHL first team in **bold** type.

First Team		1st	2nd	3rd	Pts
G	Dominik Hasek, Buf	40	6	6—	224
D	**Ray Bourque**, Bos	50	4	0—	262
D	Scott Stevens, NJ	42	11	1—	244
C	Sergei Fedorov, Det	33	19	2—	223
R	Pavel Bure, Van	33	17	2—	218
L	Brendan Shanahan, St.L.	18	19	10—	157

Second Team		1st	2nd	3rd	Pts
G	John Vanbiesbrouck, Fla	6	20	14—	104
D	Al MacInnis, Calg	8	33	7—	146
D	Brian Leetch, NYR	3	22	17—	98
C	Wayne Gretzky, LA	18	15	12—	147
R	Cam Neely, Bos	18	12	10—	136
L	Adam Graves, NYR	22	12	7—	153

All-Rookie Team

Voting by PHWA. Vote totals not released.

Pos		Pos	
G	Martin Brodeur, NJ	C	Jason Arnott, Edm
D	Chris Pronger, Hart	F	Mikael Renberg, Phil
D	Boris Mironov, Edm	F	Oleg Petrov, Mon

U.S. Division I College Hockey

Final regular season standings; overall records, including all postseason tournament games, in parentheses.

Central Collegiate Hockey Assn.

	W	L	T	Pts	GF	GA
* Michigan (33-7-1)	24	5	1	49	146	80
* Lake Superior St. (31-10-4)	18	8	4	40	129	69
* Michigan St. (23-13-5)	17	8	5	39	115	87
* Western Mich. (24-13-3)	18	10	2	38	117	101
Miami-OH (21-16-1)	17	12	1	35	112	94
Bowling Green (19-17-2)	15	13	2	32	114	105
Ferris St. (13-24-1)	12	17	1	25	110	122
Notre Dame (11-22-5)	9	16	5	23	85	121
IL-Chicago (10-27-2)	8	20	2	18	101	144
Ohio St. (7-23-5)	6	19	5	17	81	124
Kent (11-26-2)	6	22	2	14	109	172

Note: Affiliate team Alaska-Fairbanks (24-13-1) was 7-5 vs CCHA during regular season.
Conf. Tourney Final: Michigan 3, Lake Superior St. 0.
*NCAA Tourney (4-3): Lake Superior St. (4-0), Michigan (0-1) Michigan St. (0-1), Western Michigan (0-1).

Eastern Collegiate Athletic Assn.

	W	L	T	Pts	GF	GA
* Harvard (24-5-4)	16	2	4	36	107	60
Clarkson (20-9-5)	13	5	4	30	92	67
* RPI (21-11-4)	12	6	4	28	99	75
Brown (15-12-5)	12	7	3	27	91	73
Vermont (15-12-6)	10	6	6	26	88	75
Union (15-11-4)	10	9	3	23	83	89
Colgate (13-17-2)	10	10	2	22	97	90
Cornell (8-17-5)	7	10	5	19	73	89
Princeton (10-15-3)	7	12	3	17	64	80
St. Lawrence (10-21-0)	8	14	0	16	74	95
Yale (5-21-1)	5	16	1	11	58	102
Dartmouth (5-21-1)	4	17	1	9	80	111

Conf. Tourney Final: Harvard 3, RPI 0.
*NCAA Tourney (1-2): Harvard (1-1), RPI (0-1).

Hockey East Association

	W	L	T	Pts	GF	GA
* Boston University (34-7)	21	3	0	42	120	63
* UMass-Lowell (25-10-5)	14	6	4	32	91	77
* New Hampshire (25-12-3)	13	9	2	28	90	91
* Northeastern (20-12-7)	10	8	6	26	94	95
Providence (14-19-3)	9	13	2	20	74	111
Boston College (15-16-5)	7	12	5	19	85	96
Merrimack (16-19-2)	8	14	2	18	77	110
Maine (6-29-1)	3	20	1	7	92	80

Note: Maine was 17-15-4 on the ice, but was ordered by the NCAA to forfeit 21 games due to ineligible players.
Conf. Tourney Final: Boston University 3, UMass-Lowell 2.
*NCAA Tourney (4-4): Boston University (2-1), UMass-Lowell (1-1), New Hampshire (1-1), Northeastern (0-1).

Western Collegiate Hockey Assn.

	W	L	T	Pts	GF	GA
Colorado Col. (23-11-5)	18	9	5	41	135	126
* Minnesota (25-13-4)	18	10	4	40	111	109
* Wisconsin (26-15-1)	19	12	1	39	128	103
St. Cloud St. (21-13-4)	16	12	4	36	127	111
Northern Mich. (22-16-1)	17	14	1	35	129	120
AK-Anchorage (15-19-2)	14	16	2	30	110	109
Minn-Duluth (14-21-3)	12	17	3	27	125	131
North Dakota (11-23-4)	11	17	4	26	101	131
Denver (15-20-3)	11	18	3	25	116	130
Michigan Tech (13-27-5)	8	19	5	21	93	105

Conf. Tourney Final: Minnesota 3, St. Cloud St. 2 (OT).
*NCAA Tourney (2-2): Minnesota (1-1), Wisconsin (1-1).

NCAA Top 10 Poll
Taken **before** conference tournaments.

Final weekly regular season Top 10 poll conducted by *The Record* of Troy, N.Y. and taken March 7, before the start of conference tournaments. Voting panel made up of 20 Division I coaches, six national media correspondents and one pro scout. First place votes in parentheses; teams in bold type went on to reach NCAA tournament Final Four.

	League	W	L	T	Pts
1 **Boston Univ.** (17)	HEA	28	6	0	263
2 Michigan (7)	CCHA	29	6	1	254
3 **Harvard** (3)	ECAC	19	4	4	222
4 Colorado College	WCHA	22	9	5	182
5 **L. Superior St.** (1)	CCHA	24	9	4	180
6 **Minnesota**	WCHA	20	12	4	125
7 Michigan St.	CCHA	20	10	5	95
8 UMass-Lowell	HEA	21	8	5	85
9 Wisconsin	WCHA	22	13	1	66
10 RPI	ECAC	17	8	4	19

Also receiving votes: 11. **Clarkson** (17-7-4, 18 pts); 12. **Western Michigan** (21-11-3, 5 pts); 13. **New Hampshire** (22-10-2, 15 pt).

Leading Scorers
Including postseason games.

West	Cl	Pos	Gm	G	A	Pts
Steve Guolla, Mich. St.	Jr.	C	41	23	46	69
Brian Wiseman, Michigan	Sr.	C	40	19	50	69
David Oliver, Michigan	Sr.	R	41	28	40	68
Kelly Fairchild, Wisconsin	Jr.	C	42	20	44	64
Andrew Shier, Wisconsin	Sr.	R	42	17	45	62
Chris Marinucci, Min-Dul	Sr.	R	38	30	31	61
Mike Knuble, Michigan	Jr.	R	41	32	26	58
Claude Morin, Kent	Jr.	C	39	17	39	56
Sean Tallaire, Lake St	So.	R	45	23	32	55
Anson Carter, Mich. St	So.	C	39	30	24	54
Clayton Beddoes, Lake St.	Sr.	C	44	23	31	54
Rem Murray, Mich. St	Jr.	L	41	16	38	54

East	Cl	Pos	Gm	G	A	Pts
Craig Conroy, Clarkson	Sr.	C	34	26	40	66
Steve Martins, Harvard	Jr.	C	32	25	35	60
Greg Bullock, Lowell	Fr.	C	38	24	35	59
Ron Pasco, RPI	L	36	17	40	57
Brian Mueller, Clarkson	Jr.	D	34	17	39	56
Mike Pomichter, BU	Jr.	R	40	28	26	54
Bryan Richardson, RPI	So.	C	36	23	29	52
Martin St. Louis, Vermont	Fr.	R	33	15	36	51
Craig Hamelin, RPI	Jr.	C	36	19	30	49
Shane Henry, Lowell	Sr.	L	38	11	37	48

Leading Goaltenders
Including postseason games; minimum 15 games.

West	Cl	Record	Sv%	GAA
Blaine Lacher, Lake St	Jr.	20-5-4	.918	1.98
Steve Shields, Michigan	Sr.	28-6-1	.892	2.66
Mike Buzak, Mich. St	Jr.	21-12-5	.903	2.72
Craig Brown, West. Mich	Sr.	14-5-2	.905	2.86
Rich Shulmistra, Miami-OH	Sr.	13-12-1	.892	2.92

East	Cl	Record	Sv%	GAA
Aaron Israel, Harvard	So.	12-2-2	.898	2.30
Derek Herlofsky, BU	Jr.	14-4-0	.909	2.50
Dwayne Roloson, Lowell	Sr.	23-10-7	.909	2.76
J.P. McKersie, BU	Jr.	19-4-0	.896	2.90
Trent Cavicchi, New Hamp	So.	14-7-1	.896	2.95

Lake State Recaptures NCAA Title

by Mike Lucas

NCAA Visitors Center

Seniors **Kurt Miller** (left) and **Steve Barnes** flank Lake Superior St. coach **Jeff Jackson** as he holds the NCAA championship trophy.

Jeff Jackson lost some sleep after leaving his head coaching job at Lake Superior State in June of 1993 to become an assistant with the Hartford Whalers of the NHL.

Early on, when the NHL failed to live up to his expectations, Jackson had a change of heart and returned to Lake State, where he was also named the athletic director prior to the start of the 1993-94 school year.

But that didn't put an end to his insomnia (just call him Sleepless in Sault Ste. Marie).

Jackson was tossing and turning again in late March after each of his team's three consecutive overtime victories in the NCAA Division I tournament. In the opening, quarterfinal and semifinal rounds, the Soo Lakers beat Northeastern, 6-5, CCHA champion Michigan, 5-4, and ECAC champ Harvard, 3-2, respectively.

Three straight playoff wins in sudden death. "My exterior is calm, but my interior isn't," said Jackson, whose team made it to the NCAA title game for the third year in a row. Meanwhile, his All-America goaltender, junior Blaine Lacher, was losing his hair.

"A lot of our games [13] have gone into overtime this year," said Lacher, who led the nation with a goals against average of 1.98 and set an NCAA record for consecutive scoreless minutes (375:01) while tossing five straight shutouts late in the regular season.

"All these overtimes must be getting to me. I keep finding hair in my helmet. A 4-1, 5-1 game would be just great for my nerves."

How about 9-1?

In the most lopsided Division I hockey final in 33 years, Lake Superior embarrassed No. 1-ranked Boston University by eight goals at the St. Paul (Minn.) Civic Center on April 2.

Sparked by sophomore forward and tournament MVP Sean Tallaire, who set up Clayton Beddoes' winning goal against Harvard and scored twice against BU, the Lakers won their second Division I NCAA title in three years and their third since 1988.

While the LSSU victory redeemed a 5-4 loss to Maine in the 1993 final, the defending national champions skated under a cloud all season. The Black Bears were forced to forfeit 21 games after a number of NCAA eligibility violations were reported.

Maine needed a court order to be reinstated for the Hockey East playoffs but was eliminated in the first round by BU. The Terriers went on to beat Wisconsin and Minnesota by identical 4-1 scores before falling to Lake Superior in the final.

"I recruited these kids as an assistant coach, they're a part of me," said Jackson who took over as Lake State's head coach four years ago and has compiled a 129-32-17 record for a winning percentage of .772).

"No one can overestimate their value to me as players and people. I'd adopt any one of them personally as my own."

And his players have adopted Jackson's disciplined, no-nonsense, defensive-oriented coaching style.

"It takes a while to adjust to it (the structure) when you're a freshman," said senior center Clayton Beddoes. "You're always thinking out there. You just can't use your instincts. But you find you get more offensive chances this way than if you run and gun."

The results speak for themselves.

Mike Lucas is a columnist for *The Capital Times* in Madison, Wisc., and has covered college hockey since 1972.

NCAA Division I Tournament

Regional Seeds

East	West
1 **Boston U.** (30-7-1)	1 Michigan (33-6-1)
2 **Harvard** (23-4-4)	2 **Minnesota** (24-12-4)
3 Wisconsin (25-14-1)	3 **Lake Superior** (27-10-4)
4 RPI (21-9-4)	4 UMass-Lowell (22-9-7)
5 W. Michigan (24-12-3)	5 Mich. St. (23-12-5)
6 New Hamp. (22-13-3)	6 Northeastern (19-12-7)

West Regional

At Munn Arena in East Lansing, Mich., March 26-27. Single elimination, two second round winners advance.

First Round

Lake Superior St. 6 ....OT.................Northeastern 5
UMass-Lowell 4 ....Michigan St. 3
(Byes: Michigan and Minnesota)

Second Round

Minnesota 2....................2OT...............UMass-Lowell 1
Lake Superior St. 5...........OT.......................Michigan 4
(Minnesota and Lake Superior St. advance)

East Regional

At Knickerbocker Arena in Albany, N.Y., March 25-26. Single elimination, two second round winners advance.

First Round

Wisconsin 6...................................Western Michigan 3
New Hampshire 2.......................................RPI 0
(Byes: Boston University and Harvard)

Second Round

Boston University 4......................................Wisconsin 1
Harvard 7...New Hampshire 1
(Boston University and Harvard advance)

Hobey Baker Award

For College Player of the Year. Presented since 1981 by the Decathlon Athletic Club of Bloomington, Minn. Voting by 16-member panel of national media, coaches and pro scouts. Vote totals not released.

	Cl	Pos
Winner: Chris Marinucci, Minn-Duluth........Sr.		RW
Runner-up: Craig Conroy, Clarkson ....Sr.		C

Division I All-America

Regional University first team selections as chosen by the American Hockey Coaches Association. Holdover from 1992-93 All-America first teams is in **bold** type.

West Team

Pos		Yr	Hgt	Wgt
G	**Jamie Ram**, Michigan Tech ....Sr.		5-11	175
D	John Gruden, Ferris St.....................Sr.		6-0	190
D	Shawn Reid, Colorado College ....Sr.		6-0	190
F	Chris Marinucci, Minn-Duluth..........Sr.		6-0	195
F	David Oliver, Michigan ....Sr.		5-11	185
F	Brian Wiseman, Michigan ....Sr.		5-6	175

East Team

Pos		Yr	Hgt	Wgt
G	Dwayne Roloson, UMass-Lowell ......Sr.		6-1	180
D	Sean McCann, Harvard.................Sr.		6-0	195
D	Brian Mueller, Clarkson..................Jr.		5-11	200
F	Craig Conroy, Clarkson..................Sr.		6-2	195
F	Steve Martins, Harvard ....Jr.		5-9	175
F	Mike Pomichter, Boston Univ............Jr.		6-2	220

FINAL FOUR

At St. Paul (Minn.) Civic Center, March 31 and April 2. Single elimination.

Semifinals

Boston University 4 ....Minnesota 1
Lake Superior St. 3 ....OT ....Harvard 2

Championship

Lake Superior St. 9.....................Boston University 1

Final records: Lake Superior St. (31-10-4); Boston University (34-7-0); Harvard (24-5-4); Minnesota (25-13-4).

Outstanding Player: Sean Tallaire, Lake Superior St. sophomore right wing. SEMIFINAL— 1 goal, 2 assists; FINAL— 2 goals, 1 assist.

All-Tournament Team: S. Tallaire, center Clayton Beddoes, defensemen Keith Aldridge and Steve Barnes and goaltender Blaine Lacher of Lake Superior St.; left wing Mike Pomichter of Boston U.

Championship Game
Lake Superior St., 9-1

Saturday, April 2, 1994, at St. Paul (Minn.) Civic Center; Attendance: 16,085; TV Rating: 0.3/1 share (ESPN).

Lake Superior St. (CCHA) 1	5	3—**9**
Boston University (Hockey East) 0	1	0—**1**

Scoring

1st Period: LSS— Rob Valicevic (Kurt Miller, Gerald Tallaire), 13:40.
2nd Period: LSS— Matt Alvey (Wayne Strachan, Steve Barnes), 3:10; LSS— Miller (Valicevic, G.Tallaire), 5:07; BU— Rich Brennan (Chris O'Sullivan, Mike Pomichter), power play, 9:40; LSS— Jay Ness (Valicevic, G.Tallaire), power play, 14:13; LSS— Barnes (Sean Tallaire, Strachan), power play, 17:26; LSS— S.Tallaire (Strachan, Mike Morin), power play, 19:17.
3rd Period: LSS— Mike Matteucci (Clayton Beddoes), 4:40; LSS— S.Tallaire (Beddoes), 12:51.

Goaltenders

Saves: LSS— Blaine Lacher (24); BU— Derek Herlofsky (19) and J.P. McKersie (12).

Other NCAA Tournaments
Division II

Two teams selected from limited national field. Championship decided in two games with mini-game (one 15-minute period), if necessary.

Final Two

March 11-12 at Huntsville, Ala
Championship: GAME ONE— Alabama-Huntsville 5, Bemidji St. (MN) 3; GAME TWO— Bemidji St. 2, Ala-Hunsville 1; MINI-GAME—Bemidji St. 2, Ala-Huntsville (OT).

Division III
Final Four

March 18-19 at Superior, Wisc.
Semifinals— WI-River Falls 4, Fredonia St. (NY) 3; WI-Superior 3, Salem St. 2 (OT). **Third Place**— Fredonia St. 7, Salem St. 4. **Championship**— WI-River Falls 6, WI-Superior 4.

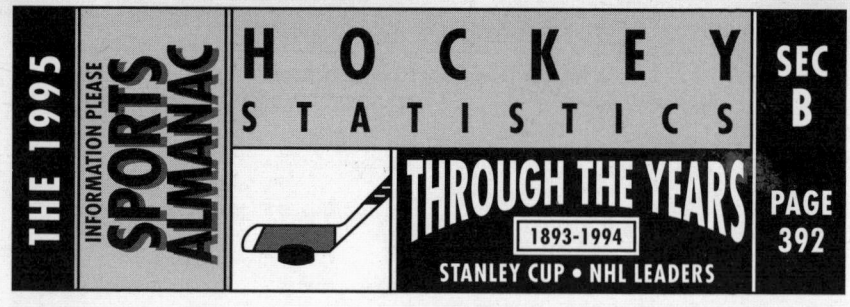

THE 1995 INFORMATION PLEASE SPORTS ALMANAC

HOCKEY STATISTICS

SEC B

THROUGH THE YEARS
1893-1994
STANLEY CUP • NHL LEADERS

PAGE 392

The Stanley Cup

The Stanley Cup was originally donated to the Canadian Amateur Hockey Association by Sir Frederick Arthur Stanley, Lord Stanley of Preston and 16th Earl of Derby, who had become interested in the sport while Governor General of Canada from 1888 to 1893. Stanley wanted the trophy to be a challenge cup, contested for each year by the best amateur hockey teams in Canada.

In 1893, the Cup was presented without a challenge to the AHA champion Montreal Amateur Athletic Association team. Every year since, however, there has been a playoff. In 1914, Cup trustees limited the field challenging for the trophy to the champion of the eastern professional National Hockey Association (NHA, organized in 1910) and the western professional Pacific Coast Hockey Association (PCHA, organized in 1912).

The NHA disbanded in 1917 and the National Hockey League (NHL) was formed. From 1918 to 1926, the NHL and PCHL champions played for the Cup with the Western Canada Hockey League (WCHL) champion joining in a three-way challenge in 1923 and '24. The PCHA disbanded in 1924, while the WCHL became the Western Hockey League (WHL) for the 1925-26 season and folded the following year. The NHL playoffs have decided the winner of the Stanley Cup ever since.

Champions, 1893-1917

Multiple winners: Montreal Victorias and Montreal Wanderers (4); Montreal Amateur Athletic Association and Ottawa Silver Seven (3); Montreal Shamrocks, Ottawa Senators, Quebec Bulldogs and Winnipeg Victorias (2).

Year		Year		Year	
1893	Montreal AAA	1901	Winnipeg Victorias	1909	Ottawa Senators
1894	Montreal AAA	1902	Montreal AAA	1910	Montreal Wanderers
1895	Montreal Victorias	1903	Ottawa Silver Seven	1911	Ottawa Senators
1896	(Feb.) Winnipeg Victorias	1904	Ottawa Silver Seven	1912	Quebec Bulldogs
	(Dec.) Montreal Victorias	1905	Ottawa Silver Seven	1913	Quebec Bulldogs
1897	Montreal Victorias	1906	Montreal Wanderers	1914	Toronto Blueshirts (NHA)
1898	Montreal Victorias	1907	(Jan.) Kenora Thistles	1915	Vancouver Millionaires (PCHA)
1899	Montreal Shamrocks		(Mar.) Montreal Wanderers	1916	Montreal Canadiens (NHA)
1900	Montreal Shamrocks	1908	Montreal Wanderers	1917	Seattle Metropolitans (PCHA)

Champions Since 1918

Multiple winners: Montreal Canadiens (23); Toronto Arenas-St.Pats-Maple Leafs (13); Detroit Red Wings (7); Boston Bruins and Edmonton Oilers (5); NY Islanders, NY Rangers and Ottawa Senators (4); Chicago Blackhawks (3); Philadelphia Flyers, Pittsburgh Penguins and Montreal Maroons (2).

Year	Winner	Head Coach	Series	Loser	Head Coach
1918	Toronto Arenas	Dick Carroll	3-2 (WLWLW)	Vancouver (PCHA)	Frank Patrick
1919	No Decision: (see below).				
1920	Ottawa	Pete Green	3-2 (WWLLW)	Seattle (PCHA)	Pete Muldoon
1921	Ottawa	Pete Green	3-2 (LWWLW)	Vancouver (PCHA)	Frank Patrick
1922	Toronto St.Pats	Eddie Powers	3-2 (LWLWW)	Vancouver (PCHA)	Frank Patrick
1923	Ottawa	Pete Green	3-1 (WLWW)	Vancouver (PCHA)	Frank Patrick
			2-0	Edmonton (WCHL)	K.C. McKenzie
1924	Montreal	Leo Dandurand	2-0	Vancouver (PCHA)	Frank Patrick
			2-0	Calgary (WCHL)	Eddie Oatman
1925	Victoria (WCHL)	Lester Patrick	3-1 (WWLW)	Montreal	Leo Dandurand
1926	Montreal Maroons	Eddie Gerard	3-1 (WWLW)	Victoria (WHL)	Lester Patrick
1927	Ottawa	Dave Gil	2-0 (TWTW)	Boston	Art Ross
1928	NY Rangers	Lester Patrick	3-2 (LWLWW)	Montreal Maroons	Eddie Gerard
1929	Boston	Art Ross	2-0	NY Rangers	Lester Patrick
1930	Montreal	Cecil Hart	2-0	Boston	Art Ross
1931	Montreal	Cecil Hart	3-2 (WLLWW)	Chicago	Art Duncan
1932	Toronto	Dick Irvin	3-0	NY Rangers	Lester Patrick
1933	NY Rangers	Lester Patrick	3-1 (WWLW)	Toronto	Dick Irvin
1934	Chicago	Tommy Gorman	3-1 (WWLW)	Detroit	Jack Adams
1935	Montreal Maroons	Lionel Conacher	3-0	Toronto	Dick Irvin
1936	Detroit	Jack Adams	3-1 (WWLW)	Toronto	Dick Irvin

Note: The 1919 Finals were cancelled after five games due to an influenza epidemic with Montreal and Seattle (PCHA) tied at 2-2-1.

Stanley Cup Champions

Year	Winner	Head Coach	Series	Loser	Head Coach
1937	Detroit	Jack Adams	3-2 (LWLWW)	NY Rangers	Lester Patrick
1938	Chicago	Bill Stewart	3-1 (WLWW)	Toronto	Dick Irvin
1939	Boston	Art Ross	4-1 (WLWWW)	Toronto	Dick Irvin
1940	NY Rangers	Frank Boucher	4-2 (WWLLWW)	Toronto	Dick Irvin
1941	Boston	Cooney Weiland	4-0	Detroit	Jack Adams
1942	Toronto	Hap Day	4-3 (LLLWWWW)	Detroit	Jack Adams
1943	Detroit	Jack Adams	4-0	Boston	Art Ross
1944	Montreal	Dick Irvin	4-0	Chicago	Paul Thompson
1945	Toronto	Hap Day	4-3 (WWWLLLW)	Detroit	Jack Adams
1946	Montreal	Dick Irvin	4-1 (WWWLW)	Boston	Dit Clapper
1947	Toronto	Hap Day	4-2 (LWWWLW)	Montreal	Dick Irvin
1948	Toronto	Hap Day	4-0	Detroit	Tommy Ivan
1949	Toronto	Hap Day	4-0	Detroit	Tommy Ivan
1950	Detroit	Tommy Ivan	4-3 (WLWLLWW)	NY Rangers	Lynn Patrick
1951	Toronto	Joe Primeau	4-1 (WLWWW)	Montreal	Dick Irvin
1952	Detroit	Tommy Ivan	4-0	Montreal	Dick Irvin
1953	Montreal	Dick Irvin	4-1 (WLWWW)	Boston	Lynn Patrick
1954	Detroit	Tommy Ivan	4-3 (WLWWLLW)	Montreal	Dick Irvin
1955	Detroit	Jimmy Skinner	4-3 (WWLLWLW)	Montreal	Dick Irvin
1956	Montreal	Toe Blake	4-1 (WWWLW)	Detroit	Jimmy Skinner
1957	Montreal	Toe Blake	4-1 (WWWLW)	Boston	Milt Schmidt
1958	Montreal	Toe Blake	4-2 (WLWLWW)	Boston	Milt Schmidt
1959	Montreal	Toe Blake	4-1 (WWLWW)	Toronto	Punch Imlach
1960	Montreal	Toe Blake	4-0	Toronto	Punch Imlach
1961	Chicago	Rudy Pilous	4-2 (WLWLWW)	Detroit	Sid Abel
1962	Toronto	Punch Imlach	4-2 (WWLLWW)	Chicago	Rudy Pilous
1963	Toronto	Punch Imlach	4-1 (WWLWW)	Detroit	Sid Abel
1964	Toronto	Punch Imlach	4-3 (WLWWLLW)	Detroit	Sid Abel
1965	Montreal	Toe Blake	4-3 (WWLLWLW)	Chicago	Billy Reay
1966	Montreal	Toe Blake	4-2 (LLWWWW)	Detroit	Sid Abel
1967	Toronto	Punch Imlach	4-2 (LWWLWW)	Montreal	Toe Blake
1968	Montreal	Toe Blake	4-0	St. Louis	Scotty Bowman
1969	Montreal	Claude Ruel	4-0	St. Louis	Scotty Bowman
1970	Boston	Harry Sinden	4-0	St. Louis	Scotty Bowman
1971	Montreal	Al MacNeil	4-3 (LLWWLWW)	Chicago	Billy Reay
1972	Boston	Tom Johnson	4-2 (WWLWLW)	NY Rangers	Emile Francis
1973	Montreal	Scotty Bowman	4-2 (WWLWLW)	Chicago	Billy Reay
1974	Philadelphia	Fred Shero	4-2 (LWWLWW)	Boston	Bep Guidolin
1975	Philadelphia	Fred Shero	4-2 (WWLLWW)	Buffalo	Floyd Smith
1976	Montreal	Scotty Bowman	4-0	Philadelphia	Fred Shero
1977	Montreal	Scotty Bowman	4-0	Boston	Don Cherry
1978	Montreal	Scotty Bowman	4-2 (WWLLWW)	Boston	Don Cherry
1979	Montreal	Scotty Bowman	4-1 (LWWWW)	NY Rangers	Fred Shero
1980	NY Islanders	Al Arbour	4-2 (WLWWLW)	Philadelphia	Pat Quinn
1981	NY Islanders	Al Arbour	4-1 (WWWLW)	Minnesota	Glen Sonmor
1982	NY Islanders	Al Arbour	4-0	Vancouver	Roger Neilson
1983	NY Islanders	Al Arbour	4-0	Edmonton	Glen Sather
1984	Edmonton	Glen Sather	4-1 (WLWWW)	NY Islanders	Al Arbour
1985	Edmonton	Glen Sather	4-1 (LWWWW)	Philadelphia	Mike Keenan
1986	Montreal	Jean Perron	4-1 (LWWWW)	Calgary	Bob Johnson
1987	Edmonton	Glen Sather	4-3 (WWLWLLW)	Philadelphia	Mike Keenan
1988	Edmonton	Glen Sather	4-0	Boston	Terry O'Reilly
1989	Calgary	Terry Crisp	4-2 (WLLWWW)	Montreal	Pat Burns
1990	Edmonton	John Muckler	4-1 (WWLWW)	Boston	Mike Milbury
1991	Pittsburgh	Bob Johnson	4-2 (LWLWLWW)	Minnesota	Bob Gainey
1992	Pittsburgh	Scotty Bowman	4-0	Chicago	Mike Keenan
1993	Montreal	Jacques Demers	4-1 (LWWWW)	Los Angeles	Barry Melrose
1994	NY Rangers	Mike Keenan	4-3 (LWWWLLW)	Vancouver	Pat Quinn

M.J. O'Brien Trophy

Donated by Canadian mining magnate M.J. O'Brien, whose son Ambrose founded the National Hockey Association in 1910. Originally presented to the NHA champion until the league's demise in 1917, the trophy then passed to the NHL champion through 1927. It was awarded to the NHL's Canadian Division winner from 1927-38 and the Stanley Cup runner-up from 1939-50 before being retired in 1950.

NHA winners included the Montreal Wanderers (1910), original Ottawa Senators (1911 and '15), Quebec Bulldogs (1912 and '13), Toronto Blueshirts (1914) and Montreal Canadiens (1916 and '17).

Conn Smythe Trophy

The Most Valuable Player of the Stanley Cup Playoffs, as selected by the Pro Hockey Writers Assn. Presented since 1965 by Maple Leaf Gardens Limited in the name of the former Toronto coach, GM and owner, Conn Smythe. Winners who did not play for the Cup champion are in **bold** type.

Multiple winners: Wayne Gretzky, Mario Lemieux, Bobby Orr, Bernie Parent and Patrick Roy (2).

Year		Year		Year	
1965	Jean Beliveau, Mon., C	1975	Bernie Parent, Phi., G	1985	Wayne Gretzky, Edm., C
1966	**Roger Crozier**, Det., G	1976	**Reggie Leach**, Phi., RW	1986	Patrick Roy, Mon., G
1967	Dave Keon, Tor., C	1977	Guy Lafleur, Mon., RW	1987	**Ron Hextall**, Phi., G
1968	**Glenn Hall**, St.L., G	1978	Larry Robinson, Mon., D	1988	Wayne Gretzky, Edm., C
1969	Serge Savard, Mon., D	1979	Bob Gainey, Mon., LW	1989	Al MacInnis, Calg., D
1970	Bobby Orr, Bos., D	1980	Bryan Trottier, NYI, C	1990	Bill Ranford, Edm., G
1971	Ken Dryden, Mon., G	1981	Butch Goring, NYI, C	1991	Mario Lemieux, Pit., C
1972	Bobby Orr, Bos., D	1982	Mike Bossy, NYI, RW	1992	Mario Lemieux, Pit., C
1973	Yvan Cournoyer, Mon., RW	1983	Billy Smith, NYI, G	1993	Patrick Roy, Mon., G
1974	Bernie Parent, Phi., G	1984	Mark Messier, Edm., LW	1994	Brian Leetch, NYR, D

Note: Ken Dryden (1971) and Patrick Roy (1986) are the only players to win as rookies.

All-Time Stanley Cup Playoff Leaders

CAREER

Stanley Cup Playoff leaders through 1994. Years listed indicate number of playoff appearances. Players active in 1994 in **bold** type; (DNP) indicates active player did not participate in 1994 playoffs.

Scoring

Points

		Yrs	Gm	G	A	Pts
1	**Wayne Gretzky** (DNP)	14	180	110	236	346
2	**Mark Messier**	14	200	99	160	259
3	**Jari Kurri** (DNP)	12	174	102	120	222
4	**Glenn Anderson**	13	208	91	116	207
5	**Bryan Trottier**	17	221	71	113	184
6	Jean Beliveau	17	162	79	97	176
7	Denis Potvin	14	185	56	108	164
8	Mike Bossy	10	129	85	75	160
	Gordie Howe	20	157	68	92	160
	Bobby Smith	13	184	64	96	160
11	**Paul Coffey**	12	137	47	107	154
12	**Denis Savard** (DNP)	13	137	58	94	152
13	Stan Mikita	18	155	59	91	150
14	**Brian Propp** (DNP)	13	160	64	84	148
15	**Doug Gilmour**	10	125	48	98	146
16	Larry Robinson	20	227	28	116	144
17	Jacques Lemaire	11	145	61	78	139
18	Phil Esposito	15	130	61	76	137
19	**Ray Bourque**	15	152	33	103	136
20	Guy Lafleur	14	128	58	76	134
21	Bobby Hull	14	119	62	67	129
	Henri Richard	18	180	49	80	129
23	Yvan Cournoyer	12	147	64	63	127
	Steve Larmer	12	130	54	73	127
25	Maurice Richard	15	133	82	44	126

Goals

		Yrs	Gm	No
1	**Wayne Gretzky** (DNP)	14	180	110
2	**Jari Kurri** (DNP)	12	174	102
3	**Mark Messier**	14	200	99
4	**Glenn Anderson**	13	208	91
5	Mike Bossy	10	129	85
6	Maurice Richard	15	133	82
7	Jean Beliveau	17	162	79
8	**Bryan Trottier**	17	221	71
9	Gordie Howe	20	157	68
10	Yvon Cournoyer	12	147	64
	Brian Propp	13	159	64
	Bobby Smith	13	184	64
13	Bobby Hull	14	119	62
14	Phil Esposito	15	130	61
	Jacques Lemaire	11	145	61

Assists

		Yrs	Gm	No
1	**Wayne Gretzky** (DNP)	14	180	236
2	**Mark Messier**	14	200	160
3	**Jari Kurri** (DNP)	12	174	120
4	**Glenn Anderson**	13	208	116
5	Larry Robinson	20	227	116
	Bryan Trottier	16	219	113
7	Denis Potvin	14	185	108
8	**Paul Coffey**	12	137	107
9	**Ray Bourque**	15	152	103
10	**Doug Gilmour**	10	125	98
11	Jean Beliveau	17	162	97
12	Bobby Smith	13	184	96
13	**Denis Savard** (DNP)	13	137	94
14	Gordie Howe	20	157	92
15	Stan Mikita	18	155	91

Goaltending

Wins

		Gm	W-L	Pct	GAA
1	Billy Smith	132	88-36	.710	2.73
2	Ken Dryden	112	80-32	.714	2.40
3	**Grant Fuhr** (DNP)	119	77-36	.681	3.06
4	Jacques Plante	112	71-37	.657	2.17
5	**Patrick Roy**	114	70-42	.625	2.46
6	Andy Moog	111	60-44	.577	3.03
7	Turk Broda	102	58-42	.580	1.98
8	Terry Sawchuk	106	54-48	.529	2.64
9	Glenn Hall	115	49-65	.430	2.79
10	**Tom Barrasso**	82	47-33	.588	3.10
	Gerry Cheevers	88	47-35	.573	2.69
12	Tony Esposito	99	45-53	.459	3.09
13	Gump Worsley	70	41-25	.621	2.82
14	**Mike Vernon**	81	43-33	.566	3.02
15	Bernie Parent	71	38-33	.535	2.43

Shutouts

		Gm	GAA	No
1	Clint Benedict	48	1.80	15
2	Jacques Plante	112	2.17	15
3	Turk Broda	102	1.98	13
4	Terry Sawchuk	106	2.64	12
5	Ken Dryden	112	2.40	10

All-Time Stanley Cup Playoff Leaders

Goaltending

Goals Against Average

Minimum of 50 games played.

		Gm	Min	GA	GAA
1	George Hainsworth	52	3486	112	1.93
2	Turk Broda	101	6389	211	1.98
3	Jacques Plante	112	6651	241	2.17
4	Ken Dryden	112	6846	274	2.40
5	Bernie Parent	71	4302	174	2.43
6	**Patrick Roy**	114	7089	285	2.46
7	Harry Lumley	76	4759	199	2.51
8	Johnny Bower	74	4350	184	2.54
9	Frankie Brimsek	68	4365	186	2.56
10	Terry Sawchuk	106	6291	267	2.64

Note: Clint Benedict had an average of 1.80 but played in only 48 games.

Games Played

		Yrs	Gm
1	Billy Smith, NY Islanders	13	132
2	**Grant Fuhr**, Edmonton-Buffalo (DNP)	10	119
3	Glenn Hall, Det-Chi-StL	17	115
4	Jacques Plante, Mon-StL-Tor-Bos	16	112
5	Ken Dryden, Montreal	8	112

Appearances in Cup Final

Standings of all teams that have reached the Stanley Cup championship round, since 1918.

App		Cups	Last Won
32	Montreal Canadiens	23*	1993
21	Toronto Maple Leafs	13†	1967
18	Detroit Red Wings	7	1955
17	Boston Bruins	5	1972
10	New York Rangers	4	1994
10	Chicago Blackhawks	3	1961
6	Edmonton Oilers	5	1990
6	Philadelphia Flyers	2	1975
5	New York Islanders	4	1983
5	Vancouver Millionaires (PCHA)	0	—
4	(original) Ottawa Senators	4	1927
3	Montreal Maroons	2	1935
3	St. Louis Blues	0	—
2	Pittsburgh Penguins	2	1992
2	Calgary Flames	1	1989
2	Victoria Cougars (WCHL-WHL)	1	1925
2	Minnesota North Stars	0	—
2	Seattle Metropolitans (PCHA)	0	—
2	Vancouver Canucks	0	—
1	Buffalo Sabres	0	—
1	Calgary Tigers (WCHL)	0	—
1	Edmonton Eskimos (WCHL)	0	—
1	Los Angeles Kings	0	—

*Les Canadiens also won the Cup in 1916 for a total of 24. Also, their final with Seattle in 1919 was cancelled due to an influenza epidemic that claimed the life of the Habs' Joe Hall.

†Toronto has won the Cup under three nicknames—Arenas (1918), St. Pats (1922) and Maple Leafs (1932,42,45,47-49,51,62-64,67).

Teams now defunct (6): Calgary Tigers, Edmonton Eskimos, Montreal Maroons, (original) Ottawa Senators, Seattle, Vancouver Millionaires and Victoria. Edmonton (1923) and Calgary (1924) represented the WCHL and later the WHL, while Vancouver (1918,1921-24) and Seattle (1919-20) played out of the PCHA.

Miscellaneous

Championships

		Yrs	Cups
1	Henri Richard, Montreal	18	11
2	Yvan Cournoyer, Montreal	15	10
3	Jean Beliveau, Montreal	17	10
4	Claude Provost, Montreal	14	9
5	Jacques Lemaire, Montreal	11	8
	Maurice Richard, Montreal	15	8
	Red Kelly, Detroit-Toronto	19	8

Years in Playoffs

		Yrs	Gm
1	Gordie Howe, Detroit-Hartford	20	157
	Larry Robinson, Montreal-Los Angeles	20	227
3	Red Kelly, Detroit-Toronto	19	164
4	Henri Richard, Montreal	18	180
	Stan Mikita, Chicago	18	155

Games Played

		Yrs	Gm
1	Larry Robinson, Montreal-Los Angeles	20	227
2	**Bryan Trottier**, NY Isles-Pittsburgh	17	221
3	**Glenn Anderson**, Edm-Tor-NY Rangers	13	208
4	**Mark Messier**, Edm-NY Rangers	14	200
5	Denis Potvin, NY Islanders	14	185

Penalty Minutes

		Yrs	Gm	PM
1	**Dale Hunter**, Que-Wash	14	133	613
2	Chris Nilan, Mon-NYR-Bos-Mon	12	111	541
3	Willi Plett, Atl-Calg-Min-Bos	10	83	466
4	Dave Williams, Tor-Van-LA	12	83	455
5	Dave Schultz, Phi-LA-Buf	6	73	412

SINGLE SEASON

Scoring

Points

		Year	Gm	G	A	Pts
1	Wayne Gretzky, Edm	1985	18	17	30	47
2	Mario Lemieux, Pit	1991	23	16	28	44
3	Wayne Gretzky, Edm	1988	19	12	31	43
4	Wayne Gretzky, LA	1993	24	15	25	40
5	Wayne Gretzky, Edm	1983	16	12	26	38
6	Paul Coffey, Edm	1985	18	12	25	37
7	Mike Bossy, NYI	1981	18	17	18	35
	Wayne Gretzky, Edm	1984	19	13	22	35
	Doug Gilmour, Tor	1993	21	10	25	35
10	Mario Lemieux, Pit	1992	15	16	18	34
	Mark Messier, Edm	1988	19	11	23	34
	Mark Recchi, Pit	1991	24	10	24	34
	Wayne Gretzky, Edm	1987	21	5	29	34
14	Brian Leetch, NYR	1994	23	11	23	34
15	Kevin Stevens, Pit	1991	24	17	16	33
	Rick Middleton, Bos	1983	17	11	22	33

Goals

		Year	Gm	No
1	Reggie Leach, Philadelphia	1976	16	19
	Jari Kurri, Edmonton	1985	18	19
3	Newsy Lalonde, Montreal	1917	10	17
	Mike Bossy, NY Islanders	1981	18	17
	Wayne Gretzky, Edmonton	1985	18	17
	Steve Payne, Minnesota	1981	19	17
	Mike Bossy, NY Islanders	1982	19	17
	Mike Bossy, NY Islanders	1983	19	17
	Kevin Stevens, Pittsburgh	1991	24	17
10	Six tied with 16 goals each.			

All-Time Stanley Cup Playoff Leaders (Cont.)

Assists

		Year	Gm	No
1	Wayne Gretzky, Edmonton	1988	19	31
2	Wayne Gretzky, Edmonton	1985	18	30
3	Wayne Gretzky, Edmonton	1987	21	29
4	Mario Lemieux, Pittsburgh	1991	23	28
5	Wayne Gretzky, Edmonton	1983	16	26
6	Paul Coffey, Edmonton	1985	18	25
	Doug Gilmour, Toronto	1993	21	25
	Wayne Gretzky, Los Angeles	1993	24	25
9	Al MacInnis, Calgary	1989	22	24
	Mark Recchi, Pittsburgh	1991	24	24

Goaltending

Wins

		Year	Gm	Min	W-L
1	Grant Fuhr, Edm	1988	19	1136	16-2
	Patrick Roy, Mon	1993	20	1293	16-4
	Mike Vernon, Calg	1989	22	1381	16-5
	Tom Barrasso, Pit	1992	21	1233	16-5
	Bill Ranford, Edm	1990	22	1401	16-6
	Mike Richter, NYR	1994	23	1417	16-7
7	Six tied with 15 wins each.				

Shutouts

		Year	Gm	No
1	Clint Benedict, Mon. Maroons	1926	8	4
	Terry Sawchuk, Detroit	1952	8	4
	Clint Benedict, Mon. Maroons	1928	9	4
	Dave Kerr, NY Rangers	1937	9	4
	Frank McCool, Toronto	1945	13	4
	Ken Dryden, Montreal	1977	14	4
	Bernie Parent, Philadelphia	1975	17	4
	Mike Richter, NY Rangers	1994	23	4
	Kirk McLean, Vancouver	1994	24	4

Goals Against Average

Minimum of eight games played.

		Year	Gm	Min	GA	GAA
1	Terry Sawchuk, Det	1952	8	480	5	0.63
2	Clint Benedict, Mon-M	1928	9	555	8	0.89
3	Turk Broda, Tor	1951	9	509	9	1.06
4	Dave Kerr, NYR	1937	9	553	10	1.11
5	Jacques Plante, Mon	1960	8	488	11	1.35
6	Rogie Vachon, Mon	1969	8	507	12	1.42
7	Jacques Plante, St.L	1969	10	589	14	1.43
8	Chuck Gardiner, Chi	1931	9	638	13	1.44
9	Frankie Brimsek, Bos	1939	12	863	18	1.50
10	Chuck Gardiner, Chi	1934	8	602	12	1.50

Note: Average determined by games played through 1942-43 season and by minutes played since then.

SINGLE SERIES

Scoring

Points

	Year	Rd	G-A-Pts
Rick Middleton, Bos vs Buf	1983	DF	5-14—19
Wayne Gretzky, Edm vs Chi	1985	CF	4-14—18
Mario Lemieux, Pit vs Wash	1992	DSF	7-10—17
Barry Pederson, Bos vs Buf	1983	DF	7-9—16
Jari Kurri, Edm vs Chi	1985	CF	12-3—15
Tim Kerr, Phi vs Pit	1989	DF	10-5—15
Mario Lemieux, Pit vs Bos	1991	CF	6-9—15
Wayne Gretzky, Edm vs LA	1987	DSF	2-13—15

Goals

	Year	Rd	No
Jari Kurri, Edm vs Chi	1985	CF	12
Newsy Lalonde, Mon vs Ott	1919	SF*	11
Tim Kerr, Phi vs Pit	1989	DF	10
Five tied with nine each.			

*NHL final prior to Stanley Cup series with Seattle.

Assists

	Year	Rd	No
Rick Middleton, Bos vs Buf	1983	DF	14
Wayne Gretzky, Edm vs Chi	1985	CF	14
Wayne Gretzky, Edm vs LA	1987	DSF	13
Four tied with 11 each.			

SINGLE GAME

Scoring

Points

	Date	G	A	Pts
Patrik Sundstrom, NJ vs Wash	4/22/88	3	5	8
Mario Lemieux, Pit. vs Phi	4/25/89	5	3	8
Wayne Gretzky, Edm. at Calg	4/17/83	4	3	7
Wayne Gretzky, Edm. vs Win	4/25/85	3	4	7
Wayne Gretzky, Edm. vs LA	4/9/87	1	6	7

Goals

	Date	No
Newsy Lalonde, Mon. vs Ott	3/1/19	5
Maurice Richard, Mon. vs Tor	3/23/44	5
Darryl Sittler, Tor. vs Phi	4/22/76	5
Reggie Leach, Phi. vs Bos	5/6/76	5
Mario Lemieux, Pit. vs Phi	4/25/89	5

Assists

	Date	No
Mikko Leinonen, NYR vs Phi	4/8/82	6
Wayne Gretzky, Edm. vs LA	4/9/87	6
Ten players tied with five each.		

Ten Longest Playoff Overtime Games

The 10 longest overtime games in Stanley Cup history. Note the following Series initials: SF (semifinals), DSF (division semifinal), QF (quarterfinal) and Final (Cup Final). Series winners are in bold type; (*) indicates deciding game of series.

		OTs	Elapsed Time	Goal Scorer	Date	Series	Location
1	**Detroit** 1, Montreal Maroons 0	6	116:30	Mud Bruneteau	3/24/36	SF, Gm 1	Montreal
2	**Toronto** 1, Boston 0	6	104:46	Ken Doraty	4/3/33	SF, Gm 5	Toronto
3	Toronto 3, **Detroit** 2	4	70:18	Jack McLean	3/23/43	SF, Gm 2	Detroit
4	**Montreal** 2, NY Rangers 1	4	68:52	Gus Rivers	3/28/30	SF, Gm 1	Montreal
5	**NY Islanders** 3, Washington 2	4	68:47	Pat LaFontaine	4/18/87	DSF, Gm 7*	Washington
6	Buffalo 1, **New Jersey** 0	4	65:43	Dave Hannan	4/27/94	QF, Gm 6	Buffalo
7	**Montreal** 3, Detroit 2	4	61:09	Maurice Richard	3/27/51	SF, Gm 1	Detroit
8	**NY Americans** 3, NY Rangers 2	4	60:40	Lorne Carr	3/27/38	QF, Gm 3*	New York
9	**NY Rangers** 4, Montreal 3	3	59:32	Fred Cook	3/26/32	SF, Gm 2	Montreal
10	**Boston** 2, NY Rangers 1	3	59:25	Mel Hill	3/21/39	SF, Gm 1	New York

NHL All-Star Game

Three benefit NHL All-Star games were staged in the 1930s for forwards Ace Bailey and the families of Howie Morenz and Babe Siebert. Bailey, of Toronto, suffered a fractured skull on a career-ending check by Boston's Eddie Shore. Morenz, the Montreal Canadiens' legend, died of a heart attack at age 35 after a severely broken leg ended his career. And Siebert, who played with both Montreal teams, drowned at age 35.

The All-Star Game was revived at the start of the 1947-48 season as an annual exhibition match between the defending Stanley Cup champion and All-Stars from the league's other five teams. The format has changed several times since then. The game was moved to midseason in 1966-67 and became an East vs. West contest. The Eastern (Wales, 1975-93) Conference leads the series, 13-5.

Benefit Games

Date	Occasion		Host	Coaches
2/14/34	Ace Bailey Benefit	Toronto 7, All-Stars 3	Toronto	Dick Irvin, Lester Patrick
11/3/37	Howie Morenz Memorial	All-Stars 6, Montreals* 5	Montreal	Jack Adams, Cecil Hart
10/29/39	Babe Siebert Memorial	All-Stars 5, Canadiens 2	Montreal	Art Ross, Pit Lepine

*Combined squad of Montreal Canadiens and Montreal Maroons.

All-Star Games

Multiple MVP winners: Mario Lemieux (3); Wayne Gretzky, Bobby Hull and Frank Mahovlich (2).

Year		Host	Coaches	Most Valuable Player
1947	All-Stars 4, Toronto 3	Toronto	Dick Irvin, Hap Day	No award
1948	All-Stars 3, Toronto 1	Chicago	Tommy Ivan, Hap Day	No award
1949	All-Stars 3, Toronto 1	Toronto	Tommy Ivan, Hap Day	No award
1950	Detroit 7, All-Stars 1	Detroit	Tommy Ivan, Lynn Patrick	No award
1951	1st Team 2, 2nd Team 2	Toronto	Joe Primeau, Hap Day	No award
1952	1st Team 1, 2nd Team 1	Detroit	Tommy Ivan, Dick Irvin	No award
1953	All-Stars 3, Montreal 1	Montreal	Lynn Patrick, Dick Irvin	No award
1954	All-Stars 2, Detroit 2	Detroit	King Clancy, Jim Skinner	No award
1955	Detroit 3, All-Stars 1	Detroit	Jim Skinner, Dick Irvin	No award
1956	All-Stars 1, Montreal 1	Montreal	Jim Skinner, Toe Blake	No award
1957	All-Stars 5, Montreal 3	Montreal	Milt Schmidt, Toe Blake	No award
1958	Montreal 6, All-Stars 3	Montreal	Toe Blake, Milt Schmidt	No award
1959	Montreal 6, All-Stars 1	Montreal	Toe Blake, Punch Imlach	No award
1960	All-Stars 2, Montreal 1	Montreal	Punch Imlach, Toe Blake	No award
1961	All-Stars 3, Chicago 1	Chicago	Sid Abel, Rudy Pilous	No award
1962	Toronto 4, All-Stars 1	Toronto	Punch Imlach, Rudy Pilous	Eddie Shack, Tor., RW
1963	All-Stars 3, Toronto 3	Toronto	Sid Abel, Punch Imlach	Frank Mahovlich, Tor., LW
1964	All-Stars 3, Toronto 2	Toronto	Sid Abel, Punch Imlach	Jean Beliveau, Mon., C
1965	All-Stars 5, Montreal 2	Montreal	Billy Reay, Toe Blake	Gordie Howe, Det., RW
1966	No game (see below)			
1967	Montreal 3, All-Stars 0	Montreal	Toe Blake, Sid Abel	Henri Richard, Mon., C
1968	Toronto 4, All-Stars 3	Toronto	Punch Imlach, Toe Blake	Bruce Gamble, Tor., G
1969	West 3, East 3	Montreal	Scotty Bowman, Toe Blake	Frank Mahovlich, Det., LW
1970	East 4, West 1	St. Louis	Claude Ruel, Scotty Bowman	Bobby Hull, Chi., LW
1971	West 2, East 1	Boston	Scotty Bowman, Harry Sinden	Bobby Hull, Chi., LW
1972	East 3, West 2	Minnesota	Al MacNeil, Billy Reay	Bobby Orr, Bos., D
1973	East 5, West 4	NY Rangers	Tom Johnson, Billy Reay	Greg Polis, Pit., LW
1974	West 6, East 4	Chicago	Billy Reay, Scotty Bowman	Garry Unger, St. L., C
1975	Wales 7, Campbell 1	Montreal	Bep Guidolin, Fred Shero	Syl Apps Jr., Pit., C
1976	Wales 7, Campbell 5	Philadelphia	Floyd Smith, Fred Shero	Peter Mahovlich, Mon., C
1977	Wales 4, Campbell 3	Vancouver	Scotty Bowman, Fred Shero	Rick Martin, Buf., LW
1978	Wales 3, Campbell 2 (OT)	Buffalo	Scotty Bowman, Fred Shero	Billy Smith, NYI, G
1979	No game (see below)			
1980	Wales 6, Campbell 3	Detroit	Scotty Bowman, Al Arbour	Reggie Leach, Phi., RW
1981	Campbell 4, Wales 1	Los Angeles	Pat Quinn, Scotty Bowman	Mike Liut, St. L., G
1982	Wales 4, Campbell 2	Washington	Al Arbour, Glen Sonmor	Mike Bossy, NYI, RW
1983	Campbell 9, Wales 3	NY Islanders	Roger Neilson, Al Arbour	Wayne Gretzky, Edm., C
1984	Wales 7, Campbell 6	New Jersey	Al Arbour, Glen Sather	Don Maloney, NYR, LW
1985	Wales 6, Campbell 4	Calgary	Al Arbour, Glen Sather	Mario Lemieux, Pit., C
1986	Wales 4, Campbell 3 (OT)	Hartford	Mike Keenan, Glen Sather	Grant Fuhr, Edm., G
1987	No game (see below)			
1988	Wales 6, Campbell 5 (OT)	St. Louis	Mike Keenan, Glen Sather	Mario Lemieux, Pit., C
1989	Campbell 9, Wales 5	Edmonton	Glen Sather, Terry O'Reilly	Wayne Gretzky, LA, C
1990	Wales 12, Campbell 7	Pittsburgh	Pat Burns, Terry Crisp	Mario Lemieux, Pit., C
1991	Campbell 11, Wales 5	Chicago	John Muckler, Mike Milbury	Vincent Damphousse, Tor., LW
1992	Campbell 10, Wales 6	Philadelphia	Bob Gainey, Scotty Bowman	Brett Hull, St. L., RW
1993	Wales 16, Campbell 6	Montreal	Scotty Bowman, Mike Keenan	Mike Gartner, NYR, RW
1994	East 9, West 8	NY Rangers	Jacques Demers, Barry Melrose	Mike Richter, NYR, G

No All-Star Game: in 1966 (moved from start of season to mid-season); in 1979 (replaced by Challenge Cup series with USSR); in 1987 (replaced by Rendez-Vous '87 series with USSR). See page 413.

NHL Franchise Origins

Here is what the current 26 teams in the National Hockey League have to show for the years they have put in as members of the NHL, the early National Hockey Association (NHA) and the more recent World Hockey Association (WHA). League titles and Stanley Cup championships are noted by year won. The Stanley Cup has automatically gone to the NHL champion since the 1926-27 season. Following the 1992-93 season, the NHL renamed the Clarence Campbell Conference the Western Conference, while the Prince of Wales Conference became the Eastern Conference.

Western Conference

	First Season	League Titles	Franchise Stops
Anaheim, Mighty Ducks of	1993-94 (NHL)	None	•Anaheim, CA (1993—)
Calgary Flames	1972-73 (NHL)	1 Cup (1989)	•Atlanta (1972-80) Calgary (1980—)
Chicago Blackhawks	1926-27 (NHL)	3 Cups (1934,38,61)	•Chicago (1926—)
Dallas Stars	1967-68 (NHL)	None	•Bloomington, MN (1967-93) Dallas (1993—)
Detroit Red Wings	1926-27 (NHL)	7 Cups (1936-37,43,50, 52,54-55)	•Detroit (1926—)
Edmonton Oilers	1973-74 (WHA)	5 Cups (1984-85,87-88,90)	•Edmonton (1972—)
Los Angeles Kings	1967-68 (NHL)	None	•Inglewood, CA (1967—)
St. Louis Blues	1967-68 (NHL)	None	•St. Louis (1967—)
San Jose Sharks	1991-92 (NHL)	None	•San Francisco (1991-93) San Jose (1993—)
Toronto Maple Leafs	1916-17 (NHA)	2 NHL (1918,22) 13 Cups (1918,22,32,42,45 47-49,51,62-64,67)	•Toronto (1916—)
Vancouver Canucks	1970-71 (NHL)	None	•Vancouver (1970—)
Winnipeg Jets	1972-73 (WHA)	3 WHA (1976,78-79)	•Winnipeg (1972—)

Eastern Conference

	First Season	League Titles	Franchise Stops
Boston Bruins	1924-25 (NHL)	5 Cups (1929,39,41,70,72)	•Boston (1924—)
Buffalo Sabres	1970-71 (NHL)	None	•Buffalo (1970—)
Florida Panthers	1993-94 (NHL)	None	•Miami (1993—)
Hartford Whalers	1972-73 (WHA)	1 WHA (1973)	•Boston (1972-74) W. Springfld, MA (1974-75) Hartford, CT (1975-78) Springfield, MA (1978-80) Hartford (1980—)
Montreal Canadiens	1909-10 (NHA)	2 NHA (1916-17) 2 NHL (1924-25) 24 Cups (1916,24,30-31,44,46, 53,56-60,65-66,68-69, 71,73,76-79,86,93)	•Montreal (1909—)
New Jersey Devils	1974-75 (NHL)	None	•Kansas City (1974-76) Denver (1976-82) E. Rutherford, NJ (1982—)
New York Islanders	1972-73 (NHL)	4 Cups (1980-83)	•Uniondale, NY (1972—)
New York Rangers	1926-27 (NHL)	4 Cups (1928,33,40,94)	•New York (1926—)
Ottawa Senators	1992-93 (NHL)	None	•Ottawa (1992—)
Philadelphia Flyers	1967-68 (NHL)	2 Cups (1974-75)	•Philadelphia (1967—)
Pittsburgh Penguins	1967-68 (NHL)	2 Cups (1991-92)	•Pittsburgh (1967—)
Quebec Nordiques	1972-73 (WHA)	1 WHA (1977)	•Quebec City (1972—)
Tampa Bay Lightning	1992-93 (NHL)	None	•Tampa, FL (1992—93) St. Petersburg, FL (1993—)
Washington Capitals	1974-75 (NHL)	None	•Landover, MD (1974—)

Note: The Hartford Civic Center roof collapsed after a snowstorm in January 1978, forcing the Whalers to move their home games to Springfield, Mass., for two years.

The Growth of the NHL

Of the four franchises that comprised the National Hockey League (NHL) at the start of the 1917-18 season, only two remain—the Montreal Canadiens and the Toronto Maple Leafs (originally the Toronto Arenas). From 1919-26, eight new teams joined the league, but only four—the Boston Bruins, Chicago Blackhawks (originally Black Hawks), Detroit Red Wings (originally Cougars) and New York Rangers—survived.

It was 41 years before the NHL expanded again, doubling in size for the 1967-68 season with new teams in Los Angeles, Minnesota, Oakland, Philadelphia, Pittsburgh and St. Louis. The league had 16 clubs by the start of the 1972-73 season, but it also had a rival in the **World Hockey Association**, which debuted that year with 12 teams.

The NHL added two more teams in 1974 and merged the struggling Cleveland Barons (originally the Oakland Seals) and Minnesota North Stars in 1978, before absorbing four WHA clubs—the Edmonton Oilers, Hartford Whalers, Quebec Nordiques and Winnipeg Jets—in time for the 1979-80 season. Five expansion teams have joined the league so far in the 1990s, giving the NHL its current 26-team roster.

Expansion/Merger Timetable

For teams currently in NHL.

1919—Quebec Bulldogs finally take the ice after sitting out NHL's first two seasons; **1924**—Boston Bruins and Montreal Maroons; **1925**—New York Americans and Pittsburgh Pirates; **1926**—Chicago Black Hawks (now Blackhawks), Detroit Cougars (now Red Wings) and New York Rangers; **1932**—Ottawa Senators return after sitting out 1931-32 season.

1967—California Seals (later Cleveland Barons), Los Angeles Kings, Minnesota North Stars, Philadelphia Flyers, Pittsburgh Penguins and St. Louis Blues.

1970—Buffalo Sabres and Vancouver Canucks; **1972**—Atlanta Flames (now Calgary) and New York Islanders; **1974**—Kansas City Scouts (now New Jersey Devils) and Washington Capitals; **1978**—Cleveland Barons merge with Minnesota North Stars and team remains in Minnesota; **1979**—added WHA's Edmonton Oilers, Hartford Whalers, Quebec Nordiques and Winnipeg Jets.

1991—San Jose Sharks; **1992**—Ottawa Senators and Tampa Bay Lightning; **1993**—Mighty Ducks of Anaheim and Florida Panthers.

City and Nickname Changes

1919—Toronto Arenas renamed St. Pats; **1920**—Quebec moves to Hamilton and becomes Tigers (will fold in 1925); **1926**—Toronto St. Pats renamed Maple Leafs; **1929**—Detroit Cougars renamed Falcons.

1930—Pittsburgh Pirates move to Philadelphia and become Quakers (will fold in 1931); **1932**—Detroit Falcons renamed Red Wings; **1934**—Ottawa Senators move to St. Louis and become Eagles (will fold in 1935); **1941**—New York Americans renamed Brooklyn Americans (will fold in 1942).

1967—California Seals renamed Oakland Seals three months into first season; **1970**—Oakland Seals renamed California Golden Seals; **1975**—California Golden Seals renamed Seals; **1976**—California Seals move to Cleveland and become Barons, while Kansas City Scouts move to Denver and become Colorado Rockies; **1978**—Cleveland Barons merge with Minnesota North Stars and become Minnesota North Stars.

1980—Atlanta Flames move to Calgary; **1982**—Colorado Rockies move to East Rutherford, N.J., and become New Jersey Devils; **1986**—Chicago Black Hawks renamed Blackhawks; **1993**—Minnesota North Stars move to Dallas and become Stars.

Defunct NHL Teams

Teams that once played in the NHL, but no longer exist.

Brooklyn—Americans (1941-42, formerly NY Americans from 1925-41); **Cleveland**—Barons (1976-78, originally California-Oakland Seals from 1967-76); **Hamilton (Ont.)**—Tigers (1920-25, originally Quebec Bulldogs from 1919-20); **Montreal**—Maroons (1924-38) and Wanderers (1917-18); **New York**—Americans (1925-42, later Brooklyn Americans for 1941-42); **Oakland**—Seals (1967-76, also known as California Seals and Golden Seals and later Cleveland Barons from 1976-78); **Ottawa**—Senators (1917-31 and 1932-34, later St. Louis Eagles for 1934-35); **Philadelphia**—Quakers (1930-31, originally Pittsburgh Pirates from 1925-30); **Pittsburgh**—Pirates (1925-30, later Philadelphia Quakers for 1930-31); **Quebec**—Bulldogs (1919-20, later Hamilton Tigers from 1920-25); **St. Louis**—Eagles (1934-35), originally Ottawa Senators (1917-31 and 1932-34).

WHA Teams (1972-79)

Baltimore—Blades (1975); **Birmingham**—Bulls (1976-78); **Calgary**—Cowboys (1975-77); **Chicago**—Cougars (1972-75); **Cincinnati**—Stingers (1975-79); **Cleveland**—Crusaders (1972-76, moved to Minnesota); **Denver**—Spurs (1975-76, moved to Ottawa); **Edmonton**—Oilers (1972-79, originally called Alberta Oilers in 1972-73); **Houston**—Aeros (1972-78); **Indianapolis**—Racers (1974-78).

Los Angeles—Sharks (1972-74, moved to Michigan); **Michigan**—Stags (1974-75, moved to Baltimore); **Minnesota**—Fighting Saints (1972-76) and New Fighting Saints (1976-77); **New England**—Whalers (1972-79, played in Boston from 1972-74, West Springfield-MA from 1974-75, Hartford from 1975-78 and Springfield-MA in 1979); **New Jersey**—Knights (1973-74, moved to San Diego); **New York**—Raiders (1972-73, renamed Golden Blades in 1973, moved to New Jersey).

Ottawa—Nationals (1972-73, moved to Toronto) and Civics (1976); **Philadelphia**—Blazers (1972-73, moved to Vancouver); **Phoenix**—Roadrunners (1974-77); **Quebec**—Nordiques (1972-79); **San Diego**—Mariners (1974-77); **Toronto**—Toros (1973-76, moved to Birmingham, AL); **Vancouver**—Blazers (1973-75, moved to Calgary); **Winnipeg**—Jets (1972-79).

Annual NHL Leaders
Art Ross Trophy (Scoring)

Given to the player who leads the league in points scored and named after the former Boston Bruins general manager-coach. First presented in 1947, names of prior leading scorers have been added retroactively. A tie for the scoring championship is broken three ways: 1. total goals; 2. fewest games played; 3. first goal scored.

Multiple winners: Wayne Gretzky (10); Gordie Howe (6); Phil Esposito (5); Mario Lemieux and Stan Mikita (4); Guy Lafleur (3); Max Bentley, Charlie Conacher, Bill Cook, Babe Dye, Bernie Geoffrion, Bobby Hull, Elmer Lach, Newsy Lalonde, Joe Malone, Dickie Moore, Howie Morenz, Bobby Orr and Sweeney Schriner (2).

Year		Gm	G	A	Pts	Year		Gm	G	A	Pts
1918	Joe Malone, Mon	20	44	0	44	1957	Gordie Howe, Det	70	44	45	89
1919	Newsy Lalonde, Mon	17	23	9	32	1958	Dickie Moore, Mon	70	36	48	84
						1959	Dickie Moore, Mon	70	41	55	96
1920	Joe Malone, Que	24	39	6	45						
1921	Newsy Lalonde, Mon	24	33	8	41	1960	Bobby Hull, Chi	70	39	42	81
1922	Punch Broadbent, Ott	24	32	14	46	1961	Bernie Geoffrion, Mon	64	50	45	95
1923	Babe Dye, Tor	22	26	11	37	1962	Bobby Hull, Chi.*	70	50	34	84
1924	Cy Denneny, Ott	21	22	1	23	1963	Gordie Howe, Det	70	38	48	86
1925	Babe Dye, Tor	29	38	6	44	1964	Stan Mikita, Chi	70	39	50	89
1926	Nels Stewart, Maroons	36	34	8	42	1965	Stan Mikita, Chi	70	28	59	87
1927	Bill Cook, NYR	44	33	4	37	1966	Bobby Hull, Chi	65	54	43	97
1928	Howie Morenz, Mon	43	33	18	51	1967	Stan Mikita, Chi	70	35	62	97
1929	Ace Bailey, Tor	44	22	10	32	1968	Stan Mikita, Chi	72	40	47	87
						1969	Phil Esposito, Bos	74	49	77	126
1930	Cooney Weiland, Bos	44	43	30	73						
1931	Howie Morenz, Mon	39	28	23	51	1970	Bobby Orr, Bos	76	33	87	120
1932	Busher Jackson, Tor	48	28	25	53	1971	Phil Esposito, Bos	78	76	76	152
1933	Bill Cook, NYR	48	28	22	50	1972	Phil Esposito, Bos	76	66	67	133
1934	Charlie Conacher, Tor	42	32	20	52	1973	Phil Esposito, Bos	78	55	75	130
1935	Charlie Conacher, Tor	47	36	21	57	1974	Phil Esposito, Bos	78	68	77	145
1936	Sweeney Schriner, NYA	48	19	26	45	1975	Bobby Orr, Bos	80	46	89	135
1937	Sweeney Schriner, NYA	48	21	25	46	1976	Guy Lafleur, Mon	80	56	69	125
1938	Gordie Drillon, Tor	48	26	26	52	1977	Guy Lafleur, Mon	80	56	80	136
1939	Toe Blake, Mon	48	24	23	47	1978	Guy Lafleur, Mon	79	60	72	132
						1979	Bryan Trottier, NYI	76	47	87	134
1940	Milt Schmidt, Bos	48	22	30	52						
1941	Bill Cowley, Bos	46	17	45	62	1980	Marcel Dionne, LA*	80	53	84	137
1942	Bryan Hextall, NYR	48	24	32	56	1981	Wayne Gretzky, Edm	80	55	109	164
1943	Doug Bentley, Chi	50	33	40	73	1982	Wayne Gretzky, Edm	80	92	120	212
1944	Herbie Cain, Bos	48	36	46	82	1983	Wayne Gretzky, Edm	80	71	125	196
1945	Elmer Lach, Mon	50	26	54	80	1984	Wayne Gretzky, Edm	74	87	118	205
1946	Max Bentley, Chi	47	31	30	61	1985	Wayne Gretzky, Edm	80	73	135	208
1947	Max Bentley, Chi	60	29	43	72	1986	Wayne Gretzky, Edm	80	52	163	215
1948	Elmer Lach, Mon	60	30	31	61	1987	Wayne Gretzky, Edm	79	62	121	183
1949	Roy Conacher, Chi	60	26	42	68	1988	Mario Lemieux, Pit	77	70	98	168
						1989	Mario Lemieux, Pit	76	85	114	199
1950	Ted Lindsay, Det	69	23	55	78						
1951	Gordie Howe, Det	70	43	43	86	1990	Wayne Gretzky, LA	73	40	102	142
1952	Gordie Howe, Det	70	47	39	86	1991	Wayne Gretzky, LA	78	41	122	163
1953	Gordie Howe, Det	70	49	46	95	1992	Mario Lemieux, Pit	64	44	87	131
1954	Gordie Howe, Det	70	33	48	81	1993	Mario Lemieux, Pit	60	69	91	160
1955	Bernie Geoffrion, Mon	70	38	37	75	1994	Wayne Gretzky, LA	81	38	92	130
1956	Jean Beliveau, Mon	70	47	41	88						

*Note: The two times players have tied for total points in one season the player with more goals has won the trophy. In 1961-62, Hull outscored Andy Bathgate of NY Rangers, 50 goals to 28. In 1979-80, Dionne outscored Wayne Gretzky of Edmonton, 53-51.

NHL 500-Goal Scorers

Detroit right wing Dino Ciccarelli became the 19th player in NHL history to score 500 regular season goals when he knocked in No. 500 against Los Angeles on Jan. 8, 1994. Two other landmark goals were scored in 1993-94: Mike Gartner's 600th on Dec. 26 and Wayne Gretzky's 800th on Mar. 20 (see page 368). Of the 500-goal scorers listed below, two (Gartner and Hull) went on to score over 600 goals, two (Dionne and Esposito) scored over 700, and two (Gretzky and Howe) have scored over 800. Players who were active in 1993-94 are in **bold** type.

	Date	Game #		Date	Game #
Maurice Richard, Mon. vs Chi	10/19/57	863	Mike Bossy, NYI vs Bos	1/2/86	647
Gordie Howe, Det. at NYR	3/14/62	1045	Gilbert Perreault, Buf. vs NJ	3/9/86	1159
Bobby Hull, Chi. vs NYR	2/21/70	861	**Wayne Gretzky,** Edm. vs Van	11/22/86	575
Jean Beliveau, Mon. vs Min	2/11/71	1101	Lanny McDonald, Calg. vs NYI	3/21/89	1107
Frank Mahovlich, Mon. vs Van	3/21/73	1105	**Bryan Trottier,** NYI vs Calg	2/13/90	1104
Phil Esposito, Bos. vs Det	12/22/74	803	**Mike Gartner,** NYR vs Wash	10/14/91	936
John Bucyk, Bos. vs St.L	10/30/74	1370	**Michel Goulet,** Chi. vs Calg	2/16/92	951
Stan Mikita, Chi vs Van	2/27/77	1221	**Jari Kurri,** LA vs Bos	10/17/92	833
Marcel Dionne, LA at Wash	12/14/82	887	**Dino Ciccarelli,** Det. at LA	1/8/94	946
Guy Lafleur, Mon. at NJ	12/20/83	918			

Goals

Multiple winners: Bobby Hull (7); Phil Esposito (6); Charlie Conacher, Wayne Gretzky, Gordie Howe and Maurice Richard (5); Bill Cook, Babe Dye and Brett Hull (3); Jean Beliveau, Doug Bentley, Mike Bossy, Bernie Geoffrion, Bryan Hextall, Mario Lemieux, Joe Malone and Nels Stewart (2).

Year		No	Year		No	Year		No
1918	Joe Malone, Mon	44	1943	Doug Bentley, Chi	33	1970	Phil Esposito, Bos	43
1919	Odie Cleghorn, Mon	23	1944	Doug Bentley, Chi	38	1971	Phil Esposito, Bos	76
	& Newsy Lalonde, Mon	23	1945	Maurice Richard, Mon	50	1972	Phil Esposito, Bos	66
			1946	Gaye Stewart, Tor	37	1973	Phil Esposito, Bos	55
1920	Joe Malone, Que	39	1947	Maurice Richard, Mon	45	1974	Phil Esposito, Bos	68
1921	Babe Dye, Ham-Tor	35	1948	Ted Lindsay, Det	33	1975	Phil Esposito, Bos	61
1922	Punch Broadbent, Ott	32	1949	Sid Abel, Det	28	1976	Reggie Leach, Phi	61
1923	Babe Dye, Tor	26				1977	Steve Shutt, Mon	60
1924	Cy Denneny, Ott	22	1950	Maurice Richard, Mon	43	1978	Guy Lafleur, Mon	60
1925	Babe Dye, Tor	38	1951	Gordie Howe, Det	43	1979	Mike Bossy, NYI	69
1926	Nels Stewart, Maroons	34	1952	Gordie Howe, Det	47			
1927	Bill Cook, NYR	33	1953	Gordie Howe, Det	49	1980	Danny Gare, Buf	56
1928	Howie Morenz, Mon	33	1954	Maurice Richard, Mon	37		Charlie Simmer, LA	56
1929	Ace Bailey, Tor	22	1955	Bernie Geoffrion, Mon	38		& Blaine Stoughton, Hart	56
1930	Cooney Weiland, Bos	43		& Maurice Richard, Mon	38	1981	Mike Bossy, NYI	68
1931	Charlie Conacher, Tor	31	1956	Jean Beliveau, Mon	47	1982	Wayne Gretzky, Edm	92
1932	Charlie Conacher, Tor	34	1957	Gordie Howe, Det	44	1983	Wayne Gretzky, Edm	71
	& Bill Cook, NYR	34	1958	Dickie Moore, Mon	36	1984	Wayne Gretzky, Edm	87
1933	Bill Cook, NYR	28	1959	Jean Beliveau, Mon	45	1985	Wayne Gretzky, Edm	73
1934	Charlie Conacher, Tor	32				1986	Jari Kurri, Edm	68
1935	Charlie Conacher, Tor	36	1960	Bronco Horvath, Bos	39	1987	Wayne Gretzky, Edm	62
1936	Charlie Conacher, Tor	23		& Bobby Hull, Chi	39	1988	Mario Lemieux, Pit	70
	& Bill Thoms, Tor	23	1961	Bernie Geoffrion, Mon	50	1989	Mario Lemieux, Pit	85
1937	Larry Aurie, Det	23	1962	Bobby Hull, Chi	50			
	& Nels Stewart, Bos-NYA	23	1963	Gordie Howe, Det	38	1990	Brett Hull, St.L	72
1938	Gordie Drillon, Tor	26	1964	Bobby Hull, Chi	43	1991	Brett Hull, St.L	86
1939	Roy Conacher, Bos	26	1965	Norm Ullman, Tor	42	1992	Brett Hull, St.L	70
			1966	Bobby Hull, Chi	54	1993	Alexander Mogilny, Buf	76
1940	Bryan Hextall, NYR	24	1967	Bobby Hull, Chi	52		& Teemu Selanne, Win	76
1941	Bryan Hextall, NYR	26	1968	Bobby Hull, Chi	44	1994	Pavel Bure, Van	60
1942	Lynn Patrick, NYR	32	1969	Bobby Hull, Chi	58			

Assists

Multiple winners: Wayne Gretzky (14); Bobby Orr (5); Frank Boucher, Bill Cowley, Phil Esposito, Gordie Howe, Elmer Lach, Stan Mikita and Joe Primeau (3); Syl Apps, Andy Bathgate, Jean Beliveau, Doug Bentley, Art Chapman, Bobby Clarke, Ted Lindsay, Bert Olmstead, Henri Richard and Bryan Trottier (2).

Year		No	Year		No	Year		No
1918	No official records kept		1944	Clint Smith, Chi	49	1970	Bobby Orr, Bos	87
1919	Newsy Lalonde, Mon	9	1945	Elmer Lach, Mon	54	1971	Bobby Orr, Bos	102
			1946	Elmer Lach, Mon	34	1972	Bobby Orr, Bos	80
1920	Corbett Denneny, Tor	12	1947	Billy Taylor, Det	46	1973	Phil Esposito, Bos	75
1921	Louis Berlinquette, Mon	9	1948	Doug Bentley, Chi	37	1974	Bobby Orr, Bos	90
	Harry Cameron, Tor	9	1949	Doug Bentley, Chi	43	1975	Bobby Clarke, Phi	89
	& Joe Matte, Ham	9					& Bobby Orr, Bos	89
1922	Punch Broadbent, Ott	14	1950	Ted Lindsay, Det	55	1976	Bobby Clarke, Phi	89
	& Leo Reise, Ham	14	1951	Gordie Howe, Det	43	1977	Guy Lafleur, Mon	80
1923	Ed Bouchard, Ham	12		& Teeder Kennedy, Tor	43	1978	Bryan Trottier, NYI	77
1924	King Clancy, Ott	8	1952	Elmer Lach, Mon	50	1979	Bryan Trottier, NYI	87
1925	Cy Denneny, Ott	15	1953	Gordie Howe, Det	46			
1926	Frank Nighbor, Ott	13	1954	Gordie Howe, Det	48	1980	Wayne Gretzky, Edm	86
1927	Dick Irvin, Chi	18	1955	Bert Olmstead, Mon	48	1981	Wayne Gretzky, Edm	109
1928	Howie Morenz, Mon	18	1956	Bert Olmstead, Mon	56	1982	Wayne Gretzky, Edm	120
1929	Frank Boucher, NYR	16	1957	Ted Lindsay, Det	55	1983	Wayne Gretzky, Edm	125
1930	Frank Boucher, NYR	36	1958	Henri Richard, Mon	52	1984	Wayne Gretzky, Edm	118
1931	Joe Primeau, Tor	32	1959	Dickie Moore, Mon	55	1985	Wayne Gretzky, Edm	135
1932	Joe Primeau, Tor	37				1986	Wayne Gretzky, Edm	163
1933	Frank Boucher, NYR	28	1960	Don McKenney, Bos	49	1987	Wayne Gretzky, Edm	121
1934	Joe Primeau, Tor	32	1961	Jean Beliveau, Mon	58	1988	Wayne Gretzky, Edm	109
1935	Art Chapman, NYA	34	1962	Andy Bathgate, NYR	56	1989	Wayne Gretzky, LA	114
1936	Art Chapman, NYA	28	1963	Henri Richard, Mon	50		& Mario Lemieux, Pit	114
1937	Syl Apps, Tor	29	1964	Andy Bathgate, NYR-Tor	58			
1938	Syl Apps, Tor	29	1965	Stan Mikita, Chi	59	1990	Wayne Gretzky, LA	102
1939	Bill Cowley, Bos	34	1966	Jean Beliveau, Mon	48	1991	Wayne Gretzky, LA	122
				Stan Mikita, Chi	48	1992	Wayne Gretzky, LA	90
1940	Milt Schmidt, Bos	30		& Bobby Rousseau, Mon	48	1993	Adam Oates, Bos	97
1941	Bill Cowley, Bos	45	1967	Stan Mikita, Chi	62	1994	Wayne Gretzky, LA	92
1942	Phil Watson, NYR	37	1968	Phil Esposito, Bos	49			
1943	Bill Cowley, Bos	45	1969	Phil Esposito, Bos	77			

Annual NHL Leaders (Cont.)

Goals Against Average

Average determined by games played through 1942-43 season and by minutes played since then. Minimum of 15 games from 1917-18 season through 1925-26; minimum of 25 games since 1926-27 season. Not to be confused with the Vezina Trophy. Goaltenders who posted the season's lowest goals against average, but did not win the Vezina are in **bold** type.

Multiple winners: Jacques Plante (9); Clint Benedict and Bill Durnan (6); Johnny Bower, Ken Dryden and Tiny Thompson (4); Patrick Roy and Georges Vezina (3); Frankie Brimsek, Turk Broda, George Hainsworth, Harry Lumley, Bernie Parent, Pete Peeters and Terry Sawchuk (2).

Year		No	Year		No	Year		No
1918	Georges Vezina, Mon	3.82	1944	Bill Durnan, Mon	2.18	1970	**Ernie Wakely**, St.L	2.11
1919	Clint Benedict, Ott	2.94	1945	Bill Durnan, Mon	2.42	1971	**Jacques Plante**, Tor	1.88
1920	Clint Benedict, Ott	2.67	1946	Bill Durnan, Mon	2.60	1972	Tony Esposito, Chi	1.77
1921	Clint Benedict, Ott	3.13	1947	Bill Durnan, Mon	2.30	1973	Ken Dryden, Mon	2.26
1922	Clint Benedict, Ott	3.50	1948	Turk Broda, Tor	2.38	1974	Bernie Parent, Phi	1.89
1923	Clint Benedict, Ott	2.25	1949	Bill Durnan, Mon	2.10	1975	Bernie Parent, Phi	2.03
1924	Georges Vezina, Mon	2.00	1950	Bill Durnan, Mon	2.20	1976	Ken Dryden, Mon	2.03
1925	Georges Vezina, Mon	1.87	1951	Al Rollins, Tor	1.77	1977	Bunny Larocque, Mon	2.09
1926	Alex Connell, Ott	1.17	1952	Terry Sawchuk, Det	1.90	1978	Ken Dryden, Mon	2.05
1927	**C. Benedict**, Mon-M	1.51	1953	Terry Sawchuk, Det	1.90	1979	Ken Dryden, Mon	2.30
1928	Geo. Hainsworth, Mon	1.09	1954	Harry Lumley, Tor	1.86			
1929	Geo. Hainsworth, Mon	0.98	1955	**Harry Lumley**, Tor	1.94	1980	Bob Sauve, Buf	2.36
1930	Tiny Thompson, Bos	2.23	1956	Jacques Plante, Mon	1.86	1981	Richard Sevigny, Mon	2.40
1931	Roy Worters, NYA	1.68	1957	Jacques Plante, Mon	2.02	1982	**Denis Herron**, Mon	2.64
1932	Chuck Gardiner, Chi	1.92	1958	Jacques Plante, Mon	2.11	1983	Pete Peeters, Bos	2.36
1933	Tiny Thompson, Bos	1.83	1959	Jacques Plante, Mon	2.16	1984	**Pat Riggin**, Wash	2.66
1934	**Wilf Cude**, Det-Mon	1.57	1960	Jacques Plante, Mon	2.54	1985	**Tom Barrasso**, Buf	2.66
1935	Lorne Chabot, Chi	1.83	1961	Johnny Bower, Tor	2.50	1986	**Bob Froese**, Phi	2.55
1936	Tiny Thompson, Bos	1.71	1962	Jacques Plante, Mon	2.37	1987	**Brian Hayward**, Mon	2.81
1937	Norm Smith, Det	2.13	1963	**Jacques Plante**, Mon	2.49	1988	Pete Peeters, Wash	2.78
1938	Tiny Thompson, Bos	1.85	1964	**Johnny Bower**, Tor	2.11	1989	Patrick Roy, Mon	2.47
1939	Frankie Brimsek, Bos	1.58	1965	Johnny Bower, Tor	2.38			
1940	Dave Kerr, NYR	1.60	1966	**Johnny Bower**, Tor	2.25	1990	**Mike Liut**, Hart-Wash	2.53
1941	Turk Broda, Tor	2.06	1967	Glenn Hall, Chi	2.38		& Patrick Roy, Mon	2.53
1942	Frankie Brimsek, Bos	2.45	1968	Gump Worsley, Mon	1.98	1991	Ed Belfour, Chi	2.47
1943	John Mowers, Det	2.48	1969	**Jacques Plante**, St.L	1.96	1992	Patrick Roy, Mon	2.36
						1993	**Felix Potvin**, Tor	2.50
						1994	Dominik Hasek, Buf	1.95

Penalty Minutes

Multiple winners: Red Horner (8); Gus Mortson and Dave Schultz (4); Bert Corbeau, Lou Fontinato and Tiger Williams (3); Billy Boucher, Carl Brewer, Red Dutton, Pat Egan, Bill Ezinicki, Tim Hunter, Keith Magnuson, Chris Nilan and Jimmy Orlando (2).

Year		Min	Year		Min	Year		Min
1918	No officials records kept.		1944	Mike McMahon, Mon	98	1970	Keith Magnuson, Chi	213
1919	Joe Hall, Mon	85	1945	Pat Egan, Bos	86	1971	Keith Magnuson, Chi	291
1920	Cully Wilson, Tor	79	1946	Jack Stewart, Det	73	1972	Bryan Watson, Pit	212
1921	Bert Corbeau, Mon	86	1947	Gus Mortson, Tor	133	1973	Dave Schultz, Phi	259
1922	Sprague Cleghorn, Mon	63	1948	Bill Barilko, Tor	147	1974	Dave Schultz, Phi	348
1923	Billy Boucher, Mon	52	1949	Bill Ezinicki, Tor	145	1975	Dave Schultz, Phi	472
1924	Bert Corbeau, Tor	55	1950	Bill Ezinicki, Tor	144	1976	Steve Durbano, Pit-KC	370
1925	Billy Boucher, Mon	92	1951	Gus Mortson, Tor	142	1977	Tiger Williams, Tor	338
1926	Bert Corbeau, Tor	121	1952	Gus Kyle, Bos	127	1978	Dave Schultz, LA-Pit	405
1927	Nels Stewart, Mon-M	133	1953	Maurice Richard, Mon	112	1979	Tiger Williams, Tor	298
1928	Eddie Shore, Bos	165	1954	Gus Mortson, Chi	132			
1929	Red Dutton, Mon-M	139	1955	Fern Flaman, Bos	150	1980	Jimmy Mann, Win	287
1930	Joe Lamb, Ott	119	1956	Lou Fontinato, NYR	202	1981	Tiger Williams, Van	343
1931	Harvey Rockburn, Det	118	1957	Gus Mortson, Chi	147	1982	Paul Baxter, Pit	409
1932	Red Dutton, NYA	107	1958	Lou Fontinato, NYR	152	1983	Randy Holt, Wash	275
1933	Red Horner, Tor	144	1959	Ted Lindsay, Chi	184	1984	Chris Nilan, Mon	338
1934	Red Horner, Tor	146	1960	Carl Brewer, Tor	150	1985	Chris Nilan, Mon	358
1935	Red Horner, Tor	125	1961	Pierre Pilot, Chi	165	1986	Joey Kocur, Det	377
1936	Red Horner, Tor	167	1962	Lou Fontinato, Mon	167	1987	Tim Hunter, Calg	361
1937	Red Horner, Tor	124	1963	Howie Young, Det	273	1988	Bob Probert, Det	398
1938	Red Horner, Tor	*82	1964	Vic Hadfield, NYR	151	1989	Tim Hunter, Calg	375
1939	Red Horner, Tor	85	1965	Carl Brewer, Tor	177			
1940	Red Horner, Tor	87	1966	Reg Fleming, Bos-NYR	166	1990	Basil McRae, Min	351
1941	Jimmy Orlando, Det	99	1967	John Ferguson, Mon	177	1991	Rob Ray, Buf	350
1942	Pat Egan, NYA	124	1968	Barclay Plager, St.L	153	1992	Mike Peluso, Chi	408
1943	Jimmy Orlando, Det	99	1969	Forbes Kennedy, Phi-Tor	219	1993	Marty McSorley, LA	399
						1994	Tie Domi, Win	347

All-Time NHL Regular Season Leaders

Through 1993-94 regular season.

CAREER

Players active during 1993-94 in **bold** type.

Points

		Yrs	Gm	G	A	Pts
1	**Wayne Gretzky**	15	1125	803	1655	2458
2	Gordie Howe	26	1767	801	1049	1850
3	Marcel Dionne	18	1348	731	1040	1771
4	Phil Esposito	18	1282	717	873	1590
5	Stan Mikita	22	1394	541	926	1467
6	**Bryan Trottier**	18	1279	524	901	1425
7	John Bucyk	23	1540	556	813	1369
8	Guy Lefleur	17	1126	560	793	1353
9	Gilbert Perreault	17	1191	512	814	1326
10	**Mark Messier**	15	1081	478	838	1316
11	**Dale Hawerchuk**	13	1032	484	814	1298
12	Alex Delvecchio	24	1549	456	825	1281
13	**Paul Coffey**	14	1033	344	934	1278
14	**Jari Kurri**	13	990	555	712	1267
	Jean Ratelle	21	1281	491	776	1267
16	**Denis Savard**	14	1020	441	797	1238
17	**Peter Stastny**	14	971	449	788	1237
18	Norm Ullman	20	1410	490	739	1229
19	Jean Beliveau	20	1125	507	712	1219
20	**Mario Lemieux**	10	599	494	717	1211
21	Bobby Clarke	15	1144	358	852	1210
22	**Ray Bourque**	15	1100	311	877	1188
23	**Mike Gartner**	15	1170	617	554	1171
24	Bobby Hull	16	1063	610	560	1170
25	**Michel Goulet**	15	1089	548	604	1152
26	Bernie Federko	14	1000	369	761	1130
27	Mike Bossy	10	752	573	553	1126
28	**Steve Yzerman**	11	815	469	653	1122
29	Darryl Sittler	15	1096	484	637	1121
30	Frank Mahovlich	18	1181	533	570	1103

Goals

		Yrs	Gm	No
1	**Wayne Gretzky**	15	1125	803
2	Gordie Howe	26	1767	801
3	Marcel Dionne	18	1348	731
4	Phil Esposito	18	1282	717
5	**Mike Gartner**	15	1170	617
6	Bobby Hull	16	1063	610
7	Mike Bossy	10	752	573
8	Guy Lafleur	17	1126	560
9	John Bucyk	23	1540	556
10	**Jari Kurri**	13	990	555
11	**Michel Goulet**	15	1089	548
12	Maurice Richard	18	978	544
13	Stan Mikita	22	1394	541
14	Frank Mahovlich	18	1181	533
15	**Bryan Trottier**	18	1279	524
16	**Dino Ciccarelli**	14	973	513
17	Gilbert Perreault	17	1191	512
18	Jean Beliveau	18	1125	507
19	Lanny McDonald	16	1111	500
20	**Mario Lemieux**	10	599	494
21	Jean Ratelle	21	1281	491
22	Norm Ullman	20	1410	490
23	**Dale Hawerchuk**	13	1032	484
	Darryl Sittler	15	1096	484
25	**Glenn Anderson**	14	1060	480
26	**Mark Messier**	15	1081	478
27	**Joe Mullen**	14	926	471
28	**Steve Yzerman**	11	815	469
29	Alex Delvecchio	24	1549	456
30	**Peter Stastny**	14	971	449

Assists

		Yrs	Gm	No
1	**Wayne Gretzky**	15	1125	1655
2	Gordie Howe	26	1767	1049
3	Marcel Dionne	18	1348	1040
4	**Paul Coffey**	14	1033	934
5	Stan Mikita	22	1394	926
6	**Bryan Trottier**	18	1279	901
7	**Ray Bourque**	15	1100	877
8	Phil Esposito	18	1281	873
9	Bobby Clarke	15	1144	852
10	**Mark Messier**	15	1081	838
11	Alex Delvecchio	24	1549	825
12	**Dale Hawerchuk**	13	1032	814
	Gilbert Perreault	17	1191	814
14	John Bucyk	23	1540	813
15	**Denis Savard**	14	1020	797
16	Guy Lafleur	17	1126	793
17	**Peter Stastny**	14	971	788
18	Jean Ratelle	21	1281	776
19	Bernie Federko	14	1000	761
20	Larry Robinson	20	1384	750

Penalty Minutes

		Yrs	Gm	PM
1	Tiger Williams	14	962	3966
2	Chris Nilan	13	688	3043
3	**Dale Hunter**	14	1054	3005
4	**Tim Hunter**	13	675	2769
5	**Marty McSorley**	11	666	2640
6	Willi Plett	12	834	2572
7	**Basil McRae**	13	529	2333
8	Dave Schultz	9	535	2294
9	**Garth Butcher**	13	852	2276
10	Laurie Boschman	14	1009	2265

NHL-WHA Top 15

All-Time regular season scoring leaders, including games played in World Hockey Association (1972-79). NHL players with WHA experience are listed in CAPITAL letters. Players active during 1993-94 are in **bold** type.

Points

		Yrs	G	A	Pts
1	**WAYNE GRETZKY**	16	849	1719	2568
2	GORDIE HOWE	32	975	1383	2358
3	BOBBY HULL	23	913	895	1808
4	Marcel Dionne	18	731	1040	1771
5	Phil Esposito	18	717	873	1590
6	Stan Mikita	22	541	926	1467
7	**Bryan Trottier**	18	524	901	1425
8	John Bucyk	23	556	813	1369
9	NORM ULLMAN	22	537	822	1359
10	Guy Lafleur	17	560	793	1353
11	FRANK MAHOVLICH	22	622	713	1335
12	**MARK MESSIER**	16	479	848	1327
13	Gilbert Perreault	17	512	814	1326
14	**Dale Hawerchuk**	13	484	814	1298
15	Alex Delvecchio	24	456	825	1281

WHA Totals: GRETZKY (1 yr, 60 gm, 46-64—110); HOWE (6 yrs, 419 gm, 174-334—508); HULL (7 yrs, 411 gm, 303-335—638); MAHOVLICH (4 yrs, 237 gm, 89-143—232); MESSIER (1 yr, 52 gm, 1-10—11); ULLMAN (2 yrs, 144 gm, 47-83—130).

All-Time NHL Regular Season Leaders (Cont.)

Years Played

		Yrs	Career	Gm
1	Gordie Howe	26	1946-71, 79-80	1767
2	Alex Delvecchio	24	1950-74	1549
	Tim Horton	24	1949-50, 51-74	1446
4	John Bucyk	23	1955-78	1540
5	Stan Mikita	22	1958-80	1394
	Doug Mohns	22	1953-75	1390
	Dean Prentice	22	1952-74	1378
8	Harry Howell	21	1952-73	1411
	Ron Stewart	21	1952-73	1353
	Jean Ratelle	21	1960-81	1281
	Allan Stanley	21	1948-69	1244
	Eric Nesterenko	21	1951-72	1219
	Marcel Pronovost	21	1950-70	1206
	George Armstrong	21	1949-50, 51-71	1187
	Terry Sawchuk	21	1949-70	971
	Gump Worsley	21	1952-53, 54-74	862

Note: Combined NHL-WHA years played: Howe (32); Howell (24); Bobby Hull (23); Norm Ullman, Nesterenko, Frank Mahovlich and Dave Keon (22).

Games Played

		Yrs	Career	Gm
1	Gordie Howe	26	1946-71, 79-80	1767
2	Alex Delvecchio	24	1950-74	1549
3	John Bucyk	23	1955-78	1540
4	Tim Horton	24	1949-50, 51-74	1446
5	Harry Howell	21	1952-73	1411
6	Norm Ullman	20	1955-75	1410
7	Stan Mikita	22	1958-80	1394
8	Doug Mohns	22	1953-75	1390
9	Larry Robinson	20	1972-92	1384
10	Dean Prentice	22	1952-74	1378
11	Ron Stewart	21	1952-73	1353
12	Marcel Dionne	18	1971-89	1348
13	Red Kelly	20	1947-67	1316
14	Dave Keon	18	1960-75, 79-82	1296
15	Phil Esposito	18	1963-81	1282

Note: Combined NHL-WHA games played: Howe (2,186), Keon (1,597), Howell (1,581), Ullman (1,554), Bobby Hull (1,474) and Frank Mahovlich (1,418).

Goaltending

Wins

		Yrs	Gm	W	L	T	Pct
1	Terry Sawchuk	21	971	435	337	188	.551
2	Jacques Plante	18	837	434	246	137	.615
3	Tony Esposito	16	886	423	307	151	.566
4	Glenn Hall	18	906	407	327	165	.544
5	Rogie Vachon	16	795	355	291	115	.542
6	Gump Worsley	21	862	335	353	150	.489
7	Harry Lumley	16	804	332	324	143	.505
8	Billy Smith	18	680	305	233	105	.556
9	**Andy Moog**	14	551	303	148	64	.654
10	Turk Broda	12	629	302	224	101	.562
11	Mike Liut	13	663	293	271	74	.517
12	Ed Giacomin	13	610	289	206	97	.570
13	**Grant Fuhr**	13	579	288	186	68	.594
14	Dan Bouchard	14	655	286	232	113	.543
15	Tiny Thompson	12	553	284	194	75	.581
16	Bernie Parent	13	608	270	197	121	.562
	Gilles Meloche	18	788	270	351	131	.446
18	**Tom Barrasso**	11	546	266	196	60	.567
19	**Patrick Roy**	9	486	260	146	59	.623
20	Ken Dryden	8	397	258	57	74	.758

Losses

		Yrs	Gm	W	L	T	Pct
1	Gump Worsley	21	862	335	353	150	.489
2	Gilles Meloche	18	788	270	351	131	.446
3	Terry Sawchuk	21	971	435	337	188	.551
4	Glenn Hall	18	906	407	327	165	.544
5	Harry Lumley	16	804	332	324	143	.505

Goals Against Average

Minimum of 300 games played.

Before 1950

		Gm	Min	GA	Avg
1	George Hainsworth	465	29,415	937	1.91
2	Alex Connell	416	26,030	837	2.01
3	Chuck Gardiner	316	19,687	664	2.02
4	Lorne Chabot	412	25,309	861	2.04
5	Tiny Thompson	552	34,174	1183	2.08

Since 1950

		Gm	Min	GA	Avg
1	Ken Dryden	397	23,352	870	2.24
2	Jacques Plante	837	49,633	1965	2.38
3	Glenn Hall	906	53,484	2239	2.51
4	Terry Sawchuk	971	57,205	2401	2.52
5	Johnny Bower	552	32,077	1347	2.52

Shutouts

		Yrs	Games	No
1	Terry Sawchuk	21	971	103
2	George Hainsworth	11	464	94
3	Glenn Hall	18	906	84
4	Jacques Plante	18	837	82
5	Alex Connell	12	417	81
	Tiny Thompson	12	553	81
7	Tony Esposito	16	886	76
8	Lorne Chabot	11	411	73
9	Harry Lumley	16	804	71
10	Roy Worters	12	484	66
11	Turk Broda	14	629	62
12	John Roach	14	492	58
13	Clint Benedict	13	362	57
14	Bernie Parent	13	608	55
15	Ed Giacomin	13	610	54

NHL-WHA Top 15

All-Time regular season wins leaders, including games played in World Hockey Association (1972-79). NHL goaltenders with WHA experience are listed in CAPITAL letters. Players active during 1993-94 are in **bold** type.

Wins

		Yrs	W	L	T	Pct
1	JACQUES PLANTE	19	449	260	138	.612
2	Terry Sawchuk	21	435	337	188	.551
3	Tony Esposito	16	423	307	151	.566
4	Glenn Hall	18	407	327	165	.544
5	Rogie Vachon	16	355	291	115	.542
6	Gump Worsley	21	335	353	150	.489
7	Harry Lumley	16	332	324	143	.505
8	GERRY CHEEVERS	16	329	172	83	.634
9	MIKE LIUT	15	324	310	78	.510
10	Billy Smith	18	305	233	105	.556
11	**Andy Moog**	14	303	148	64	.654
	BERNIE PARENT	14	303	225	121	.560
13	Turk Broda	12	302	224	101	.562
14	Ed Giacomin	13	289	206	97	.570
15	**Grant Fuhr**	13	288	186	68	.594

WHA Totals: CHEEVERS (4 yrs, 191 gm, 99-78-9); LIUT (2 yrs, 81 gm, 31-39-4); PARENT (1 yr, 63 gm, 33-28-0); PLANTE (1 yr, 31 gm, 15-14-1).

SINGLE SEASON

Scoring
Points

		Season	G	A	Pts
1	Wayne Gretzky, Edm	1985-86	52	163	215
2	Wayne Gretzky, Edm	1981-82	92	120	212
3	Wayne Gretzky, Edm	1984-85	73	135	208
4	Wayne Gretzky, Edm	1983-84	87	118	205
5	Mario Lemieux, Pit	1988-89	85	114	199
6	Wayne Gretzky, Edm	1982-83	71	125	196
7	Wayne Gretzky, Edm	1986-87	62	121	183
8	Mario Lemieux, Pit	1987-88	70	98	168
	Wayne Gretzky, LA	1988-89	54	114	168
10	Wayne Gretzky, Edm	1980-81	55	109	164
11	Wayne Gretzky, LA	1990-91	41	122	163
12	Mario Lemieux, Pit	1992-93	69	91	160
13	Steve Yzerman, Det	1988-89	65	90	155
14	Phil Esposito, Bos	1970-71	76	76	152
15	Bernie Nicholls, LA	1988-89	70	80	150
16	Wayne Gretzky, Edm	1987-88	40	109	149
17	Pat LaFontaine, Buf	1992-93	53	95	148
18	Mike Bossy, NYI	1981-82	64	83	147
19	Phil Esposito, Bos	1973-74	68	77	145
20	Adam Oates, Bos	1992-93	45	97	142
	Wayne Gretzky, LA	1989-90	40	102	142

WHA 150 points or more: 154—Marc Tardif, Que. (1977-78).

Goals

		Season	Gm	No
1	Wayne Gretzky, Edm	1981-82	80	92
2	Wayne Gretzky, Edm	1983-84	74	87
3	Brett Hull, St.L	1990-91	78	86
4	Mario Lemieux, Pit	1988-89	76	85
5	Alexander Mogilny, Buf	1992-93	77	76
	Phil Esposito, Bos	1970-71	78	76
	Teemu Selanne, Win	1992-93	84	76
8	Wayne Gretzky, Edm	1984-85	80	73
9	Brett Hull, St.L	1989-90	80	72
10	Jari Kurri, Edm	1984-85	73	71
	Wayne Gretzky, Edm	1982-83	80	71
12	Brett Hull, St.L	1991-92	73	70
	Mario Lemiuex, Pit	1987-88	77	70
	Bernie Nicholls, LA	1988-89	79	70
15	Mario Lemieux, Pit	1992-93	60	69
	Mike Bossy, NYI	1978-79	80	69
17	Phil Esposito, Bos	1973-74	78	68
	Jari Kurri, Edm	1985-86	78	68
	Mike Bossy, NYI	1980-81	79	68
20	Phil Esposito, Bos	1971-72	76	66
	Lanny McDonald, Calg	1982-83	80	66

WHA 70 goals or more: 77—Bobby Hull, Win. (1974-75); 75—Real Cloutier, Que. (1978-79); 71—Marc Tardif, Que. (1975-76); 70—Anders Hedberg, Win. (1976-77).

Assists

		Season	Gm	No
1	Wayne Gretzky, Edm	1985-86	80	163
2	Wayne Gretzky, Edm	1984-85	80	135
3	Wayne Gretzky, Edm	1982-83	80	125
4	Wayne Gretzky, LA	1990-91	78	122
5	Wayne Gretzky, Edm	1986-87	79	121
6	Wayne Gretzky, Edm	1981-82	80	120
7	Wayne Gretzky, Edm	1983-84	74	118
8	Mario Lemieux, Pit	1988-89	76	114
	Wayne Gretzky, LA	1988-89	78	114
10	Wayne Gretzky, Edm	1987-88	64	109
	Wayne Gretzky, Edm	1980-81	80	109
12	Wayne Gretzky, LA	1989-90	73	102
	Bobby Orr, Bos	1970-71	78	102
14	Mario Lemieux, Pit	1987-88	77	98
15	Adam Oates, Bos	1992-93	84	97

WHA 95 assists or more: 106—Andre Lacroix, S.Diego (1974-75).

Goaltending
Wins

		Season	Record
1	Bernie Parent, Phi	1973-74	47-13-12
2	Bernie Parent, Phi	1974-75	44-14- 9
	Terry Sawchuk, Det	1950-51	44-13-13
	Terry Sawchuk, Det	1951-52	44-14-12
5	Tom Barrasso, Pit	1992-93	43-14- 5
	Ed Belfour, Chi	1990-91	43-19- 7
7	Jacques Plante, Mon	1955-56	42-12-10
	Jacques Plante, Mon	1961-62	42-14-14
	Ken Dryden, Mon	1975-76	42-10- 8
	Mike Richter, NYR	1993-94	42-12- 6

Most WHA wins in one season: 44—Richard Brodeur, Que. (1975-76).

Losses

		Season	Record
1	Gary Smith, Cal	1970-71	19-48- 4
2	Al Rollins, Chi	1953-54	12-47- 7
3	Peter Sidorkiewicz, Ott	1992-93	8-46- 3
4	Harry Lumley, Chi	1951-52	17-44- 9
5	Harry Lumley, Chi	1950-51	12-41-10
	Craig Billington, Ott	1993-94	11-41- 4

Most WHA losses in one season: 36—Don McLeod, Van. (1974-75) and Andy Brown, Ind. (1974-75).

Shutouts

		Season	Gm	No
1	George Hainsworth, Mon	1928-29	44	22
2	Alex Connell, Ottawa	1925-26	36	15
	Alex Connell, Ottawa	1927-28	44	15
	Hal Winkler, Bos	1927-28	44	15
	Tony Esposito, Chi	1969-70	63	15

Most WHA shutouts in one season: 5—Gerry Cheevers, Cle. (1972-73) and Joe Daly, Win. (1975-76).

Goals Against Average
Before 1950

		Season	Gm	No
1	George Hainsworth, Mon	1928-29	44	0.98
2	George Hainsworth, Mon	1927-28	44	1.09
3	Alex Connell, Ottawa	1925-26	36	1.17
4	Tiny Thompson, Bos	1928-29	44	1.18
5	Roy Worters, NY Americans	1928-29	38	1.21

Since 1950

		Season	Gm	No
1	Tony Esposito, Chi	1971-72	48	1.77
2	Al Rollins, Tor	1950-51	40	1.77
3	Harry Lumley, Tor	1953-54	69	1.86
4	Jacques Plante, Mon	1955-56	64	1.86
5	Jacques Plante, Tor	1970-71	40	1.88

Penalty Minutes

		Season	PM
1	Dave Schultz, Phi	1974-75	472
2	Paul Baxter, Pit	1981-82	409
3	Mike Peluso, Chi	1991-92	408
4	Dave Schultz, LA-Pit	1977-78	405
5	Marty McSorley, LA	1992-93	399
6	Bob Probert, Det	1987-88	398
7	Basil McRae, Min	1987-88	382
8	Joey Kocur, Det	1985-86	377
9	Tim Hunter, Calg	1988-89	375
10	Steve Durbano, Pit-KC	1975-76	370
	Gino Odjick, Van	1992-93	370

WHA 355 minutes or more: 365—Curt Brackenbury, Min-Que. (1975-76).

All-Time NHL Regular Season Leaders (Cont.)
SINGLE GAME
Scoring

Points

	Date	G-A—Pts
Darryl Sittler, Tor. vs Bos.	2/7/76	6-4—10
Maurice Richard, Mon. vs Det.	12/28/44	5-3— 8
Bert Olmstead, Mon. vs Chi.	1/9/54	4-4— 8
Tom Bladon, Phi. vs Cle.	12/11/77	4-4— 8
Bryan Trottier, NYI vs NYR	12/23/78	5-3— 8
Peter Stastny, Que. at Wash.	2/22/81	4-4— 8
Anton Stastny, Que. at Wash.	2/22/81	3-5— 8
Wayne Gretzky, Edm. vs NJ.	11/19/83	3-5— 8
Wayne Gretzky, Edm. vs Min.	1/4/84	4-4— 8
Paul Coffey, Edm. vs Det.	3/14/86	2-6— 8
Mario Lemieux, Pit. vs St.L	10/15/88	2-6— 8
Bernie Nicholls, LA vs Tor.	12/1/88	2-6— 8
Mario Lemieux, Pit. vs NJ	12/31/88	5-3— 8

Goals

	Date	No
Joe Malone, Que. vs Tor.	1/31/20	7
Newsy Lalonde, Mon. vs Tor	1/10/20	6
Joe Malone, Que. vs Ott.	3/10/20	6
Corb Denneny, Tor. vs Ham.	1/26/21	6
Cy Denneny, Ott. vs Ham	3/7/21	6
Syd Howe, Det. vs NYR	2/3/44	6
Red Berenson, St.L at Phi	11/7/68	6
Darryl Sittler, Tor. vs Bos.	2/7/76	6

Assists

	Date	No
Billy Taylor, Det. at Chi.	3/16/47	7
Wayne Gretzky, Edm. vs Wash	2/15/80	7
Wayne Gretzky, Edm. at Chi	12/11/85	7
Wayne Gretzky, Edm. vs Que	2/14/86	7
22 players tied with 6 each.		

THE GREAT ONE: FOR THE RECORD

Los Angeles center Wayne Gretzky broke Gordie Howe's all-time NHL regular season goal-scoring record with his 802nd goal on Mar. 23, 1994. The record is the 60th league mark he has either tied or set outright. Gretzky ended the 1993-94 season with 38 goals (803 career), 92 assists and 130 points to win his 10th scoring title in 15 seasons. However, he missed the playoffs for the first time in his career when the Kings failed to qualify.

Year by Year Statistics

Season	Age	Club	Regular Season					Playoffs					Awards
			Gm	G	A	Pts	PM	Gm	G	A	Pts	PM	
1978-79	18	Indianapolis	8	3	3	6	0						
		Edmonton	72	43	61	104	19	13	10*	10	20*	2	WHA Top Rookie
1979-80	19	Edmonton	79	51	86*	137†	21	3	2	1	3	0	Hart, Byng
1980-81	20	Edmonton	80	55	109*	164*	28	9	7	14	21	4	Hart, Ross
1981-82	21	Edmonton	80	92*	120*	212*	26	5	5	7	12	8	Hart, Ross
1982-83	22	Edmonton	80	71*	125*	196*	59	16	12	26*	38*	4	Hart, Ross
1983-84	23	Edmonton	74	87*	118*	205*	39	19	13	22*	35*	12	Hart, Ross
1984-85	24	Edmonton	80	73*	135*	208*	52	18	17	30*	47*	4	Hart, Ross, Smythe
1985-86	25	Edmonton	80	52	163*	215*	46	10	8	11	19	2	Hart, Ross
1986-87	26	Edmonton	79	62*	121*	183*	28	21	5	29*	34*	6	Hart, Ross
1987-88	27	Edmonton	64	40	109*	149	24	19	12	31*	43*	16	Smythe
1988-89	28	Los Angeles	78	54	114*	168	26	11	5	17	22	0	Hart
1989-90	29	Los Angeles	73	40	102*	142*	42	7	3	7	10	0	Ross
1990-91	30	Los Angeles	78	41	122*	163*	16	12	4	11	15	2	Ross, Byng
1991-92	31	Los Angeles	74	31	90*	121	34	6	2	5	7	2	Byng
1992-93	32	Los Angeles	45	16	49	65	6	24	15*	25*	40*	4	—
1993-94	33	Los Angeles	81	38	92*	130*	20	—	—	—	—	—	Byng
		WHA totals	80	46	64	110	19	13	10	10	20	2	
		NHL totals	1125	803	1655	2458	467	180	110	236	346	64	

*Led league; †Tied for league lead.

Gretzky vs. Howe

The all-time records of Wayne Gretzky and Gordie Howe, pro hockey's two most prolific scorers. Below are their career records in the NHL, the WHA and the two leagues combined. Howe played with Detroit (1946-71) and Hartford (1979-80) in the NHL and with Houston (1973-77) and New England (1977-79) in the WHA.

NHL	Regular Season						Playoffs						Stanley Cups
	Yrs	Gm	G	A	Pts	PM	Yrs	Gm	G	A	Pts	PM	
Wayne Gretzky	15	1125	803	1655	2458	467	14	180	110	236	346	64	4 (1984-85,87-88)
Gordie Howe	26	1767	801	1049	1850	1685	20	157	68	92	160	220	4 (1950,52,54-55)

WHA	Regular Season						Playoffs						AVCO World Cups
	Yrs	Gm	G	A	Pts	PM	Yrs	Gm	G	A	Pts	PM	
Gordie Howe	6	419	174	334	508	399	6	78	28	43	71	115	2 (1974-75)
Wayne Gretzky	1	80	46	64	110	19	1	13	10	10	20	2	None

NHL/WHA	Regular Season						Playoffs					
	Yrs	Gm	G	A	Pts	PM	Yrs	Gm	G	A	Pts	PM
Wayne Gretzky	16	1205	849	1719	2568	486	15	193	120	246	366	66
Gordie Howe	32	2186	975	1383	2358	2084	26	235	96	135	231	335

All-Time Winningest NHL Coaches

Top 20 NHL career victories through the 1993-94 season. Career, regular season and playoff records are noted along with NHL titles won. Coaches active during 1993-94 season in **bold** type.

		Yrs	Career W	L	T	Pct	Regular Season— W	L	T	Pct	Playoffs W	L	T	Pct	Stanley Cups
1	**Scotty Bowman**	22	1020	496	234	.650	880	410	234	.654	140	86	0	.619	6 (1973,76-79,92)
2	**Al Arbour**	22	902	662	246	.566	779	576	246	.563	123	86	0	.589	4 (1980-83)
3	Dick Irvin	26	790	609	228	.556	690	521	226	.559	100	88	2	.532	4 (1932,44,46,53)
4	Billy Reay	16	599	445	175	.563	542	385	175	.571	57	60	0	.487	None
5	Toe Blake	13	582	292	159	.640	500	255	159	.634	82	37	0	.689	8 (1956-60,65-66,68)
6	Glen Sather	11	553	305	110	.628	464	268	110	.616	89	37	0	.706	4 (1984-85,87-88)
7	Bryan Murray	12	501	381	115	.560	467	337	115	.571	34	44	0	.436	None
8	**Mike Keenan**	9	476	311	77	.595	395	252	77	.599	81	59	0	.579	1 (1994)
9	Punch Imlach	15	467	421	163	.522	423	373	163	.526	44	48	0	.478	4 (1962-64,67)
10	Jack Adams	21	465	442	162	.511	413	390	161	.512	52	52	1	.500	3 (1936-37,43)
11	Fred Shero	10	451	272	119	.606	390	225	119	.612	61	47	0	.565	2 (1974-75)
12	Emile Francis	13	433	326	112	.561	393	273	112	.577	40	53	0	.430	None
13	Sid Abel	16	414	470	155	.473	382	426	155	.477	32	44	0	.421	None
14	**Jacques Demers**	10	412	388	106	.513	357	345	106	.507	55	43	0	.561	1 (1993)
15	**Pat Quinn**	11	405	328	102	.546	354	282	102	.549	51	46	0	.526	None
16	**Roger Neilson**	12	398	344	126	.531	361	304	126	.536	37	40	0	.481	None
17	**Bob Berry**	11	395	377	121	.510	384	355	121	.517	11	22	0	.333	None
18	Art Ross	18	393	310	95	.552	361	277	90	.558	32	33	5	.493	1 (1939)
19	Michel Bergeron	10	369	387	104	.490	338	350	104	.492	31	37	0	.456	None
20	Bob Pulford	11	364	348	130	.510	336	305	130	.520	28	43	0	.394	None

Note: The NHL does not recognize records from the World Hockey Association (1972-79), so the following WHA overall coaching records are not included above: **Demers** (155-164-44 in 4 yrs); **Sather** (103-97-1 in 3 yrs).

Where They Coached

Abel—Chicago (1952-54), Detroit (1957-68,69-70), St. Louis (1971-72), Kansas City (1975-76); **Adams**—Toronto (1922-23), Detroit (1927-47); **Arbour**—St. Louis (1970-73), NY Islanders (1973-86,88-94); **Bergeron**—Quebec (1980-87), NY Rangers (1987-89), Quebec (1989-90); **Berry**—Los Angeles (1978-81), Montreal (1981-84), Pittsburgh (1984-87), St. Louis (1992-94); **Blake**—Montreal (1955-68); **Bowman**—St. Louis (1967-71), Montreal (1971-79), Buffalo (1979-87), Pittsburgh (1991-93), Detroit (1993—).

Demers—Quebec (1979-80), St. Louis (1983-86), Montreal (1992—); **Francis**—NY Rangers (1965-75), St. Louis (1976-77,81-83); **Imlach**—Toronto (1958-69), Buffalo (1970-72), Toronto (1979-81); **Irvin**—Chicago (1930-31,55-56), Toronto (1931-40), Montreal (1940-55); **Keenan**—Philadelphia (1984-88), Chicago (1988-92), NY Rangers (1993-94), St. Louis (1994—); **B. Murray**—Washington (1982-90), Detroit (1990-93).

Neilson—Toronto (1977-79), Buffalo (1979-81), Vancouver (1982-83), Los Angeles (1984), NY Rangers (1989-93), Florida (1993—); **Pulford**—Los Angeles (1972-77), Chicago (1977-79,81-82,85-87); **Quinn**—Philadelphia (1978-82), Los Angeles (1984-87), Vancouver (1990-94); **Reay**—Toronto (1957-59), Chicago (1963-77); **Ross**—Montreal Wanderers (1917-18), Hamilton (1922-23), Boston (1924-28,29-34,36-39,41-45); **Sather**—Edmonton (1979-89, 93-94); **Shero**—Philadelphia (1971-78), NY Rangers (1978-81).

Top Winning Percentages

Minimum of 275 victories, including playoffs.

		Yrs	W	L	T	Pct
1	**Scotty Bowman**	22	1020	496	234	**.650**
2	Toe Blake	13	582	292	159	**.640**
3	**Glen Sather**	11	553	305	110	**.628**
4	Fred Shero	10	451	272	119	**.606**
5	Don Cherry	6	281	177	77	**.597**
6	**Mike Keenan**	9	476	311	77	**.595**
7	Tommy Ivan	9	324	205	111	**.593**
8	**Pat Burns**	6	311	207	53	**.591**
9	**Al Arbour**	22	902	662	246	**.566**
10	Billy Reay	16	599	445	175	**.563**
11	Emile Francis	13	433	326	112	**.561**
12	Bryan Murray	12	501	381	115	**.560**
13	Hap Day	10	308	237	81	**.557**
14	Dick Irvin	26	790	609	228	**.556**
15	Art Ross	18	393	310	95	**.552**
16	Lester Patrick	13	312	242	115	**.552**
17	Bob Johnson	6	275	223	58	**.547**
18	**Pat Quinn**	11	405	328	102	**.546**
19	**Roger Neilson**	12	398	344	126	**.531**
20	Punch Imlach	15	467	421	163	**.522**
21	**Jacques Demers**	10	412	388	106	**.513**
22	Jack Adams	17	465	442	162	**.511**
23	**Bob Berry**	11	395	377	121	**.510**
	Bob Pulford	14	364	348	130	**.510**
25	Michel Bergeron	10	369	387	104	**.490**

Active Coaches' Victories

Through 1993-94 season, including playoffs.

		Yrs	W	L	T	Pct
1	Scotty Bowman, Det.	22	1020	496	234	.650
2	Mike Keenan, St.L.	9	476	311	77	.595
3	Jacques Demers, Mon.	10	412	388	106	.513
4	Roger Neilson, Fla.	12	398	344	126	.531
5	Pat Burns, Tor.	6	311	207	53	.591
6	Brian Sutter, Bos.	6	272	211	63	.556
7	Terry Crisp, T.B.	5	219	175	51	.549
	John Muckler, Buf.	6	219	203	53	.517
9	Terry Murray, Phi.	5	181	155	28	.536
10	Eddie Johnston, Pit.	5	166	194	67	.467
11	Bob Gainey, Dal.	4	159	165	43	.492
12	Paul Holmgren, Hart.	4	147	198	39	.434
13	Jacques Lemaire, N.J.	3	121	83	24	.616
14	John Paddock, Win.	3	102	128	31	.450
15	Jim Schoenfeld, Wash.	5	93	96	26	.493
16	Dave King, Calg.	2	90	67	24	.564
17	Darryl Sutter, Chi.	2	88	69	21	.553
18	Barry Melrose, L.A.	2	79	91	22	.469
19	Rick Bowness, Ott.	4	76	187	28	.309
20	Rick Ley, Van.	2	74	79	20	.486
21	Lorne Henning, N.Y.I.	3	72	76	20	.488
22	Tim Constantine, S.J.	1	40	42	16	.490
23	Ron Wilson, Ana.	1	33	46	5	.423
24	George Burnett, Edm.	0	0	0	0	.000
	Colin Campbell, NYR	0	0	0	0	.000
	Marc Crawford, Que.	0	0	0	0	.000

Annual Awards

Hart Memorial Trophy

Awarded to the player "adjudged to be the most valuable to his team" and named after Cecil Hart, the former manager-coach of the Montreal Canadiens. Winners selected by Pro Hockey Writers Assn. (PHWA). Winners' scoring statistics or goaltender W-L records and goals against average are provided; (*) indicates led league.

Multiple winners: Wayne Gretzky (9); Gordie Howe (6); Eddie Shore (4); Bobby Clarke, Howie Morenz and Bobby Orr (3); Jean Beliveau, Bill Cowley, Phil Esposito, Bobby Hull, Guy Lafleur, Mario Lemieux, Mark Messier, Stan Mikita, and Nels Stewart (2).

Year		G	A	Pts	Year		G	A	Pts
1924	Frank Nighbor, Ottawa, C	10	3	13	1960	Gordie Howe, Det., RW	28	45	73
1925	Billy Burch, Hamilton, C	20	4	24	1961	Bernie Geoffrion, Mon., RW	50	45	95*
1926	Nels Stewart, Maroons, C	34	8	42*	1962	Jacques Plante, Mon., G	42-14-14; 2.37*
1927	Herb Gardiner, Mon., D	6	6	12	1963	Gordie Howe, Det., RW	38	48	86*
1928	Howie Morenz, Mon., C	33	18	51*	1964	Jean Beliveau, Mon., C	28	50	78
1929	Roy Worters, NYA, G	16-13-9; 1.21			1965	Bobby Hull, Chi., LW	39	32	71
1930	Nels Stewart, Maroons, C	39	16	55	1966	Bobby Hull, Chi., LW	54	43	97*
1931	Howie Morenz, Mon., C	28	23	51*	1967	Stan Mikita, Chi., C	35	62	97*
1932	Howie Morenz, Mon., C	24	25	49	1968	Stan Mikita, Chi., C	40	47	87*
1933	Eddie Shore, Bos., D	8	27	35	1969	Phil Esposito, Bos., C	49	77	126*
1934	Aurel Joliat, Mon., LW	22	15	37	1970	Bobby Orr, Bos., D	33	87	120*
1935	Eddie Shore, Bos., D	7	26	33	1971	Bobby Orr, Bos., D	37	102	139
1936	Eddie Shore, Bos., D	3	16	19	1972	Bobby Orr, Bos., D	37	80	117
1937	Babe Siebert, Mon., D	8	20	28	1973	Bobby Clarke, Phi., C	37	67	104
1938	Eddie Shore, Bos., D	3	14	17	1974	Phil Esposito, Bos., C	68	77	145*
1939	Toe Blake, Mon., LW	24	23	47*	1975	Bobby Clarke, Phi., C	27	89	116
1940	Ebbie Goodfellow, Det., D	11	17	28	1976	Bobby Clarke, Phi., C	30	89	119
1941	Bill Cowley, Bos., C	17	45	62*	1977	Guy Lafleur, Mon., RW	56	80	136*
1942	Tommy Anderson, NYA, D	12	29	41	1978	Guy Lafleur, Mon., RW	60	72	132*
1943	Bill Cowley, Bos., C	27	45	72	1979	Bryan Trottier, NYI., C	47	87	134*
1944	Babe Pratt, Tor., D	17	40	57	1980	Wayne Gretzky, Edm., C	51	86	137
1945	Elmer Lach, Mon., C	26	54	80*	1981	Wayne Gretzky, Edm., C	55	109	164*
1946	Max Bentley, Chi., C	31	30	61*	1982	Wayne Gretzky, Edm., C	92	120	212*
1947	Maurice Richard, Mon., RW	45	26	71	1983	Wayne Gretzky, Edm., C	71	125	196*
1948	Buddy O'Connor, NYR, C	24	36	60	1984	Wayne Gretzky, Edm., C	87	118	205*
1949	Sid Abel, Det., C	28	26	54	1985	Wayne Gretzky, Edm., C	73	135	208*
1950	Chuck Rayner, NYR, G	28-30-11; 2.62			1986	Wayne Gretzky, Edm., C	52	163	215*
1951	Milt Schmidt, Bos., C	22	39	61	1987	Wayne Gretzky, Edm., C	62	121	183*
1952	Gordie Howe, Det., RW	47	39	86*	1988	Mario Lemieux, Pit., C	70	98	168*
1953	Gordie Howe, Det., RW	49	46	95*	1989	Wayne Gretzky, LA, C	54	114	168
1954	Al Rollins, Chi., G	12-47-7; 3.23			1990	Mark Messier, Edm., C	45	84	129
1955	Ted Kennedy, Tor., C	10	42	52	1991	Brett Hull, St. L., RW	86	45	131
1956	Jean Beliveau, Mon., C	47	41	88*	1992	Mark Messier, NYR, C	35	72	107
1957	Gordie Howe, Det., RW	44	45	89*	1993	Mario Lemieux, Pit., C	69	91	160*
1958	Gordie Howe, Det., RW	33	44	77	1994	Sergei Fedorov, Det., C	56	64	120
1959	Andy Bathgate, NYR, RW	40	48	88					

Calder Memorial Trophy

Awarded to the most outstanding rookie of the year and named after Frank Calder, the late NHL president (1917-43). Since the 1990-91 season, all eligible candidates must not have attained their 26th birthday by Sept. 15 of their rookie year. Winners selected by PHWA. Winners' scoring statistics or goaltender W-L record & goals against average are provided.

Year		G	A	Pts	Year		G	A	Pts
1933	Carl Voss, NYR-Det., C	8	15	23	1950	Jack Gelineau, Bos., G	22-30-15; 3.28		
1934	Russ Blinco, Maroons, C	14	9	23	1951	Terry Sawchuk, Det., G	44-13-13; 1.99		
1935	Sweeney Schriner, NYA, LW	18	22	40	1952	Bernie Geoffrion, Mon., RW	30	24	54
1936	Mike Karakas, Chi., G	21-19-8; 1.92			1953	Gump Worsley, NYR, G	13-29-13; 3.06
1937	Syl Apps, Tor., C	16	29	45	1954	Camille Henry, NYR, LW	24	15	39
1938	Cully Dahlstrom, Chi., C	10	9	19	1955	Ed Litzenberger, Mon-Chi., RW	16	24	40
1939	Frankie Brimsek, Bos., G	33-9-1; 1.58			1956	Glenn Hall, Det., G	30-24-16; 2.11
1940	Kilby MacDonald, NYR, LW	15	13	28	1957	Larry Regan, Bos., RW	14	19	33
1941	John Quilty, Mon., C	18	16	34	1958	Frank Mahovlich, Tor., LW	20	16	36
1942	Knobby Warwick, NYR, RW	16	17	33	1959	Ralph Backstrom, Mon., C	18	22	40
1943	Gaye Stewart, Tor., LW	24	23	47	1960	Billy Hay, Chi., C	18	37	55
1944	Gus Bodnar, Tor., C	22	40	62	1961	Dave Keon, Tor., C	20	25	45
1945	Frank McCool, Tor., G	24-22-2; 3.22			1962	Bobby Rousseau, Mon., RW	21	24	45
1946	Edgar Laprade, NYR, C	15	19	34	1963	Kent Douglas, Tor., D	7	15	22
1947	Howie Meeker, NYR, RW	27	18	45	1964	Jacques Laperriere, Mon., D	2	28	30
1948	Jim McFadden, Det., C	24	24	48	1965	Roger Crozier, Det., G	40-23-7; 2.42		
1949	Penny Lund, NYR, RW	14	16	30	1966	Brit Selby, Tor., LW	14	13	27

Year		G	A	Pts	Year		G	A	Pts
1967	Bobby Orr, Bos., D	13	28	41	1982	Dale Hawerchuk, Win., C	45	58	103
1968	Derek Sanderson, Bos., C	24	25	49	1983	Steve Larmer, Chi., RW	43	47	90
1969	Danny Grant, Min., LW	34	31	65	1984	Tom Barrasso, Buf., G	26-12-3;		2.84
					1985	Mario Lemieux, Pit., C	43	57	100
1970	Tony Esposito, Chi., G	38-17-8;		2.17	1986	Gary Suter, Calg., D	18	50	68
1971	Gilbert Perreault, Buf., C	38	34	72	1987	Luc Robitaille, LA, LW	45	39	84
1972	Ken Dryden, Mon., G	39-8-15;		2.24	1988	Joe Nieuwendyk, Calg., C	51	41	92
1973	Steve Vickers, NYR, LW	30	23	53	1989	Brian Leetch, NYR, D	23	48	71
1974	Denis Potvin, NYI, D	17	37	54					
1975	Eric Vail, Atl., LW	39	21	60	1990	Sergei Makarov, Calg., RW	24	62	86
1976	Bryan Trottier, NYI, C	32	63	95	1991	Ed Belfour, Chi., G	43-19-7;		2.47
1977	Willi Plett, Atl., RW	33	23	56	1992	Pavel Bure, Van., RW	34	26	60
1978	Mike Bossy, NYI, RW	53	38	91	1993	Teemu Selanne, Win., RW	76	56	132
1979	Bobby Smith, Min., C	30	44	74	1994	Martin Brodeur, NJ, G	27-11-8;		2.40
1980	Ray Bourque, Bos., D	17	48	65					
1981	Peter Stastny, Que., C	39	70	109					

Vezina Trophy

From 1927-80, given to the principal goaltender(s) on the team allowing the fewest goals during the regular season. Trophy named after 1920's goalie Georges Vezina of the Montreal Canadiens, who died of tuberculosis in 1926. Since the 1980-81 season, the trophy has been awarded to the most outstanding goaltender of the year as selected by the league's general managers.

Multiple winners: Jacques Plante (7, one of them shared); Bill Durnan (6); Ken Dryden (5, three shared); Bunny Larocque (4, all shared); Terry Sawchuk (4, one shared); Tiny Thompson (4); Tony Esposito (3, one shared); George Hainsworth (3); Glenn Hall (3, two shared); Patrick Roy (3); Ed Belfour (2); Johnny Bower (2, one shared); Frankie Brimsek (2); Turk Broda (2); Chuck Gardiner (2); Charlie Hodge (2, one shared); Bernie Parent (2); Gump Worsley (2, both shared).

Year		Record	GAA	Year		Record	GAA
1927	George Hainsworth, Mon	28-14-2	1.52	1967	Glenn Hall, Chi	19-5-5	2.38
1928	George Hainsworth, Mon	26-11-7	1.09		& Denis Dejordy, Chi	22-12-7	2.46
1929	George Hainsworth, Mon	22-7-15	0.98	1968	Gump Worsley, Mon	19-9-8	1.98
					& Rogie Vachon, Mon	23-13-2	2.48
1930	Tiny Thompson, Bos	38-5-1	2.23	1969	Jacques Plante, St.L	18-12-6	1.96
1931	Roy Worters, NYA	18-16-10	1.68		& Glenn Hall, St.L	19-12-8	2.17
1932	Chuck Gardiner, Chi	18-19-11	2.10				
1933	Tiny Thompson, Bos	25-15-8	1.83	1970	Tony Esposito, Chi	38-17-8	2.17
1934	Chuck Gardiner, Chi	20-17-11	1.73	1971	Ed Giacomin, NYR	27-10-7	2.16
1935	Lorne Chabot, Chi	26-17-5	1.83		& Gilles Villemure, NYR	22-8-4	2.30
1936	Tiny Thompson, Bos	22-20-6	1.73	1972	Tony Esposito, Chi	31-10-6	1.77
1937	Norm Smith, Det	25-14-9	2.13		& Gary Smith, Chi	14-5-6	2.42
1938	Tiny Thompson, Bos	30-11-7	1.85	1973	Ken Dryden, Mon	33-7-13	2.26
1939	Frankie Brimsek, Bos	33-9-1	1.59	1974	(Tie) Bernie Parent, Phi	47-13-12	1.89
					Tony Esposito, Chi	34-14-21	2.04
1940	Dave Kerr, NYR	27-11-10	1.60	1975	Bernie Parent, Phi	44-14-10	2.03
1941	Turk Broda, Tor	28-14-6	2.06	1976	Ken Dryden, Mon	42-10-8	2.03
1942	Frankie Brimsek, Bos	24-17-6	2.44	1977	Ken Dryden, Mon	41-6-8	2.14
1943	Johnny Mowers, Det	25-14-11	2.48		& Bunny Larocque, Mon	19-2-4	2.09
1944	Bill Durnan, Mon	38-5-7	2.18	1978	Ken Dryden, Mon	37-7-7	2.05
1945	Bill Durnan, Mon	38-8-4	2.42		& Bunny Larocque, Mon.	22-3-4	2.67
1946	Bill Durnan, Mon	24-11-5	2.60	1979	Ken Dryden, Mon	30-10-7	2.30
1947	Bill Durnan, Mon	34-16-10	2.30		& Bunny Larocque, Mon.	22-7-4	2.84
1948	Turk Broda, Tor	32-15-13	2.38				
1949	Bill Durnan, Mon	28-23-9	2.10	1980	Bob Sauve, Buf	20-8-4	2.36
					& Don Edwards, Buf.	27-9-12	2.57
1950	Bill Durnan, Mon	26-21-17	2.20	1981	Richard Sevigny, Mon	20-4-3	2.40
1951	Al Rollins, Tor	27-5-8	1.75		Denis Herron, Mon	6-9-6	3.50
1952	Terry Sawchuk, Det	44-14-12	1.90		& Bunny Larocque, Mon.	16-9-3	3.03
1953	Terry Sawchuk, Det	32-15-16	1.90	1982	Billy Smith, NYI	32-9-4	2.97
1954	Harry Lumley, Tor	32-24-13	1.85	1983	Pete Peeters, Bos	40-11-9	2.36
1955	Terry Sawchuk, Det	40-17-11	1.94	1984	Tom Barrasso, Buf	26-12-3	2.84
1956	Jacques Plante, Mon	42-12-10	1.86	1985	Pelle Lindbergh, Phi	40-17-7	3.02
1957	Jacques Plante, Mon	31-18-12	2.02	1986	John Vanbiesbrouck, NYR	31-21-5	3.32
1958	Jacques Plante, Mon	34-14-8	2.11	1987	Ron Hextall, Phi	37-21-6	3.00
1959	Jacques Plante, Mon	38-16-13	2.18	1988	Grant Fuhr, Edm	40-24-9	3.43
				1989	Patrick Roy, Mon	33-5-6	2.47
1960	Jacques Plante, Mon	40-17-12	2.54				
1961	Johnny Bower, Tor	33-15-10	2.50	1990	Patrick Roy, Mon	31-16-5	2.53
1962	Jacques Plante, Mon	42-14-14	2.37	1991	Ed Belfour, Chi	43-19-7	2.47
1963	Glenn Hall, Chi	30-20-16	2.51	1992	Patrick Roy, Mon.	36-22-8	2.36
1964	Charlie Hodge, Mon	33-18-11	2.26	1993	Ed Belfour, Chi	41-18-11	2.59
1965	Johnny Bower, Tor	13-13-8	2.38	1994	Dominik Hasek, Buf	30-20-6	1.95
	& Terry Sawchuk, Tor	17-13-6	2.56				
1966	Gump Worsley, Mon	29-14-6	2.36				
	& Charlie Hodge, Mon	12-7-2	2.58				

Annual Awards (Cont.)
Lady Byng Memorial Trophy

Awarded to the player "adjudged to have exhibited the best type of sportsmanship and gentlemanly conduct combined with a high standard of playing ability" and named after Lady Evelyn Byng, the wife of former Canadian Governor General (1921-26) Baron Byng of Vimy. Winners selected by PHWA.

Multiple winners: Frank Boucher (7); Wayne Gretzky and Red Kelly (4); Bobby Bauer, Mike Bossy and Alex Delvecchio (3); Johnny Bucyk, Marcel Dionne, Dave Keon, Stan Mikita, Joey Mullen, Frank Nighbor, Jean Ratelle, Clint Smith and Sid Smith (2).

Year		Year		Year	
1925	Frank Nighbor, Ott., C	1949	Bill Quackenbush, Det., D	1972	Jean Ratelle, NYR, C
1926	Frank Nighbor, Ott., C	1950	Edgar Laprade, NYR, C	1973	Gilbert Perreault, Buf., C
1927	Billy Burch, NYA, C	1951	Red Kelly, Det., D	1974	Johnny Bucyk, Bos., LW
1928	Frank Boucher, NYR, C	1952	Sid Smith, Tor., LW	1975	Marcel Dionne, Det., C
1929	Frank Boucher, NYR, C	1953	Red Kelly, Det., D	1976	Jean Ratelle, NY-Bos., C
1930	Frank Boucher, NYR, C	1954	Red Kelly, Det., D	1977	Marcel Dionne, LA, C
1931	Frank Boucher, NYR, C	1955	Sid Smith, Tor., LW	1978	Butch Goring, LA, C
1932	Joe Primeau, Tor., C	1956	Earl Reibel, Det., C	1979	Bob MacMillan, Atl., RW
1933	Frank Boucher, NYR, C	1957	Andy Hebenton, NYR, RW	1980	Wayne Gretzky, Edm., C
1934	Frank Boucher, NYR, C	1958	Camille Henry, NYR, LW	1981	Rick Kehoe, Pit., RW
1935	Frank Boucher, NYR, C	1959	Alex Delvecchio, Det., LW	1982	Rick Middleton, Bos., RW
1936	Doc Romnes, Chi., F	1960	Don McKenney, Bos., C	1983	Mike Bossy, NYI, RW
1937	Marty Barry, Det., C	1961	Red Kelly, Tor., D	1984	Mike Bossy, NYI, RW
1938	Gordie Drillon, Tor., RW	1962	Dave Keon, Tor., C	1985	Jari Kurri, Edm., RW
1939	Clint Smith, NYR, C	1963	Dave Keon, Tor., C	1986	Mike Bossy, NYI, RW
1940	Bobby Bauer, Bos., RW	1964	Ken Wharram, Chi., RW	1987	Joey Mullen, Calg., RW
1941	Bobby Bauer, Bos., RW	1965	Bobby Hull, Chi., LW	1988	Mats Naslund, Mon., LW
1942	Syl Apps, Tor., C	1966	Alex Delvecchio, Det., LW	1989	Joey Mullen, Calg., RW
1943	Max Bentley, Chi., C	1967	Stan Mikita, Chi., C	1990	Brett Hull, St.L., RW
1944	Clint Smith, Chi., C	1968	Stan Mikita, Chi., C	1991	Wayne Gretzky, LA, C
1945	Bill Mosienko, Chi., RW	1969	Alex Delvecchio, Det., LW	1992	Wayne Gretzky, LA, C
1946	Toe Blake, Mon., LW	1970	Phil Goyette, St.L., C	1993	Pierre Turgeon, NYI, C
1947	Bobby Bauer, Bos., RW	1971	Johnny Bucyk, Bos., LW	1994	Wayne Gretzky, LA, C
1948	Buddy O'Connor, NYR, C				

Note: Quackenbush and Kelly are the only defensemen to win the Lady Byng.

James Norris Memorial Trophy

Awarded to the most outstanding defenseman of the year and named after James Norris, the late Detroit Red Wings owner-president. Winners selected by PHWA.

Multiple winners: Bobby Orr (8); Doug Harvey (7); Ray Bourque (5); Pierre Pilote and Denis Potvin (3); Chris Chelios, Paul Coffey, Rod Langway and Larry Robinson (2).

Year		Year		Year	
1954	Red Kelly, Detroit	1969	Bobby Orr, Boston	1982	Doug Wilson, Chicago
1955	Doug Harvey, Montreal	1970	Bobby Orr, Boston	1983	Rod Langway, Washington
1956	Doug Harvey, Montreal	1971	Bobby Orr, Boston	1984	Rod Langway, Washington
1957	Doug Harvey, Montreal	1972	Bobby Orr, Boston	1985	Paul Coffey, Edmonton
1958	Doug Harvey, Montreal	1973	Bobby Orr, Boston	1986	Paul Coffey, Edmonton
1959	Tom Johnson, Montreal	1974	Bobby Orr, Boston	1987	Ray Bourque, Boston
1960	Doug Harvey, Montreal	1975	Bobby Orr, Boston	1988	Ray Bourque, Boston
1961	Doug Harvey, Montreal	1976	Denis Potvin, NY Islanders	1989	Chris Chelios, Montreal
1962	Doug Harvey, NY Rangers	1977	Larry Robinson, Montreal	1990	Ray Bourque, Boston
1963	Pierre Pilote, Chicago	1978	Denis Potvin, NY Islanders	1991	Ray Bourque, Boston
1964	Pierre Pilote, Chicago	1979	Denis Potvin, NY Islanders	1992	Brian Leetch, NY Rangers
1965	Pierre Pilote, Chicago	1980	Larry Robinson, Montreal	1993	Chris Chelios, Chicago
1966	Jacques Laperriere, Montreal	1981	Randy Carlyle, Pittsburgh	1994	Ray Bourque, Boston
1967	Harry Howell, NY Rangers				
1968	Bobby Orr, Boston				

Frank Selke Trophy

Awarded to the outstanding defensive forward of the year and named after the late Montreal Canadiens general manager. Winners selected by the PHWA.

Multiple winners: Bob Gainey (4); Guy Carbonneau (3).

Year	Winner	Year	Winner	Year	Winner
1978	Bob Gainey, Mon., LW	1984	Doug Jarvis, Wash., C	1990	Rick Meagher, St.L., C
1979	Bob Gainey, Mon., LW	1985	Craig Ramsay, Buf., LW	1991	Dirk Graham, Chi., RW
1980	Bob Gainey, Mon., LW	1986	Troy Murray, Chi., C	1992	Guy Carbonneau, Mon., C
1981	Bob Gainey, Mon., LW	1987	Dave Poulin, Phi., C	1993	Doug Gilmour, Tor., C
1982	Steve Kasper, Bos., C	1988	Guy Carbonneau, Mon., C	1994	Sergei Fedorov, Det., C
1983	Bobby Clarke, Phi., C	1989	Guy Carbonneau, Mon., C		

Jack Adams Award

Awarded to the coach "adjudged to have contributed the most to his team's success" and named after the late Detroit Red Wings coach and general manager. Winners selected by NHL Broadcasters' Assn.; (*) indicates division champion.

Multiple winners: Jacques Demers and Pat Quinn (2).

Year	Improvement	Year	Improvement
1974	Fred Shero, Phi ....37-30-11 to 50-16-12*	1985	Mike Keenan, Phi ....44-26-10 to 53-20- 7*
1975	Bob Pulford, Chi...............41-14-23 to 37-35- 8	1986	Glen Sather, Edm............49-20-11* to 56-17- 7*
1976	Don Cherry, Bos...............40-26-14 to 48-15-17*	1987	Jacques Demers, Det ....17-57- 6 to 34-36-10
1977	Scotty Bowman, Mon ......58-11-11* to 60- 8-12*	1988	Jacques Demers, Det ....34-36-10 to 41-28-11*
1978	Bobby Kromm, Det...........16-55- 9 to 32-34-14	1989	Pat Burns, Mon ....45-22-13 to 53-18- 9*
1979	Al Arbour, NYI ....48-17-15* to 51-15-14*		
1980	Pat Quinn, Phi ....40-25-15 to 48-12-20*	1990	Bob Murdoch, Win............26-42-12 to 37-32-11
1981	Red Berenson, StL.............34-34-12 to 45-18-17*	1991	Brian Sutter, St. L............37-34- 9 to 47-22-11
1982	Tom Watt, Win................9-57-14 to 33-33-14	1992	Pat Quinn, Van ....28-43- 9 to 42-26-12*
1983	Orval Tessier, Chi ....30-38-12 to 47-23-10*	1993	Pat Burns, Tor....................30-43-7 to 44-29-11
1984	Bryan Murray, Wash........39-25-16 to 48-27- 5	1994	Jacques Lemaire, NJ..........40-37-7 to 47-25-12

Lester Pearson Award

Awarded to the season's most outstanding player and named after the former diplomat, Nobel Peace Prize winner and Canadian prime minister. Winners selected by the NHL Players Assn.

Multiple winners: Wayne Gretzky (5); Guy Lafleur and Mario Lemieux (3); Marcel Dionne, Phil Esposito and Mark Messier (2).

Year		Year		Year	
1971	Phil Esposito, Bos.	1980	Marcel Dionne, LA	1988	Mario Lemieux, Pit.
1972	Jean Ratelle, NYR	1981	Mike Liut, St.L.	1989	Steve Yzerman, Det.
1973	Phil Esposito, Bos.	1982	Wayne Gretzky, Edm.		
1974	Bobby Clarke, Phi.	1983	Wayne Gretzky, Edm.	1990	Mark Messier, Edm.
1975	Bobby Orr, Bos.	1984	Wayne Gretzky, Edm.	1991	Brett Hull, St.L.
1976	Guy Lafleur, Mon.	1985	Wayne Gretzky, Edm.	1992	Mark Messier, NYR
1977	Guy Lafleur, Mon.	1986	Mario Lemieuvx, Pit.	1993	Mario Lemieux, Pit
1978	Guy Lafleur, Mon.	1987	Wayne Gretzky, Edm.	1994	Sergei Fedorov, Det.
1979	Marcel Dionne, LA				

Bill Masterton Trophy

Awarded to the player who "best exemplifies the qualities of perseverance, sportsmanship and dedication to hockey" and named after the 29-year-old rookie center of the Minnesota North Stars who died of a head injury sustained in a 1968 NHL game. Presented by the PHWA.

Year		Year		Year	
1968	Claude Provost, Mon., RW	1977	Ed Westfall, NYI, RW	1986	Charlie Simmer, Bos., LW
1969	Ted Hampson, Oak., C	1978	Butch Goring, LA, C	1987	Doug Jarvis, Hart., C
		1979	Serge Savard, Mon., D	1988	Bob Bourne, LA, C
1970	Pit Martin, Chi., C			1989	Tim Kerr, Phi., C
1971	Jean Ratelle, NYR, C	1980	Al MacAdam, Min., RW		
1972	Bobby Clarke, Phi., C	1981	Blake Dunlop, St.L., C	1990	Gord Kluzak, Bos., D
1973	Lowell MacDonald, Pit., RW	1982	Chico Resch, Colo., G	1991	Dave Taylor, LA, RW
1974	Henri Richard, Mon., C	1983	Lanny McDonald, Calg., RW	1992	Mark Fitzpatrick, NYI, G
1975	Don Luce, Buf., C	1984	Brad Park, Det., D	1993	Mario Lemieux, Pit., C
1976	Rod Gilbert, NYR, RW	1985	Anders Hedberg, NYR, RW	1994	Cam Neely, Bos., RW

Number One Draft Choices

Overall first choices in the NHL Draft since the league staged its first universal amateur draft in 1969. Players are listed with team that selected them; those who became Rookie of the Year are in **bold** type.

Year		Year		Year	
1969	Rejean Houle, Mon., LW	1978	**Bobby Smith**, Min., C	1987	Pierre Turgeon, Buf., C
1970	**Gilbert Perreault,** Buf., C	1979	Rob Ramage, Colo., D	1988	Mike Modano, Min., C
1971	Guy Lafleur, Mon., RW			1989	Mats Sundin, Que., C
1972	Billy Harris, NYI, RW	1980	Doug Wickenheiser, Mon., C		
1973	**Denis Potvin,** NYI, D	1981	**Dale Hawerchuk,** Win., C	1990	Owen Nolan, Que., RW
1974	Greg Joly, Wash., D	1982	Gord Kluzak, Bos., D	1991	Eric Lindros, Que., C
1975	Mel Bridgman, Phi., C	1983	Brian Lawton, Min., LW	1992	Roman Hamrlik, TB, D
1976	Rick Green, Wash., D	1984	**Mario Lemieux,** Pit., C	1993	Alexandre Daigle, Ott., C
1977	Dale McCourt, Det., C	1985	Wendel Clark, Tor., LW	1994	Ed Jovanovski, Fla., D
		1986	Joe Murphy, Det., RW		

World Hockey Association
WHA Finals

The World Hockey Association began play in 1972-73 as a 12-team rival of the 56-year-old NHL. The WHA played for the Avco World Trophy in its seven playoff finals (Avco Financial Services underwrote the playoffs).

Multiple winners: Winnipeg (3); Houston (2).

Year	Winner	Head Coach	Series	Loser	Head Coach
1973	New England Whalers	Jack Kelley	4-1 (WWLWW)	Winnipeg Jets	Bobby Hull
1974	Houston Aeros	Bill Dineen	4-0	Chicago Cougars	Pat Stapleton
1975	Houston Aeros	Bill Dineen	4-0	Quebec Nordiques	Jean-Guy Gendron
1976	Winnipeg Jets	Bobby Kromm	4-0	Houston Aeros	Bill Dineen
1977	Quebec Nordiques	Marc Boileau	4-3 (LWLWWLW)	Winnipeg Jets	Bobby Kromm
1978	Winnipeg Jets	Larry Hillman	4-0	NE Whalers	Harry Neale
1979	Winnipeg Jets	Larry Hillman	4-2 (WWLWLW)	Edmonton Oilers	Glen Sather

Playoff MVPs—1973—No award; **1974**—No award; **1975**—Ron Grahame, Houston, G; **1976**—Ulf Nilsson, Winnipeg, C; **1977**—Serg Bernier, Quebec, C; **1978**—Bobby Guindon, Winnipeg, C; **1979**—Rich Preston, Winnipeg.

Most Valuable Player
(Gordie Howe Trophy, 1976-79)

Year		G	A	Pts
1973	Bobby Hull, Win., LW	51	52	103
1974	Gordie Howe, Hou., RW	31	69	100
1975	Bobby Hull, Win., LW	77	65	142
1976	Marc Tardif, Que., LW	71	77	148
1977	Robbie Ftorek, Pho., C	46	71	117
1978	Marc Tardif, Que., LW	65	89	154
1979	Dave Dryden, Edm., G	41-17-2; 2.89		

Scoring Leaders

Year		Gm	G	A	Pts
1973	Andre Lacroix, Phi	78	50	74	124
1974	Mike Walton, Min	78	57	60	117
1975	Andre Lacroix, S.Diego	78	41	106	147
1976	Marc Tardif, Que	81	71	77	148
1977	Real Cloutier, Que	76	66	75	141
1978	Marc Tardif, Que	78	65	89	154
1979	Real Cloutier, Que	77	75	54	129

Note: In 1979, 18 year-old Rookie of the Year Wayne Gretzky finished third in scoring (46-64—110).

Rookie of the Year

Year		G	A	Pts
1973	Terry Caffery, N.Eng., C	39	41	100
1974	Mark Howe, Hou., LW	38	41	79
1975	Anders Hedberg, Win., RW	53	47	100
1976	Mark Napier, Tor., RW	43	50	93
1977	George Lyle, N.Eng., LW	39	33	72
1978	Kent Nilsson, Win., C	42	65	107
1979	Wayne Gretzky, Edm., C	46	64	110

Best Goaltender

Year		Record	GAA
1973	Gerry Cheevers, Cleveland	32-20-0	2.84
1974	Don McLeod, Houston	33-13-3	2.56
1975	Ron Grahame, Houston	33-10-0	3.03
1976	Michel Dion, Indianapolis	14-15-1	2.74
1977	Ron Grahame, Houston	27-10-2	2.74
1978	Al Smith, New England	30-20-3	3.22
1979	Dave Dryden, Edmonton	41-17-2	2.89

Best Defenseman

Year	
1973	J.C. Tremblay, Quebec
1974	Pat Stapleton, Chicago
1975	J.C. Tremblay, Quebec
1976	Paul Shmyr, Cleveland
1977	Ron Plumb, Cincinnati
1978	Lars-Erik Sjoberg, Winnipeg
1979	Rick Ley, New England

Coach of the Year

Year		Improvement
1973	Jack Kelley, N. Eng	46-30-2*
1974	Billy Harris, Tor	35-39-4 to 41-33-4
1975	Sandy Hucul, Pho	Expan. to 39-31-8
1976	Bobby Kromm, Win	38-35-5 to 52-27-2*
1977	Bill Dineen, Hou	53-27-0* to 50-24-6
1978	Bill Dineen, Hou	50-24-6* to 42-34-4
1979	John Brophy, Birm	36-41-3 to 32-42-6

*Won Division.

WHA All-Star Game

The WHA All-Star Game was an Eastern Division vs Western Division contest from 1973-75. In 1976, the league's five Canadian-based teams played the nine teams in the US. Over the final three seasons—East played West in 1977; AVCO Cup champion Quebec played a WHA All-Star team in 1978; and in 1979, a full WHA All-Star team played a three-game series with Moscow Dynamo of the Soviet Union.

Year	Result	Host	Coaches	Most Valuable Player
1973	East 6, West 2	Quebec	Jack Kelley, Bobby Hull	Wayne Carleton, Ottawa
1974	East 8, West 4	St. Paul, MN	Jack Kelley, Bobby Hull	Mike Walton, Minnesota
1975	West 6, East 4	Edmonton	Bill Dineen, Ron Ryan	Rejean Houle, Quebec
1976	Canada 6, USA 1	Cleveland	Jean-Guy Gendron, Bill Dineen	Can—Real Cloutier, Que. USA—Paul Shmyr, Cleve.
1977	East 4, West 2	Hartford	Jacques Demers, Bobby Kromm	East—L. Levasseur, Min. West—W. Lindstrom, Win.
1978	Quebec 5, WHA 4	Quebec	Marc Boileau, Bill Dineen	Quebec—Marc Tardif WHA—Mark Howe, NE
1979	WHA def. Moscow Dynamo 3 games to 1 (4-2, 4-2, 4-3)	Edmonton	Larry Hillman, P. Iburtovich	No awards

World Championship

The World Hockey Championship tournament has been played regularly since 1930. The International Ice Hockey Federation (IIHF), which governs both the World and Winter Olympic tournaments, considers the Olympic champions from 1920-68 to also be the World champions. However the IIHF has not recognized an Olympic champion as World champion since 1968. The IIHF has sanctioned separate World Championships in Olympic years three times—in 1972, 1976 and again in 1992. The World championship is officially vacant for the three Olympic years from 1980-88.

Multiple winners: Soviet Union/Russia (23); Canada (20); Czechoslovakia and Sweden (6); USA (2).

Year		Year		Year		Year	
1920	Canada	1949	Czechoslovakia	1965	Soviet Union	1980	Not held
1924	Canada	1950	Canada	1966	Soviet Union	1981	Soviet Union
1928	Canada			1967	Soviet Union	1982	Soviet Union
		1951	Canada	1968	Soviet Union	1983	Soviet Union
1930	Canada	1952	Canada	1969	Soviet Union	1984	Not held
1931	Canada	1953	Sweden			1985	Czechoslovakia
1932	Canada	1954	Soviet Union	1970	Soviet Union	1986	Soviet Union
1933	United States	1955	Canada	1971	Soviet Union	1987	Sweden
1934	Canada	1956	Soviet Union	1972	Czechoslovakia	1988	Not held
1935	Canada	1957	Sweden	1973	Soviet Union	1989	Soviet Union
1936	Great Britain	1958	Canada	1974	Soviet Union		
1937	Canada	1959	Canada	1975	Soviet Union	1990	Soviet Union
1938	Canada			1976	Czechoslovakia	1991	Sweden
1939	Canada	1960	United States	1977	Czechoslovakia	1992	Sweden
		1961	Canada	1978	Soviet Union	1993	Russia
1940-46	Not held	1962	Sweden	1979	Soviet Union	1994	Canada
1947	Czechoslovakia	1963	Soviet Union				
1948	Canada	1964	Soviet Union				

Canada vs USSR Summits

The first competition between the Soviet National Team and the NHL took place Sept. 2-28, 1972. A team of NHL All-Stars emerged as the winner of the heralded 8-game series, but just barely—winning with a record of 4-3-1 after trailing 1-3-1.

Two years later a WHA All-Star team played the Soviet Nationals and could win only one game and tie three others in eight contests. Two other Canada vs USSR series took place during NHL All-Star breaks: the three-game Challenge Cup at New York in 1979, and the two-game Rendez-Vous '87 in Quebec City in 1987.

The NHL All-Stars played the USSR in a three-game Challenge Cup series in 1979.

1972 Team Canada vs USSR
NHL All-Stars vs Soviet National Team.

Date	City	Result	Goaltenders
9/2	Montreal	USSR, 7-3	Tretiak/Dryden
9/4	Toronto	Canada, 4-1	Esposito/Tretiak
9/6	Winnipeg	Tie, 4-4	Tretiak/Esposito
9/8	Vancouver	USSR, 5-4	Tretiak/Dryden
9/22	Moscow	USSR, 5-4	Tretiak/Esposito
9/24	Moscow	Canada, 3-2	Dryden/Tretiak
9/26	Moscow	Canada, 4-3	Esposito/Tretiak
9/28	Moscow	Canada, 6-5	Dryden/Tretiak

Standings

	W	L	T	Pts	GF	GA
Team Canada (NHL)	4	3	1	9	32	32
Soviet Union	3	4	1	7	32	32

Leading Scorers

1. Phil Esposito, Canada, (7-6—13); **2.** Aleksandr Yakushev, USSR (7-4—11); **3.** Paul Henderson, Canada (7-2—9); **4.** Boris Shadrin, USSR (3-5—8); **5.** Valeri Kharlamov, Canada (3-4—7) and Vladimir Petrov, USSR (3-4—7); **7.** Bobby Clarke, Canada (2-4—6).

1974 Team Canada vs USSR
WHA All-Stars vs Soviet National Team.

Date	City	Result	Goaltenders
9/17	Quebec	Tie, 3-3	Tretiak/Cheevers
9/19	Toronto	Canada, 4-1	Cheevers/Tretiak
9/21	Winnipeg	USSR, 8-5	Tretiak/McLeod
9/23	Vancouver	Tie, 5-5	Tretiak/Cheevers
10/1	Moscow	USSR, 3-2	Tretiak/Cheevers
10/3	Moscow	USSR, 5-2	Tretiak/Cheevers
10/5	Moscow	Tie, 4-4	Cheevers/Tretiak
10/6	Moscow	USSR, 3-2	Sdn'kov/Cheevers

Standings

	W	L	T	Pts	GF	GA
Soviet Union	4	1	3	11	32	27
Team Canada (WHA)	1	4	3	5	27	32

Leading Scorers

1. Bobby Hull, Canada (7-2—9); **2.** Aleksandr Yakushev, USSR (6-2—8), Ralph Backstrom, Canada (4-4—8) and Valeri Kharlamov, USSR (2-6—8); **5.** Gordie Howe, Canada (3-4—7), Andre Lacroix, Canada (1-6—7) and Vladimir Petrov, USSR (1-6—7).

1979 Challenge Cup Series
NHL All-Stars vs Soviet National Team

Date	City	Result	Goaltenders
2/8	New York	NHL, 4-2	K. Dryden/Tretiak
2/10	New York	USSR, 5-4	Tretiak/K. Dryden
2/11	New York	USSR, 6-0	Myshkin/Cheevers

Rendez-Vous '87
NHL All-Stars vs Soviet National Team

Date	City	Result	Goaltenders
2/11	Quebec	NHL, 4-3	Fuhr/Belosheykhin
2/13	Quebec	USSR, 5-3	Belosheykhin/Fuhr

The Canada Cup

After organizing the historic 8-game Team Canada-Soviet Union series of 1972, NHL Players Association executive director Alan Eagleson and the NHL created the Canada Cup in 1976. For the first time, the best players from the world's six major hockey powers—Canada, Czechoslovakia, Finland, Russia, Sweden and the USA competed together in one tournament.

1976
Round Robin Standings

	W	L	T	Pts	GF	GA
Canada	4	1	0	8	22	6
Czechoslovakia	3	1	1	7	19	9
Soviet Union	2	2	1	5	23	14
Sweden	2	2	1	5	16	18
United States	1	3	1	3	14	21
Finland	1	4	0	2	16	42

Finals (Best of 3)

Date	City	Score
9/13	Toronto	Canada 6, Czechoslovakia 0
9/15	Montreal	Canada 5, Czechoslovakia 4 (OT)

Note: Darryl Sittler scored the winning goal for Canada at 11:33 in overtime to clinch the Cup, 2 games to none.

Team MVPs

Canada—Rogie Vachon
Czech.—Milan Novy
USSR—Alexandr Maltsev
Sweden—Borje Salming
USA—Robbie Ftorek
Finland—Matti Hagman
Tournament MVP—Bobby Orr, Canada

1981
Round Robin Standings

	W	L	T	Pts	GF	GA
Canada	4	0	1	9	32	13
Soviet Union	3	1	1	7	20	13
Czechoslovakia	2	1	2	6	21	13
United States	2	2	1	5	17	19
Sweden	1	4	0	2	13	20
Finland	0	4	1	1	6	31

Semifinals

Date	City	Score
9/11	Ottawa	USSR 4, Czechoslovakia 1
9/15	Montreal	Canada 4, United States 1

Finals

Date	City	Score
9/13	Montreal	USSR 8, Canada 1

Leading Scorers

1. Wayne Gretzky, Canada (5-7—12); **2.** Mike Bossy, Canada (8-3—11), Bryan Trottier, Canada (3-8—11), Guy Lafleur, Canada (2-9—11), Alexei Kasatonov, USSR (1-10—11).

All-Star Team

Goal—Vladislav Tretiak, USSR; **Defense**—Arnold Kadlec, Czech. and Alexei Kasatonov, USSR; **Forwards**—Mike Bossy, Canada, Gil Perreault, Canada, and Sergei Shepelev, USSR. **Tournament MVP**—Tretiak.

1984
Round Robin Standings

	W	L	T	Pts	GF	GA
Soviet Union	5	0	0	10	22	7
United States	3	1	1	7	21	13
Sweden	3	2	0	6	15	16
Canada	2	2	1	5	23	18
West Germany	0	4	1	1	13	29
Czechoslovakia	0	4	1	1	10	21

Semifinals

Date	City	Score
9/12	Edmonton	Sweden 9, United States 2
9/15	Montreal	Canada 3, USSR 2 (OT)

Note: Mike Bossy scored the winning goal for Canada at 12:29 in overtime.

Finals (Best of 3)

Date	City	Score
9/16	Calgary	Canada 5, Sweden 2
9/18	Edmonton	Canada 6, Sweden 5

Leading Scorers

1. Wayne Gretzky, Canada (5-7—12); **2.** Michel Goulet, Canada (5-6—11), Kent Nilsson, Sweden (3-8—11), Paul Coffey, Canada (3-8—11); **5.** Hakan Loob, Sweden (6-4—10).

All-Star Team

Goal—Vladimir Myshkin, USSR; **Defense**—Paul Coffey, Canada and Rod Langway, USA; **Forwards**—Wayne Gretzky, Canada, John Tonelli, Canada, and Sergei Makarov, USSR. **Tournament MVP**—Tonelli.

1987
Round Robin Standings

	W	L	T	Pts	GF	GA
Canada	3	0	2	8	19	13
Soviet Union	3	1	1	7	22	13
Sweden	3	2	0	6	17	14
Czechoslovakia	2	2	1	5	12	15
United States	2	3	0	4	13	14
Finland	0	5	0	0	9	23

Semifinals

Date	City	Score
9/8	Hamilton	USSR 4, Sweden 2
9/9	Montreal	Canada 5, Czechoslovakia 3

Finals (Best of 3)

Date	City	Score
9/11	Montreal	USSR 6, Canada 5 (OT)
9/13	Hamilton	Canada 6, USSR 5 (2 OT)
9/15	Hamilton	Canada 6, USSR 5

Note: In Game 1, Alexander Semak of USSR scored at 5:33 in overtime. In Game 2, Mario Lemieux of Canada scored at 10:07 in the second overtime period. Lemieux also won Game 3 on a goal with 1:26 left in regulation time.

Leading Scorers

1. Wayne Gretzky, Canada (3-18—21); **2.** Mario Lemieux, Canada (11-7—18); **3.** Sergei Makarov, USSR (7-8—15); **4.** Vladimir Krutov, USSR (7-7—14); **5.** Viacheslav Bykov, USSR (2-7—9); **6.** Ray Bourque, Canada (2-6—8).

All-Star Team

Goal—Grant Fuhr, Canada; **Defense**—Ray Bourque, Canada and Viacheslav Fetisov, USSR; **Forwards**—Wayne Gretzky, Canada, Mario Lemieux, Canada, and Vladimir Krutov, USSR. **Tournament MVP**—Gretzky.

1991

Round Robin Standings

	W	L	T	Pts	GF	GA
Canada	3	0	2	8	21	11
United States	4	1	0	8	19	15
Finland	2	2	1	5	10	13
Sweden	2	3	0	4	13	17
Soviet Union	1	3	1	3	14	14
Czechoslovakia	1	4	0	2	11	18

Semifinals

Date	City	Score
9/11	Hamilton	United States 7, Finland 3
9/12	Toronto	Canada 4, Sweden 0

Finals (Best of 3)

Date	City	Score
9/14	Montreal	Canada 4, United States 1
9/16	Hamilton	Canada 4, United States 2

Leading Scorers

1. Wayne Gretzky, Canada (4-8—12); **2.** Steve Larmer, Canada (6-5—11); **3.** Brett Hull, USA (2-7—9); **4.** Mike Modano, USA (2-7—9); **5.** Mark Messier, Canada (2-6—8).

All-Star Team

Goal—Bill Ranford, Canada; **Defense**—Al MacInnis, Canada and Chris Chelios, USA; **Forwards**—Wayne Gretzky, Canada, Jeremy Roenick, USA and Mats Sundin, Sweden. **Tournament MVP**—Bill Ranford.

U.S. DIVISION I COLLEGE HOCKEY

NCAA Final Four

The NCAA Division I hockey tournament began in 1948 and was played at the Broadmoor Ice Palace in Colorado Springs from 1948-57. Since 1958, the tournament has moved around the country, stopping for consecutive years only at Boston Garden from 1972-74. Consolation games to determine third place were played from 1949-89 and discontinued in 1990.

Multiple Winners: Michigan (7); Denver, North Dakota and Wisconsin (5); Boston University, Lake Superior St., Michigan Tech and Minnesota (3); Colorado College, Cornell, Michigan St. and RPI (2).

Year	Champion	Head Coach	Score	Runner-up	Third Place	Score	Fourth Place
1948	Michigan	Vic Heyliger	8-4	Dartmouth	Colorado College and Boston College		

Year	Champion	Head Coach	Score	Runner-up	Third Place	Score	Fourth Place
1949	Boston College	Snooks Kelley	4-3	Dartmouth	Michigan	8-4	Colorado Col.
1950	Colorado College	Cheddy Thompson	13-4	Boston Univ.	Michigan	10-6	Boston Col.
1951	Michigan	Vic Heyliger	7-1	Brown	Boston U.	7-4	Colorado Col.
1952	Michigan	Vic Heyliger	4-1	Colorado Col.	Yale	4-1	St. Lawrence
1953	Michigan	Vic Heyliger	7-3	Minnesota	RPI	6-3	Boston Univ.
1954	RPI	Ned Harkness	5-4*	Minnesota	Michigan	7-2	Boston Col.
1955	Michigan	Vic Heyliger	5-3	Colorado Col.	Harvard	6-3	St. Lawrence
1956	Michigan	Vic Heyliger	7-5	Michigan Tech	St. Lawrence	6-2	Boston Col.
1957	Colorado College	Tom Bedecki	13-6	Michigan	Clarkson	2-1†	Harvard
1958	Denver	Murray Armstrong	6-2	North Dakota	Clarkson	5-1	Harvard
1959	North Dakota	Bob May	4-3*	Michigan St.	Boston Col.	7-6†	St. Lawrence
1960	Denver	Murray Armstrong	5-3	Michigan Tech	Boston Univ.	7-6	St. Lawrence
1961	Denver	Murray Armstrong	12-2	St. Lawrence	Minnesota	4-3	RPI
1962	Michigan Tech	John MacInnes	7-1	Clarkson	Michigan	5-1	St. Lawrence
1963	North Dakota	Barry Thorndycraft	6-5	Denver	Clarkson	5-3	Boston Col.
1964	Michigan	Allen Renfrew	6-3	Denver	RPI	2-1	Providence
1965	Michigan Tech	John MacInnes	8-2	Boston Col.	North Dakota	9-0	Brown
1966	Michigan St.	Amo Bessone	6-1	Clarkson	Denver	4-3	Boston Univ.
1967	Cornell	Ned Harkness	4-1	Boston Univ.	Michigan St.	6-1	North Dakota
1968	Denver	Murray Armstrong	4-0	North Dakota	Cornell	6-1	Boston Col.
1969	Denver	Murray Armstrong	4-3	Cornell	Harvard	6-5†	Michigan Tech
1970	Cornell	Ned Harkness	6-4	Clarkson	Wisconsin	6-5	Michigan Tech
1971	Boston Univ.	Jack Kelley	4-2	Minnesota	Denver	1-0	Harvard
1972	Boston Univ.	Jack Kelley	4-0	Cornell	Wisconsin	5-2	Denver
1973	Wisconsin	Bob Johnson	4-2	Denver	Boston Col.	3-1	Cornell
1974	Minnesota	Herb Brooks	4-2	Michigan Tech	Boston Univ.	7-5	Harvard
1975	Michigan Tech	John MacInnes	6-1	Minnesota	Boston Univ.	10-5	Harvard
1976	Minnesota	Herb Brooks	6-4	Michigan Tech	Brown	8-7	Boston Univ.
1977	Wisconsin	Bob Johnson	6-5*	Michigan	Boston Univ.	6-5	New Hampshire
1978	Boston Univ.	Jack Parker	5-3	Boston Col.	Bowling Green	4-3	Wisconsin
1979	Minnesota	Herb Brooks	4-3	North Dakota	Dartmouth	7-3	New Hampshire
1980	North Dakota	Gino Gasparini	5-2	Northern Mich.	Dartmouth	8-4	Cornell
1981	Wisconsin	Bob Johnson	6-3	Minnesota	Michigan Tech	5-2	Northern Mich.
1982	North Dakota	Gino Gasparini	5-2	Wisconsin	Northeastern	10-4	New Hampshire
1983	Wisconsin	Jeff Sauer	6-2	Harvard	Providence	4-3	Minnesota
1984	Bowling Green	Jerry York	5-4*	Minn-Duluth	North Dakota	6-5†	Michigan St.
1985	RPI	Mike Addesa	2-1	Providence	Minn-Duluth	7-6†	Boston Col.
1986	Michigan St.	Ron Mason	6-5	Harvard	Minnesota	6-4	Denver
1987	North Dakota	Gino Gasparini	5-3	Michigan St.	Minnesota	6-3	Harvard
1988	Lake Superior St.	Frank Anzalone	4-3*	St. Lawrence	Maine	5-2	Minnesota
1989	Harvard	Billy Cleary	4-3*	Minnesota	Michigan St.	7-4	Maine

†Consolation game overtimes ended in 1st OT except in 1957, '59 and '69, which all ended in 2nd OT.

U.S. Division I College Hockey (Cont.)
NCAA Final Four

Year	Champion	Head Coach	Score	Runner-up	Third Place
1990	Wisconsin	Jeff Sauer	7-3	Colgate	Boston College and Boston University
1991	Northern Michigan	Rick Comley	8-7*	Boston Univ.	Maine and Clarkson
1992	Lake Superior St.	Jeff Jackson	5-3	Wisconsin	Michigan and Michigan St.
1993	Maine	Shawn Walsh	5-4	Lake Superior	Boston University and Michigan
1994	Lake Superior St.	Jeff Jackson	9-1	Boston Univ.	Harvard and Minnesota

*Championship game overtime goals: 1954—1:54; **1959**—4:22; **1977**—0: 23; **1984**—7:11 in 4th OT; **1988**—4:46; **1989**—4:16; **1991**—1:57 in 3rd OT.

Most Outstanding Player

The Most Outstanding Players of each NCAA Div.I tournament since 1948. Winners of the award who did not play for the tournament champion are in **bold** type. In 1960, three players, none on the winning team, shared the award.
   Multiple winners: Lou Angotti and Marc Behrend (2).

Year		Year		Year	
1948	**Joe Riley**, Dartmouth, F	1963	Al McLean, N. Dakota, F	1980	Doug Smail, N. Dakota, F
1949	**Dick Desmond**, Dart., G	1964	Bob Gray, Michigan, G	1981	Marc Behrend, Wisc., G
1950	**Ralph Bevins**, Boston U., G	1965	Gary Milroy, Mich. Tech, F	1982	Phil Sykes, N. Dakota, F
1951	**Ed Whiston**, Brown, G	1966	Gaye Cooley, Mich. St., G	1983	Marc Behrend, Wisc., G
1952	**Ken Kinsley**, Colo. Col., G	1967	Walt Stanowski, Cornell, F	1984	Gary Kruzich, Bowl. Green, G
1953	John Matchefts, Mich., F	1968	Gerry Powers, Denver, G	1985	**Chris Terreri**, Prov., G
1954	Abbie Moore, RPI, F	1969	Keith Magnuson, Denver, D	1986	Mike Donnelly, Mich. St., F
1955	**Phil Hilton**, Colo. Col., D			1987	Tony Hrkac, N. Dakota, F
1956	Lorne Howes, Mich., G	1970	Dan Lodboa, Cornell, D	1988	Bruce Hoffort, Lk. Superior, G
1957	Bob McCusker, Colo. Col., F	1971	Dan Brady, Boston U., G	1989	Ted Donato, Harvard, F
1958	Murray Massier, Denver, F	1972	Tim Regan, Boston, U., G		
1959	Reg Morelli, N. Dakota, F	1973	Dean Talafous, Wisc., F	1990	Chris Tancill, Wisconsin, F
		1974	Brad Shelstad, Minn., G	1991	Scott Beattie, No. Mich., F
1960	**Lou Angotti**, Mich. Tech, F;	1975	Jim Warden, Mich. Tech, G	1992	Paul Constantin, Lk. Superior, F
	Bob Marquis, Boston U., F;	1976	Tom Vanelli, Minn., F	1993	Jim Montgomery, Maine, F
	& **Barry Urbanski**, Bos. U., G	1977	Julian Baretta, Wisc., G	1994	Sean Tallaire, Lk. Superior, F
1961	Bill Masterton, Denver, F	1978	Jack O'Callahan, Boston U., D		
1962	Lou Angotti, Mich. Tech, F	1979	Steve Janaszak, Minn., G		

Hobey Baker Award

College hockey's Player of the Year award; voted on by a national panel of sportswriters, broadcasters, college coaches and pro scouts. First presented in 1981 by the Decathlon Athletic Club of Bloomington, Minn., in the name of the Princeton collegiate hockey and football star who was killed in World War I.

Year		Class	Year		Class
1981	Neal Broten, Minnesota, F	So.	1988	Robb Stauber, Minnesota, G	So.
1982	George McPhee, Bowling Green, F	Sr.	1989	Lane MacDonald, Harvard, F	Sr.
1983	Mark Fusco, Harvard, D	Sr.	1990	Kip Miller, Michigan St., F	Sr.
1984	Tom Kurvers, Minnesota-Duluth, D	Sr.	1991	Dave Emma, Boston College, F	Sr.
1985	Bill Watson, Minnesota-Duluth, F	Jr.	1992	Scott Pellerin, Maine, F	Sr.
1986	Scott Fusco, Harvard, F	Sr.	1993	Paul Kariya, Maine, F	Fr.
1987	Tony Hrkac, North Dakota, F	So.	1994	Chris Marinucci, Minnesota-Duluth, F	Sr.

Coach of the Year

The Penrose Memorial Trophy, voted on by the American Hockey Coaches Association and first presented in 1951 in the name of Colorado gold and copper magnet Spencer T. Penrose. Penrose built the Broadmoor hotel and athletic complex in Colorado Springs, that originally hosted the NCAA hockey championship from 1948-57.
   Multiple winners: Len Ceglarski and Charlie Holt (3); Rick Comley, Eddie Jeremiah, Snooks Kelly, John MacInnes, Jack Parker, Jack Riley and Cooney Weiland (2).

Year		Year		Year	
1951	Eddie Jeremiah, Dartmouth	1966	Amo Bessone, Michigan St.	1980	Rick Comley, No. Michigan
1952	Cheedy Thompson, Colo. Col.		& Len Ceglarski, Clarkson	1981	Bill O'Flarety, Clarkson
1953	John Mariucci, Minnesota	1967	Eddie Jeremiah, Dartmouth	1982	Fern Flaman, Northeastern
1954	Vic Heyliger, Michigan	1968	Ned Harkness, Cornell	1983	Bill Cleary, Harvard
1955	Cooney Weiland, Harvard	1969	Charlie Holt, New Hampshire	1984	Mike Sertich, Minn-Duluth
1956	Bill Harrison, Clarkson	1970	John MacInnes, Michigan Tech	1985	Len Ceglarski, BC
1957	Jack Riley, Army	1971	Cooney Weiland, Harvard	1986	Ralph Backstrom, Denver
1958	Harry Cleverly, BU	1972	Snooks Kelly, BC	1987	Gino Gasparini, N. Dakota
1959	Snooks Kelly, BC	1973	Len Ceglarski, BC	1988	Frank Anzalone, Lk. Superior
1960	Jack Riley, Army	1974	Charlie Holt, New Hampshire	1989	Joe March, St. Lawrence
1961	Murray Armstrong, Denver	1975	Jack Parker, BU	1990	Terry Slater, Colgate
1962	Jack Kelley, Colby	1976	John MacInnes, Michigan Tech	1991	Rick Comley, No. Michigan
1963	Tony Frasca, Colorado Col.	1977	Jerry York, Clarkson	1992	Ron Mason, Michigan St.
1964	Tom Eccleston, Providence	1978	Jack Parker, BU	1993	George Gwozdecky, Miami-OH
1965	Jim Fullerton, Brown	1979	Charlie Holt, New Hampshire	1994	Don Lucia, Colorado Col.

Note: 1960 winner Jack Riley won the award for coaching the USA to its first hockey gold medal in the Winter Olympics at Squaw Valley.

Mobil Cotton Bowl Classic

The pursuit of money in Division I-A college football sounded the death knell in 1994 for two gridiron institutions: the Cotton Bowl and the Southwest Conference.

COLLEGE SPORTS

Tough Love

In their bid to boost profits, conference commissioners move to kill a football playoff and condemn the Cotton Bowl.

The meeting room in Kansas City on June 2 was filled with people who, for the most part, had dedicated their lives to college athletics. The objective on this day was to come up with a plan to conquer the last remaining frontier of collegiate sport— a playoff format to determine the championship of Division I-A football.

There were problems, to be sure, about tackling this monster. But the financial payoff for college athletics, maybe an extra $60 million per year, kept the special NCAA committee going. They had to try and come up with a plan, any plan, that could at least be presented to the next NCAA convention in January.

Each person on the committee had his or her turn to speak. There was genuine excitement in the room that, despite the obstacles involved, a playoff could become a reality. Maybe it wouldn't happen this year or the next, but it would happen.

Then it was Derrick Brooks' turn to speak. Brooks is an All-America linebacker at Florida State University and one of three student athletes picked for the committee. He is extremely intelligent, an Academic All-ACC selection. He folded his hands and spoke with great clarity:

"I would ask the committee that once these new revenues are generated, how will the student-athlete benefit?" he said. "What would be our share?"

Tony Barnhart is the national college sports writer for the *Atlanta Journal and Constitution*.

The room grew strangely quiet.

"It was like somebody had sucked all the air out of the place," said a participant in the meeting. "Suddenly an issue had been raised that no one was prepared to deal with."

The record will show that the day after Brooks said his piece to this committee, the Southeastern Conference voted 12-0 against the concept of a Division I-A football playoff. The next day the special NCAA committee, chaired by UCLA chancellor Charles Young, said it could not come up with a plan and agreed to continue studying the issue. A few days later the NCAA Presidents Commission disbanded the committee. The issue of a playoff was essentially dead for the forseeable future.

In many ways the Derrick Brooks incident became the perfect metaphor for the state of college athletics in 1994. For much of the news that dominated the headlines was about money— or better yet— the pursuit of money. It was also about who had control over that revenue.

And before the year was over, the pursuit of and control over that money had not only killed the idea of a Division I-A playoff, it had totally changed the landscape of college athletics.

- The Florida State football team, which beat Nebraska in the Orange Bowl in January for the school's first national championship, was hit with a major scandal in May. A *Sports Illustrated*

UCLA

Florida St.

The special NCAA committee chaired by UCLA chancellor **Charles Young** (left) was excited about the financial prospects of a Division I-A football playoff until committee member and All-America linebacker **Derrick Brooks** of Florida State asked how student-athletes would benefit.

cover story reported that at least nine players on the team had taken part in a $6,000 shopping spree which was paid for by an agent's representative— a major violation of NCAA rules. The players involved said that with schools and coaches making millions, they deserved whatever they could get from the process.

- By early August college football's Division I-A bowl coalition was restructured for the 1995 season and beyond, creating three elite, big money bowls and leaving the others to scramble for the television and monetary leftovers. One of those left out, the 58-year-old Cotton Bowl, was relegated to second class status and was considering closing up shop rather than accept its new station in life.

- The College Football Association ceased to be a major player in the TV negotiating game. The CFA had been home to 63 major football playing schools in five major conferences. But with the contract between the CFA and the various networks expiring after the '95 season, the conferences decided they could do bet-

ter by independently striking their own deals. The CFA will remain in existence in some form but will never have the same clout.

- The Southwest Conference will no longer exist after the 1995-96 school year. When the major conferences broke with the CFA and started pursuing the TV networks, the SWC and the Big Eight saw relatively fewer television dollars coming their way. The ACC, SEC, and Big East were the big winners. In order to survive and give television a more viable product, four SWC schools (Texas, Texas A&M, Texas Tech and Baylor) agreed to join the Big Eight in the fall of 1996, thus forming a new Big 12 conference. The remaining SWC schools, which did not generate sufficient revenues to be invited, were left to fend for themselves.

In the 1976 movie "Network," anchorman Howard Beale was killed because his ratings dipped too low. Likewise, the proud Southwest Conference, founded in 1914, was sacrificed to the gods of television 80 years later.

"We're at an unusual place in college ath-

419

ACC   Big East   SEC

Gene Corrigan (left) of the Atlantic Coast Conference, **Mike Tranghese** (center) of the Big East and **Roy Kramer** of the Southeastern Conference are college football's major power brokers along with Notre Dame athletic director Dick Rosenthal, who will be replaced by Michael Wadsworth on Aug. 1, 1995.

letics in that there are so many pressures—including financial— that we haven't had before," said Gene Corrigan, the commissioner of the ACC. "Change is inevitable in anything and this is no different. Some of it is good. Some of it is not fun at all."

The death of the college football playoff was the most blatant example of those in power realizing that change would not be in their best interest. The current 19-bowl system generates just under $41 million for the participating teams and their conference members. By anyone's analysis, a 16-team Division I playoff, would create at least $100 million in revenue.

But as the summer of '94 went along, the major conference commissioners started doing the math and realized a playoff would not be as beneficial to them as some might have believed.

``The only way it [a playoff] gets started is if there's more money,'' said Mike Tranghese, commissioner of the Big East. ``Is there more? Yes, but who gets it? How is it divided?''

Under a playoff, the NCAA would gain control of postseason dollars and could potentially divide the money among the 800-plus schools in three divisions. The financial pie would be significantly bigger but with more people getting a slice, the big conferences could actually get less. Plus the commissioners would give up control of the process. They do not like that.

"For a conference that sends only one or two teams to bowls, a playoff could be a good situation," said Roy Kramer, commissioner of the SEC. "But for our conference [which sometimes has as many as seven bowl teams], it could turn out to be a negative."

The commissioners also realized, thanks to Derrick Brooks, that if a playoff came to pass, generating an additional $60 million for college football, then compensation for players, long a backburner issue, would quickly be moved to the front of the stove.

"It [paying players] is a can of worms nobody wants to touch, much less open," said a member of the NCAA playoff committee. "Brooks made a compelling argument and some of the people in that room were sympathetic with his point of view. That's what scared everybody."

Ironically, Brooks would become involved in another issue dealing with money that would draw national headlines. In early August it was revealed that he had taken part in that shopping spree that had been reported by *Sports Illustrated*. The magazine had not reported that Brooks was a participant but it was discovered during an internal investigation conducted for the school by a Kansas City law firm. Brooks, who passed up a lucrative pro contract to play his senior season at FSU, was one of four Florida State players suspended for the first two games of the 1994 season (see page 422).

As 1994 drew to a close, student-athletes in the big money sports of football and basketball, were becoming more vocal in their belief that they should receive a piece of the pie. More and more, however, administrators kept explaining why in the current climate, it cannot happen.

"I can understand my guys and why they feel that way," said Gene Stallings, the football coach at Alabama. "But if they get money, why shouldn't the women's basketball team get money? And the volleyball and track teams? If football players get money then everybody gets money. And almost nobody can afford to pay a stipend to all of their athletes on scholarship. That's the reality of the situation."

With the idea of a football playoff dead, the conference commissioners continued their work of improving the bowl system and making it possible for the system to generate more revenue. What they came up with was a new alliance to replace the current Bowl Coalition that would give three bowls exclusive primetime television slots on Dec. 31, Jan. 1, and Jan. 2. The alliance will begin after the 1995 regular season.

The assurance of exclusive prime time slots during the holiday period cleared up the current glut of games on New Year's Day which had driven down TV ratings and ad revenue. TV execs promised that significant money would be generated and when the bowls were thrown open for bids, they put their money where their mouths were.

CBS, which no longer has NFL football or Major League Baseball to underwrite, put up $300 million to back the bids of the Orange, Fiesta, and Gator Bowls, hoping to lock up all three prime time slots. ABC, already the rights-holder of the non-allied Rose Bowl, put up $330 million to back the Sugar, Citrus, Peach, and Alamo Bowls.

In the end, the commissioners decided to split the risk and go with two networks instead of one— awarding the slots to the Sugar, Orange, and Fiesta bowls. The Sugar will join the Rose on ABC while the Orange and Fiesta will move over to CBS after many years on NBC. The deal is for six years with an "out" clause after three for all parties.

The new alliance will create a six-team pool from the champions of the ACC, Big East, Big 12 and SEC, plus Notre Dame and another at-large team. (Should the Irish go winless or be deemed otherwise unsuitable, another independent would be chosen.) The two highest ranked teams in the pool will play in the Jan. 2 bowl, presumably for the national title. The No. 3

New Bowl Alliance

Following the 1995 college football regular season, the top six ranked teams in the nation (except for Big 10 and Pac-10 schools) will meet in three bowls: Nos. 5-6 (Dec. 31), Nos. 3-4 (Jan. 1) and Nos. 1-2 (Jan. 2). The "A" game will rotate among the Fiesta, Orange and Sugar bowls. Estimated bids over six years: Fiesta ($116 million), Orange ($101 million) and Sugar ($100 million).

1995 Season

Bowls (3): Fiesta (Tempe, Ariz.), Orange (Miami) and Sugar (New Orleans). **Pool of teams (6):** champions of ACC, Big East, Big 8, SEC and SWC; and independent Notre Dame.

1996-2000 Seasons

Bowls (3): Fiesta (Tempe, Ariz.), Orange (Miami) and Sugar (New Orleans). **Pool of teams (6):** champions of ACC, Big East, Big 12 and SEC; independent Notre Dame; and an at-large entry.

and No. 5 teams will play in the Jan. 1 game, while Nos. 4 and 6 will play on Dec. 31. The Rose Bowl will continue to host the Big Ten and Pac-10 champions and play on New Year's Day at 5 p.m.

Obviously, if No. 1 or No. 2 is playing in the Rose Bowl, the alliance won't get its national championship. But that has only happened once in the past 15 years (on Jan. 1, 1980, when No. 3 Southern Cal upset No. 1 Ohio State, 17-16). What the new alliance does is eliminate all previous relationships between the bowls and the conferences— hence, the SEC champion will no longer be locked into the Sugar and the Big Eight (soon to be Big 12) champ won't be wedded to the Orange. The chances for a No. 1 vs. No. 2 game are thus greatly enhanced. And the guarantee of an exclusive time slot with no competition is music to television's ears.

Not everybody, however, was jumping for joy over these newly-found riches. Certainly no one in Dallas. Due to the threat of bad weather and the fact that its host conference, the Southwest, was going out of business, the Cotton Bowl simply did not have enough leverage or enough appeal when it came time to pick the Big Three.

The Holiday Bowl, where the champion of the Western Athletic Conference traditionally plays, wasn't exactly thrilled with the alliance either. It made a formal request to join the club but was rejected. While WAC lawyers have threatened legal action under antitrust law if the alliance is put into place, alliance members are confident they are within the law on this one.

The net result of all this? Money and lots of it. The largest payout by a single bowl after the 1993 season was the Rose, which paid Wisconsin and UCLA $6.5 million each for their visit to Pasadena. In the new alliance, the Fiesta Bowl will get the first national championship game (on Jan. 2, 1996) and pay in excess of $12 million per team.

Not everything that happened in college athletics in 1993-94 was about the pursuit of money. There actually was some good news.

On Nov. 5, 1993, University of Arizona athletic Cedric Dempsey became the NCAA's third executive director, replacing Dick Schultz, who had resigned on May 11. The other three finalists for the job were former Congressman and North Carolina athletic director Bill Cobey, University of California at San Diego AD Judy Sweet and University of Mississippi chancellor Gerald Turner.

The NCAA's latest study on graduation rates revealed that the success rate of black male athletes had risen 10 percentage points, to 43 percent, over the past four years. That was substantially higher than the overall graduation rates of the black male college population in the United States.

The NCAA Presidents Commission saw that as validation that its position of continuing to raise entrance standards was the correct one. For that 10 percent increase had all come in the years since a minimum standard for athletic eligibility— known as Proposition 48— had been established in 1986.

Those minimum standards— a 2.0 grade point average on 11 core curriculum subjects and a 700 SAT score— are scheduled to be increased on Aug. 1, 1995. The new standard, known as Proposition 16, will up the core courses to 13 and introduce a sliding indexing scale that factors in GPA and SAT. Prop 16 would, for instance, require a

Long, Hot Summer In Tallahassee

It was supposed to be the best summer ever in the colorful and successful life of Bobby Bowden of Tallahassee, Fla. Instead it was the longest and the hottest he has ever known.

With his first national championship finally in the trophy case after years and years of frustration, this summer was going to be Bowden's non-stop magical victory tour— a Seminole celebration that would not end until the 1994 season began on Sept. 3. Everybody's favorite grandfather would finally be allowed to enjoy the fruits of his labors.

But everything in Bobby Bowden's life changed in May when *Sports Illustrated* went national with a cover story of a $6,000 shopping spree by at least nine FSU players, paid for by agents' representatives. The now infamous visit to a Tallahassee Foot Locker store on Nov. 7, 1993, came just six days before the Notre Dame game.

The magazine told of payoffs to players and painted a picture of a program out of control. More than once *SI* suggested Bowden and his staff knew of the problems or least should have known. A subsequent article told of boosters giving bogus jobs to players which, if proven, could be a major NCAA violation.

The *SI* articles opened the floodgates for allegation upon allegation of various NCAA violations from various sources. Two players were arrested for non-related offenses, lending further credence to the suggestion that FSU had a runaway program. Suddenly a friendly press, which had always given Bowden the benefit of the doubt, seemed to turn on him.

The man once dubbed "Saint Bobby" began to see others— some of them people he knew and trusted— grab at his halo in an attempt to wrap it tightly around his throat.

"It's been the most aggravating thing I've ever dealt with in my life," said Bowden, who turned 65 in November. "It makes you mad because you feel you can't do any better than you did. I'm just really anxious to put this thing behind us and get back to work."

But that's the problem. This is a story that will not go away anytime soon. As of mid-September, the NCAA had yet to look into the allegations raised by *SI* and others. Instead, it was waiting on an internal investigation by

Bobby Bowden's Florida State football team made the cover of Sports Illustrated twice in 1994, as national football champions in January and then as an accused out of control program in May. The fall from grace took its toll on the normally buoyant Bowden, who had always enjoyed a friendly relationship with the press.

an independent law firm hired by FSU. Once that report is complete, the NCAA will review it and decide what to do next.

The fallout, however, has already been felt. In July, Bowden was forced to suspend four of his players, including All-America linebacker Derrick Brooks, for the first two games of the 1994 season. FSU President Sandy D'Alemberte is now in control of the process. Bowden admitted that the suspensions of the four "were more than I recommended, but I can live with it." He has to.

Meanwhile, three of the agents' representatives involved in the case have been arrested under a Florida law which prohibits agents from operating without registering with the state.

The knowledge that the controversy won't be over for a long time has made the most affable football coach in America testy at times. He didn't mind it when they said he wasn't a good coach. He didn't mind it that much when they kept saying he couldn't win the big one. He didn't get all that upset when, during an alumni golf outing in May, a newspaper helicopter landed in the fairway. "Right in the middle of my backswing," he laughed.

But now some folks out there are saying he's a liar. And that, he cannot stomach.

"What I'm amazed about is how big this thing has gotten," said Bowden. "They [Sports Illustrated] made me feel like I was a dadgum criminal. Let's look at it. A kid took a pair of shoes. A kid took a warmup. Maybe a kid took two pairs of shoes. It ain't murder. It ain't rape. We didn't lie to the NCAA. It ain't like we instigated this thing. It ain't like we put this deal together trying to cheat."

Bowden can say with a clear conscience that he had no knowledge of the now-infamous shopping spree. He can't understand why some people don't think that's good enough.

"They [Sports Illustrated] tried to tie us in that we knew about it and we absolutely did not know about it. Then they say we should have known about it. Well, the heck we do..."

Where and when is this all going to end, Bowden wanted to know. A coach spends most of his adult life trying to win a national title and when he finally does it, this is the payoff?

There are rumblings that Bowden will coach this last season (his 18th at FSU) and then hang it up. He has his national championship and nothing the NCAA can do will change it.

"I always said that while I wanted to win the national championship I could live without it," said Bowden, his voice growing quiet. "Because no matter how hard you work to get it you find out something. There's nothing at the top."

Wide World Photos

Former University of Arizona athletic director **Cedric Dempsey** beat out three other finalists to become the NCAA's third executive director on Nov. 5, 1993.

student with a 700 SAT score to have a grade point average of 2.5 or more in the core courses to be eligible.

The further increasing of standards, particularly the raising of the standarized test score, drew the wrath of the Black Coaches Association, which feels the SAT is biased against minority students. During the basketball season they threatened a walkout during regularly scheduled games, but their boycott never materialized (see page 276).

The BCA's position is that raising entrance standards to a higher level would deny a large group of athletes, disproportionately minorities, the access to a college scholarship. An NCAA committee was formed to review initial eligibility standards and that committee recommended delaying the implementation of the higher standards until further study could be done. It also recommended a liberalization of those standards.

But at its July meeting, the NCAA Presidents stood their ground, keeping Prop 16 in place but creating opportunities for those athletes who do not meet the revised requirements as freshmen. They will now be allowed to enroll in school, practice with the team, and receive financial aid. If the student is successful in class, he can also receive a fourth year of eligibility.

The measure must still be approved at the NCAA convention, where the BCA will again be expected to voice its disapproval.

"We don't want to be in the position of exploiting student-athletes, so we we have to be in position of making sure they succeed," said Judith Albino, president of Colorado and chairperson of the Presidents Commission.

Academic standards weren't the only thing that were set to draw fireworks in 1995.

The NCAA will take another look at the rule which allows college basketball players to enter the NBA Draft but return to school after 30 days. Two underclassmen drafted in the second round of the '94 Draft—Minnesota's Voshon Lenard (No. 46, by Milwaukee) and Georgia's Charles Claxton (No. 50, by Phoenix)— passed on the NBA and will return to school. The problem is that those same teams will retain the rights to these players through the 1995 Draft. So, no matter how well these two guys play this season, they can't improve their draft status and bargaining position. That's not what the rule was intended to do.

The gender equity question, once confined to availability of scholarships and athletic opportunities for women, was making serious inroads into the issue of coaching salaries. Andy Landers and Suzanne Yoculan, who coached women's basketball and women's gymnastics at Georgia, had their salaries almost doubled after threatening to take the school to court. Yoculan, who has won three national titles, became the highest-paid women's gymnastics coach in America with a salary of almost $80,000.

The schools with big-time athletic departments are still making noises about bolting the NCAA and forming their own organization. They will settle for more control over the legislative and administrative process which is currently too cumbersome and ineffective. It may be the single biggest battle in college athletics in 1995.

And finally, Notre Dame will remain an independent in football but will join the Big East in basketball and all other sports. The Big East gets the Chicago market and Notre Dame gets instant access to recruiting territory and players it could not previously touch. The Big East coaches are not thrilled about the new competition. ❑

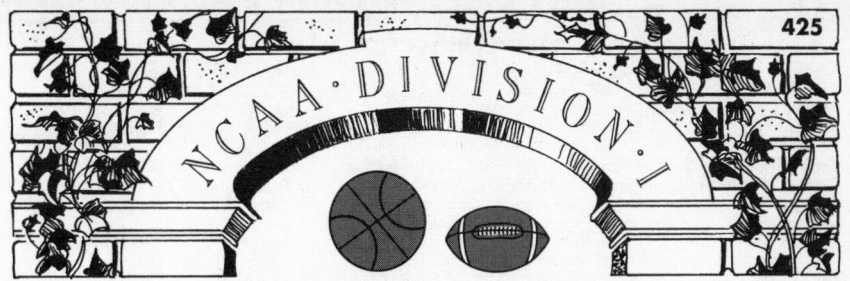

NCAA Division I Basketball Schools

Conferences and coaches as of Sept. 15, 1994.

New Conference in 1994-95: AMERICAN WEST (4 teams)— independents Cal State-Northridge, Cal State-Sacramento, Cal Poly SLO (moving up from Div. II) and Southern Utah.

Switching conferences in 1994-95 (14): CLEVELAND ST., ILLINOIS-CHICAGO, NORTHERN ILLINOIS, WISCONSIN-GREEN BAY, WISCONSIN-MILWAUKEE and WRIGHT ST. from Mid-Continent to Midwestern; BUFFALO, CENTRAL CONN. ST., CHICAGO ST., NORTHEASTERN ILLINOIS and TROY ST from East Coast to Mid-Continent; CAMPBELL from Big South to Trans America; EVANSVILLE from Midwestern to Missouri Valley; HOFSTRA from East Coast to North Atlantic.

Independent joining new conference in 1994-95: MISSOURI-KANSAS CITY to Mid-Continent.

Switching conferences in 1995-96 (4): RUTGERS and WEST VIRGINIA from Atlantic 10 to Big East; TOWSON ST. from Big South to North Atlantic; XAVIER-OH from Midwestern to Atlantic 10.

Independent joining conference in 1995-96: NOTRE DAME to Big East.

Changing conference name as of June 30, 1996: Big 8 becomes Big 12.

Breakup of Southwest Conference as of June 30, 1996: to Big 12 (4)— BAYLOR, TEXAS, TEXAS A&M and TEXAS TECH; to Western Athletic Conf. (3)— RICE, SMU and TCU; to Independent— HOUSTON.

Joining Big 12 in 1996-97 (4): BAYLOR, TEXAS, TEXAS A&M and TEXAS TECH from Southwest Conference.

Joining Western Athletic Conference in 1996-97 (6): SAN JOSE ST. and UNLV from Big West; TULSA from Mo. Valley; and RICE, SMU and TCU from Southwest Conference.

	Nickname	Conference	Head Coach	Location	Colors
Air Force	Falcons	WAC	Reggie Minton	Colo. Springs, CO	Blue/Silver
Akron	Zips	Mid-American	Coleman Crawford	Akron, OH	Blue/Gold
Alabama	Crimson Tide	SEC-West	David Hobbs	Tuscaloosa, AL	Crimson/White
Alabama St.	Hornets	Southwestern	James Oliver	Montgomery, AL	Black/Gold
Ala-Birmingham	Blazers	Great Midwest	Gene Bartow	Birmingham, AL	Green/Gold
Alcorn St.	Braves	Southwestern	Sam Weaver	Lorman, MS	Purple/Gold
American	Eagles	Colonial	Chris Knoche	Washington, DC	Red/White/Blue
Appalachian St.	Mountaineers	Southern	Tom Apke	Boone, NC	Black/Gold
Arizona	Wildcats	Pac-10	Lute Olson	Tucson, AZ	Cardinal/Navy
Arizona St.	Sun Devils	Pac-10	Bill Frieder	Tempe, AZ	Maroon/Gold
Arkansas	Razorbacks	SEC-West	Nolan Richardson	Fayetteville, AR	Cardinal/White
Arkansas-Little Rock	Trojans	Sun Belt	Wimp Sanderson	Little Rock, AR	Maroon/Gold/White
Arkansas St.	Indians	Sun Belt	Nelson Catalina	State Univ., AR	Scarlet/Black
Army	Cadets, Black Knights	Patriot	Dino Gaudio	West Point, NY	Black/Gold/Gray
Auburn	Tigers	SEC-West	Cliff Ellis	Auburn, AL	Orange/Blue
Austin Peay St.	Governors	Ohio Valley	Dave Loos	Clarksville, TN	Red/White
Ball St.	Cardinals	Mid-American	Ray McCallum	Muncie, IN	Cardinal/White
Baylor	Bears	SWC	Darrel Johnson	Waco, TX	Green/Gold
Bethune-Cookman	Wildcats	Mid-Eastern	Tony Sheals	Daytona Beach, FL	Maroon/Gold
Boise St.	Broncos	Big Sky	Bobby Dye	Boise, ID	Orange/Blue
Boston College	Eagles	Big East	Jim O'Brien	Chestnut Hill, MA	Maroon/Gold
Boston University	Terriers	North Atlantic	Dennis Wolff	Boston, MA	Scarlet/White
Bowling Green	Falcons	Mid-American	Jim Larranaga	Bowling Green, OH	Orange/Brown
Bradley	Braves	Mo. Valley	Jim Molinari	Peoria, IL	Red/White
BYU	Cougars	WAC	Roger Reid	Provo, UT	Royal Blue/White
Brown	Bears	Ivy	Frank Dobbs	Providence, RI	Brown/Cardinal/White
Bucknell	Bison	Patriot	Pat Flannery	Lewisburg, PA	Orange/Blue
Buffalo	Bulls	Mid-Continent	Tim Cohane	Buffalo, NY	Blue/Red/White
Butler	Bulldogs	Midwestern	Barry Collier	Indianapolis, IN	Blue/White
California	Golden Bears	Pac-10	Todd Bozeman	Berkeley, CA	Blue/Gold
CS-Fullerton	Titans	Big West	Bob Hawking	Fullerton, CA	Blue/Orange/White
CS-Northridge	Matadors	American West	Pete Cassidy	Northridge, CA	Red/White/Black
CS-Sacramento	Hornets	American West	Don Newman	Sacramento, CA	Green/Gold
Cal Poly SLO	Mustangs	American West	Steve Beason	San Luis Obispo, CA	Green/Gold

NCAA Division I Basketball Schools (Cont.)

	Nickname	Conference	Head Coach	Location	Colors
Campbell	Fighting Camels	Trans Am	Billy Lee	Buies Creek, NC	Orange/Black
Canisius	Golden Griffins	Metro Atlantic	John Beilein	Buffalo, NY	Blue/Gold
Centenary	Gentlemen	Trans Am	Tommy Vardeman	Shreveport, LA	Maroon/White
Central Conn. St.	Blue Devils	Mid-Continent	Mark Adams	New Britain, CT	Blue/White
Central Florida	Golden Knights	Trans Am	Ben DeVary	Orlando, FL	Black/Gold
Central Michigan	Chippewas	Mid-American	Leonard Drake	Mt. Pleasant, MI	Maroon/Gold
College of Charleston	Cougars	Trans Am	John Kresse	Charleston, SC	Maroon/White
Charleston So.	Buccaneers	Big South	Gary Edwards	Charleston, SC	Blue/Gold
Chicago St.	Cougars	Mid-Continent	Craig Hodges	Chicago, IL	Green/White
Cincinnati	Bearcats	Great Midwest	Bob Huggins	Cincinnati, OH	Red/Black
The Citadel	Bulldogs	Southern	Pat Dennis	Charleston, SC	Blue/White
Clemson	Tigers	ACC	Rick Barnes	Clemson, SC	Purple/Orange
Cleveland St.	Vikings	Midwestern	Mike Boyd	Cleveland, OH	Green/White
Coastal Carolina	Chanticleers	Big South	Michael Hopkins	Myrtle Beach, SC	Scarlet/Black
Colgate	Red Raiders	Patriot	Jack Bruen	Hamilton, NY	Maroon/Gray/White
Colorado	Golden Buffaloes	Big 8	Joe Harrington	Boulder, CO	Silver/Gold/Black
Colorado St.	Rams	WAC	Stew Morrill	Ft. Collins, CO	Green/Gold
Columbia	Lions	Ivy	Jack Rohan	New York, NY	Lt. Blue/White
Connecticut	Huskies	Big East	Jim Calhoun	Storrs, CT	Blue/White
Coppin St.	Eagles	Mid-Eastern	Ron Mitchell	Baltimore, MD	Royal Blue/Gold
Cornell	Big Red	Ivy	Al Walker	Ithaca, NY	Carnelian Red/White
Creighton	Bluejays	Mo. Valley	Dana Altman	Omaha, NE	Blue/White
Dartmouth	Big Green	Ivy	Dave Faucher	Hanover, NH	Green/White
Davidson	Wildcats	Southern	Bob McKillop	Davidson, NC	Red/Black
Dayton	Flyers	Great Midwest	Oliver Purnell	Dayton, OH	Red/Blue
DePaul	Blue Demons	Great Midwest	Joey Meyer	Chicago, IL	Scarlet/Blue
Delaware	Blue Hens	North Atlantic	Steve Steinwedel	Newark, DE	Blue/Gold
Delaware St.	Hornets	Mid-Eastern	Jeff Jones	Dover, DE	Red/Blue
Detroit Mercy	Titans	Midwestern	Perry Watson	Detroit, MI	Red/White/Blue
Drake	Bulldogs	Mo. Valley	Rudy Washington	Des Moines, IA	Blue/White
Drexel	Dragons	North Atlantic	Bill Herrion	Philadelphia, PA	Navy Blue/Gold
Duke	Blue Devils	ACC	Mike Krzyzewski	Durham, NC	Royal Blue/White
Duquesne	Dukes	Atlantic 10	John Carroll	Pittsburgh, PA	Red/Blue
East Carolina	Pirates	Colonial	Eddie Payne	Greenville, NC	Purple/Gold
East Tenn. St.	Buccaneers	Southern	Alan LeForce	Johnson City, TN	Blue/Gold
Eastern Illinois	Panthers	Mid-Continent	Rick Samuels	Charleston, IL	Blue/Gray
Eastern Kentucky	Colonels	Ohio Valley	Mike Calhoun	Richmond, KY	Maroon/White
Eastern Michigan	Eagles	Mid-American	Ben Braun	Ypsilanti, MI	Green/White
Eastern Washington	Eagles	Big Sky	John Wade	Cheney, WA	Red/White
Evansville	Aces	Mo. Valley	Jim Crews	Evansville, IN	Purple/White
Fairfield	Stags	Metro Atlantic	Paul Cormier	Fairfield, CT	Cardinal Red
Fairleigh Dickinson	Knights	Northeast	Tom Green	Teaneck, NJ	Maroon/White/Blue
Florida	Gators	SEC-East	Lon Kruger	Gainesville, FL	Orange/Blue
Florida A&M	Rattlers	Mid-Eastern	Ron Brown	Tallahassee, FL	Orange/Green
Florida Atlantic	Owls	Trans Am	Tim Loomis	Boca Raton, FL	Blue/Gray
Florida Int'l	Golden Panthers	Trans Am	Bob Weltlich	Miami, FL	Blue/Yellow
Florida St.	Seminoles	ACC	Pat Kennedy	Tallahassee, FL	Garnet/Gold
Fordham	Rams	Patriot	Nick Macarchuk	Bronx, NY	Maroon/White
Fresno St.	Bulldogs	WAC	Gary Colson	Fresno, CA	Cardinal/Blue
Furman	Paladins	Southern	Joe Cantafio	Greenville, SC	Purple/White
George Mason	Patriots	Colonial	Paul Westhead	Fairfax, VA	Green/Gold
George Washington	Colonials	Atlantic 10	Mike Jarvis	Washington, DC	Buff/Blue
Georgetown	Hoyas	Big East	John Thompson	Washington, DC	Blue/Gray
Georgia	Bulldogs, 'Dawgs	SEC-East	Hugh Durham	Athens, GA	Red/Black
Georgia Southern	Eagles	Southern	Frank Kerns	Statesboro, GA	Blue/White
Georgia St.	Panthers	Trans Am	Carter Wilson	Atlanta, GA	Royal Blue/Crimson
Georgia Tech	Yellow Jackets	ACC	Bobby Cremins	Atlanta, GA	Old Gold/White
Gonzaga	Bulldogs, Zags	West Coast	Dan Fitzgerald	Spokane, WA	Blue/White/Red
Grambling St.	Tigers	Southwestern	Aaron James	Grambling, LA	Black/Gold
Hartford	Hawks	North Atlantic	Paul Brazeau	W. Hartford, CT	Scarlet/White
Harvard	Crimson	Ivy	Frank Sullivan	Cambridge, MA	Crimson/Black/White
Hawaii	Rainbows	WAC	Riley Wallace	Honolulu, HI	Green/White
Hofstra	Flying Dutchmen	North Atlantic	Jay Wright	Hempstead, NY	Blue/White/Gold
Holy Cross	Crusaders	Patriot	Bill Raynor	Worcester, MA	Royal Purple
Houston	Cougars	SWC	Alvin Brooks	Houston, TX	Scarlet/White
Howard	Bison	Mid-Eastern	TBA	Washington, DC	Blue/White/Red

	Nickname	Conference	Head Coach	Location	Colors
Idaho	Vandals	Big Sky	Joe Cravens	Moscow, ID	Silver/Gold
Idaho St.	Bengals	Big Sky	Herb Williams	Pocatello, ID	Orange/Black
Illinois	Fighting Illini	Big 10	Lou Henson	Champaign, IL	Orange/Blue
Illinois-Chicago	Flames	Midwestern	Bob Hallberg	Chicago, IL	Indigo/Flame
Illinois St.	Redbirds	Mo. Valley	Kevin Stallings	Normal, IL	Red/White
Indiana	Hoosiers	Big 10	Bob Knight	Bloomington, IN	Cream/Crimson
Indiana St.	Sycamores	Mo. Valley	Sherman Dillard	Terre Haute, IN	Blue/White
Iona	Gaels	Metro Atlantic	Jerry Welsh	New Rochelle, NY	Maroon/Gold
Iowa	Hawkeyes	Big 10	Tom Davis	Iowa City, IA	Old Gold/Black
Iowa St.	Cyclones	Big 8	Tim Floyd	Ames, IA	Cardinal/Gold
Jackson St.	Tigers	Southwestern	Andrew Stoglin	Jackson, MS	Blue/White
Jacksonville	Dolphins	Sun Belt	George Scholtz	Jacksonville, FL	Green/Gold
James Madison	Dukes	Colonial	Lefty Driesell	Harrisonburg, VA	Purple/Gold
Kansas	Jayhawks	Big 8	Roy Williams	Lawrence, KS	Crimson/Blue
Kansas St.	Wildcats	Big 8	Tom Asbury	Manhattan, KS	Purple/White
Kent	Golden Flashes	Mid-American	Dave Grube	Kent, OH	Navy Blue/Gold
Kentucky	Wildcats	SEC-East	Rick Pitino	Lexington, KY	Blue/White
La Salle	Explorers	Midwestern	Bill Morris	Philadelphia, PA	Blue/Gold
Lafayette	Leopards	Patriot	John Leone	Easton, PA	Maroon/White
Lamar	Cardinals	Sun Belt	Grey Giovanine	Beaumont, TX	Red/White
Lehigh	Engineers	Patriot	Dave Duke	Bethlehem, PA	Brown/White
Liberty	Flames	Big South	Jeff Meyer	Lynchburg, VA	Red/White/Blue
Long Beach St.	49ers	Big West	Seth Greenberg	Long Beach, CA	Black/Gold
Long Island	Blackbirds	Northeast	Paul Lizzo	Brooklyn, NY	Blue/White
LSU	Fighting Tigers	SEC-West	Dale Brown	Baton Rouge, LA	Purple/Gold
Louisiana Tech	Bulldogs	Sun Belt	Jim Wooldridge	Ruston, LA	Red/Blue
Louisville	Cardinals	Metro	Denny Crum	Louisville, KY	Red/Black/White
Loyola-CA	Lions	West Coast	John Olive	Los Angeles, CA	Crimson/Gray/Lt.Blue
Loyola-IL	Ramblers	Midwestern	Ken Burmeister	Chicago, IL	Maroon/Gold
Loyola-MD	Greyhounds	Metro Atlantic	Brian Ellerbe	Baltimore, MD	Green/Gray
Maine	Black Bears	North Atlantic	Rudy Keeling	Orono, ME	Blue/White
Manhattan	Jaspers	Metro Atlantic	Fran Fraschilla	Riverdale, NY	Kelly Green/White
Marist	Red Foxes	Northeast	Dave Magarity	Poughkeepsie, NY	Red/White
Marquette	Golden Eagles	Great Midwest	Mike Deane	Milwaukee, WI	Blue/Gold
Marshall	Thundering Herd	Southern	Billy Donovan	Huntington, WV	Green/White
Maryland	Terrapins, Terps	ACC	Gary Williams	College Park, MD	Red/White/Black/Gold
MD-Balt. County	Retrievers	Big South	Earl Hawkins	Baltimore, MD	Black/Old Gold
MD-Eastern Shore	Hawks	Mid-Eastern	Jeff Menday	Princess Anne, MD	Maroon/Gray
Massachusetts	Minutemen	Atlantic 10	John Calipari	Amherst, MA	Maroon/White
McNeese St.	Cowboys	Southland	Ron Everhart	Lake Charles, LA	Blue/Gold
Memphis	Tigers	Great Midwest	Larry Finch	Memphis, TN	Blue/Gray
Mercer	Bears	Trans Am	Bill Hodges	Macon, GA	Orange/Black
Miami-FL	Hurricanes	Big East	Leonard Hamilton	Miami, FL	Orange/Green/White
Miami-OH	Redskins	Mid-American	Herb Sendek	Oxford, OH	Red/White
Michigan	Wolverines	Big 10	Steve Fisher	Ann Arbor, MI	Maize/Blue
Michigan St.	Spartans	Big 10	Jud Heathcote	East Lansing, MI	Green/White
Middle Tenn. St.	Blue Raiders	Ohio Valley	Dave Farrar	Murfreesboro, TN	Blue/White
Minnesota	Golden Gophers	Big 10	Clem Haskins	Minneapolis, MN	Maroon/Gold
Mississippi	Ole Miss, Rebels	SEC-West	Rob Evans	Oxford, MS	Red/Blue
Mississippi St.	Bulldogs	SEC-West	Richard Williams	Starkville, MS	Maroon/White
Miss. Valley St.	Delta Devils	Southwestern	Lafayette Stribling	Itta Bena, MS	Green/White
Missouri	Tigers	Big 8	Norm Stewart	Columbia, MO	Old Gold/Black
Missouri-KC	Kangaroos	Mid-Continent	Lee Hunt	Kansas City, MO	Blue/Gold
Monmouth	Hawks	Northeast	Wayne Szoke	W. Long Branch, NJ	Royal Blue/White
Montana	Grizzlies	Big Sky	Blaine Taylor	Missoula, MT	Copper/Silver/Gold
Montana St.	Bobcats	Big Sky	Mick Durham	Bozeman, MT	Blue/Gold
Morehead St.	Eagles	Ohio Valley	Dick Fick	Morehead, KY	Blue/Gold
Morgan St.	Bears	Mid-Eastern	Lynn Ramage	Baltimore, MD	Blue/Orange
Mt. St. Mary's	Mountaineers	Northeast	Jim Phelan	Emmitsburg, MD	Blue/White
Murray St.	Racers	Ohio Valley	Scott Edgar	Murray, KY	Blue/Gold
Navy	Midshipmen	Patriot	Don DeVoe	Annapolis, MD	Navy Blue/Gold
Nebraska	Cornhuskers	Big 8	Danny Nee	Lincoln, ME	Scarlet/Cream
Nevada	Wolf Pack	Big West	Pat Foster	Reno, NV	Silver/Blue
New Hampshire	Wildcats	North Atlantic	Gib Chapman	Durham, NH	Blue/White
New Mexico	Lobos	WAC	Dave Bliss	Albuquerque, NM	Cherry/Silver
New Mexico St.	Aggies	Big West	Neil McCarthy	Las Cruces, NM	Crimson/White
New Orleans	Privateers	Sun Belt	Tic Price	New Orleans, LA	Royal Blue/Silver
Niagara	Purple Eagles	Metro Atlantic	Jack Armstrong	Niagara, NY	Purple/White/Gold

NCAA Division I Basketball Schools (Cont.)

	Nickname	Conference	Head Coach	Location	Colors
Nicholls St.	Colonels	Southland	Rickey Broussard	Thibodaux, LA	Red/Gray
North Carolina	Tar Heels	ACC	Dean Smith	Chapel Hill, NC	Carolina Blue/White
North Carolina A&T	Aggies	Mid-Eastern	Roy Thomas	Greensboro, NC	Blue/Gold
North Carolina St.	Wolfpack	ACC	Les Robinson	Raleigh, NC	Red/White
NC-Asheville	Bulldogs	Big South	Randy Wiel	Asheville, NC	Royal Blue/White
NC-Charlotte	49ers	Metro	Jeff Mullins	Charlotte, NC	Green/White
NC-Greensboro	Spartans	Big South	Mike Dement	Greensboro, NC	Gold/White/Navy
NC-Wilmington	Seahawks	Colonial	Jerry Wainwright	Wilmington, NC	Green/Gold
North Texas	Mean Green, Eagles	Southland	Tim Jankovich	Denton, TX	Green/White
NE Illinois	Golden Eagles	Mid-Continent	Rees Johnson	Chicago, IL	Royal Blue/Gold
NE Louisiana	Indians	Southland	Mike Vining	Monroe, LA	Maroon/Gold
Northeastern	Huskies	North Atlantic	Dave Leitao	Boston, MA	Red/Black
Northern Arizona	Lumberjacks	Big Sky	Ben Howland	Flagstaff, AZ	Blue/Gold
Northern Illinois	Huskies	Midwestern	Brian Hammel	De Kalb, IL	Cardinal/Black
Northern Iowa	Panthers	Mo. Valley	Eldon Miller	Cedar Falls, IA	Purple/Old Gold
Northwestern	Wildcats	Big 10	Ricky Byrdsong	Evanston, IL	Purple/White
Northwestern St.	Demons	Southland	J.D. Barnett	Natchitoches, LA	Burnt Orange/Purple
Notre Dame	Fighting Irish	Independent	John MacLeod	South Bend, IN	Gold/Blue
Ohio University	Bobcats	Mid-American	Larry Hunter	Athens, OH	Kelly Green/White
Ohio St.	Buckeyes	Big 10	Randy Ayers	Columbus, OH	Scarlet/Gray
Oklahoma	Sooners	Big 8	Kelvin Sampson	Norman, OK	Crimson/Cream
Oklahoma St.	Cowboys	Big 8	Eddie Sutton	Stillwater, OK	Orange/Black
Old Dominion	Monarchs	Colonial	Jeff Capel	Norfolk, VA	Slate Blue/Silver
Oral Roberts	Golden Eagles	Independent	Bill Self	Tulsa, OK	Navy Blue/Gold
Oregon	Ducks	Pac-10	Jerry Green	Eugene, OR	Green/Yellow
Oregon St.	Beavers	Pac-10	Jim Anderson	Corvallis, OR	Orange/Black
Pacific	Tigers	Big West	Bob Thomason	Stockton, CA	Orange/Black
Pennsylvania	Quakers	Ivy	Fran Dunphy	Philadelphia, PA	Red/Blue
Penn St.	Nittany Lions	Big 10	Bruce Parkhill	University Park, PA	Blue/White
Pepperdine	Waves	West Coast	Tony Fuller	Malibu, CA	Blue/Orange
Pittsburgh	Panthers	Big East	Ralph Willard	Pittsburgh, PA	Gold/Blue
Portland	Pilots	West Coast	Rob Chavez	Portland, OR	Purple/White
Prairie View A&M	Panthers	Southwestern	Elwood Plummer	Prairie View, TX	Purple/Gold
Princeton	Tigers	Ivy	Pete Carril	Princeton, NJ	Orange/Black
Providence	Friars	Big East	Pete Gillen	Providence, RI	Black/White
Purdue	Boilermakers	Big 10	Gene Keady	W. Lafayette, IN	Old Gold/Black
Radford	Highlanders	Big South	Ron Bradley	Radford, VA	Blue/Red/Green
Rhode Island	Rams	Atlantic 10	Al Skinner	Kingston, RI	Blue/White
Rice	Owls	SWC	Willis Wilson	Houston, TX	Blue/Gray
Richmond	Spiders	Colonial	Bill Dooley	Richmond, VA	Red/Blue
Rider	Broncs	Northeast	Kevin Bannon	Lawrenceville, NJ	Cranberry/White
Robert Morris	Colonials	Northeast	Jarrett Durham	Coraopolis, PA	Blue/White
Rutgers	Scarlet Knights	Atlantic 10	Bob Wenzel	New Brunswick, NJ	Scarlet
St. Bonaventure	Bonnies	Atlantic 10	Tom Chapman	St. Bonaventure, NY	Brown/White
St. Francis-NY	Terriers	Northeast	Ron Ganulin	Brooklyn, NY	Red/Blue
St. Francis-PA	Red Flash	Northeast	Jim Baron	Loretto, PA	Red/White
St. John's	Red Storm	Big East	Brian Mahoney	Jamaica, NY	Red/White
St. Joseph's-PA	Hawks	Atlantic 10	John Griffin	Philadelphia, PA	Crimson/Gray
Saint Louis	Billikens	Great Midwest	Charlie Spoonhour	St. Louis, MO	Blue/White
St. Mary's-CA	Gaels	West Coast	Ernie Kent	Moraga, CA	Red/Blue
St. Peter's	Peacocks	Metro Atlantic	Ted Fiore	Jersey City, NJ	Blue/White
Sam Houston St.	Bearkats	Southland	Jerry Hopkins	Huntsville, TX	Orange/White
Samford	Bulldogs	Trans Am	John Brady	Birmingham, AL	Red/Blue
San Diego	Toreros	West Coast	Brad Holland	San Diego, CA	Lt. Blue/Navy/White
San Diego St.	Aztecs	WAC	Fred Trenkle	San Diego, CA	Scarlet/Black
San Francisco	Dons	West Coast	Jim Brovelli	San Francisco, CA	Green/Gold
San Jose St.	Spartans	Big West	Stan Morrison	San Jose, CA	Gold/White/Blue
Santa Clara	Broncos	West Coast	Dick Davey	Santa Clara, CA	Bronco Red/White
Seton Hall	Pirates	Big East	George Blaney	South Orange, NJ	Blue/White
Siena	Saints	Metro Atlantic	Bob Beyer	Loudonville, NY	Green/Gold
South Alabama	Jaguars	Sun Belt	Ronnie Arrow	Mobile, AL	Red/White/Blue
South Carolina	Gamecocks	SEC-East	Eddie Fogler	Columbia, SC	Garnet/Black
South Carolina St.	Bulldogs	Mid-Eastern	Cy Alexander	Orangeburg, SC	Garnet/Blue
South Florida	Bulls	Metro	Bobby Paschal	Tampa, FL	Green/Gold
SE Louisiana	Lions	Trans Am	John Lyles	Hammond, LA	Green/Gold
SE Missouri St.	Indians	Ohio Valley	Ron Shumate	Cape Girardeau, MO	Red/Black

	Nickname	Conference	Head Coach	Location	Colors
Southern Illinois	Salukis	Mo. Valley	Rich Herrin	Carbondale, IL	Maroon/White
SMU	Mustangs	Southwest	John Shumate	Dallas, TX	Red/Blue
Southern Miss.	Golden Eagles	Metro	M.K. Turk	Hattiesburg, MS	Black/Gold
Southern Utah	Thunderbirds	American West	Bill Evans	Cedar City, UT	Scarlet/Royal Blue
Southern-BR	Jaguars	Southwestern	Ben Jobe	Baton Rouge, LA	Blue/Gold
SW Missouri St.	Bears	Mo. Valley	Mark Bernsen	Springfield, MO	Maroon/White
SW Texas St.	Bobcats	Southland	Mike Miller	San Marcos, TX	Maroon/Gold
SW Louisiana	Ragin' Cajuns	Sun Belt	Marty Fletcher	Lafayette, LA	Vermilion/White
Stanford	Cardinal	Pac-10	Mike Montgomery	Stanford, CA	Cardinal/White
S.F. Austin St.	Lumberjacks	Southland	Ned Fowler	Nacogdoches, TX	Purple/White
Stetson	Hatters	Trans Am	Dan Hipsher	DeLand, FL	Green/White
Syracuse	Orangemen	Big East	Jim Boeheim	Syracuse, NY	Orange
Temple	Owls	Atlantic 10	John Chaney	Philadelphia, PA	Cherry/White
Tennessee	Volunteers	SEC-East	Kevin O'Neill	Knoxville, TN	Orange/White
Tenn-Chattanooga	Moccasins	Southern	Mack McCarthy	Chattanooga, TN	Navy Blue/Gold
Tenn-Martin	Pacers	Ohio Valley	Calvin Luther	Martin, TN	Orange/White/Blue
Tennessee St.	Tigers	Ohio Valley	Frankie Allen	Nashville, TN	Blue/White
Tennessee Tech	Golden Eagles	Ohio Valley	Frank Harrell	Cookeville, TN	Purple/Gold
Texas	Longhorns	SWC	Tom Penders	Austin, TX	Burnt Orange/White
Texas A&M	Aggies	SWC	Tony Barone	College Station, TX	Maroon/White
TCU	Horned Frogs	SWC	Billy Tubbs	Ft. Worth, TX	Purple/White
Texas Southern	Tigers	Southwestern	Robert Moreland	Houston, TX	Maroon/Gray
Texas Tech	Red Raiders	SWC	James Dickey	Lubbock, TX	Scarlet/Black
TX-Arlington	Mavericks	Southland	Mark Nixon	Arlington, TX	Royal Blue/White
TX-Pan American	Broncs	Sun Belt	Mark Adams	Edinburg, TX	Green/White
TX-San Antonio	Roadrunners	Southland	Stu Starner	San Antonio, TX	Orange/Navy Blue
Toledo	Rockets	Mid-American	Larry Gipson	Toledo, OH	Blue/Gold
Towson St.	Tigers	Big South	Terry Truax	Towson, MD	Gold/White/Black
Troy St.	Trojans	Mid-Continent	Don Maestri	Troy, AL	Cardinal/Gray/Black
Tulane	Green Wave	Metro	Perry Clark	New Orleans, LA	Olive Green/Sky Blue
Tulsa	Golden Hurricane	Mo. Valley	Tubby Smith	Tulsa, OK	Blue/Red/Gold
UC-Irvine	Anteaters	Big West	Rod Baker	Irvine, CA	Blue/Gold
UCLA	Bruins	Pac-10	Jim Harrick	Los Angeles, CA	Blue/Gold
UC-Santa Barbara	Gauchos	Big West	Jerry Pimm	Santa Barbara, CA	Blue/Gold
UNLV	Runnin' Rebels	Big West	Rollie Massimino	Las Vegas, NV	Scarlet/Gray
USC	Trojans	Pac-10	George Raveling	Los Angeles, CA	Cardinal/Gold
Utah	Utes	WAC	Rick Majerus	Salt Lake City, UT	Crimson/White
Utah St.	Aggies	Big West	Larry Eustachy	Logan, UT	Navy Blue/White
UTEP	Miners	WAC	Don Haskins	El Paso, TX	Orange/White/Blue
Valparaiso	Crusaders	Mid-Continent	Homer Drew	Valparaiso, IN	Brown/Gold
Vanderbilt	Commodores	SEC-East	Jan van Breda Kolff	Nashville, TN	Black/Gold
Vermont	Catamounts	North Atlantic	Tom Brennan	Burlington, VT	Green/Gold
Villanova	Wildcats	Big East	Steve Lappas	Villanova, PA	Blue/White
Virginia	Cavaliers	ACC	Jeff Jones	Charlottesville, VA	Orange/Blue
VCU	Rams	Metro	Sonny Smith	Richmond, VA	Black/Gold
VMI	Keydets	Southern	Bart Bellairs	Lexington, VA	Red/White/Yellow
Virginia Tech	Hokies, Gobblers	Metro	Bill Foster	Blacksburg, VA	Orange/Maroon
Wagner	Seahawks	Northeast	Tim Capstraw	Staten Island, NY	Green/White
Wake Forest	Demon Deacons	ACC	Dave Odom	Winston-Salem, NC	Old Gold/Black
Washington	Huskies	Pac-10	Bob Bender	Seattle, WA	Purple/Gold
Washington St.	Cougars	Pac-10	Kevin Eastman	Pullman, WA	Crimson/Gray
Weber St.	Wildcats	Big Sky	Ron Abegglen	Ogden, UT	Royal Purple/White
West Virginia	Mountaineers	Atlantic 10	Gale Catlett	Morgantown, WV	Old Gold/Blue
Western Carolina	Catamounts	Southern	Benny Dees	Cullowhee, NC	Purple/Gold
Western Illinois	Leathernecks	Mid-Continent	Jim Kerwin	Macomb, IL	Purple/Gold
Western Kentucky	Hilltoppers	Sun Belt	Matt Kilcullen	Bowling Green, KY	Red/White
Western Michigan	Broncos	Mid-American	Bob Donewald	Kalamazoo, MI	Brown/Gold
Wichita St.	Shockers	Mo. Valley	Scott Thompson	Wichita, KS	Yellow/Black
William & Mary	Tribe	Colonial	Charlie Woollum	Williamsburg, VA	Green/Gold/Silver
Winthrop	Eagles	Big South	Dan Kenney	Rock Hill, SC	Garnet/Gold
Wisconsin	Badgers	Big 10	Stu Jackson	Madison, WI	Cardinal/White
WI-Green Bay	Phoenix	Midwestern	Dick Bennett	Green Bay, WI	Green/White/Red
WI-Milwaukee	Panthers	Midwestern	Steve Antrim	Milwaukee, WI	Black/Gold
Wright St.	Raiders	Midwestern	Ralph Underhill	Dayton, OH	Green/Gold
Wyoming	Cowboys	WAC	Joby Wright	Laramie, WY	Brown/Yellow
Xavier	Musketeers	Midwestern	Skip Prosser	Cincinnati, OH	Blue/White
Yale	Bulldogs, Elis	Ivy	Dick Kuchen	New Haven, CT	Yale Blue/White
Youngstown St.	Penguins	Mid-Continent	Dan Peters	Youngstown, OH	Scarlet/White

NCAA Division I-A Football Schools
Conferences and coaches as of Sept. 15, 1994.

Moving up from Division I-AA In 1994: independent NORTHEAST LOUISIANA.
Moving up from Division I-AA in 1995: NORTH TEXAS from Southland Conference.
Changing conference name as of June 30, 1996: Big 8 becomes Big 12.
Breakup of Southwest Conference as of June 30, 1996: to Big 12 (4)— BAYLOR, TEXAS, TEXAS A&M and TEXAS TECH; to Western Athletic Conf. (3)— RICE, SMU and TCU; to Independent— HOUSTON.
Joining Big 12 in 1996 (4): BAYLOR, TEXAS, TEXAS A&M and TEXAS TECH from Southwest Conference.
Joining Western Athletic Conference in 1996 (6): SAN JOSE ST. and UNLV from Big West; RICE, SMU and TCU from Southwest Conference; and independent TULSA.

	Nickname	Conference	Head Coach	Location	Colors
Air Force	Falcons	WAC	Fisher DeBerry	Colo. Springs, CO	Blue/Silver
Akron	Zips	Mid-American	Gerry Faust	Akron, OH	Blue/Gold
Alabama	Crimson Tide	SEC-West	Gene Stallings	Tuscaloosa, AL	Crimson/White
Arizona	Wildcats	Pac-10	Dick Tomey	Tucson, AZ	Cardinal/Navy
Arizona St.	Sun Devils	Pac-10	Bruce Snyder	Tempe, AZ	Maroon/Gold
Arkansas	Razorbacks	SEC-West	Danny Ford	Fayetteville, AR	Cardinal/White
Arkansas St.	Indians	Big West	John Bobo	State Univ., AR	Scarlet/Black
Army	Cadets, Black Knights	Independent	Bob Sutton	West Point, NY	Black/Gold/Gray
Auburn	Tigers	SEC-West	Terry Bowden	Auburn, AL	Orange/Blue
Ball St.	Cardinals	Mid-American	Paul Schudel	Muncie, IN	Cardinal/White
Baylor	Bears	SWC	Chuck Reedy	Waco, TX	Green/Gold
Boston College	Eagles	Big East	Dan Henning	Chestnut Hill, MA	Maroon/Gold
Bowling Green	Falcons	Mid-American	Gary Blackney	Bowling Green, OH	Orange/Brown
BYU	Cougars	WAC	LaVell Edwards	Provo, UT	Royal Blue/White
California	Golden Bears	Pac-10	Keith Gilbertson	Berkeley, CA	Blue/Gold
Central Michigan	Chippewas	Mid-American	Dick Flynn	Mt. Pleasant, MI	Maroon/Gold
Cincinnati	Bearcats	Independent	Rick Minter	Cincinnati, OH	Red/Black
Clemson	Tigers	ACC	Tommy West	Clemson, SC	Purple/Orange
Colorado	Golden Buffaloes	Big 8	Bill McCartney	Boulder, CO	Silver/Gold/Black
Colorado St.	Rams	WAC	Sonny Lubick	Ft. Collins, CO	Green/Gold
Duke	Blue Devils	ACC	Fred Goldsmith	Durham, NC	Royal Blue/White
East Carolina	Pirates	Independent	Steve Logan	Greenville, NC	Purple/Gold
Eastern Michigan	Eagles	Mid-American	Ron Cooper	Ypsilanti, MI	Green/White
Florida	Gators	SEC-East	Steve Spurrier	Gainesville, FL	Orange/Blue
Florida St.	Seminoles	ACC	Bobby Bowden	Tallahassee, FL	Garnet/Gold
Fresno St.	Bulldogs	WAC	Jim Sweeney	Fresno, CA	Cardinal/Blue
Georgia	Bulldogs, 'Dawgs	SEC-East	Ray Goff	Athens, GA	Red/Black
Georgia Tech	Yellow Jackets	ACC	Bill Lewis	Atlanta, GA	Old Gold/White
Hawaii	Rainbow Warriors	WAC	Bob Wagner	Honolulu, HI	Green/White
Houston	Cougars	SWC	Kim Helton	Houston, TX	Scarlet/White
Illinois	Fighting Illini	Big 10	Lou Tepper	Champaign, IL	Orange/Blue
Indiana	Hoosiers	Big 10	Bill Mallory	Bloomington, IN	Cream/Crimson
Iowa	Hawkeyes	Big 10	Hayden Fry	Iowa City, IA	Old Gold/Black
Iowa St.	Cyclones	Big 8	Jim Walden	Ames, IA	Cardinal/Gold
Kansas	Jayhawks	Big 8	Glen Mason	Lawrence, KS	Crimson/Blue
Kansas St.	Wildcats	Big 8	Bill Snyder	Manhattan, KS	Purple/White
Kent	Golden Flashes	Mid-American	Jim Corrigall	Kent, OH	Navy Blue/Gold
Kentucky	Wildcats	SEC-East	Bill Curry	Lexington, KY	Blue/White
LSU	Fighting Tigers	SEC-West	Curley Hallman	Baton Rouge, LA	Purple/Gold
Louisiana Tech	Bulldogs	Big West	Joe Raymond Peace	Ruston, LA	Red/Blue
Louisville	Cardinals	Independent	H. Schnellenberger	Louisville, KY	Red/Black/White
Maryland	Terrapins, Terps	ACC	Mark Duffner	College Park, MD	Red/White/Black/Gold
Memphis	Tigers	Independent	Chuck Stobart	Memphis, TN	Blue/Gray
Miami-FL	Hurricanes	Big East	Dennis Erickson	Miami, FL	Orange/Green/White
Miami-OH	Redskins	Mid-American	Randy Walker	Oxford, OH	Red/White
Michigan	Wolverines	Big 10	Gary Moeller	Ann Arbor, MI	Maize/Blue
Michigan St.	Spartans	Big 10	George Perles	E. Lansing, MI	Green/White
Minnesota	Golden Gophers	Big 10	Jim Wacker	Minneapolis, MN	Maroon/Gold
Mississippi	Ole Miss, Rebels	SEC-West	Joe Lee Dunn	Oxford, MS	Cardinal/Navy Blue
Mississippi St.	Bulldogs	SEC-West	Jackie Sherrill	Starkville, MS	Maroon/White
Missouri	Tigers	Big 8	Larry Smith	Columbia, MO	Old Gold/Black
Navy	Midshipmen	Independent	George Chaump	Annapolis, MD	Navy Blue/Gold
Nebraska	Cornhuskers	Big 8	Tom Osborne	Lincoln, NE	Scarlet/Cream
Nevada	Wolf Pack	Big West	Chris Ault	Reno, NV	Silver/Blue
New Mexico	Lobos	WAC	Dennis Franchione	Albuquerque, NM	Cherry/Silver

	Nickname	Conference	Head Coach	Location	Colors
New Mexico St.	Aggies	Big West	Jim Hess	Las Cruces, NM	Crimson/White
North Carolina	Tar Heels	ACC	Mack Brown	Chapel Hill, NC	Carolina Blue/White
North Carolina St.	Wolfpack	ACC	Mike O'Cain	Raleigh, NC	Red/White
NE Louisiana	Indians	Independent	Ed Zaunbrecher	Monroe, LA	Maroon/Gold
Northern Illinois	Huskies	Big West	Charlie Sadler	De Kalb, IL	Cardinal/Black
Northwestern	Wildcats	Big 10	Gary Barnett	Evanston, IL	Purple/White
Notre Dame	Fighting Irish	Independent	Lou Holtz	South Bend, IN	Gold/Blue
Ohio University	Bobcats	Mid-American	Tom Lichtenberg	Athens, OH	Kelly Green/White
Ohio St.	Buckeyes	Big 10	John Cooper	Columbus, OH	Scarlet/Gray
Oklahoma	Sooners	Big 8	Gary Gibbs	Norman, OK	Crimson/Cream
Oklahoma St.	Cowboys	Big 8	Pat Jones	Stillwater, OK	Orange/Black
Oregon	Ducks	Pac-10	Rich Brooks	Eugene, OR	Green/Yellow
Oregon St.	Beavers	Pac-10	Jerry Pettibone	Corvallis, OR	Orange/Black
Pacific	Tigers	Big West	Chuck Shelton	Stockton, CA	Orange/Black
Penn St.	Nittany Lions	Big 10	Joe Paterno	University Park, PA	Blue/White
Pittsburgh	Panthers	Big East	Johnny Majors	Pittsburgh, PA	Blue/Gold
Purdue	Boilermakers	Big 10	Jim Colletto	W. Lafayette, IN	Old Gold/Black
Rice	Owls	SWC	Ken Hatfield	Houston, TX	Blue/Gray
Rutgers	Scarlet Knights	Big East	Doug Graber	New Brunswick, NJ	Scarlet
San Diego St.	Aztecs	WAC	Ted Tollner	San Diego, CA	Scarlet/Black
San Jose St.	Spartans	Big West	John Ralston	San Jose, CA	Gold/White/Blue
South Carolina	Gamecocks	SEC-East	Brad Scott	Columbia, SC	Garnet/Black
SMU	Mustangs	SWC	Tom Rossley	Dallas, TX	Red/Blue
Southern Miss.	Golden Eagles	Independent	Jeff Bower	Hattiesburg, MS	Black/Gold
SW Louisiana	Ragin' Cajuns	Big West	Nelson Stokley	Lafayette, LA	Vermilion/White
Stanford	Cardinal	Pac-10	Bill Walsh	Stanford, CA	Cardinal/White
Syracuse	Orangemen	Big East	Paul Pasqualoni	Syracuse, NY	Orange
Temple	Owls	Big East	Ron Dickerson	Philadelphia, PA	Cherry/White
Tennessee	Volunteers	SEC-East	Phillip Fulmer	Knoxville, TN	Orange/White
Texas	Longhorns	SWC	John Mackovic	Austin, TX	Burnt Orange/White
Texas A&M	Aggies	SWC	R.C. Slocum	College Station, TX	Maroon/White
TCU	Horned Frogs	SWC	Pat Sullivan	Ft. Worth, TX	Purple/White
Texas Tech	Red Raiders	SWC	Spike Dykes	Lubbock, TX	Scarlet/Black
Toledo	Rockets	Mid-American	Gary Pinkel	Toledo, OH	Blue/Gold
Tulane	Green Wave	Independent	Buddy Teevens	New Orleans, LA	Olive Green/Sky Blue
Tulsa	Golden Hurricane	Independent	Dave Rader	Tulsa, OK	Blue/Gold
UCLA	Bruins	Pac-10	Terry Donahue	Los Angeles, CA	Blue/Gold
UNLV	Runnin' Rebels	Big West	Jeff Horton	Las Vegas, NV	Scarlet/Gray
USC	Trojans	Pac-10	John Robinson	Los Angeles, CA	Cardinal/Gold
Utah	Utes	WAC	Ron McBride	Salt Lake City, UT	Crimson/White
Utah St.	Aggies	Big West	Charlie Weatherbie	Logan, UT	Navy Blue/White
UTEP	Miners	WAC	David Lee	El Paso, TX	Orange/White/Blue
Vanderbilt	Commodores	SEC-East	Gerry DiNardo	Nashville, TN	Black/Gold
Virginia	Cavaliers	ACC	George Welsh	Charlottesville, VA	Orange/Blue
Virginia Tech	Hokies, Gobblers	Big East	Frank Beamer	Blacksburg, VA	Orange/Maroon
Wake Forest	Demon Deacons	ACC	Jim Caldwell	Winston-Salem, NC	Old Gold/Black
Washington	Huskies	Pac-10	Jim Lambright	Seattle, WA	Purple/Gold
Washington St.	Cougars	Pac-10	Mike Price	Pullman, WA	Crimson/Gray
West Virginia	Mountaineers	Big East	Don Nehlen	Morgantown, WV	Old Gold/Blue
Western Michigan	Broncos	Mid-American	Al Molde	Kalamazoo, MI	Brown/Gold
Wisconsin	Badgers	Big 10	Barry Alvarez	Madison, WI	Cardinal/White
Wyoming	Cowboys	WAC	Joe Tiller	Laramie, WY	Brown/Yellow

New Conference Alignments for 1996

When the Southwest Athletic Conference ceases operation on June 30, 1996, four of its members (Baylor, Texas, Texas A&M and Texas Tech) will join the Big Eight, three (Rice, SMU and TCU) will join the Western Athletic Conference and one (Houston) will become an independent. Two current Big West schools (San Jose St. and UNLV) will also join the WAC in '96. The new Big Twelve and WAC will realign as follows:

BIG TWELVE		WESTERN ATHLETIC CONFERENCE			
North	South	Quad 1	Quad 2	Quad 3	Quad 4
Colorado	Baylor	Rice	Air Force	BYU	Fresno St.
Iowa St.	Oklahoma	SMU	Colorado St.	New Mexico	Hawaii
Kansas	Oklahoma St.	TCU	UNLV	Utah	San Diego St.
Kansas St.	Texas	Tulsa	Wyoming	UTEP	San Jose St.
Missouri	Texas A&M				
Nebraska	Texas Tech				

NCAA Division I-AA Football Schools

Conferences and coaches as of Sept. 15, 1994.

Div. I-AA independents joining conference in 1994 (2): DUQUESNE and MARIST to Metro Atlantic.
Division II teams moving up to Division I-AA in 1994 (2): CAL POLY ST. LUIS OBISPO to American West; independent MONMOUTH (N.J.).
New Division I-AA program starting in 1994: independent ROBERT MORRIS.

	Nickname	Conference	Head Coach	Location	Colors
Ala-Birmingham	Blazers	Independent	Jim Hilyer	Birmingham, AL	Green/Gold
Alabama St.	Hornets	Southwestern	Houston Markham	Montgomery, AL	Black/Gold
Alcorn St.	Braves	Southwestern	Cardell Jones	Lorman, MS	Purple/Gold
Appalachian St.	Mountaineers	Southern	Jerry Moore	Boone, NC	Black/Gold
Austin Peay St.	Governors	Ohio Valley	Roy Gregory	Clarksville, TN	Red/White
Bethune-Cookman	Wildcats	Mid-Eastern	Jack McClairen	Daytona Beach, FL	Maroon/Gold
Boise St.	Broncos	Big Sky	Pokey Allen	Boise, ID	Orange/Blue
Boston University	Terriers	Yankee	Dan Allen	Boston, MA	Scarlet/White
Brown	Bears	Ivy	Mark Whipple	Providence, RI	Brown/Red/White
Bucknell	Bison	Patriot	Lou Maranzana	Lewisburg, PA	Orange/Blue
Buffalo	Bulls	Independent	Jim Ward	Buffalo, NY	Blue/Red/White
Butler	Bulldogs	Pioneer	Ken LaRose	Indianapolis, IN	Blue/White
CS-Northridge	Matadors	American West	Bob Burt	Northridge, CA	Red/Black/White
CS-Sacramento	Hornets	American West	Mike Clemons	Sacramento, CA	Green/Gold
Cal Poly SLO	Mustangs	American West	Andre Patterson	San Luis Obispo, CA	Green/Gold
Canisius	Golden Griffins	Metro Atlantic	Barry Mynter	Buffalo, NY	Blue/Gold
Central Conn. St.	Blue Devils	Independent	Sal Cintorino	New Britain, CT	Blue/White
Central Florida	Golden Knights	Independent	Gene McDowell	Orlando, FL	Black/Gold
Charleston So.	Buccaneers	Independent	David Dowd	Charleston, SC	Blue/Gold
The Citadel	Bulldogs	Southern	Charlie Taaffe	Charleston, SC	Blue/White
Colgate	Red Raiders	Patriot	Mike Foley	Hamilton, NY	Maroon/White
Columbia	Lions	Ivy	Ray Tellier	New York, NY	Lt. Blue/White
Connecticut	Huskies	Yankee	Skip Holtz	Storrs, CT	Blue/White
Cornell	Big Red	Ivy	Jim Hofher	Ithaca, NY	Red/White
Dartmouth	Big Green	Ivy	John Lyons	Hanover, NH	Green/White
Davidson	Wildcats	Independent	Tim Landis	Davidson, NC	Red/Black
Dayton	Flyers	Pioneer	Mike Kelly	Dayton, OH	Red/Blue
Delaware	Blue Hens	Yankee	Tubby Raymond	Newark, DE	Blue/Gold
Delaware St.	Hornets	Mid-Eastern	Bill Collick	Dover, DE	Red/Blue
Drake	Bulldogs	Pioneer	Rob Ash	Des Moines, IA	Blue/White
Duquesne	Dukes	Metro Atl.('94)	Greg Gattuso	Pittsburgh, PA	Red/Blue
East Tenn. St.	Buccaneers	Southern	Mike Cavan	Johnson City, TN	Blue/Gold
Eastern Illinois	Panthers	Gateway	Bob Spoo	Charleston, IL	Blue/Gray
Eastern Kentucky	Colonels	Ohio Valley	Roy Kidd	Richmond, KY	Maroon/White
Eastern Wash.	Eagles	Big Sky	Dick Zornes	Cheney, WA	Red/White
Evansville	Aces	Pioneer	Robin Cooper	Evansville, IN	Purple/White
Florida A&M	Rattlers	Mid-Eastern	Billy Joe	Tallahassee, FL	Orange/Green
Fordham	Rams	Patriot	Nick Quartaro	New York, NY	Maroon/White
Furman	Paladins	Southern	Bobby Johnson	Greenville, SC	Purple/White
Georgetown	Hoyas	Metro Atlantic	Bob Benson	Washington, DC	Blue/Gray
Georgia Southern	Eagles	Southern	Tim Stowers	Statesboro, GA	Blue/White
Grambling St.	Tigers	Southwestern	Eddie Robinson	Grambling, LA	Black/Gold
Harvard	Crimson	Ivy	Tim Murphy	Cambridge, MA	Crimson/Black/White
Hofstra	Flying Dutchmen	Independent	Joe Gardi	Hempstead, NY	Blue/White/Gold
Holy Cross	Crusaders	Patriot	Peter Vaas	Worcester, MA	Royal Purple
Howard	Bison	Mid-Eastern	Steve Wilson	Washington, DC	Blue/White
Idaho	Vandals	Big Sky	John L. Smith	Moscow, ID	Silver/Gold
Idaho St.	Bengals	Big Sky	Brian McNeely	Pocatello, ID	Orange/Black
Illinois St.	Redbirds	Gateway	Jim Heacock	Normal, IL	Red/White
Indiana St.	Sycamores	Gateway	Dennis Raetz	Terre Haute, IN	Blue/White
Iona	Gaels	Metro Atlantic	Harold Crocker	New Rochelle, NY	Maroon/Gold
Jackson St.	Tigers	Southwestern	James Carson	Jackson, MS	Blue/White
James Madison	Dukes	Yankee	Rip Scherer	Harrisonburg, VA	Purple/Gold
Lafayette	Leopards	Patriot	Bill Russo	Easton, PA	Maroon/White
Lehigh	Engineers	Patriot	Kevin Higgins	Bethlehem, PA	Brown/White
Liberty	Flames	Independent	Sam Rutigliano	Lynchburg, VA	Red/White/Blue
Maine	Black Bears	Yankee	Kirk Ferentz	Orono, ME	Blue/White
Marist	Red Foxes	Metro Atlantic	Jim Parady	Poughkeepsie, NY	Red/White
Marshall	Thundering Herd	Southern	Jim Donnan	Huntington, WV	Green/White

	Nickname	Conference	Head Coach	Location	Colors
Massachusetts	Minutemen	Yankee	Mike Hodges	Amherst, MA	Maroon/White
McNeese St.	Cowboys	Southland	Bobby Keasler	Lake Charles, LA	Blue/Gold
Middle Tenn. St.	Blue Raiders	Ohio Valley	Boots Donnelly	Murfreesboro, TN	Blue/White
Miss. Valley St.	Delta Devils	Southwestern	Larry Dorsey	Itta Bena, MS	Green/White
Monmouth	Hawks	Independent	Kevin Callahan	W. Long Branch, NJ	Royal Blue/White
Montana	Grizzlies	Big Sky	Don Read	Missoula, MT	Copper/Silver/Gold
Montana St.	Bobcats	Big Sky	Cliff Hysell	Bozeman, MT	Blue/Gold
Morehead St.	Eagles	Ohio Valley	Matt Ballard	Morehead, KY	Blue/Gold
Morgan St.	Bears	Mid-Eastern	Ricky Diggs	Baltimore, MD	Blue/Orange
Murray St.	Racers	Ohio Valley	Mike Mahoney	Murray, KY	Blue/Gold
New Hampshire	Wildcats	Yankee	Bill Bowes	Durham, NH	Blue/White
Nicholls St.	Colonels	Southland	Phil Greco	Thibodaux, LA	Red/Gray
North Carolina A&T	Aggies	Mid-Eastern	Bill Hayes	Greensboro, NC	Blue/Gold
North Texas	Mean Green, Eagles	Southland	Matt Simon	Denton, TX	Green/White
Northeastern	Huskies	Yankee	Barry Gallup	Boston, MA	Red/Black
Northern Ariz.	Lumberjacks	Big Sky	Steve Axman	Flagstaff, AZ	Blue/Gold
Northern Iowa	Panthers	Gateway	Terry Allen	Cedar Falls, IA	Purple/Old Gold
Northwestern St.	Demons	Southland	Sam Goodwin	Natchitoches, LA	Purple/White
Pennsylvania	Quakers	Ivy	Al Bagnoli	Philadelphia, PA	Red/Blue
Prairie View A&M	Panthers	Southwestern	Ron Beard	Prairie View, TX	Purple/Gold
Princeton	Tigers	Ivy	Steve Tosches	Princeton, NJ	Orange/Black
Rhode Island	Rams	Yankee	Bob Griffin	Kingston, RI	Blue/White
Richmond	Spiders	Yankee	Jim Marshall	Richmond, VA	Red/Blue
Robert Morris	Colonials	Independent	Joe Walton	Coraopolis, PA	Blue/White
St. Francis-PA	Red Flash	Independent	Frank Pergolizzi	Loretto, PA	Red/White
St. John's-NY	Red Storm	Metro Atlantic	Bob Ricca	Jamaica, NY	Red/White
St. Mary's-CA	Gaels	Independent	Mike Rasmussen	Moraga, CA	Red/Blue
St. Peter's	Peacocks	Metro Atlantic	Mark Collins	Jersey City, NJ	Blue/White
Sam Houston St.	Bearkats	Southland	Ron Randleman	Huntsville, TX	Orange/White/Blue
Samford	Bulldogs	Independent	Pete Hurt	Birmingham, AL	Crimson/Blue
San Diego	Toreros	Pioneer	Brian Fogarty	San Diego, CA	Lt. Blue/Navy/White
Siena	Saints	Metro Atlantic	Jack DuBois	Loudonville, NY	Green/Gold
South Carolina St.	Bulldogs	Mid-Eastern	Willie Jeffries	Orangeburg, SC	Garnet/Blue
SE Missouri St.	Indians	Ohio Valley	John Mumford	Cape Girardeau, MO	Red/Black
Southern-BR	Jaguars	Southwestern	Marino Casem	Baton Rouge, LA	Blue/Gold
Southern Illinois	Salukis	Gateway	Shawn Watson	Carbondale, IL	Maroon/White
Southern Utah	Thunderbirds	American West	Jack Bishop	Cedar City, UT	Scarlet/Blue/White
SW Missouri St.	Bears	Gateway	Jesse Branch	Springfield, MO	Maroon/White
SW Texas St.	Bobcats	Southland	Jim Bob Helduser	San Marcos, TX	Maroon/Gold
S.F. Austin St.	Lumberjacks	Southland	John Pearce	Nacogdoches, TX	Purple/White
Tenn-Chattanooga	Moccasins	Southern	Buddy Green	Chattanooga, TN	Navy Blue/Gold
Tenn-Martin	Pacers	Ohio Valley	Don McLeary	Martin, TN	Orange/White/Blue
Tennessee St.	Tigers	Ohio Valley	Joe Gilliam Sr.	Nashville, TN	Blue/White
Tennessee Tech	Golden Eagles	Ohio Valley	Jim Ragland	Cookeville, TN	Purple/Gold
Texas Southern	Tigers	Southwestern	Bill Thomas	Houston, TX	Maroon/Gray
Towson St.	Tigers	Independent	Gordy Combs	Towson, MD	Gold/White
Troy St.	Trojans	Independent	Larry Blakeney	Troy, AL	Cardinal/Gray/Black
Valparaiso	Crusaders	Pioneer	Tom Horne	Valparaiso, IN	Brown/Gold
Villanova	Wildcats	Yankee	Andy Talley	Villanova, PA	Blue/White
VMI	Keydets	Southern	Bill Stewart	Lexington, VA	Red/White/Yellow
Wagner	Seahawks	Independent	Walt Hameline	Staten Island, NY	Green/White
Weber St.	Wildcats	Big Sky	Dave Arslanian	Ogden, UT	Royal Purple/White
Western Carolina	Catamounts	Southern	Steve Hodgin	Cullowhee, NC	Purple/Gold
Western Illinois	Leathernecks	Gateway	Randy Ball	Macomb, IL	Purple/Gold
Western Kentucky	Hilltoppers	Independent	Jack Harbaugh	Bowling Green, KY	Red/White
William & Mary	Tribe	Yankee	Jimmye Laycock	Williamsburg, VA	Green/Gold
Yale	Bulldogs, Elis	Ivy	Carmen Cozza	New Haven, CT	Yale Blue/White
Youngstown St.	Penguins	Independent	Jim Tressel	Youngstown, OH	Scarlet/White

---

Native American Nicknames Down to 11

The Marquette *Warriors* and St. John's *Redmen* passed into college nickname history this past spring. It's now the Marquette *Golden Eagles* and St. John's *Red Storm*. That reduced the number of Native American nickname variations to 11 in Division I basketball and football: INDIANS (3)— Arkansas St., Northeast Louisiana and Southeast Missouri St; BRAVES (2)— Alcorn St. and Bradley; CHIPPEWAS— Central Michigan; FIGHTING ILLINI— Illinois; MOCCASINS— Tennessee-Chattanooga; REDSKINS— Miami of Ohio; SEMINOLES— Florida St.; and TRIBE— William & Mary.

Coaching Changes

New head coaches were named at 51 Division I basketball schools after the 1993-94 season while 14 Division I-A football schools changed head coaches following the 1993 season. Coaching changes listed below are as of Sept. 15, 1994.

Division I Basketball

	Old Coach	Record	Why Left?	New Coach	Old Job
Ark-Little Rock	Jim Platt	13-15	Reassigned	Wimp Sanderson	ex-Coach, Alabama
Auburn	Tommy Joe Eagles	11-17	Resigned	Cliff Ellis	Coach, Clemson
Boston Univ.	Bob Brown	11-16	Fired	Dennis Wolff	Ast., Virginia
Bucknell	Charlie Woollum	10-17	to Wm. & Mary*	Pat Flannery	Coach, Leb. Valley
CS-Fullerton	Brad Holland	8-19	to San Diego*	Bob Hawking	Ast., CS-Fullerton
Chicago St.	Rick Pryor	4-23	Fired	Craig Hodges	ex-NBA player
Clemson	Cliff Ellis	18-16	Resigned	Rick Barnes	Coach, Providence
Coast Carolina	Russ Bergman	6-20	Resigned	Michael Hopkins	Ast., Appalach. St.
Creighton	Rick Johnson	7-22	Resigned	Dana Altman	Coach, Kansas St.
Dayton	Jim O'Brien	6-21	Fired	Oliver Purnell	Coach, Old Dominion
Furman	Butch Estes	10-18	Resigned	Joe Cantafio	Coach, VMI
Georgia St.	Bob Reinhart	13-14	Fired	Carter Wilson	Ast., Georgia St.
Hofstra	B. van Breda Kolff	9-20	Retired	Jay Wright	Ast., UNLV
Holy Cross	George Blaney	14-14	to Seton Hall*	Bill Raynor	Ast., Holy Cross
Howard	Butch Beard	10-17	to NBA Nets*	TBA	—
Indiana St.	Tates Locke	4-22	Fired	Sherman Dillard	Ast., Georgia Tech
Iowa St.	Johnny Orr	14-13	Retired	Tim Floyd	Coach, New Orleans
Jacksonville	Matt Kilcullen	17-11	to Western Ky.*	George Scholtz	ex-Coach, Fla. So.
Kansas St.	Dana Altman	20-14	to Creighton*	Tom Asbury	Coach, Pepperdine
Louisiana Tech	Jerry Loyd	2-25	Resigned	Jim Wooldridge	Coach, SW Texas St.
Loyola-IL	Will Rey	8-19	Resigned	Ken Burmeister	Ast., DePaul
Loyola-MD	Skip Prosser	17-13	to Xavier-OH*	Brian Ellerbe	Ast., Virginia
Marquette	Kevin O'Neill	24-9	to Tennessee*	Mike Deane	Coach, Siena
Marshall	Dwight Freeman	9-18	Resigned	Billy Donovan	Ast., Kentucky
MD-East Shore	Rob Chavez	16-12	to Portland*	Jeff Menday	Ast., MD-E. Shore
McNeese St.	Steve Welch	11-16	Resigned	Ron Everhart	Ast., Tulane

* as head coach

NCAA Division I Schools on Probation

As of Sept. 15, 1994, there were 29 Division I member institutions serving NCAA probations.

School	Sport	Yrs	Penalty To End	School	Sport	Yrs	Penalty To End
SE Louisiana	Basketball	5	10/2/94	South Carolina St	Tennis	2	7/20/95
Lock Haven	Wrestling	2	10/6/94		& M/W Track	2	7/20/95
Syracuse	Basketball	2	10/8/94	Jackson St	W. Track	3	7/28/95
	W. Basketball	2	10/8/94		& W. X-country	3	7/28/95
	Football	2	10/8/94	Texas-Pan Am	W. Basketball	3	8/20/95
	Lacrosse	2	10/8/94	Virginia Tech	M/W X-country	2	11/10/95
	& Wrestling	2	10/8/94	Auburn	Basketball	4	11/22/95
UTEP	Basketball	3	10/30/94		Tennis	4	11/22/95
Lamar	W. Basketball	2	11/21/94		& Football	4	11/22/95
Buffalo	Basketball	1	11/30/94	Pittsburgh	Football	2	11/23/95
Clemson	Basketball	2	12/9/94		& Basketball	2	11/23/95
Louisiana Tech	Basketball	1	4/12/95	New Mexico	X-country	3	12/7/95
Wake Forest	Basketball	1	4/15/95		Track	3	12/7/95
Virginia	Football	2	5/6/95		& W. Gym	3	12/7/95
Kansas St.	M/W Track	0	5/31/95	Oklahoma St.	Wrestling	3	1/5/96
	& M/W X-country	0	5/31/95	Tulsa	All sports	3	1/8/96
Idaho St.	Football	1	6/4/95	Wisconsin	Wrestling	2	1/12/96
Ohio St.	Basketball	1	6/4/95	Washington	Football	2	6/5/96
	& M/W Track	1	6/4/95	Ball St.	Basketball	2	6/3/96
Colorado College	Ice Hockey	1	6/10/95	Nevada-Las Vegas	Basketball	3	11/9/96
Washington St	Baseball	3	6/21/95	Texas A&M	Football	5	1/6/99
	X-country	3	6/21/95				
	& Track	3	6/21/95				

Remaining postseason and TV sanctions

No 1994 football postseason: Auburn, Texas A&M and Washington.

Football TV restrictions: Texas A&M (no games on TV in 1994); Washington (maximum of 4 games on TV in either 1994 or '95).

Basketball TV restrictions: UNLV (no regular season nonconference away games on TV in 1994-95).

Kansas St.

Oklahoma

Duke

Harvard

Tom Asbury
Pepperdine to Wildcats

Kelvin Sampson
Wash. St. to Sooners

Fred Goldsmith
Rice to Blue Devils

Tim Murphy
Cincinnati to Crimson

	Old Coach	Record	Why Left?	New Coach	Old Job
Morgan St.	Michael Holmes	8-21	Fired	Lynn Ramage	Ast., Morgan St.
New Orleans	Tim Floyd	20-10	to Iowa St.*	Tic Price	Ast., Auburn
N. Carolina A&T	Jeff Capel	16-14	to Old Dominion*	Roy Thomas	Coach, Tyler JC
NC-Wilmington	Kevin Eastman	18-10	to Wash. St.*	Jerry Wainwright	Ast., Wake Forest
Northeastern	Karl Fogel	5-22	Reassigned	Dave Leitao	Ast., UConn
Northwestern St.	Dan Bell	11-15	Resigned	J.D. Barnett	Coach, Tulsa (90-91)
Northern Ariz.	Harold Merritt	13-13	Resigned	Ben Howland	Ast., UC-S. Barbara
Oklahoma	Billy Tubbs	15-13	to TCU*	Kelvin Sampson	Coach, Wash. St.
Old Dominion	Oliver Purnell	21-10	to Dayton*	Jeff Capel	Coach, N.C. A&T
Pepperdine	Tom Asbury	19-11	to Kansas St.*	Tony Fuller	Coach, S. Diego St.
Pittsburgh	Paul Evans	13-14	Fired	Ralph Willard	Coach, Western Ky.
Portland	Larry Steele	13-17	Fired	Rob Chavez	Coach, MD-E.Shore
Providence	Rick Barnes	20-10	to Clemson*	Pete Gillen	Coach, Xavier-OH
San Diego	Hank Egan	18-11	to NBA Spurs†	Brad Holland	Coach, CS-Fullerton
San Diego St.	Tony Fuller	12-16	to Pepperdine*	Fred Trenkle	Coach, So. Idaho JC
Seton Hall	P.J. Carlesimo	17-13	to NBA Blazers*	George Blaney	Coach, Holy Cross
Siena	Mike Deane	25-8	to Marquette*	Bob Beyer	Ast., Wisconsin
SE Louisiana	Norm Picou	10-17	to Southern-BR†	John Lyles	Ast., SW La.
SW Texas St.	Jim Wooldridge	25-7	to La. Tech*	Mike Miller	Ast., SW Texas St.
Tennessee	Wade Houston	5-22	Resigned	Kevin O'Neill	Coach, Marquette
TCU	Moe Iba	7-20	Fired	Billy Tubbs	Coach, Oklahoma
VMI	Joe Cantafio	5-23	to Furman*	Bart Bellairs	Ast., J. Madison
Washington St.	Kelvin Sampson	20-11	to Oklahoma*	Kevin Eastman	Coach, NC-Wilmington
Western Ky.	Ralph Willard	20-11	to Pittsburgh*	Matt Kilcullen	Coach, Jacksonville
William & Mary	Chuck Swenson	4-23	Fired	Charlie Woollum	Coach, Bucknell
Wisconsin	Stu Jackson	18-11	to NBA Vanc. #	Stan Van Gundy	Ast., Wisconsin
Xavier-OH	Pete Gillen	22-8	to Providence*	Skip Prosser	Coach, Loyola-MD

*as head coach; #as general manager; †as assistant coach.
Note: New Orleans coach Tic Price replaced Tommy Joe Eagles, who died July 30, 1994.

Division I-A Football

	Old Coach	Record	Why Left?	New Coach	Old Job
Boston College	Tom Coughlin	9-3-0	to NFL Jaguars*	Dan Henning	Ast., NFL Lions
Central Mich.	Herb Deromedi	5-6-0	to Ath. Dir.	Dick Flynn	Ast., CMU
Cincinnati	Tim Murphy	8-3-0	to Harvard*	Rick Minter	Ast., Notre Dame
Clemson	Ken Hatfield	9-3-0	Resigned	Tommy West	Coach, Tenn-Chatt.
Duke	Barry Wilson	3-8-0	Resigned	Fred Goldsmith	Coach, Rice
Kent	Pete Cordelli	0-11-0	Fired	Jim Corrigall	Ast., Kent
Mississippi	Billy Brewer	5-6-0	Fired	Joe Lee Dunn	Ast., Mississippi
Missouri	Bob Stull	3-7-1	Fired	Larry Smith	ex-Coach, USC
Nevada	Jeff Horton	7-4-0	to UNLV*	Chris Ault	ex-Coach, Nevada
NE Louisiana	Dave Roberts	9-3-0	to Notre Dame†	Ed Zaunbrecher	Ast., Mich. St.
Rice	Fred Goldsmith	6-5-0	to Duke*	Ken Hatfield	Coach, Clemson
San Diego St.	Al Luginbill	6-6-0	Fired	Ted Tollner	Ast., NFL Rams
South Carolina	Sparky Woods	4-7-0	Fired	Brad Scott	Ast., Florida St.
UNLV	Jim Strong	3-8-0	Fired	Jeff Horton	Coach, Nevada

*as head coach; †as an assistant coach.

1993-94 Directors' Cup

Officially, the Sears Directors' Cup is sponsored by the National Association of Collegiate Directors of Athletics. Introduced in 1993-94 to honor the nation's best overall Division I athletic department (combining men's and women's sports).

Standings computed by NACDA with points awarded for each school's finish in 22 sports (10 core sports and one wild card sport for men and 10 core sports and one wild card for women). National champions in each sport get 64 points, runners-up get 63, etc., through tournament field. Division I-A football points based on final *USA Today*/CNN Coaches Top 25 poll. Listed below are team conferences, Final Four finishes (1st thru 4th place) for men's and women's programs and overall points.

		Men	Women				Men	Women	
	Conf	1-2-3-4	1-2-3-4	Pts		Conf	1-2-3-4	1-2-3-4	Pts
1 North Carolina	ACC	0-0-0-0	2-1-0-0	806½	14 Minnesota	Big 10	0-0-1-0	0-0-0-0	553
2 Stanford	Pac-10	3-1-0-1	1-1-1-0	786½	15 Alabama	SEC	0-0-0-0	0-2-1-0	552½
3 UCLA	Pac-10	0-1-1-0	0-0-2-0	779½	16 Clemson	ACC	0-0-0-0	0-0-0-0	546½
4 Florida	SEC	0-0-2-1	0-0-2-0	768	17 California	Pac-10	0-0-1-0	0-0-1-0	534½
5 Penn St	Big 10	1-0-1-0	0-1-1-0	756	18 Nebraska	Big 8	1-0-1-0	0-0-0-0	524½
6 Arizona	Pac-10	0-0-1-0	1-0-0-0	710	19 Virginia	ACC	1-1-0-0	0-0-1-0	513
7 Texas	SWC	0-2-0-0	0-2-1-1	697½	20 Oklahoma	Big 8	1-0-0-1	0-0-0-0	499
8 USC	Pac-10	1-1-0-0	0-1-0-0	677	21 Georgia	SEC	0-0-0-0	1-0-1-0	495½
9 Michigan	Big 10	0-0-1-0	0-0-0-0	656	22 BYU	WAC	0-1-0-0	0-0-1-0	488
10 Arizona St	Pac-10	0-0-1-0	1-0-0-0	603	23 Ohio St	Big 10	0-0-1-0	0-0-0-0	483½
11 Notre Dame	Indep.	0-1-0-0	0-0-0-0	595	24 Texas A&M	SWC	0-0-0-0	0-0-0-0	454½
12 Wisconsin	Big 10	0-0-0-0	0-0-0-0	565	25 Florida St	ACC	1-0-0-0	0-0-0-0	454
13 Tennessee	SEC	0-1-0-0	0-0-0-0	560					

Men's and Women's Athletic Programs

Unofficial ranking of Top 25 NCAA Division I men's and women's athletic programs in 1993-94, according to performances in 10 leading sports (based on participation). Points based on 20 for a national championship, 19 for runner-up, etc. Determining factors as follows:

Men's rankings— Cross-country (NCAA meet); Football (final AP postseason Top 25); Soccer (NCAA Final Four and final Soccer America regular season Top 20); Basketball (NCAA Final 16 and final AP regular season Top 25); Swimming (NCAA meet); Wrestling (NCAA meet); Baseball (College World Series Final Eight and final postseason Baseball America Top 25); Golf (NCAA meet); Tennis (NCAA Final Four and final ITA Top 20); and Outdoor Track (NCAA meet).

Women's rankings— Cross-country (NCAA meet); Field Hockey (NCAA Final Four and final NCAA regular season Top 20); Soccer (NCAA Final Four and final ISAA regular season Top 20); Volleyball (NCAA Final Four and final AVCA regular season Top 20); Basketball (NCAA Final 16 and final AP regular season Top 25); Swimming (NCAA meet); Golf (NCAA meet); Softball (NCAA Final Eight and final NCAA regular season Top 25); Tennis (NCAA Final Four and final ITA Top 20); and Outdoor Track (NCAA meet).

MEN

	Conf.	Cross-country	Football	Soccer	Basketball	Swimming	Wrestling	Baseball	Golf	Tennis	Outdoor Track	TOTAL
1 Florida	SEC	0	16	0	17½	13	0	0	18	12½	7½	84½
2 Arkansas	SEC	20	0	0	20	½	0	0	17	0	20	77½
3 Stanford	Pac-10	0	0	0	0	20	0	6	20	19	0	65
4 Clemson	ACC	0	0	11	0	0	14	17	11½	0	10	63½
5 Tennessee	SEC	3	9	0	0	12	0	13	0	8	18	63
6 Auburn	SEC	0	17	0	0	17	0	8	13½	6½	0	62
7 Michigan	Big 10	11	0	0	14½	18	16	0	0	0	0	59½
8 Texas	SWC	0	0	0	0	19	0	7	19	14	0	59
9 UCLA	Pac-10	0	3	15	3	9	0	0	0	17½	9	56½
10 USC	Pac-10	0	0	0	0	15	0	10	0	20	11	56
11 Oklahoma St.	Big 8	5	0	0	1	0	20	12	16	0	0	54
12 Georgia Tech	ACC	0	0	0	0	0	0	19	15	0	17	51
13 North Carolina	ACC	0	0	5	12	0	15	0	10	1½	0	45½
14 Arizona St.	Pac-10	0	0	0	0	7	12½	16	11½	0	0	47
15 Penn St	Big 10	7	13	8	0	18	0	0	0	0	0	46
16 Duke	ACC	0	0	13	19	0	0	0	0	12½	0	44½
17 Arizona	Pac-10	0	11	0	17½	8	0	0	7	0	0	43½
18 Florida St	ACC	0	20	0	0	0	0	14	5	0	0	39
Notre Dame	Indep.	16	19	0	0	0	0	1	0	3	0	39
20 Oklahoma	Big 8	0	4	0	0	0	12½	20	0	0	0	36½
21 CS-Fullerton	Big West	0	0	17½	0	0	0	18	0	0	0	35½
22 Iowa St	Big 8	18	0	0	0	0	11	0	0	0	5½	34½
23 Georgia	SEC	0	0	0	0	5	0	0	0	16	13	34
24 Miami-FL	Big East	0	6	0	0	3	0	15	0	9	0	33
25 Fresno St	WAC	0	0	0	0	0	9½	0	0	4	0	16	29½

WOMEN

	Conf.	Field Hockey	Soccer	Cross-country	Volleyball	Swimming	Basketball	Tennis	Golf	Softball	Outdoor Track	TOTAL
1 Stanford	Pac-10	10	0	17½	13	14½	20	14	0	19	3	111
2 UCLA	Pac-10	0	0	0	16	0	14	15	17	12	18	92
3 Texas	SWC	0	0	0	15	0	19	16	0	17½	19	86½
4 North Carolina	ACC	0	19	20	0	20	0	5	0	0	14 ½	7½
5 Penn St.	Big 10	14	17½	0	19	1 ½	0	0	0	0	0	65
6 Arizona St	Pac-10	0	0	0	10	0	8	20	0	11	10 ½	59½
7 Duke	ACC	0	14	12	1	0	0	17	0	15	0	59
8 Florida	SEC	0	0	0	17½	1	18	6	0	16	0	58½
9 USC	Pac-10	0	0	0	7	14½	15	19	0	2	0	57½
10 Alabama	SEC	7½	0	0	0	17½	12	0	0	0	9	46
11 Arizona	Pac-10	9	0	0	5	0	11	0	20	1	0	46
12 Tennessee	SEC	0	0	0	0	12	7	8	0	0	16	43
13 Villanova	Big East	20	0	0	0	0	0	0	0	0	17	37
14 Connecticut	Big East	0	9	10	0	14½	0	0	0	0	0	33½
15 UMass	Atlantic 10	0	15	17½	0	0	0	0	0	0	0	32½

Others in Top 25 standings: 16. Notre Dame (32 pts); 17. Colorado (29½ pts); 18. BYU, California and Oklahoma St. (29 pts); 21. Georgia and Michigan (28 pts); 23. George Mason, SMU and Virginia (26 pts).

1993-94 NCAA Team Champions

Arkansas and Stanford each won four national team championships in 1993-94, the most of any NCAA schools. The Razorbacks repeated as men's champions in cross-country, indoor track and outdoor track and captured their first-ever men's basketball title. The track teams were led by senior Erick Walder, who became the first athlete since Arkansas alum Mike Conley to sweep the long jump and triple jump titles at the NCAA indoor and outdoor meets in the same year. Walder ended his collegiate career with 10 individual national titles, six indoors and four outside.

Stanford, a four-time national champion in 1992-93, once again ruled the waves in men's and women's swimming while replacing lost titles in men's gymnastics and women's volleyball with new honors in water polo and men's golf. Trenton State of New Jersey was the only other school with as many as three championships, winning Division III women's titles in soccer, lacrosse and softball.

Eleven schools won two championships: DIVISION I— LSU (women's indoor and outdoor track), North Carolina (women's soccer and basketball), Princeton (men's and women's lacrosse); DIVISION II— Abilene Christian (men's and women's indoor track), Adams State (men's and women's cross-country), Oakland (men's and women's swimming); DIVISION III— Cortland State (women's cross-country and field hockey), Kenyon (men's and women's swimming), North Central-IL (men's cross-country and outdoor track), UC-San Diego (men's soccer and women's tennis), Wisconsin-Oshkosh (women's indoor track and men's baseball).

FALL

(*) indicates defending champions; total NCAA titles in parentheses.

Cross Country

MEN

Div.	Winner		Runner-Up	Score
I	Arkansas*	(7)	BYU	31-153
II	Adams St., CO*	(2)	Edinboro	25-103
III	North Central, IL*	(9)	WI-La Crosse	32-123

WOMEN

Div.	Winner		Runner-Up	Score
I	Villanova*	(5)	Arkansas	66-71
II	Adams St., CO*	(2)	Cal Poly SLO	75-106
III	Cortland St., NY*	(4)	Calvin	61-93

Field Hockey

Div.	Winner		Runner-Up	Score
I	Maryland	(2)	N. Carolina 2-1	(2OT)†
II	Bloomsburg, PA	(2)	Lock Haven 2-1	(2OT)†
III	Cortland St., NY	(4)	Mary Washington	1-0†

†decided on penalty strokes.

Football

Div.	Winner		Runner-Up	Score
I-A	Florida St.	(1)	Notre Dame	AP poll
I-AA	Youngstown St.	(2)	Marshall	17-5
II	North Alabama	(1)	Indiana-PA	41-34
III	Mount Union, OH	(1)	Rowan	34-24

Note: There is no official NCAA Div. I-A playoff.

Soccer

MEN

Div.	Winner		Runner-Up	Score
I	Virginia*	(4)	South Carolina	2-0
II	Seattle Pacific	(5)	Southern Conn St.	1-0
III	UC-San Diego	(3)	Williams	1-0

WOMEN

Div.	Winner		Runner-Up	Score
I	North Carolina*	(11)	Stanford	6-0
II	Barry, FL*	(3)	Cal Poly SLO	2-0
III	Trenton St.	(1)	Plymouth St.	4-0

Volleyball

WOMEN

Div.	Winner		Runner-Up	Score
I	Long Beach St.	(2)	Penn St.	4 sets
II	Northern Mich.	(1)	CS-Bakersfield	4 sets
III	Washington, MO*	(4)	Juniata	3 sets

Water Polo

Div.	Winner		Runner-Up	Score
National	Stanford	(7)	USC	11-9

1993-94 NCAA Team Champions (Cont.)

(*) indicates defending champions; total NCAA titles in parentheses.

WINTER

Basketball

MEN

Div.	Winner		Runner-Up	Score
I	Arkansas	(1)	Duke	76-72
II	CS-Bakersfield*	(2)	Southern Ind.	92-86
III	Lebanon Valley, PA	(1)	NYU	66-59 (OT)

WOMEN

Div.	Winner		Runner-Up	Score
I	North Carolina	(1)	Louisiana Tech	60-59
II	North Dakota St.*	(3)	CS-St. B'dino	89-56
III	Capital, OH.	(1)	Washington-MO	82-63

Fencing

Div.	Winner		Runner-Up	Score
Combined	Notre Dame	(1)	Penn St.	4350-4075

Gymnastics

Div.	Winner		Runner-Up	Score
Men	Nebraska	(8)	Stanford	by 2.325
Women	Utah	(8)	Alabama	by 0.050

Ice Hockey

Div.	Winner		Runner-Up	Score
I	Lake Superior St.	(3)	Boston Univ.	9-1
II	Bemidji St., MN*	(3)	AL-Huntsville	2-1 (OT)
III	WI-River Falls	(2)	WI-Superior	6-4

Rifle

Div.	Winner		Runner-Up	Score
Combined	AK-Fairbanks	(1)	West Va.*	6194-6187

Skiing

Div.	Winner		Runner-Up	Score
Combined	Vermont	(5)	Utah	688-667

Swimming & Diving

MEN

Div.	Winner		Runner-Up	Score
I	Stanford*	(7)	Texas	566-445
II	Oakland, MI	(2)	CS-B'field	791-718
III	Kenyon, OH*	(15)	UC-S.Diego	615-389

WOMEN

Div.	Winner		Runner-Up	Score
I	Stanford*	(5)	Texas	512-421
II	Oakland, MI*	(5)	Air Force	630-454
III	Kenyon, OH*	(11)	Hope	595-408

Indoor Track

MEN

Div.	Winner		Runner-Up	Score
I	Arkansas*	(11)	Tennessee	94-40
II	Abilene Christian*	(3)	St. Augustine's	99-54
III	WI-La Crosse	(6)	NE-Wesleyan	50-42

WOMEN

Div.	Winner		Runner-Up	Score
I	LSU*	(5)	Alabama	48-29
II	Abilene Christian*	(6)	Norfolk St.	78-42
III	WI-Oshkosh	(1)	Chris. Newport	41-36

Wrestling

Div.	Winner		Runner-Up	Score
I	Oklahoma St.	(30)	Iowa	94½—76¾
II	Central Oklahoma*	(3)	Mankato St.	127½—65¼
III	Ithaca, NY	(3)	Wartburg	77½—75¾

SPRING

Baseball

Div.	Winner		Runner-Up	Score
I	Oklahoma	(2)	Georgia Tech	13-5
II	Central Mo. St.	(1)	Fla. Southern	14-9
III	WI-Oshkosh	(2)	Wesleyan-CT	6-2

Golf

Div.	Winner		Runner-Up	Score
I	Stanford	(7)	Texas	1129-1133
II	Columbus, GA	(5)	North Fla.	1175-1179
III	Methodist, NC	(4)	UC-S.Diego	1177-1201

Lacrosse

MEN

Div.	Winner		Runner-Up	Score
I	Princeton	(2)	Virginia	9-8 (OT)
II	Springfield, MA	(1)	New York Tech	15-12
III	Salisbury St., MD	(1)	Hobart	15-9

WOMEN

Div.	Winner		Runner-Up	Score
I	Princeton	(1)	Maryland	10-7
III	Trenton St., NJ*	(6)	William Smith	29-11

Softball

Div.	Winner		Runner-Up	Score
I	Arizona*	(3)	CS-Northridge	4-0
II	Merrimack, MA	(1)	Humboldt St.	6-2
III	Trenton St., NJ	(5)	Bridgewater St.	6-5

Tennis

MEN

Div.	Winner		Runner-Up	Score
I	USC*	(15)	Stanford	4-3
II	Lander, SC*	(2)	Hampton	5-3
III	Washington, MD	(1)	Claremont-M-S	5-4

WOMEN

Div.	Winner		Runner-Up	Score
I	Georgia	(1)	Stanford	5-4
II	North Florida	(1)	Cal Poly Pomona	6-0
III	UC-San Diego	(4)	Williams	7-2

Outdoor Track

MEN

Div.	Winner		Runner-Up	Score
I	Arkansas*	(4)	UTEP	83-45
II	St. Augustine's NC*	(6)	Abilene Chrst.	118-117
III	North Central, IL	(2)	WI-La Crosse	75-74

WOMEN

Div.	Winner		Runner-Up	Score
I	LSU*	(8)	Texas	86-43
II	Alabama A&M*	(3)	Abilene Chrst.	117-81½
III	Chris. Newport, VA	(5)	WI-Oshkosh	73-53

Volleyball

MEN

Div.	Winner		Runner-Up	Score
National	Penn St.	(1)	UCLA	5 sets

Villanova
Carole Zajac
Women's Cross-country

Penn St.
Tom Strzalkowski
Fencing

Kentucky
Jenny Hansen
Women's Gymnastics

Oklahoma St.
Pat Smith
Wrestling

1993-94 Division I Individual Champions

FALL
Cross-country

Men (10,000 meters)	Time
1 Josephat Kapkory, Washington St.	29:32.4
2 Jason Bunston, Arkansas	29:40.2
3 Niall Bruton, Arkansas	29:43.6

Women (5,000 meters)	Time
1 Carole Zajac, Villanova	16:40.3
2 Jennifer Rhines, Villanova	16:44.4
3 Kay Gooch, Oklahoma	16:47.7

WINTER
Fencing
MEN

Event		Record
Sabre	Thomas Strzalkowski, Penn St.	14-2
Foil	Kwame van Leeuwen, Harvard	16-0
Epee	Harald Winkmann, Princeton	14-2

WOMEN

Event		Record
Foil	Olga Kalinovskaya, Penn St.	16-0

Gymnastics
MEN

Event		Points
All-Around	Dennis Harrison, Nebraska	58.200
Horizonal Bar	Jim Foody, UCLA	9.450
Parallel Bars	Richard Grace, Nebraska	9.575
Pommel Horse	Jason Bertram, Calif.	9.550
Rings	Chris LaMorte, New Mex.	9.900
Vault	Steve McCain, UCLA	9.675
Floor Exercise	Mark Booth, Stanford	9.300

WOMEN

Event		Points
All-Around	Jenny Hansen, Kentucky	39.450
Uneven Bars (tie)	Lori Strong, Georgia	9.950
	Sandy Woolsey, Utah	9.950
	& Beth Wymer, Michigan	9.950
Balance Beam	Jenny Hansen, Kentucky	9.975
Vault	Jenny Hansen, Kentucky	9.9375
Floor Exercise	Hope Spivey-Sheeley, Georgia	10.000

Rifle
COMBINED
Smallbore

	Pts
1 Cory Brunetti, AK-Fairbanks	1,173
2 Jean Foster, West Virginia	1,173
3 Tim Myers, AK-Fairbanks	1,168

Note: Brunetti won on inner tens (78-75).

Air Rifle

	Pts
1 Nancy Napolski, Kentucky	391
2 Robin Orth, Air Force	389
3 Jason Parker, Xavier-OH	388

Skiing
MEN

Event		Time
Slalom	Louis-Francois Gagnon, Utah	1:36.23
Giant Slalom	Erik Roland, Denver	2:13.55
10-k Classical	Harvard Solbakken, Utah	30:39.2
20-k Freestyle	Niklas Skoglund, New Mex.	52:37.0

WOMEN

Event		Time
Slalom	Gibson Lafountaine, Vermont	1:36.77
Giant Slalom	Christl Hager, Utah	2:07.06
5-k Classical	Mina Turvo, Ak-Anchorage	15:38.8
15-k Freestyle	Nina Hamilton, Vermont	46:20.1

Wrestling

Wgt	Champion	Runner-Up
108	Sam Henson, Clemson	Eric Akin, Iowa St.
126	David Hirsch, Cornell	Jody Staylor, ODU
134	T.J. Jaworsky, UNC	Babak Mohammadi, Ore.St.
142	Alan Fried, Okla. St.	Gerry Abas, Fresno St.
150	Lincoln McIlravy, Iowa	Brian Harper, Michigan
158	Pat Smith, Okla. St.	Sean Bormet, Michigan
167	Mark Branch, Okla. St.	Laszlo Molnar, CS-Full.
177	Dean Morrison, West Va.	Reese Andy, Wyoming
190	Joel Sharratt, Iowa	Andy Foster, Oklahoma
Hvy	Kerry McCoy, Penn St.	Justin Greenlee, No. Iowa

Arizona
Chad Carvin
Men's Swimming

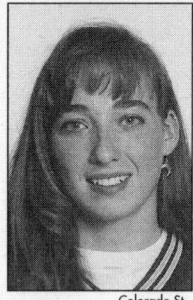
Colorado St.
Amy Van Dyken
Women's Swimming

Arizona St.
Emilee Klein
Women's Golf

Agence Shot
Erick Walder
Men's Track and Field

Swimming & Diving

(*) indicates meet record; (†) is U.S. Open record.

MEN

Event (yards)		Time
50 free	Brian Retterer, Stanford	19.45
100 free	Gustavo Borges, Michigan	42.46
200 free	Gustavo Borges, Michigan	1:34.31
500 free	Chad Carvin, Arizona	4:11.59†
1650 free	Chad Carvin, Arizona	14:34.91†
100 back	Brian Retterer, Stanford	46.07
200 back	Derek Weatherford, Stanford	1:42.18
100 breast	Tyler Mayfield, Stanford	53.73
200 breast	Kurt Grote, Stanford	1:56.79
100 butterfly	Rafal Szukala, Iowa	47.43
200 butterfly	Ugur Taner, Calif.	1:44.54
200 IM	Greg Burgess, Florida	1:43.66
400 IM	Greg Burgess, Florida	3:40.64*
200 free relay	Stanford	1:16.93*
400 free relay	Texas	2:51.07*
800 free relay	Michigan	6:21.99
200 medley relay	Stanford	1:26.17
400 medley relay	Stanford	3:09.97

Diving		Points
1-meter	Chemi Gil, Miami-FL	562.50
3-meter	Evan Stewart, Tennessee	614.65
Platform	Brian Early, USC	817.90

WOMEN

Event (yards)		Time
50 free	Amy Van Dyken, Colorado St.	21.77†
100 free	Jenny Thompson, Stanford	47.74
200 free	Nicole Haislett, Florida	1:44.51
500 free	Nicole Haislett, Florida	4:43.36
1650 free	Tobie Smith, Texas	16:07.26
100 back	Lea Loveless, Stanford	53.51
200 back	Whitney Hedgepeth, Texas	1:53.05
100 breast	Beata Kaszuba, Ariz. St.	1:00.46*
200 breast	Kristine Quance, USC	2:10.69*
100 butterfly	Jenny Thompson, Stanford	51.81
200 butterfly	Berit Puggaard, SMU	1:57.99
200 IM	Kristine Quance, USC	1:58.89
400 IM	Kristine Quance, USC	4:08.71
200 free relay	Stanford	1:30.53
400 free relay	Stanford	3:15.80
800 free relay	USC	7:11.89
200 medley relay	Auburn	1:40.12
400 medley relay	Florida	3:37.76

Diving		Points
1-meter	Vanessa Thelin, BYU	449.80
3-meter	Robin Carter, Texas	522.10
Platform	Susie Ryan, LSU	584.65

Indoor Track

(*) indicates meet record.

MEN

Event		Time
55 meters	Greg Saddler, Mississippi	6.11
200 meters	Chris Nelloms, Ohio St.	20.60
400 meters	Calvin Davis, Arkansas	46.18
800 meters	Jose Parrilla, Tennessee	1:47.77
Mile	Niall Bruton, Arkansas	3:59.34
3000 meters	Josephat Kapkory, Wash. St.	7:50.90*
5000 meters	Jason Bunston, Arkansas	13:48.07
55-m hurdles	Robert Foster, Fresno St.	7.11
4x400-m relay	Texas A&M	3:06.51
Distance medley relay	Arkansas	9:30.07*

Event		Distance
High Jump	Randy Jenkins, Tennessee	7-7
Pole Vault	Lawrence Johnson, Tennessee	19-1½*
Long Jump	Erick Walder, Arkansas	27-8
Triple Jump	Erick Walder, Arkansas	56-6¾
Shut Put	John Godina, UCLA	65-8¾
35-lb Throw	Ron Willis, S. Carolina	71-11

WOMEN

Event		Time
55 meters	Holli Hyche, Indiana St.	6.70
200 meters	Holli Hyche, Indiana St.	22.90*
400 meters	Flirtisha Harris, Seton Hall	52.11
800 meters	Amy Wickus, Wisconsin	2:02.05*
Mile	Amy Randolph, Providence	4:37.64
3000 meters	Kay Gooch, Oklahoma	8:58.85
5000 meters	Brenda Sleeuwenhoek, Arizona	16:46.54
55-m hurdles	Dionne Rose, M. Tenn. St.	7.60
4x400-m relay	Seton Hall	3:34.69
Distance medley relay	Michigan	11:08.60

Event		Distance
High Jump	Amy Acuff, UCLA	6-2¼
Long Jump	Daphnie Saunders, LSU	22-1*
Triple Jump	Telisa Young, Texas	43-3¾
Shut Put	Eileen Vanisi, Texas	58-1¾

SPRING
Golf
MEN

	Total
1 Justin Leonard, Texas	71-68-63-69—271
2 Alan Bratton, Okla. St	70-67-66-76—276
3 William Yanagisawa, Stanford	72-71-70-64—277
& Mark Swygert, Clemson	70-72-65-70—277

WOMEN

	Total
1 Emilee Klein, Arizona St	69-73-70-74—286
2 Wendy Ward, Arizona St	72-68-74-74—288
3 Caroline Peek, Furman	68-73-73-76—290

Tennis

MEN

Singles— Mark Merklein (Florida) def. Wayne Black (USC), 6-2,6-7 (8-10), 6-4.

Doubles— Laurent Miquelard & Joe Simmons (Miss. St.) def. Wayne Black & Jon Leach (USC), 7-6 (7-5), 2-6, 6-3.

WOMEN

Singles— Angela Lettiere (Georgia) def. Keri Phebus (UCLA), 7-6 (6-4), 6-2.

Doubles— Rebecca Jensen & Nora Koves (Kansas) def. Marie-Laure Bougnol & Pascale Piquemal (Mississippi), 6-4, 7-5.

Outdoor Track

(*) indicates meet record.

MEN

Event		Time
100 meters	Sam Jefferson, Houston	10.12
200 meters	Andrew Tynes, UTEP	20.20
400 meters	Derek Mills, Ga. Tech	45.06
800 meters	Jose Parrilla, Tennessee	1:46.01
1500 meters	Graham Hood, Arkansas	3:42.10
5000 meters	Brian Baker, Arkansas	14:22.09
10,000 meters	Teddy Mitchell, Arkansas	29:39.54
110-m hurdles	Robert Foster, Fresno St.	13.53
400-m hurdles	Octavius Terry, Ga. Tech	49.85
3000-m steeple	Jim Svenoy, UTEP	8:41.22
4x100-m relay	LSU	38.91
4x400-m relay	Georgia Tech	3:01.75

Event		Distance
High Jump	Randy Jenkins, Tennessee	7-7
Pole Vault	Nick Hysong, Arizona St.	18-8¼
Long Jump	Erick Walder, Arkansas	27-4½
Triple Jump	Erick Walder, Arkansas	55-5¾
Shut Put	Brent Noon, Georgia	67-9¾
Discus	John Godina, UCLA	198-5
Hammer	Balazs Kiss, USC	245-6
Javelin	Todd Reich, Fresno St.	266-9*
Decathlon	Enoch Borozinski, Nevada	7870 pts

WOMEN

Event		Time
100 meters	Holli Hyche, Indiana St.	11.23
200 meters	Merlene Frazer, Texas	22.49
400 meters	Flirtisha Harris, Seton Hall	51.65
800 meters	Inez Turner, SW Texas St.	2:01.50
1500 meters	Amy Rudolph, Providence	4:17.99
3000 meters	Karen Hecox, UCLA	9:22.63
5000 meters	Jennifer Rhines, Villanova	16:21.60
10,000 meters	Carole Zajak, Villanova	33:32.36
100-m hurdles	Gillian Russell, Miami-FL	12.97
400-m hurdles	Debbie Parris, LSU	55.54
4x100-m relay	LSU	43.26
4x400-m relay	Seton Hall	3:31.42

Event		Distance
High Jump	Gai Kapernick, LSU	6-2¼
Long Jump	Dedra Davis, Tennessee	22-5¾
Triple Jump	Nicola Martial, Nebraska	44-11¾
Shut Put	Eileen Vanisi, Texas	58-2½
Discus	Danyel Mitchell, LSU	193-10
Javelin	Valerie Tulloch, Rice	187-7
Heptathlon	Diane Guthrie, George Mason	6032 pts

Most Outstanding Players

(*) indicates won individual or all-around NCAA championship; (†) high-point winner in NCAA track meet. There were no official Outstanding Players in the men's and women's combined sports of fencing, riflery and skiing.

MEN

Baseball	Chip Glass, Oklahoma
Basketball	Corliss Williamson, Arkansas
Cross-country	Josephat Kapkory, Wash. St.*
Golf	Justin Leonard, Texas*
Gymnastics	Dennis Harrison, Nebraska*
Ice Hockey	Sean Tallaire, Lake Superior St.
Lacrosse	Scott Bacigalupo, Princeton
Soccer: Offense	Nate Friends, Virginia
Defense	Brian Bates, Virginia
Swimming & Diving	Chad Carvin, Arizona
Tennis	Mark Merklein, Florida*
Track (Indoor)	Erick Walder, Arkansas†
(Outdoor)	Erick Walder, Arkansas†
Volleyball	Ramon Hernandez, Penn St.
Water Polo	Larry Bercutt, Stanford and Uzi Hadar, USC
Wrestling	Pat Smith, Okla. St.

WOMEN

Basketball	Charlotte Smith, N. Carolina
Cross-country	Carole Zajak, Villanova*
Field Hockey	No award
Golf	Emilee Klein, Arizona St.*
Gymnastics	Jenny Hansen, Kentucky*
Lacrosse	No award
Soccer: Offense	Mia Hamm, North Carolina
Defense	Skye Eddy, George Mason
Softball	No award
Swimming & Diving	Amy Van Dyken, Colorado St.
Tennis	Angela Lettiere, Georgia*
Track (Indoor)	Flirtisha Harris, Seton Hall†
(Outdoor)	Holli Hyche, Indiana St.†
Volleyball	No award

1993-94 NAIA Team Champions

FALL

Cross Country: MEN'S— Lubbock Christian, TX (4); WOMEN'S— Puget Sound, WA (2). **Football:** MEN'S— Division I: East Central, OK (1) and Division II: Pacific Lutheran, WA (3). **Soccer:** MEN'S— Sangamon St., IL (3); WOMEN'S— Berry, GA (3). **Volleyball:** WOMEN'S— Puget Sound, WA (1).

WINTER

Basketball: MEN'S— Division I: Oklahoma City (3) and Division II: Eureka, IL (1); WOMEN'S— Division I: Southern Nazarene, OK (2) and Division II: Northern St., SD (2). **Swimming & Diving:** MEN'S— Drury, MO (10); WOMEN'S— Drury, MO (3). **Indoor Track:** MEN'S— Central St., OH (2); WOMEN'S— Wayland Baptist, TX (3). **Wrestling:** MEN'S (tie)— Southern Oregon (3) and Western Montana (1).

SPRING

Baseball: MEN'S— Kennesaw St., GA (1). **Golf:** MEN'S— Huntingdon, AL (6); WOMEN'S— Hardin-Simmons, TX (1). **Softball:** WOMEN'S— Oklahoma City (1). **Tennis:** MEN'S— Texas-Tyler (2); WOMEN'S— Mobile, AL (1). **Outdoor Track:** MEN'S— Azusa Pacific, CA (10); WOMEN'S— Central St., OH (4).

Annual NCAA Division I Team Champions

Men's and Women's NCAA Division I team champions from Cross-country to Wrestling. Rowing is included, although the NCAA does not sanction championships in the sport. Team champions in baseball, basketball, football, golf, ice hockey, soccer and tennis can be found in the appropriate chapters throughout the almanac.

CROSS-COUNTRY

Men

Paced by the 2-3-8 finish of Jason Bunston, Niall Bruton and Teddy Mitchell, Arkansas became only the second school to ever win four straight team titles, tying the mark set by UTEP from 1978-81. In all, the Razorbacks had five runners in the Top 25 and outpointed runner-up BYU, 31-153. Washington State's Josephat Kapkory won the individual title, covering the 10,000-meter course in 29:32.4. Bunston was next at 29:40.2. (*Bethlehem, Pa.; Nov. 22, 1993.*)

Multiple winners: Michigan St. (8); Arkansas and UTEP (7); Oregon and Villanova (4); Drake, Indiana, Penn St. and Wisconsin (3); San Jose St. and Western Michigan (2).

Year		Year		Year		Year		Year	
1938	Indiana	1949	Michigan St.	1960	Houston	1972	Tennessee	1984	Arkansas
1939	Michigan St.	1950	Penn St.	1961	Oregon St.	1973	Oregon	1985	Wisconsin
1940	Indiana	1951	Syracuse	1962	San Jose St.	1974	Oregon	1986	Arkansas
1941	Rhode Island	1952	Michigan St.	1963	San Jose St.	1975	UTEP	1987	Arkansas
1942	Indiana	1953	Kansas	1964	Western Mich.	1976	UTEP	1988	Wisconsin
	& Penn St.	1954	Oklahoma St.	1965	Western Mich.	1977	Oregon	1989	Iowa St.
1943	Not held	1955	Michigan St.	1966	Villanova	1978	UTEP		
1944	Drake	1956	Michigan St.	1967	Villanova	1979	UTEP	1990	Arkansas
1945	Drake	1957	Notre Dame	1968	Villanova	1980	UTEP	1991	Arkansas
1946	Drake	1958	Michigan St.	1969	UTEP	1981	UTEP	1992	Arkansas
1947	Penn St.	1959	Michigan St.	1970	Villanova	1982	Wisconsin	1993	Arkansas
1948	Michigan St.			1971	Oregon	1983	Vacated		

Women

With Carole Zajac outrunning the field for the second year in a row, Villanova was able to sweep the individual and team championships for the fifth straight year. Zajac (16:40.3) and Jennifer Rhines (16:44.4) led the way with a 1-2 finish across the 5,000-meter course, enabling the Wildcats to beat out second place Arkansas, 66-71. Zajac and former teammate Sonia O'Sullivan are the only repeat individual champs. (*Bethlehem, Pa.; Nov. 22, 1993.*)

Multiple winners: Villanova (5); Oregon, Virginia and Wisconsin (2).

Year		Year		Year		Year		Year	
1981	Virginia	1984	Wisconsin	1987	Oregon	1990	Villanova	1992	Villanova
1982	Virginia	1985	Wisconsin	1988	Kentucky	1991	Villanova	1993	Villanova
1983	Oregon	1986	Texas	1989	Villanova				

FENCING

Men & Women

Notre Dame rallied on the final day of competition to overcome a 275-point Penn State lead and win its first title since the men's and women's championships were combined in 1990. In team competition, the Irish won the men's foil, placed second in the men's epee, third in the women's foil and fourth in the men's sabre. Individually, Thomas Strzalkowski of Penn State won the men's sabre for the third straight year, while teammate Olga Kalinovskaya repeated as women's foil champion. (*Waltham, Mass.; Mar. 18-22, 1994.*)

Multiple winners: Columbia/Barnard and Penn St. (2). **Note:** Prior to 1990, men and women held separate championships. Men's multiple winners included: NYU (12); Columbia (11); Wayne St. (7); Navy, Notre Dame and Penn (3); Illinois (2). Women's multiple winners included: Wayne St. (3); Yale (2).

Year		Year		Year		Year		Year	
1990	Penn St.	1991	Penn St.	1992	Columbia/ Barnard	1993	Columbia/ Barnard	1994	Notre Dame

FIELD HOCKEY

Women

Maryland shut out Iowa, 1-0, in the semifinals and defeated ACC rival North Carolina, 2-1, on penalty strokes in the final to win its first national title since 1987. After 100 minutes of playing time ended in a 1-1 tie, the Terrapins scored three times on penalty strokes while goaltender Irene Horvat blanked UNC. (*Piscataway, N.J.; Nov. 20-21, 1993.*)

Multiple winners: Old Dominion (7); Connecticut and Maryland (2).

Year		Year		Year		Year		Year	
1981	Connecticut	1984	Old Dominion	1987	Maryland	1990	Old Dominion	1992	Old Dominion
1982	Old Dominion	1985	Connecticut	1988	Old Dominion	1991	Old Dominion	1993	Maryland
1983	Old Dominion	1986	Iowa	1989	North Carolina				

GYMNASTICS

Men

After consecutive second place finishes behind Stanford in both 1992 and '93, hometown Nebraska edged the Cardinal by a 288.250 to 285.925 score to win its eighth national title since 1980. The Cornhuskers were led by individual champions Dennis Harrison in the all-around and Richard Grace on the parallel bars. Ohio State finished third for the third consecutive year. (*Lincoln, Neb.; Apr. 22-23, 1994.*)

Multiple winners: Illinois and Penn St. (9); Nebraska (8); So. Illinois (4); Iowa St. and Oklahoma (3); California, Florida St., Michigan, Stanford and UCLA (2).

Year		Year		Year		Year		Year	
1938	Chicago	1954	Penn St.	1965	Penn St.	1975	California	1986	Arizona St.
1939	Illinois	1955	Illinois	1966	So.Illinois	1976	Penn St.	1987	UCLA
1940	Illinois	1956	Illinois	1967	So.Illinois	1977	Indiana St.	1988	Nebrasksa
1941	Illinois	1957	Penn St.	1968	California		& Oklahoma	1989	Illinois
1942	Illinois	1958	Michigan St.	1969	Iowa	1978	Oklahoma	1990	Nebraska
1943-47 Not held			& Illinois		& Michigan (T)	1979	Nebraska	1991	Oklahoma
1948	Penn St.	1959	Penn St.	1970	Michigan	1980	Nebraska	1992	Stanford
1949	Temple	1960	Penn St.		& Michigan (T)	1981	Nebraska	1993	Stanford
1950	Illinois	1961	Penn St.	1971	Iowa St.	1982	Nebraska	1994	Nebraska
1951	Florida St.	1962	USC	1972	So.Illinois	1983	Nebraska		
1952	Florida St.	1963	Michigan	1973	Iowa St.	1984	UCLA		
1953	Penn St.	1964	So. Illinois	1974	Iowa St.	1985	Ohio St.		

(T) indicates won trampoline competition (1969 and '70).

Women

Like the Nebraska men, the Utah women hosted the national championships and won their eighth national team title, edging Alabama, 196.400 to 196.350. 'Bama also placed second in 1993. Kentucky sophomore Jenny Hansen was the meet's individual star, successfully defending her all-around crown and adding titles in the vault and balance beam. Georgia's Hope Spivey-Sheeley turned in the meet's only perfect score with a 10.000 in the floor exercise. (*Salt Lake City; Apr. 21-23, 1994.*)

Multiple winners: Utah (8); Georgia (3); Alabama (2).

Year		Year		Year		Year		Year	
1982	Utah	1985	Utah	1988	Alabama	1991	Alabama	1993	Georgia
1983	Utah	1986	Utah	1989	Georgia	1992	Utah	1994	Utah
1984	Utah	1987	Georgia	1990	Utah				

LACROSSE

Men

Princeton won its second national title in three years when Kevin Lowe scored 42 seconds into overtime to defeat Virginia, 9-8. Scott Conklin (4 goals) and Scott Reinhardt (3 goals) led the way for the Tigers on offense while goalkeeper Scott Bacigalupo (14 saves in final) was named the tournament's Most Outstanding Player. Princeton beat Brown (10-7) and Virginia downed defending NCAA champ Syracuse (15-14) in the semifinals. (*College Park, Md.; May 28-30, 1994.*)

Multiple winners: Johns Hopkins (7); Syracuse (5) ; North Carolina (4); Cornell (3); Maryland and Princeton (2).

Year		Year		Year		Year		Year	
1971	Cornell	1976	Cornell	1981	North Carolina	1986	North Carolina	1991	North Carolina
1972	Virginia	1977	Cornell	1982	North Carolina	1987	Johns Hopkins	1992	Princeton
1973	Maryland	1978	Johns Hopkins	1983	Syracuse	1988	Syracuse	1993	Syracuse
1974	Johns Hopkins	1979	Johns Hopkins	1984	Johns Hopkins	1989	Syracuse	1994	Princeton
1975	Maryland	1980	Johns Hopkins	1985	Johns Hopkins	1990	Syracuse		

Women

After barely defeating Virginia, 14-13, in the semifinals, Princeton rallied from behind to upset Maryland, 10-7, in the championship game for its first national title. (A week later, Princeton would win the men's title on the same Byrd Stadium field.) Jenny Bristow, Casey Coleman, Janice Petrella and Lisa Rebane each scored twice for the Tigers, who trailed the Terrapins, 5-3 early in the first half. (*College Park, Md.; May 21-22, 1994.*)

Multiple winners: Maryland, Penn St., Temple and Virginia (2).

Year		Year		Year		Year		Year	
1982	Massachusetts	1985	New Hampshire	1988	Temple	1991	Virginia	1993	Virginia
1983	Delaware	1986	Maryland	1989	Penn St.	1992	Maryland	1994	Princeton
1984	Temple	1987	Penn St.	1990	Harvard				

Annual NCAA Division I Team Champions (Cont.)

RIFLE

Men & Women

Alaska-Fairbanks, which had finished second to West Virginia three years running, finally outshot the Mountaineers, 6,194 points to 6,187 to win its first national title. West Virginia, a nine-time champion, had won six straight titles since 1988. The Nanooks' Cory Brunetti won the individual smallbore championship, while Nancy Napolski of Kentucky won the air rifle competition. (*Murray, Ky.; Mar. 10-12, 1994.*)

Multiple winners: West Virginia (9); Tennessee Tech (3); Murray St. (2).

Year		Year		Year		Year		Year	
1980	Tenn. Tech	1983	West Virginia	1986	West Virginia	1989	West Virginia	1992	West Virginia
1981	Tenn. Tech	1984	West Virginia	1987	Murray St.	1990	West Virginia	1993	West Virginia
1982	Tenn. Tech	1985	Murray St.	1988	West Virginia	1991	West Virginia	1994	AK-Fairbanks

ROWING

The Brown University men's varsity eight crew repeated as collegiate rowing's Triple Crown champion in 1994, sweeping the Eastern Sprints, the IRA Regatta and the National Championships (see next page). No other school's crew has ever swept all three events.

Brown crew: Bow—Ludovic Hood; Seat 2—Dennis Zvegelj; Seat 3— David Filippone; Seat 4— J.C. Raby; Seat 5— Jamie Koven; Seat 6— Alec Holcombe; Seat 7- Igor Boraska; Stroke— Ben Holbrook; Cox—Rajanya Shah; Coach— Steve Gladstone (retired after season).

Intercollegiate Rowing Association Regatta
VARSITY EIGHTS
MEN

Opening up a half-length lead over Princeton after 700 meters, Brown pulled away to win the 92nd running of the IRA regatta by nearly seven seconds (more than two boat lengths). The Bears' clocking of 5:54.4 set a new record over the 2,000-meter course on Lake Onondaga. The victory was Brown's sixth IRA regatta win since 1979. (*Syracuse, N.Y.; June 4, 1994.*)

The IRA was formed in 1895 by several northeastern schools, shortly after Harvard and Yale quit the Rowing Association (established in 1871) to stage an annual race of their own. Since then the IRA Regatta has been contested over courses of varying lengths in Poughkeepsie, N.Y., Marietta, Ohio, and Onondaga Lake in Syracuse, N.Y. The race has been over a 2000-meter course in Syracuse since 1968.

Distances: 4 miles (1895-97,1899-1916,1925-41); 3 miles (1898,1921-24,1947-49,1952-63,1965-67); 2 miles (1920,1950-51); 2000 meters (1964, since 1968).

Multiple winners: Cornell (24); Navy (13); California and Washington (10); Penn (9); Wisconsin (7); Brown and Syracuse (6); Columbia (4); Northwestern (2).

Year		Year		Year		Year		Year	
1895	Columbia	1915	Cornell	1936	Washington	1959	Wisconsin	1978	Syracuse
1896	Cornell	1916	Syracuse	1937	Washington	1960	California	1979	Brown
1897	Cornell	1917-19	Not held	1938	Navy	1961	California	1980	Navy
1898	Penn			1939	California	1962	Cornell	1981	Cornell
1899	Penn	1920	Syracuse			1963	Cornell	1982	Cornell
		1921	Navy	1940	Washington	1964	California	1983	Brown
1900	Penn	1922	Navy	1941	Washington	1965	Navy	1984	Navy
1901	Cornell	1923	Washington	1942-46	Not held	1966	Wisconsin	1985	Princeton
1902	Cornell	1924	Washington	1947	Navy	1967	Penn	1986	Brown
1903	Cornell	1925	Navy	1948	Washington	1968	Penn	1987	Brown
1904	Syracuse	1926	Washington	1949	California	1969	Penn	1988	Northeastern
1905	Cornell	1927	Columbia					1989	Penn
1906	Cornell	1928	California	1950	Washington	1970	Washington		
1907	Cornell	1929	Columbia	1951	Wisconsin	1971	Cornell	1990	Wisconsin
1908	Syracuse			1952	Navy	1972	Penn	1991	Northeastern
1909	Cornell	1930	Cornell	1953	Navy	1973	Wisconsin	1992	Dartmouth,
1910	Cornell	1931	Navy	1954	Navy*	1974	Wisconsin		Navy & Penn†
		1932	California	1955	Cornell	1975	Wisconsin	1993	Brown
1911	Cornell	1933	Not held	1956	Cornell	1976	California	1994	Brown
1912	Cornell	1934	California	1957	Cornell	1977	Cornell		
1913	Syracuse	1935	California	1958	Cornell				
1914	Columbia								

*In 1954, Navy was disqualified because of an ineligble coxwain; no trophies were given. †First dead heat in history of IRA Regatta.

The Harvard-Yale Regatta

Harvard stretched its winning streak to 10 in a row on June 4, 1994, taking the 129th Harvard-Yale Regatta for varsity eights by two lengths over Yale on the Thames River at New London, Conn. The Crimson set an upstream record for the second straight year in the four-mile event, posting a winning time of 18 minutes, 52.4 seconds at New London, Conn. The Harvard-Yale Regatta is the country's oldest intercollegiate sporting event and Harvard holds a 78-51 edge.

National Rowing Championships

VARSITY EIGHTS

Brown set a record pace and held off Harvard to become only the second crew to win back-to-back national rowing titles. The Bears' blistering time of 5:24.52 beat Harvard for the Herschede Cup by half a boat-length. In the women's competition, Princeton also successfully defended its national title in record time (6:11.38), outstroking Yale for the Ferguson Bowl. (*Harsha Lake, Bantam, Ohio; June 11, 1994.*)

Men

National championship determined at Cincinnati Regatta over a 2000-meter course on Harsha Lake since 1982. Winner receives Herschede Cup.

Multiple winners: Harvard (6); Brown and Wisconsin (2).

Year	Champion	Time	Runner-up	Time	Year	Champion	Time	Runner-up	Time
1982	Yale	5:50.8	Cornell	5:54.15	1989	Harvard	5:36.6	Washington	5:38.93
1983	Harvard	5:59.6	Washington	6:00.0	1990	Wisconsin	5:52.5	Harvard	5:56.84
1984	Washington	5:51.1	Yale	5:55.6	1991	Penn	5:58.21	Northeastern	5:58.48
1985	Harvard	5:44.4	Princeton	5:44.87	1992	Harvard	5:33.97	Dartmouth	5:34.28
1986	Wisconsin	5:57.8	Brown	5:59.9	1993	Brown	5:54.15	Penn	5:56.98
1987	Harvard	5:35.17	Brown	5:35.63	1994	Brown	5:24.52	Harvard	5:25.83
1988	Harvard	5:35.98	Northeastern	5:37.07					

Women

National championship held over various distances at 10 different venues since 1979. Distances—1000 meters (1979-81); 1500 meters (1982-83); 1000 meters (1984); 1750 meters (1985); 2000 meters (1986-88, since 1991); 1852 meters (1989-90). Winner receives Ferguson Bowl.

Multiple winners: Washington (7); Princeton (3); Boston University (2).

Year	Champion	Time	Runner-up	Time	Year	Champion	Time	Runner-up	Time
1979	Yale	3:06	California	3:08.6	1987	Washington	6:33.8	Yale	6:37.4
1980	California	3:05.4	Oregon St.	3:05.8	1988	Washington	6:41.0	Yale	6:42.37
1981	Washington	3:20.6	Yale	3:22.9	1989	Cornell	5:34.9	Wisconsin	5:37.5
1982	Washington	4:56.4	Wisconsin	4:59.83	1990	Princeton	5:52.2	Radcliffe	5:54.2
1983	Washington	4:57.5	Dartmouth	5:03.02	1991	Boston Univ.	7:03.2	Cornell	7:06.21
1984	Washington	3:29.48	Radcliffe	3:31.08	1992	Boston Univ.	6:28.79	Cornell	6:32.79
1985	Washington	5:28.4	Wisconsin	5:32.0	1993	Princeton	6:40.75	Washington	6:43.86
1986	Wisconsin	6:53.28	Radcliffe	6:53.34	1994	Princeton	6:11.38	Yale	6:14.46

SKIING

Men & Women

Strong cross-country performances on the final day of competition enabled Vermont to overtake defending champion Utah, 688 to 667 and win its fourth national title in six years. Nina Hamilton led the way with a first in the 15-kilometer freestyle and a third in the 5-km classical. Gibson Lafountaine (women's slalom) also won for the Catamounts. Utah fell short despite three individual titles. (*Sugarloaf/USA, Carabassett Valley, Me.; Mar. 9-12, 1994.*)

Multiple winners: Denver (14); Colorado (12); Utah (7); Vermont (5); Dartmouth and Wyoming (2).

Year		Year		Year		Year		Year	
1954	Denver	1963	Denver	1972	Colorado	1980	Vermont	1988	Utah
1955	Denver	1964	Denver	1973	Colorado	1981	Utah	1989	Vermont
1956	Denver	1965	Denver	1974	Colorado	1982	Colorado	1990	Vermont
1957	Denver	1966	Denver	1975	Colorado	1983	Utah	1991	Colorado
1958	Dartmouth	1967	Denver	1976	Colorado	1984	Utah	1992	Vermont
1959	Colorado	1968	Wyoming		& Dartmouth	1985	Wyoming	1993	Utah
1960	Colorado	1969	Denver	1977	Colorado	1986	Utah	1994	Vermont
1961	Denver	1970	Denver	1978	Colorado	1987	Utah		
1962	Denver	1971	Denver	1979	Colorado				

SOFTBALL

Women

Susie Parra pitched Arizona to a national championship for the second year in a row as the Wildcats defeated Cal State Northridge, 4-0. In 1993, Parra two-hit UCLA, 1-0. This time she allowed only one hit (a Beth Calcante double in the 1st inning) and struck out 13. The victory was Parra's third of the tourney and 33rd of the season. (*Oklahoma City; May 26-30, 1994.*)

Multiple winners: UCLA (7); Arizona (3); Texas A&M (2).

Year		Year		Year		Year		Year	
1982	UCLA	1985	UCLA	1988	UCLA	1991	Arizona	1993	Arizona
1983	Texas A&M	1986	CS-Fullerton	1989	UCLA	1992	UCLA	1994	Arizona
1984	UCLA	1987	Texas A&M	1990	UCLA				

Annual NCAA Division I Team Champions (Cont.)

SWIMMING & DIVING

Men

Stanford captured its sixth national championship in 10 years, paced by junior Brian Retterer, who splashed to first place in the 50-yard freestyle and 100-yd backstroke and three relays. The Cardinal easily outdistanced runner-up Texas, 556 1/2 points to 445. Arizona sophomore Chad Carvin set two meet and U.S. Open records in the 500-yd freestyle (4:11.59) and 1,650-yd free (14:34.91) and placed third in the 400-yd individual medley. Michigan's Gustavo Borges won the 100-yd freestyle for the third straight year and added victories in the 200-yd free and the 800-yd freestyle relay. (*Minneapolis; Mar. 24-26, 1994.*)

Multiple winners: Ohio St. (11); Michigan (10); USC (9); Stanford (7); Indiana (6); Texas (5); Yale (4); California and Florida (2).

Year		Year		Year		Year		Year	
1937	Michigan	1949	Ohio St.	1960	USC	1972	Indiana	1984	Florida
1938	Michigan	1950	Ohio St.	1961	Michigan	1973	Indiana	1985	Stanford
1939	Michigan	1951	Yale	1962	Ohio St.	1974	USC	1986	Stanford
1940	Michigan	1952	Ohio St.	1963	USC	1975	USC	1987	Stanford
1941	Michigan	1953	Yale	1964	USC	1976	USC	1988	Texas
1942	Yale	1954	Ohio St.	1965	USC	1977	USC	1989	Texas
1943	Ohio St.	1955	Ohio St.	1966	USC	1978	Tennessee	1990	Texas
1944	Yale	1956	Ohio St.	1967	Stanford	1979	California	1991	Texas
1945	Ohio St.	1957	Michigan	1968	Indiana	1980	California	1992	Stanford
1946	Ohio St.	1958	Michigan	1969	Indiana	1981	Texas	1993	Stanford
1947	Ohio St.	1959	Michigan	1970	Indiana	1982	UCLA	1994	Stanford
1948	Michigan			1971	Indiana	1983	Florida		

Women

Stanford defended its title with a 91-point victory over runner-up Texas. Olympian Jenny Thompson paced the Cardinal with 100-yard victories in the freestyle and butterfly, a second in the 50-yd free and two winning anchor legs. Coaches' Swimmer of the Year Amy Van Dyken of Colorado State beat Thompson in the 50-yd free with a U.S. Open record time of 21.77. Meanwhile, USC freshman Kristine Quance won both individual medlays, set a meet record in the 200-yard breaststroke (2:10.69) and swam on the winning 800-yd freestyle relay team. (2:10.69). (*Bloomington, Ind.; Mar. 17-19, 1994.*)

Multiple winners: Texas (7); Stanford (5).

Year		Year		Year		Year		Year	
1982	Florida	1985	Texas	1988	Texas	1991	Texas	1993	Stanford
1983	Stanford	1986	Texas	1989	Stanford	1992	Stanford	1994	Stanford
1984	Texas	1987	Texas	1990	Texas				

INDOOR TRACK

Men

Inspired by Erick Walder's unique triple double, Arkansas scored a championship meet-record 94 points to win its 11th consecutive national title. Tennessee placed second with 40 points. Walder won the long jump (27-8) and triple jump (56-6 3/4) to become the first athlete to win both events three years in a row. Calvin Davis (400 meters) Niall Bruton (mile) and Jason Bunston (5,000 meters) also won for the Razorbacks. (*Hoosier Dome, Indianapolis; Mar. 11-12, 1994.*)

Multiple winners: Arkansas (11); UTEP (7); Kansas and Villanova (3); USC (2).

Year		Year		Year		Year		Year	
1965	Missouri	1971	Villanova	1978	UTEP	1984	Arkansas	1990	Arkansas
1966	Kansas	1972	USC	1979	Villanova	1985	Arkansas	1991	Arkansas
1967	USC	1973	Manhattan	1980	UTEP	1986	Arkansas	1992	Arkansas
1968	Villanova	1974	UTEP	1981	UTEP	1987	Arkansas	1993	Arkansas
1969	Kansas	1975	UTEP	1982	UTEP	1988	Arkansas	1994	Arkansas
1970	Kansas	1976	UTEP	1983	SMU	1989	Arkansas		
		1977	Washington St.						

(*) indicates unofficial championship.

Women

Defending champion LSU ended its even-numbered-year jinx with a comfortable 48-29 margin over runner-up Alabama. The Tigers were led by Daphnie Saunders, who repeated in the long jump with a record leap of 22-1 and placed third in the triple jump. Indiana State's Holli Hyche swept the 55- and 200-meter dashes for the second year in a row, setting a meet record (22.90) in the 200. (*Hoosier Dome, Indianapolis; Mar. 11-12, 1994.*)

Multiple winners: LSU (5); Texas (3); Nebraska (2).

Year		Year		Year		Year		Year	
1983	Nebraska	1986	Texas	1989	LSU	1991	LSU	1993	LSU
1984	Nebraska	1987	LSU	1990	Texas	1992	Florida	1994	LSU
1985	Florida St.	1988	Texas						

Wide World Photos

Indiana St. sprinter **Holli Hyche** (right) finishes in front of a lunging **Cheryl Taplin** to win the women's 100 meters at the NCAA Track & Field Championships in Boise, Idaho, on June 4.

OUTDOOR TRACK

Men

Arkansas scored 54 of its 83 points on the final day of competition to win its third straight national championship by nearly 40 points over second place UTEP. Erick Walder led the Razorbacks with victories in both the long jump (27-4 1/2) and triple jump (55-5 3/4). The long jump win was his third straight. Two other three-time champions were Jose Parrilla of Tennessee in the 800 meters and Georgia's Brent Noon in the shut put. *(Boise, Idaho; June 1-4, 1994.)*

Multiple winners: USC (26); UCLA (8); UTEP (6); Illinois and Oregon (5); Arkansas (4), Kansas, LSU and Stanford (3); SMU and Tennessee (2).

Year		Year		Year		Year		Year	
1921	Illinois	1937	USC	1952	USC	1967	USC	1980	UTEP
1922	California	1938	USC	1953	USC	1968	USC	1981	UTEP
1923	Michigan	1939	USC	1954	USC	1969	San Jose St.	1982	UTEP
1924	Not held	1940	USC	1955	USC	1970	BYU, Kansas	1983	SMU
1925	Stanford*	1941	USC	1956	UCLA		& Oregon	1984	Oregon
1926	USC*	1942	USC	1957	Villanova	1971	UCLA	1985	Arkansas
1927	Illinois*	1943	USC	1958	USC	1972	UCLA	1986	SMU
1928	Stanford	1944	Illinois	1959	Kansas	1973	UCLA	1987	UCLA
1929	Ohio St.	1945	Navy	1960	Kansas	1974	Tennessee	1988	UCLA
1930	USC	1946	Illinois	1961	USC	1975	UTEP	1989	LSU
1931	USC	1947	Illinois	1962	Oregon	1976	USC	1990	LSU
1932	Indiana	1948	Minnesota	1963	USC	1977	Arizona St.	1991	Tennessee
1933	LSU	1949	USC	1964	Oregon	1978	UCLA & UTEP	1992	Arkansas
1934	Stanford	1950	USC	1965	Oregon	1979	UTEP	1993	Arkansas
1935	USC	1951	USC		& USC			1994	Arkansas
1936	USC			1966	UCLA				

(*) indicates unofficial championship.

Women

With four individual titles, another in the 400-meter relay and five other top four efforts, LSU ran off with its eighth straight national title, doubling the score of runner-up Texas, 86-43. The Tigers' Danyell Mitchell (discus) and Debbie Parris (400-meter hurdles) joined Holli Hyche of Indiana State (100 meters), Gillian Russell (100-meter hurdles) and Carole Zajac (10,000 meters) in winning their events for the second year in a row. *(Boise, Idaho; June 1-4, 1994.)*

Multiple winners: LSU (8); UCLA (2).

Year		Year		Year		Year		Year	
1982	UCLA	1985	Oregon	1988	LSU	1991	LSU	1993	LSU
1983	UCLA	1986	Texas	1989	LSU	1992	LSU	1994	LSU
1984	Florida St.	1987	LSU	1990	LSU				

Annual NCAA Division I Team Champions (Cont.)

VOLLEYBALL

Men

Penn State became the first team from anywhere other than California to win the national title when the Nittany Lions upset top-ranked and heavily-favored UCLA in five sets— 9-15, 15-13, 4-15, 15-12, 15-12. All-America outside hitter Ramon Hernandez rallied PSU from an 11-6 deficit with 17 kills in the fourth game. (*Indianapolis; May 6-7, 1994*).

Multiple winners: UCLA (14); Pepperdine and USC (4).

Year		Year		Year		Year		Year	
1970	UCLA	1975	UCLA	1980	USC	1985	Pepperdine	1990	USC
1971	UCLA	1976	UCLA	1981	UCLA	1986	Pepperdine	1991	Long Beach St.
1972	UCLA	1977	USC	1982	UCLA	1987	UCLA	1992	Pepperdine
1973	San Diego St.	1978	Pepperdine	1983	UCLA	1988	USC	1993	UCLA
1974	UCLA	1979	UCLA	1984	UCLA	1989	UCLA	1994	Penn St.

Women

Five months before the Penn State men became the first Eastern team to win a Division I volleyball title, the Penn State women fell to Long Beach State in a four-set championship final. With Player of the Year Danielle Scott registering 21 kills, the 49ers won, 15-13, 12-15, 15-11, 16-14, before a partisan Big 10 crowd of 11,114 at Wisconsin Field House. (*Madison, Wisc.; Dec. 16-18, 1993.*)

Multiple winners: Hawaii and UCLA (3); Long Beach St. and Pacific (2).

Year		Year		Year		Year		Year	
1981	USC	1984	UCLA	1987	Hawaii	1990	UCLA	1992	Stanford
1982	Hawaii	1985	Pacific	1988	Texas	1991	UCLA	1993	Long Beach St.
1983	Hawaii	1986	Pacific	1989	Long Beach St.				

WATER POLO

Men

Stanford, a 12-11 loser to California in sudden death overtime a year ago, returned to the finals to beat Southern Cal, 11-9. The Cardinal led 9-5 after three periods then hung on to win its seventh overall title and first since 1986. USC eliminated Cal, 21-11, in overtime in the semifinals. (*Long Beach, Calif.; Nov. 26-28, 1994.*)

Multiple winners: California (11); Stanford (7); UC-Irvine and UCLA (3).

Year		Year		Year		Year		Year	
1969	UCLA	1974	California	1979	UC-S.Barbara	1984	California	1989	UC-Irvine
1970	UC-Irvine	1975	California	1980	Stanford	1985	Stanford	1990	California
1971	UCLA	1976	Stanford	1981	Stanford	1986	Stanford	1991	California
1972	UCLA	1977	California	1982	UC-Irvine	1987	California	1992	California
1973	California	1978	Stanford	1983	California	1988	California	1993	Stanford

WRESTLING

Men

Before Pat Smith came along, no wrestler had ever won four individual Division I titles— not even his brother John. Smith became the first with a 5-3 victory over Michigan's Sean Bormet in the 158-lb. division final. His victory, along with those of teammates Alan Fried (142 lbs.) and freshman Mark Branch (167 lbs.), enabled Oklahoma State to beat runner-up and defending champion Iowa, 94¾ to 76½. John Smith, the Cowboys' coach, won twice in the NCAAs, twice in the Olympics and six times in the worlds. (*Chapel Hill, N.C.; Mar. 17-19, 1994.*)

Multiple winners: Oklahoma St. (30); Iowa (14); Iowa St. (8); Oklahoma (7).

Year		Year		Year		Year		Year	
1928	Okla. A&M*	1940	Okla. A&M	1955	Okla. A&M	1968	Okla. St.	1980	Iowa
1929	Okla. A&M	1941	Okla. A&M	1956	Okla. A&M	1969	Iowa St.	1981	Iowa
1930	Okla. A&M	1942	Okla. A&M	1957	Oklahoma	1970	Iowa St.	1982	Iowa
1931	Okla. A&M*	1943-45	Not held	1958	Okla. St.	1971	Okla. St.	1983	Iowa
1932	Indiana*	1946	Okla. A&M	1959	Okla. St.	1972	Iowa St.	1984	Iowa
1933	Okla. A&M*	1947	Cornell Col.	1960	Oklahoma	1973	Iowa St.	1985	Iowa
	& Iowa St.*	1948	Okla. A&M	1961	Okla. St.	1974	Oklahoma	1986	Iowa
1934	Okla. A&M	1949	Okla. A&M	1962	Okla. St.	1975	Iowa	1987	Iowa St.
1935	Okla. A&M	1950	Northern Iowa	1963	Oklahoma	1976	Iowa	1988	Arizona St.
1936	Oklahoma	1951	Oklahoma	1964	Okla. St.	1977	Iowa St.	1989	Okla. St.
1937	Okla. A&M	1952	Oklahoma	1965	Iowa St.	1978	Iowa	1990	Okla. St.
1938	Okla. A&M	1953	Penn St.	1966	Okla. St.	1979	Iowa	1991	Iowa
1939	Okla. A&M	1954	Okla. A&M	1967	Michigan St.			1992	Iowa
								1993	Iowa
								1994	Okla. St.

(*) indicates unofficial champions. **Note:** Oklahoma A&M became Oklahoma St. in 1958.

Carol Blazejowski is one of five members of the Basketball Hall of Fame's Class of '94. An All-America at Montclair St. from 1976-78, her career scoring average of 31.7 is still a college record.

HALLS OF FAME & AWARDS

AUTO RACING

International Motorsports Hall of Fame

Established in 1990 by the International Motorsports Hall of Fame Commission. **Address:** P.O.Box 1018, Talladega, AL 35160. **Telephone:** (205) 362-5002.

Eligibility: Nominees must be retired from their specialty in motorsports for five years. Voting done by 150-member panel made up of the world-wide auto racing media.

Class of 1994 (9): DRIVERS—**Tiny Lund** (Sprints, Modifieds, NASCAR), **Benny Parsons** (ARCA, NASCAR), **Mauri Rose** (Indy car), **Herb Thomas** (NASCAR), **Joe Weatherly** (Motorcycles, NASCAR). CONTRIBUTORS—**Colin Chapman** (engineer, Lotus Co. founder), **Enzo Ferrari** (motor company founder), **John Marcum** (Automobile Racing Club of America founder), **Ralph Moody** (driver, engineer, car builder).

Members are listed with year of induction; (+) indicates deceased members.

Drivers

Allison, Bobby 1993	+ Hill, Phil..............................1991	Pearson, David 1993
+ Ascari, Alberto 1992	+ Holbert, Al............................1993	Petty, Lee 1990
Baker, Buck..........................1990	Jarrett, Ned..........................1991	Roberts, Fireball....................1990
+ Bettenhausen, Tony 1991	Johnson, Junior 1990	Roberts, Kenny 1992
Brabham, Jack......................1990	Jones, Parnelli......................1990	Rose, Mauri 1994
+ Campbell, Sir Malcolm 1990	Lauda, Niki 1993	+ Shaw, Wilbur........................1991
+ Clark, Jim..............................1990	Lorenzen, Fred 1991	Stewart, Jackie 1990
+ DePalma, Ralph 1991	+ Lund, Tiny 1994	Thomas, Herb 1994
+ Donahue, Mark 1990	+ Mays, Rex 1993	+ Turner, Curtis 1992
+ Fangio, Juan Manuel 1990	+ McLaren, Bruce 1991	Unser, Bobby 1990
Flock, Tim 1991	Meyer, Louis 1992	+ Vukovich, Bill 1991
+ Gregg, Peter..........................1992	Moss, Stirling 1990	Ward Rodger..........................1992
Gurney, Dan..........................1990	+ Oldfield, Barney 1990	+ Weatherly, Joe 1994
+ Hill, Graham..........................1990	Parsons, Benny 1994	Yarborough, Cale....................1993

Contributors

Bignotti, George......................1993	+ France, Bill Sr 1990	Parks, Wally 1992
+ Chapman, Colin......................1994	Granatelli, Andy 1992	+ Rickenbacker, Eddie 1992
+ Chevrolet, Louis......................1992	+ Hulman, Tony 1990	Shelby, Carroll 1991
+ Ferrari, Enzo..........................1994	Marcum, John 1994	+ Thompson, Mickey 1990
+ Ford, Henry 1993	Moody, Ralph 1994	Yunick, Smokey......................1990

Motorsports Hall of Fame of America

Established in 1989. **Address:** P.O.Box 194, Novi, MI 48050. **Telephone:** (313) 349-7223.

Eligibility: Nominees must be retired at least three years or engaged in their area of motor sports for at least 20 years. Areas include: open wheel, stock car, dragster, sports car, motorcycle, off road, power boat, air racing and land speed records.

Class of 1994 (10): DRIVERS—**Sir Malcolm Campbell** (land and water speed record holder), **Roger DeCosta** (motorcycles), **Bob Glidden** (drag racing), **Bobby Unser** (Indy cars), **Cale Yarborough** (stock cars). PILOT—**Bill Falck**. CONTRIBUTORS—**Jim Hall** (designer, builder), **Chris Economacki** (journalist), **Eddie Rickenbacker** (driver, track owner), **Bernie Little** (power boat owner).

Members are listed with year of induction; (+) indicates deceased members.

Drivers

Allison, Bobby 1992	Kalitta, Connie 1992	**Pilots**
Andretti, Mario 1990	Leonard, Joe 1991	+ Cochran, Jacqueline..............1993
Arfons, Art 1991	Mann, Dick............................1993	+ Curtiss, Glenn 1990
+ Baker, Cannonball................1989	Meyer, Louis 1993	+ Doolittle, Jimmy 1989
Breedlove, Craig 1993	Muldowney, Shirley 1990	+ Earhart, Amelia 1992
+ Campbell, Sir Malcolm 1994	+ Muncy, Bill 1989	+ Falck, Bill 1994
Cantrell, Bill 1992	Musson, Ron 1993	
+ Chenoweth, Dean 1991	+ Oldfield, Barney 1989	**Contributors**
+ Clark, Jim..............................1990	Parks, Wally 1993	+ Agajanian, J.C 1992
DeCosta, Roger 1994	Pearson, David 1993	Bignotti, George......................1993
+ DePalma, Ralph 1992	+ Petrali, Joe 1992	Economacki, Chris..................1994
+ Donahue, Mark 1990	Petty, Richard 1989	+ France, Bill Sr........................1990
Foyt, A.J...............................1989	Prudhomme, Don 1991	Hall, Jim................................1994
Garlits, Don 1989	Roberts, Kenny 1990	+ Hulman, Tony 1991
Glidden, Bob 1994	+ Shaw, Wilbur........................1991	Little, Bernie 1994
Gurney, Dan..........................1991	+ Thompson, Mickey 1990	+ Rickenbacker, Eddie 1994
Hill, Phil................................1989	+ Turner, Roscoe 1991	Shelby, Carroll 1992
+ Holbert, Al............................1993	Unser, Bobby 1994	
+ Horn, Ted 1993	+ Vukovich, Bill Sr 1992	
Johnson, Junior 1991	+ Wood, Gar............................1990	
Jones, Parnelli......................1992	Yarborough, Cale....................1994	

Wide World Photos

Two of the Baseball Hall of Fame's newest members, **Phil Rizzuto** (left) and **Steve Carlton** exchange pleasantries at their Cooperstown induction on July 31. Carlton was elected in his first year of eligibility, while Rizzuto and the late Leo Durocher were voted in by the Veterans' Committee.

BASEBALL

National Baseball Hall of Fame & Museum

Established in 1935 by Major League Baseball to celebrate the game's 100th anniversary. **Address:** P.O.Box 590, Cooperstown, NY 13326. **Telephone:** (607) 547-7200.

Eligibility: Nominated players must have played at least part of 10 seasons in the Major Leagues and be retired for five years. Voting done by Baseball Writers' Association of America. Any nominated player not elected after 15 years on the writers' ballot becomes eligible for consideration by the Veterans' Committee after a three-year wait. The Hall of Fame board of directors voted unanimously on Feb. 4, 1991, to exclude players on baseball's permanently ineligible list from consideration. Pete Rose is the only living ex-player on that list.

Class of 1994 (3): BBWAA vote—pitcher **Steve Carlton**, St. Louis (1965–71), Philadelphia (1972–86), San Francisco (1986), Chicago-AL (1986), Cleveland (1987), Minnesota (1987–88). VETERANS' COMMITTEE vote—shortstop **Phil Rizzuto**, New York-AL (1941–42, 1946–56); manager **Leo Durocher**, Brooklyn (1939–48), New York-NL (1948–55), Chicago-NL (1966–72), Houston (1972–73).

1994 Top 10 vote-getters (455 BBWAA ballots cast, 342 needed to elect): 1. **Steve Carlton** (396); 2. **Orlando Cepeda** (335); 3. **Phil Niekro** and **Tony Perez** (273); 5. **Don Sutton** (259); 6. **Steve Garvey** (166); 7. **Tony Oliva** (158); 8. **Ron Santo** (150); 9. **Bruce Sutter** (109); 10. **Jim Kaat** (98).

Elected first year on ballot (25): Hank Aaron, Ernie Banks, Johnny Bench, Lou Brock, **Steve Carlton**, Rod Carew, Bob Feller, Bob Gibson, Reggie Jackson, Al Kaline, Sandy Koufax, Mickey Mantle, Willie Mays, Willie McCovey, Joe Morgan, Stan Musial, Jim Palmer, Brooks Robinson, Frank Robinson, Jackie Robinson, Tom Seaver, Warren Spahn, Willie Stargell, Ted Williams and Carl Yastrzemski.

Members are listed with years of induction; (+) indicates deceased members.

1st Basemen

+ Anson, Cap	1939	+ Connor, Roger	1976		Killebrew, Harmon	1984
+ Beckley, Jake	1971	+ Foxx, Jimmie	1951		McCovey, Willie	1986
+ Bottomley, Jim	1974	+ Gehrig, Lou	1939		+ Mize, Johnny	1981
+ Brouthers, Dan	1945	+ Greenberg, Hank	1956		+ Sisler, George	1939
+ Chance, Frank	1946	+ Kelly, George	1973		+ Terry, Bill	1954

2nd Basemen

Carew, Rod	1991	+ Gehringer, Charlie	1949		Morgan, Joe	1990
+ Collins, Eddie	1939	+ Herman, Billy	1975		+ Robinson, Jackie	1962
Doerr, Bobby	1986	+ Hornsby, Rogers	1942		Schoendienst, Red	1989
+ Evers, Johnny	1946	+ Lajoie, Nap	1937			
+ Frisch, Frankie	1947	+ Lazzeri, Tony	1991			

Baseball Hall of Fame (Cont.)

Shortstops

Aparicio, Luis.........................1984
+ Appling, Luke 1964
+ Bancroft, Dave 1971
Banks, Ernie.........................1977
Boudreau, Lou.......................1970
+ Cronin, Joe 1956

+ Jackson, Travis 1982
+ Jennings, Hugh 1945
+ Maranville, Rabbit 1954
Reese, Pee Wee 1984
Rizzuto, Phil 1994
+ Sewell, Joe 1977

+ Tinker, Joe 1946
+ Vaughan, Arky 1985
+ Wagner, Honus.....................1936
+ Wallace, Bobby 1953
+ Ward, Monte 1964

+ Baker, Frank 1955
+ Collins, Jimmy......................1945
Kell, George 1983

3rd Basemen

+ Lindstrom, Fred 1976
Mathews, Eddie 1978
Robinson, Brooks 1983

+ Traynor, Pie..........................1948

Left Fielders

Brock, Lou 1985
+ Burkett, Jesse 1946
+ Clarke, Fred..........................1945
+ Delahanty, Ed 1945
+ Goslin, Goose 1968
+ Hafey, Chick 1971

+ Kelley, Joe 1971
Kiner, Ralph 1975
+ Manush, Heinie......................1964
+ Medwick, Joe 1968
Musial, Stan 1969
+ O'Rourke, Jim 1945

+ Simmons, Al 1953
Stargell, Willie.......................1988
+ Wheat, Zack 1959
Williams, Billy 1987
Williams, Ted 1966
Yastrzemski, Carl 1989

Center Fielders

+ Averill, Earl 1975
+ Carey, Max 1961
+ Cobb, Ty...............................1936
+ Combs, Earle 1970
DiMaggio, Joe 1955

+ Duffy, Hugh 1945
+ Hamilton, Billy 1961
Mantle, Mickey 1974
Mays, Willie 1979
+ Roush, Edd 1962

Snider, Duke 1980
+ Speaker, Tris 1937
+ Waner, Lloyd 1967
+ Wilson, Hack 1979

Right Fielders

Aaron, Hank...........................1982
+ Clemente, Roberto.................1973
+ Crawford, Sam 1957
+ Cuyler, Kiki 1968
+ Flick, Elmer 1963
+ Heilmann, Harry 1952
+ Hooper, Harry 1971

Jackson, Reggie 1993
Kaline, Al 1980
+ Keeler, Willie 1939
+ Kelly, King 1945
+ Klein, Chuck 1980
+ McCarthy, Tommy 1946
+ Ott, Mel................................1951

+ Rice, Sam 1963
Robinson, Frank 1982
+ Ruth, Babe 1936
Slaughter, Enos 1985
+ Thompson, Sam 1974
+ Waner, Paul 1952
+ Youngs, Ross 1972

Catchers

Bench, Johnny........................1989
Berra, Yogi 1972
+ Bresnahan, Roger...................1945
+ Campanella, Roy 1969

+ Cochrane, Mickey 1947
+ Dickey, Bill 1954
+ Ewing, Buck 1939
Ferrell, Rick 1984

+ Hartnett, Gabby 1955
+ Lombardi, Ernie 1986
+ Schalk, Ray...........................1955

Pitchers

+ Alexander, Grover 1938
+ Bender, Chief 1953
+ Brown, Mordecai 1949
Carlton, Steve 1994
+ Chesbro, Jack 1946
+ Clarkson, John 1963
+ Coveleski, Stan 1969
+ Dean, Dizzy 1953
+ Drysdale, Don 1984
+ Faber, Red 1964
Feller, Bob 1962
Fingers, Rollie 1992
Ford, Whitey 1974
+ Galvin, Pud 1965
Gibson, Bob 1981
+ Gomez, Lefty 1972
+ Grimes, Burleigh 1964
+ Grove, Lefty 1947

+ Haines, Jess 1970
+ Hoyt, Waite 1969
+ Hubbell, Carl 1947
Hunter, Catfish 1987
Jenkins, Ferguson 1991
+ Johnson, Walter 1936
+ Joss, Addie 1978
+ Keefe, Tim 1964
Koufax, Sandy 1972
Lemon, Bob 1976
+ Lyons, Ted 1955
Marichal, Juan 1983
+ Marquard, Rube 1971
+ Mathewson, Christy................1936
+ McGinnity, Joe 1946
Newhouser, Hal 1992
+ Nichols, Kid 1949
Palmer, Jim 1990

+ Pennock, Herb 1948
Perry, Gaylord 1991
+ Plank, Eddie 1946
+ Radbourne, Old Hoss 1939
+ Rixey, Eppa 1963
Roberts, Robin 1976
+ Ruffing, Red 1967
+ Rusie, Amos 1977
Seaver, Tom 1992
Spahn, Warren 1973
+ Vance, Dazzy 1955
+ Waddell, Rube 1946
+ Walsh, Ed..............................1946
+ Welch, Mickey 1973
Wilhelm, Hoyt 1985
Wynn, Early 1972
+ Young, Cy..............................1937

Managers

Lopez, Al 1977
+ Mack, Connie 1937
+ McCarthy, Joe 1957
+ McGraw, John 1937

+ McKechnie, Bill 1962
+ Robinson, Wilbert 1945
+ Stengel, Casey 1966

+ Alston, Walter 1983
+ Durocher, Leo........................1994
+ Harris, Bucky 1975
+ Huggins, Miller 1964

Umpires

Barlick, Al.............................1989
+ Conlan, Jocko 1974
+ Connolly, Tom 1953

+ Evans, Billy 1973
+ Hubbard, Cal 1976

+ Klem, Bill 1953
+ McGowan, Bill 1992

From Negro Leagues

+ Bell, Cool Papa (OF).............1974	+ Foster, Rube (P-Mgr)..............1981	Leonard, Buck (1B).................1972
+ Charleston, Oscar (1B-OF)......1976	+ Gibson, Josh (C)....................1972	+ Lloyd, Pop (SS)......................1977
+ Dandridge, Ray (3B)..............1987	Irvin, Monte (OF)..................1973	+ Paige, Satchel (P)..................1971
+ Dihigo, Martin (P-OF)............1977	+ Johnson, Judy (3B)................1975	

Pioneers and Executives

+ Barrow, Ed.........................1953	+ Frick, Ford............................1970	+ Rickey, Branch.......................1967
+ Bulkeley, Morgan.................1937	+ Giles, Warren.......................1979	+ Spalding, Al.........................1939
+ Cartwright, Alexander...........1938	+ Griffith, Clark......................1946	+ Veeck, Bill..........................1991
+ Chadwick, Henry..................1938	+ Harridge, Will......................1972	+ Weiss, George.......................1971
+ Chandler, Happy..................1982	+ Johnson, Ban.......................1937	+ Wright, George......................1937
+ Comiskey, Charles................1939	+ Landis, Kenesaw...................1944	+ Wright, Harry.......................1953
+ Cummings, Candy................1939	+ MacPhail, Larry....................1978	+ Yawkey, Tom........................1980

J.G. Taylor Spink Award

First presented in 1962 by the Baseball Writers' Association of America for meritorious contributions by members of the BBWAA. Named in honor of the late publisher of *The Sporting News*, the Spink Award does not constitute induction into the Hall of Fame. Winners are honored in the year following their selection.

Year		Year		Year	
1962	J.G. Taylor Spink	1973	Warren Brown, John Drebinger & John F. Kieran	1983	Ken Smith
1963	Ring Lardner			1984	Joe McGuff
1962	J.G. Taylor Spink	1974	John Carmichael & James Isaminger	1985	Earl Lawson
1963	Ring Lardner			1986	Jack Lang
1964	Hugh Fullerton	1975	Tom Meany & Shirley Povich	1987	Jim Murray
1965	Charley Dryden	1976	Harold Kaese & Red Smith	1988	Bob Hunter & Ray Kelly
1966	Grantland Rice	1977	Gordon Cobbledick & Edgar Munzel	1989	Jerome Holtzman
1967	Damon Runyon				
1968	H.G. Salsinger	1978	Tim Murnane & Dick Young	1990	Phil Collier
1969	Sid Mercer	1979	Bob Broeg & Tommy Holmes	1991	Ritter Collett
				1992	Leonard Koppett & Buzz Saidt
1970	Heywood C. Broun	1980	Joe Reichler & Milt Richman		
1971	Frank Graham	1981	Bob Addie & Allen Lewis	1993	John Wendall Smith
1972	Dan Daniel, Fred Lieb & J. Roy Stockton	1982	Si Burick		

Ford Frick Award

First presented in 1978 by Hall of Fame for meritorious contributions by baseball broadcasters. Named in honor of the late newspaper reporter, broadcaster, National League president and commissioner, the Frick Award does not constitute induction into the Hall of Fame.

Year		Year		Year	
1978	Mel Allen & Red Barber	1984	Curt Gowdy	1990	Byrum Saam
1979	Bob Elson	1985	Buck Canel	1991	Joe Garagiola
1980	Russ Hodges	1986	Bob Prince	1992	Milo Hamilton
1981	Ernie Harwell	1987	Jack Buck	1993	Chuck Thompson
1982	Vin Scully	1988	Lindsey Nelson	1994	Bob Murphy
1983	Jack Brickhouse	1989	Harry Caray		

BASKETBALL

Naismith Memorial Basketball Hall of Fame

Established in 1949 by the National Association of Basketball Coaches in memory of the sport's inventor, Dr. James Naismith. Original Hall opened in 1968 and current Hall in 1985. **Address:** 1150 West Columbus Avenue, Springfield, MA 01105. **Telephone:** (413) 781-6500.

Eligibility: Nominated players and referees must be retired for five years, coaches must have coached 25 years or be retired for five, and contributors must have already completed their noteworthy service to the game. Voting done by 24-member honors committee made up of media representatives, Hall of Fame members and trustees. Any nominee not elected after five years becomes eligible for consideration by the Veterans' Committee after a five-year wait.

Class of 1994 (5): PLAYERS—guard **Buddy Jeannette**, college (Washington & Jefferson, 1935–38), NBL (Warren-Cleveland-Detroit-Sheboygan-Ft. Wayne, 1938–46), BAA (Baltimore, 1947–49), NBA (Baltimore 1949–50). COACHES—**Denny Crum**, college (Louisville, 1972–93); **Chuck Daly**, college (Boston College 1969–71, Penn 1971–77), NBA (Cleveland 1981–82, Detroit 1983–92, New Jersey 1992–94); **Cesare Rubini** (Simmenthal of Milan in Italian League 1946–78). WOMAN—center **Carol Blazejowski**, college (Montclair St. 1974–78), Olympics (1980).

Note: John Wooden is the only member to be honored as both a player and a coach.

Members are listed with years of induction; (+) indicates deceased members.

Roster starts on next page. ☞

Basketball Hall of Fame (Cont.)

Men

Archibald, Nate	1991	Greer, Hal	1981	Mikan, George	1959
Arizin, Paul	1977	+ Gruenig, Robert	1963	Monroe, Earl	1990
+ Barlow, Thomas (Babe)	1980	Hagan, Cliff	1977	Murphy, Calvin	1993
Barry, Rick	1987	+ Hanson, Victor	1960	+ Murphy, Charles (Stretch)	1960
Baylor, Elgin	1976	Havlicek, John	1983	+ Page, Harlan (Pat)	1962
+ Beckman, John	1972	Hawkins, Connie	1992	Pettit, Bob	1970
Bellamy, Walt	1993	Hayes, Elvin	1990	Phillip, Andy	1961
Belov, Sergei	1992	Heinsohn, Tom	1986	+ Pollard, Jim	1977
Bing, Dave	1990	Holman, Nat	1964	Ramsey, Frank	1981
+ Borgmann, Benny	1961	Houbregs, Bob	1987	Reed, Willis	1981
Bradley, Bill	1982	+ Hyatt, Chuck	1959	Robertson, Oscar	1979
+ Brennan, Joe	1974	Issel, Dan	1993	+ Roosma, John	1961
Cervi, Al	1984	Jeannette, Buddy	1994	Russell, Bill	1974
Chamberlain, Wilt	1978	+ Johnson, Bill (Skinny)	1976	+ Russell, John (Honey)	1964
+ Cooper, Charles (Tarzan)	1976	+ Johnston, Neil	1990	Schayes, Dolph	1972
Cousy, Bob	1970	Jones, K. C	1989	+ Schmidt, Ernest J	1973
Cowens, Dave	1991	Jones, Sam	1983	+ Schommer, John	1959
Cunningham, Billy	1986	+ Krause, Edward (Moose)	1975	+ Sedran, Barney	1962
+ Davies, Bob	1969	Kurland, Bob	1961	Sharman, Bill	1975
+ DeBernardi, Forrest	1961	Lanier, Bob	1992	+ Steinmetz, Christian	1961
DeBusschere, Dave	1982	+ Lapchick, Joe	1966	+ Thompson, John (Cat)	1962
+ Dehnert, Dutch	1968	Lovellette, Clyde	1988	Thurmond, Nate	1984
Endacott, Paul	1971	Lucas, Jerry	1979	Twyman, Jack	1982
Erving, Julius (Dr. J)	1993	Luisetti, Hank	1959	Unseld, Wes	1988
Foster, Bud	1964	Macauley, Ed	1960	+ Vandivier, Robert (Fuzzy)	1974
Frazier, Walt	1987	+ Maravich, Pete	1987	+ Wachter, Ed	1961
+ Friedman, Marty	1971	Martin, Slater	1981	Walton, Bill	1993
+ Fulks, Joe	1977	+ McCracken, Branch	1960	Wanzer, Bobby	1987
Gale, Laddie	1976	+ McCracken, Jack	1962	West, Jerry	1979
Gallatin, Harry	1991	McDermott, Bobby	1988	Wilkens, Lenny	1989
Gates, William (Pop)	1989	McGuire, Dick	1993	Wooden, John	1960
Gola, Tom	1975				

Women

Blazejowski, Carol	1994	Meyers, Ann	1993	White, Nera	1992
Harris, Lucy	1992	Semenova, Juliana	1993		

Coaches

+ Anderson, Harold (Andy)	1984	+ Gill, Amory (Slats)	1967	McGuire, Frank	1976
Auerbach, Red	1968	Harshman, Marv	1984	+ Meanwell, Walter (Doc)	1959
+ Barry, Sam	1978	+ Hickey, Eddie	1978	Meyer, Ray	1978
+ Blood, Ernest (Prof)	1960	+ Hobson, Howard (Hobby)	1965	Miller, Ralph	1988
+ Cann, Howard	1967	Holzman, Red	1986	Ramsay, Jack	1992
+ Carlson, Henry (Doc)	1959	+ Iba, Hank	1968	Rubini, Cesare	1994
Carnesecca, Lou	1992	+ Julian, Alvin (Doggie)	1967	+ Rupp, Adolph	1968
Carnevale, Ben	1969	+ Keaney, Frank	1960	+ Sachs, Leonard	1961
+ Case, Everett	1981	+ Keogan, George	1961	+ Shelton, Everett	1979
Crum, Denny	1994	Knight, Bob	1991	Smith, Dean	1982
Daly, Chuck	1994	+ Lambert, Ward (Piggy)	1960	Taylor, Fred	1985
Dean, Everett	1966	Litwack, Harry	1975	Wade, Margaret	1984
+ Diddle, Ed	1971	+ Leoffler, Ken	1964	Watts, Stan	1985
+ Drake, Bruce	1972	+ Lonborg, Dutch	1972	Wooden, John	1972
Gaines, Clarence (Bighouse)	1981	+ McCutchan, Arad	1980	+ Woolpert, Phil	1992
Gardner, Jack	1983	McGuire, Al	1992		

Teams

Buffalo Germans	1961	New York Renaissance	1963	Original Celtics	1959
First Team	1959				

Referees

+ Enright, Jim	1978	+ Leith, Lloyd	1982	+ Shirley, J. Dallas	1979
+ Hepbron, George	1960	Mihalik, Red	1986	Tobey, Dave	1961
+ Hoyt, George	1961	Nucatola, John	1977	+ Walsh, David	1961
+ Kennedy, Pat	1959	+ Quigley, Ernest (Quig)	1961		

Contributors

+ Abbott, Senda Berenson 1984	+ Hinkle, Tony 1965
+ Allen, Forrest (Phog) 1959	+ Irish, Ned 1964
+ Bee, Clair 1967	+ Jones, R. William 1964
+ Brown, Walter A 1965	+ Kennedy, Walter 1980
+ Bunn, John 1964	+ Liston, Emil (Liz) 1974
+ Douglas, Bob 1971	McLendon, John 1978
+ Duer, Al 1981	+ Mokray, Bill 1965
Fagen, Clifford B..............1983	+ Morgan, Ralph 1959
+ Fisher, Harry 1973	+ Morgenweck, Frank (Pop) 1962
+ Fleisher, Larry 1991	+ Naismith, James....................1959
+ Gottlieb, Eddie 1971	Newell, Pete 1978
+ Gulick, Luther 1959	+ O'Brien, John J. (Jack) 1961
Harrison, Les......................1979	+ O'Brien, Larry 1991
+ Hepp, Ferenc 1980	+ Olsen, Harold G 1959
+ Hickox, Ed 1959	+ Podoloff, Maurice..................1973

+ Porter, Henry (H.V.) 1960
+ Reid, William A 1963
+ Ripley, Elmer 1972
+ St. John, Lynn W 1962
+ Saperstein, Abe 1970
+ Schabinger, Arthur 1961
+ Stagg, Amos Alonzo 1959
Stankovic, Boris...................1991
+ Steitz, Ed 1983
+ Taylor, Chuck 1968
+ Teague, Bertha 1984
+ Tower, Oswald 1959
+ Trester, Ather (A.L.) 1961
+ Wells, Cliff............................1971
+ Wilke, Lou 1982

Curt Gowdy Award

First presented in 1990 by the Hall of Fame Board of Trustees for meritorious contributions by the media. Named in honor of the former NBC sportscaster, the Gowdy Award does not constitute induction into the Hall of Fame.

Year		Year		Year	
1990	Curt Gowdy & Dick Herbert	1992	Sam Goldaper & Chick Hearn	1994	Leonard Koppett
1991	Dave Dorr & Marty Glickman	1993	Leonard Lewin & Johnny Most		& Cawood Ledford

---

BOWLING

National Bowling Hall of Fame & Museum

The National Bowling Hall is one museum with separate wings for honorees of the American Bowling Congress (ABC), Professional Bowlers' Association (PBA) and Women's International Bowling Congress (WIBC). **Address:** 111 Stadium Plaza, St.Louis, MO 63102. **Telephone:** (314) 231-6340.

Professional Bowlers Association

Established in 1975. **Eligibility:** Nominees must be PBA members and at least 35 years old. Voting done by 50-member panel that includes writers who have covered bowling for at least 12 years.

Class of 1994 (3): PERFORMANCE—**Brian Voss**. VETERANS—**Mike Limongello**. MERITORIOUS SERVICE—**Chuck Clemens**.

Members are listed with years of induction; (+) indicates deceased members.

Performance

Allen, Bill.............................1983	Durbin, Mike 1984	Roth, Mark 1987
Anthony, Earl.......................1986	+ Fazio, Buzz 1976	Salvino, Carmen 1975
Berardi, Joe 1990	Godman, Jim.........................1987	Smith, Harry 1975
Bluth, Ray 1975	Hardwick, Billy.......................1977	Soutar, Dave 1979
Buckley, Roy 1992	Holman, Marshall 1990	Stefanich, Jim 1980
Burton, Nelson Jr 1979	Hudson, Tommy 1989	Voss, Brian 1994
Carter, Don 1975	Johnson, Don 1977	Webb, Wayne 1993
Colwell, Paul 1991	Laub, Larry 1985	Weber, Dick...........................1975
Cook, Steve 1993	Pappas, George 1986	+ Welu, Billy 1975
Davis, Dave 1978	Petraglia, John 1982	Zahn, Wayne.........................1981
Dickinson, Gary.....................1988	Ritger, Dick 1978	

Veterans

Allison, Glenn........................1984	+ Joseph, Joe 1985	McGrath, Mike 1988
Asher, Barry 1988	Limongello, Mike....................1994	+ St. John, Jim 1989
Foremsky, Skee 1992	Marzich, Andy........................1990	Strampe, Bob.........................1987
Guenther, Johnny 1986	McCune, Don 1991	

Meritorious Service

Antenora, Joe 1993	Fisher, E.A. (Bud) 1984	Pezzano, Chuck......................1975
Archibald, John 1989	+ Frantz, Lou 1978	Reichert, Jack.........................1992
Clemens, Chuck 1994	Golden, Harry 1983	+ Richards, Joe 1976
Elias, Eddie 1976	Hoffman, Ted Jr......................1985	Schenkel, Chris 1976
Esposito, Frank 1975	Jowdy, John 1988	Stitzlein, Lorraine 1980
Evans, Dick............................1986	Kelley, Joe 1989	Thompson, Al 1991
Firestone, Raymond................1987	+ Nagy, Steve 1977	

American Bowling Congress

Established in 1941 and open to professional and amateur bowlers. **Eligibility:** Nominated bowlers must have competed in at least 20 years of ABC tournaments. Voting done by 170-member panel made up of ABC officials, Hall of Fame members and media representatives.

Class of 1994 (8): PERFORMANCE—**Mike Berlin** and **Bob Hart**. PIONEERS—**Lafayette Allen Jr.**, **Sydney Celesteine**, **Eric deFreitas**, **William Hall Sr.** and **Masao Satow**. MERITORIOUS SERVICE—**Roger Tessman**.

Members are listed with years of induction; (+) indicates deceased members.

Performance

Allison, Glenn ...1979	Golembiewski, Billy ...1979	Pappas, George ...1989
Anthony, Earl ...1986	Guenther, Johnny ...1988	+ Patterson, Pat ...1974
+ Asplund, Harold ...1978	Hardwick, Billy ...1985	Ritger, Dick ...1984
Baer, Gordy ...1987	Hart, Bob ...1994	+ Rogoznica, Andy ...1993
Beach, Bill ...1991	Hennessey, Tom ...1976	Salvino, Carmen ...1979
Benkovic, Frank ...1958	Hoover, Dick ...1974	Schissler, Les ...1991
Berlin, Mike ...1994	Horn, Bud ...1992	Schroeder, Jim ...1990
+ Billick, George ...1982	Howard, George ...1986	+ Schwoegler, Connie ...1968
+ Blouin, Jimmy ...1953	Jackson, Eddie ...1988	Semiz, Teata ...1991
Bluth, Ray ...1973	Johnson, Don ...1982	+ Sielaff, Lou ...1968
+ Bodis, Joe ...1941	Johnson, Earl ...1987	+ Sinke, Joe ...1977
+ Bomar, Buddy ...1966	+ Joseph, Joe ...1969	+ Sixty, Billy ...1961
+ Brandt, Allie ...1960	+ Jouglard, Lee ...1979	Smith, Harry ...1978
+ Brosius, Eddie ...1976	+ Kartheiser, Frank ...1967	+ Smith, Jimmy ...1941
+ Bujack, Fred ...1967	+ Kawolics, Ed ...1968	Soutar, Dave ...1985
Bunetta, Bill ...1968	+ Kissoff, Joe ...1976	+ Sparando, Tony ...1968
Burton, Nelson Jr ...1981	Klares, John ...1982	+ Spinella, Barney ...1968
+ Burton, Nelson Sr ...1964	+ Knox, Billy ...1954	+ Steers, Harry ...1941
+ Campi, Lou ...1968	+ Koster, John ...1941	Stefanich, Jim ...1983
+ Carlson, Adolph ...1941	+ Krems, Eddie ...1973	+ Stein, Otto, Jr. ...1971
Carter, Don ...1970	Kristof, Joe ...1968	Stoudt, Bud ...1991
+ Caruana, Frank ...1977	+ Krumske, Paul ...1968	Strampe, Bob ...1977
+ Cassio, Marty ...1972	+ Lange, Herb ...1941	+ Thoma, Sykes ...1971
+ Castellano, Graz. ...1976	Lauman, Hank ...1976	Toft, Rod ...1991
+ Clause, Frank ...1980	Lillard, Bill ...1972	Tountas, Pete ...1989
Cohn, Alfred ...1985	Lindenmann, Tony ...1979	Tucker, Bill ...1988
+ Crimmins, Johnny ...1962	+ Lindsey, Mort ...1941	+ Varipapa, Andy ...1957
Davis, Gene ...1990	Lippe, Harry ...1989	+ Ward, Walter ...1959
+ Daw, Charlie ...1941	Lubanski, Ed ...1971	Weber, Dick ...1970
+ Day, Ned ...1952	Lucci, Vince, Sr ...1978	+ Welu, Billy ...1975
Dickinson, Gary ...1992	+ Marino, Hank ...1941	+ Wilman, Joe ...1951
+ Easter, Sarge ...1963	+ Martino, John ...1969	+ Wolf, Phil ...1961
Ellis, Don ...1981	Marzich, Andy ...1993	Wonders, Rich ...1990
+ Falcaro, Joe ...1968	McGrath, Mike ...1993	+ Young, George ...1959
Faragalli, Lindy ...1968	+ McMahon, Junie ...1967	Zahn, Wayne ...1980
+ Fazio, Buzz ...1963	+ Mercurio, Skang ...1967	Zikes, Les ...1983
Fehr, Steve ...1993	+ Meyers, Norm ...1984	+ Zunker, Gil ...1941
+ Gersonde, Russ ...1968	+ Nagy, Steve ...1963	
+ Gibson, Therm ...1965	Norris, Joe ...1954	
Godman, Jim ...1987	O'Donnell, Chuck ...1968	

Pioneers

+ Allen, Lafayette Jr. ...1994	Hall, William Sr. ...1994	+ Schutte, Louis ...1993
+ Celesteine, Sydney ...1994	+ Karpf, Samuel ...1993	+ Thompson, William V. ...1993
+ Curtis, Thomas ...1993	+ Pasdeloup, Frank ...1993	+ Timm, Dr. Henry ...1993
deFreitas, Eric ...1994	+ Satow, Masao ...1994	

Meritorious Service

+ Allen, Harold ...1966	+ Hagerty, Jack ...1963	Pezzano, Chuck ...1982
Baker, Frank ...1975	+ Hattstrom, H.A. (Doc) ...1980	Picchietti, Remo ...1993
+ Baumgarten, Elmer ...1963	+ Hermann, Cone ...1968	Pluckhahn, Bruce ...1989
+ Bellisimo, Lou ...1986	+ Howley, Pete ...1941	+ Raymer, Milt ...1972
+ Bensinger, Bob ...1969	+ Kennedy, Bob ...1981	+ Reed, Elmer ...1978
+ Chase, LeRoy ...1972	+ Langtry, Abe ...1963	Rudo, Milt. ...1984
+ Coker, John ...1980	+ Levine, Sam ...1971	Schenkel, Chris ...1988
+ Collier, Chuck ...1963	+ Luby, David ...1969	+ Sweeney, Dennis ...1974
+ Cruchon, Steve ...1983	Luby, Mort, Jr. ...1988	Tessman, Roger ...1994
+ Ditzen, Walt ...1973	+ Luby, Mort, Sr. ...1974	+ Thum, Joe ...1980
+ Doehrman, Bill ...1968	+ McCullough, Howard ...1971	Weinstein, Sam ...1970
Elias, Eddie ...1985	+ Patterson, Morehead ...1985	+ Whitney, Eli ...1975
Evans, Dick ...1992	+ Petersen, Louie ...1963	Wolf, Fred ...1976
Franklin, Bill ...1992		

Women's International Bowling Congress

Established in 1953. **Eligibility:** Performance nominees must have won at least one WIBC Championship Tournament title, a WIBC Queens tournament title or an international competition title and have bowled in at least 15 national WIBC Championship Tournaments (unless injury or illness cut career short).

Class of 1994 (5): PERFORMANCE—**Paula Carter**, **Mary Moharsi** and **Robbie Rickard**. MERITORIOUS SERVICE—**Glady Banker** and **Mildred Spitalnick**.

Members are listed with years of induction; (+) indicates deceased members.

Performance

Abel, Joy 1984	+ Harman, Janet 1985	Norman, Edie Jo 1993
Bolt, Mae..............1978	+ Hartrick, Stella 1972	Norton, Virginia 1988
Bouvia, Gloria 1987	+ Hatch, Grayce 1953	Notaro, Phyllis 1979
Boxberger, Loa..........1984	Havlish, Jean 1987	Ortner, Bev 1972
Buckner, Pam 1990	Hoffman, Martha 1979	+ Powers, Connie 1973
Burling, Catherine 1958	Holm, Joan 1974	Rickard, Robbie 1994
+ Burns, Nina 1977	+ Humphreys, Birdie..........1979	+ Robinson, Leona 1969
Cantaline, Anita 1979	Jacobson, D.D 1981	+ Rump, Anita 1962
Carter, LaVerne 1977	+ Jaeger, Emma 1953	+ Ruschmeyer, Addie..........1961
Carter, Paula..........1994	Kelly, Annesse..........1985	+ Ryan, Esther..........1963
Coburn, Doris 1976	+ Knechtges, Doris 1983	+ Sablatnik, Ethel 1979
Costello, Pat..........1986	Kuczynski, Betty 1981	+ Schulte, Myrtle 1965
Costello, Patty 1989	Ladewig, Marion..........1964	+ Shablis, Helen 1977
Dryer, Pat..........1978	Martin, Sylvia Wene..........1966	+ Simon, Violet (Billy) 1960
Duval, Helen 1970	Martorella, Millie 1975	+ Small, Tess 1971
Fellmeth, Catherine..........1970	+ Matthews, Merle 1974	+ Smith, Grace 1968
Fothergill, Dotty..........1980	+ McCutcheon, Floretta..........1956	Soutar, Judy..........1976
+ Fritz, Deane..........1966	Merrick, Marge..........1980	+ Stockdale, Louise..........1953
Garms, Shirley..........1971	+ Mikiel, Val 1979	Toepfer, Elvira 1976
Gloor, Olga 1976	+ Miller, Dorothy 1954	+ Twyford, Sally 1964
Graham, Linda 1992	Mivelaz, Betty 1991	+ Warmbier, Marie 1953
Graham, Mary Lou 1989	Moharsi, Mary..........1994	Wilkinson, Dorothy 1990
+ Greenwald, Goldie 1953	Morris, Betty 1983	+ Winandy, Cecelia 1975
Grinfelds, Vesma..........1991	Nichols, Lorrie 1989	Zimmerman, Donna 1982

Meritorious Service

Baetz, Helen 1977	+ Haas, Dorothy 1977	+ Porter, Cora..........1986
+ Baker, Helen 1989	+ Higley, Margaret..........1969	+ Quinn, Zoe..........1979
+ Banker, Glady..........1994	+ Hochstadter, Bee 1967	+ Rishling, Gertrude 1972
+ Bayley, Clover..........1992	+ Kay, Nora 1964	Simone, Anne..........1991
+ Berger, Winifred 1976	+ Kelly, Ellen 1979	Sloan, Catherine 1985
+ Bohlen, Philena 1955	Kelone, Theresa 1978	+ Speck, Berdie..........1966
Borschuk, Lo 1988	+ Knepprath, Jeannette..........1963	Spitalnick, Mildred 1994
Botkin, Freda 1986	+ Lasher, Iolia 1967	+ Spring, Alma 1979
+ Chapman, Emily 1957	Marrs, Mabel..........1979	+ Switzer, Pearl 1973
+ Crowe, Alberta 1982	+ McBride, Bertha 1968	Todd, Trudy 1993
+ Dornblaser, Gertrude..........1979	+ Menne, Catherine 1979	+ Veatch, Georgia..........1974
Duffy, Agnes..........1987	+ Mraz, Jo..........1959	+ White, Mildred 1975
Finke, Gertrude 1990	O'Connor, Billie 1992	+ Wood, Ann 1970
+ Fisk, Rae..........1983	+ Phaler, Emma..........1965	

B'nai B'rith National Sports Hall of Fame

Established in 1991 by B'nai B'rith to recognize the achievements and contributions of Jewish athletes and sportsmen in America. **Address:** 1640 Rhode Island Ave. NW, Washington, DC 20036. A permanent museum is scheduled to open in the spring of 1995. **Telephone:** (202) 857-6580.

Eligibility: Nominees must be prominent Jewish athletes, coaches, administrators or media figures. Voting done by seven-member panel of B'nai B'rith lay persons.

Class of 1994 (9): Baseball catcher **Harry Danning** and pitchers **Ken Holtzman** and **Steve Stone;** Boxer **Barney Ross;** Football halfback **Marshall Goldberg;** Baseball and Basketball team owner **Jerry Reinsdorf;** Women's swimming pioneer **Charlotte Epstein;** and Columnists **Jerome Holtzman** and **Irv Kupcinet**.

Members are listed with year of induction; (+) indicates deceased members.

Allen, Mel 1991	Holtzman, Ken..........1994	Rosen, Al 1991
Auerbach, Red 1991	Kupcinet, Irv..........1994	+ Ross, Barney..........1994
Danning, Harry 1994	Koufax, Sandy 1991	Savitt, Dick 1991
+ Epstein, Charlotte..........1994	+ Leonard, Benny 1991	Schayes, Dolph..........1991
Goldberg, Marshall..........1994	Luckman, Sid 1991	Spitz, Mark 1991
+ Gottlieb, Eddie 1991	Pollin, Abe 1991	Stone, Steve..........1994
+ Greenberg, Hank..........1991	Povich, Shirley 1991	
Holtzman, Jerome 1994	Reinsdorf, Jerry 1994	

BOXING

International Boxing Hall of Fame

Established in 1989 and opened in 1990. **Address:** 1 Hall of Fame Drive, Canastota, NY 13032. **Telephone:** (315) 697-7095.

Eligibility: All nominees must be retired for five years. Voting done by 142-member panel made up of Boxing Writers' Association members and world-wide boxing historians.

Class of 1994 (14): MODERN ERA—**Jackie (Kid) Berg** (jr. welterweight); **Joey Maxim** (light heavyweight); **Michael Spinks** (light heavyweight & heavyweight); **Carlos Zarate** (bantamweight). OLD TIMERS—**John Henry Lewis** (light heavyweight); **Philadelphia Jack O'Brien** (light heavyweight); **Jack Sharkey** (heavyweight); **Pancho Villa** (flyweight). PIONEERS—**Ben Brain** (heavyweight); **Paddy Duffy** (welterweight). NON-PARTICIPANTS—**Chris Dundee** (promoter); **Eddie Futch** (trainer); **Ruby Goldstein** (referee); **Sam Taub** (broadcaster).

Members are listed with year of induction; (+) indicates deceased members.

Modern Era

Ali, Muhammad 1990	+ Graham, Billy 1992	Olivares, Ruben 1991
Arguello, Alexis 1992	+ Graziano, Rocky 1991	Ortiz, Carlos 1991
+ Armstrong, Henry 1990	Griffith, Emile 1990	Patterson, Floyd 1991
Basilio, Carmen 1990	Hagler, Marvelous Marvin ...1993	Pep, Willie 1990
Benvenuti, Nino 1992	Jack, Beau 1991	+ Robinson, Sugar Ray 1990
+ Berg, Jackie (Kid) 1994	Jofre, Eder 1992	Saddler, Sandy 1990
+ Burley, Charley 1992	Johnson, Harold 1993	+ Sanchez, Salvadore 1991
+ Cerdan, Marcel 1991	LaMotta, Jake 1990	Schmeling, Max 1992
+ Charles, Ezzard 1990	+ Liston, Sonny 1991	Spinks, Michael 1994
+ Conn, Billy 1990	+ Louis, Joe 1990	+ Tiger, Dick 1991
+ Elorde, Gabriel (Flash) 1993	+ Marciano, Rocky 1990	Walcott, Jersey Joe 1990
Foster, Bob 1990	Maxim, Joey 1994	Williams, Ike 1990
Frazier, Joe 1990	Monzon, Carlos 1990	Zale, Tony 1991
Fullmer, Gene 1991	Moore, Archie 1990	Zarate, Carlos 1994
Gavilan, Kid 1990	Napoles, Jose 1990	+ Zivic, Fritzie 1993
Giardello, Joey 1993	Norton, Ken 1992	

Old-Timers

Ambers, Lou 1992	+ Gans, Joe 1990	+ McFarland, Packey 1992
+ Attell, Abe 1990	+ Gibbons, Mike 1992	+ McGovern, Terry 1990
+ Britton, Jack 1990	+ Gibbons, Tommy 1993	McLarnin, Jimmy 1991
+ Brown, Panama Al 1992	+ Greb, Harry 1990	+ Nelson, Battling 1992
+ Canzoneri, Tony 1990	+ Griffo, Young 1991	+ O'Brien, Philadelphia Jack 1994
+ Carpentier, Georges 1991	+ Jackson, Peter 1990	+ Rosenbloom, Maxie 1993
+ Chocolate, Kid 1991	+ Jeffries, James J 1990	+ Ross, Barney 1990
+ Corbett, James J 1990	+ Johnson, Jack 1990	+ Ryan, Tommy 1991
+ Darcy, Les 1993	+ Ketchel, Stanley 1990	+ Sharkey, Jack 1994
+ Dempsey, Jack 1990	+ Langford, Sam 1990	+ Tunney, Gene 1990
+ Dempsey, Jack (the Nonpareil) ..1992	+ Leonard, Benny 1990	+ Villa, Pancho 1994
+ Dixon, George 1990	+ Lewis, John Henry 1994	+ Walker, Mickey 1990
+ Driscoll, Jim 1990	+ Lewis, Ted (Kid) 1992	+ Walcott, Joe 1991
+ Dundee, Johnny 1991	+ Loughran, Tommy 1991	+ Wilde, Jimmy 1990
+ Fitzsimmons, Bob 1990	+ McCoy, Charles (Kid) 1991	+ Wills, Harry 1992
+ Flowers, Theodore (Tiger) 1993		

Pioneers

+ Belcher, Jem 1992	+ Figg, James 1992	+ Pearce, Henry 1993
+ Brain, Ben 1994	+ Jackson, John 1992	+ Sayers, Tom 1990
+ Broughton, Jack 1990	+ King, Tom 1992	Spring, Tom 1992
+ Burke, James 1992	+ Langham, Nat 1992	+ Sullivan, John L 1990
+ Cribb, Tom 1991	+ Mace, Jem 1990	+ Thompson, William 1991
+ Duffy, Paddy 1994	+ Mendoza, Daniel 1990	

Non-Participants

+ Andrews, Thomas S 1992	Dundee, Chris 1994	+ Kearns, Jack (Doc) 1990
+ Arcel, Ray 1991	Dunphy, Don 1993	+ Liebling, A.J 1992
+ Blackburn, Jack 1992	+ Egan, Pierce 1991	+ Lonsdale, Lord 1990
Brenner, Teddy 1993	+ Fleischer, Nat 1990	Markson, Harry 1992
+ Chambers, John Graham 1990	Futch, Eddie 1994	+ Parnassus, George 1991
Clancy, Gil 1993	+ Goldman, Charley 1992	+ Queensberry, Marquis of 1990
+ Coffroth, James W 1991	+ Goldstein, Ruby 1994	+ Rickard, Tex 1990
+ Donovan, Arthur 1993	+ Jacobs, Jimmy 1993	+ Taub, Sam 1994
Dundee, Angelo 1992	+ Jacobs, Mike 1990	+ Walker, James J. (Jimmy) 1992

FOOTBALL

College Football Hall of Fame

Established in 1955 by the National Football Foundation. **Address:** P.O. Box 11146, South Bend, IN 46634 (moving from Kings Island, Ohio. New Hall of Fame will open in the fall of 1995). **Telephone:** (219) 235-5581.

Eligibility: Nominated players must be out of college 10 years and a first team All-America pick by a major selector during their careers; coaches must be retired three years. Voting done by 12-member panel of athletic directors, conference and bowl officials and media representatives.

Class of 1994 (14): PLAYERS—LB **Bob Babich**, Miami-OH (1966–68); RB **Tony Dorsett**, Pittsburgh (1973–76); OG **Steve Eisenhauer**, Navy (1952–53); FL-RB **Steve Elkins**, Baylor (1962–64); QB **Pete Elliott**, Michigan (1945–48); TB **Tucker Frederickson**, Auburn (1962–64); C **Jerry Groom**, Notre Dame (1948–50); QB-HB **John Hadl**, Kansas (1959–61); SE **Ozzie Newsome**, Alabama (1974–77); QB **Gifford Nielsen**, BYU (1975–77); OT **Marvin Powell**, USC (1974–76); DT **Randy White**, Maryland (1972–74). COACHES—**Vince Dooley**, Georgia (1964–88); **John Merritt**, Jackson St. (1952–62) and Tennessee St. (1963–83).

Note: Bobby Dodd and **Amos Alonzo Stagg** are the only members to be honored as both players and coaches.

Players are listed with final year they played in college and coaches are listed with year of induction; (+) indicates deceased members.

Players

+ Abell, Earl-Colgate..................1915
Agase, Alex-Purdue/Ill...........1946
+ Agganis, Harry-Boston U........1952
Albert, Frank-Stanford.............1941
+ Aldrich, Ki-TCU.....................1938
+ Aldrich, Malcolm-Yale............1921
+ Alexander, Joe-Syracuse..........1920
Alworth, Lance-Arkansas..........1961
+ Ameche, Alan-Wisconsin.........1954
+ Ames, Knowlton-Princeton........1889
Amling, Warren-Ohio St............1946
Anderson, Dick-Colorado.........1967
Anderson, Donny-Tex.Tech.......1966
+ Anderson, Hunk-N.Dame...........1921
Atkins, Doug-Tennessee...........1952

Babich, Bob-Miami-OH...........1968
Bacon, Everett-Wesleyan..........1912
Bagnell, Reds-Penn................1950
+ Baker, Hobey-Princeton............1913
+ Baker, John-USC...................1931
+ Baker, Moon-N'western...........1926
Baker, Terry-Oregon St...........1962
+ Ballin, Harold-Princeton...........1914
+ Banker, Bill-Tulane................1929
Banonis, Vince-Detroit.............1941
+ Barnes, Stan-California............1921
+ Barrett, Charles-Cornell...........1915
+ Baston, Bert-Minnesota............1916
+ Battles, Cliff-WV Wesleyan........1931
Baugh, Sammy-TCU................1936
Baughan, Maxie-Ga.Tech..........1959
+ Bausch, James-Kansas............1930
Beagle, Ron-Navy..................1955
Beban, Gary-UCLA................1967
Bechtol, Hub-Texas...............1946
+ Beckett, John-Oregon.............1916
Bednarik, Chuck-Penn.............1948
Behm, Forrest-Nebraska...........1940
Bell, Bobby-Minnesota............1962
Bellino, Joe-Navy..................1960
Below, Marty-Wisconsin...........1923
+ Benbrook, Al-Michigan...........1910
+ Berry, Charlie-Lafayette...........1924
Bertelli, Angelo-N.Dame...........1943
Berwanger, Jay-Chicago...........1935
+ Bettencourt, L.-St.Mary's..........1927
Biletnikoff, Fred-Fla.St.............1964
Blanchard, Doc-Army.............1946
+ Blozis, Al-Georgetown............1942
Bock, Ed-Iowa St...................1938
Bomar, Lynn-Vanderbilt...........1924

+ Bomeisler, Bo-Yale................1913
+ Booth, Albie-Yale 1931
+ Borries, Fred-Navy................1934
Bosely, Bruce-West Va............1955
Bosseler, Don-Miami,FL...........1956
Bottari, Vic-California..............1938
+ Boynton, Ben-Williams............1920
+ Brewer, Charles-Harvard..........1895
+ Bright, Johnny-Drake.............1951
Brodie, John-Stanford.............1956
+ Brooke, George-Penn.............1895
Brown, Bob-Nebraska............1963
Brown, Geo-Navy/S.Diego St.1947
+ Brown, Gordon-Yale..............1900
+ Brown, John, Jr.-Navy.............1913
+ Brown, Johnny Mack-Ala..........1925
Brown, Tay-USC...................1932
+ Bunker, Paul-Army................1902
Burton, Ron-N'western............1959
Butkus, Dick-Illinois...............1964
+ Butler, Robert-Wisconsin.........1912

Cafego, George-Tenn..............1939
+ Cagle, Red-SWLA/Army..........1929
+ Cain, John-Alabama..............1932
Cameron, Ed-Wash.& Lee.......1924
+ Campbell, David-Harvard.........1901
Campbell, Earl-Texas.............1977
+ Cannon, Jack-N.Dame............1929
Cappelletti, John-Penn St........1973
+ Carideo, Frank-N.Dame..........1930
+ Carney, Charles-Illinois...........1921
Caroline, J.C.-Illinois.............1954
Carpenter, Bill-Army.............1959
+ Carpenter, Hunter-Va.Tech......1905
Carroll, Chas.-Washington.......1928
+ Casey, Edward-Harvard..........1919
Cassady, Howard-Ohio St.......1955
+ Chamberlin, Guy-Neb............1915
Chapman, Sam-California.........1938
Chappuis, Bob-Michigan.........1947
+ Christman, Paul-Missouri........1940
+ Clark, Dutch-Colo. Col...........1929
Cleary, Paul-USC.................1947
+ Clevenger, Zora-Indiana.........1903
Cloud, Jack-Wm&Mary...........1948
+ Cochran, Gary-Princeton.........1897
+ Cody, Josh-Vanderbilt............1919
Coleman, Don-Mich.St...........1951
Conerly, Charlie-Miss............1947
Connor, George-HC/ND.........1947
+ Corbin, William-Yale.............1888

Corbus, William-Stanford.......1933
+ Cowan, Hector-Princeton........1889
+ Coy, Edward (Tad)-Yale..........1909
+ Crawford, Fred-Duke.............1933
Crow, John David-Tex.A&M......1957
+ Crowley, Jim-Notre Dame.......1924
Csonka, Larry-Syracuse..........1967
Cutter, Slade-Navy................1934
+ Czarobski, Ziggie-N.Dame......1947

Dale, Carroll-Va.Tech.............1959
+ Dalrymple, Gerald-Tulane........1931
Dalton, John-Navy................1911
Daly, Chas.-Harvard/Army......1902
Daniell, Averell-Pitt...............1936
+ Daniell, James-Ohio St..........1941
+ Davies, Tom-Pittsburgh..........1921
+ Davis, Ernie-Syracuse...........1961
Davis, Glenn-Army................1946
Davis, Robert-Ga.Tech...........1947
Dawkins, Pete-Army..............1958
DeLong, Steve-Tennessee........1964
DeRogatis, Al-Duke...............1948
+ DesJardien, Paul-Chicago.......1914
+ Devine, Aubrey-Iowa.............1921
+ DeWitt, John-Princeton..........1903
Dial, Buddy-Rice.................1958
Ditka, Mike-Pittsburgh..........1960
Dobbs, Glenn-Tulsa..............1942
+ Dodd, Bobby-Tennessee.........1930
Donan, Holland-Princeton.......1950
+ Donchess, Joseph-Pitt...........1929
Dorsett, Tony-Pitt...............1976
+ Dougherty, Nathan-Tenn........1909
Drahos, Nick-Cornell............1940
+ Driscoll, Paddy-N'western.......1917
+ Drury, Morley-USC..............1927
Dudley, Bill-Virginia..............1941

Easley, Kenny-UCLA.............1980
+ Eckersall, Walter-Chicago........1906
+ Edwards, Turk-Wash.St..........1931
Edwards, Wm.-Princeton........1899
+ Eichenlaub, Ray-N.Dame........1914
Eisenhauer, Steve-Navy.........1953
Elkins, Larry-Baylor..............1964
Elliott, Bump-Mich/Purdue......1947
Elliott, Pete-Michigan............1948
Evans, Ray-Kansas...............1947
+ Exendine, Albert-Carlisle........1907

Falaschi, Nello-S.Clara...........1936
Fears, Tom-S.Clara/UCLA.......1947

College Football Hall of Fame (Cont.)

Players

+ Feathers, Beattie-Tenn 1933
Fenimore, Bob-Okla.St 1946
+ Fenton, Doc-LSU 1909
Ferraro, John-USC 1944
Fesler, Wes-Ohio St 1930
+ Fincher, Bill-Ga.Tech 1920
Fischer, Bill-Notre Dame 1948
+ Fish, Hamilton-Harvard 1909
+ Fisher, Robert-Harvard 1911
+ Flowers, Allen-Ga.Tech 1920
Fortmann Danny-Colgate 1935
Francis, Sam-Nebraska 1936
Franco Ed-Fordham 1937
+ Frank, Clint-Yale 1937
Franz, Rodney-California 1949
Frederickson, Tucker-Auburn ...1964
+ Friedman, Benny-Michigan 1926

Gabriel, Roman-N.C. State 1961
Gain, Bob-Kentucky 1950
+ Galiffa, Arnold-Army 1949
Gallarneau, Hugh-Stanford.....1940
+ Garbisch, Edgar-W.& J./Army..1924
Garrett, Mike-USC 1965
+ Gelbert, Charles-Penn 1896
+ Geyer, Forest-Oklahoma.........1915
Giel, Paul-Minnesota 1953
Gifford, Frank-USC 1951
+ Gilbert, Walter-Auburn...........1936
Gilmer, Harry-Alabama 1947
+ Gipp, George-N.Dame...........1920
+ Gladchuk, Chet-Boston Col 1940
Glass, Bill-Baylor 1956
Goldberg, Marshall-Pitt 1938
Goodreault, Gene-BC 1940
+ Gordon, Walter-Calif 1918
+ Governali, Paul-Columbia.......1942
Graham, Otto-N'western.........1943
+ Grange, Red-Illinois 1925
+ Grayson, Bobby-Stanford 1935
+ Green, Jack-Tulane/Army 1945
Greene, Joe-N.Texas St 1968
Griese, Bob-Purdue 1966
Griffin, Archie-Ohio St 1975
Groom, Jerry-Notre Dame 1950
+ Gulick, Merle-Toledo/Hobart ..1929
+ Guyon, Joe-Ga.Tech 1918

Hadl, John-Kansas 1961
+ Hale, Edwin-Miss.College 1921
+ Hall, Parker-Miss.....................1938
Ham, Jack-Penn St 1970
Hamilton, Bob-Stanford 1935
+ Hamilton, Tom-Navy..............1926
+ Hanson, Vic-Syracuse 1926
+ Harder, Pat-Wisconsin 1942
+ Hardwick, Tack-Harvard.........1914
+ Hare, T.Truxton-Penn 1900
+ Harley, Chick-Ohio St.............1919
+ Harmon, Tom-Michigan 1940
+ Harpster, Howard-Carnegie 1928
+ Hart, Edward-Princeton 1911
Hart, Leon-Notre Dame 1949
Hartman, Bill-Georgia 1937
+ Hazel, Homer-Rutgers.............1924
Hazeltine, Matt-Calif 1954
+ Healey, Ed.-Dartmouth............1916
+ Heffelfinger, Pudge-Yale.........1891
+ Hein, Mel-Washington St 1930
+ Heinrich, Don-Washington......1952
Hendricks, Ted-Miami,FL.........1968

+ Henry, Pete-Wash&Jeff 1919
+ Herschberger, C.-Chicago.......1898
+ Herwig, Robert-Calif 1937
+ Heston, Willie-Michigan 1904
+ Hickman, Herman-Tenn 1931
+ Hickok, William-Yale 1894
Hill, Dan-Duke 1938
+ Hillebrand, Art-Princeton 1899
+ Hinkey, Frank-Yale 1894
Hinkle, Carl-Vanderbilt 1937
Hinkle, Clarke-Bucknell 1931
Hirsch, Elroy-Wisc./Mich........1943
+ Hitchcock, James-Auburn 1932
Hoffmann, Frank-N.Dame 1931
+ Hogan, James J.-Yale 1904
+ Holland, Brud-Cornell.............1938
+ Holleder, Don-Army 1955
+ Hollenback, Bill-Penn 1908
Holovak, Mike-Boston Col 1942
Holub, E.J.-Texas Tech 1960
Hornung, Paul-N.Dame 1956
+ Horrell, Edwin-California 1924
Horvath, Les-Ohio St 1944
+ Howe, Arthur-Yale..................1911
+ Howell, Dixie-Alabama 1934
+ Hubbard, Cal-Centenary 1926
+ Hubbard, John-Amherst 1906
+ Hubert, Pooley-Ala.................1925
Huff, Sam-West Virginia 1955
Humble, Weldon-Rice 1946
+ Hunt, Joe-Texas A&M 1927
Huntington, Ellery-Colgate 1914
Hutson, Don-Alabama 1934

+ Ingram, Jonas-Navy 1906
+ Isbell, Cecil-Purdue 1937

+ Jablonsky, J.-Army/Wash........1933
Janowicz, Vic-Ohio St 1951
+ Jenkins, Darold-Missouri.........1941
+ Jensen, Jackie-California 1948
+ Joesting, Herbert-Minn 1927
Johnson, Bob-Tennessee.........1967
+ Johnson, Jimmie-Carlisle/
                         N'western....1903
Johnson, Ron-Michigan 1968
+ Jones, Calvin-Iowa 1955
+ Jones, Gomer-Ohio St 1935
Jordan, Lee Roy-Alabama.......1962
+ Juhan, Frank-U.of South 1910
Justice, Charlie-N.Car 1949

+ Kaer, Mort-USC 1926
Karras, Alex-Iowa 1957
Kavanaugh, Ken-LSU 1939
+ Kaw, Edgar-Cornell 1922
Kazmaier, Dick-Princeton 1951
+ Keck, James-Princeton 1921
Kelley, Larry-Yale 1936
+ Kelly, Wild Bill-Montana 1926
Kenna, Doug-Army 1944
+ Kerr, George-Boston Col 1941
+ Ketcham, Henry-Yale..............1913
Keyes, Leroy-Purdue 1968
+ Killinger, Glenn-Penn St 1921
+ Kilpatrick, John-Yale..............1910
Kimbrough, John-Tex A&M......1940
+ Kinard, Frank-Mississippi.........1937
+ King, Phillip-Princeton.............1893
+ Kinnick, Nile-Iowa 1939
+ Kipke, Harry-Michigan 1923

+ Kirkpatrick, John-Yale.............1910
+ Kitzmiller, John-Oregon 1930
+ Koch, Barton-Baylor 1931
+ Koppisch, Walt-Columbia 1924
Kramer, Ron-Michigan.............1956
Krueger, Charlie-Tex.A&M 1957
Kutner, Malcolm-Texas 1941
Kwalick, Ted-Penn St...............1968

+ Lach, Steve-Duke 1941
+ Lane, Myles-Dartmouth...........1927
Lattner, Johnny-N.Dame...........1953
Lauricella, Hank-Tenn 1952
+ Lautenschlaeger-Tulane 1925
+ Layden, Elmer-N.Dame............1924
+ Layne, Bobby-Texas 1947
+ Lea, Langdon-Princeton 1895
LeBaron, Eddie-Pacific 1949
+ Leech, James-VMI 1920
+ Lester, Darrell-TCU 1935
Lilly, Bob-TCU 1960
Little, Floyd-Syracuse 1966
+ Lio, Augie-Georgetown 1940
+ Locke, Gordon-Iowa 1922
+ Lourie, Don-Princeton 1921
Lucas, Richie-Penn St 1959
Luckman, Sid-Columbia 1938
+ Lujack, Johnny-N.Dame..........1947
Lund, Pug-Minnesota 1934
Lynch, Jim-Notre Dame 1966

+ Macomber, Bart-Illinois 1915
MacLeod, Robert-Dart. 1938
Maegle, Dick-Rice 1954
+ Mahan, Eddie-Harvard 1915
Majors, John-Tennessee 1956
+ Mallory, William-Yale..............1923
Mancha, Vaughn-Ala 1947
+ Mann, Gerald-SMU 1927
Manning, Archie-Miss 1970
Manske, Edgar-N'western........1933
Marinaro, Ed-Cornell 1971
Markov, Vic-Washington 1937
+ Marshall, Bobby-Minn 1906
Matson, Ollie-San Fran 1952
Matthews, Ray-TCU 1927
+ Maulbetsch, John-Mich 1914
+ Mauthe, Pete-Penn St.............1912
+ Maxwell, Robert-Chicago/
                         Swarthmore ...1906
McAfee, George-Duke 1939
+ McClung, Thomas-Yale 1891
McColl, Bill-Stanford...............1951
+ McCormick, Jim-Princeton.......1907
McDonald, Tommy-Okla 1956
+ McDowall, Jack-N.C.State 1927
McElhenny, Hugh-Wash...........1951
+ McEver, Gene-Tennessee 1931
+ McEwan, John-Army 1916
McFadden, Banks-Clemson 1939
McFadin, Bud-Texas 1950
McGee, Mike-Duke 1959
+ McGinley, Edward-Penn 1924
+ McGovern, John-Minn.............1910
McGraw, Thurman-Colo.St 1949
+ McKeever, Mike-USC 1960
+ McLaren, George-Pitt..............1918
+ McMillan, Dan-USC/Calif........1922
McMillin, Bo-Centre.................1921
+ McWhorter, Bob-Georgia 1913
+ Mercer, LeRoy-Penn 1912

College Football Hall of Fame (Cont.)

Players

Whitmire, Don-Navy/Ala 1944
+ Wickhorst, Frank-Navy 1926
Widseth, Ed-Minnesota 1936
+ Wildung, Dick-Minnesota 1942
Williams, Bob-N.Dame 1950
Williams, Froggie-Rice 1949
Willis, Bill-Ohio St 1944
Wilson, Bobby-SMU 1935
+ Wilson, George-Wash 1925
+ Wilson, Harry-Army/Penn St...1926

Wilson, Mike-Lafayette...........1928
Wistert, Albert-Michigan 1942
Wistert, Alvin-Michigan 1949
+ Wistert, Whitey-Michigan 1933
+ Wojciechowicz, Alex-Fordham.1937
+ Wood, Barry-Harvard............1931
+ Wyant, Andy-Chicago...........1894
+ Wyatt, Bowden-Tenn 1938
+ Wyckoff, Clint-Cornell...........1895
+ Yarr, Tommy-N.Dame............1931

Yary, Ron-USC 1967
+ Yoder, Lloyd-Carnegie............1926
+ Young, Buddy-Illinois.............1946
+ Young, Harry-Wash.& Lee.......1916
+ Young, Waddy-Okla 1938
Youngblood, Jack-Florida 1970

Zarnas, Gust-Ohio State 1937

Coaches

+ Aillet, Joe..............................1989
+ Alexander, Bill 1951
+ Anderson, Ed 1971
+ Armstrong, Ike......................1957
+ Bachman, Charlie...................1978
+ Banks, Earl 1992
+ Baujan, Harry 1990
+ Bell, Matty...........................1955
+ Bezdek, Hugo........................1954
+ Bible, Dana X 1951
+ Bierman, Bernie 1955
Blackman, Bob 1987
+ Blaik, Earl (Red)....................1965
Broyles, Frank 1983
+ Bryant, Paul (Bear)................1986
+ Caldwell, Charlie...................1961
+ Camp, Walter 1951
Casanova, Len 1977
+ Cavanaugh, Frank 1954
+ Colman, Dick 1990
+ Crisler, Fritz.........................1954
+ Daugherty, Duffy 1984
Devaney, Bob 1981
Devine, Dan 1985
+ Dobie, Gil 1951
+ Dodd, Bobby 1993
+ Donohue, Michael 1951
Dooley, Vince 1994
+ Dorais, Gus 1954
+ Edwards, Bill 1986
+ Engle, Rip 1973
Faurot, Don 1961
+ Gaither, Jake 1973
Gillman, Sid 1989
+ Godfrey, Ernest.....................1972
Graves, Ray 1990
+ Gustafson, Andy 1985
+ Hall, Edward 1951
+ Harding, Jack........................1980
+ Harlow, Richard 1954

+ Harman, Harvey 1981
+ Harper, Jesse 1971
+ Haughton, Percy....................1951
+ Hayes, Woody 1983
+ Heisman, John W 1954
+ Higgins, Robert 1954
+ Hollingberry, Babe..................1979
Howard, Frank 1989
+ Ingram, Bill 1973
+ Jennings, Morley 1973
+ Jones, Biff 1954
+ Jones, Howard 1951
+ Jones, Tad 1958
+ Jordan, Lloyd 1978
+ Jordan, Ralph (Shug) 1982
+ Kerr, Andy 1951
+ Leahy, Frank 1970
+ Little, George 1955
+ Little, Lou 1960
+ Madigan, Slip 1974
Maurer, Dave 1991
McClendon, Charley 1986
McCracken, Herb 1973
+ McGugin, Dan 1951
McKay, John 1988
+ McKeen, Allyn 1991
+ McLaughry, Tuss 1962
+ Merritt, John 1994
+ Meyer, Dutch 1956
+ Mollenkopf, Jack 1988
+ Moore, Bernie 1954
+ Moore, Scrappy 1980
+ Morrison, Ray 1954
+ Munger, George 1976
+ Munn, Clarence (Biggie)..........1959
+ Murray, Bill 1974
+ Murray, Frank 1983
+ Mylin, Ed (Hooks) 1974
+ Neale, Earle (Greasy) 1967
+ Neely, Jess 1971

+ Nelson, David 1987
+ Neyland, Robert 1956
+ Norton, Homer......................1971
+ O'Neill, Frank (Buck) 1951
+ Owen, Bennie 1951
Parseghian, Ara 1980
+ Perry, Doyt 1988
+ Phelan, Jimmy 1973
Prothro, Tommy 1991
Ralston, John 1992
+ Robinson, E.N. 1955
+ Rockne, Knute 1951
+ Romney, Dick 1954
+ Roper, Bill 1951
Royal, Darrell 1983
+ Sanford, George 1971
Schembechler, Bo 1993
+ Schmidt, Francis 1971
+ Schwartzwalder, Ben...............1982
+ Shaughnessy, Clark................1968
+ Shaw, Buck 1972
+ Smith, Andy 1951
+ Snavely, Carl 1965
+ Stagg, Amos Alonzo 1951
+ Sutherland, Jock 1951
+ Tatum, Jim 1984
+ Thomas, Frank.......................1951
+ Vann, Thad 1987
Vaught, Johnny 1979
+ Wade, Wallace 1955
+ Waldorf, Lynn (Pappy)............1966
+ Warner, Glenn (Pop)..............1951
+ Wieman, E.E. (Tad)...............1956
+ Wilce, John 1954
+ Wilkinson, Bud 1969
+ Williams, Henry 1951
+ Woodruff, George 1963
Woodson, Warren 1989
+ Yost, Fielding (Hurry Up) 1951
+ Zuppke, Bob 1951

Pro Football Hall of Fame

Established in 1963 by National Football League to commemorate the sport's professional origins. **Address:** 2121 George Halas Drive NW, Canton, OH 44708. **Telephone:** (216) 456-8207.

Eligibility: Nominated players must be retired five years, coaches must be retired, and contributors can still be active. Voting done by 34-member panel made up of media representatives from all 28 NFL cities, one PFWA representative and five selectors-at-large.

Class of 1994 (6): PLAYERS—RB **Tony Dorsett**, Dallas (1977-87), Denver (1988); CB **Jimmy Johnson**, San Francisco (1961-76); RB **Leroy Kelly**, Cleveland (1964-73); TE **Jackie Smith**, St. Louis (1963-77), Dallas (1978); DT **Randy White**, Dallas (1975-88). COACH—**Bud Grant**, Minnesota (1967-83, 1985).

1994 finalists (nominated, but not elected): PLAYERS—Dan Dierdorf, Carl Eller, Charlie Joiner, Paul Krause, Tom Mack, Mel Renfro, John Stallworth, Lynn Swann and Kellen Winslow.

Members are listed with year of induction; (+) indicates deceased members.

☞

Quarterbacks

Baugh, Sammy 1963	Graham, Otto......................1965	Starr, Bart.............................1977
Blanda, George (also PK)........1981	Griese, Bob 1990	Staubach, Roger 1985
Bradshaw, Terry 1989	+ Herber, Arnie......................1966	Tarkenton, Fran 1986
+ Clark, Dutch 1963	Jurgensen, Sonny 1983	Tittle, Y.A. 1971
+ Conzelman, Jimmy................1964	+ Layne, Bobby......................1967	Unitas, Johnny 1979
Dawson, Len 1987	Luckman, Sid 1965	+ Van Brocklin, Norm.............1971
+ Driscoll, Paddy.....................1965	Namath, Joe.........................1985	+ Waterfield, Bob....................1965
Fouts, Dan 1993	Parker, Clarence (Ace)...........1972	

Running Backs

+ Battles, Cliff 1968	Hornung, Paul......................1986	Payton, Walter 1993
Brown, Jim 1971	Johnson, John Henry 1987	Perry, Joe 1969
Campbell, Earl.....................1991	Kelly, Leroy 1994	Riggins, John 1992
Canadeo, Tony 1974	+ Leemans, Tuffy 1978	Sayers, Gale 1977
Csonka, Larry 1987	Matson, Ollie 1972	Simpson, O.J 1985
Dorsett, Tony 1994	McAfee, George 1966	+ Strong, Ken 1967
Dudley, Bill 1966	McElhenny, Hugh 1970	Taylor, Jim 1976
Gifford, Frank.......................1977	+ McNally, Johnny (Blood).........1963	+ Thorpe, Jim..........................1963
+ Grange, Red.........................1963	Moore, Lenny 1975	Trippi, Charley 1968
+ Guyon, Joe 1966	Motley, Marion 1968	Van Buren, Steve 1965
Harris, Franco 1990	+ Nagurski, Bronko 1963	Walker, Doak 1986
+ Hinkle, Clarke 1964	+ Nevers, Ernie 1963	

Ends & Wide Receivers

Alworth, Lance 1978	+ Hewitt, Bill 1971	+ Millner, Wayne 1968
Badgro, Red 1981	Hirsch, Elroy (Crazylegs).........1968	Mitchell, Bobby 1983
Berry, Raymond 1973	Hutson, Don 1963	Pihos, Pete 1970
Biletnikoff, Fred....................1988	Lavelli, Dante 1975	Smith, Jackie 1994
+ Chamberlin, Guy 1965	Mackey, John 1992	Taylor, Charley 1984
Ditka, Mike 1988	Maynard, Don 1987	Warfield, Paul 1983
Fears, Tom 1970		

Linemen (pre-World War II)

+ Edwards, Turk (T) 1969	+ Hubbard, Cal (T) 1963	Musso, George (T-G) 1982
Fortmann, Dan (G) 1985	Kiesling, Walt (G)..................1966	+ Stydahar, Joe (T) 1967
+ Healey, Ed (T) 1964	+ Kinard, Bruiser (T) 1971	+ Trafton, George (C) 1964
+ Hein, Mel (C) 1963	+ Lyman, Link (T) 1964	Turner, Bulldog (C)...............1966
+ Henry, Pete (T) 1963	+ Michalske, Mike (G) 1964	+ Wojciechowicz, Alex (C)........1968

Offensive Linemen

Bednarik, Chuck (C-LB) 1967	Jones, Stan (T-G-DT)..............1991	Parker, Jim (G) 1973
Brown, Roosevelt (T) 1975	Langer, Jim (C) 1987	Ringo, Jim (C) 1981
Gatski, Frank (C)...................1985	Little, Larry (G) 1993	St. Clair, Bob (T) 1990
Gregg, Forrest (T-G) 1977	McCormack, Mike (T) 1984	Shell, Art (T) 1989
Groza, Lou (T-PK)..................1974	Mix, Ron (T-G) 1979	Upshaw, Gene (G) 1987
Hannah, John (G) 1991	Otto, Jim (C) 1980	

Defensive Linemen

Atkins, Doug.........................1982	Jones, Deacon 1980	Robustelli, Andy 1971
+ Buchanan, Buck 1990	Lilly, Bob 1980	Stautner, Ernie 1969
Davis, Willie 1981	Marchetti, Gino.....................1972	Weinmeister, Arnie................1984
Donovan, Art 1968	Nomellini, Leo.......................1969	White, Randy........................1994
+ Ford, Len 1976	Olsen, Merlin 1982	Willis, Bill 1977
Greene, Joe...........................1987	Page, Alan 1988	

Linebackers

Bell, Bobby 1983	Ham, Jack 1988	Lanier, Willie 1986
Butkus, Dick 1979	Hendricks, Ted 1990	Nitschke, Ray 1978
Connor, George (DT-OT)..........1975	Huff, Sam 1982	Schmidt, Joe 1973
+ George, Bill 1974	Lambert, Jack........................1990	

Defensive Backs

Adderley, Herb 1980	+ Christiansen, Jack 1970	Lary, Yale 1979
Barney, Lem 1992	Houston, Ken 1986	+ Tunnell, Emlen 1967
Blount, Mel 1989	Johnson, Jimmy 1994	Wilson, Larry 1978
Brown, Willie 1984	Lane, Dick (Night Train) 1974	Wood, Willie.........................1989

Placekicker

Stenerud, Jan........................1991

Pro Football Hall of Fame (Cont.)

Coaches

+ Brown, Paul	1967	+ Halas, George	1963	+ Neale, Earle (Greasy)	1969
Ewbank, Weeb	1978	+ Lambeau, Curly	1963	Noll, Chuck	1993
+ Flaherty, Ray	1976	Landry, Tom	1990	+ Owen, Steve	1966
Gillman, Sid	1983	+ Lombardi, Vince	1971	Walsh, Bill	1993
Grant, Bud	1994				

Contributors

+ Bell, Bert	1963	Hunt, Lamar	1972	+ Reeves, Dan	1967
+ Bidwill, Charles	1967	+ Mara, Tim	1963	+ Rooney, Art	1964
+ Carr, Joe	1963	+ Marshall, George	1963	Rozelle, Pete	1985
Davis, Al	1992	+ Ray, Hugh (Shorty)	1966	Schramm, Tex	1991
+ Halas, George	1963				

All-Time All-NFL Team, 1920–94

The 75th Year Anniversary All-Time NFL Team, released Sept. 1, 1994. Voting by 15-member panel of former players, NFL and Pro Football Hall of Fame officials and media representatives.

OFFENSE

Wide Receivers (4): Lance Alworth, Raymond Berry, Don Hutson and Jerry Rice
Tight Ends (2): Mike Ditka and Kellen Winslow
Tackles (3): Rosevelt Brown, Forrest Gregg and Anthony Munoz
Guards (3): John Hannah, Jim Parker and Gene Upshaw
Centers (2): Mel Hein and Mike Webster
Quarterbacks (4): Sammy Baugh, Otto Graham, Joe Montana and Johnny Unitas
Running Backs (6): Jim Brown, Marion Motley, Bronko Nagurski, Walter Payton, O.J. Simpson and Steve Van Buren

DEFENSE

Ends (3): Deacon Jones, Gino Marchetti and Reggie White
Tackles (3): Joe Greene, Bob Lilly and Merlin Olsen
Linebackers (7): Dick Butkus, Jack Ham, Ted Hendricks, Jack Lambert, Willie Lanier, Ray Nitschke and Lawrence Taylor
Cornerbacks (4): Mel Blount, Mike Haynes, Dick (Night Train) Lane and Rod Woodson
Safties (3): Ken Houston, Ronnie Lott and Larry Wilson

SPECIALISTS

Placekicker: Jan Stenerud
Punter: Ray Guy
Kick Returner: Gale Sayers
Punt Returner: Billy (White Shoes) Johnson

Dick McCann Award

First presented in 1969 by the Pro Football Writers of America for long and distinguished reporting on pro football. Named in honor of the first director of the Hall, the McCann Award does not constitute induction into the Hall of Fame.

Year		Year		Year	
1969	George Strickler	1978	Murray Olderman	1987	Jerry Magee
1970	Arthur Daley	1979	Pat Livingston	1988	Gordon Forbes
1971	Joe King	1980	Chuck Heaton	1989	Vito Stellino
1972	Lewis Atchison	1981	Norm Miller	1990	Will McDonough
1973	Dave Brady	1982	Cameron Snyder	1991	Dick Connor
1974	Bob Oates	1983	Hugh Brown	1992	Frank Luska
1975	John Steadman	1984	Larry Felser	1993	Ira Miller
1976	Jack Hand	1985	Cooper Rollow	1994	Don Pierson
1977	Art Daley	1986	Bill Wallace		

Pete Rozelle Award

First presented in 1989 by the Hall of Fame for exceptional longtime contributions to radio and TV in pro football. Named in honor of the former NFL commissioner, who was also a publicist and GM for the LA Rams, the Rozelle Award does not constitute induction into the Hall of Fame.

Year		Year		Year	
1989	Bill McPhail	1991	Ed Sabol	1993	Curt Gowdy
1990	Lindsey Nelson	1992	Chris Schenkel	1994	Pat Summerall

Canadian Football Hall of Fame

Established in 1963. Current Hall opened in 1972. **Address:** 58 Jackson Street West, Hamilton, Ontario, L8P 1L4. Telephone: (905) 528-7566.

Eligibility: Nominated players must be retired three years, but coaches and builders can still be active. Voting done by 15-member panel of Canadian pro and amateur football officials.

Class of 1994 (4): PLAYERS—DT **Bill Baker**, Saskatchewan (1968–73, 77–78), B.C. Lions (1974–76); QB **Tom Clements**, Ottawa (1975–78), Saskatchewan (1979), Hamilton (1979, 81–83), Winnipeg (1983–87); DB **Gene Gaines**, Montreal (1961–62, 70–76), Ottawa (1963–69). BUILDER—**Don McNaughton**, guiding force of postseason Schenley Awards from 1963–88 as distillery company's director of advertising and later CEO and chairman.

Members are listed with year of induction; (+) indicates deceased members.

Players

Atchison, Ron 1978	Hanson, Fritz 1963	Parker, Jackie..........1971
Bailey, Byron..........1975	Harris, Wayne 1976	Patterson, Hal 1971
Baker, Bill 1994	Harrison, Herm 1993	Perry, Gordon 1970
Barrow, John 1976	Helton, John 1986	+ Perry, Norm..........1963
+ Batstone, Harry 1963	Henley, Garney 1979	Ploen, Ken 1975
+ Beach, Ormond 1963	Hinton, Tom 1991	+ Quilty, S.P. (Silver) 1966
Box, Ab..........1965	+ Huffman, Dick..........1987	Rebholz, Russ..........1963
+ Breen, Joseph 1963	+ Isbister, Bob Sr 1965	Reed, George 1979
+ Bright, Johnny 1970	Jackson, Russ 1973	+ Reeve, Ted 1963
Brown, Tom..........1984	+ Jacobs, Jack 1963	Rigney, Frank..........1985
Casey, Tom..........1964	+ James, Eddie (Dynamite)..........1963	+ Rodden, Mike 1964
Charlton, Ken 1992	James, Gerry 1981	+ Rowe, Paul 1964
Clements, Tom..........1994	+ Kabat, Greg 1966	Ruby, Martin 1974
Coffey, Tommy Joe 1977	Kapp, Joe 1984	+ Russel, Jeff..........1963
+ Conacher, Lionel 1963	Keeling, Jerry 1989	+ Scott, Vince..........1982
Copeland, Royal 1988	Kelly, Brian 1991	Shatto, Dick 1975
Corrigall, Jim..........1990	Kelly, Ellison 1992	+ Simpson, Ben..........1963
+ Cox, Ernest 1963	Krol, Joe 1963	Simpson, Bob..........1976
+ Craig, Ross 1964	Kwong, Normie 1969	+ Sprague, David..........1963
+ Cronin, Carl 1967	Lancaster, Ron 1982	Stevenson, Art..........1969
+ Cutler, Wes 1968	+ Lawson, Smirle..........1963	Stewart, Ron 1977
Dalla Riva, Peter 1993	+ Leadlay, Frank (Pep) 1963	+ Stirling, Hugh (Bummer)..........1966
+ Dixon, George..........1974	+ Lear, Les 1974	Sutherin, Don 1992
+ Eliowitz, Abe 1969	Lewis, Leo 1973	Thelen, Dave..........1989
+ Emerson, Eddie 1963	Lunsford, Earl 1983	+ Timmis, Brian 1963
Etcheverry, Sam 1969	Luster, Marv 1990	Tinsley, Bud..........1982
Evanshen, Terry 1984	Luzzi, Don 1986	+ Tommy, Andy 1989
Faloney, Bernie 1974	+ McCance, Ches 1976	+ Trawick, Herb 1975
+ Fear, A.H. (Cap) 1967	+ McGill, Frank 1965	+ Tubman, Joe 1968
Fennell, Dave..........1990	McQuarters, Ed 1988	Tucker, Whit 1993
+ Ferraro, John 1966	Miles, Rollie 1980	Urness, Ted 1989
Fieldgate, Norm 1979	+ Molson, Percy 1963	Vaughan, Kaye 1978
Fleming, Willie..........1982	Morris, Frank 1983	Wagner, Virgil 1980
Gabriel, Tony 1985	+ Morris, Ted 1964	+ Welch, Hawley (Huck) 1964
Gaines, Gene 1994	Mosca, Angelo 1987	Wilkinson, Tom 1987
+ Gall, Hugh 1963	Nelson, Roger 1986	Wylie, Harvey 1980
Golab, Tony 1964	Neumann, Peter..........1979	Young, Jim 1991
Gray, Herbert 1983	O'Quinn, John (Red) 1981	+ Zock, Bill 1985
Griffing, Dean 1965	Pajaczkowski, Tony 1988	

Builders

+ Back, Leonard..........1971	Grant, Bud 1983	+ Newton, Jack..........1964
+ Bailey, Harold..........1965	+ Grey, Lord Earl 1963	+ Preston, Ken 1990
+ Ballard, Harold..........1987	+ Griffith, Dr. Harry 1963	+ Ritchie, Alvin 1963
+ Berger, Sam..........1993	+ Halter, Sydney 1966	+ Ryan, Joe B...........1968
+ Brook, Tom 1975	+ Hannibal, Frank 1963	Sazio, Ralph 1988
+ Brown, D.Wes..........1963	+ Hayman, Lew 1975	+ Shaughnessy, Frank (Shag) 1963
Chipman, Arthur..........1969	+ Hughes, W.P. (Billy) 1974	+ Shouldice, W.T. (Hap)..........1977
Clair, Frank..........1981	Keys, Eagle 1990	+ Simpson, Jimmie 1986
Cooper, Ralph 1992	Kimball, Norman 1991	+ Slocomb, Karl 1989
+ Crighton, Hec 1986	+ Kramer, R.A. (Bob) 1987	+ Spring, Harry 1976
+ Currie, Andrew 1974	+ Lieberman, M.I. (Moe)..........1973	Stukus, Annis 1974
+ Davies, Dr. Andrew 1969	+ McBrien, Harry 1978	+ Taylor, N.J. (Piffles) 1963
+ DeGruchy, John 1963	+ McCaffrey, Jimmy 1967	+ Tindall, Frank..........1985
Dojack, Paul 1978	+ McCann, Dave 1966	+ Warner, Clair..........1965
+ Duggan, Eck..........1981	McNaughton, Don 1994	+ Warwick, Bert..........1964
+ DuMoulin, Seppi 1963	+ McPherson, Don..........1983	+ Wilson, Seymour..........1984
+ Foulds, Wllliam 1963	+ Metras, Johnny 1980	
Gaudaur, J.G. (Jake) 1984	+ Montgomery, Ken..........1970	

GOLF

A new Golf Museum and Hall of Fame is expected to open in the spring of 1996 at the PGA Tour's World Golf Village, currently under construction in St. Johns County, Fla., between Jacksonville and St. Augustine. The new hall will incorporate the inactive PGA/World Golf Hall of Fame (formerly run by the PGA of America) and the active LPGA Hall as well as provide a role for the USGA and the Royal and Ancient Golf Club of St. Andrews. Questions concerning the new Golf Hall of Fame and Museum should be directed to the PGA Tour at (904) 285-3700.

PGA/World Golf Hall of Fame

Established in 1974, but inactive since 1993. Will become part of the PGA Tour's new Golf Museum and Hall of Fame in 1996. Members are listed with year of induction; (+) indicates deceased members.

Men

+ Anderson, Willie 1975	+ Hagen, Walter 1974	Palmer, Arnold 1974
+ Armour, Tommy 1976	+ Hilton, Harold 1978	Player, Gary 1974
+ Ball, John, Jr 1977	Hogan, Ben 1974	Runyan, Paul 1990
+ Barnes, Jim 1989	Irwin, Hale 1992	Sarazen, Gene 1974
+ Boros, Julius 1982	+ Jones, Bobby 1974	+ Smith, Horton 1990
+ Braid, James 1976	+ Little, Lawson 1980	Snead, Sam 1974
Casper, Billy 1978	Littler, Gene 1990	+ Taylor, John H 1975
Cooper, Lighthorse Harry 1992	+ Locke, Bobby 1977	Thomson, Peter 1988
+ Cotton, Thomas 1980	Middlecoff, Cary 1986	+ Travers, Jerry 1976
DeVicenzo, Roberto 1989	+ Morris, Tom, Jr 1975	+ Travis, Walter 1979
+ Evans, Chick 1975	+ Morris, Tom, Sr 1976	Trevino, Lee 1981
Floyd, Ray 1989	Nelson, Byron 1974	+ Vardon, Harry 1974
+ Guldahl, Ralph 1981	Nicklaus, Jack 1974	Watson, Tom 1988
	+ Ouimet, Francis 1974	

Women

Berg, Patty 1974	Rawls, Betsy 1987	Whitworth, Kathy 1982
Carner, JoAnne 1985	Suggs, Louise 1979	Wright, Mickey 1976
+ Howe, Dorothy C.H 1978	+ Vare, Glenna Collett 1975	+ Zaharias, Babe Didrikson 1974
Lopez, Nancy 1989	+ Wethered, Joyce 1975	

Contributors

Campbell, William 1990	+ Graffis, Herb 1977	+ Roberts, Clifford 1978
+ Corcoran, Fred 1975	+ Harlow, Robert 1988	Rodriguez, Chi Chi 1992
+ Crosby, Bing 1978	Hope, Bob 1983	+ Ross, Donald 1977
+ Dey, Joe 1975	Jones, Robert Trent 1987	+ Tufts, Richard 1992

Old PGA Hall Members Not in PGA/World Hall

The original PGA Hall of Fame was established in 1940 by the PGA of America, but abandoned after the 1982 inductions in favor of the PGA/World Golf Hall of Fame. Twenty-seven members of the old PGA Hall have been elected to the PGA/World Hall since then. Players yet to make the cut are listed below with year of induction into old PGA Hall.

+ Brady, Mike 1960	Ford, Doug 1975	+ McLeod, Fred 1960
+ Burke, Billy 1966	+ Ghezzi, Vic 1965	+ Picard, Henry 1961
Burke, Jack Jr 1975	+ Harbert, Chick 1968	+ Revolta, Johnny 1963
+ Cruickshank, Bobby 1967	Harper, Chandler 1969	+ Shute, Denny 1957
+ Diegel, Leo 1955	+ Harrison, Dutch 1962	+ Smith, Alex 1940
+ Dudley, Ed 1964	+ Hutchison, Jock, Sr 1959	+ Smith, Macdonald 1954
+ Dutra, Olin 1962	+ McDermott, John 1940	+ Wood, Craig 1956
+ Farroll, Johnny 1961	+ Mangrum, Lloyd 1964	

LPGA Hall of Fame

Established in 1967 by the LPGA to replace the old Women's Golf Hall of Fame (founded in 1950). Originally located in Augusta, GA (1967-77), the Hall has been moved to Pinehurst, NC (1977-83), Sugar Land, TX (1983-89) and Daytona Beach, FL (since 1990). Will become part of the PGA Tour's new Golf Museum and Hall of Fame in 1996. **Address:** LPGA Headquarters, 2570 Volusia Ave., Suite B, Daytona Beach, FL, 32114. **Telephone:** (904) 254-8800.

    Eligibility: Nominees must have played 10 years on the LPGA tour and won 30 official events, including two major championships; 35 official events and one major; or 40 official events and no majors.

    Latest inductee: Patty Sheehan (30 wins, three majors) gained entry by capturing her 30th tournament at the Standard Register Ping in Phoenix on Mar. 21, 1993. **Leading candidates** (through Sept. 1, 1994): Amy Alcott (29 wins, 5 majors), Beth Daniel (30 wins, 1 major) and Betsy King (29 wins, 5 majors).

    Members are listed with year of induction; (+) indicates deceased members.

Players

Berg, Patty 1951	Mann, Carol 1977	Wright, Mickey 1964
Bradley, Pat 1991	Rawls, Betsy 1960	+ Zaharias, Babe Didrikson 1951
Carner, JoAnne 1982	Sheehan, Patty 1993	
Haynie, Sandra 1977	Suggs, Louise 1951	### Contributor
Jameson, Betty 1951	Whitworth, Kathy 1975	+ Dinah Shore 1994
Lopez, Nancy 1987		

HOCKEY

Hockey Hall of Fame

Established in 1945 by the National Hockey League and opened in 1961. **Address:** BCE Place, 30 Yonge Street, Toronto, Ontario, M5E 1X8. **Telephone:** (416) 360-7735.

Eligibility: Nominated players and referees must be retired three years. Voting done by 15-member panel made up of pro and amateur hockey personalities and media representatives. A 15-member Veterans Committee selects older players.

Class of 1994 (3): VETERANS: D **Lionel Conacher**, Pittsburgh (1925-26), NY Americans (1926-30), Montreal Maroons (1930-33, 34-37), Chicago (1933-34); LW **Harry Watson**, NY Americans (1941-42), Detroit (1942-46), Toronto (1946-54), Chicago (1954-57). BUILDER: **Brian O'Neill**, an NHL administrator for 26 years (1966-92) and Executive V.P. for 16 seasons (1977-92).

Members are listed with year of induction; (+) indicates deceased members.

Forwards

Abel, Sid 1969	Gainey, Bob 1992	+ O'Connor, Buddy 1988
+ Adams, Jack..........................1959	+ Gardner, Jimmy 1962	+ Oliver, Harry 1967
Apps, Syl............................1961	Geoffrion, Bernie 1972	Olmstead, Bert 1985
Armstrong, George 1975	+ Gerard, Eddie 1945	+ Patrick, Lynn 1980
+ Bailey, Ace 1975	Gilbert, Rod.......................1982	Perreault, Gilbert................1990
+ Bain, Dan 1945	+ Gilmour, Billy 1962	+ Phillips, Tom 1945
+ Baker, Hobey 1945	+ Griffis, Si 1950	+ Primeau, Joe 1963
Barber, Bill 1990	+ Hay, George 1958	Pulford, Bob........................1991
+ Barry, Marty 1965	+ Hextall, Bryan 1969	+ Rankin, Frank 1961
Bathgate, Andy 1978	+ Hooper, Tom 1962	Ratelle, Jean 1985
Beliveau, Jean.....................1972	Howe, Gordie 1972	Richard, Henri 1979
+ Bentley, Doug........................1964	+ Howe, Syd...........................1965	Richard, Maurice (Rocket) 1961
+ Bentley, Max 1966	Hull, Bobby 1983	+ Richardson, George 1950
Blake, Toe 1966	+ Hyland, Harry 1962	+ Roberts, Gordie 1971
Bossy, Mike 1991	+ Irvin, Dick 1958	+ Russel, Blair 1965
+ Boucher, Frank 1958	+ Jackson, Busher 1971	+ Russell, Ernie 1965
+ Bowie, Dubbie 1945	+ Joliat, Aurel 1947	+ Ruttan, Jack 1962
+ Broadbent, Punch 1962	+ Keats, Duke 1958	+ Scanlan, Fred 1965
Bucyk, John (Chief).............1981	Kennedy, Ted (Teeder) 1966	Schmidt, Milt.......................1961
+ Burch, Billy 1974	Keon, Dave 1986	+ Schriner, Sweeney 1962
Clarke, Bobby.....................1987	Lach, Elmer 1966	+ Seibert, Oliver 1961
Colville, Neil 1967	Lafleur, Guy 1988	Shutt, Steve 1993
+ Conacher, Charlie 1961	+ Lalonde, Newsy 1950	+ Siebert, Babe 1964
+ Cook, Bill 1952	Laprade, Edgar 1993	Sittler, Darryl 1989
Cournoyer, Yvan 1982	Lemaire, Jacques 1984	+ Smith, Alf 1962
+ Cowley, Bill 1968	+ Lewis, Herbie 1989	Smith, Clint.........................1991
+ Crawford, Rusty 1962	Lindsay, Ted 1966	+ Smith, Hooley 1972
+ Darragh, Jack 1962	+ MacKay, Mickey 1952	+ Smith, Tommy 1973
+ Davidson, Scotty 1950	Mahovlich, Frank 1981	+ Stanley, Barney 1962
Day, Hap 1961	+ Malone, Joe 1950	+ Stewart, Nels 1962
Delvecchio, Alex 1977	+ Marshall, Jack 1965	+ Stuart, Bruce 1961
+ Denneny, Cy 1959	+ Maxwell, Fred 1962	+ Taylor, Fred (Cyclone) 1947
Dionne, Marcel 1992	McDonald, Lanny 1992	+ Trihey, Harry 1950
+ Drillon, Gordie 1975	+ McGee, Frank 1945	Ullman, Norm 1982
+ Drinkwater, Graham...............1950	+ McGimsie, Billy 1962	+ Walker, Jack 1960
Dumart, Woody 1992	Mikita, Stan 1983	+ Walsh, Marty 1962
+ Dunderdale, Tommy 1974	Moore, Dickie 1974	Watson, Harry 1994
+ Dye, Babe 1970	+ Morenz, Howie 1945	+ Watson, Harry (Moose) 1962
Esposito, Phil 1984	+ Mosienko, Bill 1965	+ Weiland, Cooney 1971
+ Farrell, Arthur 1965	+ Nighbor, Frank 1947	+ Westwick, Harry (Rat)...........1962
+ Foyston, Frank 1958	+ Noble, Reg 1962	+ Whitcroft, Fred....................1962
+ Frederickson, Frank 1958		

Goaltenders

+ Benedict, Clint.......................1965	Giacomin, Eddie 1987	Parent, Bernie 1984
Bower, Johnny......................1976	+ Hainsworth, George 1961	+ Plante, Jacques 1978
Brimsek, Frankie...................1966	Hall, Glenn 1975	Rayner, Chuck 1973
+ Broda, Turk 1967	+ Hern, Riley 1962	+ Sawchuk, Terry 1971
Cheevers, Gerry 1985	+ Holmes, Hap 1972	Smith, Billy 1993
+ Connell, Alex 1958	+ Hutton, J.B. (Bouse) 1962	+ Thompson, Tiny 1959
Dryden, Ken 1983	+ Lehman, Hughie 1958	Tretiak, Vladislav 1989
+ Durnan, Bill 1964	+ LeSueur, Percy 1961	+ Vezina, Georges 1945
Esposito, Tony 1988	Lumley, Harry 1980	Worsley, Gump 1980
+ Gardiner, Chuck 1945	+ Moran, Paddy 1958	+ Worters, Roy........................1969

Hockey Hall of Fame (Cont.)

Defensemen

Boivin, Leo 1986	+ Hall, Joe 1961	Pilote, Pierre 1975
+ Boon, Dickie 1952	+ Harvey, Doug 1973	+ Pitre, Didier 1962
Bouchard, Butch....................1966	Horner, Red 1965	Potvin, Denis........................1991
+ Boucher, George 1960	+ Horton, Tim 1977	+ Pratt, Babe..........................1966
+ Cameron, Harry 1962	Howell, Harry 1979	Pronovost, Marcel 1978
+ Clancy, King 1958	+ Johnson, Ching 1958	+ Pulford, Harvey......................1945
+ Clapper, Dit 1947	+ Johnson, Ernie 1952	Quackenbush, Bill 1976
+ Cleghorn, Sprague 1958	Johnson, Tom 1970	Reardon, Kenny 1966
+ Conacher, Lionel 1994	Kelly, Red 1969	+ Ross, Art..............................1945
Coulter, Art...........................1974	Laperriere, Jacques 1987	Savard, Serge 1986
+ Dutton, Red 1958	Lapointe, Guy 1993	Seibert, Earl 1963
Flaman, Fernie.......................1990	+ Laviolette, Jack 1962	+ Shore, Eddie.........................1947
Gadsby, Bill 1970	+ Mantha, Sylvio 1960	+ Simpson, Joe 1962
+ Gardiner, Herb 1958	+ McNamara, George...............1958	Stanley, Allan 1981
+ Goheen, F.X. (Moose) 1952	Orr, Bobby 1979	+ Stewart, Jack 1964
+ Goodfellow, Ebbie.................1963	Park, Brad 1988	+ Stuart, Hod 1945
+ Grant, Mike 1950	+ Patrick, Lester 1947	+ Wilson, Gordon (Phat)............1962
+ Green, Wilf (Shorty)...............1962		

Referees & Linesmen

Armstrong, Neil 1991	+ Hayes, George 1988	+ Rodden, Mike 1962
Ashley, John 1981	+ Hewitson, Bobby 1963	+ Smeaton, J. Cooper...............1961
Chadwick, Bill 1964	+ Ion, Mickey 1961	Storey, Red 1967
D'Amico, John 1993	Pavelich, Matt 1987	Udvari, Frank........................1973
+ Elliott, Chaucer.....................1961		

Builders

+ Adams, Charles 1960	+ Hay, Charles.........................1984	O'Neill, Brian 1994
+ Adams, Weston W. Sr 1972	+ Hendy, Jim 1968	Page, Fred 1993
+ Ahearn, Frank 1962	+ Hewitt, Foster 1965	+ Patrick, Frank 1958
+ Ahearn, J.F. (Bunny) 1977	+ Hewitt, W.A. 1945	+ Pickard, Allan 1958
+ Allan, Sir Montagu.................1945	+ Hume, Fred 1962	Pilous, Rudy 1985
Allen, Keith 1992	+ Imlach, Punch 1984	Poile, Bud 1990
+ Ballard, Harold 1977	Ivan, Tommy 1964	Pollock, Sam 1978
+ Bauer, Fr. David 1989	+ Jennings, Bill 1975	+ Raymond, Donat 1958
+ Bickell, J.P 1978	+ Johnson, Bob 1992	+ Robertson, John Ross.............1945
+ Brown, George 1961	Juckes, Gordon 1979	+ Robinson, Claude 1945
+ Brown, Walter 1962	+ Kilpatrick, John 1960	+ Ross, Philip 1976
+ Buckland, Frank 1975	Knox, Seymour III 1993	+ Selke, Frank 1960
Butterfield, Jack.....................1980	+ Leader, Al 1969	Sinden, Harry 1983
+ Calder, Frank 1945	LeBel, Bob. 1970	+ Smith, Frank 1962
+ Campbell, Angus 1964	+ Lockhart, Tom 1965	+ Smythe, Conn 1958
+ Campbell, Clarence 1966	+ Loicq, Paul 1961	Snider, Ed.............................1988
+ Cattarinich, Joseph.................1977	+ Mariucci, John 1985	+ Stanley, Lord of Preston...........1945
+ Dandurand, Leo 1963	Mathers, Frank 1992	+ Sutherland, James 1945
Dilio, Frank............................1964	+ McLaughlin, Frederic 1963	Tarasov, Anatoli 1974
+ Dudley, George 1958	+ Milford, Jake 1984	+ Turner, Lloyd 1958
+ Dunn, James.........................1968	Molson, Hartland 1973	+ Tutt, William Thayer...............1978
Eagleson, Alan 1989	+ Nelson, Francis 1945	Voss, Carl.............................1974
Francis, Emile 1982	+ Norris, Bruce 1969	+ Waghorne, Fred 1961
+ Gibson, Jack.........................1976	+ Norris, James D 1962	+ Wirtz, Arthur 1971
+ Gorman, Tommy 1963	+ Norris, James Sr 1958	Wirtz, Bill 1976
+ Griffiths, Frank A. 1993	+ Northey, William 1945	Ziegler, John 1987
+ Hanley, Bill 1986	+ O'Brien, J.A...........................1962	

Elmer Ferguson Award

First presented in 1984 by the Professional Hockey Writers' Association for meritorious contributions by members of the PHWA. Named in honor of the late Montreal newspaper reporter, the Ferguson Award does not constitute induction into the Hall of Fame and is not necessarily an annual presentation.

1984—Jacques Beauchamp, Jim Burchard, Red Burnett, Dink Carroll, Jim Coleman, Ted Damata, Marcel Desjardins, Jack Dulmage, Milt Dunnell, Elmer Ferguson, Tom Fitzgerald, Trent Frayne, Al Laney, Joe Nichols, Basil O'Meara, Jim Vipond and Lewis Walter

1985—Charlie Barton, Red Fisher, George Gross, Zotique L'Esperance, Charles Mayer & Andy O'Brien

1986—Dick Johnston, Leo Monahan & Tim Moriarty
1987—Bill Brennan, Rex MacLeod, Ben Olan & Fran Rosa
1988—Jim Proudfoot & Scott Young
1989—Claude Larochelle & Frank Orr
1990—Bertrand Raymond
1991—Hugh Delano
1992—Al Strachan

Foster Hewitt Award

First presented in 1984 by the NHL Broadcasters' Association for meritorious contributions by members of the NHLBA. Named in honor of Canada's legendary "Voice of Hockey," the Hewitt Award does not constitute induction into the Hall of Fame and is not necessarily an annual presentation.

1984—Fred Cusick, Danny Gallivan, Foster Hewitt & Rene Lecavelier
1985—Budd Lynch & Doug Smith
1986—Wes McKnight & Lloyd Pettit

1987—Bob Wilson
1988—Dick Irvin
1989—Dan Kelly
1990—Jiggs McDonald

1991—Bruce Martyn
1992—Jim Robson
1993—Al Shaver
1994—Ted Darling

U.S. Hockey Hall of Fame

Established in 1968 by the Eveleth (Minn.) Civic Association Project H Committee and opened in 1973. Address: 801 Hat Trick Ave., P.O. Box 657, Eveleth, MN 55734. **Telephone:** (218) 744-5167.

Eligibility: Nominated players and referees must be American-born and retired five years; coaches must be American-born and must have coached predominantly American teams. Voting done by 12-member panel made up of Hall of Fame members and U.S. hockey officials.

Class of 1994: (3): PLAYERS—**Joe Cavanaugh** (Harvard 1968/69–1970/71) and **Wally Grant** (Michigan 1945/46, 1947/48–1949/50). COACH—**Ned Harkness**, college at RPI, Cornell and Union; pros with Detroit Red Wings.

Members are listed with year of induction; (+) indicates deceased members.

Players

+ Abel, Clarence (Taffy)	1973
+ Baker, Hobey	1973
Bartholome, Earl	1977
+ Bessone, Peter	1978
Blake, Bob	1985
Brimsek, Frankie	1973
Cavanaugh, Joe	1994
+ Chaisson, Ray	1974
Chase, John	1973
Christian, Bill	1984
Christian, Roger	1989
Cleary, Bill	1976
Cleary, Bob	1981
+ Conroy, Tony	1975
Dahlstrom, Carl (Cully)	1973
+ DesJardins, Vic	1974
+ Desmond, Richard	1988
+ Dill, Bob	1979

Everett, Doug	1974
Ftorek, Robbie	1991
+ Garrison, John	1974
Garrity, Jack	1986
+ Goheen, Frank (Moose)	1973
Grant, Wally	1994
+ Harding, Austie	1975
Iglehart, Stewart	1975
Ikola, Willard	1990
Johnson, Virgil	1974
+ Karakas, Mike	1973
Kirrane, Jack	1987
+ Lane, Myles	1973
Langevin, Dave	1993
+ Linder, Joe	1975
+ LoPresti, Sam	1973
+ Mariucci, John	1973
Matchefts, John	1991

Mayasich, John	1976
McCartan, Jack	1983
Moe, Bill	1974
+ Moseley, Fred	1975
+ Murray, Hugh (Muzz) Sr	1987
+ Nelson, Hub	1978
Olson, Eddie	1977
+ Owen, George	1973
+ Palmer, Winthrop	1973
Paradise, Bob	1989
Purpur, Clifford (Fido)	1974
Riley, Bill	1977
+ Romnes, Elwin (Doc)	1973
Rondeau, Dick	1985
+ Williams, Tom	1981
+ Winters, Frank (Coddy)	1973
+ Yackel, Ken	1986

Coaches

+ Almquist, Oscar	1983
Bessone, Amo	1992
Brooks, Herb	1990
Ceglarski, Len	1992
+ Fullerton, James	1992
+ Gordon, Malcolm	1973
Harkness, Ned	1994

Heyliger, Vic	1974
Ikola, Willard	1990
+ Jeremiah, Eddie	1973
+ Johnson, Bob	1991
Kelley, Jack	1993
+ Kelly, John (Snooks)	1974

Pleban, Connie	1990
Riley, Jack	1979
Ross, Larry	1988
+ Thompson, Cliff	1973
+ Stewart, Bill	1982
+ Winsor, Ralph	1973

Referee

Chadwick, Bill	1974

Contributor

Schulz, Charles M.	1993

Administrators

+ Brown, George	1973
+ Brown, Walter	1973
Bush, Walter	1980
Clark, Don	1978
+ Gibson, J.L. (Doc)	1973

+ Jennings, Bill	1981
+ Kahler, Nick	1980
+ Lockhart, Tom	1973
Marvin, Cal	1982
Ridder, Bob	1976

Trumble, Hal	1970
+ Tutt, Thayer	1973
Wirtz, Bill	1967
+ Wright, Lyle	1973

Members of both Hockey and U.S. Hockey Halls of Fame
(as of Sept. 15, 1994)

Players
Hobey Baker
Frankie Brimsek
Frank (Moose) Goheen
John Mariucci

Coach
Bob Johnson

Referee
Bill Chadwick

Builders
George Brown
Walter Brown
Doc Gibson
Bill Jennings

Tom Lockhart
Thayer Tutt
Bill Wirtz

HORSE RACING

National Horse Racing Hall of Fame

Established in 1950 by the Saratoga Springs Racing Association and opened in 1955. **Address:** National Museum of Racing and Hall of Fame, Union Ave., Saratoga Springs, NY 12866. **Telephone:** (518) 584-0400.

Eligibility: Nominated horses must be retired five years; jockeys must be active at least 15 years; trainers must be active at least 25 years. Voting done by 100-member panel of horse racing media.

Class of 1994 (6): HORSES—**Arts and Letters**, **Eight 30**, **Flatterer** and **Ta Wee**. JOCKEY—**Steve Cauthen**. TRAINER—**Jimmy Croll**.

Members are listed with year of induction; (+) indicates deceased members.

Horses
Year foaled in parentheses.

+ Ack Ack (1966) 1986
  Affectionately (1960)..............1989
  Affirmed (1975).....................1980
  All-Along (1979) 1990
+ Alsab (1939) 1976
+ Alydar (1975).........................1989
  Alysheba (1984) 1993
+ American Eclipse (1814) 1970
+ Armed (1941)..........................1963
+ Artful (1902) 1956
+ Arts and Letters (1966) 1994
+ Assault (1943)........................1964

+ Battleship (1927).....................1969
+ Bed O'Roses(1947)..................1976
+ Beldame (1901).......................1956
+ Ben Brush (1893).....................1955
+ Bewitch (1945) 1977
+ Bimelech (1937).......................1990
+ Black Gold (1919)....................1989
+ Black Helen (1932)....................1991
+ Blue Larkspur (1926) 1957
+ Bold Ruler (1954) 1973
+ Bon Nouvel (1960) 1976
+ Boston (1833).........................1955
+ Broomstick (1901)....................1956
+ Buckpasser (1963) 1970
+ Busher (1942).........................1964
+ Bushranger (1930)...................1967

+ Cafe Prince (1970)...................1985
+ Carry Back (1958) 1975
+ Cavalcade (1931) 1993
+ Challendon (1936)....................1977
+ Chris Evert (1988)....................1971
+ Cicada (1959) 1967
+ Citation (1945) 1959
+ Coaltown (1945)......................1983
+ Colin (1905)...........................1956
+ Commando (1898)....................1956
+ Count Fleet (1940)...................1961

+ Dahlia (1971).........................1981
+ Damascus (1964).....................1974
+ Dark Mirage (1965)..................1974
+ Davona Dale (1976) 1985
+ Desert Vixen (1970) 1979
+ Devil Diver (1939)....................1980
+ Discovery (1931) 1969
+ Domino (1891).........................1955
+ Dr. Fager (1964)......................1971

+ Eight 30 (1936) 1994
+ Elkridge (1938).........................1966
+ Emperor of Norfolk (1885) 1988
+ Equipoise (1928) 1957
+ Exterminator (1915) 1957

+ Fairmount (1921) 1985
+ Fair Play (1905) 1956
+ Firenze (1885).........................1981
  Flatterer (1979).......................1994
+ Forego (1971) 1979

+ Gallant Bloom (1966)..............1977
+ Gallant Fox (1927)...................1957
+ Gallant Man (1954) 1987
+ Gallorette (1942) 1962
+ Gamely (1964).........................1980
  Genuine Risk (1977) 1986
+ Good and Plenty (1900) 1956
+ Grey Lag (1918) 1957

+ Hamburg (1895).......................1986
+ Hanover (1884).........................1955
+ Henry of Navarre (1891)........1985
+ Hill Prince (1947).....................1991
+ Hindoo (1878)..........................1955

+ Imp (1894) 1965

+ Jay Trump (1957).....................1971
  John Henry (1975)....................1990
+ Johnstown (1936)......................1992
+ Jolly Roger (1922)....................1965

+ Kingston (1884)........................1955
+ Kelso (1957)...........................1967
+ Kentucky (1861) 1983
  Lady's Secret (1982)................1992
+ L'Escargot (1963) 1977
+ Lexington (1850).......................1955
+ Longfellow (1867).....................1971
+ Luke Blackburn (1877)............1956

+ Majestic Prince (1966)............1988
+ Man o' War (1917)...................1957
+ Miss Woodford (1880) 1967
+ Myrtlewood (1933)...................1979

+ Nashua (1952).........................1965
+ Native Dancer (1950) 1963
+ Native Diver (1959) 1978
+ Northern Dancer (1961)..........1976
+ Neji (1950) 1966

+ Oedipus (1941) 1978
+ Old Rosebud (1911).................1968
+ Omaha (1932) 1965

+ Pan Zareta (1910)...................1972
+ Parole (1873) 1984
  Personal Ensign (1984)............1993
+ Peter Pan (1904).....................1956
  Princess Rooney (1980) 1991

+ Real Delight (1949).................1987
+ Regret (1912) 1957
+ Reigh Count (1925)..................1978
+ Roamer (1911).........................1981
+ Roseben (1901).......................1956
+ Round Table (1954) 1972
+ Ruffian (1972).........................1976
+ Ruthless (1864).......................1975

+ Salvator (1886).......................1955
+ Sarazen (1921)........................1957
+ Seabiscuit (1933)....................1958
+ Searching (1952)......................1978
  Seattle Slew (1974).................1981
+ Secretariat (1970)...................1974
+ Shuvee (1966).........................1975
+ Silver Spoon (1956) 1978
+ Sir Archy (1805)......................1955
+ Sir Barton (1916).....................1957
  Slew o'Gold (1980)..................1992
+ Stymie (1941)..........................1975
+ Susan's Girl (1969) 1976
+ Swaps (1952).........................1966
+ Sword Dancer (1956)...............1977
+ Sysonby (1902) 1956

+ Ta Wee (1966)........................1994
+ Tim Tam (1955)........................1985
+ Tom Fool (1949)......................1960
+ Top Flight (1929).....................1966
+ Tosmah (1961).........................1984
+ Twenty Grand (1928) 1957
+ Twilight Tear (1941)................1963

+ War Admiral (1934) 1958
+ Whirlaway (1938) 1959
+ Whisk Broom II (1907) 1979

  Zaccio (1976).........................1990
+ Zev (1920) 1983

Exemplars of Racing

Mellon, Paul 1989   Widener, George D................1971

+ Hanes, John W 1982
+ Jeffords, Walter M..................1973

Jockeys

+ Adams, Frank (Dooley)* 1970
+ Adams, John 1965
+ Aitcheson, Joe Jr.* 1978
    Arcaro, Eddie 1958
    Atkinson, Ted 1957
    Baeza, Braulio 1976
+ Bassett, Carroll* 1972
+ Blum, Walter 1987
+ Bostwick, George H.* 1968
+ Boulmetis, Sam 1973
+ Brooks, Steve 1963
+ Burns, Tommy 1983
+ Butwell, Jimmy 1984
    Cauthen, Steve 1994
+ Coltiletti, Frank 1970
    Cordero, Angel Jr. 1988
+ Crawford, Robert (Specs)* 1973
    Day, Pat 1991
    Delahoussaye, Eddie 1993
+ Ensor, Lavelle (Buddy) 1962
+ Fator, Laverne 1955
    Fishback, Jerry* 1992
+ Garner, Andrew (Mack) 1969
+ Garrison, Snapper 1955

*Steeplechase jockey

+ Griffin, Henry 1956
+ Guerin, Eric 1972
    Hartack, Bill 1959
    Hawley, Sandy 1992
+ Johnson, Albert 1971
+ Knapp, Willie 1969
+ Kummer, Clarence 1972
+ Kurtsinger, Charley 1967
+ Loftus, Johnny 1959
    Longden, Johnny 1958
    Maher, Danny 1955
+ McAtee, Linus 1956
    McCarron, Chris 1989
+ McCreary, Conn 1974
+ McKinney, Rigan 1968
+ McLaughlin, James 1955
+ Miller, Walter 1955
+ Murphy, Isaac 1955
+ Neves, Ralph 1960
+ Notter, Joe 1963
+ O'Connor, Winnie 1956
+ Odom, George 1955
+ O'Neill, Frank 1956

+ Parke, Ivan 1978
+ Patrick, Gil 1970
    Pincay, Laffit Jr. 1975
+ Purdy, Sam 1970
+ Reiff, John 1956
+ Robertson, Alfred 1971
    Rotz, John L. 1983
+ Sande, Earl 1955
+ Schilling, Carroll 1970
    Shoemaker, Bill 1958
+ Simms, Willie 1977
+ Sloan, Todhunter 1955
+ Smithwick, A. Patrick* 1973
+ Stout, James 1968
+ Taral, Fred 1955
+ Tuckman, Bayard Jr.* 1973
    Turcotte, Ron 1979
+ Turner, Nash 1955
    Ussery, Robert. 1980
    Velasquez, Jorge 1990
+ Woolfe, George 1955
+ Workman, Raymond 1956
    Ycaza, Manuel 1977

Trainers

+ Barrera, Laz 1979
+ Bedwell, H. Guy 1971
+ Brown, Edward D. 1984
    Burch, Elliot 1980
+ Burch, Preston M. 1963
+ Burch, W.P. 1955
+ Burlew, Fred 1973
+ Byers, J.D. (Dilly) 1967
+ Childs, Frank E. 1968
    Cocks, W. Burling 1985
    Croll, Jimmy 1994
+ Duke, William 1956
+ Feustel, Louis 1964
+ Fitzsimmons, J. (Sunny Jim) 1958
+ Gaver, John M. 1966
+ Healey, Thomas 1955
+ Hildreth, Samuel 1955
+ Hirsch, Max 1959
+ Hirsch, W.J. (Buddy) 1982
+ Hitchcock, Thomas Sr. 1973
+ Hughes, Hollie 1973

+ Hyland, John 1956
+ Jacobs, Hirsch 1958
    Jerkens, H. Allen 1975
+ Johnson, William R. 1986
+ Jolley, LeRoy 1987
+ Jones, Ben A. 1958
    Jones, H.A. (Jimmy) 1959
+ Joyner, Andrew 1955
    Kelly, Tom 1993
    Laurin, Lucien 1977
+ Lewis, J. Howard 1969
+ Luro, Horatio 1980
+ Madden, John 1983
+ Maloney, Jim 1989
    Martin, Frank (Pancho) 1981
    McAnally, Ron 1990
+ McDaniel, Henry 1956
+ Miller, MacKenzie 1987
+ Molter, William, Jr. 1960
+ Mulholland, Winbert 1967
+ Neloy, Eddie 1983

    Nerud, John 1972
+ Parke, Burley 1986
+ Penna, Angel Sr. 1988
+ Pincus, Jacob 1988
+ Rogers, John 1955
+ Rowe, James Sr. 1955
    Schulhofer, Scotty 1992
    Sheppard, Jonathan 1990
+ Smith, Robert A. 1976
+ Smithwick, Mike 1976
    Stephens, Woody 1976
+ Thompson, H.J. 1969
+ Trotsek, Harry 1984
    Van Berg, Jack 1985
+ Van Berg, Marion 1970
+ Veitch, Sylvester 1977
+ Walden, Robert. 1970
+ Ward, Sherrill 1978
    Whiteley, Frank Jr. 1978
    Whittingham, Charlie 1974
    Winfrey, W.C. (Bill) 1971

Harness Racing Living Hall of Fame

Established by the U.S. Harness Writers Association (USHWA) in 1958. **Address:** Trotting Horse Museum, 240 Main Street, P.O. Box 590, Goshen, NY 10924; **Telephone:** (914) 294-6330.

    Eligibility: Open to all harness racing drivers, trainers and executives. Voting done by USHWA membership. There are 61 members of the Living Hall of Fame, but only the 33 drivers and trainer-drivers are listed below.

    Members are listed with years of induction; (+) indicates deceased members.

Trainer-Drivers

    Abbatiello, Carmine 1986
+ Avery, Earle 1975
+ Baldwin, Ralph 1972
    Beissinger, Howard 1975
    Bostwick, Dunbar 1989
+ Cameron, Del 1975
    Campbell, Jimmy 1991
+ Chapman, John 1980
    Cruise, Jimmy 1987
    Dancer, Stanley 1970
+ Ervin, Frank 1969

    Farrington, Bob 1980
    Filion, Herve 1976
+ Garnsey, Glen 1983
    Galbraith, Clint 1990
    Gilmour, Buddy 1990
    Harner, Levi 1986
+ Haughton, Billy 1969
+ Hodgins, Clint 1973
    Insko, Del 1981
    Miller, Del 1969
+ O'Brien, Joe 1971

    O'Donnell, Bill 1991
    Patterson, John Sir 1994
+ Pownall, Harry 1971
    Riegle, Gene 1992
+ Russell, Sanders 1971
+Shively, Bion 1968
    Sholty, George 1985
    Simpson, John Sr 1972
+ Smart, Curly 1970
    Waples, Keith 1987
    Waples, Ron 1994

MEDIA

National Sportscasters and Sportswriters Hall of Fame

Established in 1959 by the National Sportscasters and Sportswriters Association. **Mailing Address:** P.O. Box 559, Salisbury, NC 28144. A permanent museum is scheduled to open in the autumn of 1995. **Telephone:** (704) 633-4275.

Eligibility: Nominees must be active for at least 25 years. Voting done by NSSA membership and other media representatives.

Class of 1994 (3): Sportscaster **Pat Summerall** and sportswriters **John P. Carmichael** and **Edwin Pope**.

Members are listed with year of induction; (+) indicates deceased members.

Sportscasters

Allen, Mel 1972	Glickman, Marty 1992	+ McNamee, Graham 1964
+ Barber, Walter (Red)..............1973	Gowdy, Curt 1981	Nelson, Lindsey.....................1979
Brickhouse, Jack...................1983	Harwell, Ernie 1989	+ Prince, Bob 1986
Buck, Jack 1990	+ Hodges, Russ 1975	Schenkel, Chris 1981
Caray, Harry 1989	+ Hoyt, Waite 1987	Scott, Ray 1982
Cosell, Howard 1993	+ Husing, Ted 1963	Scully, Vin 1991
+ Dean, Dizzy 1976	+ McCarthy, Clem 1970	+ Stern, Bill 1974
Dunphy, Don 1986	McKay, Jim 1987	Summerall, Pat......................1994

Sportswriters

Anderson, Dave 1990	+ Grimsley, Will 1987	Povich, Shirley 1984
Bisher, Furman 1989	Heinz, W.C. 1987	+ Rice, Grantland.....................1962
Burick, Si 1985	+ Kieran, John 1971	+ Runyon, Damon 1964
+ Cannon, Jimmy 1986	+ Lardner, Ring 1967	Russell, Fred 1988
+ Carmichael, John P...............1994	+ Murphy, Jack 1988	Sherrod, Blackie 1991
+ Connor, Dick 1992	Murray, Jim 1978	+ Smith, Walter (Red) 1977
+ Considine, Bob 1980	Olderman, Murray 1993	+ Spink, J.G.Taylor 1969
+ Daley, Arthur 1976	+ Parker, Dan 1975	+ Ward, Arch 1973
+ Gould, Alan.........................1990	Pope, Edwin 1994	+ Woodward, Stanley 1974

Memorable Personalities

+ Gehrig, Lou 1980	Reagan, Ronald 1989	+ Wayne, John 1979
+ Owens, Jesse 1978	+ Rockne, Knute 1990	

American Sportscasters Hall of Fame

Established in 1984 by the American Sportscasters Association. **Address:** 5 Beekman Street, New York, NY 10038. Before the end of 1994, the ASA plans to choose a city in which to build a permanent museum site.

Eligibility: Nominations made by 15-member selection committee, voting by ASA membership.

Class of 1993 (2): **Howard Cosell** and **Marty Glickman**.

Class of 1994 (1): **Keith Jackson**.

Members are listed with year of induction; (+) indicates deceased members.

Allen, Mel............................1985	Dunphy, Don 1984	+ McCarthy, Clem 1987
+ Barber, Walter (Red)..............1984	Glickman, Marty 1993	McKay, Jim 1987
Brickhouse, Jack...................1985	Gowdy, Curt 1985	+ McNamee, Graham 1984
Buck, Jack 1990	Harwell, Ernie 1991	Nelson, Lindsey......................1986
Caray, Harry 1989	+ Husing, Ted 1984	Scully, Vin 1992
Cosell, Howard 1993	Jackson, Keith 1994	+ Stern, Bill 1984

The 40 Who Changed Sports, 1946-86

Selected by the editors of *Sport* magazine for their 40th Anniversary Issue (December, 1986).

Baseball
Hank Aaron
Curt Flood
Mickey Mantle
Willie Mays
Marvin Miller
Branch Rickey
Jackie Robinson
Pete Rose
Casey Stengel
Ted Williams

Basketball
Red Auerbach
Wilt Chamberlain
Bob Cousy
Bill Russell
John Wooden

Boxing
Muhammad Ali
James D. Norris
Sugar Ray Robinson

Football
Jim Brown
Paul Brown
Bear Bryant
Al Davis
Vince Lombardi
Joe Namath
Pete Rozelle

Golf
Jack Nicklaus
Arnold Palmer

Hockey
Wayne Gretzky
Bobby Orr

Horse Racing
Willie Shoemaker

Literature
Jim Bouton

Motorsports
Bill France Sr.

Olympics
Abebe Bikila
Avery Brundage

Soccer
Pelé

Television
Roone Arledge
Howard Cosell

Tennis
Chris Evert
Billie Jean King
Martina Navratilova

OLYMPICS

U.S. Olympic Hall of Fame

Established in 1983 by the United States Olympic Committee. **Mailing Address:** U.S. Olympic Committee, 1750 East Boulder Street, Colorado Springs, CO 80909. Plans for a permanent museum site have been suspended due to lack of funding. **Telephone:** (719) 578-4529.

Eligibility: Nominated athletes must be five years removed from active competition. Voting done by National Sportscasters and Sportswriters Association, Hall of Fame members and the USOC board members of directors.

Class of 1994: Voting for membership in the Hall has been suspended until further notice.

Members are listed with year of induction; (+) indicates deceased members.

Alpine Skiing

Mahre, Phil 1992

Bobsled

+ Eagan, Eddie (see Boxing) 1983

Boxing

Clay, Cassius* 1983
+ Eagan, Eddie (see Bobsled) 1983
Foreman, George 1990
Frazier, Joe 1989
Leonard, Sugar Ray 1985
Patterson, Floyd 1987

*Clay changed name to Muhammad Ali in 1964

Cycling

Carpenter-Phinney, Connie 1992

Diving

King, Miki 1992
Lee, Sammy 1990
Louganis, Greg 1985
McCormick, Pat 1985

Figure Skating

Albright, Tenley 1988
Button, Dick 1983
Fleming, Peggy 1983
Hamill, Dorothy 1991
Hamilton, Scott 1990

Gymnastics

Conner, Bart 1991
Retton, Mary Lou 1985
Vidmar, Peter 1991

Rowing

+ Kelly, Jack Sr. 1990

Speed Skating

Heiden, Eric 1983

Swimming

Babashoff, Shirley 1987
Caulkins, Tracy 1990
+ Daniels, Charles 1988
de Varona, Donna 1987
+ Kahanamoku, Duke 1984
+ Madison, Helene 1992
Meyer, Debbie 1986
Naber, John 1984
Schollander, Don 1983
Spitz, Mark 1983
+ Weissmuller, Johnny 1983

Track & Field

Beamon, Bob 1983
Boston, Ralph 1985
+ Calhoun, Lee 1991
Campbell, Milt 1992
Davenport, Willie 1991
Davis, Glenn 1986
+ Didrikson, Babe 1983
Dillard, Harrison 1983
Evans, Lee 1989
+ Ewry, Ray 1983
Fosbury, Dick 1992
Jenner, Bruce 1986
Johnson, Rafer 1983
+ Kraenzlein, Alvin 1985
Lewis, Carl 1985
Mathias, Bob 1983

Mills, Billy 1984
Morrow, Bobby 1989
Moses, Edwin 1985
O'Brien, Parry 1984
Oerter, Al 1983
+ Owens, Jesse 1983
+ Paddock, Charley 1991
Richards, Bob 1983
Rudolph, Wilma 1983
+ Sheppard, Mel 1989
Shorter, Frank 1984
+ Thorpe, Jim 1983
Toomey, Bill 1984
Tyus, Wyomia 1985
Whitfield, Mal 1988
+ Wykoff, Frank 1984

Weight Lifting

+ Davis, John 1989
Kono, Tommy 1990

Wrestling

Gable, Dan 1985

Contributors

Arledge, Roone 1989
+ Brundage, Avery 1983
+ Bushnell, Asa 1990
Hull, Col. Don 1992
+ Iba, Hank 1985
+ Kane, Robert 1986
+ Kelly, Jack Jr. 1992
McKay, Jim 1988
Miller, Don 1984
Simon, William 1991
Walker, LeRoy 1987

Teams

1956 Basketball—Dick Boushka, Carl Cain, Chuck Darling, Bill Evans, Gib Ford, Burdy Haldorson, Bill Hougland, Bob Jeangerard, K.C. Jones, Bill Russell, Ron Tomsic, +Jim Walsh and coach +Gerald Tucker.

1960 Basketball—Jay Arnette, Walt Bellamy, Bob Boozer, Terry Dischinger, Burdy Haldorson, Darrall Imhoff, Allen Kelley, +Lester Lane, Jerry Lucas, Oscar Robertson, Adrian Smith, Jerry West and coach Pete Newell.

1964 Basketball—Jim Barnes, Bill Bradley, Larry Brown, Joe Caldwell, Mel Counts, Richard Davies, Walt Hazzard, Luke Jackson, John McCaffrey, Jeff Mullins, Jerry Shipp, George Wilson and coach +Hank Iba.

1960 Ice Hockey—Billy Christian, Roger Christian, Billy Cleary, Bob Cleary, Gene Grazia, Paul Johnson, Jack Kirrane, John Mayasich, Jack McCartan, Bob McKay, Dick Meredith, Weldon Olson, Ed Owen, Rod Paavola, Larry Palmer, Dick Rodenheiser, +Tom Williams and coach Jack Riley.

1980 Ice Hockey—Bill Baker, Neal Broten, Dave Christian, Steve Christoff, Jim Craig, Mike Eruzione, John Harrington, Steve Janaszak, Mark Johnson, Ken Morrow, Rob McClanahan, Jack O'Callahan, Mark Pavelich, Mike Ramsey, Buzz Schneider, Dave Silk, Eric Strobel, Bob Suter, Phil Verchota, Mark Wells and coach Herb Brooks.

The Olympic Order

Established in 1974 by the International Olympic Committee (IOC) to honor athletes, officials and media members who have made remarkable contributions to the Olympic movement. The IOC's Council of the Olympic Order is presided over by the IOC president and active IOC members are not eligible for consideration. Through 1992, only two American officials have received the Order's highest commendation—the gold medal:

Avery Brundage, president of USOC (1928-53) and IOC (1952-72), was given the award posthumously in 1975.
Peter Ueberroth, president of Los Angeles Olympic Organizing Committee, was given the award in 1984.

SOCCER

National Soccer Hall of Fame

Established in 1950 by the Philadelphia Oldtimers Association. First exhibit unveiled in Oneonta, NY in 1982. Moved into present building in 1987. New Hall of Fame planned at Wright National Soccer Campus in Oneonta. **Address:** 5-11 Ford Avenue, Oneonta, NY 13820. **Telephone:** (607) 432-3351.

Eligibility: Nominated players must have represented the U.S. in international competition and be retired five years; other categories include Meritorious Service and Special Commendation.

Nominations made by state organizations and a veterans' committee. Voting done by nine-member committee made up of Hall of Famers, U.S. Soccer officials and members of the national media.

Class of 1994 (3): PLAYERS—midfielder **Pat McBride**, college (Saint Louis 1963–65), NASL (St. Louis Stars 1967–76); **Lloyd Monsen**, Olympics (1952, '56). CONTRIBUTOR—**Frank Kelly**, youth soccer administrator.

Members are listed with home state and year of induction; (+) indicates deceased members.

Members

Abronzino, Umberto (CA) 1971	+ Fairfield, Harry (PA) 1951	+ Lamm, Kurt (NY).....................1979
Aimi, Milton (TX) 1991	Feibusch, Ernst (CA) 1984	Lang, Millard (MD) 1950
+ Alonso, Julie (NY)...................1972	+ Ferguson, John (PA) 1950	Larson, Bert (CT)....................1988
+ Andersen, William (NY)..........1956	+ Fernley, John A. (MA)..............1951	+ Lewis, H. Edgar (PA) 1950
+ Ardizzone, John (CA) 1971	+ Ferro, Charles (NY) 1958	Lombardo, Joe (NY)...............1984
+ Armstrong, James (NY)...........1952	+ Fishwick, George E. (IL)...........1974	Long, Denny (MO)..................1993
+ Auld, Andrew (RI)..................1986	+ Flamhaft, Jack (NY)................1964	
	+ Fleming, Harry G. (PA) 1967	+ MacEwan, John J. (MI)............1953
Bahr, Walter (PA)....................1976	+ Florie, Thomas (NJ)................1986	+ Maca, Joe (NY) 1976
Barr, George (NY) 1983	+ Foulds, Pal (MA)....................1953	+ Magnozzi, Enzo (NY) 1978
+ Barriskill, Joe (NY).................1953	+ Foulds, Sam (MA)..................1969	+ Maher, Jack (IL)....................1970
+ Beardsworth, Fred (MA)..........1965	+ Fowler, Dan (NY)...................1970	+ Manning, Dr. Randolf (NY)......1950
Bernabei, Ray (PA) 1978	+ Fowler, Peg (NY) 1979	+ Marre, John (MO) 1953
Best, John O. (CA)...................1982	Fricker, Werner (PA) 1992	McBride, Pat (MO) 1994
+ Bookie, Michael (PA)...............1986	+ Fryer, William J. (NJ)..............1951	+ McClay, Allan (MA)................1971
+ Booth, Joseph (CT) 1952		+ McGhee, Bart (NY) 1986
Borghi, Frank (MO) 1976	+ Gaetjens, Joe (NY) 1976	+ McGrath, Frank (MA) 1978
Boulos, Frenchy (PA) 1980	+ Gallagher, James (NY)............1986	+ McGuire, Jimmy (NY) 1951
+ Boxer, Matt (CA).....................1961	+ Garcia, Pete (MO)..................1964	+ McGuire, John (NY)................1951
+ Briggs, Lawrence E. (MA)........1978	+ Gentle, James (PA).................1986	+ McIlveney, Eddie (PA).............1976
+ Brittan, Harold (PA) 1951	Getzinger, Rudy (IL) 1991	McLaughlin, Bennie (PA) 1977
+ Brock, John (MA)....................1950	+ Giesler, Walter (MO) 1962	+ McSkimming, Dent (MO)..........1951
+ Brown, Andrew M. (OH).........1950	Glover, Teddy (NY) 1965	Merovich, Pete (PA) 1971
+ Brown, David (NJ) 1951	+ Gonsalves, Billy (MA)..............1950	+ Mieth, Werner (NJ).................1974
Brown, James (NY) 1986	Gormley, Bob (PA) 1989	+ Millar, Robert (NY) 1950
	+ Gould, David L. (PA)...............1953	+ Miller, Milton (NY) 1971
+ Cahill, Thomas W (NY) 1950	+ Govier, Sheldon (IL) 1950	+ Mills, Jimmy (PA) 1954
+ Carenza, Joe (MO)................1982	Greer, Don (CA) 1985	Monson, Lloyd (NY)...............1994
+ Caraffi, Ralph (OH) 1959	Gryzik, Joe (IL).......................1973	Moore, James F. (MO) 1971
Chacurian, Chico (CT) 1992	+ Guelker, Bob (MO) 1980	+ Moorehouse, George (NY) 1986
+ Chesney, Stan (NY)................1966	Guennel, Joe (CO) 1980	+ Morrison, Robert (PA) 1951
+ Coll, John (NY)......................1986		+ Morrissette, Bill (MA) 1967
+ Collins, George M. (MA)..........1951	Harker, Al (PA) 1979	
+ Colombo, Charlie (MO) 1976	+ Healy, George (MI).................1951	Nanoski, Jukey (PA) 1993
+ Commander, Colin (OH)..........1967	Heilpern, Herb (NY).................1988	+ Netto, Fred (IL) 1958
+ Cordery, Ted (CA) 1975	+ Hemmings, William (IL)............1961	Newman, Ron (CA) 1992
+ Craddock, Robert (PA) 1959	+ Hudson, Maurice (CA) 1966	+ Niotis, D.J. (IL)......................1963
+ Craggs, Edmund (WA)............1969	Hunt, Lamar (TX) 1982	
Craggs, George (WA) 1981	Hynes, John (NY) 1977	+ O'Brien, Shamus (NY) 1990
+ Cummings, Wilfred R. (IL) 1953		Olaff, Gene (NJ) 1971
	+ Iglehart, Alfredda (MD)...........1951	+ Oliver, Arnie (MA) 1968
+ Delach, Joseph (PA) 1973		
DeLuca, Enzo (NY) 1979	+ Japp, John (PA) 1953	+ Palmer, William (PA) 1952
+ Dick, Walter (CA) 1989	+ Jeffrey, William (PA) 1951	Pariani, Gino (MO) 1976
Diorio, Nick (PA) 1974	+ Johnson, Jack (IL)..................1952	+ Patenaude, Bert (MA) 1971
+ Donaghy, Edward J. (NY) 1951		+ Pearson, Eddie (GA) 1990
+ Donelli, Buff (PA) 1954	Kabanica, Mike (WI) 1987	+ Peel, Peter (IL)......................1951
+ Donnelly, George (NY)............1989	Kehoe, Bob (MO) 1990	Pelé (Brazil)...........................1993
+ Douglas, Jimmy (NJ)..............1954	Kelly, Frank (NJ) 1994	Peters, Wally (NJ)..................1967
+ Dresmich, John W. (PA) 1968	+ Kempton, George (WA) 1950	Phillipson, Don (CO)...............1987
+ Duff, Duncan (CA).................1972	Keough, Harry (MO) 1976	+ Piscopo, Giorgio (NY).............1978
+ Dugan, Thomas (NJ) 1951	+ Klein, Paul (NJ) 1953	+ Pomeroy, Edgar (CA).............1955
+ Dunn, James (MO) 1974	+ Koszma, Oscar (CA)...............1964	
	+ Kracher, Frank (IL) 1983	+ Ramsden, Arnold (TX).............1957
Edwards, Gene (WI) 1985	Kraft, Granny (MD) 1984	+ Ratican, Harry (MO)...............1950
+ Epperleim, Rudy (NJ) 1951	+ Kraus, Harry (NY) 1963	Reese, Doc (MD)....................1957
	+ Kunter, Rudy (NY) 1963	+ Renzulli, Pete (NY) 1951

Ringsdorf, Gene (MD)............1979
Roth, Werner (NY)................1989
+ Rottenberg, Jack (NJ)............1971
Roy, Willy (IL)...................1989
+ Ryan, Hun (PA)....................1958

+ Sager, Tom (PA)..................1968
Saunders, Harry (NY)............1981
Schellscheidt, Mannie (NJ)......1990
Schillinger, Emil (PA)............1960
+ Schroeder, Elmer (PA)............1951
+ Scwarcz, Erno (NY)...............1951
+ Shields, Fred (PA)................1968
+ Single, Erwin (NY)................1981
+ Slone, Philip (NY)................1986

+ Smith, Alfred (PA)..................1951
+ Souza, Ed (MA) 1976
Souza, Clarkie (MA)..............1976
+ Spalding, Dick (PA)................1951
+ Stark, Archie (NJ)................1950
+ Steelink, Nicolaas (CA)............1971
+ Steur, August (NY)................1969
+ Stewart, Douglas (PA)............1950
+ Stone, Robert T. (CO)............1971
+ Swords, Thomas (MA)............1976

+ Tintle, Joseph (NJ)................1952
+ Tracey, Ralph (MO)................1986
+ Triner, Joseph (IL)................1951

+ Vaughan, Frank (MO)............1986

+ Walder, Jimmy (PA) 1971
+ Wallace, Frank (MO)............1976
+ Washauer, Adolph (CA)............1977
+ Webb, Tom (WA) 1987
+ Weir, Alex (NY)...................1975
+ Weston, Victor (WA)..............1956
+ Wilson, Peter (NJ)................1950
+ Wood, Alex (MI)...................1986
+ Woods, John W. (IL)..............1952

Yeagley, Jerry (IN)................1989
+ Young, John (CA)................1958

+ Zampini, Dan (PA)................1963
Zerhusen, Al (CA)................1978

TENNIS

International Tennis Hall of Fame

Originally the National Tennis Hall of Fame. Established in 1953 by James Van Alen and sanctioned by the U.S. Tennis Association in 1954. Renamed the International Tennis Hall of Fame in 1976. **Address:** 194 Bellevue Ave., Newport, RI 02840. **Telephone:** (401) 846-4567.

Eligibility: Nominated players must be five years removed from being a "significant factor" in competitive tennis. Voting done by members of the international tennis media.

Class of 1994 (2): PLAYER—**Hana Mandlikova**. CONTRIBUTOR—journalist and commentator **Bud Collins**. Members are listed with year of induction; (+) indicates deceased members.

Men

+ Adee, George...................1964
+ Alexander, Fred 1961
+ Allison, Wilmer 1963
+ Alonso, Manuel.................1977
+ Ashe, Arthur 1985
+ Behr, Karl 1969
Borg, Bjorn 1987
+ Borotra, Jean 1976
Bromwich, John 1984
+ Brookes, Norman 1977
+ Brugnon, Jacques 1976
Budge, Don 1964
+ Campbell, Oliver 1955
+ Chace, Malcolm 1961
+ Clark, Clarence 1983
+ Clark, Joseph 1955
+ Clothier, William 1956
+ Cochet, Henri 1976
Cooper, Ashley 1991
+ Crawford, Jack 1979
+ Doeg, John 1962
+ Doherty, Lawrence 1980
+ Doherty, Reginald 1980
Drobny, Jaroslav 1983
+ Dwight, James 1955
Emerson, Roy 1982
+ Etchebaster, Pierre 1978
Falkenburg, Bob 1974
Fraser, Neale 1984
+ Garland, Chuck 1969
Gonzales, Pancho 1968
+ Grant, Bryan (Bitsy) 1972
+ Griffin, Clarence 1970
+ Hackett, Harold................1961

Hewitt, Bob 1992
+ Hoad, Lew 1980
+ Hovey, Fred 1974
+ Hunt, Joe 1966
+ Hunter, Frank 1961
+ Johnston, Bill 1958
+ Jones, Perry 1970
Kodes, Jan 1990
+ Kramer, Jack 1968
Lacoste, Rene 1976
+ Larned, William 1956
Larsen, Art 1969
Laver, Rod 1981
+ Lott, George 1964
Mako, Gene 1973
+ McKinley, Chuck 1986
+ McLoughlin, Maurice 1957
McMillan, Frew 1992
McNeill, Don 1965
Mulloy, Gardnar 1972
+ Murray, Lindley 1958
+ Myrick, Julian 1963
Nastase, Ilie 1991
Newcombe, John 1986
+ Nielsen, Arthur 1971
Olmedo, Alex 1987
+ Osuna, Rafael 1979
Parker, Frank 1966
+ Patterson, Gerald 1989
Patty, Budge 1977
Perry, Fred 1975
+ Pettitt, Tom 1982
Pietrangeli, Nicola 1986
+ Quist, Adrian 1984

Ralston, Dennis 1987
+ Renshaw, Ernest 1983
+ Renshaw, William 1983
+ Richards, Vincent 1961
Riggs, Bobby 1967
Roche, Tony 1986
Rosewall, Ken 1980
Santana, Manuel 1984
Savitt, Dick 1976
Schroeder, Ted 1966
+ Sears, Richard 1955
Sedgman, Frank 1979
Segura, Pancho 1984
Seixas, Vic 1971
+ Shields, Frank 1964
+ Slocum, Henry 1955
Smith, Stan 1987
Stolle, Fred 1985
Talbert, Bill 1967
+ Tilden, Bill 1959
Trabert, Tony 1970
Van Ryn, John 1963
Vilas, Guillermo 1991
+ Vines, Ellsworth 1962
+ von Cramm, Gottfried 1977
+ Ward, Holcombe 1956
+ Washburn, Watson 1965
+ Whitman, Malcolm 1955
+ Wilding, Anthony 1978
+ Williams, Richard 2nd 1957
Wood, Sidney 1964
+ Wrenn, Robert 1955
+ Wright, Beals 1956

Women

+ Atkinson, Juliette 1974
Austin, Tracy 1992
+ Barger-Wallach, Maud..........1958
Betz Addie, Pauline 1965
+ Bjurstedt Mallory, Molla..........1958

Brough Clapp, Louise 1967
+ Browne, Mary 1957
Bueno, Maria 1978
+ Cahill, Mabel...................1976
+ Connolly Brinker, Maureen......1968

+ Dod, Charlotte (Lottie)............1983
+ Douglass Chambers, Dorothy..1981
Fry Irvin, Shirley.................1970
Gibson, Althea....................1971
Goolagong Cawley, Evonne....1988

International Tennis Hall of Fame (Cont.)

+ Hansell, Ellen	1965	Mandlikova, Hana	1994	+ Round Little, Dorothy	1986
Hard, Darlene	1973	+ Marble, Alice	1964	+ Ryan, Elizabeth	1972
Hart, Doris	1969	+ McKane Godfree, Kitty	1978	+ Sears, Eleanora	1968
Hayden Jones, Ann	1985	+ Moore, Elisabeth	1971	Smith Court, Margaret	1979
Heldman, Gladys	1979	Mortimer Barrett, Angela	1993	+ Sutton Bundy, May	1956
+ Hotchkiss Wightman, Hazel	1957	+ Nuthall Shoemaker, Betty	1977	+ Townsend Toulmin, Bertha	1974
Jacobs, Helen Hull	1962	Osborne duPont, Margaret	1967	Wade, Virginia	1989
King, Billie Jean	1987	Palfrey Danzig, Sarah	1963	+ Wagner, Marie	1969
+ Lenglen, Suzanne	1978	+ Roosevelt, Ellen	1975	Wills Moody Roark, Helen	1959

Contributors

+ Baker, Lawrence, Sr	1975	+ Gustaf, V (King of Sweden)	1980	+ Outerbridge, Mary	1981
Chatrier, Philippe	1992	+ Hester, W.E. (Slew)	1981	+ Pell, Theodore	1966
Collins, Bud	1994	+ Hopman, Harry	1978	+ Tingay, Lance	1982
Cullman, Joseph F. 3rd	1990	Hunt, Lamar	1993	+ Tinling, Ted	1986
+ Danzig, Allison	1968	+ Laney, Al	1979	+ Van Alen, James	1965
+ Davis, Dwight	1956	Martin, Alastair	1973		
+ Gray, David	1985	Martin, William McC	1982		

TRACK & FIELD

National Track & Field Hall of Fame

Established in 1974 by the The Athletics Congress (now USA Track & Field). Originally located in Charleston, WV, the Hall moved to Indianapolis in 1983 and reopened at the Hoosier Dome in 1986. **Address:** One Hoosier Dome, Indianapolis, IN 46225. **Telephone:** (317) 261-0483.

Eligibility: Nominated athletes must be retired three years and coaches must have coached at least 20 years, if retired, or 35 years, if still coaching. Voting done by 800-member panel made up of Hall of Fame and USA Track & Field officials, Hall of Fame members, current U.S. champions and members of the Track & Field Writers of America.

Class of 1994: (5): MEN—high jumper **Cornelius Johnson** and hurdler **Edwin Moses**. WOMEN—discus thrower **Lillian Copeland** and javelin thrower **Kate Schmidt**. CONTRIBUTOR—New York City Marathon race director **Fred Lebow**.

Members are listed with year of induction; (+) indicates deceased members.

Men

+ Albritton, Dave	1980	Houser, Bud	1979	Richards, Bob	1975
Ashenfelter, Horace	1975	+ Hubbard, DeHart	1979	+ Rose, Ralph	1976
+ Bausch, James	1979	Jenkins, Charlie	1992	Ryun, Jim	1980
Beamon, Bob	1977	Jenner, Bruce	1980	+ Scholz, Jackson	1977
Beatty, Jim	1990	+ Johnson, Cornelius	1994	Schul, Bob	1991
Bell, Greg	1988	Johnson, Rafer	1974	Seagren, Bob	1986
+ Boeckmann, Dee	1976	Jones, Hayes	1976	+ Sheppard, Mel	1976
Boston, Ralph	1974	Kelley, John	1980	+ Sheridan, Martin	1988
+ Calhoun, Lee	1974	Kiviat, Abel	1985	Shorter, Frank	1989
Campbell, Milt	1989	+ Kraenzlein, Alvin	1974	Sime, Dave	1981
+ Clark, Ellery	1991	Laird, Ron	1986	+ Simpson, Robert	1974
Connolly, Harold	1984	Mathias, Bob	1974	Smith, Tommie	1978
Courtney, Tom	1978	Matson, Randy	1984	+ Stanfield, Andy	1977
+ Cunningham, Glenn	1974	+ Meredith, Ted	1982	Steers, Les	1974
+ Curtis, William	1979	+ Metcalfe, Ralph	1975	Thomas, John	1985
Davenport, Willie	1982	Milburn, Rod	1993	+ Thomson, Earl	1977
Davis, Glenn	1974	Mills, Billy	1976	+ Thorpe, Jim	1975
Davis, Harold	1974	Moore, Tom	1988	+ Tolan, Eddie	1982
Dillard, Harrison	1974	Morrow, Bobby	1975	Toomey, Bill	1975
Dumas, Charley	1990	+ Mortensen, Jess	1992	+ Towns, Forrest (Spec)	1976
Evans, Lee	1983	Moses, Edwin	1994	Warmerdam, Cornelius	1974
Ewell, Barney	1986	+ Myers, Lawrence	1974	White, Willye	1981
+ Ewry, Ray	1974	O'Brien, Parry	1974	Whitfield, Mal	1974
+ Flanagan, John	1975	Oerter, Al	1974	Wilkins, Mac	1993
Fosbury, Dick	1981	+ Osborn, Harold	1974	+ Williams, Archie	1992
+ Gordien, Fortune	1979	+ Owens, Jesse	1974	Wohlhuter, Rick	1990
Greene, Charlie	1992	+ Paddock, Charley	1976	Woodruff, John	1978
+ Hahn, Archie	1983	Patton, Mel	1985	Wottle, Dave	1982
+ Hardin, Glenn	1978	Peacock, Eulace	1987	+ Wykoff, Frank	1977
Hayes, Bob	1976	+ Prefontaine, Steve	1976	Young, George	1981
Held, Bud	1987	+ Ray, Joie	1976		
Hines, Jim	1979	+ Rice, Greg	1977		

Women

Coachman, Alice 1975	+ Jackson, Nell 1989	Schmidt, Kate 1994
+ Copeland, Lillian 1994	Manning, Madeline 1984	Shiley Newhouse, Jean 1993
+ Didrikson, Babe 1974	McDaniel, Mildred 1983	+ Stephens, Helen 1975
Faggs, Mae 1976	McGuire, Edith...................1979	Tyus, Wyomia 1980
Ferrell, Barbara.................1988	Robinson, Betty 1977	+ Walsh, Stella 1975
+ Hall Adams, Evelyne 1988	Rudolph, Wilma 1974	Watson, Martha..................1987
Heritage, Doris Brown 1990		

Coaches

+ Baskin, Weems 1982	+ Hamilton, Brutus 1974	+ Moakley, Jack 1988
Beard, Percy 1981	+ Haydon, Ted 1975	+ Murphy, Michael 1974
Bell, Sam 1992	+ Hayes, Billy 1976	+ Snyder, Larry 1978
Botts, Tom 1983	Haylett, Ward 1979	Temple, Ed 1989
Bowerman, Bill 1981	+ Higgins, Ralph 1982	+ Templeton, Dink 1976
Bush, Jim 1987	+ Hillman, Harry 1976	Walker, LeRoy 1983
+ Cromwell, Dean 1974	+ Hurt, Edward 1975	Wilt, Fred 1981
Doherty, Ken 1976	+ Hutsell, Wilbur 1977	+ Winter, Bud 1985
Easton, Bill 1975	+ Jones, Thomas 1977	Wright, Stan 1993
+ Elliott, Jumbo 1981	Jordan, Payton 1982	+ Yancy, Joseph 1984
+ Giegengack, Bob 1978	+ Littlefield, Clyde 1981	

Contributors

+ Abramson, Jesse 1981	+ Ferris, Dan 1974	+ Nelson, Bert....................1991
Andersen, Roxanne 1991	+ Griffith, John 1979	Nelson, Cordner 1988
+ Bakjian, Andy...................1986	Lebow, Fred 1994	+ Sullivan, James 1977
+ Brundage, Avery 1974		

WOMEN

International Women's Sports Hall of Fame

Established in 1980 by the Women's Sports Foundation. **Address:** Women's Sports Foundation, Eisenhower Park, East Meadow, NY 11554. **Telephone:** (516) 542-4700.

Eligibility: Nominees' achievements and commitment to the development of women's sports must be internationally recognized. Athletes are elected in two categories—Pioneer (before 1960) and Contemporary (since 1960). Members are divided below by sport for the sake of easy reference; (*) indicates member inducted in Pioneer category. Coaching nominees must have coached at least 10 years.

Class of 1994 (4): CONTEMPORARY—**Chi Chen** (track & field) and **Annichen Krinstad** (orienteering). PIONEER—**Lis Hartel** (equestrian). COACH— **Rusty Kanakogi** (judo).

Members are listed with year of induction; (+) indicates deceased members.

Alpine Skiing

Cranz, Christl* 1991	
Lawrence, Andrea Mead* 1983	
Moser-Proell, Annemarie 1982	

Auto Racing

Guthrie, Janet 1980

Aviation

+ Coleman, Bessie* 1992	
+ Earhart, Amelia* 1980	
+ Marvingt, Marie* 1987	

Baseball

Stone, Toni* 1993

Basketball

Meyers, Ann...........................1985	
Miller, Cheryl 1991	

Bowling

Ladewig, Marion* 1984

Cycling

Carpenter Phinney, Connie 1990

Diving

King, Micki 1983	
McCormick, Pat* 1984	
Riggin, Aileen* 1988	

Equestrian

Hartel, Lis 1994

Fencing

Schacherer-Elek, Ilona* 1989

Figure Skating

Albright, Tenley* 1983	
+ Blanchard, Theresa Weld* 1989	
Fleming, Peggy 1981	
Heiss Jenkins, Carol* 1992	
+ Henie, Sonja* 1982	
Protopopov, Ludmila...............1992	
Rodnina, Irena 1988	

Golf

Berg, Patty* 1980	
Carner, JoAnne......................1987	
Mann, Carol 1982	
Rawls, Betsy* 1986	
Suggs, Louise* 1987	
+ Vare, Glenna Collett* 1981	
Whitworth, Kathy...................1984	
Wright, Mickey 1981	

Golf/Track & Field

+ Zaharias, Babe Didrikson* 1980

Gymnastics

Caslavska, Vera 1991	
Comaneci, Nadia 1990	
Korbut, Olga 1982	
Latynina, Larissa* 1985	
Retton, Mary Lou...................1993	
Tourischeva, Lyudmila.............1987	

Shooting

Murdock, Margaret 1988

Softball

Joyce, Joan 1989

Speed Skating

+ Klein Outland, Kit* 1993	
Young, Sheila 1981	

Swimming

Caulkins, Tracy 1986	
Curtis Cuneo, Ann* 1985	
de Varona, Donna 1983	
Ederle, Gertrude* 1980	
Fraser, Dawn 1985	
Holm, Eleanor* 1980	
Meagher, Mary T...................1993	
Meyer-Reyes, Debbie 1987	

Tennis

+ Connolly, Maureen* 1987	
+ Dod, Charlotte (Lottie)* 1986	
Evert, Chris............................1981	
Gibson, Althea* 1980	
Goolagong Cawley, Evonne.....1989	
+ Hotchkiss Wightman, Hazel*...1986	
King, Billie Jean 1980	
+ Lenglen, Suzanne* 1984	
Navratilova, Martina...............1984	
+ Sears, Eleanora* 1984	
Smith Court, Margaret............1986	

International Women's Sports Hall of Fame (Cont.)

Track & Field

Blankers-Koen, Fanny*	1982
Cheng, Chi	1994
Coachman Davis, Alice*	1991
Manning Mims, Madeline	1987
Rudolph, Wilma	1980
+ Stephens, Helen*	1983
Szewinska, Irena	1992
Tyus, Wyomia	1981
White, Willye	1988

Volleyball

+ Hyman, Flo	1986

Water Skiing

McGuire, Willa Worthington*	1990

Orienteering

Krinstad, Annichen	1994

Coaches

Applebee, Constance	1991
Backus, Sharron	1993
Grossfeld, Muriel	1991
+ Jackson, Nell	1990
Kanakogi, Rusty	1994
Summitt, Pat Head	1990
Wade, Margaret	1992

OTHER

Rock And Roll Hall of Fame

Established in 1983 by the Rock and Roll Hall of Fame Foundation, Inc. **Current Address:** 1290 Avenue of the Americas, New York, NY 10104. Ground-breaking ceremonies for a permanent museum in Cleveland took place on June 7, 1993. **Telephone:** (212) 484-1755 in New York and (216) 781-7625 in Cleveland.

Eligibility: Nominated artists and groups must have released records at least 25 years prior to their induction. Voting done by worldwide panel of 600 artists, producers, journalists, music historians and record industry executives.

Class of 1994 (10): ARTISTS—**Duane Eddy, Elton John, John Lennon, Bob Marley, Rod Stewart**. GROUPS—**The Animals, The Band, The Grateful Dead**. EARLY INFLUENCE—**Willie Dixon**. NON-PERFORMER—**Johnny Otis**.

Members are listed with year of induction; (+) indicates deceased members.

Artists

Baker, LaVern	1991	Dylan, Bob	1988	+ Nelson, Ricky	1987
Ballard, Hank	1990	Eddy, Duane	1994	+ Orbison, Roy	1987
Berry, Chuck	1986	Franklin, Aretha	1987	Perkins, Carl	1987
Bland, Bobby (Blue)	1992	+ Gaye, Marvin	1987	Pickett, Wilson	1991
Brown, James	1986	+ Haley, Bill	1987	+ Presley, Elvis	1986
Brown, Ruth	1993	+ Holly, Buddy	1986	+ Reed, Jimmy	1991
Cash, Johnny	1992	Hooker, John Lee	1991	+ Redding, Otis	1989
Charles, Ray	1986	John, Elton	1994	Richard, Little	1986
+ Cochran, Eddie	1987	King, B.B.	1987	Robinson, Smokey	1987
+ Cooke, Sam	1986	+ Lennon, John	1994	Stewart, Rod	1994
+ Darin, Bobby	1990	Lewis, Jerry Lee	1986	+ Turner, Big Joe	1987
Diddley, Bo	1987	+ Marley, Bob	1994	+ Waters, Muddy	1987
Dion	1989	+ McPhatter, Clyde	1987	+ Wilson, Jackie	1987
Domino, Fats	1986	Morrison, Van	1993	Wonder, Stevie	1989

Groups

The Animals	1994	The Everly Brothers	1986	+ Frankie Lymon	
The Band	1994	The Four Seasons	1990	& the Teenagers	1993
The Beach Boys	1988	The Four Tops	1990	The Platters	1990
The Beatles	1988	The Grateful Dead	1994	The Rolling Stones	1989
Booker T. and the MG's	1992	Ike & Tina Turner	1991	Sam & Dave	1992
The Byrds	1991	The Impressions	1991	Simon & Garfunkel	1990
The Coasters	1987	The Isley Brothers	1992	Sly & the Family Stone	1993
Cream	1993	James, Etta	1993	The Supremes	1988
Creedence Clearwater Revival	1993	The Jimi Hendrix Experience	1992	The Temptations	1989
The Doors	1993	The Kinks	1990	The Who	1990
The Drifters	1988			The Yardbirds	1992

Early Influences

+ Armstrong, Louis	1990	+ Jordan, Louis	1987	+ Smith, Bessie	1989
+ Christian, Charlie	1990	+ Leadbelly	1988	Soul Stirrers, The	1989
+ Dixon, Willie	1994	+ Longhair, Professor	1992	+ Walker, T-Bone	1987
+ Elmore, James	1992	Paul, Les	1988	+ Washington, Dinah	1993
+ Freed, Alan	1986	Phillips, Sam	1986	+ Williams, Hank	1987
+ Guthrie, Woody	1988	+ Rainey, Ma	1990	+ Wolf, Howlin'	1991
The Ink Spots	1989				

Non-Performers

Bartholomew, Dave	1991	Goffin, Gerry	1990	Leiber, Jerry	1987
Bass, Ralph	1991	Gordy, Berry Jr	1988	Otis, Johnny	1994
+ Chess, Leonard	1987	+ Graham, Bill	1992	+ Pomus, Doc	1992
Clark, Dick	1993	+ Hammond, John	1986	+ Rodgers, Jimmie	1986
Dozier, Lamont	1990	Holland, Brian	1990	Spector, Phil	1989
Ertegun, Ahmet	1987	Holland, Eddie	1990	Stoller, Mike	1987
+ Fender, Leo	1992	+ Johnson, Robert	1986	Wexler, Jerry	1987
Gabler, Milt	1993	King, Carole	1990	+ Yancey, Jimmy	1986

Dale Murphy, who won back-to-back National League MVP awards with the Atlanta Braves in 1982 and '83, shows his obvious pleasure during ceremonies to retire his old number on June 13.

RETIRED NUMBERS

Major League Baseball

The New York Yankees have retired the most uniform numbers (12) in the Major Leagues; followed by Pittsburgh and the Brooklyn-Los Angeles Dodgers (8), the Chicago White Sox (7), the New York-San Francisco Giants (6) and the St.Louis Cardinals (5). Four players and a manager have had their numbers retired by two teams: **Hank Aaron**—#44 by the Boston-Milwaukee-Atlanta Braves and the Milwaukee Brewers; **Rod Carew**—#29 by Minnesota and California; **Rollie Fingers**—#34 by Milwaukee and Oakland; **Frank Robinson**—#20 by Cincinnati and Baltimore; and **Casey Stengel**—#37 by the New York Yankees and New York Mets.

Numbers retired in 1994 (4): ATLANTA—#3 worn by outfielder **Dale Murphy** (1976–90); CLEVELAND—#14 worn by outfielder **Larry Doby** (1947–55, '58); KANSAS CITY—#5 worn by infielder-DH **George Brett** (1973–93); MILWAUKEE—#19 worn by infielder-outfielder **Robin Yount** (1974–93).

American League

Three AL teams—the Seattle Mariners, Texas Rangers and Toronto Blue Jays—have not retired any numbers.

Baltimore
4 Earl Weaver
5 Brooks Robinson
20 Frank Robinson
22 Jim Palmer
33 Eddie Murray

Boston Red Sox
1 Bobby Doerr
4 Joe Cronin
8 Carl Yastrzemski
9 Ted Williams

California Angels
26 Gene Autry
29 Rod Carew
30 Nolan Ryan

Chicago White Sox
2 Nellie Fox
3 Harold Baines
4 Luke Appling
9 Minnie Minoso
11 Luis Aparicio
16 Ted Lyons
19 Billy Pierce

Cleveland Indians
3 Earl Averill
5 Lou Boudreau
14 Larry Doby
18 Mel Harder
19 Bob Feller

Detroit Tigers
2 Charlie Gehringer
5 Hank Greenberg
6 Al Kaline

Kansas City Royals
5 George Brett
10 Dick Howser

Milwaukee Brewers
19 Robin Yount
34 Rollie Fingers
44 Hank Aaron

Minnesota Twins
3 Harmon Killebrew
6 Tony Oliva
29 Rod Carew

New York Yankees
1 Billy Martin
3 Babe Ruth
4 Lou Gehrig
5 Joe DiMaggio
7 Mickey Mantle
8 Yogi Berra & Bill Dickey
9 Roger Maris
10 Phil Rizzuto
15 Thurman Munson
16 Whitey Ford
32 Elston Howard
37 Casey Stengel
44 Reggie Jackson

Oakland Athletics
27 Catfish Hunter
34 Rollie Finger

Retired Numbers (Cont.)
National League

San Francisco has honored former NY Giants Christy Mathewson and John McGraw even though they played before numbers were worn.

Atlanta Braves
3 Dale Murphy
21 Warren Spahn
35 Phil Niekro
41 Eddie Mathews
44 Hank Aaron

Chicago Cubs
14 Ernie Banks
26 Billy Williams

Cincinnati Reds
1 Fred Hutchinson
5 Johnny Bench

Houston Astros
25 Jose Cruz
32 Jim Umbricht
33 Mike Scott
40 Don Wilson

Los Angeles Dodgers
1 Pee Wee Reese
4 Duke Snider
19 Jim Gilliam
24 Walter Alston
32 Sandy Koufax
39 Roy Campanella
42 Jackie Robinson
53 Don Drysdale

Montreal Expos
8 Gary Carter
10 Rusty Staub

New York Mets
14 Gil Hodges
37 Casey Stengel
41 Tom Seaver

Philadelphia Phillies
1 Richie Ashburn
20 Mike Schmidt
32 Steve Carlton
36 Robin Roberts

Pittsburgh Pirates
1 Billy Meyer
4 Ralph Kiner
8 Willie Stargell
9 Bill Mazeroski
20 Pie Traynor
21 Roberto Clemente
33 Honus Wagner
40 Danny Murtaugh

St. Louis Cardinals
6 Stan Musial
14 Ken Boyer
17 Dizzy Dean
20 Lou Brock
45 Bob Gibson
85 August (Gussie) Busch

San Diego Padres
6 Steve Garvey

San Francisco Giants
3 Bill Terry
4 Mel Ott
11 Carl Hubbell
24 Willie Mays
27 Juan Marichal
44 Willie McCovey

National Basketball Association

Boston has retired the most numbers (16) in the NBA; followed by the New York Knicks (7); Milwaukee, Portland and the Rochester-Cincinnati Royals/Kansas City-Omaha-Sacramento Kings (6); and the Los Angeles Lakers and Syracuse Nats/Philadelphia 76ers (5). Six players have had their numbers retired by two teams: **Kareem Abdul-Jabbar**–#33 by LA Lakers and Milwaukee; **Wilt Chamberlain**–#13 by the Los Angeles Lakers and Philadelphia; **Julius Erving**–#6 by Philadelphia and #32 by New Jersey; **Bob Lanier**–#16 by Detroit and Milwaukee; **Oscar Robertson**–#1 by Milwaukee and #14 by Sacramento; and **Nate Thurmond**–#42 by Cleveland and Golden State.

Numbers retired in 1994 (7): BOSTON—#32 worn by forward **Kevin McHale** (1980–93) and #35 worn by forward **Reggie Lewis** (1987–93); CHICAGO—#10 worn by forward **Bob Love** (1969–76) and #23 worn by forward **Michael Jordan** (1984–93); DETROIT—#15 worn by guard **Vinnie Johnson** (1982–91); NEW JERSEY—#11 worn by guard **Drazen Petrovic** (1991–93); PHOENIX—#6 worn by guard **Walter Davis** (1977–88).

Eastern Conference

Three Eastern teams—the Charlotte Hornets, Miami Heat, and Orlando Magic—have not retired any numbers.

Boston Celtics
1 Walter A. Brown
2 Red Auerbach
3 Dennis Johnson
6 Bill Russell
10 Jo Jo White
14 Bob Cousy
15 Tom Heinsohn
16 Tom (Satch) Sanders
17 John Havlicek
18 Dave Cowens
19 Don Nelson
21 Bill Sharman
22 Ed Macauley
23 Frank Ramsey
24 Sam Jones
25 K.C. Jones
32 Kevin McHale
33 Larry Bird
35 Reggie Lewis
Loscy Jim Loscutoff
Radio mike Johnny Most

Atlanta Hawks
9 Bob Pettit
23 Lou Hudson

Chicago Bulls
4 Jerry Sloan
10 Bob Love
23 Michael Jordan

Cleveland Cavaliers
7 Bingo Smith
34 Austin Carr
42 Nate Thurmond

Detroit Pistons
15 Vinnie Johnson
16 Bob Lanier
21 Dave Bing

Indiana Pacers
30 George McGinnis
34 Mel Daniels
35 Roger Brown

Milwaukee Bucks
1 Oscar Robertson
2 Junior Bridgeman
4 Sidney Moncrief
14 Jon McGlocklin
16 Bob Lanier
32 Brian Winters
33 Kareem Abdul-Jabbar

New York Knicks
10 Walt Frazier
12 Dick Barnett
15 Dick McGuire
   & Earl Monroe
19 Willis Reed
22 Dave DeBusschere
24 Bill Bradley
613 Red Holzman

New Jersey Nets
4 Wendell Ladner
11 Drazen Petrovic
23 John Williamson
25 Bill Melchionni
32 Julius Erving

Philadelphia 76ers
6 Julius Erving
13 Wilt Chamberlain
15 Hal Greer
24 Bobby Jones
32 Billy Cunningham
P.A. mike Dave Zinkoff

Washington Bullets
11 Elvin Hayes
25 Gus Johnson
41 Wes Unseld

Western Conference

Two Western teams—the Los Angeles Clippers and Minnesota Timberwolves—have not retired any numbers.

Dallas Mavericks
15 Brad Davis

Denver Nuggets
2 Alex English
33 David Thompson
40 Byron Beck
44 Dan Issel

Golden St. Warriors
14 Tom Meschery
16 Al Attles
24 Rick Barry
42 Nate Thurmond

Houston Rockets
23 Calvin Murphy
45 Rudy Tomjanovich

Los Angeles Lakers
13 Wilt Chamberlain
22 Elgin Baylor
32 Magic Johnson
33 Kareem Abdul-Jabbar
44 Jerry West

Phoenix Suns
5 Dick Van Arsdale
6 Walter Davis
33 Alvan Adams
42 Connie Hawkins
44 Paul Westphal

Portland Trail Blazers
13 Dave Twardzik
15 Larry Steele
20 Maurice Lucas
32 Bill Walton
36 Lloyd Neal
45 Geoff Petrie
77 Jack Ramsay

Sacramento Kings
6 Fans ("Sixth Man")
11 Bob Davies
12 Maurice Stokes
14 Oscar Robertson
27 Jack Twyman
44 Sam Lacey

San Antonio Spurs
13 James Silas
44 George Gervin

Seattle SuperSonics
19 Lenny Wilkens
32 Fred Brown

Utah Jazz
1 Frank Layden
7 Pete Maravich

National Football League

The Chicago Bears have retired the most uniform numbers (12) in the NFL; followed by the Dallas Texans/Kansas City Chiefs and New York Giants (8); the Baltimore-Indianapolis Colts and San Francisco (7); Detroit (6); and the Boston-New England Patriots, Cleveland and Philadelphia (5). No player has ever had his number retired by more than one NFL team.

Numbers retired in 1994 (6): CHICAGO—#40 worn by running back **Gale Sayers** (1965-71) and #51 worn by linebacker **Dick Butkus** (1965-73); DALLAS—added the names of running back **Tony Dorsett** (1977–87) and defensive tackle **Randy White** (1975–88) to the "Ring of Honor"; HOUSTON—#63 worn by guard **Mike Munchak** (1982–93); NY GIANTS—#56 worn by linebacker **Lawrence Taylor**.

NFC

Atlanta and Dallas are the only teams that haven't officially retired any numbers. The Falcons haven't issued uniforms #10 (Steve Bartowski), #31 (William Andrews) and #60 (Tommy Nobis) since those three players retired; while the Cowboys have a "Ring of Honor" at Texas Stadium that includes nine players and one coach—Tony Dorsett, Chuck Howley, Lee Roy Jordan, Tom Landry, Bob Lilly, Don Meredith, Don Perkins, Mel Renfro, Roger Staubach and Randy White.

Arizona Cardinals
8 Larry Wilson
77 Stan Mauldin
88 J.V. Cain
99 Marshall Goldberg

Chicago Bears
3 Bronko Nagurski
5 George McAfee
28 Willie Galimore
34 Walter Payton
40 Gayle Sayers
41 Brian Piccolo
42 Sid Luckman
51 Dick Butkus
56 Bill Hewitt
61 Bill George
66 Bulldog Turner
77 Red Grange
GSH George Halas

Detroit Lions
7 Dutch Clark
22 Bobby Layne
37 Doak Walker
56 Joe Schmidt
85 Chuck Hughes
88 Charlie Sanders

Green Bay Packers
3 Tony Canadeo
14 Don Hutson
15 Bart Starr
66 Ray Nitschke

Los Angeles Rams
7 Bob Waterfield
74 Merlin Olsen

Minnesota Vikings
10 Fran Tarkenton
88 Alan Page

New Orleans Saints
31 Jim Taylor
81 Doug Atkins

New York Giants
1 Ray Flaherty
7 Mel Hein
14 Y.A. Tittle
32 Al Blozis
40 Joe Morrison
42 Charlie Conerly
50 Ken Strong
56 Lawrence Taylor

Philadelphia Eagles
15 Steve Van Buren
40 Tom Brookshier
44 Pete Retzlaff
60 Chuck Bednarik
70 Al Wistert
99 Jerome Brown

San Francisco 49ers
12 John Brodie
34 Joe Perry
37 Jimmy Johnson
39 Hugh McElhenny
70 Charlie Krueger
73 Lou Nomellini
87 Dwight Clark

Tampa Bay Bucs
63 Lee Roy Selmon

Wash. Redskins
33 Sammy Baugh

AFC

Three AFC teams—the Buffalo Bills, Los Angeles Raiders and Pittsburgh Steelers—have not retired any numbers.

Cincinnati Bengals
54 Bob Johnson

Cleveland Browns
14 Otto Graham
32 Jim Brown
45 Ernie Davis
46 Don Fleming
76 Lou Groza

Denver Broncos
18 Frank Tripucka
44 Floyd Little

Houston Oilers
34 Earl Campbell
43 Jim Norton
63 Mike Munchak
65 Elvin Bethea

Indianapolis Colts
19 Johnny Unitas
22 Buddy Young
24 Lenny Moore
70 Art Donovan
77 Jim Parker
82 Raymond Berry
89 Gino Marchetti

Kansas City Chiefs
3 Jan Stenerud
16 Len Dawson
28 Abner Haynes
33 Stone Johnson
36 Mack Lee Hill
63 Willie Lanier
78 Bobby Bell
86 Buck Buchanan

Miami Dolphins
12 Bob Griese

New England Patriots
20 Gino Cappelletti
57 Steve Nelson
73 John Hannah
79 Jim Hunt
89 Bob Dee

New York Jets
12 Joe Namath
13 Don Maynard

San Diego Chargers
14 Dan Fouts

Seattle Seahawks
12 Fans ("12th Man")

Retired Numbers (Cont.)
National Hockey League

The Boston Bruins have retired the most uniform numbers (7) in the NHL; followed by Montreal (6); Chicago, Detroit, St. Louis and Philadelphia (4); and the Boston-New England-Hartford Whalers and NY Islanders (3). Two players have had their numbers retired by two teams: Gordie Howe—#9 by Detroit and Hartford; and Bobby Hull—#9 by Chicago and Winnipeg.

Number retired in 1994 (2): DETROIT—#1 worn by goaltender **Terry Sawchuk** (1949–55, '57–64, '68–69); LOS ANGELES—#18 worn by forward **Dave Taylor** (1977–94).

Eastern Conference

The New Jersey Devils, Ottawa Senators, Tampa Bay Lightning and Florida Panthers are the only Eastern teams that have not retired a number.

Boston Bruins
2 Eddie Shore
3 Lionel Hitchman
4 Bobby Orr
5 Dit Clapper
7 Phil Esposito
9 John Bucyk
15 Milt Schmidt

Buffalo Sabres
11 Gilbert Perreault

Hartford Whalers
2 Rick Ley
9 Gordie Howe
19 John McKenzie

Montreal Canadiens
2 Doug Harvey
4 Jean Beliveau
   & Aurel Joliat
7 Howie Morenz
9 Maurice Richard
10 Guy Lafleur
16 Henri Richard
   & Elmer Lach

New York Islanders
5 Denis Potvin
22 Mike Bossy
31 Billy Smith

New York Rangers
1 Eddie Giacomin
7 Rod Gilbert

Philadelphia Flyers
1 Bernie Parent
4 Barry Ashbee
7 Bill Barber
16 Bobby Clarke

Pittsburgh Penguins
21 Michel Briere

Quebec Nordiques
3 J.C. Tremblay
8 Marc Tardif

Washington Capitals
7 Yvon Labre

Western Conference

The San Jose Sharks and Mighty Ducks of Anaheim are the only Western teams that have not retired a number.

Calgary Flames
9 Lanny McDonald

Chicago Blackhawks
1 Glenn Hall
9 Bobby Hull
21 Stan Mikita
35 Tony Esposito

Dallas Stars
8 Bill Goldsworthy
19 Bill Masterton

Detroit Red Wings
1 Terry Sawchuk
6 Larry Aurie
7 Ted Lindsay
9 Gordie Howe
10 Alex Delvecchio

Edmonton Oilers
3 Al Hamilton

Los Angeles Kings
16 Marcel Dionne
18 Dave Taylor
30 Rogie Vachon

St. Louis Blues
3 Bob Gassoff
8 Barclay Plager
11 Brian Sutter
24 Bernie Federko

Toronto Maple Leafs
5 Bill Barilko
6 Ace Bailey

Vancouver Canucks
11 Wayne Maki
12 Stan Smyl

Winnipeg Jets
9 Bobby Hull

Wide World Photos

Bobby Hull (far left) clowns around after banners displaying his retired number and the numbers of former teammates **Stan Mikita, Tony Esposito** and **Glenn Hall** were lowered from the Chicago Stadium rafters before the Blackhawks' final regular season game on April 14. The banners have been moved across the street to the new United Center.

AWARDS

Associated Press Athletes of the Year

Selected annually by AP newspaper sports editors since 1931.

Male

Three-time NBA Most Valuable Player Michael Jordan of the Chicago Bulls outpolled three-time NL MVP Barry Bonds of the San Francisco Giants, 28–11, in first place votes to become the first three-time winner of the AP Male Athlete of the Year Award.

The Top Five vote-getters for 1993 were as follows; numbers in parentheses indicate first place votes: 1. **Michael Jordan**, pro basketball (28), 172 points; 2. **Barry Bonds**, baseball (11), 95 pts; 3. (three-way tie) **Troy Aikman**, pro football (5), **Mario Lemieux**, hockey (5) and **Emmitt Smith**, pro football (3), 41 pts.

Multiple winners: Michael Jordan (3); Don Budge, Sandy Koufax, Carl Lewis, Joe Montana and Byron Nelson (2).

Year		Year		Year	
1931	**Pepper Martin**, baseball	1952	**Bob Mathias**, track	1973	**O.J. Simpson**, pro football
1932	**Gene Sarazen**, golf	1953	**Ben Hogan**, golf	1974	**Muhammad Ali**, boxing
1933	**Carl Hubbell**, baseball	1954	**Willie Mays**, baseball	1975	**Fred Lynn**, baseball
1934	**Dizzy Dean**, baseball	1955	**Hopalong Cassady**, col.football	1976	**Bruce Jenner**, track
1935	**Joe Louis**, boxing	1956	**Mickey Mantle**, baseball	1977	**Steve Cauthen**, horse racing
1936	**Jesse Owens**, track	1957	**Ted Williams**, baseball	1978	**Ron Guidry**, baseball
1937	**Don Budge**, tennis	1958	**Herb Elliot**, track	1979	**Willie Stargell**, baseball
1938	**Don Budge**, tennis	1959	**Ingemar Johansson**, boxing		
1939	**Nile Kinnick**, college football			1980	**U.S. Olympic hockey team**
		1960	**Rafer Johnson**, track	1981	**John McEnroe**, tennis
1940	**Tom Harmon**, college football	1961	**Roger Maris**, baseball	1982	**Wayne Gretzky**, hockey
1941	**Joe DiMaggio**, baseball	1962	**Maury Wills**, baseball	1983	**Carl Lewis**, track
1942	**Frank Sinkwich**, col. football	1963	**Sandy Koufax**, baseball	1984	**Carl Lewis**, track
1943	**Gunder Haegg**, track	1964	**Don Schollander**, swimming	1985	**Dwight Gooden**, baseball
1944	**Byron Nelson**, golf	1965	**Sandy Koufax**, baseball	1986	**Larry Bird**, pro basketball
1945	**Byron Nelson**, golf	1966	**Frank Robinson**, baseball	1987	**Ben Johnson**, track
1946	**Glenn Davis**, college football	1967	**Carl Yastrzemski**, baseball	1988	**Orel Hershiser**, baseball
1947	**Johnny Lujack**, college football	1968	**Denny McLain**, baseball	1989	**Joe Montana**, pro football
1948	**Lou Boudreau**, baseball	1969	**Tom Seaver**, baseball		
1949	**Leon Hart**, college football			1990	**Joe Montana**, pro football
		1970	**George Blanda**, pro football	1991	**Michael Jordan**, pro basketball
1950	**Jim Konstanty**, baseball	1971	**Lee Trevino**, golf	1992	**Michael Jordan**, pro basketball
1951	**Dick Kazmaier**, college football	1972	**Mark Spitz**, swimming	1993	**Michael Jordan**, pro basketball

Female

Sheryl Swoopes, who led Texas Tech to an NCAA Division I basketball title, edged Steffi Graf, winner of three tennis Grand Slam events, 26–20, in first place votes to become the first member of a true team sport to win the AP Female Athlete of the Year Award.

The Top Five vote-getters of 1993 are as follows; numbers in parentheses indicate first place votes: 1. **Sheryl Swoopes**, college basketball (26), 180 points; 2. **Steffi Graf**, tennis (20), 177 pts; 3. **Wang Junxia**, track & field (5), 60 pts; 4. **Patty Sheehan**, golf (3), 28 pts; 5. **Betsy King**, golf, 21 pts.

Multiple winners: Babe Didrikson Zaharias (6); Chris Evert (4); Patty Berg and Maureen Connolly (3); Tracy Austin, Althea Gibson, Billie Jean King, Nancy Lopez, Alice Marble, Martina Navratilova, Wilma Rudolph, Monica Seles, Kathy Whitworth and Mickey Wright (2).

Year		Year		Year	
1931	**Helene Madison**, swimming	1952	**Maureen Connolly**, tennis	1973	**Billie Jean King**, tennis
1932	**Babe Didrikson**, track	1953	**Maureen Connolly**, tennis	1974	**Chris Evert**, tennis
1933	**Helen Jacobs**, tennis	1954	**Babe Didrikson Zaharias**, golf	1975	**Chris Evert**, tennis
1934	**Virginia Van Wie**, golf	1955	**Patty Berg**, golf	1976	**Nadia Comaneci**, gymnastics
1935	**Helen Wills Moody**, tennis	1956	**Pat McCormick**, diving	1977	**Chris Evert**, tennis
1936	**Helen Stephens**, track	1957	**Althea Gibson**, tennis	1978	**Nancy Lopez**, golf
1937	**Katherine Rawls**, swimming	1958	**Althea Gibson**, tennis	1979	**Tracy Austin**, tennis
1938	**Patty Berg**, golf	1959	**Maria Bueno**, tennis		
1939	**Alice Marble**, tennis			1980	**Chris Evert Lloyd**, tennis
		1960	**Wilma Rudolph**, track	1981	**Tracy Austin**, tennis
1940	**Alice Marble**, tennis	1961	**Wilma Rudolph**, track	1982	**Mary Decker Tabb**, track
1941	**Betty Hicks Newell**, golf	1962	**Dawn Fraser**, swimming	1983	**Martina Navratilova**, tennis
1942	**Gloria Callen**, swimming	1963	**Mickey Wright**, golf	1984	**Mary Lou Retton**, gymnastics
1943	**Patty Berg**, golf	1964	**Mickey Wright**, golf	1985	**Nancy Lopez**, golf
1944	**Ann Curtis**, swimming	1965	**Kathy Whitworth**, golf	1986	**Martina Navratilova**, tennis
1945	**Babe Didrikson Zaharias**, golf	1966	**Kathy Whitworth**, golf	1987	**Jackie Joyner-Kersee**, track
1946	**Babe Didrikson Zaharias**, golf	1967	**Billie Jean King**, tennis	1988	**Florence Griffith Joyner**, track
1947	**Babe Didrikson Zaharias**, golf	1968	**Peggy Fleming**, skating	1989	**Steffi Graf**, tennis
1948	**Fanny Blankers-Koen**, track	1969	**Debbie Meyer**, swimming		
1949	**Marlene Bauer**, golf			1990	**Beth Daniel**, golf
		1970	**Chi Cheng**, track	1991	**Monica Seles**, tennis
1950	**Babe Didrikson Zaharias**, golf	1971	**Evonne Goolagong**, tennis	1992	**Monica Seles**, tennis
1951	**Maureen Connolly**, tennis	1972	**Olga Korbut**, gymnastics	1993	**Sheryl Swoopes**, basketball

UPI International Athletes of the Year

Selected annually by United Press International's European newspaper sports editors since 1974.

Male

Multiple winners: Sebastian Coe, Alberto Juantorena and Carl Lewis (2).

Year	Year	Year
1974 **Muhammad Ali**, boxing	1981 **Sebastian Coe**, track	1988 **Matt Biondi**, swimming
1975 **Joao Oliveira**, track	1982 **Daley Thompson**, track	1989 **Boris Becker**, tennis
1976 **Alberto Juantorena**, track	1983 **Carl Lewis**, track	1990 **Stefan Edberg**, tennis
1977 **Alberto Juantorena**, track	1984 **Carl Lewis**, track	1991 **Sergei Bubka**, track
1978 **Henry Rono**, track	1985 **Steve Cram**, track	1992 **Kevin Young**, track
1979 **Sebastian Coe**, track	1986 **Diego Maradona**, soccer	1993 **Miguel Induráin**, cycling
1980 **Eric Heiden**, speed skating	1987 **Ben Johnson**, track	

Female

Multiple winners: Nadia Comaneci, Steffi Graf, Marita Koch and Monica Seles (2).

Year	Year	Year
1974 **Irena Szewinska**, track	1981 **Chris Evert Lloyd**, tennis	1988 **Florence Griffith Joyner**, track
1975 **Nadia Comaneci**, gymnastics	1982 **Marita Koch**, track	1989 **Steffi Graf**, tennis
1976 **Nadia Comaneci**, gymnastics	1983 **Jarmila Kratochvilova**, track	1990 **Merlene Ottey**, track
1977 **Rosie Ackermann**, track	1984 **Martina Navratilova**, tennis	1991 **Monica Seles**, tennis
1978 **Tracy Caulkins**, swimming	1985 **Mary Decker Slaney**, track	1992 **Monica Seles**, tennis
1979 **Marita Koch**, track	1986 **Heike Drechsler**, track	1993 **Wang Junxia**, track
1980 **Hanni Wenzel**, alpine skiing	1987 **Steffi Graf**, tennis	

Jesse Owens International Trophy

Presented annually by the International Amateur Athletic Association since 1981 and selected by a worldwide panel of electors. The Jesse Owens International Trophy is named after the late American Olympic champion, who won four gold medals at the 1936 Summer Games in Berlin.

Year	Year	Year
1981 **Eric Heiden**, speed skating	1986 **Said Aouita**, track	1991 **Greg LeMond**, cycling
1982 **Sebastian Coe**, track	1987 **Greg Louganis**, diving	1992 **Mike Powell**, track
1983 **Mary Decker**, track	1988 **Ben Johnson**, track	1993 **Vitaly Scherbo**, gymnastics
1984 **Edwin Moses**, track	1990 **Roger Kingdom**, track	1994 **Wang Junxia**, track
1985 **Carl Lewis**, track		

James E. Sullivan Memorial Award

Presented annually by the Amateur Athletic Union since 1930. The Sullivan Award is named after the former AAU president and given to the athlete who, "by his or her performance, example and influence as an amateur, has done the most during the year to advance the cause of sportsmanship." An athlete cannot win the award more than once.

The 1993 winner was college football and basketball star **Charlie Ward** of Florida State, the Heisman Trophy winner who led the Seminoles to the national championship in football. The other nine finalists are listed alphabetically: **Bruce Baumgartner** (wrestling), **Brian Boitano** (figure skating), **Gail Devers** (track & field), **Bobby Hurley** (basketball), **Dan Jansen** (speedskating), **Shannon Miller** (gymnastics), **Dan O'Brien** (track & field), **Sheryl Swoopes** (basketball) and **Jenny Thompson** (swimming). Vote totals were not released.

Year	Year	Year
1930 **Bobby Jones**, golf	1951 **Bob Richards**, track	1973 **Bill Walton**, basketball
1931 **Barney Berlinger**, track	1952 **Horace Ashenfelter**, track	1974 **Rich Wohlhuter**, track
1932 **Jim Bausch**, track	1953 **Sammy Lee**, diving	1975 **Tim Shaw**, swimming
1933 **Glenn Cunningham**, track	1954 **Mal Whitfield**, track	1976 **Bruce Jenner**, track
1934 **Bill Bonthron**, track	1955 **Harrison Dillard**, track	1977 **John Naber**, swimming
1935 **Lawson Little**, golf	1956 **Pat McCormick**, diving	1978 **Tracy Caulkins**, swimming
1936 **Glenn Morris**, track	1957 **Bobby Morrow**, track	1979 **Kurt Thomas**, gymnastics
1937 **Don Budge**, tennis	1958 **Glenn Davis**, track	
1938 **Don Lash**, track	1959 **Parry O'Brien**, track	1980 **Eric Heiden**, speed skating
1939 **Joe Burk**, rowing		1981 **Carl Lewis**, track
	1960 **Rafer Johnson**, track	1982 **Mary Decker**, track
1940 **Greg Rice**, track	1961 **Wilma Rudolph**, track	1983 **Edwin Moses**, track
1941 **Leslie MacMitchell**, track	1963 **John Pennel**, track	1984 **Greg Louganis**, diving
1942 **Cornelius Warmerdam**, track	1964 **Don Schollander**, swimming	1985 **Joan B. Samuelson**, track
1943 **Gilbert Dodds**, track	1965 **Bill Bradley**, basketball	1986 **Jackie Joyner-Kersee**, track
1944 **Ann Curtis**, swimming	1966 **Jim Ryun**, track	1987 **Jim Abbott**, baseball
1945 **Doc Blanchard**, football	1967 **Randy Matson**, track	1988 **F. Griffith Joyner**, track
1946 **Arnold Tucker**, football	1968 **Debbie Meyer**, swimming	1989 **Janet Evans**, swimming
1947 **John B. Kelly, Jr.**, rowing	1969 **Bill Toomey**, track	
1948 **Bob Mathias**, track		1990 **John Smith**, wrestling
1949 **Dick Button**, skating	1970 **John Kinsella**, swimming	1991 **Mike Powell**, track
	1971 **Mark Spitz**, swimming	1992 **Bonnie Blair**, speed skating
1950 **Fred Wilt**, track	1972 **Frank Shorter**, track	1993 **Charlie Ward**, football

USOC Sportsmen & Sportswomen of the Year

To the outstanding overall male and female athletes from within the U.S. Olympic Committee member organizations. Winners are chosen from nominees of the national governing bodies for Olympic and Pan American Games sports and affiliated disabled sports organizations. Voting is done by members of the national media, USOC board of directors and Athletes' Advisory Council.

Sportsmen

Multiple winners: Eric Heiden (3); Matt Biondi and Greg Louganis (2).

Year	Year	Year
1974 **Jim Bolding**, track	1981 **Scott Hamilton**, fig. skating	1988 **Matt Biondi**, swimming
1975 **Clint Jackson**, boxing	1982 **Greg Louganis**, diving	1989 **Roger Kingdom**, track
1976 **John Naber**, swimming	1983 **Rick McKinney**, archery	1990 **John Smith**, wrestling
1977 **Eric Heiden**, speed skating	1984 **Edwin Moses**, track	1991 **Carl Lewis**, track
1978 **Bruce Davidson**, equestrian	1985 **Willie Banks**, track	1992 **Pablo Morales**, swimming
1979 **Eric Heiden**, speed skating	1986 **Matt Biondi**, swimming	1993 **Michael Johnson**, track
1980 **Eric Heiden**, speed skating	1987 **Greg Louganis**, diving	

Sportswomen

Multiple winners: Tracy Caulkins, Jackie Joyner-Kersee and Sheila Young Ochowicz (2).

Year	Year	Year
1974 **Shirley Babashoff**, swimming	1981 **Sheila Ochowicz**, speed skating & cycling	1987 **Jackie Joyner-Kersee**, track
1975 **Kathy Heddy**, swimming		1988 **F. Griffith Joyner**, track
1976 **Sheila Young**, speedskating	1982 **Melanie Smith**, equestrian	1989 **Janet Evans**, swimming
1977 **Linda Fratianne**, fig. skating	1983 **Tamara McKinney**, skiing	1990 **Lynn Jennings**, track
1978 **Tracy Caulkins**, swimming	1984 **Tracy Caulkins**, swimming	1991 **Kim Zmeskal**, gymnastics
1979 **Sippy Woodhead**, swimming	1985 **Mary Decker Slaney**, track	1992 **Bonnie Blair**, speed skating
1980 **Beth Heiden**, speed skating	1986 **Jackie Joyner-Kersee**, track	1993 **Gail Devers**, track

Honda Broderick Cup

To the outstanding collegiate woman athlete of the year in NCAA competition. Winner is chosen from nominees in each of the NCAA's 10 competitive sports. Final voting is done by member athletic directors. Award is named after founder and sportswear manufacturer Thomas Broderick.

Multiple winner: Tracy Caulkins (2).

Year		Year	
1977 **Lucy Harris,** Delta St	basketball	1985 **Jackie Joyner**, UCLA	track & field
1978 **Ann Meyers**, UCLA	basketball	1986 **Kamie Ethridge**, Texas	basketball
1979 **Nancy Lieberman**, Old Dominion	basketball	1987 **Mary T. Meagher**, California	swimming
1980 **Julie Shea**, N.C. State	track & field	1988 **Teresa Weatherspoon**, La.Tech	basketball
1981 **Jill Sterkel**, Texas	swimming	1989 **Vicki Huber**, Villanova	track
1982 **Tracy Caulkins**, Florida	swimming	1990 **Suzy Favor**, Wisconsin	track
1983 **Deitre Collins**, Hawaii	volleyball	1991 **Dawn Staley**, Virginia	basketball
1984 **Tracy Caulkins**, Florida	swimming	1992 **Missy Marlowe**, Utah	gymnastics
& **Cheryl Miller**, USC	basketball	1993 **Lisa Fernandez**, UCLA	softball

Flo Hyman Award

Presented annually since 1987 by the Women's Sports Foundation for "exemplifying dignity, spirit and commitment to excellence" and named in honor of the late captain of the 1984 U.S. Women's Volleyball team. Voting by WSF members.

Year	Year	Year
1987 **Martina Navratilova**, tennis	1990 **Chris Evert**, tennis	1993 **Lynette Woodward**, basketball
1988 **Jackie Joyner-Kersee**, track	1991 **Diana Golden**, skiing	1994 **Patty Sheehan**, golf
1989 **Evelyn Ashford**, track	1992 **Nancy Lopez**, golf	

Arthur Ashe Award for Courage

Presented since 1993 on the annual ESPN "Espys" telecast. Given to a member of the sports community who has exemplified the same courage, spirit and determination to help others despite personal hardship that characterized Arthur Ashe, the late tennis champion and humanitarian. Voting done by select 26-member committee of media and sports personalities.

Year	Year
1993 **Jim Valvano**, basketball	1994 **Steve Palermo**, baseball

Presidential Medal of Freedom

Since President John F. Kennedy established the Medal of Freedom as America's highest civilian honor in 1963, only nine sports figures have won the award. Note that (*) indicates the presentation was made posthumously.

Year		President	Year		President
1963 **Bob Kiphuth**, swimming		Kennedy	1986 **Earl (Red) Blaik**, football		Reagan
1976 **Jesse Owens**, track & field		Ford	1991 **Ted Williams**, baseball		Bush
1977 **Joe DiMaggio**, baseball		Ford	1992 **Richard Petty**, auto racing		Bush
1983 **Paul (Bear) Bryant***, football		Reagan	1993 **Arthur Ashe***, tennis		Clinton
1984 **Jackie Robinson***, baseball		Reagan			

The Hickok Belt

Officially known as the S. Rae Hickok Professional Athlete of the Year Award and presented by the Kickik Manufacturing Co. of Arlington, Texas, from 1950–76. The trophy was a large belt of gold, diamonds and other jewels, reportedly worth $30,000 in 1976, the last year it was handed out. Voting was done by 270 newspaper sports editors from around the country.

Multiple winner: Sandy Koufax (2).

Year		Year		Year	
1950	**Phil Rizzuto**, baseball	1960	**Arnold Palmer**, golf	1970	**Brooks Robinson**, baseball
1951	**Allie Reynolds**, baseball	1961	**Roger Maris**, baseball	1971	**Lee Trevino**, golf
1952	**Rocky Marciano**, boxing	1962	**Maury Wills**, baseball	1972	**Steve Carlton**, baseball
1953	**Ben Hogan**, golf	1963	**Sandy Koufax**, baseball	1973	**O.J. Simpson**, football
1954	**Willie Mays**, baseball	1964	**Jim Brown**, football	1974	**Muhammad Ali**, boxing
1955	**Otto Graham**, football	1965	**Sandy Koufax**, baseball	1975	**Pete Rose**, baseball
1956	**Mickey Mantle**, baseball	1966	**Frank Robinson**, baseball	1976	**Ken Stabler**, football
1957	**Carmen Basilio**, boxing	1967	**Carl Yastrzemski**, baseball	1977	Discontinued
1958	**Bob Turley**, baseball	1968	**Joe Namath**, football		
1959	**Ingemar Johansson**, boxing	1969	**Tom Seaver**, baseball		

Sports Illustrated Sportsman of the Year

Selected annually by the editors of *Sports Illustrated* magazine since 1954.

Year		Year		Year	
1954	**Roger Bannister**, track	1972	**Billie Jean King**, tennis	1987	**"8 Athletes Who Care"**
1955	**Johnny Podres**, baseball		& **John Wooden**, basketball		**Bob Bourne**, hockey
1956	**Bobby Morrow**, track	1973	**Jackie Stewart**, auto racing		**Kip Keino**, track
1957	**Stan Musial**, baseball	1974	**Muhammad Ali**, boxing		**Judi Brown King**, track
1958	**Rafer Johnson**, track	1975	**Pete Rose**, baseball		**Dale Murphy**, baseball
1959	**Ingemar Johansson**, boxing	1976	**Chris Evert**, tennis		**Chip Rives**, football
		1977	**Steve Cauthen**, horse racing		**Patty Sheehan**, golf
1960	**Arnold Palmer**, golf	1978	**Jack Nicklaus**, golf		**Rory Sparrow**, basketball
1961	**Jerry Lucas**, basketball	1979	**Terry Bradshaw**, football		**Reggie Williams**, football
1962	**Terry Baker**, football		& **Willie Stargell**, baseball	1988	**Orel Hershiser**, baseball
1963	**Pete Rozelle**, pro football			1989	**Greg LeMond**, cycling
1964	**Ken Venturi**, golf	1980	**U.S. Olympic hockey team**		
1965	**Sandy Koufax**, baseball	1981	**Sugar Ray Leonard**, boxing	1990	**Joe Montana**, football
1966	**Jim Ryun**, track	1982	**Wayne Gretzky**, hockey	1991	**Michael Jordan**, basketball
1967	**Carl Yastrzemski**, baseball	1983	**Mary Decker**, track	1992	**Arthur Ashe**, tennis
1968	**Bill Russell**, basketball	1984	**Mary Lou Retton**, gymnastics	1993	**Don Shula**, football
1969	**Tom Seaver**, baseball		& **Edwin Moses**, track		
		1985	**K. Abdul-Jabbar**, basketball		
1970	**Bobby Orr**, hockey	1986	**Joe Paterno**, football		
1971	**Lee Trevino**, golf				

The Sporting News Man of the Year

Selected annually by the editors of *The Sporting News* since 1968.

Year		Year		Year	
1968	**Denny McLain**, baseball	1977	**Steve Cauthen**, horse racing	1986	**Larry Bird**, pro basketball
1969	**Tom Seaver**, baseball	1978	**Ron Guidry**, baseball	1987	No award
		1979	**Willie Stargell**, baseball	1988	**Jackie Joyner-Kersee**, track
1970	**John Wooden**, basketball			1989	**Joe Montana**, football
1971	**Lee Trevino**, golf	1980	**George Brett**, baseball		
1972	**Charles O. Finley**, baseball	1981	**Wayne Gretzky**, hockey	1990	**Nolan Ryan**, baseball
1973	**O.J. Simpson**, pro football	1982	**Whitey Herzog**, baseball	1991	**Michael Jordan**, basketball
1974	**Lou Brock**, baseball	1983	**Bowie Kuhn**, baseball	1992	**Mike Krzyzewski**, col. bask.
1975	**Archie Griffin**, football	1984	**Peter Ueberroth**, LA Olympics	1993	**Cito Gaston**
1976	**Larry O'Brien**, basketball	1985	**Pete Rose**, baseball		& **Pat Gillick**, baseball

Time Man of the Year

Since Charles Lindbergh was named *Time* magazine's first Man of the Year for 1927, two individuals with significant sports credentials have won the honor.

Year	
1984	**Peter Ueberroth**, president of the Los Angeles Olympic Organizing Committee.
1991	**Ted Turner**, owner-president of Turner Broadcasting System, founder of CNN cable news network, owner of the Atlanta Braves (NL) and Atlanta Hawks (NBA), and former winning America's Cup skipper.

TROPHY CASE

From the first organized track meet at Olympia in 776 B.C., to the Lillehammer Winter Olympics over 2,700 years later, championships have been officially recognized with prizes that are symbolically rich and eagerly pursued. Here are 15 of the most coveted trophies in America.

(Illustrations by Lynn Mercer Michaud.)

America's Cup

First presented by England's Royal Yacht Squadron to the winner of an invitational race around the Isle of Wight on Aug. 22, 1851 . . . . originally called the Hundred Guinea Cup . . . . renamed after the U.S. boat America, winner of the first race . . . . made of sterling silver and designed by London jewelers R. & G. Garrard . . . . measures 2 feet, 3 inches high and weighs 16 lbs . . . . originally cost 100 guineas ($500), now valued at $250,000 . . . . bell-shaped base added in 1958 . . . . challenged for every three to four years . . . . trophy held by yacht club sponsoring winning boat.

Vince Lombardi Trophy

First presented at the AFL-NFL World Championship Game (now Super Bowl) on Jan. 15, 1967 . . . . originally called the World Championship Game Trophy . . . . renamed in 1971 in honor of former Green Bay Packers GM-coach and two-time Super Bowl winner Vince Lombardi, who died in 1970 as coach of Washington . . . . made of sterling silver and designed by Tiffany & Co. of New York . . . . measures 21 inches high and weighs 7 lbs (football depicted is regulation size) . . . . valued at $12,500 . . . . competed for annually. . . . winning team keeps trophy.

Olympic Gold Medal

First presented by International Olympic Committee in 1908 (until then winners received silver medals) . . . . second and third place finishers also got medals of silver and bronze for first time in 1908 . . . . each medal must be at least 2.4 inches in diameter and 0.12 inches thick . . . . the gold medal is actually made of silver, but must be gilded with at least 6 grams (0.21 ounces) of pure gold . . . . the gold medal for the 1994 Winter Games at Lillehammer, Norway, was made of stone and metal and designed by Ingjerd Hanevold of Oslo . . . . each contains 6 grams of pure gold in the rings . . . . 155 were made for approximately $486 each . . . . competed for every two years as Winter and Summer Games alternate . . . . winners keep medals.

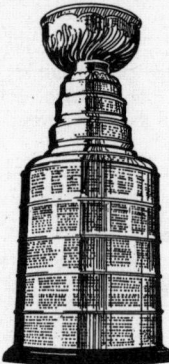

Stanley Cup

Donated by Lord Stanley of Preston, the Governor General of Canada and first presented in 1893 .... original cup was made of sterling silver by an unknown London silversmith and measured 7 inches high with an 11½-inch diameter .... in order to accommodate all the rosters of winning teams, the cup now measures 35½ inches high with a base 54 inches around and weighs 32 lbs .... originally bought for 10 guineas ($48.67), it is now insured for $75,000 .... actual cup retired to Hall of Fame and replaced in 1970 .... presented to NHL playoff champion since 1918 .... trophy loaned to winning team for one year.

World Cup

First presented by the Federation Internationale de Football Association (FIFA) .... originally called the World Cup Trophy .... renamed the Jules Rimet Cup (after the then FIFA president) in 1946, but retired by Brazil after that country's third title in 1970 .... new World Cup trophy created in 1974 .... designed by Italian sculptor Silvio Gazzaniga and made of solid 18 carat gold with two malachite rings inlaid at the base .... measures 14.2 inches high and weighs 11 lbs .... insured for $200,000 (U.S.) .... competed for every four years .... winning team gets gold-plated replica.

Commissioner's Trophy

First presented by the Commissioner of baseball to the winner of the 1967 World Series .... also known as the World Championship Trophy .... made of brass and gold plate with an ebony base and a baseball in the center made of pewter with a silver finish .... designed by Balfour & Co. of Attleboro, Mass .... 28 pennants represent 14 AL and 14 NL teams .... measures 30 inches high and 36 inches around at the base and weighs 30 lbs .... valued at $15,000 .... competed for annually .... winning team keeps trophy.

Larry O'Brien Trophy

First presented in 1978 to winner of NBA Finals .... originally called the Walter A. Brown Trophy after the league pioneer and Boston Celtics owner (an earlier NBA championship bowl was also named after Brown) .... renamed in 1984 in honor of outgoing commissioner O'Brien, who served from 1975-84 .... made of sterling silver with 24 carat gold overlay and designed by Tiffany & Co. of New York .... measures 2 feet high and weighs 14½ lbs (basketball depicted is regulation size) .... valued at $13,500 .... competed for annually .... winning team keeps trophy.

Heisman Trophy

First presented in 1935 to the best college football player east of the Mississippi by the Downtown Athletic Club of New York . . . . players across the entire country eligible since 1936 . . . . originally called the DAC Trophy . . . . renamed in 1936 following the death of DAC athletic director and former college coach John W. Heisman . . . . made of bronze and designed by New York sculptor Frank Eliscu, it measures 13 ½ in. high, 6 ½ in. wide and 14 in. long at the base and weighs 25 lbs . . . . valued at $2,000 . . . . voting done by national media and former Heisman winners . . . . awarded annually . . . . winner keeps trophy.

James E. Sullivan Memorial Award

First presented by the Amateur Athletic Union (AAU) in 1930 as a gold medal and given to the nation's outstanding amateur athlete . . . . trophy given since 1933 . . . . named after the amateur sports movement pioneer, who was a founder and past president of AAU and the director of the 1904 Olympic Games in St. Louis . . . . made of bronze with a marble base, it measures 17 ½ in. high and 11 in. wide at the base and weighs 13 ½ lbs . . . . valued at $2,500 . . . . voting done by AAU and USOC officials, former winners and selected media . . . . awarded annually . . . . winner keeps trophy.

Ryder Cup

Donated in 1927 by English seed merchant Samuel Ryder, who offered the gold cup for a biennial match between teams of golfing pros from Great Britain and the United States . . . . the format changed in 1977 to include the best players on the European PGA Tour . . . . made of 14 carat gold on a wood base and designed by Mappin and Webb of London . . . . the golfer depicted on the top of the trophy is Ryder's friend and teaching pro Abe Mitchell . . . . the cup measures 16 in. high and weighs 4 lbs . . . . insured for $50,000 . . . . competed for every two years at alternating British and U.S. sites . . . . the cup is held by the PGA headquarters of the winning side.

Davis Cup

Donated by American college student and U.S. doubles champion Dwight F. Davis in 1900 and presented by the International Tennis Federation (ITF) to the winner of the annual 16-team men's competition . . . . officially called the International Lawn Tennis Challenge Trophy . . . . made of sterling silver and designed by Shreve, Crump and Low of Boston, the cup has a matching tray (added in 1921) and a very heavy two-tiered base containing rosters of past winning teams . . . . it stands 34 ½ in. high and 108 in. around at the base and weighs 400 lbs . . . . insured for $150,000 . . . . competed for annually . . . . trophy loaned to winning country for one year.

Borg-Warner Trophy

First presented by the Borg-Warner Automotive Co. of Chicago in 1936 to the winner of the Indianapolis 500 .... replaced the Wheeler-Schebler Trophy which went to the 400-mile leader from 1911-32 .... made of sterling silver with bas-relief sculptured heads of each winning driver and a gold bas-relief head of Tony Hulman, the owner of the Indy Speedway from 1945-77 .... designed by Robert J. Hill and made by Gorham, Inc. of Rhode Island .... measures 51 ½ in. high and weighs over 80 lbs .... new base added in 1988 and the entire trophy restored in 1991 .... competed for annually .... insured for $1 million .... trophy stays at Speedway Hall of Fame .... winner gets a 14-in. high replica valued at $30,000.

NCAA Championship Trophy

First presented in 1952 by the NCAA to all 1st, 2nd and 3rd place teams in sports with sanctioned tournaments .... 1st place teams receive gold-plated awards, 2nd place award is silver-plated and 3rd is bronze .... replaced silver cup given to championship teams from 1939-1951 .... made of walnut, the trophy stands 24 ¾ in. high, 14 ⅛ in. wide and 4 ½ in. deep at the base and weighs 15 lbs .... designed by Medallic Art Co. of Danbury, Conn. and made by House of Usher of Kansas City since 1990 .... valued at $500 .... competed for annually .... winning teams keep trophies.

World Championship Belt

First presented in 1921 by the World Boxing Association, one of the three organizations (the World Boxing Council and International Boxing Federation are the others) generally accepted as sanctioning legitimate world championship fights .... belt weighs 8 lbs. and is made of hand tanned leather .... the outsized buckle measures 10 ½ in. high and 8 in. wide, is made of pewter with 24 carat gold plate and contains crystal and semi-precious stones .... side panels of polished brass are for engraving title bout results .... currently made by Phil Valentino Originals of Jersey City, N.J. .... champions keep belts even if they lose their title.

World Championship Ring

Rings decorated with gems and engraving date back to ancient Egypt where the wealthy wore heavy gold and silver rings to indicate social status .... championship rings in sports serve much the same purpose, indicating the wearer is a champion .... the 1994 Dallas Cowboys' ring for winning Super Bowl XXVIII was designed by the Balfour Co. of North Attleboro, Mass .... each ring is made of 10 carat yellow gold and contains four marquis shape diamonds— two weighing 60 points (for the team's back-to-back Super Bowls) and two weighing 45 points (for Super Bowls won in the 1970s) .... those large diamonds are surrounded by 24 smaller diamonds with another six diamonds at the top and bottom .... 120 were made for players and team personnel and cost in excess of $10,000 each.

Bettmann Archive

Babe Ruth's 100th birthday will be celebrated Feb. 6, 1995. Seen here during ceremonies marking the 25th anniversary of Yankee Stadium, he died two months later on Aug. 16, 1948. This photo, by Nat Fein of the *New York Herald Tribune,* won a Pulitzer Prize.

WHO'S WHO

Sports Personalities

Eight hundred and eight noteworthy names dating back to the turn of the century. Pages updated through Sept. 15, 1994.

Hank Aaron (b.2/5/1934): Baseball OF; led NL in HRs and RBI 4 times each and batting twice with Milwaukee and Atlanta Braves; MVP in 1957; played in 24 All-Star Games, all-time leader in HRs (755) and RBI (2,297), 3rd in hits (3,771); executive with Braves and TBS, Inc.

Jim Abbott (b.9/19/1967): Baseball LHP; born without a right hand; All-America hurler at Michigan; won Sullivan Award in 1987; threw 4-0 no-hitter for NY Yankees vs Cleveland (Sept. 4, 1993).

Kareem Abdul-Jabbar (b.Lew Alcindor, 4/16/1947): Basketball C; led UCLA to 3 NCAA titles (1967-69); tourney MVP 3 times; Player of Year twice; led Milwaukee (1) and LA Lakers (5) to 6 NBA titles; playoff MVP twice (1971,85); regular season MVP 6 times (1971-72, 74,76-77, 80); retired after 20 seasons as all-time leader in over 20 categories.

Andre Agassi (b.4/29/1970): Tennis; entered 1994 with 19 career tournament wins; helped U.S. win 2 Davis Cup finals (1990, 92); won 1st Grand Slam title at Wimbledon in 1992; defeated Michael Stich in three sets to win 1994 U.S. Open as unseeded entry; Nick Bollettieri Academy classmate of Jim Courier.

Troy Aikman (b.11/21/1966): Football QB; consensus All-America at UCLA (1988); 1st overall pick in 1989 NFL Draft (by Dallas); has led Cowboys to 2 straight Super Bowl titles (1992 and '93 seasons); MVP in Super Bowl XXVII; entered 1994 season as highest-paid player in NFL ($50 million over 8 years).

Tenley Albright (b.7/18/1935): Figure skater; 2-time world champion (1953,55), won Olympic silver (1952) and gold (1956) medals; became a surgeon.

Grover Cleveland Alexander (1887-1950): Baseball RHP; won 20 or more games 9 times; 373 career wins and 90 shutouts.

Muhammad Ali (b.Cassius Clay, 1/17/1942): Boxer; 1960 Olympic lightheavyweight champion; only 3-time world heavyweight champ (1964-67,1974-78,1978-79); defeated Sonny Liston (1964), George Foreman (1974) and Leon Spinks (1978) for title; fought Joe Frazier in 3 memorable bouts (1971-75), winning twice; adopted Black Muslim faith in 1964 and changed name; stripped of title in 1967 after conviction for refusing induction into U.S. Army; verdict reversed by Supreme Court in 1971; career record of 56-5 with 37 KOs and 19 successful title defenses.

Forrest (Phog) Allen (1885-74): Basketball; college coach 48 years; directed Kansas to NCAA title (1952); 5th on all-time list with 746 career wins.

Bobby Allison (b.12/3/1937): Auto racer; 3-time winner of Daytona 500 (1978,82,88); NASCAR national champ in 1983; father of Davey.

Davey Allison (1961-93): Auto racer; stock car Rookie of Year (1987); winner of 19 NASCAR races including 1992 Daytona 500; killed at age 32 in helicopter accident at Talladega Superspeedway on July 13, 1993; son of Bobby.

Walter Alston (1911-84): Baseball; managed Brooklyn-LA Dodgers 23 years, won 7 pennants and 4 World Series (1955,59,63,65).

Sparky Anderson (b.2/22/1934): Baseball; only manager to win World Series in each league—Cincinnati in NL (1975-76) and Detroit in AL (1984); moved past Joe McCarthy in 1994 to become 4th-ranked skipper on all-time career list with 2,168 wins (2,134 regular season and 34 postseason).

Willie Anderson (1880-1910): Scottish golfer, who became an American citizen and won 4 U.S. Open titles, including an unmatched 3 straight from 1903-05; also won four Western Opens from 1902-09.

Mario Andretti (b.2/28/1940): Auto racer; 4-time USAC/CART national champion (1965-66,69,84); only driver to win Daytona 500 (1967), Indy 500 (1969) and Formula One world title (1978); Indy 500 Rookie of Year (1965); entered final season in 1994 ranked 1st in poles (67) and 2nd in wins (52) on all-time IndyCar list; father of Michael and Jeff, uncle of John.

Michael Andretti (b.10/5/1962): Auto racer; 1992 CART national champion with singleseason record 8 wins; Indy 500 Rookie of Year (1984); left IndyCar circuit for ill-fated Formula One try in 1993; returned to IndyCar in '94; entered 1994 with 27 career wins; son of Mario.

Earl Anthony (b.4/27/1938): Bowler; 6-time PBA Bowler of Year; 41 career titles; first to earn $100,000 in 1 season (1975); first to earn $1 million in career.

Said Aouita (b.11/2/1959): Moroccan runner; won gold (5000m) and bronze (800m) in 1984 Olympics; won 5000m at 1987 World Championships; entered 1993 holding 2 world records recognized by IAAF—2000m and 5000m.

Luis Aparicio (b.4/29/1934): Baseball SS; all-time leader in most games, assists, chances and double plays by shortstop; led AL in stolen bases 9 times (1956-64); 506 career steals.

Al Arbour (b.11/1/1932): Hockey; coached NY Islanders to 4 straight Stanley Cup titles (1980-83); retired after 1993-94 season 2nd on all-time career list with 902 wins (779 regular season and 123 postseason).

Eddie Arcaro (b.2/19/1916): Jockey; 2-time Triple Crown winner (Whirlaway in 1941, Citation in '48); won Kentucky Derby 5 times, Preakness and Belmont 6 times each.

Roone Arledge (b.7/8/1931): Sports TV innovator of live events, anthology shows, Olympic coverage and "Monday Night Football;" ran ABC Sports from 1968-86; has run ABC News since 1977.

Henry Armstrong (1912-88): Boxer; held feather-, light- and welterweight titles simultaneously in 1938; pro record 145-20-9 with 98 KOs.

Arthur Ashe (1943-93): Tennis; first black man to win U.S. Championship (1968) and Wimbledon (1975); 1st U.S. player to earn $100,000 in 1 year (1970); won Davis Cup as player (1968-70) and captain (1981-82); wrote black sports history, *Hard Road to Glory*; announced in 1992 that he was infected with AIDS virus from a blood transfusion during 1983 heart surgery; died Feb. 6, 1993 at age 49.

Evelyn Ashford (b.4/16/1957): Track & Field; winner of 4 Olympic gold medals—including 100m in 1984, and 4x100m in 1984, '88 and '92; also won silver medal in 100m in '88; member of 5 U.S. Olympic teams (1976-92).

Red Auerbach (b.9/20/1917): Basketball; winningest coach in NBA history; won 1,037 times (including playoffs) in 20 years; as coach-GM, led Boston to 9 NBA titles, including 8 in a row (1959-66); also coached defunct Washington Capitols (1946-49); NBA Coach of the Year award named after him; retired as Celtics' coach in 1966 and as GM in '84; club president since 1970.

Tracy Austin (b.12/12/1962): Tennis; youngest player ever to win U.S. Open (age 16 in 1979); won 2nd U.S. Open in '81; named AP Female Athlete of Year twice before she was 20; recurring neck and back injuries shortened her career after June, 1983; youngest player ever inducted into Tennis Hall of Fame (age 29 in 1992).

Paul Azinger (b.1/6/1960): Golf; PGA Player of Year in 1987; entered 1994 with 11 career wins, including '93 PGA Championship; missed 1st 7 months of '94 season overcoming lymphoma (a form of cancer) in right shoulder blade.

Oksana Baiul (b.2/26/1977): Ukrainian figure skater; 1993 world champion at age 15; edged Nancy Kerrigan by a 5-4 judges' vote for 1994 Olympic gold medal.

Hobey Baker (1892-1918): Football and hockey star at Princeton (1911-14); member of college football and pro hockey halls of fame; college hockey Player of Year award named after him; killed in WWI plane crash.

Seve Ballesteros (b.4/9/1957): Spanish golfer; has won British Open 3 times (1979,84,88) and Masters twice (1980,83); 3-time European Golfer of Year (1986,88,91); entered 1994 with 68 world-wide victories.

Ernie Banks (b.1/31/1931): Baseball SS-1B; led NL in home runs and RBI twice each; 2-time MVP (1958-59) with Chicago Cubs; 512 career HRs.

Roger Bannister (b.3/23/1929): British runner; first to run mile in less than 4 minutes (3:59.4 on May 6, 1954).

Walter (Red) Barber (1908-92): Radio-TV; renowned baseball play-by-play broadcaster for Cincinnati, Brooklyn and N.Y. Yankees from 1934-66; won Peabody Award for radio commentary in 1991.

Charles Barkley (b.2/20/1963): Basketball F; 5-time All-NBA 1st team with Philadelphia and Phoenix; traded to Suns for 3 players (June 17, 1992); U.S. Olympic Dream Team member in '92; NBA regular season MVP in 1993.

Rick Barry (b.3/28/1944): Basketball F; only player to lead both NBA and ABA in scoring; 5-time All-NBA 1st team; playoff MVP with Golden St. in 1975.

Sammy Baugh (b.3/17/1914): Football QB-DB-P; led Washington to NFL titles in 1937 (his rookie year) and '42; led league in passing 6 times, punting 4 times and interceptions once.

Elgin Baylor (b.9/16/1934): Basketball F; MVP of NCAA tournament in 1958; led Mpls.-LA Lakers to 8 NBA Finals; 10-time All-NBA 1st team (1959-65,67-69).

Bob Beamon (b.8/29/1946): Track & Field; won 1968 Olympic gold medal in long jump with world record (29-ft, 2½ in.) that shattered old mark by nearly 2 feet; record finally broken by 2 inches in 1991 by Mike Powell.

Franz Beckenbauer (b.9/11/1945): Soccer; captain of West German World Cup champions in 1974 then coached West Germany to World Cup title in 1990; invented sweeper position; played in U.S. for NY Cosmos (1977-80,83).

Boris Becker (b.11/22/1967): German tennis player; 3-time Wimbledon champ (1985-86,89); youngest male (17) to win Wimbledon; led country to 1st Davis Cup win in 1988; has also won U.S. (1989) and Australian (1991) Opens.

Chuck Bednarik (b.5/1/1925): Football C-LB; 2-time All-America at Penn and 7-time All-Pro with NFL Philadelphia Eagles as center (1950) and linebacker (1951-56); knocked NY Giants' Frank Gifford out of commission for over a year with epic 1960 tackle; missed only 3 games in 14 seasons; led Eagles to 1960 NFL title as a 35-year-old two-way player.

Clair Bee (1896-1983): Basketball coach who led LIU to 2 undefeated seasons (1936,39) and 2 NIT titles (1939,41); his teams won 95 percent of their games between 1931-51, including 43 in a row from 1935-37; coached NBA Baltimore Bullets from 1952-54, but was only 34-116; contributions to game include 1-3-1 zone defense, 3-second rule and NBA 24-second clock; also authored sports manuals and fictional Chip Hilton sports books for kids.

Jean Beliveau (b.8/31/1931): Hockey C; led Montreal to 10 Stanley Cups in 17 playoffs; playoff MVP (1965); 2-time regular season MVP (1956,64).

Bert Bell (1895-1959): Football; team owner and 2nd NFL commissioner (1946-59); proposed college draft in 1935 and instituted TV blackout rule.

Deane Beman (b.4/22/1938): Golf; 1st commissioner of PGA Tour (1974-94); introduced "stadium golf;" as player, won U.S. Amateur twice and British Amateur once.

Johnny Bench (b.12/7/1947): Baseball C; led NL in HRs twice and RBI 3 times; 2-time regular season MVP (1970,72) with Cincinnati, World Series MVP in 1976; 389 career HRs.

Patty Berg (b.2/13/1918): Golfer; 57 career pro wins including 15 Majors; 3-time AP Female Athlete of Year (1938,43,55).

Chris Berman (b.5/10/1955): Radio-TV; 3-time Sportscaster of Year known for his nicknames and jovial studio anchoring; play-by-play man only year Brown University football team won Ivy League (1976).

Yogi Berra (b.5/12/1925): Baseball C; played on 10 World Series winners with NY Yankees; 3-time AL MVP (1951,54-55); managed both Yankees (1964) and NY Mets (1973) to pennants.

Jay Berwanger (b.3/19/1914): Football HB; University of Chicago star; won 1st Heisman Trophy in 1935.

Gary Bettman (b.6/2/1952): Hockey; former NBA executive, who was named first commissioner of NHL on Dec. 11, 1992; took office on Feb. 1, 1993.

Abebe Bikila (1932-73): Ethiopian runner; 1st to win consecutive Olympic marathons (1960,64).

Matt Biondi (b.10/8/1965): Swimmer; won 7 medals in 1988 Olympics, including 5 gold (2 individual, 3 relay); has won a total of 11 medals (8 gold, 2 silver and a bronze) in 3 Olympics (1984,88,92).

Larry Bird (b.12/7/1956): Basketball F; college Player of Year (1979) at Indiana St.; 9-time All-NBA 1st team; 3-time regular season MVP (1984-86); led Boston to 3 NBA titles; 2-time playoff MVP (1984,86); U.S. Olympic Dream Team member in '92.

The Black Sox—Eight Chicago White Sox players who were banned from baseball for life in 1921 for allegedly throwing the 1919 World Series: RHP **Eddie Cicotte** (1884-1969), OF **Happy Felsch** (1891-1964), 1B **Chick Gandil** (1887-1970), OF **Shoeless Joe Jackson**, INF **Fred McMullin** (1891-1952), SS **Swede Risberg** (1894-1975), 3B-SS **Buck Weaver** (1890-1956), and LHP **Lefty Williams** (1893-1959).

Earl (Red) Blaik (1897-1989): Football; coached Army to consecutive national titles in 1944-45; 166 career wins and 3 Heisman winners (Blanchard, Davis, Dawkins).

Bonnie Blair (b.3/18/1964): Speedskater; only American woman to win 5 Olympic gold medals in Winter or Summer Games; won 500-meters in 1988, then 500m and 1,000m in both 1992 and '94; added 1,000m bronze in 1988; Sullivan Award winner (1992).

Toe Blake (b.8/21/1912): Hockey LW; led Montreal to 2 Stanley Cups as a player and 8 more as coach; regular season MVP in 1939.

Felix (Doc) Blanchard (b12/11/1924): Football FB; 3-time All-America; led Army to national titles in 1944-45; Glenn Davis' running mate; won Heisman Trophy and Sullivan Award in 1945.

George Blanda (b.9/17/1927): Football QB-PK; NFL's all-time leading scorer (2,002 points); led Houston to 2 AFL titles (1960-61); played 26 pro seasons; retired at 48.

Fanny Blankers-Koen (b.4/26/1918): Dutch sprinter; 30-year-old mother of two, who won 4 gold medals (100m, 200m, 800m hurdles and 4x100m relay) at 1948 Olympics.

Wade Boggs (b.6/15/1958): Baseball 3B; entered 1994 season with 5 AL batting titles (1983,85-88) at Boston and .335 career average in 12 seasons.

Barry Bonds (b.7/24/1964): Baseball OF; 3-time NL MVP, twice with Pittsburgh (1990,92) and once with San Francisco (1993); NL's HR and RBI leader in 1993; signed 6-year deal with Giants worth $43.75 million following '92 season; son of Bobby.

Bjorn Borg (b.6/6/1956): Swedish tennis player; 2-time Player of Year (1979-80); won 6 French Opens and 5 straight Wimbledons (1976-80); led Sweden to 1st Davis Cup win in 1975; retired in 1983 at age 26; attempted unsuccessful comeback in 1991.

Mike Bossy (b.1/22/1957): Hockey RW; led NY Islanders to 4 Stanley Cups; playoff MVP in 1982; scored 50 goals or more 9 straight years; 573 career goals.

Ralph Boston (b.5/9/1939): Track & Field; medaled in 3 consecutive Olympic long jumps—gold (1960), silver (1964), bronze (1968).

Ray Bourque (b.12/28/1960): Hockey D; 11-time All-NHL 1st team, has won Norris Trophy 5 times (1987-88,1990-91,94) with Boston.

Bobby Bowden (b.11/8/1929): Football; coached Florida St. to a national title in 1993; entered '94 regular season 5th on all-time career list with 239 wins, including a 13-3-1 bowl record in 28 years as coach at Samford, West Va. and FSU; father of Terry.

Terry Bowden (b.2/24/1956): Football; led Auburn to 11-0 record in his first season as Division I-A head coach; NCAA probation earned under previous staff prevented bowl appearance; son of Bobby.

Riddick Bowe (b.8/10/1967): Boxing; won world heavyweight title with unanimous decision over champion Evander Holyfield on Nov. 13, 1992; lost title to Holyfield on majority decision Nov. 6, 1993; entered 1994 with pro record of 34-1 and 29 KOs.

Scotty Bowman (b.9/8/1933): Hockey; all-time winningest NHL coach in both regular season (880 wins) and playoffs (140) over 22 seasons; led Montreal to 5 Stanley Cups (1973,76-79) and Pittsburgh to another (1992); entered 1994-95 season with Detroit.

Jack Brabham (b.1926): Australian auto racer; 3-time Formula One champion (1959-60,66); 14 career wins.

Bill Bradley (b.7/28/1943): Basketball F; 3-time All-America at Princeton, Player of Year and NCAA tourney MVP in 1965; captain of gold medal-winning 1964 U.S. Olympic team; Sullivan Award winner (1965); led NY Knicks to 2 NBA titles (1970,73); U.S. Senator (D,NJ) since 1979.

Pat Bradley (b.3/24/1951): Golfer; 2-time LPGA Player of Year (1986,91); has won all four majors on LPGA tour, including 3 du Maurier Classics; entered 1994 as all-time LPGA money leader and 12th in wins (30).

Terry Bradshaw (b.9/2/1948): Football QB; led Pittsburgh to 4 Super Bowl titles (1975-76,79-80); 2-time Super Bowl MVP (1979-80).

George Brett (b.5/15/1953): Baseball 3B-1B; AL batting champion in 3 different decades (1976,80,90); MVP in 1980; led KC to World Series title in 1985; retired after 1993 season with 3,154 hits and .305 career average.

Lou Brock (b.6/18/1939): Baseball OF; former all-time stolen base leader (938); led NL in steals 8 times; led St.Louis to 2 World Series titles (1964,67); had 3,023 career hits.

Herb Brooks (b.8/5/1937): Hockey; former U.S. Olympic player (1964,68) who coached 1980 team to gold medal; coached Minnesota to 3 NCAA titles (1974,76,78); also coached NY Rangers, Minnesota and New Jersey in NHL.

Dr. Bobby Brown (b.10/25/1924): Baseball; cardiologist and 6th AL president (1983-1994); as player, hit .279 in 8 years as NY Yankees 3B; also hit .439 with 3 pinch hits in 41 World Series at bats (1947-51).

Jim Brown (b.2/17/1936): Football FB; led NFL in rushing 8 times; 8-time All-Pro (1957-61,63-65); 3-time MVP (1958,63,65) with Cleveland; ran for 12,312 yards and scored 756 points in just 9 seasons.

Larry Brown (b.9/14/1940): Basketball; played in ACC, AAU, 1964 Olympics and ABA; has coached in college at UCLA and Kansas and pros with ABA's Carolina and Denver and NBA's Denver, New Jersey, San Antonio, LA Clippers and Indiana; 3-time assist leader (1968-70) and 3-time Coach of Year (1973,75-76) in ABA; led UCLA to Final Four (1980) and Kansas to NCAA title (1988).

Paul Brown (1908-91): Football innovator; coached Ohio St. to national title in 1942; in pros, directed Cleveland Browns to 4 straight AAFC titles (1946-49) and 3 NFL titles (1950,54-55); formed Cincinnati Bengals in 1968 (reached playoffs in '70).

Sergei Bruguera (b.1/16/1971): Spanish tennis player; winner of back-to-back French Opens in 1993 and '94.

Valery Brumel (b.1942): Soviet high jumper; dominated event from 1961-64; broke world record 5 times; won silver medal in 1960 Olympics and gold in 1964; highest jump was 7-5.

Avery Brundage (1887-1975): Amateur sports czar for over 40 years as president of AAU (1928-35), U.S. Olympic Committee (1929-53) and International Olympic Committee (1952-72).

Paul (Bear) Bryant (1913-83): Football; coached at 4 colleges over 38 years; directed Alabama to 5 national titles (1961,64-65,78-79); 323 career wins; 15 bowl wins including 8 Sugar Bowls.

Sergey Bubka (b.12/4/1963): Ukrainian pole vaulter; 1st man to clear 20 feet both indoors and out (1991); holder of indoor (20-2) and outdoor (20-1¾) world records as of Sept. 1, 1994; 4-time world champion (1983, 87,91,93); won Olympic gold medal in 1988, but failed to clear any height in 1992 Games.

Don Budge (b.6/13/1915): Tennis; in 1938 became 1st player to win the Grand Slam—the French, Wimbledon, U.S. and Australian titles in 1 year; led U.S. to 2 Davis Cups (1937-38); turned pro in late '38.

Maria Bueno (b.10/11/1939): Brazilian tennis player; won 4 U.S. Championships (1959,63-64,66) and 3 Wimbledons (1959-60,64).

Leroy Burrell (b.2/21/1967): Track & Field; world's fastest human after setting world record of 9.85 in 100 meters, July 6, 1994; previously held record (9.90) in 1991; member of 4 world record-breaking 4 x 100m relay teams.

George Bush (b.6/12/1924): 41st President of U.S. (1989-93) and avid sportsman; played 1B on 1947 and '48 Yale baseball teams that placed 2nd in College World Series; captain of 1948 team.

Susan Butcher (b.12/26/1956): Sled Dog racer; 4-time winner of Iditarod Trail race (1986-88,90).

Dick Butkus (b.12/9/1942): Football LB; 2-time All-America at Illinois (1963-64); All-Pro 7 of 9 NFL seasons with Chicago Bears.

Dick Button (b.7/18/1929): Figure skater; 5-time world champion (1948-52); 2-time Olympic champ (1948,52); Sullivan Award winner (1949); won Emmy Award as Best Analyst for 1980-81 TV season.

Walter Byers (b.3/13/1922): College athletics; 1st executive director of NCAA, serving from 1951-88.

Frank Calder (1877-1943): Hockey; 1st NHL president (1917-43); guided league through its formative years; NHL's rookie of the year award named after him.

Lee Calhoun (1933-89): Track & Field; won consecutive Olympic gold medals in the 110m hurdles (1956,60).

Walter Camp (1859-1925): Football coach and innovator; established scrimmage line, center snap, downs, 11 players per side; named 1st All-America team (1889).

Roy Campanella (1921-93): Baseball C; 3-time NL MVP (1951,53,55); led Brooklyn to 5 pennants and 1st World Series title (1955); career cut short when 1958 car accident left him paralyzed.

Clarence Campbell (1905-84): Hockey; 3rd NHL president (1946-77); league tripled in size from 6 to 18 teams during his tenure.

Earl Campbell (b.3/29/1955): Football RB; won Heisman Trophy in 1977; led NFL in rushing 3 times; 3-time All-Pro; 2-time MVP (1978-80) at Houston.

John Campbell (b.4/8/1955): Harness racing; 3-time winner of Hambletonian; 3-time Driver of Year; first driver to go over $100 million in career winnings; entered 1994 with 6,308 career wins.

Milt Campbell (b.12/9/1933): Track & field; won silver medal in 1952 Olympic decathlon and gold medal in '56.

Jimmy Cannon (1910-73): Tough, opinionated New York sportswriter and essayist who viewed sports as an extension of show business; protégé of Damon Runyon; covered World War II for *Stars & Stripes*.

Tony Canzoneri (1908-59): Boxer; 2-time world lightweight champion (1930-33,35-36); pro record 141-24-10 with 44 KOs.

Jennifer Capriati (b.3/29/1976): Tennis; youngest Grand Slam semifinalist ever (age 14 in 1990 French Open); also youngest to win a match at Wimbledon (1990); upset Steffi Graf to win gold medal in 1992 Olympics; entered 1994 with 5 career tournament wins; left tour in May 1994 after being charged with marijuana possession.

Harry Caray (b.3/1/1917): Radio-TV; baseball play-by-play broadcaster for St. Louis Cardinals, Oakland, Chicago White Sox and Cubs since 1945; father of sportscaster Skip and grandfather of sportscaster Chip.

Rod Carew (b.10/1/1945): Baseball 2B-1B; led AL in batting 7 times (1969,72-75,77-78) with Minnesota; MVP in 1977; had 3,053 career hits.

Steve Carlton (b.12/22/1944): Baseball LHP; won 20 or more games 6 times; 4-time Cy Young winner (1972,77, 80,82) with Philadelphia; 329 career wins.

JoAnne Carner (b.4/4/1939): Golfer; 5-time U.S. Amateur champion; 2-time U.S. Open champ; 3-time LPGA Player of Year (1974,81-82); 7th in career wins (42).

Don Carter (b.7/29/1926): Bowler; 6-time Bowler of Year (1953-54,57-58,60-61); voted Greatest of All-Time in 1970.

Joe Carter (b.3/7/1960): Baseball OF; 3-time All-America at Wichita St.(1979-81); won 1993 World Series for Toronto with 3-run HR in bottom of the 9th of Game 6; entered 1994 season with 275 HRs and 994 RBI in 11 years.

Alexander Cartwright (1820-92): Baseball; engineer and draftsman who is widely regarded as father of modern game; his guidelines set bases 90 feet apart, 3 outs per side, 9 innings per game, 9 men per team, unalterable batting order and ended practice of throwing ball at runner to retire him.

Billy Casper (b.6/24/1931): Golfer; 2-time PGA Player of Year (1966,70); has won U.S. Open (1959,66), Masters (1970), U.S. Senior Open (1983); entered 1993 with 51 PGA wins and 9 on Senior Tour.

Tracy Caulkins (b.1/11/1963): Swimmer; won 3 gold medals (2 individual) at 1984 Olympics; set 5 world records and won 48 U.S. national titles from 1978-84; Sullivan Award winner (1978); 2-time Honda Broderick Cup winner (1982,84).

Evonne Goolagong Cawley (b.7/31/1951): Australian tennis player; won Australian Open 4 times, Wimbledon twice (1971-79), French once.

Florence Chadwick (b.11/9/1917): Dominant distance swimmer of 1950s; set English Channel records from France to England (1950) and England to France (1951 and '55).

Wilt Chamberlain (b.8/21/1936): Basketball C; consensus All-America in 1957 and '58 at Kansas; Final Four MVP in 1957; led NBA in scoring 7 times and rebounding 11 times; 7-time All-NBA first team; 4-time MVP (1960,66-68) in Philadelphia; scored 100 points vs. NY Knicks in Hershey, Pa., Mar. 2, 1962; led Philadelphia 76ers (1967) and LA Lakers (1972) to NBA titles; playoff MVP in 1972.

A.B. (Happy) Chandler (1898-1991): Baseball; former Kentucky governor and U.S. Senator who succeeded Judge Landis as commissioner in 1945; backed Branch Rickey's move in 1947 to make Jackie Robinson 1st black player in major leagues; deemed too pro-player and ousted by owners in 1951.

Julio Cesar Chavez (b.7/12/1962): Mexican boxer; world jr. welterweight champ; also held titles as jr. lightweight (1984-87) and lightweight (1987-89); fought Pernell Whitaker to controversial draw for welterweight title on Sept. 10, 1993; entered 1994 with 87-0-1 record with 69 KOs; unbeaten streak ended Jan. 29 when Frankie Randall won title on split decision; Chavez won title back May 7 when controversial, 8th round head butt by Randall stopped fight with Chavez ahead on two judges' cards.

Linford Christie (b.4/2/1960): British sprinter; won 100-meter gold medals at both 1992 Olympics (9.96) and '93 World Championships (9.87).

Jim Clark (1936-68): Scottish auto racer; 2-time Formula One world champion (1963,65); won Indy 500 in 1965; killed in car crash.

Bobby Clarke (b.8/13/1949): Hockey C; led Philadelphia Flyers to consecutive Stanley Cups in 1974-75; 3-time regular season MVP (1973,75-76).

Ron Clarke (b.1937): Australian runner; from 1963-70 set 17 world records in races from 2 miles to 20,000 meters; never won Olympic gold medal.

Roger Clemens (b.8/4/1962): Baseball RHP; fanned record 20 batters in 9-inning game (1986); 3 Cy Young Awards (1986-87,91) with Boston; AL MVP in 1986; entered 1994 season with 163 wins in 10 seasons.

Roberto Clemente (1934-72): Baseball OF; hit .300 or better 13 times with Pittsburgh; led NL in batting 4 times; World Series MVP in 1971; regular season MVP in 1966; had 3,000 career hits; killed in plane crash.

Ty Cobb (1886-1961): Baseball OF; all-time highest career batting average (.367); hit .400 or better 3 times; led AL in batting 12 times and stolen bases 6 times with Detroit; MVP in 1911; had 4,191 career hits and 892 steals.

Mickey Cochrane (1903-62): Baseball C; led Philadelphia A's (1929-30) and Detroit (1935) to 3 World Series titles; 2-time AL MVP (1928,34).

Sebastian Coe (b.9/29/1956): British runner; won gold medal in 1500m and silver medal in 800m at both 1980 and '84 Olympics; although retired, still holds world records in 800m and 1000m; elected to Parliament as Conservative in 1992.

Eddie Collins (1887-1951): Baseball 2B; led Philadelphia A's (1910-11) and Chicago White Sox (1917) to 3 World Series titles; AL MVP in 1914; had 3,311 career hits and 743 stolen bases.

Nadia Comaneci (b.11/12/1961): Romanian gymnast; 1st to record perfect 10 in Olympics; won 3 individual gold medals at 1976 Olympics and 2 more in '80.

Lionel Conacher (1902-54): Canada's greatest all-around athlete; NHL hockey (2 Stanley Cups), CFL football (1 Grey Cup), minor league baseball, soccer, lacrosse, track, amateur boxing champion; also member of Parliament (1949-54).

Gene Conley (b.11/10/1930): played for World Series and NBA champions with Milwaukee Braves (1957) and Boston Celtics (1959-61); winning pitcher in 1954 All-Star Game; won 91 games in 11 seasons.

Billy Conn (1917-93): Boxer; Pittsburgh native and world light heavyweight champion from 1939-41; nearly upset heavyweight champ Joe Louis in 1941 title bout, but was knocked out in 13th round; pro record 63-11-1 with 14 KOs.

Dennis Conner (b.9/16/1942): Sailing; 3-time America's Cup-winning skipper aboard *Freedom* (1980), *Stars & Stripes* (1987) and the *Stars & Stripes* catamaran (1988); became first and only American skipper to lose Cup in 1983 when *Australia II* beat *Liberty*.

Maureen Connolly (1934-69): Tennis; in 1953 1st woman to win Grand Slam (at age 19); riding accident ended her career in '54; won both Wimbledon and U.S. titles 3 times (1951-53); 3-time AP Female Athlete of Year (1951-53).

Jimmy Connors (b.9/2/1952): Tennis; No.1 player in world 5 times (1974-78); won 5 U.S. Opens, 2 Wimbledons and 1 Australian; rose from No. 936 at the close of 1990 to U.S. Open semifinals in 1991 at age 39; NCAA singles champ (1971); all-time leader in pro singles titles (109) and matches won at U.S. Open (98) and Wimbledon (84).

Jack Kent Cooke (b.10/25/1912): Football; sole owner of NFL Washington Redskins since 1985; teams have won 2 Super Bowls (1987,91); also owned NBA Lakers and NHL Kings in LA; built LA Forum for $12 million in 1967.

Angel Cordero, Jr. (b.11/8/1942): Jockey; third on all-time list with 7,057 wins in 38,646 starts; won Kentucky Derby 3 times, Preakness twice and Belmont 2; 2-time Eclipse Award winner (1982-83).

Howard Cosell (b.3/25/1920): Radio-TV; former ABC commentator on "Monday Night Football" and "Wide World of Sports," who energized TV sports journalism with abrasive "Tell it like it is" style.

Bob Costas (b.3/22/1952): Radio-TV; NBC anchor for NBA, NFL and Summer Olympics as well as baseball play-by-play man; 5-time Emmy winner and 5-time Sportscaster of Year.

James (Doc) Counsilman (b.12/28/1920): coached Indiana men's swim team to 6 NCAA championships (1968-73); coached the 1964 and '76 U.S. men's Olympic teams that won a combined 21 of 24 gold medals (the Hoosiers' Mark Spitz won 7 in 1976); in 1979 became oldest person (59) to swim English Channel; retired in 1990 with dual meet record of 287-36-1.

Jim Courier (b.8/17/1970): Tennis; No. 1 player in world in 1992, has won two Australian Opens (1992-93) and two French (1991-92); played on 1992 Davis Cup winner; Nick Bollettieri Academy classmate of Andre Agassi.

Margaret Smith Court (b.7/16/1942): Australian tennis player; won Grand Slam in both singles (1970) and mixed doubles (1963 with Ken Fletcher); 26 Grand Slam singles titles—11 Australian, 7 U.S., 5 French and 3 Wimbledon.

Bob Cousy (b.8/9/1928): Basketball G; led NBA in assists 8 times; 10-time All-NBA 1st team (1952-61); MVP in 1957; led Boston to 6 NBA titles (1957,59-63).

Buster Crabb (1910-83): Swimmer; 2-time Olympic freestyle medalist with bronze in 1928 (1500m) and gold in '32 (400m); became movie star and King of Serials as Flash Gordon and Buck Rogers.

Joe Cronin (1906-84): Baseball SS; hit over .300 and drove in over 100 runs 8 times each, MVP in 1930; player-manager in Washington and Boston (1933-47); AL president (1959-73).

Ann Curtis (b.3/6/1926): Swimming; won 2 gold medals and 1 silver in 1948 Olympics; set 4 world and 18 U.S. records during career; 1st woman and swimmer to win Sullivan Award (1944).

Betty Cuthbert (b.4/20/1938): Australian runner; won gold medals in 100 and 200 meters and 4x100m relay at 1956 Olympics; also won 400m gold at 1964 Olympics.

Chuck Daly (b.7/20/1930): Basketball; coached Detroit to two NBA titles (1989-90) before leaving in 1992 to coach New Jersey; retired after 1993-94 season with 638 career wins (including playoffs) in 12 years; coached NBA "Dream Team" to gold medal in 1992 Olympics.

Stanley Dancer (b.7/25/1927): Harness racing; winner of 4 Hambletonians; trainer-driver of Triple Crown winners in Trotting (Nevele Pride in 1968 and Super Bowl in '72) and Pacing (Most Happy Fella in 1970); entered 1994 with 3,778 career wins.

Tamás Darnyi (b.6/3/1967): Hungarian swimmer; 2-time double gold medal winner in 200m and 400m individual medley at 1988 and '92 Olympics; also won both events in 1986 and '91 world championships; set world records in both at '91 worlds; 1st swimmer to break 2 minutes in 200m IM (1:59:36).

Al Davis (b.7/4/1929): Football; GM-coach of Oakland 1963-66; helped force AFL-NFL merger as AFL commissioner (April-July,1966); returned to Oakland as managing general partner and directed club to 3 Super Bowl wins (1977,81,84); moved Raiders to LA in 1982.

Dwight Davis (1879-1945): Tennis; donor of Davis Cup; played for winning U.S. team in 1st two Cup finals (1900,02); won U.S. and Wimbledon doubles titles in 1901; Secretary of War (1925-29) under Coolidge.

Glenn Davis (b.12/26/1924): Football HB; 3-time All-America; led Army to national titles in 1944-45; Doc Blanchard's running mate; won Heisman Trophy in 1946.

John Davis (1921-84): Weightlifting; 6-time world champion; 2-time Olympic super-heavyweight champ (1948,52), undefeated 1938-53.

Dizzy Dean (1911-74): Baseball RHP; led NL in strikeouts and complete games 4 times; last NL pitcher to win 30 games (30-7 in 1934); MVP in 1934 with St. Louis; 150 career wins.

Dave DeBusschere (b.10/16/1940): Basketball F; 3-time All-America at Detroit; youngest coach in NBA history (24 in 1964); player-coach of Detroit Pistons (1964-67); played in 8 All-Star games; won 2 NBA titles as player with NY Knicks; ABA commissioner (1975-76); also pitched 2 seasons for Chicago White Sox (1962-63) with 3-4 record.

Pierre de Coubertin (1863-1937): French educator; father of the Modern Olympic Games; IOC president from 1896-1925.

Anita DeFrantz (b.10/4/1952): Olympics; attorney who is one of 2 American delegates to the International Olympic Committee (James Easton is the other); first woman to represent U.S. on IOC; member of USOC Executive Committee; member of bronze medal U.S. women's eight-oared shell at Montreal in 1976.

Cedric Dempsey (b.4/14/1932): College sports; named to succeed Dick Schultz as NCAA executive director on Nov. 5, 1993; served as athletic director at Pacific (1967-79), San Diego St. (1979), Houston (1979-82) and Arizona (1983-93).

Jack Dempsey (1895-1983): Boxer; world heavyweight champion from 1919-26; lost title to Gene Tunney, then lost "Long Count" rematch in 1927 when he floored Tunney in 7th round but failed to retreat to neutral corner; pro record 62-6-10 with 49 KOs.

Donna de Varona (b.4/26/1947): Swimming; won gold medals in 400 IM and 400 freestyle relay at 1964 Olympics; set 18 world records during career; co-founder of Women's Sports Foundation in 1974.

Gail Devers (b.11/19/1966): Track & Field; fastest ever woman sprinter-hurdler; overcame thyroid disorder (Graves' disease) that sidelined her in 1989-90 and nearly resulted in having both feet amputated; won 1992 Olympic gold medal in 100 meters (10.82), then took 100-meter (10.82) and 100-meter hurdles (12.46) titles at 1993 World Championships.

Klaus Dibiasi (b.10/6/1947): Italian diver; won 3 consecutive Olympic gold medals in platform event (1968,72,76).

Eric Dickerson (b.9/2/1960): Football RB; led NFL in rushing 4 times (1983-84,86,88); NFC Rookie of Year in 1983; All-Pro 5 times, traded from LA Rams to Indianapolis (Oct. 31, 1987) in 3-team, 10-player deal (including draft picks) that also involved Buffalo; 2nd on all-time career rushing list with 13,259 yards in 11 seasons.

Harrison Dillard (b.7/8/1923): Track & Field; only man to win Olympic gold medals in both sprints (100m in 1948) and hurdles (110m in 1952).

Joe DiMaggio (b.11/25/1914): Baseball OF; hit safely in 56 straight games (1941), led AL in batting, HRs and RBI twice each; 3-time MVP (1939,41,47); hit .325 with 361 HRs over 13 seasons; led NY Yankees to 10 World Series titles.

Charlotte (Lottie) Dod (1871-1962): British athlete, who was 5-time Wimbledon singles champion (1887-88,91-93); youngest player ever to win Wimbledon (15 in 1887), archery silver medalist at 1908 Olympics, member of national field hockey team in 1899, and British Amateur golf champ in 1904.

Tony Dorsett (b.4/7/1954): Football RB; won Heisman Trophy leading Pitt to national championship in 1976; all-time NCAA Div. I-A rushing leader with 6,082 yards; led Dallas to Super Bowl title as NFC Rookie of Year (1977); NFC Player of Year (1981); ranks 3rd on all-time NFL list with 12,739 yards gained in 12 years; holds NFL record for run from scrimmage (99 yards vs Min. in 1983).

James (Buster) Douglas (b.4/7/1960): Boxing; 50-1 shot who knocked out undefeated Mike Tyson in 10th round on Feb.10, 1990 to win heavyweight title in Tokyo; 10 months later, lost 1st title defense to Evander Holyfield by KO in 3rd round.

The Dream Team—Head coach **Chuck Daly's** "Best Ever" 12-member NBA All-Star squad that easily won the basketball gold medal in 1992 Olympics: co-captains **Magic Johnson** and **Larry Bird**, veterans **Charles Barkley, Clyde Drexler** (b.6/22/1962), **Patrick Ewing, Michael Jordan, Karl Malone, Chris Mullin** (b.7/30/1963), **Scottie Pippen** (b.9/25/1965), **David Robinson, John Stockton** (b.3/26/1962) and rookie **Christian Laettner** (b.8/17/1969).

Dream Team II— Head coach **Don Nelson's** 12-man NBA All-Star squad that easily won the gold medal at the 1994 World Basketball Championships in Toronto: **Derrick Coleman** (b.6/21/1967), **Joe Dumars** (b.5/24/1963), **Kevin Johnson** (b.3/4/1966), **Larry Johnson** (b.3/14/1969), **Shawn Kemp** (b.11/26/1969), **Dan Majerle** (b.9/9/1965), **Reggie Miller** (b.8/24/1965), **Alonzo Mourning** (b.2/8/1970), **Shaquille O'Neal, Mark Price** (b.2/15/1964), **Steve Smith** (b.3/31/1969) and **Dominique Wilkins.**

Heike Drechsler (b.12/16/1964): German long jumper and sprinter; East German before reunification in 1991; set world long jump record (24-2 1/4) in 1988; won long jump gold medals at 1992 Olympics and 1983 and '93 World Championships; won silver medal in long jump and bronze medals in both 100- and 200-meter sprints at 1988 Olympics.

Ken Dryden (b.8/8/1947): Hockey G; led Montreal to 6 Stanley Cup titles; playoff MVP as rookie in 1971; won or shared 5 Vezina Trophies.

Don Drysdale (1936-93): Baseball RHP; led NL in strikeouts 3 times and games started 4 straight years; pitched and won record 6 shutouts in a row in 1968; Cy Young Award winner in 1962; won 209 games and hit 29 HRs in 14 years.

Charley Dumas (b.2/12/1937): U.S. high jumper; first man to clear 7 feet (7-0½) on June 29, 1956; won gold medal at 1956 Olympics.

Margaret Osborne du Pont (b.3/4/1918): Tennis; won 5 French, 7 Wimbledon and an unprecedented 24 U.S. national titles in singles, doubles and mixed doubles from 1941-62.

Roberto Duran (b.6/16/1951): Panamanian boxer; one of only 3 fighters to hold 4 different world titles—lightweight (1972-79); welterweight (1980) junior middleweight (1983) and middleweight (1989-90); lost famous "No Mas" welterweight title bout when he quit in 8th round against Sugar Ray Leonard (1980); entered 1994 with pro record of 91-9 and 63 KOs.

Leo Durocher (1905-91): Baseball; managed in NL 24 years; won 2,015 games, including postseason; 3 pennants with Brooklyn (1941) and NY Giants (1951,54); won World Series in 1954.

Eddie Eagan (1898-1967): Only athlete to win gold medals in both Summer and Winter Olympics (Boxing in 1920, Bobsled in 1932).

Alan Eagleson (b.4/24/1933): Hockey; Toronto lawyer, agent and 1st executive director of NHL Players Assn. (1967-90); midwived Team Canada vs Soviet series (1972) and Canada Cup; charged with racketeering and defrauding NHLPA in 32-count indictment handed down by U.S. grand jury on Mar. 3, 1994.

Dale Earnhardt (b.4/29/1952): Auto racer; 6-time NASCAR national champion (1980,86-87,90-91,93); Rookie of Year in 1979; entered 1994 as all-time NASCAR money leader with $19,513,571 and 6th on career wins list with 59; in 19 years, has never won Daytona 500.

James Easton (b.7/26/1935): Olympics; archer and sporting goods manufacturer (Easton softball bats); one of 2 American delegates to the International Olympic Committee; president of International Archery Federation (FITA); member of LA Olympic Organizing Committee in 1984.

Stefan Edberg (b.1/19/1966): Swedish tennis player; 2-time No.1 player (1990-91); 2-time winner of Australian Open (1985, 87), Wimbledon (1988, 90) and U.S. Open (1991-92); has never won French.

Gertrude Ederle (b.10/23/1906): Swimmer; 1st woman to swim English Channel, breaking men's record by 2 hours in 1926; won 3 medals in 1924 Olympics.

Krisztina Egerszegi (b.1974): Hungarian swimmer; 3-time gold medal winner (100m and 200m backstroke and 400m IM) in 1992 Olympics; also won a gold (200m back) and silver (100m back) in 1988 Games; youngest (age 14) ever to win swimming gold.

Bill Elliott (b.10/8/1955): Auto racer; 2-time winner of Daytona 500 (1985,87); NASCAR national champ in 1988; entered 1994 with 39 NASCAR wins.

Herb Elliott (b.2/25/1938): Australian runner; undefeated from 1958-60; ran 17 sub-4:00 miles; 3 world records; won gold medal in 1500 meters at 1960 Olympics; retired at age 22.

Roy Emerson (b.11/3/1936): Australian tennis player; won 12 Majors in singles—6 Australian, 2 French, 2 Wimbledon and 2 U.S. from 1961-67.

Kornelia Ender (b.10/25/1958): East German swimmer; 1st woman to win 4 gold medals at one Olympics (1976), all in world-record time.

Julius Erving (b.2/22/1950): Basketball F; in ABA (1972-76)—3-time MVP, 2-time playoff MVP, led NY Nets to 2 titles (1974-76); in NBA (1977-87)—5-time All-NBA 1st team, MVP in 1981, led Philadelphia 76ers to title in 1983.

Phil Esposito (b.2/20/1942): Hockey C; 1st NHL player to score 100 points in a season (126 in 1969); 6-time All-NHL 1st team with Boston; 2-time MVP (1969,74); 5-time scoring champ; star of 1972 Canada-Soviet series; president-GM of NHL's Tampa Bay Lightning.

Janet Evans (b.8/28/1971): Swimmer; won 3 individual gold medals (400m & 800m freestyle, 400m IM) at 1988 Olympics; 1989 Sullivan Award winner; entered 1993 as world record-holder in 400m, 800m and 1500m freestyles; won 1 gold (800m) and 1 silver (400m) at 1992 Olympics.

Lee Evans (b.2/25/1947): Track & Field; dominant quarter-miler in world from 1966-72; world record in 400m at 1968 Olympics stood 20 years.

Chris Evert (b.12/21/1954): Tennis; No.1 player in world 5 times (1975-77,80-81); won at least 1 Grand Slam singles title every year from 1974-86; 18 Majors in all—7 French, 6 U.S., 3 Wimbledon and 2 Australian.

Wide World Photos

The celebrated **Four Horsemen** backfield of Notre Dame's 1924 national championship team (from left to right): halfback **Don Miller**, fullback **Elmer Layden**, halfback **Jim Crowley** and quarterback **Harry Stuhldreher**.

Weeb Ewbank (b.5/6/1907): Football; only coach to win NFL and AFL titles; led Baltimore to 2 NFL titles (1958-59) and NY Jets to Super Bowl III win.

Patrick Ewing (b.8/5/1962): Basketball C; 3-time All-America; led Georgetown to 3 NCAA Finals and 1984 title; tourney MVP in '84; NBA Rookie of Year with New York in '86; All-NBA in 1990; led U.S. Olympic team to gold medals in 1984 and '92.

Ray Ewry (1873-1937): Track & Field; won 10 gold medals over 4 consecutive Olympics (1900,04,06,08); all events he won (Standing HJ,LJ and TJ) were discontinued in 1912.

Nick Faldo (b.7/18/1957): British golfer; 3-time winner of British Open (1987,90,92) and 2-time winner of Masters (1989-90); 3-time European Golfer of Year (1989-90, 92); PGA Player of Year in 1990.

Juan Manuel Fangio (b.6/24/1911): Argentine auto racer; 5-time Formula One world champion (1951,54-57); 24 career wins, retired in 1958.

Sergei Fedorov (b.12/13/1969): Hockey C; first Russian to win NHL Hart Trophy as 1993-94 regular season MVP; 2-time All-Star with Detroit.

Donald Fehr (b.7/18/1948): Baseball labor leader; protege of Marvin Miller; executive director and general counsel of Major League Players Assn. since 1983; led players in 1994 "salary cap" strike that lasted 34 days before owners cancelled regular season and World Series on Sept. 14.

Bob Feller (b.11/3/1918): Baseball RHP; led AL in strikeouts 7 times and wins 6 times with Cleveland; threw 3 no-hitters and 12 one-hitters; 266 career wins.

Tom Ferguson (b.12/20/1950): Rodeo; 6-time All-Around champion (1974-79); 1st cowboy to win $100,000 in one season (1978); 1st to win $1 million in career (1986).

Cecil Fielder (b.9/21/1963): Baseball 1B; returned from one season with Hanshin Tigers in Japan to hit 51 HRs for Detroit Tigers in 1990; led AL in RBI 3 straight years (1990-92); AL MVP runner-up in 1990 and '91.

Herve Filion (b.2/1/1940): Harness racing; 10-time Driver of Year; entered 1994 season as all-time leader in races won with 14,084 in 33 years.

Rollie Fingers (b.8/25/1946): Baseball RHP; relief ace with 341 career saves; won AL MVP and Cy Young awards in 1981 with Milwaukee; World Series MVP in 1974 with Oakland.

Charles O. Finley (b.2/22/1918): Baseball owner; moved KC A's to Oakland in 1968; won 3 straight World Series from 1972-74; also owned teams in NHL and ABA.

Bobby Fischer (b.3/9/1943): Chess; only American to hold world championship (1972-75); resigned title in 1975 and became recluse; re-emerged to defeat old foe and former world champion Boris Spassky in 1992.

Carlton Fisk (b.12/26/1947): Baseball C; set all-time major league record at age 45 for games caught (2,226); also all-time HR leader for catchers (376); AL Rookie of Year (1972) and 10-time All-Star; hit epic, 12th-inning Game 6 homer for Boston Red Sox in 1975 World Series.

Emerson Fittipaldi (b.12/12/1946): Brazilian auto racer; 2-time Formula One world champion (1972,74); 2-time winner of Indy 500 (1989,93); won overall IndyCar title in 1989.

Bob Fitzsimmons (1863-1917): British boxer; held three world titles—middleweight (1981-97), heavyweight (1897-99) and light heavyweight (1903-05); pro record 40-11 with 32 KOs.

James (Sunny Jim) Fitzsimmons (1874-1966): Horse racing; trained horses that won over 2,275 races, including 2 Triple Crown winners—Gallant Fox in 1930 and Omaha in '35.

Larry Fleisher (1930-89): Basketball; led NBA players union from 1961-89; increased average yearly salary from $9,400 in 1967 to $600,000 without a strike.

Peggy Fleming (b.7/27/1948): Figure skating; 3-time world champion (1966-68); won Olympic gold medal in 1968.

Curt Flood (b.1/18/1938): Baseball OF; played 15 years (1956-71) mainly with St. Louis; hit over .300 6 times with 7 gold gloves; refused trade to Phillies in 1969; lost challenge to baseball's reserve clause in Supreme Court in 1972 (see Peter Seitz).

Ray Floyd (b.9/4/1942): Golfer; entered 1994 with 22 PGA victories in 4 decades; has won Masters (1976), U.S. Open (1986) and PGA twice (1969,82); only player to ever win on PGA and Senior tours in same year (1992); member of 8 Ryder Cup teams and captain in 1989.

Doug Flutie (b.10/23/1962): Football QB; won Heisman Trophy with Boston College (1984); has played in USFL, NFL and CFL since then; 3-time CFL MVP with B.C. Lions (1991) and Calgary (1992-93); led Calgary to Grey Cup title in '92.

Gerald Ford (b.7/14/1913): 38th President of the U.S.; lettered as center on undefeated Michigan football teams in 1932 and '33; team MVP of 1934 squad.

Whitey Ford (b.10/21/1928): Baseball LHP; all-time leader in World Series wins (10); led AL in wins 3 times; won both Cy Young and World Series MVP in 1961 with NY Yankees.

George Foreman (b.1/10/1948): Boxer; Olympic heavyweight champ (1968); world heavyweight champ (1973-74); lost title to Muhammad Ali (KO-8th) in '74; lost comeback bid for title at age 42 to Evander Holyfield (D-12) in 1991; entered 1994 with pro record of 72-4 and 67 KOs.

Dick Fosbury (b.3/6/1947): Track & Field; revolutionized high jump with back-first "Fosbury Flop;" won gold medal at 1968 Olympics.

Greg Foster (b.8/4/1958): Track & Field; 3-time winner of World Championship gold medal in 110-meter hurdles (1983,87,91); best Olympic performance a silver in 1984; world indoor champion in 1991; made world Top 10 rankings 15 years (a record for running events).

The Four Horsemen—Senior backfield that led Notre Dame to national collegiate football championship in 1924: put together as sophomores by Irish coach Knute Rockne, immortalized by sportswriter Grantland Rice, whose report of the Oct. 19, 1924, Notre Dame-Army game began: "Outlined against a blue, October sky the Four Horsemen rode again..."; HB **Jim Crowley** (1902-86), FB **Elmer Layden** (1903-73), HB **Don Miller** (1902-79) and QB **Harry Stuhldreher** (1901-65).

The Four Musketeers—French quartet that dominated men's world tennis in 1920s and '30s, winning 8 straight French singles titles (1925-32), 6 Wimbledons in a row (1924-29) and 6 consecutive Davis Cups (1927-32): **Jean Borotra** (1898-1994), **Jacques Brugnon** (1895-1978), **Henri Cochet** (1901-1987), **Rene Lacoste** (b.7/2/1905).

Jimmie Foxx (1907-67): Baseball 1B; led AL in HRs 4 times and batting twice; won Triple Crown in 1933; 3-time MVP (1932-33,38) with Philadelphia and Boston; hit 30 HRs or more 12 years in a row; 534 career HRs.

A.J. Foyt (b.1/16/1935): Auto racer; 7-time USAC/CART national champion (1960-61,63-64,67,75,79); 4-time Indy 500 winner (1961,64,67,77); only driver in history to win Indy 500, Daytona 500 (1972) and 24 Hours of LeMans (1967 with Dan Gurney); retired in 1993 as all-time IndyCar wins leader with 67.

Bill France Sr. (1909-92): stock car pioneer and promoter; founded NASCAR in 1948; guided race circuit through formative years; built both Daytona (Fla.) Int'l Speedway and Talladega (Ala.) Superspeedway.

Dawn Fraser (b.9/4/1937): Australian swimmer; won gold medals in 100m freestyle at 3 consecutive Olympics (1956,60,64).

Joe Frazier (b.1/12/1944): Boxer; 1964 Olympic heavyweight champion; world heavyweight champ (1970-73); fought Muhammad Ali 3 times and won once; pro record 32-4-1 with 27 KOs.

Ford Frick (1894-1978): Baseball; sportswriter and radio announcer who served as NL president (1934-51) and commissioner (1951-65); put asterisk next to Roger Maris' 61 HRs in 162 games in 1961; major leagues moved to west coast and expanded from 16 to 20 teams during his tenure.

Frankie Frisch (1898-1973): Baseball 2B; played on 8 NL pennant winners in 19 years with NY and St.Louis; hit .300 or better 11 years in a row (1921-31); MVP in 1931; player-manager from 1933-37.

Dan Gable (b.10/25/1948): Wrestling; career college wrestling record of 118-1 at Iowa St., where he was a 2-time NCAA champ (1968,69) and tourney MVP in 1969 (137 lbs.); won gold medal (149 lbs) at 1972 Olympics; coach U.S. freestyle team in 1988; coached Iowa to 9 straight NCAA titles (1978-86) and has added three more from 1991-93.

Eddie Gaedel (1925-61): Baseball pinch hitter; St. Louis Browns' midget whose career lasted one at bat (he walked) on Aug.19,1951 (see Bill Veeck).

Clarence (Bighouse) Gaines (b.5/21/1924): Basketball; retired as coach of Div. II Winston-Salem after 1992-93 season with 828-446 record in 47 years; ranks 2nd on all-time NCAA list behind Adolph Rupp's 876.

Alonzo (Jake) Gaither (1903-94): Football; head coach at Florida A&M for 25 years; led Rattlers to 6 national black college titles; retired after 1969 season with record of 203-36-4 and a winning percentage of .844; coined phrase, "I like my boys agile, mobile and hostile."

Cito Gaston (b.3/17/1944): Baseball; has managed Toronto to consecutive World Series titles (1992-93); first black manager to win Series; shared the Sporting News' 1993 Man of Year award with Blue Jays GM Pat Gillick.

Dave Gavitt (b.10/26/1937): Basketball; former Dartmouth and Providence coach who formed Big East Conference in 1979; U.S. Olympic coach in 1980; chairman of NCAA tournament committee (1981-84); as president of USA Basketball (1988-92), he was primary force behind sending Dream Team to '92 Olympics; executive with NBA Boston Celtics (1990-94).

Lou Gehrig (1903-41): Baseball 1B; played in major league-record 2,130 consecutive games from 1923-39; led AL in RBI 5 times and HRs 3 times; drove in 100 runs or more 13 years in a row; 2-time MVP (1927,36); hit .340 with 493 HRs over 17 seasons; led NY Yankees to 7 World Series titles; died at age 37 of Amyotrophic lateral sclerosis (ALS), a rare and incurable disease of the nervous system better known as Lou Gehrig's disease.

Charlie Gehringer (1903-93): Baseball 2B; hit .300 or better 13 times; AL batting champion and MVP with Detroit in 1937.

A. Bartlett Giamatti (1938-89): Scholar and 7th commissioner of baseball; banned Pete Rose for life for betting on Major League games and associating with known gamblers and drug dealers; also served as president of Yale (1978-86) and National League (1986-89).

Joe Gibbs (b.11/25/1940): Football; coached Washington to 140 victories and 3 Super Bowl titles in 12 seasons before retiring on Mar. 5, 1993; owner of NASCAR racing team that won 1993 Daytona 500.

Althea Gibson (b.8/25/1927): Tennis; won both Wimbledon and U.S. championships in 1957 and '58; 1st black to play in either tourney and 1st to win each title.

Bob Gibson (b.11/9/1935): Baseball RHP; won 20 or more games 5 times; won 2 NL Cy Young Awards (1968,70), MVP in 1968; led St. Louis to 2 World Series titles; Series MVP twice (1964,67); 251 career wins.

Josh Gibson (1911-47): Baseball C; the "Babe Ruth of the Negro Leagues;" Satchel Paige's battery mate with Pittsburgh Crawfords.

Kirk Gibson (b.5/28/1957): All-America flanker at Michigan St. in 1978; chose baseball career and was AL playoff MVP with Detroit in 1984 and NL regular season MVP with Los Angeles in 1988.

Frank Gifford (b.8/16/1930): Football HB; 4-time All-Pro (1955-57,59); NFL MVP in 1956; led NY Giants to 3 NFL title games; TV sportscaster since 1958, beginning career while still a player.

Sid Gillman (b.10/26/1911): Football innovator; only coach in both College and Pro Football halls of fame; led college teams at Miami-OH and Cincinnati to combined 81-19-2 record from 1944-54; coached LA Rams (1955-59) in NFL, then led Los Angeles and San Diego Chargers of AFL to 5 Western titles and 1 championship in the league's 1st six years.

George Gipp (1895-1920): Football FB; died of throat infection (Dec.14) 2 weeks before he made All-America (Notre Dame's 1st); rushed for 2,341 yards, scored 156 points and averaged 38 yards a punt in 4 years (1917-20).

Marc Girardelli (b.7/18/1963): Luxembourg Alpine skier; Austrian native who refused to join Austrian Ski Federation because he wanted to be coached by his father; won unprecedented 5th overall World Cup title in 1993; winless at Olympics, although he won 2 silver medals in 1992.

Tom Glavine (b.3/25/1966): Baseball LHP; 3-time 20-game winner with Atlanta; won Cy Young Award in 1991.

Tom Gola (b.1/13/1933): Basketball F; 4-time All-America and 1955 Player of Year at La Salle; MVP in 1952 NIT and '54 NCAA tournaments, leading Pioneers to both titles; won NBA title as rookie with Philadelphia Warriors in 1956; 4-time NBA All-Star.

Marshall Goldberg (b.10/24/1917): Football HB; 2-time consensus All-America at Pittsburgh (1937-38); led Pitt to national championship in 1937; played with NFL champion Chicago Cardinals 10 years later.

Lefty Gomez (1908-89): Baseball LHP, 4-time 20-game winner with NY Yankees; holds World Series record for most wins (6) without a defeat; pitched on 5 world championship clubs in 1930s.

Pancho Gonzales (b.5/9/1928): Tennis; won consecutive U.S. Championships in 1947-48 before turning pro at 21; dominated pro tour from 1950-61; in 1969 at age 41, played longest Wimbledon match ever (5:12) beating Charlie Pasarell 22-24,1-6,16-14,6-3,11-9.

Bob Goodenow (b.10/29/1952): Hockey; succeeded Alan Eagleson as executive director of NHL Players Assn. in 1990; led players out on 10-day strike (Apr. 1-10) in 1992.

Shane Gould (b.11/23/1956): Australian swimmer; set world records in 5 different freestyle events between July,1971 and Jan,1972; won 3 gold medals, a silver and bronze in 1972 Olympics then retired at age 16.

Alf Goullet (b.4/5/1891): Cycling; Australian who gained fame and fortune early in century as premier performer on U.S. 6-day bike race circuit; won 8 annual races at Madison Square Garden with 6 different partners from 1913-23.

Curt Gowdy (b.7/31/1919): Radio-TV; former radio voice of NY Yankees and then Boston Red Sox from 1949-66; TV play-by-play man for AFL, NFL and major league baseball; has broadcast World Series, All-Star Games, Rose Bowls, Super Bowls, Olympics and NCAA Final Fours for all 3 networks; also hosted "The American Sportsman."

Steffi Graf (b.6/14/1969): German tennis player; won Grand Slam and Olympic gold medal in 1988 at age 19; won three of four majors in 1993 and Australian Open in '94; her 15 Grand Slam titles include 5 at Wimbledon, 4 Australian, plus 3 French and U.S. Opens.

Otto Graham (b.12/6/1921): Football QB and basketball All-America at Northwestern; in pro ball, led Cleveland Browns to 7 league titles in 10 years, winning 4 AAFC championships (1946-50) and 3 NFL (1950,54-55); 5-time All-Pro; 2-time NFL MVP (1953,55).

Red Grange (1903-91): Football HB; 3-time All-America at Illinois who brought 1st huge crowds to pro football when he signed with Chicago Bears in 1925; formed 1st AFL with manager-promoter C.C. Pyle in 1926, but league folded and he returned to NFL.

Bud Grant (b.5/20/1927): Football and basketball; only coach to win 100 games in both CFL and NFL and only member of both CFL and U.S. Pro Football halls of fame; led Winnipeg to 4 Grey Cup titles (1958-59,61-62) in 6 appearances, but his Minnesota Vikings lost all 4 Super Bowl attempts in 1970s; all-time rank of 3rd in CFL wins (122) and 8th in NFL wins (168); also All-Big 10 at Minnesota in both football and basketball in late 1940s; a 3-time CFL All-Star offensive end; also member of 1950 NBA champion Minneapolis Lakers.

Charles Grantham (b.9/3/1943): Basketball; succeeded Larry Fleischer as executive director of NBA Players Assn. in 1988.

Rocky Graziano (1921-90): Boxer; world middleweight champion (1946-47); fought Tony Zale for title 3 times in 21 months, losing twice; pro record 67-10-6 with 52 KOs; movie "Somebody Up There Likes Me" based on his life.

Hank Greenberg (1911-86): Baseball 1B; led AL in HRs and RBI 4 times each; 2-time MVP (1935,40) with Detroit; 331 career HRs.

Joe Greene (b.9/24/1946): Football DT; 5-time All-Pro (1972-74,77,79); led Pittsburgh to 4 Super Bowl titles.

Bud Greenspan (b.9/18/1926): Filmmaker specializing in the Olympic Games; has won Emmy awards for 22-part "The Olympiad" (1976-77) and historical vignettes for ABC-TV's coverage of 1980 Winter Games; most recent documentary "16 Days of Glory" on 1992 Barcelona Summer Games; official filmmaker for 1994 Lillehammer Winter Games.

Wayne Gretzky (b.1/26/1961): Hockey C; 10-time NHL scoring champion; 9-time regular season MVP (1979-87,89) and 9-time All-NHL first team; has scored 200 points or more in a season 4 times; led Edmonton to 4 Stanley Cups (1984-85,87-88); 2-time playoff MVP (1985,88); traded to LA Kings (Aug. 9, 1988); broke Gordie Howe's all-time NHL goal scoring record of 801 on Mar. 23, 1994; entered 1994-95 regular season as all-time NHL leader in points (2,458), goals (803) and assists (1,655); also all-time Stanley Cup leader in points (346), goals (110) and assists (236).

Bob Griese (b.2/3/1945): Football QB; 2-time All-Pro (1971,77); led Miami to undefeated season (17-0) in 1972 and consecutive Super Bowl titles (1973-74).

Ken Griffey Jr. (b.11/21/1969): Baseball OF; overall 1st pick of 1987 Draft by Seattle; 4-time gold glove winner in 1st 5 seasons; MVP of 1992 All-Star game at age 23; hit home runs in 8 consecutive games in 1993; entered 1994 with 132 HRs and led AL with 40 on Aug. 12 when players' strike began; son of Ken Sr.

Archie Griffin (b.8/21/1954): Football RB; only college player to win two Heisman Trophies (1974-75); rushed for 5,177 yards in career at Ohio St.

Emile Griffith (b.2/3/1938): Boxer; world welterweight champion (1961,62-63,63-65); world middleweight champ (1966-67,67-68); pro record 85-24-2 with 23 KOs.

Dick Groat (b.11/4/1930): Two-time basketball All-America at Duke and college Player of Year in 1951; won NL MVP award as shortstop with Pittsburgh in 1960; won World Series with Pirates (1960) and St. Louis (1964).

Lefty Grove (1900-75): Baseball LHP; won 20 or more games 8 times; led AL in ERA 9 times and strikeouts 7 times; 31-4 record and MVP in 1931 with Philadelphia; 300 career wins.

Lou Groza (b.1/25/1924): Football T-PK; 6-time All-Pro; played in 13 championship games for Cleveland from 1946-67; kicked winning field goal in 1950 NFL title game; 1,608 career points (1,349 in NFL).

Sally Gunnell (b.7/29/1966): British hurdler; set world record in 400-meter hurdles (52.74) at 1993 World Championships; won gold medal in same event at '92 Olympics.

Janet Guthrie (b.3/7/1938): Auto racer; in 1977, became 1st woman to race in Indianapolis 500; placed 9th at Indy in 1978.

Tony Gwynn (b.5/7/1960): Baseball OF; 4-time NL batting champion (1984,87-89) at San Diego; entered 1994 with .329 career average in 12 seasons; was hitting .394 on Aug. 12 when players' strike began.

Harvey Haddix (1925-94): Baseball LHP; pitched 12 perfect innings for Pittsburgh, but lost to Milwaukee in the 13th, 1-0 (May 26,1959).

Walter Hagen (1892-1969): Pro golf pioneer; won 2 U.S. Opens (1914,19), 4 British Opens (1922,24,28-29), 5 PGA Championships (1921,24-27) and 5 Western Opens; retired with 40 PGA wins; 6-time U.S. Ryder Cup captain.

Marvin Hagler (b.5/23/1954): Boxer; world middleweight champion 1980-87; pro record 62-3-2 with 52 KOs.

George Halas (1895-1983): Football pioneer; MVP in 1919 Rose Bowl; player-coach-owner of Chicago Bears from 1920-83; signed Red Grange in 1925; coached Bears for 40 seasons and won 7 NFL titles (1932-33,40-41,43,46,63); 2nd on all-time career list with 324 wins.

Dorothy Hamill (b.7/26/1956): Figure skater; won Olympic gold medal and world championship in 1976; Ice Capades headliner from 1977-84; bought financially strapped Ice Capades in 1993.

Scott Hamilton (b.8/28/1958): Figure skater; 4-time world champion (1981-84); won gold medal at 1984 Olympics.

Tonya Harding (b.11/12/1970): Figure skater; 1991 U.S. women's champion; involved in bizarre plot hatched by ex-husband Jeff Gillooly to injure rival Nancy Kerrigan on Jan. 6, 1994 and keep her off Olympic team; won '94 U.S. women's title in Kerrigan's absence; denied any role in assault and sued USOC when her berth on Olympic team was threatened; finished 8th at Lillehammer (Kerrigan recovered and won silver medal); pleaded guilty on Mar. 16 to conspiracy to hinder investigation; stripped of 1994 title by U.S. Figure Skating Assn.

Tom Harmon (1919-90): Football HB; 2-time All-America at Michigan; won Heisman Trophy in 1940; played with AFL NY Americans in 1941 and NFL LA Rams (1946-47); World War II fighter pilot who won Silver Star and Purple Heart; became radio-TV commentator.

Franco Harris (b.3/7/1950): Football RB; ran for over 1,000 yards a season 8 times; rushed for 12,120 yards in 13 years; led Pittsburgh to 4 Super Bowl titles.

Leon Hart (b.11/2/1928): Football E; only player to win 3 national championships in college and 3 more in the NFL; won his titles at Notre Dame (1946-47,49) and with Detroit Lions (1952-53,57); 3-time All-America and last lineman to win Heisman Trophy (1949); All-Pro on both offense and defense in 1951.

Bill Hartack (b.12/9/1932): Jockey; won Kentucky Derby 5 times (1957,60,62,64,69), Preakness 3 times (1956,64,69), but the Belmont only once (1960).

Doug Harvey (1924-90): Hockey D; 10-time All-NHL 1st team; won Norris Trophy 7 times (1955-58,60-62); led Montreal to 6 Stanley Cups.

Billy Haughton (1923-86): Harness racing; 4-time winner of Hambletonian; trainer-driver of pacing Triple Crown winner (1968); winner of 4,910 races in career.

Joao Havelange (b.5/8/1916): Soccer; Brazilian-born president of Federation Internationale de Football Assoc. (FIFA) since 1974; also member of International Olympic Committee.

John Havlicek (b.4/8/1940): Basketball; played in 3 NCAA Finals at Ohio St. (1960-62); led Boston to 8 NBA titles (1963-66,68-69,74,76); playoff MVP in 1974; 4-time All-NBA 1st team.

Bob Hayes (b.12/20/1942): Track & Field/Football; won gold medal in 100m at 1964 Olympics; All-Pro SE for Dallas in 1966; convicted of drug trafficking in 1979 and served 18 months of a 5-year sentence.

Woody Hayes (1913-87): Football; coached Ohio St. to 3 national titles (1954,57,68) and 4 Rose Bowl victories; 238 career wins.

Thomas Hearns (b.10/15/1958): Boxer; has held recognized world titles as welterweight, light middleweight, middleweight and light heavyweight; four career losses have come against Sugar Ray Leonard, Marvin Hagler and twice to Iran Barkley; entered 1994 with pro record of 51-4-1 and 42 KOs.

Eric Heiden (b.6/14/1958): Speedskater; 3-time overall world champion (1977-79), won all 5 men's gold medals at 1980 Olympics setting new records in each; Sullivan Award winner (1980).

Mel Hein (1909-92): Football C; NFL All-Pro 8 straight years (1933-40); MVP in 1938 with NY Giants; didn't miss a game in 15 seasons.

John W. Heisman (1869-1936): Football; coached at 9 colleges from 1892-1927; won 185 games; Director of Athletics at Downtown Athletic Club in NYC (1928-36); DAC named Heisman Trophy after him.

Carol Heiss (b.1/20/1940): Figure skater; 5-time world champion (1956-60); won Olympic silver medal in 1956 and gold in '60; married 1956 men's gold medalist Hayes Jenkins.

Rickey Henderson (b.12/25/1958): Baseball OF; AL playoff MVP (1989) and AL regular season MVP (1990); set single season base stealing record of 130 in 1982; has led AL in steals 11 times; broke Lou Brock's all-time record of 938 on May 1, 1991; entered 1994 season as all-time leader in steals (1,095) and HRs as leadoff batter (63).

Sonja Henie (1912-69): Norwegian figure skater; 10-time world champion (1927-36); won 3 consecutive Olympic gold medals (1928,32,36); became movie star.

Foster Hewitt (1902-85): Radio-TV; Canada's premier hockey play-by-play broadcaster from 1923-81; coined phrase, "He shoots...he scores!"

Graham Hill (1929-75): British auto racer; 2-time Formula One world champion (1962,68); won Indy 500 in 1966; killed in plane crash; father of Damon.

Phil Hill (b.4/20/1927): Auto racer; first U.S. driver to win Formula One championship (1961); 3 career wins (1958-64).

Max Hirsch (1880-1969): Horse racing; trained 1,933 winners from 1908-68; won Triple Crown with Assault in 1946.

Tommy Hitchcock (1900-44): Polo; world class player at 20; achieved 10-goal rating 18 times from 1922-40.

Lew Hoad (1934-94): Australian tennis player; 2-time Wimbledon winner (1956-57); won Aussie, French and Wimbledon titles in 1956, but missed capturing Grand Slam at Forest Hills when beaten by Ken Rosewall in 4-set final.

Ben Hogan (b.8/13/1912): Golfer; 4-time PGA Player of Year; one of only four players to win all four Grand Slam titles (others are Nicklaus, Player and Sarazen); won 4 U.S. Opens, 2 Masters, 2 PGAs and 1 British Open between 1946-53; only player to win three majors in one year when he won Masters, U.S. Open and British Open in 1953; nearly killed in Feb. 13, 1949 car accident, but came back to win U.S. Open in '50; third on all-time list with 63 career wins.

Eleanor Holm (b.12/6/1913): Swimmer; won gold medal in 100m backstroke at 1932 Olympics; thrown off '36 U.S. team for drinking champagne in public and shooting craps on boat to Germany.

Nat Holman (b.10/18/1896): Basketball pioneer; played pro with Original Celtics (1920-28); coached CCNY to both NCAA and NIT titles in 1950 (a year later, several of his players were caught up in a point-shaving scandal); 423 career wins.

Larry Holmes (b.11/3/1949): Boxer; heavyweight champion (WBC or IBF) from 1978-85; successfully defended title 20 times before losing to Michael Spinks; returned from first retirement in 1988 and was KO'd in 4th by then champ Mike Tyson; launched second comeback in 1991; was 42 years and 7 months old when he fought 29-year-old champion Evander Holyfield in 1992, and lost a 12-round decision; entered 1994 with pro record of 59-4 and 40 KOs.

Lou Holtz (b.1/6/1937): Football; coached Notre Dame to national title in 1988; 2-time Coach of Year (1977,88) entered 1994 season with 193-84-6 record in 24 seasons with 5 schools— Wm. & Mary (3 years), N.C. State (4), Arkansas (7), Minnesota (2) and ND (8); also coached NY Jets for 13 games (3-10) in 1976.

Evander Holyfield (b.10/19/1962): Boxer; missed shot at Olympic gold medal in 1984 when he lost controversial light heavy semifinal after knocking his opponent out (referee ruled it was a late hit); knocked out Buster Douglas in 3rd round to become world heavyweight champion on Oct. 25, 1990; 2 of 4 title defenses included decisions over 42-year-old ex-champs George Foreman and Larry Holmes; lost title to Riddick Bowe by unanimous decision on Nov. 13, 1992; beat Bowe by majority decision to reclaim title on Nov. 6, 1993; entered 1994 with pro record of 30-1 and 22 KOs, but lost title to Michael Moorer by majority decision on Apr. 22, 1994.

Red Holzman (b.8/10/1920): Basketball; played for NBL and NBA champions at Rochester (1946,51); coached NY Knicks to 2 NBA titles (1970,73); Coach of Year (1970); ranks 10th on all-time NBA list with 754 wins (including playoffs).

Rogers Hornsby (1896-1963): Baseball 2B; hit .400 three times, including .424 in 1924; led NL in batting 7 times; 2-time MVP (1925,29) with St. Louis; career average of .358 over 23 years is third highest.

Paul Hornung (b.12/23/1935): Football HB-PK; only Heisman Trophy winner to play for losing team (2-8 Notre Dame in 1956); 3-time NFL scoring leader (1959-61) at Green Bay; 176 points in 1960 all-time record; MVP in 1961; suspended by NFL for 1963 season for betting on his own team.

Gordie Howe (b.3/31/1928): Hockey RW; played 32 seasons in NHL and WHA from 1946-80; led NHL in scoring 6 times; All-NHL 1st team 12 times; MVP 6 times in NHL (1952-53,57-58,60,63) with Detroit and once in WHA (1974) with Houston; ranks 2nd on all-time NHL list in goals (801) and points (1,850) to Wayne Gretzky; played with sons Mark and Marty at Houston (1973-77) and New England-Hartford (1977-80).

Cal Hubbard (1900-77): Member of college football, pro football and baseball halls of fame; 9 years in NFL; 4-time All-Pro at end and tackle; AL umpire for 15 years (1936-51).

Carl Hubbell (1903-88): Baseball LHP; led NL in wins and ERA 3 times each; 2-time MVP (1933,36) with NY Giants; fanned Ruth, Gehrig, Foxx, Simmons and Cronin in succession in 1934 All-Star Game; 253 career wins.

Sam Huff (b.10/4/1934): Football LB; glamorized NFL's middle linebacker position with NY Giants from 1956-63; subject of "The Violent World of Sam Huff" TV special in 1961; helped lead club to 6 division titles and a world championship (1956).

Miller Huggins (1880-1929): Baseball; managed NY Yankees from 1918 until his death late in '29 season; led Yanks to 6 pennants and 3 World Series titles from 1921-28.

Wayne Huizenga (b.12/29/1937): Baseball, hockey and football owner; chairman of Blockbuster Entertainment, the video/music store powerhouse; paid $95 million for 1993 expansion Florida Marlins of NL; $50 million for 1993-94 expansion Florida Panthers of NHL; and $138 million for remaining 85% of NFL Miami Dolphins in 1994; also owns Joe Robbie Stadium.

Bobby Hull (b.1/3/1939): Hockey LW; led NHL in scoring 3 times; 2-time MVP (1965-66) with Chicago; All-NHL first team 10 times; jumped to WHA in 1972, 2-time MVP there (1973,75) with Winnipeg; scored 913 goals in both leagues; father of Brett.

Brett Hull (b.8/9/1964): Hockey RW; named NHL MVP in 1991 with St. Louis; holds single season RW scoring record with 86 goals; he and father Bobby have both won Hart (MVP), Lady Byng (sportsmanship) and All-Star Game MVP trophies.

Jim (Catfish) Hunter (b.4/8/1946): Baseball RHP; won 20 games or more 5 times (1971-75); played on 5 World Series winners with Oakland, NY Yankees; threw perfect game in 1968; won Cy Young Award in '74.

Ibrahim Hussein (b.6/3/1958): Kenyan distance runner; 3-time winner of Boston Marathon (1988,91-92) and 1st African runner to win in Boston; won New York Marathon in 1987.

Don Hutson (b.1/31/1913): Football E-PK; led NFL in receptions 8 times and interceptions once; 9-time All-Pro (1936, 38-45) for Green Bay; 99 career TD catches.

Flo Hyman (1954-86): Volleyball; 3-time All-America spiker at Houston and captain of 1984 U.S. Women's Olympic team; died of heart attack caused by Marfan Syndrome during a match in Japan in 1986; Women's Sports Foundation's Hyman Award for excellence and dedication named after her.

Hank Iba (1904-93): Basketball; coached Oklahoma A&M to 2 straight NCAA titles (1945-46); 767 career wins in 41 years; coached U.S. Olympic team to 2 gold medals (1964,68), but lost to Soviets in controversial '72 final.

Mike Ilitch (b.1929): Baseball and hockey owner; chairman of Little Caesar's, the international pizza chain; bought Detroit Red Wings of NHL for $8 milllion in 1982 and AL Detroit Tigers for $85 million in 1992.

Punch Imlach (1918-1987): Hockey; directed Toronto to 4 Stanley Cups (1962-64,67) in 11 seasons as GM-coach.

Miguel Indurain (b.7/16/1964): Spanish cyclist; won 4th straight Tour de France in 1994, equaling deeds of legends Jacques Anquetil of France and Eddy Merckx of Belgium; only Anquetil, Merckx and Bernard Hinault of France have won Tour 5 times.

Hale Irwin (b.6/3/1945): Golf; oldest player ever to win U.S. Open (45 in 1990); NCAA champion in 1967; entered 1994 with 19 PGA victories, including 3 U.S. Opens (1974,79,90); 5-time Ryder Cup team member.

Bo Jackson (b.11/30/1962): Baseball OF and Football RB; won Heisman Trophy in 1985 and MVP of baseball All-Star Game in 1989; starter for both baseball's KC Royals and NFL's LA Raiders in 1988 and '89; severely injured left hip Jan. 13, 1991, in NFL playoffs; waived by Royals but signed by Chicago White Sox in 1991; missed entire 1992 season recovering from hip surgery; played for White Sox in 1993 and California in '94.

Joe Jackson (1887-1951): Baseball OF; hit .300 or better 11 times; career average of .356 (see Black Sox).

Phil Jackson (b.9/17/1945): Basketball; NBA champion as reserve forward with New York in 1973 (injured when Knicks won in '70); coached Chicago to three straight NBA titles (1991-93); entered 1994-95 season with 356 wins (including playoffs) in just 5 seasons.

Reggie Jackson (b.5/18/1946): Baseball OF; led AL in HRs 4 times; MVP in 1973; played on 5 World Series winners with Oakland, NY Yankees; 1977 Series MVP with 5 HRs; 563 career HRs; all-time strikeout leader (2,597).

Helen Jacobs (b.8/8/1908): Tennis; 4-time winner of U.S. Championship (1932-35); Wimbledon winner in 1936; lost 4 Wimbledon finals to arch-rival Helen Wills Moody.

Jim Jacobs (1930-88): Handball/Boxing; won 12 U.S. Handball titles (6 singles and 6 doubles) from 1955-68; also managed 4 world champion boxers, including Mike Tyson from 1985-88.

Dan Jansen (b.6/17/1965): Speedskater; 1993 world record-holder in 500m; fell in 500m and 1,000m in 1988 Olympics at Calgary after learning of death of sister Jane; placed 4th in 500m and didn't attempt 1,000m 4 years later in Albertville; fell in 500m in '94 Games in Lillehammer, then finally won an Olympic medal with world record (1:12.43) effort in 1,000m; took victory lap with baby daughter Jane in his arms.

James J. Jeffries (1875-1953): Boxer; world heavyweight champion (1899-1905); retired undefeated but came back to fight Jack Johnson in 1910 and lost (KO,15th).

David Jenkins (b.6/29/1936): Figure skater; brother of Hayes; 3-time world champion (1957-59); won gold medal at 1960 Olympics.

Hayes Jenkins (b.3/23/1933): Figure skater; 4-time world champion (1953-56), won gold medal at 1956 Olympics; married 1960 women's gold medalist Carol Heiss.

Bruce Jenner (b.10/28/1949): Track & Field; won gold medal in 1976 Olympic decathlon.

Jackie Jensen (1927-82): Football RB and Baseball OF; consensus All-America at California in 1948; American League MVP with Boston Red Sox in 1958.

Bob Johnson (1931-91): Hockey; coached Pittsburgh Penguins to 1st Stanley Cup title in 1991; led Wisconsin to 3 NCAA titles (1973,77,81) in 15 years; also coached 1976 U.S. Olympic team and NHL Calgary (1982-87).

Ben Johnson (b.12/30/1961): Canadian sprinter; set 100m world record (9.83) at 1987 World Championships; won 100m at 1988 Olympics, but flunked drug test and forfeited gold medal; 1987 world record revoked in '89 for admitted steroid use; returned drug-free in 1991, but performed poorly; banned for life by IAAF in 1993 for testing positive after a meet in Montreal.

Earvin (Magic) Johnson (b.8/14/1959): Basketball G; led Michigan St. to NCAA title in 1979 and was tourney MVP; All-NBA 1st team 9 times; all-time NBA assist leader with 9,921; 3-time MVP (1987,89-90); led LA Lakers to 5 NBA titles; 3-time playoff MVP (1980, 82, 87); retired on Nov. 7, 1991, stating he was HIV-positive for AIDS; returned to score 25 points in 1992 NBA All-Star game and win 2nd MVP award; U.S. Olympic Dream Team member in '92; announced NBA comeback then retired again before start of 1992-93 season; named head coach of Lakers on Mar. 23, 1994; won first game, 110-101, over Milwaukee at soldout LA Forum, but finished season at 5-11 and quit; later named minority owner of team.

Jack Johnson (1878-1946): Boxer; controversial heavyweight champion (1908-15) and 1st black to hold title; defeated Tommy Burns for crown at age 30; fled to Europe in 1913 after Mann Act conviction; lost title to Jess Willard in Havana, but claimed to have taken a dive; pro record 78-8-12 with 45 KOs.

Jimmy Johnson (b.7/16/1943): Football; All-SWC defensive lineman on Arkansas' 1964 national championship team; coached Miami of Florida to national title in 1987; college record of 81-34-3 in 10 years; hired by old friend and new Dallas owner Jerry Jones to succeed Tom Landry in February 1989; went 1-15 in '89, then led Cowboys to consecutive Super Bowl victories in 1992 and '93 seasons; quit on Mar. 29, 1994 after feuding with Jones; became TV analyst.

Rafer Johnson (b.8/18/1935): Track & Field; won silver medal in 1956 Olympic decathlon and gold medal in 1960.

Walter Johnson (1887-1946): Baseball RHP; won 20 games or more 10 straight years; led AL in ERA 5 times, wins 6 times and strikeouts 12 times; twice MVP (1913, 24) with Washington; all-time leader in shutouts (113) and 2nd in wins (416).

Ben A. Jones (1882-1961): Horse racing; Calumet Farm trainer (1939-47); saddled 6 Kentucky Derby champions and 2 Triple Crown winners—Whirlaway in 1941 and Citation in '48.

Bobby Jones (1902-71): Won U.S. and British Opens plus U.S. and British Amateurs in 1930 to become golf's only Grand Slam winner ever; from 1922-30, won 4 U.S. Opens, 5 U.S. Amateurs, 3 British Opens, and played in 6 Walker Cups; founded Masters tournament in 1934.

Deacon Jones (b.12/9/1938): Football DE; 5-time All-Pro (1965-69) with LA Rams; all-time NFL sack leader with 172 in 14 years.

Jerry Jones (b.10/13/1942): Football; owner-GM of Dallas Cowboys; bought declining team (3-13) and Texas Stadium for $140 million in 1989; hired old friend and Univ. of Arkansas teammate Jimmy Johnson to replace legendary Tom Landry as coach; their partnership led Cowboys to back-to-back Super Bowl titles in 1992 and '93 seasons; when feud developed between the two, Jones accepted Johnson's resignation on Mar. 29, 1994 and hired Barry Switzer the next day.

Michael Jordan (b.2/17/1963): Basketball G; College Player of Year with North Carolina in 1984; has led NBA in scoring 7 years in a row (1987-93); 7-time All-NBA 1st team; 3-time regular season MVP (1988,91-92) and 3-time MVP of NBA Finals (1991-93); led U.S. Olympic team to gold medals in 1984 and '92; stunned sports world when he retired at age 30 on Oct. 6, 1993; signed as OF with Chicago White Sox and spent summer of '94 in Double A with Birmingham; barely hit his weight with .204 average.

Florence Griffith Joyner (b.12/21/1959): Track & Field; set world records in 100 and 200 meters in 1988; won 3 gold medals at '88 Olympics (100m, 200m, 4x100m relay); Sullivan Award winner (1988); retired in 1989; designed NBA Indiana Pacers uniforms (1990); named as co-chairperson of President's Council on Physical Fitness and Sports in 1993.

Jackie Joyner-Kersee (b.3/3/1962): Track & Field; 2-time world champion in both long jump (1987,91) and heptathlon (1987,93); won heptathlon gold medals at 1988 and '92 Olympics and LJ gold at '88 Games; has also won Olympic silver (1984) in heptathlon and bronze (1992) in LJ; Sullivan Award winner (1986); only woman to receive *The Sporting News* Man of Year award.

Alberto Juantorena (b.3/12/1951): Cuban runner; won both 400m and 800m gold medals at 1976 Olympics.

Sonny Jurgensen (b.8/23/1934): Football QB; played 18 seasons with Philadelphia and Washington; led NFL in passing twice (1967,69); All-Pro in 1961; 255 career TD passes.

Duke Kahanamoku (1890-1968): Swimmer; won 3 gold medals and 2 silver over 3 Olympics (1912, 20, 24); also surfing pioneer.

Al Kaline (b.12/19/1934): Baseball; youngest player (at age 20) to win batting title (led AL with .340 in 1955); had 3,007 hits, 399 HRs in 22 years with Detroit.

Anatoly Karpov (b.5/23/1951): Chess; Russian world champion from 1975-85; regained International Chess Federation (FIDE) version of championship in 1993 when countryman Garry Kasparov was stripped of title after forming new Professional Chess Association.

Garry Kasparov (b.4/13/1963): Chess; Azerbaijani who became youngest player (22 years, 210 days) ever to win world championship as Russian in 1985; defeated countryman Anatoly Karpov for title; split with International Chess Federation (FIDE) to form Professional Chess Association (PCA) in 1993; stripped of FIDE title in '93 but successfully defended PCA title against Briton Nigel Short.

Mike Keenan (b.10/21/1949): Hockey; coach who finally led NY Rangers to 1994 Stanley Cup title after 54 unsuccessful years; quit a month later in pay dispute and signed with St. Louis as coach-GM; entered 1994-95 season with 476 wins (including playoffs); also reached Stanley Cup finals with Philadelphia (1987) and Chicago (1992); coached Team Canada to Canada Cup wins in 1987 and '91.

Kipchoge (Kip) Keino (b.1/17/1940): Kenyan runner; young policeman who beat USA's Jim Ryun to win 1,500m gold medal at 1968 Olympics; won again in steeplechase at 1972 Summer Games; his success spawned long line of international distance champions from Kenya.

Johnny Kelley (b.9/6/1907): Distance runner, ran in his 61st and final Boston Marathon at age 84 in 1992, finishing in 5:58:36; won Boston twice (1935,45) and was 2nd 7 times.

Jim Kelly (b.2/14/1960): Football QB; has led Buffalo to four consecutive Super Bowl appearances, and is only QB to lose four times; named to AFC Pro Bowl team 5 times; entered 1994 season ranked 4th on all-time list with passer rating of 86.0.

Walter Kennedy (1912-77): Basketball; 2nd NBA commissioner (1963-75), league doubled in size to 18 teams during his term of office.

Nancy Kerrigan (b.10/13/1969): Figure skating; 1993 U.S. women's champion and '92 Olympic bronze medalist; victim of Jan. 6, 1994 assault at U.S. nationals in Detroit when Shane Stant clubbed her in right knee with a metal baton after a practice session; conspiracy hatched by Jeff Gillooly, ex-husband of rival Tonya Harding; unable to compete in nationals, she is granted a berth on the Olympic team by the U.S. Figure Skating Assn.; 7 weeks later in Lillehammer, she wins the silver medal, losing to Oksana Baiul by a 5-4 judges' vote.

Stanley Ketchel (1886-1910): Boxer; claimed 3 world titles—welterweight (1908,08-10), middleweight (1908-10) and light heavyweight (1909-10); murdered at age 24; pro record 53-4-5 with 50 KOs.

Harmon Killebrew (b.6/29/1936): Baseball 3B-1B; led AL in HRs 6 times and RBI 4 times; MVP in 1969 with Minnesota; 573 career HRs.

Jean-Claude Killy (b.8/30/1943): French alpine skier; 2-time World Cup champion (1967-68); won 3 gold medals at 1968 Olympics in Grenoble; co-president of 1992 Winter Games in Albertville.

Ralph Kiner (b.10/27/1922): Baseball OF; led NL in home runs 7 straight years (1946-52) with Pittsburgh; 369 career HRs.

Billie Jean King (b.11/22/1943): Tennis; women's rights pioneer; Wimbledon singles champ 6 times, U.S. champ 4 times; first woman athlete to earn $100,000 in one year (1971); beat 55-year-old Bobby Riggs 6-4, 6-3, 6-3, to win $100,000 in 1973.

Don King (b.8/20/1931): Boxing promoter; controlled heavyweight title from 1978-90 while Larry Holmes and Mike Tyson were champions; 1st major bout was Muhammad Ali's comeback fight in 1970; former numbers operator who served 4 years for manslaughter (1967-70); acquitted of tax evasion and fraud in 1985; indicted July 14, 1994 for allegedly bilking Lloyd's of London out of $350,000 on a false insurance claim involving a training injury to Julio Cesar Chavez in June 1991.

Tom Kite (b.12/9/1949): Golfer; entered 1994 as all-time PGA Tour money leader with over $8.5 million; finally won 1st major with victory in 1992 U.S. Open at Pebble Beach; NCAA champion (1972); PGA Rookie of Year (1973); PGA Player of Year (1989).

Gene Klein (1921-1990): Horseman; won 3 Eclipse awards as top owner (1985-87); filly Winning Colors won 1988 Kentucky Derby; also owned San Diego Chargers football team (1966-84).

Bob Knight (b.10/25/1940): Basketball; has coached Indiana to 3 NCAA titles (1976,81,87); 3-time Coach of Year (1975-76,89); 640 career wins in 29 years; coached 1984 U.S. Olympic team to gold medal.

Phillip Knight (b.2/24/1938): founder and chairman of Nike, Inc., the 23-year-old, $4 billion shoe and fitness company based in Beaverton, Ore.; named "The Most Powerful Man in Sports" by *The Sporting News* in 1992.

Olga Korbut (b.5/16/1955): Soviet gymnast; 3 gold medals at 1972 Olympics; first to perform back somersault on balance beam.

Johann Olav Koss (b.10/29/1968): Norwegian speedskater; won three gold medals at 1994 Olympics in Lillehammer with world records in the 1,500m, 5,000m and 10,000m; also won 1,500m gold and 10,000m silver in 1992 Games; retired shortly after Olympics.

Sandy Koufax (b.12/30/1935): Baseball LHP; led NL in strikeouts 4 times and ERA 5 straight years; won 3 Cy Young Awards (1963,65,66) with LA Dodgers; MVP in 1963; 2-time World Series MVP (1963,65); pitched 1 perfect game and 3 other no-hitters.

Alvin Kraenzlein (1876-1928): Track & Field; won 4 individual gold medals in 1900 Olympics (60m, long jump, and 110m & 200m hurdles).

Jack Kramer (b.8/1/1921): Tennis; Wimbledon singles champ 1947; U.S. champ 1946-47; promoter and Open pioneer.

Ingrid Kristiansen (b.3/21/1956): Norwegian runner; 2-time Boston Marathon winner (1986,89); won New York City Marathon in 1989; entered 1994 holding 2 world records recognized by IAAF- 5,000m and marathon.

Julie Krone (b.7/24/1963): jockey; only woman to ride winning horse in a Triple Crown race when she captured Belmont Stakes aboard Colonial Affair in 1993; entered 1994 as all-time winningest female jockey with 2,762 wins.

Mike Krzyzewski (b.2/13/1947): Basketball; has coached Duke to 7 Final Four appearances in last 9 years; won consecutive NCAA titles in 1991 and '92; entered 1994-95 season with 19-year record of 422-183.

Alan Kulwicki (1954-93): Auto racer; 1992 NASCAR national champion; 1st college grad and Northerner to win title; NASCAR Rookie of Year in 1986; famous for driving car backwards on victory lap; killed at age 38 in plane crash near Bristol, Tenn., on April 1, 1993.

Marion Ladewig (b.10/30/1914): named Woman Bowler of the Year 9 times, (1950-54,57-59,63).

Guy Lafleur (b.9/20/1951): Hockey RW; led NHL in scoring 3 times (1975-78); 2-time MVP (1977-78), played for 5 Stanley Cup winners in Montreal; playoff MVP in 1977; returned to NHL as player in 1988 after election to Hall of Fame; retired again in 1991.

Napoleon (Nap) Lajoie (1875-1959): Baseball 2B; led AL in batting 3 times (1901,03-04); batted .422 in 1901; hit .338 for career with 3,244 hits.

Jack Lambert (b.7/8/1952): Football LB; 6-time All-Pro (1975-76,79-82); led Pittsburgh to 4 Super Bowl titles.

Kenesaw Mountain Landis (1866-1944): U.S. District Court judge who became first baseball commissioner (1920-44); banned Black Sox for life.

Tom Landry (b.9/11/1924): Football; coached Dallas for 29 years (1960-88); won 2 Super Bowls (1972,78); 271 career wins.

Steve Largent (b.9/28/1954): Football WR; retired in 1989 after 14 years in Seattle with then NFL records in passes caught (819) and TD passes caught (100).

Don Larsen (b.8/7/1929): Baseball RHP; pitched only perfect game in World Series history—NY Yankees 2, Brooklyn 0 (Oct.8,1956); Series MVP that year.

Tommy Lasorda (b.9/22/1927): Baseball; has managed LA Dodgers to 2 World Series titles (1981,88) in 4 appearances; entered 1994 season with 1,422 regular-season wins in 18 years.

Larissa Latynina (b.1934): Soviet gymnast; won total of 18 medals, (9 gold) in 3 Olympics (1956,60,64).

Nikki Lauda (b.2/22/1949): Austrian auto racer; 3-time world Formula One champion (1975,77,84), 25 career wins from 1971-85.

Rod Laver (b.8/9/1938): Australian tennis player; only player to win Grand Slam twice (1962,69); Wimbledon champion 4 times; 1st to earn $1 million in prize money.

Andrea Mead Lawrence (b.4/19/1932): Alpine skier; won 2 gold medals at 1952 Olympics.

Bobby Layne (1926-86): Football QB; college star at Texas; master of 2-minute offense; led Detroit to 4 divisional titles and 3 NFL championships in 1950s.

Frank Leahy (1908-73): Football; coached Notre Dame to four national titles (1943,46-47,49); career record of 107-13-9 for a winning pct. of .864.

Brian Leetch (b.3/3/1968): Hockey D; NHL Rookie of Year in 1989; won Norris Trophy as top defenseman in 1992; Conn Smythe Trophy winner as playoffs' MVP in 1994 when he helped lead NY Rangers to 1st Stanley Cup title in 54 years.

Mario Lemieux (b.10/5/1965): Hockey C; 4-time NHL scoring leader (1988-89,92-93); Rookie of Year (1985); 3-time All-NHL 1st team (1988-89,93); 2-time regular season MVP (1988,93); 3-time All-Star Game MVP; led Pittsburgh to consecutive Stanley Cup titles (1991 and '92) and was playoff MVP both years; won 1993 scoring title despite missing 24 games to undergo radiation treatments for Hodgkin's disease; missed 62 games during 1993-94 season mostly due to back injuries; announced on Aug. 29, 1994 he would sit out 1994-95 season due to fatigue.

Greg LeMond (b.6/26/1961): Cyclist; 3-time Tour de France winner (1986,89-90); only American to win the event.

Ivan Lendl (b.3/7/1960): Tennis; No.1 player in world 4 times (1985-87,89); has won both French and U.S. Opens 3 times and Australian twice; entered 1994 with 94 career tournament wins.

Suzanne Lenglen (1899-1938): French tennis player; dominated women's tennis from 1919-26; won both Wimbledon and French singles titles 6 times.

Sugar Ray Leonard (b.5/17/1956): Boxer; light welterweight Olympic champ (1976); won world welterweight title 1979 and four more titles; retired after losing to Terry Norris on Feb. 9, 1991, with record of 36-2-1 and 25 KOs.

Marv Levy (b.8/3/1928): Football; has coached Buffalo to four consecutive Super Bowls, but is one of two coaches who are 0-4 (Bud Grant is the other); won two CFL Grey Cups with Montreal in 1974 and '77; entered 1994 season with 120 NFL wins in 13 years and 50 in 5 CFL seasons.

Carl Lewis (b.7/1/1961): Track & Field; won 4 Olympic gold medals in 1984 (100m, 200m, 4x100m, LJ), 2 more in '88 (100m, LJ) and 2 more in '92 (4x100m, LJ) for a career total of 8; has record 8 World Championship titles and 9 medals in all; Sullivan Award winner in 1981; entered 1994 as world record-holder in 100m (9.86) and with 67 long jumps over 28 feet.

Lennox Lewis (b.9/2/1965): British boxer; declared WBC heavyweight champion on Dec. 14, 1992, when world champion Riddick Bowe renounced WBC belt; defeated Bowe for super heavyweight gold medal at 1988 Olympics; entered 1994 undefeated in 24 fights with 20 KOs.

Nancy Lieberman-Cline (b.7/1/1958): Basketball; 3-time All-America and 2-time Player of Year (1979-80); led Old Dominion to consecutive AIAW titles in 1979 and '80; played in defunct WPBL and WABA and became 1st woman to play in men's pro league (USBL) in 1986.

Sonny Liston (1932-70): Boxer; heavyweight champ (1962-64); lost title to Muhammad Ali (then Cassius Clay) in 1964; pro record 50-4 with 39 KOs.

Vince Lombardi (1913-70): Football; coached Green Bay to 5 NFL titles; won first 2 Super Bowls (1967-68); career 105-35-6 record and all-time win percentage of .740; Super Bowl trophy named in his honor.

Johnny Longden (b.2/14/1907): Jockey; first to win 6,000 races; rode Count Fleet to Triple Crown in 1943.

Nancy Lopez (b.1/6/1957): Golfer; 4-time LPGA Player of the Year (1978-79,85,88); Rookie of Year (1977); 3-time winner of LPGA Championship; reached Hall of Fame by age 30 with 35 victories; entered 1994 with 47 career wins.

Donna Lopiano (b.9/11/1946): former basketball and softball star who was women's athletic director at Texas for 18 years before leaving to become executive director of Women's Sports Foundation in 1992.

Greg Louganis (b.1/29/1960): U.S. diver; won platform and springboard gold medals at both 1984 and '88 Olympics.

Joe Louis (1914-81): Boxer; world heavyweight champion (1937-49); reign of 11 years, 8 months longest in division history; pro record 63-3 with 49 KOs.

Sid Luckman (b.11/21/1916): Football QB; 6-time All-Pro; led Chicago Bears to 4 NFL titles (1940-41,43,46); MVP in 1943.

Hank Luisetti (b.6/16/1916): Basketball F; 3-time All-America at Stanford (1935-38); revolutionized game with one-handed shot.

Johnny Lujack (b.1/4/1925): Football QB; led Notre Dame to three national titles (1943,46-47); won Heisman Trophy in 1947.

D. Wayne Lukas (b.9/2/1935): Horse racing; 3-time Eclipse Award-winning trainer who has saddled two Horses of Year— Lady's Secret (1988) and Criminal Type (1990); led all trainers in money won 10 straight years (1983-92); won 2nd Preakness and 2nd Belmont in 1994 with Tabasco Cat.

Gen. Douglas MacArthur (1880-1964): Controversial U.S. general of World War II and Korea; president of U.S. Olympic Committee (1927-28); college football devotee; National Football Foundation MacArthur Bowl (for No.1 team) named after him.

Connie Mack (1862-1956): Baseball owner; managed Philadelphia A's until he was 87 (1901-50); all-time major league wins leader with 3,755, including postseason; won 9 AL pennants and 5 World Series (1910-11,13,29-30); also finished last 18 times.

Andy MacPhail (b.4/5/1953): Baseball; general manager of 2 World Series champions in Minnesota (1987,91), the first title coming at age 34; son of Lee.

Larry MacPhail (1890-1975): Baseball executive and innovator; introduced major leagues to night games at Cincinnati (May 24, 1935); won pennant in Brooklyn (1941) and World Series with NY Yankees (1947); father of Lee.

Lee MacPhail (b.10/25/1917): Baseball; AL president (1974-83); president of owners' Player Relations Committee (1984-85); also GM of Baltimore (1959-65) and NY Yankees (1967-74); father of Andy.

John Madden (b.4/10/1936): Football; won 112 games and a Super Bowl (1976 season) as coach of Oakland Raiders; won 9 Emmy Awards as television analyst with CBS; he and partner Pat Summerall moved over to Fox in 1994 after CBS lost NFL rights; signed 4-year, $32 million deal with Fox on Jan. 24— a richer contract than any NFL player.

Greg Maddux (b.4/14/1966): Baseball RHP; won back-to-back NL Cy Young Awards with Cubs (1992) and Atlanta (1993); led NL in wins (16) and ERA (1.56) on Aug. 12 when 1994 players' strike began.

Larry Mahan (b.11/21/1943): Rodeo; 6-time All-Around world champion (1966-70,73).

Phil Mahre (b.5/10/1957): Alpine skier; 3-time World Cup overall champ (1981-83); finished 1-2 with twin brother Steve in 1984 Olympic slalom.

Karl Malone (b.7/24/1963): Basketball F; 6-time All-NBA 1st team (1989-93) with Utah; member of the 1992 Olympic Dream Team.

Moses Malone (b.3/23/1955): Basketball C; signed with Utah of ABA at age 19; has led NBA in rebounding 6 times; 4-time All-NBA 1st team; 3-time NBA MVP (1979,82-83); playoff MVP with Philadelphia in 1983.

Nigel Mansell (b.8/8/1953): British auto racer; won 1992 Formula One driving championship with record 9 victories and 14 poles; quit Grand Prix circuit to race Indy cars in 1993; 1st rookie to win IndyCar title; 3rd driver to win IndyCar and F1 titles; will return to F1 circuit after 1994 IndyCar season.

Mickey Mantle (b.10/20/1931): Baseball OF; led AL in home runs 4 times; won Triple Crown in 1956; 3-time MVP (1956-57,62); 536 career HRs; played on 7 World Series winners with NY Yankees.

Diego Maradona (b.10/30/1960): Soccer F; captain and MVP of 1986 World Cup champion Argentina; also led national team to 1990 World Cup final; consensus Player of Decade in 1980s; led Napoli to 2 Italian League titles (1987,90) and UEFA Cup (1989); tested positive for cocaine and suspended 15 months by FIFA in March, 1991; overcame fitness problems and two failed comebacks to return to World Cup as Argentine captain in 1994, but was kicked out of tournament after two games when doping test found 5 banned substances in his urine; suspended 15 months by FIFA on Aug. 24, 1994; announced retirement two days later.

Pete Maravich (1948-88): Basketball; NCAA scoring leader 3 times (1968-70); averaged 44.2 points a game over career; Player of Year in 1970; NBA scoring champ in 1977.

Alice Marble (1913-90): Tennis; 4-time U.S. champion (1936,38-40); won Wimbledon in 1939; swept U.S. singles, doubles and mixed doubles from 1938-40.

Gino Marchetti (b.1/2/1927): Football DE; 8-time NFL All-Pro (1957-64) with Baltimore Colts.

Rocky Marciano (1923-69): Boxer; heavyweight champion (1952-56); retired undefeated; pro record of 49-0 with 43 KOs; killed in plane crash.

Juan Marichal (b.10/24/1937): Baseball RHP; won 21 or more games 6 times for S.F. Giants from 1963-69; ended 16-year career with 243 wins.

Dan Marino (b.9/15/1961): Football QB; 4-time leading passer in AFC (1983-84,86,89); set NFL singleseason records for TD passes (48) and passing yards (5,084) with Miami in 1984; entered 1994 season ranked 2nd in career TD passes (298) and 3rd in passing yards (40,720).

Roger Maris (1934-85): Baseball OF; broke Babe Ruth's single season HR record with 61 in 1961; 2-time AL MVP (1960-61) with NY Yankees.

Billy Martin (1928-89): Baseball; 5-time manager of NY Yankees; won 2 pennants and 1 World Series (1977); also managed Minnesota, Detroit, Texas and Oakland; played 2B on 4 Yankee world champions in 1950s.

Eddie Mathews (b.10/13/1931): Baseball 3B; led NL in HRs twice (1953,59); hit 30 or more home runs 9 straight years; 512 career HRs.

Christy Mathewson (1880-1925): Baseball RHP; won 22 or more games 12 straight years (1903-14); 373 career wins; pitched 3 shutouts in 1905 World Series.

Bob Mathias (b.11/17/1930): Track & Field; youngest winner of decathlon with gold medal in 1948 Olympics at age 17; first to repeat as decathlon champ in 1952; Sullivan Award winner (1948); 4-term member of U.S. Congress (R,Calif.) from 1967-74.

Ollie Matson (b.5/1/1930): Football HB; All-America at San Francisco (1951); bronze medal winner in 400m at 1952 Olympics; 4-time All-Pro for NFL Chicago Cardinals (1954-57); traded to LA Rams for 9 players in 1959; accounted for 12,884 all-purpose yards and scored 73 TDs in 14 seasons.

Willie Mays (b.5/6/1931): Baseball OF; led NL in HRs and stolen bases 4 times each; 2-time MVP (1954,65) with NY-SF Giants; played in 24 All-Star Games; 660 HRs and 3,283 hits in career.

Bill Mazeroski (b.9/5/1936): Baseball 2B; career .260 hitter who won the 1960 World Series for Pittsburgh with a lead-off HR in the bottom of the 9th inning of Game 7; the pitcher was Ralph Terry of the NY Yankees, the count was 1-0 and the score was tied 9-9; also a sure-fielder, Maz won 8 gold gloves in 17 seasons.

Joe McCarthy (1887-1978): Baseball; managed NY Yankees to 8 pennants and 7 World Series titles (1931-46).

Mark McCormack (b.11/6/1930): founder and CEO of International Management Group, the sports management conglomerate.

Pat McCormick (b.5/12/1930): U.S. diver; won women's platform and springboard gold medals in both 1952 and '56 Olympics.

Willie McCovey (b.1/10/1938): Baseball 1B; led NL in HRs 3 times and RBI twice; MVP in 1969 with SF; 521 career HRs.

Jack McDowell (b.1/16/1966): Baseball RHP; 2-time 20-game winner (1992-93) and '93 Cy Young winner with Chicago White Sox; won championship game for Stanford in 1987 College World Series; member of progressive rock group Magenta (formerly V.I.E.W.).

John McEnroe (b.2/16/1959): Tennis; No.1 player in the world 4 times (1981-84); 4-time U.S. Open singles champ (1979-81,84); 3-time Wimbledon champ (1981,83-84); has played on 5 Davis Cup winners (1978-79,81-82,92); won NCAA singles title (1978); entered 1993 with 77 championships in singles, 77 more in doubles (including 9 Grand Slam titles), and American Davis Cup records for years played (13) and singles matches won (41).

John McGraw (1873-1934): Baseball; managed NY Giants to 10 NL pennants and 3 World Series titles in 30 years; 2,810 career wins, including postseason.

Frank McGuire (b.11/8/1916): Basketball; winner of 731 games as high school, college and pro coach; only coach to win 100 games at 3 colleges—St. John's (103), North Carolina (164) and South Carolina (283); won 550 games in 30 college seasons; 1957 UNC team went 32-0 and beat Kansas 54-53 in triple OT to win NCAA title; coached NBA Philadelphia Warriors to 49-31 record in 1961-62 season but refused to move with team to San Francisco.

Jim McKay (b.9/24/1921): Radio-TV; host and commentator of ABC's Olympic coverage and "Wide World of Sports" show since 1961; 12-time Emmy winner; also given Peabody Award in 1988 and Life Achievement Emmy in 1990; became part owner of Baltimore Orioles in 1993.

John McKay (b.7/5/1923): Football; coached USC to 3 national titles (1962,67,72); won Rose Bowl 5 times; reached NFL playoffs 3 times with Tampa Bay.

Denny McLain (b.3/29/1944): Baseball RHP; last pitcher to win 30 games (1968); 2-time Cy Young winner (1968-69) with Detroit; convicted of racketeering, extortion and drug possession in 1985, served 29 months of 25-year jail term, sentence overturned when court ruled he had not received a fair trial.

Rick Mears (b.12/3/1951): Auto racer; 3-time CART national champ (1979,81-82); 4-time winner of Indianapolis 500 (1979,84,88,91) and only driver to win 6 Indy 500 poles; Indy 500 Rookie of Year (1978); retired after 1992 season with 29 IndyCar wins and 40 poles.

Mark Messier (b.1/18/1961): Hockey C; 2-time Hart Trophy winner as MVP with Edmonton (1990) and NY Rangers (1992); captain of Rangers team that finally won 1st Stanley Cup since 1940; entered 1994-95 season with 478 regular season goals; ranked 2nd (behind Gretzky) in all-time playoff points with 259.

Debbie Meyer (b.8/14/1952): Swimmer; 1st swimmer to win 3 individual gold medals at one Olympics (1968).

George Mikan (b.6/18/1924): Basketball C; 3-time All-America (1944-46); led DePaul to NIT title (1945); led Minneapolis Lakers to 5 NBA titles in 6 years (1949-54); Commissioner of ABA (1967-69).

Stan Mikita (b.5/20/1940): Hockey C; led NHL in scoring 4 times; won both MVP and Lady Byng awards in 1967 and '68 with Chicago.

Cheryl Miller (b.1/3/1964): Basketball; 3-time college Player of Year (1984-86); led USC to NCAA title and U.S. to Olympic gold medal in 1984; returned to lead USC to 26-4 record as 1st-year head coach in 1993-94.

Del Miller (b.7/5/1913): Harness racing; driver, trainer, owner, breeder, seller and track owner; drove to 2,441 wins from 1939-90.

Marvin Miller (b.4/14/1917): Baseball labor leader; executive director of Players' Assn. from 1966-82; increased average salary from $19,000 to over $240,000; led 13-day strike in 1972 and 50-day walkout in '81.

Shannon Miller (b.3/10/1977): Gymnast; won 5 medals in 1992 Olympics; All-Around women's world champion in 1993 and '94.

Billy Mills (b.6/30/1938): Track & Field; upset winner of 10,000m gold medal at 1964 Olympics.

Bora Milutinovic (b.9/7/1944): Soccer; Serbian coach who has run U.S. national team since 1991; led Americans into 2nd round of 1994 World Cup where they lost to eventual winner Brazil, 1-0; also coached Costa Rica to 2nd round of 1990 World Cup and Mexico to 6th place finish in 1986 World Cup.

Tommy Moe (b.2/17/1970): Alpine skier; won Downhill and placed 2nd in Super-G at 1994 Winter Olympics; 1st U.S. man to win 2 Olympic alpine medals in one year.

Paul Molitor (b.8/22/1956): Baseball DH/OF; All-America SS at Minnesota in 1976; signed as free agent by Toronto on Dec. 7, 1992, after 15 years with Milwaukee; led Blue Jays to 2nd straight World Series title as MVP; has hit .418 in 2 Series appearances (1982,93); entered 1994 season with lifetime .306 average.

Joe Montana (b.6/11/1956): Football QB: led Notre Dame to national title in 1977; led San Francisco to 4 Super Bowl titles in 1980s; only 3-time Super Bowl MVP; 2-time NFL MVP (1989-90); has led NFL in passing 5 times; missed all of 1991 season and nearly all of '92 after elbow surgery; traded to Kansas City on Apr. 20, 1993; entered '94 season ranked 1st in all-time passing efficiency (93.1), 4th in TD passes (257) and 5th in yards passing (37,268).

Helen Wills Moody (b.10/6/1905): Tennis; won 8 Wimbledon singles titles, 7 U.S. and 4 French from 1923-38.

Warren Moon (b.11/18/1956): Football QB; MVP of 1978 Rose Bowl with Washington; MVP of CFL with Edmonton in 1983; led Eskimos to 5 consecutive Grey Cup titles (1978-82) and was playoff MVP twice (1980,82); joined Houston of NFL in 1984; led NFL in attempts, completions and yards in 1990 and '91; picked for 7 Pro Bowls; traded to Minnesota in 1994.

Archie Moore (b.12/13/1913): Boxer; world light-heavyweight champion (1952-60); pro record 199-26-8 with 145 KOs.

Michael Moorer (b.11/12/1967): Boxing; won world heavyweight title with majority decision over champion Evander Holyfield on Apr. 11, 1994; undefeated record as of then was 35-0 with 30 KOs.

Noureddine Morceli (b.2/28/1970): Algerian runner; 2-time world champion at 1,500 meters (1991,93); set world records in 1,500m (3:28.82) in 1992, mile (3:44.39) in '93 and 3,000m (7:25.11) in '94.

Howie Morenz (1902-37): Hockey C; 3-time NHL MVP (1928,31-32); led Montreal Canadiens to 3 Stanley Cups; voted Outstanding Player of the Half-Century in 1950.

Joe Morgan (b.9/19/1943): Baseball 2B; led NL in walks 4 times; regular season MVP both years he led Cincinnati to World Series titles (1975-76).

Bobby Morrow (b.10/15/1935): Track & Field; won 3 gold medals at 1956 Olympics (100m, 200m and 4x400m relay).

Willie Mosconi (b.6/27/1913): Pocket Billiards; 14-time world champion from 1941-57.

Annemarie Moser-Pröll (b.3/27/1953): Austrian alpine skier; won World Cup overall title 6 times (1971-75,79); won Downhill in 1980 Olympics.

Edwin Moses (b.8/31/1955): Track & Field; won 400m hurdles at 1976 and '84 Olympics, bronze medal in '88; also winner of 122 consecutive races from 1977-87.

Stirling Moss (b.9/17/1929): Auto racer; won 194 of 466 career races and 16 Formula One events, but was never world champion.

Marion Motley (b.6/5/1920): Football FB; all-time leading AAFC rusher; rushed for over 4,700 yards and 31 TDs for Cleveland Browns (1946-53).

Dale Murphy (b.3/12/1956): Baseball OF; led NL in RBI 3 times and HRs twice; 2-time MVP (1982-83) with Atlanta; also played with Philadelphia and Colorado; retired May 27, 1993, with 398 HRs.

Jim Murray (b.12/29/1919): sports columnist for LA Times since 1961; 14-time Sportswriter of the Year; won Pulitzer Prize for commentary in 1990.

Ty Murray (b.10/11/1969): Rodeo cowboy; 5-time All-Around world champion (1989-93); Rookie of Year in 1988; youngest (age 20) to win All-Around title; set single season earnings mark with $297,896 in 1993.

Stan Musial (b.11/21/1920): Baseball OF-1B; led NL in batting 7 times; 3-time MVP (1943,46,48) with St. Louis; played in 24 All-Star Games; had 3,630 career hits and .331 average.

John Naber (b.1/20/1956): Swimmer; won 4 gold medals and a silver in 1976 Olympics.

Bronko Nagurski (1908-90): Football FB-T; All-America at Minnesota (1929); All-Pro with Chicago Bears (1932-34); charter member of college and pro halls of fame.

James Naismith (1861-1939): Canadian physical education instructor who invented basketball in 1891 at the YMCA Training School (now Springfield College) in Springfield, Mass.

Joe Namath (b.5/31/1943): Football QB; signed for unheard-of $400,000 as rookie with AFL's NY Jets in 1965; 2-time All-AFL (1968-69) and All-NFL (1972); led Jets to Super Bowl as MVP in '69.

Ilie Nastase (b.7/19/1946): Romanian tennis player; No.1 in the world twice (1972-73); won U.S. (1972) and French (1973) Opens.

Martina Navratilova (b.10/18/1956): Tennis; No.1 player in the world 7 times (1978-79,82-86); won her record 9th Wimbledon singles title in 1990; also won 4 U.S. Opens, 3 Australian and 2 French; in all, won 18 Grand Slam singles titles and 38 Grand Slam doubles titles; had 861 match record in singles in 1983; entered 1994 as all-time women's leader in singles titles (166) and money won ($19.4 million) over 20 years; reached 12th Wimbledon final in '94, losing to Conchita Martinez; will retire after '94 season.

Earle (Greasy) Neale (1891-1973): Hit .357 for Cincinnati in 1919 World Series; also played with pre-NFL Canton Bulldogs; later coached Philadelphia Eagles to 2 NFL titles (1948-49).

Primo Nebiolo (b.7/14/1923): Italian president of International Amateur Athletic Federation (IAAF) since 1981; also an at-large member of International Olympic Committee; regarded as dictatorial, but credited with elevating track & field to world class financial status.

Byron Nelson (b.2/14/1912): Golfer; won Masters and PGA twice, U.S. Open once; also won 11 consecutive tournaments (19 overall) in 1945.

Lindsey Nelson (b.5/25/1919): Radio-TV; all-purpose play-by-play broadcaster for CBS, NBC and others; 4-time Sportscaster of the Year (1959-62); voice of Cotton Bowl for 25 years and NY Mets from 1962-78; given Life Achievement Emmy Award in 1991.

Ernie Nevers (1903-76): Football FB; earned 11 letters in four sports at Stanford; played pro football, baseball and basketball; scored 40 points for Chicago Cardinals in one NFL game (1929).

Paula Newby-Fraser (b.6/2/1962): Zimbabwean triathlete; 5-time winner of Ironman Triathlon in Hawaii; holds women's record of 8:55:28.

John Newcombe (b.5/23/1943): Australian tennis player; No.1 player in world 3 times (1967,70-71); won Wimbledon 3 times and U.S. and Australian championships twice each.

Bob Neyland (1892-1962): Football; 3-time coach at Tennessee; had 173-31-12 record in 21 years; won national title in 1951; Vols' stadium named for him; also Army general who won Distinguished Service Cross as supply officer in World War II.

Jack Nicklaus (b.1/21/1940): Golfer; all-time leader in major tournament wins with 20—including 6 Masters, 5 PGAs, 4 U.S. Opens and 3 British Opens; oldest player to win Masters (46 in 1986); PGA Player of Year 5 times (1967,72-73,75-76); named Golfer of Century by PGA in 1988; 6-time Ryder Cup player and 2-time captain (1983,87); won NCAA title (1961) and 2 U.S. Amateurs (1959,61); entered 1994 with 70 PGA Tour wins (2nd to Sam Snead's 81); won 2nd U.S. Senior Open in 1993.

Chuck Noll (b.1/5/1932): Football; coached Pittsburgh to 4 Super Bowl titles (1975-76,79-80); retired after 1991 season ranked 5th on all-time list with 209 wins (including playoffs) in 23 years.

Greg Norman (b.2/10/1955): Australian golfer; 2-time leading money winner on PGA Tour (1986,90); entered 1994 with 63 tournament wins worldwide; 2-time British Open winner (1986,93); lost Masters by a stroke in both 1986 (to Jack Nicklaus) and '87 (to Larry Mize) in sudden death).

James D. Norris (1906-66): boxing promoter and NHL owner; president of International Boxing Club from 1949 until U.S. Supreme Court ordered its break-up (for anti-trust violations) in 1958; only NHL owner to win Stanley Cups in two cities—Detroit (1936-37,43) and Chicago (1961).

Paavo Nurmi (1897-1973): Finnish runner; won 9 gold medals (6 individual) in 1920, '24 and '28 Olympics; from 1921-31 broke 23 world outdoor records in events ranging from 1500 to 20,000 meters.

Dan O'Brien (b.7/18/1966): Track & Field; set world record in decathlon (8,891 pts) on Sept. 4-5, 1992, after failing to qualify for event at U.S. Olympic Trials; two-time gold medalist at World Championships (1991,93).

Larry O'Brien (1917-90): Basketball; former U.S. Postmaster General and 3rd NBA commissioner (1975-84), league absorbed 4 ABA teams and created salary cap during his term in office.

Parry O'Brien (b.1/28/1932): Track & field; in 4 consecutive Olympics, won two gold medals, a silver and placed 4th in the shot put (1952-64).

Al Oerter (b.8/19/1936): Track & Field; his 4 discus gold medals in consecutive Olympics from 1956-68 is an unmatched Olympic record.

Sadaharu Oh (b.5/20/1940): Baseball 1B; led Japan League in HRs 15 times; 9-time MVP for Tokyo Giants; hit 868 HRs in 22 years.

Hakeem Olajuwon (b.1/21/1963): Basketball C; Nigerian native who was consensus All-America in 1984 and Final Four MVP in 1983 for Houston; overall 1st pick by Houston Rockets in 1984 NBA Draft; led Rockets to 1994 NBA championship as regular season and playoff MVP; 5-time All-NBA 1st team (1987-89,93-94).

Jose Maria Olazabal (b.2/5/1966): Spanish golfer; entered 1994 season with 11 worldwide victories; won 1st major at '94 Masters.

Barney Oldfield (1878-1946): Auto racing pioneer; drove cars built by Henry Ford; first man to drive car a mile per minute (1903).

Walter O'Malley (1903-79): Baseball owner; moved Brooklyn Dodgers to Los Angeles after 1957 season; won 4 World Series (1955,59,63,65).

Shaquille O'Neal (b.3/6/1972): Basketball C; 2-time All-America at LSU (1991-92); overall 1st pick (as a junior) by Orlando in 1992 NBA Draft; Rookie of Year in 1993; helped led Dream Team II to world championship in 1994.

Bobby Orr (b.3/20/1948): Hockey D; 8-time Norris Trophy winner as best defenseman; led NHL in scoring twice and assists 5 times; All-NHL 1st team 8 times; regular season MVP 3 times (1970-72); playoff MVP twice (1970,72) with Boston.

Tom Osborne (b.2/23/1937): Football; entered 1994 season with record of 206-47-3 in 21 seasons as coach at Nebraska; his win percentage of .811 is best of any active coach in Division I-A; yet to win national championship.

Mel Ott (1909-58): Baseball OF; joined NY Giants at age 16; led NL in HRs 6 times; had 511 HRs and 1,860 RBI in 22 years.

Kristin Otto (b.1966): East German swimmer; 1st woman to win 6 gold medals (4 individual) at one Olympics (1988).

Francis Ouimet (1893-1967): Golfer; won 1913 U.S. Open as 20-year-old amateur playing on Brookline, Mass. course where he used to caddie; won U.S. Amateur twice; 8-time Walker Cup player.

Steve Owen (1898-1964): Football; All-Pro guard (1927); coached NY Giants for 23 years (1931-53); won 153 career games and 2 NFL titles (1934,38).

Jesse Owens (1913-80): Track & Field; broke 5 world records at Big 10 Championships (May 25, 1935); a year later, won 4 gold medals (100m, 200m, 4x100m relay and long jump) at Berlin Olympics.

Alan Page (b.8/7/1945): Football DE; consensus All-America at Notre Dame in 1966 and member of two national championship teams; 6-time NFL All-Pro and 1971 Player of Year with Minnesota Vikings; also a lawyer who was elected to Minnesota Supreme Court in 1992.

Satchel Paige (1906-82): Baseball RHP; pitched 55 career no-hitters over 20 seasons in Negro Leagues, entered Major Leagues with Cleveland in 1948 at age 42; had 28-31 record in 5 years; returned to AL at age 59 to start 1 game for Kansas City in 1965; went 3 innings, gave up a hit and got a strikeout.

Arnold Palmer (b.9/10/1929): Golf; winner of 4 Masters, 2 British Opens and 1 U.S. Open; 2-time PGA Player of Year (1960,62); 1st player to earn over $1 million in career (1968); annual PGA Tour money leader award named after him; entered 1994 with 60 wins on PGA Tour and 10 more on Senior Tour.

Jim Palmer (b.10/15/1945): Baseball RHP; 3-time Cy Young Award winner (1973,75-76); won 20 or more games 8 times with Baltimore; 1991 comeback attempt at age 45 scrubbed in spring training.

Bill Parcells (b.8/22/1941): Football; coached NY Giants to 2 Super Bowl titles (1986,90); retired after 1990 season then returned in '93 as coach of New England; entered 1994 season with 9-year record of 90-63-1.

Bernie Parent (b.4/3/1945): Hockey G; led Philadelphia Flyers to 2 Stanley Cups as playoff MVP (1974,75); 2-time Vezina Trophy winner.

Joe Paterno (b.12/21/1926): Football; has coached Penn State to 2 national titles (1982,86) and 15-8-1 bowl record in 28 years; 4-time Coach of Year (1968,78,82,86); entered 1994 season with 257 career wins (including bowls).

Craig Patrick (b.5/20/1946): Hockey; 3rd generation Patrick to have name inscribed on Stanley Cup; GM of 2-time Cup champion Pittsburgh Penguins (1991-92); also captain of 1969 NCAA champion at Denver, assistant coach/GM of 1980 gold medal-winning U.S. Olympic team; scored 72 goals in 8 NHL seasons and won 69 games in 3 years as coach; grandson of Lester.

Lester Patrick (1883-1960): Pro hockey pioneer as player, coach and general manager for 43 years; led NY Rangers to their only Stanley Cups as coach (1928,33) and GM (1940); grandfather of Craig.

Floyd Patterson (b.1/4/1935): Boxer; Olympic middleweight champ in 1952; world heavyweight champion (1956-59,60-62); 1st to regain heavyweight crown; pro record 55-8-1 with 40 KOs.

Walter Payton (b.7/25/1954): Football RB; NFL's all-time leading rusher with 16,726 yards; scored 109 career TDs; All-Pro 7 times with Chicago; MVP in 1977; led Bears to Super Bowl title in 1986.

Pelé (b.10/23/1940): Brazilian soccer F; given name—Edson Arantes do Nascimento; led Brazil to 3 World Cup titles (1958,62,70); came to U.S. in 1975 to play for NY Cosmos in NASL; scored 1,281 goals in 22 years.

Roger Penske (b.2/20/1937): Auto racing; national sports car driving champion (1964); established racing team in 1961; co-founder of Championship Auto Racing Teams (CART); Penske Racing entered 1994 with a record 79 IndyCar victories, including 9 Indianapolis 500s and 8 IndyCar points championships; won 10th Indy 500 in '94.

Willie Pep (b.9/19/1922): Boxer; 2-time world featherweight champion (1942-48,49-50); pro record 230-11-1 with 65 KOs.

Fred Perry (b.5/18/1909): British tennis player; 3-time Wimbledon champ (1934-36), last native to win All-England men's title.

Gaylord Perry (b.9/15/1938): Baseball RHP; only pitcher to win a Cy Young Award in both leagues; retired in 1983 with 314 wins and 3,534 strikeouts over 22 years and with 8 teams; brother Jim won 215 games for family total of 529.

Bob Pettit (b.12/12/1932): Basketball F; All-NBA 1st team 10 times (1955-64); 2-time MVP (1956,59) with St. Louis Hawks; first player to score 20,000 points.

Richard Petty (b.7/2/1937): Auto racer; 7-time winner of Daytona 500; 7-time NASCAR national champ (1964, 67,71-72,74-75,79); first stock car driver to win $1 million in career; all-time NASCAR leader in races won (200), poles (127) and wins in a single season (27 in 1967); retired after 1992 season; son of Lee (54 career wins) and father of Kyle (7 wins entering 1994).

Laffit Pincay Jr. (b.12/29/1946): Jockey; 5-time Eclipse Award winner (1971,73-74,79,85); winner of 3 Belmonts and 1 Kentucky Derby (aboard Swale in 1984); entered 1994 with 8,055 career wins, trailing only Bill Shoemaker's 8,833.

Nelson Piquet (b.8/17/1952): Brazilian auto racer; 3-time Formula One world champion (1981,83,87); left circuit in 1991 with 23 career wins.

Jacques Plante (1929-86): Hockey G; led Montreal to 6 Stanley Cups (1953,56-60); won 7 Vezina Trophies; MVP in 1962; first goalie to regularly wear a mask.

Gary Player (b.11/1/1936): South African golfer; 3-time winner of Masters and British Open; only player in 20th century to win British Open in three different decades (1959,68,74); one of only four players to win all four Grand Slam titles (others are Hogan, Nicklaus and Sarazen); has also won 2 PGAs, a U.S. Open and 2 U.S. Senior Opens; entered 1994 with 21 wins on PGA Tour and 17 more on Senior Tour.

Jim Plunkett (b.12/5/1947): Football QB; Heisman Trophy winner in 1970; led Oakland-LA Raiders to Super Bowl wins in 1981 and '84; MVP in '81.

Maurice Podoloff (1890-85): Basketball; engineered merger of Basketball Assn. of America and National Basketball League into NBA in 1949; NBA commissioner (1949-63); league MVP trophy named after him.

Sam Pollack (b.12/15/1925): Hockey GM; managed NHL Montreal Canadiens to 9 Stanley Cups in 14 years (1965-78).

Fritz Pollard (1894-1986): Football; 1st black All-America RB (1916 at Brown); 1st black to play in Rose Bowl; 7-year NFL pro (1920-26); 1st black NFL coach, at Milwaukee and Hammond, Ind.

Denis Potvin (b.10/29/1953): Hockey D; won Norris Trophy 3 times (1976,78-79); 5-time All-NHL 1st-team; led NY Islanders to 4 Stanley Cups.

Mike Powell (b.11/10/1963): Track and Field; broke Bob Beamon's 23-year-old long jump world record by 2 inches with leap of 29-ft., 4½ in., on Aug. 30, 1991, at the World Championships in Tokyo; Sullivan Award winner (1991); won long jump silver medals in 1988 and '92 Olympics; repeated as world champ in 1993.

Nick Price (b.1/28/1957): Zimbabwean golfer; PGA Tour Player of Year in 1993; winner of 1994 British Open and PGA Championship; 1st player to win 2 Grand Slam titles in same year since Faldo in 1990; also won PGA Championship in 1992.

Alain Prost (b.2/24/1955): French auto racer; 4-time Formula One world champion (1985-86,89,93); sat out 1992 then returned to win 4th driver's title in 1993 at age 38; retired after '93 season as all-time F1 wins leader with 51.

Kirby Puckett (b.3/14/1961): Baseball OF; led Minnesota to 2 World Series titles (1987,'91); entered 1994 season with a batting title (1989) and .318 career average.

C.C. Pyle (1884-1939): Promoter; known as "Cash and Carry;" hyped Red Grange's pro football debut by arranging 1925 barnstorming tour with Chicago Bears; had Grange bolt NFL for new AFL in 1926 (AFL folded in '27); also staged 2 Transcontinental Races (1928-29), known as "Bunion Derbies."

Jack Ramsay (b.2/21/1925): Basketball; coach who won 239 college games with St. Joseph's-PA in 11 seasons and 906 NBA games (including playoffs) with 4 teams over 21 years; placed 3rd in 1961 Final Four; led Portland to NBA title in 1977.

Richard Ravitch (b.7/7/1933): President and CEO of Major League Baseball's Player Relations Committee since 1992; rallied owners around salary cap demand that provoked 1994 players' strike.

Willis Reed (b.6/25/1942): Basketball C; led NY Knicks to NBA titles in 1970 and '73, playoff MVP both years; regular season MVP 1970.

Mary Lou Retton (b.1/24/1968): Gymnast; won gold medal in women's All-Around at the 1984 Olympics, also won 2 silvers and 2 bronzes.

Butch Reynolds (b.6/8/1964): Track & Field; set current world record in 400 meters (43.29) in 1988; banned for 2½ years for allegedly failing drug test in 1990; sued IAAF and won $27.3 million judgement in 1992; won silver medal in 400 meters and ran 3rd leg of world record 4x400-meter relay (2:54.29) at 1993 World Championships.

Grantland Rice (1880-54): first celebrated American sportswriter; chronicled the Golden Age of Sport in 1920s; immortalized Notre Dame's "Four Horsemen."

Jerry Rice (b.10/13/1962): Football WR; 2-time Div. I-AA All-America at Mississippi Valley St. (1983-84); 6-time All-Pro, regular season MVP in 1987 and Super Bowl MVP in 1989 with San Francisco; opened 1994 season with 3 TDs (2 catches, 1 run), making him NFL's all-time touchdown leader with 127.

Henri Richard (b.2/29/1936): Hockey C; leap year baby, who played on more Stanley Cup championship teams (11) than anybody else; at 5-foot-7, known as the "Pocket Rocket;" brother of Maurice.

Maurice Richard (b.8/4/1921): Hockey RW; the "Rocket;" 8-time NHL 1st team All-Star; MVP in 1947; 1st to score 50 goals in one season (1945); 544 career goals; played on 8 Stanley Cup winners in Montreal.

Bob Richards (b.2/2/1926): Track & Field; only 2-time Olympic gold medalist in pole vault (1952,56).

Nolan Richardson (b.12/27/1941): Basketball; coached Arkansas to 1994 NCAA title, beating Duke, 76-72, in final; entered 1994-95 season with career record of 339-112 in 14 years; also won 1981 NIT at Tulsa.

Tex Rickard (1870-1929): Promoter who handled boxing's first $1 million gate (Dempsey vs Carpentier in 1921); built Madison Square Garden in 1925; founded NY Rangers as Garden tenant in 1926 and named NHL team after himself (Tex's Rangers).

Eddie Rickenbacker (1890-1973): Mechanic and auto racer; became America's top flying ace (22 kills) in World War I; owned Indianapolis Speedway (1927-45) and ran Eastern Air Lines (1938-59).

Branch Rickey (1881-1965): Baseball innovator; revolutionized game with creation of modern farm system while general manager of St. Louis Cardinals (1917-42); integrated Major Leagues in 1947 as president-GM of Brooklyn Dodgers when he brought up Jackie Robinson (who he had signed on Oct. 23, 1945); later GM of Pittsburgh Pirates.

Leni Riefenstahl (b.8/22/1902): German filmmaker of 1930's, who directed classic sports documentary "Olympia" on 1936 Berlin Summer Olympics; infamous, however, for also making 1934 Hitler propaganda film "Triumph of the Will."

Roy Riegels (1908-93): Football; California center who picked up fumble in 2nd quarter of 1929 Rose Bowl and raced 70 yards in the wrong direction to set up a 2-point safety in 8-7 loss to Georgia Tech.

Bobby Riggs (b.2/25/1918): Tennis; won Wimbledon once (1939) and U.S. title twice (1939,41) before turning pro in 1941; beat Margaret Smith Court but lost to Billie Jean King in 1973 exhibition matches.

Pat Riley (b.3/20/1945): Basketball; coached LA Lakers to 4 of their 5 NBA titles in 1980s (1982,85,87-88); quit after 1989-90 season, then returned to coach NY Knicks in 1991; NBA Coach of the Year (1990,93); reached 8th NBA Finals with Knicks in 1994, but lost to Houston in 7 games; entered 1994-95 season as all-time leader in playoff wins (131).

Cal Ripken Jr. (b.8/24/1961): Baseball SS; 2-time AL MVP (1983,91) for Baltimore; AL Rookie of Year (1982); AL starting SS in All-Star Game since 1984; entered 1994 season 297 HRs in 13 seasons, the most ever by a shortstop; consecutive game playing streak reached 2,009 when '94 players' strike interrupted season on Aug. 12; the streak, which began on May 30, 1982, is 2nd only to Gehrig's 2,130.

Joe Robbie (1916-90): Football; original owner of Miami Dolphins (1966-90); won 2 Super Bowls (1972-73); built $115-million Robbie Stadium with private funds in 1987.

Oscar Robertson (b.11/24/1938): Basketball G; 3-time college Player of Year (1958-60) at Cincinnati; led 1960 U.S. Olympic team to gold medal; NBA Rookie of Year (1961); 9-time All-NBA 1st team; MVP in 1964 with Cincinnati Royals; NBA champion in 1971 with Milwaukee Bucks; 2nd in career assists with 9,887.

Paul Robeson (1898-1976): Black 4-sport star and 2-time football All-America (1917-18) at Rutgers; 3-year NFL pro; also scholar, lawyer, singer, actor and political activist.

Brooks Robinson (b.5/18/1937): Baseball 3B; led AL in fielding 12 times from 1960-72 with Baltimore; regular season MVP in 1964; World Series MVP in 1970.

David Robinson (b.8/6/1965): Basketball C; college Player of Year at Navy in 1987; overall 1st pick by San Antonio in 1987 NBA Draft; served in military from 1987-89; NBA Rookie of Year in 1990; 2-time All-NBA 1st team (1991,92); led NBA in scoring in 1994; played on bronze medal-winning Olympic team in 1988 and Dream Team gold medal winner in '92.

Eddie Robinson (b.2/13/1919): Football; head coach at Div. I-AA Grambling State for 51 years; winningest coach in college history; has led Tigers to 8 national black college titles; entered 1994 season with career record of 388-140-15.

Frank Robinson (b.8/31/1935): Baseball OF; won MVP in NL (1961) and AL (1966); Triple Crown winner and World Series MVP in 1966 with Baltimore; 1st black manager in Major Leagues with Cleveland in 1975; also managed in SF and Baltimore.

Jackie Robinson (1919-72): Baseball 2B; 4-sport athlete at UCLA; 1st black player in Majors with Brooklyn in 1947; Rookie of the Year in 1947; NL MVP in 1949.

Sugar Ray Robinson (1921-89): Boxer; world welterweight champion (1946-51); 5-time middleweight champ; retired at age 45 after 25 years in the ring; pro record 174-19-6 with 109 KOs.

Knute Rockne (1888-1931): Football; coached Notre Dame to 3 consensus national titles (1924,29,30), career record of 105-12-5 and winning pct. of .881 in 13 years; killed in plane crash.

Bill Rodgers (b.12/23/1947): Track & Field; won Boston and New York City marathons 4 times each from 1975-80.

Irina Rodnina (b.1953): Soviet figure skater; won 10 world championships and 3 Olympic gold medals in pairs competition from 1971-80.

Diann Roffe-Steinrotter (b.3/24/1967): Alpine skier; 2-time Olympic medalist in Super-G; won silver at Albertville in 1992, then gold at Lillehammer in '94.

Art Rooney (1901-1988): Sportsman, race track legend and pro football pioneer; bought Pittsburgh Steelers franchise in 1933 for $2,500; finally won NFL championship with 1st of 4 Super Bowl titles in 1974 season.

Theodore Roosevelt (1838-1919): 26th President of the U.S.; physical fitness buff who boxed as undergraduate at Harvard; credited with presidential assist in forming of Intercollegiate Athletic Assn. (now NCAA) in 1905-06.

Mauri Rose (1906-81): Auto racer; 3-time winner of Indy 500 (1941,47-48).

Murray Rose (b.1/6/1939): Australian swimmer; won 3 gold medals at 1956 Olympics; added a gold, silver and bronze in 1960.

Pete Rose (b.4/14/1941): Baseball OF-Inf.; all-time hits leader with 4,256; led NL in batting 3 times; regular season MVP in 1973; World Series MVP in 1975; had 44-game hitting streak in '78; managed Cincinnati (1984-89); banned for life in '89 for betting on baseball and associating with known gamblers and drug dealers; convicted of tax evasion in 1990 and sentenced to 5 months in prison; released Jan. 7, 1991.

Ken Rosewall (b.11/2/1934): Tennis; won French and Australian singles titles at age 18; U.S. champ twice, but never won Wimbledon.

Mark Roth (b.4/10/1951): Bowler; 4-time PBA Player of Year (1977-79,84); entered 1994 season with 33 tournament wins, including 1984 U.S. Open.

Alan Rothenberg (b.4/10/1939): Soccer; president of U.S. Soccer since 1990; surprised European skeptics by presiding over hugely successful 1994 World Cup tournament; faces challenge of getting outdoor U.S. Division I league off ground in 1995.

Patrick Roy (b.10/5/1965): Hockey G; led Montreal to 2 Stanley Cup titles; playoff MVP as rookie in 1986 and again in '93; has won Vezina Trophy 3 times (1989-90,92).

Pete Rozelle (b.3/1/1926): Football; NFL Commissioner from 1960-89; presided over growth of league from 12 to 28 teams, merger with AFL, creation of Super Bowl and advent of huge TV rights fees.

Wilma Rudolph (b.6/23/1940): Track & Field; won 3 gold medals (100m,200m and 4x400m relay) at 1960 Olympics; also won relay silver in '56 Games.

Damon Runyon (1880-1946): Kansas native who gained fame as New York journalist, sports columnist and short-story writer; best known for 1932 story collection, "Guys and Dolls."

Adolph Rupp (1901-77): Basketball; all-time college wins leader with 876; coached Kentucky to 4 NCAA championships (1948-49,51,58) and an NIT title (1946).

Bill Russell (b.2/12/1934): Basketball C; won titles in college, Olympics and pros; 5-time NBA MVP; led Boston to 11 titles from 1957-69; also became first big league black head coach in 1966.

Babe Ruth (1895-1948): Baseball LHP-OF; 2-time 20-game winner with Boston Red Sox (1916-17); had a 94-46 regular season record with a 2.28 ERA, while he was 3-0 in the World Series with an ERA of 0.87; sold to NY Yankees for $100,000 in 1920; AL MVP in 1923; led AL in slugging average 13 times, HRs 12 times, RBI 6 times and batting once (.378 in 1924); hit 60 HRs in 1927 and 50 or more 3 other times; ended career with Boston Braves in 1935 with 714 HRs, 2,211 RBI and a batting average of .342; remains all-time leader in times walked (2,056) and slugging average (.692).

Johnny Rutherford (b.3/12/1938): Auto racer; 3-time winner of Indy 500 (1974,76,80); CART national champion in 1980.

Nolan Ryan (b.1/31/1947): Baseball RHP; author of record 7 no-hitters against Kansas City A's and Detroit (1973), Minnesota (1974), Baltimore (1975), LA Dodgers (1981), Oakland A's (1990) and Texas (at age 44); 2-time 20-game winner (1973-74); 2-time NL leader in ERA (1981,87); led AL in strikeouts 9 times and NL twice in 27 years; retired after 1993 season with 324 wins, 292 losses and all-time records for strikeouts (5,714) and walks (2,795); never won Cy Young Award.

Samuel Ryder (1859-1936): Golf; English seed merchant who donated the Ryder Cup in 1927 for competition between pro golfers from Great Britain and the U.S.; made his fortune by coming up with idea of selling seeds to public in small packages.

Toni Sailer (b.11/17/1935): Austrian skier; 1st to win 3 alpine gold medals in Winter Olympics—taking downhill, slalom and giant slalom events in 1956.

Juan Antonio Samaranch (b.7/17/1920): Native of Barcelona, Spain; President of International Olympic Committee since 1980.

Pete Sampras (b.8/12/1971): Tennis; No.1 player in world in 1993; youngest ever U.S. Open men's champion (19 years, 28 days) in 1990; won Wimbledon and U.S. Open titles in 1993; then won Australian Open and repeated at Wimbledon and U.S. Open in '94; won 5-set doubles match with John McEnroe to help win 1992 Davis Cup final.

Joan Benoit Samuelson (b.5/16/1957): Track & Field; has won Boston Marathon twice (1979,83); winner of first women's Olympic marathon in 1984; won Sullivan Award in 1985.

Arantxa Sanchez Vicario (b.12/18/1971): Spanish tennis player; entered 1994 season with 12 tour victories, including 1989 French Open; won French and U.S. Opens in 1994; teamed with '94 Wimbledon champion Conchita Martinez to win 3 of last 4 Federation Cups (1991,93-94).

Earl Sande (1889-1968): Jockey; rode Gallant Fox to Triple Crown in 1930; won 5 Belmonts and 3 Kentucky Derbys.

Barry Sanders (b.7/16/1968): Football RB; won 1988 Heisman Trophy as junior at Oklahoma St.; all-time NCAA single season leader in rushing (2,628 yards), scoring (234 points) and TDs (39); 2-time NFC rushing leader with Detroit (1989-90); NFC Rookie of Year (1988); NFL Player of the Year (1991).

Deion Sanders (b.8/9/1967): Baseball OF and Football DB-KR; 2-time consensus All-America at Florida St. in football (1987-88); 3-time NFL All-Pro with Atlanta Falcons (1991-93); led Major Leagues in triples (14) with Atlanta in 1992 and hit .533 in World Series the same year; traded to Cincinnati Reds on May 29, 1994 for OF Roberto Kelly and a minor leaguer; signed with SF 49ers after beginning '94 NFL season as unsigned free agent.

Abe Saperstein (1902-66): Basketball; founded all-black, Harlem Globetrotters barnstorming team in 1927; coached sharpshooting comedians to 1940 world pro title in Chicago and established troupe as game's foremost goodwill ambassadors; also served as 1st commissioner of American Basketball League (1961-62).

Gene Sarazen (b.2/27/1902): Golfer; one of only four players to win all four Grand Slam titles (others are Hogan, Nicklaus and Player); won Masters, British Open, 2 U.S. Opens and 3 PGA titles between 1922-35; invented sand wedge in 1930.

Glen Sather (b.9/2/1943): Hockey; GM-coach of 4 Stanley Cup winners in Edmonton (1984-85,87-88) and GM-only for another in 1990; ranks 6th on all-time NHL list with 553 wins (including playoffs).

Terry Sawchuk (1929-70): Hockey G; recorded 103 shutouts in 21 NHL seasons; 4-time Vezina Trophy winner; played on 4 Stanley Cup winners at Detroit and Toronto.

Gale Sayers (b.5/30/1943): Football HB; 2-time All-America at Kansas; NFL Rookie of Year (1965) and 5-time All-Pro with Chicago; scored then-record 22 TDs in rookie year.

Bo Schembechler (b.9/1/1929): Football; retired in 1989 as 5th winningest Div. I college coach ever; 234-65-8 record in 27 years; coached Michigan from 1969-89; 10 Rose Bowls but only 2 wins.

Chris Schenkel (b.8/21/1923): Radio-TV; 4-time Sportscaster of Year; easy-going baritone who has covered basketball, bowling, football, golf and the Olympics for ABC and CBS; host of ABC's Pro Bowlers Tour for 33 years; received lifetime achievement Emmy Award in 1993.

Vitaly Scherbo (b.1973): Russian gymnast; winner of unprecedented 6 gold medals in gymnastics, including men's All-Around, for Unified Team in 1992 Olympics.

Mike Schmidt (b.9/27/1949): Baseball 3B; led NL in HRs 8 times; 3-time MVP (1980,81,86) with Philadelphia; 548 career HRs and 10 gold gloves.

Don Schollander (b.4/30/1946): Swimming; won 4 gold medals at 1964 Olympics, plus one gold and one silver in 1968; won Sullivan Award in 1964.

Dick Schultz (b.9/5/1929): reform-minded executive director of NCAA from 1988-93; announced resignation on May, 11, 1993, in wake of special investigator's report citing Univ. of Virginia with improper student-athlete loan program during Schultz's tenure as athletic director (1981-87).

Bob Seagren (b.10/17/1946): Track & Field; won gold medal in pole vault at 1968 Olympics; broke world outdoor record 5 times.

Tom Seaver (b.11/17/1944): Baseball RHP; won 3 Cy Young Awards (1969,73,75); had 311 wins and 3,640 strikeouts over 20 years.

Peter Seitz (b.1905): Baseball arbitrator; ruled in 1975 (Dec.23) that players who perform for one season without a signed contract can become free agents; decision ushered in big money era for players.

Wide World Photos

Sam Snead (left) shakes hands with **Ben Hogan** (right) after beating Hogan in an 18-hole playoff to win the 1954 Masters. Between them is Masters founder and golf's only Grand Slam winner **Bobby Jones**.

Monica Seles (b.12/2/1973): Yugoslav tennis player; No.1 in the world in 1991 and '92 after winning Australian, French and U.S. opens both years; 3-time winner of both Australian and French; youngest to win Grand Slam title this century when she won French at age 16 in 1990; entered 1993 with 30 singles titles in just 5 years; stabbed in back by male assailant on Apr. 30, 1993, during match in Hamburg, Germany; spent remainder of 1993 and all of '94 recovering.

Bud Selig (b.7/30/1934): Baseball; car dealer who bought AL Seattle Pilots for $10.8 million in 1970 and moved team to midwest; chairman of owners' executive council and de facto commissioner since he and colleagues forced Fay Vincent to resign on Sept. 7, 1992; cancelled World Series for 1st time since 1904 after owners voted 26-2 on Sept. 14, 1994 to call off remainder of regular season in wake of 34-day players' strike over proposed salary cap.

Frank Selke (1893-1985): Hockey; GM of 6 Stanley Cup champions in Montreal (1953,56-60).

Ayrton Senna (1960-94): Brazilian auto racer; 3-time Formula One champion (1988,90-91); entered 1994 season as all-time F1 leader in poles (62) and 2nd in wins (41); killed May 1, 1994 in crash at Imola, Italy during San Marino Grand Prix.

Sterling Sharpe (b.4/6/1965): Football WR; 2-time All-Pro with Green Bay (1992-93); holds single season reception record with 112 catches in 1993; brother of Shannon, Denver TE who made All-Pro in '93.

Wilbur Shaw (1902-54): Auto racer; 3-time winner and 3-time runner-up of Indy 500 from 1933-1940.

Patty Sheehan (b.10/27/1956): Golfer; LPGA Player of Year in 1983; clinched entry into LPGA Hall of Fame with 30th career win at Phoenix on Mar. 21, 1993; entered 1994 season with 3 LPGA titles (1983-84,93) and a U.S. Open (1992); won 2nd U.S. Open in '94.

Art Shell (b.11/26/1946): Football; 3-time All-NFL tackle with Oakland (1973-74,77); teamed with guard Gene Upshaw on left side of Raiders' offensive line; played on 2 Super Bowl-winning teams; named Raiders' head coach in 1989; entered 1994 with record of 47-34 in 5 years.

Fred Shero (1925-90): Hockey; former NY Rangers defenseman who led Philadelphia Flyers to consecutive Stanley Cup titles (1974-75); also took Rangers to Cup final in 1979; ranks 10th on all-time NHL list with 451 wins (including playoffs).

Bill Shoemaker (b.8/19/1931): Jockey; all-time career wins leader with 8,833; 3-time Eclipse Award winner as Jockey (1981) and special award recipient (1976,81); won Belmont 5 times, Kentucky Derby 4 times and Preakness twice; oldest jockey to win Kentucky Derby (age 54, aboard Ferdinand in 1986; retired in 1990 to become trainer; paralyzed in 1991 auto accident but continues to train horses.

Eddie Shore (1902-85): Hockey D; only NHL defenseman (including Bobby Orr) to win MVP trophy 4 times (1933,35-36,38), all with Boston.

Frank Shorter (b.10/31/1947): Track & Field; won gold medal in marathon at 1972 Olympics, 1st U.S. marathoner to win in 64 years.

Don Shula (b.1/4/1930): Football; one of only two NFL coaches with 300 wins (George Halas is the other); has taken 6 teams to Super Bowls and won twice with Miami (1973-74); 4-time Coach of Year, twice with Baltimore (1964,68) and twice with Miami (1970-71); entered 1994 regular season with 327 career wins (including playoffs) and a winning percentage of .672; father of Cincinnati head coach David.

Al Simmons (1902-56): Baseball OF; led AL in batting twice (1930-31) and knocked in 100 runs or more 11 straight years (1924-34).

O.J. Simpson (b.7/9/1947): Football RB; won Heisman Trophy in 1968 at USC; ran for 2,003 yards in NFL in 1973; All-Pro 5 times; MVP in 1973; rushed for 11,236 career yards; TV analyst and actor after career ended; arrested June 17, 1994 and held without bail as only suspect in double murder of ex-wife Nicole Brown Simpson and her friend Ronald Goldman.

Harry Sinden (b.9/14/1932): Hockey; in 1970, coached Boston to 1st Stanley Cup title since 1941; came out of retirement in 1972 to coach victorious Team Canada in landmark, 8-game summit with USSR; Boston GM since 1972.

George Sisler (1893-73): Baseball 1B; hit over .400 twice (1920,22); 257 hits in 1920 still a major league record.

Mary Decker Slaney (b.8/4/1958): U.S. middle distance runner; has held 7 separate American track & field records from the 800 to 10,000 meters; won both 1,500 and 3,000 meters at 1983 World Championships in Helsinki, but no Olympic medals.

Raisa Smetanina (b.1953): Russian Nordic skier; all-time Winter Olympics medalist with 10 cross-country medals (4 gold, 5 silver and a bronze) in 5 appearances (1976,80,84,88,92) for USSR and Unified Team.

Billy Smith (b.12/12/1950): Hockey G; led NY Islanders to 4 consecutive Stanley Cups (1980-83); won Vezina Trophy in 1982; Stanley Cup MVP in 1983.

Dean Smith (b.2/28/1931): Basketball; has coached North Carolina to 24 NCAA tournaments in 33 years, reaching Final Four 9 times and winning championship twice (1982,93); has also led Tar Heels to 13 ACC tourney titles; coached U.S. Olympic team to gold medal in 1976; entered 1994-95 season ranked 2nd on all-time Div. I victory list with 802.

Emmitt Smith (b.5/15/1969): Football RB; consensus All-America (1989) at Florida; 3-time NFL rushing leader (1991-93); 2-time All-Pro (1992-93); regular season and Super Bowl MVP in 1993; played in two Super Bowl champions (1992 and '93 seasons).

John Smith (b.8/9/1965): Wrestler; 2-time NCAA champion for Oklahoma State at 134 lbs. (1987-88) and Most Outstanding Wrestler of '88 championships; 3-time world champion; gold medal winner at 1988 and '92 Olympics at 137 lbs; only wrestler ever to win Sullivan Award (1990); coached Oklahoma St. to 1994 NCAA title and brother Pat was Most Outstanding Wrestler.

Lee Smith (b.12/4/1957): Baseball RHP; 3-time NL saves leader (1983,91-92); all-time major league saves leader with 434 when 1994 players' strike interrupted season on Aug. 12.

Ozzie Smith (b.12/26/1954): Baseball SS; won 13 straight gold gloves from 1980-92; 10-time starter for NL in All-Star Game.

Walter (Red) Smith (1905-82): Sportswriter for newspapers in Philadelphia and New York from 1936-82; won Pulitzer Prize for commentary in 1976.

Conn Smythe (1895-1980): Hockey pioneer; built Maple Leaf Gardens in 1931; managed Toronto to 7 Stanley Cups before retiring in 1961.

Sam Snead (b.5/27/1912): Golfer; won both Masters and PGA 3 times and British Open once; runner-up in U.S. Open 4 times; PGA Player of Year in 1949; oldest player (52 years, 10 months) to win PGA event with Greater Greensboro Open title in 1965; all-time PGA Tour career victory leader with 81.

Peter Snell (b.12/17/1939): New Zealander who won gold medal in 800m at 1960 Olympics, then won both the 800m and 1,500m at 1964 Games.

Javier Sotomayor (b.10/13/1967): Cuban high jumper; first man to clear 8 feet (8-0) on July 29, 1989; won gold medal at 1992 Olympics with jump of only 7-ft, 8-in.; broke world record with leap of 8-0½ in 1993.

Warren Spahn (b.4/23/1921): Baseball LHP; led NL in wins 8 times; won 20 or more games 13 times; Cy Young winner in 1957; most career wins (363) by a left-hander.

Tris Speaker (1888-1958): Baseball OF; all-time leader in outfield assists (449) and doubles (793); had .344 career batting average and 3,515 hits.

J.G. Taylor Spink (1888-1962): Publisher of The Sporting News from 1914-62; Baseball Writers' Assn. annual meritorious service award named after him.

Mark Spitz (b.2/10/1950): set 23 world and 35 U.S. records; won all-time record 7 gold medals (4 individual, 3 relay) in 1972 Olympics; also won 4 medals (2 gold, a silver and a bronze) in 1968 Games for a total of 11; comeback attempt at age 41 foundered in 1991.

Amos Alonzo Stagg (1862-1965): Football innovator; coached at U. of Chicago for 41 seasons and College of the Pacific for 14 more; won 314 games; elected to both college football and basketball halls of fame.

Willie Stargell (b.3/6/1940): Baseball OF-1B; led NL in home runs twice (1971,73); 475 career HRs; regular season and World Series MVP in 1979.

Bart Starr (b.1/9/1934): Football QB; led Green Bay to 5 NFL titles and 2 Super Bowl wins from 1961-67; regular season MVP in 1966; 2-time Super Bowl MVP (1967,68).

Roger Staubach (b.2/5/1942): Football QB; Heisman Trophy winner as Navy junior in 1963; led Dallas to 2 Super Bowl titles (1972,78) and was Super Bowl MVP in 1972; 5-time leading passer in NFC (1971,73,77-79).

George Steinbrenner (b.7/4/1930): principal owner of NY Yankees since 1973; teams have won 4 pennants and 2 World Series (1977-78); has changed managers 18 times, pitching coaches 15 times and GMs 10 times in 21 years; ordered by baseball commissioner Fay Vincent in 1990 to surrender control of club for dealings with small-time gambler; reinstated on Mar. 1, 1993; also serves as one of 3 VPs of U.S. Olympic Committee.

Casey Stengel (1890-1975): Baseball; player for 14 years and manager for 25; outfielder and lifetime .284 hitter with 5 clubs (1912-25); guided NY Yankees to 10 AL pennants and 7 World Series titles from 1949-60; 1st NY Mets skipper from 1962-65.

Ingemar Stenmark (b.3/18/1956): Swedish alpine skier; 3-time World Cup overall champ (1976-78); 86 World Cup wins in 16 years; won 2 gold medals at 1980 Olympics.

Helen Stephens (1918-94): Track & Field; set 3 world records in 100-yard dash and 4 more at 100 meters in 1935-36; won gold medals in 100 meters and 4x100-meter relay in 1936 Olympics; retired in 1937.

Woody Stephens (b.9/1/1913): Horse racing; trainer who saddled an unprecedented 5 straight winners in Belmont Stakes (1982-86); also had two Kentucky Derby winners (1974,84); trained 1982 Horse of Year Conquistador Cielo.

David Stern (b.9/22/1942): Basketball; marketing expert and NBA commissioner since 1984; took office the year Michael Jordan turned pro; has presided over stunning artistic and financial success of NBA both nationally and internationally, best demonstrated by reception of the Dream Team at 1992 Olympics; league has grown from 23 teams to 27 during his watch and will expand to 29 in 1995 with arrival of Toronto and Vancouver; received unprecedented 5-year, $27.5 million contract extension in 1990.

Teofilo Stevenson (b.1951): Cuban boxer; won 3 consecutive gold medals as Olympic heavyweight (1972,76,80); did not turn pro.

Jackie Stewart (b.6/11/1939): Auto racer; won 27 Formula One races and 3 world driving titles from 1965-73.

Curtis Strange (b.1/30/1955): Golfer; won consecutive U.S. Open titles (1988-89); 3-time leading money winner on PGA Tour (1985,87-88); first PGA player to win $1 million in one year (1988).

Louise Suggs (b.9/7/1923): Golfer; won 11 Majors and 50 LPGA events overall from 1949-62.

James E. Sullivan (1860-1914): Track and field pioneer, who founded Amateur Athletic Union (AAU) in 1888; director of St. Louis Olympic Games in 1904; AAU's annual Sullivan Award for performance and sportsmanship named after him.

John L. Sullivan (1858-1918): Boxer; world heavyweight champion (1882-92); last of bare-knuckle champions.

Barry Switzer (b.10/5/1937): Football; coached Oklahoma to 3 national titles (1974-75,85); 4th on all-time winningest list with 157-29-4 record and .837 win percentage; resigned in 1989 after OU was slapped with 3-year NCAA probation and 5 players were brought up on criminal charges; hired as Dallas Cowboys head coach on Mar. 30, 1994.

Paul Tagliabue (b.11/24/1940): Football; NFL attorney who was elected league's 4th commissioner in 1989; ushered in salary cap in 1994; league will expand for 1st time since 1976 with arrival of Carolina and Jacksonville in 1995.

Anatoli Tarasov (b.1918): Hockey; coached USSR to 9 straight world championships and 3 Olympic gold medals (1964,68,72).

Jerry Tarkanian (b.8/30/1930): Basketball; all-time winningest college coach with .837 winning percentage; had record 625-122 over 24 years at Long Beach State and UNLV; led UNLV to 4 Final Fours and one national championship (1990); fought 16-year battle with NCAA over purity of UNLV program; quit as coach after going 26-2 in 1991-92; fired after 20 games (9-11) as coach of NBA San Antonio Spurs in 1992.

Fran Tarkenton (b.2/3/1940): Football QB; 2-time All-Pro (1973,75); Player of Year (1975); threw for 47,003 yards and 342 TDs (both NFL records) in 18 seasons with Minnesota and NY Giants.

Chuck Taylor (1901-69): Converse traveling salesman whose name came to grace the classic, high-top canvas basketball sneakers known as "Chucks"; over 500 million pairs have been sold since 1917; he also ran clinics worldwide and edited *Converse Basketball Yearbook* from 1922-68.

Lawrence Taylor (b.2/4/1959): Football LB; All-America at North Carolina (1980); only defensive player in NFL history to be consensus Player of Year (1986); led NY Giants to Super Bowl titles in 1986 and '90 seasons; played in a record 10 Pro Bowls (1981-90); retired after 1993 season with 132½ sacks.

Gustave Thoeni (b.2/28/1951): Italian alpine skier; 4-time World Cup overall champion (1971-73,75); won Giant Slalom at 1972 Olympics.

Frank Thomas (b.5/27/1968): Baseball 1B; All-America 1B at Auburn in 1989; AL MVP with Chicago White Sox in 1993; batting .353 with 38 HRs and 101 RBI when 1994 players' strike began on Aug. 12.

Isiah Thomas (b.4/30/1961): Basketball; led Indiana to NCAA title as sophomore and tourney MVP in 1981; consensus All-America guard in '81; led Detroit to 2 NBA titles in 1989 and '90; NBA Finals MVP in 1990; 3-time All-NBA 1st team (1984-86); retired at age 33 on May 11, 1994 after tearing his right Achilles tendon on Apr. 19; named GM of expansion Toronto Raptors on May 24.

Thurman Thomas (b.5/16/1966): Football RB; 3-time AFC rushing leader (1990-91,93); 2-time All-Pro (1990-91); NFL Player of Year (1991); has led Buffalo to 4 straight Super Bowls (1991-94).

Daley Thompson (b.7/30/1958): British track & field; won consecutive gold medals in decathlon at 1980 and '84 Olympics.

John Thompson (b.9/2/1941): Basketball; has coached centers Patrick Ewing, Alonzo Mourning and Dikembe Mutombo at Georgetown; reached NCAA tourney final 3 out of 4 years with Ewing, winning title in 1984; also led Hoyas to 6 Big East tourney titles; coached 1988 U.S. Olympic team to bronze medal; entered 1994-95 season with 503 wins in 22 years.

Bobby Thomson (b.10/25/1923): Baseball OF; career .270 hitter who won the 1951 NL pennant for the NY Giants with a 1-out, 3-run HR in the bottom of the 9th inning of Game 3 of a best-of-3 playoff with Brooklyn; the pitcher was Ralph Branca, the count was 0-1 and the Dodgers were ahead 4-2; the Giants had trailed Brooklyn by 13 games on Aug. 11th.

Jim Thorpe (1888-1953): 2-time All-America in football; won both pentathlon and decathlon at 1912 Olympics; played major league baseball (1913-19) and pro football (1920-26,28); chosen "Athlete of the Half Century" by AP in 1950.

Bill Tilden (1893-1953): Tennis; won 7 U.S. and 3 Wimbledon titles in 1920s; led U.S. to 7 straight Davis Cup victories (1920-26).

Tinker to Evers to Chance—Chicago Cubs double play combination from 1903-08; immortalized in poem by New York sportswriter Franklin P. Adams: SS **Joe Tinker** (1880-1948), 2B **Johnny Evers** (1883-1947) and 1B **Frank Chance** (1877-1924); all 3 managed the Cubs and made the Hall of Fame.

Y.A. Tittle (b.10/24/1926): Football QB; played 17 years in AFC and NFL; All-Pro 4 times; league MVP with San Francisco (1957) and NY Giants (1962); passed for 28,339 career yards.

Alberto Tomba (b.12/19/1966): Italian alpine skier; all-time alpine medalist with 5 (3 gold, 2 silver); became 1st alpine skier to win gold medals in 2 consecutive Olympics when he won the slalom and giant slalom in 1988 then repeated in the GS in '92; also won silvers in slalom in 1992 and '94.

Torvill and Dean— Jayne Torvill (b.10/7/1957) and Christopher Dean (7/27/1958): British figure skaters; won 4 straight world ice dancing titles (1981-84); won Olympic gold medal at Sarajevo in 1988 then turned pro; returned to take bronze medal at 1992 Olympics in Lillehammer.

Vladislav Tretiak (b.4/25/1952): Hockey G; led USSR to Olympic gold medals in 1972 and '76; starred for Soviets against Team Canada in 1972, and again in 2 Canada Cups (1976,81).

Lee Trevino (b.12/1/1939): Golfer; 2-time winner of 3 Majors — U.S. Open (1968,71), British Open (1971-72) and PGA (1974,84); Player of Year once on PGA Tour (1971) and twice on Seniors (1990,92); entered 1994 with 27 PGA Tour wins and 18 on Senior Tour; all-time money leader on combined tours ($7.4 million).

Bryan Trottier (b.7/17/1956): Hockey C; led NY Islanders to 4 straight Stanley Cups (1980-83); Rookie of Year (1976); scoring champion (134 points) and regular season MVP in 1979; playoff MVP (1980); added 5th and 6th Cups with Pittsburgh in 1991 and '92.

Gene Tunney (b.1897-78): Boxer; world heavyweight champion (1926-28); defeated Jack Dempsey twice on points; pro record 65-2-1 with 43 KOs.

Ted Turner (b.11/19/1938): Sportsman and TV mogul, skippered *Courageous* to America's Cup win in 1977; owner of both Atlanta Braves and Hawks; owner of superstation WTBS, and cable stations CNN and TNT; founder of Goodwill Games; 1991 *Time* Man of Year.

Mike Tyson (b.6/30/1965): Boxer; youngest (age 19) to win heavyweight title (WBC in 1986); undisputed champ from 1987 until upset loss to 50-1 shot Buster Douglas on Feb. 10, 1990, in Tokyo; pro record of 41-1-0 with 36 KOs through 1991; found guilty on Feb. 10, 1992, of raping 18-year-old Miss Black America contestant Desiree Washington in Indianapolis on July 19, 1991; sentenced to 6-year prison term; release date set for May 9, 1995.

Wyomia Tyus (b.8/29/1945): Track & Field; 1st woman to win consecutive Olympic gold medals in 100m (1964-68).

Peter Ueberroth (b.9/2/1937): Organizer of 1984 Summer Olympics in LA; 1984 *Time* Man of Year; baseball commissioner from 1984-89; headed Rebuild Los Angeles for one year after 1992 riots.

Johnny Unitas (b.5/7/1933): Football QB; led Baltimore Colts to 2 NFL titles (1958-59) and a Super Bowl win (1971); All-Pro 5 times; 3-time MVP (1959,64,67); passed for 40,239 career yards and 290 TDs.

Al Unser Jr. (b.4/19/1962): Auto racer; 2-time CART/IndyCar national champion, clinching 2nd title on Sept. 11, 1994; previously won in 1990; captured Indy 500 for 2nd time in 3 years in '94, giving Unser family 9 overall titles at the Brickyard; entered 1994 with 19 IndyCar wins in 12 years; son of Al and nephew of Bobby.

Al Unser Sr. (b.5/29/1939): Auto racer; 3-time USAC/CART national champion (1970,83,85); 4-time winner of Indy 500 (1970-71,78,87); retired in 1994 ranked 3rd on all-time IndyCar list with 39 wins; younger brother of Bobby and father of Little Al.

Bobby Unser (b.2/20/1934): Auto racer; 2-time USAC/CART national champion (1968,74); 3-time winner of Indy 500 (1968,75,81); retired after 1981 season; ranks 4th on all-time IndyCar list with 35 wins.

Gene Upshaw (b.8/15/1945): Football G; 2-time All-AFL and 3-time All-NFL selection with Oakland; helped lead Raiders to 2 Super Bowl titles in 1976 and '80 seasons; executive director of NFL Players Assn. since 1987; agreed to application of salary cap in 1994.

Norm Van Brocklin (1926-83): Football QB; led NFL in passing 3 times and punting twice; led LA Rams (1951) and Philadelphia (1960) to NFL titles; MVP in 1960.

Steve Van Buren (b.12/28/1920): Football HB; led Philadelphia to 2 NFL titles (1948-49); league's top rusher 4 times.

Johnny Vander Meer (b.11/2/1914): Baseball LHP; only major leaguer to pitch consecutive no-hitters (June 11 & 15, 1938).

Harold S. Vanderbilt (1884-70): Sportsman; successfully defended America's Cup 3 times (1930, 34,37); also invented contract bridge in 1926.

Glenna Collett Vare (1903-89): Golfer; won record 6 U.S. Women's Amateur titles from 1922-35; known as "the female Bobby Jones."

Andy Varipapa (1891-1984): Bowler; trick-shot artist; won consecutive All-Star match game titles (1947-48) at age 53.

Bill Veeck (1914-86): Maverick baseball executive; owned AL teams in Cleveland, St. Louis and Chicago from 1946-80; introduced ballpark giveaways, exploding scoreboards, and midget Eddie Gaedel; won World Series with Indians (1948) and pennant with White Sox (1959).

Fay Vincent (b.5/29/1938): Baseball; became 8th commissioner after death of A. Bartlett Giamatti in 1989; presided over World Series earthquake, owners' lockout and banishment of NY Yankees owner George Steinbrenner in his first year on the job; contentious relationship with owners resulted in his resignation on Sept. 7, 1992, four days after 18-9 "no confidence" vote; office has been vacant since then.

Lasse Viren (b.7/22/1949): Finnish runner; won gold medals in 5000m and 10,000m at both the 1972 and '76 Olympics.

Honus Wagner (1874-1955): Baseball SS; hit .300 for 17 consecutive seasons (1897-1913) with Pittsburgh; led NL in batting 8 times; ended career with 3,418 career hits, a .327 average and 722 stolen bases.

Lisa Wagner (b.5/19/1961): Bowler; 3-time LPBT Player of Year (1983,88,93); 1980s Bowler of Decade; entered 1994 season with 28 pro titles.

Grete Waitz (b.10/1/1953): Norwegian runner; 9-time winner of New York City Marathon from 1978-88; won silver medal at 1984 Olympics.

Doak Walker (b.1/1/1927): Football HB; won Heisman Trophy as SMU junior in 1948; led Detroit to 2 NFL titles (1952-53); All-Pro 4 times in 6 years.

Herschel Walker (b.3/3/1962): Football RB; led Georgia to national title as freshman in 1980; won Heisman as junior in 1982 then jumped to USFL in '83; signed by Dallas of NFL after USFL folded; led NFL in rushing in 1988; traded by Cowboys to Minnesota in 1989 for 5 players and 6 draft picks.

Bill Walsh (b.11/30/1931): Football; coached San Francisco to 3 Super Bowl titles (1982,85,89); retired after 1988 season with 102 wins in 10 seasons; returned to college coaching in 1992 at Stanford where he was from 1977-78.

Bill Walton (b.11/5/1950): Basketball C; 3-time college Player of Year (1972-74); led UCLA to 2 national titles (1972-73); led Portland to NBA title as MVP in 1977, regular season MVP in 1978.

Arch Ward (1896-1955): Promoter and sports editor of *Chicago Tribune* from 1930-55; founder of baseball All-Star Game (1933), Chicago College All-Star Football Game (1934) and the All-America Football Conference (1946-49).

Charlie Ward (b.10/12/1970): Football QB and Basketball G; led Florida St. to national football championship in 1993; 1st Heisman Trophy winner to play for national champs since Tony Dorsett in 1976; also won Sullivan Award as nation's top amateur athlete; 3-year starter for FSU basketball team; not taken in NFL Draft; 1st round pick (26th overall) of NY Knicks in NBA Draft.

Glenn (Pop) Warner (1871-1954): Football innovator; coached at 7 colleges over 49 years; 319 career wins 2nd only to Bear Bryant's 323 in Div. I-A; produced 47 All-Americas, including Jim Thorpe and Ernie Nevers.

Tom Watson (b.9/4/1949): Golfer; 6-time PGA player of the Year (1977-80,82,84); has won 5 British Opens, 2 Masters and a U.S. Open; 4-time Ryder Cup member and captain of 1993 team; entered 1994 with 32 tour wins.

Dick Weber (b.12/23/1929): Bowler; 3-time PBA Bowler of the Year (1961,63,65); won 30 PBA titles in 4 decades.

Johnny Weissmuller (1904-84): Swimmer; won 3 gold medals at 1924 Olympics and 2 more at 1928 Games; became Hollywood's most famous Tarzan.

Jerry West (b.5/28/1938): Basketball G; 2-time All-America and NCAA tourney MVP (1959) at West Virginia; led 1960 U.S. Olympic team to gold medal; 10-time All-NBA 1st-team; NBA finals MVP (1969); led LA Lakers to NBA title once as player (1972) and 5 times as GM in 1980s.

Pernell Whitaker (b.1/2/1964): Boxer; won WBC welterweight championship in 1993; has also held jr. welterweight and lightweight titles; outfought but failed to beat Julio Cesar Chavez when Sept. 10, 1993 welterweight title defense ended in controversial draw; entered 1994 with pro record of 32-1-1 and 15 KOs; won Olympic gold medal as lightweight in 1984.

Bill White (b./18/1934): Baseball; NL president and highest ranking black executive in sports from 1989-94; as 1st baseman, won 7 gold gloves and hit .286 with 202 HRs in 13 seasons; helped lead St. Louis to World Series title in 1964.

Byron (Whizzer) White (b.6/8/1918): Football; All-America HB at Colorado (1935-37); signed with Pittsburgh in 1938 for the then largest contract in pro history ($15,800); took Rhodes scholarship in 1939; returned to NFL in 1940 to lead league in rushing and retired in 1941; named to U.S. Supreme Court by President Kennedy in 1962 and stepped down in 1993.

Reggie White (b.12/19/1961): Football DE; consensus All-America in 1983 at Tennessee; 7-time All-NFL (1986-92) with Philadelphia; signed as free agent with Green Bay in 1993 for $17 million over 4 years; entered 1994 season with 137 sacks.

Kathy Whitworth (b.9/27/1939): Golf; 7-time LPGA Player of the Year (1966-69,71-73); won 6 Majors; 88 tour wins most on LPGA or PGA tour.

Hazel Hotchkiss Wightman (1886-1974): Tennis; won 16 U.S. national titles; 4-time U.S. Women's champion (1909-11,19); donor of Wightman Cup.

Mats Wilander (b.8/22/1964): Swedish tennis player; 1988 Player of Year; has won Australian and French Opens 3 times each and U.S. Open in 1988.

Hoyt Wilhelm (b.7/26/1923): Baseball RHP; 1st relief pitcher inducted into Hall of Fame (1985); knuckleballer and all-time leader in games pitched (1,070), games finished (651) and games won in relief (124); had career ERA of 2.52 and 227 saves; threw no-hitter vs NY Yankees (1958); also hit one and only HR of career in first major league at bat (1952).

Lenny Wilkens (b.10/28/1937): Basketball; MVP of 1960 NIT as Providence guard; played 15 years in NBA, including 4 as player-coach; MVP of 1971 All-Star Game; coached Seattle to NBA title in 1979; Coach of Year in 1994 with Atlanta; entered 1994-95 season with 986 wins (including playoffs), 2nd only to Red Auerbach's 1,037.

Dominique Wilkins (b.1/12/1960): Basketball F; last player to lead NBA in scoring (1986) before Michael Jordan's reign; All-NBA 1st team in '86; traded from Atlanta to LA Clippers in 1994; later signed as free agent with Boston; elder statesman of Dream Team II; entered 1994-95 season with 26.5 scoring average.

Bud Wilkinson (1916-94): Football; played on 1936 national championship team at Minnesota; coached Oklahoma to 3 national titles (1950,55,56); won 4 Orange and 2 Sugar Bowls; teams had winning streaks of 47 (1953-57) and 31 (1948-50); retired after 1963 season with 145-29-4 record in 17 years; also coached St. Louis of NFL to 9-20 record in 1978-79.

Matt Williams (b.11/28/1965): Baseball 3B; All-America SS in 1986 at UNLV; 2-time Gold Glove 3B with San Francisco (1991,93); leading majors in HRs with 43 when 1994 players' strike began on Aug. 12.

Ted Williams (b.8/30/1918): Baseball OF; led AL in batting 6 times, and HRs and RBI 4 times each; won Triple Crown twice (1942,47); 2-time MVP (1946,49); last player to bat .400 when he hit .406 in 1941; Marine Corps combat pilot who missed three full seasons during World War II (1943-45) and most of two others (1952-53) during Korean War; hit .344 lifetime with 521 HRs in 19 years with Boston Red Sox.

Dave Winfield (b.10/3/1951): Baseball OF-DH; selected in 4 major sports league drafts in 1973— NFL, NBA, ABA, and MLB; chose baseball and has played in 12 All-Star Games over 20-year career; at age 41, helped lead Toronto to World Series title in 1992; reached 3,000 hits in 1993; entered 1994 as leading active player in hits, HRs and RBI among others.

Katarina Witt (b.12/3/1965): East German figure skater; 4-time world champion (1984-85,87-88); won consecutive Olympic gold medals (1984,88).

John Wooden (b.10/14/1910): Basketball; college Player of Year at Purdue in 1932; coached UCLA to 10 national titles (1964-65,67-73,75); only member of Basketball Hall of Fame inducted as player and coach.

Mickey Wright (b.2/14/1935): Golfer; won 3 of 4 Majors (LPGA, U.S. Open, Titleholders) in 1961; 4-time winner of both U.S. Open and LPGA titles; 82 career wins including 13 Majors.

Early Wynn (b.1/6/1920): Baseball RHP; won 20 games 5 times; Cy Young winner in 1959; 300 career wins in 23 years.

Cale Yarborough (b.3/20/1939): Auto racer; 3-time NASCAR national champion (1976-78); 4-time winner of Daytona 500 (1968,77,83-84); ranks 4th on NASCAR all-time list with 83 wins.

Carl Yastrzemski (b.8/22/1939): Baseball OF; led AL in batting 3 times; won Triple Crown and MVP in 1967; had 3,419 hits and 452 HRs in 23 years with Boston.

Cy Young (1867-1955): Baseball RHP; all-time leader in wins (511), losses (315), complete games (750) and innings pitched (7,355); had career 2.63 ERA in 22 years (1890-1911); 30-game winner 5 times and 20-game winner 10 other times; threw 3 no-hitters and perfect game (1904); AL and NL pitching awards named after him.

Dick Young (1917-87): confrontational sportswriter for 44 years with New York tabloids; as baseball beat writer and columnist, he spearheaded change in daily coverage from flowery prose to hard-nosed reporting.

Sheila Young (b.10/14/1950): Speed skater-cyclist; 1st U.S. athlete to win 3 medals at Winter Olympics (1976); won speed skating overall and sprint cycling world titles in 1976.

Steve Young (b.10/11/1961): Football QB; consensus All-America at BYU (1983); NFL Player of Year (1992) with S.F. 49ers; only QB to lead NFL in passer rating 3 straight years (1991-93).

Robin Yount (b.9/16/1955): Baseball SS-OF; AL MVP at 2 positions— as SS in 1982 and OF in '89; retired after 1993 season with 3,142 hits, 251 HRs and a major league record 123 sacrifice flies after 20 seasons with Milwaukee Brewers.

Mario Zagalo (b.8/9/1931): Soccer; Brazilian forward who is one of only two men (Franz Beckenbauer is the other) to serve as both captain (1962) and coach (1970) of World Cup champion; served as advisor for Brazil's 1994 World Cup champion.

Babe Didrikson Zaharias (1914-56): All-around athlete who was chosen AP Female Athlete of the Year 6 times from 1932-54; won 2 gold medals (javelin and 80-meter hurdles) and a silver (high jump) at 1932 Olympics; took up golf in 1935 and went on to win 55 pro and amateur events; won 10 majors, including 3 U.S. Opens (1948,50,54); helped found LPGA in 1949; chosen female "Athlete of the Half Century" by AP in 1950.

Tony Zale (b.5/29/1913): Boxer; 2-time world middleweight champion (1941-47,48); fought Rocky Graziano for title 3 times in 21 months in 1947-48, winning twice; pro record 67-18-2 with 44 KOs.

Frank Zamboni (1901-88): mechanic, ice salesman and skating rink owner in Paramount, Calif.; invented 1st ice-resurfacing machine in 1949; over 4,000 sold in more than 33 countries since then.

Emil Zatopek (b.9/19/1922): Czech distance runner; winner of 1948 Olympic gold medal at 10,000 meters; 4 years later, won unprecedented Olympic triple (5000 meters, 10,000 meters and marathon) at 1952 Games in Helsinki.

John Ziegler (b.2/9/1934): Hockey; NHL president from 1977-92; negotiated settlement with rival WHA in 1979 that led to inviting four WHA teams (Edmonton, Hartford, Quebec and Winnipeg) to join NHL; stepped down June 12, 1992, 2 months after settling 10-day players' strike.

Pirmin Zurbriggen (b.1963): Swiss alpine skier; 4-time World Cup overall champ (1984,87,88,90) and 3-time runner-up; 40 World Cup wins in 10 years; won gold and bronze medals at 1988 Olympics.

Jim Rackwitz/St. Louis Post-Dispatch

The new, $260 million domed football stadium under construction in St. Louis as it looked in July. As of October, however, the city still didn't have an NFL team to play there.

BALLPARKS & ARENAS

Home Alone

St. Louis is building a domed stadium for an NFL team it didn't get, but at least the new arena has the Blues.

From the outset, officials involved in the St. Louis domed stadium project pointed out that this would be more than a football stadium.

For one thing, with its flatter roof, designed to blend in with the neighboring architecture, it wouldn't even look like a football stadium.

Perhaps that's a good thing. Because on Nov. 30, 1993, St. Louisans learned much to their shock that they weren't getting an NFL expansion team. That was the day the NFL selected Jacksonville, Fla. to join Charlotte, N.C. as the league's first new teams since Seattle and Tampa Bay joined its ranks in 1976. St. Louis still had the football Cardinals back then, but lost them after the 1987 season when owner Bill Bidwill up and moved the club to Phoenix.

Meanwhile, construction was well underway on the St. Louis project, which anchors the north end of downtown, when the expansion decision came down. So there was no turning back.

City, county and state tax money is being used to finance the $260 million project. The local stadium authority is legally obligated to build the facility as originally outlined to buyers of bonds sold to finance the project.

NFL team or not, St. Louis is getting a 70,000-seat pleasure dome with all the perks: 100 luxury boxes, 6,300 club seats,

state-of-the-art video replay boards, artificial turf and three locker rooms.

The only way taxpayers and state legislators would go for the project is if the stadium was tied to the city's existing convention center.

Not only is the stadium tied into the convention center, it's physically attached to it. The stadium, scheduled to be completed by September 1995, was designed to accommodate even larger conventions:

- At floor level, 7,500 retractable seats can be removed and stored, leaving 180,000 square feet of convention space on the stadium floor.

- A movable light grid can be lowered from football level 140 feet above the floor to convention level of 55 feet.

- The light grid can be lowered in quadrants or halves, providing flexibility for conventions. Divider curtains and aisle markers provide a more intimate atmosphere.

The football stadium is "the sexy part" of the building, according to Robert J. Baer, chairman of the St. Louis Regional Convention and Sports Complex Authority. "But what drove the deal from day one was the convention activities and the tourists they bring in."

Try as they might, however, it's hard for embarrassed local officials to get around the fact that this is a football stadium without a football team.

Jim Thomas is the pro football writer for the *St. Louis Post-Dispatch.*

An artists' rendering of the new $170 million **Kiel Center**, new home of the NHL's St. Louis Blues and the Saint Louis University Billikens basketball team. The 12-story building, which was built in just 21 months, will hold 18,500 for hockey and 20,000 for basketball.

Nonetheless, it's a football stadium unlike anything in the country.

"It's going to be the finest state-of-the-art stadium, in my judgment," said Don Poss, a stadium consultant on the St. Louis project who previously was involved with the Metrodome in Minneapolis and Joe Robbie Stadium in Miami.

"That's the trick with each generation of stadium that comes on board," he said. "It plagiarizes the best from the past and does a little bit of advancing into the future."

How St. Louis managed to fumble away cinch status in the expansion franchise sweepstakes is a story of greed and ego mixed in with the colossal blunder of signing over the lease to what turned out to be an underfinanced ownership group *before the franchise was awarded.*

Not that the city has given up the hope of landing another team.

"Now we'll have to do it the old-fashioned way: Go steal one," said St. Louis comptroller Virvus Jones, a one-time critic of the stadium project.

St. Louis made overtures to the New England Patriots before interim owner and St. Louis native James Orthwein sold the club to local Boston businessman Bob Kraft on Jan. 21, 1994. Ever since then, the city has been ardently wooing Los Angeles Rams owner Georgia Frontiere, who has activated an escape clause in her lease at Anaheim Stadium.

The lures are twofold: first, St. Louis is the largest metropolitan area in the nation (2.5 million people) without an NFL franchise; and second, there's a lucrative stadium lease, chock full of goodies in terms of premium-seat revenues that most existing stadiums can't match.

But the real story in St. Louis is that the football stadium folly is only half the story. At the same time the football fiasco has unfolded, another facility has quietly been built less than two miles away on the western edge of downtown.

And if the domed stadium saga was a case study in "Murphy's Law," the $170-million Kiel Center is a testament to public and private sector cooperation, compromise and a can-do attitude.

Or as Ed Calcaterra, president of J.S. Alberici Construction Co., puts it: "This is something St. Louis has done right."

The Alberici firm is construction manager

for the Kiel Center, which is scheduled to open the week of Oct. 10 as the new home of the NHL's St. Louis Blues and the Saint Louis University's revived basketball Billikens. The building, in fact, will open ahead of schedule.

"The typical construction period for an arena like this is anywhere from 24 to 30 months," said Jud Perkins, president and chief executive officer for the Kiel Center Partners, a group of St. Louis area businesses and business leaders that own the building.

Kiel went up in just 21 months.

"The new arenas in Chicago [the United Center] and Cleveland [Gateway Arena] will open up this fall, too, but both of those buildings started six to eight months ahead of Kiel Center," Perkins said. "So we've been charging from behind and have managed to catch both of those projects."

The hurry-up drill means the Blues will avoid the hassle of playing part of the 1994-95 season at the 65-year-old St. Louis Arena, their home since joining the NHL in 1967-68. The 12-story Kiel Center, its exterior accented by glass and granite, will seat 18,500 for hockey and 20,000 for basketball.

Inside are themed food courts, 80 luxury boxes priced at $37,500 to $120,000 a year, and 1,640 club seats priced at $3,800 a year. Luxury box and club seat holders will have exclusive access to a 400-seat restaurant.

The Kiel Center was built on the site of the demolished 10,000-seat Kiel Auditorium, which like the St. Louis Arena was another senior citizen at age 62. (Both the old and new Kiel were named after former mayor Henry Kiel, who served from 1913-25.)

But a direct link to the past remains at Kiel, because the charming 3,600-seat Kiel Opera House still stands. Long a home for classical concerts, dance programs and Broadway productions, the Opera House has undergone a renovation to coincide with the opening of the Kiel Center.

Once the Fat Lady sings at the Opera House, she can head immediately to the Kiel Center to watch Brett Hull and the Blues because the new arena and the old Opera House are attached to one another.

There was some sticker shock for Blues fans making the switch to the new building: ticket prices were raised an average of 30 percent. But the Blues quickly showed they intended to shovel at least some of the profits back into the product by going after every free agent that moved— from Calgary's All-Star defenseman Al MacInnis to the New York Rangers' Stanley Cup-winning coach Mike Keenan.

Despite the considerable civic embarrassment over the failed expansion effort in football, St. Louisans still take a great deal of pride in the construction of both buildings. Throw in the new light-rail mass transit system (Metro Link) and the start of riverboat gaming on the Mississippi River, and the downtown area is receiving an economic shot in the arm that should boost tourism and ease the city's unemployment picture.

Nationally, St. Louis' $430-million investment in sports facilities is the rule rather than the exception. The '90s' stadium boom continues.

As previewed in this chapter last year, the city of Cleveland led the way in grand openings in 1994 with the debutes of both Jacobs Field and Gateway Arena.

Jacobs Field, the 42,400-seat cousin of Baltimore's Camden Yards, is named after Indians' owner Richard Jacobs and his late brother David. It attracted President Clinton for Opening Day and 1,995,174 paying customers in just 51 home dates before the player's strike. Gateway Arena, with its 20,592 seats, will officially become the NBA Cavaliers' new home when they host league champion Houston on Nov. 8.

In Texas, the baseball Rangers christened the Ballpark at Arlington and its 49,292 seats on April 11, with the pride of Fort Worth, pianist Van Cliburn, at the keyboard for the national anthem. The Rangers lost the opener to Milwaukee, 4-3, but had broken their season attendance record well before the strike.

And in Chicago, the NHL Blackhawks have left venerable Chicago Stadium, their home since 1929, for the new $175 million United Center across Madison Street. And while they won't be bringing the famous Barton organ with them, they will be accompanied by the NBA Bulls.

That will bring to 16 the number of new stadiums and arenas that have gone up so far in the 90's in the four major league team sports.

And there are more on the way.

Wide World Photos

A construction worker looks up at the ceiling of the **Kingdome** in Seattle shortly after the building was closed to repair falling tiles.

In 1995 alone, six new buildings will open up for business—the Shawmut Center in Boston (for the NBA Celtics and NHL Bruins), General Motors Place in Vancouver (for the NHL Canucks and new NBA Grizzlies), Coors Field in Denver (for baseball's Colorado Rockies), The Rose Garden in the Rose City of Portland (for the NBA Trail Blazers), and two completely renovated structures— the Seattle Center Coliseum (for the NBA Sonics) and the Gator Bowl (for the new NFL Jaguars).

All of these projects are fueled by the latest fad in revenue producers—luxury boxes and club seats. Luxury suites have been around for a while, but not to such a degree of luxury. Club seats are a cross between luxury boxes and regulation seats. Designed for the middle class of pro sports fans, they usually include wider seats, waiter or waitress service and exclusive membership in a restaurant and/or upscale sports bar on the stadium site.

These premium seats usually are snapped up quickly by local corporate bigwigs, business tycoons and would-be business tycoons. The money they generate usually takes care of the light bill—and then some.

In St. Louis, for example, the luxury suites and club seats at the domed stadium would generate more than $12-million a year in revenue for football (although some of that money would be shared with visiting teams). Compare this with about $2 million a year that luxury boxes bring in at Anaheim Stadium and it's no wonder the Rams have spent a good chunk of 1994 deciding whether to move.

At the moment, the domed stadium in St. Louis is unnamed. But unlike the Kiel Center, odds are the naming rights will be sold to a local corporation at the going rate of $20 million or so over 20 years. The new buildings in Boston, Vancouver and Colorado have already sold their names to, respectively, a local bank, an automobile maker and a brewery. Chicago's United Center is named after an airline and in Indianapolis the Hoosier Dome was renamed the RCA Dome after the locally-owned electronics company.

Elsewhere, gravity and an earthquake shook up stadiums in Seattle and Los Angeles in 1994.

In Seattle, four unstable ceiling tiles fell 180 feet on July 19, forcing officials to close the Kingdome until all 40,000 ceiling tiles were replaced. Two workers were killed making the repairs on Aug. 17 and the dome was closed indefinitely. Deprived of a home field, the baseball Mariners were forced to play 15 extra games on the road and the NFL Seahawks had to rent Husky Stadium at the University of Washington for their first few home games.

In Los Angeles, the Jan. 17 earthquake that pulled a 6.6 on the Richter scale knocked down the left field scoreboard at Anaheim Stadium, and caused extensive damage at both L.A. Memorial Coliseum and the L.A. Sports Arena. All three have been repaired at considerable expense.

Finally, New York's Madison Square Garden, once the world's most glamourous sports venue, was sold by Viacom in the biggest sports transaction ever on August 28 (see "Business & Media"). ITT Corporation and Cablevision Systems Inc. acquired the Garden along with the NBA Knicks, the NHL-champion Rangers and the MSG Sports TV Network for $1.075 billion.

Pretty steep for a building that opened back in 1968. But at least it has a tenant. Two, in fact.   ❑

BALLPARKS & ARENAS
COMING ATTRACTIONS

1994

BASEBALL

Cleveland (AL): Jacobs Field (named after Indians' owner Richard Jacobs) officially opened April 4 with President Clinton throwing out the first pitch; Indians beat Seattle, 4-3; park situated on downtown site that includes new Gund Arena for NBA Cavaliers (which opens in fall); seats 42,400 for baseball; facility includes 118 luxury suites; open air, grass playing surface; cost: $166 million. Attendance for 51 home dates was 1,995,174 for an average of 39,121.

Texas (AL): The Ballpark at Arlington officially opened April 11 with world reknowned Texas pianist Van Cliburn leading the Fort Worth Symphony Orchestra in *The Star Spangled Banner;* Rangers lost to Milwaukee, 4-3; park situated a quarter mile south of old Arlington Stadium; seats 49,292 for baseball; facility includes 112 luxury suites; open air, grass playing surface; cost: $189 million. Attendance for 62 home dates was 2,502,538 for an average of 40,364.

NBA BASKETBALL

Chicago (East): Grand opening of the United Center was Aug. 29 for World Wrestling Federation Summer Slam; situated across Madison Street from old Chicago Stadium; United Airlines paid for the title sponsorship; seats 21,500 for basketball and 20,500 for NHL Blackhawks; facility includes 216 luxury suites; Bulls' home opener vs. Charlotte scheduled for Nov. 4; cost: $175 million, including land and opening costs.

Cleveland (East): Gund Arena (named after Cavaliers' owner Gordon Gund) is scheduled to open with Billy Joel concert on Oct. 17; situated on downtown site adjacent to Jacobs Field, the Indians' new ballpark (which opened April 4); seats 20,592 for basketball; facility includes 92 luxury suites; Cavs' home opener vs. Houston scheduled for Nov. 8; cost: $133 million.

NHL HOCKEY

Chicago (West): Grand opening of the United Center was Aug. 29 for World Wrestling Federation Summer Slam; situated across Madison Street from old Chicago Stadium; United Airlines paid for the title sponsorship; seats 20,500 for hockey and 21,500 for NBA Bulls; facility includes 216 luxury suites; Blackhawks' home opener vs. St. Louis scheduled for Oct. 2; cost: $175 million, including land and opening costs.

St. Louis (West): Grand opening of Kiel Center scheduled for Oct. 8 with dedication ceremony; situated on downtown site of old Kiel Auditorium near St. Louis Arena; named after Henry Kiel, who was mayor of St. Louis from 1913-25; seats 18,500 for hockey and 20,000 for college basketball; facility includes 80 luxury suites; Blues' home opener vs. Chicago scheduled for Oct. 11; cost: $170 million, including razing the old auditorium and construction of parking faciltiy.

1995

BASEBALL

Colorado (NL): Construction nearing completion in downtown Denver; to be called Coors Field (after the brewery which paid for the title sponsorship); will seat 50,100 for baseball; facility will include 60 luxury boxes; open air, grass playing surface; Rockies' opener scheduled for April 1995; estimated cost: $160 million.

NBA BASKETBALL

Boston (East): Construction nearing completion behind Boston Garden; to be called the Shawmut Center (after the Boston bank which paid for the title sponsorship); will seat 18,400 for basketball and 17,200 for NHL Bruins; facility will include 104 luxury suites; Celtics' home opener scheduled for November 1995; estimated cost: $160 million.

Portland (West): Construction nearing completion next to Memorial Coliseum in downtown Portland; will be called The Rose Garden (Portland is known as the City of Roses); will seat 20,340 for basketball; facility will include 70 luxury suites; Trail Blazers' home opener scheduled for November 1995; estimated cost: $262 million for new arena, office building and entertainment complex, three new garages and renovation of old Coliseum.

Seattle (West): Complete renovation of Seattle Center Coliseum started in May 1994 with new construction commencing in September; working title of new building is New Seattle Center Coliseum, will seat 17,800 for basketball; facility will include 58 luxury suites; Sonics' home opener scheduled for November 1995; estimated cost: $73.5 million; Sonics will play 1994-95 NBA schedule at Tacoma Dome (19,000).

Vancouver (expansion team): Construction nearing completion at downtown Vancouver site adjacent to B.C. Place (home of the CFL Lions); to be called General Motors Place (after the GM Canada which paid for the title sponsorship); will seat 20,000 for basketball and 19,000 for NHL Canucks; facility will include 88 luxury suites; Grizzlies' home opener scheduled for November 1995; estimated cost: $120 million (US).

NFL FOOTBALL

Jacksonville (expansion team): Complete renovation of Gator Bowl (only west upper deck and 10,000 seats will remain from old structure); working name is the New Stadium at Jacksonville; will seat 73,000 for football; facility will include 74 luxury boxes; open air, grass playing surface; Jaguars' home opener scheduled for September 1995; estimated cost: $135 million.

St. Louis (franchise hopeful): Construction nearing completion on indoor facility in downtown St. Louis adjoining America's Center convention complex; originally envisioned as home for one of two 1995 NFL expansion teams, but not contingent on city getting NFL franchise; as yet unnamed; will seat 70,000 for football; facility will include 100 luxury boxes; artificial playing surface; scheduled to open by September 1995; estimated cost: $259 million.

NHL HOCKEY

Boston (East): Construction nearing completion behind Boston Garden; to be called the Shawmut Center (after the Boston bank which paid for the title sponsorship); will seat 17,200 for hockey and 18,400 for NBA Celtics; facility will include 104 luxury suites; Bruins' home opener scheduled for October 1995; estimated cost: $160 million.

Vancouver (West): Construction nearing completion at downtown Vancouver site adjacent to B.C. Place (home of the CFL Lions); to be called General Motors Place (GM Canada which paid for the title sponsorship); will seat 19,000 for hockey and 20,000 for NBA Grizzlies; facility will include 88 luxury suites; Canucks' home opener scheduled for October 1995; estimated cost: $120 million (US).

1996

NBA BASKETBALL

Philadelphia (East): Ground broken in August 1994 on site of razed JFK Stadium adjacent to the current Spectrum; to be called the CoreStates Spectrum (after the local financial institution which paid for the title sponsorship); will seat 21,000 for basketball and 19,500 for NHL Flyer; facility will include 139 luxury suites; 76ers' home opener scheduled for November 1996; estimated cost: $217 million.

NFL FOOTBALL

Carolina (expansion team): Construction underway in downtown Charlotte, N.C.; to be called Carolinas Stadium; will seat 72,300 for football; facility will include 135 luxury suites; open air, grass playing surface; Panthers' home opener scheduled for September, 1996; estimated cost: $160 million. Panthers will play at Memorial Stadium (81,473) in Clemson, S.C. in 1995.

Washington (NFC): Groundbreaking scheduled for December, 1994 on site adjacent to Laurel (Md.) Race Course midway between Washington and Baltimore; to be called Redskins Stadium; will seat 78,600 for football; facility will include 331 luxury suites; open air, grass playing surface; Redskins' home opener scheduled for September, 1996; estimated cost: $203 million, including local infrastructure.

NHL HOCKEY

Buffalo (East): Groundbreaking scheduled for early October, 1994 on site three blocks from Buffalo Auditorium (the Aud); to be called Crossroads Arena (after the part of downtown where the waterfront meets the intersection of South Park and Main St.); will seat 19,500 for hockey and 20,500 for college basketball; facility will include 80 luxury suites; Sabres' home opener scheduled for October 1996; estimated cost: $125 million.

Montreal (East): Construction underway on site at Windsor Station in downtown Montreal; to be called the Montreal Forum (same as the current building); will seat 21,400 for hockey; facility will include 136 luxury suites; Canadiens' home opener scheduled for March 1996; estimated cost: $160 million (US).

Ottawa (East): Construction underway on site in suburban Kanata, Ontario; to be called the Palladium; will seat 18,500 for hockey; facility will include 103 luxury suites; Senators' home opener scheduled for October 1996; estimated cost: $150 million (US) for arena, office tower, hotel, roads and highway interchange.

Philadelphia (East): Ground broken in August 1994 on site of razed JFK Stadium adjacent to the current Spectrum; to be called the CoreStates Spectrum (after the local financial institution which paid for the title sponsorship); will seat 19,500 for hockey and 21,000 for NBA 76ers; facility will include 139 luxury suites; Flyers' home opener scheduled for October 1996; estimated cost: $217 million.

Tampa Bay (East): Groundbreaking scheduled for fall of 1994 on waterfront site near new Tampa Aquarium; as yet unnamed; will seat 20,000 for hockey; facility will include 71 luxury suites; Lightning's home opener scheduled for fall of 1995; estimated cost: $115 million.

1997

BASEBALL

Atlanta (NL): Construction underway on main Olympic stadium for 1996 Summer Games; as yet unnamed; stadium will be converted to a 49,000-seat park immediately after conclusion of '96 Olympics; facility will include approximately 60 luxury boxes; open air, grass playing surface; Braves' home opener scheduled for April 1997; estimated cost: $207 million (to build Olympic stadium and renovate as baseball park).

Milwaukee (AL): Still in planning stages; to be built across centerfield fence from County Stadium; will feature convertible roof (not retractable like SkyDome); will seat 48,000 for baseball and expand to 60,000 for NFL Green Bay Packers; facility will include 100 luxury suites; open air, grass playing surface; earliest Brewers' home opener would be April 1997; estimated cost: $180-190 million.

NBA BASKETBALL

Toronto (East): In planning stages; likely site adjacent to Eaton Center in downtown Toronto; as yet unnamed; will seat 20,500 for basketball (18,000 for hockey if NHL Maple Leafs decide to leave Maple Leaf Gardens, but not to construct a new building of their own); facility will include 150 luxury suites; earliest Raptors' home opener would be November 1997; estimated cost: $150 million (US). Raptors will play their first two seasons in SkyDome (20,000).

Washington (East): In planning stages; likely site at Gallery Place Metro Station near National Mall; as yet unnamed; will seat 21,000 for basketball and 20,000 for NHL Capitals; facility will include 150 luxury suites; earliest Bullets' home opener would be November 1997; estimated cost: $200 million.

NHL HOCKEY

Florida (East): In planning stages; part of projected Blockbuster Park entertainment village that would include a new baseball stadium for the NL Marlins (Blockbuster Viedo owner Wayne Huizenga owns the Panthers and Marlins); will seat 20,000 for hockey with an unspecified number of luxury suites; earliest Panthers' home opener would be October 1997.

Washington (East): In planning stages; likely site at Gallery Place Metro Station near National Mall; as yet unnamed; will seat 20,000 for hockey and 21,000 for NBA Bullets; facility will include 150 luxury suites; earliest Capitals' home opener would be October 1997; estimated cost: $200 million.

Winnipeg (West): In planning stages; to be built at a yet to be determined site in downtown Winnipeg; working name is the Manitoba Entertainment Complex; will seat 16,500 for hockey; facility will include 30-50 luxury suites; earliest Jets' home opener would be start of 1997-98 season; estimated cost: $85 million (US).

Home, Sweet Home

The home fields, home courts and home ice of the AL, NL, NBA, NFL, CFL, NHL, NCAA Division I-A college football and Division I basketball. Also included are Formula One, IndyCar and NASCAR auto racing tracks.

Attendance figures for the 1993 NFL regular season and the 1993-94 NBA and NHL regular seasons are provided. See Baseball chapter for 1994 AL and NL attendance figures.

MAJOR LEAGUE BASEBALL

American League

		Built	Capacity	LF	LCF	CF	RCF	RF	Field
Baltimore Orioles	Oriole Park at Camden Yards	1992	**48,262**	333	410	400	373	318	Grass
Boston Red Sox	Fenway Park	1912	**33,871**	315	379	420	380	302	Grass
California Angels	Anaheim Stadium	1966	**64,593**	333	386	404	386	333	Grass
Chicago White Sox	Comiskey Park	1991	**44,321**	347	383	400	383	347	Grass
Cleveland Indians	Jacobs Field	1994	**42,400**	325	378	405	375	325	Grass
Detroit Tigers	Tiger Stadium	1912	**52,416**	340	365	440	375	325	Grass
Kansas City Royals	Ewing Kauffman Stadium	1973	**40,625**	330	385	410	385	330	Turf
Milwaukee Brewers	County Stadium	1953	**53,192**	315	392	402	392	315	Grass
Minnesota Twins	Hubert H. Humphrey Metrodome	1982	**56,783**	343	385	408	367	327	Turf
New York Yankees	Yankee Stadium	1923	**57,545**	318	399	408	385	314	Grass
Oakland Athletics	Oakland-Alameda County Coliseum	1966	**47,313**	330	375	400	375	330	Grass
Seattle Mariners	The Kingdome	1976	**59,166**	331	372	405	349	312	Turf
Texas Rangers	New Arlington Stadium	1994	**49,292**	334	388	400	377	325	Grass
Toronto Blue Jays	SkyDome	1989	**50,516**	328	375	400	375	328	Turf

Note: After four tiles fell from the Kingdome ceiling on July 19, the Seattle Mariners had two home games cancelled then had to play their next 13 home games on the road from July 21 until the players' strike began on August 12.

National League

		Built	Capacity	LF	LCF	CF	RCF	RF	Field
Atlanta Braves	Atlanta-Fulton County Stadium	1965	**52,710**	330	385	402	385	330	Grass
Chicago Cubs	Wrigley Field	1914	**38,765**	355	368	400	368	353	Grass
Cincinnati Reds	Riverfront Stadium	1970	**52,952**	330	375	404	375	330	Turf
Colorado Rockies	Coors Field	1995	**50,100**	347	389	415	387	350	Grass
Florida Marlins	Joe Robbie Stadium	1987	**49,662**	330	385	405	385	345	Grass
Houston Astros	The Astrodome	1965	**54,313**	325	375	400	375	325	Turf
Los Angeles Dodgers	Dodger Stadium	1962	**56,000**	330	385	395	385	330	Grass
Montreal Expos	Olympic Stadium	1976	**46,500**	325	375	404	375	325	Turf
New York Mets	Shea Stadium	1964	**55,601**	338	378	410	378	338	Grass
Philadelphia Phillies	Veterans Stadium	1971	**62,530**	330	371	408	371	330	Turf
Pittsburgh Pirates	Three Rivers Stadium	1970	**47,972**	335	375	400	375	335	Turf
St. Louis Cardinals	Busch Stadium	1966	**57,076**	330	375	402	375	330	Turf
San Diego Padres	San Diego/ Jack Murphy Stadium	1967	**46,510**	327	370	405	370	327	Grass
San Francisco Giants	Candlestick Park	1960	**60,000**	335	365	400	365	328	Grass

Rank by Capacity

AL
California	64,593
Seattle	59,166
New York	57,545
Minnesota	56,783
Milwaukee	53,192
Detroit	52,416
Toronto	50,516
Texas	49,292
Baltimore	48,262
Oakland	47,313
Chicago	44,321
Cleveland	42,400
Kansas City	40,625
Boston	33,871

NL
Philadelphia	62,530
San Francisco	60,000
St. Louis	57,076
Los Angeles	56,000
New York	55,601
Houston	54,313
Cincinnati	52,952
Atlanta	52,710
Colorado (new)	50,100
Florida	49,662
Pittsburgh	47,972
San Diego	46,510
Montreal	46,500
Chicago	38,765

Rank by Age

AL
Boston	1912
Detroit	1912
New York	1923
Milwaukee	1953
California	1966
Oakland	1966
Kansas City	1973
Seattle	1977
Minnesota	1982
Toronto	1989
Chicago	1991
Baltimore	1992
Texas	1994
Cleveland	1994

NL
Chicago	1914
San Francisco	1960
Los Angeles	1962
New York	1964
Houston	1965
Atlanta	1965
St. Louis	1966
San Diego	1967
Cincinnati	1970
Pittsburgh	1970
Philadelphia	1971
Montreal	1976
Florida	1987
Colorado (new)	1995

Note: Yankee Stadium (New York, AL) was rebuilt in 1976.

Home Fields

Listed below are the principal home fields used through the years by current American and National League teams. The NL became a major league in 1876, the AL in 1901.

The capacity figures in the right-hand column indicate the largest seating capacity of the ballpark while the club played there. Capacity figures before 1915 (and the introduction of concrete grandstands) are sketchy at best and have been left blank.

American League

Baltimore Orioles

1901	Lloyd Street Grounds (Milwaukee)	—
1902-53	Sportsman's Park II (St. Louis)	30,500
1954-91	Memorial Stadium (Baltimore)	53,371
1992-	Camden Yards	48,262

Boston Red Sox

1901-11	Huntington Ave. Grounds	—
1912-	Fenway Park	33,871
	(1934 capacity–27,000)	

California Angels

1961	Wrigley Field (Los Angeles)	20,457
1962-65	Dodger Stadium	56,000
1966-	Anaheim Stadium	64,593
	(1966 capacity–43,250)	

Chicago White Sox

1901-10	Southside Park	—
1910-90	Comiskey Park I	43,931
1991-	Comiskey Park II	44,321

Cleveland Indians

1901-09	League Park I	—
1910-46	League Park II	21,414
1932-93	Cleveland Stadium	74,483
1994-	Jacobs Field	42,400

Detroit Tigers

1901-11	Bennett Park	—
1912-	Tiger Stadium	52,416
	(1912 capacity–23,000)	

Kansas City Royals

1969-72	Municipal Stadium	35,020
1973-	Kauffman Stadium	40,625
	(1973 capacity–40,762)	

Milwaukee Brewers

1969	Sick's Stadium (Seattle)	25,420
1970-	County Stadium (Milwaukee)	53,192
	(1970 capacity–46,62)	

Minnesota Twins

1901-02	American League Park (Washington, DC)	—
1903-60	Griffith Stadium	27,410
1960-81	Metropolitan Stadium (Bloomington, MN)	45,919
1982-	HHH Metrodome (Minneapolis)	56,783
	(1982 capacity–54,000)	

New York Yankees

1901-02	Oriole Park (Baltimore)	—
1903-12	Hilltop Park (New York)	—
1913-22	Polo Grounds II	38,000
1923-73	Yankee Stadium I	67,224
1974-75	Shea Stadium	55,101
1976-	Yankee Stadium II	57,545
	(1976 capacity–57,145)	

Oakland Athletics

1901-08	Columbia Park (Philadelphia)	—
1909-54	Shibe Park	33,608
1955-67	Municipal Stadium (Kansas City)	35,020
1968-	Oakland Alameda County Coliseum	47,313
	(1968 capacity–48,621)	

Seattle Mariners

1977-	The Kingdome	59,166
	(1977 capacity–59,438)	

Texas Rangers

1961	Griffith Stadium (Washington, DC)	27,410
1962-71	RFK Stadium	45,016
1972-93	Arlington Stadium (Texas)	43,521
1994	The Ballpark at Arlington	49,292

Toronto Blue Jays

1977-89	Exhibition Stadium	43,737
1989-	SkyDome	50,516
	(1989 capacity–49,500)	

Ballpark Name Changes: CHICAGO–**Comiskey Park I** originally White Sox Park (1910-12), then Comiskey Park in 1913, then White Sox Park again in 1962, then Comiskey Park again in 1976; CLEVELAND–**League Park** renamed Dunn Field in 1920, then League Park again in 1928; Cleveland Stadium originally Municipal Stadium (1932-74); DETROIT–**Tiger Stadium** originally Navin Field (1912-37), then Briggs Stadium (1938-60); KANSAS CITY—**Kauffman Stadium** originally Royals Stadium (1973-93); LOS ANGELES–**Dodger Stadium** referred to as Chavez Ravine by AL while Angels played there (1962-65); PHILADELPHIA–**Shibe Park** renamed Connie Mack Stadium in 1953; ST. LOUIS–**Sportsman's Park** renamed Busch Stadium in 1953; WASHINGTON–**Griffith Stadium** originally National Park (1892-20), **RFK Stadium** originally D.C. Stadium (1961-68).

National League

Atlanta Braves

1876-94	South End Grounds I (Boston)	—
1894-1914	South End Grounds II	—
1915-52	Braves Field	40,000
1953-65	County Stadium (Milwaukee)	43,394
1966-	Atlanta-Fulton County Stadium	52,710
	(1966 capacity–50,000)	

Chicago Cubs

1876-77	State Street Grounds	—
1878-84	Lakefront Park	—
1885-91	West Side Park	—
1891-93	Brotherhood Park	—
1893-1915	West Side Grounds	—
1916-	Wrigley Field	38,765
	(1916 capacity–16,000)	

Major League Baseball (Cont.)
Home Fields

Cincinnati Reds

1876-79	Avenue Grounds	—
1880	Bank Street Grounds	—
1890-1901	Redland Field I	—
1902-11	Palace of the Fans	—
1912-70	Crosley Field	29,603
1970-	Riverfront Stadium	52,952
	(1970 capacity–52,000)	

Colorado Rockies

1993-1994	Mile High Stadium (Denver)	76,100
1995-	Coors Field	50,100

Florida Marlins

1993-	Joe Robbie Stadium (Miami)	49,662

Houston Astros

1962-64	Colt Stadium	32,601
1965-	The Astrodome	54,313
	(1965 capacity–45,011)	

Los Angeles Dodgers

1890	Washington Park I (Brooklyn)	—
1891-97	Eastern Park	—
1898-1912	Washington Park II	—
1913-56	Ebbets Field	31,497
1957	Ebbets Field	31,497
	& Roosevelt Stadium (Jersey City)	24,167
1958-61	Memorial Coliseum (Los Angeles)	93,600
1962-	Dodger Stadium	56,000

Montreal Expos

1969-76	Jarry Park	28,000
1977-	Olympic Stadium	46,500
	(1977 capacity–58,500)	

New York Mets

1962-63	Polo Grounds	55,987
1964-	Shea Stadium	55,601
	(1964 capacity–55,101)	

Philadelphia Phillies

1883-86	Recreation Park	—
1887-94	Huntingdon Ave.Grounds	—
1895-1938	Baker Bowl	18,800
1938-70	Shibe Park	33,608
1971-	Veterans Stadium	62,530
	(1971 capacity–56,371)	

Pittsburgh Pirates

1887-90	Recreation Park	—
1891-1909	Exposition Park	—
1909-70	Forbes Field	35,000
1970-	Three Rivers Stadium	47,972
	(1970 capacity–50,235)	

St. Louis Cardinals

1876-77	Sportsman's Park I	—
1885-86	Vandeventer Lot	—
1892-1920	Robison Field	18,000
1920-66	Sportsman's Park II	30,500
1966-	Busch Stadium	56,076
	(1966 capacity–50,126)	

San Diego Padres

1969-	San Diego/Jack Murphy Stadium	46,510
	(1969 capacity–47,634)	

San Francisco Giants

1876	Union Grounds (Brooklyn)	—
1883-88	Polo Grounds I (New York)	—
1889-90	Manhattan Field	—
1891-1957	Polo Grounds II	55,987
1958-59	Seals Stadium (San Francisco)	22,900
1960-	Candlestick Park	60,000
	(1960 capacity–42,553)	

Ballpark Name Changes: ATLANTA–**Atlanta-Fulton County Stadium** originally Atlanta Stadium (1966-1974); CHICAGO–**Wrigley Field** originally Weeghman Park (1914-17), then Cubs Park (1918-25); CINCINNATI–**Redland Field** originally League Park (1890-93) and **Crosley Field** originally Redland Field II (1912-33); HOUSTON–**Astrodome** originally Harris County Domed Stadium before it opened in 1965; PHILADELPHIA–**Shibe Park** renamed Connie Mack Stadium in 1953; ST. LOUIS–**Robison Field** originally Vandeventer Lot, then League Park, then Cardinal Park all before becoming Robison Field in 1901, **Sportsman's Park** renamed Busch Stadium in 1953, and **Busch Stadium** originally Busch Memorial Stadium (1966-82); SAN DIEGO–**San Diego/Jack Murphy Stadium** originally San Diego Stadium (1967-81).

NATIONAL BASKETBALL ASSOCIATION

Western Conference

		Location	Built	Capacity
Dallas Mavericks	**Reunion Arena**	Dallas, Texas	1980	**17,502**
Denver Nuggets	**McNichols Arena**	Denver, Colo.	1975	**17,022**
Golden State Warriors	**Oakland Coliseum Arena**	Oakland, Calif.	1966	**15,025**
Houston Rockets	**The Summit**	Houston, Texas	1975	**16,279**
Los Angeles Clippers	**Los Angeles Sports Arena**	Los Angeles, Calif.	1959	**16,005**
	& The Arrowhead Pond	Anaheim, Calif.	1993	**18,198**
Los Angeles Lakers	**Great Western Forum**	Inglewood, Calif.	1967	**17,505**
Minnesota Timberwolves	**Target Center**	Minneapolis, Minn.	1990	**19,006**
Phoenix Suns	**America West Arena**	Phoenix, Ariz.	1992	**19,023**
Portland Trail Blazers	**Memorial Coliseum**	Portland, Ore.	1960	**12,888**
Sacramento Kings	**ARCO Arena**	Sacramento, Calif.	1988	**17,317**
San Antonio Spurs	**Alamodome**	San Antonio, Texas	1993	**20,500**
Seattle SuperSonics	**Tacoma Dome**	Tacoma, Wash.	1962	**19,000**
Utah Jazz	**Delta Center**	Salt Lake City, Utah	1991	**19,911**

Note: San Antonio's Alamodome seating is expandable to hold 32,500. The Los Angeles Clippers are scheduled to play six of 41 regular season home games at the Arrowhead Pond in Anaheim in 1994-95.

Eastern Conference

		Location	Built	Capacity
Atlanta Hawks	**The Omni**	Atlanta, Ga.	1972	**16,368**
Boston Celtics	**Boston Garden**	Boston, Mass.	1928	**14,890**
	& **Hartford Civic Center**	Hartford, Conn.	1975	**15,418**
Charlotte Hornets	**Charlotte Coliseum**	Charlotte, N.C.	1988	**23,698**
Chicago Bulls	**United Center**	Chicago, Ill.	1994	**21,500**
Cleveland Cavaliers	**Gund Arena**	Cleveland, Ohio	1994	**20,592**
Detroit Pistons	**The Palace of Auburn Hills**	Auburn Hills, Mich.	1988	**21,454**
Indiana Pacers	**Market Square Arena**	Indianapolis, Ind.	1974	**16,530**
Miami Heat	**Miami Arena**	Miami, Fla.	1988	**15,200**
Milwaukee Bucks	**Bradley Center**	Milwaukee, Wisc.	1988	**18,633**
New Jersey Nets	**Meadowlands Arena**	E. Rutherford, N.J.	1981	**20,029**
New York Knicks	**Madison Square Garden**	New York, N.Y.	1968	**19,763**
Orlando Magic	**Orlando Arena**	Orlando, Fla.	1989	**15,291**
Philadelphia 76ers	**The Spectrum**	Philadelphia, Pa.	1967	**18,168**
Washington Bullets	**USAir Arena**	Landover, Md.	1973	**18,756**
	& **Baltimore Arena**	Baltimore, Md.	1962	**12,654**

Notes: Boston is scheduled to play three of 41 regular season home games at Hartford Civic Center and Washington is scheduled to play four of 41 regular season home games at Baltimore Arena in 1994-95.

1995-96 Expansion Teams

		Location	Built	Capacity
Toronto Raptors	**SkyDome**	Toronto, Ont.	1986	**20,000**
Vancouver Grizzlies	**General Motors Place**	Vancouver, B.C.	1995	**20,000**

Rank by Capacity

West		East	
San Antonio	20,500	Charlotte	23,698
Utah	19,911	Chicago	21,500
Phoenix	19,023	Detroit	21,454
Minnesota	19,006	Cleveland	20,592
LA Lakers	17,505	New Jersey	20,029
Dallas	17,502	New York	19,763
Sacramento	17,317	Washington	18,756
Denver	17,022	Milwaukee	18,633
Houston	16,279	Philadelphia	18,168
LA Clippers	16,005	Indiana	16,530
Golden St	15,025	Atlanta	16,368
Seattle	14,252	Orlando	15,291
Portland	12,888	Miami	15,200
		Boston	14,890

Note: Alamodome seating is expandable to 32,500.

Rank by Age

West		East	
LA Clippers	1959	Boston	1928
Portland	1960	Philadelphia	1967
Seattle	1962	New York	1968
Golden St	1966	Atlanta	1972
LA Lakers	1967	Washington	1973
Denver	1975	Cleveland	1974
Houston	1975	Indiana	1974
Dallas	1980	New Jersey	1981
Sacramento	1988	Milwaukee	1988
Minnesota	1990	Charlotte	1988
Utah	1991	Miami	1988
Phoenix	1992	Detroit	1988
San Antonio	1993	Orlando	1989
		Chicago	1994

1993-94 NBA Attendance

Official overall attendance in the NBA for the 1993-94 season was 17,984,014 for an average per game crowd of 16,246 over 1,107 games. Teams in each conference are ranked by attendance over 41 home games based on total tickets distributed; sellouts are listed in S/O column. Numbers in parentheses indicate rank in 1992-93.

Western Conference

		Attendance	S/O	Average
1	San Antonio (5)	904,167	14	22,053
2	Utah (1)	814,502	38	19,866
3	Phoenix (2)	779,943	41	19,023
4	Minnesota (3)	733,419	4	17,888
5	Sacramento (4)	709,997	41	17,317
6	Denver (9)	673,738	27	16,433
7	Golden St.(8)	616,025	41	15,025
8	Houston (11)	615,224	19	15,005
9	Seattle (6)	601,969	41	14,682
10	LA Lakers (7)	545,915	4	13,315
11	Portland (13)	528,408	41	12,888
12	Dallas (10)	526,414	3	12,839
13	LA Clippers (12)	471,034	4	11,489
	TOTAL	8,520,755	318	15,986

Eastern Conference

		Attendance	S/O	Average
1	Charlotte (1)	971,618	41	23,698
2	New York (3)	810,283	41	19,763
3	Detroit (2)	806,641	18	19,674
4	Chicago (4)	759,816	41	18,532
5	Cleveland (5)	753,686	12	18,383
6	New Jersey (8)	658,304	17	16,056
7	Milwaukee (6)	634,107	5	15,466
8	Orlando (7)	626,931	41	15,291
9	Washington (11)	619,756	18	15,116
10	Miami (9)	617,242	18	15,055
11	Boston (10)	604,867	38	14,753
12	Atlanta (14)	546,749	0	13,335
13	Indiana (12)	543,815	6	13,264
14	Philadelphia (13)	509,444	3	12,425
	TOTAL	9,463,259	299	16,487

Note: In the Eastern Conference—Boston played 38 games at Boston Garden (38 sellouts and 14,890 avg.) and three at Hartford Civic Center (no sellouts and 12,979 avg.); Washington played 37 games at USAir Arena (12 sellouts and 15,371 avg.) and three at Baltimore Arena (4 sellouts, 12,756 avg.).

National Basketball Association (Cont.)
Home Courts

Listed below are the principal home courts used through the years by current NBA teams. The largest capacity of each arena is noted in the right-hand column. ABA arenas (1972-76) are included for Denver, Indiana, New Jersey and San Antonio.

Western Conference

Dallas Mavericks

1980-	Reunion Arena	17,502
	(1980 capacity–17,828)	

Denver Nuggets

1967-75	Auditorium Arena	6,841
1975-	McNichols Sports Arena	17,022
	(1975 capacity–16,700)	

Golden State Warriors

1946-52	Philadelphia Arena	7,777
1952-62	Convention Hall (Philadelphia)	9,200
	& Philadelphia Arena	7,777
1962-64	Cow Palace (San Francisco)	13,862
1964-66	Civic Auditorium	7,500
	& (USF Memorial Gym)	6,000
1966-67	Cow Palace, Civic Auditorium	
	& Oakland Coliseum Arena	15,000
1967-71	Cow Palace	14,500
1971-	Oakland Coliseum Arena	15,025
	(1971 capacity–12,905)	

Houston Rockets

1967-71	San Diego Sports Arena	14,000
1971-72	Hofheinz Pavilion (Houston)	10,218
	& six other sites	
1972-73	Hofheinz Pavilion	10,218
	& HemisFair Arena (San Antonio)	10,446
1973-75	Hofheinz Pavilion	10,218
1975-	The Summit	16,279
	(1975 capacity–15,600)	

Los Angeles Clippers

1970-78	Memorial Auditorium (Buffalo)	17,300
1978-84	San Diego Sports Arena	12,167
1985-94	Los Angeles Sports Arena	16,005
1994-	Los Angeles Sports Arena	16,005
	& Arrowhead Pond	18,198

Los Angeles Lakers

1948-60	Minneapolis Auditorium	10,000
1960-67	Los Angeles Sports Arena	14,781
1967-	Great Western Forum (Inglewood, CA)	17,505
	(1967 capacity–17,086)	

Minnesota Timberwolves

1989-90	Hubert H. Humphrey Metrodome	23,000
1990-	Target Center	19,006

Phoenix Suns

1968-92	Arizona Veterans' Memorial Coliseum	14,487
1992-	America West Arena	19,023

Portland Trail Blazers

1970-	Memorial Coliseum	12,888
	(1970 capacity–12,366)	

Sacramento Kings

1948-55	Edgarton Park Arena (Rochester, NY)	5,000
1955-58	Rochester War Memorial	10,000
1958-72	Cincinnati Gardens	11,438
1972-74	Municipal Auditorium (Kansas City)	9,929
	& Omaha (NE) Civic Auditorium	9,136
1974-78	Kemper Arena (Kansas City)	16,785
	& Omaha Civic Auditorium	9,136
1978-85	Kemper Arena	16,785
1985-88	ARCO Arena I	10,333
1988-	ARCO Arena II	17,317
	(1988 capacity–16,517)	

San Antonio Spurs

1967-70	Memorial Auditorium (Dallas)	8,088
	& Moody Coliseum (Dallas)	8,500
1970-71	Three courts–Moody Coliseum	8,500
	Tarrant Convention Center (Ft. Worth)	13,500
	& Municipal Coliseum (Lubbock)	10,400
1971-73	Two courts–Moody Coliseum	9,500
	& Memorial Coliseum	8,088
1973-93	HemisFair Arena (San Antonio)	16,057
1993-	The Alamodome	20,500

Seattle SuperSonics

1967-78	Seattle Center Coliseum	14,098
1978-85	Kingdome	40,192
1985-94	Seattle Center Coliseum	14,252
1994-	Tacoma Dome	19,000

Utah Jazz

1974-75	Municipal Auditorium	7,853
	& Louisiana Superdome	47,284
1975-79	Superdome	47,284
1979-83	Salt Palace (Salt Lake City)	12,519
1983-84	Salt Palace	12,519
	& Thomas-Mack Center (Las Vegas)	18,500
1985-91	Salt Palace	12,616
1991-	Delta Center	19,911

Eastern Conference

Atlanta Hawks

1949-51	Wheaton Field House (Moline, IL)	6,000
1951-55	Milwaukee Arena	11,000
1955-68	Kiel Auditorium (St. Louis)	10,000
1968-72	Alexander Mem. Coliseum (Atlanta)	7,166
1972-	The Omni	16,368
	(1972 capacity–16,818)	

Boston Celtics

1946-	Boston Garden	14,890
	(1946 capacity–13,909)	

Note: Since 1975-76, the Celtics have played some regular season games at the Hartford Civic Center (15,418).

Charlotte Hornets

1988-	Charlotte Coliseum	23,698
	(1988 capacity–23,500)	

Chicago Bulls

1966-67	Chicago Amphitheater	11,002
1967-94	Chicago Stadium	18,676
1994-	United Center	21,500

Cleveland Cavaliers

1970-74	Cleveland Arena	11,000
1974-94	The Coliseum (Richfield, OH)	20,273
1994-	Gund Arena	20,592

Detroit Pistons

1948-52	North Side H.S.Gym (Ft. Wayne, IN)	3,800
1952-57	Memorial Coliseum (Ft. Wayne)	9,306
1957-61	Olympia Stadium (Detroit)	14,000
1961-78	Cobo Arena	11,147
1978-88	Silverdome (Pontiac, MI)	22,366
1988-	The Palace of Auburn Hills	21,454

Indiana Pacers

1967-74	State Fairgrounds (Indianapolis)	9,479
1974-	Market Square Arena	16,530
	(1974 capacity–17,287)	

Miami Heat

1988-	Miami Arena	15,200

Milwaukee Bucks

1968-88	Milwaukee Arena (The Mecca)	11,052
1988-	Bradley Center	18,633

New Jersey Nets

1967-68	Teaneck (NJ) Armory	3,500
1968-69	Long Island Arena (Commack, NY)	6,500
1969-71	Island Garden (W. Hempstead, NY)	5,200
1971-77	Nassau Coliseum (Uniondale, NY)	15,500
1977-81	Rutgers Ath.Center (Piscataway, NJ)	9,050
1981-	Meadowlands Arena (E. Rutherford, NJ)	20,029

New York Knicks

1946-68	Madison Sq. Garden III (50th St)	18,496
1968-	Madison Sq. Garden IV (33rd St.)	19,763
	(1968 capacity–19,694)	

Orlando Magic

1989-	Orlando Arena	15,291

Philadelphia 76ers

1949-51	State Fair Coliseum (Syracuse, NY)	7,500
1951-63	Onondaga County (NY) War Memorial	8,000
1963-67	Convention Hall (Philadelphia)	12,000
	& Philadelphia Arena	7,777
1967-	The Spectrum	18,168
	(1967 capacity–15,205)	

Washington Bullets

1961-62	Chicago Amphitheater	11,000
1962-63	Chicago Coliseum	7,100
1963-73	Baltimore Civic Center	12,289
1973-	USAir Arena (Landover, MD)	18,756
	(1973 capacity–17,500)	

Note: Since 1988-89, the Bullets have played four regular season games at Baltimore Arena (12,654).

Building Name Change: WASHINGTON—**USAir Arena** originally Capital Centre (1973–93).

NATIONAL FOOTBALL LEAGUE

American Conference

		Location	Built	Capacity	Field
Buffalo Bills	**Rich Stadium**	Orchard Park, N.Y.	1973	**80,091**	Turf
Cincinnati Bengals	**Riverfront Stadium**	Cincinnati, Ohio	1970	**60,389**	Turf
Cleveland Browns	**Cleveland Stadium**	Cleveland, Ohio	1931	**78,512**	Grass
Denver Broncos	**Mile High Stadium**	Denver, Colo.	1948	**76,273**	Grass
Houston Oilers	**The Astrodome**	Houston, Texas	1965	**59,905**	Turf
Indianapolis Colts	**RCA Dome**	Indianapolis, Ind.	1984	**60,127**	Turf
Kansas City Chiefs	**Arrowhead Stadium**	Kansas City, Mo.	1972	**77,872**	Grass
Los Angeles Raiders	**LA Memorial Coliseum**	Los Angeles, Calif.	1923	**67,800**	Grass
Miami Dolphins	**Joe Robbie Stadium**	Miami, Fla.	1987	**74,916**	Grass
New England Patriots	**Foxboro Stadium**	Foxboro, Mass.	1971	**60,290**	Grass
New York Jets	**Giants Stadium**	E. Rutherford, N.J.	1976	**77,121**	Turf
Pittsburgh Steelers	**Three Rivers Stadium**	Pittsburgh, Pa.	1970	**59,600**	Turf
San Diego Chargers	**San Diego/Jack Murphy Stadium**	San Diego, Calif.	1967	**60,789**	Grass
Seattle Seahawks	**The Kingdome**	Seattle, Wash.	1976	**66,400**	Turf
	& **Husky Stadium**	Seattle, Wash.	1920	**72,500**	Turf

Note: The Seattle Seahawks had to start the 1994 season at Husky Stadium while the Kingdome ceiling was repaired.

National Conference

		Location	Built	Capacity	Field
Arizona Cardinals	**Sun Devil Stadium**	Tempe, Ariz.	1958	**73,521**	Grass
Atlanta Falcons	**Georgia Dome**	Atlanta, Ga.	1992	**71,280**	Turf
Chicago Bears	**Soldier Field**	Chicago, Ill.	1924	**66,950**	Grass
Dallas Cowboys	**Texas Stadium**	Irving, Texas	1971	**65,024**	Turf
Detroit Lions	**Pontiac Silverdome**	Pontiac, Mich.	1975	**80,365**	Turf
Green Bay Packers	**Lambeau Field**	Green Bay, Wisc.	1957	**59,543**	Grass
	& **County Stadium**	Milwaukee, Wisc.	1953	**56,051**	Grass
Los Angeles Rams	**Anaheim Stadium**	Anaheim, Calif.	1966	**69,008**	Grass
Minnesota Vikings	**Hubert H. Humphrey Metrodome**	Minneapolis, Minn.	1982	**63,000**	Turf
New Orleans Saints	**Louisiana Superdome**	New Orleans, La.	1975	**69,065**	Turf
New York Giants	**Giants Stadium**	E. Rutherford, N.J.	1976	**77,541**	Turf
Philadelphia Eagles	**Veterans Stadium**	Philadelphia, Pa.	1971	**65,178**	Turf
San Francisco 49ers	**Candlestick Park**	San Francisco, Calif.	1960	**68,491**	Grass
Tampa Bay Buccaneers	**Tampa Stadium**	Tampa, Fla.	1967	**74,296**	Grass
Washington Redskins	**Robert F. Kennedy Stadium**	Washington, D.C.	1961	**56,454**	Grass

Note: Green Bay was scheduled to play three of eight home games in Milwaukee in 1992.

1995 Expansion Teams

		Location	Built	Capacity	Field
Jacksonville Jaguars	**New Stadium for Jacksonville**	Jacksonville, Fla.	1995	**73,000**	Grass
Carolina Panthers	**Memorial Stadium**	Clemson, S.C.	1942	**81,473**	Grass

National Football League (Cont.)

Rank by Capacity

AFC		NFC	
Buffalo	80,091	Detroit	80,365
Cleveland	78,512	NY Giants	77,541
Kansas City	77,872	Tampa Bay	74,296
NY Jets	77,121	Arizona	73,521
Denver	76,273	Atlanta	71,280
Miami	74,916	New Orleans	69,065
LA Raiders	67,800	LA Rams	69,008
Seattle	66,400	San Francisco	68,491
San Diego	60,789	Chicago	66,950
Cincinnati	60,389	Philadelphia	65,178
New England	60,270	Dallas	65,024
Indianapolis	60,127	Minnesota	63,000
Houston	59,905	Green Bay	59,543
Pittsburgh	59,600	Washington	56,454

Rank by Age

AFC		NFC	
LA Raiders	1923	Chicago	1924
Cleveland	1931	Green Bay	1957
Denver	1948	Arizona	1958
Houston	1965	San Francisco	1960
San Diego	1967	Washington	1961
Cincinnati	1970	LA Rams	1966
Pittsburgh	1970	Tampa Bay	1967
New England	1971	Dallas	1971
Kansas City	1972	Philadelphia	1971
Buffalo	1973	Detroit	1975
NY Jets	1976	New Orleans	1975
Seattle	1976	NY Giants	1976
Indianapolis	1984	Minnesota	1982
Miami	1987	Atlanta	1992

1993 NFL Attendance

Official overall paid attendance in the NFL for the 1993 season was 13,966,843 for an average per game crowd of 62,352 over 224 games. Cumulative announced (day of game) attendance figures listed by *The Sporting News* in its 1994 Pro Football Guide show an overall NFL attendance of 13,328,760 for an average per game crowd of 59,503. Teams in each conference are ranked by attendance over eight home games. NFL Rank column indicates rank in entire league. Numbers in parentheses indicate conference rank in 1992.

AFC

		Attendance	Rank	Average
1	Buffalo (1)	626,784	1st	78,348
2	Kansas City (2)	606,321	2nd	75,790
3	Denver (4)	590,808	3rd	73,851
4	Cleveland (5)	568,768	5th	71,096
5	Miami (6)	541,541	6th	67,696
6	NY Jets (3)	531,578	9th	66,447
7	San Diego (13)	474,835	13th	59,354
8	Seattle (7)	463,530	15th	57,941
9	Houston (8)	456,818	17th	57,102
10	Pittsburgh (9)	440,927	20th	55,116
11	Indianapolis (12)	407,928	21st	50,991
12	LA Raiders (11)	397,516	23rd	49,690
13	New England (14)	362,964	26th	45,371
14	Cincinnati (10)	353,273	28th	44,159
	TOTAL	6,823,620	—	60,925

NFC

		Attendance	Rank	Average
1	NY Giants (1)	584,165	4th	73,021
2	New Orleans (4)	541,300	7th	67,663
3	Detroit (3)	533,969	8th	66,746
4	Dallas (8)	510,068	10th	63,759
5	San Francisco (7)	501,476	11th	62,685
6	Philadelphia (6)	489,760	12th	61,220
7	Chicago (5)	465,832	14th	58,229
8	Atlanta (2)	460,453	16th	57,557
9	Minnesota (9)	455,210	18th	56,901
10	Green Bay (10)	452,966	19th	56,621
11	Washington (11)	406,766	22nd	50,846
12	Tampa Bay (12)	377,498	24th	47,187
13	LA Rams (13)	363,211	25th	45,401
14	Phoenix (14)	362,466	27th	45,308
	TOTAL	6,505,140	—	58,082

Note: Green Bay played 5 games at Lambeau Field (57,685 avg.) and 3 at County Stadium in Milwaukee (54,847 avg.).

Home Fields

Listed below are the principal home fields used through the years by current NFL teams. The largest capacity of each stadium is noted in the right-hand column. All-America Football Conference stadiums (1946-49) are included for Cleveland and San Francisco; and American Football League stadiums (1960-69) are included for Buffalo, Cincinnati, Denver, Houston, Kansas City, LA (Oakland) Raiders, Miami, New England (Boston), NY Jets and San Diego.

AFC

Buffalo Bills

1960-72	War Memorial Stadium	45,748
1973-	Rich Stadium (Orchard Park, NY)	80,091
	(1973 capacity–80,020)	

Cincinnati Bengals

1968-69	Nippert Stadium (Univ. of Cincinnati)	26,500
1970-	Riverfront Stadium	60,389
	(1970 capacity–56,200)	

Cleveland Browns

1946-	Cleveland Stadium	78,512
	(1946 capacity–85,703)	

Denver Broncos

1960-	Mile High Stadium	76,273
	(1960 capacity–34,000)	

Houston Oilers

1960-64	Jeppesen Stadium	23,500
1965-67	Rice Stadium (Rice Univ.)	70,000
1968-	Astrodome	59,905
	(1968 capacity–52,000)	

Indianapolis Colts

1953-83	Memorial Stadium (Baltimore)	60,020
1984-	RCA Dome (Indianapolis)	60,127
	(1984 capacity–60,127)	

Kansas City Chiefs

1960-62	Cotton Bowl (Dallas)	72,000
1963-71	Municipal Stadium (Kansas City)	47,000
1972-	Arrowhead Stadium	77,872
	(1972 capacity–78,097)	

Los Angeles Raiders

1960	Kesar Stadium (San Francisco)	59,636
1961	Candlestick Park	42,500
1962-65	Frank Youell Field (Oakland)	20,000
1666-81	Oakland-Alameda County Coliseum	54,587
1982-	Memorial Coliseum (Los Angeles)	67,800
	(1982 capacity–92,604)	

Miami Dolphins

1966-86	Orange Bowl	75,206
1987-	Joe Robbie Stadium	74,916
	(1987 capacity–75,500)	

New England Patriots

1960-62	Nickerson Field (Boston Univ.)	17,369
1963-68	Fenway Park	33,379
1969	Alumni Stadium (Boston College)	26,000
1970	Harvard Stadium	37,300
1971-	Foxboro Stadium	60,290
	(1971 capacity–61,114)	

New York Jets

1960-63	Polo Grounds	55,987
1964-83	Shea Stadium	60,372
1984-	Giants Stadium (E.Rutherford, NJ)	77,121

Pittsburgh Steelers

1933-57	Forbes Field	35,000
1958-63	Forbes Field	35,000
	& Pitt Stadium	54,500
1964-69	Pitt Stadium	54,500
1970-	Three Rivers Stadium	59,600
	(1970 capacity–49,000)	

San Diego Chargers

1960	Memorial Coliseum (Los Angeles)	92,604
1961-66	Balboa Stadium (San Diego)	34,000
1967-	San Diego/Jack Murphy Stadium	60,789
	(1967 capacity–54,000)	

Seattle Seahawks

1976-94	Kingdome	66,000
1994-	Kingdome	66,400
	& Husky Stadium	72,500

Ballpark Name Changes: CLEVELAND–**Cleveland Stadium** originally Municipal Stadium (1932-74); DENVER–**Mile High Stadium** originally Bears Stadium (1948-66); INDIANAPOLIS–**RCA Dome** originally Hoosier Dome (1984-94); NEW ENGLAND–**Foxboro Stadium** originally Schaefer Stadium (1971-82), then Sullivan Stadium (1983-89); SAN DIEGO–**San Diego/Jack Murphy Stadium** originally San Diego Stadium (1967-81).

NFC

Arizona Cardinals

1920-21	Normal Field (Chicago)	7,500
1922-25	Comiskey Park	28,000
1926-28	Normal Field	7,500
1929-59	Comiskey Park	52,000
1960-65	Busch Stadium (St. Louis)	34,000
1966-87	Busch Memorial Stadium	54,392
1988-	Sun Devil Stadium (Tempe, AZ)	73,521

Atlanta Falcons

1966-91	Atlanta-Fulton County Stadium	59,643
1992-	Georgia Dome	71,280

Chicago Bears

1920	Staley Field (Decatur, IL)	—
1921-70	Wrigley Field (Chicago)	37,741
1971-	Soldier Field	66,950
	(1971 capacity–55,049)	

Dallas Cowboys

1960-70	Cotton Bowl	72,132
1971-	Texas Stadium (Irving, TX)	65,024
	(1971 capacity–65,101)	

Detroit Lions

1930-33	Spartan Stadium (Portsmouth, OH)	8,200
1934-37	Univ. of Detroit Stadium	25,000
1938-74	Tiger Stadium	54,468
1975-	Pontiac Silverdome	80,365
	(1975 capacity–80,638)	

Green Bay Packers

1921-22	Hagemeister Brewery Park	—
1923-24	Bellevue Park	—
1925-56	City Stadium I	24,800
1957-	Lambeau Field	59,543
	(1957 capacity–32,150)	

Note: The Packers have played some games in Milwaukee each season since 1933: at Borchert Field, State Fair Park and Marquette Stadium (1933-52), and County Stadium (56,051) since 1953.

Los Angeles Rams

1937-42	Municipal Stadium (Cleveland)	85,703
1945	Suspended operations for one year	
1944-45	Municipal Stadium	85,703
1946-79	Memorial Coliseum (Los Angeles)	92,604
1980-	Anaheim Stadium	69,008

Minnesota Vikings

1961-81	Metropolitan Stadium (Bloomington)	48,446
1982-	HHH Metrodome (Minneapolis)	63,000
	(1982 capacity–62,220)	

New Orleans Saints

1967-74	Tulane Stadium	80,997
1975-	Louisiana Superdome	69,065
	(1975 capacity–74,472)	

New York Giants

1925-55	Polo Grounds II	55,200
1956-73	Yankee Stadium I	63,800
1973-74	Yale Bowl (New Haven, CT)	70,896
1975	Shea Stadium	60,372
1976-	Giants Stadium (E. Rutherford, NJ)	77,541
	(1976 capacity–76,800)	

Philadelphia Eagles

1933-35	Baker Bowl	18,800
1936-39	Municipal Stadium	73,702
1940	Shibe Park	33,608
1941	Municipal Stadium	73,702
1942	Shibe Park	33,608
1943	Forbes Field (Pittsburgh)	34,528
1944-57	Shibe Park	33,608
1958-70	Franklin Field (Univ. of Penn.)	60,546
1971-	Veterans Stadium	65,178
	(1971 capacity–65,000)	

National Football League (Cont.)
Home Fields

San Francisco 49ers

1946-70	Kezar Stadium	59,636
1971-	Candlestick Park	68,491
	(1971 capacity–61,246)	

Tampa Bay Buccaneers

1976-	Tampa Stadium	74,296
	(1976 capacity–71,951)	

Washington Redskins

1932	Braves Field (Boston)	40,000
1933-36	Fenway Park	27,000
1937-60	Griffith Stadium (Washington, DC)	35,000
1961-	RFK Stadium	56,454
	(1961 capacity–55,004)	

Ballpark Name Changes: ATLANTA–**Atlanta-Fulton County Stadium** originally Atlanta Stadium (1966-74); CHICAGO–**Wrigley Field** originally Cubs Park (1916-25), also, Comiskey Park originally White Sox Park (1910-12); DETROIT– **Tiger Stadium** originally Navin Field (1912-37), then Briggs Stadium (1938-60); also, **Pontiac Silverdome** originally Pontiac Metropolitan Stadium (1975); GREEN BAY–**Lambeau Field** originally City Stadium II (1957-64); PHILADELPHIA–**Shibe Park** renamed Connie Mack Stadium in 1953; ST. LOUIS–**Busch Memorial Stadium** renamed Busch Stadium in 1983; WASHINGTON–**RFK Stadium** originally D.C. Stadium (1961-68).

CANADIAN FOOTBALL LEAGUE

Western Division

		Location	Built	Capacity	Field
British Columbia Lions	**B.C. Place**	Vancouver, B.C.	1983	40,800	Turf
Calgary Stampeders	**McMahon Stadium**	Calgary, Alb.	1960	37,217	Turf
Edmonton Eskimos	**Commonwealth Stadium**	Edmonton, Alb	1978	60,081	Grass
Las Vegas Posse	**Sam Boyd Stadium**	Las Vegas, Nev.	1971	32,000	Turf
Sacramento Gold Miners	**Hornet Field**	Sacramento, Calif.	1959	22,500	Grass
Saskatchewan Roughriders	**Taylor Field**	Regina, Sask.	1948	27,637	Turf

Eastern Division

		Location	Built	Capacity	Field
Baltimore CFL Fball Club	**Memorial Stadium**	Baltimore, Md.	1954	54,600	Grass
Hamilton Tiger-Cats	**Ivor Wynne Stadium**	Hamilton, Ont.	1932	29,123	Turf
Ottawa Rough Riders	**Frank Clair Stadium**	Ottawa, Ont.	1967	30,927	Turf
Shreveport Pirates	**Independence Stadium**	Shreveport, La.	1965	40,000	Grass
Toronto Argos	**SkyDome**	Toronto, Ont.	1989	53,595	Turf
Winnipeg Blue Bombers	**Winnipeg Stadium**	Winnipeg, Man.	1953	32,648	Turf

Wide World Photos

After 65 years at Chicago Stadium, the NHL Blackhawks were scheduled to move across Madison Street to the new **United Center** in October.

NATIONAL HOCKEY LEAGUE

Western Conference

		Location	Built	Capacity	Rink
Anaheim Mighty Ducks	Anaheim Arena (The Pond)	Anaheim, Calif.	1993	**17,250**	200 x 85
Calgary Flames	Olympic Saddledome	Calgary, Alb.	1983	**20,230**	200 x 85
Chicago Blackhawks	United Center	Chicago, Ill.	1994	**20,500**	200 x 85
Dallas Stars	Reunion Arena	Dallas, Texas	1980	**16,914**	200 x 85
Detroit Red Wings	Joe Louis Arena	Detroit, Mich.	1979	**19,275**	200 x 85
Edmonton Oilers	Northlands Coliseum	Edmonton, Alb.	1974	**17,503**	200 x 85
Los Angeles Kings	Great Western Forum	Inglewood, Calif.	1967	**16,005**	200 x 85
St. Louis Blues	Kiel Center	St. Louis, Mo.	1994	**18,500**	200 x 85
San Jose Sharks	San Jose Arena	San Jose, Calif.	1993	**17,190**	200 x 85
Toronto Maple Leafs	Maple Leaf Gardens	Toronto, Ont.	1931	**15,842***	200 x 85
Vancouver Canucks	Pacific Coliseum	Vancouver, B.C.	1968	**16,150**	200 x 85
Winnipeg Jets	Winnipeg Arena	Winnipeg, Man.	1954	**15,393**	200 x 85

*Including Standing Room.

Eastern Conference

		Location	Built	Capacity	Rink
Boston Bruins	Boston Garden	Boston, Mass.	1928	**14,448**	191 x 83
Buffalo Sabres	Memorial Auditorium	Buffalo, N.Y.	1940	**16,284***	193 x 84
Florida Panthers	Miami Arena	Miami, Fla.	1988	**14,503**	200 x 85
Hartford Whalers	Civic Center Coliseum	Hartford, Conn.	1975	**15,635**	200 x 85
Montreal Canadiens	Montreal Forum	Montreal, Que.	1924	**17,959***	200 x 85
New Jersey Devils	Byrne Meadowlands Arena	E. Rutherford, N.J.	1981	**19,040**	200 x 85
New York Islanders	Veterans' Coliseum	Uniondale, N.Y.	1971	**16,297**	200 x 85
New York Rangers	Madison Square Garden	New York, N.Y.	1968	**18,200**	200 x 85
Ottawa Senators	Ottawa Civic Center	Ottawa, Ont.	1967	**10,585**	200 x 85
Philadelphia Flyers	The Spectrum	Philadelphia, Pa.	1967	**17,380**	200 x 85
Pittsburgh Penguins	Civic Arena	Pittsburgh, Pa.	1961	**17,537**	200 x 85
Quebec Nordiques	Colisee de Quebec	Quebec City, Que.	1951	**15,399**	200 x 85
Tampa Bay Lightning	ThunderDome	St. Petersburg, Fla.	1990	**26,000**	200 x 85
Washington Capitals	USAir Arena	Landover, Md.	1973	**18,130**	200 x 85

*Including Standing Room.

Rank by Capacity

Western		Eastern	
Chicago	20,500	Tampa Bay	26,000
Calgary	20,230	New Jersey	19,040
Detroit	19,275	NY Rangers	18,200
St. Louis	18,500	Washington	18,130
Edmonton	17,503	Montreal	17,959*
Anaheim	17,250	Pittsburgh	17,537
San Jose	17,190	Philadelphia	17,380
Dallas	16,914	Buffalo	16,284*
Vancouver	16,150	NY Islanders	16,297
Los Angeles	16,005	Hartford	15,635
Toronto	15,842*	Quebec	15,399
Winnipeg	15,393	Florida	14,503
		Boston	14,448
		Ottawa	10,585

* Including Standing Room.

Rank by Age

Western		Eastern	
Toronto	1931	Montreal	1924
Winnipeg	1954	Boston	1928
Los Angeles	1967	Buffalo	1940
Vancouver	1968	Quebec	1951
Edmonton	1974	Pittsburgh	1961
Detroit	1979	Ottawa	1967
Dallas	1980	Philadelphia	1967
Saddledome	1983	NY Rangers	1968
Anaheim	1993	NY Islanders	1971
San Jose	1993	Washington	1973
Chicago	1994	Hartford	1975
St. Louis	1994	Meadowlands	1981
		Florida	1988
		Tampa Bay	1990

Note: Montreal's Forum (1968) and Hartford's Civic Center (1980) have both been rebuilt.

Neutral Site Arenas

For the third season in a row, each NHL team will play two neutral site games in 1994-95. Those 26 games will be played in nine arenas listed below.

	Locations	Seats		Locations	Seats
America West Arena	Phoenix, Ariz.	18,028	**Metro Centre**	Halifax, N. S.	9,655
Alamodome	San Antonio, Tex.	35,000	**MGM Grand**	Las Vegas, Nev.	18,000
Copps Coliseum	Hamilton, Ont.	17,100	**Saskatchewan Place**	Saskatoon, Sask.	11,300
McNichols Arena	Denver, Colo.	16,271	**Target Center**	Minneapolis, Minn.	16,700
Memorial Coliseum	Portland, Ore.	11,500			

1994-95 Games: Phoenix (6); Hamilton (4); Denver and Saskatoon (3); Halifax, Las Vegas, Minneapolis, Portland and San Antonio (2).

Built; Denver (1975), Halifax (1978), Hamilton (1985), Las Vegas (1992), Minneapolis (1990), Phoenix (1992), Portland (1960), San Antonio (1993) and Saskatoon (1988).

National Hockey League (Cont.)
1993-94 NHL Attendance

Official overall paid attendance in the NHL for the 1993-94 season was 15,937,624 for an average per game crowd of 14,595 over 1,092 games. These figures include 26 neutral site games that officially drew 286,202 in seven cities for an 11,008 per game average. Cumulative announced (day of game) attendance figures listed by *The Hockey News* in its April 29, 1994 edition show an overall NHL attendance of 16,653,794 (including standing room) for an average per game crowd of 15,251. Teams in each conference are ranked by attendance over 41 home games. Neutral site games are not included. Number of sellouts are listed in S/O column. Numbers in parentheses indicate rank in 1992-93.

Western Conference

		Attendance	S/O	Average
1	Detroit (1)	812,640	40	19,820
2	Calgary (2)	792,307	13	19,325
3	Chicago (3)	729,314	38	17,788
4	St. Louis (4)	720,004	31	17,561
5	Anaheim*	694,473	27	16,938
6	San Jose (11)	680,325	28	16,593
7	Dallas (9)	661,089	21	16,124
8	Toronto (6)	644,609	36	15,722
9	Los Angeles (5)	641,868	32	15,655
10	Vancouver (7)	624,490	21	15,231
11	Edmonton (8)	552,581	3	13,478
12	Winnipeg (10)	545,196	6	13,297
	TOTAL	8,098,896	298	16,461

*Anaheim was an expansion team in 1993-94.

Eastern Conference

		Attendance	S/O	Average
1	Tampa Bay*	805,904	3	19,656
2	NY Rangers (1)	738,330	21	18,008
3	Philadelphia (2)	706,454	10	17,231
4	Montreal (3)	696,430	41	16,986
5	Pittsburgh (4)	684,923	11	16,705
6	New Jersey (9)	606,366	8	14,789
7	Buffalo (6)	603,274	11	14,714
8	Washington (5)	600,622	4	14,649
9	Quebec (7)	600,317	12	14,642
10	Florida*	579,899	25	14,144
11	Boston (8)	576,996	22	14,073
12	NY Islanders (10)	498,994	5	12,171
13	Hartford (12)	430,159	3	10,492
14	Ottawa (11)	426,230	11	10,396
	TOTAL	8,554,898	178	14,904

*Tampa Bay played in the Western (Campbell) Conference in 1992-93 and Florida was an expansion team in 1993-94.

Note: Tampa Bay played 36 games at ThunderDome (1 sellout and 20,988 avg.) and five at Orlando Arena (no sellouts and 10,068 avg.).

Home Ice

Listed below are the principal home buildings used through the years by current NHL teams. The largest capacity of each arena is noted in the right hand column. World Hockey Association arenas (1972-76) are included for Edmonton, Hartford, Quebec and Winnipeg.

Western Conference

Anaheim, Mighty Ducks of

1993	The Arrowhead Pond	17,250

Calgary Flames

1972-80	The Omni (Atlanta)	15,278
1980-83	Calgary Corral	7,424
1983-	Olympic Saddledome	20,230
	(1983 capacity–16,674)	

Chicago Blackhawks

1926-29	Chicago Coliseum	5,000
1929-94	Chicago Stadium	17,317
1994-	United Center	20,500

Dallas Stars

1967-93	Met Center (Bloomington, MN)	15,174
1993-	Reunion Arena (Dallas)	16,914

Detroit Red Wings

1926-27	Border Cities Arena (Windsor, Ont.)	3,200
1927-79	Olympia Stadium (Detroit)	16,700
1979-	Joe Louis Arena	19,275
	(1979 capacity–19,275)	

Edmonton Oilers

1972-74	Edmonton Gardens	7,200
1974-	Northlands Coliseum	17,503
	(1974 capacity–15,513)	

Los Angeles Kings

1967-	Great Western Forum	16,005
	(1967 capacity–15,651)	

Note: The Kings played 17 games at Long Beach Sports Arena and LA Sports Arena at the start of the 1967-68 season.

St. Louis Blues

1967-94	St. Louis Arena	17,188
1994-	Kiel Center	18,500

San Jose Sharks

1991-93	Cow Palace (Daly City, CA)	11,100
1993-	San Jose Arena	17,190

Toronto Maple Leafs

1917-31	Mutual Street Arena	8,000
1931-	Maple Leaf Gardens	15,842
	(1931 capacity–13,542)	

Vancouver Canucks

1970-	Pacific Coliseum	16,150
	(1970 capacity–15,760)	

Winnipeg Jets

1972-	Winnipeg Arena	15,393
	(1972 capacity–10,177)	

Building Name Changes: LOS ANGELES–**Great Western Forum** originally The Forum (1967-88); MINNESOTA–**Met Center** originally Metropolitan Sports Center (1967-82); ST. LOUIS–**St. Louis Arena** renamed The Checkerdome in 1977, then St. Louis Arena again in 1982.

Eastern Conference

Boston Bruins

1924-28	Boston Arena	6,200
1928-	Boston Garden	14,448
	(1928 capacity–14,500)	

Buffalo Sabres

1970-	Memorial Auditorium (The Aud)	16,284
	(1970 capacity–10,429)	

Florida Panthers

1993-	Miami Arena	14,503

Hartford Whalers

1972-73	Boston Garden	14,442
1973-74	Boston Garden (regular season)	14,442
	West Springfield (MA) Big E (playoffs)	5,513
1974-75	West Springfield Big E	5,513
	& Hartford (CT) Civic Center	10,507
1975-77	Hartford Civic Center	10,507
1977-78	Hartford Civic Center	10,507
	& Springfield (MA) Civic Center	7,725
1978-79	Springfield Civic Center	7,725
1979-80	Springfield Civic Center	7,725
	& Hartford Civic Center II	14,250
1980-	Hartford Civic Center II	15,635
	(1980 capacity–14,460)	

Note: The Hartford Civic Center roof caved in Jan, 1978, forcing the Whalers to move their home games to Springfield, MA, for two years.

Montreal Canadiens

1910-20	Jubilee Arena	3,200
1913-18	Montreal Arena (Westmount)	6,000
1918-26	Mount Royal Arena	6,750
1926-68	Montreal Forum I	15,500
1968-	Montreal Forum II	17,959
	(1968 capacity–16,074)	

Note: The Forum (original capacity: 9,200) was built in 1924 for Montreal's other NHL team, the Maroons, who were its only tenant from 1924-26. The Maroons, who folded after the 1937-38 season, shared the Forum with the Canadiens from 1924-38.

New Jersey Devils

1974-76	Kemper Arena (Kansas City)	16,300
1976-82	McNichols Arena (Denver)	15,900
1982-	Meadowlands Arena	
	(E. Rutherford, NJ)	19,040
	(1982 capacity–19,023)	

New York Islanders

1972-	Nassau Veterans' Mem. Coliseum	16,297
	(1972 capacity–14,500)	

New York Rangers

1925-68	Madison Square Garden III	15,925
1968-	Madison Square Garden IV	18,200
	(1968 capacity–17,250)	

Ottawa Senators

1992-	Ottawa Civic Center	10,585

Philadelphia Flyers

1967-	The Spectrum	17,380
	(1967 capacity–14,558)	

Pittsburgh Penguins

1967-	Civic Arena	17,537
	(1967 capacity–12,508)	

Quebec Nordiques

1972-	Le Colisée de Quebec	15,399
	(1972 capacity–10,004)	

Tampa Bay Lightning

1992-93	Expo Hall (Tampa)	10,500
1993-	ThunderDome (St. Petersburg)	26,000

Washington Capitals

1974-	USAir Arena (Landover, MD)	18,130

Building Name Change: WASHINGTON—**USAir Arena** originally Capital Centre (1974-93).

MISCELLANEOUS

World's Largest Soccer Stadiums

The world's 10 largest soccer stadiums and other major national venues with approximate capacities, according to FIFA.

Top 10

	Stadium	Location	Capacity
1	Rungnado	Pyongyang, N.Korea	150,000
2	Magalhaes Pinto	Belo Horizonte, Brazil	125,000
	Maracana	Rio de Janeiro, Brazil	125,000
4	Castelao	Fortaleza, Brazil	120,000
	Morumbi	Sao Paulo, Brazil	120,000
	Senajan Main	Jakarta, Indonesia	120,000
	SL Benfica	Lisbon, Portugal	120,000
8	Arrudao	Recife, Brazil	115,000
	Azteca	Mexico City, Mexico	115,000
	Camp Nou	Barcelona, Spain	115,000

Others

Stadium	Location	Capacity
Lenin	Moscow, Russia	100,350
Rose Bowl	Pasadena, USA	95,000
Olimpico	Rome, Italy	82,650
Nepstadion	Budapest, Hungary	80,000
Wembley	London, England	80,000
Hampton Park	Glasgow, Scotland	73,150
Vasil Levski	Sofia, Bulgaria	70,000
Olympia	Munich, Germany	69,250
Feyenoord	Rotterdam, Holland	55,000
Pac des Princes	Paris, France	48,750

Horse Racing

Triple Crown race tracks

Race	Racetrack	Seats	Infield
Kentucky Derby	Churchill Downs	51,500	100,000
Preakness	Pimlico Race Course	40,000	50,000
Belmont Sakes	Belmont Park	32,491	50,000

Record crowds: Kentucky Derby— 163,628 (1974); Preakness—98,896 (1989); Belmont— 82,694 (1971).

Tennis

Grand Slam center courts

Event	Main Stadium	Seats
Australian Open	National Tennis Center	15,000
French Open	Stade Roland Garros	16,500
Wimbledon	Centre Court	13,107
U.S. Open	National Tennis Center	18,000

AUTO RACING

Formula One, IndyCar and NASCAR Winston Cup racing circuits. Qualifying records accurate as of Sept. 10, 1994. Capacity figures for IndyCar and NASCAR tracks areapproximate and pertain to grandstand seating only. Standing room and hillside terrain seating featured at most road courses are not included.

Formula One

Race track capacity figures unavailable.

Grand Prix	Miles	Qual.mph Record	Set By
Australian ....**Adelaide** (South Australia)	2.347	114.680	Nigel Mansell (1992)
Belgian ....**Spa-Francorchamps**	4.333	141.123	Nigel Mansell (1992)
Brazilian ....**Interlagos** (Sao Paulo)	2.687	127.799	Nigel Mansell (1992)
British ....**Silverstone** (Towcester)	3.247	148.043	Nigel Mansell (1992)
Canadian................**Circuit Gilles Villeneuve** (Montreal)	2.753	125.459	Alain Prost (1993)
European..................**Donington Park** (Derby, England)	2.5	127.724	Alain Prost (1993)
French ....**Magny Cours** (Nevers)	2.641	128.709	Nigel Mansell (1992)
German ....**Hockenheimring** (Hockenheim)	4.235	156.722	Nigel Mansell (1991)
Hungarian...............**Hungaroring** (Budapest)	2.465	117.602	Riccardo Patrese (1992)
Italian ....**Autodromo di Nazionale, Monza** (Milan)	3.604	159.951	Ayrton Senna (1991)
Japanese......................**Suzuka** (Nagoya)	3.641	138.515	Gerhard Berger (1991)
Monaco.........................**Monte Carlo**	2.068	94.811	Michael Schumacher (1994)
Pacific ....**T1 Circuit Aida** (Japan)	2.301	117.978	Ayrton Senna (1994)
Portuguese.......................**Autodromo do Estoril**	2.703	133.224	Nigel Mansell (1992)
San Marino...............**Ferrari Cicuit** (Imola, Italy)	3.132	137.755	Nigel Mansell (1992)
South African ....**Kyalami** (Johannesburg)	2.647	126.270	Nigel Mansell (1992)
Spanish ....**Catalunya** (Barcelona)	2.950	136.472	Alain Prost (1993)

IndyCar

	Location	Miles	Qual.mph Record	Set By	Seats
Belle Isle Park ....Detroit, Mich.	2.1**	108.649	Nigel Mansell (1994)	18,000
Burke Lakefront Airport.........................Cleveland, Ohio	2.37**	143.072	Emerson Fittipaldi (1993)	36,000
Exhibition Place ....Toronto, Ont.	1.78**	110.191	Robby Gordon (1994)	60,000
Indianapolis Motor Speedway.............Indianapolis, Ind.	2.5	232.618	Roberto Guerrero (1992)	265,000
Laguna Seca Raceway...........................Monterey, Calif.	2.21*	111.967	Michael Andretti (1992)	8,000
Long Beach..................................Long Beach, Calif.	1.59**	108.450	Paul Tracy (1994)	45,000
Miami..Miami, Fla.	1.84**	—	First race in 1995	50,000
Michigan International Speedway..........Brooklyn, Mich.	2.0	234.275	Mario Andretti (1993)	70,000
Mid-Ohio Sports Car Course ....Lexington, Ohio	2.25*	119.517	Al Unser Jr. (1994)	6,000
The Milwaukee Mile...........................West Allis, Wisc.	1.0	165.752	Raul Boesel (1993)	36,800
Nazareth Speedway...............................Nazareth, Pa.	1.0	181.435	Michael Andretti (1992)	35,000
New Hampshire Intl. Speedway ....Loudon, N.H.	1.06	175.091	Emerson Fittipaldi (1994)	60,000
Pacific Place ....Vancouver, B.C.	1.65**	109.049	Robby Gordon (1994)	65,000
Phoenix International Raceway ....Phoenix, Ariz.	1.0	176.266	Paul Tracy (1994)	50,000
Portland International Raceway ....Portland, Ore.	1.95	116.861	Al Unser Jr. (1994)	27,000
Road America ....Elkhart Lake, Wisc.	4.0*	134.466	Bobby Rahal (1991)	10,000
Surfers Paradise ....Gold Coast, Australia	2.8**	106.053	Nigel Mansell (1994)	55,000

*Road courses (not ovals). **Temporary street circuits.

NASCAR

	Location	Miles	Qual.mph Record	Set By	Seats
Atlanta Motor Speedway ....Hampton, Ga.	1.52	180.207	Loy Allen Jr. (1994)	78,000
Bristol International Raceway......................Bristol, Tenn.	0.53	124.946	Chuck Bown (1994)	65,000
Charlotte Motor Speedway ....Concord, N.C.	1.5	181.439	Jeff Gordon (1994)	140,000
Darlington International Raceway ....Darlington, N.C.	1.37	165.533	Bill Elliott (1994)	55,000
Daytona International Speedway ....Daytona Beach, Fla.	2.5	210.364	Bill Elliott (1987)	97,900
Dover Downs International Speedway..........Dover, Del.	1.0	151.956	Ernie Irvan (1994)	55,000
Indianapolis Motor Speedway ....Indianapolis, Ind.	2.5	172.414	Rick Mast (1994)	265,000
Martinsville Speedway..........................Martinsville, Va.	0.53	93.887	Geoff Bodine (1993)	56,000
Michigan International Speedway..........Brooklyn, Mich.	2.0	180.750	Ken Schrader (1993)	70,000
New Hampshire Int'l Speedway ....Louden, N.H.	1.06	126.871	Mark Martin (1993)	60,000
North Carolina Motor Speedway......Rockingham, N.C.	1.02	151.716	Geoff Bodine (1994)	55,000
North Wilkesboro Speedway............N.Wilkesboro, N.C.	0.63	119.016	Ernie Irvan (1994)	45,000
Phoenix International Raceway ....Phoenix, Ariz.	1.0	128.141	Rusty Wallace (1992)	50,000
Pocono International Raceway ....Long Pond, Pa.	2.5	164.558	Rusty Wallace (1994)	77,000
Richmond International Raceway ....Richmond, Va.	0.75	123.474	Ted Musgrave (1994)	71,350
Sears Point International Raceway ....Sonoma, Calif.	2.52*	91.838	Dale Earnhardt (1993)	00,000
Talladega Superspeedway ....Talladega, Ala.	2.66	212.809	Bill Elliott (1987)	85,000
Watkins Glen ....Watkins Glen, N.Y.	2.45*	119.118	Mark Martin (1993)	35,000

*Road courses (not ovals). **Note:** Richmond sells reserved seats only (no infield) for Winston Cup races.

COLLEGE BASKETBALL

The 50 Largest Arenas

The 50 largest arenas in Division I college basketball for the 1994-95 regular season. Note that (*) indicates part-time home court.

		Seats	Home Team			Seats	Home Team
1	Carrier Dome	33,000	Syracuse	26	LA Sports Arena	15,509	USC
2	Thompson-Boling Center	24,535	Tennessee	27	Knickerbocker Arena	15,500	Siena*
3	Rupp Arena	24,000	Kentucky	28	Memorial Gymnasium	15,378	Vanderbilt
4	Marriott Center	22,700	BYU	29	Breslin Student Events Center	15,138	Michigan St.
5	Dean Smith Center	21,572	N. Carolina	30	Coleman Coliseum	15,043	Alabama
6	The Pyramid	20,142	Memphis	31	Arena-Auditorium	15,028	Wyoming
7	Meadowlands Arena	20,029	Seton Hall*	32	Oakland Coliseum Arena	15,025	California*
8	Kiel Center	20,000	Saint Louis	33	Huntsman Center	15,000	Utah
9	USAir Arena	19,035	Georgetown	34	Cole Fieldhouse	14,500	Maryland
10	Madison Square Garden	18,876	St. John's*	35	Joel Coliseum	14,407	Wake Forest
11	Freedom Hall	18,865	Louisville	36	Devaney Sports Center	14,302	Nebraska
12	Bradley Center	18,633	Marquette	37	Williams Arena	14,300	Minnesota
13	Bud Walton Arena	18,600	Arkansas	38	University Center	14,287	Arizona St.
14	Thomas & Mack Center	18,500	UNLV	39	Maravich Center	14,164	LSU
15	The Spectrum	18,060	Villanova*	40	The McKale Center	14,140	Arizona
16	Rosemont Horizon	17,500	DePaul* & Loyola-IL*	41	Mackey Arena	14,123	Purdue
				42	Hilton Coliseum	14,020	Iowa St.
17	Assembly Hall	17,357	Indiana	43	WVU Coliseum	14,000	West Va.
18	University Arena (The Pit)	17,126	New Mexico	44	CSU Convention Center	13,610	Cleveland St.
19	Pittsburgh Civic Arena	16,725	Pittsburgh*	45	Crisler Arena	13,609	Michigan
20	Assembly Hall	16,321	Illinois	46	Bramlage Coliseum	13,500	Kansas St.
21	Hartford Civic Center	16,294	UConn*	47	Univ. of Dayton Arena	13,455	Dayton
22	Erwin Center	16,231	Texas	48	Hearnes Center	13,343	Missouri
23	Miami Arena	15,826	Miami	49	St. John Arena	13,276	Ohio St.
24	Allen Field House	15,800	Kansas	50	Providence Civic Center	13,106	Providence & Rhode Island
25	Carver-Hawkeye Arena	15,550	Iowa				

Division I Conference Home Courts

Division I conference by conference listing includes member teams for 1994-95 season. Teams with home games in more than one arena are noted.

American West

	Home Floor	Seats
CS-Northridge	The Matadome	2,000
CS-Sacramento	Hornet Gym	1,800
	& ARCO Arena	17,300
Cal Poly SLO	Mott Gym	3,500
Southern Utah	Centrum	5,300

Atlantic Coast

	Home Floor	Seats
Clemson	Littlejohn Coliseum	11,020
Duke	Cameron Indoor Stadium	9,314
Florida St	Tallahassee Civic Center	12,500
Georgia Tech	Alexander Mem. Coliseum	10,000
Maryland	Cole Field House	14,500
North Carolina	Dean Smith Center	21,572
N.C. State	Reynolds Coliseum	12,400
Virginia	University Hall	8,864
Wake Forest	Joel Coliseum	14,407

Atlantic 10

	Home Floor	Seats
Duquesne	Palumbo Center	6,200
G. Washington	Smith Center	5,000
Massachusetts	Mullins Center	9,493
Rhode Island	Keaney Gymnasium	4,000
	& Providence Civic Center	13,106
Rutgers	Brown Athletic Center	9,000
St. Bonaventure	Reilly Center	6,000
St. Joseph's-PA	Alumni Mem. Fieldhouse	3,200
Temple	McGonigle Hall	3,900
West Virginia	WVU Coliseum	14,000

Note: There are only nine schools in the Atlantic 10.

Big East

	Home Floor	Seats
Boston College	Conte Forum	8,606
Connecticut	Gampel Pavilion	8,241
	& Hartford Civic Center	16,294
Georgetown	USAir Arena	19,035
Miami-FL	Miami Arena	15,826
Pittsburgh	Fitzgerald Field House	6,798
	& Pittsburgh Civic Arena	16,725
Providence	Providence Civic Center	13,106
St. John's	Alumni Hall	6,008
	& Madison Sqare Garden	18,876
Seton Hall	Walsh Gymnasium	3,200
	& Meadowlands Arena	20,029
Syracuse	Carrier Dome	33,000
Villanova	duPont Pavilion	6,500
	& The Spectrum	18,060

Note: Big East football members Rutgers and West Virginia, who currently play basketball in the Atlantic 10, will join the Big East in basketball along with independent Notre Dame in 1995-96.

Big Eight

	Home Floor	Seats
Colorado	Coors Events Center	11,199
Iowa St	Hilton Coliseum	14,020
Kansas	Allen Fieldhouse	15,800
Kansas St	Bramlage Coliseum	13,500
Missouri	Hearnes Center	13,343
Nebraska	Devaney Sports Center	14,302
Oklahoma	Lloyd Noble Center	11,100
Oklahoma St	Gallagher-Iba Arena	6,381

Note: The Big Eight will become the Big 12 in 1996-97 with the addition of Baylor, Texas, Texas A&M and Texas Tech from the SWC which will fold after the 1995-96 school year.

College Basketball (Cont.)
Division I Conference Home Courts

Big Sky

Home Floor		Seats
Boise St	BSU Pavilion	12,480
Eastern Wash	Reese Court	5,000
Idaho	Kibbie Dome	10,000
Idaho St	Holt Arena	7,938
Montana	Dahlberg Arena	9,029
Montana St	Worthington Arena	7,287
Northern Ariz	Walkup Skydome	9,500
Weber St	Dee Events Center	12,000

Big South

Home Floor		Seats
Charleston So	CSU Fieldhouse	2,500
	& N. Charleston Coliseum	12,700
Coastal Carolina	Kimbel Gym	1,800
Liberty	Vines Center	9,000
MD-Balt.County	UMBC Fieldhouse	4,024
NC-Asheville	Justice Center	2,500
	& Asheville Civic Center	6,800
NC-Greensboro	Spectator Gymnasium	2,320
Radford	Dedmon Center	5,000
Towson St	Towson Center	5,000
Winthrop	Winthrop Coliseum	6,100

Note: Campbell moved into the TAAC after 1993-94 Season.

Big Ten

Home Floor		Seats
Illinois	Assembly Hall	16,321
Indiana	Assembly Hall	17,357
Iowa	Carver-Hawkeye Arena	15,550
Michigan	Crisler Arena	13,609
Michigan St	Breslin Events Center	15,138
Minnesota	Williams Arena	14,300
Northwestern	Welsh-Ryan Arena	8,117
Ohio St	St. John Arena	13,276
Penn St	Rec Hall	6,846
Purdue	Mackey Arena	14,123
Wisconsin	Wisconsin Field House	11,500

Note: There are eleven schools in the Big 10.

Big West

Home Floor		Seats
CS-Fullerton	Titan Gym	4,000
Long Beach St	The Pyramid	7,500
Nevada	Lawlor Events Center	11,200
New Mexico St	Pan American Center	13,071
Pacific	Spanos Center	6,000
San Jose St	The Event Center	5,000
UC-Irvine	Bren Events Center	5,000
UC-Santa Barbara	The Thunderdome	6,000
UNLV	Thomas & Mack Center	18,500
Utah St	The Smith Spectrum	10,270

Colonial

Home Floor		Seats
American	Bender Arena	5,000
East Carolina	Minges Coliseum	10,800
George Mason	Patriot Center	10,000
James Madison	JMU Convocation Center	7,612
NC-Wilmington	Trask Coliseum	6,100
Old Dominion	Norfolk Scope	10,253
Richmond	Robins Center	9,171
Wm. & Mary	William & Mary Hall	10,000

Great Midwest

Home Floor		Seats
Ala-Birmingham	UAB Arena	8,500
Cincinnati	Shoemaker Center	13,176
Dayton	Univ. of Dayton Arena	13,455
DePaul	Rosemont Horizon	17,500
	& Alumni Hall	5,229
Marquette	Bradley Center	18,633
Memphis	The Pyramid	20,142
Saint Louis	Kiel Center	20,000

Ivy League

Home Floor		Seats
Brown	Pizzitola Sports Center	2,500
Columbia	Levien Gymnasium	3,200
Cornell	Alberding Field House	4,473
Dartmouth	Leede Arena	2,100
Harvard	Briggs Athletic Center	3,000
Penn	The Palestra	8,722
Princeton	Jadwin Gymnasium	7,200
Yale	Payne Whitney Gymnasium	3,000

Metro

Home Floor		Seats
Louisville	Freedom Hall	18,865
NC-Charlotte	Independence Arena	9,575
South Florida	Sun Dome	10,411
Southern Miss	Green Coliseum	8,095
Tulane	Fogelman Arena	3,600
VCU	Richmond Coliseum	12,500
Virginia Tech	Cassell Coliseum	9,971

Metro Atlantic

Home Floor		Seats
Canisius	Memorial Auditorium	11,500
	& Koessler Athletic Center	1,800
Fairfield	Alumni Hall	2,479
Iona	Mulcahy Center	3,200
Loyola-MD	Reitz Arena	3,000
Manhattan	Draddy Gymnasium	3,000
Niagara	Niagara Falls Conv. Center	6,000
	& Gallagher Center	3,200
St. Peter's	Yanitelli Center	3,200
Siena	Alumni Recreation Center	4,000
	& Knickerbocker Arena	15,500

Mid-American

Home Floor		Seats
Akron	JAR Arena	5,500
Ball St	University Arena	11,500
Bowling Green	Anderson Arena	5,000
Central Mich	Rose Arena	6,000
Eastern Mich	Bowen Field House	5,600
Kent	Memorial Athletic Center	6,327
Miami-OH	Millett Hall	9,200
Ohio Univ	Convocation Center	13,080
Toledo	Savage Hall	9,000
Western Mich	Read Fieldhouse	8,250

Dome, Sweet Dome

There are 10 domes in Division I basketball (in alphabetical order): Baby Dome (Prairie View); Cajundome (SW Louisiana); Carrier Dome (Syracuse); Gold Dome (Centenary); Joe Reed Acadome (Alabama St.); Kibbie Dome (Idaho); Sun Dome (South Fla.); Thunderdome (Santa Barbara); UNI Dome (No. Iowa) and Walkup Skydome (No. Ariz.).

Mid-Continent

	Home Floor	Seats
Buffalo	Alumni Arena	8,464
Central Conn. St	Dietrick Gym	4,500
Chicago St	Phys. Ed. & Athletics Bldg.	2,000
Eastern Ill	Lantz Gym	6,500
Missouri-K.C	Municipal Auditorium	10,000
NE Illinois	Phys. Ed. Complex	2,000
Troy St	Sartain Hall	3,500
Valparaiso	Athletics-Recreation Center	4,500
Western Ill	Western Hall	5,139
Youngstown St	Beeghly Center	8,000

Note: former East Coast members Buffalo, Central Conn St., Chicago St., NE Illinois and Troy St. and independant Missouri-KC joined conference after 1993-94 season.

Mid-Eastern

	Home Floor	Seats
Bethune-Cookman	Moore Gym	2,000
Coppin St	Pullen Gym	3,000
Delaware St	Memorial Hall	4,000
Florida A&M	Gaither Gym	6,000
Howard	Burr Gym	3,000
MD-East.Shore	Tawes Gym	3,500
Morgan St	Hill Field House	7,500
N. Carolina A&T	Corbett Sports Center	7,500
S. Carolina St	Smith-Hammond-Middleton	3,200

Midwestern

	Home Floor	Seats
Butler	Hinkle Fieldhouse	11,000
Cleveland St	CSU Convocation Center	13,610
Detroit Mercy	Cobo Arena	11,143
IL-Chicago	UIC Pavilion	10,000
La Salle	Philadelphia Civic Center	10,000
Loyola-IL	Rosemont Horizon	17,500
	& Alumni Gym	1,500
Northern Illinois	Chick Evans Field House	6,044
WI-Green Bay	Brown County Arena	5,600
WI-Milwaukee	The Mecca	11,052
Wright St	Nutter Center	10,500
Xavier-OH	Cincinnati Gardens	10,400

Note: former Mid-Continent members Cleveland St., IL-Chicago, Northern Ill., WI-Green Bay, WI-Milwaukee and Wright St. joined conference after 1993-94 season.

Missouri Valley

	Home Floor	Seats
Bradley	Carver Arena	10,474
Creighton	Omaha Civic Auditorium	9,481
Drake	Knapp Center	7,002
Evansville	Roberts Stadium	12,300
Illinois St	Redbird Arena	10,500
Indiana St	Hulman Center	10,200
Northern Iowa	UNI-Dome	10-20,000
Southern Ill	SIU Arena	10,014
SW Missouri St	Hammons Student Center	8,858
Tulsa	Maxwell Convention Center	8,659
Wichita St	Levitt Arena	10,656

Note: former Midwestern member Evansville joined conference after 1993-94 season.

North Atlantic

	Home Floor	Seats
Boston University	Case Center	2,500
	& Walter Brown Arena	4,400
Delaware	Bob Carpenter Center	5,000
Drexel	Phys. Education Center	2,300
Hartford	The Sports Center	4,475
Hofstra	Physical Fitness Center	3,500
Maine	Alfond Arena	6,000
New Hampshire	Lundholm Gym	3,500
Northeastern	Matthews Arena	6,000
Vermont	Patrick Gym	3,200

Northeast

	Home Floor	Seats
FDU-Teaneck	Rothman Center	5,000
LIU-Brooklyn	Schwartz Athletic Center	1,700
Marist	McCann Center	3,944
Monmouth	Boylan Gym	3,000
Mt. St. Mary's	Knott Arena	3,500
Rider	Alumni Gymnasium	2,000
Robert Morris	Sewall Center	3,056
St. Francis-NY	Phys. Ed. Center	1,400
St. Francis-PA	Maurice Stokes Center	3,500
Wagner	Sutter Gym	1,650

Ohio Valley

	Home Floor	Seats
Austin Peay	Dunn Center	9,000
Eastern Ky	McBrayer Arena	6,500
Middle Tenn.St	Murphy Center	11,520
Morehead St	Johnson Arena	6,500
Murray St	Racer Arena	5,550
SE Missouri St	Show Me Center	7,000
Tennessee-Martin	Pacer Arena	6,700
Tennessee St	Gentry Center	10,500
Tennessee Tech	Eblen Center	10,150

Pacific-10

	Home Floor	Seats
Arizona	McKale Center	14,140
Arizona St	University Activity Center	14,287
California	Harmon Arena	6,578
	& Oakland Coliseum	15,025
Oregon	McArthur Court	10,063
Oregon St	Gill Coliseum	10,400
Stanford	Maples Pavilion	7,500
UCLA	Pauley Pavilion	12,819
USC	LA Sports Arena	15,509
Washington	Hec Edmundson Pavilion	7,870
Washington St	Friel Court	12,058

Patriot League

	Home Floor	Seats
Army	Christl Arena	5,043
Bucknell	Davis Gym	2,300
Colgate	Cotterell Court	3,000
Fordham	Rose Hill Gymnasium	3,470
Holy Cross	Hart Center	4,000
	& Worcester Centrum	13,150
Lafayette	Kirby Field House	3,500
Lehigh	Stabler Arena	5,600
Navy	Alumni Hall	5,710

Southeastern

WESTERN	Home Floor	Seats	EASTERN	Home Floor	Seats
Alabama	Coleman Coliseum	15,043	Florida	O'Connell Center	12,000
Arkansas	Bud Walton Arena	18,600	Georgia	Georgia Coliseum	10,512
Auburn	Eaves Memorial Coliseum	12,500	Kentucky	Rupp Arena	24,000
LSU	Maravich Assembly Center	14,164	South Carolina	Carolina Coliseum	12,401
Mississippi	Tad Smith Coliseum	8,135	Tennessee	Thompson-Boling Arena	24,535
Mississippi St	Humphrey Coliseum	10,000	Vanderbilt	Memorial Gymnasium	15,378

College Basketball (Cont.)
Division I Conference Home Courts

Southern

	Home Floor	Seats
Appalachian St	Varsity Gymnasium	8,000
The Citadel	McAlister Field House	6,200
Davidson	Belk Arena	6,000
E.Tenn.St	Memorial Center	12,000
Furman	Greenville Mem. Auditorium	6,000
Ga. Southern	Hanner Fieldhouse	5,500
Marshall	Henderson Center	10,250
Tenn-Chatt	UTC Arena	11,218
VMI	Cameron Hall	5,029
W. Carolina	Ramsey Center	7,826

Southland

	Home Floor	Seats
McNeese St.	Burton Coliseum	8,000
Nicholls St	Stopher Gym	3,800
North Texas	UNT Super Pit	9,885
NE Louisiana	Ewing Coliseum	8,000
N'western St	Prather Coliseum	3,900
Sam Houston St	Johnson Coliseum	6,172
SW Texas St	Strahan Coliseum	7,200
S.F. Austin	SFA Coliseum	7,050
TX-Arlington	Texas Hall	4,200
TX-San Antonio	Convocation Center	5,100

Southwest

	Home Floor	Seats
Baylor	Ferrell Center	10,084
Houston	Hofheinz Pavilion	10,145
Rice	Autry Court	5,000
SMU	Moody Coliseum	9,007
Texas	Erwin Center	16,231
Texas A&M	G. Rollie White Coliseum	7,500
TCU	Daniel-Meyer Coliseum	7,166
Texas Tech	Lubbock Municipal Coliseum	8,174

Southwestern

	Home Floor	Seats
Alabama St	Joe Reed Acadome	7,000
Alcorn St	The Scalpin' Grounds	7,000
Grambling	Memorial Gym	5,000
Jackson St	Williams Assembly Center	8,000
Miss. Valley	Harrison Athletic Complex	6,000
Prairie View	The Baby Dome	6,600
Southern-BR	Clark Activity Center	7,500
TX Southern	Health & P.E. Building	7,500

Independent

	Home Floor	Seats
Notre Dame	JACC Arena	11,418

Note: former independents CS-Northridge, CS Sacramento and Southern Utah joined new American West Conf. for 1994-95 season.

Sun Belt

	Home Floor	Seats
Ark-Little Rock	Barton Coliseum	8,303
Arkansas St	Convocation Center	10,563
Jacksonville	Memorial Coliseum	10,000
Lamar	Montagne Center	10,080
Louisiana Tech	Thomas Assembly Center	8,000
New Orleans	Lakefront Arena	10,000
South Alabama	Mobile Civic Center	10,000
SW Louisiana	The Cajundome	12,000
Texas-Pan Am	UTPA Field House	5,000
Western Ky	E.A. Diddle Arena	11,300

Trans America

	Home Floor	Seats
Campbell	Carter Gym	1,050
	& Cumberland County CC	5,000
Centenary	Gold Dome	4,000
Central Fla	UCF Arena	5,100
Charleston	Johnson Center	3,052
Fla. Atlantic	FAU Gym	5,000
Florida Int'l	Golden Panther Arena	4,661
Georgia St	GSU Athletic Complex	5,500
Mercer	Macon Coliseum	8,500
Samford	Seibert Hall	4,000
SE Louisiana	University Center	7,500
Stetson	Edmunds Center	5,000

Note: former Big South member Campbell joined conference after 1993-94 season.

West Coast Athletic

	Home Floor	Seats
Gonzaga	Martin Centre	4,000
Loyola-CA	Gersten Pavilion	4,156
Pepperdine	Firestone Fieldhouse	3,104
Portland	Chiles Center	5,000
St. Mary's-CA	McKeon Pavilion	3,500
San Diego	USD Sports Center	2,500
San Francisco	Memorial Gym	5,300
Santa Clara	Toso Pavilion	5,000

Western Athletic

	Home Floor	Seats
Air Force	Cadet Field House	6,000
BYU	Marriott Center	22,700
Colorado St	Moby Arena	9,000
Fresno St	Selland Arena	10,132
Hawaii	Blaisdell Center	7,575
New Mexico	University Arena (The Pit)	17,126
San Diego St	Peterson Gym	3,800
UTEP	Special Events Center	12,200
Utah	Jon Huntsman Center	15,000
Wyoming	Arena-Auditorium	15,028

Future NCAA Final Four Sites

Year	Arena	Seats	Location	Year	Arena	Seats	Location
1995	Kingdome	38,000	Seattle	1999	ThunderDome	32,351	St. Petersburg
1996	Meadowlands Arena	20,029	E. Rutherford	2000	RCA Dome	47,100	Indianapolis
1997	RCA Dome	47,100	Indianapolis	2001	Metrodome	50,000	Minneapolis
1998	Alamodome	32,500	San Antonio	2002	Georgia Dome	40,000	Atlanta

COLLEGE FOOTBALL

The 35 Largest Stadiums

The 35 largest stadiums in Division I college football. Note that (*) indicates stadium not on campus.

		Location	Seats	Home Team	Conference	Built	Field
1	Michigan Stadium	Ann Arbor, Mich.	**102,501**	Michigan	Big Ten	1927	Grass
2	Rose Bowl*	Pasadena, Calif.	**98,101**	UCLA	Pac-10	1922	Grass
3	Beaver Stadium	University Park, Pa.	**93,967**	Penn St.	Big Ten	1960	Grass
4	Neyland Stadium	Knoxville, Tenn.	**91,902**	Tennessee	SEC-East	1921	Grass
5	Ohio Stadium	Columbus, Ohio	**91,470**	Ohio St.	Big Ten	1922	Grass
6	Sanford Stadium	Athens, Ga.	**86,117**	Georgia	SEC-East	1929	Grass
7	Stanford Stadium	Stanford, Calif.	**85,500**	Stanford	Pac-10	1921	Grass
8	Jordan-Hare Stadium	Auburn, Ala.	**85,214**	Auburn	SEC-West	1939	Grass
9	Legion Field*	Birmingham, Ala.	**83,091**	Alabama*	SEC-West	1927	Turf
10	Florida Field	Gainesville, Fla.	**83,000**	Florida	SEC-East	1929	Turf
11	Memorial Stadium	Clemson, S.C.	**81,473**	Clemson	ACC	1942	Grass
12	Tiger Stadium	Baton Rouge, La.	**80,150**	LSU	SEC-West	1924	Grass
13	Memorial Stadium	Austin, Texas	**77,809**	Texas	SWC	1924	Turf
14	Camp Randall Stadium	Madison, Wisc.	**77,745**	Wisconsin	Big Ten	1917	Turf
15	Spartan Stadium	East Lansing, Mich.	**76,000**	Michigan St.	Big Ten	1957	Turf
16	Memorial Stadium	Berkeley, Calif.	**75,662**	California	Pac-10	1923	Turf
17	Owen Field	Norman, Okla.	**75,004**	Oklahoma	Big Eight	1924	Turf
18	Doak Campbell Stadium	Tallahasse, Fla.	**75,000**	Florida St.	ACC	1950	Grass
19	Orange Bowl*	Miami, Fla.	**74,712**	Miami-FL	Big East	1935	Grass
20	Sun Devil Stadium	Tempe, Ariz.	**73,656**	Arizona St.	Pac-10	1959	Grass
21	Memorial Stadium	Lincoln, Neb.	**72,700**	Nebraska	Big Eight	1923	Turf
22	Husky Stadium	Seattle, Wash.	**72,500**	Washington	Pac-10	1920	Turf
23	Williams-Brice Stadium	Columbia, S.C.	**72,400**	South Carolina	SEC	1934	Grass
24	Cotton Bowl	Dallas, Tex.	**71,456**	SMU, Oklahoma	SWC/Big 8	1932	Grass
25	Memorial Stadium	Champaign, Ill.	**70,904**	Illinois	Big 10	1923	Turf
26	Yale Bowl	New Haven, Conn.	**70,896**	Yale	Ivy League	1914	Grass
27	Kinnick Stadium	Iowa City, Iowa	**70,397**	Iowa	Big Ten	1929	Grass
28	Kyle Field	College Station, Texas	**70,210**	Texas A&M	SWC	1925	Turf
29	Bryant-Denny Stadium	Tuscaloosa, Ala.	**70,123**	Alabama	SEC	1929	Turf
30	Rice Stadium	Houston, Tex.	**70,000**	Rice	SWC	1950	Turf
31	Superdome	New Orleans, La.	**65,056**	Tulane	Independant	1975	Turf
32	Ross-Ade Stadium	W. Lafayette, Ind.	**67,861**	Purdue	Big Ten	1924	Grass
33	LA Memorial Coliseum*	Los Angeles, Calif.	**67,800**	USC	Pac-10	1923	Grass
34	Veterans Stadium	Philedphia, Pa.	**66,592**	Temple	Big East	1971	Turf
35	Alamodome*	San Antonio, Tex.	**65,000**	SMU, Texas Tech	SWC	1993	Turf
	Cougar Stadium	Provo, Utah	**65,000**	BYU	WAC	1964	Grass

Note: LA Memorial Coliseum will expand to seat 92,516 for USC-UCLA and USC-Notre Dame games in 1994.

Division I-A Conference Home Fields

Division I-A conference by conference listing includes member teams for 1994 season. Note that (*) indicates stadium is not on campus of home team.

Atlantic Coast

	Stadium	Built	Seats	Field
Clemson	Memorial	1942	81,473	Grass
Clemson	Memorial	1942	81,473	Grass
Duke	Wallace Wade	1929	33,941	Grass
Florida St.	Doak Campbell	1950	75,000	Grass
Ga. Tech	Dodd/Grant	1913	46,000	Turf
Maryland	Byrd	1950	45,000	Grass
N. Carolina	Kenan	1927	52,000	Grass
N.C. State	Carter-Finley	1966	50,000t	Grass
Virginia	Scott	1931	40,000	Turf
Wake Forest	Groves	1968	31,500	Grass

t Grass bank holds additional 10,000.

Big East

	Stadium	Built	Seats	Field
Boston Col	Alumni	1957	44,500	Turf
Miami-FL	Orange Bowl*	1935	74,712	Grass
Pittsburgh	Pitt	1925	56,500	Turf
Rutgers	Rutgers	1994	41,500	Grass
Syracuse	Carrier Dome	1980	50,000	Turf
Temple	Veterans*	1971	66,592	Turf
Va. Tech	Lane	1965	51,000	Grass
West Va.	Mountaineer Field	1980	63,500	Turf

Big Eight

	Stadium	Built	Seats	Field
Colorado	Folsom Field	1924	51,748	Turf
Iowa St	Trice Field	1975	50,000	Turf
Kansas	Memorial	1921	50,250	Turf
Kansas St.	KSU	1968	42,000	Turf
Missouri	Faurot Field	1926	62,000	Turf
Nebraska	Memorial	1923	72,700	Turf
Oklahoma	Owen Field	1924	75,004	Turf
Oklahoma St.	Lewis Field	1920	50,614	Turf

Big Ten

	Stadium	Built	Seats	Field
Illinois	Memorial	1923	70,904	Turf
Indiana	Memorial	1960	52,354	Turf
Iowa	Kinnick	1929	70,397	Grass
Michigan	Michigan	1927	102,501	Grass
Michigan St.	Spartan	1957	76,000	Turf
Minnesota	Metrodome*	1982	62,345	Turf
Northwestern	Dyche	1926	49,256	Turf
Ohio St.	Ohio	1922	91,470	Grass
Penn St.	Beaver	1960	93,967	Grass
Purdue	Ross-Ade	1924	67,861	Grass
Wisconsin	Camp Randall	1917	77,745	Turf

College Football (Cont.)
Division I-A Conference Home Fields

Big West

	Stadium	Built	Seats	Field
Arkansas St	Indian	1974	33,410	Grass
Louisiana Tech	Joe Aillet	1968	30,200	Grass
Nevada	Mackay	1965	31,545	Grass
New Mexico St	Aggie Memorial	1978	30,343	Grass
Northern Ill	Huskie	1965	30,998	Turf
Pacific	Stagg Memorial	1950	30,000	Grass
San Jose St	Spartan	1933	31,218	Grass
SW Louisiana	Cajun Field	1971	31,000	Grass
UNLV	Silver Bowl*	1971	32,000	Turf
Utah St	Dick Romney	1968	30,257	Grass

Mid-American

	Stadium	Built	Seats	Field
Akron	Rubber Bowl*	1940	35,202	Turf
Ball St	Ball State	1967	16,319	Grass
Bowling Green	Doyt Perry	1966	30,599	Grass
Central Mich	Kelly/Shorts	1972	20,086	Turf
Eastern Mich	Rynearson	1969	30,200	Turf
Kent	Dix	1969	30,520	Grass
Miami-OH	Fred Yager	1983	25,183	Grass
Ohio Univ	Peden	1929	20,000	Grass
Toledo	Glass Bowl	1937	26,248	Turf
Western Mich	Waldo	1939	30,000	Grass

Pacific-10

	Stadium	Built	Seats	Field
Arizona	Arizona	1928	56,167	Grass
Arizona St	Sun Devil	1959	73,656	Grass
California	Memorial	1923	75,662	Turf
Oregon	Autzen	1967	41,678	Turf
Oregon St	Parker	1953	35,547	Turf
Stanford	Stanford	1921	85,500	Grass
UCLA	Rose Bowl*	1922	98,101	Grass
USC	LA Coliseum*	1923	67,800	Grass
Washington	Husky	1920	72,500	Turf
Washington St	Martin	1972	40,000	Turf

Note: LA Memorial Coliseum was scheduled to expand to 92,516 seats for USC-UCLA and USC-Notre Dame games in 1994.

Southeastern

EASTERN	Stadium	Built	Seats	Field
Florida	Florida Field	1929	83,000	Grass
Georgia	Sanford	1929	86,117	Grass
Kentucky	Commonwealth	1973	57,800	Grass
S. Carolina	Williams-Brice	1934	72,400	Grass
Tennessee	Neyland	1921	91,902	Grass
Vanderbilt	Vanderbilt	1922	41,000	Turf

WESTERN	Stadium	Built	Seats	Field
Alabama	Bryant-Denny	1929	70,123	Grass
	& Legion Field*	1927	83,091	Turf
Arkansas	Razorback	1938	50,019	Turf
	& War Memorial*	1948	53,727	Grass
Auburn	Jordan-Hare	1939	85,214	Grass
LSU	Tiger	1924	80,150	Grass
Mississippi	Vaught-Hem'way	1941	42,577	Grass
Miss. St.	Scott Field	1915	40,656	Grass

Notes: EAST— Vanderbilt Stadium was rebuilt in 1981. WEST— at Alabama, Bryant-Denny Stadium is in Tuscaloosa and Legion Field is in Birmingham.

SEC Championship Game
The first two SEC Championship Games were played at Legion Field in Birmingham, Ala., in 1992 and '93. The game was moved to Atlanta's 71,280-seat Georgia Dome in 1994.

Southwest

	Stadium	Built	Seats	Field
Baylor	Floyd Casey	1950	48,500	Turf
Houston	Astrodome*	1965	60,000	Turf
Rice	Rice	1950	70,000	Turf
SMU	Ownby	1926	23,783	Turf
Texas	Memorial	1924	77,809	Turf
Texas A&M	Kyle Field	1925	70,210	Turf
TCU	Amon Carter	1929	46,000	Grass
Texas Tech	Jones	1947	50,500	Turf

Western Athletic

	Stadium	Built	Seats	Field
Air Force	Falcon	1962	50,049	Grass
BYU	Cougar	1964	65,000	Grass
Colorado St	Hughes	1968	30,000	Grass
Fresno St	Bulldog	1980	41,031	Grass
Hawaii	Aloha*	1975	50,000	Turf
New Mexico	University	1960	30,646	Grass
San Diego St	SD/Murphy*	1967	60,049	Grass
Utah	Robert Rice	1927	32,500	Grass
UTEP	Sun Bowl*	1963	51,270	Turf
Wyoming	War Memorial	1950	33,500	Grass

I-A Independents

	Stadium	Built	Seats	Field
Army	Michie	1924	39,929	Turf
Cincinnati	Nippert	1916	35,000	Turf
E. Carolina	Ficklin	1963	35,000	Grass
Louisville	Cardinal*	1956	35,500	Grass
Memphis	Liberty Bowl*	1965	62,405	Grass
Navy	Navy-Marine Corps Memorial	1959	30,000	Grass
Notre Dame	Notre Dame	1930	59,075	Grass
Southern Miss	Roberts	1976	33,000	Grass
Tulane	Superdome*	1975	69,056	Turf
Tulsa	Skelly	1930	40,385	Turf

Bowl Games

	Stadium	Built	Seats	Field
Alamo	Alamodome	1993	65,000	Turf
Aloha	Aloha	1975	50,000	Grass
Carquest	Joe Robbie	1986	73,000	Grass
Copper	Arizona	1928	56,167	Grass
Cotton	Cotton	1932	71,456	Turf
Fiesta	Sun Devil	1958	73,656	Grass
Fla. Citrus	Fla. Citrus Bowl	1936	70,349	Grass
Freedom	Anaheim	1966	70,962	Grass
Gator	Florida Field*	1949	83,000	Grass
Hall of Fame	Tampa	1967	74,350	Grass
Holiday	SD/Jack Murphy	1967	60,049	Grass
Independence	Independence	1936	60,128	Grass
John Hancock	Sun Bowl	1963	51,270	Turf
Las Vegas	Silver Bowl	1971	32,000	Turf
Liberty	Liberty Bowl	1965	62,405	Grass
Orange	Orange Bowl	1935	74,712	Grass
Peach	Georgia Dome	1992	71,596	Turf
Rose	Rose Bowl	1922	98,101	Grass
Sugar	Superdome	1975	72,704	Turf

*Gator Bowl scheduled to be played in Gainesville in 1995 while old Gator Bowl stadium is rebuilt in Jacksonville.

Playing Sites
Alamo— San Antonio; **Aloha**— Honolulu; **Carquest**— Miami; **Copper**— Tucson; **Cotton**— Dallas; **Fiesta**— Tempe; **Florida Citrus**— Orlando; **Freedom**— Anaheim; **Gator**— Gainesville; **Hall of Fame**— Tampa; **Holiday**— San Diego; **Independence**— Shreveport; **John Hancock**— El Paso; **Las Vegas**— Las Vegas; **Liberty**—Memphis; **Orange**— Miami; **Peach**— Atlanta; **Rose**— Pasadena; **Sugar**— New Orleans.

As America watched on TV, a white Ford Bronco with murder suspect **O.J. Simpson** in the back seat passes under the Manchester Boulevard overpass with a fleet of L.A. police cars in pursuit.

BUSINESS & MEDIA

BUSINESS AND MEDIA
by Richard Sandomir

Tuned In

*American viewers OD on O.J. and Nancy & Tonya stories
as line between sports and network TV soap opera blurs.*

How did it happen? How did such landmark events in the sports industry like the Fox Network wresting NFL Football away from CBS and the first cancelled World Series in 90 years end up taking supporting roles in 1994?

Well, it could have been the bizarre sight of O.J. Simpson, accused murderer and fugitive, leading a fleet of police cars in a slow-motion chase over the freeways of Los Angeles as supporters rooted him on from off-ramps and overpasses.

On June 17, sitting in the back seat of a white Ford Bronco with a gun to his head while a friend drove, O.J. captivated viewers in a way that his ethereal abilities as a Hall of Fame running back could never match.

Once he was a sports hero, a black man who had not only succeeded in a white world, but effortlessly climbed the ladder of American celebrity. In a less media-driven time, he was Michael Jordan before there was a Michael Jordan.

The police and local news helicopter cameras tracked him relentlessly—from the freeway, to his Brentwood estate, to jail and then into a courtroom. As a result, O.J. became the most celebrated murder suspect the world has ever known, accused of brutally murdering his ex-wife, Nicole Brown Simpson, and her friend, Ronald Goldman. Simpson became the postmodern TV ideal:

a hopelessly famous, handsome, rich man, tailor-made for Court TV as well as "Hard Copy," the *Los Angeles Times* as well as the *National Enquirer*, and of course, a Fox Network made-for-TV movie.

It was prime time in the east and midwest as the cops closed in on the Bronco carrying O.J. and his boyhood friend Al Cowlings, and 95 million Americans watched. All the networks cut away from regular programming to pick up live local coverage of the pursuit.

At Madison Square Garden, reporters covering Game 5 of the NBA Finals between New York and Houston were torn between watching the game or scurrying back to the media room to await the latest Simpson news. NBC Sports president Dick Ebersol sat at courtside, a phone in one hand and a miniature TV between his knees, coordinating with NBC News the times to break into the game with Simpson updates.

ABC News deemed the event so significant that Peter Jennings was called in to co-anchor the coverage on "20/20" with Barbara Walters. ABC sportscaster Al Michaels, a close friend of Simpson's, became the network's designated O.J. expert. But like his TV colleagues, Michaels couldn't square the smooth, garrulous O.J. he knew with the savagery of the allegations. Said Michaels: "Nobody's private persona can be the same as the public one. But he was as seamless a big name personality as I've ever known."

Richard Sandomir writes the television sports column for *The New York Times*.

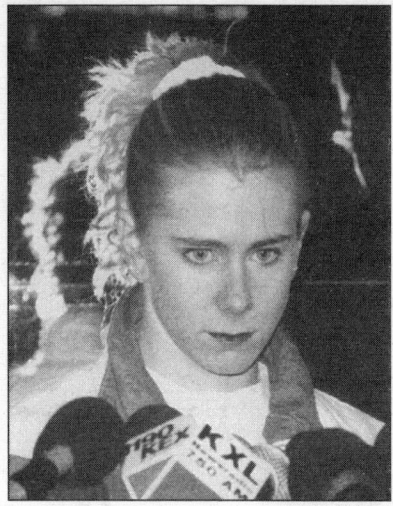
Wide World Photos

Wide World Photos

The media-driven soap opera involving U.S. figure skaters **Tonya Harding** (left) and **Nancy Kerrigan** helped propel CBS to unprecedented prime time TV ratings with its coverage of the 1994 Winter Olympics.

From the moment his preliminary hearing began a month after his arrest, any observer could see that Simpson had become a purely TV creature: he dominated the four broadcast networks, CNN and Court TV. We saw O.J. transform from a haggard, dazed wreck at his first court appearance to a more assured, involved defendant.

Showboat defense lawyer Robert Shapiro squabbled with prosecutor Marcia Clark, who proved that enough evidence existed to put Simpson on trial. We saw it all on TV. But was it an education, or merely appalling?

The networks forfeited millions of dollars in lost daytime advertising to stay with the story, but how could they ignore this real-life soap opera? By mid-summer, Simpson was no longer the former Heisman Trophy winner and All-Pro, the actor and Hertz pitchman, or the NBC pal of Bob Costas. There he was in an L.A. courtroom with nowhere to run. Right or wrong, he was linked by blood stains to the murderous likes of the Menendez brothers, Charles Manson and Fatty Arbuckle.

Network and local TV, national and local press, print and electronic tabloids, all participated in a summer-long feeding frenzy that only intensified as jury selection began

on Sept. 26. We found out, among other things, that O.J. was a wife-beater, and even heard the tape of a 911 call by Nicole to the police.

In a rare interview on ABC Radio, a faint-voiced Howard Cosell, said: "The whole thing is such a horrible mess that we'll have to wait to see what happens to an American hero."

Was it sports or was it news?

The same question could be asked about the strange case of Tonya Harding, the hardscrabble figure skater and sometime auto mechanic, whose husband, Jeff Gillooly, and three comically inept friends, conspired to whack rival Nancy Kerrigan on the right knee Jan. 6.

Within hours of the assault at the U.S. Figure Skating Championships in Detroit, a tape of the attack's aftermath appeared on TV. Kerrigan's plaintive wail, "Why me? Why me?," recorded by the independent production house, Innersport, transformed the 1992 Olympic bronze medalist into everybody's victimized sweetheart.

Meanwhile, Tonya—like O.J., her surname soon became unnecessary—became a staple of every media outlet available. Everybody wanted to know if she was in on the hit. She may have wept for CBS anchor Connie Chung, but she became closest to

Opening Day of the 1994 NFL season found **Fox Sports** instead of CBS covering the NFC game between Philadelphia and New York.

"Inside Edition," for whose crew she occasionally cooked dinners.

Naturally, the whole bizarre tale unfolded on TV. Would Nancy recover in time to make the Olympic team? Yes. Would Tonya, who won the U.S. women's title in Kerrigan's absence, be kicked off the team? No.

By the time the Winter Olympics began on Feb. 12, the question was: Would the whole unseemly mess overwhelm CBS's coverage of the Games? "No matter how we cover it, be assured that people will say we're exploiting it," said Mike Pearl, CBS's coordinating producer in Lillehammer.

By the second week, CBS was reaping the astounding dividends of this white trash drama: on Feb. 23, the night of the women's short program, CBS registered a 48.5 Nielsen rating and a 64 share. That translates into 126.6 million viewers, making it the third highest-rated sports show and sixth highest-rated overall show in history. Only the final episode of "M*A*S*H," the "Who Shot J.R.?" episode of "Dallas," part eight of "Roots" and Super Bowls XVI and XVII ever pulled better numbers (see page 551).

Two nights later, the women's long program produced a 44.1 rating, making it the 16th highest-rated sports show ever and 30th overall.

Neither woman won. Tonya faltered badly and finished eighth, while Nancy missed a gold medal by the slimmest of margins—placing second to Ukrainian teenager Oksana Baiul by one judge's vote. Later, a CBS camera caught a disappointed Nancy making disparaging remarks about Oksana's tardiness to the medal stand.

CBS rode "Tonya and Nancy" to a 27.8 prime time average rating for the 16-day Winter Games, far beyond the 18.6 it expected and 49 percent greater than the 18.7 achieved by CBS two years before in Albertville, France.

The unexpectedly spectacular performance in Norway solidified CBS's belief that, just a month before, it had bid wisely for the rights to the 1998 Winter Olympics in Nagano, Japan. At $375 million, the most ever paid by a TV network for the Winter Games, CBS chairman Laurence Tisch insisted he had not overbid, although NBC, ABC and Fox had pulled out well below his winning offer. Said Tisch: "I don't think we paid attention to ABC, NBC or Fox. The price was right for CBS. We're big boys." He predicted CBS would break even.

Winning the rights to Nagano was the first step in the remaking of CBS Sports. On Dec. 17, 1993, in a blow far more embarrassing than the loss of $500 million on its 1990-93 major league baseball TV deal, CBS lost its National Football Conference NFL package to Rupert Murdoch's still-fledgling Fox Network. Fox also grabbed John Madden, Pat Summerall, Terry Bradshaw, James Brown, Matt Millen and Dick Stockton. When "NFL Today" anchor Greg Gumbel left for NBC the cupboard was practically bare.

After wrapping up Nagano, CBS moved quickly to sign up Big East and Southeastern Conference football starting in 1996, returning to the college sport for the first time since 1990. Then came the May hiring of USA Network's David Kenin to replace CBS Sports president Neal Pilson, on whose watch the baseball deal went south and the NFL went elsewhere.

In August, CBS increased its stake in college football by grabbing NBC's two biggest bowl games—the Fiesta and Orange—starting with the 1995 postseason. Together with ABC's Sugar Bowl, the Fiesta and Orange bowls will headline the new bowl alliance, rotating as the site of the

A Welcome Antidote To Lost Season

The baseball season ended Sept. 14, but the "Baseball" season began Sept. 18. That was Opening Day for Ken Burns's nine-part, 18½-hour documentary, an even more ambitious work than his Emmy and Peabody-winning series, "The Civil War," which aired in 1989.

"Baseball is an apt segue from the Civil War," Burns said. "By studying baseball you can figure out what has happened to us since then."

Burns and his staff labored for nearly 5 years, conducting 65 interviews, poring over thousands of photographs, unearthing all-but-forgotten vintage film, recording 250 versions of "Take Me Out to the Ballgame" and matching sound effects to action.

The game's well-recorded past provided "Baseball" with materials, especially vintage film and more recent videotape, that he had no access to in "The Civil War." Interviews with players like Mickey Mantle, Ted Williams and Hank Aaron, and announcers like Vin Scully and the late Red Barber, allowed Burns to interview people who either made baseball history or were there when it happened.

For baseball fans faced with an autumn of no pennant races and no Fall Classic, "Baseball" was a PBS antidote for the season-cancellation blues, a chance to look back on better days rather than stew in the present. It is reverential history, not one swaddled in gushy melodrama.

Burns adopted an unsentimental edge by focusing on two recurring themes: racism and labor relations. The sport's heroes and villains are profiled, its great and ignominious moments recalled, but Burns returned to the leitmotifs. Racism was his core theme and could have been a documentary unto itself; his treatment culminates in Jackie Robinson's 1947 entry into the major leagues.

Robinson was Burns's Lincolnesque hero, but the star of "Baseball" was John (Buck) O'Neil, the former Negro Leagues player-manager for the Kansas City Monarchs, who later scouted Lou Brock and Ernie Banks for the majors. A delightful, elegant man of 82,

Lou Charno/General Motors

Ken Burns's nine-part "Baseball" documentary starred 82-year-old **Buck O'Neil**, a former player and manager in the Negro Leagues.

O'Neil reappeared like a loving genie throughout the series, leading viewers to an eye-opening revelry of the cultural splendor of the Negro Leagues.

"He's like family now," said Burns, who toured the country with O'Neil to publicize the series. "I'm traveling with my two girls and an 82-year-old black man. I love him."

Well before "Baseball's" debut, Burns knew his work would generate mixed reaction because of the standards set by "The Civil War." "'Nice guy continues to make good films' isn't a good enough story anymore," he said.

The length and leisurely pace was certain to be a target. Would ESPN's Chris Berman watch all 18½-hours? "Sure. That's not much longer than the average A.L. game," he said. Burns wasn't worried; some would watch live, but the 9-tape set (for $179.98) was released just as the series aired.

There were plenty of raves ("Ken Burns has come in just the nick of time," glowed *USA Today*), but there were dollops of negativity, too. Burns "has succumbed to a case of Heavy Meaning-itis," said *Newsweek*. His "rhapsodic tone becomes wearying, even for a diehard fan," moaned *Time*.

Added *Newsday*: "The weakness of the documentary is that baseball is not the Civil War."

national championship game between the top two-ranked teams in the nation—unless one or both of those teams comes from the Big 10 or Pac-10 (and is thus ticketed for ABC's Rose Bowl). The Fiesta Bowl will get the first national title game on Jan. 2, 1996. Said Kenin: "This indicates we'll be there competitively when big events are offered."

As CBS recovered, Fox grew. By offering a staggering $395 million a year, Murdoch not only blindsided CBS but kicked them out of pro football for the first time in 38 years. The deal also increased total compensation to the NFL from Fox, NBC, ABC, ESPN and TNT by 22 percent to $4.4 billion. Led by Fox Sports president David Hill, a talented eccentric from Australia, the home of Bart Simpson and Al Bundy set out to build a sports division from football.

Fox made Madden the highest-paid performer on or off the gridiron at $8 million a year (outbidding NBC, which offered $4.8 million and a General Electric train) and reunited him with Summerall. It formed a one-hour pregame studio show starring Bradshaw and Brown as co-hosts, plus former Dallas Cowboys coach Jimmy Johnson and former Los Angeles Raider Howie Long as analysts. It then hired a coterie of mostly young, little-known announcers to call the games beneath the Madden-Summerall and Stockton-Millen teams. Under Hill, the division's goal was to produce NFL games as well as CBS, then go beyond it.

Murdoch's goal, however, was broader. The NFL deal guaranteed huge losses for Fox, perhaps as high as half the value of the package. But Murdoch looked hopefully beyond that, to building his network of mostly UHF stations into a programming power to rival CBS, NBC and ABC.

Football motivated some big city stations to align with Fox, and others to boost their weak signals. But it required another raid against CBS to truly strengthen the Fox lineup. On May 23, Murdoch spent $500 million for a 20 percent interest in New World Communications, whose 12 powerful VHF stations—eight of them CBS affiliates—would switch their allegiances to Fox within 18 months.

Fox tweaked CBS's nose a third time on Sept. 13, outbidding them for the network rights to NHL hockey. The deal called for $155 million over five years. CBS had offered $150 million.

One of CBS's former properties, major league baseball, returned, if only briefly, to its old haunts on NBC and ABC. The Baseball Network, as the ABC-NBC-MLB joint venture is called, started in July with NBC's telecast of the All-Star Game (Costas back on baseball for the first time since 1989), and continued for four prime time telecasts on ABC (with old pals Michaels, Tim McCarver and Jim Palmer) before the Aug. 12 players' strike.

The first four games confirmed the goal of the partners, to raise ratings, when you combined the numbers of up to 14 local games. ABC's overall 7.1 rating was nearly double what CBS got on Saturday afternoon.

But despite TBN's sharp productions, there were complaints that the games started late, commercial breaks were lengthened to add more updates, and that fans in two-team markets like New York and Chicago could only see one team play. Advocates of the old Game of the Week format argued that the absence of a truly national game provided fans with nothing more than the same local game they would see otherwise—only the game popped up on a network affiliate, not the local broadcast station or cable outlet.

"We hope what we do will enhance, not offend," said TBN coordinating producer John Fillipelli.

Plans for TBN's coverage of the 1994 World Series went up in smoke on Sept. 14, when acting baseball commissioner Bud Selig announced that since there was no hope of reaching a settlement in the 34-day-old players' strike, baseball owners had decided by a 26-2 vote to cancel the rest of the season. The World Series would go unplayed for the first time since 1904.

Projected losses caused by the strike came to 52 days and nights, 669 regular season games, $442 million in owners' revenues and $236,636,700 in player salaries. And that's not counting the postseason.

The owners and players refused to give an inch on the two major issues of the stalemate—revenue sharing and a salary cap. The owners demanded both and the players refused to consider either. The inability of both sides to negotiate not only scuttled an exciting 1994 season, but jeopardized 1995 as well (see "Baseball" chapter).

And labor unrest wasn't just limited to

Hollywood producer **Jeff Lurie** (right), who paid a record $175 million to acquire the Philadelphia Eagles in April, watches his new team during practice with general manager **Harry Gamble**. Veterans Stadium is in the background.

baseball. On Sept. 22, NHL commissioner Gary Bettman announced that the Oct. 1 opening of the 1994-95 regular season would be delayed if a new collective bargaining agreement between owners and players wasn't reached before then. "What I learned from baseball," said Bettman, "is that you can turn a season into a complete disaster if you start without an agreement."

Bettman didn't use the word "lockout," but everybody else did. As preseason games wound down, the major issues were—surprise—revenue sharing and a salary cap as well as salary arbitration (players for it, owners against) and a rookie salary limit (owners for it, players against).

Whatever happened, the impass threatened to trash all the positive feedback hockey had received in the spring of '94 when Mark Messier and the New York Rangers captured sports fans' imaginations by winning the team's first Stanley Cup in over 50 years.

Preparations for a lockout were also being made in the NBA where contract talks had broken down as the Oct. 7 opening of training camps approached. The

salary cap was born in the NBA back in 1983 and generally credited with saving the league when most of its 23 teams were losing money.

That was before the playing skills of Larry Bird, Magic Johnson and Michael Jordan combined with the marketing acumen of commissioner David Stern to lead the NBA to the Promised Land of unimagined riches. Now, the union wants to get rid of the cap as an unwelcome encumbrance upon free agents seeking the best possible deal. "It was always supposed to be a stopgap," said Charles Grantham, executive director of the players' union.

Easier said than done. "Baseball has all but destroyed itself to get a cap," said Orlando Magic president Pat Williams. "We already have it and there is no way the owners [will] relinquish it."

The only major league at peace in 1994 seemed to be the NFL, which stumbled into its first season under a five-year agreement that included a salary cap starting at $34.6 million per team. The NFL's cap was part of a 1993 deal that settled years of litigation between owners and the players union.

The surprising highlight of World Cup soccer coverage was Univision's play-by-play man **Andres Cantor**.

Players receive 64 percent of defined revenues, which are then split evenly among teams for salaries.

But the advent of the cap, one year after enhanced free agency had ballooned salaries, meant that teams started shedding mainly older stars like New York Giants' quarterback Phil Simms (who retired), Washington receiver Art Monk (who signed for much less with the New York Jets) and the Arizona receiver Gary Clark (who took a 30 percent paycut to stay in Tempe).

Simms ripped NFL Commissioner Paul Tagliabue for suggesting that reasons other than the salary cap were responsible for the Giants' decision to rid itself of the Pro Bowl quarterback's $2.25 million salary. If Tagliabue really believed what he said, Simms replied, then he "needed a drug test."

Simms landed on his feet, taking a studio analyst's job at ESPN and turning down a midseason invitation by Buddy Ryan to resume his career in Arizona with the quarterback-challenged Cardinals. Earlier in the year, Ryan had suggested that the Giants helped themselves by dumping Simms.

Meanwhile, as the NFL readied to celebrate its 75th season in 1994, franchise values went through the roof. In April, *Financial World* magazine released its annual survey of what major league clubs are worth and the Dallas Cowboys topped the list at $190 million. At the other end of the spectrum, the league granted 1995 expansion teams to Charlotte, N.C. and Jacksonville, Fla., for $140 million apiece.

In between, the New England Patriots were sold to Boston businessman Bob Kraft for $170 million, the Philadelphia Eagles went to Hollywood producer Jeff Lurie for $185 million, and Wayne Huizenga, the Florida media tycoon who already owns baseball's Marlins, hockey's Panthers and Joe Robbie Stadium, upped his stake in the Miami Dolphins from 15 to 100 percent for $138 million.

Prior to 1994, the record purchase price for an established major league team in any sport was the $173 million it took to buy the Baltimore Orioles in 1993.

Meanwhile, new owners in Toronto and Vancouver forked over $125 million to gain 1995-96 expansion teams in the NBA, while basketball's New York Knicks and hockey's New York Rangers were bought by ITT Corporation and Cablevision Systems Inc. as part of a $1.075 billion sale that included Madison Square Garden and MSG Cable TV Network.

Bruce McNall's selling off of 72% of the Los Angeles Kings for $60 million was also among the most significant deals of the year.

Awash in debt and facing an FBI investigation into borrowing practices connected with his coin business, McNall was forced into liquidation in May for defaulting on $160 million in loans. He also sold the Toronto Argonauts of the CFL and resigned as chairman of the NHL's powerful board of governors.

Finally, World Cup soccer exceeded expectations as a national TV draw. ABC televised 11 World Cup games, including a 9.3 rating for the quarterfinal round match between the U.S. and Brazil and a 12.4 for the Italy-Brazil final.

But the real TV story was not the ratings, not the running time, score and sponsor logos seen on screen at all times, and not even the lack of commercials. The real story was Univision's sublime play-by-play man Andres Cantor, who turned listening to soccer into a Spanish aria, even for people who understood only one of his words: GOOOOAAAAALLLL!

1993-94 Top 20 Prime Time TV Series

Final 1993-94 prime time network television ratings, according to Nielsen Media Research. Covers period from Sept. 20, 1993 through April 17, 1994, and includes all series of 10 episodes or more. Events are listed with ratings points and audience share; each ratings point represents 942,000 households and shares indicate percentage of TV sets in use. Note that (*) indicates new show.

Overall network standings: 1. **CBS** (14.0 rating/23 share); 2. **ABC** (12.4 rating/20 share); 3. **NBC** (11.0 rating/18 share); 4. **FOX** (7.2/11 share).

	Series	Net	Rating	Share		Series	Net	Rating	Share
1	Home Improvement	ABC	21.9	33	11	CBS Sunday Movie	CBS	16.1	25
2	60 Minutes	CBS	20.8	34	12	20/20	ABC	14.8	26
3	Seinfeld	NBC	19.3	29	13	Love & War	CBS	14.5	22
4	Roseanne	ABC	19.2	29	14	Northern Exposure	CBS	14.4	23
5	Grace Under Fire*	ABC	18.0	27	15	Wings	NBC	14.3	22
6	Frasier*	NBC	17.5	27	16	Full House	ABC	14.2	23
7	Coach	ABC	17.4	27	17	PrimeTime Live	ABC	14.2	24
8	Murder, She Wrote	CBS	16.9	25	18	Dave's World*	CBS	14.0	21
9	**Monday Night Football**	ABC	16.8	28	19	Dr. Quinn, Medicine Woman	CBS	13.9	24
10	Murphy Brown	CBS	16.4	24		NYPD Blue	ABC	13.9	23

1993-94 Top 75 TV Sports Events

Final 1993-94 network television ratings for nationally-telecast sports events, according to Nielsen Media Research. Covers period from Sept. 20, 1993 through Aug. 31, 1994, including 15 Monday Night Football games but not including pregame, halftime and post-game shows. Events are listed with ratings points and audience share; each ratings point represents 942,000 households and shares indicate percentage of TV sets in use.

		Date	Net	Rtg/Sh			Date	Net	Rtg/Sh
1	**Winter Olympics** (Nancy vs Tonya in Women's technical program; Bonnie Blair wins 1000m; Men's GS, Hockey report)	2/23	CBS	48.5/64	13	**Winter Olympics** (Bonnie Blair 1st in 500m; Picabo Street wins silver in Women's Downhill; Men's Figure Skating final; Sweden beats USA, 6-3)	2/19	CBS	25.9/43
2	**Super Bowl XXVIII** (Cowboys vs Bills)	1/30	NBC	45.5/66	14	**NFC Semifinal** (Packers at Cowboys)	1/16	CBS	25.5/53
3	**Winter Olympics** (Nancy vs Oksana in Women's long program; Hockey Semifinals; Men's Combined; Small Hill Ski Jumping)	2/25	CBS	44.1/64	15	**Winter Olympics** (Women's Figure Skating preview; Men's X-country 4x10k Relay; Short Track; Team Ski Jumping)	2/22	CBS	24.9/36
4	**NFC Championship** (49ers at Cowboys)	1/23	CBS	31.6/54	16	**Winter Olympics** (Cathy Turner 1st in Short Track 500m; Women's GS; Cross-country, Women's Figure Skating preview)	2/24	CBS	23.1/34
5	**Winter Olympics** (Tommy Moe wins Downhill; Pairs Fig. Skating; Luge; Men's 5000m; Hockey)	2/13	CBS	29.4/41	17	**Winter Olympics** (Closing ceremonies; Sweden beats Canada 3-2 in gold medal shootout; wrap-up of Games)	2/27	CBS	22.9/34
6	**Winter Olympics** (Ice Dancing; 2-Man Bobsled; Women's Combined Downhill; Large Hill Ski Jumping)	2/20	CBS	29.3/44	18	**Winter Olympics** (Figure Skating exhibition; Women's Slalom; Hockey report, 4-man Bobsled)	2/26	CBS	22.8/38
7	**AFC Championship** (Chiefs at Bills)	1/23	NBC	28.6/58		**Winter Olympics** (Nancy & Tonya practice together; Johann Olav Koss wins 2nd gold; Men's Figure Skating preview; Luge)	2/16	CBS	22.8/34
8	**Winter Olympics** (Torvill & Dean 3rd in Ice Dancing, Blair 4th in 1500m; USA Hockey in medal round; Women's Combined Slalom)	2/21	CBS	27.9/42	20	**AFC Wild Card** (Broncos at Raiders)	1/9	NBC	22.2/40
9	**Winter Olympics** (Jansen wins 1000m gold; Ice Dancing; Luge; Nordic Combined)	2/18	CBS	27.7/43	21	**AFC Semifinal** (Raiders at Buffalo)	1/15	NBC	22.0/48
10	**AFC Semifinal** (Chiefs at Oilers)	1/16	NBC	27.3/48	22	**Winter Olympics** (Jansen falls in 500m; Men's Downhill Combined; Luge; Men's 30k X-country)	2/14	CBS	21.8/34
11	**Winter Olympics** (Roffe-Steinrotter wins Women's Super G; Luge; Pairs Skating final; Freestyle Skiing)	2/15	CBS	26.8/40	23	**NCAA Basketball Championship** (Arkansas vs Duke)	4/4	CBS	21.6/33
12	**Winter Olympics** (USA ties Canada, 3-3; Moe wins silver in Men's Super G; Speed Skating; Cross-country Skiing)	2/17	CBS	26.2/39	24	**NFC Wild Card** (Vikings at Giants)	1/9	CBS	21.3/48

Top 75 TV Sports Events of 1993-94 (Cont.)

	Date	Net	Rtg/Sh
25 **Winter Olympics**			
(Opening ceremony; Hockey;			
Men's Downhill practice)..........2/12		CBS	20.9/34
26 **NFC Semifinal**			
(Giants at 49ers)....................1/15		CBS	19.4/38
27 **World Series Game 6**			
(Phillies at Blue Jays)..............10/23		CBS	19.1/35
28 **NFL Thanksgiving**			
(Dolphins at Cowboys)..........11/25		NBC	18.6/48
NFC Wild Card			
(Packers at Lions)....................1/8		ABC	18.6/38
30 **World Series Game 5**			
(Blue Jays at Phillies)..............10/21		CBS	18.4/30
31 **World Series Game 4**			
(Blue Jays at Phillies)..............10/20		CBS	18.0/31
32 **NBA Finals Game 7**			
(Knicks at Rockets)..................6/22		NBC	17.9/31
World Series Game 2			
(Phillies at Blue Jays)..............10/17		CBS	17.9/29
34 **Orange Bowl**			
(Fla. St. vs Nebraska) 1/1		NBC	17.8/31
35 **Baseball NLCS Game 6**			
(Braves at Phillies)..................10/13		CBS	17.4/28
36 **AFC Wild Card**			
(Steelers at Chiefs)..................1/8		ABC	16.9/40
37 **Monday Night Football**			
(Various teams)....................16 wks		ABC	16.5/27
38 **NFL Thanksgiving**			
(Bears at Lions)....................11/25		CBS	15.8/41
39 **Baseball All-Star Game**			
(at Pittsburgh) 7/12		NBC	15.7/28
40 **World Series Game 1**			
(Phillies at Blue Jays)..............10/16		CBS	15.5/29
41 **NFL Christmas**			
(Oilers at 49ers)....................12/25		NBC	15.2/39
World Series Game 3			
(Blue Jays at Phillies)..............10/19		CBS	15.2/28
Baseball NLCS Game 1			
(Braves at Phillies) 10/6		CBS	15.2/25
44 **Baseball ALCS Game 6**			
(Blue Jays at White Sox) 10/12		CBS	14.8/25
45 **NFL Regular Season Early Game**			
(various teams) ....15 wks		CBS	14.4/33
46 **NFL Late Season Saturday**			
(Cowboys at Jets) 12/18		CBS	14.2/33
Baseball NLCS Game 4			
(Phillies at Braves)..................10/10		CBS	14.2/24
48 **U.S. Figure Skating Championships**			
(Women's Final) 1/8		ABC	14.1/23
49 **NCAA Basketball Semifinal**			
(Duke vs Florida)......................4/2		CBS	14.0/26
50 **Winter Olympics**			
(Ice Dancing preview;			
Hockey; Women's Downhill			
Combined; Biathlon)................2/20		CBS	13.3/30

	Date	Net	Rtg/Sh
NFL Regular Season Late Game			
(Various teams)........................7 wks		NBC	13.3/27
52 **NCAA Basketball Semifinal**			
(Arkansas vs Arizona) 4/2		CBS	13.2/31
53 **NFL '94 Preseason Special**			
(Bears vs Chiefs)....................8/22		ABC	13.1/22
54 **NFL Late Season Saturday**			
(49ers at Falcons)..................12/11		CBS	13.0/29
55 **NBA Finals Game 4**			
(Rockets at Knicks)..................6/15		NBC	12.9/23
56 **NBA Finals Game 2**			
(Knicks at Rockets)..................6/8		NBC	12.6/23
Pro Figure Skating Championships			
(Women and Pairs) 1/28		NBC	12.6/20
58 **NBA Eastern Final Game 7**			
(Pacers at Knicks)....................6/5		NBC	12.5/24
59 **NBA Finals Game 3**			
(Rockets at Knicks)..................6/12		NBC	12.4/24
60 **World Fig. Skating Championships**			
(Women's Final)......................3/26		NBC	12.3/22
61 **Winter Olympics**			
(USA ties France, 4-4; Pairs			
Figure Skating; Koss wins			
1st gold medal in 5000m)......2/13		CBS	12.2/27
62 **NFL Regular Season Early Game**			
(Various teams)........................8 wks		NBC	11.9/27
63 **NCAA Basketball Regional Final**			
(Arkansas vs Michigan) 3/27		CBS	11.7/27
64 **Baseball NLCS Game 2**			
(Braves at Phillies)....................10/7		CBS	11.5/20
65 **NBA Finals Game 6**			
(Knicks at Rockets)..................6/19		NBC	11.3/24
Cotton Bowl			
(Notre Dame vs Texas A&M) 1/1		NBC	11.3/22
Rose Bowl			
(Wisconsin vs UCLA) 1/1		ABC	11.3/22
Baseball ALCS Game 1			
Blue Jays at White Sox) 10/5		CBS	11.3/19
U.S. Fig. Skating Championships			
(Kerrigan attack report) 1/6		ABC	11.3/17
70 **NFL Late Season Saturday**			
(Broncos at Bears) 12/18		NBC	11.2/32
71 **Figure Skating Exhibition**			
("Artistry on Ice")....................5/7		CBS	11.1/20
72 **NFL Late Season Friday**			
(Vikings at Redskins)..............12/31		CBS	10.9/26
73 **World Fig. Skating Championships**			
(Women's 1st round) 3/25		NBC	10.9/19
74 **Winter Olympics**			
(Sweden beats USA 6-3; 2-Man			
Bobsled, Women's Downhill;			
Men's Figure Skating) 2/19		CBS	10.8/30
Baseball ALCS Game 3			
(White Sox at Blue Jays) 10/8		CBS	10.8/20

1993-94 Top-Rated Cable TV Sports Events

Final 1993-94 cable television ratings for nationally-telecast sports events, according to ESPN, Turner Sports and USA Network research. Covers period from Sept. 7, 1993 through Aug. 31, 1994.

NFL Telecasts

		Date	Net	Rtg
1	Chiefs at Vikings....................12/26		ESPN	11.3
2	Cowboys at Cardinals..............9/19		TNT	11.0
3	Jets at Oilers 1/2		ESPN	10.9
4	Steelers at Oilers 11/28		ESPN	10.0
5	Bengals at 49ers....................12/5		ESPN	9.4
6	Lions at Vikings......................10/31		TNT	9.1

Non-NFL Telecasts

		Date	Net	Rtg
1	MLB: Giants at Dodgers 10/3		ESPN	5.8
2	CFA: West Va. at BC................11/26		ESPN	5.6
3	MLB: Astros at Braves 9/30		TBS	5.4
4	NHL: Cup Final, Game 7 ......6/14		ESPN	5.2
	NBA: Bulls at Knicks 5/18		TNT	5.2
	NBA: Jazz at Nuggets 5/19		TNT	5.2

All-Time Top-Rated TV Programs

NFL Football dominates television's All-Time Top-Rated 50 Programs with 18 Super Bowls and the 1981 NFC Championship Game making the list. Rankings based on surveys taken from July, 1960 through August 1994; include only sponsored programs seen on individual networks; and programs under 30 minutes scheduled duration are excluded. Programs are listed with ratings points, audience share and number of households watching, according to Nielsen Media Research.

Multiple entries: The Super Bowl (19); "The Beverly Hillbillies" and "Roots" (7); "The Thorn Birds" (3); "The Bob Hope Christmas Show," "The Ed Sullivan Show" and "Gone With The Wind" (2).

	Program	Episode/Game	Net	Date	Rating	Share	Households
1	M*A*S*H (series)	Final episode	CBS	2/28/83	**60.2**	77	50,150,000
2	Dallas (series)	"Who Shot J.R.?"	CBS	11/21/80	**53.3**	76	41,470,000
3	Roots (mini-series)	Part 8	ABC	1/30/77	**51.1**	71	36,380,000
4	**Super Bowl XVI**	49ers 26, Bengals 21	CBS	1/24/82	**49.1**	73	40,020,000
5	**Super Bowl XVII**	Redskins 27, Dolphins 17	NBC	1/30/83	**48.6**	69	40,480,000
6	XVII Winter Olympics	Women's Figure Skating	CBS	2/23/94	**48.5**	64	45,690,000
7	**Super Bowl XX**	Bears 46, Patriots 10	NBC	1/26/86	**48.3**	70	41,490,000
8	Gone With the Wind (movie)	Part 1	NBC	11/7/76	**47.7**	65	33,960,000
9	Gone with the Wind (movie)	Part 2	NBC	11/8/76	**47.4**	64	33,750,000
10	**Super Bowl XII**	Cowboys 27, Broncos 10	CBS	1/15/78	**47.2**	67	34,410,000
11	**Super Bowl XIII**	Steelers 35, Cowboys 31	NBC	1/21/79	**47.1**	74	35,090,000
12	Bob Hope Special	Christmas Show	NBC	1/15/70	**46.6**	64	27,260,000
13	**Super Bowl XVIII**	Raiders 38, Redskins 9	CBS	1/22/84	**46.4**	71	38,800,000
	Super Bowl XIX	49ers 38, Dolphins 16	ABC	1/20/85	**46.4**	63	39,390,000
15	**Super Bowl XIV**	Steelers 31, Rams 19	CBS	1/20/80	**46.3**	67	35,330,000
16	ABC Theater (special)	"The Day After"	ABC	11/20/83	**46.0**	62	38,550,000
17	Roots (mini-series)	Part 6	ABC	1/28/77	**45.9**	66	32,680,000
	The Fugitive (series)	Final episode	ABC	8/29/67	**45.9**	72	25,700,000
19	**Super Bowl XXI**	Giants 39, Broncos 20	CBS	1/25/87	**45.8**	66	40,030,000
20	Roots (mini-series)	Part 5	ABC	1/27/77	**45.7**	71	32,540,000
21	**Super Bowl XXVIII**	Cowboys 30, Bills 13	NBC	1/29/94	**45.5**	66	42,860,000
	Cheers	Final episode	NBC	5/20/93	**45.5**	64	42,360,500
23	The Ed Sullivan Show	Beatles' 1st appearence	CBS	2/9/64	**45.3**	60	23,240,000
24	**Super Bowl XXVII**	Cowboys 52, Bills 17	NBC	1/31/93	**45.1**	66	41,988,100
25	Bob Hope Special	Christmas Show	NBC	1/14/71	**45.0**	61	27,050,000
26	Roots (mini-series)	Part 3	ABC	1/25/77	**44.8**	68	31,900,000
27	**Super Bowl XI**	Raiders 32, Vikings 14	NBC	1/9/77	**44.4**	73	31,610,000
	Super Bowl XV	Raiders 27, Eagles 10	NBC	1/25/81	**44.4**	63	34,540,000
29	**Super Bowl VI**	Cowboys 24, Dolphins 3	CBS	1/16/72	**44.2**	74	27,450,000
30	XVII Winter Olympics	Women's Figure Skating	CBS	2/25/94	**44.1**	64	41,540,000
	Roots (mini-series)	Part 2	ABC	1/24/77	**44.1**	62	31,400,000
32	The Beverly Hillbillies	Regular episode	CBS	1/8/64	**44.0**	65	22,570,000
33	Roots (mini-series)	Part 4	ABC	1/26/77	**43.8**	66	31,190,000
	The Ed Sullivan Show	Beatles' 2nd appearence	CBS	2/16/64	**43.8**	60	22,445,000
35	**Super Bowl XXIII**	49ers 20, Bengals 16	NBC	1/22/89	**43.5**	68	39,320,000
36	The Academy Awards	John Wayne wins Oscar	ABC	4/7/70	**43.4**	78	25,390,000
37	Thorn Birds (mini-series)	Part 3	ABC	3/29/83	**43.2**	62	35,990,000
38	Thorn Birds (mini-series)	Part 4	ABC	3/30/83	**43.1**	62	35,900,000
39	**NFC Championship Game**	49ers 28, Cowboys 27	CBS	1/10/82	**42.9**	62	34,940,000
40	The Beverly Hillbillies	Regular episode	CBS	1/15/64	**42.8**	62	21,960,000
41	**Super Bowl VII**	Dolphins 14, Redskins 7	NBC	1/14/73	**42.7**	72	27,670,000
42	Thorn Birds (mini-series)	Part 2	ABC	3/28/83	**42.5**	59	35,400,000
43	**Super Bowl IX**	Steelers 16, Vikings 6	NBC	1/12/75	**42.4**	72	29,040,000
	The Beverly Hillbillies	Regular episode	CBS	2/26/64	**42.4**	60	21,750,000
45	**Super Bowl X**	Steelers 21, Cowboys 17	CBS	1/18/76	**42.3**	78	29,440,000
	ABC Sunday Night Movie	"Airport"	ABC	11/11/73	**42.3**	63	28,000,000
	ABC Sunday Night Movie	"Love Story"	ABC	10/1/72	**42.3**	62	27,410,000
	Cinderella	Musical special	CBS	2/22/65	**42.3**	59	22,250,000
	Roots (mini-series)	Part 7	ABC	1/29/77	**42.3**	65	30,120,000
50	The Beverly Hillbillies	Regular episode	CBS	3/25/64	**42.2**	59	21,650,000

All-Time Top-Rated Cable and TV Sports Events

All-time cable television for sports events, according to ESPN and Turner Sports research. Covers period from Sept. 1, 1980 through Aug. 31, 1994.

NFL Telecasts

		Date	Net	Rtg
1	Chicago at Minnesota	12/6/87	ESPN	17.6
2	Chicago at Minnesota	12/3/89	ESPN	14.7
3	Cleveland at San Fran.	11/29/87	ESPN	14.2
4	Pittsburgh at Houston	12/30/90	ESPN	13.8
5	Three games tied		ESPN	13.1

Non-NFL Telecasts

		Date	Net	Rtg
1	NBA: Detroit-Boston	6/1/88	TBS	8.8
2	NBA: Chicago-Detroit	5/31/89	TBS	8.2
3	NBA: Detroit-Boston	5/26/88	TBS	8.1
4	NCAA: G'town-St. John's	2/27/85	ESPN	8.0
5	MLB: SF-Atlanta	9/27/83	TBS	7.7

The Rights Stuff

The network-by-network roster of major 1994-95 television rights on network and cable TV as of Sept. 15, 1994.

ABC

Auto Racing— Indianapolis 500 and NASCAR Brickyard 400.

Major League Baseball— six regular season games; 1996 and '98 World Series; 1995, '97 and '99 LCS and All-Star Games.

College Basketball— regular season games.

Bowling— PBA Winter Tour.

College Football— Big 10/Pac-10 and CFA regular season (except Notre Dame home games); Army Navy Game (1994 only); SEC Championship Game; Aloha, Citrus, Rose and Sugar bowls.

Figure Skating— U.S. Championships.

NFL Football— Monday Night Football; two Wild Card playoff games; Pro Bowl; 1995 Super Bowl.

Golf— British Open; British Senior Open; LPGA Dinah Shore; PGA, LPGA and Seniors Skins games.

Horse Racing— Kentucky Derby; Preakness; Belmont Stakes.

Soccer— Major League Soccer championship game.

CBS

Auto Racing— Daytona 500.

College Basketball— regular season, conference tournaments, NCAA tournament, Men's and Women's Final Fours.

College Football— 1994 season Hancock and Carquest bowls; 1995 season Orange, Fiesta, Hancock and Carquest bowls; 1996 season Big East, SEC games and Orange and Fiesta bowls.

Golf— PGA Tour; Masters; PGA Championship; Presidents Cup.

Olympics— 1998 Nagano Winter Games.

Tennis— U.S. Open.

ESPN (and ESPN2)

Auto Racing— IndyCar, NASCAR and Formula One.

Major League Baseball— regular season.

College Basketball— regular season and conference tournaments; pre- and postseason NIT.

Bowling— PBA and LPBT tours.

Boxing— Top Rank series.

College Football— Big 10/Pac-10 and CFA regular season (except Notre Dame home games); Heisman Trophy Show; Copper, Hall of Fame, Holiday, Independence, Las Vegas, Liberty and Peach bowls.

NFL Football— Sunday Night Football (2nd half of season); College Draft.

Golf— U.S. Open and British Open (early rounds); PGA, Senior and LPGA tour events.

NHL Hockey— regular season and Stanley Cup playoffs.

Soccer— Major League Soccer regular season and playoffs.

Tennis— ATP Tour; Australian Open; Davis Cup; Grand Slam Cup; Federation Cup.

Yachting— 1995 America's Cup.

Turner (TBS and TNT)

Auto Racing— Coca-Cola 600 and NASCAR circuit on TBS.

Major League Baseball— Atlanta Braves on TBS.

NBA Basketball— regular season and playoffs on TBS and TNT; NBA Draft on TNT.

College Football— Gator Bowl on TBS.

NFL Football— Sunday Night Football (1st half of season) on TNT.

Golf— PGA Championship (early rounds, partial 3rd and 4th) and Grand Slam of Golf on TBS.

NBC

Major League Baseball— six regular season games; 1995, '97 and '99 World Series; 1996 and '98 LCS and All-Star Games.

NBA Basketball— regular season and playoffs; NBA Finals; All-Star Game.

Figure Skating— World and European Championships.

College Football— Notre Dame home games; 1995 Cotton, 1995 Fiesta and 1995 Orange bowls.

NFL Football— AFC regular season and playoffs; 1996 and '98 Super Bowls.

Golf— U.S. Open; U.S. Women's Open; U.S. Senior Open; Players Championship; PGA Seniors Championship; 1995 Ryder Cup.

Horse Racing— Breeders' Cup.

Olympics— 1996 Atlanta Summer Games; '96 Olympic Trials.

Tennis— French Open.

FOX

NFL Football— NFC regular season and playoffs; 1997 Super Bowl.

NHL Hockey— All-Star Game; selected regular season and Stanley Cup playoff games.

USA Network

Boxing— Tuesday Night fights.

Dog Shows— Westminster Dog Show.

Golf— 1995 Ryder Cup (early rounds); Masters (early rounds); PGA Seniors (early rounds).

Tennis— French Open (thru semifinals); U.S. Open (thru quarters).

Olympics TV Rights

The reported cost of securing exclusive U.S. television rights for the Olympic Games has skyrocketed over the last 35 years. In 1960, CBS paid $50,000 for the Winter Olympics. In 1994, CBS agreed to pay $375 million for the 1998 Winter Games—an increase of 7,500 percent. In the same time, the cost of the Summer Games has gone from just under $400,000 to $456 million.

Year	Games	Location	Rights Fee	Net	TV Hrs
1960	Winter	Squaw Valley	$ 50,000	CBS	15
	Summer	Rome	394,000	CBS	20
1964	Winter	Innsbruck	$597,000	ABC	17¼
	Summer	Tokyo	1.5 mil.	NBC	14
1968	Winter	Grenoble	$2.5 mil.	ABC	27
	Summer	Mexico City	4.5 mil.	ABC	43¾
1972	Winter	Sapporo	$6.4 mil.	NBC	37
	Summer	Munich	7.5 mil.	ABC	62¾
1976	Winter	Innsbruck	$10 mil.	ABC	43½
	Summer	Montreal	25 mil.	ABC	76½
1980	Winter	Lake Placid	$15.5 mil.	ABC	53¼
	Summer	Moscow	87 mil.	NBC	150*
1984	Winter	Sarajevo	$91.5 mil.	ABC	63
	Summer	Los Angeles	225 mil.	ABC	180
1988	Winter	Calgary	$309 mil.	ABC	94½
	Summer	Seoul	300 mil.	NBC	179½
1992	Winter	Albertville	$243 mil.	CBS	116
	Summer	Barcelona	401 mil.	NBC	161
1994	Winter	Lillehammer	$300 mil.	CBS	120
1996	Summer	Atlanta	$456 mil.	NBC	168
1998	Winter	Nagano	$375 mil.	CBS	TBA

*NBC planned 150 hours of coverage for the 1980 Summer Olympics, but since the U.S. boycotted the Games, NBC did not cover them and did not pay the rights fee.

What Major League Franchises Are Worth

The estimated total market value of the 107 major league baseball, basketball, football and hockey franchises operating in the U.S. and Canada in 1992-93. Figures according to *Financial World* magazine's fourth annual survey, released May 10, 1994. Franchise values are estimates of what a team would have been worth if put up for sale in early 1994. Values are based on gate receipts, radio and TV revenues, stadium/arena income (luxury suites, concessions, parking, etc.), operating income, player salaries and other expenses. Figures are in millions of dollars; (*) indicates expansion team.

BASEBALL	Value 1993	1992	NBA	Value 1993	1992	NFL	Value 1993	1992	NHL	Value 1993	1992
NY Yankees	$166	$160	LA Lakers	$168	$155	Dallas	$190	$165	Detroit	$104	$ 87
Toronto	150	155	Detroit	154	132	NY Giants	176	146	Boston	88	79
NY Mets	147	145	Chicago	149	102	Philadelphia	172	149	Los Angeles	85	71
Boston	141	136	New York	136	87	San Francisco	167	139	Montreal	82	73
LA Dodgers	138	135	Portland	122	84	Cleveland	165	133	NY Rangers	81	76
Chicago-AL	133	123	Cleveland	118	81	Buffalo	164	138	Chicago	80	67
Texas	132	106	Boston	117	91	Miami	161	145	Toronto	77	63
Baltimore	129	130	Phoenix	108	71	Chicago	160	136	Philadelphia	69	58
Chicago-NL	120	101	Charlotte	104	77	Washington	158	123	Vancouver	69	61
Oakland	114	124	San Antonio	100	65	Houston	157	132	Pittsburgh	62	53
Colorado	110	*	Utah	98	72	New Orleans	154	130	St. Louis	59	52
St. Louis	105	98	Seattle	96	51	Kansas City	153	130	Buffalo	55	44
Cleveland	100	81	Minnesota	92	65	Atlanta	148	125	NY Islanders	53	55
Philadelphia	96	96	Golden St	85	62	LA Rams	148	128	San Jose	52	43
Atlanta	96	88	Houston	84	58	Seattle	148	137	New Jersey	51	47
Milwaukee	96	86	Orlando	84	60	Denver	147	119	Ottawa	50	*
Kansas City	94	111	Sacramento	84	66	Minnesota	147	123	Calgary	50	52
California	93	105	LA Clippers	83	54	Arizona	146	125	Washington	47	45
San Francisco	93	103	Philadelphia	83	59	LA Raiders	146	124	Dallas	46	42
Detroit	89	97	Dallas	79	56	Pittsburgh	143	120	Edmonton	46	51
Cincinnati	86	103	New Jersey	79	54	Cincinnati	142	128	Hartford	46	48
San Diego	85	103	Washington	78	53	New England	142	102	Quebec	43	48
Houston	85	87	Milwaukee	77	54	NY Jets	142	119	Tampa Bay	39	*
Minnesota	83	95	Miami	76	58	San Diego	142	119	Winnipeg	35	35
Florida	81	*	Atlanta	72	54	Tampa Bay	142	118			
Seattle	80	86	Denver	69	50	Green Bay	141	116			
Pittsburgh	79	95	Indiana	67	45	Indianapolis	141	122			
Montreal	75	86				Detroit	138	118			

Note: the NHL expanded by two teams (Anaheim and Florida) in 1993-94.

Teams Bought in 1994

Ten major league clubs changed hands from September 1, 1993 through August 31, 1994, while four expansion franchises were awarded to well-heeled backers in football and basketball. Hollywood producer Jeff Lurie led the way to the bank, shelling out a record $185 million for the NFL's Philadelphia Eagles— $12 million more than the previous major league high water mark of $173 million paid for the Baltimore Orioles in 1993.

Wayne Huizenga, the Blockbuster Video baron who recently bought Florida expansion teams in baseball and hockey for a combined $145 million, added the NFL's Miami Dolphins to his collection— upping his 15% stake to a full 100% for $138 million. The Dolphins originally cost $7.5 million, which is what Joe Robbie and actor Danny Thomas paid the AFL for the expansion rights in 1965. Twenty-nine years later, you needed well over $100 million to land a new franchise in either the NFL or NBA. In football, the NFL expanded south, welcoming Charlotte, N.C. and Jacksonville, Fla. for $140 million apiece. In basketball, the NBA headed north finding buyers in Toronto and Vancouver willing to ante up $125 million each.

MAJOR LEAGUE BASEBALL

Boston Red Sox: General Partner Haywood Sullivan sold his 10% of the club to JRY Corporation for $12 million. He originally invested $200,000 in the team in 1977 after the death of owner Tom Yawkey. JRY Corp. now owns 100% of the team.

NBA BASKETBALL

Miami Heat: Fort Lauderdale trash hauler (and Wayne Huizenga brother-in-law) Whit Hudson bought controlling interest (40-50%) of the Heat from minority owners Lewis Schaffel and Billy Cunningham for $60 million. He also guaranteed majority owners Ted and Micky Arison $60 million for their 50-60% of the team if they sell within two years. The Heat cost $32.5 million as a 1988 expansion team.

Minnesota Timberwolves: Mankato (Minn.) businessman Glen Taylor bought the T-wolves from Harvey Ratner and Marv Wolfenson for $88 million after the NBA's board of governors vetoed sale of the team to a New Orleans syndicate headed by boxing promoter Bob Arum. Arum's group had agreed to pay $152 million, which would have included paying off Ratner and Wolfenson's debt on the Target Center in Minneapolis. Ratner and Wolfenson, who would have held on to Target Center in the New Orleans deal, later sold the arena to the state's Metropolitan Sports Commission for $42 million. The T-wolves cost $32.5 million as a 1989 expansion team.

New York Knicks: sold along with the NHL Rangers, Madison Square Garden and the MSG cable TV network by Viacom to ITT Corporation and Cablevision Systems Inc. for $1.075 billion.

Toronto Raptors: 1995-96 expansion team awarded to limited partnership headed by Toronto businessman John Bitove for $125 million.

Vancouver Grizzlies: 1995-96 expansion team awarded to limited partnership headed up by NHL Canucks owner Arthur Griffiths for $125 million.

Major League Teams Bought in 1994 (Cont.)

NFL FOOTBALL

Carolina Panthers: 1995 expansion team awarded to Spartanburg, S.C. food service mogul (Denny's, Hardee's, etc.) Jerry Richardson for $140 million. Richardson, a flanker for the Baltimore Colts in 1959-60, took his 1959 NFL championship bonus of $4,864 and started the first Hardee's in Spartanburg in 1961.

Jacksonville Jaguars: 1995 expansion team awarded to limited partnership headed up by Stamford, Ct. women's shoe retailer Wayne Weaver for $140 million. **Miami Dolphins:** 15% minority owner Wayne Huizenga bought the remaining 85% of the team from the family of Joe Robbie for $138 million (Huizenga already owns Joe Robbie Stadium).

New England Patriots: Boston businessman and Foxboro Stadium owner Bob Kraft bought the Pats from interim owner and St. Louis native James Orthwein for $170 million. Orthwein, who toyed with the idea of moving the team to St. Louis, bought it for $105 million in 1992.

Philadelphia Eagles: Hollywood producer Jeff Lurie bought the Eagles for $185 million from Norman Braman, who paid $65 million for the team in 1985.

NHL HOCKEY

Hartford Whalers: KTR Limited Partnership (Peter Karmanos, Tom Thewes and former NHL goaltender Jim Rutherford) bought 100% of Whalers for $47.5 million from Richard Gordon, who paid $31 million for three-quarters of the club in 1988.

Los Angeles Kings: Jeffrey Sudikoff and Joe Cohen bought 72% of the Kings from owner Bruce McNall for $60 million. McNall, deep in debt and under federal investigation for allegedly falsifying loan documents, originally bought majority control of the the club for $20 million in 1988. He retained 28% of the club.

New York Rangers: sold along with the NBA Knicks, Madison Square Garden and the MSG cable TV network by Viacom to ITT Corporation and Cablevision Systems Inc. for 1.075 billion.

The 1993 *Forbes* Top 40

The 40 highest-paid athletes of 1993 (including salary, winnings, endorsements, etc.), according to the Dec. 20, 1993 issue of *Forbes* magazine. Nationality, birth date, and each athlete's rank on the 1992 list are also given. Age refers to athlete's age as of Dec. 31, 1993.

		Sport	Salary/ Winnings	Other Income	Total	Nat	Birthdate (Age)	1992 Rank
1	Michael Jordan	Basketball	$ 4.0	$32.0	$36.0	USA	Feb. 17, 1963 (30)	1
2	Riddick Bowe	Boxing	23.0	2.0	25.0	USA	Aug. 10, 1967 (26)	NR
3	Ayrton Senna	Auto Racing	14.0	4.5	18.5	BRA	Mar. 21, 1960 (33)	3
4	Alain Prost	Auto Racing	12.0	4.0	16.0	FRA	Feb. 24, 1955 (38)	NR
5	George Foreman	Boxing	12.5	3.3	15.8	USA	Jan. 10, 1949 (44)	17†
6	Shaquille O'Neal	Basketball	3.3	11.9	15.2	USA	Mar. 6, 1972 (21)	NR
7	Lennox Lewis	Boxing	14.0	1.0	15.0	GBR	Sept. 2, 1965 (28)	NR
8	Cecil Fielder	Baseball	12.4*	0.3	12.7	USA	Sept. 21, 1963 (30)	40
9	Jim Courier	Tennis	3.6	9.0	12.6	USA	Aug. 17, 1970 (23)	9
10	Joe Montana	Football	5.0	6.5	11.5	USA	June 11, 1956 (37)	7
11	Arnold Palmer	Golf	0.1	11.0	11.1	USA	Sept. 10, 1929 (64)	6
12	Evander Holyfield	Boxing	9.5	1.2	10.7	USA	Oct. 19, 1962 (31)	2
13	Jack Nicklaus	Golf	0.2	10.0	10.2	USA	Jan. 21, 1940 (53)	8
14	Emerson Fittipaldi	Auto Racing	5.5	4.5	10.0	BRA	Dec. 12, 1946 (47)	NR
15	Steffi Graf	Tennis	2.8	7.0	9.8	GER	June 14, 1969 (24)	20
16	Pete Sampras	Tennis	3.6	6.0	9.6	USA	Aug. 12, 1971 (22)	28
17	Reggie White	Football	9.0*	0.5	9.5	USA	Dec. 19, 1961 (32)	NR
18	David Robinson	Basketball	5.7	3.5	9.2	USA	Aug. 6, 1965 (28)	21
19	Nigel Mansell	Auto Racing	7.0	2.0	9.0	GBR	Aug. 8, 1953 (40)	4
20	Andre Agassi	Tennis	0.4	8.0	8.4	USA	Apr. 29, 1970 (23)	5
21	Greg Norman	Golf	1.4	7.0	8.4	AUS	Feb. 10, 1955 (38)	16
22	Wayne Gretzky	Hockey	4.3	4.0	8.3	CAN	Jan. 26, 1961 (32)	14†
23	Julio Cesar Chavez	Boxing	7.5	0.5	8.0	MEX	July 12, 1962 (31)	17†
24	Stefan Edberg	Tennis	2.3	5.3	7.8	SWE	Jan. 19, 1966 (26)	24†
25	Michael Chang	Tennis	1.7	5.8	7.5	USA	Feb. 22, 1972 (21)	12†
26	Ryne Sandberg	Baseball	7.1	0.3	7.4	USA	Sept. 18, 1959 (34)	NR
27	Emmitt Smith	Football	7.0*	0.3	7.3	USA	May 15, 1969 (24)	NR
28	Barry Bonds	Baseball	6.5	0.7	7.2	USA	July 24, 1964 (29)	38
29	Gerhard Berger	Auto Racing	6.5	0.5	7.0	AUT	Aug. 27, 1959 (34)	12†
	Ken Griffey Jr	Baseball	6.0	1.0	7.0	USA	Feb. 10, 1955 (38)	16
	Cal Ripken Jr	Baseball	6.6	0.4	7.0	USA	Aug. 24, 1961 (32)	NR
32	Boris Becker	Tennis	1.8	5.0	6.8	GER	Nov. 22, 1967 (26)	NR
33	Bobby Bonilla	Baseball	6.2	0.4	6.6	USA	Feb. 23, 1963 (30)	24†
34	Charles Barkley	Basketball	3.0	3.5	6.5	USA	Feb. 20, 1963 (30)	NR
	Riccardo Patrese	Auto Racing	6.0	0.5	6.5	ITA	Apr. 17, 1954 (39)	14†
	Gabriela Sabatini	Tennis	1.0	5.5	6.5	ARG	May 16, 1970 (23)	22†
37	Drew Bledsoe	Football	5.9*	0.2	6.1	USA	Feb. 14, 1972 (21)	NR
	Dwight Gooden	Baseball	5.9	0.2	6.1	USA	Nov. 16, 1964 (29)	30†
	Nolan Ryan	Baseball	4.0	2.1	6.1	USA	Jan. 31, 1947 (46)	NR
40	Steve Young	Football	5.8	0.2	6.0	USA	Oct. 11, 1961 (32)	NR

*Includes signing bonus.

AWARDS

The Peabody Award

Presented annually since 1940 for outstanding achievement in radio and television broadcasting. Only 13 Peabodys have been given for sports programming. Named after Georgia banker and philanthropist George Foster Peabody, the awards are administered by the Henry W. Grady College of Journalism and Mass Communication at the University of Georgia.

Television

Year
1960 **CBS** for coverage of 1960 Winter and Summer Olympic Games (for Outstanding Contribution to International Understanding).
1966 ABC's **"Wide World of Sports"** (for Outstanding Achievement in Promotion of International Understanding).
1968 **ABC Sports** coverage of both the 1968 Winter and Summer Olympic Games.
1972 **ABC Sports** coverage of the 1972 Summer Olympics in Munich.
1973 **Joe Garagiola** of NBC Sports (for "The Baseball World of Joe Garagiola").
1976 **ABC Sports** coverage of both the 1976 Winter and Summer Olympic Games.
1984 **Roone Arledge**, president of ABC News & Sports (for significant contributions to television news and sports programming).
1986 **WFAA-TV**, Dallas for its investigation of the Southern Methodist University football program.
1988 **Jim McKay** of ABC Sports (for pioneering efforts and career accomplishments in the world of TV sports).
1991 **CBS Sports** coverage of the 1991 Masters golf tournament
& **HBO Sports** and Black Canyon Productions for the baseball special "When It Was A Game."

Radio

Year
1974 **WSB** radio in Atlanta for "Henry Aaron: A Man with a Mission."
1991 **Red Barber** of National Public Radio (for his six decades as a broadcaster and his 10 years as a commentator on NPR's "Morning Edition").

National Emmy Awards
Sports Programming

Presented by the Academy of Television Arts and Sciences since 1948. Eligibility period covered the calendar year from 1948-57 and since 1988.
  Multiple Major Award Winners: ABC "Wide World of Sports" (18); ABC Olympic Coverage (9); CBS NFL Coverage (8); NFL Films Football Coverage (7); ABC "Monday Night Football" (5); CBS NCAA Basketball Coverage and ESPN "Outside the Lines" series (4); ABC "The American Sportsman" and ABC Indianapolis 500 Coverage (3); ABC Kentucky Derby Coverage, NBC Olympic Coverage and NBC World Series Coverage (2).

1949
Coverage—"Wrestling"(KTLA, Los Angeles)

1950
Program—"Rams Football" (KNBH-TV, Los Angeles)

1954
Program—"Gillette Cavalcade of Sports" (NBC)

1965-66
Programs—"Wide World of Sports" (ABC), "Shell's Wonderful World of Golf" (NBC) and "CBS Golf Classic" (CBS)

1966-67
Program—"Wide World of Sports" (ABC)

1967-68
Program—"Wide World of Sports" (ABC)

1968-69
Program—"1968 Summer Olympics" (ABC)

1969-70
Programs—"NFL Football" (CBS) and "Wide World of Sports" (ABC)

1970-71
Program—"Wide World of Sports" (ABC)

1971-72
Program—"Wide World of Sports" (ABC)

1972-73
News Special—"Coverage of Munich Olympic Tragedy" (ABC)
Sports Programs—"1972 Summer Olympics" (ABC) and "Wide World of Sports" (ABC)

1973-74
Program—"Wide World of Sports" (ABC)

1974-75
Non-Edited Program—"Jimmy Connors vs Rod Laver Tennis Challenge" (CBS)
Edited Program—"Wide World of Sports" (ABC)

1975-76
Live Special—"1975 World Series: Cincinnati vs Boston" (NBC)
Live Series—"NFL Monday Night Football" (ABC)
Edited Specials—"1976 Winter Olympics" (ABC)
and "Triumph and Tragedy: The Olympic Experience" (ABC)
Edited Series—"Wide World of Sports" (ABC)

1976-77
Live Special—"1976 Summer Olympics" (ABC)
Live Series—"The NFL Today/NFL Football" (CBS)
Edited Special—"1976 Summer Olympics Preview" (ABC)
Edited Series—"The Olympiad" (PBS)

National Emmy Awards (Cont.)
Sports Programming

1977-78
Live Special—"Muhammad Ali vs Leon Spinks Heavyweight Championship Fight (CBS)
Live Series—"The NFL Today/NFL Football" (CBS)
Edited Special—"The Impossible Dream: Ballooning Across the Atlantic" (CBS)
Edited Series—"The Way It Was" (PBS)

1978-79
Live Special—"Super Bowl XIII: Pittsburgh vs Dallas" (NBC)
Live Series—"NFL Monday Night Football" (ABC)
Edited Special—"Spirit of '78: The Flight of Double Eagle II" (ABC)
Edited Series—"The American Sportsman" (ABC)

1979-80
Live Special—"1980 Winter Olympics" (ABC)
Live Series—"NCAA College Football" (ABC)
Edited Special—"Gossamer Albatross: Flight of Imagination" (CBS)
Edited Series—"NFL Game of the Week" (NFL Films)

1980-81
Live Special—"1981 Kentucky Derby" (ABC)
Live Series—"PGA Golf Tour" (CBS)
Edited Special—"Wide World of Sports 20th Anniversary Show" (ABC)
Edited Series—"The American Sportsman" (ABC)

1981-82
Live Special—"1982 NCAA Basketball Final: North Carolina vs Georgetown" (CBS)
Live Series—"NFL Football" (CBS)
Edited Special—"1982 Indianapolis 500" (ABC)
Edited Series—"Wide World of Sports" (ABC)

1982-83
Live Special—"1982 World Series: St. Louis vs Milwaukee" (NBC)
Live Series—"NFL Football" (CBS)
Edited Special—"Wimbledon '83" (NBC)
Edited Series—"Wide World of Sports" (ABC)
Journalism—"ABC Sportsbeat" (ABC)

1983-84
No awards given

1984-85
Live Special—"1984 Summer Olympics" (ABC)
Live Series—No award given
Edited Special—"Road to the Super Bowl '85" (NFL Films)
Edited Series—"The American Sportsman" (ABC)
Journalism—"ABC Sportsbeat" (ABC), "CBS Sports Sunday" (CBS), Dick Schaap features (ABC) and 1984 Summer Olympic features (ABC)

1985-86
No awards given

1986-87
Live Special—"1987 Daytona 500" (CBS)
Live Series—"NFL Football" (CBS)
Edited Special—"Wide World of Sports 25th Anniversary Special" (ABC)
Edited Series—"Wide World of Sports" (ABC)

1987-88
Live Special—"1987 Kentucky Derby" (ABC)
Live Series—"NFL Monday Night Football" (ABC)
Edited Special—"Paris-Roubaix Bike Race" (CBS)
Edited Series—"Wide World of Sports" (ABC)

1988
Live Special—"1988 Summer Olympics" (NBC)
Live Series—"1988 NCAA Basketball" (CBS)
Edited Special—"Road to the Super Bowl '88" (NFL Films)
Edited Series—"Wide World of Sports" (ABC)
Studio Show—"NFL GameDay" (ESPN)
Journalism—1988 Summer Olympic reporting (NBC)

1989
Live Special—"1989 Indianapolis 500" (ABC)
Live Series—"NFL Monday Night Football" (ABC)
Edited Special—"Trans-Antarctica! The International Expedition" (ABC)
Edited Series—"This is the NFL" (NFL Films)
Studio Show—"NFL Today" (CBS)
Journalism—1989 World Series Game 3 earthquake coverage (ABC)

1990
Live Special—"1990 Indianapolis 500" (ABC)
Live Series—"1990 NCAA Basketball Tournament" (CBS)
Edited Special—"Road to Super Bowl XXIV" (NFL Films)
Edited Series—"Wide World of Sports" (ABC)
Studio Show—"SportsCenter" (ESPN)
Journalism—"Outside the Lines: The Autograph Game" (ESPN)

1991
Live Special—"1991 NBA Finals: Chicago vs LA Lakers" (NBC)
Live Series—"1991 NCAA Basketball Tournament" (CBS)
Edited Special—"Wide World of Sports 30th Anniversary Special" (ABC)
Edited Series—"This is the NFL" (NFL Films)
Studio Show—"NFL Game Day" (ESPN) and "NFL Live" (NBC)
Journalism—"Outside the Lines: Steroids—Whatever It Takes" (ESPN)

1992
Live Special—"1992 Breeders' Cup" (NBC)
Live Series—"1992 NCAA Basketball Tournament" (CBS)
Edited Special—"1992 Summer Olympics" (NBC)
Edited Series—"MTV Sports" (MTV)
Studio Show—"The NFL Today" (CBS)
Journalism—"Outside the Lines: Portraits in Black and White" (ESPN)

1993
Live Special—"1993 World Series" (CBS)
Live Series—"Monday Night Football" (ABC)
Edited Special—"Road to the Super Bowl" (NFL Films)
Edited Series—"This is the NFL" (NFL Films)
Studio Show—"The NFL Today" (CBS)
Journalism (TIE)—"Outside the Lines: Mitch Ivey Feature" (ESPN) and "SportsCenter: University of Houston Football" (ESPN).
Feature—"Arthur Ashe: His Life, His Legacy" (NBC).

Sportscasters of the Year
National Emmy Awards

An Emmy Award for Sportscasters was first introduced in 1968 and given for Outstanding Host/Commentator for the 1967-68 TV season. Two awards, one for Outstanding Host or Play-by-Play and the other for Outstanding Analyst, were first presented in 1981 for the 1980-81 season. Three awards, for Outstanding Studio Host, Play-by-Play and Analyst, have been given since the 1993 season

Multiple winners: John Madden and Jim McKay (9); Bob Costas (5); Dick Enberg (4); Al Michaels (2). Note that Jim McKay has won a total of 12 Emmy awards: 9 for Host/Commentator, two for Sports Writing, and one for News Commentary.

Season	Host/Commentator	Season	Host/Play-by-Play	Season	Analyst
1967-68	Jim McKay, ABC	1980-81	Dick Enberg, NBC	1980-81	Dick Button, ABC
1968-69	No award	1981-82	Jim McKay, ABC	1981-82	John Madden, CBS
1969-70	No award	1982-83	Dick Enberg, NBC	1982-83	John Madden, CBS
1970-71	Jim McKay, ABC	1983-84	No award	1983-84	No award
	& Don Meredith, ABC	1984-85	George Michael, NBC	1984-85	No award
1971-72	No award	1985-86	No award	1985-86	No award
1972-73	Jim McKay, ABC	1986-87	Al Michaels, ABC	1986-87	John Madden, CBS
1973-74	Jim McKay, ABC	1987-88	Bob Costas, NBC	1987-88	John Madden, CBS
1974-75	Jim McKay, ABC	1988	Bob Costas, NBC	1988	John Madden, CBS
1975-76	Jim McKay, ABC	1989	Al Michaels, ABC	1989	John Madden, CBS
1976-77	Frank Gifford, ABC	1990	Dick Enberg, NBC	1990	John Madden, CBS
1977-78	Jack Whitaker, CBS	1991	Bob Costas, NBC	1991	John Madden, CBS
1978-79	Jim McKay, ABC	1992	Bob Costas, NBC	1992	John Madden, CBS
1979-80	Jim McKay, ABC				

Year	Studio Host	Year	Play-by-Play	Year	Analyst
1993	Bob Costas	1993	Dick Enberg	1993	Billy Packer

Life Achievement Emmy Award

For outstanding work as an exemplary television sportscaster over many years.

Year		Year		Year		Year	
1989	Jim McKay	1991	Curt Gowdy	1992	Chris Schenkel	1993	Pat Summerall
1990	Lindsey Nelson						

National Sportscasters and Sportswriters Assn. Award

Sportscaster of the Year presented annually since 1959 by the National Sportscasters and Sportswriters Association, based in Salisbury, N.C. Voting is done by NSSA members and selected national media.

Multiple winners: Keith Jackson and Bob Costas (5); Lindsey Nelson and Chris Schenkel (4); Chris Berman, Dick Enberg, Al Michaels and Vin Scully (3); Curt Gowdy and Ray Scott (2).

Year		Year		Year		Year	
1959	Lindsey Nelson	1968	Ray Scott	1977	Pat Summerall	1985	Bob Costas
1960	Lindsey Nelson	1969	Curt Gowdy	1978	Vin Scully	1986	Al Michaels
1961	Lindsey Nelson	1970	Chris Schenkel	1979	Dick Enberg	1987	Bob Costas
1962	Lindsey Nelson	1971	Ray Scott	1980	Dick Enberg	1988	Bob Costas
1963	Chris Schenkel	1972	Keith Jackson		& Al Michaels	1989	Chris Berman
1964	Chris Schenkel	1973	Keith Jackson	1981	Dick Enberg		
1965	Vin Scully	1974	Keith Jackson	1982	Vin Scully	1990	Chris Berman
1966	Curt Gowdy	1975	Keith Jackson	1983	Al Michaels	1991	Bob Costas
1967	Chris Schenkel	1976	Keith Jackson	1984	John Madden	1992	Bob Costas
						1993	Chris Berman

American Sportscasters Association Award

Sportscaster of the Year presented annually since 1984 by the New York-based American Sportscasters Association. Voting done by ASA members and officials. At the urging of Bob Costas, all three-time winners become ineligible for subsequent awards.

Multiple winners: Dick Enberg (4); Bob Costas (3).

Year		Year		Year		Year	
1984	Dick Enberg	1987	Dick Enberg	1990	Dick Enberg	1993	Pat Summerall
1985	Vin Scully	1988	No award	1991	Bob Costas		
1986	Dick Enberg	1989	Bob Costas	1992	Bob Costas		

The Pulitzer Prize

The Pulitzer Prizes for journalism, letters and music have been presented annually since 1917 in the name of Joseph Pulitzer (1847-1911), the publisher of the *New York World*. Prizes are awarded by the president of Columbia University on the recommendation of a board of review. Fourteen Pulitzers have been awarded for newspaper sports reporting, sports commentary and sports photography.

News Coverage

1935 **Bill Taylor,** *NY Herald Tribune,* for his reporting on the 1934 America's Cup yacht races.

Special Citation

1952 **Max Kase,** *NY Journal-American,* for his reporting on the 1951 college basketball point-shaving scandal.

Meritorious Public Service

1954 *Newsday* (Garden City, N.Y.) for its exposé of New York State's race track scandals and labor racketeering.

General Reporting

1956 **Arthur Daley,** *NY Times,* for his 1955 columns.

Investigative Reporting

1981 **Clark Hallas** & **Robert Lowe,** (Tucson) Arizona *Daily Star,* for their 1980 investigation of the University of Arizona athletic department.

1986 **Jeffrey Marx** & **Michael York,** Lexington (Ky.) *Herald-Leader,* for their 1985 investigation of the basketball program at the University of Kentucky and other major colleges.

Specialized Reporting

1985 **Randall Savage** & **Jackie Crosby,** Macon (Ga.) *Telegraph and News,* for their 1984 investigation of athletics and academics at the University of Georgia and Georgia Tech.

Commentary

1976 **Red Smith,** *NY Times,* for his 1975 columns.
1981 **Dave Anderson,** *NY Times,* for his 1980 columns.
1990 **Jim Murray,** *LA Times,* for his 1989 columns.

Photography

1949 **Nat Fein,** *NY Herald Tribune,* for his photo, "Babe Ruth Bows Out."

1952 **John Robinson** & **Don Ultang,** Des Moines (Iowa) *Register and Tribune,* for their sequence of six pictures of the 1951 Drake-Oklahoma A&M football game, in which Drake's Johnny Bright had his jaw broken.

1985 **The Photography Staff** of the Orange County (Calif.) *Register,* for their coverage of the 1984 Summer Olympics in Los Angeles.

1993 **William Snyder** & **Ken Geiger,** *The Dallas Morning News,* for their coverage of the 1992 Summer Olympics in Barcelona, Spain.

Sportswriter of the Year
NSSA Award

Presented annually since 1959 by the National Sportscasters and Sportswriters Association, based in Salisbury, N.C. Voting is done by NSSA members and selected national media.

Multiple winners: Jim Murray (14); Frank Deford (6); Red Smith (5); Will Grimsley (4); Peter Gammons (3); Rick Reilly (2).

Year	Year	Year
1959 Red Smith, *NY Herald-Tribune*	1972 Jim Murray, *LA Times*	1983 Will Grimsley, AP
1960 Red Smith, *NY Herald-Tribune*	1973 Jim Murray, *LA Times*	1984 Frank Deford, *Sports Ill.*
1961 Red Smith, *NY Herald-Tribune*	1974 Jim Murray, *LA Times*	1985 Frank Deford, *Sports Ill.*
1962 Red Smith, *NY Herald-Tribune*	1975 Jim Murray, *LA Times*	1986 Frank Deford, *Sports Ill.*
1963 Arthur Daley, *NY Times*	1976 Jim Murray, *LA Times*	1987 Frank Deford, *Sports Ill.*
1964 Jim Murray, *LA Times*	1977 Jim Murray, *LA Times*	1988 Frank Deford, *Sports Ill.*
1965 Red Smith, *NY Herald-Tribune*	1978 Will Grimsley, AP	1989 Peter Gammons, *Sports Ill.*
1966 Jim Murray, *LA Times*	1979 Jim Murray, *LA Times*	
1967 Jim Murray, *LA Times*		1990 Peter Gammons, *Boston Globe*
1968 Jim Murray, *LA Times*	1980 Will Grimsley, AP	1991 Rick Reilly, *Sports Ill.*
1969 Jim Murray, *LA Times*	1981 Will Grimsley, AP	1992 Rick Reilly, *Sports Ill.*
	1982 Frank Deford, *Sports Ill.*	1993 Peter Gammons, *Boston Globe*
1970 Jim Murray, *LA Times*		
1971 Jim Murray, *LA Times*		

Best Newspaper Sports Sections of 1993

Winners of the annual Associated Press Sports Editors' contest for best daily and Sunday sports sections in newspapers of 175,000 circulation or more. Selections made by a committee of APSE members and released March 11, 1994.

Top 10 Dailies

Atlanta Journal-Constitution	Dallas Morning News
Baltimore Sun	Detroit Free Press
Boston Globe	Los Angeles Times
Chicago Sun-Times	Philadelphia Inquirer
Chicago Tribune	USA Today

Honorable mention: Arizona Republic; Denver Post; Ft. Lauderdale Sun-Sentinel; Miami Herald; Minneapolis Star-Tribune; New York Times; Newsday; Orlando Sentinel; Philadelphia Daily News; Washington Post.

Top 10 Sunday

Atlanta Journal-Constitution	New Orleans Times-Picayune
Boston Globe	New York Times
Chicago Sun-Times	Newsday
Dallas Morning News	Philadelphia Inquirer
Miami Herald	San Jose Mercury News

Honorable mention: Arizona Republic; Baltimore Sun; Ft. Lauderdale Sun-Sentinel; Ft. Worth Star-Telegram; Los Angeles Times; Minneapolis Star Tribune; New York Daily News; Palm Beach (Fla.) Post; St. Paul (Minn.) Pioneer Press; Washington Post.

Directory of Organizations
Listing of the major sports organizations, teams and media addresses and officials as of Sept. 15, 1994.

AUTO RACING

IndyCar
(Championship Auto Racing Teams, Inc.)
390 Enterprise Court, Bloomfield Hills, MI 48302
(810) 334-8500
President-CEO ....Andrew Craig
Director of Publicity..David Elshoff

FISA— Formula One
(Federation Internationale de Sport Automobile)
8 Plade de la Concorde, 75008 Paris, France
TEL: 011-33-1-4265-9951
President..Max Mosley
Secretary General....................................Pierre de Coninck
Director of Public Relations ....Francesco Longanesi

NASCAR
(National Assn. of Stock Car Auto Racing)
P.O. Box 2875, Daytona Beach, FL 32120
(904) 253-0611
President..Bill France Jr.
Director of Public Relations ....Andy Hall

MAJOR LEAGUE BASEBALL

Office of the Commissioner
350 Park Ave., New York, NY 10022
(212) 339-7800
Commissioner ....vacant
            (Fay Vincent resigned Sept. 7, 1992)
Chairman, Executive Council ....Bud Selig
Special Assistants to Chairman ....Dick Wagner
                                    & Peter Widdrington
General Counsel.....................................Thomas Ostertag
Executive Dir. of Public Relatons.........................Rich Levin

Player Relations Committee
350 Park Ave., New York, NY 10022
(212) 339-7400
President & COO ....Richard Ravitch
General Counsel....................................Charles O'Connor

Major League Baseball Players Association
12 East 49th St., 24th Floor, New York, NY 10017
(212) 826-0808
Exec. Director & General Counsel ....Donald Fehr
Special Assistant ....Mark Belanger

AL

American League Office
350 Park Ave., New York, NY 10022
(212) 339-7600
President...Gene Budig
V.P., Admin. & Media Affairs.......................Phyllis Merhige

Baltimore Orioles
333 West Camden St., Baltimore, MD 21201
(410) 685-9800
Managing General Partner............................Peter Angelos
Vice Chairman, Business Operations.................Joseph Foss
Exec. V.P. & General Manager ....Roland Hemond
Director of Public Relations ....Charles Steinberg

Boston Red Sox
Fenway Park, 4 Yawkey Way, Boston MA 02215
(617) 267-9440
General Partner...JRY Corporation
President-CEO ....John Harrington
Exec. V.P. & General Manager.......................Dan Duquette
V.P., Public Relations ....Dick Bresciani

California Angels
P. O. Box 2000, Anaheim, CA 92803
(714) 937-7200 or (213) 625-1123
Owners ....Gene and Jackie Autry
President & CEO ....Richard Brown
V.P. & General Manager...................................Bill Bavasi
V.P. of Media Relations & Broadcasting...........John Sevano

Chicago White Sox
Comiskey Park, 333 W. 35th St., Chicago, IL 60616
(312) 924-1000
Chairman..Jerry Reinsdorf
Vice Chairman...Eddie Einhorn
Senior V.P. & General Manager ....Ron Schueler
Director of Public Relations ....Doug Abel

Cleveland Indians
Jacobs Field, 2401 Ontario, Cleveland, OH 44115
(216) 861-1200
Owner-Chairman-CEO ....Richard Jacobs
Exec. V.P. & General Manager ....John Hart
V.P., Public Relations.......................................Bob DiBiasio

Detroit Tigers
Tiger Stadium, Detroit, MI 48216
(313) 962-4000
Owner-Chairman-President ....Mike Ilitch
Owner-Secretary-Treasurer ....Marian Ilitch
Sr. Director, General Manager.............................Joe Klein
Sr. Director, Public Relations..............................Dan Ewald

Kansas City Royals
P.O. Box 419969, Kansas City, MO 64141
(816) 921-2200
Owner ....Ewing Kauffman Estate
Chairman-CEO...David Glass
Exec. V.P. & General Manager ....Herk Robinson
V.P., Public Relations ....Dean Vogelaar

Milwaukee Brewers
County Stadium, 201 S. 46th St., Milwaukee, WI 53214
(414) 933-4114
President-CEO ....Bud Selig
Senior V.P., Baseball Operations ....Sal Bando
V.P. & General Counsel ....Wendy Selig-Prieb
Director of Media Relations ....Tom Skibosh

Minnesota Twins
Hubert H. Humphrey Metrodome
501 Chicago Ave. South, Minneapolis, MN 55415
(612) 375-1366
Owner..Carl Pohlad
President..Jerry Bell
General Manager ....Terry Ryan
Director of Media Relations ....Rob Antony

New York Yankees
Yankee Stadium, Bronx, NY 10451
(718) 293-4300
Principal Owner.................................George Steinbrenner
General Partner..Joe Malloy
V.P. & General Manager...............................Gene Michael
Director of Media Relations ....Rob Butcher

Oakland Athletics
Oakland-Alameda County Coliseum, Oakland, CA 94621
(510) 638-4900
Managing General Partner....................Walter A. Haas Jr.
Chairman-CEO.......................................Walter J. Haas
President & General Manager ....Sandy Alderson
Director of Baseball Information ....Jay Alves

GRANLUND 1994 MIDDLESEX NEWS.
Dave Granlund/Middlesex (Mass.) News

Seattle Mariners
P.O. Box 4100, Seattle, WA 98104
(206) 628-3555
Chairman-CEO ....John Ellis
President-COO ....Chuck Armstrong
V.P., Baseball Operations ....Woody Woodward
Director of Public Relations ....Dave Aust

Texas Rangers
P.O. Box 90111, Arlington, TX 76004
(817) 273-5222
General Partners ....George W. Bush and Rusty Rose
President ....Tom Schieffer
General Manager ....Sandy Johnson
V.P., Public Relations...John Blake

Toronto Blue Jays
SkyDome, One Blue Jay Way, Suite 3200,
Toronto, Ontario M5V 1J1
(416) 341-1000
Chairman..Peter Widdrington
President-CEO ....Paul Beeston
Exec. V.P. & General Manager ....Pat Gillick
Director of Public Relations ....Howie Starkman

NL

National League Office
350 Park Ave., New York, NY 10022
(212) 339-7700
President & Treasurer ....Leonard Coleman
V.P., Media & Public Affairs..........................Ricky Clemons

Atlanta Braves
P.O. Box 4064, Atlanta, GA 30302
(404) 522-7630
Owner ....Ted Turner
President..Stan Kasten
Exec. V.P. & General Manager..................John Schuerholz
Director of Public Relations ....Jim Schultz

Chicago Cubs
1060 West Addison St., Chicago, IL 60613
(312) 404-2827
Owner ....The Tribune Company
Chairman ....Stanton Cook
President-CEO ....Andy MacPhail
Director of Media Relations ....Sharon Pannozzo

Cincinnati Reds
100 Riverfront Stadium, Cincinnati, OH 45202
(513) 421-4510
General Partner-President-CEO ....Marge Schott
General Manager ....Jim Bowden
Director of Publicity ....Jon Braude

Colorado Rockies
1700 Broadway, Suite 2100, Denver, CO 80290
(303) 292-0200
President-CEO..Jerry McMorris
Exec. V.P., Baseball Operations...................John McHale Jr.
Senior V.P. & General Manager ....Bob Gebhard
Director of Public Relations ....Mike Swanson

Florida Marlins
2269 N.W. 199th St., Miami, FL 33056
(305) 626-7400
Owner-Chairman.......................................Wayne Huizenga
Exec. V.P. & General Manager ....Dave Dombrowski
Director of Media Relations ....Chuck Pool

Houston Astros
The Astrodome, P.O. Box 288, Houston, TX 77001
(713) 799-9500
Owner-Chairman-CEO ....Drayton McLane Jr.
General Manager ....Bob Watson
Director of Public Relations ....Rob Matwick

Los Angeles Dodgers
1000 Elysian Park Ave., Los Angeles, CA 90012
(213) 224-1500
President ....Peter O'Malley
Exec. V.P. & General Manager ....Fred Claire
Director of Publicity ....Jay Lucas

Montreal Expos
P.O. Box 500, Station M, Montreal, Quebec H1V 3P2
(514) 253-3434
General Partner-President ....Claude Brochu
V.P., Baseball Operations................................Bill Stoneman
Director of Media Relations..........................Richard Griffin

New York Mets
Shea Stadium, Flushing, NY 11368
(718) 507-6387
Chairman ....Nelson Doubleday
President-CEO...Fred Wilpon
Exec. V.P., Baseball Operations ....Joe McIlvaine
Director of Media Relations ....Jay Horwitz

Philadelphia Phillies
P.O. Box 7575, Philadelphia, PA 19101
(215) 463-6000
General Partner-President-CEO...........................Bill Giles
Senior V.P. & General Manager ....Lee Thomas
Manager, Public Relations ....Gene Dias

Pittsburgh Pirates
P.O. Box 7000, Pittsburgh, PA 15212
(412) 323-5000
Chairman ....Vincent Sarni
President-CEO..Mark Sauer
Senior V.P. & General Manager ....Cam Bonifay
Director of Media Relations ....Jim Trdinich

St. Louis Cardinals
250 Stadium Plaza, St. Louis, MO 63102
(314) 421-3060
Chairman ....August A. Busch III
Vice Chairman ....Fred Kuhlmann
President-CEO...Mark Lamping
General Manager ....TBA
Director of Public Relations ....Brian Bartow

San Diego Padres
P.O. Box 2000, San Diego, CA 92112
(619) 283-4494
Managing Partner..Tom Werner
President...Dick Freeman
V.P., Baseball Operations & G.M ....Randy Smith
Director of Media Relations ....Jim Ferguson

San Francisco Giants
Candlestick Park, San Francisco, CA 94124
(415) 468-3700
President & Managing Gen. Partner............Peter Magowan
Senior V.P. & General Manager ....Bob Quinn
Director of Public Relations..................................Bob Rose

---

PRO BASKETBALL

NBA

League Office
Olympic Tower, 645 Fifth Ave., New York, NY 10022
(212) 826-7000
Commissioner..David Stern
Deputy Commissioner..................................Russell Granik
V.P., Public Relations ....Brian McIntyre
Director of Media Relations ....Jan Hubbard

NBA Players Association
1775 Broadway, Suite 2401, New York, NY 10019
(212) 333-7510
Executive Director ....Charles Grantham
General Counsel..Simon Gourdine

Atlanta Hawks
One CNN Center, South Tower, Suite 405
Atlanta, GA 30303
(404) 827-3800
Owner...Ted Turner
President...Stan Kasten
V.P. & General Manager ....Pete Babcock
Director of Media Relations............................Arthur Triche

Boston Celtics
151 Merrimac St., 5th Floor, Boston, MA 02114
(617) 523-6050
Owners.................Don Gaston, Paul Dupee & Alan Cohen
President ....Red Auerbach
Exec. V.P. & General Manager ....Jan Volk
Exec. V.P., Basketball Operations ........................M.L. Carr
Director of Public Relations.................................Jeff Twiss

Charlotte Hornets
100 Hive Drive, Charlotte, NC 28217
(704) 357-0252
Owner..George Shinn
President ....Spencer Stolpen
Player Personnel Director.............................Dave Twardzik
Director of Media Relations ....Harold Kaufman

Chicago Bulls
United Center, 1901 West Madison St., Chicago, IL 60612
(312) 455-4000
Chairman ....Jerry Reinsdorf
V.P., Basketball Operations.............................Jerry Krause
Director of Media Services ....Tim Hallam

Cleveland Cavaliers
One Centre Court, Cleveland OH 44115
(216) 420-2000
Owner-Chairman ....Gordon Gund
Owner-Vice Chairman ....George Gund III
Exec. V.P. & General Manager.....................Wayne Embry
Director of Public Relations ....Bob Price

Dallas Mavericks
Reunion Arena, 777 Sports St., Dallas, TX 75207
(214) 988-0117
Owner-President...Donald Carter
COO-General Manager ....Norm Sonju
Dir. of Player Personnel ....Keith Grant
Director of Media Services ....Kevin Sullivan

Denver Nuggets
1635 Clay St., Denver, CO 80204
(303) 893-6700
Owner ....COMSAT Denver, Inc.
Senior Exec. V.P. & GM ....Bernie Bickerstaff
President ....Tim Leiweke
Director of Media Services ....Tommy Sheppard

Detroit Pistons
The Palace of Auburn Hills
Two Championship Dr., Auburn Hills, MI 48326
(313) 377-0100
Managing Partner ....William Davidson
President...Tom Wilson
V.P. of Basketball Operations......................Billy McKinney
V.P. of Public Relations....................................Matt Dobek

Golden State Warriors
Oakland Coliseum Arena, Oakland, CA 94621
(510) 638-6300
Chairman ....James Fitzgerald
President...Daniel Finnane
General Manager & Head Coach....................Don Nelson
Director of Media Relations..............................Julie Marvel

Houston Rockets
The Summit, 10 Greenway Plaza, Houston, TX 77046
(713) 627-0600
Owner ....Les Alexander
Exec. V.P. of Business Operations ....John Thomas
Manager of Media Relations ....Rose Pietrzak

Indiana Pacers
300 East Market St., Indianapolis, IN 46204
(317) 263-2100
Owners ....Melvin Simon & Herb Simon
President & General Manager......................Donnie Walsh
Director of Media Relations............................David Benner

Los Angeles Clippers
L.A. Sports Arena
3939 S. Figueroa St., Los Angeles, CA 90037
(213) 748-8000
Owner-Chairman.......................................Donald Sterling
V.P. of Basketball Operations...........................Elgin Baylor
Manager of Media Relations ....Cary Collins

Los Angeles Lakers
Great Western Forum
3900 W. Manchester Blvd., Inglewood, CA 90305
(310) 419-3100
Owner ....Jerry Buss
General Manager ....Jerry West
Director of Public Relations...................................John Black

Miami Heat
Miami Arena, Miami, FL 33136
(305) 577-4328
Owner...Harris (Whit) Hudson
Managing Partner ....Lewis Schaffel
Director of Public Relations.................................Mark Pray

Milwaukee Bucks
Bradley Center, 1001 N. Fourth St., Milwaukee, WI 53203
(414) 227-0500
President ....Sen. Herb Kohl (D., Wisc.)
V.P., Basketball Ops. & Head Coach ....Mike Dunleavy
Director of Publicity ....Bill King II

Minnesota Timberwolves
Target Center, 600 First Ave. North,
Minneapolis, MN 55403
(612) 673-1600
Owner ....Glen Taylor
President ....Rob Moor
General Manager..Jack McCloskey
Director of Media Relations.................................Kent Wipf

New Jersey Nets
Meadowlands Arena, East Rutherford, NJ 07073
(201) 935-8888
Chairman-CEO ....Alan Aufzien
President-COO ....Jon Spoelstra
Exec. V.P. & General Manager ....Willis Reed
Director of Public Relations...............................John Mertz

New York Knickerbockers
Madison Square Garden
2 Penn Plaza, 3rd Floor, New York, NY 10121
(212) 465-6499
Owner ....ITT Corp./Cablevision Systems Inc.
President..Dave Checketts
V.P. & General Manager ....Ernie Grunfeld
Manager Media Relations ....Tim Donovan

Orlando Magic
Orlando Arena, 1 Magic Place, Orlando, FL 32801
(407) 649-3200
Owner..Rich DeVos
President-CEO ....Dick DeVos
General Manager & COO ....Pat Williams
Dir. of Publicity/Media Relations ....Alex Martins

Philadelphia 76ers
Veterans Stadium
Broad St. and Pattison Ave., Philadelphia, PA 19148
(215) 339-7600
Owner-President ....Harold Katz
General Manager & Head Coach ....John Lucas
Director of Public Relations ....Joe Favorito
Dir. of Statistical Information ....Harvey Pollack

Phoenix Suns
P.O. Box 1369, Phoenix, AZ 85001
(602) 379-7900
President-CEO...Jerry Colangelo
Sr. Executive V.P ....Cotton Fitzsimmons
V.P., Dir. of Player Personnel ....Dick Van Arsdale
Public Relations Director ....Julie Fie

Portland Trail Blazers
Suite 600 Lloyd Building
700 N.E. Multnomah St., Portland, OR 97232
(503) 234-9291
Owner-Chairman...Paul Allen
President & General Manager.........................Bob Whitsitt
Director of Communications ....John Lashway

Sacramento Kings
One Sports Parkway, Sacramento, CA 95834
(916) 928-0000
Managing General Partner..............................Jim Thomas
President..Rick Benner
Dir. of Player Personnel ....Jerry Reynolds
Director of Media Relations............................Travis Stanley

San Antonio Spurs
Alamodome, 100 Montana St., San Antonio, TX 78203
(210) 554-7700
Chairman......................................Gen. Robert McDermott
President-CEO ....John Diller
Exec. V.P., Basketball Operations................Gregg Popovich
Director of Media Relations.............................Tom James

Seattle Supersonics
190 Queen Anne Ave. North, Suite 200,
Seattle, WA 98109
(206) 281-5800
Owner-Chairman...Barry Ackerley
President & General Manager ....Wally Walker
Director of Media Relations............................Cheri White

Utah Jazz
Delta Center, 301 West South Temple,
Salt Lake City, UT 84101
(801) 325-2500
Owner ....Larry Miller
General Manager ....Tim Howells
President ....Frank Layden
Director of Media Services..................................Kim Turner

Washington Bullets
One Harry S. Truman Dr., Landover, MD 20785
(301) 773-2255
Chairman...Abe Pollin
President...Susan O'Malley
V.P. & General Manager..................................John Nash
Director of Public Relations.............................Matt Williams

1995-96 NBA Expansion Teams

Toronto Raptors
150 York St., Suite 1100, Toronto Ontario M5H 3S5
(416) 214-2255
President ....John Bitove Jr.
V.P. Basketball Operations ....Isiah Thomas
Director of Communications ....Tom Mayenknecht

Vancouver Grizzlies
788 Beatty St., Suite 201, Vancouver BC V6B 2M1
(604) 688-5867
Chairman-CEO ....Arthur Griffiths
V.P., Basketball Operations ....Stu Jackson
Director of Public Relations ....John Rocha

ABC
(American Bowling Congress)
5301 South 76th St., Greendale, WI 53129
(414) 421-6400
Executive Director..Darold Dobs
Public Relations Manager ....Dave DeLorenzo

BPAA
(Bowling Proprietors' Assn. of America)
P.O. Box 5802, Arlington, TX 76005
(817) 649-5105
Chief Executive Officer ....William Blue
President...Kurt Brose
Director of Public Relations ....Rosie Crews

LPBT
(Ladies Professional Bowlers Tour)
7171 Cherryvale Blvd., Rockford, IL 61112
(815) 332-5756
President...John Falzone
Media Director ....Linda Thomas

PBA
(Professional Bowlers Association)
1720 Merriman Road, P.O. Box 5118, Akron, OH 44334
(216) 836-5568
Commissioner...Mike Connor
Public Relations Director.................................Kevin Shippy

WIBC
(Women's International Bowling Congress)
5301 South 76th St., Greendale, WI 53129
(414) 421-9000
President...Joyce Deitch
Public Relations Manager ....Karen Systma

BOXING

IBF
(International Boxing Federation)
134 Evergreen Place, 9th Floor,
East Orange, NJ 07018
(201) 414-0300
President ....Robert (Bob) Lee
Executive Secretary ....Marian Muhammad
Championship Chairman ....Bill Brennan
               P.O. Box 224, Warsaw, VA 22572
               (804) 333-4541
Ratings Chairman....................................Douglas Beavers
         1601 Holiday St., Portsmouth, VA 23704
               (804) 399-4503

WBA
(World Boxing Association)
Centro Comercial Ciudad Turmero, Local #21, Piso #2
Calle Petion Cruce Con Urdaneta,
Turmero, 2115 Estado Aragua, Venezuela
TEL: 011-58-44-61645
President ....Gilberto Mendoza
General Counsel/U.S. Spokesman ....Jimmy Binns
          300 Walnut St., Philadelphia, PA 19106
               (215) 922-4000
Championship Chairman.......................Alberto Sarmiento
      P.O. Box 87-1022, Panama 1, Rep. de Panama
               TEL: 011-507-64-5363
Ratings Chairman......................................Rodolfo Fortich
      P.O. Box 69675, Caracus 1060A, Venezuela
               TEL: 011-58-2-682-3353

WBC
(World Boxing Council)
Genova 33-503, Col. Juarez,
Delegacion Cuauhtemoc, MEXICO, 06600, D.F.
011-525-533-6546
President ....Jose Sulaiman
Executive Secretary ....Eduardo Lamazon
Ratings Chairman ....Robert Busse
        4003 Brandy Court, Austin, TX 78759
               (512) 345-4761
Press Information/U.S. Spokesman...................John Brister
      402 Ocean View Ave., Santa Cruz, CA 95062
               (408) 423-2631

COLLEGE SPORTS

CCA
(Collegiate Commissioners Association)
800 South Broadway, Suite 400, Walnut Creek, CA 94596
(510) 932-4411
President..Gene Corrigan (ACC)
Executive V.P. ....Wright Waters (Southern)
Secretary-Treasurer ....David Price

CFA
(College Football Association)
6688 Gunpark Drive, Suite 201, Boulder CO 80301
(303) 530-5566
Executive Director......................................Charles Neinas
Director of Marketing ....Mike Bohn

NAIA
(National Assn. of Intercollegiate Athletics)
6120 South Yale, Suite 1450, Tulsa, OK 74136
(918) 494-8828
President-CEO..James Chasteen
Public Relations Contact.................................Amy Douglas

NCAA
(National Collegiate Athletic Association)
6201 College Blvd., Overland Park, KS 66211
(913) 339-1906
President ....Joe Crowley (Nevada)
              (term expires January, 1995)
Executive Director ....Cedric Dempsey
Asst. Exec. Dir. for Enforcement.........................David Berst
Director of Public Information ....Kathryn Reith

WSF
Women's Sports Foundation
Eisenhower Park, East Meadow, NY 11554
(516) 542-4700
Executive Director......................................Donna Lopiano
Communications Director............................Lynnore Lawton

Major NCAA Conferences

See pages 425-433 for basketball coaches, football coaches, nicknames and colors of all Division I basketball schools and Division I-A and I-AA football schools.

ATLANTIC COAST CONFERENCE

P.O. Drawer ACC, Greensboro, NC 27419
(910) 854-8787   Founded: 1953
Commissioner ....Gene Corrigan
Director of Media Relations ....Brian Morrison
   1994 members: BASKETBALL & FOOTBALL (9)— Clemson, Duke, Florida St., Georgia Tech, Maryland, North Carolina, North Carolina St., Virginia and Wake Forest.

Clemson University
Clemson, SC 29633   Founded: 1889
SID: (803) 656-2114   Enrollment: 16,000
Acting President ....Phil Prince
Athletic Director ....Bobby Robinson
Sports Information Director ....Tim Bourret

Duke University
Durham, NC 27708   Founded: 1838
SID: (919) 684-2633   Enrollment: 6,100
President ....Nannerl Koehane
Athletic Director ....Tom Butters
Sports Information Director ....Mike Cragg

Florida State University
Tallahassee, FL 32316   Founded: 1857
SID: (904) 644-1403   Enrollment: 28,500
President..................................Talbot (Sandy) D'Alemberte
Interim Athletic Director ....Wayne Hogan
Interim Sports Information Director ....Rob Wilson

Georgia Tech
Atlanta, GA 30332   Founded: 1885
SID: (404) 894-5445   Enrollment: 13,000
President ....Wayne Clough
Athletic Director ....Homer Rice
Sports Information Director ....Mike Finn

University of Maryland
College Park, MD 20741   Founded: 1807
SID: (301) 314-7064   Enrollment: 25,900
President ....William E. Kirwan
Athletic Director ....Debbi Yow
Sports Information Director ....Herb Hartnett

University of North Carolina
Chapel Hill, NC 27514   Founded: 1789
SID: (919) 962-2123   Enrollment: 24,300
Chancellor ....Paul Hardin
Athletic Director ....John Swofford
Sports Information Director................................Rick Brewer

North Carolina State University
Raleigh, NC 27695   Founded: 1887
SID: (919) 515-2102   Enrollment: 25,500
Chancellor ....Larry Monteith
Athletic Director...Todd Turner
Sports Information Director ....Mark Bockelman

University of Virginia
Charlottesville, VA 22903   Founded: 1819
SID: (804) 982-5500   Enrollment: 18,100
President..John T. Casteen III
Athletic Director...Jim Copeland
Sports Information Director.................................Rich Murray

Wake Forest University
Winston-Salem, NC 27109   Founded: 1834
SID: (910) 759-5640   Enrollment: 3,600
President...Thomas K. Hearn Jr.
Athletic Director ....Ron Wellman
Sports Information Director................................John Justus

BIG EAST CONFERENCE

56 Exchange Terrace, Providence, RI 02903
(401) 272-9108   Founded: 1979
Commissioner..Mike Tranghese
Asst. Commissioner/P.R ....John Paquette
   1994 members: BASKETBALL (10)— Boston College, Connecticut, Georgetown, Miami-FL, Pittsburgh, Providence, St. John's, Seton Hall, Syracuse and Villanova; FOOTBALL (8)— Boston College, Miami-FL, Pittsburgh, Rutgers, Syracuse, Temple, Virginia Tech and West Virginia.

Boston College
Chestnut Hill, MA 02167   Founded: 1863
SID: (617) 552-3004   Enrollment: 9,000
President......................................Rev. J. Donald Monan, SJ
Athletic Director ....Chet Gladchuk
Sports Information Director...................................Reid Oslin

University of Connecticut
Storrs, CT 06269   Founded: 1881
SID: (203) 486-3531   Enrollment: 11,000
President...Harry J. Hartley
Athletic Director ....Lew Perkins
Sports Information Director...............................Tim Tolokan

Georgetown University
Washington, DC 20057   Founded: 1798
SID: (202) 687-2492   Enrollment: 6,300
President.............................Rev. Leo J. O'Donovan, SJ
Athletic Director......................................Francis X. Rienzo
Sports Information Director ....Bill Hurd

University of Miami
Coral Gables, FL 33124   Founded: 1926
SID: (305) 284-3244   Enrollment: 13,200
President..Edward T. Foote II
Athletic Director...Paul Dee
Sports Information Director ....John Hahn

University of Pittsburgh
Pittsburgh, PA 15213   Founded: 1787
SID: (412) 648-8240   Enrollment: 13,500
President ....J. Dennis O'Connor
Athletic Director..Oval Jaynes
Sports Information Director ....Larry Eldridge

Providence College
Providence, RI 02918   Founded: 1917
SID: (401) 865-2272   Enrollment: 3,800
President...Philip A. Smith OP
Athletic Director...John Marinatto
Sports Information Director ....Gregg Burke

Rutgers University
New Brunswick, NJ 08903   Founded: 1766
SID: (908) 445-4200   Enrollment: 34,000
President...Francis L. Lawrence
Athletic Director ....Fred Gruninger
Sports Information Director...........................Pete Kowalski

St. John's University
Jamaica, NY 11439   Founded: 1870
SID: (718) 990-6367   Enrollment: 18,000
President ....Rev. Donald J. Harrington, CM
Athletic Director...John Kaiser
Sports Information Director ....Frank Racaniello

Seton Hall University
South Orange, NJ 07079   Founded: 1856
SID: (201) 761-9493   Enrollment: 10,200
President ....Rev. Thomas R. Peterson, OP
Athletic Director ....Larry Keating
Sports Information Director ....John Wooding

Syracuse University
Syracuse, NY 13244
SID: (315) 443-2608
Chancellor...Kenneth Shaw
Athletic Director ....Jake Crouthamel
Sports Information Director ....Larry Kimball
Founded: 1870
Enrollment: 10,200

Temple University
Philadelphia, PA 19122
SID: (215) 204-7445
President...Peter J. Liacouras
Athletic Director...R.C. Johnson
Sports Information Director ....Al Shrier
Founded: 1884
Enrollment: 32,000

Villanova University
Villanova, PA 19085
SID: (215) 519-4120
President ....Rev. Edmund Dobbin, OSA
Athletic Director...Gene DeFilippo
Sports Information Director ....Jim DeLorenzo
Founded: 1842
Enrollment: 5,900

Virginia Tech
Blacksburg, VA 24061
SID: (703) 231-6726
President...Paul Torgersen
Athletic Director...Dave Braine
Sports Information Director ....Dave Smith
Founded: 1872
Enrollment: 22,200

West Virginia University
Morgantown, WV 26507
SID: (304) 293-2821
President...Neil Bucklew
Athletic Director...Ed Pastilong
Sports Information Director...............................Shelly Poe
Founded: 1867
Enrollment: 23,000

~

BIG EIGHT CONFERENCE
104 West 9th Street, Suite 408
Kansas City, MO 64105-1755
(816) 471-5088
Commissioner ....Carl James
Service Bureau Director.......................................Jeff Bollig
Founded: 1907

1994 members: BASKETBALL & FOOTBALL (8)—
Colorado, Iowa St., Kansas, Kansas St., Missouri, Nebraska, Oklahoma and Oklahoma St.,

University of Colorado
Boulder, CO 80309
SID: (303) 492-5626
President ....Judith E.N. Albino
Athletic Director...Bill Marolt
Sports Information Director ....Dave Plati
Founded: 1876
Enrollment: 25,000

Iowa State University
Ames, IA 50011
SID: (515) 294-3372
President ....Martin Jischke
Athletic Director...Eugene Smith
Sports Information Director ....Tom Kroeschell
Founded: 1858
Enrollment: 25,000

University of Kansas
Lawrence, KS 66045
SID: (913) 864-3417
Acting Chancellor ....Delbert Schankel
Athletic Director...Bob Frederick
Sports Information Director ....Dean Buchan
Founded: 1866
Enrollment: 29,200

Kansas State University
Manhattan, KS 66502
SID: (913) 532-6735
President ....Jon Wefald
Athletic Director...Max Urick
Sports Information Director ....Ben Boyle
Founded: 1863
Enrollment: 20,100

University of Missouri
Columbia, MO 65205
SID: (314) 882-3241
President ....George Russell
Athletic Director...Joe Castiglione
Sports Information Director ....Bob Brendel
Founded: 1839
Enrollment: 26,200

University of Nebraska
Lincoln, NE 68588
SID: (402) 472-2263
President...Martin Massengale
Athletic Director...Bill Byrne
Sports Information Director ....Chris Anderson
Founded: 1869
Enrollment: 24,000

University of Oklahoma
Norman, OK 73019
SID: (405) 325-8231
President...David Boren
Athletic Director...Donnie Duncan
Sports Information Director ....Mike Prusinski
Founded: 1890
Enrollment: 24,000

Oklahoma State University
Stillwater, OK 74078
SID: (405) 744-5749
President...James Halligan
Interim Athletic Director..................................Dave Martin
Sports Information Director ....Steve Buzzard
Founded: 1890
Enrollment: 18,500

~

BIG TEN CONFERENCE
1500 West Higgins Road
Park Ridge, IL 60068-6300
(708) 696-1010
Commissioner..Jim Delany
Dir. of Information Services....................Dennis LaBissonier
Founded: 1895

1994 members: BASKETBALL & FOOTBALL (11)—
Illinois, Indiana, Iowa, Michigan, Michigan St., Minnesota,
Northwestern, Ohio St., Penn St., Purdue and Wisconsin.

University of Illinois
Champaign, IL 61820
SID: (217) 333-1390
President...Stanley O. Ikenberry
Athletic Director...Ron Guenther
Sports Information Director ....Mike Pearson
Founded: 1867
Enrollment: 34,000

Indiana University
Bloomington, IN 47405
SID: (812) 855-2421
President...Myles Brand
Athletic Director..................................Clarence Doninger
Sports Information Director ....Kit Klingelhoffer
Founded: 1820
Enrollment: 35,600

University of Iowa
Iowa City, IA 52242
SID: (319) 335-9411
President...Hunter Rawlings III
Athletic Director...Bob Bowlsby
Sports Information Director................................Phil Haddy
Founded: 1847
Enrollment: 28,000

University of Michigan
Ann Arbor, MI 48109
SID: (313) 763-1381
President...James J. Duderstadt
Athletic Director...Joe Roberson
Sports Information Director ....Bruce Madej
Founded: 1817
Enrollment: 36,900

Michigan State University
East Lansing, MI 48824
SID: (517) 355-2271
President...Peter McPherson
Athletic Director..................................Merrily Dean Baker
Sports Information Director..............................Ken Hoffman
Founded: 1855
Enrollment: 39,700

University of Minnesota
Minneapolis, MN 55455
SID: (612) 625-4090
President ....Nils Hasselmo
Athletic Director.....................................McKinley Boston
Sports Information Director.................................Marc Ryan

Founded: 1851
Enrollment: 38,000

Northwestern University
Evanston, IL 60208
SID: (708) 491-7503
President ....Arnold Weber
Athletic Director ....Rick Taylor
Sports Information Director ....Greg Shea

Founded: 1851
Enrollment: 15,700

Ohio State University
Columbus, OH 43210
SID: (614) 292-6861
President...E. Gordon Gee
Athletic Director..Andy Geiger
Sports Information Director.............................Steve Snapp

Founded: 1870
Enrollment: 50,600

Penn State University
University Park, PA 16802
SID: (814) 865-1757
President..Joab Thomas
Athletic Director ....Tim Curley
Sports Information Director.................................Jeff Nelson

Founded: 1855
Enrollment: 30,500

Purdue University
West Lafayette, IN 47907
SID: (317) 494-3200
President....................................Steven C. Beering
Athletic Director.......................................Morgan Burke
Sports Information Director.............................Mark Adams

Founded: 1869
Enrollment: 35,200

University of Wisconsin
Madison, WI 53711
SID: (608) 262-1811
Chancellor ....David Ward
Athletic Director ....Pat Richter
Sports Information Director.........................Steve Malchow

Founded: 1848
Enrollment: 40,900

⁂

BIG WEST CONFERENCE
2 Corporate Park, Suite 206
Irvine, CA 92714
(714) 261-2525
Commissioner ....Dennis Farrell
Director of Information ....Dennis Bickmeier

Founded: 1969

1994 members: BASKETBALL (10)— CS-Fullerton, Long Beach St., Nevada, New Mexico St., Pacific, San Jose St., UC-Irvine, UC-Santa Barbara, UNLV and Utah St.; FOOTBALL (10)— Arkansas St., Louisiana Tech, Nevada, New Mexico St., Northern Illinois, Pacific, San Jose St., SW Louisiana, UNLV and Utah St.

Arkansas State University
State University AK 72467
SID: (501) 972-2541
Acting President..Eugene Smith
Athletic Director ....Brad Hovious
Sports Information Director...........................Gina Bowman

Founded: 1909
Enrollment: 10,300

Cal State-Fullerton
Fullerton, CA 92634
SID: (714) 773-3970
President..Milton A. Gordon
Athletic Director..John Easterbrook
Sports Information Director...............................Mel Franks

Founded: 1957
Enrollment: 22,500

Long Beach State
Long Beach, CA 90840
SID: (310) 985-7978
President...Robert Maxson
Athletic Director...Dave O'Brien
Sports Information Director ....Scott Cathcart

Founded: 1949
Enrollment: 27,500

Louisiana Tech
Ruston, LA 71272
SID: (318) 257-3144
President ....Dan Reneau
Interim Athletic Director ....Pat Patterson
Sports Information Director ....Brian McCallum

Founded: 1894
Enrollment: 10,200

University of Nevada
Reno, NV 89557
SID: (702) 784-4600
President...Joe Crowley
Athletic Director ....Chris Ault
Sports Information Director ....Paul Stuart

Founded: 1874
Enrollment: 12,500

New Mexico State University
Las Cruces, NM 88003
SID: (505) 646-3929
Interim President..William Conroy
Athletic Director...Al Gonzales
Sports Information Director ....Steve Shutt

Founded: 1888
Enrollment: 15,800

Northern Illinois University
De Kalb, IL 60115
SID: (815) 753-1706
President...John E. La Tourette
Athletic Director ....Cary Groth
Sports Information Director...............................Mike Korcek

Founded: 1895
Enrollment: 23,200

University of the Pacific
Stockton, CA 95211
SID: (209) 946-2479
President..Bill Atchley
Athletic Director ....Bob Lee
Sports Information Director ....Kevin Messenger

Founded: 1851
Enrollment: 4,000

San Jose State University
San Jose, CA 95192
SID: (408) 924-1216
President..J. Handel Evans
Athletic Director...Tom Brennan
Sports Information Director.............................Lawrence Fan

Founded: 1857
Enrollment: 27,000

University of Southwestern Louisiana
Lafayette, LA 70506
SID: (318) 231-6331
President...Ray Authement
Athletic Director...................................Nelson Schexnayder
Sports Information Director.........................Dan McDonald

Founded: 1898
Enrollment: 16,700

University of California, Irvine
Irvine, CA 92717
SID: (714) 856-5814
Chancellor...Laurel Wilkening
Athletic Director ....Dan Guerrero
Sports Information Director ....Bob Olson

Founded: 1962
Enrollment: 15,600

University of California, Santa Barbara
Santa Barbara, CA 93106
SID: (805) 893-3428
Chancellor ....Henry Yang
Acting Athletic Director.....................................Jim Romeo
Sports Information Director.............................Bill Mahoney

Founded: 1944
Enrollment: 18,200

UNLV— University of Nevada, Las Vegas
Las Vegas, NV 89154
SID: (702) 895-3207
Interim President..Kenny Guinn
Athletic Director ....Jim Weaver
Sports Information Director ....Tommy Sheppard

Founded: 1957
Enrollment: 19,500

Utah State University
Logan, UT 84322
SID: (801) 797-1361
President...George Emert
Athletic Director..Chuck Bell
Sports Information Director ....Craig Hislop

Founded: 1888
Enrollment: 16,800

MID-AMERICAN CONFERENCE
Four SeaGate, Suite 102
Toledo, OH 43604
(419) 249-7177 — Founded: 1946
Commissioner ....Jerry Ippoliti
Director of Communications ....Sue Wagner
1994 members: BASKETBALL & FOOTBALL (10)—
Akron, Ball St., Bowling Green, Central Michigan, Eastern
Michigan, Kent, Miami-OH, Ohio University, Toledo and
Western Michigan.

University of Akron
Akron, OH 44325 — Founded: 1870
SID: (216) 972-7468 — Enrollment: 26,000
President...Peggy Gordon Elliott
Athletic Director ....Mike Bobinski
Sports Information Director ....Mac Yates

Ball State University
Muncie, IN 47306 — Founded: 1918
SID: (317) 285-8242 — Enrollment: 20,700
President...John Worthen
Athletic Director ....Don Purvis
Sports Information Director.........................Joe Hernandez

Bowling Green State University
Bowling Green, OH 43403 — Founded: 1910
SID: (419) 372-7075 — Enrollment: 17,000
President...Paul Olscamp
Athletic Director ....Ron Zwierlein
Sports Information Director ....Steve Barr

Central Michigan University
Mt. Pleasant, MI 48859 — Founded: 1892
SID: (517) 774-3277 — Enrollment: 16,300
President...Leonard Plachta
Athletic Director ....Herb Deromedi Jr.
Sports Information Director ....Fred Stabley

Eastern Michigan University
Ypsilanti, MI 48197 — Founded: 1849
SID: (313) 487-0317 — Enrollment: 25,800
President...William Shelton
Athletic Director ....Tim Weiser
Sports Information Director ....Jim Streeter

Kent State University
Kent, OH 44242 — Founded: 1910
SID: (216) 672-2110 — Enrollment: 30,200
President...Carol Cartwright
Athletic Director ....Laing Kennedy
Sports Information Director ....Dale Gallagher

Miami University
Oxford, OH 45056 — Founded: 1809
SID: (513) 529-4327 — Enrollment: 16,000
President ....Paul Risser
Interim Athletic Director ....Darrell Hedric
Sports Information Director ....Brian Teter

Ohio University
Athens, OH 45701 — Founded: 1804
SID: (614) 593-1298 — Enrollment: 18,500
President...Robert Glidden
Athletic Director.......................................Harold McElhaney
Sports Information Director ....Glenn Coble

University of Toledo
Toledo, OH 43606 — Founded: 1872
SID: (419) 537-3790 — Enrollment: 24,200
President...Frank Horton
Athletic Director ....Allen Bohl
Sports Information Director ....Rod Brandt

Western Michigan University
Kalamazoo, MI 49008 — Founded: 1903
SID: (616) 387-4104 — Enrollment: 26,500
President...Diether Haenicke
Athletic Director ....Dan Meinert
Sports Information Director ....John Beatty

PACIFIC-10 CONFERENCE
800 South Broadway, Suite 400
Walnut Creek, CA 94596
(510) 932-4411 — Founded: 1915
Commissioner...Tom Hansen
Director of Information ....Jim Muldoon
1994 members: BASKETBALL & FOOTBALL (10)—
Arizona, Arizona St., California, Oregon, Oregon St.,
Stanford, UCLA, USC, Washington and Washington St.

University of Arizona
Tucson, AZ 85721 — Founded: 1885
SID: (602) 621-4163 — Enrollment: 35,100
President...Manuel Pacheco
Athletic Director ....Jim Livengood
Sports Information Director.........................Tom Duddleston

Arizona State University
Tempe, AZ 85287 — Founded: 1885
SID: (602) 965-6592 — Enrollment: 42,600
President...Lattie F. Coor
Athletic Director ....Charles Harris
Sports Information Director ....Mark Brand

University of California
Berkeley, CA 94720 — Founded: 1868
SID: (510) 642-5363 — Enrollment: 30,000
Chancellor ....Chang-Lin Tien
Athletic Director ....John Kaffer
Sports Information Director ....Kevin Reneau

University of Oregon
Eugene, OR 97401 — Founded: 1876
SID: (503) 346-5488 — Enrollment: 16,700
President...Dave Frohnmeyer
Athletic Director ....Rich Brooks
Sports Information Director ....Steve Hellyer

Oregon State University
Corvallis, OR 97331 — Founded: 1868
SID: (503) 737-3720 — Enrollment: 14,500
President...John Byrne
Athletic Director ....Dutch Bauchman
Sports Information Director ....Hal Cowan

Stanford University
Stanford, CA 94305 — Founded: 1891
SID: (415) 723-4418 — Enrollment: 13,900
President...Gerhard Casper
Athletic Director ....Ted Leyland
Sports Information Director ....Gary Migdol

UCLA— Univ. of California, Los Angeles
Los Angeles, CA 90024 — Founded: 1919
SID: (310) 206-6831 — Enrollment: 34,000
Chancellor ....Charles Young
Athletic Director ....Pete Dalis
Sports Information Director ....Marc Dellins

USC— Univ. of Southern California
Los Angeles, CA 90089 — Founded: 1880
SID: (213) 740-8480 — Enrollment: 27,700
President...Steven Sample
Athletic Director ....Mike Garrett
Sports Information Director ....Tim Tessalone

University of Washington
Seattle, WA 98195 — Founded: 1861
SID: (206) 543-2230 — Enrollment: 34,000
President ....William P. Gerberding
Athletic Director.......................................Barbara Hedges
Sports Information Director ....Jim Daves

Washington State University
Pullman, WA 99164 — Founded: 1890
SID: (509) 335-0270 — Enrollment: 18,500
President...Samuel Smith
Athletic Director ....Rick Dickson
Sports Information Director.........................Rod Commons

SOUTHEASTERN CONFERENCE

2201 Civic Center Blvd.
Birmingham, AL 35203
(205) 458-3010   Founded: 1933
Commissioner ....Roy Kramer
Director of Communications ....Mark Whitworth
   1994 members: BASKETBALL & FOOTBALL (12)—
Alabama, Arkansas, Auburn, Florida, Georgia, Kentucky,
LSU, Mississippi, Mississippi St., South Carolina, Tennessee
and Vanderbilt.

University of Alabama

Tuscaloosa, AL 35487   Founded: 1831
SID: (205) 348-6084   Enrollment: 20,000
President...Roger Sayers
Athletic Director ....Hootie Ingram
Sports Information Director ....Larry White

University of Arkansas

Fayetteville, AR 72701   Founded: 1871
SID: (501) 575-2751   Enrollment: 14,000
President ....Daniel Ferritor
Athletic Director ....Frank Broyles
Sports Information Director ....Rick Schaeffer

Auburn University

Auburn, AL 36831   Founded: 1856
SID: (205) 844-9800   Enrollment: 21,500
President ....William V. Muse
Athletic Director ....David Housel
Sports Information Director ....Kent Partridge

University of Florida

Gainesville, FL 32604   Founded: 1853
SID: (904) 375-4683   Enrollment: 34,500
President ....John Lombardi
Athletic Director ....Jeremy Foley
Sports Information Director ....John Humenik

University of Georgia

Athens, GA 30613   Founded: 1785
SID: (706) 542-1621   Enrollment: 28,800
President ....Charles Knapp
Athletic Director ....Vince Dooley
Sports Information Director ....Claude Felton

University of Kentucky

Lexington, KY 40506   Founded: 1865
SID: (606) 257-3838   Enrollment: 24,200
President....................................Charles T. Wethington Jr.
Athletic Director ....C.M. Newton
Sports Information Director ....Tony Neely

LSU— Louisiana State University

Baton Rouge, LA 70894   Founded: 1860
SID: (504) 388-8226   Enrollment: 23,600
Chancellor ....William (Bud) Davis
Athletic Director ....Joe Dean
Sports Information Director ....Herb Vincent

University of Mississippi

Oxford, MS 38677   Founded: 1848
SID: (601) 232-7522   Enrollment: 10,400
Chancellor ....R. Gerald Turner
Athletic Director..TBA Sept 15
Sports Information Director ....Langston Rogers

Mississippi State University

Starkville, MS 39759   Founded: 1878
SID: (601) 325-2703   Enrollment: 13,600
President...Donald Zacharias
Athletic Director...Larry Templeton
Sports Information Director ....Mike Nemeth

University of South Carolina

Columbia, SC 29208   Founded: 1801
SID: (803) 777-5204   Enrollment: 25,600
President ....John Palms
Athletic Director ....Mike McGee
Sports Information Director ....Kerry Tharp

University of Tennessee

Knoxville, TN 37901   Founded: 1794
SID: (615) 974-1212   Enrollment: 25,900
President ....Joe Johnson
Athletic Director ....Doug Dickie
Sports Information Director ....Bud Ford

Vanderbilt University

Nashville, TN 37212   Founded: 1873
SID: (615) 322-4121   Enrollment: 9,300
Chancellor ....Joe B. Wyatt
Athletic Director ....Paul Hoolahan
Sports Information Director ....Rod Williamson

🕸

SOUTHWEST CONFERENCE

P.O. Box 569420, Dallas, TX 75356-9420
(214) 634-7353   Founded: 1914
Commissioner ....Steve Hatchell
Director of Information ....Bo Carter
   1994 members: BASKETBALL & FOOTBALL (8)—
Baylor, Houston, Rice, SMU, TCU, Texas, Texas A&M and
Texas Tech. The SWC will disband on June 30, 1996.

Baylor University

Waco, TX 76711   Founded: 1845
SID: (817) 755-2743   Enrollment: 12,000
President....................................Herbert H. Reynolds
Athletic Director..Dick Ellis
Sports Information Director ....Maxey Parrish

University of Houston

Houston, TX 77204   Founded: 1927
SID: (713) 743-9404   Enrollment: 34,000
President ....James H. Pickering
Athletic Director..Bill Carr
Sports Information Director ....Donna Turner

Rice University

Houston, TX 77005   Founded: 1912
SID: (713) 527-4034   Enrollment: 2,700
President ....Malcolm Gillis
Athletic Director ....Bobby May
Sports Information Director ....Bill Cousins

SMU— Southern Methodist University

Dallas, TX 75275   Founded: 1911
SID: (214) 768-2883   Enrollment: 5,300
Interim President ....James Kirby
Interim Athletic Director......................................Bill Lively
Sports Information Director ....Ed Wisneski

University of Texas

Austin, TX 78713   Founded: 1883
SID: (512) 471-7437   Enrollment: 49,300
President ....Robert Berdahl
Athletic Director ....DeLoss Dodds
Sports Information Director ....Bill Little

Texas A&M University

College Station, TX 77843   Founded: 1876
SID: (409) 845-5725   Enrollment: 43,900
President...Ray Bowen
Athletic Director ....Wally Groff
Sports Information Director ....Alan Cannon

TCU— Texas Christian University

Fort Worth, TX 76129   Founded: 1873
SID: (817) 921-7969   Enrollment: 7,000
Chancellor ....William Tucker
Athletic Director..Frank Windegger
Sports Information Director ....Glen Stone

Texas Tech University

Lubbock, TX 79409   Founded: 1923
SID: (806) 742-2770   Enrollment: 24,000
President..Robert Lawless
Athletic Director ....Bob Bokrath
Sports Information Director ....Joe Hornaday

WESTERN ATHLETIC CONFERENCE
14 West Dry Creek Circle
Littleton, CO 80120
(303) 795-1962   Founded: 1962
Commissioner ....Karl Benson
Director of Information...Jeff Hurd
   1994 members: BASKETBALL & FOOTBALL (10)—
Air Force, BYU, Colorado St., Fresno St., Hawaii, New
Mexico, San Diego St., Utah, UTEP and Wyoming.

U.S. Air Force Academy
Colorado Springs, CO 80840   Founded: 1959
SID: (719) 472-2313   Enrollment: 4,100
Superintendent.............................Lt. Gen. Paul Stein
Athletic Director ....Col. Kenneth Schweitzer
Sports Information Director ....Dave Kellogg

Brigham Young University
Provo, UT 84602   Founded: 1875
SID: (801) 378-4911   Enrollment: 27,000
President...Rex E. Lee
Athletic Director ....Clayne Jensen
Sports Information Director ....Ralph Zobell

Colorado State University
Fort Collins, CO 80523   Founded: 1870
SID: (303) 491-5067   Enrollment: 20,000
President...Albert Yates
Athletic Director ....Tom Jurich
Sports Information Director...........................Gary Ozzello

Fresno State University
Fresno, CA 93740   Founded: 1911
SID: (209) 278-2509   Enrollment: 18,900
President...John D. Welty
Athletic Director ....Gary Cunningham
Sports Information Director ....Scott Johnson

University of Hawaii
Honolulu, HI 96822   Founded: 1907
SID: (808) 956-7523   Enrollment: 20,300
President..Kenneth Mortimer
Athletic Director ....Hugh Yoshida
Sports Information Director...........................Eddie Inouye

University of New Mexico
Albuquerque, NM 87131   Founded: 1889
SID: (505) 277-2026   Enrollment: 25,300
President...Richard Peck
Athletic Director ....Rudy Davalos
Sports Information Director.....................Greg Remington

San Diego State University
San Diego, CA 92182   Founded: 1897
SID: (619) 594-5547   Enrollment: 29,000
President...Thomas Day
Athletic Director ....Fred Miller
Sports Information Director ....John Rosenthal

University of Utah
Salt Lake City, UT 84112   Founded: 1850
SID: (801) 581-3510   Enrollment: 27,100
President..Arthur Smith
Athletic Director ....Chris Hill
Sports Information Director......................Bruce Woodbury

UTEP— University of Texas at El Paso
El Paso, TX 79968   Founded: 1913
SID: (915) 747-5330   Enrollment: 17,200
President...Diana Natalicio
Athletic Director ....John Thompson
Sports Information Director ....Eddie Mullens

University of Wyoming
Laramie, WY 82071   Founded: 1886
SID: (307) 766-2256   Enrollment: 11,000
President...Terry Roark
Athletic Director ....Paul Roach
Sports Information Director ....Kevin McKinney

MAJOR INDEPENDENTS
Ten schools that are Division I-A football independents.

Army— U.S. Military Academy
West Point, NY 10996   Founded: 1802
SID: (914) 938-3303   Enrollment: 4,200
Superintendent ....Lt. Gen. Howard D. Graves
Athletic Director ....Al Vanderbush
Sports Information Director ....Bob Kinney

University of Cincinnati
Cincinnati, OH 45221   Founded: 1819
SID: (513) 556-5191   Enrollment: 36,000
President ....Joseph A. Steger
Athletic Director ....Gerald O'Dell
Sports Information Director ....Tom Hathaway

East Carolina University
Greenville, NC 27858   Founded: 1907
SID: (919) 757-4522   Enrollment: 17,800
Chancellor..Richard Eakin
Athletic Director..Dave Hart, Jr.
Sports Information Director.......................Charles Bloom

University of Louisville
Louisville, KY 40292   Founded: 1798
SID: (502) 852-6581   Enrollment: 23,000
President ....Donald C. Swain
Athletic Director...Bill Olsen
Sports Information Director ....Kenny Klein

Memphis University
Memphis, TN 38152   Founded: 1912
SID: (901) 678-2337   Enrollment: 21,500
President ....V. Lane Rawlins
Athletic Director ....Charles Cavagnaro
Sports Information Director ....Bob Winn

Navy— U.S. Naval Academy
Annapolis, MD 21402   Founded: 1845
SID: (410) 268-6226   Enrollment: 4,000
Superintendent...............................Adm. Charles R. Larson
Athletic Director ....Jack Lengyel
Sports Information Director ....Tom Bates

University of Notre Dame
Notre Dame, IN 46556   Founded: 1842
SID: (219) 631-7516   Enrollment: 10,100
President....................................Rev. Edward (Monk) Malloy
Athletic Director ....Dick Rosenthal
Sports Information Director ....John Heisler

University of Southern Mississippi
Hattiesburg, MS 39406   Founded: 1910
SID: (601) 266-4503   Enrollment: 13,000
President ....Aubrey K. Lucas
Athletic Director ....Bill McLellan
Sports Information Director...........................Regiel Napier

Tulane University
New Orleans, LA 70118   Founded: 1834
SID: (504) 865-5506   Enrollment: 10,800
President...Eamon M. Kelly
Athletic Director ....Kevin White
Sports Information Director ....Lenny Vangilder

University of Tulsa
Tulsa, OK 74104   Founded: 1894
SID: (918) 631-2395   Enrollment: 4,900
President...Robert Donaldson
Athletic Director ....Chris Small
Sports Information Director ....Don Tomkalski

---

11 National Titles
Since 1936, Army (twice) and Notre Dame (nine times)
are the only currently independent football schools to
win a national championship.

OTHER MAJOR DIVISION I CONFERENCES
Conferences that play either Division I basketball or Division I-AA football, or both.

American West Conference
5855 Brookline Lane
San Luis Obispo, CA 93401
(805) 756-1412
Commissioner..Vic Buccola
Director of Information ....Mike Robles
1994 members: BASKETBALL & FOOTBALL (4)— Cal Poly St. Luis Obispo, CS-Northridge, CS-Sacramento and Southern Utah.

Atlantic 10 Conference
101 Interchange Plaza, Suite 202
Cranbury, N.J. 08512
(609) 860-9100   Founded: 1976
Commissioner ....Linda Bruno
Director of Communications................................Ray Cella
  1994 members: BASKETBALL (9)— Duquesne, George Washington, Massachusetts, Rhode Island, Rutgers, St.Bonaventure, St.Joseph's-PA, Temple and West Virginia.

Big Sky Conference
P.O. Box 1736
Boise, ID 83701
(208) 345-0281   Founded: 1963
Commissioner ....Ron Stephenson
Director of Information....................................Arnie Sgalio
  1994 members: BASKETBALL & FOOTBALL (8)— Boise St., Eastern Washington, Idaho, Idaho St., Montana, Montana St., Northern Arizona and Weber St.

Big South Conference
1551 21st Avenue North, Suite 11
Myrtle Beach, SC 29577
(803) 448-9998   Founded: 1983
Commissioner ....Buddy Sasser
Director of Public Relations ....Carl McAloose
  1994 members: BASKETBALL (9)— Charleston Southern, Coastal Carolina, Liberty, MD-Baltimore County, NC-Asheville, NC-Greensboro, Radford, Towson St. and Winthrop.

Note: NC-Greensboro will not compete for conference title until the 1994-95 season.

Colonial Athletic Association
8625 Patterson Ave.
Richmond, VA 23229
(804) 754-1616   Founded: 1985
Commissioner...Tom Yeager
Director of Information ....Tripp Sheppard
  1994 members: BASKETBALL (8)— American, East Carolina, George Mason, James Madison, NC-Wilmington, Old Dominion, Richmond and William & Mary.

Gateway Football Conference
1000 Union Station, Suite 333
St.Louis, MO 63103
(314) 421-2268   Founded: 1982
Commissioner ....Patty Viverito
Director of Information ....Mike Kern
  1994 members: (7): Eastern Illinois, Illinois St., Indiana St., Northern Iowa, Southern Illinois, SW Missouri St. and Western Illinois.

Great Midwest Conference
35 East Wacker Drive, Suite 650,
Chicago, IL 60601
(312) 553-0483   Founded: 1990
Commissioner ....Mike Slive
Director of Media Relations...........................Erika Amstadt
  1994 members: BASKETBALL (7)— Ala-Birmingham, Cincinnati, Dayton, DePaul, Marquette, Memphis St. and St.Louis.

Ivy League
120 Alexander Street
Princeton, NJ 08544
(609) 258-6426   Founded: 1954
Executive Director.......................................Jeffrey Orleans
Director of Information ....Chuck Yrigoyen
  1994 members: BASKETBALL & FOOTBALL (8)— Brown, Columbia, Cornell, Dartmouth, Harvard, Pennsylvania, Princeton and Yale.

Metro Conference
Two Ravinia Drive, Suite 210
Atlanta, GA 30346
(404) 395-6444   Founded: 1975
Commissioner ....Ralph McFillen
Director of Communications ....Jamie Kimbrough
  1994 members: BASKETBALL (7)— Louisville, NC-Charlotte, South Florida, Southern Mississippi, Tulane, VCU and Virginia Tech.

Metro Atlantic Athletic Conference
1090 Amboy Avenue,
Edison, NJ 08837
(908) 225-0202   Founded: 1980
Commissioner ....Richard Ensor
Director of Media Relations...........................Jaye Cavallo
  1994 members: BASKETBALL (8)— Canisius, Fairfield, Iona, Loyola-MD, Manhattan, Niagara, St.Peter's and Siena. FOOTBALL (6)— Canisius, Georgetown, Iona, St. John's, St. Peter's and Siena. Note: Duquesne and Marist will join for football in 1994.

Mid-Continent Conference
40 Shuman Blvd., Suite 118,
Naperville, IL 60563
(708) 416-7560   Founded: 1982
Acting Commissioner ....Jon Steinbrecher
Director of Publicity ....Tom Lessig
  1994 members: BASKETBALL (10)— Buffalo, Central Connecticut St., Chicago St., Eastern Illinois, Missouri/K.C., NE Illinois, Troy St., Valparaiso, Western Illinois, Youngstown St.

Mid-Eastern Athletic Conference
102 North Elm St. SE Building, Suite 401
Greensboro, NC 27401
(910) 275-9961   Founded:1970
Commissioner..Ken Free
Director of Service Bureau...............................Larry Barber
  1994 members: BASKETBALL (9)— Bethune-Cookman, Coppin St., Delaware St., Florida A&M, Howard, MD-Eastern Shore, Morgan St., North Carolina A&T and South Carolina St.; FOOTBALL (7)— all but Coppin St. and MD-Eastern Shore.

Midwestern Collegiate Conference
201 South Capitol Ave., Suite 500
Indianapolis, IN 46225
(317) 237-5622   Founded: 1979
Commissioner...John LeCrone
Director of Communications ....Will Hancock
  1994 members: BASKETBALL (11)— Butler, Cleveland St., Detroit Mercy, Illinois-Chicago, La Salle, Loyola-IL, Northern Illinois, Wisconsin-Green Bay, Wisconsin-Milwaukee, Wright St. and Xavier-OH.

Missouri Valley Conference
1000 St. Louis Union Station, Suite 333
St. Louis, MO 63103
(314) 421-0339   Founded: 1907
Commissioner ....Doug Elgin
Asst. Commissioner for Comm ....Jack Watkins
  1994 members: BASKETBALL (11)— Bradley, Creighton, Drake, Evansville, Illinois St., Indiana St., Northern Iowa, Southern Illinois, SW Missouri St., Tulsa and Wichita St.

North Atlantic Conference
P.O. Box 69 — 28 Main Street
Orono, ME 04473
(207) 866-2383
Commissioner..Stuart Haskell
Director of Information.....................................Julie Power
    Founded: 1979

1994 members: BASKETBALL (9)— Boston University, Delaware, Drexel, Hartford, Hofstra University, Maine, New Hampshire, Northeastern and Vermont. (Towson St. will be added for 1995-96 season)

Northeast Conference
900 Route 9, Suite 120
Woodbridge, NJ 07095
(908) 636-9119
Commissioner..Chris Monasch
Director of Information ....Dave Siroty
    Founded: 1981

1994 members: BASKETBALL (8)— Fairleigh Dickinson, LIU-Brooklyn, Marist, Monmouth, Mount St.Mary's, Rider, Robert Morris, St.Francis-NY, St.Francis-PA and Wagner.

Ohio Valley Conference
278 Franklin Road, Suite 103
Brentwood, TN 37027
(615) 371-1698 Founded: 1948
Commissioner...Dan Beebe
Director of Information ....Rob Washburn

1994 members: BASKETBALL & FOOTBALL (9)— Austin Peay St., Eastern Kentucky, Middle Tennessee St., Morehead St., Murray St., SE Missouri St., Tennessee-Martin, Tennessee St. and Tennessee Tech.
Note: Tenn-Martin will not compete for conference title in basketball until the 2000-2001 season.

Patriot League
3897 Adler Place, Building C, Suite 310
Bethlehem, PA 18017
(215) 691-2414
Executive Director ....Constance Hurlbut
Director of Information ....Todd Newcomb
    Founded: 1984

1994 members: BASKETBALL (8)— Army, Bucknell, Colgate, Fordham, Holy Cross, Lafayette, Lehigh and Navy; FOOTBALL (6)— all except Army and Navy, who play independent Div.I-A schedules.

Pioneer Football League
c/o Midwestern Collegiate Conference
201 South Capitol Ave., Suite 500
Indianapolis, IN 46225
(317) 237-5622
Commissioner...John LeCrone
Director of Information ....Will Hancock
    Founded: 1993

1994 members: FOOTBALL (6): Butler, Dayton, Drake, Evansville, San Diego and Valparaiso.

Southern Conference
1 West Pack Square, Suite 1508
Asheville, NC 28801
(704) 255-7872
Commissioner..Wright Waters
Director of Information ....Geoff Cabe
    Founded: 1921

1994 members: BASKETBALL (10)— Appalachian St., The Citadel, Davidson, East Tennessee St., Furman, Georgia Southern, Marshall, Tennessee-Chattanooga, VMI and Western Carolina; FOOTBALL (9)—all except Davidson.

Southland Conference
1309 West 15th Street, Suite 303
Plano, TX 75075
(214) 424-4833
Executive Director ....Britton Banowski
Director of Information ....Tammy Broz
    Founded: 1963

1994 members: BASKETBALL (10)— McNeese St., Nicholls St., North Texas, NE Louisiana, Northwestern St., Sam Houston St., Southwest Texas St., Stephen F.Austin St., Texas-Arlington and Texas-San Antonio; FOOTBALL (7)— all except NE Louisiana, Texas-Arlington and Texas-San Antonio.

Southwestern Athletic Conference
1500 Sugar Bowl Drive, Superdome
New Orleans, LA 70112
(504) 523-7574
Commissioner ....James Frank
Director of Publicity....................................Lonza Hardy Jr.
    Founded: 1920

1994 members: BASKETBALL & FOOTBALL (8)— Alabama St., Alcorn St., Grambling St., Jackson St., Mississippi Valley St., Prairie View A&M, Southern-Baton Rouge and Texas Southern.

Sun Belt Conference
One Galleria Boulevard, Suite 2115
Metairie, LA 70001
(504) 834-6600
Commissioner ....Craig Thompson
Director of Communications.............................Tom Burnett
    Founded: 1976

1994 members: BASKETBALL (10)— Arkansas-Little Rock, Arkansas St., Jacksonville, Lamar, Louisiana Tech, New Orleans, South Alabama, SW Louisiana, Texas-Pan American and Western Kentucky.

Trans America Conference
The Commons, 3370 Vineville Ave., Suite 108-B
Macon, GA 31204
(912) 474-3394
Commissioner...Bill Bibb
Director of Information ....Ted Gumbart
    Founded: 1978

1994 members: BASKETBALL (11)— Campbell, Centenary, Central Florida, College of Charleston, Florida Atlantic, Florida International, Georgia St., Mercer, Samford, SE Louisiana and Stetson. Note: Florida Atlantic ineligible for conference title until 1995-96 season. College of Charleston will not play in tournament in 1995.

West Coast Conference
400 Oyster Point Blvd., Suite 221
South San Francisco, CA 94080
(415) 873-8622
Commissioner ....Michael Gilleran
Director of Information ....Don Ott
    Founded: 1952

1994 members: BASKETBALL (8)— Gonzaga, Loyola Marymount, Pepperdine, Portland, St.Mary's, San Diego, San Francisco and Santa Clara.

Yankee Conference
University of Richmond, P.O. Box 8
Richmond, VA 23173
(804) 289-8371
Executive Director...Chuck Boone
Director of Information ....Pat McCarthy
    Founded: 1946

1994 members: FOOTBALL (12)— Boston University, Connecticut, Delaware, James Madison, Maine, Massachusetts, New Hampshire, Northeastern, Rhode Island, Richmond, Villanova and William & Mary.

Division I Hockey Conferences
The four Division I hockey conferences are the Eastern Collegiate Athletic Conference (ECAC) in Centerville, Mass., (508) 771-5060; the Central Collegiate Hockey Assn. (CCHA) in Ann Arbor, Mich., (313) 764-2590; Hockey East in Orono, Me., (207) 866-2244; and the Western Collegiate Hockey Assn. (WCHA) in Madison, Wisc., (608) 251-4007.

PRO FOOTBALL

National Football League

League Office
410 Park Ave., New York, NY 10022
(212) 758-1500
Commissioner ....Paul Tagliabue
President...Neil Austrian
Exec. V.P. & League Counsel...............................Jay Moyer
Director of Information, AFC....................Leslie Hammond
Director of Information, NFC.......................Reggie Roberts

NFL Management Council
410 Park Ave., New York, NY 10022
(212) 758-1500
Chairman...Harold Henderson
V.P. & General Counsel ....Dennis Curran

NFL Players Association
2021 L Street NW, Suite 600, Washington, DC 20036
(202) 463-2200
Executive Director ....Gene Upshaw
Asst. Exec. Director ....Doug Allen
General Counsel.....................................Richard Berthelsen
Director of Public Relations..........................Frank Woschitz

AFC

Buffalo Bills
One Bills Drive, Orchard Park, NY 14127
(716) 648-1800
Owner-President ....Ralph Wilson
Exec. V.P. & General Manager..........................John Butler
V.P. & Head Coach ....Marv Levy
Director of Media Relations..........................Scott Berchtold

Cincinnati Bengals
200 Riverfront Stadium, Cincinnati, OH 45202
(513) 621-3550
Chairman...Austin Knowlton
President & General Manager ....Mike Brown
Public Relations Directors ....Al Heim & Jack Brennan

Cleveland Browns
80 First Avenue, Berea, OH 44017
(216) 891-5000
Owner-President ....Art Modell
Exec. V.P., Legal & Administration ....Jim Bailey
V.P., Assistant to President..............................David Modell
V.P., Public Relations ....Kevin Byrne

Denver Broncos
13655 Broncos Parkway, Englewood, CO 80112
(303) 649-9000
Owner-President-CEO.......................................Pat Bowlen
General Manager ....John Beake
Director of Media Relations........................Jim Saccomano

Houston Oilers
6910 Fannin St., Houston, TX 77030
(713) 797-9111
Owner-President..................................K.S. (Bud) Adams Jr.
Exec. V.P. & General Manager ....Floyd Reese
Director of Media Relations ....Dave Pearson

Indianapolis Colts
P.O. Box 535000, Indianapolis, IN 46253
(317) 297-2658
Owner-President-Treasurer..............................Robert Irsay
V.P. & General Manager...Jim Irsay
V.P., Dir. Football Operations ....Bill Tobin
Director of Public Relations ....Craig Kelley

Kansas City Chiefs
One Arrowhead Drive, Kansas City, MO 64129
(816) 924-9300
Owner-Founder...Lamar Hunt
President-CEO-General Manager ....Carl Peterson
Director of Public Relations................................Bob Moore

Los Angeles Raiders
332 Center St., El Segundo, CA 90245
(310) 322-3451
Managing General Partner ....Al Davis
Executive Assistant..Al LoCasale
Publications Director ....Mike Taylor

Miami Dolphins
Joe Robbie Stadium
2269 NW 199th Street, Miami, FL 33056
(305) 620-5000
Owner-Chairman..Wayne Huizenga
Exec. V.P. & General Manager ....Eddie Jones
Director of Media Relations........................Harvey Greene

New England Patriots
Foxboro Stadium, 60 Washington St., Foxboro, MA 02035
(508) 543-8200
Owner-President-CEO ....Robert Kraft
V.P., Football Operations ....Patrick Forte
Director of Public Relations...............................Don Lowery

New York Jets
1000 Fulton Ave., Hempstead, NY 11550
(516) 538-6600
Owner-Chairman..Leon Hess
President...Steve Gutman
V.P. & General Manager ....Dick Steinberg
Director of Public Relations ....Frank Ramos

Pittsburgh Steelers
300 Stadium Circle, Pittsburgh, PA 15212
(412) 323-1200
Owner-President...Dan Rooney
Vice Presidents..................John McGinley & Art Rooney Jr.
Director of Media Relations ....Rob Boulware

San Diego Chargers
Box 609609, San Diego, CA 92160
(619) 280-2111
Owner-Chairman-President.............................Alex Spanos
Vice Chairman...Dean Spanos
General Manager ....Bobby Beathard
Director of Public Relations ....Bill Johnston

Seattle Seahawks
11220 NE 53rd Street, Kirkland, WA 98033
(206) 827-9777
Owner..Ken Behring
President ....David Behring
General Manager & Head Coach.....................Tom Flores
Publicity Director ....Dave Neubert

NFC

Arizona Cardinals
P.O. Box 888, Phoenix, AZ 85001
(602) 379-0101
Owner-President..Bill Bidwill
General Manager & Head Coach....................Buddy Ryan
Public Relations Director ....Paul Jensen

Atlanta Falcons
2745 Burnett Road, Suwanee, GA 30174
(404) 945-1111
Owner-Chairman.......................................Rankin Smith Sr.
President ....Taylor Smith
V.P., Player Personnel ....Ken Herock
Director of Public Relations...........................Charlie Taylor

Chicago Bears
Halas Hall, 250 N. Washington, Lake Forest, IL 60045
(708) 295-6600
Owner-Chairman ....Edward McCaskey
President-CEO...Mike McCaskey
V.P., Football Operations ....Ted Phillips
Director of Public Relations ....Bryan Harlan

Dallas Cowboys
Cowboys Center
One Cowboys Parkway, Irving, TX 75063
(214) 556-9900
Owner-President-GM...Jerry Jones
Public Relations Director...............................Rich Dalrymple

Detroit Lions
Pontiac Silverdome
1200 Featherstone Rd., Pontiac, MI 48342
(313) 335-4131
Owner-President.....................................William Clay Ford
Executive V.P. & COO...................................Chuck Schmidt
Media Relations Coordinator ....Mike Murray

Green Bay Packers
1265 Lombardi Ave., Green Bay, WI 54304
(414) 496-5700
President-CEO ....Bob Harlan
Exec. V.P. & General Manager ....Ron Wolf
Exec. Dir. of Public Relations..............................Lee Remmel

Los Angeles Rams
2327 West Lincoln Ave., Anaheim, CA 92801
(714) 535-7267
Owner-President......................................Georgia Frontiere
Executive V.P ....John Shaw
V.P. & Head Coach...Chuck Knox
Director of Public Relations ....Rick Smith

Minnesota Vikings
9520 Viking Drive, Eden Prairie, MN 55344
(612) 828-6500
Owner-Chairman..John Skoglund
President-CEO ....Roger Headrick
V.P., Team Operations......................................Jeff Diamond
Director of Public Relations ....David Pelletier

New Orleans Saints
6928 Saints Drive, Metairie, LA 70003
(504) 733-0255
Owner-President...Tom Benson
V.P., Football Operations.................................Bill Kuharich
V.P. & Head Coach ....Jim Mora
Director of Media Relations ....Rusty Kasmiersky

New York Giants
Giants Stadium, East Rutherford, NJ 07073
(201) 935-8111
President/co-CEO...................................Wellington Mara
Chairman/co-CEO.............................Preston Robert Tisch
V.P. & General Manager ....George Young
Director of Public Relations ....Pat Hanlon

Philadelphia Eagles
Veterans Stadium, Broad St. & Pattison Ave.
Philadelphia, PA 19148
(215) 463-2500
Owner..Jeff Lurie
President & COO ....Harry Gamble
V.P. of Player Personnel ....John Wooten
Director of Public Relations.................................Ron Howard

San Francisco 49ers
4949 Centennial Blvd., Santa Clara, CA 95054
(408) 562-4949
Owner..Edward DeBartolo Jr.
President...Carmen Policy
V.P., Football Administration ....John McVay
Director of Public Relations..............................Rodney Knox

Tampa Bay Buccanners
1 Buccaneer Place, Tampa, FL 33607
(813) 870-2700
Owner ....Hugh Culverhouse
V.P., Football Adminsitration.............................Rich McKay
Director of Public Relations...........................Chip Namias

Washington Redskins
Redskin Park, P.O. Box 17247, Washington D.C. 20041
(703) 478-8900
Owner-Chairman-CEO ....Jack Kent Cooke
Executive V.P...John Kent Cooke
General Manager ....Charley Casserly
Director of Communications ....Rick Vaughn

1995 NFL Expansion Teams

Carolina Cougars
227 West Trade Street, Suite 1600, Charlotte, NC 28202
(704) 358-7000
Owner..Jerry Richardson
President ....Mike McCormack
General Manager...Bill Polian
Director of Communications........................Charlie Dayton

Jacksonville Jaguars
One Stadium Place, Jacksonville, FL 32202
(904) 633-6000
Owner-Chairman-CEO ....Wayne Weaver
President-COO...David Seldon
General Manager & Head Coach ....Tom Coughlin
Exec. Dir. of Communications.........................Dan Edwards

Canadian Football League

League Office
CFL Building, 110 Eglinton Avenue West, 5th Floor,
Toronto, Ontario M4R 1A3
(416) 322-9650
Commissioner ....Larry Smith
Chairman...John Tory
V.P., Football Operations ....Ed Chalupka
Communications Co-ordinators....................Diane Milhalek
                                    and Jim Neish

Baltimore CFL Football Club
Memorial Stadium, 1000 E 33rd St.,
Baltimore MD 21218
(410) 554-1010
Owner ....Jim Speros
General Manager & Head Coach ....Don Matthews
Dir. of Public Relations................................Mike Gathagan

British Columbia Lions
10605 135th St., Surrey, B.C. V3T 4C8
(604) 583-7747
Owner..Bill Comrie
President ....Peter Classon
General Manager...Eric Tillman
Dir. of Media/Public Relations...........................Roger Kelly

Calgary Stampeders
McMahon Stadium, 1817 Crowchild Trail, NW
Calgary, Alberta T2M 4R6
(403) 289-0205
Owner-President ....Larry Ryckman
General Manager & Head Coach ....Wally Buono
Media Relations Coordinator ....Tania Van Brunt

Edmonton Eskimos
9023 — 11th Ave., Edmonton, Alberta T5B 0C3
(403) 448-1525
Owner...Community-owned
President ....John Ramsey
General Manager ....Hugh Campbell
Dir. of Communications ....Allan Watt

Hamilton Tiger-Cats
2 King Street West, Hamilton, Ontario L8P 1A1
(905) 521-5666
Chairman..Roger Yachetti
President-CEO...John Michaluk
General Manager & Head Coach ....John Gregory
Communications Director................................Norm Miller

Las Vegas Posse
1204 E. Desert Inn Road, Las Vegas, NV 89109
(702) 242-4200
Owner-Chairman-CEO ....Glenn Goldenberg
Majority Owner-President..................................Nick Mileti
General Manager & Head Coach ....Ron Meyer
Media Coordinator ....Amy Slade

Ottawa Rough Riders
301 Moodie Drive, Suite 102, Nepean, Ontario K2H 9C4
(613) 721-2255
Owner-Chairman ....Bruce Firestone
President & General Manager........................Phil Kershaw
Director of Communications ....Rob Gialloreto

Sacramento Gold Miners
14670 Cantova Way, Suite 200,
Rancho Murieta, CA 95683
(916) 354-1000
Managing General Partner ....Fred Anderson
General Manager ....Tom Huiskens
Director of Media Relations ....Tim McDowd

Saskatchewan Roughriders
2940 — 10th Avenue, P.O. Box 1277,
Regina, Saskatchewan S4P 3B8
(306) 569-2323
Owner...Community-owned
President ....John Lipp
COO & General Manager................................Alan Ford
Media Coordinator...Tony Playter

Shreveport Pirates
505 Travis St., Suite 602, Shreveport, LA 71101
(318) 222-3000
Owner...Bernard Glieberman
President ....Lonie Glieberman
General Manager & Head Coach ....Forrest Gregg
Dir. of Public/Media Relations........................Missy Setters

Toronto Argonauts
SkyDome Gate 7, P.O. Box 188, Station C,
Toronto, Ontario M6J 3M9
(416) 595-9600
Owners...TSN Enterprises
President ....Paul Beesten
General Manager & Head Coach................Bob O'Billovich
Manager of Media Relations ....Mike Cosentino

Winnipeg Blue Bombers
1465 Maroons Road, Winnipeg, Manitoba R3G 0L6
(204) 784-2583
Owner...Community-owned
President ....Reg Lowe
General Manager & Head Coach....................Cal Murphy
Dir. of Public/Media Relations ....Kevin O'Donovan

WLAF

World League of American Football
Mellier House, 26-A Albemarle St.,
London W1X 2FA England
TEL: 011-44-71-629-1300
President-CEO ....Marc Lory
Director of Public Relations ....TBA
   Member teams (6): Amsterdam Admirals, Barcelona
Dragons, Frankfurt Galaxy, London Monarchs, Rhein Fire
(Dusseldorf), Scottish Claymores (Edinburgh).

GOLF

LPGA Tour
(Ladies Professional Golf Association)
2570 West International Speedway Blvd., Suite B,
Daytona Beach, FL 32114
(904) 254-8800
Commissioner ....Charles Mechem
Deputy Commissioner...Jim Webb
Director of Communications..............................Elaine Scott

PGA of America
100 Avenue of the Champions,
Palm Beach Gardens, FL 33418
(407) 624-8400
President ....Gary Schaal
Executive Director ....Jim Awtrey
Director of Communications ....Terry McSweeney

PGA European Tour
Wentworth Drive, Virginia Water,
Surrey, England GU25 4LX
TEL: 011-44-344-842881
Executive Director ....Ken Schofield
Director of Communications ....Mitchell Platts

PGA Tour
Sawgrass, Ponte Vedra, FL 32082
(904) 285-3700
Commissioner ....Tim Finchem
Director of Information ....Dave Lancer

Royal & Ancient Golf Club of St. Andrews
St. Andrews, Fife, Scotland KY16 9JD
TEL: 011-44-334-472112
Secretary ....Michael Bonallack
Deputy Secretary...George Wilson

USGA
(United States Golf Association)
P.O. Box 708, Liberty Corner Road, Far Hills, NJ 07931
TEL: (908) 234-2300
President ....Reg Murphy
Executive Director ....David Fay
Director of Communications............................Mark Carlson

PRO HOCKEY

NHL

Commissioner ....Gary Bettman
Senior V.P., Hockey Operations........................Brian Burke
Senior V.P., COO ....Stephen Solomon
V.P., Public Relations ....Arthur Pincus

League Offices
Montreal:.................1800 McGill College Ave., Suite 2600
Montreal, Quebec H3A 3J6
(514) 288-9220
New York:....................................650 Fifth Ave., 33rd Floor
New York, NY 10019
(212) 789-2000
Toronto .... 75 International Blvd., Suite 300
Rexdale, Ontario M9W 6L9
(416) 798-0809

NHL Players' Association
1 Dundas St. West, Suite 2300, Toronto, Ontario M5G 1Z3
(416) 408-4040
Executive Director ....Bob Goodenow
Associate Counsel ....Ian Pulver

Anaheim, Mighty Ducks of
Arrowhead Pond of Anaheim, P.O. Box 61077,
Anaheim, CA 92803
(714) 704-2700
Owner ....Walt Disney Co.
Governor ....Michael Eisner
General Manager ....Jack Ferreira
Director of Public Relations ....Bill Robertson

Boston Bruins
Boston Garden, 150 Causeway St., Boston, MA 02114
(617) 557-1310
Owner ....Jeremy Jacobs
President & General Manager.......................Harry Sinden
Director of Media Relations ....Heidi Holland

Buffalo Sabres
Memorial Auditorium, 140 Main St., Buffalo, NY 14202
(716) 856-7300
Chairman-President...................................Seymour Knox III
General Manager & Head Coach..................John Muckler
Director of Public Relations ....Steve Rossi

Calgary Flames
Olympic Saddledome, P.O. Box 1540 Station M,
Calgary, Alberta T2P 3B9
(403) 261-0475
Owners ....Harley Hotchkiss, Norman Kwong,
                Sonia Scurfield, Byron and Daryl Seamen
President ....W.C. (Bill) Hay
V.P. & General Manager ....Doug Risebrough
Director of Public Relations..............................Rick Skaggs

Chicago Blackhawks
United Center, 1901 West Madison St., Chicago, IL 60612
(312) 455-7000
Owner-President.....................................William Wirtz
Senior V.P. & General Manager ....Bob Pulford
Director of Public Relations ....Jim DeMaria

Dallas Stars
901 Main St., Suite 2301, Dallas, TX 75202
(214) 712-2890
Owner..Norman Green
General Manager & Head Coach....................Bob Gainey
Director of Public Relations..................................Larry Kelly

Detroit Red Wings
Joe Louis Arena
600 Civic Center Drive, Detroit, MI 48226
(313) 396-7544
Owner/President ....Mike Ilitch
Owner/Secretary-Treasurer ....Marian Ilitch
Senior V.P ....Jim Devellano
Dir. of Player Personnel & Head Coach ....Scott Bowman
Director of Public Relations ....Bill Jamieson

Edmonton Oilers
Northlands Coliseum, 7424 118th Ave.,
Edmonton, Alberta, T5B 4M9
(403) 474-8561
Owner ....Peter Pocklington
President & General Manager ....Glen Sather
Exec. V.P. & Assistant GM ....Bruce MacGregor
Director of Public Relations....................................Bill Tuele

Florida Panthers
100 North East Third Ave., 10th Floor,
Fort Lauderdale, FL 33301
(305) 768-1900
Owner ....Wayne Huizenga
President ....Bill Torrey
General Manager ....Bryan Murray
Dir. of Public & Media Relations ....Greg Bouris

Hartford Whalers
242 Trumbull St., 8th Floor, Hartford, CT 06103
(203) 728-3366
Owner-CEO..Peter Karmanos Jr.
General Partner...Thomas Thewes
President & General Manager ....Jim Rutherford
Director of Public Relations ....John Forslund

Los Angeles Kings
Great Western Forum, 3900 West Manchester Blvd.,
Inglewood, CA 90306
(310) 419-3160
Majority Owners ....Jeffrey Sudikoff & Joseph Cohen
President ....Bruce McNall
General Manager..Sam McMaster
Director of Media Relations ....Rick Minch

Montreal Canadiens
Montreal Forum, 2313 St. Catherine St. West,
Montreal, Quebec H3H 1N2
(514) 932-2582
Owner ....Molson Companies, Ltd.
Chairman-President ....Ronald Corey
V.P. & Managing Director ....Serge Savard
Director of Communications ....Don Beauchamp

New Jersey Devils
Meadowlands Arena
P.O. Box 504, East Rutherford, NJ 07073
(201) 935-6050
Chairman ....John McMullen
President & General Manager ....Lou Lamoriello
Director of Media Relations ....Mike Levine

New York Islanders
Nassau Veterans' Memorial Coliseum
Uniondale, NY 11553
(516) 794-4100
Owner ....John Pickett
V.P. & General Manager...............................Don Maloney
Director of Media Relations ....Ginger Killian

New York Rangers
4 Penn Plaza, 4th Floor, New York, NY 10001
(212) 465-6486
Owner ....ITT Corp./Cablevision Systems Inc.
President & General Manager ....Neil Smith
Director of Communications.........................Barry Watkins

Ottawa Senators
301 Moodie Dr., Suite 200, Nepean, Ontario, K2H 9C4
(613) 721-0115
Chief Operating Officer ....Rod Bryden
President & General Manager ....Randy Sexton
Director of Media Relations...........................Laurent Benoit

Philadelphia Flyers
The Spectrum, Philadelphia, PA 19148
(215) 465-4500
Majority Owner..Ed Snider
President & General Manager ....Bob Clarke
Director of Public Relations.............................Mark Piazza

Pittsburgh Penguins
Civic Arena, Pittsburgh, PA 15219
(412) 642-1800
Owners ....Howard Baldwin, Morris Belzberg
                                            and Thomas Ruta
Exec. V.P. & General Manager.......................Craig Patrick
Director of Public Relations............................Cindy Himes

Quebec Nordiques
Coliseé de Quebec, 2205 Avenue du Coliseé,
Quebec City, Quebec G1L 4W7
(418) 529-8441
Part Owner-President ....Marcel Aubut
General Manager ....Pierre Lacroix
Director of Press Relations..........................Jean Martineau

St. Louis Blues
Kiel Center, 1401 Clark Ave., St. Louis, MO 63110
(314) 781-5300
Chairman ....Michael Shanahan
President ....Jack Quinn
General Manager & Head Coach ....Mike Keenan
V.P. & Dir. of Public Relations.........................Susie Mathieu

San Jose Sharks
525 West Santa Clara St., San Jose, CA 95113
(408) 287-7070
Owner-Chairman......................................George Gund III
Co-Owner ....Gordon Gund
President-CEO ....Art Savage
V.P.& Dir. of Hockey Operations ....Dean Lombardi
Director of Media Relations..............................Ken Arnold

Tampa Bay Lightning
501 East Kennedy Blvd., Suite 175, Tampa, FL 33602
(813) 229-2658
Owners ....Lightning Partners, Inc.
President & General Manager ....Phil Esposito
Director of Hockey Operations ....Tony Esposito
V.P., Communications.....................................Gerry Helper

Toronto Maple Leafs
Maple Leaf Gardens
60 Carlton Street, Toronto, Ontario M5B 1L1
(416) 977-1641
Chairman-CEO ....Steve Stavro
President-COO-GM.......................................Cliff Fletcher
Public Relations Coordinator...................................Pat Park

Vancouver Canucks
Pacific Coliseum, 100 North Renfrew St.,
Vancouver, British Columbia V5K 3N7
(604) 254-5141
Owner-Chairman ....Arthur Griffiths
President & General Manager............................Pat Quinn
Dir. of Public & Media Relations.................Steve Tambellini

Washington Capitals
USAir Arena, Landover, MD 20785
(301) 386-7000
Chairman...Abe Pollin
President...Dick Patrick
V.P. & General Manager ....Dave Poile
V.P. of Communications ....Ed Quinlan

Winnipeg Jets
Winnipeg Arena, 15-1430 Maroons Road,
Winnipeg, Manitoba R3G 0L5
(204) 982-5387
Owner-President ....Barry Shenkarow
General Manager & Head Coach.................John Paddock
Director of Information ....Igor Kuperman

IIHF

International Ice Hockey Federation
Todistrasse 23, CH-8002 Zurich, Switzerland
TEL: 011-411-281-1430
President ....Rene Fasel
General Secretary ....Jan-Ake Edvinsson

HORSE RACING

Breeders' Cup Limited
2525 Harrodsburg Road, Suite 500, Lexington, KY 40504
(606) 223-5444
President ....James E. (Ted) Bassett III
Executive Director....................................D.G. Van Clief, Jr.
Director of Communications ....Dan Metzger

The Jockeys' Guild
250 West Main Street, Suite 1820, Lexington, KY 40507
(606) 259-3211
President ....Jerry Bailey
National Manager.......................................John Giovanni

TRA
(Thoroughbred Racing Associations)
420 Fair Hill Drive, Suite 1, Elkton, MD 21921
(410) 392-9200
President ....David Vance
Executive V.P ....Chris Scherf
Racing Commissioner............................J. Brian McGrath
Director of Services................................Conrad Sobkowiak

TRC
(Thoroughbred Racing Communications)
40 East 52nd Street, New York, NY 10022
(212) 371-5910
Executive Director...Tom Merritt
Director of Media Relations ....Bob Curran

USTA
(United States Trotting Association)
750 Michigan Ave., Columbus, OH 43215
(614) 224-2291
President ....Corwin Nixon
Executive V.P ....Fred Noe
Director of Public Relations............................John Pawlak

MEDIA

PERIODICALS

Sports Illustrated
Time & Life Bldg., Rockefeller Center, New York, NY 10020
(212) 586-1212
Publisher ....David Long
Managing Editor ....Mark Mulvoy
Executive Editor ....Peter Carry

The Sporting News
1212 North Lindbergh Blvd., St. Louis, MO 63132
(314) 997-7111
Publisher...Nicholas Niles
Editor...John Rawlings

USA Today
1000 Wilson Blvd., Arlington, VA 22229
(703) 276-3400
Owner ....Gannett Company
President-Publisher ....Thomas Curley
Managing Editor/Sports ....Gene Policinski

WIRE SERVICES

Associated Press
50 Rockefeller Plaza, New York, NY 10020
(212) 621-1630
Sports Editor..Terry Taylor
Deputy Sports Editor ....Ron Sirak

United Press International
1400 Eye Street NW, Washington, DC 20005
(202) 898-8000
Sports Editor ....Ian Love

The Sports Network
701 Mason's Mill Business Park,
Huntington Valley, PA 19006
(215) 947-2400
President..Mickey Charles
Director of Operations ....Phil Sokol
Managing Editor...Steve Abbott

Sportsticker
600 Plaza Two, Jersey City, NJ 07311
(201) 309-1200
President ....Peter Bavasi
Vice President ....Rick Alessandri
Managing Editor............................Joe Carnicelli

TV NETWORKS

ABC Sports
47 West 66th St., 13th Floor, New York, NY 10023
(212) 456-4867
President ....Dennis Swanson
Senior V.P., Production ....Dennis Lewin
Executive Producer ....Jack O'Hara
Director of Information ....Mark Mandel

The Baseball Network
1301 Ave. of the Americas, New York, NY 10019
(212) 977-7300
President-CEO...............................Ken Schanzer
Coordinating Producer ....John Filippelli
Director of Communications............Ray Stallone

CBC Sports
P.O. Box 500 Station A 5H 100,
Toronto, Ontario M5W 1E6
(416) 205-6523
Head of Sports ....Alan Clark
Sr. Executive Producer ....Doug Sellars
Publicist ....Susan Proctor

Classic Sports Network
35 East 21st. St., 4th Floor, New York, NY 10010
(212) 529-8000
President ....Steve Greenberg
Executive Producer................Douglas Warshaw
Director of Communications..............Lisa Grimes

CBS Sports
51 West 52nd St., 25th Floor, New York, NY 10019
(212) 975-4321
President..David Kenin
Senior V.P., Production....................Rick Gentile
V.P., Programming...........................Len DeLuca
Director of Public Relations............Robin Brendle

ESPN
ESPN Plaza, Bristol, CT 06010
(203) 585-2000
President-CEO.............................Steve Bornstein
V.P., Programming...........................David Zucker
Executive Editor ....John Walsh
Managing Editor........................Steve Anderson
Managing Editor, ESPN2 ....Vince Doria
Director of Communications ....Mike Soltys

FOX Sports
5746 Sunset Blvd., Sunset Bldg., 2nd Floor,
Los Angeles, CA 90029
(213) 856-2128
President..David Hill
Exec. Producer-NFL ....Ed Goren
Director of Public Relations (NYC) ....Vince Wladika
                                             (212) 556-2472

HBO Sports
1100 Ave. of the Americas, New York, NY 10036
(212) 512-1066
President.......................................Seth Abraham
V.P., Executive Producer ....Ross Greenburg
Director of Publicity ....Ross Levinsohn

MTV Sports
1515 Broadway, New York, NY 10036
(212) 713-7400
Executive Producer ....Scott Messick
Director of Publicity.........................Tina Exarhos

NBC Sports
30 Rockefeller Plaza, New York, NY 10112
(212) 664-4444
President.......................................Dick Ebersol
Executive Producer ....Tommy Roy
Director of Public Relations ....Ed Markey

Prime SportsChannel Networks
Prime Network: 5251 Gulfton St., Houston, TX 77081
(713) 661-0078
NewSport: 3 Crossways Park West, Woodbury, NY 11797
(516) 921-3764
CEO ....James Dolan
COO ....Josh Sapan
V.P., Programming/Prime Network.................Dan Wilhelm
Media Relations Manager......................Denise Seomin
Exec. Producer/NewSport.............................Mike Lardner
Dir. of Public Relations ....Tom Cosentino
                                             (510) 364-2222

TSN-The Sports Network
2225 Shepherd Ave. East, Suite 100,
Willowdale, Ontario, MZJ-5C2
(416) 494-1212
President-CEO ....Gordon Craig
V.P. & General Manager............................Jim Thompson
Public Relations Officer ....Steve Rayment

Turner Sports
One CNN Center, 13th Floor, Atlanta, GA 30303
(404) 827-1735
President....................................Harvey Schiller
Sr. V.P., Executive Producer ....Don McGuire
Sr. V.P., Programming...................Kevin O'Malley
Director of Media Relations.........................Greg Hughes

Univision (Spanish)
9405 NW 41st St., Miami FL 33178
(305) 471-4008
Sports Director.............................Jorge Hidalgo
Publicity Coordinator ....Rosaly Espinosa

USA Network
1230 Ave. of the Americas, New York, NY 10020
(212) 408-9100
V.P., Executive Producer.....................Gordon Beck
V.P., Programming ....Rob Korrea
Sports Publicist......................Dan Schoenberg

OLYMPICS

**IOC
(International Olympic Committee)**
Chateau de Vidy, CH-1007 Lausanne, Switzerland
TEL: 011-41-21-621-6111
President.........................Juan Antonio Samaranch
Director General.......................Francois Carrard
Secretary General ....Francoise Zweifel
Public Relations Director ....Andrew Napier
Director of Information ....Michele Verdier

1996 SUMMER GAMES

Atlanta Committee for the Olympic Games
250 Williams St., Suite 6000, (P.O. Box 1996)
Atlanta, GA 30303
(404) 224-1996
President-CEO ....Billy Payne
Chief Operating Officer .............A.D. Frazier Jr.
Press Chief ....Bob Brennan
Director of Public Information ....Harry Shuman
Managing Dir. of Communications ....Dick Yarbrough
(Games of XXVIth Olympiad, July 20-Aug. 4, 1996)

1998 WINTER GAMES

Nagano Olympic Organizing Committee
KT Building, 3109-63 Kawaishinden
Nagano City 380, Japan
TEL: 011-81-262-25-1998
Time difference: 13 hours ahead of New York (EDT)
President..Eishiro Saito
Director General ....Makoto Kobayashi
Director of Public Relations...................Naokichi Nishimura
(XVIIIth Olympic Winter Games, Feb. 7-22, 1998)

2000 SUMMER GAMES

Sydney Olympic Organizing Committee
Level 14, Maritime Center, 207 Kent St.
Sydney, Australia NSW 2000
TEL: 011-612-931-2000
Time difference: 14 hours ahead of New York (EDT)
President..Gary Pemberton
Director General ....Bob Elphinston
Director of Information ....Ian Dose
(Games of XXVIIth Olympiad, Sept. 16-Oct. 1, 2000)

2002 WINTER GAMES

Salt Lake City Organizing Committee (U.S. Bid City)
215 South State, Suite 2002, Second Floor
Salt Lake City, UT 84111
(801) 322-2002
Chairman ....Frank Joklik
President ....Tom Welch
Vice President ....Dave Johnson
Dir. of Communications ....Robert Hunter

COA
(Canadian Olympic Association)
2380 Avenue Pierre Dupuy, Montreal, Quebec H3C-3R4
(514) 861-3371
CEO & General Secretary ....Carol Anne Letheren
Interim President ....Wayne Hellquist
IOC members......................................Carol Anne Letheren
& Richard Pound
Director of Communications ....Frank Ratcliffe

USOC
(United States Olympic Committee)
One Olympic Plaza, Colorado Springs, CO 80909
(719) 632-5551
President...LeRoy Walker
Interim Exec. Director...................................John Krimsky Jr.
IOC members..Anita DeFrantz
& James Easton
Director of Public/Media Relations..................Mike Moran

1995 PAN AMERICAN GAMES

Argentina Organizing Committee
COPAN '95, Gascon 27,
7600 Mar del Plata, Argentina
TEL: 011-54-23-51-3347
Managing Director....................................Gen. Dante Seva
Director of Public Relations ....Pablo Baques
(XIIth Pan American Games, March 11-26, 1995)

1995 U.S. OLYMPIC FESTIVAL

Denver Organizing Committee
Colorado Sports Council,
1391 Steer Blvd., Suite 700, Denver, CO 80205
(303) 573-1995
President-CEO................................Edmond (Buddy) Noel
Executive Director ....Jim Warsinske
(Festival '95 at Boulder-Denver-Colorado Springs,
July 21-30, 1995)

1998 GOODWILL GAMES

New York Organizing Committee
Two World Trade Center, Suite 2164, New York, NY 10048
(212) 321-1998
Chairman ....Bob Johnson
President ....Michael Rowe
V.P., Communications......................................Don Smith
Project Director ....Stephen Chriss
(4th Goodwill Games, July 25-Aug 9, 1998)

U.S. OLYMPICS TRAINING CENTERS

Colorado Springs Training Center
One Olympic Plaza, Colorado Springs, CO 80909
(719) 578-4500 ext. 5500
Interim Director ....John Smyth

Lake Placid Training Center
421 Old Military Road, Lake Placid, NY 12946
(518) 523-2600
Director...Gloria Chadwick

San Diego Training Center
c/o San Diego National Sports Training Foundation
1650 Hotel Circle N., Suite 125, San Diego, CA 92108
Director...David Armstrong

U.S. OLYMPIC ORGANIZATIONS

National Archery Association
One Olympic Plaza, Colorado Springs, CO 80909
(719) 578-4576
President...Robert C.W. Smith
Executive Director ....Christine McCartney

U.S. Badminton Association
One Olympic Plaza, Colorado Springs, CO 80909
(719) 578-4808
President...Cynthia Kelly
Executive Director ....Jim Hadley

USA Baseball
2160 Greenwood Avenue, Trenton, NJ 08609
(609) 586-2381
President...Mark Marquess
Executive Director & CEO ....Richard Case
Dir. of Public Relations......................................Mike Lantz

USA Basketball
5465 Mark Dabling Blvd., Colorado Springs, CO 80918
(719) 590-4800
President...C.M. Newton
Executive Director..Warren Brown
Director of Public Relations...............................Craig Miller

U.S. Biathlon Association
421 Old Military Rd., Lake Placid, NY 12946
(518) 523-3836
Director of Summer Biathlon.......................Kyle Woodlief
Assistant Director...Julie Jorling

U.S. Bobsled and Skeleton Federation
P.O. Box 828, 421 Old Military Road,
Lake Placid, NY 12946
(518) 523-1842
President..Jim Morris
Executive Director ....Matt Roy

USA Boxing
One Olympic Plaza, Colorado Springs, CO 80909
(719) 578-4506
President ....Jerry Dusenberry
Executive Director ....Bruce Mathis
Communications Director ....Kurt Stenerson

U.S. Canoe and Kayak Team
Pan American Plaza, Suite 610,
201 South Capitol Avenue, Indianapolis, IN 46225
(317) 237-5690
Chairman ....Eric Haught
Executive Director ....Chuck Wielgus
Communications Director ....Craig Bohnert

U.S. Cycling Federation
One Olympic Plaza, Colorado Springs, CO 80909
(719) 578-4581
President ....Mike Fraysse
Executive Director ....Lisa Voight
Director of Communications ....Steve Penny

United States Diving, Inc.
Pan American Plaza, Suite 430,
201 South Capitol Avenue, Indianapolis, IN 46225
(317) 237-5252
President ....Micki King
Executive Director ....Todd Smith
Director of Communications ....Dave Shatkowski

U.S. Equestrian Team
Pottersville Road, Gladstone, NJ 07934
(908) 234-1251
President...Finn Caspersen
Executive Director ....Bob Standish
Director of Public Relations ....Marty Bauman

U.S. Fencing Association
One Olympic Plaza, Colorado Springs, CO 80909
(719) 578-4511
President ....Steve Sobel
Executive Director ....Selden Fritschner
Media Contact ....Jeff Dimond

U.S. Field Hockey Association
One Olympic Plaza, Colorado Springs, CO 80909
(719) 578-4567
President ....Jenepher Shillingford
Executive Director...Carrie Haag
Director of Public Relations ....Interviewing

U.S. Figure Skating Association
20 First Street, Colorado Springs, CO 80906
(719) 635-5200
President...Claire Ferguson
Executive Director ....Jerry Lace
Director of Communications ....Kristin Matta

USA Gymnastics
Pan American Plaza, Suite 300,
201 South Capitol Avenue, Indianapolis, IN 46225
(317) 237-5050
President-Exec. Director...............................Kathy Scanlan
Director of Public Relations ....Luan Peszek

USA Hockey
4965 North 30th St., Colorado Springs, CO 80919
(719) 599-5500
President ....Walter Bush
Executive Director ....Dave Ogrean
Dir. of Public Relations & Media......................Darryl Seibel

United States Judo, Inc.
P.O. Box 10013, El Paso, TX 79991
(915) 771-6699
President & Media Contact ....Frank Fullerton

U.S. Luge Association
P.O. Box 651, Lake Placid, NY 12946
(518) 523-2071
President...Dwight Bell
Executive Director ....Ron Rossi
Public Relations Manager ....Dmitry Feld

U.S. Modern Pentathlon Association
530 McCullough, Suite 619, San Antonio, TX 78215
(210) 246-3000
Acting President ....Robert Marbut Jr.
Executive Director ....Dean Billick

U.S. Rowing
Pan American Plaza, Suite 400,
201 South Capitol Avenue, Indianapolis, IN 46225
(317) 237-5656
President ....Frank J. Coyle
Executive Director....................................Sandra R. Hughes
Media Contact ....Terry Friel

U.S. Sailing Association
P.O. Box 209, Newport, RI 02840
(401) 849-5200
President ....Robert Hobbs
Executive Director ....Terry D. Harper
Media Contact ....Barby MacGowan

U.S. Shooting Team
One Olympic Plaza, Colorado Springs, CO 80909
(719) 578-4670
Program Administrator...................................Steven Ducoff
Director of Operations...................................Joseph Berry
Public Relations Director................................Nancy Moore

U.S. Skiing
P.O. Box 100, 1500 Kearns Blvd., Park City, UT 84060
(801) 649-9090
Chairman...Nick Badami
President & CEO ....Mike Jacki
President U.S. Ski Association ....Bill Slattery
Director of Communications ....Tom Kelly

U.S. Soccer Federation
U.S. Soccer House
1801-1811 South Prairie Ave., Chicago, IL 60616
(312) 808-1300
President ....Alan Rothenberg
Executive Director ....Hank Steinbrecher
Director of Communications ....Tom Lange

Amateur Softball Association
2801 N.E. 50th Street, Oklahoma City, OK 73111
(405) 424-5266
President ....Jack Aaron
Executive Director ....Don Porter
Dir. Media Relations/Hall of Fame ....Bill Plummer
Director of Communications ....Ron Babb

U.S. International Speedskating Assn.
P.O. Box 16157, Rocky River, OH 44116
(216) 899-0128
President ....Bill Cushman
Executive Director ....Katie Marquard
Media Relations Director................................Susan Polakoff

U.S. Swimming, Inc.
One Olympic Plaza, Colorado Springs, CO 80909
(719) 578-4578
President ....Bill Maxson
Executive Director ....Ray Essick
Director of Communications ....Charlie Snyder

U.S. Synchronized Swimming, Inc.
Pan American Plaza, Suite 510,
201 South Capitol Avenue, Indianapolis, IN 46225
(317) 237-5700
President..Nancy Wightman
Executive Director ....Debbie Hesse
Communications Coordinator ....Laura LaMarca

U.S. Table Tennis Association
One Olympic Plaza, Colorado Springs, CO 80909
(719) 578-4583
President..Dan Seemiller
Executive Director...Paul Montville

U.S. Team Handball Federation
One Olympic Plaza, Colorado Springs, CO 80909
(719) 578-4582
President...Peter Buehning
Executive Director................................Michael Cavanaugh
Media Contact ....Evelyn Anderson

U.S. Tennis Association
70 West Red Oak Lane, White Plains, NY 10604
(914) 696-7000
President ....J. Howard Frazer
Executive Director ....M. Marshall Happer III
Dir. of Communications.........................Page Dahl Crosland

USA Track and Field
P.O. Box 120, Indianapolis, IN 46206
(317)261-0500
President...Larry Ellis
Executive Director...Ollan Cassell
Press Information Director ....Pete Cava

U.S. Volleyball Association
3595 East Fountain Blvd., Suite I-2,
Colorado Springs, CO 80910
(719) 637-8300
President...Jerry Sherman
Executive Director-CEO ....John Carroll
Director Media Relations ....Tony Lovitt

United States Water Polo
Pan American Plaza, Suite 520,
201 South Capitol Avenue, Indianapolis, IN 46225
(317) 237-5599
President ....Richard Foster
Executive Director...Bruce Wigo
Dir. of Media/Public Relations.......................Eileen Sexton

U.S. Weightlifting Federation
One Olympic Plaza, Colorado Springs, CO 80909
(719) 578-4508
President...Jim Schmitz
Executive Director................................George Greenway
Communications Director ....John Halpin

USA Wrestling
6155 Lehman Drive, Colorado Springs, CO 80918
(719) 598-8181
President...Arthur Martori
Executive Director ....Jim Scherr
Dir. of Communications...................................Gary Abbott

AFFILIATED ORGANIZATIONS

U.S. Curling Association
1100 Center Point Drive, Box 866,
Stevens Point, WI 54481
(715) 344-1199
President...Evelyn Nostrand
Exec. Dir. & Media Contact ....David Garber

Triathlon Federation USA
3595 East Fountain Blvd., Suite F-1
Colorado Springs, CO 80910
(719) 597-9090
President...David Backer
Executive Director...Steven Locke
Media Contact...Sean Phelps

American Water Ski Association
799 Overlook Drive, SE, Winter Haven, FL 33884
(813) 324-4341
President ....Tony Baggiano
Executive Director....................................Duke Cullimore
Director of Communications.........................Don Cullimore

SOCCER

FIFA
(Federation Internationale de Football Assn.)
P.O. Box 85, 8030 Zurich, Switzerland
TEL: 011-41-1-384-9595
President ....Joao Havelange
General Secretary ....Joseph Blatter
Head of Public Relations/Media ....Guido Tognoni

1998 WORLD CUP

French Organizing Committee
90 Avenue des Champs Elysees, F-75008 Paris France
TEL: 011-33-1-44-95-1998
Co-Presidents ....Ferdnand Sastre
                        and Michel Platini
General Director..Jacques Lambert
Dir. of Press & Communications...................Gerard Ernault
(16th World Cup, June/July, 1998)

CONCACAF
(Confederation of North, Central American & Caribbean Association Football)
725 Fifth Ave., 17th Floor, New York, NY 10022
(212) 308-0044
President ....Jack Austin Warner
General Secretary ....Chuck Blazer

U.S. Soccer
(United States Soccer Federation)
Soccer House, 1801-1811 South Prairie Ave.,
Chicago, IL 60616
(312) 808-1300
President ....Alan Rothenberg
Exec. Director/Sec. General ....Hank Steinbrecher
Director of Communications ....Tom Lange

APSL
(American Professional Soccer League)
3702 Pender Dr., Suite 210, Fairfax, VA 22030
(703) 273-7767
Commissioner..Richard Groff
Operations Director ....Emily Ballus
Co-Directors of Media Relations ....Steve Winter
                       and Kerry Lynn Bohen
                       (202) 296-2775
Member teams (7): Colorado Foxes, Ft. Lauderdale Strikers, Los Angeles Salsa, Montreal Impact, Seattle Sounders, Toronto Rockets and Vancouver 86ers. 1995 Altanta Magic and Detroit Wheels

CISL
(Continental Indoor Soccer League)
16027 Ventura Blvd., Suite 605, Encino, CA 91436
(818) 906-7627
Commissioner..Ron Weinstein
League Counsel ....Dan Grigsby
Director of Public Relations...................Dan Courtemanche
Member teams (14): Anaheim Splash, Arizona Sandsharks, Carolina Vipers, Dallas Sidekicks, Detroit Neon, Houson Hotshots, Las Vegas Dustdevils, Monterrey La Raza, Pittsburgh Stingers, Portland Pride, Sacramento Knights, San Diego Sockers, San Jose Grizzlies and Washington Warthogs.

MLS
(Major League Soccer)
2049 Century Park East, Suite 4390,
Los Angeles CA 90067
(310) 772-2600
Chairman ....Alan Rothenberg
COO ....Bill Sage
   Member cities (12): Boston, Columbus (OH), Los
Angeles, New Jersey, New York (Long Island), San Jose,
Washington D.C., and five cities to be named later.

NPSL
(National Professional Soccer League)
229 Third Street, NW, Canton OH 44702
(216) 455-4625
Commissioner ....Steve M. Paxos
Director of Operations.................................Paul Luchowski
Public Relations Assistant ....Jay Holby
   Member teams (12): American Division—Baltimore
Spirit, Buffalo Blizzard, Canton Invaders, Cleveland Crunch,
Dayton Dynamo and Harrisburg Heat. National Division—
Chicago Power, Detroit Rockers, Kansas City Attack,
Milwaukee Wave, St. Louis Ambush and Wichita Wings.

USISL
(United States Interregional Soccer League)
4322 N. Beltline Rd., Suite B-205, Irving, TX 75038
(214) 570-7575
Commissioner ....Francisco Marcos
Administrative Manager ....Beverly Wright
Director of Public Relations..............................Mike Agnew

TENNIS

ATP
(Association of Tennis Professionals)
200 ATP Tour Blvd., Ponte Verde Beach, FL 32082
(904) 285-8000
Chief Executive Officer ....Mark Miles
V.P., Communications ....Pete Alfano

ITF
(International Tennis Federation)
Pallisert, Barons Court, London, England W14 9EN
TEL: 011-44-71-3818060
President ....Brian Tobin
General Manager ....Mike Davies
Media Administrator ....Ian Barnes

USTA
(United States Tennis Association)
70 West Red Oak Lane, White Plains, NY 10604
(914) 696-7000
President ....J. Howard Frazer
Executive Director ....Marshall Happer
Dir. of Communications.......................Page Dahl Crosland

WTA Tour
(Women's Tennis Association)
133 First Street NE, St. Petersburg, FL 33701
(813) 895-5000
Executive Director & CEO...............Anne Person Worcester
Director of Public Relations ....Ana Leaird

TRACK & FIELD

AAU
(Amateur Athletic Union)
3400 West 86th St., Indianapolis, IN 46268
(317) 872-2900
President...Bobby Dodd
Executive Director...Louis Marciani
Director of Communications.........................David Dececco

IAAF
(International Ameteur Athletics Federation)
17 Rue Princesse Florestine, BP 359, MC-98007, Monaco
TEL: 011-33-93-30-7070
President ....Primo Nebiolo
General Secretary ....Istvan Gyulai
Director of Information ....Christopher Winner

USA Track & Field
(formerly The Athletics Congress)
P.O. Box 120, Indianapolis, IN 46225
(317) 261-0500
Executive Director..Ollan Cassell
Director of Information ....Pete Cava

YACHTING

1995 America's Cup

America's Cup '95
2727 Shelter Island Drive, San Diego, CA 92106
(619) 221-1995
Chairman ....Frank Hope Jr.
Public Information Officer ....Gayle Storrza-Gill
Defense Committee:
   Chairman ....Bill Munster
   Media Liason..Ann Sandison

MISCELLANEOUS

All-American Soap Box Derby
P.O.Box 7233, Akron, OH 44306
(216) 733-8723
President ....Bob Otterman
Chairman of the Board and Dir. PR ....Bob Proyer

Arena Football League
2200 East Devon, Suite 247, Des Plaines, IL 60018
(708) 390-7400
Founder & Consultant ....Jim Foster
Commissioner ....Joseph O'Hara
Coordinator, Media Services ....Howard Balzer
   Member teams (10): American Conference—
Albany (NY) Firebirds, Arizona Rattlers, Cleveland
Thunderbolds, Las Vegas Sting, Massachusetts Marauders
and Milwaukee Mustangs. National Conference— Charlotte
Rage, Fort Worth Calvalry, Miami Hooters, Orlando
Predators, Tampa Bay Storm.

Association of Volleyball Professionals
15260 Ventura Blvd., Suite 2250,
Sherman Oaks, CA 91403
(818) 386-2486
President...Jon Stevenson
Director of Public Relations ....Debbie Rubio

CBA
Continental Basketball League
701 Market St., St. Louis, MO 63101
(314) 621 7222
Commissioner ....Tom Valdiserri
V.P. of Basketball Operations ....Clay Moser
Director of Public Relations ....Brett Meister
   Member teams (16): Chicago (IL) Rockers, Ft. Wayne
(IN) Fury, Grand Rapids (MI) Mackers, Harrisburg (PA)
Hammerheads, Hartford (CT) Hellcats, Mexico (Mexico)
Aztecas, Oklahoma City (OK) Cavalry, Omaha (NE)
Racers, Pittsburgh (PA) Piranhas, Quad City (IL) Thunder,
Rapid City (SD) Thrillers, Rockford (IL) Lightning, Shreveport
(LA) Crawdads, Sioux Falls (SD) Skyforce, Tri-City (WA)
Chinook and Yakima (WA) Sun Kings.

International Game Fish Association
1301 East Atlantic Blvd., Pompano Beach, FL 33060
(305) 941-3474
Chairman...George Matthews
President ....Mike Leach
Editor ....Ray Crawford

Little League Baseball Incorporated
P.O.Box 3485, Williamsport, PA 17701
(717) 326-1921
President-CEO..C.J. Hale
Director of Communications ....Dennis Sullivan

Major Indoor Lacrosse League
2310 West 75th St., Prairie Village, KS 66208
(913) 384-8960
Chairman-CEO...Chris Fritz
President ....Russ Cline
Director of Public Relations ....Mary Havel
  Member teams (7): Baltimore Thunder, Boston Blazers, Buffalo Bandits, Detroit Turbos, New York Saints, Philadelphia Wings, Pittsburgh Bulls.

National Hot Rod Association
2035 Financial Way, Glendora, CA 91740
(818) 914-4761
President ....Dallas Gardner
Director of Communications........................Denny Darnell

National Rifle Association
11250 Waples Mill Road, Fairfax, VA 22030
(703) 267-1000
Executive VP...Wayne LaPierre
Public Relations Director ....Deborah Nauser

National Sports Foundation
1314 North Hayworth Ave., Suite 402,
Los Angeles, CA 90046
(213) 851-5773
Executive Director ....Ed Harris

National Wheelchair Athletic Association
3595 East Fountain Blvd., Suite L-10
Colorado Springs, CO 80910
(719) 574-9840
Chairman ....Paul DePace
Operations Manager ....Patricia Long

Professional Rodeo Cowboys Association
101 Pro Rodeo Drive, Colorado Springs, CO 80919
(719) 593-8840
Commissioner...Lewis Cryer
Director of Public Relations ....Steve Fleming

Roller Hockey International
5182 Katella Ave., Suite 106, Los Alamitos, CA 90720
(310) 430-2423
Commissioner ....Ralph Backstrom
COO ....David B. McLane
Public Relations Director..................................Nancy King

TeamTennis
445 North Wells, Suite 404, Chicago, IL 60610
(312) 245-5300
Chief Executive Officer...............................Billie Jean King
Executive Director ....Ilana Kloss
Communications Director..............................Mike Shapiro

---

Commissioners & Presidents
Chief executives of established major sports organizations since 1876.

Major League Baseball

Commissioner	Tenure
Kanesaw Mountain Landis*	1920-44
Albert (Happy) Chandler	1945-51
Ford Frick	1951-65
William Eckert	1965-68
Bowie Kuhn	1969-84
Peter Ueberroth	1984-89
A. Bartlett Giamatti*	1989
Fay Vincent	1989-92
Bud Selig†	1992–

*Died in office.
†Chairman of Executive Committee.

National League

President	Tenure
Morgan G. Bulkeley	1876
William A. Hulbart*	1877-82
A.G. Mills	1883-84
Nicholas Young	1885-1902
Henry Pulliam*	1903-09
Thomas J. Lynch	1910-13
John K. Tener	1914-18
John A. Heydler	1918-34
Ford Frick	1935-51
Warren Giles	1951-69
Charles (Chub) Feeney	1970-86
A. Bartlett Giamatti	1987-89
Bill White	1989-94
Leonard Coleman	1994–

*Died in office.

American League

President	Tenure
Bancroft (Ban) Johnson	1901-27
Ernest Barnard*	1927-31
William Harridge	1931-59
Joe Cronin	1959-73
Lee McPhail	1974-83
Bobby Brown	1984-94
Gene Budig	1994—

*Died in office.

NBA

Commissioner	Tenure
Maurice Podoloff	1949-63
Walter Kennedy	1963-75
Larry O'Brien	1975-84
David Stern	1984—

NFL

President	Tenure
Jim Thorpe	1920
Joe Carr	1921-39
Carl Storck	1939-41

Commissioner	Tenure
Elmer Layden	1941-46
Bert Bell*	1946-59
Austin Gunsel†	1959-60
Pete Rozelle	1960-89
Paul Tagliabue	1989—

*Died in office.
†Acting Commissioner.

NHL

President	Tenure
Frank Calder*	1917-43
Red Dutton	1943-46
Clarence Campbell	1946-77
John Ziegler	1977-92
Gil Stein	1992-93

Commissioner	Tenure
Gary Bettman	1993–

*Died in office.

NCAA

Executive Director	Tenure
Walter Byers	1951-88
Dick Schultz	1988-93
Cedric Dempsey	1993—

IOC

President	Tenure
Demetrius Vikelas Greece	1894-96
Baron Pierre de Coubertin, France	1896-1925
Count Henri de Baillet-Latour, Belgium	1925-42
Vacant	1942-46
J. Sigfried Edstrom, Sweden	1946-52
Avery Brundage, USA	1952-72
Lord Michael Killanin, Ireland	1972-80
Juan Antonio Samaranch, Spain	1980–

Clive Brunskill/Allsport

American speed skater **Dan Jansen** with daughter **Jane** after winning the 1,000-meter gold medal at the Winter Olympics in Lillehammer.

OLYMPICS

WINTER OLYMPICS
by Philip Hersh

Picture Perfect

*Dan Jansen's overdue gold medal and victory lap
epitomizes the true spirit of the Lillehammer Olympics.*

Speed skater Dan Jansen carried the American flag in the closing ceremonies for the XVII Winter Olympics, which will be forever remembered for the moment when he carried something far more precious—his infant daughter, Jane, around the Viking Ship speed skating oval.

The sight of Jane Jansen in her father's arms symbolized everything right about an Olympics in which fallout from the wrong done to U.S. figure skater Nancy Kerrigan threatened to contaminate the lasting image of these picture-perfect Winter Games.

The Jan. 6 attack on Kerrigan by associates of rival Tonya Harding, including ex-husband Jeff Gillooly (see p. 590), led to pictures that ran from sad to stupid to sordid: Harding sobbing to the judges when her shoelace broke in the free skate; silver medalist Kerrigan, made an instant millionairess by the fame that followed her bruised knee; sniping at Olympic champion Oksana Baiul's tears; reporters interviewing garbage collectors while awaiting Harding's arrival in Norway; Harding cutting grass and serving meals to the elderly as part of her plea bargain for withholding ex-post facto knowledge of the attack; and, finally, intimate pictures of Harding's wedding night splashed across nine pages of Penthouse magazine.

Since the Battle of Wounded Knee

attracted more worldwide viewers than ever to the Olympics, hundreds of millions saw the healing of Jansen's spirit. When he finished his Olympic career with the medal that previously had eluded him, Jansen gave a heavenward salute to his late sister, who had died hours before his fateful performance (two falls) in the 1988 Olympics at Calgary. Then he took her namesake, 8-month old Jane, on a victory lap around the arena as the Norwegians delightedly shared his joy.

Norway gave joy to the world, and an Olympics to savor in millions of ways. Having the first Winter Olympics of the new cycle—midway between the Summer Games—in a country for which winter sports are part competition and part folk festival assured their success.

The Norwegians excelled at both, leading the overall medal count with 26 and acting as such good winners no one could help but be happy for them. In a country so egalitarian that the notion of heroes is anathema even if heroic deeds are not, speedskater Johan Olav Koss became a golden symbol of his homeland. After winning three gold medals, each with a world record, Koss dwelled more on what he could do for Lillehammer Olympic Aid than what he had done on the ice.

One of Olympic Aid's beneficiaries is the tortured city of Sarajevo, host to the 1984 Winter Games. International Olympic Committee president Juan Antonio Samaranch made haunting references to

Philip Hersh covers international sports for the *Chicago Tribune* and has been the *Tribune's* full-time Olympic writer since 1986.

100 m

Relay anchors **Silvio Fauner** of Italy (left) and **Bjorn Dählie** of Norway battle down the stretch in the men's 4 x 10-kilometer cross-country race which finished at Birkebeiner Stadium. A crowd of more than 120,000 lined the course to see Italy win the gold.

Sarajevo in both the opening and closing ceremonies. And the presence of nine competitors from Bosnia-Herzegovina, athletes of ethnic and religious diversity, helped remind everyone of the horrors continuing in their homeland. They also recalled those wondrous days of 10 years past, when the Sarajevo Games, ever so briefly, carried the torch for humanity.

Figure Skating. Fittingly, the soap operatic Olympic women's championship ended in controversy. The judges' 5-4 split decision in the free skate that gave 16-year-old Oksana Baiul of Ukraine the gold medal over Nancy Kerrigan, 24, of Stoneham, Mass., seemed the proper conclusion to the event after seven weeks of buildup in which controversy was the recurrent theme.

Each skated well enough to be Olympic champion, especially considering what they had both overcome. Baiul, a virtual orphan, needed pain-killing injections in her right leg an hour before the Feb. 25 final as a result of a practice collision the day before. She became the youngest Olympic women's champion since Norway's Sonja Henie won her first of a record three golds in 1928.

Kerrigan had been clubbed in the leg by associates of rival Tonya Harding on Jan. 6 and all-but-assaulted by tabloid journalists in the aftermath of the attack.

Harding, whom the U.S. Olympic Committee tried vainly to dump from the team, ended up where she had spent most of her skating career—in the twilight zone. She finished eighth after being granted a reskate of the free program because of shoelace problems.

Kerrigan led after the technical program, the telecast of which earned a 48.5 Nielsen TV rating to become the highest-rated sports event in 11 years and the sixth highest-rated TV show ever.

The technical phase was also a triumph for two-time Olympic champion Katarina Witt of Germany, whose artistry overcame her relatively weak jumps to put her in medal contention in sixth place. Witt, a reinstated pro, placed seventh after a desultory free skate. In the other three events, the question was how reinstated pros would do against quasi-amateurs in this first Olympics with a virtually open figure skating competition, were mixed.

In pairs skating, ex-pros Ekaterina

Wide World Photos

Wide World Photos

U.S. speed skater **Bonnie Blair** (left) holds up five fingers to signify her fifth career gold medal after winning the women's 1,000-meter event, while Norway's **Johan Olav Koss** flashes three speed skating gold medals of his own, all won in world record time.

Gordeeva and Sergey Grinkov (Olympic champions in 1988) and Natalia Mishkutenok and Artur Dmitriev (Olympic gold medalists in '92), both of Russia, finished 1-2. But in the men's competition, 1988 champion Brian Boitano of the U.S. and '92 champion Viktor Petrenko of Ukraine, both reinstatees, bombed in the technical phase and finished sixth and fourth, respectively. The eventual winner, 20-year-old Alexei Urmanov of Russia, became the youngest men's Olympic figure skating champion ever.

The oldest pros, 1984 dance champions Jayne Torvill (36) and Christopher Dean (35), wound up as bronze medalists to Oksana Gritschuk and Evgeny Platov of Russia, although many felt T&D deserved better. Some judges penalized them for an apparently illegal lift during a free skate program that was purposefully staid, a far cry from their lubricious rendering of Bolero (that earned nine perfect 6.0s) in Sarajevo.

Speed Skating. It was an Olympics for apotheosis. Johan Olav Koss, merely "the Boss" when the meet began, became super-

man. Bonnie Blair, the peanut butter-and-jelly kid, became The Golden Girl (or, to be more politically correct, The Golden Woman) of U.S. Olympic sports. And Jansen became one of the best-loved champions in Olympic history, when his decade-long, often tragic chase for gold ended in a triumph so emotionally fulfilling that few would have dared script it.

Home boy Koss also fell into the too-good-to-be-true realm, as both athlete and humanitarian. He won the 1,500, 5,000 and 10,000 meters, setting world records in each, the last by a stunning 12.99 seconds. "That record will stand 30 years," said 10,000 bronze medalist Bart Veldkamp. Koss donated his $30,000 bonus for winning the 1,500 to Olympic Aid and, in May, announced his retirement to concentrate on medical school.

Blair won two more golds—her third straight Olympic title in the 500 and second straight in the 1,000. The total of five makes her the most gilded female athlete in U.S. Olympic history, Winter or Summer.

Perhaps the simplest way to describe the

impact Jansen's story had on the world's sporting consciousness was a sign placed alongside the main road between Lillehammer and Hamar on the night of Feb. 18. The sign simply said, "Dan," and that was enough to honor the man who had the last word on his career.

Through four Olympics, Jansen had been one of the world's best skaters, yet until Feb. 18, he had not won an Olympic medal in seven races. In 1988, his heart and feet were yanked out from under him when his sister, Jane Beres, died a few hours before his first race. In '92, with the memory of the 1988 falls still weighing on him, he skated too conservatively. And in the first race of 1994, the 500 meters, he nearly fell again, keeping his balance but placing eighth. "I guess I'm going to have to live my life without an Olympic gold medal," Jansen said.

Four days later, destiny finally took Jansen's side. He won the 1,000 meters in world-record time. Standing atop the medals stand, Jansen looked heavenward, in a salute to his late sister. When he took a victory lap with 8-month-old daughter Jane, named in his sister's memory, a circle had been completed. Jansen first thought of competing again in 1995, but retired a few months later.

Alpine Skiing. *Sports Illustrated* chuckled that the U.S. ski team would be an underdog to any Swiss Holstein, but Team USA was not cowed by such naysaying. In the first four races, the U.S. won four medals—including golds by Tommy Moe in the downhill and Diann Roffe-Steinrotter in the Super-G. Picabo Street took a silver in women's downhill, while Moe added a silver in Super-G, becoming the first U.S. skier since Jean Saubert in 1964 to win more than one medal in a single Olympics.

After that, the alpine triumphs all belonged to more likely sources, if occasionally unlikely athletes.

Germany's Markus Wasmeier, who had not won a championship race since 1985, took both the Super-G and giant slalom. Italy's Deborah Compagnoni (giant slalom) and Sweden's Pernilla Wiberg (combined) both completed comebacks from knee injuries. And Norwegian men, led by Lasse Kjus, swept the combined, the first alpine sweep since Austria in the 1956 giant slalom.

Switzerland's Vreni Schneider, a double winner at the 1988 Winter Games but a disappointment in '92, etched her place in Olympic history with gold (slalom), silver (combined) and bronze (giant slalom) in 1994. Her five career alpine medals is a women's Olympic record.

And what of Alberto Tomba, skiing's best-known personality? Once again, he managed to steal the show with a dramatic silver medal in slalom.

Experts' predictions that Tomba no longer could cut it in giant slalom proved correct, as he stood 13th after the first run and missed a gate in the second. After the first run of the slalom, his medal chances seemed equally slim—Tomba was 12th and a whopping 1.84 seconds behind leader Thomas Stangassinger of Austria. Then the magic returned. Tomba put together a stunning second run, then watched the next 10 men either fail to match his time or miss gates. With the pressure on, Stangassinger all-but-walked through the second run to beat Tomba's combined time by .15 seconds.

Cross-country skiing. This event was so popular among Norwegians that 200,000 ticket requests could not be filled for the men's 30-kilometer race. And the home country did not disappoint its fans, winning three of the four men's individual races—two by Bjorn Dählie—and taking second to Italy in a relay that many felt, on purely competitive terms, was the most extraordinary event of the Olympics.

More than 120,000 people lined the course and filled Birkebeiner Stadium for the 4 x 10-kilometer relay, which became a bitterly contested race. Vegard Ulvang accused Italy's Marco Albarello of breaking Harri Kirvesniemi's pole during the second leg. The anchor skiers, Dählie and Silvio Fauner of Italy, were only feet apart for most of the final leg, with Fauner doggedly hanging on until a final surge gave him victory by .4 seconds. Also worth noting: Italy's first leg was skied by 43-year-old Maurilio DeZolt.

Russia's Lyubov Egorova, toughened by a childhood in Siberia, tied the Winter Olympic record for career gold medals with six—adding three to the three she had won in 1992. While Italy's Manuela Di Centa won the other two golds, another skiing ancient embellished her remarkable record. Finland's Marja-Liisa

592 ➤

Figure Skating Becomes A Contact Sport

Chronology of key events in the attack on Nancy Kerrigan, based on interviews, news conferences and court documents reported by the Associated Press and other sources.

THE PLOT

Dec. 26— A meeting is held at the Portland, Ore. home of Tonya Harding's would-be bodyguard, the 310-pound Shawn Eckardt. Attending are Eckardt, Harding's ex-husband Jeff Gillooly, plus bodybuilder Shane Stant and Stant's uncle Derrick Smith, both of Phoenix. Plans are made to attack Harding's main rival Nancy Kerrigan, the reigning U.S. champion and Olympic favorite. Gillooly agrees to pay Smith and Stant $6,500 if they knock Kerrigan out of the 1994 championships scheduled for Jan. 4-9 in Detroit.

Dec. 27— Gillooly cashes a check at his bank for $3,000 and gives $2,000 in $100 bills to Eckardt. Eckardt passes the money along to Smith.

Dec. 28— According to Eckardt, Harding makes four telephone calls from Portland to Kerrigan's home rink on Cape Cod, Mass. to find out Kerrigan's practice schedule. Stant flies to Boston to carry out the assault.

THE ASSAULT

Dec. 31— After arriving in Boston on Dec. 29, Stant checks into a Yarmouth, Mass. motel near the Tony Kent Arena in Dennis.

Kerrigan practices for four hours in the afternoon, but is not hit.

Jan. 2-4— Eckardt confesses to Eugene Saunders, pastor of the Foursquare Church in Gresham, Ore. that he, Gillooly, and a man from Arizona have arranged to hurt Nancy Kerrigan before the National Figure Skating Championships.

Jan. 3— After taking Jan. 1-2 off, Kerrigan skates for an hour in the morning in her last practice session before leaving for the nationals. Missing his chance, Stant climbs on a bus for Detroit.

Jan. 4— As Kerrigan arrives in Detroit by plane, Stant checks into a Romulus, Mich. motel near Detroit. Back in Oregon, Eckardt wires $750 to Smith in Phoenix.

Jan. 5— Smith flies to Detroit from Phoenix to help Stant carry out the assault.

Jan. 6— Kerrigan is attacked by Stant following an afternoon practice at Cobo Arena. Stant clubs her in the right knee with a collapsible metal baton then makes his escape by running head first through a locked plexi-glass door and jumping into a getaway car driven by Smith. Gillooly withdraws another $3,000, gives Eckardt $1,300 to wire to Smith in Dearborn Heights, Mich. Eckardt, who says he threw up after seeing the injured Kerrigan crying on TV, tells Rev. Saunders the plan has been carried out.

Jan. 7— Smith and Stant fly back to Phoenix.

Jan. 8— With Kerrigan out of the way, Harding wins the national title for the second time. She had previously won in 1991.

THE AFTERMATH

Jan. 10— Harding and Gillooly return to Portland. Gillooly then meets with Eckardt to hammer out an alibi for the FBI explaining why they sent money to Smith. According to Eckardt, they would say Smith was helping them set up a security service for figure skaters.

Jan. 11— FBI agents interview Rev. Saunders.

Jan. 12— Eckardt's mother tells FBI about the Dec. 26 meeting. Eckardt confesses, giving FBI a signed statement. Smith also gives FBI a signed confession.

Jan. 14— Eckardt and Smith are arraigned in Portland and charged with conspiracy to commit assault. Eckardt is released on bail. Stant turns himself in to the FBI in Phoenix.

Jan. 16— Ten days after the attack, Kerrigan skates for the first time in Stoneham, Mass. Back in Portland, Diane and Dennis Rawlinson defend Harding at a press conference. Dennis, one of Harding's lawyers, reads a statement from Harding claiming she is innocent. Diane, who is Harding's coach, says Tonya will distance herself from Gillooly if he is shown to be involved.

Jan. 18— Stant is charged in Portland with conspiracy and a warrant is issued for Gillooly's arrest. The FBI and the Multnomah County DA's office question Harding for 10½ hours. Harding says she and Gillooly, who are already divorced, are separating but insists he is innocent.

Jan. 19— Gillooly surrenders to police and is charged with conspiracy to commit assault. In a statement released by her lawyers, Harding denies making the Dec. 28 phone calls to determine Kerrigan's practice schedule. Kerrigan resumes her jumping routine for the first time since the attack.

Jan. 20— Harding holds her first public practice session in Portland and lands several triple axels without a miss. An FBI spokesman in Portland announces that no federal charges will be filed in the attack.

Jan. 26— Gillooly meets for the first time with investigators amid speculation that he will implicate Harding in exchange for a lesser sentence.

Pascal Rondeau/Allsport

Nancy Kerrigan (left) and **Tonya Harding** do their best to avoid each other at an Olympic figure skating practice session in Hamar on Feb. 17.

Jan. 27— At a press conference attended by over 100 news media, Harding admits she knew about the attack on Kerrigan after it happened, but failed to notify the authorities. Her teary confession includes a plea to keep her place on the Olympic team.

Jan. 31— The U.S. Olympic Committee formally names Kerrigan and Harding to the team that will compete in Lillehammer.

Feb. 1— Gillooly pleads guilty to one count of racketeering in exchange for his testimony. The deal includes a two-year prison term and a $100,000 fine. He says Harding was in on the conspiracy from the beginning.

Feb. 5— The U.S. Figure Skating Assn., meeting in Colorado Springs, says there are "reasonable grounds" to believe Harding violated standards of ethics, fairness and sportsmanship.

Feb. 8— The USOC announces it will convene its Games Administrative Board on Feb. 15 to determine whether Harding violated several ethical standards.

Feb. 9— Harding's lawyers file a $25 million suit aimed at preventing the USOC from conducting hearings into whether their client should be kicked off the Olympic team.

Feb. 13— XVIIth Winter Olympics open in Lillehammer. Less than 12 hours later, the USOC agrees to keep Harding on the team if she will drop her lawsuit.

Feb. 23— Kerrigan wins technical program portion of the Women's Figure Skating competition, leads Ukrainian teenager and world champion Oksana Baiul and France's

Surya Bonaly with only long program remaining. Harding is 10th. Event pulls a 48.5 Nielsen rating on CBS, making it the sixth top-rated TV show of all time.

Feb. 25— Baiul edges Kerrigan for gold medal and Harding places 8th in women's final. Event gets a 44.1 rating. Baiul's late arrival for medal ceremony prompts impatient Kerrigan to say, "Oh, come on. She's just going to get out here and cry again." Unfortunately, the comment is overheard by tens of million of CBS viewers.

Feb. 27— While closing ceremonies are taking place in Lillehammer, Kerrigan is honored with a parade at Disney World where she is overheard telling Mickey Mouse, "This is corny. It's dumb. This is the corniest thing I've ever done."

Feb. 28— Over 200 fans and a mobilized media greet Harding on her return to Portland from Lillehammer.

Mar. 12— Kerrigan appears as guest host on NBC's "Saturday Night Live." Critics advise her to keep skating.

Mar. 16— Harding pleads guilty to conspiracy to hinder investigation which carries a $160,000 fine, three years probation, 500 hours of community service and an agreement to undergo psychological counseling. She also agrees to resign her membership in the U.S. Figure Skating Assn. and withdraw from the World Championships in Japan, Mar. 22-27.

May 2— Kerrigan and the U.S. Olympic team visit President Clinton at the White House. Harding blasts USOC for not inviting her to reception.

May 16— Hit man Stant and getaway driver Smith are each sentenced to 18 months in prison after pleading guilty to conspiracy to commit second degree assault.

June 30— The U.S. Figure Skating Association disciplinary panel strips Harding of her 1994 Women's title and bans her from membership in the USFSA for life.

July 11— Harding bodyguard Eckardt sentenced to 18 months in prison after pleading guilty to racketeering.

July 13— Despite the district attorney's recommendation for a more lenient penalty, judge Donald Londer sentences Gillooly to two years in prison for racketeering and fines him $100,000. Londer says Gillooly was "the primary moving force which led to the assault," adding that his actions were a blot on Portland's reputation that would linger long after his name is forgotten.

Aug. 2— The 25th anniversary edition of *Penthouse* magazine hits the newsstands with intimate pictures of Harding's wedding night splashed across nine pages. *Penthouse*, which acquired the photos from a third party, is also selling a copy of the video from which the stills were lifted.

Agence Vandystadt

Tommy Moe of the U.S. shows off his gold medal after winning the men's downhill on the first full day of medal competition at Lillehammer.

Kirvesniemi, 38, mother of two and husband of Harri, competed in her record-tying sixth Olympics and won two individual bronze medals. A decade ago, she had won three golds in Sarajevo.

Ski Jumping. After the 1992 Games, Espen Bredesen of Norway was mocked as "Espen the Eagle," a reference to myopic 1988 Olympian Eddie "The Eagle" Edwards of Great Britain, who was dead last in both jumping events. Bredesen had not done much better in 1992, when he was learning the sport's new "V" jumping form. He finished last in one event and third to last in another at Albertville.

Nonetheless, it became "V for Victory" for Bredesen, winner of the small hill and silver medalist to 1984 Olympic champion Jens Weissflog of Germany on the large hill. Weissflog became an anti-hero when his shameless attempt to psyche out a Japanese jumper worked well enough to beat Japan in the team event.

Ice Hockey. The Big Red Machine, which had hung together for one Olympics after the breakup of the Soviet Union, could not do it again. After winning three straight Olympic titles—and eight of 10 from 1956

to 1992—the Russian successor to the Soviet hockey team lost to Sweden 4-3 in the semifinals.

Sweden went on to beat Canada in the sudden-death phase of a penalty shootout after perhaps the most dramatic final match in Olympic history. The Canadians were 1:49 from winning their first hockey gold in 42 years when Sweden's Magnus Svensson tied the score at 2-2.

A 10-minute overtime and the first phase of the shootout—five shots for each team—failed to break the tie. On the second round of alternating sudden-death shots, Peter Forsberg scored for Sweden, and Paul Kariya of Canada was stopped by goalie Tommy Salo. Sweden (6-1-1) had its first Olympic hockey gold, a final-day performance that helped the country forget its worst overall Olympic performance (just three medals) in 18 years.

The U.S. was also miserable, finishing a woeful eighth with a 1-4-3 record.

Freestyle Skiing. Presumably unbeatable moguls defending champion Donna Weinbrecht of the U.S., whose comeback from knee surgery had become a CBS miniseries, finished seventh behind Stine Lise Hattestad of Norway.

Bobsled. In 1992, Harald Czudaj was a controversial member of the unified German team because he had been revealed as having served as an informer for the former East German secret police. Czudaj repaid those who supported him with an upset win over Swiss super pilot Gustav Weder in the four-man. Weder's sled won the two-man event.

Reigning World Cup champion Brian Shimer, who went into the Olympics with high hopes of winning the USA's first medal in 38 years, ended the Games in ignominy and defeat. After finishing 13th in the two-man, Shimer was disqualified from four-man for having overheated his sled runners. And the final blow: Jamaica, writing its own version of "Cool Runnings," beat both American sleds with its 14th place in four-man.

Luge. For the second straight Olympics, U.S. medal hopes proved false. Duncan Kennedy, a consistent World Cup medalist for three years, was fourth after two of the four runs but crashed on the third. Wendell Suckow, reigning world champion, struggled to place fifth after a poor start.

Swedish forward **Peter Forsberg** sweeps puck past Canadian goaltender **Corey Hirsch** for the winning goal in the hockey gold medal game. Sweden won in a sudden-death shootout on the final day of the Olympics.

Meanwhile, Germany's George Hackl won his second straight gold.

In women's singles, won by Italy's Gerda Weissensteiner, contender Cammy Myler, who carried the U.S. flag in the opening ceremonies, placed a disappointing 11th.

Biathlon. Myriam Bedard of Canada took both individual races, becoming the first North American athlete of either sex to win a gold medal.

Short Track. For years, short-trackers bristled when their sport was compared to roller derby. After the antics that took place in these Olympics, roller derby should take umbrage at being likened to short track.

One gold medalist and two silver medalists were disqualified for interference, pushing and general nastiness. The thing turned into such a circus that Samaranch told the sport to clean up its act or be booted from the Olympics.

Cathy Turner of the U.S., former lounge singer and author of the apparently autobiographical song, "Sexy, Kinky Tomboy," was at the center of two controversies and a member of the U.S. relay team that benefitted from a third.

Turner successfully defended her Olympic title in the 500 meters despite a protest by silver medalist Zhang Yanmei of China, who stormed off the awards stand because she thought Turner should have been disqualified for pushing. Later, in the 1,000 meters, Turner was disqualified for obstructing another skater.

South Korea won four of the six medals, with 13-year-old relay member Kim Yoon-Mi becoming the youngest medalist in Winter Olympic history. The silver medal won by the U.S. men's relay on the penultimate day of the Games became the record-breaking 13th medal for Uncle Sam, topping its previous highs of 12 at the Lake Placid Games of 1932 and '80. This achievement gets an asterisk, however, because there were 57 medal events in 1994—far more than the 38 of 1980 and the 14 of 1932. ❑

The Olympic flag being carried into the ski jumping stadium during opening ceremonies on Feb. 12, 1994.

Nathan Bilow/Allsport

THE 1995 SPORTS ALMANAC
INFORMATION PLEASE

OLYMPICS
STATISTICS

SEC
A

THE GAMES IN REVIEW
1994
LILLEHAMMER

PAGE
595

Final Medal Standings

Final results of XVIIth Olympic Winter Games at Lillehammer, Norway, Feb. 12-27, 1992. National medal standings are not recognized by the IOC. The unofficial point totals are based on 3 points for a gold medal, 2 for a silver and 1 for a bronze. Sixty-seven nations participated in the Games, but only 22 medaled.

		G	S	B	Medals	Pts			G	S	B	Medals	Pts
1	Norway	10	11	5	26	57	12	Finland	0	1	5	6	7
2	Russia	11	8	4	23	53		Kazakhstan	1	2	0	3	7
3	Germany	9	7	8	24	49	14	France	0	1	4	5	6
4	Italy	7	5	8	20	39	15	Holland	0	1	3	4	5
5	**United States**	6	5	2	13	30	16	China	0	1	2	3	4
6	Canada	3	6	4	13	25		Ukraine	1	0	1	2	4
7	Switzerland	3	4	2	9	19		Belarus	0	2	0	2	4
8	Austria	2	3	4	9	16	19	Slovenia	0	0	3	3	3
9	South Korea	4	1	1	6	15		Uzbekistan	1	0	0	1	3
10	Japan	1	2	2	5	9	20	Great Britain	0	0	2	2	2
11	Sweden	2	1	0	3	8	22	Australia	0	0	1	1	1
								TOTALS	61	61	61	183	366

1992 Albertville Top 10: 1. **Germany** (26 medals, 56 points); 2. **Unified Team** (23 medals, 47 pts); 3. **Norway** (20 medals, 44 pts); 4. **Austria** (21 medals, 40 pts); 5. **Italy** (14 medals, 28 pts); 6. **USA** (11 medals, 25 pts); 7. **France** (9 medals, 20 pts); 8. **Finland** and **Canada** (7 medals, 14 pts); 10. **Japan** (7 medals, 11 pts).

Leading Medal Winners

Number of individual medals won on the left; gold, silver and bronze medal breakdown on the right.

MEN

No		Sport	G-S-B
4	Bjorn Dählie, NOR	Cross-country	2-2-0
3	Johann Olav Koss, NOR	Speed Skating	3-0-0
3	Vladimir Smirnov, KAZ	Cross-country	1-2-0
3	Sergei Tarasov, RUS	Biathlon	1-1-1
3	Kjetil Andre Aamodt, NOR	Alpine	0-2-1
3	Mika Myllyla, FIN	Cross-country	0-1-2
2	Markus Wasmeier, GER	Alpine	2-0-0
2	Jens Weissflog, GER	Ski Jumping	2-0-0
2	Donat Acklin, SWI	Bobsled	1-1-0
2	Thomas Alsgaard, NOR	Cross-country	1-1-0
2	Espen Bredesen, NOR	Ski Jumping	1-1-0
2	Ji-Hoon Chae, S.Kor	ST Sp. Skating	1-1-0
2	Ricco Gross, GER	Biathlon	1-1-0
2	Takanori Kono, JPN	Nordic Comb.	1-1-0
2	Frank Luck, GER	Biathlon	1-1-0
2	Fred Borre Lundberg, NOR	Nordic Comb.	1-1-0
2	**Tommy Moe**, USA	Alpine	1-1-0
2	Sergei Chepikov, RUS	Biathlon	1-1-0
2	Mirko Vuillermin, ITA	ST Sp. Skating	1-1-0
2	Gustav Weder, SWI	Bobsled	1-1-0
2	Marco Albarello, ITA	Cross-country	1-0-1
2	Silvio Fauner, ITA	Cross-country	1-0-1
2	Sven Fischer, GER	Biathlon	1-0-1
2	Dieter Thoma, GER	Ski Jumping	1-0-1
2	Kjell Storelid, NOR	Speed Skating	0-2-0
2	Sergei Klevchenya, RUS	Speed Skating	0-1-1
2	Rintje Ritsma, HOL	Speed Skating	0-1-1
2	Sture Sivertsen, NOR	Cross-country	0-1-1
2	Bjarte Engen Vik, NOR	Nordic Comb.	0-1-1
2	Andreas Goldberger, AUT	Ski Jumping	0-0-2

WOMEN

No		Sport	G-S-B
5	Manuela Di Centa, ITA	Cross-country	2-2-1
4	Lyubov Egorova, RUS	Cross-country	3-1-0
3	Vreni Schneider, SWI	Alpine	1-1-1
2	Myriam Bedard, CAN	Biathlon	2-0-0
2	**Bonnie Blair,** USA	Speed Skating	2-0-0
2	Lee-Kyung Chun, S.Kor	ST Sp. Skating	2-0-0
2	Emese Hunyady, AUT	Speed Skating	1-1-0
2	Nina Gavriluk, RUS	Cross-country	1-0-1
2	So-Hee Kim, S.Kor	ST Sp. Skating	1-0-1
2	Claudia Pechstein, GER	Speed Skating	1-0-1
2	**Cathy Turner,** USA	ST Sp. Skating	1-0-1
2	Ann Briand, FRA	Biathlon	0-1-1
2	Ursula Disl, GER	Biathlon	0-1-1
2	Gunda Niemann, GER	Speed Skating	0-1-1
2	Stefina Belmondo, ITA	Cross-country	0-0-2
2	M.L. Kirvesniemi, FIN	Cross-country	0-0-2
2	Isolde Kostner, ITA	Alpine	0-0-2
2	**Amy Peterson,** USA	ST Sp. Skating	0-0-2

U.S. Medal Winners

The United States won 13 medals at Lillehammer.

Gold (6): Bonnie Blair (2), Dan Jansen, Tommy Moe, Diann Roffe-Steinrotter and Cathy Turner.

Silver (5): Nancy Kerrigan, Liz McIntyre, Tommy Moe, Picabo Street and Men's Short Track relay (Randy Bartz, John Coyle Eric Flaim, Andy Gabel).

Bronze (2): Amy Peterson and Women's Short Track relay (Karen Cashman, Amy Peterson, Cathy Turner, Nikki Ziegelmeyer).

MEDAL SPORTS

Medal winners in individual and team sports at Lillehammer, Norway, Feb. 12-27, 1994. Demonstration sports not included.

ALPINE SKIING

Medal breakdown (10 events): **Five medals**— Norway (1-2-2); **Four**— Germany (3-1-0), USA (2-2-0), Switzerland (1-2-1) and Italy (1-1-2); **Three**— Austria (1-1-1) and Slovenia (0-0-3); **One**— Sweden (1-0-0), Russia (0-1-0) and Canada (0-0-1).

MEN

Downhill

		Time
1	Tommy Moe, USA	1:45.75
2	Kjetil Andre Aamodt, NOR	1:45.79
3	Ed Podivinsky, CAN	1:45.87

Next best USA: 11th, Kyle Rasmussen (1:46.35).

Slalom

		Time
1	Thomas Stangassinger, AUT	2:02.02
2	Alberto Tomba, ITA	2:02.17
3	Jure Kosir, SLO	2:02.53

Top 10 USA: 7th, Casey Puckett (2:03.47).

Giant Slalom

		Time
1	Markus Wasmeier, GER	2:52.46
2	Urs Kaelin, SWI	2:52.48
3	Christian Mayer, AUT	2:52.58

Top 10 USA: 9th, Jeremy Nobis (2:53.60).

Super G

		Time
1	Markus Wasmeier, GER	1:32.53
2	Tommy Moe, USA	1:32.61
3	Kjetil Andre Aamodt, NOR	1:32.93

Next best USA: none.

Combined

Downhill (Feb. 14) and Slalom (Feb. 25)

		DH	SL	Time
1	Lasse Kjus, NOR	1st	7th	3:17.53
2	Kjetil Andre Aamodt, NOR	6th	9th	3:18.55
3	Harald Strand Nilsen, NOR	21st	4th	3:19.14

Top 10 USA: 5th Tommy Moe (3rd; 15th, 3:19.41).

WOMEN

Downhill

		Time
1	Katja Seizinger, GER	1:35.93
2	Picabo Street, USA	1:36.59
3	Isolde Kostner, ITA	1:36.85

Other Top 10 USA: 7th, Hilary Lindh (1:37.44).

Slalom

		Time
1	Vreni Schneider, SWI	1:56.01
2	Elfriede Eder, AUT	1:56.35
3	Katja Koren, SLO	1:56.61

Best USA: 18th, Carrie Sheinberg (2:00.16).

Giant Slalom

		Time
1	Deborah Compagnoni, ITA	2:30.97
2	Martina Ertl, GER	2:32.19
3	Vreni Schneider, SWI	2:32.97

Top 10 USA: 6th, Eva Twardokens (2:34.41).

Super G

		Time
1	Diann Roffe-Steinrotter, USA	1:22.15
2	Svetlana Gladischeva, RUS	1:22.44
3	Isolda Kostner, ITA	1:22.45

Other Top 10 USA: 10th, Shannon Nobis (1:23.02).

Combined

Downhill (Feb. 20) and Slalom (Feb. 21)

		DH	SL	Time
1	Pernilla Wiberg, SWE	5th	2nd	3:05.16
2	Vreni Schneider, SWI	7th	1st	3:05.29
3	Alenka Dovzan, SLO	4th	3rd	3:06.64

Top 10 USA: 10th, Picabo Street (2nd, 14th; 3:10.15).

FIGURE SKATING

All four events consist of a short program (two minutes and 40 seconds) and a long program (4:30 for men and 4:00 for women). Skaters are ranked on technical merit and artistic impression in a consensus vote by nine judges. Factored placements (FP) are determined by multiplying the final short program rank by 0.5 and then adding that number to the final long program rank.

Medal breakdown (4 events): **Five medals**— Russia (3-2-0); **Two**— Canada (0-1-1); **One**— Ukraine (1-0-0), USA (0-1-0), China (0-0-1), France (0-0-1) and Great Britain (0-0-1).

MEN

		FP
1	Alexei Urmanov, RUS	1.5
2	Elvis Stojko, CAN	3.0
3	Philippe Candeloro, FRA	6.5

Top 10 USA: 6th, Brian Boitano (10.0); 8th, Scott Davis (10.0).

PAIRS

		FP
1	Ekaterina Gordeeva & Sergei Grinkov, RUS	1.5
2	Natalya Mishkutienok & Artur Dmitriev, UT	3.0
3	Isabelle Brasseur & Lloyd Eisler, CAN	4.5

Top 10 USA: 5th, Jenni Meno & Todd Sand (8.0); 9th, Kyoka Ina & Jason Dungjen (14.5).

WOMEN

		FP
1	Oksana Baiul, UKR	2.0
2	Nancy Kerrigan, USA	2.5
3	Chen Lu, CHN	5.0

Other Top 10 USA: 8th, Tonya Harding (12.0).

ICE DANCING

		FP
1	Oksana Gritschuk & Yevgeny Platov, RUS	3.0
2	Maia Usova & Alexander Zhulin, UT	3.8
3	Jayne Torvill & Christopher Dean, GBR	4.8

Best USA: 15th, Elizabeth Punsalan & Jerod Swallow (29.0).

Wide World Photos

Women's figure skating winners (from left to right): bronze medalist **Chen Lu** of China, champion **Oksana Baiul** of the Ukraine and silver medal winner **Nancy Kerrigan** of the U.S.

BIATHLON

Cross-country (any style) and rifle shooting (.22 caliber, small-bore, standing and prone). MT indicates missed targets.

Medal breakdown (6 events): **Six medals**— Germany (1-3-2); **Five**— Russia (3-1-1); **Three**— France (0-1-2); **Two**— Canada (2-0-0); **One**— Belarus (0-1-0) and Ukraine (0-0-1).

MEN

10 kilometers

		MT	Time
1	Sergei Chepikov, RUS	0	28:07.0
2	Ricco Gross, GER	0	28:13.0
3	Sergei Tarasov, RUS	1	28:27.4

Best USA: 64th, David Jareckie (4 MTs; 33:15.6).

20 kilometers

		MT	Time
1	Sergei Tarasov, RUS	3	57:25.3
2	Frank Luck, GER	3	57:28.7
3	Sven Fischer, GER	2	57:41.9

Best USA: 64th, Jon Engen (4 MTs; 1:06:39.7).

4 x 7.5-km Relay

		MT	Time
1	Germany	0	1:30:22.1
2	Russia	2	1:31:23.6
3	France	1	1:32:31.3

GER— Ricco Gross, Frank Luck, Mark Kirchner, Sven Fischer; **RUS**— Valeri Kirienko, Vladimir Dratchev, Sergei Tarasov, Sergei Chepikov; **FRA**— Thierry Dusserre, Patrice Bailly-Salins, Lionel Laurent, Herve Flandin.
  USA entry: 14th; Curt Schreiner, David Jareckie, Jon Engen, Duncan Douglas; (0 MTs; 1:35:43.7).

WOMEN

7.5 kilometers

		MT	Time
1	Myriam Bedard, CAN	2	26:08.8
2	Svetlana Paramygina, BLR	2	26:09.9
3	Valentyna Tserbe, UKR	0	26:10.0

Best USA: 24th, Joan Smith (2 MTs; 27:39.1).

15 kilometers

		MT	Time
1	Myriam Bedard, CAN	2	52:06.6
2	Anne Briand, FRA	3	52:53.3
3	Ursula Disl, GER	3	53:15.3

Best USA: 14th, Joan Smith (3 MTs; 54:46.7).

4 x 7.5-km Relay

		MT	Time
1	Russia	0	1:47:19.5
2	Germany	0	1:51:16.5
3	France	1	1:52:28.3

RUS— Nadejda Talanova, Natalya Snytina, Louiza Noskova, Anfisa Reztsova; **GER**— Ursula Disl, Harvey, Simone Greiner-Petter-Memm, Petra Schaaf; **FRA**— Corinne Niogret, Veronique Claudel, Delphyne Heymann, Anne Briand.
  USA entry: 8th; Beth Coats, Joan Smith, Laura Tavares, Joan Guetschow (0 MTs; 1:57:35.9).

CROSS-COUNTRY SKIING

There are two techniques in cross-country: classical (diagonal stride) and freestyle (skating style). The Freestyle Pursuit consists of a classical race (10 km for men, 5 km for women) followed the next day by a freestyle race (15 km for men, 10 km for women). The starting order in the Freestyle Pursuit is determined by the finish of the classical leg. Relays consist of two classical and two freestyle legs.

Medal breakdown (10 events): **Nine medals**— Italy (3-2-4); **Eight**— Norway (3-4-1); **Five**— Russia (3-1-1) and Finland (0-1-4); **Three**— Kazakhstan (1-2-0).

MEN
10-km Classical

		Time
1	Bjorn Dählie, NOR	24:20.1
2	Vladimir Smirnov, KAZ	24:38.3
3	Marco Albarello, ITA	24:42.3

Best USA: 41st, Todd Boonstra (26:56.3).

15-km Freestyle Pursuit

		Overall Time
1	Bjorn Dählie, NOR	1:00:08.8
2	Vladimir Smirnov, KAZ	1:00:38.0
3	Silvio Fauner, ITA	1:01:48.6

Best USA: 33rd, John Aalberg (1:05:33.4).

30-km Freestyle

		Time
1	Thomas Alsgaard, NOR	1:12:26.4
2	Bjorn Dählie, NOR	1:13:13.6
3	Mika Myllyla, FIN	1:14:14.0

Best USA: 36th, Luke Bodensteiner (1:20:13.0).

50-km Classical

		Time
1	Vladimir Smirnov, KAZ	2:07:20.3
2	Mika Myllyla, FIN	2:08:41.9
3	Sture Sivertsen, NOR	2:08:49.0

Best USA: 35th, Justin Wadsworth (2:19:49.1).

4 x 10-km Mixed Relay

		Time
1	Italy	1:41:15.0
2	Norway	1:41:15.4
3	Finland	1:42:15.6

ITA— Maurilio De Zolt, Marco Albarello, Giorgio Vanzetta, Silvio Fauner; **NOR**— Sture Sivertsen, Vegard Ulvang, Thomas Alsgaard, Bjorn Dählie; **FIN**— Mika Myllyla, Harri Kirvesniemi, Jari Rasanen, Jari Isometsa.
USA entry: 13th; John Aalberg, Ben Husaby, Todd Boonstra, Luke Bodensteiner (1:49:40.5).

Wide World Photos

Norwegian cross-country skier **Thomas Alsgaard** on the shoulders of silver medalist and teammate **Bjorn Dählie** after winning the men's 30-kilometer freestyle.

WOMEN

5-km Classical

		Time
1	Lyubov Egorova, RUS	14:08.8
2	Manuela Di Centa, ITA	14:28.3
3	Marja-Liisa Kirvesniemi, FIN	14:36.0

Best USA: 28th, Nina Kemppel (15:44.8).

10-km Freestyle Pursuit

		Overall Time
1	Lyubov Egorova, RUS	41:38.1
2	Manuela Di Centa, ITA	41:46.4
3	Stefania Belmondo, ITA	42:21.1

Best USA: 31st, Nina Kemppel (46:21.8).

15-km Freestyle

		Time
1	Manuela Di Centa, ITA	39:44.5
2	Lyubov Egorova, RUS	41:03.0
3	Nina Gavriluk, RUS	41:10.4

Best USA: 34th, Laura McCabe (45:51.1).

30-km Classical

		Time
1	Manuela Di Centa, ITA	1:25:41.6
2	Marit Wold, NOR	1:25:57.8
3	Marja-Liisa Kirvesniemi, FIN	1:26:13.6

Note: Russia's Lyubov Egorova finished 5th (1:26:54.8).
Best USA: 27th, Nina Kemppel (1:32:55.3).

4 x 5-km Mixed Relay

		Time
1	Russia	57:12.5
2	Norway	57:42.6
3	Italy	58:42.6

RUS— Elena Valbe, Larisa Lazutina, Nina Gavriluk, Lyubov Egorova; **NOR**— Trude Dybendahl, Inger Helene Nybraaten, Elin Nilsen, Anita Moen; **ITA**— Bice Vanzetta, Manuela Di Centa, Gabriella Paruzzi, Stefania Belmondo.
USA entry: 10th; Laura Wilson, Nina Kemppel, Laura McCabe, Leslie Thompson (1:02:28.4).

ICE HOCKEY

Medal breakdown (1 event): **One medal**— Sweden (1-0-0), Canada (0-1-0) and Finland (0-0-1).

Round Robin Standings

First four teams in each group advanced to medal round.

Group A	Gm	W-L-T	Pts	GF	GA
* Finland	5	5-0-0	10	25	4
* Germany	5	3-2-0	6	11	14
* Czech Republic	5	3-2-0	6	16	11
* Russia	5	3-2-0	6	20	14
Austria	5	1-4-0	2	13	28
Norway	5	0-5-0	0	5	19

Note: Second place tie broken by goal differential in three common games. Germany (+1) beat Russia, 4-2, and lost to Czechs, 0-1; Czechs (0) beat Germany, 1-0, and lost to Russia, 3-4; and Russia (-1) beat Czechs 4-3, and lost to Germany, 2-4.

Group B	Gm	W-L-T	Pts	GF	GA
* Slovakia	5	3-0-2	8	26	14
* Canada	5	3-1-1	7	17	11
* Sweden	5	3-1-1	7	23	13
* United States	5	1-1-3	5	21	17
Italy	5	1-4-0	2	15	31
France	5	0-4-1	1	11	27

Note: Second place tie broken by goal differential in one common game between Canada and Sweden. Canada won, 3-2.

Quarterfinals

Sweden 3		Germany 0
Canada 3	OT	Czech Republic 2
Finland 6		United States 1
Russia 3	OT	Slovakia 2

Semifinals

Sweden 4	Russia 3
Canada 5	Finland 3

Bronze Medal

Finland 4	Russia 0

Gold Medal

Sweden 2	OT	Canada 2

(Sweden wins shootout, 3-2)

Leading Scorers

Includes all games; goals scored in Sweden-Canada shootout periods not included.

	Gm	G	A	Pts	PM
Zigmund Palffy, SLO	8	3	7	10	8
Miroslav Satan, SLO	8	9	0	9	0
Peter Stastny, SLO	8	5	4	9	9
Hakan Loob, SWE	8	4	5	9	2
Gaets Orlando, ITA	7	3	6	9	4
Patrik Juhlin, SWE	8	7	1	8	16
Jiri Kucera, CZE	8	6	2	8	4
Marty Dallman, AUT	7	4	4	8	8
Mika Nieminen, FIN	8	3	5	8	0
David Sacco, USA	8	3	5	8	12
Peter Forsberg, SWE	8	2	6	8	6
Brian Rolston, USA	8	7	0	7	8
Roger Hansson, SWE	8	5	2	7	4
Saku Koivu, FIN	8	4	3	7	12
Ville Peltonen, FIN	8	4	3	7	0
Paul Kariya, CAN	8	3	4	7	2
Richard Zemlicka, CZE	8	3	4	7	6
Otakar Janecky, CZE	8	2	5	7	6
Andrei Nikolishin, RUS	8	2	5	7	6
Oto Hascak, SLO	8	1	6	7	4
Robert Petrovicky, SLO	8	1	6	7	18

Gold Medal Game

	1	2	3	OT	F
Canada	0	0	2	0	2
Sweden	1	0	1	0	2

Scoring: 1ST PERIOD— Tomas Jonsson, SWE (Hakan Loob, Peter Forsberg), 6:10 (pp). 3RD PERIOD— Paul Kariya, CAN (Chris Kontos, Greg Johnson), 9:08; Derek Mayer, CAN (unassisted), 11:43; Magnus Svensson, SWE (Forsberg, T. Jonsson), 18:11 (pp).

Goaltenders: CANADA— Corey Hirsch (42 shots, 40 saves); SWEDEN— Tommy Salo (21 shots, 19 saves).

Shootout

	1st Round						Sudden Death		
	1	2	3	4	5	T		1	2	T
Canada	1	1	0	0		2	Sweden	0	1	1
Sweden	0	1	0	1		2	Canada	0	0	0

1st Round— 1. Peter Nedved, CAN (goal); 2. Haken Loob, SWE (miss); 3. Paul Kariya, CAN (goal); 4. Magnus Svensson, SWE (goal); 5. Dwayne Norris, CAN (miss); 6. Mats Naslund, SWE (miss); 7. Greg Parks, CAN (miss); 8. Peter Forsberg, SWE (goal); 9. Greg Johnson, CAN (miss); 10. Roger Hansson, SWE (miss).
Sudden Death— 1. Magnus Svensson, SWE (miss); 2. Peter Nedved, CAN (miss); 3. Peter Forsberg, SWE (goal); 4. Paul Kariya, CAN (miss).

Leading Goaltenders

Minimum 180 minutes.

	Gm	Min	SV%	GAA	Record
Jarmo Myllys, FIN	5	300	.967	0.60	5-0-0
Corey Hirsch, CAN	8	495	.930	2.06	5-2-1
Tommy Salo, SWE	6	370	.896	2.11	5-1-0
Petr Briza, CZE	7	381	.899	2.36	4-2-0
Klaus Merk, GER	3	180	.916	2.67	3-0-0
Andrei Zuev, RUS	5	288	.866	3.13	3-2-0
Eduard Hartmann, SLO	5	309	.861	3.29	1-2-2

Shutouts: Finland 3 (Myllys 2, Jukka Tammi); Czech Rep. (Briza); Sweden (Salo).

LUGE

MEN

Medal breakdown (3 events): **Four medals**— Italy (2-1-1); **Three**— Germany (1-1-1); **Two**— Austria (0-1-1).

Singles

		Time
1	Georg Hackl, GER	3:21.571
2	Markus Prock, AUT	3:21.584
3	Armin Zoggeler, ITA	3:21.833

Top 10 USA: 5th, Wendel Suckow (3:22.424).

Doubles

		Time
1	Kurt Brugger & Wilfried Huber, ITA	1:36.720
2	Hansjorg Raffl & Norbert Huber, ITA	1:36.769
3	Stefan Krausse & Jan Behrendt, GER	1:36.945

Top 10 USA: 4th, Mark Grimmette & Jonathan Edwards (1:37.289); 5th, Chris Thorpe & Gordy Sheer (1:37.296).

WOMEN

Singles

		Time
1	Gerda Weissensteiner, ITA	3:15.517
2	Susi Erdmann, GER	3:16.276
2	Andrea Tagwerker, AUT	3:16.652

Best USA: 11th, Cammy Myler (3:17.834).

SPEED SKATING

The long track oval measures 400-meters (1,312 feet). Distance laps: 500m (1¼ laps); 1,000m (2½ laps); 1,500m (3¾ laps); 3,000m (7½ laps); 5,000m (12½ laps); 10,000m (25 laps).

Medal breakdown (10 events): **Six medals**— Germany (1-2-3); **Five**— Norway (3-2-0) and Russia (2-2-1); **Four**— Holland (0-1-3); **Three**— USA (3-0-0); **Two**— Austria (1-1-0) and Japan (0-0-2); **One**— Belarus (0-1-0), Canada (0-1-0) and China (0-0-1).

MEN
500 meters

		Time	
1	Aleksandr Golubev, RUS	36.33	OR
2	Sergei Klevchenya, RUS	36.39	
3	Manabu Horii, JPN	36.53	

Top 10 USA: 8th, Dan Jansen (36.68).

1000 meters

		Time	
1	Dan Jansen, USA	1:12.43	WR
2	Igor Zhelezovsky, BLR	1:12.72	
3	Sergei Klevchenya, RUS	1:12.85	

Next best USA: 21st, Nathaniel Mills (1:15.11).

1500 meters

		Time	
1	Johann Olav Koss, NOR	1:51.29	WR
2	Rintje Ritsma, HOL	1:51.99	
3	Falko Zandstra, HOL	1:52.38	

Best USA: 22nd (tie), David Tamburrino (1:55.78).

5000 meters

		Time	
1	Johann Olav Koss, NOR	6:34.96	WR
2	Kjell Storelid, NOR	6:42.68	
3	Rintje Ritsma, HOL	6:43.94	

Best USA: 30th, Brian Wanek (7:05.95).

10,000 meters

		Time	
1	Johann Olav Koss, NOR	13:30.55	WR
2	Kjell Storelid, NOR	13:49.25	
3	Bart Veldkamp, HOL	13:56.73	

Best USA: No entries in final round.

WOMEN
500 meters

		Time
1	Bonnie Blair, USA	39.25
2	Susan Auch, CAN	39.61
3	Franziska Schenk, GER	39.70

Next Best USA: 20th, Kristen Talbot (41.05).

1000 meters

		Time
1	Bonnie Blair, USA	1:18.74
2	Anke Baier, GER	1:20.12
3	Ye Qiaobo, CHN	1:20.22

Next Best USA: 23rd, Christine Witty (1:22.42).

1500 meters

		Time
1	Emese Hunyady, AUT	2:02.19
2	Svetlana Fedotkina, RUS	2:02.69
3	Gunda Niemann, GER	2:03.41

Top 10 USA: 4th, Bonnie Blair (2:03.44).

3000 meters

		Time
1	Svetlana Bazhanova, RUS	4:17.43
2	Emese Hunyady, AUT	4:18.14
3	Claudia Pechstein, GER	4:18.34

Best USA: 19th, Angela Zuckerman (4:33.08).

5000 meters

		Time
1	Claudia Pechstein, GER	7:14.37
2	Gunda Niemann, GER	7:14.88
2	Hiromi Yamamoto, JPN	7:19.68

Best USA: No Americans qualified for final.

SHORT TRACK SPEED SKATING

The short track oval is 111 meters (364 feet).

Medal breakdown (6 events): **Six medals**— South Korea (4-1-1); **Four**— USA (1-1-2); **Three**— Canada (0-2-1); **Two**— Italy (1-1-0); **One**— China (0-1-0), Australia (0-0-1) and Great Britain (0-0-1).

MEN
500 meters

		Time
1	Ji-Hoon Chae, S.Kor	43.45
2	Mirko Vuillermin, ITA	43.47
3	Nicholas Gooch, GBR	43.68

Best USA: No Americans qualified for final.

1000 meters

		Time
1	Ki-Hoon Kim, S.Kor	1:34.57
2	Ji-Hoon Chae, S.Kor	1:34.92
3	Marc Gagnon, CAN	DNF

Best USA: No Americans qualified for final.

5000M Relay

		Time	
1	Italy	7:11.74	OR
2	United States	7:13.37	
3	Australia	7:13.68	

USA— Randy Bartz, John Coyle, Eric Flaim, Andy Gabel.

WOMEN
500 meters

		Time	
1	Cathy Turner, USA	45.98	OR
2	Yanmei Zhang, CHN	46.44	
3	Amy Peterson, USA	46.76	

Next best USA: No other Americans qualified for final.

1000 meters

		Time
1	Lee-Kyung Chun, S.Kor	1:36.87
2	Nathalie Lambert, CAN	1:36.97
3	So-Hee Kim, S.Kor	1:37.09

Best USA: Cathy Turner was disqualified in semifinals.

3000M Relay

		Time	
1	South Korea	4:26.64	WR
2	Canada	4:32.04	
3	United States	4:39.34	

USA: Peterson, Turner, Nikki Ziegelmeyer, Karen Cashman.
Note: China was stripped of silver medal after officials ruled they interfered with U.S. skaters.

FREESTYLE SKIING

Aerials consist of two jumps with points awarded for execution and precision (50%), height and distance (20%) and landing (30%). Moguls consist of turns executed on bumpy course (50%), two aerials (25%) and elapsed time (25%).

Medal breakdown (4 events): **Three medals**— Canada (1-1-1); **Two**— Norway (1-0-1) and Russia (0-1-1); **One**— Switzerland (1-0-0), Uzbekistan (1-0-0), Sweden (0-1-0), USA (0-1-0) and France (0-0-1).

MEN
Aerials
		Pts
1	Andreas Schoenbaechler, SWI	234.67
2	Philippe Laroche, CAN	228.63
3	Lloyd Langlois, CAN	222.44

Top 10 USA: 5th, Trace Worthington (218.19 pts).

Moguls
		Pts
1	Jean-Luc Brassard, CAN	27.24
2	Sergei Shoupletsov, RUS	26.90
3	Edgar Grospiron, FRA	26.64

Top 10 USA: 8th, Troy Benson (24.86 pts).

WOMEN
Aerials
		Pts
1	Lina Cherjazova, UZB	166.84
2	Marie Lindgren, SWE	165.88
3	Hilde Synnove Lid, NOR	164.13

Top 10 USA: 7th, Tracy Evans (139.77 pts).

Moguls
		Pts
1	Stine Lise Hattestad, NOR	25.97
2	Liz McIntyre, USA	25.89
3	Elizaveta Kojevnikova, RUS	25.81

Other Top 10 USA: 7th, Donna Weinbrecht (24.38 pts); 8th, Ann Battelle (23.71 pts).

NORDIC COMBINED

Three jumps off normal hill (best two count) followed the next day by a 15-km cross-country race. The cross-country starting order determined by finish of ski jump.

Medal breakdown (2 events): **Three medals**— Norway (1-1-1); **Two**— Japan (1-1-0); **One**— Switzerland (0-0-1).

Individual
		Jump	15km	Points
1	Fred Borre Lundberg, NOR	1st	8th	457.970
2	Takanori Kono, JPN	4th	13th	446.345
3	Bjarte Engen Vik, NOR	3rd	15th	446.175

Best USA: 13th, Todd Lodwick (5th, 43rd, 410.975 pts).

Team
		Jump	3x10km	Points
1	Japan	1st	3rd	1368.860
2	Norway	2nd	2nd	1310.940
3	Switzerland	3rd	4th	1275.240

JPN— Takanori Kono, Masashi Abe, Kenji Ogiwara; **NOR**— Knut Tore Apeland, Bjarte Engen Vik, Fred Borre Lundberg; **SWI**— Hippolyt Kempf, Jean-Yves Cuendet, Andreas Schaad.
USA entry: 7th; David Jarrett, Ryan Heckman, Todd Lodwick (7th, 8th, 1209.640 pts).

BOBSLED

Medal breakdown (2 events): **Three medals**— Switzerland (1-2-0); **Two**— Germany (1-0-1); **One**— Italy (0-0-1).

Two-Man
		Time
1	Switzerland I	3:30.81
2	Switzerland II	3:30.86
3	Italy I	3:31.01

SWI I— Gustav Weder & Donat Acklin; **SWI II**— Reto Goetschi & Guido Acklin; **ITA I**— Gunther Huber & Stefano Ticci.
Best USA: 13th, USA I— Brian Shimer & Randy Jones (3:32.85).

Four-Man
		Time
1	Germany II	3:27.78
2	Switzerland I	3:27.84
3	Germany I	3:28.01

GER II— Harald Czudaj (driver), Karsten Brannasch, Olaf Hampel, Alexander Szelig; **SWI I**— Gustav Weder (driver), Donat Acklin, Kurt Meier, Domenico Semeraro; **GER I**— Wolfgang Hoppe (driver), Ulf Hielscher, Rene Hannemann, Carsten Embach.
Top 10 USA: 15th, USA I— Randy Will (driver), Jeff Woodward, Joe Sawyer, Chris Coleman, (3:29.97).

SKI JUMPING

Each contestant gets two jumps with points awarded for distance and style. The normal hill is 90 meters (295 feet) and the large hill is 120 meters (394 feet).

Medal breakdown (3 events): **Four medals**— Germany (2-1-1); **Two**— Norway (1-1-0) and Austria (0-0-2); Japan (0-1-0).

Normal Hill
		1st (ft)	2nd (ft)	Pts
1	Espen Bredesen, NOR	329-8	341-2	282.0
2	Lasse Ottesen, NOR	336-3	321-6	268.0
3	Dieter Thoma, GER	323-1	336-3	260.5

Best USA: 33rd, Tad Langlois (287-0; 255-10: 197.0 pts).

Large Hill
		1st (ft)	2nd (ft)	Pts
1	Jens Weissflog, GER	424-10	436-4	274.5
2	Espen Bredesen, NOR	444-6	400-3	266.5
3	Andreas Goldberger, AUT	421-7	398-7	255.0

Best USA: 35th, Tad Langlois (318-2, 310-0; 135.2 pts).

Team (Large Hill)
		Pts
1	Germany	970.1
2	Japan	956.9
3	Austria	918.9

GER— Hansjorg Jaekle, Christof Duffner, Dieter Thoma, Jens Weissflog; **JPN**— Jinya Nishikata, Takanobu Okabe, Noriaki Kasai, Masahiko Harada; **AUT**— Heinz Kuttin, Christian Moser, Stefan Horngacher, Andreas Goldberger.
USA entry: 11th; Randy Weber, Greg Boester, Kurt Stein, Tad Langlois (505.0 pts).

Olympic Postscript

• Luger **Cammy Myler** carried the American flag at the head of the U.S. team in the parade of nations.
• Norwegian ski jumper **Stein Gruben** replaced injured **Ole Gunnar Fidjestol** and soared into the Olympic stadium and landed safely holding the Olympic torch aloft. Fidjestol had crashed and suffered a concussion during rehearsals two days before.
• On the 10th anniversary of the Winter Games in wartorn Sarajevo, nine athletes represented Bosnia-Herzegovina.

OLYMPICS STATISTICS

THROUGH THE YEARS
1924-1994
WINTER GAMES

THE 1995 INFORMATION PLEASE SPORTS ALMANAC

SEC B

PAGE 602

The Winter Olympics

The move toward a winter version of the Olympics began in 1908 when figure skating made an appearance at the Summer Games in London. Ten-time world champion Ulrich Salchow of Sweden, who originated the backwards, one revolution jump that bears his name, and Madge Syers of Britain were the first singles champions. Germans Anna Hubler and Heinrich Berger won the pairs competition.

Organizers of the 1916 Summer Games in Berlin planned to introduce a "Skiing Olympia," featuring nordic events in the Black Forest, but the Games were cancelled after the outbreak of World War I in 1914.

The Games resumed in 1920 at Antwerp, Belgium, where figure skating returned and ice hockey was added as a medal event. Sweden's Gillis Grafstrom and Magda Julin took individual honors, while Ludovika and Walter Jakobsson were the top pair. In hockey, Canada won the gold medal with the United States second and Czechoslovakia third.

Despite the objections of Modern Olympics' founder Baron Pierre de Coubertin and the resistance of the Scandinavian countries, which had staged their own Nordic championships every four or five years from 1901-26 in Sweden, the International Olympic Committee sanctioned an "International Winter Sports Week" at Chamonix, France, in 1924. The 11-day event, which included nordic skiing, speed skating, figure skating, ice hockey and bobsledding, was a huge success and was retroactively called the First Olympic Winter Games.

Seventy years after those first cold weather Games, the 17th edition of the Winter Olympics took place in Lillehammer, Norway, in 1994. The event ended the four-year Olympic cycle of staging both Winter and Summer Games in the same year and began a new schedule that calls for the two Games to alternate every two years.

Year	No	Location	Dates	Nations	Most medals	USA Medals
1924	I	Chamonix, FRA	Jan. 25-Feb. 4	16	Norway (4-7-6—17)	1-2-1— 4 (3rd)
1928	II	St. Moritz, SWI	Feb. 11-19	25	Norway (6-4-5—15)	2-2-2— 6 (2nd)
1932	III	Lake Placid, NY	Feb. 4-15	17	USA (6-4-2—12)	6-4-2—12 (1st)
1936	IV	Garmisch-Partenkirchen, GER	Feb. 6-16	28	Norway (7-5-3—15)	1-0-3— 4 (T-5th)
1940-a	—	Sapporo, JPN	Cancelled (WWII)			
1944	—	Cortina d'Ampezzo, ITA	Cancelled (WWII)			
1948	V	St. Moritz, SWI	Jan. 30-Feb. 8	28	Norway (4-3-3—10), Sweden (4-3-3—10) & Switzerland (3-4-3—10)	3-4-2— 9 (4th)
1952-b	VI	Oslo, NOR	Feb. 14-25	30	Norway (7-3-6—16)	4-6-1—11 (2nd)
1956-c	VII	Cortina d'Ampezzo, ITA	Jan. 26-Feb. 5	32	USSR (7-3-6—16)	2-3-2— 7 (T-4th)
1960	VIII	Squaw Valley, CA	Feb. 18-28	30	USSR (7-5-9—21)	3-4-3—10 (2nd)
1964	IX	Innsbruck, AUT	Jan. 29-Feb. 9	36	USSR (11-8-6—25)	1-2-3— 6 (7th)
1968-d	X	Grenoble, FRA	Feb. 6-18	37	Norway (6-6-2—14)	1-5-1— 7 (T-7th)
1972	XI	Sapporo, JPN	Feb. 3-13	35	USSR (8-5-3—16)	3-2-3— 8 (6th)
1976-e	XII	Innsbruck, AUT	Feb. 4-15	37	USSR (13-6-8—27)	3-3-4—10 (T-3rd)
1980	XIII	Lake Placid, NY	Feb. 14-23	37	E.Germany (9-7-7—23)	6-4-2—12 (3rd)
1984	XIV	Sarajevo, YUG	Feb. 7-19	49	USSR (6-10-9—25)	4-4-0— 8 (T-5th)
1988	XV	Calgary, CAN	Feb. 13-28	57	USSR (11-9-9—29)	2-1-3— 6 (T-8th)
1992-f	XVI	Albertville, FRA	Feb. 8-23	63	Germany (10-10-6—26)	5-4-2—11 (6th)
1994-g	XVII	Lillehammer, NOR	Feb. 12-27	67	Norway (10-11-5—26)	6-5-2—13 (T-5th)
1998	XVIII	Nagano, JPN	Feb. 7-22			

a—The 1940 Winter Games are originally scheduled for Sapporo, but Japan resigns as host in 1937 when the Sino-Japanese war breaks out. St. Moritz is the next choice, but the Swiss feel that ski instructors should not be considered professionals and the IOC withdraws its offer. Finally, Garmisch-Partenkirchen is asked to serve again as host, but the Germans invade Poland in 1939 and the Games are eventually cancelled.

b—Germany and Japan are allowed to rejoin the Olympic community for the first time since World War II. Though a divided country, the Germans send a joint East-West team.

c—The Soviet Union (USSR) participates in its first Winter Olympics and takes home the most medals, including the gold medal in ice hockey.

d—East Germany and West Germany officially send separate teams for the first time and will continue to do so through 1988.

e—The IOC grants the 1976 Winter Games to Denver in May 1970, but in 1972 Colorado voters reject a $5 million bond issue to finance the undertaking. Denver immediately withdraws as host and the IOC selects Innsbruck, the site of the 1964 Games, to take over.

f—Germany sends a single team after East and West German reunification in 1990 and the USSR competes as the Unified Team after the breakup of the Soviet Union in 1991.

g—In 1988, the IOC votes to move the Winter Games' four-year cycle ahead two years in order to separate them from the Summer Games and alternate Olympics every two years.

As of Sept. 1, 1994, the following nine cities were bidding to host the 2002 Winter Games (in alphabetical order): Graz, Austria; Jaca, Spain; Oestersund, Sweden; Poprad-Tatry, Slovakia; Quebec City, Canada; **Salt Lake City, USA;** Sion, Switzerland; Sochi, Russia; Tarvisio, Italy. The winner will be announced at the IOC 104th Session, June 15-17, 1995 in Budapest, Hungary.

Event-by-Event

Gold medal winners from 1924-94 in the following events: Alpine Skiing, Biathlon, Bobsled, Cross-country Skiing, Figure Skating, Ice Hockey, Luge, Nordic Combined, Ski Jumping and Speed Skating.

ALPINE SKIING

MEN

Multiple gold medals: Jean-Claude Killy, Toni Sailer and Alberto Tomba (3); Henri Oreiller, Ingemar Stenmark and Markus Wasmeier (2).

Downhill

Year		Time	Year		Time
1948	Henri Oreiller, FRA	2:55.0	1976	Franz Klammer AUT	1:45.73
1952	Zeno Colò, ITA	2:30.8	1980	Leonhard Stock, AUS	1:45.50
1956	Toni Sailer, AUT	2:52.2	1984	Bill Johnson, USA	1:45.59
1960	Jean Vuarnet, FRA	2:06.0	1988	Pirmin Zurbriggen, SWI	1:59.63
1964	Egon Zimmermann, AUT	2:18.16	1992	Patrick Ortlieb, AUT	1:50.37
1968	Jean-Claude Killy, FRA	1:59.85	1994	Tommy Moe, USA	1:45.75
1972	Bernhard Russi, SWI	1:51.43			

Slalom

Year		Time	Year		Time
1948	Edi Reinalter, SWI	2:10.3	1976	Piero Gros, ITA	2:03.29
1952	Othmar Schneider, AUT	2:00.0	1980	Ingemar Stenmark, SWE	1:44.26
1956	Toni Sailer, AUT	3:14.7	1984	Phil Mahre, USA	1:39.41
1960	Ernst Hinterseer, AUT	2:08.9	1988	Alberto Tomba, ITA	1:39.47
1964	Pepi Stiegler, AUT	2:11.13	1992	Finn Christian Jagge, NOR	1:44.39
1968	Jean-Claude Killy, FRA	1:39.73	1994	Thomas Stangassinger, AUT	2:02.02
1972	Francisco Ochoa, SPA	1:49.27			

Giant Slalom

Year		Time	Year		Time
1952	Stein Eriksen, NOR	2:25.0	1976	Heini Hemmi, SWI	3:26.97
1956	Toni Sailer, AUS	3:00.1	1980	Ingemar Stenmark, SWE	2:40.74
1960	Roger Staub, SWI	1:48.3	1984	Max Julen, SWI	2:41.18
1964	Francois Bonlieu, FRA	1:46.71	1988	Alberto Tomba, ITA	2:06.37
1968	Jean-Claude Killy, FRA	3:29.28	1992	Alberto Tomba, ITA	2:06.98
1972	Gustav Thöni, ITA	3:09.62	1994	Markus Wasmeier, GER	2:52.46

Super Giant Slalom

Year		Time	Year		Time
1988	Frank Piccard, FRA	1:39.66	1994	Markus Wasmeier, GER	1:32.53
1992	Kjetil Andre Aamodt, NOR	1:13.04			

Alpine Combined

Year		Points	Year		Points
1936	Franz Pfnür, GER	99.25	1992	Josef Polig, ITA	14.58
1948	Henri Oreiller, FRA	3.27	**Year**		**Time**
1952-84	Not held		1994	Lasse Kjus, NOR	3:17.53
1988	Hubert Strolz, AUT	36.55			

WOMEN

Multiple gold medals: Vreni Schneider (3); Deborah Compagnoni, Marielle Goitschel, Trude Jochum-Beiser, Petra Kronberger, Andrea Mead Lawrence, Rosi Mittermaier, Marie-Theres Nadig, Hanni Wenzel and Pernilla Wiberg (2).

Downhill

Year		Time	Year		Time
1948	Hedy Schlunegger, SWI	2:28.3	1976	Rosi Mittermaier, W.Ger	1:46.16
1952	Trude Jochum-Beiser, AUT	1:47.1	1980	Annemarie Moser-Pröll, AUT	1:37.52
1956	Madeleine Berthod, SWI	1:40.7	1984	Michela Figini, SWI	1:13.36
1960	Heidi Biebl, GER	1:37.6	1988	Marina Kiehl, W.Ger	1:25.86
1964	Christl Haas, AUT	1:55.39	1992	Kerrin Lee-Gartner, CAN	1:52.55
1968	Olga Pall, AUT	1:40.87	1994	Katja Seizinger, GER	1:35.93
1972	Marie-Theres Nadig, SWI	1:36.68			

Slalom

Year		Time	Year		Time
1948	Gretchen Fraser, USA	1:57.2	1976	Rosi Mittermaier, W.Ger	1:30.54
1952	Andrea Mead Lawrence, USA	2:10.6	1980	Hanni Wenzel, LIE	1:25.09
1956	Renée Colliard, SWI	1:52.3	1984	Paoletta Magoni, ITA	1:36.47
1960	Anne Heggtveit, CAN	1:49.6	1988	Vreni Schneider, SWI	1:36.69
1964	Christine Goitschel, FRA	1:29.86	1992	Petra Kronberger, AUT	1:32.68
1968	Marielle Goitschel, FRA	1:25.86	1994	Vreni Schneider, SWI	1:56.01
1972	Barbara Cochran, USA	1:31.24			

Alpine Skiing (Cont.)
WOMEN
Giant Slalom

Year		Time	Year		Time
1952	Andrea Mead Lawrence, USA	2:06.8	1976	Kathy Kreiner, CAN	1:29.13
1956	Ossi Reichert, GER	1:56.5	1980	Hanni Wenzel, LIE	2:41.66
1960	Yvonne Rügg, SWI	1:39.9	1984	Debbie Armstrong, USA	2:20.98
1964	Marielle Goitschel, FRA	1:52.24	1988	Vreni Schneider, SWI	2:06.49
1968	Nancy Greene, CAN	1:51.97	1992	Pernilla Wiberg, SWE	2:12.74
1972	Marie-Theres Nadig, SWI	1:29.90	1994	Deborah Compagnoni, ITA	2:30.97

Super Giant Slalom

Year		Time	Year		Time
1988	Sigrid Wolf, AUT	1:19.03	1994	Diann Roffe-Steinrotter, USA	1:22.15
1992	Deborah Compagnoni, ITA	1:21.22			

Alpine Combined

Year		Points	Year		Points
1936	Christl Cranz, GER	97.06	1992	Petra Kronberger, AUT	2.55
1948	Trude Jochum-Beiser, AUT	6.58	**Year**		**Time**
1952-84	Not held		1994	Pernilla Wiberg, SWE	3:05.16
1988	Anita Wachter, AUT	29.25			

BIATHLON

MEN

Multiple gold medals (including relays): Aleksandr Tikhonov (4); Mark Kirchner (3); Anatoly Alyabyev, Ivan Biakov, Sergei Chepikov, Viktor Mamatov, Frank-Peter Roetsch, Magnar Solberg and Dmitri Vasilyev (2).

10 kilometers

Year		Time	Year		Time
1980	Frank Ullrich, E.Ger	32:10.69	1992	Mark Kirchner, GER	26:02.3
1984	Erik Kvalfoss, NOR	30:53.8	1994	Sergei Chepikov, RUS	28:07.0
1988	Frank-Peter Roetsch, E.Ger	25:08.1			

20 kilometers

Year		Time	Year		Time
1960	Klas Lestander, SWE	1:33:21.6	1980	Anatoly Alyabyev, USSR	1:08:16.31
1964	Vladimir Melanin, USSR	1:20:26.8	1984	Peter Angerer, W.Ger	1:11:52.7
1968	Magnar Solberg, NOR	1:13:45.9	1988	Frank-Peter Roetsch, E.Ger	56:33.3
1972	Magnar Solberg, NOR	1:15:55.50	1992	Yevgeny Redkine, UT	57:34.4
1976	Nikolai Kruglov, USSR	1:14:12.26	1994	Sergei Tarasov, RUS	57:25.3

4x7.5-kilometer Relay

Year		Time	Year		Time	Year		Time
1968	Soviet Union	2:13:02.4	1980	Soviet Union	1:34:03.27	1992	Germany	1:24:43.5
1972	Soviet Union	1:51:44.92	1984	Soviet Union	1:38:51.7	1994	Germany	1:30:22.1
1976	Soviet Union	1:57:55.64	1988	Soviet Union	1:22:30.0			

WOMEN

Multiple gold medals (including relays): Myriam Bedard and Anfisa Reztsova (2). Note that Reztsova won a third gold medal in 1988 in the Cross-country 4x5-kilometer Relay.

7.5 kilometers

Year		Time	Year		Time
1992	Anfisa Reztsova, UT	24:29.2	1994	Myriam Bedard, CAN	26:08.8

15 kilometers

Year		Time	Year		Time
1992	Antje Misersky, GER	51:47.2	1994	Myriam Bedard, CAN	52:06.6

4 x 7.5 kilometer Relay

Year		Time	Year		Time
1992	France	1:15:55.6	1994	Russia	1:47:19.5

Note: Event featured three skiers per team in 1992.

Youngest and Oldest Gold Medalists in an Individual Event

Youngest: MEN— Toni Nieminen, Finland, Large Hill Ski Jumping, 1992 (16 years, 261 days); WOMEN—Sonja Henie, Norway, Figure Skating, 1928 (15 years, 315 days).
Oldest: MEN— Magnar Solberg, NOR, 20-km Biathlon, 1972 (35 years, 4 days); WOMEN— Christina Baas-Kaiser, Holland, 3,000m Speed Skating, 1972 (33 years, 268 days).

BOBSLED

Multiple gold medals: DRIVERS—Meinhard Nehmer (3); Billy Fiske, Wolfgang Hoppe, Eugenio Monti, Andreas Ostler and Gustav Weder (2). CREW—Bernard Germeshausen (3); Donat Acklin, Luciano De Paolis, Cliff Gray, Lorenz Nieberl and Dietmar Schauerhammer (2).

Two-Man

Year		Time	Year		Time
1932	United States (Hubert Stevens)	8:14.74	1972	West Germany (Wolfgang Zimmerer)	4:57.07
1936	United States (Ivan Brown)	5:29.29	1976	East Germany (Meinhard Nehmer)	3:44.42
1948	Switzerland (Felix Endrich)	5:29.2	1980	Switzerland (Erich Schärer)	4:09.36
1952	Germany (Andreas Ostler)	5:24.54	1984	East Germany (Wolfgang Hoppe)	3:25.56
1956	Italy (Lamberto Dalla Costa)	5:30.14	1988	Soviet Union (Jānis Ķipurs)	3:54.19
1960	Not held		1992	Switzerland I (Gustav Weder)	4:03.26
1964	Great Britain (Anthony Nash)	4:21.90	1994	Switzerland I (Gustav Weder)	3:30.81
1968	Italy (Eugenio Monti)	4:41.54			

Four-Man

Year		Time	Year		Time
1924	Switzerland (Eduard Scherrer)	5:45.54	1968	Italy (Eugenio Monti)	2:17.39
1928	United States (Billy Fiske)	3:20.5	1972	Switzerland (Jean Wicki)	4:43.07
1932	United States (Billy Fiske)	7:53.68	1976	East Germany (Meinhard Nehmer)	3:40.43
1936	Switzerland (Pierre Musy)	5:19.85	1980	East Germany (Meinhard Nehmer)	3:59.92
1948	United States (Francis Tyler)	5:20.1	1984	East Germany (Wolfgang Hoppe)	3:20.22
1952	Germany (Andreas Ostler)	5:07.84	1988	Switzerland (Ekkehard Fasser)	3:47.51
1956	Switzerland (Franz Kapus)	5:10.44	1992	Austria I (Ingo Appelt)	3:53.90
1960	Not held		1994	Germany II (Harald Czudaj)	3:27.78
1964	Canada (Vic Emery)	4:14.46			

Note: Five-man sleds were used in 1928.

CROSS-COUNTRY SKIING

There have been two significant changes in men's and women's Cross-country racing since the end of the 1984 Winter Games in Sarajevo. First, the classical and freestyle (i.e., skating) techniques were designated for specific events beginning in 1988, and the Pursuit race was introduced in 1992.

MEN

Multiple gold medals (including relays): Bjorn Dählie (5); Sixten Jernberg, Gunde Svan, Thomas Wassberg and Nikolai Zimyatov (4); Veikko Hakulinen, Eero Mäntyranta and Vegard Ulvang (3); Hallgeir Brenden, Harald Grönningen, Thorlief Haug, Jan Ottoson, Pål Tyldum and Vyacheslav Vedenine (2).
Multiple gold medals (including Nordic Combined): Johan Gröttumsbråten and Thorlief Haug (3).

10-kilometer Classical

Year		Time	Year		Time
1924-88	Not held		1994	Bjorn Dählie, NOR	24:20.1
1992	Vegard Ulvang, NOR	27:36.0			

15-kilometer Freestyle Pursuit

A 15-km Freestyle race in which the starting order is determined by order of finish in the 10-km Classical race. Time given is combined time of both events.

Year		Time	Year		Time
1924-88	Not held		1994	Bjorn Dählie, NOR	1:00.08.8
1992	Bjorn Dählie, NOR	1:05:37.9			

15-kilometer Classical (Discont.)

Discontinued in 1992 and replaced by 15-km Freestyle Pursuit. Event was held over 18 kilometers from 1924-52.

Year		Time	Year		Time
1924	Thorlief Haug, NOR	1:14:31.0	1964	Eero Mäntyranta, FIN	50:54.1
1928	Johan Gröttumsbråten, NOR	1:37:01.0	1968	Harald Grönningen, NOR	47:54.2
1932	Sven Utterström, SWE	1:23:07.0	1972	Sven-Ake Lundbäck, SWE	45:28.24
1936	Erik-August Larsson, SWE	1:14:38.0	1976	Nikolai Bazhukov, USSR	43:58.47
1948	Martin Lundström, SWE	1:13:50.0	1980	Thomas Wassberg, SWE	41:57.63
1952	Hallgeir Brenden, NOR	1:01:34.0	1984	Gunde Svan, SWE	41:25.6
1956	Hallgeir Brenden, NOR	49:39.0	1988	Mikhail Devyatyarov, USSR	41:18.9
1960	Håkon Brusveen NOR	51:55.5			

30-kilometer Freestyle

Year		Time	Year		Time
1924-52	Not held		1976	Sergei Saveliev, USSR	1:30:29.38
1956	Veikko Hakulinen, FIN	1:44:06.0	1980	Nikolai Zimyatov, USSR	1:27:02.80
1960	Sixten Jernberg, SWE	1:51:03.9	1984	Nikolai Zimyatov, USSR	1:28:56.3
1964	Eero Mäntyranta, FIN	1:30:50.7	1988	Alexi Prokurorov, USSR	1:24:26.3
1968	Franco Nones, ITA	1:35:39.2	1992	Vegard Ulvang, NOR	1:22:27.8
1972	Vyacheslav Vedenine, USSR	1:36:31.15	1994	Thomas Alsgaard, NOR	1:12:26.4

Cross-country Skiing (Cont.)
MEN
50-kilometer Classical

Year		Time	Year		Time
1924	Thorleif Haug, NOR	3:44:32.0	1968	Ole Ellefsaeter, NOR	2:28:45.8
1928	Per Erik Hedlund, SWE	4:52:03.0	1972	Päl Tyldum, NOR	2:43:14.75
1932	Veli Saarinen, FIN	4:28:00.0	1976	Ivar Formo, NOR	2:37:30.05
1936	Elis Wiklund, SWE	3:30:11.0	1980	Nikolai Zimyatov, USSR	2:27:24.60
1948	Nils Karlsson, SWE	3:47:48.0	1984	Thomas Wassberg, SWE	2:15:55.8
1952	Veikko Hakulinen, FIN	3:33:33.0	1988	Gunde Svan, SWE	2:04:30.9
1956	Sixten Jernberg, SWE	2:50:27.0	1992	Bjorn Dählie, NOR	2:03:41.5
1960	Kalevi Hämäläinen, FIN	2:59:06.3	1994	Vladimir Smirnov, KAZ	2:07:20.3
1964	Sixten Jernberg, SWE	2:43:52.6			

4x10-kilometer Mixed Relay
Two Classical and two Freestyle legs.

Year		Time	Year		Time	Year		Time
1936	Finland	2:41:33.0	1964	Sweden	2:18:34.6	1984	Sweden	1:55:06.3
1948	Sweden	2:32:08.0	1968	Norway	2:08:33.5	1988	Sweden	1:43:58.6
1952	Finland	2:20:16.0	1972	Soviet Union	2:04:47.94	1992	Norway	1:39:26.0
1956	Soviet Union	2:15:30.0	1976	Finland	2:07:59.72	1994	Italy	1:41:15.0
1960	Finland	2:18:45.6	1980	Soviet Union	1:57:03.46			

WOMEN

Multiple gold medals (including relays): Lyubov Egorova (6); Galina Kulakova and Raisa Smetanina (4); Claudia Boyarskikh and Marja-Liisa Hämäläinen (3); Manuela Di Centa, Toini Gustafsson, Larisa Lazutina, Barbara Petzold and Elena Valbe (2).
Multiple gold medals (including relays and Biathlon): Anfisa Reztsova (2).

5-kilometer Classical

Year		Time	Year		Time
1952-60	Not held		1980	Raisa Smetanina, USSR	15:06.92
1964	Claudia Boyarskikh, USSR	17:50.5	1984	Marja-Liisa Hämäläinen, FIN	17:04.0
1968	Toini Gustafsson, SWE	16:45.2	1988	Marjo Matikainen, FIN	15:04.0
1972	Galina Kulakova, USSR	17:00.50	1992	Marjut Lukkarinen, FIN	14:13.8
1976	Helena Takalo, FIN	15:48.69	1994	Lyubov Egorova, RUS	14:08.8

10-kilometer Freestyle Pursuit
A 10-km Freestyle race in which the starting order is determined by order of finish in the 5-km Classical race. Time given is combined time of both events.

Year		Time	Year		Time
1952-88	Not held		1994	Lyubov Egorova, RUS	41:38.1
1992	Lyubov Egorova, UT	40:07.7			

10-kilometer Classical (Discont.)
Discontinued in 1992 and replaced by 10-km Freestyle Pursuit. Event was held over 18 kilometers from 1924-52.

Year		Time	Year		Time
1952	Lydia Wideman, FIN	41:40.0	1972	Galina Kulakova, USSR	34:17.82
1956	Lyubov Kosyreva, USSR	38:11.0	1976	Raisa Smetanina, USSR	30:13.41
1960	Maria Gusakova, USSR	39:46.6	1980	Barbara Petzold, E.Ger	30:31.54
1964	Claudia Boyarskikh, USSR	40:24.3	1984	Marja-Liisa Hämäläinen, FIN	31:44.2
1968	Toini Gustafsson, SWE	36:46.5	1988	Vida Venciene, USSR	30:08.3

15-kilometer Freestyle

Year		Time	Year		Time
1952-88	Not held		1994	Manuela Di Centa, ITA	39:44.5
1992	Lyubov Egorova, UT	42:20.8			

30-kilometer Classical
Event was held over 20 kilometers from 1984-88.

Year		Time	Year		Time
1984	Marja-Liisa Hämäläinen, FIN	1:01:45.0	1992	Stefania Belmondo, ITA	1:22:30.1
1988	Tamara Tikhonova, USSR	55:53.6	1994	Manuela Di Centa, ITA	1:25:41.6

4x5-kilometer Mixed Relay
Two Classical and two Freestyle legs. Event featured three skiers per team from 1956-72.

Year		Time	Year		Time	Year		Time
1956	Finland	1:09:01.0	1972	Soviet Union	48:46.15	1988	Soviet Union	59:51.1
1960	Sweden	1:04:21.4	1976	Soviet Union	1:07:49.75	1992	Unified Team	59:34.8
1964	Soviet Union	59:20.2	1980	East Germany	1:02:11.10	1994	Russia	57:12.5
1968	Norway	57:30.0	1984	Norway	1:06:49.7			

FIGURE SKATING

MEN

Multiple gold medals: Gillis Grafström (3); Dick Button and Karl Schäfer (2).

Year			Year			Year		
1908	Ulrich Salchow	SWE	1948	Dick Button	USA	1976	John Curry	GBR
1912	Not held		1952	Dick Button	USA	1980	Robin Cousins	GBR
1920	Gillis Grafström	SWE	1956	Hayes Alan Jenkins	USA	1984	Scott Hamilton	USA
1924	Gillis Grafström	SWE	1960	David Jenkins	USA	1988	Brian Boitano	USA
1928	Gillis Grafström	SWE	1964	Manfred Schnelldorfer	GER	1992	Victor Petrenko	UT
1932	Karl Schäfer	AUT	1968	Wolfgang Schwarz	AUT	1994	Alexei Urmanov	RUS
1936	Karl Schäfer	AUT	1972	Ondrej Nepela	CZE			

WOMEN

Multiple gold medals: Sonja Henie (3); Katarina Witt (2).

Year			Year			Year		
1908	Madge Syers	GBR	1948	Barbara Ann Scott	CAN	1976	Dorothy Hamill	USA
1912	Not held		1952	Jeanette Altwegg	GBR	1980	Anett Pötzsch	E.Ger
1920	Magda Julin-Mauroy	SWE	1956	Tenley Albright	USA	1984	Katarina Witt	E.Ger
1924	Herma Planck-Szabö	AUT	1960	Carol Heiss	USA	1988	Katarina Witt	E.Ger
1928	Sonja Henie	NOR	1964	Sjoukje Dijkstra	HOL	1992	Kristi Yamaguchi	USA
1932	Sonja Henie	NOR	1968	Peggy Fleming	USA	1994	Oksana Baiul	UKR
1936	Sonja Henie	NOR	1972	Beatrix Schuba	AUT			

PAIRS

Multiple gold medals: MEN—Pierre Brunet, Sergei Grinkov, Oleg Protopopov and Aleksandr Zaitsev (2). WOMEN—Irina Rodnina (3); Ludmila Belousova, Ekaterina Gordeeva and Andrée Joly Brunet (2).

Year			Year		
1908	Anna Hübler & Heinrich Burger	Germany	1960	Barbara Wagner & Robert Paul	Canada
1912	Not held		1964	Ludmila Belousova & Oleg Protopopov	USSR
1920	Ludovika & Walter Jakobsson	Finland	1968	Ludmila Belousova & Oleg Protopopov	USSR
1924	Helene Engelmann & Alfred Berger	Austria	1972	Irina Rodnina & Aleksei Ulanov	USSR
1928	Andrée Joly & Pierre Brunet	France	1976	Irina Rodnina & Aleksandr Zaitsev	USSR
1932	Andrée & Pierre Brunet	France	1980	Irina Rodnina & Aleksandr Zaitsev	USSR
1936	Maxi Herber & Ernst Baier	Germany	1984	Elena Valova & Oleg Vasiliev	USSR
1948	Micheline Lannoy & Pierre Baugniet	Belgium	1988	Ekaterina Gordeeva & Sergei Grinkov	USSR
1952	Ria & Paul Falk	Germany	1992	Natalya Mishkutienok & Arthur Dmitriev	UT
1956	Elisabeth Schwartz & Kurt Oppelt	Austria	1994	Ekaterina Gordeeva & Sergei Grinkov	RUS

ICE DANCING

Year			Year		
1976	Lyudmila Pakhomova & Aleksandr Gorshkov	USSR	1988	Natalia Bestemianova & Andrei Bukin	USSR
1980	Natalia Linichuk & Gennady Karponosov	USSR	1992	Marina Klimova & Sergei Ponomarenko	UT
1984	Jayne Torvill & Christopher Dean	Great Britain	1994	Oksana Gritschuk & Yevgeny Platov	RUS

ICE HOCKEY

Multiple gold medals: Soviet Union/Unified Team (8); Canada (6); United States (2).

Year		Year	
1920	**Canada**, United States Czechoslovakia	1964	**Soviet Union**, Sweden, Czechoslovakia
1924	**Canada**, United States, Great Britain	1968	**Soviet Union**, Czechoslovakia, Canada
1928	**Canada**, Sweden, Switzerland	1972	**Soviet Union**, United States, Czechoslovakia
1932	**Canada**, United States, Germany	1976	**Soviet Union**, Czechoslovakia, West Germany
1936	**Great Britain**, Canada, United States	1980	**United States**, Soviet Union, Sweden
1948	**Canada**, Czechoslovakia, Switzerland	1984	**Soviet Union**, Czechoslovakia, Sweden
1952	**Canada**, United States, Sweden	1988	**Soviet Union**, Finland, Sweden
1956	**Soviet Union**, United States, Canada	1992	**Unified Team**, Canada, Czechoslovakia
1960	**United States**, Canada, Soviet Union	1994	**Sweden**, Canada, Finland

U.S. Gold Medal Hockey Teams
1960

Forwards: Billy Christian, Roger Christian, Billy Cleary, Gene Grazia, Paul Johnson, Bob McVey, Dick Meredith, Weldy Olson, Dick Rodenheiser and Tom Williams. **Defensemen:** Bob Cleary, Jack Kirrane (captain), John Mayasich, Bob Owen and Rod Paavola. **Goaltenders:** Jack McCartan and Larry Palmer. **Coach:** Jack Riley.

1980

Forwards: Neal Broten, Steve Christoff, Mike Eruzione (captain), John Harrington, Mark Johnson, Rob McClanahan, Mark Pavelich, Buzz Schneider, Dave Silk, Eric Strobel, Phil Verchota and Mark Wells. **Defensemen:** Bill Baker, Dave Christian, Ken Morrow, Jack O'Callahan, Mike Ramsey and Bob Suter. **Goaltenders:** Jim Craig and Steve Janaszak. **Coach:** Herb Brooks.

LUGE

MEN

Multiple gold medals: (including doubles): Norbert Hahn, Georg Hackl, Paul Hildgartner, Thomas Köhler and Hans Rinn (2).

Singles

Year		Time	Year		Time
1964	Thomas Köhler, GER	3:26.77	1984	Paul Hildgartner, ITA	3:04.258
1968	Manfred Schmid, AUT	2:52.48	1988	Jens Müller, E.Ger	3:05.548
1972	Wolfgang Scheidel, E.Ger	3:27.58	1992	Georg Hackl, GER	3:02.363
1976	Dettlef Günther, E.Ger	3:27.688	1994	Georg Hackl, GER	3:21.571
1980	Bernhard Glass, E.Ger	2:54.796			

Doubles

Year		Time	Year		Time	Year		Time
1964	Austria	1:41.62	1976	East Germany	1:25.604	1988	East Germany	1:31.940
1968	East Germany	1:35.85	1980	East Germany	1:19.331	1992	Germany	1:32.053
1972	(TIE) East Germany	1:28.35	1984	West Germany	1:23.620	1994	Italy	1:36.720
	& Italy	1.28.35						

WOMEN

Multiple gold medals: Steffi Martin Walter (2).

Singles

Year		Time	Year		Time
1964	Ortrun Enderlein, GER	3:24.67	1984	Steffi Martin, E.Ger	2:46.570
1968	Erica Lechner, ITA	2:28.66	1988	Steffi Martin Walter, E.Ger	3:03.973
1972	Anna-Maria Müller, E.Ger	2:59.18	1992	Doris Neuner, AUT	3:06.696
1976	Margit Schumann, E.Ger	2:50.621	1994	Gerda Weissensteiner, ITA	3:15.517
1980	Vera Zozulya, USSR	2:36.537			

NORDIC COMBINED

Multiple gold medals: Ulrich Wehling (3); Johan Gröttumsbråten (2).

Individual

Year		Points	Year		Points
1924	Thorleif Haug, NOR	18.906	1968	Franz Keller, W.Ger	449.04
1928	Johan Gröttumsbråten, NOR	17.833	1972	Ulrich Wehling, E.Ger	413.340
1932	Johan Gröttumsbråten, NOR	446.00	1976	Ulrich Wehling, E.Ger	423.39
1936	Oddbjörn Hagen, NOR	430.3	1980	Ulrich Wehling, E.Ger	432.200
1948	Heikki Hasu, FIN	448.80	1984	Tom Sandberg, NOR	422.595
1952	Simon Slattvik, NOR	451.621	1988	Hippolyt Kempf, SWI	432.230
1956	Sverre Stenersen, NOR	455.000	1992	Fabrice Guy, FRA	426.470
1960	Georg Thoma, GER	457.952	1994	Fred Borre Lundberg, NOR	457.970
1964	Tormod Knutsen, NOR	469.28			

Team

Year		Points	Year		Points
1924-84	Not held		1992	Japan	1247.180
1988	West Germany	792.08	1994	Japan	1368.860

SKI JUMPING

Multiple gold medals (including team jumping): Matti Nykänen (4); Jens Weissflog (3); Birger Ruud and Toni Nieminen (2).

Normal Hill—70 Meters

Year		Points	Year		Points
1924-60	Not held		1980	Anton Innauer, AUT	266.3
1964	Veikko Kankkonen, FIN	229.9	1984	Jens Weissflog, E.Ger	215.2
1968	Jiri Raska, CZE	216.5	1988	Matti Nykänen, FIN	229.1
1972	Yukio Kasaya, JPN	244.2	1992	Ernst Vettori, AUT	222.8
1976	Hans-Georg Aschenbach, E.Ger	252.0	1994	Espen Bredesen, NOR	282.0

Large Hill—90 Meters

Year		Points	Year		Points
1924	Jacob Tullin Thams, NOR	18.960	1968	Vladimir Beloussov, USSR	231.3
1928	Alf Andersen, NOR	19.208	1972	Wojciech Fortuna, POL	219.9
1932	Birger Ruud, NOR	228.1	1976	Karl Schnabl, AUT	234.8
1936	Birger Ruud, NOR	232.0	1980	Jouko Törmänen, FIN	271.0
1948	Petter Hugsted, NOR	228.1	1984	Matti Nykänen, FIN	231.2
1952	Arnfinn Bergmann, NOR	226.0	1988	Matti Nykänen, FIN	224.0
1956	Antti Hyvärinen, FIN	227.0	1992	Toni Nieminen, FIN	239.5
1960	Helmut Recknagel, GER	227.2	1994	Jens Weissflog, GER	274.5
1964	Toralf Engan, NOR	230.7			

Note: Jump held at various lengths from 1924-56; at 80 meters from 1960-64; at 90 meters from 1968-88; and at 120 meters in 1992.

Team Large Hill

Year		Points	Year		Points
1924-84 Not held			1992	Finland	644.4
1988	Finland	634.4	1994	Germany	970.1

SPEED SKATING

MEN

Multiple gold medals: Eric Heiden and Clas Thunberg (5); Ivar Ballangrud, Yevgeny Grishin and Johann Olav Koss (4); Hjalmar Andersen, Tomas Gustafson, Irving Jaffee and Ard Schenk (3); Gaétan Boucher, Knut Johannesen, Erhard Keller, Uwe-Jens Mey and Jack Shea (2). Note that Thunberg's total includes the All-Around, which was contested for the only time in 1924.

500 meters

Year		Time		Year		Time	
1924	Charles Jewtraw, USA	44.0		1964	Terry McDermott, USA	40.1	OR
1928	(TIE) Bernt Evensen, NOR	43.4	OR	1968	Erhard Keller, W.Ger	40.3	
	& Clas Thunberg, FIN	43.4	OR	1972	Erhard Keller, W.Ger	39.44	OR
1932	Jack Shea, USA	43.4	=OR	1976	Yevgeny Kulikov, USSR	39.17	OR
1936	Ivar Ballangrud, NOR	43.4	=OR	1980	Eric Heiden, USA	38.03	OR
1948	Finn Helgesen, NOR	43.1	OR	1984	Sergei Fokichev, USSR	38.19	
1952	Ken Henry, USA	43.2		1988	Uwe-Jens Mey, E.Ger	36.45	WR
1956	Yevgeny Grishin, USSR	40.2	=WR	1992	Uwe-Jens Mey, GER	37.14	
1960	Yevgeny Grishin, USSR	40.2	=WR	1994	Aleksandr Golubev, RUS	36.33	OR

1000 meters

Year		Time		Year		Time	
1924-72 Not held				1988	Nikolai Gulyaev, USSR	1:13.03	OR
1976	Peter Mueller, USA	1:19.32		1992	Olaf Zinke, GER	1:14.85	
1980	Eric Heiden, USA	1:15.18	OR	1994	Dan Jansen, USA	1:12.43	WR
1984	Gaétan Boucher, CAN	1:15.80					

1500 meters

Year		Time		Year		Time	
1924	Clas Thunberg, FIN	2:20.8		1964	Ants Antson, USSR	2:10.3	
1928	Clas Thunberg, FIN	2:21.1		1968	Kees Verkerk, HOL	2:03.4	OR
1932	Jack Shea, USA	2:57.5		1972	Ard Schenk, HOL	2:02.96	OR
1936	Charles Mathisen, NOR	2:19.2	OR	1976	Jan Egil Storholt, NOR	1:59.38	OR
1948	Sverre Farstad, NOR	2:17.6	OR	1980	Eric Heiden, USA	1:55.44	OR
1952	Hjalmar Andersen, NOR	2:20.4		1984	Gaétan Boucher, CAN	1:58.36	
1956	(TIE) Yevgeny Grishin, USSR	2:08.6	WR	1988	André Hoffman, E.Ger	1:52.06	WR
	& Yuri Mikhailov, USSR	2:08.6	WR	1992	Johann Olav Koss, NOR	1:54.81	
1960	(TIE) Roald Aas, NOR	2:10.4		1994	Johann Olav Koss, NOR	1:51.29	WR
	& Yevgeny Grishin, USSR	2:10.4					

5000 meters

Year		Time		Year		Time	
1924	Clas Thunberg, FIN	8:39.0		1968	Fred Anton Maier, NOR	7:22.4	WR
1928	Ivar Ballangrud, NOR	8:50.5		1972	Ard Schenk, HOL	7:23.61	
1932	Irving Jaffee, USA	9:40.8		1976	Sten Stensen, NOR	7:24.48	
1936	Ivar Ballangrud, NOR	8:19.6	OR	1980	Eric Heiden, USA	7:02.29	OR
1948	Reidar Liaklev, NOR	8:29.4		1984	Tomas Gustafson, SWE	7:12.28	
1952	Hjalmar Andersen, NOR	8:10.6	OR	1988	Tomas Gustafson, SWE	6:44.63	WR
1956	Boris Shilkov, USSR	7:48.7	OR	1992	Geir Karlstad, NOR	6:59.97	
1960	Viktor Kosichkin, USSR	7:51.3		1994	Johann Olev Koss, NOR	6:34.96	WR
1964	Knut Johannesen, NOR	7:38.4	OR				

Speed Skating (Cont.)
MEN
10,000 meters

Year		Time		Year		Time	
1924	Julius Skutnabb, FIN	18:04.8		1968	Johnny Höglin, SWE	15:23.6	OR
1928	Irving Jaffee, USA*	18:36.5		1972	Ard Schenk, HOL	15:01.35	OR
1932	Irving Jaffee, USA	19:13.6		1976	Piet Kleine, HOL	14:50.59	OR
1936	Ivar Ballangrud, NOR	17:24.3	OR	1980	Eric Heiden, USA	14:28.13	WR
1948	Ake Seyffarth, SWE	17:26.3		1984	Igor Malkov, USSR	14:39.90	
1952	Hjalmar Andersen, NOR	16:45.8	OR	1988	Tomas Gustafson, SWE	13:48.20	WR
1956	Sigvard Ericsson, SWE	16:35.9	OR	1992	Bart Veldkamp, HOL	14:12.12	
1960	Knut Johannesen, NOR	15:46.6	WR	1994	Johann Olav Koss, NOR	13:30.55	WR
1964	Jonny Nilsson, SWE	15:50.1					

*Unofficial, according to the IOC. Jaffee recorded the fastest time, but the event was called off in progress due to thawing ice.

WOMEN

Multiple gold medals: Lydia Skoblikova (6); Bonnie Blair (5); Karin Enke and Yvonne van Gennip (3); Tatiana Averina, Gunda Niemann and Christa Rothenburger (2).

500 meters

Year		Time		Year		Time	
1960	Helga Haase, GER	45.9		1980	Karin Enke, E.Ger	41.78	OR
1964	Lydia Skoblikova, USSR	45.0	OR	1984	Christa Rothenburger, E.Ger	41.02	OR
1968	Lyudmila Titova, USSR	46.1		1988	Bonnie Blair, USA	39.10	WR
1972	Anne Henning, USA	43.33	OR	1992	Bonnie Blair, USA	40.33	
1976	Sheila Young, USA	42.76	OR	1994	Bonnie Blair, USA	39.25	

1000 meters

Year		Time		Year		Time	
1960	Klara Guseva, USSR	1:34.1		1980	Natalia Petruseva, USSR	1:24.10	OR
1964	Lydia Skoblikova, USSR	1:33.2	OR	1984	Karin Enke, E.Ger	1:21.61	OR
1968	Carolina Geijssen, HOL	1:32.6	OR	1988	Christa Rothenburger, E.Ger	1:17.65	WR
1972	Monika Pflug, W.Ger	1:31.40	OR	1992	Bonnie Blair, USA	1:21.90	
1976	Tatiana Averina, USSR	1:28.43	OR	1994	Bonnie Blair, USA	1:18.74	

1500 meters

Year		Time		Year		Time	
1960	Lydia Skoblikova, USSR	2:25.2	WR	1980	Annie Borckink, HOL	2:10.95	OR
1964	Lydia Skoblikova, USSR	2:22.6	OR	1984	Karin Enke, E.Ger	2:03.42	WR
1968	Kaija Mustonen, FIN	2:22.4	OR	1988	Yvonne van Gennip, HOL	2:00.68	OR
1972	Dianne Holum, USA	2:20.85	OR	1992	Jacqueline Börner, GER	2:05.87	
1976	Galina Stepanskaya, USSR	2:16.58	OR	1994	Emese Hunyady, AUT	2:02.19	

3000 meters

Year		Time		Year		Time	
1960	Lydia Skoblikova, USSR	5:14.3		1980	Bjorg Eva Jensen, NOR	4:32.13	OR
1964	Lydia Skoblikova, USSR	5:14.9		1984	Andrea Schöne, E.Ger	4:24.79	OR
1968	Johanna Schut, HOL	4:56.2	OR	1988	Yvonne van Gennip, HOL	4:11.94	WR
1972	Christina Baas-Kaiser, HOL	4:52.14	OR	1992	Gunda Niemann, GER	4:19.90	
1976	Tatiana Averina, USSR	4:45.19	OR	1994	Svetlana Bazhanova, RUS	4:17.43	

5000 meters

Year		Time		Year		Time	
1988	Yvonne van Gennip, HOL	7:14.13	WR	1992	Gunda Niemann, GER	7:31.57	
1960-84	Not held			1994	Claudia Pechstein, GER	7:14.37	

Athletes with Winter and Summer Medals

Only three athletes have won medals in both the Winter and Summer Olympics:

Eddie Eagan, USA— Light Heavyweight Boxing gold (1920) and Four-man Bobsled gold (1932).

Jacob Tullin Thams, Norway— Ski Jumping gold (1924) and 8-meter Yachting silver (1936).

Christa Luding-Rothenburger, East Germany— Speed Skating gold at 500 meters (1984) and 1,000m (1988), silver at 500m (1988) and bronze at 500m (1992) and Match Sprint Cycling silver (1988). Luding-Rothenburger is the only athlete to ever win medals in both Winter and Summer Games in the same year.

All-Time Leading Medal Winners
MEN

No		Sport	G-S-B
9	Sixten Jernberg, SWE	Cross-country	4-3-2
8	Bjorn Dählie, NOR	Cross-country	5-3-0
7	Clas Thunberg, FIN	Speed Skating	5-1-1
7	Ivar Ballangrud, NOR	Speed Skating	4-2-1
7	Veikko Hakulinen, FIN	Cross-country	3-3-1
7	Eero Mäntyranta, FIN	Cross-country	3-2-2
7	Bogdan Musiol, E.Ger/GER	Bobsled	1-5-1
6	Gunde Svan, SWE	Cross-country	4-1-1
6	Vegard Ulvang, NOR	Cross-country	3-2-1
6	Johan Gröttumsbraten, NOR	Nordic	3-1-2
6	Wolfgang Hoppe, E.Ger/GER	Bobsled	2-3-1
6	Eugenio Monti, ITA	Bobsled	2-2-2
6	Roald Larsen, NOR	Speed Skating	0-2-4
6	**Eric Heiden, USA**	Speed Skating	5-0-0
5	Yevgeny Grishin, USSR	Speed Skating	4-1-0
5	Johann Olav Koss, NOR	Speed Skating	4-1-0
5	Matti Nykänen, FIN	Ski Jumping	4-1-0
5	Aleksandr Tikhonov, USSR	Biathlon	4-1-0
5	Nikolai Zimyatov, USSR	Cross-country	4-1-0
5	Alberto Tomba, ITA	Alpine	3-2-0
5	Harald Grönningen, NOR	Cross-country	2-3-0
5	Pål Tyldum, NOR	Cross-country	2-3-0
5	Knut Johannesen, NOR	Speed Skating	2-2-1
5	Vladimir Smirnov, USSR/UT/KAZ	X-country	1-4-0
5	Kjetil André Aamodt, NOR	Alpine	1-2-2
5	Peter Angerer, W.Ger/GER	Biathlon	1-2-2
5	Juha Mieto, FIN	Cross-country	1-2-2
5	Fritz Feierabend, SWI	Bobsled	0-3-2

WOMEN

No		Sport	G-S-B
10	Raisa Smetanina, USSR/UT	Cross-country	4-5-1
9	Lyubov Egorova, UT/RUS	Cross-country	6-3-0
8	Galina Kulakova, USSR	Cross-country	4-2-2
8	Karin (Enke) Kania, E.Ger	Speed Skating	3-4-1
7	Marja-Liisa (Hämäläinen) Kirvesniemi, FIN	Cross-country	3-0-4
7	Andrea (Mitscherlich, Schöne) Ehrig, E.Ger	Speed Skating	1-5-1
7	Lydia Skoblikova, USSR	Speed Skating	6-0-0
6	**Bonnie Blair, USA**	Speed Skating	5-0-1
6	Manuela Di Centa, ITA	Cross-country	2-2-2
6	Elena Valbe, UT/RUS	Cross-country	2-0-4
5	Anfisa Reztsova, USSR/UT	CC/Biathlon	3-1-1
5	Vreni Schneider, SWI	Alpine	3-1-1
5	Gunda Neimann, GER	Speed Skating	2-2-1
5	Helena Takalo, FIN	Cross-country	1-3-1
5	Stefania Belmondo, ITA	Cross-country	1-1-3
5	Alevtina Kolchina, USSR	Cross-country	1-1-3

Games Medaled In

MEN— **Aamodt** (1992,94); **Angerer** (1980,84,88); **Ballangrud** (1928,32,36); **Dählie** (1992,94); **Feierabend** (1936,48,52); **Grishin** (1956,60,64); **Gröttumsbraten** (1924,28,32); **Grönningen** (1960,64,68); **Hakulinen** (1952,56,60); **Heiden** (1980); **Hoppe** (1984,88,92,94); **Jernberg** (1956,60,64); **Johannesen** (1956,60,64); **Koss** (1992,94). **Larsen** (1924,28); **Mäntyranta** (1960,64,68); **Mieto** (1976,80,84); **Monti** (1956,60,64,68); **Musiol** (1980,84,88,92); **Nykänen** (1984,88); **Smirnov** (1988,92,94); **Svan** (1984,88); **Thunberg** (1924,28); **Tikhonov** (1968,72,76); **Tomba** (1988,92,94); **Tyldum** (1968,72,76); **Ulvang** (1988,92,94); **Zimyatov** (1980,84).

WOMEN— **Belmondo** (1992,94); **Blair** (1988,92,94); **Di Centa** (1992,94); **Egorova** (1992,94); **Ehrig** (1976,80,84,88); **Kania** (1980,84,88); **Kirvesniemi** (1984,88,94); **Kolchina** (1956,64,68); **Kulakova** (1968,72,76,80); **Niemann** (1992-94); **Reztsova** (1988,92,94); **Schneider** (1988,92,94); **Skoblikova** (1960,64); **Smetanina** (1976,80,84,88,92); **Takalo** (1972,76,80); **Valbe** (1992,94).

Most Gold Medals
MEN

No		Sport	G-S-B
5	Bjorn Dählie, NOR	Cross-country	5-3-0
5	Clas Thunberg, FIN	Speed Skating	5-1-1
5	**Eric Heiden, USA**	Speed Skating	5-0-0
4	Sixten Jernberg, SWE	Cross-country	4-3-2
4	Ivar Ballangrud, NOR	Speed Skating	4-2-1
4	Gunde Svan, SWE	Cross-country	4-1-1
4	Yevgeny Grishin, USSR	Speed Skating	4-1-0
4	Johann Olav Koss, NOR	Speed Skating	4-1-0
4	Matti Nykänen, FIN	Ski Jumping	4-1-0
4	Aleksandr Tikhonov, USSR	Biathlon	4-1-0
4	Nikolai Zimyatov, USSR	Cross-country	4-1-0
4	Thomas Wassberg, SWE	Cross-country	4-0-0
3	Veikko Hakulinen, FIN	Cross-country	3-3-1
3	Eero Mäntyranta, FIN	Cross-country	3-2-2
3	Vegard Ulvang, NOR	Cross-country	3-2-1
3	Alberto Tomba, ITA	Alpine	3-2-0
3	Johan Gröttumsbråten, NOR	Nordic	3-1-2
3	Bernhard Germeshausen, E.Ger	Bobsled	3-1-0
3	Gillis Grafström, SWE	Figure Skating	3-1-0
3	Tomas Gustafson, SWE	Speed Skating	3-1-0
3	Vladislav Tretiak, USSR	Ice Hockey	3-1-0
3	Jens Weissflog, E.Ger/GER	Ski Jumping	3-1-0
3	Meinhard Nehmer, E.Ger	Bobsled	3-0-1
3	Hjalmar Andersen, NOR	Speed Skating	3-0-0
3	Vitaly Davydov, USSR	Ice Hockey	3-0-0
3	Anatoly Firsov, USSR	Ice Hockey	3-0-0
3	Thorleif Haug, NOR	Cross-country	3-0-0
3	**Irving Jaffee, USA**	Speed Skating	3-0-0
3	Andrei Khomoutov, USSR/UT	Ice Hockey	3-0-0
3	Jean-Claude Killy, FRA	Alpine	3-0-0
3	Viktor Kuzkin, USSR	Ice Hockey	3-0-0
3	Aleksandr Ragulin, USSR	Ice Hockey	3-0-0
3	Toni Sailer, AUT	Alpine	3-0-0
3	Ard Schenk, HOL	Speed Skating	3-0-0
3	Ulrich Wehling, E.Ger	Ski Jumping	3-0-0

WOMEN

No		Sport	G-S-B
6	Lyubov Egorova, UT/RUS	Cross-country	6-3-0
6	Lydia Skoblikova, USSR	Speed Skating	6-0-0
5	**Bonnie Blair, USA**	Speed Skating	5-0-1
4	Raisa Smetanina, USSR/UT	Cross-country	4-5-1
4	Galina Kulakova, USSR	Cross-country	4-2-2
3	Karin (Enke) Kania, E.Ger	Speed Skating	3-4-1
3	Anfisa Reztsova, USSR/UT	CC/Biathlon	3-1-1
3	Vreni Schneider, SWI	Alpine	3-1-1
3	Marja-Liisa Hämäläinen, FIN	Cross-country	3-0-4
3	Claudia Boyarskikh, USSR	Cross-country	3-0-0
3	Sonja Henie, NOR	Figure Skating	3-0-0
3	Irina Rodnina, USSR	Figure Skating	3-0-0
3	Yvonne van Gennip, HOL	Speed Skating	3-0-0

All-Time Leading USA Medalists

MEN

No		Sport	G-S-B
5	Eric Heiden	Speed Skating	5-0-0
3*	Irving Jaffee	Speed Skating	3-0-0
3	Pat Martin	Bobsled	1-2-0
3	John Heaton	Bobsled/Cresta	0-2-1
2	Dick Button	Figure Skating	2-0-0
2†	Eddie Eagan	Boxing/Bobsled	2-0-0
2	Billy Fiske	Bobsled	2-0-0
2	Cliff Gray	Bobsled	2-0-0
2	Jack Shea	Speed Skating	2-0-0
2	Billy Cleary	Ice Hockey	1-1-0
2	Jennison Heaton	Bobsled/Cresta	1-1-0
2	John Mayasich	Ice Hockey	1-1-0
2	Terry McDermott	Speed Skating	1-1-0
2	Dick Meredith	Ice Hockey	1-1-0
2	Tommy Moe	Alpine	1-1-0
2	Weldy Olson	Ice Hockey	1-1-0
2	Dick Rodenheiser	Ice Hockey	1-1-0
2	David Jenkins	Figure Skating	1-1-0
2	Stan Benham	Bobsled	0-2-0
2	Herb Drury	Ice Hockey	0-2-0
2	Frank Synott	Ice Hockey	0-2-0
2	John Garrison	Ice Hockey	0-1-1

WOMEN

No		Sport	G-S-B
5	Bonnie Blair	Speed Skating	5-0-1
4	Cathy Turner	ST Sp. Skating	2-1-1
4	Dianne Holum	Speed Skating	1-2-1
3	Sheila Young	Speed Skating	1-1-1
3	Leah Poulos Mueller	Speed Skating	0-3-0
3	Beatrix Loughran	Figure Skating	0-2-1
3	Amy Peterson	ST Sp. Skating	0-2-1
2	Andrea Mead Lawrence	Alpine	2-0-0
2	Tenley Albright	Figure Skating	1-1-0
2	Gretchen Fraser	Alpine	1-1-0
2	Carol Heiss	Figure Skating	1-1-0
2	Diann Roffe-Steinrotter	Alpine	1-1-0
2	Anne Henning	Speed Skating	1-0-1
2	Penny Pitou	Alpine	0-2-0
2	Nancy Kerrigan	Figure Skating	0-1-1
2	Jean Saubert	Alpine	0-1-1
2	Nikki Ziegelmeyer	ST Sp. Skating	0-1-1

*Jaffee is generally given credit for a third gold medal in the 10,000-meter Speed Skating race of 1928. He had the fastest time before the race was cancelled due to thawing ice. The IOC considers the race unofficial.

†Eagan won the Light Heavyweight boxing title at the 1920 Summer Games in Antwerp and the four-man Bobsled at the 1932 Winter Games in Lake Placid. He is the only athlete ever to win gold medals in both the Winter and Summer Olympics.

All-Time Medal Standings, (1924-94)

All-time Winter Games medal standings, according to *The Golden Book of the Olympic Games* and updated through 1994. Medal counts include figure skating medals (1908 and '20) and hockey medals (1920) awarded at the Summer Games. National medal standings for the Winter and Summer Games are not recognized by the IOC.

		G	S	B	Total
1	Norway	73	77	64	214
2	Soviet Union (1956-88)	78	57	59	194
3	**United States**	53	56	37	146
4	Austria	36	48	44	128
5	East Germany (1956-88)	43	39	36	118
6	Finland	36	45	42	123
7	Sweden	39	26	34	99
8	Switzerland	27	29	29	85
9	Italy	25	21	21	67
10	Germany (1928-36,92—)	23	21	17	61
11	Canada	19	20	25	64
12	West Germany (1952-88)	18	20	19	57
13	France	16	16	21	53
14	Holland	14	19	17	50
15	Russia (1994—)	12	8	4	24
16	Unified Team (1992)	9	6	8	23
17	Great Britain	7	4	12	23
18	Czechoslovakia (1924-92)	2	8	16	26
19	Japan	3	8	8	19
20	South Korea	6	2	2	10
21	Liechtenstein	2	2	5	9

		G	S	B	Total
21	Liechtenstein	2	2	5	9
22	China	0	4	2	6
23	Hungary	0	2	4	6
24	Belgium	1	1	2	4
	Poland	1	1	2	4
	Yugoslavia (1924-88)	0	3	1	4
	Kazakhstan (1994—)	1	2	0	3
28	Spain	1	0	1	2
	Ukraine (1994—)	1	0	1	2
	Belarus (1994—)	0	2	0	2
	Luxembourg	2	0	0	2
32	Slovenia (1992—)	0	0	3	3
	North Korea	0	1	1	2
	Uzbekistan (1994—)	1	0	0	1
35	New Zealand	0	1	0	1
36	Australia	0	0	1	1
	Bulgaria	0	0	1	1
	Romania	0	0	1	1
	Note:				
	USSR/UT/Russia	99	71	71	241
	Germany/E.Ger/W.Ger	84	80	72	236

Athletes from the USSR participated in the Winter Games from 1956-88, returned as the Unified Team in 1992 after the breakup of the Soviet Union (in 1991) and then competed for the independent republics of Belarus, Kazakhstan, Russia, Ukraine, Uzbekistan and three others in 1994. Yugoslavia divided into Croatia and Bosnia-Herzegovina in 1991, while Czechoslovakia split into Slovenia and the Czech Republic the same year.

Germany was barred from the Olympics in 1924 and 1948 as an aggressor nation in both World Wars I and II. Divided into East and West Germany after WWII, both countries competed under one flag from 1952-64, then as separate teams from 1968-88. Germany was reunified in 1990.

The Summer Olympics

The original Olympic Games were celebrated as a religious festival from 776 B.C. to 393 A.D., when Roman emperor Theodosius I banned all pagan festivals (the Olympics celebrated the Greek god Zeus).

On June 23, 1894, French educator Baron Pierre de Coubertin, speaking at the Sorbonne in Paris to a gathering of international sports leaders, proposed that the ancient games be revived on an international scale. The idea was enthusiastically received and the Modern Olympics were born.

The first Olympics were held two years later in Athens, where 311 athletes from 14 nations competed in the ancient Panathenaic stadium to large and enthusiastic crowds. Americans captured nine out of 12 track and field events, but Greece won the most medals with 50.

Year	No	Location	Dates	Nations	Most medals	USA Medals
1896	I	Athens, GRE	Apr. 6-15	14	Greece (10-18-22—50)	11- 7- 1— 19 (2nd)
1900	II	Paris, FRA	May 20-Oct. 28	26	France (26-37-32—95)	18-14-15— 47 (2nd)
1904	III	St. Louis, Mo.	July 1-Nov. 23	13	USA (78-84-82—244)	78-84-82—244 (1st)
1906-a	—	Athens, GRE	Apr. 22-May 2	20	France (15-9-16—40)	12- 6- 6— 24 (3rd)
1908	IV	London, GBR	Apr. 27-Oct. 31	22	Britain (54-46-38—138)	23-12-12— 47 (2nd)
1912	V	Stockholm, SWE	May 5-July 22	28	Sweden (23-24-17—64)	25-18-20— 63 (2nd)
1916	VI	Berlin, GER	Cancelled (WWI)			
1920	VII	Antwerp, BEL	Apr. 20-Sept. 12	29	USA (41-26-26—93)	41-26-26— 93 (1st)
1924	VIII	Paris, FRA	May 4-July 27	44	USA (45-27-27—99)	45-27-27— 99 (1st)
1928	IX	Amsterdam, HOL	May 17-Aug. 12	46	USA (22-18-16—56)	22-18-16— 56 (1st)
1932	X	Los Angeles, Calif.	July 30-Aug. 14	37	USA (41-32-30—103)	41-32-30—103 (1st)
1936	XI	Berlin, GER	Aug. 1-16	49	Germany (33-26-30-89)	24-20-12— 56 (2nd)
1940-b	XII	Tokyo, JPN	Cancelled (WWII)			
1944	XIII	London, GBR	Cancelled (WWII)			
1948	XIV	London, GBR	July 29-Aug. 14	59	USA (38-27-19—84)	38-27-19— 84 (1st)
1952-cd	XV	Helsinki, FIN	July 19-Aug. 3	69	USA (40-19-17—76)	40-19-17— 76 (1st)
1956-e	XVI	Melbourne, AUS	Nov. 22-Dec .8	72	USSR (37-29-32—98)	32-25-17— 74 (2nd)
1960	XVII	Rome, ITA	Aug. 25-Sept. 11	83	USSR (43-29-31—103)	34-21-16— 71 (2nd)
1964	XVIII	Tokyo, JPN	Oct. 10-24	93	USA (36-26-28—90)	36-26-28— 90 (1st)
1968-f	XIX	Mexico City, MEX	Oct. 12-27	112	USA (45-28-34—107)	45-28-34—107 (1st)
1972	XX	Munich, W.GER	Aug. 26-Sept. 10	121	USSR (50-27-22-99)	33-31-30— 94 (2nd)
1976-g	XXI	Montreal, CAN	July 17-Aug. 1	92	USSR (49-41-35—125)	34-35-25— 94 (3rd)
1980-h	XXII	Moscow, USSR	July 19-Aug. 3	80	USSR (80-69-46—195)	Boycotted Games
1984-i	XXIII	Los Angeles, Calif.	July 28-Aug. 12	140	USA (83-61-30—174)	83-61-30—174 (1st)
1988	XXIV	Seoul, S.KOR	Sept. 17-Oct. 2	159	USSR (55-31-46—132)	36-31-27— 94 (3rd)
1992-j	XXV	Barcelona, SPA	July 25-Aug. 9	169	UT (45-38-29—112)	37-34-37—108 (2nd)
1996	XXVI	Atlanta, Ga.	July 20-Aug. 4			
2000	XXVII	Sydney, AUS	Sept. 16-Oct. 1			

a—The 1906 Intercalated Games in Athens are considered unofficial by the IOC because they did not take place in the four-year cycle established in 1896. However, most record books include these interim games with the others.

b—The 1940 Summer Games are originally scheduled for Tokyo, but Japan resigns as host after the outbreak of the Sino-Japanese war in 1937. Helsinki is the next choice, but the IOC cancels the Games after Russian troops invade Finland in 1939.

c—Germany and Japan are allowed to rejoin Olympic community for first Summer Games since 1936. Though a divided country, the Germans send a joint East-West team.

d—The Soviet Union (USSR) participates in its first Olympics, Winter or Summer, since the Russian revolution in 1917 and takes home the second most medals (22-30-19—71).

e—Due to Australian quarantine laws, the equestrian events for the 1956 Games are held in Stockholm, June 10-17.

f—East Germany and West Germany send separate teams for the first time and will continue to do so through 1988.

g—The 1976 Games are boycotted by 32 nations, most of them from black Africa, because the IOC will not ban New Zealand. Earlier that year, a rugby team from New Zealand had toured racially-segregated South Africa.

h—The 1980 Games are boycotted by 64 nations, led by the USA, to protest the Russian invasion of Afghanistan on Dec. 27, 1979.

i—The 1984 Games are boycotted by 14 Eastern Bloc nations, led by the USSR, to protest America's overcommercialization of the Games, inadequate security and an anti-Soviet attitude by the U.S. government. Most believe, however, the communist walkout is simply revenge for 1980.

j—Germany sends a single team after East and West German reunification in 1990 and the USSR competes as the Unified Team after the breakup of the Soviet Union in 1991.

Event-by-Event

Gold medal winners from 1896-1992 in the following events: Baseball, Basketball, Boxing, Diving, Field Hockey, Gymnastics, Soccer, Swimming, Tennis, and Track & Field.

BASEBALL

Year
1992 **Cuba**, Taiwan, Japan

BASKETBALL

MEN

Multiple gold medals: USA (10); USSR (2).

Year		Year	
1936	**United States**, Canada, Mexico	1972	**Soviet Union**, United States, Cuba
1948	**United States**, France, Brazil	1976	**United States**, Yugoslavia, Soviet Union
1952	**United States**, Soviet Union, Uruguay	1980	**Yugoslavia**, Italy, Soviet Union
1956	**United States**, Soviet Union, Uruguay	1984	**United States**, Spain, Yugoslavia
1960	**United States**, Soviet Union, Brazil	1988	**Soviet Union**, Yugoslavia, United States
1964	**United States**, Soviet Union, Brazil	1992	**United States**, Croatia, Lithuania
1968	**United States**, Yugoslavia, Soviet Union		

U.S. Medal-Winning Men's Basketball Teams

1936 (gold medal): Sam Balter, Ralph Bishop, Joe Fortenberry, Tex Gibbons, Francis Johnson, Carl Knowles, Frank Lubin, Art Mollner, Don Piper, Jack Ragland, Carl Shy, Willard Schmidt, Duane Swanson and William Wheatley. Coach—Jim Needles; Assistant—Gene Johnson. Final: USA over Canada, 19-8.

1948 (gold medal): Cliff Barker, Don Barksdale, Ralph Beard, Louis Beck, Vince Boryla, Gordon Carpenter, Alex Groza, Wallace Jones, Bob Kurland, Ray Lumpp, R.C. Pitts, Jesse Renick, Robert (Jackie) Robinson and Ken Rollins. Coach—Omar Browning; Assistant—Adolph Rupp. Final: USA over France, 65-21.

1952 (gold medal): Ron Bontemps, Mark Freiberger, Wayne Glasgow, Charlie Hoag, Bill Hougland, John Keller, Dean Kelley, Bob Kenney, Bob Kurland, Bill Lienhard, Clyde Lovellette, Frank McCabe, Dan Pippin and Howie Williams. Coach—Warren Womble; Assistant—Forrest (Phog) Allen. Final: USA over USSR, 36-25.

1956 (gold medal): Dick Boushka, Carl Cain, Chuck Darling, Bill Evans, Gib Ford, Burdy Haldorson, Bill Hougland, Bob Jeangerard, K.C. Jones, Bill Russell, Ron Tomsic, Jim Walsh. Coach—Gerald Tucker; Assistant—Bruce Drake. Final: USA over USSR, 89-55.

1960 (gold medal): Jay Arnette, Walt Bellamy, Bob Boozer, Terry Dischinger, Jerry Lucas, Oscar Robertson, Adrian Smith, Burdy Haldorson, Darrall Imhoff, Allen Kelley, Lester Lane and Jerry West. Coach—Pete Newell; Assistant—Warren Womble. Final: USA over Brazil, 90-63.

1964 (gold medal): Jim (Bad News) Barnes, Bill Bradley, Larry Brown, Joe Caldwell, Mel Counts, Dick Davies, Walt Hazzard, Lucius Jackson, Pete McCaffrey, Jeff Mullins, Jerry Shipp and George Wilson. Coach—Hank Iba; Assistant—Henry Vaughn. Final: USA over USSR, 73-59.

1968 (gold medal): Mike Barrett, John Clawson, Don Dee, Cal Fowler, Spencer Haywood, Bill Hosket, Jim King, Glynn Saulters, Charlie Scott, Mike Silliman, Ken Spain, and JoJo White. Coach—Hank Iba; Assistant—Henry Vaughn. USA over Yugoslavia, 65-50.

1972 (silver medal refused): Mike Bantom, Jim Brewer, Tom Burleson, Doug Collins, Kenny Davis, Jim Forbes, Tom Henderson, Bobby Jones, Dwight Jones, Kevin Joyce, Tom McMillen and Ed Ratleff. Coach—Hank Iba; Assistants— John Bach and Don Haskins. Final: USSR over USA, 51-50.

1976 (gold medal): Tate Armstrong, Quinn Buckner, Kenny Carr, Adrian Dantley, Walter Davis, Phil Ford, Ernie Grunfeld, Phil Hubbard, Mitch Kupchak, Tommy LaGarde, Scott May and Steve Sheppard. Coach—Dean Smith; Assistants—Bill Guthridge and John Thompson. Final: USA over Yugoslavia, 95-74.

1980 (no medal): USA boycotted Moscow Games. Final: Yugoslavia over Italy, 86-77.

1984 (gold medal): Steve Alford, Patrick Ewing, Vern Fleming, Michael Jordan; Joe Kleine, Jon Koncak, Chris Mullin, Sam Perkins, Alvin Robertson, Wayman Tisdale, Jeff Turner and Leon Wood. Coach—Bobby Knight; Assistants— Don Donoher and George Raveling. Final: USA over Spain, 96-65.

1988 (bronze medal): Stacey Augmon, Willie Anderson, Bimbo Coles, Jeff Grayer, Hersey Hawkins, Dan Majerle, Danny Manning, Mitch Richmond, J.R. Reid, David Robinson, Charles D. Smith and Charles E. Smith. Coach—John Thompson; Assistants—George Raveling and Mary Fenlon. Final: USSR over Yugoslavia, 76-63.

1992 (gold medal): Charles Barkley, Larry Bird, Clyde Drexler, Patrick Ewing, Magic Johnson, Michael Jordan, Christian Laettner, Karl Malone, Chris Mullin, Scottie Pippen, David Robinson and John Stockton. Coach—Chuck Daly; Assistants—Lenny Wilkens, Mike Krzyzewski and P.J. Carlesimo. Final: USA over Croatia, 117-85.

WOMEN

Multiple gold medals: USSR/UT (3); USA (2).

Year		Year	
1976	**Soviet Union**, United States, Bulgaria	1988	**United States**, Yugoslavia, Soviet Union
1980	**Soviet Union**, Bulgaria, Yugoslavia	1992	**Unified Team**, China, United States
1984	**United States**, South Korea, China		

U.S. Gold Medal-Winning Women's Basketball Teams

1984: Cathy Boswell, Denise Curry, Anne Donovan, Teresa Edwards, Lea Henry, Janice Lawrence, Pamela McGee, Carol Menken-Schaudt, Cheryl Miller, Kim Mulkey, Cindy Noble, Lynette Woodard. Coach—Pat Summitt; Assistant—Kay Yow. Final: USA over South Korea, 85–55.

1988: Cindy Brown, Vicky Bullett, Cynthia Cooper, Anne Donovan, Teresa Edwards, Kamie Ethridge, Jennifer Gillom, Bridgette Gordon, Andrea Lloyd, Katrina McClain, Suzie McConnell, Teresa Weatherspoon. Coach—Kay Yow; Assistants— Sylvia Hatchell and Susan Yow. Final: USA over Yugoslavia, 77–70.

BOXING

Multiple gold medals: László Papp and Teofilo Stevenson (3); Angel Herrera, Oliver Kirk, Jerzy Kulej, Boris Lagutin and Harry Mallin (2). All fighters won titles in consecutive Olympics, except Kirk, who won both the Bantam and Featherweight titles in 1904 (he only had to fight once in each division).

Light Flyweight (106 lbs)

Year		Final Match	Year		Final Match
1968	Francisco Rodriguez, VEN	Decision, 3-2	1984	Paul Gonzales, USA	Default
1972	György Gedó, HUN	Decision, 5-0	1988	Ivailo Hristov, BUL	Decision, 5-0
1976	Jorge Hernandez, CUB	Decision, 4-1	1992	Rogelio Marcelo, CUB	Decision, 24-10
1980	Shamil Sabyrov, USSR	Decision, 3-2			

Flyweight (112 lbs)

Year		Final Match	Year		Final Match
1904	George Finnegan, USA	Stopped, 1st	1960	Gyula Török, HUN	Decision, 3-2
1920	Frank Di Gennara, USA	Decision	1964	Fernando Atzori, ITA	Decision, 4-1
1924	Fidel LaBarba, USA	Decision	1968	Ricardo Delgado, MEX	Decision, 5-0
1928	Antal Kocsis, HUN	Decision	1972	Georgi Kostadinov, BUL	Decision, 5-0
1932	István Énekes, HUN	Decision	1976	Leo Randolph, USA	Decision, 3-2
1936	Willi Kaiser, GER	Decision	1980	Peter Lessov, BUL	Stopped, 2nd
1948	Pascual Perez, ARG	Decision	1984	Steven McCrory, USA	Decision, 4-1
1952	Nathan Brooks, USA	Decision, 3-0	1988	Kim Swang-Sun, KOR	Decision, 4-1
1956	Terence Spinks, GBR	Decision	1992	Su Choi-Chol, N.Kor	Decision, 12-2

Bantamweight (119 lbs)

Year		Final Match	Year		Final Match
1904	Oliver Kirk, USA	Stopped, 3rd	1960	Oleg Grigoryev, USSR	Decision
1908	Henry Thomas, GBR	Decision	1964	Takao Sakurai, JPN	Stopped, 2nd
1920	Clarence Walker, SAF	Decision	1968	Valery Sokolov, USSR	Stopped, 2nd
1924	William Smith, SAF	Decision	1972	Orlando Martinez, CUB	Decision, 5-0
1928	Vittorio Tamagnini, ITA	Decision	1976	Gu Yong-Ju, N.Kor	Decision, 5-0
1932	Horace Gwynne, CAN	Decision	1980	Juan Hernandez, CUB	Decision, 5-0
1936	Ulderico Sergo, ITA	Decision	1984	Maurizio Stecca, ITA	Decision, 4-1
1948	Tibor Csik, HUN	Decision	1988	Kennedy McKinney, USA	Decision, 5-0
1952	Pentti Hämäläinen, FIN	Decision, 2-1	1992	Joel Casamayor, CUB	Decision, 14-8
1956	Wolfgang Behrendt, GER	Decision			

Featherweight (125 lbs)

Year		Final Match	Year		Final Match
1904	Oliver Kirk, USA	Decision	1960	Francesco Musso, ITA	Decision, 4-1
1908	Richard Gunn, GBR	Decision	1964	Stanislav Stepashkin, USSR	Decision, 3-2
1920	Paul Fritsch, FRA	Decision	1968	Antonio Roldan, MEX	Won on Disq.
1924	John Fields, USA	Decision	1972	Boris Kousnetsov, USSR	Decision, 3-2
1928	Lambertus van Klaveren, HOL	Decision	1976	Angel Herrera, CUB	KO, 2nd
1932	Carmelo Robledo, ARG	Decision	1980	Rudi Fink, E.Ger	Decision, 4-1
1936	Oscar Casanovas, ARG	Decision	1984	Meldrick Taylor, USA	Decision, 5-0
1948	Ernesto Formenti, ITA	Decision	1988	Giovanni Parisi, ITA	Stopped, 1st
1952	Jan Zachara, CZE	Decision, 2-1	1992	Andreas Tews, GER	Decision, 16-7
1956	Vladimir Safronov, USSR	Decision			

Lightweight (132 lbs)

Year		Final Match	Year		Final Match
1904	Harry Spanger, USA	Decision	1960	Kazimierz Pazdzior, POL	Decision, 4-1
1908	Frederick Grace, GBR	Decision	1964	Józef Grudzien, POL	Decision
1920	Samuel Mosberg, USA	Decision	1968	Ronnie Harris, USA	Decision, 5-0
1924	Hans Nielsen, DEN	Decision	1972	Jan Szczepanski, POL	Decision, 5-0
1928	Carlo Orlandi, ITA	Decision	1976	Howard Davis, USA	Decision, 5-0
1932	Lawrence Stevens, SAF	Decision	1980	Angel Herrera, CUB	Stopped, 3rd
1936	Imre Harangi, HUN	Decision	1984	Pernell Whitaker, USA	Foe quit, 2nd
1948	Gerald Dreyer, SAF	Decision	1988	Andreas Zuelow, E.Ger	Decision, 5-0
1952	Aureliano Bolognesi, ITA	Decision, 2-1	1992	Oscar De La Hoya, USA	Decision, 7-2
1956	Richard McTaggart, GBR	Decision			

Light Welterweight (139 lbs)

Year		Final Match	Year		Final Match
1952	Charles Adkins, USA	Decision, 2-1	1976	Ray Leonard, USA	Decision, 5-0
1956	Vladimir Yengibaryan, USSR	Decision	1980	Patrizio Oliva, ITA	Decision, 4-1
1960	Bohumil Nemecek CZE	Decision, 5-0	1984	Jerry Page, USA	Decision, 5-0
1964	Jerzy Kulej, POL	Decision, 5-0	1988	Vyacheslav Yanovsky, USSR	Decision, 5-0
1968	Jerzy Kulej, POL	Decision, 3-2	1992	Hector Vinent, CUB	Decision, 11-1
1972	Ray Seales, USA	Decision, 3-2			

Boxing (Cont.)

Welterweight (147 lbs)

Year		Final Match	Year		Final Match
1904	Albert Young, USA	Decision	1960	Nino Benvenuti, ITA	Decision, 4-1
1920	Albert Schneider, CAN	Decision	1964	Marian Kasprzyk, POL	Decision, 4-1
1924	Jean Delarge, BEL	Decision	1968	Manfred Wolke, E.Ger	Decision, 4-1
1928	Edward Morgan, NZE	Decision	1972	Emilio Correa, CUB	Decision, 5-0
1932	Edward Flynn, USA	Decision	1976	Jochen Bachfeld, E.Ger	Decision, 3-2
1936	Sten Suvio, FIN	Decision	1980	Andrés Aldama, CUB	Decision, 4-1
1948	Julius Torma, CZE	Decision	1984	Mark Breland, USA	Decision, 5-0
1952	Zygmunt Chychla, POL	Decision, 3-0	1988	Robert Wangila, KEN	KO, 2nd
1956	Nicolae Linca, ROM	Decision, 3-2	1992	Michael Carruth, IRE	Decision, 13-10

Light Middleweight (156 lbs)

Year		Final Match	Year		Final Match
1952	László Papp, HUN	Decision, 3-0	1976	Jerzy Rybicki, POL	Decision, 5-0
1956	László Papp, HUN	Decision	1980	Armando Martinez, CUB	Decision, 4-1
1960	Skeeter McClure, USA	Decision, 4-1	1984	Frank Tate, USA	Decision, 5-0
1964	Boris Lagutin, USSR	Decision, 4-1	1988	Park Si-Hun, S.Kor	Decision, 3-2
1968	Boris Lagutin, USSR	Decision, 5-0	1992	Juan Lemus, CUB	Decision, 6-1
1972	Dieter Kottysch, W.Ger	Decision, 3-2			

Middleweight (165 lbs)

Year		Final Match	Year		Final Match
1904	Charles Mayer, USA	Stopped, 3rd	1960	Edward Crook, USA	Decision, 3-2
1908	John Douglas, GBR	Decision	1964	Valery Popenchenko, USSR	Stopped, 1st
1920	Harry Mallin, GBR	Decision	1968	Christopher Finnegan, GBR	Decision, 3-2
1924	Harry Mallin, GBR	Decision	1972	Vyacheslav Lemechev, USSR	KO, 1st
1928	Piero Toscani, ITA	Decision	1976	Michael Spinks, USA	Stopped, 3rd
1932	Carmen Barth, USA	Decision	1980	José Gomez, CUB	Decision, 4-1
1936	Jean Despeaux, FRA	Decision	1984	Shin Joon-Sup, S.Kor	Decision, 3-2
1948	László Papp, HUN	Decision	1988	Henry Maske, E.Ger	Decision, 5-0
1952	Floyd Patterson, USA	KO, 1st	1992	Ariel Hernandez, CUB	Decision, 12-7
1956	Gennady Schatkov, USSR	KO, 1st			

Light Heavyweight (178 lbs)

Year		Final Match	Year		Final Match
1920	Eddie Eagan, USA	Decision	1964	Cosimo Pinto, ITA	Decision, 3-2
1924	Harry Mitchell, GBR	Decision	1968	Dan Poznjak, USSR	Default
1928	Victor Avendaño, ARG	Decision	1972	Mate Parlov, YUG	Stopped, 2nd
1932	David Carstens, SAF	Decision	1976	Leon Spinks, USA	Stopped, 3rd
1936	Roger Michelot, FRA	Decision	1980	Slobodan Kacar, YUG	Decision, 4-1
1948	George Hunter, SAF	Decision	1984	Anton Josipovic, YUG	Default
1952	Norvel Lee, USA	Decision, 3-0	1988	Andrew Maynard, USA	Decision, 5-0
1956	James Boyd, USA	Decision	1992	Torsten May, GER	Decision, 8-3
1960	Cassius Clay, USA	Decision, 5-0			

Note: Cassius Clay changed his name to Muhammad Ali after winning the world heavyweight championship in 1964.

Heavyweight (201 lbs)

Year		Final Match	Year		Final Match
1984	Henry Tillman, USA	Decision, 5-0	1992	Felix Savon, CUB	Decision, 14-1
1988	Ray Mercer, USA	KO, 1st			

Super Heavyweight (Unlimited)

Year		Final Match	Year		Final Match
1904	Samuel Berger, USA	Decision	1960	Franco De Piccoli, ITA	KO, 1st
1908	Albert Oldham, GBR	KO, 1st	1964	Joe Frazier, USA	Decision, 3-2
1920	Ronald Rawson, GBR	Decision	1968	George Foreman, USA	Stopped, 2nd
1924	Otto von Porat, NOR	Decision	1972	Teófilo Stevenson, CUB	Default
1928	Arturo Rodriguez Jurado, ARG	Stopped, 1st	1976	Teófilo Stevenson, CUB	KO, 3rd
1932	Santiago Lovell, ARG	Decision	1980	Teófilo Stevenson, CUB	Decision, 4-1
1936	Herbert Runge, GER	Decision	1984	Tyrell Biggs, USA	Decision, 4-1
1948	Rafael Iglesias, ARG	KO, 2nd	1988	Lennox Lewis, CAN	Stopped, 2nd
1952	Ed Sanders, USA	Won on Disq.	1992	Roberto Balado, CUB	Decision, 13-2
1956	Pete Rademacher, USA	Stopped, 1st			

Note: Heavyweight division until 1984.

Future World Heavyweight Champions

Six Olympic gold medal winners eventually went on to become heavyweight champion of the world.

Middleweights	Light Heavyweights	Heavyweights
Floyd Patterson	Cassius Clay	Joe Frazier
Michael Spinks	Leon Spinks	George Foreman

DIVING

MEN

Multiple gold medals: Greg Louganis (4); Klaus Dibiasi (3); Pete Desjardins, Sammy Lee, Bob Webster and Albert White (2).

Springboard

Year		Points	Year		Points
1908	Albert Zürner, GER	85.5	1960	Gary Tobian, USA	170.00
1912	Paul Günther, GER	79.23	1964	Ken Sitzberger, USA	159.90
1920	Louis Kuehn, USA	675.4	1968	Bernie Wrightson, USA	170.15
1924	Albert White, USA	696.4	1972	Vladimir Vasin, USSR	594.09
1928	Pete Desjardins, USA	185.04	1976	Phil Boggs, USA	619.05
1932	Michael Galitzen, USA	161.38	1980	Aleksandr Portnov, USSR	905.03
1936	Richard Degener, USA	163.57	1984	Greg Louganis, USA	754.41
1948	Bruce Harlan, USA	163.64	1988	Greg Louganis, USA	730.80
1952	David Browning, USA	205.29	1992	Mark Lenzi, USA	676.53
1956	Bob Clotworthy, USA	159.56			

Platform

Year		Points	Year		Points
1904	George Sheldon, USA	12.66	1956	Joaquin Capilla, MEX	152.44
1906	Gottlob Walz, GER	156.0	1960	Bob Webster, USA	165.56
1908	Hjalmar Johansson, SWE	83.75	1964	Bob Webster, USA	148.58
1912	Erik Adlerz, SWE	73.94	1968	Klaus Dibiasi, ITA	164.18
1920	Clarence Pinkston, USA	100.67	1972	Klaus Dibiasi, ITA	504.12
1924	Albert White, USA	97.46	1976	Klaus Dibiasi, ITA	600.51
1928	Pete Desjardins, USA	98.74	1980	Falk Hoffmann, E.Ger	835.65
1932	Harold Smith, USA	124.80	1984	Greg Louganis, USA	710.91
1936	Marshall Wayne, USA	113.58	1988	Greg Louganis, USA	638.61
1948	Sammy Lee, USA	130.05	1992	Sun Shuwei, CHN	677.31
1952	Sammy Lee, USA	156.28			

WOMEN

Multiple gold medals: Pat McCormick (4); Ingrid Engel-Krämer (3); Vicki Draves, Dorothy Poynton Hill and Gao Min (2).

Springboard

Year		Points	Year		Points
1920	Aileen Riggin, USA	539.9	1964	Ingrid Engel-Krämer, GER	145.00
1924	Elizabeth Becker, USA	474.5	1968	Sue Gossick, USA	150.77
1928	Helen Meany, USA	78.62	1972	Micki King, USA	450.03
1932	Georgia Coleman, USA	87.52	1976	Jennifer Chandler, USA	506.19
1936	Marjorie Gestring, USA	89.27	1980	Irina Kalinina, USSR	725.91
1948	Vicki Draves, USA	108.74	1984	Sylvie Bernier, CAN	530.70
1952	Pat McCormick, USA	147.30	1988	Gao Min, CHN	580.23
1956	Pat McCormick, USA	142.36	1992	Gao Min, CHN	572.40
1960	Ingrid Krämer, GER	155.81			

Platform

Year		Points	Year		Points
1912	Greta Johansson, SWE	39.9	1960	Ingrid Krämer, GER	91.28
1920	Stefani Fryland-Clausen, DEN	34.6	1964	Lesley Bush, USA	99.80
1924	Caroline Smith, USA	33.2	1968	Milena Duchková, CZE	109.59
1928	Elizabeth Becker Pinkston, USA	31.6	1972	Ulrika Knape, SWE	390.00
1932	Dorothy Poynton, USA	40.26	1976	Elena Vaytsekhovskaya, USSR	406.59
1936	Dorothy Poynton Hill, USA	33.93	1980	Martina Jäschke, E.Ger	596.25
1948	Vicki Draves, USA	68.87	1984	Zhou Jihong, CHN	435.51
1952	Pat McCormick, USA	79.37	1988	Xu Yanmei, CHN	445.20
1956	Pat McCormick, USA	84.85	1992	Fu Mingxia, CHN	461.43

FIELD HOCKEY

MEN

Multiple gold medals: India (8); Great Britain and Pakistan (3); West Germany/Germany (2).

Year		Year	
1908	**Great Britain**, Ireland, Scotland	1964	**India**, Pakistan, Australia
1920	**Great Britain**, Denmark, Belgium	1968	**Pakistan**, Australia, India
1928	**India**, Holland, Germany	1972	**West Germany**, Pakistan, India
1932	**India**, Japan, United States	1976	**New Zealand**, Australia, Pakistan
1936	**India**, Germany, Holland	1980	**India**, Spain, Soviet Union
1948	**India**, Great Britain, Holland	1984	**Pakistan**, West Germany, Great Britain
1952	**India**, Holland, Great Britain	1988	**Great Britain**, West Germany, Holland
1956	**India**, Pakistan, Germany	1992	**Germany**, Australia, Pakistan
1960	**Pakistan**, India, Spain		

Field Hockey (Cont.)
WOMEN

Year		Year	
1980	**Zimbabwe**, Czechoslovakia, Soviet Union	1988	**Australia**, South Korea, Holland
1984	**Holland**, West Germany, United States	1992	**Spain**, Germany, Great Britain

GYMNASTICS

MEN

At least 4 gold medals (including team events): Sawao Kato (8); Nikolai Andrianov, Viktor Chukarin and Boris Shakhlin (7); Akinori Nakayama and Vitaly Scherbo (6); Yukio Endo, Anton Heida, Mitsuo Tsukahara and Takashi Ono (5); Vladimir Artemov, Georges Miez and Valentin Muratov (4).

All-Around

Year		Points	Year		Points
1900	Gustave Sandras, FRA	302.0	1952	Viktor Chukarin, USSR	115.7
1904	Julius Lenhart, AUT	69.80	1956	Viktor Chukarin, USSR	114.25
1906	Pierre Payssé, FRA	97.0	1960	Boris Shakhlin, USSR	115.95
1908	Alberto Braglia, ITA	317.0	1964	Yukio Endo, JPN	115.95
1912	Alberto Braglia, ITA	135.0	1968	Sawao Kato, JPN	115.9
1920	Giorgio Zampori, ITA	88.35	1972	Sawao Kato, JPN	114.650
1924	Leon Stukelj, YUG	110.340	1976	Nikolai Andrianov, USSR	116.65
1928	Georges Miez, SWI	247.500	1980	Aleksandr Dityatin, USSR	118.65
1932	Romeo Neri, ITA	140.625	1984	Koji Gushiken, JPN	118.7
1936	Alfred Schwarzmann, GER	113.100	1988	Vladimir Artemov, USSR	119.125
1948	Veikko Huhtanen, FIN	229.7	1992	Vitaly Scherbo, UT	59.025

Horizontal Bar

Year		Points	Year		Points
1896	Hermann Weingartner, GER	—	1964	Boris Shakhlin, USSR	19.625
1904	(TIE) Anton Heida, USA	40.0	1968	(TIE) Akinori Nakayama, JPN	19.55
	& Edward Hennig, USA	40.0		& Mikhail Voronin, USSR	19.55
1924	Leon Stukelj, YUG	19.73	1972	Mitsuo Tsukahara, JPN	19.725
1928	Georges Miez, SWI	19.17	1976	Mitsuo Tsukahara, JPN	19.675
1932	Dallas Bixler, USA	18.33	1980	Stoyan Deltchev, BUL	19.825
1936	Aleksanteri Saarvala, FIN	19.367	1984	Shinji Morisue, JPN	20.00
1948	Josef Stalder, SWI	19.85	1988	(TIE) Vladimir Artemov, USSR	19.900
1952	Jack Günthard, SWI	19.55		& Valeri Lyukin, USSR	19.900
1956	Takashi Ono, JPN	19.60	1992	Trent Dimas, USA	9.875
1960	Takashi Ono, JPN	19.60			

Parallel Bars

Year		Points	Year		Points
1896	Alfred Flatow, GER	—	1960	Boris Shakhlin, USSR	19.40
1904	George Eyser, USA	44.0	1964	Yukio Endo, JPN	19.675
1924	August Güttinger, SWI	21.63	1968	Akinori Nakayama, JPN	19.475
1928	Ladislav Vácha, CZE	18.83	1972	Sawao Kato, JPN	19.475
1932	Romeo Neri, ITA	18.97	1976	Sawao Kato, JPN	19.675
1936	Konrad Frey, GER	19.067	1980	Aleksandr Tkachyov, USSR	19.775
1948	Michael Reusch, SWI	19.75	1984	Bart Conner, USA	19.95
1952	Hans Eugster, SWI	19.65	1988	Vladimir Artemov, USSR	19.925
1956	Viktor Chukarin, USSR	19.20	1992	Vitaly Scherbo, UT	9.900

Vault

Year		Points	Year		Points
1896	Karl Schumann, GER	—	1960	(TIE) Takashi Ono, JPN	19.35
1904	(TIE) George Eyser, USA	36.0		& Boris Shakhlin, USSR	19.35
	& Anton Heida, USA	36.0	1964	Haruhiro Yamashita, JPN	19.60
1924	Frank Kriz, USA	9.98	1968	Mikhail Voronin, USSR	19.00
1928	Eugen Mack, SWI	9.58	1972	Klaus Köste, E.Ger	18.85
1932	Savino Guglielmetti, ITA	18.03	1976	Nikolai Andrianov, USSR	19.45
1936	Alfred Schwarzmann, GER	19.20	1980	Nikolai Andrianov, USSR	19.825
1948	Paavo Aaltonen, FIN	19.55	1984	Lou Yun, CHN	19.95
1952	Viktor Chukarin, USSR	19.20	1988	Lou Yun, CHN	19.875
1956	(TIE) Helmut Bantz, GER	18.85	1992	Vitaly Scherbo, UT	9.856
	& Valentin Muratov, USSR	18.85			

Pommel Horse

Year		Points	Year		Points
1896	Louis Zutter, SWI	—	1964	Miroslav Cerar, YUG	19.525
1904	Anton Heida, USA	42.	1968	Miroslav Cerar, YUG	19.325
1924	Josef Wilhelm, SWI	21.23	1972	Viktor Klimenko, SOV	19.125
1928	Hermann Hänggi, SWI	19.75	1976	Zoltán Magyar, HUN	19.70
1932	István Pelle, HUN	19.07	1980	Zoltán Magyar, HUN	19.925
1936	Konrad Frey, GER	19.333	1984	(TIE) Li Ning, CHN	19.95
1948	(TIE) Paavo Aaltonen, FIN	19.35		& Peter Vidmar, USA	19.95
	Veikko Huhtanen, FIN	19.35	1988	(TIE) Dmitri Bilozerchev, USSR	19.95
	& Heikki Savolainen, FIN	19.35		Zsolt Borkai, HUN	19.95
1952	Viktor Chukarin, USSR	19.50		& Lyubomir Geraskov, BUL	19.95
1956	Boris Shakhlin, USSR	19.25	1992	(TIE) Pae Gil-Su, N.Kor	9.925
1960	(TIE) Eugen Ekman, FIN	19.375		& Vitaly Scherbo, UT	9.925
	& Boris Shakhlin, USSR	19.375			

Rings

Year		Points	Year		Points
1896	Ioannis Mitropoulos, GRE	—	1968	Akinori Nakayama, JPN	19.45
1904	Hermann Glass, USA	45.	1972	Akinori Nakayama, JPN	19.35
1924	Francesco Martino, ITA	21.553	1976	Nikolai Andrianov, USSR	19.65
1928	Leon Stukelj, YUG	19.25	1980	Aleksandr Dityatin, USSR	19.875
1932	George Gulack, USA	18.97	1984	(TIE) Koji Gushiken, JPN	19.85
1936	Alois Hudec, CZE	19.433		& Li Ning, CHN	19.85
1948	Karl Frei, SWI	19.80	1988	(TIE) Holger Behrendt, E.Ger	19.925
1952	Grant Shaginyan, USSR	19.75		& Dmitri Bilozerchev, USSR	19.925
1956	Albert Azaryan, USSR	19.35	1992	Vitaly Scherbo, UT	9.937
1960	Albert Azaryan, USSR	19.725			
1964	Takuji Haytta, JPN	19.475			

Floor Exercise

Year		Points	Year		Points
1932	Istvän Pelle, HUN	9.60	1968	Sawao Kato, JPN	19.475
1936	Georges Miez, SWI	18.666	1972	Nikolai Andrianov, USSR	19.175
1948	Ferenc Pataki, HUN	19.35	1976	Nikolai Andrianov, USSR	19.45
1952	William Thoresson, SWE	19.25	1980	Roland Brückner, E.Ger	19.75
1956	Valentin Muratov, USSR	19.20	1984	Li Ning, CHN	19.925
1960	Nobuyuki Aihara, JPN	19.45	1988	Sergei Kharkov, USSR	19.925
1964	Franco Menichelli, ITA	19.45	1992	Li Xiaosahuang, CHN	9.925

Team Combined Exercises

Year		Points	Year		Points
1904	United States	374.43	1956	Soviet Union	568.25
1906	Norway	19.00	1960	Japan	575.20
1908	Sweden	438	1964	Japan	577.95
1912	Italy	265.75	1968	Japan	575.90
1920	Italy	359.855	1972	Japan	571.25
1924	Italy	839.058	1976	Japan	576.85
1928	Switzerland	1718.625	1980	Soviet Union	598.60
1932	Italy	541.850	1984	United States	591.40
1936	Germany	657.430	1988	Soviet Union	593.35
1948	Finland	1358.30	1992	Unified Team	585.45
1952	Soviet Union	574.40			

WOMEN

At least 4 gold medals (including team events): Larissa Latynina (9); Vera Cáslavská (7); Polina Astakhova, Nadia Comaneci, Agnes Keleti and Nelli Kim (5); Olga Korbut, Ecaterina Szabó and Lyudmila Tourischeva (4).

All-Around

Year		Points	Year		Points
1952	Maria Gorokhovskaya, USSR	76.78	1976	Nadia Comaneci, ROM	79.275
1956	Larissa Latynina, USSR	74.933	1980	Yelena Davydova, USSR	79.15
1960	Larissa Latynina, USSR	77.031	1984	Mary Lou Retton, USA	79.175
1964	Vera Cáslavská, CZE	77.564	1988	Yelena Shushunova, USSR	79.662
1968	Vera Cáslavská, CZE	78.25	1992	Tatiana Gutsu, UT	39.737
1972	Lyudmila Tourischeva, USSR	77.025			

Vault

Year		Points	Year		Points
1952	Yekaterina Kalinchuk, USSR	19.20	1976	Nelli Kim, USSR	19.80
1956	Larissa Latynina, USSR	18.833	1980	Natalia Shaposhnikova, USSR	19.725
1960	Margarita Nikolayeva, USSR	19.316	1984	Ecaterina Szabó, ROM	19.875
1964	Vera Cáslavská, CZE	19.483	1988	Svetlana Boginskaya, USSR	19.905
1968	Vera Cáslavská, CZE	19.775	1992	(TIE) Henrietta Onodi, HUN	9.925
1972	Karin Janz, E.Ger	19.525		& Lavinia Milosovici, ROM	9.925

Gymnastics (Cont.)
WOMEN
Uneven Bars

Year		Points	Year		Points
1952	Margit Korondi, HUN	19.40	1976	Nadia Comaneci, ROM	20.00
1956	Agnes Keleti, HUN	18.966	1980	Maxi Gnauck, E.Ger	19.875
1960	Polina Astakhova, USSR	19.616	1984	Ma Yanhong, CHN	19.95
1964	Polina Astakhova, USSR	19.332	1988	Daniela Silivas, ROM	20.00
1968	Vera Cáslavská, CZE	19.65	1992	Lu Li, CHN	10.00
1972	Karin Janz, E.Ger	19.675			

Balance Beam

Year		Points	Year		Points
1952	Nina Bocharova, USSR	19.22	1976	Nadia Comaneci, ROM	19.95
1956	Agnes Keleti, HUN	18.80	1980	Nadia Comaneci, ROM	19.80
1960	Eva Bosáková, CZE	19.283	1984	(TIE) Simona Pauca, ROM	19.80
1964	Vera Cáslavská, CZE	19.449		& Ecaterina Szabó, ROM	19.80
1968	Natalya Kuchinskaya, USSR	19.65	1988	Daniela Silivas, ROM	19.924
1972	Olga Korbut, USSR	19.40	1992	Tatiana Lysenko, UT	9.975

Floor Exercise

Year		Points	Year		Points
1952	Agnes Keleti, HUN	19.36	1972	Olga Korbut, USSR	19.575
1956	(TIE) Agnes Keleti, HUN	18.733	1976	Nelli Kim, USSR	19.85
	& Larissa Latynina, USSR	18.733	1980	(TIE) Nadia Comaneci, ROM	19.875
1960	Larissa Latynina, USSR	19.583		& Nelli Kim, USSR	19.875
1964	Larissa Latynina, USSR	19.599	1984	Ecaterina Szabó, ROM	19.975
1968	(TIE) Vera Cáslavská, CZE	19.675	1988	Daniela Silivas, ROM	19.937
	& Larissa Petrik, USSR	19.675	1992	Lavinia Milosovici, ROM	10.000

Team Combined Exercises

Year		Points	Year		Points
1928	Holland	316.75	1968	Soviet Union	382.85
1936	Germany	506.50	1972	Soviet Union	380.50
1948	Czechoslovakia	445.45	1976	Soviet Union	466.00
1952	Soviet Union	527.03	1980	Soviet Union	394.90
1956	Soviet Union	444.800	1984	Romania	392.02
1960	Soviet Union	382.320	1988	Soviet Union	395.475
1964	Soviet Union	280.890	1992	Unified Team	395.666

SOCCER

Multiple gold medals: Great Britain and Hungary (3); Uruguay and USSR (2).

Year		Year	
1900	**Great Britain**, France, Belgium	1956	**Soviet Union**, Yugoslavia, Bulgaria
1904	**Canada**, USA I, USA II	1960	**Yugoslavia**, Denmark, Hungary
1906	**Denmark**, Smyrna (Int'l entry), Greece	1964	**Hungary**, Czechoslovakia, Germany
1908	**Great Britain**, Denmark, Holland	1968	**Hungary**, Bulgaria, Japan
1912	**Great Britain**, Denmark, Holland	1972	**Poland**, Hungary, East Germany
1920	**Belgium**, Spain, Holland	1976	**East Germany**, Poland, Soviet Union
1924	**Uruguay**, Switzerland, Sweden	1980	**Czechoslovakia**, East Germany, Soviet Union
1928	**Uruguay**, Argentina, Italy	1984	**France**, Brazil, Yugoslavia
1936	**Italy**, Austria, Norway	1988	**Soviet Union**, Brazil, West Germany
1948	**Sweden**, Yugoslavia, Denmark	1992	**Spain**, Poland, Ghana
1952	**Hungary**, Yugoslavia, Sweden		

SWIMMING

World and Olympic records below that appear to be broken or equalled by winning times, heights and distances in subsequent years, but are not so indicated, were all broken in preliminary races and field events leading up to the finals.

MEN

At least 4 gold medals (including relays): Mark Spitz (9); Matt Biondi (8); Charles Daniels, Tom Jager, Don Schollander, and Johnny Weissmuller (5); Tamás Darnyi, Roland Matthes, John Naber, Murray Rose, Vladimir Salnikov and Henry Taylor (4).

50-meter Freestyle

Year		Time	Year		Time	
1904	Zoltán Halmay, HUN	28.0	1988	Matt Biondi, USA	22.14	WR
1906-84 Not held			1992	Aleksandr Popov, UT	21.91	OR

100-meter Freestyle

Year		Time		Year		Time	
1896	Alfréd Hajós, HUN	1:22.2	OR	1952	Clarke Scholes, USA	57.4	
1904	Zoltán Halmay, HUN	1:02.8		1956	Jon Henricks, AUS	55.4	OR
1906	Charles Daniels, USA	1:13.4		1960	John Devitt, AUS	55.2	OR
1908	Charles Daniels, USA	1:05.6	WR	1964	Don Schollander, USA	53.4	OR
1912	Duke Kahanamoku, USA	1:03.4		1968	Michael Wenden, AUS	52.2	WR
1920	Duke Kahanamoku, USA	1:00.4	WR	1972	Mark Spitz, USA	51.22	WR
1924	Johnny Weissmuller, USA	59.0	OR	1976	Jim Montgomery, USA	49.99	WR
1928	Johnny Weissmuller, USA	58.6	OR	1980	Jorg Woithe, E.Ger	50.40	
1932	Yasuji Miyazaki, JPN	58.2		1984	Rowdy Gaines, USA	49.80	OR
1936	Ferenc Csik, HUN	57.6		1988	Matt Biondi, USA	48.63	OR
1948	Wally Ris, USA	57.3	OR	1992	Aleksandr Popov, UT	49.02	

200-meter Freestyle

Year		Time		Year		Time	
1900	Frederick Lane, AUS	2:25.2	OR	1980	Sergei Kopliakov, USSR	1:49.81	OR
1904	Charles Daniels, USA	2:44.2		1984	Michael Gross, W.Ger	1:47.44	WR
1968	Michael Wenden, AUS	1:55.2	OR	1988	Duncan Armstrong, AUS	1:47.25	WR
1972	Mark Spitz, USA	1:52.78	WR	1992	Yevgeny Sadovyi, UT	1:46.70	WR
1976	Bruce Furniss, USA	1:50.29	WR				

400-meter Freestyle

Year		Time		Year		Time	
1896	Paul Neumann, AUT	8:12.6		1952	Jean Boiteux, FRA	4:30.7	OR
1904	Charles Daniels, USA	6:16.2		1956	Murray Rose, AUS	4:27.3	OR
1906	Otto Scheff, AUT	6:23.8		1960	Murray Rose, AUS	4:18.3	OR
1908	Henry Taylor, GBR	5:36.8		1964	Don Schollander, USA	4:12.2	WR
1912	George Hodgson, CAN	5:24.4		1968	Mike Burton, USA	4:09.0	OR
1920	Norman Ross, USA	5:26.8		1972	Bradford Cooper, AUS*	4:00.27	OR
1924	Johnny Weissmuller, USA	5:04.2	OR	1976	Brian Goodell, USA	3:51.93	WR
1928	Alberto Zorilla, ARG	5:01.6	OR	1980	Vladimir Salnikov, USSR	3:51.31	OR
1932	Buster Crabbe, USA	4:48.4	OR	1984	George DiCarlo, USA	3:51.23	OR
1936	Jack Medica, USA	4:44.5	OR	1988	Uwe Dassler, E.Ger	3:46.95	WR
1948	Bill Smith, USA	4:41.0	OR	1992	Yevgeny Sadovyi, UT	3:45.00	WR

*Australian Cooper finished second to Rick DeMont of the U.S. who was disqualified when he flunked the post-race drug test (his asthma medication was on the IOC's banned list).

1500-meter Freestyle

Year		Time		Year		Time	
1896	Alfréd Hajós, HUN	18:22.2	OR	1952	Ford Konno, USA	18:30.3	OR
1900	John Arthur Jarvis, GBR	13:40.2		1956	Murray Rose, AUS	17:58.9	
1904	Emil Rausch, GER	27:18.2		1960	Jon Konrads, AUS	17:19.6	OR
1906	Henry Taylor, GBR	28:28.0		1964	Robert Windle, AUS	17:01.7	OR
1908	Henry Taylor, GBR	22:48.4	WR	1968	Mike Burton, USA	16:38.9	OR
1912	George Hodgson, CAN	22:00.0	WR	1972	Mike Burton, USA	15:52.58	WR
1920	Norman Ross, USA	22:23.2		1976	Brian Goodell, USA	15:02.40	WR
1924	Andrew (Boy) Charlton, AUS	20:06.6	WR	1980	Vladimir Salnikov, USSR	14:58.27	WR
1928	Arne Borge, SWE	19:51.8	OR	1984	Mike O'Brien, USA	15:05.20	
1932	Kusuo Kitamura, JPN	19:12.4	OR	1988	Vladimir Salnikov, USSR	15:00.40	
1936	Noboru Terada, JPN	19:13.7		1992	Kieren Perkins, AUS	14:43.48	WR
1948	James McLane, USA	19:18.5					

100-meter Backstroke

Year		Time		Year		Time	
1904	Walter Brack, GER	1:16.8		1956	David Theile, AUS	1:02.2	OR
1908	Arno Bieberstein, GER	1:24.6	WR	1960	David Theile, AUS	1:01.9	OR
1912	Harry Hebner, USA	1:21.2		1968	Roland Matthes, E.Ger	58.7	OR
1920	Warren Kealoha, USA	1:15.2		1972	Roland Matthes, E.Ger	56.58	OR
1924	Warren Kealoha, USA	1:13.2	OR	1976	John Naber, USA	55.49	WR
1928	George Kojac, USA	1:08.2	WR	1980	Bengt Baron, SWE	56.33	
1932	Masaji Kiyokawa, JPN	1:08.6		1984	Rick Carey, USA	55.79	
1936	Adolf Kiefer, USA	1:05.9	OR	1988	Daichi Suzuki, JPN	55.05	
1948	Allen Stack, USA	1:06.4		1992	Mark Tewksbury, CAN	53.98	OR
1952	Yoshinobu Oyakawa, USA	1:05.4	OR				

Note: Event covered 100 yards in 1904.

200-meter Backstroke

Year		Time		Year		Time	
1900	Ernst Hoppenberg, GER	2:47.0		1980	Sándor Wladár, HUN	2:01.93	
1964	Jed Graef, USA	2:10.3	WR	1984	Rick Carey, USA	2:00.23	
1968	Roland Matthes, E.Ger	2:09.6	WR	1988	Igor Poliansky, USSR	1:59.37	
1972	Roland Matthes, E.Ger	2:02.82	=WR	1992	Martin Lopez-Zubero, SPA	1:58.47	OR
1976	John Naber, USA	1:59.19	WR				

Swimming (Cont.)
MEN
100-meter Breaststroke

Year		Time		Year		Time	
1968	Don McKenzie, USA	1:07.7	OR	1984	Steve Lundquist, USA	1:01.65	WR
1972	Nobutaka Taguchi, JPN	1:04.94	WR	1988	Adrian Moorhouse, GBR	1:02.04	
1976	John Hencken, USA	1:03.11	WR	1992	Nelson Diebel, USA	1:01.50	OR
1980	Duncan Goodhew, GBR	1:03.44					

200-meter Breaststroke

Year		Time		Year		Time	
1908	Frederick Holman, GBR	3:09.2	WR	1960	Bill Mulliken, USA	2:37.4	
1912	Walter Bathe, GER	3:01.8	OR	1964	Ian O'Brien, AUS	2:27.8	WR
1920	Hakan Malmroth, SWE	3:04.4		1968	Felipe Muñoz, MEX	2:28.7	
1924	Robert Skelton, USA	2:56.6		1972	John Hencken, USA	2:21.55	WR
1928	Yoshiyuki Tsuruta, JPN	2:48.8	OR	1976	David Wilkie, GBR	2:15.11	WR
1932	Yoshiyuki Tsuruta, JPN	2:45.4		1980	Robertas Zhulpa, USSR	2:15.85	
1936	Tetsuo Hamuro, JPN	2:41.5	OR	1984	Victor Davis, CAN	2:13.34	WR
1948	Joseph Verdeur, USA	2:39.3	OR	1988	József Szabó, HUN	2:13.52	
1952	John Davies, AUS	2:34.4	OR	1992	Mike Barrowman, USA	2:10.16	WR
1956	Masaru Furukawa, JPN	2:34.7*	OR				

*In 1956, the butterfly stroke and breaststroke were separated into two different events.

100-meter Butterfly

Year		Time		Year		Time	
1968	Doug Russell, USA	55.9	OR	1984	Michael Gross, W.Ger	53.08	WR
1972	Mark Spitz, USA	54.27	WR	1988	Anthony Nesty, SUR	53.0	OR
1976	Matt Vogel, USA	54.35		1992	Pablo Morales, USA	53.32	
1980	Pär Arvidsson, SWE	54.92					

200-meter Butterfly

Year		Time		Year		Time	
1956	Bill Yorzyk, USA	2:19.3	OR	1976	Mike Bruner, USA	1:59.23	WR
1960	Mike Troy, USA	2:12.8	WR	1980	Sergei Fesenko, USSR	1:59.76	
1964	Kevin Berry, AUS	2:06.6	WR	1984	Jon Sieben, AUS	1:57.04	WR
1968	Carl Robie, USA	2:08.7		1988	Michael Gross, W.Ger	1:56.94	OR
1972	Mark Spitz, USA	2:00.70	WR	1992	Melvin Stewart, USA	1:56.26	OR

200-meter Individual Medley

Year		Time		Year		Time	
1968	Charles Hickcox, USA	2:12.0	OR	1988	Tamás Darnyi, HUN	2:00.17	WR
1972	Gunnar Larsson, SWE	2:07.17	WR	1992	Tamás Darnyi, HUN	2:00.76	
1984	Alex Baumann, CAN	2:01.42	WR				

400-meter Individual Medley

Year		Time		Year		Time	
1964	Richard Roth, USA	4:45.4	WR	1980	Aleksandr Sidorenko, USSR	4:22.89	OR
1968	Charles Hickcox, USA	4:48.4		1984	Alex Baumann, CAN	4:17.41	WR
1972	Gunnar Larsson, SWE	4:31.98	OR	1988	Tamás Darnyi, HUN	4:14.75	WR
1976	Rod Strachan, USA	4:23.68	WR	1992	Tamás Darnyi, HUN	4:14.23	OR

4x100-meter Freestyle Relay

Year		Time		Year		Time	
1964	United States	3:32.2	WR	1984	United States	3:19.03	WR
1968	United States	3:31.7	WR	1988	United States	3:16.53	WR
1972	United States	3:26.42	WR	1992	United States	3:16.74	
1976-80	Not held						

4x200-meter Freestyle Relay

Year		Time		Year		Time	
1906	Hungary	16:52.4		1956	Australia	8:23.6	WR
1908	Great Britain	10:55.6	WR	1960	United States	8:10.2	WR
1912	Australia/New Zealand	10:11.6	WR	1964	United States	7:52.1	WR
1920	United States	10:04.4	WR	1968	United States	7:52.33	
1924	United States	9:53.4	WR	1972	United States	7:35.78	WR
1928	United States	9:36.2	WR	1976	United States	7:23.22	WR
1932	Japan	8:58.4	WR	1980	Soviet Union	7:23.50	
1936	Japan	8:51.5	WR	1984	United States	7:15.69	WR
1948	United States	8:46.0	WR	1988	United States	7:12.51	WR
1952	United States	8:31.1	OR	1992	Unified Team	7:11.95	WR

Note: Event was a 4x250-meter competition in 1906.

4x100-meter Medley Relay

Year		Time		Year		Time	
1960	United States	4:05.4	WR	1980	Australia	3:45.70	
1964	United States	3:58.4	WR	1984	United States	3:39.30	WR
1968	United States	3:54.9	WR	1988	United States	3:36.93	WR
1972	United States	3:48.16	WR	1992	United States	3:36.93	=WR
1976	United States	3:42.22	WR				

WOMEN

At least 4 gold medals (including relays): Kristin Otto (6); Krisztina Egerszegi, Kornelia Ender, Janet Evans and Dawn Fraser (4).

50-meter Freestyle

Year		Time		Year		Time	
1988	Kristin Otto, E.Ger	25.49	OR	1992	Yang Wenyi, CHN	24.79	WR

100-meter Freestyle

Year		Time		Year		Time	
1912	Fanny Durack, AUS	1:22.2		1964	Dawn Fraser, AUS	59.5	OR
1920	Ethelda Bleibtrey, USA	1:13.6	WR	1968	Jan Henne, USA	1:00.0	
1924	Ethel Lackie, USA	1:12.4		1972	Sandra Neilson, USA	58.59	OR
1928	Albina Osipowich, USA	1:11.0	OR	1976	Kornelia Ender, E.Ger	55.65	WR
1932	Helene Madison, USA	1:06.8	OR	1980	Barbara Krause, E.Ger	54.79	WR
1936	Rie Mastenbroek, HOL	1:05.9	OR	1984	(TIE) Nancy Hogshead, USA	55.92	
1948	Greta Andersen, DEN	1:06.3			& Carrie Steinseifer, USA	55.92	
1952	Katalin Szöke, HUN	1:06.8		1988	Kristin Otto, E.Ger	54.93	
1956	Dawn Fraser, AUS	1:02.0	WR	1992	Zhuang Yong, CHN	54.65	OR
1960	Dawn Fraser, AUS	1:01.2	OR				

200-meter Freestyle

Year		Time		Year		Time	
1968	Debbie Meyer, USA	2:10.5	OR	1984	Mary Wayte, USA	1:59.23	
1972	Shane Gould, AUS	2:03.56	WR	1988	Heike Friedrich, E.Ger	1:57.65	OR
1976	Kornelia Ender, E.Ger	1:59.26	WR	1992	Nicole Haislett, USA	1:57.90	
1980	Barbara Krause, E.Ger	1:58.33	OR				

400-meter Freestyle

Year		Time		Year		Time	
1920	Ethelda Bleibtrey, USA	4:34.0	WR	1964	Ginny Duenkel, USA	4:43.3	OR
1924	Martha Norelius, USA	6:02.2	OR	1968	Debbie Meyer, USA	4:31.8	OR
1928	Martha Norelius, USA	5:42.8	WR	1972	Shane Gould, AUS	4:19.44	WR
1932	Helene Madison, USA	5:28.5	WR	1976	Petra Thümer, E.Ger	4:09.89	WR
1936	Rie Mastenbroek, HOL	5:26.4	OR	1980	Ines Diers, E.Ger	4:08.76	OR
1948	Ann Curtis, USA	5:17.8	OR	1984	Tiffany Cohen, USA	4:07.10	OR
1952	Valéria Gyenge, HUN	5:12.1	OR	1988	Janet Evans, USA	4:03.85	WR
1956	Lorraine Crapp, AUS	4:54.6	OR	1992	Dagmar Hase, GER	4:07.18	
1960	Chris von Saltza, USA	4:50.6	OR				

Note: Event covered 300 meters in 1920.

800-meter Freestyle

Year		Time		Year		Time	
1968	Debbie Meyer, USA	9:24.0	OR	1984	Tiffany Cohen, USA	8:24.95	OR
1972	Keena Rothhammer, USA	8:53.68	WR	1988	Janet Evans, USA	8:20.20	OR
1976	Petra Thümer, E.Ger	8:37.14	WR	1992	Janet Evans, USA	8:25.52	
1980	Michelle Ford, AUS	8:28.90	OR				

100-meter Backstroke

Year		Time		Year		Time	
1924	Sybil Bauer, USA	1:23.2	OR	1964	Cathy Ferguson, USA	1:07.7	WR
1928	Maria Braun, HOL	1:22.0		1968	Kaye Hall, USA	1:06.2	WR
1932	Eleanor Holm, USA	1:19.4		1972	Melissa Belote, USA	1:05.78	OR
1936	Dina Senff, HOL	1:18.9		1976	Ulrike Richter, E.Ger	1:01.83	OR
1948	Karen-Margrete Harup, DEN	1:14.4	OR	1980	Rica Reinisch, E.Ger	1:00.86	WR
1952	Joan Harrison, SAF	1:14.3		1984	Theresa Andrews, USA	1:02.55	
1956	Judy Grinham, GBR	1:12.9	OR	1988	Kristin Otto, E.Ger	1:00.89	
1960	Lynn Burke, USA	1:09.3	OR	1992	Krisztina Egerszegi, HUN	1:00.68	OR

200-meter Backstroke

Year		Time		Year		Time	
1968	Pokey Watson, USA	2:24.8	OR	1984	Jolanda de Rover, HOL	2:12.38	
1972	Melissa Belote, USA	2:19.19	WR	1988	Krisztina Egerszegi, HUN	2:09.29	OR
1976	Ulrike Richter, E.Ger	2:13.43	OR	1992	Krisztina Egerszegi, HUN	2:07.06	OR
1980	Rica Reinisch, E.Ger	2:11.77	WR				

Swimming (Cont.)
WOMEN
100-meter Breaststroke

Year		Time		Year		Time	
1968	Djurdjica Bjedov, YUG	1:15.8	OR	1984	Petra van Staveren, HOL	1:09.88	OR
1972	Cathy Carr, USA	1:13.58	WR	1988	Tania Dangalakova, BUL	1:07.95	OR
1976	Hannelore Anke, E.Ger	1:11.16		1992	Yelena Rudkovskaya, UT	1:08.00	
1980	Ute Geweniger, E.Ger	1:10.22					

200-meter Breaststroke

Year		Time		Year		Time	
1924	Lucy Morton, GBR	3:33.2	OR	1964	Galina Prozumenshikova, USSR	2:46.4	OR
1928	Hilde Schrader, GER	3:12.6		1968	Sharon Wichman, USA	2:44.4	OR
1932	Clare Dennis, AUS	3:06.3	OR	1972	Beverley Whitfield, AUS	2:41.71	OR
1936	Hideko Maehata, JPN	3:03.6		1976	Marina Koshevaya, USSR	2:33.35	WR
1948	Petronella van Vliet, HOL	2:57.2		1980	Lina Kaciusyte, USSR	2:29.54	OR
1952	Éva Székely, HUN	2:51.7	OR	1984	Anne Ottenbrite, CAN	2:30.38	
1956	Ursula Happe, GER	2:53.1	OR	1988	Silke Hörner, E.Ger	2:26.71	WR
1960	Anita Lonsbrough, GBR	2:49.5	OR	1992	Kyoko Iwasaki, JPN	2:26.65	OR

100-meter Butterfly

Year		Time		Year		Time	
1956	Shelly Mann, USA	1:11.0	OR	1976	Kornelia Ender, E.Ger	1:00.13	=WR
1960	Carolyn Schuler, USA	1:09.5	OR	1980	Caren Metschuck, E.Ger	1:00.42	
1964	Sharon Stouder, USA	1:04.7	WR	1984	Mary T. Meagher, USA	59.26	
1968	Lynn McClements, AUS	1:05.5		1988	Kristin Otto, E.Ger	59.00	OR
1972	Mayumi Aoki, JPN	1:03.34	WR	1992	Qian Hong, CHN	58.62	OR

200-meter Butterfly

Year		Time		Year		Time	
1968	Ada Kok, HOL	2:24.7	OR	1984	Mary T. Meagher, USA	2:06.90	OR
1972	Karen Moe, USA	2:15.57	WR	1988	Kathleen Nord, E.Ger	2:09.51	
1976	Andrea Pollack, E.Ger	2:11.41	OR	1992	Summer Sanders, USA	2:08.67	
1980	Ines Geissler, E.Ger	2:10.44	OR				

200-meter Individual Medley

Year		Time		Year		Time	
1968	Claudia Kolb, USA	2:24.7	OR	1988	Daniela Hunger, E.Ger	2:12.59	OR
1972	Shane Gould, AUS	2:23.07	WR	1992	Lin Li, CHN	2:11.65	WR
1984	Tracy Caulkins, USA	2:12.64	OR				

400-meter Individual Medley

Year		Time		Year		Time	
1964	Donna de Varona, USA	5:18.7	OR	1980	Petra Schneider, E.Ger	4:36.29	WR
1968	Claudia Kolb, USA	5:08.5	OR	1984	Tracy Caulkins, USA	4:39.24	
1972	Gail Neall, AUS	5:02.97	WR	1988	Janet Evans, USA	4:37.76	
1976	Ulrike Tauber, E.Ger	4:42.77	WR	1992	Krisztina Egerszegi, HUN	4:36.54	

4x100-meter Freestyle Relay

Year		Time		Year		Time	
1912	Great Britain	5:52.8	WR	1960	United States	4:08.9	WR
1920	United States	5:11.6	WR	1964	United States	4:03.8	WR
1924	United States	4:58.8	WR	1968	United States	4:02.5	OR
1928	United States	4:47.6	WR	1972	United States	3:55.19	WR
1932	United States	4:38.0	WR	1976	United States	3:44.82	WR
1936	Holland	4:36.0	OR	1980	East Germany	3:42.71	WR
1948	United States	4:29.2	WR	1984	United States	3:43.43	
1952	Hungary	4:24.4	WR	1988	East Germany	3:40.63	OR
1956	Australia	4:17.1	WR	1992	United States	3:39.46	WR

4x100-meter Medley Relay

Year		Time		Year		Time	
1960	United States	4:41.1	WR	1980	East Germany	4:06.67	WR
1964	United States	4:33.9	WR	1984	United States	4:08.34	
1968	United States	4:28.3	OR	1988	East Germany	4:03.74	OR
1972	United States	4:20.75	WR	1992	United States	4:02.54	WR
1976	East Germany	4:07.95	WR				

TENNIS
MEN

Multiple gold medals (including doubles): John Boland, Max Decugis, Laurie Doherty, Reggie Doherty, Arthur Gore, André Grobert, Vincent Richards, Charles Winslow and Beals Wright (2).

Singles

Year			Year		
1896	John Boland	Great Britain/Ireland	1920	Louis Raymond	South Africa
1900	Laurie Doherty,	Great Britain	1924	Vincent Richards	United States
1904	Beals Wright	United States	1928-84	Not held	
1906	Max Decugis	France	1988	Miloslav Mecir	Czechoslovakia
1908	Josiah Ritchie	Great Britain	1992	Marc Rosset	Switzerland
	(Indoor) Arthur Gore	Great Britain			
1912	Charles Winslow	South Africa			
	(Indoor) André Gobert	France			

Doubles

Year		Year	
1896	John Boland, IRL & Fritz Traun, GER	1920	Noel Turnbull & Max Woosnam, GBR
1900	Laurie and Reggie Doherty	1924	Vincent Richards & Frank Hunter, USA
1904	Edgar Leonard & Beals Wright, USA	1928-84	Not held
1906	Max Decugis & Maurice Germot, FRA	1988	Ken Flach & Robert Seguso, USA
1908	George Hillyard & Reggie Doherty, GRB	1992	Boris Becker & Michael Stich, GER
	(Indoor) Arthur Gore & Herbert Barrett, GBR		
1912	Charles Winslow & Harold Kitson, SAF		
	(Indoor) André Gobert & Maurice Germot, FRA		

WOMEN
Multiple gold medals (including doubles): Helen Wills (2).

Singles

Year			Year		
1900	Charlotte Cooper	Great Britain	1920	Suzanne Lenglen	France
1906	Esmee Simiriotou	Greece	1924	Helen Wills	United States
1908	Dorothea Chambers	Great Britain	1928-84	Not held	
	(Indoor) Gwen Eastlake-Smith	Great Britain	1988	Steffi Graf	West Germany
1912	Marguerite Broquedis	France	1992	Jennifer Capriati	USA
	(Indoor) Edith Hannam	Great Britain			

Doubles

Year		Year	
1920	Winifred McNair & Kitty McKane, GBR	1988	Pam Shriver & Zina Garrison, USA
1924	Hazel Wightman & Helen Wills, USA	1992	Gigi Fernandez & Mary Joe Fernandez, USA
1928-84	Not held		

TRACK & FIELD

World and Olympic records below that appear to be broken or equalled by winning times, heights and distances in subsequent years, but are not so indicated, were all broken in preliminary races and field events leading up to the finals.

MEN

At least 4 gold medals (including relays and discontinued events): Ray Ewry (10); Paavo Nurmi (9); Carl Lewis (8); Ville Ritola and Martin Sheridan (5); Harrison Dillard, Archie Hahn, Hannes Kolehmainen, Alvin Kraenzlein, Eric Lemming, Jim Lightbody, Al Oerter, Jesse Owens, Meyer Prinstein, Mel Sheppard, Lasse Viren and Emil Zátopek (4). Note that all of Ewry's gold medals came before 1912, in the Standing High, Long and Triple jumps.

100 meters

Year		Time		Year		Time	
1896	Tom Burke, USA	12.0		1952	Lindy Remigino, USA	10.4	
1900	Frank Jarvis, USA	11.0		1956	Bobby Morrow, USA	10.5	
1904	Archie Hahn, USA	11.0		1960	Armin Hary, GER	10.2	**OR**
1906	Archie Hahn, USA	11.2		1964	Bob Hayes, USA	10.0	**=WR**
1908	Reggie Walker, SAF	10.8	**=OR**	1968	Jim Hines, USA	9.95	**WR**
1912	Ralph Craig, USA	10.8		1972	Valery Borzov, USSR	10.14	
1920	Charley Paddock, USA	10.8		1976	Hasely Crawford, TRI	10.06	
1924	Harold Abrahams, GBR	10.6	**=OR**	1980	Allan Wells, GBR	10.25	
1928	Percy Williams, CAN	10.8		1984	Carl Lewis, USA	9.99	
1932	Eddie Tolan, USA	10.3	**OR**	1988	Carl Lewis, USA*	9.92	**WR**
1936	Jesse Owens, USA	10.3w		1992	Linford Christie, GBR	9.96	
1948	Harrison Dillard, USA	10.3	**=OR**				

w indicates wind-aided.

*Lewis finished second to Ben Johnson of Canada, who set a world record of 9.79 seconds. A day later, Johnson was stripped of his gold medal and his record when he tested positive for steroid use in a post-race drug test.

Track & Field (Cont.)
MEN
200 meters

Year		Time		Year		Time	
1900	John Walter Tewksbury, USA	22.2		1956	Bobby Morrow, USA	20.6	OR
1904	Archie Hahn, USA	21.6	OR	1960	Livio Berruti, ITA	20.5	=WR
1908	Bobby Kerr, CAN	22.6		1964	Henry Carr, USA	20.3	OR
1912	Ralph Craig, USA	21.7		1968	Tommie Smith, USA	19.83	WR
1920	Allen Woodring, USA	22.0		1972	Valery Borzov, USSR	20.00	
1924	Jackson Scholz, USA	21.6		1976	Donald Quarrie, JAM	20.23	
1928	Percy Williams, CAN	21.8		1980	Pietro Mennea, ITA	20.19	
1932	Eddie Tolan, USA	21.2	OR	1984	Carl Lewis, USA	19.80	OR
1936	Jesse Owens, USA	20.7	OR	1988	Joe DeLoach, USA	19.75	OR
1948	Mel Patton, USA	21.1		1992	Mike Marsh, USA	20.01	
1952	Andy Stanfield, USA	20.7					

400 meters

Year		Time		Year		Time	
1896	Tom Burke, USA	54.2		1952	George Rhoden, JAM	45.9	OR
1900	Maxey Long, USA	49.4	OR	1956	Charley Jenkins, USA	46.7	
1904	Harry Hillman, USA	49.2	OR	1960	Otis Davis, USA	44.9	WR
1906	Paul Pilgrim, USA	53.2		1964	Mike Larrabee, USA	45.1	
1908	Wyndham Halswelle, GBR	50.0		1968	Lee Evans, USA	43.86	WR
1912	Charlie Reidpath, USA	48.2	OR	1972	Vince Matthews, USA	44.66	
1920	Bevil Rudd, SAF	49.6		1976	Alberto Juantorena, CUB	44.26	
1924	Eric Liddell, GBR	47.6	OR	1980	Viktor Markin, USSR	44.60	
1928	Ray Barbuti, USA	47.8		1984	Alonzo Babers, USA	44.27	
1932	Bill Carr, USA	46.2	WR	1988	Steve Lewis, USA	43.87	
1936	Archie Williams, USA	46.5		1992	Quincy Watts, USA	43.50	OR
1948	Arthur Wint, JAM	46.2					

800 meters

Year		Time		Year		Time	
1896	Teddy Flack, AUS	2:11.0		1952	Mal Whitfield, USA	1:49.2	=OR
1900	Alfred Tysoe, GBR	2:01.2		1956	Tom Courtney, USA	1:47.7	OR
1904	Jim Lightbody, USA	1:56.0	OR	1960	Peter Snell, NZE	1:46.3	OR
1906	Paul Pilgrim, USA	2:01.5		1964	Peter Snell, NZE	1:45.1	OR
1908	Mel Sheppard, USA	1:52.8	WR	1968	Ralph Doubell, AUS	1:44.3	=WR
1912	Ted Meredith, USA	1:51.9	WR	1972	Dave Wottle, USA	1:45.9	
1920	Albert Hill, GBR	1:53.4		1976	Alberto Juantorena, CUB	1:43.50	WR
1924	Douglas Lowe, GBR	1:52.4		1980	Steve Ovett, GBR	1:45.4	
1928	Douglas Lowe, GBR	1:51.8	OR	1984	Joaquim Cruz, BRA	1:43.00	OR
1932	Tommy Hampson, GBR	1:49.7	WR	1988	Paul Ereng, KEN	1:43.45	
1936	John Woodruff, USA	1:52.9		1992	William Tanui, KEN	1:43.66	
1948	Mal Whitfield, USA	1:49.2	OR				

1500 meters

Year		Time		Year		Time	
1896	Teddy Flack, AUS	4:33.2		1952	Josy Barthel, LUX	3:45.1	OR
1900	Charles Bennett, GBR	4:06.2	WR	1956	Ron Delany, IRL	3:41.2	OR
1904	Jim Lightbody, USA	4:05.4	WR	1960	Herb Elliott, AUS	3:35.6	WR
1906	Jim Lightbody, USA	4:12.0		1964	Peter Snell, NZE	3:38.1	
1908	Mel Sheppard, USA	4:03.4	OR	1968	Kip Keino, KEN	3:34.9	OR
1912	Arnold Jackson, GBR	3:56.8	OR	1972	Pekka Vasala, FIN	3:36.3	
1920	Albert Hill, GBR	4:01.8		1976	John Walker, NZE	3:39.17	
1924	Paavo Nurmi, FIN	3:53.6	OR	1980	Sebastian Coe, GBR	3:38.4	
1928	Harry Larva, FIN	3:53.2	OR	1984	Sebastian Coe, GBR	3:32.53	OR
1932	Luigi Beccali, ITA	3:51.2	OR	1988	Peter Rono, KEN	3:35.96	
1936	John Lovelock, NZE	3:47.8	WR	1992	Fermin Cacho, SPA	3:40.12	
1948	Henry Eriksson, SWE	3:49.8					

5000 meters

Year		Time		Year		Time	
1912	Hannes Kolehmainen, FIN	14:36.6	WR	1960	Murray Halberg, NZE	13:43.4	
1920	Joseph Guillemot, FRA	14:55.6		1964	Bob Schul, USA	13:48.8	
1924	Paavo Nurmi, FIN	14:31.2	OR	1968	Mohamed Gammoudi, TUN	14:05.0	
1928	Ville Ritola, FIN	14:38.0		1972	Lasse Viren, FIN	13:26.4	OR
1932	Lauri Lehtinen, FIN	14:30.0	OR	1976	Lasse Viren, FIN	13:24.76	
1936	Gunnar Höckert, FIN	14:22.2	OR	1980	Miruts Yifter, ETH	13:21.0	
1948	Gaston Reiff, BEL	14:17.6	OR	1984	Said Aouita, MOR	13:05.59	OR
1952	Emil Zátopek, CZE	14:06.6	OR	1988	John Ngugi, KEN	13:11.70	
1956	Vladimir Kuts, USSR	13:39.6	OR	1992	Dieter Baumann, GER	13:12.52	

10,000 meters

Year		Time		Year		Time	
1912	Hannes Kolehmainen, FIN	31:20.8		1960	Pyotr Bolotnikov, USSR	28:32.2	OR
1920	Paavo Nurmi, FIN	31:45.8		1964	Billy Mills, USA	28:24.4	OR
1924	Ville Ritola, FIN	30:23.2	WR	1968	Naftali Temu, KEN	29:27.4	
1928	Paavo Nurmi, FIN	30:18.8	OR	1972	Lasse Viren, FIN	27:38.4	WR
1932	Janusz Kusocinski, POL	30:11.4	OR	1976	Lasse Viren, FIN	27:40.38	
1936	Ilmari Salminen, FIN	30:15.4		1980	Miruts Yifter, ETH	27:42.7	
1948	Emil Zátopek, CZE	29:59.6	OR	1984	Alberto Cova, ITA	27:47.54	
1952	Emil Zátopek, CZE	29:17.0	OR	1988	Brahim Boutaib, MOR	27:21.46	OR
1956	Vladimir Kuts, USSR	28:45.6	OR	1992	Khalid Skah, MOR	27:46.70	

Marathon

Year		Time		Year		Time	
1896	Spiridon Louis, GRE	2:58:50		1952	Emil Zátopek, CZE	2:23:03.2	OR
1900	Michel Théato, FRA	2:59:45		1956	Alain Mimoun, FRA	2:25:00.0	
1904	Thomas Hicks, USA	3:28:53		1960	Abebe Bikila, ETH	2:15:16.2	WB
1906	Billy Sherring, CAN	2:51:23.6		1964	Abebe Bikila, ETH	2:12:11.2	WB
1908	Johnny Hayes, USA*	2:55:18.4	OR	1968	Mamo Wolde, ETH	2:20:26.4	
1912	Kenneth McArthur, SAF	2:36:54.8		1972	Frank Shorter, USA	2:12:19.8	
1920	Hannes Kolehmainen, FIN	2:32:35.8	WB	1976	Waldemar Cierpinski, E.Ger	2:09:55.0	OR
1924	Albin Stenroos, FIN	2:41:22.6		1980	Waldemar Cierpinski, E.Ger	2:11:03.0	
1928	Boughèra El Ouafi, FRA	2:32:57.0		1984	Carlos Lopes, POR	2:09:21.0	OR
1932	Juan Carlos Zabala, ARG	2:31:36.0	OR	1988	Gelindo Bordin, ITA	2:10:32	
1936	Sohn Kee-Chung, JPN†	2:29:19.2	OR	1992	Hwang Young-Cho, S.Kor	2:13:23	
1948	Delfo Cabrera, ARG	2:34:51.6					

*Dorando Pietri of Italy placed first, but was disqualified for being helped across the finish line.
†Sohn was a Korean, but he was forced to compete under the name Kitei Son by Japan, which occupied Korea at the time.
Note: Marathon distances—40,000 meters (1896,1904); 40,260 meters (1900); 41,860 meters (1906); 42,195 meters (1908 and since 1924); 40,200 meters (1912); 42,750 meters (1920). Current distance of 42,195 meters measures 26 miles, 385 yards.

110-meter Hurdles

Year		Time		Year		Time	
1896	Tom Curtis, USA	17.6		1952	Harrison Dillard, USA	13.7	OR
1900	Alvin Kraenzlein, USA	15.4	OR	1956	Lee Calhoun, USA	13.5	OR
1904	Frederick Schule, USA	16.0		1960	Lee Calhoun, USA	13.8	
1906	Robert Leavitt, USA	16.2		1964	Hayes Jones, USA	13.6	
1908	Forrest Smithson, USA	15.0	WR	1968	Willie Davenport, USA	13.3	OR
1912	Frederick Kelly, USA	15.1		1972	Rod Milburn, USA	13.24	=WR
1920	Earl Thomson, CAN	14.8	WR	1976	Guy Drut, FRA	13.30	
1924	Daniel Kinsey, USA	15.0		1980	Thomas Munkelt, E.Ger	13.39	
1928	Syd Atkinson, SAF	14.8		1984	Roger Kingdom, USA	13.20	OR
1932	George Saling, USA	14.6		1988	Roger Kingdom, USA	12.98	OR
1936	Forrest (Spec) Towns, USA	14.2		1992	Mark McKoy, CAN	13.12	
1948	William Porter, USA	13.9	OR				

400-meter Hurdles

Year		Time		Year		Time	
1900	John Walter Tewksbury, USA	57.6		1956	Glenn Davis, USA	50.1	=OR
1904	Harry Hillman, USA	53.0		1960	Glenn Davis, USA	49.3	OR
1908	Charley Bacon, USA	55.0	WR	1964	Rex Cawley, USA	49.6	
1920	Frank Loomis, USA	54.0	WR	1968	David Hemery, GBR	48.12	WR
1924	Morgan Taylor, USA	52.6		1972	John Akii-Bua, UGA	47.82	WR
1928	David Burghley, GBR	53.4	OR	1976	Edwin Moses, USA	47.64	WR
1932	Bob Tisdall, IRL	51.7		1980	Volker Beck, E.Ger	48.70	
1936	Glenn Hardin, USA	52.4		1984	Edwin Moses, USA	47.75	
1948	Roy Cochran, USA	51.1	OR	1988	Andre Phillips, USA	47.19	OR
1952	Charley Moore, USA	50.8	OR	1992	Kevin Young, USA	46.78	WR

3000-meter Steeplechase

Year		Time		Year		Time	
1900	George Orton, CAN	7:34.4		1956	Chris Brasher, GBR	8:41.2	OR
1904	Jim Lightbody, USA	7:39.6		1960	Zdzislaw Krzyszkowiak, POL	8:34.2	OR
1908	Arthur Russell, GBR	10:47.8		1964	Gaston Roelants, BEL	8:30.8	OR
1920	Percy Hodge, GBR	10:00.4	OR	1968	Amos Biwott, KEN	8:51.0	
1924	Ville Ritola, FIN	9:33.6	OR	1972	Kip Keino, KEN	8:23.6	OR
1928	Toivo Loukola, FIN	9:21.8	WR	1976	Anders Gärderud, SWE	8:08.2	WR
1932	Volmari Iso-Hollo, FIN*	10:33.4		1980	Bronislaw Malinowski, POL	8:09.7	
1936	Volmari Iso-Hollo, FIN	9:03.8	WR	1984	Julius Korir, KEN	8:11.80	
1948	Thore Sjöstrand, SWE	9:04.6		1988	Julius Kariuki, KEN	8:05.51	OR
1952	Horace Ashenfelter, USA	8:45.4	WR	1992	Matthew Birir, KEN	8:08.84	

*Iso-Hollo ran one extra lap due to lap counter's mistake.
Note: Other steeplechase distances—2500 meters (1900); 2590 meters (1904); 3200 meters (1908) and 3460 meters (1936).

Track & Field (Cont.)
MEN
4x100-meter Relay

Year		Time		Year		Time	
1912	Great Britain	42.4		1960	Germany	39.5	=WR
1920	United States	42.2	WR	1964	United States	39.0	WR
1924	United States	41.0	=WR	1968	United States	38.23	WR
1928	United States	41.0	=WR	1972	United States	38.19	WR
1932	United States	40.0	WR	1976	United States	38.33	
1936	United States	39.8	WR	1980	Soviet Union	38.26	
1948	United States	40.6		1984	United States	37.83	WR
1952	United States	40.1		1988	Soviet Union	38.19	
1956	United States	39.5	WR	1992	United States	37.40	WR

4x400-meter Relay

Year		Time		Year		Time	
1908	United States	3:29.4		1960	United States	3:02.2	WR
1912	United States	3:16.6	WR	1964	United States	3:00.7	WR
1920	Great Britain	3:22.2		1968	United States	2:56.16	WR
1924	United States	3:16.0	WR	1972	Kenya	2:59.8	
1928	United States	3:14.2	WR	1976	United States	2:58.65	
1932	United States	3:08.2	WR	1980	Soviet Union	3:01.1	
1936	Great Britain	3:09.0		1984	United States	2:57.91	
1948	United States	3:10.4		1988	United States	2:56.16	=WR
1952	Jamaica	3:03.9	WR	1992	United States	2:55.74	WR
1956	United States	3:04.8					

20-kilometer Walk

Year		Time		Year		Time	
1956	Leonid Spirin, USSR	1:31:27.4		1976	Daniel Bautista, MEX	1:24:40.6	OR
1960	Vladimir Golubnichiy, USSR	1:34:07.2		1980	Maurizio Damilano, ITA	1:23:35.5	OR
1964	Ken Matthews, GBR	1:29:34.0	OR	1984	Ernesto Canto, MEX	1:23:13	OR
1968	Vladimir Golubnichiy, USSR	1:33:58.4		1988	Jozef Pribilinec, CZE	1:19:57	OR
1972	Peter Frenkel, E.Ger	1:26:42.4	OR	1992	Daniel Plaza Montero, SPA	1:21:45	

50-kilometer Walk

Year		Time		Year		Time	
1932	Thomas Green, GBR	4:50:10		1968	Christoph Höhne, E.Ger	4:20:13.6	
1936	Harold Whitlock, GBR	4:30:41.4	OR	1972	Bernd Kannenberg, W.Ger	3:56:11.6	OR
1948	John Ljunggren, SWE	4:41:52		1976	Not held		
1952	Giuseppe Dordoni, ITA	4:28:07.8		1980	Hartwig Gauder, E.Ger	3:49:24.0	OR
1956	Norman Read, NZE	4:30:42.8		1984	Raúl González, MEX	3:47:26	OR
1960	Don Thompson, GBR	4:25:30.0	OR	1988	Vyacheslav Ivanenko, USSR	3:38:29	OR
1964	Abdon Pamich, ITA	4:11:12.4	OR	1992	Andrei Perlov, UT	3:50:13	

High Jump

Year		Height		Year		Height	
1896	Ellery Clark, USA	5-11¼		1952	Walt Davis, USA	6- 8½	OR
1900	Irving Baxter, USA	6- 2¾	OR	1956	Charley Dumas, USA	6-11½	OR
1904	Sam Jones, USA	5-11		1960	Robert Shavlakadze, USSR	7- 1	OR
1906	Cornelius Leahy, GBR/IRL	5-10		1964	Valery Brumel, USSR	7- 1¾	OR
1908	Harry Porter, USA	6- 3	OR	1968	Dick Fosbury, USA	7- 4¼	OR
1912	Alma Richards, USA	6- 4	OR	1972	Yuri Tarmak, USSR	7- 3¾	
1920	Richmond Landon, USA	6- 4	=OR	1976	Jacek Wszola, POL	7- 4½	OR
1924	Harold Osborn, USA	6- 6	OR	1980	Gerd Wessig, E.Ger	7- 8¾	WR
1928	Bob King, USA	6- 4½		1984	Dietmar Mögenburg, W.Ger	7- 8½	
1932	Duncan McNaughton, CAN	6- 5½		1988	Gennady Avdeyenko, USSR	7- 9¾	OR
1936	Cornelius Johnson, USA	6- 8	OR	1992	Javier Sotomayor, CUB	7- 8	
1948	John Winter, AUS	6- 6					

Pole Vault

Year		Height		Year		Height	
1896	William Hoyt, USA	10-10		1948	Guinn Smith, USA	14- 1¼	
1900	Irving Baxter, USA	10-10		1952	Bob Richards, USA	14-11	OR
1904	Charles Dvorak, USA	11- 5¾		1956	Bob Richards, USA	14-11½	OR
1906	Fernand Gonder, FRA	11- 5¾		1960	Don Bragg, USA	15- 5	OR
1908	(TIE) Edward Cooke, USA	12- 2		1964	Fred Hansen, USA	16- 8¾	OR
	& Alfred Gilbert, USA	12- 2	OR	1968	Bob Seagren, USA	17- 8½	OR
1912	Harry Babcock, USA	12-11½	OR	1972	Wolfgang Nordwig, E.Ger	18- 0½	OR
1920	Frank Foss, USA	13- 5	WR	1976	Tadeusz Slusarski, POL	18- 0½	=OR
1924	Lee Barnes, USA	12-11½		1980	Wladyslaw Kozakiewicz, POL	18-11½	WR
1928	Sabin Carr, USA	13- 9¼	OR	1984	Pierre Quinon, FRA	18-10¼	
1932	Bill Miller, USA	14- 1¾	OR	1988	Sergei Bubka, USSR	19- 4¼	OR
1936	Earle Meadows, USA	14- 3¼	OR	1992	Maksim Tarasov, UT	19- 0¼	

Long Jump

Year		Distance		Year		Distance	
1896	Ellery Clark, USA	20-10		1952	Jerome Biffle, USA	24-10	
1900	Alvin Kraenzlein, USA	23- 6¾	OR	1956	Greg Bell, USA	25- 8¼	
1904	Meyer Prinstein, USA	24- 1	OR	1960	Ralph Boston, USA	26- 7¾	OR
1906	Meyer Prinstein, USA	23- 7½		1964	Lynn Davies, GBR	26- 5¾	
1908	Frank Irons, USA	24- 6½	OR	1968	Bob Beamon, USA	29- 2½	WR
1912	Albert Gutterson, USA	24-11¼	OR	1972	Randy Williams, USA	27- 0½	
1920	William Petersson, SWE	23- 5½		1976	Arnie Robinson, USA	27- 4¾	
1924	De Hart Hubbard, USA	24- 5		1980	Lutz Dombrowski, E.Ger	28- 0¼	
1928	Ed Hamm, USA	25- 4½	OR	1984	Carl Lewis, USA	28- 0¼	
1932	Ed Gordon, USA	25- 0¾		1988	Carl Lewis, USA	28- 7¼	
1936	Jesse Owens, USA	26- 5½	OR	1992	Carl Lewis, USA	28- 5½	
1948	Willie Steele, USA	25- 8					

Triple Jump

Year		Distance		Year		Distance	
1896	James Connolly, USA	44-11¾		1952	Adhemar da Silva, BRA	53- 2¾	WR
1900	Meyer Prinstein, USA	47- 5¾	OR	1956	Adhemar da Silva, BRA	53- 7¾	OR
1904	Meyer Prinstein, USA	47- 1		1960	Józef Schmidt, POL	55- 2	
1906	Peter O'Connor, GBR/IRL	46- 2¼		1964	Józef Schmidt, POL	55- 3½	OR
1908	Timothy Ahearne, GBR/IRL	48-11¼	OR	1968	Viktor Saneyev, USSR	57- 0¾	WR
1912	Gustaf Lindblom, SWE	48- 5¼		1972	Viktor Saneyev, USSR	56-11¼	
1920	Vilho Tuulos, FIN	47- 7		1976	Viktor Saneyev, USSR	56- 8¾	
1924	Nick Winter, AUS	50-11¼	WR	1980	Jaak Uudmäe, USSR	56-11¼	
1928	Mikio Oda, JPN	49-11		1984	Al Joyner, USA	56- 7½	
1932	Chuhei Nambu, JPN	51- 7	WR	1988	Khristo Markov, BUL	57- 9¼	OR
1936	Naoto Tajima, JPN	52- 6	WR	1992	Mike Conley, USA	57-10¼	OR
1948	Arne Ahman, SWE	50- 6¼					

Shot Put

Year		Distance		Year		Distance	
1896	Bob Garrett, USA	36- 9¾		1952	Parry O'Brien, USA	57- 1½	OR
1900	Richard Sheldon, USA	46- 3¼	OR	1956	Parry O'Brien, USA	60-11¼	OR
1904	Ralph Rose, USA	48- 7	WR	1960	Bill Nieder, USA	64- 6¾	OR
1906	Martin Sheridan, USA	40- 5¼		1964	Dallas Long, USA	66- 8½	OR
1908	Ralph Rose, USA	46- 7½		1968	Randy Matson, USA	67- 4¾	
1912	Patrick McDonald, USA	50- 4	OR	1972	Wladyslaw Komar, POL	69- 6	OR
1920	Ville Pörhölä, FIN	48- 7¼		1976	Udo Beyer, E.Ger	69- 0¾	
1924	Bud Houser, USA	49- 2¼		1980	Vladimir Kiselyov, USSR	70- 0½	OR
1928	John Kuck, USA	52- 0¾	WR	1984	Alessandro Andrei, ITA	69- 9	
1932	Leo Sexton, USA	52- 6	OR	1988	Ulf Timmermann, E.Ger	73- 8¾	OR
1936	Hans Woellke, GER	53- 1¾	OR	1992	Mike Stulce, USA	71- 2½	
1948	Wilbur Thompson, USA	56- 2	OR				

Discus Throw

Year		Distance		Year		Distance	
1896	Bob Garrett, USA	95- 7½		1952	Sim Iness, USA	180- 6	OR
1900	Rudolf Bauer, HUN	118- 3	OR	1956	Al Oerter, USA	184-11	OR
1904	Martin Sheridan, USA	128-10½	OR	1960	Al Oerter, USA	194- 2	OR
1906	Martin Sheridan, USA	136- 0		1964	Al Oerter, USA	200- 1	OR
1908	Martin Sheridan, USA	134- 2	OR	1968	Al Oerter, USA	212- 6	OR
1912	Armas Taipale, FIN	148- 3	OR	1972	Ludvik Danek, CZE	211- 3	
1920	Elmer Niklander, FIN	146- 7		1976	Mac Wilkins, USA	221- 5	
1924	Bud Houser, USA	151- 4	OR	1980	Viktor Rashchupkin, USSR	218- 8	
1928	Bud Houser, USA	155- 3	OR	1984	Rolf Danneberg, W.Ger	218- 6	
1932	John Anderson, USA	162- 4	OR	1988	Jürgen Schult, E.Ger	225- 9	OR
1936	Ken Carpenter, USA	165- 7	OR	1992	Romas Ubartas, LIT	213- 8	
1948	Adolfo Consolini, ITA	173- 2	OR				

Hammer Throw

Year		Distance		Year		Distance	
1900	John Flanagan, USA	163- 1		1956	Harold Connolly, USA	207- 3	OR
1904	John Flanagan, USA	168- 1	OR	1960	Vasily Rudenkov, USSR	220- 2	OR
1908	John Flanagan, USA	170- 4	OR	1964	Romuald Klim, USSR	228-10	OR
1912	Matt McGrath, USA	179- 7	OR	1968	Gyula Zsivótzky, HUN	240- 8	OR
1920	Pat Ryan, USA	173- 5		1972	Anatoly Bondarchuk, USSR	247- 8	OR
1924	Fred Tootell, USA	174-10		1976	Yuri Sedykh, USSR	254- 4	OR
1928	Pat O'Callaghan, IRL	168- 7		1980	Yuri Sedykh, USSR	268- 4	WR
1932	Pat O'Callaghan, IRL	176-11		1984	Juha Tiainen, FIN	256- 2	
1936	Karl Hein, GER	185- 4	OR	1988	Sergei Litvinov, USSR	278- 2	OR
1948	Imre Németh, HUN	183-11		1992	Andrei Abduvaliyev, UT	270- 9	
1952	József Csérmák, HUN	197-11	WR				

Track & Field (Cont.)
MEN
Javelin Throw

Year		Distance		Year		Distance	
1908	Eric Lemming, SWE	179-10	WR	1960	Viktor Tsibulenko, USSR	277- 8	
1912	Eric Lemming, SWE	198-11	WR	1964	Pauli Nevala, FIN	271- 2	
1920	Jonni Myyrä, FIN	215-10		1968	Jänis Lüsis, USSR	295- 7	OR
1924	Jonni Myyrä, FIN	206- 7		1972	Klaus Wolfermann, W.Ger	296-10	OR
1928	Erik Lundkvist, SWE	218- 6	OR	1976	Miklos Németh, HUN	310- 4	WR
1932	Matti Järvinen, FIN	238- 6		1980	Dainis Küla, USSR	299- 2	
1936	Gerhard Stöck, GER	235- 8		1984	Arto Härkönen, FIN	284- 8	
1948	Kai Tapio Rautavaara, FIN	228-10		1988	Tapio Korjus, FIN	276- 6	
1952	Cy Young, USA	242- 1	OR	1992	Jan Zelezny, CZE	294- 2*	OR
1956	Egil Danielson, NOR	281- 2	WR				

*In 1986 the balance point of the javelin was modified and new records have been kept since.

Decathlon

Year		Points		Year		Points	
1904	Thomas Kiely, IRL	6036		1956	Milt Campbell, USA	7937	OR
1906-08	Not held			1960	Rafer Johnson, USA	8392	OR
1912	Jim Thrope, USA	8412	WR	1964	Willi Holdorf, GER	7887	
1920	Helge Lövland, NOR	6803		1968	Bill Toomey, USA	8193	OR
1924	Harold Osborn, USA	7711	WR	1972	Nikolai Avilov, USSR	8454	WR
1928	Paavo Yrjölä, FIN	8053	WR	1976	Bruce Jenner, USA	8617	WR
1932	Jim Bausch, USA	8462	WR	1980	Daley Thompson, GBR	8495	
1936	Glenn Morris, USA	7900	WR	1984	Daley Thompson, GBR	8798	=WR
1948	Bob Mathias, USA	7139		1988	Christian Schenk, E.Ger	8488	
1952	Bob Mathias, USA	7887	WR	1992	Robert Zmelik, CZE	8611	

WOMEN

At least 3 gold medals (including relays): Evelyn Ashford, Fanny Blankers-Koen, Betty Cuthbert and Bärbel Eckert Wöckel (4); Valerie Brisco-Hooks, Olga Bryzgina, Florence Griffith Joyner, Jackie Joyner-Kersee, Tamara Press, Wilma Rudolph, Renate Stecher, Shirley Strickland, Irena Kirszenstein Szewinska and Wyomia Tyus (3).

100 meters

Year		Time		Year		Time	
1928	Betty Robinson, USA	12.2	=WR	1968	Wyomia Tyus, USA	11.08	WR
1932	Stella Walsh, POL*	11.9	=WR	1972	Renate Stecher, E.Ger	11.07	
1936	Helen Stephens, USA	11.5W		1976	Annegret Richter, W.Ger	11.08	
1948	Fanny Blankers-Koen, HOL	11.9		1980	Lyudmila Kondratyeva, USSR	11.06	
1952	Marjorie Jackson, AUS	11.5	=WR	1984	Evelyn Ashford, USA	10.97	OR
1956	Betty Cuthbert, AUS	11.5		1988	Florence Griffith Joyner, USA	10.54W	
1960	Wilma Rudolph, USA	11.0W		1992	Gail Devers, USA	10.82	OR
1964	Wyomia Tyus, USA	11.4					

*An autopsy performed after Walsh's death in 1980 revealed that she was a man.
W indicates wind-aided.

200 meters

Year		Time		Year		Time	
1948	Fanny Blankers-Koen, HOL	24.4		1972	Renate Stecher, E.Ger	22.40	=WR
1952	Marjorie Jackson, AUS	23.7	OR	1976	Bärbel Eckert, E.Ger	22.37	OR
1956	Betty Cuthbert, AUS	23.4	=OR	1980	Bärbel Eckert Wöckel, E.Ger	22.03	OR
1960	Wilma Rudolph, USA	24.0		1984	Valerie Brisco-Hooks, USA	21.81	OR
1964	Edith McGuire, USA	23.0	OR	1988	Florence Griffith Joyner, USA	21.34	WR
1968	Irena Szewinska, POL	22.5	WR	1992	Gwen Torrence, USA	21.81	

400 meters

Year		Time		Year		Time	
1964	Betty Cuthbert, AUS	52.0		1980	Marita Koch, E.Ger	48.88	OR
1968	Colette Besson, FRA	52.03	=OR	1984	Valerie Brisco-Hooks, USA	48.83	OR
1972	Monika Zehrt, E.Ger	51.08	OR	1988	Olga Bryzgina, USSR	48.65	OR
1976	Irena Szewinska, POL	49.29	WR	1992	Marie-Jose Perec, FRA	48.83	

800 meters

Year		Time		Year		Time	
1928	Lina Radke, GER	2:16.8	WR	1976	Tatyana Kazankina, USSR	1:54.94	WR
1960	Lyudmila Shevtsova, USSR	2:04.3	=WR	1980	Nadezhda Olizarenko, USSR	1:53.42	WR
1964	Ann Packer, GBR	2:01.1	OR	1984	Doina Melinte, ROM	1:57.60	
1968	Madeline Manning, USA	2:00.9	OR	1988	Sigrun Wodars, E.Ger	1:56.10	
1972	Hildegard Falck, W.Ger	1:58.55	OR	1992	Ellen van Langen, HOL	1:55.54	

1500 meters

Year		Time		Year		Time	
1972	Lyudmila Bragina, USSR	4:01.4	WR	1984	Gabriella Dorio, ITA	4:03.25	
1976	Tatyana Kazankina, USSR	4:05.48		1988	Paula Ivan, ROM	3:53.96	OR
1980	Tatyana Kazankina, USSR	3:56.6	OR	1992	Hassiba Boulmerka, ALG	3:55.30	

3000 meters

Year		Time		Year		Time
1984	Maricica Puica, ROM	8:35.96		1992	Elena Romanova, UT	8:46.04
1988	Tatyana Samolenko, USSR	8:26.53	OR			

10,000 meters

Year		Time		Year		Time
1988	Olga Bondarenko, USSR	31:05.21	OR	1992	Derartu Tulu, ETH	31:06.02

Marathon

Year		Time	Year		Time
1984	Joan Benoit, USA	2:24:52	1992	Valentina Yegorova, UT	2:32:41
1988	Rosa Mota, POR	2:25:40			

100-meter Hurdles

Year		Time		Year		Time	
1932	Babe Didrikson, USA	11.7	WR	1968	Maureen Caird, AUS	10.3	OR
1936	Trebisonda Valla, ITA	11.7		1972	Annelie Ehrhardt, E.Ger	12.59	WR
1948	Fanny Blankers-Koen, HOL	11.2	OR	1976	Johanna Schaller, E.Ger	12.77	
1952	Shirley Strickland, AUS	10.9	WR	1980	Vera Komisova, USSR	12.56	OR
1956	Shirley Strickland, AUS	10.7	OR	1984	Benita Fitzgerald-Brown, USA	12.84	
1960	Irina Press, USSR	10.8		1988	Yordanka Donkova, BUL	12.38	OR
1964	Karin Balzer, GER	10.5w		1992	Paraskevi Patoulidou, GRE	12.64	

w indicates wind-aided.   **Note:** Event held over 80 meters from 1932-68.

400-meter Hurdles

Year		Time		Year		Time	
1984	Nawal El Moutawakel, MOR	54.61	OR	1992	Sally Gunnell, GBR	53.23	
1988	Debra Flintoff-King, AUS	53.17	OR				

4x100-meter Relay

Year		Time		Year		Time	
1928	Canada	48.4	WR	1968	United States	42.87	WR
1932	United States	46.9	WR	1972	West Germany	42.81	WR
1936	United States	46.9		1976	East Germany	42.55	OR
1948	Holland	47.5		1980	East Germany	41.60	WR
1952	United States	45.9	WR	1984	United States	41.65	
1956	Australia	44.5	WR	1988	United States	41.98	
1960	United States	44.5		1992	United States	42.11	
1964	Poland	43.6					

4x400-meter Relay

Year		Time		Year		Time	
1972	East Germany	3:23.0	WR	1984	United States	3:18.29	OR
1976	East Germany	3:19.23	WR	1988	Soviet Union	3:15.18	WR
1980	Soviet Union	3:20.2		1992	Unified Team	3:20.20	

10-kilometer Walk

Year		Time
1992	Chen Yueling, CHN	44.32

High Jump

Year		Height		Year		Height	
1928	Ethel Catherwood, CAN	5- 2½		1968	Miloslava Režková, CZE	5-11½	
1932	Jean Shiley, USA	5- 5¼	WR	1972	Ulrike Meyfarth, W.Ger	6- 3½	=WR
1936	Ibolya Csák, HUN	5- 3		1976	Rosemarie Ackermann, E.Ger	6- 4	OR
1948	Alice Coachman, USA	5- 6	OR	1980	Sara Simeoni, ITA	6- 5½	OR
1952	Esther Brand, SAF	5- 5¾		1984	Ulrike Meyfarth, W.Ger	6- 7½	OR
1956	Mildred McDaniel, USA	5- 9¼	WR	1988	Louise Ritter, USA	6- 8	OR
1960	Iolanda Balas, ROM	6- 0¾	OR	1992	Heike Henkel, GER	6- 7½	
1964	Iolanda Balas, ROM	6- 2¾	OR				

Long Jump

Year		Distance		Year		Distance	
1948	Olga Gyarmati, HUN	18- 8¼		1972	Heidemarie Rosendahl, W.Ger	22- 3	
1952	Yvette Williams, NZE	20- 5¾	OR	1976	Angela Voigt, E.Ger	22- 0¾	
1956	Elzbieta Krzesinska, POL	20-10	=WR	1980	Tatyana Kolpakova, USSR	23- 2	OR
1960	Vyera Krepkina, USSR	20-10¾	OR	1984	Anisoara Cusmir-Stanciu, ROM	22-10	
1964	Mary Rand, GBR	22- 2¼	WR	1988	Jackie Joyner-Kersee, USA	24- 3¼	OR
1968	Viorica Viscopoleanu, ROM	22- 4½	WR	1992	Heike Drechsler, GER	23- 5¼	

Track & Field (Cont.)
WOMEN
Shot Put

Year		Distance		Year		Distance	
1948	Micheline Ostermeyer, FRA	45- 1½		1972	Nadezhda Chizhova, USSR	69- 0	WR
1952	Galina Zybina, USSR	50- 1¾	WR	1976	Ivanka Hristova, BUL	69- 5¼	OR
1956	Tamara Tyshkevich, USSR	54- 5		1980	Ilona Slupianek, E.Ger	73- 6¼	OR
1960	Tamara Press, USSR	56-10	OR	1984	Claudia Losch, W.Ger	67- 2¼	
1964	Tamara Press, USSR	59- 6¼	OR	1988	Natalia Lisovskaya, USSR	72-11¾	
1968	Margitta Gummel, E.Ger	64- 4	WR	1992	Svetlana Krivaleva, UT	69- 1¼	

Discus Throw

Year		Distance		Year		Distance	
1928	Halina Konopacka, POL	129-11¾	WR	1968	Lia Manoliu, ROM	191- 2	OR
1932	Lillian Copeland, USA	133- 2	OR	1972	Faina Melnik, USSR	218- 7	OR
1936	Gisela Mauermayer, GER	156- 3	OR	1976	Evelin Schlaak, E.Ger	226- 4	OR
1948	Micheline Ostermeyer, FRA	137- 6		1980	Evelin Schlaak Jahl, E.Ger	229- 6	OR
1952	Nina Romaschkova, USSR	168- 8	OR	1984	Ria Stalman, HOL	214- 5	
1956	Olga Fikotová, CZE	176- 1	OR	1988	Martina Hellmann, E.Ger	237- 2½	OR
1960	Nina Ponomaryeva, USSR	180- 9	OR	1992	Maritza Marten, CUB	229-10	
1964	Tamara Press, USSR	187-10	OR				

Javelin Throw

Year		Distance		Year		Distance	
1932	Babe Didrikson, USA	143- 4		1968	Angéla Németh, HUN	198- 0	
1936	Tilly Fleischer, GER	148- 3	OR	1972	Ruth Fuchs, E.Ger	209- 7	OR
1948	Herma Bauma, AUT	149- 6	OR	1976	Ruth Fuchs, E.Ger	216- 4	OR
1952	Dana Zátopková, CZE	165- 7	OR	1980	Maria Colon Rueñes, CUB	224- 5	OR
1956	Ineze Jaunzeme, USSR	176- 8	OR	1984	Tessa Sanderson, GBR	228- 2	OR
1960	Elvira Ozolina, USSR	183- 8	OR	1988	Petra Felke, E.Ger	245- 0	OR
1964	Mihaela Penes, ROM	198- 7	OR	1992	Silke Renk, GER	224- 2	

Heptathlon

Year		Points		Year		Points	
1964	Irina Press, USSR	5246	WR	1980	Nadezhda Tkachenko, USSR	5083	WR
1968	Ingrid Becker, W.Ger	5098		1984	Glynis Nunn, AUS	6390	OR
1972	Mary Peters, GBR	4801	WR	1988	Jackie Joyner-Kersee, USA	7291	WR
1976	Siegrun Siegl, E.Ger	4745		1992	Jackie Joyner Kersee, USA	7044	

Note: Seven-event Heptathlon replaced five-event Pentathlon in 1984.

All-Time Top 35 Medal Standings, 1986-1992

All-time Summer Games medal standings, according to *The Golden Book of the Olympic Games*. Medal counts include the 1906 Intercalated Games which are not recognized by the IOC.

		G	S	B	Total			G	S	B	Total
1	United States	788	602	528	1918	20	Czechoslovakia (1924-92)	49	49	44	142
2	USSR (1952-88)	395	319	296	1010	21	Denmark	34	59	56	149
3	Great Britain	168	215	212	595	22	Belgium	35	47	47	117
4	France	160	172	191	523	23	Norway	43	39	35	117
5	E. Germany (1956-88)	159	150	136	445	24	Unified Team (1992)	45	38	29	112
6	Sweden	130	147	172	449	25	China	36	41	37	114
7	Italy	153	125	132	410	26	Greece	24	38	43	105
8	Hungary	135	125	145	405	27	South Korea	31	27	41	99
9	Germany (1896-36,92—)	104	103	107	314	28	Cuba	35	25	23	83
10	W. Germany (1952-88)	77	104	120	301	29	Yugoslavia (1924-88)	26	30	30	86
11	Finland	98	78	112	288	30	Austria	18	30	32	80
12	Japan	89	83	92	264	31	New Zealand	26	10	28	64
13	Australia	77	76	98	251	32	Turkey	26	15	12	53
14	Romania	59	70	90	219	33	South Africa	16	17	20	53
15	Poland	43	62	105	210	34	Spain	17	19	11	47
16	Canada	45	67	82	194	35	Argentina	13	19	15	47
17	Switzerland	42	66	59	167		**Note:**				
18	Bulgaria	40	69	58	167		USSR/UT/Russia	440	360	327	1127
19	Holland	45	53	71	169		Germany/E.Ger/W.Ger	340	357	363	1060

Athletes from the USSR participated in the Summer Games from 1952-88, returned as the Unified Team in 1992 after the breakup of the Soviet Union (in 1991) and then competed for the independent republics of Belarus, Kazakhstan, Russia, Ukraine, Uzbekistan and three others in 1994. Yugoslavia divided into Croatia and Bosnia-Herzegovina in 1991, while Czechoslovakia split into Slovenia and the Czech Republic the same year.

Germany was barred from the Olympics in 1924 and '48 following World Wars I and II. Divided into East and West Germany after WWII, both countries competed together from 1952-64, then separately from 1968-88. Germany was reunified in 1990.

All-Time Leading Medal Winners
All Nations

Most Overall Medals
MEN

No		Sport	G-S-B
15	Nikolai Andrianov, USSR	Gymnastics	7-5-3
13	Boris Shakhlin, USSR	Gymnastics	7-4-2
13	Edoardo Mangiarotti, ITA	Fencing	6-5-2
13	Takashi Ono, JPN	Gymnastics	5-4-4
12	Paavo Nurmi, FIN	Track/Field	9-3-0
12	Sawao Kato, JPN	Gymnastics	8-3-1
11	**Mark Spitz**, USA	Swimming	9-1-1
11*	**Matt Biondi**, USA	Swimming	8-2-1
11	Viktor Chukarin, USSR	Gymnastics	7-3-1
11	**Carl Osburn**, USA	Shooting	5-4-2
10	**Ray Ewry**, USA	Track/Field	10-0-0
10	Aladár Gerevich, HUN	Fencing	7-1-2
10	Akinori Nakayama, JPN	Gymnastics	6-2-2
10	Aleksandr Dityatin, USSR	Gymnastics	3-6-1
9	**Carl Lewis**, USA	Track/Field	8-1-0
9	**Martin Sheridan**, USA	Track/Field	5-3-1
9	Zoltán Halmay, HUN	Swimming	3-5-1
9	Giulio Gaudini, ITA	Fencing	3-4-2
9	Mikhail Voronin, USSR	Gymnastics	2-6-1
9	Heikki Savolainen, FIN	Gymnastics	2-1-6
9	Yuri Titov, USSR	Gymnastics	1-5-3

*Includes gold medal as preliminary member of 1st-place relay team.

Games Participated In

Andrianov (1972,76,80); **Biondi** (1984,88,92); **Chukarin** (1952,56); **Dityatin** (1976,80); **Ewry** (1900,04,06,08); **Gerevich** (1932,36,48,52,56,60); **Gaudini** (1928,32,36); **Halmay** (1900,04,06,08); **Kato** (1968,72,76); **Lewis** (1984,88,92); **Mangiarotti** (1936,48,52,56,60); **Nakayama** (1968,72); **Nurmi** (1920,24,28); **Ono** (1952,56,60,64); **Osburn** (1912,20, 24); **Savolainen** (1928,32,36,48,52); **Shakhlin** (1956,60,64); **Sheridan** (1904,06,08); **Spitz** (1968,72); **Titov** (1956,60,64); **Voronin** (1968,72).

WOMEN

No		Sport	G-S-B
18	Larissa Latynina, USSR	Gymnastics	9-5-4
11	Vera Cáslavská, CZE	Gymnastics	7-4-0
10	Agnes Keleti, HUN	Gymnastics	5-3-2
10	Polina Astaknova, USSR	Gymnastics	5-2-3
9	Nadia Comaneci, ROM	Gymnastics	5-3-1
9	Lyudmila Tourischeva, USSR	Gymnastics	4-3-2
8	Kornelia Ender, E.Ger	Swimming	4-4-0
8	Dawn Fraser, AUS	Swimming	4-4-0
8	**Shirley Babashoff**, USA	Swimming	2-6-0
8	Sofia Muratova, USSR	Gymnastics	2-2-4
7	Irena Kirszenstein Szewinska, POL	Track/Field	3-2-2
7	Shirley Strickland, AUS	Track/Field	3-1-3
7	Maria Gorokhovskaya, USSR	Gymnastics	2-5-0
7	Ildikó Ságiné-Ujlaki-Rejtö, HUN	Fencing	2-3-2

Games Participated In

Astaknova (1956,60,64); **Babashoff** (1972,76); **Cáslavská** (1960,64,68); **Comaneci** (1976,80); **Ender** (1972,76); **Fraser** (1956,60,64); **Gorokhovskaya** (1952); **Keleti** (1952,56); **Latynina** (1956,60,64); **Muratova** (1956,60); **Ságiné-Ujlaki-Rejtö** (1960,64, 68,72,76); **Strickland** (1948,52,56); **Szewinska** (1964,68,72,76,80); **Tourischeva** (1968, 72,76).

Most Medals—Single Games

	Medals
Men: Aleksandr Dityatin, USSR (1980)	8 (3-4-1)
Women: Maria Gorokhovskaya, USSR (1952)	7 (2-5-0)

Most Gold Medals
MEN

No		Sport	G-S-B
10	**Ray Ewry**, USA	Track/Field	10-0-0
9	Paavo Nurmi, FIN	Track/Field	9-3-0
9	**Mark Spitz**, USA	Swimming	9-1-1
8	Sawao Kato, JPN	Gymnastics	8-3-1
8*	**Matt Biondi**, USA	Swimming	8-2-1
8	**Carl Lewis**, USA	Track/Field	8-1-0
7	Nikolai Andrianov, USSR	Gymnastics	7-5-3
7	Boris Shakhlin, USSR	Gymnastics	7-4-2
7	Viktor Chukarin, USSR	Gymnastics	7-3-1
7	Aladar Gerevich, HUN	Fencing	7-1-2

*Includes gold medal as preliminary member of 1st-place relay team.

WOMEN

No		Sport	G-S-B
9	Larissa Latynina, USSR	Gymnastics	9-5-4
7	Vera Cáslavská, CZE	Gymnastics	7-4-0
6	Kristin Otto, E.Ger	Swimming	6-0-0
5	Agnes Keleti, HUN	Gymnastics	5-3-2
5	Nadia Comaneci, ROM	Gymnastics	5-3-1
5	Polina Astaknova, USSR	Gymnastics	5-2-3
4	Kornelia Ender, E.Ger	Swimming	4-4-0
4	Dawn Fraser, AUS	Swimming	4-4-0
4	Lyudmila Tourischeva, USSR	Gymnastics	4-3-2
4	**Evelyn Ashford**, USA	Track/Field	4-1-0
4	Krisztina Egerszegi, HUN	Swimming	4-1-0
4	**Janet Evans**, USA	Swimming	4-1-0
4	Fanny Blankers-Koen, HOL	Track/Field	4-0-0
4	Betty Cuthbert, AUS	Track/Field	4-0-0
4	**Pat McCormick**, USA	Diving	4-0-0
4	Bärbel Eckert Wöckel, E.Ger.	Track/Field	4-0-0

Most Silver Medals
MEN

No		Sport	G-S-B
6	Alexandr Dityatin, USSR	Gymnastics	3-6-1
6	Mikhail Voronin, USSR	Gymnastics	2-6-1
5	Nikolai Andrianov, USSR	Gymnastics	7-5-3
5	Edoardo Mangiarotti, ITA	Fencing	6-5-2
5	Zoltán Halmay, HUN	Swimming	3-5-1
5	Philippe Cattiau, FRA	Fencing	3-4-1
5	Gustavo Marzi, ITA	Fencing	2-5-0
5	Yuri Titov, USSR	Gymnastics	1-5-3
5	Viktor Lisitsky, USSR	Gymnastics	0-5-1

WOMEN

No		Sport	G-S-B
6	**Shirley Babashoff**, USA	Swimming	2-6-0
5	Larissa Latynina, USSR	Gymnastics	9-5-4
5	Maria Gorokhovskaya, USSR	Gymnastics	2-5-0
4	Vera Cáslavská, CZE	Gymnastics	7-4-0
4	Kornelia Ender, E.Ger	Swimming	4-4-0
4	Dawn Fraser, AUS	Swimming	4-4-0
4	Erica Zuchold, E.Ger	Gymnastics	0-4-1

Most Bronze Medals
MEN

No		Sport	G-S-B
6	Heikki Savolainen, FIN	Gymnastics	2-1-6
5	Daniel Revenu, FRA	Fencing	1-0-5
5	Philip Edwards, CAN	Track/Field	0-0-5
5	Adrianus Jong, HOL	Fencing	0-0-5

WOMEN

No		Sport	G-S-B
4	Larissa Latynina, USSR	Gymnastics	9-5-4
4	Sofia Muratova, USSR	Gymnastics	2-2-4
4	Merlene Ottey, JAM	Track/Field	0-0-4

All-Time Leading USA Medal Winners

Most Overall Medals
MEN

No		Sport	G-S-B
11	Mark Spitz	Swimming	9-1-1
11*	Matt Biondi	Swimming	8-2-1
11	Carl Osburn	Shooting	5-4-2
10	Ray Ewry	Track/Field	10-0-0
9	Carl Lewis	Track/Field	8-1-0
9	Martin Sheridan	Track/Field	5-3-1
8	Charles Daniels	Swimming	5-1-2
7†	Tom Jager	Swimming	5-1-1
7	Willis Lee	Shooting	5-1-1
7	Lloyd Spooner	Shooting	4-1-2
6	Anton Heida	Gymnastics	5-1-0
6	Don Schollander	Swimming	5-1-0
6	Johnny Weissmuller	Swim/Water Polo	5-0-1
6	Alfred Lane	Shooting	5-0-1
6	Jim Lightbody	Track/Field	4-2-0
6	George Eyser	Gymnastics	3-2-1
6	Michael Plumb	Equestrian	2-4-0
6	Burton Downing	Cycling	2-3-1
6	Bob Garrett	Track/Field	2-2-2

*Includes gold medal as prelim. member of 1st-place relay team.
†Includes 3 gold medals as prelim. member of 1st-place relay teams.

Games Participated In
Biondi (1984,88,92); **Daniels** (1904,06,08); **Downing** (1904); **Ewry** (1900,04,06,08); **Eyser** (1904); **Garrett** (1896,1900); **Heida** (1904); **Jager** (1984,88,92); **Lane** (1912,20); **Lee** (1920); **Lewis** (1984,88,92); **Lightbody** (1904,06); **Osburn** (1912,20,24); **Plumb** (1960, 64,68,72,76,84); **Schollander** (1964, 68); **Sheridan** (1904,06,08); **Spitz** (1968,72); **Spooner** (1920); **Weissmuller** (1924,28).

WOMEN

No		Sport	G-S-B
8	Shirley Babashoff	Swimming	2-6-0
5	Evelyn Ashford	Track/Field	4-1-0
5	Janet Evans	Swimming	4-1-0
5*	Mary T. Meagher	Swimming	3-1-1
5	Florence Griffith Joyner	Track/Field	3-2-0
5	Jackie Joyner-Kersee	Track/Field	3-1-1
5	Mary Lou Retton	Gymnastics	1-2-2
5	Shannon Miller	Gymnastics	0-2-3
4	Pat McCormick	Diving	4-0-0
4	Valerie Brisco-Hooks	Track/Field	3-1-0
4	Nancy Hogshead	Swimming	3-1-0
4	Sharon Stouder	Swimming	3-1-0
4	Wyomia Tyus	Track/Field	3-1-0
4	Wilma Rudolph	Track/Field	3-0-1
4	Chris von Saltza	Swimming	3-1-0
4	Sue Pederson	Swimming	2-2-0
4	Jan Henne	Swimming	2-1-1
4	Dorothy Poynton Hill	Diving	2-1-1
4*	Summer Sanders	Swimming	2-1-1
4*	Dara Torres	Swimming	2-1-1
4	Kathy Ellis	Swimming	2-0-2
4	Georgia Coleman	Diving	1-2-1

*Includes silver medal as prelim. member of 2nd-place relay team.

Games Participated In
Ashford (1976,84,88,92); **Babashoff** (1972,76); **Brisco-Hooks** (1984,88); **Coleman** (1928,32); **Ellis** (1964); **Evans** (1988,92); **Griffith Joyner** (1984,88); **Henne** (1968); **Hogshead** (1984); **Joyner-Kersee** (1984,88,92); **McCormick** (1952,56); **Meagher** (1984,88); **Miller** (1992); **Pederson** (1968); **Poynton Hill** (1928,32,36); **Retton** (1984); **Rudolph** (1956,60); **Sanders** (1992); **Stouder** (1964); **Torres** (1984,88,92); **Tyus** (1964,68); **von Saltza** (1960).

Most Gold Medals
MEN

No		Sport	G-S-B
10	Raymond Ewry	Track/Field	10-0-0
9	Mark Spitz	Swimming	9-1-1
8	Carl Lewis	Track/Field	8-1-0
8*	Matt Biondi	Swimming	8-2-1
5	Carl Osburn	Shooting	5-4-2
5	Martin Sheridan	Track/Field	5-3-1
5	Charles Daniels	Swimming	5-1-2
5†	Tom Jager	Swimming	5-1-1
5	Willis Lee	Shooting	5-1-1
5	Anton Heida	Gymnastics	5-1-0
5	Don Schollander	Swimming	5-1-0
5	Johnny Weissmuller	Swim/Water Polo	5-0-1
5	Alfred Lane	Shooting	5-0-1
5	Morris Fisher	Shooting	5-0-0
4	Jim Lightbody	Track/Field	4-2-0
4	Lloyd Spooner	Shooting	4-1-2
4	Greg Louganis	Diving	4-1-0
4	John Naber	Swimming	4-1-0
4	Meyer Prinstein	Track/Field	4-1-0
4	Mel Sheppard	Track/Field	4-1-0
4	Marcus Hurley	Cycling	4-0-1
4	Harrison Dillard	Track/Field	4-0-0
4	Archie Hahn	Track/Field	4-0-0
4	Alvin Kraenzlein	Track/Field	4-0-0
4	Al Oerter	Track/Field	4-0-0
4	Jesse Owens	Track/Field	4-0-0

*Includes gold medal as prelim. member of 1st-place relay team.
†Includes 3 gold medals as prelim. member of 1st-place relay teams.

WOMEN

No		Sport	G-S-B
4	Evelyn Ashford	Track/Field	4-1-0
4	Janet Evans	Swimming	4-1-0
4	Pat McCormick	Diving	4-0-0
3	Florence Griffith Joyner	Track/Field	3-2-0
3	Jackie Joyner-Kersee	Track/Field	3-1-1
3*	Mary T. Meagher	Swimming	3-1-1
3	Valerie Brisco-Hooks	Track/Field	3-1-0
3	Nancy Hogshead	Swimming	3-1-0
3	Sharon Stouder	Swimming	3-1-0
3	Wyomia Tyus	Track/Field	3-1-0
3	Chris von Saltza	Swimming	3-1-0
3	Wilma Rudolph	Track/Field	3-0-1
3	Melissa Belote	Swimming	3-0-0
3	Ethelda Bleibtrey	Swimming	3-0-0
3	Tracy Caulkins	Swimming	3-0-0
3*	Nicole Haislett	Swimming	3-0-0
3	Helen Madison	Swimming	3-0-0
3	Debbie Meyer	Swimming	3-0-0
3	Sandra Neilson	Swimming	3-0-0
3	Martha Norelius	Swimming	3-0-0
3*	Carrie Steinseifer	Swimming	3-0-0

*Includes gold medal as prelim. member of 1st-place relay team.

Most Silver Medals
MEN

No		Sport	G-S-B
4	Carl Osburn	Shooting	5-4-2
4	Michael Plumb	Equestrian	2-4-0
3	Martin Sheridan	Track/Field	5-3-1
3	Burton Downing	Cycling	2-3-1
3	Irving Baxter	Track/Field	2-3-0
3	Earl Thomson	Equestrian	2-3-0

WOMEN

No		Sport	G-S-B
6	Shirley Babashoff	Swimming	2-6-0

Le Jingyi of China raises her fist in triumph after setting a world record in the 50-meter freestyle at the World Swimming Championships in Rome in September.

INTERNATIONAL SPORTS

Tidal Wave

Chinese women swimmers dominate world meet in Rome, but leave suspicions of rampant drug use in their wake.

One year after Chinese women distance runners shocked the track and field world with three gold medals at the World Championships in Stuttgart and four subsequent world records at their national meet in Beijing, Chinese women swimmers set five world records and won 12 of 16 events at the 7th World Swimming Championships in Rome.

China's performance raised questions about how they have come to dominate world swimming only six years after winning their first world or Olympic medal.

Those questions led to an unprecedented action by coaches and administrators from 18 nations, who signed a statement blasting "the apparent reemergence of the extensive use of performance-enhancing drugs, especially in women's competition." Although that statement did not mention China by name, many of the coaches individually aired their suspicions that drug use was a key to Chinese success.

U.S. women's coach Richard Quick was blunt in his assessment, saying: "I think the results of the Chinese are a sham."

The Chinese tidal wave swept aside 1994 Olympic stars like Janet Evans of the U. S. (fifth in the 400-meter freestyle) and Krisztina Egerszegi of Hungary (fifth in the 100-meter backstroke, second in the 200 back). Evans, however, did maintain her

eight-year unbeaten streak in the 800.

China's Le Jingyi, 19, who set world records in the 50 and 100-meter freestyles and anchored two world-record-setting relays, was the meet's most outstanding swimmer. Five other world records were set, but only one by an American swimmer—Tom Dolan, in the 400 individual medley. The U.S. performance of four gold medals and 21 overall was its worst in meet history.

The Chinese also cleaned up in diving, winning four of six gold medals and nine of 18 overall. Their diving success raised no eyebrows because it was nothing new.

Baseball. Cuba went 10-0 for its fifth straight world championship in Nicaragua. The Cubans batters hit a combined .397 while their pitchers had a collective ERA of 0.92 ERA. The U.S. finished in a tie for seventh after losing to Cuba 15-2 in the quarterfinals.

Basketball. Dream Team II plowed through the 1994 World Championships in Toronto, pounding Russia, 137-91, in the final. This second group of NBA All-Stars to represent the U.S. in international competition outscored opponents by 38 points per game, six fewer than Dream Team I's winning margin in the 1992 Olympics. Shaquille O'Neal lead the Dreamers with 18 points and 8.5 rebounds per game. Croatia beat Greece, 78-60, for the bronze.

Brazil won the 1994 women's world title in Australia after upsetting the defending champion U.S. in the semis and China in the finals. The U.S., which had won 21

Philip Hersh covers international sports for the *Chicago Tribune* and has been the *Tribune's* full-time Olympics writer since 1986.

Wide World Photos

Distance runner **Nourredine Morceli** of Morocco poses with the time clock after setting a new world record of 7 minutes 25.11 in the 3,000 meters at the Hercules Grand Prix in Monaco on Aug. 2. Morceli also holds world marks in the mile and 1,500.

straight games at the worlds (dating back to the 1983 final) prior to losing to the Brazilians, beat Australia for the bronze.

Cycling. After his third-place finish in the Giro d'Italia (won by Yevgeni Berzin of Russia), Miguel Indurain of Spain seemed vulnerable in the 81st Tour de France. Tony Rominger of Switzerland figured to mount the strongest challenge but, once again, "Big Mig" proved too much, riding to a fourth straight win by almost six minutes in what was a Tour of Hades because of brutally hot weather.

Among those who did not finish the 2,467-mile, 23-day race were Rominger, three-time winner Greg LeMond of the U.S., two-time world champion Gianni Bugno of Italy, and two-time Tour runner-up Claudio Chiappucci of Italy.

At the World Championships at Palermo, Sicily in late August, Marty Nothstein, 23, of Trexlertown, Pa., became the first U.S. rider since 1912 to win a world sprint title. Nothstein later became the first U.S. winner of the keirin event, contested since 1981.

In the road race, defending champion Lance Armstrong of Dallas became trapped in a sprint battle between the French and Italian teams and wound up seventh, 48 seconds behind winner Luc LeBlanc of France. Under a broiling sun, LeBlanc, 28, gave France its first men's road title since the legendary Bernard Hinault in 1980.

Gymnastics. Shannon Miller, 17, of Edmond, Okla., won her second straight all-around title and another gold medal in the balance beam at the April world championships in Birmingham, England.

After tumbling to third in the all-around, won by Ivan Ivanov of Belarus, Olympic champion Vitaly Scherbo won three gold medals on individual apparatus. Paul O'Neill of Mandan, N.D., was second on rings, becoming the first U.S. man to win a world medal since 1979.

Marathons. Germany's Uta Pipping won the 1993 New York City Marathon and the '94 Boston Marathon. Despite an unseasonably warm Nov. 14 in New York, she knocked 28 seconds off her personal best to run a 2:26:24. Five months later, she took advantage of a tailwind to set a course record of 2:21:45 in Boston. That tailwind also enabled defending Boston champion

Cosmas Ndeti of Kenya to shatter the men's record with a 2:07.15.

Rowing. The first World Championships hosted in the United States were held at Eagle Creek Park outside Indianapolis in mid-September and wound up with a melting pot of results. Italy won the most gold medals with four; Germany the most overall medals with nine; the United States regained the men's heavyweight eight title for the first time since 1987; and Croatia won its first world title in any sport with a first in the men's pairs with coxwain.

Track & Field. Seven individual world records were set in this "off" year, beginning with the 5,000-meter mark of 12:56.96 set on June 4 by Haile Gebresilasie, the first Ethiopian to hold a world record. That was followed on July 6 by Leroy Burrell's 100-meter mark of 9.85 at Lausanne, Switzerland, lowering Carl Lewis' mark by .01 second.

Other breakers were William Sigei of Kenya, whose 26:52.23 in the 10,000 lopped a stunning six seconds off countryman Yobes Ondieki's mark; Sergey Bubka of Ukraine, whose outdoor pole vault mark of 20 feet, 1¾ inches was his 35th world record; Noureddine Morceli of Algeria, who added the 3,000 meters record (7:25.11) to a collection that already includes the 1,500 and mile marks; and race walkers Bernardo Segura of Mexico (20-km) and Rene Piller of France (50 km).

In an otherwise desultory European Championships at Helsinki, (no world or Euro records for the first time since 1966 in this quadrennial meet), Olympic champion Linford Christie of Great Britain reaffirmed his continental superiority by winning his third straight 100-meter title. Christie then beat all comers at the Zurich Grand Prix.

Other Euro Championship highlights: Spain's historic medal sweep in the men's marathon, the first time that had happened in any major championship; Norway's first gold medal in a track event (Geir Moen in the 200 meters) at a major championship; and Sally Gunnell's win in the 400-meter hurdles, making the 28-year-old Briton the first woman to hold simultaneously the world, Olympic, European and Commonwealth titles in the same event.

Weightlifting. The 1993 World Championships in Melbourne were mired in controversies over doping as resurgent Bulgaria took four of the 10 men's titles. As usual China dominated the women's events, winning 19 of 27 gold medals. In seven women's world championships, China has won an incredible 156 of 171 golds.

Wrestling. After winning its first-ever freestyle team title at the 1993 World Championships, the U.S. slipped to its worst performance in two decades (a silver and one bronze) at the '94 worlds in Istanbul, Turkey. Reigning heavyweight champion Bruce Baumgartner, 33, lost in the final to Turkey's Mahmut Demir.

Winter Sports

Alpine Skiing. The season wore a shroud after Austria's Ulrike Maier, 26, died in a horrifying crash during the Jan. 29 World Cup downhill at Garmisch-Partenkirchen, Germany. Maier, the only mother on the World Cup circuit, was killed when she lost her balance at 65 miles per hour and appeared to hit a timing post. The impact snapped her head backward and broke her neck. Maier, double world champion and an Olympic gold medal favorite, is one of 16 athletes who have died in international ski racing since 1959.

Vreni Schneider, 29, of Switzerland, had a banner year, winning her second overall title and third straight slalom crown, plus gold, silver and bronze medals at the Olympics. Seven World Cup race victories, all in slalom, hiked her career total to 51, putting her within reach of Annemarie Moser-Proell's career record of 62.

Kjetil Andre-Aamodt became the first Norwegian to win a World Cup overall title. By winning the super-G at Whistler, Canada, Olympic downhill champion Tommy Moe of Palmer, Alaska gave the U.S. men their first World Cup race win since 1991 and only the second since 1983.

Diann Roffe-Steinrotter of Potsdam, N.Y., the Olympic super-G champion, ended her 11-season international career with a flourish by taking the World Cup Finals super-G at Vail, Colorado. Roffe, 26, had been the youngest world champion ever when she won the giant slalom at the 1985 worlds.

Bobsled. Brian Shimer of the U.S., four-man and overall World Cup champion in 1992-93, never could get untracked in 1993-94. He finished 12th in four-man and 11th overall. Pierre Lueders of Canada, a

Snafus And Apathy Plague Goodwill III

Take murky water, thin ice, fickle wind, computer snafus, underwhelming competition and an idea that has become an anachronism, and what do you have? The Goodwill Games.

In 1994, the third edition of the Goodwill Games generated pathetic TV ratings and lost $39 million. It also raised more questions about whether this 16-day "mini-Olympics" has outlived its viability and credibility.

The only man who expressed no doubts about the future of the Games was Ted Turner, who has bankrolled the quadrennial event since he thought it up in 1986. The idea was to repair superpower sports relations after the tit-for-tat Summer Olympic boycotts of 1980 and '84. However, communism soon collapsed under its own weight and the old Soviet Union ceased to exist in 1991.

Well, the Red Menace may have died, but the Goodwill Games still have a pulse. And even though the first three Games have lost Turner some $109 million, he insists Goodwill IV will be held as scheduled in New York in 1998.

After that, the Games may go to to a city in Siberia. That would be the most appropriate venue, since the event already has been exiled to the Siberia of the U.S. sporting consciousness.

Goodwill III, which took place from July 23 to Aug. 7 in St. Petersburg, Russia, managed an average TV rating of just 1.4, meaning it reached barely 1 million U.S. homes. Live interest in the 24 sports on the program was equally sparse in St. Petersburg, owing partly to both an inadequate ticket-sale system and high ticket prices in a country stuggling to make the transition from communism to capitalism.

From start to finish, Goodwill III was plagued by serious organizational problems. A filtration problem turned the swimming pool into what Spanish swimmer Martin Zubero called, "the black lagoon." The first day of events had to be postponed while the Russians frantically tried to clear the water with chemicals. By the time the

Phil Cole/Allsport

Goodwill Games founder and benefactor **Ted Turner** (right) with **Anatoli Sobchak** the mayor of St. Petersburg.

contents of the pool had turned an acceptable shade of green the entire swim program had to be compressed into one day. Not impressed, the Swedish team pulled out because it felt the conditions imperiled swimmers' health.

Because a computer was incorrectly programmed, officials had to use hand calculaters to figure the results of the women's gymnastics all-around, in which Shannon Miller of the U.S. lost for the first time in two years.

Both figure skating and short-track speed skating endured postponements due to poor ice preparation. "You would think ice is one thing Russians could make," grumbled rink general contractor Aleksandr Shlykov.

What men couldn't screw up, nature did. The absence of wind wiped out part of the sailing schedule.

The competition lived down to the ambiance. The U.S. men lost to Italy in the basketball semifinals, although the U.S. women beat France for their first international gold medal since 1990. Sergey Bubka was third in the pole vault and decathlon winner Dan O'Brien wimped out on a world-record attempt by virtually walking the final 1,500 meters.

Despite all that. St. Petersburg wants to make a bid to host the 2004 Summer Olympics and Turner is talking about a Goodwill Winter Games. Siberia is waiting.

disappointment (7th place) at the Olympics, drove to the two-man and overall titles, while Hubert Schoesser of Austria was four-man champion.

Figure Skating. The return of 1988 Olympic champion Brian Boitano figured to be the highlight of the U.S. Championships in Detroit. But the men's final came only a few hours after the assault on Nancy Kerrigan, so Boitano's loss to Scott Davis went largely unnoticed. In Kerrigan's absence, Tonya Harding went on to win her second U.S. title, but was stripped of the championship on June 30 by the U.S. Figure Skating Association because of her link to the Kerrigan attack.

The World Championships, always an anticlimax in Olympic years, were even more so this time. Held in Chiba, Japan, the event was missing all three women's Olympic medalists and the top two pairs medalists. Only the men's competition was memorable, as Canada's Elvis Stojko, the runner-up in Lillehammer, won with a dazzling free skate—including a historic quad-triple jump combination. Olympic champion Alexi Urmanov of Russia was fourth.

The meet ended with a sour-grapes display by France's Surya Bonaly, who needed to be coaxed onto the medal stand to receive her silver medal and then removed it immediately from her neck. Bonaly was upset by the 5-4 judges decision that made Japan's Yuka Sato the winner. The U.S., minus Boitano, Kerrigan and Harding (whose plea bargain forced her off the world team), failed to win a medal for the second straight world championship. That had not happened since 1963-64, when U.S. skating was recovering from the 1961 plane crash that killed all its top athletes.

Ice Hockey. Canada won its first World Championship in 33 years, although its significance was reduced by having so many top players absent due to commitments in the National Hockey League. Canada beat Finland, 2-1, in a shootout for the gold medal. The United States wound up fourth, but was crushed, 8-0, by Finland in the semifinals, and 7-2 by Sweden in the bronze medal game. Canada also won the women's world title, beating the U.S., 6-3, in the final.

In late July, the NHL and International Hockey Federation agreed to work toward NHL player participation in the 1998 Olympics.

Luge. The sport attracted an unusual amount of attention this year because of an Oct. 29 incident in Oberhof, Germany, where neo-Nazi skinheads attacked U.S. luger Robert Pipkins at a local nightspot. Simpkins, who is black, escaped serious injury thanks to the courageous intervention of teammate Duncan Kennedy, who stood off the attackers while Simpkins had time to escape. Kennedy suffered cuts and bruises. Three men later were convicted in the attack, which had brought an apology from the German government.

On the track, Markus Prock of Austria won his fourth straight World Cup overall title, with Kennedy second. Germany, led by Gabi Kohlisch, finished 1-2-3 in the women's standings.

Nordic Skiing. Norway's Espen Bredesen presaged his Olympic performance (gold and silver medals) by winning the Four Hills Tournament in January and went on to capture the World Cup jumping title. In Nordic Combined, Kenjo Ogiwara of Japan won five of the season's first six World Cup events and a second straight World Cup title. Russia's Vladimir Smirnov and Italy's Manuela Di Centa took the World Cup cross-country titles.

Speed Skating. American stars Dan Jansen and Bonnie Blair each won their second World Sprint Championships and set barrier-breaking world records in the 500 meters. Blair, whose previous sprint title was in 1989, won all four races in the Jan. 29-30 meet at Calgary.

Back on the Calgary Olympic oval March 26, Blair clocked 38.99 in the 500 meters, breaking her six-year-old mark of 39.10. On Dec. 4 at the Hamar Olympic Oval, Jansen became the first man under 36 seconds (35.92), a mark he lowered to 35.76 while winning his first World Sprint title since 1988.

Norway's Olympic hero, Johann Olav Koss, won his third World All-Around title March 12-13 in Goteborg, Sweden, while Emese Hunyady of Austria took the women's title Feb. 5-6 at Butte, Montana.

Germany's Gunda Niemann, who surprisingly failed to win gold at the Olympics, finished the season by breaking her own world records in the 3,000 and 5,000 meters on the Calgary oval. ❑

WATER SPORTS

VIIth FINA World Championships

The 7th FINA World Championship in swimming, diving, water polo and synchronized swimming at Rome, Italy (Sept. 1-11). Note that WR indicates world record.

Final Medal Standings

Unofficial point totals based on three points for every gold medal, two for each silver and one for each bronze.

	G	S	B	Total	Pts		G	S	B	Total	Pts
1 China	16	10	2	28	70	12 New Zealand	0	1	2	3	4
2 United States	6	10	8	24	46	Japan	0	2	0	2	4
3 Russia	5	7	5	17	34	14 Poland	1	0	0	1	3
4 Australia	5	3	4	12	25	Zimbabwe	1	0	0	1	3
5 Hungary	3	3	4	10	19	16 Belgium	0	0	2	2	2
6 Germany	1	1	6	8	11	Brazil	0	0	2	2	2
7 Finland	2	2	0	4	10	Costa Rica	0	0	2	2	2
8 Spain	1	2	0	3	7	Holland	0	1	0	1	2
Sweden	1	2	0	3	7	20 Lithuania	0	0	1	1	1
10 Canada	1	0	3	4	6	Mexico	0	0	1	1	1
11 Italy	1	0	2	3	5	TOTALS	44	44	44	132	264

Swimming

MEN

Multiple medals: Four—Gary Hall (2-2-0), Aleksandr Popov (2-2-0) and Denis Pankratov (1-2-1). **Three**—Norbert Rozsa (2-0-1). **Two**—Kieren Perkins (2-0-0), Lars Frolander (1-1-0), Anders Holmertz (1-1-0), Antti Kasvio (1-1-0), Martin Lopez-Zubero (1-1-0), Jeff Rouse (1-1-0), Vladimir Selkov (1-1-0), Jan Sievinen (1-1-0), Eric Wunderlich (1-1-0), Roman Chegolev (0-2-0), Karoly Guttler (0-1-1), Danyon Loader (0-1-1), Gustavo Borges (0-0-2), Attila Czene (0-0-2), Tamas Deutsch (0-0-2) and Steffen Zesner (0-0-2).

50-meter Freestyle

	Time
1 Aleksandr Popov, RUS	22.17
2 Gary Hall, USA	22.44
3 Raimundas Majolis, LIT	22.52

100-meter Freestyle

	Time
1 Aleksandr Popov, RUS	49.12
2 Gary Hall, USA	49.41
3 Gustavo Borges, BRA	49.52

Other Top 10 USA: 4th—Jon Olsen (49.90).

200-meter Freestyle

	Time
1 Antti Kasvio, FIN	1:47.32
2 Anders Holmertz, SWE	1:48.24
3 Danyon Loader, NZE	1:48.49

Top 10 USA: 8th—Chad Carvin (1:49.86).

400-meter Freestyle

	Time	
1 Kieren Perkins, AUS	3:43.80	WR
2 Antti Kasvio, FIN	3:48.55	
3 Danyon Loader, NZE	3:48.62	

Top 10 USA: 8th—Tom Dolan (3:54.26).

1500-meter Freestyle

	Time
1 Kieren Perkins, AUS	14:50.52
2 Daniel Kowalski, AUS	14:53.42
3 Steffen Zesner, GER	15:09.20

Top 10 USA: 5th—Carlton Brunner (15:15.64).

100-meter Backstroke

	Time
1 Martin Lopez-Zubero, SPA	55.17
2 Jeff Rouse, USA	55.51
3 Tamas Deutsch, HUN	55.69

Other Top 10 USA: 5th—Brian Retterer (55.77).

200-meter Backstroke

	Time
1 Vladimir Selkov, RUS	1:57.42
2 Martin Lopez-Zubero, SPA	1:58.75
3 Royce Sharp, USA	1:58.86

Other Top 10 USA: 9th—Brad Bridgewater (2:01.37).

100-meter Breaststroke

	Time
1 Norbert Rozsa, HUN	1:01.24
2 Karoly Guttler, HUN	1:01.44
3 Frederic Deburghgraevr, BEL	1:01.79

Top 10 USA: 6th—Eric Wunderlich (1:01.91); 8th—Seth Van Neerden (1:02.59).

VIIth FINA World Championships (Cont.)

MEN

200-meter Breaststroke

		Time
1	Norbert Rozsa, HUN	2:12.81
2	Eric Wunderlich, USA	2:12.87
3	Karoly Guttler, HUN	2:14.12

Other Top 10 USA: 8th—Seth Van Neerden (2:15.43).

100-meter Butterfly

		Time
1	Rafal Szukala, POL	53.51
2	Lars Frolander, SWE	53.65
3	Denis Pankratov, RUS	53.68

Top 10 USA: 5th—Mark Henderson (53.95).

200-meter Butterfly

		Time
1	Denis Pankratov, RUS	1:56.54
2	Danyon Loader, NZE	1:57.99
3	Chris-Carol Bremer, GER	1:58.11

Top 10 USA: 4th—Ugur Taner (1:58.42).

200-meter Individual Medley

		Time	
1	Jani Sievinen, FIN	1:58.16	WR
2	Greg Burgess, USA	2:00.86	
3	Attila Czene, HUN	2:01.84	

Other Top 10 USA: 4th—Eric Namesnik (2:02.01).

400-meter Individual Medley

		Time	
1	Tom Dolan, USA	4:12.30	WR
2	Jani Sievinen, FIN	4:13.29	
3	Eric Namesnik, USA	4:15.69	

4 x 100-meter Freestyle Relay

		Time
1	United States	3:16.90
2	Russia	3:18.12
3	Brazil	3:19.35

USA—Jon Olsen, Josh Davis, Ugur Taner, Gary Hall; **RUS**—Roman Chegolev, Vladimir Predkin, Vladimir Pyshnenko, Aleksandr Popov; **BRA**—Fernando Scherer, Teofilio Ferreria, Andre Teixeira, Gustavo Borges.

4 x 200-meter Freestyle Relay

		Time
1	Sweden	7:17.34
2	Russia	7:18.13
3	Germany	7:19.10

SWE—Christer Waller, Tommy Werner, Lars Frolander, Anders Holmertz; **RUS**—Yuri Mukhin, Vladimir Pyshnenko, Denis Pankratov, Roman Chegolev; **GER**—Andreas Szigat, Christian Keller, Oliver Lampe, Steffen Zesner.

Top 10 USA: 4th—Chad Carvin, Ugur Taner, Chris Eckerman, Josh Davis (7:19.54).

4 x 100-meter Medley Relay

		Time
1	United States	3:37.74
2	Russia	3:38.28
3	Hungary	3:39.47

USA—Jeff Rouse, Eric Wunderlich, Mark Henderson, Gary Hall; **RUS**—Vladimir Selkov, Vasily Ivanov, Denis Pankratov, Aleksandr Popov; **HUN**—Tamas Deutsch, Norbert Rozsa, Peter Horvath, Attila Czene.

WOMEN

Multiple medals: Five—Lu Bin (3-2-0). **Four**—Le Jingyi (4-0-0) and Franziska Van Almsick (1-1-2). **Three**—He Cihong (3-0-0), Liu Limin (3-0-0), Dai Guohong (2-1-0), Jenny Thompson (0-2-1) and Amy Van Dyken (0-2-1). **Two**—Yang Aihua (2-0-0), Samantha Riley (2-0-0), Le Ying (2-0-0), Janet Evans (1-0-1), Qu Yun (0-2-0), Allison Wagner (0-2-0), Nicole Haislett (0-1-1), Kerstin Kielglass (0-1-1), Natalia Mesheryakova (0-1-1), Kristine Quance (0-1-1), Cristina Teuscher (0-1-1), Yuan Yuan (0-1-1), Nina Zhivanevskaya (0-1-1), Susan O'Neil (0-0-2) and Claudia Poll (0-0-2).

50-meter Freestyle

		Time	
1	Le Jingyi, CHN	24.51	WR
2	Natalia Mesheryakova, RUS	25.10	
3	Amy Van Dyken, USA	25.18	

Other Top 10 USA: 5th—Angel Martino (25.46).

100-meter Freestyle

		Time	
1	Le Jingyi, CHN	54.01	WR
2	Lu Bin, CHN	54.15	
3	Franziska Van Almsick, GER	54.77	

Top 10 USA: 4th—Jenny Thompson (55.16); 6th—Angel Martino (55.77).

200-meter Freestyle

		Time	
1	Franziska Van Almsick, GER	1:56.78	WR
2	Lu Bin, CHN	1:56.89	
3	Claudia Poll, CRC	1:57.61	

Top 10 USA: 4th—Cristina Teuscher (2:00.18); 5th—Nicole Haislett (2:00.30).

400-meter Freestyle

		Time
1	Yang Aihua, CHN	4:09.64
2	Cristina Teuscher, USA	4:10.21
3	Claudia Poll, CRC	4:10.61

Other Top 10 USA: 5th—Janet Evans (4:11.75).

800-meter Freestyle

		Time
1	Janet Evans, USA	8:29.85
2	Hayley Lewis, AUS	8:29.94
3	Brooke Bennett, USA	8:31.30

100-meter Backstroke

		Time	
1	He Cihong, CHN	1:00.57	WR
2	Nina Zhivanevskaya, RUS	1:00.83	
3	Barbara Bedford, USA	1:01.32	

Other Top 10 USA: 4th—Lea Loveless (1:01.44).

200-meter Backstroke

		Time
1	He Cihong, CHN	2:07.40
2	Krisztina Egerszegi, HUN	2:09.10
3	Lorenza Vigarani, ITA	2:10.92

Top 10 USA: 4th—Barbara Bedford (2:11.01).

100-meter Breaststroke

		Time	
1	Samantha Riley, AUS	1:07.69	WR
2	Dai Guohong, CHN	1:09.26	
3	Yuan Yuan, CHN	1:10.19	

200-meter Breaststroke

		Time
1	Samantha Riley, AUS	2:26.87
2	Yuan Yuan, CHN	2:27.38
3	Brigitte Becue, BEL	2:28.85

Other Top 10 USA: 6th—Kristine Quance (2:29.64).

100-meter Butterfly

		Time
1	Liu Limin, CHN	58.98
2	Qu Yun, CHN	59.69
3	Susan O'Neil, AUS	1:00.11

Top 10 USA: 6th—Jenny Thompson (1:00.84); 9th—Amy Van Dyken (1:00.90).

200-meter Butterfly

		Time
1	Liu Limin, CHN	2:07.25
2	Qu Yun, CHN	2:07.42
3	Susan O'Neil, AUS	2:09.54

Top 10 USA: 9th—Whitney Phelps (2:12.16).

200-meter Individual Medley

		Time
1	Lu Bin, CHN	2:12.34
2	Allison Wagner, USA	2:14.40
3	Elli Overton, AUS	2:15.26

Other Top 10 USA: 6th—Nicole Haislett (2:16.58).

400-meter Individual Medley

		Time
1	Dai Guohong, CHN	4:39.14
2	Allison Wagner, USA	4:39.98
3	Kristine Quance, USA	4:42.21

4 x 100-meter Freestyle Relay

		Time	
1	China	3:37.91	WR
2	United States	3:41.50	
3	Germany	3:42.92	

CHN—Le Jingyi, Shan Ying, Le Ying, Lu Bin; **USA**—Angel Martino, Amy Van Dyken, Nicole Haislett, Jenny Thompson; **GER**—Franziska Van Almsick, Katrin Meissner, Kerstin Kielgass, Daniela Hunger.

4 x 200-meter Freestyle Relay

		Time
1	China	7:57.96
2	Germany	8:01.37
3	United States	8:03.16

CHN—Le Ying, Yang Aihua, Zhou Guambin, Lu Bin; **GER**—Kerstin Kielglass, Franziska Van Almsick, Julia Jung, Dagmar Hase; **USA**—Cristina Teusher, Jenny Thompson, Janet Evans, Nicole Haislett.

4 x 100-meter Medley Relay

		Time	
1	China	4:01.67	WR
2	United States	4:06.53	
3	Russia	4:06.70	

CHN—He Cihong, Dai Guohong, Liu Limin, Le Jingyi; **USA**—Lea Loveless, Kristine Quance, Amy Van Dyken, Jenny Thompson; **RUS**—Nina Zhivanevskaya, Olga Prokhorova, Svetlana Pozdeeva, Natalia Mesheryakova.

Diving

MEN

Multiple medals: Two—Dmitri Sautin (1-1-0).

1-meter Springboard

		Pts
1	Evan Stewart, ZIM	382.14
2	Lan Wei, CHN	375.96
3	Brian Earley, USA	361.59

3-meter Springboard

		Pts
1	Yu Zhuocheng, CHN	655.44
2	Dmitri Sautin, RUS	646.59
3	Wang Tianling, CHN	638.22

Top 10 USA: 4th—Mark Bradshaw (616.92); 10th—Dean Panaro (560.07).

Platform

		Pts
1	Dmitri Sautin, RUS	634.71
2	Sun Shuwei, CHN	630.03
3	Vladimir Timoshinin, RUS	607.32

WOMEN

Multiple medals: Two—Tan Shuping (1-1-0).

1-meter Springboard

		Pts
1	Chen Lixia, CHN	279.30
2	Tan Shuping, CHN	276.00
3	Annie Pelletier, CAN	273.84

Top 10 USA: 4th—Cheril Santini (261.72).

3-meter Springboard

		Pts
1	Tan Shuping, CHN	548.49
2	Vera Ilyina, RUS	498.60
3	Claudia Bockner, GER	480.15

Top 10 USA: 4th—Karen Dalton (471.42).

Platform

		Pts
1	Fu Mingxia, CHN	434.04
2	Chi Bin, CHN	420.24
3	Maria Jose Alcala, MEX	396.48

Top 10 USA: 4th—Eileen Richetelli (395.88); 7th—Mary Ellen Clark (388.05).

Synchronized Swimming

Multiple medals: Two—Becky Dyroen-Lancer (2-0-0), Fumiko Okuno (0-2-0) and Lisa Alexander (0-0-2).

Solo

		Pts
1	Becky Dyroen-Lancer, USA	191.040
2	Fumiko Okuno, JPN	187.306
3	Lisa Alexander, CAN	186.826

Duet

		Pts
1	B. Dyroen-Lancer & Jill Sudduth, USA	187.009
2	Fumiko Okuno & Myia Tachibana, JPN	186.259
3	Lisa Alexander & Erin Woodley, CAN	186.259

VIIth FINA World Championships (Cont.)
Water Polo

MEN		WOMEN	
Semifinals		**Semifinals**	
Italy 8 ....Croatia 5		Holland 10 ....United States 7	
Spain 9 ....Russia 6		Hungary 7 ....Italy 5	
Bronze Medal		**Bronze Medal**	
Russia 14.....................OT...........Croatia 13		Italy 14 ....United States 9	
Gold Medal		**Gold Medal**	
Italy 10 ....Spain 5		Hungary 7..Holland 5	

Note: USA def. Greece (8-7) for 7th place.

■ SWIMMING ■

World, Olympic and American Records
As of Sept. 15, 1994

World long course records officially recognized by the Federation Internationale de Natation Amateur (FINA). Note that (ph) indicates preliminary heat; (r) relay leadoff split; and (s) indicates split time.

MEN
Freestyle

Distance		Time		Date Set	Location
50 meters:	**World**	21.81	**Tom Jager**, USA	Mar. 24, 1990	Nashville
	Olympic	21.91	Aleksandr Popov, Unified Team	July 30, 1992	Barcelona
	American	21.81	Jager (see World)		
100 meters:	**World**	48.21	**Alexander Popov**, Russia	June 18, 1994	Monte Carlo
	Olympic	48.63	Matt Biondi, USA	Sept. 22, 1988	Seoul
	American	48.42	Biondi (same as World)		
200 meters:	**World**	1:46.69	**Giorgio Lamberti**, Italy	Aug. 15, 1989	Bonn, W.Ger.
	Olympic	1:46.70	Yevgeny Sadovyi, Unified Team	July 26, 1992	Barcelona
	American	1:47.72ph	Matt Biondi	Aug. 8, 1988	Austin, TX
400 meters:	**World**	3:43.80	**Kieren Perkins**, Australia	Sept. 9, 1994	Rome
	Olympic	3:45.00	Sadovyi (same as World)	—	
	American	3:48.06	Matt Cetlinski	Aug. 11, 1988	Austin, TX
800 meters:	**World**	7:46.00	**Kieren Perkins**, Australia	Aug. 24, 1994	Victoria, CAN
	Olympic		Not an event	—	
	American	7:52.45	Sean Killion	July 27, 1987	Clovis, CA
1500 meters:	**World**	14:41.66	**Kieren Perkins**, Australia	Aug. 24, 1994	Victoria, CAN
	Olympic	14:43.48	Perkins (same as World)	—	
	American	15:01.51	George DiCarlo	June 30, 1984	Indianapolis

Backstroke

Distance		Time		Date Set	Location
100 meters:	**World**	53.86r	**Jeff Rouse**, USA	July 31, 1992	Barcelona
	Olympic	53.98	Mark Tewksbury, Canada	July 30, 1992	Barcelona
	American	53.86r	Rouse (same as World)		
200 meters:	**World**	1:56.57	**Martin Zubero**, Spain	Nov. 23, 1991	Tuscaloosa, AL
	Olympic	1:58.47	Martin Zubero, Spain	July 28, 1992	Barcelona
	American	1:58.66	Royce Sharp	Mar. 3, 1992	Indianapolis

Breaststroke

Distance		Time		Date Set	Location
100 meters:	**World**	1:00.95ph	**Karoly Guttler**, Hungary	Aug. 5, 1993	Sheffield, ENG
	Olympic	1:01.50	Nelson Diebel, USA	July 26, 1992	Barcelona
	American	1:01.40	Nelson Diebel, USA	Mar. 1, 1992	Indianapolis
		1:01.40	Seth van Neerden	Aug. 14, 1994	Indianapolis
200 meters:	**World**	2:10.16	**Mike Barrowman**, USA	July 29, 1992	Barcelona
	Olympic	2:10.16	Barrowman (same as World)	—	—
	American	2:10.16	Barrowman (same as World)	—	—

Butterfly

Distance		Time		Date Set	Location
100 meters:	**World**	52.84	**Pablo Morales**, USA	June 23, 1986	Orlando
	Olympic	53.00	Anthony Nesty, Suriname	Sept. 21, 1988	Seoul
	American	52.84	Morales (same as World)		
200 meters:	**World**	1:55.69	**Melvin Stewart**, USA	Jan. 12, 1991	Perth
	Olympic	1:56.26	Melvin Stewart, USA	July 30, 1992	Barcelona
	American	1:55.69	Stewart (same as World)		

Individual Medley

Distance		Time		Date Set	Location
200 meters:	**World**	1:58.16	**Jani Sievinen,** Finland	Sept. 11, 1994	Rome
	Olympic	2:00.17	Tamas Darnyi, Hungary	Sept. 25, 1988	Seoul
	American	2:00.11	David Wharton	Aug. 20, 1989	Tokyo
400 meters:	**World**	4:12.30	**Tom Dolan,** USA	Sept. 6 1994	
	Olympic	4:14.23	Tamas Darnyi, Hungary	July 27, 1992	Barcelona
	American	4:12.30	Tom Dolan (same as World)	—	—

Relays

Distance		Time		Date Set	Location
4x100m free:	**World**	3:16.53	**USA** (Jacobs, Dalbey, Jager, Biondi)	Sept. 25, 1988	Seoul
	Olympic	3:16.53	USA (same as World)	—	—
	American	3:16.53	USA (same as World)	—	—
4x200m free:	**World**	7:11.95	**Unified Team** (Lepikov, Pychnenka, Taianovitch, Sadovyi)	July 27, 1992	Barcelona
	Olympic	7:11.95	Unified Team (same as World)	—	—
	American	7:12.51	USA (Dalbey, Cetlinski, Gjertsen, Biondi)	Sept. 21, 1988	Seoul
4x100m medley:	**World**	3:36.93	**USA** (Berkoff, Schroeder, Biondi, Jacobs)	Sept. 23, 1988	Seoul
			USA (Rouse, Diebel, Morales, Olsen)	July 31, 1992	Barcelona
	Olympic	3:36.93	USA (same as World)	—	—
	American	3:36.93	USA (same as World)	—	—

WOMEN
Freestyle

Distance		Time		Date Set	Location
50 meters:	**World**	24.51	**Le Jingyi,** China	Sept. 11, 1994	Rome
	Olympic	24.79	Yang Wenyi, China	July 31, 1992	Barcelona
	American	25.18	Amy Van Dyken	Sept. 11, 1994	Rome
100 meters:	**World**	54.01	**Le Jingyi,** China	Sept. 5, 1994	Rome
	Olympic	54.65	Zhaung Yong, China	July 26, 1992	Barcelona
	American	54.48	Jenny Thompson	Mar. 1, 1992	Indianapolis

World Swimming Records Set in 1994
World long course records set between Sept. 30, 1993 and Oct. 1, 1994.

MEN

Event		Record	Old Mark	Former Holder
100-meter Free	Aleksandr Popov, Russia	48.21	48.42	Matt Biondi, USA (1988)
400-meter Free	Kieren Perkins, Australia	3:43.80	3:45.00	Yevgeny Sadovyi, UT (1992)
800-meter Free	Kieren Perkins, Australia	7:46.00	7:46.60	Kieren Perkins, AUS (1992)
1500-meter Free	Kieren Perkins, Australia	14:41.66	14:43.48	Kieren Perkins, AUS (1992)
200-meter I.M.	Jani Sievinen, Finland	1:58.16	1:59.36	Tamas Darnyi, HUN (1991)
400-meter I.M.	Tom Dolan, USA	4:12.30	4:12.36	Tamas Darnyi, HUN (1991)

WOMEN

Event		Record	Old Mark	Former Holder
50-meter Free	Le Jingyi, China	24.51	24.79	Yang Wenyi, CHN (1992)
100-meter Free	Le Jingyi, China	54.01	54.48	Jenny Thompson, USA (1992)
200-meter Free	Franziska van Almsick, Germany	1:56.78	1:57.55	Heike Friedrich, E.Ger (1986)
100-meter Back	He Cihong, China	1:00.16	1:00.31	Krisztina Egerszegi, HUN (1991)
100-meter Breast	Samantha Riley, Australia	1:07.69	1:07.91	Silke Horner, E.Ger (1987)
200-meter Breast	Rebecca Brown, Australia	2:24.76	2:25.35	Anita Nall, USA (1992)
4 x 100m Medley	China World Champ. Team (Le Jingyi, Shan Ying, Le Ying, Lu Bin)	4:01.67	4:02.54	USA (Lea Loveless, Anita Nall, Crissy Ahmann-Leighton, Jenny Thompson), 1992
4 x 100m Free	China World Champ. Team (He Cihong, Dai Guohong, Liu Limin, Le Jingyi)	3:37.91	3:39.46	USA (Nicole Haislett, Dara Torrez, Angel Martino, Jenny Thompson), 1992

Swimming (Cont.)
World, Olympic and American Records
WOMEN
Freestyle

Distance		Time		Date Set	Location
200 meters	World	1:56.78	**Franziska Van Almsick,** Germany	Sept. 6, 1994	Rome
	Olympic	1:57.65	Heike Friedrich, East Germany	Sept. 21, 1988	Seoul
	American	1:57.90	Nicole Haislett	July 27, 1992	Barcelona
400 meters	World	4:03.85	**Janet Evans,** USA	Sept. 22, 1988	Seoul
	Olympic	4:03.85	Evans (same as World)	—	—
	American	4:03.85	Evans (same as World)	—	—
800 meters	World	8:16.22	**Janet Evans,** USA	Aug. 20, 1989	Tokyo
	Olympic	8:20.20	Janet Evans, USA	Sept. 24, 1988	Seoul
	American	8:16.22	Evans (same as World)	—	—
1500 meters	World	15:52.10	**Janet Evans,** USA	Mar. 26, 1988	Orlando
	Olympic		Not an event	—	—
	American	15:52.10	Evans (same as World)	—	—

Backstroke

Distance		Time		Date Set	Location
100 meters	World	1:00.57	**He Cihong,** China	Sept. 10, 1994	Rome
	Olympic	1:00.68	Krisztina Egerszegi, Hungary	July 28, 1992	Barcelona
	American	1:00.82r	Lea Loveless	July 30, 1992	Barcelona
200 meters	World	2:06.62	**Krisztina Egerszegi,** Hungary	Aug. 26, 1991	Athens
	Olympic	2:07.06	Krisztina Egerszegi, Hungary	July 31, 1992	Barcelona
	American	2:08.60	Betsy Mitchell	June 27, 1986	Orlando

Breaststroke

Distance		Time		Date Set	Location
100 meters	World	1:07.69	**Samantha Riley,** Australia	Sept. 9, 1994	Rome
	Olympic	1:07.95	Tania Dangalakova, Bulgaria	Sept. 23, 1988	Seoul
	American	1:08.17	Anita Nall	July 29, 1992	Barcelona
200 meters	World	2:24.76	**Rebecca Brown,** Australia	Mar. 16 1994	Queensland, AUS
	Olympic	2:26.65	Kyoko Iwasaki, Japan	July 27, 1992	Barcelona
	American	2:25.35	Anita Nall	Mar. 2, 1992	Indianapolis

Butterfly

Distance		Time		Date Set	Location
100 meters	World	57.93	**Mary T. Meagher,** USA	Aug. 16, 1981	Brown Deer, WI
	Olympic	58.62	Qian Hong, China	July 29, 1992	Barcelona
	American	57.93	Meagher (same as World)	—	—
200 meters	World	2:05.96	**Mary T. Meagher,** USA	Aug. 13, 1981	Brown Deer, WI
	Olympic	2:06.90	Mary T. Meagher, USA	Aug. 4, 1984	Los Angeles
	American	2:05.96	Meagher (same as World)	—	—

Individual Medley

Distance		Time		Date Set	Location
200 meters	World	2:11.65	**Lin Li,** China	July 30, 1992	Barcelona
	Olympic	2:11.65	Li (same as World)	—	—
	American	2:11.91	Summer Sanders	July 30, 1992	Barcelona
400 meters	World	4:36.10	**Petra Schneider,** East Germany	Aug. 1, 1982	Guayaquil, EQU
	Olympic	4:36.29	Petra Schneider, East Germany	July 26, 1980	Moscow
	American	4:37.58	Summer Sanders	July 26, 1992	Barcelona

Relays

Distance		Time		Date Set	Location
4x100m free:	World	3:37.91	**China** (Jingyi , Ying, Shan, Lu)	Sept. 7, 1994	Rome
	Olympic	3:39.46	USA (Haislett, Torres, Martino, Thompson)	July 28, 1992	Barcelona
	American	3:39.46	USA (same as Olympic)	—	—
4x200m free:	World	7:55.47	**E.Germany** (Stellmach, Strauss, Mohring, Friedrich)	Aug. 18, 1987	Strasbourg, FRA
	Olympic		Not an event	—	—
	American	8:02.12	USA (Mitchell, Meagher, Brown, Wayte)	Aug. 22, 1986	Madrid
4x100m medley:	World	4:01.67	**China** (Cihong, Guohong, Limin, Jingyi)	Sept. 10, 1994	Rome
	Olympic	4:02.54	USA (Loveless, Nall, Ahmann-Leighton, Thompson)	July 30, 1992	Barcelona
	American	4:02.54	USA (same as Olympic)	—	—

TRACK & FIELD

OUTDOOR
IAAF Mobil Grand Prix Final

The final meeting of the International Amateur Athletic Federation's Grand Prix season, which includes the world's 16 leading outdoor invitational meets. Athletes earn points throughout the season with the leading point winners invited to the Grand Prix Final. The 1994 final was held Sept. 3, 1994 at the new Charlety Stadium in Paris.

MEN

Event	Time	Event	Hgt/Dist
100m	Dennis Mitchell, USA — 10.12	High Jump (TIE)	Javier Sotomayor, CUB — 7- 7¾
400m	Derrick Mills, USA — 45.22		& Troy Kemp, BAH — 7- 7¾
1500m	Noureddine Morceli, ALG — 3:40.89	Pole Vault	Sergey Bubka, UKR — 19- 4¼
5000m	Khalid Skah, MOR — 13:14.63	Triple Jump	Mike Conley, USA — 58- 0¼
110m Hurdles	Colin Jackson, GBR — 13.08	Shot Put	Randy Barnes, USA — 67- 7
400m Hurdles	Samuel Matet, ZAM — 48.02	Hammer Throw	Andrei Abduvaliyev, TAJ — 267- 3

WOMEN

Event	Time	Event	Hgt/Dist
100m	Merlene Ottey, JAM — 10.78	Long Jump	Jackie Joyner-Kersee, USA — 23- 8
400m	Marie-Jose Perec, FRA — 49.77	Discus	Ilke Wyludda, GER — 216- 0
1500m	Angela Chalmers, CAN — 4:01.61	Javelin	Natalya Shikolenko, BEL — 223-11
5000m	Sonia O'Sullivan, IRE — 15:12.94		
100m Hurdles	Svetlana Dimitrova, BUL — 12.66		

Final Overall Standings

Overall Men's and Women's winners receive $130,000 (US) each; all ties broken by complex Grand Prix scoring system.

MEN

1. Noureddine Morceli, ALG (78 points); 2. Samuel Matete, Zambia (72 pts); 3. Mike Conley, USA (72 pts); 4. Dennis Mitchell, USA (72 pts); 5. Javier Sotomayer, Cuba (72 pts); 6. Andrei Abduvaliyev (68 pts); 7. Derrick Adkins, USA (66 pts); 8. Venuste Niyongabo, BUR (66 pts); 9. Khalid Skah, MOR (64 pts); 10. Troy Kemp, BAH (60 pts).

WOMEN

1. Jackie Joyner-Kersee, USA (72 points); 2. Svetlana Dimitrova, Bulgaria (72 pts); 3. Sonia O'Sullivan, Ireland (72 pts); 4. Natalya Shikolenko, Belarus (70 pts); 5. Gwen Torrence, USA (66 pts); 6. Ilka Wyludda, Germany (66 pts); 7. Heike Drechsler, Germany (63 pts); 8. Angela Chalmers, Canada (62 pts); 9. Trine Hattestad, Norway (62 pts); 10. Yekaterina Podkopayeva, Russia (61 pts).

Goodwill Games

Founded in 1986 by American media entrepreneur and sportsman Ted Turner to help improve relations between the U.S. and the former USSR after the boycotted Olympics of 1980 and '84. The third Goodwill Games were held in St. Petersburg, Russia, from July 23 to Aug. 3, 1994. The track and field events were held July 24-29. Note that (*) indicates world record and (w) indicates wind-aided.

MEN

Event	Time
100m	Dennis Mitchell, USA — 10.07
200m	Michael Johnson, USA — 20.10
400m	Quincy Watts, USA — 45.21
800m	Andrei Loginov, RUS — 1:46.65
Mile	Noureddine Morceli, ALG — 3:48.67
5000m	Moses Kiptanui, KEN — 13:10.76
10,000m	Hammou Boutayeb, MOR — 28:10.89
110m Hurdles	Colin Jackson, GBR — 13.29
400m Hurdles	Derrick Adkins, USA — 47.86
3000m Steeple	Marc Davis, USA — 8:14.30
20km Walk	Bernardo Segura, MEX — 1:23:28.88
4x100m Relay	USA (Marsh, Burrell, Jefferson, C.Lewis) — 38.30
4x400m Relay	USA (Mills, Valmon, Rouser, Johnson) — 2:59.42

Event	Hgt/Dist
High Jump	Javier Sotomayor, CUB — 7-10½
Pole Vault	Igor Trandenkov, RUS — 19- 4¼
Long Jump	Mike Powell, USA — 27- 8¾w
Triple Jump	Kenny Harrison, USA — 57- 2¼
Shot Put	Cottrell Hunter, USA — 66- 9¼
Discus	Dmitri Shevchenko, RUS — 212- 2
Hammer Throw	Lance Deal, USA — 263- 1
Javelin	Andrei Shevchuk, RUS — 272- 0
Decathlon	Dan O'Brien, USA — 8715 pts

WOMEN

Event	Time
100m	Gwen Torrence, USA — 10.95
200m	Gwen Torrence, USA — 22.09
400m	Jearl Miles, USA — 50.60
800m	Maria Mutola, MOZ — 1:57.63
1500m	Yekaterina Podkopayeva, RUS — 4:04.92
3000m	Yelena Romanova, RUS — 8:41.06
5000m	Yelena Romanova, RUS — 15:28.69
10,000m	Tecla Lorupe, KEN — 31:52.39
100m Hurdles	Brigitta Bukovec, SLO — 12.83
400m Hurdles	Sally Gunnell, GBR — 53.51
2000m Steeple	Marina Pluzhnikova, RUS — 6:11.84*
10km Walk	Olimpiada Ivanova, RUS — 42:30.31
4x100m Relay	USA (Taplin, Young, Collins, Torrence) — 42.98
4x400m Relay	USA (Kaiser-Brown, Malone, Miles, Collins) — 3:22.27

Event	Hgt/Dist
High Jump	Silvia Costa, CUB — 6- 4¾
Pole Vault	Caiyun Sun, CHN — 13- 1½
Long Jump	Heike Drechsler, GER — 23- 4½
Triple Jump	Anna Biryukova, RUS — 47- 9¾
Shot Put	Xinmei Sui, CHN — 66- 1½
Discus	Barbara Echevarria, CUB — 212- 9
Javelin	Trine Hattestad, NOR — 215- 8
Decathlon	Jackie Joyner-Kersee, USA — 6606 pts

Track & Field (cont.)
OUTDOOR
World, Olympic and American Records
As of Sept. 15, 1994
World outdoor records officially recognized by the International Amateur Athletics Federation (IAAF).
MEN
Running

Event		Time		Date Set	Location
100 meters:	**World**	9.85	**Leroy Burrell,** USA	July 6, 1994	Lausanne, SWI
	Olympic	9.92	Carl Lewis, USA	Sept. 24, 1988	Seoul
	American	9.86	Burrell (same as World)	—	—
200 meters:	**World**	19.72	**Pietro Mennea,** Italy	Sept.12, 1979	Mexico City
	Olympic	19.75	Joe DeLoach, USA	Sept. 28, 1988	Seoul
	American	19.73	Mike Marsh	Aug. 5, 1992	Barcelona
400 meters:	**World**	43.29	**Butch Reynolds,** USA	Aug. 17, 1988	Zurich
	Olympic	43.50	Quincy Watts, USA	Aug. 5, 1992	Barcelona
	American	43.29	Reynolds (same as World)	—	—
800 meters:	**World**	1:41.73	**Sebastian Coe,** Great Britain	June 10, 1981	Florence
	Olympic	1:43.00	Joaquim Cruz, Brazil	Aug. 6, 1984	Los Angeles
	American	1:42.60	Johnny Gray	Aug. 28, 1985	Koblenz, W.Ger.
1000 meters:	**World**	2:12.18	**Sebastian Coe,** Great Britain	July 11, 1981	Oslo
	Olympic		Not an event	—	—
	American	2:13.9	Rick Wohlhuter	July 30, 1974	Oslo
1500 meters:	**World**	3:28.86	**Noureddine Morceli,** Algeria	Sept. 6, 1992	Rieti, ITA
	Olympic	3:32.53	Sebastian Coe, Great Britain	Aug. 11, 1984	Los Angeles
	American	3:29.77	Sydney Maree	Aug. 25, 1985	Cologne
Mile:	**World**	3:44.39	**Noureddine Morceli,** Algeria	Sept. 5, 1993	Rieti, ITA
	Olympic		Not an event	—	—
	American	3:47.69	Steve Scott	July 7, 1982	Oslo
2000 meters:	**World**	4:50.81	**Said Aouita,** Morocco	July 16, 1987	Paris
	Olympic		Not an event	—	—
	American	4:52.44	Jim Spivey	Sept.15, 1987	Lausanne
3000 meters:	**World**	7:25.11	**Noureddine Morceli,** Algeria	Aug. 2 1994	Monte Carlo, MON
	Olympic		Not an event	—	—
	American	7:35.33	Bob Kennedy	July 18, 1994	Nice, FRA
5000 meters:	**World**	12:56.96	**Haile Gebresilasie,** Ethiopia	June 4, 1994	Hengelo, HOL
	Olympic	13:05.59	Said Aouita, Morocco	Aug. 11, 1984	Los Angeles
	American	13:01.15	Sydney Maree	July 27, 1985	Oslo
10,000 meters:	**World**	26:52.23	**William Sigei,** Kenya	July 22, 1994	Oslo
	Olympic	27:21.46	Brahim Boutaib, Morocco	Sept. 26, 1988	Seoul
	American	27:20.56	Mark Nenow	Sept. 5, 1986	Brussels
20,000 meters:	**World**	56:55.6	**Arturo Barrios,** Mexico	Mar. 30, 1991	La Flèche, FRA
	Olympic		Not an event	—	—
	American	58:25.0	Bill Rodgers	Aug. 9, 1977	Boston
25,000 meters:	**World**	1:13:55.8	**Toshihiko Seko,** Japan	Mar. 22, 1981	Christchurch
	Olympic		Not an event	—	—
	American	1:14:11.8	Bill Rodgers	Feb. 21, 1979	Saratoga, Calif.
30,000 meters:	**World**	1:29:18.8	**Toshihiko Seko,** Japan	Mar. 22, 1991	Christchurch
	Olympic		Not an event	—	—
	American	1:31:49	Bill Rodgers	Feb. 21, 1979	Saratoga, Calif.

World Outdoor Records Set in 1994
World outdoor records set between Oct. 1, 1993 and Sept. 15, 1994.
MEN

Event		Record	Old Mark	Former Holder
100 meters	Leroy Burrell, USA	9.85	9.86	Carl Lewis, USA (1991)
3000 meters	Noureddine Morceli, ALG	7:25.11	7:28.96	Moses Kiptanui, KEN (1992)
5000 meters	Haile Gebresilasie, ETH	12:56.96	12:58.39	Said Aouita, MOR (1987)
10,000 meters	William Sigei, KEN	26:52.23	26:58.38	Yobes Ondieki, KEN (1993)
20-kilometer Walk	Bernado Segura, MEX	1:17:25.5	1:18:35.2	Stefan Johansson, SWE (1992)
50-kilometer Walk	René Piller, FRA	3:41:28.2	3:41:38.4	Raul Gonzales, MEX (1979)
4 x 200-meter Relay	Santa Monica Track Club, USA (Mike Marsh, Leroy Burrell, Floyd Heard, Carl Lewis)	1:18.68	1:19.11	USA (Mike Marsh, Leroy Burrell, Floyd Heard, Carl Lewis), 1992
Pole Vault	Sergey Bubka, UKR	20- 1¾p	20- 1½	Sergey Bubka, UKR (1992)

WOMEN

Event		Record	Old Mark	Former Holder
2000 meter	Sonia O'Sullivan, IRE	5:25.36p	5:28.69	Maricica Puica, ROM (1986)

Event		Time		Date Set	Location
Marathon:	World	2:06.50	Belayneh Densimo, Ethiopia	Apr. 17, 1988	Rotterdam
	Olympic	2:09.21	Carlos Lopes, Portugal	Aug. 12, 1984	Los Angeles
	American	2:10.04	Pat Petersen	Apr. 23, 1989	London
		2:08.52*	Alberto Salazar	Apr. 19, 1982	Boston

Note: The Mile run is 1,609.344 meters and the Marathon is 42,194.988 meters (26 miles, 385 yards).
*Former American record no longer officially recognized.

Hurdles

Event		Time		Date Set	Location
110 meters:	World	12.91	Colin Jackson, Great Britain	Aug. 20, 1993	Stuttgart
	Olympic	12.98	Roger Kingdom, USA	Sept. 28, 1988	Seoul
	American	12.92	Kingdom (same as World)	—	
400 meters:	World	46.78	Kevin Young, USA	Aug. 6, 1992	Barcelona
	Olympic	46.78	Young (same as World)	—	
	American	46.78	Young (same as World)	—	

Note: The hurdles at 110 meters are 3 feet, 6 inches high and the hurdles at 400 meters are 3 feet. There are 10 hurdles in both races.

Steeplechase

Event		Time		Date Set	Location
3000 meters:	World	8:02.08	Moses Kiptanui, Kenya	Aug. 19, 1992	Zurich
	Olympic	8:05.51	Julius Kariuki, Kenya	Sept. 30, 1988	Seoul
	American	8:09.17	Henry Marsh	Aug. 28, 1985	Koblenz

Note: A Steeplechase course consists of 28 hurdles (3 feet high) and seven water jumps (12 feet long).

Walking

Event		Time		Date Set	Location
20 km:	World	1:17:25.5	Bernardo Segura, Mexico	May 7, 1994	Fana, NOR
	Olympic	1:19:57	Jozef Pribilinec, Czechoslovakia	Sept. 23, 1988	Seoul
	American	1:24:26.9	Allen James	May 7, 1994	Fana, NOR
30 km:	World	2:01:44.1p	Maurizio Damilano, Italy	Oct. 4, 1992	Cuneo, ITA
	Olympic		Not an event		
	American	2:21:40	Herm Nelson	Sept. 7, 1991	Bellevue, Wash.
50 km:	World	3:41:28.2	René Piller, France	May 7, 1994	Fana, NOR
	Olympic	3:38:29	Vyacheslav Ivanenko, USSR	Sept. 30, 1988	Seoul
	American	3:55:39	Allen James	Mar. 13, 1994	Palo Alto, Calif.

Relays

Event		Time		Date Set	Location
4 x 100m:	World	37.40	USA (Marsh, Burrell, Mitchell, C.Lewis)	Aug. 8, 1992	Barcelona
		37.40p	USA (Drummond, Cason, Mitchell, Burrell)	Aug. 21, 1993	Stuttgart
	Olympic	37.40	USA (same as World)	—	
	American	37.40	USA (same as World)	—	
4 x 200m:	World	1:18.68	USA (Marsh, Burrell, Heard, C.Lewis)	Apr.17, 1994	Walnut, Calif.
	Olympic		Not an event		
	American	1:18.68	USA (same as World)	—	
4 x 400m:	World	2:54.29p	USA (Valmon, Watts, Reynolds, Johnson)	Aug. 22, 1993	Stuttgart
	Olympic	2:55.74	USA (Valmon, Watts, Johnson, S.Lewis)	Aug. 8, 1992	Barcelona
	American	2:54.29p	USA (same as World)	—	
4 x 800m:	World	7:03.89	Great Britain (Elliott, Cook, Cram, Coe)	Aug. 30, 1982	London
	Olympic		Not an event	—	
	American	7:06.5	SMTC (J.Robinson, Mack, E.Jones, Gray)	Apr. 26, 1986	Walnut, Calif.
4 x 1500m:	World	14:38.8	West Germany (Wessinghage, Hudak, Lederer, Fleschen)	Aug. 17, 1977	Cologne
	Olympic		Not an event		
	American	14:46.3	USA (Aldredge, Clifford, Harbour, Duits)	June 24, 1979	Bourges, FRA

Decathlon

Event		Points		Date Set	Location
Ten Events:	World	8891	Dan O'Brien, USA	Sept. 4-5, 1992	Talence, FRA
	Olympic	8847	Daley Thompson, Great Britain	Aug. 8-9, 1984	Los Angeles
	American	8891	O'Brien (same as World)	—	

Note: O'Brien's WR times and distances, in order over two days—**100m** (10.43); **LJ** (26-6¼); **SP** (54-9¼); **HJ** (6-9½); **400m** (48.51); **110m H** (13.98); **Discus** (159-4); **PV** (16-4¾); **Jav** (205-4); **1500m** (4:42.10).

Track and Field (Cont.)
MEN
Field Events

Events	Mark		Date Set	Location
High Jump: World	8- 0½	**Javier Sotomayor,** Cuba	July 27, 1993	Salamanca, SPA
Olympic	7- 9¾	Gennady Avdeyenko, USSR	Sept. 25, 1988	Seoul
American	7-10½	Charles Austin	Aug. 7, 1991	Zurich
Pole Vault: World	20- 1¾	**Sergey Bubka,** Ukraine	July 31, 1994	Sestriere, ITA
Olympic	19- 4¼	Sergey Bubka, USSR	Sept. 28, 1988	Seoul
American	19- 7	Scott Huffman	June 18, 1984	Knoxville, Tenn.
Long Jump: World	29- 4½	**Mike Powell,** USA	Aug. 30, 1991	Tokyo
Olympic	29- 2½	Bob Beamon, USA	Oct. 18, 1968	Mexico City
American	29- 4½	Powell (same as World)	—	
Triple Jump: World	58-11½	**Willie Banks,** USA	June 16, 1985	Indianapolis
Olympic	57-10¼	Mike Conley, USA	Aug. 3, 1992	Barcelona
American	58-11½	Banks (same as World)	—	
Shot Put: World	75-10¼	**Randy Barnes,** USA	May 20, 1990	Los Angeles
Olympic	73- 8¾	Ulf Timmermann, East Germany	Sept. 23, 1988	Seoul
American	75-10¼	Barnes (same as World)	—	
Discus: World	243- 0	**Jurgen Schult,** East Germany	June 6, 1986	Neubrandenburg
Olympic	225- 9	Jurgen Schult, East Germany	Oct. 1, 1988	Seoul
American	237- 4	Ben Plucknett	July 7, 1981	Stockholm
Javelin: World	313-10	**Jan Zelezny,** Czech Republic	Aug. 29, 1993	Sheffield, ENG
Olympic	294- 2	Jan Zelezny, Czechoslovakia	Aug. 8, 1992	Barcelona
American	281- 2	Tom Pukstys	June 26, 1993	Kuortane, FIN
Hammer: World	284- 7	**Yuri Sedykh,** USSR	Aug. 30, 1986	Stuttgart
Olympic	278- 2	Sergey Litvinov, USSR	Sept. 26, 1988	Seoul
American	270- 8	Lance Deal	June 17, 1994	Knoxville, Tenn.

Note: The international weights for men—**Shot** (16 lbs); **Discus** (4 lbs/6.55 oz); **Hammer** (16 lbs); **Javelin** (minimum 1 lb/124¼ oz).

WOMEN
Running

Event	Time		Date Set	Location
100 meters: World	10.49	**Florence Griffith Joyner,** USA	July 16, 1988	Indianapolis
Olympic	10.62	Florence Griffith Joyner, USA	Sept. 24, 1988	Seoul
American	10.49	Griffith Joyner (same as World)	—	
200 meters: World	21.34	**Florence Griffith Joyner,** USA	Sept. 29, 1988	Seoul
Olympic	21.34	Griffith Joyner (same as World)	—	
American	21.34	Griffith Joyner (same as World)	—	
400 meters: World	47.60	**Marita Koch,** East Germany	Oct. 6, 1985	Canberra, AUS
Olympic	48.65	Olga Bryzgina, USSR	Sept. 26, 1988	Seoul
American	48.83	Valerie Brisco	Aug. 6, 1984	Los Angeles
800 meters: World	1:53.28	**Jarmila Kratochvilova,** Czech.	July 26, 1983	Munich
Olympic	1:53.42	Nadezhda Olizarenko, USSR	July 27, 1980	Moscow
American	1:56.90	Mary Decker Slaney	Aug. 16, 1985	Bern
1000 meters: World	2:30.67	**Tatyana Providokhina,** USSR	Aug. 20, 1978	Pololsk, USSR
Olympic		Not an event		
American	2:34.04	Julie Jenkins	Aug. 17, 1990	Berlin
1500 meters: World	3:52.47	**Tatyana Kazankina,** USSR	Aug. 13, 1980	Zurich
Olympic	3:53.96	Paula Ivan, Romania	Oct. 1, 1988	Seoul
American	3:57.12	Mary Decker	July 26, 1983	Stockholm
Mile: World	4:15.61	**Paula Ivan,** Romania	July 10, 1989	Nice
Olympic		Not an event		
American	4:16.71	Mary Decker Slaney	Aug. 21, 1985	Zurich
2000 meters: World	5:25.36	**Sonia O'Sullivan,** Ireland	July 8, 1994	Edinburgh
Olympic		Not an event		
American	5:32.7	Mary Decker	Aug. 3, 1984	Eugene
3000 meters: World	8:22.62	**Tatyana Kazankina,** USSR	Aug. 26, 1984	Leningrad
Olympic	8:26.53	Tatyana Samolenko, USSR	Sept. 25, 1988	Seoul
American	8:25.83	Mary Decker Slaney	Sept. 7, 1985	Rome
5000 meters: World	14:37.33	**Ingrid Kristiansen,** Norway	Aug. 5, 1986	Stockholm
Olympic		Not an event		
American	15:00.00	PattiSue Plumer	July 3, 1989	Stockholm
10,000 meters: World	30:13.74	**Ingrid Kristiansen,** Norway	July 5, 1986	Oslo
Olympic	31:05.21	Olga Bondarenko, USSR	Sept. 30, 1988	Seoul
American	31:19.89	Lynn Jennings	Aug. 7, 1992	Barcelona
Marathon: World	2:21.06	**Ingrid Kristiansen,** Norway	Apr. 21, 1985	London
Olympic	2:24.52	Joan Benoit, USA	Aug. 5, 1984	Los Angeles
American	2:21.21	Joan Benoit Samuelson	Oct. 20, 1985	Chicago

Note: The Mile run is 1,609.344 meters and the Marathon is 42,194.988 meters (26 miles, 385 yards).

Hurdles

Event		Time		Date Set	Location
100 meters:	**World**	12.21	**Yordanka Donkova,** Bulgaria	Aug. 20, 1988	Stara Zagora, BUL
	Olympic	12.38	Yordanka Donkova, Bulgaria	Sept. 30, 1988	Seoul
	American	12.46	Gail Devers	Aug. 20, 1993	Stuttgart
400 meters:	**World**	52.74	**Sally Gunnell,** Great Britain	Aug. 19, 1993	Stuttgart
	Olympic	53.17	Debra Flintoff-King, Australia	Sept. 28, 1988	Seoul
	American	52.79	Sandra Farmer-Patrick	Aug. 19, 1993	Stuttgart

Note: The hurdles at 110 meters are 3 feet, 6 inches high and the hurdles at 400 meters are 3 feet. There are 10 hurdles in both races.

Walking

Event		Time		Date Set	Location
10 km:	**World**	41:37.9	**Gao Hongmiao,** China	Apr. 7 1994	Beijing, CHN
	Olympic	44:32	Chen Yueling, China	Aug. 3, 1992	Barcelona
	American	44:41.87	Michelle Rohl	July 26, 1994	St. Petersburg, RUS

Relays

Event		Time		Date Set	Location
4 x 100m:	**World**	41.37	**East Germany** (Gladisch, Reiger, Auerswald, Gohr)	Oct. 6, 1985	Canberra, AUS
	Olympic	41.60	East Germany (Muller, Wockel, Auerswald, Gohr)	Aug. 1, 1980	Moscow
	American	41.49	USA (Finn, Torrence, Vereen, Devers)	Aug. 22, 1993	Stuttgart
4 x 200m:	**World**	1:28.15	**East Germany** (Gohr, Muller, Wockel, Koch)	Aug. 9, 1980	Jena, E.Ger.
	Olympic		Not an event	—	—
	American	1:32.57	LSU (Stanley, Brydson, Jones, Sowell)	Apr. 28, 1989	Des Moines
	American	1:32.57	LSU (Hill, Boone, Hall, Taplin)	Apr. 30, 1994	Phildelphia
4 x 400m:	**World**	3:15.17	**USSR** (Ledovskaya, Nazarova, Pinigina, Bryzgina)	Oct. 1, 1988	Seoul
	Olympic	3:15.17	USSR (same as World)	—	—
	American	3:15.51	USA (Howard, Dixon, Brisco, Griffith Joyner)	Oct. 1, 1988	Seoul

Heptathlon

		Points		Date Set	Location
Seven Events:	**World**	7291	**Jackie Joyner-Kersee,** USA	Sept. 23-24, 1988	Seoul
	Olympic	7291	Joyner-Kersee (same as World)	—	—
	American	7291	Joyner-Kersee (same as World)	—	—

Note: Joyner-Kersee's WR times and distances, in order over two days—**100m H** (12.69); **HJ** (61¼); **SP** (5110); **200m** (22.56); **LJ** (2310¼); **Jav** (14910); **800m** (2:08.51).

Field Events

Events		Mark		Date Set	Location
High Jump:	**World**	6-10¼	**Stefka Kostadinova,** Bulgaria	Aug. 30, 1987	Rome
	Olympic	6- 8	Louise Ritter, USA	Sept. 30, 1988	Seoul
	American	6- 8	Louise Ritter	July 8, 1988	Austin
		6- 8	Ritter (see Olympic)		
Long Jump:	**World**	24- 8¼	**Galina Chistyakova,** USSR	June 11, 1988	Leningrad
	Olympic	24- 3¼	Jackie Joyner-Kersee, USA	Sept. 29, 1988	Seoul
	American	24- 7	Jackie Joyner-Kersee	May 22, 1994	New York City
	American	24- 7	Jackie Joyner-Kersee	July 31, 1994	Sestriere, ITA
Triple Jump:	**World**	49- 6¼	**Ann Biryukova,** Russia	Aug. 21, 1993	Stuttgart
	Olympic		Not an event	—	—
	American	46- 8¼	Sheila Hudson	June 20, 1992	New Orleans
		46- 8¼	Sheila Hudson-Strudwick	June 16, 1994	Knoxville, Tenn.
Shot Put:	**World**	74- 3	**Natalya Lisovskaya,** USSR	June 7, 1987	Moscow
	Olympic	73- 6¼	Ilona Slupianek, E.Germany	July 24, 1980	Moscow
	American	66- 2½	Ramona Pagel	June 25, 1989	San Diego
Discus:	**World**	252- 0	**Gabriele Reinsch,** E.Germany	July 9, 1988	Neubrandenburg
	Olympic	237- 2½	Martina Hellmann, E.Germany	Sept. 29, 1988	Seoul
	American	216-10	Carol Cady	May 31, 1986	San Jose
Javelin:	**World**	262- 5	**Petra Felke,** East Germany	Sept. 9, 1988	Potsdam, E.Ger.
	Olympic	245- 0	Petra Felke, East Germany	Sept. 26, 1988	Seoul
	American	227- 5	Kate Schmidt	Sept. 10, 1977	Furth, W.Ger.

Note: The international weights for women—**Shot** (8 lbs/13 oz); **Discus** (2 lbs/3.27 oz); **Javelin** (minimum 1 lb/5.16 oz).

Track and Field (Cont.)
INDOOR
World and American Records
As of Sept. 15, 1994

World indoor records officially recognized by the International Amateur Athletics Federation (IAAF).

MEN

Running

Event		Time		Date Set	Location
50 meters:	World	5.61	**Manfred Kokot,** East Germany	Feb. 4, 1973	East Berlin
		5.61	James Sanford, USA	Feb. 20, 1981	San Diego
	American	5.61	Sanford (same as World)	—	
60 meters:	World	6.41	**Andre Cason,** USA	Feb. 14, 1992	Madrid
	American	6.41	Cason (same as World)	—	
200 meters:	World	20.36	**Bruno MarieRose,** France	Feb. 22, 1987	Lievin, FRA
	American	20.55	Michael Johnson	Jan. 26, 1991	Lievin, FRA
400 meters:	World	45.02	**Danny Everett,** USA	Feb. 2, 1992	Stuttgart
	American	45.02	Everett (same as World)	—	
800 meters:	World	1:44.84	**Paul Ereng,** Kenya	Mar. 4, 1989	Budapest
	American	1:45.00	Johnny Gray	Mar. 8, 1992	Sindelfingen, GER
1000 meters:	World	2:15.26	**Noureddine Morceli,** Algeria	Feb. 22, 1992	Birmingham, ENG
	American	2:18.19	Ocky Clark	Feb. 12, 1989	Stuttgart
1500 meters:	World	3:34.16	**Noureddine Morceli,** Algeria	Feb. 28, 1991	Seville
	American	3:38.12	Jeff Atkinson	Mar. 5, 1989	Budapest
Mile:	World	3:49.78	**Eamonn Coghlan,** Ireland	Feb. 27, 1983	E. Rutherford
	American	3:51.8	Steve Scott	Feb. 20, 1981	San Diego
3000 meters:	World	7:37.31	**Moses Kiptanui,** Kenya	Feb. 20, 1992	Seville
	American	7:39.94	Steve Scott	Feb. 10, 1989	E. Rutherford
5000 meters:	World	13:20.4	**Suleiman Nyambui,** Tanzania	Feb. 6, 1981	New York City
	American	13:20.55	Doug Padilla	Feb. 12, 1982	New York City

Note: The Mile run is 1,609.344 meters.

Hurdles

Event		Time		Date Set	Location
50 meters:	World	6.25	**Mark McKoy,** Canada	Mar. 5, 1986	Kobe, JPN
	American	6.35	Greg Foster	Jan. 27, 1985	Rosemont, Ill.
		6.35	Greg Foster	Jan. 31, 1987	Ottawa
60 meters:	World	7.30	**Colin Jackson,** GBR	Mar. 6, 1994	Sindelfingen, GER
	American	7.36	Greg Foster	Jan. 16, 1987	Los Angeles

Note: The hurdles for both distances are 3 feet, 6 inches high. There are four hurdles in the 50 meters and five in the 60.

Relays

Event		Time		Date Set	Location
4x200 meters:	World	1:22.11	**Great Britain**	Mar. 3, 1991	Glasgow
	American	1:22.71	National Team	Mar. 3, 1991	Glasgow
4x400 meters:	World	3:03.05	**Germany**	Mar. 10, 1991	Seville
	American	3:03.24	National Team	Mar. 10, 1991	Seville

Heptathlon

Points				Date Set	Location
Seven Events:	World	6476	**Dan O'Brien,** USA	Mar.13-14, 1993	Toronto
	American	6476	O'Brien (same as World)	—	

Note: O'Brien's WR times and distances, in order over two days—**60m** (6.67); **LJ** (25-8¾); **SP** (52-6¾); **HJ** (6-11¾); **60m H** (7.85); **PV** (17-0¾); **1000m** (2:57.96).

Field Events

Events		Mark		Date Set	Location
High Jump:	World	7-11¼	**Javier Sotomayor,** Cuba	Mar. 4, 1989	Budapest
	American	7-10½	Hollis Conway	Mar. 10, 1991	Seville
Pole Vault:	World	20- 2	**Sergey Bubka,** Ukraine	Feb. 21, 1993	Donyetsk, UKR
	American	19- 3¾	Billy Olson	Jan. 25, 1986	Albuquerque
Long Jump:	World	28-10¼	**Carl Lewis,** USA	Jan. 27, 1984	New York City
	American	28-10¼	Lewis (same as World)	—	
Triple Jump:	World	58- 3¾	**Leonid Voloshin,** RUS	Feb. 6, 1994	Grenoble, FRA
	American	58- 3¼	Mike Conley	Feb. 27, 1987	New York City
Shot Put:	World	74- 4¼	**Randy Barnes,** USA	Jan. 20, 1989	Los Angeles
	American	74- 4¼	Barnes (same as World)	—	

Note: The international shot put weight for men is 16 lbs.

WOMEN
Running

Event		Time		Date Set	Location
50 meters:	**World**	6.00	**Merlene Ottey,** Jamaica	Feb. 4, 1994	Moscow
	American	6.10	Gail Devers	Feb. 20, 1993	Los Angeles
60 meters:	**World**	6.92	**Irina Privalova,** Russia	Feb. 11, 1993	Madrid
	American	6.95	Gail Devers	Mar. 12 1993	Toronto
200 meters:	**World**	21.87	**Merlene Ottey,** Jamaica	Feb. 13, 1993	Lievin, FRA
	American	22.74	Gwen Torrence	Mar. 5, 1994	Atlanta
400 meters:	**World**	49.59	**Jarmila Kratochvilova,** Czech.	Mar. 7, 1982	Milan
	American	50.64	Diane Dixon	Mar. 10, 1991	Seville
800 meters:	**World**	1:56.40	**Christine Wachtel,** E.Germany	Feb. 14, 1988	Vienna
	American	1:58.9	Mary Decker	Feb. 22, 1980	San Diego
1000 meters:	**World**	2:33.93	**Inna Yevseyeva,** Ukraine	Feb. 7, 1992	Moscow
	American	2:37.6	Mary Decker Slaney	Jan. 21, 1989	Portland
1500 meters:	**World**	4:00.27	**Doina Melinte,** Romania	Feb. 9, 1990	E. Rutherford
	American	4:00.8	Mary Decker	Feb. 8, 1980	New York City
Mile:	**World**	4:17.13	**Doina Melinte,** Romania	Feb. 9, 1990	E. Rutherford
	American	4:20.5	Mary Decker	Feb. 19, 1982	San Diego
3000 meters:	**World**	8:33.82	**Elly van Hulst,** Holland	Mar. 4, 1989	Budapest
	American	8:40.45	Lynn Jennings	Feb. 23, 1990	New York City
5000 meters:	**World**	15:03.17	**Liz McGolgan,** Great Britain	Feb. 22, 1992	Birmingham, ENG
	American	15:22.64	Lynn Jennings	Jan. 7, 1990	Hanover, N.H.

Note: The Mile run is 1,609.344 meters.

Hurdles

Event		Time		Date Set	Location
50 meters:	**World**	6.58	**Cornelia Oschkenat,** E.Ger.	Feb. 20, 1988	East Berlin
	American	6.84	Kim McKenzie	Jan. 20, 1989	Ottawa
		6.84	Jackie JoynerKersee	Feb. 20, 1993	Los Angeles
60 meters:	**World**	7.63	**Lyudmila Narozhilenko,** Russia	Mar. 4, 1993	Seville
	American	7.81	Jackie JoynerKersee	Feb. 5, 1989	Fairfax, Va.

Note: The hurdles for both distances are 2 feet, 9 inches high. There are four hurdles in the 50 meters and five in the 60.

Walking

Event		Time		Date Set	Location
3000 meters:	**World**	11:44.00	**Alina Ivanova,** RUS	Feb. 7, 1992	Moscow
	American	12:20.79	Debbi Lawrence	Mar. 12, 1993	Toronto

Relays

Event		Time		Date Set	Location
4x200 meters:	**World**	1:32.55	**West Germany**	Feb. 20, 1988	Dortmund, W.Ger.
	American	1:33.24	National Team	Feb. 12, 1994	Glasgow
4x400 meters:	**World**	3:27.22	**Germany**	Mar. 10, 1991	Seville
	American	3:29.0	National Team	Mar. 10, 1991	Seville
4x800 meters:	**World**	8:18.71	**Russia Team**	Feb. 4, 1994	Moscow
	American	8:25.5	Villanova	Feb. 7, 1987	Gainesville

Pentathlon

Event		Points		Date Set	Location
Five Events:	**World**	4991	**Irina Belova,** Russia	Feb.14-15, 1993	Berlin
	American	4566	Kym Carter	Mar. 12, 1993	Toronto

Note: Belova's WR times and distances, in order over two days—**60m H** (8.22); **HJ** (6-4); **SP** (43-5¾); **LJ** (21-10¾); **800m** (2:10.26).

Field Events

Events		Mark		Date Set	Location
High Jump:	**World**	6- 9½	**Heike Henkel,** Germany	Feb. 9, 1992	Karlsruhe, GER
	American	6- 6¾	Coleen Sommer	Feb. 13, 1982	Ottawa
Long Jump:	**World**	24- 2¾	**Heike Drechsler,** E.Germany	Feb. 13, 1988	Vienna
	American	23- 4⅔	Jackie Joyner-Kersee	Mar. 5, 1992	Atlanta
Triple Jump:	**World**	48-10¾	**Inna Lasovskaya,** Russia	Jan. 13, 1994	Lievin, FRA
	American	45- 9	Sheila Hudson	Mar. 10, 1990	Indianapolis
Shot Put:	**World**	73-10	**Helena Fibingerova,** Czech.	Feb. 19, 1977	Jablonec, CZE
	American	65- 0¾	Ramona Pagel	Feb. 20, 1987	Inglewood

Note: The international shot put weight for women is 8 lbs. and 13 oz.

1995 World Indoor Championships
Both the indoor and outdoor World Track & Field Championships will be held in Europe in 1995. The World Indoors will be in Barcelona (March 10-12), followed by the World Outdoors in Goteborg, Sweden (Aug. 5-13).

Other 1993-94 Champions

WINTER SPORTS

Alpine Skiing
World Cup Champions
MEN

Overall	Kjetil Andre Aamodt, NOR
Downhill	Marc Girardelli, LUX
Slalom	Alberto Tomba, ITA
Giant Slalom	Christian Mayer, AUT
Super G	Jan Einar Thorsen, NOR
Combined	Kjetil Andre Aamodt, NOR
Nation's Cup	Austria

WOMEN

Overall	Vreni Schneider, SWI
Downhill	Katja Seizinger, GER
Slalom	Vreni Schneider, SWI
Giant Slalom	Anita Wachter, AUT
Super G	Katja Seizinger, GER
Combined	Pernilla Wiberg, SWE
Nation's Cup	Germany

U.S. Alpine Championships
at Winter Park, Colo. (Mar. 23-27)
MEN

Downhill	Raff Socher, Canada
Slalom	Thomas Grandi, Canada
Giant Slalom	Thomas Grandi, Canada
Super G	Tommy Moe, Palmer, Alaska
Combined	Jeremy Nobis, Park City, Utah

WOMEN

Downhill	Picabo Street, Sun Valley, Idaho
Slalom	Kristi Terzian, Park City, Utah
Giant Slalom	Eva Twardokens, Santa Cruz, Calif
Super G	Shannon Nobis, Park City, Utah
Combined	Melanie Turgeon, Canada

Bobsled
World Cup Champion Drivers

Two-Man	Pierre Lueders, Canada I
Four-Man	Hubert Schosser, Austria I
Combined	Pierre Lueders

Luge
World Cup Champions
MEN

Singles	Marcus Prock, AUT
Doubles	Jan Behrendt & Stefan Krause, GER

WOMEN

Singles	Gabi Kolisch, GER

Figure Skating
World Championships
at Chiba Makuhari, Japan (Mar. 22-27)

Men's	Elvis Stojko, CAN
Women's	Yuka Sato, JPN
Pairs	Evgenia Shishkova & Vadim Naumov, RUS
Ice Dance	Oksana Gritschuk & Yevgeny Platov, RUS

European Championships
at Copenhagen, Denmark (Jan. 18-23)

Men's	Victor Petrenko, UKR
Women's	Surya Bonaly, FRA
Pairs	Ekaterina Gordeeva & Sergey Grinkov, RUS
Ice Dance	Jayne Torvill & Christopher Dean, GBR

U.S. Championships
at Detroit (Jan. 2-9)

Men's	Scott Davis, Great Falls, Mont.
Women's	Tonya Harding, Portland, Ore.*
Pairs	Jenni Menno, Westlake, Ohio & Todd Sand, Thousand Oakes, Calif.
Ice Dance	Elizabeth Punsalan, Sheffield Lake, Ohio & Jerod Swallow, Northville, Mich.

*Harding was stripped of 1994 women's title and banned from membership in U.S. Figure Skating Assn. for life on June 30, for violating USFSA Code of Ethics after she pleaded guilty to a charge of conspiracy to hinder prosecution related to the Jan. 6 attack on Nancy Kerrigan.

Freestyle Skiing
World Cup Champions
MEN

Overall	Sergey Shupletsov, RUS
Aerials	Philippe LaRoche, CAN
Moguls	Edgar Grospiron, FRA
Ballet	Fabrice Becker, FRA
Combined	David Belhumeur, CAN

WOMEN

Overall	Kristean Porter, USA
Aerials	Lina Cherjazova, UZB
Moguls	Donna Weinbrecht, USA
Ballet	Ellen Breen, USA
Combined	Maja Schmid, SWI

Nordic Skiing
World Cup Champions
MEN

Cross-country	Vladimir Smirnov, KAZ
Ski Jumping	Espen Bredesen, NOR
Nordic Combined	Kenji Ogiwara, JPN

WOMEN

Cross-country	Manuela DiCenta, ITA

Speed Skating
World Cup Champions
MEN

500 meters	Dan Jansen, USA
1000 meters	Dan Jansen, USA
1500 meters	Falko Zandstra, HOL
5000 meters	Johann Olav Koss, NOR

WOMEN

500 meters	Bonnie Blair, USA
1000 meters	Bonnie Blair, USA
1500 meters	Emese Hunyady, AUT
3000 meters	Gunda Niemann, GER

World Sprint Championships
at Calgary (Jan. 29-30)

Men's Overall	Dan Jansen, USA
Women's Overall	Bonnie Blair, USA

Biathlon
World Cup Champions

Men's Overall	Patrice Bailly-Salins, FRA
Women's Overall	Svetlana Paramygina, RUS

SUMMER SPORTS

Basketball
World Championship
at Toronto (Aug. 4-14)

Semifinals: USA 97 ....Greece 58
Russia 66..................................Croatia 64
Bronze medal: Croatia 78 ....Greece 60
Gold medal: USA 137 ....Russia 91

Other Champions

Goodwill Games ....Puerto Rico
European Champion..................Joventut Badalona (Spain)
French League ....CSP Limoges
German League...Bayer Leverkusen
Italian League ....Buckler Bologna
Spanish League ....Real Madrid

CBA Finals.............Quad City Thunder def. Omaha Racers
(4 games to 1)

Cycling
Tour de France

81st Tour de France (July 2-24); 21 stages plus prologue covering 2,474 miles from Lille to Paris; 117 out of 189 riders finished the race.
Winning time: 103 hours, 38 minutes, 38 seconds (an average hourly speed of 24 mph). **Winner's share:** two million francs (about $400,000).

		Team	Behind
1	Miguel Indurain, SPA ....Banesto		—
2	Pyotr Ugrumov, LAT ....Gewiss		5:39
3	Marco Pantani, ITA ....Carrera		7:19
4	Luc Leblanc, FRA..........................Festina		10:03
5	Richard Virenque, FRA ....Festina		10:10
6	Roberto Conti, ITA........................GB-MG		12:29
7	Alberto Elli, ITA...........................GB-MB		20:17
8	Alex Zulle, SWI............................Once		20:35
9	Udo Bolts, GER.............................Telekom		25:19
10	Vladimir Poulnikov, UKR...............Carrera		25:28

Best USA: 89th—Frankie Andreu, Dearborn, Mich., Team Motorola, 2:26:24 behind.

Worldwide Champions
MEN

Tour de France ....Miguel Indurain, SPA
Giro d'Italia (Italy)...............................Yevgeni Berzin, RUS
Vuelta de Espana (Spain) ....Tony Rominger, SWI
World Pro Road Race ....Luc Leblanc, FRA*
Paris-to-Roubaix..................................Andrei Chmil, RUS
Tour du Pont (USA) ....Viacheslav Ekimov, RUS
CoreStates U.S. Pro ....Sean Yates, GBR

*Defending champion Lance Armstrong (USA) finished 7th.

WOMEN

Ore-ida Challenge (USA)....................Clara Hughes, CAN
Tour Cycliste Feminin ....Valentina Polhanova, RUS
World Pro Road Race........................Monika Valvik, NOR

Gymnastics
World Championships
at Brisbane, Australia (Apr. 19-24)
MEN

All-Around...Ivan Ivankov, BLR
Horizontal Bar...Vitaly Scherbo, BLR
Parallel Bars...Huang Liping, CHN
Vault ....Vitaly Scherbo, BLR
Pommel Horse..Marius Urzica, ROM
Rings ....Yuri Chechi, ITA
Floor Exercise..Vitaly Scherbo, BLR

WOMEN

All-Around ....Shannon Miller, USA
Vault...Gina Gogean, ROM
Uneven Bars ....Lou Li, CHN
Balance Beam......................................Shannon Miller, USA
Floor Exercise ....Dina Kochjetkova, RUS

U.S. Championships
at Nashville, Tenn. (Aug. 24-27)
MEN

All-Around ....Scott Kefwick, Las Vegas
Horizontal Bar ....Scott Kefwick, Las Vegas
Parallel Bars ....Steve McCain, Houston
Vault ....Keith Wiley, Vero Beach, Fla.
Pommel Horse ....Mihai Bagiu, Albuquerque, N.M.
Rings ....Scott Kefwick, Las Vegas
Floor Exercise ....Jeremy Killen, Phoenix

WOMEN

All-Around ....Dominique Dawes, Silver Spring, Md.
Vault...Dominique Dawes
Uneven Bars ....Dominique Dawes
Balance Beam......................................Dominique Dawes
Floor Exercise ....Dominique Dawes

Marathons
1994 Winners
(*) indicates course record.

		Time
Boston		
Men...................................Cosmas Ndeti, KEN		2:07.15*
Women...Uta Pippig, GER		2:21:45*
London		
Men ....Dionisio Ceron, MEX		2:08:53
Women...........................Katrin Dorre, GER		2:32:34
Los Angeles		
Men ....Paul Pilkington, USA		2:12:13
Women...........................Olga Appell, USA		2:28:12
Osaka		
Women (only) ....Tomoe Abe, JPN		2:26:09
Rotterdam		
Men ....Vincent Rousseau, BEL		2:07:51
Women.......................Miyoko Asahina, JPN		2:25:52*

Late 1993

Chicago		Time
Men ....Luis Dos Santos, BRA		2:13:14
Women...........................Ritva Lemettinen, FIN		2:33:18
Fukuoka		
Men (only) ....Dionisio Ceron, MEX		2:08:51
New York City		
Men ....Andres Espinosa, MEX		2:10:04
Women...........................Uta Pippig, GER		2:26:24

Rowing
World Championships
at Indianapolis (Sept. 11-18)
MEN

Lightweight Single Sculls ....Peter Haining, GBR
Lightweight Eights ....Britain (USA 5th)
Single Sculls..Andre Willms, GER
Eights ....United States

WOMEN

Lightweight Single Sculls ....Constanta Pipota, ROM
Lightweight Fours without Coxswain ....United States
Single Sculls ....Trine Hansen, DEN
Eights ....Germany (USA 2nd)

THE 1995 SPORTS ALMANAC INFORMATION PLEASE

INT'L SPORTS STATISTICS

THROUGH THE YEARS
1896-1994
WINNERS • RECORDS

SEC B

PAGE 656

TRACK & FIELD

IAAF World Championships

While the Summer Olympics have served as the unofficial world outdoor championships for track and field throughout the century, a separate World Championship meet was started in 1983 by the International Amateur Athletic Federation (IAAF). The meet was held every four years from 1983-91, but began an every-other-year cycle in 1993. World Championship sites include Helsinki (1983), Rome (1987), Tokyo (1991), Stuttgart (1993) and Göteborg, Sweden (1995).

MEN

Multiple gold medals: Carl Lewis (8); Sergey Bubka (4); Greg Foster, Werner Gunthor, Michael Johnson and Calvin Smith (3); Leroy Burrell, Andre Cason, Maurizio Damilano, Moses Kiptanui, Billy Konchellah, Sergey Litvinov, Dennis Mitchell, Noureddine Morceli, Edwin Moses, Dan O'Brien, Mike Powell, Butch Reynolds and Lars Riedel (2).

100 meters

Year		Time	
1983	Carl Lewis, USA	10.07	
1987	Carl Lewis, USA	9.93	
1991	Carl Lewis, USA	9.86	**WR**
1993	Linford Christie, GBR	9.87	

Note: Ben Johnson was the original winner in 1987, but was stripped of his title and world record time (9.83) following his 1989 admission of drug taking.

200 meters

Year		Time
1983	Calvin Smith, USA	20.14
1987	Calvin Smith, USA	20.16
1991	Michael Johnson, USA	20.01
1993	Frank Fredericks, NAM	19.85

400 meters

Year		Time
1983	Bert Cameron, JAM	45.05
1987	Thomas Schonlebe, E.Ger	44.33
1991	Antonio Pettigrew, USA	44.57
1993	Michael Johnson, USA	43.65

800 meters

Year		Time
1983	Willi Wülbeck, W.Ger	1:43.65
1987	Billy Konchellah, KEN	1:43.06
1991	Billy Konchellah, KEN	1:43.99
1993	Paul Ruto, KEN	1:44.71

1500 meters

Year		Time
1983	Steve Cram, GBR	3:41.59
1987	Abdi Bile, SOM	3:36.80
1991	Noureddine Morceli, ALG	3:32.84
1993	Noureddine Morceli, ALG	3:34.24

5000 meters

Year		Time
1983	Eammon Coghlan, IRE	13:28.53
1987	Said Aoutia, MOR	13:26.44
1991	Yobes Ondieki, KEN	13:14.45
1993	Ismael Kirui, KEN	13:02.75

10,000 meters

Year		Time
1983	Alberto Cova, ITA	28:01.04
1987	Paul Kipkoech, KEN	27:38.63
1991	Moses Tanui, KEN	27:38.74
1993	Haile Gebresilasie, ETH	27:46.02

Marathon

Year		Time
1983	Rob de Castella, AUS	2:10:03
1987	Douglas Wakiihuri, KEN	2:11:48
1991	Hiromi Taniguchi, JPN	2:14:57
1993	Mark Plaatjes, USA	2:13:57

110-meter Hurdles

Year		Time	
1983	Greg Foster, USA	13.42	
1987	Greg Foster, USA	13.21	
1991	Greg Foster, USA	13.06	
1993	Colin Jackson, GBR	12.91	**WR**

400-meter Hurdles

Year		Time
1983	Edwin Moses, USA	47.50
1987	Edwin Moses, USA	47.46
1991	Samuel Matete, ZAM	47.64
1993	Kevin Young, USA	47.18

3000-meter Steeplechase

Year		Time
1983	Patriz Ilg, W.Ger	8:15.06
1987	Francesco Panetta, ITA	8:08.57
1991	Moses Kiptanui, KEN	8:12.59
1993	Moses Kiptanui, KEN	8:06.36

4x100-meter Relay

Year		Time	
1983	United States	37.86	**WR**
1987	United States	37.90	
1991	United States	37.50	**WR**
1993	United States	37.48	

4x400-meter Relay

Year		Time	
1983	Soviet Union	3:00.79	
1987	United States	2:57.29	
1991	Great Britain	2:57.53	
1993	Great Britain	2:54.29	**WR**

Triple Jump

Year		Distance
1983	Zdzislaw Hoffmann, POL	57- 2
1987	Khristo Markov, BUL	58- 9
1991	Kenny Harrison, USA	58- 4
1993	Mike Conley, USA	58- 7¼

20-kilometer Walk

Year		Time
1983	Ernesto Canto, MEX	1:20:49
1987	Maurizio Damilano, ITA	1:20:45
1991	Maurizio Damilano, ITA	1:19:37
1993	Valentin Massana, SPA	1:22.31

Shot Put

Year		Distance
1983	Edward Sarul, POL	70- 2¼
1987	Werner Günthör, SWI	72-11¼
1991	Werner Günthör, SWI	71- 1¼
1993	Werner Günthör, SWI	72- 1

50-kilometer Walk

Year		Time
1983	Ronald Weigel, E. Ger	3:43:08
1987	Hartwig Gauder, E. Ger	3:40:53
1991	Aleksandr Potashov, USSR	3:53:09
1993	Jesus Angel Garcia, SPA	3:41:41

Discus

Year		Distance
1983	Imrich Bugar, CZE	222- 2
1987	Jurgen Schult, E. Ger	225- 6
1991	Lars Riedel, GER	217- 2
1993	Lars Riedel, GER	222- 2

High Jump

Year		Height
1983	Gennedy Avdeyenko, USSR	7- 7¼
1987	Patrik Sjoberg, SWE	7- 9¾
1991	Charles Austin, USA	7- 9¾
1993	Javier Sotomayor, CUB	7-10½

Hammer Throw

Year		Distance
1983	Sergey Litvinov, USSR	271- 3
1987	Sergey Litvinov, USSR	272- 6
1991	Yuri Sedykh, USSR	268- 0
1993	Andrey Abduvaliyev, TAJ	267-10

Pole Vault

Year		Height
1983	Sergey Bubka, USSR	18- 8¼
1987	Sergey Bubka, USSR	19- 2¼
1991	Sergey Bubka, USSR	19- 6¼
1993	Sergey Bubka, USSR	19- 8¼

Javelin

Year		Distance	
1983	Detlef Michel, E. Ger	293- 7	**OLD**
1987	Seppo Raty, FIN	274- 1	**NEW**
1991	Kimmo Kinnunen, FIN	297-11	
1993	Jan Zelezny, CZE	282- 1	

Long Jump

Year		Distance	
1983	Carl Lewis, USA	28- 0¾	
1987	Carl Lewis, USA	28- ¼	
1991	Mike Powell, USA	29- 4½	**WR**
1993	Mike Powell, USA	28- 2¼	

Decathlon

Year		Points
1983	Daley Thompson, GBR	8714
1987	Torsten Voss, E. Ger	8680
1991	Dan O'Brien, USA	8812
1993	Dan O'Brien, USA	8817

WOMEN

Multiple gold medals: Jackie Joyner-Kersee (4); Tatyana Samolenko Dorovskikh, Silke Gladisch and Marita Koch (3); Olga Bryzgina, Mary Decker, Gail Devers, Heike Daute Drechsler, Martina Optiz Hellmann, Katrin Krabbe, Jarmila Kratochvilova, Jearl Miles, Merlene Ottey and Huang Zhihong (2).

100 meters

Year		Time
1983	Marlies Gohr, E. Ger	10.97
1987	Silke Gladisch, E. Ger	10.90
1991	Katrin Krabbe, GER	10.99
1993	Gail Devers, USA	10.81

1500 meters

Year		Time
1983	Mary Decker, USA	4:00.90
1987	Tatiana Samolenko, USSR	3:58.56
1991	Hassiba Boulmerka, ALG	4:02.21
1993	Liu Dong, CHN	4:00.50

200 meters

Year		Time
1983	Marita Koch, E. Ger	22.13
1987	Silke Gladisch, E. Ger	21.74
1991	Katrin Krabbe, GER	22.09
1993	Merlene Ottey, JAM	21.98

3000 meters

Year		Time
1983	Mary Decker, USA	8:34.62
1987	Tatyana Samolenko, USSR	8:38.73
1991	T. Samolenko Dorovskikh, USSR	8:35.82
1993	Qu Yunxia, CHN	8:28.71

400 meters

Year		Time	
1983	Jarmila Kratochvilova, CZE	47.99	**WR**
1987	Olga Bryzgina, USSR	49.38	
1991	Marie-Jose Perec, FRA	49.13	
1993	Jearl Miles, USA	49.82	

10,000 meters

Year		Time
1983	Not held	
1987	Ingrid Kristiansen, NOR	31:05.85
1991	Liz McColgan, GBR	31:14.31
1993	Wang Junxia, CHN	30:49.30

800 meters

Year		Time
1983	Jarmila Kratochvilova, CZE	1:54.68
1987	Sigrun Wodars, E. Ger	1:55.26
1991	Lilia Nurutdinova, USSR	1:57.50
1993	Maria Mutola, MOZ	1:55.43

Marathon

Year		Time
1983	Grete Waitz, NOR	2:28:09
1987	Rose Mota, POR	2:25:17
1991	Wanda Panfil, POL	2:29:53
1993	Junko Asari, JPN	2:30:03

Track & Field Championships (Cont.)
Women

100-meter Hurdles

Year		Time
1983	Bettine Jahn, E. Ger	12.35 ʷ
1987	Ginka Zagorcheva, BUL	12.34
1991	Lyudmila Narozhilenko, USSR	12.59
1993	Gail Devers, USA	12.46

ʷ indicates wind-aided.

400-meter Hurdles

Year		Time	
1983	Yekaterina Fesenko, USSR	54.14	
1987	Sabine Busch, E. Ger	53.62	
1991	Tatiana Ledovskaya, USSR	53.11	
1993	Sally Gunnell, GBR	52.74	**WR**

4x100-meter Relay

Year		Time
1983	East Germany	41.76
1987	United States	41.58
1991	Jamaica	41.94
1993	Russia	41.49

4x400-meter Relay

Year		Time
1983	East Germany	3:19.73
1987	East Germany	3:18.63
1991	Soviet Union	3:18.43
1993	United States	3:16.71

10-kilometer Walk

Year		Time
1983	Not held	
1987	Irina Strakhova, USSR	44:12
1991	Alina Ivanova, USSR	42:57
1993	Sari Essayah, FIN	42.59

High Jump

Year		Height	
1983	Tamara Bykova, USSR	6- 7	
1987	Stefka Kostadinova, BUL	6-10¼	**WR**
1991	Heike Henkel, GER	6- 8¾	
1993	Ioamnet Quintero, CUB	6- 6¼	

Long Jump

Year		Distance
1983	Heike Daute, E. Ger	23-10¼ ʷ
1987	Jackie Joyner-Kersee, USA	24- 1¾
1991	Jackie Joyner-Kersee, USA	24- 0¼
1993	Heike Drechsler, GER	23- 4

ʷ indicates wind-aided.

Triple Jump

Year		Distance	
1983	Not held		
1987	Not held		
1991	Not held		
1993	Ana Biryukova, RUS	46- 6¼	**WR**

Shot Put

Year		Distance
1983	Helena Fibingerova, CZE	69- 0
1987	Natalia Lisovskaya, USSR	69- 8
1991	Huang Zhihong, CHN	68- 4
1991	Huang Zhihong, CHN	67- 6

Discus

Year		Distance
1983	Martina Opitz, E. Ger	226- 2
1987	Martina Opitz Hellmann, E. Ger	235- 0
1991	Tsvetanka Khristova, BUL	233- 0
1993	Olga Burova, RUS	221- 1

Javelin

Year		Distance
1983	Tiina Lillak, FIN	232- 4
1987	Fatima Whitbread, GBR	251- 5
1991	Xu Demei, CHN	225- 8
1993	Trine Hattestad, NOR	227- 0

Heptathlon

Year		Points
1983	Ramona Neubert, E. Ger	6770
1987	Jackie Joyner-Kersee, USA	7128
1991	Sabine Braun, GER	6672
1993	Jackie Joyner-Kersee, USA	6837

Marathons

Boston Marathon

America's oldest regularly contested foot race, the Boston Marathon is held on Patriots' Day every April. It has been run at four different distances: 24 miles, 1232 yards (1897-1923); 26 miles, 209 yards (1924-26); 26 miles, 385 yards (1927-52); 25 miles, 958 yards (1953-56); and 26 miles, 385 yards (since 1957).

Men

Multiple winners: Clarence DeMar (7); Gerard Cote and Bill Rodgers (4); Ibrahim Hussein and Leslie Pawson (3); Tarzan Brown, Jim Caffrey, John A. Kelley, John Miles, Cosmas Ndeti, Eino Oksanen, Toshihiko Seko, Geoff Smith and Aurele Vandendriessche (2).

Year		Time	Year		Time
1897	John McDermott, New York	2:55:10	1907	Tom Longboat, Canada	2:24:24
1898	Ronald McDonald, Massachusetts	2:42:00	1908	Tom Morrissey, New York	2:25:43
1899	Lawrence Brignolia, Massachusetts	2:54:38	1909	Henri Renaud, New Hampshire	2:53:36
1900	Jim Caffrey, Canada	2:39:44	1910	Fred Cameron, Nova Scotia	2:28:52
1901	Jim Caffrey, Canada	2:29:23	1911	Clarence DeMar, Massachusetts	2:21:39
1902	Sam Mellor, New York	2:43:12	1912	Mike Ryan, Illinois	2:21:18
1903	J.C. Lorden, Massachusetts	2:41:29	1913	Fritz Carlson, Minnesota	2:25:14
1904	Mike Spring, New York	2:38:04	1914	James Duffy, Canada	2:25:01
1905	Fred Lorz, New York	2:38:25	1915	Edouard Fabre, Canada	2:31:41
1906	Tim Ford, Massachusetts	2:45:45	1916	Arthur Roth, Massachusetts	2:27:16

Year		Time	Year		Time
1917	Bill Kennedy, New York	2:28:37	1957	John J. Kelley, Connecticut	2:20:05
1918	World War relay race		1958	Franjo Mihalic, Yugoslavia	2:25:54
1919	Carl Linder, Massachusetts	2:29:13	1959	Eino Oksanen, Finland	2:22:42
1920	Peter Trivoulidas, New York	2:29:31	1960	Paavo Kotila, Finland	2:20:54
1921	Frank Zuna, New Jersey	2:18:57	1961	Eino Oksanen, Finland	2:23:39
1922	Clarence DeMar, Massachusetts	2:18:10	1962	Eino Oksanen, Finland	2:23:48
1923	Clarence DeMar, Massachusetts	2:23:37	1963	Aurele Vandendriessche, Belgium	2:18:58
1924	Clarence DeMar, Massachusetts	2:29:40	1964	Aurele Vandendriessche, Belgium	2:19:59
1925	Charles Mellor, Illinois	2:33:00	1965	Morio Shigematsu, Japan	2:16:33
1926	John Miles, Nova Scotia	2:25:40	1966	Kenji Kimihara, Japan	2:17:11
1927	Clarence DeMar, Massachusetts	2:40:22	1967	David McKenzie, New Zealand	2:15:45
1928	Clarence DeMar, Massachusetts	2:37:07	1968	Amby Burfoot, Connecticut	2:22:17
1929	John Miles, Nova Scotia	2:33:08	1969	Yoshiaki Unetani, Japan	2:13:49
1930	Clarence DeMar, Massachusetts	2:34:48	1970	Ron Hill, England	2:10:30
1931	James Henigan, Massachusetts	2:46:45	1971	Alvaro Mejia, Colombia	2:18:45
1932	Paul deBruyn, Germany	2:33:36	1972	Olavi Suomalainen, Finland	2:15:39
1933	Leslie Pawson, Rhode Island	2:31:01	1973	Jon Anderson, Oregon	2:16:03
1934	Dave Komonen, Canada	2:32:53	1974	Neil Cusack, Ireland	2:13:39
1935	John A. Kelley, Massachusetts	2:32:07	1975	Bill Rodgers, Massachusetts	2:09:55
1936	Ellison (Tarzan) Brown, Rhode Island	2:33:40	1976	Jack Fultz, Pennsylvania	2:20:19
1937	Walter Young, Canada	2:33:20	1977	Jerome Drayton, Canada	2:14:46
1938	Leslie Pawson, Rhode Island	2:35:34	1978	Bill Rodgers, Massachusetts	2:10:13
1939	Ellison (Tarzan) Brown, Rhode Island	2:28:51	1979	Bill Rodgers, Massachusetts	2:09:27
1940	Gerard Cote, Canada	2:28:28	1980	Bill Rodgers, Massachusetts	2:12:11
1941	Leslie Pawson, Rhode Island	2:30:38	1981	Toshihiko Seko, Japan	2:09:26
1942	Joe Smith, Massachusetts	2:26:51	1982	Alberto Salazar, Oregon	2:08:52
1943	Gerard Cote, Canada	2:28:25	1983	Greg Meyer, New Jersey	2:09:00
1944	Gerard Cote, Canada	2:31:50	1984	Geoff Smith, England	2:10:34
1945	John A. Kelley, Massachusetts	2:30:40	1985	Geoff Smith, England	2:14:05
1946	Stylianos Kyriakides, Greece	2:29:27	1986	Rob de Castella, Australia	2:07:51
1947	Yun Bok Suh, Korea	2:25:39	1987	Toshihiko Seko, Japan	2:11:50
1948	Gerard Cote, Canada	2:31:02	1988	Ibrahim Hussein, Kenya	2:08:43
1949	Karle Leandersson, Sweden	2:31:50	1989	Abebe Mekonnen, Ethiopia	2:09:06
1950	Kee Yonh Ham, Korea	2:32:39	1990	Gelindo Bordin, Italy	2:08:19
1951	Shigeki Tanaka, Japan	2:27:45	1991	Ibrahim Hussein, Kenya	2:11:06
1952	Doroteo Flores, Guatemala	2:31:53	1992	Ibrahim Hussein, Kenya	2:08:14
1953	Keizo Yamada, Japan	2:18:51	1993	Cosmas Ndeti, Kenya	2:09:33
1954	Veiko Karvonen, Finland	2:20:39	1994	Cosmas Ndeti, Kenya	2:07:15*
1955	Hideo Hamamura, Japan	2:18:22			
1956	Antti Viskari, Finland	2:14:14	*Course record.		

WOMEN

Multiple winners: Rosa Mota (3); Joan Benoit, Miki Gorman, Ingrid Kristiansen and Olga Markova (2).

Year		Time	Year		Time
1972	Nina Kuscsik, New York	3:08:58	1984	Lorraine Moller, New Zealand	2:29:28
1973	Jacqueline Hansen, California	3:05:59	1985	Lisa Larsen Weidenbach, Mass	2:34:06
1974	Miki Gorman, California	2:47:11	1986	Ingrid Kristiansen, Norway	2:24:55
1975	Liane Winter, West Germany	2:42:24	1987	Rosa Mota, Portugal	2:25:21
1976	Kim Merritt, Wisconsin	2:47:10	1988	Rosa Mota, Portugal	2:24:30
1977	Miki Gorman, California	2:48:33	1989	Ingrid Kristiansen, Norway	2:24:33
1978	Gayle Barron, Georgia	2:44:52			
1979	Joan Benoit, Maine	2:35:15	1990	Rosa Mota, Portugal	2:25:23
			1991	Wanda Panfil, Poland	2:24:18
1980	Jacqueline Gareau, Canada	2:34:28	1992	Olga Markova, CIS	2:23:43
1981	Allison Roe, New Zealand	2:26:46	1993	Olga Markova, Russia	2:25:27
1982	Charlotte Teske, West Germany	2:29:33	1994	Uta Pippig, Germany	2:21:45*
1983	Joan Benoit, Maine	2:22:43	*Course record.		

New York City Marathon

Started in 1970, the New York City Marathon is run in the fall, usually on the first Sunday in November. The route winds through all of the city's five boroughs and finishes in Central Park.

MEN

Multiple winners: Bill Rodgers (4); Alberto Salazar (3); Tom Fleming and Orlando Pizzolato (2).

Year		Time	Year		Time
1970	Gary Muhrcke, USA	2:31:38	1975	Tom Fleming, USA	2:19:27
1971	Norman Higgins, USA	2:22:54	1976	Bill Rodgers, USA	2:10:09
1972	Sheldon Karlin, USA	2:27:52	1977	Bill Rodgers, USA	2:11:28
1973	Tom Fleming, USA	2:21:54	1978	Bill Rodgers, USA	2:12:12
1974	Norbert Sander, USA	2:26:30	1979	Bill Rodgers, USA	2:11:42

New York City Marathon (Cont.)

Year		Time
1980	Alberto Salazar, USA	2:09:41
1981	Alberto Salazar, USA	2:08:13
1982	Alberto Salazar, USA	2:09:29
1983	Rod Dixon, New Zealand	2:08:59
1984	Orlando Pizzolato, Italy	2:14:53
1985	Orlando Pizzolato, Italy	2:11:34
1986	Gianni Poli, Italy	2:11:06
1987	Ibrahim Hussein, Kenya	2:11:01

Year		Time
1988	Steve Jones, Wales	2:08:20
1989	Juma Ikangaa, Tanzania	2:08:01*
1990	Douglas Wakiihuri, Kenya	2:12:39
1991	Salvador Garcia, Mexico	2:09:28
1992	Willie Mtolo, South Africa	2:09:29
1993	Andres Espinosa, Mexico	2:10:04

*Course record.

WOMEN

Multiple winners: Grete Waitz (9); Miki Gorman and Nina Kuscsik (2).

Year		Time
1970	No Finisher	
1971	Beth Bonner, USA	2:55:22
1972	Nina Kuscsik, USA	3:08:41
1973	Nina Kuscsik, USA	2:57:07
1974	Katherine Switzer, USA	3:07:29
1975	Kim Merritt, USA	2:46:14
1976	Miki Gorman, USA	2:39:11
1977	Miki Gorman, USA	2:43:10
1978	Grete Waitz, Norway	2:32:30
1979	Grete Waitz, Norway	2:27:33
1980	Grete Waitz, Norway	2:25:41
1981	Allison Roe, New Zealand	2:25:29

Year		Time
1982	Grete Waitz, Norway	2:27:14
1983	Grete Waitz, Norway	2:27:00
1984	Grete Waitz, Norway	2:29:30
1985	Grete Waitz, Norway	2:28:34
1986	Grete Waitz, Norway	2:28:06
1987	Priscilla Welch, Britain	2:30:17
1988	Grete Waitz, Norway	2:28:07
1989	Ingrid Kristiansen, Norway	2:25:30
1990	Wanda Panfil, Poland	2:30:45
1991	Liz McColgan, Scotland	2:27:23
1992	Lisa Ondieki, Australia	2:24:40*
1993	Uta Pippig, Germany	2:26:24

*Course record.

Annual Awards

Track & Field News Athletes of the Year

Voted on by an international panel of track and field experts and presented since 1959 (men) and 1974 (women) by *Track & Field News*.

MEN

Multiple winners: Carl Lewis (3); Sergey Bubka, Sebastian Coe, Alberto Juantorena, Jim Ryun, Peter Snell (2).

Year		Event
1959	Martin Lauer, W. Germany	110H/Decathlon
1960	Rafer Johnson, USA	Decathlon
1961	Ralph Boston, USA	Long Jump/110 Hurdles
1962	Peter Snell, New Zealand	800/1500
1963	C.K. Yang, Taiwan	Decathlon/Pole Vault
1964	Peter Snell, New Zealand	800/1500
1965	Ron Clarke, Australia	5000/10,000
1966	Jim Ryun, USA	800/1500
1967	Jim Ryun, USA	1500
1968	Bob Beamon, USA	Long Jump
1969	Bill Toomey, USA	Decathlon
1970	Randy Matson, USA	Shot Put
1971	Rod Milburn, USA	110 Hurdles
1972	Lasse Viren, Finland	5000/10,000
1973	Ben Jipcho, Kenya	1500/5000/Steeplechase
1974	Rick Wohlhuter, USA	800/1500
1975	John Walker, New Zealand	800/1500
1976	Alberto Juantorena, Cuba	400/800

Year		Event
1977	Alberto Juantorena, Cuba	400/800
1978	Henry Rono, Kenya	5000/10,000/Steeplechase
1979	Sebastian Coe, Great Britain	800/1500
1980	Edwin Moses, USA	400 Hurdles
1981	Sebastian Coe, Great Britain	800/1500
1982	Carl Lewis, USA	100/200/Long Jump
1983	Carl Lewis, USA	100/200/Long Jump
1984	Carl Lewis, USA	100/200/Long Jump
1985	Said Aouita, Morocco	1500/5000
1986	Yuri Sedykh, USSR	Hammer Throw
1987	Ben Johnson, Canada	100
1988	Sergey Bubka, USSR	Pole Vault
1989	Roger Kingdom, USA	110 Hurdles
1990	Michael Johnson, USA	200/400
1991	Sergey Bubka, USSR	Pole Vault
1992	Kevin Young, USA	400 Hurdles
1993	Noureddine Morceli, Algeria	Mile/1500/3000

WOMEN

Multiple winners: Marita Koch (4); Evelyn Ashford and Jackie Joyner-Kersee (2).

Year		Event
1974	Irena Szewinska, Poland	100/200/400
1975	Faina Melnik, USSR	Shot Put/Discus
1976	Tatiana Kazankina, USSR	800/1500
1977	Rosemarie Ackermann, E. Germany	High Jump
1978	Marita Koch, E. Germany	100/200/400
1979	Marita Koch, E. Germany	100/200/400
1980	Ilona Briesenick, E. Germany	Shot Put
1981	Evelyn Ashford, USA	100/200
1982	Marita Koch, E. Germany	100/200/400
1983	Jarmila Kratochvilova, Czech	200/400/800

Year		Event
1984	Evelyn Ashford, USA	100
1985	Marita Koch, E. Germany	100/200/400
1986	Jackie Joyner-Kersee, USA	Heptathlon/Long Jump
1987	Jackie Joyner-Kersee, USA	100h/Heptathlon/LJ
1988	Florence Griffith Joyner, USA	100/200
1989	Ana Quirot, Cuba	400/800
1990	Merlene Ottey, Jamaica	100/200
1991	Heike Henkel, Germany	High Jump
1992	Heike Drechsler, Germany	Long Jump
1993	Wang Junxia, China	1500/3000/10,000

SWIMMING & DIVING
FINA World Championships

While the Summer Olympics have served as the unofficial world championships for swimming and diving throughout the century, a separate World Championship meet was started in 1973 by the International Amateur Swimming Federation (FINA). The meet was held three times between 1973-78, then every four years since then. Sites have included Belgrade (1973); Cali, COL (1975); West Berlin (1978); Guayaquil, ECU (1982); Madrid (1986); Perth (1991) and Rome (1994).

Swimming
MEN

Most gold medals (including relays): Jim Montgomery (7); Matt Biondi (6); Rowdy Gaines (5); Joe Bottom, Tamas Darnyi, Michael Gross, Tom Jager, David McCagg, Vladimir Salnikov and Tim Shaw (4); Billy Forrester, Andras Hargitay, Roland Matthes, John Murphy, Jeff Rouse, Norbert Rozsa and David Wilkie (3).

50-meter Freestyle

Year		Time
1973-82 Not held.		
1986	Tom Jager, USA	22.49
1991	Tom Jager, USA	22.16
1994	Aleksandr Popov, RUS	22.17

100-meter Freestyle

Year		Time
1973	Jim Montgomery, USA	51.70
1975	Tim Shaw, USA	51.25
1978	David McCagg, USA	50.24
1982	Jorg Woithe, E.Ger	50.18
1986	Matt Biondi, USA	48.94
1991	Matt Biondi, USA	49.18
1994	Aleksandr Popov, RUS	49.12

200-meter Freestyle

Year		Time
1973	Jim Montgomery, USA	1:53.02
1975	Tim Shaw, USA	1:52.04
1978	Billy Forrester, USA	1:51.02
1982	Michael Gross, W.Ger	1:49.84
1986	Michael Gross, W.Ger	1:47.92
1991	Giorgio Lamberti, ITA	1:47.27
1994	Antti Kasvio, FIN	1:47.32

400-meter Freestyle

Year		Time	
1973	Rick DeMont, USA	3:58.18	
1975	Tim Shaw, USA	3:54.88	
1978	Vladimir Salnikov, USSR	3:51.94	
1982	Vladimir Salnikov, USSR	3:51.30	
1986	Rainer Henkel, W.Ger	3:50.05	
1991	Jorg Hoffman, GER	3:48.04	
1994	Kieren Perkins, AUS	3:43.80	**WR**

1500-meter Freestyle

Year		Time	
1973	Stephen Holland, AUS	15:31.85	
1975	Tim Shaw, USA	15.28.92	
1978	Vladimir Salnikov, USSR	15:03.99	
1982	Vladimir Salnikov, USSR	15:01.77	
1986	Rainer Henkel, W.Ger	15:05.31	
1991	Jorg Hoffman, GER	14:50.36	**WR**
1994	Kieren Perkins, AUS	14:50.52	

100-meter Backstroke

Year		Time
1973	Roland Matthes, E.Ger	57.47
1975	Roland Matthes, E.Ger	58.15
1978	Bob Jackson, USA	56.36
1982	Dirk Richter, E.Ger	55.95
1986	Igor Polianski, USSR	55.58
1991	Jeff Rouse, USA	55.23
1994	Martin Lopez-Zubero, SPA	55.17

200-meter Backstroke

Year		Time
1973	Roland Matthes, E.Ger	2:01.87
1975	Zoltan Varraszto, HUN	2:05.05
1978	Jesse Vassallo, USA	2:02.16
1982	Rick Carey, USA	2:00.82
1986	Igor Polianski, USSR	1:58.78
1991	Martin Zubero, SPA	1:59.52
1994	Vladimir Selkov, RUS	1:57.42

100-meter Breaststroke

Year		Time	
1973	John Hencken, USA	1:04.02	
1975	David Wilkie, GBR	1:04.26	
1978	Walter Kusch, W.Ger	1:03.56	
1982	Steve Lundquist, USA	1:02.75	
1986	Victor Davis, CAN	1:02.71	
1991	Norbert Rozsa, HUN	1:01.45	**WR**
1994	Norbert Rozsa, HUN	1:10.24	

200-meter Breaststroke

Year		Time	
1973	David Wilkie, GBR	2:19.28	
1975	David Wilkie, GBR	2:18.23	
1978	Nick Nevid, USA	2:18.37	
1982	Victor Davis, CAN	2:14.77	**WR**
1986	Jozsef Szabo, HUN	2:14.27	
1991	Mike Barrowman, USA	2:11.23	**WR**
1994	Norbert Rozsa, HUN	2:12.81	

100-meter Butterfly

Year		Time
1973	Bruce Robertson, CAN	55.69
1975	Greg Jagenburg, USA	55.63
1978	Joe Bottom, USA	54.30
1982	Matt Gribble, USA	53.88
1986	Pablo Morales, USA	53.54
1991	Anthony Nesty, SUR	53.29
1994	Rafal Szukala, POL	53.51

200-meter Butterfly

Year		Time	
1973	Robin Backhaus, USA	2:03.32	
1975	Billy Forrester, USA	2:01.95	
1978	Mike Bruner, USA	1:59.38	
1982	Michael Gross, W.Ger	1:58.85	
1986	Michael Gross, W.Ger	1:56.53	
1991	Melvin Stewart, USA	1:55.69	**WR**
1994	Denis Pankratov, RUS	1:56.54	

200-meter Individual Medley

Year		Time	
1973	Gunnar Larsson, SWE	2:08.36	
1975	Andras Hargitay, HUN	2:07.72	
1978	Graham Smith, CAN	2:03.65	**WR**
1982	Alexander Sidorenko, USSR	2:03.30	
1986	Tamás Darnyi, HUN	2:01.57	
1991	Tamás Darnyi, HUN	1:59.36	**WR**
1994	Janis Sievinen, FIN	1:58.16	**WR**

Swimming World Champions (Cont.)
MEN

400-meter Individual Medley

Year		Time	
1973	Andras Hargitay, HUN	4:31.11	
1975	Andras Hargitay, HUN	4:32.57	
1978	Jesse Vassallo, USA	4:20.05	WR
1982	Ricardo Prado, BRA	4:19.78	WR
1986	Tamás Darnyl, HUN	4.18.98	
1991	Tamás Darnyl, HUN	4:12.36	WR
1994	Tom Dolan, USA	4:12.30	WR

4 x 100-meter Freestyle Relay

Year		Time	
1973	United States	3:27.18	
1975	United States	3:24.85	
1978	United States	3:19.74	
1982	United States	3:19.26	WR
1986	United States	3:19.98	
1991	United States	3:17.15	
1994	United States	3:16.90	

4 x 200-meter Freestyle Relay

Year		Time	
1973	United States	7:33.22	WR
1975	West Germany	7:39.44	
1978	United States	7:20.82	
1982	United States	7:21.09	
1986	East Germany	7:15.91	
1991	Germany	7:13.50	
1994	Sweden	7:17.34	

4 x 100-meter Medley Relay

Year		Time	
1973	United States	3:49.49	
1975	United States	3:49.00	
1978	United States	3:44.63	
1982	United States	3:40.84	WR
1986	United States	3:41.25	
1991	United States	3:39.66	
1994	United States	3:37.74	

WOMEN

Most gold medals (including relays): Kornelia Ender (8); Kristin Otto (7); Tracy Caulkins, Heike Friedrich, Le Jingyi, Rosemarie Kother and Ulrike Richter (4); Hannalore Anke, Lu Bin, He Cihong, Janet Evans, Nicole Haislett, Lui Limin, Birgit Meineke, Joan Pennington, Manuela Stellmach, Renate Vogel and Cynthia Woodhead (3).

50-meter Freesstyle

Year		Time	
1973-82 Not held.			
1986	Tamara Costache, ROM	25.28	WR
1991	Zhuang Yong, CHN	25.47	
1994	Le Jingyi, CHN	24.51 WR	

100-meter Freestyle

Year		Time	
1973	Kornelia Ender, E.Ger	57.54	
1975	Kornelai Ender, E.Ger	56.50	
1978	Barbara Krause, E.Ger	55.68	
1982	Birgit Meineke, E.Ger	55.79	
1986	Kristin Otto, E.Ger	55.05	
1991	Nicole Haislett, USA	55.17	
1994	Le Jingyi, CHN	54.01 WR	

200-meter Freestyle

Year		Time	
1973	Keena Rothhammer, USA	2:04.99	
1975	Shirley Babashoff, USA	2:02.50	
1978	Cynthia Woodhead, USA	1:58.53	WR
1982	Annemarie Verstappen, HOL	1:59.53	
1986	Heike Friedrich, E.Ger	1:58.26	
1991	Hayley Lewis, AUS	2:00.48	
1994	Franziska Van Almsick, GER	1:56.78	WR

400-meter Freestyle

Year		Time	
1973	Heather Greenwood, USA	4:20.28	
1975	Shirley Babashoff, USA	4:22.70	
1978	Tracey Wickham, AUS	4:06.28	WR
1982	Carmela Schmidt. E.Ger	4:08.98	
1986	Heike Friedrich, E.Ger	4:07.45	
1991	Janet Evans, USA	4:08.63	
1994	Yang Aihua, CHN	4:09.64	

800-meter Freestyle

Year		Time	
1973	Novella Calligaris, ITA	8:52.97	
1975	Jenny Turrall, AUS	8:44.75	
1978	Tracey Wickham, AUS	8:25.94	
1982	Kim Linehan, USA	8:27.48	
1986	Astrid Strauss, E.Ger	8:28.24	
1991	Janet Evans, USA	8:24.05	
1994	Janet Evans, USA	8:29.85	

100-meter Backstroke

Year		Time	
1973	Ulrike Richter, E.Ger	1:05.42	
1975	Ulrike Richter, E.Ger	1:03.30	
1978	Linda Jezek, USA	1:02.55	
1982	Kristin Otto, E.Ger	1:01.30	
1986	Betsy Mitchell, USA	1:01.74	
1991	Krisztina Egerszegi, HUN	1:01.78	
1994	He Cihong, CHN	1:00.57	WR

200-meter Backstroke

Year		Time	
1973	Melissa Belote, USA	2:20.52	
1975	Birgit Treiber, E.Ger	2:15.46	WR
1978	Linda Jezek, USA	2:11.93	WR
1982	Cornelia Sirch, E.Ger	2:09.91	WR
1986	Cornelia Sirch, E.Ger	2:11.37	
1991	Krisztina Egerszegi, HUN	2:09.15	
1994	He Cihong, CHN	2:07.40	

100-meter Breaststroke

Year		Time	
1973	Renate Vogel, E.Ger	1:13.74	
1975	Hannalore Anke, E.Ger	1:12.72	
1978	Julia Bogdanova, USSR	1:10.31	WR
1982	Ute Geweniger, E.Ger	1:09.14	
1986	Sylvia Gerasch, E.Ger	1:08.11	WR
1991	Linley Frame, AUS	1:08.81	
1994	Samantha Riley, AUS	1:07.69	WR

200-meter Breaststroke

Year		Time	
1973	Renate Vogel, E.Ger	2:40.01	
1975	Hannalore Anke, E.Ger	2:37.25	
1978	Lina Kachushite, USSR	2:31.42	WR
1982	Svetlana Varganova, USSR	2:28.82	
1986	Silke Hoerner, E.Ger	2:27.40	WR
1991	Elena Volkova, USSR	2:29.53	
1994	Samantha Riley, AUS	2:26.87	

100-meter Butterfly

Year		Time	
1973	Kornelia Ender, E.Ger	1:02.53	
1975	Kornelia Ender, E.Ger	1:01.24	WR
1978	Joan Pennington, USA	1:00.20	
1982	Mary T. Meagher, USA	59.41	
1986	Kornelai Gressler, E.Ger	59.51	
1991	Qian Hong, CHN	59.68	
1994	Liu Limin, CHN	58.98	

200-meter Butterfly

Year		Time	
1973	Rosemarie Kother, E.Ger	2:13.76	
1975	Rosemarie Kother, E.Ger	2:15.92	
1978	Tracy Caulkins, USA	2:09.78	WR
1982	Ines Geissler, E.Ger	2:08.66	
1986	Mary T. Meagher, USA	2:08.41	
1991	Summer Sanders, USA	2:09.24	
1994	Liu Limin, CHN	2:07.25	

200-meter Individual Medley

Year		Time	
1973	Andre Huebner, E.Ger	2:20.51	
1975	Kathy Heddy, USA	2:19.80	
1978	Tracy Caulkins, USA	2:19.80	WR
1982	Petra Schneider, E.Ger	2:11.79	
1986	Kristin Otto, E.Ger	2:15.56	
1991	Lin Li, CHN	2:13.40	
1994	Lu Bin, CHN	2:12.34	

400-meter Individual Medley

Year		Time	
1973	Gudrun Wegner, E.Ger	4:57.71	
1975	Ulrike Tauber, E.Ger	4:52.76	
1978	Tracy Caulkins, USA	4:40.83	WR
1982	Petra Schneider, E.Ger	4:36.10	WR
1986	Kathleen Nord, E.Ger	4:43.75	
1991	Lin Li, CHN	4:41.45	
1994	Dai Guohong, CHN	4:39.14	

4 x 100-meter Freestyle Relay

Year		Time	
1973	East Germany	3:52.45	
1975	East Germany	3:49.37	
1978	United States	3:43.43	WR
1982	East Germany	3:43.97	
1986	East Germany	3:40.57	
1991	United States	3:43.26	
1994	China	3:37.91	WR

4 x 200-meter Freestyle Relay

Year		Time	
1973-82 Not held.			
1986	East Germany	7:59.33	WR
1991	Germany	8:02.56	
1994	China	7:57.96	

4 x 100-meter Medley Relay

Year		Time	
1973	East Germany	4:16.84	
1975	East Germany	4:14.74	
1978	United States	4:08.21	
1982	East Germany	4:05. 8	WR
1986	East Germany	4:04.82	
1991	United States	4:06.51	
1994	China	4:01.67	

Diving

MEN

1-meter Springboard

Year		Pts
1991	Edwin Jongejans, HOL	588.51
1994	Evan Stewart, ZIM	382.14

3-meter Springboard

Year		Pts
1973	Phil Boggs, USA	618.57
1975	Phil Boggs, USA	597.12
1978	Phil Boggs, USA	913.95
1982	Greg Louganis, USA	752.67
1986	Greg Louganis, USA	750.06
1991	Kent Ferguson, USA	650.25
1994	Yu Zhuocheng, CHN	655.44

Platform

Year		Pts
1973	Klaus Dibiasi, ITA	559.53
1975	Klaus Dibiasi, ITA	547.98
1978	Greg Louganis, USA	844.11
1982	Greg Louganis, USA	634.26
1986	Greg Louganis, USA	668.58
1991	Sun Shuwei, CHN	626.79
1994	Dmitri Sautin, RUS	634.71

WOMEN

1-meter Springboard

Year		Pts
1991	Gao Min, CHN	478.26
1994	Chen Lixia, CHN	279.30

3-meter Springboard

Year		Pts
1973	Christa Koehler, E.Ger	442.17
1975	Irina Kalinina, USSR	489.81
1978	Irina Kalinina, USSR	691.43
1982	Megan Neyer, USA	501.03
1986	Gao Min, CHN	582.90
1991	Gao Min, CHN	539.01
1994	Tan Shuping, CHN	548.49

Platform

Year		Pts
1973	Ulrike Knape, SWE	406.77
1975	Janet Ely, USA	403.89
1978	Irina Kalinina, USSR	412.71
1982	Wendy Wyland, USA	438.79
1986	Chen Lin, CHN	449.67
1991	Fu Mingxia, CHN	426.51
1994	Fu Mingxia, CHN	434.04

CYCLING
Tour de France

The world's premier cycling event, the Tour de France is staged throughout the country (sometimes passing through neighboring countries) over four weeks. The 1946 Tour, however, the first after World War II, was only a five-day race.

Multiple winners: Jacques Anquetil, Bernard Hinault and Eddy Merckx (5); Miguel Induráin (4); Louison Bobet, Greg LeMond and Philippe Thys (3); Gino Bartali, Ottavio Bottecchia, Fausto Coppi, Laurent Fignon, Nicholas Frantz, Firmin Lambot, André Leducq, Sylvere Maes, Antonin Magne, Lucien Petit-Breton and Bernard Thevenet (2).

Year		Year		Year	
1903	Maurice Garin, France	1934	Antonin Magne, France	1967	Roger Pingeon, France
1904	Henri Cornet, France	1935	Romain Maes, Belgium	1968	Jan Janssen, Holland
1905	Louis Trousselier, France	1936	Sylvere Maes, Belgium	1969	Eddy Merckx, Belgium
1906	René Pottier, France	1937	Roger Lapebie, France		
1907	Lucien Petit-Breton, France	1938	Gino Bartali, Italy	1970	Eddy Merckx, Belgium
1908	Lucien Petit-Breton, France	1939	Sylvere Maes, Belgium	1971	Eddy Merckx, Belgium
1909	Francois Faber, Luxembourg			1972	Eddy Merckx, Belgium
		1940-45	Not held	1973	Luis Ocana, Spain
1910	Octave Lapize, France	1946	Jean Lazarides, France	1974	Eddy Merckx, Belgium
1911	Gustave Garrigou, France	1947	Jean Robic, France	1975	Bernard Thevenet, France
1912	Odile Defraye, Belgium	1948	Gino Bartali, Italy	1976	Lucien van Impe, Belgium
1913	Philippe Thys, Belgium	1949	Fausto Coppi, Italy	1977	Bernard Thevenet, France
1914	Philippe Thys, Belgium			1978	Bernard Hinault, France
1915-18	Not held	1950	Ferdinand Kubler, Switzerland	1979	Bernard Hinault, France
1919	Firmin Lambot, Belgium	1951	Hugo Koblet, Switzerland		
		1952	Fausto Coppi, Italy	1980	Joop Zoetemelk, Holland
1920	Philippe Thys, Belgium	1953	Louison Bobet, France	1981	Bernard Hinault, France
1921	Léon Scieur, Belgium	1954	Louison Bobet, France	1982	Bernard Hinault, France
1922	Firmin Lambot, Belgium	1955	Louison Bobet, France	1983	Laurent Fignon, France
1923	Henri Pelissier, France	1956	Roger Walkowiak, France	1984	Laurent Fignon, France
1924	Ottavio Bottecchia, Italy	1957	Jacques Anquetil, France	1985	Bernard Hinault, France
1925	Ottavio Bottecchia, Italy	1958	Charly Gaul, Luxembourg	1986	Greg LeMond, USA
1926	Lucien Buysse, Belgium	1959	Federico Bahamontes, Spain	1987	Stephen Roche, Ireland
1927	Nicholas Frantz, Luxembourg			1988	Pedro Delgado, Spain
1928	Nicholas Frantz, Luxembourg	1960	Gastone Nencini, Italy	1989	Greg LeMond, USA
1929	Maurice Dewaele, Belgium	1961	Jacques Anquetil, France		
		1962	Jacques Anquetil, France	1990	Greg LeMond, USA
1930	André Leducq, France	1963	Jacques Anquetil, France	1991	Miguel Induráin, Spain
1931	Antonin Magne, France	1964	Jacques Anquetil, France	1992	Miguel Induráin, Spain
1932	André Leducq, France	1965	Felice Gimondi, Italy	1993	Miguel Induráin, Spain
1933	Georges Speicher, France	1966	Lucien Aimar, France	1994	Miguel Induráin, Spain

ALPINE SKIING
World Cup Overall Champions

World Cup Overall Champions (downhill and slalom events combined) since the tour was organized in 1967.

MEN

Multiple winners: Marc Girardelli (5), Gustavo Thoeni and Pirmin Zurbriggen (4); Phil Mahre, and Ingemar Stenmark (3); Jean-Claude Killy and Karl Schranz (2).

Year		Year		Year	
1967	Jean-Claude Killy, France	1977	Ingemar Stenmark, Sweden	1987	Pirmin Zurbriggen, Switzerland
1968	Jean-Claude Killy, France	1978	Ingemar Stenmark, Sweden	1988	Pirmin Zurbriggen, Switzerland
1969	Karl Schranz, Austria	1979	Peter Luescher, Switzerland	1989	Marc Girardelli, Luxembourg
1970	Karl Schranz, Austria	1980	Andreas Wenzel, Lichtenstein	1990	Pirmin Zurbriggen, Switzerland
1971	Gustavo Thoeni, Italy	1981	Phil Mahre, USA	1991	Marc Girardelli, Luxembourg
1972	Gustavo Thoeni, Italy	1982	Phil Mahre, USA	1992	Paul Accola, Switzerland
1973	Gustavo Thoeni, Italy	1983	Phil Mahre, USA	1993	Marc Girardelli, Luxembourg
1974	Piero Gros, Italy	1984	Pirmin Zurbriggen, Switzerland	1994	Kjetil Andre Aamodt, Norway
1975	Gustavo Thoeni, Italy	1985	Marc Girardelli, Luxembourg		
1976	Ingemar Stenmark, Sweden	1986	Marc Girardelli, Luxembourg		

WOMEN

Multiple winners: Annemarie Moser-Proell (6); Petra Kronberger (3); Michela Figini, Nancy Greene, Erika Hess, Vreni Schneider, Maria Walliser and Hanni Wenzel (2).

Year		Year		Year	
1967	Nancy Greene, Canada	1977	Lise-Marie Morerod, Switzerland	1987	Maria Walliser, Switzerland
1968	Nancy Greene, Canada	1978	Hanni Wenzel, Lichtenstein	1988	Michela Figini, Switzerland
1969	Gertrud Gabi, Austria	1979	Annemarie Moser-Proell, Austria	1989	Vreni Schneider, Switzerland
1970	Michele Jacot, France	1980	Hanni Wenzel, Lichtenstein	1990	Petra Kronberger, Austria
1971	Annemarie Proell, Austria	1981	Marie-Theres Nadig, Switzerland	1991	Petra Kronberger, Austria
1972	Annemarie Proell, Austria	1982	Erika Hess, Switzerland	1992	Petra Kronberger, Austria
1973	Annemarie Proell, Austria	1983	Tamara McKinney, USA	1993	Anita Wachter, Austria
1974	Annemarie Proell, Austria	1984	Erika Hess, Switzerland	1994	Vreni Schneider, Switzerland
1975	Annemarie Moser-Proell, Austria	1985	Michela Figini, Switzerland		
1976	Rosi Mittermaier, W. Germany	1986	Maria Walliser, Switzerland		

FIGURE SKATING

World Champions

Skaters who won World and Olympic championships in the same year are listed in **bold** type.

MEN

Multiple winners: Ulrich Salchow (10); Karl Schafer (7); Dick Button (5); Willy Bockl, Kurt Browning, Scott Hamilton and Hayes Jenkins (4); Emmerich Danzor, Gillis Grafstrom, Gustav Hugel, David Jenkins, Fritz Kachler and Ondrej Nepela (3); Brian Boitano, Gilbert Fuchs, Jan Hoffmann, Felix Kaspar, Vladimir Kovalev and Tim Wood (2).

Year		Year		Year	
1896	Gilbert Fuchs, Germany	1932	**Karl Schafer**, Austria	1968	Emmerich Danzer, Austria
1897	Gustav Hugel, Austria	1933	Karl Schafer, Austria	1969	Tim Wood, USA
1898	Henning Grenander, Sweden	1934	Karl Schafer, Austria	1970	Tim Wood, USA
1899	Gustav Hugel, Austria	1935	Karl Schafer, Austria	1971	Ondrej Nepela, Czechoslovakia
1900	Gustav Hugel, Austria	1936	**Karl Schafer**, Austria	1972	**Ondrej Nepela**, Czechoslovakia
1901	Ulrich Salchow, Sweden	1937	Felix Kaspar, Austria	1973	Ondrej Nepela, Czechoslovakia
1902	Ulrich Salchow, Sweden	1938	Felix Kaspar, Austria	1974	Jan Hoffmann, E. Germany
1903	Ulrich Salchow, Sweden	1939	Graham Sharp, Britain	1975	Sergie Volkov, USSR
1904	Ulrich Salchow, Sweden	1940-46	Not held	1976	**John Curry**, Britain
1905	Ulrich Salchow, Sweden	1947	Hans Gerschwiler, Switzerland	1977	Vladimir Kovalev, USSR
1906	Gilbert Fuchs, Germany	1948	**Dick Button**, USA	1978	Charles Tickner, USA
1907	Ulrich Salchow, Sweden	1949	Dick Button, USA	1979	Vladimir Kovalev, USSR
1908	**Ulrich Salchow**, Sweden	1950	Dick Button, USA	1980	Jan Hoffmann, E. Germany
1909	Ulrich Salchow, Sweden	1951	Dick Button, USA	1981	Scott Hamilton, USA
1910	Ulrich Salchow, Sweden	1952	**Dick Button**, USA	1982	Scott Hamilton, USA
1911	Ulrich Salchow, Sweden	1953	Hayes Jenkins, USA	1983	Scott Hamilton, USA
1912	Fritz Kachler, Austria	1954	Hayes Jenkins, USA	1984	**Scott Hamilton**, USA
1913	Fritz Kachler, Austria	1955	Hayes Jenkins, USA	1985	Alexander Fadeev, USSR
1914	Gosta Sandhal, Sweden	1956	**Hayes Jenkins**, USA	1986	Brian Boitano, USA
1915-21	Not held	1957	David Jenkins, USA	1987	Brian Orser, Canada
1922	Gillis Grafstrom, Sweden	1958	David Jenkins, USA	1988	**Brian Boitano**, USA
1923	Fritz Kachler, Austria	1959	David Jenkins, USA	1989	Kurt Browning, Canada
1924	**Gillis Grafstrom**, Sweden	1960	Alan Giletti, France	1990	Kurt Browning, Canada
1925	Willy Bockl, Austria	1961	Not held	1991	Kurt Browning, Canada
1926	Willy Bockl, Austria	1962	Donald Jackson, Canada	1992	**Viktor Petrenko**, CIS
1927	Willy Bockl, Austria	1963	Donald McPherson, Canada	1993	Kurt Browning, Canada
1928	Willy Bockl, Austria	1964	**Manfred Schnelldorfer**, W.Ger	1994	Elvis Stojko, Canada
1929	Gillis Grafstrom, Sweden	1965	Alain Calmat, France		
1930	Karl Schafer, Austria	1966	Emmerich Danzer, Austria		
1931	Karl Schafer, Austria	1967	Emmerich Danzer, Austria		

WOMEN

Multiple winners: Sonja Henie (10); Carol Heiss and Herma Planck Szabo (5); Lily Kronberger and Katarina Witt (4); Sjoukje Dijkstra, Peggy Fleming, Meray Horvath (3); Tenley Albright, Linda Fratianne, Anett Poetzsch, Beatrix Schuba, Barbara Ann Scott, Gabriele Seyfert, Megan Taylor, Alena Vrzanova, and Kristi Yamaguchi (2).

Year		Year		Year	
1906	Madge Syers, Britain	1932	**Sonja Henie**, Norway	1958	Carol Heiss, USA
1907	Madge Syers, Britian	1933	Sonja Henie, Norway	1959	Carol Heiss, USA
1908	Lily Kronberger, Hungary	1934	Sonja Henie, Norway	1960	**Carol Heiss**, USA
1909	Lily Kronberger, Hungary	1935	Sonja Henie, Norway	1961	Not held
1910	Lily Kronberger, Hungary	1936	**Sonja Henie**, Norway	1962	Sjoukje Dijkstra, Holland
1911	Lily Kronberger, Hungary	1937	Cecilia Colledge, Britain	1963	Sjoukje Dijkstra, Holland
1912	Meray Horvath, Hungary	1938	Megan Taylor, Britain	1964	**Sjoukje Dijkstra**, Holland
1913	Meray Horvath, Hungary	1939	Megan Taylor, Britain	1965	Petra Burka, Canada
1914	Meray Horvath, Hungary	1940-46	Not held	1966	Peggy Fleming, USA
1915-21	Not held	1947	Barbara Ann Scott, Canada	1967	Peggy Fleming, USA
1922	Herma Planck-Szabo, Austria	1948	**Barbara Ann Scott**, Canada	1968	**Peggy Fleming**, USA
1923	Herma Planck-Szabo, Austria	1949	Alena Vrzanova, Czechoslovakia	1969	Gabriele Seyfert, E. Germany
1924	**Herma Planck-Szabo**, Austria	1950	Alena Vrzanova, Czechoslovakia	1970	Gabriele Seyfert, E. Germany
1925	Herma Planck-Szabo, Austria	1951	Jeannette Altwegg, Britain	1971	Beatrix Schuba, Austria
1926	Herma Planck-Szabo, Austria	1952	Jacqueline Du Bief, France	1972	**Beatrix Schuba**, Austria
1927	Sonja Henie, Norway	1953	Tenley Albright, USA	1973	Karen Magnussen, Canada
1928	**Sonja Henie**, Norway	1954	Gundi Busch, W. Germany	1974	Christine Errath, E. Germany
1929	Sonja Henie, Norway	1955	Tenley Albright, USA	1975	Dianne DeLeeuw, Holland
1930	Sonja Henie, Norway	1956	Carol Heiss, USA	1976	**Dorothy Hamill**, USA
1931	Sonja Henie, Norway	1957	Carol Heiss, USA	1977	Linda Fratianne, USA

Figure Skating (Cont.)
World Champions
WOMEN

Year		Year		Year	
1978	Anett Poetzsch, E. Germany	1984	**Katarina Witt**, E. Germany	1990	Jill Trenary, USA
1979	Linda Fratianne, USA	1985	Katarina Witt, E. Germany	1991	Kristi Yamaguchi, USA
1980	**Anett Poetzsch**, E. Germany	1986	Debi Thomas, USA	1992	**Kristi Yamaguchi**, USA
1981	Denise Biellmann, Switzerland	1987	Katarina Witt, E. Germany	1993	Oksana Baiul, Ukraine
1982	Elaine Zayak, USA	1988	**Katarina Witt**, E. Germany	1994	Yuka Sato, Japan
1983	Rosalyn Sumners, USA	1989	Midori Ito, Japan		

U.S. Champions
Skaters who won U.S., World and Olympic championships in same year are in **bold** type.

MEN

Multiple winners: Dick Button and Roger Turner (7); Sherwin Badger, Robin Lee (5); Brian Boitano, Scott Hamilton, David Jenkins, Hayes Jenkins and Charles Tickner (4); Gordon McKellen, Nathaniel Niles and Tim Wood (3); Scott Allen, Christopher Bowman, Scott Davis, Todd Eldredge, Eugene Turner and Gary Visconti (2).

Year		Year		Year		Year	
1914	Norman Scott	1936	Robin Lee	1957	David Jenkins	1977	Charles Tickner
1915-17	Not held	1937	Robin Lee	1958	David Jenkins	1978	Charles Tickner
1918	Nathaniel Niles	1938	Robin Lee	1959	David Jenkins	1979	Charles Tickner
1919	Not held	1939	Robin Lee	1960	David Jenkins	1980	Charles Tickner
1920	Sherwin Badger	1940	Eugene Turner	1961	Bradley Lord	1981	Scott Hamilton
1921	Sherwin Badger	1941	Eugene Turner	1962	Monty Hoyt	1982	Scott Hamilton
1922	Sherwin Badger	1942	Robert Specht	1963	Thomas Litz	1983	Scott Hamilton
1923	Sherwin Badger	1943	Arthur Vaughn	1964	Scott Allen	1984	**Scott Hamilton**
1924	Sherwin Badger	1944-45	Not held	1965	Gary Visconti	1985	Brian Boitano
1925	Nathaniel Niles	1946	Dick Button	1966	Scott Allen	1986	Brian Boitano
1926	Chris Christenson	1947	Dick Button	1967	Gary Visconti	1987	Brian Boitano
1927	Nathaniel Niles	1948	**Dick Button**	1968	Tim Wood	1988	**Brian Boitano**
1928	Roger Turner	1949	Dick Button	1969	Tim Wood	1989	Christopher Bowman
1929	Roger Turner	1950	Dick Button	1970	Tim Wood	1990	Todd Eldredge
1930	Roger Turner	1951	Dick Button	1971	John (Misha) Petkevich	1991	Todd Eldredge
1931	Roger Turner	1952	**Dick Button**	1972	Ken Shelley	1992	Christopher Bowman
1932	Roger Turner	1953	Hayes Jenkins	1973	Gordon McKellen	1993	Scott Davis
1933	Roger Turner	1954	Hayes Jenkins	1974	Gordon McKellen	1994	Scott Davis
1934	Roger Turner	1955	Hayes Jenkins	1975	Gordon McKellen		
1935	Robin Lee	1956	**Hayes Jenkins**	1976	Terry Kubicka		

WOMEN

Multiple winners: Maribel Vinson (9); Theresa Weld Blanchard and Gretchen Merrill (6); Tenley Albright, Peggy Fleming, and Janet Lynn (5); Linda Fratianne and Carol Heiss (4); Dorothy Hamill, Beatrix Loughran, Rosalyn Summers, Joan Tozzer and Jill Trenary (3); Yvonne Sherman and Debi Thomas (2).

Year		Year		Year		Year	
1914	Theresa Weld	1936	Maribel Vinson	1956	Tenley Albright	1976	**Dorothy Hamill**
1915-17	Not held	1937	Maribel Vinson	1957	Carol Heiss	1977	Linda Fratianne
1918	Rosemary Beresford	1938	Joan Tozzer	1958	Carol Heiss	1978	Linda Fratianne
1919	Not held	1939	Joan Tozzer	1959	Carol Heiss	1979	Linda Fratianne
1920	Theresa Weld	1940	Joan Tozzer	1960	**Carol Heiss**	1980	Linda Fratianne
1921	Theresa Blanchard	1941	Jane Vaughn	1961	Laurence Owen	1981	Elaine Zayak
1922	Theresa Blanchard	1942	Jane Sullivan	1962	Barbara Pursley	1982	Rosalyn Sumners
1923	Theresa Blanchard	1943	Gretchen Merrill	1963	Lorraine Hanlon	1983	Rosalyn Sumners
1924	Theresa Blanchard	1944	Gretchen Merrill	1964	Peggy Fleming	1984	Rosalyn Sumners
1925	Beatrix Loughran	1945	Gretchen Merrill	1965	Peggy Fleming	1985	Tiffany Chin
1926	Beatrix Loughran	1946	Gretchen Merrill	1966	Peggy Fleming	1986	Debi Thomas
1927	Beatrix Loughran	1947	Gretchen Merrill	1967	Peggy Fleming	1987	Jill Trenary
1928	Maribel Vinson	1948	Gretchen Merrill	1968	**Peggy Fleming**	1988	Debi Thomas
1929	Maribel Vinson	1949	Yvonne Sherman	1969	Janet Lynn	1989	Jill Trenary
1930	Maribel Vinson	1950	Yvonne Sherman	1970	Janet Lynn	1990	Jill Trenary
1931	Maribel Vinson	1951	Sonya Klopfer	1971	Janet Lynn	1991	Tonya Harding
1932	Maribel Vinson	1952	Tenley Albright	1972	Janet Lynn	1992	**Kristi Yamaguchi**
1933	Maribel Vinson	1953	Tenley Albright	1973	Janet Lynn	1993	Nancy Kerrigan
1934	Suzanne Davis	1954	Tenley Albright	1974	Dorothy Hamill	1994	vacated*
1935	Maribel Vinson	1955	Tenley Albright	1975	Dorothy Hamill		

*Tonya Harding was stripped of the 1994 women's title and banned from membership in the U.S. Figure Skating Assn. for life on June 30, for violating the USFSA Code of Ethics after she pleaded guilty to a charge of conspiracy to hinder the prosecution related to the Jan. 6 attack on Nancy Kerrigan.

Billy Stickland/Allsport

Midfielder **Mazinho** holds World Cup trophy aloft after Brazil's shootout victory over Italy in the Cup final at the Rose Bowl on July 17.

SOCCER

Samba Time

*Brazil wins unprecedented 4th World Cup championship,
as the United States hosts best-attended tournament ever.*

"It will be the greatest World Cup ever." Thus spake Alan Rothenberg, the man in charge of World Cup USA '94.

"The United States is underwhelmed about soccer. The World Cup will be played in half-empty stadia." That was the view of English sportswriter Michael Herd, one of the many skeptics who felt that staging the tournament in the U.S., not a traditional soccer country, was a huge mistake, doomed to failure.

Rothenberg came out on top of this one. By almost every measure the 1994 World Cup was a resounding success. Far from stadiums being half empty, the tournament set a new World Cup record: a total of 3,567,415 spectators watched the 52 games, over 1 million more than the previous record set in Italy in 1990.

Evidently, the soccer Gods were smiling on the USA. The organizers got lucky when both Iraq and Iran—seen as bringing potential terrorist problems with them—failed to qualify.

But the big break came when, against all expectations, England failed to make it. The dreaded English fans, the hooligans who had caused mayhem all over Europe, would not be coming. Security costs, always

likely to be the biggest expense, would be substantially reduced.

In fact, little security was needed. It was smiles all around as a party atmosphere took over and the rival fans did their thing: the orange-clad Dutch in their clogs, the blue-and-white Argentines throwing their confetti, the yellow-and-blue Brazilians beating out their samba rhythms, the Norwegians with their horned viking helmets, the Irish with their banners and their songs.

Actually, the Irish did have a complaint. About the heat. Their coach, Jack Charlton, thought it possible that "players will die out there." Then the team went out and—on a suffocatingly steamy afternoon in New Jersey's Giants Stadium—upset Italy 1-0.

There were bigger surprises to come. Colombia, rated by many as a possible World Cup champion, went down 3-1 to Romania in its first game. That brought on a must-win game against the USA—which the Americans, playing defensively but intelligently, won 2-1.

The Colombians were out, amid sinister controversy. Death threats had been issued to the coaching staff before the USA game. Veteran midfielder Gabriel Gomez must not play, said the threats—and Gomez was duly banished to the bench.

Much worse was to come. The first American goal came off the foot of Colombian defender Andres Escobar when he inadvertently put the ball into his own net. Soon after his return to Colombia with

Paul Gardner has been the columnist for *Soccer America* since 1982. He has covered international soccer as a writer and broadcaster in Europe and the U.S. since 1964 and has written four books on the sport.

Brazil's starting lineup in Cup final against Italy (left to right): front row— **Mazinho, Romario, Dunga, Bebeto, Zinho;** back row— **Taffarel, Jorginho, Aldair, Mauro Silva, Marcio Santos** and **Branco.**

his defeated teammates, Escobar was shot dead outside a Medellín restaurant— apparently in reprisal for his error.

For Argentina there was tragedy of a different kind. After convincing victories over Greece and Nigeria, the team was being hailed as a serious candidate for the title. Not least because Diego Maradona was back as captain. Back after a 15-month suspension for cocaine use and a host of other troubles that included discharging an air gun at journalists near his home. He looked—if not as quick at age 33—certainly as wily as ever.

But just before Argentina's final first round game against Bulgaria, the rumors started that an unidentified player had shown a positive drug test. (Two randomly-selected players from each team are tested after every game). Attention quickly focused on Maradona. Journalists besieged the team's hotel until Julio Grondona, president of the Argentine Soccer Federation, admitted that Maradona was the culprit.

The test revealed a range of ephedrine-related drugs in Maradona's urine sample. The drugs are commonly used as weight-reducers (Maradona had shed over 20 pounds in preparation for the World Cup), but also have stimulant properties. "Maradona must have taken a cocktail of drugs," said Belgian Michel D'Hooghe, head of FIFA's medical committee. "These substances are not found together in one medicine."

Grondona grumbled "I can't follow every player to the bathroom, they know what they're doing." Fearing that his team might be punished along with his captain, Grondona voluntarily withdrew Maradona from the tournament. It was a decision that surely marked a sad end to the career of one of the sport's greatest players.

Without Maradona, Argentina played poorly and lost to Bulgaria, but advanced to the second round anyway. Against Romania—in what many rated as the most spectacular game of the entire tournament—Argentina recovered to play brilliantly, and was unlucky to go down, and out of the tournament, by a 3-2 score.

Italy, Germany and Brazil—all among the pre-tournament favorites—advanced. But the Germans looked very ordinary and almost succumbed to a determined South Korean team that fought back from 3-0

Shaun Botterill/Allsport

Ben Radford/Allsport

Italy's **Roberto Baggio** (left) and Brazil's **Romario** carried their teams to the World Cup final. But while Romario won the MVP award, Baggio had to overcome his disbelief at missing a do-or-die penalty kick at the end of the game.

down to make the score 3-2. "They played hara-kiri soccer," said a stunned Berti Vogts, the German coach. "They really played attacking soccer." The German cause was not helped by midfielder Stefan Effenberg, who flipped his finger at heckling fans in Dallas. After the game, Vogts told Effenberg to pack his bags and leave the team.

Brazil was the most impressive team of the first round, with comfortable wins over Russia and Cameroon, and a tie with Sweden. In forwards Romario and Bebeto they had the deadliest attackers in the competition.

The Italians had a deadly attacker too, in the pony-tailed 1993 Player of the Year Roberto Baggio; but their tradition of playing poorly in the first round continued, and they squeaked through as a third place team.

The USA also made it as a third place team, despite a 1-0 loss to Romania in its final first round game. A 1-1 tie against Switzerland and the victory over Colombia saw the Americans through.

Relying on a packed defense of Marcelo Balboa, Alexi Lalas, Paul Caligiuri and either Fernando Clavijo or Cle Kooiman, plus midfielders Mike Sorber, Tom Dooley and John Harkes playing essentially defensive roles, coach Bora Milutinovic's cautious tactics achieved what was always the USA's minimum aim: a place in the second round. As midfielder Tom Dooley put it: "For the U.S. to reach the second round is the same as Germany winning the World Cup."

The next opponent was Brazil—now firmly positioned as the tournament favorite—on July 4 at Stanford Stadium in Palo Alto. Two days before the game, President Clinton telephoned good luck wishes to Milutinovic, saying "We're all going to sit here on pins and needles and cheer for you. All of America is. We're very proud of you."

A sunlit afternoon, a crowd of 84,147 fans full of noisy support for the Americans, a nationwide television audience on ABC—but there was to be no upset.

Milutinovic had joked that his players "should not ask for autographs from the Brazilians before the game." Certainly the Americans were not in awe, but they did little more than make life difficult for Brazil.

Milutinovic's cautious tactics almost

ensured this. Second round games, if tied after overtime, used the penalty kick shoot-out as a tiebreaker. Milutinovic had openly talked of frustrating the Brazilians and taking the game to the tiebreaker.

The USA kept the score down but there were those who would have liked to see the Americans playing a more enterprising game. Even when Brazil was reduced to 10 men after defender Leonardo was ejected in the 44th minute of the game for elbowing Tab Ramos in the face, the USA could make little impression. Brazil continued its domination, and Bebeto got the inevitable goal (on an assist from Romario) after 74 minutes.

"Nobody is going to take us for granted any more," said defender Marcelo Balboa, the star of the game for the USA. "We've proved throughout this World Cup that we're a very good team."

Still, the Americans took the defeat hard. "Five years back, maybe a 1-0 loss to Brazil was considered really good for the U.S.," said forward Ernie Stewart. "But today, everybody is really disappointed."

Not everybody. American fans, who had managed to hold their own against the samba-drumming Brazilian rooters all afternoon, saluted their team with a roaring "U-S-A" chant as the players left the field.

Meanwhile, Bulgaria was becoming the unsung longshot of the tournament. Before USA '94, the Bulgarians had played in just five World Cups, and had yet to record a win. After an opening game 3-0 loss to Nigeria, the Bulgarians' overall Cup record was a dismal 10 losses and six ties.

Things changed when striker Hristo Stoitchkov scored twice in a 4-0 win over Greece. He scored again in wins over Argentina and Mexico, and the Bulgarians found themselves in the quarterfinals.

They did have an unusual problem. Exalted after the victory against Argentina, the players had hit the town in Dallas and photographs of them posing with female friends had been published back home in Bulgaria. In no time, a charter flight had been organized, and the players' wives arrived in the U.S. "Playing the Mexicans didn't worry me," said coach Dimitar Penev. "I was more worried about what the wives would do to us."

Bulgaria's quarterfinal opponent was Germany, the reigning world champions.

Ben Radford/Allsport

Hristo Stoitchkov scored six goals in seven games to lead unsung Bulgaria past Germany and into the semifinals.

With only 15 minutes left in the game, the Germans were leading 1-0 on a penalty kick from captain Lothar Matthaus. But in four dramatic minutes, they were undone. First, Stoitchkov hooked a vicious left foot free kick over the German defensive wall and into the goal. Then the balding Yordan Letchkov launched himself in a spectacular forward dive to head in the winner in the 79th minute.

Germany was out, and God, said Stoitchkov, was Bulgarian.

On to the semifinals went Bulgaria, there to face Italy. The Italians had continued their death-defying heroics. Coach Arrigo Sacchi had never used the same lineup twice, because of player suspensions, or injuries, or for tactical reasons. The biggest blow had come when defender and team captain Franco Baresi had to undergo arthroscopic surgery for a knee injury.

But Baggio had come through. Against Nigeria he had scored the tying goal with only two minutes left, then hit the winner in overtime. He got another winner against Spain, again with only two minutes left in the game.

Against Bulgaria he was on target again, scoring twice in the 21st and 26th minutes. The Bulgarians, who gave the impression that beating Germany had been their high for the tournament, could reply with only a penalty kick goal from Nasko Sirakov.

Stoitchkov was not happy with French referee Joel Quiniou, recalling that Bulgaria had eliminated France in the qualifying rounds. "God is still Bulgarian," he said, "but today the referee was French."

The excitement of getting to the final was clouded for the Italians by yet another setback. Central defender Alessandro Costacurta was out of the game, suspended for receiving his second yellow card caution.

Meanwhile, Brazil marched inexorably on. Wins against Holland (3-2) and Sweden (1-0) saw them into the final at the Rose Bowl in Pasadena. By now, it was clear that all the other teams were scared of the Brazilians. Both the Dutch and the Swedes played defensively (as had the USA), and Brazil found it difficult to break down the massed defenses.

The Italians proved no different. The field was crowded with top class players, but it was the coaches' tactics that dominated the day.

Coach Sacchi opted for defense and left his top scorer, Giuseppe Signori, on the bench. But he did play the questionably-fit Baggio as well as Baresi, who had miraculously recovered only 18 days after his knee surgery.

For Brazil, coach Carlos Alberto Parreira continued with his hard-working, hard-running midfield of Dunga, Mazinho, Mauro Silva and Zinho. The artistry and creativity that had traditionally distinguished Brazilian play was missing.

It was more like chess than a soccer game. Move and countermove, and ultimately stalemate: 0-0 after 90 minutes and still scoreless after 30 minutes of overtime. For the first time in World Cup history, a scoreless final.

Also for the first time, a final decided on penalty kicks. Brazil took the tiebreaker 3-2. For Italy, the big misses in the shoot-out came from the top stars: Baggio, who struggled throughout the game, and Baresi, who had played magnificently. "We emerged from hell and came within touching distance of paradise," said Sacchi.

The victory made Brazil the World Cup's first four-time winner, having won previously in 1958, 1962 and 1970. Parreira had withstood the batterings of those who accused him of deserting the traditional Brazilian attacking game. There was truth in the criticisms; the Brazilians ended up in the unfamiliar position of having the tournament's best defense, with only three goals conceded in seven games.

But Parreira's tactics had triumphed. "I did

What Now For Soccer In U.S.?

When Alan Rothenberg first stood for president of the United States Soccer Federation in 1990, he was an outsider not previously involved in soccer politics. His chances of election seemed slim, but he swept to power on the first ballot.

Four years later, Rothenberg sought reelection as the man who had run the massively successful World Cup USA '94, and who had just announced that the tournament would turn over a profit of $50 million that would go towards the development of the sport.

A shoo-in? Not at all. This time it took two ballots, as his opponent—USSF treasurer Richard Groff—got 46 per cent of the votes.

What was the problem here? The opposition to Rothenberg centered on his plans for creating a national professional league. This league—to be called Major League Soccer, or MLS—is scheduled to begin operations in April 1995.

To start with, the pro division of the USSF already includes four leagues. The American Professional Soccer League—which has seven teams, including three in Canada—believes it is already the nation's pro league. Said APSL chairman William De La Pena: "The APSL offers the highest level of professional soccer in North America and our goal is to remain at the top of the sport." Not unreasonably, the APSL felt threatened by the MLS plan.

The APSL found anti-Rothenberg allies in the two indoor leagues, the Continental Indoor Soccer League and the National Professional Soccer League. All three leagues strongly objected to the fact that Rothenberg not only wanted to be USSF president, but that he intended to run MLS as well. Not only that, he would have a financial involvement in MLS.

"Other people have contributed to the growth of soccer in this country," said candidate Groff. "I don't think Rothenberg should be in charge of everything."

But the opposition to Rothenberg went deeper than accusations of power-grabbing. His insistence on being both USSF president and CEO of MLS was seen by many as a clear conflict of interest. Could he operate impartially as head of the USSF, which is the supervisory body of all the pro leagues—including his own MLS?

Wide World Photos

One of the many problems facing fledgling Major League Soccer is holding on to home-grown stars, like defender **Alexi Lalas**, who have already signed to play with first division clubs in Europe.

Rothenberg said he could, and would recuse himself from any involvement when conflict threatened. Otherwise, Rothenberg saw not a conflict but rather "a confluence of interests. Just as my dual position as USSF president and head of the World Cup helped both organizations."

Unease about the situation among USSF voters accounted for Rothenberg's narrow margin of victory. And from the APSL came mumblings of possible legal action.

But the immediate business for Rothenberg after his victory was not to defend MLS in the courts, but to make sure that the new league actually began operating in April 1995.

A daunting task. There were obstacles at every turn. Money, for a start. Rothenberg had originally announced that $100 million would be needed to float the league. But at the time of the USSF election on Aug. 10, no investors had been announced. Work on the league was being financed by a loan of $5 million from the World Cup profits.

MLS was planned as a 12-team league, but only seven cities had been announced by election time. One of the thorniest problems was finding suitable stadiums. MLS believed that "the ideal venue for pro soccer in the United States should have a capacity of between 20,000 and 30,000." As there were

virtually no such stadiums of the necessary quality, the answer was to "downsize" larger stadiums "by, among other things, attractively draping off upper decks."

Finding players was not going to be easy either. MLS is committed to developing American players, and will have a limit of four or five foreigners per team—which means that something like 200 top-caliber American pros have to be signed before April 1995.

The pessimists insist that the players just aren't there. Even the optimists admit that there will be problems finding that number of players who are free from commitments to other clubs. There was also the awkward fact that the best U.S. players—like Tab Ramos, John Harkes, Eric Wynalda and Kasey Keller—were all playing for European clubs.

But even as MLS claimed that it would "commit funds to bring home many of those U.S. players currently playing abroad," players from the younger generation—Alexi Lalas, Cobi Jones, Brad Friedel and Claudio Reyna—were signing contracts to play in Europe.

Such challenges are exactly what Rothenberg seems to thrive on. MLS, he says, will be a league that "will soon rank with the finest in the world."

Wide World Photos

Diego Maradona addresses the media following his dismissal from Argentina's World Cup squad on June 30, after testing positive for banned drugs.

it my way," he told the press after the final. Bebeto made the crucial point: "We were the best team—that is proved, because everyone we played changed their style against us."

Bebeto's forward partner Romario, a feisty character whom Parreira had originally left off the team until immense popular pressure forced his recall, said: "I'm a winner. Wherever I go I win titles—I knew this would be Romario's World Cup."

Sure enough, Romario was voted the tournament's Most Valuable Player. He was not the top scorer, however. That honor was shared by Stoichkov and Russia's Oleg Salenko with six goals each. Five of Salenko's tally had come in a 6-1 rout of Cameroon—a new World Cup single-game record.

But the final had not been the sparkling game that this lively tournament deserved. There was general disappointment that it had to end in a scoreless tie, and something approaching outrage at the use of penalty kicks to decide a world championship. FIFA promised to rethink things, but its immediate decision to make the 30-minute overtime period sudden-death smacked of panic. Cautious coaches, afraid of conceding a goal, are a major part of soccer's problem. Sudden death would surely make them even more cautious.

But overall FIFA was delighted with the tournament: record crowds, record profits, and a great improvement on Italia '90, both

in quality of play and in goal-scoring, which went up from 2.21 per game to 2.76.

The gate receipts for the final were $43.5 million—a record for a sporting event—and the ratings for the ABC telecast showed over 35 million viewers in the U.S., the highest-ever for a soccer game. "These numbers continue to excite us," said FIFA general Secretary Sepp Blatter.

There was open discussion of the World Cup returning to the United States as soon as 2006. For Alan Rothenberg, however, there was little time to enjoy the euphoria. The huge task of exploiting the soccer enthusiasm and launching a national pro league by April 1995 beckoned.

On the eve of the World Cup, the 78-year-old president of FIFA Joao Havelange had mercilessly quashed a move to replace him, and had been re-elected for his sixth four-year term. He announced that, starting with the next World Cup, in France in 1998, the number of finalists would be increased from 24 to 32.

In other FIFA matters: the number of FIFA member nations went up to 191; Japan pressed its bid to stage the 2002 World Cup, but was now challenged by a bid from South Korea; and Sweden was officially named as the venue for the second FIFA Women's World Championship in 1995. The United States won the first Women's World Championship, played in China in 1991, beating Norway, 2-1, in the final.

Of course, there was soccer life beyond the World Cup. São Paulo of Brazil took the world club championship for the second year running, beating AC Milan, 3-2, in the Intercontinental Cup on Dec. 12, 1993. Nigeria won the African Nations' Cup with a 2-1 victory over surprising Zambia, which had rebuilt its squad after its first team was virtually wiped out in an air crash in 1993.

Franz Beckenbauer shocked everyone by returning—temporarily—to coaching duties with Bayern Munich, and leading them to the German championship.

And Paul Gascoigne, England's wayward star, forever in the news and forever in trouble, broke his leg in a practice session for his Italian club Lazio. The Italian press calculated that Gascoigne's irregular appearances for the club were costing it $600 per minute. ❑

THE 1995 INFORMATION PLEASE SPORTS ALMANAC

SOCCER STATISTICS

THE SEASON IN REVIEW
1993-1994
WORLD • EUROPE • AMERICA

SEC A

PAGE 675

World Cup USA '94
Final Qualifying

Each team played every other team in it's group twice over two years (Mar. 1, 1992 to Nov. 17, 1993). Note that (*) indicates team qualified for 24-team World Cup tournament, and (†) indicates team advanced to sectional playoff.

EUROPE

Qualifiers (12): Belgium, Bulgaria, Greece, Holland, Ireland, Italy, Norway, Romania, Russia, Spain, Sweden and Switzerland. **Automatic berth:** Germany (as defending champion).

Group 1	Gm	W	L	T	Pts	GF	GA
* Italy	10	7	1	2	16	22	7
* Switzerland	10	6	1	3	15	23	6
Portugal	10	6	2	2	14	18	5
Scotland	10	4	3	3	11	14	13
Malta	10	1	8	1	3	3	23
Estonia	10	0	9	1	1	1	27

Group 2	Gm	W	L	T	Pts	GF	GA
* Norway	10	7	1	2	16	25	5
* Holland	10	6	1	3	15	29	9
England	10	5	2	3	13	26	9
Poland	10	3	5	2	8	10	15
Turkey	10	3	6	1	7	11	19
San Marino	10	0	9	1	1	2	46

Group 3	Gm	W	L	T	Pts	GF	GA
* Spain	12	8	1	3	19	27	4
* Ireland	12	7	1	4	18	19	6
Denmark	12	7	1	4	18	15	2
Northern Ireland	12	5	4	3	13	14	13
Lithuania	12	2	7	3	7	8	21
Latvia	12	0	7	5	5	4	21
Albania	12	1	9	2	4	6	26

Group 4	Gm	W	L	T	Pts	GF	GA
* Romania	10	7	2	1	15	29	12
* Belgium	10	7	2	1	15	16	5
Czechs/Slovaks	10	4	1	5	13	21	9
Wales	10	5	3	2	12	19	12
Cyprus	10	2	7	1	5	8	18
Faeroe Islands	10	0	10	0	0	1	38

Group 5	Gm	W	L	T	Pts	GF	GA
* Greece	8	6	0	2	14	10	2
* Russia	8	5	1	2	12	15	4
Iceland	8	3	3	2	8	7	6
Hungary	8	2	5	1	5	6	11
Luxembourg	8	0	7	1	1	2	17

Group 6	Gm	W	L	T	Pts	GF	GA
* Sweden	10	6	1	3	15	19	8
* Bulgaria	10	6	2	2	14	19	10
France	10	6	3	1	13	17	10
Austria	10	3	5	2	8	15	16
Finland	10	2	7	1	5	9	18
Israel	10	1	6	3	5	10	27

Note: In Group 3, Ireland qualified over Denmark by virtue of total goals (19-15). Otherwise, the Irish and Danes tied in goal differential (+13).

SOUTH AMERICA

Qualifiers (4): Argentina, Bolivia, Brazil and Colombia. Group B runner-up Argentina qualified via inter-regional playoff round, beating Oceania champion Australia (1-1 at Sydney and 1-0 at Buenos Aires).

Group A	Gm	W	L	T	Pts	GF	GA
* Colombia	6	4	0	2	10	13	2
Argentina	6	3	1	2	8	7	9
Paraguay	6	1	2	3	5	6	7
Peru	6	0	5	1	1	4	12

Note: Runner-up Argentina advanced to playoff vs. winner of playoff between Oceania champion and CONCACAF runner-up.

Group B	Gm	W	L	T	Pts	GF	GA
* Brazil	8	5	1	2	12	20	4
* Bolivia	8	5	2	1	11	22	11
Uruguay	8	4	2	2	10	10	7
Ecuador	8	1	4	3	5	7	7
Venezuela	8	1	7	0	2	4	34

CONCACAF

Qualifier: Mexico. **Automatic berth:** United States (as host country).

Final Round	Gm	W	L	T	Pts	GF	GA
* Mexico	6	5	1	0	10	17	5
† Canada	6	3	2	1	7	10	10
El Salvador	6	2	4	0	4	6	11
Honduras	6	1	4	1	3	7	14

ASIA

Qualifiers (2): Saudi Arabia and South Korea.

Final Round	Gm	W	L	T	Pts	GF	GA
* Saudi Arabia	5	2	0	3	7	8	7
* South Korea	5	2	1	2	6	9	4
Japan	5	2	1	2	6	7	4
Iraq	5	1	1	3	5	9	9
Iran	5	2	3	0	4	8	11
North Korea	5	1	4	0	2	5	12

Notes: All matches played in Doha, Qatar. South Korea qualified over Japan by virtue of goal differential (+5 to +3).

World Cup USA '94 (Cont.)
Final Qualifying

AFRICA

Qualifiers (3): Cameroon, Morocco and Nigeria.

Group A	Gm	W	L	T	Pts	GF	GA
*Nigeria	4	2	1	1	5	10	5
Ivory Coast	4	2	1	1	5	6	5
Algeria	4	0	2	2	1	3	7

Group B	Gm	W	L	T	Pts	GF	GA
*Morocco	4	3	1	0	6	6	3
Zambia	4	2	1	1	5	6	2
Senegal	4	0	3	1	1	1	8

Group C	Gm	W	L	T	Pts	GF	GA
*Cameroon	4	3	1	0	6	7	3
Zimbabwe	4	2	2	0	4	3	6
Guinea	4	1	3	0	2	4	5

OCEANIA

Qualifiers: none.

Final	Gm	W	L	T	Pts	GF	GA
†Australia	2	2	0	0	4	4	0
New Zealand	2	0	2	0	0	0	4

SECTIONAL PLAYOFFS
(Home team in CAPITAL letters)

First round: CANADA def. Australia, 2-1; AUSTRALIA def. Canada, 2-1 (Australia advances on PKs, 4-1).
Qualifier round: AUSTRALIA tied Argentina, 1-1; ARGENTINA def. Australia, 1-0 (Argentina advances on total goals).

WORLD CUP TOURNAMENT

The 15th World Cup, hosted by the United States from June 17 to July 17, 1994.

FIRST ROUND

Round Robin; each team played the other three teams in its group once. Note that three points were awarded for a win and one point for a tie and (*) indicates team advanced to second round.

Group A	Gm	W	L	T	Pts	GF	GA
*Romania	3	2	1	0	6	5	5
*Switzerland	3	1	1	1	4	5	4
*United States	3	1	1	1	4	3	3
Colombia	3	1	2	0	3	4	5

Results

6/18	Pontiac (73,425)	USA 1, Switzerland 1
6/18	Pasadena (91,856)	Romania 3, Colombia 1
6/22	Pontiac (61,428)	Switzerland 4, Romania 1
6/22	Pasadena (93,124)	USA 2, Colombia 1
6/26	Pasadena (93,869)	Romania 1, USA 0
6/26	Stanford (83,769)	Colombia 2, Switzerland 0

Group B	Gm	W	L	T	Pts	GF	GA
*Brazil	3	2	0	1	7	6	1
*Sweden	3	1	0	2	5	6	4
Russia	3	1	2	0	3	7	6
Cameroon	3	0	2	1	1	3	11

Results

6/19	Pasadena (83,959)	Cameroon 2, Sweden 2
6/20	Stanford (81,061)	Brazil 2, Russia 0
6/24	Stanford (83,401)	Brazil 3, Cameroon 0
6/24	Pontiac (71,528)	Sweden 3, Russia 1
6/28	Stanford (74,914)	Russia 6, Cameroon 1
6/28	Pontiac (77,217)	Brazil 1, Sweden 1

Group C	Gm	W	L	T	Pts	GF	GA
*Germany	3	2	0	1	7	5	3
*Spain	3	1	0	2	5	6	4
South Korea	3	0	1	2	2	4	5
Bolivia	3	0	2	1	1	1	4

Results

6/17	Chicago (62,000)	Germany 1, Bolivia 0
6/17	Dallas (56,247)	South Korea 2, Spain 2
6/21	Chicago (63,113)	Germany 1, Spain 1
6/23	Foxboro (53,500)	Bolivia 0, South Korea 0
6/27	Chicago (63,089)	Spain 3, Bolivia 1
6/27	Dallas (63,998)	Germany 3, South Korea 2

Group D	Gm	W	L	T	Pts	GF	GA
*Nigeria	3	2	1	0	6	6	2
*Bulgaria	3	2	1	0	6	6	3
*Argentina	3	2	1	0	6	6	3
Greece	3	0	3	0	0	0	10

Results

6/21	Foxboro (53,644)	Argentina 4, Greece 0
6/21	Dallas (44,132)	Nigeria 3, Bulgaria 0
6/25	Foxboro (54,453)	Argentina 2, Nigeria 1
6/26	Chicago (63,160)	Bulgaria 4, Greece 0
6/30	Foxboro (53,001)	Nigeria 2, Greece 0
6/30	Dallas (63,998)	Bulgaria 2, Argentina 0

Group E	Gm	W	L	T	Pts	GF	GA
*Mexico	3	1	1	1	4	3	3
*Ireland	3	1	1	1	4	2	2
*Italy	3	1	1	1	4	2	2
Norway	3	1	1	1	4	1	1

Results

6/18	E. Rutherford (73,511)	Ireland 1, Italy 0
6/19	Washington (52,359)	Norway 1, Mexico 0
6/23	E. Rutherford (74,624)	Italy 1, Norway 0
6/24	Orlando (61,219)	Mexico 2, Ireland 1
6/28	E. Rutherford (76,322)	Ireland 0, Norway 0
6/28	Washington (53,186)	Italy 1, Mexico 1

Group F	Gm	W	L	T	Pts	GF	GA
*Holland	3	2	1	0	6	4	3
*Saudi Arabia	3	2	1	0	6	4	3
*Belgium	3	2	1	0	6	2	1
Morocco	3	0	3	0	0	2	5

Results

6/19	Orlando (60,790)	Belgium 1, Morocco 0
6/20	Washington (52,535)	Holland 2, S. Arabia 1
6/25	Orlando (61,219)	Belgium 1, Holland 0
6/25	E. Rutherford (72,404)	S. Arabia 2, Morocco 1
6/29	Orlando (60,578)	Holland 2, Morocco 1
6/29	Washington (52,959)	S. Arabia 1, Belgium 0

1994 WORLD CUP

ROUND OF 16	QUARTER-FINALS	SEMIFINALS	FINAL	SEMIFINALS	QUARTER-FINALS	ROUND OF 16

Romania 3 / Argentina 2 → Romania 2 → Sweden 0 → Brazil 0* / Italy 0 *Brazil won shootout, 3-2 ← Bulgaria 1 ← Germany 1 ← Germany 3 / Belgium 2

Sweden 3 / Saudi Arabia 1 → Sweden 2* → Brazil 1 ← Bulgaria 2 ← Mexico 1 / Bulgaria 1*

Brazil 1 / USA 0 → Brazil 3 → Italy 2 ← Spain 1 ← Switzerland 0 / Spain 3

Holland 2 / Ireland 0 → Holland 2 *Sweden won shootout, 5-4 → 3rd Place Sweden 4, Bulgaria 0 ← Italy 2 *Bulgaria won shootout, 3-1 ← Nigeria 1 / Italy 2 (OT)

WorldCup **USA94**

Round of 16

7/2   Chicago (60,246) .... Germany 3, Belgium 2
7/2   Washington (53,141) .... Spain 3, Switzerland 0
7/3   Dallas (60,277) .... Sweden 3, Saudi Arabia 1
7/3   Pasadena (90,469) .... Romania 3, Argentina 2
7/4   Orlando (61,355) .... Holland 2, Ireland 0
7/4   Stanford (84,147) .... Brazil 1, USA 0
7/5   Foxboro (54,367) .... Italy 2, Nigeria 1 (OT)
7/5   E. Ruth. (71,030) .... Bulgaria 1, Mexico 1 (SO)*
*Bulgaria won shootout, 3-1.

Quarterfinals

7/9   Foxboro (54,605) .... Italy 2, Spain 1
7/9   Dallas (63,998) .... Brazil 3, Holland 2
7/10 E. Rutherford (74,147) .... Bulgaria 2, Germany 1
7/10 Stanford (81,715) .... Sweden 2, Romania 2 (SO)*
*Sweden won shootout, 5-4.

Semifinals

7/13 E. Rutherford (77,094) .... Italy 2, Bulgaria 1
7/13 Pasadena (84,569) .... Brazil 1, Sweden 0

Third Place

7/16 Pasadena (84,716) .... Sweden 4, Bulgaria 0

Final

7/17 Pasadena (94,194) .... Brazil 0, Italy 0 (SO)*
*Brazil won shootout, 3-2.

World Cup All-Star Team

Voting done by international media, FIFA Technical Study Group and FIFA media officers.

G	Michel Preud'homme, BEL	M	Dunga, BRA
D	Jorginho, BRA	M	Gheorghe Hagi, ROM
D	Paolo Maldini, ITA	F	Roberto Baggio, ITA
D	Marcio Santos, BRA	F	Romario, BRA
M	Krassimir Balakov, BUL	F	Hristo Stoitchkov, BUL
M	Tomas Brolin, SWE		

Honorable Mention

Goalkeeper—Thomas Ravelli, SWE. **Defenders**—Miodrag Belodedici, ROM and Alexi Lalas, USA. **Midfielders**—Juan Goikoetxea, SPA; Fernando Redondo, ARG. **Forwards**—Bebeto, BRA; Dennis Bergkamp, HOL; Jurgen Klinsmann, GER and Rashidi Yekini, NGR.

Final

Brazil 0, Italy 0*

*Brazil wins shootout, 3-2
Rose Bowl, Pasadena, Calif.

Lineups

Italy: G—Gianluca Pagliuca; D—Roberto Mussi (Luigi Apolloni, 35th minute), Franco Baresi, Antonio Benarrivo, Paolo Maldini; M—Demetrio Albertini, Dino Baggio (Alberigo Evani, 95th), Nicola Berti, Roberto Donadoni; F—Roberto Baggio, Daniele Massaro. Coach—Arrigo Sacchi.

Brazil: G—Claudio Taffarel; D—Jorginho (Cafu, 21st minute), Branco, Aldair, Marcio Santos; M—Mazinho, Mauro Silva, Dunga, Zinho (Viola, 106th); F—Bebeto, Romario. Coach—Carlos Alberto Parreira.

	1	2	OT—T	(SO)
July 17 Italy (4-2-1)	0	0	0—0	2
Brazil (6-0-1)	0	0	0—0	3

Shots on goal: Brazil 22, Italy 8. **Fouls:** Brazil 18, Italy 18. **Corner kicks:** Brazil 5, Italy 3. **Offsides:** Brazil 9, Italy 3. **Yellow cards:** Brazil 2 (Mazinho, Cafu); Italy 2 (Luigi Apolloni, Demetrio Albertini).

Shootout (five shots each, alternating): ITA—Baresi (miss, 0-0); BRA—Santos (blocked, 0-0); ITA—Albertini (goal, 1-0); BRA—Romario (goal, 1-1); ITA—Evani (goal, 2-1); BRA—Branco (goal, 2-2); ITA—Massaro (blocked, 2-2); BRA—Dunga (goal, 2-3); ITA—R. Baggio (miss, 2-3). **Goalkeepers:** BRA—Taffarel (1 save, 2 misses, 2 goals); ITA—Pagliuca (1 save, 3 goals).

Referee: Sandor Puhl (Hungary). **Linesmen:** Venancio Zarate (Paraguay), Mohammed Fanei (Iran). **Attendance:** 94,194. **TV Rating:** 9.5/24 share (ABC). **Worldwide TV audience:** 2 billion (est.).

Golden Ball Award (MVP)

Voting done by over 1,000 international media, FIFA Technical Study Group and FIFA media officers. The top 3 vote-getters:

	Points
Romario, Brazil, F	2,402
Roberto Baggio, Italy, F	1,507
Hristo Stoitchkov, Bulgaria, F	450

World Cup USA (Cont.)

Final World Cup Standings

First 16 teams advanced past opening round. The following knockout matches were decided by shootouts and officially counted as draws: Bulgaria-Mexico (2nd Round), Sweden-Romania (Quarterfinals) and Brazil-Italy (Final).

	Gm	W	L	T	Pts	GF	GA	Dif
1 Brazil	7	5	0	2	17	11	3	+8
2 Italy	7	4	1	2	14	8	5	+3
3 Sweden	7	3	1	3	12	15	8	+7
4 Bulgaria	7	3	3	1	10	10	11	-1
5 Germany	5	3	1	1	10	9	7	+2
6 Romania	5	3	1	1	10	10	9	+1
7 Holland	5	3	2	0	9	8	6	+2
8 Spain	5	2	1	2	8	10	6	+4
9 Nigeria	4	2	2	0	6	7	4	+3
10 Argentina	4	2	2	0	6	8	6	+2
11 Belgium	4	2	2	0	6	4	4	E
12 Mexico	4	1	1	2	5	4	4	E
13 Saudi Arabia	4	2	2	0	6	5	6	-1
14 United States	4	1	2	1	4	3	4	-1
15 Switzerland	4	1	2	1	4	5	7	-2
16 Ireland	4	1	2	1	4	2	4	-2
17 Norway	3	1	1	1	4	1	1	E
18 Russia	3	1	2	0	3	7	6	+1
19 Colombia	3	1	2	0	3	4	5	-1
20 South Korea	3	0	1	2	2	4	5	-1
21 Bolivia	3	0	2	1	1	1	4	-3
22 Cameroon	3	0	2	1	1	3	11	-8
23 Morocco	3	0	3	0	0	2	5	-3
24 Greece	3	0	3	0	0	0	10	-10

Scoring Leaders

Two points for a goal, one for an assist; shootout goals not included. Winners share Golden Shoe Award.

	Gm	G	A	Pts
Oleg Salenko, Russia	3	6	1	13
Hristo Stoitchkov, Bulgaria	7	6	1	13
Kennet Andersson, Sweden	7	5	2	12
Romario, Brazil	6	5	1	11
Juergen Klinsmann, Germany	5	5	0	10
Roberto Baggio, Italy	6	5	0	10
Gheorghe Hagi, Romania	5	3	4	10
Gabriel Batistuta, Argentina	4	4	1	9
Martin Dahlin, Sweden	6	4	1	9
Tomas Brolin, Sweden	7	4	1	9

Three players tied with 8 each.

Leading Goalkeepers

At least 300 minutes played; shootout goals not included.

	Gm	Min	GA	Sv	GAA
Claudio Taffarel, Brazil	7	660	3	21	0.41
Gianluca Pagliuca, Italy	5	410	3	43	0.66
Peter Rufai, Nigeria	4	390	4	28	0.92
Jorge Campos, Mexico	4	390	4	19	0.92
Tony Meola, USA	4	360	4	38	1.00
Michel Preud'homme, Belgium	4	360	4	25	1.00
Andoni Zubizarreta, Spain	4	360	4	22	1.00
Pat Bonner, Ireland	4	360	4	17	1.00
Thomas Ravelli, Sweden	7	660	8	61	1.09
Ed DeGoej, Holland	5	450	6	19	1.20

FIFA Top 30 World Rankings

As of July 31, after completion of the 1994 World Cup. Note that the '94 World Cup Final Four teams are in **bold** type. FIFA introduced its monthly world ranking system on Aug. 13, 1993, designed to provide a constant international comparison of national team performances. The rankings are based on a mathematical formula that weighs strength of schedule, importance of matches and goals scored for and against. Games considered include World Cup qualifying and final rounds, Continental championship qualifying and final rounds and friendly matches. Note that (DNQ) indicates team did not qualify for World Cup final tournament.

		Points	Lead Up Matches	World Cup Recap	Head Coach	Ranking 12/93	6/94
1	**Brazil**	65.21	4-0-1	6-0-1	Carlos Alberto Parreira	3	3
2	**Italy**	62.89	3-2-0	4-2-1 (Brazil)	Arrigo Sacchi	2	4
3	**Sweden**	61.28	4-2-2	4-1-2 (Brazil)	Tommy Svensson	9	10
4	Germany	61.14	4-1-0	3-1-1 (Bulgaria)	Berti Vogts	1	1
5	Holland	60.97	3-1-1	3-2-0 (Brazil)	Dick Advocaat	7	2
6	Spain	59.74	2-1-2	2-1-2 (Italy)	Javier Clemente	5	5
7	Romania	58.20	4-1-3	3-2-0 (Sweden)	Anghel Iordanescu	13	7
8	Norway	57.52	2-2-3	1-1-1 (1st Round)	Egil Olsen	4	6
9	Argentina	57.46	2-2-2	2-2-0 (Romania)	Alfio Basile	8	8
10	Nigeria	56.28	1-3-1	2-2-0 (Italy)	Clemence Westeroff	18	11
11	Switzerland	55.80	4-1-2	1-2-1 (Spain)	Roy Hodgson	12	12
12	Denmark	54.88	3-2-1	DNQ	Richard Moeller Nielsen	6	9
13	Ireland	53.68	3-1-1	1-2-1 (Holland)	Jack Charlton	10	14
14	**Bulgaria**	53.40	0-0-4	4-3-0 (Italy)	Dimitar Penev	31	29
15	Mexico	53.10	2-3-2	1-2-1 (Bulgaria)	Miguel Mejia Baron	16	16
16	France	52.82	4-0-1	DNQ	Aime Jacquet	15	13
17	Colombia	52.72	6-1-4	1-2-0 (1st round)	Francisco Maturana	21	17
18	England	52.15	2-0-1	DNQ	Terry Venables	11	15
19	Russia	52.02	3-0-2	1-2-0 (1st round)	Pavel Sadyrin	14	19
20	Belgium	50.17	2-1-0	2-2-0 (1st round)	Paul Van Himst	25	27
21	Zambia	48.28	3-2-1	DNQ	Ian Porterfield	27	20
22	United States	47.68	6-4-9	1-2-1 (Brazil)	Bora Milutinovic	22	23
23	Uruguay	47.23	0-0-0	DNQ	No coach	17	18
24	Ivory Coast	45.23	2-0-0	DNQ	Henry Kazperczak	33	21
25	Portugal	44.73	0-0-2	DNQ	Nelo Vingada	20	22
26	Egypt	44.65	2-1-2	DNQ	Taha Ismail	26	25
27	Cameroon	44.02	1-1-3	0-2-1 (1st round)	Henri Michel	23	24
28	Ghana	43.32	1-0-2	DNQ	Emmanuel Aggrey-Fynn	37	26
29	Saudi Arabia	42.93	3-5-4	2-2-0 (1st round)	Jorge Solari	38	34
30	Morocco	42.71	2-0-4	0-3-0 (1st round)	Abdellah Ajri	30	28

U.S. National Team
1994 Schedule and Results

Through Sept. 7, 1994. Note the following match references: Carlsberg Cup (CC) and Robbie Cup (JR). In addition, (*) indicates opponent was a World Cup qualifier, while all World Cup match opponents are in **bold** type. All other matches are international friendlies.

Date		Result	USA Goals	Site	Crowd
Jan. 15	Norway*	W, 2-1	Marcelo Balboa, Cobi Jones	Tempe, Ariz.	15,386
Jan. 22	Switzerland*	T, 1-1	(Own goal)	Fullerton, Calif.	10,173
Jan. 29	Russia*	T, 1-1	Alexi Lalas	Seattle	43,651
Feb. 10	Denmark (CC)	T, 0-0†	none	Hong Kong	9,000
Feb. 13	Romania* (CC)	L, 2-1	Balboa	Hong Kong	9,000
Feb. 18	Bolivia* (JRC)	T, 1-1	Jones	Miami	15,676
Feb. 20	Sweden* (JRC)	L, 3-1	Hugo Perez	Miami	20,171
Mar. 12	South Korea*	T, 1-1	Balboa	Fullerton, Calif.	10,319
Mar. 26	Bolivia*	T, 2-2	Perez (2)	Dallas	26,835
Apr. 16	Moldova	T, 1-1	Mike Sorber	Jacksonville, Fla.	6,103
Apr. 20	Moldova	W, 3-0	Frank Klopas, Mike Lapper, Claudio Reyna	Davidson, N.C.	4,790
Apr. 24	Iceland	L, 2-1	Klopas	San Diego	3,017
Apr. 30	Chile	L, 2-0	none	Albuquerque, N.M.	15,610
May. 7	Estonia	W, 4-0	Klopas, Reyna, Balboa, Joe-Max Moore	Fullerton, Calif.	2,158
May 15	Armenia	W, 1-0	Klopas	Fullerton, Calif.	9,753
May 25	Saudi Arabia*	T, 0-0	none	Piscataway, N.J.	5,576
May 28	Greece*	L, 2-1	Klopas	New Haven, Conn.	21,317
June 4	Mexico*	W, 1-0	Roy Wegerle	Pasadena	91,123
June 18	**Switzerland**	T, 1-1	Eric Wynalda	Pontiac, Mich	73,425
June 22	**Colombia**	W, 2-1	(own goal), Ernie Stewart	Pasadena	93,194
June 26	**Romania**	L, 1-0	none	Pasadena	93,869
July 4	**Brazil**	L, 1-0	none	Stanford, Calif.	84,177
Sept. 7	**England**	L, 2-0	none	London	38,629

† Denmark won match, 4-2, on penalty kicks.

Overall record: 6-7-10. **World Cup record:** 1-2-1. **Team scoring:** Goals for—25; Goals against—24. **Individual scoring:** Klopas (5); Balboa (4); Perez (3); Jones and Reyna (2); Lalas, Lapper, Moore; Sorber, Stewart, Wegerle and Wynalda.

1994 World Cup Roster

Individual statistics through Sept. 7, 1994. Note that the column labeled Career C/G refers to career caps and goals. (Red cards are listed below.)

Strikers	GP	GS	Mins	G	A	Pts	Career C/G
Frank Klopas	12	9	625	5	0	10	32/9
Joe-Max Moore	11	7	485	1	1	3	35/9
Ernie Stewart	7	5	495	1	0	2	21/3
Roy Wegerle	7	0	173	1	0	2	21/2
Eric Wynalda	8	3	435	1	1	3	58/15

Midfielders	GP	GS	Mins	G	A	Pts	Career C/G
Mike Burns	17	13	1250	0	2	2	18/0
John Harkes	3	3	270	0	0	0	52/4
Cobi Jones	22	18	1602	2	0	4	55/5
Hugo Perez	17	16	1206	3	3	9	79/16
Tab Ramos	7	6	514	0	1	1	54/3
Claudio Reyna	18	8	973	2	1	5	18/2
Mike Sorber	14	10	910	1	0	2	41/2

Defenders	GP	GS	Mins	G	A	Pts	Career C/G
Marcelo Balboa	20	18	1518	4	0	8	95/10
Paul Caligiuri	17	13	1263	0	2	2	88/4
Fernando Clavijo	8	6	591	0	0	0	61/0
Thomas Dooley	22	21	1829	0	0	0	44/4
Cle Kooiman	2	2	180	0	0	0	12/1
Alexi Lalas	22	22	1929	1	1	3	51/5
Mike Lapper	10	8	694	1	1	3	40/1

Goalkeepers	GP	GS	Mins	Record	GA	SO	Career Caps
Brad Friedel	9	9	800	1-3-5	11	2	26
Tony Meola	14	14	1260	5-4-5	13	4	89
Juergen Sommer	1	0	10	0-0-0	0	0	1

Red cards: Balboa, Clavijo, Lalas, Lapper. **Yellow cards** (more than one): Burns 5; Lalas 4, Clavijo and Klopas 3; Harkes 2. **World Cup minutes:** Balboa, Caligiuri, Dooley, Lalas and Meola (360); Sorber (345); Stewart (327); Ramos (289); Harkes (270), Clavijo (267); Wynalda (255); Jones (149); Wegerle (99); Kooiman (90); Perez (66).

Head coach: Bora Milutinovic; **Assistant coaches:** Timo Liekoski, Steve Sampson, Sigi Schmid; **Goalkeeping coach:** Milutin Soskic; **General Manager:** Bill Nuttall; **Captain:** Tony Meola.

World Cup Playing Venues

Chicago—Soldier Field (65,000); **Dallas**—Cotton Bowl (67,000); **East Rutherford**—Giants Stadium (76,000); **Foxboro**—Foxboro Stadium (54,500); **Orlando**—Bowl (64,000); **Pasadena**—Rose Bowl (94,000); **Pontiac**—Silverdome (76,000); **Stanford**—Stanford Stadium (84,000); **Washington**—RFK Stadium (53,000).

Club Team Competition
1993 Intercontinental Cup

The 34th Intercontinental (Toyota) Cup World Club Championship between the 1993 European Cup and Copa Libertadores winners at Tokyo's National Stadium. Italy's AC Milan lost the '93 European Cup final to Marseille, but replaced the French club because of its involvement in the match-rigging scandal.

Final
(Dec. 12, 1993, at Tokyo; Att—52,000)

São Paulo (Brazil) 3 ....AC Milan (Italy) 2
   Scoring: São Paulo—Palhinha, Toninho, Cerezo, Muller; AC Milan—Daniele Massaro, Jean-Pierre Papin.

EUROPE

There are three European club competitions sanctioned by the Union of European Football Associations (UEFA). The European Cup (officially, the Champions' Cup) is a knockout contest between national league champions of UEFA member countries; the Cup Winners' Cup is between winners of domestic cup competitions (note that a double winner—league and cup titles—would play for the European Cup and be replaced in the Cup Winners' Cup by the team it defeated in the domestic cup final); and the UEFA Cup is between the so-called best of the rest, usually the national league runners-up. Note that home teams are listed first.

1994 European Cup

   Six-game double round-robin in two 4-team groups (Nov.24-Apr.13); top two teams in each group meet in one-game playoff to determine who advances to one-game Cup final.

ROUND ROBIN STANDINGS

Group A	Gm	W	L	T	Pts	GF	GA
*Barcelona (SPA)	6	4	0	2	10	13	3
*Monaco (FRA)	6	3	2	1	7	9	4
Spartak (RUS)	6	1	2	3	5	6	12
Galatasaray (TUR)	6	0	4	2	2	1	10

Group B	Gm	W	L	T	Pts	GF	GA
*AC Milan (ITA)	6	2	0	4	8	6	2
*FC Porto (POR)	6	3	2	1	7	10	6
Werder Breman (GER)	6	2	3	1	5	11	15
Anderlecht (BEL)	6	1	3	2	4	5	9

SEMIFINALS
(April 27)

AC Milan 3 ....Monaco 0
Barcelona 3 ....FC Porto 0

FINAL
(May 18 at Athens; Att—75,000)

AC Milan 4 ....Barcelona 0
   Scoring: AC Milan—Daniele Massaro (2), Dejan Savicevic and Marcel Desailly.

1994 Cup Winners' Cup
Two-leg Semifinals; one-game Final.

SEMIFINALS
Paris St. Germain (FRA) vs **Arsenal** (ENG)
Mar. 30— Paris St. Germain 1 ....Arsenal 1
Apr. 13— Arsenal 1 ....Paris St. Germain 0
(Arsenal wins, 2-1)

Benfica (POR) vs **Parma** (ITA)
Mar. 30— Benfica 2 ....Parma 1
Apr. 13— Parma 1 ....Benfica 0
(Aggregate 2-2; Parma wins on away goals)

FINAL
(May 4 at Copenhagen; Att—33,765)

Arsenal 1 ....Parma 0
   Scoring: Arsenal—Alan Smith.

1994 UEFA Cup
Two-leg Semifinals and two-leg Final.

SEMIFINALS
Cagliari (ITA) vs **Inter-Milan** (ITA)
Mar. 30— Cagliari 3 ....Inter-Milan 2
Apr. 13— Inter-Milan 3 ....Cagliari 0
(Inter wins, 5-3)

Austria Salzburg (AUT) vs. **Karlsruhe** (GER)
Mar. 30— Austria Salzburg 0 ....Karlsruhe 0
Apr. 13— Karlsruhe 1 ....Austria Salzburg 1
(Aggregate 1-1; Salzburg wins on away goals)

FINAL
Apr. 24— Austria Salzburg 0.........................Inter-Milan 1
May 11— Inter-Milan 1 ....Austria Salzburg 0
(Inter wins, 2-0)

National Champions
1994 European league champions and cup winners.

Country	League Champion	Cup Winner
Austria	Casino Salzburg	Austria Vienna
Belgium	Anderlecht	Anderlecht
Bulgaria	Levski Sofia	Levski Sofia
Croatia	Hajduk Split	Croatia Zagreb
Czech Rep	Sparta Prague	Viktoria Zizkov
Denmark	Silkeborg	Broendby
England	Manchester United	Manchester United
France	Paris St. Germain	Auxerre
Germany	Bayern Munich	Werder Bremen
Greece	AEK Athens	Panathinaikos
Holland	Ajax	Feyernoord
Hungary	VAC	Ferencvaros
Ireland	Shamrock Rovers	Sligo Rovers
Italy	AC Milan	Sampdoria
No. Ireland	Linfield	Linfield
Poland	Legia Warsaw	Legia Warsaw
Portugal	Benfica	FC Porto
Romania	Steaua Bucharest	Gloria Bistrita
Russia	Spartak Moscow*	CSKA Moscow
Scotland	Rangers	Dundee United
Slovakia	Slovan Bratislava	Slovan Bratislava
Spain	Barcelona	Real Zaragoza
Sweden	IFK Gothenburg*	IFK Norrkoeping*
Switzerland	Servette	Grasshoppers
Turkey	Galatasaray	Besiktas

*1993 champion; country plays spring-fall season.

SOUTH AMERICA

1994 Copa Libertadores

Contested by league champions of South America's football union. Two-leg Semifinals and Final; home teams listed first.

SEMIFINALS

Velez Sarsfield (ARG) vs **Atletico Junior** (COL)

Aug. 10— Atletico Junior 2 .... Velez Sarsfield 1
Aug. 17— Velez Sarsfield 2 .... Atletico Junior 1
(Aggregate 3-3; Velez wins shootout, 5-4)

São Paulo (BRA) vs **Olimpia** (PAR)

Aug. 10— São Paulo 2 .... Olimpia 1
Aug. 17— Olimpia 1 .... São Paulo 0
(Aggregate 2-2, São Paulo wins shootout, 4-3)

FINAL

Aug. 24— Velez Sarsfield 1 .... São Paulo 0
Aug. 31— São Paulo 1 .... Velez Sarsfield 0
(Aggregate 1-1, Velez wins shootout, 5-3)

U.S. Pro Leagues

Division champions (*) and playoff qualifiers (†) are noted.

NPSL Final Standings (Indoor)

American Division

	W	L	Pct.	GB	GF	GA
* Baltimore Spirit	26	14	.660	—	594	553
†Cleveland Crunch	23	17	.575	3	717	613
†Buffalo Blizzard	19	21	.475	7	499	515
†Harrisburg Heat	19	21	.475	7	557	585
Canton Invaders	18	22	.450	8	537	584
Dayton Dynamo	15	25	.375	11	644	665

National Division

	W	L	Pct.	GB	GF	GA
* St. Louis Ambush	25	15	.625	—	676	566
†Detroit Rockers	24	16	.600	1	575	577
†Wichita Wings	22	18	.550	3	598	572
†Milwaukee Wave	20	20	.500	5	496	486
Chicago Power	15	25	.375	10	501	616
Kansas City Attack	14	26	.350	11	566	628

Playoffs

Division Semifinals (Best of 3): Cleveland over Buffalo (2-1); Detroit over Wichita (2-0); Harrisburg over Baltimore (2-0); St. Louis over Milwaukee (2-1).

Division Finals (Best of 3): Cleveland over Harrisburg (2-1); St. Louis over Detroit (2-0).

Final (Best of 5): Cleveland over St. Louis (3-1).

APSL Final Standings (Outdoor)

	W	L	Pts	GF	GA
Seattle Sounders	14	6	121	38	16
Los Angeles Salsa	12	8	106	36	22
Montreal Impact	12	8	93	27	18
Colorado Foxes	12	8	92	26	26
Ft. Lauderdale Strikers	8	12	72	23	33
Vancouver 86ers	7	13	65	25	41
Toronto Blizzard	5	15	44	14	33

Teams earn six points for a win and one point per goal up to a maximum of three per game. No points are given for goals scored in overtime. In shootout tie-breakers, the winning team earns four points and the loser gets two.

Playoffs

Semifinals (2 legs with mini-game): Colorado over Seattle (2-0, 1-4, 2-1 in shootout); Montreal over Los Angeles (2-1, 0-3, 2-1 in shootout).
Final: Montreal 1, Colorado 0.

CISL Final Standings (Indoor)

Eastern Division

	W	L	Pct.	GB	GF	GA
* Dallas Sidekicks	24	4	.857	—	255	160
†Monterrey La Raza	17	11	.607	7	271	210
†Wash. Warthogs	14	14	.500	10	215	193
†Pittsburgh Stingers	13	15	.464	11	165	189
Detroit Neon	11	17	.393	13	188	204
Houston Hotshots	7	21	.250	17	150	223
Carolina Vipers	3	25	.107	21	126	245

National Division

	W	L	Pct.	GB	GF	GA
* Anaheim Splash	20	8	.714	—	227	172
†San Diego Sockers	18	10	.643	1	222	178
†Las Vegas Dustdevils	17	11	.607	3	200	198
†Sacramento Knights	15	13	.536	5	163	179
Portland Pride	14	14	.500	6	176	189
San Jose Grizzlies	12	16	.429	8	177	181
Arizona Sandsharks	11	17	.393	9	200	214

Playoffs

Division Semifinals (Best of 3): Dallas over Pittsburgh (2-0); Washington over Monterrey (2-1); Las Vegas over San Diego (2-1); Anaheim over Sacramento (2-1).

Division Finals (Best of 3): Dallas over Washington (2-0); Las Vegas over Anaheim (2-0).

Final (Best of 3): Las Vegas over Dallas (2-1)

U.S. Foreign Legion

U.S. National Team members playing overseas as of Sept. 7, 1994. Note following first division abbreviations: Bund.—German Bundesliga; and Prem.— English Premier Division.

	Foreign Club	Div.
Tom Dooley	Bayer Leverkusen (Ger.)	Bund.
John Harkes	Derby County (England)	1st
Cobi Jones	Coventry City (England)	Prem.
Cle Kooiman	Morelia (Mexico)	1st
Alexi Lalas	Calcio Padova (Italy)	1st
Joe-Max Moore	FC Saarbruecken (Ger.)	2nd
Tab Ramos	Real Betis (Spain)	1st
Claudio Reyna	Bayer Leverkusen (Ger.)	Bund.
Juergen Sommer	Luton Town (England)	1st
Ernie Stewart	Willem II (Holland)	1st
Roy Wegerle	Coventry City (England)	Prem.
Eric Wynalda	VFB Bochum (Germany)	Bund.

Colleges
MEN

1993 Final *Soccer America* Top 20

Final 1993 regular season poll including games through Nov. 7. Conducted by the national weekly *Soccer America* and released in the Nov. 22nd issue. Listing includes records through conference playoffs as well as NCAA tournament record and team lost to. Teams in **bold** type went on to reach NCAA Final Four. All tournament games decided by penalty kicks are considered ties.

		Nov. 8 Record	NCAA Recap
1	Creighton	19-0-0	0-1 (Air Force)
2	UCLA	18-2-0	0-1 (San Diego)
3	**Virginia**	17-3-0	5-0
4	Indiana	16-2-1	1-1 (Wisconsin)
5	Duke	15-4-0	0-1 (N.Carolina)
6	James Madison	19-1-1	0-1 (Loyola-MD)
7	Clemson	17-4-1	1-1 (S.Carolina)
8	St. John's	18-0-3	0-1 (Boston U.)
9	San Francisco	11-3-4	2-1 (CS-Fullerton)
10	Penn St	16-3-2	1-1 (Princeton)
11	Saint Louis	16-4-0	0-1-1* (San Fran.)
12	Santa Clara	14-2-2	0-1 (San Fran.)
13	**South Carolina**	12-3-4	4-1 (Virginia)
14	North Carolina	12-6-2	1-1 (Air Force)
15	Rutgers	17-4-1	0-1 (Hartwick)
16	Loyola-MD	18-2-1	1-1 (Virginia)
17	**Princeton**	10-4-0	3-1 (Virginia)
18	Hartwick	14-3-2	2-1 (Princeton)
19	Wisconsin	13-3-4	2-1 (Virginia)
20	Boston Univ.	13-6-1	1-1 (Hartwick)

Note: Unranked **CS-Fullerton**, 16-6 and 3-1 (South Carolina), was the fourth entry in the NCAA tournament Final Four.

NCAA Division I Tournament
First Round

Air Force 2	OT	at Creighton 1
Boston Univ. 2		at St. John's 1
CS-Fullerton 4		at Fresno St. 0
at Clemson 2		NC-Greensboro 0
at Hartwick 2		Rutgers 1
at Indiana 6		Memphis St. 0
at Loyola-MD 1		James Madison 0
at North Carolina 3		Duke 2
at Penn St. 3		Robert Morris 0
at Princeton 2		Columbia 0
Saint Louis 0	2 OT	at Portland St. 0

(Saint Louis advances on PKs, 3-2)

San Diego 4	OT	at UCLA 2
San Francisco 2	OT	at Santa Clara 1
at South Carolina 1		Furman 0
at Virginia 3		William & Mary 1
at Wisconsin 3		Notre Dame 1

Second Round

Air Force 2		at North Carolina 1
CS-Fullerton 3		at San Diego 2
at Hartwick 2	OT	Boston Univ. 1
at Princeton 5		Penn St. 2
at San Francisco 2		Saint Louis 1
South Carolina 3		at Clemson 2
at Virginia 2		Loyola-MD 1
Wisconsin 1		at Indiana 0

Quarterfinals

CS-Fullerton 1	at San Francisco 0
at Princeton 3	Hartwick 0
at South Carolina 6	Air Force 0
at Virginia 3	Wisconsin 0

WOMEN
1993 Final ISAA Top 15

Final 1993 regular season poll including games through Nov. 7. Coaches poll conducted by the Intercollegiate Soccer Assn. of America. Listing includes records through conference playoffs as well as NCAA tournament record and team lost to. Teams in **bold** type went on to reach NCAA Final Four. All tournament games decided by penalty kicks are considered ties.

		Nov.8 Record	NCAA Recap
1	**North Carolina**	19-0-0	4-0
2	**Stanford**	16-2-1	2-0-1* (G.Mason)
3	Notre Dame	19-2-0	0-1 (G.Mason)
4	Santa Clara	15-4-0	0-1 (Portland)
5	**Massachusetts**	15-2-3	2-1 (N.Carolina)
6	William & Mary	12-4-1	0-1 (Wisconsin)
7	Portland	15-3-1	1-1 (Stanford)
8	Duke	12-6-2	0-0-1* (Fla.Intl)
9	Wisconsin	15-3-0	1-1 (G.Mason)
10	**George Mason**	16-2-1	2-1-1* (N.Carolina)
11	Connecticut	16-5-1	1-1 (UMass)
12	SMU	13-6-1	0-1 (N.Carolina)
13	California	10-3-4	0-1 (Stanford)
14	Dartmouth	12-2-1	0-1 (UConn)
15	Florida Intl	13-2-2	0-1-1* (N.Carolina)

Note: Unranked Providence, 10-8-2 and 0-1 (UMass), was the remaining entry in the 16-team NCAA tournament.

NCAA Division I Tournament
Regional Finals

East	UMass 1, Connecticut 0
	(3rd place: Dartmouth, Providence)
South	North Carolina 3, Florida Int'l. 0
	(3rd place: Duke, SMU)
Midwest	George Mason 3, Wisconsin 1
	(3rd place: Notre Dame, Wm. & Mary)
West	Stanford 1, Portland 0
	(3rd place: California, Santa Clara)

ACC Teams Dominating College Game

By Paul Kennedy

College soccer ended the 1993 season with two dynasties in the Atlantic Coast Conference.

The North Carolina women's team won its eighth straight NCAA Division I championship on Nov. 21, and two weeks later, Virginia became the first men's team to capture three straight NCAA Division I titles.

UVA beat South Carolina, 2-0, before a sellout crowd of 10,549 at Davidson College's Richardson Field. The Cavaliers then celebrated with a trip to nearby Lake Norman, where coach Bruce Arena took a swim.

In 1992, Arena had promised to jump in the lake if the NCAA final between Virginia and the University of San Diego, also played at Davidson, did not produce a goal. He was spared when Virginia won 2-0. A year later, before the showdown with South Carolina, Arena said, "If we win, I'm in." After the victory, he chose a section of the lake near the McGuire power plant where the water was the warmest to take his plunge.

Virginia has become quite familiar with the Davidson area the last two years, winning all four games in the two Final Fours and scoring 10 goals en route to its triple (the 1991 Final Four was held in Tampa).

Once again, UVA was led by junior midfielder Claudio Reyna, the two-time College Player of the Year who would announce shortly after the Final Four that he was foregoing his senior year for a shot at the U.S. World Cup team.

"When I came [to Virginia]," said Reyna, "I wanted to be lucky enough to win one championship."

Reyna, who quickly made the U.S. starting lineup but missed the 1994 World Cup because of a hamstring pull, left college as perhaps its best playmaker ever. His ability to beat defenders on the dribble and spring his teammates with long passes made him an unstoppable force on the college scene.

Virginia could also rely on Friends—striker Nate Friends, who had the winning goal against San Diego in 1992. Friends topped

Tony Quinn

Forward **Nate Friends** scored all five goals for three-time NCAA champion Virginia in the 1994 Men's Final Four.

himself in '93 by scoring all five of the Cavaliers' goals in the Final Four. He netted a hat trick against Princeton and two more against South Carolina. "We were worried Nate might announce he's going pro, too," joked Arena afterward.

UVA's wide-open offense won a lot of friends at Davidson, where for the second straight year the finals were sold out months ahead of time. Said Charlotte *Observer* sports columnist Tom Sorenson: "If everybody played soccer like Virginia does, the sport would be so popular that soccer fans could finally stop talking about how popular it is going to be."

North Carolina's women's team was even more convincing than Virginia in 1993, hardly a surprise considering the Tar Heels have won 11 of 12 NCAA titles since 1982.

Led by senior forward and two-time Player of the Year Mia Hamm, who broke numerous career scoring records along the way, the Tar Heels beat George Mason, 6-0, in the final. That followed up on their 9-1 rout of Duke the year before.

"They are secure until the end of time," said North Carolina coach Anson Dorrance of Hamm's records, which included most overall Division I goals in a career (103) and in the NCAA tournament (16).

Paul Kennedy has been the managing editor of *Soccer America* since 1985.

Colleges (Cont.)

1993 All-America Teams
MEN

As selected by the National Soccer Coaches Assn. of America (NSCAA). The one holdover from 1992 team is in **bold** type.

First Team

Pos		Cl	Hgt	Wgt
G	....................Tim Deck, Wisconsin	Sr.	6-1	180
D	............Shane Battelle, Saint Louis	Sr.	5-11	175
D	.....................Pedro Lopes, Rutgers	Jr.	5-8	150
D	....................Jorge Salcedo, UCLA	Sr.	6-1	175
M	...............Brian Kamler, Creighton	Sr.	6-1	165
M	........................Jason Kreis, Duke	Jr.	5-7	155
M	..........**Claudio Reyna,** Virginia	Jr.	5-10	160
F	................Keith DeFini, Creighton	Sr.	6-1	190
F	................Jimmy Glenn, Clemson	Sr.	5-11	180
F	............Brian McBride, Saint Louis	Sr.	6-0	175
F	.......Staale Soebye, San Francisco	Jr.	6-1	170

WOMEN

As selected by the National Soccer Coaches Assn. of America (NSCAA). Most schools do not list heights and weights of women athletes. The four holdovers from 1992 All-America team are in **bold** type.

GOALTENDER—**Karen Ferguson,** George Mason, Sr. DEFENDERS—**Karen Ferguson,** UConn, Sr.; Jessica Fischer, Stanford, So.; Paula Wilkins, UMass., Sr. MIDFIELDERS—Cindy Daws, Notre Dame, Fr.; Jennifer Lalor, Santa Clara, So.; **Tisha Venturini,** N.Carolina, Jr.; Kelly Walbert, Duke, So. FORWARDS—**Mia Hamm,** N.Carolina, Sr.; Kara Lee, SMU, Sr.; Shannon MacMillan, Portland, So.; **Sarah Rafanelli,** Stanford, Sr.

Annual Awards
Men's Player of the Year

Hermann Trophy	..............Claudio Reyna, Virginia, M
MAC Award	....Claudio Reyna
Soccer America	...................................Claudio Reyna

Women's Player of the Year

Hermann Trophy	...........Mia Hamm, North Carolina, F
MAC Award	....Mia Hamm
Soccer America	....Mia Hamm

NSCAA Coaches of the Year

Division I:	Men's	...................Bob Bradley, Princeton
	Women's	.........Jac Cicala, George Mason

Other Tournament Finals
NCAA

MEN
Div. II	..............................Seattle Pacific 1, So. Conn. St. 0
Div. III	...................................UC-San Diego 1, Williams 0

WOMEN
Div. II	....Barry 2, Cal Poly SLO 0
Div. III	....................................Trenton St. 4, Plymouth St. 0

NAIA

MEN ....Sangamon St. 4, Lynn 3
(winning goal at 0:23 of 2nd sudden death period)
WOMEN ....Berry 1, Lynn 0
(winning goal at 39:14 of 1st sudden death period)

U.S. Women's National Team

1994 CONCACAF Qualifying roster: G—Mary Harvey, Briana Scurry and Saskia Webber; **D**—Amanda Cromwell, Linda Hamilton, Carla Overbeck, Thori Staples; **D/M**—Joy Fawcett, Mia Hamm; **M**—Julie Foudy, Jennifer Lalor, Kristine Lilly, Tiffany Roberts, Tisha Venturini; **F**—Michelle Akers-Stahl, Carin Gabarra, Tiffeny Milbrett, Sarah Rafanelli; **Coach**—Anson Dorrance (resigned, effective Aug. 22, and succeeded by assistant Tony DiCicco); **Captain:** Carla Overbeck.

1994 Schedule and Results

Through Aug. 21, 1994. Note the following match references: Chiquita Cup (CC); CONCACAF qualifying tournament for 1995 World Championship (Q). All other opponents are international friendly matches.

Date		Result	USA Goals	Site	Crowd
Mar. 16	Portugal	.....................W, 5-0	Gabarra (2), Lilly, Milbrett, Foudy	Silves, Portugal	2,000
Mar. 18	Sweden	.....................W, 1-0	Hamm	San Antonio, Portugal	450
Mar. 20	Norway	.......................L, 1-0	none	Faro, Portugal	1,200
Apr. 10	Trinidad/Tobago	.......W, 3-1	Lilly, Foudy, Roberts	Scarborough, Tobago	250
Apr. 14	Canada	.....................W, 4-1	Akers-Stahl (2), Gabarra (2)	San Fernando, Trinidad	1,000
Apr. 17	Canada	.....................W, 3-0	Venturini, Akers-Stahl, MacMillan	Port of Spain, Trinidad	500
July 31	Germany (CC)	............W, 2-1	Hamm, Akers-Stahl	Fairfax, Va.	5,731
Aug. 3	China (CC)	...............W, 1-0	Foudy	Piscataway, N.J.	5,826
Aug. 7	Norway (CC)	..............W, 4-1	own goal, Akers-Stahl, Hamm (2)	Worcester, Mass.	6,511
Aug. 13	Mexico (Q)	................W, 9-0	Lilly (2), Venturini, Hamm, Lalor, Akers-Stahl (2), Roberts, Gabarra	Montreal	1,821
Aug. 17	Trin./Tobago (Q)	.......W,11-0	Hamm (4), Gabarra (2), Cromwell, Akers-Stahl, Venturini (2), Roberts	Montreal	1,900
Aug. 19	Jamaica (Q)	..............W,10-0	Roberts, Gabarra, Overbeck (2), Lilly (2), Rafanelli, Milbrett, Akers-Stahl (2)	Montreal	1,087
Aug. 21	Canada (Q)	..............W, 6-0	Hamm, Gabarra, Akers-Stahl, Roberts, Foudy, own goal	Montreal	2,160

Overall record: 12-1-0. **Team scoring:** Goals for—59; Goals against—6.

Leading scorers: Michelle Akers-Stahl (11); Mia Hamm (10); Carin Gabarra (9); Kristine Lilly (7); Julie Foudy, Tiffany Roberts and Tisha Venturini (4); Tiffeny Milbrett and Carla Overbeck (2); Amanda Cromwell, Jennifer Lalor, Shannon MacMillan and Sarah Rafanelli. Own goals (2).

THE 1995 SPORTS ALMANAC — INFORMATION PLEASE — SOCCER STATISTICS — THROUGH THE YEARS 1900-1994 — WORLD • U.S. • COLLEGE — SEC B — PAGE 685

The World Cup

The Federation Internationale de Football Association (FIFA) began the World Cup championship tournament in 1930 with a 13-team field in Uruguay. Sixty-four years later, 138 countries competed in qualifying rounds to fill 24 berths in the 1994 World Cup finals.

The United States hosted the World Cup for the first time in '94 and American crowds shattered tournament attendance records (see page 687). Tournaments have now been played three times in North America (Mexico 2 and U.S.), four times in South America (Argentina, Chile, Brazil and Uruguay) and eight times in Europe (Italy 2, England, France, Spain, Sweden, Switzerland and West Germany). France will host the tournament again in 1998.

Brazil retired the first World Cup (called the Jules Rimet Trophy after FIFA's first president) in 1970 after winning it for the third time. The new trophy, first presented in 1974, is known as simply the World Cup.

Multiple winners: Brazil (4); Italy and West Germany (3); Argentina and Uruguay (2).

Year	Champion	Manager	Score	Runner-up	Host Country	Third Place
1930	Uruguay	Alberto Supicci	4-2	Argentina	Uruguay	No game
1934	Italy	Vittorio Pozzo	2-1*	Czechoslovakia	Italy	Germany 3, Austria 2
1938	Italy	Vittorio Pozzo	4-2	Hungary	France	Brazil 4, Sweden 2
1942-46	Not held					
1950	Uruguay	Juan Lopez	2-1	Brazil	Brazil	No game
1954	West Germany	Sepp Herberger	3-2	Hungary	Switzerland	Austria 3, Uruguay 1
1958	Brazil	Vicente Feola	5-2	Sweden	Sweden	France 6, W.Germany 3
1962	Brazil	Aymore Moreira	3-1	Czechoslovakia	Chile	Chile 1, Yugoslavia 0
1966	England	Alf Ramsey	4-2*	W. Germany	England	Portugal 2, USSR 1
1970	Brazil	Mario Zagalo	4-1	Italy	Mexico	W.Ger. 1, Uruguay 0
1974	West Germany	Helmut Schoen	2-1	Holland	W. Germany	Poland 1, Brazil 0
1978	Argentina	Cesar Menotti	3-1*	Holland	Argentina	Brazil 2, Italy 1
1982	Italy	Enzo Bearzot	3-1	W. Germany	Spain	Poland 3, France 2
1986	Argentina	Carlos Bilardo	3-2	W. Germany	Mexico	France 4, Belgium 2*
1990	West Germany	Franz Beckenbauer	1-0	Argentina	Italy	Italy 2, England 1
1994	Brazil	Carlos A. Parreira	0-0†	Italy	USA	Sweden 4, Bulgaria 0
1998	at France (June-July)					

*Winning goals scored in overtime (no sudden death); †Brazil defeated Italy in shootout (3-2) after scoreless overtime period (30 minutes).

All-Time World Cup Leaders

Career Goals

World Cup scoring leaders through 1994. Years listed are years played in World Cup.

	No
Gerd Müller, West Germany (1970,74)	14
Just Fontaine, France (1958)	13
Pelé, Brazil (1958, 62, 66, 70)	12
Sandor Kocsis, Hungary (1954)	11
Teofilo Cubillas, Peru (1970, 78)	10
Gregorz Lato, Poland (1974, 78, 82)	10
Gary Lineker, England (1986,90)	10
Helmut Rahn, West Germany (1954,58)	10

Most Valuable Player

Officially, the Golden Ball Award, the Most Valuable Player of the World Cup tournament has been selected since 1982 by a panel of international soccer journalists.

Year		Year	
1982	Paolo Rossi, Italy	1990	Toto Schillaci, Italy
1986	Diego Maradona, Arg.	1994	Romario, Brazil

Single Tournament Goals

World Cup tournament scoring leaders through 1994.

Year		Gm	No
1930	Guillermo Stabile, Argentina	4	8
1934	Angelo Schiavio, Italy	3	4
	Oldrich Nejedly, Czechoslovakia	4	4
	& Edmund Conen, Germany	4	4
1938	Leonidas, Brazil	3	8
1950	Ademir, Brazil	6	7
1954	Sandor Kocsis, Hungary	5	11
1958	Just Fontaine, France	6	13
1962	Drazen Jerkovic, Yugoslavia	6	5
1966	Eusebio, Portugal	6	9
1970	Gerd Müller, West Germany	6	10
1974	Grzegorz Lato, Poland	7	7
1978	Mario Kempes, Argentina	7	6
1982	Paolo Rossi, Italy	7	6
1986	Gary Lineker, England	5	6
1990	Toto Schillaci, Italy	7	6
1994	Oleg Salenko, Russia	3	6
	Hristo Stoichkov, Bulgaria	7	6

All-Time World Cup Ranking Table

Since the first World Cup in 1930, Brazil is the only country to play in all 15 final tournaments and win the championship four times. The FIFA All-Time Table below ranks all nations that have ever qualified for a World Cup final tournament by points earned through 1994. Victories, which earned two points from 1930-90, were awarded three points starting in 1996. Note that Germany's appearances include 10 made by West Germany from 1954-90. Participants in the 1994 World Cup final are in **bold** type.

	App	Gm	W	L	T	Pts	GF	GA
1 **Brazil**	15	73	49	11	13	111	159	68
2 **Germany**	13	73	42	15	16	100	154	97
3 **Italy**	13	61	35	12	14	84	97	59
4 **Argentina**	11	52	26	17	9	61	90	65
5 **England**	9	41	18	11	12	48	55	38
6 **Spain**	9	37	15	13	9	39	53	44
7 Uruguay	9	37	15	14	8	38	61	52
Russia	8	34	16	12	6	38	60	40
9 **Sweden**	9	38	14	15	9	37	66	60
10 France	9	34	15	14	5	35	71	56
Yugoslavia	8	33	14	12	7	35	55	42
12 Hungary	9	32	15	14	3	33	87	57
13 Poland	5	25	13	7	5	31	39	29
14 **Holland**	6	25	11	8	6	28	43	29
15 Czech Rep.	8	30	11	14	5	27	44	45
16 Austria	6	26	12	12	2	26	40	43
17 **Mexico**	10	33	7	18	8	22	31	68
Belgium	9	29	9	16	4	22	37	53
19 Chile	6	21	7	11	3	17	26	32
20 **Romania**	6	17	6	7	4	16	26	29
21 **Switzerland**	7	22	6	13	3	15	33	51
22 Scotland	7	20	4	10	6	14	23	35
23 **Bulgaria**	6	23	3	13	7	13	21	46
24 Portugal	2	9	6	3	0	12	19	12
25 Peru	4	15	4	8	3	11	19	31
No. Ireland	3	13	3	5	5	11	13	23
27 Paraguay	4	11	3	4	4	10	16	25
Cameroon	3	11	3	4	4	10	11	21
29 **USA**	5	14	4	9	1	9	17	33
30 **Ireland**	2	9	1	3	5	7	4	7

	App	Gm	W	L	T	Pts	GF	GA
31 **Colombia**	3	10	2	6	2	6	13	20
Denmark	1	4	3	1	0	6	10	6
East Germany	1	6	2	2	2	6	5	5
34 **Morocco**	3	10	1	6	3	5	7	13
Algeria	2	6	2	3	1	5	6	10
Wales	1	5	1	1	3	5	4	4
37 Costa Rica	1	4	2	2	0	4	4	6
Nigeria	1	4	2	2	0	4	7	4
Saudi Arabia	1	4	2	2	0	4	5	6
40 **South Korea**	4	11	0	8	3	3	9	34
Norway	2	4	1	2	1	3	2	3
Cuba	1	3	1	1	1	3	5	12
North Korea	1	4	1	2	1	3	5	9
Tunisia	1	3	1	1	1	3	3	2
45 Egypt	2	4	0	2	2	2	3	6
Honduras	1	3	0	1	2	2	2	3
Israel	1	3	0	1	2	2	1	3
Turkey	1	3	1	2	0	2	10	11
49 **Bolivia**	3	6	0	5	1	1	1	20
Australia	1	3	0	2	1	1	0	5
Iran	1	3	0	1	2	1	2	8
Kuwait	1	3	0	2	1	1	2	6
53 El Salvador	2	6	0	6	0	0	1	22
Canada	1	3	0	3	0	0	0	5
East Indies	1	1	0	1	0	0	0	6
Greece	1	3	0	3	0	0	0	10
Haiti	1	3	0	3	0	0	2	14
Iraq	1	3	0	3	0	0	1	4
New Zealand	1	3	0	3	0	0	2	12
UAE	1	3	0	3	0	0	2	11
Zaire	1	3	0	3	0	0	0	14

The United States in the World Cup

While the United States has fielded a national team every year of the World Cup, only four of those teams have been able to make it past the preliminary competition and qualify for the final World Cup tournament. The 1994 national team automatically qualified because the U.S. served as host of the event for the first time. The U.S. has played in three of the first four World Cups (1930, '34 and '50) and each of the last two (1990, '94). The Americans have a record of 4-9-1 in 14 World Cup matches, with two victories in 1930, a 1-0 upset of England in 1950, and a 2-1 shocker over Colombia in 1994.

1930
1st Round Matches

United States 3..Belgium 0
United States 3...Paraguay 0

Semifinals

Argentina 6...United States 1
U.S. Scoring—Bert Patenaude (3), Bart McGhee (2), James Brown, Thomas Florie.

1934
1st Round Match

Italy 7...United States 1
U.S. Scoring—Buff Donelli (who later became a noted college and NFL football coach).

1950
1st Round Matches

Spain 3...United States 1
United States 1...England 0
Chile 5...United States 2
U.S. Scoring—Joe Gaetjens, Joe Maca, Gino Pariani, Frank Wallace.

1990
1st Round Matches

Czechoslovakia 5..United States 1
Italy 1..United States 0
Austria 2..United States 1
U.S. Scoring—Paul Caligiuri, Bruce Murray.

1994

1st Round Matches

United States 1..Switzerland 1
United States 2...Colombia 1
Romania 1...United States 0

Round of 16

Brazil 1..United States 0
Overall U.S. Scoring— Eric Wynalda, Ernie Stewart, own goal (Colombia defender Andres Escobar).

World Cup Finals

Current World Cup champion Brazil and finalist Italy each appeared in their fifth Cup championship game in 1994 and played to the first scoreless overtime draw in the history of the Cup final. The match was also the first decided by a shootout (Brazil winning, 3-2). West Germany (now Germany) has played in the most Cup finals with six. Note that a four-team round robin determined the 1950 championship—the deciding game turned out to be the last one of the tournament between Uruguay and Brazil.

1930

Uruguay 4, Argentina 2

(at Montevideo, Uruguay)

		1	2—T
July 30	Uruguay (4-0)	1	3—4
	Argentina (4-1)	2	0—2

Goals: Uruguay—Pablo Dorado (12th minute), Pedro Cea (54th), Santos Iriarte (68th), Castro (89th); Argentina—Carlos Peucelle (20th), Guillermo Stabile (37th).

Uruguay—Ballesteros, Nasazzi, Mascheroni, Andrade, Fernandez, Gestido, Dorado, Scarone, Castro, Cea, Iriarte.

Argentina—Botasso, Della Torre, Paternoster, J. Evaristo, Monti, Suarez, Peucelle, Varallo, Stabile, Ferreira, M. Evaristo.

Attendance: 90,000. **Referee:** Langenus (Belgium).

1934

Italy 2, Czechoslovakia 1 (OT)

(at Rome)

		1	2	OT—T
June 10	Italy (4-0-1)	0	1	1—2
	Czechoslovakia (3-1)	0	1	0—1

Goals: Italy—Raimondo Orsi (80th minute), Angelo Schiavio (95th); Czechoslovakia—Puc (70th).

Italy—Combi, Monzeglio, Allemandi, Ferraris IV, Monti, Bertolini, Guaita, Meazza, Schiavio, Ferrari, Orsi.

Czechoslovakia—Planicka, Zenisek, Ctyroky, Kostalek, Cambal, Krcil, Junek, Svoboda, Sobotka, Nejedly, Puc.

Attendance: 55,000. **Referee:** Eklind (Sweden).

1938

Italy 4, Hungary 2

(at Paris)

		1	2—T
June 19	Italy (4-0)	3	1—4
	Hungary (3-1)	1	1—2

Goals: Italy—Gino Colaussi (5th minute), Silvio Piola (16th), Colassi (35th), Piola (82nd); Hungary—Titkos (7th), Georges Sarosi (70th).

Italy—Olivieri, Foni, Rava, Serantoni, Andreolo, Locatelli, Biavati, Meazza, Piola, Ferrari, Colaussi.

Hungary—Szabo, Polgar, Biro, Szalay, Szucs, Lazar, Sas, Vincze, G. Sarosi, Szengeller, Titkos.

Attendance: 65,000. **Referee:** Capdeville (France).

1950

Uruguay 2, Brazil 1

(at Rio de Janeiro)

		1	2—T
July 16	Uruguay (3-0-1)	0	2—2
	Brazil (4-1-1)	0	1—1

Goals: Uruguay—Juan Schiaffino (66th minute), Chico Ghiggia (79th); Brazil—Friaça (47th).

Uruguay—Maspoli, M. Gonzales, Tejera, Gambetta, Varela, Andrade, Ghiggia, Perez, Miguez, Schiaffino, Moran.

Brazil—Barbosa, Augusto, Juvenal, Bauer, Danilo, Bigode, Friaça, Zizinho, Ademir, Jair, Chico.

Attendance: 199,854. **Referee:** Reader (England).

1954

West Germany 3, Hungary 2

(at Berne, Switzerland)

		1	2—T
July 4	West Germany (4-1)	2	1—3
	Hungary (4-1)	2	0—2

Goals: West Germany—Max Morlock (10th minute), Helmut Rahn (18th), Rahn (84th); Hungary—Ferenc Puskas (4th), Zoltan Czibor (9th).

West Germany—Turek, Posipal, Liebrich, Kohlmeyer, Eckel, Mai, Rahn, Morlock, O. Walter, F. Walter, Schaefer.

Hungary—Grosics, Buzansky, Lorant, Lantos, Bozsik, Zakarias, Czibor, Kocsis, Hidegkuti, Puskas, J. Toth.

Attendance: 60,000. **Referee:** Ling (England).

1958

Brazil 5, Sweden 2

(at Stockholm)

		1	2—T
June 29	Brazil (5-0-1)	2	3—5
	Sweden (4-1-1)	1	1—2

Goals: Brazil—Vavà (9th minute), Vavà (32nd), Pelé (55th), Mario Zagalo (68th), Pelé (90th); Sweden—Nils Liedholm (3rd), Agne Simonsson (80th).

Brazil—Gilmar, D. Santos, N. Santos, Zito, Bellini, Orlando, Garrincha, Didi, Vavà, Pelé, Zagalo.

Sweden—Svensson, Bergmark, Axbom, Boerjesson, Gustavsson, Parling, Hamrin, Gren, Simonsson, Liedholm, Skoglund.

Attendance: 49,737. **Referee:** Guigue (France).

1962

Brazil 3, Czechoslovakia 1

(at Santiago, Chile)

		1	2—T
June 17	Brazil (5-0-1)	1	2—3
	Czechoslovakia (3-2-1)	1	0—1

Goals: Brazil—Amarildo (17th minute), Zito (68th), Vavà (77th); Czechoslovakia—Josef Masopust (15th).

Brazil—Gilmar, D. Santos, N. Santos, Zito, Mauro, Zozimo, Garrincha, Didi, Vavà, Amarildo, Zagalo.

Czechoslovakia—Schroiff, Tichy, Novak, Pluskal, Popluhar, Masopust, Pospichal, Scherer, Kvasniak, Kadraba, Jelinek.

Attendance: 68,679. **Referee:** Latishev (USSR).

1966

England 4, West Germany 2 (OT)

(at London)

		1	2	OT—T
July 30	England (5-0-1)	1	1	2—4
	West Germany (4-1-1)	1	1	0—2

Goals: England—Geoff Hurst (18th minute), Martin Peters (78th), Hurst (101st), Hurst (120th); West Germany—Helmut Haller (12th), Wolfgang Weber (90th).

England—Banks, Cohen, Wilson, Stiles, J. Charlton, Moore, Ball, Hurst, B. Charlton, Hunt, Peters.

West Germany—Tilkowski, Hottges, Schnellinger, Beckenbauer, Schulz, Weber, Haller, Seeler, Held, Overath, Emmerich.

Attendance: 93,802. **Referee:** Dienst (Switzerland).

World Cup Finals (Cont.)

1970

Brazil 4, Italy 1
(at Mexico City)

	1	2—T
June 21 Brazil (6-0)	1	3—4
Italy (3-1-2)	1	0—1

Goals: Brazil—Pelé (18th minute), Gerson (65th), Jairzinho (70th), Carlos Alberto (86th); Italy—Roberto Boninsegna (37th).

Brazil—Felix, C. Alberto, Everaldo, Clodoaldo, Brito, Piazza, Jairzinho, Gerson, Tostao, Pelé, Rivelino.

Italy—Albertosi, Burgnich, Facchetti, Bertini (Juliano, 73rd), Rosato, Cera, Domenghini, Mazzola, Boninsegna (Rivera, 84th), De Sisti, Riva.

Attendance: 107,412. **Referee:** Glockner (E. Germany).

1974

West Germany 2, Holland 1
(at Munich)

	1	2—T
July 7 West Germany (6-1)	2	0—2
Holland (5-1-1)	1	0—1

Goals: West Germany—Paul Breitner (25th minute, penalty kick), Gerd Müller (43rd); Holland—Johan Neeskens (1st, penalty kick).

West Germany—Maier, Beckenbauer, Vogts, Breitner, Schwarzenbeck, Overath, Bonhof, Hoeness, Grabowski, Müller, Holzenbein.

Holland—Jongbloed, Suurbier, Rijsbergen (De Jong, 58th), Krol, Haan, Jansen, Van Hanegem, Neeskens, Rep, Cruyff, Rensenbrink (R. Van de Kerkhof, 46th).

Attendance: 77,833. **Referee:** Taylor (England).

1978

Argentina 3, Holland 1 (OT)
(at Buenos Aires)

	1	2	OT—T
June 25 Argentina (5-1-1)	1	0	2—3
Holland (3-2-2)	0	1	0—1

Goals: Argentina—Mario Kempes (37th minute), Kempes (104th), Daniel Bertoni (114th); Holland—Dirk Nanninga (81st).

Argentina—Fillol, Olguin, L. Galvan, Passarella, Tarantini, Ardiles (Larrosa, 65th), Gallego, Kempes, Luque, Bertoni, Ortiz (Houseman, 77th).

Holland—Jongbloed, Jansen (Suurbier, 72nd), Brandts, Krol, Poortvliet, Haan, Neeskens, W. Van de Kerkhof, R. Van de Kerkhof, Rep (Nanninga, 58th), Rensenbrink.

Attendance: 77,260. **Referee:** Gonella (Italy).

1982

Italy 3, West Germany 1
(at Madrid)

	1	2—T
July 11 Italy (4-0-3)	0	3—3
West Germany (4-2-1)	0	1—1

Goals: Italy—Paolo Rossi (57th minute), Marco Tardelli (68th), Alessandro Altobelli (81st); West Germany—Paul Breitner (83rd).

Italy—Zoff, Scirea, Gentile, Cabrini, Collovati, Bergomi, Tardelli, Oriali, Conti, Rossi, Graziani (Altobelli, 8th, and Causio, 89th).

West Germany—Schumacher, Stielike, Kaltz, Briegel, K.H. Foerster, B. Foerster, Breitner, Dremmler (Hrubesch, 61st), Littbarski, Fischer, Rummenigge (Müller, 69th).

Attendance: 90,080. **Referee:** Coelho (Brazil).

1986

Argentina 3, West Germany 2
(at Mexico City)

	1	2—T
June 29 Argentina (6-0-1)	1	2—3
West Germany (4-2-1)	0	2—2

Goals: Argentina—Jose Brown (22nd minute), Jorge Valdano (55th), Jorge Burruchaga (83rd); West Germany—Karl-Heinz Rummenigge (73rd), Rudi Voeller (81st).

Argentina—Pumpido, Cuciuffo, Olarticoechea, Ruggeri, Brown, Batista, Burruchaga (Trobbiani, 89th), Giusti, Enrique, Maradona, Valdano.

West Germany—Schumacher, Jakobs, Foerster, Berthold, Briegel, Eder, Brehme, Matthäus, Rummenigge, Magath (Hoeness, 61st), Allofs (Völler, 46th).

Attendance: 114,590. **Referee:** Filho (Brazil).

1990

West Germany 1, Argentina 0
(at Rome)

	1	2—T
July 8 West Germany (6-0-1)	0	1—1
Argentina (4-2-1)	0	0—0

Goals: West Germany—Andreas Brehme (85th minute, penalty kick).

West Germany—Illgner, Berthold (Reuter, 73rd), Kohler, Augenthaler, Buchwald, Brehme, Haessler, Matthäus, Littbarski, Klinsmann, Völler.

Argentina—Goycoechea, Ruggeri (Monzon, 46th), Simon, Serrizuela, Lorenzo, Basualdo, Troglio, Burruchaga (Calderon, 53rd), Sensini, Dezotti, Maradona.

Attendance: 73,603. **Referee:** Codesal (Mexico).

1994

Brazil 0, Italy 0 (SO)
(at Pasadena, Calif.)

	1	2	OT—T
July 17 Italy (4-2-1)	0	0	0—0
Brazil (6-0-1)	0	0	0—0*

*Brazil wins shootout, 3-2.

Shootout (five shots each, alternating): ITA— Baresi (miss, 0-0); BRA— Santos (blocked, 0-0); ITA— Albertini (goal, 1-0); BRA—Romario (goal, 1-1); ITA— Evani (goal, 2-1); BRA— Branco (goal, 2-2); ITA— Massaro (blocked, 2-2); BRA— Dunga (goal, 2-3); ITA—R. Baggio (miss, 2-3).

Italy—Pagliuca, Mussi (Apolloni, 35th minute), Baresi, Benarrivo, Maldini, Albertini, D. Baggio (Evani, 95th), Berti, Donadoni, R. Baggio, Massaro.

Brazil—Taffarel, Jorginho (Cafu, 21st minute), Branco, Aldair, Santos, Mazinho, Silva, Dunga, Zinho (Viola, 106th), Bebeto, Romario.

Attendance: 94,194. **Referee:** Puhl (Hungary).

World Cup Shootouts

Introduced in 1982; winning sides in **bold** type.

Year	Round		Final	SO
1982	Semi	**W. Germany** vs France	3-3	(5-4)
1986	Quarter	**Belgium** vs Spain	1-1	(5-4)
	Quarter	**France** vs Brazil	1-1	(4-3)
	Quarter	**W. Germany** vs Mexico	0-0	(4-1)
1990	Second	**Ireland** vs Romania	0-0	(5-4)
	Quarter	**Argentina** vs Yugoslavia	0-0	(3-2)
	Semi	**Argentina** vs Italy	1-1	(4-3)
	Semi	**W. Germany** vs England	1-1	(4-3)
1994	Second	**Bulgaria** vs Mexico	1-1	(3-1)
	Quarter	**Sweden** vs Romania	2-2	(5-4)
	Final	**Brazil** vs Italy	0-0	(3-2)

Year-by-Year Comparisons

How the 15 World Cup tournaments have compared in nations qualifying, matches played, players participating, goals scored, average goals per game, overall attendance and attendance per game.

Year	Host	Continent	Nations	Matches	Players	Goals Scored	Goals Per Game	Attendance Overall	Attendance Per Game
1930	Uruguay	So. America	13	18	189	70	3.8	434,500	24,138
1934	Italy	Europe	16	17	208	70	4.1	395,000	23,235
1938	France	Europe	15	18	210	84	4.7	483,000	26,833
1942-46		Not held							
1950	Brazil	So. America	13	22	192	88	4.0	1,337,000	60,772
1954	Switzerland	Europe	16	26	233	140	5.3	943,000	36,270
1958	Sweden	Europe	16	35	241	126	3.9	868,000	24,800
1962	Chile	So. America	16	32	252	89	2.8	776,000	24,250
1966	England	Europe	16	32	254	89	2.8	1,614,677	50,458
1970	Mexico	No. America	16	32	270	95	3.0	1,673,975	52,311
1974	West Germany	Europe	16	38	264	97	2.6	1,774,022	46,684
1978	Argentina	So. America	16	38	277	102	2.7	1,610,215	42,374
1982	Spain	Europe	24	52	396	146	2.8	1,856,277	33,967
1986	Mexico	No. America	24	52	414	132	2.5	2,402,951	46,211
1990	Italy	Europe	24	52	413	115	2.2	2,517,348	48,411
1994	United States	No. America	24	52	437	140	2.7	3,567,415	68,102
1998	France	Europe	32	—	—	—	—	—	—

OTHER WORLDWIDE COMPETITION

The Olympic Games

Held every four years since 1896, except during World War I (1916) and World War II (1940-44). Soccer was not a medal sport in 1896 at Athens or in 1932 at Los Angeles. By agreement between FIFA and the IOC, Olympic soccer competition is currently limited to players 23 years old and under.

Multiple winners: England and Hungary (3); Soviet Union and Uruguay (2).

Year		Year	
1900	**England,** France, Belgium	1956	**Soviet Union,** Yugoslavia, Bulgaria
1904	**Canada,** USA I, USA II	1960	**Yugoslavia,** Denmark, Hungary
1906	**Denmark,** Smyrna (Int'l entry), Greece	1964	**Hungary,** Czechoslovakia, East Germany
1908	**England,** Denmark, Holland	1968	**Hungary,** Bulgaria, Japan
1912	**England,** Denmark, Holland	1972	**Poland,** Hungary, East Germany
1920	**Belgium,** Spain, Holland	1976	**East Germany,** Poland, Soviet Union
1924	**Uruguay,** Switzerland, Sweden	1980	**Czechoslovakia,** East Germany, Soviet Union
1928	**Uruguay,** Argentina, Italy	1984	**France,** Brazil, Yugoslavia
1936	**Italy,** Austria, Norway	1988	**Soviet Union,** Brazil, West Germany
1948	**Sweden,** Yugoslavia, Denmark	1992	**Spain,** Poland, Ghana
1952	**Hungary,** Yugoslavia, Sweden		

The Under-20 World Cup

Held every two years since 1977. Officially, The World Youth Championship for the FIFA/Coca-Cola Cup.

Multiple winners: Brazil (3); Portugal (2).

Year		Year	
1977	Soviet Union	1987	Yugoslavia
1979	Argentina	1989	Portugal
1981	West Germany	1991	Portugal
1983	Brazil	1993	Brazil
1985	Brazil	1995	(at Nigeria)

The Under-17 World Cup

Held every two years since 1985. Officially, The FIFA U-17 World Tournament for the JVC Cup.

Multiple winners: Nigeria (2).

Year		Year	
1985	Nigeria	1991	Ghana
1987	Soviet Union	1993	Nigeri
1989	Saudi Arabia	1995	(at Ecuador)

Indoor World Championship

First held in 1989. FIFA's only Five-a-Side tournament.
Multiple winners: Brazil (2).

Year		Year	
1989	Brazil	1996	(at Spain)
1992	Brazil		

Women's World Championship

First held in 1991. Officially, the FIFA World Championship for Women's Football for the M&M's Cup.

Year		Year	
1991	United States	1995	(at Sweden)

CONTINENTAL COMPETITION

European Championship

Held every four years since 1960. Officially, the European Football Championship.
Multiple winner: West Germany (2).

Year		Year		Year		Year	
1960	Soviet Union	1972	West Germany	1980	West Germany	1988	Holland
1964	Spain	1976	Czechoslovakia	1984	France	1992	Denmark
1968	Italy						

Copa America

Held irregularly since 1916. Unofficially, the Championship of South America.
Multiple winners: Argentina (14); Uruguay (13); Brazil (4); Paraguay and Peru (2).

Year		Year		Year		Year	
1916	Uruguay	1926	Uruguay	1946	Argentina	1963	Bolivia
1917	Uruguay	1927	Argentina	1947	Argentina	1967	Uruguay
1919	Brazil	1929	Argentina	1949	Brazil	1975	Peru
1920	Uruguay	1935	Uruguay	1953	Paraguay	1979	Paraguay
1921	Argentina	1937	Argentina	1955	Argentina	1983	Uruguay
1922	Brazil	1939	Peru	1956	Uruguay	1987	Uruguay
1923	Uruguay	1941	Argentina	1957	Argentina	1989	Brazil
1924	Uruguay	1942	Uruguay	1958	Argentina	1991	Argentina
1925	Argentina	1945	Argentina	1959	Uruguay	1993	Argentina

African Nations' Cup

Contested since 1957 and held every two years since 1968.
Multiple winners: Ghana (4); Congo/Zaire and Egypt (3); Cameroon and Nigeria (2).

Year		Year		Year		Year	
1957	Egypt	1968	Congo	1978	Ghana	1988	Cameroon
1959	Egypt	1970	Sudan	1980	Nigeria	1990	Algeria
1962	Ethiopia	1972	Zaire	1982	Ghana	1992	Ivory Coast
1963	Ghana	1974	Zaire	1984	Cameroon	1994	Nigeria
1965	Ghana	1976	Morocco	1986	Egypt		

CONCACAF Gold Cup

The Confederation of North, Central American and Caribbean Football Championship. Contested irregularly from 1963-81 and revived as CONCACAF Gold Cup in 1991.
Multiple winners: Mexico (4); Costa Rica (2).

Year		Year		Year		Year	
1963	Costa Rica	1969	Costa Rica	1977	Mexico	1991	United States
1965	Mexico	1971	Mexico	1981	Honduras	1993	Mexico
1967	Guatemala	1973	Haiti				

CLUB COMPETITION

Intercontinental Cup

Also known as the Toyota Cup. Contested annually in December between the winners of the European Cup and South America's Copa Libertadores. Four European Cup winners refused to participate in the championship match in the 1970s and were replaced each time by the European Cup runner-up: Panathinaikos (Greece) for Ajax Amsterdam (Holland) in 1971; Juventus (Italy) for Ajax in 1973; Atlético Madrid (Spain) for Bayern Munich (West Germany) in 1974; and Malmo (Sweden) for Nottingham Forest (England) in 1979. Another European Cup winner, Marseille of France, was prohibited by the Union of European Football Associations (UEFA) from playing for the 1993 Intercontinental Cup because of its involvement in the match-rigging scandal.

Best-of-three game format from 1960-68, then a two-game/total goals format from 1969-79. Toyota became Cup sponsor in 1980, changed the format to a one-game championship and moved it to Toyko.
Multiple winners: AC Milan, Nacional and Peñarol (3); Independiente, Inter-Milan, Santos and São Paulo (2).

Year		Year		Year	
1960	Real Madrid (Spain)	1972	Ajax Amsterdam (Holland)	1983	Gremio (Brazil)
1961	Peñarol (Uruguay)	1973	Independiente (Argentina)	1984	Independiente (Argentina)
1962	Santos (Brazil)	1974	Atlético Madrid (Spain)	1985	Juventus (Italy)
1963	Santos (Brazil)	1975	Not held	1986	River Plate (Argentina)
1964	Inter-Milan (Italy)	1976	Bayern Munich W.Germany)	1987	FC Porto (Portugal)
1965	Inter-Milan (Italy)	1977	Boca Juniors (Argentina)	1988	Nacional (Uruguay)
1966	Peñarol (Uruguay)	1978	Not held	1989	AC Milan (Italy)
1967	Racing Club (Argentina)	1979	Olimpia (Paraguay)	1990	AC Milan (Italy)
1968	Estudiantes (Argentina)	1980	Nacional (Uruguay)	1991	Red Star (Yugoslavia)
1969	AC Milan (Italy)	1981	Flamengo (Brazil)	1992	São Paulo (Brazil)
1970	Feyenoord (Holland)	1982	Peñarol (Uruguay)	1993	São Paulo (Brazil)
1971	Nacional (Uruguay)				

European Cup

Contested annually since the 1955-56 season by the league champions of the member countries of the Union of European Football Associations (UEFA).

Multiple winners: Real Madrid (6); AC Milan (5); Liverpool (4); Ajax Amsterdam and Bayern Munich (3); Benfica, Inter-Milan and Nottingham Forest (2).

Year		Year		Year	
1956	Real Madrid (Spain)	1970	Feyenoord (Holland)	1983	SV Hamburg (W. Germany)
1957	Real Madrid (Spain)	1971	Ajax Amsterdam (Holland)	1984	Liverpool (England)
1958	Real Madrid (Spain)	1972	Ajax Amsterdam (Holland)	1985	Juventus (Italy)
1959	Real Madrid (Spain)	1973	Ajax Amsterdam (Holland)	1986	Steaua Bucharest (Romania)
1960	Real Madrid (Spain)	1974	Bayern Munich (W. Germany)	1987	FC Porto (Portugal)
1961	Benfica (Portugal)	1975	Bayern Munich (W. Germany)	1988	PSV Eindhoven (Holland)
1962	Benfica (Portugal)	1976	Bayern Munich (W. Germany)	1989	AC Milan (Italy)
1963	AC Milan (Italy)	1977	Liverpool (England)	1990	AC Milan (Italy)
1964	Inter-Milan (Italy)	1978	Liverpool (England)	1991	Red Star Belgrade (Yugo.)
1965	Inter-Milan (Italy)	1979	Nottingham Forest (England)	1992	Barcelona (Spain)
1966	Real Madrid (Spain)	1980	Nottingham Forest (England)	1993	Marseille (France)
1967	Glasgow Celtic (Scotland)	1981	Liverpool (England)	1994	AC Milan (Italy)
1968	Manchester United (England)	1982	Aston Villa (England)		
1969	AC Milan (Italy)				

European Cup Winners' Cup

Contested annually since the 1960-61 season by the cup winners of the member countries of the Union of European Football Associations (UEFA).

Multiple winners: Barcelona (3); AC Milan, RSC Anderlecht and Dynamo Kiev (2).

Year		Year		Year	
1961	Fiorentina (Italy)	1973	AC Milan (Italy)	1985	Everton (England)
1962	Atlético Madrid (Spain)	1974	FC Magdeburg (E. Germany)	1986	Dynamo Kiev (USSR)
1963	Tottenham Hotspur (England)	1975	Dynamo Kiev (USSR)	1987	Ajax Amsterdam (Holland)
1964	Sporting Lisbon (Portugal)	1976	RSC Anderlecht (Belgium)	1988	Mechelen (Belgium)
1965	West Ham United (England)	1977	SV Hamburg (W. Germany)	1989	Barcelona (Spain)
1966	Borussia Dortmund (W. Germany)	1978	RSC Anderlecht (Belgium)	1990	Sampdoria (Italy)
1967	Bayern Munich (W. Germany)	1979	Barcelona (Spain)	1991	Manchester United (England)
1968	AC Milan (Italy)	1980	Valencia (Spain)	1992	Werder Bremen (Germany)
1969	Slovan Bratislava (Czech.)	1981	Dynamo Tbilisi (USSR)	1993	Parma (Italy)
1970	Manchester City (England)	1982	Barcelona (Spain)	1994	Arsenal (England)
1971	Chelsea (England)	1983	Aberdeen (Scotland)		
1972	Glasgow Rangers (Scotland)	1984	Juventus (Italy)		

UEFA Cup

Contested annually since the 1957-58 season by teams other than league champions and cup winners of the Union of European Football Associations (UEFA). Teams selected by UEFA based on each country's previous performance in the tournament. Teams from England were banned from UEFA Cup play from 1985-90 for the criminal behavior of their supporters.

Multiple winners: Barcelona and Juventus (3); Borussia Moenchengladbach, IFL Gothenburg, Leeds United, Liverpool, Real Madrid, Tottenham Hotspur and Valencia (2).

Year		Year		Year	
1958	Barcelona (Spain)	1972	Tottenham Hotspur (England)	1983	RSC Anderlecht (Belgium)
1959	Not held	1973	Liverpool (England)	1984	Tottenham Hotspur (England)
1960	Barcelona (Spain)	1974	Feyenoord (Holland)	1985	Real Madrid (Spain)
1961	AS Roma (Italy)	1975	Borussia Mönchengladbach (W. Germany)	1986	Real Madrid (Spain)
1962	Valencia (Spain)	1976	Liverpool (England)	1987	IFK Gothenburg (Sweden)
1963	Valencia (Spain)	1977	Juventus (Italy)	1988	Bayer Leverkusen (W. Germany)
1964	Real Zaragoza (Spain)	1978	PSV Eindhoven (Holland)	1989	Napoli (Italy)
1965	Ferencvaros (Hungary)	1979	Borussia Mönchengladbach (W. Germany)	1990	Juventus (Italy)
1966	Barcelona (Spain)	1980	Eintracht Frankfurt (W. Germany)	1991	Inter-Milan (Italy)
1967	Dynamo Zagreb (Yugoslavia)	1981	Ipswich Town (England)	1992	Ajax Amsterdam (Holland)
1968	Leeds United (England)	1982	IFK Gothenburg (Sweden)	1993	Juventus (Italy)
1969	Newcastle United (England)			1994	Inter-Milan (Italy)
1970	Arsenal (England)				
1971	Leeds United (England)				

Club Competition (Cont.)
Copa Libertadores

Contested annually since the 1955-56 season by the league champions of South America's football union.

Multiple winners: Independiente (7); Peñarol (5); Estudiantes and Nacional-Uruguay (3); Boca Juniors, Olimpia, Santos and São Paulo (2).

Year		Year		Year	
1960	Peñarol (Uruguay)	1972	Independiente (Argentina)	1984	Independiente (Argentina)
1961	Peñarol (Uruguay)	1973	Independiente (Argentina)	1985	Argentinos Jrs. (Argentina)
1962	Santos (Brazil)	1974	Independiente (Argentina)	1986	River Plate (Argentina)
1963	Santos (Brazil)	1975	Independiente (Argentina)	1987	Peñarol (Uruguay)
1964	Independiente (Argentina)	1976	Cruzeiro (Brazil)	1988	Nacional (Uruguay)
1965	Independiente (Argentina)	1977	Boca Juniors (Argentina)	1989	Nacional Medellin (Colombia)
1966	Peñarol (Uruguay)	1978	Boca Juniors (Argentina)		
1967	Racing Club (Argentina)	1979	Olimpia (Paraguay)	1990	Olimpia (Paraguay)
1968	Estudiantes de la Plata (Argentina)			1991	Colo Colo (Chile)
1969	Estudiantes de la Plata (Argentina)	1980	Nacional (Uruguay)	1992	São Paulo (Brazil)
		1981	Flamengo (Brazil)	1993	São Paulo (Brazil)
1970	Estudiantes de la Plata (Argentina)	1982	Peñarol (Uruguay)	1994	Velez Sarsfield (Argentina)
1971	Nacional (Uruguay)	1983	Gremio (Brazil)		

Annual Awards

World Player of the Year

Presented by FIFA, the European Sports Magazine Association (ESM) and Adidas, the sports equipment manufacturer, since 1991. Winners are selected by national team coaches from around the world.

Year		Nat'l Team	Year		Nat'l Team
1991	Lothar Matthäus, Inter-Milan	Germany	1993	Roberto Baggio, Juventus	Italy
1992	Marco Van Basten, AC Milan	Holland			

European Player of the Year

Officially, the "Ballon d'Or" and presented by *France Football* magazine since 1956. Candidates are limited to European players in European leagues and winners are selected by a panel of 29 European soccer journalists.

Multiple winners: Johan Cruyff, Michel Platini and Marco Van Basten (3); Franz Beckenbauer, Alfredo di Stéfano, Kevin Keegan and Karl-Heinz Rummenigge (2).

Year		Nat'l Team	Year		Nat'l Team
1956	Stanley Matthews, Blackpool	England	1975	Oleg Blokhin, Dynamo Kiev	Soviet Union
1957	Alfredo di Stéfano, Real Madrid	Arg./Spain	1976	Franz Beckenbauer, Bayern Munich	W.Ger.
1958	Raymond Kopa, Real Madrid	France	1977	Allan Simonsen, B. Mönchengladbach	Denmark
1959	Alfredo di Stéfano, Real Madrid	Arg./Spain	1978	Kevin Keegan, SV Hamburg	England
1960	Luis Suarez, Barcelona	Spain	1979	Kevin Keegan, SV Hamburg	England
1961	Enrique Sivori, Juventus	Arg./Italy	1980	K.H. Rummenigge, Bayern Munich	W.Ger.
1962	Josef Masopust, Dukla Prague	Czech.	1981	K.H. Rummenigge, Bayern Munich	W.Ger.
1963	Lev Yashin, Dynamo Moscow	Soviet Union	1982	Paolo Rossi, Juventus	Italy
1964	Denis Law, Manchester United	Scotland	1983	Michel Platini, Juventus	France
1965	Eusebio, Benfica	Portugal	1984	Michel Platini, Juventus	France
1966	Bobby Charlton, Manchester United	England	1985	Michel Platini, Juventus	France
1967	Florian Albert, Ferencvaros	Hungary	1986	Igor Belanov, Dynamo Kiev	Soviet Union
1968	George Best, Manchester United	No. Ireland	1987	Ruud Gullit, AC Milan	Holland
1969	Gianni Rivera, AC Milan	Italy	1988	Marco Van Basten, AC Milan	Holland
1970	Gerd Müller, Bayern Munich	W.Ger.	1989	Marco Van Basten, AC Milan	Holland
1971	Johan Cruyff, Ajax Amsterdam	Holland	1990	Lothar Matthäus, Inter-Milan	W.Ger.
1972	Franz Beckenbauer, Bayern Munich	W.Ger.	1991	Jean-Pierre Papin, Marseille	France
1973	Johan Cruyff, Barcelona	Holland	1992	Marco Van Basten, AC Milan	Holland
1974	Johan Cruyff, Barcelona	Holland	1993	Roberto Baggio, Juventus	Italy

South American Player of the Year

Presented by *El Pais* of Uruguay since 1971. Candidates are limited to South American players in South American leagues and winners are selected by a panel of 80 Latin American sports editors.

Multiple winners: Elias Figueroa and Zico (3); Diego Maradona and Carlos Valderrama (2).

Year		Nat'l Team	Year		Nat'l Team
1971	Tostão, Cruzeiro	Brazil	1978	Mario Kempes, Valencia	Argentina
1972	Teofilo Cubillas, Alianza Lima	Peru	1979	Diego Maradona, Argentinos Juniors	Argentina
1973	Pelé, Santos	Brazil	1980	Diego Maradona, Boca Juniors	Argentina
1974	Elias Figueroa, Internacional	Chile	1981	Zico, Flamengo	Brazil
1975	Elias Figueroa, Internacional	Chile	1982	Zico, Flamengo	Brazil
1976	Elias Figueroa, Internacional	Chile	1983	Socrates, Corinthians	Brazil
1977	Zico, Flamengo	Brazil	1984	Enzo Francescoli, River Plate	Uruguay

Year	Nat'l Team
1985	Julio Cesar Romero, Fluminense.................Paraguay
1986	Antonio Alzamendi, River Plate.................Uruguay
1987	Carlos Valderrama, Deportivo Cali ....Colombia
1988	Ruben Paz, Racing Buenos Aires ....Uruguay
1989	Bebeto, Vasco da Gama ....Brazil

Year	Nat'l Team
1990	Raul Amarilla, Olimpia ....Paraguay
1991	Oscar Ruggeri, Velez Sarsfield ....Argentina
1992	Rai, São Paulo ....Brazil
1993	Carlos Valderrama, Atl. Junior ....Colombia

African Player of the Year

Officially, the African "Ballon d'Or" and presented by *France Football* magazine since 1970. All African players are eligible for the award and winners are selected by a panel of 41 African soccer journalists.

Multiple winners: Abedi Pele (3); Roger Milla and Thomas N'kona (2).

Year	
1970	Salif Keita, Mali
1971	Ibrahim Sunday, Ghana
1972	Cherif Souleymane, Guinea
1973	Tshimimu Bwanga, Zaire
1974	Paul Moukila, Congo
1975	Ahmed Faras, Morocco
1976	Roger Milla, Cameroon
1977	Dhiab Tarak, Tunisia
1978	Abdul Razak, Ghana

Year	
1979	Thomas N'Kono, Cameroon
1980	Jean Manga Onguene, Cameroon
1981	Lakhdar Belloumi, Algeria
1982	Thomas N'Kono, Cameroon
1983	Mahmoud Al-Khatib, Egypt
1984	Theophile Abega, Cameroon
1985	Mohamed Timoumi, Morocco
1986	Badou Zaki, Morocco

Year	
1987	Rabah Madjer, Algeria
1988	Kalusha Bwalya, Zambia
1989	George Weah, Liberia
1990	Roger Milla, Cameroon
1991	Abedi Pele, Ghana
1992	Abedi Pele, Ghana
1993	Abedi Pele, Ghana

U.S. Player of the Year

Presented by Honda and the Spanish-speaking radio show "Futbol de Primera" since 1991. Candidates are limited to American players who have played at least five games in the APSL or with the U.S. National Team and winners are selected by a panel of U.S. soccer journalists.

Year	
1991	Hugo Perez

Year	
1992	Eric Wynalda

Year	
1993	Thomas Dooley

The Century Club

Players who have made at least 100 international appearances. Each appearance is considered one cap. Players active in 1994—World Cup goalkeeper Thomas Ravelli (age 35) of Sweden and German national team captain Lothar Matthäus (age 33) are in **bold** type.

		Caps
1	Peter Shilton, England 125
2	Pat Jennings, Northern Ireland..............................119
3	**Thomas Ravelli,** Sweden 118
4	Heinz Hermann, Switzerland..................................117
	Lothar Matthäus, Germany 117
6	Bjorn Nordqvist, Sweden.....................................115
7	Dino Zoff, Italy 112
8	Hector Chumpitaz, Peru 111
9	Oleg Blochin, Russia 109
10	Ladislau Boloni, Romania 108
	Bobby Moore, England 108
12	Bobby Charlton, England 106
	Billy Wright, England 106

		Caps
14	Grzegorz Lato, Poland 104
	Torbjorn Svensson, Norway...................................104
16	Franz Beckenbauer, West Germany 103
17	Soon-Ho Choi, South Korea 102
	Kenny Dalglish, Scotland......................................102
	Kazimierz Deyna, Poland......................................102
	Morten Olsen, Denmark..102
	Joachim Steich, East Germany 102
22	Joszef Bozsik, Hungary 100
	Hans J. Dorner, East Germany 100
	Djalma Santos, Brazil...100

U.S. PRO LEAGUES

OUTDOOR

National Professional Soccer League (1967)

Not sanctioned by FIFA, the international soccer federation. The NPSL recruited individual players to fill the rosters of its 10 teams. The league lasted only one season.

	Playoff Final			Regular Season			
Year	Winner	Score(s)	Loser	Leading Scorer	G	A	Pts
1967	Oakland Clippers	0-1, 4-1	Baltimore Bays	Yanko Daucik, Toronto 20	8	48

United Soccer Association (1967)

Sanctioned by FIFA. Originally called the North American Soccer League, it became the USA to avoid being confused with the National Professional Soccer League (see above). Instead of recruiting individual players, the USA imported 12 entire teams from Europe to represent its 12 franchises. It, too, only lasted a season. The league champion Los Angeles Wolves were actually Wolverhampton of England and the runner-up Washington Whips were Aberdeen of Scotland.

	Playoff Final			Regular Season			
Year	Winner	Score	Loser	Leading Scorer	G	A	Pts
1967	Los Angeles Wolves	6-5 (OT)	Washington Whips	Roberto Boninsegna, Chicago.......................10	1	21

U.S. Pro Leagues (Cont.)
North American Soccer League (1968-84)

The NPSL and USA merged to form the NASL in 1968 and the new league lasted until 1985. The NASL championship was known as the Soccer Bowl from 1975-84. One game decided the NASL title every year but five. There were no playoffs in 1969; a two-game/aggregate goals format was used in 1968 and '70; and a best-of-three games format was used in 1971 and '84; (*) indicates overtime and (†) indicates tie-breaker.

Multiple winners: NY Cosmos (5); Chicago (2).

	Playoff Final			**Regular Season**			
Year	Winner	Score(s)	Loser	Leading Scorer	G	A	Pts
1968	Atlanta Chiefs	0-0,3-0	San Diego Toros	John Kowalik, Chicago	30	9	69
1969	Kansas City Spurs	No game	Atlanta Chiefs	Kaiser Motaung, Atlanta	16	4	36
1970	Rochester Lancers	3-0,1-3	Washington Darts	Kirk Apostolidis, Dallas	16	3	35
1971	Dallas Tornado	1-2*,4-1,2-0	Atlanta Chiefs	Carlos Metidieri, Rochester	19	8	46
1972	New York Cosmos	2-1	St. Louis Stars	Randy Horton, New York	9	4	22
1973	Philadelphia Atoms	2-0	Dallas Tornado	Kyle Rote, Jr., Dallas	10	10	30
1974	Los Angeles Aztecs	4-3†	Miami Toros	Paul Child, San Jose	15	6	36
1975	Tampa Bay Rowdies	2-0	Portland Timbers	Steve David, Miami	23	6	52
1976	Toronto Metros	3-0	Minnesota Kicks	Giorgio Chinaglia, New York	19	11	49
1977	New York Cosmos	2-1	Seattle Sounders	Steve David, Los Angeles	26	6	58
1978	New York Cosmos	3-1	Tampa Bay Rowdies	Giorgio Chinaglia, New York	34	11	79
1979	Vancouver Whitecaps	2-1	Tampa Bay Rowdies	Oscar Fabbiani, Tampa Bay	25	8	58
1980	New York Cosmos	3-0	Ft.Laud. Strikers	Giorgio Chinaglia, New York	32	13	77
1981	Chicago Sting	1-0†	New York Cosmos	Giorgio Chinaglia, New York	29	16	74
1982	New York Cosmos	1-0	Seattle Sounders	Giorgio Chinaglia, New York	20	15	55
1983	Tulsa Roughnecks	2-0	Toronto Blizzard	Roberto Cabanas, New York	25	16	66
1984	Chicago Sting	2-1,3-2	Toronto Blizzard	Steve Zungul, Golden Bay	20	10	50

Regular Season MVP

Regular season Most Valuable Player as designated by the NASL.

Multiple winner: Carlos Metidieri (2).

Year		Year		Year	
1967	Rueben Navarro, Phila (NPSL)	1973	Warren Archibald, Miami	1979	Johan Cruyff, LA
1968	John Kowalik, Chicago	1974	Peter Silvester, Baltimore	1980	Roger Davis, Seattle
1969	Cirilio Fernandez, KC	1975	Steve David, Miami	1981	Giorgio Chinaglia, NY
1970	Carlos Metidieri, Rochester	1976	Pelé, New York	1982	Peter Ward, Seattle
1971	Carlos Metidieri, Rochester	1977	Franz Beckenbauer, NY	1983	Roberto Cabanas, NY
1972	Randy Horton, New York	1978	Mike Flanagan, New England	1984	Steve Zungul, San Jose

American Professional Soccer League

Formed in 1990 after the merger of the Western Soccer League (WSL) and New American Soccer League (NASL). The APSL was officially sanctioned as an outdoor professional league in 1992.

Year		Year		Year		Year	
1990	Maryland Bays	1992	Colorado Foxes	1993	Colorado Foxes	1994	Montreal Impact
1991	SF Bay Blackhawks						

INDOOR
Major Soccer League (1978-92)

Originally the Major Indoor Soccer League from 1978-79 season through 1989-90. The MISL championship was decided by one game in 1980 and 1981; a best-of-three games series in 1979, best-of-five games in 1982 and 1983; and best-of-seven games since 1984. MSL folded after the 1991-92 season.

Multiple winners: San Diego (8); New York (4).

	Playoff Final			**Regular Season**			
Year	Winner	Series	Loser	Leading Scorer	G	A	Pts
1979	New York Arrows	2-0 (WW)	Philadelphia	Fred Grgurev, Philadelphia	46	28	74
1980	New York Arrows	7-4 (1 game)	Houston	Steve Zungul, New York	90	46	136
1981	New York Arrows	6-5 (1 game)	St. Louis	Steve Zungul, New York	108	44	152
1982	New York Arrows	3-2 (LWWLW)	St. Louis	Steve Zungul, New York	103	60	163
1983	San Diego Sockers	3-2 (WWLLW)	Baltimore	Steve Zungul, NY/Golden Bay	75	47	122
1984	Baltimore Blast	4-1 (LWWWW)	St. Louis	Stan Stamenkovic, Baltimore	34	63	97
1985	San Diego Sockers	4-1 (WWLWW)	Baltimore	Steve Zungul, San Diego	68	68	136
1986	San Diego Sockers	4-3 (WLLLWWW)	Minnesota	Steve Zungul, Tacoma	55	60	115
1987	Dallas Sidekicks	4-3 (LLWWLWW)	Tacoma	Tatu, Dallas	73	38	111
1988	San Diego Sockers	4-0	Cleveland	Eric Rasmussen, Wichita	55	57	112
1989	San Diego Sockers	4-3 (LWWWLLW)	Baltimore	Preki, Tacoma	51	53	104
1990	San Diego Sockers	4-2 (LWWWLW)	Baltimore	Tatu, Dallas	64	49	113
1991	San Diego Sockers	4-2 (WLWLWW)	Cleveland	Tatu, Dallas	78	66	144
1992	San Diego Sockers	4-2 (WWWLLW)	Dallas	Zoran Karic, Cleveland	39	63	102

MSL Playoff MVPs

MSL playoff Most Valuable Players, selected by a panel of soccer media covering the playoffs.
Multiple winners: Zungul (4); Quinn (2).

Year		Year	
1979	Shep Messing, NY	1986	Brian Quinn, SD
1980	Steve Zungul, NY	1987	Tatu, Dallas
1981	Steve Zungul, NY	1988	Hugo Perez, SD
1982	Steve Zungul, NY	1989	Victor Nogueira, SD
1983	Juli Veee, SD	1990	Brian Quinn, SD
1984	Scott Manning, Bal.	1991	Ben Collins, SD
1985	Steve Zungul, SD	1992	Thompson Usiyan, SD

MSL Regular Season MVPs

MSL regular season Most Valuable Players, selected by a panel of soccer media from every city in the MISL.
Multiple winner: Zungul (6); Nogueira (2).

Year		Year	
1979	Steve Zungul, NY	1986	Steve Zungul, SD/Tac.
1980	Steve Zungul, NY	1987	Tatu, Dallas
1981	Steve Zungul, NY	1988	Erik Rasmussen, Wich.
1982	Steve Zungul, NY	1989	Preki, Tacoma
	& Stan Terlecki, Pit.	1990	Tatu, Dallas
1983	Alan Mayer, G, SD	1991	Victor Nogueira, SD
1984	Stan Stamenkovic, Bal.	1992	Victor Nogueira, SD
1985	Steve Zungul, SD		

NASL Indoor Champions (1980-84)

The North American Soccer League started an indoor league in the fall of 1979. The indoor NASL, which featured many of the same teams and players who played in the outdoor NASL, crowned champions from 1980-82 before suspending play. It was revived for the 1983-84 indoor season but folded for good in 1984.
Multiple winners: San Diego (2).

Year		Year		Year		Year	
1980	Tampa Bay Rowdies	1982	San Diego Sockers	1983	Play suspended	1984	San Diego Sockers
1981	Edmonton Drillers						

NPSL

The National Professional Soccer League. Winter indoor league which played its first season in 1992-93.

Year		Year	
1993	Kansas City Attack	1994	Cleveland Crunch

CISL

The Continental Indoor Soccer League. Summer indoor league which played its first season in 1993.

Year		Year	
1993	Dallas Sidekicks	1994	Las Vegas Dustdevils

U.S. COLLEGES

NCAA Division I Champions

NCAA Division I champions since the first title was contested in 1959. The championship has been shared three times—in 1967, 1968 and 1989. There was playoff for third place from 1974-81.
Multiple winners: Saint Louis (10); San Francisco (5); Virginia (4); Indiana (3); Clemson, Howard, and Michigan St. (2).

Year	Winner	Head Coach	Score	Runner-up	Host/Site	Semifinalists
1959	Saint Louis	Bob Guelker	5-2	Bridgeport	UConn	West Chester, CCNY
1960	Saint Louis	Bob Guelker	3-2	Maryland	Brooklyn	West Chester, UConn
1961	West Chester	Mel Lorback	2-0	Saint Louis	Saint Louis	Bridgeport, Rutgers
1962	Saint Louis	Bob Guelker	4-3	Maryland	Saint Louis	Mich. St., Springfield
1963	Saint Louis	Bob Guelker	3-0	Navy	Rutgers	Army, Maryland
1964	Navy	F.H. Warner	1-0	Michigan St.	Brown	Army, Saint Louis
1965	Saint Louis	Bob Guelker	1-0	Michigan St.	Saint Louis	Army, Navy
1966	San Francisco	Steve Negoesco	5-2	LIU-Brooklyn	California	Army, Mich. St.
1967-a	Michigan St. & Saint Louis	Gene Kenney Harry Keough	0-0	—	Saint Louis	LIU-Bklyn, Navy
1968-b	Michigan St. & Maryland	Gene Kenney Doyle Royal	2-2 (2 OT)	—	Ga.Tech	Brown, San Jose St.
1969	Saint Louis	Harry Keough	4-0	San Francisco	San Jose St.	Harvard, Maryland
1970	Saint Louis	Harry Keough	1-0	UCLA	SIU-Ed'sville	Hartwick, Howard
1971-c	Howard	Lincoln Phillips	3-2	Saint Louis	Miami	Harvard, San Fran.
1972	Saint Louis	Harry Keough	4-2	UCLA	Miami	Cornell, Howard
1973	Saint Louis	Harry Keough	2-1 (OT)	UCLA	Miami	Brown, Clemson

Year	Winner	Head Coach	Score	Runner-up	Host/Site	Third Place
1974	Howard	Lincoln Phillips	2-1 (4OT)	Saint Louis	Saint Louis	Hartwick 3, UCLA 1
1975	San Francisco	Steve Negoesco	4-0	SIU-Ed'sville	SIU-Ed'sville	Brown 2, Howard 0
1976	San Francisco	Steve Negoesco	1-0	Indiana	Penn	Hartwick 4, Clemson 3
1977	Hartwick	Jim Lennox	2-1	San Francisco	California	SIU-Ed'sville 3, Brown 2
1978-d	San Francisco	Steve Negoesco	4-3 (OT)	Indiana	Tampa	Clemson 6, Phi. Textile 2
1979	SIU-Ed'sville	Bob Guelker	3-2	Clemson	Tampa	Penn St. 2, Columbia 1
1980	San Francisco	Steve Negoesco	4-3 (OT)	Indiana	Tampa	Ala.A&M 2, Hartwick 0
1981	Connecticut	Joe Morrone	2-1 (OT)	Alabama A&M	Stanford	East. Ill. 4, Phi. Textile 2

Year	Winner	Head Coach	Score	Runner-up	Host/Site	Semifinalists
1982	Indiana	Jerry Yeagley	2-1 (8 OT)	Duke	Ft. Lauderdale	UConn, SIU-Ed'sville
1983	Indiana	Jerry Yeagley	1-0 (2 OT)	Columbia	Ft. Lauderdale	UConn, Virginia
1984	Clemson	I.M. Ibrahim	2-1	Indiana	Seattle	Hartwick, UCLA

U.S. Colleges (Cont.)

Year	Winner	Head Coach	Score	Runner-up	Host/Site	Semifinalists
1985	UCLA	Sigi Schmid	1-0 (8 OT)	American	Seattle	Evansville, Hartwick
1986	Duke	John Rennie	1-0	Akron	Tacoma	Fresno St., Harvard
1987	Clemson	I.M. Ibrahim	2-0	San Diego St.	Clemson	Harvard, N. Carolina
1988	Indiana	Jerry Yeagley	1-0	Howard	Indiana	Portland, S. Carolina
1989-e	Santa Clara & Virginia	Steve Sampson Bruce Arena	1-1 (2 OT)	— —	Rutgers	Indiana, Rutgers
1990-f	UCLA	Sigi Schmid	0-0 (PKs)	Rutgers	South Fla.	Evansville, N.C. State
1991-g	Virginia	Bruce Arena	0-0 (PKs)	Santa Clara	Tampa	Indiana, Saint Louis
1992	Virginia	Bruce Arena	2-0	San Diego	Davidson	Davidson, Duke
1993	Virginia	Bruce Arena	2-0	South Carolina	Davidson	CS-Fullerton, Princeton

Notes: a—game declared a draw due to inclement weather after regulation time; **b**—game declared a draw after two overtimes; **c**—Howard vacated title for using ineligible player; **d**—San Francisco vacated title for using ineligible player; **e**—game declared a draw due to inclement weather after two overtimes; **f**—UCLA wins on penalty kicks (4-3) after four overtimes; **g**—Virginia wins on penalty kicks (3-1) after four overtimes.

Women's NCAA Division I Champions

NCAA Division I women's champions since the first title was contested in 1982.
    Multiple winner: North Carolina (11).

Year	Winner	Score	Runner-up	Year	Winner	Score	Runner-up
1982	North Carolina	2-0	Central Florida	1988	North Carolina	4-1	N.C. State
1983	North Carolina	4-0	George Mason	1989	North Carolina	2-0	Colorado College
1984	North Carolina	2-0	Connecticut	1990	North Carolina	6-0	Connecticut
1985	George Mason	2-0	North Carolina	1991	North Carolina	3-1	Wisconsin
1986	North Carolina	2-0	Colorado College	1992	North Carolina	9-1	Duke
1987	North Carolina	1-0	Massachusetts	1993	North Carolina	6-0	George Mason

Annual Awards

MEN

Hermann Trophy

College Player of the Year. Voted on by Division I college coaches and selected sportswriters and first presented in 1967 in the name of Robert Hermann, one of the founders of the North American Soccer League.
    Multiple winners: Mike Seerey, Ken Snow and Al Trost (2).

Year		Year		Year	
1967	Dov Markus, LIU	1976	Glenn Myernick, Hartwick	1985	Tom Kain, Duke
1968	Manuel Hernandez, San Jose St.	1977	Billy Gazonas, Hartwick	1986	John Kerr, Duke
1969	Al Trost, Saint Louis	1978	Angelo DiBernardo, Indiana	1987	Bruce Murray, Clemson
1970	Al Trost, Saint Louis	1979	Jim Stamatis, Penn St.	1988	Ken Snow, Indiana
1971	Mike Seerey, Saint Louis			1989	Tony Meola, Virginia
1972	Mike Seerey, Saint Louis	1980	Joe Morrone, Jr. UConn		
1973	Dan Counce, Saint Louis	1981	Armando Betancourt, Indiana	1990	Ken Snow, Indiana
1974	Farrukh Quraishi, Oneonta St.	1982	Joe Ulrich, Duke	1991	Alexi Lalas, Rutgers
1975	Steve Ralbovsky, Brown	1983	Mike Jeffries, Duke	1992	Brad Friedel, UCLA
		1984	Amr Aly, Columbia	1993	Claudio Reyna, Virginia

Missouri Athletic Club Award

College Player of the Year. Voted on by men's team coaches around the country from Division I to junior college level and first presented in 1986 by the Missouri Athletic Club of St. Louis.
    Multiple winner: Claudio Reyna and Ken Snow (2).

Year		Year		Year	
1986	John Kerr, Duke	1989	Tony Meola, Virginia	1992	Claudio Reyna, Virginia
1987	John Harkes, Virginia	1990	Ken Snow, Indiana	1993	Claudio Reyna, Virginia
1988	Ken Snow, Indiana	1991	Alexi Lalas, Rutgers		

WOMEN

Hermann Trophy

Women's College Player of the year. Voted on by Division I college coaches and selected sportswriters and first presented in 1988 in the name of Robert Hermann, one of the founders of the North American Soccer League.
    Multiple winner: Mia Hamm (2).

Year		Year		Year	
1988	Michelle Akers, Central Fla.	1990	April Kater, Massachusetts	1992	Mia Hamm, N. Carolina
1989	Shannon Higgins, N. Carolina	1991	Kristine Lilly, N. Carolina	1993	Mia Hamm, N. Carolina

Missouri Athletic Club Award

Women's College Player of the Year. Voted on by women's team coaches around the country from Division I to junior college level and first presented in 1991 by the Missouri Athletic Club of St. Louis.
    Multiple winner: Mia Hamm (2).

Year		Year		Year	
1991	Kristine Lilly, N. Carolina	1992	Mia Hamm, N. Carolina	1993	Mia Hamm, N. Carolina

Chris Faytok

Thirty-year-old **Norm Duke** ran away from the field on the PBA Winter Tour with four victories, including the Tournament of Champions in Akron.

BOWLING

Duke Rules

Norm Duke wins Tournament of Champions and 3 other events to succeed Walter Ray Williams Jr. as the PBA's hot hand.

In 1994, the sport of bowling began to get a clearer picture of its future—and liked only some of what it saw.

On the positive side came news that the National Bowling Stadium being constructed in Reno, Nev., was on schedule and would be completed in time to play host to the American Bowling Congress Tournament in January 1995.

The state-of-the-art stadium, with a seating capacity of 1,200 and all the modern conveniences, is being counted upon to be the centerpiece of an entire sport and industry. It is also being seen as a symbol that the sport has turned away from being a beer-and-cigar, bowling alley proposition.

On a similar note, the sport's primary national showcase, the Professional Bowlers Tour, tried an innovation that it hopes will increase audience awareness and participation in the future. The PBA moved the Saturday-afternoon finals of the Flagship City Open in Erie, Pa., from the bowling center to the city's convention center. The crowd of about 4,000 cheered like they were at a basketball game. The PBA loved it and is looking into doing it at other tour stops.

On the other hand, the PBA—and, consequently, bowling fans—got plenty of bad news in '94. ABC-TV did not televise the PBA's fall tour for the first time in years,

leaving it for ESPN. The same situation will exist in 1995—and probably for many years to come.

The PBA also suffered a major blow in September when it lost the sponsor of its biggest tournament, the Tournament of Champions, which has been held for 30 straight years in the PBA's hometown of Akron, Ohio. General Tire, which had signed a three-year agreement in April 1993, withdrew its support and bought out the last two years of the contract. This came 16 months after Firestone had dropped out as sponsor after 29 years.

Those setbacks were somewhat ironic because the PBA had one of its greatest on-the-lanes seasons in 1994.

When the year began, all the talk was about the 1993 performance of PBA Player of the Year Walter Ray Williams Jr., who came close to breaking two of the PBA's most cherished records: titles and earnings won in a single season. Williams won seven championships in '93—just one behind the record set by Mark Roth in 1978—and he earned $296,370—less than $2,000 short of Mike Aulby's 1989 record of $298,237.

But when the 1994 Winter Tour began heating up, it was the breaded Norm Duke, not Williams, who got out of the gate fast.

Duke, a 30-year-old right-hander from Edmond, Okla., who joined the pro tour in 1983, began the year with four career PBA national titles. He quickly won four more on the Winter Tour alone.

Duke's first victory came in the first stop of

Tom Gaffney has covered bowling, golf and college sports for the *Akron Beacon Journal* since 1987.

Dave Zapotosky/The Toledo Blade

David Traber (left) is congratulated by older brother **Dale** after winning the PBA National in Toledo. Their duel marked the first time in PBA tournament history that two brothers squared off in the championship finals.

the year—the AC-Delco Classic in Lakewood, Calif., where he finished qualifying as the second seed. In the televised concluding round, he beat Steve Wilson in the semifinal, 276-213, then defeated amateur Robert Smith in the final, 247-223. Duke collected $44,000 for his efforts and was on his way.

Three weeks later, Duke was at it again in the Choice Hotels Classic in his hometown of Edmond. The final came down to a battle between Duke and Walter Ray Williams Jr. with Duke prevailing in the final, 226-213, to win the $38,000.

Two weeks later, in the True Value Open at Peoria, Ill., Duke rolled a 280 in the championship game with Bryan Goebel—and lost! Goebel, 33, of Merriam, Kan., was one strike away from a perfect game and a $100,000 bonus, but he missed. Goebel settled for a 296 and Duke took solace in having the highest losing score ever in a televised final game.

But two weeks after that Duke got his revenge. In the Johnny Petraglia Open in North Brunswick, N.J., Duke edged Goebel

in the title match, 244-211, to pocket $34,000.

Duke's final victory of the Winter Tour was the one he and all pro bowlers want most—the Tournament of Champions at Riviera Lanes in Akron. In this case, it was the one and only General Tire Tournament of Champions.

Duke finished second in qualifying to 33-year-old lefty Eric Forkel of Chatsworth, Calif. In the televised semifinals, he edged Randy Pedersen, 205-186. In a close final, Forkel had a chance to take the lead in the eighth frame, but he put his first ball into the gutter. Duke got a needed mark late in the game and won the biggest title of his career, 217-194.

Before the Tournament of Champions, Duke's biggest win was the 1993 ABC Masters which is not an official PBA event.

The $65,000 first prize gave Duke a Winter Tour total of $215,160 and a commanding lead in the standings. It also put him in a mood to predict the future.

"This absolutely locks me as the 1994 PBA Player of the Year. If somebody else

Dave Zapotosky/The Toledo Blade

PBA Hall of Famer **Johnny Petraglia** leaps into the air after rolling a perfect game in the PBA National championship round that brought him a $100,000 bonus.

would have won here, there would still be competition. This means everything to me," said Duke.

Sitting in second place in the money standings, over $100,000 behind Duke, was Johnny Petraglia, a PBA Hall of Famer who hadn't registered a tour victory since 1980. On Mar. 5, two days after he turned 47, Petraglia received the biggest paycheck of his career at the PBA National Championship in Toledo, Ohio. He didn't win the tournament, he merely rolled a perfect game in the second match of the televised finals to beat Walter Ray Williams Jr., 300-194, and collect a $100,000 bonus from sponsor True Value.

"When I reached seven in a row I knew 300 was possible," said Petragalia. "After that, the adrenaline was really flowing."

Asked what the $100,000 windfall meant to him, Petraglia gave a refreshing reply league bowlers everywhere could relate to. "The main thing," he said, "is that now my kids don't have to worry much about college. This money is going right now into their college fund."

In that same tournament, David Traber, 31, defeated his older brother Dale, who is 36, to win the championship and $27,000. The final score was 196-187. It was the first time in PBA tournament history that two brothers had faced each other in the championship finals. David was the first seeded player after qualifying and Dale was second. Dale defeated Petraglia, 193-188, to reach the final.

A week after his thrilling perfect game, Petraglia finished 26th in the tournament that bears his name in North Brunswick, N.J., and missed qualifying for match play by just four pins.

Elsewhere on the pro tour, Pete Weber set PBA records for 24 games (5,855 pins) and 32 games (7,794) at the Showboat Invitational in Las Vegas. Weber finished as the top seed but lost to Walter Ray Williams Jr. in the final, 215-213.

The BPAA U.S. Open was won by 27-year-old Austin Hromek of Andover, Kan., who beat Parker Bohn III in the championship game, 267-230. Not only was it Hromek's first major, but his first pro title as well.

The PBA's less-celebrated Summer Tour—with far smaller purses and less TV exposure than in Winter stops—made eight stops.

The highlights were Amleto Monacelli winning his 15th career title, at the Greater Lexington (Ky.) Classic, and Dave Husted and Pedersen each winning their 10th championships. Ten titles is significant, in that it is usually the benchmark for entry into the PBA Hall of Fame.

Duke had foot surgery early in the summer and missed most of the action. He still led in earnings—$221,010 to $148,615 for runner-up Williams—heading into the seven-stop Fall Tour. While Duke still led the field with four victories, four other players—Goebel, Monacelli, Husted and Steve Hoskins—each had two wins.

Williams, meanwhile, won his sixth World Horseshoe Pitching Championship on Aug. 6 in Syracuse—beating Jim Walters of Troy, Ohio, 40-28.

Also of note during 1994, Ernie Schlegel, 51, of Vancouver, Wash., set a PBA record for national tournaments entered at 701. That broke the record of 700 held by Carmen Salvino.

The ABC-PBA Senior Masters was played in March at Greenacres, Fla., where Delano Harmon (Hobo) Boothe beat Rich

The new $35 million, state-of-the-art **National Bowling Stadium** nearing completion in Reno, Nev., will feature 80 Brunswick lanes and permanent seating for 1,200 spectators. The stadium will be open in January 1995.

Moores, 194-184, to win a record $38,000.

On the PBA Senior Tour, 56-year-old John Handegard of Las Vegas won two consecutive titles—capturing the Springfield (Mo.) Open on July 28 and the Rocky Mountain Classic in Littleton, Colo., on Aug. 6. That gave Handegard a Senior Tour-record 10 career titles.

The Showboat Invitational in Las Vegas saw a high-scoring final as Tommy Evans defeated Frankie May, 278-237. Evans won $24,000 for the victory.

Ironically, the Ladies Pro Bowlers Tour was also paced by a bowler from Edmond, Okla. Norm Duke did it in the PBA, and in the LPBT, the dominant bowler for much of 1994 was 32-year-old Anne Marie Duggan.

Through the 14-event Winter and Spring-Summer tours, Duggan was at the top of most statistical categories. She was the only player with three titles, winning the Texas Border Shoot-out in McAllen, Texas, the Santa Maria (Calif.) Classic and the prestigious WIBC Queens tournament in Salt Lake City, Utah.

With $80,832 in earnings so far in '94, Duggan entered the fall well on the pace to break Robin Romeo's all-time LPBT record of $113,750, set in 1989. Duggan was also first in points with 8,450 and her 214.44 average was second only to Dana Miller-Mackie's 215.51.

Cheryl Daniels, 34, of Detroit, Mich., was the only other multiple winner on the circuit, defeating Duggan at both the Arlington Heights (Ill.) Open and the Hammond (Ind.) Open, by respective scores of 215-174 and 259-194 in the championship finals.

Lisa Wagner, the 1993 LPBT Player of the Year, got off to a slow start in '94. She won only $12,240 in her first 14 starts. Wagner, who was also the LPBT's Bowler of the Decade in the 1980s, finished third in earnings (51,663) and second in points (8,515) in 1993.

The LPBT, which is headquartered in Rockford, Ill., got some good news in 1994 when Sam Town's Hotel in Las Vegas signed a three-year agreement to be an umbrella sponsor for the entire tour.

Even with all the excitement generated by the pros, much of the talk in bowling in 1994 was about the new National Bowling Center in Reno. The first major event in the stadium will be the 100th American Bowling Congress tournament, which will begin in January.

Anne Marie Duggan, another resident of Edmond, Okla., won the WIBC Queens title and was the only player on the women's pro tour with three victories heading into the fall.

The stadium was built at a cost of about $35 million and is a full 330,000 square feet. It has 80 Brunswick lanes and 1,200 permanent seats. The bowling area has a 44-foot ceiling, roughly 30 feet higher than most bowling centers, and the square-footage is 120,000. It also has a high-definition TV scoring system that is 8-feet high and 11-feet wide over each pair of lanes.

That's staggering enough, but it also has plenty of other amenities—440 lockers, 6,000 square feet of exhibition space, a restaurant, and a 10,000 square-foot pro shop.

"The bowlers will now have a facility unlike any other in the world," said Jay Milligan, president of the Reno Sparks Convention and Visitors Authority, the organization at the forefront of building the stadium.

Said stadium architect Peter Wilday: "The stadium is going to be a real statement for the sport. Bowlers are going to be knocked out by it."

The ABC and Women's International Bowling Congress thought so much of the stadium that both made long-term commit-ments to it. Each signed a 15-year contract to hold its annual tournament there every three years, starting with the ABC in 1995. The WIBC tournament will come to Reno for the first time in 1997.

Meanwhile, the ABC and WIBC members had to "settle" for having their tournaments elsewhere in 1994. And few minded, as the competition was once again fierce.

The WIBC Tournament was held in Salt Lake City and ran from March 30-May 31. The All-Events team title was won by Strike Zone Pro Shop of Rolling Meadows, Ill., led by Duggan, the LPBT star. It was Strike Zone's second consecutive team title, something that hadn't been done in 31 years.

Individually, Wendy McPherson-Papanos of Las Vegas won the All-Events championship and Vicki Fifield of El Paso won Classic Division singles (in a big upset over Cheryl Daniels 716-703). Lucy Giovinco and Cindy Coburn-Carroll won the All-Events doubles.

The ABC Tournament was held in Mobile, Ala., from Feb. 5-June 12. An entry composed of members from northern New York State, National Clean Way, won the All-Events team title. Two of its members, Dean Distin and Mike Tryniski, won the All-Events doubles. John Weltzien of Boca Raton, Fla., won Regular singles (with an outstanding 810 for three games) and Thomas Holt of Abilene, Texas, won All-Events singles.

The ABC Bud Light Masters, held in conjunction with the ABC Tournament, was won by 39-year-old Steve Fehr of Cincinnati, a member of the ABC Hall of Fame. Fehr defeated Steve Anderson 224-206 in the final to win $43,700.

One of bowling's longest-standing records was broken in 1994. On Feb. 23, the Hurst Bowling Supplies team in Luzerne, Pa., shot a 3,868 to break the five-man series record of 3,858 set by the Budweiser's of St. Louis in 1958. Team members were Jeff Piatt, Brian Snear, Carmen Marsit, Bob Buckery and Howard Holly.

In the Brunswick World Team Challenge Championship in Reno, the Ebonite Nitro/R team of Hopkinsville, Ky., beat Rhino Pro II of Buffalo for the team title. Members were Lonnie Waliczek, Billy Murphy, Sean Swanson, Paul Fleming, and Chad Murphy.

Wichita State won both the men's and women's titles in the Intercollegiate Bowling Championships held in Carson City, Nev. ❑

THE 1995
INFORMATION PLEASE
SPORTS ALMANAC
B O W L I N G
S T A T I S T I C S
SEC A
THE SEASON IN REVIEW
1993-1994
PBA • SENIORS • LPBT
PAGE 703

Tournament Results

Winners of stepladder finals in all PBA, Seniors and LPBT tournaments from November, 1993, through the Summer Tour of 1994; major tournaments in **bold** type. Note that (*) indicates winner was top seeded player entering championship round; and (a) indicates amateur. See "Updates" for later results.

PBA

Late 1993 Fall Tour

Final	Event	Winner	Earnings	Score	Runner-up
Nov. 3	Touring Players Championship	Jason Couch	$27,000	238-214	Parker Bohn III
Nov.10	Brunswick World Open	Dave Husted	46,440	192-183	Brian Voss
Dec. 5	Merit Mixed Doubles	Parker Bohn III/	40,000	15,305	David Ozio/
		Aleta Sill		to 14,995	Tish Johnson
Dec. 12	National Resident Pro	Jeff Richgels	6,000	257-185	Lenny Blakey

1994 Winter Tour

The King of the Hill competition, introduced at the Phoenix Open on Jan. 16, paired newly-crowned tournament champion Parker Bohn III in a one-game match against the previous week's winner Ron Williams. Williams won to become the tour's first King of the Hill. The reigning King then met the next week's champion through the Tournament of Champions.

Final	Event	Winner	Earnings	Score	Runner-up
Jan. 22	AC-Delco Classic	Norm Duke	$44,000	247-223	Robert Smith
Jan. 29	Showboat Invitational	Walter R. Williams Jr.	37,000	215-213	Pete Weber
Feb. 5	Quaker State Open	Steve Hoskins	41,000	253-219	Pete Weber
Feb. 12	Choice Hotel Open	Norm Duke	38,000	226-213	W.R. Williams Jr.
Feb. 19	Bud Light Hall of Fame	Andy Neuer	30,000	276-238	W.R. Williams Jr.
Feb. 26	True Value Open	Bryan Goebel	43,000	296-280	Norm Duke
Mar. 5	**PBA National Championship**	David Traber	27,000	196-187	Dale Traber
Mar.12	Johnny Petraglia Open	Norm Duke	34,000	244-211	Bryan Goebel
Mar.19	Leisure's Long Island Open	Amleto Monacelli	24,000	217-217*	Steve Wilson
Mar.26	Tums Classic	Harry Sullins	23,000	248-203	Jess Stayrook
Apr. 2	SplitFire Spark Plug Open	Dennis Horan	39,000	267-235	Brian Voss
Apr. 9	**BPAA U.S. Open**	Justin Hromek	46,000	267-230	Parker Bohn III
Apr. 16	Bowling for Miracles Open	Mike Edwards	43,000	203-192	Pete Weber
Apr. 23	**Tournament of Champions**	Norm Duke	65,000	217-194	Eric Forkel
May 7	**ABC Masters**	Steve Fehr	43,700	224-206	Steve Anderson

*Monacelli defeated Wilson in two-frame roll-off, 40-39.
Note: The American Bowling Congress Masters tournament is not a PBA Tour event.

1994 Spring/Summer Tour

Final	Event	Winner	Earnings	Score	Runner-up
June 28	Northwest Classic	David Husted	$16,000	239-203	W.R. Williams Jr.
July 5	Oregon Open	Dave D'Entremont	16,000	235-214	Joe Firpo
July 12	Hilton Hotels Classic	John Mazza	27,000	267-233	W.R. Williams Jr.
July 19	Active West Open	Bryan Goebel	14,000	247-201	Steve Hoskins
July 26	Tucson Open	Steve Hoskins	14,000	207-195	W.R. Williams Jr.
Aug.16	Sherwin-Williams Classic	David Husted	27,000	279-238	George Branham III
Aug.23	Greater Harrisburg Open	Randy Pedersen	16,000	210-166	Bob Vespi
Aug.30	Lexington Classic	Amleto Monacelli	16,000	257-193	Brian Voss

Tournament Results (Cont.)

SENIORS

Late 1993 Fall Tour

Final	Event	Winner	Earnings	Score	Runner-up
Nov. 3	Ebonite Senior Championship	Gene Stus	$25,000	224-199	Gary Dickinson

1994 Spring/Summer Tour

Final	Event	Winner	Earnings	Score	Runner-up
Mar.30	ABC/PBA Senior Masters	Hobo Boothe	$38,000	194-184	Rich Moores
May 18	Jackson (Miss.) Open	Dave Soutar	13,000	239-209	Gary Dickinson
May 25	Chicagoland Open	Gene Stus	8,000	267-189	Dave Soutar
June 2	Lansing Open	Dave Davis	7,500	256-205	Lon Marshall
June 9	Greater Providence Open	Rich Holden	6,500	by 64 pins*	Tommy Evans
June 16	Canadian Open.............................	Mel Wolf	6,500	214-213	Gene Stus
June 23	Wyoming Valley Open....................	Sam Flanagan	9,000	214-193	John Handegard
July 28	Springfield Senior Open.................	John Handegard	9,000	199-181	Dave Davis
Aug. 6	Rocky Mountain Open....................	John Handegard	8,000	226-215	Gene Stus
Aug.13	Showboat Invitational	Tommy Evans	24,000	278-237	Frankie May

*No stepladder finals, Holden def. Evans, 9,779 to 9,715.

LPBT

Late 1993 Fall Tour

Final	Event	Winner	Earnings	Score	Runner-up
Nov. 4	Hammer Midwest Open	Lisa Wagner	9,000	257-192	Debbie McMullen
Nov.12	LPBT National Doubles	Aleta Sill/ Laurie Soto	11,000	242-233	Wendy Macpherson/ Darris Street
Nov.21	**Sam's Town Invitational**..........	Robin Romeo	20,000	194-191	a-Tammy Turner
Dec. 5	Merit Mixed Doubles	Aleta Sill/ Parker Bohn III	40,000	15,305 to 14,995	Tish Johnson/ David Ozio

1994 Winter Tour

Final	Event	Winner	Earnings	Score	Runner-up
Feb. 10	Lady Ebonite Classic.....................	Carolyn Dorin	$12,600	216-207	Aleta Sill
Feb. 17	Alexandria Louisiana Open	Leanne Barrette	9,000	254-194	Jeanne Naccarato
Feb. 24	New Orleans Classic......................	Debbie McMullen	9,000	177-167	Marianne DiRupo
Mar. 3	Claremore Classic	Tammy Turner	9,000	227-162	Michelle Mullen
Mar.10	AMF Ninja Challenge	Kim Couture	10,800	182-182*	Darris Street
Mar.17	Texas Border Shoot-Out	Anne Marie Duggan	9,000	182-177	Tammy Turner

*Couture defeated Street in two-frame roll-off, 50-49.

1994 Spring/Summer Tour

Final	Event	Winner	Earnings	Score	Runner-up
Apr. 28	Greater San Diego Open.................	Sandra Jo Shiery	$ 9,000	265-218	Aleta Sill
May 5	Santa Maria Classic	Anne Marie Duggan	9,000	201-156	Aleta Sill
May 12	**WIBC Queens**............................	Anne Marie Duggan	12,510	238-218	Aleta Sill
May 19	Omaha Classic	Marianne DiRupo	9,000	269-196	Kim Couture
May 26	Arlington Heights Open..................	Cheryl Daniels	9,000	215-174	Anne Marie Duggan
June 9	Hammond Open	Cheryl Daniels	9,000	259-194	Anne Marie Duggan
June 16	Rocket City Challenge.....................	Aleta Sill	9,000	194-188	Robin Romeo
June 23	Tunica Classic..............................	Dana Miller-Mackie	9,000	194-162	Tish Johnson

Note: The Women's International Bowling Congress Queens tournament is not an LPBT Tour event.

1994 Fall Tour Schedules

PBA

Events (7): Dick Weber Classic (Oct. 1-5); Greater Detroit Open (Oct. 8-12); Indianapolis Open (Oct. 15-19); Rochester Open (Oct. 22-26); Greater Grand Rapids (Oct. 29-Nov. 2); Brunswick Memorial World Open (Nov. 3-9); PBA/LPBT Merit Mixed Doubles (Dec. 8-11).

LPBT

Events (8): **BPAA U.S. Open** (Sept. 30-Oct. 7); Hammer Midwest Open (Oct. 8-13); Brunswick Three Rivers Open (Oct. 16-20); Columbia 300 Delaware Open (Oct 22-27); Hammer Eastern Open (Oct. 29-Nov. 3); South Bend Open (Nov. 6-10); **Sam's Town Invitational** (Nov. 12-19); PBA/LPBT Merit Mixed Doubles (Dec. 8-11).

SENIORS

Events (3): Naples Senior Open (Sept. 15-20); St. Petersburg/Clearwater Senior Championship (Sept. 22-27); Palm Beach Senior Classic (Sept. 30-Oct. 5).

Tour Leaders

Official standings for 1993 and unofficial standings (through summer tours) for 1994. Note that (TB) indicates Tournaments Bowled; (CR) Championship Rounds as Stepladder Finalist; and (1st) Titles Won.

Final 1993
PBA
Top 10 Money Winners

		TB	CR	1st	Earnings
1	Walter R. Williams Jr	33	15	7	$296,370
2	Parker Bohn III	30	4	2	175,827
3	Pete Weber	30	3	2	156,080
4	Ron Williams	34	4	2	148,010
5	Brian Voss	27	5	1	147,735
6	Mike Aulby	30	7	2	142,550
7	Norm Duke	25	4	1	140,275
8	George Branham III	31	5	2	132,463
9	Dave Arnold	35	3	1	126,825
10	Dave Husted	24	3	1	118,885

Top 10 Averages

		Gm	Pins	Avg
1	Walter R. Williams Jr	1300	289,885	222.98
2	Brian Voss	902	198,516	220.08
3	Amleto Monacelli	932	205,048	220.01
4	Dave Arnold	1221	268,436	219.85
5	Dave Ferraro	959	209,184	218.13
6	Norm Duke	789	172,060	218.07
7	Ron Williams	1046	228,020	217.99
8	Parker Bohn III	993	215,946	217.47
9	Peter Weber	962	209,028	217.28
10	David Ozio	1013	219,913	217.01

SENIOR PBA
Top 5 Money Winners

		TB	CR	1st	Earnings
1	Gary Dickinson	13	6	2	$75,520
2	Gene Stus	14	8	1	74,940
3	John Handegard	13	7	2	66,893
4	Frankie May	13	3	1	50,128
5	Ron Winger	14	3	2	43,425

Top 5 Averages

		Gm	Pins	Avg
1	Gary Dickinson	573	125,130	218.38
2	John Handegard	509	110,829	217.74
3	Gene Stus	576	124,596	216.31
4	Denny Torgerson	297	63,963	215.36
5	John Hricsina	508	109,117	214.80

LPBT
Top 10 Money Winners

		TB	CR	1st	Earnings
1	Aleta Sill	16	4	2	$57,995
2	Tish Johnson	17	6	0	57,824
3	Lisa Wagner	17	5	2	51,663
4	Wendy Macpherson	16	6	1	50,511
5	Dana Miller-Mackie	17	4	1	49,755
6	Kim Couture	17	5	1	49,365
7	Anne Marie Duggan	17	5	2	48,560
8	Robin Romeo	17	2	1	45,649
9	Dede Davidson	17	3	1	43,644
10	Leanne Barrette	17	7	0	41,760

Top 5 Averages

		Gm	Pins	Avg
1	Tish Johnson	672	144,742	215.39
2	Wendy Macpherson	657	141,347	215.14
3	Leanne Barrette	630	135,261	214.70
4	Kim Couture	704	150,550	213.85
5	Dana Miller-Mackie	624	133,380	213.75

1994 (through Aug. 30)
PBA
Top 10 Money Winners

		TB	CR	1st	Earnings
1	Norm Duke	13	6	4	$221,010
2	Walter R. Williams Jr	20	9	1	148,615
3	Bryan Goebel	22	4	2	125,213
4	Johnny Petraglia	14	1	0	114,410*
5	Justin Hromek	20	3	1	100,888
6	Pete Weber	20	5	0	98,165
7	Steve Hoskins	22	3	2	94,731
8	Amleto Monacelli	14	4	2	86,155
9	Randy Pedersen	21	3	1	83,035
10	Parker Bohn III	20	3	0	70,655

*Includes $100,000 bonus for championship round 300 game.

Top 10 Averages

		Gm	Pins	Avg
1	Norm Duke	465	103,928	223.50
2	Walter R. Williams Jr	751	167,481	223.01
3	Amleto Monacelli	502	111,745	222.60
4	John Mazza	571	125,323	219.48
5	Bryan Goebel	707	555,031	219.28
6	Parker Bohn III	637	139,618	219.18
7	Dave Arnold	664	144,918	218.25
8	Justin Hromek	659	143,735	218.11
9	Randy Pedersen	660	143,946	218.10
10	Eric Forkel	553	120,355	217.64

SENIOR PBA
Top 5 Money Winners

		TB	CR	1st	Earnings
1	Delano Boothe	10	1	1	$44,208
2	Tommy Evans	10	3	1	38,103
3	John Handegard	10	5	2	37,430
4	Gene Stus	10	7	1	34,180
5	Rich Moores	9	2	0	32,538

Top 5 Averages

		Gm	Pins	Avg
1	John Handegard	367	82,667	225.25
2	Gene Stus	403	90,271	224.00
3	Dave Davis	267	59,581	223.15
4	Dave Soutar	310	68,938	222.38
5	Larry Laub	234	51,935	221.94

LPBT
Top 10 Money Winners

		TB	CR	1st	Earnings
1	Anne Marie Duggan	14	7	3	$80,033
2	Aleta Sill	14	4	1	55,965
3	Leanne Barrette	14	4	1	46,647
4	Kim Couture	14	4	1	42,837
5	Tammy Turner	14	4	1	40,643
6	Cheryl Daniels	13	3	2	37,195
7	Carolyn Dorin	14	2	1	36,902
8	Debbie McMullen	14	2	1	30,058
9	Marianne DiRupo	14	2	1	29,693
10	Sandra Jo Shiery	14	1	1	27,793

Top 5 Averages

		Gm	Pins	Avg
1	Dana Miller-Mackie	303	65,300	215.51
2	Anne Marie Duggan	485	104,004	214.44
3	Cheryl Daniels	411	86,997	211.67
4	Leanne Barrette	483	101,711	210.58
5	Kim Couture	491	103,258	210.30

THE 1995 SPORTS ALMANAC
INFORMATION PLEASE
BOWLING STATISTICS
THROUGH THE YEARS
1942-1994
CHAMPIONS • AWARDS
SEC B
PAGE 706

Major Championships
MEN
BPAA U.S. Open

Started in 1941 by the Bowling Proprietors' Association of America, 18 years before the founding of the Professional Bowlers Association. Originally the BPAA All-Star Tournament, it became the U.S. Open in 1971. There were two BPAA All-Star tournaments in 1955, in January and December.

Multiple winners: Don Carter and Dick Weber (4); Del Ballard, Jr., Marshall Holman, Junie McMahon, Connie Schwoegler, Andy Varipapa and Pete Weber (2).

Year		Year		Year		Year	
1942	John Crimmons	1956	Bill Lillard	1970	Bobby Cooper	1984	Mark Roth
1943	Connie Schwoegler	1957	Don Carter	1971	Mike Limongello	1985	Marshall Holman
1944	Ned Day	1958	Don Carter	1972	Don Johnson	1986	Steve Cook
1945	Buddy Bomar	1959	Billy Welu	1973	Mike McGrath	1987	Del Ballard Jr.
1946	Joe Wilman			1974	Larry Laub	1988	Pete Weber
1947	Andy Varipapa	1960	Harry Smith	1975	Steve Neff	1989	Mike Aulby
1948	Andy Varipapa	1961	Bill Tucker	1976	Paul Moser		
1949	Connie Schwoegler	1962	Dick Weber	1977	Johnny Petraglia	1990	Ron Palombi Jr.
		1963	Dick Weber	1978	Nelson Burton Jr.	1991	Pete Weber
1950	Junie McMahon	1964	Bob Strampe	1979	Joe Berardi	1992	Robert Lawrence
1951	Dick Hoover	1965	Dick Weber			1993	Del Ballard Jr.
1952	Junie McMahon	1966	Dick Weber	1980	Steve Martin	1994	Justin Hromek
1953	Don Carter	1967	Les Schissler	1981	Marshall Holman		
1954	Don Carter	1968	Jim Stefanich	1982	Dave Husted		
1955	Steve Nagy	1969	Billy Hardwick	1983	Gary Dickinson		

PBA Tournament of Champions

Originally the Firestone Tournament of Champions from 1965–93 and held annually in Akron, Ohio.
Multiple winners: Mike Durbin (3); Earl Anthony, Jim Godman, Marshall Holman and Mark Williams (2).

Year		Year		Year		Year	
1965	Billy Hardwick	1973	Jim Godman	1981	Steve Cook	1990	Dave Ferraro
1966	Wayne Zahn	1974	Earl Anthony	1982	Mike Durbin	1991	David Ozio
1967	Jim Stefanich	1975	Dave Davis	1983	Joe Berardi	1992	Marc McDowell
1968	Dave Davis	1976	Marshall Holman	1984	Mike Durbin	1993	George Branham III
1969	Jim Godman	1977	Mike Berlin	1985	Mark Williams	1994	Norm Duke
		1978	Earl Anthony	1986	Marshall Holman		
1970	Don Johnson	1979	George Pappas	1987	Pete Weber		
1971	Johnny Petraglia	1980	Wayne Webb	1988	Mark Williams		
1972	Mike Durbin			1989	Del Ballard Jr.		

PBA National Championship

The Professional Bowlers Association was formed in 1958 and its first national championship tournament was held in Memphis in 1960. The tournament has been held in Toledo, Ohio, since 1981.
Multiple winners: Earl Anthony (6); Mike Aulby, Dave Davis, Mike McGrath and Wayne Zahn (2).

Year		Year		Year		Year	
1960	Don Carter	1970	Mike McGrath	1980	Johnny Petraglia	1990	Jim Pencak
1961	Dave Soutar	1971	Mike Limongello	1981	Earl Anthony	1991	Mike Miller
1962	Carmen Salvino	1972	Johnny Guenther	1982	Earl Anthony	1992	Eric Forkel
1963	Billy Hardwick	1973	Earl Anthony	1983	Earl Anthony	1993	Ron Palombi Jr.
1964	Bob Strampe	1974	Earl Anthony	1984	Bob Chamberlain	1994	David Traber
1965	Dave Davis	1975	Earl Anthony	1985	Mike Aulby		
1966	Wayne Zahn	1976	Paul Colwell	1986	Tom Crites		
1967	Dave Davis	1977	Tommy Hudson	1987	Randy Pedersen		
1968	Wayne Zahn	1978	Warren Nelson	1988	Brian Voss		
1969	Mike McGrath	1979	Mike Aulby	1989	Pete Weber		

ABC Masters Tournament

Sponsored by the American Bowling Congress. The Masters is not a PBA event, but is considered one of the four major tournaments on the men's tour and is open to qualified pros and amateurs.

Multiple winners: Earl Anthony, Billy Golembiewski, Dick Hoover and Billy Welu (2).

Year		Year		Year		Year	
1951	Lee Jouglard	1962	Billy Golembiewski	1973	Dave Soutar	1984	Earl Anthony
1952	Willard Taylor	1963	Harry Smith	1974	Paul Colwell	1985	Steve Wunderlich
1953	Rudy Habetler	1964	Billy Welu	1975	Eddie Ressler	1986	Mark Fahy
1954	Red Elkins	1965	Billy Welu	1976	Nelson Burton Jr.	1987	Rick Steelsmith
1955	Buzz Fazio	1966	Bob Strampe	1977	Earl Anthony	1988	Del Ballard Jr.
1956	Dick Hoover	1967	Lou Scalia	1978	Frank Ellenburg	1989	Mike Aulby
1957	Dick Hoover	1968	Pete Tountas	1979	Doug Myers	1990	Chris Warren
1958	Tom Hennessey	1969	Jim Chestney	1980	Neil Burton	1991	Doug Kent
1959	Ray Bluth	1970	Don Glover	1981	Randy Lightfoot	1992	Ken Johnson
1960	Billy Golembiewski	1971	Jim Godman	1982	Joe Berardi	1993	Norm Duke
1961	Don Carter	1972	Bill Beach	1983	Mike Lastowski	1994	Steve Fehr

WOMEN
BPAA U.S. Open

Started by the Bowling Proprietors' Association of America in 1949, 11 years before the founding of the Professional Women's Bowling Association. Originally the BPAA Women's All-Star Tournament, it became the U.S. Open in 1971. There were two BPAA All-Star tournaments in 1955, in January and December. Note that (a) indicates amateur.

Multiple winners: Marion Ladewig (8); Donna Adamek, Paula Sperber Carter, Pat Costello, Dotty Fothergill, Dana Miller-Mackie and Sylvia Wene (2).

Year		Year		Year		Year	
1949	Marion Ladewig	1960	Sylvia Wene	1972	a-Lorrie Koch	1984	Karen Ellingsworth
1950	Marion Ladewig	1961	Phyllis Notaro	1973	Millie Martorella	1985	Pat Mercatanti
1951	Marion Ladewig	1962	Shirley Garms	1974	Pat Costello	1986	Wendy Macpherson
1952	Marion Ladewig	1963	Marion Ladewig	1975	Paula Sperber Carter	1987	Carol Norman
1953	Not held	1964	LaVerne Carter	1976	Patty Costello	1988	Lisa Wagner
1954	Marion Ladewig	1965	Ann Slattery	1977	Betty Morris	1989	Robin Romeo
1955	Sylvia Wene	1966	Joy Abel	1978	Donna Adamek	1990	Dana Miller-Mackie
1955	Anita Cantaline	1967	Gloria Simon	1979	Diana Silva	1991	Anne Marie Duggan
1956	Marion Ladewig	1968	Dotty Fothergill	1980	Pat Costello	1992	Tish Johnson
1957	Not held	1969	Dotty Fothergill	1981	Donna Adamek	1993	Dede Davidson
1958	Merle Matthews	1970	Mary Baker	1982	Shinobu Saitoh	1994	Aleta Sill
1959	Marion Ladewig	1971	a-Paula Sperber	1983	Dana Miller		

WIBC Queens

Sponsored by the Women's International Bowling Congress, the Queens is a double elimination, match play tournament. It is not an LPBT event, but is open to qualified pros and amateurs. Note that (a) indicates amateur.

Multiple winners: Mille Martorella (3); Donna Adamek, Dotty Fothergill, Aleta Sill and Katsuko Sugimoto (2).

Year		Year		Year		Year	
1961	Janet Harman	1970	Millie Martorella	1979	Donna Adamek	1987	Cathy Almeida
1962	Dorothy Wilkinson	1971	Millie Martorella	1980	Donna Adamek	1988	Wendy Macpherson
1963	Irene Monterosso	1972	Dotty Fothergill	1981	Katsuko Sugimoto	1989	Carol Gianotti
1964	D.D. Jacobson	1973	Dotty Fothergill	1982	Katsuko Sugimoto	1990	a-Patty Ann
1965	Betty Kuczynski	1974	Judy Soutar	1983	Aleta Sill	1991	Dede Davidson
1966	Judy Lee	1975	Cindy Powell	1984	Kazue Inahashi	1992	Cindy Coburn-Carroll
1967	Millie Martorella	1976	Pam Rutherford	1985	Aleta Sill	1993	Jan Schmidt
1968	Phyllis Massey	1977	Dana Stewart	1986	Cora Fiebig	1994	Anne Marie Duggan
1969	Ann Feigel	1978	Loa Boxberger				

Sam's Town Invitational

Originally held in Milwaukee as the Pabst Tournament of Champions, but discontinued after one year (1981). The event was revived in 1984, moved to Las Vegas and renamed Sam's Town Tournament of Champions. Since then it has been known as the LPBT Tournament of Champions (1985), the Sam's Town National Pro/Am (1986-88) and the Sam's Town Invitational (since 1989).

Multiple winners: Tish Johnson and Aleta Sill (2).

Year		Year		Year		Year	
1981	Cindy Coburn	1986	Aleta Sill	1989	Tish Johnson	1992	Tish Johnson
1982-83	Not held	1987	Debbie Bennett	1990	Wendy Macpherson	1993	Robin Romeo
1984	Aleta Sill	1988	Donna Adamek	1991	Lorrie Nichols	1994	Ends Nov. 19
1985	Patty Costello						

Major Championships (Cont.)
WOMEN
WPBA National Championship (1960-1980)

The Women's Professional Bowling Association National Championship tournament was discontinued when the WPBA broke up in 1981. The WPBA changed its name from the Professional Women Bowlers Association (PWBA) in 1978.

Multiple winners: Patty Costello (3); Dotty Fothergill (2).

Year		Year		Year		Year	
1960	Marion Ladewig	1966	Judy Lee	1971	Patty Costello	1976	Patty Costello
1961	Shirley Garms	1967	Betty Mivelaz	1972	Patty Costello	1977	Vesma Grinfelds
1962	Stephanie Balogh	1968	Dotty Fothergill	1973	Betty Morris	1978	Toni Gillard
1963	Janet Harman	1969	Dotty Fothergill	1974	Pat Costello	1979	Cindy Coburn
1964	Betty Kuczynski	1970	Bobbe North	1975	Pam Buckner	1980	Donna Adamek
1965	Helen Duval						

Annual Leaders
Average
PBA Tour

The George Young Memorial Award, named after the late ABC Hall of Fame bowler. Based on at least 16 national PBA tournaments from 1959-78, and at least 400 games of tour competition since 1979.

Multiple winners: Mark Roth (6); Earl Anthony (5); Marshall Holman (3); Billy Hardwick, Don Johnson and Wayne Zahn (2).

Year		Avg	Year		Avg	Year		Avg
1962	Don Carter	212.84	1973	Earl Anthony	215.80	1984	Marshall Holman	213.91
1963	Bill Hardwick	210.35	1974	Earl Anthony	219.34	1985	Mark Baker	213.72
1964	Ray Bluth	210.51	1975	Earl Anthony	219.06	1986	John Gant	214.38
1965	Dick Weber	211.90	1976	Mark Roth	215.97	1987	Marshall Holman	216.80
1966	Wayne Zahn	208.63	1977	Mark Roth	218.17	1988	Mark Roth	218.04
1967	Wayne Zahn	212.14	1978	Mark Roth	219.83	1989	Pete Weber	215.43
1968	Jim Stefanich	211.90	1979	Mark Roth	221.66			
1969	Billy Hardwick	212.96				1990	Amleto Monacelli	218.16
			1980	Earl Anthony	218.54	1991	Norm Duke	218.21
1970	Nelson Burton Jr	214.91	1981	Mark Roth	216.70	1992	Dave Ferraro	219.70
1971	Don Johnson	213.98	1982	Marshall Holman	216.15	1993	Walter R. Williams Jr.	222.98
1972	Don Johnson	215.29	1983	Earl Anthony	216.65			

LPBT Tour

Based on at least 282 games of tour competition.

Multiple winners: Leanne Barrette, Nikki Gianulias and Lisa Rathgeber Wagner (3); and Aleta Sill (2).

Year		Avg	Year		Avg	Year		Avg
1981	Nikki Gianulias	213.71	1986	Nikki Gianulias	213.89	1990	Leanne Barrette	211.53
1982	Nikki Gianulias	210.63	1987	Wendy Macpherson	211.11	1991	Leanne Barrette	211.48
1983	Lisa Rathgeber	208.50	1988	Lisa Wagner	213.02	1992	Leanne Barrette	211.36
1984	Aleta Sill	210.68	1989	Lisa Wagner	211.87	1993	Tish Johnson	215.39
1985	Aleta Sill	211.10						

Money Won
PBA Tour

Multiple winners: Earl Anthony (6); Dick Weber and Mark Roth (4); Mike Aulby, Don Carter and Walter Ray Williams Jr. (2).

Year		Earnings	Year		Earnings
1959	Dick Weber	$ 7,672	1977	Mark Roth	$105,583
			1978	Mark Roth	134,500
1960	Don Carter	22,525	1979	Mark Roth	124,517
1961	Dick Weber	26,280			
1962	Don Carter	49,972	1980	Wayne Webb	116,700
1963	Dick Weber	46,333	1981	Earl Anthony	164,735
1964	Bob Strampe	33,592	1982	Earl Anthony	134,760
1965	Dick Weber	47,675	1983	Earl Anthony	135,605
1966	Wayne Zahn	54,720	1984	Mark Roth	158,712
1967	Dave Davis	54,165	1985	Mike Aulby	201,200
1968	Jim Stefanich	67,375	1988	Walter Ray Williams Jr.	145,550
1969	Billy Hardwick	64,160	1987	Pete Weber	179,516
			1988	Brian Voss	225,485
1970	Mike McGrath	52,049	1989	Mike Aulby	298,237
1971	Johnny Petraglia	85,065			
1972	Don Johnson	56,648	1990	Amleto Monacelli	204,775
1973	Don McCune	69,000	1991	David Ozio	225,585
1974	Earl Anthony	99,585	1992	Marc McDowell	176,215
1975	Earl Anthony	107,585	1993	Walter Ray Williams Jr.	296,370
1976	Earl Anthony	110,833			

WPBA and LPBT Tours

WPBA leaders through 1980; LPBT leaders since 1981.

Multiple winners: Aleta Sill (5); Donna Adamek (4); Patty Costello and Betty Morris (3); Dotty Fothergill and Tish Johnson (2).

Year		Earnings	Year		Earnings	Year		Earnings
1965	Betty Kuczynski	$ 3,792	1975	Judy Soutar	$20,395	1985	Aleta Sill	$ 52,655
1966	Joy Abel	5,795	1976	Patty Costello	39,585	1986	Aleta Sill	36,962
1967	Shirley Garms	4,920	1977	Betty Morris	23,802	1987	Betty Morris	63,735
1968	Dotty Fothergill	16,170	1978	Donna Adamek	31,000	1988	Lisa Wagner	105,500
1969	Dotty Fothergill	9,220	1979	Donna Adamek	26,280	1989	Robin Romeo	113,750
1970	Patty Costello	9,317	1980	Donna Adamek	31,907	1990	Tish Johnson	94,420
1971	Vesma Grinfelds	4,925	1981	Donna Adamek	41,270	1991	Leanne Barrette	87,618
1972	Patty Costello	11,350	1982	Nikki Gianulias	45,875	1992	Tish Johnson	96,872
1973	Judy Cook	11,200	1983	Aleta Sill	42,525	1993	Aleta Sill	57,995
1974	Betty Morris	30,037	1984	Aleta Sill	81,452			

All-Time Leaders

All-time leading money winners on the PBA and LPBT tours, through 1993. PBA figures date back to 1959, while LPBT figures include Women's Pro Bowlers Association (WPBA) earnings through 1980. National tour titles are also listed. Note that (ret.) indicates bowler has retired.

Money Winners

PBA Top 15

		Titles	Earnings
1	Marshall Holman	21	$1,606,961
2	Pete Weber	21	1,584,443
3	Mark Roth	33	1,417,487
4	Mike Aulby	22	1,404,710
5	Earl Anthony (ret.)	41	1,361,931
6	Walter Ray Williams Jr	13	1,229,114
7	Amleto Monacelli	12	1,214,801
8	Brian Voss	13	1,183,143
9	Dave Husted	8	1,139,136
10	Wayne Webb	17	1,060,436
11	Del Ballard Jr	12	988,332
12	Dave Ferraro	8	960,148
13	Gary Dickinson	8	910,695
14	David Ozio	10	908,057
15	Dick Weber	26	887,051

WPBA-LPBT Top 15

		Titles	Earnings
1	Lisa Wagner	28	$543,277
2	Aleta Sill	19	530,606
3	Tish Johnson	18	515,690
4	Robin Romeo	14	476,422
5	Donna Adamek	19	473,984
6	Nikki Gianulias	18	458,671
7	Lorrie Nichols	15	445,906
8	Leanne Barrette	14	392,766
9	Cindy Coburn-Carroll	14	357,084
10	Jeanne Maiden Naccarato	9	337,235
11	Betty Morris	17	335,417
12	Dana Miller-Mackie	11	331,806
13	Cheryl Daniels	5	305,122
14	Wendy Macpherson	5	293,321
15	Anne Marie Duggan	8	289,207

Annual Awards
MEN
BWAA Bowler of the Year

Winners selected by Bowling Writers Association of America.

Multiple winners: Earl Anthony and Don Carter (6); Mark Roth (4); Dick Weber (3); Mike Aulby, Buddy Bomar, Ned Day, Billy Hardwick, Don Johnson, Steve Nagy and Walter Ray Williams Jr. (2).

Year		Year		Year		Year	
1942	Johnny Crimmins	1956	Bill Lillard	1970	Nelson Burton Jr.	1982	Earl Anthony
1943	Ned Day	1957	Don Carter	1971	Don Johnson	1983	Earl Anthony
1944	Ned Day	1958	Don Carter	1972	Don Johnson	1984	Mark Roth
1945	Buddy Bomar	1959	Ed Lubanski	1973	Don McCune	1985	Mike Aulby
1946	Joe Wilman			1974	Earl Anthony	1986	Walter Ray Williams Jr.
1947	Buddy Bomar	1960	Don Carter	1975	Earl Anthony	1987	Marshall Holman
1948	Andy Varipapa	1961	Dick Weber	1976	Earl Anthony	1988	Brian Voss
1949	Connie Schwoegler	1962	Don Carter	1977	Mark Roth	1989	Mike Aulby
		1963	Dick Weber	1978	Mark Roth		
1950	Junie McMahon	1964	Billy Hardwick	1979	Mark Roth	1990	Amleto Monacelli
1951	Lee Jouglard	1965	Dick Weber			1991	David Ozio
1952	Steve Nagy	1966	Wayne Zahn	1980	Wayne Webb	1992	Marc McDowell
1953	Don Carter	1967	Dave Davis	1981	Earl Anthony	1993	Walter Ray Williams Jr.
1954	Don Carter	1968	Jim Stefanich				
1955	Steve Nagy	1969	Billy Hardwick				

Annual Awards (Cont.)
PBA Player of the Year

Winners selected by members of Professional Bowlers Association. The PBA Player of the Year has differed from the BWAA Bowler of the Year four times—in 1963, '64, '89 and '92.

Multiple winners: Earl Anthony (6); Mark Roth (4); Billy Hardwick, Don Johnson, Amleto Monacelli and Walter Ray Williams Jr. (2).

Year		Year		Year		Year	
1963	Billy Hardwick	1971	Don Johnson	1980	Wayne Webb	1988	Brian Voss
1964	Bob Strampe	1972	Don Johnson	1981	Earl Anthony	1989	Amleto Monacelli
1965	Dick Weber	1973	Don McCune	1982	Earl Anthony		
1966	Wayne Zahn	1974	Earl Anthony	1983	Earl Anthony	1990	Amleto Monacelli
1967	Dave Davis	1975	Earl Anthony	1984	Mark Roth	1991	David Ozio
1968	Jim Stefanich	1976	Earl Anthony	1985	Mike Aulby	1992	Dave Ferraro
1969	Billy Hardwick	1977	Mark Roth	1986	Walter Ray Williams Jr.	1993	Walter Ray Williams Jr.
1970	Nelson Burton Jr.	1978	Mark Roth	1987	Marshall Holman		
		1979	Mark Roth				

PBA Rookie of the Year

Winners selected by members of Professional Bowlers Association.

Year		Year		Year		Year	
1964	Jerry McCoy	1972	Tommy Hudson	1980	Pete Weber	1988	Rick Steelsmith
1965	Jim Godman	1973	Steve Neff	1981	Mark Fahy	1989	Steve Hoskins
1966	Bobby Cooper	1974	Cliff McNealy	1982	Mike Steinbach		
1967	Mike Durbin	1975	Guy Rowbury	1983	Toby Contreras	1990	Brad Kiszewski
1968	Bob McGregor	1976	Mike Berlin	1984	John Gant	1991	Ricky Ward
1969	Larry Lichstein	1977	Steve Martin	1985	Tom Crites	1992	Jason Crouch
		1978	Joseph Groskind	1986	Marc McDowell	1993	Mark Scroggins
1970	Denny Krick	1979	Mike Aulby	1987	Ryan Shafer		
1971	Tye Critchlow						

WOMEN
BWAA Bowler of the Year

Winners selected by Bowling Writers Association of America.

Multiple winners: Marion Ladewig (9); Donna Adamek and Lisa Rathgeber Wagner (4); Betty Morris (3); Patty Costello, Dotty Forthergill, Shirley Garms, Tish Johnson, Val Mikiel, Aleta Sill, Judy Soutar and Sylvia Wene (2).

Year		Year		Year		Year	
1948	Val Mikiel	1960	Sylvia Wene	1972	Patty Costello	1983	Lisa Rathgeber
1949	Val Mikiel	1961	Shirley Garms	1973	Judy Soutar	1984	Aleta Sill
		1962	Shirley Garms	1974	Betty Morris	1985	Aleta Sill
1950	Marion Ladewig	1963	Marion Ladewig	1975	Judy Soutar	1986	Lisa Wagner
1951	Marion Ladewig	1964	LaVerne Carter	1976	Patty Costello	1987	Betty Morris
1952	Marion Ladewig	1965	Betty Kuczynski	1977	Betty Morris	1988	Lisa Wagner
1953	Marion Ladewig	1966	Joy Abel	1978	Donna Adamek	1989	Robin Romeo
1954	Marion Ladewig	1967	Millie Martorella	1979	Donna Adamek		
1955	Sylvia Wene	1968	Dotty Forthergill			1990	Tish Johnson
1956	Anita Cantaline	1969	Dotty Forthergill	1980	Donna Adamek	1991	Leanne Barrette
1957	Marion Ladewig			1981	Donna Adamek	1992	Tish Johnson
1958	Marion Ladewig	1970	Mary Baker	1982	Nikki Gianulias	1993	Lisa Wagner
1959	Marion Ladewig	1971	Paula Sperber				

LPBT Player of the Year

Winners selected by members of Ladies Professional Bowlers Tour. The LPBT Player of the Year has differed from the BWAA Bowler of the Year twice—in 1985 and '86.

Multiple winners: Lisa Rathgeber Wagner (3); Leanne Barrette (2).

Year		Year		Year		Year	
1983	Lisa Rathgeber	1986	Jeanne Maiden	1989	Robin Romeo	1992	Tish Johnson
1984	Aleta Sill	1987	Betty Morris	1990	Leanne Barrette	1993	Lisa Wagner
1985	Patty Costello	1988	Lisa Wagner	1991	Leanne Barrette		

WPBA and LPBT Rookie of the Year

Winners selected by members of Women's Professional Bowlers Association (1978–80) and the Ladies Professional Bowlers Tour (since 1981).

Year		Year		Year		Year	
1978	Toni Gillard	1982	Carol Norman	1986	Wendy Macpherson	1990	Debbie McMullen
1979	Nikki Gianulias	1983	Anne Marie Pike	1987	Paula Drake	1991	Kim Kahrman
1980	Lisa Rathgeber	1984	Paula Vidad	1988	Mary Martha Cerniglia	1992	Marianne DiRupo
1981	Cindy Mason	1985	Dede Davidson	1989	Kim Terrell	1993	Kathy Zielke

Kentucky Derby favorite **Holy Bull** finished 12th at Churchill Downs, but rebounded during the summer to become one of racing's top thoroughbreds.

HORSE RACING

HORSE RACING
by Sharon Smith

Comebacks

*Older horses command more attention than usual in 1994,
while Holy Bull and Tabasco Cat vie for top 3-year-old.*

There is no more anticipated or appreciated circumstance in sport than the comeback. It may be an athlete returning to action after an injury or to top form after a slump, or it may be a team winning a championship after a disastrous previous season. Whichever it is, it's a comeback and we love it.

Horse racing enjoys each kind of comeback, plus another less dramatic but probably more important kind. Both the economics and the rigors of the sport encourage early retirements of the best horses, and any good horse who stays in training after the age of three is honored and admired for just being there.

There was plenty to admire among the thoroughbreds set to race in 1994. There had never been a season with so many good, older horses coming back to race again, mostly horses who could have been lucratively retired to the breeding farms— as 1993 Horse of the Year and male turf champion Kotashaan was by his Japanese purchasers.

Two-time Breeders' Cup winner Lure was back to race at the age of five, even though as one of the best-bred horses in training he could have commanded a huge stud fee. Six-year-old Best Pal was back, as were the five-year-olds Paradise Creek, The Wicked

North, Devil His Due, and Bien Bien. The seven-year-old Grand Flotilla came back too. All enjoyed important wins or at least good performances during the year, including Grand Flotilla's Sunset Handicap and Hollywood Turf Cup, Devil His Due's Brooklyn Handicap, The Wicked North's Santa Anita Handicap, and Bien Bien's San Juan Capistrano.

But best of all through the summer were Lure and his archrival Paradise Creek, the grass specialists whose abilities seem only to improve with age. Paradise Creek beat Lure twice in May, then Lure came back with an impressive victory over Paradise Creek in the Bernard Baruch at Saratoga on Aug. 12. Each horse won a rich race in the absence of the other during the summer— Paradise Creek at the Arlington Million and Lure at the Caesar's International— leaving racing fans hoping for more during the rest of the year.

"If you look up champion in the dictionary, you'll find a picture of him," said Lure's jockey Mike Smith after his Saratoga win. But you'd probably find a picture of Paradise Creek right alongside.

Older fillies and mares came back as well. Sky Beauty has, remarkably, never been an official champion, having run almost but not quite as well as two different fillies at the ages of two and three. But her return to race as a four-year-old in 1994 was greeted with pleasure by everyone in racing, including the people who own, train, and ride other fillies and mares.

Sharon Smith has covered horse racing for ESPN, NBC and *Horse Illustrated* and is the author of *The Performance Mare* and *The Affordable Horse* (Howell Book House).

Jockey Mike Smith exults as **Lure** beats archrival **Paradise Creek** by a length in the Bernard Baruch Handicap on Aug. 12. In the six meetings between the two 5-year-olds over the years, Lure has prevailed four times.

Trainer Mack Miller sent out You'd Be Surprised to face Sky Beauty in Belmont's Hempstead Handicap, insisting that he was just honored to have a horse in the same race with her. Miller, habitually modest, saw his mare run the race of her life, carrying ten pounds less than Sky Beauty, only to lose anyway. But people tend not to mind losing to an admired champion, official or not. Sky Beauty ended the summer unbeaten for the season.

Another female champion, official this time, returned to race in 1994. This was the two-time Eclipse Award winner Paseana, now seven years old, who found success slow in coming at first. But come it did with a win in the Chula Vista Handicap at Del Mar in late August. The 1994 racing season is expected to be her last, but Paseana has raced three or four years longer than almost every other well-bred mare of her generation and earned the respect and honor of the entire sport for coming back so many times and so very well.

The nature of the jockey's trade is such that comebacks are inevitable in a long

career. It's a dangerous sport for both man and horse, and no successful jockey has ever completed a career unscathed. Julie Krone's shattered right ankle, suffered in a spill on August 30th, 1993, threatened her ability to ever ride a horse again. Only a protective vest kept the accident from being worse; she suffered a bruised heart where she might have suffered fatal chest injuries.

But Krone returned with her courage and enthusiasm intact. She rode again on May 25, 1994, won again on May 26, and had won a number of stakes by the end of the summer. The pleasure found in winning was greater than ever for Krone. "When something is nearly taken away, it means so much more to you," she said after her comeback ride.

Trainer Jeff Lukas very nearly lost more than a career late in 1993. On Dec. 15, Lukas, son of and assistant to D. Wayne Lukas, was knocked over by a runaway horse in the barn area at Santa Anita. A fractured skull left him in a coma for weeks, and a severe case of pneumonia further threatened his life. Over the next several

Wide World Photos

Jockey **Julie Krone**, wearing a protective vest like the one that probably saved her life in a spill on Aug. 30, 1993, jokes with reporters the morning of her May 25 comeback race.

months, he slowly emerged from the coma and began the long and arduous comeback to a normal life.

The process was helped along by the developments of the 1994 Triple Crown season, and the very horse who caused all the damage played a major role. The Lukas-trained Tabasco Cat won the Jan. 22 El Camino Real Derby at Bay Meadows in California, leaving himself behind only 1993's top two-year-olds Dehere and Brocco on the list of Triple Crown prospects.

Champion Dehere was out of the hunt early with an injury, but Brocco, coming off a win in the Santa Anita Derby, arrived at Churchill Downs in May with the credentials to be second choice. Tabasco Cat had plenty of support himself, having added a San Rafael Stakes win and a Santa Anita Derby second place finish to his record.

But the favorite's role went to Holy Bull, who had won the Florida Derby and the Blue Grass Stakes on the way to the Kentucky Derby. To be sure, the favorite is not something you necessarily want to have the first Saturday in May. Thirteen straight favorites had lost going into the '94 edition of the Run for the Roses. Still, it shows that a lot of people are convinced you have the best horse, and nobody minds going into a race with that. Besides, Holy Bull's 74-year-old owner and trainer Jimmy Kroll, a recent electee to the Hall of Fame, had never won the race.

But Derby Day brought rain and mud—lots of it— and a big, rowdy 14-horse field. Holy Bull handled the track well enough, but not the field. A rough start, then pushing and shoving on the turns left the favorite in 12th place. After the disappointing finish, Holy Bull's jockey Mike Smith said, "Nothing went right. It just wasn't meant to be."

Nor was it meant to be for Brocco, who ran fourth, or Tabasco Cat, who finished sixth. But for Go for Gin, it was the race of a lifetime. The New York-based colt took the lead just after the quarter pole and never looked back, comfortably holding off Strodes Creek and Blumin Affair. Jockey Chris McCarron, who had hoped to be at the Derby with two-year-old champion Dehere, was on Go for Gin instead. McCarron's early season disappointment at the injury of his top prospect turned into the joy of a second Kentucky Derby win.

Go for Gin headed toward Pimlico for the Preakness surrounded by optimistic handlers, while Brocco and Holy Bull opted for a rest. Tabasco Cat traveled on to Maryland in spite of the disappointment in Kentucky, and his people were almost as optimistic as Go for Gin's. "He has a lot more talent than he showed," Cat's jockey Pat Day said, while a Lukas assistant promised a Preakness win.

They were both right. Go for Gin ran well at Pimlico, finishing second, but Tabasco Cat ran better, winning by nearly a length. "Everything went absolutely right," Day said of his Preakness run. "We had a picture perfect trip."

It was a victory of enormous importance to Wayne Lukas. First, it was watched on television by his recovering son Jeff, and, second, it occurred on the same racetrack where the Lukas-trained Union City suffered a fatal breakdown in the previous year's Preakness.

"I just don't know how to express what this means," Lukas said after the race. What it meant was that Lukas again had a championship contender, a fact that became even clearer three weeks later in

Tabasco Cat (left), with **Pat Day** aboard, takes the last turn of the Belmont Stakes in pursuit of **Go for Gin**. Tabasco Cat, who finished sixth in the Kentucky Derby, came back to win the Preakness and the Belmont.

the Belmont Stakes. Tabasco Cat repeated his victory over Go for Gin, with Strodes Creek finishing third.

Unfortunately for both Tabasco Cat and Go for Gin, the Chrysler Corporation ended its Triple Crown Challenge in 1994 and the $1 million bonus that went with it. From 1987-93, the horse with the best finishes in all three Triple Crown races received a $1 million bonus. Tabasco Cat, with two wins, and Go for Gin, with a win and two seconds, would have each earned 20 points in 1994 and split the money. But the bonus was cancelled by Chrysler after the 1993 races in favor of an annual $300,000 donation to an equine-related charity.

With wins at Pimlico and Belmont, Wayne Lukas was now enjoying his greatest success in nearly three years, while Jeff Lukas was continuing to recover. Still, Wayne Lukas felt after the Belmont that he had to keep his turnaround in fortune in perspective.

"The good is never as good as the bad is bad," he said, something that probably lurks in the mind of anybody enjoying a comeback. But the good was pretty good, since Lukas was now the trainer of the best three-year-old in the country.

Not for long, though. Holy Bull, after running unplaced in the Kentucky Derby, was sent into the supposedly more difficult older horse division. The result: a win by 5 1/2 lengths in the Metropolitan Handicap. Then it was back to the three-year-old division, and a 6 3/4-length victory in the Dwyer Stakes. After that came wins in the Haskell and the Travers Stakes. Tabasco Cat also ran in the Travers, but finished third which put Holy Bull securely atop the three-year-old division. By summer's end Bull was also the top-ranked horse in the National Thoroughbred Poll.

The three-year-old filly division was not nearly so well defined. Sardula beat Lakeway in the Kentucky Oaks at Churchill Downs in May, but Lakeway beat Sardula in the Hollywood Oaks in California in July. Added to her victory in New York's classic Mother Goose Stakes, Lakeway's conquest of Sardula made her the star of her division. She impressed her trainer, certainly.

Wide World Photos

Kotashaan, thoroughbred Horse of the Year as a 5-year-old in 1993, was one of the few highly-regarded older horses that didn't race in 1994. His owners retired him to stud.

"I think she's the best filly to come along since Ruffian," Gary Jones said before Lakeway's attempt to win Saratoga's revered Alabama stakes.

Mistake. The gods of racing do not take kindly to people who compare their fillies to the sport's most legendary female performer. Lakeway finished seven lengths behind Heavenly Prize, whose later win in Belmont Park's Gazelle assured a three-way competition for year-end honors among three-year-old fillies.

Canada's Triple Crown events were shared by two horses. The Queen's Plate and the Breeders' Stakes were taken by Basqueian, while the middle jewel, the Prince of Wales Stakes, went to Bruce's Mill.

The star of the 1994 English classic season may have been the 12-year-old American stallion Chief's Crown. Two of his offspring, Erhaab and Hrand Lodge, either won and placed second in two of the year's major races. Erhaab won in the English Derby at Epsom and Hrand Lodge was second in the Two Thousand Guineas.

It was a comeback of sorts for Chief's Crown, the 1984 two-year-old champion of North America. Although he won four Grade One races at three, Chief's Crown

retired under a slight shadow of disappointment. In the 1985 Triple Crown he finished second in the Preakness and third in both the Kentucky Derby and Belmont. At the time, detractors sniffed at the accomplishment believing he couldn't quite go a classic distance. His offspring certainly can.

Another Triple Crown veteran, eight-year-old Easy Goer, collapsed and died May 12 in his paddock at Claiborne Farm. In 1989, Easy Goer finished second to Sunday Silence in both the Kentucky Derby and Preakness before coming back to finally beat him in the Belmont. Fourth on the all-time money list, Easy Goer was the two-year-old champion of 1988 and retired in 1990 after 20 starts and 14 wins.

The pacing colt Cam's Card Shark had been far too steady as a two-year-old in 1993 to qualify for any kind of a comeback at three. But from a winner of five of fourteen races at two years old he turned into a winning machine at three.

"It's just maturity," said driver John Campbell of Cam's Card Shark's new-found dominance.

"We never expected this," said owner Jeffrey Snyder. "It's beyond our wildest dreams." What they, along with trainer Bill Robinson, enjoyed in 1994 were wins in two different million dollar races— the Meadowlands Pace and the North America Cup— as well as the Adios, the Messenger, and more than a dozen other races. His September win in the James B. Dancer at Freehold gave Cam's Card Shark the standardbred single season earnings record.

Nearly as accomplished, although much more lightly raced, was the '94 Hambletonian winner Victory Dream. The three-year-old trotter won his sport's most famous race so easily that he had trainer Ron Gurfein saying, "I think he's the greatest trotter ever."

Quarter horse racing's most famous event, the All-American Futurity at Ruidoso, New Mexico, featured a million dollar first place purse and a victory by a gelding who sold for $23,000 at the same track a year earlier.

The two-year-old Noblesse Six, gelded halfway through the 1994 racing season, kept his mind on his work on Labor Day, winning the Futurity by 3/4 length in 21.35 seconds, a race record for the 440-yard event. ❑

HORSE RACING
S T A T I S T I C S

THE SEASON IN REVIEW
1993-1994
THOROUGHBRED • HARNESS

THE 1995 SPORTS ALMANAC
INFORMATION PLEASE

SEC A

PAGE 717

Thoroughbred Racing
Major Stakes Races

Winners of major stakes races from Oct. 2, 1993 through Sept. 24, 1994; (T) indicates turf race course; (F) indicates furlongs. See "Updates" for later results.

Late 1993

Date	Race	Location	Miles	Winner	Jockey	Purse
Oct. 2	Super Derby XIV	La. Downs	1¼	Wallenda	William McCauley	$ 750,000
Oct. 3	L'arc de Triomphe	Longchamp	1½ (T)	Urban Sea	Eric St. Martin	1,519,205
Oct. 9	Turf Classic	Belmont	1½ (T)	Apple Tree (FRA)	Mike Smith	500,000
Oct. 10	Oak Tree Invitational	Santa Anita	1½	Kotashaan (FRA)	Kent Desormeaux	300,000
Oct. 15	Meadowlands Cup	Meadowlands	1⅛	Marquetry	Kent Desormeaux	500,000
Oct. 16	Champagne Stakes	Belmont	1	Dehere	Chris McCarron	500,000
Oct. 16	Jockey Club Gold Cup	Belmont	1¼	Miner's Mark	Chris McCarron	850,000
Oct. 23	Wash. D.C. International	Laurel	1 (T)	Buckhar	Jean Cruguet	600,000
Oct. 17	Rothmans International	Woodbine	1½ (T)	Husband	Cash Asmussen	1,000,000
Nov. 6	Breeders' Cup Classic	Santa Anita	1¼	Arcanques	Jerry Bailey	3,000,000
Nov. 6	Breeders' Cup Turf	Santa Anita	1½ (T)	Kotashaan (FRA)	Kent Desormeaux	2,000,000
Nov. 6	Breeders' Cup Distaff	Santa Anita	1⅛	Hollywood Wildcat	Eddie Delahoussaye	1,000,000
Nov. 6	Breeders' Cup Mile	Santa Anita	1	Lure	Mike Smith	1,000,000
Nov. 6	Breeders' Cup Juvenile	Santa Anita	1 1/16	Brocco	Gary Stevens	1,000,000
Nov. 6	Breeders' Cup Juv. Fil	Santa Anita	1 1/16	Phone Chatter	Laffit Pincay Jr.	1,000,000
Nov. 6	Breeders' Cup Sprint	Santa Anita	6 F	Cardmania	Eddie Delahoussaye	1,000,000
Nov. 20	Hawthorne Cup Gold	Hawthorne	1¼	Evanescent	Aaron Gryder	400,000
Nov. 28	Japan Cup	Tokyo Racecourse	1½ (T)	Legacy World (JPN)	H. Kawachi	3,123,779
Dec. 12	Hollywood Turf Cup	Hollywood	1½ (T)	Fraise	Chris McCarron	500,000
Dec. 18	Hollywood Starlet	Hollywood	1 1/16	Sardula	Eddie Delahoussaye	250,000
Dec. 19	Hollywood Futurity	Hollywood	1 1/16	Valiant Nature	Laffit Pincay Jr.	500,000

1994 (through Sept. 24)

Date	Race	Location	Miles	Winner	Jockey	Purse
Jan. 22	El Camino Real Derby	Bay Meadows	1 1/16	Tabasco Cat	Pat Day	$ 200,000
Feb. 5	Donn Handicap	Gulfstream	1⅛	Pistols and Roses	Heberto Castillo Jr.	300,000
Feb. 6	Charles H. Strub Stakes	Santa Anita	1¼	Diazo	Laffit Pincay Jr.	500,000
Feb. 19	Fountain of Youth	Gulfstream	1 1/16	Dehere	Craig Perret	200,000
Mar. 5	Santa Anita Handicap	Santa Anita	1¼	Stuka	Chris Antley	1,000,000
Mar. 6	Gulfstream Park Hand.	Gulfstream	1¼	Scuffleburg	Craig Perret	500,000
Mar. 12	Florida Derby	Gulfstream	1⅛	Holy Bull	Mike Smith	500,000
Mar. 27	San Luis Rey Stakes	Santa Anita	1½ (T)	Bien Bien	Chris McCarron	250,000
Apr. 2	Jim Beam Stakes	Turfway	1⅛	Polar Expedition	Curt Bourque	600,000
Apr. 3	Flamingo Stakes	Hialeah	1⅛	Meadow Flight	Craig Perret	200,000
Apr. 9	Santa Anita Derby	Santa Anita	1⅛	Brocco	Gary Stevens	500,000
Apr. 16	Blue Grass Stakes	Keeneland	1⅛	Holy Bull	Mike Smith	500,000
Apr. 16	California Derby	Golden Gate	1⅛	Screaming Don	Adalberto Lopez	200,000
Apr. 16	Oaklawn Handicap	Oaklawn	1⅛	The Wicked North	Kent Desormeaux	750,000
Apr. 16	Wood Memorial Invit.	Aqueduct	1⅛	Irgun	Gary Stevens	500,000
Apr. 22	Apple Blossom Handicap	Oaklawn	1 1/16	Nine Keys	Mike Smith	500,000
Apr. 23	Arkansas Derby	Oaklawn	1⅛	Concern	Garrett Gomez	500,000
Apr. 24	San Juan Capistrano	Santa Anita	1¾ (T)	Bien Bien	Chris McCarron	400,000
May 4	Kentucky Oaks	Churchill Downs	1⅛	Sardula	Eddie Delahoussaye	250,000
May 7	**Kentucky Derby**	Churchill Downs	1¼	Go for Gin	Chris McCarron	500,000
May 8	Acorn Stakes	Belmont	1	Inside Information	Mike Smith	150,000

Thoroughbred Racing (Cont.)
Major Stakes Races
1994 (through Sept. 24)

Date	Race	Location	Miles	Winner	Jockey	Purse
May 14	Pimlico Special	Pimlico	1 3/16	As Indicated	Robbie Davis	$ 600,000
May 21	**Preakness Stakes**	Pimlico	1 3/16	Tabasco Cat	Pat Day	500,000
May 28	Jersey Derby	Garden State	1 1/16(T)	Zuno Star	Mike Smith	150,000
May 30	Hollywood Turf Handicap	Hollywood	1 1/4 (T)	Grand Flotilla	Gary Stevens	500,000
May 30	Metropolitan Handicap	Belmont	1	Holy Bull	Mike Smith	500,000
June 1	Ever Ready English Derby	Epsom Downs	1 1/2 (T)	Erhaab	Willie Carson	1,162,714
June 5	Californian Stakes	Hollywood Park	1 1/8	The Wicked North	Kent Desormeaux	300,000
June 11	**Belmont Stakes**	Belmont	1 1/2	Tabasco Cat	Pat Day	500,000
June 12	Mother Goose Stakes	Belmont	1 1/8	Lakeway	Kent Desormeaux	200,000
June 26	Caesars Int'l Handicap	Atlantic City	1 3/16(T)	Lure	Mike Smith	500,000
June 26	Budweiser Irish Derby	Curragh	1 1/2 (T)	Balanchine	Lafranco Dettori	842,460
July 2	Hollywood Gold Cup	Hollywood	1 1/4	Slew of Damascus	Gary Stevens	750,000
July 4	Suburban Handicap	Belmont	1 1/4	Devil His Due	Mike Smith	350,000
July 10	Queen's Plate	Woodbine	1 1/4	Basqueian	Jim Lauzon	375,000
July 9	Coaching Club Am. Oaks	Belmont	1 1/4	Two Altazano	Jose Santos	250,000
July 23	King George VI and Queen Elizabeth Diamond Stakes	Ascot	1 1/2 (T)	King's Theatre	Mick Kinane	666,022
July 31	Prince of Wales Stakes	Fort Erie	1 3/16	Bruce's Mill	Craig Perret	150,000
July 31	Haskell Invitational	Monmouth	1 1/8	Holy Bull	Mike Smith	500,000
Aug. 13	Alabama Stakes	Saratoga	1 1/4	Heavenly Prize	Mike Smith	200,000
Aug. 13	Pacific Classic	Del Mar	1 1/4	Tinners Way	Eddie Delahoussaye	1,000,000
Aug. 20	Travers Stakes	Saratoga	1 1/4	Holy Bull	Mike Smith	750,000
Aug. 21	Breeders' Stakes	Fort Erie	1 1/2 (T)	Basquean	Jim Lauzon	250,000
Aug. 21	Philip Iselin Handicap	Monmouth	1 1/8	Taking Risks	Mark Johnston	250,000
Aug. 27	Whitney Handicap	Saratoga	1 1/8	Colonial Affair	Jose Santos	350,000
Aug. 27	Beverly D. Stakes	Arlington	1 3/16(T)	Hatoof	Walter Swinburn	500,000
Aug. 28	Arlington Million	Arlington	1 1/4 (T)	Paradise Creek	Pat Day	1,000,000
Sept.17	Woodward Stakes	Belmont	1 1/8	Holy Bull	Mike Smith	500,000
Sept.17	Man o' War Stakes	Belmont	1 3/8 (T)	Royal Mountain Inn	Julie Krone	400,000
Sept.17	Ruffian Handicap	Belmont	1 1/16	Sky Beauty	Mike Smith	200,000
Sept.18	Molson Export Million	Woodbine	1 1/8	Dramatic Gold	Corey Nakatani	1,000,000
Sept.24	Kentucky Cup Classic	Turfway	1 1/8	Tabasco Cat	Pat Day	400,000

TRC National Thoroughbred Poll

(Sept. 26, 1994)

Through Week 30 of the 1994 racing season. Poll taken by Thoroughbred Communications, Inc., and based on the votes of sports and Thoroughbred racing media. First place votes are in parentheses.

	Pts	Owner (Trainer)	'94 Record Sts—1-2-3	Earnings	Last Start (Date, Distance)
1. Holy Bull (32)	320	Jimmy Croll (Jimmy Croll)	10—8-0-0	$2,095,000	1st— Woodward Handicap (9/17, 1 1/8 mi.)
2. Paradise Creek	279	Masayuki Nishiyama (Bill Mott)	8—7-1-0	1,320,872	1st— Arlington Million (8/28, 1 1/4 mi.-T)
3. Sky Beauty	230	Georgia Hofmann (Allen Jerkens)	5—5-0-0	438,855	1st— Ruffian Handicap (9/17, 1 1/16 mi.)
4. Lure	212	Claiborne Farm (Shug McGaughey)	5—3-2-0	508,236	1st— Baruch Handicap (8/12, 1 1/8 mi.-T)
5. Tabasco Cat	196	Overbrook & Reynolds (D. Wayne Lukas)	9—5-2-1	1,519,334	1st— Ky. Cup Classic (9/24, 1 1/8 mi.)
6. Devil His Due	162	Lion Crest Stable (Allen Jerkins)	9—3-4-1	922,000	2nd— Woodward Handicap (9/17, 1 1/8 mi.)
7. Lakeway	88	Mike Rutherford (Gary Jones)	7—5-2-0	579,520	2nd— Alabama Stakes (8/13, 1 1/4 mi.)
8. The Wicked North	64	Philip & Sophie Hersh (David Bernstein)	6—3-1-0	921,750	4th— Hollywood Gold Cup (7/2, 1 1/4 mi.)
9. Paseana	29	Sidney Craig (Ron McAnally)	3—2-1-0	327,100	1st— Chula Hista H'cap (8/28, 1 1/16 mi.)
10. Bien Bien	27	Toffan & McCaffery (Paco Gonzalez)	6—3-3-0	785,350	2nd— Hollywood Turf H'cap (5/30, 1 1/4 mi.-T)

Others receiving votes: 11. Heavenly Prize (26 points); **12.** Go for Gin (20); **13.** Flanders, Flawlessly and Royal Mountain Inn (17); **16.** Colonial Affair (16); **17.** Fanmore (11); **18.** Hollywood Wildcat (8); **19.** As Indicated (7); **20.** Dramatic Gold (5); **21.** Hatoof (4); **22.** Montreal Red (3); **23.** Call Now and Tinners Way (1).

The 1994 Triple Crown

Thoroughbred racing's Triple Crown for 3-year-olds consists of the Kentucky Derby, Preakness Stakes and Belmont Stakes run over six weeks in May and June. After a disappointed sixth place finish in the Derby, Tabasco Cat came back to win both the Preakness and Belmont. Derby winner Go for Gin placed second in both the Preakness and Belmont.

120TH KENTUCKY DERBY

Grade I for three-year-olds. **Date**—May 7, 1994; **Distance**—1¼ miles; **Stakes Purse**—$878,800 ($628,800 to winner); **Track**—Sloppy; **Off**—5:34 p.m. EDT; **Favorite**—Holy Bull (8-5).

Winner—Go for Gin; **Time**—2:03⅗; **Won**—Driving; **Sire**—Cormorant; **Dam**—Never Knock (by Stage Door Johnny); **Breeder**—Darmstadt Pamela Du Pont (Ky.).

Order of Finish	Jockey	PP	1/4	1/2	3/4	1-Mile	Stretch	Finish	To $1
Go for Gin	Chris McCarron	8	2-½	1-½	1-1½	1-4	1-2	1-2	9.90
Strodes Creek	Eddie Delahoussaye	7	7-½	8-head	9-1	7-head	2-head	2-2½	7.90
Blumin Affair	Jerry Bailey	13	10-½	11-3	8-½	6-1	5-½	3-¾	14.90
Brocco	Gary Stevens	10	9-1½	6-1	7-½	4-½	3-½	4-1¼	4.30
Soul of the Matter	Kent Desormeaux	1	12-5	10-½	10-½	4-½	4-head	5-head	16.90
Tabasco Cat	Pat Day	9	4-½	4-1	5-1	5-1½	7-2	6-1¼	6.10
Southern Rhythm	Garrett Gomez	12	14	13-4	13-3½	10-½	9-3	7-1½	20.00
Powis Castle	Chris Antley	3	3-1	3-½	3-1	2-1	4-head	8-2	20.30
Mahogany Hall	Wilfredo Martinez	6	12-½	14	14	12-1½	11-½	9-½	16.70
Smilin Singin Sam	Larry Melancon	11	11-head	9-1	2-head	3-1½	3-½	10-2	16.70
Meadow Flight	Shane Sellers	14	8-1	12-2	11-½	11-1½	10-½	11-2	16.70
Holy Bull	Mike Smith	4	6-1½	5-1½	6-1½	9-2	12-4	12-2	2.20
Valiant Nature	Laffit Pincay Jr.	2	5-½	7-½	12-3	13-8	13-6	13-15	12.00
Ulises	Jorge Chavez	5	5-½	7-½	12-3	13-8	13-6	13-15	12.00

Times—0:22⅘; 0:47⅕; 1:11⅘; 1:37⅗; 2:03⅗.
$2 Mutual Prices—#6 Go for Gin ($20.20, $8.40, $5.80); #5 Strodes Creek ($7.80, $6.00); #10 Blumin Affair ($8.00).
Scratched—Kandaly. **Overweights**—None. **Attendance**—130,594. **TV Rating**—8.5/23 share (ABC).
Trainers & Owners (by finish): **1**—Nick Zito & William Condren and Joseph Cornacchia; **2**—Charlie Whittingham & Arthur Hancock III, Rose Hill Stable and Whittingham; **3**—Jack Van Berg & Leroy Bowman and Art Vogel; **4**—Randy Winick & Mr. and Mrs. Albert Broccoli; **5**—Richard Mandella & Burt Bacharach; **6**—D. Wayne Lukas & Overbrook Farm and David Reynolds; **7**—Jim Keefer & Ted Keefer, Buddy New and Bill Heiligbrodt; **8**—Rodney Rash & Vistas Stables (Berry Gordy); **9**—Jim Baker & Robert Hoeweler; **10**—Niall O'Callaghan & Dogwood Stable; **11**—Jim Ryerson & Aliyuee Ben J. Stables; **12**—Jimmy Croll & Jimmy Croll; **13**—Ron McAnally & Winchell Stable; **14**—Alfredo Callejas & Robert Perez.

119TH PREAKNESS STAKES

Grade I for three-year-olds; 10th race at Pimlico in Baltimore. **Date**—May 21, 1994; **Distance**—1$\frac{3}{16}$ miles; **Stakes Purse**—$686,800 ($447,720 to winner); **Track**—Fast; **Off**—5:32 p.m. EDT. **Favorite**—Go for Gin (2-1).

Winner—Tabasco Cat; **Time**—1:56⅖; **Won**—Driving; **Sire**—Storm Cat; **Dam**—Barbicue Sauce (by Sauce Boat); **Breeder**—Overbrook Farm and David Reynolds (Ky.).

Order of Finish	Jockey	PP	1/4	1/2	3/4	Stretch	Finish	To $1
Tabasco Cat	Pat Day	1	4-4	4-2	3-head	1-head	1-¾	3.60
Go for Gin	Chris McCarron	2	2-1½	1-head	1-½	2-5	2-6	2.80
a-Concern	Garrett Gomez	3	10	9-2	9-head	7-½	3-½	10.20
Kandaly	Craig Perret	7	8-10	8-7	8-4	5-1	4-1¾	11.80
Numerous	Pat Valenzuela	10	6-1½	5-½	5-1	3-head	5-½	9.10
Blumin Affair	Jerry Bailey	6	7-4	6-1	6-3	4-1	6-2	3.10
a-Looming	Andrea Seefeldt	9	9-1	10	10	9-8	7-½	10.20
Silver Goblin	Dale Cordova	4	3-1	3-1½	4-1½	6-head	8-¾	9.90
Powis Castle	Brent Bartram	5	5-head	7-4	7-1½	8-½	9-11	11.30
Polar Expedition	Curt Bourque	8	1-1	2-1½	2-1	10	10	18.10

Note: (a) indicates horses were coupled.

Times—0:23⅗; 0:47⅖; 1:11⅘; 1:37; 1:56⅖.
$2 Mutual Prices—#2 Tabasco Cat ($9.20, $4.60, $4.60); #3 Go for Gin ($4.60, $4.40); #1 Concern ($6.40).
Scratched—None. **Overweights**—None. **Attendance**—86,343. **TV Rating**—5.0/15 share (ABC).
Trainers & Owners (by finish): **1**—D. Wayne Lukas & Overbrook Farm and David Reynolds; **2**—Nick Zito & William Condren and Joseph Cornacchia; **3**—Richard Small & Robert Meyerhoff; **4**—Louie Roussell III & Roz Cole, Ronnie Lamarque and Roussell; **5**—Charlie Whittingham & Howard Keck; **6**—Jack Van Berg & Leroy Bowman and Art Vogel; **7**—Richard Small & Robert Meyerhoff; **8**—Kenny Smith & Al Horton; **9**—Rodney Rash & Vistas Stables (Berry Gordy); **10**—Hugh Robertson & James Cody.

1994 Triple Crown (Cont.)

126TH BELMONT STAKES

Grade I for three-year-olds; **Date**—June 11, 1994; **Distance**—1½ miles;
Stakes Purse—$653,800 ($392,280 to winner); **Track**—Fast; **Off**—5:31 p.m. EDT. **Favorite**—Go for Gin (9-5).
Winner—Tabasco Cat; **Time**—2:26⅘; **Won**—Driving; **Sire**—Storm Cat; **Dam**—Barbicue Sauce (by Sauce Boat); **Breeder**—Overbrook Farm and David Reynolds (Ky.).

Order of Finish	Jockey	PP	1/4	1/2	1-Mile	1 1/4-M	Stretch	Finish	To $1
Tabasco Cat	Pat Day	2	3-head	2-head	2-2½	2-3	1-½	1-2	3.40
Go for Gin	Chris McCarron	1	1-1	1-1	1-1½	1-1½	2-3	2-½	1.50
Strodes Creek	Jerry Bailey	6	2-head	4-1½	3-1½	3-head	3-1	3-3½	1.30
Signal Tap	Jose Santos	3	5-1	6	4-½	4-4	4-4	4-5	13.50
Amathos	Mike Smith	4	6	5-½	5-6	5-14	5-24	5-35	13.30
Ulises	Craig Perret	5	4-1	3-1½	6	6	6	6	28.80

Times—0:23⅘; 0:47⅖; 1:11⅕; 1:35⅘; 2:00⅖; 2:26⅘.
$2 Mutual Prices—#2 Tabasco Cat ($8.80, $3.80, $2.40); #1 Go for Gin ($3.00, $2.20); #6 Strodes Creek ($2.20).
Scratched—Brocco. **Overweights**—None. **Attendance**—42,695. **TV Rating**—4.5/14 share (ABC).
Trainers & Owners (by finish): 1—D. Wayne Lukas & Overbrook Farm and David Reynolds; **2**—Nick Zito & William Condren and Joseph Cornacchia; **3**—Charlie Whittingham & Arthur Hancock, Rose Hill Stable and Whittingham; **4**—Scotty Schulhofer & Centennial Farms; **5**—Bill Mott & Mohammed al Maktoum; **6**—Alfredo Callejas & Robert Perez.

1993-94 Money Leaders

Official Top 10 standings for 1993 and unofficial Top 10 standings for 1994, through Sept.25, as compiled by *The Daily Racing Form.*

Final 1993

HORSES	Age	Sts	1-2-3	Earnings
Kotashaan (FRA)	5	10	6-3-0	$2,619,014
Sea Hero	3	9	2-0-2	2,484,190
Bertrando	4	9	3-4-1	2,217,800
Devil His Due	4	11	4-2-1	1,939,120
Star of Cozzene	5	12	6-4-0	1,776,071
Arcangues	5	1	1-0-0	1,560,000
Prairie Bayou	3	8	5-2-0	1,405,521
Kissin Kris	3	12	2-4-2	1,341,292
Peteski	3	10	7-2-1	1,287,150
Lure	4	8	6-2-0	1,212,323

JOCKEYS	Mts	1st	Earnings
Mike Smith	1510	343	$14,008,148
Kent Desormeaux	1214	279	13,206,031
Jerry Bailey	1104	209	12,360,114
Chris McCarron	963	157	11,673,795
†Gary Stevens	1236	248	11,598,946
Eddie Delahoussaye	1213	228	10,315,419
Pat Day	1049	263	8,901,194
Jose Santos	1169	191	8,729,705
Corey Nakatani	1226	206	8,210,269
Laffit Pincay Jr	1222	166	6,743,689

†Includes foreign racing.

TRAINERS	Sts	1st	Earnings
Bobby Frankel	346	79	$8,883,252
Richard Mandella	344	65	6,586,592
Shug McGaughey	290	82	5,766,492
Ron McAnally	572	82	5,586,326
Bill Mott	535	133	5,148,163
Allen Jerkens	354	79	4,709,862
Gary Jones	354	70	4,539,925
Roger Attfield	355	82	4,475,843
D. Wayne Lukas	756	135	4,122,153
Mark Henning	233	48	4,068,857

1994 (through Sept. 25)

HORSES	Age	Sts	1-2-3	Earnings
Holy Bull	3	10	8-0-0	$2,095,000
Tabasco Cat	3	9	5-2-1	1,519,334
Paradise Creek	5	8	7-1-0	1,320,872
Go for Gin	3	9	2-4-1	1,178,596
Devil His Due	5	9	3-4-1	922,000
The Wicked North	5	6	3-1-0	921,750
Dramatic Gold	3	8	4-1-1	894,850
Concern	3	12	2-4-6	831,670
Bien Bien	5	6	3-3-0	785,350
Tinners Way	4	10	2-4-1	756,050

JOCKEYS	Mts	1st	Earnings
Mike Smith	1191	251	$11,837,249
Pat Day	911	249	9,315,968
Gary Stevens	1044	193	8,957,425
Chris McCarron	671	123	8,312,012
Kent Desormeaux	892	192	8,069,915
Jerry Bailey	1030	217	7,825,995
Corey Nakatani	760	136	6,396,122
Eddie Delahoussaye	721	129	6,364,782
Jose Santos	967	163	5,978,713
Alex Solis	1049	176	5,876,977

TRAINERS	Sts	1st	Earnings
Bill Mott	439	96	$5,206,055
D. Wayne Lukas	486	92	4,742,344
Allen Jerkens	320	75	3,655,363
Bobby Frankel	217	40	3,639,480
Ron McAnally	339	59	3,491,463
Gary Jones	224	53	3,427,650
Jack Van Berg	830	101	3,123,438
Shug McGaughey	207	60	3,053,623
Richard Mandella	238	45	2,704,920
Scotty Schulhofer	321	55	2,570,008

Harness Racing

1993-94 Major Stakes Races

Winners of major stakes races from Sept. 23, 1993 through Sept. 22, 1994; all paces and trots cover one mile; (BC) indicates year-end Breeders' Crown series.

LATE 1993

Date	Race	Raceway	Winner	Time	Driver	Purse
Sept.23	Little Brown Jug	Delaware	Life Sign	1:52	John Campbell	$465,500
Oct. 8	Kentucky Futurity	Red Mile	Pine Chip	1:52 3/5	John Campbell	157,000
Oct. 8	BC 3 & Up F/M Pace	Mohawk	Swing Back	1:52 2/5	Kelly Sheppard	330,675
Oct. 8	BC 3 & Up F/M Trot	Mohawk	Lifetime Dream	1:55 4/5	Paul MacDonell	330,675
Oct. 8	BC 3 & Up Open Pace	Mohawk	Staying Together	1:51 1/5	Bill O'Donnell	396,810
Oct. 8	BC 3 & Up Open Trot	Mohawk	Earl	1:56	C. Christoforou	396,810
Oct. 23	BC 2-Yr-Old Colt Pace	Freehold	Expensive Scooter	1:54 2/5	Jack Moiseyev	300,000
Oct. 23	BC 2-Yr-Old Filly Pace	Freehold	Electric Slide	1:57 4/5	Michel Lachance	300,000
Oct. 23	BC 3-Yr-Old Colt Pace	Freehold	Life Sign	1:54 2/5	John Campbell	300,000
Oct. 23	BC 3-Yr-Old Filly Pace	Freehold	Immortality	1:55 3/5	John Campbell	300,000
Oct. 29	BC 2-Yr-Old Colt Trot	Pompano	Wesgate Crown	1:57 1/5	John Campbell	300,000
Oct. 29	BC 2-Yr-Old Filly Trot	Pompano	Gleam	1:58 4/5	Jimmy Takter	300,000
Oct. 29	BC 3-Yr-Old Colt Trot	Pompano	Pine Chip	1:54 2/5	John Campbell	300,000
Oct. 29	BC 3-Yr-Old Filly Trot	Pompano	Expressway Hanover	1:55 4/5	Per Henriksen	300,000
Nov.20	Governor's Cup	Garden St.	Magical Mike	1:54 3/5	John Campbell	550,000

1994 (through Sept. 22)

Date	Race	Raceway	Winner	Time	Driver	Purse
June 26	North America Cup	Woodbine	Cam's Card Shark	1:51 4/5	John Campbell	$1,000,000
July 2	Messenger Stakes	Rosecroft	Cam's Card Shark	1:51	John Campbell	342,595
July 9	Yonkers Trot	Yonkers	Bullville Victory	1:58 2/5	Cat Manzi	286,280
July 17	Meadowlands Pace	Meadowlands	Cam's Card Shark	1:50	John Campbell	1,000,000
Aug. 6	**Hambletonian**	Meadowlands	Victory Dream	1:54 1/5	Michel Lachance	1,200,000
Aug.13	Sweetheart Pace	Meadowlands	Efishnc	1:54 3/5	Ron Waples	567,500
Aug.13	Woodrow Wilson Pace	Meadowlands	Dontgetinmyway	1:53 4/5	John Campbell	774,750
Aug.27	Cane Pace	Yonkers	Falcon's Future	1:53 2/5	Ken Holliday	391,780
Sept. 3	World Trotting Derby	Du Quoin	Bullville Victory	1:57 2/5	Bill Fahy	650,000
Sept.22	Little Brown Jug	Delaware	Magical Mike	1:52 3/5	Michel Lachance	512,830

1993-94 Money Leaders

Official Top 10 standings for 1993 and unofficial Top 10 standings for 1994 through Sept. 22, as compiled by the U.S. Trotting Association.

Final 1993

HORSES	Age	Sts	1-2-3	Earnings
Presidential Ball	3pc	25	17-5-2	$2,222,166
Pine Chip	3tc	24	16-3-1	1,363,483
Life Sign	3pc	22	13-6-3	1,354,911
American Winner	3tc	22	15-4-2	1,299,468
Staying Together	apg	26	21-1-0	1,169,155
Riyadh	3pc	25	14-6-2	1,124,309
Magical Mike	2pc	16	13-1-0	769,408
Wesgate Crown	2tc	8	7-0-1	766,626
Expensive Scooter	2pc	18	11-2-1	674,845
Freedoms Friend	2pf	11	6-3-0	600,412

DRIVERS	Sts	1st	Earnings
John Campbell	1811	370	$9,926,482
Jack Moiseyev	3159	645	8,202,270
Ron Pierce	2546	362	4,940,990
Cat Manzi	3042	437	4,727,416
Doug Brown	1994	386	4,446,467
Dave Magee	2809	553	4,020,128
Michel Lachance	2061	247	3,912,458
Ron Waples	1627	202	3,858,663
Steve Condren	1555	193	3,212,218
Bill O'Donnell	920	125	3,210,542

1994 (through Sept. 25)

HORSES	Age	Sts	1-2-3	Earnings
Cam's Card Shark	3pc	18	15-2-0	$2,264,714
Pacific Rocket	3pc	19	5-9-2	945,825
Victory Dream	3tc	12	8-1-0	844,295
Falcons Future	3pc	22	10-5-0	741,254
Magical Mike	3pc	15	7-2-4	672,038
Bullville Victory	3tc	18	6-4-2	645,846
Mr Lavec	3tc	15	6-4-5	590,529
Historic	3pc	17	3-3-2	562,197
Arrive At Five	aph	21	17-1-2	529,005
Dontgetinmyway	2pc	12	6-5-0	522,872

DRIVERS	Sts	1st	Earnings
John Campbell	1648	342	$8,453,977
Jack Moiseyev	2138	397	5,373,207
Michel Lachance	1820	253	4,708,705
Ron Waples	2056	250	4,132,298
Cat Manzi	2326	314	3,894,728
Doug Brown	1498	324	3,537,157
Dave Magee	2066	448	3,352,781
Steve Condren	1250	201	2,510,429
Luc Ouellette	1655	376	2,254,234
Ron Pierce	1331	151	2,216,272

THE 1995 INFORMATION PLEASE SPORTS ALMANAC

HORSE RACING STATISTICS

THROUGH THE YEARS
1867-1994
THOROUGHBRED • HARNESS

SEC B

PAGE 722

Thoroughbred Racing

The Triple Crown

The term "Triple Crown" was coined by sportswriter Charles Hatton while covering the 1930 victories of Gallant Fox in the Kentucky Derby, Preakness Stakes and Belmont Stakes. Before then, only Sir Barton (1919) had won all three races in the same year. Since then, nine horses have won the Triple Crown. Two trainers, James (Sunny Jim) Fitzsimmons and Ben A. Jones, have saddled two Triple Crown champions, while Eddie Arcaro is the only jockey to ride two champions.

Year		Jockey	Trainer	Owner	Sire/Dam
1919	**Sir Barton**	Johnny Loftus	H. Guy Bedwell	J.K.L. Ross	Star Shoot/Lady Sterling
1930	**Gallant Fox**	Earl Sande	J.E. Fitzsimmons	Belair Stud	Sir Gallahad III/Marguerite
1935	**Omaha**	Willie Saunders	J.E. Fitzsimmons	Belair Stud	Gallant Fox/Flambino
1937	**War Admiral**	Charley Kurtsinger	George Conway	Samuel Riddle	Man o'War/Brushup
1941	**Whirlaway**	Eddie Arcaro	Ben A. Jones	Calumet Farm	Blenheim II/Dustwhirl
1943	**Count Fleet**	Johnny Longden	Don Cameron	Mrs. J.D. Hertz	Reigh Count/Quickly
1946	**Assault**	Warren Mehrtens	Max Hirsch	King Ranch	Bold Venture/Igual
1948	**Citation**	Eddie Arcaro	Ben A. Jones	Calumet Farm	Bull Lea/Hydroplane II
1973	**Secretariat**	Ron Turcotte	Lucien Laurin	Meadow Stable	Bold Ruler/Somethingroyal
1977	**Seattle Slew**	Jean Cruguet	Billy Turner	Karen Taylor	Bold Reasoning/My Charmer
1978	**Affirmed**	Steve Cauthen	Laz Barrera	Harbor View Farm	Exclusive Native/Won't Tell You

Note: Gallant Fox (1930) is the only Triple Crown winner to sire another Triple Crown winner, Omaha (1935). Wm. Woodward Sr., owner of Belair Stud, was breeder-owner of both horses and both were trained by Sunny Jim Fitzsimmons.

Triple Crown Near Misses

Forty horses have won two legs of the Triple Crown. Of those, a dozen won the Kentucky Derby (KD) and Preakness Stakes (PS) only to be beaten in the Belmont Stakes (BS). Two others, Burgoo King (1932) and Bold Venture (1936), each won the Derby and Preakness but were forced out of the Belmont with the same injury—a bowed tendon—that effectively ended their racing careers. In 1978, Alydar finished second to Affirmed in all three races, the only time that has happened. Note that the Preakness preceeded the Kentucky Derby in 1922, '23 and '31; (*) indicates won on disqualification.

Year		KD	PS	BS	Year		KD	PS	BS
1877	**Cloverbrook**	DNS	won	won	1961	**Carry Back**	won	won	7th
1878	**Duke of Magenta**	DNS	won	won	1963	**Chateaugay**	won	2nd	won
1880	**Grenada**	DNS	won	won	1964	**Northern Dancer**	won	won	3rd
1881	**Saunterer**	DNS	won	won	1966	**Kauai King**	won	won	4th
1895	**Belmar**	DNS	won	won	1967	**Damascus**	3rd	won	won
1920	**Man o'War**	DNS	won	won	1968	**Forward Pass**	won*	won	2nd
1922	**Pillory**	DNS	won	won	1969	**Majestic Prince**	won	won	2nd
1923	**Zev**	won	12th	won	1971	**Canonero II**	won	won	4th
1931	**Twenty Grand**	won	2nd	won	1972	**Riva Ridge**	won	4th	won
1932	**Burgoo King**	won	won	DNS	1974	**Little Current**	5th	won	won
1936	**Bold Venture**	won	won	DNS	1976	**Bold Forbes**	won	3rd	won
1939	**Johnstown**	won	5th	won	1979	**Spectacular Bid**	won	won	3rd
1940	**Bimelech**	2nd	won	won	1981	**Pleasant Colony**	won	won	3rd
1942	**Shut Out**	won	5th	won	1984	**Swale**	won	7th	won
1944	**Pensive**	won	won	2nd	1987	**Alysheba**	won	won	4th
1949	**Capot**	2nd	won	won	1988	**Risen Star**	3rd	won	won
1950	**Middleground**	won	2nd	won	1989	**Sunday Silence**	won	won	2nd
1953	**Native Dancer**	2nd	won	won	1991	**Hansel**	10th	won	won
1955	**Nashua**	2nd	won	won	1994	**Tabasco Cat**	6th	won	won
1956	**Needles**	won	2nd	won					
1958	**Tim Tam**	won	won	2nd					

The Triple Crown Challenge (1987-93)

Seeking to make the Triple Crown more than just a media event and to insure that owners would not be attracted to more lucrative races, officials at Churchill Downs, the Maryland Jockey Club and the New York Racing Association created Triple Crown Productions in 1985 and announced that a $1 million bonus would be given to the horse that performs best in the Kentucky Derby, Preakness Stakes and Belmont Stakes. Furthermore, a bonus of $5 million would be presented to any horse winning all three races.

Revised in 1991, the rules stated that the winning horse must: 1. finish all three races; 2. earn points by finishing first, second, third or fourth in at least one of the three races; and 3. earn the highest number of points based on the following system—10 points to win, five to place, three to show and one to finish fourth. In the event of a tie, the $1 million is distributed equally among the top point-getters. From 1987-90, the system was five points to win, three to place and one to show. The Triple Crown Challenge was discontinued in 1994.

Year		KD	PS	BS	Pts	Year		KD	PS	BS	Pts
1987	1 **Bet Twice**	2nd	2nd	1st	11	1991	1 **Hansel**	10th	1st	1st	20
	2 Alysheba	1st	1st	4th	10		2 Strike the Gold	1st	6th	2nd	15
	3 Cryptoclearance	4th	3rd	2nd	4		3 Mane Minister	3rd	3rd	3rd	9
1988	1 **Risen Star**	3rd	1st	1st	11	1992	1 **Pine Bluff**	5th	1st	3rd	13
	2 Winning Colors	1st	3rd	6th	6		2 Casual Lies	2nd	3rd	5th	8
	3 Brian's Time	6th	2nd	3rd	4		(No other horses ran all three races.)					
1989	1 **Sunday Silence**	1st	1st	2nd	13	1993	1 **Sea Hero**	1st	5th	7th	10
	2 Easy Goer	2nd	2nd	1st	11		2 Wild Gale	3rd	8th	3rd	6
	3 Hawkster	5th	5th	5th	0		(No other horses ran all three races.)					
1990	1 **Unbridled**	1st	2nd	4th	8						
	2 Summer Squall	2nd	1st	DNR	8						
	3 Go and Go	DNR	DNR	1st	5						
	(Unbridled was only horse to run all three races.)										

Kentucky Derby

For three-year-olds. Held the first Saturday in May at Churchill Downs in Louisville, Ky. Inaugurated in 1875. Originally run at 1½ miles (1875-95), shortened to present 1¼ miles in 1896.

Trainers with most wins: Ben Jones (6); Dick Thompson (4); Sunny Jim Fitzsimmons and Max Hirsch (3).

Jockeys with most wins: Eddie Arcaro and Bill Hartack (5); Bill Shoemaker (4); Angel Cordero Jr, Issac Murphy and Earl Sande (3).

Winning fillies: Regret (1915), Genuine Risk (1980) and Winning Colors (1988).

Year		Time	Jockey	Trainer	2nd place	3rd place
1875	**Aristides**	2:37¾	Oliver Lewis	Ansel Anderson	Volcano	Verdigris
1876	**Vagrant**	2:38¼	Bobby Swim	James Williams	Creedmore	Harry Hill
1877	**Baden-Baden**	2:38	Billy Walker	Ed Brown	Leonard	King William
1878	**Day Star**	2:37¼	Jimmy Carter	Lee Paul	Himyar	Leveler
1879	**Lord Murphy**	2:37	Charlie Shauer	George Rice	Falsetto	Strathmore
1880	**Fonso**	2:37½	George Lewis	Tice Hutsell	Kimball	Bancroft
1881	**Hindoo**	2:40	Jim McLaughlin	James Rowe Sr.	Lelex	Alfambra
1882	**Apollo**	2:40¼	Babe Hurd	Green Morris	Runnymede	Bengal
1883	**Leonatus**	2:43	Billy Donohue	John McGinty	Drake Carter	Lord Raglan
1884	**Buchanan**	2:40¼	Isaac Murphy	William Bird	Loftin	Audrain
1885	**Joe Cotton**	2:37¼	Babe Henderson	Alex Perry	Bersan	Ten Booker
1886	**Ben Ali**	2:36½	Paul Duffy	Jim Murphy	Blue Wing	Free Knight
1887	**Montrose**	2:39¼	Isaac Lewis	John McGinty	Jim Gore	Jacobin
1888	**MacBeth II**	2:38¼	George Covington	John Campbell	Gallifet	White
1889	**Spokane**	2:34½	Thomas Kiley	John Rodegap	Proctor Knott	Once Again
1890	**Riley**	2:45	Isaac Murphy	Edward Corrigan	Bill Letcher	Robespierre
1891	**Kingman**	2:52¼	Isaac Murphy	Dud Allen	Balgowan	High Tariff
1892	**Azra**	2:41½	Lonnie Clayton	John Morris	Huron	Phil Dwyer
1893	**Lookout**	2:39¼	Eddie Kunze	Wm. McDaniel	Plutus	Boundless
1894	**Chant**	2:41	Frank Goodale	Eugene Leigh	Pearl Song	Sigurd
1895	**Halma**	2:37½	Soup Perkins	Byron McClelland	Basso	Laureate
1896	**Ben Brush**	2:07¾	Willie Simms	Hardy Campbell	Ben Eder	Semper Ego
1897	**Typhoon II**	2:12½	Buttons Garner	J.C. Cahn	Ornament	Dr. Catlett
1898	**Plaudit**	2:09	Willie Simms	John E. Madden	Lieber Karl	Isabey
1899	**Manuel**	2:12	Fred Taral	Robert Walden	Corsini	Mazo
1900	**Lieut. Gibson**	2:06¼	Jimmy Boland	Charles Hughes	Florizar	Thrive
1901	**His Eminence**	2:07¾	Jimmy Winkfield	F.B. Van Meter	Sannazarro	Driscoll
1902	**Alan-a-Dale**	2:08¾	Jimmy Winkfield	T.C. McDowell	Inventor	The Rival
1903	**Judge Himes**	2:09	Hal Booker	J.P. Mayberry	Early	Bourbon
1904	**Elwood**	2:08½	Shorty Prior	C.E. Durnell	Ed Tierney	Brancas
1905	**Agile**	2:10¾	Jack Martin	Robert Tucker	Ram's Horn	Layson
1906	**Sir Huon**	2:08⅘	Roscoe Troxler	Pete Coyne	Lady Navarre	James Reddick
1907	**Pink Star**	2:12⅗	Andy Minder	W.H. Fizer	Zal	Ovelando

Kentucky Derby (Cont.)

Year		Time	Jockey	Trainer	2nd place	3rd place
1908	**Stone Street**	2:15⅕	Arthur Pickens	J.W. Hall	Sir Cleges	Dunvegan
1909	**Wintergreen**	2:08⅕	Vincent Powers	Charles Mack	Miami	Dr. Barkley
1910	**Donau**	2:06⅖	Fred Herbert	George Ham	Joe Morris	Fighting Bob
1911	**Meridian**	2:05	George Archibald	Albert Ewing	Governor Gray	Colston
1912	**Worth**	2:09⅖	C.H. Shilling	Frank Taylor	Duval	Flamma
1913	**Donerail**	2:04⅘	Roscoe Goose	Thomas Hayes	Ten Point	Gowell
1914	**Old Rosebud**	2:03⅖	John McCabe	F.D. Weir	Hodge	Bronzewing
1915	**Regret**	2:05⅖	Joe Notter	James Rowe Sr.	Pebbles	Sharpshooter
1916	**George Smith**	2:04	Johnny Loftus	Hollie Hughes	Star Hawk	Franklin
1917	**Omar Khayyam**	2:04⅗	Charles Borel	C.T. Patterson	Ticket	Midway
1918	**Exterminator**	2:10⅘	William Knapp	Henry McDaniel	Escoba	Viva America
1919	**SIR BARTON**	2:09⅘	Johnny Loftus	H. Guy Bedwell	Billy Kelly	Under Fire
1920	**Paul Jones**	2:09	Ted Rice	Billy Garth	Upset	On Watch
1921	**Behave Yourself**	2:04⅕	Charles Thompson	Dick Thompson	Black Servant	Prudery
1922	**Morvich**	2:04⅗	Albert Johnson	Fred Burlew	Bet Mosie	John Finn
1923	**Zev**	2:05⅖	Earl Sande	David Leary	Martingale	Vigil
1924	**Black Gold**	2:05⅕	John Mooney	Hanly Webb	Chilhowee	Beau Butler
1925	**Flying Ebony**	2:07⅗	Earl Sande	William Duke	Captain Hal	Son of John
1926	**Bubbling Over**	2:03⅘	Albert Johnson	Dick Thompson	Bagenbaggage	Rock Man
1927	**Whiskery**	2:06	Linus McAtee	Fred Hopkins	Osmand	Jock
1928	**Reigh Count**	2:10⅖	Chick Lang	Bert Michell	Misstep	Toro
1929	**Clyde Van Dusen**	2:10⅘	Linus McAtee	Clyde Van Dusen	Naishapur	Panchio
1930	**GALLANT FOX**	2:07⅗	Earl Sande	Jim Fitzsimmons	Gallant Knight	Ned O.
1931	**Twenty Grand**	2:01⅘	Charley Kurtsinger	James Rowe Jr.	Sweep All	Mate
1932	**Burgoo King**	2:05⅕	Eugene James	Dick Thompson	Economic	Stepenfetchit
1933	**Brokers Tip**	2:06⅘	Don Meade	Dick Thompson	Head Play	Charley O.
1934	**Cavalcade**	2:04	Mack Garner	Bob Smith	Discovery	Agrarian
1935	**OMAHA**	2:05	Willie Saunders	Jim Fitzsimmons	Roman Soldier	Whiskolo
1936	**Bold Venture**	2:03⅗	Ira Hanford	Max Hirsch	Brevity	Indian Broom
1937	**WAR ADMIRAL**	2:03⅕	Charley Kurtsinger	George Conway	Pompoon	Reaping Reward
1938	**Lawrin**	2:04⅘	Eddie Arcaro	Ben Jones	Dauber	Can't Wait
1939	**Johnstown**	2:03⅖	James Stout	Jim Fitzsimmons	Challedon	Heather Broom
1940	**Gallahadion**	2:05	Carroll Bierman	Roy Waldron	Bimelech	Dit
1941	**WHIRLAWAY**	2:01⅖	Eddie Arcaro	Ben Jones	Staretor	Market Wise
1942	**Shut Out**	2:04⅖	Wayne Wright	John Gaver	Alsab	Valdina Orphan
1943	**COUNT FLEET**	2:04	Johnny Longden	Don Cameron	Blue Swords	Slide Rule
1944	**Pensive**	2:04⅕	Conn McCreary	Ben Jones	Broadcloth	Stir Up
1945	**Hoop Jr**	2:07	Eddie Arcaro	Ivan Parke	Pot O'Luck	Darby Dieppe
1946	**ASSAULT**	2:06⅗	Warren Mehrtens	Max Hirsch	Spy Song	Hampden
1947	**Jet Pilot**	2:06⅘	Eric Guerin	Tom Smith	Phalanx	Faultless
1948	**CITATION**	2:05⅖	Eddie Arcaro	Ben Jones	Coaltown	My Request
1949	**Ponder**	2:04⅕	Steve Brooks	Ben Jones	Capot	Palestinian
1950	**Middleground**	2:01⅗	William Boland	Max Hirsch	Hill Prince	Mr. Trouble
1951	**Count Turf**	2:02⅗	Conn McCreary	Sol Rutchick	Royal Mustang	Ruhe
1952	**Hill Gail**	2:01⅗	Eddie Arcaro	Ben Jones	Sub Fleet	Blue Man
1953	**Dark Star**	2:02	Hank Moreno	Eddie Hayward	Native Dancer	Invigorator
1954	**Determine**	2:03	Raymond York	Willie Molter	Hasty Road	Hasseyampa
1955	**Swaps**	2:01⅘	Bill Shoemaker	Mesh Tenney	Nashua	Summer Tan
1956	**Needles**	2:03⅖	David Erb	Hugh Fontaine	Fabius	Come On Red
1957	**Iron Liege**	2:02⅕	Bill Hartack	Jimmy Jones	Gallant Man	Round Table
1958	**Tim Tam**	2:05	Ismael Valenzuela	Jimmy Jones	Lincoln Road	Noureddin
1959	**Tomy Lee**	2:02⅕	Bill Shoemaker	Frank Childs	Sword Dancer	First Landing
1960	**Venetian Way**	2:02⅖	Bill Hartack	Victor Sovinski	Bally Ache	Victoria Park
1961	**Carry Back**	2:04	John Sellers	Jack Price	Crozier	Bass Clef
1962	**Decidedly**	2:00⅖	Bill Hartack	Horatio Luro	Roman Line	Ridan
1963	**Chateaugay**	2:01⅘	Braulio Baeza	James Conway	Never Bend	Candy Spots
1964	**Northern Dancer**	2:00	Bill Hartack	Horatio Luro	Hill Rise	The Scoundrel
1965	**Lucky Debonair**	2:01⅕	Bill Shoemaker	Frank Catrone	Dapper Dan	Tom Rolfe
1966	**Kauai King**	2:02	Don Brumfield	Henry Forrest	Advocator	Blue Skyer
1967	**Proud Clarion**	2:00⅗	Bobby Ussery	Loyd Gentry	Barbs Delight	Damascus
1968	**Forward Pass***	—	Ismael Valenzuela	Henry Forrest	Francie's Hat	T.V. Commercial
1969	**Majestic Prince**	2:01⅘	Bill Hartack	Johnny Longden	Arts and Letters	Dike
1970	**Dust Commander**	2:03⅖	Mike Manganello	Don Combs	My Dad George	High Echelon
1971	**Canonero II**	2:03⅕	Gustavo Avila	Juan Arias	Jim French	Bold Reason
1972	**Riva Ridge**	2:01⅘	Ron Turcotte	Lucien Laurin	No Le Hace	Hold Your Peace

Year		Time	Jockey	Trainer	2nd place	3rd place
1973	**SECRETARIAT**	1:59⅖	Ron Turcotte	Lucien Laurin	Sham	Our Native
1974	**Cannonade**	2:04	Angel Cordero Jr.	Woody Stephens	Hudson County	Agitate
1975	**Foolish Pleasure**	2:02	Jacinto Vasquez	LeRoy Jolley	Avatar	Diabolo
1976	**Bold Forbes**	2:01⅗	Angel Cordero Jr.	Laz Barrera	Honest Pleasure	Elocutionist
1977	**SEATTLE SLEW**	2:02⅕	Jean Cruguet	Billy Turner	Run Dusty Run	Sanhedrin
1978	**AFFIRMED**	2:01⅕	Steve Cauthen	Laz Barrera	Alydar	Believe It
1979	**Spectacular Bid**	2:02⅖	Ron Franklin	Bud Delp	General Assembly	Golden Act
1980	**Genuine Risk**	2:02	Jacinto Vasquez	LeRoy Jolley	Rumbo	Jaklin Klugman
1981	**Pleasant Colony**	2:02	Jorge Velasquez	John Campo	Woodchopper	Partez
1982	**Gato Del Sol**	2:02⅖	E. Delahoussaye	Eddie Gregson	Laser Light	Reinvested
1983	**Sunny's Halo**	2:02⅕	E. Delahoussaye	David Cross Jr.	Desert Wine	Caveat
1984	**Swale**	2:02⅖	Laffit Pincay Jr.	Woody Stephens	Coax Me Chad	At The Threshold
1985	**Spend A Buck**	2:00⅕	Angel Cordero Jr.	Cam Gambolati	Stephan's Odyssey	Chief's Crown
1986	**Ferdinand**	2:02⅘	Bill Shoemaker	Chas. Whittingham	Bold Arrangement	Broad Brush
1987	**Alysheba**	2:03⅖	Chris McCarron	Jack Van Berg	Bet Twice	Avies Copy
1988	**Winning Colors**	2:02⅕	Gary Stevens	D. Wayne Lukas	Forty Niner	Risen Star
1989	**Sunday Silence**	2:05	Pat Valenzuela	Chas. Whittingham	Easy Goer	Awe Inspiring
1990	**Unbridled**	2:02	Craig Perret	Carl Nafzger	Summer Squall	Pleasant Tap
1991	**Strike the Gold**	2:03	Chris Antley	Nick Zito	Best Pal	Mane Minister
1992	**Lil E. Tee**	2:03	Pat Day	Lynn Whiting	Casual Lies	Dance Floor
1993	**Sea Hero**	2:02⅖	Jerry Bailey	Mack Miller	Prairie Bayou	Wild Gale
1994	**Go For Gin**	2:03⅗	Chris McCarron	Nick Zito	Strodes Creek	Blumin Affair

*Dancer's Image finished first (in 2:02½), but was disqualified after traces of prohibited medication were found in his system.

Preakness Stakes

For three-year-olds. Held two weeks after the Kentucky Derby at Pimlico Race Course in Baltimore, Md. Inaugurated 1873. Originally run at 1½ miles (1873-88), then at 1¼ miles (1889), 1½ miles (1890), 1¹⁄₁₆ miles (1894-1900), 1 mile & 70 yards (1901-07), 1¹⁄₁₆ miles (1908), 1 mile (1909-10), 1⅛ miles (1911-24), and the present 13/16 miles since 1925

Trainers with most wins: Robert W. Walden (7); T.J. Healey (5); Sunny Jim Fitzsimmons and Jimmy Jones (4); D. Wayne Lukas and J. Whalen (3).

Jockeys with most wins: Eddie Arcaro (6); G. Barbee, Pat Day, Bill Hartack and Lloyd Hughes (3).

Winning fillies: Flocarline (1903), Whimsical (1906), Rhine Maiden (1915) and Nellie Morse (1924).

Year		Time	Jockey	Trainer	2nd place	3rd place
1873	**Survivor**	2:43	G. Barbee	A.D. Pryor	John Boulger	Artist
1874	**Culpepper**	2:56½	W. Donohue	H. Gaffney	King Amadeus	Scratch
1875	**Tom Ochiltree**	2:43½	L. Hughes	R.W. Walden	Viator	Bay Final
1876	**Shirley**	2:44¾	G. Barbee	W. Brown	Rappahannock	Compliment
1877	**Cloverbrook**	2:45½	C. Holloway	J. Walden	Bombast	Lucifer
1878	**Duke of Magenta**	2:41¾	C. Holloway	R.W. Walden	Bayard	Albert
1879	**Harold**	2:40½	L. Hughes	R.W. Walden	Jericho	Rochester
1880	**Grenada**	2:40½	L. Hughes	R.W. Walden	Oden	Emily F.
1881	**Saunterer**	2:40½	T. Costello	R.W. Walden	Compensation	Baltic
1882	**Vanguard**	2:44½	T. Costello	R.W. Walden	Heck	Col. Watson
1883	**Jacobus**	2:42½	G. Barbee	R. Dwyer	Parnell	(2-horse race)
1884	**Knight of Ellerslie**	2:39½	S. Fisher	T.B. Doswell	Welcher	(2-horse race)
1885	**Tecumseh**	2:49	Jim McLaughlin	C. Littlefield	Wickham	John C.
1886	**The Bard**	2:45	S. Fisher	J. Huggins	Eurus	Elkwood
1887	**Dunboyne**	2:39½	W. Donohue	W. Jennings	Mahoney	Raymond
1888	**Refund**	2:49	F. Littlefield	R.W. Walden	Bertha B.*	Glendale
1889	**Buddhist**	2:17½	W. Anderson	J. Rogers	Japhet	(2-horse race)
1890	**Montague**	2:36¾	W. Martin	E. Feakes	Philosophy	Barrister
1891-93	Not held					
1894	**Assignee**	1:49¼	F. Taral	W. Lakeland	Potentate	Ed Kearney
1895	**Belmar**	1:50½	F. Taral	E. Feakes	April Fool	Sue Kittie
1896	**Margrave**	1:51	H. Griffin	Byron McClelland	Hamilton II	Intermission
1897	**Paul Kauvar**	1:51¼	T. Thorpe	T.P. Hayes	Elkins	On Deck
1898	**Sly Fox**	1:49¾	W. Simms	H. Campbell	The Huguenot	Nuto
1899	**Half Time**	1:47	R. Clawson	F. McCabe	Filigrane	Lackland
1900	**Hindus**	1:48⅖	H. Spencer	J.H. Morris	Sarmatian	Ten Candles
1901	**The Parader**	1:47⅕	F. Landry	T.J. Healey	Sadie S.	Dr. Barlow
1902	**Old England**	1:45⅘	L. Jackson	G.B. Morris	Maj. Daingerfield	Namtor
1903	**Flocarline**	1:44⅘	W. Gannon	H.C. Riddle	Mackey Dwyer	Rightful
1904	**Bryn Mawr**	1:44⅕	E. Hildebrand	W.F. Presgrave	Wotan	Dolly Spanker
1905	**Cairngorm**	1:45⅘	W. Davis	A.J. Joyner	Kiamesha	Coy Maid
1906	**Whimsical**	1:45	Walter Miller	T.J. Gaynor	Content	Larabie
1907	**Don Enrique**	1:45⅖	G. Mountain	J. Whalen	Ethon	Zambesi

* Later named Judge Murray.

Preakness Stakes (Cont.)

Year		Time	Jockey	Trainer	2nd place	3rd place
1908	**Royal Tourist**	1:46⅖	Eddie Dugan	A.J. Joyner	Live Wire	Robert Cooper
1909	**Effendi**	1:39⅘	Willie Doyle	F.C. Frisbie	Fashion Plate	Hill Top
1910	**Layminster**	1:40⅗	R. Estep	J.S. Healy	Dalhousie	Sager
1911	**Watervale**	1:51	Eddie Dugan	J. Whalen	Zeus	The Nigger
1912	**Colonel Holloway**	1:56⅗	C. Turner	D. Woodford	Bwana Tumbo	Tipsand
1913	**Buskin**	1:53⅖	James Butwell	J. Whalen	Kleburne	Barnegat
1914	**Holiday**	1:53⅘	A. Schuttinger	J.S. Healy	Brave Cunarder	Defendum
1915	**Rhine Maiden**	1:58	Douglas Hoffman	F. Devers	Half Rock	Runes
1916	**Damrosch**	1:54⅘	Linus McAtee	A.G. Weston	Greenwood	Achievement
1917	**Kalitan**	1:54⅖	E. Haynes	Bill Hurley	Al M. Dick	Kentucky Boy
1918	**War Cloud**	1:53⅗	Johnny Loftus	W.B. Jennings	Sunny Slope	Lanius
1918	**Jack Hare Jr**	1:53⅖	Charles Peak	F.D. Weir	The Porter	Kate Bright
1919	**SIR BARTON**	1:53	Johnny Loftus	H. Guy Bedwell	Eternal	Sweep On
1920	**Man o'War**	1:51⅗	Clarence Kummer	L. Feustel	Upset	Wildair
1921	**Broomspun**	1:54⅕	F. Coltiletti	James Rowe Sr.	Polly Ann	Jeg
1922	**Pillory**	1:51⅗	L. Morris	Thomas Healey	Hea	June Grass
1923	**Vigil**	1:53⅗	B. Marinelli	Thomas Healey	General Thatcher	Rialto
1924	**Nellie Morse**	1:57⅕	John Merimee	A.B. Gordon	Transmute	Mad Play
1925	**Coventry**	1:59	Clarence Kummer	William Duke	Backbone	Almadel
1926	**Display**	1:59⅘	John Maiben	Thomas Healey	Blondin	Mars
1927	**Bostonian**	2:01⅗	Whitey Abel	Fred Hopkins	Sir Harry	Whiskery
1928	**Victorian**	2:00⅕	Sonny Workman	James Rowe Jr.	Toro	Solace
1929	**Dr. Freeland**	2:01⅗	Louis Schaefer	Thomas Healey	Minotaur	African
1930	**GALLANT FOX**	2:00⅗	Earl Sande	Jim Fitzsimmons	Crack Brigade	Snowflake
1931	**Mate**	1:59	George Ellis	J.W. Healy	Twenty Grand	Ladder
1932	**Burgoo King**	1:59⅘	Eugene James	Dick Thompson	Tick On	Boatswain
1933	**Head Play**	2:02	Charley Kurtsinger	Thomas Hayes	Ladysman	Utopian
1934	**High Quest**	1:58⅕	Robert Jones	Bob Smith	Cavalcade	Discovery
1935	**OMAHA**	1:58⅖	Willie Saunders	Jim Fitzsimmons	Firethorn	Psychic Bid
1936	**Bold Venture**	1:59	George Woolf	Max Hirsch	Granville	Jean Bart
1937	**WAR ADMIRAL**	1:58⅖	Charley Kurtsinger	George Conway	Pompoon	Flying Scot
1938	**Dauber**	1:59⅘	Maurice Peters	Dick Handlen	Cravat	Menow
1939	**Challedon**	1:59⅘	George Seabo	Louis Schaefer	Gilded Knight	Volitant
1940	**Bimelech**	1:58⅗	F.A. Smith	Bill Hurley	Mioland	Gallahadion
1941	**WHIRLAWAY**	1:58⅘	Eddie Arcaro	Ben Jones	King Cole	Our Boots
1942	**Alsab**	1:57	Basil James	Sarge Swenke	Requested & Sun Again (dead heat)	
1943	**COUNT FLEET**	1:57⅖	Johnny Longden	Don Cameron	Blue Swords	Vincentive
1944	**Pensive**	1:59⅕	Conn McCreary	Ben Jones	Platter	Stir Up
1945	**Polynesian**	1:58⅘	W.D. Wright	Morris Dixon	Hoop Jr.	Darby Dieppe
1946	**ASSAULT**	2:01⅖	Warren Mehrtens	Max Hirsch	Lord Boswell	Hampden
1947	**Faultless**	1:59	Doug Dodson	Jimmy Jones	On Trust	Phalanx
1948	**CITATION**	2:02⅖	Eddie Arcaro	Jimmy Jones	Vulcan's Forge	Bovard
1949	**Capot**	1:56	Ted Atkinson	J.M. Gaver	Palestinian	Noble Impulse
1950	**Hill Prince**	1:59⅕	Eddie Arcaro	Casey Hayes	Middleground	Dooly
1951	**Bold**	1:56⅖	Eddie Arcaro	Preston Burch	Counterpoint	Alerted
1952	**Blue Man**	1:57⅖	Conn McCreary	Woody Stephens	Jampol	One Count
1953	**Native Dancer**	1:57⅘	Eric Guerin	Bill Winfrey	Jamie K.	Royal Bay Gem
1954	**Hasty Road**	1:57⅖	Johnny Adams	Harry Trotsek	Correlation	Hasseyampa
1955	**Nashua**	1:54⅗	Eddie Arcaro	Jim Fitzsimmons	Saratoga	Traffic Judge
1956	**Fabius**	1:58⅖	Bill Hartack	Jimmy Jones	Needles	No Regrets
1957	**Bold Ruler**	1:56⅕	Eddie Arcaro	Jim Fitzsimmons	Iron Liege	Inside Tract
1958	**Tim Tam**	1:57⅕	Ismael Valenzuela	Jimmy Jones	Lincoln Road	Gone Fishin'
1959	**Royal Orbit**	1:57	William Harmatz	R. Cornell	Sword Dancer	Dunce
1960	**Bally Ache**	1:57⅗	Bobby Ussery	Jimmy Pitt	Victoria Park	Celtic Ash
1961	**Carry Back**	1:57⅗	Johnny Sellers	Jack Price	Globemaster	Crozier
1962	**Greek Money**	1:56⅕	John Rotz	V.W. Raines	Ridan	Roman Line
1963	**Candy Spots**	1:56⅕	Bill Shoemaker	Mesh Tenney	Chateaugay	Never Bend
1964	**Northern Dancer**	1:56⅘	Bill Hartack	Horatio Luro	The Scoundrel	Hill Rise
1965	**Tom Rolfe**	1:56⅕	Ron Turcotte	Frank Whiteley	Dapper Dan	Hail To All
1966	**Kauai King**	1:55⅖	Don Brumfield	Henry Forrest	Stupendous	Amberoid
1967	**Damascus**	1:55⅕	Bill Shoemaker	Frank Whiteley	In Reality	Proud Clarion
1968	**Forward Pass**	1:56⅘	Ismael Valenzuela	Henry Forrest	Out Of the Way	Nodouble
1969	**Majestic Prince**	1:55⅗	Bill Hartack	Johnny Longden	Arts and Letters	Jay Ray
1970	**Personality**	1:56⅕	Eddie Belmonte	John Jacobs	My Dad George	Silent Screen
1971	**Canonero II**	1:54	Gustavo Avila	Juan Arias	Eastern Fleet	Jim French
1972	**Bee Bee Bee**	1:55⅗	Eldon Nelson	Red Carroll	No Le Hace	Key To The Mint

Year		Time	Jockey	Trainer	2nd place	3rd place
1973	**SECRETARIAT**	1:54⅖	Ron Turcotte	Lucien Laurin	Sham	Our Native
1974	**Little Current**	1:54⅗	Miguel Rivera	Lou Rondinello	Neapolitan Way	Cannonade
1975	**Master Derby**	1:56⅖	Darrel McHargue	Smiley Adams	Foolish Pleasure	Diabolo
1976	**Elocutionist**	1:55	John Lively	Paul Adwell	Play The Red	Bold Forbes
1977	**SEATTLE SLEW**	1:54⅖	Jean Cruguet	Billy Turner	Iron Constitution	Run Dusty Run
1978	**AFFIRMED**	1:54⅖	Steve Cauthen	Laz Barrera	Alydar	Believe It
1979	**Spectacular Bid**	1:54⅕	Ron Franklin	Bud Delp	Golden Act	Screen King
1980	**Codex**	1:54⅕	Angel Cordero Jr.	D. Wayne Lukas	Genuine Risk	Colonel Moran
1981	**Pleasant Colony**	1:54⅗	Jorge Velasquez	John Campo	Bold Ego	Paristo
1982	**Aloma's Ruler**	1:55⅖	Jack Kaenel	John Lenzini Jr.	Linkage	Cut Away
1983	**Deputed Testamony**	1:55⅖	Donald Miller Jr.	Bill Boniface	Desert Wine	High Honors
1984	**Gate Dancer**	1:53⅗	Angel Cordero Jr.	Jack Van Berg	Play On	Fight Over
1985	**Tank's Prospect**	1:53⅖	Pat Day	D. Wayne Lukas	Chief's Crown	Eternal Prince
1986	**Snow Chief**	1:54⅘	Alex Solis	Melvin Stute	Ferdinand	Broad Brush
1987	**Alysheba**	1:55⅘	Chris McCarron	Jack Van Berg	Bet Twice	Cryptoclearance
1988	**Risen Star**	1:56⅕	E. Delahoussaye	Louie Roussel III	Brian's Time	Winning Colors
1989	**Sunday Silence**	1:53⅘	Pat Valenzuela	Chas. Whittingham	Easy Goer	Rock Point
1990	**Summer Squall**	1:53⅗	Pat Day	Neil Howard	Unbridled	Mister Frisky
1991	**Hansel**	1:54	Jerry Bailey	Frank Brothers	Corporate Report	Mane Minister
1992	**Pine Bluff**	1:55⅗	Chris McCarron	Tom Bohannan	Alydeed	Casual Lies
1993	**Prairie Bayou**	1:56⅗	Mike Smith	Tom Bohannon	Cherokee Run	El Bakan
1994	**Tabasco Cat**	1:56⅖	Pat Day	D. Wayne Lukas	Go For Gin	Concern

Belmont Stakes

For three-year-olds. Held three weeks after Preakness Stakes at Belmont Park in Elmont, N.Y. Inaugurated in 1867 at Jerome Park, moved to Morris Park in 1890 and Belmont Park in 1905.

Originally run at 1 mile and 5 furlongs (1867-89), then 1¼ miles (1890-1905), 1⅜ miles (1906-25), and the present 1½ miles since 1926.

Trainers with most wins: James Rowe, Sr.(8); Sam Hildreth (7); Sunny Jim Fitzsimmons (6); Woody Stephens (5); Max Hirsch and Robert W. Walden (4); Elliott Burch, Lucien Laurin, F. McCabe and D. McDaniel (3).

Jockeys with most wins: Eddie Arcaro and Jim McLaughlin (6); Earl Sande and Bill Shoemaker (5); Braulio Baeza, Laffit Pincay, Jr and James Stout (3).

Winning fillies: Ruthless (1867) and Tanya (1905).

Year		Time	Jockey	Trainer	2nd place	3rd place
1867	**Ruthless**	3:05	J. Gilpatrick	A.J. Minor	DeCourcey	Rivoli
1868	**General Duke**	3:02	Bobby Swim	A. Thompson	Northumberland	Fanny Ludlow
1869	**Fenian**	3:04¼	C. Miller	J. Pincus	Glenelg	Invercauld
1870	**Kingfisher**	2:59½	W. Dick	R. Colston	Foster	Midday
1871	**Harry Bassett**	2:56	W. Miller	D. McDaniel	Stockwood	By the Sea
1872	**Joe Daniels**	2:58¼	James Roe	D. McDaniel	Meteor	Shylock
1873	**Springbok**	3:01¾	James Roe	D. McDaniel	Count d'Orsay	Strachino
1874	**Saxon**	2:39½	G. Barbee	W. Prior	Grinstead	Aaron Pennington
1875	**Calvin**	2:42¼	Bobby Swim	A. Williams	Aristides	Milner
1876	**Algerine**	2:40½	Billy Donohue	Major Doswell	Fiddlesticks	Barricade
1877	**Cloverbrook**	2:46	C. Holloway	J. Walden	Loiterer	Baden-Baden
1878	**Duke of Magenta**	2:43½	L. Hughes	R.W. Walden	Bramble	Sparta
1879	**Spendthrift**	2:42¾	George Evans	T. Puryear	Monitor	Jericho
1880	**Grenada**	2:47	L. Hughes	R.W. Walden	Ferncliffe	Turenne
1881	**Saunterer**	2:47	T. Costello	R.W. Walden	Eole	Baltic
1882	**Forester**	2:43	Jim McLaughlin	L. Stuart	Babcock	Wyoming
1883	**George Kinney**	2:42½	Jim McLaughlin	James Rowe Sr.	Trombone	Renegade
1884	**Panique**	2:42	Jim McLaughlin	James Rowe Sr.	Knight of Ellerslie	Himalaya
1885	**Tyrant**	2:43	Paul Duffy	W. Claypool	St. Augustine	Tecumseh
1886	**Inspector B**	2:41	Jim McLaughlin	F. McCabe	The Bard	Linden
1887	**Hanover**	2:43½	Jim McLaughlin	F. McCabe	Oneko	(2-horse race)
1888	**Sir Dixon**	2:40¼	Jim McLaughlin	F. McCabe	Prince Royal	(2-horse race)
1889	**Eric**	2:47¼	W. Hayward	J. Huggins	Diablo	Zephyrus
1890	**Burlington**	2:07¾	Pike Barnes	A. Cooper	Devotee	Padishah
1891	**Foxford**	2:08¾	Ed Garrison	M. Donavan	Montana	Laurestan
1892	**Patron**	2:12	W. Hayward	L. Stuart	Shellbark	(2-horse race)
1893	**Commanche**	1:53¼	Willie Simms	G. Hannon	Dr. Rice	Rainbow
1894	**Henry of Navarre**	1:56½	Willie Simms	B. McClelland	Prig	Assignee
1895	**Belmar**	2:11½	Fred Taral	E. Feakes	Counter Tenor	Nanki Poo
1896	**Hastings**	2:24½	H. Griffin	J.J. Hyland	Handspring	Hamilton II
1897	**Scottish Chieftain**	2:23¼	J. Scherrer	M. Byrnes	On Deck	Octagon
1898	**Bowling Brook**	2:32	F. Littlefield	R.W. Walden	Previous	Hamburg
1899	**Jean Beraud**	2:23	R. Clawson	Sam Hildreth	Half Time	Glengar

Belmont Stakes (Cont.)

Year		Time	Jockey	Trainer	2nd place	3rd place
1900	**Ildrim**	2:21¼	Nash Turner	H.E. Leigh	Petruchio	Missionary
1901	**Commando**	2:21	H. Spencer	James Rowe Sr.	The Parader	All Green
1902	**Masterman**	2:22⅗	John Bullman	J.J. Hyland	Renald	King Hanover
1903	**Africander**	2:21¾	John Bullman	R. Miller	Whorler	Red Knight
1904	**Delhi**	2:06⅗	George Odom	James Rowe Sr.	Graziallo	Rapid Water
1905	**Tanya**	2:08	E. Hildebrand	J.W. Rogers	Blandy	Hot Shot
1906	**Burgomaster**	2:20	Lucien Lyne	J.W. Rogers	The Quail	Accountant
1907	**Peter Pan**	N/A	G. Mountain	James Rowe Sr.	Superman	Frank Gill
1908	**Colin**	N/A	Joe Notter	James Rowe Sr.	Fair Play	King James
1909	**Joe Madden**	2:21⅗	E. Dugan	Sam Hildreth	Wise Mason	Donald MacDonald
1910	**Sweep**	2:22	James Butwell	James Rowe Sr.	Duke of Ormonde	(2-horse race)
1911-12	Not held					
1913	**Prince Eugene**	2:18	Roscoe Troxler	James Rowe Sr.	Rock View	Flying Fairy
1914	**Luke McLuke**	2:20	Merritt Buxton	J.F. Schorr	Gainer	Charlestonian
1915	**The Finn**	2:18⅖	George Byrne	E.W. Heffner	Half Rock	Pebbles
1916	**Friar Rock**	2:22	E. Haynes	Sam Hildreth	Spur	Churchill
1917	**Hourless**	2:17⅘	James Butwell	Sam Hildreth	Skeptic	Wonderful
1918	**Johren**	2:20⅖	Frank Robinson	A. Simons	War Cloud	Cum Sah
1919	**SIR BARTON**	2:17⅖	John Loftus	H. Guy Bedwell	Sweep On	Natural Bridge
1920	**Man o'War**	2:14⅕	Clarence Kummer	L. Feustel	Donnacona	(2-horse race)
1921	**Grey Lag**	2:16⅘	Earl Sande	Sam Hildreth	Sporting Blood	Leonardo II
1922	**Pillory**	2:18⅘	C.H. Miller	T.J. Healey	Snob II	Hea
1923	**Zev**	2:19	Earl Sande	Sam Hildreth	Chickvale	Rialto
1924	**Mad Play**	2:18⅘	Earl Sande	Sam Hildreth	Mr. Mutt	Modest
1925	**American Flag**	2:16⅘	Albert Johnson	G.R. Tompkins	Dangerous	Swope
1926	**Crusader**	2:32⅕	Albert Johnson	George Conway	Espino	Haste
1927	**Chance Shot**	2:32⅖	Earl Sande	Pete Coyne	Bois de Rose	Flambino
1928	**Vito**	2:33⅕	Clarence Kummer	Max Hirsch	Genie	Diavolo
1929	**Blue Larkspur**	2:32⅘	Mack Garner	C. Hastings	African	Jack High
1930	**GALLANT FOX**	2:31⅗	Earl Sande	Jim Fitzsimmons	Whichone	Questionnaire
1931	**Twenty Grand**	2:29⅗	Charley Kurtsinger	James Rowe Jr.	Sun Meadow	Jamestown
1932	**Faireno**	2:32⅘	Tom Malley	Jim Fitzsimmons	Osculator	Flag Pole
1933	**Hurryoff**	2:32⅗	Mack Garner	H. McDaniel	Nimbus	Union
1934	**Peace Chance**	2:29⅕	W.D. Wright	Pete Coyne	High Quest	Good Goods
1935	**OMAHA**	2:30⅗	Willie Saunders	Jim Fitzsimmons	Firethorn	Rosemont
1936	**Granville**	2:30	James Stout	Jim Fitzsimmons	Mr. Bones	Hollyrood
1937	**WAR ADMIRAL**	2:28⅗	Charley Kurtsinger	George Conway	Sceneshifter	Vamoose
1938	**Pasteurized**	2:29⅖	James Stout	George Odom	Dauber	Cravat
1939	**Johnstown**	2:29⅗	James Stout	Jim Fitzsimmons	Belay	Gilded Knight
1940	**Bimelech**	2:29⅗	Fred Smith	Bill Hurley	Your Chance	Andy K.
1941	**WHIRLAWAY**	2:31	Eddie Arcaro	Ben Jones	Robert Morris	Yankee Chance
1942	**Shut Out**	2:29⅕	Eddie Arcaro	John Gaver	Alsab	Lochinvar
1943	**COUNT FLEET**	2:28⅕	Johnny Longden	Don Cameron	Fairy Manhurst	Deseronto
1944	**Bounding Home**	2:32⅕	G.L. Smith	Matt Brady	Pensive	Bull Dandy
1945	**Pavot**	2:30⅕	Eddie Arcaro	Oscar White	Wildlife	Jeep
1946	**ASSAULT**	2:30⅘	Warren Mehrtens	Max Hirsch	Natchez	Cable
1947	**Phalanx**	2:29⅖	R. Donoso	Syl Veitch	Tide Rips	Tailspin
1948	**CITATION**	2:28⅕	Eddie Arcaro	Jimmy Jones	Better Self	Escadru
1949	**Capot**	2:30⅕	Ted Atkinson	John Gaver	Ponder	Palestinian
1950	**Middleground**	2:28⅗	William Boland	Max Hirsch	Lights Up	Mr. Trouble
1951	**Counterpoint**	2:29	David Gorman	Syl Veitch	Battlefield	Battle Morn
1952	**One Count**	2:30⅕	Eddie Arcaro	Oscar White	Blue Man	Armageddon
1953	**Native Dancer**	2:28⅗	Eric Guerin	Bill Winfrey	Jamie K.	Royal Bay Gem
1954	**High Gun**	2:30⅘	Eric Guerin	Max Hirsch	Fisherman	Limelight
1955	**Nashua**	2:29	Eddie Arcaro	Jim Fitzsimmons	Blazing Count	Portersville
1956	**Needles**	2:29⅘	David Erb	Hugh Fontaine	Career Boy	Fabius
1957	**Gallant Man**	2:26⅗	Bill Shoemaker	John Nerud	Inside Tract	Bold Ruler
1958	**Cavan**	2:30⅕	Pete Anderson	Tom Barry	Tim Tam	Flamingo
1959	**Sword Dancer**	2:28⅖	Bill Shoemaker	Elliott Burch	Bagdad	Royal Orbit
1960	**Celtic Ash**	2:29⅕	Bill Hartack	Tom Barry	Venetian Way	Disperse
1961	**Sherluck**	2:29⅕	Braulio Baeza	Harold Young	Globemaster	Guadalcanal
1962	**Jaipur**	2:28⅘	Bill Shoemaker	B. Mulholland	Admiral's Voyage	Crimson Satan
1963	**Chateaugay**	2:30⅕	Braulio Baeza	James Conway	Candy Spots	Choker
1964	**Quadrangle**	2:28⅖	Manuel Ycaza	Elliott Burch	Roman Brother	Northern Dancer
1965	**Hail to All**	2:28⅖	John Sellers	Eddie Yowell	Tom Rolfe	First Family
1966	**Amberoid**	2:29⅗	William Boland	Lucien Laurin	Buffle	Advocator

Wide World Photos

Jockey **Ron Turcotte** glances back at the field as Secretariat rounds the turn en route to a 31-length victory and the Triple Crown in the 1973 Belmont Stakes. The winning time of 2:24 is still a world record for a mile and a half on dirt.

Year		Time	Jockey	Trainer	2nd place	3rd place
1967	**Damascus**	2:28⅘	Bill Shoemaker	F.Y. Whiteley Jr.	Cool Reception	Gentleman James
1968	**Stage Door Johnny**	2:27⅕	Gus Gustines	John Gaver	Forward Pass	Call Me Prince
1969	**Arts and Letters**	2:28⅘	Braulio Baeza	Elliott Burch	Majestic Prince	Dike
1970	**High Echelon**	2:34	John Rotz	John Jacobs	Needles N Pens	Naskra
1971	**Pass Catcher**	2:30⅖	Walter Blum	Eddie Yowell	Jim French	Bold Reason
1972	**Riva Ridge**	2:28	Ron Turcotte	Lucien Laurin	Ruritania	Cloudy Dawn
1973	**SECRETARIAT**	2:24	Ron Turcotte	Lucien Laurin	Twice A Prince	My Gallant
1974	**Little Current**	2:29⅕	Miguel Rivera	Lou Rondinello	Jolly Johu	Cannonade
1975	**Avatar**	2:28⅕	Bill Shoemaker	Tommy Doyle	Foolish Pleasure	Master Derby
1976	**Bold Forbes**	2:29	Angel Cordero Jr.	Laz Barrera	McKenzie Bridge	Great Contractor
1977	**SEATTLE SLEW**	2:29⅗	Jean Cruguet	Billy Turner	Run Dusty Run	Sanhedrin
1978	**AFFIRMED**	2:26⅘	Steve Cauthen	Laz Barrera	Alydar	Darby Creek Road
1979	**Coastal**	2:28⅗	Ruben Hernandez	David Whiteley	Golden Act	Spectacular Bid
1980	**Temperence Hill**	2:29⅘	Eddie Maple	Joseph Cantey	Genuine Risk	Rockhill Native
1981	**Summing**	2:29	George Martens	Luis Barerra	Highland Blade	Pleasant Colony
1982	**Conquistador Cielo**	2:28⅕	Laffit Pincay Jr.	Woody Stephens	Gato Del Sol	Illuminate
1983	**Caveat**	2:27⅘	Laffit Pincay Jr.	Woody Stephens	Slew o' Gold	Barberstown
1984	**Swale**	2:27⅕	Laffit Pincay Jr.	Woody Stephens	Pine Circle	Morning Bob
1985	**Creme Fraiche**	2:27	Eddie Maple	Woody Stephens	Stephan's Odyssey	Chief's Crown
1986	**Danzig Connection**	2:29⅘	Chris McCarron	Woody Stephens	Johns Treasure	Ferdinand
1987	**Bet Twice**	2:28⅕	Craig Perret	Jimmy Croll	Cryptoclearance	Gulch
1988	**Risen Star**	2:26⅖	E. Delahoussaye	Louie Roussel III	Kingpost	Brian's Time
1989	**Easy Goer**	2:26	Pat Day	Shug McGaughey	Sunday Silence	Le Voyageur
1990	**Go And Go**	2:27⅕	Michael Kinane	Dermot Weld	Thirty Six Red	Baron de Vaux
1991	**Hansel**	2:28	Jerry Bailey	Frank Brothers	Strike the Gold	Mane Minister
1992	**A.P. Indy**	2:26	E. Delahoussaye	Neil Drysdale	My Memoirs	Pine Bluff
1993	**Colonial Affair**	2:29⅘	Julie Krone	Scotty Schulhofer	Kissin Kris	Wild Gale
1994	**Tabasco Cat**	2:26⅘	Pat Day	D. Wayne Lukas	Go For Gin	Strodes Creek

Breeders' Cup

Inaugurated on Nov. 10, 1984, the Breeders' Cup consists of seven races at one track on one day late in the year to determine thoroughbred racing's principal champions.

Breeders' Cup Day has been held at Hollywood Park (Calif.) in 1984, Aqueduct Racetrack (N.Y.) in 1985, Santa Anita Park (Calif.) in 1986, Hollywood Park in 1987, Churchill Downs (Ky.) in 1988 and '91, Gulfstream Park (Fla.) in 1989 and 1992, and Belmont Park (N.Y.) in 1990.

The steeplechase was added to the Breeders' Cup championship roster in 1986, and has been held at Fair Hill Race Course (Md.) in 1986-88 and '91, Moreland Farms (N.J.) in 1989 and Belmont Park in 1990 and '92.

Trainers with most wins: D.Wayne Lukas (10); Neil Drysdale and Shug McGaughey (5); Francois Boutin, Ron McAnally and J.E. Sheppard (3).

Jockeys with most wins: Eddie Delzhoussaye and Laffit Pincay Jr. (7); Pat Day and Pat Valenzuela (6); Chris McCarron and Jose Santos (5); Angel Cordero Jr. (4); Craig Perret and Randy Romero (3).

Juvenile

Distances: one mile (1984-85, 87); 1 1/16 miles (1986 and since 1988).

Year		Time	Jockey	Trainer	2nd place	3rd place
1984	**Chief's Crown**	1:36⅕	Don MacBeth	Roger Laurin	Tank's Prospect	Spend A Buck
1985	**Tasso**	1:36⅕	Laffit Pincay Jr.	Neil Drysdale	Storm Cat	Scat Dancer
1986	**Capote**	1:43⅘	Laffit Pincay Jr.	D. Wayne Lukas	Qualify	Alysheba
1987	**Success Express**	1:35⅕	Jose Santos	D. Wayne Lukas	Regal Classic	Tejano
1988	**Is It True**	1:46⅗	Laffit Pincay Jr.	D. Wayne Lukas	Easy Goer	Tagel
1989	**Rhythm**	1:43⅗	Craig Perret	Shug McGaughey	Grand Canyon	Slavic
1990	**Fly So Free**	1:43⅖	Jose Santos	Scotty Schulhofer	Take Me Out	Lost Mountain
1991	**Arazi**	1:44⅗	Pat Valenzuela	Francois Boutin	Bertrando	Snappy Landing
1992	**Gilded Time**	1:43⅖	Chris McCarron	Darrell Vienna	It'sali'lknownfact	River Special
1993	**Brocco**	1:42⅘	Gary Stevens	Randy Winick	Blumin Affair	Tabasco Cat

Juvenile Fillies

Distances: one mile (1984-85, 87); 1 1/16 miles (1986 and since 1988).

Year		Time	Jockey	Trainer	2nd place	3rd place
1984	**Outstandingly**	1:37⅘	Walter Guerra	Pancho Martin	Dusty Heart	Fine Spirit
1985	**Twilight Ridge**	1:35⅘	Jorge Velasquez	D. Wayne Lukas	Family Style	Steal A Kiss
1986	**Brave Raj**	1:43⅕	Pat Valenzuela	Melvin Stute	Tappiano	Saros Brig
1987	**Epitome**	1:36⅖	Pat Day	Phil Hauswald	Jeanne Jones	Dream Team
1988	**Open Mind**	1:46⅗	Angel Cordero Jr.	D. Wayne Lukas	Darby Shuffle	Lea Lucinda
1989	**Go for Wand**	1:44⅕	Randy Romero	Wm. Badgett, Jr.	Sweet Roberta	Stella Madrid
1990	**Meadow Star**	1:44	Jose Santos	LeRoy Jolley	Private Treasure	Dance Smartly
1991	**Pleasant Stage**	1:46⅖	Eddie Delahoussaye	Chris Speckert	La Spia	Cadillac Women
1992	**Liza**	1:42⅘	Pat Valenzuela	Alex Hassingfer	Educated Risk	Boots 'n Jackie
1993	**Phone Chatter**	1:43	Laffit Pincay Jr.	Richard Mandella	Sardula	Heavenly Prize

Note: In 1984, winner Fran's Valentine was disqualified for interference in the stretch and placed 10th.

Sprint

Distance: six furlongs (since 1984).

Year		Time	Jockey	Trainer	2nd place	3rd place
1984	**Eillo**	1:10⅕	Craig Perret	Budd Lepman	Commemorate	Fighting Fit
1985	**Precisionist**	1:08⅖	Chris McCarron	L.R. Fenstermaker	Smile	Mt. Livermore
1986	**Smile**	1:08⅖	Jacinto Vasquez	Scotty Schulhofer	Pine Tree Lane	Bedside Promise
1987	**Very Subtle**	1:08⅘	Pat Valenzuela	Melvin Stute	Groovy	Exclusive Enough
1988	**Gulch**	1:10⅖	Angel Cordero Jr.	D. Wayne Lukas	Play The King	Afleet
1989	**Dancing Spree**	1:09	Angel Cordero Jr.	Shug McGaughey	Safely Kept	Dispersal
1990	**Safely Kept**	1:09⅗	Craig Perret	Alan Goldberg	Dayjur	Black Tie Affair
1991	**Sheikh Albadou**	1:09⅕	Pat Eddery	Alexander Scott	Pleasant Tap	Robyn Dancer
1992	**Thirty Slews**	1:08⅕	Eddie Delahoussaye	Bob Baffert	Meafara	Rubiano
1993	**Cardmania**	1:08⅗	Eddie Delahoussaye	Derek Meredith	Meafara	Gilded Time

Mile

Year		Time	Jockey	Trainer	2nd place	3rd place
1984	**Royal Heroine**	1:32⅗	Fernando Toro	John Gosden	Star Choice	Cozzene
1985	**Cozzene**	1:35	Walter Guerra	Jan Nerud	Al Mamoon	Shadeed
1986	**Last Tycoon**	1:35⅕	Yves St.-Martin	Robert Collet	Palace Music	Fred Astaire
1987	**Miesque**	1:32⅘	Freddie Head	Francois Boutin	Show Dancer	Sonic Lady
1988	**Miesque**	1:38⅗	Freddie Head	Francois Boutin	Steinlen	Simply Majestic
1989	**Steinlen**	1:37⅕	Jose Santos	D. Wayne Lukas	Sabona	Most Welcome
1990	**Royal Academy**	1:35⅕	Lester Piggott	M.V. O'Brien	Itsallgreektome	Priolo
1991	**Opening Verse**	1:37⅖	Pat Valenzuela	Dick Lundy	Val des Bois	Star of Cozzene
1992	**Lure**	1:32⅘	Mike Smith	Shug McGaughey	Paradise Creek	Brief Truce
1993	**Lure**	1:33⅖	Mike Smith	Shug McGaughey	Ski Paradise	Fourstars Allstar

Note: In 1985, 2nd place finisher Palace Music was disqualified for interference and placed 9th.

Distaff

Distances: 1¼ miles (1984-87); 1⅛ miles (since 1988).

Year		Time	Jockey	Trainer	2nd place	3rd place
1984	**Princess Rooney**	2:02⅖	Eddie Delahoussaye	Neil Drysdale	Life's Magic	Adored
1985	**Life's Magic**	2:02	Angel Cordero Jr.	D. Wayne Lukas	Lady's Secret	DontstopThemusic
1986	**Lady's Secret**	2:01⅕	Pat Day	D. Wayne Lukas	Fran's Valentine	Outstandingly
1987	**Sacahuista**	2:02⅘	Randy Romero	D. Wayne Lukas	Clabber Girl	Oueee Bebe
1988	**Personal Ensign**	1:52	Randy Romero	Shug McGaughey	Winning Colors	Goodbye Halo
1989	**Bayakoa**	1:47⅖	Laffit Pincay Jr.	Ron McAnally	Gorgeous	Open Mind
1990	**Bayakoa**	1:49⅕	Laffit Pincay Jr.	Ron McAnally	Colonial Waters	Valay Maid
1991	**Dance Smartly**	1:50⅘	Pat Day	Jim Day	Versailles Treaty	Brought to Mind
1992	**Paseana**	1:48	Chris McCarron	Ron McAnally	Versailles Treaty	Magical Maiden
1993	Hollywood Wildcat	1:48⅕	Eddie Delahoussaye	Neil Drysdale	Paseana	Re Toss

Turf

Distance: 1½ miles (since 1984).

Year		Time	Jockey	Trainer	2nd place	3rd place
1984	**Lashkari**	2:25⅕	Yves St.-Martin	de Royer-Dupre	All Along	Raami
1985	**Pebbles**	2:27	Pat Eddery	Clive Brittain	Strawberry Road II	Mourjane
1986	**Manila**	2:25⅖	Jose Santos	Leroy Jolley	Theatrical	Estrapade
1987	**Theatrical**	2:24⅖	Pat Day	Bill Mott	Trempolino	Village Star II
1988	Gt. Communicator	2:35⅕	Ray Sibille	Thad Ackel	Sunshine Forever	Indian Skimmer
1989	**Prized**	2:28	Eddie Delahoussaye	Neil Drysdale	Sierra Roberta	Star Lift
1990	**In The Wings**	2:29⅗	Gary Stevens	Andre Fabre	With Approval	El Senor
1991	**Miss Alleged**	2:30⅘	Eric Legrix	Pascal Bary	Itsallgreektome	Quest for Fame
1992	**Fraise**	2:24	Pat Valenzuela	Bill Mott	Sky Classic	Quest for Fame
1993	**Kotashaan**	2:25	Kent Desormeaux	Richard Mandella	Bien Bien	Luazur

Classic

Distance: 1¼ miles (since 1984).

Year		Time	Jockey	Trainer	2nd place	3rd place
1984	**Wild Again**	2:03⅖	Pat Day	Vincent Timphony	Slew o' Gold	Gate Dancer
1985	**Proud Truth**	2:00⅘	Jorge Velasquez	John Veitch	Gate Dancer	Turkoman
1986	**Skywalker**	2:00⅖	Laffit Pincay Jr.	M. Whittingham	Turkoman	Precisionist
1987	**Ferdinand**	2:01⅖	Bill Shoemaker	C. Whittingham	Alysheba	Judge Angelucci
1988	**Alysheba**	2:04⅘	Chris McCarron	Jack Van Berg	Seeking the Gold	Waquoit
1989	**Sunday Silence**	2:00⅕	Chris McCarron	C. Whittingham	Easy Goer	Blushing John
1990	**Unbridled**	2:02⅕	Pat Day	Carl Nafzger	Ibn Bey	Thirty Six Red
1991	**Black Tie Affair**	2:02⅘	Jerry Bailey	Ernie Poulos	Twilight Agenda	Unbridled
1992	**A.P. Indy**	2:00⅕	Eddie Delahoussaye	Neil Drysdale	Pleasant Tap	Jolypha
1993	**Arcangues**	2:00⅘	Jerry Bailey	Andre Fabre	Bertrando	Kissin Kris

Note: In 1984, 2nd place finisher Gate Dancer was disqualified for interference and placed 3rd.

Steeplechase

Distances: 2⅜ miles (1986); 2⅝ miles (since 1987).

Year		Time	Jockey	Trainer	2nd place	3rd place
1986	**Census**	4:27⅗	Jeff Teter	Janet Elliott	Kesslin	Pont du Loup
1987	**Gacko**	5:15⅕	Roger Duchene	Xavier Guigand	Inlander	Gateshead
1988	**Jimmy Lorenzo**	5:12⅖	Graham McCourt	J.E. Sheppard	Kalankoe	Polar Pleasure
1989	**Highland Bud**	4:58⅘	Richard Dunwoody	J.E. Sheppard	Polar Pleasure	Victorian Hill
1990	**Morley Street**	4:53⅕	Jimmy Frost	Toby Balding	Summer Colony	Moonstruck
1991	**Morley Street**	5:10⅗	Jimmy Frost	Toby Balding	Declare Your Wish	Cheering News
1992	**Highland Bud**	4:56⅖	Richard Dunwoody	J.E. Sheppard	Mistico	Sassello
1993	**Lonesome Glory**	4:53⅖	Blythe Miller	Bruce Miller	Highland Bud	Mistico

Breeders' Cup Leaders

The all-time money-winning horses and race winning jockeys in the history of the Breeders' Cup since it began in 1984.

Top 10 Horse—Money Won

		Sts	1-2-3	Earnings
1	Alysheba	3	1–1–1	$2,133,000
2	Unbridled	2	1–0–1	1,710,000
3	Black Tie Affair (IRE)	3	1–0–1	1,668,000
4	A.P. Indy	1	1–0–0	1,560,000
	Arcangues	1	1–0–0	1,560,000
5	Ferdinand	1	1–0–0	1,350,000
	Proud Truth	1	1–0–0	1,350,000
	Skywalker	2	1–0–0	1,350,000
	Sunday Silence	1	1–0–0	1,350,000
	Theatrical (IRE)	3	1–1–0	1,350,000
	Wild Again	1	1–0–0	1,350,000

Top 10 Jockeys—Races Won

		Sts	1-2-3	Earnings
1	Pat Day	53	6–7–5	$9,551,000
2	Chris McCarron	55	5–10–5	8,742,000
3	Eddie Delahoussaye	49	7–3–4	7,359,000
4	Laffit Pincay Jr.	56	7–4–9	6,811,000
5	Angel Cordero Jr.	48	4–7–7	6,020,000
6	Gary Stevens	38	2–7–5	5,073,000
7	Jose Santos	34	5–1–3	4,295,000
8	Pat Valenzuela	32	6–0–1	4,202,000
9	Jerry Bailey	21	2–3–0	3,871,000
10	Pad Eddery	23	2–2–3	3,370,000

Annual Money Leaders
Horses

Annual money-leading horses since 1910, according to *The American Racing Manual*.

Multiple leaders: Round Table, Buckpasser and Alysheba (2)

Year		Age	Sts	1st	Earnings	Year		Age	Sts	1st	Earnings
1910	Novelty	2	16	11	$ 72,630	1952	Crafty Admiral	4	16	9	$ 277,225
1911	Worth	2	13	10	16,645	1953	Native Dancer	3	10	9	513,425
1912	Star Charter	4	17	6	14,655	1954	Determine	3	15	10	328,700
1913	Old Rosebud	2	14	12	19,057	1955	Nashua	3	12	10	752,550
1914	Roamer	3	16	12	29,105	1956	Needles	3	8	4	440,850
1915	Borrow	7	9	4	20,195	1957	Round Table	3	22	15	600,383
1916	Campfire	2	9	6	49,735	1958	Round Table	4	20	14	662,780
1917	Sun Briar	2	9	5	59,505	1959	Sword Dancer	3	13	8	537,004
1918	Eternal	2	8	6	56,173	1960	Bally Ache	3	15	10	445,045
1919	Sir Barton	3	13	8	88,250	1961	Carry Back	3	16	9	565,349
1920	Man o' War	3	11	11	166,140	1962	Never Bend	2	10	7	402,969
1921	Morvich	2	11	11	115,234	1963	Candy Spots	3	12	7	604,481
1922	Pillory	3	7	4	95,654	1964	Gun Bow	4	16	8	580,100
1923	Zev	3	14	12	272,008	1965	Buckpasser	2	11	9	568,096
1924	Sarzen	3	12	8	95,640	1966	Buckpasser	3	14	13	669,078
1925	Pompey	2	10	7	121,630	1967	Damascus	3	16	12	817,941
1926	Crusader	3	15	9	166,033	1968	Forward Pass	3	13	7	546,674
1927	Anita Peabody	2	7	6	111,905	1969	Arts and Letters	3	14	8	555,604
1928	High Strung	2	6	5	153,590	1970	Personality	3	18	8	444,049
1929	Blue Larkspur	3	6	4	153,450	1971	Riva Ridge	2	9	7	503,263
1930	Gallant Fox	3	10	9	308,275	1972	Droll Role	4	19	7	471,633
1931	Gallant Flight	2	7	7	219,000	1973	Secretariat	3	12	9	860,404
1932	Gusto	3	16	4	145,940	1974	Chris Evert	3	8	5	551,063
1933	Singing Wood	2	9	3	88,050	1975	Foolish Pleasure	3	11	5	716,278
1934	Cavalcade	3	7	6	111,235	1976	Forego	6	8	6	401,701
1935	Omaha	3	9	6	142,255	1977	Seattle Slew	3	7	6	641,370
1936	Granville	3	11	7	110,295	1978	Affirmed	3	11	8	901,541
1937	Seabiscuit	4	15	11	168,580	1979	Spectacular Bid	3	12	10	1,279,334
1938	Stagehand	3	15	8	189,710	1980	Temperence Hill	3	17	8	1,130,452
1939	Challedon	3	15	9	184,535	1981	John Henry	6	10	8	1,798,030
1940	Bimelech	3	7	4	110,005	1982	Perrault (GB)	5	8	4	1,197,400
1941	Whirlaway	3	20	13	272,386	1983	All Along (FRA)	4	7	4	2,138,963
1942	Shut Out	3	12	8	238,872	1984	Slew o' Gold	4	6	5	2,627,944
1943	Count Fleet	3	6	6	174,055	1985	Spend A Buck	3	7	5	3,552,704
1944	Pavot	2	8	8	179,040	1986	Snow Chief	3	9	6	1,875,200
1945	Busher	3	13	10	273,735	1987	Alysheba	3	10	3	2,511,156
1946	Assault	3	15	8	424,195	1988	Alysheba	4	9	7	3,808,600
1947	Armed	6	17	11	376,325	1989	Sunday Silence	3	9	7	4,578,454
1948	Citation	3	20	19	709,470	1990	Unbridled	3	11	4	3,718,149
1949	Ponder	3	21	9	321,825	1991	Dance Smartly	3	8	8	2,876,821
1950	Noor	5	12	7	346,940	1992	A.P. Indy	3	7	5	2,622,560
1951	Counterpoint	3	15	7	250,525	1993	Kotashaan (FRA)	5	10	6	2,619,014

Jockeys

Annual money-leading jockeys since 1910, according to *The American Racing Manual*.

Multiple leaders: Bill Shoemaker (10); Laffit Pincay Jr. (7); Eddie Arcaro (6); Braulio Baeza (5); Chris McCarron and Jose Santos (4); Angel Cordero Jr. and Earl Sande (3); Ted Atkinson, Laverne Fator, Mack Garner, Bill Hartack, Charles Kurtsinger, Johnny Longden, Sonny Workman and Wayne Wright (2).

Year		Mts	Wins	Earnings	Year		Mts	Wins	Earnings
1910	Carroll Shilling	506	172	$176,030	1924	Ivan Parke	844	205	$290,395
1911	Ted Koerner	813	162	88,308	1925	Laverne Fator	315	81	305,775
1912	Jimmy Butwell	684	144	79,843	1926	Laverne Fator	511	143	361,435
1913	Merritt Buxton	887	146	82,552	1927	Earl Sande	179	49	277,877
1914	J. McCahey	824	155	121,845	1928	Linus McAtee	235	55	301,295
1915	Mack Garner	775	151	96,628	1929	Mack Garner	274	57	314,975
1916	John McTaggart	832	150	155,055	1930	Sonny Workman	571	152	420,438
1917	Frank Robinson	731	147	148,057	1931	Charley Kurtsinger	519	93	392,095
1918	Lucien Luke	756	178	201,864	1932	Sonny Workman	378	87	385,070
1919	John Loftus	177	65	252,707	1933	Robert Jones	471	63	226,285
1920	Clarence Kummer	353	87	292,376	1934	Wayne Wright	919	174	287,185
1921	Earl Sande	340	112	263,043	1935	Silvio Coucci	749	141	319,760
1922	Albert Johnson	297	43	345,054	1936	Wayne Wright	670	100	264,000
1923	Earl Sande	430	122	569,394	1937	Charley Kurtsinger	765	120	384,202

Year		Mts	Wins	Earnings	Year		Mts	Wins	Earnings
1938	Nick Wall	658	97	$ 385,161	1966	Braulio Baeza	1341	298	$ 2,951,022
1939	Basil James	904	191	353,333	1967	Braulio Baeza	1064	256	3,088,888
					1968	Braulio Baeza	1089	201	2,835,108
1940	Eddie Arcaro	783	132	343,661	1969	Jorge Velasquez	1442	258	2,542,315
1941	Don Meade	1164	210	398,627					
1942	Eddie Arcaro	687	123	481,949	1970	Laffit Pincay Jr.	1328	269	2,626,526
1943	Johnny Longden	871	173	573,276	1971	Laffit Pincay Jr.	1627	380	3,784,377
1944	Ted Atkinson	1539	287	899,101	1972	Laffit Pincay Jr.	1388	289	3,225,827
1945	Johnny Longden	778	180	981,977	1973	Laffit Pincay Jr.	1444	350	4,093,492
1946	Ted Atkinson	1377	233	1,036,825	1974	Laffit PincayJr.	1278	341	4,251,060
1947	Douglas Dodson	646	141	1,429,949	1975	Braulio Baeza	1190	196	3,674,398
1948	Eddie Arcaro	726	188	1,686,230	1976	Angel Cordero Jr.	1534	274	4,709,500
1949	Steve Brooks	906	209	1,316,817	1977	Steve Cauthen	2075	487	6,151,750
					1978	Darrel McHargue	1762	375	6,188,353
1950	Eddie Arcaro	888	195	1,410,160	1979	Laffit Pincay Jr.	1708	420	8,183,535
1951	Bill Shoemaker	1161	257	1,329,890					
1952	Eddie Arcaro	807	188	1,859,591	1980	Chris McCarron	1964	405	7,666,100
1953	Bill Shoemaker	1683	485	1,784,187	1981	Chris McCarron	1494	326	8,397,604
1954	Bill Shoemaker	1251	380	1,876,760	1982	Angel Cordero Jr.	1838	397	9,702,520
1955	Eddie Arcaro	820	158	1,864,796	1983	Angel Cordero Jr.	1792	362	10,116,807
1956	Bill Hartack	1387	347	2,343,955	1984	Chris McCarron	1565	356	12,038,213
1957	Bill Hartack	1238	341	3,060,501	1985	Laffit Pincay Jr.	1409	289	13,415,049
1958	Bill Shoemaker	1133	300	2,961,693	1986	Jose Santos	1636	329	11,329,297
1959	Bill Shoemaker	1285	347	2,843,133	1987	Jose Santos	1639	305	12,407,355
					1988	Jose Santos	1867	370	14,877,298
1960	Bill Shoemaker	1227	274	2,123,961	1989	Jose Santos	1459	285	13,847,003
1961	Bill Shoemaker	1256	304	2,690,819					
1962	Bill Shoemaker	1126	311	2,916,844	1990	Gary Stevens	1504	283	13,881,198
1963	Bill Shoemaker	1203	271	2,526,925	1991	Chris McCarron	1440	265	14,456,073
1964	Bill Shoemaker	1056	246	2,649,553	1992	Kent Desormeaux	1568	361	14,193,006
1965	Braulio Baeza	1245	270	2,582,702	1993	Mike Smith	1510	343	14,024,815

Annual Money-Leading Female Jockeys

Annual money-leading female jockeys since 1979, according to *The American Racing Manual*.
Multiple Leaders: Julie Krone (9); Patty Cooksey and Karen Rogers (2).

Year		Mts	Wins	Earnings	Year		Mts	Wins	Earnings
1979	Karen Rogers	550	77	$590,469	1987	Julie Krone	1698	324	4,522,191
1980	Karen Rogers	622	65	$894,878	1988	Julie Krone	1958	363	7,770,314
1981	Patty Cooksey	1469	197	895,951	1989	Julie Krone	1673	368	8,031,445
1982	Mary Russ	952	84	1,319,363	1990	Julie Krone	649	144	2,846,237
1983	Julie Krone	1024	151	1,095,622	1991	Julie Krone	1414	230	7,748,077
1984	Patty Cooksey	955	116	803,189	1992	Julie Krone	1462	282	9,220,824
1985	Abby Fuller	883	145	1,452,576	1993	Julie Krone	1012	212	6,415,462
1986	Julie Krone	1442	199	2,357,136					

Trainers

Annual money-leading trainers since 1908, according to *The American Racing Manual*.
Multiple winners: D. Wayne Lukas (10); Sam Hildreth (9), Charlie Whittingham (7); Sunny Jim Fitzsimmons and Jimmy Jones (5); Laz Barrera, Ben Jones and Willie Molter (4); Hirsch Jacobs, Eddie Neloy and James Rowe Sr. (3); H. Guy Bedwell, Jack Gaver, John Schorr, Humming Bob Smith, Silent Tom Smith, and Mesh Tenney (2).

Year		Wins	Earnings	Year		Wins	Earnings
1908	James Rowe Sr.	50	$284,335	1925	G.R. Tompkins	30	$199,245
1909	Sam Hildreth	73	123,942	1926	Scott Harlan	21	205,681
				1927	W.H. Bringloe	63	216,563
1910	Sam Hildreth	84	148,010	1928	John Schorr	65	258,425
1911	Sam Hildreth	67	49,418	1929	James Rowe Jr.	25	314,881
1912	John Schorr	63	58,110				
1913	James Rowe Sr.	18	45,936	1930	Sunny Jim Fitzsimmons	47	397,355
1914	R.C. Benson	45	59,315	1931	Big Jim Healy	33	297,300
1915	James Rowe Sr.	19	75,596	1932	Sunny Jim Fitzsimmons	68	266,650
1916	Sam Hildreth	39	70,950	1933	Humming Bob Smith	53	135,720
1917	Sam Hildreth	23	61,698	1934	Humming Bob Smith	43	249,938
1918	H. Guy Bedwell	53	80,296	1935	Bud Stotler	87	303,005
1919	H. Guy Bedwell	63	208,728	1936	Sunny Jim Fitzsimmons	42	193,415
				1937	Robert McGarvey	46	209,925
1920	Louis Feustal	22	186,087	1938	Earl Sande	15	226,495
1921	Sam Hildreth	85	262,768	1939	Sunny Jim Fitzsimmons	45	266,205
1922	Sam Hildreth	74	247,014				
1923	Sam Hildreth	75	392,124	1940	Silent Tom Smith	14	269,200
1924	Sam Hildreth	77	255,608	1941	Ben Jones	70	475,318

Annual Money Leaders (Cont.)
Trainers

Year		Wins	Earnings	Year		Sts	Wins	Earnings
1942	Jack Gaver	48	$ 406,547	1968	Eddie Neloy	212	52	$1,233,101
1943	Ben Jones	73	267,915	1969	Elliott Burch	156	26	1,067,936
1944	Ben Jones	60	601,660	1970	Charlie Whittingham	551	82	1,302,354
1945	Silent Tom Smith	52	510,655	1971	Charlie Whittingham	393	77	1,737,115
1946	Hirsch Jacobs	99	560,077	1972	Charlie Whittingham	429	79	1,734,020
1947	Jimmy Jones	85	1,334,805	1973	Charlie Whittingham	423	85	1,865,385
1948	Jimmy Jones	81	1,118,670	1974	Pancho Martin	846	166	2,408,419
1949	Jimmy Jones	76	978,587	1975	Charlie Whittingham	487	3	2,437,244
1950	Preston Burch	96	637,754	1976	Jack Van Berg	2362	496	2,976,196
1951	Jack Gaver	42	616,392	1977	Laz Barrera	781	127	2,715,848
1952	Ben Jones	29	662,137	1978	Laz Barrera	592	100	3,307,164
1953	Harry Trotsek	54	1,028,873	1979	Laz Barrera	492	98	3,608,517
1954	Willie Molter	136	1,107,860	1980	Laz Barrera	559	99	2,969,151
1955	Sunny Jim Fitzsimmons	66	1,270,055	1981	Charlie Whittingham	376	74	3,993,302
1956	Willie Molter	142	1,227,402	1982	Charlie Whittingham	410	63	4,587,457
1957	Jimmy Jones	70	1,150,910	1983	D. Wayne Lukas	595	78	4,267,261
1958	Willie Molter	69	1,116,544	1984	D. Wayne Lukas	805	131	5,835,921
1959	Willie Molter	71	847,290	1985	D. Wayne Lukas	1140	218	11,155,188

Year		Sts	Wins	Earnings
1960	Hirsch Jacobs	—	97	$ 748,349
1961	Jimmy Jones	—	62	759,856
1962	Mesh Tenney	—	58	1,099,474
1963	Mesh Tenney	192	40	860,703
1964	Bill Winfrey	287	61	1,350,534
1965	Hirsch Jacobs	610	91	1,331,628
1966	Eddie Neloy	282	93	2,456,250
1967	Eddie Neloy	262	72	1,776,089

Year		Sts	Wins	Earnings
1986	D. Wayne Lukas	1510	259	12,345,180
1987	D. Wayne Lukas	1735	343	17,502,110
1988	D. Wayne Lukas	1500	318	17,842,358
1989	D. Wayne Lukas	1398	305	16,103,998
1990	D. Wayne Lukas	1396	267	14,508,871
1991	D. Wayne Lukas	1497	289	15,942,223
1992	D. Wayne Lukas	1349	230	9,806,436
1993	Bobby Frankel	345	79	8,933,252

Wide World Photos

Alysheba, racing's all-time money-winning horse, carries jockey **Chris McCarron** to victory in the darkness of the 1988 Breeders' Cup Classic at Churchill Downs.

All-Time Leaders

The all-time money-winning horses and race-winning jockeys of North America through 1993, according to *The American Racing Manual*. Records include all available information on races in foreign countries.

Top 35 Horses—Money Won

Note that horses who raced in 1993 are in **bold** type; (†) indicates foreign-bred; and (f) indicates female.

	Sts	1st	2nd	3rd	Earnings
1 Alysheba	26	11	8	2	$6,679,242
2 John Henry	83	39	15	9	6,597,947
3 Sunday Silence	14	9	5	0	4,968,554
4 Easy Goer	20	14	5	1	4,873,770
5 **Best Pal**	31	14	7	3	4,709,445
6 Unbridled	24	8	6	6	4,489,475
7 Spend a Buck	15	10	3	2	4,220,689
8 Creme Fraiche	64	17	12	13	4,024,727
9 Ferdinand	29	8	9	6	3,777,978
10 Slew o' Gold	21	12	5	1	3,533,534
11 Precisionist	46	20	10	4	3,485,393
12 **Strike the Gold**	31	6	8	5	3,457,026
13 Snow Chief	24	13	3	5	3,383,210
14 Cryptoclearance	44	12	10	7	3,376,327
15 Black Tie Affair	45	18	9	6	3,370,694
16 Bet Twice	26	10	6	4	3,308,599
17 Steinlen	45	20	10	7	3,300,100
18 Dance Smartly (f)	17	12	2	3	3,263,836
19 Sky Classic	29	15	6	1	3,240,398
20 Gulch	32	13	8	4	3,095,521
21 **Bertrando**	16	7	6	2	3,024,465
22 Lady's Secret (f)	45	25	9	3	3,021,425
23 All Along (f)	21	9	4	2	3,015,764
24 A.P. Indy	11	8	0	1	2,979,815
25 Theatrical	22	10	4	2	2,943,627
26 Hansel	14	7	2	3	2,936,586
27 Great Communicator	56	14	10	7	2,922,615
28 Symboli Rudolf	16	13	1	1	2,909,593
29 Farma Way	23	8	5	1	2,897,176
30 With Approval	23	13	5	1	2,863,540
31 **Marquetry**	36	10	9	4	2,856,811
32 **Sea Hero**	16	5	1	2	2,823,910
33 Bayakoa (f)	39	21	9	0	2,817,524
34 **Kotashaan**	21	10	4	2	2,810,520
35 Triptych (f)	41	14	5	11	2,792,246

Top 35 Jockeys—Races Won

Note that jockeys active in 1993 are in **bold** type.

	Yrs	Wins	Earnings
1 Bill Shoemaker	42	8833	$123,375,524
2 **Laffit Pincay Jr.**	28	8055	177,071,603
3 Angel Cordero Jr.	31	7057	164,526,217
4 **Jorge Velasquez**	31	6611	122,043,875
5 **David Gall**	37	6395	19,493,195
6 **Larry Snyder**	34	6359	46,791,078
7 **Carl Gambardella**	38	6263	28,661,142
8 **Sandy Hawley**	26	6051	79,294,344
9 Johnny Longden	40	6032	24,665,800
10 **Pat Day**	22	5990	135,153,578
11 Chris McCarron	18	5919	166,817,558
12 **Earlie Fires**	29	5484	62,468,215
13 Eddie Delahoussaye	24	5191	129,485,541
14 **Jacinto Vasquez**	34	5146	78,306,194
15 Eddie Arcaro	31	4779	30,039,543
16 Don Brumfield	37	4573	43,567,861
17 Steve Brooks	34	4451	18,239,817
18 Walter Blum	22	4382	26,497,189
19 **Russell Baze**	20	4334	58,093,078
20 Bill Hartack	22	4272	26,466,758
21 **Eddie Maple**	26	4115	94,082,886
22 Avelino Gomez	34	4081	11,777,297
23 Hugo Dittfach	33	4000	13,506,052
24 **Craig Perret**	28	3856	79,615,463
25 **Philip Grove**	27	3847	15,279,023
26 **Randy Romero**	20	3803	62,592,233
27 Ted Atkinson	22	3795	17,449,360
28 **David Whited**	36	3784	25,067,466
29 Ralph Neves	21	3772	13,786,239
30 Leroy Moyers	34	3771	21,492,940
31 Bobby Baird	39	3749	12,592,611
32 **Ron Hansen**	16	3693	42,635,184
33 **Daniel Weiler**	37	3680	12,134,026
34 **Steve Neff**	23	3640	15,250,246
35 Bobby Ussery	24	3611	22,714,074

Retired: Arcaro (1961), Atkinson (1959), Baird (1982), Blum (1975), Brooks (1975), Brumfield (1989), Cordero (1992), Dittfach (1989), Gomez (1980), Hartack (1974), Longden (1966), Neves (1964), Shoemaker (1990), Toro (1990) and Ussery (1974).

Horse of the Year (1936-70)

In 1971, the *Daily Racing Form,* the Thoroughbred Racing Associations, and the National Turf Writers Assn. joined forces to create the Eclipse Awards. Before then, however, the Racing Form (1936-70) and the TRA (1950-70) issued separate selections for Horse of the Year. Their picks differed only four times from 1950-70 and are so noted. Horses listed in CAPITAL letters are Triple Crown winners; (f) indicates female.

Multiple winners: Kelso (5); Challedon, Native Dancer and Whirlaway (2).

Year		Year		Year		Year	
1936	Granville	1946	ASSAULT	1955	Nashua	1964	Kelso
1937	WAR ADMIRAL	1947	Armed	1956	Swaps	1965	Roman Brother (DRF)
1938	Seabiscuit	1948	CITATION	1957	Bold Ruler (DRF)		Moccasin (TRA)
1939	Challedon	1949	Capot		Dedicate (TRA)	1966	Buckpasser
1940	Challedon	1950	Hill Prince	1958	Round Table	1967	Damascus
1941	WHIRLAWAY	1951	Counterpoint	1959	Sword Dancer	1968	Dr. Fager
1942	Whirlaway	1952	One Count (DRF)	1960	Kelso	1969	Arts and Letters
1943	COUNT FLEET		Native Dancer (TRA)	1961	Kelso	1970	Fort Marcy (DRF)
1944	Twilight Tear (f)	1953	Tom Fool	1962	Kelso		Personality (TRA)
1945	Busher (f)	1954	Native Dancer	1963	Kelso		

Eclipse Awards

The Eclipse Awards, honoring the Horse of the Year and other champions of the sport, are sponsored by the *Daily Racing Form*, the Thoroughbred Racing Associations and the National Turf Writers Assn.

The awards are named after the 18th century racehorse and sire, Eclipse, who began racing at age five and was unbeaten in 18 starts (eight wins were walkovers). As a stallion, Eclipse sired winners of 344 races, including three Epsom Derby champions.

Horses listed in CAPITAL letters won the Triple Crown that year. Age of horse in parentheses where necessary.

Multiple winners (horses): Forego (8); John Henry (7); Affirmed and Secretariat (5); Flatterer, Seattle Slew and Spectacular Bid (4); Ack Ack, Susan's Girl and Zaccio (3); All Along, Alysheba, Bayakoa, Black Tie Affair, Cafe Prince, Conquistador Cielo, Desert Vixen, Ferdinand, Flawlessly, Go for Wand, Housebuster, Kotashaan, Lady's Secret, Life's Magic, Lonesome Glory, Miesque, Morley Street, Open Mind, Paseana, Riva Ridge, Slew o'Gold and Spend A Buck (2).

Multiple winners (people): Laffit Pincay Jr. (5); Laz Barrera and Pat Day (4); Steve Cauthen, Pat Day, Harbor View Farm, John Franks, Fred W. Hooper, Nelson Bunker Hunt, Mr. & Mrs. Gene Klein, Dan Lasater, D.Wayne Lucas, Ogden Phipps, Bill Shoemaker, Edward Taylor and Charlie Whittingham (3); Braulio Baeza, C.T. Chenery, Claiborne Farm, Angel Cordero Jr., Kent Desormeaux, John W. Galbreath, Chris McCarron and Paul Mellon (2).

Horse of the Year

Year		Year		Year		Year	
1971	Ack Ack (5)	1977	SEATTLE SLEW (3)	1983	All Along (4)	1989	Sunday Silence (3)
1972	Secretariat (2)	1978	AFFIRMED (3)	1984	John Henry (9)	1990	Criminal Type (5)
1973	SECRETARIAT (3)	1979	Affirmed (4)	1985	Spend A Buck (3)	1991	Black Tie Affair (5)
1974	Forego (4)	1980	Spectacular Bid (4)	1986	Lady's Secret (4)	1992	A.P. Indy (3)
1975	Forego (5)	1981	John Henry (6)	1987	Ferdinand (4)	1993	Kotashaan (5)
1976	Forego (6)	1982	Conquistador Cielo (3)	1988	Alysheba (4)		

Older Male

Year		Year		Year		Year	
1971	Ack Ack (5)	1977	Forego (7)	1983	Bates Motel (4)	1989	Blushing John (4)
1972	Autobiography (4)	1978	Seattle Slew (4)	1984	Slew o' Gold (4)	1990	Criminal Type (5)
1973	Riva Ridge (4)	1979	Affirmed (4)	1985	Vanlandingham (4)	1991	Black Tie Affair (5)
1974	Forego (4)	1980	Spectacular Bid (4)	1986	Turkoman (4)	1992	Pleasant Tap (5)
1975	Forego (5)	1981	John Henry (6)	1987	Ferdinand (4)	1993	Bertrando (4)
1976	Forego (6)	1982	Lemhi Gold (4)	1988	Alysheba (4)		

Older Filly or Mare

Year		Year		Year		Year	
1971	Shuvee (5)	1977	Cascapedia (4)	1983	Amb. of Luck (4)	1989	Bayakoa (5)
1972	Typecast (6)	1978	Late Bloomer (4)	1984	Princess Rooney (4)	1990	Bayakoa (6)
1973	Susan's Girl (4)	1979	Waya (5)	1985	Life's Magic (4)	1991	Queena (5)
1974	Desert Vixen (4)	1980	Glorious Song (4)	1986	Lady's Secret (4)	1992	Paseana (5)
1975	Susan's Girl (6)	1981	Relaxing (5)	1987	North Sider (5)	1993	Paseana (6)
1976	Proud Delta (4)	1982	Track Robbery (6)	1988	Personal Ensign (4)		

3-Year-Old Colt or Gelding

Year		Year		Year		Year	
1971	Canonero II	1977	SEATTLE SLEW	1983	Slew o' Gold	1989	Sunday Silence
1972	Key to the Mint	1978	AFFIRMED	1984	Swale	1990	Unbridled
1973	SECRETARIAT	1979	Spectacular Bid	1985	Spend A Buck	1991	Hansel
1974	Little Current	1980	Temperence Hill	1986	Snow Chief	1992	A.P. Indy
1975	Wajima	1981	Pleasant Colony	1987	Alysheba	1993	Prairie Bayou
1976	Bold Forbes	1982	Conquistador Cielo	1988	Risen Star		

3-Year-Old Filly

Year		Year		Year		Year	
1971	Turkish Trousers	1977	Our Mims	1983	Heartlight No. One	1989	Open Mind
1972	Susan's Girl	1978	Tempest Queen	1984	Life's Magic	1990	Go for Wand
1973	Desert Vixen	1979	Davona Dale	1985	Mom's Command	1991	Dance Smartly
1974	Chris Evert	1980	Genuine Risk	1986	Tiffany Lass	1992	Saratoga Slew
1975	Ruffian	1981	Wayward Lass	1987	Sacahuista	1993	Hollywood Wildcat
1976	Revidere	1982	Christmas Past	1988	Winning Colors		

2-Year-Old Colt or Gelding

Year		Year		Year		Year	
1971	Riva Ridge	1977	Affirmed	1983	Devil's Bag	1989	Rhythm
1972	Secretariat	1978	Spectacular Bid	1984	Chief's Crown	1990	Fly So Free
1973	Protagonist	1979	Rockhill Native	1985	Tasso	1991	Arazi
1974	Foolish Pleasure	1980	Lord Avie	1986	Capote	1992	Gilded Time
1975	Honest Pleasure	1981	Deputy Minister	1987	Forty Niner	1993	Dehere
1976	Seattle Slew	1982	Roving Boy	1988	Easy Goer		

2-Year-Old Filly

Year		Year		Year		Year	
1971	Numbered Account	1977	Lakeville Miss	1982	Landaluce	1988	Open Mind
1972	La Prevoyante	1978	(tie) Candy Eclair	1983	Althea	1989	Go for Wand
1973	Talking Picture		& It's in the Air	1984	Outstandingly	1990	Meadow Star
1974	Ruffian	1979	Smart Angle	1985	Family Style	1991	Pleasant Stage
1975	Dearly Precious	1980	Heavenly Cause	1986	Brave Raj	1992	Eliza
1976	Sensational	1981	Before Dawn	1987	Epitome	1993	Phone Chatter

Champion Turf Horse

Year		Year		Year		Year	
1971	Run the Gantlet (3)	1973	Secretariat (3)	1975	Snow Knight (4)	1977	Johnny D (3)
1972	Cougar II (6)	1974	Dahlia (4)	1976	Youth (3)	1978	Mac Diarmida (3)

Champion Male Turf Horse

Year		Year		Year		Year	
1979	Bowl Game (5)	1983	John Henry (8)	1987	Theatrical (5)	1991	Tight Spot (4)
1980	John Henry (5)	1984	John Henry (9)	1988	Sunshine Forever (3)	1992	Sky Classic (5)
1981	John Henry (6)	1985	Cozzene (4)	1989	Steinlen (6)	1993	Kotashaan (5)
1982	Perrault (5)	1986	Manila (3)	1990	Itsallgreektome (3)		

Champion Female Turf Horse

Year		Year		Year		Year	
1979	Trillion (5)	1983	All Along (4)	1987	Miesque (3)	1991	Miss Alleged (4)
1980	Just A Game II (4)	1984	Royal Heroine (4)	1988	Miesque (4)	1992	Flawlessly (4)
1981	De La Rose (3)	1985	Pebbles (4)	1989	Brown Bess (7)	1993	Flawlessly (5)
1982	April Run (4)	1986	Estrapade (6)	1990	Laugh and Be Merry (5)		

Sprinter

Year		Year		Year		Year	
1971	Ack Ack (5)	1977	What a Summer (4)	1983	Chinook Pass (4)	1989	Safely Kept (3)
1972	Chou Croute (4)	1978	(tie) Dr. Patches (4)	1984	Eillo (4)	1990	Housebuster (3)
1973	Shecky Greene (3)		& J.O. Tobin (4)	1985	Precisionist (4)	1991	Housebuster (4)
1974	Forego (4)	1979	Star de Naskra (4)	1986	Smile (4)	1992	Rubiano (5)
1975	Gallant Bob (3)	1980	Plugged Nickle (3)	1987	Groovy (4)	1993	Cardmania (7)
1976	My Juliet (4)	1981	Guilty Conscience (5)	1988	Gulch (4)		
		1982	Gold Beauty (3)				

Steeplechase or Hurdle Horse

Year		Year		Year		Year	
1971	Shadow Brook (7)	1977	Cafe Prince (7)	1983	Flatterer (4)	1989	Highland Bud (4)
1972	Soothsayer (5)	1978	Cafe Prince (8)	1984	Flatterer (5)	1990	Morley Street (6)
1973	Athenian Idol (5)	1979	Martie's Anger (4)	1985	Flatterer (6)	1991	Morley Street (7)
1974	Gran Kan (8)	1980	Zaccio (4)	1986	Flatterer (7)	1992	Lonesome Glory (4)
1975	Life's Illusion (4)	1981	Zaccio (5)	1987	Inlander (6)	1993	Lonesome Glory (5)
1976	Straight and True (6)	1982	Zaccio (6)	1988	Jimmy Lorenzo (6)		

Outstanding Jockey

Year		Year		Year		Year	
1971	Laffit Pincay Jr.	1977	Steve Cauthen	1983	Angel Cordero Jr.	1989	Kent Desormeaux
1972	Braulio Baeza	1978	Darrel McHargue	1984	Pat Day	1990	Craig Perret
1973	Laffit Pincay Jr.	1979	Laffit Pincay Jr.	1985	Laffit Pincay Jr.	1991	Pat Day
1974	Laffit Pincay Jr.	1980	Chris McCarron	1986	Pat Day	1992	Kent Desormeaux
1975	Braulio Baeza	1981	Bill Shoemaker	1987	Pat Day	1993	Mike Smith
1976	Sandy Hawley	1982	Angel Cordero Jr.	1988	Jose Santos		

Outstanding Apprentice Jockey

Year		Year		Year		Year	
1971	Gene St. Leon	1977	Steve Cauthen	1983	Declan Murphy	1989	Michael Luzzi
1972	Thomas Wallis	1978	Ron Franklin	1984	Wesley Ward	1990	Mark Johnston
1973	Steve Valdez	1979	Cash Asmussen	1985	Art Madrid Jr.	1991	Mickey Walls
1974	Chris McCarron	1980	Frank Lovato Jr.	1986	Allen Stacy	1992	Jesus A. Bracho
1975	Jimmy Edwards	1981	Richard Migliore	1987	Kent Desormeaux	1993	Juan Umana
1976	George Martens	1982	Alberto Delgado	1988	Steve Capanas		

Eclipse Awards (Cont.)

Outstanding Trainer

Year		Year		Year		Year	
1971	Charlie Whittingham	1977	Laz Barrera	1983	Woody Stephens	1989	Charlie Whittingham
1972	Lucien Laurin	1978	Laz Barrera	1984	Jack Van Berg	1990	Carl Nafzger
1973	H. Allen Jerkens	1979	Laz Barrera	1985	D. Wayne Lukas	1991	Ron McAnally
1974	Sherill Ward	1980	Bud Delp	1986	D. Wayne Lukas	1992	Ron McAnally
1975	Steve DiMauro	1981	Ron McAnally	1987	D. Wayne Lukas	1993	Bobby Frankel
1976	Laz Barrera	1982	Charlie Whittingham	1988	Shug McGaughey		

Outstanding Owner

Year		Year		Year		Year	
1971	Mr. & Mrs. E.E. Fogleson	1977	Maxwell Gluck	1982	Viola Sommer	1988	Ogden Phipps
1972-73	No award	1978	Harbor View Farm	1983	John Franks	1989	Ogden Phipps
1974	Dan Lasater	1979	Harbor View Farm	1984	John Franks	1990	Frances Genter
1975	Dan Lasater	1980	Mr. & Mrs. Bertram Firestone	1985	Mr. & Mrs. Gene Klein	1991	Sam-Son Farms
1976	Dan Lasater	1981	Dotsam Stable	1986	Mr. & Mrs. Gene Klein	1992	Juddmonta Farms
				1987	Mr. & Mrs. Gene Klein	1993	John Franks

Outstanding Owner-Breeder

Year		Year		Year	
1971	Paul Mellon	1972	C.T. Chenery	1973	C.T. Chenery

Outstanding Breeder

Year		Year		Year		Year	
1974	John W. Galbreath	1979	Claiborne Farm	1984	Claiborne Farm	1989	North Ridge Farm
1975	Fred W. Hooper	1980	Mrs. Henry Paxson	1985	Nelson Bunker Hunt	1990	Calumet Farm
1976	Nelson Bunker Hunt	1981	Golden Chance Farm	1986	Paul Mellon	1991	Mr. & Mrs. John Mabee
1977	Edward P. Taylor	1982	Fred W. Hooper	1987	Nelson Bunker Hunt	1992	William S. Farish
1978	Harbor View Farm	1983	Edward P. Taylor	1988	Ogden Phipps	1993	Allan Paulson

Outstanding Achievement

Year		Year	
1971	Charles Engelhard*	1972	Arthur B. Hancock Jr.*

*Awarded posthumously.

Man of the Year

Year		Year	
1972	John W. Galbreath	1974	William L. McKnight
1973	Edward P. Taylor	1975	John A. Morris

Award of Merit

Year		Year		Year		Year	
1976	Jack J. Dreyfus	1980	John D. Shapiro	1986	Herman Cohen	1990	Warner L. Jones
1977	Steve Cauthen	1981	Bill Shoemaker	1987	J.B. Faulconer	1991	Fred W. Hooper
1978	Dinny Phipps	1984	John Gaines	1988	John Forsythe	1992	Joe Hirsch & Robert P. Strub
1979	Jimmy Kilroe	1985	Keene Daingerfield	1989	Michael Sandler		

Special Award

Year		Year		Year		Year	
1971	Robert J. Kleberg	1980	John T. Landry & Pierre E. Bellocq	1985	Arlington Park	1988	Edward J. DeBartolo Sr.
1974	Charles Hatton	1984	C.V. Whitney	1987	Anheuser-Busch	1989	Richard Duchossois
1976	Bill Shoemaker						

HARNESS RACING

Triple Crown Winners
PACERS

Seven 3-year-olds have won the Cane Pace, Little Brown Jug and Messenger Stakes in the same year since the Pacing Triple Crown was established in 1956. No trainer or driver has won it more than once.

Year		Driver	Trainer	Owner
1959	**Adios Butler**	Clint Hodgins	Paige West	Paige West & Angelo Pellillo
1965	**Bret Hanover**	Frank Ervin	Frank Ervin	Richard Downing
1966	**Romeo Hanover**	Bill Meyer & George Sholty*	Jerry Silverman	Lucky Star Stables & Morton Finder
1968	**Rum Customer**	Billy Haughton	Billy Haughton	Kennilworth Farms & L.C. Mancuso
1970	**Most Happy Fella**	Stanley Dancer	Stanley Dancer	Egyptian Acres Stable
1980	**Niatross**	Clint Galbraith	Clint Galbraith	Niagara Acres, Niatross Stables & Clint Galbraith
1983	**Ralph Hanover**	Ron Waples	Stew Firlotte	Waples Stable, Pointsetta Stable, Grant's Direct Stable & P.J. Baugh

*Myer drove Romeo Hanover in the Cane, Sholty in the other two races.

TROTTERS

Six 3-year-olds have won the Yonkers Trot, Hambletonian and Kentucky Futurity in the same year since the Trotting Triple Crown was established in 1955. Stanley Dancer is the only driver/trainer to win it twice.

Year		Driver/Trainer	Owner
1955	**Scott Frost**	Joe O'Brien	S.A. Camp Farms
1963	**Speedy Scot**	Ralph Baldwin	Castleton Farms
1964	**Ayres**	John Simpson Sr.	Charlotte Sheppard
1968	**Nevele Pride**	Stanley Dancer	Nevele Acres & Lou Resnick
1969	**Lindy's Pride**	Howard Beissinger	Lindy Farms
1972	**Super Bowl**	Stanley Dancer	Rachel Dancer & Rose Hild Breeding Farm

Triple Crown Near Misses

PACERS

Seven horses have won the first two legs of the Triple Crown, but not the third. The Cane Pace (CP), Little Brown Jug (LBJ), and Messenger Stakes (MS) have not always been run in the same order so numbers after races won indicate sequence for that year.

Year		CP	LBJ	MS
1957	**Torpid**	won, 1	won, 2	DNF
1960	**Countess Adios**	won, 2	NE	won, 1
1971	**Albatross**	won, 2	2nd*	won, 1
1976	**Keystone Ore**	won, 1	won, 2	2nd*
1986	**Barberry Spur**	won, 1	won, 2	2nd*
1990	**Jake and Elwood**	won, 1	NE	won, 2
1992	**Western Hanover**	won, 1	2nd*	won, 2
1993	**Rijadh**	won, 1	2nd*	won, 2

TROTTERS

Six horses have won the first two legs of the Triple Crown—the Yonkers Trot (YT) and the Hambletonian (Ham)—but not the third. The eventual winner of the Ky. Futurity (KF) is listed.

Year		YT	Ham	KF
1962	**A.C.'s Viking**	won	won	Safe Mission
1976	**Steve Lobell**	won	won	Quick Pay
1977	**Green Speed**	won	won	Texas
1978	**Speedy Somolli**	won	won	Doublemint
1987	**Mack Lobell**	won	won	Napoletano
1993	**American Winner**	won	won	Pine Chip

Note: Green Speed (1977) not eligible for Ky. Futurity.

***Winning horses:** Nansemond (1971), Windshield Wiper (1976), Amity Chef (1986), Fake Left (1992), Life Sign (1993).

Note: Torpid (1957) scratched before the final heat; Countess Adios (1960) not eligible for Messenger; Jake and Elwood (1990) not eligible for Little Brown Jug.

The Hambletonian

For three-year-old trotters. Inaugurated in 1926 and has been held in Syracuse, N.Y.; Lexington, Ky.; Goshen, N.Y, Yonkers, N.Y.; Du Quoin, Ill.; and, since 1981 at The Meadowlands in East Rutherford, N.J.

Run at one mile since 1947. Winning horse must win two heats.

Drivers with most wins: Ben White, Stanley Dancer and Billy Haughton (4); Howard Beissinger, Del Cameron, John Campbell and Henry Thomas (3).

Year		Driver	Fastest Heat
1926	**Guy McKinney**	Nat Ray	2:04¾
1927	**Iosola's Worthy**	Marvin Childs	2:03¾
1928	**Spencer**	W.H. Lessee	2:02½
1929	**Walter Dear**	Walter Cox	2:02¾
1930	**Hanover's Bertha**	Tom Berry	2:03
1931	**Calumet Butler**	R.D. McMahon	2:03¼
1932	**The Marchioness**	Will Caton	2:01¼
1933	**Mary Reynolds**	Ben White	2:03¾
1934	**Lord Jim**	Doc Parshall	2:02¾
1935	**Greyhound**	Sep Palin	2:02¼
1936	**Rosalind**	Ben White	2:01¾
1937	**Shirley Hanover**	Henry Thomas	2:01½
1938	**McLin Hanover**	Henry Tomas	2:02¼
1939	**Peter Astra**	Doc Parshall	2:04¼
1940	**Spencer Scott**	Fred Egan	2:02
1941	**Bill Gallon**	Lee Smith	2:05
1942	**The Ambassador**	Ben White	2:04
1943	**Volo Song**	Ben White	2:02½
1944	**Yankee Maid**	Henry Thomas	2:04
1945	**Titan Hanover**	Harry Pownall Sr.	2:04
1946	**Chestertown**	Thomas Berry	2:02½
1947	**Hoot Mon**	Sep Palin	2:00
1948	**Demon Hanover**	Harrison Hoyt	2:02
1949	**Miss Tilly**	Fred Egan	2:01⅖
1950	**Lusty Song**	Del Miller	2:02
1951	**Mainliner**	Guy Crippen	2:02⅗
1952	**Sharp Note**	Bion Shively	2:02⅗
1953	**Helicopter**	Harry Harvey	2:01⅗
1954	**Newport Dream**	Del Cameron	2:02⅘
1955	**Scott Frost**	Joe O'Brien	2:00⅗
1956	**The Intruder**	Ned Bower	2:01⅖
1957	**Hickory Smoke**	John Simpson Sr.	2:00⅕
1958	**Emily's Pride**	Flave Nipe	1:59⅘
1959	**Diller Hanover**	Frank Ervin	2:01⅕
1960	**Blaze Hanover**	Joe O'Brien	1:59⅗
1961	**Harlan Dean**	James Arthur	1:58⅖
1962	**A.C.'s Viking**	Sanders Russell	1:59⅗
1963	**Speedy Scot**	Ralph Baldwin	1:57⅗
1964	**Ayres**	John Simpson Sr.	1:56⅘
1965	**Egyptian Candor**	Del Cameron	2:03⅘
1966	**Kerry Way**	Frank Ervin	1:58⅘
1967	**Speedy Streak**	Del Cameron	2:00
1968	**Nevele Pride**	Stanley Dancer	1:59⅖
1969	**Lindys Pride**	Howard Beissinger	1:57⅗
1970	**Timothy T**	John Simpson Jr.	1:58⅖
1971	**Speedy Crown**	Howard Beissinger	1:57⅖
1972	**Super Bowl**	Stanley Dancer	1:56⅖
1973	**Flirth**	Ralph Baldwin	1:57⅕
1974	**Christopher T**	Billy Haughton	1:58⅗
1975	**Bonefish**	Stanley Dancer	1:59
1976	**Steve Lobell**	Billy Haughton	1:56⅖
1977	**Green Speed**	Billy Haughton	1:55⅗
1978	**Speedy Somolli**	Howard Beissinger	1:55
1979	**Legend Hanover**	George Sholty	1:56⅕
1980	**Burgomeister**	Billy Haughton	1:56⅗
1981	**Shiaway St. Pat**	Ray Remmen	2:01⅕
1982	**Speed Bowl**	Tommy Haughton	1:56⅘
1983	**Duenna**	Stanley Dancer	1:57⅖
1984	**Historic Freight**	Ben Webster	1:56⅖
1985	**Prakas**	Bill O'Donnell	1:54⅗
1986	**Nuclear Kosmos**	Ulf Thoresen	1:55⅖
1987	**Mack Lobell**	John Campbell	1:53⅗

The Hambletonian (Cont.)

Year		Driver	Fastest Heat	Year		Driver	Fastest Heat
1988	**Armbro Goal**	John Campbell	1:54⅗	1992	**Alf Palema**	Mickey McNichol	1:56⅖
1989	**Park Avenue Joe**	Ron Waples	1:54⅖	1993	**American Winner**	Ron Pierce	1:53⅕
	& Probe	Bill Fahy		1994	**Victory Dream**	Michel Lachance	1:54⅕
1990	**Harmonious**	John Campbell	1:54⅕				
1991	**Giant Victory**	Jack Moiseyev	1:54⅖				

Note: In 1989, Park Avenue Joe and Probe finished in a dead heat in the race-off. They were later declared co-winners, but Park Avenue Joe was awarded 1st place money because his three-race summary (2-1-1) was better than Probe's (1-9-1).

All-Time Leaders

The all-time winning trotters, pacers and drivers through 1993 according to *The Trotting and Pacing Guide.* Purses for horses include races in foreign countries. Purses, starts and wins for drivers include only races held in North America.

Top 15 Horses—Money Won

Note that (*) indicates horse raced in 1993.

		T/P	Sts	1st	Earnings
1	Peace Corps*.....................	T	42	35	$4,907,307
2	Ourasi (FRA).....................	T	N/A	32	4,010,105
3	Mack Lobell	T	86	65	3,917,594
4	Reve d'Udon*	T	23	18	3,611,351
5	Nihilator..........................	P	38	35	3,225,653
6	Artsplace*	P	49	37	3,085,083
7	Presidential Ball	P	38	26	3,021,363
8	Matt's Scooter	P	61	37	2,944,591
9	On the Road Again............	P	61	44	2,819,102
10	Ideal du Gazeau (FRA)	T	N/A	21	2,744,777
11	Vrai Lutin (FRA)................	T	N/A	N/A	2,612,429
12	Grades Singing.................	T	101	66	2,607,552
13	Beach Towel....................	P	36	29	2,570,357
14	Embassy Lobell (FRA).........	T	21	8	2,566,370
15	Western Hanover*..............	P	42	27	2,541,647

Top 15 Drivers — Races Won

All drivers were active in 1993.

		Yrs	Wins	Earnings	(Rk)
1	Herve Filion	33	14,084	$ 80,668,478	(2)
2	Carmine Abbatiello	38	7,100	49,315,634	(6)
3	Michel Lachance.........	26	6,740	70,083,387	(4)
4	John Campbell............	22	6,308	118,951,088	(1)
5	Walter Case Jr............	17	6,144	23,496,265	(33)
6	Dave Magee	21	5,889	40,639,574	(12)
7	Cat Manzi	26	5,877	46,197,533	(7)
8	Walter Paisley	36	5,712	34,655,715	(14)
9	Joe Marsh Jr...............	39	5,649	34,567,520	(15)
10	Ron Waples	28	5,648	54,451,262	(5)
11	Eddie Davis	30	5,565	27,086,844	(29)
12	Bill Gale	23	5,563	30,100,637	(19)
13	Leigh Fitch	32	5,523	5,277,497	(262)
14	Gilles Gendron...........	27	5,464	23,248,301	(34)
15	Jack Moiseyev............	18	5,428	43,670,264	(10)

Annual Awards
Horse of the Year

Selected since 1947 by U.S. Trotting Association and the U.S. Harness Writers Association; age of winning horse is noted; (t) indicates trotter and (p) indicates pacer. USTA added Trotter and Pacer of the Year awards in 1970.

Multiple winners: Bret Hanover and Nevele Pride (3); Adios Butler, Albatross, Cam Fella, Good Time, Mack Lobell, Niatross and Scott Frost (2).

Year		Year		Year		Year	
1947	Victory Song (4t)	1960	Adios Butler (4p)	1972	Albatross (4p)	1984	Fancy Crown (3t)
1948	Rodney (4t)	1961	Adios Butler (5p)	1973	Sir Dalrai (4p)	1985	Nihilator (3p)
1949	Good Time (3p)	1962	Su Mac Lad (8t)	1974	Delmonica Hanover(5t)	1986	Forrest Skipper (4p)
1950	Proximity (8t)	1963	Speedy Scot (3t)	1975	Savoir (7t)	1987	Mack Lobell (3t)
1951	Pronto Don (6t)	1964	Bret Hanover (2p)	1976	Keystone Ore (3p)	1988	Mack Lobell (4t)
1952	Good Time (6t)	1965	Bret Hanover (3p)	1977	Green Speed (3t)	1989	Matt's Scooter (4p)
1953	Hi Lo's Forbes (5p)	1966	Bret Hanover (4p)	1978	Abercrombie (3p)		
1954	Stenographer (3t)	1967	Nevele Pride (2t)	1979	Niatross (2p)	1990	Beach Towel (3p)
1955	Scott Frost (3t)	1968	Nevele Pride (3t)			1991	Precious Bunny (3p)
1956	Scott Frost (4t)	1969	Nevele Pride (4t)	1980	Niatross (3p)	1992	Artsplace (4p)
1957	Torpid (3p)			1981	Fan Hanover (3p)	1993	Staying Together (4p)
1958	Emily's Pride (3t)	1970	Fresh Yankee (7t)	1982	Cam Fella (3p)		
1959	Bye Bye Byrd (4p)	1971	Albatross (3p)	1983	Cam Fella (4p)		

Driver of the Year

Determined by Universal Driving Rating System (UDR) and presented by the Harness Tracks of America since 1968. Eligible drivers must have at least 1000 starts for the season.

Multiple winners: Herve Filion (10); John Campbell and Michel Lachance (3); Walter Case Jr., Bill O'Donnell and Ron Waples (2).

Year		Year		Year		Year	
1968	Stanley Dancer	1976	Herve Filion	1983	John Campbell	1990	John Campbell
1969	Herve Filion	1977	Donald Dancer	1984	Bill O'Donnell	1991	Walter Case Jr.
		1978	Carmine Abbatiello	1985	Michel Lachance	1992	Walter Case Jr.
1970	Herve Filion		& Herve Filion	1986	Michel Lachance	1993	Jack Moiseyeu
1971	Herve Filion	1979	Ron Waples	1987	Michel Lachance		
1972	Herve Filion			1988	John Campbell		
1973	Herve Filion	1980	Ron Waples	1989	Herve Filion		
1974	Herve Filion	1981	Herve Filion				
1975	Joe O'Brien	1982	Bill O'Donnell				

Nine-time Wimbledon winner **Martina Navratilova** (left) shares a laugh with new champion **Conchita Martinez** after their three-set final.

TENNIS

Martina Exits

*In a year where Sampras, Agassi and Spain starred,
Navratilova walked away with the loudest cheers.*

This year should belong to Pete Sampras, lord of Wimbledon and Australia, but he fell victim to a case of exhaustion at home and got bounced from the U.S. Open in the fourth round.

So maybe the year belongs to Andre Agassi, the wild-haired, multi-colored curiosity who entered the U.S. Open unseeded then proceeded to beat five seeded players to win the title.

Or maybe it was the Year of the Spanish. After all, they won half of the eight majors and the Federation Cup and turned June 5 into a national holiday when Arantxa Sanchez Vicario and Sergi Bruguera swept the French Open singles titles in front of their beaming king, Juan Carlos.

The king had no trouble rooting for Sanchez, who beat Mary Pierce, 6-4, 6-4, but the men's final was a different story. That match was the first All-Spanish final in Grand Slam history and defending champion Sergi Bruguera outlasted Alberto Berasategui in four sets.

Then there was Conchita Martinez, who had lost to Sanchez in the French semifinals. In July, she astounded everybody, including herself, by winning the Wimbledon title. In September, Sanchez astounded everybody, except herself, and won the U.S. Open. The first Spanish woman ever to ever win the Open, Sanchez

Diane Pucin is a columnist for the *The Philadelphia Inquirer* where she has covered international tennis since 1988.

did it the hard way—upsetting Steffi Graf in the finals, 1-6, 7-6 (7-3), 6-4.

Or maybe this year should belong to nobody. If there was a single theme running through the sport in 1994, it was boredom. The question was posed, over and over: What's wrong with tennis?

The sport sorely missed personalities like Jimmy Connors and John McEnroe, as well as old rivalries like Borg-McEnroe, Borg-Connors, Connors-McEnroe and Navratilova-Evert.

Graf, the fine German woman with the athletic skills of a track star and the steely focus of a chess champion, won her first 32 matches this season and fans yawned. Where was the competition?

And where was Monica Seles? Ever since she was stabbed by a crazed Graf devotee named Gunther Parche at a tournament in Hamburg on April 30, 1993, Seles has virtually disappeared. Over a year later, she was still sidelined—physically okay it seemed, but unwilling to play in public.

Women's tennis lost another star in Jennifer Capriati, the young pixie with a brilliant smile and killer forehand, who became the youngest Grand Slam semifinalist ever at 13 and won an Olympic gold medal at 16. But in May, Capriati was arrested in a seedy Miami hotel room filled with drugs and disaffected teens. She was 18 years old and sullen. She hadn't played tennis since losing in the first round of the 1993 U.S. Open and had been picked up for shoplifting the previous December.

Spaniards **Arantxa Sanchez Vicario** (left) and **Sergi Bruguera** show off their trophies after sweeping both singles titles at the French Open.

Capriati's precipitous and public fall from grace and stardom forced the Women's Tennis Association to look at its rules allowing girls as young as 13 to turn pro. The WTA announced at the U.S. Open a curious and complicated policy that is supposed to gradually let women play pro tournaments until, at age 18, they can handle a full schedule.

But the WTA also made immediate exceptions. Martina Hingis, a long-legged, fragile-looking 13-year-old from Switzerland, who won the French Open and Wimbledon junior titles, can play a full schedule as soon as she turns 14 in October. So can Anna Kournikova, a 12-year-old Nick Bollettieri prodigy, and Venus Williams, a 13-year-old American.

So leaderless is women's tennis that at the U.S. Open, on the afternoon that defending champion and No. 1 seed Pete Sampras was stunned by Peru's Jaime Yzaga in five sets, releases were handed out along press row announcing that a 9:30 a.m. press conference would be held the next morning to announce the formation of a new women's tour. Billie Jean King and representatives from IMG, the powerful Mark McCormack management group that represents many tennis players and that runs many tennis tournaments, were to be the featured speakers.

Ten minutes after the releases were handed out the same messenger returned to take them back. The press conference had been cancelled.

Meanwhile, Martina Navratilova, who turned 38 in October, defeated her former doubles partner Pam Shriver for the presidency of the WTA and promised to reorganize the group.

It was Navratilova, in fact, who provided the most excitement to this tennis year. She began the season by announcing that 1994 would be her last year on the tour. She even played in the French Open for the first time since 1988 as part of her farewell tour.

The year had been almost worthless—no titles and a first-round loss at the French—when Navratilova moved on to the lawns of Wimbledon and one more shot at the singles title she had already won nine times.

AFP Photo

Fourteen-year-old **Martina Hingis** of Switzerland made her first pro tournament appearance in friendly surroundings at the Zürich Open in October.

There was a little hope in everybody that maybe Martina could get a few breaks, win her 10th and walk away in glory.

It almost happened.

Defending champion and top seed Graf lost in the first round to Lori McNeil. Then Sanchez, seeded second, went out in the fourth against Zina Garrison Jackson. Another threat, Pierce, had bowed out before the tournament started, fearful that her abusive father might show up.

Navratilova, the fourth seed, just kept winning. She crushed Jana Novotna in the quarters and did the same to Gigi Fernandez in the semis. Meanwhile, in the top half of the draw, seeds kept falling away. All except one—Conchita Martinez.

The 22-year-old Martinez, known primarily as a clay court player, was competing in only her third Wimbledon. Seeded third, she had reached the final only after three-set victories over Lindsay Davenport in the quarters and Graf-killer McNeil in the semis.

Martinez made the most of her Centre Court opportunity even though she had to do it before a reverential crowd, including Princess Diana, that was clearly pulling for Navratilova. After splitting the first two sets, Martinez won the third and her first Grand Slam title, 6-4, 3-6, 6-3.

At the awards ceremony, Martina gave Conchita a gentle shove. Go, she seemed to be saying, take your big, shiny winner's plate and enjoy this moment. Leave the nest. I won't be here next time so learn your way around Centre Court, love it, treasure it, always come back to it.

Navratilova waved good-bye and she cried. She cried, she said, not because she lost, but because it was her last Wimbledon singles match.

No one has treasured Wimbledon more than Martina. Not ever. It's where she learned to play on grass and where she established her serve and volley. It's also where she gained respect from the fans and finally gained love. After she had curtsied to the assembled royalty and as the applause grew and grew, Navratilova walked back to the court and bent over. She picked a fingerful of grass and carried it off with her towels and her rackets.

No other Grand Slam final was as dramatic. Sampras was dominating in winning the Australian Open in straight sets over Todd Martin and even more forceful in his straight-set Wimbledon final win over Goran Ivanisevic.

One suspects Sampras might have won his third U.S. Open just as easily had an ankle injury not kept him out of the summer hardcourt season and brought him to Flushing Meadows out of shape and unable to win that fourth-round five-setter against Yzaga.

Sampras did decide to continue to play Davis Cup for the United States and announced on the last day of the Open that he would join the American team in Göteborg, Sweden, the weekend of Sept. 23-25, and face the Swedes in the semifinals.

It might have been the wrong decision. The U.S. jumped out to a 2-0 lead the first day as Martin and Sampras defeated Stefan Edberg and Magnus Larsson, respectively, in singles.

Not good enough.

U.S. coach Tom Guillikson elected to field

Wide World Photos

Wide World Photos

Top-seeded **Pete Sampras** (left) won his first Australian Open and his second Wimbledon in 1994, but unseeded **Andre Agassi** captured the U.S. Open title.

a doubles team of Jonathan Stark and Jared Palmer, who are highly-ranked doubles players but who don't usually play together. They lost to Jan Apell and Jonas Bjorkman in four sets.

On Sunday morning, Sampras was hobbling with a strained right hamstring, related to his previous tendinitis. He began his reverse singles match with Edberg, but had to retire after losing the first set. Martin, with all the pressure shifted to his shoulders, couldn't beat Larsson and the U.S. was eliminated.

More amazing than the Swedish comeback was the fact that they wouldn't be challenging defending Cup holder Germany in the final. Instead, they would meet Russia for the Cup in Moscow in December.

The Russians, led by 20-year-old Yvegeny Kafelnikov, upset Michael Stich and the Germans, 4-1, in Hamburg.

The very fact that Agassi finally won a second Slam to go with his 1992 Wimbledon title made the buildup to the U.S. Open final more dramatic than usual. Not only did Agassi have a chance to become the first unseeded male since Fred Stolle in 1966 to win the Open but he was

following in a line of unseeded finalists that began with girlfriend Brooke Shields' grandfather Frank Shields in 1930.

In the end, it was no contest as Agassi destroyed Stich, 6-1, 7-6 (7-5) 7-5. The best thing about the victory is that it seems to mean that Agassi, with the help of his new coach Brad Gilbert, is finally committing to tennis in a way that might make him a worthy rival for Sampras.

Agassi's Open breakthrough came at the same time that Jim Courier, who was ranked No. 1 in the world just a year ago, seemed to have lost all his desire to play the game. Courier had played brilliantly in July to clinch a 3-2 U.S. win over Holland in the Davis Cup quarterfinals where Sampras actually lost a match. But Courier's year had otherwise been filled with first and second-round losses.

It got so bad that two weeks before the U.S. Open, where he had been seeded No. 1 in 1993, Courier packed up his gear and went home to Florida leaving behind the statement that he might be back in a day, a week, a month, a year, or 10 years.

Courier came back two weeks later as the 11th seed in the Open, but was eliminated by Andrea Gaudenzi of Italy in the second

Monica Seles, the former No. 1 women's player in the world who has virtually disappeared since being attacked at a tournament in April 1993, surfaced in Monaco on Aug. 27, as a guest at a Monte Carlo celebrity tournament.

round and quickly returned home.

Graf won the Australian Open easily, but it was to be her only major. She was listless in losing to Pierce in the French semis and sullen in losing to McNeil at Wimbledon. She came to the U.S. Open enthusiastic but physically fragile. Her back was sore and it was her back that ultimately betrayed her. In the final against Sanchez, Graf needed just 22 minutes to win the first set, 6-1, then her back stiffened and she couldn't hit out on her forehand. Sanchez rallied and won the 2-hour, 7-minute match 1-6, 7-6, 6-4.

Two days after the U.S. Open, Capriati announced she would start a tentative comeback at tournaments in Zürich and Filderstadt, Germany. A few weeks later, she had to pull out of those tournaments with a groin pull but was adamant in saying she planned to return to tennis as soon as possible.

Elsewhere, the thin, 6-foot-6 Martin, who went to Northwestern University for two years, reached at least the semifinals of three men's Grand Slam tournaments. At the U.S. Open, where he made it to the semis despite playing with a tender groin pull, Martin took the tournament bus every day from his Manhattan hotel to Queens.

Sometimes he took the same bus as his parents. At 24, Martin is just reaching his prime. He didn't burn out on the junior circuit or spend his life at some Florida tennis camp.

Russia's Kafelnikov also seemed to arrive in 1994, as he came close to cracking the Top 10. He can come to the net and he has fluid groundstrokes that remind one of Sampras four years ago.

As it becomes clear that aging tour regulars like Edberg and Boris Becker have probably won their last majors, Martin and Kafelnikov showed they might challenge Sampras and Agassi in the 1995 Grand Slam events.

Pierce and Davenport might provide desperately needed oomph to the women's game in 1995.

With Nick Bollettieri telling Pierce to quit thinking on the court and just hit the ball hard, she proved with her win over Graf in the French Open that she has the game to be No. 1. Pierce hits groundstrokes harder than anyone, though she needs to improve her fitness and her mental toughness. Everybody knows about her abusive father and former coach Jim Pierce, which may be why fans everywhere seem to love her. They also love her emotional openness on the court where she will laugh aloud at her own mistakes.

Davenport, a 6-foot-2 teenager, who didn't get to Wimbledon until two days before the tournament began because she wanted to attend senior week at her high school in California, also needs to get fitter. At the U.S. Open, Pam Shriver said the beefy Davenport could stand to "drop a few pounds" and Davenport agreed, saying she plans to commit herself to a rigorous fitness program.

Shriver noticed something else about Davenport.

"Lindsay's parents are my favorite parents," Shriver said, "and I've never even met them."

Good point.

Thanks to her parents, Davenport waited until she was 18 to join the circuit full-time. She was able to grow up at home and in private instead of on the road and in the spotlight.

Hopefully, that means she will have the longevity and happiness that has so far eluded Capriati. □

THE 1995 INFORMATION PLEASE SPORTS ALMANAC

TENNIS STATISTICS

SEC A

THE SEASON IN REVIEW
1993-1994
MEN • WOMEN • LEADERS

PAGE 747

Tournament Results

Winners of men's and women's pro singles championships from Oct. 31, 1993 through Sept. 18, 1994. See "Updates" for later results.

Men's ATP Tour

LATE 1993

Finals	Tournament	Winner	Earnings	Loser	Score
Oct. 31	Stockholm Open	Michael Stich	$229,000	G. Ivanisevic	46 76 76 62
Nov. 7	Paris Indoor	Goren Ivanisevic	314,000	A. Medvedev	64 62 76
Nov. 7	Sul America Open (São Paulo)	Alberto Berasategui	25,000	C. Dosedel	64 63
Nov. 14	European Community Champs. (Antwerp)	Pete Sampras	155,000	M. Gustafsson	61 64
Nov. 14	Kremlin Cup (Moscow)	Marc Rosset	47,000	P. Kuhnen	64 63
Nov. 14	South American Open (Buenos Aires)	Carlos Costa	42,000	A. Berasategui	36 61 64
Nov. 21	IBM/ATP World Champs. (Frankfort)	Michael Stich	1,240,000	P. Sampras	76 26 76 62
Nov. 28	ATP Doubles Champs. (Johannesburg)	Jacco Eltingh/ Paul Haarhuis	300,000	T. Woodbridge/ M. Woodforde	76 76 64
Dec. 12	ITF Grand Slam Cup (Munich)	Petr Korda	1,625,000	M. Stich	26 64 76 26 119

Note: The Grand Slam Cup is not an ATP Tour event.

1994 (through Sept. 19)

Finals	Tournament	Winner	Earnings	Loser	Score
Jan. 9	Qatar Open (Doha)	Stefan Edberg	$71,000	P. Haarhuis	63 62
Jan. 9	Hawaii Open (Kuala Lumpur)	Wayne Ferreira	42,000	R. Reneberg	64 67 61
Jan. 9	Australian Hardcourt (Adelaide)	Yevgeny Kafelnikov	42,000	A. Volkov	64 63
Jan. 16	The Peters N.S.W. Open T.O.C.(Sydney)	Pete Sampras	42,000	I. Lendl	76 64
Jan. 16	Indonesian Open (Jakarta)	Michael Chang	42,000	D. Rikl	63 63
Jan. 16	Benson & Hedges Open (Auckland)	Magnus Gustafsson	42,000	P. McEnroe	64 60
Jan. 30	Ford **Australian Open** (Melbourne)	Pete Sampras	460,000	T. Martin	76 64 64
Feb. 6	San Jose Open (San Jose)	Renzo Furlan	42,000	M. Chang	36 62 75
Feb. 6	Open 13 (Marseille)	Marc Rosset	73,000	A. Boetsh	76 76
Feb. 6	Dubai Duty Free/BMW Open (UAE)	Magnus Gustafsson	144,000	S. Bruguera	64 62
Feb. 13	Kroger/St.Jude International (Memphis)	Todd Martin	110,500	B. Gilbert	64 75
Feb. 13	Muratti Time Indoor (Milan)	Boris Becker	115,000	P. Korda	62 36 63
Feb. 20	Eurocard Open (Stuttgart)	Stefan Edberg	335,000	G. Ivanisevic	46 64 62 62
Feb. 20	Comcast U.S.Indoor (Philadelphia)	Michael Chang	96,000	P. Haarhuis	63 62
Feb. 27	ABN/AMRO World (Rotterdam)	Michael Stich	82,000	W. Ferreira	46 63 60
Feb. 27	Nuveen Championships (Scottsdale)	Andre Agassi	42,000	L. Mattar	64 63
Feb. 27	Abierto Mexicano (Mexico City)	Thomas Muster	43,000	R. Jabali	63 61
Mar. 6	Newsweek Champions Cup (Indian Wells)	Pete Sampras	244,000	P. Korda	46 63 36 63 62
Mar. 6	Copenhagen Open	Yevgeny Kafelnikov	27,000	D. Vacek	63 75
Mar. 20	Lipton Championships (Key Biscayne)	Pete Sampras	242,000	A. Agassi	57 63 63
Apr. 3	Estoril Open (Lisbon)	Carlos Costa	71,000	A. Medvedev	46 75 64
Apr. 3	Salem Open (Osaka)	Pete Sampras	89,000	L. Roux	62 62
Apr. 3	South African Open (Johannesburg)	Markus Zoecke	42,000	H. Dreekmann	64 61
Apr. 10	Japan Open (Tokyo)	Pete Sampras	156,000	M. Chang	64 62
Apr. 10	Trofeo Conde de Godo (Barcelona)	Richard Krajicek	130,000	C. Costa	64 76 62
Apr. 17	Salem Open (Hong Kong)	Michael Chang	42,600	P. Rafter	61 63
Apr. 17	Philips Open (Nice)	Alberto Berasategui	42,000	J. Courier	64 62
Apr. 17	Diet Pepsi/U.S. Clay Court (Charlotte)	Jason Stoltenberg	42,000	G. Markus	63 64
Apr. 25	Volvo Monte Carlo Open	Andrei Medvedev	235,000	S. Bruguera	75 61 63
Apr. 25	KAL Cup Korea Open (Seoul)	Jeremy Bates	27,000	J. Renzenbrink	64 67 63
May 1	XXII Trofeo Grupo Zeta (Madrid)	Thomas Muster	110,500	S. Bruguera	62 36 64 75
May 1	BMW Open (Munich)	Michael Stich	57,600	P. Korda	62 26 63
May 1	AT&T Challenge (Atlanta)	Michael Chang	42,000	T. Martin	67 76 60

Tournament Results (Cont.)

Finals	Tournament	Winner	Earnings	Loser	Score
May 8	Panasonic German Open (Hamburg)............Andrei Medvedev		$245,000	Y. Kafelnikov	64 64 36 63
May 8	USTA Clay Courts of Tampa.......................Jared Palmer		36,000	T. Martin	64 76
May 15	Mercedes Italian Open (Rome) ....Pete Sampras		280,000	B. Becker	61 62 62
May 15	Americas Red Clay Champ. (Coral Springs)	Luiz Mattar	31,000	J. Morgan	64 36 63
May 22	Peugeot World Team Cup (Dusseldorf)........Germany		450,000	Spain	2-1
May 22	Cassa di Risparmio (Bologna) ....Javier Sanchez		42,000	A. Berasategui	76 46 63
June 5	**French Open** (Paris)...............................Sergi Bruguera		585,185	A. Berasategui	63 75 26 61
June 12	Stella Artois Grass Court (London) ....Todd Martin		86,000	P. Sampras	76 76
June 12	Continental Grass Court (Rosmalen)............Richard Krajicek		42,000	K. Braasch	63 64
June 12	Torneo Internazionale (Florence)................Marcelo Filippini		42,000	R. Fromberg	36 63 63
June 18	The Manchester Open.................................Patrick Rafter		42,000	W. Ferreira	76 76
June 19	Gary Weber Open (Halle) ....Michael Stich		71,000	M. Larsson	64 46 63
June 19	International ÖTV Raiffeisen Grand Prix........Thomas Muster		43,000	T. Carbonell	46 62 64
July 3	**Wimbledon** (London) ....Pete Sampras		504,252	G. Ivanisevic	76 76 60
July 10	Hall of Fame Championships (Newport).......David Wheaton		43,000	T. Woodbridge	64 36 76
July 10	Swedish Open (Bastad)..............................Bernd Karbacher		42,000	H. Skoff	64 63
July 10	Rado Swiss Open (Gstaad)........................Sergi Bruguera		65,000	G. Forget	36 75 62 61
July 24	Mercedes Cup (Stuttgart)...........................Alberto Berasategui		150,000	A. Gaudenzi	75 63 76
July 24	Legg Mason Classic (Washington, D.C.).......Stefan Edberg		87,500	J. Stoltenberg	64 62
July 31	Player's Ltd. Canadian Open (Montreal) ......Andre Agassi		245,000	J. Stoltenberg	64 64
July 31	Dutch Open (Hilversum)............................Karel Novacek		39,600	R. Fromberg	75 64 76
Aug. 7	EA Generali Open (Kitzbuhel).....................Goran Ivanisevic		53,000	F. Santoro	62 46 46 63 62
Aug. 7	Skoda Czechoslovak Open (Prague) ....Sergi Bruguera		49,000	A. Medvedev	63 64
Aug. 7	Los Angeles Open ....Boris Becker		42,000	M. Woodforde	62 62
Aug. 14	San Marino Open ....Carlos Costa		39,600	O. Gross	61 63
Aug. 14	Thriftway ATP Championship (Cincinnati)......Michael Chang		245,000	S. Edberg	62 75
Aug. 21	RCA/U.S. Hardcourts (Indianapolis)............Wayne Ferreira		152,500	O. Delaitre	62 61
Aug. 21	Volvo International (New Haven)..................Boris Becker		152,500	M. Rosset	63 75
Aug. 28	Croatia Open (Umag)................................Alberto Berasategui		54,000	K. Kucera	06 64 63
Aug. 28	Waldbaum's Hamlet Cup (Long Island) ....Yevgeny Kafelnikov		42,000	C. Pioline	57 61 62
Aug. 28	OTB International (Schenectady)..................Jacco Eltingh		42,000	C. Adams	63 64
Sept.12	**U.S. Open** (New York)..........................Andre Agassi		550,000	M. Stich	63 46 62 63
Sept.19	Romanian Open (Bucharest)........................Franco Davin		75,000	G. Ivanisevic	62 64
Sept.19	Grand Prix Passing Shot (Bordeaux) ....Wayne Ferreira		54,000	J. Tarango	60 75

Women's WTA Tour
LATE 1993

Finals	Tournament	Winner	Earnings	Loser	Score
Oct. 31	Nokia Grand Prix (Germany) ....Natalia Medvedeva		$ 75,000	C. Martinez	67 75 64
Oct. 31	Bancesa Classic (Brazil) ....Sabine Hack		18,000	F. Labat	62 60
Nov. 7	Bank of the West Classic (Oakland) ....Martina Navratilova		75,000	Z.G. Jackson	62 76
Nov. 7	Bell Challenge (Quebec City).......................Nathalie Tauziat		27,000	K. Maleeva	64 61
Nov. 15	Va. Slims of Philadelphia ....Conchita Martinez		150,000	S. Graf	63 63
Nov. 20	Va. Slims Doubles Champs. (New York)........Gigi Fernandez/ Natalia Zvereva		90,000	L. Neiland/ J. Novotna	63 75
Nov. 21	Va. Slims Championships (New York) ....Steffi Graf		250,000	A. S. Vicario	61 64 36 61

1994 (through Sept. 19)

Finals	Tournament	Winner	Earnings	Loser	Score
Jan. 9	Danone Australian Hardcourt (Brisbane) ....Lindsay Davenport		$ 27,000	F. Labat	61 26 63
Jan. 15	Tasmanian International Open ....Mana Endo		18,000	R. McQuillan	61 67 64
Jan. 16	New South Wales Open (Sydney) ....Kimiko Date		60,000	M. J. Fernandez	64 62
Jan. 30	Ford **Australian Open** (Melbourne)..........Steffi Graf		309,833	A. Sanchez Vicario	60 62
Feb. 6	Toray Pan Pacific Open (Tokyo)..................Steffi Graf		150,000	M. Navratilova	62 64
Feb. 6	Amway Classic (Auckland)........................Ginger Helgeson		18,000	I. Gorrochategui	76 63
Feb. 13	Va. Slims/Chicago ....Natalia Zvereva		80,000	C. Rubin	63 75
Feb. 13	Asia Open in Osaka ....Man. Maleeva-Fragniere		27,000	I. Majoli	61 46 75
Feb. 13	EA Generali (Linz) ....Sabine Appelmans		27,000	M. Babel	61 46 76
Feb. 20	Open Gaz de France (Paris)........................Martina Navratilova		80,000	J. Halard	75 63
Feb. 20	IGA Classic (Oklahoma City)......................Meredith McGrath		18,000	B. Shultz	76 76
Feb. 20	Nokia Open (Beijing)................................Yayuk Basuki		18,000	K. Nagatsuka	64 62
Feb. 27	The Evert Cup (Indian Wells).....................Steffi Graf		80,000	A. Coetzer	60 64
Mar. 6	Va. Slims/Florida (Delray Beach).................Steffi Graf		80,000	A. S. Vicario	63 75
Mar. 20	Lipton Championships (Key Biscayne) ....Steffi Graf		150,000	N. Zvereva	46 61 62
Mar. 27	Va. Slims/Houston ....Sabine Hack		80,000	M. Pierce	75 64
Mar. 27	Light n' Lively Doubles (Saddlebrook)............Jana Novotna/ A. Sanchez Vicario		65,000	G. Fernandez/ N. Zvereva	62 75

Finals	Tournament	Winner	Earnings	Loser	Score
Apr. 3	Family Circle Cup (Hilton Head)	Conchita Martinez	150,000	N. Zvereva	64 60
Apr. 10	Bausch & Lomb Champs.(Amelia Island)	A. Sanchez Vicario	80,000	G. Sabatini	61 64
Apr. 10	Japan Open (Tokyo)	Kimiko Date	27,000	A. Frazier	75 60
Apr. 17	Volvo Open (Pattaya City, Thailand)	Sabine Appelmans	18,000	P. Fendick	67 76 62
Apr. 24	Internat'l Champ. of Spain (Barcelona)	A. Sanchez Vicario	80,000	I. Majoli	60 62
May 1	Citizen Cup (Hamburg)	A. Sanchez Vicario	80,000	S. Graf	46 76 76
May 1	Ilva Trophy (Taranto, Italy)	Julie Halard	18,000	I. Spirlea	62 63
May 8	Italian Open (Rome)	Conchita Martinez	150,000	M. Navratilova	76 64
May 15	German Open (Berlin)	Steffi Graf	150,000	B. Schultz	76 64
May 15	BVV Prague Open (Prague)	Amanda Coetzer	18,000	A. Carlson	61 76
May 23	Eurocard Open (Lucerne)	Lindsay Davenport	27,000	L. Raymond	76 64
May 23	Strasbourg International	Mary Joe Fernandez	27,000	G. Sabatini	26 64 60
June 5	**French Open** (Paris)	A. Sanchez Vicario	502,857	M. Pierce	64 64
June 12	DFS Classic (Birmingham)	Lori McNeil	27,000	Z.G. Jackson	62 62
June 18	Volkswagen Cup (Eastbourne)	Meredith McGrath	80,000	L. Harvey-Wild	62 64
July 3	**Wimbledon** (London)	Conchita Martinez	464,282	M. Navratilova	64 36 63
July 16	European Champions Cup	A. Sanchez Vicario	120,000	C. Martinez	62 67 63
July 31	Acura/U.S. Hardcourts (Stratton, VT)	Conchita Martinez	80,000	A.S. Vicario	46 63 64
July 31	Styria Open	Anke Huber	18,000	J. Wiesner	63 63
Aug. 7	Toshiba Classic (San Diego)	Steffi Graf	80,000	A.S. Vicario	62 61
Aug. 14	Va. Slims/Los Angeles	Amy Frazier	80,000	A. Grossman	61 63
Aug. 21	Matinee Ltd. Canadian Open (Toronto)	A. Sanchez Vicario	150,000	S. Graff	75 16 76
Aug. 28	OTB Open (Schenectady)	Judith Wiesner	27,000	L. Neiland	75 36 64
Sept.11	**U.S. Open** (New York)	A. Sanchez Vicario	550,000	S. Graf	16 76 64
Sept.19	Digital Open (Hong Kong)				

1994 Grand Slam Tournaments

Australian Open
MEN'S SINGLES

FINAL EIGHT—#1 Pete Sampras; #3 Jim Courier; #4 Stefan Edberg; #5 Goran Ivanisevic; #8 Thomas Muster; #9 Todd Martin; #10 Magnus Gustafsson; plus unseeded MaliVai Washington.

Quarterfinals
Sampras def. Gustafsson		76 (7-4) 26 63 76 (7-4)
Courier def. Ivanisevic		76 (9-7) 64 62
Edberg def. Muster		62 63 64
Martin def. Washington	62 76 (7-4) 76 (7-5)	

Semifinals
Sampras def. Courier	63 64 64
Martin def. Edberg	36 76 (9-7) 76 (9-7) 76 (7-4)

Final
Sampras def. Martin	76 (7-4) 64 64

WOMEN'S SINGLES

FINAL EIGHT— #1 Steffi Graf; #2 Arantxa Sanchez Vicario; #3 Conchita Martinez; #4 Gabriela Sabatini; #5 Jana Novotna; #8 Manuela Maleeva-Fragniere; #10 Kimiko Date; #16 Lindsay Davenport.

Quarterfinals
Graf def. Davenport		63 62
Sanchez Vicario def. Maleeva-Fragniere	76 (7-3) 64	
Sabatini def. Novotna		63 64
Date def. Martinez		62 46 63

Semifinals
Graf def. Date	63 63
Sanchez Vicario def. Sabatini	61 62

Final
Graf def. Sanchez Vicario	60 62

DOUBLES FINALS

Men— #3 Jacco Eltingh & Paul Haarhuis def. #2 Byron Black & Jonathon Stark, 6-7(3-7), 6-3, 6-4, 6-3.

Women— #1 Gigi Fernandez & Natalia Zvereva def. #7 Patty Fendick & Meredith McGrath, 6-3, 4-6, 6-4.

Mixed— #6 Andrei Olhovskiy & Larisa Neiland def. #1 Todd Woodbridge & Helena Sukova, 7-5, 6-7(0-7), 6-2.

French Open
MEN'S SINGLES

FINAL EIGHT—#1 Pete Sampras; #4 Andrei Medvedev; #5 Goran Ivanisevic; #6 Sergi Bruguera; #7 Jim Courier; plus unseeded Alberto Berasategui, Hendrik Dreekmann and Magnus Larsson.

Quarterfinals
Courier def. Sampras	64 57 64 64
Bruguera def. Medvedev	63 62 75
Berasategui def. Ivanisevic	64 63 63
Larsson def. Dreekmann	36 67 (1-7) 76 (7-3) 60 61

Semifinals
Bruguera def. Courier	63 57 63 63
Berasategui def. Larsson	63 64 61

Final
Bruguera def. Berasategui	63 75 26 61

WOMEN'S SINGLES

FINAL EIGHT—#1 Steffi Graf; #2 Arantxa Sanchez Vicario; #3 Conchita Martinez; #12 Mary Pierce; #16 Sabine Hack; plus unseeded Ines Gorrochategui, Julie Halard and Petra Ritter.

Quarterfinals
Graf def. Gorrochategui	64 61
Sanchez Vicario def. Halard	61 76 (8-6)
Martinez def. Hack	26 60 62
Pierce def. Ritter	60 62

Semifinals
Pierce def. Graf	62 62
Sanchez Vicario def. Martinez	63 61

Final
Sanchez Vicario def. Pierce	64 64

DOUBLES FINALS

Men— #2 Byron Black & Jonathan Stark def. #12 Jan Apell & Jonas Bjorkman, 6-4, 7-6 (7-5).

Women— #1 Gigi Fernandez & Natalia Zvereva def. #11 Lindsay Davenport & Lisa Raymond, 6-2, 6-2.

Mixed— (Unseeded) Kristie Boogert & Ned Oosting def. #7 Larisa Neiland & Andrei Olhovskiy, 7-5, 3-6, 7-5.

1994 Grand Slam Tournaments (Cont.)

Wimbledon

MEN'S SINGLES

FINAL EIGHT—#1 Pete Sampras; #4 Goran Ivanisevic; #6 Todd Martin; #7 Boris Becker; #10 Michael Chang; plus unseeded Christian Bergstrom, Wayne Ferreira and Guy Forget.

Quarterfinals

Sampras def. Chang	64 61 63
Ivanisevic def. Forget	76 (7-3) 76 (7-3) 64
Martin def. Ferriera	63 62 36 57 75
Becker def. Bergstrom	76 (7-5) 64 63

Semifinals

Sampras def. Martin	64 64 36 63
Ivanisevic def. Becker	62 76 (8-6) 64

Final

Sampras def. Ivanisevic	76 (7-2) 76 (7-5) 60

WOMEN'S SINGLES

FINAL EIGHT—#3 Conchita Martinez; #4 Martina Navratilova; #5 Jana Novotna; #9 Lindsay Davenport; #13 Zina Garrison Jackson; plus unseeded Gigi Fernandez, Lori McNeil and Larisa Neiland.

Quarterfinals

McNeil def. Neiland	63 64
Martinez def. Davenport	62 67 (4-7) 63
Navratilova def. Novotna	57 60 61
Fernandez def. Garrison Jackson	64 64

Semifinals

Martinez def. McNeil	36 62 108
Navratilova def. Fernandez	64 76 (8-6)

Final

Martinez def. Navratilova	64 36 63

DOUBLES FINALS

Men— #5 Todd Woodbridge & Mark Woodforde def. #2 Grant Connell & Patric Galbraith, 7-6(7-3), 6-3, 6-1.

Women— #1 Gigi Fernandez & Natalia Zvereva def. #2 Jana Novotna & Arantxa Sanchez Vicario, 6-4, 6-1.

Mixed— #4 Todd Woodbridge & Helena Sukova def. (unseeded) T.J. Middleton & Lori McNeil, 3-6, 7-5, 6-3.

U.S. Open

MEN'S SINGLES

FINAL EIGHT— #4 Michael Stich; #9 Todd Martin; #13 Thomas Muster; plus unseeded Andre Agassi, Jonas Bjorkman, Bernd Karbacher, Karel Novacek and Jaime Yzaga.

Quarterfinals

Stich def. Bjorkman	64 64 67 (7-9) 63
Martin def. Karbacher	62 46 63 62
Agassi def. Muster	76 (7-5) 63 60
Novacek def. Yzaga	62 67 (7-9) 61 57 63

Semifinals

Stich def. Novacek	75 63 76 (7-4)
Agassi def. Martin	63 46 62 63

Final

Agassi def. Stich	61 76 (7-5) 75

WOMEN'S SINGLES

FINAL EIGHT—#1 Steffi Graf; #2 Arantxa Sanchez Vicario; #4 Mary Pierce; #5 Kimiko Date; #7 Jana Novotna; #8 Gabriela Sabatini; #11 Amanda Coetzer; plus unseated Gigi Fernandez.

Quarterfinals

Graf def. Coetzer	60 62
Sanchez Vicario def. Date	63 60
Novotna def. Pierce	64 60
Sabatini def. Fernandez	62 75

Semifinals

Graf def. Novotna	63 75
Sanchez Vicario def. Sabatini	61 76 (8-6)

Final

Sanchez Vicario def. Graf	16 76 (7-3) 64

DOUBLES FINALS

Men—#3 Jacco Eltingh & Paul Haarhuis def. #4 Todd Woodbridge & Mark Woodforde 6-3, 7-6 (7-4).

Women—#2 Jana Novotna & Arantxa Sanchez Vicario def. Katerina Maleeva & Robin White 7-6 (7-3), 6-2.

Mixed— #8 Elna Reinach & Patrick Galbraith def. #1 Jana Novotna & Todd Woodbridge 6-2, 6-4.

Clive Brunskill/Allsport

Martina Navratilova waves goodbye to Wimbledon's centre court after failing in her bid to win a 10th women's singles title against Conchita Martinez on July 2.

Singles Leaders

Official Top 20 computer rankings and money leaders of men's and women's tours for 1993 and unofficial rankings and money leaders for 1994 (through Sept.19), as compiled by the ATP (Association of Tennis Professionals) and WTA (Women's Tennis Association). Note that money list includes doubles earnings.

Final 1993 Computer Rankings and Money Won

Listed are tournaments won and times a finalist and semifinalist (Finish, 1-2-SF), match record (W-L), and earnings for the year.

MEN

	Finish 1-2-SF	W-L	Earnings
1 Pete Sampras	8-1-6	83-15	$3,648,075
2 Michael Stich	6-2-1	73-24	2,936,521
3 Jim Courier	5-3-1	58-17	3,584,321
4 Sergi Bruguera	5-4-0	64-24	1,447,484
5 Stefan Edberg	1-3-6	59-25	2,309,509
6 Andrei Medvedev	3-2-4	57-24	1,301,143
7 Goran Ivanisevic	3-3-3	54-21	1,818,897
8 Michael Chang	6-2-0	65-20	1,743,524
9 Thomas Muster	7-2-5	77-20	805,066
10 Cedric Pioline	0-5-2	51-26	841,239
11 Boris Becker	2-1-3	41-19	1,765,839
12 Petr Korda	0-2-5	50-23	1,517,229
13 Todd Martin	1-4-2	45-22	642,108
14 Magnus Gustafsson	1-3-4	52-30	605,490
15 Richard Krajicek	1-1-1	35-22	729,753
16 Marc Rosset	3-0-3	49-22	622,733
17 Karel Novacek	2-3-1	43-25	682,306
18 Alexander Volkov	1-0-5	44-29	568,300
19 Ivan Lendl	2-2-0	33-23	1,075,876
20 Arnaud Boetsch	2-0-2	46-26	532,831

WOMEN

	Finish 1-2-SF	W-L	Earnings
1 Steffi Graf	10-4-1	76-6	$2,821,337
2 A. Sanchez Vicario	4-5-7	77-14	1,938,239
3 Martina Navratilova	5-2-1	46-8	1,036,119
4 Conchita Martinez	5-3-5	71-13	1,208,795
5 Gabriela Sabatini	0-3-6	51-18	957,680
6 Jana Novotna	2-2-5	47-17	926,646
7 Mary Joe Fernandez	1-1-3	34-13	611,681
8 Monica Seles	2-1-0	17-2	437,588
9 Jennifer Capriati	1-1-1	29-11	357,108
10 Anke Huber	1-2-3	42-15	469,327
11 M. Maleeva-Fragniere	2-0-4	36-16	561,320
12 Mary Pierce	1-1-2	38-15	347,360
13 Kimiko Date	1-2-1	24-11	229,326
14 Zina Garrison Jackson	2-3-1	43-19	438,797
15 Amanda Coetzer	2-1-3	42-19	478,108
16 Magdalena Maleeva	0-1-2	38-16	286,034
17 Helena Sukova	0-1-1	26-16	655,573
18 Nathalie Tauziat	1-0-2	44-19	351,208
19 Natalia Zvereva	0-1-0	37-19	857,160
20 Lindsay Davenport	1-0-1	38-16	201,409

Note: ITF Grand Slam Cup statistics are considered unofficial by the ATP and not included here.

1994 Computer Rankings (through Sept.19)

For Men's Tour, listed are tournaments won and times a finalist and semifinalist (Finish, 1-2-SF), match record (W-L), and computer points earned (Pts). For Women's Tour, listed are tournaments won and times a finalist and semifinalist (Finish, 1-2-SF), match record (W-L), and average computer points per game (Avg).

MEN

ATP/IBM singles rankings based on total computer points from each player's 14 best tournaments covering the last 12 months. Tournaments, titles and match won-lost records, however, are for 1994 only.

Rank 94 (93)	Finish 1-2-SF	W-L	Pts
1 (1) Pete Sampras	8-1-0	61-8	4884
2 (2) Michael Stich	3-1-4	52-19	3272
3 (7) Goran Ivanisevic	1-3-3	49-19	3170
4 (4) Sergi Bruguera	3-3-2	58-18	2776
5 (5) Stefan Edberg	3-1-3	52-18	2767
6 (13) Todd Martin	2-3-3	46-15	2492
7 (11) Boris Becker	3-1-3	33-12	2374
8 (8) Michael Chang	5-2-0	52-15	2364
9 (36) Alberto Berasategui	3-2-1	43-20	2163
10 (24) Andre Agassi	3-1-1	36-11	2132
11 (6) Andrei Medvedev	2-2-0	31-13	2069
12 (104) Yevgeny Kafelnikov	3-1-4	57-21	1992
13 (22) Wayne Ferreira	3-2-3	55-21	1901
14 (3) Jim Courier	0-1-5	42-16	1811
15 (9) Thomas Muster	3-0-0	51-18	1744
16 (12) Petr Korda	0-3-0	31-17	1536
17 (14) Marc Rosset	1-1-2	33-22	1485
18 (14) Magnus Gustafsson	1-0-0	30-11	1433
19 (30) Jaime Yzaga	0-0-2	32-23	1389
20 (26) Carlos Costa	2-1-0	37-21	1310

WOMEN

WTA/Va.Slims Slimstat singles rankings based on average computer points awarded for each tournament played during the last 12 months. Tournaments, titles and match won-lost records, however, are for 1994 only.

Rank 94 (93)	Finish 1-2-SF	W-L	Pts
1 (1) Steffi Graf	7-3-1	57-5	351.5
2 (2) A.Sanchez Vicario	7-4-0	70-8	302.6
3 (4) Conchita Martinez	4-0-3	50-10	214.2
4 (3) Martina Navratilova	1-3-1	26-10	155.9
5 (12) Mary Pierce	0-2-2	29-13	142.1
6 (6) Jana Novotna	0-0-3	27-10	140.1
7 (20) Lindsay Davenport	2-0-3	42-12	122.7
8 (5) Gabriela Sabatini	0-2-4	35-15	120.2
9 (13) Kimiko Date	2-0-3	31-13	114.8
10 (19) Natalia Zvereva	1-2-1	23-8	111.8
11 (7) Mary Joe Fernandez	1-1-0	25-9	97.8
12 (14) Z. Garrison-Jackson	0-1-1	21-12	88.1
13 (16) Magdalena Maleeva	0-0-3	28-12	81.1
14 (39) Amy Frazier	1-2-2	26-13	78.2
15 (15) Amanda Coetzer	1-1-2	35-15	77.1
16 (24) Sabine Hack	1-0-2	34-15	72.6
17 (25) Lori McNeil	1-0-2	23-12	71.8
18 (10) Anke Huber	1-0-1	23-12	71.5
19 (36) Sabine Appelmans	2-0-3	28-13	66.4
20 (56) Ines Gorrochategui	0-1-0	23-10	65.9

Singles Leaders (Cont.)
1994 Money Winners
Amounts include singles and doubles earnings.

MEN

	Earnings		Earnings		Earnings
1 Pete Sampras	$2,106,312	8 Wayne Ferreira	$847,041	15 Paul Haarhuis	$612,016
2 Sergi Bruguera	1,421,074	9 Boris Becker	836,223	16 Jacco Eltingh	610,994
3 Michael Stich	1,216,591	10 Yevgeny Kafelnikov	810,093	17 Thomas Muster	581,604
4 Andre Agassi	1,106,300	11 Todd Martin	799,717	18 Mark Woodforde	547,004
5 Stefan Edberg	1,100,686	12 Andrei Medvedev	753,434	19 Carlos Costa	540,818
6 Goran Ivanisevic	975,703	13 Alberto Berasategui	725,951	20 Karel Novacek	538,114
7 Michael Chang	847,095	14 Jim Courier	631,084		

WOMEN

	Earnings		Earnings		Earnings
1 A. Sanchez Vicario	$2,054,665	8 Mary Pierce	$455,414	15 Larisa Neiland	$281,637
2 Steffi Graf	1,461,980	9 Gabriela Sabatini	425,070	16 Julie Halard	276,273
3 Conchita Martinez	1,055,692	10 Lindsay Davenport	391,120	17 Sabine Hack	264,296
4 Natalia Zvereva	650,567	11 Kimiko Date	323,904	18 Amy Frazier	222,742
5 Gigi Fernandez	590,050	12 Amanda Coetzer	307,741	19 Iva Majoli	222,652
6 Jana Novotna	567,119	13 Meredith McGrath	306,592	20 Brenda Schultz	221,746
7 Martina Navratilova	525,132	14 Lori McNeil	299,246		

National Team Competition
Davis Cup

Germany won its third Davis Cup in 1993, beating Australia by a 4-1 score in Dusseldorf, Dec. 3-5. Michael Stich led the way for the Germans, clinching the championship with a 6-4, 6-2, 6-2, victory over Richard Fromberg for an unbeatable 3-1 lead. Boris Becker, who sparked West Germany to back-to-back wins in 1988-89, did not compete in 1993.

1993 Final

Germany 4, Australia 1
(December 3-5, at Dusseldorf, Germany)

Day One— Michael Stich (GER) def. Jason Stoltenberg (AUS), 6-7 (2-7), 6-3, 6-1, 4-6, 6-3; Richard Fromberg (AUS) def. Marc Goellner (GER), 3-6, 5-7, 7-6 (9-7), 6-2, 9-7.

Day Two— Patrik Kuhnen & Michael Stich (GER) def. Todd Woodbridge & Mark Woodforde (AUS), 7-6 (7-4), 4-6, 6-3, 7-6 (7-4).

Day Three— Stich (GER) def. Fromberg (AUS), 6-4, 6-2, 6-2; Goellner (GER) def. Stoltenberg (AUS), 6-1, 6-7 (2-7), 7-6 (7-3).

1994 Early Rounds

Russia will host Sweden in the Davis Cup final, Dec. 2-4, in Moscow. The Swedes have won the Cup four times (1975, 1984-85 and 1987) while the Russians have never reached the final round before.

1st ROUND
(Mar. 25-27)

Winner	Loser
United States 5	at India 0
Netherlands 5	at Belgium 0
Sweden 5	at Denmark 0
France 4	at Hungary 1
at Czech. Republic 4	Israel 1
Russia 4	Australia 1
at Spain 4	Italy 1
at Germany 3	Austria 2

QUARTERFINALS
(July 15-17)

Winner	Loser
United States 3	at Netherlands 2
Sweden 3	at France 2
at Russia 3	Czech. Republic 2
at Germany 3	Spain 2

SEMIFINALS

Sweden 3, United States 2
(Sept. 23-25, at Göteborg, Sweden)

Day One— Todd Martin (USA) def. Stephan Edberg (SWE), 6-2, 2-6, 6-4, 6-3; Pete Sampras (USA) def. Magnus Larsson (SWE), 6-7 (3-7), 6-4, 6-2, 7-6 (7-3).

Day Two— Jan Apell & Jonas Bjorkman (SWE) def. Jared Palmer & Jonathan Stark (USA), 6-4, 6-4, 3-6, 6-2.

Day Three— Edberg (SWE) def. Sampras (USA), 6-3, retired; Larsson (SWE) def. Martin (USA) 5-7, 6-2, 6-2, 6-4.

Russia 4, Germany 1
(Sept. 23-25, at Hamburg, Germany)

Day One— Yevgeny Kafelnikov (RUS) def. Bernd Karbacher (GER), 7-6(7-2), 6-1, 2-6, 6-4; Alexander Volkov(RUS) def. Michael Stich (GER), 7-5, 1-6, 7-6 (7-5), 6-4.

Day Two— Kafelnikov & Andrei Olhovskiy (RUS) def. Stich & Karsten Braasch (GER), 6-4, 7-6 (7-1), 3-6, 6-7(3-7), 10-8.

Day Three— Kafelnikov (RUS) def. Stich (GER), 7-5, 6-3; Karbacher (GER) def. Volkov (RUS), 6-4, 6-1.

FINAL
Moscow, Russia (Dec. 2-4)

1994 Federation Cup

Spain defeated the United States, 3-0, to win the Women's Federation Cup for the third time. This week-long tournament featuring 32 international teams was held in Frankfurt, July 18-24.

FINAL

Spain 3, United States 0

Singles— Conchita Martinez (SPA) def. Mary Joe Fernandez (USA), 6-2, 6-2; Arantxa Sanchez Vicario (SPA) def. Lindsay Davenport (USA), 6-2, 6-1.

Doubles— Conchita Martinez & Arantxa Sanchez Vicario (SPA) def. Gigi Fernandez & Mary Joe Fernandez (USA), 6-3, 6-4.

Grand Slam Championships
Australian Open
MEN

Became an Open Championship in 1969. Two tournaments were held in 1977; the first in January, the second in December. Tournament moved back to January in 1987, so no championship was decided in 1986.

Surface: Synpave Rebound Ace (hardcourt surface composed of polyurethane and synthetic rubber).

Multiple winners: Roy Emerson (6); Jack Crawford and Ken Rosewall (4); James Anderson, Rod Laver, Adrian Quist, Mats Wilander and Pat Wood (3); Jack Bromwich, Ashley Cooper, Jim Courier, Stefan Edberg, Rodney Heath, Johan Kriek, Ivan Lendl, John Newcombe, Frank Sedgman, Guillermo Vilas and Tony Wilding (2).

Year	Winner	Loser	Score	Year	Winner	Loser	Score
1905	Rodney Heath	A. Curtis	46 63 64 64	1954	Mervyn Rose	R. Hartwig	62 06 64 62
1906	Tony Wilding	H. Parker	60 64 64	1955	Ken Rosewall	L. Hoad	97 64 64
1907	Horace Rice	H. Parker	63 64 64	1956	Lew Hoad	K. Rosewall	64 36 64 75
1908	Fred Alexander	A. Dunlop	36 36 60 62 63	1957	Ashley Cooper	N. Fraser	63 9-11 64 62
1909	Tony Wilding	E. Parker	61 75 62	1958	Ashley Cooper	M. Anderson	75 63 64
				1959	Alex Olmedo	N. Fraser	61 63 63
1910	Rodney Heath	H. Rice	64 63 62	1960	Rod Laver	N. Fraser	57 36 63 86 86
1911	Norman Brookes	H. Rice	61 62 63	1961	Roy Emerson	R. Laver	16 63 75 64
1912	J. Cecil Parke	A. Beamish	36 63 16 61 75	1962	Rod Laver	R. Emerson	86 06 64 64
1913	Ernie Parker	H. Parker	26 61 62 63	1963	Roy Emerson	K. Fletcher	63 63 61
1914	Pat Wood	G. Patterson	64 63 57 61	1964	Roy Emerson	F. Stolle	63 64 62
1915	Francis Lowe	H. Rice	46 61 61 64	1965	Roy Emerson	F. Stolle	79 26 64 75 61
1916-18	Not held	World War I		1966	Roy Emerson	A. Ashe	64 68 62 63
1919	A.R.F. Kingscote	E. Pockley	64 60 63	1967	Roy Emerson	A. Ashe	64 61 61
				1968	Bill Bowrey	J. Gisbert	75 26 97 64
1920	Pat Wood	R. Thomas	63 46 68 61 63	1969	Rod Laver	A. Gimeno	63 64 75
1921	Rhys Gemmell	A. Hedeman	75 61 64	1970	Arthur Ashe	D. Crealy	64 97 62
1922	James Anderson	G. Patterson	60 36 36 63 62	1971	Ken Rosewall	A. Ashe	61 75 63
1923	Pat Wood	C.B. St. John	61 61 63	1972	Ken Rosewall	M. Anderson	76 63 75
1924	James Anderson	R. Schlesinger	63 64 36 57 63	1973	John Newcombe	O. Parun	63 67 75 61
1925	James Anderson	G. Patterson	11-9 26 62 63	1974	Jimmy Connors	P. Dent	76 64 46 63
1926	John Hawkes	J. Willard	61 63 61	1975	John Newcombe	J. Connors	75 36 64 75
1927	Gerald Patterson	J. Hawkes	36 64 36 18-16 63	1976	Mark Edmondson	J. Newcombe	67 63 76 61
1928	Jean Borotra	R.O. Cummings	64 61 46 57 63	1977	Roscoe Tanner	G. Vilas	63 63 63
1929	John Gregory	R. Schlesinger	62 62 57 75		Vitas Gerulaitis	J. Lloyd	63 76 57 36 62
1930	Gar Moon	H. Hopman	63 61 63	1978	Guillermo Vilas	J. Marks	64 64 36 63
1931	Jack Crawford	H. Hopman	64 62 26 61	1979	Guillermo Vilas	J. Sadri	76 63 62
1932	Jack Crawford	H. Hopman	46 63 36 63 61	1980	Brian Teacher	K. Warwick	75 76 63
1933	Jack Crawford	K. Gledhill	26 75 63 62	1981	Johan Kriek	S. Denton	62 76 67 64
1934	Fred Perry	J. Crawford	63 75 61	1982	Johan Kriek	S. Denton	63 63 62
1935	Jack Crawford	F. Perry	26 64 64 64	1983	Mats Wilander	I. Lendl	61 64 64
1936	Adrian Quist	J. Crawford	62 63 46 36 97	1984	Mats Wilander	K. Curren	67 64 76 62
1937	Viv McGrath	J. Bromwich	63 16 60 26 61	1985	Stefan Edberg	M. Wilander	64 63 63
1938	Don Budge	J. Bromwich	64 62 61	1986	Not held		
1939	Jack Bromwich	A. Quist	64 61 63	1987	Stefan Edberg	P. Cash	63 64 36 57 63
1940	Adrian Quist	J. Crawford	63 61 62	1988	Mats Wilander	P. Cash	63 67 36 61 86
1941-45	Not held	World War II		1989	Ivan Lendl	M. Mecir	62 62 62
1946	Jack Bromwich	D. Pails	57 63 75 36 62	1990	Ivan Lendl	S. Edberg	46 76 52 (ret)
1947	Dinny Pails	J. Bromwich	46 64 36 75 86	1991	Boris Becker	I. Lendl	16 64 64 64
1948	Adrian Quist	J. Bromwich	64 36 63 26 63	1992	Jim Courier	S. Edberg	63 36 64 62
1949	Frank Sedgman	J. Bromwich	63 63 62	1993	Jim Courier	S. Edberg	62 61 26 75
1950	Frank Sedgman	K. McGregor	63 64 46 61	1994	Pete Sampras	T. Martin	76 64 64
1951	Dick Savitt	K. McGregor	63 26 63 61				
1952	Ken McGregor	F. Sedgman	75 12-10 26 62				
1953	Ken Rosewall	M. Rose	60 63 64				

Grand Slam Championships (Cont.)
Australian Open
WOMEN

Became an Open Championship in 1969. Two tournaments were held in 1977, the first in January, the second in December. Tournament moved back to January in 1987, so no championship was decided in 1986.

Multiple winners: Margaret Smith Court (11); Nancye Wynne Bolton (6); Daphne Akhurst (5); Evonne Goolagong Cawley and Steffi Graf (4); Jean Hartigan, Martina Navratilova and Monica Seles (3); Coral Buttsworth, Chris Evert Lloyd, Thelma Long, Hana Mandlikova, Mall Molesworth and Mary Carter Reitano (2).

Year	Winner	Loser	Score	Year	Winner	Loser	Score
1922	Mall Molesworth	E. Boyd	63 10-8	1962	Margaret Smith	J. Lehane	60 62
1923	Mall Molesworth	E. Boyd	61 75	1963	Margaret Smith	J. Lehane	62 62
1924	Sylvia Lance	E. Boyd	63 36 64	1964	Margaret Smith	L. Turner	63 62
1925	Daphne Akhurst	E. Boyd	16 86 64	1965	Margaret Smith	M. Bueno	57 64 52 (ret)
1926	Daphne Akhurst	E. Boyd	61 63	1966	Margaret Smith	N. Richey	walkover
1927	Esna Boyd	S. Harper	57 61 62	1967	Nancy Richey	L. Turner	61 64
1928	Daphne Akhurst	E. Boyd	75 62	1968	Billie Jean King	M. Smith	61 62
1929	Daphne Akhurst	L. Bickerton	61 57 62	1969	Margaret Court	B.J. King	64 61
1930	Daphne Akhurst	S. Harper	10-8 26 75	1970	Margaret Court	K. Melville	61 63
1931	Coral Buttsworth	M. Crawford	16 63 64	1971	Margaret Court	E. Goolagong	26 76 75
1932	Coral Buttsworth	K. Le Messurier	97 64	1972	Virginia Wade	E. Goolagong	64 64
1933	Joan Hartigan	C. Buttsworth	64 63	1973	Margaret Court	E. Goolagong	64 75
1934	Joan Hartigan	M. Molesworth	61 64	1974	Evonne Goolagong	C. Evert	76 46 60
1935	Dorothy Round	N. Lyle	16 61 63	1975	Evonne Goolagong	M. Navratilova	63 62
1936	Joan Hartigan	N. Bolton	64 64	1976	Evonne Cawley	R. Tomanova	62 62
1937	Nancye Wynne	E. Westacott	63 57 64	1977	Kerry Reid	D. Balestrat	75 62
1938	Dorothy Bundy	D. Stevenson	63 62		Evonne Cawley	H. Gourlay	63 60
1939	Emily Westacott	N. Hopman	61 62	1978	Chris O'Neill	B. Nagelsen	63 76
				1979	Barbara Jordan	S. Walsh	63 63
1940	Nancye Wynne	T. Coyne	57 64 60				
1941-45	Not held	World War II		1980	Hana Mandlikova	W. Turnbull	60 75
1946	Nancye Bolton	J. Fitch	64 64	1981	Martina Navratilova	C. Evert Lloyd	67 64 75
1947	Nancye Bolton	N. Hopman	63 62	1982	Chris Evert Lloyd	M. Navratilova	63 26 63
1948	Nancye Bolton	M. Toomey	63 61	1983	Martina Navratilova	K. Jordan	62 76
1949	Doris Hart	N. Bolton	63 64	1984	Chris Evert Lloyd	H. Sukova	67 61 63
				1985	Martina Navratilova	C. Evert Lloyd	62 46 62
1950	Louise Brough	D. Hart	64 36 64	1986	Not held		
1951	Nancye Bolton	T. Long	61 75	1987	Hana Mandlikova	M. Navratilova	75 76
1952	Thelma Long	H. Angwin	62 63	1988	Steffi Graf	C. Evert	61 76
1953	Maureen Connolly	J. Sampson	63 62	1989	Steffi Graf	H. Sukova	64 64
1954	Thelma Long	J. Staley	63 64				
1955	Beryl Penrose	T. Long	64 63	1990	Steffi Graf	M.J. Fernandez	63 64
1956	Mary Carter	T. Long	36 62 97	1991	Monica Seles	J. Novotna	57 63 61
1957	Shirley Fry	A. Gibson	63 64	1992	Monica Seles	M.J. Fernandez	62 63
1958	Angela Mortimer	L. Coghlan	63 64	1993	Monica Seles	S. Graf	46 63 62
1959	Mary Reitano	T. Schuurman	62 63	1994	Steffi Graf	A.S. Vicario	60 62
1960	Margaret Smith	J. Lehane	75 62				
1961	Margaret Smith	J. Lehane	61 64				

French Open
MEN

Prior to 1925, entry was restricted to members of French clubs. Became an Open Championship in 1968, but closed to contract pros in 1972.

Surface: Red clay.

First year: 1891. **Most wins:** Max Decugis (8).

Multiple winners (since 1925): Bjorn Borg (6); Henri Cochet (4); Rene Lacoste, Ivan Lendl and Mats Wilander (3); Sergi Bruguera, Jim Courier, Jaroslav Drobny, Roy Emerson, Jan Kodes, Rod Laver, Frank Parker, Nicola Pietrangeli, Ken Rosewall, Manuel Santana, Tony Trabert and Gottfried von Cramm (2).

Year	Winner	Loser	Score	Year	Winner	Loser	Score
1925	Rene Lacoste	J. Borotra	75 61 64	1935	Fred Perry	G. von Cramm	63 36 61 63
1926	Henri Cochet	R. Lacoste	62 64 63	1936	Gottfried von Cramm	F. Perry	60 26 62 26 60
1927	Rene Lacoste	B. Tilden	64 46 57 63 11-9	1937	Henner Henkel	H. Austin	61 64 63
1928	Henri Cochet	R. Lacoste	57 63 61 63	1938	Don Budge	R. Menzel	63 62 64
1929	Rene Lacoste	J. Borotra	63 26 60 26 86	1939	Don McNeill	B. Riggs	75 60 63
1930	Henri Cochet	B. Tilden	36 86 63 61	1940-45	Not held	World War II	
1931	Jean Borotra	C. Boussus	26 64 75 64	1946	Marcel Bernard	J. Drobny	36 26 61 64 63
1932	Henri Cochet	G. de Stefani	60 64 46 63	1947	Joseph Asboth	E. Sturgess	86 75 64
1933	Jack Crawford	H. Cochet	86 61 63	1948	Frank Parker	J. Drobny	64 75 57 86
1934	Gottfried von Cramm	J. Crawford	64 79 36 75 63	1949	Frank Parker	B. Patty	63 16 61 64

Year	Winner	Loser	Score	Year	Winner	Loser	Score
1950	Budge Patty	J. Drobny	61 62 36 57 75	1973	Ilie Nastase	N. Pilic	63 63 60
1951	Jaroslav Drobny	E. Sturgess	63 63 63	1974	Bjorn Borg	M. Orantes	26 67 60 61 61
1952	Jaroslav Drobny	F. Sedgman	62 60 36 64	1975	Bjorn Borg	G. Vilas	62 63 64
1953	Ken Rosewall	V. Seixas	63 64 16 62	1976	Adriano Panatta	H. Solomon	61 64 46 76
1954	Tony Trabert	A. Larsen	64 75 61	1977	Guillermo Vilas	B. Gottfried	60 63 60
1955	Tony Trabert	S. Davidson	26 61 64 62	1978	Bjorn Borg	G. Vilas	61 61 63
1956	Lew Hoad	S. Davidson	64 86 63	1979	Bjorn Borg	V. Pecci	63 61 67 64
1957	Sven Davidson	H. Flam	63 64 64				
1958	Mervyn Rose	L. Ayala	63 64 64	1980	Bjorn Borg	V. Gerulaitis	64 61 62
1959	Nicola Pietrangeli	I. Vermaak	36 63 64 61	1981	Bjorn Borg	I. Lendl	61 46 62 36 61
				1982	Mats Wilander	G. Vilas	16 76 60 64
1960	Nicola Pietrangeli	L. Ayala	36 63 64 46 63	1983	Yannick Noah	M. Wilander	62 75 76
1961	Manuel Santana	N. Pietrangeli	46 61 36 60 62	1984	Ivan Lendl	J. McEnroe	36 26 64 75 75
1962	Rod Laver	R. Emerson	36 26 63 97 62	1985	Mats Wilander	I. Lendl	36 64 62 62
1963	Roy Emerson	P. Darmon	36 61 64 64	1986	Ivan Lendl	M. Pernfors	63 62 64
1964	Manuel Santana	N. Pietrangeli	63 61 46 75	1987	Ivan Lendl	M. Wilander	75 62 36 76
1965	Fred Stolle	T. Roche	36 60 62 63	1988	Mats Wilander	H. Leconte	75 62 61
1966	Tony Roche	I. Gulyas	61 64 75	1989	Michael Chang	S. Edberg	61 36 46 64 62
1967	Roy Emerson	T. Roche	61 64 26 62				
1968	Ken Rosewall	R. Laver	63 61 26 62	1990	Andres Gomez	A. Agassi	63 26 64 64
1969	Rod Laver	K. Rosewall	64 63 64	1991	Jim Courier	A. Agassi	36 64 26 61 64
				1992	Jim Courier	P. Korda	75 62 61
1970	Jan Kodes	Z. Franulovic	62 64 60	1993	Sergi Bruguera	J. Courier	64 26 62 36 63
1971	Jan Kodes	I. Nastase	86 62 26 75	1994	Sergi Bruguera	A. Berasategui	63 75 26 61
1972	Andres Gimeno	P. Proisy	46 63 61 61				

WOMEN

Prior to 1925, entry was restricted to members of French clubs. Became an Open Championship in 1968, but closed to contract pros in 1972.

First year: 1897. **Most wins:** Chris Evert Lloyd (7) and Suzanne Lenglen (6).

Multiple winners (since 1920): Chris Evert Lloyd (7); Margaret Smith Court (5); Helen Wills Moody (4); Steffi Graf, Monica Seles and Hilde Sperling (3); Maureen Connolly, Margaret Osborne duPont, Doris Hart, Ann Haydon Jones, Suzanne Lenglen, Simone Mathieu, Margaret Scriven, Martina Navratilova, Lesley Turner and Arantxa Sanchez Vicario (2).

Year	Winner	Loser	Score	Year	Winner	Loser	Score
1925	Suzanne Lenglen	K. McKane	61 62	1963	Lesley Turner	A. Jones	26 63 75
1926	Suzanne Lenglen	M. Browne	61 60	1964	Margaret Smith	M. Bueno	57 61 62
1927	Kea Bouman	I. Peacock	62 64	1965	Lesley Turner	M. Smith	63 64
1928	Helen Wills	E. Bennett	61 62	1966	Ann Jones	N. Richey	63 61
1929	Helen Wills	S. Mathieu	63 64	1967	Francoise Durr	L. Turner	46 63 64
				1968	Nancy Richey	A. Jones	57 64 61
1930	Helen Moody	H. Jacobs	62 61	1969	Margaret Court	A. Jones	61 46 63
1931	Cilly Aussem	B. Nuthall	86 61				
1932	Helen Moody	S. Mathieu	75 61	1970	Margaret Court	H. Niessen	62 64
1933	Margaret Scriven	S. Mathieu	62 46 64	1971	Evonne Goolagong	H. Gourlay	63 75
1934	Margaret Scriven	H. Jacobs	75 46 61	1972	Billie Jean King	E. Goolagong	63 63
1935	Hilde Sperling	S. Mathieu	62 61	1973	Margaret Court	C. Evert	67 76 64
1936	Hilde Sperling	S. Mathieu	63 64	1974	Chris Evert	O. Morozova	61 62
1937	Hilde Sperling	S. Mathieu	62 64	1975	Chris Evert	M. Navratilova	26 62 61
1938	Simone Mathieu	N. Landry	60 63	1976	Sue Barker	R. Tomanova	62 06 62
1939	Simone Mathieu	J. Jedrzejowska	63 86	1977	Mima Jausovec	F. Mihai	62 67 61
				1978	Virginia Ruzici	M. Jausovec	62 62
1940-45	Not held	World War II		1979	Chris Evert Lloyd	W. Turnbull	62 60
1946	Margaret Osborne	P. Betz	16 86 75				
1947	Patricia Todd	D. Hart	63 36 64	1980	Chris Evert Lloyd	V. Ruzici	60 63
1948	Nelly Landry	S. Fry	62 06 60	1981	Hana Mandlikova	S. Hanika	62 64
1949	Margaret duPont	N. Adamson	75 62	1982	Martina Navratilova	A. Jaeger	76 61
				1983	Chris Evert Lloyd	M. Jausovec	61 62
1950	Doris Hart	P. Todd	64 46 62	1984	Martina Navratilova	C. Evert Lloyd	63 61
1951	Shirley Fry	D. Hart	63 36 63	1985	Chris Evert Lloyd	M. Navratilova	63 67 75
1952	Doris Hart	S. Fry	64 64	1986	Chris Evert Lloyd	M. Navratilova	26 63 63
1953	Maureen Connolly	D. Hart	62 64	1987	Steffi Graf	M. Navratilova	64 46 86
1954	Maureen Connolly	G. Bucaille	64 61	1988	Steffi Graf	N. Zvereva	60 60
1955	Angela Mortimer	D. Knode	26 75 10-8	1989	A. Sanchez Vicario	S. Graf	76 36 75
1956	Althea Gibson	A. Mortimer	60 12-10				
1957	Shirley Bloomer	D. Knode	61 63	1990	Monica Seles	S. Graf	76 64
1958	Susi Kormoczi	S. Bloomer	64 16 62	1991	Monica Seles	A.S. Vicario	63 64
1959	Christine Truman	S. Kormoczi	64 75	1992	Monica Seles	S. Graf	62 36 10-8
				1993	Steffi Graf	M.J. Fernandez	46 62 64
1960	Darlene Hard	Y. Ramirez	63 64	1994	A. Sanchez Vicario	M. Pierce	64 64
1961	Ann Haydon	Y. Ramirez	62 61				
1962	Margaret Smith	L. Turner	63 36 75				

Grand Slam Champions (Cont.)
Wimbledon
MEN

Officially called "The Lawn Tennis Championships" at the All England Club, Wimbledon. Challenge round system (defending champion qualified for following year's final) used from 1877–1921. Became an Open Championship in 1968, but closed to contract pros in 1972.

Surface: Grass.

Multiple winners: Willie Renshaw (7); Bjorn Borg and Laurie Doherty (5); Reggie Doherty, Rod Laver and Tony Wilding (4); Wilfred Baddeley, Boris Becker, Arthur Gore, John McEnroe, John Newcombe, Fred Perry and Bill Tilden (3); Jean Borotra, Norman Brookes, Don Budge, Henri Cochet, Jimmy Connors, Stefan Edberg, Roy Emerson, John Hartley, Lew Hoad, Rene Lacoste, Gerald Patterson, Joshua Pim and Pete Sampras (2).

Year	Winner	Loser	Score	Year	Winner	Loser	Score
1877	Spencer Gore	W. Marshall	61 62 64	1935	Fred Perry	G. von Cramm	62 64 64
1878	Frank Hadow	S. Gore	75 61 97	1936	Fred Perry	G. von Cramm	61 61 60
1879	John Hartley	V. St.L. Gould	62 64 62	1937	Don Budge	G. von Cramm	63 64 62
1880	John Hartley	H. Lawford	60 62 26 63	1938	Don Budge	H. Austin	61 60 63
1881	Willie Renshaw	J. Hartley	60 62 61	1939	Bobby Riggs	E. Cooke	26 86 36 63 62
1882	Willie Renshaw	E. Renshaw	61 26 46 62 62	1940-45	Not held	World War II	
1883	Willie Renshaw	E. Renshaw	26 63 63 46 63	1946	Yvon Petra	G. Brown	62 64 79 57 64
1884	Willie Renshaw	H. Lawford	60 64 97	1947	Jack Kramer	T. Brown	61 63 62
1885	Willie Renshaw	H. Lawford	75 62 46 75	1948	Bob Falkenburg	J. Bromwich	75 06 62 36 75
1886	Willie Renshaw	H. Lawford	60 57 63 64	1949	Ted Schroeder	J. Drobny	36 60 63 46 64
1887	Herbert Lawford	E. Renshaw	16 63 36 64 64	1950	Budge Patty	F. Sedgman	61 8-10 62 63
1888	Ernest Renshaw	H. Lawford	63 75 60	1951	Dick Savitt	K. McGregor	64 64 64
1889	Willie Renshaw	E. Renshaw	64 61 36 60	1952	Frank Sedgman	J. Drobny	46 62 63 62
1890	William Hamilton	W. Renshaw	68 62 36 61 61	1953	Vic Seixas	K. Nielsen	97 63 64
1891	Wilfred Baddeley	J. Pim	64 16 75 60	1954	Jaroslav Drobny	K. Rosewall	13-11 46 62 97
1892	Wilfred Baddeley	J. Pim	46 63 63 62	1955	Tony Trabert	K. Nielsen	63 75 61
1893	Joshua Pim	W. Baddeley	36 61 63 62	1956	Lew Hoad	K. Rosewall	62 46 75 64
1894	Joshua Pim	W. Baddeley	10-8 62 86	1957	Lew Hoad	A. Cooper	62 61 62
1895	Wilfred Baddeley	W. Eaves	46 26 86 62 63	1958	Ashley Cooper	N. Fraser	36 63 64 13-11
1896	Harold Mahony	W. Baddeley	62 68 57 86 63	1959	Alex Olmedo	R. Laver	64 63 64
1897	Reggie Doherty	H. Mahony	64 64 63	1960	Neale Fraser	R. Laver	64 36 97 75
1898	Reggie Doherty	L. Doherty	63 63 26 57 61	1961	Rod Laver	C. McKinley	63 61 64
1899	Reggie Doherty	A. Gore	16 46 62 63 63	1962	Rod Laver	M. Mulligan	62 62 61
1900	Reggie Doherty	S. Smith	68 63 61 62	1963	Chuck McKinley	F. Stolle	97 61 64
1901	Arthur Gore	R. Doherty	46 75 64 64	1964	Roy Emerson	F. Stolle	64 12-10 46 63
1902	Laurie Doherty	A. Gore	64 63 36 60	1965	Roy Emerson	F. Stolle	62 64 64
1903	Laurie Doherty	F. Riseley	75 63 60	1966	Manuel Santana	D. Ralston	64 11-9 64
1904	Laurie Doherty	F. Riseley	61 75 86	1967	John Newcombe	W. Bungert	63 61 61
1905	Laurie Doherty	N. Brookes	86 62 64	1968	Rod Laver	T. Roche	63 64 62
1906	Laurie Doherty	F. Riseley	64 46 62 63	1969	Rod Laver	J. Newcombe	64 57 64 64
1907	Norman Brookes	A. Gore	64 62 62	1970	John Newcombe	K. Rosewall	57 63 62 36 61
1908	Arthur Gore	R. Barrett	63 62 46 36 64	1971	John Newcombe	S. Smith	63 57 26 64 64
1909	Arthur Gore	M. Ritchie	68 16 62 62 62	1972	Stan Smith	I. Nastase	46 63 63 46 75
1910	Tony Wilding	A. Gore	64 75 46 62	1973	Jan Kodes	A. Metreveli	61 98 63
1911	Tony Wilding	R. Barrett	64 46 26 62 (ret)	1974	Jimmy Connors	K. Rosewall	61 61 64
1912	Tony Wilding	A. Gore	64 64 46 64	1975	Arthur Ashe	J. Connors	61 61 57 64
1913	Tony Wilding	M. McLoughlin	86 63 10-8	1976	Bjorn Borg	I. Nastase	64 62 97
1914	Norman Brookes	T. Wilding	64 64 75	1977	Bjorn Borg	J. Connors	36 62 61 57 64
1915-18	Not held	World War I		1978	Bjorn Borg	J. Connors	62 62 63
1919	Gerald Patterson	N. Brookes	63 75 62	1979	Bjorn Borg	R. Tanner	67 61 36 63 64
1920	Bill Tilden	G. Patterson	26 63 62 64	1980	Bjorn Borg	J. McEnroe	16 75 63 67 86
1921	Bill Tilden	B. Norton	46 26 61 60 75	1981	John McEnroe	B. Borg	46 76 76 64
1922	Gerald Patterson	R. Lycett	63 64 62	1982	Jimmy Connors	J. McEnroe	36 63 67 76 64
1923	Bill Johnston	F. Hunter	60 63 61	1983	John McEnroe	C. Lewis	62 62 62
1924	Jean Borotra	R. Lacoste	61 36 61 36 64	1984	John McEnroe	J. Connors	61 61 62
1925	Rene Lacoste	J. Borotra	63 63 46 86	1985	Boris Becker	K. Curren	63 67 76 64
1926	Jean Borotra	H. Kinsey	86 61 63	1986	Boris Becker	I. Lendl	64 63 75
1927	Henri Cochet	J. Borotra	46 46 63 64 75	1987	Pat Cash	I. Lendl	76 62 75
1928	Rene Lacoste	H. Cochet	61 46 64 62	1988	Stefan Edberg	B. Becker	46 76 64 62
1929	Henri Cochet	J. Borotra	64 63 64	1989	Boris Becker	S. Edberg	60 76 64
1930	Bill Tilden	W. Allison	63 97 64	1990	Stefan Edberg	B. Becker	62 62 36 36 64
1931	Sidney Wood	F. Shields	walkover	1991	Michael Stich	B. Becker	64 76 64
1932	Ellsworth Vines	H. Austin	64 62 60	1992	Andre Agassi	G. Ivanisevic	67 64 64 16 64
1933	Jack Crawford	E. Vines	46 11-9 62 26 64	1993	Pete Sampras	J. Courier	76 76 36 63
1934	Fred Perry	J. Crawford	63 60 75	1994	Pete Sampras	G. Ivanisevic	76 76 60

WOMEN

Officially called "The Lawn Tennis Championships" at the All England Club, Wimbledon. Challenge round system (defending champion qualified for following year's final) used from 1886-1921. Became an Open Championship in 1968, but closed to contract pros in 1972.

Multiple winners: Martina Navratilova (9); Helen Wills Moody (8); Dorothea Douglass Chambers (7); Blanche Bingley Hillyard, Billie Jean King and Suzanne Lenglen (6); Lottie Dod, Steffi Graf and Charlotte Cooper Sterry (5); Louise Brough (4); Maria Bueno, Maureen Connolly, Margaret Smith Court and Chris Evert Lloyd (3); Evonne Goolagong Cawley, Althea Gibson, Dorothy Round, May Sutton and Maud Watson (2).

Year	Winner	Loser	Score	Year	Winner	Loser	Score
1884	Maud Watson	L. Watson	68 63 63	1940-45	Not held	World War II	
1885	Maud Watson	B. Bingley	61 75	1946	Pauline Betz	L. Brough	62 64
1886	Blanche Bingley	M. Watson	63 63	1947	Margaret Osborne	D. Hart	62 64
1887	Lottie Dod	B. Bingley	62 60	1948	Louise Brough	D. Hart	63 86
1888	Lottie Dod	B. Hillyard	63 63	1949	Louise Brough	M. duPont	10-8 16 10-8
1889	Blanche Hillyard	L. Rice	46 86 64	1950	Louise Brough	M. duPont	61 36 61
1890	Lena Rice	M. Jacks	64 61	1951	Doris Hart	S. Fry	61 60
1891	Lottie Dod	B. Hillyard	62 61	1952	Maureen Connolly	L. Brough	75 63
1892	Lottie Dod	B. Hillyard	61 61	1953	Maureen Connolly	D. Hart	86 75
1893	Lottie Dod	B. Hillyard	68 61 64	1954	Maureen Connolly	L. Brough	62 75
1894	Blanche Hillyard	E. Austin	61 61	1955	Louise Brough	B. Fleitz	75 86
1895	Charlotte Cooper	H. Jackson	75 86	1956	Shirley Fry	A. Buxton	63 61
1896	Charlotte Cooper	W. Pickering	62 63	1957	Althea Gibson	D. Hard	63 62
1897	Blanche Hillyard	C. Cooper	57 75 62	1958	Althea Gibson	A. Mortimer	86 62
1898	Charlotte Cooper	L. Martin	64 64	1959	Maria Bueno	D. Hard	64 63
1899	Blanche Hillyard	C. Cooper	62 63	1960	Maria Bueno	S. Reynolds	86 60
1900	Blanche Hillyard	C. Cooper	46 64 64	1961	Angela Mortimer	C. Truman	46 64 75
1901	Charlotte Sterry	B. Hillyard	62 62	1962	Karen Susman	V. Sukova	64 64
1902	Muriel Robb	C. Sterry	75 61	1963	Margaret Smith	B.J. Moffitt	63 64
1903	Dorothea Douglass	E. Thomson	46 64 62	1964	Maria Bueno	M. Smith	64 79 63
1904	Dorothea Douglass	C. Sterry	60 63	1965	Margaret Smith	M. Bueno	64 75
1905	May Sutton	D. Douglass	63 64	1966	Billie Jean King	M. Bueno	63 36 61
1906	Dorothea Douglass	M. Sutton	63 97	1967	Billie Jean King	A. Jones	63 64
1907	May Sutton	D. Chambers	61 64	1968	Billie Jean King	J. Tegart	97 75
1908	Charlotte Sterry	A. Morton	64 64	1969	Ann Jones	B.J. King	36 63 62
1909	Dora Boothby	A. Morton	64 46 86	1970	Margaret Court	B.J. King	14-12 11-9
1910	Dorothea Chambers	D. Boothby	62 62	1971	Evonne Goolagong	M. Court	64 61
1911	Dorothea Chambers	D. Boothby	60 60	1972	Billie Jean King	E. Goolagong	63 63
1912	Ethel Larcombe	C. Sterry	63 61	1973	Billie Jean King	C. Evert	60 75
1913	Dorothea Chambers	R. McNair	60 64	1974	Chris Evert	O. Morzova	60 64
1914	Dorothea Chambers	E. Larcombe	75 64	1975	Billie Jean King	E. Cawley	60 61
1915-18	Not held	World War I		1976	Chris Evert	E. Cawley	63 46 86
1919	Suzanne Lenglen	D. Chambers	10-8 46 97	1977	Virginia Wade	B. Stove	46 63 61
1920	Suzanne Lenglen	D. Chambers	63 60	1978	Martina Navratilova	C. Evert	26 64 75
1921	Suzanne Lenglen	E. Ryan	62 60	1979	Martina Navratilova	C. Evert Lloyd	64 64
1922	Suzanne Lenglen	M. Mallory	62 60	1980	Evonne Cawley	C. Evert Lloyd	61 76
1923	Suzanne Lenglen	K. McKane	62 62	1981	Chris Evert Lloyd	H. Mandlikova	62 62
1924	Kathleen McKane	H. Wills	46 64 64	1982	Martina Navratilova	C. Evert Lloyd	61 36 62
1925	Suzanne Lenglen	J. Fry	62 60	1983	Martina Navratilova	A. Jaeger	60 63
1926	Kathleen Godfree	L. de Alvarez	62 46 63	1984	Martina Navratilova	C. Evert Lloyd	76 62
1927	Helen Wills	L. de Alvarez	62 64	1985	Martina Navratilova	C. Evert Lloyd	46 63 62
1928	Helen Wills	L. de Alvarez	62 63	1986	Martina Navratilova	H. Mandlikova	76 63
1929	Helen Wills	H. Jacobs	61 62	1987	Martina Navratilova	S. Graf	75 63
1930	Helen Moody	E. Ryan	62 62	1988	Steffi Graf	M. Navratilova	57 62 61
1931	Cilly Aussem	H. Kranwinkel	62 75	1989	Steffi Graf	M. Navratilova	62 67 61
1932	Helen Moody	H. Jacobs	63 61	1990	Martina Navratilova	Z. Garrison	64 61
1933	Helen Moody	D. Round	64 68 63	1991	Steffi Graf	G. Sabatini	64 36 86
1934	Dorothy Round	H. Jacobs	62 57 63	1992	Steffi Graf	M. Seles	62 61
1935	Helen Moody	H. Jacobs	63 36 75	1993	Steffi Graf	J. Novotna	76 16 64
1936	Helen Jacobs	H.K. Sperling	62 46 75	1994	Conchita Martinez	M. Navratilova	64 36 63
1937	Dorothy Round	J. Jedrzejowska	62 26 75				
1938	Helen Moody	H. Jacobs	64 60				
1939	Alice Marble	K. Stammers	62 60				

Grand Slam Champions (Cont.)
U.S. Open
MEN

Challenge round system (defending champion qualified for following year's final) used from 1884-1911. Known as the Patriotic Tournament in 1917 during World War I. Amateur and Open Championships held in 1968 and '69. Became an exclusively Open Championship in 1970.

Surface: Decoturf II (acrylic cement).

Multiple winners: Bill Larned, Richard Sears and Bill Tilden (7); Jimmy Connors (5); John McEnroe and Robert Wrenn (4); Oliver Campbell, Ivan Lendl, Fred Perry and Malcolm Whitman (3); Don Budge, Stefan Edberg, Roy Emerson, Neale Fraser, Pancho Gonzalez, Bill Johnston, Jack Kramer, Rene Lacoste, Rod Laver, Maurice McLoughlin, Lindley Murray, John Newcombe, Frank Parker, Bobby Riggs, Ken Rosewall, Frank Sedgman, Pete Sampras, Henry Slocum Jr., Tony Trabert, Ellsworth Vines and Dick Williams (2).

Year	Winner	Loser	Score	Year	Winner	Loser	Score
1881	Richard Sears	W. Glyn	60 63 62	1937	Don Budge	G. von Cramm	61 79 61 36 61
1882	Richard Sears	C. Clark	61 64 60	1938	Don Budge	G. Mako	63 68 62 61
1883	Richard Sears	J. Dwight	62 60 97	1939	Bobby Riggs	S.W. van Horn	64 62 64
1884	Richard Sears	H. Taylor	60 16 60 62	1940	Don McNeill	B. Riggs	46 68 63 63 75
1885	Richard Sears	G. Brinley	63 46 60 63	1941	Bobby Riggs	F. Kovacs	57 61 63 63
1886	Richard Sears	R. Beeckman	46 61 63 64	1942	Fred Schroeder	F. Parker	86 75 36 46 62
1887	Richard Sears	H. Slocum Jr.	61 63 62	1943	Joe Hunt	J. Kramer	63 68 10-8 60
1888	Henry Slocum Jr.	H. Taylor	64 61 60	1944	Frank Parker	B. Talbert	64 36 63 63
1889	Henry Slocum Jr.	Q. Shaw	63 61 46 62	1945	Frank Parker	B. Talbert	14-12 61 62
1890	Oliver Campbell	H. Slocum Jr.	62 46 63 61	1946	Jack Kramer	T. Brown, Jr.	97 63 60
1891	Oliver Campbell	C. Hobart	26 75 79 61 62	1947	Jack Kramer	F. Parker	46 26 61 60 63
1892	Oliver Campbell	F. Hovey	75 36 63 75	1948	Pancho Gonzalez	E. Sturgess	62 63 14-12
1893	Robert Wrenn	F. Hovey	64 36 64 64	1949	Pancho Gonzalez	F. Schroeder	16-18 26 61 62 64
1894	Robert Wrenn	M. Goodbody	68 61 64 64	1950	Arthur Larsen	H. Flam	63 46 57 64 63
1895	Fred Hovey	R. Wrenn	63 62 64	1951	Frank Sedgman	V. Seixas	64 61 61
1896	Robert Wrenn	F. Hovey	75 36 60 16 61	1952	Frank Sedgman	G. Mulloy	61 62 63
1897	Robert Wrenn	W. Eaves	46 86 63 26 62	1953	Tony Trabert	V. Seixas	63 62 63
1898	Malcolm Whitman	D. Davis	36 62 62 61	1954	Vic Seixas	R. Hartwig	36 62 64 64
1899	Malcolm Whitman	P. Paret	61 62 36 75	1955	Tony Trabert	K. Rosewall	97 63 63
1900	Malcolm Whitman	B. Larned	64 16 62 62	1956	Ken Rosewall	L. Hoad	46 62 63 63
1901	Bill Larned	B. Wright	62 68 64 64	1957	Mal Anderson	A. Cooper	10-8 75 64
1902	Bill Larned	R. Doherty	46 62 64 86	1958	Ashley Cooper	M. Anderson	62 36 46 10-8 86
1903	Laurie Doherty	B. Larned	60 63 10-8	1959	Neale Fraser	A. Olmedo	63 57 62 64
1904	Holcombe Ward	B. Clothier	10-8 64 97	1960	Neale Fraser	R. Laver	64 64 97
1905	Beals Wright	H. Ward	62 61 11-9	1961	Roy Emerson	R. Laver	75 63 62
1906	Bill Clothier	B. Wright	63 60 64	1962	Rod Laver	R. Emerson	62 64 57 64
1907	Bill Larned	B. LeRoy	62 62 64	1963	Rafael Osuna	F. Froehling	75 64 62
1908	Bill Larned	B. Wright	61 62 86	1964	Roy Emerson	F. Stolle	64 62 64
1909	Bill Larned	B. Clothier	61 62 57 16 61	1965	Manuel Santana	C. Drysdale	62 79 75 61
1910	Bill Larned	T. Bundy	61 57 60 68 61	1966	Fred Stolle	J. Newcombe	46 12-10 63 64
1911	Bill Larned	M. McLoughlin	64 64 62	1967	John Newcombe	C. Graebner	64 64 86
1912	Maurice McLoughlin	W. F. Johnson	36 26 62 64 62	1968	Am-Arthur Ashe	B. Lutz	46 63 8-10 60 64
1913	Maurice McLoughlin	R. Williams	64 57 63 61		Op-Arthur Ashe	T. Okker	14-12 57 63 36 63
1914	Dick Williams	M. McLoughlin	63 86 10-8	1969	Am-Stan Smith	B. Lutz	97 63 61
1915	Bill Johnston	M. McLoughlin	16 60 75 10-8		Op-Rod Laver	T. Roche	79 61 63 62
1916	Dick Williams	B. Johnston	46 64 06 62 64	1970	Ken Rosewall	T. Roche	26 64 76 63
1917	Lindley Murray	N. Niles	57 86 63 63	1971	Stan Smith	J. Kodes	36 63 62 76
1918	Lindley Murray	B. Tilden	63 61 75	1972	Ilie Nastase	A. Ashe	36 63 67 64 63
1919	Bill Johnston	B. Tilden	64 64 63	1973	John Newcombe	J. Kodes	64 16 46 62 63
1920	Bill Tilden	B. Johnston	61 16 75 57 63	1974	Jimmy Connors	K. Rosewall	61 60 61
1921	Bill Tilden	W. Johnson	61 63 61	1975	Manuel Orantes	J. Connors	64 63 63
1922	Bill Tilden	B. Johnston	46 36 62 63 64	1976	Jimmy Connors	B. Borg	64 36 76 64
1923	Bill Tilden	B. Johnston	64 61 64	1977	Guillermo Vilas	J. Connors	26 63 76 60
1924	Bill Tilden	B. Johnston	61 97 62	1978	Jimmy Connors	B. Borg	64 62 62
1925	Bill Tilden	B. Johnston	46 11-9 63 46 63	1979	John McEnroe	V. Gerulaitis	75 63 63
1926	Rene Lacoste	J. Borotra	64 60 64	1980	John McEnroe	B. Borg	76 61 67 57 64
1927	Rene Lacoste	B. Tilden	11-9 63 11-9	1981	John McEnroe	B. Borg	46 62 64 63
1928	Henri Cochet	F. Hunter	46 64 36 75 63	1982	Jimmy Connors	I. Lendl	63 62 46 64
1929	Bill Tilden	F. Hunter	36 63 46 62 64	1983	Jimmy Connors	I. Lendl	63 67 75 60
1930	John Doeg	F. Shields	10-8 16 64 16-14	1984	John McEnroe	I. Lendl	63 64 61
1931	Ellsworth Vines	G. Lott Jr.	79 63 97 75	1985	Ivan Lendl	J. McEnroe	76 63 64
1932	Ellsworth Vines	H. Cochet	64 64 64	1986	Ivan Lendl	M. Mecir	64 62 60
1933	Fred Perry	J. Crawford	63 11-13 46 60 61	1987	Ivan Lendl	M. Wilander	67 60 76 64
1934	Fred Perry	W. Allison	64 63 16 86	1988	Mats Wilander	I. Lendl	64 46 63 57 64
1935	Wilmer Allison	S. Wood	62 62 63	1989	Boris Becker	I. Lendl	76 16 63 76
1936	Fred Perry	D. Budge	26 62 86 16 10-8				

Year	Winner	Loser	Score	Year	Winner	Loser	Score
1990	Pete Sampras	A. Agassi	64 63 62	1993	Pete Sampras	C. Pioline	64 64 63
1991	Stefan Edberg	J. Courier	62 64 60	1994	Andre Agassi	M. Stich	61 76 75
1992	Stefan Edberg	P. Sampras	36 64 76 62				

WOMEN

Challenge round system used from 1887-1918. Five set final played from 1887-1901. Amateur and Open Championships held in 1968 and '69. Became an exclusively Open Championship in 1970.

Multiple winners: Molla Mallory Bjurstedt (8); Helen Wills Moody (7); Chris Evert Lloyd (6); Margaret Smith Court (5); Pauline Betz, Mario Bueno, Helen Jacobs, Billie Jean King, Alice Marble, Elisabeth Moore, Martina Navratilova and Hazel Hotchkiss Wightman (4); Juliette Atkinson, Mary Browne, Maureen Connolly, Margaret Osborne duPont and Steffi Graf (3); Tracy Austin, Mabel Cahill, Sarah Palfrey Cooke, Darlene Hard, Doris Hart, Althea Gibson, Monica Seles and Bertha Townsend (2).

Year	Winner	Loser	Score	Year	Winner	Loser	Score
1887	Ellen Hansell	L. Knight	61 60	1942	Pauline Betz	L. Brough	46 61 64
1888	Bertha Townsend	E. Hansell	63 65	1943	Pauline Betz	L. Brough	63 57 63
1889	Bertha Townsend	L. Voorhes	75 62	1944	Pauline Betz	M. Osborne	63 86
				1945	Sarah Cooke	P. Betz	36 86 64
1890	Ellen Roosevelt	B. Townsend	62 62	1946	Pauline Betz	P. Canning	11-9 63
1891	Mabel Cahill	E. Roosevelt	64 61 46 63	1947	Louise Brough	M. Osborne	86 46 61
1892	Mabel Cahill	E. Moore	57 63 64 46 62	1948	Margaret duPont	L. Brough	46 64 15-13
1893	Aline Terry	M. Cahill	default	1949	Margaret duPont	D. Hart	64 61
1894	Helen Hellwig	A. Terry	75 36 60 36 63	1950	Margaret duPont	D. Hart	64 63
1895	Juliette Atkinson	H. Hellwig	64 62 61	1951	Maureen Connolly	S. Fry	63 16 64
1896	Elisabeth Moore	J. Atkinson	64 46 62 62	1952	Maureen Connolly	D. Hart	63 75
1897	Juliette Atkinson	E. Moore	63 63 46 36 63	1953	Maureen Connolly	D. Hart	62 64
1898	Juliette Atkinson	M. Jones	63 57 64 26 75	1954	Doris Hart	L. Brough	68 61 86
1899	Marion Jones	M. Banks	61 61 75	1955	Doris Hart	P. Ward	64 62
				1956	Shirley Fry	A. Gibson	63 64
1900	Myrtle McAteer	E. Parker	62 62 60	1957	Althea Gibson	L. Brough	63 62
1901	Elizabeth Moore	M. McAteer	64 36 75 26 62	1958	Althea Gibson	D. Hard	36 61 62
1902	Marion Jones	E. Moore	61 10(ret)	1959	Maria Bueno	C. Truman	61 64
1903	Elizabeth Moore	M. Jones	75 86	1960	Darlene Hard	M. Bueno	64 10-12 64
1904	May Sutton	E. Moore	61 62	1961	Darlene Hard	A. Haydon	63 64
1905	Elizabeth Moore	H. Homans	64 57 61	1962	Margaret Smith	D. Hard	97 64
1906	Helen Homans	M. Barger-Wallach	64 63	1963	Maria Bueno	M. Smith	75 64
1907	Evelyn Sears	C. Neely	63 62	1964	Maria Bueno	C. Graebner	61 60
1908	Maud B. Wallach	Ev. Sears	63 16 63	1965	Margaret Smith	B.J. Moffitt	86 75
1909	Hazel Hotchkiss	M. Wallach	60 61	1966	Maria Bueno	N. Richey	63 61
				1967	Billie Jean King	A. Jones	11-9 64
1910	Hazel Hotchkiss	L. Hammond	64 62	1968	Am-Margaret Court	M. Bueno	62 62
1911	Hazel Hotchkiss	F. Sutton	8-10 61 97		Op-Virginia Wade	B.J. King	64 62
1912	Mary Browne	E. Sears	64 62	1969	Am-Margaret Court	V. Wade	46 63 60
1913	Mary Browne	D. Green	62 75		Op-Margaret Court	N. Richey	62 62
1914	Mary Browne	M. Wagner	62 16 61				
1915	Molla Bjurstedt	H. Wightman	46 62 60	1970	Margaret Court	R. Casals	62 26 61
1916	Molla Bjurstedt	L. Raymond	60 61	1971	Billie Jean King	R. Casals	64 76
1917	Molla Bjurstedt	M. Vanderhoef	46 60 62	1972	Billie Jean King	K. Melville	63 75
1918	Molla Bjurstedt	E. Goss	64 63	1973	Margaret Court	E. Goolagong	76 57 62
1919	Hazel Wightman	M. Zinderstein	61 62	1974	Billie Jean King	E. Goolagong	36 63 75
				1975	Chris Evert	E. Cawley	57 64 62
1920	Molla Mallory	M. Zinderstein	63 61	1976	Chris Evert	E. Cawley	63 60
1921	Molla Mallory	M. Browne	46 64 62	1977	Chris Evert	W. Turnbull	76 62
1922	Molla Mallory	H. Wills	63 61	1978	Chris Evert	P. Shriver	75 64
1923	Helen Wills	M. Mallory	62 61	1979	Tracy Austin	C. Evert Lloyd	64 63
1924	Helen Wills	M. Mallory	61 63	1980	Chris Evert Lloyd	H. Mandlikova	57 61 61
1925	Helen Wills	K. McKane	36 60 62	1981	Tracy Austin	M. Navratilova	16 76 76
1926	Molla Mallory	E. Ryan	46 64 97	1982	Chris Evert Lloyd	H. Mandlikova	63 61
1927	Helen Wills	B. Nuthall	61 64	1983	Martina Navratilova	C. Evert Lloyd	61 63
1928	Helen Wills	H. Jacobs	62 61	1984	Martina Navratilova	C. Evert Lloyd	46 64 64
1929	Helen Wills	P. Watson	64 62	1985	Hana Mandlikova	M. Navratilova	76 16 76
				1986	Martina Navratilova	H. Sukova	63 62
1930	Betty Nuthall	A. Harper	61 64	1987	Martina Navratilova	S. Graf	76 61
1931	Helen Moody	E. Whitingstall	64 61	1988	Steffi Graf	G. Sabatini	63 36 61
1932	Helen Jacobs	C. Babcock	62 62	1989	Steffi Graf	M. Navratilova	36 75 61
1933	Helen Jacobs	H. Moody	86 36 30(ret)	1990	Gabriela Sabatini	S. Graf	62 76
1934	Helen Jacobs	S. Palfrey	61 64	1991	Monica Seles	M. Navratilova	76 61
1935	Helen Jacobs	S. Fabyan	62 64	1992	Monica Seles	A.S. Vicario	63 63
1936	Alice Marble	H. Jacobs	46 63 62	1993	Steffi Graf	H. Sukova	63 63
1937	Anita Lizana	J. Jedrzejowska	64 62	1994	A. Sanchez Vicario	S. Graf	16 76 64
1938	Alice Marble	N. Wynne	60 63				
1939	Alice Marble	H. Jacobs	60 8-10 64				
1940	Alice Marble	H. Jacobs	62 63				
1941	Sarah Cooke	P. Betz	75 62				

Grand Slam Summary

Men's and Women's singles winners of the four Grand Slam tournaments—Australian, French, Wimbledon and United States—since the French was opened to all comers in 1925. Note that there were two Australian Open championships in 1977 and none in 1986.

MEN

Only two men have won the Grand Slam—all four events in a single year: Don Budge in 1938 and Rod Laver in both 1962 and 1969.

Three wins in one year: Jack Crawford (1933); Fred Perry (1934); Tony Trabert (1955); Lew Hoad (1956); Ashley Cooper (1958); Roy Emerson (1964); Jimmy Connors (1974); Mats Wilander (1988).

Two wins in one year: Roy Emerson (4 times); Bjorn Borg (3 times); Rene Lacoste, Ivan Lendl, John Newcombe, Fred Perry and Pete Sampras (twice); Boris Becker, Don Budge, Henri Cochet, Jimmy Connors, Jim Courier, Neale Fraser, Jack Kramer, John McEnroe, Alex Olmedo, Budge Patty, Bobby Riggs, Ken Rosewall, Dick Savitt, Frank Sedgman and Guillermo Vilas (once).

Year	Australia	French	Wimbledon	U.S.
1925	Anderson	Lacoste	Lacoste	Tilden
1926	Hawkes	Cochet	Borotra	Lacoste
1927	Patterson	Lacoste	Cochet	Lacoste
1928	Borotra	Cochet	Lacoste	Cochet
1929	Gregory	Lacoste	Cochet	Tilden
1930	Moon	Cochet	Tilden	Doeg
1931	Crawford	Borotra	Wood	Vines
1932	Crawford	Cochet	Vines	Vines
1933	Crawford	Crawford	Crawford	Perry
1934	Perry	von Cramm	Perry	Perry
1935	Crawford	Perry	Perry	Allison
1936	Quist	von Cramm	Perry	Perry
1937	McGrath	Henkel	Budge	Budge
1938	**Budge**	**Budge**	**Budge**	**Budge**
1939	Bromwich	McNeill	Riggs	Riggs
1940	Quist	—	—	McNeill
1941	—	Destremau	—	Riggs
1942	—	Destremau	—	Schroeder
1943	—	Petra	—	Hunt
1944	—	Petra	—	Parker
1945	—	Petra	—	Parker
1946	Bromwich	Bernard	Petra	Kramer
1947	Pails	Asboth	Kramer	Kramer
1948	Quist	Parker	Falkenburg	Gonzales
1949	Sedgman	Parker	Schroeder	Gonzales
1950	Sedgman	Patty	Patty	Larsen
1951	Savitt	Drobny	Savitt	Sedgman
1952	McGregor	Drobny	Sedgman	Sedgman
1953	Rosewall	Rosewall	Seixas	Trabert
1954	Rose	Trabert	Drobny	Seixas
1955	Rosewall	Trabert	Trabert	Trabert
1956	Hoad	Hoad	Hoad	Rosewall
1957	Cooper	Davidson	Hoad	Anderson
1958	Cooper	Rose	Cooper	Cooper
1959	Olmedo	Pietrangeli	Olmedo	Fraser
1960	Laver	Pietrangeli	Fraser	Fraser
1961	Emerson	Santana	Laver	Emerson

Year	Australia	French	Wimbledon	U.S.
1962	**Laver**	**Laver**	**Laver**	**Laver**
1963	Emerson	Emerson	McKinley	Osuna
1964	Emerson	Santana	Emerson	Emerson
1965	Emerson	Stolle	Emerson	Santana
1966	Emerson	Roche	Santana	Stolle
1967	Emerson	Emerson	Newcombe	Newcombe
1968	Bowrey	Rosewall	Laver	Ashe
1969	**Laver**	**Laver**	**Laver**	**Laver**
1970	Ashe	Kodes	Newcombe	Rosewall
1971	Rosewall	Kodes	Newcombe	Smith
1972	Rosewall	Gimeno	Smith	Nastase
1973	Newcombe	Nastase	Kodes	Newcombe
1974	Connors	Borg	Connors	Connors
1975	Newcombe	Borg	Ashe	Orantes
1976	Edmondson	Panatta	Borg	Connors
1977	Tanner & Gerulaitis	Vilas	Borg	Vilas
1978	Vilas	Borg	Borg	Connors
1979	Vilas	Borg	Borg	McEnroe
1980	Teacher	Borg	Borg	McEnroe
1981	Kriek	Borg	McEnroe	McEnroe
1982	Kriek	Wilander	Connors	Connors
1983	Wilander	Noah	McEnroe	Connors
1984	Wilander	Lendl	McEnroe	McEnroe
1985	Edberg	Wilander	Becker	Lendl
1986	—	Lendl	Becker	Lendl
1987	Edberg	Lendl	Cash	Lendl
1988	Wilander	Wilander	Edberg	Wilander
1989	Lendl	Chang	Becker	Becker
1990	Lendl	Gomez	Edberg	Sampras
1991	Becker	Courier	Stich	Edberg
1992	Courier	Courier	Agassi	Edberg
1993	Courier	Bruguera	Sampras	Sampras
1994	Sampras	Bruguera	Sampras	Agassi

All-Time Grand Slam Singles Titles

Men and women with the most singles championships in the Australian, French, Wimbledon and U.S. championships, through 1994. Note that (*) indicates player never played in that particular Grand Slam event; and players active in 1994 are in **bold** type.

Top 10 Men

	Aus	Fre	Wim	US		Total
1 Roy Emerson	6	2	2	2	—	12
2 Bjorn Borg	0	6	5	0	—	11
Rod Laver	3	2	4	2	—	11
4 Bill Tilden	*	0	3	7	—	10
5 Jimmy Connors	1	0	2	5	—	8
Ivan Lendl	2	3	0	3	—	8
Fred Perry	1	1	3	3	—	8
Ken Rosewall	4	2	0	2	—	8
9 Seven tied with 7 titles each.						

Top 10 Women

	Aus	Fre	Wim	US		Total
1 Margaret Smith Court	11	5	3	7	—	26
2 Helen Wills Moody	*	4	8	7	—	19
3 Chris Evert Lloyd	2	7	3	6	—	18
Martina Navratilova	3	2	9	4	—	18
5 **Steffi Graf**	4	3	5	3	—	15
6 Billie Jean King	1	1	6	4	—	12
Suzanne Lenglen	*	6	6	0	—	12
8 Maureen Connelly	1	2	3	3	—	9
9 Molla Bjurstedt Mallory	*	*	0	8	—	8
Monica Seles	3	3	0	2	—	8

WOMEN

Only three women have won the Grand Slam—all four events in a single year: Maureen Connolly in 1953, Margaret Smith Court in 1970 and Steffi Graf in 1988.

Three in one year: Helen Wills Moody (1928 and '29); Margaret Smith Court (1962, '65, '69 and '73); Billie Jean King (1972); Martina Navratilova (1983 and '84); Steffi Graf (1989 and '93); and Monica Seles (1991 and '92).

Two in one year: Chris Evert Lloyd (5 times); Helen Wills Moody and Martina Navratilova (3 times); Maria Bueno, Maureen Connolly, Margaret Smith Court, Althea Gibson, Billie Jean King (twice); Cilly Aussem, Pauline Betz, Louise Brough, Evonne Goolagong Cawley, Shirley Fry, Darlene Hard, Margaret Osborne duPont, Suzanne Lenglen, Alice Marble and Arantxa Sanchez Vicario (once).

Year	Australia	French	Wimbledon	U.S.
1925	Akhurst	Lenglen	Lenglen	Wills
1926	Akhurst	Lenglen	Godfree	Mallory
1927	Boyd	Bouman	Wills	Wills
1928	Akhurst	Wills	Wills	Wills
1929	Akhurst	Wills	Wills	Wills
1930	Akhurst	Moody	Moody	Nuthall
1931	Buttsworth	Aussem	Aussem	Moody
1932	Buttsworth	Moody	Moody	Jacobs
1933	Hartigan	Scriven	Moody	Jacobs
1934	Hartigan	Scriven	Round	Jacobs
1935	Round	Sperling	Moody	Jacobs
1936	Hartigan	Sperling	Jacobs	Marble
1937	Bolton	Sperling	Round	Lizana
1938	Bundy	Mathieu	Moody	Marble
1939	Westacott	Mathieu	Marble	Marble
1940	Bolton	—	—	Marble
1941	—	—	—	Cooke
1942	—	—	—	Betz
1943	—	—	—	Betz
1944	—	—	—	Betz
1945	—	—	—	Cooke
1946	Bolton	Osborne	Betz	Betz
1947	Bolton	Todd	Osborne	Brough
1948	Bolton	Landry	Brough	du Pont
1949	Hart	du Pont	Brough	du Pont
1950	Brough	Hart	Brough	du Pont
1951	Bolton	Fry	Hart	Connolly
1952	Long	Hart	Connolly	Connolly
1953	**Connolly**	**Connolly**	**Connolly**	**Connolly**
1954	Long	Connolly	Connolly	Hart
1955	Penrose	Mortimer	Brough	Hart
1956	Carter	Gibson	Fry	Fry
1957	Fry	Bloomer	Gibson	Gibson
1958	Mortimer	Kormoczi	Gibson	Gibson
1959	Reitano	Truman	Bueno	Bueno
1960	Smith	Hard	Bueno	Hard
1961	Smith	Haydon	Mortimer	Hard

Year	Australia	French	Wimbledon	U.S.
1962	Smith	Smith	Susman	Smith
1963	Smith	Turner	Smith	Bueno
1964	Smith	Smith	Bueno	Bueno
1965	Smith	Turner	Smith	Smith
1966	Smith	Jones	King	Bueno
1967	Richey	Durr	King	King
1968	King	Richey	King	Wade
1969	Court	Court	Jones	Court
1970	**Court**	**Court**	**Court**	**Court**
1971	Court	Goolagong	Goolagong	King
1972	Wade	King	King	King
1973	Court	Court	King	Court
1974	Goolagong	Evert	Evert	King
1975	Goolagong	Evert	King	Evert
1976	Cawley	Barker	Evert	Evert
1977	Reid & Cawley	Jausovec	Wade	Evert Lloyd
1978	O'Neil	Ruzici	Navratilova	Evert Lloyd
1979	Jordan	Evert Lloyd	Navratilova	Austin
1980	Mandlikova	Evert Lloyd	Cawley	Evert Lloyd
1981	Navratilova	Mandlikova	Evert Lloyd	Austin
1982	Evert Lloyd	Navratilova	Navratilova	Evert Lloyd
1983	Navratilova	Evert Lloyd	Navratilova	Navratilova
1984	Evert Lloyd	Navratilova	Navratilova	Navratilova
1985	Navratilova	Evert Lloyd	Navratilova	Mandlikova
1986	—	Evert Lloyd	Navratilova	Navratilova
1987	Mandlikova	Graf	Navratilova	Navratilova
1988	**Graf**	**Graf**	**Graf**	**Graf**
1989	Graf	Vicario	Graf	Graf
1990	Graf	Seles	Navratilova	Sabatini
1991	Seles	Seles	Graf	Seles
1992	Seles	Seles	Graf	Seles
1993	Seles	Graf	Graf	Graf
1994	Graf	Vicario	Martinez	Vicario

Overall Leaders

All-Time Grand Slam titlists including all singles and doubles championships at the four major tournaments. Titles listed under each heading are singles, doubles and mixed doubles. Players active in 1994 are in **bold** type.

MEN

		Career	Australian	French	Wimbledon	U.S.	Titles S-D-M	Titles
1	Roy Emerson	1959-71	6-3-0	2-6-0	2-3-0	2-4-0	12-16-0	28
2	John Newcombe	1965-76	2-5-0	0-3-0	3-6-0	2-3-1	7-17-1	25
3	Frank Sedgman	1949-52	2-2-2	0-2-2	1-3-2	2-2-2	5-9-8	22
4	Bill Tilden	1913-30	*	0-0-1	3-1-0	7-5-4	10-6-5	21
5	Rod Laver	1959-71	3-4-0	2-1-1	4-1-2	2-0-0	11-6-3	20
6	Jack Bromwich	1938-50	2-8-1	0-0-0	0-2-2	0-3-1	2-13-4	19
7	Ken Rosewall	1953-72	4-3-0	2-2-0	0-2-2	2-2-1	8-9-1	18
	Neale Fraser	1957-62	0-3-1	0-3-0	1-2-0	2-3-3	3-11-4	18
	Jean Borotra	1925-36	1-1-1	1-5-2	2-3-1	0-0-1	4-9-5	18
	Fred Stolle	1962-69	0-3-1	1-2-0	0-2-3	1-3-2	2-10-6	18
11	John McEnroe	1977-93	0-0-0	0-0-1	3-5-0	4-4-0	7-9-1	17
	Jack Crawford	1929-35	4-4-3	1-1-1	1-1-1	0-0-0	6-6-5	17
	Adrian Quist	1936-50	3-10-0	0-1-0	0-2-0	0-1-0	3-14-0	17
14	Laurie Doherty	1897-1906	*	*	5-8-0	1-2-0	6-10-0	16
15	Henri Cochet	1922-32	*	4-3-2	2-2-0	1-0-1	7-5-3	15
	Vic Seixas	1952-56	0-1-0	0-2-1	1-0-4	1-2-3	2-5-8	15
	Bob Hewitt	1961-79	0-2-1	0-1-2	0-5-2	0-1-1	0-9-6	15

Grand Slam Summary (Cont.)
Overall Leaders
WOMEN

	Career	Australian	French	Wimbledon	U.S.	S-D-M	Total Titles
1 Margaret Court Smith	1960-75	11-8-2	5-4-4	3-2-5	7-7-8	26-21-19	66
2 **Martina Navratilova**	1974—	3-8-0	2-7-2	9-7-2	4-9-2	18-31-6	55
3 Billie Jean King	1961-81	1-0-1	1-1-2	6-10-4	4-5-4	12-16-11	39
4 Margaret du Pont	1941-60	*	2-3-0	1-5-1	3-13-9	6-21-10	37
5 Louise Brough	1942-57	1-1-0	0-3-0	4-5-4	1-12-4	6-21-8	35
Doris Hart	1948-55	1-1-2	2-5-3	1-4-5	2-4-5	6-14-15	35
7 Helen Wills Moody	1923-38	*	4-2-0	8-3-1	7-4-2	19-9-3	31
8 Elizabeth Ryan	1914-34	*	0-4-0	0-12-7	0-1-2	0-17-9	26
9 Suzanne Lenglen	1919-26	*	6-2-2	6-6-3	0-0-0	12-8-5	25
10 **Pam Shriver**	1981—	0-7-0	0-4-1	0-5-0	0-5-0	0-21-1	22
11 Chris Evert Lloyd	1974-89	2-0-0	7-2-0	3-1-0	6-0-0	18-3-0	21
Darlene Hard	1958-69	*	1-3-2	0-4-3	2-6-0	3-13-5	21
13 Nancye Wynne Bolton	1935-52	6-10-4	0-0-0	0-0-0	0-0-0	6-10-4	20
14 Maria Bueno	1958-68	0-1-0	0-1-1	3-5-0	4-4-0	7-11-1	19
Thelma Coyne Long	1936-58	2-12-4	0-0-1	0-0-0	0-0-0	2-12-5	19

Annual Number One Players

Unofficial world rankings for men and women determined by the *London Daily Telegraph* from 1914-72. Since then, official world rankings computed by men's and women's tours. Rankings included only amateur players from 1914 until the arrival of open (professional) tennis in 1968. No rankings were released during World Wars I and II.

MEN

Multiple winners: Bill Tilden (6); Jimmy Connors (5); Henri Cochet, Rod Laver, Ivan Lendl and John McEnroe (4); John Newcombe and Fred Perry (3); Bjorn Borg, Don Budge, Ashley Cooper, Stefan Edberg, Roy Emerson, Neale Fraser, Jack Kramer, Rene Lacoste, Ilie Nastase, Frank Sedgman and Tony Trabert (2).

Year		Year		Year		Year	
1914	Maurice McLoughlin	1935	Fred Perry	1958	Ashley Cooper	1976	Jimmy Connors
1915-18	No rankings	1936	Fred Perry	1959	Neale Fraser	1977	Jimmy Connors
1919	Gerald Patterson	1937	Don Budge	1960	Neale Fraser	1978	Jimmy Connors
1920	Bill Tilden	1938	Don Budge	1961	Rod Laver	1979	Bjorn Borg
1921	Bill Tilden	1939	Bobby Riggs	1962	Rod Laver	1980	Bjorn Borg
1922	Bill Tilden	1940-45	No rankings	1963	Rafael Osuna	1981	John McEnroe
1923	Bill Tilden	1946	Jack Kramer	1964	Roy Emerson	1982	John McEnroe
1924	Bill Tilden	1947	Jack Kramer	1965	Roy Emerson	1983	John McEnroe
1925	Bill Tilden	1948	Frank Parker	1966	Manuel Santana	1984	John McEnroe
1926	Rene Lacoste	1949	Pancho Gonzalez	1967	John Newcombe	1985	Ivan Lendl
1927	Rene Lacoste	1950	Budge Patty	1968	Rod Laver	1986	Ivan Lendl
1928	Henri Cochet	1951	Frank Sedgman	1969	Rod Laver	1987	Ivan Lendl
1929	Henri Cochet	1952	Frank Sedgman	1970	John Newcombe	1988	Mats Wilander
1930	Henri Cochet	1953	Tony Trabert	1971	John Newcombe	1989	Ivan Lendl
1931	Henri Cochet	1954	Jaroslav Drobny	1972	Ilie Nastase	1990	Stefan Edberg
1932	Ellsworth Vines	1955	Tony Trabert	1973	Ilie Nastase	1991	Stefan Edberg
1933	Jack Crawford	1956	Lew Hoad	1974	Jimmy Connors	1992	Jim Courier
1934	Fred Perry	1957	Ashley Cooper	1975	Jimmy Connors	1993	Pete Sampras

WOMEN

Multiple winners: Helen Wills Moody (9); Margaret Smith Court and Martina Navratilova (7); Steffi Graf and Chris Evert Lloyd (5); Margaret Osborne duPont and Billie Jean King (4); Maureen Connolly (3); Maria Bueno, Althea Gibson, Suzanne Lenglen and Monica Seles (2).

Year		Year		Year		Year	
1925	Suzanne Lenglen	1946	Pauline Betz	1962	Margaret Smith	1978	Martina Navratilova
1926	Suzanne Lenglen	1947	Margaret Osborne	1963	Margaret Smith	1979	Martina Navratilova
1927	Helen Wills	1948	Margaret duPont	1964	Margaret Smith	1980	Chris Evert Lloyd
1928	Helen Wills	1949	Margaret duPont	1965	Margaret Smith	1981	Chris Evert Lloyd
1929	Helen Wills	1950	Margaret duPont	1966	Billie Jean King	1982	Martina Navratilova
1930	Helen Wills Moody	1951	Doris Hart	1967	Billie Jean King	1983	Martina Navratilova
1931	Helen Wills Moody	1952	Maureen Connolly	1968	Billie Jean King	1984	Martina Navratilova
1932	Helen Wills Moody	1953	Maureen Connolly	1969	Margaret Court	1985	Martina Navratilova
1933	Helen Wills Moody	1954	Maureen Connolly	1970	Margaret Court	1986	Martina Navratilova
1934	Dorothy Round	1955	Louise Brough	1971	Evonne Goolagong	1987	Steffi Graf
1935	Helen Wills Moody	1956	Shirley Fry	1972	Billie Jean King	1988	Steffi Graf
1936	Helen Jacobs	1957	Althea Gibson	1973	Margaret Court	1989	Steffi Graf
1937	Anita Lizana	1958	Althea Gibson	1974	Billie Jean King	1990	Steffi Graf
1938	Helen Wills Moody	1959	Maria Bueno	1975	Chris Evert	1991	Monica Seles
1939	Alice Marble	1960	Maria Bueno	1976	Chris Evert	1992	Monica Seles
1940-45	No rankings	1961	Angela Mortimer	1977	Chris Evert	1993	Steffi Graf

Annual Top 10 World Rankings (since 1968)

Year by year Top 10 world computer rankings for Men (ATP Tour) and Women (WTA Tour) since the arrival of open tennis in 1968. Rankings from 1968-72 made by Lance Tingay of the *London Daily Telegraph*. Since 1973, computerized rankings by ATP Tour (men) and WTA Tour (women).

MEN

1968	1973	1978	1983
1 Rod Laver	1 Ilie Nastase	1 Jimmy Connors	1 John McEnroe
2 Arthur Ashe	2 John Newcombe	2 Bjorn Borg	2 Ivan Lendl
3 Ken Rosewall	3 Jimmy Connors	3 Guillermo Vilas	3 Jimmy Connors
4 Tom Okker	4 Tom Okker	4 John McEnroe	4 Mats Wilander
5 Tony Roche	5 Stan Smith	5 Vitas Gerulaitis	5 Yannick Noah
6 John Newcombe	6 Ken Rosewall	6 Eddie Dibbs	6 Jimmy Arias
7 Clark Graebner	7 Manuel Orantes	7 Brian Gottfried	7 Jose Higueras
8 Dennis Ralston	8 Rod Laver	8 Raul Ramirez	8 Jose-Luis Clerc
Cliff Drysdale	Jan Kodes	9 Harold Solomon	9 Kevin Curren
10 Pancho Gonzalez	10 Arthur Ashe	10 Corrado Barazzutti	10 Gene Mayer

1969	1974	1979	1984
1 Rod Laver	1 Jimmy Connors	1 Bjorn Borg	1 John McEnroe
2 Tony Roche	2 John Newcombe	2 Jimmy Connors	2 Jimmy Connors
3 John Newcombe	3 Bjorn Borg	3 John McEnroe	3 Ivan Lendl
4 Tom Okker	4 Rod Laver	4 Vitas Gerulaitis	4 Mats Wilander
5 Ken Rosewall	5 Guillermo Vilas	Roscoe Tanner	5 Andres Gomez
6 Arthur Ashe	6 Tom Okker	Guillermo Vilas	6 Anders Jarryd
7 Cliff Drysdale	7 Arthur Ashe	7 Arthur Ashe	7 Henrik Sundstrom
8 Pancho Gonzalez	8 Ken Rosewall	8 Harold Solomon	8 Pat Cash
9 Andres Gimeno	9 Stan Smith	9 Jose Higueras	9 Eliot Teltscher
10 Fred Stolle	10 Ilie Nastase	10 Eddie Dibbs	10 Yannick Noah

1970	1975	1980	1985
1 John Newcombe	1 Jimmy Connors	1 Bjorn Borg	1 Ivan Lendl
2 Ken Rosewall	2 Guillermo Vilas	2 John McEnroe	2 John McEnroe
3 Tony Roche	3 Bjorn Borg	3 Jimmy Connors	3 Mats Wilander
4 Rod Laver	4 Arthur Ashe	4 Gene Mayer	4 Jimmy Connors
5 Arthur Ashe	5 Manuel Orantes	5 Guillermo Vilas	5 Stefan Edberg
6 Ilie Nastase	6 Ken Rosewall	6 Ivan Lendl	6 Boris Becker
7 Tom Okker	7 Ilie Nastase	Harold Solomon	7 Yannick Noah
8 Roger Taylor	8 John Alexander	8 Jose-Luis Clerc	8 Anders Jarryd
9 Jan Kodes	9 Roscoe Tanner	9 Vitas Gerulaitis	9 Miloslav Mecir
10 Cliff Richey	10 Rod Laver	10 Eliot Teltscher	10 Kevin Curren

1971	1976	1981	1986
1 John Newcombe	1 Jimmy Connors	1 John McEnroe	1 Ivan Lendl
2 Stan Smith	2 Bjorn Borg	2 Ivan Lendl	2 Boris Becker
3 Rod Laver	3 Ilie Nastase	3 Jimmy Connors	3 Mats Wilander
4 Ken Rosewall	4 Manuel Orantes	4 Bjorn Borg	4 Yannick Noah
5 Jan Kodes	5 Raul Ramirez	5 Jose-Luis Clerc	5 Stefan Edberg
6 Arthur Ashe	6 Guillermo Vilas	6 Guillermo Vilas	6 Henri Leconte
7 Tom Okker	7 Adriano Panatta	7 Gene Mayer	7 Joakim Nystrom
8 Marty Riessen	8 Harold Solomon	8 Eliot Teltscher	8 Jimmy Connors
9 Cliff Drysdale	9 Eddie Dibbs	9 Vitas Gerulaitis	9 Miloslav Mecir
10 Ilie Nastase	10 Brian Gottfried	10 Peter McNamara	10 Andres Gomez

1972	1977	1982	1987
1 Stan Smith	1 Jimmy Connors	1 John McEnroe	1 Ivan Lendl
2 Ken Rosewall	2 Guillermo Vilas	2 Jimmy Connors	2 Stefan Edberg
3 Ilie Nastase	3 Bjorn Borg	3 Ivan Lendl	3 Mats Wilander
4 Rod Laver	4 Vitas Gerulaitis	4 Guillermo Vilas	4 Jimmy Connors
5 Arthur Ashe	5 Brian Gottfried	5 Vitas Gerulaitis	5 Boris Becker
6 John Newcombe	6 Eddie Dibbs	6 Jose-Luis Clerc	6 Miloslav Mecir
7 Bob Lutz	7 Manuel Orantes	7 Mats Wilander	7 Pat Cash
8 Tom Okker	8 Raul Ramirez	8 Gene Mayer	8 Yannick Noah
9 Marty Riessen	9 Ilie Nastase	9 Yannick Noah	9 Tim Mayotte
10 Andres Gimeno	10 Dick Stockton	10 Peter McNamara	10 John McEnroe

Annual Top 10 World Rankings (Cont.)
MEN

1988	1989	1990	1991
1 Mats Wilander	1 Ivan Lendl	1 Stefan Edberg	1 Stefan Edberg
2 Ivan Lendl	2 Boris Becker	2 Boris Becker	2 Jim Courier
3 Andre Agassi	3 Stefan Edberg	3 Ivan Lendl	3 Boris Becker
4 Boris Becker	4 John McEnroe	4 Andre Agassi	4 Michael Stich
5 Stefan Edberg	5 Michael Chang	5 Pete Sampras	5 Ivan Lendl
6 Kent Carlsson	6 Brad Gilbert	6 Andres Gomez	6 Pete Sampras
7 Jimmy Connors	7 Andre Agassi	7 Thomas Muster	7 Guy Forget
8 Jakob Hlasek	8 Aaron Krickstein	8 Emilio Sanchez	8 Karel Novacek
9 Henri Leconte	9 Alberto Mancini	9 Goran Ivanisevic	9 Petr Korda
10 Tim Mayotte	10 Jay Berger	10 Brad Gilbert	10 Andre Agassi

1992		1993	
1 Jim Courier	6 Michael Chang	1 Pete Sampras	6 Andrei Medvedev
2 Stefan Edberg	7 Petr Korda	2 Michael Stich	7 Goren Ivanisevic
3 Pete Sampras	8 Ivan Lendl	3 Jim Courier	8 Michael Chang
4 Goren Ivanisevic	9 Andre Agassi	4 Sergi Bruguera	9 Thomas Muster
5 Boris Becker	10 Richard Krajicek	5 Stefan Edberg	10 Cedric Pioline

WOMEN

1968	1972	1976	1980
1 Billie Jean King	1 Billie Jean King	1 Chris Evert	1 Chris Evert
Virginia Wade	2 Evonne Goolagong	2 Evonne G. Cawley	2 Tracy Austin
3 Nancy Richey	3 Chris Evert	3 Virginia Wade	3 Martina Navratilova
4 Maria Bueno	4 Margaret Court	4 Martina Navratilova	4 Hana Mandlikova
5 Margaret Court	5 Kerry Melville	5 Sue Barker	5 Evonne G. Cawley
6 Ann Jones	6 Virginia Wade	6 Betty Stove	6 Billie Jean King
7 Judy Tegart	7 Rosie Casals	7 Dianne Balestrat	7 Andrea Jaeger
8 Annette du Plooy	8 Nancy R. Gunter	8 Mima Jausovec	8 Wendy Turnbull
9 Leslie Bowrey	9 Francoise Durr	9 Rosie Casals	9 Pam Shriver
10 Rosie Casals	10 Linda Tuero	10 Francoise Durr	10 Greer Stevens

1969	1973	1977	1981
1 Margaret Court	1 Margaret S. Court	1 Chris Evert	1 Chris Evert
2 Ann Jones	2 Billie Jean King	2 Billie Jean King	2 Tracy Austin
3 Billie Jean King	3 Evonne G. Cawley	3 Martina Navratilova	3 Martina Navratilova
4 Nancy Richey	4 Chris Evert	4 Virginia Wade	4 Andrea Jaeger
5 Julie Heldman	5 Rosie Casals	5 Sue Barker	5 Hana Mandlikova
6 Rosie Casals	6 Virginia Wade	6 Rosie Casals	6 Sylvia Hanika
7 Kerry Melville	7 Kerry Reid	7 Betty Stove	7 Pam Shriver
8 Peaches Barkowicz	8 Nancy Richey	8 Dianne Balestrat	8 Wendy Turnbull
9 Virginia Wade	9 Julie Heldman	9 Wendy Turnbull	9 Bettina Bunge
10 Leslie Bowrey	10 Helga Masthoff	10 Kerry Reid	10 Barbara Potter

1970	1974	1978	1982
1 Margaret Court	1 Billie Jean King	1 Martina Navratilova	1 Martina Navratilova
2 Billie Jean King	2 Evonne G. Cawley	2 Chris Evert	2 Chris Evert
3 Rosie Casals	3 Chris Evert	3 Evonne G. Cawley	3 Andrea Jaeger
4 Virginia Wade	4 Virginia Wade	4 Virginia Wade	4 Tracy Austin
5 Helga Niessen	5 Julie Heldman	5 Billie Jean King	5 Wendy Turnbull
6 Kerry Melville	6 Rosie Casals	6 Tracy Austin	6 Pam Shriver
7 Julie Heldman	7 Kerry Reid	7 Wendy Turnbull	7 Hana Mandlikova
8 Karen Krantczke	8 Olga Morozova	8 Kerry Reid	8 Barbara Potter
9 Francoise Durr	9 Lesley Hunt	9 Betty Stove	9 Bettina Bunge
10 Nancy R. Gunter	10 Francoise Durr	10 Dianne Balestrat	10 Sylvia Hanika

1971	1975	1979	1983
1 Evonne Goolagong	1 Chris Evert	1 Martina Navratilova	1 Martina Navratilova
2 Billie Jean King	2 Billie Jean King	2 Chris Evert	2 Chris Evert
3 Margaret Court	3 Evonne G. Cawley	3 Tracy Austin	3 Andrea Jaeger
4 Rosie Casals	4 Martina Navratilova	4 Evonne G. Cawley	4 Pam Shriver
5 Kerry Melville	5 Virginia Wade	5 Billie Jean King	5 Sylvia Hanika
6 Virginia Wade	6 Margaret S. Court	6 Dianne Balestrat	6 Jo Durie
7 Judy Tagert	7 Olga Morozova	7 Wendy Turnbull	7 Bettina Bunge
8 Francoise Durr	8 Nancy Richey	8 Virginia Wade	8 Wendy Turnbull
9 Helga N. Masthoff	9 Francoise Durr	9 Kerry Reid	9 Tracy Austin
10 Chris Evert	10 Rosie Casals	10 Sue Barker	10 Zina Garrison

1984
1 Martina Navratilova
2 Chris Evert
3 Hana Mandlikova
4 Pam Shriver
5 Wendy Turnbull
6 Manuela Maleeva
7 Helena Sukova
8 Claudia Kohde-Kilsch
9 Zina Garrison
10 Kathy Jordan

1985
1 Martina Navratilova
2 Chris Evert
3 Hana Mandlikova
4 Pam Shriver
5 Claudia Kohde-Kilsch
6 Steffi Graf
7 Manuela Maleeva
8 Zina Garrison
9 Helena Sukova
10 Bonnie Gadusek

1986
1 Martina Navratilova
2 Chris Evert
3 Steffi Graf
4 Hana Mandlikova
5 Helena Sukova
6 Pam Shriver
7 Claudia Kohde-Kilsch
8 M. Maleeva-Fragniere
9 Zina Garrison
10 Claudia Kohde-Kilsch

1987
1 Steffi Graf
2 Martina Navratilova
3 Chris Evert
4 Pam Shriver
5 Hana Mandlikova
6 Gabriela Sabatini
7 Helena Sukova
8 M. Maleeva-Fragniere
9 Zina Garrison
10 Claudia Kohde-Kilsch

1988
1 Steffi Graf
2 Martina Navratilova
3 Chris Evert
4 Gabriela Sabatini
5 Pam Shriver
6 M. Maleeva-Fragniere
7 Natalia Zvereva
8 Helena Sukova
9 Zina Garrison
10 Barbara Potter

1989
1 Steffi Graf
2 Martina Navratilova
3 Gabriela Sabatini
4 Z. Garrison-Jackson
5 A. Sanchez Vicario
6 Monica Seles
7 Conchita Martinez
8 Helena Sukova
9 M. Maleeva-Fragniere
10 Chris Evert

1990
1 Steffi Graf
2 Monica Seles
3 Martina Navratilova
4 Mary Joe Fernandez
5 Gabriela Sabatini
6 Katerina Maleeva
7 A. Sanchez Vicario
8 Jennifer Capriati
9 M. Maleeva-Fragniere
10 Z. Garrison-Jackson

1991
1 Monica Seles
2 Steffi Graf
3 Gabriela Sabatini
4 Martina Navratilova
5 A. Sanchez Vicario
6 Jennifer Capriati
7 Jana Novotna
8 Mary Joe Fernandez
9 Conchita Martinez
10 M. Maleeva-Fragniere

1992
1 Monica Seles
2 Steffi Graf
3 Gabriela Sabatini
4 A. Sanchez Vicario
5 Martina Navratilova
6 Mary Joe Fernandez
7 Jennifer Capriati
8 Conchita Martinez
9 M. Maleeva-Fragniere
10 Jana Novotna

1993
1 Steffi Graf
2 A. Sanchez Vicario
3 Martina Navratilova
4 Conchita Martinez
5 Gabriela Sabatini
6 Jana Novotna
7 Mary Joe Fernandez
8 Monica Seles
9 Jennifer Capriati
10 Anke Huber

All-Time Leaders

Tournaments Won

All-time tournament wins from the arrival of open tennis in 1968 through 1993. Players active in 1993 are in **bold** type.

MEN

	Total		Total		Total
1 Jimmy Connors	109	6 Ilie Nastase	57	11 Arthur Ashe	33
2 **Ivan Lendl**	94	7 Rod Laver	47	**Mats Wilander**	33
3 John McEnroe	77	8 Stan Smith	39	13 John Newcombe	32
4 Bjorn Borg	62	9 **Boris Becker**	38	Manuel Orantes	32
5 Guillermo Vilas	61	**Stefan Edberg**	37	Ken Rosewall	32

WOMEN

	Total		Total		Total
1 **Martina Navratilova**	166	6 Billie Jean King	71	11 Tracy Austin	29
Chris Evert	157	7 Virginia Wade	55	12 Hana Mandlikova	27
3 Evonne G. Cawley	88	8 Helga Masthoff	37	13 Nancy Richey	25
4 Margaret Smith Court	79	9 Monica Seles	32	**Gabriela Sabatini**	25
5 **Steffi Graf**	79	10 Olga Morozova	31	15 Kerry Melville Reid	22

Money Won

All-time money winners from the arrival of open tennis in 1968 through 1993. Totals include doubles earnings.

MEN

	Earnings		Earnings		Earnings
1 Ivan Lendl	$20,248,503	6 Jim Courier	$8,430,780	11 Guillermo Vilas	$4,923,452
2 Stefan Edberg	15,648,584	7 Pete Sampras	8,205,300	12 Anders Jarryd	4,817,454
3 Boris Becker	13,436,281	8 Mats Wilander	7,422,048	13 Goran Ivanisevic	4,727,155
4 John McEnroe	12,227,622	9 Andre Agassi	5,759,038	14 Michael Chang	4,421,345
5 Jimmy Connors	8,498,820	10 Michael Stich	5,329,524	15 Emilio Sanchez	4,409,660

All-Time Leaders (Cont.)
Money Won
WOMEN

		Earnings			Earnings			Earnings
1	Martina Navratilova	$19,432,645	6	A. Sanchez Vicario	$5,374,351	11	Hana Mandlikova	$3,340,959
2	Steffi Graf	13,154,010	7	Pam Shriver	5,072,125	12	Natalia Zvereva	3,220,989
3	Chris Evert	8,896,195	8	Helena Sukova	4,998,606	13	M.Maleeva-Fragniere	3,135,352
4	Monica Seles	7,408,981	9	Zina Garrison-Jackson	4,013,373	14	Mary Joe Fernandez	2,865,202
5	Gabriela Sabatini	7,014,352	10	Jana Novotna	3,554,303	15	Wendy Turnbull	2,769,024

Year-end Tournaments
MEN
Masters/ATP Tour World Championship

The year-end championship of the ATP men's tour since 1970. Contested by the year's top eight players. Originally a round-robin, the Masters was revised in 1972 to include a round-robin to decide the four semifinalists then a single elimination format after that. Held at Madison Square Garden in New York from 1978-89. Replaced by ATP Tour World Championship in 1990 and held in Frankfurt, Germany since then.

Multiple Winners: Ivan Lendl (5); Ilie Nastase (4); John McEnroe (3); Boris Becker and Bjorn Borg (2).

Year	Winner		Runner-Up
1970	Stan Smith (4-1)		Rod Laver (4-1)
1971	Ilie Nastase (6-0)		Stan Smith (4-2)

Year	Winner	Loser	Score
1972	Ilie Nastase	S. Smith	63 62 36 26 63
1973	Ilie Nastase	T. Okker	63 75 46 63
1974	Guillermo Vilas	I. Nastase	76 62 36 36 64
1975	Ilie Nastase	B. Borg	62 62 61
1976	Manuel Orantes	W. Fibak	57 62 06 76 61
1978	Jimmy Connors	B. Borg	64 16 64
1979	John McEnroe	A. Ashe	67 63 75
1980	Bjorn Borg	V. Gerulaitis	62 62
1981	Bjorn Borg	I. Lendl	64 62 62
1982	Ivan Lendl	V. Gerulaitis	67 26 76 62 64

Year	Winner	Loser	Score
1983	Ivan Lendl	J. McEnroe	64 64 62
1984	John McEnroe	I. Lendl	63 64 64
1985	John McEnroe	I. Lendl	75 60 64
1986	Ivan Lendl	B. Becker	62 76 63
1986	Ivan Lendl	B. Becker	64 64 64
1987	Ivan Lendl	M. Wilander	62 62 63
1988	Boris Becker	I. Lendl	57 76 36 62 76
1989	Stefan Edberg	B. Becker	46 76 63 61
1990	Andre Agassi	S.Edberg	57 76 75 62
1991	Pete Sampras	J. Courier	36 76 63 64
1992	Boris Becker	J. Courier	64 63 75
1993	Michael Stich	P. Sampras	76 26 76 62

*Tournament switched from December to January in 1977-78, then back to December in 1986.
Note: In 1970, Smith was declared the winner because he beat Laver in their round-robin match (4-6, 6-3, 6-4).

WOMEN
Virginia Slims Championships

The year-end championship of the WTA women's tour since 1977. Contested by the year's top 16 players. Since 1983, the tournament has featured the tour's only best-of-five set final.

Multiple winners: Martina Navratilova (6); Monica Seles (3); Tracy Austin, Steffi Graf and Chris Evert Lloyd (2).

Year	Winner	Loser	Score
1977	Chris Evert	B.J. King	62 62
1978	Chris Evert	M. Navratilova	63 63
1979	M. Navratilova	T. Austin	62 61
1980	Tracy Austin	A. Jaeger	62 62
1981	Tracy Austin	M. Navratilova	26 64 62
1982	M. Navratilova	C. Evert Lloyd	46 61 62
1983	M. Navratilova	C. Evert Lloyd	63 75 64
1984	M. Navratilova	H. Sukova	63 75 64
1985	M. Navratilova	H. Mandlikova	62 60 36 61

Year	Winner	Loser	Score
1986	M. Navratilova	S. Graf	76 63 62
1987	Steffi Graf	G. Sabatini	46 64 60 64
1988	Gabriela Sabatini	P. Shriver	75 62 62
1989	Steffi Graf	M. Navratilova	64 75 26 62
1990	Monica Seles	G. Sabatini	64 57 36 64 62
1991	Monica Seles	M. Navratilova	64 36 75 60
1992	Monica Seles	M. Navratilova	75 63 61
1993	Steffi Graf	A.S. Vicario	61 64 36 61

National Team Competition
Davis Cup

Established in 1900 as an annual international tournament by American player Dwight Davis. Originally called the International Lawn Tennis Challenge Trophy. Challenge round system until 1972. Since 1981, the top 16 nations in the world have played a straight knockout tournament over the course of a year. The format is a best-of-five match of two singles, one doubles and two singles over three days.

Multiple winners: USA (30); Australia (20); France (7); Australasia (6); British Isles (5); Britain and Sweden (4); Germany (3).

Challenge Rounds

Year	Winner	Loser	Score	Site
1900	USA	British Isles	3-0	Boston
1901	Not held			
1902	USA	British Isles	3-2	New York
1903	British Isles	USA	4-1	Boston
1904	British Isles	Belgium	5-0	Wimbledon

Year	Winner	Loser	Score	Site
1905	British Isles	USA	5-0	Wimbledon
1906	British Isles	USA	5-0	Wimbledon
1907	Australasia	British Isles	3-2	Wimbledon
1908	Australasia	USA	3-2	Melbourne
1909	Australasia	USA	5-0	Sydney

Year	Winner	Loser	Score	Site	Year	Winner	Loser	Score	Site
1910	Not held				1938	USA	Australia	3-2	Philadelphia
1911	Australasia	USA	5-0	Christchurch,NZ	1939	Australia	USA	3-2	Philadelphia
1912	British Isles	Australasia	3-2	Melbourne	1940-45	Not held		World War II	
1913	USA	British Isles	3-2	Wimbledon	1946	USA	Australia	5-0	Melbourne
1914	Australasia	USA	3-2	New York	1947	USA	Australia	4-1	New York
1915-18	Not held	World War I			1948	USA	Australia	5-0	New York
1919	Australasia	British Isles	4-1	Sydney	1949	USA	Australia	4-1	New York
1920	USA	Australasia	5-0	Auckland, NZ	1950	Australia	USA	4-1	New York
1921	USA	Japan	5-0	New York	1951	Australia	USA	3-2	Sydney
1922	USA	Australasia	4-1	New York	1952	Australia	USA	4-1	Adelaide
1923	USA	Australasia	4-1	New York	1953	Australia	USA	3-2	Melbourne
1924	USA	Australia	5-0	Philadelphia	1954	USA	Australia	3-2	Sydney
1925	USA	France	5-0	Philadelphia	1955	Australia	USA	5-0	New York
1926	USA	France	4-1	Philadelphia	1956	Australia	USA	5-0	Adelaide
1927	France	USA	3-2	Philadelphia	1957	Australia	USA	3-2	Melbourne
1928	France	USA	4-1	Paris	1958	USA	Australia	3-2	Brisbane
1929	France	USA	3-2	Paris	1959	Australia	USA	3-2	New York
1930	France	USA	4-1	Paris	1960	Australia	Italy	4-1	Sydney
1931	France	Britain	3-2	Paris	1961	Australia	Italy	5-0	Melbourne
1932	France	USA	3-2	Paris	1962	Australia	Mexico	5-0	Brisbane
1933	Britain	France	3-2	Paris	1963	USA	Australia	3-2	Adelaide
1934	Britain	USA	4-1	Wimbledon	1964	Australia	USA	3-2	Cleveland
1935	Britain	USA	5-0	Wimbledon	1965	Australia	Spain	4-1	Sydney
1936	Britain	Australia	3-2	Wimbledon	1966	Australia	India	4-1	Melbourne
1937	USA	Britain	4-1	Wimbledon	1967	Australia	Spain	4-1	Brisbane

Final Rounds

Year	Winner	Loser	Score	Site	Year	Winner	Loser	Score	Site
1968	USA	Australia	4-1	Adelaide	1981	USA	Argentina	3-1	Cincinnati
1969	USA	Romania	5-0	Cleveland	1982	USA	France	4-1	Grenoble
1970	USA	W. Germany	5-0	Cleveland	1983	Australia	Sweden	3-2	Melbourne
1971	USA	Romania	3-2	Charlotte	1984	Sweden	USA	4-1	Gothenburg
1972	USA	Romania	3-2	Bucharest	1985	Sweden	W. Germany	3-2	Munich
1973	Australia	USA	5-0	Cleveland	1986	Australia	Sweden	3-2	Melbourne
1974	So. Africa	India	walkover —		1987	Sweden	India	5-0	Gothenburg
1975	Sweden	Czech.	3-2	Stockholm	1988	W.Germany	Sweden	4-1	Gothenburg
1976	Italy	Chile	4-1	Santiago	1989	W.Germany	Sweden	3-2	Stuttgart
1977	Australia	Italy	3-1	Sydney	1990	USA	Australia	3-2	St. Petersburg
1978	USA	Britain	4-1	Palm Springs	1991	France	USA	3-1	Lyon
1979	USA	Italy	5-0	San Francisco	1992	USA	Switzerland	3-1	Ft. Worth
1980	Czech.	Italy	4-1	Prague	1993	Germany	Australia	4-1	Dusseldorf

Note: In 1974, India refused to play the final as a protest against the South African government's policies of apartheid.

Federation Cup

Started in 1963 by the International Lawn Tennis Federation as the Davis Cup of women's tennis. The major difference is that all competing countries gather at one site to decide the Cup winner in one week.
Multiple winners: USA (14); Australia (7); Czechoslovakia (5); Spain (3); Germany (2).

Year	Winner	Loser	Score	Site	Year	Winner	Loser	Score	Site
1963	USA	Australia	2-1	London	1980	USA	Australia	3-0	W. Germany
1964	Australia	USA	2-1	Philadelphia	1981	USA	Britain	3-0	Tokyo
1965	Australia	USA	2-1	Melbourne	1982	USA	W. Germany	3-0	Santa Clara
1966	USA	W. Germany	3-0	Italy	1983	Czech.	W. Germany	2-1	Zurich
1967	USA	Britain	2-0	W. Germany	1984	Czech.	Australia	2-1	Brazil
1968	Australia	Holland	3-0	Paris	1985	Czech.	USA	2-1	Japan
1969	USA	Australia	2-1	Athens	1986	USA	Czech.	3-0	Prague
1970	Australia	Britain	3-0	W. Germany	1987	W. Germany	USA	2-1	Vancouver
1971	Australia	Britain	3-0	Perth	1988	Czech.	USSR	2-1	Melbourne
1972	So. Africa	Britain	2-1	Africa	1989	USA	Spain	3-0	Tokyo
1973	Australia	So. Africa	3-0	W. Germany	1990	USA	USSR	2-1	Atlanta
1974	Australia	USA	2-1	Italy	1991	Spain	USA	2-1	Nottingham
1975	Czech.	Australia	3-0	France	1992	Germany	Spain	2-1	Frankfurt
1976	USA	Australia	2-1	Philadelphia	1993	Spain	Australia	3-0	Frankfurt
1977	USA	Australia	2-1	Eastbourne	1994	Spain	USA	3-0	Frankfurt
1978	USA	Australia	2-1	Melbourne					
1979	USA	Australia	3-0	Spain					

COLLEGES

The NCAA recognizes men's individual tennis champions since 1883, but team titles were not sanctioned until 1946. NCAA women's individual and team championships started in 1982.

Men's NCAA Individual Champions (1883-1945)

Multiple winners: Malcolm Chace and Pancho Segura (3); Edward Chandler, George Church, E.B. Dewhurst, Fred Hovey, Frank Guernsey, W.P. Knapp, Robert LeRoy, P.S. Sears, Cliff Sutter, Ernest Sutter and Richard Williams (2).

Year		Year		Year	
1883	J. Clark, Harvard (spring)	1903	E.B. Dewhurst, Penn	1925	Edward Chandler, Calif.
	H. Taylor, Harvard (fall)	1904	Robert LeRoy, Columbia	1926	Edward Chandler, Calif.
1884	W.P. Knapp, Yale	1905	E.B. Dewhurst, Penn	1927	Wilmer Allison, Texas
1885	W.P. Knapp, Yale	1906	Robert LeRoy, Columbia	1928	Julius Seligson, Lehigh
1886	G.M. Brinley, Trinity, CT	1907	G.P. Gardner Jr, Harvard	1929	Berkeley Bell, Texas
1887	P.S. Sears, Harvard	1908	Nat Niles, Harvard		
1888	P.S. Sears, Harvard	1909	Wallace Johnson, Penn	1930	Cliff Sutter, Tulane
1889	R.P. Huntington Jr, Yale			1931	Keith Gledhill, Stanford
		1910	R.A. Holden Jr, Yale	1932	Cliff Sutter, Tulane
1890	Fred Hovey, Harvard	1911	E.H. Whitney, Harvard	1933	Jack Tidball, UCLA
1891	Fred Hovey, Harvard	1912	George Church, Princeton	1934	Gene Mako, USC
1892	William Larned, Cornell	1913	Richard Williams, Harv.	1935	Wilbur Hess, Rice
1893	Malcolm Chace, Brown	1914	George Church, Princeton	1936	Ernest Sutter, Tulane
1894	Malcolm Chace, Yale	1915	Richard Williams, Harv.	1937	Ernest Sutter, Tulane
1895	Malcolm Chace, Yale	1916	G.C. Caner, Harvard	1938	Frank Guernsey, Rice
1896	Malcolm Whitman, Harvard	1917-1918	Not held	1939	Frank Guernsey, Rice
1897	S.G. Thompson, Princeton	1919	Charles Garland, Yale		
1898	Leo Ware, Harvard			1940	Don McNeill, Kenyon
1899	Dwight Davis, Harvard	1920	Lascelles Banks, Yale	1941	Joseph Hunt, Navy
		1921	Philip Neer, Stanford	1942	Fred Schroeder, Stanford
1900	Ray Little, Princeton	1922	Lucien Williams, Yale	1943	Pancho Segura, Miami-FL
1901	Fred Alexander, Princeton	1923	Carl Fischer, Phi.Osteo.	1944	Pancho Segura, Miami-FL
1902	William Clothier, Harvard	1924	Wallace Scott, Wash.	1945	Pancho Segura, Miami-FL

NCAA Division I Champions

Multiple winners (teams): UCLA and USC (15); Stanford (12); Georgia and William & Mary (2).
Multiple winners (players): Alex Olmedo, Mikael Pernfors, Dennis Ralston and Ham Richardson (2).

Year	Team winner	Individual Champion	Year	Team winner	Individual Champion
1946	USC	Bob Falkenburg, USC	1970	UCLA	Jeff Borowiak, UCLA
1947	Wm. & Mary	Garner Larned, Wm.& Mary	1971	UCLA	Jimmy Connors, UCLA
1948	Wm. & Mary	Harry Likas, San Francisco	1972	Trinity-TX	Dick Stockton, Trinity-TX
1949	San Francisco	Jack Tuero, Tulane	1973	Stanford	Alex Mayer, Stanford
1950	UCLA	Herbert Flam, UCLA	1974	Stanford	John Whitlinger, Stanford
1951	USC	Tony Trabert, Cinncinati	1975	UCLA	Bill Martin, UCLA
1952	UCLA	Hugh Stewart, USC	1976	USC & UCLA	Bill Scanlon, Trinity-TX
1953	UCLA	Ham Richardson, Tulane	1977	Stanford	Matt Mitchell, Stanford
1954	UCLA	Ham Richardson, Tulane	1978	Stanford	John McEnroe, Stanford
1955	USC	Jose Aguero, Tulane	1979	UCLA	Kevin Curren, Texas
1956	UCLA	Alex Olmedo, USC	1980	Stanford	Robert Van't Hof, USC
1957	Michigan	Barry MacKay, Michigan	1981	Stanford	Tim Mayotte, Stanford
1958	USC	Alex Olmedo, USC	1982	UCLA	Mike Leach, Michigan
1959	Tulane & Notre Dame	Whitney Reed, San Jose St.	1983	Stanford	Greg Holmes, Utah
			1984	UCLA	Mikael Pernfors, Georgia
1960	UCLA	Larry Nagler, UCLA	1985	Georgia	Mikael Pernfors, Georgia
1961	UCLA	Allen Fox, UCLA	1986	Stanford	Dan Goldie, Stanford
1962	USC	Rafael Osuna, USC	1987	Georgia	Andrew Burrow, Miami-FL
1963	USC	Dennis Ralston, USC	1988	Stanford	Robby Weiss, Pepperdine
1964	USC	Dennis Ralston, USC	1989	Stanford	Donni Leaycraft, LSU
1965	UCLA	Arthur Ashe, UCLA			
1966	USC	Charlie Pasarell, UCLA	1990	Stanford	Steve Bryan, Texas
1967	USC	Bob Lutz, USC	1991	USC	Jared Palmer, Stanford
1968	USC	Stan Smith, USC	1992	Stanford	Alex O'Brien, Stanford
1969	USC	Joaquin Loyo-Mayo, USC	1993	USC	Chris Woodruff, Tennessee
			1994	USC	Mark Merklein, Florida

Women's NCAA Champions

Multiple winners (teams): Stanford (8); USC (2).
Multiple winners (players): Sandra Birch, Patty Fendick and Lisa Raymond (2).

Year	Team winner	Individual Champion	Year	Team winner	Individual Champion
1982	Stanford	Alycia Moulton, Stanford	1989	Stanford	Sandra Birch, Stanford
1983	USC	Beth Herr, USC	1990	Stanford	Debbie Graham, Stanford
1984	Stanford	Lisa Spain, Georgia	1991	Stanford	Sandra Birch, Stanford
1985	USC	Linda Gates, Stanford	1992	Florida	Lisa Raymond, Florida
1986	Stanford	Patty Fendick, Stanford	1993	Texas	Lisa Raymond, Florida
1987	Stanford	Patty Fendick, Stanford	1994	Georgia	Angela Lettiere, Georgia
1988	Stanford	Shaun Stafford, Florida			

Nick Price became the first player in four years to win two majors, claiming his second PGA Championship and his first British Open in 1994.

GOLF

by Marino Parascenzo

The Predator

*Nick Price wins British Open and PGA Championship
on his way to becoming golf's most dominant player.*

If you can forget that they found cancer in 'Zinger, it was a dynamite year. Start with Nick Price. The dominant player everyone was looking for had been standing there all along, only nobody really noticed—even after he was named Player of the Year in 1993.

The world was waiting for a predator, and Price seems too nice a guy to dominate. But if what he's achieved isn't domination, it must be two guys. By mid-September, Price had seven victories in 1994—six on the PGA Tour, including the PGA Championship, plus the British Open, plus nearly $1.5 million in U.S. winnings.

In the last three years, he has had 16 wins in 54 starts worldwide, and 33 Top-10 finishes. Since joining the PGA Tour in 1983, he has won a total of 14 titles—13 of them coming in the last four seasons. He also leads the world in newspaper headline puns: "Price Is Right," "Can't Beat This Price," "Price Fixing for More," etc., etc.

Price had been the best for about two years, but never admitted it. Now? "From the way I played the last month and a half, plus the way I've played since the beginning of '93, maybe the Sony Ranking is right," he said. Maybe.

Back to the year.

U.S. players were shut out of the four

Marino Parascenzo has been the Pittsburgh *Post-Gazette's* golf writer since 1975. He has also been a contributing editor to *Golf Digest.*

men's majors for the first time ever in 1994—which sent jingoists off to light candles for American golf.

Spain's Jose Maria Olazabal, the 28-year-old son of a greens superintendent, led off by taking the Masters (nothing new there, foreigners have won six of the last seven green blazers). But then Ernie Els, the big South African, was the last man standing in the U.S. Open at Oakmont. And Price, the 37-year-old native of Zimbabwe who now lives in Orlando, walked off with his first British Open and his second PGA Championship. All four majors were boffo box office, except for folks who don't like foreign films.

Elsewhere, there was great theater of various kinds. There was sore-kneed Johnny Miller, 46, climbing down from the TV booth and winning the AT&T National Pro-Am at Pebble Beach in February. And LPGA golfer Kim Williams adding new meaning to the phrase "playing hurt," or, better yet, "playing shot." John Daly continued to career back and forth across the deck. Deane Beman up and quit the commissioner's job. Fred Couples sat out awhile with his bad back. Rocco Mediate had his back operated on. Phil Mickelson crashed on the ski slopes in late winter and broke his right thigh and left ankle. And in a different kind of crash, Sweden's Helen Alfredsson went down in flames at the U.S. Women's Open.

But first, all eyes were on Paul Azinger. The stubborn pain in his right shoulder that

New Masters champion **Jose Maria Olazabal** (right) of Spain is helped into his green jacket by 1993 winner **Bernhard Langer** of Germany. Foreign players, who have won the Masters six out of the last seven years, swept all four major tournaments on the men's tour for the first time ever in 1994.

plagued him in 1993 was diagnosed as lymphoma. Don't panic, they said, there's a 90 percent rate of recovery. After chemotherapy and radiation treatment, Zinger returned to the PGA Tour in August, at the Buick Open, and missed the cut. "Teeing off was the big victory for me," he said.

He also missed the cut the following week in defense of his title at the PGA Championship in Tulsa, then decided to leave the tour again. "I think it might be a little longer before I can make a full comeback," he said.

The Masters came down to a duel of fatalists. Big, likeable Tom Lehman lost by a total of about 15 inches on the last four holes. Twelve inches was how far above the water Olazabal's ball clung to the tight-shaved (did someone say "bikini-waxed"?) banked green at the 15th. Everyone else who hit that bank was reaching for a new ball. The remaining three inches was the total distance by which Lehman's putts were rejected at the 15th, 16th, and 17th.

"When you see things like that happen, you think maybe it's your time to win," said Olazabal, whose eagle on the 15th provided his two-stroke margin of victory. Added Lehman, the 35-year-old journeyman who led after three rounds: "Maybe I'm not fated to win this tournament."

In Els, the U.S. Open got its first foreign champion since 1981 and its first South African since Gary Player in '65, but in a Bill Murray finish.

In the fourth round, Els hooked his tee shot at No. 1 and got a huge, maybe decisive, break. Dr. Trey Holland, the U.S. Golf Association's rules expert, apparently not noticing its big wheels, concluded that the TV crane in Els' line was an immovable obstruction. He awarded a free drop, which took Els out of heavy rough and into friendlier stuff.

Els bogeyed, but some thought he might have done worse from the original lie. Sometime later, the crane was moved to another location. "I made a mistake," Holland said.

Later, frazzled American Loren Roberts had an uphill four-footer at the 18th for a par and the Open championship. But he never touched the hole. "I won't lie to you,"

Gary Newkirk/Allsport

An emotional **Arnold Palmer** waves to the crowd at Oakmont Country Club as he finishes competing in his final U.S. Open. Palmer won the Open in 1960 and was second four times.

he said. "I had trouble getting the putter back."

Els, meanwhile, was back at the 18th tee thinking he needed a birdie to win. The nearby leaderboard would have told him a par was enough, and to hit a safe iron, but he never looked at the board. He hit the driver, and hooked into the jungle. His bogey for a 73 tied him with Roberts (70) and Scotland's Colin Montgomery (70) at 5-under 279.

Off they went on Monday in an 18-hole playoff. If this were the Indy 500 and not the Open, the caution flags would have come out in first turn. At No. 2, a fairly easy par-4, Els flew the green, then pitched back over the green and triple-bogeyed. Montgomery needed three chips just to get on. He doubled. Roberts won the hole with a bogey. They staggered on. Eventually Monty, flushed from heat and bewildered by Oakmont, fell out with a 78. Els and Roberts tied at 74 and Els won with a par on the second extra hole.

The Open was also the scene of one of the most poignant moments ever in sports.

Arnold Palmer, who won the Open in 1960 and finished second four times, was playing the tournament by special invitation for the final time at age 64. After he missed the cut on Friday, he came to the media tent for a farewell interview. But he couldn't speak. He broke down and cried into a towel. He managed about three sentences, and then abruptly got up and left, to a standing ovation from a surprisingly teary press corps.

At the British Open at Turnberry, Sweden's Jesper Parnevik, like Els at Oakmont, refused to peek at the leaderboard and paid for it. He thought he needed a birdie on the 18th, misclubbed, missed the green and bogeyed. Price finished birdie-eagle-par—the eagle putt went in from 50 feet—and won by a shot. Price had previously blown opportunities to win the Open in 1982 and '88, but finished second.

By the time of the PGA Championship in mid-August, ideas on how to stop Price ranged from "Stick an extra club in his bag" (John Cook) to "Take him skiing" (Phil Mickelson).

In the PGA at Southern Hills, the closest anyone got to him was a first-round tie. Price led the second round by five and the third by three. Corey Pavin finished at 5-under and was second by six shots. Said Pavin: "I feel like I won the B Flight."

Price did not have the summer to himself. Not with John Daly walking around loose. Daly came off suspension, his second, early in the spring, and some two months later won the BellSouth Classic. That was the good news. Then, in a newspaper interview at the Scottish Open, he accused unnamed pros of using drugs. He later tried to back off, but that didn't save him from an audience with new PGA Tour commissioner Tim Finchem.

Not long after that, Daly, 28, got into a scuffle with the 62-year-old father of a competitor at the World Series of Golf in Akron. Bob Roth took exception to Daly's hitting into his son Jeffrey's twosome, told him so, Daly said something back to him and they wrestled until spectators separated them.

Finchem summoned Daly back to the principal's office, and in mid-September, announced that the 1991 PGA champion was voluntarily taking the rest of the year off.

Things were quieter on the LPGA Tour, but they had their moments. At the Youngstown-

David Cannon/Allsport

Gary Newkirk/Allsport

Ernie Els (left) of South Africa and **Paul Azinger** each made news during the year, Els by winning the U.S. Open in a three-way playoff and Azinger by bouncing back from cancer treatment to defend his PGA Championship title.

Warren (Ohio) Classic in July, a funny thing happened to Kim Williams on the way to the drugstore. She got shot.

Police believed that it was a stray bullet from someone target-shooting a mile away from the shopping plaza. Nevertheless, it hit the left side of Williams' neck, plowed down—somehow missing everything vital—and lodged below her right collarbone. Doctors decided to leave the bullet where it was, and a few days later, she was playing in the Jamie Farr Toledo Classic, stiff and hurting.

"I've got bills to pay," said Williams. "I'm here because I need to work." Besides, there was always the chance of making some side money. "Maybe I can get an endorsement deal," she cracked. "With Bullet Golf. Or Target Stores."

After Williams, the LPGA's most celebrated victim was Sweden's Helen Alfredsson, the tour's 1992 Rookie of the Year. At the U.S. Women's Open in Lake Orion, Mich., Alfredsson set the Indianwood course on fire with an Open-record 63 in the first round. After 43

holes—through No. 7 in the third-round—she was 13 under par and leading by seven. Then she sprang a leak. After opening 63-69, she went 76-77 and plunged to a tie for ninth, eight strokes behind eventual Patty Sheehan.

What do you do at a time like this? someone asked the volatile, 29-year-old Swede. "You scream at everybody near you," Alfredsson said.

Sheehan understood. She had blown an 11-shot lead in the 1990 Women's Open then bounced back to win it in '92. This time she stuck to her fairways-and-greens game plan and fended off the ambitious Tammie Green for her fifth major and the 32nd victory of her Hall of Fame career.

Alfredsson, meanwhile, didn't dwell on her misfortune. She went out and won the Ping/Welch's Championship the following week.

The LPGA's four majors started on a muted note with the Nabisco Dinah Shore in March. Shore, the Bing Crosby of women's golf, died of cancer at age 76 a month before her tournament was played.

LPGA Hall of Famer **Patty Sheehan** won her second U.S. Women's Open in three years, beating runner-up Tammie Green by a stroke. The title was the 32nd of Sheehan's career and her fifth major.

Donna Andrews birdied the last hole to edge big-hitting Englishwoman Laura Davies for her first major. She then paid tribute to Dinah by jumping into the water near the 18th green, as Dinah had done with Amy Alcott when Alcott won in '91.

Davies wouldn't be put off for long. Two weeks later she won the Sara Lee Classic, and the week after that the second major of the season, the McDonald's LPGA Championship.

The final major of the year, the du Maurier Classic late in August, slayed a personal dragon for Martha Nause, 39, a 17-year veteran with two previous victories. "I don't think I believed in myself until now," Nause said.

The LPGA Tour, home to so many top Europeans, became a rehearsal for the Solheim Cup, the women's version of the Ryder Cup. You had England's Davies winning three times and topping the money list by mid-September, and Sweden's Liselotte Neumann winning twice. For the Americans, Andrews and the resurrected Beth Daniel won three times each. The Yanks and Euros would go head-to-head at the Greenbrier in October to break a 1-1 tie in the biennial series.

Also on the U.S. vs. Them scene was the first Presidents Cup, a Ryder Cup copycat featuring the best American golfers against the best from everywhere else in the world except Europe. The competition debuted Sept. 16-18 on the Robert Trent Jones course at Lake Manassas, Va., but it wasn't a true test. Greg Norman couldn't play, Els didn't want to play and Price was inconsistent. So the Yanks won easily, 20-12.

On the Senior PGA Tour, Lee Trevino was running amok. By mid-September, he had won six times, including the PGA Seniors, and had rung up nearly $1.5 million to stay ahead of 1993 Player of the Year Dave Stockton.

But death struck here, too. Bert Yancey, whose emotional troubles early in his career were traced to an imbalance in body chemicals, collapsed and died just before the Franklin Quest Championship late in August. Tom Weiskopf, an old friend, won the tournament—his first as a Senior—and dedicated it to Yancey.

Simon Hobday made it a South African sweep of the Opens when he survived a closing 75 to take the U.S. Senior Open in July at Pinehurst No. 2 in North Carolina. "By 18, I was just hoping to get into a playoff," he said. "I was definitely choking."

While Els has been all but crowned as the next great player, that role might be filled by a California kid who isn't out of golf's short pants yet. He's Tiger Woods, the hottest amateur in the land—maybe the world.

In the U.S. Amateur, Woods, an 18-year-old who started his freshman year at Stanford in the fall, came back from six down after 13 holes in the 36-hole final and beat collegian Trip Kuehne. In doing so, Woods made tournament history four times: biggest comeback, youngest winner, first black winner, and first player to win both the U.S. Junior and U.S. Amateur.

Two months later, Woods and teammates Allen Doyle, John Harris and Todd Dempsey won the World Amateur Team Championship in LaBoulie, France, by 11 strokes over Great Britain and Ireland. ❑

GOLF STATISTICS

THE SEASON IN REVIEW
1993-1994
PGA • SENIORS • LPGA

THE 1995 INFORMATION PLEASE SPORTS ALMANAC

SEC A

PAGE 775

Tournament Results

Winners of PGA, European PGA, PGA Seniors and LPGA tournaments from Oct. 31, 1993 through Sept. 25, 1994.

PGA Tour
LATE 1993

Last Rd	Tournament	Winner	Earnings	Runner-Up
Oct. 31	The Tour Championship	Jim Gallagher Jr. (277)	$540,000	4-way tie (278)
Nov. 7	Kapalua International	Fred Couples (274)	180,000	B. McCallister (278)
Nov. 14	World Cup of Golf (Orlando)	USA— Fred Couples/	130,000	ZIM— N. Price/
		Davis Love III (556)	130,000	M. McNulty (561)
Nov. 21	Franklin Funds Shark Shootout	Steve Elkington/	150,000	4-way tie (189)
		Ray Floyd (188)	150,000	
Nov. 28	Skins Game #11	Payne Stewart (9)	280,000	F. Couples (9)
Dec. 5	JCPenney Classic	Mike Springer/	120,000	5-way tie (269)
		Melissa McNamara (265)	120,000	

Second place ties (3 players or more): 5-WAY— JCPenney Classic (J. Huston/A. Benz, R. Gamez/H. Alfredsson, F. Funk/T. Barrett, K. Perry/S. Steinhauer, T. Sieckmann/D. McHaffie). 4-WAY— Tour Championship (D. Frost, J. Huston, G. Norman, S. Simpson); **Shark Shootout** (H. Irwin/B. Lietzke, M. O'Meara/C. Strange, M. Calcavecchia/B. Faxon, T. Kite/D. Love III).

1994 (through Sept. 25)

Last Rd	Tournament	Winner	Earnings	Runner-Up
Jan. 9	Mercedes Championships	Phil Mickelson (276)*	$180,000	F. Couples (276)
Jan. 16	United Airlines Hawaiian Open	Brett Ogle (269)	216,000	D. Love III (270)
Jan. 23	Northern Telecom Open	Andrew Magee (270)	198,000	4-way tie (272)
Jan. 30	Phoenix Open	Bill Glasson (268)	216,000	B. Estes (271)
Feb. 6	AT&T Pebble Beach National Pro-Am	Johnny Miller (281)	225,000	4-way tie (282)
Feb. 13	Nissan Los Angeles Open	Corey Pavin (271)	180,000	F. Couples (273)
Feb. 20	Bob Hope Chrysler Classic	Scott Hoch (334)	198,000	3-way tie (337)
Feb. 27	Buick Invitational of California	Craig Stadler (268)	198,000	S. Lowery (269)
Mar. 6	Doral Ryder Open	John Huston (274)	252,000	B. Bryant
				& B. Andrade (277)
Mar. 13	Honda Classic	Nick Price (276)	198,000	C. Perry (277)
Mar. 20	Nestle Invitational	Loren Roberts (275)	216,000	3-way tie (276)
Mar. 27	The Players Championship	Greg Norman (264)	450,000	F. Zoeller (268)
Apr. 3	Freeport-McMoRan Classic	Ben Crenshaw (273)	216,000	J.M. Olazabal (276)
Apr. 10	**The Masters** (Augusta)	Jose Maria Olazabal (279)	360,000	T. Lehman (281)
Apr. 17	MCI Heritage Classic	Hale Irwin (266)	225,000	G. Norman (268)
Apr. 24	Kmart Greater Greensboro Open	Mike Springer (275)	270,000	3-way tie (278)
May 1	Shell Houston Open	Mike Heinen (272)	234,000	3-way tie (275)
May 8	BellSouth Atlanta Classic	John Daly (274)	216,000	N. Henke (275)
				& B. Henninger
May 15	GTE Byron Nelson Classic	Neal Lancaster (132)*	216,000	5-way tie (132)
May 22	Memorial Tournament	Tom Lehman (268)	270,000	G. Norman (273)
May 30	Southwestern Bell Colonial	Nick Price (266)*	252,000	M. Calcavecchia
				& B. Crenshaw (275)
June 5	Kemper Open	Mark Brooks (271)	234,000	D.A. Weibring
				& B. Wadkins (274)
June 12	Buick Classic	Lee Janzen (268)	216,000	E. Els (271)
June 19	**U.S. Open** (Springfield, NJ)	Ernie Els (279)*	320,000	C. Montgomerie
				& L. Roberts (279)
June 26	Canon Greater Hartford Open	David Frost (268)	216,000	G. Norman (269)
July 3	Motorola Western Open	Nick Price (277)	216,000	G. Kraft (278)
July 10	Anheuser-Busch Classic	Mark McCumber (267)	198,000	G. Day (270)
July 17	**British Open** (Turnberry)	Nick Price (268)	178,200	J. Parnevik (269)
July 17	Deposit Guaranty Classic	Brian Henninger (135)*	126,000	M. Sullivan (135)

Tournament Results (Cont.)
PGA Tour

Last Rd	Tournament	Winner	Earnings	Runner-Up
July 24	New England Classic	Kenny Perry (268)	$180,000	D. Feherty (269)
July 31	Federal Express St. Jude Classic	Dicky Pride (267)*	198,000	G. Sauers & H. Sutton (267)
Aug. 7	Buick Open	Fred Couples (270)	198,000	C. Pavin (272)
Aug. 14	**PGA Championship** (Toledo)	Nick Price (269)	310,000	C. Pavin (275)
Aug. 21	The International	Steve Lowery (35 pts.)*	252,000	R. Fehr (35 pts.)
Aug. 28	NEC World Series of Golf	Jose Maria Olazabal (269)	360,000	S. Hoch (270)
Sept. 4	Greater Milwaukee Open	Mike Springer (268)	180,000	L. Roberts (269)
Sept. 11	Canadian Open	Nick Price (275)	234,000	M. Calcavecchia (276)
Sept. 18	B.C. Open	Mike Sullivan (266)	162,000	J. Sluman (270)
Sept. 18	President's Cup (Lake Manassas)	United States (20)	(none)	Internationals (12)
Sept. 25	Hardee's Golf Classic	Mark McCumber (265)	180,000	K. Perry (266)

(See "Updates" for later results.)

*Playoffs (4): Mercedes— Mickelson won on 2nd hole; **Byron Nelson—** Lancaster won on 1st hole; **Colonial—** Price won on 1st hole; **U.S. Open—** Els won on 2nd extra hole after he and Roberts shot 74 and Montgomerie shot 78 in playoff round; **Deposit Guaranty—** Henninger won on 1st hole; **St. Jude—** Pride won on 1st hole; **International—** Lowery won on 1st hole.

Second place ties (3 players or more): 5-way— **Byron Nelson** (T. Byrum, M. Carnevale, D. Edwards, Y. Mizumaki, D. Ogrin). 4-WAY— **Northern Telecom** (J. D. Blake, L. Roberts, V. Singh, S. Stricker); **Pebble Beach** (J. Maggert, C. Pavin, K. Triplett, T. Watson). 3-WAY— **Bob Hope** (L. Clements, J. Gallagher Jr., F. Zoeller); **Nestle** (N. Price, V. Singh, F. Zoeller); **Greater Greensboro** (B. Bryant, E. Humenik, H. Irwin,); **Houston** (H. Sutton, T. Kite, J. Maggert).

PGA Majors

The Masters

Edition: 58th   **Dates:** April 7-10
Site: Augusta National GC, Augusta, Ga.
Par: 36-36—72 (6905 yards)   **Purse:** $1,500,000

	1 2 3 4 Tot	Earnings
1 Jose Maria Olazabal	74-67-69-69—279	$360,000
2 Tom Lehman	70-70-69-72—281	216,000
3 Larry Mize	68-71-72-71—282	136,000
4 Tom Kite	69-72-71-71—283	96,000
5 Jay Haas	72-72-72-69—285	73,000
Jim McGovern	72-70-71-72—285	73,000
Loren Roberts	75-68-72-70—285	73,000
8 Ernie Els	74-67-74-71—286	60,000
Corey Pavin	71-72-73-70—286	60,000
10 Ian Baker-Finch	71-71-71-74—287	50,000
Ray Floyd	70-74-71-72—287	50,000
John Huston	72-72-74-69—287	50,000

Early round leaders: 1st— Mize (68); 2nd— Mize (139); 3rd— Lehman (209).

Top amateur: John Harris (305).

U.S. Open

Edition: 94th   **Dates:** June 16-20
Site: Oakmont CC, Oakmont, Pa.
Par: 36-35—71 (6946 yards)   **Purse:** $1,700,000

	1 2 3 4 Tot	Earnings
1 Ernie Els	69-71-66-73—279	$320,000
2 Loren Roberts	76-69-64-70—279	141,827
Colin Montgomerie	71-65-73-70—279	141,827
4 Curtis Strange	70-70-70-70—280	108,655
5 John Cook	73-65-73-71—282	75,728
6 Clark Dennis	71-71-70-71—283	54,839
Greg Norman	71-71-69-72—283	54,839
Tom Watson	68-73-68-74—283	54,839
9 Frank Nobilo	69-71-68-76—284	40,133
Duffy Waldorf	74-68-73-69—284	40,133

Playoff: Els won on 2nd extra hole after he and Roberts shot 74 and Montgomerie shot 78 of playoff round.
Early round leaders: 1st— Watson (68); 2nd— Montgomerie (136); 3rd— Els (206).
Top amateur: none.

British Open

Edition: 123rd   **Dates:** July 14-17
Site: Turnberry Hotel, Scotland
Par: 35-35—70 (6957 yards)   **Purse:** $1,672,000 (US)

	1 2 3 4 Tot	Earnings
1 Nick Price	69-66-67-66—268	$178,200
2 Jesper Parnevik	68-66-68-67—269	142,560
3 Fuzzy Zoeller	71-66-64-70—271	119,880
4 Mark James	72-67-66-68—273	82,080
David Feherty	68-69-66-70—273	82,080
Andes Forsbrand	72-71-66-64—273	82,080
7 Brad Faxon	69-65-67-73—274	58,320
8 Nick Faldo	75-66-70-64—275	48,600
Tom Kite	71-69-66-69—275	48,600
Colin Montgomerie	72-69-65-69—275	48,600

Early round leaders: 1st— Greg Turner (65); 2nd— Tom Watson (133); 3rd— Faxon, Zoeller (201).
Top amateur: Warren Bennett (286).

PGA Championship

Edition: 76th   **Dates:** Aug. 11-14
Site: Southern Hills CC, Tulsa, Okla.
Par: 35-35—70 (6834 yards)   **Purse:** $1,800,000

	1 2 3 4 Tot	Earnings
1 Nick Price	67-65-70-67—269	$310,000
2 Corey Pavin	70-67-69-69—275	160,000
3 Phil Mickelson	68-71-67-70—276	110,000
4 Nick Faldo	73-67-71-66—277	76,667
Greg Norman	71-69-67-70—277	76,667
John Cook	71-69-67-70—277	76,667
7 Steve Elkington	73-70-66-69—278	57,500
Jose M. Olazabal	72-66-70-70—278	57,500
9 Tom Kite	72-68-69-70—279	41,000
Tom Watson	69-72-67-71—279	41,000
Loren Roberts	69-72-69-71—279	41,000
Ben Crenshaw	70-67-70-72—279	41,000
Ian Woosnam	68-72-73-66—279	41,000

Early round leaders: 1st— Colin Montgomerie, Price (67); 2nd— Price (132); 3rd— Price (202).
Top amateur: none.

European PGA Tour

Earnings listed in pounds sterling (£) unless otherwise indicated.

1994 (through Sept. 25)

Last Rd	Tournament	Winner	Earnings	Runner-Up
Jan. 16	Madeira Island Classic	Mats Lanner (206)	£ 41,660	3-way tie (208)
Jan. 23	Moroccan Open	Anders Forsbrand (276)	58,330	H. Clark (280)
Jan. 30	Dubai Desert Classic	Ernie Els (268)	75,000	G. Norman (274)
Feb. 6	Johnny Walker Classic (Phuket)	Greg Norman (277)	100,000	F. Couples (278)
Feb. 13	Iberia Open de Tenerife	David Gilford (278)	41,660	3-way tie (280)
Feb. 20	Open de Extremadura	Paul Eales (281)	41,660	P. Hedblom (282)
Feb. 27	Masters Open de Andalucia	Carl Mason (278)	50,536	J. M. Olazabal (280)
Feb. 6	Open Mediterrania (Valencia)	Jose Maria Olazabal (276)*	50,000	P. McGinley (276)
Mar. 13	Iberia Open de Baleares	Barry Lane (269)	41,616	J. Payne (271)
Mar. 20	Portuguese Open	Phillip Price (278)	50,000	3-way tie (282)
Apr. 4	Open V33 du Grand Lyon	Stephen Ames (282)	37,500	P. Lenhart (284) & G. Hjertstedt
Apr. 17	Tournoi Perrier de Paris	Peter Baker (260)	35,000	M. Mouland (261)
Apr. 24	Heineken Open Catalonia	José Coceres (275)	50,000	J. L. Guepy (278)
May 1	Air France Cannes Open	Ian Woosnam (271)	50,000	C. Montgomerie (276)
May 8	Benson & Hedges Intl. Open	Steve Ballesteros (281)	108,330	N. Faldo (284)
May 15	Peugeot Spanish Open	Colin Montgomerie (277)	83,330	3-way tie (278)
May 22	Tisettanta Italian Open	Eduardo Romero (272)	75,000	G. Turner (273)
May 30	Volvo PGA Championship	José Maria Olazabal (271)	133,330	E. Els (272)
June 5	Alfred Dunhill Open (Knokke)	Nick Faldo (279)*	100,000	J. Haeggman (279)
June 12	Honda Open	Robert Allenby (276)*	83,330	M. A. Jiménez (276)
June 19	Jersey European Airways Open	Paul Curry (266)	58,330	M. James (269)
June 26	Peugeot French Open	Mark Roe (274)	91,660	G. Hjertstedt (275)
July 3	Murphy's Irish Open	Berhard Langer (275)	98,765	R. Allenby (276) & J. Daly
July 9	Bell's Scottish Open	C. Mason (265)	100,000	P. Mitchell (266)
July 17	**British Open** (Turnberry)	Nick Price (268)	110,000	J. Parnevik (269)
July 24	Heineken Dutch Open	Miguel Angel Jiménez (270)	108,330	H. Clark (272)
July 31	Scandinavian Masters	Vijay Singh (268)	108,330	M. McNulty (271)
Aug. 7	BMW International Open	Mark McNulty (274)	87,500	S. Ballesteros (275)
Aug 15	Hohe Brucke Austrian Open	Mark Davis (270)	41,660	P. Walton (272)
Aug. 22	Murphy's English Open	Colin Montgomerie (274)	100,000	B. Lane (275)
Aug. 29	Volvo German Open	Colin Montgomerie (269)	108,330	B. Langer (270)
Sept. 5	Canon European Masters	Eduardo Romero (266)	111,290	P. Fulke (267)
Sept. 12	GA European Open	David Gilford (275)	100,000	C. Rocca (280)
Sept. 19	British Masters	Ian Woosnam (271)	108,330	S. Ballesteros (275)
Sept. 19	Lancome Trophy	Vijay Singh (263)	100,000	M. A. Jimenez (264)

(See "Updates" for later results.)

*Playoffs (3): **Open Mediterrania**—Olazabal won on 2nd hole; **Alfred Dunhill Open**—Faldo won on 1st hole; **Honda Open**—Allenby won on 2nd hole.
   Second place ties (3 players or more): 3-WAY— **Madeira Island** (M. Grönberg, P. Hedblom, H. Clark); **Iberia Open** (W. Riley, A. Murray, J. Quiros); **Portuguese Open** (D. Gilford, R. Goosen, P. Eales); **Spanish Open** (M. Roe, R. Boxall, M. McNulty).

Sony World Rankings

Begun in 1986, the Sony World Rankings combine the best golfers on the PGA and European PGA tours. Rankings are based on a rolling three-year period and weighted in favor of more recent results. Points are awarded after each worldwide tournament according to finish. Final point averages are determined by dividing a player's total points by the number of tournaments played in.

Through Sept. 25, 1994

	Avg		Avg		Avg
1 Nick Price	21.79	9 Corey Pavin	10.75	15 Vijay Singh	8.28
2 Greg Norman	20.83	10 David Frost	10.50	16 Mark McNulty	8.26
3 Nick Faldo	16.53	11 Masashi Ozaki	9.69	17 Davis Love III	7.77
4 Bernhard Langer	16.21	12 Tom Kite	9.59	18 Paul Azinger	7.76
5 Jose Maria Olazabal	14.50	13 Ian Woosnam	9.07	19 Fuzzy Zoeller	7.68
6 Fred Couples	13.88	14 Tom Lehman	8.64	20 Loren Roberts	7.62
7 Colin Montgomerie	12.48				
Ernie Els	12.48				

Tournament Results (Cont.)
Senior PGA Tour

LATE 1993

Last Rd	Tournament	Winner	Earnings	Runner-Up
Oct. 31	Kaanapali Classic	George Archer (199)*	$ 82,500	D.Stockton (199)
				& L. Trevino
Nov. 14	Du Pont Cup (Sawara City, Japan)	USA (26 pts)	360,000†	Zimbabwe (6)
Dec. 12	Senior Tour Championship	Simon Hobday (199)	150,000	L. Gilbert
				& R. Floyd (201)

†Each team member received $45,000.

*Playoffs (1): **Kaanapali Classic**—George Archer won on first hole.

1994 (through Sept. 25)

Last Rd	Tournament	Winner	Earnings	Runner-Up
Jan. 9	Mercedes Championships	Jack Nicklaus (279)	$100,000	B. Murphy (280)
Jan. 30	Senior Skins Game #6	Ray Floyd (8)	240,000	A. Palmer (5)
Feb. 6	Royal Caribbean Classic	Lee Trevino (205)*	120,000	K. Zarley (205)
Feb. 8	Senior Slam at Queretaro	Tom Shaw (139)	250,000	J. Colbert (139)
Feb. 13	GTE Suncoast Classic	Rocky Thompson (201)	105,000	R. Floyd (202)
Feb. 20	The Intellinet Challenge	Mike Hill (201)	75,000	T. Wargo (204)
Feb. 27	Chrysler Cup	International Team (-58)	360,000	USA (-60)
Mar. 6	GTE West Classic	Jay Sigel (198)*	82,500	J. Colbert (198)
Mar. 13	Vantage at The Dominion	Jim Albus (208)	97,500	3-way tie (209)
Mar. 27	Doug Sanders Celebrity Classic	Tom Wargo (207)	75,000	B. Murphy (208)
Mar. 28	Fuji Electric Grand Slam	Lee Trevino (207)	77,600	G.Cowan (209)
Apr. 3	**The Tradition** at Desert Mountain	Ray Floyd (271)*	127,500	D. Douglass (271)
Apr. 17	**PGA Seniors** (Palm Beach Gardens)	Lee Trevino (279)	115,000	J. Colbert (280)
Apr. 24	Dallas Reunion Pro-Am	Larry Gilbert (202)	75,000	G. Archer
				& R. Thompson (203)
May 1	Las Vegas Classic	Ray Floyd (204)	135,000	T. Wargo (207)
May 8	Liberty Mutual Legends of Golf	Dale Douglass/	200,000	2-way tie (189)
		Charles Coody (188)		
May 15	PaineWebber Invitational	Lee Trevino (203)	112,500	J. Colbert
				& J. Powell (204)
May 22	Cadillac NFL Classic	Ray Floyd (206)	135,000	B. Murphy
				& G. Player (207)
May 29	Bell Atlantic Classic	Lee Trevino (206)	105,000	M. Hill (208)
June 5	Bruno's Memorial Classic	Jim Dent (201)	150,000	3-way tie (203)
June 12	Nationwide Championship	Dave Stockton (198)	172,500	B. Murphy
June 19	BellSouth Classic	Lee Trevino (199)	157,500	D. Stockton (199)
				& J. Albus (200)
June 26	**Senior Players Champs** (Dearborn)	Dave Stockton (271)	210,000	J. Albus (277)
July 3	**U.S. Senior Open** (Pinehurst)	Simon Hobday (274)	145,000	J. Albus
				& G. Marsh (275)
July 10	Kroger Classic	Jim Colbert (199)	127,500	R. Floyd (201)
July 17	Ameritech Open	John Paul Cain (202)	97,500	S. Hobday
				& J. Colbert (203)
July 24	Southwestern Bell Classic	Jim Colbert (196)	105,000	I. Aoki
				& L. Gilbert (197)
July 31	Northville Long Island Classic	Lee Trevino (200)	97,500	J. Colbert (207)
Aug. 7	Bank of Boston Classic	Jim Albus (203)	112,500	B. Brue
				& R. Floyd (205)
Aug. 14	First of America Classic	Tony Jacklin (136)#	97,500	D. Stockton (137)
Aug. 21	Burnet Classic	Dave Stockton (203)	157,500	J. Albus (204)
Aug. 28	Franklin Quest Classic	Tom Weiskopf (204)*	75,000	D. Stockton (204)
Sept. 4	GTE Northwest Classic	Simon Hobday (209)*	82,500	J. Albus (209)
Sept. 11	Quicksilver Classic	Dave Eichelberger (209)	157,500	H. Blancas
				& R. Floyd (211)
Sept. 18	Bank One Classic	Isao Aoki (202)	82,500	C.C. Rodriguez (205)
Sept. 25	Brickyard Crossing Championship	Isao Aoki (133)#	105,000	J. Powell
				& T. Wargo (134)

(See "Updates" for later results.)

#Rain-shortened.

*Playoffs (5): **Royal Caribbean**—Trevino won on 4th hole; **GTE West**—Sigel won on 4th hole; **The Tradition**—Floyd won on 1st hole; **Franklin**—Weiskopf won on 1st hole; **GTE Northwest**—Hobday won on 3rd hole.
Second place ties (3 players or more): 3-WAY— **The Dominion** (G. Archer, G. Marsh, L. Trevino); **Bruno's Memorial Classic** (B. Charles, L. Gilbert, K. Zarley); 2-WAY— **Legends of Golf** (C.C. Rodriguez/J. Dent and B. Murphy/J. Colbert).

Senior PGA Majors

The Tradition

Edition: 6th   **Dates:** Mar. 31-Apr. 3
Site: Desert Mt. Cochise Course, Scottsdale, Ariz.
Par: 36-36—72 (6869 yards)   **Purse:** $850,000

	1 2 3 4 Tot	Earnings
1 Ray Floyd	65-70-68-68—271	$127,500
2 Dale Douglass	68-68-69-66—271	74,800
3 Jim Colbert	70-66-68-70—274	61,200
4 Jack Nicklaus	70-71-69-68—278	41,933
Jimmy Powell	67-69-72-70—278	41,933
Tom Weiskopf	68-70-70-70—278	41,933
7 Gibby Gilbert	66-69-73-71—279	28,900
Mike Hill	70-70-68-71—279	28,900
9 Dave Stockton	68-70-72-70—280	22,100
Tom Wargo	68-75-65-72—280	22,100
Isao Aoki	67-69-71-73—280	22,100

Playoff: Floyd won on 1st hole of sudden death.
Early round leaders: 1st— Floyd (65); 2nd— Floyd, G. Gilbert, Charles Coody (135); 3rd— Floyd (203).

PGA Seniors' Championship

Edition: 56th   **Dates:** April 11-17
Site: PGA National GC, Palm Springs Gardens, Fla.
Par: 36-36—72 (6718 yards)   **Purse:** $800,000

	1 2 3 4 Tot	Earnings
1 Lee Trevino	70-69-70-70—279	$115,000
2 Jim Colbert	68-71-74-67—280	85,000
3 Ray Floyd	69-69-69-75—282	57,500
Dave Stockton	70-69-71-72—282	57,500
Isao Aoki	71-71-75-66—283	32,500
Dewitt Weaver	72-73-70-68—283	32,500
Dale Douglass	70-71-70-72—283	32,500
Chi Chi Rodriguez	73-72-69-69—283	32,500
9 Jack Nicklaus	71-71-72-72—286	20,500
10 Tom Wargo	72-80-70-65—287	16,500
Bob Murphy	69-75-73-70—287	16,500
Bob Charles	69-74-71-73—287	16,500

Early round leaders: 1st— Dent (66); 2nd— Larry Mowry (138); 3rd— Floyd (207).

PGA Senior Players Championship

Edition: 12th   **Dates:** June 23-26
Site: The Players Club of Michigan, Dearborn, Mich.
Par: 36-36—72 (6876 yards)   **Purse:** $1,400,000

	1 2 3 4 Tot	Earnings
1 Dave Stockton	66-66-71-68—271	$210,000
2 Jim Albus	67-69-72-69—277	123,200
3 Isao Aoki	67-70-73-68—278	84,000
Ray Floyd	72-68-71-67—278	84,000
Lee Trevino	66-69-74-69—278	84,000
6 Jack Nicklaus	68-72-73-67—280	50,400
Harold Henning	69-67-74-70—280	50,400
Jim Dent	72-67-70-71—280	50,400
9 Jay Sigel	67-71-73-70—281	39,200
10 Tom Wargo	70-73-71-68—282	32,200
Jerry McGee	69-69-74-70—282	32,200
Bob Murphy	69-68-73-72—282	32,200
Tom Weiskopf	65-71-74-72—282	32,200

Early round leaders: 1st— Weiskopf (65); 2nd— Stockton (132); 3rd— Stockton (203).

U.S. Senior Open

Edition: 15th   **Dates:** June 30-July 3
Site: Pinehurst CC, Pinehurst, N.C.
Par: 35-36—71 (6771 yards)   **Purse:** $800,000

	1 2 3 4 Tot	Earnings
1 Simon Hobday	66-67-66-75—274	$145,330
2 Jim Albus	66-69-66-74—275	63,419
Graham Marsh	68-68-69-70—275	63,419
4 Tom Weiskopf	72-66-72-67—277	30,608
Tom Wargo	69-70-68-70—277	30,608
Dave Stockton	74-67-68-68—277	30,608
7 Bob Murphy	71-70-71-67—279	21,651
Jay Sigel	73-66-70-70—279	21,651
Jack Nicklaus	69-68-70-72—279	21,651
10 Isao Aoki	69-71-73-67—280	18,313

Early round leaders: 1st— Albus, Hobday (66); 2nd— Hobday (133); 3rd— Hobday (199).

LPGA Tour
LATE 1993

Last Rd	Tournament	Winner	Earnings	Runner-Up
Oct. 31	Nichirei International (Japan)	USA (23 pts)	$500,000	Japan (9)
Nov. 7	Toray Japan Queens Cup	Betsy King (205)	97,500	J. Geddes (206)
Dec. 5	JCPenney Classic	Melissa McNamara/	120,000	5-way tie
		Mike Springer (265)	120,000	
Dec. 27	Wendy's Three-Tour Challenge	Senior PGA (206)@	300,000	PGA (211)
				LPGA (218)

*Playoff: Japan— King won on 4th hole.
Second place ties (3 players or more): 5-WAY— **JCPenney Classic** (J. Huston/A. Benz, R. Gamez/H. Alfredsson, F. Funk/T. Barrett, K. Perry/S. Steinhauer, T. Sieckmann/D. McHaffie).
@Three-Tour Teams: Senior PGA (Ray Floyd, Jack Nicklaus, Chi Chi Rodriguez); LPGA (Nancy Lopez, Lauri Merten, Patty Sheehan); PGA (Greg Norman, Paul Azinger, Lee Jansen).

1994 (through Sept. 26)

Last Rd	Tournament	Winner	Earnings	Runner-Up
Feb. 6	HealthSouth Palm Beach Classic	Dawn Coe-Jones (201)	$ 60,000	L. Merten (202)
Feb. 13	Mos Bruger Honolulu Super Pro-Am	Hollis Stacy (138)	7,500	E. Crosby & S. Steinhauer (139)
Feb. 19	Cuo Noodles Hawaiian Ladies Open	Marta Figueras-Dotti (209)	75,000	J. Geddes (210)
Mar. 5	Chrysler-Plymouth Tourn. of Champs	Dottie Mochrie (287)	115,000	N. Lopez & L. Merten (289)
Mar. 13	Ping-Welch's Championship	Donna Andrews (276)	63,750	J. Dickinson & B. Burton (279)
Mar. 20	Standard Register Ping	Laura Davies (277)	105,000	B. Daniel & E. Crosby (281)
Mar. 28	**Nabisco Dinah Shore** (Rancho Mirage)	Donna Andrews (276)	105,000	L. Davies (277)
Apr. 17	Atlanta Women's Championship	Val Skinner (206)	97,500	L. Neumann (207)
May 1	Sprint Championship	Sherri Steinhauer (273)	180,000	K. Robbins (274)
May 8	Sara Lee Classic	Laura Davies (203)	78,750	M. Mallon (204)

Tournament Results (Cont.)
LPGA

Last Rd	Tournament	Winner	Earnings	Runner-Up
May 15	**LPGA Championship** (Wilmington)	Laura Davies (279)	165,000	A. Ritzman (282)
May 22	Lady Keystone Open	Elaine Crosby (211)	60,000	L. Davies (212)
May 29	JCPenney Skins Game	Patty Sheehan (13)	285,000	B. King (5)
May 29	Corning Classic	Beth Daniel (278)	75,000	S. Farwig & N. Ramsbottom (279)
June 5	Oldsmobile Classic	Beth Daniel (268)	90,000	L. Kiggens (272)
June 12	LPGA Classic (Minnesota)	Liselotte Neumann (205)	75,000	H. Kobayashi (207)
June 19	Rochester International	Lisa Kiggens (273)	75,000	D. Coe-Jones (274)
June 26	ShopRite Classic	Donna Andrews (207)	75,000	M. Estill (209)
July 3	Youngstown-Warren Classic	Tammie Green (206)	82,500	T. Green (208)
July 10	Jamie Farr Toledo Classic	Kellie Robbins (204)*	75,000	T. Green (204)
July 17	JAL Big Apple Classic	Beth Daniel (276)*	97,500	L. Davies (276)
July 25	**U.S. Women's Open** (Lake Orion)	Patty Sheehan (277)	155,000	T. Green (278)
July 31	Ping/Welch's Classic	Helen Alfredsson (274)	67,500	P. Bradley & J. Inkster (278)
Aug. 7	McCall's Classic at Stratton Mt.	Carolyn Hill (275)	75,000	N. Ramsbottom (278)
Aug. 14	Women's British Open	Liselotte Neumann (280)	80,325	D. Mochrie & A. Sorenstam (283)
Aug. 14	Children's Medical Center Classic	Maggie Will (210)	52,500	J. Briles-Hinton & A. Dibos (210)
Aug. 21	Chicago Challenge	Jane Geddes (272)	75,000	D. Eggeling & R. Walton (275)
Aug. 28	**du Maurier Classic** (Ottawa, Ont.)	Martha Nause (279)	120,000	M. McGann (280)
Sept. 6	State Farm Rail Classic	Barb Mucha (203)	78,750	K. Shipman (204)
Sept. 12	Ping-Cellular One Championship	Missie McGeorge (207)	75,000	B. King (210)
Sept. 19	Safeco Classic	Deb Richard (276)	75,000	4-way tie (277)

* Playoffs (3): Toledo—Robbins won on 1st hole; **Big Apple**—Daniel won on 1st hole; **Children's**—Will won on 2nd hole.
Second place ties (3 players or more): 4—WAY—**Safeco** (M. Estill, T. Green, C. Johnson, R. Jones).

LPGA Majors

Dinah Shore

Edition: 23rd   **Dates:** March 24-27
Site: Mission Hills CC, Rancho Mirage, Calif.
Par: 36-36—72 (6446 yards)   **Purse:** $700,000

		1	2	3	4	Tot	Earnings
1	Donna Andrews	70	69	67	70	—276	$105,000
2	Laura Davies	70	68	69	70	—277	65,165
3	Tammie Green	70	72	69	68	—279	47,553
4	Jan Stephenson	70	69	70	71	—280	36,985
5	Michelle McGann	70	68	70	73	—281	29,940
6	Gail Graham	73	71	71	68	—283	21,251
	Kelly Robbins	73	70	69	71	—283	21,251
	Brandie Burton	73	73	65	72	—283	21,251
9	Hollis Stacy	72	72	70	70	—284	15,674
	Nancy Lopez	68	72	73	71	—284	15,674

Early round leaders: 1st— Lopez, Alice Miller, Lisa Walters (68); **2nd**— Davies, McGann (138); **3rd**— Andrews (206).
Top amateur: Emilee Klein (300).

U.S. Women's Open

Edition: 49th   **Dates:** July 21-24
Site: Indianwood GC, Lake Orion, Mich.
Par: 35-36—71 (6244 yards)   **Purse:** $850,000

		1	2	3	4	Tot	Earnings
1	Patty Sheehan	66	71	69	71	—277	$155,000
2	Tammie Green	66	72	69	71	—278	85,000
3	Liselotte Neumann	69	72	71	69	—281	47,752
4	Tania Abitbol	72	68	73	70	—283	31,133
	Alicia Dibos	69	68	73	73	—283	31,133
6	Amy Alcott	71	67	77	69	—284	21,487
	Meg Mallon	70	72	73	69	—284	21,487
	Betsy King	69	71	72	72	—284	21,487
8	Kelly Robbins	71	72	70	72	—285	16,446
	Donna Andrews	67	72	70	76	—285	16,446
	Helen Alfredsson	63	69	76	77	—285	16,446

Early round leaders: 1st— Alfredsson (63); **2nd**— Alfredsson (132); **3rd**— Sheehan (206). **Top amateur:** Carol Thompson (291).

LPGA Championship

Edition: 40th   **Dates:** May 12-15
Site: Du Pont CC, Wilmington, Del.
Par: 35-36—71 (6386 yards)   **Purse:** $1,100,000

		1	2	3	4	Tot	Earnings
1	Laura Davies	70	72	69	68	—279	$165,000
2	Alice Ritzman	68	73	71	70	—282	102,402
3	Elaine Crosby	76	71	69	67	—283	54,660
	Pat Bradley	73	73	70	67	—283	54,660
	Hiromi Kobayashi	72	73	71	67	—283	54,660
	Liselotte Neumann	74	73	67	69	—283	54,660
7	Sherri Steinhauer	75	70	72	68	—285	27,676
	Amy Alcott	71	75	70	69	—285	27,676
	Beth Daniel	72	74	68	71	—285	27,676
	Patty Sheehan	72	68	72	73	—285	27,676

Early round leaders: 1st— Ritzman, Mochrie (68); **2nd**— Sheehan, Robin Walton (140); **3rd**— Meg Mallon, Davies (211). **Top amateur:** None.

du Maurier Classic

Edition: 22nd   **Dates:** August 26-29
Site: Ottawa Hunt Club, Ottawa, Ontario
Par: 36-36—72 (6400 yards)   **Purse:** $800,000

		1	2	3	4	Tot	Earnings
1	Martha Nause	65	71	72	71	—279	$120,000
2	Michelle McGann	66	71	71	72	—280	74,474
3	Liselotte Neumann	70	67	71	73	—281	54,346
4	Jane Geddes	74	67	70	72	—283	34,888
	Betsy King	67	69	74	73	—283	34,888
	Meg Mallon	70	72	68	73	—283	34,888
7	Dawn Coe-Jones	72	70	71	71	—284	20,128
	Judy Dickinson	72	68	70	74	—284	20,128
	Marianne Morris	69	72	70	73	—284	20,128
	Kelly Robbins	66	70	73	75	—284	20,128

Early round leaders: 1st— Nause (65); **2nd**— King, Nause, Robbins (136); **3rd**— McGann, Nause, Neumann (208). **Top amateur:** None.

Money Leaders

Official money leaders of PGA, European PGA, Senior PGA and LPGA tours for 1993 and unofficial money leaders for 1994 (through Sept. 25), as compiled by the PGA, European PGA and LPGA. All European amounts are in pound sterling (£). Listed are tournaments played (TP); cuts made (CM); 1st, 2nd and 3rd place finishes; and earnings for the year.

PGA

Final 1993

	TP	CM	Finish 1-2-3	Earnings
1 Nick Price	18	17	4-2-0	$1,478,557
2 Paul Azinger	24	17	3-1-6	1,458,456
3 Greg Norman	15	14	1-4-2	1,359,653
4 Jim Gallagher Jr	27	18	2-1-1	1,078,870
5 David Frost	22	15	2-2-1	1,030,717
6 Payne Stewart	26	22	0-4-3	982,875
7 Lee Janzen	26	23	2-0-1	932,335
8 Tom Kite	20	14	2-2-0	887,811
9 Fulton Allem	28	18	2-0-0	851,345
10 Fred Couples	19	17	1-2-0	796,579

1994 (through Sept. 25)

	TP	CM	Finish 1-2-3	Earnings
1 Nick Price	16	12	5-1-0	$1,442,927
2 Greg Norman	14	14	1-3-0	1,255,164
3 Tom Lehman	20	18	1-1-1	978,689
4 Jose-Maria Olazabal	8	6	2-1-0	969,900
5 Loren Roberts	19	16	1-3-1	920,570
6 Corey Pavin	18	14	1-3-1	825,305
7 Hale Irwin	20	17	1-1-1	759,836
8 Jeff Maggert	21	20	0-2-2	712,475
9 Mike Springer	21	16	2-0-1	710,717
10 Scott Hoch	23	18	1-1-2	705,559

Note: Olazabal and Els are European PGA Tour members.

EUROPEAN PGA

Final 1993

	TP	CM	Finish 1-2-3	Earnings
1 Colin Montgomerie	24	21	2-2-0	£613,683
2 Nick Faldo	14	13	2-3-1	558,738
3 Ian Woosnam	15	15	2-2-0	501,353
4 Bernhard Langer	13	13	2-0-2	469,570
5 Sam Torrance	30	25	3-2-0	421,328
6 Constantino Rocca	30	22	2-1-2	403,866
7 Peter Baker	30	23	2-1-0	378,989
8 Darren Clarke	30	23	1-1-0	369,675
9 Gordon Brand Jr	29	25	1-2-0	367,589
10 Barry Lane	31	24	1-1-3	339,218

1994 (through Sept. 25)

	TP	CM	Finish 1-2-3	Earnings
1 Colin Montgomerie	19	18	3-1-2	£602,920
2 Bernhard Langer	15	15	1-1-4	418,946
3 Jose Marie Olazabal	14	14	2-2-1	399,608
4 Miguel Angel Jiminez	24	20	1-2-0	368,353
5 Seve Ballesteros	14	11	1-2-1	350,724
6 David Gilford	25	19	2-1-0	294,779
7 Mark Roe	24	21	1-1-1	289,140
8 Nick Faldo	9	8	1-1-0	269,143
9 Ernie Els	11	9	1-1-0	257,600
10 Eduardo Romero	22	16	2-0-0	253,197

SENIOR PGA

Final 1993

	TP	CM	Finish 1-2-3	Earnings
1 Dave Stockton	34	34	5-5-2	$1,175,944
2 Bob Charles	29	29	3-4-2	1,046,823
3 George Archer	32	32	4-3-2	963,124
4 Lee Trevino	25	25	3-3-1	956,591
5 Chi Chi Rodriguez	32	32	1-4-1	798,857
6 Mike Hill	29	29	2-3-2	798,116
7 Jim Colbert	31	31	2-3-1	779,889
8 Bob Murphy	27	27	2-2-2	768,743
9 Ray Floyd	14	14	2-4-2	713,168
10 Simon Hobday	34	34	2-2-0	670,417

1994 (through Sept. 25)

	TP	CM	Finish 1-2-3	Earnings
1 Lee Trevino	21	21	6-1-3	$1,183,919
2 Dave Stockton	26	26	3-3-3	1,169,885
3 Jim Albus	29	29	2-5-2	1,015,883
4 Ray Floyd	16	16	3-4-2	989,074
5 Jim Colbert	27	27	2-5-1	878,045
6 Tom Wargo	30	30	1-3-0	821,282
7 Jim Dent	24	24	1-0-4	688,672
8 Bob Murphy	24	24	0-4-3	619,892
9 George Archer	25	25	0-2-2	590,470
10 Simon Hobday	26	26	2-1-0	584,199

LPGA

Final 1993

	TP	CM	Finish 1-2-3	Earnings
1 Betsy King	27	25	1-5-1	$595,992
2 Patty Sheehan	21	20	2-1-2	540,547
3 Brandie Burton	26	25	3-0-2	517,741
4 Dottie Mochrie	25	24	1-2-1	429,118
5 Helen Alfredsson	22	19	1-1-2	402,685
6 Lauri Merten	23	18	1-1-1	394,744
7 Tammy Green	23	21	2-1-0	356,579
8 Hiromi Kobayashi	24	21	2-0-0	347,060
9 Donna Andrews	23	22	1-3-0	334,285
10 Trish Johnson	16	15	2-1-1	331,745

1994 (through Sept. 25)

	TP	CM	Finish 1-2-3	Earnings
1 Laura Davies	19	18	3-3-0	$631,910
2 Beth Daniel	22	19	3-1-1	551,687
3 Dottie Mochrie	25	25	1-1-2	443,285
4 Liselotte Neumann	19	16	2-1-2	408,201
5 Donna Andrews	21	20	3-0-0	407,103
6 Tammie Green	21	19	1-3-1	406,884
7 Sherri Steinhauer	25	22	1-0-1	382,604
8 Kelly Robbins	23	18	1-1-0	380,770
9 Meg Mallon	24	21	0-1-1	320,984
10 Patty Sheehan	17	15	1-0-0	310,462

THE 1995 INFORMATION PLEASE SPORTS ALMANAC

GOLF STATISTICS

SEC B

THROUGH THE YEARS
1860-1994
MAJOR TITLES • LEADERS

PAGE 782

Major Championships
MEN
The Masters

The Masters has been played every year since 1934 at the Augusta National Golf Club in Augusta, GA. Both the course (6905 yards, par 72) and the tournament were created by Bobby Jones; (*) indicates playoff winner.

Multiple winners: Jack Nicklaus (6); Arnold Palmer (4); Jimmy Demaret, Gary Player and Sam Snead (3); Seve Ballesteros, Nick Faldo, Ben Hogan, Bernhard Langer, Byron Nelson, Horton Smith and Tom Watson (2).

Year	Winner	Score	Runner-up
1934	Horton Smith	284	Craig Wood (285)
1935	Gene Sarazen*	282	Craig Wood (282)
1936	Horton Smith	285	Harry Cooper (286)
1937	Byron Nelson	283	Ralph Guldahl (285)
1938	Henry Picard	285	Ralph Guldahl & Harry Cooper (287)
1939	Ralph Guldahl	279	Sam Snead (280)
1940	Jimmy Demaret	280	Lloyd Mangrum (284)
1941	Craig Wood	280	Byron Nelson (283)
1942	Byron Nelson*	280	Ben Hogan (280)
1943-45	Not held		World War II
1946	Herman Keiser	282	Ben Hogan (283)
1947	Jimmy Demaret	281	Frank Stranahan & Byron Nelson (283)
1948	Claude Harmon	279	Cary Middlecoff (284)
1949	Sam Snead	282	Lloyd Mangrum & Johnny Bulla (285)
1950	Jimmy Demaret	283	Jim Ferrier (285)
1951	Ben Hogan	280	Skee Riegel (282)
1952	Sam Snead	286	Jack Burke, Jr. (290)
1953	Ben Hogan	274	Ed Oliver (279)
1954	Sam Snead*	289	Ben Hogan (289)
1955	Cary Middlecoff	279	Ben Hogan (286)
1956	Jack Burke, Jr.	289	Ken Venturi (290)
1957	Doug Ford	283	Sam Snead (286)
1958	Arnold Palmer	284	Doug Ford, & Fred Hawkins (285)
1959	Art Wall, Jr.	284	Cary Middlecoff (285)
1960	Arnold Palmer	282	Ken Venturi (283)
1961	Gary Player	280	Arnold Palmer & Charles R. Coe (281)
1962	Arnold Palmer*	280	Dow Finsterwald & Gary Player (280)
1963	Jack Nicklaus	286	Tony Lema (287)
1964	Arnold Palmer	276	Jack Nicklaus & Dave Marr (282)
1965	Jack Nicklaus	271	Arnold Palmer & Gary Player (280)
1966	Jack Nicklaus*	288	Gay Brewer, Jr. & Tommy Jacobs (288)
1967	Gay Brewer, Jr.	280	Bobby Nichols (281)
1968	Bob Goalby	277	Roberto DeVicenzo (278)
1969	George Archer	281	Billy Casper, George Knudson & Tom Weiskopf (282)
1970	Billy Casper*	279	Gene Littler (279)
1971	Charles Coody	279	Jack Nicklaus & Johnny Miller (281)
1972	Jack Nicklaus	286	Bruce Crampton, Bobby Mitchell, & Tom Weiskopf (289)
1973	Tommy Aaron	283	J.C. Snead (284)
1974	Gary Player	278	Tom Weiskopf, & Dave Stockton (280)
1975	Jack Nicklaus	276	Johnny Miller & Tom Weiskopf (277)
1976	Ray Floyd	271	Ben Crenshaw (279)
1977	Tom Watson	276	Jack Nicklaus (278)
1978	Gary Player	277	Hubert Green, Rod Funseth, & Tom Watson (278)
1979	Fuzzy Zoeller*	280	Ed Sneed & Tom Watson (280)
1980	Seve Ballesteros	275	Gibby Gilbert & Jack Newton (279)
1981	Tom Watson	280	Jack Nicklaus & Johnny Miller (282)
1982	Craig Stadler*	284	Dan Pohl (284)
1983	Seve Ballesteros	280	Ben Crenshaw, & Tom Kite (284)
1984	Ben Crenshaw	277	Tom Watson (279)
1985	Bernhard Langer	282	Curtis Strange, Seve Ballesteros & Ray Floyd (284)
1986	Jack Nicklaus	279	Greg Norman (280)
1987	Larry Mize*	285	Seve Ballesteros & Greg Norman (285)
1988	Sandy Lyle	281	Mark Calcavecchia (282)
1989	Nick Faldo*	283	Scott Hoch (283)
1990	Nick Faldo*	278	Ray Floyd (278)
1991	Ian Woosnam	277	J.M. Olazabal (278)
1992	Fred Couples	275	Ray Floyd (277)
1993	Bernhard Langer	277	Chip Beck (281)
1994	J.M. Olazabal	279	Tom Lehman (281)

*PLAYOFFS

1935: Gene Sarazen (144) def. Craig Wood (149) in 36 holes. **1942:** Byron Nelson (69) def. Ben Hogan (70) in 18 holes. **1954:** Sam Snead (70) def. Ben Hogan (71) in 18 holes. **1962:** Arnold Palmer (68) def. Gary Player (71) and Dow Finsterwald (77) in 18 holes. **1966:** Jack Nicklaus (70) def. Tommy Jacobs (72) and Gay Brewer (78) in 18 holes. **1970:** Billy Casper (69) def. Gene Littler (74) in 18 holes. **1979:** Fuzzy Zoeller (4-3) def. Ed Sneed (4-4) and Tom Watson (4-4) on 2nd hole of sudden death. **1982:** Craig Stadler (4) def. Dan Pohl (5) on 1st hole of sudden death. **1987:** Larry Mize (4-3) def. Greg Norman (4-4) and Seve Ballesteros (5) on 2nd hole of sudden death. **1989:** Nick Faldo (5-3) def. Scott Hoch (5-4) on 2nd hole of sudden death. **1990:** Nick Faldo (4-4) def. Raymond Floyd (4-x) on second hole of sudden death.

U.S. Open

Played at a different course each year, the U.S. Open was launched by the new U.S. Golf Association in 1895. The Open was a 36-hole event from 1895-97 and has been 72 holes since then. It switched from a 3-day, 36-hole Saturday finish to 4 days of play in 1965. Note that (*) indicates playoff winner and (a) indicates amateur winner.

Multiple winners: Willie Anderson, Ben Hogan, Bobby Jones and Jack Nicklaus (4); Hale Irwin (3); Julius Boros, Billy Casper, Ralph Guldahl, Walter Hagen, John McDermott, Cary Middlecoff, Andy North, Gene Sarazen, Alex Smith, Curtis Strange and Lee Trevino (2).

Year	Winner	Score	Runner-up	Course	Location
1895	Horace Rawlins	173	Willie Dunn (175)	Newport GC	Newport, R.I.
1896	James Foulis	152	Horace Rawlins (155)	Shinnecock Hills GC	Southampton, N.Y.
1897	Joe Lloyd	162	Willie Anderson (163)	Chicago GC	Wheaton, Ill.
1898	Fred Herd	328	Alex Smith (335)	Myopia Hunt Club	Hamilton, Mass.
1899	Willie Smith	315	George Low, W.H. Way & Val Fitzjohn (326)	Baltimore CC	Baltimore
1900	Harry Vardon	313	J.H. Taylor (315)	Chicago GC	Wheaton, Ill.
1901	Willie Anderson*	331	Alex Smith (331)	Myopia Hunt Club	Hamilton, Mass.
1902	Laurie Auchterlonie	307	Stewart Gardner (313)	Garden City GC	Garden City, N.Y.
1903	Willie Anderson*	307	David Brown (307)	Baltusrol GC	Springfield, N.J.
1904	Willie Anderson*	303	Gil Nicholls (308)	Glen View Club	Golf, Ill.
1905	Willie Anderson	314	Alex Smith (316)	Myopia Hunt Club	Hamilton, Mass.
1906	Alex Smith	295	Willie Smith (302)	Onwentsia Club	Lake Forest, Ill.
1907	Alec Ross	302	Gil Nicholls (304)	Phila. Cricket Club	Chestnut Hill, Pa.
1908	Fred McLeod*	322	Willie Smith (322)	Myopia Hunt Club	Hamilton, Mass.
1909	George Sargent	290	Tom McNamara (294)	Englewood GC	Englewood, N.J.
1910	Alex Smith*	298	Macdonald Smith & John McDermott (298)	Phila. Cricket Club	Chestnut Hill, Pa.
1911	John McDermott*	307	George Simpson & Mike Brady (307)	Chicago GC	Wheaton, Ill.
1912	John McDermott	294	Tom McNamara (296)	CC of Buffalo	Buffalo
1913	a-Francis Ouimet*	304	Harry Vardon & Ted Ray (304)	The Country Club	Brookline, Mass.
1914	Walter Hagen	290	a-Chick Evans (291)	Midlothian CC	Blue Island, Ill.
1915	a-John Travers	297	Tom McNamara (298)	Baltusrol GC	Springfield, N.J.
1916	a-Chick Evans	286	Jock Hutchinson (288)	Minikahda Club	Minneapolis
1917-18	Not held		World War I		
1919	Walter Hagen*	301	Mike Brady (301)	Brae Burn CC	West Newton, Mass.
1920	Ted Ray	295	Jock Hutchinson, Jack Burke, Leo Diegel & Harry Vardon (296)	Inverness Club	Toledo, Ohio
1921	Jim Barnes	289	Walter Hagen & Fred McLeod (298)	Columbia CC	Chevy Chase, Md.
1922	Gene Sarazen	288	a-Bobby Jones & John Black (289)	Skokie CC	Glencoe, Ill.
1923	a-Bobby Jones*	296	Bobby Cruickshank (296)	Inwood CC	Far Rockaway, N.Y.
1924	Cyril Walker	297	a-Bobby Jones (300)	Oakland Hills CC	Birmingham, Mich.
1925	Willie Macfarlane*	291	a-Bobby Jones (291)	Worcester CC	Worcester, Mass.
1926	a-Bobby Jones	293	Joe Turnesa (294)	Scioto CC	Columbus, Ohio
1927	Tommy Armour*	301	Harry Cooper (301)	Oakmont CC	Oakmont, Pa.
1928	Johnny Farrell*	294	a-Bobby Jones (294)	Olympia Fields CC	Matteson, Ill.
1929	a-Bobby Jones*	294	Al Espinosa (294)	Winged Foot CC	Mamaroneck, N.Y.
1930	a-Bobby Jones	287	Macdonald Smith (289)	Interlachen CC	Hopkins, Minn.
1931	Billy Burke*	292	George Von Elm (292)	Inverness Club	Toledo, Ohio
1932	Gene Sarazen	286	Bobby Cruickshank & Phil Perkins (289)	Fresh Meadow CC	Flushing, N.Y.
1933	a-Johnny Goodman	287	Ralph Guldahl (288)	North Shore GC	Glenview, Ill.
1934	Olin Dutra	293	Gene Sarazen (294)	Merion Cricket Club	Ardmore, Pa.
1935	Sam Parks, Jr.	299	Jimmy Thomson (301)	Oakmont CC	Oakmont, Pa.
1936	Tony Manero	282	Harry E. Cooper (284)	Baltusrol GC	Springfield, N.J.
1937	Ralph Guldahl	281	Sam Snead (283)	Oakland Hills CC	Birmingham, Mich.
1938	Ralph Guldahl	284	Dick Metz (290)	Cherry Hills CC	Denver

Major Championships (Cont.)
U.S. Open

Year	Winner	Score	Runner-up	Course	Location
1939	Byron Nelson*	284	Craig Wood & Denny Shute (284)	Philadelphia CC	Philadelphia
1940	Lawson Little*	287	Gene Sarazen (287)	Canterbury GC	Cleveland
1941	Craig Wood	284	Denny Shute (287)	Colonial Club	Ft. Worth
1942-45	Not held		World War II		
1946	Lloyd Mangrum*	284	Byron Nelson & Vic Ghezzi (284)	Canterbury GC	Cleveland
1947	Lew Worsham*	282	Sam Snead (282)	St. Louis CC	Clayton, Mo.
1948	Ben Hogan	276	Jimmy Demaret (278)	Riviera CC	Los Angeles
1949	Cary Middlecoff	286	Clayton Heafner & Sam Snead (287)	Medinah CC	Medinah, Ill.
1950	Ben Hogan*	287	Lloyd Mangrum & George Fazio (287)	Merion Golf Club	Ardmore, Pa.
1951	Ben Hogan	287	Clayton Heafner (289)	Oakland Hills CC	Birmingham, Mich.
1952	Julius Boros	281	Ed Oliver (285)	Northwood Club	Dallas
1953	Ben Hogan	283	Sam Snead (289)	Oakmont CC	Oakmont, Pa.
1954	Ed Furgol	284	Gene Littler (285)	Baltusrol GC	Springfield, N.J.
1955	Jack Fleck*	287	Ben Hogan (287)	Olympic CC	San Francisco
1956	Cary Middlecoff	281	Ben Hogan & Julius Boros (282)	Oak Hill CC	Rochester, N.Y.
1957	Dick Mayer*	282	Cary Middlecoff (282)	Inverness Club	Toledo, Ohio
1958	Tommy Bolt	283	Gary Player (287)	Southern Hills CC	Tulsa
1959	Billy Casper	282	Bob Rosburg (283)	Winged Foot GC	Marmaroneck, N.Y.
1960	Arnold Palmer	280	Jack Nicklaus (282)	Cherry Hills CC	Denver
1961	Gene Littler	281	Doug Sanders & Bob Goalby (282)	Oakland Hills CC	Birmingham, Mich.
1962	Jack Nicklaus*	283	Arnold Palmer (283)	Oakmont CC	Oakmont, Pa.
1963	Julius Boros*	293	Arnold Palmer & Jacky Cupit (293)	The Country Club	Brookline, Mass.
1964	Ken Venturi	278	Tommy Jacobs (282)	Congressional CC	Bethesda, Md.
1965	Gary Player*	282	Kel Nagle (282)	Bellerive CC	St. Louis
1966	Billy Casper*	278	Arnold Palmer (278)	Olympic CC	San Francisco
1967	Jack Nicklaus	275	Arnold Palmer (279)	Baltusrol GC	Springfield, N.J.
1968	Lee Trevino	275	Jack Nicklaus (279)	Oak Hill CC	Rochester, N.Y.
1969	Orville Moody	281	Al Geiberger, Deane Beman & Bob Rosburg (282)	Champions GC	Houston
1970	Tony Jacklin	281	Dave Hill (288)	Hazeltine National GC	Chaska, Minn.
1971	Lee Trevino*	280	Jack Nicklaus (280)	Merion GC	Ardmore, Pa.
1972	Jack Nicklaus	290	Bruce Crampton (293)	Pebble Beach GL	Pebble Beach, Calif.
1973	Johnny Miller	279	John Schlee (280)	Oakmont CC	Oakmont, Pa.
1974	Hale Irwin	287	Forest Fezler (289)	Winged Foot GC	Mamaroneck, N.Y.
1975	Lou Graham*	287	John Mahaffey (287)	Medinah CC	Medinah, Ill.
1976	Jerry Pate	277	Al Geiberger & Tom Weiskopf (279)	Atlanta AC	Duluth, Ga.
1977	Hubert Green	278	Lou Graham (279)	Southern Hills CC	Tulsa
1978	Andy North	285	Dave Stockton & J.C. Snead (286)	Cherry Hills CC	Denver
1979	Hale Irwin	284	Gary Player & Jerry Pate (286)	Inverness Club	Toledo, Ohio
1980	Jack Nicklaus	272	Isao Aoki (274)	Baltusrol GC	Springfield, N.J.
1981	David Graham	273	George Burns & Bill Rogers (276)	Merion GC	Ardmore, Pa.
1982	Tom Watson	282	Jack Nicklaus (284)	Pebble Beach GL	Pebble Beach, Calif.
1983	Larry Nelson	280	Tom Watson (281)	Oakmont CC	Oakmont, Pa.
1984	Fuzzy Zoeller*	276	Greg Norman (276)	Winged Foot GC	Mamaroneck, N.Y.
1985	Andy North	279	Dave Barr, T.C. Chen & Denis Watson (280)	Oakland Hills CC	Birmingham, Mich.
1986	Ray Floyd	279	Lanny Wadkins & Chip Beck (281)	Shinnecock Hills GC	Southampton, N.Y.
1987	Scott Simpson	277	Tom Watson (278)	Olympic Club	San Francisco
1988	Curtis Strange*	278	Nick Faldo (278)	The Country Club	Brookline, Mass.
1989	Curtis Strange	278	Chip Beck, Ian Woosnam & Mark McCumber (279)	Oak Hill CC	Rochester, N.Y.

Year	Winner	Score	Runner-up	Course	Location
1990	Hale Irwin*	280	Mike Donald (280)	Medinah CC	Medinah, Ill.
1991	Payne Stewart*	282	Scott Simpson (282)	Hazeline National GC	Chaska, Minn.
1992	Tom Kite	285	Jeff Sluman (287)	Pebble Beach GL	Pebble Beach, Calif.
1993	Lee Janzen	272	Payne Stewart (274)	Baltusrol GC	Springfield, N.J.
1994	Ernie Els*	279	Colin Montgomerie (279) & Loren Roberts (279)	Oakmont CC	Oakmont, Pa.

*PLAYOFFS

1901: Willie Anderson (85) def. Alex Smith (86) in 18 holes. **1903:** Willie Anderson (82) def. David Brown (84) in 18 holes. **1908:** Fred McLeod (77) def. Willie Smith (83) in 18 holes. **1910:** Alex Smith (71) def. John McDermott (75) & Macdonald Smith (77) in 18 holes. **1911:** John McDermott (80) def. Mike Brady (82) & George Simpson (85) in 18 holes. **1913:** Francis Ouimet (72) def. Harry Vardon (77) & Edward Ray (78) in 18 holes. **1919:** Walter Hagen (77) def. Mike Brady (78) in 18 holes. **1923:** Bobby Jones (76) def. Bobby Cruickshank (78) in 18 holes. **1925:** Willie Macfarlane (75-72—147) def. Bobby Jones (75-73—148) in 36 holes. **1927:** Tommy Armour (76) def. Harry Cooper (79) in 18 holes. **1928:** Johnny Farrell (70-73—143) def. Bobby Jones (73-71—144) in 36 holes. **1929:** Bobby Jones (141) def. Al Espinosa (164) in 36 holes. **1931:** Billy Burke (149-148) def. George Von Elm (149-149) in 72 holes. **1939:** Byron Nelson (68-70) def. Craig Wood (68-73) and Denny Shute (76) in 36 holes. **1940:** Lawson Little (70) def. Gene Sarazen (73) in 18 holes. **1946:** Lloyd Mangrum (72-72—144) def. Byron Nelson (72-73—145) and Vic Ghezzi (72-73—145) in 36 holes. **1947:** Lew Worsham (69) def. Sam Snead (70) in 18 holes. **1950:** Ben Hogan (69) def. Lloyd Mangrum (73) & George Fazio (75) in 18 holes. **1955:** Jack Fleck (69) def. Ben Hogan (72) in 18 holes. **1957:** Dick Mayer (72) def. Cary Middlecoff (79) in 18 holes. **1962:** Jack Nicklaus (71) def. Arnold Palmer (74) in 18 holes. **1963:** Julius Boros (70) def. Jacky Cupit (73) & Arnold Palmer (76) in 18 holes. **1965:** Gary Player (71) def. Kel Nagle (74) in 18 holes. **1966:** Billy Casper (69) def. Arnold Palmer (73) in 18 holes. **1971:** Lee Trevino (68) def. Jack Nicklaus (71) in 18 holes. **1975:** Lou Graham (71) def. John Mahaffey (73) in 18 holes. **1984:** Fuzzy Zoeller (67) def. Greg Norman (75) in 18 holes. **1988:** Curtis Strange (71) def. Nick Faldo (75) in 18 holes. **1990:** Hale Irwin (74-3) def. Mike Donald (74-4) on 1st hole of sudden death after 18 holes. **1991:** Payne Stewart (75) def. Scott Simpson (77) in 18 holes. **1994:** Ernie Els (74-4-4) def. Loren Roberts (74-4-5) and Colin Montgomerie (78-x-x) on 2nd hole of sudden death after 18 holes.

British Open

The oldest of the Majors, The Open began in 1860 to determine "the champion golfer of the world." Conducted by the Royal and Ancient Golf Club of St. Andrews, The Open is rotated among select golf courses in England and Scotland. Note that (*) indicates playoff winner and (a) indicates amateur winner.

Multiple winners: Harry Vardon (6); James Braid, J.H.Taylor, Peter Thomson and Tom Watson (5); Walter Hagen, Bobby Locke, Tom Morris, Sr., Tom Morris, Jr., and Willie Park (4); Jamie Anderson, Seve Ballesteros, Henry Cotton, Nick Faldo, Robert Ferguson, Bobby Jones, Jack Nicklaus and Gary Player (3); Harold Hilton, Bob Martin, Greg Norman, Arnold Palmer, Willie Park, Jr., and Lee Trevino (2).

Year	Winner	Score	Runner-up	Course	Location
1860	Willie Park	174	Tom Morris Sr. (176)	Prestwick Club	Ayrshire, Scotland
1861	Tom Morris Sr.	163	Willie Park (167)	Prestwick Club	Ayrshire, Scotland
1862	Tom Morris Sr.	163	Willie Park (176)	Prestwick Club	Ayrshire, Scotland
1863	Willie Park	168	Tom Morris Sr. (170)	Prestwick Club	Ayrshire, Scotland
1864	Tom Morris Sr.	167	Andrew Strath (169)	Prestwick Club	Ayrshire, Scotland
1865	Andrew Strath	162	Willie Park (164)	Prestwick Club	Ayrshire, Scotland
1866	Willie Park	169	David Park (171)	Prestwick Club	Ayrshire, Scotland
1867	Tom Morris Sr.	170	Willie Park (172)	Prestwick Club	Ayrshire, Scotland
1868	Tom Morris Jr.	157	Robert Andrew (159)	Prestwick Club	Ayrshire, Scotland
1869	Tom Morris Jr.	154	Tom Morris Sr. (157)	Prestwick Club	Ayrshire, Scotland
1870	Tom Morris Jr.	149	Bob Kirk (161)	Prestwick Club	Ayrshire, Scotland
1871	Not held				
1872	Tom Morris Jr.	166	David Strath (169)	Prestwick Club	Ayrshire, Scotland
1873	Tom Kidd	179	Jamie Anderson (180)	St. Andrews	St. Andrews, Scotland
1874	Mungo Park	159	Tom Morris Jr. (161)	Musselburgh	Musselburgh, Scotland
1875	Willie Park	166	Bob Martin (168)	Prestwick Club	Ayrshire, Scotland
1876	Bob Martin*	176	David Strath (176)	St. Andrews	St. Andrews, Scotland
1877	Jamie Anderson	160	Bob Pringle (162)	Musselburgh	Musselburgh, Scotland
1878	Jamie Anderson	157	Bob Kirk (159)	Prestwick Club	Ayrshire, Scotland
1879	Jamie Anderson	169	Andrew Kirkaldy & James Allan (172)	St. Andrews	St. Andrews, Scotland
1880	Bob Ferguson	162	Peter Paxton (167)	Musselburgh	Musselburgh, Scotland
1881	Bob Ferguson	170	Jamie Anderson (173)	Prestwick Club	Ayrshire, Scotland
1882	Bob Ferguson	171	Willie Fernie (174)	St. Andrews	St. Andrews, Scotland
1883	Willie Fernie*	159	Bob Ferguson (159)	Musselburgh	Musselburgh, Scotland
1884	Jack Simpson	160	David Rollan & Willie Fernie (164)	Prestwick Club	Ayrshire, Scotland
1885	Bob Martin	171	Archie Simpson (172)	St. Andrews	St. Andrews, Scotland
1886	David Brown	157	Willie Campbell (159)	Musselburgh	Musselburgh, Scotland

Major Championships (Cont.)
British Open

Year	Winner	Score	Runner-up	Course	Location
1887	Willie Park Jr.	161	Bob Martin (162)	Prestwick Club	Ayrshire, Scotland
1888	Jack Burns	171	David Anderson & Ben Sayers (172)	St. Andrews	St. Andrews, Scotland
1889	Willie Park Jr.*	155	Andrew Kirkaldy (155)	Musselburgh	Musselburgh, Scotland
1890	a-John Ball	164	Willie Fernie (167) & A. Simpson (167)	Prestwick Club	Ayrshire, Scotland
1891	Hugh Kirkaldy	166	Andrew Kirkaldy & Willie Fernie (168)	St. Andrews	St. Andrews, Scotland
1892	a-Harold Hilton	305	John Ball, Sandy Herd & Hugh Kirkaldy (308)	Muirfield	Gullane, Scotland
1893	Willie Auchterlonie	322	Johnny Laidlay (324)	Prestwick Club	Ayrshire, Scotland
1894	J.H. Taylor	326	Douglas Rolland (331)	Royal St. George's	Sandwich, England
1895	J.H. Taylor	322	Sandy Herd (326)	St. Andrews	St. Andrews, Scotland
1896	Harry Vardon*	316	J.H. Taylor (316)	Muirfield	Gullane, Scotland
1897	a-Harold Hilton	314	James Braid (315)	Hoylake	Hoylake, England
1898	Harry Vardon	307	Willie Park Jr. (308)	Prestwick Club	Ayrshire, Scotland
1899	Harry Vardon	310	Jack White (315)	Royal St. George's	Sandwich, England
1900	J.H. Taylor	309	Harry Vardon (317)	St. Andrews	St. Andrews, Scotland
1901	James Braid	309	Harry Vardon (312)	Muirfield	Gullane, Scotland
1902	Sandy Herd	307	Harry Vardon (308)	Hoylake	Hoylake, England
1903	Harry Vardon	300	Tom Vardon (306)	Prestwick Club	Ayrshire, Scotland
1904	Jack White	296	James Braid (297)	Royal St. George's	Sandwich, England
1905	James Braid	318	J.H. Taylor (323) & Rolland Jones (323)	St. Andrews	St. Andrews, Scotland
1906	James Braid	300	J.H. Taylor (304)	Muirfield	Gullane, Scotland
1907	Arnaud Massy	312	J.H. Taylor (314)	Hoylake	Hoylake, England
1908	James Braid	291	Tom Ball (299)	Prestwick Club	Ayrshire, Scotland
1909	J.H. Taylor	295	James Braid (299)	Deal	Deal, England
1910	James Braid	299	Sandy Herd (303)	St. Andrews	St. Andrews, Scotland
1911	Harry Vardon*	303	Arnaud Massy (303)	Royal St. George's	Sandwich, England
1912	Ted Ray	295	Harry Vardon (299)	Muirfield	Gullane, Scotland
1913	J.H. Taylor	304	Ted Ray (312)	Hoylake	Hoylake, England
1914	Harry Vardon	306	J.H. Taylor (309)	Prestwick Club	Ayrshire, Scotland
1915-19	Not held		World War I		
1920	George Duncan	303	Sandy Herd (305)	Deal	Deal, England
1921	Jock Hutchison*	296	Roger Wethered (296)	St. Andrews	St. Andrews, Scotland
1922	Walter Hagen	300	George Duncan & Jim Barnes (301)	Royal St. George's	Sandwich, England
1923	Arthur Havers	295	Walter Hagen (296)	Troon	Troon, Scotland
1924	Walter Hagen	301	Ernest Whitcombe (302)	Hoylake	Hoylake, England
1925	Jim Barnes	300	Archie Compston & Ted Ray (301)	Prestwick Club	Ayrshire, Scotland
1926	a-Bobby Jones	291	Al Watrous (293)	Royal Lytham	Lytham, England
1927	a-Bobby Jones	285	Aubrey Boomer (291)	St. Andrews	St. Andrews, Scotland
1928	Walter Hagen	292	Gene Sarazen (294)	Royal St. George's	Sandwich, England
1929	Walter Hagen	292	Johnny Farrell (298)	Muirfield	Gullane, Scotland
1930	a-Bobby Jones	291	Macdonald Smith & Leo Diegel (293)	Hoylake	Hoylake, England
1931	Tommy Armour	296	Jose Jurado (297)	Carnoustie	Carnoustie, Scotland
1932	Gene Sarazen	283	Macdonald Smith (288)	Prince's	Prince's, England
1933	Denny Shute*	292	Craig Wood (292)	St. Andrews	St. Andrews, Scotland
1934	Henry Cotton	283	Sid Brews (288)	Royal St. George's	Sandwich, England
1935	Alf Perry	283	Alf Padgham (287)	Muirfield	Gullane, Scotland
1936	Alf Padgham	287	Jimmy Adams (288)	Hoylake	Hoylake, England
1937	Henry Cotton	290	Reg Whitcombe (292)	Carnoustie	Carnoustie, Scotland
1938	Reg Whitcombe	295	Jimmy Adams (297)	Royal St. George's	Sandwich, England
1939	Dick Burton	290	Johnny Bulla (292)	St. Andrews	St. Andrews, Scotland
1940-45	Not held		World War II		
1946	Sam Snead	290	Bobby Locke (294) & Johnny Bulla (294)	St. Andrews	St. Andrews, Scotland
1947	Fred Daly	293	Frank Stranahan & Reg Horne (294)	Hoylake	Hoylake, England

Year	Winner	Score	Runner-up	Course	Location
1948	Henry Cotton	284	Fred Daly (289)	Muirfield	Gullane, Scotland
1949	Bobby Locke*	283	Harry Bradshaw (283)	Royal St. George's	Sandwich, England
1950	Bobby Locke	279	Roberto de Vicenzo (281)	Royal Troon	Troon, Scotland
1951	Max Faulkner	285	Tony Cerda (287)	Royal Portrush	Portrush, Ireland
1952	Bobby Locke	287	Peter Thomson (288)	Royal Lytham	Lytham, England
1953	Ben Hogan	282	Frank Stranahan Dai Rees, Tony Cerda & Peter Thomson (286)	Carnoustie	Carnoustie, Scotland
1954	Peter Thomson	283	Sid Scott, Dai Rees & Bobby Locke (284)	Royal Birkdale	Southport, England
1955	Peter Thomson	281	Johny Fallon (283)	St. Andrews	St. Andrews, Scotland
1956	Peter Thomson	286	Flory Van Donck (289)	Hoylake	Hoylake, England
1957	Bobby Locke	279	Peter Thomson (282)	St. Andrews	St. Andrews, Scotland
1958	Peter Thomson*	278	Dave Thomas (278)	Royal Lytham	Lytham, England
1959	Gary Player	284	Flory Van Donck & Fred Bullock (286)	Muirfield	Gullane, Scotland
1960	Kel Nagle	278	Arnold Palmer (279)	St. Andrews	St. Andrews, Scotland
1961	Arnold Palmer	284	Dai Rees (285)	Royal Birkdale	Southport, England
1962	Arnold Palmer	276	Kel Nagle (282)	Royal Troon	Troon, Scotland
1963	Bob Charles*	277	Phil Rodgers (277)	Royal Lytham	Lytham, England
1964	Tony Lema	279	Jack Nicklaus (284)	St. Andrews	St. Andrews, Scotland
1965	Peter Thomson	285	Christy O'Connor & Brian Huggett (287)	Royal Birkdale	Southport, England
1966	Jack Nicklaus	282	Doug Sanders & Dave Thomas (283)	Muirfield	Gullane, Scotland
1967	Roberto de Vicenzo	278	Jack Nicklaus (280)	Hoylake	Hoylake, England
1968	Gary Player	289	Jack Nicklaus & Bob Charles (291)	Carnoustie	Carnoustie, Scotland
1969	Tony Jacklin	280	Bob Charles (282)	Royal Lytham	Lytham, England
1970	Jack Nicklaus*	283	Doug Sanders (283)	St. Andrews	St. Andrews, Scotland
1971	Lee Trevino	278	Lu Liang Huan (279)	Royal Birkdale	Southport, England
1972	Lee Trevino	278	Jack Nicklaus (279)	Muirfield	Gullane, Scotland
1973	Tom Weiskopf	276	Johnny Miller & Neil Coles (279)	Royal Troon	Troon, Scotland
1974	Gary Player	282	Peter Oosterhuis (286)	Royal Lytham	Lytham, England
1975	Tom Watson*	279	Jack Newton (279)	Carnoustie	Carnoustie, Scotland
1976	Johnny Miller	279	Seve Ballesteros & Jack Nicklaus (285)	Royal Birkdale	Southport, England
1977	Tom Watson	268	Jack Nicklaus (269)	Turnberry	Turnberry, Scotland
1978	Jack Nicklaus	281	Tom Kite, Ray Floyd, Ben Crenshaw & Simon Owen (283)	St. Andrews	St. Andrews, Scotland
1979	Seve Ballesteros	283	Jack Nicklaus & Ben Crenshaw (286)	Royal Lytham	Lytham, England
1980	Tom Watson	271	Lee Trevino (275)	Muirfield	Gullane, Scotland
1981	Bill Rogers	276	Bernhard Langer (280)	Royal St. George's	Sandwich, England
1982	Tom Watson	284	Peter Oosterhuis & Nick Price (285)	Royal Troon	Troon, Scotland
1983	Tom Watson	275	Hale Irwin & Andy Bean (276)	Royal Birkdale	Southport, England
1984	Seve Ballesteros	276	Bernhard Langer & Tom Watson (278)	St. Andrews	St. Andrews, Scotland
1985	Sandy Lyle	282	Payne Stewart (283)	Royal St. George's	Sandwich, England
1986	Greg Norman	280	Gordon J. Brand (285)	Turnberry	Turnberry, Scotland
1987	Nick Faldo	279	Paul Azinger & Rodger Davis (280)	Muirfield	Gullane, Scotland
1988	Seve Ballesteros	273	Nick Price (275)	Royal Lytham	Lytham, England
1989	Mark Calcavecchia*	275	Greg Norman & Wayne Grady (275)	Royal Troon	Troon, Scotland
1990	Nick Faldo	270	Payne Stewart & Mark McNulty (275)	St. Andrews	St. Andrews, Scotland
1991	Ian Baker-Finch	272	Mike Harwood (274)	Royal Birkdale	Southport, England
1992	Nick Faldo	272	John Cook (273)	Muirfield	Gullane, Scotland
1993	Greg Norman	267	Nick Faldo (269)	Royal St. George's	Sandwich, England
1994	Nick Price	268	Jesper Parnevik (269)	Turnberry	Turnberry, Scotland

Major Championships (Cont.)

British Open
*PLAYOFFS

1876: Bob Martin awarded title when David Strath refused playoff. **1883:** Willie Fernie (158) def. Robert Ferguson (159) in 36 holes. **1889:** Willie Park Jr. (158) def. Andrew Kirkaldy (163) in 36 holes. **1896:** Harry Vardon (157) def. John H. Taylor (161) in 36 holes. **1911:** Harry Vardon won when Arnaud Massy conceded at 35th hole. **1921:** Jack Hutchison (150) def. Roger Wethered (159) in 36 holes. **1933:** Denny Shute (149) def. Craig Wood (154) in 36 holes. **1949:** Bobby Locke (135) def. Harry Bradshaw (147) in 36 holes. **1958:** Peter Thomson (139) def. Dave Thomas (143) in 36 holes. **1963:** Bob Charles (140) def. Phil Rodgers (148) in 36 holes. **1970:** Jack Nicklaus (72) def. Doug Sanders (73) in 18 holes. **1975:** Tom Watson (71) def. Jack Newton (72) in 18 holes. **1989:** Mark Calcavecchia (4-3-3—13) def. Wayne Grady (4-4-4-4—16) and Greg Norman (3-3-4-x) in 4 holes.

PGA Championship

The PGA Championship began in 1916 as a professional golfers match play tournament, but switched to stroke play in 1958. Conducted by the PGA of America, the tournament is played on a different course each year.

Multiple winners: Walter Hagen and Jack Nicklaus (5); Gene Sarazen and Sam Snead (3); Jim Barnes, Leo Diegel, Raymond Floyd, Ben Hogan, Byron Nelson, Larry Nelson, Gary Player, Paul Runyan, Denny Shute, Dave Stockton and Lee Trevino (2).

Year	Winner	Score	Runner-up	Course	Location
1916	Jim Barnes	1-up	Jock Hutchison	Siwanoy CC	Bronxville, N.Y.
1917-18	Not held		World War I		
1919	Jim Barnes	6 & 5	Fred McLeod	Engineers CC	Roslyn, N.Y.
1920	Jock Hutchison	1-up	J. Douglas Edgar	Flossmoor CC	Flossmoor, Ill.
1921	Walter Hagen	3 & 2	Jim Barnes	Inwood CC	Far Rockaway, N.Y.
1922	Gene Sarazen	4 & 3	Emmet French	Oakmont CC	Oakmont, Pa.
1923	Gene Sarazen	1-up/38	Walter Hagen	Pelham CC	Pelham, N.Y.
1924	Walter Hagen	2-up	Jim Barnes	French Lick CC	French Lick, Ind.
1925	Walter Hagen	6 & 5	Bill Mehlhorn	Olympia Fields CC	Matteson, Ill.
1926	Walter Hagen	5 & 3	Leo Diegel	Salisbury GC	Westbury, N.Y.
1927	Water Hagen	1-up	Joe Turnesa	Cedar Crest CC	Dallas
1928	Leo Diegel	6 & 5	Al Espinosa	Five Farms CC	Baltimore
1929	Leo Diegel	6 & 4	John Farrell	Hillcrest CC	Los Angeles
1930	Tommy Armour	1-up	Gene Sarazen	Fresh Meadow CC	Flushing, N.Y.
1931	Tom Creavy	2 & 1	Denny Shute	Wannamoisett CC	Rumford, R.I.
1932	Olin Dutra	4 & 3	Frank Walsh	Keller GC	St. Paul, Minn.
1933	Gene Sarazen	5 & 4	Willie Goggin	Blue Mound CC	Milwaukee
1934	Paul Runyan	1-up/38	Craig Wood	Park CC	Williamsville, N.Y.
1935	Johnny Revolta	5 & 4	Tommy Armour	Twin Hills CC	Oklahoma City
1936	Denny Shute	3 & 2	Jimmy Thomson	Pinehurst CC	Pinehurst, N.C.
1937	Denny Shute	1-up/37	Harold McSpaden	Pittsburgh FC	Aspinwall, Pa.
1938	Paul Runyan	8 & 7	Sam Snead	Shawnee CC	Shawnee-on-Del, Pa.
1939	Henry Picard	1-up/37	Byron Nelson	Pomonok CC	Flushing, N.Y.
1940	Byron Nelson	1-up	Sam Snead	Hershey CC	Hershey, Pa.
1941	Vic Ghezzi	1-up/38	Byron Nelson	Cherry Hills CC	Denver
1942	Sam Snead	2 & 1	Jim Turnesa	Seaview CC	Atlantic City, N.J.
1943	Not held		World War II		
1944	Bob Hamilton	1-up	Byron Nelson	Manito G & CC	Spokane, Wash.
1945	Byron Nelson	4 & 3	Sam Byrd	Morraine CC	Dayton, Ohio
1946	Ben Hogan	6 & 4	Ed Oliver	Portland GC	Portland, Ore.
1947	Jim Ferrier	2 & 1	Chick Harbert	Plum Hollow CC	Detroit
1948	Ben Hogan	7 & 6	Mike Turnesa	Norwood Hills CC	St. Louis
1949	Sam Snead	3 & 2	John Palmer	Hermitage CC	Richmond, Va.
1950	Chandler Harper	4 & 3	Henry Williams Jr.	Scioto CC	Columbus, Ohio
1951	Sam Snead	7 & 6	Walter Burkemo	Oakmont CC	Oakmont, Pa.
1952	Jim Turnesa	1-up	Chick Harbert	Big Spring CC	Louisville
1953	Walter Burkemo	2 & 1	Felice Torza	Birmingham CC	Birmingham, Mich.
1954	Chick Harbert	4 & 3	Walter Burkemo	Keller GC	St. Paul, Minn.
1955	Doug Ford	4 & 3	Cary Middlecoff	Meadowbrook CC	Detroit
1956	Jack Burke	3 & 2	Ted Kroll	Blue Hill CC	Boston
1957	Lionel Hebert	2 & 1	Dow Finsterwald	Miami Valley GC	Dayton, Ohio
1958	Dow Finsterwald	276	Billy Casper (278)	Llanerch CC	Havertown, Pa.
1959	Bob Rosburg	277	Jerry Barber & Doug Sanders (278)	Minneapolis GC	St. Louis Park, Minn.
1960	Jay Hebert	281	Jim Ferrier (282)	Firestone CC	Akron, Ohio
1961	Jerry Barber*	277	Don January (277)	Olympia Fields CC	Matteson, Ill.
1962	Gary Player	278	Bob Goalby (279)	Aronimink GC	Newtown Square, Pa.
1963	Jack Nicklaus	279	Dave Ragan (281)	Dallas AC	Dallas
1964	Bobby Nichols	271	Jack Nicklaus & Arnold Palmer (274)	Columbus CC	Columbus, Ohio

Year	Winner	Score	Runner-up	Course	Location
1965	Dave Marr	280	Jack Nicklaus & Billy Casper (282)	Laurel Valley GC	Ligonier, Pa.
1966	Al Geiberger	280	Dudley Wysong (284)	Firestone CC	Akron, Ohio
1967	Don January*	281	Don Massengale (281)	Columbine CC	Littleton, Colo.
1968	Julius Boros	281	Arnold Palmer & Bob Charles (282)	Pecan Valley CC	San Antonio
1969	Ray Floyd	276	Gary Player (277)	NCR GC	Dayton, Ohio
1970	Dave Stockton	279	Arnold Palmer & Bob Murphy (281)	Southern Hills CC	Tulsa
1971	Jack Nicklaus	281	Billy Casper (283)	PGA National GC	Palm Beach Gardens, Fla.
1972	Gary Player	281	Jim Jamieson & Tommy Aaron (283)	Oakland Hills GC	Birmingham, Mich.
1973	Jack Nicklaus	277	Bruce Crampton (281)	Canterbury GC	Cleveland
1974	Lee Trevino	276	Jack Nicklaus (277)	Tanglewood GC	Winston-Salem, N.C.
1975	Jack Nicklaus	276	Bruce Crampton (278)	Firestone CC	Akron, Ohio
1976	Dave Stockton	281	Don January & Ray Floyd (282)	Congressional CC	Bethesda, Md.
1977	Lanny Wadkins*	282	Gene Littler (282)	Pebble Beach GL	Pebble Beach, Calif.
1978	John Mahaffey*	276	Jerry Pate & Tom Watson (276)	Oakmont CC	Oakmont, Pa.
1979	David Graham*	272	Ben Crenshaw (272)	Oakland Hills CC	Birmingham, Mich.
1980	Jack Nicklaus	274	Andy Bean (281)	Oak Hill CC	Rochester, N.Y.
1981	Larry Nelson	273	Fuzzy Zoeller (277)	Atlanta AC	Duluth, Ga.
1982	Ray Floyd	272	Lanny Wadkins (275)	Southern Hills CC	Tulsa
1983	Hal Sutton	274	Jack Nicklaus (275)	Riviera CC	Los Angeles
1984	Lee Trevino	273	Lanny Wadkins & Gary Player (277)	Shoal Creek	Birmingham, Ala.
1985	Hubert Green	278	Lee Trevino (280)	Cherry Hills CC	Denver
1986	Bob Tway	276	Greg Norman (278)	Inverness Club	Toledo, Ohio
1987	Larry Nelson*	287	Lanny Wadkins (287)	PGA National	Palm Beach Gardens, Fla.
1988	Jeff Sluman	272	Paul Azinger (275)	Oak Tree GC	Edmond, Okla.
1989	Payne Stewart	276	Andy Bean, Mike Reid & Curtis Strange (277)	Kemper Lakes GC	Hawthorn Woods, Ill.
1990	Wayne Grady	282	Fred Couples (285)	Shoal Creek	Birmingham, Ala.
1991	John Daly	276	Bruce Lietzke (279)	Crooked Stick GC	Carmel, Ind.
1992	Nick Price	278	Nick Faldo, John Cook, Jim Gallagher & Gene Sauers (281)	Bellerive CC	St. Louis
1993	Paul Azinger*	272	Greg Norman (272)	Inverness Club	Toledo, Ohio
1994	Nick Price	269	Corey Pavin (275)	Southern Hills CC	Tulsa

*PLAYOFFS

1961: Jerry Barber (67) def. Don January (68) in 18 holes. **1967:** Don January (69) def. Don Massengale (71) in 18 holes. **1977:** Lanny Wadkins (4-4-4) def. Gene Littler (4-4-5) on 3rd hole of sudden death. **1978:** John Mahaffey (4-3) def. Jerry Pate (4-4) and Tom Watson (4-5) on 2nd hole of sudden death. **1979:** David Graham (4-4-2) def. Ben Crenshaw (4-4-4) on 3rd hole of sudden death. **1987:** Larry Nelson (4) def. Lanny Wadkins (5) on 1st hole of sudden death. **1993:** Paul Azinger (4-4) def. Greg Norman (4-5) on 2nd hole of sudden death.

Major Championship Leaders

Through 1994; active players in **bold** type.

	US Open	British Open	PGA	Masters	US Am	British Am	Total
Jack Nicklaus	4	3	5	6	2	0	**20**
Bobby Jones	4	3	0	0	5	1	13
Walter Hagen	2	4	5	0	0	0	11
Ben Hogan	4	1	2	2	0	0	9
Gary Player	1	3	2	3	0	0	9
John Ball	0	1	0	0	0	8	9
Arnold Palmer	1	2	0	4	1	0	8
Tom Watson	1	5	0	2	0	0	8
Harold Hilton	0	2	0	0	1	4	7
Gene Sarazen	2	1	3	1	0	0	7
Sam Snead	0	1	3	3	0	0	7
Harry Vardon	1	6	0	0	0	0	7
Lee Trevino	2	2	2	0	0	0	6

Tournaments: U.S. Open, British Open, PGA Championship, Masters, U.S. Amateur, and British Amateur.

Grand Slam Summary

The only golfer ever to win a recognized Grand Slam—four major championships in a single season—was Bobby Jones in 1930. That year, Jones won the U.S. and British Opens as well as the U.S. and British Amateurs.

The men's professional Grand Slam—the Masters, U.S. Open, British Open and PGA Championship—did not gain acceptance until 30 years later when Arnold Palmer won the 1960 Masters and U.S. Open. The media wrote that the popular Palmer was chasing the "new" Grand Slam and would have to win the British Open and the PGA to claim it. He did not, but then nobody has before or since.

Three wins in one year: Ben Hogan (1953). **Two wins in one year** (15): Jack Nicklaus (5 times); Ben Hogan, Arnold Palmer and Tom Watson (twice); Nick Faldo, Gary Player, Nick Price, Sam Snead, Lee Trevino and Craig Wood (once).

Year	Masters	US Open	Brit.Open	PGA
1934	H. Smith	Dutra	Cotton	Runyan
1935	Sarazen	Parks	Perry	Revolta
1936	H. Smith	Manero	Padgham	Shute
1937	B. Nelson	Guldahl	Cotton	Shute
1938	Picard	Guldahl	Whitcombe	Runyan
1939	Guldahl	B. Nelson	Burton	Picard
1940	Demaret	Little	—	B. Nelson
1941	Wood	Wood	—	Ghezzi
1942	B. Nelson	—	—	Snead
1943	—	—	—	—
1944	—	—	—	Hamilton
1945	—	—	—	B. Nelson
1946	Keiser	Mangrum	Snead	Hogan
1947	Demaret	Worsham	F. Daly	Ferrier
1948	Harmon	Hogan	Cotton	Hogan
1949	Snead	Middlecoff	Locke	Snead
1950	Demaret	Hogan	Locke	Harper
1951	Hogan	Hogan	Faulkner	Snead
1952	Snead	Boros	Locke	Turnesa
1953	Hogan	Hogan	Hogan	Burkemo
1954	Snead	Furgol	Thomson	Harbert
1955	Middlecoff	Fleck	Thomson	Ford
1956	Burke	Middlecoff	Thomson	Burke
1957	Ford	Mayer	Locke	L. Hebert
1958	Palmer	Bolt	Thomson	Finsterwald
1959	Wall	Casper	Player	Rosburg
1960	Palmer	Palmer	Nagle	J. Hebert
1961	Player	Littler	Palmer	J. Barber
1962	Palmer	Nicklaus	Palmer	Player
1963	Nicklaus	Boros	Charles	Nicklaus
1964	Palmer	Venturi	Lema	Nichols
1965	Nicklaus	Player	Thomson	Marr
1966	Nicklaus	Casper	Nicklaus	Geiberger
1967	Brewer	Nicklaus	DeVicenzo	January
1968	Goalby	Trevino	Player	Boros
1969	Archer	Moody	Jacklin	Floyd
1970	Casper	Jacklin	Nicklaus	Stockton
1971	Coody	Trevino	Trevino	Nicklaus
1972	Nicklaus	Nicklaus	Trevino	Player
1973	Aaron	J. Miller	Weiskopf	Nicklaus
1974	Player	Irwin	Player	Trevino
1975	Nicklaus	L. Graham	T. Watson	Nicklaus
1976	Floyd	J. Pate	Miller	Stockton
1977	T. Watson	H. Green	T. Watson	L. Wadkins
1978	Player	North	Nicklaus	Mahaffey
1979	Zoeller	Irwin	Ballesteros	D. Graham
1980	Ballesteros	Nicklaus	T. Watson	Nicklaus
1981	T. Watson	D. Graham	Rogers	L. Nelson
1982	Stadler	T. Watson	T. Watson	Floyd
1983	Ballesteros	L. Nelson	T. Watson	Sutton
1984	Crenshaw	Zoeller	Ballesteros	Trevino
1985	Langer	North	Lyle	H. Green
1986	Nicklaus	Floyd	Norman	Tway
1987	Mize	S. Simpson	Faldo	L. Nelson
1988	Lyle	Strange	Ballesteros	Sluman
1989	Faldo	Strange	Calcavecchia	Stewart
1990	Faldo	Irwin	Faldo	Grady
1991	Woosnam	Stewart	Baker-Finch	J. Daly
1992	Couples	Kite	Faldo	Price
1993	Langer	Janzen	Norman	Azinger
1994	Olazabal	Els	Price	Price

Vardon Trophy

Awarded since 1937 by the PGA of America to the PGA Tour regular with the lowest scoring average. The award is named after Harry Vardon, the six-time British Open champion, who won the U.S. Open in 1900. A point system was used from 1937-41.

Multiple winners: Billy Casper and Lee Trevino (5); Arnold Palmer and Sam Snead (4); Ben Hogan and Tom Watson (3); Fred Couples, Bruce Crampton, Tom Kite, Lloyd Mangrum and Greg Norman (2).

Year		Pts
1937	Harry Cooper	500
1938	Sam Snead	520
1939	Byron Nelson	473
1940	Ben Hogan	423
1941	Ben Hogan	494
1942-46	No award	

Year		Avg
1947	Jimmy Demaret	69.90
1948	Ben Hogan	69.30
1949	Sam Snead	69.37
1950	Sam Snead	69.23
1951	Lloyd Mangrum	70.05
1952	Jack Burke	70.54
1953	Lloyd Mangrum	70.22
1954	E.J. Harrison	70.41
1955	Sam Snead	69.86
1956	Cary Middlecoff	70.35
1957	Dow Finsterwald	70.30

Year		Avg
1958	Bob Rosburg	70.11
1959	Art Wall	70.35
1960	Billy Casper	69.95
1961	Arnold Palmer	69.85
1962	Arnold Palmer	70.27
1963	Billy Casper	70.58
1964	Arnold Palmer	70.01
1965	Billy Casper	70.85
1966	Billy Casper	70.27
1967	Arnold Palmer	70.18
1968	Billy Casper	69.82
1969	Dave Hill	70.34
1970	Lee Trevino	70.64
1971	Lee Trevino	70.27
1972	Lee Trevino	70.89
1973	Bruce Crampton	70.57
1974	Lee Trevino	70.53
1975	Bruce Crampton	70.51

Year		Avg
1976	Don January	70.56
1977	Tom Watson	70.32
1978	Tom Watson	70.16
1979	Tom Watson	70.27
1980	Lee Trevino	69.73
1981	Tom Kite	69.80
1982	Tom Kite	70.21
1983	Ray Floyd	70.61
1984	Calvin Peete	70.56
1985	Don Pooley	70.36
1986	Scott Hoch	70.08
1987	Dan Pohl	70.25
1988	Chip Beck	69.46
1989	Greg Norman	69.49
1990	Greg Norman	69.10
1991	Fred Couples	69.59
1992	Fred Couples	69.38
1993	Nick Price	69.11

U.S. Amateur

Match play from 1895-64, stroke play from 1965-72, match play since 1972.

Multiple winners: Bobby Jones (5); Jerry Travers (4); Walter Travis (3); Deane Beman, Charles Coe, Gary Cowan, H. Chandler Egan, Chick Evans, Lawson Little, Jack Nicklaus, Francis Ouimet, Jay Sigel, William Turnesa, Bud Ward, Harvie Ward and H.J. Whigham (2).

Year		Year		Year		Year	
1895	Charles Macdonald	1922	Jess Sweetser	1950	Sam Urzetta	1975	Fred Ridley
1896	H.J. Whigham	1923	Max Marston	1951	Billy Maxwell	1976	Bill Sander
1897	H.J. Whigham	1924	Bobby Jones	1952	Jack Westland	1977	John Fought
1898	Findlay Douglas	1925	Bobby Jones	1953	Gene Littler	1978	John Cook
1899	H.M. Harriman	1926	George Von Elm	1954	Arnold Palmer	1979	Mark O'Meara
		1927	Bobby Jones	1955	Harvie Ward		
1900	Walter Travis	1928	Bobby Jones	1956	Harvie Ward	1980	Hal Sutton
1901	Walter Travis	1929	Harrison Johnston	1957	Hillman Robbins	1981	Nathanial Crosby
1902	Louis James			1958	Charles Coe	1982	Jay Sigel
1903	Walter Travis	1930	Bobby Jones	1959	Jack Nicklaus	1983	Jay Sigel
1904	H. Chandler Egan	1931	Francis Ouimet			1984	Scott Verplank
1905	H. Chandler Egan	1932	Ross Somerville	1960	Deane Beman	1985	Sam Randolph
1906	Eben Byers	1933	George Dunlap	1961	Jack Nicklaus	1986	Buddy Alexander
1907	Jerry Travers	1934	Lawson Little	1962	Labron Harris	1987	Billy Mayfair
1908	Jerry Travers	1935	Lawson Little	1963	Deane Beman	1988	Eric Meeks
1909	Robert Gardner	1936	John Fischer	1964	Bill Campbell	1989	Chris Patton
		1937	John Goodman	1965	Bob Murphy		
1910	W.C. Fownes Jr.	1938	William Turnesa	1966	Gary Cowan	1990	Phil Mickelson
1911	Harold Hilton	1939	Bud Ward	1967	Bob Dickson	1991	Mitch Voges
1912	Jerry Travers			1968	Bruce Fleisher	1992	Justin Leonard
1913	Jerry Travers	1940	Richard Chapman	1969	Steve Melnyk	1993	John Harris
1914	Francis Ouimet	1941	Bud Ward			1994	Tiger Woods
1915	Robert Gardner	1942-45	Not held	1970	Lanny Wadkins		
1916	Chick Evans	1946	Ted Bishop	1971	Gary Cowan		
1917-18	Not held	1947	Skee Riegel	1972	Vinny Giles		
1919	Davidson Herron	1948	William Turnesa	1973	Craig Stadler		
		1949	Charles Coe	1974	Jerry Pate		
1920	Chick Evans						
1921	Jesse Guilford						

British Amateur

Match play since 1885.

Multiple winners: John Ball (8); Michael Bonallack (5); Harold Hilton (4); Joe Carr (3); Horace Hutchinson, Ernest Holderness, Trevor Homer, Johnny Laidley, Lawson Little, Peter McEvoy, Dick Siderowf, Frank Stranahan, Freddie Tait and Cyril Tolley (2).

Year		Year		Year		Year	
1885	Allen MacFie	1912	John Ball	1948	Frank Stranahan	1976	Dick Siderowf
1886	Horace Hutchinson	1913	Harold Hilton	1949	Samuel McCready	1977	Peter McEvoy
1887	Horace Hutchinson	1914	J.L.C. Jenkins			1978	Peter McEvoy
1888	John Ball	1915-19	Not held	1950	Frank Stranahan	1979	Jay Sigel
1889	Johnny Laidley			1951	Richard Chapman		
		1920	Cyril Tolley	1952	Harvie Ward	1980	Duncan Evans
1890	John Ball	1921	William Hunter	1953	Joe Carr	1981	Phillipe Ploujoux
1891	Johnny Laidlay	1922	Ernest Holderness	1954	Douglas Bachli	1982	Martin Thompson
1892	John Ball	1923	Roger Wethered	1955	Joe Conrad	1983	Philip Parkin
1893	Peter Anderson	1924	Ernest Holderness	1956	John Beharrell	1984	Jose-Maria Olazabal
1894	John Ball	1925	Robert Harris	1957	Reid Jack	1985	Garth McGimpsey
1895	Leslie Balfour-Melville	1926	Jesse Sweetser	1958	Joe Carr	1986	David Curry
1896	Freddie Tait	1927	William Tweddell	1959	Deane Beman	1987	Paul Mayo
1897	Jack Allan	1928	Thomas Perkins			1988	Christian Hardin
1898	Freddie Tait	1929	Cyril Tolley	1960	Joe Carr	1989	Stephen Dodd
1899	John Ball			1961	Michael Bonallack		
		1930	Bobby Jones	1962	Richard Davies	1990	Rolf Muntz
1900	Harold Hilton	1931	Eric Smith	1963	Michael Lunt	1991	Gary Wolstenholme
1901	Harold Hilton	1932	John deForest	1964	Gordon Clark	1992	Stephen Dundas
1902	Charles Hutchings	1933	Michael Scott	1965	Michael Bonallack	1993	Ian Pyman
1903	Robert Maxwell	1934	Lawson Little	1966	Bobby Cole	1994	Lee James
1904	Walter Travis	1935	Lawson Little	1967	Bob Dickson		
1905	Arthur Barry	1936	Hector Thomson	1968	Michael Bonallack		
1906	James Robb	1937	Robert Sweeny, Jr.	1969	Michael Bonallack		
1907	John Ball	1938	Charles Yates				
1908	E.A. Lassen	1939	Alexander Kyle	1970	Michael Bonallack		
1909	Robert Maxwell			1971	Steve Melnyk		
		1940-45	Not held	1972	Trevor Homer		
1910	John Ball	1946	James Bruen	1973	Dick Siderowf		
1911	Harold Hilton	1947	William Turnesa	1974	Trevor Homer		
				1975	Vinny Giles		

Major Championships
WOMEN
U.S. Women's Open

The U.S. Women's Open began under the direction of the defunct Women's Professional Golfers Assn. in 1946, passed to the LPGA in 1949 and to the USGA in 1953. The tournament used a match play format its first year then switched to stroke play; (*) indicates playoff winner and (a) indicates amateur winner.

Multiple winners: Betsy Rawls and Mickey Wright (4); Susie Maxwell Berning, Hollis Stacy and Babe Zaharias (3); JoAnne Carner, Donna Caponi, Betsy King, Patty Sheehan and Louise Suggs (2).

Year		Year		Year		Year	
1946	Patty Berg	1960	Betsy Rawls	1972	Susie M. Berning	1984	Hollis Stacy
1947	Betty Jameson	1961	Mickey Wright	1973	Susie M. Berning	1985	Kathy Baker
1948	Babe Zaharias	1962	Murle Lindstrom	1974	Sandra Haynie	1986	Jane Geddes*
1949	Louise Suggs	1963	Mary Mills	1975	Sandra Palmer	1987	Laura Davies*
1950	Babe Zaharias	1964	Mickey Wright*	1976	JoAnne Carner*	1988	Liselotte Neumann
1951	Betsy Rawls	1965	Carol Mann	1977	Hollis Stacy	1989	Betsy King
1952	Louise Suggs	1966	Sandra Spuzich	1978	Hollis Stacy	1990	Betsy King
1953	Betsy Rawls*	1967	a-Catherine Lacoste	1979	Jerilyn Britz	1991	Meg Mallon
1954	Babe Zaharias	1968	Susie M. Berning	1980	Amy Alcott	1992	Patty Sheehan
1955	Fay Crocker	1969	Donna Caponi	1981	Pat Bradley	1993	Lauri Merten
1956	Kathy Cornelius*	1970	Donna Caponi	1982	Janet Anderson	1994	Patty Sheehan
1957	Betsy Rawls	1971	JoAnne Carner	1983	Jan Stephenson		
1958	Mickey Wright						
1959	Mickey Wright						

*PLAYOFFS

1953: Betsy Rawls (71) def. Jackie Pung (77) in 18 holes. **1956:** Kathy Cornelius (75) def. Barbara McIntire (82) in 18 holes. **1964:** Mickey Wright (70) def. Ruth Jessen (72) in 18 holes. **1976:** JoAnne Carner (76) def. Sandra Palmer (78) in 18 holes. **1986:** Jane Geddes (71) def. Sally Little (73) in 18 holes. **1987:** Laura Davies (71) def. Ayako Okamoto (73) and JoAnne Carner (74) in 18 holes. **1992:** Patty Sheehan (72) def. Juli Inkster (74) in 18 holes.

LPGA Championship

Officially the McDonald's LPGA Championship since 1994 (Mazda sponsored from 1987-93), the tournament began in 1955 and has had extended stays at the Stardust CC in Las Vegas (1961-66), Pleasant Valley CC in Sutton, Mass. (1967-68,70-74); the Jack Nicklaus Sports Center at Kings Island, Ohio (1978-89) and Bethesda CC in Maryland (since 1990); (*) indicates playoff winner.

Multiple winners: Mickey Wright (4); Nancy Lopez, Patty Sheehan and Kathy Whitworth (3); Donna Caponi, Sandra Haynie, Mary Mills and Betsy Rawls (2).

Year		Year		Year		Year	
1955	Beverly Hanson	1965	Sandra Haynie	1975	Kathy Whitworth	1985	Nancy Lopez
1956	Marlene Hagge*	1966	Gloria Ehret	1976	Betty Burfeindt	1986	Pat Bradley
1957	Louise Suggs	1967	Kathy Whitworth	1977	Chako Higuchi	1987	Jane Geddes
1958	Mickey Wright	1968	Sandra Post*	1978	Nancy Lopez	1988	Sherri Turner
1959	Betsy Rawls	1969	Betsy Rawls	1979	Donna Caponi	1989	Nancy Lopez
1960	Mickey Wright	1970	Shirley Englehorn*	1980	Sally Little	1990	Beth Daniel
1961	Mickey Wright	1971	Kathy Whitworth	1981	Donna Caponi	1991	Meg Mallon
1962	Judy Kimball	1972	Kathy Ahern	1982	Jan Stephenson	1992	Betsy King
1963	Mickey Wright	1973	Mary Mills	1983	Patty Sheehan	1993	Patty Sheehan
1964	Mary Mills	1974	Sandra Haynie	1984	Patty Sheehan	1994	Laura Davies

*PLAYOFFS

1956: Marlene Hagge def. Patti Berg in sudden death. **1968:** Sandra Post (68) def. Kathy Whitworth (75) in 18-holes. **1970:** Shirley Englehorn def. Kathy Whitworth in sudden death.

Nabisco Dinah Shore

Formerly known as the Colgate Dinah Shore from 1972-81, the tournament become the LPGA's fourth designated major championship in 1983. Named after the entertainer, this tourney has been played at Mission Hills CC in Rancho Mirage, Calif., since it began; (*) indicates playoff winner.

Multiple winners (as a major): Amy Alcott (3); Juli Inkster and Betsy King (2).

Year		Year		Year		Year	
1972	Jane Blalock	1978	Sandra Post	1984	Juli Inkster*	1990	Betsy King
1973	Mickey Wright	1979	Sandra Post	1985	Alice Miller	1991	Amy Alcott
1974	Jo Ann Prentice	1980	Donna Caponi	1986	Pat Bradley	1992	Dottie Mochrie*
1975	Sandra Palmer	1981	Nancy Lopez	1987	Betsy King*	1993	Helen Alfredsson
1976	Judy Rankin	1982	Sally Little	1988	Amy Alcott	1994	Donna Andrews
1977	Kathy Whitworth	1983	Amy Alcott	1989	Juli Inkster		

*PLAYOFFS

1984: Juli Inkster def. Pat Bradley in sudden death. **1987:** Betsy King def. Patty Sheehan in sudden death. **1992:** Dottie Mochrie def. Juli Inkster in sudden death.

du Maurier Classic

Formerly known as La Canadienne in 1973 and the Peter Jackson Classic from 1974-83, this Canadian stop on the LPGA Tour became the third designated major championship in 1979; (*) indicates playoff winner.

Multiple winners (as a major): Pat Bradley (3); JoAnne Carner (2).

Year		Year		Year		Year	
1973	Jocelyne Bourassa	1979	Amy Alcott	1984	Juli Inkster	1990	Cathy Johnston
1974	Carole Jo Skala	1980	Pat Bradley	1985	Pat Bradley	1991	Nancy Scranton
1975	JoAnne Carner	1981	Jan Stephenson	1986	Pat Bradley*	1992	Sherri Steinhauer
1976	Donna Caponi	1982	Sandra Haynie	1987	Jody Rosenthal	1993	Brandie Burton
1977	Judy Rankin	1983	Hollis Stacy	1988	Sally Little	1994	Martha Nause
1978	JoAnne Carner			1989	Tammie Green		

*PLAYOFF

1986: Pat Bradley def. Ayako Okamoto in sudden death. **1993:** Brandie Burton def. Betsy King in sudden death.

Titleholders Championship (1937-72)

The Titleholders was considered a major title on the women's tour until it was discontinued after the 1972 tournament.

Multiple winners: Patty Berg (7); Louise Suggs (4); Babe Zaharias (3); Dorothy Kirby, Marilynn Smith, Kathy Whitworth and Mickey Wright (2).

Year		Year		Year		Year	
1937	Patty Berg	1947	Babe Zaharias	1955	Patty Berg	1963	Marilynn Smith
1938	Patty Berg	1948	Patty Berg	1956	Louise Suggs	1964	Marilynn Smith
1939	Patty Berg	1949	Peggy Kirk	1957	Patty Berg	1965	Kathy Whitworth
1940	Betty Hicks	1950	Babe Zaharias	1958	Beverly Hanson	1966	Kathy Whitworth
1941	Dorothy Kirby	1951	Pat O'Sullivan	1959	Louise Suggs	1967-71	Not held
1942	Dorothy Kirby	1952	Babe Zaharias	1960	Fay Crocker	1972	Sandra Palmer
1943-45	Not held	1953	Patty Berg	1961	Mickey Wright		
1946	Louise Suggs	1954	Louise Suggs	1962	Mickey Wright		

Western Open (1930-67)

The Western Open was considered a major title on the women's tour until it was discontinued after the 1967 tournament.

Multiple winners: Patty Berg (7); Louise Suggs and Babe Zaharias (4); Mickey Wright (3); June Beebe; Opal Hill; Betty Jameson and Betsy Rawls (2).

Year		Year		Year		Year	
1930	Mrs. Lee Mida	1940	Babe Zaharias	1950	Babe Zaharias	1960	Joyce Ziske
1931	June Beebe	1941	Patty Berg	1951	Patty Berg	1961	Mary Lena Faulk
1932	Jane Weiller	1942	Betty Jameson	1952	Betsy Rawls	1962	Mickey Wright
1933	June Beebe	1943	Patty Berg	1953	Louise Suggs	1963	Mickey Wright
1934	Marian McDougall	1944	Babe Zaharias	1954	Betty Jameson	1964	Carol Mann
1935	Opal Hill	1945	Babe Zaharias	1955	Patty Berg	1965	Susie Maxwell
1936	Opal Hill	1946	Louise Suggs	1956	Beverly Hanson	1966	Mickey Wright
1937	Betty Hicks	1947	Louise Suggs	1957	Patty Berg	1967	Kathy Whitworth
1938	Bea Barrett	1948	Patty Berg	1958	Patty Berg		
1939	Helen Dettweiler	1949	Louise Suggs	1959	Betsy Rawls		

Major Championship Leaders

Through 1994; active players in **bold** type.

	US Open	LPGA	duM	Dinah	Title-holders	Western	US Am	Brit Am	Total
Patty Berg	1	0	0	0	7	7	1	0	**16**
Mickey Wright	4	4	0	0	2	3	0	0	**13**
Louise Suggs	2	1	0	0	4	4	1	1	**13**
Babe Zaharias	3	0	0	0	3	4	1	1	**12**
Betsy Rawls	4	2	0	0	0	2	0	0	**8**
JoAnne Carner	2	0	0	0	0	0	5	0	**7**
Kathy Whitworth	0	3	0	0	2	1	0	0	**6**
Pat Bradley	1	1	3	1	0	0	0	0	**6**
Juli Inkster	0	0	1	2	0	0	3	0	**6**
Glenna C. Vare	0	0	0	0	0	0	6	0	**6**

Tournaments: U.S. Open, LPGA Championship, du Maurier Classic, Nabisco Dinah Shore, Titleholders (1937-72), Western Open (1937-67), U.S. Amateur, and British Amateur.

Grand Slam Summary

The Women's Grand Slam has consisted of four tournaments only 19 years. From 1955-66, the U.S. Open, LPGA Championship, Western Open and Titleholders tournaments served as the major events. Since 1983, the U.S. Open, LPGA, du Maurier Classic in Canada and Nabisco Dinah Shore have been the major events. No one has won a four-event Grand Slam on the women's tour.

Three wins in one year (3): Babe Zaharias (1950), Mickey Wright (1961) and Pat Bradley (1986).

Two wins in one year (14): Patty Berg and Mickey Wright (3 times); Louise Suggs (twice); Sandra Haynie, Juli Inkster, Betsy King, Meg Mallon, Betsy Rawls and Kathy Whitworth (once).

Year	LPGA	US Open	T'holders	Western
1937	—	—	Berg	Hicks
1938	—	—	Berg	Barrett
1939	—	—	Berg	Dettweiler
1940	—	—	Hicks	Zaharias
1941	—	—	Kirby	Berg
1942	—	—	Kirby	Jameson
1943	—	—	—	Berg
1944	—	—	—	Zaharias
1945	—	—	—	Zaharias
1946	—	Berg	Suggs	Suggs
1947	—	Jameson	Zaharias	Suggs
1948	—	Zaharias	Berg	Berg
1949	—	Suggs	Kirk	Suggs
1950	—	Zaharias	Zaharias	Zaharias
1951	—	Rawls	O'Sullivan	Berg
1952	—	Suggs	Zaharias	Rawls
1953	—	Rawls	Berg	Suggs
1954	—	Zaharias	Suggs	Jameson
1955	Hanson	Crocker	Berg	Berg
1956	Hagge	Cornelius	Suggs	Hanson
1957	Suggs	Rawls	Berg	Berg
1958	Wright	Wright	Hanson	Berg
1959	Rawls	Wright	Suggs	Rawls
1960	Wright	Rawls	Crocker	Ziske
1961	Wright	Wright	Wright	Faulk
1962	Kimball	Lindstrom	Wright	Wright
1963	Wright	Mills	M.Smith	Wright
1964	Mills	Wright	M.Smith	Mann
1965	Haynie	Mann	Whitworth	Maxwell
1966	Ehret	Spuzich	Whitworth	Wright

Year	LPGA	US Open	T'holders	Western
1967	Whitworth	a-LaCoste	—	Whitworth
1968	Post	Berning	—	—
1969	Rawls	Caponi	—	—
1970	Englehorn	Caponi	—	—
1971	Whitworth	Carner	—	—
1972	Ahern	Berning	Palmer	—
1973	Mills	Berning	—	—
1974	Haynie	Haynie	—	—
1975	Whitworth	Palmer	—	—
1976	Burfeindt	Carner	—	—
1977	Higuchi	Stacy	—	—
1978	Lopez	Stacy	—	—

Year	LPGA	US Open	duMaurier	D. Shore
1979	Caponi	Britz	Alcott	—
1980	Little	Alcott	Bradley	—
1981	Caponi	Bradley	Stephenson	—
1982	Stephenson	Anderson	Haynie	—
1983	Sheehan	Stephenson	Stacy	Alcott
1984	Sheehan	Stacy	Inkster	Inkster
1985	Lopez	Baker	Bradley	Miller
1986	Bradley	Geddes	Bradley	Bradley
1987	Geddes	Davies	Rosenthal	King
1988	Turner	Neumann	Little	Alcott
1989	Lopez	King	Green	Inkster
1990	Daniel	King	Johnston	King
1991	Mallon	Mallon	Scranton	Alcott
1992	King	Sheehan	Steinhaur	Mochrie
1993	Sheehan	Merten	Burton	Alfredsson
1994	Davies	Sheehan	Nause	Andrews

Vare Trophy

The Vare Trophy for best scoring average by a player on the LPGA Tour has been awarded since 1937 by the LPGA. The award is named after Glenna Collett Vare, winner of six U.S. women's amateur titles from 1922-35.

Multiple winners: Kathy Whitworth (7); JoAnne Carner and Mickey Wright (5); Patty Berg, Nancy Lopez and Judy Rankin (3); Pat Bradley, Beth Daniel and Betsy King (2).

Year		Avg	Year		Avg	Year		Avg
1953	Patty Berg	75.00	1967	Kathy Whitworth	72.73	1980	Amy Alcott	71.51
1954	Babe Zaharias	75.48	1968	Carol Mann	72.04	1981	JoAnne Carner	71.75
1955	Patty Berg	74.47	1969	Kathy Whitworth	72.38	1982	JoAnne Carner	71.49
1956	Patty Berg	74.57	1970	Kathy Whitworth	72.26	1983	JoAnne Carner	71.41
1957	Louise Suggs	74.64	1971	Kathy Whitworth	72.88	1984	Patty Sheehan	71.40
1958	Beverly Hanson	74.92	1972	Kathy Whitworth	72.38	1985	Nancy Lopez	70.73
1959	Betsy Rawls	74.03	1973	Judy Rankin	73.08	1986	Pat Bradley	71.10
1960	Mickey Wright	73.25	1974	JoAnne Carner	72.87	1987	Betsy King	71.14
1961	Mickey Wright	73.55	1975	JoAnne Carner	72.40	1988	Colleen Walker	71.26
1962	Mickey Wright	73.67	1976	Judy Rankin	72.25	1989	Beth Daniel	70.38
1963	Mickey Wright	72.81	1977	Judy Rankin	72.16	1990	Beth Daniel	70.54
1964	Mickey Wright	72.46	1978	Nancy Lopez	71.76	1991	Pat Bradley	70.66
1965	Kathy Whitworth	72.61	1979	Nancy Lopez	71.20	1992	Dottie Mochrie	70.80
1966	Kathy Whitworth	72.60				1993	Betsy King	70.85

U.S. Women's Amateur

Stroke play in 1895, match play since 1896.

Multiple winners: Glenna Collett Vare (6); JoAnne Gunderson Carner (5); Margaret Curtis, Beatrix Hoyt, Dorothy Campbell Hurd, Juli Inkster, Alexa Stirling, Virginia Van Wie, Anne Quast Decker Welts (3); Kay Cockerill, Beth Daniel, Vicki Goetze, Katherine Harley, Genevieve Hecker, Betty Jameson and Barbara McIntire (2).

Year		Year		Year		Year	
1895	Mrs. C.S. Brown	1922	Glenna Collett	1950	Beverly Hanson	1975	Beth Daniel
1896	Beatrix Hoyt	1923	Edith Cummings	1951	Dorothy Kirby	1976	Donna Horton
1897	Beatrix Hoyt	1924	Dorothy C. Hurd	1952	Jacqueline Pung	1977	Beth Daniel
1898	Beatrix Hoyt	1925	Glenna Collett	1953	Mary Lena Faulk	1978	Cathy Sherk
1899	Ruth Underhill	1926	Helen Stetson	1954	Barbara Romack	1979	Carolyn Hill
		1927	Miriam Burns Horn	1955	Patricia Lesser		
1900	Frances Griscom	1928	Glenna Collett	1956	Marlene Stewart	1980	Juli Inkster
1901	Genevieve Hecker	1929	Glenna Collett	1957	JoAnne Gunderson	1981	Juli Inkster
1902	Genevieve Hecker			1958	Anne Quast	1982	Juli Inkster
1903	Bessie Anthony	1930	Glenna Collett	1959	Barbara McIntire	1983	Joanne Pacillo
1904	Georgianna Bishop	1931	Helen Hicks			1984	Deb Richard
1905	Pauline Mackay	1932	Virginia Van Wie	1960	JoAnne Gunderson	1985	Michiko Hattori
1906	Harriot Curtis	1933	Virginia Van Wie	1961	Anne Quast Decker	1986	Kay Cockerill
1907	Margaret Curtis	1934	Virginia Van Wie	1962	JoAnne Gunderson	1987	Kay Cockerill
1908	Katherine Harley	1935	Glenna Collett Vare	1963	Anne Quast Welts	1988	Pearl Sinn
1909	Dorothy Campbell	1936	Pamela Barton	1964	Barbara McIntire	1989	Vicki Goetze
		1937	Estelle Lawson	1965	Jean Ashley		
1910	Dorothy Campbell	1938	Patty Berg	1966	JoAnne G. Carner	1990	Pat Hurst
1911	Margaret Curtis	1939	Betty Jameson	1967	Mary Lou Dill	1991	Amy Fruhwirth
1912	Margaret Curtis			1968	JoAnne G. Carner	1992	Vicki Goetze
1913	Gladys Ravenscroft	1940	Betty Jameson	1969	Catherine Lacoste	1993	Jill McGill
1914	Katherine Harley	1941	Elizabeth Hicks			1994	Wendy Ward
1915	Florence Vanderbeck	1942-45	Not held	1970	Martha Wilkinson		
1916	Alexa Stirling	1946	Babe D. Zaharias	1971	Laura Baugh		
1917-18	Not held	1947	Louise Suggs	1972	Mary Budke		
1919	Alexa Stirling	1948	Grace Lenczyk	1973	Carol Semple		
		1949	Dorothy Porter	1974	Cynthia Hill		
1920	Alexa Stirling						
1921	Marion Hollins						

British Women's Amateur Championship

Match play since 1893.

Multiple winners: Cecil Leitch and Joyce Wethered (4); May Hezlet, Lady Margaret Scott, Brigitte Varangot and Enid Wilson (3); Rhona Adair, Pam Barton, Dorothy Campbell, Elizabeth Chadwick, Helen Holm, Marley Spearman, Frances Stephens, Jessie Valentine and Michelle Walker.

Year		Year		Year		Year	
1893	Lady Margaret Scott	1922	Joyce Wethered	1952	Moira Paterson	1977	Angela Uzielli
1894	Lady Margaret Scott	1923	Doris Chambers	1953	Marlene Stewart	1978	Edwina Kennedy
1895	Lady Margaret Scott	1924	Joyce Wethered	1954	Frances Stephens	1979	Maureen Madill
1896	Amy Pascoe	1925	Joyce Wethered	1955	Jessie Valentine		
1897	Edith Orr	1926	Cecil Leitch	1956	Wiffi Smith	1980	Anne Quast Sander
1898	Lena Thomson	1927	Simone de la Chaume	1957	Philomena Garvey	1981	Belle Robertson
1899	May Hezlet	1928	Nanette le Blan	1958	Jessie Valentine	1982	Kitrina Douglas
		1929	Joyce Wethered	1959	Elizabeth Price	1983	Jill Thornhill
1900	Rhona Adair					1984	Jody Rosenthal
1901	Mary Graham	1930	Diana Fishwick	1960	Barbara McIntire	1985	Lillian Behan
1902	May Hezlet	1931	Enid Wilson	1961	Marley Spearman	1986	Marnie McGuire
1903	Rhona Adair	1932	Enid Wilson	1962	Marley Spearman	1987	Janet Collingham
1904	Lottie Dod	1933	Enid Wilson	1963	Brigitte Varangot	1988	Joanne Furby
1905	Bertha Thompson	1934	Helen Holm	1964	Carol Sorenson	1989	Helen Dobson
1906	Mrs. W. Kennion	1935	Wanda Morgan	1965	Brigitte Varangot		
1907	May Hezlet	1936	Pam Barton	1966	Elizabeth Chadwick	1990	Julie Wade Hall
1908	Maud Titterton	1937	Jessie Anderson	1967	Elizabeth Chadwick	1991	Valerie Michaud
1909	Dorothy Campbell	1938	Helen Holm	1968	Brigitte Varangot	1992	Bernille Pedersen
		1939	Pam Barton	1969	Catherine Lacoste	1993	Catriona Lambert
1910	Elsie Grant-Suttie					1994	Emma Duggleby
1911	Dorothy Campbell	1940-45	Not held	1970	Dinah Oxley		
1912	Gladys Ravenscroft	1946	Jean Hetherington	1971	Michelle Walker		
1913	Muriel Dodd	1947	Babe Zaharias	1972	Michelle Walker		
1914	Cecil Leitch	1948	Louise Suggs	1973	Ann Irvin		
1915-19	Not held	1949	Frances Stephens	1974	Carol Semple		
				1975	Nancy Roth Syms		
1920	Cecil Leitch	1950	Lally de St. Sauveur	1976	Cathy Panton		
1921	Cecil Leitch	1951	Catherine MacCann				

Major Championships (Cont.)
SENIOR PGA
PGA Seniors' Championship

First played in 1937. Two championships played in 1979 and 1984.
Multiple winners: Sam Snead (6); Gary Player, Al Watrous and Eddie Williams (3); Julius Boros, Jock Hutchison, Don January, Arnold Palmer, Paul Runyan, Gene Sarazen and Lee Trevino (2).

Year		Year		Year		Year	
1937	Jock Hutchison	1953	Harry Schwab	1969	Tommy Bolt	1983	Not held
1938	Fred McLeod*	1954	Gene Sarazen	1970	Sam Snead	1984	Arnold Palmer
1939	Not held	1955	Mortie Dutra	1971	Julius Boros	1984	Peter Thomson
1940	Otto Hackbarth*	1956	Pete Burke	1972	Sam Snead	1985	Not held
1941	Jack Burke	1957	Al Watrous	1973	Sam Snead	1986	Gary Player
1942	Eddie Williams	1958	Gene Sarazen	1974	Robert de Vicenzo	1987	Chi Chi Rodriguez
1943-44	Not held	1959	Willie Goggin	1975	Charlie Sifford*	1988	Gary Player
1945	Eddie Williams	1960	Dick Metz	1976	Pete Cooper	1989	Larry Mowry
1946	Eddie Williams*	1961	Paul Runyan	1977	Julius Boros	1990	Gary Player
1947	Jock Hutchison	1962	Paul Runyan	1978	Joe Jiminez*	1991	Jack Nicklaus
1948	Charles McKenna	1963	Herman Barron	1979	Jack Fleck*	1992	Lee Trevino
1949	Marshall Crichton	1964	Sam Snead	1979	Don January	1993	Tom Wargo*
1950	Al Watrous	1965	Sam Snead	1980	Arnold Palmer*	1994	Lee Trevino
1951	Al Watrous*	1966	Fred Haas	1981	Miller Barber		
1952	Ernest Newnham	1967	Sam Snead	1982	Don January		
		1968	Chandler Harper				

*PLAYOFFS

1938: Fred McLeod def. Otto Hackbarth in 18 holes. **1940:** Otto Hackbarth def. Jock Hutchison in 36 holes. **1946:** Eddie Williams def. Jock Hutchison in 18 holes. **1951:** Al Watrous def. Jock Hutchison in 18 holes. **1975:** Charlie Sifford def. Fred Wampler on 1st extra hole. **1978:** Joe Jiminez def. Joe Cheves and M.de la Torre on 1st extra hole. **1979:** Jack Fleck def. Bill Johnston on 1st extra hole. **1980:** Arnold Palmer def. Paul Harney on 1st extra hole. **1993:** Tom Wargo def. Bruce Crampton on 2nd extra hole.

U.S. Senior Open

Established in 1980 for senior players 55 years old and over, the minimum age was dropped to 50 (the PGA Seniors Tour entry age) in 1981. Arnold Palmer, Billy Casper, Orville Moody, Jack Nicklaus and Lee Trevino are the only golfers who have won both the U.S. Open and U.S. Senior Open.
Multiple winners: Miller Barber (3); Jack Nicklaus and Gary Player (2).

Year		Year		Year		Year	
1980	Roberto deVicenzo	1984	Miller Barber	1988	Gary Player*	1992	Larry Laoretti
1981	Arnold Palmer*	1985	Miller Barber	1989	Orville Moody	1993	Jack Nicklaus
1982	Miller Barber	1986	Dale Douglass	1990	Lee Trevino	1994	Simon Hobday
1983	Bill Casper*	1987	Gary Player	1991	Jack Nicklaus*		

*PLAYOFFS

1981: Arnold Palmer (70) def. Bob Stone (74) and Billy Casper (77) in 18 holes. **1983:** Tied at 75 after 18-hole playoff, Casper def. Rod Funseth with a birdie on the 1st extra hole. **1988:** Gary Player (68) def. Bob Charles (70) in 18 holes. **1991:** Jack Nicklaus (65) def. Chi Chi Rodriguez (69) in 18 holes.

Senior Players Championship

First played in 1983 and contested in Cleveland (1983-86), Ponte Vedra, Fla. (1987-89), and Dearborn, Mich. (since1990).
Multiple winner: Arnold Palmer and Dave Stockton (2).

Year		Year		Year		Year	
1983	Miller Barber	1986	Chi Chi Rodriguez	1989	Orville Moody	1992	Dave Stockton
1984	Arnold Palmer	1987	Gary Player	1990	Jack Nicklaus	1993	Jim Colbert
1985	Arnold Palmer	1988	Billy Casper	1991	Jim Albus	1994	Dave Stockton

The Tradition

First played in 1989 and played every year since at the Golf Club at Desert Mountain in Scottsdale, Ariz.
Multiple winner: Jack Nicklaus (2).

Year		Year		Year		Year	
1989	Don Bies	1991	Jack Nicklaus	1993	Tom Shaw	1994	Ray Floyd
1990	Jack Nicklaus	1992	Lee Trevino				

*PLAYOFF

1994: Ray Floyd def. Dale Douglass on 1st extra hole.

Grand Slam Summary

The Senior Grand Slam has officially consisted of The Tradition, the PGA Senior Championship, the Senior Players Championship and the U.S. Senior Open since 1990. Jack Nicklaus won three of the four events in 1991, but no one has won all four in one season.

Three wins in one year: Jack Nicklaus (1991).
Two wins in one year: Gary Player (twice); Orville Moody, Jack Nicklaus, Arnold Palmer and Lee Trevino (once).

Year	Tradition	PGA Sr.	Players	US Open	Year	Tradition	PGA Sr.	Players	US Open
1983	—	—	M. Barber	Casper	1989	Bies	Mowry	Moody	Moody
1984	—	Palmer*	Palmer	M. Barber	1990	Nicklaus	Player	Nicklaus	Trevino
1985	—	Thomson	Palmer	M. Barber	1991	Nicklaus	Nicklaus	Albus	Nicklaus
1986	—	Player	Rodriguez	Douglass	1992	Trevino	Trevino	Stockton	Laoretti
1987	—	Rodriguez	Player	Player	1993	Shaw	Wargo	Colbert	Nicklaus
1988	—	Player	Casper	Player	1994	Floyd	Trevino	Stockton	Hobday

Annual Money Leaders

Official annual money leaders on the PGA, European PGA, Senior PGA and LPGA tours. European PGA earnings listed in pounds sterling (£).

PGA

Multiple leaders: Jack Nicklaus (8); Ben Hogan and Tom Watson (5); Arnold Palmer (4); Sam Snead and Curtis Strange (3); Julius Boros, Billy Casper, Tom Kite and Byron Nelson (2).

Year		Earnings	Year		Earnings	Year		Earnings
1934	Paul Runyan	$ 6,767	1954	Bob Toski	$ 65,820	1974	Johnny Miller	$353,022
1935	Johnny Revolta	9,543	1955	Julius Boros	63,122	1975	Jack Nicklaus	298,149
1936	Horton Smith	7,682	1956	Ted Kroll	72,836	1976	Jack Nicklaus	266,439
1937	Harry Cooper	14,139	1957	Dick Mayer	65,835	1977	Tom Watson	310,653
1938	Sam Snead	19,534	1958	Arnold Palmer	42,608	1978	Tom Watson	362,429
1939	Henry Picard	10,303	1959	Art Wall	53,168	1979	Tom Watson	462,636
1940	Ben Hogan	10,655	1960	Arnold Palmer	75,263	1980	Tom Watson	530,808
1941	Ben Hogan	18,358	1961	Gary Player	64,540	1981	Tom Kite	375,699
1942	Ben Hogan	13,143	1962	Arnold Palmer	81,448	1982	Craig Stadler	446,462
1943	No records kept		1963	Arnold Palmer	128,230	1983	Hal Sutton	426,668
1944	Byron Nelson	37,968	1964	Jack Nicklaus	113,285	1984	Tom Watson	476,260
1945	Byron Nelson	63,336	1965	Jack Nicklaus	140,752	1985	Curtis Strange	542,321
1946	Ben Hogan	42,556	1966	Billy Casper	121,945	1986	Greg Norman	653,296
1947	Jimmy Demaret	27,937	1967	Jack Nicklaus	188,998	1987	Curtis Strange	925,941
1948	Ben Hogan	32,112	1968	Billy Casper	205,169	1988	Curtis Strange	1,147,644
1949	Sam Snead	31,594	1969	Frank Beard	164,707	1989	Tom Kite	1,395,278
1950	Sam Snead	35,759	1970	Lee Trevino	157,037	1990	Greg Norman	1,165,477
1951	Lloyd Mangrum	26,089	1971	Jack Nicklaus	244,491	1991	Corey Pavin	979,430
1952	Julius Boros	37,033	1972	Jack Nicklaus	320,542	1992	Fred Couples	1,344,188
1953	Lew Worsham	34,002	1973	Jack Nicklaus	308,362	1993	Nick Price	1,478,557

Note: In 1944-45, Nelson's winnings were in War Bonds.

European PGA

Multiple leaders: Seve Ballesteros (6); Sandy Lyle (3); Gay Brewer, Nick Faldo, Bernard Hunt, Bernhard Langer, Peter Thomson and Ian Woosnam (2).

Year		Earnings	Year		Earnings	Year		Earnings
1961	Bernard Hunt	£ 4,492	1972	Bob Charles	£18,538	1983	Nick Faldo	£140,761
1962	Peter Thomson	5,764	1973	Tony Jacklin	24,839	1984	Bernhard Langer	160,883
1963	Bernard Hunt	7,209	1974	Peter Oosterhuis	32,127	1985	Sandy Lyle	199,020
1964	Neil Coles	7,890	1975	Dale Hayes	20,507	1986	Seve Ballesteros	259,275
1965	Peter Thomson	7,011	1976	Seve Ballesteros	39,504	1987	Ian Woosnam	439,075
1966	Bruce Devlin	13,205	1977	Seve Ballesteros	46,436	1988	Seve Ballesteros	502,000
1967	Gay Brewer	20,235	1978	Seve Ballesteros	54,348	1989	Ronan Rafferty	465,981
1968	Gay Brewer	23,107	1979	Sandy Lyle	49,233			
1969	Billy Casper	23,483	1980	Greg Norman	74,829	1990	Ian Woosnam	737,977
1970	Christy O'Connor	31,532	1981	Bernhard Langer	95,991	1991	Seve Ballesteros	744,236
1971	Gary Player	11,281	1982	Sandy Lyle	86,141	1992	Nick Faldo	871,777
						1993	Colin Montgomerie	710,897

Senior PGA

Multiple leaders: Don January (3); Miller Barber, Bob Charles and Lee Trevino (2).

Year		Earnings	Year		Earnings	Year		Earnings
1980	Don January	$44,100	1985	Peter Thomson	$386,724	1990	Lee Trevino	$1,190,518
1981	Miller Barber	83,136	1986	Bruce Crampton	454,299	1991	Mike Hill	1,065,657
1982	Miller Barber	106,890	1987	Chi Chi Rodriguez	509,145	1992	Lee Trevino	1,027,002
1983	Don January	237,571	1988	Bob Charles	533,929	1993	Dave Stockton	1,175,944
1984	Don January	328,597	1989	Bob Charles	725,887			

Annual Money Leaders (Cont.)
LPGA

Multiple leaders: Kathy Whitworth (8); Mickey Wright (4); Patty Berg, JoAnne Carner, Betsy King and Nancy Lopez (3); Pat Bradley, Beth Daniel, Judy Rankin, Betsy Rawls, Louise Suggs and Babe Zaharias (2).

Year		Earnings	Year		Earnings	Year		Earnings
1950	Babe Zaharias	$14,800	1965	Kathy Whitworth	$ 28,658	1980	Beth Daniel	$231,000
1951	Babe Zaharias	15,087	1966	Kathy Whitworth	33,517	1981	Beth Daniel	206,998
1952	Betsy Rawls	14,505	1967	Kathy Whitworth	32,937	1982	JoAnne Carner	310,400
1953	Louise Suggs	19,816	1968	Kathy Whitworth	48,379	1983	JoAnne Carner	291,404
1954	Patty Berg	16,011	1969	Carol Mann	49,152	1984	Betsy King	266,771
1955	Patty Berg	16,492				1985	Nancy Lopez	416,472
1956	Marlene Hagge	20,235	1970	Kathy Whitworth	30,235	1986	Pat Bradley	492,021
1957	Patty Berg	16,272	1971	Kathy Whitworth	41,181	1987	Ayako Okamoto	466,034
1958	Beverly Hanson	12,639	1972	Kathy Whitworth	65,063	1988	Sherri Turner	350,851
1959	Betsy Rawls	26,774	1973	Kathy Whitworth	82,864	1989	Betsy King	654,132
			1974	JoAnne Carner	87,094			
1960	Louise Suggs	16,892	1975	Sandra Palmer	76,374	1990	Beth Daniel	863,578
1961	Mickey Wright	22,236	1976	Judy Rankin	150,734	1991	Pat Bradley	763,118
1962	Mickey Wright	21,641	1977	Judy Rankin	122,890	1992	Dottie Mochrie	693,335
1963	Mickey Wright	31,269	1978	Nancy Lopez	189,814	1993	Betsy King	595,992
1964	Mickey Wright	29,800	1979	Nancy Lopez	197,489			

All-Time Leaders
PGA, Senior PGA and LPGA leaders through 1993.

Tournaments Won

	PGA	No		Senior PGA	No		LPGA	No
1	Sam Snead	81	1	Miller Barber	24	1	Kathy Whitworth	88
2	Jack Nicklaus	70	2	Don January	22	2	Mickey Wright	82
3	Ben Hogan	63		Chi Chi Rodriguez	22	3	Patty Berg	57
4	Arnold Palmer	60	4	Bob Charles	21	4	Betsy Rawls	55
5	Byron Nelson	52	5	Bruce Crampton	19	5	Louise Suggs	50
6	Billy Casper	51	6	Lee Trevino	18	6	Nancy Lopez	47
7	Walter Hagen	40	7	Gary Player	17	7	JoAnne Carner	42
	Cary Middlecoff	40	8	George Archer	15		Sandra Haynie	42
9	Gene Sarazen	38		Mike Hill	15	9	Carol Mann	38
10	Lloyd Mangrum	36	10	Peter Thomson	11	10	Babe Zaharias	31
11	Horton Smith	32		Orville Moody	11		Patty Sheehan	31
	Tom Watson	32	12	Dale Douglass	10	12	Pat Bradley	30
13	Harry Cooper	31		Arnold Palmer	10	13	Amy Alcott	29
	Jimmy Demaret	31	14	Billy Casper	9		Jane Blalock	29
15	Leo Diegel	30	15	Gene Littler	8		Betsy King	29
				Lee Elder	8			

Note: Patty Berg's total includes 13 official pro wins prior to formation of LPGA in 1950.

Money Won

	PGA	Earnings		Senior PGA	Earnings		LPGA	Earnings
1	Tom Kite	$8,500,729	1	Bob Charles	$4,689,368	1	Pat Bradley	$4,535,841
2	Paul Azinger	6,761,306	2	Chi Chi Rodriguez	4,539,124	2	Betsy King	4,502,635
3	Greg Norman	6,607,562	3	Mike Hill	3,973,978	3	Patty Sheehan	4,131,837
4	Payne Stewart	6,377,573	4	Lee Trevino	3,906,533	4	Nancy Lopez	3,866,851
5	Tom Watson	6,370,949	5	George Archer	3,634,508	5	Beth Daniel	3,832,666
6	Fred Couples	6,263,494	6	Dale Douglass	3,569,491	6	Amy Alcott	2,910,706
7	Curtis Strange	6,042,561	7	Bruce Crampton	3,500,675	7	JoAnne Carner	2,784,598
8	Lanny Wadkins	5,877,256	8	Miller Barber	3,267,325	8	Ayako Okamoto	2,683,361
9	Ben Crenshaw	5,448,507	9	Gary Player	3,156,251	9	Jan Stephenson	2,175,309
10	Jack Nicklaus	5,360,662	10	Al Geiberger	3,028,331	10	Dottie Mochrie	2,099,753
11	Chip Beck	5,304,632	11	Orville Moody	2,848,834	11	Rosie Jones	2,069,366
12	Nick Price	5,226,491	12	Harold Henning	2,815,179	12	Jane Geddes	1,995,654
13	Craig Stadler	5,131,605	13	Don January	2,679,715	13	Juli Inkster	1,956,589
14	Ray Floyd	5,033,996	14	Jim Dent	2,667,715	14	Hollis Stacy	1,908,964
15	Mark O'Meara	4,998,267	15	Jim Colbert	2,486,406	15	Colleen Walker	1,850,124

PGA/Seniors Tours Combined

		Earnings
1	Lee Trevino	$7,384,983
2	Jack Nicklaus	6,364,972
3	Ray Floyd	6,184,155
4	Chi Chi Rodriguez	5,576,229
5	George Archer	5,516,749
6	Bob Charles	$5,228,486
7	Gary Player	4,971,201
8	Bruce Crampton	4,876,868
9	Miller Barber	4,869,733
10	Mike Hill	4,547,702
11	Al Geiberger	$4,293,518
12	Dale Douglass	4,147,442
13	Jim Colbert	4,039,541
14	Don January	3,820,141
15	Charles Coody	3,684,723

European PGA

		Earnings
1	Nick Faldo	£4,163,697
2	Ian Woosnam	3,643,241
3	Bernhard Langer	3,412,563
4	Seve Ballesteros	3,374,240
5	Jose Maria Olazabal	2,454,703
6	Ronan Rafferty	£2,210,231
7	Sandy Lyle	2,196,195
8	Sam Torrance	2,193,466
9	Colin Montgomerie	2,113,343
10	Mark James	1,975,901
11	Mark McNulty	£1,972,121
12	Gordon Brand Jr	1,909,203
13	Rodger Davis	1,795,265
14	Anders Forsbrand	1,741,212
15	David Feherty	1,495,279

The Skins Game

The Skins Game is a made-for-TV, $450,000 shootout between four premier golfers playing 18 holes over two days (nine each day). Each hole is counted as a skin with the first six skins worth $15,000 apiece, the second six worth $25,000, and the last six worth $35,000. If a hole is tied, the money is added to the worth of the next hole. The PGA Skins Game was started in 1983, followed by the Senior Skins in 1988 and the LPGA Skins in 1990. Due to scheduling conflicts, the LPGA Skins was not played in 1991.

PGA Skins

Played in late November.

Total winnings: 1. Payne Stewart ($760,000); 2. Fuzzy Zoeller ($695,000); 3. Jack Nicklaus ($650,000); 4. Curtis Strange ($605,000); 5. Fred Couples ($470,000); 6. Lee Trevino ($435,000); 7. Ray Floyd ($350,000); 8. Arnold Palmer ($245,000); 9. Tom Watson ($230,000); 10. Greg Norman ($200,000); 11. Gary Player ($170,000); 12. John Daly ($160,000); 13. Nick Faldo ($70,000); 14. Paul Azinger and Tom Kite ($0).

Year	Winner	Earnings	Outskinned	
1983	Gary Player	$170,000	Palmer	$140,000
			Nicklaus	40,000
			Watson	10,000
1984	Jack Nicklaus	$240,000	Watson	$120,000
			Palmer	0
			Player	0
1985	Fuzzy Zoeller	$255,000	Watson	$100,000
			Palmer	80,000
			Nicklaus	15,000
1986	Fuzzy Zoeller	$370,000	Trevino	$55,000
			Palmer	25,000
			Nicklaus	0
1987	Lee Trevino	$310,000	Nicklaus	$70,000
			Zoeller	70,000
			Palmer	0
1988	Ray Floyd	$290,000	Nicklaus	$125,000
			Trevino	35,000
			Strange	0
1989	Curtis Strange	$265,000	Nicklaus	$90,000
			Floyd	60,000
			Trevino	35,000
1990	Curtis Strange	$220,000	Norman	$90,000
			Faldo	70,000
			Nicklaus	70,000
1991	Payne Stewart	$260,000	Daly	$160,000
			Strange	120,000
			Nicklaus	0
1992	Payne Stewart	$220,000	Couples	$210,000
			Norman	110,000
			Kite	0
1993	Payne Stewart	$280,000	Couples	$260,000
			Palmer	0
			Azinger	0

Senior Skins

Played in late January.

Total winnings: 1. Arnold Palmer ($855,000); 2. Chi Chi Rodriguez ($685,000); 3. Jack Nicklaus ($615,000); 4. Lee Trevino ($305,000); 5. Ray Floyd ($300,000); 6. Gary Player ($130,000); 7. Billy Casper ($80,000); Sam Snead ($0).

Year	Winner	Earnings	Outskinned	
1988	C.C.Rodriguez	$300,000	Player	$40,000
			Palmer	20,000
			Snead	0
1989	C.C.Rodriguez	$120,000	Player	$90,000
			Casper	80,000
			Palmer	70,000
1990	Arnold Palmer	$240,000	Nicklaus	$140,000
			Trevino	70,000
			Player	0
1991	Jack Nicklaus	$310,000	Trevino	$125,000
			Palmer	15,000
			Player	0
			Rodriguez	0
1992	Arnold Palmer	$205,000	Rodriguez	$120,000
			Nicklaus	95,000
			Trevino	30,000
1993	Arnold Palmer	$190,000	Rodriguez	$145,000
			Floyd	60,000
			Nicklaus	55,000
1994	Ray Floyd	$240,000	Palmer	$115,000
			Trevino	80,000
			Nicklaus	15,000

LPGA Skins

Played in late May.

Year	Winner	Earnings	Outskinned	
1990	Jan Stephenson	$200,000	Carner	$110,000
			Lopez	95,000
			King	45,000
1991	Not held.			
1992	Pat Bradley	$200,000	Lopez	$115,000
			Stephenson	70,000
			Mallon	65,000
1992	Betsy King	$185,000	Lopez	$110,000
			Bradley	85,000
			Mochrie	70,000
1994	Patty Sheehan	$285,000	King	$165,000
			Burton	0
			Lopez	0

Annual Awards
PGA of America Player of the Year

Awarded by the PGA of America; based on points scale that weighs performance in major tournaments, regular events, money earned and scoring average.
Multiple winners: Tom Watson (6); Jack Nicklaus (5); Ben Hogan (4); Julius Boros, Billy Casper and Arnold Palmer (2).

Year		Year		Year		Year	
1948	Ben Hogan	1960	Arnold Palmer	1972	Jack Nicklaus	1983	Hal Sutton
1949	Sam Snead	1961	Jerry Barber	1973	Jack Nicklaus	1984	Tom Watson
1950	Ben Hogan	1962	Arnold Palmer	1974	Johnny Miller	1985	Lanny Wadkins
1951	Ben Hogan	1963	Julius Boros	1975	Jack Nicklaus	1986	Bob Tway
1952	Julius Boros	1964	Ken Venturi	1976	Jack Nicklaus	1987	Paul Azinger
1953	Ben Hogan	1965	Dave Marr	1977	Tom Watson	1988	Curtis Strange
1954	Ed Furgol	1966	Billy Casper	1978	Tom Watson	1989	Tom Kite
1955	Doug Ford	1967	Jack Nicklaus	1979	Tom Watson	1990	Nick Faldo
1956	Jack Burke	1968	No award	1980	Tom Watson	1991	Corey Pavin
1957	Dick Mayer	1969	Orville Moody	1981	Bill Rogers	1992	Fred Couples
1958	Dow Finsterwald	1970	Billy Casper	1982	Tom Watson	1993	Nick Price
1959	Art Wall	1971	Lee Trevino				

PGA Tour Player of the Year

Awarded by the PGA Tour starting in 1990. Winner voted on by tour members from list of nominees.
Multiple winner: Fred Couples (2).

Year		Year		Year		Year	
1990	Wayne Levi	1991	Fred Couples	1992	Fred Couples	1993	Nick Price

PGA Senior Player of the Year

Awarded by the PGA Seniors Tour starting in 1990. Winner voted on by tour members from list of nominees.
Multiple winner: Lee Trevino (2).

Year		Year		Year		Year	
1990	Lee Trevino	1991	George Archer & Mike Hill	1992	Lee Trevino	1993	Dave Stockton

European Golfer of the Year

Officially, the Ritz Club Trophy; voting done by panel of European golf writers and tour members.
Multiple winners: Seve Ballesteros and Nick Faldo (3); Bernhard Langer (2).

Year		Year		Year		Year	
1985	Bernhard Langer	1988	Seve Ballesteros	1990	Nick Faldo	1992	Nick Faldo
1986	Seve Ballesteros	1989	Nick Faldo	1991	Seve Ballesteros	1993	Bernhard Langer
1987	Ian Woosnam						

LPGA Player of the Year

Awarded by the LPGA; based on performance points accumulated during the year.
Multiple winners: Kathy Whitworth (7); Nancy Lopez (4); JoAnne Carner and Betsy King (3); Pat Bradley, Beth Daniel and Judy Rankin (2).

Year		Year		Year		Year	
1966	Kathy Whitworth	1973	Kathy Whitworth	1980	Beth Daniel	1987	Ayako Okamoto
1967	Kathy Whitworth	1974	JoAnne Carner	1981	JoAnne Carner	1988	Nancy Lopez
1968	Kathy Whitworth	1975	Sandra Palmer	1982	JoAnne Carner	1989	Betsy King
1969	Kathy Whitworth	1976	Judy Rankin	1983	Patty Sheehan	1990	Beth Daniel
1970	Sandra Haynie	1977	Judy Rankin	1984	Betsy King	1991	Pat Bradley
1971	Kathy Whitworth	1978	Nancy Lopez	1985	Nancy Lopez	1992	Dottie Mochrie
1972	Kathy Whitworth	1979	Nancy Lopez	1986	Pat Bradley	1993	Betsy King

Sony World Rankings

Begun in 1986, the Sony World Rankings combine the best golfers on the PGA and European PGA tours. Rankings are based on a rolling three-year period and weighed in favor of more recent results. While annual winners are not announced, certain players reaching No. 1 have dominated each year.
No. 1 players (through Sept., 1993): Greg Norman (6 times for 181 weeks); Seve Ballesteros (5 times, 60 weeks); Nick Faldo (4 times, 56 weeks); Ian Woosnam (1 time, 50 weeks); Fred Couples (2 times, 16 weeks); Bernhard Langer (1 time, 3 weeks).

Year		Year		Year		Year	
1986	Seve Ballesteros	1989	Seve Ballesteros & Greg Norman	1990	Nick Faldo & Greg Norman	1992	Fred Couples & Nick Faldo
1987	Greg Norman			1991	Ian Woosnam	1993	Nick Faldo
1988	Greg Norman						

National Team Competition
MEN
Ryder Cup

The Ryder Cup was presented by British businessman Samuel Ryder in 1927 for competition between professional golfers from Great Britain and the United States. Since 1979, the British have been joined by the rest of Europe in challenging the U.S. The U.S. leads the series with a 23-5-2 record after 30 matches.

Year		Year		Year	
1927	United States, 9½-2½	1955	United States, 8-4	1975	United States, 21-11
1929	Britain-Ireland, 7-5	1957	Britain-Ireland, 7½-4½	1977	United States, 12½-7½
1931	United States, 9-3	1959	United States, 8½-3½	1979	United States, 17-11
1933	Britain-Ireland, 6½-5½	1961	United States, 14½-9½	1981	United States, 18½-9½
1935	United States, 9-3	1963	United States, 23-9	1983	United States, 14½-13½
1937	United States, 8-4	1965	United States, 19½-12½	1985	Europe, 16½-11½
1939-45	Not held	1967	United States, 23½-8½	1987	Europe, 15-13
1947	United States, 11-1	1969	Draw, 16-16	1989	Draw, 14-14
1949	United States, 7-5	1971	United States, 18½-13½	1991	United States, 14½-13½
1951	United States, 9½-2½	1973	United States, 19-13	1993	United States, 15-13
1953	United States, 6½-5½				

Playing Sites

1927—Worcester CC (Mass.); **1929**—Moortown, England; **1931**—Scioto CC (Ohio); **1933**—Southport & Ainsdale, England; **1935**—Ridgewood CC (N.J.); **1937**—Southport & Ainsdale, England; **1939-45**—Not held.
1947—Portland CC (Ore.); **1949**—Ganton GC, England; **1951**—Pinehurst CC (N.C.); **1953**—Wentworth, England; **1955**—Thunderbird Ranch & CC (Calif.); **1957**—Lindrick GC, England; **1959**—Eldorado CC (Calif.).
1961—Royal Lytham & St. Annes, England; **1963**—East Lake CC (Ga.); **1965**—Royal Birkdale, England; **1967**—Champions GC (Tex.); **1969**—Royal Birkdale, England; **1971**—Old Warson CC (Mo.); **1973**—Muirfield, Scotland; **1975**—Laurel Valley GC (Pa.); **1977**—Royal Lytham & St. Annes, England; **1979**—Greenbrier (W.Va.).
1981—Walton Heath GC, England; **1983**—PGA National GC (Fla.); **1985**—The Belfry, England; **1987**—Muirfield Village GC (Ohio); **1989**—The Belfry, England; **1991**—Ocean Course (S.C.); **1993**—The Belfry, England.

Walker Cup

The Walker Cup was presented by American businessman George Herbert Walker in 1922 for competition between amateur golfers from Great Britain and the United States. The U.S. leads the series with a 30-3-1 record after 34 matches.

Year		Year		Year	
1922	United States, 8-4	1949	United States, 10-2	1973	United States, 14-10
1923	United States, 6½-5½	1951	United States, 7½-4½	1975	United States, 15½-8½
1924	United States, 9-3	1953	United States, 9-3	1977	United States, 16-8
1926	United States, 6½-5½	1955	United States, 10-2	1979	United States, 15½-8½
1928	United States, 11-1	1957	United States, 8½-3½	1981	United States, 15-9
1930	United States, 10-2	1959	United States, 9-3	1983	United States, 13½-10½
1932	United States, 9½-2½	1961	United States, 11-1	1985	United States, 13-11
1934	United States, 9½-2½	1963	United States, 14-10	1987	United States, 16½-7½
1936	United States, 10½-1½	1965	Draw, 12-12	1989	Britain-Ireland, 12½-11½
1938	Britain-Ireland, 7½-4½	1967	United States, 15-9	1991	United States, 14-10
1940-46	Not held	1969	United States, 13-11	1993	United States, 19-5
1947	United States, 8-4	1971	Britain-Ireland, 13-11		

WOMEN
Solheim Cup

The Solheim Cup was presented by the Karsten Manufacturing Co. in 1990 for competition between women professional golfers from Europe and the United States. The Cup was contested for the first time in 1990 in Orlando.

Year		Year		Year	
1990	United States, 11½-4½	1992	Europe, 11½-6½	1994	Oct. 21-23

Curtis Cup

Named after British golfing sisters Harriot and Margaret Curtis, the Curtis Cup was first contested in 1932 between teams of women amateurs from the United States and the British Isles.

Competed for every other year since 1932 (except during World War II). The U.S. leads the series with a 20-5-3 record after 27 matches.

Year		Year		Year	
1932	United States, 5½-3½	1958	Draw, 4½-4½	1978	United States, 12-6
1934	United States, 6½-2½	1960	United States, 6½-2½	1980	United States, 13-5
1936	Draw, 4½-4½	1962	United States, 8-1	1982	United States, 14½-3½
1938	United States, 5½-3½	1964	United States, 10½-7½	1984	United States, 9½-8½
1940-46	Not held	1966	United States, 13-5	1986	British Isles, 13-5
1948	United States, 6½-2½	1968	United States, 10½-7½	1988	British Isles, 11-7
1950	United States, 7½-1½	1970	United States, 11½-6½	1990	United States, 14-4
1952	British Isles, 5-4	1972	United States, 10-8	1992	British Isles, 10-8
1954	United States, 6-3	1974	United States, 13-5	1994	Draw, 9-9
1956	British Isles, 5-4	1976	United States, 11½-6½		

COLLEGES

Men's NCAA Division I Champions

College championships decided by match play from 1897-1964, and stroke play since 1965.

Multiple winners (teams): Yale (21); Houston (16); Princeton (12); Oklahoma St. and Stanford (7); Harvard (6); LSU and North Texas (4); Florida and Wake Forest (3); Michigan, Ohio St. and Texas (2).

Multiple winners (individuals): Ben Crenshaw and Phil Mickelson (3); Dick Crawford, Dexter Cummings, G.T. Dunlop, Fred Lamprecht, and Scott Simpson (2).

Year	Team winner	Individual champion	Year	Team winner	Individual champion
1897	Yale	Louis Bayard, Princeton	1946	Stanford	George Hamer, Georgia
1898	Harvard (spring)	John Reid, Yale	1947	LSU	Dave Barclay, Michigan
1898	Yale (fall)	James Curtis, Harvard	1948	San Jose St.	Bob Harris, San Jose St.
1899	Harvard	Percy Pyne, Princeton	1949	North Texas	Harvie Ward, N.Carolina
1900	Not held		1950	North Texas	Fred Wampler, Purdue
1901	Harvard	H. Lindsley, Harvard	1951	North Texas	Tom Nieporte, Ohio St.
1902	Yale (spring)	Chas.Hitchcock, Jr., Yale	1952	North Texas	Jim Vichers, Oklahoma
1902	Harvard (fall)	Chandler Egan, Harvard	1953	Stanford	Earl Moeller, Oklahoma St.
1903	Harvard	F.O. Reinhart, Princeton	1954	SMU	Hillman Robbins, Memphis St.
1904	Harvard	A.L. White, Harvard	1955	LSU	Joe Campbell, Purdue
1905	Yale	Robert Abbott, Yale	1956	Houston	Rick Jones, Ohio St.
1906	Yale	W.E. Clow Jr., Yale	1957	Houston	Rex Baxter Jr., Houston
1907	Yale	Ellis Knowles, Yale	1958	Houston	Phil Rodgers, Houston
1908	Yale	H.H. Wilder, Harvard	1959	Houston	Dick Crawford, Houston
1909	Yale	Albert Seckel, Princeton	1960	Houston	Dick Crawford, Houston
1910	Yale	Robert Hunter, Yale	1961	Purdue	Jack Nicklaus, Ohio St.
1911	Yale	George Stanley, Yale	1962	Houston	Kermit Zarley, Houston
1912	Yale	F.C. Davison, Harvard	1963	Oklahoma St.	R.H. Sikes, Arkansas
1913	Yale	Nathaniel Wheeler, Yale	1964	Houston	Terry Small, San Jose St.
1914	Princeton	Edward Allis, Harvard	1965	Houston	Marty Fleckman, Houston
1915	Yale	Francis Blossom, Yale	1966	Houston	Bob Murphy, Florida
1916	Princeton	J.W. Hubbell, Harvard	1967	Houston	Hale Irwin, Colorado
1917-18	Not held		1968	Florida	Grier Jones, Oklahoma St.
1919	Princeton	A.L. Walker, Jr., Columbia	1969	Houston	Bob Clark, Cal St.-LA
1920	Princeton	Jess Sweetster, Yale	1970	Houston	John Mahaffey, Houston
1921	Dartmouth	Simpson Dean, Princeton	1971	Texas	Ben Crenshaw, Texas
1922	Princeton	Pollack Boyd, Dartmouth	1972	Texas	Ben Crenshaw, Texas
1923	Princeton	Dexter Cummings, Yale			& Tom Kite, Texas
1924	Yale	Dexter Cummings, Yale	1973	Florida	Ben Crenshaw, Texas
1925	Yale	Fred Lamprecht, Tulane	1974	Wake Forest	Curtis Strange, W.Forest
1926	Yale	Fred Lamprecht, Tulane	1975	Wake Forest	Jay Haas, Wake Forest
1927	Princeton	Watts Gunn, Georgia Tech	1976	Oklahoma St.	Scott Simpson, U.S.C
1928	Princeton	Maurice McCarthy, G'town	1977	Houston	Scott Simpson, U.S.C
1929	Princeton	Tom Aycock, Yale	1978	Oklahoma St.	David Edwards, Okla. St.
1930	Princeton	G.T. Dunlap Jr., Princeton	1979	Ohio St.	Gary Hallberg, Wake Forest
1931	Yale	G.T. Dunlap Jr., Princeton	1980	Oklahoma St.	Jay Don Blake, Utah St.
1932	Yale	J.W. Fischer, Michigan	1981	Brigham Young	Ron Commans, U.S.C
1933	Yale	Walter Emery, Oklahoma	1982	Houston	Billy Ray Brown, Houston
1934	Michigan	Charles Yates, Ga.Tech	1983	Oklahoma St.	Jim Carter, Arizona St.
1935	Michigan	Ed White, Texas	1984	Houston	John Inman, N.Carolina
1936	Yale	Charles Kocsis, Michigan	1985	Houston	Clark Burroughs, Ohio St.
1937	Princeton	Fred Haas, Jr., LSU	1986	Wake Forest	Scott Verplank, Okla. St.
1938	Stanford	John Burke, Georgetown	1987	Oklahoma St.	Brian Watts, Oklahoma St.
1939	Stanford	Vincent D'Antoni, Tulane	1988	UCLA	E.J. Pfister, Oklahoma St.
1940	Princeton & LSU	Dixon Brooke, Virginia	1989	Oklahoma	Phil Mickelson, Ariz. St.
1941	Stanford	Earl Stewart, LSU	1990	Arizona St.	Phil Mickelson, Ariz. St.
1942	LSU & Stanford	Frank Tatum Jr., Stanford	1991	Oklahoma St.	Warren Schuette, UNLV
1943	Yale	Wallace Ulrich, Carleton	1992	Arizona	Phil Mickelson, Ariz. St.
1944	Notre Dame	Louis Lick, Minnesota	1993	Florida	Todd Demsey, Ariz. St.
1945	Ohio State	John Lorms, Ohio St.	1994	Stanford	Justin Leonard, Texas

Women's NCAA Champions

College championships decided by stroke play since 1982.

Multiple winners (teams): Arizona St. (3); Florida, San Jose St. and Tulsa (2).

Year	Team winner	Individual champion	Year	Team winner	Individual champion
1982	Tulsa	Kathy Baker, Tulsa	1989	San Jose St.	Pat Hurst, San Jose St.
1983	TCU	Penny Hammel, Miami	1990	Arizona St.	Susan Slaughter, Arizona
1984	Miami-FL	Cindy Schreyer, Georgia	1991	UCLA	Annika Sorenstam, Arizona
1985	Florida	Danielle Ammaccapane, Ariz.St.	1992	San Jose St.	Vicki Goetze, Georgia
1986	Florida	Page Dunlap, Florida	1993	Arizona St.	Charlotta Sorenstam, Ariz. St.
1987	San Jose St.	Caroline Keggi, New Mexico	1994	Arizona St.	Emilee Klein, Ariz. St.
1988	Tulsa	Melissa McNamara, Tulsa			

Roger Penske (top left) and three generations of **Al Unsers** all show how many wins they have after this year's running of the Indianapolis 500.

AUTO RACING

Transition

The on track deaths of Ayrton Senna and Neil Bonnett overshadow an otherwise fascinating year of change.

The 1994 season in auto racing was a transitional one darkened by the tragic on track deaths of Formula One's Ayrton Senna, NASCAR's Neil Bonnett and two others.

Ernie Irvan, one of the Winston Cup circuit's rising stars, was critically injured in another crash in August, but his story had a happy ending when he regained consciousness after seven days and began a slow-but-steady recovery from head and lung injuries.

The year saw the official retirements of four greats—Mario Andretti, Al Unser Sr. and Johnny Rutherford in Indy-car and NASCAR favorite Harry Gant. And the blossoming of four youngsters—Jeff Gordon, 23, in NASCAR and Indy-car's Jacques Villeneuve, 23, Robby Gordon, 25, and Paul Tracy, 25.

Meanwhile, Al Unser Jr., in his first season driving for powerful Team Penske, stole the competitive show, overwhelming the field with eight victories—including his second Indianapolis 500—on the way to his second Indy-car PPG Cup championship.

The 32-year-old Unser, whose family has now won nine Indy 500s and seven Indy-car series, was considered a slumbering superstar after two somewhat mediocre seasons under his long-time boss and friend Rick Galles.

Mike Harris covered his first Indianapolis 500 in 1969 and has been Motorsports Editor for the Associated Press since 1980.

"It was just time to make a change," Unser said. "Rick and I both knew it. And my dad and Uncle Bobby both drove for Roger [Penske] at one time. They always told me, `If you get a chance to drive for Penske, you take it, period.'"

Little Al, who won his first Indy-car with Galles in 1990, wrapped up the '94 title with two of 16 races remaining, the earliest clincher since former Penske star Rick Mears in 1981. The title gave Penske a record 10 series championships, but the first since Danny Sullivan won it for him in 1988.

Teammates Emerson Fittipaldi and Tracy helped make it a Penske parade most of the season as they combined with Unser for 12 victories through the season-finale at Monterey, Calif. Fittipaldi, who had one win (at Phoenix), clinched second in the points chase, while Tracy, with three wins, finished third after a season-long battle with Gordon and former champion Michael Andretti.

"The whole thing is how hard the Team Penske people work," Unser said. "And that goes along with all the testing. I've never driven so many miles in my life, or enjoyed it more."

Unser's second victory at Indianapolis was considerably different than his first, when he beat Scott Goodyear by .0043-seconds in 1992—the closest finish in Indy history.

A loophole in the Indianapolis engine rules allowed the Penske team to commission Ilmor Engineering—25 percent of which is owned by Penske—to build a spe-

The wreckage of **Ayrton Senna's** Williams-Renault after the May 1 crash that killed the 34-year-old Brazilian driver at the San Marino Grand Prix in Imola, Italy. The three-time world champion had won 41 races in 10 years.

cial pushrod-style Mercedes-Benz engine for that one event. With an obvious horse-power advantage, Unser and Fittipaldi totally controlled the 500-mile race with one or the other leading for 193 of the 200 laps.

It appeared to be Fittipaldi's victory until he made an uncharacteristic mistake just 16 laps and one turn from the end. Coming off turn four high on the 2.5-mile oval, he skated up into the wall in an attempt to put Unser a lap down.

It was redemption for Unser, who saw Fittipaldi take the checkered flag at Indy in 1989 after the two bumped wheels while battling for the lead at 210 mph, sending Unser into the wall just a lap and a half from the finish.

Unser's victory brought a record check of $1,373,813 from a record purse of $7,864,800.

Then there was the struggle of 1993 Driver of the Year Nigel Mansell to regain the edge which had given him five victories and the PPG Cup championship the year after winning the '92 Formula One title.

Mansell was hampered throughout the season by mechanical demons, crashes and the dominance of the Penske cars. And it was apparent that the British Lion still longed for his roots in F-1. He drove in the French Grand Prix between Indy-car week-ends early in the summer, then announced in September that he would return to Formula One at the close of the Indy-car season on Oct. 9. That would allow him to drive in the final three races of 1994 on the European-based circuit and to negotiate a huge contract—reportedly somewhere between $15 and $18 million—with Williams or Ferrari for 1995.

While the elder Unser and three-time Indy 500 winner Rutherford, both of whom have been relatively inactive as drivers in recent years, announced their retirements at Indianapolis in May, the 54-year-old Andretti made one last trip through the series, calling it his "Arrivederci, Mario" Tour.

Andretti, whose most recent of 52 Indy-car victories was at Phoenix in April of 1993, still showed flashes of his old ability and lots of his competitive nature as he raced to three Top-5 finishes including a third in the season-opener in Australia.

"I think I could probably be effective for another year or so, but I'm looking for satis-faction," said Andretti, a three-time

A disappointed **Mario Andretti** waves to spectators after a fuel system malfunction on the 23rd lap forced him to exit his 29th and final Indianapolis 500 on May 30.

Indy-car champion and the 1978 Formula One champ. "Satisfaction comes from being competitive."

Still, Andretti wasn't quite ready to quit entirely, leaving the door open to the possibility of some sports car endurance racing in 1995.

"I've won the Indianapolis 500 (1969) and the Daytona 500 (1967) and I've won championships, but I've never won LeMans," he said, referring to the famed 24-hour race in France. "I'd like to have that on my resume, and there's a possibility of a factory deal for maybe Daytona (the Rolex 24-Hour race) and LeMans next year. But I won't be back in an Indy-car."

Meanwhile, Villeneuve, the son of Gilles Villeneuve, a Formula One star who was killed in a crash during qualifying in Belgium in 1982, burst upon the Indy-car scene in '94. His second place finish earned him Rookie of the Year at the Indy 500 and he won his first Indy-car race later in the season at Road America.

NASCAR entered 1994 still reeling from a grim season in '93, when defending Winston Cup champion Alan Kulwicki and rising star Davey Allison both died in aviation crashes. Then it happened again. On Feb. 11, a Daytona 500 practice crash claimed the life of 47-year-old Neil Bonnett.

After sustaining a serious head injury in a 1990 crash at Darlington, S.C., Bonnett had successfully made the transition to the TV broadcast booth, but still longed to be behind the wheel. His attempted comeback began in July 1993 when he drove in a race at Talladega, Ala., and walked away from a spectacular crash. He came back to drive in the Daytona 500 and was killed during the first day of practice.

Three days later, hours before Bonnett was buried in his native Alabama, rookie Rodney Orr was killed in another practice crash at Daytona.

When racing resumed, rookie Loy Allen Jr. surprised everyone by winning the Daytona pole as the latest version of NASCAR's "Tire Wars" began with Hoosier, the small Indiana independent racing tire company, winning the first round against established giant Goodyear.

The Hoosier tire, however, was good only for a fast lap or two and not for the long haul. The company decided to withdraw from the race and Sterling Marlin, driving on Goodyears, made the Daytona 500 his first visit to Victory Lane after 17 years and 279 races.

Gambling on making it to the finish line with a near-empty gas tank, Marlin just beat Irvan to the finish line. Marlin drove a Chevrolet campaigned by Morgan-McClure Racing, the team that Irvan had left midway through the 1993 season when he bought out his contract for a reported $400,000 to take the ride vacant at Robert Yates Racing by the death of Allison.

"It gives me a lot of satisfaction to win a race," said Marlin, whose father, former stock car racer Clifton (Coo Coo) Marlin was on hand to watch the race. "I knew I could do it if I got with the right team."

Dale Earnhardt, the defending and six-time Winston Cup champion, came away from Daytona frustrated again by his failure to win NASCAR's biggest race. He has failed to win Daytona 16 times. This time, hampered by late handling problems, Earnhardt wound up seventh.

But "The Intimidator" didn't let his Daytona problems keep him down. He got off to a quick start, winning three races before midseason and fighting off the tenacious Irvan in what was shaping up to be a great late-season points battle before

Sterling Marlin, driving the Kodak Film Chevrolet, takes the checkered flag in front of **Ernie Irvan** to win the Daytona 500 on Feb. 20. The victory was Marlin's first in 17 years and 279 races on the Winston Cup circuit.

Irvan's nearly fatal crash on Aug. 20 during practice at Michigan International Speedway.

Irvan was just 27 points behind Earnhardt going into that event, the 21st on the 31-race calendar. That left Earnhardt firmly in charge as he attempted to tie retired Richard Petty for the all-time lead with seven Winston Cup championships.

But Rusty Wallace, driving for Roger Penske's NASCAR team, wasn't willing to concede a thing to old nemesis and friend Earnhardt, whom he beat for his only series title in 1989. Wallace went into the last four races of the season with a series-leading eight victories and still within striking range—209 points—of overtaking Earnhardt in the standings.

"All we can do is keep winning," said Wallace, who continued his winning ways despite making an offseason switch from Pontiacs to Fords after a 10-win season and a runner-up finish to Earnhardt in 1993.

Wallace's Thunderbird victories helped Ford wrap up the NASCAR Manufacturers' Championship early, beating Chevrolet for the second time in three years.

Despite the consistency of Earnhardt and Irvan, prior to his crash, it was a very competitive stock car season, with plenty of different winners including new team-owners Geoff Bodine and Ricky Rudd.

Bodine, who bought the team that had won the 1992 title for Kulwicki, had won five poles—tying Irvan for the series lead—and three races late in the season. Those victories were the only ones enjoyed by Hoosier in the battle of the radial tires.

Gordon, who was the circuit's 1993 Rookie of the Year, continued to blossom into a full-fledged star, winning two major races. His first win came on May 29—the same day as the Indy 500—in the Coca-Cola 600 at Charlotte, N.C. His second was on Aug. 6 at Indianapolis, when he won the inaugural Brickyard 400, the richest race in NASCAR history and the first time in more than 75 years that a second race has been run at the Indianapolis Motor Speedway.

Gordon, who lives about 10 miles down the road in Pittsboro, Ind., won after a great battle with Irvan that ended with the latter forced to pit with a flat tire. A crowd estimated at more than 300,000—the biggest in stock car history—saw Gordon earn a record $613,000 from the $3.2 million Brickyard payoff.

Germany's **Michael Schumacher** (fore-ground) led the Formula One circuit throughout the year, with Britain's **Damon Hill** (second row) right behind him.

In Formula One, the death of Senna at Imola, Italy on May 1, was the worst incident of a turbulent year. The brilliant, 34-year-old Brazilian, who had won 41 races and 65 poles in his 10-year career, died instantly when his Williams-Renault careened off course at high speed, skidded across a grassy area and slammed into a wall during the San Marino Grand Prix.

"It is a tragedy of the worst kind," said long-time bitter rival Alain Prost. "He was one of the greatest drivers of all time. It should not have happened."

Senna's death sparked national mourning in Brazil, where he was the country's biggest sports hero. He was buried with full military honors.

Just two days before Senna died, Austrian driver Roland Ratzenberger was killed at Imola in a similar crash during practice. Before that, Formula One hadn't had a fatal accident since rookie Riccardo Paletti was killed in Canada in 1982.

A month later, on the streets of Monaco, Karl Wendlinger of Austria was critically injured in a crash. He came to after spending nine days in a coma and, like Irvan, is beginning an extended period of recovery in almost miraculous fashion.

This series of accidents caused near panic among Formula One officials, who instituted a number of safety-related changes to their cars, some of them immediate and some for 1995.

On the competition side of F1, it was almost as chaotic. With Prost retired and Mansell in America, the death of Senna left the series without a former champion.

Relative newcomer Michael Schumacher of Germany drove his Benetton to four straight victories and won six of the first seven. Then, on July 10 at Silverstone, England, Schumacher passed the Williams of top rival Damon Hill on the warm-up lap. He was later black-flagged for the violation, but ignored the flag long enough for Formula One officials to decide to ban him for two races and take away his second-place finish at Silverstone.

Hill, the son of former champion Graham Hill of England, won that race, and while the appeals process was going on, Ferrari's Gerhard Berger of Austria, Schumacher and Hill each won a race, the latter at Spa, Belgium, where Schumacher was disqualified for an illegal skid pad after running away with an apparent win.

Finally, the German had to sit out the two races, both of which Hill won, leaving Schumacher with a bare one-point lead and three races remaining.

In other racing news, the team of New Zealander Steve Millen and Americans Scott Pruett, Paul Gentilozzi and Butch Leitziner ran away with the Daytona 24-hour race in a Nissan 300ZX.

Pruett, who also was the test driver for the Patrick Racing team, which spent the year testing the new Firestone Indy radials that will make their competition debut in 1995, drove the full SCCA Trans-Am season and won his second series championship.

At LeMans, American Hurley Haywood won for the third time, sharing a Porsche 962 with Yannick Dalmas of France and Mauro Baldi of Italy. It was the 13th victory for Porsche at LeMans and ended Peugot's string of wins at two. ❏

AUTO RACING
S T A T I S T I C S

THE 1995 SPORTS ALMANAC — INFORMATION PLEASE

SEC A

THE SEASON IN REVIEW
1993-1994
NASCAR • INDYCAR • FORMULA 1

PAGE 809

NASCAR Results

Winners of NASCAR Winston Cup races from Feb. 20 through Oct. 9, 1994.

1994 SEASON (through Oct. 9)

Date	Event	Location	Winner (Pos.)	Avg.mph	Earnings	Pole	Qual.mph
Feb. 20	**Daytona 500**............Daytona		Sterling Marlin (4)	156.931	$253,575	L. Allen Jr.	190.158
Feb. 27	Goodwrench 500 ....Rockingham		Rusty Wallace (15)	125.239	50,385	M. Martin	149.547†
Mar. 6	Pontiac 400 ....Richmond		Ernie Irvan (7)	98.334	66,175	T. Musgrave	123.474†
Mar. 13	Purolator 500 ....Atlanta		Ernie Irvan (7)	146.136	86,100	L. Allen Jr.	180.207†
Mar. 27	TranSouth 500.............Darlington		Dale Earnhardt (9)	132.432	70,190	B. Elliott	165.553†
Apr. 10	Food City 500 ....Bristol		Dale Earnhardt (24)	89.647	72,500	C. Brown	124.946†
Apr. 17	First Union 400.............N.Wilkesboro		Terry Labonte (10)	95.816	61,640	E. Irvan	119.016†
Apr. 24	Hanes 500 ....Martinsville		Rusty Wallace (1)	76.700	173,675*	R. Wallace	92.942
May 1	**Winston 500**.............Talladega		Dale Earnhardt (3)	157.478	94,865	E. Irvan	193.298
May 15	Save Mart 300 ....Sonoma		Ernie Irvan (1)	77.458	78,810*	E. Irvan	91.514
May 21	The Winston Select.......Charlotte		Geoff Bodine (4)	115.561	250,000	J. Gordon	130.372
May 29	**Coca-Cola 600**..........Charlotte		Jeff Gordon (3)	139.445	196,500*	J. Gordon	181.439†
June 5	Budweiser 500.............Dover		Rusty Wallace (6)	102.529	70,605	E. Irvan	151.956†
June 12	UAW-GM Teamwork 500 .Pocono		Rusty Wallace (1)	128.801	84,525*	R. Wallace	164.558†
June 19	Miller Draft 400 ....Michigan		Rusty Wallace (5)	125.022	66,980	L. Allen Jr.	180.641
July 2	Pepsi 400 ....Daytona		Jimmy Spencer (3)	155.558	75,880	D. Earnhardt	191.339
July 10	Slick 50 300................Loudon		Ricky Rudd (3)	87.599	91,875	E. Irvan	127.197†
July 17	Miller Draft 500...........Pocono		Geoff Bodine (1)	136.075	103,270	G. Bodine	163.869
July 24	DieHard 500 ....Talladega		Jimmy Spencer (3)	163.217	81,450	D. Earnhardt	193.470
Aug. 6	Brickyard 400..............Indianapolis		Jeff Gordon (3)	131.977†	613,000	R. Mast	172.414†
Aug. 14	Bud at the Glen............Watkins Glen		Mark Martin (1)	93.752	85,100	M. Martin	118.326
Aug. 21	GM Goodwrench 400....Michigan		Geoff Bodine (1)	139.914	89,595	G. Bodine	181.082
Aug. 27	Goody's 500 ....Martinsville		Rusty Wallace (4)	91.363	53,015	H. Gant	124.186
Sept. 4	**Southern 500**...........Darlington		Bill Elliott (9)	127.915	68,330	G. Bodine	166.998†
Sept.11	Miller Draft 400 ....Richmond		Terry Labonte (3)	104.156	67,765	T. Musgrave	124.052†
Sept.18	Split Fire 500..............Dover		Rusty Wallace (10)	112.556	55,055	G. Bodine	152.840†
Sept.25	Goody's 500 ....Martinsville		Rusty Wallace (7)	77.139	69,125	T. Musgrave	94.129
Oct. 2	Holly Farms 400 ....N.Wilkesboro		Geoff Bodine (18)	98.522	61,440	J. Spencer	118.558
Oct. 9	Mello Yello 500 ....Charlotte		Dale Jarrett (22)	145.922	106,800	W. Burton	185.759†

Note: The Winston Select (May 21) is a non-points race.

†Track record.
*Includes carryover Unocal 76 bonus of $7,600 for winning race from the pole: **Hanes 500**—R. Wallace ($98,800); **Save Mart 500**—Irvan ($15,200); **Coca-Cola 600**—Gordon ($7,600); **Teamwork 500**—R. Wallace ($15,200); **Miller Genuine Draft 500**—Bodine ($30,400); **Bud at the Glen**—Martin ($22,800); **GM Goodwrench 400**—G. Bodine ($7,600).
Winning Cars: FORD THUNDERBIRD (19)—R. Wallace (8), G. Bodine (3), Irvan (3), J. Spencer (2), Elliott, Martin, Rudd; CHEVY LUMINA (9)—Earnhardt (3), Gordon (2), T. Labonte (2), Jarrett and Marlin.
Remaining Races (3): AC Delco 500 at Rockingham (Oct. 23); Slick 50 500 at Phoenix (Oct.30); Hooters 500 at Atlanta (Nov. 13).

1994 Race Locations

February—DAYTONA 500 by STP at Daytona International Speedway in Daytona Beach, Fla.; GOODWRENCH 500 at North Carolina Motor Speedway in Rockingham, N.C. **March**—PONTIAC EXCITEMENT 400 at Richmond (Va.) International Raceway; PUROLATOR 500 at Atlanta International Speedway in Hampton, Ga.; TRANSOUTH 500 at Darlington (S.C.) International Raceway. **April**—FOOD CITY 500 at Bristol (Tenn.) International Raceway; FIRST UNION 400 at North Wilkesboro (N.C.) Speedway; HANES 500 at Martinsville (Va.) Speedway. **May**—WINSTON SELECT 500 at Talladega (Ala.) Superspeedway; SAVE MART 300 at Sears Point International Raceway in Sonoma, Calif.; THE WINSTON SELECT at Charlotte Motor Speedway in Concord, N.C.; COCA-COLA 600 at Charlotte.

June—BUDWEISER 500 at Dover (Del.) Downs International Speedway; POCONO 500 at Pocono International Raceway in Long Pond, Pa.; MILLER GENUINE DRAFT 400 at Michigan International Speedway in Brooklyn, Mich. **July**—PEPSI 400 at Daytona; SLICK 50 300 at New Hampshire International Speedway in Loudon, N.H.; MILLER GENUINE DRAFT 500 at Pocono; DIEHARD 500 at Talladega. **August**—BRICKYARD 400 at Indianapolis Motor Speedway; BUD AT THE GLEN in Watkins Glen, N.Y.; GM GOODWRENCH 400 at Brooklyn, Mich.; GOODY'S 500 at Bristol, Mich.; **September**—MOUNTAIN DEW SOUTHERN 500 at Darlington; MILLER GENUINE DRAFT 400 at Richmond; SPLIT FIRE 500 at Dover; GOODY'S 500 at Martinsville. **October**—HOLLY FARMS 400 at North Wilkesboro; MELLO YELLO 500 at Charlotte; AC DELCO 500 at Rockingham; Slick 50 500 at Phoenix International Raceway. **November**—HOOTERS 500 at Atlanta.

NASCAR Results (Cont.)

1994 Daytona 500

Date—Sunday, Feb. 20, 1994, at Daytona, FL International Speedway. **Distance**—500 miles; **Course**—2.5 miles; **Field**—42 cars; **Average speed**—154.972 mph; **Margin of victory**—0.23 seconds; **Time of race**—3 hours, 11 minutes, 10 seconds; **Caution flags**—4 for 22 laps; **Lead changes**—33 among 14 drivers; **Lap leaders**—Ernie Irvan (84 laps), Dale Earnhardt (46), Marlin (30), T. Bodine, Cope, Gordon, and Shepherd (7), Martin (4), Jarrett (3), Hamilton (2), G. Bodine, T. Labonte, and Little (1); **Pole sitter**—Loy Allen Jr. at 190.158 mph; **Attendance**—140,000 (estimated); **TV Rating**—9.6/26 share (CBS).

	Driver (start pos.)	Hometown	Car	Laps	Ended	Earnings
1	Sterling Marlin (4)	Franklin, Tenn.	Chevy Lumina	200	Running	$253,575
2	Ernie Irvan (3)	Modesto, Calif.	Ford Thunderbird	200	Running	190,750
3	Terry Labonte (9)	Corpus Christi, Tex.	Chevy Lumina	200	Running	138,475
4	Jeff Gordon (6)	Vallejo, Calif.	Chevy Lumina	200	Running	112,525
5	Morgan Shepherd (12)	Conover, N.C.	Ford Thunderbird	200	Running	92,805
6	Greg Sacks (31)	Mattituck, N.Y.	Ford Thunderbird	200	Running	70,480
7	Dale Earnhardt (2)	Kannapolis, N.C.	Chevy Lumina	200	Running	110,340
8	Ricky Rudd (20)	Chesapeake, Va.	Ford Thunderbird	200	Running	56,465
9	Bill Elliott (8)	Cumming, Va.	Ford Thunderbird	200	Running	65,615
10	Ken Schrader (13)	St. Louis, Mo.	Chevy Lumina	200	Running	59,565
11	Geoff Bodine (39)	Elmira, N.Y.	Ford Thunderbird	200	Running	52,065
12	Bobby Hamilton (23)	Nashville, Tenn.	Pontiac Grand Prix	200	Running	51,265
DNF	Mark Martin (7)	Batesville, Ark.	Ford Thunderbird	199	Out of gas	65,670
14	Lake Speed (22)	Jackson, Miss.	Ford Thunderbird	199	Running	50,530
15	Jimmy Hensley (25)	Ridgeway, Va.	Ford Thunderbird	199	Running	42,215
16	Bobby Labonte (42)	Corpus Christi, Tex.	Pontiac Grand Prix	199	Running	43,195
17	Wally Dallenbach Jr. (18)	Brunswick, N.J.	Pontiac Grand Prix	199	Running	39,175
18	Joe Ruttman (34)	Franklin, Tenn.	Ford Thunderbird	199	Running	34,005
19	Jimmy Horton (28)	Hammonton, N.J.	Ford Thunderbird	199	Running	33,485
20	Dick Trickle (29)	Wisconsin Rapids	Chevy Lumina	198	Running	33,475
21	Derrike Cope (16)	San Diego, Calif.	Ford Thunderbird	198	Running	36,220
22	Loy Allen Jr. (1)	Raleigh, N.C.	Ford Thunderbird	198	Running	43,515
23	Chuck Brown (37)	Portland, Oreg.	Ford Thunderbird	198	Running	36,860
24	Bobby Hillin (33)	Midland, Tex.	Ford Thunderbird	198	Running	29,955
25	Dave Marcis (27)	Wausau, Wisc.	Chevy Lumina	198	Running	31,150
26	Jeff Burton (35)	South Boston, Va.	Ford Thunderbird	197	Running	37,145
27	Rick Mast (30)	Lexington, Va.	Ford Thunderbird	197	Running	36,540
28	Darrell Waltrip (32)	Owensboro, Ky.	Chevy Lumina	197	Running	35,435
29	Chad Little (17)	Charlotte, NC	Ford Thunderbird	196	Running	30,805
DNF	Jeremy Mayfield (40)	Nashville, Ky.	Ford Thunderbird	195	Out of gas	27,645
31	Michael Waltrip (14)	Owensboro, Ky.	Pontiac Grand Prix	194	Running	36,545
32	Brett Bodine (10)	Elmira, N.Y.	Ford Thunderbird	185	Running	39,865
33	Hut Stricklin (38)	Calera, Ala.	Ford Thunderbird	174	Running	28,235
34	Harry Gant (36)	Taylorsville, N.C.	Chevy Lumina	165	Running	34,630
DNF	Dale Jarrett (41)	Newton, N.C.	Chevy Lumina	146	Engine	38,325
DNF	Todd Bodine (11)	Elmira, N.Y.	Ford Thunderbird	79	Crash	35,870
DNF	Jimmy Spencer (21)	Berwick, Penn.	Ford Thunderbird	79	Crash	28,790
DNF	Ted Musgrave (24)	Evenston, Wisc.	Ford Thunderbird	79	Crash	32,360
DNF	Kyle Petty (26)	Randleman, N.C.	Pontiac Grand Prix	64	Crash	39,075
DNF	Robert Pressley (19)	Asheville, N.C.	Chevy Lumina	62	Crash	28,490
DNF	Rusty Wallace (5)	St. Louis, Mo.	Ford Thunderbird	61	Crash	57,865
DNF	John Andretti (15)	Bethlehem, Penn.	Chevy Lumina	47	Crash	32,365

NASCAR Point Standings

Official Top 10 NASCAR Winston Cup point leaders and Top 15 money leaders for 1993 and unofficial Top 15 point leaders and Top 15 money leaders for 1994 (through Oct. 9). Points awarded for all qualifying drivers (winner receives 175) and lap leaders. Earnings include bonuses. Listed are starts (Sts), Top 5 finishes (1-2-3-4-5), poles won (PW) and points (Pts).

FINAL 1993

		Sts	Finishes 1-2-3-4-5	PW	Pts
1	Dale Earnhardt	30	6-5-3-3-0	2	4526
2	Rusty Wallace	30	10-4-2-1-2	3	4446
3	Mark Martin	30	5-3-1-1-2	5	4150
4	Dale Jarrett	30	1-1-4-5-2	0	4000
5	Kyle Petty	30	1-1-2-2-3	1	3860
6	Ernie Irvan	30	3-4-3-0-2	4	3834
7	Morgan Shepherd	30	1-1-0-1-0	0	3807
8	Bill Elliott	30	0-1-2-2-1	2	3774
9	Ken Schrader	30	0-2-2-3-2	6	3715
10	Ricky Rudd	30	1-1-1-3-3	0	3644

Note: Alan Kulwicki and Davey Allison were killed in aviation accidents in 1993.

1994 SEASON (through Oct. 9)

		Sts	Finishes 1-2-3-4-5	PW	Pts
1	Dale Earnhardt	28	3-6-6-1-2	2	4291
2	Rusty Wallace	28	8-3-1-4-1	2	3970
3	Mark Martin	28	1-3-2-4-3	1	3744
4	Ken Schrader	28	0-1-2-4-2	0	3740
5	Ricky Rudd	28	1-0-0-2-2	0	3613
6	Morgan Shepherd	28	0-2-1-1-4	0	3582
7	Jeff Gordon	28	2-1-1-1-1	1	3412
8	Terry Labonte	28	2-1-1-0-0	0	3389
9	Darrell Waltrip	28	0-0-2-2-0	0	3360
10	Bill Elliott	28	1-1-3-0-1	1	3350

Other wins (10): Geoff Bodine and Ernie Irvan (3); Jimmy Spencer (2); Dale Jarrett and Sterling Marlin.

Top 5 + Pole Finishing Order
1994 SEASON (through Oct. 9)

No.	Event	Winner	2nd	3rd	4th	5th	Pole
1	Daytona 500	S. Marlin	E. Irvan	T. Labonte	J. Gordon	M. Shepherd	L. Allen Jr.
2	Goodwrench 500	R. Wallace	S. Marlin	R. Mast	M. Martin	E. Irvan	G. Bodine
3	Pontiac 400	E. Irvan	R. Wallace	J. Gordon	D. Earnhardt	K. Petty	T. Musgrave
4	Purolator 500	E. Irvan	M. Shepherd	D. Waltrip	J. Burton	M. Martin	L. Allen
5	TranSouth 500	D. Earnhardt	M. Martin	B. Elliott	D. Jarrett	L. Speed	B. Elliott
6	Food City 500	D. Earnhardt	K. Schrader	L. Speed	G. Bodine	M. Waltrip	C. Brown
7	First Union 400	T. Labonte	R. Wallace	E. Irvan	K. Petty	D. Earnhardt	E. Irvan
8	Hanes 500	R. Wallace	E. Irvan	M. Martin	D. Waltrip	M. Shepherd	R. Wallace
9	Winston Select 500	D. Earnhardt	E. Irvan	M. Waltrip	J. Spencer	K. Schrader	E. Irvan
10	Save Mart 300	E. Irvan	G. Bodine	D. Earnhardt	W. Dallenbach	R. Wallace	E. Irvan
11	Coca-Cola 600	J. Gordon	R. Wallace	G. Bodine	D. Jarrett	E. Irvan	J. Gordon
12	Budweiser 500	R. Wallace	E. Irvan	K. Schrader	M. Martin	J. Gordon	E. Irvan
13	Teamwork 500	R. Wallace	D. Earnhardt	K. Schrader	M. Shepherd	M. Martin	R. Wallace
14	Miller 400	R. Wallace	D. Earnhardt	M. Martin	R. Rudd	M. Shepherd	L. Allen
15	Pepsi 400	J. Spencer	E. Irvan	D. Earnhardt	M. Martin	K. Schrader	D. Earnhardt
16	Slick 50 300	R. Rudd	D. Earnhardt	R. Wallace	M. Martin	T. Bodine	E. Irvan
17	Miller GD 500	G. Bodine	W. Burton	J. Nemechek	J. Burton	M. Shepherd	G. Bodine
18	DieHard 500	J. Spencer	B. Elliott	E. Irvan	K. Schrader	S. Marlin	D. Earnhardt
19	Brickyard 400	J. Gordon	B. Bodine	B. Elliott	R. Wallace	D. Earnhardt	R. Mast
20	Bud at the Glen	M. Martin	E. Irvan	D. Earnhardt	K. Schrader	R. Rudd	M. Martin
21	GM Goodwrench 400	G. Bodine	M. Martin	R. Mast	R. Wallace	B. Labonte	G. Bodine
22	Goody's 500	R. Wallace	M. Martin	D. Earnhardt	D. Waltrip	B. Elliott	H. Gant
23	Southern 500	B. Elliot	D. Earnhardt	M. Shepherd	R. Rudd	S. Marlin	G. Bodine
24	Miller 400	T. Labonte	J. Gordon	D. Earnhardt	R. Wallace	R. Rudd	T. Musgrave
25	Split Fire 500	R. Wallace	D. Earnhardt	D. Waltrip	K. Schrader	G. Bodine	G. Bodine
26	Goody's 500	R. Wallace	D. Earnhardt	B. Elliott	R. Wallace	D. Jarrett	T. Musgrave
27	Holly Farms 400	G. Bodine	T. Labonte	R. Mast	R. Wallace	M. Martin	J. Spencer
28	Mello Yello 500	D. Jarrett	M. Shepherd	D. Earnhardt	K. Schrader	L. Speed	W. Burton

Money Leaders
FINAL 1993

	Earnings			Earnings			Earnings
1 Dale Earnhardt	$3,353,789		6 Bill Elliott	$955,859		11 Harry Gant	$772,832
2 Rusty Wallace	1,702,154		7 Ken Schrader	952,748		12 Jeff Gordon	765,168
3 Mark Martin	1,657,662		8 Kyle Petty	914,662		13 Ricky Rudd	752,562
4 Ernie Irvan	1,400,468		9 Geoff Bodine	783,762		14 Darrell Waltrip	746,646
5 Dale Jarrett	1,242,394		10 Morgan Shepherd	782,523		15 Jimmy Spencer	686,026

1994 SEASON (through Oct. 9)

	Earnings			Earnings			Earnings
1 Jeff Gordon	$1,533,805		6 Sterling Marlin	$948,830		11 Bill Elliott	$799,610
2 Rusty Wallace	1,437,330		7 Mark Martin	922,032		12 Dale Jarrett	748,810
3 Dale Earnhardt	1,392,770		8 Terry Labonte	855,660		13 Brett Bodine	686,600
4 Ernie Irvan	1,164,455		9 Ken Schrader	817,690		14 Lake Speed	674,235
5 Geoff Bodine	1,097,478		10 Morgan Shepherd	811,025		15 Kyle Petty	669,596

IndyCar Results
1994 SEASON

Date	Event	Location	Winner (Pos)	Time	Avg.mpg	Pole	Qual.mph
Mar. 20	Australian GP	Queensland	Michael Andretti (2)	1:53:52.700	80.994	N. Mansell	106.053†
Apr. 10	Slick 50 200	Phoenix	Emerson Fittipaldi (6)	1:51:41.615	107.437	P. Tracy	176.266†
Apr. 17	Toyota GP	Long Beach	Al Unser Jr. (2)	1:40:53.582	99.283†	P. Tracy	108.450†
May 29	**Indianapolis 500**	Indianapolis	Al Unser Jr. (1)	3:06:29.006	160.872	A. Unser Jr.	228.785
June 5	Miller 200	West Allis	Al Unser Jr. (11)	1:36:57.964*	118.804	R. Boesel	161.364
June 12	Detroit GP	Belle Isle	Paul Tracy (3)	1:52:29.642	86.245†	N. Mansell	108.649†
June 26	Bud/GI Joe's 200	Portland	Al Unser Jr. (1)	1:50:43.706	107.777†	A. Unser Jr.	116.861†
July 10	Budweiser GP	Cleveland	Al Unser Jr. (1)	1:27:32.000	138.026†	A. Unser Jr.	143.983
July 17	Molson Indy	Toronto	Michael Andretti (6)	1:48:15.978	96.673	R. Gordon	110.191†
July 31	Marlboro 500	Michigan	Scott Goodyear (12)	3:07:44.099	159.800	N. Mansell	233.738
Aug. 14	Miller Draft 200	Mid-Ohio	Al Unser Jr. (1)	1:40:59.436	110.387†	A. Unser Jr.	119.517†
Aug. 21	Slick 50 200	Loudon	Al Unser Jr. (10)	1:43:31.594	122.635	E. Fittipaldi	175.091†
Sept. 4	Molson Indy	Vancouver	Al Unser Jr. (8)	1:53:27.345	89.166†	R. Gordon	109.049†
Sept.11	Texaco/Havoline 200	Elkhart Lake	Jacques Villeneuve (2)	1:42:37.930	116.922	P. Tracy	136.602†
Sept.18	Bosch GP	Nazareth	Paul Tracy (2)	1:31:30.292	131.141	E. Fittipaldi	185.600†
Oct. 9	Toyota GP	Laguna Seca	Paul Tracy (1)	2:00:00.763	92.978	P. Tracy	113.768†

†Track record. *Race distance shortened due to rain

Winning cars: MARLBORO PENSKE (12)—Unser Jr. (8), Tracy (3), Fittipaldi. GANASSI REYNARD-FORD (2)—Mi. Andretti (2). BUDWEISER LOLA-FORD (1)—Goodyear. FORSYTHE-GREEN REYNARD-FORD (1)—Villeneuve.

IndyCar Results (Cont.)

1994 Race Locations

March—AUSTRALIAN FAI INDYCAR GP at Surfers Paradise, Queensland. **April**—SLICK 50 200 at Phoenix International Raceway; TOYOTA GP AT LONG BEACH, Calif. **May**—INDIANAPOLIS 500 at Indianapolis Motor Speedway. **June**—MILLER GENUINE DRAFT 200 at Wisconsin State Fair Park in West Allis, Wisc.; ITT AUTOMOTIVE DETROIT GP at Belle Isle Park; BUDWEISER/G.I. JOE'S 200 at Portland (Ore.) International Raceway. **July**—BUDWEISER GP OF CLEVELAND at Burke Lakefront Airport; MOLSON INDY TORONTO at Exhibition Place; MARLBORO 500 at Michigan International Speedway in Brooklyn, Mich.

August—MILLER GENUINE DRAFT 200 at Mid-Ohio Sports Car Course in Lexington; SLICK 50 200 at New Hampshire International Speedway in Loudon. **September**—MOLSON INDY VANCOUVER at Pacific Place; TEXACO/HAVOLINE 200 at Road America in Elkhart Lake, Wisc.; BOSCH SPARK PLUG GP at Nazareth (Pa.) Speedway. **October**—TOYOTA MONTEREY (Calif.) GP at Laguna Seca Raceway.

1994 Indianapolis 500

Date—Sunday, May 29, 1994, at Indianapolis Motor Speedway. **Distance**—500 miles; **Course**—2.5 mile oval; **Field**—33 cars; **Winner's average speed**—160.872 mph; **Margin of victory**—8.600 seconds; **Time of race**—3 hours, 6 minutes, 29.006 seconds; **Caution flags**—7 for 43 laps; **Lead changes**—10 by three drivers; **Lap leaders**—Fittipaldi (145 laps), Unser Jr. (48), Villeneuve (7); **Pole sitter**—Al Unser Jr. at 228.011 mph; **Attendance**—400,000 (estimated); **TV Rating**—8.3/29 share (ABC). Note that (r) indicates rookie driver.

Driver (start pos.)	Hometown	Car	Laps	Ended	Earnings
1 Al Unser Jr (1)	Albuquerque	Penske-Mercedes	200	Running	$1,373,813
2 r-Jacques Villeneuve (4)	Monte Carlo	Reynard-Ford	200	Running	622,713
3 Bobby Rahal (28)	Dublin, Ohio	Penske-Ilmor	199	Running	411,163
4 Jimmy Vasser (16)	Discovery Bay, Calif.	Reynard-Ford	199	Running	295,163
5 Robby Gordon (19)	Orange, Calif.	Lola-Ford	199	Running	277,563
6 Michael Andretti (5)	Nazareth, Pa.	Reynard-Ford	198	Running	245,563
7 Teo Fabi (24)	Milan, Italy	Reynard-Ilmor	198	Running	216,563
8 Eddie Cheever (11)	Aspen, Colo.	Lola-Menard	197	Running	238,563
9 r-Bryan Herta (22)	Dublin, Ohio	Lola-Ford	197	Running	212,213
10 John Andretti (10)	Indianapolis, Ind.	Lola-Ford	196	Running	191,750
11 r-Mauricio Gugelmin (29)	Curitiba, Brazil	Reynard-Ford	196	Running	182,063
12 r-Brian Till (21)	Columbus, Ohio	Lola-Ford	194	Running	180,763
13 Stan Fox (13)	Janesville, Wisc.	Reynard-Ford	193	Crash	186,313
14 Hiro Matsushita (18)	San Clemente, Calif.	Lola-Ford	193	Running	177,013
15 Stefan Johansson (27)	Monte Carlo	Penske-Ilmor	192	Running	164,113
16 r-Scott Sharp (17)	Wilton, Conn.	Lola-Ford	186	Running	161,663
17 Emerson Fittipaldi (3)	Key Biscayne, Fla.	Penske-Mercedes	184	Crash	298,163
18 Arie Luyendyk (8)	Scottsdale, Ariz.	Lola-Ilmor	179	Engine	161,412
19 Lyn St. James (6)	Daytona Beach, Fla.	Lola-Ford	170	Running	161,212
20 Scott Brayton (23)	Coldwater, Mich.	Lola-Menard	116	Engine	177,112
21 Raul Boesel (2)	Key Biscayne, Fla.	Lola-Ford	100	Water pump	173,112
22 Nigel Mansell (7)	Clearwater, Fla.	Lola-Ford	92	Crash	153,312
23 Paul Tracy (25)	West Hill, Ontario	Penske-Mercedes	92	Turbocharger	151,612
24 r-Hideshi Matsuda (14)	Kawasaki, Japan	Lola-Ford	90	Crash	150,362
25 John Paul Jr. (30)	Lantana, Fla.	Lola-Ilmor	89	Crash	168,812
26 r-Dennis Vitolo (15)	Ft. Lauderdale, Fla.	Lola-Ford	89	Crash	143,862
27 r-Marco Greco (32)	Sao Paulo, Brazil	Lola-Ford	53	Electrical	171,762
28 r-Adrian Fernandez (26)	Costa Mesa, Calif	Reynard-Ilmor	30	Suspension	146,612
29 Dominic Dobson (12)	Bellevue, Wash.	Lola-Ford	29	Crash	139,912
30 Scott Goodyear (33)	Toronto	Lola-Ford	29	Engine	159,312
31 Mike Groff (31)	Worthington, Ohio	Penske-Ilmor	28	Crash	138,812
32 Mario Andretti (9)	Nazareth, Pa.	Lola-Ford	23	Fuel system	138,512
33 Roberto Guerrero (20)	S.J. Capistrano, Calif.	Lola-Buick	20	Crash	143,912

IndyCar Point Standings

Official Top 10 PPG Cup point leaders and Top 15 money leaders for 1993 and 1994. Points awarded for places 1 to 12, fastest qualifier and overall lap leader. Listed are starts (Sts), Top 5 finishes, poles won (PW) and points (Pts).

FINAL 1993

	Sts	Finishes 1-2-3-4-5	PW	Pts
1 Nigel Mansell	15	5-2-3-0-0	7*	191
2 Emerson Fittipaldi	16	3-4-2-0-2	2	183
3 Paul Tracy	16	5-1-2-0-0	2	157
4 Bobby Rahal	15	0-2-1-3-1	0	133
5 Raul Boesel	16	0-3-0-4-0	1	132
6 Mario Andretti	16	1-1-1-1-3	1	117
7 Al Unser Jr	16	1-0-0-1-4	0	100
8 Arie Luyendyk	16	0-1-2-0-2	1	90
9 Scott Goodyear	16	0-1-1-2-1	2	86
10 Robby Gordon	16	0-1-1-1-1	0	84

FINAL 1994

	Sts	Finishes 1-2-3-4-5	PW	Pts
1 Al Unser Jr	16	8-3-0-0-0	4	225
2 Emerson Fittipaldi	16	1-4-5-1-0	2	178
3 Paul Tracy	16	3-2-3-0-1	4	152
4 Michael Andretti	16	2-0-1-1-3	0	118
5 Robby Gordon	16	0-1-2-2-1	2	104
6 Jacques Villeneuve	16	1-1-1-1-0	0	94
7 Raul Boesel	16	0-1-0-3-0	1	90
8 Nigel Mansell	16	0-2-1-0-2	3	88
9 Teo Fabi	16	0-0-0-3-0	0	79
10 Bobby Rahal	16	0-1-1-0-0	0	59

*One pole determined by championship points due to rainout.

Top 5 + Pole Finishing Order

No.	Event	Winner	2nd	3rd	4th	5th	Pole
1	Australian GP	Mi. Andretti	E. Fittipaldi	J. Vasser	Ma. Andretti	S. Johansson	N. Mansell
2	Slick 50 200	E. Fittipaldi	A. Unser Jr.	N. Mansell	S. Johansson	J. Vasser	P. Tracy
3	Toyota GP	A. Unser Jr.	N. Mansell	R. Gordon	R. Boesel	Ma. Andretti	P. Tracy
4	Indianapolis 500	A. Unser Jr.	J. Villeneuve	B. Rahal	J. Vasser	R. Gordon	A. Unser Jr.
5	Miller 200	A. Unser Jr.	E. Fittipaldi	P. Tracy	Mi. Andretti	N. Mansell	R. Boesel
6	Detroit GP	P. Tracy	E. Fittipaldi	R. Gordon	T. Fabi	Mi. Andretti	N. Mansell
7	Bud/Gl Joe's 200	A. Unser Jr.	E. Fittipaldi	P. Tracy	R. Gordon	N. Mansell	A. Unser Jr.
8	GP of Cleveland	A. Unser Jr.	N. Mansell	P. Tracy	G. Villenevue	S. Johansson	A. Unser Jr.
9	Molson Toronto	Mi. Andretti	B. Rahal	E. Fittipaldi	Ma. Andretti	P. Tracy	R. Gordon
10	Marlboro 500	S. Goodyear	A. Luyendyk	D. Dobson	T. Fabi	M. Smith	N. Mansell
11	Miller GD 200	A. Unser Jr.	P. Tracy	E. Fittipaldi	R. Gordon	Mi. Andretti	A. Unser Jr.
12	Slick 50 200	A. Unser Jr.	P. Tracy	E. Fittipaldi	R. Boesel	Mi. Andretti	E. Fittipali
13	Molson Vancouver	A. Unser Jr.	P. Tracy	R. Gordon	Mi. Andretti	S. Goodyear	M. Gugelmin / R. Gordon
14	Texaco/Havoline 200	J. Villeneuve	A. Unser Jr.	E. Fittipaldi	T. Fabi	A. Fernandez	P. Tracy
15	Bosch GP	P. Tracy	A. Unser Jr.	E. Fittipaldi	R. Boesel	S. Johansson	E. Fittipaldi
16	Toyota GP	P. Tracy	R. Boesel	J. Villeneuve	E. Fittipaldi	A. Luyendyk	P. Tracy

Money Leaders

FINAL 1993

		Earnings			Earnings			Earnings
1	Emerson Fittipaldi	$2,575,554	6	Mario Andretti	$1,111,453	11	Teo Fabi	$753,453
2	Nigel Mansell	2,526,953	7	Al Unser, Jr	932,503	12	Scott Brayton	729,003
3	Paul Tracy	1,422,253	8	Scott Goodyear	920,203	13	Stefan Johansson	656,020
4	Arie Luyendyk	1,294,053	9	Bobby Rahal	858,250	14	Hiro Matsushita	634,253
5	Raul Boesel	1,163,653	10	Robby Gordon	796,203	15	Danny Sullivan	630,703

FINAL 1994

		Earnings			Earnings			Earnings
1	Al Unser Jr	$3,535,813	6	Robby Gordon	$1,034,063	11	Jimmy Vasser	$753,163
2	Emerson Fittipaldi	1,604,163	7	Bobby Rahal	978,413	12	Scott Goodyear	724,062
3	Paul Tracy	1,267,862	8	Raul Boesel	881,612	13	Stefan Johansson	710,613
4	Michael Andretti	1,135,063	9	Teo Fabi	875,813	14	Mauricio Gugelmin	694,563
5	Jacques Villeneuve	1,101,463	10	Nigel Mansell	866,562	15	Adrian Fernandez	676,112

Formula One Results

Winners of Formula One Grand Prix races from Mar. 27, through Sept. 25, 1994. See "Updates" for later results.

1994 SEASON (through Oct. 9)

Date	Grand Prix	Location	Winner (Pos)	Time	Avg. mpg	Pole	Qual.mph
Mar. 27	Brazilian	São Paulo	M. Schumacher (1)	1:35:38.759	119.677	A. Senna	127.366
Apr. 17	Pacific	Aida	M. Schumacher (10)	1:46:01.693	108.075†	A. Senna	117.978†
May 1	San Marino	Imola	M. Schumacher (20)	1:28:28.642	122.88	A. Senna*	138.256†
May 15	Monaco	Monte Carlo	M. Schumacher (1)	1:49:55.372	88.824	M. Schumacher	94.811†
May 29	Spanish	Barcelona	Damon Hill (2)	1:36:14.374	118.768	M. Schumacher	129.646
June 12	Canadian	Montreal	M. Schumacher (1)	1:44:31.887	109.27	M. Schumacher	115.512
July 3	French	Magny-Cours	M. Schumacher (3)	1:38:35.704	115.711	D. Hill	124.633
July 10	British	Silverstone	Damon Hill (1)	1:30:03.640	126.339	D. Hill	133.151
July 31	German	Hockenheim	Gerhard Berger (1)	1:22:37.272	138.241	G. Berger	147.352
Aug. 14	Hungarian	Hungaroring	M. Schumacher (1)	1:48:00.185	105.237	M. Schumacher	113.425
Aug. 28	Belgian	Spa-Francorchamps	Damon Hill (3)	1:28:47.170	129.379	R. Barrichello	110.944
Sept. 11	Italian	Monza	Damon Hill (3)	1:18:02.754	154.169	J. Alesi	154.747
Sept. 25	Portuguese	Estoril	Damon Hill (2)	1:43:10.165	114.080	G. Berger	120.997

†Track record. *Senna was killed May 1 in a crash at the San Marino Grand Prix.
Winning Constructors: BENETTON-FORD (7)—Schumacher (7); WILLIAMS-RENAULT (5)—Hill (5); FERRARI (1)—Berger.
Remaining Races (3): European GP at Jerez, Spain (Oct. 16); Japanese GP at Suzuka (Nov. 6); Australian GP at Adelaide (Nov. 13).

1994 Race Locations

March—BRAZILIAN GP at Interlagos in São Paulo. **April**—PACIFIC GP at TI Circuit in Aida, Japan. **May**—SAN MARINO GP at Imola, Italy; MONACO GP at Monte Carlo; SPANISH GP at Barcelona. **June**—CANADIAN GP at Circuit Gilles Villenueve in Montreal. **July**—FRENCH GP at Magny-Cours; BRITISH GP at Silverstone in Towcester; GERMAN GP at Hockenheimring in Hockenheim. **August**—HUNGARIAN GP at Hungaroring in Budapest; BELGIAN GP at Spa-Francorchamps. **September**—ITALIAN GP at Monza in Milan; PORTUGUESE GP at Estoril. **October**—European GP at Jerez. **November**—JAPANESE GP at Suzuka; AUSTRALIAN GP at Adelaide.

Formula One Results (Cont.)

Formula One Point Standings

Official Top 10 Formula One World Championship point leaders for 1993 and unofficial Top 15 point leaders for 1994 (through Oct. 9). Points awarded for places 1 through 6 only (i.e., 10-6-4-3-2-1). Listed are starts (Sts), Top 6 finishes, poles won (PW) and points (Pts).

Note: Formula One does not keep Money Leader standings.

FINAL 1993

	Sts	Finishes 1-2-3-4-5-6	PW	Pts
1 Alain Prost	16	7-3-2-1-0-0	13	99
2 Ayrton Senna	16	5-2-0-3-1-0	1	73
3 Damon Hill	16	3-4-3-1-0-0	2	69
4 Michael Schumacher	16	1-5-3-0-0-0	0	52
5 Ricardo Patrese	16	0-1-1-1-3-1	0	20
6 Jean Alesi	16	0-1-1-2-0-0	0	16
7 Martin Brundle	16	0-0-1-0-3-3	0	13
8 Gerhard Berger	16	0-0-1-1-1-3	0	12
9 Johnny Herbert	16	0-0-0-3-1-0	0	11
10 Mark Blundell	16	0-0-2-0-1-0	0	10

1994 SEASON (thru Sept. 25)

	Sts	Finishes 1-2-3-4-5-6	PW	Pts
1 Michael Schumacher	11	7-1-0-0-0-0	4	76
2 Damon Hill	13	5-4-0-0-0-1	2	75
3 Gerhard Berger	13	1-2-2-1-0-0	2	33
4 Mika Hakkinen	13	0-1-4-0-0-0	0	22
5 Jean Alesi	13	0-1-2-1-1-0	1	19
6 Rubens Barrichello	13	0-0-1-4-0-0	1	16
7 David Coulthard	13	0-1-0-1-2-1	0	14
8 Martin Brundle	13	0-0-1-1-1-1	0	12
9 Jos Verstappen	13	0-0-2-0-1-0	0	10
10 Mark Blundell	13	0-0-1-0-2-0	0	8

Other poles (3): Ayrton Senna (3). Senna was killed May 1 in a crash at the San Marino Grand Prix in Imola, Italy.

Top 5 + Pole Finishing Order

1994 SEASON (through Sept. 26)

No.	Event	Winner	2nd	3rd	4th	5th	Pole
1	Brazil	M. Schumacher	D. Hill	J. Alesi	R.Barrichello	V. Katayama	A. Senna
2	Pacific	M. Schumacher	G. Berger	R.Barrichello	C. Fittipaldi	H .H. Frentzen	A. Senna
3	S.Marino	M. Schumacher	N. Larini	M. Hakkinen	K. Wendlinger	V. Katayama	A. Senna
4	Monaco	M. Schumacher	M. Brundle	G. Berger	A. de Cesaris	J. Alesi	M.Schumacher
5	Spain	D. Hill	M. Schumacher	M. Blundell	J. Alesi	P.L. Martini	M.Schumacher
6	Canada	M. Schumacher	D. Hill	J. Alesi	G. Berger	D. Coulthard	M.Schumacher
7	France	M. Schumacher	D. Hill	G. Berger	H.H. Frentzen	P.L. Martini	D. HIll
8	Britain	D. Hill	J. Alesi	M. Hakkinen	R. Barrichello	D. Coulthard	D. Hill
9	Germany	G. Berger	O. Panis	E. Bernard	C. Fittipaldi	G. Morbidelli	G. Berger
10	Hungary	M. Schumacher	D. Hill	J. Verstappen	M. Brundle	M. Blundell	M.Schumacher
11	Belgium	D. Hill	M. Hakkinen	J. Verstappen	D. Coulthard	M. Blundell	R. Barrichello
12	Italy	D. Hill	G. Berger	M. Hakkinen	R. Barrichello	M. Brundle	J. Alesi
13	Portugal	D. Hill	D. Coulthard	M. Hakkinen	R. Barrichello	J. Verstappen	G. Berger

1994 ENDURANCE RACES

24 Hours of Daytona

Feb. 5-6, at Daytona Beach, Fla.

Officially the Rolex 24 Hours of Daytona and first held in 1962 (as a 3-hour race). An IMSA Camel GT race for exotic prototype sports cars and contested over a 3.56-mile road course at Daytona International Speedway. Listed are drivers, home countries, chassis, and laps completed.

1 Paul Gentilozzi (USA), Scott Pruett (USA), Butch Leitzinger (USA), Steve Millen (USA); Nissan 300 ZXT, 707 laps (2,516.92 miles at 104.80 mph).

2 Dominique Dupuy (F), Jesus Pareja (E), Jack Leconte (F), Jugern Barth (D), Bob Wollek (F); Porsche 911T; 683 laps.

3 Dirk Ebeling (D), Karl Wlazik (D), Ulrich Richter (D), Gunter Doebler (D); Porsche 911 RSR; 671 laps.

4 Mark Sandbridge (USA), Haorl Grohs (D), Bernd Maylaender (D), Frank Katthoefer (D); Porsche 911 RSR; 670 laps.

5 Irv Hoert (US), Tommy Riggins (USA), R.K. Smith (USA), Price Cobb (USA); Olds Cutlass; 665 laps.

Fastest lap: John Morton (USA); Nissan 200 ZX T; 1:51.829 (114.603 mph).

24 Hours of Le Mans

June 18-19, at LeMans, France

Officially the Le Mans Grand Prix d'Endurance and first held in 1923. Contested over the 8.451-mile circuit in Le Mans, France. Listed are drivers, countries, car, and laps completed.

1 Hurley Haywood (I), Mauro Baldi (I), Yannick Dalmas (F); Dauer Porsche 962LM ; 344 laps (2,907.64 miles at 121.4 mph).

2 Mauro Martini (I), Jeff Krosnoff (USA), Eddie Irvine(GB); Nippondenso Toyota; 343 laps.

3 Hans Stuck (D), Danny Sullivan (USA) Thierry Boutsen (BEL); Dauer Porsche 962LM; 343 laps.

4 Georges Fouche (ZA), Steve Andskar (S), Lionel Rovert (FR); Nisso Toyota; 328 laps.

5 Steve Millen (USA), Johnny O'Connell (USA), John Morton (USA); Nissan 300ZX; 317 laps.

Fastest lap: Thierry Boutsen (BEL); Dauer Porsche 962LM; 3:52.54 (130.83 mph).

THE 1995 INFORMATION PLEASE SPORTS ALMANAC

AUTO RACING
STATISTICS
THROUGH THE YEARS
1911-1994
MAJOR RACES • LEADERS

SEC B
PAGE 815

NASCAR Circuit
The Crown Jewels

The four biggest races on the NASCAR circuit are the Daytona 500, the Winston Select 500, the Coca-Cola 600 and the Mountain Dew Southern 500. The Winston Cup Media Guide lists them as the richest (Daytona), the fastest (Winston), the longest (Coca-Cola) and the oldest (Southern). Winston has offered a $1 million bonus since 1985 to any driver who can win three of the four races. The only drivers to win three of the races in a single year are Lee Roy Yarbrough (1969), David Pearson (1976) and Bill Elliott (1985).

Daytona 500

Held early in the NASCAR season; 200 laps around a 2.5-mile high-banked oval at Daytona International Speedway in Daytona Beach, FL. First race in 1959, although stock car racing at Daytona dates back to 1936. Winning drivers who started from pole positions are in **bold** type.

   Multiple winners: Richard Petty (7); Cale Yarborough (4); Bobby Allison (3); Bill Elliott (2).
   Multiple poles: Buddy Baker and Cale Yarborough (4); Bill Elliott, Fireball Roberts and Ken Schrader (3); Donnie Allison (2).

Year	Winner	Car	Owner	MPH	Pole Sitter	MPH
1959	Lee Petty	Oldsmobile	Petty Enterprises	135.521	Bob Welborn	140.121
1960	Junior Johnson	Chevrolet	Ray Fox	124.740	Cotton Owens	149.892
1961	Marvin Panch	Pontiac	Smokey Yunick	149.601	Fireball Roberts	155.709
1962	**Fireball Roberts**	Pontiac	Smokey Yunick	152.529	Fireball Roberts	156.999
1963	Tiny Lund	Ford	Wood Brothers	151.566	Fireball Roberts	160.943
1964	Richard Petty	Plymouth	Petty Enterprises	154.344	Paul Goldsmith	174.910
1965-a	Fred Lorenzen	Ford	Holman-Moody	141.539	Darel Dieringer	171.151
1966-b	**Richard Petty**	Plymouth	Petty Enterprises	160.627	Richard Petty	175.165
1967	Mario Andretti	Ford	Holman-Moody	149.926	Curtis Turner	180.831
1968	**Cale Yarborough**	Mercury	Wood Brothers	143.251	Cale Yarborough	189.222
1969	Lee Roy Yarbrough	Ford	Junior Johnson	157.950	Buddy Baker	188.901
1970	Pete Hamilton	Plymouth	Petty Enterprises	149.601	Cale Yarborough	194.015
1971	Richard Petty	Plymouth	Petty Enterprises	144.462	A.J. Foyt	182.744
1972	A.J. Foyt	Mercury	Wood Brothers	161.550	Bobby Issac	186.632
1973	Richard Petty	Dodge	Petty Enterprises	157.205	Buddy Baker	185.662
1974-c	Richard Petty	Dodge	Petty Enterprises	140.894	David Pearson	185.017
1975	Benny Parsons	Chevrolet	L.G. DeWitt	153.649	Donnie Allison	185.827
1976	David Pearson	Mercury	Wood Brothers	152.181	Ramo Stott	183.456
1977	Cale Yarborough	Chevrolet	Junior Johnson	153.218	Donnie Allison	188.048
1978	Bobby Allison	Ford	Bud Moore	159.730	Cale Yarborough	187.536
1979	Richard Petty	Oldsmobile	Petty Enterprises	143.977	Buddy Baker	196.049
1980	**Buddy Baker**	Oldsmobile	Ranier Racing	177.602*	Buddy Baker	194.009
1981	Richard Petty	Buick	Petty Enterprises	169.651	Bobby Allison	194.624
1982	Bobby Allison	Buick	DiGard Racing	153.991	Benny Parsons	196.317
1983	Cale Yarborough	Pontiac	Ranier Racing	155.979	Ricky Rudd	198.864
1984	**Cale Yarborough**	Chevrolet	Ranier Racing	150.994	Cale Yarborough	201.848
1985	**Bill Elliott**	Ford	Melling Racing	172.265	Bill Elliott	205.114
1986	Geoff Bodine	Chevrolet	Hendrick Motorsports	148.124	Bill Elliott	205.039
1987	**Bill Elliott**	Ford	Melling Racing	176.263	Bill Elliott	210.364†
1988	Bobby Allison	Buick	Stavola Brothers	137.531	Ken Schrader	198.823
1989	Darrell Waltrip	Chevrolet	Hendrick Motorsports	148.466	Ken Schrader	196.996
1990	Derrike Cope	Chevrolet	Bob Whitcomb	165.761	Ken Schrader	196.515
1991	Ernie Irvan	Chevrolet	Morgan-McClure	148.148	Davey Allison	195.955
1992	Davey Allison	Ford	Robert Yates	160.256	Sterling Martin	192.213
1993	Dale Jarrett	Chevrolet	Joe Gibbs Racing	154.972	Kyle Petty	189.426
1994	Sterling Marlin	Chevrolet	Morgan-McClure	156.931	Loy Allen	190.158

*Track and race record for Winning Time.   †Track and race record for Qualifying Time.
Notes: a—rain shortened 1965 to 332+ miles; **b**—rain shortened 1966 race to 495 miles; **c**—in 1974, race shortened 50 miles due to energy crisis. **Also:** Pole sitters determined by pole qualifying race (1959-65); by two-lap average (1966-68); by fastest single lap (since 1969).

NASCAR Circuit (Cont.)

Winston Select 500

Held at Talladega (Ala.) Superspeedway. **Multiple winners:** Bobby Allison, Davey Allison, Buddy Baker and David Pearson (3); Dale Earnhardt, Darrell Waltrip and Cale Yarborough (2).

Year		Year		Year		Year	
1970	Pete Hamilton	1977	Darrell Waltrip	1983	Richard Petty	1990	Dale Earnhardt
1971	Donnie Allison	1978	Cale Yarborough	1984	Cale Yarborough	1991	Harry Gant
1972	David Pearson	1979	Bobby Allison	1985	Bill Elliott	1992	Davey Allison
1973	David Pearson	1980	Buddy Baker	1986	Bobby Allison	1993	Ernie Irvan
1974	David Pearson	1981	Bobby Allison	1987	Davey Allison	1994	Dale Earnhardt
1975	Buddy Baker	1982	Darrell Waltrip	1988	Phil Parsons		
1976	Buddy Baker			1989	Davey Allison		

Coca-Cola 600

Held at Charlotte (N.C.) Motor Speedway. **Multiple winners:** Darrell Waltrip (5); Bobby Allison, Buddy Baker, Dale Earnhardt and David Pearson (3); Neil Bonnett, Fred Lorenzen, Jim Paschal and Richard Petty (2).

Year		Year		Year		Year	
1960	Joe Lee Johnson	1969	Lee Roy Yarbrough	1978	Darrell Waltrip	1987	Kyle Petty
1961	David Pearson	1970	Donnie Allison	1979	Darrell Waltrip	1988	Darrell Waltrip
1962	Nelson Stacy	1971	Bobby Allison	1980	Benny Parsons	1989	Darrell Waltrip
1963	Fred Lorenzen	1972	Buddy Baker	1981	Bobby Allison	1990	Rusty Wallace
1964	Jim Paschal	1973	Buddy Baker	1982	Neil Bonnett	1991	Davey Allison
1965	Fred Lorenzen	1974	David Pearson	1983	Neil Bonnett	1992	Dale Earnhardt
1966	Marvin Panch	1975	Richard Petty	1984	Bobby Allison	1993	Dale Earnhardt
1967	Jim Paschal	1976	David Pearson	1985	Darrell Waltrip	1994	Jeff Gordon
1968	Buddy Baker	1977	Richard Petty	1986	Dale Earnhardt		

Southern 500

Held at Darlington (S.C.) International Raceway. **Multiple winners:** Cale Yarborough (5); Bobby Allison (4); Buck Baker, Dale Earnhardt, Bill Elliott, David Pearson and Herb Thomas (3); Harry Gant and Fireball Roberts (2).

Year		Year		Year		Year	
1950	Johnny Mantz	1962	Larry Frank	1973	Cale Yarborough	1984	Harry Gant
1951	Herb Thomas	1963	Fireball Roberts	1974	Cale Yarborough	1985	Bill Elliott
1952	Fonty Flock	1964	Buck Baker	1975	Bobby Allison	1986	Tim Richmond
1953	Buck Baker	1965	Ned Jarrett	1976	David Pearson	1987	Dale Earnhardt
1954	Herb Thomas	1966	Darel Dieringer	1977	David Pearson	1988	Bill Elliott
1955	Herb Thomas	1967	Richard Petty	1978	Cale Yarborough	1989	Dale Earnhardt
1956	Curtis Turner	1968	Cale Yarborough	1979	David Pearson	1990	Dale Earnhardt
1957	Speedy Thompson	1969	Lee Roy Yarbrough	1980	Terry Labonte	1991	Harry Gant
1958	Fireball Roberts	1970	Buddy Baker	1981	Neil Bonnett	1992	Darrell Waltrip
1959	Jim Reed	1971	Bobby Allison	1982	Cale Yarborough	1993	Mark Martin
1960	Buck Baker	1972	Bobby Allison	1983	Bobby Allison	1994	Bill Elliott
1961	Nelson Stacy						

All-Time Leaders

NASCAR's all-time Top 20 drivers in victories, pole positions and earnings, based on records through 1993. Drivers active in 1994 are in **bold** type.

Victories

1	Richard Petty	200
2	David Pearson	105
3	Bobby Allison	84
	Darrell Waltrip	84
5	Cale Yarborough	83
6	**Dale Earnhardt**	59
7	Lee Petty	54
8	Ned Jarrett	50
	Junior Johnson	50
10	Herb Thomas	48
11	Buck Baker	46
12	Tim Flock	40
13	**Bill Elliott**	39
14	Bobby Isaac	37
15	Fireball Roberts	34
16	**Rusty Wallace**	31
17	Red White	28
18	Fred Lorenzen	26
19	Jim Paschal	25
20	Joe Weatherly	24

Pole Positions

1	Richard Petty	127
2	David Pearson	113
3	Cale Yarborough	70
4	**Darrell Waltrip**	58
5	Bobby Allison	57
6	Bobby Isaac	51
7	Junior Johnson	47
8	**Bill Elliott**	45
9	Buck Baker	44
10	Buddy Baker	40
11	Herb Thomas	38
12	Tim Flock	37
	Fireball Roberts	37
14	Ned Jarrett	36
	Rex White	36
16	Fred Lorenzen	33
17	Fonty Flock	30
	Geoff Bodine	30
19	Marvin Panch	25
20	Alan Kulwicki	24
	Jack Smith	24

Earnings

1	**Dale Earnhardt**	$19,513,571
2	**Bill Elliott**	13,606,884
3	**Darrell Waltrip**	12,753,279
4	**Rusty Wallace**	9,197,811
5	**Harry Gant**	7,882,084
6	**Terry Labonte**	7,770,175
7	Richard Petty	7,755,409
8	**Ricky Rudd**	7,641,170
9	**Geoff Bodine**	7,125,572
10	Bobby Allison	7,102,233
11	Davey Allison	6,726,974
12	**Mark Martin**	6,508,387
13	**Kyle Petty**	5,682,492
14	**Ken Schrader**	5,645,555
15	Alan Kulwicki	5,061,202
16	Cale Yarborough	5,003,716
17	**Morgan Shepherd**	4,626,778
18	**Ernie Irvan**	4,287,599
19	**Dave Marcis**	4,015,779
20	**Sterling Marlin**	3,971,047

Wide World Photos

Richard Petty, who retired in 1992 as NASCAR's all-time leader in victories (200) and pole positions (127), was Rookie of the Year in 1959 and a seven-time Winston Cup champion.

Winston Cup Champions

Originally the Grand National Championship, 1949-70, and based on official NASCAR (National Association for Stock Car Auto Racing) records.

Multiple winners: Richard Petty (7); Dale Earnhardt (6); David Pearson, Lee Petty, Darrell Waltrip and Cale Yarborough (3); Buck Baker, Tim Flock, Ned Jarrett, Herb Thomas and Joe Weatherly (2).

Year		Year		Year		Year	
1949	Red Byron	1960	Rex White	1972	Richard Petty	1984	Terry Labonte
		1961	Ned Jarrett	1973	Benny Parsons	1985	Darrell Waltrip
1950	Bill Rexford	1962	Joe Weatherly	1974	Richard Petty	1986	Dale Earnhardt
1951	Herb Thomas	1963	Joe Weatherly	1975	Richard Petty	1987	Dale Earnhardt
1952	Tim Flock	1964	Richard Petty	1976	Cale Yarborough	1988	Bill Elliott
1953	Herb Thomas	1965	Ned Jarrett	1977	Cale Yarborough	1989	Rusty Wallace
1954	Lee Petty	1966	David Pearson	1978	Cale Yarborough		
1955	Tim Flock	1967	Richard Petty	1979	Richard Petty	1990	Dale Earnhardt
1956	Buck Baker	1968	David Pearson			1991	Dale Earnhardt
1957	Buck Baker	1969	David Pearson	1980	Dale Earnhardt	1992	Alan Kulwicki
1958	Lee Petty			1981	Darrell Waltrip	1993	Dale Earnhardt
1959	Lee Petty	1970	Bobby Issac	1982	Darrell Waltrip		
		1971	Richard Petty	1983	Bobby Allison		

NASCAR Rookie of the Year

Award presented to rookie driver who accumulates the most Winston Cup points based on his best 15 finishes.

Year		Year		Year		Year	
1958	Shorty Rollins	1967	Donnie Allison	1976	Skip Manning	1985	Ken Schrader
1959	Richard Petty	1968	Pete Hamilton	1977	Ricky Rudd	1986	Alan Kulwicki
		1969	Dick Brooks	1978	Ronnie Thomas	1987	Davey Allison
1960	David Pearson			1979	Dale Earnhardt	1988	Ken Bouchard
1961	Woodie Wilson	1970	Bill Dennis			1989	Dick Trickle
1962	Tom Cox	1971	Walter Ballard	1980	Jody Ridley		
1963	Billy Wade	1972	Larry Smith	1981	Ron Bouchard	1990	Rob Moroso
1964	Doug Cooper	1973	Lennie Pond	1982	Geoff Bodine	1991	Bobby Hamilton
1965	Sam McQuagg	1974	Earl Ross	1983	Sterling Marlin	1992	Jimmy Hensley
1966	James Hylton	1975	Bruce Hill	1984	Rusty Wallace	1993	Jeff Gordon

IndyCar Circuit

Indianapolis 500

Held every Memorial Day weekend; 200 laps around a 2.5-mile oval at Indianapolis Motor Speedway. First race was held in 1911. Winning drivers are listed with starting positions. Winners who started from pole position are in **bold** type.

Multiple wins: A.J.Foyt, Rick Mears and Al Unser (4); Louis Meyer, Mauri Rose, Johnny Rutherford, Wilbur Shaw and Bobby Unser (3); Gordon Johncock, Tommy Milton, Bill Vukovich and Rodger Ward (2).

Multiple poles: Rick Mears (6); Mario Andretti, A.J.Foyt and Tom Sneva (4); Rex Mays (3); Billy Arnold, Ralph DePalma, Walt Faulkner, Parnelli Jones, Jack McGrath, Jimmy Murphy, Duke Nalon, Johnny Rutherford and Jimmy Snyder (2).

Year	Winner (Pos.)	Car	MPH	Pole Sitter	MPH
1911	Ray Harroun (28)	Marmon Wasp	74.602	Lewis Strang	—
1912	Joe Dawson (7)	National	78.719	Gil Anderson	—
1913	Jules Goux (7)	Peugeot	75.933	Caleb Bragg	—
1914	Rene Thomas (15)	Delage	82.474	Jean Chassagne	—
1915	Ralph DePalma (2)	Mercedes	89.840	Howard Wilcox	98.90
1916-a	Dario Resta (4)	Peugeot	84.001	John Aitken	96.69
1917-18	Not held				
1919	Howdy Wilcox (2)	Peugeot	88.050	Rene Thomas	104.78
1920	Gaston Chevrolet (6)	Monroe	88.618	Ralph DePalma	99.15
1921	Tommy Milton (20)	Frontenac	89.621	Ralph DePalma	100.75
1922	**Jimmy Murphy** (1)	Murphy Special	94.484	Jimmy Murphy	100.50
1923	**Tommy Milton** (1)	H.C.S. Special	90.954	Tommy Milton	108.17
1924	L.L. Corum & Joe Boyer (21)	Duesenberg Special	98.234	Jimmy Murphy	108.037
1925	Peter DePaolo (2)	Duesenberg Special	101.127	Leon Duray	113.196
1926-b	Frank Lockhart (20)	Miller Special	95.904	Earl Cooper	111.735
1927	George Souders (22)	Duesenberg	97.545	Frank Lockhart	120.100
1928	Louie Meyer (13)	Miller Special	99.482	Leon Duray	122.391
1929	Ray Keech (6)	Simplex Piston Ring Special	97.585	Cliff Woodbury	120.599
1930	**Billy Arnold** (1)	Miller-Hartz Special	100.448	Billy Arnold	113.268
1931	Louis Schneider (13)	Bowes Seal Fast Special	96.629	Russ Snowberger	112.796
1932	Fred Frame (27)	Miller-Hartz Special	104.144	Lou Moore	117.363
1933	Louie Meyer (6)	Tydol Special	104.162	Bill Cummings	118.530
1934	Bill Cummings (10)	Boyle Products Special	104.863	Kelly Petillo	119.329
1935	Kelly Petillo (22)	Gilmore Speedway Special	106.240	Rex Mays	120.736
1936	Louie Meyer (28)	Ring Free Special	109.069	Rex Mays	119.644
1937	Wilbur Shaw (2)	Shaw-Gilmore Special	113.580	Bill Cummings	123.343
1938	**Floyd Roberts** (1)	Burd Piston Ring Special	117.200	Floyd Roberts	125.681
1939	Wilbur Shaw (3)	Boyle Special	115.035	Jimmy Snyder	130.138
1940	Wilbur Shaw (2)	Boyle Special	114.277	Rex Mays	127.850
1941	Floyd Davis & Mauri Rose (17)	Noc-Out Hose Clamp Special	115.117	Mauri Rose	128.691
1942-45	Not held				
1946	George Robson (15)	Thorne Engineering Special	114.820	Cliff Bergere	126.471
1947	Mauri Rose (3)	Blue Crown Spark Plug Special	116.338	Ted Horn	126.564
1948	Mauri Rose (3)	Blue Crown Spark Plug Special	119.814	Duke Nalon	131.603
1949	Bill Holland (4)	Blue Crown Spark Plug Special	121.327	Duke Nalon	132.939
1950-c	Johnnie Parsons (5)	Wynn's Friction Proofing	124.002	Walt Faulkner	134.343
1951	Lee Wallard (2)	Belanger Special	126.244	Duke Nalon	136.498
1952	Troy Ruttman (7)	Agajanian Special	128.922	Fred Agabashian	138.010
1953	**Bill Vukovich** (1)	Fuel Injection Special	128.740	Bill Vukovich	138.392
1954	Bill Vukovich (19)	Fuel Injection Special	130.840	Jack McGrath	141.033
1955	Bob Sweikert (14)	John Zink Special	128.213	Jerry Hoyt	140.045
1956	**Pat Flaherty** (1)	John Zink Special	128.490	Pat Flaherty	145.596
1957	Sam Hanks (13)	Belond Exhaust Special	135.601	Pat O'Connor	143.948
1958	Jimmy Bryan (7)	Belond AP Parts Special	133.791	Dick Rathmann	145.974
1959	Rodger Ward (6)	Leader Card 500 Roadster	135.857	Johnny Thomson	145.908
1960	Jim Rathmann (2)	Ken-Paul Special	138.767	Eddie Sachs	146.592
1961	A.J. Foyt (7)	Bowes Seal Fast Special	139.130	Eddie Sachs	147.481
1962	Rodger Ward (2)	Leader Card 500 Roadster	140.293	Parnelli Jones	150.370
1963	**Parnelli Jones** (1)	Agajanian-Willard Special	143.137	Parnelli Jones	151.153
1964	A.J. Foyt (5)	Sheraton-Thompson Special	147.350	Jim Clark	158.828
1965	Jim Clark (2)	Lotus Ford	150.686	A.J. Foyt	161.233

Year	Winner (Pos.)	Car	MPH	Pole Sitter	MPH
1966	Graham Hill (15)	American Red Ball Special	144.317	Mario Andretti	165.899
1967-d	A.J. Foyt (4)	Sheraton-Thompson Special	151.207	Mario Andretti	168.982
1968	Bobby Unser (3)	Rislone Special	152.882	Joe Leonard	171.559
1969	Mario Andretti (2)	STP Oil Treatment Special	156.867	A.J. Foyt	170.568
1970	**Al Unser** (1)	Johnny Lightning 500 Spl.	155.749	Al Unser	170.221
1971	Al Unser (5)	Johnny Lightning Special	157.735	Peter Revson	178.696
1972	Mark Donohue (3)	Sunoco McLaren	162.962	Bobby Unser	195.940
1973-e	Gordon Johncock (11)	STP Double Oil Filters	159.036	Johnny Rutherford	198.413
1974	Johnny Rutherford (25)	McLaren	158.589	A.J. Foyt	191.632
1975-f	Bobby Unser (3)	Jorgensen Eagle	149.213	A.J. Foyt	193.976
1976-g	**Johnny Rutherford** (1)	Hy-Gain McLaren/Goodyear	148.725	Johnny Rutherford	188.957
1977	A.J. Foyt (4)	Gilmore Racing Team	161.331	Tom Sneva	198.884
1978	Al Unser (5)	FNCTC Chaparral Lola	161.363	Tom Sneva	202.156
1979	**Rick Mears** (1)	The Gould Charge	158.899	Rick Mears	193.736
1980	**Johnny Rutherford** (1)	Pennzoil Chaparral	142.862	Johnny Rutherford	192.256
1981-h	**Bobby Unser** (1)	Norton Spirit Penske PC-9B	139.084	Bobby Unser	200.546
1982	Gordon Johncock (5)	STP Oil Treatment	162.029	Rick Mears	207.004
1983	Tom Sneva (4)	Texaco Star	162.117	Teo Fabi	207.395
1984	Rick Mears (3)	Pennzoil Z-7	163.612	Tom Sneva	210.029
1985	Danny Sullivan (8)	Miller American Special	152.982	Pancho Carter	212.583
1986	Bobby Rahal (4)	Budweiser/Truesports/March	170.722	Rick Mears	216.828
1987	Al Unser (20)	Cummins Holset Turbo	162.175	Mario Andretti	215.390
1988	**Rick Mears** (1)	Pennzoil Z-7/Penske Chevy V-8	149.809	Rick Mears	219.198
1989	Emerson Fittipaldi (3)	Marlboro/Penske Chevy V-8	167.581	Rick Mears	223.885
1990	Arie Luyendyk (3)	Domino's Pizza Chevrolet	185.981*	Emerson Fittipaldi	225.301
1991	**Rick Mears** (1)	Marlboro Penske Chevy	176.457	Rick Mears	224.113
1992	Al Unser Jr. (12)	Valvoline Galmer '92	134.477	Roberto Guerrero	232.482†
1993	Emerson Fittipaldi (9)	Marlboro Penske Chevy	157.207	Arie Luyendyk	223.967
1994	**Al Unser Jr.** (1)	Marlboro Penske Mercedes	160.872	Al Unser Jr.	228.011

*Track record for Winning Time. †Track record for Qualifying Time.
Notes: a—1916 race scheduled for 300 miles; **b**—rain shortened 1926 race to 400 miles; **c**—rain shortened 1950 race to 345 miles; **d**—1967 race postponed due to rain after 18 laps (May 30), resumed next day (May 31); **e**—rain shortened 1973 race to 332.5 miles; **f**—rain shortened 1975 race to 435 miles; **g**—rain shortened 1976 race to 255 miles; **h**—in 1981, runner-up Mario Andretti was awarded 1st place when winner Bobby Unser was penalized a lap after the race was completed for passing cars illegally under the caution flag. Unser and car-owner Roger Penske appealed the race stewards' decision to the U.S. Auto Club. Four months later, USAC overturned the ruling, saying that the penalty was too harsh and Unser should be fined $40,000 rather than stripped of his championship.

Indy 500 Rookie of the Year

Voted on by a panel of auto racing media. Award does not necessarily go to highest-finishing first-year driver. Graham Hill won the race on his first try in 1966, but the rookie award went to Jackie Stewart, who led with 10 laps to go only to lose oil pressure and finish 6th.

Father and son winners: Mario and Michael Andretti (1965 and 1984); Bill and Billy Vukovich (1968 and 1988).

Year		Year		Year		Year	
1952	Art Cross	1963	Jim Clark	1975	Bill Puterbaugh	1985	Arie Luyendyk
1953	Jimmy Daywalt	1964	Johnny White	1976	Vern Schuppan	1986	Randy Lanier
1954	Larry Crockett	1965	Mario Andretti	1977	Jerry Sneva	1987	Fabrizio Barbazza
1955	Al Herman	1966	Jackie Stewart	1978	Rick Mears	1988	Billy Vukovich III
1956	Bob Veith	1967	Denis Hulme		& Larry Rice	1989	Bernard Jourdain
1957	Don Edmunds	1968	Bill Vukovich	1979	Howdy Holmes		& Scott Pruett
1958	George Amick	1969	Mark Donohue				
1959	Bobby Grim	1970	Donnie Allison	1980	Tim Richmond	1990	Eddie Cheever
		1971	Denny Zimmerman	1981	Josele Garza	1991	Jeff Andretti
1960	Jim Hurtubise	1972	Mike Hiss	1982	Jim Hickman	1992	Lyn St. James
1961	Parnelli Jones	1973	Graham McRae	1983	Teo Fabi	1993	Nigel Mansell
	& Bobby Marshman	1974	Pancho Carter	1984	Michael Andretti	1994	Jacques Villeneuve
1962	Jimmy McElreath				& Roberto Guerrero		

CART/IndyCar Rookie of the Year

Award presented to rookie who accumulates the most PPG Cup points among first year drivers. Originally the CART Rookie of the Year; CART was renamed IndyCar in 1992.

Year		Year		Year		Year	
1979	Bill Alsup	1983	Teo Fabi	1987	Fabrizio Barbazza	1991	Jeff Andretti
1980	Dennis Firestone	1984	Roberto Guerrero	1988	John Jones	1992	Stefan Johansson
1981	Bob Lazier	1985	Arie Luyendyk	1989	Bernard Jourdain	1993	Nigel Mansell
1982	Bobby Rahal	1986	Dominic Dobson	1990	Eddie Cheever	1994	Jacques Villeneuve

Wide World Photos	Wide World Photos	Wide World Photos	Wide World Photos
A. J. Foyt	**Bobby Unser**	**Al Unser**	**Mario Andretti**

All-Time Leaders

IndyCar's all-time Top 20 drivers in victories, pole positions and earnings, based on records through 1993. Drivers active in 1994 are in **bold** type.

Victories

1 A.J. Foyt 67
2 **Mario Andretti** 52
3 **Al Unser** 39
4 Bobby Unser 35
5 Rick Mears............................29
6 **Michael Andretti** 27
  Johnny Rutherford...............27
8 Rodger Ward.........................26
9 Gordon Johncock 25
10 Ralph DePalma......................24
  Bobby Rahal......................24
12 Tommy Milton........................23
13 Tony Bettenhausen 21
  Earl Cooper 21
15 **Emerson Fittipaldi**............20
16 Jimmy Bryan 19
  Jimmy Murphy 19
  Al Unser, Jr 19
19 Ralph Mulford 17
  Danny Sullivan.......................17

Pole Positions

1 **Mario Andretti** 67
2 A.J. Foyt 53
3 Bobby Unser 49
4 Rick Mears............................40
5 **Michael Andretti** 27
  Al Unser 27
7 Johnny Rutherford...............23
8 Gordon Johncock 20
9 Rex Mays...............................19
  Danny Sullivan.......................19
11 **Bobby Rahal**......................18
12 Don Branson 15
  Emerson Fittipaldi............15
14 Tony Bettenhausen 14
  Tom Sneva 14
16 Parnelli Jones........................12
17 Danny Ongais........................11
  Rodger Ward.........................11
19 Dan Gurney 10
  Johnny Thomson....................10

Earnings

1 **Bobby Rahal**.......$12,024,828
2 **Emerson Fittipaldi** 11,668,712
3 **Al Unser, Jr** 11,644,093
4 Rick Mears...............11,050,807
5 **Mario Andretti** 10,887,392
6 **Michael Andretti** 10,197,503
7 Danny Sullivan...........8,254,673
8 **Al Unser** 6,740,843
9 Arie Luyendyk........6,503,359
10 A.J. Foyt 5,357,589
11 Tom Sneva 4,392,993
12 **Raul Boesel**............4,391,972
13 **Scott Brayton**........4,323,599
14 Johnny Rutherford 4,209,232
15 **Roberto Guerrero** 4,131,251
16 **Scott Goodyear**...3,488,236
17 Gordon Johncock 3,431,414
18 **Kevin Cogan**..........3,202,106
19 **Teo Fabi**.................3,115,465
20 **John Andretti** 2,983,624

PPG Cup Champions

Officially the PPG Indy Car World Series Championship since 1979 and based on official AAA (American Automobile Assn., 1909-55), USAC (U.S. Auto Club, 1956-79), and CART (Championship Auto Racing Teams, 1979-91). CART was renamed IndyCar in 1992.

Multiple titles: A.J. Foyt (7); Mario Andretti (4); Jimmy Bryan, Earl Cooper, Ted Horn, Rick Mears, Louie Meyer Bobby Rahal and Al Unser (3); Tony Bettenhausen, Ralph DePalma, Peter DePaolo, Joe Leonard, Rex Mays, Tommy Milton, Jimmy Murphy, Wilbur Shaw, Tom Sneva, Al Unser Jr., Bobby Unser and Rodger Ward (2).

AAA

Year		Year		Year		Year	
1909	George Robertson	1920	Tommy Milton	1931	Louis Schneider	1942-45	No racing
1910	Ray Harroun	1921	Tommy Milton	1932	Bob Carey	1946	Ted Horn
1911	Ralph Mulford	1922	Jimmy Murphy	1933	Louie Meyer	1947	Ted Horn
1912	Ralph DePalma	1923	Eddie Hearne	1934	Bill Cummings	1948	Ted Horn
1913	Earl Cooper	1924	Jimmy Murphy	1935	Kelly Petillo	1949	Johnnie Parsons
1914	Ralph DePalma	1925	Peter DePaolo	1936	Mauri Rose		
1915	Earl Cooper	1926	Harry Hartz	1937	Wilbur Shaw	1950	Henry Banks
1916	Dario Resta	1927	Peter DePaolo	1938	Floyd Roberts	1951	Tony Bettenhausen
1917	Earl Cooper	1928	Louie Meyer	1939	Wilbur Shaw	1952	Chuck Stevenson
1918	Ralph Mulford	1929	Louie Meyer			1953	Sam Hanks
1919	Howard Wilcox	1930	Billy Arnold	1940	Rex Mays	1954	Jimmy Bryan
				1941	Rex Mays	1955	Bob Sweikert

USAC

Year		Year		Year		Year	
1956	Jimmy Bryan	1962	Rodger Ward	1968	Bobby Unser	1974	Bobby Unser
1957	Jimmy Bryan	1963	A.J. Foyt	1969	Mario Andretti	1975	A.J. Foyt
1958	Tony Bettenhausen	1964	A.J. Foyt			1976	Gordon Johncock
1959	Rodger Ward	1965	Mario Andretti	1970	Al Unser	1977	Tom Sneva
		1966	Mario Andretti	1971	Joe Leonard	1978	Tom Sneva
1960	A.J. Foyt	1967	A.J. Foyt	1972	Joe Leonard	1979	A.J. Foyt
1961	A.J. Foyt			1973	Roger McCluskey		

CART/IndyCar

Year		Year		Year		Year	
1979	Rick Mears	1983	Al Unser	1987	Bobby Rahal	1991	Michael Andretti
1980	Johnny Rutherford	1984	Mario Andretti	1988	Danny Sullivan	1992	Bobby Rahal
1981	Rick Mears	1985	Al Unser	1989	Emerson Fittipaldi	1993	Nigel Mansell
1982	Rick Mears	1986	Bobby Rahal	1990	Al Unser Jr.	1994	Al Unser Jr.

Formula One Circuit
United States Grand Prix

There have been 54 official Formula One races held in the United States since 1950, including the Indianapolis 500 from 1950-60. FISA sanctioned two annual U.S. Grand Prix—USA/East and USA/West—from 1976-80 and 1983. Phoenix was the site of the U.S. Grand Prix from 1989-91.

Indianapolis 500

Officially sanctioned as Grand Prix race from 1950-60 only. See page 818 for details.

U.S. Grand Prix—East

Held from 1959-80 and 1981-88 at the following locations: Sebring, Fla. (1959); Riverside, Calif. (1960); Watkins Glen, N.Y. (1961-80); and Detroit (1982-88). There was no race in 1981. Race discontinued in 1989.
Multiple winners: Jim Clark, Graham Hill and Ayrton Senna (3); James Hunt, Carlos Reutemann and Jackie Stewart (2).

Year		Car	Year		Car
1959	Bruce McLaren, NZE	Cooper Climax	1974	Carlos Reutemann, ARG	Brabham Ford
			1975	Niki Lauda, AUT	Ferrari
1960	Stirling Moss, GBR	Lotus Climax	1976	James Hunt, GBR	McLaren Ford
1961	Innes Ireland, GBR	Lotus Climax	1977	James Hunt, GBR	McLaren Ford
1962	Jim Clark, GBR	Lotus Climax	1978	Carlos Reutemann, ARG	Ferrari
1963	Graham Hill, GBR	BRM	1979	Gilles Villeneuve, CAN	Ferrari
1964	Graham Hill, GBR	BRM	1980	Alan Jones, AUS	Williams Ford
1965	Graham Hill, GBR	BRM	1981	Not held	
1966	Jim Clark, GBR	Lotus BRM	1982	John Watson, GBR	McLaren Ford
1967	Jim Clark, GBR	Lotus Ford	1983	Michele Alboreto, ITA	Tyrrell Ford
1968	Jackie Stewart, GBR	Matra Ford	1984	Nelson Piquet, BRA	Brabham BMW Turbo
1969	Jochen Rindt, AUT	Lotus Ford	1985	Keke Rosberg, FIN	Williams Honda Turbo
			1986	Ayrton Senna, BRA	Lotus Renault Turbo
1970	Emerson Fittipaldi, BRA	Lotus Ford	1987	Ayrton Senna, BRA	Lotus Honda Turbo
1971	Francois Cevert, FRA	Tyrrell Ford	1988	Ayrton Senna, BRA	McLaren Honda Turbo
1972	Jackie Stewart, GBR	Tyrrell Ford			
1973	Ronnie Peterson, SWE	Lotus Ford			

U.S. Grand Prix—West

Held from 1976-83 at Long Beach, Calf. Races also held in Las Vegas (1981-82), Dallas (1984) and Phoenix (1989-91). Race discontinued in 1992.
Multiple winners: Ayrton Senna (2) at Phoenix.

Long Beach

Year		Car
1976	Clay Regazzoni, SWI	Ferrari
1977	Mario Andretti, USA	Lotus Ford
1978	Carlos Reutemann, ARG	Ferrari
1979	Gilles Villeneuve, CAN	Ferrari
1980	Nelson Piquet, BRA	Brabham Ford
1981	Alan Jones, AUS	Williams Ford
1982	Niki Lauda, AUT	McLaren Ford
1983	John Watson, GBR	McLaren Ford

Las Vegas

Year		Car
1981	Alan Jones, AUS	Williams Ford
1982	Michele Alboreto, ITA	Tyrrell Ford

Dallas

Year		Car
1984	Keke Rosberg, FIN	Williams Honda Turbo

Phoenix

Year		Car
1989	Alain Prost, FRA	McLaren Honda
1990	Ayrton Senna, BRA	McLaren Honda
1991	Ayrton Senna, BRA	McLaren Honda

Formula One Circuit (Cont.)
All-Time Leaders

The all-time Top 20 Grand Prix winning drivers, based on records through 1993. Listed are starts (Sts), poles won (Pole), wins (1st), second place finishes (2nd), and thirds (3rd). Drivers active in 1994 and career victories are in **bold** type.

	Sts	Pole	1st	2nd	3rd		Sts	Pole	1st	2nd	3rd
1 Alain Prost	199	33	51	35	20	Graham Hill	176	13	**14**	15	7
2 **Ayrton Senna**	158	62	**41**	23	16	13 Alberto Ascari	32	14	**13**	4	0
3 **Nigel Mansell**	181	31	**30**	17	11	14 Mario Andretti	128	18	**12**	2	5
4 Jackie Stewart	99	17	**27**	11	5	Alan Jones	116	6	**12**	7	5
5 Jim Clark	72	33	**25**	1	6	Carlos Reutemann	146	6	**12**	13	20
Niki Lauda	171	24	**25**	20	9	17 James Hunt	92	14	**10**	6	7
7 Juan-Manuel Fangio	51	28	**24**	10	1	Ronnie Peterson	123	14	**10**	10	6
8 Nelson Piquet	204	24	**23**	20	17	Jody Scheckter	112	3	**10**	14	9
9 Stirling Moss	66	16	**16**	5	3	20 **Gerhard Berger**	147	8	**8**	12	12
10 Jack Brabham	126	13	**14**	10	7	Denis Hulme	112	1	**8**	9	16
Emerson Fittipaldi	144	6	**14**	13	8	Jacky Ickx	116	13	**8**	7	10

Note: The following five drivers either died or were killed in their final year of competition—Clark in a Formula Two race in West Germany in 1968; Hill in a plane crash in 1975; Ascari in a private practice run in 1955; Peterson following a crash in the 1978 Italian GP; and Senna following a crash in the 1994 San Marino GP.

World Champions

Officially called the World Championship of Drivers and based on Formula One (Grand Prix) records through the 1993 racing season. **Multiple winners:** Juan-Manuel Fangio (5); Alain Prost (4); Jack Brabham, Niki Lauda, Nelson Piquet, Ayrton Senna and Jackie Stewart (3); Alberto Ascari, Jim Clark, Emerson Fittipaldi and Graham Hill (2).

Year		Car	Year		Car
1950	Guiseppe Farina, ITA	Alfa Romeo	1972	Emerson Fittipaldi, BRA	Lotus Ford
1951	Juan-Manuel Fangio, ARG	Alfa Romeo	1973	Jackie Stewart, GBR	Tyrrell Ford
1952	Alberto Ascari, ITA	Ferrari	1974	Emerson Fittipaldi, BRA	McLaren Ford
1953	Alberto Ascari, ITA	Ferrari	1975	Niki Lauda, AUT	Ferrari
1954	Juan-Manuel Fangio, ARG	Maserati/Mercedes	1976	James Hunt, GBR	McLaren Ford
1955	Juan-Manuel Fangio, ARG	Mercedes	1977	Niki Lauda, AUT	Ferrari
1956	Juan-Manuel Fangio, ARG	Ferrari	1978	Mario Andretti, USA	Lotus Ford
1957	Juan-Manuel Fangio, ARG	Maserati	1979	Jody Scheckter, SAF	Ferrari
1958	Mike Hawthorn, GBR	Ferrari			
1959	Jack Brabham, AUS	Cooper Climax	1980	Alan Jones, AUS	Williams Ford
			1981	Nelson Piquet, BRA	Brabham Ford
1960	Jack Brabham, AUS	Cooper Climax	1982	Keke Rosberg, FIN	Williams Ford
1961	Phil Hill, USA	Ferrari	1983	Nelson Piquet, BRA	Brabham BMW Turbo
1962	Graham Hill, GBR	BRM	1984	Niki Lauda, AUT	McL. TAG Porsche Turbo
1963	Jim Clark, GBR	Lotus Climax	1985	Alain Prost, FRA	McL. TAG Porsche Turbo
1964	John Surtees, GBR	Ferrari	1986	Alain Prost, FRA	McL. TAG Porsche Turbo
1965	Jim Clark, GBR	Lotus Climax	1987	Nelson Piquet, BRA	Williams Honda Turbo
1966	Jack Brabham, AUS	Brabham Repco	1988	Ayrton Senna, BRA	McLaren Honda Turbo
1967	Denis Hulme, NZE	Brabham Repco	1989	Alain Prost, FRA	McLaren Honda
1968	Graham Hill, GBR	Lotus Ford			
1969	Jackie Stewart, GBR	Matra Ford	1990	Ayrton Senna, BRA	McLaren Honda
			1991	Ayrton Senna, BRA	McLaren Honda
1970	Jochen Rindt, AUT	Lotus Ford	1992	Nigel Mansell, GBR	Williams Renault
1971	Jackie Stewart, GBR	Tyrrell Ford	1993	Alain Prost, FRA	Williams-Renault

Wide World Photos

ENDURANCE RACES

The 24 Hours at Le Mans

Officially, the Le Mans Grand Prix d'Endurance. First run May 22-23, 1923, and won by Andre Lagache and Rene Leonard in a 3-litre Chenard & Walcker. All subsequent races have been held in June, except in 1956 (July) and 1968 (September). Originally contested over a 10.73-mile track, the circuit was shortened to its present 8.451-mile distance in 1932. The original start of Le Mans, where drivers raced across the track to their unstarted cars, was discontinued in 1970.

Multiple winners: Jacky Ickx (6); Derek Bell (5); Oliver Gendebien and Henri Pescarolo (4); Woolf Barnato, Luigi Chinetti, Hurley Haywood, Phil Hill, Klaus Ludwig and Al Holbert (3); Sir Henry Birkin, Ivoe Bueb, Yannick Dalmas, Ron Flockhart, Jean-Pierre Jaussaud, Gerard Larrousse, Andre Rossignol, Raymond Sommer, Hans Stuck, Gijs van Lennep and Jean-Pierre Wimille (2).

Year	Drivers	Car	MPH
1923	Andre Lagache & Rene Leonard	Chenard & Walcker	57.21
1924	John Duff & Francis Clement	Bentley	53.78
1925	Gerard de Courcelles & Andre Rossignol	La Lorraine	57.84
1926	Robert Bloch & Andre Rossignol	La Lorraine	66.08
1927	J.D. Benjafield & Sammy Davis	Bentley	61.35
1928	Woolf Barnato & Bernard Rubin	Bentley	69.11
1929	Woolf Barnato & Sir Henry Birkin	Bentley	73.63
1930	Woolf Barnato & Glen Kidston	Bentley	75.88
1931	Earl Howe & Sir Henry Birkin	Alfa Romeo	78.13
1932	Raymond Sommer & Luigi Chinetti	Alfa Romeo	76.48
1933	Raymond Sommer & Tazio Nuvolari	Alfa Romeo	81.40
1934	Luigi Chinetti & Philippe Etancelin	Alfa Romeo	74.74
1935	John Hindmarsh & Louis Fontes	Lagonda	77.85
1936	Not held		
1937	Jean-Pierre Wimille & Robert Benoist	Bugatti	85.13
1938	Eugene Chaboud & Jean Tremoulet	Delahaye	82.36
1939	Jean-Pierre Wimille & Pierre Veyron	Bugatti	86.86
1940-48		Not held	
1949	Luigi Chinetti & Lord Selsdon	Ferrari	82.28
1950	Louis Rosier & Jean-Louis Rosier	Talbot-Lago	89.71
1951	Peter Walker & Peter Whitehead	Jaguar	93.50
1952	Hermann Lang & Fritz Reiss	Mercedes-Benz	96.67
1953	Tony Rolt & Duncan Hamilton	Jaguar	98.65
1954	Froilan Gonzalez & Maurice Trintignant	Ferrari	105.13
1955	Mike Hawthorn & Ivor Bueb	Jaguar	107.05
1956	Ron Flockhart Ninian Sanderson	Jaguar	104.47
1957	Ron Flockhart & Ivor Bueb	Jaguar	113.83
1958	Oliver Gendebien & Phil Hill	Ferrari	106.18
1959	Roy Salvadori & Carroll Shelby	Aston Martin	112.55
1960	Oliver Gendebien & Paul Fräre	Ferrari	109.17
1961	Oliver Gendebien & Phil Hill	Ferrari	115.88
1962	Oliver Gendebien & Phil Hill	Ferrari	115.22
1963	Lodovico Scarfiotti & Lorenzo Bandini	Ferrari	118.08
1964	Jean Guichel & Nino Vaccarella	Ferrari	121.54
1965	Masten Gregory & Jochen Rindt	Ferrari	121.07
1966	Bruce McLaren & Chris Amon	Ford	125.37
1967	A.J. Foyt & Dan Gurney	Ford	135.46
1968	Pedro Rodriguez & Lucien Bianchi	Ford	115.27
1969	Jacky Ickx & Jackie Oliver	Ford	129.38
1970	Hans Herrmann & Richard Attwood	Porsche	119.28
1971	Gijs van Lennep & Helmut Marko	Porsche	138.13
1972	Graham Hill & Henri Pescarolo	Matra-Simca	121.45
1973	Henri Pescarolo & Gerard Larrousse	Matra-Simca	125.67
1974	Henri Pescarolo & Gerard Larrousse	Matra-Simca	119.27
1975	Derek Bell & Jacky Ickx	Mirage-Ford	118.98
1976	Jacky Ickx & Gijs van Lennep	Porsche	123.49
1977	Jacky Ickx, Jurgen Barth & Hurley Haywood	Porsche	120.95
1978	Jean-Pierre Jaussaud & Didier Pironi	Renault-Alpine	130.60
1979	Klaus Ludwig, Bill Wittington & Don Whittington	Porsche	108.10
1980	Jean-Pierre Jaussaud & Jean Rondeau	Rondeau-Cosworth	119.23
1981	Jacky Ickx & Derek Bell	Porsche	124.94
1982	Jacky Ickx & Derek Bell	Porsche	126.85
1983	Vern Schuppan, Hurley Haywood & Al Holbert	Porsche	130.70
1984	Klaus Ludwig & Henri Pescarolo	Porsche	126.88
1985	Klaus Ludwig, Paolo Barilla & John Winter	Porsche	131.75
1986	Derek Bell, Hans Stuck & Al Holbert	Porsche	128.75

Endurance Races (Cont.)
The 24 Hours at Le Mans

Year	Drivers	Car	MPH	Year	Drivers	Car	MPH
1987	Derek Bell, Hans Stuck & Al Holbert	Porsche	124.06	1991	Volker Weider, Johnny Herbert & Bertrand Gachof	Mazda	127.31
1988	Jan Lammers, Johnny Dumfries & Andy Wallace	Jaguar	137.75	1992	Derek Warwick, Yannick Dalmas & Mark Blundell	Peugeot	123.89
1989	Jochen Mass, Manuel Reuter & Stanley Dickens	Sauber-Mercedes	136.39	1993	Geoff Brabham, Christophe Bouchut & Eric Helary	Peugeot	132.58
1990	John Nielsen, Price Cobb & Martin Brundle	Jaguar	126.71	1994	Yannick Dalmas, Hurley Haywood & Mauro Baldi	Porsche	129.82

The 24 Hours of Daytona

Officially, the Rolex 24 at Daytona. First run in 1962 as a three-hour race and won by Dan Gurney in a Lotus 19 Ford. Contested over a 3.56-mile course at Daytona (Fla.) International Speedway. There have been several distance changes since 1962: the event was a three-hour race (1962-63); a 2,000-kilometer race (1964-65); a 24-hour race (1966-71); a six-hour race (1972) and a 24-hour race again since 1973. The race was canceled in 1974 due to the national energy crisis.

Multiple winners: Hurley Haywood (5); Peter Gregg, Pedro Rodriguez and Bob Wollek (4); Derek Bell and Rolf Stommelen (3); A.J. Foyt, Al Holbert, Ken Miles, Brian Redman, Lloyd Ruby and Al Unser, Jr. (2).

Year	Drivers	Car	MPH	Year	Drivers	Car	MPH
1962	Dan Gurney	Lotus Ford	104.101	1982	John Paul Sr., John Paul Jr. & Rolf Stommelen	Porsche	114.794
1963	Pedro Rodriguez	Ferrari	102.074	1983	A.J. Foyt, Preston Henn, Bob Wollek & Claude Ballot-Lena	Porsche	98.781
1964	Pedro Rodriguez & Phil Hill	Ferrari	98.230	1984	Sarel van der Merwe, Tony Martin & Graham Duxbury	Porsche	103.119
1965	Ken Miles & Lloyd Ruby	Ford	99.944	1985	A.J. Foyt, Bob Wollek, Al Unser Sr. & Thierry Boutsen	Porsche 962	104.162
1966	Ken Miles & Lloyd Ruby	Ford	108.020	1986	Al Holbert, Derek Bell & Al Unser Jr	Porsche 962	105.484
1967	Lorenzo Bandini & Chris Amon	Ferrari	105.688	1987	Al Holbert, Derek Bell, Chip Robinson & Al Unser Jr	Porsche 962	111.599
1968	Vic Elford & Jochen Neerpasch	Porsche	106.697	1988	Raul Boesel, Martin Brundle & John Nielsen	Jaguar XJR-9	107.943
1969	Mark Donohue & Chuck Parsons	Lola Chevrolet	99.268	1989	John Andretti, Derek Bell & Bob Wollek	Porsche 962	92.009
1970	Pedro Rodriguez & Leo Kinnunen	Porsche	114.866	1990	Davy Jones, Jan Lammers & Andy Wallace	Jaguar XJR-12	112.857
1971	Pedro Rodriguez & Jackie Oliver	Porsche	109.203	1991	Hurley Haywood, John Winter, Frank Jelinski, Henri Pescarolo & Bob Wollek	Porsche 962-C	106.633
1972	Mario Andretti & Jacky Ickx	Ferrari	122.573				
1973	Peter Gregg & Hurley Haywood	Porsche	106.225	1992	Masahiro Hasemi, Kazuyoshi Hoshino & Toshio Suzuki	Nissan R-91	112.897
1974	Not held						
1975	Peter Gregg & Hurley Haywood	Porsche	108.531	1993	P.J. Jones, Mark Dismore & Rocky Moran	Eagle MKIII	103.537
1976	Peter Gregg, Brian Redman & John Fitzpatrick	BMW	104.040	1994	Paul Gentilozzi, Scott Pruett, Butch Leitzinger & Steve Millen	Nissan 300 ZXT	104.80
1977	Hurley Haywood, John Graves & Dave Helmick	Porsche	108.801				
1978	Peter Gregg, Rolf Stommelen & Antoine Hezemans	Porsche	108.743				
1979	Hurley Haywood, Ted Field & Danny Ongais	Porsche	109.249				
1980	Rolf Stommelen, Volkert Merl & Reinhold Joest	Porsche	114.303				
1981	Bobby Rahal, Brian Redman & Bob Garretson	Porsche	113.153				

Wide World Photos

Newly-crowned WBC heavyweight champion **Oliver McCall** celebrates with promoter **Don King** after knocking out Lennox Lewis on Sept. 24.

BOXING

BOXING

by Bernard Fernandez

Train Wreck

Oliver McCall's upset victory over Lennox Lewis is another unexpected derailment in boxing's volatile glamour division.

The heavyweight division is the locomotive that pulls boxing's train, which explains all those wrecked boxcars currently littering the landscape.

Oliver McCall's second-round knockout of WBC champion Lennox Lewis Sept. 24 in London marked only the latest and most spectacular derailment in a year which, in retrospect, seemed like a continuous showing of the escape scene from "The Fugitive." Lots of surprises, to be sure, but is the common good being served?

The occasional upset can be a reassuring thing, affirming a sport's integrity and raising the hopes of its downtrodden. But too many deviations from the status quo can create a parallel universe in which up is down, left is right, black is white and confusion reigns.

Fight fans who were looking forward to a showdown of Lewis and former champion Riddick Bowe in the spring of 1995 must now resign themselves to the likelihood that the widely anticipated matchup—like the Mike Tyson-Evander Holyfield megabout of a few years back, which twice was scheduled but never happened—permanently has fallen victim to greed, stupidity and capricious winds of fate.

What the public has been left with is the uneasy hope that Tyson—who has spent the last three years in an Indiana prison while serving time on a rape conviction—can save boxing from itself shortly after his scheduled May 5, 1995, release.

With or without a title to defend, Tyson presumably would be reanointed as the most charismatic and compelling figure in a field that, collectively speaking, does not constitute a new golden age of heavyweights. But Tyson's personal timetable might not coincide with the hurried agenda envisioned for him by the public.

On the morning after his former sparring partner, McCall, starched Lewis with a textbook-perfect counter right, Tyson telephoned *New York Daily News* sportswriter Vic Ziegel to detail his plans to climb back to the top from a starting point of ground zero. "I'd like to do what George Foreman did—have 20 fights before I go for the title," Tyson told Ziegel.

"[Promoter Don King] might want to throw me in quicker. I'll resist it. The quickest way to fail is to try to please everybody. When I enter the ring again, it'll be like my professional debut ... Who am I to think that layoff won't affect me? Look what it did to Muhammad Ali and Joe Louis."

If Tyson is sincere in his intentions to gradually work off the ring rust brought on by nearly four years of inactivity, we can only wonder as to who'll be waiting when he finally deems himself ready.

Will it be the reluctant southpaw, Michael Moorer, current holder of the WBA and IBF championships? Instant-cult figure McCall? The peripatetic Bowe? A retooled Lewis?

Bernard Fernandez has been a sports reporter at *The Philadelphia Daily News* for 20 years and the boxing writer since 1987.

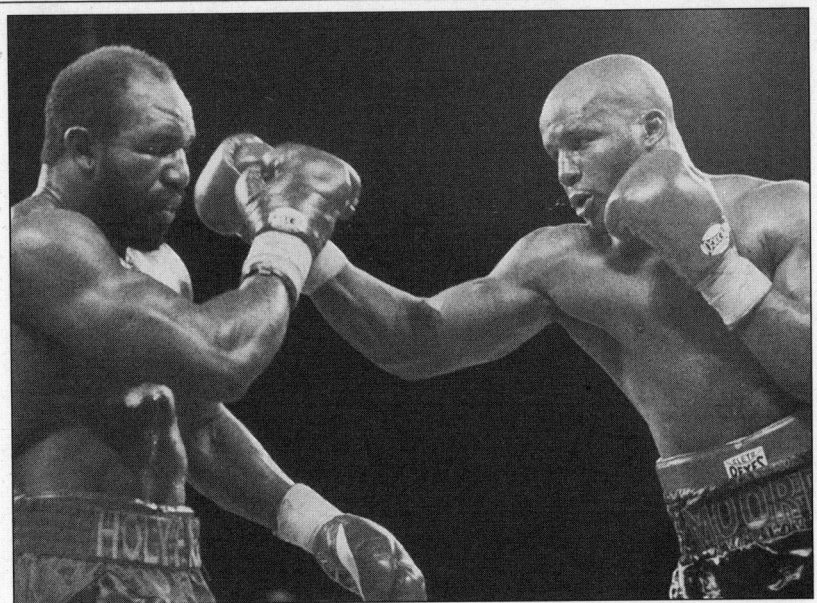

Holly Stein/Allsport

Lefthanded challenger **Michael Moorer** (right) jabs the swollen face of champion **Evander Holyfield** on his way to a 12-round unanimous decision in their April 22 WBA and IBF heavyweight championship bout.

Crystal-chinned (Not So) Great White Hope Tommy Morrison? Senior citizen George Foreman? Any one of another dozen or so quasi-contenders, all of whom possess similarly thin credentials?

Dating back to Oct. 1, 1993, the upheaval among the top tier of heavyweights has been as profound as, say, the political changes within the former Soviet Union following the fall of communism.

Bowe, the most widely recognized heavyweight champion, lost his WBA and IBF titles to the man he had won them from a year earlier, Holyfield, on a 12-round majority decision Nov. 6, 1993, in Las Vegas. Holyfield, in turn, was dethroned by Moorer, who became the first lefthanded heavyweight champion ever when he jabbed his way to a majority decision April 22, also in Vegas. After the fight it was learned that Holyfield has a congenital heart defect which in all likelihood has ended his career.

Lewis, the first British heavyweight king since Bob Fitzsimmons' two-year reign ended in 1899, was something of a paper champion in that he never actually won the WBC title in the ring. It was awarded to him by decree in 1992 after Bowe dissed the Mexico City-based sanctioning body by dumping its belt in a trash can. The London-born Lewis, who won the 1988 Olympic super-heavyweight gold medal while representing Canada, had won three desultory defenses—against Tony Tucker, Frank Bruno and Phil Jackson—before his flaws were fully revealed by McCall, a 5½-to-1 underdog.

Morrison had hoped to be the one to upend Lewis, but he had problems of his own. A $7.5 million payday against Lewis went sailing out the window when Morrison, despite manager Bill Cayton's objections, opted to take a tuneup fight against Michael Bentt on Oct. 29, 1993, in Tulsa. Bentt, of course, knocked Morrison down three times en route to a first-round TKO, capturing Morrison's lightly regarded WBO title in the process. Herbie Hide promptly won the WBO belt and sent Bentt into retirement on a savage, seventh-round TKO March 19 in London.

Demonstrating that the wheel does indeed go round and round, Morrison, despite being dropped twice and forced to settle for a draw against journeyman Ross Puritty in another tuneup bout filled with sour notes, was scheduled to challenge Hide for the WBO title Oct. 22, 1994, in Hong Kong. One might presume that another loss would finish Morrison as a credible contender, but, in these uncertain times, the trip between outhouse to penthouse can be remarkably swift.

"When you're in the heavyweight division, you're always one punch away from stardom," Morrison reasoned. "Oliver McCall proved that."

Yes, he did. Despite a No. 1 rating from the WBC, WBA and IBF, McCall was widely perceived to be just another member of Don King's stable of rent-a-pugs. For all the toughness he exhibited in the gym—he had knocked down Tyson in training prior to Tyson's 1989 bout with Michael Spinks—the self-proclaimed "greatest sparring partner the world has ever seen" was viewed as a colorful miscreant whose nocturnal habits were of more interest than anything he did inside the ropes.

One-time aide de camp Bruce Blair, recalling the time when McCall served as a sparring partner for Ray Mercer, said McCall would "toss down shots and beers for three or four hours, leave at midnight with a couple of babes in tow, roll in at 4 a.m. and give Mercer hell in sparring at noon. I always said that if the guy ever harnessed all that physical ability, he could be something special."

Toward that end, King opted to sequester McCall in various out-of-the-way sites during his preparations for the Lewis fight. McCall's training base in England was Henlow Grange Health Farm, a luxurious spa 60 miles from the glitz and glitter of downtown London.

"You look out the window and see lambs in the field!" King said excitedly of the rural setting. "Little sheep! You got streams and brooks and meadows! This is a wonderful place."

In terrific shape and perhaps a tad irritable at being around four-legged lambs instead of two-legged babes, McCall, well prepared by trainers Emanuel Steward and Greg Page, waited for the moment when Lewis would flick a lazy jab and attempt to follow it with his favorite punch—a big, telegraphed overhand right.

He didn't have to wait long. Lewis gave McCall the opening he was anticipating and the champion went crashing, face first, to the canvas after catching a thunderous right to the jaw early in the second round. Lewis beat the count, barely, but he was wobbling and glassy-eyed as he lurched into the arms of Mexican referee Lupe Garcia. Garcia did the right thing by signalling the fight to an end.

Not surprisingly, Lewis' manager, Frank Maloney, and American promoter, Dan Duva, vehemently protested that their man should have been allowed to continue. "Lennox Lewis isn't some four-round preliminary fighter," Maloney said. "He was fighting for the heavyweight title. He should have been given the benefit of the doubt."

Lewis' defeat ended talk of a multimillion-dollar showdown with Bowe in 1995. Lewis-Bowe was a matchup that could and probably should have been made two years earlier, when both fighters were undefeated and very hot commodities. The blown opportunity recalls the hesitation that prevented an even more lucrative fight, Tyson-Holyfield, from becoming reality.

Tyson, the undisputed champion, was to have taken on No. 1 contender Holyfield in the summer of 1990. All Tyson had to do was dispose of a 42-1 longshot named Buster Douglas in February of that year.

Douglas' shocking victory in Tokyo, the biggest upset in boxing history, put everything on hold. Then, after Holyfield had won the title from Douglas, he was scheduled to defend against Tyson on Nov. 8, 1991. But Tyson injured his ribs in training, forcing a postponement that became a cancellation after an Indiana jury came in with a guilty verdict on the rape charge.

Now that Tyson is close to gaining his freedom, Holyfield, who has been diagnosed as having a noncompliant left ventricle, sometimes referred to as a "stiff heart," might not be allowed to fight any more. And so it goes.

It could turn out that McCall is better than his sparring-partner reputation, that his conquest of Lewis in time will cease to be thought of as a fluke. In the short term, though, don't count on McCall risking his title against quality opposition: the short list of possible opponents being mentioned by King includes such fringe contenders as Peter McNeeley, Bruce Seldon and Frans Botha, all of whom, not surprisingly, are

Julio Cesar Chavez hits the canvas for the first time in his pro career after being knocked down in the 11th round by challenger Frankie Randall in their Jan. 29 WBC super-lightweight title bout in Las Vegas.

promoted by King.

What McCall would like most to do is to test himself against his former employer, Tyson, in a fight that isn't in practice.

"Once he gets out [of prison], believe me, I know I can knock him out," McCall said. "I hurt him a lot of times with those big pillows [18-ounce gloves used in sparring]. I still have pictures at home of him with a big, old icepack on his eye after I swole it up."

No one ever claimed that Moorer was as quick with a quip as McCall, but, given that he is the linear descendant of a regal line of champions that dates back to John L. Sullivan, his claim to being the world's premier non-incarcerated heavyweight probably is more legitimate.

Knocked down in the second round by Holyfield, Moorer began to gain momentum in the middle rounds with a right jab the champion never seemed to figure out. But Moorer fought with a curious lack of passion, obliging his trainer, Teddy Atlas, to spend the one-minute break between rounds giving variations of the same pep talk.

"There is something wrong with him; go get him," Atlas repeatedly said. Moorer appeared not to pay heed. This so exasperated Atlas that when Moorer returned to his corner after the eighth round, he found the trainer perched on the stool and snarling a challenge.

"Do you want to fight?" Atlas screamed. "Do you? Or do you want me to change places with you? This guy is finished. There comes a time in every man's life when he makes a decision—just live and survive, or he wants to win.

"You're doing just enough to keep him off you and you'll cry tomorrow. You're lying to yourself and I'd be lying if I let you get away with that. You want to cry tomorrow?"

Perhaps Moorer's inner fires will be burning hotter in his first defense, a scheduled Nov. 5 date against Foreman, the 46-year-old former champion. Big George has not fought since losing a decision to Morrison for the vacant WBO title on June 6, 1993, but, hey, he sells tickets. Never underestimate the power of a muffler commercial.

The WBA initially had declined to approve Foreman as an opponent for Moorer, but an injunction granted by a Nevada judge got him back on the card. Legal action is as much a part of boxing as sequined trunks, and this might have been an even busier year than usual in the courtroom.

A federal indictment against King,

Wide World Photos

Pernell Whitaker, the WBC welterweight champ, renewed his claim as the world's best pound-for-pound fighter with a convincing Oct. 1 win over Buddy McGirt in Norfolk, Va.

accused of bilking Lloyds of London out of $350,000 on a false insurance claim for a June 28, 1991, Julio Cesar Chavez—Frankie Randall fight that never took place, could have consequential effects should boxing's most prominent promoter replace Tyson as a member of America's penal population. The case is expected to be heard in January.

McCall's rise and the federal indictment were only part of a busy year for King, who, as always, was an integral figure in any number of major events, several of which included Julio Cesar Chavez.

Chavez fought five times from Oct. 30, 1993 through Sept. 17, 1994. The most notable of those bouts saw him lose his WBC super-lightweight title on a split decision to unheralded Frankie Randall Jan. 29 in Las Vegas. Not only was it the first official loss in 91 pro bouts for Mexico's El Gran Campeon, but he was knocked down for the first time ever, by an overhand right in the 11th round.

Randall held the championship for three months. On May 7, Chavez reclaimed it on a controversial eight-round technical deci-

sion after an unintentional head butt opened a deep cut over Chavez' right eye. Many believed Randall deserved a better shake in the scoring, but he got a consolation prize when he wrested the WBA junior middleweight crown from Juan Coggi Sept. 17 on a unanimous decision.

After two trials by combat with Randall, Chavez turned his attention to an old foe, Meldrick Taylor, whom he had defeated on a hotly disputed 12th-round TKO in 1990. The long-awaited rematch, on Sept. 17, on the same card as Coggi-Randall, vindicated Chavez as he pounded out an eighth-round TKO.

McCall and Randall might have been the most obvious members of the club, but the Year of the Upset featured other unlikely winners: Steve Little over Michael Nunn for the WBA super-middleweight title; Jake Rodriguez over Charles "The Natural" Murray for the IBF junior welterweight title; Jesse James Leija over Azumah Nelson for the WBC super-featherweight title; John Michael Johnson over Junior Jones for the WBA bantamweight title; Vuyani Bungu over Kennedy McKinney for the IBF junior featherweight title; Hector Acero-Sanchez over Tracy Harris Patterson for the WBC super-bantamweight title.

It wasn't an upset, exactly, but Humberto Gonzalez took back the IBF/WBC junior flyweight championships from Michael Carbajal Feb. 19 in Inglewood, Calif., on a rousing split decision.

Some favorites were as dominating as ever, principally IBF super-middleweight champion James Toney and WBC welterweight champ Pernell Whitaker, whose names crop up most often in any discussions concerning the best pound-for-pound fighter in the world.

Toney stated his case for that designation with three victories, the most impressive of which was a 12th-round TKO of former IBF light-heavyweight champion "Prince" Charles Williams July 29 in Las Vegas, while Whitaker countered by impressively winning a pair of decisions, the second a near-shutout of former two-time titlist Buddy McGirt Oct. 1 in Norfolk, Va.

Finally, on a sad note, 1988 Olympic champion Wangila Napunyi, who fought in America under the name Robert Wangila, died following a fifth-round knockout loss to David Gonzales. □

THE 1995 INFORMATION PLEASE SPORTS ALMANAC

BOXING STATISTICS

SEC A

THE SEASON IN REVIEW
1993-1994
CHAMPIONS • TITLE BOUTS

PAGE 831

Current Champions

WBA, WBC and IBF Titleholders (through Oct. 15, 1994)

The champions of professional boxing's 17 principal weight divisions, as recognized by the World Boxing Association (WBA), World Boxing Council (WBC) and International Boxing Federation (IBF).

	Weight Limit	WBA Champion	WBC Champion	IBF Champion
Heavyweight	—	Michael Moorer 35-0-0, 30 KO	Oliver McCall 25-5-0, 18 KO	Michael Moorer 35-0-0, 30 KO
Jr. Heavyweight	190 lbs	Orlin Norris 41-3-0, 23 KO	Anaclet Wamba 42-2-1, 20 KO	Alfred Cole 25-1-0, 12 KO
Light Heavyweight	175 lbs	Virgil Hill 39-1-0, 20 KO	Mike McCallum 47-2-1, 35 KO	Henry Maske 25-0-0, 11 KO
Super Middleweight	168 lbs	Frank Liles 25-1-0, 16 KO	Nigel Benn 39-2-1, 32 KO	James Toney 43-0-2, 29 KO
Middleweight	160 lbs	Jorge Castro 94-4-2, 65 KO	Gerald McClellan 31-2-0, 28 KO	Vacant
Jr. Middleweight	154 lbs	Julio C. Vasquez 52-1-0, 35 KO	Terry Norris 38-4-0, 23 KO	Vincent Pettway 37-4-1, 30 KO
Welterweight	147 lbs	Ike Quartey 27-0-0, 23 KO	Pernell Whitaker 34-1-1, 15 KO	Felix Trinidad 24-0-0, 20 KO
Jr. Welterweight	140 lbs	Frankie Randall 50-3-1, 39 KO	Julio Cesar Chavez 91-1-1, 75 KO	Jake Rodriguez 26-2-2, 7 KO
Lightweight	135 lbs	Gussie Nazarov 19-0-0, 14 KO	Miguel A. Gonzalez 34-0-0, 28 KO	Rafael Ruelas 41-1-0, 32 KO
Jr. Lightweight	130 lbs	Genaro Hernandez 30-0-1, 15 KO	Gabriel Ruelas 39-2-0, 21 KO	John-John Molina 35-3-0, 25 KO
Featherweight	126 lbs	Eloy Rojas 28-1-1, 24 KO	Kevin Kelley 40-0-0, 28 KO	Tom Johnson 36-2-1, 22 KO
Jr. Featherweight	122 lbs	Wilfredo Vazquez 41-6-3, 32 KO	Hector Acero-Sanchez 30-2-2, 20 KO	Vuyani Bungu 24-2-0 17 KO
Bantamweight	118 lbs	Daorung Chuvatana 53-4-2, 32 KO	Yasuei Yakushiji 22-2-1, 16 KO	Orlando Canizales 38-1-1, 28 KO
Jr. Bantamweight	115 lbs	Hyung-Chul Lee 18-4-0, 14 KO	Hiroshi Kawashima 15-2-1, 12 KO	Harold Gray 17-0-0, 15 KO
Flyweight	112 lbs	San Sow Ploenchit 19-0-0, 5 KO	Yuri Arbachakov 19-0-0, 15 KO	Phichit Sithbangprachan 20-0-0, 15 KO
Jr. Flyweight	108 lbs	Leo Gamez 26-3-1, 19 KO	Humberto Gonzalez 39-2-0, 28 KO	Humberto Gonzalez 39-2-0, 28 KO
Strawweight	105 lbs	Chana Porpaoin 32-0-0, 13 KO	Ricardo Lopez 37-0-0, 26 KO	Ratanapol Vorapin 19-2-1, 14 KO

Note: The following weight divisions are also known by these names—**Jr. Heavyweight** as Cruiserweight; **Jr. Middleweight** as Super Welterweight; **Jr. Welterweight** as Super Lightweight; **Jr. Lightweight** as Super Featherweight; **Jr. Featherweight** as Super Bantamweight; **Jr. Bantamweight** as Super Flyweight; **Jr. Flyweight** as Light Flyweight; and **Strawweight** as Minimum.

Heavyweight Champions' Records

The career pro records of current heavyweight champions Michael Moorer and Oliver McCall as of Oct. 15, 1994.

Michael Moorer

Born: Nov. 12, 1967   **Pro record:** 35-0-0, 30 KO
Height: 6'2"   **Trainer:** Teddy Atlas
Weight: 214 lbs   **Manager:** John Davimos

No	Date	Opponent, location	Result
1	3/4/88	Adrian Riggs, Las Vegas	TKO 1
2	3/25/88	Bill Lee, Detroit	TKO 1
3	4/29/88	Brett Zywcewinsk, Detroit	KO 1
4	5/10/88	Dennis Fikes, Phoenix	TKO 2
5	6/6/88	Keith McMurray, Las Vegas	TKO 2
6	6/25/88	Lavelle Stanley, Detroit	TKO 2
7	8/6/88	Terrance Walker, Las Vegas	KO 4
8	8/12/88	Jordan Keepers, Milwaukee	TKO 2
9	10/7/88	Jorge Suero, Auburn Hills	KO 2
10	10/17/88	Carl Williams, Tucson	TKO 1
11	11/4/88	Glenn Kennedy, Las Vegas	KO 1
12	12/3/88	Ramzi Hassan, Cleveland	TKO 4
13	12/8/86	Victor Claudio, Auburn Hills	TKO 2
14	1/14/89	Frankie Swindell, Monessen, Pa	TKO 6
15	2/19/89	Fred Delgado, Auburn Hills	TKO 1
16	6/25/89	Leslie Stewart, Atlantic City	TKO 8
17	11/16/89	Jeff Thompson, Atlantic City	TKO 1
18	12/22/89	Mike Sedillo, Auburn Hills	TKO 6
19	2/3/90	Marcellus Allen, Atlantic City	TKO 9
20	4/28/90	Mario Melo, Atlantic City	KO 1
21	8/21/90	Jim MacDonald, Auburn Hills	TKO 3
22	12/15/90	Danny Lindstrom, Pittsburgh	TKO 8
23	4/19/91	Terry Davis, Atlantic City	TKO 2
24	6/25/91	Levi Billups, Auburn Hills	TKO 3
25	7/27/91	Alex Stewart, Norfolk, Va	TKO 4
26	11/23/91	Bobby Crabtree, Atlanta	TKO 1
27	2/1/92	Mike White, Las Vegas	Wu 10
28	3/17/92	Big Foot Martin, Auburn Hills	Wu 10
29	5/15/92	Bert Cooper, Atlantic City	TKO 5
30	11/13/92	Billy Wright, Las Vegas	TKO 2
31	2/27/93	Bonecrusher Smith, Atl. City	Wu 10
32	4/26/93	Frankie Swindell, Detroit	TKO 3
33	6/22/93	James Pritchard, Atlantic City	TKO 3
34	12/4/93	Mike Evans, Reno	Wu 10
35	4/22/94	Evander Holyfield, Las Vegas	Wm 12

(won IBF/WBA titles)

Oliver McCall

Born: April 21, 1965   **Pro Record:** 25-5-0, 19 KO
Height: 6'2½"   **Weight:** 231 lbs.
Trainer: Emanuel Steward   **Manager:** Jimmy Adams

No	Date	Opponent, location	Result
1	11/2/85	Lou Bailey, Villa Park, Ill.	TKO 1
2	12/6/85	Joey Christjohn, Las Vegas	L 4
3	1/18/86	Felix Shorter, Chicago	TKO 2
4	6/21/86	Kimmuel Odum, Chicago	W 4
5	8/14/86	James Churn, Chicago	KO 1
6	9/13/86	Larry Roberson, Chicago	TKO 1
7	10/25/86	Bashir Wadud, Chicago	W 6
8	12/16/86	Al Evans, Alsip, Ill.	W 6
9	3/21/87	Fred Whitaker, Chicago	W 6
10	5/30/87	Tim Morrison, Chicago	KO 1
11	8/11/87	Richard Scott, Chicago	KO 2
12	8/30/87	Kim Adams, Chicago	TKO 2
13	1/22/88	Mike Hunter, Atlantic City	L 10
14	6/30/88	David Jaco, Virginia Beach	W 10
15	9/16/88	Wes Smith, Winston-Salem	TKO 2
16	10/1/88	Bruce Johnson, Chicago	KO 1
17	7/21/89	Buster Douglas, Atlantic City	L 10
18	7/16/90	Lionel Butler, Oklahoma City	W 10
19	11/17/90	Orlin Norris, Fort Myers, Fla.	L 10
20	4/18/91	Bruce Seldon, Atlantic City	TKO 9
21	6/8/91	Dan Wofford, Salem, Va.	TKO 5
22	8/8/91	Jesse Ferguson, Atlantic City	W 10
23	2/15/92	Mike Rouse, Las Vegas	TKO 4
24	6/26/92	Tony Tucker, Cleveland	L 12
25	12/13/92	Lawrence Carter, Las Vegas	KO 3
26	1/30/93	Mike Dixon, Memphis	KO 2
27	4/23/93	Francesco Damiani, Memphis	TKO 8
28	12/18/93	Art Card, Puebla, Mexico	KO 1
29	2/26/94	Dan Murphy, London	TKO 1
30	9/24/94	Lennox Lewis, London	TKO 2

(won WBC heavyweight title)

Mike Tyson's Record

Born: June 30, 1966   **Height:** 5'11½"   **Weight:** 216 lbs   **Pro record:** 42-1-0, 36 KO
Tyson has been in jail on a rape conviction since Feb. 10, 1992. His release date is set for May 9, 1995.

No	Date	Opponent, location	Result
1	3/6/85	Hector Mercedes, Albany, N.Y.	KO 1
2	4/10/85	Trent Singleton, Albany, N.Y.	TKO 1
3	5/23/85	Don Halpin, Albany, N.Y.	KO 4
4	6/20/85	Rick Spain, Atlantic City	KO 1
5	7/11/85	John Anderson, Atlantic City	TKO 2
6	7/19/85	Larry Sims, Poughkeepsie, N.Y.	KO 3
7	8/15/85	Lorenzo Canady, Atlantic City	TKO 1
8	9/5/85	Michael Johnson, Atlantic City	KO 1
9	10/9/85	Donnie Long, Atlantic City	KO 1
10	10/25/85	Robert Colay, Atlantic City	KO 1
11	11/1/85	Sterling Benjamin, Latham, N.Y.	TKO 1
12	11/13/85	Eddie Richardson, Houston	KO 1
13	11/22/85	Conroy Nelson, Latham, N.Y.	KO 2
14	12/6/85	Sammy Scaff, New York City	KO 1
15	12/27/85	Mark Young, Latham, N.Y.	KO 1
16	1/10/86	Dave Jaco, Albany, N.Y.	TKO 1
17	1/24/86	Mike Jameson, Atlantic City	TKO 5
18	2/16/86	Jesse Ferguson, Atlantic City	TKO 6
19	3/10/86	Steve Zouski, Uniondale, N.Y.	KO 3
20	5/3/86	James Tillis, Glens Falls, N.Y.	Wu 10
21	5/20/86	Mitchell Green, New York City	Wu 10
22	6/13/86	Reggie Gross, New York City	TKO 1
23	6/28/86	William Hosea, Troy, N.Y.	KO 1
24	7/11/86	Lorenzo Boyd, Swan Lake, N.Y.	KO 2
25	7/26/86	Marvis Frazier, Glens Falls, N.Y.	KO 1
26	8/17/86	Jose Ribalta, Atlantic City	TKO 10
27	9/6/86	Alfonzo Ratliff, Las Vegas	KO 2
28	11/22/86	Trevor Berbick, Las Vegas	KO 2
		(won WBC heavyweight title)	
29	3/7/87	Bonecrusher Smith, Las Vegas	Wu 12
		(won WBA heavyweight title)	
30	5/30/87	Pinklon Thomas, Las Vegas	TKO 6
31	8/1/87	Tony Tucker, Las Vegas	Wu 12
		(won IBF heavyweight title)	
32	10/16/87	Tyrell Biggs, Atlantic City	TKO 7
33	1/22/88	Larry Holmes, Atlantic City	KO 4
34	3/21/88	Tony Tubbs, Tokyo	TKO 2
35	6/27/88	Michael Spinks, Atlantic City	KO 1
36	2/25/89	Frank Bruno, Las Vegas	TKO 5
37	7/21/89	Carl Williams, Atlantic City	TKO 1
38	2/10/90	Buster Douglas, Tokyo	KO by 10
		(lost world heavyweight title)	
39	6/16/90	Henry Tillman, Las Vegas	KO 1
40	12/8/90	Alex Stewart, Atlantic City	TKO 1
41	3/18/91	Razor Ruddock, Las Vegas	TKO 7
42	6/28/91	Razor Ruddock, Las Vegas	Wu 12

Major Bouts, 1993-94

Division by division, from Oct. 1, 1993 through Oct. 15, 1994.

WBA, WBC and IBF champions are listed in **bold** type. Note the following Result column abbreviations (in alphabetical order): Disq. (won by disqualification); KO (knockout); MDraw (majority draw); NC (no contest)); SDraw (split draw); TDraw (technical draw); TKO (technical knockout); TWs (won by technical split decision); TWu (won by technical unanimous decision); Wm (won by majority decision); Ws (won by split decision); Wu (won by unanimous decision).

Heavyweights

Date	Winner	Loser	Result		Title	Site
Oct. 1	Lennox Lewis	Frank Bruno	TKO	7	WBC	Cardiff, Wales
Oct. 29	Michael Bentt	Tommy Morrison	KO	1	(WBO)	Tulsa
Nov. 6	Evander Holyfield	Riddick Bowe	Wm	12	IBF/WBA	Las Vegas
Nov. 6	Herbie Hide	Mike Dixon	TKO	9	Non-title	London
Nov. 19	Ray Mercer	Jesse Ferguson	Ws	10	Non-title	Atlantic City
Dec. 4	Michael Moorer	Mike Evans	Wu	10	Non-title	Reno
Dec. 4	Herbie Hide	Jeff Lampkin	TKO	2	Non-title	Sun City, S.A.
Jan. 29	Razor Ruddock	Anthony Wade	Wu	10	Non-title	Las Vegas
Feb. 20	Tommy Morrison	Tui Toia	KO	3	Non-title	Biloxi, Miss.
Feb. 22	Tony Tubbs	Big Foot Martin	Wu	10	Non-title	Auburn Hills
Mar. 8	Larry Holmes	Garing Lane	Wu	10	Non-title	Ledyard, Conn.
Mar. 16	Frank Bruno	Jesse Ferguson	TKO	1	Non-title	Birmingham, Eng.
Mar. 19	Herbie Hide	Michael Bentt	TKO	7	(WBO)	London
Mar. 27	Tommy Morrison	Bryan Scott	TKO	2	Non-title	Tokyo
Apr. 2	Buster Mathis Jr.	Sherman Griffin	Wm	10	Non-title	Bay St. Louis, Miss.
Apr. 14	Larry Donald	Bert Cooper	TKO	7	Non-title	Bay St. Louis, Miss.
Apr. 22	Michael Moorer	**Evander Holyfield**	Wm	12	**IBF/WBA**	Las Vegas
May 6	**Lennox Lewis**	Phil Jackson	TKO	8	**WBC**	Atlantic City
May 24	Tommy Morrison	Sherman Griffin	Wu	10	Non-title	Tulsa
June 4	Larry Donald	Juan Antonio Diaz	TKO	6	Non-title	Reno
July 5	Larry Donald	Dan Murphy	Wu	10	Non-title	Washington, D.C.
July 28	Tommy Morrison	Ross Puritty	SDraw	10	Non-title	Atlantic City
July 28	Ray Mercer	Marion Wilson	SDraw	10	Non-title	Atlantic City
Aug. 9	Larry Holmes	Jesse Ferguson	Wu	10	Non-title	Prior Lake, Minn.
Aug. 12	Tim Witherspoon	Sherman Griffin	TKO	3	Non-title	South Padre Is., Tex.
Aug. 13	Riddick Bowe	Buster Mathis Jr.	NC	4*	Non-title	Atlantic City
Sept. 24	Oliver McCall	Lennox Lewis	TKO	2	**WBC**	London

Note: On Dec. 3, Tony Tubbs won four bouts in one night to claim the ill-fated Heavyweight SuperFights title in a 16-man tournament held in Bay St. Louis, Miss. Tubbs defeated Willie Jackson (KO-1), Jose Ribalta (Decision-3 rounds), Tyrell Biggs (D-3) and Daniel Dancuta of Romania (D-3) winning only $170,000 of a promised $1 million.

*Bowe leveled Mathis with a right at 2:11 of the 4th round while Mathis was down on one knee.

Junior Heavyweights

(Cruiserweights)

Date	Winner	Loser	Result		Title	Site
Oct. 16	**Anaclet Wamba**	Akim Tafer	TKO	7	**WBC**	Levallois, France
Oct. 22	George O'Mara	Troy Boudoin	Wu	12	Non-title	Boise, Idaho
Nov. 6	Orlin Norris	Marcelo Figueroa	TKO	6	vacant **WBA**	Paris
Nov. 6	Thomas Hearns	Andrew Maynard	KO	1	Non-title	Las Vegas
Nov. 17	**Al Cole**	Vincent Boulware	TKO	5	**IBF**	Atlantic City
Nov. 20	Nestor Giovannini	Markus Bott	Wu	12	(WBO)	Hamburg, Germany
Jan. 9	**Orlin Norris**	Art Jimmerson	TKO	3	Non-title	Lakeside, Calif.
Jan. 29	Thomas Hearns	Dan Ward	TKO	1	(NABF)	Las Vegas
Feb. 19	Thomas Hearns	Freddie Delgado	Wu	12	(NABF)	Charlotte, N.C.
Feb. 19	Bobby Czyz	George O'Mara	Wu	10	Non-title	Charlotte, N.C.
Mar. 4	Orlin Norris	Arthur Williams	Ws	12	**WBA**	Las Vegas
Apr. 2	Nestor Giovannini	Joa Dos Santoz	KO	5	Non-title	Sunchales, Arg.
Apr. 24	**Anaclet Wamba**	Mike De Vito	TKO	4	Non-title	Limoges, France
May 24	Iran Barkley	Rick Enis	TKO	4	Non-title	Tulsa
July 2	**Orlin Norris**	Art Williams	TKO	3	**WBA**	Las Vegas
July 14	**Anaclet Wamba**	Adolpho Washington	MDraw	12	**WBC**	Monte Carlo
July 23	**Al Cole**	Nate Miller	Wu	12	**IBF**	Bismarck, N.D.
Aug. 4	David Izeqwire	Bobby Czyz	TKO	4	Non-title	Ledyard, Conn.

Light Heavyweights

Date	Winner	Loser	Result		Title	Site
Nov. 9	**Virgil Hill**	Saul Montana	TKO	10	**WBA**	Fargo, N.D.
Dec. 11	**Henry Maske**	David Vedder	Wu	12	**IBF**	Dusseldorf
Dec. 17	**Virgil Hill**	Guy Waters	Wu	12	**WBA**	Minot, N.D.
Jan. 16	James Toney*	Anthony Hembrick	TKO	7	Non-title	Bushkill, Pa.
Jan. 29	Leeonzer Barber	Nicky Piper	TKO	9	(WBO)	Cardiff, Wales
Mar. 4	Mike McCallum	Randall Yonker	TKO	5	Interim WBC	Las Vegas

Major Bouts 1993-94 (Cont.)
Light Heavyweights

Date	Winner	Loser	Result	Title	Site
Mar. 26	**Henry Maske**	Ernesto Magdaleno	TKO 9	IBF	Dortmund, Germany
May 18	James Toney	Vince Durham	Wu 10	Non-title	Rosemont, Ill.
June 4	**Henry Maske**	Andrea Magi	Wu 12	IBF	Dortmund, Germany
July 23	**Virgil Hill**	Frank Tate	Wu 12	WBA	Bismarck, N.D.
July 23	Mike McCallum	Jeff Harding	Wu 12	WBC	Bismarck, N.D.
Sept. 9	Dariusz Michalczewski	Leeonzer Barber	Wu 12	(WBO)	Hamburg, Germany
Oct. 8	**Henry Maske**	Iran Barkley	—	IBF	Dusseldorf, Germany

*Toney, the IBF super middleweight champion, stepped up in weight class to fight Hembrick.
†McCallum named interim champion in May by WBC following victory over Yonker. WBC world champion Jeff Harding, inactive since Dec. 2, 1992, cancelled his scheduled Mar. 4, 1992, defense against Yonker when he suffered a cut eye while sparring.

Super Middleweights

Date	Winner	Loser	Result	Title	Site
Oct. 9	**Nigel Benn**	Chris Eubank	SDraw 12	WBC	Manchester, England
Oct. 26	Vinny Pazienza	Robbie Sims	Wu 10	Non-title	Ledyard, Conn.
Oct. 29	**James Toney**	Tony Thornton	Wu 12	IBF	Tulsa
Nov. 30	Roy Jones Jr.*	Fermin Chirino	Wu 10	Non-title	Pensacola, Fla.
Dec. 3	Tim Littles	James Williamson	TKO 7	Non-title	Biloxi, Miss.
Dec. 14	Roberto Duran	Tony Menefee	TKO 8	Non-title	Bay St. Louis, Miss.
Dec. 18	**Michael Nunn**	Merqui Sosa	Wu 12	WBA	Puebla, Mexico
Dec. 28	Vinny Pazienza	Dan Sherry	KO 11	Non-title	Ledyard, Conn.
Feb. 5	Chris Eubank	Graciano Rocchigiani	Wu 12	(WBO)	Berlin
Feb. 22	Roberto Duran	Carlos Montero	Wu 10	Non-title	Marseille, France
Feb. 26	**Nigel Benn**	Henry Wharton	Wu 12	WBC	London
Feb. 26	Steve Little	**Michael Nunn**	Wm 12	WBA	London
Mar. 5	**James Toney**	Tim Littles	TKO 4	IBF	Los Angeles
Mar. 29	Roberto Duran	Terry Thomas	TKO 4	Non-title	Bay St. Louis, Miss.
Apr. 5	Vinny Pazienza	Jacques LeBlanc	Wu 10	Non-title	Ledyard, Conn.
May 21	Chris Eubank	Ray Close	Ws 12	(WBO)	Belfast
June 25	Vinny Pazienza	Roberto Duran	Wu 12	Non-title	Las Vegas
July 9	Chris Eubank	Mauricio Amaral	Wu 12	(WBO)	London
July 29	**James Toney**	Prince Chas. Williams	KO 12	IBF	Las Vegas
Aug. 13	Frank Liles	**Steve Little**	Wu 12	WBA	Tucuman, Argentina
Aug. 27	Chris Eubank	Sam Storey	TKO 7	(WBO)	Cardiff, Wales
Sept. 10	**Nigel Benn**	Juan Carlos Gimenez	Wu 12	WBC	Birmingham, England
Oct. 15	**Chris Eubank**	Dan Schommer	—	(WBO)	Sun City, S.A.

*Jones, the IBF middleweight champion, stepped up in weight class to fight Chirino.
**Jones renounced IBF middleweight crown to fight Toney for IBF super middleweight title.

Middleweights

Date	Winner	Loser	Result	Title	Site
Oct. 1	John David Jackson	**Reggie Johnson**	Wu 12	WBA	Buenos Aires
Feb. 19	Reggie Johnson	Ramon Felix	KO 1	Non-title	Charlotte, N.C.
Mar. 4	**Gerald McClellan**	Gilbert Baptist	KO 1	WBC	Las Vegas
Mar. 22	Roy Jones Jr.	Danny Garcia	TKO 6	Non-title	Pensacola, Fla.
May 6	John David Jackson*	Jeff Johnson	TKO 7	Non-title	Atlantic City
May 7	**Gerald McClellan**	Julian Jackson	KO 1	WBC	Las Vegas
May 27	Roy Jones Jr.**	Thomas Tate	KO 2	IBF	Las Vegas
Aug. 13	Jorge Castro	Reggie Johnson	Ws 12	vacant WBA	Tucuman, Argentina

*The WBA stripped Jackson of his title for not paying a sanctioning fee for this non-title fight and avoiding mandatory challenger Jorge Castro. On Aug. 11, however, a federal court in New Jersey ordered the WBA to give back Jackson's title.
**Jones renounced IBF middleweight crown to fight Toney for IBF super middleweight title.

Junior Middleweights
(Super Welterweights)

Date	Winner	Loser	Result	Title	Site
Dec. 18	Simon Brown	**Terry Norris**	KO 4	WBC	Puebla, Mexico
Jan. 22	**Julio C. Vasquez**	Juan Medina-Padilla	Wu 12	WBA	Alma-Ata, Kazakhstan
Jan. 29	**Simon Brown**	Troy Waters	Wm 12	WBC	Las Vegas
Mar. 4	**Gianfranco Rosi**	Vincent Pettway	TDraw*	IBF	Las Vegas
Mar. 4	**Julio C. Vasquez**	Armand Picar	TKO 2	WBA	Las Vegas
Mar. 18	Terry Norris	Armando Campas	KO 4	Non-title	Las Vegas
Apr. 8	**Julio C. Vasquez**	Ricardo Nunez	Wu 12	WBA	Buenos Aires
May 7	Terry Norris	**Simon Brown**	Wu 12	WBC	Las Vegas
May 21	**Julio C. Vasquez**	Ahmet Dottouev	TKO 10	WBA	Belfast
Aug. 21	**Julio C. Vasquez**	Ronald (Winky) Wright	Wu 12	WBA	St. Jean De Luz, France
Sept. 17	Vincent Pettway	**Gianfranco Rosi**	TKO 4	IBF	Las Vegas

*The Rosi-Pettway bout was ruled a Technical Draw after being stopped in the 6th round due to a headbutt (Rosi retained title).

Welterweights

Date	Winner	Loser	Result	Title	Site
Oct. 9	**Crisanto Espana**	Donovan Boucher	TKO 10	WBA	Manchester, Eng.
Oct. 23	**Felix Trinidad**	Anthony Stevens	KO 10	IBF	Ft. Lauderdale
Nov. 2	Buddy McGirt	Nick Rupa	Wu 10	Non-title	Atlantic City
Dec. 18	Hector (Macho) Camacho	Lee Fortune	KO 1	Non-title	Puebla, Mexico
Jan. 4	Buddy McGirt	James Hughes	Wu 12	Non-title	Ft. Lauderdale
Jan. 29	**Felix Trinidad**	Hector (Macho) Camacho	Wu 12	IBF	Las Vegas
Jan. 29	Meldrick Taylor	Craig Houk	KO 3	Non-title	Las Vegas
Apr. 9	**Pernell Whitaker**	Santos Cardona	Wu 12	WBC	Norfolk, Va.
Apr. 9	Buddy McGirt	Livingstone Bramble	Wu 12	Non-title	Norfolk, Va.
May 3	Hector (Macho) Camacho	Franco DiOrio	Wu 10	Non-title	Bay St. Louis, Miss.
May 7	Meldrick Taylor	Chad Broussard	KO 2	non-title	Las Vegas
June 4	Ike (Bazooka) Quartey	Crisanto Espana	TKO 11	WBA	Paris, France
June 9	Hector (Macho) Camacho	Craig Snyder	Wu 10	Non-title	Rosemont, Ill.
June 28	Buddy McGirt	Kevin Pompey	Wu 10	Non-title	Secaucus, N.J.
Aug. 7	Buddy McGirt	Patrick Coleman	Ws 10	Non-title	Callicoon, N.Y.
Sept. 1	**Felix Trinidad**	Yuri Boy Campas	TKO 4	IBF	Las Vegas
Sept. 27	**Hector (Macho) Camacho**	Pat Lawlor	Wu 10	Non-title	Bay St. Louis, Miss.
Oct. 1	**Pernell Whitaker**	Buddy McGirt	Wu 12	WBC	Norfolk, Va.

Junior Welterweights

(Super Lightweights)

Date	Winner	Loser	Result	Title	Site
Oct. 30	**Julio Cesar Chavez**	Mike Powell	TKO 4	Non-title	Juarez, Mexico
Nov. 19	**Charles Murray**	Courtney Hooper	TKO 5	IBF	Atlantic City
Nov. 19	Zack Padilla	Efrem Calamati	TKO 7	(WBO)	Arezzo, Italy
Dec. 16	Zack Padilla	Ray Oliveira	Wu 12	(WBO)	Ledyard, Conn.
Dec. 17	**Juan Martin Coggi**	Eder Gonzalez	TKO 7	WBA	Tucuman, Argentina
Dec. 17	**Julio Cesar Chavez**	Andy Holligan	TKO 5	WBC	Puebla, Mexico
Jan. 29	Joey Gamache	Jeff Mayweather	Wu 10	Non-title	Lewiston, Me.
Jan. 29	Frankie Randall	**Julio Cesar Chavez**	Ws 12	WBC	Las Vegas
Feb. 19	Jake Rodriguez	**Charles Murray**	Wm 12	IBF	Atlantic City
Mar. 18	**Juan Martin Coggi**	Eder Gonzalez	TKO 3	WBA	Las Vegas
Apr. 18	Zack Padilla	Harold Miller	TKO 6	(WBO)	Rotterdam, Holland
Apr. 21	**Jake Rodriguez**	Ray Oliveira	Wu 12	IBF	Ledyard, Conn.
May 7	Julio Cesar Chavez	**Frankie Randall**	TWs 8*	WBC	Las Vegas
July 17	**Juan Martin Coggi**	Mario Morales	KO 3	Non-title	Buenos Aires
July 24	Zack Padilla	Juan LaPorte	TKO 10	(WBO)	Los Angeles
July 28	Charles Murray	Lyndon Walker	Wu 10	Non-title	Atlantic City
Aug. 27	**Jake Rodriguez**	George Scott	TKO 9	IBF	Atlantic City
Aug. 27	Alexis Arguello	Jorge Palomares	Wm 10	Non-title	Miami Beach
Sept. 17	**Julio Cesar Chavez**	Meldrick Taylor	TKO 8	WBC	Las Vegas
Sept. 17	Frankie Randall	**Juan Martin Coggi**	Wu 12	WBA	Las Vegas

*Fight was stopped at 2:57 of 8th round after a Brown headbutt opened a gash over Chavez's right eye. Under WBC rules a point was deducted from Brown and the fight went to scorecards. Judges: Tamotsu Tomihara (Randall, 76-75), Ray Solis (Chavez, 77-74) and Dalby Shirley (Chavez, 76-75).

Lightweights

Date	Winner	Loser	Result	Title	Site
Oct. 22	Rafael Ruelas	Mike Hernandez	TKO 1	Non-title	Boise, Idaho
Oct. 22	Gabriel Ruelas	Mike Grow	TKO 8	Non-title	Boise, Idaho
Oct. 30	Gussie Nazarov	**Dingaan Thobela**	Wu 12	WBA	Johannesburg
Nov. 27	**Miguel A. Gonzalez**	Wilfrido Rocha	TKO 11	WBC	Mexico City
Dec. 8	Joey Gamache	Kyu-Han Park	TKO 1	Non-title	Augusta, Me.
Jan. 28	Joey Gamache	Jeff Mayweather	Wu 12	Non-title	Lewiston, Me.
Feb. 19	Rafael Ruelas	**Fred Pendleton**	Wu 12	IBF	Inglewood
Mar. 4	Leavander Johnson	Sharmba Mitchell	KO 8	Non-title	Las Vegas
Mar. 19	**Gussie Nazarov**	Dingaan Thobela	Wu 12	WBA	Pretoria, S.A.
Mar. 29	**Miguel A. Gonzalez**	Jean Baptiste Mendy	TKO 5	WBC	Levallois, France
May 27	**Rafael Ruelas**	Mike Evgen	TKO 3	IBF	Las Vegas
June 11	Jorge Paez	Juan Gomez	Wu 10	Non-title	Inglewood
June 15	**Miguel A. Gonzalez**	Kenny Baysmore	TKO 6	Non-title	Juarez, Mexico
July 29	Oscar De La Hoya*	Jorge Paez	KO 2	(vacant WBO)	Las Vegas
Aug. 6	**Miguel A. Gonzalez**	Leavander Johnson	TKO 8	WBC	Juarez, Mexico

*De La Hoya, the WBO junior lightweight champion, stepped up in weight class to fight Paez.

Major Bouts 1993-94 (Cont.)
Junior Lightweights
(Super Featherweights)

Date	Winner	Loser	Result	Title	Site
Oct. 9	**John-John Molina**	Bernard Taylor	TKO 8	IBF	San Juan
Oct. 11	**Genaro Hernandez**	Harold Warren	Wu 12	**WBA**	Inglewood
Oct. 30	Oscar De La Hoya	Narciso Valenzuela	KO 1	Non-title	Phoenix
Jan. 22	**John-John Molina**	Floyd Havard	TKO 6	IBF	Cardiff, Wales
Jan. 31	**Genaro Hernandez**	Cocas Ramirez	TKO 8	**WBA**	Inglewood
Mar. 5	Oscar De La Hoya	Jimmy Bredahl	TKO 10	(WBO)	Los Angeles
Mar. 23	Jesse James Leija	Tomas Valdez	TKO 3	Non-title	San Antonio
Apr. 22	**John-John Molina**	Gregorio Vargas	Wu 12	IBF	Las Vegas
May 7	Jesse James Leija	**Azuma Nelson**	Wu 12	**WBC**	Las Vegas
May 25	Oscar De La Hoya	Giorgio Campanela	TKO 3	(WBO)	Las Vegas
Sept. 17	Gabriel Ruelas	**Jesse James Leija**	Wu 12	**WBC**	Las Vegas

Featherweights

Date	Winner	Loser	Result	Title	Site
Nov. 30	**Tom Johnson**	Stephane Haccoun	TKO 9	IBF	Marseilles, France
Dec. 4	Kevin Kelley	Goyo Vargas	Wu 12	**WBC**	Reno
Dec. 5	Eloy Rojas	Yung-Kyun Park	Ws 12	**WBA**	Seoul
Jan. 8	Tracy Patterson*	Steve Young	TKO 5	Non-title	Catskill, N.Y.
Feb. 12	**Tom Johnson**	Orlando Soto	Wu 12	IBF	St. Louis
Mar. 12	Steve Robinson	Paul Hodkinson	KO 12	(WBO)	Cardiff, Wales
Mar. 19	**Eloy Rojas**	Seiji Asakawa	TKO 5	**WBA**	Kobe, Japan
May 6	**Kevin Kelley**	Jesse Benavides	Wu 12	**WBC**	Atlantic City
June 4	Steve Robinson	Freddy Cruz	Wu 12	(WBO)	Cardiff, Wales
June 11	**Tom Johnson**	Benny Amparo	TKO 12	IBF	Atlantic City
June 26	Kevin Kelley	George Navarro	TKO 6	Non-title	McKee City, N.J.
Aug. 6	Alejandro Gonzalez	Cesar Soto	Ws 10	Non-title	Juarez, Mexico
Sept. 11	**Eloy Rojas**	Samart Payakarun	KO 8	**WBA**	Bangkok
Sept. 24	**Kevin Kelley**	Jose Vida Ramos	TKO 2	**WBC**	Atlantic City

*Patterson, the WBC super bantamweight champion, stepped up in weight class to fight Young.

Junior Featherweights
(Super Bantamweights)

Date	Winner	Loser	Result	Title	Site
Oct. 16	**Kennedy McKinney**	Jesus Salud	Wu 12	IBF	Lake Tahoe
Nov. 18	**Wilfredo Vazquez**	Hiroaki Yokota	Wu 12	**WBA**	Tokyo
Feb. 19	**Kennedy McKinney**	Jose Rincones	KO 5	IBF	Johannesburg
Mar. 2	**Wilfredo Vazquez**	Yuichi Kasai	KO 1	**WBA**	Tokyo
Apr. 9	**Tracy Patterson**	Richard Duran	Wu 12	**WBC**	Reno
Apr. 16	**Kennedy McKinney**	Welcome Ncita	Ws 12	IBF	South Padre Is., Tex.
June 12	Junior Jones	Orlando Fernandez	Wu 10	Non-title	Atlantic City
July 2	**Wilfredo Vazquez**	Jae-Won Choi	TKO 2	**WBA**	Las Vegas
Aug. 20	Vuyani Bungu	**Kennedy McKinney**	Wu 12	IBF	Pretoria, S.A.
Aug. 26	Hector Acero-Sanchez	**Tracy Patterson**	Ws 12	**WBC**	Atlantic City
Oct. 13	**Wilfredo Vazquez**	Juan Polo Perez	Wu 12	**WBA**	Paris

Bantamweights

Date	Winner	Loser	Result	Title	Site
Oct. 23	Junior Jones	**Jorge Julio**	Wu 12	**WBA**	Atlantic City
Nov. 20	**Orlando Canizales**	Juvenal Berrio	Wu 12	IBF	Sun City, S.A.
Dec. 22	John Michael Johnson	Arturo Estrada	TKO 8	Non-title	San Antonio
Dec. 23	Yasuei Yakushiji	**Jung-Il Byun**	Ws 12	**WBC**	Nagoya, Japan
Jan. 8	**Junior Jones**	Elvis Alvarez	Wu 12	**WBA**	Catskill, N.Y.
Feb. 26	**Orlando Canizales**	Gerardo Martinez	TKO 4	IBF	San Jose
Apr. 16	**Yasuei Yakushiji**	Josefino Suarez	KO 10	**WBC**	Nagoya, Japan
Apr. 22	John M. Johnson	**Junior Jones**	TKO 11	**WBA**	Las Vegas
June 7	**Orlando Canizales**	Rolando Bohol	KO 5	IBF	South Padre Is., Tex.
June 12	Junior Jones	Orlando Fernandez	Wu 10	Non-title	Atlantic City
June 17	Wayne McCullough	Victor Rabanales	Wu 12	Non-title	Atlantic City
July 16	Daorung Chuvatana	**John M. Johnson**	TKO 1	**WBA**	Bangkok
July 31	**Yasuei Yakushiji**	Jung-Il Byun	TKO 11	**WBC**	Nagoya, Japan
Oct. 15	**Orlando Canizales**	Sergio Reyes	Wu 12	IBF	Laredo, TX

Junior Bantamweights
(Super Flyweights)

Date	Winner	Loser	Result	Title	Site
Oct. 29	Johnni Bredahl	Eduardo Nazario	Disq 4	(WBO)	Korsor, Denmark
Nov. 5	**Katsuya Onizuka**	Khaoyai Mahasarakam	Wu 12	**WBA**	Tokyo
Nov. 13	Jose Luis Bueno	**Sung-Kil Moon**	Ws 12	**WBC**	Seoul
Nov. 26	**Julio Cesar Borboa**	Rolando Pascua	TKO 5	**IBF**	Hermosillo, Mexico
Mar. 25	Johnni Bredahl	Eduardo Nazario	Wu 12	(WBO)	Akirkeby, Denmark
Apr. 3	**Katsuya Onizuka**	Seung-Loo Lee	Wu 12	**WBA**	Tokyo
Apr. 25	**Julio Cesar Borboa**	Jorge Roman	KO 4	**IBF**	Inglewood
May 4	Hiroshi Kawashima	**Jose Luis Bueno**	Wu 12	**WBC**	Yokohama, Japan
May 21	**Julio Cesar Borboa**	Jaji Sibali	TKO 9	**IBF**	Johannesburg
Aug. 7	**Hiroshi Kawashima**	Carlos Salazar	Wu 12	**WBC**	Tokyo
Aug. 29	Harold Grey	**Julio Cesar Borboa**	WS 12	**IBF**	Inglewood
Sept. 18	Hyun-chul Lee	**Katsuya Onizuka**	TKO 9	**WBA**	Tokyo

Flyweights

Date	Winner	Loser	Result	Title	Site
Oct. 3	**Phi. Sithbangprachan**	Miguel Martinez	TKO 9	**IBF**	Bangkok
Oct. 3	**David Griman**	Alvaro Mercado	Wu 12	**WBA**	Puerto la Cruz, Ven.
Dec. 13	Yuri Arbachakov	Nam-Hoon Cha	Wu 12	**WBC**	Kyoto, Japan
Jan. 23	**Phi. Sithbangprachen**	Arthur Johnson	Wu 12	**IBF**	Bangkok
Feb. 13	San Sow Ploenchit	**David Griman**	Wu 12	**WBA**	Bangkok
Feb. 19	Jorge Luis Roman	Scotty Olson	Ws 10	Non-title	Inglewood
Apr. 8	Michael Carbajal*	Abner Barajas	TKO 3	Non-title	Laughlin, Nev.
Apr. 10	**San Sow Ploenchit**	Kiki Rojas	Wu 12	**WBA**	Bangkok
May 8	**Phi. Sithbangprachen**	Jose Luis Zepeda	Ws 12	**IBF**	Bangkok
May 16	**Yuri Arbachakov**	Hiroshi Kobayashi	TKO 9	Non-title	Tokyo
June 12	**San Sow Ploenchit**	Aquiles Guzman	Wm 12	**WBA**	Sakaew, Thailand
Aug. 1	**Yuri Arbachakov**	Hugo Soto	KO 8	**WBC**	Tokyo
Sept. 24	**San Sow Ploenchit**	Yong-Kang Kim	Wu 12	**WBA**	Bangkok

*Carbajal stepped up in weight class after losing his IBF and WBC junior flyweight titles to Chiquito Gonzalez on a Feb. 19 split decision.

Junior Flyweights
(Light Flyweights)

Date	Winner	Loser	Result	Title	Site
Oct. 21	Leo Gamez	Shiro Yahiro	TKO 9	vacant WBA	Tokyo
Oct. 30	**Michael Carbajal**	Domingo Sosa	TKO 5	IBF/WBC	Phoenix
Nov. 17	Humberto Gonzalez	Armando Diaz	Wu 12	Non-title	Atlantic City
Feb. 5	**Leo Gamez**	Juan Torres	TKO 7	**WBA**	Panama City
Feb. 19	Humberto Gonzalez	**Michael Carbajal**	Ws 12	IBF/WBC	Inglewood
June 27	**Leo Gamez**	Kaaj Chartibandit	SDraw 12	**WBA**	Bangkok
July 8	**Humberto Gonzalez**	Armando Diaz	TKO 3	Non-title	Inglewood
July 15	Michael Carbajal	Josue Camacho	Wu 12	(WBO)	Phoenix
Sept. 10	**Humberto Gonzalez**	Juan Domingo Cordoba	KO 7	IBF/WBC	Stateline, Nev.
Oct. 9	Leo Gamez	P'noi Sithbangprachen	TKO 6	**WBA**	Bangkok

Minimumweights
(Strawweights or Mini-Flyweights)

Date	Winner	Loser	Result	Title	Site
Nov. 28	**Chana Porpaoin**	Rafael Torres	KO 4	**WBA**	Bangkok
Dec. 10	**Ratanapol Vorapin**	Felix Naranjo	TKO 2	**IBF**	Bangkok
Dec. 18	**Ricardo Lopez**	Manny Melchor	KO 11	**WBC**	Lake Tahoe
Feb. 27	**Ratanapol Vorapin**	Ronnie Magrano	Wu 12	**IBF**	Bangkok
Mar. 26	**Chana Porpaoin**	Carlos Murillo	Wm 12	**WBA**	Bangkok
May 7	**Ricardo Lopez**	Kermin Guardia	Wu 12	**WBC**	Las Vegas
May 8	P'noi Sithbangprachen	Nico Thomas	TKO 3	Non-title	Bangkok
May 14	**Ratanapol Vorapin**	Roger Espanola	TKO 6	**IBF**	Bangkok
Aug. 20	**Ratanapol Vorapin**	Marcelino Bolivar	KO 4	**IBF**	Bangkok
Sept. 3	**Chana Porpaoin**	Keum-Young Kang	Wu 12	**WBA**	Pattalung, Thailand
Sept. 17	**Ricardo Lopez**	Yodsingh Saengmorokot	TKO 1	**WBC**	Las Vegas

B O X I N G
S T A T I S T I C S

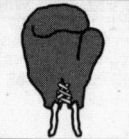

THROUGH THE YEARS
1884-1994
WORLD CHAMPIONS

THE 1995 SPORTS ALMANAC INFORMATION PLEASE

SEC B

PAGE 838

World Heavyweight Championship Fights

Widely accepted world champions in **bold** type. Note following result abbreviations: KO (knockout), TKO (technical knockout), Wu (unanimous decision), Wm (majority decision), Ws (split decision), Ref (referee's decision), ND (no decision), Disq (won on disqualification).

Year	Date	Winner	Age	Wgt	Loser	Wgt	Result	Location
1892	Sept. 7	James J. Corbett	26	178	John L. Sullivan	212	KO 21	New Orleans
1894	Jan. 25	**James J. Corbett**	27	184	Charley Mitchell	158	KO 3	Jacksonville, FL
1897	Mar. 17	Bob Fitzsimmons	34	167	**James J. Corbett**	183	KO 14	Carson City, NV
1899	June 9	James J. Jeffries	24	206	**Bob Fitzsimmons**	167	KO 11	Coney Island, NY
1899	Nov. 3	**James J. Jeffries**	24	215	Tom Sharkey	183	Ref 25	Coney Island, NY
1900	Apr. 6	James J. Jeffries	24	NA	Jack Finnegan	NA	KO 1	Detroit
1900	May 11	**James J. Jeffries**	25	218	James J. Corbett	188	KO 23	Coney Island, NY
1901	Nov. 15	James J. Jeffries	26	211	Gus Ruhlin	194	TKO 6	San Francisco
1902	July 25	James J. Jeffries	27	219	Bob Fitzsimmons	172	KO 8	San Francisco
1903	Aug. 14	James J. Jeffries	28	220	James J. Corbett	190	KO 10	San Francisco
1904	Aug. 25	**James J. Jeffries***	29	219	Jack Munroe	186	TKO 2	San Francisco
1905	July 3	Marvin Hart	28	190	Jack Root	171	KO 12	Reno, NV
1906	Feb. 23	Tommy Burns	24	180	**Marvin Hart**	188	Ref 20	Los Angeles
1906	Oct. 2	**Tommy Burns**	25	NA	Jim Flynn	NA	KO 15	Los Angeles
1906	Nov. 28	**Tommy Burns**	25	172	Phila. Jack O'Brien	163½	Draw 20	Los Angeles
1907	May 8	**Tommy Burns**	25	180	Phila. Jack O'Brien	167	Ref 20	Los Angeles
1907	July 4	**Tommy Burns**	26	181	Bill Squires	180	KO 1	Colma, Calif
1907	Dec. 2	**Tommy Burns**	26	177	Gunner Moir	204	KO 10	London
1908	Feb. 10	**Tommy Burns**	26	NA	Jack Palmer	NA	KO 4	London
1908	Mar. 17	**Tommy Burns**	26	NA	Jem Roche	NA	KO 1	Dublin
1908	Apr. 18	**Tommy Burns**	26	NA	Jewey Smith	NA	KO 5	Paris
1908	June 13	**Tommy Burns**	26	184	Bill Squires	183	KO 8	Paris
1908	Aug. 24	**Tommy Burns**	27	181	Bill Squires	184	KO 13	Sydney
1908	Sept. 2	**Tommy Burns**	27	183	Bill Lang	187	KO 6	Melbourne
1908	Dec. 26	Jack Johnson	30	192	**Tommy Burns**	168	TKO 14	Sydney
1909	Mar. 10	**Jack Johnson**	30	NA	Victor McLaglen	NA	ND 6	Vancouver
1909	May 19	**Jack Johnson**	31	205	Phila. Jack O'Brien	161	ND 6	Philadelphia
1909	June 30	**Jack Johnson**	31	207	Tony Ross	214	ND 6	Pittsburgh
1909	Sept. 9	**Jack Johnson**	31	209	Al Kaufman	191	ND 10	San Francisco
1909	Oct. 16	**Jack Johnson**	31	205½	Stanley Ketchel	170¼	KO 12	Colma, Calif.
1910	July 4	**Jack Johnson**	32	208	James J. Jeffries	227	KO 15	Reno, Nev.
1912	July 4	**Jack Johnson**	34	195½	Jim Flynn	175	TKO 9	Las Vegas, NM
1913	Dec. 19	**Jack Johnson**	35	NA	Jim Johnson	NA	Draw 10	Paris
1914	June 27	**Jack Johnson**	36	221	Frank Moran	203	Ref 20	Paris
1915	Apr. 5	Jess Willard	33	230	**Jack Johnson**	205½	KO 26	Havana
1916	Mar. 25	**Jess Willard**	34	225	Frank Moran	203	ND 10	NYC (Mad.Sq.Garden)
1919	July 4	Jack Dempsey	24	187	**Jess Willard**	245	TKO 4	Toledo, Ohio
1920	Sept. 6	**Jack Dempsey**	25	185	Billy Miske	187	KO 3	Benton Harbor, Mich.
1920	Dec. 14	**Jack Dempsey**	25	188¼	Bill Brennan	197	KO 12	NYC (Mad. Sq. Garden)

*James J. Jeffries retired as champion on May 13, 1905, then came out of retirement to fight Jack Johnson for the title in 1910.

Year	Date	Winner	Age	Wgt	Loser	Wgt	Result	Location
1921	July 2	**Jack Dempsey**	26	188	Georges Carpentier	172	KO 4	Jersey City, N.J.
1923	July 4	**Jack Dempsey**	28	188	Tommy Gibbons	175½	Ref 15	Shelby, Montana
1923	Sept. 14	**Jack Dempsey**	28	192½	Luis Firpo	216½	KO 2	NYC (Polo Grounds)
1926	Sept. 23	Gene Tunney	29	189½	**Jack Dempsey**	190	Wu 10	Philadelphia
1927	Sept. 22	**Gene Tunney**	30	189½	Jack Dempsey	192½	Wu 10	Chicago
1928	July 26	**Gene Tunney***	31	192	Tom Heeney	203	TKO 11	NYC (Yankee Stadium)
1930	June 12	Max Schmeling	24	188	Jack Sharkey	197	Foul 4	NYC (Yankee Stadium)
1931	July 3	**Max Schmeling**	25	189	Young Stribling	186½	TKO 15	Cleveland
1932	June 21	Jack Sharkey	29	205	**Max Schmeling**	188	Ws 15	Long Island City, N.Y.
1933	June 29	Primo Carnera	26	260½	**Jack Sharkey**	201	KO 6	Long Island City, N.Y.
1933	Oct. 22	**Primo Carnera**	26	259½	Paulino Uzcudun	229¼	Wu 15	Rome
1934	Mar. 1	**Primo Carnera**	27	270	Tommy Loughran	184	Wu 15	Miami
1934	June 14	Max Baer	25	209½	**Primo Carnera**	263¼	TKO 11	Long Island City, N.Y.
1935	June 13	James J. Braddock	29	193¾	**Max Baer**	209½	Wu 15	Long Island City, N.Y.
1937	June 22	Joe Louis	23	197¼	**James J. Braddock**	197	KO 8	Chicago
1937	Aug. 30	**Joe Louis**	23	197	Tommy Farr	204¼	Wu 15	NYC (Yankee Stadium)
1938	Feb. 23	**Joe Louis**	23	200	Nathan Mann	193½	KO 3	NYC (Mad. Sq. Garden)
1938	Apr. 1	**Joe Louis**	23	202½	Harry Thomas	196	KO 5	Chicago
1938	June 22	**Joe Louis**	24	198¾	Max Schmeling	193	KO 1	NYC (Yankee Stadium)
1939	Jan. 25	**Joe Louis**	24	200¼	John Henry Lewis	180¾	KO 1	NYC (Mad. Sq. Garden)
1939	Apr. 17	**Joe Louis**	24	201¼	Jack Roper	204¾	KO 1	Los Angeles
1939	June 28	**Joe Louis**	25	200¾	Tony Galento	233¾	TKO 4	NYC (Yankee Stadium)
1939	Sept. 20	**Joe Louis**	25	200	Bob Pastor	183	KO 11	Detroit
1940	Feb. 9	**Joe Louis**	25	203	Arturo Godoy	202	Ws 15	NYC (Mad. Sq. Garden)
1940	Mar. 29	**Joe Louis**	25	201½	Johnny Paychek	187½	KO 2	NYC (Mad. Sq. Garden)
1940	June 20	**Joe Louis**	26	199	Arturo Godoy	201¼	TKO 8	NYC (Yankee Stad.)
1940	Dec. 16	**Joe Louis**	26	202¼	Al McCoy	180¾	TKO 6	Boston
1941	Jan. 31	**Joe Louis**	26	202½	Red Burman	188	KO 5	NYC (Mad. Sq. Garden)
1941	Feb. 17	**Joe Louis**	26	203½	Gus Dorazio	193½	KO 2	Philadelphia
1941	Mar. 21	**Joe Louis**	26	202	Abe Simon	254½	TKO 13	Detroit
1941	Apr. 8	**Joe Louis**	26	203½	Tony Musto	199½	TKO 9	St. Louis
1941	May 23	**Joe Louis**	27	201½	Buddy Baer	237½	Disq 7	Washington, DC
1941	June 18	**Joe Louis**	27	199½	Billy Conn	174	KO 13	NYC (Polo Grounds)
1941	Sept. 29	**Joe Louis**	27	202¼	Lou Nova	202½	TKO 6	NYC (Polo Grounds)
1942	Jan. 9	**Joe Louis**	27	206¾	Buddy Baer	250	KO 1	NYC (Mad. Sq. Garden)
1942	Mar. 27	**Joe Louis**	27	207½	Abe Simon	255½	KO 6	NYC (Mad. Sq. Garden)
1942-45	World War II							
1946	June 9	**Joe Louis**	32	207	Billy Conn	187	KO 8	NYC (Yankee Stadium)
1946	Sept. 18	**Joe Louis**	32	211	Tami Mauriello	198½	KO 1	NYC (Yankee Stadium)
1947	Dec. 5	**Joe Louis**	33	211½	Jersey Joe Walcott	194½	Ws 15	NYC (Mad. Sq. Garden)
1948	June 25	**Joe Louis****	34	213½	Jersey Joe Walcott	194¾	KO 11	NYC (Yankee Stadium)
1949	June 22	**Ezzard Charles**	27	181¾	Jersey Joe Walcott	195½	Wu 15	Chicago
1949	Aug. 10	**Ezzard Charles**	28	180	Gus Lesnevich	182	TKO 8	NYC (Yankee Stadium)
1949	Oct. 14	**Ezzard Charles**	28	182	Pat Valentino	188½	KO 8	San Francisco
1950	Aug. 15	**Ezzard Charles**	29	183¼	Freddie Beshore	184½	TKO 14	Buffalo
1950	Sept. 27	**Ezzard Charles**	29	184½	Joe Louis	218	Wu 15	NYC (Yankee Stadium)
1950	Dec. 5	**Ezzard Charles**	29	185	Nick Barone	178½	KO 11	Cincinnati
1951	Jan. 12	**Ezzard Charles**	29	185	Lee Oma	193	TKO 10	NYC (Mad. Sq. Garden)
1951	Mar. 7	**Ezzard Charles**	29	186	Jersey Joe Walcott	193	Wu 15	Detroit
1951	May 30	**Ezzard Charles**	29	182	Joey Maxim	181½	Wu 15	Chicago
1951	July 18	Jersey Joe Walcott	37	194	**Ezzard Charles**	182	KO 7	Pittsburgh
1952	June 5	**Jersey Joe Walcott**	38	196	Ezzard Charles	191½	Wu 15	Philadelphia
1952	Sept. 23	Rocky Marciano	29	184	**Jersey Joe Walcott**	196	KO 13	Philadelphia
1953	May 15	**Rocky Marciano**	29	184½	Jersey Joe Walcott	197¾	KO 1	Chicago
1953	Sept. 24	**Rocky Marciano**	30	185	Roland LaStarza	184¾	TKO 11	NYC (Polo Grounds)

*Gene Tunney retired as undefeated champion in 1928.

**Joe Louis retired as undefeated champion on Mar. 1, 1949, then came out of retirement to fight Ezzard Charles for the title in 1950.

World Heavyweight Championship Fights (Cont.)

Year	Date	Winner	Age	Wgt	Loser	Wgt	Result	Location
1954	June 17	**Rocky Marciano**	30	187½	Ezzard Charles	185½	Wu 15	NYC (Yankee Stadium)
1954	Sept. 17	**Rocky Marciano**	31	187	Ezzard Charles	192½	KO 8	NYC (Yankee Stadium)
1955	May 16	**Rocky Marciano**	31	189	Don Cockell	205	TKO 9	San Francisco
1955	Sept. 21	**Rocky Marciano***	32	188¼	Archie Moore	188	KO 9	NYC (Yankee Stadium)
1956	Nov. 30	Floyd Patterson	21	182¼	Archie Moore	187¾	KO 5	Chicago
1957	July 29	**Floyd Patterson**	22	184	Tommy Jackson	192½	TKO 10	NYC (Polo Grounds)
1957	Aug. 22	**Floyd Patterson**	22	187¼	Pete Rademacher	202	KO 6	Seattle
1958	Aug. 18	**Floyd Patterson**	23	184½	Roy Harris	194	TKO 13	Los Angeles
1959	May 1	**Floyd Patterson**	24	182½	Brian London	206	KO 11	Indianapolis
1959	June 26	Ingemar Johansson	26	196	**Floyd Patterson**	182	TKO 3	NYC (Yankee Stadium)
1960	June 20	Floyd Patterson	25	190	**Ingemar Johansson**	194¾	KO 5	NYC (Polo Grounds)
1961	Mar. 13	**Floyd Patterson**	26	194¾	Ingemar Johansson	206½	KO 6	Miami Beach
1961	Dec. 4	**Floyd Patterson**	26	188½	Tom McNeeley	197	KO 4	Toronto
1962	Sept. 25	Sonny Liston	30	214	**Floyd Patterson**	189	KO 1	Chicago
1963	July 22	**Sonny Liston**	31	215	Floyd Patterson	194½	KO 1	Las Vegas
1964	Feb. 25	Cassius Clay**	22	210½	**Sonny Liston**	218	TKO 7	Miami Beach
1965	Mar. 5	Ernie Terrell WBA	25	199	Eddie Machen	192	Wu 15	Chicago
1965	May 25	**Muhammad Ali**	23	206	Sonny Liston	215¼	KO 1	Lewiston, Me.
1965	Nov. 1	Ernie Terrell WBA	26	206	George Chuvalo	209	Wu 15	Toronto
1965	Nov. 22	**Muhammad Ali**	23	210	Floyd Patterson	196¾	TKO 12	Las Vegas
1966	Mar. 29	**Muhammad Ali**	24	214½	George Chuvalo	216	Wu 15	Toronto
1966	May 21	**Muhammad Ali**	24	201½	Henry Cooper	188	TKO 6	London
1966	June 28	Ernie Terrell WBA	27	209½	Doug Jones	187½	Wu 15	Houston
1966	Aug. 6	**Muhammad Ali**	24	209½	Brian London	201½	KO 3	London
1966	Sept. 10	**Muhammad Ali**	24	203½	Karl Mildenberger	194¼	TKO 12	Frankfurt, W. Ger.
1966	Nov. 14	**Muhammad Ali**	24	212¾	Cleveland Williams	210½	TKO 3	Houston
1967	Feb. 6	**Muhammad Ali**	25	212¼	Ernie Terrell WBA	212½	Wu 15	Houston
1967	Mar. 22	**Muhammad Ali**	25	211½	Zora Folley	202½	KO 7	NYC (Mad. Sq. Garden)
1968	Mar. 4	Joe Frazier	24	204½	Buster Mathis	243½	TKO 11	NYC (Mad. Sq. Garden)
1968	Apr. 27	Jimmy Ellis	28	197	Jerry Quarry	195	Wm 15	Oakland
1968	June 24	Joe Frazier NY	24	203½	Manuel Ramos	208	TKO 2	NYC (Mad. Sq. Garden)
1968	Aug. 14	Jimmy Ellis WBA	24	198	Floyd Patterson	188	Ref 5	Stockholm
1968	Dec. 10	Joe Frazier NY	24	203	Oscar Bonavena	207	Wu 15	Philadelphia
1969	Apr. 22	Joe Frazier NY	25	204½	Dave Zyglewicz	190½	KO 1	Houston
1969	June 23	Joe Frazier NY	25	203½	Jerry Quarry	198½	TKO 8	NYC (Mad. Sq. Garden)
1970	Feb. 16	Joe Frazier NY	26	205	Jimmy Ellis WBA	201	TKO 5	NYC (Mad. Sq. Garden)
1970	Nov. 18	Joe Frazier	26	209	Bob Foster	188	KO 2	Detroit
1971	Mar. 8	Joe Frazier	27	205½	**Muhammad Ali**	215	Wu 15	NYC (Mad. Sq. Garden)
1972	Jan. 15	**Joe Frazier**	28	215½	Terry Daniels	195	TKO 4	New Orleans
1972	May 26	**Joe Frazier**	28	217½	Ron Stander	218	TKO 5	Omaha, Neb.
1973	Jan. 22	George Foreman	24	217½	**Joe Frazier**	214	TKO 2	Kingston, Jamaica
1973	Sept. 1	**George Foreman**	24	219½	Jose (King) Roman	196½	KO 1	Tokyo
1974	Mar. 26	**George Foreman**	24	224¾	Ken Norton	212¾	TKO 2	Caracas, Venezuela
1974	Oct. 30	Muhammad Ali	32	216½	**George Foreman**	220	KO 8	Kinshasa, Zaire
1975	Mar. 24	**Muhammad Ali**	33	223½	Chuck Wepner	225	TKO 15	Cleveland
1975	May 16	**Muhammad Ali**	33	224½	Ron Lyle	219	TKO 11	Las Vegas
1975	July 1	**Muhammad Ali**	33	224½	Joe Bugner	230	Wu 15	Kuala Lumpur, Malaysia
1975	Oct. 1	**Muhammad Ali**	33	224½	Joe Frazier	215	TKO 15	Manila, Philippines
1976	Feb. 20	**Muhammad Ali**	34	226	Jean Pierre Coopman	206	KO 5	San Juan, P.R.
1976	Apr. 30	**Muhammad Ali**	34	230	Jimmy Young	209	Wu 15	Landover, Md.
1976	May 24	**Muhammad Ali**	34	220	Richard Dunn	206½	TKO 5	Munich, W. Ger.
1976	Sept. 28	**Muhammad Ali**	34	221	Ken Norton	217½	Wu 15	NYC (Yankee Stadium)
1977	May 16	**Muhammad Ali**	35	221¼	Alfredo Evangelista	209¼	Wu 15	Landover, Md.
1977	Sept. 29	**Muhammad Ali**	35	225	Earnie Shavers	211¼	Wu 15	NYC (Mad. Sq. Garden)

*Rocky Marciano retired as undefeated champion on Apr. 27, 1956.
**After defeating Liston, Cassius Clay announced that he had changed his name to Muhammad Ali. He was later stripped of his title by the WBA and most state boxing commissions after refusing induction into the U.S. Army on Apr. 28, 1967.

Year	Date	Winner	Age	Wgt	Loser	Wgt	Result	Location
1978	Feb. 15	Leon Spinks	24	197¼	**Muhammad Ali**	224¼	Ws 15	Las Vegas
1978	June 9	Larry Holmes	28	209	Ken Norton WBC†	220	Ws 15	Las Vegas
1978	Sept. 15	Muhammad Ali*	36	221	**Leon Spinks**	201	Wu 15	New Orleans
1978	Nov. 10	Larry Holmes WBC	29	214	Alfredo Evangelista	208¼	KO 7	Las Vegas
1979	Mar. 23	Larry Holmes WBC	29	214	Osvaldo Ocasio	207	TKO 7	Las Vegas
1979	June 22	Larry Holmes WBC	29	215	Mike Weaver	202	TKO 12	NYC (Mad. Sq. Garden)
1979	Sept. 28	Larry Holmes WBC	29	210	Earnie Shavers	211	TKO 11	Las Vegas
1979	Oct. 20	John Tate	24	240	Gerrie Coetzee	222	Wu 15	Pretoria, S. Africa
1980	Feb. 3	Larry Holmes WBC	30	213½	Lorenzo Zanon	215	TKO 6	Las Vegas
1980	Mar. 31	Mike Weaver	27	232	John Tate WBA	232	KO 15	Knoxville, Tenn.
1980	Mar. 31	Larry Holmes WBC	30	211	Leroy Jones	254½	TKO 8	Las Vegas
1980	July 7	Larry Holmes WBC	30	214¼	Scott LeDoux	226	TKO 7	Minneapolis
1980	Oct. 2	Larry Holmes WBC	30	211½	Muhammad Ali	217½	TKO 11	Las Vegas
1980	Oct. 25	Mike Weaver WBA	28	210	Gerrie Coetzee	226½	KO 13	Sun City, Boph'swana
1981	Apr. 11	**Larry Holmes**	31	215	Trevor Berbick	215½	Wu 15	Las Vegas
1981	June 12	**Larry Holmes**	31	212¼	Leon Spinks	200¼	TKO 3	Detroit
1981	Oct. 3	Mike Weaver WBA	29	215	Quick Tillis	209	Wu 15	Rosemont, Ill.
1981	Nov. 6	**Larry Holmes**	32	213¼	Renaldo Snipes	215¾	TKO 11	Pittsburgh
1982	June 11	**Larry Holmes**	32	212½	Gerry Cooney	225½	TKO 13	Las Vegas
1982	Nov. 26	**Larry Holmes**	33	217½	Randall (Tex) Cobb	234¼	Wu 15	Houston
1982	Dec. 10	Michael Dokes	24	216	Mike Weaver WBA	209¾	TKO 1	Las Vegas
1983	Mar. 27	**Larry Holmes**	33	221	Lucien Rodriguez	209	Wu 12	Scranton, Pa.
1983	May 20	Michael Dokes WBA	24	223	Mike Weaver	218½	Draw 15	Las Vegas
1983	May 20	**Larry Holmes**	33	213	Tim Witherspoon	219½	Ws 12	Las Vegas
1983	Sept. 10	**Larry Holmes**	33	223	Scott Frank	211¼	TKO 5	Atlantic City
1983	Sept. 23	Gerrie Coetzee	28	215	Michael Dokes WBA	217	KO 10	Richfield, Ohio
1983	Nov. 25	**Larry Holmes**	34	219	Marvis Frazier	200	TKO 1	Las Vegas
1984	Mar. 9	Tim Witherspoon††	26	220¼	Greg Page	239½	Wm 12	Las Vegas
1984	Aug. 31	Pinklon Thomas	26	216	Tim Witherspoon WBC	217	Wm 12	Las Vegas
1984	Nov. 9	**Larry Holmes** IBF	35	221½	Bonecrusher Smith	227	TKO 12	Las Vegas
1984	Dec. 1	Greg Page	26	236½	Gerrie Coetzee WBA	218	KO 8	Sun City, Boph'swana
1985	Mar. 15	**Larry Holmes**	35	223½	David Bey	233¼	TKO 10	Las Vegas
1985	Apr. 29	Tony Tubbs	26	229	Greg Page WBA	239½	Wu 15	Buffalo
1985	May 20	**Larry Holmes**	35	222¼	Carl Williams	215	Wu 15	Las Vegas
1985	June 15	Pinklon Thomas	27	220¼	Mike Weaver	221¼	KO 8	Las Vegas
1985	Sept. 21	Michael Spinks	29	200	**Larry Holmes** IBF	221½	Wu 15	Las Vegas
1986	Jan. 17	Tim Witherspoon	28	227	Tony Tubbs WBA	229	Wm 15	Atlanta
1986	Mar. 22	Trevor Berbick	33	218½	Pinklon Thomas WBC	222¾	Wu 15	Las Vegas
1986	Apr. 19	**Michael Spinks**	29	205	Larry Holmes	223	Ws 15	Las Vegas
1986	July 19	Tim Witherspoon WBA	28	234¾	Frank Bruno	228	TKO 11	Wembley, England
1986	Sept. 6	**Michael Spinks**	30	201	Steffen Tangstad	214¾	TKO 4	Las Vegas
1986	Nov. 22	Mike Tyson	20	221¼	Trevor Berbick WBC	218½	TKO 2	Las Vegas
1986	Dec. 12	Bonecrusher Smith	33	228½	Tim Witherspoon WBA	233½	TKO 1	NYC (Mad. Sq. Garden)
1987	Mar. 7	Mike Tyson WBC	20	219	Bonecrusher Smith WBA	233	Wu 12	Las Vegas
1987	May 30	Mike Tyson	20	218¾	Pinklon Thomas	217¾	KO 6	Las Vegas
1987	May 30	Tony Tucker‡	28	222¼	Buster Douglas	227¼	TKO 10	Las Vegas
1987	June 15	**Michael Spinks**	30	208¾	Gerry Cooney	238	TKO 5	Atlantic City
1987	Aug. 1	Mike Tyson	21	221	Tony Tucker IBF	221	Wu 12	Las Vegas
1987	Oct. 16	Mike Tyson	21	216	Tyrell Biggs	228¾	TKO 7	Atlantic City
1988	Jan. 22	Mike Tyson	21	215¾	Larry Holmes	225¾	TKO 4	Atlantic City
1988	Mar. 20	Mike Tyson	21	216¼	Tony Tubbs	238¼	KO 2	Tokyo
1988	June 27	Mike Tyson	21	218¼	**Michael Spinks**	212¼	KO 1	Atlantic City
1989	Feb. 25	**Mike Tyson**	22	218	Frank Bruno	228	TKO 5	Las Vegas
1989	July 21	**Mike Tyson**	23	219¼	Carl Williams	218	TKO 1	Atlantic City
1990	Feb. 10	Buster Douglas	29	231½	**Mike Tyson**	220½	KO 10	Tokyo
1990	Oct. 25	Evander Holyfield	28	208	**Buster Douglas**	246	KO 3	Las Vegas
1991	Apr. 19	**Evander Holyfield**	28	208	George Foreman	257	Wu 12	Atlantic City
1991	Nov. 23	**Evander Holyfield**	29	210	Bert Cooper	215	TKO 7	Atlanta

*Muhammad Ali retired as champion on June 27, 1979, then came out of retirement to fight Larry Holmes for the title in 1980.
†WBC recognized Ken Norton as world champion when Leon Spinks refused to meet Norton before Spinks' rematch with Muhammad Ali. Norton had scored a 15-round split decision over Jimmy Young on Nov. 5, 1977 in Las Vegas.
††WBC recognized winner of Mar. 9, 1984 fight between Tim Witherspoon and Greg Page as world champion after Larry Holmes relinquished title in dispute. IBF then recognized Holmes.
‡IBF recognized winner of May 30, 1987 fight between Tony Tucker and James (Buster) Douglas as world champion after Michael Spinks relinquished title in dispute.

World Heavyweight Championship Fights (Cont.)

Year	Date	Winner	Age	Wgt	Loser	Wgt	Result	Location
1992	June 19	**Evander Holyfield**	29	210	Larry Holmes	233	Wu 12	Las Vegas
1992	Nov. 13	Riddick Bowe	25	235	**Evander Holyfield**	205	Wu 12	Las Vegas
1993	Feb. 6	**Riddick Bowe**	25	243	Michael Dokes	244	TKO 1	NYC (Mad. Sq. Garden)
1993	May 8	Lennox Lewis WBC*	27	235	Tony Tucker	235	Wu 12	Las Vegas
1993	May 22	**Riddick Bowe**	25	244	Jesse Ferguson	224	TKO 2	Washington, D.C.
1993	Oct. 1	Lennox Lewis WBC	28	233	Frank Bruno	238	TKO 7	Cardiff, Wales
1993	Nov. 6	Evander Holyfield	31	217	**Riddick Bowe**	246	Wm 12	Las Vegas
1994	Apr. 22	Michael Moorer	26	214	**Evander Holyfield**	214	Wm 12	Las Vegas
1994	May 6	Lennox Lewis WBC	28	235	Phil Jackson	218	TKO 8	Atlantic City
1994	Sept. 25	Oliver McCall	29	231¼	**Lennox Lewis** WBC	238	TKO 2	London

*WBC recognized Lennox Lewis as world champion when Riddick Bowe gave up that portion of his title on Dec. 14, 1992, rather than fight Lewis, the WBC's mandatory challenger.

Wide World Photos

Cassius Clay (left) stunned the boxing world in 1964 when he beat champion Sonny Liston in a seventh round TKO. Clay changed his name to **Muhammad Ali** after winning the title.

All-Time Heavyweight Upsets

Buster Douglas' Feb. 10, 1990, knockout of unbeaten heavyweight champion Mike Tyson ranks as the biggest upset in boxing history. It tops 11 other well-known upsets in the annals of the heavyweight division. All were fights for the world championship except the Max Schmeling-Joe Louis bout.

Note the following abbreviations: KO (knockout), Wu (unanimous decision), TKO (technical knockout, fight stopped), WS (split decision).

Date	Winner	Loser	Result	KO Time	Location
9/7/1892	James J. Corbett	John L. Sullivan	KO 21	1:30	Olympic Club, New Orleans
4/5/1915	Jess Willard	Jack Johnson	KO 26	1:26	Mariano Race Track, Havana
9/23/26	Gene Tunney	Jack Dempsey	Wu 10	—	Sesquicentennial Stadium, Phila.
6/13/35	James J.Braddock	Max Baer	Wu 15	—	Mad.Sq.Garden Bowl, L.I.City
6/19/36	Max Schmeling	Joe Louis	KO 12	2:29	Yankee Stadium, New York
7/18/51	Jersey Joe Walcott	Ezzard Charles	KO 7	0:55	Forbes Field, Pittsburgh
6/26/59	Ingemar Johansson	Floyd Patterson	TKO 3	2:03	Yankee Stadium, New York
2/25/64	Cassius Clay	Sonny Liston	TKO 7	*	Convention Hall, Miami Beach
10/30/74	Muhammad Ali	George Foreman	KO 8	2:58	20th of May Stadium, Zaire
2/15/78	Leon Spinks	Muhammad Ali	Ws 15	—	Hilton Pavilion, Las Vegas
9/21/85	Michael Spinks	Larry Holmes	Wu 15	—	Riviera Hotel, Las Vegas
2/10/90	Buster Douglas	Mike Tyson	KO 10	1:23	Tokyo Dome, Tokyo

*Liston failed to answer bell for Round 7.

Muhammad Ali's Career Pro Record

Born Cassius Marcellus Clay, Jr. on Jan. 17, 1942, in Louisville; Amateur record of 100-5; won light-heavyweight gold medal at 1960 Olympic Games; Pro record of 56-5-0 with 37 KOs in 61 fights.

1960

Date	Opponent (location)	Result
Oct. 29	Tunney Hunsaker, Louisville	Wu 6
Dec. 27	Herb Siler, Miami Beach	TKO 4

1961

Date	Opponent (location)	Result
Jan. 17	Tony Esperti, Miami Beach	TKO 3
Feb. 7	Jim Robinson, Miami Beach	TKO 1
Feb. 21	Donnie Fleeman, Miami Beach	TKO 7
Apr. 19	Lamar Clark, Louisville	KO 2
June 26	Duke Sabedong, Las Vegas	Wu 10
July 22	Alonzo Johnson, Louisville	Wu 10
Oct. 7	Alex Miteff, Louisville	TKO 6
Nov. 29	Willi Besmanoff, Louisville	TKO 7

1962

Date	Opponent (location)	Result
Feb. 10	Sonny Banks, New York	TKO 4
Feb. 28	Don Warner, Miami Beach	TKO 4
Apr. 23	George Logan, Los Angeles	TKO 4
May 19	Billy Daniels, Los Angeles	TKO 7
July 20	Alejandro Lavorante, Los Angeles	KO 5
Nov. 15	Archie Moore, Los Angeles	KO 4

1963

Date	Opponent (location)	Result
Jan. 24	Charlie Powell, Pittsburgh	KO 3
Mar. 13	Doug Jones, New York	Wu 10
June 18	Henry Cooper, London	TKO 5

1964

Date	Opponent (location)	Result
Feb. 25	Sonny Liston, Miami Beach	TKO 7

(won World Heavyweight title)

After the fight, Clay announces he is a member of the Black Muslim religious sect and has changed his name to Muhammad Ali.

1965

Date	Opponent (location)	Result
May 25	Sonny Liston, Lewiston, Me.	KO 1
Nov. 22	Floyd Patterson, Las Vegas	TKO 12

1966

Date	Opponent (location)	Result
Mar. 29	George Chuvalo, Toronto	Wu 15
May 21	Henry Cooper, London	TKO 6
Aug. 6	Brian London, London	KO 3
Sept.10	Karl Mildenberger, Frankfurt	TKO 12
Nov. 12	Cleveland Williams, Houston	TKO 3

1967

Date	Opponent (location)	Result
Feb. 6	Ernie Terrell, Houston	Wu 15
Mar. 22	Zora Folley, New York	KO 7
Apr. 28	Refuses induction into U.S. Army and is stripped of world title by WBA and most state commissions the next day.	
June 20	Found guilty of draft evasion in Houston; fined $10,000 and sentenced to 5 years; remains free pending appeals, but is barred from the ring.	

1968-69
(Inactive)

1970

Date	Opponent (location)	Result
Feb. 3	Announces retirement.	
Oct. 26	Jerry Quarry, Atlanta	TKO 3
Dec. 7	Oscar Bonavena, New York	TKO 15

1971

Date	Opponent (location)	Result
Mar. 8	Joe Frazier, New York	Lu 15

(for World Heavyweight title)

June 28	U.S. Supreme Court reverses Ali's 1967 conviction saying he had been drafted improperly.	
July 26	Jimmy Ellis, Houston	TKO 12

(won vacant NABF Heavyweight title)

Nov. 17	Buster Mathis, Houston	Wu 12
Dec. 26	Jurgen Blin, Zurich	KO 7

1972

Date	Opponent (location)	Result
Apr. 1	Mac Foster, Tokyo	Wu 15
May 1	George Chuvalo, Vancouver	Wu 12
June 27	Jerry Quarry, Las Vegas	TKO 7
July 19	Al (Blue) Lewis, Dublin, Ire.	TKO 11
Sept.20	Floyd Patterson, New York	TKO 7
Nov. 21	Bob Foster, Stateline, Nev.	TKO 8

1973

Date	Opponent (location)	Result
Feb. 14	Joe Bugner, Las Vegas	Wu 12
Mar. 31	Ken Norton, San Diego	Ls 12

(lost NABF Heavyweight title)

Sept.10	Ken Norton, Inglewood, Calif.	Ws 12

(regained NABF Heavyweight title)

Oct. 20	Rudi Lubbers, Jakarta, Indonesia	Wu 12

1974

Date	Opponent (location)	Result
Jan. 28	Joe Frazier, New York	Wu 12
Oct. 30	George Foreman, Kinshasa, Zaire	KO 8

(regained World Heavyweight title)

1975

Date	Opponent (location)	Result
Mar. 24	Chuck Wepner, Cleveland	TKO 15
May 16	Ron Lyle, Las Vegas	TKO 11
June 30	Joe Bugner, Kuala Lumpur, Malaysia	Wu 15
Sept.30	Joe Frazier, Manila	TKO 14

1976

Date	Opponent (location)	Result
Feb. 20	Jean-Pierre Coopman, San Juan	KO 5
Apr. 30	Jimmy Young, Landover, Md	Wu 15
May 24	Richard Dunn, Munich	TKO 5
Sept.28	Ken Norton, New York	Wu 15

1977

Date	Opponent (location)	Result
May 16	Alfredo Evangelista, Landover	Wu 15
Sept.29	Earnie Shavers, New York	Wu 15

1978

Date	Opponent (location)	Result
Feb. 15	Leon Spinks, Las Vegas	Ls 15

(lost World Heavyweight title)

Sept.15	Leon Spinks, New Orleans	Wu 15

(regained World Heavyweight title)

1979

Date		
June 27	Announces retirement.	

1980

Date	Opponent (location)	Result
Oct. 2	Larry Holmes, Las Vegas	TKO by 11

1981

Date	Opponent (location)	Result
Dec. 11	Trevor Berbick, Nassau	Lu 10
	(retires after fight)	

Major Titleholders

Note the following sanctioning body abbreviations: NBA (National Boxing Association), WBA (World Boxing Association), WBC (World Boxing Council), GBR (Great Britain), IBF (International Boxing Federation), plus other national and state commissions.

Fighters who retired as champion are indicated by (*) and champions who abandoned or relinquished their titles are indicated by (†).

Heavyweights

Widely accepted champions in CAPITAL letters. Current champions in **bold** type.

Champion	Held Title	Champion	Held Title
JOHN L. SULLIVAN	1885-92	MUHAMMAD ALI	1974-78
JAMES J. CORBETT	1892-97	LEON SPINKS	1978
BOB FITZSIMMONS	1897-99	Ken Norton (WBC)	1978
JAMES J. JEFFRIES	1899-1905*	Larry Holmes (WBC)	1978-80
MARVIN HART	1905-06	MUHAMMAD ALI	1978-79*
TOMMY BURNS	1906-08	John Tate (WBA)	1979-80
JACK JOHNSON	1908-15	Mike Weaver (WBA)	1980-82
JESS WILLARD	1915-19	LARRY HOLMES	1980-85
JACK DEMPSEY	1919-26	Michael Dokes (WBA)	1982-83
GENE TUNNEY	1926-28*	Gerrie Coetzee (WBA)	1983-84
MAX SCHMELING	1930-32	Tim Witherspoon (WBC)	1984
JACK SHARKEY	1932-33	Pinklon Thomas (WBC)	1984-86
PRIMO CARNERA	1933-34	Greg Page (WBA)	1984-85
MAX BAER	1934-35	MICHAEL SPINKS	1985-87
JAMES J. BRADDOCK	1935-37	Tim Witherspoon (WBA)	1986
JOE LOUIS	1937-49*	Trevor Berbick (WBC)	1986
EZZARD CHARLES	1949-51	Mike Tyson (WBC)	1986-87
JERSEY JOE WALCOTT	1951-52	James (Bonecrusher) Smith (WBA)	1986-87
ROCKY MARCIANO	1952-56*	Tony Tucker (IBF)	1987
FLOYD PATTERSON	1956-59	Mike Tyson (WBC, WBA, IBF)	1987-88
INGEMAR JOHANSSON	1959-60	MIKE TYSON	1988-90
FLOYD PATTERSON	1960-62	BUSTER DOUGLAS (WBC, WBA, IBF)	1990
SONNY LISTON	1962-64	EVANDER HOLYFIELD (WBC, WBA, IBF)	1990-92
CASSIUS CLAY (MUHAMMAD ALI)	1964-70	RIDDICK BOWE (WBA, IBF)	1992-93
Ernie Terrell (WBA)	1965-67	Lennox Lewis (WBC)	1992-94
Joe Frazier (NY)	1968-70	EVANDER HOLYFIELD (WBA, IBF)	1993-94
Jimmy Ellis (WBA)	1968-70	**MICHAEL MOORER** (WBA, IBF)	1994—
JOE FRAZIER	1970-73	**Oliver McCall** (WBC)	1994—
GEORGE FOREMAN	1973-74		

Note: John L. Sullivan held the Bare Knuckle championship from 1882-85.

Light Heavyweights

Widely accepted champions in CAPITAL letters. Current champions in **bold** type.

Champion	Held Title	Champion	Held Title
JACK ROOT	1903	ARCHIE MOORE	1952-62
GEORGE GARDNER	1903	Harold Johnson (NBA)	1961
BOB FITZSIMMONS	1903-05	HAROLD JOHNSON	1962-63
PHILADELPHIA JACK O'BRIEN	1905-12*	WILLIE PASTRANO	1963-65
JACK DILLON	1914-16	Eddie Cotton (Mich.)	1963-64
BATTLING LEVINSKY	1916-20	JOSE TORRES	1965-66
GEORGES CARPENTIER	1920-22	DICK TIGER	1966-68
BATTLING SIKI	1922-23	BOB FOSTER	1968-74 *
MIKE McTIGUE	1923-25	Vicente Rondon (WBA)	1971-72
PAUL BERLENBACH	1925-26	John Conteh (WBC)	1974-77
JACK DELANEY	1926-27†	Victor Galindez (WBA)	1974-78
Jimmy Slattery (NBA)	1927	Miguel A. Cuello (WBC)	1977-78
TOMMY LOUGHRAN	1927-29	Mate Parlov (WBC)	1978
JIMMY SLATTERY	1930	Mike Rossman (WBA)	1978-79
MAXIE ROSENBLOOM	1930-34	Marvin Johnson (WBC)	1978-79
George Nichols (NBA)	1932	Matthew (Franklin) Saad Muhammad (WBC)	1979-81
Bob Godwin (NBA)	1933	Marvin Johnson (WBA)	1979-80
BOB OLIN	1934-35	Eddie (Gregory)	
JOHN HENRY LEWIS	1935-38	Mustapha Muhammad (WBA)	1980-81
MELIO BETTINA (NY)	1939	Michael Spinks (WBA)	1981-83
Len Harvey (GBR)	1939-42	Dwight (Braxton) Muhammad Qawi (WBC)	1981-83
BILLY CONN	1939-40†	MICHAEL SPINKS	1983-85†
ANTON CHRISTOFORIDIS (NBA)	1941	J.B. Williamson (WBC)	1985-86
GUS LESNEVICH	1941-48	Slobodan Kacar (IBF)	1985-86
Freddie Mills (GBR)	1942-46	Marvin Johnson (WBA)	1986-87
FREDDIE MILLS	1948-50	Dennis Andries (WBC)	1986-87
JOEY MAXIM	1950-52	Bobby Czyz (IBF)	1986-87

Champion	Held Title
Leslie Stewart (WBA)	1987
Virgil Hill (WBA)	1987-91
Prince Charles Williams (IBF)	1987-93
Thomas Hearns (WBC)	1987
Donny Lalonde (WBC)	1987-88
Sugar Ray Leonard (WBC)	1988
Dennis Andries (WBC)	1989
Jeff Harding (WBC)	1989-90

Champion	Held Title
Dennis Andries (WBC)	1990-91
Jeff Harding (WBC)	1991-94
Thomas Hearns (WBA)	1991-92
Iran Barkley (WBA)	1992†
Virgil Hill (WBA)	1992—
Henry Maske (IBF)	1993—
Mike McCallum (WBC)	1994—

Middleweights

Widely accepted champions in CAPITAL letters. Current champions in **bold** type.

Champion	Held Title
JACK (NONPAREIL) DEMPSEY	1884-91
BOB FITZSIMMONS	1891-97
CHARLES (KID) McCOY	1897-98
TOMMY RYAN	1898-1907
STANLEY KETCHEL	1908
BILLY PAPKE	1908
STANLEY KETCHEL	1908-10
FRANK KLAUS	1913
GEORGE CHIP	1913-14
AL McCOY	1914-17
Jeff Smith (AUS)	1914
Mick King (AUS)	1914
Jeff Smith (AUS)	1914-15
Lee Darcy (AUS)	1915-17
MIKE O'DOWD	1917-20
JOHNNY WILSON	1920-23
Wm. Bryan Downey (Ohio)	1921-22
Dave Rosenberg (NY)	1922
Jock Malone (Ohio)	1922-23
Mike O'Dowd (NY)	1922
Lou Bogash (NY)	1923
HARRY GREB	1923-26
TIGER FLOWERS	1926
MICKEY WALKER	1926-31†
GORILLA JONES	1931-32
MARCEL THIL	1932-37
Ben Jeby (NY)	1932-33
Lou Brouillard (NBA, NY)	1933
Vince Dundee (NBA, NY)	1933-34
Teddy Yarosz (NBA, NY)	1934-35
Babe Risko (NBA, NY)	1935-36
Freddie Steele (NBA, NY)	1936-38
FRED APOSTOLI	1937-39
Al Hostak (NBA)	1938
Solly Krieger (NBA)	1938-39
Al Hostak (NBA)	1939-40
CEFERINO GARCIA	1939-40
KEN OVERLIN	1940-41
Tony Zale (NBA)	1940-41
BILLY SOOSE	1941
TONY ZALE	1941-47
ROCKY GRAZIANO	1947-48
TONY ZALE	1948
MARCEL CERDAN	1948-49

Champion	Held Title
JAKE LA MOTTA	1949-51
SUGAR RAY ROBINSON	1951
RANDY TURPIN	1951
SUGAR RAY ROBINSON	1951-52 *
CARL (BOBO) OLSON	1953-55
SUGAR RAY ROBINSON	1955-57
GENE FULLMER	1957
SUGAR RAY ROBINSON	1957
CARMEN BASILIO	1957-58
SUGAR RAY ROBINSON	1958-60
Gene Fullmer (NBA)	1959-62
PAUL PENDER	1960-61
TERRY DOWNES	1961-62
PAUL PENDER	1962-63
Dick Tiger (WBA)	1962-63
DICK TIGER	1963
JOEY GIARDELLO	1963-65
DICK TIGER	1965-66
EMILE GRIFFITH	1966-67
NINO BENVENUTI	1967
EMILE GRIFFITH	1967-68
NINO BENVENUTI	1968-70
CARLOS MONZON	1970-77 *
Rodrigo Valdez (WBC)	1974-76
RODRIGO VALDEZ	1977-78
HUGO CORRO	1978-79
VITO ANTUOFERMO	1979-80
ALAN MINTER	1980
MARVELOUS MARVIN HAGLER	1980-87
SUGAR RAY LEONARD	1987
Frank Tate (IBF)	1987-88
Sumbu Kalambay (WBA)	1987-89
Thomas Hearns (WBC)	1987-88
Iran Barkley (WBC)	1988-89
Michael Nunn (IBF)	1988-91
Roberto Duran (WBC)	1989-90 *
Mike McCallum (WBA)	1989-91
Julian Jackson (WBC)	1990-93
James Toney (IBF)	1991-93†
Reggie Johnson (WBA)	1992-93
Roy Jones Jr. (IBF)	1993-94†
Gerald McClellan (WBC)	1993—
John David Jackson (WBA)	1993-94
Jorge Castro (WBA)	1994—

Welterweights

Widely accepted champions in CAPITAL letters. Current champions in **bold** type.

Champion	Held Title
PADDY DUFFY	1888-90
MYSTERIOUS BILLY SMITH	1892-94
TOMMY RYAN	1894-98
MYSTERIOUS BILLY SMITH	1898-1900
MATTY MATTHEWS	1900
EDDIE CONNOLLY	1900
JAMES (RUBE) FERNS	1900
MATTY MATHEWS	1900-01
JAMES (RUBE) FERNS	1901
JOE WALCOTT	1901-04
THE DIXIE KID	1904-05

Champion	Held Title
HONEY MELLODY	1906-07
MIKE (TWIN) SULLIVAN	1907-08†
Harry Lewis	1908-11
Jimmy Gardner	1908
Jimmy Clabby	1910-11
WALDEMAR HOLBERG	1914
TOM McCORMICK	1914
MATT WELLS	1914-15
MIKE GLOVER	1915
JACK BRITTON	1915
TED (KID) LEWIS	1915-16

Major Titleholders (Cont.)
Welterweights

Champion	Held Title
JACK BRITTON	1916-17
TED (KID) LEWIS	1917-19
JACK BRITTON	1919-22
MICKEY WALKER	1922-26
PETE LATZO	1926-27
JOE DUNDEE	1927-29
JACKIE FIELDS	1929-30
YOUNG JACK THOMPSON	1930
TOMMY FREEMAN	1930-31
YOUNG JACK THOMPSON	1931
LOU BROUILLARD	1931-32
JACKIE FIELDS	1932-33
YOUNG CORBETT III	1933
JIMMY McLARNIN	1933-34
BARNEY ROSS	1934
JIMMY McLARNIN	1934-35
BARNEY ROSS	1935-38
HENRY ARMSTRONG	1938-40
FRITZIE ZIVIC	1940-41
Izzy Jannazzo (Md.)	1940-41
FREDDIE (RED) COCHRANE	1941-46
MARTY SERVO	1946 *
SUGAR RAY ROBINSON	1946-51†
Johnny Bratton	1951
KID GAVILAN	1951-54
JOHNNY SAXTON	1954-55
TONY DeMARCO	1955
CARMEN BASILIO	1955-56
JOHNNY SAXTON	1956
CARMEN BASILIO	1956-57†
VIRGIL AKINS	1958
DON JORDAN	1958-60
BENNY (KID) PARET	1960-61
EMILE GRIFFITH	1961
BENNY (KID) PARET	1961-62
EMILE GRIFFITH	1962-63
LUIS RODRIGUEZ	1963
EMILE GRIFFITH	1963-66†
Charlie Shipes (Calif.)	1966-67

Champion	Held Title
CURTIS COKES	1966-69
JOSE NAPOLES	1969-70
BILLY BACKUS	1970-71
JOSE NAPOLES	1971-75
Hedgemon Lewis (NY)	1972-73
Angel Espada (WBA)	1975-76
JOHN H. STRACEY	1975-76
CARLOS PALOMINO	1976-79
Pipino Cuevas (WBA)	1976-80
WILFREDO BENITEZ	1979
SUGAR RAY LEONARD	1979-80
ROBERTO DURAN	1980
Thomas Hearns (WBA)	1980-81
SUGAR RAY LEONARD	1980-82
Donald Curry (WBA)	1983-85
Milton McCrory (WBC)	1983-85
DONALD CURRY	1985-86
LLOYD HONEYGHAN	1986-87
JORGE VACA (WBC)	1987-88
LLOYD HONEYGHAN (WBC)	1988-89
Mark Breland (WBA)	1987
Marlon Starling (WBA)	1987-88
Tomas Molinares (WBA)	1988-89
Simon Brown (IBF)	1988-91
Mark Breland (WBA)	1989-90
MARLON STARLING (WBC)	1989-90
Aaron Davis (WBA)	1990-91
Maurice Blocker (WBC)	1990-91
Meldrick Taylor (WBA)	1991-92
Simon Brown (WBC)	1991
Maurice Blocker (IBF)	1991-93
Buddy McGirt (WBC)	1991-93
Crisanto Espana (WBA)	1992-94
Pernell Whitaker (WBC)	1993—
Felix Trinidad (IBF)	1993—
Ike Quartey (WBA)	1994—

Lightweights

Widely accepted champions in CAPITAL letters. Current champions in **bold** type.

Champion	Held Title
JACK McAULIFFE	1886-94
GEORGE (KID) LAVIGNE	1896-99
FRANK ERNE	1899-02
JOE GANS	1902-04
JIMMY BRITT	1904-05
BATTLING NELSON	1905-06
JOE GANS	1906-08
BATTLING NELSON	1908-10
AD WOLGAST	1910-12
WILLIE RITCHIE	1912-14
FREDDIE WELSH	1915-17
BENNY LEONARD	1917-25 *
JIMMY GOODRICH	1925
ROCKY KANSAS	1925-26
SAMMY MANDELL	1926-30
AL SINGER	1930
TONY CANZONERI	1930-33
BARNEY ROSS	1933-35†
TONY CANZONERI	1935-36
LOU AMBERS	1936-38
HENRY ARMSTRONG	1938-39
LOU AMBERS	1939-40
Sammy Angott (NBA)	1940-41
LEW JENKINS	1940-41
SAMMY ANGOTT	1941-42

Champion	Held Title
Beau Jack (NY)	1942-43
Slugger White (Md.)	1943
Bob Montgomery (NY)	1943
Sammy Angott (NBA)	1943-44
Beau Jack (NY)	1943-44
Bob Montgomery (NY)	1944-47
Juan Zurita (NBA)	1944-45
IKE WILLIAMS	1947-51
JAMES CARTER	1951-52
LAURO SALAS	1952
JAMES CARTER	1952-54
PADDY DeMARCO	1954
JAMES CARTER	1954-55
WALLACE (BUD) SMITH	1955-56
JOE BROWN	1956-62
CARLOS ORTIZ	1962-65
Kenny Lane (Mich.)	1963-64
ISMAEL LAGUNA	1965
CARLOS ORTIZ	1965-68
CARLOS TEO CRUZ	1968-69
MANDO RAMOS	1969-70
ISMAEL LAGUNA	1970
KEN BUCHANAN	1970-72
Pedro Carrasco (WBC)	1971-72
Mando Ramos (WBC)	1972

Champion	Held Title
ROBERTO DURAN	1972-79†
Chango Carmona (WBC)	1972
Rodolfo Gonzalez (WBC)	1972-74
Ishimatsu Suzuki (WBC)	1974-76
Esteban DeJesus (WBC)	1976-78
Jim Watt (WBC)	1979-81
Ernesto Espana (WBA)	1979-80
Hilmer Kenty (WBA)	1980-81
Sean O'Grady (WBA,WAA)	1981
Alexis Arguello (WBC)	1981-82
Claude Noel (WBA)	1981
Andrew Ganigan (WAA)	1981-82
Arturo Frias (WBA)	1981-82
Ray Mancini (WBA)	1982-84
ALEXIS ARGUELLO	1982-83
Edwin Rosario (WBC)	1983-84
Choo Choo Brown (IBF)	1984
Livingstone Bramble (WBA)	1984-86
Harry Arroyo (IBF)	1984-85
Jose Luis Ramirez (WBC)	1984-85

Champion	Held Title
Jimmy Paul (IBF)	1985-86
Hector Camacho (WBC)	1985-86
Edwin Rosario (WBA)	1986-87
Greg Haugen (IBF)	1986-87
Julio Cesar Chavez (WBA)	1987-88
Jose Luis Ramirez (WBC)	1987-88
JULIO CESAR CHAVEZ (WBC,WBA)	1988-89
Vinny Pazienza (IBF)	1987-88
Greg Haugen (IBF)	1988-89
Pernell Whitaker (IBF,WBC)	1989-90
Edwin Rosario (WBA)	1989-90
Juan Nazario (WBA)	1990
PERNELL WHITAKER (IBF, WBC, WBA)	1990-92†
Joey Gamache (WBA)	1992
Miguel A. Gonzalez (WBC)	1992—
Tony Lopez (WBA)	1992-93
Dingaan Thobela (WBA)	1993
Fred Pendleton (IBF)	1993-94
Gussie Nazarov (WBA)	1993—
Rafael Ruelas (IBF)	1994—

Featherweights

Widely accepted champions in CAPITAL letters. Current champions in **bold** type.

Champion	Held Title
TORPEDO BILLY MURPHY	1890
YOUNG GRIFFO	1890-92
GEORGE DIXON	1892-97
SOLLY SMITH	1897-98
Ben Jordan (GBR)	1898-99
Eddie Santry (GBR)	1899-1900
DAVE SULLIVAN	1898
GEORGE DIXON	1898-1900
TERRY McGOVERN	1900-01
YOUNG CORBETT II	1901-04
ABE ATTELL	1904
BROOKLYN TOMMY SULLIVAN	1904-05
ABE ATTELL	1906-12
JOHNNY KILBANE	1912-23
Jem Driscoll (GBR)	1912-13
EUGENE CRIQUI	1923
JOHNNY DUNDEE	1923-24†
LOUIS (KID) KAPLAN	1925-26†
Dick Finnegan (Mass.)	1926-27
BENNY BASS	1927-28
TONY CANZONERI	1928
ANDRE ROUTIS	1928-29
BATTLING BATTALINO	1929-32†
Tommy Paul (NBA)	1932-33
Kid Chocolate (NY)	1932-33
Freddie Miller (NBA)	1933-36
Baby Arizmendi (MEX)	1935-36
Mike Belloise (NY)	1936-37
Petey Sarron (NBA)	1936-37
HENRY ARMSTRONG	1937-38†
Joey Archibald (NY)	1938-39
Leo Rodak (NBA)	1938-39
JOEY ARCHIBALD	1939-40
Petey Scalzo (NBA)	1940-41
Jimmy Perrin (La.)	1940-41
HARRY JEFFRA	1940-41
JOEY ARCHIBALD	1941
Richie Lemos (NBA)	1941
CHALKY WRIGHT	1941-42
Jackie Wilson (NBA)	1941-43
WILLIE PEP	1942-48
Jackie Callura (NBA)	1943
Phil Terranova (NBA)	1943-44
Sal Bartolo (NBA)	1944-46
SANDY SADDLER	1948-49
WILLIE PEP	1949-50
SANDY SADDLER	1950-57 *

Champion	Held Title
HOGAN (KID) BASSEY	1957-59
DAVEY MOORE	1959-63
ULTIMINIO (SUGAR) RAMOS	1963-64
VICENTE SALDIVAR	1964-67 *
Howard Winstone (GBR)	1968
Raul Rojas (WBA)	1968
Jose Legra (WBC)	1968-69
Shozo Saijyo (WBA)	1968-71
JOHNNY FAMECHON (WBC)	1969-70
VICENTE SALDIVAR (WBC)	1970
KUNIAKI SHIBATA (WBC)	1970-72
Antonio Gomez (WBA)	1971-72
CLEMENTE SANCHEZ (WBC)	1972
Ernesto Marcel (WBA)	1972-74
JOSE LEGRA (WBC)	1972-73
EDER JOFRE (WBC)	1973-74
Ruben Olivares (WBA)	1974
Bobby Chacon (WBC)	1974-75
ALEXIS ARGUELLO (WBA)	1974-76†
Ruben Olivares (WBC)	1975
David (Poison) Kotey (WBC)	1975-76
DANNY (LITTLE RED) LOPEZ (WBC)	1976-80
Rafael Ortega (WBA)	1977
Cecilio Lastra (WBA)	1977-78
Eusebio Pedroza (WBA)	1978-85
SALVADOR SANCHEZ (WBC)	1980-82
Juan LaPorte (WBC)	1982-84
Wilfredo Gomez (WBC)	1984
Min-Keun Oh (IBF)	1984-85
Azumah Nelson (WBC)	1984-88
Barry McGuigan (WBA)	1985-86
Ki-Young Chung (IBF)	1985-86
Steve Cruz (WBA)	1986-87
Antonio Rivera (IBF)	1986-88
Antonio Esparragoza (WBA)	1987-91
Calvin Grove (IBF)	1988
Jorge Paez (IBF)	1988-91†
Jeff Fenech (WBC)	1988-90†
Marcos Villasana (WBC)	1990-91
Yung-Kyun Park (WBA)	1991-93
Troy Dorsey (IBF)	1991
Manuel Medina (IBF)	1991-93
Paul Hodkinson (WBC)	1991-93
Tom Johnson (IBF)	1993—
Goyo Vargas (WBC)	1993
Kevin Kelley (WBC)	1993—
Eloy Rojas (WBA)	1993—

Major Titleholders (Cont.)
Bantamweights

Widely accepted champions in CAPITAL letters. Current champions in **bold** type.

Champion	Held Title	Champion	Held Title
HUGHEY BOYLE	1887-88	MARIO D'AGATA	1956-57
CHAPPIE MORAN	1889-90	ALPHONSE HALIMI	1957-59
TOMMY (SPIDER) KELLY	1890-92	JOE BECERRA	1959-60*
BILLY PLIMMER	1892-95	Johnny Caldwell (EBU)	1961-62
PEDLAR PALMER	1895-99	EDER JOFRE	1961-65
TERRY McGOVERN	1899-1900	MASAHIKO FIGHTING HARADA	1965-68
DANNY DOUGHERTY	1900-01	LIONEL ROSE	1968-69
HARRY FORBES	1901-03	RUBEN OLIVARES	1969-70
FRANKIE NEIL	1903-04	CHUCHO CASTILLO	1970-71
JOE BOWKER	1904-05	RUBEN OLIVARES	1971-72
JIMMY WALSH	1905-06†	RAFAEL HERRERA	1972
OWEN MORAN	1907-08	ENRIQUE PINDER	1972-73
MONTE ATTELL	1909-10	ROMEO ANAYA	1973
FRANKIE CONLEY	1910-11	Rafael Herrera (WBC)	1973-74
JOHNNY COULON	1911-14	ARNOLD TAYLOR	1973-74
Digger Stanley (GBR)	1910-12	SOO-HWAN HONG	1974-75
Charles Ledoux (GBR)	1912-13	Rodolfo Martinez (WBC)	1974-76
Eddie Campi (GBR)	1913-14	ALFONSO ZAMORA	1975-77
KID WILLIAMS	1914-17	Carlos Zarate (WBC)	1976-79
Johnny Ertle	1915-18	JORGE LUJAN	1977-80
PETE HERMAN	1917-20	Lupe Pintor (WBC)	1979-83
Memphis Pal Moore	1918-19	JULIAN SOLIS	1980
JOE LYNCH	1920-21	JEFF CHANDLER	1980-84
PETE HERMAN	1921	Albert Davila (WBC)	1983-85
JOHNNY BUFF	1921-22	RICHARD SANDOVAL	1984-86
JOE LYNCH	1922-24	Satoshi Shingaki (IBF)	1984-85
ABE GOLDSTEIN	1924	Jeff Fenech (IBF)	1985
CANNONBALL EDDIE MARTIN	1924-25	Daniel Zaragoza (WBC)	1985
PHIL ROSENBERG	1925-27	Miguel (Happy) Lora (WBC)	1985-88
Teddy Baldock (GBR)	1927	GABY CANIZALES	1986
BUD TAYLOR (NBA)	1927-28†	BERNARDO PINANGO	1986-87
Willie Smith (GBR)	1927-28	Wilfredo Vasquez (WBA)	1987-88
Bushy Graham (NY)	1928-29	Kevin Seabrooks (IBF)	1987-88
PANAMA AL BROWN	1929-35	Kaokor Galaxy (WBA)	1988
Sixto Escobar (NBA)	1934-35	Moon Sung-Kil (WBA)	1988-89
BALTAZAR SANGCHILLI	1935-36	Kaokor Galaxy (WBA)	1989
Lou Salica (NBA)	1935	Raul Perez (WBC)	1988-91
Sixto Escobar (NBA)	1935-36	**Orlando Canizales** (IBF)	1988—
TONY MARINO	1936	Luisito Espinosa (WBA)	1989-91
SIXTO ESCOBAR	1936-37	Greg Richardson	1991
HARRY JEFFRA	1937-38	Joichiro Tatsuyoshi (WBC)	1991-92
SIXTO ESCOBAR	1938-39 *	Israel Contreras (WBA)	1991-92
Georgie Pace (NBA)	1939-40	Eddie Cook (WBA)	1992
LOU SALICA	1940-42	Victor Rabanales (WBC)	1992-93
MANUEL ORTIZ	1942-47	Jorge Julio (WBA)	1992-93
HAROLD DADE	1947	Jung-Il Byun (WBC)	1993
MANUEL ORTIZ	1947-50	Junior Jones (WBA)	1993-94
VIC TOWEEL	1950-52	**Yasuei Yakushiji** (WBC)	1993—
JIMMY CARRUTHERS	1952-54 *	John M. Johnson (WBA)	1994
ROBERT COHEN	1954-56	**Daorung Chuvatana** (WBA)	1994—
Raul Macias (NBA)	1955-57		

Flyweights

Widely accepted champions in CAPITAL letters. Current champions in **bold** type.

Champion	Held Title	Champion	Held Title
Sid Smith (GBR)	1913	Newsboy Brown (Calif.)	1928
Bill Ladbury (GBR)	1913-14	FRANKIE GENARO (NBA,IBU)	1928-29
Percy Jones (GBR)	1914	Johnny Hill (GBR)	1928-29
Joe Symonds (GBR)	1914-16	SPIDER PLADNER (NBA,IBU)	1929
JIMMY WILDE	1916-23	FRANKIE GENARO (NBA,IBU)	1929-31
PANCHO VILLA	1923-25	Willie LaMorte (NY)	1929-30
FIDEL LaBARBA	1925-27*	Midget Wolgast (NY)	1930-35
FRENCHY BELANGER (NBA,IBU)	1927-28	YOUNG PEREZ (NBA,IBU)	1931-32
Izzy Schwartz (NY)	1927-29	JACKIE BROWN (NBA,IBU)	1932-35
Johnny McCoy (Calif.)	1927-28	BENNY LYNCH	1935-38†

Champion	Held Title
Small Montana (NY,Calif.)	1935-37
PETER KANE	1938-43
Little Dado (NBA,Calif.)	1938-40
JACKIE PATERSON	1943-48
RINTY MONAGHAN	1948-50 *
TERRY ALLEN	195
SALVADOR (DADO) MARINO	1950-52
YOSHIO SHIRAI	1953-54
PASCUAL PEREZ	1954-60
PONE KINGPETCH	1960-62
MASAHIKO (FIGHTING) HARADA	1962-63
PONE KINGPETCH	1963
HIROYUKI EBIHARA	1963-64
PONE KINGPETCH	1964-65
SALVATORE BURRINI	1965-66
Horacio Accavallo (WBA)	1966-68
WALTER McGOWAN	1966
CHARTCHAI CHIONOI	1966-69
EFREN TORRES	1969-70
Hiroyuki Ebihara (WBA)	1969
Bernabe Villacampo (WBA)	1969-70
CHARTCHAI CHIONOI	1970
Berkrerk Chartvanchai (WBA)	1970
Masao Ohba (WBA)	1970-73
ERBITO SALAVARRIA	1970-73
Betulio Gonzalez (WBC)	1972
Venice Borkorsor (WBC)	1972-73
VENICE BORKORSOR	1973
Chartchai Chionoi (WBA)	1973-74
Betulio Gonzalez (WBA)	1973-74
Shoji Oguma (WBC)	1974-75
Susumu Hanagata (WBA)	1974-75
Miguel Canto (WBC)	1975-79
Erbito Salavarria (WBA)	1975-76
Alfonso Lopez (WBA)	1976
Guty Espadas (WBA)	1976-78
Betulio Gonzalez (WBA)	1978-79
Chan-Hee Park (WBC)	1979-80
Luis Ibarra (WBA)	1979-80
Tae-Shik Kim (WBA)	1980

Champion	Held Title
Shoji Oguma (WBC)	1980-81
Peter Mathebula (WBA)	1980-81
Santos Laciar (WBA)	1981
Antonio Avelar (WBC)	1981-82
Luis Ibarra (WBA)	1981
Juan Herrera (WBA)	1981-82
Prudencio Cardona (WBC)	1982
Santos Laciar (WBA)	1982-85
Freddie Castillo (WBC)	1982
Eleoncio Mercedes (WBC)	1982-83
Charlie Magri (WBC)	1983
Frank Cedeno (WBC)	1983-84
Soon-Chun Kwon (IBF)	1983-85
Koji Kobayashi (WBC)	1984
Gabriel Bernal (WBC)	1984
Sot Chitalada (WBC)	1984-88
Hilario Zapate (WBA)	1985-87
Chong-Kwan Chung (IBF)	1985-86
Bi-Won Chung (IBF)	1986
Hi-Sup Shin (IBF)	1986-87
Dodie Penalosa (IBF)	1987
Fidel Bassa (WBA)	1987-89
Choi Chang-Ho (IBF)	1987-88
Rolando Bohol (IBF)	1988
Yong-Kang Kim (WBC)	1988-89
Duke McKenzie (IBF)	1988-89
Dave McAuley (IBF)	1989-92
Sot Chitalada (WBC)	1989-91
Jesus Rojas (WBA)	1989-90
Yul-Woo Lee (WBA)	1990
Leopard Tamakuma (WBA)	1990-91
Muangchai Kittikasem (WBC)	1991-92
Yong-Kang Kim (WBA)	1991-92
Rodolfo Blanco (IBF)	1992
Yuri Arbachakov (WBC)	1992—
Aquiles Guzman (WBA)	1992
Phichit Sithbangprachan (IBF)	1992—
David Griman (WBA)	1992-94
San Sow Ploenchit (WBA)	1994—

Annual Awards

Ring Magazine Fighter of the Year

First presented in 1928 by Nat Fleischer, who started *The Ring* magazine in 1922.

Multiple winners: Muhammad Ali (5); Joe Louis (4); Joe Frazier and Rocky Marciano (3); Ezzard Charles, George Foreman, Marvin Hagler, Thomas Hearns, Ingemar Johansson, Sugar Ray Leonard, Tommy Loughran, Floyd Patterson, Sugar Ray Robinson, Barney Ross, Dick Tiger and Mike Tyson (2).

Year		Year		Year		Year	
1928	Gene Tunney	1945	Willie Pep	1963	Cassius Clay*	1980	Thomas Hearns
1929	Tommy Loughran	1946	Tony Zale	1964	Emile Griffith	1981	Sugar Ray Leonard
		1947	Gus Lesnevich	1965	Dick Tiger		& Salvador Sanchez
1930	Max Schmeling	1948	Ike Williams	1966	No award	1982	Larry Holmes
1931	Tommy Loughran	1949	Ezzard Charles	1967	Joe Frazier	1983	Marvin Hagler
1932	Jack Sharkey			1968	Nino Benvenuti	1984	Thomas Hearns
1933	No award	1950	Ezzard Charles	1969	Jose Napoles	1985	Donald Curry
1934	Tony Canzoneri	1951	Sugar Ray Robinson				& Marvin Hagler
	& Barney Ross	1952	Rocky Marciano	1970	Joe Frazier	1986	Mike Tyson
1935	Barney Ross	1953	Carl (Bobo) Olson	1971	Joe Frazier	1987	Evander Holyfield
1936	Joe Louis	1954	Rocky Marciano	1972	Muhammad Ali	1988	Mike Tyson
1937	Henry Armstrong	1955	Rocky Marciano		& Carlos Monzon	1989	Pernell Whitaker
1938	Joe Louis	1956	Floyd Patterson	1973	George Foreman		
1939	Joe Louis	1957	Carmen Basilio	1974	Muhammad Ali	1990	Julio Cesar Chavez
		1958	Ingemar Johansson	1975	Muhammad Ali	1991	James Toney
1940	Billy Conn	1959	Ingemar Johansson	1976	George Foreman	1992	Riddick Bowe
1941	Joe Louis	1960	Floyd Patterson	1977	Carlos Zarate	1993	Michael Carbajal
1942	Sugar Ray Robinson	1961	Joe Brown	1978	Muhammad Ali		
1943	Fred Apostoli	1962	Dick Tiger	1979	Sugar Ray Leonard		
1944	Beau Jack						

*Changed name to Muhammad Ali in 1964.

Annual Awards (Cont.)
Ring Magazine Fight of the Year

First presented in 1945.

Multiple matchups: Muhammad Ali vs. Joe Frazier, Carmen Basilio vs. Sugar Ray Robinson and Graziano vs. Tony Zale (2).

Multiple fights: Muhammad Ali (6); Carmen Basilio (5); George Foreman and Joe Frazier (4); Rocky Graziano, Rocky Marciano and Tony Zale (3); Nino Benvenuti, Bobby Chacon, Ezzard Charles, Marvin Hagler, Thomas Hearns, Sugar Ray Leonard, Floyd Patterson, Sugar Ray Robinson and Jersey Joe Walcott (2).

Year	Winner	Loser	Result	Year	Winner	Loser	Result
1945	Rocky Graziano	Red Cochrane	KO 10	1970	Carlos Monzon	Nino Benvenuti	KO 12
1946	Tony Zale	Rocky Graziano	KO 6	1971	Joe Frazier	Muhammad Ali	W 15
1947	Rocky Graziano	Tony Zale	KO 6	1972	Bob Foster	Chris Finnegan	KO 14
1948	Marcel Cerdan	Tony Zale	KO 12	1973	George Foreman	Joe Frazier	KO 2
1949	Willie Pep	Sandy Saddler	W 15	1974	Muhammad Ali	George Foreman	KO 8
1950	Jake LaMotta	Laurent Dauthuille	KO 15	1975	Muhammad Ali	Joe Frazier	KO 14
1951	Jersey Joe Walcott	Ezzard Charles	KO 7	1976	George Foreman	Ron Lyle	KO 4
1952	Rocky Marciano	Jersey Joe Walcott	KO 13	1977	Jimmy Young	George Foreman	W 12
1953	Rocky Marciano	Roland LaStarza	KO 11	1978	Leon Spinks	Muhammad Ali	W 15
1954	Rocky Marciano	Ezzard Charles	KO 8	1979	Danny Lopez	Mike Ayala	KO 15
1955	Carmen Basilio	Tony DeMarco	KO 12	1980	Saad Muhammad	Yaqui Lopez	KO 14
1956	Carmen Basilio	Johnny Saxton	KO 9	1981	Sugar Ray Leonard	Thomas Hearns	KO 14
1957	Carmen Basilio	Sugar Ray Robinson	W 15	1982	Bobby Chacon	Rafael Limon	W 15
1958	Sugar Ray Robinson	Carmen Basilio	W 15	1983	Bobby Chacon	C. Boza-Edwards	W 12
1959	Gene Fullmer	Carmen Basilio	KO 14	1984	Jose Luis Ramirez	Edwin Rosario	KO 4
1960	Floyd Patterson	Ingemar Johansson	KO 5	1985	Marvin Hagler	Thomas Hearns	KO 3
1961	Joe Brown	Dave Charnley	W 15	1986	Stevie Cruz	Barry McGuigan	W 15
1962	Joey Giardello	Henry Hank	W 10	1987	Sugar Ray Leonard	Marvin Hagler	W 12
1963	Cassius Clay	Doug Jones	W 10	1988	Tony Lopez	Rocky Lockridge	W 12
1964	Cassius Clay	Sonny Liston	KO 7	1989	Roberto Duran	Iran Barkley	W 12
1965	Floyd Patterson	George Chuvalo	W 12	1990	Julio Cesar Chavez	Meldrick Taylor	KO 12
1966	Jose Torres	Eddie Cotton	W 15	1991	Robert Quiroga	Akeem Anifowoshe	W 12
1967	Nino Benvenuti	Emile Griffith	W 15	1992	Riddick Bowe	Evander Holyfield	W 12
1968	Dick Tiger	Frank DePaula	W 10	1993	Michael Carbajal	Humberto Gonzalez	KO 7
1969	Joe Frazier	Jerry Quarry	KO 7				

Triple Champions

Fighters who have won world championships in more than one division. Note that (*) indicates title claimant.

Sugar Ray Leonard (5)—WBC Welterweight (1979-80,80-82); WBA Jr. Middleweight (1981); WBC Middleweight (1987); WBC Super Middleweight (1988-90); WBC Light Heavyweight (1988).

Thomas Hearns (5)—WBA Welterweight (1980-81); WBC Jr. Middleweight (1982-84); WBC Light Heavyweight (1987); WBC Middleweight (1987-88); WBA Light Heavyweight (1991).

Roberto Duran (4)—Lightweight (1972-79); WBC Welterweight (1980); WBA Jr. Middleweight (1983-84); WBC Middleweight (1989-90).

Alexis Arguello (3)—WBA Featherweight (1974-77); WBC Jr. Lightweight (1978-80); WBC Lightweight (1981-83).

Henry Armstrong (3)—Featherweight (1937-38); Welterweight (1938-40); Lightweight (1938-39).

Iran Barkley (3)—WBC Middleweight (1988-89); IBF Super Middleweight (1992-93); WBA Light Heavyweight (1992).

Wilfredo Benitez (3)—Jr. Welterweight (1976-79); Welterweight (1979); WBC Jr. Middleweight (1981-82).

Tony Canzoneri (3)—Featherweight (1928); Lightweight (1930-33); Jr. Welterweight (1931-32,33).

Julio Cesar Chavez (3)—WBC Jr. Lightweight (1984-87); WBA/WBC Lightweight (1987-89); WBC/IBF Jr. Welterweight (1989-91); WBC Jr. Welterweight (1991-94, 1994—).

Jeff Fenech (3)—IBF Bantamweight (1985); WBC Jr. Featherweight (1986-88); WBC Featherweight (1988-90).

Bob Fitzsimmons (3)—Middleweight (1891-97); Light Heavyweight (1903-05); Heavyweight (1897-99).

Wilfredo Gomez (3)—WBC Super Bantamweight (1977-83); WBC Featherweight (1984); WBA Jr. Lightweight (1985-86).

Emile Griffith (3)—Welterweight (1961,62-63,63-66); Jr. Middleweight (1962-63); Middleweight (1966-67,67-68).

Stanley Ketchel (3)—Welterweight* (1908,08-10); Middleweight (1908-10); Light Heavyweight (1909-10).

Terry McGovern (3)—Bantamweight (1899-1900); Featherweight (1900-01); Lightweight* (1900-01).

Barney Ross (3)—Lightweight (1933-35); Jr. Welterweight (1933-35); Welterweight (1934, 35-38).

Pernell Whitaker (3)—IBF/WBC/WBA Lightweight (1989-92); IBF Jr. Welterweight (1992-93); WBC Welterweight (1993—).

Paula Newby-Fraser, who became the first woman to break the nine-hour barrier at the Ironman Triathlon in 1993, won the event for the seventh time in nine years in 1994.

MISCELLANEOUS SPORTS

CHESS

World Champions

Both the International Chess Federation (FIDE) and the breakaway Professional Chess Association (PCA) will stage world championship matches in 1995. Azerbaijan's Garry Kasparov, 31, who was FIDE world champion until he quit to join the PCA, became the PCA's first world champion in 1993. He will defend his title in the fall against the winner of the challenger final between 20-year-old former U.S. champion Gata Kamsky of Brooklyn and Viswanathan Anand, 24, of India. Kasparov's old rival, Anatoly Karpov, who reclaimed the FIDE title in 1993, will also defend.

Years		Years		Years	
1866-94	Wilhelm Steinitz, Austria	1937-46	Alexander Alekhine, France	1963-69	Tigran Petrosian, USSR
1894-		1948-57	Mikhail Botvinnik, USSR	1969-72	Boris Spassky, USSR
1921	Emanuel Lasker, Germany	1957-58	Vassily Smyslov, USSR	1972-75	Bobby Fischer, USA*
1921-27	Jose Capablanca, Cuba	1958-59	Mikhail Botvinnik, USSR	1975-85	Anatoly Karpov, USSR
1927-35	Alexander Alekhine, France	1960-61	Mikhail Tal, USSR	1985-	Garry Kasparov, AZR
1935-37	Max Euwe, Holland	1961-63	Mikhail Botvinnik, USSR		

*Fischer defaulted championship in 1975

U.S. Champions (since 1900)

Twenty-seven-year-old Alexander Shabalov and Alex Yermolinsky, 36, emerged from the 1993 U.S. Championships in Long Beach, Calif., as co-champions. Shabalov of Pittsburgh and Yermolinsky of Edison, N.J. each had 8-3 records in the 12-player round robin. The 1994 championship was scheduled for Oct. 10-26, in Key West, Fla.

Years		Years		Years	
1857-71	Paul Morphy	1948-51	Herman Steiner	1983	Roman Dzindzichashvili,
1871-76	George Mackenzie	1951-54	Larry Evans		Larry Christiansen
1876-80	James Mason	1954-57	Arthur Bisguier		& Walter Browne
1880-89	George Mackenzie	1957-61	Bobby Fischer	1984-85	Lev Alburt
1889-90	Samuel Lipschutz	1961-62	Larry Evans	1986	Yasser Seirawan
1890	Jackson Showalter	1962-68	Bobby Fischer	1987	Joel Benjamin
1890-91	Max Judd	1968-69	Larry Evans		& Nick DeFirmian
1891-92	Jackson Showalter	1969-72	Samuel Reshevsky	1988	Michael Wilder
1892-94	Samuel Lipschutz	1972-73	Robert Byrne	1989	Roman Dzindzichashvili,
1894	Jackson Showalter	1973-74	Lubomir Kavalek		Stuart Rachels
1894-95	Albert Hodges		& John Grefe		& Yasser Seirawan
1895-97	Jackson Showalter	1974-78	Walter Browne	1990	Lev Alburt
1897-1906	Harry Pillsbury	1978-80	Lubomir Kabalek	1991	Gata Kamsky
1906-09	Vacant	1980-81	Larry Evans,	1992	Patrick Wolff
1909-36	Frank Marshall		Larry Christiansen	1993	Alexander Shabalov
1936-44	Samuel Reshevsky		& Walter Browne		& Alex Yermolinsky
1944-46	Arnold Denker	1981-83	Walter Browne		
1946-48	Samuel Reshevsky		& Yasser Seirawan		

World chess champion **Garry Kasparov** (left) and U.S. grandmaster **Patrick Wolff** play a game of "speed chess" during a Feb. 1 exhibition to announce that Intel Corp. had signed on as a sponsor for the Professional Chess Association.

DOGS

Iditarod Trail Sled Dog Race

Martin Buser of Big Lake, Alaska, won the Iditarod Trail Sled Dog Race for the second time in three years on March 15, 1994. He and his 10-dog team won the 22nd edition of the race in the record time of 10 days, 13 hours, two minutes and 39 seconds. Buser, 35, received $50,000 and a new pickup truck for the victory.

The annual 1,151-mile race stretches from Anchorage to Nome, Alaska. Begun in 1973, the course follows an old frozen river mail route and is named after a deserted mining town along the way. The Iditarod also commemorates a famous midwinter emergency mission to get medical supplies to Nome during a 1925 diptheria epidemic. Men and women mushers compete together.

Multiple winners: Rick Swenson (5); Susan Butcher (4); Martin Buser and Rick Mackey (2).

Year		Elapsed Time	Year		Elapsed Time
1973	Dick Wilmarth	20 days, 00:49:41	1985	Libby Riddles	18 days, 00:20:17
1974	Carl Huntington	20 days, 15:02:07	1986	Susan Butcher	11 days, 15:06:00
1975	Emmit Peters	14 days, 14:43:45	1987	Susan Butcher	11 days, 02:05:13
1976	Gerald Riley	18 days, 22:58:17	1988	Susan Butcher	11 days, 11:41:40
1977	Rick Swenson	16 days, 16:27:13	1989	Joe Runyan	11 days, 05:24:34
1978	Dick Mackey	14 days, 18:52:24			
1979	Rick Swenson	15 days, 10:37:47	1990	Susan Butcher	11 days, 01:53:23
			1991	Rick Swenson	12 days, 16:34:39
1980	Joe May	14 days, 07:11:51	1992	Martin Buser	10 days, 19:17:00
1981	Rick Swenson	12 days, 08:45:02	1993	Jeff King	10 days, 15:38:00
1982	Rick Swenson	16 days, 04:40:10	1994	Martin Buser	10 days, 13:02:39*
1983	Rick Mackey	12 days, 14:10:44			
1984	Dean Osmar	12 days, 15:07:33	*Course record.		

Westminster Kennel Club
Best in Show

Ch. Chidley Willum, a 4-year-old black-and-tan Norwich terrier, was judged Best-in-Show, Feb. 15, 1994, at the 118th Westminster Kennel Club show at Madison Square Garden in New York. It marked the first time in one of the country's longest-running sporting events that a representative of the breed had won the top prize—defeating a field of 2,580 champions for the title. He is owned by Ruth Cooper of Glenview, Ill., and Patricia Lussier of Lake Placid, N.Y., and handled by Peter Green. The judge was Walter Goodman.

The Westminster show is the most prestigious canine event in America. Held every year since 1877, it is one of the oldest annual sporting events in the country.

Multiple winners: Ch.Warren Remedy (3); Ch.Chinoe's Adamant James, Ch.Comejo Wycollar Boy, Ch.Flornell Spicy Piece of Halleston; Ch.Matford Vic, Ch.My Own Brucie, Ch.Pendley Calling of Blarney, Ch.Rancho Dobe's Storm (2).

Year		Breed	Year		Breed
1907	Warren Remedy	Fox Terrier	1938	Daro of Maridor	English Setter
1908	Warren Remedy	Fox Terrier	1939	Ferry v.Rauhfelsen of Giralda	Doberman
1909	Warren Remedy	Fox Terrier			
			1940	My Own Brucie	Cocker Spaniel
1910	Sabine Rarebit	Fox Terrier	1941	My Own Brucie	Cocker Spaniel
1911	Tickle Em Jock	Scottish Terrier	1942	Wolvey Pattern of Edgerstoune	W.Highland Terrier
1912	Kenmore Sorceress	Airedale	1943	Pitter Patter of Piperscroft	Miniature Poodle
1913	Strathway Prince Albert	Bulldog	1944	Flornell Rarebit of Twin Ponds	Welsh Terrier
1914	Brentwood Hero	Old English Sheepdog	1945	Shieling's Signature	Scottish Terrier
1915	Matford Vic	Old English Sheepdog	1946	Hetherington Model Rhythm	Fox Terrier
1916	Matford Vic	Old English Sheepdog	1947	Warlord of Mazelaine	Boxer
1917	Comejo Wycollar Boy	Fox Terrier	1948	Rock Ridge Night Rocket	Bedling. Terrier
1918	Haymarket Faultless	Bull Terrier	1949	Mazelaine's Zazarac Brandy	Boxer
1919	Briergate Bright Beauty	Airedale			
			1950	Walsing Winning Trick of Edgerstoune	Scot. Terrier
1920	Comejo Wycollar Boy	Fox Terrier	1951	Bang Away of Sirrah Crest	Boxer
1921	Midkiff Seductive	Cocker Spaniel	1952	Rancho Dobe's Storm	Doberman
1922	Boxwood Barkentine	Airedale	1953	Rancho Dobe's Storm	Doberman
1923	No best-in-show award		1954	Carmor's Rise and Shine	Cocker Spaniel
1924	Barberryhill Bootlegger	Sealyham	1955	Kippax Fearnought	Bulldog
1925	Governor Moscow	Pointer	1956	Wilber White Swan	Toy Poodle
1926	Signal Circuit	Fox Terrier	1957	Shirkhan of Grandeur	Afghan Hound
1927	Pinegrade Perfection	Sealyham	1958	Puttencove Promise	Standard Poodle
1928	Talavera Margaret	Fox Terrier	1959	Fontclair Festoon	Miniature Poodle
1929	Land Loyalty of Bellhaven	Collie			
			1960	Chick T'Sun of Caversham	Pekingese
1930	Pendley Calling of Blarney	Fox Terrier	1961	Cappoquin Little Sister	Toy Poodle
1931	Pendley Calling of Blarney	Fox Terrier	1962	Elfinbrook Simon	W.Highland Terrier
1932	Nancolleth Markable	Pointer	1963	Wakefield's Black Knight	English Springer Spaniel
1933	Warland Protector of Shelterock	Airedale	1964	Courtenay Fleetfoot of Pennyworth	Whippet
1934	Flornell Spicy Bit of Halleston	Fox Terrier	1965	Carmichaels Fanfare	Scottish Terrier
1935	Nunsoe Duc de la Terrace of Blakeen	Standard Poodle	1966	Zeloy Mooremaides Magic	Fox Terrier
1936	St.Margaret Magnificent of Clairedale	Sealyham	1967	Bardene Bingo	Scottish Terrier
1937	Flornell Spicy Bit of Halleston	Fox Terrier	1968	Stingray of Derryabah	Lakeland Terrier

Dogs (Cont.)
Westminster Kennel Club
Best in Show

Year	Breed	Year	Breed
1969 Glamoor Good News	Skye Terrier	1982 St.Aubrey Dragonora of Elsdon	Pekingese
1970 Arriba's Prima Donna	Boxer	1983 Kabik's The Challenger	Afghan Hound
1971 Chinoe's Adamant James	E.S. Spaniel	1984 Seaward's Blackbeard	Newfoundland
1972 Chinoe's Adamant James	E.S. Spaniel	1985 Braeburn's Close Encounter	Scottish Terrier
1973 Acadia Command Performance	Standard Poodle	1986 Marjetta National Acclaim	Pointer
1974 Gretchenhof Columbia River	German SH Pointer	1987 Covy Tucker Hill's Manhattan	German Shepherd
1975 Sir Lancelot of Barvan	Old Eng. Sheepdog	1988 Great Elms Prince Charming II	Pomeranian
1976 Jo Ni's Red Baron of Crofton	Lakeland Terrier	1989 Royal Tudor's Wild As The Wind	Doberman
1977 Dersade Bobby's Girl	Sealyham		
1978 Cede Higgens	Yorkshire Terrier	1990 Wendessa Crown Prince	Pekingese
1979 Oak Tree's Irishtocrat	Irish Water Spaniel	1991 Whisperwind on a Carousel	Stan. Poodle
		1992 Lonesome Dove	Fox Terrier
1980 Sierra Cinnar	Siberian Husky	1993 Salilyn's Condor	E.S. Spaniel
1981 Dhandy Favorite Woodchuck	Pug	1994 Chidley Willum	Norwich Terrier

FISHING

IGFA All-Tackle World Records

All-tackle records are maintained for the heaviest fish of any species caught on any line up to 130-lb (60 kg) class and certified by the International Game Fish Association. Records logged through Oct. 1, 1994. **Address:** 3000 East Las Olas Blvd., Ft. Lauderdale, FL, 33316. **Telephone:** 305-941-3474.

FRESHWATER FISH

Species	Lbs-Oz	Where Caught	Date	Angler
Barramundi	63- 2	Queensland, Australia	Apr. 28,1991	Scott Barnsley
Bass, Guadalupe	3-11	Lake Travis, TX	Sept. 25, 1983	Allen Christenson Jr.
Bass, largemouth	22- 4	Montgomery Lake, GA	June 2,1932	George W. Perry
Bass, peacock	26- 8	Matevini River, Colombia	Jan. 26,1982	Rod Neubert
Bass, peacock butterfly	9- 8	Kendale Lakes, FL	Mar. 11, 1993	Jerry Gomez
Bass, redeye	8- 3	Flint River, GA	Oct. 23, 1977	David A. Hubbard
Bass, Roanoke	1- 5	Nottoway River, VA	Nov. 11, 1991	Tom Elkins
Bass, rock	3- 0	York River, Ontario	Aug. 1,1974	Peter Gulgin
Bass, smallmouth	11-15	Dale Hollow Lake, KY	July 9,1955	David L. Hayes
Bass, spotted	9- 7	Pine Flat Lake, CA	Feb. 25, 1994	Bob E. Shelton
Bass, striped (landlocked)	67- 8	O'Neill Forebay, San Luis, CA	May 7,1992	Hank Ferguson
Bass, Suwannee	3-14	Suwannee River, FL	Mar. 2,1985	Ronnie Everett
Bass, white	6-13	Lake Orange, VA	July 31,1989	Ronald L. Sprouse
Bass, whiterock	24- 3	Leesville Lake, VA	May 12,1989	David N. Lambert
Bass, yellow	2- 4	Lake Monroe, IN	Mar. 27,1977	Donald L. Stalker
Bass, yellow hybrid	2- 5	Kiamichi River, OK	Mar. 26, 1991	George Edwards
Bluegill	4-12	Ketona Lake, AL	Apr. 9,1950	T.S. Hudson
Bowfin	21- 8	Florence, SC	Jan. 29,1980	Robert L. Harmon
Buffalo, bigmouth	70- 5	Bussey Brake, Bastrop, LA	Apr. 21,1980	Delbert Sisk
Buffalo, black	55- 8	Cherokee Lake, TN	May 3,1984	Edward H. McLain
Buffalo, smallmouth	68- 8	Lake Hamilton, AR	May 16,1984	Jerry L. Dolezal
Bullhead, black	8- 0	Lake Waccabuc, NY	Aug. 1,1951	Kani Evans
Bullhead, brown	5- 8	Veal Pond, GA	May 22,1975	Jimmy Andrews
Bullhead, yellow	4- 4	Mormon Lake, AZ	May 11,1984	Emily Williams
Burbot	18- 4	Pickford, MI	Jan. 31,1980	Tom Courtemanche
Carp	75-11	Lac de St. Cassien, France	May 21,1987	Leo van der Gugten
Catfish, blue	109- 4	Cooper River, SC	Mar. 14,1991	George Lijewski
Catfish, channel	58- 0	Santee-Cooper Res., SC	July 7,1964	W.B. Whaley
Catfish, flathead	91- 4	Lake Lewisville, TX	Mar. 28,1982	Mike Rogers
Catfish, flatwhiskered	5-13	Cuiaba River, Brazil	June 28, 1992	Sergio Roberto Rothier
Catfish, gilded	85- 8	Amazon River, Brazil	Nov. 15, 1986	Gilberto Fernandes
Catfish, redtail	97- 7	Amazon River, Brazil	July 16, 1988	Gilberto Fernandes
Catfish, sharptoothed	79- 5	Orange River, S. Africa	Dec. 5, 1992	Hennie Moller
Catfish, white	18-14	Inverness, FL	Sept. 21,1991	Jim Miller
Char, Arctic	32- 9	Tree River, Canada	July 30,1981	Jeffery Ward
Crappie, black	4- 8	Kerr Lake, VA	Mar. 1,1981	L. Carl Herring Jr.
Crappie, white	5- 3	Enid Dam, MS	July 31,1957	Fred L. Bright
Dolly Varden	16- 9	Mashutuk River, AK	July 13,1993	Richard B. Evans
Dorado	51- 5	Corrientes, Argentina	Sept. 27,1984	Armando Giudice
Drum, freshwater	54- 8	Nickajack Lake, TN	Apr. 20,1972	Benny E. Hull

Species	Lbs-Oz	Where Caught	Date	Angler
Gar, alligator	279- 0	Rio Grande, TX	Dec. 2,1951	Bill Valverde
Gar, Florida	21- 3	Boca Raton, FL	June 3,1981	Jeff Sabol
Gar, longnose	50- 5	Trinity River, TX	July 30,1954	Townsend Miller
Gar, shortnose	5- 0	Sally Jones Lake, OK	Apr. 26,1985	Buddy Croslin
Gar, spotted	8-12	Tennessee River, AL	Aug. 26,1987	Winston H. Baker
Goldfish	3- 0	Southland Pk., Livingston, TX	May 8,1988	Kenneth R. Kinsey
Grayling, Arctic	5-15	Katseyedie River, N.W.T.	Aug. 16,1967	Jeanne P. Branson
Inconnu	53- 0	Pah River, AK	Aug. 20,1986	Lawrence E. Hudnall
Kokanee	9- 6	Okanagan Lake, Brit.Columbia	June 18,1988	Norm Kuhn
Muskellunge	65- 0	Blackstone Harbor, Ontario	Oct. 16,1988	Kenneth J. O'Brien
Muskellunge, tiger	51- 3	Lac Vieux-Desert, WI-MI	July 16,1919	John A. Knobla
Perch, Nile	191- 8	Lake Victoria, Kenya	Sept. 5,1991	Andy Davison
Perch, white	4-12	Messalonskee Lake, ME	June 4,1949	Mrs. Earl Small
Perch, yellow	4- 3	Bordentown, NJ	May, 1865	Dr. C.C. Abbot
Pickerel, chain	9- 6	Homerville, GA	Feb. 17,1961	Baxley McQuaig Jr.
Pickerel, grass	1- 0	Dewart Lake, Indiana	June 9, 1990	Mike Berg
Pickerel, redfin	1-15	Redhook, NY	Oct. 16, 1988	Bill Stagias
Pike, northern	55- 1	Lake of Grefeern, W.Germany	Oct.16,1986	Lothar Louis
Redhorse, greater	9- 3	Salmon River, Pulaski, NY	May 11,1985	Jason Wilson
Redhorse, silver	11- 7	Plum Creek, WI	May 29,1985	Neal D.G. Long
Salmon, Atlantic	79- 2	Tana River, Norway	1928	Henrik Henriksen
Salmon, chinook	97- 4	Kenai River, AK	May 17,1985	Les Anderson
Salmon, chum	32- 0	Behm Canal, AK	June 7,1985	Fredrick Thynes
Salmon, coho	33- 4	Salmon River, Pulaski, NY	Sept. 27,1989	Jerry Lifton
Salmon, lake	18- 4	Lake Tanganyika, Zambia	Dec. 1, 1987	Steve Robinson
Salmon, pink	13- 1	St. Mary's River, Ontario	Sept. 23,1992	Ray Higaki
Salmon, sockeye	15- 3	Kenai River, AK	Aug. 9,1987	Stan Roach
Sauger	8-12	Lake Sakakawea, ND	Oct. 6,1971	Mike Fischer
Shad, American	11- 4	Conn.River, S.Hadley, MA	May 19,1986	Bob Thibodo
Shad, gizzard	4- 0	Lake Michigan, IN	Jan. 15, 1993	Mike Berg
Sturgeon, lake	92- 4	Kettle River, MN	Sept. 11,1986	James M. DeOtis
Sturgeon, white	468- 0	Benicia, CA	July 9,1983	Joey Pallotta 3rd
Tigerfish	97- 0	Zaire River, Kinshasa, Zaire	July 9,1988	Raymond Houtmans
Tilapia	6- 0	Lake Okeechobee, FL	June 24,1989	Joseph M. Tucker
Trout, Apache	5- 3	White Mountain, AZ	May 29,1991	John Baldwin
Trout, brook	14- 8	Nipigon River, Ontario	July, 1916	Dr. W.J. Cook
Trout, brown	40- 4	Little Red River, AR	May 9,1992	Rip Collins
Trout, bull	32- 0	Lake Pond Orielle, ID	Oct. 27,1949	N.L. Higgins
Trout, cutthroat	41- 0	Pyramid Lake, NV	Dec., 1925	John Skimmerhorn
Trout, golden	11- 0	Cooks Lake, WY	Aug. 5,1948	Charles S. Reed
Trout, lake	66- 8	Great Bear Lake, N.W.T.	July 19,1991	Rodney Harback
Trout, rainbow	42- 2	Bell Island, AK	June 22,1970	David Robert White
Trout, tiger	20-13	Lake Michigan, WI	Aug. 12,1978	Peter M. Friedland
Walleye	25- 0	Old Hickory Lake, TN	Apr. 1,1960	Mabry Harper
Warmouth	2- 7	Guess Lake, Holt, FL	Oct. 19,1985	Tony D. Dempsey
Whitefish, lake	14- 6	Meaford, Ontario	May 21,1984	Dennis M.Laycock
Whitefish, mountain	5- 6	Rioh River, Saskatchewan	June 15,1988	John R. Bell
Whitefish, river	11- 2	Skrabean, Nymoua, Sweden	Dec. 9,1984	Jorgen Larsson
Whitefish, round	6- 0	Putahow River, Manitoba	June 14,1984	Allan J. Ristori
Zander	25- 2	Trosa, Sweden	June 12,1986	Harry Lee Tennison

SALTWATER FISH

Species	Lbs-Oz	Where Caught	Date	Angler
Albacore	88- 2	Gran Canaria, Canary Islands	Nov. 19,1977	Siegfried Dickemann
Amberjack, greater	155-10	Challenger Bank, Bermuda	June 24,1981	Joseph Dawson
Amberjack, pacific	104- 0	Baja Calif., Mexico	July 4,1984	Richard Cresswell
Barracuda, great	85- 0	Christmas Is., Rep. of Kiribati	Apr. 11,1992	John W. Helfrich
Barracuda, Mexican	21- 0	Phantom Island, Costa Rica	Mar. 27,1987	E. Greg Kent
Barracuda, slender	17- 4	Sitra Channel, Bahrain	Nov. 21,1985	Roger Cranswick
Bass, barred sand	13- 3	Huntington Beach, CA	Aug. 29,1988	Robert Halal
Bass, black sea	9- 8	Virginia Beach, VA	Jan. 9,1987	Joe Mizelle Jr.
Bass, European	20-11	Stes Maries de la Mer, France	May 6,1986	Jean Baptiste Bayle
Bass, giant sea	563- 8	Anacapa Island, CA	Aug. 20,1968	J.D. McAdam Jr.
Bass, striped	78- 8	Atlantic City, NJ	Sept. 21,1982	Albert R. McReynolds
Bluefish	31-12	Hatteras, NC	Jan. 30,1972	James M. Hussey
Bonefish	19- 0	Zululand, South Africa	May 26,1962	Brian W. Batchelor
Bonito, Atlantic	18- 4	Faial Island, Azores	July 8,1953	D. Gama Higgs
Bonito, Pacific	14-12	San Benitos Is., Baja Calif., Mexico	Oct. 12,1980	Jerome H. Rilling
Cabezon	23- 0	Juan de Fuca Strait, WA	Aug. 4,1990	Wesley Hunter
Cobia	135- 9	Shark Bay, W. Australia	July 9,1985	Peter W. Goulding
Cod, Atlantic	98-12	Isle of Shoals, NH	June 8,1969	Alphonse Bielevich

Fishing (Cont.)

SALTWATER FISH

Species	Lbs-Oz	Where Caught	Date	Angler
Cod, Pacific	30- 0	Andrew Bay, AK	July 7,1984	Donald R. Vaughn
Conger	110- 8	English Channel, Plymouth	Aug. 20,1991	Hans Christian Clausen
Dolphin	87- 0	Papagallo Gulf, Costa Rica	Sept. 25,1976	Manuel Salazar
Drum, black	113- 1	Lewes, DE	Sept. 15,1975	Gerald M. Townsend
Drum, red	94- 2	Avon, NC	Nov. 7,1984	David G. Deuel
Eel, African mottled	36- 1	Durban, S. Africa	June 10,1984	Ferdie van Nooten
Eel, American	8- 8	Cliff Pond, Brewster, MA	May 17,1992	Gerald G. Lapierre Sr.
Flounder, southern	20- 9	Nassau Sound, FL	Dec. 23,1983	Larenza Mungin
Flounder, summer	22- 7	Montauk, NY	Sept. 15,1975	Charles Nappi
Grouper, warsaw	436-12	Gulf of Mexico, Destin, FL	Dec. 22,1985	Steve Haeusler
Haddock	11-11	Perkins Cove, Ogunquit, ME	Sept. 12,1991	Jim Mailea
Halibut, Atlantic	255- 4	Gloucester, MA	July 28,1989	Sonny Manley
Halibut, California	53- 4	Santa Rosa Island, CA	July 7,1988	Russell J. Harmon
Halibut, Pacific	368- 0	Gustavus, AL	July 5,1991	Celia H. Dueitt
Jack, almaco (Pacific)	132- 0	La Paz, Baja Calif., Mexico	July 21,1964	Howard H. Hahn
Jack, crevalle	57- 5	Barra do Bwanza, Angola	Oct. 10,1992	Cam Nicolson
Jack, horse-eye	24- 8	Miami, FL	Dec. 20,1982	Tito Schnau
Jewfish	680- 0	Fernandina Beach, FL	May 20,1961	Lynn Joyner
Kawakawa	29- 0	Clarion Island, Mexico	Dec. 17,1986	Ronald Nakamura
Lingcod	69- 0	Langara Is., Brit. Columbia	June 16,1992	Murray M.Romer
Mackerel, cero	17- 2	Islamorada, FL	Apr. 5,1986	G. Michael Mills
Mackerel, king	90- 0	Key West, FL	Feb. 16,1976	Norton I. Thomton
Mackerel, Spanish	13- 0	Ocracoke Inlet, NC	Nov. 4,1987	Robert Cranton
Marlin, Atlantic blue	1402- 2	Vitoria, Brazil	Feb. 29,1992	Paulo R.A. Amorim
Marlin, Black	1560- 0	Cabo Blanco, Peru	Aug. 4,1953	A.C. Glassell Jr.
Marlin, Pacific blue	1376- 0	Kaaiwi Point, Kona, HI	May 31,1982	Jay W. deBeaubien
Marlin, striped	494- 0	Tutakaka, New Zealand	Jan. 16,1986	Bill Boniface
Marlin, white	181-14	Vitoria, Brazil	Dec. 8,1979	Evandro Luiz Coser
Permit	53- 4	Lake Worth, FL	Mar. 25, 1994	Roy Brooker
Pollack	27- 6	Salcombe, Devon, England	Jan. 16,1986	Robert S. Milkins
Pollock	46-10	Perkins Cove, Ogunquit, ME	Oct. 24,1990	Linda M. Paul
Pompano, African	50- 8	Daytona Beach, FL	Apr. 21,1990	Tom Sargent
Roosterfish	114- 0	La Paz, Baja Calif., Mexico	June 1,1960	Abe Sackheim
Runner, blue	8- 4	Bimini, Bahamas	Sept. 9,1990	Brent Rowland
Runner, rainbow	37- 9	Clarion Island, Mexico	Nov. 21,1991	Tom Pfleger
Sailfish, Atlantic	135- 5	Lago, Nigeria	Nov. 10,1991	Ron King
Sailfish, Pacific	221- 0	Santa Cruz Is., Ecuador	Feb. 12,1947	C.W. Stewart
Seabass, white	83-12	San Felipe, Mexico	Mar. 31,1953	L.C. Baumgardner
Seatrout, spotted	16- 0	Mason's Beach, VA	May 28,1977	William Katko
Shark, blue	437- 0	Catherine Bay, NSW, Australia	Oct. 2,1976	Peter Hyde
Shark, great white	2664- 0	Ceduna, S. Australia	Apr. 21,1959	Alfred Dean
Shark, greenland	1708- 9	Trondheimsfjord, Norway	Oct.18,1987	Terje Nordtvedt
Shark, hammerhead	991- 0	Sarasota, FL	May 30,1982	Allen Ogle
Shark, mako	1115- 0	Black River, Mauritius	Nov. 16,1988	Patrick Guillanton
Shark, porbeagle	507- 0	Pentland Firth, Scotland	Mar. 9, 1993	Christopher Bennet
Shark, thresher	802- 0	Tutakaka, New Zealand	Feb. 8,1981	Dianne North
Shark, tiger	1780- 0	Cherry Grove, SC	June 14,1964	Walter Maxwell
Snapper, cubera	121- 8	Cameron, LA	July 5,1982	Mike Hebert
Snapper, red	46- 8	Destin, FL	Oct. 1,1985	E. Lane Nichols III
Snook	53-10	Parismina Ranch, Costa Rica	Oct. 18,1978	Gilbert Ponzi
Spearfish	90-13	Madeira Island, Portugal	June 2,1980	Joseph Larkin
Swordfish	1182- 0	Iquique, Chile	May 7,1953	L. Marron
Tarpon	283- 4	Sherbro Is., Sierra Leone	Apr. 16, 1991	Yvon Victor Sebag
Tautog	24- 0	Wachapreague, VA	Aug. 25,1987	Gregory R. Bell
Tuna, Atlantic bigeye	375- 8	Ocean City, MD	Aug. 26,1977	Cecil Browne
Tuna, blackfin	42- 0	Bermuda	June 2,1978	Alan J. Card
	42- 0	Challenger Bank, Bermuda	July 18,1989	Gilbert C. Pearman
Tuna, bluefin	1496- 0	Aulds Cove, Nova Scotia	Oct. 26,1979	Ken Fraser
Tuna, longtail	79- 0	Montague Is., NSW, Australia	Apr. 12,1982	Tim Simpson
Tuna, Pacific bigeye	435- 0	Cabo Blanco, Peru	Apr. 17,1957	Dr. Russell Lee
Tuna, skipjack	41-14	Pearl Beach, Mauritius	Nov. 12,1985	Edmund Heinzen
Tuna, southern bluefin	348- 5	Whakatane, New Zealand	Jan. 16,1981	Rex Wood
Tuna, yellowfin	388-12	San Benedicto Island, Mexico	Apr. 1,1977	Curt Wiesenhutter
Tunny, little	35- 2	Cape de Garde, Algeria	Dec. 14,1988	Jean Yves Chatard
Wahoo	155- 8	San Salvador, Bahamas	Apr. 3,1990	William Bourne
Weakfish	19- 2	Jones Beach, Long Island, NY	Oct. 11,1984	Dennis R. Rooney
	19- 2	Delaware Bay, DE	May 20,1989	William E. Thomas

Bass Anglers Sportsman Society

Amateur fisherman **Bryan Kerchal** of Newtown, Conn., won the prestigious BASS Masters Classic in July. His three-day catch of 15 largemouth bass weighed 36 pounds, 7 ounces.

Amateur Wins BASS Masters

Bryan Kerchal became the first amateur to win the BASS Masters Classic when he captured the 24th edition of the $200,000 "Super Bowl of freshwater fishing," July 28-30, in Greensboro, N.C. The 23-year-old cook from Newtown, Conn., who is also the event's youngest winner, boated a three-day total of 15 High Rock Lake largemouth bass weighing 36 pounds, 7 ounces. He beat Oklahoma touring pro Tommy Biffle by just four ounces.

Kerchal, who qualified for the tournament for the second straight year through the Bass Anglers Sportsman Society's club federation ranks, accepted his winner's check of $50,000 in front of 23,500 spectators at Greesboro Coliseum, the site of the weigh-in. He can expect to earn as much as $1 million more in endorsements and speaking engagements.

BASS Masters Classic

The BASS Masters Classic is fishing's version of the Masters golf tournament. Invitees to the three-day event include the 36 top-ranked pros on the BASS tour and five top-ranked amateurs. Anglers may weigh only seven bass per day and each bass must be at least 12 inches long. Competitors are allowed only seven rods and reels and are limited to the tackle they can pack into two tournament-approved tackleboxes. Only artificial lures are permitted. The first Classic, held at Lake Mead, Nevada in 1971, was a $10,000 winner-take-all event.

Multiple winners: Rick Clunn (4); Bobby Murray and Hank Parker (2).

Year		Weight	Year		Weight
1971	Bobby Murray, Hot Springs, Ark	43-11	1983	Larry Nixon, Hemphill, Tex	18- 1
1972	Don Butler, Tulsa, Okla	38-11	1984	Rick Clunn, Montgomery, Tex	75- 9
1973	Rayo Breckenridge, Paragould, Ark	52- 8	1985	Jack Chancellor, Phenix City, Ala	45- 0
1974	Tommy Martin, Hemphill, Tex	33- 7	1986	Charlie Reed, Broken Bow, Okla	23- 9
1975	Jack Hains, Rayne, La	45- 4	1987	George Cochran, N. Little Rock, Ark	15- 5
1976	Rick Clunn, Montgomery, Tex	59-15	1988	Guido Hibdon, Gravois Mills, Mo	28- 8
1977	Rick Clunn, Montgomery, Tex	27- 7	1989	Hank Parker, Denver, N.C	31- 6
1978	Bobby Murray, Nashville, Tenn	37- 9			
1979	Hank Parker, Clover, S.C	31- 0	1990	Rick Clunn, Montgomery, Tex	34- 5
			1991	Ken Cook, Meers, Okla	33- 2
1980	Bo Dowden, Natchitoches, La	54-10	1992	Robert Hamilton Jr., Brandon, Miss	59- 6
1981	Stanley Mitchell, Fitzgerald, Ga	35- 2	1993	David Fritts, Lexington, N.C	48- 6
1982	Paul Elias, Laurel, Miss	32- 8	1994	Bryan Kerchal, Newtown, Conn	36- 7

LITTLE LEAGUE BASEBALL

World Series

Maracaibo, Venezuela, overcame a three-hour rain delay to become the first Latin American team in 36 years to win the Little League World Series. They defeated Northridge, Calif., 4-3, for the championship on Aug. 27. Pitchers Cesar Hidalgo of Maracaibo and Justin Gentile of Northridge were locked in a scoreless duel when the rains came in the top of the third inning. After the game was restarted, Gentile threw five wild pitches and gave up seven hits over the next three innings. Northridge, represented the California city that was ravaged by an earthquake in January.

Multiple winners: Taiwan (15); California (5); Connecticut and Pennsylvania (4); Japan and New Jersey (3); Mexico, New York, South Korea and Texas (2).

Year	Winner	Score	Loser	Year	Winner	Score	Loser
1947	Williamsport, PA	16-7	Lock Haven, PA	1972	Taipei, Taiwan	6-0	Hammond, IN
1948	Lock Haven, PA	6-5	St. Petersburg, FL	1973	Tainan City, Taiwan	12-0	Tucson, AZ
1949	Hammonton, NJ	5-0	Pensacola, FL	1974	Kao Hsiung, Taiwan	7-2	El Cajun, CA
				1975	Lakewood, NJ	4-3*	Tampa, FL
1950	Houston, TX	2-1	Bridgeport, CT	1976	Tokyo, Japan	10-3	Campbell, CA
1951	Stamford, CT	3-0	Austin, TX	1977	Kao Hsiung, Taiwan	7-2	El Cajun, CA
1952	Norwalk, CT	4-3	Monongahela, PA	1978	Pin-Tung, Taiwan	11-1	Danville, CA
1953	Birmingham, AL	1-0	Schenectady, NY	1979	Hsien, Taiwan	2-1	Campbell, CA
1954	Schenectady, NY	7-5	Colton, CA				
1955	Morrisville, PA	4-3	Merchantville, NJ	1980	Hua Lian, Taiwan	4-3	Tampa, FL
1956	Roswell, NM	3-1	Merchantville, NJ	1981	Tai-Chung, Taiwan	4-2	Tampa, FL
1957	Monterrey, Mexico	4-0	LaMesa, CA	1982	Kirkland, WA	6-0	Hsien, Taiwan
1958	Monterrey, Mexico	10-1	Kankakee, IL	1983	Marietta, GA	3-1	Barahona, D.Rep.
1959	Hamtramck, MI	12-0	Auburn, CA	1984	Seoul, S.Korea	6-2	Altamonte Sgs, FL
				1985	Seoul, S.Korea	7-1	Mexicali, Mex.
1960	Levittown, PA	5-0	Ft. Worth, TX	1986	Tainan Park, Taiwan	12-0	Tucson, AZ
1961	El Cajon, CA	4-2	El Campo, TX	1987	Hua Lian, Taiwan	21-1	Irvine, CA
1962	San Jose, CA	3-0	Kankakee, IL	1988	Tai-Chung, Taiwan	10-0	Pearl City, HI
1963	Granada Hills, CA	2-1	Stratford, CT	1989	Trumbull, CT	5-2	Kaohsiung, Taiwan
1964	Staten Island, NY	4-0	Monterrey, Mex.				
1965	Windsor Locks, CT	3-1	Stoney Creek, Can.	1990	Taipei, Taiwan	9-0	Shippensburg, PA
1966	Houston, TX	8-2	W.New York, NJ	1991	Taichung, Taiwan	11-0	San Ramon Vly, CA
1967	West Tokyo, Japan	4-1	Chicago, IL	1992	Long Beach, CA	6-0	Zamboanga, Phil.
1968	Osaka, Japan	1-0	Richmond, VA	1993	Long Beach, CA	3-2	Panama
1969	Taipei, Taiwan	5-0	Santa Clara,CA	1994	Maracaibo, Venezuela	4-3	Northridge, CA
1970	Wayne, NJ	2-0	Campbell, CA				
1971	Tainan, Taiwan	2-3	Gary, IN				

* Foreign teams were banned from the tournament in 1975. The ban was lifted the next year.

POWER BOAT RACING

APBA Gold Cup

Hometown favorite Mark Tate, won his second APBA Gold Cup championship on June 5, piloting Smokin' Joe's to victory over runner-up Nate Brown in The Tide. Tate, from nearby Wayne, Mich., who first won the race in 1991, covered the 2½-mile Detroit River course in 145.532 mph. Nine-time winner Chip Hanauer was unable to go after his 10th Gold Cup after suffering four fractured lumbar vertebrae when the escape hatch on the bottom of Miss Budweiser tore off in a practice run sending a wall of water into the cockpit.

The American Power Boat Association Gold Cup for unlimited hydroplane racing is the oldest active motor sports trophy in North America. The first Gold Cup was competed for on the Hudson River in New York in June and September of 1904. Since then several cities have hosted the race, led by Detroit (28 times, including 1990) and Seattle (14). Note that (*) indicates driver was also owner of the winning boat.

Drivers with multiple wins: Chip Hanauer (9); Bill Muncey (8); Gar Wood (5); Dean Chenoweth (4); Caleb Bragg, Tom D'Eath, Lou Fageol, Ron Musson, George Reis and Jonathon Wainwright (3); Danny Foster, George Henley, Vic Kliesrath, E.J. Schroeder, Bill Schumacher, Zalmon G.Simmons Jr., Joe Taggart, Mark Tate, and George Townsend (2).

Year	Boat	Driver	Avg. MPH	Year	Boat	Driver	Avg. MPH
1904	Standard (June)	*Carl Riotte	23.160	1915	Miss Detroit	Johnny Milot & Jack Beebe	37.656
1904	Vingt-Et-Un II (Sept.)	*W. Sharpe Kilmer	24.900	1916	Miss Minneapolis	Bernard Smith	48.860
1905	Chip I	*J. Wainwright	15.000	1917	Miss Detroit II	*Gar Wood	54.410
1906	Chip II	*J. Wainwright	25.000	1918	Miss Detroit II	Gar Wood	51.619
1907	Chip II	*J. Wainwright	23.903	1919	Miss Detroit III	*Gar Wood	42.748
1908	Dixie II	*E.J. Schroeder	29.938				
1909	Dixie II	*E.J. Schroeder	29.590	1920	Miss America I	*Gar Wood	62.022
1910	Dixie III	*F.K. Burnham	32.473	1921	Miss America I	*Gar Wood	52.825
1911	MIT II	*J.H. Hayden	37.000	1922	Packard Chriscraft	*J.G.Vincent	40.253
1912	P.D.Q. II	*A.G. Miles	39.462	1923	Packard Chriscraft	Caleb Bragg	43.867
1913	Ankle Deep	*Cas Mankowski	42.779	1924	Baby Bootlegger	*Caleb Bragg	45.302
1914	Baby Speed Demon II	Jim Blackton & Bob Edgren	48.458	1925	Baby Bootlegger	*Caleb Bragg	47.240
				1926	Greenwich Folly	*Geo.Townsend	47.984
				1927	Greenwich Folly	*Geo.Townsend	47.662

Year	Boat	Driver	Avg. MPH	Year	Boat	Driver	Avg. MPH
1928	Not held			1962	Miss Century 21	Bill Muncey	100.710
1929	Imp	*Richard Hoyt	48.662	1963	Miss Bardahl	Ron Musson	105.124
				1964	Miss Bardahl	Ron Musson	103.433
1930	Hotsy Totsy	*Vic Kliesrath	52.673	1965	Miss Bardahl	Ron Musson	103.132
1931	Hotsy Totsy	*Vic Kliesrath	53.602	1966	Tahoe Miss	Mira Slovak	93.019
1932	Delphine IV	Bill Horn	57.775	1967	Miss Bardahl	Bill Shumacher	101.484
1933	El Lagarto	*George Reis	56.260	1968	Miss Bardahl	Bill Shumacher	108.173
1934	El Lagarto	*George Reis	55.000	1969	Miss Budweiser	Bill Sterett	98.504
1935	El Lagarto	*George Reis	55.056	1970	Miss Budweiser	Dean Chenoweth	99.562
1936	Impshi	Kaye Don	45.735	1971	Miss Madison	Jim McCormick	98.043
1937	Notre Dame	Clell Perry	63.675	1972	Atlas Van Lines	Bill Muncey	104.277
1938	Alagi	*Theo Rossi	64.340	1973	Miss Budweiser	Dean Chenoweth	99.043
1939	My Sin	*Z.G. Simmons Jr.	66.133	1974	Pay 'n Pak	George Henley	104.428
1940	Hotsy Totsy III	*Sidney Allen	48.295	1975	Pay 'n Pak	George Henley	108.921
1941	My Sin	*Z.G. Simmons Jr.	52.509	1976	Miss U.S.	Tom D'Eath	100.412
1942-45	Not held			1977	Atlas Van Lines	*Bill Muncey	111.822
1946	Tempo VI	*Guy Lombardo	68.132	1978	Atlas Van Lines	*Bill Muncey	111.412
1947	Miss Peps V	Danny Foster	57.000	1979	Atlas Van Lines	*Bill Muncey	100.765
1948	Miss Great Lakes	Danny Foster	46.845	1980	Miss Budweiser	Dean Chenoweth	106.932
1949	My Sweetie	Bill Cantrell	73.612	1981	Miss Budweiser	Dean Chenoweth	116.932
1950	Slo-Mo-Shun IV	Ted Jones	78.216	1982	Atlas Van Lines	Chip Hanauer	120.050
1951	Slo-Mo-Shun V	Lou Fageol	90.871	1983	Atlas Van Lines	Chip Hanauer	118.507
1952	Slo-Mo-Shun IV	Stan Dollar	79.923	1984	Atlas Van Lines	Chip Hanauer	130.175
1953	Slo-Mo-Shun IV	Joe Taggart & Lou Fageol	99.108	1985	Miller American	Chip Hanauer	120.643
				1986	Miller American	Chip Hanauer	116.523
1954	Slo-Mo-Shun IV	Joe Taggart & Lou Fageol	92.613	1987	Miller American	Chip Hanauer	127.620
				1988	Miss Circus Circus	Chip Hanauer & Jim Prevost	123.756
1955	Gale V	Lee Schoenith	99.552				
1956	Miss Thriftaway	Bill Muncey	96.552	1989	Miss Budweiser	Tom D'Eath	131.209
1957	Miss Thriftaway	Bill Muncey	101.787	1990	Miss Budweiser	Tom D'Eath	143.176
1958	Hawaii Kai III	Jack Regas	103.000	1991	Winston Eagle	Mark Tate	137.771
1959	Maverick	Bill Stead	104.481	1992	Miss Budweiser	Chip Hanauer	136.282
1960	Not held			1993	Miss Budweiser	Chip Hanauer	141.296
1961	Miss Century 21	Bill Muncey	99.678	1994	Smokin' Joe's	Mark Tate	145.532

PRO RODEO

All-Around Champion Cowboy

Ty Murray, of Stephenville, Texas, won his fifth consecutive professional rodeo cowboy All-Around championship on Dec. 13, 1993, at the National Finals Rodeo in Las Vegas. Murray, 24, also won the NFR bareback riding average championship, his first world bull riding title, a NFR earnings record of $124,821, and a single-season earnings record of $297,896.

The Professional Rodeo Cowboys Association (PRCA) title of All-Around World Champion Cowboy goes to the rodeo athlete who wins the most prize money in a single year in two or more events. Only prize money earned in sanctioned PRCA rodeos is counted. From 1929-44, All-Around champions were named by the Rodeo Association of America (earnings for those years is not available).

Multiple winners: Tom Ferguson and Larry Mahan (6); Ty Murray and Jim Shoulders (5); Lewis Feild and Dean Oliver (3); Everett Bowman, Lewis Brooks, Clay Carr, Bill Linderman, Phil Lyne, Gerald Roberts, Casey Tibbs and Harry Tompkins (2).

Year		Year		Year		Year	
1929	Earl Thode	1934	Leonard Ward	1938	Burel Mulkey	1942	Gerald Roberts
1930	Clay Carr	1935	Everett Bowman	1939	Paul Carney	1943	Louis Brooks
1931	John Schneider	1936	John Bowman	1940	Fritz Truan	1944	Louis Brooks
1932	Donald Nesbit	1937	Everett Bowman	1941	Homer Pettigrew	1945-46	No award
1933	Clay Carr						

Year		Earnings	Year		Earnings	Year		Earnings
1947	Todd Whatley	$18,642	1958	Jim Shoulders	$32,212	1969	Larry Mahan	$57,726
1948	Gerald Roberts	21,766	1959	Jim Shoulders	32,905	1970	Larry Mahan	41,493
1949	Jim Shoulders	21,495	1960	Harry Tompkins	32,522	1971	Phil Lyne	49,245
1950	Bill Linderman	30,715	1961	Benny Reynolds	31,309	1972	Phil Lyne	60,852
1951	Casey Tibbs	29,104	1962	Tom Nesmith	32,611	1973	Larry Mahan	64,447
1952	Harry Tompkins	30,934	1963	Dean Oliver	31,329	1974	Tom Ferguson	66,929
1953	Bill Linderman	33,674	1964	Dean Oliver	31,150	1975	Tom Ferguson	50,300
1954	Buck Rutherford	40,404	1965	Dean Oliver	33,163	1976	Tom Ferguson	87,908
1955	Casey Tibbs	42,065	1966	Larry Mahan	40,358	1977	Tom Ferguson	65,981
1956	Jim Shoulders	43,381	1967	Larry Mahan	51,996	1978	Tom Ferguson	83,734
1957	Jim Shoulders	33,299	1968	Larry Mahan	49,129	1979	Tom Ferguson	96,272

Pro Rodeo (Cont.)
All Around Cowboy

Year		Earnings	Year		Earnings	Year		Earnings
1980	Paul Tierney	$105,568	1985	Lewis Feild	$130,347	1990	Ty Murray	$213,772
1981	Jimmie Cooper	105,861	1986	Lewis Feild	166,042	1991	Ty Murray	258,750
1982	Chris Lybbert	123,709	1987	Lewis Feild	144,335	1992	Ty Murray	225,992
1983	Roy Cooper	153,391	1988	Dave Appleton	121,546	1993	Ty Murray	297,896
1984	Dee Picket	122,618	1989	Ty Murray	134,806			

SOAP BOX DERBY

All-American Soap Box Derby

Thirteen-year-old Danielle Del Ferraro of Akron became the first two-time winner in the 57-year history of the All-American Soap Box Derby on Aug. 7. Del Ferraro, who won the Kit division in 1993, was victorious in the Masters division in '94. She was joined in the winners' circle by Kit winner Joel Endres, 14, of Akron and Stock division champion Kristine Damond, 13, of Jamestown, N.Y. A field of 249 regional champions from as far away as Australia competed in the races.

The All-American Soap Box Derby is a coasting race for small gravity-powered cars built by their drivers and assembled within strict guidelines on size, weight and cost. The Derby got its name in the 1930s when most cars were built from wooden soap boxes. Held every summer on the second Saturday of August at Derby Downs in Akron, the Soap Box Derby is open to all boys and girls from 9 to 16 years old who qualify.

There are three competitive divisions: Stock Cars (ages 9-16), made up of generic, prefab racers that come in Derby-approved kits and can be assembled in four hours; Kit Cars (ages 9-16), made up of racers assembled from Derby-approved kits that do not include wood shells; and Masters (ages 11-16), made up of racers designed by drivers, but constructed with Derby-approved hardware. The racing ramp at Derby Downs is 953.75 feet with an 11 percent grade.

One champion reigned at the All-American Soap Box Derby each year from 1934-75; Junior and Senior division champions from 1976-87; Kit and Masters champions from 1988-91; and Stock, Kit and Masters champions starting in 1992.

Year		Hometown	Age	Year		Hometown	Age
1934	Robert Turner	Muncie, IN	11	1976	JR: Phil Raber	Sugarcreek, OH	11
1935	Maurice Bale Jr.	Anderson, IN	13		SR: Joan Ferdinand	Canton, OH	14
1936	Herbert Muench Jr.	St. Louis	14	1977	JR: Mark Ferdinand	Canton, OH	10
1937	Robert Ballard	White Plains, NY	12		SR: Steve Washburn	Bristol, CT	15
1938	Robert Berger	Omaha, NE	14	1978	JR: Darren Hart	Salem, OR	11
1939	Clifton Hardesty	White Plains, NY	11		SR: Greg Cardinal	Flint, MI	13
1940	Thomas Fisher	Detroit	12	1979	JR: Russell Yurk	Flint, MI	10
1941	Claude Smith	Akron, OH	14		SR: Craig Kitchen	Akron, OH	14
1942-45	Not held			1980	JR: Chris Fulton	Indianapolis	11
1946	Gilbert Klecan	San Diego	14		SR: Dan Porul	Sherman Oaks, CA	12
1947	Kenneth Holmboe	Charleston, WV	14	1981	JR: Howie Fraley	Portsmouth, OH	11
1948	Donald Strub	Akron, OH	13		SR: Tonia Schlegel	Hamilton, OH	13
1949	Fred Derks	Akron, OH	15	1982	JR: Carol A. Sullivan	Rochester, NH	10
1950	Harold Williamson	Charleston, WV	15		SR: Matt Wolfgang	Lehigh Val., PA	12
1951	Darwin Cooper	Williamsport, PA	15	1983	JR: Tony Carlini	Del Mar, CA	10
1952	Joe Lunn	Columbus, GA	11		SR: Mike Burdgick	Flint, MI	14
1953	Fred Mohler	Muncie, IN	14	1984	JR: Chris Hess	Hamilton, OH	11
1954	Richard Kemp	Los Angeles	14		SR: Anita Jackson	St. Louis	15
1955	Richard Rohrer	Rochester, NY	14	1985	JR: Michael Gallo	Danbury, CT	12
1956	Norman Westfall	Rochester, NY	14		SR: Matt Sheffer	York, PA	14
1957	Terry Townsend	Anderson, IN	14	1986	JR: Marc Behan	Dover, NH	9
1958	James Miley	Muncie, IN	15		SR: Tami Jo Sullivan	Lancaster, OH	13
1959	Barney Townsend	Anderson, IN	13	1987	JR: Matt Margules	Danbury, CT	11
					SR: Brian Drinkwater	Bristol, CT	14
1960	Fredric Lake	South Bend, IN	11	1988	KIT: Jason Lamb	Des Moines, IA	10
1961	Dick Dawson	Wichita, KS	13		MAS: David Duffield	Kansas City	13
1962	David Mann	Gary, IN	14	1989	KIT: David Schiller	Dayton, OH	12
1963	Harold Conrad	Duluth, MN	12		MAS: Faith Chavarria	Ventura, CA	12
1964	Gregory Schumacher	Tacoma, WA	14	1990	KIT: Mark Mihal	Valparaiso, IN	12
1965	Robert Logan	Santa Ana, CA	12		MAS: Sami Jones	Salem, OR	13
1966	David Krussow	Tacoma, WA	12	1991	KIT: Paul Greenwald	Saginaw, MI	13
1967	Kenneth Cline	Lincoln, NE	13		MAS: Danny Garland	San Diego, CA	14
1968	Branch Lew	Muncie, IN	11	1992	KIT: Carolyn Fox	Sublimity, OR	11
1969	Steve Souter	Midland, TX	12		MAS: Bonnie Thornton	Redding, CA	12
					STK: Loren Hurst	Hudson, OH	10
1970	Samuel Gupton	Durham, NC	13	1993	KIT: D.M. Del Ferraro	Stow, OH	12
1971	Larry Blair	Oroville, CA	13		MAS: Dean Lutton	Delta, OH	14
1972	Robert Lange Jr.	Boulder, CO	14		STK: Owen Yuda	Boiling Springs, PA	10
1973	Bret Yarborough	Elk Grove, CA	11	1994	KIT: Joel Endres	Akron, OH	14
1974	Curt Yarborough	Elk Grove, CA	11		MAS: D.M. Del Ferraro	Akron, OH	13
1975	Karren Stead	Lower Bucks, PA	11		STK: Kristina Damond	Jamestown, NY	13

Jeff Iula

The three winners in the 1994 All-American Soap Box Derby (from left to right): **Danielle Del Ferraro** (Masters division), **Joel Endres** (Kit division) and **Kristina Damond** (Stock division).

SOFTBALL

Men's and women's national champions since 1933 in Major Fast Pitch, Major Slow Pitch and Super Slow Pitch (men only). Sanctioned by the Amateur Softball Association of America.

MEN

Major Fast Pitch

Multiple winners: Clearwater Bombers (10); Raybestos Cardinals (5); Sealmasters (4); Briggs Beautyware, Pay'n Pak and Zollner Pistons (3); Billard Barbell, Hammer Air Field, National Health Care, Penn Corp and Peterbilt Western (2).

Year		Year		Year	
1933	J.L. Gill Boosters, Chicago	1955	Raybestos Cardinals, Stratford, CT	1977	Billard Barbell, Reading, PA
1934	Ke-Nash-A, Kenosha, WI			1978	Billard Barbell
1935	Crimson Coaches, Toledo, OH	1956	Clearwater Bombers	1979	McArdle Pontiac/Cadillac, Midland, MI
1936	Kodak Park, Rochester, NY	1957	Clearwater Bombers		
1937	Briggs Body Team, Detroit	1958	Raybestos Cardinals	1980	Peterbilt Western, Seattle
1938	The Pohlers, Cincinnati	1959	Sealmasters, Aurora, IL	1981	Archer Daniels Midland, Decatur, IL
1939	Carr's Boosters, Covington, KY	1960	Clearwater Bombers		
1940	Kodak Park, Rochester, NY	1961	Sealmasters	1982	Peterbilt Western
1941	Bendix Brakes, South Bend, IN	1962	Clearwater Bombers	1983	Franklin Cardinals, Stratford, CT
1942	Deep Rock Oilers, Tulsa, OK	1963	Clearwater Bombers		
1943	Hammer Air Field, Fresno, CA	1964	Burch Tool, Detroit	1984	California Kings, Merced, CA
1944	Hammer Air Field	1965	Sealmasters	1985	Pay'n Pak, Seattle
1945	Zollner Pistons, Ft. Wayne, IN	1966	Clearwater Bombers	1986	Pay'n Pak
1946	Zollner Pistons	1967	Sealmasters	1987	Pay'n Pak
1947	Zollner Pistons	1968	Clearwater Bombers	1988	TransAire, Elkhart, IN
1948	Briggs Beautyware, Detroit	1969	Raybestos Cardinals	1989	Penn Corp, Sioux City, IA
1949	Tip Top Tailors, Toronto	1970	Raybestos Cardinals	1990	Penn Corp
1950	Clearwater (FL) Bombers	1971	Welty Way, Cedar Rapids, IA	1991	Gianella Bros., Rohnert Park, CA
1951	Dow Chemical, Midland, MI	1972	Raybestos Cardinals	1992	National Health Care, Sioux City, IA
1952	Briggs Beautyware	1973	Clearwater Bombers		
1953	Briggs Beautyware	1974	Gianella Bros, Santa Rosa, CA	1993	National Health Care
1954	Clearwater Bombers	1975	Rising Sun Hotel, Reading, PA	1994	Decatur (IL) Pride
		1976	Raybestos Cardinals		

Softball (Cont.)

MEN
Major Slow Pitch

Multiple winners: Gatliff Auto Sales and Skip Hogan A.C. (3); Campbell Carpets, Hamilton Tailoring, Howard's Furniture and Riverside Paving (2).

Year		Year		Year	
1953	Shields Construction, Newport, KY	1966	Michael's Lounge, Detroit	1981	Elite Coating, Gordon, CA
1954	Waldneck's Tavern, Cincinnati	1967	Jim's Sport Shop, Pittsburgh	1982	Triangle Sports, Minneapolis
1955	Lang Pet Shop, Covington, KY	1968	County Sports, Levittown, NY	1983	No.1 Electric & Heating, Gastonia, NC
1956	Gatliff Auto Sales, Newport, KY	1969	Copper Hearth, Milwaukee	1984	Lilly Air Systems, Chicago
1957	Gatliff Auto Sales	1970	Little Caesar's, Southgate, MI	1985	Blanton's Fayetteville, NC
1958	East Side Sports, Detroit	1971	Pile Drivers, Va.Beach, VA	1986	Non-Ferrous Metals, Cleveland
1959	Yorkshire Restaurant, Newport, KY	1972	Jiffy Club, Louisville, KY	1987	Stapath, Monticello, KY
		1973	Howard's Furniture, Denver, NC	1988	Bell Corp/FAF, Tampa, FL
1960	Hamilton Tailoring, Cincinnati	1974	Howard's Furniture	1989	Ritch's Salvage, Harrisburg, NC
1961	Hamilton Tailoring	1975	Pyramid Cafe, Lakewood, OH	1990	New Construction, Shelbyville,IN
1962	Skip Hogan A.C., Pittsburgh	1976	Warren Motors, J'ville, FL	1991	Riverside Paving, Louisville
1963	Gatliff Auto Sales	1977	Nelson Painting, Okla.City	1992	Vernon's, Jacksonville, FL
1964	Skip Hogan A.C.	1978	Campbell Carpets, Concord, CA	1993	Back Porch/Destin (FL) Roofing
1965	Skip Hogan A.C.	1979	Nelco Mfg.Co., Okla.City	1994	Riverside Paving, Louisville
		1980	Campbell Carpets		

Super Slow Pitch

Multiple winners: Howard's/Western Steer and Steele's Sports (3); Rich's/Superior (2).

Year		Year		Year	
1981	Howard's/Western Steer, Denver, NC	1986	Steele's Sports	1991	Sun Belt/Worth, Atlanta
1982	Jerry's Catering, Miami	1987	Steele's Sports	1992	Rich's/Superior, Windsor Locks, CT
1983	Howard's/Western Steer	1988	Starpath, Monticello, KY	1993	Rich's/Superior
1984	Howard's/Western Steer	1989	Ritch's Salvage, Harrisburg, NC	1994	Bellcorp., Tampa
1985	Steele's Sports, Grafton, OH	1990	Steele's Silver Bullets		

WOMEN
Major Fast Pitch

Multiple winners: Raybestos Brakettes (21); Orange Lionettes (9); Jax Maids (4); Arizona Ramblers (3); Hi-Ho Brakettes, J.J. Krieg's, National Screw & Manufacturing and Redding Rebels (2).

Year		Year		Year	
1933	Great Northerns, Chicago	1955	Orange Lionettes	1977	Raybestos Brakettes
1934	Hart Motors, Chicago	1956	Orange Lionettes	1978	Raybestos Brakettes
1935	Bloomer Girls, Cleveland	1957	Hacienda Rockets, Fresno, CA	1979	Sun City (AZ) Saints
1936	Nat'l Screw & Mfg., Cleveland	1958	Raybestos Brakettes, Stratford, CT	1980	Raybestos Brakettes
1937	Nat'l Screw & Mfg.	1959	Raybestos Brakettes	1981	Orlando (FL) Rebels
1938	J.J. Krieg's, Alameda, CA	1960	Raybestos Brakettes	1982	Raybestos Brakettes
1939	J.J. Krieg's	1961	Gold Sox, Whittier, CA	1983	Raybestos Brakettes
1940	Arizona Ramblers, Phoenix	1962	Orange Lionettes	1984	Los Angeles Diamonds
1941	Higgins Midgets, Tulsa, OK	1963	Raybestos Brakettes	1985	Hi-Ho Brakettes, Stratford, CT
1942	Jax Maids, New Orleans	1964	Erv Lind Florists, Portland, OR	1986	So. California Invasion, LA
1943	Jax Maids	1965	Orange Lionettes	1987	Orange County Majestics, Anaheim, CA
1944	Lind & Pomeroy, Portland, OR	1966	Raybestos Brakettes	1988	Hi-Ho Brakettes (CT)
1945	Jax Maids	1967	Raybestos Brakettes	1989	Whittier (CA) Raiders
1946	Jax Maids	1968	Raybestos Brakettes		
1947	Jax Maids	1969	Orange Lionettes	1990	Raybestos Brakettes
1948	Arizona Ramblers	1970	Orange Lionettes	1991	Raybestos Brakettes
1949	Arizona Ramblers	1971	Raybestos Brakettes	1992	Raybestos Brakettes
1950	Orange (CA) Lionettes	1972	Raybestos Brakettes	1993	Redding (CA) Rebels
1951	Orange Lionettes	1973	Raybestos Brakettes	1994	Redding (CA) Rebels
1952	Orange Lionettes	1974	Raybestos Brakettes		
1953	Betsy Ross Rockets, Fresno, CA	1975	Raybestos Brakettes		
1954	Leach Motor Rockets, Fresno, CA	1976	Raybestos Brakettes		

Major Slow Pitch

Multiple winners: Dana Gardens and Spooks (4); Universal Plastics (3); Cannan's Illusions, Bob Hoffman's Dots and Marks Brothers Dots (2).

Year		Year		Year	
1959	Pearl Laundry, Richmond, VA	1972	Riverside Ford, Cincinnati	1983	Spooks, Anoka, MN
1960	Carolina Rockets, High Pt., NC	1973	Sweeney Chevrolet, Cincinnati	1984	Spooks
1961	Dairy Cottage, Covington, KY	1974	Marks Brothers Dots, Miami	1985	Key Ford Mustangs, Pensacola, FL
1962	Dana Gardens, Cincinnati	1975	Marks Brothers Dots	1986	Sur-Way Tomboys, Tifton, GA
1963	Dana Gardens	1976	Sorrento's Pizza, Cincinnati	1987	Key Ford Mustangs
1964	Dana Gardens	1977	Fox Valley Lassies, St.Charles, IL	1988	Spooks
1965	Art's Acres, Omaha, NE			1989	Cannan's Illusions, Houston
1966	Dana Gardens	1978	Bob Hoffman's Dots, Miami		
1967	Ridge Maintenance, Cleveland	1979	Bob Hoffman's Dots	1990	Spooks
1968	Escue Pontiac, Cincinnati	1980	Howard's Rubi-Otts, Graham, NC	1991	Cannan's Illusions, San Antonio
1969	Converse Dots, Hialeah, FL			1992	Universal Plastics, Cookeville, TN
1970	Rutenschruder Floral, Cincinnati	1981	Tifton (GA) Tomboys	1993	Universal Plastics
1971	Gators, Ft.Lauderdale, FL	1982	Richmond (VA) Stompers	1994	Universal Plastics

TRIATHLON

Ironman Championship

Contested in Hawaii since 1978, the Ironman Triathlon Championship consists of a 2.4-mile swim, a 112-mile bike ride and 26.2-mile run. The race begins at 7 A.M. and continues all day until the course is closed at midnight.

MEN

Multiple winners: Dave Scott (6); Mark Allen (5); Scott Tinley (2).

Year	Date	Winner	Time	Runner-up	Margin	Start	Finish	Location
I	2/18/78	Gordon Haller	11:46	John Dunbar	34:00	15	12	Waikiki Beach
II	1/14/79	Tom Warren	11:15:56	John Dunbar	48:00	15	12	Waikiki Beach
III	1/10/80	Dave Scott	9:24:33	Chuck Neumann	1:08	108	95	Ala Moana Park
IV	2/14/81	John Howard	9:38:29	Tom Warren	26:00	326	299	Kailua-Kona
V	2/6/82	Scott Tinley	9:19:41	Dave Scott	17:16	580	541	Kailua-Kona
VI	10/9/82	Dave Scott	9:08:23	Scott Tinley	20:05	850	775	Kailua-Kona
VII	10/22/83	Dave Scott	9:05:57	Scott Tinley	0:33	964	835	Kailua-Kona
VIII	10/6/84	Dave Scott	8:54:20	Scott Tinley	24:25	1036	903	Kailua-Kona
IX	10/25/85	Scott Tinley	8:50:54	Chris Hinshaw	25:46	1018	965	Kailua-Kona
X	10/18/86	Dave Scott	8:28:37	Mark Allen	9:47	1039	951	Kailua-Kona
XI	10/10/87	Dave Scott	8:34:13	Mark Allen	11:06	1380	1284	Kailua-Kona
XII	10/22/88	Scott Molina	8:31:00	Mike Pigg	2:11	1277	1189	Kailua-Kona
XIII	10/15/89	Mark Allen	8:09:15	Dave Scott	0:58	1285	1231	Kailua-Kona
XIV	10/6/90	Mark Allen	8:28:17	Scott Tinley	9:23	1386	1255	Kailua-Kona
XV	10/19/91	Mark Allen	8:18:32	Greg Welch	6:01	1386	1235	Kailua-Kona
XVI	10/10/92	Mark Allen	8:09:08	Cristian Bustos	7:21	1364	1298	Kailua-Kona
XVII	10/30/93	Mark Allen	8:07:45	Paulli Kiuru	6:37	1438	1353	Kailua-Kona
XVIII	10/15/94	Greg Welch	8:20:27	Dave Scott	4:05	1405	1290	Kailua-Kona

WOMEN

Multiple winners: Paula Newby-Fraser (7); Erin Baker and Sylviane Puntous (2).

Year	Winner	Time	Runner-up	Year	Winner	Time	Runner-up
1978	No finishers			1986	Paula Newby-Fraser	9:49:14	Sylviane Puntous
1979	Lyn Lemaire	12:55.00	None	1987	Erin Baker	9:35:25	Sylviane Puntous
1980	Robin Beck	11:21:24	Eve Anderson	1988	Paula Newby-Fraser	9:01:01	Erin Baker
1981	Linda Sweeney	12:00:32	Sally Edwards	1989	Paula Newby-Fraser	9:00:56	Sylviane Puntous
1982	Kathleen McCartney	11:09:40	Julie Moss	1990	Erin Baker	9:13:42	P.Newby-Fraser
1982	Julie Leach	10:54:08	Joann Dahlkoetter	1991	Paula Newby-Fraser	9:07:52	Erin Baker
1983	Sylviane Puntous	10:43:36	Patricia Puntous	1992	Paula Newby-Fraser	8:55:28	Julie Anne White
1984	Sylviane Puntous	10:25:13	Patricia Puntous	1993	Paula Newby-Fraser	8:58:23	Erin Baker
1985	Joanne Ernst	10:25:22	Liz Bulman	1994	Paula Newby-Fraser	9:20:14	Karen Smyers

World Championship

Contested since 1989, the Triathlon World Championship consists of a 1.5 kilometer swim, a 40-kilometer bike ride and a 10-kilometer run. The 1994 championship was scheduled for Nov. 27 at Wellington, New Zealand.

	MEN			WOMEN	
Year		Time	Year		Time
1989	Mark Allen, United States	1:58:46	1989	Erin Baker, New Zealand	2:10:01
1990	Greg Welch, Australia	1:51:37	1990	Karen Smyers, United States	2:03:33
1991	Miles Stewart, Australia	1:48:20	1991	Joanne Ritchie, Canada	2:02:04
1992	Simon Lessing, Great Britain	1:49:04	1992	Michellie Jones, Australia	2:02:08
1993	Spencer Smith, Great Britain	1:51:20	1993	Michellie Jones, Australia	2:07:41

YACHTING

The America's Cup

International yacht racing was launched in 1851 when England's Royal Yacht Squadron staged a 60-mile regatta around the Isle of Wight and offered a silver trophy to the winner. The 101-foot schooner *America*, sent over by the New York Yacht Club, won the race and the prize. Originally called the Hundred-Guinea Cup, the trophy was renamed The America's Cup after the winning boat's owners deeded it to the NYYC with instructions to defend it whenever challenged.

From 1870-1980, the NYYC successfully defended the Cup 25 straight times; first in large schooners and J-class boats that measured up to 140 feet in overall length, then in 12-meter boats. A foreign yacht finally won the Cup in 1983 when *Australia II* beat defender *Liberty* in the seventh and deciding race off Newport, R.I. Four years later, the San Diego Yacht Club's *Stars & Stripes* won the Cup back, sweeping the four races of the final series off Fremantle, Australia.

Then in 1988, New Zealand's Mercury Bay Boating Club, unwilling to wait the usual three- to four-year period between Cup defenses, challenged the SDYC to a match race, citing the Cup's 102-year-old Deed of Gift, which clearly stated that every challenge had to be honored. Mercury Bay announced it would race a 133-foot monohull. San Diego countered with a 60-foot catamaran. The resulting best-of-three series (Sept. 7-8) was a mismatch as the SDYC's catamaran *Stars & Stripes* won two straight by margins of better than 18 and 21 minutes.

Mercury Bay syndicate leader Michael Fay protested the outcome and took the SDYC to court in New York State (where the Deed of Gift was first filed) claiming San Diego had violated the spirit of the deed by racing a catamaran instead of a monohull. N.Y. State Supreme Court judge Carmen Ciparick agreed and on March 28, 1989, ordered the SDYC to hand the Cup over to Mercury Bay. The SDYC refused, but did consent to the court's appointment of the New York Yacht Club as custodian of the Cup until an appeal was ruled on.

On Sept.19, 1989, the Appellate Division of the N.Y.Supreme Court overturned Ciparick's decision and awarded the Cup back to the SDYC. An appeal by Mercury Bay was denied by the N.Y.Court of Appeals on April 26, 1990, ending three years of legal wrangling. To avoid the chaos of 1988-90, a new class of boat—75-foot monohulls with 110-foot masts—was used by all competing countries in the 1992 races.

The America's Cup will be contested again in 1995 off San Diego.

Note that (*) indicates skipper was also owner of the boat.

Schooners and J-Class Boats

Year	Winner	Skipper	Series	Loser	Skipper
1851	*America*	Richard Brown	—	—	—
1870	*Magic*	Andrew Comstock	1-0	*Cambria*, GBR	J. Tannock
1871	*Columbia* (2-1)	Nelson Comstock	4-0	*Livonia*, GBR	J.R. Woods
	& *Sappho* (2-0)	Sam Greenwood			
1876	*Madeleine*	Josephus Williams	2-0	*Countess of Dufferin*, CAN	J.E. Ellsworth
1881	*Mischief*	Nathanael Clock	2-0	*Atalanta*, CAN	Alexander Cuthbert*
1885	*Puritan*	Aubrey Crocker	2-0	*Genesta*, GBR	John Carter
1886	*Mayflower*	Martin Stone	2-0	*Galatea*, GBR	Dan Bradford
1887	*Volunteer*	Henry Haff	2-0	*Thistle*, GBR	John Barr
1893	*Vigilant*	William Hansen	3-0	*Valkyrie II*, GBR	Wm. Granfield
1895	*Defender*	HenryHaff	3-0	*Valkyrie III*, GBR	Wm. Granfield
1899	*Columbia*	Charles Barr	3-0	*Shamrock I*, GBR	Archie Hogarth
1901	*Columbia*	Charles Barr	3-0	*Shamrock II*, GBR	E.A. Sycamore
1903	*Reliance*	Charles Barr	3-0	*Shamrock III*, GBR	Bob Wringe
1920	*Resolute*	Charles F. Adams	3-2	*Shamrock IV*, GBR	William Burton
1930	*Enterprise*	Harold Vanderbilt*	4-0	*Shamrock V*, GBR	Ned Heard
1934	*Rainbow*	Harold Vanderbilt*	4-2	*Endeavour*, GBR	T.O.M. Sopwith
1937	*Ranger*	Harold Vanderbilt*	4-0	*Endeavour II*, GBR	T.O.M. Sopwith

12-Meter Boats

Year	Winner	Skipper	Series	Loser	Skipper
1958	*Columbia*	Briggs Cunningham	4-0	*Sceptre*, GBR	Graham Mann
1962	*Weatherly*	Bus Mosbacher	4-1	*Gretel*, AUS	Jock Sturrock
1964	*Constellation*	Bob Bavier & Eric Ridder	4-0	*Sovereign*, AUS	Peter Scott
1967	*Intrepid*	Bus Mosbacher	4-0	*Dame Pattie*, AUS	Jock Sturrock
1970	*Intrepid*	Bill Ficker	4-1	*Gretel II*, AUS	Jim Hardy
1974	*Courageous*	Ted Hood	4-0	*Southern Cross*, AUS	John Cuneo
1977	*Courageous*	Ted Turner	4-0	*Australia*	Noel Robins
1980	*Freedom*	Dennis Conner	4-1	*Australia*	Jim Hardy
1983	*Australia II*	John Bertrand	4-3	*Liberty*, USA	Dennis Conner
1987	*Stars & Stripes*	Dennis Conner	4-0	*Kookaburra III*, AUS	Iain Murray

60-ft Catamaran vs 133-ft Monohull

Year	Winner	Skipper	Series	Loser	Skipper
1988	*Stars & Stripes*	Dennis Conner	2-0	*New Zealand*, NZE	David Barnes

75-ft International America's Cup Class

Year	Winner	Skipper	Series	Loser	Skipper
1992	*America*[3]	Bill Koch* & Buddy Melges	4-1	*Il Moro di Venezia*, ITA	Paul Cayard

Other 1994 Champions
Championships decided in 1994, unless otherwise indicated.

ARENA FOOTBALL
Final AFL Standings
(*) indicates Conference champion; (†) indicates playoff wild card.

American Conf.	W	L	T	Pct	PF	PA
*Albany Firebirds	11	1	0	.917	595	341
†Arizona Rattlers	7	5	0	.583	561	564
†Mass Marauders	5	7	0	.417	442	521
†Las Vegas Sting	5	7	0	.417	559	490
Milwaukee Mustangs	5	7	0	.417	398	491

National Conf.	W	L	T	Pct	PF	PA
*Orlando Predators	11	1	0	.917	595	341
†Tampa Bay Storm	7	5	0	.583	561	564
†Charlotte Rage	5	7	0	.417	442	521
†Ft. Worth Cavalry	5	7	0	.417	559	490
Miami Hooters	5	7	0	.417	398	491

Quarterfinals
at Arizona 52...Charlotte 24
at Albany 49...Las Vegas 30
at Orlando 34..Fort Worth 13
at Massachusetts 58....................................Tampa Bay 51

Semifinals
at Orlando 51...Massachusetts 42
Arizona 40..at Albany 33

Arena Bowl VIII
(at Orlando, Att—14,368)
Arizona 36...Orlando 31

AUSTRALIAN RULES FOOTBALL
AFL Grand Final
West Coast Eagles 143............................Geelong Cats 63

BILLIARDS
PBT World Championships
Pro 9-Ball......................Earl Strickland, Greensboro, N.C.
PBT U.S. Open
Pro 9-Ball...................................Efrem Reyes, Manila, PHI
WPBA World Championships
Pro 9-Ball..........................Ewe Mataya-Laurance, Sweden
1993 BCA U.S. Open Straight Pool
Men..Takeshi Okumura, Japan
Women............................Ewa Mataya-Laurence, Sweden

CRICKET
1996 World Cup Final
at India, Pakistan & Sri Lanka (Sept.-Oct.)
England vs New Zealand
(Best of 3 Tests)
1st— NZE: 251 & 226........................ENG: 8/567 dec.
(England wins by an innings and 90 runs)
2nd— NZE: 476 & 5/211 dec. ....ENG: 281 & 8/254
(match drawn)
3rd— ENG: 382 ....NZE: 151 & 7/308
(match drawn; England wins 3-test series, 1-0

England vs South Africa
(Best of 3 Tests)
1st— SAF: 357 & 8/278 dec.; ....ENG: 180 & 99
(South Africa wins by 356 runs)
2nd— ENG: 9/477 dec. & 5/267 dec; SAF: 447 & 3/116
(match drawn)
3rd— SAF: 332 & 175 ....ENG: 304 & 2/205
(England won by 8 wickets; series drawn)

Australia vs Pakistan
Best of 3 Tests...Sept. 20-Nov. 7

CURLING
World Champions
Men ....Canada (skip: Rick Folk)
Women ....Canada (skip: Sandra Peterson)
U.S. Champions
Men...................................Bemidji, Minn. (skip: Scott Baird)
Women ....Denver (skip: Bev Behnke)

DRAG RACING
NHRA U.S. Nationals
Top Fuel ....Connie Kalitta
Funny Car ....Cruz Pedregon
Pro Stock...Warren Johnson
NHRA Overall Champions
Top Fuel ....Scott Kalitta
Funny Car ....John Force
Pro Stock ....undecided

EQUESTRIAN
World Equestrian Games
at The Hague, HOL
Individual Champions
Special Dressage ....Isabell Werth, Germany
Freestyle Dressage ....Anky van Grunsven, Holland
Show Jumping..........................Franke Sloothaak, Germany
3-Day Event ....Vaughan Jefferis, New Zealand
Endurance Riding...............................Valerie Kanavy, USA
Four-in-Hand ....Michael Freund, Germany
Team Champions
Dressage: Germany   Endurance Riding: France
Show Jumping: Germany   Four-in-Hand: Germany
3-Day Event: Great Britain

HANDBALL
World Four-Wall Championships
Men ....David Chapman, USA
Women...Lisa Fraser, Canada
U.S. Four-Wall Championships
Men ....Octavio Silveyra, Los Angeles
Women ....Anna Engele, St. Paul, MN
Open doubles..................................John Bike, Tucson, Ariz.
& Octavio Silveyra, Los Angeles

Other 1994 Champions (Cont.)

HORSESHOE PITCHING

World Champions

Men .... Walter Ray Williams Jr., Stockton, Calif.
Women .... Sue Snyder, Grandview, Ind.

LACROSSE

Men's World Cup

at Manchester, England

Final: USA 21 .... Australia 7
3rd place: Canada 25 .... England 10
5th place: Iroquois Nationals 19 .... Japan 13

1997 Women's World Championship

at Tokyo

Major Indoor Lacrosse

Final MILL Standings

(*) indicates Conference champion; (†) indicates playoff wild card.

American Div.	W	L	GB	Pct	GF	GA
*Phila. Wings	6	2	—	.917	595	341
†New York Saints	5	3	1	.583	561	564
Baltimore Thunder	4	4	2	.417	442	521

National Div.	W	L	T	Pct	PF	PA
*Buffalo Bandits	1	1	0	.917	595	341
†Detroit Turbos	7	5	0	.583	561	564
Boston Blazers	5	7	0	.417	442	521

Division Finals

at Buffalo 16 .... Detroit 10
at Philadelphia 17 .... New York 7

Championship

(at Buffalo, Att— 16,284)

Philadelphia 26 .... Buffalo 15

MOTORCYCLE RACING

ROAD RACING

Grand Prix Champions

125 cc .... Kazuto Sakata, Japan
250 cc .... Max Biaggi, Italy
500 cc .... Michael Doohan, Australia
1993 Super Bike .... Scott Russell, USA

MOTOCROSS

Motorcross des Nations

Team .... England (Paul Malin, Rob Herring
and Kurt Nicoll)

Grand Prix Champions

125 cc .... Bob Moore, USA
250 cc .... Greg Albertyn, South Africa
500 cc .... Marcus Hansson, Sweden

RACQUETBALL

U.S. Amateur Champions

Men .... Michael Bronfeld, Monterey, Calif.
Women .... Robin Levine, Sacramento

IRT Pro Tour Champions

Men .... Cliff Swain, Braintree, Mass.
Women .... Michelle Gould, Boise, Idaho

RODEO

1994 PRCA Champion Cowboys

All-Around Cowboy .... Ty Murray, Stephenville, Tex.
Bareback Riding .... Deb Greenough, Red Lodge, Mont.
Bull Riding .... Ty Murray
Calf Roping .... Joe Beaver, Huntsville, Tex.
Saddle Bronc Riding .... Dan Mortensen, Billings, Mont.
Steer Roping .... Guy Allen, Vinita, Okla.
Steer Wrestling .... Steve Duhon, Opelousas, La.
Team Roping .... Bobby Hurley, Clarksville, Ark.

RUGBY

Rugby League (Pro)

Grand Final

Camberra Raiders 36 .... Canterbury Bulldogs 12

Rugby Union (Amateur)

International Champions

1995 Men's World Cup .... at South Africa
1994 Women's World Cup Final .... England 38, USA 23
1994 Five Nations* .... Wales

*England, Wales, Scotland, Ireland and France.

U.S. Champions

Club .... Old Mission Beach A.C., La Jolla, CA
College .... California (Berkeley)

VOLLEYBALL

World Champions

Men's Final .... Italy over Holland
(15-10, 11-15, 15-11, 15-1)
Women .... at Brazil (Oct. 19-29)

U.S. Open Champions

Men's Gold Div .... Asics/Paul Mitchell, So. Calif.
Women's Gold Div .... Nick's/Gold's, Chicago

Pro Beach Tours

Goodwill Games

Men .... Jan Kvalagim/Bjorn Maaseide, NOR
Women .... Karolyn Kirby/Liz Masakayan, USA

MEN (AVP)

Manhattan Beach Open .... Karch Kiraly/Kent Steffes
U.S. Championships .... Karch Kiraly/Kent Steffes
Tourn. of Champions .... Karch Kiraly/Kent Steffes

WOMEN (WPVA)

Newport Shoot-out .... Karolyn Kirby/Liz Masakayan
Reebok Nationals .... Karolyn Kirby/Liz Masakayan
U.S. Open .... Karolyn Kirby/Liz Masakayan

WATER SKIING

1995 World Championships

Men/Women .... at Roquebrune, France (Sept. 11-17)

U.S. Open Champions

Overall: Men .... Patrice Martin, France
Women .... Julie Shull-Petrus, Hartville, Mo.

Bud Water Ski Tour

Men's Slalom .... Andy Mapple, England
Men's Freestyle .... Dave Reinhart, Defiance, Ohio
Men's Jump .... Sammy Duvall, Greenville, S.C.
Women's Slalom .... Kristi Overton, Greenville, N.C.

Andres Escobar, a defender on Colombia's highly-regarded 1994 World Cup team, was gunned down in Medellin on July 2. His accidental "own goal" in a 2-1 loss to the United States helped eliminate Colombia in the first round of competition.

DEATHS

Wide World Photos

Hank Aguirre

Wide World Photos

Paul Anderson

Wide World Photos

Ray Arcel

Hank Aguirre, 62; former three-time all-star pitcher who spent most of his career with the Detroit Tigers; career record was 75-72 with a 3.25 ERA between 1955 and 1970; spent 10 seasons with the Tigers and also hurled for Cleveland, Los Angeles and the Chicago Cubs; best season was in 1962 with Detroit when he went 16-8 with a league-leading 2.21 ERA; known as a poor hitter (.085 lifetime) who only improved after becoming a switch hitter; served as pitching coach with the Cubs and also coached in minors before going into auto parts manufacturing; of cancer; in Detroit, Sept. 5.

Dave Albritton, 82; won a silver medal in high jumping at the 1936 Olympics in Berlin by clearing 6 feet, 7¾ inches; also set a world record that year with a leap of 6 feet, 9⅞ inches; a close friend of Jesse Owens, the two grew up together and developed into track stars at Ohio State; cause of death not reported; in Dayton, Ohio, May 14.

Jeff Alm, 25; defensive tackle for the Houston Oilers; played on the 1988 national-champion Notre Dame squad; drafted in the second-round by the Oilers in 1990; of gunshot wounds in an apparent suicide minutes after a friend riding in his car was killed in a crash; in Houston, Dec. 14, 1993.

H.V. (Shorty) Almquist, 90; quarterbacked the Minnesota football team to an undefeated season in 1927; coached Augustana (Illinois) football to a 67-31-10 record, including one undefeated season, from 1928 to 1940; coached football and basketball and served as AD at Rock Island (Illinois) High, where he retired in 1969; of natural causes; in Moline, Ill., Apr. 5.

Thomas Alston, 67; first black baseball player for the St. Louis Cardinals; played first base during his three-year pro career in St. Louis and finished with four home runs and 36 RBI in 91 games; struggled to find work following retirement in 1958 and spent time in two mental institutions; honored by the Cardinals three years ago at Busch Stadium when he threw out the first ball in a game; graduate of North Carolina A&T; of prostate cancer; in Winston-Salem, N.C., Jan. 4.

Paul Anderson, 61; once recognized as the world's strongest man, won an Olympic gold medal at Melbourne in 1956 and set three Olympic records; is the last American heavyweight to win an Olympic gold medal; listed in the Guinness Book of World Records for having lifted the most weight with his back - 6,270 pounds in 1957; once had a 23½ inch neck; of kidney failure and arthritis; in Vidalia, Georgia, Aug. 15.

Ray Arcel, 94; incredibly successful and resilient boxing trainer who handled numerous champions during a career that spanned six decades; trained 19 champions in all, including Roberto Duran; first champion was Frankie Genaro, who captured the American flyweight title in 1923;

last appearance in the corner of a titlist was in 1982, when Larry Holmes stopped Gerry Cooney; known as "The Meat Wagon" because 13 of his 14 fighters were defeated by heavyweight Joe Louis; did train Ezzard Charles to a victory over Louis in 1950, a win that helped signature Arcel's career; matchmaker and producer for television's "Saturday Night Fights" from 1953-1955; purchasing agent for the Meehanite Metal Corporation; of natural causes; in Manhattan, Mar. 7.

Roberto Balado, 25; a Cuban super heavyweight champion considered by some experts to be the world's second best amateur fighter; won Caribbean, Pan American, world and Olympic titles; in a car crash; in Havana, July 2.

Jerry Barber, 78; PGA Player of the Year in 1961, who won the '61 PGA Championship in a playoff with Don January; full-time member of the PGA tour from 1948-62; member of the 1955 and '62 Ryder Cup teams as well as captain in '62; of heart failure after suffering a stroke; in Glendale, Calif., Sept. 23.

Ray Bare, 44; former Tiger pitcher who snapped Detroit's longest losing streak (19 games) ever by throwing a two-hitter against the Angels on Aug. 16, 1975; righthander went 16-26 over five major league seasons; of leukemia; in Miami, Mar. 29.

Vince Beall, 21; outfielder for Cal State Sacramento; came to Cal State Sacramento from Sacramento City College, where he was the 1992 Camino Norte Conference Player of the Year; of liver and lung cancer; in San Diego, May 14.

Cally Belcher, 22; linebacker for Stephen F. Austin who was twice named All-Southland Conference at strong safety; helped lead the Lumberjacks to an 8-4 record and a berth in the Division I-AA playoffs; after collapsing during spring practice due to neurological complications; in Nacogdoches, Tex., Mar. 29.

Marcel Bernard, 89; won the French Open men's singles title in 1946; only one other French national since Bernard - Yannick Noah (1983) - has captured the French Open since; paired with Jean Borotra in 1936 to win the French Open doubles title; president of French tennis association from 1968 to 1974 and was the organization's president of honor; of a heart attack; in Paris, Apr. 29.

Marcel Bich, 79; businessman who built an empire on pens, razors and lighters but was also well-known for his repeated entries in the America's Cup; his fortunes made it possible to keep entering the race, in which his yachts were never too successful until 1980, when France III reached the semifinals; cause of death not reported; in Paris, May 30.

Paul Bienz, 68; a former world record sprinter and All-America track star at Tulane; tied the world record in the 100 in 1948 with a time of 9.4 seconds and tied Jesse

Wide World Photos

International Speedway Corp./NASCAR

PGA Tour

Verlon Biggs   **Neil Bonnett**   **Julius Boros**

Owens' 200 mark of 20.3 the following year; following a stint in the Air Force Bienz played football and ran track at Tulane; member of the Green Wave's SEC champion football team in 1949; member of the Tulane Hall of Fame and Indiana Track Hall of Fame; after a lomg illness; in Fort Wayne, Ind., Aug. 31.

Verlon Biggs, 51; defensive end on the New York Jets' 1969 Super Bowl champion team who was known for making big plays; spent five seasons with the Jets and five with the Washington Redskins before retiring with an injury in 1975; three-time All-Star who was voted the most outstanding defensive player in the 1966 AFL All-Star game; of leukemia; in Moss Point, Miss., June 7.

Lewis Billups, 30; former Cincinnati Bengals defensive back who experienced legal troubles after leaving the NFL in 1991; drafted by the Bengals out of North Alabama in 1985; was named by a Seattle woman as one of several Bengals who allegedly sexually assaulted her; in 1993, pleaded guilty to and was sentenced to a year in jail for making threatening phone calls to NBA player Rex Chapman, who dated Billups' sister; in a 100-mph car crash; in Orlando, Apr. 9.

Bob Bjorklund, 75; co-captain of the undefeated 1940 University of Minnesota football team; played for the Philadelphia Eagles in 1941 and 1946 and served in the Navy during WWII; Bjorklund's son, Dick, said his father's work with both the Gophers and the US Olympic Committee, of which he was fundraising chairman in Minnesota, North Dakota, South Dakota and Iowa, "were his pride and joy;" of pulmonary fibrosis; in Hopkins, Minn., Jan. 28.

Neil Bonnett, 47; raced in 46 Daytona races in Winston Cup cars, winning three times; registered 18 Winston Cup victories; 26th person killed at Daytona International Speedway; in addition to being a prominent NASCAR driver, was also a TV personality; career that began in 1973 was checkered with dangerous crashes - suffered a serious concussion in 1990 and crashed again in '93 during a comeback attempt; earned $3.5 million in winnings, placing him 25th on the career list despite never finishing higher than fourth in the annual Winston Cup standings; in a car crash during a practice run for the Daytona 500; in Daytona, Fla., Feb. 11.

Julius Boros, 74; two-time US Open and PGA champion; managed to create a name for himself during the same era in which golfing legends Ben Hogan, Sam Snead, Arnold Palmer, Gary Player and Jack Nicklaus competed; PGA player of the year in 1952 and 1963; won the Open in 1952 and 1963 and the PGA in 1968; of a heart attack while riding in a cart on one of his favorite courses - the Coral Ridge Country Club in Fort Lauderdale; in Ft. Lauderdale, Fla., May 28.

Jean Borotra, 95; legendary French tennis champion who was a force during France's golden years of tennis in the

1920's and 1930's; was dubbed a "Four Musketeer" along with countrymen Rene Lacoste, Jacques Brunon and Henri Cochet; won Wimbledon in 1924 and 1926, lost it three times to other Musketeers and won the doubles title in 1925; captured the French Open singles title once and the doubles title three times and, in 1928, won the Australian Open singles, doubles and mixed doubles titles; has the record for third-most appearances in the Davis Cup finals, with nine, and played in the tournament a record 17 years; Borotra's squads won the Davis Cup from 1927 through 1932; cause of death not reported; in Biarritz, France, July 17.

Ed Bozik, 64; athletic director at the University of Pittsburgh for 10 years before retiring in 1991; headed Pitt athletics during some of its most controversial years: months after he was hired the basketball program was reprimanded for a recruiting violation, one football coach— Foge Fazio—was fired and another—Mike Gottfried—retired under pressure and a top aide, Bob Heddleston, was placed on four years probation for misapplying booster funds and bribery; also oversaw improvements to Pitt Stadium and Fitzgerald Field House and the construction of the Cost Sports Center; of heart problems; in Pittsburgh, July 21.

Ray (Muscles) Bray Sr., 76; guard for Chicago Bears from 1939-1951 and helped the Bears to championships in 1940, 1943 and 1946; also was a member of the Green Bay Packers in 1952; may be remembered most for an illegal play in 1951: during a game against the Rams Bray was standing on the sidelines when LA intercepted a pass, so Bray jumped in bounds and tackled the player without getting whistled for a penalty; in Chicago, Dec. 26, 1994.

Jim Brock, 57; one of college baseball's winningest coaches, Brock compiled a 1,100-440 record during 23 years with Arizona State; sent an average of more than seven players per year into the pros, including Barry Bonds, Hubie Brooks and Pat Listach; won 60 or more games four times; won national championships in 1977 and 1981; of liver and colon cancer; in Mesa, Ariz., June 12.

Joel Broering, 17; teenager who became friends with golfer Payne Stewart through the A Special Wish Foundation, which meets the requests of seriously ill children; the MVP of his high school golf team, Broering idolized Stewart, who presented the youngster with the Skins Game trophy he won in Nov., 1993; of leukemia; in St. Henry, Ohio, Dec. 11, 1993.

Raymond (Tay) Brown, 82; tackle who starred for USC's 1931 and 1932 national championship football teams; inducted into the College Football Hall of Fame in 1981; captained the '32 Trojan squad that went unbeaten and shut out Pitt, 35-0, in the Rose Bowl; after coaching both football and basketball at the University of Cincinnati, Brown coached football at Compton College, where he amassed a 140-33-9 record; of cancer; in Los Angeles, July 16.

Arizona State

Wide World Photos

Jean Borotra   **Jim Brock**   **John Candy**

Matt Busby, 84; coach of Manchester (England) United from 1945-1969, leading it to Football Association Cup titles in 1948 and 1963; in 1968, 10 years after an air crash that seriously injured Busby and killed eight of his players, he coached United to one of British soccer's greatest triumphs, a 4-1 win over Benfica of Lisbon in the European Champions Cup; was knighted by Queen Elizabeth II later that year; also guided United to Football League titles in 1952, 1956, 1957, 1965 and 1967; of blood cancer; in Manchester, England, Jan. 20.

Lee Roy Caffey, 52; linebacker for three NFL Super Bowl champions; played on the Green Bay Packer teams under Vince Lombardi that won the first two Super Bowls, and played for Tom Landry on Dallas' 1972 Super Bowl champion; finished with the San Diego Chargers; member of both the Packer and Texas A&M Hall of Fames; of colon cancer; in Houston, Jan. 18.

Jim Callanan, 67; former lineman for Southern Cal who scored the quickest touchdown in Rose Bowl history when, as a sophomore in 1945, he blocked a Tennessee punt, picked it up and ran 32 yards for a touchdown after just 1:50 had elapsed; the Trojans went on to win, 25-0; USC's lineman of the year in 1946; of a heart attack; in Santa Ana, Calif., Jan. 21.

John Candy, 43; famous actor and comedian who was also a passionate sports fan; co-owner of the Toronto Argonauts of the Canadian Football League; in one of his final films, "Cool Runnings," he played the coach of a Jamaican bobsled team; of a heart attack; in Mexico, Mar. 5.

Tim Capaldi, 31; first to race a blown alcohol hydro boat over 200 mph; three-time IHBA blown alcohol hydro world champion; won 30 races and set 32 speed records during his drag boat competition; in a crash at the International Hot Boat Association Spring nationals, which he won in 5.741 seconds before his fatal crash; in San Dimas, Calif., Apr. 10.

Margaret Chenery Carmichael, 74; once part-owner of the famous racehorse Secretariat, which won horse racing's Triple Crown in 1973; Carmichael's father, Christopher Chenery, owned The Meadows, a horse farm where Secretariat was born; cause of death not reported; in Tucson, Ariz., Nov. 7, 1993.

Hugo Castello, 79; coached New York University to ten national championships in fencing; coached the Violets from 1947 to 1975; while his father, Julio, was the NYU fencing coach, Hugo won three National Intercollegiate Foil Fencing Championships (1935-1937); of cancer; in New York, Mar. 28.

Nev Chandler, 47; long-time radio voice of the Cleveland Browns who also broadcast Indian games; Ohio's sportscaster of the year in 1987, 1988, 1989 and 1992; of colon cancer; in Rocky River, Ohio, Aug. 7.

Lynne Chuvalo, 50; wife of former boxing star George Chuvalo, the Canadian heavyweight champion in the 1960's who fought Muhammad Ali, Joe Frazier and George Foreman; since the 55-year-old Chuvalo retired from boxing, his life has been riddled with tragedy: four days before his wife's death, Chuvalo's son, George Jr., died of a heroin overdose, and in 1985, Chuvalo's youngest son, Jesse, shot himself; of an apparent overdose with the intention of suicide; in Toronto, Nov. 4, 1993.

Walt Chyzowych, 57; Wake Forest soccer coach since 1986; played for the U.S. national team in 1965 and coached it from 1976 to 1981; director of coaching of the U.S. Soccer Federation from 1975 to 1981 and from '84-'86; coached ten years at Philadelphia Textile, taking it to five NCAA tournaments and compiling a record of 122-37-14; guided Wake Forest to its first ACC title in 1989; of a heart attack; in Winston-Salem, N.C., Sept. 2.

Ben Cohen, 94; co-owner of Pimlico Race Course from 1952-1986; under Cohen's management, Pimlico—the home of the Preakness Stakes, the middle jewel in the Triple Crown of thoroughbred racing—was modernized and seating was expanded; of natural causes at Sinai Hospital, less than a mile from the Pimlico backstretch; in Baltimore, Mar. 21.

Gordy Coleman, 59; former Cincinnati Reds first baseman who later went on to become a broadcaster for the team; broke into the majors with Cleveland in 1959 and played first for the Reds between 1960-1967; hit .273 lifetime with 98 homers and 387 runs batted in; was part of the Reds TV team for SportsChannel cable; of a heart attack; in Cincinnati, Mar. 12.

Mary Washburn Conklin, 86; ran the first leg on the US' silver medal-winning 400-meter relay team at the 1928 Amsterdam Olympics; a track and field star for both DePauw and New York Universities, Conklin set national collegiate records and won the 80-meter hurdles in international competition; was inducted into both school's Hall of Fame; served as a national field hockey and lacrosse official; of natural causes; in Braintree, Mass., Feb. 2.

Eugenia Conner, 30; standout basketball player at Missisippi in the 1980's; only player in school history to be named to the all-Southeastern Conference team four times; the 6-foot-2-inch center finished as Ole Miss's third-leading scorer with 1,993 points; after college played professionally in Europe for four years; of a heart attack related to a hyperactive thyroid; in Gulfport, Miss., Mar. 3.

Huey Cranford, 66; men's basketball coach at Northwestern State from 1957-1965; led the Demons to a 116-98 record during those eight years, as well as Gulf States Conference championships in 1957-58 and 1959-60; that '59-'60 team had a 23-5 record; his career .542 winning percentage is third among the seven men who

Tampa Bay Buccaneers

Hugh Culverhouse

Wide World Photos

John Curry

UPI/Bettmann

Bill Dickey

have coached basketball at Northwestern since 1913; in a fire that destroyed his home; in Converse, La., Feb. 21.

Pat Crawford, 91; a substitute infielder who was the last living member of the "Gashouse Gang," a nickname for the 1934 World Series champion St. Louis Cardinals; real name was Clifford; batted .280 in a 318-game career that began with the New York Giants in 1929 and ended that season with the Cardinals; first hit was a grand slam against the Boston Braves; of natural causes; in Morehead City, N.C., Jan. 25.

Hugh Culverhouse, 75; the only owner the Tampa Bay Buccaneers ever had; head of the NFL's Financial Committee during the strikes of 1982 and 1987; credited with forming the league's bargaining policy; of lung cancer; in New Orleans, Aug. 25.

John Curry, 44; English figure skater who, in 1976, won an Olympic Gold medal and a world championship; his artistry on ice was said to have revolutionized figure skating by mixing classical ballet with acrobatics; nicknamed "Nureyev on Ice;" contracted the HIV virus in 1987 and was told he had full-blown AIDS in 1991; is considered the most prominent figure skater to have died from AIDS; other notable fatalaties include former Canadian champion Brian Pockar and 1988 Olympic dance bronze medalist Rob McCall, also a Canadian; of an AIDS-related illness; in Stratford-Upon-Avon, England, Apr. 15.

Francis Dale, 72; former president of the Cincinnati Reds and former commissioner of the Major Indoor Soccer League; as president of the Reds from 1967-1973, was a catalyst in getting the downtown Riverfront Stadium—where the Reds now play—built; former publisher of both The Cincinnati Enquirer and the Los Angeles Herald; in 1972 President Nixon appointed Dale a U.S. ambassador in Geneva, Switzerland; also served as chairman of Nixon's re-election committee; in 1979, performed at the Cotton Bowl; of a heart attack; in Victoria Falls, Zimbabwe, Nov. 28, 1993.

Ray Dandridge, 79; Hall of Fame third baseman who was inducted in 1987; began career with the Detroit Stars of the Negro Leagues in 1933 and went on to play for the Newark Eagles; spent five years in the minor leagues after Jackie Robinson broke baseball's color barrier in 1947; cause of death not reported; in Palm Bay, Fla., Feb. 12.

Gussie Nell Davis, 87; founder of the Kilgore College Rangerettes—the nation's first dance-drill team to perform at halftime of a college football game; retired in 1979 after heading the 65-member dance team for 40 years; performed at the Cotton Bowl for the past 43 New Year's Day games, and the team also danced in some of the most prominent movies, parades and athletic events in the country; in 1979, said of her troupe, "...There's nobody in the world...that does routines as precise and as perfect as we do. They don't make mistakes;" of respiratory complications; in Kilgore, Texas, Dec. 20.

Saul Davis, 92; played third base, second base and shortstop in the Negro League from 1921-1931; was the oldest living player from the Negro League's National League; credited with discovering Hall of Fame pitcher Satchel Paige; of cancer; in Minot, N.D., Feb. 10.

Helen Dell, 71; former Dodger Stadium organist who entertained fans from 1971 until her retirement in 1987; was the first organist to play for an Olympic baseball game when Dodger Stadium hosted the event in 1984; in Los Angeles, Dec. 16, 1993.

Dener, 23; Brazilian soccer star with the club Vasco da Gama; compared by some to a young Pelé, Dener quickly earned the respect of the soccer world with his ball-handling prowess; in a car crash; in Rio de Janeiro, Brazil, Apr. 19.

Walt Dette, 86; a renowned fly tyer from the Catskill Mountains who passed his art on to several generations; along with his wife, Winnie, and their daughter, Mary, the Dette's were known as "the first family of fly fishing;" during a time when dressing flies was a guarded secret, once Dette learned the trade he shared it with anyone who inquired and is credited with directly or indirectly affecting all those who fish with the fly today; of a heart attack; in Roscoe, N.Y., Mar. 31.

Bill Dickey, 86; Hall of Fame catcher who spent three decades with the New York Yankees as a player, manager and coach; the Yankees reached the World Series eight times with Dickey and won seven; batted .313 with 202 homers in 1,712 games from 1928 to 1946; was Lou Gehrig's road roommate; played himself in "Pride of the Yankees," a classic film about Gehrig; an eight-time all-star whose No. 8 is retired in a shared status along with Yogi Berra, who replaced Dickey behind the plate; his best seasons were in 1936-37: in '36 he hit .362 with 22 homers and 107 RBI's, then followed that in '37 by hitting .332 with 29 homers and 133 RBI's; caught 38 World Series games, a record later broken by Berra; remembered for a single in the 1934 All-Star Game that broke Carl Hubbell's record of striking out five straight future Hall of Famers; took over as Yankee manager in 1946, resigned at the end of the season and then was a coach for New York until 1957; in 1932, drew a 30-day suspension and $1,000 fine for breaking the jaw of Washington's Carl Reynolds with a single punch after a collision at home plate; cause of death not reported; in Little Rock, Ark., Nov. 12, 1993.

Trent DiGiuro, 20; an offensive guard on Kentucky's football team; mysteriously shot while attending his own birthday-party just three days before turning 21; in Lexington, Ky., July 17.

Wide World Photos

Buff Donelli

Wide World Photos

Chub Feeney

New Orleans Saints

Jim Finks

Joe Dobson, 77; former Red Sox pitcher who compiled a lifetime record of 137-103 in 14 seasons; also pitched with the Indians and White Sox; won Game 5 of the 1946 World Series for Boston, pitching a four-hitter against St. Louis; had a 13-7 record that season and registered a career-best 18-8 mark the next; was GM of Boston's Winter Haven farm team following his retirement in 1954; following a lengthy illness; in Jacksonville, Fla., June 23.

Jim Donaghy, 37; national baseball writer for The Associated Press who covered six of the last seven World Series; acclaimed for his reporting during an earthquake at the 1989 Series in San Francisco between the Giants and A's: as Candlestick Park shook, Donaghy remained in the press box and dictated the story to editors in New York; a 13-year veteran of the AP; of cancer; in New York, Apr. 9.

Aldo (Buff) Donelli, 87; once coached the Pittsburgh Steelers and the Duquesne University football teams at the same time; also coached at BU and Columbia and played soccer for the U.S. in the 1934 World Cup; while coaching at Duquesne in 1941, also led the Steelers for five games—all losses—before receiving an order from NFL commissioner Elmer Layden to choose one or the other: Donelli chose Duquesne; compiled a 29-4-2 record at Duquesne, 46-36-4 mark at BU and a 30-76-2 record at Columbia; member of the U.S. Soccer Hall of Fame; during the 1934 World Cup he scored the lone U.S. goal in a loss to Italy, making him the last U.S. player to score against the Italians in the World Cup; following a long illness; in Fort Lauderdale, Fla., Aug. 9.

Pierre Dorion, 49; director of scouting for the Toronto Maple Leafs; joined the Leafs in 1990 after 10 years with the NHL's scouting bureau; of a massive heart attack; in Orleans, Ont., June 25.

Herbert Dorricott, 80; served two terms as NCAA president from 1959 to 1961; former chairman of the NCAA's first Television Committee, which negotiated with networks and designed policy on how television income would be distributed; worked for his alma mater, Western State College, for 33 years and was one of the few persons from a small college to head the NCAA; served as a timer and judge for ski events at the 1962 Winter Olympics; of diabetes; in Gunnison, Colo., Mar. 14.

Dick Dozer, 68; former sportswriter for The Phoenix Gazette and the Chicago Tribune; left the Tribune in 1981 and retired from The Gazette in 1986; former president of the Baseball Writers Association of America; father of Phoenix Suns vice president and chief operating officer Richard Dozer; of internal injuries suffered when he fell a day earlier off the roof of his home; in Phoenix, Jan. 4.

Lee Dubose, 27; former star quarterback for Howard University who was the 1988 Mid-Eastern Athletic Conference Player of the Year after throwing for 49 touchdowns and accumulating over 5,800 yards in total offense; of carbon monoxide poisoning; in Gainesville, Fla., Dec. 8, 1993.

Tommy Eagles, 45; former Auburn basketball coach who took over the University of New Orleans program in May; played for and coached at Louisiana Tech, where he compiled a 97-40 record; resigned under pressure in Auburn after finishing with a 64-78 record in five seasons; after collapsing while playing basketball; in Salt Lake City, Utah, July 30.

Don Earle, 64; television broadcaster of the Boston Bruins between 1967-1971, when the team was known as "The Big, Bad Bruins"; considered too much of a "homer" even by not-so-objective Bruins fans and was dismissed from his post; later became the TV voice of the Philadelphia Flyers and was also a weekend sports announcer for CBS radio network; for several years Earle co-hosted muscular dystrophy TV telethons in Boston and Philadelphia; cause of death not reported; in Westfield, Mass., Dec. 15, 1993.

Easy Goer, 8; one of New York's most exciting horse racing champions; career totals are astounding: 14 victories in 20 races, five second-place finishes, one third place finish and $4,873,770 million in winnings, the fourth-highest total ever in racing; trained by Shug McGaughey, owned by Ogden Phipps; biggest rival was Sunday Silence, which won a legendary duel over Easy Goer by a nose in the 1989 Preakness; career was ended by a bone chip in his right foreleg; of a heart attack; at Claiborne Farm, Kentucky, May 12.

Andres Escobar, 27; a defender on Colombia's highly-regarded 1994 World Cup team, who accidently kicked the ball into his own net while attempting to deflect a pass in a 2-1 opening round loss to the United States on June 22; the own goal gave the U.S. a 1-0 lead in the 35th minute of the game; two weeks later, after returning to Medellin, Colombia, Escobar was shot 12 times by an unknown assailant as he left a nightclub; witnesses said the killer shouted "Goal! Goal!" as he fired each shot; of gunshot wounds; in Medellin, July 2.

Dernell Every, 88; former national fencing champion and Olympic medalist; member of U.S. Olympic fencing team in 1928, 1932 and 1948; the 1932 team won the bronze; first undisputed Intercollegiate Fencing Association foil champion while at Yale in 1927 and 1928; from 1928-1951 won three national individual foil titles and was a member of 10 national championship foil teams while competing for the Fencers Club of New York and the New York Athletic Club; of complications suffered in a fall at his home; in Mt. Kisco, N.Y., Sept. 11.

Heather Farr, 28; professional golfer who made a courageous attempt to rejoin the game despite a battle with cancer; two-time all-American at Arizona State and the

UPI/Bettmann

Wide World Photos

UPI/Bettmann

Gretchen Fraser

Jake Gaither

Vitas Gerulaitis

youngest player ever to qualify for the LPGA tour—at age 20—in 1976; won $170,038 in 3½ years before being diagnosed with breast cancer; stated in February 1992 that she felt she was cured of cancer and would return to the game in 1993, but several medical setbacks wouldn't allow it; of cancer; in Scottsdale, Ariz., Nov. 20, 1993.

John O'Neil Farrell, 87; bronze-medal winning speed skater in the 500-meter event in the 1928 Winter Olympics; finished sixth in the 500 meters at the 1932 Olympics; member of the Speed Skating Hall of Fame; coached the U.S. men's team at the 1936 Olympics; of complications from abdominal surgery; in Evergreen Park, Ill., June 20.

Charles S. (Chub) Feeney, 72; the National League president from 1970-86 and a former general manager of the New York Giants; "one of baseball's most endearing figures," Feeney was regarded as a purist who was opposed to the designated hitter rule because he perceived it as a gimmick; was instrumental in getting the National League to split into two divisions; worked for the Giants from 1946 until 1970, rising to general manager before taking over for Warren Giles as NL president; was with the Giants when they won the World Series in 1954; finished his career as president of the San Diego Padres, where he stayed just one year; came quite close to being named baseball commissioner in 1969, but when owners were deadlocked in deciding between the final two candidates—Feeney and Yankees executive Michael Burke—they compromised and named Bowie Kuhn, who at the time was the NL general counsel; nicknamed "Chub" by his mother; of a heart attack; in San Francisco, Jan. 10.

Sherm Feller, 75; Boston Red Sox PA announcer for 26 seasons whose distinctive voice developed into a symbol of the Fenway Park legend; known internationally as a songwriter and composer; two of his more famous tunes were "Summertime, Summertime" and "My Baby's Coming Home;" the Boston Pops regularly performed his "Snow, Beautiful Snow;" of natural causes; in Stoughton, Mass., Jan. 27.

Neal (Doc) Fenkell, 71; longtime employee of the Detroit Tigers; joined the Tigers' PR staff in 1954 and later became director of broadcasting and a consultant; retired in 1992; of cancer; in Detroit, Jan. 7.

Rui Filipe, 26; member of the Portuguese national soccer team; quality midfielder for FC Porto of the Portuguese first division; was not available for what would have been his final game because of a red card suspension the previous week; in a car accident; near Oporto, Portugal, Aug. 28.

Jim Finks, 66; rose in pro football from player to coach to general manager to club president and, in 1989, nearly to commissioner; well known in recent years for helping turn a sagging New Orleans Saints franchise into a perennial contender; in their 20th season, the Saints, under Finks and the coach he hired, Jim Mora, had their first winning season ever; in 1989, was the apparent choice to succeed Pete Rozelle as NFL commissioner but was shut out by a group of younger owners who felt the selection of Finks was being forced upon them by the older, more established owners; named by new commissioner Paul Tagliabue as the chairman of the league's competition committee; was general manager of the Minnesota Vikings for nine years and directed the Chicago Bears' operations for another nine; in 1984, took a one-year respite from football and became president of the division-winning Chicago Cubs; was a 12th-round draft choice of the Pittsburgh Steelers in 1949; of lung cancer; in Metairie, La., May 8.

George (Showboat) Fisher, 95; major league outfielder in the 1920's and 1930's who played on the 1930 St. Louis Cardinal World Series team; also played for the St. Louis Browns and Washington Senators; after surgery to repair a broken hip; in St. Cloud, Minn., May 15.

Ray Flaherty, 89; Hall of Fame end who played on two NFL championship teams with the N.Y. Giants and coached the Washington Redskins to the 1937 title; credited with introducing the screen pass; also coached New York and Boston in the All-American Football Conference; inducted into the Pro Football Hall of Fame in 1976; of natural causes; in Coeur d'Alene, Idaho, July 19.

Elbie Fletcher, 77; first baseman for the Boston Braves and Pittsburgh Pirates in the 1930's and 1940's; career was interrupted for two years in the '40's when he served in WWII; hit 79 home runs during his career and finished with a batting average of .271; cause of death not reported; in Milton, Mass., Mar. 9.

Barbara Flowers, 45; choreographer for champion figure skaters Rosalyn Sumners and Tonya Harding; Sumners went on to win three U.S. titles and a silver medal at the 1984 Olympics, while Harding won the U.S. title in 1991; of cancer; in Brier, Wash., Nov. 23, 1993.

Bob Fontaine, 70; former Padres general manager and former scouting director for the Padres and Giants who spent 51 years in baseball; drafted Dave Winfield for San Diego on the first round in 1973; signed with the Brooklyn Dodgers in 1941 but never made it to the big leagues as a player; first scouting director in Padres history, and in 1977 rose to GM; his son, Bob Jr., is scouting director for the Angels; cause of death not reported; in Poway, Calif., Mar. 25.

Phil Fox, 80; NBA referee during the league's early years; officiated games on the Harlem Globetrotter tours and in the Basketball Association of America, which later became the NBA; of a heart attack; in New York, Apr. 13.

Vancouver Canucks

Frank A. Griffiths

U.S. Naval Academy

Alton Grizzard

The Atlanta Journal & Constitution

Lewis Grizzard

Samuel T.N. Foulds, 88; member of the United States Soccer Hall of Fame; authored "America's Soccer Heritage," a comprehensive history of the sport in America; historian of the U.S. Soccer Federation for 25 years; coached at Brandeis University in Waltham, Mass., and served as a columnist for *Soccer America* magazine; of natural causes; in Derry, N.H., Jan. 9.

Oscar Fraley, 79; former sports reporter who penned "The Untouchables" with Eliot Ness, the federal agent who brought down Al Capone; that story sold 1.5 million copies; author of 31 books; employed by United Press International from 1940 to 1965; of heart failure after surgery for a strangulated hernia; in Fort Lauderdale, Fla., Jan. 6.

Gretchen Fraser, 75; in 1948, became the first American to win an Olympic gold medal for skiing by taking first in the special slalom (known today as the giant slalom) at St. Moritz, Switzerland; also won a silver in the combined slalom and downhill; inducted into the U.S. National Ski Hall of Fame in 1960; of natural causes; in Sun Valley, Idaho, Feb. 17.

Ivan Fuqua, 84; won an Olympic gold medal in 1932 by running the opening leg on a world record-breaking 1,600-meter relay team; member of the Indiana Hoosiers track team; coached Brown University's track and field program from 1946 until 1974, leading it to three New England titles; served as president of the New England Track Coaches Association and the IC4A's Track Coaches Association; of heart failure following a bout with cancer; in Providence, RI, Jan. 14.

L. Damon Gadd, 67; founder of Vermont's Sugarbush ski resort (1958); credited with several ski mountain innovations, such as improved safety standards on ski lifts; one of the first resorts to have a cocktail lounge in the lodge; sold his property in 1977; of cancer; in Palm Beach, Fla., Nov. 7, 1993.

Alonzo Gaither, 90; highly successful football coach at Florida A&M University who compiled a 203-36-4 (.844) record between 1945 and 1969; sent 42 players to the National Football League from FAMU, a historically black school; coached the Rattlers to undefeated seasons in 1957, 1959 and 1961, and between 1953 and 1962 Gaither's squads rolled to a 93-7-1 record; once remarked that "I can teach a lot more character winning than I can losing;" in 1960 Gaither's Rattlers blew out intrastate rival Bethune-Cookman, 97-0; of natural causes; in Tallahassee, Fla., Feb. 18.

Augie Galan, 81; the first National League player to hit switch-hit homers during the same game; during 16-year career Galan played with the Chicago Cubs, Brooklyn Dodgers, Cincinnati Reds, New York Giants and Philadelphia Athletics; played in three World Series; hit .300 or more six times and finished with a .287 career

average and 100 home runs; in 1935, while playing for the pennant-winning Cubs, Galan hit .314, led the league with 133 runs and 22 stolen bases and set a major league record by playing every game and not hitting into a double play; of an aneurism; in Fairfield, Calif., Dec. 28, 1993.

Harry Gamage, 94; coached Kentucky football to a 32-25-5 record from 1927-1933 and is the winningest coach ever at South Dakota with an 18-year mark of 82-67-7; his South Dakota teams won four North Central Conference championships; cause of death not reported; in Mesa, Ariz., Aug. 22.

Vitas Gerulaitis, 40; at one time was one of the world's best and best known tennis players; won the Australian Open in 1977, his lone grand slam title, and was ranked No. 4 in the world in 1984; won 27 singles titles on the ATP tour and his career earnings eclipsed two million dollars; played on the U.S. Davis Cup team from 1977-1980; after unknowingly being exposed to lethal gas at a friend's home; in Southampton Village, N.Y., Sept. 18.

Leroy (Spike) Gibson, 57; spent five years with the Harlem Globetrotters during the 1960's; during a world tour that spanned 92 nations, Gibson played before a crowd of 150,000 (in Berlin) and of one (Pope Paul VI); following his Globetrotter years Gibson settled in South Miami and became a police officer, and in 1970 was the first South Miami black ever elected to public office - as city commissioner; member of Florida A&M's Sports Hall of Fame; of cancer; in South Miami, Fla., Feb. 12.

George Gregory Jr., 88; 1931, became first black All America basketball player while starring for Columbia University; 6-4 team captain led his school to a 21-2 mark that season; later became a New York City civil service commissioner and respected community leader in Harlem; of colon cancer; in Manhattan, May 11.

Frank Griffiths Sr., 77; member of the Hockey Hall of Fame and owner of the Vancouver Canucks; often cited as the individual who saved hockey in that city after purchasing the club in 1974; assembled a broadcasting empire in Western Canada; after a long illness; in Vancouver, Apr. 7.

Alton Grizzard, 24; former Navy quarterback (1987-1990) who was the school's all-time career total offense leader with a combination of 5,666 rushing and passing yards; set a Navy record with 12 touchdown tosses and 1,438 passing yards during his senior season; Navy SEAL commando and a lieutenant who had already completed missions in Somalia; shot to death (along with Navy Ensign Kerryn O'Neill) by Navy Ensign George Smith, who was apparently upset about his recent breakup with O'Neill; in Coronado, Calif., Dec. 1, 1993.

Lewis Grizzard, 47; popular syndicated columnist for the Atlanta Journal-Constitution who also served as sports

Harvey Haddix

Tom Hamilton

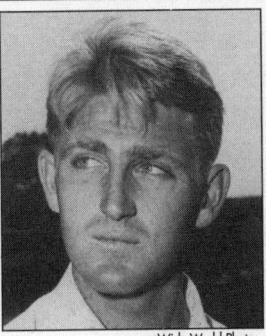

Lew Hoad

editor of that paper and the Chicago Sun-Times; a humorist recognized for his "Son of the South" characteristics and "good 'ol boy" writing style, Grizzard also authored 20 books, many with offbeat titles such as "Don't Bend Over in the Garden, Granny, You Know Them Taters Got Eyes;" column was syndicated to nearly 450 newspapers nationwide; of complications following open-heart surgery; in Emory University Hospital, in Atlanta, Mar. 20.

Matt Goukas Sr., 78; radio voice of the Philadelphia Eagles for over 30 years; played for the NBA champion Philadelphia Warriors in 1946-47, but career ended when he lost his right leg in a car accident; father of Matt Goukas Jr., who played and coached for the Phila. 76ers; of an illness following a broken hip; in Fourtown, Pa., Dec. 9, 1993.

Jayson Gwinn, 20; sophomore defensive end for Ohio State who made 14 solo tackles and assisted on 11 others during the 1993 season; in a car crash after leaving a club where a teammate had been shot; in Columbus, Ohio, Dec. 12, 1993.

Harvey Haddix, 68; in 1959, while pitching for Pittsburgh, hurled a perfect game for 12 innings—retiring the first 36 Milwaukee Braves he faced—but eventually lost the contest in the 13th; played for the Cardinals, Phillies, Reds, Pirates and Orioles and amassed a career record of 136-113; followed his 14-year stint in the majors with 13 years as a pitching coach; of emphysema; in Springfield, Ohio, Jan. 9.

Lee Halfpenny, 87; a hall of fame boxer who held the amateur lightweight world championship between 1928 and 1931; professional record was 45-2; helped coach the U.S.Olympic team in 1932; known throughout Baltimore for teaching young boxers at the Central YMCA; of a heart attack; in Baltimore, Dec. 29, 1993.

Harry T. Hall, 60; spent over a decade serving as commissioner of the NAIA's Arkansas Intercollegiate Conference; in 1991, led an investigation into the University of Arkansas at Pine Bluff's football program that revealed nearly 100 violations and resulted in that school being given the "death penalty"; known for his ability to evaluate NAIA basketball officials; served 23 years in the Army; of cancer; in Atlanta, Dec. 31, 1993.

Tom Hamilton, 88; former Navy football star and coach who, while coaching in 1946, justified not attempting a field goal against Army despite being down by three during the game's final moments by saying, "A tie is like kissing your sister;" halfback for Navy's undefeated squad in 1926; retired from the Navy in 1948 and served as AD at Pitt from 1949-59; of pneumonia; in Chula Vista, Calif., Apr. 3.

Sam Hanks, 79; won the 1957 Indy 500; was director of racing for the Indianapolis Motor Speedway; after a long illness; in Pacific Palisades, Calif., June 27.

Ron Hansen, 33; Northern California jockey who amassed nearly 3,700 career victories; apparently after injuries suffered from a hit-and-run car accident on Oct. 1; near San Francisco Bay, body found on Jan. 20.

Merle Hapes, 75; former NY Giants fullback who was suspended following a betting scandal involving the 1946 championship game; admitted he had been offered a bribe to fix that game against the Bears, but maintained he never accepted; suspended for that game and later indefinitely by commissioner Bert Bell, Hapes went on to play for seven seasons in the Canadian Football League; played for the University of Mississippi from 1939-42 and is a member of the Ole Miss Hall of Fame; of complications associated with Alzheimer's disease; in Biloxi, Miss., July 18.

Robert (Bubbles) Hawkins, 39; former Illinois State basketball standout who played just over three seasons in the NBA for Golden State, the New York Nets and Detroit; from a gunshot in a suspected crack house; in Detroit, Nov. 28, 1993.

Christy Henrich, 22; missed qualifying for the 1988 Olympics by 0.188 points; fourth on the uneven parallel bars in the 1989 World Championships; after battling anorexia nervosa and bulimia; in Kansas City, Mo., July 26.

Robert Lee Herron, 69; former Negro League slugger who played in the Canadian Baseball League and the National Colored League; won several batting titles during the 1950's; nicknamed "Big Daddy," Herron was once a teammate of Satchel Paige; cause of death not reported; in Wichita Falls, Texas, Jan. 17.

Ralph Hill, 85; uncomplaining Olympic silver medalist at the 1932 Summer Games in Los Angeles, who lost the 5,000 meters to Lauri Lehtinen of Finland when Lehtinen cut in front of him twice over the final 200 meters to prevent him from passing; although the crowd at the L.A. Coliseum howled in protest, the U.S. did not contest the outcome; said humorist Will Rogers at the time: "It looked as if Lehtinen made the mistake of zigging when he should have zagged"; after a long illness; in Klamath Falls, Ore., Oct. 17.

Hugh Hindman, 67; former Ohio State athletic director best known as the man who fired football coaching legend Woody Hayes after he punched a Clemson player in the closing minutes of the 1978 Gator Bowl; was a former assistant under Hayes; in 1970 became associate athletic director under Ed Weaver; succeeded Weaver in 1977; retired in 1984; of complications from pneumonia; in Columbus, Ohio, Oct. 12.

Lew Hoad, 59; Australian who won five Wimbledon crowns during the 1950's; was singles champion in 1956 and 1957 and doubles champion in 1953, 1955 and 1956; finished as either singles or doubles champion in 13 Grand Slam events; inducted into the International Tennis Hall of Fame in 1980; of a heart attack; in London, July 3.

New York Road Runners Club

Fred Lebow

Reuters/Bettmann

Ulrike Maier

UPI/ Bettmann

Bob Matheson

Bobby Hofman, 68; the New York Giants infielder played in 341 major league games between 1949 and 1957, finishing with a career batting average of .248; New York Yankees farm director for eight seasons during the 1980's; of cancer; in Chesterfield, Mo., Apr. 5.

Jim Honochick, 76; umpired in the American League for 25 years before retiring in 1973; worked six All-Star games and six World Series; earned fame during the late 1970's for his role in a series of Miller Lite beer commercials with Boog Powell; cause of death not reported; in Allentown, Pa., Mar. 10.

Paul Hornung, 78; former sports editor of *The Columbus Dispatch* who covered 326 consecutive Ohio State football games; Hornung's remarkable streak was stopped in 1975 when he covered the Cincinnati Reds in the World Series; wrote several books, including "Woody Hayes: A Remembrance;" of cancer; in upper Arlington, Ohio, May 2.

Martinez Jackson, 89; father of Hall of Fame slugger Reggie Jackson; played second base for the Newark Eagles in the Negro League; the proprietor of a tailor shop, the elder Jackson carried business cards that read: "Marty the Tailor, Father of Famous Reggie Jackson;" of complications from a stroke suffered several months prior; in Philadelphia, Apr. 27.

George (Lefty) James, 88; coach of Cornell football from 1947-60; some of his Cornell teams were dubbed the "James Boys" because of their reputation as giant killers: James' 1948 squad stopped Syracuse and Navy and in 1951 Cornell defeated defending Rose Bowl champion Michigan; record at Cornell was 66-58-2; coached Cornell baseball from 1943-45; elected president of the American Football Coaches Association in 1957 and was inducted into both the Cornell and Bucknell (his alma mater) Halls of Fame; of a stroke; in Sarasota, Fla., Jan. 9.

Robert L. (Jet) Johnson, 58; coached South Carolina State's track team to a national title in 1982; led the Bulldogs to a 99-32-5 record over a 12-season span and in 18 years compiled 24 conference championships; also served as an assistant football coach; following a brief illness; in Orangeburg, S.C., July 13.

Warner Jones Jr., 78; Churchill Downs chairman for eight years before stepping down in 1992; considered the "guardian" to Kentucky's racing industry, Jones was originally elected to the Churchill board in 1941; only person to breed champions of the Kentucky Derby, Kentucky Oaks and a Breeders Cup race; of lung cancer; in Louisville, Ky., Feb. 7.

Irving B. Kahn, 76; founder of Cable TV and Teleprompter machine; among his accomplishments were introducing closed circuit television in 1956, which enabled him to begin arranging for rights to championship boxing matches and auto races; served a 20-month prison term after his Teleprompter company was convicted of bribery to city officials in Johnstown, Pa.; of a heart attack; in Boston, Jan. 25.

Virginia Kelley, 70; mother of President Clinton; was a $2 bettor for 53 years at the Oaklawn Park racetrack in Hot Springs, Ark.; of complications from breast cancer; in Arkansas, Jan. 6.

Page Crosley Kess, 81; former Cincinnati Reds president who directed the team for just a year, between 1961-62, following the death of her father, Powel Crosley Jr.; following a stroke; in Cincinnati, May 9.

Chad Kinch, 35; Cleveland Cavaliers No. 1 draft choice in 1980 who spent that season with the Cavs and Dallas Mavericks; spent just one year in the NBA; former UNC-Charlotte star who helped lead it to the 1977 NCAA Final Four before bowing in the semifinal game to eventual champion Marquette; averaged 18.3 ppg during his career with the 49ers; of AIDS; in Carteret, N.J., Apr. 3.

August Kirsch, 68; council member of the world track's governing body since 1981; also served as vice-president of the German Olympic Committee; cause of death not reported; in Darmstadt, Germany, Dec. 22, 1993.

Dan Klepper, 64; spent 37 years as outdoor editor of the *San Antonio Express-News*; in 1992 he was recognized by the Game Wardens Association of Texas for his contributions to hunting, fishing and wildlife; described as "the voice for sportsmen of the Southwest" by Texas Gov. Ann Richards; authored a book of his columns entitled "The 13th Month;" of cancer; in Boerne, Texas, Dec. 4, 1993.

Michael Kochel, 78; a guard on Fordham University's well-known teams of the 1930's; backup on the 1936 team whose line was known as the "Seven Blocks of Granite;" started the next two years and later played for the NFL's Chicago Cardinals; an Air Force colonel during WWII who flew bombers; of a heart attack; in Bellevue, Nebraska, Aug. 21.

Marvin Kohn, 70; spent over 30 years as Secretary-Treasurer for the Boxing Writers Association of America; served on the New York State Athletic Commission - which regulate professional boxing and wrestling in New York State—for 38 years; following a stroke; in New York City, Feb. 8.

Jack Krol, 57; managed at all levels of professional baseball; was 1-1 as interim skipper of the St. Louis Cardinals in 1978; spent 10 years as third base coach for St. Louis and San Diego; lifetime managerial record was 1,135-1,130 over 18 seasons; of cancer; in Winston-Salem, NC, May 30.

Maurice (Lefty) Lachance, 72; successful featherweight boxer who finished with a career record of

Wide World Photos

Frank McGuire

Hockey Hall

Bill Mosienko

UPI/Bettmann

Ira Murchison

151 wins, 52 losses and 17 draws; known for his wicked left hand; once the fourth-ranked featherweight in the world, Lachance fought four world champions during his career and won a nontitle bout in 1943 against champion Phil Terranova; after a one-month hospital stay; in Lewiston, Me., Apr. 29.

Ray Lamanno, 74; played five seasons with the Cincinnati Reds during the 1940's; appeared in 442 games and compiled a .252 career batting average; of cancer; in Berkeley, Calif., Feb. 9.

Stan Landes, 70; former National League umpire; served with the U.S. Marines during WWII and the Korean War; cause of death not reported; in Peoria, Ariz., Jan. 23.

Don Lash, 82; Indiana University distance runner from 1934-37, who won the Sullivan Award as the country's top amateur athlete in 1938; held the world record in the 2-mile run, both indoors and outdoors, as well as anchoring Indiana's world record holding 4-mile and medley relay teams; was later an FBI special agent for 21 years; of cancer; in Terre Haute, Ind., Sept. 19.

Fred Lebow, 62; founder of the New York Road Runners Club, who started the New York City Marathon in 1970; under Lebow's direction, the race grew from a four-loop circuit around Central Park involving just 127 runners to a world-class event staged through all five boroughs of the city that attracts over 25,000 entrants annually while turning away thousands more; first diagnosed with brain cancer in 1990, but rallied to enter and complete the '92 NYC Marathon along side nine-time women's champion Grete Waitz; inducted into the Track & Field Hall of Fame in 1994; of brain cancer; in New York, Oct. 9.

Hank Leiber, 82; played nine baseball seasons as an outfielder for the New York Giants, beginning in 1933, and finished his career with a .288 average and 101 HRs; hit over .300 three times; participated in the World Series—both against the New York Yankees—in 1936 and 1937; his infamous plate-crowding stance resulted in two serious beanings that sliced significant chunks from his career; of complications following kidney failure; in Tucson, Ariz., Nov. 8, 1993.

James R. (J.R.) Leonard Sr., 83; lettered in football and baseball at Notre Dame during the early 1930's and later played fullback for the Philadelphia Eagles (1935-36) and later served as coach of the Pittsburgh Steelers (1945-46); cause of death not reported; in Woodbury, N.J., Nov. 28, 1993.

Bobby Lewis, 63; coached former heavyweight champion George Foreman to an Olympic gold medal in 1968 and is often credited with launching Foreman's career; coached the U.S. Olympic boxing team in 1972; spent many years as a professional trainer; cause of death not reported; in Denver, Nov. 13, 1993.

Alfred Loomis, 81; won a gold medal in the 1948 Olympics while sailing a 6-meter yacht; in 1977 managed the *Independence-Courageous* syndicate, the yachting squad that defended the America's Cup that year; cause of death not reported; in Manhattan, Sept. 7.

Francis (Pug) Lund, 81; star halfback on the 1934 Minnesota team that was unbeaten and the consensus national champion; member of the National College Football Hall of Fame; triple threat who could run, pass and kick; of heart failure; in Minneapolis, May 26.

Bill Lynn, 69; coached Auburn basketball from 1963-73; career record was 130-124; played for Auburn from 1948-50 and led it in scoring twice; cause of death not reported; in Auburn, Ala., Nov. 8, 1993.

Ulrike Maier, 26; Austrian downhill skiier who was the winner of two world titles—in 1989 and 1991; was in her 10th World Cup season and had five World Cup victories overall; fourth in overall standings at the time of her death; of a broken neck suffered during a violent World Cup ski crash; in Garmisch-Partenkirchen, Germany, Jan. 29.

Tony Mason, 66; former head football coach at the University of Cincinnati and the University of Arizona; coached the Bearcats from 1973-76 and compiled a 26-18 record; then coach the Wildcats until the spring of 1980 and finished with a record of 16-18-1; of a heart attack; in Cleveland, July 23.

Eddie Mast, 46; star basketball player at Temple who led the Owls to the 1969 NIT title; drafted in the third round that year by New York; played 70 games for the Knicks over two years; traded to Atlanta in 1972; of an apparent heart attack while playing basketball; in Easton, Pa., Oct. 18.

Bob Matheson, 49; pivotal member of the Miami Dolphins' "No Name" defense that led the franchise to three straight Super Bowls—two of which were Dolphin victories—during the early 1970's; first-team all-American for Duke who was a first round pick of the Cleveland Browns; Dolphins "53" defense was named after his uniform number; of Hodgkins disease; in Durham, N.C., Sept. 5.

Carl (Red) Mayes, 63; two-sport athlete at Texas in the 1950's who was best known for his track and field accomplishments; key member of Texas' 440-yard relay teams that set world records at the 1950 Kansas Relays and at the California Coliseum in 1952; also played football at Texas and spent one season with both the Los Angeles Rams and the British Columbia Lions of the Canadian Football League; cause of death not reported; in Nacogdoches, Texas, Feb. 24.

Jerry Mays, 54; defensive lineman who retired from the Kansas City Chiefs following its 1970 Super Bowl victory; was all-Southwest Conference for Southern Methodist during the late 1950's; became a member of the American Football League's Dallas Texans and remained with the franchise in Kansas City from 1963 to 1970; of cancer; in Lewisville, Texas, July 17.

Hockey Hall

Wide World Photos

Wide World Photos

Marguerite Norris   **Bill Pellington**   **Jimmie Reese**

James McCurdy, 72; innovative designer in the sailing field who devoted much of his life's work to creating modern sailboats; during the late 1950's he was chief of design at Philip L. Rhodes, the firm that designed *Weatherly*, the 1962 defender of the America's Cup; of complications from heart failure, in Huntington, N.Y., Aug. 21.

Frank McGuire, 80; former college and pro basketball coach, who led North Carolina to the 1957 NCAA championship in an epic, three-overtime, 54-53 victory over Wilt Chamberlain and Kansas; lost the 1952 NCAA final to Kansas as coach at St. John's; helped popularize basketball down South when he left New York to take the UNC job in 1953; left college ball to coach Chamberlain and the Philadelphia Warriors for the 1961-62 NBA season, but quit rather than follow the Warriors to San Francisco; returned to college ranks and coached South Carolina from 1965-80; retired with 724 coaching victories— 549 at the college level— in his 41-year career; inducted into Basketball Hall of Fame in 1977; after a long illness; in Columbia, S.C., Oct. 11.

John V. McManmon, 88; offensive tackle who captained the Notre Dame football team; one of the "seven mules" who blocked for the legendary "four horsemen" under coach Knute Rockne during the 1920's; served as an assistant coach at ND, Boston College and Boston University; cause of death not reported; in Lowell, Mass., Dec. 24, 1993.

Bill Mosienko, 72; member of Hockey's Hall of Fame and the record-holder for the quickest three goals scored in National Hockey League history; playing for Chicago in 1952, Mosienko beat goalie Lorne Anderson in the third period at 6:09, 6:20 and 6:30 in the Blackhawks' 7-6 win over the New York Rangers; played entire career (1941 to 1955) with Chicago, finishing with 258 goals and 282 assists in 711 games; of cancer; in Winnipeg, July 9.

George Munger, 84; assumed football head coaching duties at the University of Pennsylvania in 1938 at the age of 28; retired 16 seasons later with a record of 82-42-10; member of college football's Hall of Fame; three of his teams finished in the Top 10 but Munger retired when Penn joined the Ivy League rather than compete against the nation's powerhouse programs, which Penn was considered during his tenure; served on the President's Council for Physical Fitness; of heart failure; in Philadelphia, July 21.

Ira Murchison, 61; sprinter who set world records on two continents and captured an Olympic gold medal in 1956; member of the American 400-meter relay team that finished in 39.5 seconds to win the gold in Melbourne, Australia; earlier that year he matched Jesse Owen's 20-year record in the 100 at 10.2, and later bested that in another meet with a time of 10.1; the 5-foot-4-inch Murchison was the collegiate champion in the 100 at Western Michigan; of bone cancer; in Harvey, Ill., Mar. 28.

Steve Myhra, 60; kicker who played six seasons with the Baltimore Colts in the NFL; remembered most for his 20-yard field goal that forced overtime in the Colts' 1958 championship game against the New York Giants, a game the Colts, led by Johnny Unitas, eventually won; Myhra's crucial kick made the cover of *Life* magazine; also played offensive line, linebacker and special teams for the Colts; played college football for the University of North Dakota and the University of Minnesota; of a heart attack; in Detroit Lakes, Minn., Aug. 4.

Wangila Napunyi, 26; 1988 Olympic boxing gold medalist from Kenya; turned professional one year later and lived in Las Vegas; of head injuries sustained in a fight two days earlier against David Gonzales; in Las Vegas, July 24.

Bert Nelson, 72; member of the National Track and Field Hall of Fame who co-founded, with his brother Cordner, the magazine "Track and Field News" in 1948; of Parkinson's Disease; in Mountain View, Calif., Jan. 10.

Jimmy Nix, 55; member of the National Hot Rod Association Division 4 Hall of Fame; considered a force among top fuel dragsters from 1959 to 1966; when his top fuel dragster crashed during an exhibition race at the Texas Motorplex; in Ennis, Texas, May 21.

Marguerite Norris, 67; first female chief executive in the National Hockey League and the only woman to have her name engraved on the Stanley Cup; was the Detroit Red Wings' president from 1952 to 1955; the Red Wings finished first during each of those three seasons and won the Stanley Cup twice during that time; of heart failure; in Waterbury, Conn., May 12.

Harry O'Boyle, 89; member of Notre Dame's "Four Horsemen" backfield and a part of the Irish's 1924 national champion team; played three seasons with the Green Bay Packers and one with the Philadelphia Eagles; of cancer; in Wheeling, Ill., May 5.

George Oliver, 83; one of the top professional polo players between the 1930's and 1960's; began playing the sport at age 23 and maintained a nine-goal handicap into his 50's; of pneumonia; in Sparta, N.C., Apr. 25.

Kerryn O'Neill, 21; former Naval Academy track star; set several academy records in cross country and track and field; graduated in 1993; fatally shot along with former Navy quarterback Alton Grizzard by Navy ensign George P. Smith, O'Neill's former boyfriend, who then turned the gun on himself; in Coronado, Calif., Dec. 1, 1993.

Rodney Orr, 31; race car driver who was the defending champion in NASCAR's Goody's Dash sedan racing series; veteran of Florida's short tracks; had a stellar season in 1993, when he won two races and finished in the top five during 11 of 16 starts; killed in a one-car crash during practice for the Daytona 500; in Daytona Beach, Fla., Feb. 14.

California Angels

Bob Reynolds

Buena Vista Television

Amy Sacks

UPI/Bettmann

George Sauer

James Wilfred (Bill) Orwig, 87; former Indiana athletic director who spent 14 years as AD, beginning in 1961; saw the Hoosiers win a total of 39 Big Ten titles and six NCAA championships; named to the Indiana University athletics Hall of Fame in 1987; of cancer; July 30.

Joe Paparella, 85; American League umpire who worked five World Series and four All-Star games during his 22-year career before retiring in 1968; cause of death not reported; in Sebastian, Fla., Oct. 17.

Leo Paquin, 83; member of the Fordham University Hall of Fame who played with Vince Lombardi along the offensive line during the 1930's; those two, along with five other linemen, formed what was known as the "Seven Blocks of Granite;" in his sleep; in Rutherford, N.J., Dec. 2, 1993.

Park Avenue Kathy, 7; one of the world's top racing horses that had accounted for nearly $1.2 million in career earnings; was to have soon finished her racing career and returned to Sweden, where she was trained, to become a broodmare; in a fire that broke out in a horse van; in Italy, Dec. 26, 1993.

Bill Pearce, 73; chairman of the National Football Foundation and College Hall of Fame; helped expand the National Football Foundation and acquired a new site—in South Bend, Ind.—for its Hall of Fame; played football at Miami of Ohio in 1939-40; of a heart attack; in Hilton Head, S.C., May 20.

Bill Pellington, 66; linebacker for the Baltimore Colts from 1953 to 1964; member of two NFL championship teams in 1958 and 1959; compiled 21 interceptions; "He was famous for 'clotheslining' wide receivers and running backs. I think he broke his arm two or three times doing that," former teammate Dick Szymanski said; of complications from Alzheimer's disease; in Baltimore, Apr. 26.

Ed Periard, 44; member of the 1970 Nebraska wire-service national champion; the middle guard was all-Big Eight Conference and third-team All-American that season; from injuries sustained in a traffic accident; in Birch Run, Mich., Dec. 21, 1993.

William Haggin Perry, 85; well-known owner of prominent thoroughbreds since 1952; some of his more famous horses were Alanesian, Gamely, Lamb Chop, 1979 Belmont Stakes winner Coastal and Princessnesian; following a long illness; in Oakwood, Va., Nov. 12, 1993.

Charles Price, 68; journalist who spent nearly 50 years covering golf; reported for Golf World and Golf Digest and was the founding editor of Golf Magazine; wrote or contributed to 17 books; stopped competing in professional golf at age 27; of lung cancer; in Pinehurst, N.C., Jan. 29.

Dr. Ernesto Punsalan, 54; father of United States Olympic ice dancer Elizabeth Punsalan; Elizabeth and her husband, Jerod Swallow, qualified as the only American dance entrants at the 1994 Winter Games in Lillehammer; of stab wounds inflicted by his 20-year-old son, Rickey; in Sheffield Lake, Ohio, Feb. 4.

A. Kenneth Pye, 62; former president of Southern Methodist University who took over following numerous and devastating scandals were discovered in the football program; the Mustangs football program was banned for the 1987 season and part of the 1988 season and chose to sit out the entire 1988 campaign; credited with helping to rebuild the university's athletic program; of cancer; in Lake City, Colo., July 11.

Roland Ratzenberger, 31; the Austrian was a rookie in Forumla One racing; of injuries sustained in a high speed crash during qualifying at the San Marino Grand Prix; in Imola, Italy, Apr. 30.

Jimmie Reese, 92; known as the best fungo hitter in baseball, Reese was a mentor and friend to many players from different eras—such as Babe Ruth, Nolan Ryan, Reggie Jackson and Jim Abbott—during his 78-year professional baseball career; began his career in 1917 as a batboy for the Los Angeles Angels of the Pacific Coast League; played two seasons with the New York Yankees and one with the St. Louis Cardinals; most notably, he had 15 pinch hits in 33 at-bats; long-time minor league player and coach; served as the Angels' conditioning coach since 1972; cause of death not reported; in Santa Ana, Calif., July 13.

Bob (Horse) Reynolds, 79; standout tackle for Stanford during the 1930's who played in three Rose Bowls; set a Rose Bowl record by playing every minute of every game on both sides of the ball; member of the Stanford All-Century Team, the Rose Bowl Hall of Fame and the National Football Foundation College Hall of Fame; played two seasons with the Detroit Lions; founded Golden West Broadcasters with California Angels owner Gene Autry, who later employed Reynolds as Angels president from 1961 to 1975; served as vice president and director of the Los Angeles Rams from 1963 to 1972; member of the 1984 Los Angeles Olympic Organizing Committee; cause of death not reported; in San Rafael, Calif., Feb. 8.

Bailey Robertson, 58; played four seasons at the University of Indianapolis and holds the school's career scoring record at 2,280 points and the school record for scoring average at 23.3; older brother of NBA Hall of Famer Oscar Robertson; cause of death not reported; in Indianapolis, Jan. 6.

Buddy Rosar, 78; catcher who spent thirteen years in the major leagues from 1939 to 1951; set a major-league record for consecutive errorless games (147) by a catcher, including all 117 games he caught for the Philadelphia A's in 1946; played on five all-star teams; hit .261 for his career; cause of death not reported; in Rochester, N.Y., Mar. 13.

UPI/Bettmann

Jack Sharkey

Wide World Photos

Dinah Shore

UPI/Bettmann

Helen Stephens

Goody Rosen, 81; broke in as an outfielder with the Brooklyn Dodgers in 1937 and was traded to the New York Giants in 1946, his last season in the majors; career batting average of .291, including a .325 campaign—good for a third-place finish in the National League—in 1945; of pneumonia; in Toronto, Apr. 6.

Eric Ross, 24; running back from Pacific University who lapsed into a coma in Nov., 1991, after suffering a severe head injury during a game against Washington State; of head injuries that caused the coma; in Hillsboro, Ore., Mar. 15.

Amy Jill Sacks, 39; television producer who won 13 Emmys, many for her contributions to ABC Sports; some of her more notable achievements were capturing Emmys for ABC's coverage of the 1984 Summer Olympics and for a pair of specials during the 1988 Winter Olympics; considered an innovator because she set sports to music, and considered a pioneer for paving the way for women in her industry; of complications from lupus; in Philadelphia, Aug. 8.

Ed Sadowski, 62; catcher who spent five years during the 1960's with the Red Sox, Angels and Braves; his brothers, Bob and Ted, and his nephew, Jim Sadowski, all played in the majors; of Lou Gehrig's disease; in Garden Grove, Calif., Nov. 6, 1993.

Michel Sansen, 59; veteran Belgian motorcyclist; 30th competitor to die during the Paris-Dakar-Paris rally since 1979; of injuries suffered when his bike skidded just before the race began; in Paris, Jan. 5.

George Sauer, 83; coached at the University of New Hampshire for five years, beginning in 1937, and later became the first player personnel director of the New York Jets; compiled a 22-18-1 record at UNH; an All-American running back at Nebraska; played one year with the Green Bay Packers; of Alzheimer's disease; in Waco, Texas, Feb. 5.

Tom Scott, 85; former head basketball coach at North Carolina and Davidson, where he also served as AD; coached at Concordia and Central Missouri State before taking over the Tar Heels in 1947; had a five-year record of 100-65 at UNC; while at Davidson, where he also coached golf, Scott was chair of the NCAA Division 1 Men's Basketball Committee; cause of death not reported; in Charlotte, N.C., Nov. 24, 1993.

Ayrton Senna, 34; considered the world's most outstanding race car driver at the time of his death; won the Grand Prix circuit's world championship in 1988, 1990 and 1991; fearless, intimidating driver began 65 Formula One races on the pole position, a record number; accumulated 41 Grand Prix race victories, the second highest total ever; "He might have been the greatest driver of all time," said Michael Andretti, who was a 1993 Formula One teammate of Senna; in his native Brazil, Senna was considered a national hero on par with soccer stars such as Pelé; annual salary was believed to be more than $10 million; of injuries sustained during a crash in the San Marino Grand Prix, where Senna's car barrelled head-on into a wall and one of its tires apparently ricocheted back and struck him in the head; in Imola, Italy, May 1.

Jeff Seymour, 20; junior walk-on defensive back for Tennessee who never played in a game; three-time state wrestling champion at Dulaney (Md.) High; of a ruptured cerebral aneurysm; in Knoxville, Tenn., Feb. 1.

Billy Shantz, 66; played three seasons in big league baseball with the Philadelphia/Kansas City Athletics and the New York Yankees; the catcher's final big league totals were a .257 average, 2 home runs and 29 RBI's; of cancer; in Lauderhill, Fla., Dec. 13, 1993.

Jack Sharkey, 91; former heavyweight champion who fought during boxing's golden era of the 1930's; had 55 professional fights and won the title in 1932 after a 15-round decision against Max Schmeling; lost the belt the following year to Primo Carnera; career record was 38-13-3 with one no-decision; cause of death not reported; in Beverly, Mass., Aug. 17.

Sergei Shcherbakov, 75; Russian boxer who won the silver medal at the 1952 Olympics; 10-time Soviet champion between 1944 and 1953; won 207 of 227 bouts; cause of death not reported; in Moscow, Jan. 27.

Dr. George Sheehan, 74; nationally known runner who gave up his medical practice in 1984 to focus all his energies toward running, speaking (about running) and writing (about running); set a world age-group record at 50 when he ran the mile in 4 minutes, 47 seconds; beginning in his late 40's, ran in 21 consecutive Boston Marathons; of prostate cancer, a disease he coped with by running between radiation treatments; in Ocean Grove, N.J., Nov. 1, 1993.

Alvin (Tex) Shirley, 75; pitched for the only St. Louis Browns team to reach the World Series; pitched five years in the big leagues, beginning in 1941, with the Philadelphia A's and Browns; career record was 19-30 with a 4.25 ERA in 102 games; of lung cancer; in DeSoto, Texas, Nov. 7, 1993.

Dinah Shore, 76; entertainer known as "The First Lady of Golf;" first person ever to be named an Honorary Member of the LPGA; earned the honor through her contributions to the game and by her involvement in and hosting of the Nabisco Dinah Shore, one of the LPGA's four major golf championships; was named four times in a Gallup Poll as one of the most admired women in the world; won 10 Emmy awards; of cancer; in Beverly Hills, Calif., Feb. 24.

Ayrton Senna

1960-94

by Mike Harris

The auto racing world changed dramatically on May 1. That was the day that even the best in the business found out just how vulnerable they really are.

It was the day that Ayrton Senna, acclaimed by many as the greatest driver of his time, and perhaps the best ever, died in a devastating crash on the historic race track in Imola, Italy, during the San Marino Grand Prix.

Senna's Williams-Renault went off the track at the end of a fast straightaway, slid across a long grassy area and made violent contact with a concrete wall. Authorities said he was killed instantly.

The 34-year-old Senna was one of long list of brilliant Brazilian Formula One racers that includes two-time world champion Emerson Fittipaldi and three-time title winner Nelson Piquet as well as youngsters Christian Fittipaldi and Rubens Barrichello.

His fans could always find Senna on the race track. His trademark yellow helmet stood out clearly despite the blazing speed, and he was nearly always at or near the front of the pack.

In his 10 years of Formula One racing, Senna won 41 races—second only to often bitter rival Alain Prost of France—and a record 65 pole positions, a sure testament to his love of speed and his ability to find it.

Senna, the Formula One champion in 1988, 1990 and 1991, was so revered that his sudden and unexpected death brought sadness and gloom to all of Brazil.

President Itamar Franco declared three days of national mourning for the country's biggest sports hero and schools were closed on the day of the funeral. An estimated 250,000 people filed past his coffin as it lay in state, and Senna's body was carried to its final resting place at the Morumbi cemetery outside Sao Paulo on a fire engine as thousands of his countrymen lined the streets to watch the procession go past.

Among Senna's pall bearers were 16 of his former competitors, including Prost.

The final and perhaps greatest public tribute came on July 17, when the Brazilian soccer team beat Italy in the World Cup final and solemnly dedicated the coveted title to Senna.

Prost, whose battles with Senna on and off the track were well-documented, was as

Pascal Rondeau/Allsport

Ayrton Senna celebrates after clinching his third World Formula One Driving Championship in 1991.

shocked as anyone by the tragedy. "Professionally, Ayrton Senna was the only driver I respected," Prost said. "He was a great, great driver, the sort of driver you thought nothing could ever happen to.

"We were enemies at one stage, but at the same time we were very close. We had a high mutual respect for each other and we each knew that one without the other would not be the same. My career records mean more because I had to beat Senna. I was proud to compete against him."

Emerson Fittipaldi, who at 47 was like an older brother to Senna, has run the Indy-car circuit and lived in the United States in recent years, but still kept in close touch. Senna's death came as a tremendous blow.

"The world has lost the greatest athlete in the history of motor racing and I have lost a great friend," Fittipaldi said. "You can never understand such a thing. He was so good and his equipment was so good, nothing like this is expected. When these things happen, we all begin to question ourselves and wonder why we do what we do.

"But the answer is that we love what we do, and Ayrton loved motor racing as much as anybody."

Mike Harris is the Motorsports Editor for the Associated Press.

Ken Levine/Allsport

Earl Strom

UPI/Bettmann

Johnny Temple

Wide World Photos

Marv Throneberry

Eric Show, 37; pitcher for the San Diego Padres from 1981-1990 who helped the franchise into the World Series in 1984; career record was 101-89 with an ERA of 3.66; in 1985 surrendered the pitch to Pete Rose that Rose roped for a single to break Ty Cobb's career hit mark of 4,191; known as somewhat of an eccentric, Show was a member of the right-wing John Birch Society; found dead in his bed at a drug rehab; in Dulzura, Calif., Mar. 16.

Clyde Silvey, 75; first public address announcer for the San Francisco Giants; following a long illness; in Oakland, May 23.

Edgar Smith, 80; as a lefthanded pitcher with the White Sox, Smith led the American League in losses in 1942 with 20; pitched in the majors for 10 seasons with the Philadelphia A's, the White Sox and Red Sox; finished with a 73-113 record and 3.82 ERA; cause of death not reported; in Willingboro, N.J., Jan. 2.

William Earle Smith, 86; only athlete in Alabama history to major in four major sports—baseball, basketball, football and track and field; played on the 1926 Crimson Tide team that was the wire-service national champion, started on Alabama's undefeated baseball team in 1930 and set annual school records in track; cause of death not reported; in Atlanta, July 3.

Vern Smith, 70; Toledo University athletic director for 15 years who retired in 1986; credited with expanding Toledo's sports programs and its athletic facilities; of a stroke; in Toledo, Jan. 20.

Fred Snowden, 57; former basketball coach at Arizona who was the first black to head a NCAA Division 1 program; coached the Wildcats from 1972-1982 and is credited with turning the program around, leading them to a 167-108 record during his tenure, which saw Arizona move into the Pacific 10 conference six years after he arrived; twice led his team into the NCAA tournament; civic-minded activist worked for the Supermarkets Foundation, a charitable group developed by two California food chains; of a heart attack; in Washington, D.C., Jan. 17.

Howard Snyder, 64; veteran harness driver; of injuries sustained during a racing accident at Northfield Park; in Cleveland, June 1.

Jim Snyder, 75; coached Ohio University basketball from 1949 to 1974, compiling 20 winning seasons and a 355-244 record; his Bobcat teams won seven Mid-American Athletic Conference championships and appeared in seven postseason tournaments; after a long illness; in Palatine, Ill., Apr. 27.

Paul Sommerkamp, 71; radio sportscaster and PA announcer for the Cincinnati Reds who missed just one game—opening day, 1983, with the flu—during his 34-year career; of cancer; in Cincinnati, Aug. 23.

Dr. Paul E. Spangler, 95; Naval doctor who began running at age 67 in order to prolong his life; completed 10 marathons, including the New York City marathon in 1991 at 92 years old; held 85 national age group records at various distances; in San Luis Obispo, Calif., Mar. 29.

Jack Spinks, 64; the first black man from the state of Mississippi to be drafted by the NFL; a running back at Alcorn A&M (now Alcorn State) from 1948 to 1952; led Alcorn to a 29-11-3 mark and three Southern College Athletic Conference titles; drafted by Pittsburgh in 1953; later played with Green Bay, the Chicago Cardinals and New York Giants; member of the Mississippi sports Hall of Fame; Alcorn State named its new football stadium after him in 1992; of a stroke; in Jackson, Miss., Sept. 29.

Art Spinney, 66; played eight years as a lineman with the Baltimore Colts and was part of two championship teams in 1958 and 1959; member of the Boston College Hall of Fame; in Lynn, Mass., May 29.

Joe (Mule) Sprinz, 91; played 26 professional baseball seasons as a catcher, three in the big leagues with the Indians and Cardinals between 1930 and 1933; well known for trying to catch a baseball dropped from a blimp 800 feet high in 1939, an attempt that left him with a fractured jaw, ripped lips and four missing teeth; cause of death not reported; in Fremont, Calif., Jan. 11.

Robbie Stanley, 26; three-time national sprint car champion who was vying to win an unprecedented fourth straight title; was leading the USAC national sprint car series in points; in a crash during a race at the Winchester Speedway; in Winchester, Ind., May 26.

Helen Stephens, 75; gold medal winner at the 1936 Summer Olympic games in two track and field events - the 100, in which she set a world record that stood until 1960, and the relay team; known as "The Fulton Flash" and "The Missouri Express," Stephens set American indoor records for 50 meters, the shot put and the standing broad jump; outdoor records were in the 100 and 220; inducted in the National Track and Field Hall of Fame, the U.S. Track and Field Hall of Fame and the National Women's Hall of Fame; of a stroke; in St. Louis, Jan. 17.

John Kershaw Stevenson, 79; co-owned the Detroit Lions from 1948-65, winning three NFL championships; in Bloomfield Hills, Mich., Aug. 8.

Bradley Stone, 23; British boxer who fought Richie Wenton for the British super-bantamweight title; while in a coma, two days after suffering brain damage during that fight; in London, Apr. 28.

Rob Strasser, 46; former Nike executive who helped introduce the Air Jordan shoe line, a move that catapulted the athletic shoe and apparel company into an elite corporate stratosphere; later worked for Adidas; of a heart attack; in Munich, Germany, Nov. 1, 1993.

Wide World Photos   Wide World Photos   Wide World Photos

Cesar Tovar   **Ellsworth Vines**   **Jersey Joe Walcott**

Earl Strom, 66; highly respected NBA referee known for his flamboyant personaility; beginning in 1957, Strom worked the NBA courts for 32 years; Strom was discovered during a college game, no doubt because of his fearless style with the whistle; of cancer; in Pottstown, Pa., July 10.

Jack Stroud, 66; former All-Pro offensive lineman with the New York Giants between 1951-63; the three-time Pro-Bowler played on Giant teams that won six conference titles and one NFL championship (1956); cause of death not reported; in Flemington, N.J., June 1.

Philip Strubing 2d, 86; president of the United States Golf Association in 1970 and 1971; following a series of strokes; in Memphis, Jan. 2.

Billy Sullivan Jr., 83; played 12 seasons in the big leagues with seven teams during the '30's and '40's; catcher and infielder finished with a .289 average after tours of duty with the White Sox, Reds, Indians, St. Louis Browns, Tigers, Brooklyn Dodgers and Pirates; of heart failure; in Sarasota, Fla., Jan. 4.

Tampa Bay Rowdies, 19; oldest franchise in pro soccer; guided since 1986 by owner Cornelia Corbett; won the NASL's first Soccer Bowl championship in '75; clung to professional soccer through difficult financial times, surviving in 1984 by playing indoors; became a member of the American Soccer League in 1988 and remained after the ASL merged with the Western Soccer League in 1990; of massive financial problems; in Tampa, Jan. 31.

Chuck Taylor, 74; former football player, football coach and athletic director at Stanford; all-America offensive lineman in 1942; coached Stanford to a 40-29-2 record during the 1950's; athletic director for the Cardinal from 1963-71; of cancer; in Stanford, Calif., May 7.

Johnny Temple, 66; four-time all-star second basemen for the Cincinnati Reds during the 1950's; leadoff man also played for Cleveland, Baltimore and Houston; retired in 1964 with 1,484 hits and a .284 career average; of pancreatic cancer; in Anderson, S.C., Jan. 9.

Hank Thomson, 86; well-known horseman and publisher of The Delaware Gazette; co-founded the Little Brown Jug in 1940, a Triple Crown race for 3-year-old pacers; chosen for the U.S. Harness Writers Living Hall of Fame in 1988; of cancer; in Delaware, Ohio, Jan. 24.

Marv Throneberry, 60; first baseman between 1958-63 for the Yankees, Kansas City A's, Baltimore Orioles and Mets; known as a symbol of the expansion 1962 Mets, which went 40-120, because of his penchant for making humorous mistakes; career numbers are .237 with 53 homers and 170 RBI's; starred in Miller Lite beer commercials; of cancer; in Fisherville, Tenn., June 23.

Cesar Tovar, 54; one of only two major league ballplayers (Bert Campaneris being the other) to play all nine positions in a game; 12-year career that spanned through the '60's and '70's was spent with Minnesota, Philadelphia, Texas, Oakland and the Yankees; led the American league in doubles (36) and triples (13) in 1970; finished his career with a .278 average, 46 home runs and 435 RBI's; of pancreatic cancer; in Caracas, Venezuela, July 14.

(Pappa) John Venturello, 105; took a job in New York City in 1903 as a pin boy and kept bowling for the next 90 years; recognized by the American Bowling Congress as the world's oldest living bowler; failing eyesight forced him to quit in 1993; in Plantation, Fla., Apr. 4.

George Vico, 70; homered in his first major league at-bat for the Tigers in 1948; a first baseman, spent two years (48-49) with Detroit, compiling career stats of .250, 12 homers and 211 RBI's in 211 games; cause of death not reported; in Redondo Beach, Calif., Jan. 13.

Ellsworth Vines, 82; three-time Grand Slam titlist, who won the U.S. National championship at Forest Hills as a 19-year-old in 1931; the following year he captured both Wimbledon and Forest Hills; turned pro in 1933; considered one of the best players of his era but abruptly left the game at age 28 and attempted golf on the PGA tour; never won a golf tournament between 1940 and 1957, but of the 100 tourneys he participated in Vines had 87 top-20 finishes; of complications from kidney disease; in La Quinta, Calif., Mar. 17.

Jersey Joe Walcott, 80; oldest fighter, at 38 years, to win the heavyweight championship; historic bout was against then-champion Ezzard Charles in 1951; knocked down Joe Louis three times in two separate fights, but only came away with a controversial split-decision from the first bout and a Lewis knockout punch in the second; lost his title to Rocky Marciano one year later; lost more heavyweight title fights—six—than any other fighter; later became a fight referee and served as chairman of the New Jersey State Boxing Commission, retiring in 1984; real name was Arnold Cream; of complications from diabetes; in Camden, N.J., Feb. 27.

Randy Walkowe, 13; AIDS-infected teenager who was befriended by former Michigan player Juwan Howard; often visited the Michigan locker room and travelled with team in 1993 to New Orleans for the NCAA Final Four; a hemophiliac, Walkowe contracted AIDS through a tainted blood transfusion; in Tipton, Mich., Jan. 10.

Charles Dunlap (Chic) Werner, 91; coached cross country at Penn State from 1933 to 1962; his Nittany Lions won three NCAA Division 1 national titles; ran for Illinois in the 1920's and set a world record in the high hurdles at 7.5 seconds during a Big Ten indoor championship; set four world records as a runner for the Illinois Athletic Club; cause of death not reported; May 3.

UPI/Bettmann

Bud Wilkinson

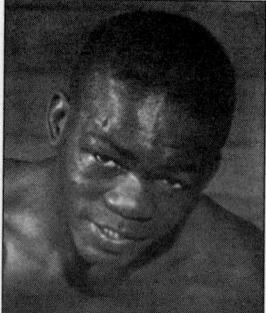

Wide World Photos

Ike Williams

PGA Tour

Bert Yancey

John Wheeler, 29; 7-1 center who played for Baylor during the early-to-mid 1980's who is best remembered for taping a conversation with Bears coach Jim Haller that eventually forced Haller to resign; on the tape, Haller agreed to give Wheeler a check for $172 for car payments; this revelation left the Baylor program on probation; Wheeler played very sparingly for Baylor between 1983-85; after a long illness that resulted in complications from heart ailments and Marfan syndrome; in Dallas, Nov. 6, 1993.

William Whetsell, 76; coached Marietta College basketball coach for 13 years, compiling a career record of 148-115; during 1954-55, Marietta went 22-0 in the Ohio Athletic Conference championships; member of the National Basketball Hall of Fame; served as AD at Marietta, where he also coached football, cross country and golf and chaired the physical education department during his 41 years at the school; of cancer; in Marietta, Ohio, Jan. 5.

Frank Whitham, 62; Kansas horse breeder whose best-known horse was Bayakoa, which won the 1990 Breeders' Cup Distaff in 1989 and 1990; in a plane crash; in Goodland, Kan., Dec. 15, 1993.

Bud Wilkinson, 77; University of Oklahoma football coach whose teams won three national titles during the 1950's and a record 47 straight games during a five-season span; in 17 seasons Wilkinson amassed a record of 145-29-4; won 14 conference titles and his Sooner teams scored in 123 consecutive games; later coached the St.Louis Cardinals and was also a broadcaster for ABC and ESPN; "I've only known one genius in my lifetime. His name was Bud Wilkinson," Eddie Crowder, a Sooner QB during 1951-52, once said; the football dormitory at Oklahoma is named in Wilkinson's honor; first director of the President's Physical Fitness Council that was created by President Kennedy in 1961; of congestive heart failure brought on after recent heart surgery; in Oklahoma City, Feb. 9.

Clarence Williams, 38; former NFL running back with San Diego and Washington; played at University of South Carolina from 1974 to 1976; of gunshot wounds suffered while driving with a friend; in Columbia, S.C., Sept. 17.

Ike Williams, 71; one of boxing's leading lightweights ever who compiled a 123-25-5 record, along with 60 knockouts, over a 15-year career; recognized as the undisputed world lightweight champion in 1947 and made five successful defenses of this title; often fought junior welterweights and welterweights; of natural causes; in Los Angeles, Sept. 5.

Frank C. Wilson, 61; was president and CEO of North Carolina Motor Speedway, where he had worked since its inception in 1965; following a stroke; in Greenville, N.C., Aug. 20.

Fred Wilt, 73; NCAA two-mile and cross-country champion in 1941, who won eight national titles for the New York Athletic Club after graduating from Indiana University; won the Sullivan Award as the nation's top amateur athlete in 1950; served as women's track & field coach at Purdue from 1978-89; inducted into the Track & Field Hall of Fame in 1981; cause of death not reported; in Anderson, Ind., Sept. 5.

Roger Wolff, 82; righthander who spent seven years in the majors (1941-47) with the Philadelphia A's, Washington Senators, Cleveland Indians and Pittsburgh Pirates; best season was in 1945 with Washington when Wolff went 20-10 with a 2.12 ERA and had 21 complete games and four shutouts; finished career with a 52-69 record and 3.41 ERA; cause of death not reported; in Chester, Ill., Mar. 23.

Gary Wood, 52; a baseball and football star at Cornell during the early 1960's who set five Ivy League offensive records as a quarterback and is a member of the school's Hall of Fame; spent five seasons with the New York Giants, mostly as a backup, and one season with the New Orleans Saints; also played for Ottawa in the CFL; of a heart attack; in Melville, N.Y., Mar. 1.

Bob Woolf, 65; Boston-based agent who represented some of the most recognizable athletic (and entertainment) figures in the country; known as a force in earning huge contracts for his clients; represented Larry Bird, Carl Yastrzemski, New Kids on the Block and Larry King, among others; of heart failure; in Hallandale, Fla., Nov. 29, 1993.

Catherine (Katy) Rodolph Wyatt, 63; former national champion skier who broke her neck in a fall just days before the 1956 Winter Olympics, but recovered fully by staying conscious and holding her neck in place until she was taken to the hospital; took fifth in the downhill at the 1950 world championships; worked with tennis star Pancho Gonzalez at Caesars Palace and won the 1975 and 1978 state tennis titles; with her husband opened the first-ever ski facility at what is now Lee Canyon; owner-operator of Rainbow Properties; of complications from a rare blood disease; in Las Vegas, Sept. 17.

Bert Yancey, 56; seven-time winner on the PGA tour who also enjoyed good fortune on the Senior PGA tour; career almost evaporated after a highly publicized struggle with manic depression; turned professional in 1961 and joined the PGA tour in 1962 after golfing for the US Military Academy; of a heart attack just minutes before teeing off at the Park Meadows (Utah) Golf Course; in Park City, Utah, Aug. 26.

James Zachery, 36; former Texas A&M football player who also played for Montreal and Edmonton of the CFL; after being attacked by several men; in Midland, Texas, Jan. 25.

Hawaiian swimmer **Duke Kahanamoku** is decorated by New York City mayor **John Hylan** after returning from the 1920 Olympics with two gold medals.

TIME-OUT

Roaring '20

A tumultuous decade began 75 years ago with Prohibition, the Antwerp Olympics and the Jack Dempsey "Slacker" trial.

Seventy-five years ago, the headline events of the country could hardly measure up to the astonishing era that was at hand in American sports. In the next 10 years, legends like Ruth, Dempsey, Grange, Jones, Nurmi, Ederle, Lenglen, Man o' War and others would help to make the 1920s "the golden age of sports."

The decade got off to a gloomy start when, at midnight on Jan. 16, the 18th Amendment went into effect establishing prohibition. Also in January, the Palmer Raids—named after U.S. attorney general A. Mitchell Palmer—jailed thousands of anarchists and Communists, both real and imagined, with little regard for their consitutional rights.

In Boston, two Italian anarchists named Sacco and Vanzetti were arrested for murder. And, although women had finally secured the vote, their first opportunity to exercise the privilege came in an uninspiring Presidential campaign between Republican Warren Harding and the Democrats' James M. Cox. Harding and running mate Calvin Coolidge won the election, running on the slogan of "Return to Normalcy."

F. Scott Fitzgerald published his first novel, *This Side of Paradise* in 1920, but the bestsellers for the year were Zane Grey's *The Man of the Forest* and World

War I stories of the reporter Phillip Gibbs, called *Now It Can be Told*. And just after noon on Sept. 16 a horse cart filled with dynamite and sash weights exploded near the Wall Street offices of J.P. Morgan. Morgan himself was out of town, but 20 people were killed along the street and dozens injured in the blast.

Meanwhile, a subway ride away, Babe Ruth was taking frightening advantage of that year's livelier baseball and Brooklyn was on its way to the World Series with Cleveland.

After four years of trench warfare, mortar strikes and German occupation, the Belgian city of Antwerp recovered enough to host the 1920 Olympics—an austere festival which nonetheless introduced the Olympic flag and the Olympic oath and for the first time released hundreds of homing pigeons as a symbol of peace.

The United States team dominated the Games, winning 41 gold medals and 95 in all. There were 20 shooting events on the program and American marksmen Willis Lee and Lloyd Spooner cleaned up with seven medals each. Hawaiian swimmer Duke Kahanamoku, who won the 100-meter freestyle at the last Olympics, at Stockholm in 1912, captured the event again and anchored the winning 800-meter relay. But Antwerp will be best remembered for the debut of distance runner Paavo Nurmi, "the Flying Finn," who won three events and placed second in a fourth. He would go on to win five more

Nathan Ward is an associate editor at *American Heritage* magazine and is working on a history of Gleason's boxing gym.

Jack Dempsey (left) and manager **Jack (Doc) Kearns** were acquitted of all draft evasion charges in the heavyweight champion's celebrated "slacker" trial of 1920.

gold medals at Paris in 1924 and a gold and two silver medals at Amsterdam in 1928.

❧

On May 25, Gov. Al Smith signed the Walker bill to make professional boxing legal in the state of New York. The governor, who also approved the accompanying Walker beer bill—giving his blessing to a 2.75 percent brew—had declined to sign the boxing bill until state senator Jimmy Walker could demonstrate the support of some clergymen. Walker delivered enthusiastic telegrams from a thousand men of the cloth.

In a June 7 editorial, the *New York Times* added its own unqualified approval: "Restored under the Walker law . . . the sport will experience a revivification which will be both welcome and wholesome." The new law, hoped the editors, "should eliminate the evils of the past."

Boxing, which had been thriving elsewhere in the country, was now able to come East. Promoter Tex Rickard, who the year before had staged Jack Dempsey's butchery of heavyweight champion Jess Willard under a hot sun in Toledo, could, with the law's passage, soon put on his boxing shows at Madison Square Garden. Within two months he had bought the building.

❧

On June 16, Jack Dempsey and his manager, Jack (Doc) Kearns were acquitted in their so-called "slacker trial." The controversy had really begun that January, when the *San Francisco Chronicle* published a letter by Dempsey's former wife, Maxine, charging he had evaded the draft. While alleging she had once actually supported the future heavyweight champion on her dancehall girl earnings, Mrs. Dempsey also claimed to have "positive proofs of a letter in his [Dempsey's] own handwriting, naming his manager, Jack Kearns, and two others, and telling me how they succeeded in having him put in class 4-A."

A San Francisco grand jury indicted Dempsey in February. Although neither

Maxine nor the scheming Kearns seemed especially trustworthy, a feeling took hold with the public that Dempsey's draft exemption was, at best, very questionable. As one writer put it, "Dempsey, whose profession is fighting, whose living is combat...did not go to war, while weak-armed, strong-hearted clerks reeled under pack and rifle."

Even if he actually had all the legal dependents he had claimed on his government questionaire and had raised hundreds of thousands of dollars through his appearances for the war effort, why hadn't the "Manassa Mauler" gone to fight the Hun? (In fact, even one of Dempsey's war effort publicity photos shot in a shipyard had backfired when readers spotted the patent leather shoes beneath his rugged overalls.)

After days of tantalizing testimony by Maxine, two prostitute friends of hers, Dempsey's mother, Dempsey and his Navy recruiter, the jury took ten minutes to acquit the champion of all charges. The country as a whole took longer to forget.

"A funny thing," Dempsey remembered of the thousands of calls of 'slacker' he heard for years, "Nobody ever called me a slacker to my face." Despite his troubles, Dempsey would successfully defend his title twice in a four-month period in 1920.

Seeing a sensible and profitable solution to the problems of independent barnstorming baseball teams, black ballplayer and entrepreneur Rube Foster devised the Negro National League in the winter of 1919 to "keep Colored baseball from the control of whites." On Feb. 13, he announced his league's creation in the Kansas City YMCA, accompanied by the new league's six other owners.

Foster, who had answered to "Andrew" until his celebrated defeat of Rube Wardell in 1902, was the acknowledged premier black pitcher of the century's first decade. Later, as a manager, his Chicago Leland Giants dominated on a par with Ruth's Yankees, compiling 128 wins in the 1910 season alone. The following season Foster became partners with John Schorling, the son-in-law of Charles Comiskey, and their renamed Chicago American Giants played at old Comiskey Park. The team was successful and popular, with Foster himself still taking the mound a few times each season as a special attraction.

Yet Foster recognized that if black baseball was to be anywhere near the equal of the white game, it had to be organized similarly. "We are the ship, all else the sea," was the Negro National League's inspiring slogan the year it began. A rival, the East Coast League, emerged in 1924 and for three years a Negro World Series thrived, to the benefit of both. In 1926, Foster suffered a nervous breakdown and entered an asylum in Kankahee, Illinois. When he died four years later, his body lay in state in Chicago for three days. He was elected to the Hall of Fame in 1981.

On Nov. 12, Judge Kenesaw Mountain Landis became the first commissioner of Baseball. The new office, which Landis himself named, replaced Ban Johnson's comparatively weak administration, which had been unable to keep the sport free of gamblers.

Landis had dropped out of high school in Logansport, Indiana, but later achieved a law degree through YMCA and Union law classes, without ever going to college. He was a dramatic but undistinguished judge in Illinois' Northern District when he took the baseball job. His reputation for legal strictness was attractive, but the owners also remembered that in 1915 Landis had so long delayed his decision in the new Federal League's anti-trust suit against the two recognized major leagues that the F.L. went bankrupt waiting.

Although he had fined the monopolist Standard Oil Company almost $30 million in a 1907 anti-trust suit, Landis said he could not rule "against the national institution" of baseball. Here was the man the owners needed. They had looked favorably at Landis for the post even before the 1919 World Series scandal created the demand for an Old Testament-style lawgiver who would drive at least the illegal money changers from the game.

Landis was a peculiar combination of lifelong Cubs fan and grim, unsmiling defender of baseball's purity. In 1921 he banned the eight White Sox defendants from the sport despite their 1920 jury acquittal and banned another player merely for publicly considering changing baseball clubs, let alone for fraternizing with gamblers.

The judge insisted he have exclusive pow-

Federal court judge **Kenesaw Mountain Landis,** who was named baseball's first commissioner on Nov. 12, 1920, prepares to throw out the first ball of the 1921 season at Brooklyn's Ebbets Field.

ers for seven years, but was reappointed not just in 1926, but in 1933, and 1940, despite the animosity of some owners and many players. He served until his death in 1944. (His salutary effect on the sport inspired Hollywood to create a film czar when it had its own public relations problem in the twenties.)

However, without the simultaneous arrival of Babe Ruth, who was far from a clean liver, baseball's revival under Landis would have been far more difficult. The conduct of the game was one thing, but the sport's real savior may have been the whoring, hard-drinking, moonfaced pitcher-turned-outfielder.

In July, 6-foot-2, William T. (Big Bill) Tilden became, at age 27, the first American men's tennis player to win the All England singles championship at Wimbledon, overcoming Australia's Gerald Patterson in four sets. He followed that feat by leading the United States to its first Davis Cup title since 1913, then outlasted fellow American William M. (Little Bill) Johnston in five sets to claim the U.S. Lawn Tennis Championship at Forest Hills.

Far from the polite country club style of his upbringing, Tilden had a complete pow-

erful game; he could serve with force, attack with a battery of cruel slice shots; rally steadily from the base line or end things quickly at the net.

Tilden had known a privileged childhood in Philadelphia, where he grew up taught by tutors and often kept indoors by a mother who feared illness. It wasn't until the death of his father and older brother in 1915 that Tilden applied himself fully to the sport he would dominate within five years.

He was haughty and aristocratic by the standards of American athletes, but could back up what he said. Tilden won seven American titles during his twenties reign, took Wimbledon again in 1921 and a third time in 1930 as an old man of 37. He then toured for decades as a professional.

His very last years were sad ones, often living off his Hollywood friends and being periodically jailed for indiscretions with teenaged boys. Tilden died of a heart attack in 1953.

The war just ended had known its bad executive decisions, but jaded Boston fans would marvel for generations at the short-sightedness of Red Sox owner Harry Frazee, who traded his star pitcher, out-fielder and home run attraction, Babe Ruth,

Bill Tilden with the men's singles trophy he won three times in the 1920s at the U.S. Championships at Forest Hills.

to the Yankees for $125,000 cash in order to support his own Broadway ventures. In fairness to Frazee, although Ruth had led his team to three world championships, and had set a major league record by clubbing 29 homers in 1919, no one could have known that the next year he would almost double that output.

In 1920, Ruth hit 54 home runs for New York with his uppercut lefthanded swing. Only the Philadelphia Phillies managed to hit that many homers as a team.

Although he won 26 games for the Yankees in 1920 and led the league in shutouts, an outing on August 16th made pitcher Carl Mays notorious. Cleveland's Ray Chapman, arguably the best shortstop in the American League at the time, had just stood in against Mays to lead off the fifth inning when Mays's third pitch, a rising submarine ball, found Chapman's temple. Mays started to field the ball to first, then saw Chapman had dropped unconscious. He died 12 hours later.

It was baseball's only playing fatality and Mays, although he had thrown a near-strike to the crouching Chapman, suffered abuse from players and fans for years afterwards. The mourning Indians neverthe-less rallied that year to win their first World Championship, beating Brooklyn in seven games.

Man o' War did not enter the Kentucky Derby in 1920, but the 3-year-old did take the other two thirds of racing's Triple Crown—the Preakness and Belmont Stakes. Man 'o War had earned nearly $250,000 when he retired later that year, victorious in 20 of 21 races as a 2 and 3-year-old. He raced for the final time on Oct. 12 at Ontario, outrunning Sir Barton, the Triple Crown winner of 1919, by six lengths in a one-on-one contest for a $75,000 purse. The champion's only loss came at Saratoga the year before to a horse named, appropriately, Upset.

On Sept. 17, Ralph Hay's auto dealership in Canton, Ohio, served as the cheerful, humble birthplace for the American Professional Football League. The 10 team owners (four more franchises would join during the 1920 season) had each paid a $100 entrance fee.

They now gathered around Jim Thorpe, the 1912 Olympic hero, N.Y. Giants' outfielder, and Canton Bulldogs running back on whose celebrity the new league depended. He had agreed to become the new league's president, which meant chiefly that his name would appear on its stationery.

Unlike the two major league baseball organizations, with their clusters of teams in Eastern cities, the APFLA had the bulk of its franchises in the heartland of Illinois, Indiana and Ohio.

The organization had been brought about in part to secure professional players and control salaries: College players were joining pro teams for a game or two and moving on, leaving fans only to hope their favorites would be on the field the next week. (College coaches hadn't been too fond of this practice either.)

Many of the new league's players would continue to change teams as freely as they had before, however, and after the 1921 season, the troubled APFLA became the National Football League. The reorganization came at the suggestion of league president Joe Carr and Chicago Staleys' owner, player and coach, George Halas, whose team would be renamed the Chicago Bears. ❏

Other Milestones

1895
(100 years ago)

William G. Morgan invents the game of **volleyball** in Holyoke, Mass. Morgan had originally devised the game for middle-aged men for whom basketball was too physically demanding. Early on, a basketball was used but it proved too heavy and the smaller and lighter volleyball was developed.

In an attempt to lift the game from the gutter, the **American Bowling Congress** (ABC) is formed in New York City on Sept. 9. The once popular game had been dominated by gamblers and thugs in recent years. The ABC becomes the sport's governing body, standardizing rules and equipment and staging national tournaments.

Golf's first **U.S. Open** is held in Newport, R.I. on the nine-hole course at the Newport Golf Club on Oct. 4. Briton Horace Rawlins, a 21-year-old employee at the club, wins the 36-hole, one-day competition, scoring 91-88–173 to beat nine other professional and one amateur entrant. Rawlins wins $150 and a gold medal.

1905
(90 years ago)

President Theodore Roosevelt threatens to ban the play of college football after 18 players are killed and another 159 seriously injured in 1905 alone. In an effort to save the game, a branch of the newly founded Intercollegiate Athletic Association of the United States (IAAUS), known as the American Intercollegiate Football Rules Committee, convenes on Dec. 28 in New York City. Several rules changes come about, including the legalization of the forward pass. The IAAUS, founded to establish guidelines for all college sports, will change its name to the National Collegiate Athletic Association in 1910.

1915
(80 years ago)

Jess Willard defeats controversial black heavyweight champion Jack Johnson under a blazing Havana, Cuba sun for the world title on Apr. 5. Willard, a 6-foot-6, 250-pound white slugger outdistances Johnson, finally knocking him out, to win the title in 26 rounds.

The men's tournament of the **U.S. Tennis Championships** is moved from Newport, R.I., to the West Side Tennis Club in Forest Hills, N.Y. The women's tournament will move to Forest Hills from the Philadelphia Cricket Club in 1921. The Championships will become known as the U.S. Open in 1968 and move to its present location in Flushing, N.Y. in 1978.

1920
(75 years ago)

On Jan. 5, the New York Yankees announce they have bought **Babe Ruth** from the Boston Red Sox for $125,000. The deal was actually made on Dec. 26, 1919 and included a $300,000 loan to Boston owner Harry Frazee with Fenway Park as collateral.

Cleveland Indian shortstop **Ray Chapman** is beaned by New York Yankees' pitcher Carl Mays on Aug. 16 at the Polo Grounds. Chapman is carried off the field and dies the next day. His death is major league baseball's first and only game-related fatality.

Federal Judge **Kenesaw Mountain Landis** is named baseball's first commissioner on Nov. 12, in the wake of the infamous "Black Sox" sandal. The previous three-man National Commission is disbanded and Landis is given absolute authority over players and owners. He will rule the game until his death in November 1944.

1930
(65 years ago)

Gallant Fox becomes the second horse to win thoroughbred racing's Triple Crown. Five years later, he will become the only Triple Crown winner to sire another Triple Crown winner, Omaha, who sweeps in 1935.

On Sept. 27, golfer **Bobby Jones** wins the U.S. Amateur to go along with his British Open, British Amateur and U.S. Open titles, and becomes the first and only golfer ever to win four majors in one year. Jones is also awarded the first James E. Sullivan Award for "his performance, example, and influence as an amateur."

1935
(60 years ago)

Major league baseball's **first night game** is played at Cincinnati's Crosley Field on May 24 and draws 20,422 fans. The floodlights, flicked on by President Franklin D. Roosevelt in Washington, illuminate a 2-1 Cincinnati victory over the Philadelphia Phillies.

University of Chicago halfback **Jay Berwanger** wins the first Downtown Athletic Club award as the best college football player east of the Mississippi. After the death of DAC athletic director John W. Heisman in 1936, the award is renamed the Heisman Trophy and eligibility broadened from coast to coast.

1945
(50 years ago)

U.S. Senator **Albert B. (Happy) Chandler** of Kentucky is named the second commissioner of baseball on Apr. 24. Chandler succeeds the late Judge Landis following a unanimous vote by major league club owners at a meeting in Cleveland. The owners will replace him with NL president Ford Frick in September 1951.

Byron Nelson dominates the pro golf tour, winning 19 of the 31 tournaments he enters, including 11 straight. On July 15, he wins his second PGA championship, defeating Sam Byrd in the final round. Due to World War II, it is the only major tournament played that year. Nelson, who was prevented from serving due to a blood disorder, is paid his one-year record earnings of $63,336 in war bonds.

The **Chicago Cardinals** end the NFL's longest losing streak with a 16-7 victory over the crosstown Bears. The Cardinals had lost a record 29 consecutive games before their first and last victory of the year on Oct. 14.

On Oct. 23, **Branch Rickey**, the general manager of the Brooklyn Dodgers, announces the signing of Jackie Robinson to a minor league contract with Montreal of the International League for the 1946 season. In 1947, Robinson will become the first black man to play major league baseball.

Rookie quarterback **Bob Waterfield** and the Cleveland Rams defeat Washington, 15-14, in the NFL championship game on Dec. 16. It will prove to be the final home game for the Rams in Cleveland and the first time a rookie QB leads his team to an NFL title. Owner Dan Reeves will move his club to Los Angeles before the start of 1946 season.

1950
(45 years ago)

The unranked **City College of New York** stuns all of college basketball, winning both the NCAA Tournament and the NIT in the same season. CCNY defeats No. 1-ranked Bradley at Madison Square Garden in the finals of both tournaments. The next year seven CCNY players are among those implicated in a widespread point-shaving scandal that centered around the New York City tournaments. The NCAA championship is never played in New York again.

1950 (Cont.)

George Mikan leads the Minneapolis Lakers over the Syracuse Nationals for the first championship of the new National Basketball Association. The NBA was created with the merger of the National Basketball League and Basketball Association of America after the 1948-49 season.

On June 29, the **United States** shocks England, 1-0, in a first round match at the World Cup in Brazil. Haitian-born Joe Gaetjens scores the winning goal in what is still considered the biggest upset in international soccer history.

1955
(40 years ago)

Race car driver **Bill Vukovich** is killed in a fiery, five-car crash at the Indianapolis 500. Vukovich, who entered the race seeking his record-breaking third straight win at Indy, was leading when the accident occurred on the 57th lap.

Beverly Hanson wins the first **LPGA Championship** on July 17. Hanson was tied with Louise Suggs after the 54-hole event and went on to win the playoff by three strokes.

1960
(35 years ago)

The **U.S. Olympic hockey team** pulls off a startling upset by winning the gold medal at the Winter Olympics in Squaw Valley, Calif. The lightly-regarded Americans go undefeated in five games, beating Canada (2-1), the USSR (3-2) and Czechoslovakia (9-4) in their last three games.

Floyd Patterson becomes the first fighter in history to regain the heavyweight title when he stops Ingemar Johansson in the fifth round of their June 20th bout at New York's Polo Grounds. He knocks out the previously unbeaten Swede with a smashing left hook.

On Sept. 26 at Fenway Park, Boston's **Ted Williams** hits his 521st homer in the last at bat of his career.

1965
(30 years ago)

The **Harris County Domed Stadium,** which cost over $30 million to build, opens in Houston with the newly-renamed Astros beating the New York Yankees, 2-1, in an exhibition game. The stadium would soon be renamed the Astrodome.

1970
(25 years ago)

The **Boston Bruins** capture their first Stanley Cup since 1941 as 22-year-old defenseman Bobby Orr scores the winning goal just 40 seconds into overtime on May 10. Orr's photo finish gave Boston a 4-3 victory and a four-game sweep over the St. Louis Blues.

The **National League** wins its eighth straight All-Star game, 5-4, at Cincinnati's Riverfront Stadium when hometown hero Pete Rose bowls over AL catcher Ray Fosse to score the winning run with two out in the bottom of the 12th inning.

It is a summer of milestones for some of baseball's greatest. On May 12, **Ernie Banks** belts career home run number 500. Five days later, **Hank Aaron** hammers his 3,000th career hit (and 570th home run), becoming the first player in baseball to amass 3,000 hits and 500 homers. And on July 18, **Willie Mays** collects his 3,000th hit.

On Aug. 12, **Curt Flood** loses his $4.1 million anti-trust suit against baseball. The suit was initiated after Flood refused to report to Philadelphia after being traded by St. Louis in the off-season (Tim McCarver and Dick Allen were also involved in the deal). While federal judge Irving Ben Cooper upholds the legality of baseball's reserve clause, the case sets the stage for free agency in baseball.

New Orleans Saints placekicker **Tom Dempsey** sets an NFL record on Nov. 8, by booting a 63-yard field goal to beat Detroit, 19-17, with three seconds left in the game. Dempsey, who was born missing both a right hand and all the toes on his right foot, makes the kick with with a specially-designed, league-approved shoe.

Tragedy strikes college football for the second time in six weeks on Nov. 14 when 36 Marshall University football players and five coaches are among 75 persons killed in a West Virginia plane crash. On Oct. 2, a plane carrying 13 Wichita State players, their head coach and athletic director went down near Silver Plume, Colo., killing all aboard.

1975
(20 years ago)

UCLA coach **John Wooden** retires after the Bruins defeat Kentucky, 92-85, to win their 10th NCAA college basketball championship in 12 years. Wooden leaves the game with 10 national titles and a career coaching record of 664-162. UCLA won a record 88 straight games from 1971-1974.

On Apr. 8, **Frank Robinson** debuts as the first black manager in major league history. The Cleveland player-manager belts a dramatic first inning home run to lead the Indians to a 5-3 win over the visiting Yankees before 56,204 at Municipal Stadium.

Arthur Ashe upsets Jimmy Connors in the men's finals at Wimbledon on July 5. Using a slow-down strategy to rattle Connors, Ashe wins in four sets to become the first black man to win the All-England singles title.

Muhammad Ali retains his world heavyweight title on Oct. 1, defeating former champion Joe Frazier in the "Thrilla in Manila" before 25,000 in the Philippines. Frazier, his right eye swollen shut, fails to answer the bell for the 15th round in this, the third meeting between the two fighters.

Boston catcher **Carlton Fisk** homers in the bottom of the 12th inning of Game 6 to lift the Red Sox to a 7-6 win over Cincinnati and force a deciding seventh game. A day later, the Reds would win Game 7 and the series, 4-3.

In a landmark ruling, pitchers **Andy Messersmith** and Dave McNally are given their unqualified free agency by labor arbitrator Peter Seitz on Dec. 23.

1980
(15 years ago)

Speed skater **Eric Heiden** and the **U.S. hockey team** are the stars of the Winter Olympics as the Games return to Lake Placid for the first time since 1932. Heiden wins five gold medals and the hockey team shocks the world and the USSR, 4-3, on its way to the gold.

President Jimmy Carter calls for a boycott of the Summer Olympic Games in Moscow to protest the Soviets' recent invasion of Afghanistan. On Apr. 12, the U.S. Olympic Committee votes to endorse the boycott, shattering the hopes of American athletes hoping to compete.

The **Philadelphia Phillies** win the World Series for the first time in their 98-year history, defeating Kansas City in five games.

1985
(10 years ago)

Bill Shoemaker becomes the first jockey to win $100 million in career purses, riding Lord at War to a win in the Santa Anita Handicap on Mar. 3. Shoemaker will retire in 1990 with 8,833 victories in 40,350 races.

Pete Rose becomes baseball's all-time hit leader on Sept. 11, driving a single into left field off San Diego pitcher Eric Show for career hit No. 4,192. Rose surpasses Ty Cobb's mark 57 years to the day that Cobb played in his final game.

Research Material

Many sources were used in the gathering of information for this almanac. Day to day material was almost always found in copies of **USA Today**, **The Boston Globe**, and **The New York Times**.

Several weekly and bi-weekly periodicals were also used in the past year's pursuit of facts and figures, among them— **Baseball America, Boxing Illustrated, The European, FIFA (Soccer) News, The Hockey News, The NCAA News, On Track, Soccer America, Sports Illustrated, The Sporting News, Track & Field News,** and **USA Today Baseball Weekly**.

In addition, the following books provided background material for one or more chapters of the almanac.

Arenas & Ballparks

The Ballparks, by Bill Shannon and George Kalinsky; Hawthorn Books, Inc. (1975); New York.

Diamonds, by Michael Gershman; Houghton Mifflin Co. (1993); Boston.

Green Cathedrals (Revised Edition), by Philip Lowry; Addison-Wesley Publishing Co. (1992); Reading, Mass.

The NFL's Encyclopedic History of Professional Football, Macmillan Publishing Co. (1977); New York.

Take Me Out to the Ballpark, by Lowell Reidenbaugh; The Sporting News Publishing Co. (1983); St. Louis.

24 Seconds to Shoot (An Informal History of the NBA), by Leonard Koppett; Macmillan Publishing Co. (1968); New York.

Plus major league baseball, NBA, NFL, NHL league guides, and major college football and basketball guides.

Auto Racing

1994 IndyCar Media Guide, edited by Dave Elshoff; Championship Auto Racing Teams; Bloomfield Hills, Mich.

1994 Indianapolis 500 Media Fact Book, compiled Bob Laycock, Jan Shaffer and Lee Driggers; Indianapolis Motor Speedway; Indianapolis.

Indy: 75 Years of Racing's Greatest Spectacle, by Rich Taylor; St. Martin's Press (1991); New York.

Marlboro Grand Prix Guide, 1950-93 (1994 Edition), compiled by Jacques Deschenaux; Charles Stewart & Company Ltd; Brentford, England.

1994 Winston Cup Media Guide, compiled and edited by Ty Norris; NASCAR Winston Cup Series; Winston-Salem, N.C.

Baseball

The All-Star Game (A Pictorial History, 1933 to Present), by Donald Honig; The Sporting News Publishing Co. (1987); St. Louis.

1994 American League Red Book, published by The Sporting News Publishing Co.; St. Louis.

Baseball America's 1994 Almanac, edited by Allan Simpson; Baseball America, Inc.; Durham, N.C.

Baseball America's 1994 Directory, edited by Allan Simpson; Baseball America, Inc.; Durham, N.C.

The Baseball Chronology, edited by James Charlton; Macmillian Publishing Co. (1991); New York.

The Baseball Encyclopedia (Ninth Edition), editorial director, Rick Wolff; Macmillan Publishing Co. (1993); New York.

The Complete 1994 Baseball Record Book, edited by Craig Carter; The Sporting News Publishing Co.; St. Louis.

Daguerreotypes (Eighth Edition), edited by Craig Carter; The Sporting News Publishing Co.; St. Louis.

1994 National League Green Book, published by The Sporting News Publishing Co.; St. Louis.

1994 NCAA Baseball and Softball, compiled by John Painter, Sean Straziscar and James Wright; edited by Ted Breidenthal; NCAA Books; Overland Park, Kan.

The Scrapbook History of Baseball, by Jordan Deutsch, Richard Cohen, Roland Johnson and David Neft; Bobbs-Merrill Co., Inc. (1975); Indianapolis/New York.

1994 Sporting News Official Baseball Guide, edited by Craig Carter and Dave Sloan; The Sporting News Publishing Co.; St. Louis.

1994 Sporting News Official Baseball Register, edited by Mark Shimabukuro; The Sporting News Publishing Co.; St. Louis.

The Sports Encyclopedia: Baseball (1994 Edition), edited by David Neft and Richard Cohen; St. Martin's Press; New York.

Total Baseball (Third Edition), edited by John Thorn and Pete Palmer; HarperPerennial (1993); New York.

College Basketball

All the Moves (A History of College Basketball), by Neil D. Issacs; J.B. Lippincott Company (1975); New York.

1993-94 Blue Ribbon College Basketball Yearbook, edited by Chris Wallace; Christopher Publishing; Buckhannon, W.Va.

College Basketball, U.S.A. (Since 1892), by John D. McCallum; Stein and Day (1978); New York.

Collegiate Basketball: Facts and Figures on the Cage Sport, by Edwin C. Caudle; The Paragon Press (1960); Montgomery, Ala.

The Encyclopedia of the NCAA Basketball Tournament, written and compiled by Jim Savage; Dell Publishing (1990); New York.

The Final Four (Reliving America's Basketball Classic), compiled by Billy Reed; Host Communications, Inc. (1988); Lexington, Ky.

Final Four Records, 1939-93, compiled by Gary Johnson; edited by Steven Hagwell; NCAA Books; Overland Park, Kan.

The Modern Encyclopedia of Basketball (Second Revised Edition), edited by Zander Hollander; Dolphins Books (1979); Doubleday & Co., Inc.; Garden City, N.Y.

1994 NCAA Basketball, compiled by Gary Johnson, Richard Campbell, John Painter, Sean Straziscar and James Wright; edited by Laura Bollig; NCAA Books; Overland Park, Kan.

Plus many 1993-94 NCAA Division I conference guides from the ACC to the WAC.

Pro Basketball

The Official NBA Basketball Encyclopedia, edited by Zander Hollander and Alex Sachere; Villard Books (1989); New York.

1993-94 Philadelphia 76ers Statistical Yearbook, edited by Harvey Pollack; Philadelphia 76ers; Philadelphia.

1993-94 Sporting News Official NBA Guide, edited by Craig Carter and Alex Sachare; The Sporting News Publishing Co.; St. Louis.

1993-94 Sporting News Official NBA Register, edited by Alex Sachare and Mark Shimabukuro; The Sporting News Publishing Co.; St. Louis.

Bowling

Bowlers Journal Annual, January, 1994; Chicago.

1994 LPBT Guide, Ladies Professional Bowlers Tour; Rockford, Ill.

1994 PBA Press-Radio-TV Guide; Professional Bowlers Association; Akron, Ohio.

Boxing

1994 Computer Boxing Update (volumes 7-11), edited by Phill Marder; Fight Fax Inc.; Sicklerville, N.J.

The Ring 1985 Record Book & Boxing Encyclopedia, edited by Herbert G. Goldman; The Ring Publishing Corp.; New York.

The Ring: Boxing, The 20th Century, Steven Farhood, editor-in-chief; BDD Illustrated Books (1993); New York.

College Sports

1992-93 National Collegiate Championships, edited by Ted Breidenthal; NCAA Books; Overland Park, Kan.

1994 NCAA Basketball, compiled by Gary Johnson, Richard Campbell, John Painter, Sean Straziscar and James Wright; edited by Laura Bollig; NCAA Books; Overland Park, Kan.

1993 NCAA Football, compiled by Richard Campbell, John Painter, Sean Straziscar and James Van Valkenburg; edited by J. Gregory Summers; NCAA Books; Overland Park, Kan.

1993-94 National Directory of College Athletics, edited by Kevin Cleary; Collegiate Directories, Inc.; Cleveland.

College Football

Football: A College History, by Tom Perrin; McFarland & Company, Inc. (1987); Jefferson, N.C.

Football: Facts & Figures, by Dr. L.H. Baker; Farrar & Rinehart, Inc. (1945); New York.

Great College Football Coaches of the Twenties and Thirties, by Tim Cohane; Arlington House (1973); New Rochelle, N.Y.

1993 NCAA Football, compiled by Richard Campbell, John Painter and Sean Straziscar; edited by Gregory Summers; NCAA Books; Overland Park, Kan.

Saturday Afternoon, by Richard Whittingham; Workman Publishing Co., Inc. (1985); New York.

Saturday's America, by Dan Jenkins; Sports Illustrated Books; Little, Brown & Company (1970); Boston.

Tournament of Roses, The First 100 Years, by Joe Hendrickson; Knapp Press (1989); Los Angeles.

Plus numerous college football team and conference guides, especially the 1993 guides compiled by Notre Dame, the Atlantic Coast Conference, Southeastern Conference and Southwest Conference.

Pro Football

1993 Canadian Football League Guide, compiled by the CFL Communications Dept.; Toronto.

The Football Encyclopedia (The Complete History of NFL Football from 1892 to the Present), compiled by David Neft and Richard Cohen; St. Martin's Press (1991); New York.

The Official NFL Encyclopedia, by Beau Riffenburgh; New American Library (1986); New York.

Official NFL 1993 Record and Fact Book, edited by Reggie Roberts and Chuck Garrity, Jr.; produced by NFL Properties, Inc.; New York.

The Scrapbook History of Pro Football, by Richard Cohen, Jordan Deutsch, Roland Johnson and David Neft; Bobbs-Merrill Company, Inc. (1976); Indianapolis/New York.

1993 Sporting News Football Guide, edited by Craig Carter; The Sporting News Publishing Co.; St. Louis.

1993 Sporting News Football Register, edited Mark Shimabukuro; The Sporting News Publishing Co.; St. Louis.

1994 Sporting News Super Bowl Book, edited by Tom Dienhart, Joe Hoppel and Dave Sloan; The Sporting News Publishing Co.; St. Louis.

Golf

The Encyclopedia of Golf (Revised Edition), compiled by Nevin H. Gibson; A.S. Barnes and Company (1964); New York.

Guinness Golf Records: Facts and Champions, by Donald Steel; Guinness Superlatives Ltd. (1987); Middlesex, England.

The History of the PGA Tour, by Al Barkow; Doubleday (1989); New York.

The Illustrated History of Women's Golf, by Rhonda Glenn, Taylor Publishing Co. (1991); Dallas.

The PGA World Golf Hall of Fame Book, by Gerald Astor, Prentice Hall Press (1991); New York.

1994 LPGA Player Guide, produced by LPGA Communications Dept.; Ladies Professional Golf Assn. Tour; Daytona Beach, Fla.

1994 Official PGA Tour Book, produced by PGA Tour Creative Services; Professional Golfers Assn. Tour; Ponte Vedra, Fla.

1994 Official Senior PGA Tour Book, produced by PGA Tour Creative Services; Professional Golfers Assn. Tour; Ponte Vedra, Fla.

Pro-Golf '94, PGA European Tour Media Guide, Virginia Water, Surrey, England.

The Random House International Encyclopedia of Golf, by Malcolm Campbell; Random House (1991); New York.

USGA Record Books (1895-1959, 1960-80 and 1981-90); U.S. Golf Association; Far Hills, N.J.

Hockey

Canada Cup '87: The Official History, No.1 Publications Ltd.; Toronto.

Checking Back (A History of the National Hockey League), by Neil D. Issacs; W.W. Norton & Company, Inc. (1977); New York.

The Hockey Encyclopedia, by Stan Fischler and Shirley Walton Fischler; research editor, Bob Duff; Macmillan Publishing Co. (1983); New York.

Hockey Hall of Fame (The Official History of the Game and Its Greatest Stars), by Dan Diamond and Joseph Romain; Doubleday (1988); New York.

The National Hockey League, by Edward F. Dolan Jr.; W H Smith Publishers Inc. (1986); New York.

The Official National Hockey League 75th Anniversary Commemorative Book, edited by Dan Diamond; McClelland & Stewart, Inc. (1991); Toronto.

The Official National Hockey League Stanley Cup Centennial Book, edited by Dan Diamond; Firefly Books (1992); Buffalo, NY.

1993-94 Official NHL Guide & Record Book, compiled by the NHL Communications Dept.; New York/Montreal.

1994-95 Sporting News Complete Hockey Book, edited Craig Carter, George Puro and Kyle Veltrop; The Sporting News Publishing Co.; St. Louis.

The Stanley Cup, by Joseph Romain and James Duplacey; Gallery Books (1989); New York.

The Trail of the Stanley Cup (Volumns I-III), by Charles L. Coleman; Progressive Publications Inc. (1969); Sherbrooke, Quebec.

Horse Racing

1994 American Racing Manual, compiled by the Daily Racing Form; Hightstown, N.J.

1994 Breeders' Cup Statistics; Breeders' Cup Limited; Lexington, Ky.

1994 Directory and Record Book, Thoroughbred Racing Associations of North America Inc.; Elkton, Md.

1994 Kentucky Derby Media Guide, compiled by Churchill Downs Public Relations Dept.; Louisville, Ky.

1994 NYRA Media Guide, The New York Racing

Association Inc.; Jamaica, N.Y.

1994 Preakness Press Guide, compiled and edited by Dale Austin, Craig Sculos and Joe Kelly; Maryland Jockey Club; Baltimore, Md.

1994 Trotting and Pacing Guide, compiled and edited by John Pawlak; United States Trotting Association; Columbus, Ohio.

International Sports

Athletics: A History of Modern Track and Field (1860-1990, Men and Women), by Roberto Quercetani; Vallardi & Associati (1990); Milan, Italy.

1994 International Track & Field Annual, Association of Track & Field Statisticians; edited by Peter Matthews; Lyons & Burford; New York.

Track & Field News' Little Blue Book; Metric conversion tables; From the editors of Track & Field News (1989); Los Altos, Calif.

Miscellaneous

The America's Cup 1851-1987 (Sailing for Supremacy), by Gary Lester and Richard Sleeman; Lester-Townsend Publishing (1986); Sydney, Australia.

The Encyclopedia of Sports (Fifth Revised Edition), by Frank G. Menke; revisions by Suzanne Treat; A.S. Barnes and Co., Inc. (1975); Cranbury, N.J.

The Great American Sports Book, by George Gipe; Doubleday & Company, Inc. (1978); Garden City, N.Y.

The 1994 Information Please Almanac, edited by Otto Johnson; Houghton Mifflin Co.; Boston.

1994 Official PRCA Media Guide, edited by Steve Fleming; Professional Rodeo Cowboys Association; Colorado Springs.

The Sail Magazine Book of Sailing, by Peter Johnson; Alfred A. Knopf (1989); New York.

1994 Sports Illustrated Sports Almanac, by the editors of Sports Illustrated; Little, Brown and Co.; Boston.

"Ten Years of the Ironman," Triathlete Magazine; October, 1988; Santa Monica, Calif.

The 1994 World Almanac and Book of Facts, edited by Robert Famighetti; Funk & Wagnalls; Mahwah, N.J.

Olympics

An Approved History of the Olympic Games, by Bill Henry and Patricia Henry Yeomans; Alfred Publishing Co., Inc. (1984); Sherman Oaks, Calif.

An Illustrated History of the Olympics (Third Edition); by Dick Schaap; Alfred A. Knopf (1975); New York.

The Complete Book of the Olympics (1992 Edition); by David Wallechinsky; Little, Brown and Co.; Boston.

The Games Must Go On (Avery Brundage and the Olympic Movement), by Allen Guttmann; Columbia University Press (1984); New York.

The Golden Book of the Olympic Games, edited by Erich Kamper and Bill Mallon; Vallardi & Associati (1992); Milan, Italy.

Hitler's Games (The 1936 Olympics), by Duff Hart-Davis; Harper & Row (1986); New York/London.

The Nazi Olympics, by Richard D. Mandell; Souvenir Press (1972); London.

The Official USOC Book of the 1984 Olympic Games, by Dick Schaap; Random House/ABC Sports; New York.

The Olympic Games Handbook, by David Chester; Charles Scribner's Sons (1975); New York.

Pursuit of Excellence (The Olympic Story), by The Associated Press and Grolier; Grolier Enterprises Inc. (1979); Danbury, Conn.

The Story of the Olympic Games (776 B.C. to 1948 A.D.), by John Kieran and Arthur Daley; J.B. Lippincott Company (1948); Philadelphia/New York.

United States Olympic Books (Seven Editions): 1936,48,52,56,60,61-65,68; U.S. Olympic Association; New York.

The USA and the Olympic Movement, produced by the USOC Information Dept.; edited by Gayle Plant; U.S. Olympic Committee (1988); Colorado Springs.

Plus official IOC and USOC records from the 1994 Winter Olympics in Lillehammer, Norway.

Soccer

The American Encyclopedia of Soccer, edited by Zander Hollander; Everest House Publishers (1980); New York.

The European Football Yearbook (1992-93 Edition), edited by Mike Hammond; Sports Projects Ltd; West Midlands, England.

The Guinness Book of Soccer Facts & Feats, by Jack Rollin; Guinness Superlatives Ltd. (1978); Middlesex, England.

History of Soccer's World Cup, by Michael Archer; Chartwell Books, Inc. (1978); Secaucus, N.J.

The Simplest Game, by Paul Gardner; Collier Books (1994); New York.

The Story of the World Cup, by Brian Glanville; Faber and Faber Limited (1993); London/Boston.

1991-92 MSL Official Guide, Major (Indoor) Soccer League; Overland Park, Kan.

U.S. Soccer 1993 Media Guide, edited by Jim Froslid; U.S. Soccer Federation; Chicago.

Tennis

Bud Collins' Modern Encyclopedia of Tennis, edited by Bud Collins and Zander Hollander; Visible Ink Press (1994); Detroit.

The Illustrated Encyclopedia of World Tennis, by John Haylett and Richard Evans; Exeter Books (1989); New York.

Official Encyclopedia of Tennis, edited by the staff of the U.S. Lawn Tennis Assn.; Harper & Row (1972); New York.

1994 Official ATP Tour Player Guide, compiled by ATP Tour Communications Dept.; Association of Tennis Professionals; Ponte Vedra Beach, Fla.

1994 Official WTA Tour Media Guide, compiled by WTA Public Relations staff; edited by Renee Bloch Shallouf; St. Petersburg, Fla.

Who's Who

The Encyclopedia of North American Sports History, by Ralph Hickok; Facts on File (1992); New York.

The Guiness International Who's Who of Sport, edited by Peter Mathews, Ian Buchanan and Bill Mallon; Guiness Publishing (1993); Middlesex, England

101 Greatest Athletes of the Century, by Will Grimsley and the Associated Press Sports Staff; Bonanza Books (1987); Crown Publishers, Inc.; New York.

Superstars, by Frank Litsky; Vineyard Books, Inc. (1975); Secaucus, N.J.

Other Reference Books

Facts & Dates of American Sports, by Gorton Carruth & Eugene Ehrlich; Harper & Row, Publishers, Inc. (1988); New York.

Sports Market Place 1994 (July edition), edited by Richard A. Lipsey; Sportsguide Inc.; Princeton N.J.

The World Book Encyclopedia (1988 Edition); World Book, Inc.; Chicago.

The World Book Yearbook (Annual Supplements, 1954-93); World Book, Inc.; Chicago.

Olympics

Winter Games

Year	No.	Host City	Dates
1998	XVIII	Nagano, Japan	Feb. 7-22

Summer Games

Year	No.	Host City	Dates
1996	XXVI	Atlanta, Georgia	July 19-Aug. 4
2000	XXVII	Sydney, Australia	Sept. 16-Oct. 1

All-Star Games

Baseball

Year	Site	Date
1995	The Ballpark in Arlington	July 11
1996	Veterans Stadium, Philadelphia	July 9
1997	Not decided	

NBA Basketball

Year	Site	Date
1995	America West Arena, Phoenix	Feb. 12
1996	Alamodome, San Antonio	Feb. 11

NFL Pro Bowl

Year	Site	Date
1995	Aloha Stadium, Honolulu	Feb. 5
1996	Aloha Stadium, Honolulu	Feb. 4
1997	Aloha Stadium, Honolulu	Feb. 2

NHL Hockey

Year	Site	Date
1995	San Jose Arena	TBA
1996	Shawmut Center, Boston	Jan. 21

Auto Racing

The Daytona 500 stock car race is usually held on the Sunday before the third Monday in February, while the Indianapolis 500 is usually held on the Sunday of Memorial Day weekend in May. Except for 1994, the following dates are tentative.

Year	Daytona 50	Indianapolis 500
1995	Feb. 19	May 28
1996	Feb. 18	May 26
1997	Feb. 16	May 25
1998	Feb. 15	May 24

NCAA Basketball

Men's Final Four

Year	Site	Date
1995	The Kingdome, Seattle	April 1-3
1996	Meadowlands (N.J.) Arena	Mar. 30-Apr. 1
1997	RCA Dome, Indianapolis	March 29-31
1998	Alamodome, San Antonio	March 28-30
1999	ThunderDome, St. Petersburg	March 27-29
2000	RCA Dome, Indianapolis	April 1-3
2001	Metrodome, Minneapolis	Mar. 31-Apr. 2
2002	Georgia Dome, Atlanta	Mar. 30-Apr. 1

Women's Final Four

Year	Site	Date
1995	Target Center, Minneapolis	April 1-2
1996	Charlotte (N.C.) Coliseum	March 30-31
1997	Riverfront Coliseum	March 28-29
1998	Kemper Arena	March 28-29

NFL Football

Super Bowls

No.	Site	Date
XXVIX	Joe Robbie Stadium, Miami	Jan. 29, 1995
XXX	Sun Devil Stadium, Tempe	Jan. 28, 1996
XXXI	Superdome, New Orleans	Jan. 26, 1997
XXXII	Jack Murphy Stadium, San Diego	Jan. 25, 1998

Golf

The Masters

Year	Site	Date
1995	Augusta National Ga	April 6-9
1996	Augusta National Ga	April 11-14
1997	Augusta National Ga	April 10-13

U.S. Open

Year	Site	Date
1995	Shinnecock Hills (N.Y.) GC	June 15-18
1996	Oakland Hills CC, Birmingham, Mich	June 13-16
1997	Congressional CC, Bethesda, Md	TBA

U.S. Women's Open

Year	Site	Date
1995	Broadmoor GC, Colorado Springs	July 13-16
1996	Pine Needles Resort, So. Pines, N.C	May 23-26

U.S. Senior Open

Year	Site	Date
1995	Congressional CC, Bethesda, Md	June 29-July 2
1996	Canterbury GC, Cleveland	July 11-14

PGA Championship

Year	Site	Date
1995	Riviera CC, Pacific Palisades, Cailf	Aug. 10-13
1996	Valhalla GC, Louisville	Aug. 8-11
1997	Winged Foot CC, Mamaroneck, N.Y.	TBA

British Open

Year	Site	Date
1995	St. Andrews, Scotland	July 20-23
1996	Royal Lytham & St. Annes, England	July 18-21
1997	Royal Troon, Scotland	July 17-20

Ryder Cup

Year	Site	Date
1995	Oak Hill CC, Rochester, N.Y.	Sept. 22-24
1997	Valderrama, Spain	Sept. 20-28
1999	The Country Club, Brookline, Mass.	TBA

Horse Racing

Triple Crown

The Kentucky Derby is always held at Churchill Downs in Louisville on the first Saturday in May, followed two weeks later by the Preakness Stakes at Pimlico Race Course in Baltimore and three weeks after that by the Belmont Stakes at Belmont Park in Elmont, N.Y.

Year	Ky Derby	Preakness	Belmont
1995	May 6	May 20	June 10
1996	May 4	May 18	June 8
1997	May 3	May 17	June 7

Tennis

U.S. Open

Usually held from the last Monday in August through the second Sunday in September, with Labor Day weekend the midway point in the tournament.

Year	Site	Dates
1995	U.S. Tennis Center, NYC	Aug. 28-Sept. 10
1996	U.S. Tennis Center, NYC	Aug. 26-Sept. 8
1997	U.S. Tennis Center, NYC	Aug. 25-Sept. 7

Yachting

America's Cup

All racing held off San Diego

Year		Dates
1995	Defender Selection Trials	Jan. 12- Apr. 22
	Challenger Selection Trials	Jan. 14- Apr. 22
	Final (Best-of-7)	starts May 6
	Races 1-4 scheduled for May 6-8-9-11	